The Consumer Credit and Sales
Legal Practice Series

COLLECTION ACTIONS

Defending Consumers and Their Assests

Third Edition

WITH ONLINE UPDATES

Keyword Search Entire Book

www.nclc.org/library

See *page ix* for details.

Jonathan Sheldon
Carolyn L. Carter
Chi Chi Wu

Contributing Authors: Dwain Alexander, Jeremiah Battle, Jr., Leah Davenport, Robert J. Hobbs, Mary Kingsley, Darlene R. Wong

National Consumer Law Center®
7 Winthrop Square, 4th Floor Boston, MA 02110 www.nclc.org/library

About NCLC®

The National Consumer Law Center®, a nonprofit corporation founded in 1969, assists consumers, advocates, and public policy makers nationwide who use the powerful and complex tools of consumer law to ensure justice and fair treatment for all, particularly those whose poverty renders them powerless to demand accountability from the economic marketplace. For more information, go to www.nclc.org.

Ordering NCLC Publications

Order online at www.nclc.org/library, or contact Publications Department, National Consumer Law Center, 7 Winthrop Square, 4th Floor, Boston, MA 02110, (617) 542-9595, FAX: (617) 542-8028, e-mail: publications@nclc.org.

Training, Conferences, and Webinars

NCLC participates in numerous national, regional, and local consumer law trainings. Its annual fall conference is a forum for consumer rights attorneys from legal services programs, private practice, government, and nonprofit organizations to share insights into common problems and explore novel and tested approaches that promote consumer justice in the marketplace. Contact NCLC for more information or see our website. NCLC offers free webinars and views of past webinars. Go to www.nclc.org/webinars.html for more information.

Case Consulting

Case analysis, consulting and co-counseling for lawyers representing vulnerable consumers are among NCLC's important activities. Administration on Aging funds allow us to provide free consulting to legal services advocates representing elderly consumers on many types of cases. Massachusetts Legal Assistance Corporation funds permit case assistance to advocates representing low-income Massachusetts consumers. Other funding may allow NCLC to provide very brief consultations to other advocates without charge. See our website for more information at www.nclc.org.

Charitable Donations and Cy Pres *Awards*

NCLC's work depends in part on the support of private donors. Tax-deductible donations should be made payable to National Consumer Law Center, Inc. For more information, contact Gerald Tuckman of NCLC's Development Office at (617) 542-8010 or gtuckman@nclc.org. NCLC has also received generous court-approved *cy pres* awards arising from consumer class actions to advance the interests of class members. For more information, contact Rich Dubois (rdubois@nclc.org) or Gerald Tuckman (gtuckman@nclc.org) at (617) 542-8010.

Comments and Corrections

Write to the above address to the attention of the Editorial Department or e-mail consumerlaw@nclc.org.

About This Volume

This is the Third Edition of *Collection Actions*. Discard prior editions and supplements.

Cite This Volume As

National Consumer Law Center, Collection Actions (3d ed. 2014), *updated at* www.nclc.org/library.

Attention

Copyright

ISBN: 978-1-60248-146-6 (this volume)
ISBN: 978-0-943116-10-5 (Series)

Library of Congress Control Number: 2014940592

About the Authors

Jonathan Sheldon has been an NCLC staff attorney writing and consulting on a number of consumer law topics since 1976. Previously he was a staff attorney with the Federal Trade Commission. His other publications include *Unfair and Deceptive Acts and Practices, Consumer Warranty Law, Consumer Arbitration Agreements, Automobile Fraud,* and *Repossessions*. He is also a contributing author to a number of other NCLC publications.

Carolyn L. Carter is NCLC's director of advocacy and was formerly co-director of Legal Services, Inc., in Gettysburg, Pennsylvania, and director of the Law Reform Office of the Cleveland Legal Aid Society. She is the editor of *Pennsylvania Consumer Law,* editor of the first edition of *Ohio Consumer Law,* co-author of *Consumer Warranty Law, Unfair and Deceptive Acts and Practices, Repossessions,* and *Automobile Fraud,* and a contributing author to *Fair Debt Collection* and other NCLC publications. She is a recipient of the Vern Countryman Consumer Law Award.

Chi Chi Wu is an NCLC staff attorney working on medical debt collection, consumer credit, and credit reporting issues. She is author of *Fair Credit Reporting* and a contributing author to *Consumer Credit Regulation, Credit Discrimination,* and *Truth in Lending*. She was formerly an assistant attorney general with the Consumer Protection Division of the Massachusetts attorney general's office and an attorney with the Asian Outreach Unit of Greater Boston Legal Services.

Dwain Alexander, II is a retired navy captain and the senior supervising civilian attorney for the Region Legal Service Office, Mid Atlantic. In addition to providing retail legal assistance for servicemembers and their families, he mentors and trains attorneys at the Navy's largest Region Legal Service Office. Mr. Alexander is a frequent speaker at conferences and continuing legal education courses on the Servicemembers Civil Relief Act, automobile transactions, and servicemember's rights. He has testified before the Senate Commerce Committee and the Senate Sub-Committee on Oversight, Federal Rights, and Agency Actions. Mr. Alexander serves as chair of the National Association of Consumer Advocates, Military Consumer Justice Project.

Jeremiah Battle, Jr. is an NCLC staff attorney. He is the author of NCLC's *Credit Discrimination* and a contributing author to several NCLC publications, including *Consumer Credit Regulation, Unfair and Deceptive Acts and Practices,* and *Repossessions*. He also works on NCLC's *Working Cars for Working Families* initiative. Previously, he was a staff attorney with Northeast New Jersey Legal Services and a managing attorney with what is now Disability Rights New Jersey.

Robert J. Hobbs is NCLC's deputy director. He has written and consulted since 1972 on debt collection and other consumer credit issues. Prior to that, he was a staff attorney with New Orleans Legal Assistance. He is the author of *Fair Debt Collection,* co-author of *The Practice of Consumer Law,* and editor of *Consumer Law Pleadings*. He has served on the FRB's Consumer Advisory Council, is a founder of the National Association of Consumer Advocates, and coordinates NCLC's annual Fair Debt Collection Practices and Consumer Rights Litigation conferences.

Mary Kingsley is a 1971 graduate of Harvard Law School and a Massachusetts attorney. She has contributed to a number of NCLC publications in addition to this volume, including *Fair Debt Collection* and *Repossessions*.

Leah M. Davenport is a legal assistance attorney with the United States Air Force at Joint Base Langley-Eustis in Virginia, where she provides legal assistance to servicemembers, retirees, and their families. She has been a speaker at continuing legal education courses on the Servicemembers Civil Relief Act. Prior to her entry into civil service, she was a civil litigation attorney in Norfolk, Virginia. She is also an adjunct professor of Law at William and Mary Law School.

Acknowledgments

We want to especially thank Lynn Drysdale, Joanne S. Faulkner, and Richard Rubin for their many contributions to this and the prior edition. Thanks also to Carol Kenner, Deanne Loonin, Sharon Dietrich, Annie Chan, and Peter Holland for substantive contributions to this edition; Nate Player and Allen Agnitti for legal research; Dorothy Tan for editorial supervision; Kim Calvi for editorial assistance; Shirlron Williams for assistance checking citations; Shannon Halbrook for assistance with the online companion materials; Mary McLean for indexing; and Scribe for composition services.

What Your Library Should Contain

The Consumer Credit and Sales Legal Practice Series contains twenty titles, continuously updated, and designed to be an attorney's primary practice guide and legal resource for use in all fifty states. Titles are available individually or as part of the complete twenty-title series. Every NCLC treatise includes online companion material, allowing rapid access to appendices, pleadings, primary sources, and other practice aids. Search for documents by category or with a table of contents or various keyword search options. All documents can be downloaded, printed, and copy-pasted into a word processing document. Pleadings are also available in Word format.

In 2015, NCLC also plans to offer online the full text of each title (chapters and appendices), so that subscribers may read, download, print, e-mail, and copy/paste the online material, with live links and advanced search functions.

Debtor Rights

Consumer Bankruptcy Law and Practice

2012 Tenth Edition (Two Volumes)

The definitive personal bankruptcy manual, from the initial interview to final discharge, including consumer rights when a company files for bankruptcy. This practice package contains the leading expert analysis of individual bankruptcy law and such practice aids as over 150 pleadings and forms, a client questionnaire and handout, the latest Bankruptcy Code, Rules, and fee schedules, a date calculator, and means test data.

Fair Debt Collection

2014 Eighth Edition (Two Volumes)

The leading reference covering the Fair Debt Collection Practices Act and common law, state statutory and other federal debt collection protections. Over 5000 unique case summaries cover reported and unreported FDCPA cases by category. The online companion material contains sample pleadings and discovery, the FTC Commentary, an index to and the full text of all FTC staff opinion letters, and other practice aids.

Foreclosures and Mortgage Servicing

2014 Fifth Edition

Examines RESPA and other federal and state requirements placed on mortgage loan servicers, including the new CFPB regulations, and details on loan modification and mediation programs implemented by federal and state governments. The volume features standing and substantive and procedural defenses to foreclosure and tactics after the foreclosure sale. Special chapters cover reverse mortgages, tax liens, land installment sales contracts, manufactured home and condominium foreclosures, and other topics.

Repossessions

2013 Eighth Edition

A unique guide to motor vehicle and mobile home repossessions, threatened seizures of household goods, statutory liens, and automobile lease and rent-to-own default remedies. The volume examines UCC Article 9 and hundreds of other federal and state statutes regulating repossessions.

Student Loan Law

2010 Fourth Edition

Collection harassment; closed school, disability, and other discharges; tax intercepts, wage garnishment, and offset of social security benefits; and repayment plans, consolidation loans, deferments, private student loans, and non-payment of loan based on school fraud.

Access to Utility Service

2011 Fifth Edition

Consumer rights as to regulated and unregulated utilities, including telecommunications, terminations, billing errors, low-income payment plans, utility allowances in subsidized housing, LIHEAP, and weatherization.

Credit and Banking

Truth in Lending

2012 Eighth Edition (Two Volumes)

Details the CFPB's comprehensive new mortgage rules in effect in 2014, all aspects of TILA, the Consumer Leasing Act, the Fair Credit Billing Act, the Home Ownership and Equity Protection Act (HOEPA), and the Credit CARD Act. Appendices and the website contain the Acts, Reg. Z, Reg. M, and their official staff commentaries, numerous sample pleadings, rescission notices, two programs to compute APRs, TILA legislative history, and a unique compilation of all Federal Register notices and supplementary information on Regulation Z since 1969. The text references to both FRB and CFPB versions of Regulation Z.

Fair Credit Reporting

2013 Eighth Edition

The key resource for handling any type of credit reporting issue, from cleaning up blemished credit records to suing reporting agencies and creditors for inaccurate reports. Covers the new FACTA changes, identity theft, creditor liability for failing to properly reinvestigate disputed information, credit scoring, privacy issues, the Credit Repair Organizations Act, state credit reporting and repair statutes, and common law claims.

Mortgage Lending

2014 Second Edition

A litigation manual covering federal and state regulation (and federal preemption) of the origination and the terms of mortgage loans, including ability to pay, steering, churning, flipping, appraisals, loan broker compensation, insurance, adjustable rates, negative amortization, interest rate limitations, late fees, reverse mortgages, holder-in-due course, mortgage litigation, and claims against failed banks.

Consumer Credit Regulation

2012 First Edition

Examines federal and state regulation (and federal preemption of state regulation) concerning credit cards, payday loans, automobile finance and installment sales, auto title pawns, rent-to-own, refund anticipation loans, "sale" of the consumer's future income stream and other non-mortgage lending. Special chapters on credit math, what is interest, and credit insurance.

Consumer Banking and Payments Law

2013 Fifth Edition

Covers checks, telechecks, electronic fund transfers, electronic check conversions, money orders, and debit, payroll, unemployment, and other prepaid cards. The treatise also covers new federal regulations on remittances, banker's right of setoff, electronic transfers of federal and state benefit payments, and a special chapter on electronic records an signatures.

Credit Discrimination

2013 Sixth Edition

Analyzes the Equal Credit Opportunity Act, Fair Housing Act, Civil Rights Acts, and state credit discrimination statutes, including reprints of all relevant federal interpretations, government enforcement actions, and numerous sample pleadings.

Consumer Litigation

Collection Actions

2014 Third Edition

A complete guide to consumer defenses and counterclaims to collection lawsuits filed in court or in arbitration, with extensive discussion of setting aside default judgments and limitations on a collector's post-judgment remedies. Special chapters include the rights of active duty military, and unique issues involving medical debt, government collections, collector's attorney fees, and bad check laws.

Consumer Arbitration Agreements

2011 Sixth Edition

Successful approaches to challenge arbitration agreements' enforceability and waivers of class arbitration, the interrelation of the Federal Arbitration Act and state law, class actions and punitive damages in arbitration, implications of NAF's withdrawal from consumer arbitrations, the right to discovery, import of recent Supreme Court rulings, and other topics.

Consumer Class Actions

2013 Eighth Edition

Makes class litigation manageable even for small offices, including numerous sample pleadings, class certification memoranda, discovery, class notices, settlement materials, and much more online as companion material. Includes a detailed analysis of the Class Action Fairness Act, state class action rules and case law, NACA class action guidelines, and other topics.

Consumer Law Pleadings

2013 Index Guide: ALL pleadings from ALL NCLC treatises, including Consumer Law Pleadings Numbers One through Nineteen

Over 2000 notable pleadings from all types of consumer cases, including predatory lending, foreclosures, automobile fraud, lemon laws, debt collection, fair credit reporting, home improvement fraud, student loans, and lender liability. Finding aids pinpoint desired pleading in seconds, ready to paste into a word processor.

Deception and Warranties

Unfair and Deceptive Acts and Practices

2012 Eighth Edition

The only practice manual covering all aspects of a deceptive practices case in every state. Citations to tens of thousands of state UDAP and FTC cases. Special sections on automobile sales, unfair insurance practices, unfair and deceptive credit practices, third party liability, attorney fees, and many other topics.

Automobile Fraud

2011 Fourth Edition

Examination of title law, "yo-yo" sales, odometer tampering, lemon laundering, sale of salvage and wrecked cars, undisclosed prior use, and prior damage to new cars. The website contains numerous sample pleadings and title search techniques.

Consumer Warranty Law

2010 Fourth Edition

Comprehensive treatment of new and used car lemon laws, the Magnuson-Moss Warranty Act, UCC Articles 2 and 2A, mobile home, new home, and assistive device warranty laws, FTC Used Car Rule, tort theories, car repair and home improvement statutes, service contract and lease laws, with numerous sample pleadings.

Federal Deception Law

2012 First Edition

New treatise covering FTC and CFPB rulemaking, special chapters on the FTC Holder and Telemarketing Sales Rules, federal restrictions on unwanted calls and texts, junk faxes and spam, federal and state RICO, the federal False Claims Act, federal and state regulation of debt relief services, and more.

Other NCLC Publications for Lawyers

Foreclosure Prevention Counseling: Preserving the American Dream

2013 Third Edition and Companion Website

Explains how to obtain a loan modification or workout, with advice specifically tailored for Fannie Mae, Freddie Mac, subprime, FHA-insured, VA, and Rural Housing Service loans. The book also details advice on foreclosure defense, dealing with servicers, and on new government foreclosure mediation programs.

Bankruptcy Basics: A Step-by-Step Guide for Pro Bono Attorneys, General Practitioners, and Legal Services Offices

2013 Second Edition and Companion Website

Provides everything attorneys new to bankruptcy need to file their first case. Companion website contains software, sample pleadings, and other practice aids that greatly simplify handling a bankruptcy case.

Instant Evidence: A Quick Guide to Federal Evidence and Objections

2013 Second Edition

Facilitates objection by rule number and includes common objections and motions at every stage of a case—all in 21 pages! Spiral-bound to lay flat, all pages are laminated, allowing new notations for each trial with a dry-erase pen.

The Practice of Consumer Law: Seeking Economic Justice

Second Edition with CD-Rom

Contains an essential overview to consumer law and explains how to get started in a private or legal services consumer practice. Packed with invaluable sample pleadings and practice pointers for even experienced consumer attorneys.

National Consumer Law Center Guide Series

are books designed for consumers, counselors, and attorneys new to consumer law:

NCLC Guide to Surviving Debt

2013 Edition

A great overview of consumer law. Everything a paralegal, new attorney, or client needs to know about home foreclosures and mortgage modifications, debt collectors, managing credit card debt, whether to refinance, credit card problems, evictions, repossessions, credit reporting, utility terminations, student loans, budgeting, and bankruptcy.

NCLC Guide to the Rights of Utility Consumers

First Edition

Explains consumer rights concerning electric, gas, and other utility services: shut off protections, rights to restore terminated service, bill payment options, weatherization tips, rights to government assistance, and much more.

NCLC Guide to Consumer Rights for Domestic Violence Survivors

First Edition

Provides practical advice to help survivors get back on their feet financially and safely establish their economic independence.

Visit www.nclc.org/library to order online or for more information on all NCLC publications and online companion material, including the full tables of contents, indices, and web-based searches of the publications' full text.

About the Companion Online Resources

IMPORTANT NOTE: In 2015, we will launch the NCLC Digital Library, an all-new website offering full digital versions of the full text of all of our consumer law treatises. Material from the existing companion websites will be available on the new site as well, but the instructions in this section will no longer apply. Purchasers and subscribers to this title will be provided additional information on accessing and using the new website prior to launch.

The Companion Websites: www.nclc.org/library

NCLC companion websites offer the treatises' appendices plus hundreds of additional documents in PDF and Microsoft Word formats—pleadings, forms, statutes, regulations, agency interpretations, legislative and regulatory history, and much more—all easily located with flexible, powerful search tools. The sites can be easily viewed on a smartphone or tablet, and documents can be electronically searched, printed, downloaded, and copy-pasted into a word processor.

We highly recommend reading the Help page on the website, found at the top of the left toolbar once you are logged in.

Registering for the Companion Website

Until the new NCLC Digital Library launches in 2015, users only need to register once; companion sites for subsequent treatise purchases will be added to users' accounts. To register for the first time, go to *www.nclc.org/library, click on companion websites*, and click "Register as a New User." Enter the Companion Website Registration Number found on the packing statement or invoice accompanying this book. Then enter the requested information to create your account.

Locating Documents on the Companion Website

The companion website provides three ways to locate documents:

1. **The search page** (the home page) uses keyword searches to find documents—full text searches of all documents on the website or searches of just the documents' titles. Enter text in the appropriate field and click the Search button. You may also specify Document Type or Appendix section. When searching documents' full text, each entry in your search results will include excerpts of the document, showing your search terms highlighted in context.

2. **The contents page** (click the "Contents" tab at the top of the page) is a traditional nested table of contents. Click a branch to expand it into a list of sub-branches or documents. Each document appears once in this contents tree.

3. **The pleading finder page** (click the "Pleading Finder" link at the top of the search page, if available) allows pleadings to be located using one or more menus, such as "Type of Pleading" or "Subject." **Select more than one item from a menu, or deselect items, by holding the Ctrl key while clicking.** This page also includes optional fields to specify terms to be found in the documents' text or titles, to further narrow search results.

Over 2000 pleadings are also available at NCLC's *Consumer Law Pleadings* website using the same search techniques discussed above. Pleadings can also be located using *Consumer Law Pleadings*' index guide, which lists pleadings organized by type, subject area, legal claim, title, and other categories identical to those on the website.

How to Use the Documents and Download Microsoft Word Versions

Click a document title in your search results or on the contents page to view the document in your web browser. Text may be copy-pasted directly from the page or the full document may be downloaded as a PDF file for easier printing. (You will need a PDF reader to open PDF documents; the free Adobe Reader is available at www.adobe.com.) Additionally, pleadings and certain other documents can be downloaded in Microsoft Word format, enabling the opening of entire documents in a word processor. Icons to download PDF and Word versions are found at the top of the page.

NCLC Digital Library

As discussed above, early 2015 will see the launch of NCLC's Digital Library, **where the complete contents of treatises, including the chapters, will be made available online on a subscription basis**. Pleadings, practice aids, and primary source materials found on the companion websites discussed above will also be available and fully searchable on the new site, but the new site's operation and appearance will differ dramatically. Furthermore, the new site will incorporate all the functions described in the rest of this section: full text search of NCLC's treatises, bookstore, and Quick Reference. The full-text search will be a particularly useful tool, as subscribers will be able to search all treatises or only the treatises they own, then jump straight to the given book section of interest. Material from the treatises will be able to be copy-pasted, printed, or emailed, and the site will be optimized for mobile devices as well as desktop computers.

Users with companion website accounts must re-register for the new site once it is launched.

Other NCLC Online Resources Available Through 2014

In the meantime, the following sites will remain available until the end of 2014. Visit **www.nclc.org/library** for links to all the online resources listed below, including the treatises' companion websites, *NCLC eReports*, a search engine to search the full text of all treatises, the Quick Reference, and our online bookstore.

- Search the full text of NCLC's treatises at **www.nclc.org/keyword**. This free search utility allows users to search the full text of NCLC treatises for a word or phrase without registration or log-in. While the chapters' text will not be available online until the launch of the Digital Library, this web-based search engine points readers to the page(s) of print treatises where search terms can be found. Search results are shown in context, enabling selection of the most relevant pages.
- *NCLC eReports*, found alongside the treatises' companion websites at **www.nclc.org/webaccess**, is a collection of short articles by NCLC's experts discussing recent consumer law developments. About ten new articles are published each month, with older articles available in a searchable archive. Treatise subscribers are provided free access to *NCLC eReports*. NCLC sends occasional eAlerts to inform our readers about new *eReports* articles and other news items; visit **www.nclc.org/ealerts** to sign up.
- Our online bookstore at **www.nclc.org/shop** provides information about all twenty NCLC treatises and our other titles, including current tables of contents, indices, sample pages, and more. The PDF-format documents found there can be quickly searched for a word or phrase.
- The Quick Reference, found at **www.nclc.org/qr**, is an alphabetical index spanning all twenty NCLC treatises. It lists over 1000 subjects and indicates the book(s) and section(s) where each subject is discussed.

If you cannot locate this number, contact NCLC Publications at (617) 542-9595 or publications@nclc.org.

Summary Contents

Contents

Chapter 1 Introduction

1.1 About This Treatise

This treatise assists attorneys in the representation of consumers sued on credit card, medical, and other debts. Recent years have seen an explosion in not just the number of consumer debts being enforced in the courts but also in the number of such actions in which the consumer does not owe the debt or has substantial defenses, or in which the collector has no reliable evidence whether the consumer owes the debt or not. Moreover, the entity bringing most consumer collection actions today is not an original creditor but a debt buyer represented by a collection law firm that brings huge numbers of cases in state courts. These realities color all aspects of consumer collection actions and point to the need for a comprehensive treatise to assist attorneys in representing consumers in such cases.

This treatise examines consumer defenses and counterclaims, the elements of the collector's causes of action, evidentiary issues, and other practical considerations. It also contains chapters covering a number of specialized issues: the rights of active duty military personnel, the collection of medical debt, debts owed the federal government, and debts arising from dishonored checks.

The treatise also details consumer protections when the collector seeks to enforce the judgment and details consumer rights to set aside or discharge that judgment. Finally, this treatise presents steps that a prevailing consumer should consider taking after a judgment is issued in favor of the consumer.

1.2 This Treatise's Organization

1.2.1 Chapters 2–6: General Consumer Defenses

Chapter 2, *infra*, is a practical chapter focusing on the reasons why attorneys should represent consumers in collection actions, tips on setting up a practice in this area, and pointers on conducting the client interview and other preliminary investigative steps. The chapter lists case selection considerations, litigation tactics, and alternatives to representing the consumer in the collection action.

Chapter 3, *infra*, examines defenses to a collection action that are not based upon the merits of the collector's claims. These defenses can be used to support a motion to dismiss and can also be used later in the proceeding. The most important such defense is the statute of limitations, which has taken on increasing importance as debt buyers bring collection actions years after a consumer defaults on the credit account. Another important group of defenses relate to the adequacy of the complaint and the supporting documents, because a number of states require the complaint to be verified or to include certain documentation. In addition, there may be issues as to whether the plaintiff is qualified to bring an action in the state's courts, whether the action is brought in the correct venue, whether there is jurisdiction to hear the case, and whether the action can be forced into arbitration.

Chapter 4, *infra*, covers the collector's proof of the merits of its allegations, both the elements of its causes of action and the evidentiary requirements as to the proof of those elements. Collectors often seek to prove their case not with their own evidence but by sending lengthy requests for admissions to the consumer, that are deemed admitted if the consumer fails to timely respond. The chapter provides advice on how to respond to such requests for admissions and how to withdraw an admission that is based solely upon the consumer's failure to answer.

Collectors also seek to prove their case at summary judgment with documentary evidence. The chapter examines the admissibility and weight to be given to two types of documentary evidence commonly submitted with such motions—affidavits and business records.

A key issue in many collection actions is whether the collector in fact owns the debt and has the right to collect on it. With the advent of debt buyers who aggressively buy and sell portfolios, the consumer's account may have passed through two, three, or even more hands before it is sold to the entity bringing the collection action. Chapter 4, *infra*, also examines the collector's burden to prove that a continuous chain of ownership has properly transferred the debt to that entity.

The chapter then turns to the elements of the collector's cause of action. Collectors often bring claims for breach of contract or for the balance owed on a credit card or other open-end account. Another common collector cause of action is "account stated," which is not based upon the contract but upon a consumer's implicit promise to pay an amount delineated in a statement of account. Other possible causes of action treated in the chapter are *quantum meruit*, money lent, goods and services, and sworn account.

Chapter 5, *infra*, focuses on basic consumer defenses and counterclaims to the collector's action. These defenses include that the debt has already been paid, settled, or discharged in bankruptcy. Other defenses relate to when someone else owes the debt (such as when the collector mistakenly sues the wrong consumer), when the consumer is the victim of identity theft or other unauthorized charges, when the consumer is only an authorized user, or when the consumer's spouse owes the money, not the consumer. The chapter also examines defenses related to the consumer's incapacity based on minority, mental incompetence, or intoxication. The chapter also considers an important consumer defense when the collector seeks a deficiency action after a car's repossession and sale—that the collector has offered insufficient proof of a commercially reasonable sale of the repossessed vehicle.

A consumer may have numerous counterclaims to a collection action. Chapter 5, *infra*, also focuses on what types of counterclaims are available and tactical considerations as to whether they should be raised in the collection action or brought as affirmative claims in a separate lawsuit brought by the consumer. The chapter looks in particular at such considerations when the counterclaim relates to the collector's litigation misconduct. The chapter concludes with a discussion of some advantages to bringing a counterclaim on a classwide basis.

Chapter 6, *infra*, reviews the collector's attempt in the collection action to recover attorney fees and other collection expenses. The chapter analyzes whether the collector has a contractual right to those fees and whether state law overrides that contract. The chapter also examines state law that allows prevailing collectors to recover attorney fees regardless of the contract terms and also considers state law that limits the size of an attorney fee award.

1.2.2 Chapters 7–10: Special Topics

Chapter 7, *infra*, looks at special rights that the Servicemembers Civil Relief Act provides for active duty military personnel in defending collection actions. The Act limits the ability of a collector to take a default judgment and also gives the servicemember the right to stay a collector's action. Military service tolls statutes of limitations, reduces the interest rate to 6% on obligations incurred before active duty, and restricts a creditor's right to self-help repossession, foreclosure, and lien enforcement. Other special rights for active duty personnel relate to automobile and residential leases and cell phone contracts. The Act provides consumer remedies for violations.

Chapter 8, *infra*, looks at criminal and civil proceedings against consumers concerning dishonored checks, including limitations on criminal prosecutions for a consumer presenting a check with insufficient funds. The chapter also looks at the operation of civil dishonored check laws and details the consumer's remedies for a collector's abuse of dishonored check laws.

Chapter 9, *infra*, is a thorough analysis of consumer law claims and defenses involving medical debt. It provides an overview of special issues raised by medical debt cases, including discriminatory or chargemaster pricing, availability of charity care, overbilling, and billing errors. The chapter also examines a number of federal and state statutes, such as the Affordable Care Act, that specifically address medical debt or can be used to protect medical debtors. It also analyzes statutory and common law defenses to medical collection actions. The chapter considers the applicability of family necessaries statutes that would impose liability on other family members and statutes that allow hospitals to place liens on the tort recoveries of consumers.

Chapter 10, *infra*, examines federal agency collection actions, including such non-litigation collection methods as administrative offset, wage garnishment, tax refund intercepts, and other remedies under the Claims Collection Act. The chapter also considers private remedies for illegal government collection actions and government prejudgment and postjudgment remedies under the Federal Debt Collection Procedures Act. While the chapter considers collection by most federal agencies, a more thorough discussion of student loan collections is found in NCLC's *Student Loan Law*.[1]

1.2.3 Chapters 11–13: Collector and Consumer Postjudgment Rights

Chapter 11, *infra*, details approaches consumers can take to set aside or discharge a judgment in the collection action that is in favor of the collector. The chapter reviews the grounds to set aside both default and stipulated judgments and then considers the relief a bankruptcy filing can offer a judgment debtor. The chapter concludes with a discussion of the advisability of an affirmative action challenging collector litigation misconduct after a judgment for the collector.

Chapter 12, *infra*, may be the most important chapter in the treatise. It considers consumer protections against the collector's postjudgment remedies. These include federal and state limits on wage garnishment and bank account seizures and exemption laws that prevent seizure of the consumer's property to satisfy a court judgment. These exemptions may apply to the consumer's homestead, personal property, benefit payments, and other assets. An important discussion is the protection from seizure of exempt federal benefits electronically deposited into the consumer's bank account. Also covered are limits on a collector's ability to seize funds in a joint bank account and prohibitions on a consumer's waiver of exemptions. The chapter also reviews interstate collection efforts, debtor's examinations, and imprisonment for debt.

Chapter 13, *infra*, reviews actions a *consumer* can take after the *consumer* prevails in the collector's collection action. The chapter discusses various theories allowing the consumer to recover attorney fees from the collector. It also examines how consumers can improve their credit reports after prevailing in the collection action. Also considered are consumer remedies in the surprising number of cases in which collectors either sell the debt to another debt buyer or continue to seek collection on the debt, even though the court has dismissed the collector's action with prejudice. The chapter concludes with a discussion of what types of litigation the consumer should consider to challenge the collector's litigation misconduct that occurred during what is now a dismissed collection action.

1 (4th ed. 2010), *updated at* www.nclc.org/library.

1.2.4 *The Appendices*

This volume contains eight appendices. Appendix A, *infra*, reprints selected portions of the Servicemembers Civil Relief Act. Appendix B, *infra*, reprints the Debt Collection Improvement Act and portions of the Debt Collection Procedures Act that regulate the collection of debts owed to the federal government. Appendix C, *infra*, reprints the federal statute and regulations protecting a portion of a consumer's wages from garnishment. Appendix D, *infra*, is the Treasury rule protecting exempt federal benefits in a consumer's bank account. Appendix E, *infra*, excerpts provisions from various federal statutes that exempt federal benefit payments from seizure to satisfy a debt, including Social Security, SSI, veteran's benefits, and civil service and federal employee retirement and disability payments.

Appendix F, *infra*, reprints the Federal Trade Commission's Credit Practices Rule that limits certain creditor remedies, such as cognovit notes, non-purchase money security interests in certain household goods, certain co-signer practices, and the waiver of exemptions. Appendix G, *infra*, summarizes each state's exemption statutes, which protect property and income from a collector's postjudgment remedies. Finally, Appendix H, *infra*, provides information on over 100 additional pleadings and primary source materials available to subscribers to this treatise.

1.2.5 *Additional Pleadings, Practice Tools, and Primary Source Materials Found Online*

NCLC has placed online for subscribers to this treatise a number of legal pleadings, practice tools, and primary source materials relevant to collection actions. Most are various types of pleadings in response to a collection lawsuit and are collected from ten of the more populous states. Other pleadings involve challenges to collection misconduct or specifically relate to hospital collections. The additional materials include statutes, regulations, and agency interpretations, as well as manuals on the Servicemembers Civil Relief Act and on hospital collections.

During 2014, this material can be accessed at www.nclc.org/webaccess, following instructions found on page ix, *supra*. In 2015, NCLC plans on providing upgraded online access to this and additional material. Information will be forthcoming, and subscribers should also go to www.nclc.org for announcements and access to this material.

1.3 Topics Covered in Other NCLC Treatises

This treatise comprehensively covers a consumer's rights when the consumer is sued in a collection action. But this volume cannot cover in detail all areas of consumer law. Consequently, this treatise should be read in conjunction with other NCLC treatises, which cover in far more detail certain types of collections or consumer rights.

A common collection lawsuit seeks a deficiency, that is, the remaining balance after a creditor forecloses on the consumer's home, repossesses the consumer's car or manufactured home, or otherwise seizes and sells the consumer's property. The creditor sells the property and deducts the sale price and other fees from the amount due on the loan. The creditor (or a debt buyer) then sues for the remainder of the original balance due, called a deficiency.

Deficiency actions raise many unique defenses and counterclaims that are examined in detail in two other NCLC treatises. *Foreclosures*[2] focuses on foreclosure of real property, including a chapter on manufactured homes. *Repossessions*[3] comprehensively covers repossessions of motor vehicles, manufactured homes, and household goods.

Chapter 10, *infra*, reviews general consumer defenses to a collection action brought by the federal government. Collection actions on student loans are so pervasive, and involve so many special issues, that they require a volume of their own: NCLC's *Student Loan Law*.[4]

This volume frequently refers to the federal Fair Debt Collection Practices Act, state debt collection law, and tort law in discussing consumer counterclaims and independent affirmative actions against the collector or collection attorney. These subjects are examined in great detail in NCLC's *Fair Debt Collection*.[5] Reference should also be made to NCLC's *Unfair and Deceptive Acts and Practices*[6] and *Consumer Class Actions*.[7]

One of the recurring themes in this treatise is the importance of the consumer's credit report in a collection action. The credit report is a key investigative tool and can be particularly helpful in cases involving identity theft, mistaken identity, or disputes over the amount owed. A review of the consumer's credit report can also indicate if it has been reviewed by the collector. If so, this information will reveal what the collector should have known about the debt and can thus help prove that a collector was seeking payment on a debt it should have known was not owed (for example, because the debt was discharged in bankruptcy). Moreover, consumers being sued upon a debt will invariably have negative information on their report. An important step for a consumer prevailing in the collection action will be to try to clean up that credit report. All these issues are examined in more detail in NCLC's *Fair Credit Reporting*.[8]

Bankruptcy can be an important consumer strategy in dealing with a collection action and a court judgment. In addition, a complete defense on a debt is that the debt has been previously discharged in bankruptcy. For a complete analysis

2 (5th ed. 2014), *updated at* www.nclc.org/library.
3 (8th ed. 2013), *updated at* www.nclc.org/library.
4 (4th ed. 2010), *updated at* www.nclc.org/library.
5 (8th ed. 2014), *updated at* www.nclc.org/library.
6 (8th ed. 2012), *updated at* www.nclc.org/library.
7 (8th ed. 2013), *updated at* www.nclc.org/library.
8 (8th ed. 2013), *updated at* www.nclc.org/library.

of all consumer bankruptcy issues, see NCLC's *Consumer Bankruptcy Law and Practice*.[9] For a step-by-step guide to assist an attorney in filing a first bankruptcy case, see NCLC's *Bankruptcy Basics*.[10]

The federal Fair Credit Billing Act and other Truth in Lending Act provisions have an impact on a collection action involving credit cards or other open-end credit. These issues are discussed in Chapters 4 and 5, *infra*, but are described in more detail in another NCLC volume, *Truth in Lending*.[11]

Chapter 11, *infra*, briefly touches on challenging the enforcement of arbitration awards obtained by collectors who used arbitration as an alternative to a court proceeding. These issues are examined in far more detail in NCLC's *Consumer Arbitration Agreements*.[12]

Other relevant NCLC publications include *Surviving Debt*[13] and *Instant Evidence*.[14] *Instant Evidence* is a handy guide to the Federal Rules of Evidence and raising objections and motions in court. Many state evidence rules parallel the federal rules.

Instant Evidence is designed to sit on the attorney's table at trial—it is twenty-one pages, spiral-bound to lay flat, and laminated to hold up to constant use. It can also be annotated with a dry-erase pen. *Surviving Debt* is an inexpensive 500-page guide for a lay audience (and paralegals and attorneys new to consumer law) on steps that families can take to deal with financial distress—everything from which debts to pay first, whether to refinance, and dealing with debt collectors to how to respond to threats of utility termination, foreclosure, repossession, or eviction.

1.4 Debt Buyers and Collection Lawsuits

1.4.1 Dramatic Growth in Debt Buying

Attorneys representing consumers in collection cases must consider the implications of the dramatic growth of the debt buying industry. A large portion of collection lawsuits are brought not by the original creditor but by a debt buyer.

Debt buying is a big business. Testimony from the Office of the Comptroller of the Currency in 2013 indicated that, in recent years, the nineteen largest banks sold about $37 billion a year in debt.[15] Estimates of total debt buyer purchases a year from all creditors far exceed $100 billion.[16]

The Comptroller of the Currency also found that the vast majority of debt sold by the nation's nineteen largest banks was credit card debt, but other debt involved automobile, home equity, mortgage, and student loans. Of course, other non-bank entities sell different types of debt, such as cell phone, utilities, and medical debt.[17] A 2013 FTC study cites industry estimates that 75% of all debt purchased involves credit card debt.[18] Recent trends indicate that non-credit-card debt purchases (for example, medical, cell phone, utilities, health spas) have been growing faster than credit card debt purchases.

Debt buyers purchase debt for pennies on the dollar. The Federal Trade Commission analyzed 3400 debt portfolios sold in 2009 and found four cents on the dollar to be the average price paid.[19] In 2013, the Office of the Comptroller of the Currency indicated that the price at which the nation's nineteen largest banks sold debt ranged from five to ten cents on the dollar, the prices having increased due to an improved economy.[20] Of course, debt sold by banks is relatively "fresh" debt, and the price that one debt buyer sells debt to another is typically much less.[21] A 2009 GAO study found that, during the economic downturn, the price to purchase debt more than three years old and/or previously placed with three collection agencies fell from one to two-and-a-half cents on the dollar to less than half a cent to a cent on the dollar.[22]

But the large amount of debt purchased at low face value is only half the story. The other half is that the same debt is often then sold from one debt buyer to another, even resold again and again between debt buyers. A chain of ownership might have four, five, or even more links. A GAO report detailed estimates that almost half of all credit card debts purchased by debt buyers are then resold to other debt buyers.[23]

Debt sold multiple times may result in ambiguities as to ownership and increasing difficulty for a debt buyer plaintiff to prove that it has an unbroken chain of ownership stretching from the original creditor. The increased separation between the entity suing on a debt and the original creditor means that the debt buyer plaintiff will also have difficulty obtaining documentation proving the underlying debt.

9 (10th ed. 2012), *updated at* www.nclc.org/library.

10 (2d ed. 2013), *updated at* www.nclc.org/library.

11 (8th ed. 2012), *updated at* www.nclc.org/library.

12 (6th ed. 2011), *updated at* www.nclc.org/library.

13 (2013).

14 (2d ed. 2013), *updated at* www.nclc.org/library.

15 *Shining a Light on the Consumer Debt Industry: Hearing Before the Subcomm. on Financial Institutions & Consumer Prot., Senate Comm. on Banking, Hous., and Urban Affairs*, 113th Cong. (July 17, 2013) (statement of the Office of the Comptroller of the Currency), *available online as companion material to this treatise*.

16 Robert Hunt, *Collecting Consumer Debt in America*, Philadelphia Fed. Reserve Bank Bus. Rev. (2d Qtr. 2007).

17 *Shining a Light on the Consumer Debt Industry: Hearing Before the Subcomm. on Financial Institutions & Consumer Prot., Senate Comm. on Banking, Hous., and Urban Affairs*, 113th Cong. (July 17, 2013) (statement of the Office of the Comptroller of the Currency), *available online as companion material to this treatise*.

18 Fed. Trade Comm'n, The Structure and Practices of the Debt Buying Industry at 12 (2013).

19 Fed. Trade Comm'n, The Structure and Practices of the Debt Buying Industry (2013).

20 *Shining a Light on the Consumer Debt Industry: Hearing Before the Subcomm. on Financial Institutions & Consumer Prot., Senate Comm. on Banking, Hous., and Urban Affairs*, 113th Cong. (July 17, 2013) (statement of the Office of the Comptroller of the Currency), *available online as companion material to this treatise*.

21 Fed. Trade Comm'n, The Structure and Practices of the Debt Buying Industry (2013).

22 U.S. Gov't Accountability Office, Credit Cards, GAO–09–748, at 29 (Sept. 2009).

23 U.S. Gov't Accountability Office, Credit Cards, GAO–09–748, at 29 (Sept. 2009).

1.4.2 Debt Buyers Identified

While debt buyers come in all shapes and sizes, and there are many small debt buyers, most collection lawsuits are brought by debt buyers who are large corporations that do business on an enormous scale, often collecting debts under a variety of names. In 2009, the ten largest debt buyers accounted for over 80% of all debt purchased.[24] These ten debt buyers were: Sherman Financial Group (purchased $11 billion in debt in 2012), Asset Acceptance Corp. (now purchased by Encore Capital Group), Encore Capital Group (presently the nation's largest debt buyer, often operating under the name Midland, purchasing $18 billion in debt in 2012), eCAST Settlement Corp., NCO Portfolio Recovery Associates, Arrow Financial Group, Portfolio Recovery Associates, Unifund Corp., B-Line, L.L.C., and Asta Funding.

But the names of top debt buyers are in constant flux. For example a number of debt buyers exited the industry in 2012, including B-Line, NCO, Arrow Financial, West Corp., and Zenith. Presumably these companies sold their debt to other debt buyers before exiting the industry. More recently, other debt buyers have been included in the list of top companies, including Square Two Financial, Ophrys, and Fourscore.

Moreover, many of the top debt buyers operate under multiple names. For example, Sherman Financial Group also does business under the names LVNV Funding, Resurgent Capital Services, Sherman Acquisitions, Alegis Corporation Group, Ventus Capital Services, Performance Recovery Group, and Ascent Card Services.

1.4.3 The Nature of Debt Sales to Debt Buyers

A debt buyer purchases thousands of accounts from a creditor or another debt buyer in one bulk sale. Usually, the actual assignment of ownership will be accomplished by the creation of three separate documents. First is a signed "forward flow" agreement—a lengthy document that will set out the terms of sale of debt in general between the creditor and debt buyer. Typically the seller will disclaim any representation as to the accuracy of the information provided and limits the buyer's access to additional information about the individual debtor's account. One forward flow agreement typically sets out the terms for multiple sales of portfolios of debt.

When a particular portfolio of debt (typically thousands of accounts) is sold, the parties execute a bill or sale or other short assignment document. That document will reference the portfolio and the forward flow agreement for the terms of the sale. That short assignment document will be accompanied by a "sale data file" or "final data file," which is an electronic spreadsheet that lists the specific consumer accounts being transferred, which will typically be numbered in the thousands.

24 Fed. Trade Comm'n, The Structure and Practices of the Debt Buying Industry (2013) (nine of the top ten accounted for 77% and one of the largest, Asset Acceptance, was not counted because it was under FTC investigation at the time).

The sale data file will have minimal information on each account. Sometimes the sale data file only includes the consumer's name, social security number, account number, and account balance. Other debt sellers provide the consumer's last known address, identity of a co-debtor, the date and amount of the last payment, the charge-off date, and/or the date and amount of the last purchase on an account.[25] This is all the debt buyer will initially receive concerning an individual debt. The debt buyer will not receive business records concerning the account, such as the contract, the credit card application, or billing statements.

The forward flow agreement will spell out what if any right the debt buyer has to go back to the debt seller to obtain additional information about an account. There may be a limit on what information on an account will be provided, or the seller will limit the number of accounts for which it is obligated to provide information. The buyer may also have to pay for such additional information.

1.4.4 Resulting Explosion in Collection Litigation

Debt buyers aggressively use state courts to collect on their purchased debt. Thus one study found that 195,000 collection lawsuits were filed in New York in 2011, most by debt buyers.[26] An analysis of over 150,000 collection actions filed in Cook County, Illinois, in 2007 found that more than half were filed by debt buyers.[27]

Consumer debt cases are clogging up state courts. One study looked at the percentage of civil cases filed in city courts in New York state that were collection filings and found the following percentages: 76% in Buffalo, 77% in Albany, and 89% in Rochester.[28] New York City Civil Court had the lowest at 36%, in large part due to new protections and requirements instituted in New York City.[29] Other studies also find that over 50% of the dockets in some courts are collection cases.[30] Just one debt buyer, Encore Capital Group, filed nearly 450,000 lawsuits around the country in 2008.[31]

25 Fed. Trade Comm'n, The Structure and Practices of the Debt Buying Industry C–7 (2013); Robert Hunt, *Collecting Consumer Debt in America*, Philadelphia Fed. Reserve Bank Bus. Rev. (2d Qtr. 2007).

26 New Economy Project, The Debt Collection Racket in New York (June 2013).

27 Brief of Amici Curiae Legal Assistance Found. of Metro. Chi., Nat'l Ass'n of Consumer Advocates, and Am. Ass'n of Retired Persons in Support of Defendant-Appellee, Portfolio Acquisitions, L.L.C. v. Feltman, 909 N.E.2d 876 (Ill. App. Ct. 2009).

28 New Economy Project, The Debt Collection Racket in New York (June 2013).

29 *Id.*

30 Richard M. Hynes, *Broke But Not Bankrupt: Consumer Debt Collection in State Courts*, 60 Fla. L. Rev. 1 (Jan. 2008); Urban Justice, Debt Weight, the Consumer Credit Crisis in New York City and Its Impact on the Working Poor (Oct. 2007).

31 As listed in Encore Capital Group's 2008 10K statement filed with the Securities Exchange Commission, which is available at www.sec.gov/Archives/edgar/data/1084961/000119312509024779/d10k.htm.

1.4.5 Characteristics of Debt Buyer Collection Lawsuits

Consumer debt is sold for pennies on the dollar because it does not make economic sense for a creditor to prepare a case for litigation, litigate a case, and collect a resulting judgment for the amount at stake. Instead, debt buyers develop a mass production model, somewhat akin to manufacturing widgets, to inexpensively collect on these consumer debts. Debts from many creditors are consolidated with one debt buyer who produces affidavits and related information on a mass production basis and forwards this information to a large collection law firm. The law firm also works on a mass production basis, producing complaints in bulk, filing many complaints on the same day in the same court, and appearing for hearings for many cases in the same court on the same day.

For example, over 70% of the 320,000 collection actions brought in New York City in 2006 were brought by just four law firms: Pressler & Pressler, Cohen & Slamowitz, Mel S. Harris & Associates, and Wolpoff & Abramson.[32] In New York City alone, on average *each* of these four firms *each week* filed over 1000 new cases and obtained over 800 default judgments in other cases. Interestingly, shortly after 2006 Wolpoff & Abramson sought even larger economies of scale and merged with another huge collection firm, Mann Bracken.

It is no coincidence that this system results in robo-signing abuses wherein affiants rubber-stamp affidavits without reading them and notaries notarize signatures without seeing an individual actually sign the document. Nor is it a coincidence that there are so many errors in the affidavits, attachments that are not attached, and glaring errors in the legal complaints.

Even this model does not make economic sense if the collector's attorney has to produce adequate evidence and participate in a contested case. Instead the large majority of cases result in default judgments. If the collection attorney cannot obtain a default judgment, the attorney may seek to convince the unrepresented consumer to settle the case for most of the amount due. If neither approach succeeds, the collection attorney may even dismiss the case if the consumer contests the matter and refuses to settle. One sampling of debt buyer lawsuits found none went to trial or were resolved on the merits.[33]

In virtually none of the cases filed by debt buyers does the collection attorney face a consumer represented by an attorney. A Maryland study found that in only 2% of collection lawsuits was the consumer represented by an attorney.[34] Another study found that attorneys represented consumers in only 2% of the 195,000 collection cases filed in New York in 2011.[35] Before a number of pro bono programs were instituted, an earlier study had found the percentage was well under 1%.[36]

It is thus not surprising that this system works for debt buyers. Estimates are as high as 90% of collection lawsuits resulting in default judgments,[37] and very few of these are ever set aside. One study found only about 2% of the default judgments in New York City are later set aside.[38] And of course many of the cases not resulting in default judgments resulted in settlements very favorable to the collector. As a result, collectors in New York City in one year recovered about $800 million of the almost $1 billion sought.[39]

The fact that cases are never contested also means the debt buyers do not have to worry about adequate legal pleadings. A New York City study also found that in 99% of the cases in which default judgments were entered, the materials underlying those applications constituted inadmissible hearsay and did not meet New York's standards for the entry of a default judgment.[40] In 85% of the cases, the supporting evidence was an affidavit from the debt buyer's own employee, and in another 12% it was from an employee of an unidentified entity.[41] Another study concluded that, among the sample of cases reviewed, no application by a debt buyer for a default judgment complied with New York law.[42]

32 Urban Justice, Debt Weight, the Consumer Credit Crisis in New York City and Its Impact on the Working Poor (Oct. 2007).

33 New Economy Project, The Debt Collection Racket in New York (June 2013).

34 Peter Holland, *Junk Justice: A Statistical Analysis of 4400 Lawsuits Filed by Debt Buyers*, 26 Loy. Consumer L. Rev. 179 (2014).

35 New Economy Project, The Debt Collection Racket in New York (June 2013).

36 Urban Justice, Debt Weight, the Consumer Credit Crisis in New York City and Its Impact on the Working Poor (Oct. 2007).

37 McCollough v. Johnson, Rodenburg & Lauinger, L.L.C., 637 F.3d 939 (9th Cir. 2011) (Montana collection attorney estimated that 90% of collection lawsuits result in a default); Fed. Trade Comm'n, Repairing a Broken System 7 (July 2010) (most panelists from around the country at FTC hearings indicated that the 90% figure was about right; also citing a number of studies); The Legal Aid Soc'y, Debt Deception 6 (May 2010) (study of New York City collection lawsuits found that 94.3% of cases in sample resulted in a default judgment or a settlement); *Dignity Faces a Steamroller: Small-Claims Proceedings Ignore Rights, Tilt to Collectors*, Boston Globe, July 31, 2006 (study of collection actions in Massachusetts found an 80% default rate).

38 Urban Justice, Debt Weight, the Consumer Credit Crisis in New York City and Its Impact on the Working Poor (Oct. 2007).

39 *Id.*

40 *Id.*

41 *Id.*

42 New Economy Project, The Debt Collection Racket in New York (June 2013).

Chapter 2 Case Selection, Advising the Client, and Litigation Strategy

2.1 Ten Reasons to Defend Consumer Collection Actions

2.1.1 Reason #1: Consumers Often Have Dispositive Defenses

Many people, including some judges, assume that when a collector sues on a debt the consumer almost always owes the money. Whatever the accuracy of this view in times past, changed practices in the marketplace have dramatically altered the facts. Today, consumers have complete defenses in a significant number of collection cases.

The major reason for this change is the explosive expansion of the multi-billion dollar distressed-debt-buying industry, in which debt collectors purchase literally millions of old consumer debts for pennies on the dollar from the original creditors. The debt buyers receive minimal information on each account and certainly do not receive the contract or copies of any communications in which the consumer might have disputed the amount owed. Debt buyers also regularly resell repackaged portfolios of debts to other debt buyers whose connection to the original creditor—and to original documentation and proof—is even more attenuated.

Because debt buyers purchase very old debt, the statute of limitations is an important consumer defense. Debt buyers who cannot produce the written contract often bring the case on an account stated or other claim not based upon a written contract.[1] In many states, such causes of action have a shorter limitations period than a claim based upon a written contract.[2] Credit card collection cases, even when brought on a contract theory, may have to be brought within a shorter limitations period applying to non-written contracts.[3] Moreover, the action may have to be brought within a shorter limitations period found in the law of some state other than the forum state.[4]

Because the debts are old, the consumer often will have moved after the credit account was closed, and the debt buyer must first try to locate the consumer's present residence. Debt buyers may try to serve the consumer at the wrong address[5] or even sue the wrong consumer.[6] Debt buyers rely on credit reports to locate the consumer, but the credit reports themselves are filled with errors, including "mismerged" information that mixes the credit reports of two or more people with similar names and other identifying information, which results in the collector then suing the wrong person.

Quite often, the debt buyer does not have sufficient evidence to prove its case, relies on business records that are not properly introduced into evidence, or tries to prove its case based on clearly defective affidavits.[7] Debt buyers frequently cannot even prove that they own the debt they are collecting.[8] Debt buyers may not have access to better evidence or may not want to expend the resources acquiring that evidence, so they try to win cases by default without an ability to prove that money is owed.

Creditors also may commit billing errors which may be the reason the creditor stopped collection efforts—the consumer did not owe all or part of the money claimed. When these debts are sold, the debt buyer does not receive or retain this information concerning consumer defenses. The consumer can then defend the collection action based upon the original dispute the consumer had with the creditor.[9]

Too often debt buyers will bring actions against spouses and other parties knowing these defendants do not owe the debt but hoping to either pressure them into payment or obtain a default judgment against them.[10] Examples include suits against authorized users not liable on the account and against family members of a deceased debtor. The debt buying business model is to cast a wide net without consideration as to whether the consumer owes the money and see what money is recovered.

At the same time that debt buyers are suing people without sufficient knowledge whether they actually owe the money or whether the statute of limitations has run, there has also been an explosion of identity theft and unauthorized use of credit cards. While federal law states that consumers in these situations do not owe the money,[11] collectors frequently sue the consumer regardless.

Another factor leading to the recent increase in valid consumer defenses is that creditors have aggressively offered credit to almost anyone, including college and even high school students. Credit is being thrust upon not only the young but also upon others who traditionally would not have been eligible. This practice leads to the increased relevance of the defense of lack of capacity, including that the consumer was underage, had mental disabilities, or was intoxicated at the time of the credit offer.[12]

1 *See* Ch. 4, *infra*.
2 *See* § 3.5.4.2, *infra*.
3 *See* § 3.5.6.3.2, *infra*.
4 *See* § 3.5.3, *infra*.
5 *See* § 11.3.10.1, *infra*.
6 *See* § 5.3.1, *infra*.
7 *See* § 4.2, *infra*.
8 *See* § 4.3, *infra*.
9 *See* Ch. 5, *infra*.
10 *See* § 5.3, *infra*.
11 *See* § 5.3.2, *infra*.
12 *See* § 5.4.1, *infra*.

Another change in the marketplace is that many creditors base their profitability on consumers *not* paying their debts. Creditors are content to load up interest charges and fees on those who pay less than the minimum amount due. Collectors also seek enormous extra charges when suing on the debt, including finance charges at jacked up rates and unreasonable or even illegal attorney fees. Because most cases end in unexamined default judgments, there is little incentive for the collector to limit the amount requested in such fees in addition to the original debt. But such fees may not even be available based upon the legal theories the collector utilized in the case, or the amount sought may be more than is authorized by state law.[13]

The bottom line is that attorneys, judges, and the public must readjust their expectations. When consumers are sued, the operating assumption, more likely than not, is that the consumer does not owe the amount sought or that the collector will not be able to prove its case against the consumer. Certainly the assumption should never be that the consumer owes the amount the collector is seeking.

2.1.2 Reason #2: Stopping Systematic Abuse of the Justice System

Debt buyers today are using the courts to engage in wholesale litigation abuse. They sue huge numbers of consumers with no real knowledge of whether the consumer owes the debt or whether the statute of limitations has run. Debt buyers sue with little or no evidence to prove that the consumer owes the money, that the debt buyer in fact owns the debt, or even that they are suing the right consumer. This litigation strategy is effective because very few consumers obtain legal representation, and the overwhelming majority of consumer defendants default in the collection action.

When the consumer contests an action, the collector utilizes various techniques to win without having to produce admissible evidence to prove its claim. The collector may take advantage of the unrepresented consumer by working out a stipulated judgment without disclosing that the collector cannot prove the debt. Another technique is to send the consumer a long list of requests for admission to which the consumer does not timely respond. The requests are deemed admitted, and the collector needs no other evidence to prove its case.[14] Alternatively, collectors seek summary judgment on junk evidence—attachments that are not attached, affidavits from employees (or even non-employees) of a debt buyer who state conclusory facts about which the affiant has no personal knowledge, or about pretend business records created years after the fact.

Consumers fare much better in court when they obtain legal representation. Many debt buyers will not even pursue the case once they realize the consumer has legal representation. Such an individual consumer victory has no adverse impact on a debt buyer that has purchased the debt for pennies on the dollar. But that strategy may educate the court as to the shoddy practices of certain debt buyers and collection attorneys. The next time the collector or collection attorney brings a series of cases asking that court to enter default judgments, the court may look more closely at the collector's evidence, throw out large numbers of uncontested collection actions, or establish standards for when default judgments will be allowed in uncontested consumer collection matters. For example, courts and legislatures have enacted rules or statutes, respectively, to deal with these abuses in Delaware, Maryland, Massachusetts, North Carolina, and other states.

Individual collection litigation can be the vehicle that creates a jurisdiction's controlling standards. A collector or collection attorney who brings cases that are clearly not actionable under those established standards runs a significant risk that a Fair Debt Collection Practices Act (FDCPA) class action will succeed in producing a large award for the class.

For example, individual litigation in a collection case may establish the state's rule recognizing, for example, a three-year limitations period for an account stated claim or barring an account stated claim on an "account statement" that the debt buyer created and sent to the consumer years after the creditor wrote off the account, thereby resulting in FDCPA liability for future actions.[15]

2.1.3 Reason #3: Counterclaims Can Result in the Recovery of Damages and Attorney Fees

In many collection actions the consumer will have significant counterclaims. Being able to raise consumer claims as counterclaims has both advantages and disadvantages. Some of the advantages are that filing fees may be avoided and federal claims can stay in state court. Disadvantages include that the collector may be less willing to dismiss its claims and may prosecute the collection case more aggressively in order to vigorously contest the counterclaim.

A good example of a collection case that raises numerous potential counterclaims is when the collector is seeking to recover a deficiency after a car repossession and sale. The consumer may have counterclaims under Uniform Commercial Code (UCC) Article 9 and other state laws relating to the repossession and sale or to the original sale and performance of the vehicle. In many collection cases, consumers can also raise counterclaims based upon the FDCPA and related debt harassment theories.[16] It may even be possible to raise counterclaims related to the collector's litigation misconduct.[17] Legal representation can thus result not only in dismissal of the collector's case but also in the consumer's recovery of significant damages and attorney fees.

13 *See* Ch. 6, *infra*.

14 *See* § 4.2.2, *infra*.

15 *See* § 13.4, *infra*.

16 *See* § 5.5.4, *infra*.

17 *See* § 5.5.5, *infra*.

2.1.4 Reason #4: Prevailing in the Collection Action Can Improve a Consumer's Credit Rating

Consumers are rightfully concerned about their credit rating, and prevailing in the collection action can have an impact on their credit record. If the case is dismissed, the consumer can take action to ensure that credit reports indicate that the current balance of that debt is now reported as zero.[18] If the judge also rules that the consumer never owed the money (for example, because the collector sued the wrong consumer), then the consumer can seek to delete information in their consumer report that the debt had been in default in the past.[19] In addition the consumer attorney can help the consumer dispute inaccurate information in a credit report, and the consumer has a cause of action under the Fair Credit Reporting Act (FCRA) if that information is not properly investigated and corrected.[20]

2.1.5 Reason #5: Alleviation of Emotional Distress

Being sued can be extremely upsetting for some clients, particularly older and vulnerable consumers. Some may never have been sued in their whole lives and can become very distressed over a suit, even for a relatively minor debt. That distress can have medical consequences, which can be accentuated when the consumer cannot obtain legal representation to explain to them what is happening and to defend the consumer's interests.

2.1.6 Reason #6: Protection of the Consumer's Assets and Income

A judgment for a collector can have serious consequences for the consumer's assets and income, particularly for lower-income consumers.[21] Assets in bank accounts are likely to be seized. Wages can be garnished. Cars and other property can be seized. Defeating a collection action can eliminate these threats. Even if a default judgment has already been entered, an attorney can assist the consumer either in setting aside the default judgment or in minimizing the impact of these creditor remedies.

2.1.7 Reason #7: Collection Clients Often Have FDCPA, FCRA, and Other Consumer Claims

Representing consumers in collection actions can lead an attorney to discover that the consumer has separate affirmative actions under the FDCPA, FCRA, and other federal and state statutes, resulting in significant actual and statutory damages and attorney fees, either on an individual or class-wide basis. Investigating the facts relating to the collection action will often uncover various systematic law violations. Consumer attorneys taking collection defense cases find this an effective way to grow their practices.

The consumer's attorney should normally not pursue these affirmative claims without first resolving the individual collection action, as there will be legal and tactical reasons to complete the collection action first.[22] Moreover, the client is unlikely to be interested in retaining an attorney to handle an affirmative action while that attorney turns down the request for representation in the collection action.

2.1.8 Reason # 8: Debt Collector May Have to Pay the Consumer's Attorney Fees

Attorneys often shy away from collection cases for fear their time will be uncompensated. The consumer may be willing to offer a modest retainer, which still may not cover the attorney's time and expenses. Nevertheless, there are a number of ways that a prevailing consumer can recover attorney fees from the collector, as set out in § 13.1, *infra*. Fees may be recovered by statute in about twenty states. Fees are also available to the consumer for prevailing on certain counterclaims, or as a result of the collector's bringing an action without adequate facts.

2.1.9 Reason #9: Development of Expertise and a Name in the Community

Attorneys report very good results representing consumers in collection actions, particularly those brought by debt buyers. Many attorneys build on this success to develop expertise in this area. That capability in turn enhances one's reputation as a consumer attorney among judges, other attorneys, and the community at large, thus leading to increased referrals of other collection cases and also other consumer law matters.

2.1.10 Reason #10: Defending a Collection Action Allows for a Class Action to Stay in State Court

The Class Action Fairness Act (CAFA) has resulted in many state court consumer class actions being removed to federal court.[23] Class actions can avoid removal and stay in state court only if they allege state law causes of action and include fewer than 100 class members or seek less than $5 million. Otherwise they can be removed to federal court unless two-thirds of the class members and all the primary defendants are residents of the state.[24]

Defense of a consumer collection action provides an exception. A class counterclaim brought in the collection action

18 *See* § 13.2, *infra*.
19 *Id.*
20 *Id.*
21 *See* § 2.4, Ch. 12, *infra*.
22 *See* § 5.5, *infra*.
23 *See* § 5.5.1.3, *infra*.
24 *See* National Consumer Law Center, Consumer Class Actions § 2.4 (8th ed. 2013), *updated at* www.nclc.org/library.

cannot be removed to federal court, even if it could be removed if brought as an affirmative action.[25] CAFA allows only the defendant to remove a case, not the plaintiff. Class counterclaims thus can stay in state court even if they allege federal causes of action.[26]

2.2 Setting Up a Consumer Collection Defense Legal Practice

2.2.1 Obtaining Clients

There is an almost unlimited number of consumers being sued in collection actions needing representation. With effective marketing attorneys wishing to take these cases will typically find they have too many consumers seeking representation, not too few. Traditional sources of marketing are effective, such as the yellow pages, websites, and the like. Bar associations also have referral panels. Legal aid offices may welcome the ability to refer these cases to private attorneys.

Private attorneys are particularly happy to provide referrals. Most attorneys view consumer collection defense cases as economic drains and have no interest in either pursuing them or receiving compensation for the referral. They are thrilled to be able to refer the consumer to someone who makes known a willingness to take these cases.

Consumers who have been sued may try to consult lawyers in general practice, family law attorneys, personal injury attorneys, and others. For example, personal injury lawyers will have clients with unpaid medical bills. Family law lawyers will often have clients who were supporting one household and are now supporting two households. Getting one's name around to these attorneys should produce a steady supply of clients. Advertising or placing articles in the local bar association periodical can heighten the attorney's exposure.

A key referral source is bankruptcy attorneys, whom the consumer attorney should consider contacting in person. Consumers being sued, or those with serious debt delinquencies, often go to bankruptcy attorneys, and many of these consumers are dissuaded from proceeding with a bankruptcy because their debt load is too low, relative to the costs of filing bankruptcy, or bankruptcy is not a good option for some other reason. Bankruptcy attorneys should be only too happy to refer such cases to a consumer attorney willing to explore other debt defense options. Bankruptcy trustees are another potential referral source.

Other sources of referrals are court clerks and even judges who on a daily basis see unrepresented consumers unable to adequately represent their interests in court. Effectively handling a few cases in a court can lead to many others. It is also worth exploring whether you can assist the local court in providing education to consumers and court personnel about collection actions. An attorney can even offer to hold a debtors' defense clinic.

25 *See* § 5.5.1.3, *infra*.
26 *Id.*

2.2.2 Office Resources

The consumer attorney should obtain copies of all court rules for the courts in which collection actions are traditionally brought in that state. The attorney should also start collecting and organizing copies of all relevant statutes and case law. This library will slowly grow and will pay enormous dividends in the long run. Also included should be selected law treatises, including any state-specific manual on collection cases. Other particularly good choices are NCLC's *Fair Debt Collection*[27] and *Fair Credit Reporting*.[28] For deficiency cases following repossessions, an essential resource is NCLC's *Repossessions*.[29] For student loan cases, NCLC's *Student Loan Law*[30] is indispensable. NCLC's *Truth in Lending*[31] details important new consumer substantive rights concerning credit cards and credit card collection cases.

A useful office resource is a client brochure (containing the attorney's contact information) that explains what to do if the consumer has been sued. This is helpful if the attorney decides not to represent the consumer, in that the consumer is at least provided some assistance and the consumer leaves with a more favorable impression of the attorney. The brochure can also discuss the advantages of an attorney and cost issues, and this brochure circulated in the community may be a source of referrals for the attorney.

NCLC's *Surviving Debt*[32] is a comprehensive guide for families in financial distress, covering everything from defending collection actions to the bankruptcy option, budgeting, staving off foreclosures, and much more. The book may be helpful for paralegals in the office, and some consumer attorneys purchase *Surviving Debt* in quantities of 100 at very low prices and then distribute the book to clients or to counselors, clergy, social workers, and others in the community.

2.3 First Steps in Meeting with a Client

2.3.1 When the Consumer Has Not Yet Been Sued

Consumers may seek legal representation before they are sued on a debt. Debt collection contacts can be stopped by the consumer sending a "cease communication" letter to a collection agency or a debt buyer.[33] If that fails, an attorney letter should succeed.[34] The consumer can also be advised about how to document abusive collection contacts.[35]

27 (8th ed. 2014).
28 (8th ed. 2013), *updated at* www.nclc.org/library.
29 (8th ed. 2013), *updated at* www.nclc.org/library.
30 (4th ed. 2010), *updated at* www.nclc.org/library.
31 (8th ed. 2012), *updated at* www.nclc.org/library.
32 (2013) (504 pages).
33 *See* National Consumer Law Center, Fair Debt Collection § 5.9 (8th ed. 2014), *updated at* www.nclc.org/library.
34 *Id.* § 5.3.3.
35 *Id.* § 2.4.1.

The attorney should also explain to the consumer what a summons and complaint look like and how they are served. It is probably a good idea to advise the consumer to accept all certified mail, because failure to do so will likely shorten the time the consumer has to respond to a summons and increase the likelihood of a default. Upon receipt of a complaint the consumer should be advised to contact the attorney immediately.

The attorney can also warn the client of the risks of various quick fixes, such as debt elimination, debt settlement scams, or refinancing unsecured debt into a home mortgage or other secured debt. Other offers to avoid include credit repair agencies and Internet offers to help consumers defend collection actions brought against them. These are described briefly at § 2.7, *infra*.

2.3.2 What the Client Should Bring to the First Interview

The decision whether to take a case will be greatly facilitated by the consumer bringing to the first interview all relevant documentation. When talking to a prospective client on the phone, before almost anything else, tell the consumer not to write on any documents relating to the case. Too often consumers will have the original of such documents in front of them when calling the attorney and will take notes of their conversation on the originals of the documents!

Consumers should be told to bring in absolutely everything that has been sent to them regarding the matter, including envelopes. Consumers should also bring in all debt collection correspondence, any answering machine that has messages from collectors, any and all statements and paperwork relating to the account, any canceled checks or bank statements reflecting payments, and even the credit card itself. Consumers who have already received a credit report should bring it in too; but consumers who have not yet obtained their report should be told to wait to do so until they come to the attorney's office, when the report can be accessed using the precautions discussed in the next subsection.

A consumer who has defaulted on one debt likely has others. The attorney should consider having the consumer bring in this information concerning *all* of the consumer's debts. Such an over-inclusive request may also be the only way to insure that the consumer brings in all the documents related to the debt at issue, as the consumer is unlikely to have separate files for each debt. Finding out about all of the consumer's debts also will help the attorney formulate a strategy to protect the consumer's assets. Fighting off one judgment will not do much good for consumers who already have, or in the near future will have, other judgments entered against them. The documents relating to other debts may also uncover Fair Debt Collection Practices Act or other consumer law violations that the attorney may decide are worth pursuing.

2.3.3 Reviewing the Consumer's Credit Report

A consumer's credit report is a key document that can help the attorney unravel many aspects of a case. It will usually show the current status of an account, the amount owed, and who provided that information. It will also show the history of the account and who reported that historical information.

The report will show the last payment, the date of the account's charge-off, which is usually six months after the date of the last payment, and may show the date a debt buyer purchased the debt. The report will indicate public record information, such as bankruptcies. The report can provide evidence of identity theft, or that the collector has mistakenly sued the wrong consumer. The credit report itself will also disclose who has obtained a credit report on the consumer in the past year. As a result the report may show that a particular collector knew or should have known of the exculpatory information reported and that the collector still pursued its predetermined course of action, thus proving that it engaged in the misconduct willfully, intentionally, and with full knowledge of its wrongdoing.

The consumer is entitled to one free report a year from each of the three major reporting agencies. While a report can easily be accessed over the Internet, Internet reports may not be as complete as hard copy reports mailed to the client. Also, there is always the risk in dealing with Internet sites that the consumer will click an agreement to terms that may include a hidden arbitration requirement. Details on obtaining a report are found in § 13.2.4, *infra*. A good strategy may be to obtain only one free report at first and save the other two free reports for a later time.

It makes sense for the consumer to obtain the report in the attorney's office with the assistance of the attorney or the attorney's staff and with the aid of the attorney's Internet connection and printers. Unskilled consumers who attempt to access their reports on their own may mistakenly purchase extra services that the credit bureaus foist on them, seek more than one credit report, or fail to properly print out the report or save it electronically. The consumer attorney should not only obtain the consumer's permission to order the report but should have the consumer present when this is done, because the reporting agency may require various identifying information concerning the consumer before providing the report. Obtaining the report with the consumer shows the consumer how to do it in the future and also eliminates any question as to whether the attorney had authority to obtain the report.

Letting the consumer go home with a copy of the report is also a positive in developing a relationship with the attorney. The consumer has left the office with something concrete.

Some attorneys prefer that potential clients obtain the report on their own, using the toll free number for a free report (1–877–322–8228). Using this number prevents the client from clicking the wrong box on an Internet site when, for example, the consumer might agree to arbitration. The attorney explains how to order a report over the phone, and, if the client is unwilling to do this, then the attorney has to decide whether this is a suitable client. Of course, when a disability or special circumstances make it difficult for the potential client to perform this task, then that is another matter.

Another option is to have hard copies in the office of the form used to request a credit report that is very easy to fill out. The client fills it out on the spot and mails it in. Usually the report is received in two weeks, and the client is asked to return with the results. Whether the client in fact returns is considered by some attorneys to be a good screening tactic to ensure the client's seriousness.

2.3.4 The Client Interview and Questions to Ask

An attorney should develop a system to obtain basic information from the client without taking up too much of the attorney's time, so that the attorney can focus on the important parts of the interview. This habit is particularly important when the attorney follows the useful practice of obtaining information not just about the debt in question but about all of the consumer's debt issues. While all that information may be invaluable in effectively representing the consumer, it can also take a long time to review all of this information.

One approach is to have a paralegal or office assistant work with the consumer in recording basic information. Another approach is to develop a standard questionnaire that the consumer can be asked to fill out with or without the assistance of office staff. Some questions can be sent to the consumer in advance, or asked over the telephone.

The attorney can then focus on the more important parts of the interview. An essential part of any client interview is to lower client expectations if they are too high. It is much better for a client to be pleasantly surprised by an outcome than to be disappointed by an outcome that the consumer's own attorney believes to be a good one.

Another key issue is to determine the procedural status of a case. Besides talking to the consumer and reviewing the documents the consumer brings in, this task may require contacting the opponent's attorney or the court. Has the consumer just been served with the complaint? Is an answer or response to admissions due imminently or overdue? Has the collector moved for summary judgment? Has the consumer defaulted? Has the collector obtained a default judgment? How long ago? Has the collector begun instituting postjudgment remedies?

In particular, note all deadlines, such as those to answer the complaint or respond to requests for admissions. Determine whether the court in which the action is brought is in the judicial district where the consumer resides or where the contract was signed. Otherwise, venue may not be proper.[36]

Also, listen to and hear everything the consumer has to say. Potentially material information includes anything about the consumer's health, job, and age, as well as any debt collection contacts prior to the collection action and even the nature of the transaction underlying the debt. Look for any evidence of identity theft and anything that might lead to a counterclaim. Check to see if the consumer is in, or recently was on, active duty in the military, as this status provides special defenses.[37]

A collection case can drag on for some time and can be further extended if there is any follow-up litigation.[38] It is important for the attorney to be able to communicate with the client over that period, even if the client has moved or changed phone numbers. Thus it is useful to obtain additional contact information for the client, such as all telephone and cell phone numbers, e-mail addresses, and work and home addresses, as well as contact information for two or three other people who will always know how to reach the consumer.

A key issue in any collection action will be the consequences for the consumer of a judgment for the collector. In particular, what assets and wages can the collector seize pursuant to the judgment? This issue is explored in § 2.3.6, *infra*.

Carefully read the complaint and all attachments. If attachments are missing, do not assume the consumer lost them. Debt buyers frequently fail to attach those attachments referenced in the complaint. Note whether the plaintiff is the original creditor or a debt buyer. See what evidence is attached to the complaint that a debt buyer in fact owns the debt. If a contract is available, review the choice of law provision.

Compute whether the limitations period has run. A key factor will be determining when the last payment was made on the account. Another factor will be whether the forum state's limitations period applies or whether a shorter limitations period is applicable under the law of the state chosen in the contract's choice of law provision or the state where the credit agreement arose. Also determine from the complaint exactly what causes of action the collector is alleging, and see what evidence the collector may have for each cause of action. Look at the attorney fees and finance charges being sought, determine if they are legal under existing law for the specific claims being brought, and determine whether the collector can justify them.

Ask the consumer in detail about the underlying transaction that resulted in the debt. Did it involve medical debt, a student loan, a dishonored check, a credit card, a cell phone bill, or the like? Each different type of debt may present different defenses and counterclaims.[39] For example, if the collector is seeking a deficiency after an automobile repossession, then the attorney should explore with the consumer the nature of the default (did the creditor suddenly repossess after customarily allowing late payment, thus possibly waiving default), whether the creditor complied with a state right to cure or right to reinstate law, whether the repossession breached the peace, what notices of sale and of a deficiency the consumer received, and other aspects of the repossession. The attorney should even ask about the underlying sale of the vehicle to see if there were unfair sales tactics, credit violations, or problems with the vehicle.

---

36 *See* § 3.2.2, *infra*.

37 *See* Ch. 7, *infra*.

38 *See* § 13.4, *infra*.

39 *See, e.g.*, Chs. 4, 8–10, *infra*.

Explore whether the consumer was the principal owner of a credit account, or only an authorized user. What is the basis for the consumer's alleged liability? Does the consumer believe payments were made that are not reflected in the account balance? Are there unauthorized charges involved?

2.3.5 Evaluating the Collector and the Collector's Attorney

A key factor in any collection action will be an appraisal of the litigation tactics that are typical of both the collector and the collector's attorney. Do the collector and collection attorney typically pursue cases aggressively, or do they drop them upon the first hint that the matter will be contested? Is the collector's attorney even familiar with what is necessary to prevail in a contested action?

Other attorneys are probably the best source of information on the litigation tendencies of the collector and the collector's attorney. The collector and collector's attorney can also be the subject of a Westlaw or Lexis search, or a search of a state-specific litigation database, similar to the federal PACER system.

2.3.6 Do Judgment-Proof Debtors Need Representation?

An important part of a client interview is to understand the client's assets and income that are at risk if the collector prevails in the court action. A debtor who possesses *only* exempt assets is referred to as "judgment proof" or "collection proof." While a judgment may be taken against such a person, the creditor cannot compel collection of the judgment from the debtor's income or assets, unless the debtor fails to properly claim the exemption or circumstances change.

Judgment-proof debtors formerly were unlikely to be sued except by high-volume collection firms that do not make any pre-suit assessment of the prospects of collection. The growth of the debt buying industry, however, is making suits against judgment-proof debtors more common, since debt buyers do not evaluate individual cases but instead use a scattershot approach.

Creditors also may pursue a judgment because the debtor's or the exempt property's status may change in the future. For example, in many states a homestead loses that status when the owner-occupant dies, and a judgment lien will generally be paid by the decedent's estate to clear the title. The debtor may receive training that makes employment viable. Also the creditor may need to obtain a judgment in order to protect the debt from being barred by the statute of limitations.

A client's limited vulnerability to judgment is often the key factor in devising a strategy of representation. Although bankruptcy is often not a prudent option to deal with a limited number of minor debts, the advisability of the bankruptcy option will depend in part on the consumer's vulnerability to postjudgment remedies. The advocate must first determine which of the low-income client's assets are available to creditors. A debtor who has nonexempt wages may want to consider a chapter 7 (liquidating) bankruptcy if there are substantial debts and little other property available to creditors.[40] Nonexempt equity in a home threatened by creditors presents yet a different scenario and suggests that consideration should be given to a chapter 13 (installment payment plan) bankruptcy.[41] While property exemption laws are fundamental to bankruptcy cases, many exemptions are also available outside of bankruptcy, and a truly judgment-proof debtor is not likely to need bankruptcy at all.

Some attorneys consider defense of a debt collection suit brought against a judgment-proof client to be a low priority unless there is a substantial potential counterclaim. Remember, however, that judgment-proof individuals are sometimes targets for debt collection abuse. Because ordinary legal tactics are not effective, collectors attempt to scare these judgment debtors into paying "voluntarily." Representing a consumer in an affirmative suit against a debt collector for collection abuse may remove a source of grave stress for the client and provide some relief for the client's financial hardship. In addition an unsatisfied judgment can stay on the consumer's credit record until the statute of limitations for the judgment has expired, but no less than seven years.[42] Finally, the growth of the debt buyer industry means that judgment debts are rarely abandoned. Debt buyers may invoke postjudgment remedies repeatedly over a period of years until they find some asset that the debtor cannot protect or fails to protect.

2.3.7 Case Selection

2.3.7.1 Procedural Status of the Case

The first criterion in deciding whether to take a case is the procedural status of the litigation. Sometimes the consumer comes to the attorney years after a default or stipulated judgment was entered, when the collector is just getting around to garnishing wages or bank accounts. The first step (after making sure the consumer asserts all available exemptions concerning garnishment) will require the consumer to set aside a default judgment and then successfully defend the collection action. Most jurisdictions establish special hurdles to set aside a default judgment entered more than one year earlier, but even then relief is still possible.[43] At this point the attorney will have to decide whether setting aside the judgment is the appropriate approach, whether the consumer should file bankruptcy, or whether the attorney should help the consumer resist the creditor's remedies.[44] If a default judgment has not been entered in a case, then the factors discussed in the succeeding subsections will determine case selection.

---

40 *See generally* National Consumer Law Center, Consumer Bankruptcy Law and Practice Ch. 3 (10th ed. 2012), *updated at* www.nclc.org/library.

41 *Id.* Ch. 4.

42 15 U.S.C. § 1681c(a)(2). *See* National Consumer Law Center, Fair Credit Reporting § 5.2.3.4 (8th ed. 2013), *updated at* www.nclc.org/library.

43 *See* § 11.3, *infra*.

44 *See* §§ 11.3, 11.5, Ch. 12, *infra*.

2.3.7.2 The Client

An important consideration in the decision whether to take the case is the client. Is the client likely to stay in touch throughout the whole length of the case, or is the client likely to lose interest and fail to attend a critical hearing? Are the client's expectations unreasonably high, indicating it may be difficult to conclude the case to the client's satisfaction? Of course, as in any litigation, an important factor may be how sympathetic the client is. Does the client have a compelling story to explain why the debt has not been paid? Does the client have a solid defense to payment? Does the client have viable counterclaims?

Of course, the client's credibility will be important when the client is a witness. Beware of the client who believes he understands the law, particularly when that understanding includes some popular but bizarre legal theories, such as "no money lent," "illegally monetized" debt, or "vapor money," or when the client thinks he can pick a bogus arbitration company to rule the debt is not owed. The client may aggravate not only his own attorney but also the court.

The attorney must also warn the client of the risks of litigation, including the fact that the collector's attorney fees may be higher if the collector wins after a contested case than if the collector prevailed without a contest. A potential client's response to that warning should be a factor in case selection.

2.3.7.3 The Collector

Probably no factor will be as determinative of the nature of the litigation as the identity of the collector and, in particular, whether the collector is a debt buyer or the original creditor. A debt buyer will have purchased a debt for pennies on the dollar, a debt that the original creditor had decided was not worth pursuing. The debt buyer is using the state's courts to play a numbers game. A high percentage of cases will proceed to default judgment without the collector having to expend time marshalling evidence or otherwise incurring significant expenses. The debt buyer is betting that postjudgment remedies for all those cases will bring in more money than the debt buyer expended on purchasing and litigating all its debts. Such a debt buyer is unlikely to expend significant resources either coming to court with solid evidence or actually trying the case. The debt buyer may not even be able to prove it owns the debt with admissible evidence, if challenged by the consumer.

The original creditor, on the other hand, may have easy access to employee affidavits and will usually be able to produce account statements and the credit contract, though not always.[45] The original creditor will have less of a problem proving it owns the debt.

45 *See, e.g.*, Johnson v. MBNA Am. Bank, 357 F.3d 426 (4th Cir. 2004); *In re* Vee Vinhnee, 336 B.R. 437 (B.A.P. 9th Cir. 2005).

2.3.7.4 Other Factors

Good facts make good law. Do not try to make new law in a case in which the consumer clearly owes the money. It is much better to raise new legal theories when there is a good argument that the consumer does not owe the money and when the consumer is otherwise sympathetic.

Obviously the strength of the consumer's defense and the availability of counterclaims will be factors in taking a case, as will the availability of an attorney fee award for a prevailing consumer. An attorney must consider how much time a case will require in traveling to the court and waiting around for the case to be heard. The attorney must also consider how many court appearances will be necessary and how often those court dates will be put off at the last minute by the collector. On the other hand, the consumer may be able to attend certain hearings instead of the attorney, depending on state procedure. For example, a consumer might attend an initial hearing to see if the action is disputed and merely state that a defense will be raised, with the court setting a later trial date.

Related to those factors is the type of court which will hear the action. In a small claims court, pleadings may be minimal or nonexistent and the consumer or attorney can just appear at the trial date. A key question then is whether the court customarily grants the collector's continuance motions when someone appears for the defense and whether the particular collection attorney routinely asks for a continuance only if an attorney shows up, or if even a consumer makes an appearance. In some situations, one solution might be for the client to attend and obtain a definite trial date at which the attorney can attend.

Another factor that varies depending on the court and a state's court system is the nature of the appeal from the trial court's decision. In some states there is the right to an appeal de novo to a higher court, meaning there is less incentive for the consumer attorney to attend the first trial.

2.4 Minimizing the Impact of Creditor Postjudgment Remedies

2.4.1 Introduction

Whether or not an attorney takes a consumer's case, the attorney can offer basic advice concerning minimizing the impact of the collector's postjudgment remedies. This advice will have immediate utility if a default or other judgment has already been entered and can also educate the consumer as to the stakes involved in defending a collection action *pro se* and steps to take to avoid the worst consequences of losing the case.

Sometimes there is a fine line between exemption planning and fraudulent transfers, and this line varies from jurisdiction to jurisdiction. To the extent that the exemption planning is legal and ethical, the attorney can explore with the client converting nonexempt assets into exempt assets or transferring assets to others. The discussion in the rest of this section considers consumer actions that can protect income or property without involving such transfers.

2.4.2 *Bank Accounts*

A collector with a judgment can seize nonexempt funds from the consumer's bank account, and certain exempt funds may be subject to a freeze. Procedures to "unfreeze" an account vary by state. In some states the consumer must fill out, file with the court, and serve on the collector a form stating that the funds in the account are exempt and provide accompanying proof. A collector agreeing to release the funds sends a release to the bank, and it often takes days or even weeks before the funds are actually released. If the collector does not agree to release the funds, the consumer must seek a court hearing. The collector may later seek to seize funds from the same account again, requiring the consumer to repeat the same process.

A U.S. Treasury Rule now protects from both seizure and freeze all exempt federal benefits electronically deposited in a bank account over the prior two months.[46] This rule does not protect funds exempt under state law, federal benefits deposited by check, or exempt federal benefits that exceed the federal benefit payments deposited in the last two months.

When a consumer may accumulate in the account exempt federal benefits exceeding the amounts deposited in the last two months, a safer alternative is to receive the federal benefits loaded onto a Direct Express card. The Direct Express card is a stored value card on which the funds will be electronically deposited and which can be used like a debit card to access cash and to make purchases. Funds deposited onto the Direct Express card will not be subject to garnishment *or* freezing.[47] This arrangement is generally also a better alternative than a consumer taking a paper check and paying a check casher to cash the payment.

If the consumer is going to keep in a bank account exempt funds not protected by the U.S. Treasury Rule, one option is to create two accounts, one account holding only exempt funds. This should facilitate the consumer being able to protect those funds from seizure and perhaps a freeze, but it is important for the consumer to spend down the non-exempt account before using the exempt funds.

Of course, if funds are not deposited in a bank, they cannot be seized. Thus, a consumer can immediately cash small checks or endorse them over to others, for consideration. Consumers should avoid highly-priced check cashers.

Collectors will also seek to seize any bank account with the consumer's name on it. Consumers who have or expect to have a judgment entered against them should remove their names from any account that holds someone else's money (for example, accounts containing funds owned by another family member, such as an elderly parent or a child). If the owner of the funds needs the consumer to manage the account, a power of attorney should be used or the account should be clearly designated as a trust.

46 *See* 76 Fed. Reg. 9939 (Feb. 23, 2011), *to be codified at* 31 C.F.R. §§ 212.1 through 212.12. *See also* § 12.6.3, *infra*.

47 There are very narrow situations in which these funds may be garnished. Social Security—but not SSI—funds may be garnished to pay child support and alimony, and can also be administratively offset to satisfy debts owed to the federal government, such as taxes or student loans. Administrative offsets are deducted from the funds before payment is even made, whether it is made by direct deposit, by paper check, or onto the Direct Express card.

2.4.3 *Wages*

State law may provide for more protections beyond the minimum limits on wage garnishment that federal law imposes.[48] At present, the federal minimum wage is $7.25 per hour, and no garnishment is allowed if an employee's disposable earnings are $217.50 or less for the week in question. If an employee's disposable earnings exceed $217.50 but are less than $290.00, under federal law only the amount over $217.50 can be garnished. When an employee's disposable earnings are $290.00 or more in a given week, federal law allows up to 25% of those earnings to be garnished. Some states protect a larger portion of a consumer's wages, and these greater protections will apply instead of the federal standard.

The wages that are exempt are the "disposable earnings," that is, the wages available after applicable taxes and other "amounts required by law to be withheld" are deducted.[49] As a result, consumers who under-withhold taxes expose themselves to greater garnishment while at the same time do not pay down their tax liability. Consumers who pay child support should consider having those payments made by way of wage deduction. Each dollar of a child support wage deduction reduces the consumer's disposable earnings that could otherwise be subject to garnishment by judgment creditors. Some states do not allow more than one garnishment at a time, so that child support protects the balance of the wages.

2.4.4 *Property*

A consumer's property can be seized to pay a judgment to the extent to which the equity in that property is not exempt. For example, if a state has a $100,000 homestead exemption and the consumer's home is valued at $200,000 and is subject to a $105,000 mortgage, then the home is exempt from seizure. The consumer has $95,000 in equity in the home and there is a $100,000 exemption.

Some states require that a homestead declaration be recorded before the exemption is effective.[50] This declaration should be recorded before judgment is entered, at the first meeting with the attorney. Whether this declaration will be effective as to preexisting debts that have not yet been reduced to a judgment is a question of state law, but the sooner the homestead declaration is recorded, the better.

If a judgment is against one spouse, the attorney can make sure that assets that are in fact held as tenancies by the entirety are properly labeled as such. Property held in such a tenancy

48 *See* § 12.4.3, *infra*.

49 *See* 15 U.S.C. § 1672(b).

50 *See* § 12.5.1, *infra*.

by the entirety cannot be seized to pay the debts of only one of the owners.[51] Although an attorney may not advise a consumer to fraudulently transfer assets, property that is in fact owned by another should not have the consumer's name associated with that property.

2.5 The Bankruptcy Alternative

A chapter 7 bankruptcy filing wipes out unsecured debts and eliminates the need to defend the collection action. Because nonexempt assets will be lost in a chapter 7 bankruptcy, and because of the cost involved, bankruptcy may not make sense to discharge one small debt. It is a powerful remedy when a consumer has a significant amount of unsecured debt and minimal nonexempt assets. When a consumer has significant nonexempt assets, filing under chapter 13 may be a better alternative, as it typically will significantly reduce the portion of an unsecured debt that must be repaid and allows that amount to be paid out over a period of years.

There is no rush to file bankruptcy, as the bankruptcy can discharge the obligation even after a judgment has been entered and often can even avoid liens that a creditor places on the consumer's property after judgment. Bankruptcy will not discharge debts incurred after the bankruptcy filing, so the timing of a bankruptcy filing is important. Absent the immediate loss of property or income, it is usually premature to file bankruptcy until the consumer's financial picture has stabilized. Any additional debts that are expected to mount up can only be discharged by waiting to file bankruptcy. Probably the best course of action is to consider the bankruptcy option early but let the bankruptcy attorney determine the appropriate time to actually file. The consumer might consider starting credit counseling, which is a precondition to filing bankruptcy (cost ranges from $30 to $50, but can be waived for indigency), but counseling must be completed no more than 180 days before the bankruptcy filing.

More on the bankruptcy option is found in § 11.5, *infra*. A good chapter explaining bankruptcy to the consumer is found in NCLC's *Guide to Surviving Debt*,[52] and a brochure on bankruptcy rights may be found at www.nclc.org. Other NCLC publications provide information on bankruptcy for the consumer attorney, as described below.

If bankruptcy is an option, the attorney can refer the consumer to a bankruptcy specialist or to a bar association pro bono bankruptcy program. A relationship between a bankruptcy attorney and a consumer attorney can be mutually beneficial. The bankruptcy specialist can refer clients to the consumer attorney when a bankruptcy is not appropriate or when the consumer has substantial consumer law claims. The consumer attorney refers clients to the bankruptcy attorney when bankruptcy may be the best course of action.

The consumer attorney can also handle the bankruptcy for the client. An initial intake interview has already been conducted and a relationship established. Bankruptcy is not nearly as intimidating as many think. NCLC's *Bankruptcy Basics*[53] takes the attorney through all the necessary steps with clear guidance. NCLC's *Consumer Bankruptcy Law and Practice*[54] is an even more comprehensive practice guide.

2.6 *Pro Se* Representation

Attorneys who decide not to represent the consumer can still give the consumer information on *pro se* representation. The attorney can explain the importance of not missing court dates and of responding to requests for admission in a timely fashion.

A strict warning can be given about the dangers of communications with the collector's attorney. The collector's attorney is representing the interests of the collector—no matter how helpful the attorney seems, statements by the attorney should not be seen as being in the consumer's best interest.

Sample settlement language can be spelled out. The consumer should be advised to check with the court clerk regarding the status of a case, particularly after settlement, in order to prevent the collector's attorney from obtaining a default judgment after the consumer believed the case was settled.

The consumer should retain any settlement documents. It is very possible that the same collector or another debt buyer will sue the consumer on the same debt, even though the debt has been settled.[55]

The consumer will also need specific information on how to appear and defend a collection action for the particular court and the particular jurisdiction. In many states the bar association or a legal services office may have already created a step-by-step written guide that can be given to the consumer. If the collection action has been filed in a small claims court that does not require pleadings, then the attorney may be able to provide sufficient advice during a brief interview.

2.7 Scams to Avoid

Attorneys should advise consumers as to certain scams to avoid. The marketplace is rife with companies preying on those in debt, and consumers compound their difficulties by signing up for one of these pitches.

One common scam is the debt elimination company that, for a fee, promises to explain how to eliminate debt. Some offer various instruments, such as a "bond for discharge of debt" or a "redemption certificate," that the debtor is to present to the creditor supposedly to force the creditor to relinquish the debt. These scams are not only ineffective, but their use may be a federal crime. Another useless scheme sets up an

51 *See* §§ 12.7.9, 12.8.5, *infra*.

52 NCLC Guide to Surviving Debt Ch. 20 (2013 ed.).

53 (2013).

54 National Consumer Law Center, Consumer Bankruptcy Law and Practice (10th ed. 2012), *updated at* www.nclc.org/library.

55 *See* Burke v. Messerli & Kramer P.A., 2010 WL 3167403 (D. Minn. Aug. 9, 2010); Overcash v. United Abstract Group, Inc., 549 F. Supp. 2d 193 (N.D.N.Y. 2008); Chiverton v. Fed. Fin. Group, Inc., 399 F. Supp. 2d 96 (D. Conn. 2005).

arbitration proceeding that is programmed to produce a ruling that the debt is invalid.

Just as problematic are debt settlement companies that require consumers to make their payments to the debt settlement company or to some other account and not to the creditor. The company takes an up-front fee and a percentage of each payment and puts the rest of the payment in a segregated account. At a later point, if enough money is accumulated, the debt settlement company promises to negotiate with creditors and satisfy the debt with part payment using the accumulated sums. Typically the fees are so high that the consumer never accumulates enough money, and the only winner is the debt settlement company. Even when settlements are arranged, the fees are so high that consumers might have been better off negotiating settlements on their own.

Other scams involve debt consolidation and home equity loans that result in large fees, high interest rates, and eventually the consumer losing far more than would have been lost based upon the simple collection action. Payday and auto title loans also will just sink the consumer deeper in debt and are not a solution. Consumers should be warned about overdrawing their bank account through use of a check, debit card, or ATM withdrawal, which can result in astronomical bank fees and effective interest rates that exceed even payday loan rates.

2.8 Collection Litigation

2.8.1 Tactical Considerations

Different consumer attorneys utilize very different tactics in collection defense cases, depending on their jurisdiction, the applicable court, and the attorney's own preferences. One approach is to litigate the case aggressively from the start, sending extensive discovery to the collector, filing motions, and raising counterclaims. This approach will often lead to the collector voluntarily dismissing the case, leaving the case in limbo or, at some point, bringing a summary judgment motion, seeking to dispose of the case without a trial. This summary judgment motion is examined in § 2.8.4, *infra*. When the summary judgment motion fails, the collector may stop pursuing the case.

The opposite approach is to minimize the consumer attorney's time and pre-trial discovery and just appear at trial and see if the collector is prepared to prove its case. Collectors usually show up with either insufficient or inadmissible evidence, because they are used to an unrepresented consumer either defaulting or presenting an ineffective challenge at trial.

In choosing between these two models, one factor will be local rules. For example, some court rules require the consumer's attorney to file an appearance prior to trial. The necessity to respond to requests for admissions or to file an answer may force the consumer attorney to expend resources prior to the trial, as will the necessity to move to set aside a default judgment.

A consumer's litigation tactics will also be shaped by the nature of the collector. A debt buyer is unlikely to have access to the credit contract or to affidavits from the original creditor's employees to authenticate business records. On the other hand, the original creditor may have access to this evidence; yet the creditor's cost-benefit determination may still prevent it from producing this information at trial.

Another factor affecting litigation tactics will be the probability of the consumer recovering an attorney fee. When the likelihood is low, then the attorney may wish to minimize the number of hours devoted to the case, including minimizing pre-trial motions. This will minimize how much the consumer will have to pay to his or her own attorney.

2.8.2 First Litigation Steps

The consumer's answer should admit as little as possible, because the collector will have trouble proving facts on its own.[56] Depending on local rules, failure to plead an affirmative defense in the consumer's answer may constitute waiver of that defense. It is thus critical in many courts to affirmatively plead that the statute of limitations has expired and the like. These defenses may also lead to the consumer filing a motion to dismiss. A motion to dismiss is appropriate if the collector's own pleadings indicate the date of default and that the applicable limitations period has expired.

The plaintiff's failure to obey local rules (particularly in "code" pleading states) that require it to append to the complaint documents substantiating its claim can also lead to a motion to dismiss. One example is when a collector pleads breach of contract and fails to attach a copy of the contract as required by local rule. On the other hand, the consumer can raise this objection later at trial. Making the motion at the start of the trial may just educate the collector and help the collector prepare its case.

It is critical to determine from the collector's complaint exactly what legal theories are being pleaded in order to know, among other things, the elements the collector must prove, the applicable statute of limitations, whether the collector is entitled to attorney fees or finance charges, and which state's law applies.[57] The consumer should request a more definite statement or seek dismissal for failure to state a claim if there is any uncertainty, or if there is sufficient ambiguity that the collector may try to swap theories midway through the case.

Pay careful attention to a collector's request for admissions. If the consumer fails to timely respond, the statements will be deemed admitted.[58] If the time to respond has already passed, then immediately ask the collector's attorney for an extension and, if denied, then make a request to the judge. When a consumer was not represented at the time a response was due to a request for admissions, the consumer can often withdraw

56 *See* § 4.2, *infra*.
57 *See* § 4.4, *infra*.
58 See § 4.2.2.1, *infra*.

such an admission and ask for additional time to respond.[59] If there is still an opportunity to respond to the request for admissions in a timely manner, then § 4.2.2.2, *infra*, provides advice on how to do so. When the consumer's memory and the facts allow, there is little additional risk to denying core requests that ask the consumer to admit liability. If a collector does not prevail, then the consumer will not have to pay the collector's attorney fees for refusing to admit to the requests. And if the collector does prevail, the consumer typically will have to pay the collector's attorney fees whether or not the consumer denied the requests for admissions.

2.8.3 The Consumer's Discovery

Discovery in a collection case has a tactical component. Refraining from taking discovery at all may be appropriate when the collector assumes the case will result in a default judgment or a simple trial and therefore may not be prepared with sufficient evidence to meet its burden of proof. Discovery may in fact force the collector to pull together its evidence and be more prepared for trial, when it otherwise would not be.

On the other hand, sending extensive discovery can delay a case, or even convince the collector that the case is not worth pursuing.[60] The collector may ignore the discovery request and refrain from prosecuting the case. The consumer can attempt to compel discovery, send a series of letters to the collector reminding the collector that discovery is overdue, and then ask the court to dismiss the case for failure to respond to discovery.[61] Alternatively, the consumer can just do nothing and wait for developments.

This standoff between the parties can keep a case in limbo for years. In this situation, it is important for the consumer attorney to make sure that the consumer keeps in touch with the attorney the whole time. The consumer will still need legal representation if the same or another collector revives the old case or brings a new case. Bringing a second case on the same debt without first resolving the first case may be a Fair Debt Collection Practices Act (FDCPA) violation, emphasizing the need for the consumer to stay in touch with the attorney. One technique is for the consumer's attorney to periodically update the client as to the status of the case, even if it is just by a form letter stating that the case is still pending.

Discovery in a collection case can also be used to develop evidence as to the nature of collection contacts and related actions that may lead to FDCPA claims. Ask for collection notes and communications from the debt collector to the consumer. In other words, the collector's lawsuit can provide the vehicle to find evidence to determine whether an FDCPA case is worth bringing.

2.8.4 The Collector's Summary Judgment Motion

In an attempt to avoid a time-consuming trial, collectors may resort to a summary judgment motion. The motion may be based on statements deemed admitted by the consumer because the consumer failed to timely respond to a request for admissions. Or the motion can be based on an affidavit from an employee of the collector and various "business records" attached to the motion.

When the consumer's discovery requests are outstanding, the consumer should argue that summary judgment is premature until the consumer receives all of the requested discovery. The collector cannot argue that there are no facts in dispute if the consumer has not had a chance to obtain all the facts.

Carefully review the affidavits and records supporting a summary judgment motion. Look for inconsistencies between the affidavits and documents and even between the facts alleged in the summary judgment motion and in the attachments. Of course, documents referenced in the motion but not attached should have no weight. For example, debt buyers often seek to prove they own a debt by attaching a bulk transfer agreement and referencing a computer tape or document that allegedly shows that the contract at issue was part of that bulk transfer, but no computer tape or document is in fact attached.[62]

Determine if attached records meet all of the requirements of the business records exception to the hearsay rule. In particular, there must be an affidavit from someone who on personal knowledge can attest that the record was made at or near the time of the occurrence set forth in the record and that the record was kept in the regular course of business.[63] Employees of a debt buyer should not be able to introduce business records produced by the original creditor.[64] Debt buyers also often seek to prove a fact by a conclusory affidavit, which is no substitute for the actual business records.

The consumer can present counter-affidavits and documents to create a factual dispute to defeat the summary judgment motion. Certainly the court should not utilize a different standard for acceptable affidavits from the consumer than from the collector.

A court should not order summary judgment for the total amount the collector seeks if there are factual disputes as to certain elements. The consumer can present facts showing that some or the entire amount sought has been paid, that the collector agreed to accept payments in full satisfaction of the debt, that certain charges were unauthorized, that the consumer never received a proffered contract, and the like.

2.8.5 The Trial

Sometimes the best course of action is for only the consumer's attorney and not the consumer to appear at trial. A common collector technique when it has insufficient evidence

59 *See* § 4.2.2, *infra*.

60 *See, e.g.*, Palisades Collection, L.L.C. v. Coleman, 2009 WL 2882940 (Tex. App. Sept. 9, 2009).

61 *See* Capital One Bank v. Maners, 909 N.E.2d 517 (Ind. Ct. App. 2009) (unpublished).

62 *See* § 4.3, *infra*.

63 *See* § 4.2.4, *infra*.

64 *Id.*

to prove its case is to call the consumer to the stand and to try to prove its case using the consumer's own testimony. For example, it can ask the consumer to authenticate various documents when it has not brought its own witness to trial. If it is unclear whether the consumer will be needed to testify in his own defense, one option is for the consumer to wait nearby, but not so close that the collector can call the consumer to the stand in the case in chief.

If the judge asks where the consumer is, one response might be that the consumer is at work and the consumer's attorney has no questions for the consumer. The collector has the burden of proof and the consumer need not disprove the debt. If the collector wants the consumer to testify, depending on local procedure, it has subpoena power or can send a notice to appear.

If the case is to be heard by a jury or before certain judges, it may be better to have the consumer testify or at least appear in the courtroom, even if the result is that the collector can then prove some of the elements of its case through the consumer. Otherwise the jury will be wondering why the consumer did not appear. Even if the consumer's attorney does not plan to call the consumer as a witness, if the consumer does appear in the courtroom, the consumer should be prepared to testify. The consumer's attorney should explain how cross-examination works and what are proper responses to such questioning (in other words, yes or no answers).

When the collector produces a witness, make sure the hearsay rules are enforced and that the witness testifies based upon firsthand knowledge. Business records should be introduced only if they meet the exceptions to the hearsay rules. The consumer's attorney may even come into court with a few short "pocket briefs" arguing why certain business records or testimony is inadmissible as hearsay. The attorney should be prepared with a copy of the applicable rules of evidence, particularly the rules regarding admissibility of documents, hearsay, and the business records exception to the hearsay rule. NCLC publishes *Instant Evidence*, a handy guide that summarizes the federal rules of evidence in only twenty-one pages, is laminated to withstand abuse and to allow dry-erase pen notations, and is spiral bound to lay flat.[65] State rules often are patterned after the federal rules summarized in this guide.

The consumer's attorney should give some consideration to having a court reporter present. Some courts automatically provide a court reporter, but in others arrangements have to be made for a court reporter to be hired. A number of factors must be weighed in deciding whether to incur this expense. When an appeal is possible, there may be little for the appellate court to review if there is no transcript.[66] The trial court decision may simply specify the amount the collector is to recover.

If the consumer has a right to a trial de novo, the trial transcript will be useful as a tool to remind the consumer's attorney as to testimony and argument in the first trial and for impeachment. A trial transcript may also have the effect of formalizing the proceeding so that it is more likely that the collector will have to follow the rules of evidence in introducing records and the like, and the court may be more detailed in its rulings.

2.9 Settlement, the Court's Decision, Postjudgment Actions

2.9.1 The Court's Order for the Consumer

Consumers who assert that they never owed the debt—for example, because of identity theft, because the wrong consumer has been sued, or because of a valid dispute on the debt—should seek more than just dismissal of the case with prejudice. The consumer ultimately will want to clean up their credit report so that it contains no evidence of the debt. It will not be enough to show that the current balance is zero. The report should delete all historical record of the debt being overdue.

A decision that states that the consumer never owed the debt will facilitate deleting this historical information.[67] The court might even order the collector to correct the consumer's credit report as part of its judgment.

2.9.2 Settlement

2.9.2.1 General

Dismissing the consumer's counterclaims with prejudice along with the collector's claims will constitute res judicata, barring a subsequent action. If the consumer wishes to bring the counterclaims in a subsequent action, the settlement must dismiss the collector's claim with prejudice but not the counterclaims.

Any settlement of the action should dismiss the lawsuit with prejudice using a court order or a document filed with the court. Possible options for settlement include: a written consent order to judgment, a voluntary or involuntary dismissal, or the court can issue a written order, or orally state "on the record" that the case is dismissed. The case can be dismissed with conditions, which can presented to the court or not; the court can include the conditions in an order; or the conditions can just be filed with the court. The important point is that the case has been formally dismissed, the consumer cannot be sued on the debt again, and the consumer has a certified document to use in cleaning up the credit report. The consumer may also want to include a paragraph in the settlement agreement in which the collector certifies that it has not already assigned, hypothecated, or transferred the debt.

The consumer should retain any settlement documents. It is very possible that the same collector or another debt buyer will sue the consumer on the same debt, even though the debt has been settled.[68]

---

65 (2d ed. 2013), *updated at* www.nclc.org/library.

66 *Cf.* Asset Acceptance, L.L.C. v. Lemon, 2007 WL 3408304 (Ohio Ct. App. Nov. 5, 2007).

67 *See* § 13.2, *infra*.

68 *See* Burke v. Messerli & Kramer P.A., 2010 WL 3167403 (D. Minn. Aug. 9, 2010); Overcash v. United Abstract Group, Inc., 549 F. Supp. 2d 193 (N.D.N.Y. 2008); Chiverton v. Fed. Fin. Group, Inc., 399 F. Supp. 2d 96 (D. Conn. 2005).

Assignees of the original creditor and the original creditor itself may change the account number of the debt at issue. The settlement thus should cover all different account numbers that have been associated with the consumer's credit obligation.

Sometimes a settlement will require the consumer to make payments, and failure to do so may result in a judgment against the consumer. In that case, the settlement should include at least two provisions. One is that, before the collector seeks a judgment for the non-payment, the collector provide notice of the default and a grace period to cure the default. With notice, the consumer can then contest the collector's default judgment action, asserting in defense that payments have in fact been made.[69] Otherwise the collector may obtain a default judgment without any notice to the consumer, and it may be difficult to vacate this default.[70] Stipulated settlements are judicially favored and courts are resistant to set them aside.[71]

The other provision to include is that the settlement explicitly states that the consumer's attorney will continue to represent the consumer until the case concludes. This may allow for court documents to be sent to the attorney and prevents the other side's attorney from contacting the consumer.

2.9.2.2 Settlement Language Requiring the Collector to Completely Remove Disputed Debt from Credit Report

Any settlement of the debt should include a provision requiring the collector to clean up the consumer's credit report. Reproduced below is a sample settlement provision that requires the creditor to withdraw the entire report of the disputed debt. This withdrawal is sometimes referred to as a "hard delete." The credit record will then be altogether silent about the debt and will not even provide a basis for another creditor, interested in the creditworthiness of the consumer, to inquire further. This approach is often the simplest solution for the consumer and the safest. When a debt buyer brings the action, the language will have to be modified to only require deletion of information provided by that entity.

> It is further agreed that [*creditor*] shall take all steps necessary to ensure that no credit report or credit reference that is unfavorable or that may be construed unfavorably to [*consumer*] shall be made by it or by any consumer reporting agency with regard to any debts or claims as between [*creditor*] and [*consumer*]. Without limiting the effect of the foregoing obligation, [*creditor*] shall also within ten days hereof send notice [*in writing or electronically or both*] [*in the form attached hereto as Appendix A*], to each consumer reporting agency to which [*creditor*] has reported any information about [*consumer*], deleting from their files all references to the [*alleged*] debt which is the subject of this settlement agreement. To that end, [*creditor*] shall submit a Metro II form coded with "DA" (delete account) [*and/or*] a Universal Data Form with the "Delete Tradeline" option box checked to each consumer reporting agency to which [*creditor*] has reported any information about [*consumer*]. Prior to any execution of any release of claims by [*consumer*], [*creditor*] shall submit to counsel for [*consumer*] clear and complete copies of these forms (with [*creditor's*] subscriber/password code redacted if [*creditor*] chooses) and proof that [*creditor*] has submitted these forms. Each required "Universal Data Form" or the equivalent must contain [*creditor's*] certification that it has modified its internal records so that the information to be deleted is not re-reported. In the event Plaintiffs discover, more than forty-five (45) days following [*creditor's*] submission of the Metro II form/Universal Data form as described, that any consumer reporting agency still reports the alleged debt, [*consumer*] may notify [*creditor*] in writing, and [*creditor*] will within ten business days resubmit a request for deletion of all reference to the debt.
>
> [*Creditor*] shall adjust its relevant internal records in a manner that will permanently reflect the agreed-upon status of the debt. [*Creditor*] agrees to take all steps necessary or appropriate to prevent the re-reporting of any information about the [*alleged*] debt. In the event any such information is re-reported to any consumer reporting agency, [*creditor*] agrees to take all steps necessary or appropriate to ensure that the re-reported information is deleted from the files of every consumer reporting agency to which the information was re-reported. Further, should a consumer reporting agency ever notify [*creditor*] that [*consumer*] is disputing the tradeline, [*creditor*] will not verify the tradeline or will confirm that the tradeline should be deleted; in such an event, [*creditor*] will also submit to counsel for [*consumer*], within forty-five (45) days after receiving the notification of the dispute from the consumer reporting agency, clear and complete copies of the notification of the dispute and any and all forms (including electronic forms) by which it responds to such notification (with [*creditor's*] subscriber/password code redacted if [*creditor*] chooses). [*Creditor*] further agrees that it will not assign, hypothecate, or transfer the [*alleged*] debt to another creditor, a collection agency, or any other third party, and that it will not alter the account number or otherwise re-label the account. The parties agree that time is of the essence for this contract. This release shall not extend to the obligations created by this Agreement, or to any claim or cause of action based in whole or in part upon a communication to a consumer reporting agency after the date of this agreement.

69 *See, e.g.*, Midland Funding, L.L.C. v. Dort, 2013 WL 3111297 (N.Y. Sup. App. Term June 6, 2013).

70 *See, e.g.*, Cach L.L.C. v. Woodsnajac, 2013 WL 6645003 (N.Y. Sup. Ct. App. Term, Dec. 17, 2013).

71 *See, e.g.*, Cavalry Portfolio Servs., L.L.C. v. Williams, 2013 WL 518705 (N.Y. Sup. Ct. Feb. 1, 2013).

2.9.2.3 Settlement Language Requiring Collector to Withdraw Only Adverse Information from Credit Report

Sometimes the consumer wishes to keep information about an account in the credit report to show a history of payments and only wishes to delete adverse information supplied about the account. To accomplish this goal the settlement provisions must carefully delineate what information cannot be furnished to an agency because it might be construed unfavorably to the client. Relevant sample settlement language is found below. Even so, there is always the risk that even the limited information reported, though accurate in a narrow sense, will permit another creditor using the report to fill in the gaps incorrectly or to draw its own negative inferences. For example, if there was a dispute, a creditor might suppose there was a default as well.

The following is proposed settlement language that would require the creditor to request correction of a disputed credit account but would leave the account listed in the consumer's credit reporting file. This option is recommended only when there is a significant benefit to the client in maintaining information about the account, for it is far more likely to raise post-settlement problems.

> It is further agreed that [*creditor*] shall take all steps necessary to ensure that no credit report or credit reference that is unfavorable or that may be construed unfavorably to [*consumer*] shall be made by it or by any consumer reporting agency with regard to any debts or claims as between [*creditor*] and [*consumer*]. Without limiting the foregoing obligation, the [*creditor*] shall, within ten (10) days hereof, send written or electronic notice of the current status of the debt which is the subject of this settlement agreement to each consumer reporting agency to which [*creditor*] has reported any information about [*consumer*], such notice to be in a form approved by counsel for [*consumer*] [*or attached hereto as Appendix A*], and shall cause the deletion of all information that is unfavorable or may be construed unfavorably to [*consumer*]. For this purpose, the parties agree that the current status of the debt is [*describe*]. [*Creditor*] shall submit a Metro II form coded with [*describe codes*] [*and/or*] a Universal Data Form [*describe marks to be made on Form*] to each credit reporting agency to which [*creditor*] has reported any information about [*consumer*]. Prior to any execution of any release of claims by [*consumer*], [*creditor*] shall submit to counsel for [*consumer*] clear and complete copies of these forms, with [*creditor's*] subscriber/password code redacted if [*creditor*] so chooses, and proof that [*creditor*] has submitted these forms. In the event Plaintiffs discover, more than forty-five (45) days following [*creditor's*] submission of the [*Metro II form/Universal Data form*] as described, that any consumer reporting agency still reports the [*alleged*] debt other than as described above, [*consumer*] may notify [*creditor*] in writing, and [*creditor*] will, within ten (10) business days, re-submit a request for reporting of the [*alleged*] debt as described above. Furthermore, should a consumer reporting agency ever notify [*creditor*] that [*consumer*] is disputing the [*alleged*] debt, [*creditor*] will re-report the [*alleged*] debt only as described above; in such an event, [*creditor*] will also submit to counsel for [*consumer*], within forty-five (45) days after receiving the notification of the dispute from the consumer reporting agency, clear and complete copies of the notification of the dispute and any and all forms (including electronic forms) by which it responds to such notification, with [*creditor's*] subscriber password code redacted if [*creditor*] so chooses.
>
> [*Creditor*] shall further refrain from reporting any information that is unfavorable or may be construed unfavorably to [*consumer*] about said debt, so long as [*consumer*] remains in compliance with [*specify any paragraphs of the settlement that deal with future payments*].
>
> [*Creditor*] shall adjust its relevant internal records in a manner that will permanently reflect the agreed-upon status of the debt. [*Creditor*] agrees to take all steps necessary or appropriate to prevent the re-reporting of any information about the debt that is inconsistent with the current status of the debt or the payment history from the date of this settlement agreement. In the event any such information is re-reported to any consumer reporting agency, [*creditor*] agrees to take all steps necessary or appropriate to ensure that the re-reported information is deleted from the files of every consumer reporting agency to which the information was re-reported. [*Creditor*] further agrees that it will not assign, hypothecate, or transfer the [*alleged*] debt to another creditor, a collection agency, or any other third party, and that it will not alter the account number or otherwise re-label the account. The parties agree that time is of the essence of this contract. This release shall not extend to the obligations created by this Agreement or to any claim or cause of action based in whole or in part upon a communication to a consumer reporting agency after the date of this agreement.
>
> If [*Creditor*] receives inquiries about said debt from anyone not a party to this settlement agreement, [*creditor*] will report only the current status of the debt as described above and the payment history from the date of this settlement. [*Creditor*] shall not provide, directly or indirectly, any information regarding the status of the debt before the date of this settlement, including [*delinquencies/repossessions/deficiencies/judgments/foreclosures/collection efforts*].

2.9.3 Attorney Fee Awards for a Prevailing Consumer

The prevailing consumer's attorney should file a request for attorney fees, when available, together with adequate documentation. Procedures will vary by state and may also depend on the basis for the attorney fee award.

As described in § 13.1, *infra*, there are a number of bases on which a prevailing consumer can recover fees in a collection action. Surprisingly some contracts actually call for fees, not just for the collector but for the prevailing party. About twenty states have statutes that allow the consumer to recover fees, at least in certain collection actions. Another basis may be a counterclaim under the Fair Debt Collection Practices Act (FDCPA), a deceptive practices (UDAP) statute, or other statute with fee provisions. A collector's bringing a lawsuit without evidence may also provide a basis to recover fees. In addition, the consumer may recover fees as actual damages in follow-up litigation under the FDCPA or a related claim for the collector's litigation misconduct.[72]

72 *See* § 13.4, *infra.*

Chapter 3 Dismissal Before Reaching the Merits

3.1 Introduction

This chapter focuses on consumer defenses that may precede litigation of the merits of the collector's claim: whether the action is brought in the proper court, whether the collector is qualified to bring the action, whether pleading requirements have been met, and whether the action is brought within the applicable statute of limitations. Typically these defenses are raised at the beginning of litigation, before the merits are decided. But sometimes they are raised later in the proceeding.

For example, the statute of limitations may be raised immediately in a motion to dismiss, if the defect is apparent from the pleadings, but may also be raised later in a summary judgment motion after the facts have been clarified. Moreover for tactical reasons, as discussed in Chapter 2, *supra*, the consumer may wish to wait until trial before raising defenses. This chapter focuses on defenses that do not go to the merits of the collector's claims, no matter when the defense is raised.

One exception is service of process. Typically, when process is defective, the consumer never even becomes aware that a suit has been brought until after a default judgment has been entered. Setting aside a default judgment based upon defective service of process is examined in § 11.3.10.1, *infra*.

Standing to sue is another preliminary issue that is treated elsewhere. This chapter examines whether a collector is properly licensed or otherwise eligible to use a state's courts to bring a collection action. Section 4.3, *infra*, considers the important question of whether the collector bringing the lawsuit in fact has proven that it owns the debt.

3.2 Has the Collector Chosen an Appropriate Forum?

3.2.1 Does the Court Have Jurisdiction?

Except in unusual circumstances there is no federal jurisdiction for a collection action, and collectors must bring the case in state court. This also means that consumers cannot successfully remove the case to federal court. Raising a federal claim in a counterclaim is not a basis to remove a case to federal court.[1]

The collector must bring the action in the proper state court. Determine if the action seeks an amount above any jurisdictional maximum for the court selected,[2] or whether state law requires that cases seeking such amount be brought in a different court.[3] If a collection action seeks to confirm an arbitration award, a state may also limit in which court the confirmation proceeding may be brought. State and constitutional limits on long-arm jurisdiction may also prevent an out-of-state creditor from suing a debtor in the creditor's home state.[4]

3.2.2 Venue

3.2.2.1 Limitations on State Court Venue

A collector's action must comply with state venue rules and also with the federal Fair Debt Collection Practices Act (FDCPA). The FDCPA requires that a debt collector bring a lawsuit only in the judicial district in which the consumer signed the contract or resides at the time of the lawsuit.[5] The judicial district refers to the state district and not the federal district.[6]

The FDCPA venue provision applies to actions brought by debt buyers and also by collection attorneys and collection agencies bringing the court action on behalf of the original creditor. The provision does not apply to the original creditor bringing an action *pro se*, but that exception has little practical significance.[7] In any event, *pro se* creditors and others that are exempt from the FDCPA must still meet state law and constitutional limits on long-arm jurisdiction when suing debtors.[8] In addition, bringing an action in an inconvenient venue to

---

1 *See* § 5.5.1.1, *infra*.

2 *See, e.g.*, Citibank v. Bowen, 671 S.E.2d 596 (table), 2008 WL 5225857 (N.C. Ct. App. Dec. 16, 2008) (unpublished) (under N.C. Gen. Stat. § 7A-243, cases seeking more than $10,000 should be brought in superior court, not district court—statute since amended to increase amount to $25,000).

3 *Cf.* Unifund CCR Partners v. Kyle, 2009 WL 1442870 (Mich. Ct. App. May 21, 2009) (Mich. Comp. Laws § 600.8301 provides that district courts have exclusive jurisdiction of claims for less than $25,000; when a location does not have a district court but only a municipal court that can only hear matters up to $3000, then the matter can be brought before a circuit court).

4 *See, e.g.*, Thai v. Nguyen, 2012 WL 2449903 (D. Mass. June 26, 2012) (Massachusetts lender cannot bring contract claim in his home state against Florida business borrower when terms were negotiated in Florida). *See generally* § 3.2.2.1, *infra* (FDCPA limits on suit in distant forum); National Consumer Law Center, Consumer Credit Regulation § 7.9.2 (2012), *updated at* www.nclc.org/library (long-arm jurisdiction).

5 15 U.S.C. § 1692i. One exception is that an action to enforce an interest in real property securing the consumer's obligation must be brought in the district where the real property is located.

6 *See* Fox v. Citicorp Credit Servs. Inc., 15 F.3d 1507 (9th Cir. 1994); Nichols v. Byrd, 435 F. Supp. 2d 1101 (D. Nev. 2006).

7 If the creditor files *pro se* but an attorney enters an appearance retaining control over the case, the FDCPA provision applies to that attorney. *See* John F. LeFevre, Att'y, Fed. Trade Comm'n, Informal Staff Letter to Milton P. Goldfarb, Att'y, Newman, Goldfarb, Freyman & Stevens, P.C. (Nov. 23, 1988), *available online as companion material to this treatise*. Moreover, state law may prevent a corporation from appearing *pro se*. In any event, the creditor may also be violating a state deceptive practices statute that should prohibit the same practice.

8 *See* § 3.2.1, *supra*.

collect from a consumer may also be a violation of a state deceptive practices statute.[9] It is likely that a court will find that the deceptive practices statute places the same restrictions on inconvenient venue as does the FDCPA.[10]

Although the FDCPA allows the collector to bring the action where the contract was signed, the collector must prove where the contract was signed and that there is a contract. Debt buyers in particular may not be able to produce the contract and will find it even more difficult to prove where the contract was signed. As a result, in most cases the collector is limited to suing in the state judicial district where the consumer presently resides.[11] If there are joint debtors on an obligation, residing in different judicial districts, the collector must bring two separate actions, each complying with the FDCPA venue rule. More on the FDCPA and venue requirements is found in NCLC's *Fair Debt Collection*.[12]

3.2.2.2 Implications of a Collection Suit Brought in Violation of Federal or State Limits

If a collection action is brought in a venue violating the FDCPA, the consumer has an action for actual and statutory damages and attorney fees under the FDCPA[13] and may also have a cause of action under the state deceptive practices statute. But the availability of such a damage action does not resolve the question of whether the federal or state law violation can be grounds to dismiss or move a collection action brought in a venue violating the federal or state standard.

Language in the state's venue statute or rules may imply that it is improper to bring an action in a venue prohibited by federal or state law—the language may even say so explicitly, that venue is improper if an action is brought "in violation of federal or state law." Even if there is no such explicit language in a venue provision, the collection lawsuit can still be dismissed or moved pursuant to the common law doctrine of *forum non conveniens*.

The United States Supreme Court has stated that a case can be dismissed on *forum non conveniens* grounds "when an alternative forum has jurisdiction to hear [the] case and . . . trial in the chosen forum would establish . . . oppressiveness and vexation to the defendant . . . out of all proportion to plaintiff's convenience."[14] This reasoning should certainly apply to a case brought in violation of federal or state law in an inconvenient judicial district. The case can easily be refiled in the judicial district where the consumer resides, the consumer is harmed by the action brought in a distant forum, and the collector's convenience cannot be considered when it seeks to bring a case in violation of federal or state law. The Supreme Court has made clear that *forum non conveniens* applies to damages actions in law and not just actions in equity.[15]

3.2.3 When a Collection Action Is Brought Before an Arbitrator

Until 2009, hundreds of thousands of collection actions were brought before the National Arbitration Forum (NAF), instead of in court. The NAF is a private arbitration forum with no governmental connection. An arbitrator selected by the NAF, pursuant to NAF rules, would issue an award (invariably for the collector). When the collector confirmed that award in court, the award had the same effect as a court judgment, allowing the collector to garnish wages and seize bank accounts.

A good rule of thumb is that, if a collector wishes to bring a collection action before an arbitrator, the consumer will want to resist that forum, since the collector has decided it will be a favorable forum for it to quickly process its claim. At least if past history is any guide, the arbitrator will give short shrift to consumer defenses and will almost always quickly rule for the collector.

For all practical purposes, new collection actions via arbitration ceased in July 2009, when the NAF agreed in a law enforcement action to stop consumer collection arbitrations and the American Arbitration Association (AAA) stated it would not conduct such arbitration proceedings until standards were put in place.[16] As a result, at the moment there is limited practical relevance to the question of how a consumer should respond to a collector's action in arbitration to collect on a debt.

This topic is treated at some length in National Consumer Law Center's *Consumer Arbitration Agreements*.[17] Because it is treated elsewhere and because of the limited practical significance, it is not discussed here. But see *Consumer Arbitration Agreements* for the procedure the consumer should utilize to object to the arbitration and for legal grounds to resist the arbitration forum.

3.2.4 Forcing the Collector to Bring the Action Before an Arbitrator

As described in the prior subsection, collection actions via arbitration are no longer being held before the major arbitration forums designated in most consumer contracts, but many credit agreements still allow parties to remove court actions to arbitration. Creditors seek this right in the credit agreement to immunize themselves from class actions, punitive damage

9 National Consumer Law Center, Unfair and Deceptive Acts and Practices § 6.10.9 (8th ed. 2012), *updated at* www.nclc.org/library.

10 *Id.*

11 *See also* Ohio Rev. Code Ann. § 1319.12(D) (West) (collection action must be in county where consumer resides).

12 National Consumer Law Center, Fair Debt Collection § 5.9 (8th ed. 2014), *updated at* www.nclc.org/library.

13 *See id. See also* Harrington v. CACV of Colo., L.L.C., 508 F. Supp. 2d 128 (D. Mass. 2007).

14 Sinochem Int'l Co. v. Malaysia Int'l Shipping Corp., 549 U.S. 422, 127 S. Ct. 1184, 167 L. Ed. 2d 15 (2007) (quoting Am. Dredging Co. v. Miller, 510 U.S. 443, 114 S. Ct. 981, 127 L. Ed. 2d 285 (1994)).

15 Quackenbush v. Allstate Ins. Co., 517 U.S. 706, 116 S. Ct. 1712, 135 L. Ed. 2d 1 (1996).

16 *See* National Consumer Law Center, Consumer Arbitration Agreements § 11.1 (6th ed. 2011), *updated at* www.nclc.org/library.

17 (6th ed. 2011), *updated at* www.nclc.org/library.

awards issued by juries, and court-ordered discovery. This same arbitration agreement can be used by the consumer to turn the tables on a collector and force the collector to drop its lawsuit in court and instead bring the collection action in an arbitration proceeding.

Often arbitration clauses will give either party the right to insist that a lawsuit be moved to arbitration. If the consumer initiates litigation in court, the creditor or collector will seek to remove the case to arbitration but is counting on the consumer not to raise this right when the collector brings a court action. Consequently, a simple appearance in the case, requesting the matter be referred to arbitration, will surprise the collector, who may be unprepared to arbitrate the dispute. High arbitration fees may also discourage the collector from pursuing the claim in arbitration. Some arbitration agreements even specify that the creditor will pay all the arbitration costs.

In addition, the arbitration forum designated in the arbitration agreement—such as the AAA and NAF—may not presently be administering consumer collection arbitrations.[18] This puts the collector in a difficult position. It cannot select an alternative forum without the consumer's consent and so would have to go into court either to ask the judge to designate an arbitrator or argue that the arbitration requirement is unenforceable as to the collector because it cannot be carried out according to its terms.

In a bizarre turn of events, some credit card collectors are so put off by consumer demands that collection actions be removed to arbitration, that they are inserting change-in-terms notices in their collection letters. The change-in-terms notice purports to nullify the arbitration clause in the original credit contract. Such a unilateral change is unlikely to be legally binding; among other reasons, the consumer is no longer allowed to use the credit card, so the collector cannot rely on the consumer's continued use of the card to signify acceptance of the changed terms.[19] But a collector's attempt to change the terms, while certainly not legally binding, does indicate the consternation that some collectors feel when required to arbitrate, instead of going to court, to collect on a debt.

The consumer must be aware, however, of certain risks of arbitration. If the arbitration agreement does not provide otherwise, there may be significant added costs to the consumer—arbitration involves very high payments to the arbitrator, and the consumer may have to share in those payments up front or pay all of them if the collector prevails. Arbitration may also significantly abbreviate the consumer's discovery. Moreover, the arbitrator need not follow the law or the facts, and there is very limited judicial review of an arbitration decision.[20]

If the consumer does decide to try to force the case into arbitration, review the arbitration clause to see if it covers creditor disputes with the consumer and not just consumer disputes with the creditor. If it covers lawsuits brought by the creditor, it should also cover any lawsuit brought by the creditor's assignee.[21] Watch out for any exceptions in the arbitration requirement for actions under a certain dollar amount or cases brought in small claims court. The motivation of such an exception is to force class actions and punitive damages claims into arbitration, while allowing small collection actions to remain in court. Any ambiguity must be interpreted against the drafter and *in favor of* arbitration.[22]

To force a collection action into arbitration, the consumer's attorney should appear before the court hearing the collection action and file a motion with the court to either dismiss the case or stay the judicial action until after the creditor has submitted its case to arbitration. In either case the consumer's attorney should do so immediately, before any extensive participation in the court action. Participation in the court case may be viewed as waiving the right to arbitrate the dispute.[23]

3.3 Is the Collector Qualified to Bring an Action in the State's Courts?

3.3.1 Introduction

This section considers a number of reasons why the collector may not be qualified to bring the collection action in a state's courts. The entity bringing the action may not be entitled to bring any type of action in the state's courts. Or the entity may be unqualified to bring consumer collection actions. Or the entity may not be qualified to bring an action without representation from an attorney.

Another reason why the collector may have no right to pursue the action is examined in the next chapter: that the collector has insufficient proof that it owns the obligation or that it is properly bringing the action for the owner. This contention will often turn on whether there is proof of an unbroken chain of assignment from the original creditor to the party collecting on the debt. This reason why the collector cannot pursue the collection action is examined in detail at § 4.3, *infra*.

3.3.2 When Collector or Its Assignor Is a Foreign Corporation

3.3.2.1 When Collector Is a Foreign Corporation

Some states require that companies incorporated out-of-state obtain certification, registration, or licensure before they can bring actions in the state's courts.[24] Nevertheless, a special

18 *See* National Consumer Law Center, Consumer Arbitration Agreements § 5.8 (6th ed. 2011), *updated at* www.nclc.org/library.

19 *See* National Consumer Law Center, Consumer Arbitration Agreements § 5.6 (6th ed. 2011), *updated at* www.nclc.org/library.

20 *See* National Consumer Law Center, Consumer Arbitration Agreements Ch. 10 (6th ed. 2011), *updated at* www.nclc.org/library.

21 *See id.* § 7.5.1.

22 *See id.* § 3.1.

23 *See id.* Ch. 8.

24 *See, e.g.*, Ohio Rev. Code Ann. § 1703.29 (West); 15 Pa. Cons. Stat. § 4141(a). *See also* Evans v. Midland Funding, L.L.C., 574 F. Supp. 2d 808 (S.D. Ohio 2008); Centurion Capital Corp. v. Guarino, 951 N.Y.S.2d 85 (table), 2012 WL 1543286 (N.Y. Civ. Ct. Apr. 30, 2012); Discover Bank v. Sweeney, 2012 WL 5872746 (Ohio Ct. App.

rule applies to national banks. National banks by statute have authority to sue in any court as fully as natural persons.[25] Thus state registration requirements for out-of-state corporations will not apply to national banks.[26] Of course, for a bank to take advantage of this exemption, the bank must produce evidence that it is, in fact, a national bank.[27] Moreover, a debt buyer that purchases debt from a national bank cannot take advantage of this exception, which only applies to national banks.

Another possible exception for the registration requirement, at least in some states, is that an unregistered entity can still use the state's courts if that is the only business the entity is conducting in the state.[28] This language has been interpreted by Michigan and Pennsylvania courts as exempting a debt buyer suing on a debt,[29] but a federal court interpreting similar language in the Ohio statutes disagreed.[30] In New York, the requirement for registration is not a precondition to litigation if the litigation is an isolated transaction, but this isolated transaction exception does not apply to a debt buyer regularly bringing suit in the state.[31]

An out-of-state, unregistered corporation may attempt to sue under the auspices of an in-state or registered corporation. But this should not succeed since the debt is not assigned to that other entity or otherwise owned by that other entity.[32]

3.3.2.2 When Registered Collector Buys Debt from Unregistered Foreign Corporation

A state statute may provide that if an entity owning a debt fails to register, not only can it not sue in a state's courts, but anyone taking assignment of that debt cannot sue upon that debt in the state's courts either.[33] Such a rule prevents a non-qualifying corporation from merely assigning the action to another. These rules have important implications for collection actions, because what is at issue is not only whether the collector is qualified to bring an action but whether every owner up the chain of ownership is qualified.

For example, in states with this rule, if a creditor is qualified and assigns the debt to unqualified debt buyer A that assigns the debt to qualified debt buyer B, then B cannot bring an action in the state's courts, even though it could have if it had been assigned the debt directly from the creditor. The consumer's attorney in such a state should look not just at the collector's qualification to sue but at the qualifications of every entity in the chain of ownership.

3.3.3 Can Collector Sue Under a Fictitious Name?

Some states have a statute pertaining to fictitious business names that requires filing of a business name before the entity is granted the capacity to sue under that name in the state's courts. Until then, neither the business nor its assignee can bring suit. For example, California, Ohio, and Pennsylvania have such requirements.[34]

3.3.4 Partnership's Capacity to Sue in Its Own Name

The common-law aggregate theory of partnership holds that a general partnership has no legal existence separate from its members.[35] Thus, in states adopting this theory, a general partnership has no authority to sue in the firm name alone.[36] Significantly, debt buyers often are partnerships and thus cannot sue solely in their own name in these states.[37]

3.3.5 Licensure As a Precondition to a Collection Action

3.3.5.1 Must Debt Collectors Be Licensed?

The failure of a debt buyer to be licensed as a debt collection agency may prevent it from bringing suit.[38] A number of

---

Nov. 21, 2012); Atlantic Credit & Finance, Inc. v. Giuliana, 829 A.2d 340 (Pa. Super. Ct. 2003); Talented IT, Inc. v. Data Group, Inc., 2009 WL 3488465 (N.J. Super. Ct. App. Div. Oct. 28, 2009).

25 *See* 12 U.S.C. § 24.

26 *See* Williams v. Chase Bank, 390 S.W.3d 824 (Ky. Ct. App. 2012); Citibank v. Bowen, 671 S.E.2d 596 (table), 2008 WL 5225857 (N.C. Ct. App. Dec. 16, 2008) (unpublished); Citibank v. Eckmeyer, 2009 WL 1452614 (Ohio Ct. App. May 8, 2009).

27 *See* Citibank v. Rowe, 2013 WL 601600 (Ohio Ct. App. Feb. 19, 2013); Discover Bank v. Sweeney, 2012 WL 5872746 (Ohio Ct. App. Nov. 21, 2012).

28 *See* Mich. Comp. Laws § 450.2012; 15 Pa. Cons. Stat. § 4122(a)(8).

29 Cadle Co. II, Inc. v. Wechsler, 2006 WL 2959698 (Mich. Ct. App. Oct. 17, 2006); Atlantic Credit & Finance, Inc. v. Gardner (Pa. Ct. Com. Pl. May 14, 2008), *available at* www.nclc.org/unreported; Cavalry Portfolio Servs., L.L.C. v. Rowan (Pa. Ct. Com. Pl. Feb. 6, 2008), *available at* www.nclc.org/unreported.

30 Evans v. Midland Funding, L.L.C., 574 F. Supp. 2d 808 (S.D. Ohio 2008). *But see* Premier Capital, L.L.C. v. Baker, 972 N.E.2d 1125 (Ohio Ct. App. 2012).

31 Centurion Capital Corp. v. Guarino, 951 N.Y.S.2d 85 (table), 2012 WL 1543286 (N.Y. Civ. Ct. Apr. 30, 2012).

32 Discover Bank v. Sweeney, 2012 WL 5872746 (Ohio Ct. App. Nov. 21, 2012).

33 *See, e.g.*, 15 Pa. Cons. Stat. § 4141(a).

34 *See* Cal. Bus. & Prof. Code § 17918 (West); 54 Pa. Cons. Stat. §§ 301–332; Foster v. D.B.S. Collection Agency, 463 F. Supp. 2d 783 (S.D. Ohio 2006).

35 *See* Unifund CCR Partners v. Kinnamon, 384 S.W.3d 703 (Mo. Ct. App. 2012).

36 *Id.*

37 *Id.*

38 *See* N.C. Gen. Stat. §§ 58–70–145; Commercial Serv. of Perry, Inc. v. Fitzgerald, 856 P.2d 58 (Colo. App. 1993); B.C. Inv. Co. v. Throm, 650 P.2d 1333 (Colo. App. 1982); LVNV Funding, L.L.C. v. Trice, 952 N.E.2d 1232 (Ill. App. Ct. 2011) (any judgment obtained by such an entity is void ab initio); Centurion Capital Corp. v. Guarino, 951 N.Y.S.2d 85 (table), 2012 WL 1543286 (N.Y. Civ. Ct. Apr. 30, 2012); PRA III, L.L.C. v. MacDowell, 841 N.Y.S.2d 822 (N.Y. Civ. Ct. 2007); Centurion Capital Corp. v. Druce, 828 N.Y.S.2d 851 (N.Y. Civ. Ct. 2006); Rushmore Recoveries XI, L.L.C. v. Morningstar (N.Y. Civ. Ct. May 7, 2007), *available at* www.nclc.org/unreported; Tri-City Bldg. Ctr., Inc. v. Williams, 562 P.2d 1218 (Or. 1977); Settlement Agreement, In the Matter of LVNV (Office of Comm'r of Financial Regulation June 28, 2012), *available at* www.nclc.org/unreported. *See also* Great

states require that only licensed debt collection agencies can bring suit.[39] For example, the statute may say that a debt collector must be licensed prior to collecting any debts[40] or that a court complaint must allege that the collector is licensed.[41] Alternatively, a state's courts may interpret compliance with the debt collection licensing statute as a precondition to bringing suit.[42] A judgment obtained by an unlicensed collector may even be void.[43]

Other states have a more general rule that any entity that must be licensed cannot bring suit unless properly licensed,[44] which rule certainly includes unlicensed debt collectors. A state may even generally require that, whenever a plaintiff is required to be licensed, the plaintiff must allege in its complaint that it is licensed and include its licensing information in its complaint.[45]

While national banks may be immune to state credit regulation, an assignee of a national bank should still be subject to a licensing requirement. In addition, courts are not impressed with the argument that application of the state licensing requirement to an out-of-state debt buyer suing in a state's courts somehow conflicts with the Commerce Clause.[46]

3.3.5.2 Is a Debt Buyer a Debt Collector?

It is clear in such states that an unlicensed collection agency cannot sue on debts for which it is collecting for another—when the assignment is a device to allow the agency to sue but the assignor still retains ownership.[47] When the assignor still retains control over a debt, the assignee is a collection agency and must be licensed.[48]

An important question, though, is whether the state debt collection agency licensing requirement applies to a debt buyer suing on a debt it owns itself. Is an entity in the business of buying and suing on defaulted loans a debt collection agency within the meaning of the state debt collection licensing statute?

Often the answer will be found in the definition of debt collection agency applicable to the state licensing requirement. For example, a statutory definition of debt collector may explicitly apply to anyone regularly collecting debts on behalf of itself,[49] anyone who is a debt buyer,[50] or anyone whose principal business is the collection of debts.[51]

Debt buyers will also be covered by statutory language applying to anyone who acquires a debt after the debt is in default.[52] Of course, such statutory language does not require licensure when a debt buyer purchases a debt prior to the consumer's default.[53] Similarly, if the originating creditor brings suit, it need not be licensed as a debt collection agency.[54]

Other times, the statutory language will be less clear, and much will depend on a court's interpretation of that language. When the statutory definition is ambiguous or conflicting, courts often find that a debt buyer falls within the definition of a debt collection agency and must be licensed,[55] and thus cannot sue if not licensed.

Seneca Fin. Corp. v. Dowd, No. 12627–05 (N.Y. Civ. Ct. Jan. 24, 2008), *available at* www.nclc.org/unreported; Dep't of Consumer Affairs v. Asset Acceptance, L.L.C. (N.Y.C. Dep't of Consumer Affairs July 24, 2006), *on appeal* (N.Y.C. Dep't of Consumer Affairs Feb. 23, 2007), *both available at* www.nclc.org/unreported.

39 *See, e.g.*, Haw. Rev. Stat §§ 443B-3, 443B-3.5; N.C. Gen. Stat. §§ 58–70–145; Or. Rev Stat. § 697.015; Wash. Rev. Code § 19.16.260.

40 *See, e.g.*, Haw. Rev. Stat § 443B-3; Or. Rev Stat. § 697.015.

41 N.C. Gen. Stat. §§ 58–70–145.

42 *See, e.g.*, LeBlanc v. Unifund CCR Partners, 601 F.3d 1185 (11th Cir. 2010) (interpreting Florida law; since suing without registration is a misdemeanor, registration is a precondition to bringing suit); B.C. Inv. Co. v. Throm, 650 P.2d 1333 (Colo. App. 1982).

43 *See* LVNV Funding, L.L.C. v. Trice, 952 N.E.2d 1232 (Ill. App. Ct. 2011); Finch v. LVNV Funding, 71 A.3d 193 (Md. Ct. Spec. App. 2013). *See also* McDonald v. Baranowski, 19 A.3d 927 (Md. 2011).

44 *See, e.g.*, Golt v. Phillips, 517 A.2d 328 (Md. 1986); DeReggi Constr. Co. v. Mate, 747 A.2d 743 (Md. Ct. Spec. App. 2000).

45 *See* N.Y. C.P.L.R. 3015(e) (McKinney); N.C. Gen. Stat. §§ 58–70–145. *See also* Centurion Capital Corp. v. Druce, 828 N.Y.S.2d 851 (N.Y. Civ. Ct. 2006); PRA III, L.L.C. v. MacDowell, 841 N.Y.S.2d 822 (N.Y. Civ. Ct. 2007).

46 Hauk v. LVNV Funding, L.L.C., 749 F. Supp. 2d 358 (D. Md. 2010).

47 *See In re* Wilson, 311 B.R. 566 (D. Or. 2004), *aff'd sub nom.* Shelton v. Wilson, 185 Fed. Appx. 696 (9th Cir. 2006).

48 *See* Purco Fleet Servs., Inc. v. Idaho State Dep't of Fin., 90 P.3d 346 (Idaho 2004).

---

49 *See* 225 Ill. Comp. Stat. § 425/2. *See also* N.Y. City Admin. Code § 20–489; LVNV Funding, L.L.C. v. Trice, 952 N.E.2d 1232 (Ill. App. Ct. 2011).

50 *See* N.C. Gen. Stat. 58–70–15.

51 *See* Winemiller v. Worldwide Asset Purchasing, L.L.C., 2011 WL 1457749 (D. Md. Apr. 15, 2011); Commercial Serv. of Perry, Inc. v. Fitzgerald, 856 P.2d 58 (Colo. App. 1993); Settlement Agreement, In the Matter of LVNV (Office of Comm'r of Financial Regulation June 28, 2012), *available at* www.nclc.org/unreported. *See also* Fiorenzano v. LVNV Funding, L.L.C., 2012 WL 2562415 (D.R.I. June 29, 2012) (debt buyer is someone engaged in the business of a debt collector within the scope of the state registration statute).

52 *See* Bradshaw v. Hilco Receivables, L.L.C., 765 F. Supp. 2d 719 (D. Md. Feb. 23, 2011); Winemiller v. Worldwide Asset Purchasing, L.L.C., 2011 WL 1457749 (D. Md. Apr. 15, 2011); Settlement Agreement, In the Matter of LVNV (Office of Comm'r of Financial Regulation June 28, 2012), *available at* www.nclc.org/unreported.

53 PurCo Fleet Servs., Inc. v. Koenig, 240 P.3d 435 (Colo. App. 2010) (company that took assignment of debt for damages to rental car not a debt collector because debt not in default when assigned), *aff'd on other grounds*, 285 P.3d 979 (Colo. 2012).

54 Household Fin. Corp. III v. Leslie, 2005 WL 2277040 (Conn. Super. Ct. Aug. 19, 2005).

55 LeBlanc v. Unifund CCR Partners, 601 F.3d 1185 (11th Cir. 2010) (interpreting Florida law); Wisniewski v. Asset Acceptance Capital Corp., 2009 WL 212155 (N.D. Ill. Jan. 29, 2009); McCorriston v. L.W.T., Inc., 536 F. Supp. 2d 1268 (M.D. Fla. 2008); Goray v. Unifund CCR Partners, 2007 WL 4260017 (D. Haw. Dec. 4, 2007); Kim v. Riscuity, Inc., 2006 WL 2192121 (N.D. Ill. July 31, 2006); Cross v. Receivables Mgmt. Solutions, 2006 WL 446083 (D. Colo. Feb. 21, 2006); Gibson v. Grupo de Ariel, L.L.C., 2006 WL 42369 (N.D. Tex. Jan. 9, 2006) (Texas definition of third-party debt collector same as FDCPA; fact question whether debt buyer acquired debt after default); Commercial Serv. of Perry, Inc. v. Fitzgerald, 856 P.2d 58 (Colo. App. 1993); B.C. Inv. Co. v. Throm, 650 P.2d 1333 (Colo. App. 1982); Centurion Capital Corp. v. Guarino, 951 N.Y.S.2d 85 (table), 2012 WL 1543286 (N.Y. Civ. Ct. Apr. 30, 2012); Centurion Capital Corp. v. Druce, 828 N.Y.S.2d 851 (N.Y. Civ. Ct. 2006). *See also* Mass. Div. of Banks, Selected Opinion 06–060, "Passive" Debt Buyer Exemption from Debt Collector License (Oct. 13, 2006), *available at* www.mass.gov, search for "selected opinion 06–060"

When a debt collector is defined as only someone who collects the debts of another,[56] courts may interpret this language as not applying to a debt buyer suing on debt it owns.[57] But even then there is an alternative interpretation that the statute applies to a debt buyer collecting debts that were *originally* owned by another but have since been assigned.

Courts are divided whether a collection licensure statute applies to a debt buyer that is merely a "passive" collector that has no contact with the consumer, and contracts with others to perform all collection activity.[58] Sometimes a debt buyer who is not licensed will argue that it can still bring actions if it does so represented by an attorney licensed in the state where the action is brought.[59] Even if this is the case, do not assume that the attorneys of record are properly licensed in that state.[60]

3.3.5.3 State Law Requiring Debt Buyers to Be Licensed as Debt Buyers

Some states require debt buyers to be licensed not as debt collectors, but as debt buyers. States adopting the 1974 Uniform Consumer Credit Code (UCCC) require any assignee of a "supervised loan" to be licensed;[61] an unlicensed assignee is barred from enforcing the loan.[62] Thus, in these states, the assignee of a supervised loan must be licensed even if the assignee is not characterized as a collection agency pursuant to the state debt collection licensing statute. The UCCC licensing requirement only applies, however, to supervised loans, not to credit sales—such as cell phone or medical bills. The UCCC defines a supervised loan as including open end credit (credit cards) with an interest rate over 18%.[63]

Similarly, Pennsylvania has a number of licensing and related requirements that apply to debt buyers. Assignees of creditors must be licensed just as the assignor was, and, in addition, the debt buyer must have an office in the state.[64] Failure to comply makes a contract void, so the debt buyer cannot sue upon it.[65] In addition, a licensee must provide the state banking department notice before it assigns a debt to a non-licensee.[66]

3.3.6 Champerty and Other Limits on Suits on Assigned Debt

State law may prohibit certain suits on assigned debt. Connecticut prohibits a licensed collection agency from purchasing or receiving assignments of an obligation with the purpose of collection or instituting suit on the obligation.[67] This provision in effect prevents licensed collection agencies from becoming debt buyers and bringing collection actions on the debts they purchase. But some courts have been convinced that this statute applies only to licensed collection agencies collecting debts owned by others and not debts purchased and thus owned by the agency.[68]

New York Judiciary Law § 489[69] prohibits any person engaged even indirectly in the business of collection of claims and any corporation or association from buying a "book debt, or other thing in action, or any claim or demand, with the intent and for the purpose of bringing an action or proceeding thereon." Arguably, this statute prohibits certain forms of debt

(debt buyers must be licensed as debt collectors if they do any collection activity); Great Seneca Fin. Corp. v. Dowd, No. 12627–05 (N.Y. Civ. Ct. Richmond Cnty. Jan. 24, 2008), *available at* www.nclc.org/unreported; PRA III, L.L.C. v. MacDowell, 841 N.Y.S.2d 822 (N.Y. Civ. Ct. 2007); Rushmore Recoveries XI, L.L.C. v. Morninstar (N.Y. Civ. Ct. May 7, 2007), *available at* www.nclc.org/unreported; Dep't of Consumer Affairs v. Asset Acceptance, L.L.C. (N.Y.C. Dep't of Consumer Affairs July 24, 2006), *on appeal* (N.Y.C. Dep't of Consumer Affairs Feb. 23, 2007), *both available at* www.nclc.org/unreported; Centurion Capital Corp. v. Druce, 828 N.Y.S.2d 851 (N.Y. Civ. Ct. 2006); Tri-City Bldg. Ctr., Inc. v. Williams, 562 P.2d 1218 (Or. 1977); CA Partners v. Spears, 274 S.W.3d 51 (Tex. App. 2008) (Texas definition of third-party debt collector same as FDCPA; fact question whether debt buyer acquired debt after default). *Cf.* McCorriston v. L.W.T., Inc., 536 F. Supp. 2d 1268 (M.D. Fla. 2008) (noting that debt buyer may be in the business "of soliciting consumer debts for collection" under Fla. Stat. § 559.55(7), and thus required to register with state). *But see* Grismore v. RJM Acquisitions, L.L.C., 2009 WL 806627 (D. Ariz. Mar. 26, 2009) (debt buyer not required to register as debt collector if it buys debts outright without time payments or any kind of contingency arrangement), *aff'd*, 399 Fed. Appx. 217 (9th Cir. 2010).

56 *See* Ind. Code § 25–11-1-1(b); Ohio Rev. Code Ann. § 1319.12(A)(1) (West); Wash. Rev. Code § 19.16.100(4).

57 Quick Recovery Servs. v. Zehm, 2008 WL 2408090 (Wash. Ct. App. June 16, 2008). *See also* Hernandez v. Palisades Collection, L.L.C., 2008 WL 4426890 (D. Conn. Sept. 29, 2008); Barcosh, Ltd. v. Dumas, 2010 WL 2638516 (Ohio Ct. App. June 30, 2010). *Cf.* Fausset v. Mortgage First, L.L.C., 2010 WL 987169 (N.D. Ind. Mar. 12, 2010) (no summary judgment for consumer's FDCPA claim when debt buyer claimed it need not be licensed because only filed suits on own debt).

58 *Compare In re* Rogers, 2008 WL 1902050 (Bankr. E.D. Tenn. Apr. 25, 2008) (passive debt buyer not a debt collector), Kuhne v. Cohen & Slamowitz, L.L.P., 2008 WL 608607 (S.D.N.Y. Mar. 5, 2008) (passive debt buyer not a collector), *and* Mass. Div. of Banks, Selected Opinion 06–060, "Passive" Debt Buyer Exemption from Debt Collector License (Oct. 13, 2006), *available at* www.mass.gov, search for "selected opinion 06–060" (debt buyers must be licensed as debt collectors if they do any collection activity), *with* Winemiller v. Worldwide Asset Purchasing, L.L.C., 2011 WL 1457749 (D. Md. Apr. 15, 2011) (even a passive debt buyer is a collection agency); Bradshaw v. Hilco Receivables, L.L.C., ___ F. Supp. 2d ___, 2011 WL 652476 (D. Md. Feb. 23, 2011) (same).

59 *But see* Tri-City Bldg. Ctr., Inc. v. Williams, 562 P.2d 1218 (Or. 1977).

60 *See* § 3.3.9, *infra*.

61 Uniform Consumer Credit Code § 2.302 (1974).

62 *See, e.g.*, Indep. Fin., Inc. v. Wanna, 186 P.3d 196 (Kan. Ct. App. 2008).

63 *See* Unif. Consumer Credit Code § 1.301(43).

64 Letter of David H. Bleiken, Deputy Chief Counsel, Pennsylvania Dep't of Banking (Nov. 19, 2001), *available online as companion material to this treatise*.

65 *Id.*

66 *Id.*

67 *See, e.g.*, Conn. Gen. Stat. § 36a-805(a)(3).

68 *See* Hernandez v. Palisades Collection, L.L.C., 2008 WL 4426890 (D. Conn. Sept. 29, 2008); LVNV Funding, L.L.C. v. Jones, 2011 WL 2177195 (Conn. Super. Ct. May 11, 2011); Unifund CCR Partners v. Coyle, 2009 WL 1873878 (Conn. Super. Ct. June 5, 2009); Asset Acceptance Corp. v. Robinson, 625 N.W.2d 804 (Mich. Ct. App. 2001).

69 (McKinney).

buying in the state of New York. There is a similar statute, New York Judiciary Law § 488,[70] that prohibits lawyers from engaging in the same practice.

New York's highest court has found that buying a debt to enforce the obligation is not champerty in violation of the statute if the party simply intends to do so via litigation.[71] What is prohibited is buying debt with the intent and purpose of litigation "where such claims would not be prosecuted if not stirred up . . . in [an] effort to secure costs."[72] Thus, whether a debt buyer or attorney is covered by the champerty law is a matter of fact, depending on the party's intent.[73]

3.3.7 Can an Attorney Function As a Debt Buyer?

State law or state legal ethics rulings may prohibit a law firm from purchasing and suing upon debt in its own name.[74] If the law firm does so in violation of the state law, a court may find that the firm is not entitled to bring a legal action to collect on the debt.[75]

3.3.8 Requirement that a Collector Retain an Attorney to Bring Suit

A number of states require that a corporation only appear in court through counsel and not through a non-attorney employee.[76] A corporate collector's officer or employee cannot represent the collector in court unless that person is authorized to practice law in that jurisdiction.[77] Other state law may limit the ability of "debt collectors" to pursue actions without an attorney,[78] which raises the question of whether a debt buyer is a debt collector for purposes of this restriction.[79]

3.3.9 Requirements Concerning the Collection Attorney

Even if a debt buyer can properly institute a suit, a case may be dismissed if the attorney of record does not meet state requirements. A state may have a requirement that the collection attorney be licensed as a collector, and failure to comply may be enough to dismiss an action.[80] Out-of-state law firms may have to comply with registration or similar requirements to appear as counsel of record.[81]

Even apart from registration requirements, law firms may get very sloppy in complying with court requirements as to identification of the counsel of record. The largest collection firm in the country, Mann-Bracken, has dissolved, and it would not be unusual for other collection firms to cease business. Of course, a dissolved firm cannot be listed as counsel of record.

When a collector seeks to change attorneys in a pending case, then all aspects of the change must comport with state procedure. Any sloppiness in the identification of the previous attorney or designation of the new attorney may prevent the change in representation.[82]

3.4 Defects on the Face of the Complaint

3.4.1 Introduction

Consumer collection actions bear little resemblance to normal litigation. Some law firms literally file over one thousand collection complaints a week. Their focus is on volume, not precision. The collection attorney is relying on the fact that

---

70 *Id.*

71 Trust for the Certificate Holders of Merrill Lynch Mortgage Investors, Inc. v. Love Funding Corp., 918 N.E.2d 889 (N.Y. 2009). *See also* Bluebird Partners v. First Fid. Bank, 731 N.E.2d 581 (N.Y. 2000). *But see* Elliott Assocs., L.P. v. Banco de la Nacion, 194 F.3d 363 (2d Cir. 1999).

72 Trust for the Certificate Holders of Merrill Lynch Mortgage Investors, Inc. v. Love Funding Corp., 918 N.E.2d 889 (N.Y. 2009) (citing Wightman v. Catlin, 98 N.Y.S. 1071 (N.Y. App. Div. 1906)).

73 *See* Centurion Capital Corp. v. Guarino, 951 N.Y.S.2d 85 (table), 2012 WL 1543286 (N.Y. Civ. Ct. Apr. 30, 2012). *See also* DNS Equity Group Inc. v. Lavallee, 907 N.Y.S.2d 436 (table), 2010 WL 682466 (N.Y. Dist. Ct. 2010).

74 *See* Cal. Bus. & Prof. Code § 6129 (West) (misdemeanor for attorney to buy debt to sue thereon); Chulsky v. Hudson Law Offices, P.C., 777 F. Supp. 2d 811 (D.N.J. 2011), *amended in part by* 777 F. Supp. 2d 823 (D.N.J. 2011).

75 Chulsky v. Hudson Law Offices, P.C., 777 F. Supp. 2d 811 (D.N.J. 2011), *amended in part by* 777 F. Supp. 2d 823 (D.N.J. 2011).

76 *See* Miller v. Account Mgmt. Servs., 2008 WL 4415502 (N.D. Ind. Sept. 25, 2008).

77 *See, e.g., In re* Fifarek, 370 B.R. 754 (Bankr. W.D. Mich. 2007) (non-lawyer debt buyer, a single proprietor, could go to court and move to extend a judgment; if business were corporation, partnership, or other fictitious entity, licensed attorney would be required); Merco Constr. Eng'rs, Inc. v. Mun. Ct. for Long Beach Judicial Dist., 581 P.2d 636 (Cal. 1978); Remole Soil Serv., Inc. v. Benson, 215 N.E.2d 678 (Ill. App. Ct. 1966). *See also* Cleveland Bar Ass'n v. Picklo, 772 N.E.2d 1187 (Ohio 2002) (statute allowing landlords' non-lawyer agents to file eviction actions was unconstitutional violation of separation of powers); Cole v. Price, 758 A.2d 231 (Pa. Super. Ct. 2000) (creditor engaged in unauthorized practice of law when, after filing suit *pro se* he transferred his interest in claim to another; former creditor enjoined from further court appearances but case not dismissed), *rev'd in part on other grounds*, 778 A.2d 621 (Pa. 2001). *Cf. In re* Thomas, 387 B.R. 808 (D. Colo. 2008) (assignee for collection purposes may retain counsel and sue as real party in interest, but non-attorney debt buyer who agreed to split proceeds fifty-fifty with original creditor was impermissibly acting in representative capacity for original creditor). *But cf.* Harper v. Collection Bureau of Walla Walla, Inc., 2007 WL 4287293 (W.D. Wash. Dec. 4, 2007) (neither unauthorized practice nor simulated process, when president of corporate collector signed summons, which may be signed either by party or its attorney).

78 *See, e.g.*, 225 Ill. Comp. Stat. § 425/8b(e) (attorney must represent collector whether collector sues on debt it owns or collects for another); Ohio Rev. Code Ann. § 1319.12(E) (West) (debt collection agency must use attorney to sue). *See also* Wiesenfeld v. Kennedy (Pa. Ct. Com. Pl. Dec. 31, 2007), *available at* www.nclc.org/unreported (debt collector who takes assignment on a contingency basis must be represented by attorney).

79 *See* Haley v. DCO Int'l, Inc., 2010 WL 1228783 (Ohio Ct. App. Mar. 31, 2010).

80 Centurion Capital Corp. v. Guarino, 951 N.Y.S.2d 85 (table), 2012 WL 1543286 (N.Y. Civ. Ct. Apr. 30, 2012).

81 *Id.*

82 *Id.*

consumers are unlikely to contest a matter, so the form of the pleading is irrelevant. If the consumer does contest the action, the collection firm may drop the suit, so the form of the pleading is not even important to the collector if the consumer contests the action. Thus, there is little incentive for such a collection attorney to follow state requirements as to filing complaints.

It is therefore incumbent on the consumer practitioner to carefully analyze the collector's complaint for defects on its face. Such defects in the complaint and its attachments may be grounds to dismiss the case, although perhaps not with prejudice. In some states, the proper consumer response is not a motion to dismiss but a motion for a more definite statement.[83]

This section explores defects found on the face of a complaint and its attachments, and discusses applicable case law. But it is critical to realize that requirements vary by state so that case law from other states may have limited applicability.

3.4.2 Required Pleading that Collector Entitled to Bring the Action

3.4.2.1 Allegations Present in the Complaint

Some state laws require that, if the plaintiff is required to have a license, the plaintiff must allege in its complaint that it is licensed and include its licensing information in its complaint.[84] For example, if a debt buyer must be licensed, then the debt buyer's complaint is only proper in some states if the complaint alleges that the debt buyer is licensed and attaches the licensing information to the complaint.[85]

State law may also require that the complaint sufficiently demonstrate that the plaintiff owns the debt it is suing upon. North Carolina has special requirements when a plaintiff is a debt buyer. The complaint must indicate proof of the assignment that shows an unbroken chain of title, with each document evidencing the assignment containing the original account number with the debtor's name associated with the account.[86]

Delaware Justice of the Peace Courts and Courts of Common Pleas require that, when a collection agency brings suit after being assigned all rights in a claim, it must file with the court the actual assignment before the case can proceed.[87] If there has been more than one assignment, each assignment must be attached, showing at least the last four digits of the original account number and the debtor's name associated with the account number.[88]

Illinois has a somewhat complicated requirement.[89] One debt buyer challenged the Illinois statute as violating the Constitution's Commerce Clause, but a federal court found no merit in this argument.[90] Illinois courts interpret the Illinois statute as distinguishing between sale of an account to a debt buyer (where both equitable and legal ownership are transferred) and an assignment of a debt to a collector solely for collection (where the collection agency is given legal but not equitable title).

If equitable and legal title are transferred, then the debt buyer's complaint need only be verified and allege that the plaintiff is the bona fide owner and set forth how and when title was acquired, including any chain of title from the original creditor.[91] On the other hand, if the account is assigned for collection where only legal title is transferred, in addition to these requirements, the complaint must attach a document identifying the account transferred, the consideration paid, and the effective date of the transfer.[92]

An Illinois appellate court considered a case of a complex chain of title in which legal and equitable title is transferred several times, and then the legal title is transferred more than once for collection. The collector with legal title only bringing the lawsuit has multiple requirements. It first must produce a verified complaint alleging a complete chain of ownership from the original creditor through all transfers, whether of both legal and equitable title or just of legal title. Then the collector must produce evidence identifying the account transferred, the consideration paid, and the effective date of the transfer for each of the multiple transfers of legal title only, but not for the transfers that involved both legal and equitable title.[93]

In that case, the appellate court found the action should be dismissed when the collector redacted the file containing all of the accounts transferred and the consideration paid and only presented minimal information about the consumer's account on an otherwise blank piece of paper. There was no evidence that the account description on that paper related to the file containing the accounts transferred.[94]

3.4.2.2 Requirements As to Attachments to the Complaint

When a state rule requires that a writing be attached to a complaint in which a claim is based upon that writing, courts often find that this requires attaching to a debt buyer's complaint a written assignment from the original creditor to the assignee bringing the action.[95] State law may require the actual

83 Ohio Civ. R. 12(E); Capital One Bank v. Toney, 2007 WL 969420 (Ohio Ct. App. Mar. 28, 2007).

84 *See* N.Y. C.P.L.R. § 3015(e) (McKinney).

85 Centurion Capital Corp. v. Druce, 828 N.Y.S.2d 851 (N.Y. Civ. Ct. 2006). *See also* N.C. Gen. Stat. §§ 58–70–145; PRA III, L.L.C. v. MacDowell, 841 N.Y.S.2d 822 (N.Y. Civ. Ct. 2007).

86 N.C. Gen. Stat. §§ 58–70–145, 58–70–150, 58–70–155.

87 Delaware Justice of the Peace Court Directive 14(2); Administrative Directive of the Chief Judge of the Court of Common Pleas for the State of Delaware, No. 2011–1 (Mar. 16, 2011) (effective July 1, 2011).

88 Administrative Directive of the Chief Judge of the Court of Common Pleas for the State of Delaware, No. 2011–1 (Mar. 16, 2011) (effective July 1, 2011).

89 225 Ill. Comp. Stat. § 425/8b.

90 Grant-Hall v. Cavalry Portfolio Serv., L.L.C., 856 F. Supp. 2d 929 (N.D. Ill. 2012).

91 Unifund CCR Partners v. Shah, 993 NE 2d 518 (Ill. App. Ct. 2013).

92 *Id.*

93 *Id.*

94 *Id.*

95 New Century Financial Servs., Inc. v. Sanchez (N.J. Super. Ct. Law Div. Apr. 12, 2002), *available at* www.nclc.org/unreported; Midland Funding v. Snyder (Pa. Commw. Ct. Jan. 11, 2008), *available at* www.nclc.org/unreported; Portfolio Recovery Assocs. v. Gilbert (Pa. Ct.

assignment document to be attached to the complaint, and it is not sufficient for an employee of the assignee to produce an affidavit attesting to ownership of the debt.[96]

Debt buyers must produce an assignment document that shows assignment of the particular account at issue.[97] As described at §§ 3.5 and 4.3.4.2.2, *infra*, this will pose significant problems for a debt buyer that obtains thousands of accounts in one purchase transaction. The debt buyer may have to attach the "forward flow agreement" specifying the general agreements between the seller and buyer, the bill of sale for a group of accounts, and evidence that the consumer's account is in that group of accounts.

When the chain of ownership involves multiple owners, the complaint must specify the complete chain of assignments.[98] An affidavit concerning the assignment from the originating creditor is inadequate when the plaintiff did not take assignment from the creditor but from an assignee of the creditor.[99]

The requirement of obtaining documentation of the complete chain of ownership cannot be waived just because the collector is unable to obtain assignments earlier in the chain at the time it files the complaint.[100] It is clearly not adequate for a debt buyer to merely state that the assignment is currently unavailable because it is in the debt buyer's archives.[101] Even if the court were to find that the plaintiff need not immediately produce the actual assignment as an attachment to the pleadings, the complaint must at least state the fact and date of the assignment and the parties thereto.[102] Of course, additional proof will be required later. Section 4.3.4.2, *infra*, examines what a proper documentation of assignment must include. Section 3.5, *infra*, examines more generally problems with collector attachments to their complaints.

3.4.3 Pleading Requirements As to the Nature of the Collector's Claim

There are significant variations between states' requirements for legal pleadings. Most states have adopted notice pleading for civil litigation, often modeled after the Federal Rules of Civil Procedure. Other states, such as Florida, Illinois, Nebraska, and Pennsylvania, adopt "code" pleading that places more requirements on filing a complaint than is present in notice pleading states.

In reviewing the requirements for the appropriate form of pleading, be sure to look at the rules of procedure for the court in which the action is being brought. For example, a small claims court may have its own rules as to the form of the complaint and required attachments that are different from the state's general rules of civil procedure.

In addition, both "notice" and "code" states supplement general pleading requirements with special rules or statutes relating to consumer collection cases. These rules may apply only to licensed collection agencies or to debt buyers.

For example, California has enacted a Fair Debt Buyer Practices Act that is effective as of January 1, 2014, and requires that a debt buyer's complaint seeking recovery on a debt allege nine items.[103] These nine items are: that the plaintiff is a debt buyer; the nature of the debt and the consumer transaction from which it derives; the debt buyer is the sole owner of the debt; the debt balance at charge off and the amount, nature, and reason of all post-charge-off interest and fees; the date of default or last payment; the creditor's name and address and account number; the debtor's name and address as they appeared in the creditor's records prior to the first sale of the debt; the complete chain of title of the debt with names and addresses; and that the debt buyer has complied with certain requirements concerning collection contacts. The debt buyer must also attach a copy of the contract.[104]

Nevada requires that a complaint on a credit card debt include the name of the card issuer, the account number originally assigned by the issuer, any subsequent account number assigned to the account, and the date of the last transaction.[105] North Carolina and Michigan have similar rules.[106]

Com. Pl. Venango Cnty. Sept. 10, 2013), *available at* www.nclc.org/unreported; Velocity Invs., L.L.C. v. Kahanic (Pa. Ct. Com. Pl. May 1, 2012), *available at* www.nclc.org/unreported; Asset Acceptance, L.L.C. v. Jones (Pa. Ct. Com. Pl. June 10, 2011), *available at* www.nclc.org/unreported; Atlantic Credit & Finance, Inc. v. Spangler, 13 Pa. D & C.5th 339 (Pa. Ct. Com. Pl. 2010); Commonwealth Financial Systems v. Hartzell, 17 Pa. D. & C.5th 176 (Pa. Ct. Com. Pl. 2010); Discover Bank v. Winfree, 11 Pa. D. & C.5th 3212 (Pa. Ct. Com. Pl. 2010); LVNV Funding, L.L.C. v. Johns (Pa. Ct. Com. Pl. Nov. 5, 2010), *available at* www.nclc.org/unreported; Arrow Fin. Servs., L.L.C. v. Witmer (Pa. Ct. Com. Pl. May 13, 2010), *available at* www.nclc.org/unreported; Unifund CCR Partners v. Vo (Pa. Ct. Com. Pl. Feb. 17, 2009), *available at* www.nclc.org/unreported; Remit Corp. v. Miller, 5 Pa. D. & C.5th 43 (Pa. Ct. Com. Pl. 2008); Atlantic Credit & Fin., Inc. v. Gardner (Pa. Ct. Com. Pl. May 14, 2008), *available at* www.nclc.org/unreported; Cavalry Portfolio Servs., L.L.C. v. Rowan (Pa. Ct. Com. Pl. Feb. 6, 2008), *available at* www.nclc.org/unreported; Palisades Collection, L.L.C. v. Grassmyer (Pa. Ct. Com. Pl. Jan. 15, 2008), *available at* www.nclc.org/unreported; Worldwide Asset Purchasing, L.L.C. v. Stern (Pa. Ct. Com. Pl. May 13, 2005), *available at* www.nclc.org/unreported. *See also* LVNV Funding, L.L.C. v. Theurer (Pa. Ct. Com. Pl. Feb. 2, 2009), *available at* www.nclc.org/unreported. *But see* Hudson & Keyse, L.L.C. v. Carson, 2008 WL 2221968 (Ohio Ct. App. May 29, 2008).

96 Asset Acceptance, L.L.C. v. Jones (Pa. Ct. Com. Pl. June 10, 2011), *available at* www.nclc.org/unreported; Atlantic Credit & Finance, Inc. v. Spangler, 13 Pa. D & C.5th 339 (Pa. Ct. Com. Pl. 2010).

97 Portfolio Recovery Assocs. v. Gilbert (Pa. Ct. Com. Pl. Venango Cnty. Sept. 10, 2013), *available at* www.nclc.org/unreported.

98 Cach, L.L.C. v. Craig (Pa. Ct. Com. Pl. Dec. 15, 2010), *available at* www.nclc.org/unreported.

99 *Id.*

100 *See* Four Seasons Invs., L.L.C. v. Petrucci (Pa. Ct. Com. Pl. May 10, 2011), *available at* www.nclc.org/unreported.

101 Cavalry Portfolio Servs., L.L.C. v. Rowan (Pa. Ct. Com. Pl. Feb. 6, 2008), *available at* www.nclc.org/unreported.

102 Cach, L.L.C. v. Abbott (Pa. Ct. Com. Pl. Mar. 15, 2010), *available at* www.nclc.org/unreported; LVNV Funding, L.L.C. v. Theurer (Pa. Ct. Com. Pl. Feb. 2, 2009), *available at* www.nclc.org/unreported; Cavalry Portfolio Servs., L.L.C. v. Rowan (Pa. Ct. Com. Pl. Feb. 6, 2008), *available at* www.nclc.org/unreported.

103 *See* Cal. Civ. Code § 1788.58(a) (West).

104 Cal Civ. Code § 1788.58(b) (West).

105 Nev. Rev. Stat. § 97A.165.

106 Mich. Ct. R. 3.101; N.C. Gen. Stat. §§ 58-70-145, 58-70-150, 58-70-155.

In Delaware, in any action suing on a consumer loan or a credit card, the following information must be set forth with specificity: the original creditor and the assignee, the last four digits of the original account number, the full chain of assignment, and the amounts being sought for principal, interest, fees, and other charges, broken down separately.[107] A Massachusetts small claims court rule does not allow a default to be entered unless a collector has included in the claim the name of the original creditor, the last four digits of the account number assigned by the original creditor, and the amount and date of the consumer's last payment.[108] Iowa requires that the complaint allege the facts of the consumer's default, the amount to which the creditor is entitled, and an indication of how that amount was determined.[109]

The Federal Trade Commission has stated that a consumer collection complaint should include the following information: the name of the original creditor, the last four digits of the account number, the date of default and the amount due at that time, the name of the current owner of the debt, the total amount due and a breakdown by principal, interest and fees.[110] While this finding is not binding on a court, it provides guidance as to what information an adequate complaint should include.

3.4.4 *Defective Summons and Service*

Often a state's technical requirements for a summons must be strictly construed and followed. Any non-compliance should be grounds to dismiss the action.[111] Thus, an action should be dismissed when the plaintiff's attorney's address is not included as required by state rules or when the summons does not mention that it is from the state.[112]

Even if a consumer has actual notice of a summons and appears in the case, defective service of the summons may be grounds to dismiss the case, because the court does not have jurisdiction over the defendant.[113] In one case, delivery of the summons by FedEx was found not in compliance with state rules, nor was delivery only to the defendant's husband, when state rules required delivery to the defendant personally.[114]

3.4.5 *Signature and Verification of the Complaint*

Federal Rule of Civil Procedure 11(a) requires that a complaint be signed by the attorney of record in the attorney's name or by a party personally if the party is unrepresented. Thus, in states following the federal rule, the pleading is improper if signed by someone other than the attorney of record.

Under federal rules, the complaint need not be verified or accompanied by an affidavit. Some states, however, require that a complaint be verified and specify how a corporation is to verify the complaint. Failure to meet such state requirements as to verification should suffice to get the case dismissed.[115] For example, facts stated in a complaint may have to be stated as true upon the signer's personal knowledge or information and belief. This requirement is not met when the complaint is signed with an unreadable signature by an otherwise unnamed paralegal for the collector with no personal knowledge of the facts and not an officer of the plaintiff.[116]

In Pennsylvania, with certain exceptions, the verification must be by a party and not the party's attorney. A complaint is improper when verified by the attorney, and none of the exceptions apply.[117] The same is the case when the verification is signed by an employee of the creditor's service provider.[118] In Pennsylvania, the individual verifying the complaint for a corporation must be an officer of the corporation and not just a records custodian.[119] The verification must also set forth the source of information for the individual signing the verification as to matters not stated upon that person's knowledge.[120]

3.4.6 *False or Vague Pleadings*

Claims based upon obviously false statements in the pleadings are subject to dismissal. Collection law firms that file hundreds of cases a day may be producing pleadings by filling in the blanks within one standard form complaint without bothering to analyze how a particular case's facts fit that form pleading. For example, the pleadings may allege that the contract was between the consumer and the debt buyer, instead of between the consumer and the original creditor. The debt buyer may also allege that it supplied goods and services to the consumer, even though it clearly did not do so as an assignee.

Other times, the pleading is not false on its face but will be vague as to what is being alleged. For example, the complaint may not identify the originating creditor or the account that is allegedly in default. The complaint may not specify the legal basis for the recovery being sought.

---

107 Administrative Directive of the Chief Judge of the Court of Common Pleas for the State of Delaware, No. 2011–1 (Mar. 16, 2011) (effective July 1, 2011).

108 Mass. Unif. Small Claims Rule 2(b) (effective Oct. 1, 2009).

109 Iowa Code § 537.5114. *See also* Capital One Bank v. Denboer, 791 N.W.2d 264 (Iowa Ct. App. 2010).

110 Fed. Trade Comm'n, Repairing a Broken System 17 (July 2010).

111 *See* Dobbs v. Discover Bank, ___ S.W.3d ___, 2012 Ark. App. 678 (Ark. Ct. App. 2012).

112 *Id.*

113 *Id.*

114 *Id.*

115 Portfolio Recovery Assocs. v. Gilbert (Pa. Ct. Com. Pl. Venango Cnty. Sept. 10, 2013), *available at* www.nclc.org/unreported.

116 Atlantic Credit & Finance, Inc. v. Giuliana, 829 A.2d 340 (Pa. Super. Ct. 2003). *See also* Worldwide Asset Purchasing, L.L.C. v. Stern (Pa. Ct. Com. Pl. May 13, 2005), *available at* www.nclc.org/unreported.

117 Discover Bank v. Winfree, 11 Pa. D & C 5th 321 (Pa. Ct. Com. Pl. 2010); LVNV Funding, L.L.C. v. Johns (Pa. Ct. Com. Pl. Nov. 5, 2010), *available at* www.nclc.org/unreported; Arrow Fin. Servs., L.L.C. v. Witmer (Pa. Ct. Com. Pl. May 13, 2010), *available at* www.nclc.org/unreported.

118 Citibank v. Mszyco (Pa. Ct. Com. Pl. Mar. 15, 2011), *available at* www.nclc.org/unreported.

119 Portfolio Recovery Assocs. v. Gilbert (Pa. Ct. Com. Pl. Venango Cnty. Sept. 10, 2013), *available at* www.nclc.org/unreported.

120 Citibank v. Mszyco (Pa. Ct. Com. Pl. Mar. 15, 2011), *available at* www.nclc.org/unreported.

Even in notice pleading states, a vague pleading is not sufficient. Federal Rule of Civil Procedure 12(e) allows a defendant to move that the plaintiff file a more definite statement when the complaint is "so vague or ambiguous that the [defendant] cannot reasonably prepare a response." The U.S. Supreme Court has stated that a complaint must "give the defendant fair notice of what the . . . claim is and the grounds upon which it rests."[121] Moreover, the Supreme Court has said that in a complaint "the plaintiff pleads factual content that allows the court to draw the reasonable inference that the defendant is liable for the misconduct alleged."[122]

3.5 Problems with Attachments to the Complaint

3.5.1 Required Attachments to the Complaint

Besides standards as to the complaint itself, a collection action often has to comply with state procedural rules specifying documents that must be attached to the complaint. (Subsection 3.4.2.2, *supra*, discusses the special requirement that a debt buyer has the right to bring an action on the debt—this subsection focuses instead on required attachments relating to the consumer's obligation to pay the amount sought.)

Debt buyer compliance with these rules is often sloppy. If rules require a document to be attached and it is not, this may be grounds to dismiss the case.[123] Nevertheless, at least in Ohio, the consumer must first file a motion for a more definite statement before bringing a motion to dismiss.[124]

A number of state court rules specify that, if a claim is based upon a written document, then a copy of the document shall be attached to the complaint; if the writing is not accessible to the pleader, then it is sufficient to state the reason it is not accessible and the substance of the writing.[125] Other state law may require the same for debt buyers. California has enacted a Fair Debt Buyer Practices Act that is effective as of January 1, 2014, and that requires the debt buyer to attach a copy of the contract to any complaint.[126]

When a collection case is based upon a credit agreement, then non-compliance with the rules concerning the attachments to the complaint should be grounds for dismissal.[127] It may not even be enough to later provide the document. If the required document is not attached to the initial complaint, the case should be dismissed for non-compliance with pleading rules.[128]

To take advantage of an exception that a document is not accessible, the collector must at least state the reason that it is not accessible and provide the substance of the writing.[129] The purpose of this provision is to permit a party to proceed when the writing is in the possession of an opposing party or when the party can state the contents of the writing from his or her own recollection.[130] These rationales are clearly inapplicable to

121 Bell Atl. Corp. v. Twombly, 550 U.S. 544, 555, 127 S. Ct. 1955, 167 L. Ed. 2d 929 (2007).

122 Ashcroft v. Iqbal, 129 S. Ct. 1937, 1949, 173 L. Ed. 2d 868, 556 U.S. 662 (2009).

123 *See, e.g.*, LVNV Funding, L.L.C. v. Nardi, 2012 Ark. 460 (Ark. 2012); Four Seasons Invs., L.L.C. v. Petrucci (Pa. Ct. Com. Pl. May 10, 2011), *available at* www.nclc.org/unreported; Worldwide Asset Purchasing, L.L.C. v. Stern (Pa. Ct. Com. Pl. May 13, 2005), *available at* www.nclc.org/unreported.

124 *See* Midland Funding L.L.C. v. Biehl, 2013 WL 5407593 (Ohio Ct. App Sept. 23, 2013).

125 *See, e.g.*, Ark. R. Civ. P. 10(d); Fla. Small Cl. R. 7.050(a); Fla. R. Civ. P. 1.130; 735 Ill. Comp. Stat. § 5/2–606; N.J. R. Civ. P. 6:6–3(a); N.M. R. Civ. P. 1–009(I); Ohio Civ. R. 10(D); Pa. R. Civ. P. 1019(i); Administrative Directive of the Chief Judge of the Court of Common Pleas for the State of Delaware, No. 2011–1 (Mar. 16, 2011) (effective July 1, 2011); LVNV Funding, L.L.C. v. Nardi, 2012 Ark. 460 (Ark. 2012). *See also* Ind. Proc. R. 9.2(A).

126 Cal Civ. Code § 1788.58(b) (West).

127 Fla. Credit Research, Inc. v. Felicien (Fla. Duval Cnty. Ct. Apr. 15, 2008), *available at* www.nclc.org/unreported; N. Star Capitol Acquisition, L.L.C. v. Lewis (Fla. Duval Cnty. Ct. Oct. 23, 2007), *available at* www.nclc.org/unreported (illegible contract, without the defendant's name or other indication that it relates to the complaint, no dates, and exhibit not attached); LVNV Funding, L.L.C. v. Matthews (Fla. Duval Cnty. Ct. Oct. 4, 2007), *available at* www.nclc.org/unreported; LVNV Funding, L.L.C. v. Moeherlin (Fla. Volusia Cnty. Ct. Aug. 2006), *available at* www.nclc.org/unreported; Velocity Invs., L.L.C. v. Alston, 922 N.E.2d 538 (Ill. App. Ct. 2010); New Century Fin. Servs., Inc. v. Sanchez (N.J. Super. Ct. Law Div. Apr. 12, 2002), *available at* www.nclc.org/unreported; Citibank v. Martin, 807 N.Y.S.2d 284 (N.Y. Civ. Ct. 2005); Capital One Bank v. Toney, 2007 WL 969420 (Ohio Ct. App. Mar. 28, 2007); Administrative Directive of the Chief Judge of the Court of Common Pleas for the State of Delaware, No. 2011–1 (Mar. 16, 2011) (effective July 1, 2011); Atlantic Credit & Fin., Inc. v. Giuliana, 829 A.2d 340 (Pa. Super. Ct. 2003); Asset Acceptance, L.L.C. v. Jones (Pa. Ct. Com. Pl. June 10, 2011), *available at* www.nclc.org/unreported; Cach, L.L.C. v. Craig (Pa. Ct. Com. Pl. Dec. 15, 2010), *available at* www.nclc.org/unreported; Discover Bank v. Winfree, 11 Pa. D & C 5th 321 (Pa. Ct. Com. Pl. 2010); Cavalry Portfolio Servs., L.L.C. v. Mostyn (Pa. Ct. Com. Pl. Feb. 2011), *available at* www.nclc.org/unreported; Arrow Financial Servs., L.L.C. v. Witmer (Pa. Ct. Com. Pl. May 13, 2010), *available at* www.nclc.org/unreported; Midland Funding v. Snyder (Pa. Commw. Ct. Jan. 11, 2008), *available at* www.nclc.org/unreported; Asset Acceptance, L.L.C. v. Madden (Pa. Ct. Com. Pl. Mar. 19, 2009), *available at* www.nclc.org/unreported; LVNV Funding, L.L.C. v. Theurer (Pa. Ct. Com. Pl. Feb. 2, 2009), *available at* www.nclc.org/unreported; Cach, L.L.C. v. Myers (Pa. Ct. Com. Pl. Oct. 6, 2008), *available at* www.nclc.org/unreported; Belmont Fin. Servs. Group, Inc. v. Hawkins (Pa. Ct. Com. Pl. July 24, 2008), *available at* www.nclc.org/unreported; Atlantic Credit & Fin., Inc. v. Gardner (Pa. Ct. Com. Pl. May 14, 2008), *available at* www.nclc.org/unreported; Cavalry Portfolio Servs., L.L.C. v. Rowan (Pa. Ct. Com. Pl. Feb. 6, 2008), *available at* www.nclc.org/unreported; Palisades Collection, L.L.C. v. Grassmyer (Pa. Ct. Com. Pl. Jan. 15, 2008), *available at* www.nclc.org/unreported; FIA Card Servs. v. Kirasic (Pa. Ct. Com. Pl. Nov. 7, 2007), *available at* www.nclc.org/unreported; Preston State Bank v. Jordan, 692 S.W.2d 740 (Tex. App. 1985). *See also In re* Tran, 369 B.R. 312 (Bankr. S.D. Tex. 2007). *But see* Nat'l Check Bureau v. Buerger, 2006 WL 3702638 (Ohio Ct. App. Dec. 18, 2006).

128 *See* LVNV Funding, L.L.C. v. Nardi, 2012 WL 6218481 (Ark. Dec. 13, 2012).

129 Asset Acceptance, L.L.C. v. Madden (Pa. Ct. Com. Pl. Mar. 19, 2009), *available at* www.nclc.org/unreported; Cavalry Portfolio Servs., L.L.C. v. Rowan (Pa. Ct. Com. Pl. Feb. 6, 2008), *available at* www.nclc.org/unreported.

130 Belmont Fin. Servs. Group, Inc. v. Hawkins (Pa. Ct. Com. Pl. July 24, 2008), *available at* www.nclc.org/unreported.

a debt buyer who never saw the contract between the original creditor and consumer.[131]

It is also insufficient for the collector to state that the defendant at one time was sent a copy and thus should have the document.[132] Similarly, to claim that the documents cannot be provided because they "may be" voluminous is not a valid reason. This claim implies the collector has the documents, and it must so state and then describe with some specificity the size of the documents to justify why they are not attached.

3.5.2 *Is the Attachment Actually Attached?*

Debt buyers sometimes pretend to comply with rules as to the form of attachments, without really doing so. If the complaint claims there is an attachment, make sure the attachment is actually attached. If the attachment refers to attachments to itself, make sure those attachments are attached.[133] A complaint cannot refer to exhibits "A" and "B," when there is only one illegible attachment, labeled neither "A" nor "B," that does not contain the defendant's name or relate in any other way to the case.[134]

3.5.3 *Sufficiency of an Attached Document*

When state rules require that a breach of contract claim attach a copy of the contract to the complaint, there must be more than just an unsigned, standard form contract attached to the complaint. Some connection between that form contract and the defendant and the defendant's account number must be provided.[135]

For example, credit card issuers utilize different standard form contracts and these are often amended over time. The collector has not attached the operative contract when the contract attached is the original version that does not include any subsequent amendments applicable to the consumer.[136] It is not sufficient to attach an unsigned standard form agreement from 2002 when the consumer first obtained credit in 2006.[137] Similarly, appending the current contract should not suffice if the consumer's account has been closed since well before that form of the standard form contract was ever used.

Pennsylvania courts require that the credit card agreement include the "Schumer Box" that specifies the annual percentage rate (APR) and other key terms of the transaction. The complaint is inadequate if that information is not attached to the complaint.[138]

The specificity of what the collector attaches to the complaint as the contract should be considered in relationship to a federal regulation provision requiring the originating card issuer to provide consumers with a copy of their contract when requested.[139] The card issuer must post and maintain the consumer's agreement on its website or provide a copy upon request. Thus, federal law requires that the contract be retained and accessible.

A court had little problem finding inadequate an unsigned and undated ledger card that did not reference the account number, the name of the plaintiff, or the original account holder.[140] The complaint may also have to attach a copy of the consumer's signed application.[141] Attaching the application and some monthly statements is not enough when the collector submits a version of the application in which the back of the application, instead of containing the terms and conditions of the agreement, is left blank.[142] It is insufficient to attach a copy of an account statement generated by the debt buyer and not even by the card issuer.[143] A final bill is also not sufficient.[144]

This requirement that the contract be attached cannot be met by a report and affidavit from a legal specialist of the plaintiff debt buyer, particularly when that person is not

131 *Id.*

132 Point Rental Co. v. Posani, 368 N.E.2d 1267 (Ohio Ct. App. 1976); Midland Funding, L.L.C. v. Snyder (Pa. Ct. Com. Pl. Jan. 11, 2008), *available at* www.nclc.org/unreported.

133 *See* §§ 4.2.3, 4.3.4, *infra.*

134 N. Star Capital Acquisition, L.L.C. v. Lewis (Fla. Duval Cnty. Ct. Oct. 23, 2007), *available at* www.nclc.org/unreported.

135 *See, e.g.*, Velocity Invs., L.L.C. v. Alston, 922 N.E.2d 538 (Ill. App. Ct. 2010); Target Nat'l Bank v. Kilbride (Pa. Ct. Com. Pl. Feb. 5, 2010), *available at* www.nclc.org/unreported; Midland Funding, L.L.C. v. Snyder (Pa. Ct. Com. Pl. Jan. 11, 2008), *available at* www.nclc.org/unreported.

136 Target Nat'l Bank v. Greiner (Pa. Commw. Ct. Sept. 30, 2009), *available at* www.nclc.org/unreported; Remit Corp. v. Miller, 5 Pa. D. & C.5th 43 (Pa. Ct. Com. Pl. 2008); FIA Card Servs. v. Kirasic (Pa. Ct. Com. Pl. Nov. 7, 2007), *available at* www.nclc.org/unreported; Worldwide Asset Purchasing, L.L.C. v. Stern (Pa. Ct. Com. Pl. May 13, 2005), *available at* www.nclc.org/unreported. *See also* Midland Funding v. Snyder (Pa. Commw. Ct. Jan. 11, 2008), *available at* www.nclc.org/unreported (date of contract is unstated).

137 Capital One Bank v. Clevenstine, 2009 WL 1245043 (Pa. Ct. Com. Pl. Jan. 30, 2009). *See also* Target Nat'l Bank v. Kilbride (Pa. Ct. Com. Pl. Feb. 5, 2010), *available at* www.nclc.org/unreported.

138 Portfolio Recovery Assocs. v. Gilbert (Pa. Ct. Com. Pl. Venango Cnty. Sept. 10, 2013), *available at* www.nclc.org/unreported.

139 12 C.F.R. § 1026.58(e).

140 LVNV Funding, L.L.C. v. Matthews (Fla. Duval Cnty. Ct. Oct. 4, 2007), *available at* www.nclc.org/unreported; Capital One Bank v. Clevenstine (Pa. Ct. Com. Pl. Jan. 30, 2009), *available at* www.nclc.org/unreported. *See also* Fla. Credit Research, Inc. v. Stromberg (Fla. Duval Cnty. Ct. June 22, 2007), *available at* www.nclc.org/unreported; Target Nat'l Bank v. Greiner (Pa. Commw. Ct. Sept. 30, 2009), *available at* www.nclc.org/unreported; Remit Corp. v. Miller, 5 Pa. D. & C.5th 43 (Pa. Ct. Com. Pl. 2008); Cach, L.L.C. v. Myers (Pa. Ct. Com. Pl. Oct. 6, 2008), *available at* www.nclc.org/unreported; Cavalry Portfolio Servs., L.L.C. v. Rowan (Pa. Ct. Com. Pl. Feb. 6, 2008), *available at* www.nclc.org/unreported; Worldwide Asset Purchasing, L.L.C. v. Stern (Pa. Ct. Com. Pl. May 13, 2005), *available at* www.nclc.org/unreported.

141 Target Nat'l Bank v. Greiner (Pa. Commw. Ct. Sept. 30, 2009), *available at* www.nclc.org/unreported.

142 Cach, L.L.C. v. Abbott (Pa. Ct. Com. Pl. Mar. 15, 2010), *available at* www.nclc.org/unreported.

143 Velocity Invs., L.L.C. v. Alston, 922 N.E.2d 538 (Ill. App. Ct. 2010). *See also* Discover Bank v. Winfree, 11 Pa. C & D 5th 321 (Pa. Ct. Com. Pl. 2010) (account statement not sufficient to prove a contract).

144 Cach, L.L.C. v. Myers (Pa. Ct. Com. Pl. Oct. 6, 2008), *available at* www.nclc.org/unreported.

familiar with the business records of the original creditor.[145] An affidavit certainly is not sufficient if it does not identify the account number[146] or has the wrong account number. Nor is it sufficient to state that a copy of the contract has been requested and will be provided upon receipt.[147]

When the collector is suing on the contract or on an "open account" theory, then the collector should also attach to the complaint monthly statements or other documentation showing how the amount owed was computed.[148] Moreover, when a collector seeks interest and other fees under the credit agreement, the contract that must be appended to the complaint must include the collector's basis for the claimed fees and interest. If these charges are set out in a separate disclosure, that disclosure must also be appended.[149]

In Illinois, the collector must attach appropriate documents even when suing on a non-written agreement.[150] Thus, even if the agreement is based upon the card issuer sending terms to the consumer and the consumer's subsequent use of the credit card, the collector's complaint must attach the terms of the agreement and tie those terms to the consumer—that is, show that those terms were sent to the consumer.[151] This must not only be proven at trial but produced with the initial complaint.[152]

145 Velocity Invs., L.L.C. v. Alston, 922 N.E.2d 538 (Ill. App. Ct. 2010); PRA III, L.L.C. v. MacDowell, 841 N.Y.S.2d 822 (N.Y. Civ. Ct. 2007).

146 Hudson & Keyse, L.L.C. v. Carson, 2008 WL 2221968 (Ohio Ct. App. May 29, 2008).

147 *See* LVNV Funding, L.L.C. v. Theurer (Pa. Ct. Com. Pl. Feb. 2, 2009), *available at* www.nclc.org/unreported.

148 Fla. Credit Research, Inc. v. Felicien (Fla. Duval Cnty. Ct. Apr. 15, 2008), *available at* www.nclc.org/unreported; Hudson & Keyse, L.L.C. v. Carson, 2008 WL 2221968 (Ohio Ct. App. May 29, 2008); Asset Acceptance, L.L.C. v. Jones (Pa. Ct. Com. Pl. June 10, 2011), *available at* www.nclc.org/unreported; LVNV Funding, L.L.C. v. Johns (Pa. Ct. Com. Pl. Nov. 5, 2010), *available at* www.nclc.org/unreported; Unifund CCR Partners v. Vo (Pa. Ct. Com. Pl. Feb. 17, 2009), *available at* www.nclc.org/unreported (insufficient to show just recent statements showing interest and other charges but not original purchases); LVNV Funding, L.L.C. v. Theurer (Pa. Ct. Com. Pl. Feb. 2, 2009), *available at* www.nclc.org/unreported; Midland Funding, L.L.C. v. Snyder (Pa. Ct. Com. Pl. Jan. 11, 2008), *available at* www.nclc.org/unreported; Worldwide Asset Purchasing, L.L.C. v. Stern (Pa. Ct. Com. Pl. May 13, 2005), *available at* www.nclc.org/unreported. *See also* Remit Corp. v. Miller, 5 Pa. D. & C.5th 43 (Pa. Ct. Com. Pl. 2008). *Cf.* Capital One Bank v. Day, 892 N.E.2d 932 (Ohio Ct. App. 2008) (following *Nolan*); Capital One Bank v. Nolan, 2008 WL 1758892 (Ohio Ct. App. Apr. 15, 2008) (at the complaint stage, the account must start with a provable balance, but not necessarily one that is proven at that stage of the litigation); Capital One Bank v. Clevenstine (Pa. Ct. Com. Pl. Jan. 30, 2009), *available at* www.nclc.org/unreported (sufficient to attach all monthly billing statements from the opening of the account to the present, reflecting individual charges and fees).

149 Unifund CCR Partners v. Vo (Pa. Ct. Com. Pl. Feb. 17, 2009), *available at* www.nclc.org/unreported.

150 Razor Capital v. Antaal, 972 N.E.2d 1238 (Ill. App. Ct. 2012).

151 *Id.*

152 *Id.*

3.5.4 Attachments for Account Stated Claims

Collectors often seek to recover based upon an account stated cause of action.[153] The claim is that the consumer has been sent a statement of the account, and the consumer has implicitly agreed to pay that amount. Thus, the action is not upon the original contract or the individual charges making up the statement of account, but on the promise to pay the amount included in the statement.[154]

An account stated claim may allow the plaintiff to avoid proving each of the underlying obligations making up the statement of account, but it does not mean the plaintiff can avoid the obligation to show that there is in fact a statement of account that has been agreed to. The collector must allege that there is an account stated and that there is evidence that the consumer has agreed to that account stated.[155]

Thus if state law requires that, when a claim is based upon a writing, that the writing be attached to the complaint,[156] then the collector must attach the actual account stated to which the consumer allegedly has agreed. The attachment must be more than a memorandum but must show on its face that it was intended to be a final settlement up to that date,[157] and show individual items, amount due, and dates.[158] Pennsylvania

153 This cause of action is examined in more detail in § 4.7, *infra*.

154 *See* § 4.7, *infra*.

155 Cavalry Portfolio Servs., L.L.C. v. Mostyn (Pa. Ct. Com. Pl. Feb. 2011), *available at* www.nclc.org/unreported; Capital One Bank v. Clevenstine (Pa. Ct. Com. Pl. Jan. 30, 2009), *available at* www.nclc.org/unreported.

156 *See, e.g.*, Ark. R. Civ. P. 10(d); Fla. Small Cl. R. 7.050(a); Fla. R. Civ. P. 1.1.30; 735 Ill. Comp. Stat. § 5/2–606; N.J. R. Civ. P. 6:6–3(a); N.M. R. Civ. P. 1–009(I); Ohio Civ. R. 10(D); Pa. R. Civ. P. 1019(i). *See also* Ind. Proc. R. 9.2(A).

157 *See* Ahlbin v. Crescent Commercial Corp., 224 P.2d 131 (Cal. Ct. App. 1950); Capital One Bank v. Toney, 2007 WL 969420 (Ohio Ct. App. Mar. 28, 2007). *But see* Citibank v. Kessler, 2004 WL 795689 (Ohio Ct. App. Apr. 15, 2004); Cavalry Portfolio Servs., L.L.C. v. Mostyn (Pa. Ct. Com. Pl. Feb. 2011), *available at* www.nclc.org/unreported.

158 *See* Nevilles v. Citigroup, Inc., 2007 WL 1879427 (S.D. Fla. June 27, 2007); Fla. Credit Research, Inc. v. Felicien (Fla. Duval Cnty. Ct. Apr. 15, 2008), *available at* www.nclc.org/unreported; N. Star Capital Acquisition, L.L.C. v. Lewis (Fla. Duval Cnty. Ct. Oct. 23, 2007), *available at* www.nclc.org/unreported; LVNV Funding, L.L.C. v. Matthews (Fla. Duval Cnty. Ct. Oct. 4, 2007), *available at* www.nclc.org/unreported; Capital One Bank v. Gelsey (Fla. Duval Cnty. Ct. July 3, 2007), *available at* www.nclc.org/unreported; New Century Fin. Servs., Inc. v. Sanchez (N.J. Super. Ct. Law Div. Apr. 12, 2002), *available at* www.nclc.org/unreported; Cach, L.L.C. v. Craig (Pa. Ct. Com. Pl. Dec. 15, 2010), *available at* www.nclc.org/unreported; Arrow Financial Servs., L.L.C. v. Witmer (Pa. Ct. Com. Pl. May 13, 2010), *available at* www.nclc.org/unreported; Cavalry Portfolio Servs., L.L.C. v. Mostyn (Pa. Ct. Com. Pl. Feb. 2011), *available at* www.nclc.org/unreported; Palisades Collection, L.L.C. v. Grassmyer (Pa. Ct. Com. Pl. Jan. 15, 2008), *available at* www.nclc.org/unreported; FIA Card Servs. v. Kirasic (Pa. Ct. Com. Pl. Nov. 7, 2007), *available at* www.nclc.org/unreported. *See also* Mercy Franciscan Hosp. v. Willis, 2004 Ohio App. LEXIS 4595 (Ohio Ct. App. Sept. 24, 2004); Asset Acceptance, L.L.C. v. Madden (Pa. Ct. Com. Pl. Mar. 19, 2009), *available at* www.nclc.org/unreported; Unifund CCR Partners v. Vo (Pa. Ct. Com. Pl. Feb. 17, 2009), *available at* www.nclc.org/unreported (insufficient to show just recent statements showing interest and other charges but not original purchases); Atlantic Credit & Fin., Inc. v. Gardner (Pa. Ct. Com.

courts also require that a copy of the contract itself be attached even in an account-stated cause of action, because an element of an account stated is that there is an agreement between the parties underlying the statement of account.[159]

3.6 Statute of Limitations

3.6.1 Raising the Defense

Particularly when a debt buyer is bringing a collection action, the statute of limitations is a key consumer defense. A statute of limitations defense can be raised as an affirmative defense and as grounds for a motion to dismiss, or later through a summary judgment motion or at the trial. The consumer may also bring a Fair Debt Collection Practices Act (FDCPA) counterclaim or a separate affirmative action based upon the collector's filing of a lawsuit outside the applicable statutes of limitations.[160] This section focuses on what statute of limitations applies to a case and how the limitations period is computed—irrespective of whether expiration of the limitations period is raised in a motion to dismiss, at trial, or in an FDCPA action.

Determining whether the statute of limitations has run turns out to be a surprisingly complicated process. The first questions deal with whether a federal or state limitations period applies and, if a state law period applies, then which state's law applies—the law of the forum state or some other state.[161] The next question is which limitations period in the appropriate state applies to each separate collector cause of action. A state will have limitations periods of varying length that apply to different causes of action, and there is often uncertainty concerning which limitations period applies to a particular claim.[162] Finally, there are issues as to how to compute a particular limitations period—when it starts running and whether the running is tolled or revived.[163] Statutes of limitations on judgments are discussed in § 12.15, *infra*.

3.6.2 Federal Statutes of Limitations

3.6.2.1 General

In general, collection actions are governed by state statutes of limitations, but there are several important situations in which federal law determines the limitations period. Collection actions on debts owed to the United States are governed by federal limitations periods, as described in Chapter 10, *infra*. As discussed *infra*, federal law also tolls state statutes of limitations when the defendant is on active duty in the military[164] and during the pendency of a bankruptcy proceeding.[165] Federal law may also determine the limitations periods for actions to collect debt emanating from cell phone and long-distance charges, considered immediately below.[166]

3.6.2.2 Two-Year Federal Limitations for Cell Phone and Long Distance Phone Charges

3.6.2.2.1 General

Federal law appears to specify a two-year statute of limitations for actions to recover on cell phone charges and on interstate or foreign landline communication charges.[167] 47 U.S.C. § 415(a) states that: "All actions at law by carriers for recovery of their lawful charges . . . shall be begun, within two years from the time the cause of action accrues, and not after." This language, by its own terms, applies to all actions and not just to causes of action brought under the federal telecommunications statutes or pursuant to federally regulated tariffs. Thus, it applies to actions to collect the carrier's charges from a consumer. If this short limitations period is enforced (as described *infra*, some courts refuse to do so), it has significant practical import because a large number of collection lawsuits are based upon such charges but are brought beyond this two-year limitations period.

In addition, while the federal limitation does not apply to state-regulated local phone charges, local telephone bills often include charges for long-distance or cell phone service. For debts more than two years old, the collector will have to specify the amount of the total outstanding balance (including any interest charges) which relates solely to local service and that which relates to interstate, foreign, or cell phone usage. This may impose an impossible burden on a debt buyer with limited access to the original monthly billing statements. Similarly, the same bill may bundle local and long-distance charges with cable television and even internet access. When two years have elapsed, the collector will have to specify what portion of the bill is subject to the two year limitations period and what portion does not.

Pl. May 14, 2008), *available at* www.nclc.org/unreported; Cavalry Portfolio Servs., L.L.C. v. Rowan (Pa. Ct. Com. Pl. Feb. 6, 2008), *available at* www.nclc.org/unreported. *But see* Capital One Bank v. Nolan, 2008 WL 1758892 (Ohio Ct. App. Apr. 15, 2008) (there are limits as to the specificity required at the pleading stage, as opposed to the proof stage).

159 Velocity Invs., L.L.C. v. Kahanic (Pa. Ct. Com. Pl. May 1, 2012), *available at* www.nclc.org/unreported.

160 *See* §§ 5.5, 13.4, *infra*.

161 *See* §§ 3.6.2, 3.6.3, *infra*.

162 *See* §§ 3.6.4–3.6.6, *infra*.

163 *See* §§ 3.6.7, 3.6.8, *infra*.

164 *See* § 3.6.8.2.1, *infra*.

165 *See* § 3.6.8.2.2, *infra*.

166 *See* § 3.6.2.2, *infra*.

167 47 U.S.C. § 415(a). *But see* Castro v. Collecto, Inc., 634 F.3d 779 (5th Cir. 2011) (federal limitations period only applies to tariffed charges); Rose v. Asset Acceptance, L.L.C., 2012 WL 603263 (Cal. Ct. App. Feb. 24, 2012) (unpublished). *Cf.* Cotton v. Asset Acceptance, L.L.C., 2008 WL 2561103 (N.D. Ill. June 26, 2008) (certifying FDCPA class action challenge to carriers bringing actions beyond the two-year limitations period; debt buyer had argued that common questions did not predominate because individual class members would have different mixes of charges subject to the federal two-year limitations period and intrastate charges subject to state limitations periods).

3.6.2.2.2 Scope of the two-year limitations provision

The federal limitations period applies to common carriers. 47 U.S.C. § 153(10) defines "common carrier" or "carrier" as "any person engaged as a common carrier for hire, in interstate or foreign communication by wire or radio or interstate or foreign radio transmission of energy, except when reference is made to common carriers not subject to this chapter." Thus the definition of carrier includes cell phone, interstate, and foreign communications operators.

47 U.S.C. § 332(c)(1)(A) itemizes when cell phone services are not treated as carriers. It states that mobile services shall be treated as carriers except for those provisions of subchapter II in which the Federal Communications Commission specifies through regulation that the provision is inapplicable to such mobile services. Subchapter II includes only 47 U.S.C. §§ 201–276, while 47 U.S.C. § 415(a) creating the two-year limitations period is in Subchapter IV. As a result, a cell phone service is treated as a carrier for purposes of the statute of limitations.

This federal statute of limitations should apply even though cell phone service and long-distance service are not subject to federal tariffs. Tariffing and federal regulation are two different things.[168] A practice can be federally regulated even if there is no federal tariff.

3.6.2.2.3 Fifth Circuit denies applicability of the federal limitations period

A federal statute of limitations that is shorter than a state limitations period should govern, not the longer state period. Federal law preempts state law. Nevertheless, the Fifth Circuit has held otherwise in the case of a collector seeking to recover cell phone charges.[169]

The court disapproved of a federal limitations period affecting state court collections by a federally regulated industry that has been de-tariffed. The court recognized the direct conflict between a four-year state period in Texas and the federal two-year period and that the federal period should apply if applicable. But it got around this preemption by finding that the collector was not seeking "lawful charges," since the federal act applies the two year period to actions "by carriers for recovery of their lawful charges."[170]

The court found two possible interpretations of "lawful charges." One was based upon the ordinary meaning of the phrase, which would encompass a carrier's charges, whether tariffed or not. The other interpretation is that in this context "lawful" means "tariffed." Since cell phone charges are not pursuant to a tariff filed with the Federal Communications Commission, such an interpretation would mean that the federal limitations period does not apply to the collection of cell phone charges.[171]

Because the Fifth Circuit found two possible interpretations of the phrase "lawful charges," it decided to use the interpretation when there would be no conflict with state law, because Congress must clearly specify when it wants to preempt the "historic policy powers of the states."[172] Of course, in the context of commercial litigation, courts have found no problem applying the two-year federal limitations period.[173]

Moreover, Congress has no trouble using the term tariffed when it wishes to limit a communications statute just to tariffed charges. Tariffed and lawful are two different things, and it is hard to see how a collector can seek charges that are not "lawful."

Nor does the Fifth Circuit focus on the language that the federal limitations period applies to "*all* actions at law by carriers for recovery of their lawful charges."[174] The term "all" implies a broad scope.

3.6.2.2.4 Federal limitations period applies to assignees

If a court were to disagree with the Fifth Circuit and find that the federal limitations period applies to a cell phone carrier, the federal limitations period applies to any assignee of that carrier. The assignee steps into the shoes of the assignor and has no greater rights. The assignor cannot revive an action simply by selling it to someone else. Thus a federal court has stated:

> Congress could not have been clearer. To suggest a carrier could otherwise assign its contract to a third-party debt collector to bypass the requirements of section 415 and bring a state action pursuant to a four-year limitations period would undermine the express language and purpose of the statute. Therefore, the clear language of section 415 states a two-year statute of limitations applies.[175]

168 *See* Dreamscape Design, Inc. v. Affinity Network, Inc., 414 F.3d 665 (7th Cir. 2005). *See also* Boomer v. AT & T Corp., 309 F.3d 404 (7th Cir. 2002); Ramette v. AT & T Corp., 812 N.E.2d 504 (Ill. App. Ct. 2004).

169 Castro v. Collecto, Inc., 634 F.3d 779 (5th Cir. 2011). *See also* Rose v. Asset Acceptance, L.L.C., 2012 WL 603263 (Cal. Ct. App. Feb. 24, 2012) (unpublished). *But cf.* Cotton v. Asset Acceptance, L.L.C., 2008 WL 2561103 (N.D. Ill. June 26, 2008) (certifying FDCPA class action challenge to carriers bringing actions beyond the two-year limitations period; debt buyer had argued that common questions did not predominate because individual class members would have different mixes of charges subject to the federal two-year limitations period and intrastate charges subject to state limitations periods).

170 47 U.S.C. § 415(a).

171 *See* Castro v. Collecto, Inc., 634 F.3d 779 (5th Cir. 2011). *See also* Asset Acceptance, L.L.C. v. Brown, 2010 WL 1369256 (Cal. Super. Ct. Apr. 5, 2010).

172 *Id.*

173 Global Crossing Bandwidth, Inc. v. Locus Telecomm., Inc., 632 F. Supp. 2d 224 (W.D.N.Y. 2009); MFS Int'l v. Int'l Telecom Ltd., 50 F. Supp. 2d 517 (E.D. Va. 1999).

174 47 U.S.C. § 415(a).

175 Castro v. Collecto, Inc., 256 F.R.D. 534, 539–40 (W.D. Tex. 2009), *related case*, 668 F. Supp. 2d 950 (not ruling on assignee liability but reversing itself on applicability of two year limitations period), *related case affirmed on grounds unrelated to assignee liability*, 634 F.3d 779 (5th Cir. 2011).

3.6.3 *Which State's Statute of Limitations Applies?*

3.6.3.1 Introduction

Except in those limited situations when federal law applies,[176] state law determines the applicable limitations period. Questions often arise, however, as to which state's law applies to the determination of the limitations period. Because limitations periods vary significantly by state, it matters whether the limitations period is determined by the law of the forum state or by some other state's law.

There are at least two situations in which a limitations period other than that of the forum state may apply. The first is when the credit contract has a choice of law provision that specifies that the contract will be governed by the law of a particular state other than the forum state, such as Delaware. This situation is examined in §§ 3.6.3.2 and 3.6.3.3, *infra*.

The second situation in which another state's law may apply is when the cause of action arose in a state other the forum state. Some courts, for example, rule that a credit card collection action arose where the card issuer resides, not where the consumer resides. This situation is considered in § 3.6.3.4, *infra*.

3.6.3.2 The Forum State or the State Selected in the Credit Agreement?

3.6.3.2.1 General

Surprisingly, the law selected in a credit contract may have a shorter limitations period than the forum state. For example, Chase, Bank of America, Discover, and Barclays agreements specify Delaware law, which has a three-year limitation period even for written contracts, a period significantly shorter than many other states. (On the other hand, Citi and Wells Fargo use South Dakota law, which has a six-year limitations period even for non-written contracts.)

Creditors, in selecting the state's law to be used in interpreting the credit agreement, typically have legal issues in mind other than the statute of limitations—which has more significance for those purchasing debts than it does for the original creditor. As a result the consumer, in some cases, may wish to argue for the applicability of the statute of limitations of the state selected in the contract whose limitations period is shorter than that of the forum state. The consumer need not admit to the enforceability of the contract in arguing for the use of the contractual choice of law. The consumer can simply state that, if the contract is enforceable, then by its own terms the limitations period has expired.

Courts typically follow the limitation period of the forum state when it is the shorter of the two.[177] When the forum's limitation period is the longer of the two, courts are divided as to whether they will utilize the limitations period of the longer forum or that of the state selected in the contractual choice of law provision.[178] This confusion is largely caused by the dual purpose of a statute of limitations—to prevent a state's courts from having to hear stale evidence (an interest of the forum state no matter the law specified in a contract) and to protect parties from having to preserve evidence for long periods of time (an interest that might be specified in the contract).

3.6.3.2.2 Use of the forum state's limitations period when it is the shortest

Although not followed by all states, both the 1971 and 1988 versions of *Restatement (Second) of Conflict of Laws* clearly state that the forum's limitations period will be selected when it is the shorter of the two.[179] Forum states have an important interest in avoiding limitations periods that extend the time period beyond that established by their own legislature, because the period protects the state's courts from having to hear stale evidence. States also have policies that a contract cannot extend the limitations period,[180] which is exactly what the contract would do if its provision was given effect selecting the law of another state with a longer limitations period.

3.6.3.2.3 States using the forum state's period even when it is the longest

When the law selected in the contract has a shorter limitations period than the forum state, some states use the forum's longer limitation period because their courts view the statute of limitations as a procedural matter for the courts, not a substantive one determined by contract.[181] Some states alternatively simply rule that the forum state's statute of limitations is always to be applied.[182] These courts are generally following the same

176 *See* § 3.6.2, *supra*.

177 *See* § 3.6.3.2.2, *infra*.

178 *See* §§ 3.6.3.2.3, 3.6.3.2.4, *infra*.

179 Restatement (Second) of Conflict of Laws § 142 (1971, 1988). *See also In re* W. Group Nurseries, Inc., 2000 WL 34446155 (D. Ariz. July 3, 2000), *vacated in part on other grounds*, 2000 WL 34448963 (D. Ariz. Sept. 29, 2000).

180 *See* § 3.6.5, *infra*.

181 MedCap Corp. v. Betsy Johnson Health Care Systems, Inc., 16 Fed. Appx. 180 (4th Cir. 2001) (North Carolina law); Cole v. Mileti, 133 F.3d 433 (6th Cir. 1998) (Michigan law); Phelps v. McClellan, 30 F.3d 658 (6th Cir. 1994) (Michigan law); Telular Corp. v. Mentor Graphics Corp., 282 F. Supp. 2d 869 (N.D. Ill. 2003) (Illinois law treats the statute of limitations as procedural, requiring use of the forum's law); Sharp-Richardson v. Boyds Collection, Ltd., 1999 WL 33656875 (N.D. Iowa Sept. 30, 1999) (interpreting Iowa law as to choice of laws); Smither v. Asset Acceptance, L.L.C., 919 N.E.2d 1153 (Ind. Ct. App. 2010); Hemar Ins. Corp. of Am. v. Ryerson, 108 S.W.3d 90 (Mo. Ct. App. 2003); Portfolio Recovery Assocs., L.L.C. v. King, 927 N.E.2d 1059 (N.Y. 2010); Educ. Res. Inst., Inc. v. Piazza, 794 N.Y.S.2d 65 (N.Y. App. Div. 2005); Educ. Res. Inst., Inc. v. Czarnik, 803 N.Y.S.2d 18 (table), 2005 WL 1862721 (N.Y. App. Term 2005) (unpublished).

182 Boon v. Professional Collection Consultants, 2013 WL 5687374 (S.D. Cal. Oct. 17, 2013); Nez v. Forney, 783 P.2d 471 (N.M. 1989); Capital One Bank v. Rodgers, 2010 WL 3620304 (Ohio Ct. App. Sept. 14, 2010); Unifund CCR Partners v. Childs, 2010 WL 703274 (Ohio Ct. App. Feb. 26, 2010); D.A.N. Joint Venture III, L.P. v. Armstrong, 2007 WL 634457 (Ohio Ct. App. Mar. 2, 2007); Unifund CCR Partners v. Bonfigli, 2010 Vt. Super. LEXIS 24 (Vt. Super Ct. May 5, 2010). *See also* Dudek v. Thomas & Thomas Attorneys & Counselors at Law, L.L.C., 702 F. Supp. 2d 826 (N.D. Ohio 2010).

approach as the 1971 version of the *Restatement (Second) of Conflict of Laws*, which took the position that the limitations period of the forum state always applies.[183]

Rhode Island uses a balancing test and, in at least one credit card case, a federal court determined the balancing in favor of Rhode Island's longer limitations period and not the state law mentioned in the credit card agreement.[184] Minnesota's rule is that Minnesota's statute of limitations applies unless the choice of law provision not only specifies another state's law but also explicitly provides that another state's law is applicable for procedure and remedies.[185] Arizona, by statute, states that, when more than one state's limitations period could apply, it is Arizona's limitations period that applies to actions for a debt founded on a written contract or a credit card.[186]

3.6.3.2.4 States adopting modern view applying a shorter limitations period of contractually chosen state

Courts increasingly utilize what the United States Supreme Court has termed the more "modern" view,[187] that the statute of limitations is a substantive concern, and thus the limitations period of the contractually chosen state applies when it is shorter than that of the forum state.[188] The 1988 version of the *Restatement (Second) of Conflict of Laws* takes this position if maintenance of the claim serves no substantial interest of the forum and the chosen state has "a more significant relationship to the parties and the occurrence."[189] The comments state: "Speaking generally, a claim . . . should not be entertained if no interest of the forum state would be served by entertaining the claim and the claim would be barred by the statute of limitations of the alternative forum. Entertainment of the claim under such circumstances would add to the burden of the local courts and bring no countervailing advantage."[190]

Minnesota and Oregon, by statute, apply the limitations period of the state whose substantive law applies.[191] Nevertheless, the Oregon middle level appellate court has used odd reasoning in deciding to use Oregon's limitations period instead of Delaware's, even though the contract specified Delaware law as the substantive law that applies to the collector's claim.[192] The Oregon statute also specifies that, when another state's statute of limitations applies, the tolling rules of that state also apply.[193] Delaware's statute of limitations provides for tolling when the defendant is not in the state, and, since the Oregon defendant will never be in Delaware, the limitations period will never end.

To avoid this result, the court decided to use Oregon law, despite the Oregon statute providing that Delaware law should apply.[194] But the court did not consider that the Delaware courts interpreting their own tolling rule would not apply it to a situation in which the plaintiff had no problem serving the defendant in Oregon. The Delaware legislature has no interest in extending its limitations period just because Delaware law was selected in resolving a lawsuit in Oregon and the parties were in Oregon, not in Delaware.[195]

Other jurisdictions resolve the issue by seeking to interpret the language of the choice of law provision itself and then read it as referring to all of the chosen state's laws (not just substantive laws), including the statute of limitations of the chosen state.[196] Having decided that the contractual choice of

183 Restatement (Second) of Conflict of Laws § 142 (1971).

184 *See* Fiorenzano v. LVNV Funding, L.L.C., 2012 WL 2562415 (D.R.I. June 29, 2012).

185 *See* Midland Funding v. Schlick, 2013 WL 6223571 (Minn. Ct. App. Dec. 2, 2013).

186 Ariz. Rev. Stat. Ann. § 12–548(B).

187 Sun Oil Co. v. Wortman, 486 U.S. 717, 108 S. Ct. 2117, 100 L. Ed. 2d 743 (1988) (while terming this view as more modern, the Court refused to overturn a state decision holding the limitations period procedural, finding no violation of the Full Faith and Credit Clause).

188 Lopez v. Capital One Bank, 2009 WL 6713593 (Fla. Cir. Ct. Aug. 18, 2009); Delrey v. Capital One Bank, 2009 WL 5103229 (Fla. Cir. Ct. July 7, 2009; Capital One Bank v. Pincus (Fla. Palm Beach Cnty. Ct. Sept. 8, 2008), *available at* www.nclc.org/unreported (Virginia law); Fla. Credit Research, Inc. v. Felicien (Fla. Duval Cnty. Ct. Apr. 15, 2008), *available at* www.nclc.org/unreported; Fla. Credit Research, Inc. v. Stromberg (Fla. Duval Cnty. Ct. Feb. 20, 2008), *available at* www.nclc.org/unreported; Capital One Bank v. Gregorich (Fla. Miami-Dade Cnty. Ct. June 17, 2008), *available at* www.nclc.org/unreported; Capital One Bank v. Gelsey (Fla. Duval Cnty. Ct. July 3, 2007), *available at* www.nclc.org/unreported; L.W.T. v. Brodsky, 14 Fla. L. Weekly Supp. 188a (Fla. Broward Cnty. Ct. Dec. 8, 2006). *See also* Fulton Cnty. Adm'r v. Sullivan, 753 So. 2d 549 (Fla. 1999).

189 Restatement (Second) of Conflict of Laws § 142 (1988).

190 *Id.*, § 142 cmt. (g).

191 Minn. Stat. § 541.31(1); Or. Rev. Stat. § 12.430(1)(a).

192 Unifund CCR Partners v. Deboer, 277 P.3d 562 (Or. Ct. App. 2012); Unifund CCR Partners v. Porras, 275 P.3d 992 (Or. Ct. App. 2012); CACV of Colo., L.L.C. v. Stevens, 274 P.3d 859 (Or. Ct. App. 2012).

193 Or. Rev. Stat. § 12.440.

194 Unifund CCR Partners v. Deboer, 277 P.3d 562 (Or. Ct. App. 2012); Unifund CCR Partners v. Porras, 275 P.3d 992 (Or. Ct. App. 2012); CACV of Colo., L.L.C. v. Stevens, 274 P.3d 859 (Or. Ct. App. 2012).

195 *See* § 3.6.8.2.4, *infra* (discussing issue).

196 Avery v. First Resolution Mgmt. Corp., 568 F.3d 1018 (9th Cir. 2009) (Oregon law); Wang Laboratories, Inc. v. Kagan, 990 F.2d 1126 (9th Cir. 1993); Gaisser v. Portfolio Recovery Assocs., L.L.C., 571 F. Supp. 2d 1273 (S.D. Fla. 2008) (applying New Hampshire choice-of-law rules and not forum state Florida's statute of limitations); McCorriston v. L.W.T., Inc., 536 F. Supp. 2d 1268 (M.D. Fla. 2008); Avery v. First Resolution Mgmt. Corp., 2007 WL 1560653 (D. Or. May 25, 2007) (but court refused to use non-forum state's law when court's odd interpretation of non-forum state's tolling rules would mean there would never be a limitations period); Jahn v. 1–800-Flowers.Com, Inc., 2002 WL 32362244 (W.D. Wis. Oct. 21, 2002); W. Group Nurseries, Inc. v. Ergas, 211 F. Supp. 2d 1362 (S.D. Fla. 2002); W. Group Nurseries, Inc. v. Adams, 2000 WL 34446155 (D. Ariz. July 3, 2000), *vacated in part on other grounds*, 2000 WL 34448963 (D. Ariz. Sept. 29, 2000); Resurgence Fin., L.L.C. v. Chambers, 92 Cal. Rptr. 3d 844 (Cal. Ct. App. 2009); ABF Capital Corp. v. Costello & Lanahan, 2005 WL 3514288 (Cal. Ct. App. Dec. 23, 2005); Hambrecht & Quist Venture Partners v. Am. Med. Int'l, Inc., 46 Cal. Rptr. 2d 33 (Cal. Ct. App. 1995); Discover Bank v. Eschwege (N.Y. Sup. Ct. Mar. 5, 2008), *available at* www.nclc.org/unreported. *See also* Maxcess, Inc. v. Lucent Technologies, Inc., 433 F.3d 1337 (11th Cir. 2005) (Florida law); Boracchia v. Biomet, Inc., 2008 WL 512721 (N.D. Cal. Feb. 25, 2008), *aff'd in part on this ground and rev'd in part on other grounds by* 348 Fed. Appx. 269 (9th Cir. 2009); Hughes Electronics Corp. v. Citibank Del., 15 Cal. Rptr. 3d 244 (Cal. Ct. App. 2004). *But see* Ashland Chem. Co. v. Provence, 181 Cal. Rptr. 340 (Cal. Ct. App. 1982).

law includes that state's statute of limitations, courts generally find no fundamental state policy to use their own statute of limitations, which might override the contractual choice of law provision, and therefore utilize the chosen state's limitation period.[197]

3.6.3.3 Only the Consumer Can Take Advantage of the Limitations Period of the State Chosen in the Contract

A collector may attempt to use the limitations period of the state selected in the contract when it is longer than that of the forum state. Of course, this will not work in states that always use the forum state's limitations period. But even in other states, this flies in the face of both the 1971 and 1988 *Restatement (Second) of Conflict of Laws*, which provide that the forum limitations period should always be used if it is shorter—the state has an interest in its own courts not having to hear stale claims.[198]

In addition, the collector will have to prove that there is a choice of law provision that is binding on the consumer, which will require proof of a binding contract and proof of the version of the contract in effect at the time of the lawsuit. Otherwise there is no basis for that state's law being applied to any of the collector's causes of action. As described in § 4.5.3, *infra*, collectors in consumer collection cases may have difficulty producing such proof.

Compare this with the consumer's position that the contractually chosen state's law should apply to the limitations period. The consumer is just taking the position that, when the collector alleges there is a contract, then if there is such an enforceable contract, then by its own terms, the contact claim should be dismissed by the very language of the contract. But the consumer is not admitting that there is a contract.

The consumer can use the contract's choice of law provision even when the collector's causes of action are not based upon the contract, as long as the collector alleges there is a contract. By alleging that there is a contract, the collector is estopped from arguing that the contract, and the contract's choice of law, do not apply. By choosing to allege that a binding contract exists, the collector cannot avoid application of the contract's choice of law provisions and the statute of limitations chosen in this document.[199] The plaintiff is the "master of its complaint" and cannot avoid the choice of law provision found in the contract referenced in its complaint.

If the non-forum state's limitations period has clearly expired, then the consumer should also consider introducing the contract into evidence if the collector does not. A new federal right provides that the originating card issuer must provide consumers a copy of their contract when requested.[200] The card issuer must post and maintain the consumer's agreement on its website or provide a copy upon request.

3.6.3.4 Borrowing Statutes: Using the Shorter Limitations Period of the State Where the Action Arose

3.6.3.4.1 General

Over half the states have borrowing statutes that require, when an action arose elsewhere than the forum state, that the action can only be brought if within the limitations period which applies under the law of the state where the action arose. These borrowing statutes apply when the consumer resided in one state when incurring the debt but is sued in a second state where the consumer has since moved.[201] This is a fairly common situation in which the debt being sued upon is a number of years old.

Even if a state does not have a borrowing statute, it is likely to use the limitations period of the state where the consumer resided at the time of the transaction, not the state to which the consumer later moved,[202] at least when that limitations period is shorter.

Almost all borrowing statutes also apply when the cause of action arose in another state, even when the consumer has always resided in the forum state.[203] That is, when state law

197 Gaisser v. Portfolio Recovery Assocs., L.L.C., 571 F. Supp. 2d 1273 (S.D. Fla. 2008) (applying New Hampshire choice-of-law rules and not forum state Florida's statute of limitations); W. Group Nurseries, Inc. v. Ergas, 211 F. Supp. 2d 1362 (S.D. Fla. 2002); Hambrecht & Quist Venture Partners v. Am. Med. Int'l, Inc., 46 Cal. Rptr. 2d 33 (Cal. Ct. App. 1995). *See also* Maxcess, Inc. v. Lucent Technologies, Inc., 433 F.3d 1337 (11th Cir. 2005) (Fla. law); Burroughs Corp. v. Suntogs of Miami, Inc., 472 So. 2d 1166 (Fla. 1985) (contractual provision shortening the period of time for filing a suit was not contrary to a strong public policy).

198 *See* § 3.6.3.2, *supra*.

199 Fla. Credit Research, Inc. v. Felicien (Fla. Duval Cnty. Ct. Jan. 17, 2008), *available at* www.nclc.org/unreported; Capital One Bank v. Gelsey (Fla. Duval Cnty. Ct. July 3, 2007), *available at* www.nclc.org/unreported.

200 12 C.F.R. § 1026.58(e).

201 *See, e.g.*, Ala. Code § 6-2-17; Alaska Stat. § 09.10.220; Ariz. Rev. Stat. Ann. § 12-506; Cal. Civ. Proc. Code § 361 (West); Colo. Rev. Stat. § 13-80-110; Del. Code Ann. tit. 10, § 8121; Fla. Stat. § 95.10; Haw. Rev. Stat. § 657-9; Idaho Code Ann. § 5-239; 735 Ill. Comp. Stat. § 5/13-210; Kan. Stat. Ann. § 60-516; Ky. Rev. Stat. Ann. § 413.320 (West); La. Civ. Code Ann. art. 3537; Mich. Comp. Laws § 600.5869; Minn. Stat. § 541.31; Mo. Rev. Stat. § 516.190. Mont. Code Ann. § 27-2-503; Nev. Rev. Stat. § 11.020; N.Y. C.P.L.R. 202 (McKinney); Ohio Rev. Code Ann. § 2305.03(B) (West); Or. Rev. Stat. § 12.430; 42 Pa. Cons. Stat. § 5521 (b); Tenn. Code Ann. § 28-1-112; Tex. Civ. Prac. & Rem. Code § 16.066(a) (West); Utah Code Ann. § 78B-2-103 (West); Va. Code Ann. § 8.01-247; W. Va. Code § 55-2A-2; Wis. Stat. § 893.07; Wyo. Stat. Ann. § 1-3-117. *See also* Wash. Rev. Code § 4.26.290 (use limitations period when accrued elsewhere between non-residents).

202 Jackson v. Midland Funding, L.L.C., 468 Fed. Appx. 123 (3d Cir. Feb. 16, 2012).

203 *See, e.g.*, Cal. Civ. Proc. Code § 361 (West); Colo. Rev. Stat. § 13-80-110; Del. Code Ann. tit. 10, § 8121; Fla. Stat. § 95.10; Haw. Rev. Stat. § 657-9; Idaho Code Ann. § 5-239; 735 Ill. Comp. Stat. § 5/13-210; Kan. Stat. Ann. § 60-516; Ky. Rev. Stat. Ann. § 413.320 (West); La. Civ. Code Ann. art. 3537; Mich. Comp. Laws § 600.5869; Minn. Stat. § 541.31; Mo. Rev. Stat. § 516.190. Mont. Code Ann. § 27-2-503; N.Y. C.P.L.R. 202 (McKinney); Nev. Rev. Stat. § 11.020; Ohio Rev. Code Ann. § 2305.03(B) (West); Or. Rev. Stat. § 12.430; 42 Pa. Cons. Stat. § 5521 (b); Utah Code Ann. § 78B-2-103 (West); Va. Code Ann. § 8.01-247; W. Va. Code § 55-2A-2; Wis. Stat. § 893.07; Wyo. Stat. Ann. § 1-3-117. The California, Hawaii, Idaho, Minnesota, Nevada, and Utah statutes have an exception when the person holding the

determines that a debt arose in another state, then the limitations period of that other state acts as a bar to collection. This has significant practical import, as described in § 3.6.3.4.2, *infra*, because state law may determine that the cause of action arose where the creditor resides.

An important question is whether the borrowing statute can only shorten the applicable imitations period (when the period of the state where the action arose is shorter than forum state's period), or whether the non-forum state's period should always be used, even if this extends the forum state's limitations period. The most common borrowing statute states that, when an action cannot be maintained where the cause of action arose, then it cannot be maintained in the forum state.[204] The borrowing statute does not state that the forum state's limitation is replaced.

The language's clear implication is that the forum state's statute of limitations continues to apply but that the plaintiff must also bring the action within the limitations period of the state where the action arose.[205] That is, the action must be brought within the shortest of the two periods. This interpretation is consistent with the forum state's interest in not having its courts hear claims when the state legislature has determined that a claim is too stale for its own courts to hear.

A few borrowing statutes make this explicit. Several statutes provide that the shortest of the two states' limitations periods is to be applied.[206] A few others seem to imply that only the out-of-state period is to apply,[207] although even some of these states allow the forum state's courts to use their own limitations period if fairness requires.[208]

Some borrowing statutes have been enacted recently, and questions arise as to whether the statutes apply to credit agreements entered into before the statute's effective date. A federal court predicted that Ohio state courts would not apply Ohio's borrowing statute to credit extended before the effective date of the borrowing statute, even if the collection action was filed after that date.[209] Similarly, a Minnesota court refused to apply the borrowing statute to a cause of action accruing before the statute's enactment in 2004.[210]

3.6.3.4.2 *Borrowing statutes may limit actions by out-of-state creditors*

Borrowing statutes most dramatic use may be when state law determines that a credit transaction arises not where the consumer resides, but where the creditor resides and extends the credit. For example, New York's highest court has found that a Delaware credit card issuer's collection action against a New York resident in New York arises in Delaware.[211] The card issuer suffered the economic injury in Delaware; the card issuer was incorporated in Delaware and was not a New York resident.

As a result, even though the consumer had always lived in New York, the New York borrowing statute required application of the Delaware limitations period. Since the Delaware limitations period had expired even though New York's had not, the case must be dismissed.

Similarly, an Ohio appellate court has found that a Delaware credit card issuer's claim against an Ohio cardholder accrued in Delaware, so the Ohio borrowing statute applied and Delaware's short statute of limitations governs the action.[212] A federal court has also interpreted where an action accrued for purposes of the Pennsylvania borrowing statute when a Pennsylvania consumer failed to mail a payment to a Delaware credit card issuer. The court ruled that the breach occurred in Delaware, because that is where the card issuer failed to receive payment. Thus, the Pennsylvania borrowing statute required the Pennsylvania action be brought within Delaware's three-year limitations period.[213]

Where a borrowing statute is to be applied because the creditor is out-of-state, it does so whether or not the collection action is brought by the originating creditor or by an assignee, and it does not matter whether the assignee is a resident of the forum state. The assignee is not entitled to stand in a better position than the assignor.[214]

---

cause of action was a resident of the forum state at the time the action accrued. But the original creditor will almost never be a resident of the forum state and should not be able to take advantage of this exception.

204 *See, e.g.*, Ala. Code § 6–2-17; Alaska Stat. § 09.10.220; Ariz. Rev. Stat. Ann. § 12–506; Cal. Civ. Proc. Code § 361 (West); Colo. Rev. Stat. § 13–80–110; Fla. Stat. § 95.10; Haw. Rev. Stat. § 657–9; Idaho Code Ann. § 5–239; 735 Ill. Comp. Stat. § 5/13–210; Kan. Stat. Ann. § 60–516; Mo. Rev. Stat. § 516.190. Nev. Rev. Stat. § 11.020; N.Y. C.P.L.R. 202 (McKinney); Ohio Rev. Code Ann. § 2305.03(B) (West); Tenn. Code Ann. § 28–1–112; Tex. Civ. Prac. and Rem. Code § 16.066(a) (West); Utah Code Ann. § 78B-2–103 (West); Va. Code Ann. § 8.01–247; W. Va. Code § 55–2A-2.

205 *See* CMACO Automotive Systems, Inc. v. Wanxiang America Corp., 589 F.3d 235 (6th Cir. 2009) (Ohio law); Combs v. Int'l Ins. Co., 354 F.3d 568 (6th Cir. 2004) (Ohio law); Dudek v. Thomas & Thomas Attorneys & Counselors at Law, L.L.C., 702 F. Supp. 2d 826 (N.D. Ohio 2010); Global Fin. Corp. v. Triarc Corp., 715 N.E.2d 482 (N.Y. 1999); American Express Bank, FSB v. Dalbis, 2011 WL 873512 (NY City Civ. Ct. Mar. 14, 2011).

206 Del. Code Ann. tit. 10, § 8121; Ky. Rev. Stat. Ann. § 413.320; 42 Pa. Cons. Stat. § 5521 (b); Wis. Stat. § 893.07; Wyo. Stat. Ann. § 1–3–117.

207 La. Civ. Code Ann. art. 3537; Mich. Comp. Laws § 600.5869; Minn. Stat. § 541.31; Mont. Code Ann. § 27–2–503; Or. Rev. Stat. § 12.430.

208 Mont. Code Ann. § 27–2–503; Or. Rev. Stat. § 12.430.

209 Dudek v. Thomas & Thomas Attorneys & Counselors at Law, L.L.C., 702 F. Supp. 2d 826 (N.D. Ohio 2010). *See also* Jarvis v. First Resolution Mgmt. Corp., 983 N.E.2d 380 (Ohio Ct. App. 2012) (finding cause of action accrued after borrowing statute's effective date); D.A.N. Joint Venture III, L.P. v. Armstrong, 2007 WL 634457 (Ohio Ct. App. Mar. 2, 2007).

210 *See* Midland Funding v. Schlick, 2013 WL 6223571 (Minn. Ct. App. Dec. 2, 2013).

211 Portfolio Recovery Assocs., L.L.C. v. King, 927 N.E.2d 1059 (N.Y. 2010). *See also* Capital One Bank v. McGurk, 932 N.Y.S.2d 420 (N.Y. Civ. Ct. June 3, 2010).

212 Jarvis v. First Resolution Mgmt. Corp., 983 N.E.2d 380 (Ohio Ct. App. 2012).

213 Hamid v. Stock & Grimes, 2011 WL 3802859 (E.D. Pa. Aug. 26, 2011).

214 Portfolio Recovery Assocs., L.L.C. v. King, 927 N.E.2d 1059 (N.Y. 2010).

3.6.4 Differing Statutes of Limitation Within a State

3.6.4.1 General

States typically establish several statutes of limitations, of varying lengths that are applicable to different causes of action. These statutes of limitations are often found in the state's code section governing courts and judicial proceedings for personal actions and in the state's version of the Uniform Commercial Code (UCC).

There is enormous variation in statutes of limitations from state to state and in how the state organizes and applies its different statutes of limitations. The one exception are the statutes of limitations found in the UCC, described in §§ 3.6.4.3 and 3.6.4.4, *infra*. Although there are some state variations even in UCC provisions, in general there is uniformity among the states as to the limitations period for cases related to the sale of goods, leases, dishonored checks, and promissory notes, which are all found in the state's version of the UCC.

Every state also has a limitations periods for claims based on a written contract, but the time periods vary significantly from state to state.[215] Statutes of limitations for a claim on a non-written contract are often shorter than those for written contracts, but this is not always the case.[216] In states in which the period is shorter for non-written than written contracts, an important issue is whether a collector's claim—for example, a claim on a credit card debt or an account stated cause of action—should be characterized as a written or a non-written contract claim.[217] Sometimes this issue will be resolved by the statute's language, such as when there is an explicit limitations periods for a claim based upon an account stated,[218] an open account,[219] or a contract implied in law (for example, *quantum meruit* or unjust enrichment).[220]

States also have default limitations periods that apply when no other limitations period is applicable—in some states a claim for *quantum meruit* may be covered under this default limitations period.[221] Default limitation periods can be quite short[222] but can be quite long in other states.[223]

3.6.4.2 State-by-State Listing of Limitations Periods for Breach of Contract

Every state has a limitations periods for claims based on a written contract, but the time periods vary significantly from state to state. In some states it is only three, four, or five years, while six years is more common. A handful of states have limitations periods of eight or ten years. Statutes of limitations for a claim on a non-written contract are usually shorter than those for a written contract, varying by state from three to ten years. In a number of states, though, the limitations period is the same for non-written and written contracts.

State limitations periods for written and non-written contracts are listed below:

- Alabama: six years for written contracts[224] and three years for non-written contracts;[225]
- Alaska: three years for written contracts and three years for non-written contracts;[226]
- Arizona: six years for written contracts[227] and three years for non-written contracts;[228]
- Arkansas: five years for written contracts and three years for non-written contracts;[229]
- California: four years for written contracts[230] and two years for non-written contracts;[231]
- Colorado: six years for written contracts and six years for non-written contracts;[232]
- Connecticut: six years for written contracts[233] and three years for non-written contracts;[234]
- Delaware: three years for written contracts and three years for non-written contracts;[235]

215 *See* § 3.6.4.2, *infra*.
216 *Id.*
217 *See* § 3.6.6, *infra*.
218 Ariz. Rev. Stat. Ann. § 12–543 (three years); Cal. Civ. Proc. Code § 337 (West) (four years); Del. Code Ann. tit. 10, § 8106 (three years); Tex. Civ. Prac. & Rem. Code Ann. § 16.004(c) (West) (four years).
219 Ala. Code § 6–2-37(1) (three years); Ariz. Rev. Stat. Ann. § 12–543 (three years); Cal. Civ. Proc. Code § 337(2) (West) (four years); Conn. Gen. Stat. § 52–576 (six years); La. Civ. Code art. 3494 (three years); Utah Code Ann. § 78B-2–307 (West) (four years); Nev. Rev. Stat. § 11.190 (four years); Tex. Civ. Prac. & Rem. Code Ann. § 16.004(c) (West) (four years). *See also* Bourdier v. Dermatology & Aesthetic Institute, L.L.C., 2013 WL 486971 (M.D. La. Feb. 6, 2013); Ayers v. Cavalry SVP I, L.L.C., 876 So. 2d 474 (Ala. Civ. App. 2003).
220 Cal. Civ. Proc. Code § 339 (West) (two years); 42 Pa. Cons. Stat. § 5525(a)(4) (four years); HECI Exploration Co. v. Neel, 982 S.W.2d 881 (Tex. 1998); Pepi Corp. v. Galliford, 254 S.W.3d 457 (Tex. App. 2007) (four years for *quantum meruit* but two years for unjust enrichment). *See also* Elledge v. Friberg-Cooper Water Supply Corp., 240 S.W.3d 869 (Tex. 2007) (two-year limitations period for unjust enrichment); C.M. Asfahl Agency v. Tensor, Inc., 135 S.W.3d 768 (Tex. App. 2004) (four-year limitations period for *quantum meruit*); Thomason v. Freberg, 588 S.W.2d 821 (Tex. App. 1979) (*quantum meruit* claim accrues when goods delivered or services performed for each transaction).
221 *See* Capital One Bank v. Gelsey (Fla. Duval Cnty. Ct. July 3, 2007), *available at* www.nclc.org/unreported.
222 *E.g.*, Va. Code Ann. § 8.01–248 (two years).
223 *E.g.*, 42 Pa. Cons. Stat. § 5527(b) (six years).
224 Ala. Code § 6–2-34.
225 Ala. Code § 6–2-37.
226 Alaska Stat. § 09.10.053.
227 Ariz. Rev. Stat. Ann. § 12–548.
228 Ariz. Rev. Stat. Ann. § 12–543.
229 Ark. Code Ann. §§ 16–56–105, 111.
230 Cal. Civ. Proc. Code § 337 (West).
231 Cal. Civ. Proc. Code § 339 (West).
232 Colo. Rev. Stat. § 13–80–103.5. Colorado has a three-year limitations for unliquidated obligations and six years for liquidated obligations, and defines a liquidated debt as one on which the amount owed is ascertainable either by reference to the agreement or by simple computation using extrinsic evidence if necessary. *See* Portercare Adventist Health Sys. v. Lego, 286 P.3d 525 (Colo. 2012).
233 Conn. Gen. Stat. § 52–576.
234 Conn. Gen. Stat. § 52–581.
235 Del. Code Ann. tit. 10 § 8106.

- District of Columbia: three years for written contracts and three years for non-written contracts;[236]
- Florida: five years for written contracts[237] and four years for non-written contracts;[238]
- Georgia: six years for written contracts[239] and four years for non-written contracts;[240]
- Hawaii: six years for written contracts and six years for non-written contracts;[241]
- Idaho: five years for written contracts[242] and four years for non-written contracts;[243]
- Illinois: ten years for written contracts and five years for non-written contracts;[244]
- Indiana: six years for written contracts for money and six years for non-written contract;[245]
- Iowa: ten years for written contracts[246] and five years for non-written contracts;[247]
- Kansas: five years for written contracts and three years for non-written contracts;[248]
- Kentucky: fifteen years for written contracts[249] and five years for non-written contracts;[250]
- Louisiana: ten years for written contracts;[251] ten years for non-written contracts;[252] three years for an action on money lent or an open account.[253]
- Maine: six years for written contracts and six years for non-written contracts;[254]
- Maryland: three years for written contracts and three years for non-written contracts;[255]
- Massachusetts: six years for written contracts and six years for non-written contracts;[256]
- Michigan: six years for written contracts and six years for non-written contracts;[257]
- Minnesota: six years for written contracts and six years for non-written contracts;[258]
- Mississippi: three years for written contracts and three years for non-written contracts;[259]
- Missouri: ten years for written contracts[260] and five years for non-written contracts;[261]
- Montana: eight years for written contracts and five years for non-written contracts;[262]
- Nebraska: five years for written contracts and four years for non-written contracts;[263]
- Nevada: six years for written contracts and four years for non-written contracts;[264]
- New Hampshire: three years for written contracts and three years for non-written contracts;[265]
- New Jersey: six years for written contracts and six years for non-written contracts;[266]
- New Mexico: six years for written contracts[267] and four years for non-written contracts;[268]
- New York: six years for written contracts and six years for non-written contracts;[269]
- North Carolina: three years for written contracts and three years for non-written contracts;[270]
- North Dakota: six years for written contracts and six years for non-written contracts;[271]
- Ohio: effective September 28, 2012, eight years for written contracts for money and six years for non-written contract;[272]
- Oklahoma: five years for written contracts and three years for non-written contracts;[273]
- Oregon: six years for written contracts and six years for non-written contracts;[274]
- Pennsylvania: four years for written contracts and four years for non-written contracts;[275]
- Rhode Island: ten years for written contracts and ten years for non-written contracts;[276]
- South Carolina: three years for written contracts and three years for non-written contracts;[277]

---

236 D.C. Code § 12–301.
237 Fla. Stat. § 95.11(2)(b).
238 Fla. Stat. § 95.11(3)(k).
239 Ga. Code Ann. § 9–3–24.
240 Ga. Code Ann. § 9-3-25.
241 Haw. Rev. Stat. § 657–1.
242 Idaho Code Ann. § 5–216.
243 Idaho Code Ann. § 5–217.
244 735 Ill. Comp. Stat. §§ 5/13–205, 5/13–206.
245 Ind. Code §§ 34–11–2-9 (contract in writing for money), 34–11–2-7 (non-written contracts).
246 Iowa Code § 614.1(5).
247 Iowa Code § 614.1(4).
248 Kan. Stat. Ann. §§ 60–511, 60–512.
249 Ky. Rev. Stat. Ann. § 413.090 (West).
250 Ky. Rev. Stat. Ann. § 413.120 (West).
251 La. Civ. Code Ann. art. 3499.
252 La. Civ. Code Ann. art. 3498.
253 La. Civ. Code Ann. art. 3494(4). *See also* Bourdier v. Dermatology & Aesthetic Inst., L.L.C., 2013 WL 486971 (M.D. La. Feb. 6, 2013).
254 Me. Rev. Stat. tit. 14 § 752.
255 Md. Code Ann., Cts. & Jud. Proc. § 5–101 (West). *See also In re* Dorsey, 2008 WL 2511897 (Bankr. D. Md. June 20, 2008) (applying Maryland's three-year limitations period to credit card debt, when statutory period is the same whether written or implied contract involved).
256 Mass. Gen. Laws ch. 260, § 2.
257 Mich. Comp. Laws § 600.5807.
258 Minn. Stat. § 541.05.
259 Miss. Code Ann. § 15–1–29.
260 Mo. Rev. Stat. § 516.110(1).
261 Mo. Rev. Stat. § 516.120.
262 Mont. Code Ann. § 27–2–202.
263 Neb. Rev. Stat. §§ 25–205, 206.
264 Nev. Rev. Stat. § 11.190.
265 N.H. Rev. Stat. Ann. § 508:4.
266 N.J. Stat. Ann. § 2A:14–1 (West).
267 N.M. Stat. Ann. § 37–1–3.
268 N.M. Stat. Ann. § 37–1–4.
269 N.Y. C.P.L.R. § 213 (McKinney).
270 N.C. Gen. Stat § 1–52(1).
271 N.D. Cent. Code § 28–01–16.
272 Ohio Rev. Code Ann. §§ 2305.06, 2305.07 (West).
273 Okla. Stat. tit. 12, § 95.
274 Or. Rev. Stat. § 12.080.
275 42 Pa. Cons. Stat. § 5525.
276 R.I. Gen. Laws § 9–1–13(a).
277 S.C. Code Ann. § 15–3–530.

- South Dakota: six years for written contracts and six years for non-written contracts;[278]
- Tennessee: six years for written contracts and six years for non-written contracts;[279]
- Texas: four years for written contracts and four years for non-written contracts;[280]
- Utah: six years for written contracts[281] and four years for non-written contracts;[282]
- Vermont: six years for written contracts and six years for non-written contracts;[283]
- Virginia: five years for written contracts and three years for non-written contracts;[284]
- Washington: six years for written contracts[285] and three years for non-written contracts;[286]
- West Virginia: ten years for written contracts and five years for non-written contracts;[287]
- Wisconsin: six years for written contracts and six years for non-written contracts;[288]
- Wyoming: ten years for written contracts and eight years for non-written contracts.[289]

3.6.4.3 UCC Limitations Period for Credit Sales and Leases

Every state but Louisiana has adopted UCC Article 2,[290] which provides that an action for breach of any contract for the sale of goods must be brought within four years after the cause of action accrues.[291] Eight states have adopted variations to this period, most of these lengthening the period to five or six years.[292]

Every state but Louisiana has adopted UCC Article 2A on leases. UCC § 2A-506(1) provides for a four-year limitations period after the cause of action accrues on default of a lease.

As described in § 3.6.6.2, *infra*, these UCC statute of limitations periods are important because, for the causes of action these periods cover, they generally take precedence over other state limitations periods, such as for a written contract. This should be the case even when goods are sold via a store credit card, but this may not be the case for a general-purpose, bank-issued credit card, since the bank is extending a loan and not a credit sale.[293] When a seller or lessor of goods (or that entity's assignee) is seeking to collect on a debt, the UCC four-year limitations period generally controls, even when some other statute of limitations could apply.[294] Of some significance, goods covered by the UCC Article 2 definition include the delivery of natural gas via a pipeline, so actions for collection of past-due gas bills have a four-year limitations period.[295]

3.6.4.4 UCC Limitations Period for Dishonored Checks and Defaulted Promissory Notes

If a consumer pays for goods or services with a personal check that is later dishonored, the collector can sue for nonpayment of the goods or services and/or for nonpayment of the check. Each claim has a separate statute of limitations. If a creditor sues for nonpayment of goods, the four-year UCC Article 2 limitations period applies.[296] If the creditor sues on the dishonored check, UCC § 3–118(c) requires that the action be commenced within three years after the check's dishonor.[297]

A separate UCC Article 3 statute of limitations applies to actions to collect on promissory notes that are negotiable instruments. UCC § 3–118(a) states that an action to enforce the obligation of a party to pay a note payable at a definite time must be commenced within six years of the due date. If the note is accelerated, then the six years commences with the accelerated due date. Arkansas and Louisiana shorten both six-year periods to five years; Montana, Oregon, and Washington shorten it to three years; and Illinois and Iowa omit this provision entirely.

A promissory note is a negotiable instrument if it meets certain UCC Article 3 requirements.[298] Often, a note evidencing a direct loan from a credit union or a bank will qualify as a negotiable instrument—even if the proceeds are used to purchase goods. But a note does not qualify as a negotiable

278 S.D. Codified Laws § 15–2–13.

279 Tenn. Code Ann. § 28–3–109.

280 Tex. Civ. Prac. & Rem. Code Ann. § 16.004 (West).

281 Utah Code Ann. § 78B-2-309–12–23 (West). *But cf.* American Express Bank, F.S.B. v. Dalbis, 2011 WL 873512 (N.Y. City Civ. Ct. Mar. 14, 2011) (arguing that one-year limitations period found in Utah Consumer Credit Code applies to an action to collect a credit card debt).

282 Utah Code Ann. § 78B-2-307 (West).

283 Vt. Stat. Ann. tit. 12, § 511.

In contrast, the U.C.C. Article 2A limitations period for leases accrues when the default occurs or when the lessor should have discovered the default, whichever is later. U.C.C. § 2A-506(2).

284 Va. Code Ann. § 8.01–246.

285 Wash. Rev. Code § 4.16.040.

286 Wash. Rev. Code § 4.16.080.

287 W. Va. Code § 55–2–6.

288 Wis. Stat. § 893.43.

289 Wyo. Stat. Ann. § 1–3–105.

290 Although U.C.C. Article 2 was amended in 2003, no state has adopted this revised version, so the pre-2003 version of Article 2 that is enacted in every state but Louisiana is discussed here.

291 U.C.C. § 2–725.

292 The following states have variations that would affect consumer collection actions: the Colorado U.C.C. refers to Colo. Rev. Stat. § 13–80–101, which imposes a three-year period for U.C.C. actions but also in turn refers to Colo. Rev. Stat. § 13–80–103.5, which imposes a six-year period for actions to recover a liquidated debt or an unliquidated determinable amount; Florida omits the section; Iowa omits the four-year period; Mississippi substitutes six years for four; Oklahoma substitutes five years for four; South Carolina substitutes six years for four; South Dakota deletes the provision prohibiting lengthening of the period by agreement; and Wisconsin substitutes six years for four.

293 *See* § 3.6.6.3, *infra*.

294 *See* § 3.6.6.2, *infra*.

295 Phillips v. Asset Acceptance, 736 F.3d 1076 (7th Cir. 2013).

296 *See* § 3.6.4.2, *supra*.

297 There are unusual situations in which the three-year period can be even further shortened when the collector holds onto the check for a number of years before it seeks to cash it. The U.C.C. Article 3 limitations period for dishonored checks has been uniformly adopted in every state but Iowa.

298 *See* U.C.C. § 3–104(a), (b), (e).

instrument if it does not meet the UCC's strict requirements.[299] Installment sales agreements will not meet these requirements because they include too many duties in addition to the duty to pay. In that case, the Article 3 limitations period will not apply.

3.6.5 The Statute of Limitations Cannot Be Extended by Contract

It would be unusual for a consumer credit agreement to *lengthen* a statute of limitations, and any such attempt should be unenforceable. The statute of limitations is the legislature's attempt to achieve a balance between protecting the courts and defendants against stale claims and providing plaintiffs a reasonable period in which to bring an action. As such, the private parties cannot waive the courts' interest in not hearing stale claims. A contract provision seeking to extend that period should be unenforceable.[300] The UCC Article 2 statute of limitations explicitly states that its limitations period may not be extended by agreement.[301]

3.6.6 Determining Which Statute of Limitations in a State Applies

3.6.6.1 General

As described in § 3.6.4, *supra*, a state may have a number of different statutes of limitations of different lengths, such as for written contracts, non-written contracts, sales of goods, leases, dishonored checks, and promissory notes. It is often critical to determine which limitations period applies to each of the collection causes of action. Different limitations periods may apply to different causes of action.

Sometimes, two limitations periods appear to apply to the *same* cause of action, such as when a merchant sues for breach of a written agreement to pay for goods purchased. Does the limitations period for written contracts apply or that for the sale of goods? Another issue is determining which limitations period applies to a claim when the scope of a statute is not precise. For example, is a claim on an account stated a claim on a written contract or on a non-written contract?

Each cause of action in a collection lawsuit must be analyzed separately to determine which statute of limitations applies to that cause of action. An action being brought on only one debt can have multiple statutes of limitations, each applying to a different cause of action and each specifying a different limitations period.

When the collector's complaint has not sufficiently clarified the nature of a claim so as to allow the consumer to determine which limitations period applies, the consumer should ask the court to require a more definite statement or seek the claim's dismissal for failure to state a claim. Ambiguity in the nature of the claim being sued upon not only confuses what elements the collector must prove but also confuses the applicable limitations period. In fact, the collector's ambiguity as to the nature of its claim may be a deliberate attempt to seek to prove one cause of action while adopting the longer limitations period of a different cause of action.

3.6.6.2 Application of UCC "Sales" Limitations Period to Credit Sales, Store Credit Cards, and Utilities

The UCC Article 2 four-year limitations period for the sale of goods overrides a state's limitations period for a claim based upon a written contract, which is often longer than UCC Article 2's four-year period.[302]

The official comment to UCC section 2–725 states:

> **Purposes**: To introduce a uniform statute of limitations for sales contracts, thus eliminating the jurisdictional variations and providing needed relief for concerns doing business on a nationwide scale whose contracts have heretofore been governed by several different periods of limitation depending upon the state in which the transaction occurred. This Article takes sales contracts out of the general laws limiting the time for commencing contractual actions and selects a four year period as the most appropriate to modern business practice. This is within the normal commercial record keeping period.

Thus, the UCC's Article 2 four-year limitations period, and not the period for written contracts, applies to installment agreements for the sale of goods, such as automobile installment sales initiated by a dealer and sold to a bank.[303] This rule applies even when the vehicle is repossessed and the collector is seeking a deficiency.[304] Creditors sometimes argue that they are suing upon a "secured transaction" or a "deficiency suit," and not on a contract for the sale of goods. This argument has

299 *See* National Consumer Law Center, Mortgage Lending § 10.7 (2d ed. 2014), *updated at* www.nclc.org/library (discussion of when a note qualifies as a negotiable instrument).

300 W. Gate Vill. Ass'n v. Dubois, 761 A.2d 1066 (N.H. 2000).

301 U.C.C. § 2–725.

302 *See* Va. Code Ann. § 8.01–246 (specifying that the UCC § 2–725 limitations period controls); Phillips v. Asset Acceptance, 736 F.3d 1076 (7th Cir. 2013); Taylor v. Unifund Corp., 2001 WL 1035717 (N.D. Ill. Sept. 1, 2001) (applying four-year UCC period instead of ten-year period for written contracts, including promises to pay); D.A.N. Joint Venture III, L.P. v. Armstrong, 2007 WL 634457 (Ohio Ct. App. Mar. 2, 2007). As described in § 3.6.4.2, *supra*, most states have limitations periods for written contracts that are five years or longer, but three states have four-year limitations periods and six (plus the District of Columbia) have three-year periods for written contract claims.

303 When a credit union, for example, makes a direct loan to the consumer to pay for a vehicle, and the loan note qualifies as a negotiable instrument, then U.C.C. Article 3's six-year limitations period for notes would apply.

304 *See* National Consumer Law Center, Repossessions § 12.7 (8th ed. 2013), *updated at* www.nclc.org/library. *See also* Jack Heskett Lincoln-Mercury, Inc. v. Metcalf, 204 Cal. Rptr. 355 (Cal. Ct. App. 1984); Citizen's Nat'l Bank of Decatur v. Farmer, 395 NE 2d 1121 (Ill App. Ct. 1979); Barnes v. Community Trust Bank, 121 SW 3d 520 (Ky. Ct. App. 2003); Calvary Portfolio Serv. v. Stout (Minn. Dist. Ct. Wash. Cnty. Oct. 8, 2010), *available at* www.nclc.org/unreported; D.A.N. Joint Venture, III v. Clark, 218 S.W.3d 455 (Mo. Ct. App. 2006); Ford Motor Credit Co. v. Arce, 791 A.2d 1041 (N.J. Super. Ct. App. Div. 2002).

long been rejected.[305] Similarly, the UCC Article 2, not the UCC Article 3, limitations period applies to promissory notes when the buyer pays for goods with a promissory note.[306]

The UCC Article 2 limitations period also applies to a collection action on a single purpose credit card (a card that can only be used at one merchant)[307] or when a merchant otherwise agrees to defer payment.[308] This transaction is a contract for the sale of goods, with payment deferred. The same logic may not, however, apply to a general purpose, bank-issued credit card (such as a VISA or MasterCard imprinted card), when the bank is loaning money to the consumer to make a purchase with a third party.[309] The applicable period for such a card is examined at § 3.6.6.3, *infra*.

The distinction between a bank-issued card and a store card has become less clear in recent years. Consider a store arranging for a bank to issue a credit card that can only be used to make purchases at that store.[310] The UCC limitations period should apply to an action to collect on a Sears credit card used to purchase goods at Sears. But what about goods purchased at Sears with a Discover Card during the years when Sears owned the Discover Card?

UCC case law also holds that water, electricity, and gas are goods,[311] so that the UCC Article 2 four-year limitations period applies to actions to collect delinquent utility bills for water, electricity, and gas.[312] Even if cell phone, internet, and cable charges are generally not treated as goods, part of the amount owed might involve the purchase of a phone or other equipment which portion of the amount owed would have a four-year limitations period. Note that cell phone charges may be subject to a federal statute of limitations that preempts state law periods.[313]

The UCC Article 2 limitations period does not apply to the sale of services. UCC § 2–102 states "unless the context otherwise requires, this Article applies to transactions in goods." When a series of sales, some for goods and some for services or cash advances, is combined in the same open-end account with a merchant, then two different statutes of limitations may apply. If an action is brought after the four-year period has expired, but before the limitations period for sale of services has expired, the collector should only be able to collect on the amount owed for the services, if it can collect anything.

If a purchase is a mixed sale of goods and services (for example, the sale of flooring which is also installed as part of the purchase), then UCC Article 2 case law has developed rules as to how the purchase is to be treated—as the sale of goods, services, or both. These rules are set out in NCLC's *Consumer Warranty Law § 19.3*.[314]

3.6.6.3 Applicable Limitations Period for Bank-Issued Credit Cards

3.6.6.3.1 General

A number of possible limitations periods might apply to claims concerning breach of a contract concerning a bank-issued, general purpose credit card. Typically a state limitations period will not specifically reference credit card debt,[315] so that courts must determine the applicable period. Occasionally collectors claim that a credit card obligation is based upon a promissory note and that the UCC's six-year limitations period applies.[316] There is no merit to this argument, as a credit card obligation is not a negotiable instrument because there is not a promise to pay a fixed amount and there are conditions on the promise to pay.[317]

More commonly collectors argue that a state's limitations period for written contracts applies to a credit card debt. This is advantageous to the collector in about half the states because the period applicable to written contracts is longer than other limitations periods in the state.[318] (In the other half of the states, the limitations period for claims based upon a written contract is the same as for a claim based upon a non-written contract or an open account, so this issue does not

305 *See* Associates Discount Corp. v. Palmer, 219 A.2d 858 (N.J. 1966) (Pa. law); Ford Motor Credit Co. v. Arce, 791 A.2d 1041 (N.J. Super. Ct. App. Div. 2002); D.A.N. Joint Venture III, L.P. v. Armstrong, 2007 WL 634457 (Ohio Ct. App. Mar. 2, 2007).

306 Fallimento C.Op.M.A. v. Fischer Crane Co., 995 F.2d 789 (7th Cir. 1993).

307 *See* Hamid v. Blatt, Hasenmiller, Leibsker, Moore & Pellettieri, 2001 WL 1035726 (N.D. Ill. Sept. 4, 2001); Taylor v. Unifund Corp., 2001 WL 1035717 (N.D. Ill. Sept. 1, 2001); Gimbel Bros., Inc. v. Cohen, 46 Pa. D. & C.2d 747 (Pa. Ct. Com. Pl. 1969). *See also* Sliger v. R.H. Macy & Co., 283 A.2d 904 (N.J. 1971) (store charge account is a contract for sale of goods). *But see* Asset Acceptance, L.L.C. v. Witten, 2008 WL 2837304 (Ohio Ct. App. July 24, 2008) (U.C.C. limitations period does not apply when merchant only arranges a credit card under its name and obligation was always owed to a third-party lender).

308 Fallimento C.Op.M.A. v. Fischer Crane Co., 995 F.2d 789 (7th Cir. 1993); Ford Motor Credit Co. v. Arce, 791 A.2d 1041 (N.J. Super. Ct. App. Div. 2002); May Co. v. Trusnik, 375 N.E.2d 72 (Ohio Ct. App. 1977).

309 Harris Trust & Sav. Bank v. McCray, 316 N.E.2d 209 (Ill. App. Ct. 1974); Unifund CCR Partners v. Hemm, 2009 WL 2106289 (Ohio Ct. App. July 17, 2009).

310 *See* Asset Acceptance, L.L.C. v. Witten, 2008 WL 2837304 (Ohio Ct. App. July 24, 2008) (merchant just arranged credit card under its name and credit was extended by a third party). *Cf.* Phoenix Recovery Group, Inc. v. Mehta, 663 S.E.2d 290 (Ga. Ct. App. 2008) (U.C.C. limitations period never considered for Best Buy card issued by bank).

311 *See* National Consumer Law Center, Consumer Warranty Law § 1.5.7 (4th ed. 2010), *updated at* www.nclc.org/library.

312 *See* Phillips v. Asset Acceptance, 736 F.3d 1076 (7th Cir. 2013).

313 *See* § 3.6.2.2, *supra*.

314 (4th ed. 2010 and Supp.).

315 *But see* Ariz. Rev. Stat. Ann. § 12–548(A)(2) (effective Apr. 12, 2011) (six-year limitations period for credit card debt). In Arizona, no statute is retroactive unless expressly declared therein. *See* Ariz. Rev. Stat. Ann. § 1–244.

Since the Arizona statute does not expressly provide for retroactivity, the provision for a six-year limitations period for credit card debt does not apply to limitations periods that have expired prior to April 12, 2011. As a result, even in Arizona, it will be important for courts to resolve whether a three or six year period applies to credit card debt, at least for debts that went into default more than three and less than six years from the new legislation's effective date.

316 *See* § 3.6.4.4, *infra*.

317 *See* McLane v. MRC Receivables Corp., 2007 WL 19435 (Ky. Ct. App. Jan. 5, 2007).

318 *See* § 3.6.4.2, *supra*.

arise.)[319] Subsections 3.6.6.3.2 and 3.6.6.3.3, *infra*, explain that the period for a written contract should generally not apply to credit card obligations.

3.6.6.3.2 *Written contract limitations period inapplicable if claim not for breach of written contract*

The statute of limitations for written contracts only applies to causes of action for breach of a written contract. Because debt buyers often cannot produce the written credit card agreement, they often look for causes of action to include in their collection complaints that are *not* based upon that agreement. If a cause of action is not based upon a written contract, the statute of limitations for a written contract claim does not apply to that cause of action.[320] This rule applies even if the cause of action relies in part upon the existence of a written contract, when the written instrument is a link in the chain of evidence to prove the cause of action but does not on its face establish all of the elements of plaintiff's claim.[321]

A collector's counts for *quantum meruit* or money lent are not based on a written contract,[322] and this limitations period will not apply.[323] *Quantum meruit*, by its very nature, is a claim based upon a contract implied in law, not an actual contract.

A claim for account stated is not a claim based upon a written contract either, but instead is based on a statement of account to which the consumer has implicitly assented.[324] Instead of a written, signed contract, there is only a statement identifying an account, itemizing certain charges. The statement of account supersedes the contract and the collector is suing not upon the contract but upon the consumer's implicit promise to pay the statement. In fact, some states have an explicit limitations period for an account stated claim.[325] Other states use the limitations period for a non-written contract or a contract implied in law.[326]

If a collector's cause of action is based upon a written contract, then an essential element of the collector's case must be proof of a binding written contract. The collector cannot fudge the two and claim that its cause of action is founded on a written contract, when in fact the collector cannot produce the written contract or can only produce a form contract that may not even apply to the consumer. Thus one court has found:

> The "Customer Agreement" attached to the Complaint does not identify the Defendant or his account, show the amount lent to Defendant or the terms of repayment, or otherwise establish that Defendant is liable to Plaintiff. When a document does not on its face establish all the elements of Plaintiff's claim, that claim is not "founded on a written instrument" so as to extend the statute of limitations.[327]

3.6.6.3.3 *Is a written credit card agreement a "contract in writing"?*

Even if the collector is able to produce the agreement and bring an action for breach of the written contract, a credit card agreement may not qualify as a written agreement for purposes of a state statute of limitations.[328] Credit card agreements

319 *See id.* Every state listed in that section as having the same limitations period for both written and non-written contracts also has the same limitations period for open accounts, with the exception of two states, Alabama and Louisiana. Ala. Code §§ 6–2–34, 6–2–37 (the same six-year limitation period for written and non-written contract claims, but three years for claims on open accounts); La. Civ. Code arts. 3494, 3499 (ten years for written or non-written contracts, but three years for claims on open accounts).

320 *See* Rawson v. Credigy Receivables, Inc., 2006 WL 418665 (N.D. Ill. Feb. 16, 2006). *See also* Basile v. Blatt, Hasenmiller, Leibsker & Moore, L.L.C., 632 F. Supp. 2d 842 (N.D. Ill. 2009) (no evidence of written contract so claim based upon unwritten contract); Union Labor Life Ins. Co. v. Sheet Metal Workers Nat'l Health Plan, 1991 WL 212232 (D.D.C. Sept. 30, 1991); Capital One Bank v. Creed, 220 S.W.3d 874 (Mo. Ct. App. 2007) (failure to produce agreement signed by consumer precluded creditor from bringing action based on a "writing for the payment of money or property," which has a ten-year statute of limitations under Missouri law, versus a breach of implied contract claim, which has a five-year limitations period). *Cf.* Capital One Bank v. Rodgers, 2010 WL 3620304 (Ohio Ct. App. Sept. 14, 2010).

321 Kersten v. Continental Bank, 628 P.2d 592 (Ariz. 1981); ARDC Corp. v. Hogan, 656 So. 2d 1371, 1374 (Fla. Dist. Ct. App. 1995).

322 *See* Tao of Systems Integration, Inc. v. Analytical Servs. & Materials, Inc., 299 F. Supp. 2d 565 (E.D. Va. 2004); Union Labor Life Ins. Co. v. Sheet Metal Workers Nat'l Health Plan, 1991 WL 212232 (D.D.C. Sept. 30, 1991); Capital One Bank v. Gelsey (Fla. Duval Cnty. Ct. July 3, 2007), *available at* www.nclc.org/unreported.

323 *See* Unifund CCR Partners v. Childs, 2010 WL 703274 (Ohio Ct. App. Feb. 26, 2010); Unifund CCR Partners v. Hemm, 2009 WL 2106289 (Ohio Ct. App. July 17, 2009). *See also* Capital One Bank v. Gregorich (Fla. Miami-Dade Cnty. Ct. June 17, 2008) (applying Virginia's two year default limitations period to a claim for money lent), *available at* www.nclc.org/unreported.

324 *See* § 4.7, *infra*.

325 *See* § 3.6.4.1, *supra*.

326 Richburg v. Palisades Collection, L.L.C., 247 F.R.D. 457 (E.D. Pa. 2008); Capital One Bank v. Gelsey (Fla. Duval Cnty. Ct. July 3, 2007), *available at* www.nclc.org/unreported; Nicolai v. Mason, 454 N.E.2d 1049 (Ill. App. Ct. 1983).

327 Capital One Bank v. Sawyer, 15 Fla. L. Weekly Supp. 170a (Fla. Duval Cnty. Ct. Dec. 17, 2007) (Cox, J.). *See also* Ramirez v. Palisades Collection, L.L.C., 2008 WL 2512679 (N.D. Ill. June 23, 2008); Parkis v. Arrow Fin. Servs., L.L.S., 2008 WL 94798 (N.D. Ill. Jan. 8, 2008); Capital One Bank v. Ruffcorn (Ariz. Super. Ct. Apr. 19, 2010), *available at* www.nclc.org/unreported; Capital One Bank v. Gelsey (Fla. Duval Cnty. Ct. July 3, 2007), *available at* www.nclc.org/unreported.

328 Gemini Capital Group v. New, 807 N.W.2d 157 (Iowa Ct. App. 2011). *See* Rawson v. Credigy Receivables, Inc., 2006 WL 418665 (N.D. Ill. Feb. 16, 2006); Delrey v. Capital One Bank, 2009 WL 5103229 (Fla. Cir. Ct. July 7, 2009) (interpreting Virginia law); Capital One Bank v. Mohammed, 2009 WL 1370834 (Fla. Cir. Ct. Apr. 29, 2009) (unreported) (trial order); Capital One Bank v. Gregorich (Fla. Miami-Dade Cnty. Ct. June 17, 2008) (interpreting Virginia law), *available at* www.nclc.org/unreported; Capital One Bank v. Pincus (Fla. Palm Beach Cnty. Ct. Sept. 8, 2008), *available at* www.nclc.org/unreported; Portfolio Acquisitions, L.L.C. v. Feltman, 909 N.E.2d 876 (Ill. App. Ct. 2009); Smither v. Asset Acceptance, L.L.C., 919 N.E.2d 1153 (Ind. Ct. App. 2010); Capital One Bank v. Creed, 220 S.W.3d 874 (Mo. Ct. App. 2007); Unifund CCR Partners v. Childs, 2010 WL 703274 (Ohio Ct. App. Feb. 26, 2010); Unifund CCR Partners v. Hemm, 2009 WL 2106289 (Ohio Ct. App. July 17, 2009). *See also* Herkert v. MRC Receivables Corp., 655 F. Supp. 2d 870 (N.D. Ill. 2009); Capital One Bank v. McGurk, 932 N.Y.S.2d 420 (N.Y. Civ. Ct. 2010) (Virginia law). *Cf.* Dudek v. Thomas & Thomas Attorneys & Counselors at Law, L.L.C., 702 F. Supp. 2d 826 (N.D. Ohio 2010). *But see* Ariz. Rev. Stat. Ann. § 12–548(A)(2) (effective Apr. 12, 2011) (six-year limitations

are subject to change unilaterally, are generally not signed by either party, and there often is not a "complete writing," but an initial writing plus a series of standard form amendments whose enforceability is contingent on the consumer's continued use of the credit card.[329]

Thus, Virginia's limitations period for written agreements refers to a writing that is signed by the defendant.[330] Virginia's attorney general and one court have interpreted the Virginia limitations period for written contracts only to apply when there is a signed document and that document references all the other documents which make up the agreement. When a consumer credit card account does not contain a signed writing, then the shorter limitations period for non-written contracts applies.[331]

In addition, credit card obligations are open ended, and the amount owed is not fixed in the contract but is instead determined by a series of charges and payments. The interest rate may not be shown in the writing and it will be subject to change in any event.[332] A shorter limitations period for non-written contracts is most appropriate:

> "[S]tatute of limitations are designed to prevent undue delay in bringing suit on claim and to suppress fraudulent and stale claims from being asserted, to the surprise of parties or their representatives, when all the proper vouchers and evidence are lost, or the facts have become obscure from the lapse of time or the defective memory or death or removal of [a] witness" citing *Foremost Properties, Inc. v. Gladman*, 100 So. 2d 669 (Fla. Dist. Ct. App. 1958), *cert den.* 102 So. 2d 728 (Fla. 1958). A review of the statute shows, consistent with common sense, that those actions on which proof is less likely to deteriorate over time are subject to longer limitation periods; those actions on which proof is more likely to deteriorate because of faulty memory or otherwise are subject of shorter limitations periods. Unlike a written contract containing all the terms sued on, proof of the balance due under a store credit card depends on the correctness of the store's books. We know, though, that record keepers come and go; purchased items are returned or exchanged; and partial payments are made. Proof of the amount due under a store credit card is simply not as secure as proof of the amount due on, for example, a promissory note that contains in writing all the terms of the parties' undertakings. *See Nardone v. Reynolds*, 333 So. 2d 25, 36 (Fla. 1976), *mod. on other grds., Tanner v. Hartog*, 618 So. 2d 177 (Fla. 1993) (unfair to allow one who has slept on his rights to sue a party "'. . . who is left to shield himself from liability with nothing more than tattered or faded memories, misplaced or discarded records, and missing or deceased witnesses'"); *Allie v. Ionata*, 503 So. 2d 1237 (Fla. 1987).[333]

In Illinois it may even be the case that an action by a debt buyer does not involve a written contract, within the meaning of the statute of limitations, because the debt buyer is not mentioned in the original contract but only in subsequent writings.[334] The parties must be identified in the contract to qualify as a written contract within the meaning of the statute of limitations.

3.6.7 When Does the Limitations Period Start Running?

3.6.7.1 The Date Triggering the Limitations Period

UCC Article 3's limitations period for suit on a dishonored check begins to run from the date of dishonor.[335] The limitations period for promissory notes begins on the date of acceleration.[336] Under most other statutes of limitations, the period begins from the date of default.[337]

---

period for credit card debt); *In re* Brown, 403 B.R. 1 (Bankr. E.D. Ark. 2009); Phoenix Recovery Group, Inc. v. Mehta, 663 S.E.2d 290 (Ga. Ct. App. 2008); Hill v. Am. Express, 657 S.E.2d 547 (Ga. Ct. App. Jan. 24, 2008); Unifund CCR Partners v. Hemm, 2009 WL 2106289 (Ohio Ct. App. July 17, 2009).

329 Gemini Capital Group v. New, 807 N.W.2d 157 (Iowa Ct. App. 2011). *See* Ramirez v. Palisades Collection, L.L.C., 2008 WL 2512679 (N.D. Ill. June 23, 2008); Parkis v. Arrow Fin. Servs., L.L.S., 2008 WL 94798 (N.D. Ill. Jan. 8, 2008); Rawson v. Credigy Receivables, Inc., 2006 WL 418665 (N.D. Ill. Feb. 16, 2006); Delrey v. Capital One Bank, 2009 WL 5103229 (Fla. Cir. Ct. July 7, 2009) (interpreting Virginia law); Capital One Bank v. Mohammed, 2009 WL 1370834 (Fla. Cir. Ct. Apr. 29, 2009) (unreported) (trial order); Capital One Bank v. Gregorich (Fla. Miami-Dade Cnty. Ct. June 17, 2008), *available at* www.nclc.org/unreported; Capital One Bank v. Pincus (Fla. Palm Beach Cnty. Ct. Sept. 8, 2008) (Va. law), *available at* www.nclc.org/unreported; Capital One Bank v. Gelsey (Fla. Duval Cnty. Ct. July 3, 2007), *available at* www.nclc.org/unreported; Portfolio Acquisitions, L.L.C. v. Feltman, 909 N.E.2d 876 (Ill. App. Ct. 2009); Smither v. Asset Acceptance, L.L.C., 919 N.E.2d 1153 (Ind. Ct. App. 2010). *See also* Capital One Bank v. Creed, 220 S.W.3d 874 (Mo. Ct. App. 2007). *But see In re* Brown, 403 B.R. 1 (Bankr. E.D. Ark. 2009); Asset Acceptance, L.L.C. v. Witten, 2008 WL 2837304 (Ohio Ct. App. July 24, 2008).

330 Va. Code Ann. § 8.01–246(2).

331 Capital One Bank v. Bassham (Cal. Super. Ct. July 25, 2012), *available at* www.nclc.org/unreported. *But see* Capital One Bank v. Chiu (Cal. Super. Ct. Dec. 21, 2012), *available at* www.nclc.org/unreported (without discussion, finding that Virginia's written contract limitation period applies).

332 Delrey v. Capital One Bank, 2009 WL 5103229 (Fla. Cir. Ct. July 7, 2009) (interpreting Virginia law).

333 Portfolio Recovery Assocs., L.L.C. v. Fernandes, 13 Fla. L. Weekly Supp. 506a (Fla. Palm Beach Cnty. Ct. Mar. 6, 2006) (Perez, J.). *See also* Delrey v. Capital One Bank, 2009 WL 5103229 (Fla. Cir. Ct. July 7, 2009) (interpreting Virginia law); Capital One Bank v. Mohammed, 2009 WL 1370834 (Fla. Cir. Ct. Apr. 29, 2009) (unreported) (trial order); Portfolio Acquisitions, L.L.C. v. Feltman, 909 N.E.2d 876 (Ill. App. Ct. 2009); Smither v. Asset Acceptance, L.L.C., 919 N.E.2d 1153 (Ind. Ct. App. 2010). *Cf.* ARDC Corp. v. Hogan, 656 So. 2d 1371 (Fla. Dist. Ct. App. 1995) (when writing does not contain all the terms, the statute of limitations for a written contract does not apply). *But see* Phoenix Recovery Group, Inc. v. Mehta, 663 S.E.2d 290 (Ga. Ct. App. 2008).

334 *See* Brown v. Goodman, 498 N.E.2d 854 (Ill. App. Ct. 1986).

335 U.C.C. § 3–118(c).

336 U.C.C. § 3–118(a).

337 Isaacson, Stolper & Co. v. Artisans' Sav. Bank, 330 A.2d 130, 132 (Del. 1974).

Using the date of default is consistent with the rule that, for a breach of contract action, the statute of limitations "runs from the time of the breach, although no damage occurs until later."[338] UCC Article 2's limitations period explicitly states that it begins running when the breach occurs, regardless of the aggrieved party's lack of knowledge of the breach.[339] In other words, the four years begin running as soon as the consumer has breached the agreement, even if the creditor has not realized the breach has occurred, and certainly not when the creditor decides to declare a breach or when the debt buyer acquires an account. When a contract for services indicates that payment is due when the services are completed, then the statute of limitations should begin running when the services are completed and payment is not made on that date.[340]

New Hampshire has a very short three-year limitations period for breach of contract, and its period begins when the creditor discovers or should have reasonably discovered the act or omission.[341] Nevertheless, even New Hampshire typically considers the date of reasonable discovery in a contract case to be the date of breach.[342]

Another approach, particularly for an open account, is to start the limitations period from the date the last payment was made or the date after that when the minimum payment was due but unpaid. The card issuer continuing to send new statements with additional late or interest charges does not trigger the beginning of a new limitations period.[343] Yet another approach, particularly for account stated or open account causes of action, is to start the period running from the date of the last item purchased on the account,[344] indicating that it begins to run not from the occurrence of any default but from the date the last charge was incurred.

Collectors on credit card debt often claim that the date of default for purposes of the statute of limitations is when the creditor unilaterally decides to cancel the card and accelerate the debt. This claim may be inconsistent with how a state's statute of limitations is worded or how the credit agreement defines default. A common default provision of a credit card agreement states: "You will be in default under this agreement upon: (a) your failure to make at least the minimum payment by the date specified on your statement; (b) your violation of any other provision of this agreement. . . ." Default clauses generally provide that a party has a right to sue immediately upon the occurrence of any of the "default contingencies," and thus the default should be the trigger date for the starting of the running of the limitations period.

On the other hand, a credit card agreement may state that, if the card issuer considers the consumer delinquent, the issuer can close the account and demand payment immediately. Florida federal courts, interpreting Delaware law, view this as triggering the statute of limitations when the issuer closes the account and demands payment.[345] But most courts find that the statute of limitations on a credit card account starts from when the last payment is made.[346]

Collectors may also claim that the statute of limitations begins to run on the charge-off date. But this date is only a matter of accounting practice dictated by banking regulators, such as the Office of the Comptroller of the Currency (OCC).[347] For example, the OCC defines "charge off" as the date when a company using the accrual method must stop recording putative income from the loan and treat it as non-performing. In open-end credit accounts such as credit cards, the account must be "charged off" 180 days after the delinquency. The charge-off date is not the date of default; a creditor would not take the position that it would have to wait 180 days after the debtor stopped making payments before it could file a lawsuit.[348] A debt is charged off after repeated collection attempts *post-default* are unsuccessful, and the charge-off signifies to the creditor's investors that this account receivable has diminished value on the creditor's books. Only if a credit agreement defines default as occurring when an account is closed and only when that occurs on the charge-off date should that dated be treated as triggering the limitations period.

Finally, some debt buyers go so far as to claim that the limitations period begins to run when they purchase the debt. This

338 31 Richard A. Lord, Williston on Contracts § 79.14 (4th ed. 2004). *See also* Med. Jet, S.A. v. Signature Flight Support-Palm Beach, Inc., 941 So. 2d 576 (Fla. Dist. Ct. App. 2006).

339 U.C.C. § 2-725(2).

340 Person Earth Movers, Inc. v. Buckland, 525 S.E.2d 239 (N.C. Ct. App. 2000).

341 N.H. Rev. Stat. Ann. § 508:4.

342 W. Gate Vill. Ass'n v. Dubois, 761 A.2d 1066 (N.H. 2000).

343 *See* Smither v. Asset Acceptance, L.L.C., 919 N.E.2d 1153 (Ind. Ct. App. 2010). *See also* Jarvis v. First Resolution Mgmt. Corp., 983 N.E.2d 380 (Ohio Ct. App. 2012). *But see* Capital One Bank v. Conti, 345 S.W.3d 490 (Tex. App. 2011) (consumer has burden of proving when dealings between parties conclusively ended, and mere allegation of last payment date is not sufficient).

344 *See* Cal. Civ. Proc. Code § 337 (West); Mich. Comp. Laws § 600.5831.

345 Mercado v. HFC Collection Ctr., Inc., 2013 WL 645988 (M.D. Fla. Jan. 28, 2013), *report and recommendation adopted by* 2013 WL 654419 (M.D. Fla. Feb. 21, 2013); Carter v. Athena Funding Group Assets, L.L.C., 2012 WL 3947344 (M.D. Fla. Sept. 10, 2012). *But see* Gonzalez v. Asset Acceptance, L.L.C., 2008 WL 2694895 (M.D. Fla. July 2, 2008), *aff'd on other grounds*, 308 Fed. Appx. 429 (11th Cir. Jan. 26, 2009).

346 *See* Eckert v. LVNV Funding, L.L.C., 647 F. Supp. 2d 1096 (E.D. Mo. 2009); McCollough v. Johnson, Rodenberg & Lauinger, 587 F. Supp. 2d 1170 (D. Mont. 2008), *aff'd on other grounds*, 637 F.3d 939 (9th Cir. 2011); Jenkins v. General Collection Co., 538 F. Supp. 2d 1165 (D. Neb. 2008); Dunlap v. Friedman's, Inc., 582 S.E.2d 841 (W. Va. 2003).

347 Office of the Comptroller of the Currency, OCC 2000-20, OCC Bulletin; Fed. Fin. Insts. Examinations Council, Uniform Retail Credit Classification and Account Management Policy, 65 Fed. Reg. 36,903 (June 12, 2000); Fed. Fin. Insts. Examinations Council, Uniform Retail Credit Classification and Account Management Policy, 64 Fed. Reg. 6655 (Feb. 10, 1999). *See also* Smither v. Asset Acceptance, L.L.C., 919 N.E.2d 1153 (Ind. Ct. App. 2010) (charge-off date not relevant to when limitations period begins to run).

348 *See* Rochholz v. Farrar, 547 F.2d 63, 64 n.2 (8th Cir. 1976) ("A 'charge off' occurs when a loan is determined to be uncollectible. The amount charged off is then carried in the bad debt account and not as a general ledger asset on the books of the bank."); Fla. Credit Research, Inc. v. Felicien (Fla. Duval Cnty. Ct. Apr. 15, 2008), *available at* www.nclc.org/unreported.

position is clearly wrong, because the date of default generally triggers the limitations period, not the date the collector discovers the default. And even if a limitations period begins to run when the creditor discovers the default, this rule applies to the original creditor's discovery. Subsequent purchases of the debt do not start the period running anew. If that were the case, the limitations period could go on forever. Assignees step into the shoes of the assignor.

Whatever the legal standard is with regard to when the limitations period begins to run, there can be factual questions as to when the event triggering the limitations period actually took place. While the consumer may bear the burden of proving that the limitations period has run, the consumer should be able to survive a summary judgment motion when (1) there is a factual dispute as to when the limitations period began to run, and (2) the consumer's statement of the facts is consistent with the limitations period expiring.[349]

3.6.7.2 Determining the Date of Default

In computing whether the statute of limitations has run, it is not always easy to determine the date of default. The consumer is unlikely to have records, and a debt buyer's records will not be reliable.

The consumer can start investigating the date of default by closely examining the collector's pleadings and any attached documents. Even if the collector is claiming a later date of default, its own pleadings, affidavits, and other documents may indicate an earlier date of default.[350] Never underestimate the sloppiness of debt buyer documentation. The date on which a consumer stopped payments on a credit card account can also be inferred from the charge-off date,[351] if the collector provides that date in any of its documents—something collectors do surprisingly often. The charge-off date, under the OCC standards, is supposed to be 180 days after the account becomes delinquent. Thus, a reasonable assumption of a delinquency date is 180 days *before* the charge-off date.[352]

Another approach is to look at the consumer's credit report to determine the last payment on the account reflected in the report. Again, do not confuse the charge-off date, which may be indicated there, with the date when the consumer stopped paying.[353] Also be alert to certain collectors seeking to "re-age" a debt by reporting an incorrect date of first delinquency, which is a potential violation of the FCRA (albeit without a federal private right of action unless first disputed with the credit reporting agency),[354] as well as the Fair Debt Collection Practices Act.

3.6.8 *Is the Limitations Period Tolled or Revived?*

3.6.8.1 Terminology

Although courts use varying terminology, this chapter uses the term "tolling" to mean suspension of the running of the limitations period and "reviving" to mean restarting the running of the limitations period from the beginning. When the limitations period is five years and two years remain on the period, and the period is *tolled*, then two years continue to remain left in the period until the tolling of the period ceases. When the occurrence that tolled the period ends, the counting begins anew, with only two years left in the period. If the action is *revived*, then the counting goes back to zero, and the limitations period does not expire for five more years.

3.6.8.2 Tolling the Limitations Period

3.6.8.2.1 Military service

Federal law specifies that the period of a servicemember's military service is not included in the computing any limitations period under federal or state law.[355] The provision applies to the period in which the consumer is on active duty military service and applies to debts incurred before and during the period of active duty military service. This increased risk of a collection lawsuit is offset to some extent by the fact that servicemembers have certain protections against collection actions not available to others, examined in Chapter 7, *infra*. The tolling, though, can extend the limitations period of a collection suit until well after the consumer leaves active duty, at which time the servicemember may no longer qualify for special protections.

The tolling provision applies to the servicemember and the servicemember's heirs, executors, administrators, or assigns. It does not apply to those jointly liable with the servicemember.[356] Thus, the statute of limitations may run against a spouse while it is still tolled against the servicemember.

3.6.8.2.2 Bankruptcy

A bankruptcy proceeding tolls the limitations period, but a successful chapter 7 or chapter 13 bankruptcy filing moots the tolling effect of the bankruptcy proceeding on a collection action for an unsecured debt. The successful bankruptcy discharges the debt and eliminates any collection action. But if a chapter 7 filing is dismissed or if a chapter 13 plan fails, then the collector can sue for the unpaid portion of a debt, and

349 *See* Midland Funding v. Schlick, 2013 WL 6223571 (Minn. Ct. App. Dec. 2, 2013).

350 *See* Fla. Credit Research, Inc. v. Felicien (Fla. Duval Cnty. Ct. Apr. 15, 2008), *available at* www.nclc.org/unreported; Capital One Bank v. Gelsey (Fla. Duval Cnty. Ct. July 3, 2007), *available at* www.nclc.org/unreported.

351 *See* § 3.6.7.1, *supra*.

352 *See* Fla. Credit Research, Inc. v. Felicien (Fla. Duval Cnty. Ct. Apr. 15, 2008), *available at* www.nclc.org/unreported; Capital One Bank v. Gelsey (Fla. Duval Cnty. Ct. July 3, 2007), *available at* www.nclc.org/unreported.

353 *See* § 3.6.7.1, *supra*.

354 *See* National Consumer Law Center, Fair Credit Reporting § 5.2.3.4.4 (8th ed. 2013), *updated at* www.nclc.org/library.

355 50 U.S.C. app. § 526(a).

356 50 U.S.C. app. § 526(a).

the statute of limitations will be tolled during the pendency of the bankruptcy.[357] As soon as the bankruptcy is dismissed or the plan fails, then the statute of limitations starts running again.[358]

3.6.8.2.3 Time spent out of state

Other grounds for tolling the statute of limitations will be based on state law. A common ground for such tolling is if the consumer moves out of state for some of the period. The period of the absence is not counted in computing the limitations period.[359] The burden will be on the collector to show the dates the consumer was absent from the state. If the collector cannot meet this burden, then the limitations period will not be tolled.

A number of courts find that the tolling rule for time out of state does not apply when service of process is available out of state.[360] The premise of the tolling statute is that the defendant's personal absence from the jurisdiction makes service on the defendant difficult. This premise is no longer applicable, because of modern notions of long-arm statutes and the like, and thus the tolling statute should not apply.[361] Some courts simply define "absent" or "out of state" as meaning a defendant who is beyond personal jurisdiction and process of the court, thus denying tolling when an action is possible against the out-of-state defendant.[362]

Moreover, it is very possible that a rule tolling the limitations period when the defendant is out of state is unconstitutional. The courts seem to be in agreement that leaving the state to engage in commerce should not be discriminated against, and that lengthening a statute of limitations period for those engaging in interstate commerce would be unconstitutional.[363] Courts have found the tolling to be unconstitutional when the consumer went out of state for employment,[364] or to change residences,[365] but not for a vacation.[366]

3.6.8.2.4 Non-applicability of time spent out of the state chosen in contract's choice of law provision

When the law of the state selected in the credit agreement controls the statute of limitations, collectors sometimes point to the statutory provision in the non-forum state specifying that the limitations period does not run when the consumer does not reside in that state. As the consumer has never resided in the non-forum state, collectors argue, the limitations period never begins to run. Courts have no problem rejecting this argument that would otherwise make a sham of the limitations period.[367]

Among other reasons, the purpose of the provision is to protect a plaintiff when the defendant cannot be served with the complaint, but there is no question that the collector can serve the consumer in the consumer's home state where the action is being brought.[368] In addition, providing a statute of limitations applicable to residents, but not to non-residents, raises serious constitutional questions, as discussed in part at § 3.6.8.2.3, *supra*.

Nevertheless the Ninth Circuit, in *Avery*, interpreting New Hampshire law, came to the opposite conclusion.[369] This holding can be criticized for a number of reasons. First, it claims that several New Hampshire cases support its position—

357 11 U.S.C. § 108(c). *See also* Person Earth Movers, Inc. v. Buckland, 525 S.E.2d 239 (N.C. Ct. App. 2000).

358 Person Earth Movers, Inc. v. Buckland, 525 S.E.2d 239 (N.C. Ct. App. 2000).

359 Alaska Stat. § 09.10.130; Cal. Civ. Proc. Code § 351 (West); Idaho Code Ann. § 5–229; Me. Rev. Stat. tit. 14, § 866; Miss. Code Ann. § 15–1–63; Mo. Rev. Stat. § 516.200; Neb. Rev. Stat. § 25–214; Ohio Rev. Code Ann. § 2305.15(A) (West); Or. Rev. Stat. § 12.150; S.C. Code Ann. § 15–3–30; S.D. Codified Laws § 15–2–20; Tenn. Code Ann. § 28–1–111; Tex. Civ. Prac. & Rem. Code Ann. § 16.063 (West); Utah Code Ann. § 78B-2–104 (West); Wash. Rev. Code § 4.16.180; Wyo. Stat. Ann. § 1–3–116.

360 Kuk v. Nalley, 166 P.3d 47 (Alaska 2007); Shin v. McLaughlin, 967 P.2d 1059 (Haw. 1998); Meyer v. Paschal, 498 S.E.2d 635 (S.C. 1998). *See also* Hurwitch v. Adams, 155 A.2d 591 (Del. 1959). *But see* Dew v. Appleberry, 591 P.2d 509 (Cal. 1979); Couts v. Rose, 90 N.E.2d 139 (Ohio 1950); Vaughn v. Deitz, 430 S.W.2d 487 (Tex. 1968); Olseth v. Larson, 158 P.3d 532 (Utah 2007).

361 Kuk v. Nalley, 166 P.3d 47 (Alaska 2007); Ashley v. Hawkins, 293 S.W.3d 175 (Tex. 2009).

362 Peters v. Tuell Dairy Co., 35 So. 2d 344 (Ala. 1948); Byrne v. Ogle, 488 P.2d 716 (Alaska 1971); Meyer v. Paschal, 498 S.E.2d 635 (S.C. 1998).

363 Bendix Autolite Corp. v. Midwesco Enterprises, 486 U.S. 888, 108 S. Ct. 2218, 100 L. Ed. 2d 896 (1988); Abramson v. Brownstein, 897 F.2d 389 (9th Cir. 1990); Tesar v. Hallas, 738 F. Supp. 240 (N.D. Ohio 1990); Heritage Mktg. & Ins. Servs., Inc. v. Chrustawka, 73 Cal. Rptr. 3d 126 (Cal. Ct. App. 2008); McFadden v. Battifora, 2004 WL 103353 (Cal. Ct. App. Jan. 23, 2004); Filet Menu, Inc. v. Cheng, 84 Cal. Rptr. 2d 384 (Cal. Ct. App. 1999); State *ex rel.* Bloomquist v. Schneider, 244 S.W.3d 139 (Mo. 2008); Grover v. Bartsch, 866 N.E.2d 547 (Ohio Ct. App. 2006).

364 Tesar v. Hallas, 738 F. Supp. 240 (N.D. Ohio 1990); McFadden v. Battifora, 2004 WL 103353 (Cal. Ct. App. Jan. 23, 2004). *See also* Filet Menu, Inc. v. Cheng, 84 Cal. Rptr. 2d 384 (Cal. Ct. App. 1999).

365 Heritage Mktg. & Ins. Servs., Inc. v. Chrustawka, 73 Cal. Rptr. 3d 126 (Cal. Ct. App. 2008); Filet Menu, Inc. v. Cheng, 84 Cal. Rptr. 2d 384 (Cal. Ct. App. 1999); State *ex rel.* Bloomquist v. Schneider, 244 S.W.3d 139 (Mo. 2008).

366 Johnson v. Rhodes, 733 N.E.2d 1132 (Ohio 2000).

367 Gaisser v. Portfolio Recovery Assocs., L.L.C., 571 F. Supp. 2d 1273 (S.D. Fla. 2008); McCorriston v. L.W.T., Inc., 536 F. Supp. 2d 1268 (M.D. Fla. 2008) (interpreting the Delaware tolling provision); Resurgence Fin., L.L.C. v. Chambers, 92 Cal. Rptr. 3d 844 (Cal. Ct. App. 2009); Hurwitch v. Adams, 155 A.2d 591 (Del. 1959); L.W.T. v. Brodsky, 14 Fla. L. Weekly Supp. 188a (Fla. Broward Cnty. Ct. Dec. 8, 2006); Portfolio Recovery Assocs., L.L.C. v. King, 927 N.E.2d 1059 (N.Y. 2010). *But cf.* Unifund CCR Partners v. Deboer, 277 P.3d 562 (Or. Ct. App. 2012) (refusing to apply the law selected in the contract because the court was concerned that application of that state's tolling rules would extend the limitations period indefinitely); Unifund CCR Partners v. Porras, 275 P.3d 992 (Or. Ct. App. 2012) (same); CACV of Colo., L.L.C. v. Stevens, 274 P.3d 859 (Or. Ct. App. 2012) (same).

368 Resurgence Fin., L.L.C. v. Chambers, 92 Cal. Rptr. 3d 844 (Cal. Ct. App. 2009).

369 Avery v. First Resolution Mgmt. Corp., 568 F.3d 1018 (9th Cir. 2009) (N.H. law). *See also* Unifund CCR Partners v. Deboer, 277 P.3d 562 (Or. Ct. App. 2012) (refusing to apply the law selected in the contract because the court was concerned that application of that state's tolling rules would extend the limitations period indefinitely); Unifund CCR Partners v. Porras, 275 P.3d 992 (Or. Ct. App. 2012) (same); CACV of Colo., L.L.C. v. Stevens, 274 P.3d 859 (Or. Ct. App. 2012) (same).

however, these cases not only hold the reverse, but the court's own description of the cases indicates that they hold the reverse. The cases state that New Hampshire's tolling provision does *not* apply when the plaintiff can successfully serve the defendant while the defendant is not in New Hampshire, which was clearly the case in *Avery*.[370]

The Ninth Circuit opinion also ignores the obvious question of whether the New Hampshire legislature intended such a bizarre result—that the statute of limitations would never run, that out-of-state parties opting for New Hampshire law would be completely waiving the statute of limitations. The purpose of the tolling statute is to protect plaintiffs when it is difficult to serve the defendant while the defendant is out of state. That clearly does not apply to a situation in which the defendant resides in the state where the action is brought but the choice of law rules specify another state's laws.

As described in §§ 3.6.3 and 3.6.5, *supra*, courts will not apply a choice of law provision to extend the limitations period beyond what would be allowed in the forum state. (In the Ninth Circuit case, the collector's case was brought within the forum state's statute of limitations, and it is unlikely that even the Ninth Circuit would allow an out-of-state tolling rule to extend the limitations period beyond that applicable in the forum state.) Fortunately, the Ninth Circuit's interpretation of New Hampshire law should not be binding precedent as to the tolling rules for other states' law and should also be far less persuasive as to New Hampshire law than a New Hampshire state court decision, including the very New Hampshire state court decisions cited in *Avery*.

The other set of decisions that is confused on this point is a series of Oregon middle level appellate court decisions refusing to apply the law selected in the contract because the courts were concerned that application of that state's tolling rules would extend the limitations period indefinitely.[371] Those cases rely principally on a Delaware case tolling the limitations period when the defendants in a Delaware court raised counterclaims against the government of Saudi Arabia outside the limitations period. The court found the limitations period tolled because it would have been impossible to bring the claims against Saudi Arabia in a Delaware court before then.[372] But this is exactly the situation in which the Delaware legislature intended its tolling provision to apply, not to litigation brought in another state wherein the plaintiff never had a problem finding the defendant to serve process.

3.6.8.2.5 Voluntary dismissal of a case does not toll the period

Consider a situation in which a collector brings an action, and then the case is voluntarily dismissed or dismissed for lack of prosecution. If the collector then seeks to bring a new action, the period of time when the first case was pending typically does *not* toll the running of the limitations period.[373]

On the other hand, state law may provide otherwise, that the time during which a prior action on the same debt was pending does not count toward the running of the statute of limitations.[374]

3.6.8.3 Reviving the Limitations Period

3.6.8.3.1 Part payment

Certain actions by the consumer can revive the statute of limitations—that is start the statute running again from the beginning. In many states, one such action is making a payment on the debt.[375] Of course, the payment must be directed at the debt in question. For example, if a collector seeks payment on two different accounts, even two accounts with the same creditor, payment on one account does not revive the limitations period on the other account.[376]

Moreover, to revive the action, the consumer's intent in making part payment must be to acknowledge that the remainder is also due. Thus, the Supreme Court over one hundred years ago stated:

> [A] promise to pay cannot be inferred from the mere fact of payment of part of a debt, there being nothing to raise a presumption that it was a payment on account of this debt. The principle on which part payment takes a case out of the statute is, that the party paying intended by it to acknowledge and admit the greater debt to be due. If it was not in the mind of

370 The court cites *Bolduc v. Richards*, 142 A.2d 156 (N.H. 1958) with the following parenthetical: "(holding that the statute of limitations is only tolled when a defendant could not otherwise be served in New Hampshire due to lack of personal jurisdiction)." The court also cites *Quarles v. Bickford*, 13 A. 642 (N.H. 1888) and describes its holding as "(same)." These cases more precisely state that the limitations period is *not* tolled if service of process is possible while the defendant is out of state. Obviously, in *Avery*, the defendant could be served, and so the limitations period should not have been tolled. It is irrelevant that the defendant cannot be served in New Hampshire when the plaintiff wishes, and successfully manages, to serve the defendant in Oregon. In fact, it would be illegal under the FDCPA to try to sue the consumer defendant in New Hampshire.

371 CACV of Colo., L.L.C. v. Stevens, 274 P.3d 859 (Or. Ct. App. 2012). *See also* Unifund CCR Partners v. Deboer, 277 P.3d 562 (Or. Ct. App. 2012); Unifund CCR Partners v. Porras, 275 P.3d 992 (Or. Ct. App. 2012).

372 Saudi Basic Indus. v. Mobil Yanbu Petrochemical Co., 866 A.2d 1 (Del. 2005).

373 See Wood v. Elling Corp., 572 P.2d 755 (Cal. 1977); Thomas v. Gilliland, 115 Cal. Rptr. 2d 520 (Cal. Ct. App. 2002).

374 *See, e.g.*, Va. Code Ann. § 8.01–229(E)(1).

375 *See* Kan. Stat. Ann. § 60–520(a); Krawczyk v. Centurion Capital Corp., 2009 WL 395458 (N.D. Ill. Feb. 18, 2009); Martindell v. Bodrero, 63 Cal. Rptr. 774 (Cal. Ct. App. 1967); Portfolio Recovery Assocs., L.L.C. v. Neska, 2010 WL 696649 (Minn. Ct. App. Mar. 2, 2010); Dodeka, L.L.C. v. Campos, 377 SW 3d 726 (Tex. App. 2012); Citibank v. Cramer, 139 Wash. App. 1089 (Wash. Ct. App. 2007); Annotation, *Payment on Account, or Claimed to be on Account, as Removing or Tolling Statute of Limitations*, 156 A.L.R. 1082 (1945). *See also* Davis v. World Credit Fund I, L.L.C., 543 F. Supp. 2d 953 (N.D. Ill. 2008); Davis v. Unifund CCR Partners, 2008 WL 191272 (N.D. Cal. Jan. 22, 2008).

376 H.A. Wood, Annotation, *Necessity and sufficiency of identification of part payment with the particular debt in question, for purposes of tolling, or removing bar of, statute of limitations*, 142 A.L.R. 389 (1943).

the debtor to do this, then the statute, having begun to run, will not be stopped by reason of such payment.[377]

If the consumer intended a payment to be the final amount, even if the collector believes more is due, then the statute of limitations on the remainder due is not revived by the part payment.[378] Payment of principal does not revive the limitations period for interest payments that are disputed.[379] If the consumer makes a payment indicating an obligation for part of the debt alleged but disputing the remainder of the debt, the payment does not revive the limitations period for the disputed portion of the debt.[380]

An interesting question is whether partial payment by a debt adjustment company on behalf of the consumer acknowledges an obligation to pay the remainder of the debt.[381] In fact, such payments are often an attempt to settle the total amount due, and the payment certainly evidences no intent by the consumer that the remainder is due.

There must also be proof that payment was in fact made. A debt buyer wishing to revive the limitations period cannot just claim that a part payment has been made recently.[382] It must provide evidence of that payment, particularly if the consumer denies making the payment. Some states disallow an alleged payment the only proof of which is a note of payment in the creditor's books—additional proof must be produced.[383]

Payment by one co-debtor may not revive the limitations period in an action against the other co-debtor.[384] The same is the case for a payment by a bankruptcy trustee. This payment does not revive the limitations period against the consumer.[385] The reason that payment revives the limitation period is that it implies that the consumer acknowledges the debt. If the consumer did not make the payment, or if the consumer made the payment with a different intent, then the payment does not imply this acknowledgment.[386]

Because the collector has the burden of proof to show that a consumer's action has revived the limitations period, the collector will have the burden of proof to show that a payment was made, that the consumer being sued in fact made the payment, that the payment was directed to the account in question, and that the payment was made with the intent to acknowledge the remainder of the debt.[387]

Debt buyers sometimes purchase debts outside the statute of limitations, dun the consumer with the intent to obtain a small payment toward the debt, and then use that payment to revive the statute of limitations. Questions arise as to whether the dunning on a debt with the intent to trick the consumer into reviving a time-barred debt is an unfair or deceptive practice or a violation of the federal FDCPA, particularly when the collector does not disclose that the debt is time-barred.[388]

Thus, in one case, the collector threatened the consumer with a lawsuit that it could not bring because the limitations period had expired. Nevertheless, the collector tricked the consumers into making a payment and then sued for the remainder of the debt. The court found that the collector was equitably estopped from arguing the limitations period had revived and also found that suing on a time-barred debt violated the FDCPA. The court ordered the collector's action dismissed and the amount of the consumer's payment returned to the consumer.[389]

If a partial payment does revive the limitations period, then the limitations period begins running again from that date of partial payment (not thirty days from that date).[390] As of the date of the partial payment, the consumer is still behind in payments and thus is still in default on that date.

3.6.8.3.2 Acknowledgment of the debt

The consumer's acknowledgment of the obligation may revive the statute of limitations. States establish standards as to what type of acknowledgment is sufficient to revive the limitations period. Typically an oral statement that the money is owed is *not* enough. Some states require the acknowledgment be in writing and signed.[391] Other states find that it is not enough that the debtor recognize the debt. The debtor must also admit liability and agree to pay the remainder due.[392]

In Pennsylvania, a simple declaration of an intent to discharge an obligation is not enough. There must not only be a willingness to pay at a future time, but a willingness to pay upon demand.[393]

---

377 United States v. Wilder, 80 U.S. 254, 256, 20 L. Ed. 681 (1872).

378 Huntingdon Fin. Corp. v. Newtown Artesian Water Co., 659 A.2d 1052 (Pa. Super. Ct. 1995).

379 *Id.*

380 O'Malley v. Frazier, 49 P.3d 438 (Kan. 2002).

381 *See* Charbonneau v. Mary Jane Elliott P.C., 611 F. Supp. 2d 736 (E.D. Mich. 2009).

382 *Cf.* McCollough v. Johnson, Rodenburg & Lavinger, L.L.C., 637 F.3d 939 (9th Cir. Mar. 4, 2011).

383 *E.g.*, N.J. Stat. Ann. § 2A:14–25 (West).

384 *See* N.J. Stat. Ann. § 2A:14–24 (West); Elmore v. Fanning, 117 P. 1019 (Kan. 1911).

385 Person Earth Movers, Inc. v. Buckland, 525 S.E.2d 239 (N.C. Ct. App. 2000).

386 *Id.*

387 Huntingdon Fin. Corp. v. Newtown Artesian Water Co., 659 A.2d 1052 (Pa. Super. Ct. 1995).

388 *Cf.* Asset Acceptance, L.L.C. v. Hanson, 2009 WL 840047 (Cal. Ct. App. Apr. 1, 2009) (unpublished) (declining to certify class when allegations made that this practice violated state and federal law).

389 Calvary Portfolio Serv. v. Stout (Minn. Dist. Ct. Wash. Cnty. Feb. 11, 2011), *available at* www.nclc.org/unreported.

390 Capital One Bank v. Creed, 220 S.W.3d 874 (Mo. Ct. App. 2007).

391 *See* Cal. Civ. Proc. Code § 360 (West) (no acknowledgment or promise is sufficient evidence of a new or continuing contract, by which to take the case out of the operation of this title, unless the same is contained in some writing, signed by the party to be charged thereby); Kan. Stat. Ann. § 60–520(a); N.J. Stat. Ann. § 2A:14–24 (West); S.D. Codified Laws § 15–2–29; Va. Code Ann. § 8.01–229(G); Asset Acceptance, L.L.C. v. Morgan, 2007 WL 949251 (Mich. Ct. App. Mar. 29, 2007). *Cf.* Charbonneau v. Mary Jane Elliott P.C., 611 F. Supp. 2d 736 (E.D. Mich. 2009) (written acknowledgment revives the limitations period).

392 A & B Lumber Co., L.L.C. v. Vrusho, 871 A.2d 64 (N.H. 2005); Gurenlian v. Gurenlian, 595 A.2d 145 (Pa. Super. Ct. 1991).

393 Gurenlian v. Gurenlian, 595 A.2d 145 (Pa. Super. Ct. 1991). *See also In re* Pagnotti, 269 B.R. 326 (Bankr. M.D. Pa. 2001).

The acknowledgment must be "clear, distinct, and unequivocal."[394] An acknowledgment of the principal amount due on a debt may not be an acknowledgment that the claimed finance charges and other fees are also owed.[395] In addition, when there are joint debtors and one of the debtors admits to the debt sufficient to restart the limitations period, that admission may not be sufficient to restart the limitations period for claims against the other debtor.[396] Nor is it enough to acknowledge that the amount due was owed as of the time of the default. The consumer must admit that the amount is still presently owed.[397]

394 Gurenlian v. Gurenlian, 595 A.2d 145 (Pa. Super. Ct. 1991).

395 Huntingdon Fin. Corp. v. Newtown Artesian Water Co., 659 A.2d 1052 (Pa. Super. Ct. 1995).

396 N.J. Stat. Ann. § 2A:14–24 (West); A & B Lumber Co., L.L.C. v. Vrusho, 871 A.2d 64 (N.H. 2005).

397 Nicolai v. Mason, 454 N.E.2d 1049 (Ill. App. Ct. 1983).

Chapter 4 Proof of the Merits of the Collector's Claims

4.1 Introduction

This chapter examines the debt collector's proof as to the merits of its causes of action. As the burden is on the plaintiff to prove its claims, no recovery can be had, either at trial or on summary judgment, unless the collector presents proper evidence satisfying the elements of the collector's cause of action. As a general rule, debt buyers assume virtually all complaints will end in a default judgment. As a result debt buyers will not produce this level of evidence, and the consumer is in a strong position to defend against the claim.

This chapter first analyzes the adequacy of the types of evidence collectors typically submit in consumer collection cases—requests for admissions deemed admitted, affidavits, and business records.[1] Then the chapter turns to the application of these evidentiary rules to the various elements of the collector's claims. The first and often most important element of any claim is whether the collector is the real party in interest or otherwise has standing to sue upon the debt.[2]

Assuming the collector can establish standing, it can only recover under one or more delineated causes of action. Section 4.4, *infra*, explains that the collector must clearly specify which causes of action it is bringing in a case and that the court should rule only on those claims and not on any others. The chapter then turns to the collector's proof as to various possible causes of action:

- Breach of contract;[3]
- On account or open account;[4]
- Account stated;[5]
- *Quantum meruit*;[6] and
- Other causes of action, including money lent, a sworn account, and materials and services supplied.

4.2 Sufficiency of the Collector's Evidence

4.2.1 Introduction

Most contested consumer collection actions do not involve extensive testimony but are largely decided based upon documents submitted to the court. The collector may move for summary judgment, attaching admissions, affidavits, and purported business records. Even at trial, the collector may seek to rely on similar documentation, with only limited witness testimony. The sufficiency of witness testimony will often raise similar issues as the sufficiency of the collector's affidavits presented to the court.

This section focuses on three forms of evidence collectors commonly use: the consumer's admissions, affidavits, and business records. This section provides merely an overview of the subject as it relates to collection actions. It does not replace a thorough knowledge of a state's rules of evidence. The discussion should also be supplemented with review of general treatises on evidence.

4.2.2 Collector's Request for Admissions

4.2.2.1 General

Debt buyers in particular may have little evidence to establish their case and little interest in obtaining the evidence. Instead they may try to win their case using the consumer's own admissions. Along with the complaint, or shortly thereafter, the collector will send the consumer a lengthy list of statements, asking the consumer to admit to them, hoping the consumer will not respond in a timely manner.

Failure to respond is treated as an admission to all the requested statements.[7] The failure to respond may even be treated as an admission even if that party denies the same facts in the complaint.

When the consumer does not respond, the collector appends its request for admissions, which are now deemed admitted, to a summary judgment motion. The collector will then seek to prevail on summary judgment without presenting its own evidence.[8] By serving requests for admission, collectors

1 *See* § 4.2, *infra*.
2 *See* § 4.3, *infra*.
3 *See* §§ 4.5, 4.6, *infra*.
4 *See* § 4.6, *infra*.
5 *See* § 4.7, *infra*.
6 *See* § 4.8, *infra*.

7 *See* McLane v. MRC Receivables Corp., 2007 WL 29435 (Ky. Ct. App. Jan. 5, 2007); Hickman v. Citibank (South Dakota), 89 So. 3d 691 (Miss. 2012); LVNV Funding, L.L.C. v. Kaminsky, 2011 WL 2519228 (Ohio Ct. App. June 23, 2011); Unifund CCR Partners v. Childs, 2010 WL 703274 (Ohio Ct. App. Feb. 26, 2010); Capital One Bank v. Rodgers, 2010 WL 3620304 (Ohio Ct. App. Sept. 14, 2010); Capital One Bank v. Zavatchen, 2008 WL 3870619 (Ohio Ct. App. Aug. 21, 2008); Asset Acceptance, L.L.C. v. Witten, 2008 WL 2837304 (Ohio Ct. App. July 24, 2008); Nat'l Check Bureau, Inc. v. Esque, 2008 WL 458431 (Ohio Ct. App. Feb. 21, 2008); Great Seneca Fin. Corp. v. Lee, 2006 WL 1132473 (Ohio Ct. App. Apr. 28, 2006); Asset Acceptance, L.L.C. v. Rees, 2006 WL 416373 (Ohio Ct. App. Feb. 23, 2006); Discover Bank v. Andresen, 4 Pa. D. & C.5th 353 (Pa. Ct. Com. Pl. 2008); Hewitt v. Roberts, 2013 WL 398940 (Tex. App. Jan. 31, 2013); Lee v. Unifund CCR Partners, 2008 WL 3539938 (Tex. App. Aug. 15, 2008); Sherman Acquisition II, L.P. v. Garcia, 229 S.W.3d 802 (Tex. App. 2007); Luke v. Unifund CCR Partners, 2007 WL 2460327 (Tex. App. Aug. 31, 2007). *See also* Unifund CCR Partners v. Weaver, 262 S.W.3d 796 (Tex. 2008); Gellatly v. Unifund CCR Partners, 2008 WL 2611894 (Tex. App. July 3, 2008).

8 *See* Unifund CCR Partners v. Childs, 2010 WL 703274 (Ohio Ct. App. Feb. 26, 2010) (even though collector apparently sued wrong person); Capital One Bank v. Zavatchen, 2008 WL 3870619 (Ohio Ct. App. Aug. 21, 2008); Great Seneca Fin. Corp. v. Lee, 2006 WL 1132473

prey on unrepresented consumers' lack of legal knowledge, attempting to prove their cases by sleight of hand when they cannot do so with evidence. Of course, if a summary judgment motion relies on the request for admissions being admitted, the motion should not be granted if the request for admissions is not appended to the motion.[9]

This section examines two related questions. The first is how to respond to requests for admission when there is still an opportunity to timely do so.[10] The second is what should be done if the consumer has failed to timely respond to the requests.[11]

The rules as to requests for admissions vary by state and even by court within the same state. Some small claims court rules do not even allow discovery and thus should not allow requests for admission.[12] This section focuses on the rules set out by Federal Rules of Civil Procedure 36 and 37, because many state rules of procedure are patterned after the federal rules. But practitioners must compare the federal rules with their own state's rules and the procedures that apply for the court in which the action is brought.

For example, Maine rules of civil procedure provide that improper responses to a request for admissions are not deemed admitted for purposes of summary judgment unless supported by record citations.[13] The collector must provide a properly supported statement of material facts. Similarly, small claims courts may not even allow requests for admission or will not provide for any negative consequences if the consumer fails to respond. If a court's rules do not establish any negative consequences, there will be little reason to respond.

Federal Rule of Civil Procedure 36 states that parties can seek admissions as to the facts, the application of law to the facts, and the genuineness of described documents. Matters are admitted unless there is a response within thirty days.[14] If the consumer admits to the statement, then the collector need not prove that statement in court by its own evidence and the matter is deemed proven. If the consumer timely responds to the requests but denies the statement without good cause to do so, Federal Rule of Civil Procedure 37(c)(2) provides that, if the collector later proves the statement to be true, the consumer is liable for the reasonable expenses of the collector's proof—which would include attorney fees and other expenses.

This section does not examine sanctions for a party's failure to respond to other forms of discovery. For example, collectors may try to obtain a default judgment on the basis that the consumer has not responded to interrogatories. But the collector cannot restyle the request for admissions as interrogatories and obtain a judgment for the consumer's failure to comply with a discovery request.[15] Moreover, collectors must be able to prove that the discovery and motions to compel discovery were properly mailed to the consumer.[16]

4.2.2.2 How to Respond to Requests for Admissions

4.2.2.2.1 General

If a request for admissions contains statements meeting all the elements of the causes of action the collector is raising, the collector can prevail on summary judgment based solely upon the consumer's failure to respond.[17] Consequently, the worst thing that the consumer can do is fail to respond to the request for admissions. The consumer's options as to each requested admission are to admit (in whole or in part), deny (in whole or in part), neither admit nor deny (with explanation), or object.

In responding, the consumer should not admit to matters that are not true or that the collector could not prove or will not seek to prove. On the other hand, there is risk in denying matters which are true and that the collector will be able to prove to be true. The consumer can be ordered to pay the costs required to prove those matters—both attorney fees and other costs associated with developing that evidence.

4.2.2.2.2 Neither admitting nor denying

One option is to neither admit nor deny the matter. Federal Rule of Civil Procedure 36 allows the consumer to state in detail why the answering party cannot truthfully admit or deny the matter. For example, the consumer cannot truthfully deny or admit a fact if the consumer has no records or no recollection of that fact. Lack of knowledge can be a basis for the inability to admit or deny only if the party states he or she has first made a reasonable inquiry and that the information known or readily obtainable by the party is insufficient to enable the party to admit or deny the matter.[18] The consumer cannot be expected to admit or deny information outside the consumer's control, or about which the consumer has no personal knowledge.[19]

If the lack of knowledge is reasonable, then the consumer is not liable under Rule 36 for the collector's expenses in proving that fact.[20] For example, the consumer does not have to go to the trouble or expense of trying to get records from the original creditor; that is up to the debt buyer that has to prove its case.

(Ohio Ct. App. Apr. 28, 2006); Sherman Acquisition II, L.P. v. Garcia, 229 S.W.3d 802 (Tex. App. 2007).

9 Cach, L.L.C. v. Fisher, 2013 WL 498726 (N.Y. Sup. Ct. Feb. 5, 2013).

10 *See* § 4.2.2.2, *infra*.

11 *See* § 4.2.2.3–4.2.2.5, *infra*.

12 *See, e.g.*, Mass. Unif. Small Claims Rule 5.

13 Cach, L.L.C. v. Kulas, 21 A.3d 1015 (Me. 2011).

14 Fed. R. Civ. P. 36. *See also* McLane v. MRC Receivables Corp., 2007 WL 29435 (Ky. Ct. App. Jan. 5, 2007); Great Seneca Fin. Corp. v. Lee, 2006 WL 1132473 (Ohio Ct. App. Apr. 28, 2006); Asset Acceptance, L.L.C. v. Rees, 2006 WL 416373 (Ohio Ct. App. Feb. 23, 2006); Luke v. Unifund CCR Partners, 2007 WL 2460327 (Tex. App. Aug. 31, 2007).

15 Cach, L.L.C. v. Fisher, 2013 WL 498726 (N.Y. Sup. Ct. Feb. 5, 2013);

16 Unifund CCR Partners v. Lindsey, 275 P.3d 1020 (Utah Ct. App. 2012). *See also* Cach, L.L.C. v. Fisher, 2013 WL 498726 (N.Y. Sup. Ct. Feb. 5, 2013).

17 *See* LVNV Funding, L.L.C. v. Kaminsky, 2011 WL 2519228 (Ohio Ct. App. June 23, 2011); Great Seneca Fin. Corp. v. Lee, 2006 WL 1132473 (Ohio Ct. App. Apr. 28, 2006); Luke v. Unifund CCR Partners, 2007 WL 2460327 (Tex. App. Aug. 31, 2007).

18 Fed. R. Civ. P. 36.

19 United States *ex rel.* Englund v. Los Angeles Cnty., 235 F.R.D. 675 (E.D. Cal. 2006).

20 Fed. R. Civ. P. 36.

The consumer can also reasonably state he or she is neither admitting nor denying that a debt buyer is the owner of an indebtedness, because to do so would require knowledge of facts not known to the consumer. The consumer can also refuse to admit or deny that the collector's "predecessor in interest" made the loan, because the consumer does not know who is being referred to or that the card issuer is the collector's predecessor in interest. The consumer should also be able to reasonably refuse to admit or deny that a standard form contract is identical to the one the consumer received, if the consumer no longer possesses the consumer's copy. The consumer can also state that he or she is neither admitting nor denying that various documents generated by the debt buyer are genuine business records of the debt buyer. For all of these requests, the consumer has no ability to obtain sufficient information on which to base a response. And the consumer will face no adverse consequences by refusing to admit or deny.

4.2.2.2.3 Objecting to requests for admissions

The consumer is also allowed to object to a request for admissions, stating the grounds for the objection.[21] At that point, the collector can request that the court determine the sufficiency of the objection and the court, if it overrules the objection, can then order that an amended answer be made.[22] Possible grounds for objection are that the statement calls for a purely legal opinion,[23] or that the requested statement is irrelevant or burdensome.[24] The consumer can also object to vague or ambiguous requests. The Third Circuit has said that requests for admissions "should not be used unless a statement of fact sought to be admitted is phrased so that it can be admitted or denied without explanation."[25]

The consumer can also ask the court to strike the request for admissions because the requests for admissions go to the heart of the matter at issue and also to the ultimate conclusions that must be drawn in the litigation.[26] The consumer should not be asked to admit to all of the elements of the collector's case.[27] Nor should the consumer be asked to admit to facts that the consumer would not know or have any way of knowing, such as whether a credit card debt was assigned from one entity to another.[28]

Local state rules may specify additional grounds to object. In New York a request for admission must ask about information within the party's knowledge and cannot ask about matters that go to the ultimate issue of the case.[29] For example, it would be objectionable to ask the consumer to admit that the debt has been assigned to the plaintiff (no firsthand knowledge) or to admit that the consumer is liable for the amount sought (ultimate issue of the case).

4.2.2.2.4 Denying requests for admissions

When good faith permits, the consumer can deny a request for admission. However good faith may require that the consumer admit to a specific part of a statement and deny the rest. Even if the statement is later proven to be true, the consumer is not liable for the collector's expenses of proof if there were reasonable grounds for the consumer to deny the matter.[30] The consumer need not win the case to avoid paying for the collector's costs—for the particular statement requested, the consumer need only have reasonable grounds for believing that the statement is not true. For example, the consumer can safely deny a statement that a $5000 amount is due even when $4950 is clearly owed, if there is a reasonable issue as to the remaining $50, and even if the full $5000 is eventually proven.

When it is not certain that the consumer has reasonable grounds to deny a statement, tactical considerations come into play as to the safest response. If the consumer denies the statement, what are the odds that the collector will in fact try to prove that statement, and what are the odds that it will in fact prove that statement? If the statement is proven, will the collector go back to court to seek the expenses of proving that statement, necessitating a showing that the consumer did not have reasonable grounds for the denial, and also requiring proof of the amount of the expenses involved?

Even if the consumer has to pay the collector's expenses necessary to prove a statement, pursuant to Federal Rule of Civil Procedure 37, those expenses may not be as costly as one might suppose. If the consumer loses the case, the consumer may be liable for the collector's attorney fees and for costs in any case. Of course, these fees and costs may be lower if the consumer admits to certain matters, shortening the trial. In addition, certain expenses to prove a statement may be recoverable under Federal Rule of Civil Procedure 37 that would not otherwise be awarded as court costs.

4.2.2.2.5 Admitting to certain parts of a statement and denying other parts

In general, the consumer must be wary of admitting to anything that the collector cannot easily prove on its own. The consumer does not want to lose a case that the collector would not have been able to prove if it had been forced to develop its own evidence at trial. Nevertheless, the consumer can admit to certain aspects of a statement but deny other aspects that

21 Fed. R. Civ. P. 36(a)(5). *See also* ADC Telecomms. Inc. v. Telect, Inc., 143 F.R.D. 214 (D. Minn. 1992).

22 Fed. R. Civ. P. 36(a)(6).

23 *See* Cedyco Corp. v. Whitehead, 253 S.W. 3d 877 (Tex. App. 2008).

24 Federal Rule of Civil Procedure 36 incorporates Federal Rule of Civil Procedure 26(b) which indicates that a request's burden should not outweigh its likely benefit.

25 United Coal Companies v. Powell Constr. Co., 839 F.2d 958 (3d Cir. 1988).

26 Tolchin v. Glaser, 849 N.Y.S.2d 439 (N.Y. App. Div. 2008); Midland Funding, L.L.C. v. Valentin, 40 Misc. 3d 266 (N.Y. Dist. Ct. 2013). *See also* Chase Bank v. Hershkovits, 28 Misc. 3d 1202(A) (N.Y. Civ. Ct. 2010).

27 Midland Funding, L.L.C. v. Valentin, 40 Misc. 3d 266 (N.Y. Dist. Ct. 2013).

28 Midland Funding, L.L.C. v. Valentin, 40 Misc. 3d 266 (N.Y. Dist. Ct. 2013).

29 N.Y. C.P.L.R. Law § 3123 (McKinney).

30 Fed. R. Civ. P. 37(c)(2).

are central to the collector's proof. For example, the consumer might admit to applying for and using a credit card but deny the amount being sought on the card, on the grounds that payments were not credited, that fees were unfair or improperly assessed, or that the finance charges are not accurate.

4.2.2.3 Requesting Relief When Time Period to Respond Has Lapsed

A consumer who has failed to respond to admissions in a timely manner is in peril. The request specifies a due date and the court has discretion, if there is no response by that date, to deem the requested statements to be admitted.[31]

Do not assume that a collector has sent the requests for admissions just because it says it has, or that it sent the requests on the date it specifies. Many debt buyers and collection attorneys work more on volume than on precision. Thus, the date to respond has not lapsed when the consumer never received the request for admissions.

If the consumer has received the request for admissions, and the consumer has missed the deadline for responding, immediately approach the collector's attorney and request additional time. If the request is denied, promptly seek relief from the court. The court has discretion to accept a late-filed response.[32] Under Federal Rule of Civil Procedure 6(b), the court can extend time to respond because of excusable neglect. Waiting will only lessen the chances that the court will grant the requested relief, because delay will make the neglect less excusable and may increase the prejudice to the collector of withdrawing the admissions.

Rule 36(b) offers an alternative standard to Rule 6(b) and one that courts are more likely to utilize in deciding when to grant a party leave to submit otherwise untimely answers to requests for admission.[33] The standard set out in Rule 36(b) is also more advantageous to consumer defendants than the standard found in Rule 6(b). Rule 36(b) deals with withdrawal of admissions, and its provisions apply to withdrawal of admissions that were deemed admitted based upon the failure to answer.[34]

Rule 36(b) provides: "[T]he court may permit withdrawal or amendment if it would promote the presentation of the merits of the action and if the court is not persuaded that it would prejudice the requesting party in maintaining or defending the action on the merits."[35] The consumer has the burden of showing that leave to file an untimely answer will promote the presentation of the merits, and the collector will have the burden of showing prejudice from the delay.[36] When the consumer shows the answer will promote presentation of the merits, and the collector fails to prove prejudice, the court must allow withdrawal of the admission. This is not a matter of court discretion.[37]

The collector's prejudice that the Rule refers to is not that the collector will now have to prove to the fact finder that the statement previously admitted is true. Instead, the prejudice must concern how the delay will make it more difficult for the collector to prove its case as compared to if the consumer had denied the admissions on a timely basis. Examples might be the sudden unavailability of key witnesses or the difficulty in obtaining evidence for trial at short notice.[38] Prejudice to the collector is more likely to be present when the admission is withdrawn during trial than before trial.[39]

The consumer's burden to show that withdrawal of the admission will promote the presentation of the merits is "satisfied when upholding the admissions would practically eliminate any presentation of the merits of the case."[40] The Eleventh Circuit required that admissions be withdrawn when a party uses the rule "with the wild-eyed hope that the other side will fail to answer and therefore admit essential elements."[41] The Rule's purpose is to establish uncontested facts in order to narrow the issues at trial, not to be used as a weapon to take advantage of unrepresented consumers.[42] Courts can strike requests for admissions if the requests for admissions go to the heart of the matter at issue and also to the ultimate conclusions that must be drawn in the litigation.[43]

Always explain the reason for the consumer's neglect. In one case, relief was granted when the consumer asked for a more definite statement of the complaint and did not respond to the request for admissions while waiting for that more definite statement.[44] In another case, relief was granted when the consumer had consistently disputed the bill over

31 *See* § 4.2.2.1, *supra*.

32 *See* United States v. Petroff-Kline, 557 F.3d 285 (6th Cir. 2009).

33 *See* 8B Charles A. Wright et al., Federal Practice and Procedure § 2257 (3d ed. 2010) (preferring the Rule 36 standard over the Rule 6 standard). *See also* Skoczylas v. Atlantic Credit & Fin., Inc., 2002 WL 55298 (E.D. Pa. Jan. 15, 2002).

34 Perez v. Miami-Dade Cnty., 297 F.3d 1255 (11th Cir. 2002); Gutting v. Falstaff Brewing Corp., 710 F.2d 1309 (8th Cir. 1983); McLane v. MRC Receivables Corp., 2007 WL 29435 (Ky. Ct. App. Jan. 5, 2007).

35 *See also* Skoczylas v. Atlantic Credit & Fin., Inc., 2002 WL 55298 (E.D. Pa. Jan. 15, 2002); Asset Acceptance, L.L.C. v. Lemon, 2006 WL 2474355 (Ohio Ct. App. Aug. 25, 2006) (citing Balson v. Dodds, 405 N.E.2d 293 (Ohio 1980)).

36 Skoczylas v. Atlantic Credit & Fin., Inc., 2002 WL 55298 (E.D. Pa. Jan. 15, 2002); Revlon Consumer Prods. Corp. v. L'Oreal S.A., 170 F.R.D. 391 (D. Del. 1997).

37 Perez v. Miami-Dade Cnty., 297 F.3d 1255 (11th Cir. 2002).

38 *Id. See also* Skoczylas v. Atlantic Credit & Fin., Inc., 2002 WL 55298 (E.D. Pa. Jan. 15, 2002).

39 Perez v. Miami-Dade Cnty., 297 F.3d 1255 (11th Cir. 2002).

40 Hadley v. United States, 45 F.3d 1345, 1348 (9th Cir. 1995). *See also* Perez v. Miami-Dade Cnty., 297 F.3d 1255 (11th Cir. 2002); Skoczylas v. Atlantic Credit & Fin., Inc., 2002 WL 55298 (E.D. Pa. Jan. 15, 2002).

41 Perez v. Miami-Dade Cnty., 297 F.3d 1255, 1268 (11th Cir. 2002).

42 Cach, L.L.C. v. Fisher, 2013 WL 498726 (N.Y. Sup. Ct. Feb. 5, 2013); Capital One Bank v. Toney, 2007 WL 969420 (Ohio Ct. App. Mar. 28, 2007) (time extended because consumer had requested a more definite statement of the complaint, which was not forthcoming); Asset Acceptance, L.L.C. v. Lemon, 2006 WL 2474355 (Ohio Ct. App. Aug. 25, 2006) (consumer had consistently disputed the amount owed). *See also* Human Res. Dev. Press, Inc. v. IKON Office Solutions, Inc., 246 F.R.D. 82 (D. Mass. 2007); McLane v. MRC Receivables Corp., 2007 WL 29435 (Ky. Ct. App. Jan. 5, 2007).

43 Tolchin v. Glaser, 849 N.Y.S.2d 439 (N.Y. App. Div. 2008).

44 Capital One Bank v. Toney, 2007 WL 969420 (Ohio Ct. App. Mar. 28, 2007).

a period of years and had requested information from the creditor.[45] The unrepresented consumer may have thought a response was unnecessary because the consumer already had so clearly disputed many of the statements. Of course, courts also consider the fact that the consumer was unrepresented at the time.[46] On the other hand, a court will be less sympathetic to a defendant who consistently fails to respond to litigation deadlines.[47]

4.2.2.4 Limiting the Impact of Facts Deemed Admitted

4.2.2.4.1 Introduction

If admissions cannot be withdrawn, there are still steps to take. Carefully review all the statements that are being treated as admitted. Debt buyers and other collectors may be sloppy in their drafting of admissions.

4.2.2.4.2 Admissions conflicting with other admissions or with the collector's evidence

See if any of the statements requested to be admitted conflict with each other. If the request asks the consumer to admit "X" and also "not X," and the consumer fails to respond to the requests, then the collector cannot rely on the admissions to prove either X or not X.[48] Contradictory admissions are a nullity.

The same may be the case when the collector produces evidence that contradicts the fact deemed admitted. Courts may rule that even when a fact is deemed admitted, that fact becomes a disputed piece of evidence to be determined by the trier of fact if the collector introduces evidence contrary to that fact.[49] For example, when a collector introduces into evidence a document that places into question whether the collector owns the debt, the court must determine whether the collector owns the debt, even if the consumer had been deemed to have admitted that fact by failing to respond to the request for admissions.[50]

4.2.2.4.3 Narrowly interpret admissions and point out ambiguities

Another approach to limit the impact of facts deemed admitted is to narrowly interpret the admissions. For example, consider the admission that the consumer promised to pay the debt buyer *or* the original creditor. A strict reading of the admission does *not* admit that the consumer promised to pay the debt buyer and does *not* admit that the creditor assigned the obligation to the debt buyer. Thus, the admission is not sufficient for the debt buyer to recover when the debt buyer proffers insufficient evidence that it had been assigned the debt.[51]

Look also to see if the debt buyer listed in the requests for admissions is the same debt buyer seeking a judgment—accounts are sold between debt buyers so frequently that this may happen while a case is still pending. Then, even if the consumer's failure to respond to requests for admissions is deemed to admit that the debt buyer propounding the requests for admissions owns the debt, the consumer can still contest whether the second debt buyer has standing to sue on the debt.[52]

Similarly, if a matter to be admitted is not drafted well or contains a typographical error, such that its meaning is unclear, the failure to respond should not be taken as an admission of anything.[53] A state appellate court has found that a failure to respond should not be deemed an admission when the collector's request for admissions cited the wrong rule of civil procedure number.[54] The collector stated that, pursuant to Rule 33, each item not responded to would be deemed admitted. The correct rule citation was to Rule 36.

4.2.2.4.4 Consumer can admit only to the facts, not to legal opinions

Unanswered requests for admissions should have no effect on a case if the requests solely ask for a legal opinion or ask the party to admit a matter of law as opposed to a fact.[55] Admissions are to facilitate proof at trial by obviating the need to adduce testimony or documents as to matters that are not really in controversy. "Such requests should not be confused with pure requests for opinions of law, which are not contemplated by the rule. Nor are requests seeking legal conclusions appropriate when proceeding under Rule 36."[56]

4.2.2.4.5 Technical defects with the request for admissions

Look for technical problems in the requests for admissions. Requests for admissions may not be deemed admitted if the certificate of service is not signed.[57]

When the collector's complaint was found insufficient and a new complaint was filed after the requests for admissions had been submitted, a court has found that the consumer need

45 Asset Acceptance, L.L.C. v. Lemon, 2006 WL 2474355 (Ohio Ct. App. Aug. 25, 2006).

46 Spencer v. Dearborn Cnty. Sheriff's Dep't, 2007 WL 1729752 (S.D. Ind. June 6, 2007).

47 *See* FIA Card Servs. v. Marshall, 2010 WL 3503497 (Ohio Ct. App. Sept. 7, 2010).

48 Luke v. Unifund CCR Partners, 2007 WL 2460327 (Tex. App. Aug. 31, 2007).

49 Ray Klein, Inc. v. Kerr, 272 S.W.3d 896 (Mo. Ct. App. 2008).

50 *Id.*

51 Rolen v. LVNV Funding, L.L.C., 2010 WL 1633402 (Tex. App. Apr. 22, 2010).

52 Gentry v. Great Seneca Fin. Corp., 2009 WL 3444936 (Tex. App. Oct. 27, 2009).

53 Luke v. Unifund CCR Partners, 2007 WL 2460327 (Tex. App. Aug. 31, 2007).

54 Bullock v. Worldwide Asset Purchasing, L.L.C., 2008 WL 3159921 (Ky. Ct. App. Sept. 5, 2008).

55 Cedyco Corp. v. Whitehead, 253 S.W. 3d 877 (Tex. App. 2008).

56 7 James Wm. Moore et al., Moore's Federal Practice and Procedure § 36.10[8] (3d. ed. 2008). *See also* United States v. Petroff-Kline, 557 F.3d 285 (6th Cir. 2009); 8B Charles A. Wright et al., Federal Practice and Procedure § 2255, at 334–36 nn.7–8 (3d ed. 2010).

57 Hudson & Keyse, L.L.C. v. Carson, 2009 WL 1611252 (Ohio Ct. App. June 9, 2009).

not reply to the initial requests for admissions.[58] This seems only just, because the consumer should have an opportunity to understand the nature of the complaint before being required to respond to requests for admissions and thus should not have to respond to admissions before the collector files a sufficient complaint.

4.2.2.4.6 When consumer's failure to respond properly was a matter of form, not substance

If a consumer does respond to the requests for admission, but improperly labels the response as an answer and counterclaims, the court should not view the requests for admissions as unanswered. The consumer's intent can be found by examining the nature of the document.[59]

Also courts will likely not hold a *pro se* defendant to strict technical compliance with the rules. Thus in one case the court found no admission when the consumer stated that he had no knowledge as to a request for admission when the proper response would have been that the consumer had no knowledge after making a reasonable inquiry and that the information known or readily obtainable by him was insufficient to enable him to deny or admit.[60]

4.2.2.5 Suit Against Collector for Abuses Related to Requests for Admissions

When a collector is abusing requests for admissions to take unfair advantage of unrepresented consumers, one approach is to sue the collector's attorney for violating the federal Fair Debt Collection Practices Act (FDCPA). For example, in a case in which the collection attorney's file indicated that the consumer had not made a payment in 2004, the requests for admission asked the consumer to admit that a $75 payment was made in 2004 (which would have revived the statute of limitations). And when the consumer's defense pleaded the statute of limitations, the attorney asked the consumer to admit that there were no facts supporting the defense.

The federal court found that to ask a *pro se* defendant to admit to false information was an FDCPA violation.[61] The Ninth Circuit on appeal found that it was an FDCPA violation for a collector to serve requests for admission containing false information on a *pro se* defendant without an explanation that requests would be deemed admitted after thirty days.[62]

58 *Id.*

59 Robinson v. Global Res., Inc., 684 S.E.2d 104 (Ga. Ct. App. 2009).

60 *See* ANJ Corp. v. Ross, 2014 WL 721389 (Mass. App. Div. Feb. 20, 2014).

61 McCollough v. Johnson, Rodenberg & Lauinger, 610 F. Supp. 2d 1247 (D. Mont. 2009), *aff'd*, 637 F.3d 939 (9th Cir. Mar. 4, 2011).

62 McCollough v. Johnson, Rodenberg & Lauinger, 637 F.3d 939 (9th Cir. Mar. 4, 2011) (Assoc. Justice Sandra Day O'Connor (ret.) sat on the panel by designation).

4.2.3 Collector's Use of Affidavits As Evidence

4.2.3.1 Introduction

This section focuses on collectors' use of affidavits to proffer evidence found in the affidavits themselves. Section 4.2.4, *infra*, examines the use of affidavits to authenticate or certify business records that are introduced into evidence. This section instead examines affidavits meant to constitute evidence, rather than those used just to authenticate other documentary evidence.

4.2.3.2 Use of Affidavits at Trial

The general rule is that live testimony is required at trial and that affidavits are not allowed.[63] This rule typically still applies in small claims courts and other lower courts.[64] Affidavits are generally used instead as evidence for summary judgment motions.

4.2.3.3 Based Upon the Affiant's Personal Knowledge

4.2.3.3.1 General

Debt buyers in particular may seek to conceal their inability to produce the best evidence of a factual allegation by having an employee of the debt buyer state in an affidavit that the factual allegation is true. Affidavits must be made on personal knowledge and show affirmatively that the affiant is competent to testify as to the matters stated therein.[65] Thus, an affidavit is not admissible if it states that it is made "on information and belief" or "to the best of my knowledge and belief."[66]

The affidavit must be based upon personal knowledge, and the affidavit itself must indicate the source of the affiant's

63 *See, e.g.*, Cal. Evidence Code §§ 711, 1200 (West). *See also* Cach, L.L.C. v. Jones (Cal. Super. Ct. Mar. 12, 2012), *available at* www.nclc.org/unreported; LHR, Inc. v. Ayree (Md. Cir. Ct. July 26, 2010), *available at* www.nclc.org/unreported. *But see* Investment Receivers, Inc. v. Marshall, 2009 WL 2411668 (Ariz. Ct. App. Aug. 6, 2009) (affidavit from creditor that debt assigned to debt buyer not hearsay because statement was against the creditor's interest).

64 *See, e.g.*, Cal. Civ. Proc. Code § 90 (West); Cach, L.L.C. v. Jones (Cal. Super. Ct. Mar. 12, 2012), *available at* www.nclc.org/unreported.

65 Vassalle v. Midland Funding, L.L.C. (N.D. Ohio Apr. 25, 2012) (special master findings; collecting cases), *available at* www.nclc.org/unreported; Midland Funding, L.L.C. v. Edwards (Cal. App. Dep't Super Ct. Dec. 13, 2013), *available at* www.nclc.org/unreported; Palisades Collection, L.L.C. v. Gonzalez, 809 N.Y.S.2d 482 (table), 2005 WL 3372971 (N.Y. Civ. Ct. Dec. 12, 2005); Citibank v. Martin, 807 N.Y.S.2d 284 (N.Y. Civ. Ct. 2005); Unifund CCR Partners v. Dover, 681 S.E.2d 565 (N.C. Ct. App. 2009); Luke v. Unifund CCR Partners, 2007 WL 2460327 (Tex. App. Aug. 31, 2007).

66 *See, e.g.*, Lopez-Carrasquillo v. Rubianes, 230 F.3d 409 (1st Cir. 2000); Sellers v. M.C. Floor Crafters, Inc., 842 F.2d 639 (2d Cir. 1988); Chandler v. Coughlin, 763 F.2d 110 (2d Cir. 1985); Vassalle v. Midland Funding, L.L.C. (N.D. Ohio Apr. 25, 2012) (special master findings; collecting cases), *available at* www.nclc.org/unreported.

knowledge.[67] The source of the personal knowledge is important as it allows the court to make a determination whether in fact the affiant has such knowledge.[68] The affiant must have perceived or observed what the affiant purports to assert; recollections of what the affiant has been told are inadmissible hearsay.[69]

Thus, when an affiant asserts that a statement was mailed to the consumer, the affiant must either attest to personal knowledge that the statement was mailed or describe a regular office practice for mailing documents of that type.[70] It is clearly inadequate for a debt buyer's employee to state in an affidavit, without more, that the originating creditor had mailed out a contract to the consumer, as the debt buyer's employee has no personal knowledge whether the originating creditor mailed the contract to the consumer.

4.2.3.3.2 Robo-signed affidavits

There is a growing resistance to accepting robo-signed affidavits. In one case, the court refused to rule for a collector based on an affidavit that was prepared in advance of knowing who would sign it.[71] The affiant's name was simply rubber stamped into the opening sentence. The specific name of the employer was not even mentioned, and the affidavit stated only that the affiant was employed by the creditor "or an affiliate." The robo-stamping of the affidavit does not automatically disqualify the affidavit, but the court stated that the robo-stamping caused the court to take a closer look at whether the affiant did have personal knowledge with regard to the consumer's account.[72] A careful review of the affidavit and related documents convinced the court that the affiant did not have personal knowledge.[73]

In a case involving United Credit Recovery, the Minnesota attorney general alleged that, in one case, United Credit Recovery created about 1600 affidavits involving Minnesota consumers and bearing the identical pasted-in April 29, 2008, signature of an officer of the originating creditor. The signatures were all supposedly witnessed by a notary on March 19, 2008—over a month before the officer supposedly signed the affidavit![74]

In the typical debt buyer situation, the affiant has no personal knowledge of many facts of the case, and the affiant will not even have reviewed the file but will have relied upon the fact that others have determined the accuracy of the information in the affidavit. The affiant does little more than sign a stack of affidavits, without any knowledge of an individual consumer's account or even any knowledge of what type of information the collector might store on its consumer accounts or what support there might be for the information the affiant is swearing to.

A federal court explained how one debt buyer's affidavits were not based upon personal knowledge.[75] The office fulfills about 200 to 400 affidavits a day. One of ten specialists sign each affidavit, after finding a stack of affidavits on a printer. After signing the affidavit, it is sent on to a notary located in a different office to be notarized. The specialist has no idea where the affidavit comes from and rarely checks the information found on the affidavit, although the specialist has access to certain data to check information in the affidavit. The affidavit is then sent on to a law firm to attach to a complaint.

Despite the affidavit claiming personal knowledge, the specialist has no knowledge of the debtor or the debtor's account. The specialist signing a particular affidavit is fairly random. While the affidavit claims that the affiant or one of the affiant's employees was the one who hired the law firm to process the case, in fact the affiant has no employees and has no knowledge as to how the law firm was chosen.

The affiant claims personal knowledge of the debt buyer purchasing the account, but the affiant also admits to having no role in the purchase of the account and to not knowing any of the terms of the purchase. Finally, the affiant claims that the debtor is not a minor or mentally incapacitated, when the affiant has had no contact with the debtor. And of course the affiant's signature is not properly notarized, because the notary did not witness the signature.

Collectors will often have professional testifiers or affiants who travel from court to court. A deposition may reveal that the individual "custodian of records" is almost never in the office and that the number of large files the individual processes a month may require several hours each and cannot possibly be reviewed in that time.

4.2.3.3.3 Attorney affirmations and verified complaints

Similarly, an attorney's affirmation that is not based upon personal knowledge of the fact has no probative value.[76] Nor

67 Midland Funding, L.L.C. v. Edwards (Cal. App. Dep't Super Ct. Dec. 13, 2013), *available at* www.nclc.org/unreported; Sherman Acquisition II, L.P. v. Garcia, 229 S.W.3d 802 (Tex. App. 2007).

68 Unifund CCR Partners v. Perkins 2013 WL 5350941 (La. Ct. App. Sept. 25, 2013).

69 Vassalle v. Midland Funding, L.L.C. (N.D. Ohio Apr. 25, 2012) (special master findings; collecting cases), *available at* www.nclc.org/unreported.

70 Palisades Collection, L.L.C. v. Gonzalez, 809 N.Y.S.2d 482 (table), 2005 WL 3372971 (N.Y. Civ. Ct. Dec. 12, 2005). *See also* Norfolk Fin. Corp. v. MacDonald, 2003 Mass. App. Div. 153 (Ma. Dist. Ct. 2003) (debt buyer's employee could not prove that contract had been sent by creditor to consumer); Unifund CCR Partners v. Dover, 681 S.E.2d 565 (N.C. Ct. App. 2009) (debt buyer's affidavit cannot attest to the creation or maintenance of a credit card account).

71 Citibank v. Majka (N.Y. Sup. Ct. July 18, 2012), *available at* www.nclc.org/unreported.

72 *Id.*

73 *Id.*

74 *See* Press Release, Minnesota Att'y Gen., Attorney General Lori Swanson Sues Florida Company for Creating Manufactured Affidavits to Aid in Collection of Overdraft Debt Purchased from Large Banks (Oct. 30, 2013).

75 Midland Funding, L.L.C. v. Brent, 644 F. Supp. 2d 961 (N.D. Ohio 2009), *related rulings*, 2009 WL 3086560 (N.D. Ohio Sept. 23, 2009) and 2010 WL 703066 (N.D. Ohio Feb. 22, 2010).

76 Citibank v. Beckerman, 856 N.Y.S.2d 496 (N.Y. App. Term. 2008).

can a verified complaint be the basis for summary judgment when the plaintiff only verifies that the facts are true based on the plaintiff's own knowledge, and, for those matters that are alleged "upon information and belief," that the plaintiff believes them to be true.[77]

4.2.3.4 Conclusory Affidavits; Missing Attachments

The affidavit should not be conclusory.[78] General statements in an affidavit which are only conclusions of law do not prove a case.[79] Good examples of inadequate affidavits are those that state that the consumer owes a certain amount without attaching any documentation to support that conclusion,[80] and an affidavit claiming that an assignment has been made without attaching the actual assignment document.[81] It is hearsay and incompetent for an affidavit to state that the affiant has reviewed a loan file and that the debt is in default without in fact attaching the actual loan documentation.[82]

An affidavit clearly provides no evidence as to the nature of account statements, contracts, or other documents that are allegedly attached to the affidavit when the documents in fact are not attached.[83] Such omissions occur surprisingly often, particularly with debt buyers.

Thus, an affidavit is inadequate when it references various documents as Exhibit A concerning the debt but when Exhibit A is not attached to the affidavit.[84] Debt buyer affidavits often reference a computer tape or schedule of accounts assigned to the debt buyer but fail to attach the tape or schedule.[85]

77 Dawkins v. Fields, 580 S.E.2d 433 (S.C. 2003).

78 Luke v. Unifund CCR Partners, 2007 WL 2460327 (Tex. App. Aug. 31, 2007). *See also* Hay v. Citibank, 2006 WL 2620089 (Tex. App. Sept. 14, 2006). *Cf.* Wood v. Pharia, L.L.C., 2010 WL 5060621 (Tex. App. Dec. 9, 2010) (affidavits found to be conclusory).

79 Thomas v. OSI Funding Group, Inc., 2004 WL 541519 (Fla. Cir. Ct. Feb. 2, 2004). *See also* American Express Bank, FSB v. Dalbis, 2011 WL 873512 (N.Y. Civ. Ct. Mar. 14, 2011).

80 *See* LVNV Funding, L.L.C. v. Reilly, 2009 WL 2506362 (Conn. Super. Ct. July 17, 2009); Suggs v. Sherman Acquisition, L.P., 13 Fla. L. Weekly Supp. 301a (Fla. Cir. Ct. Sept. 28, 2005); Capital One Bank v. Toney, 2007 WL 969420 (Ohio Ct. App. Mar. 28, 2007); Luke v. Unifund CCR Partners, 2007 WL 2460327 (Tex. App. Aug. 31, 2007). *See also* American Express Bank, FSB v. Dalbis, 2011 WL 873512 (N.Y. Civ. Ct. Mar. 14, 2011).

81 *See* § 4.3.4.2.1, *infra*.

82 *See* New England Sav. Bank v. Bedford Realty Corp., 680 A.2d 301 (Conn. 1996); Haw. Cmty. Fed. Credit Union v. Keka, 11 P.3d 1 (Haw. 2000); *In re* A.B., 719 N.E.2d 348 (Ill. App. Ct. 1999); Topps v. Unicorn Ins. Co., 648 N.E.2d 214 (Ill. App. Ct. 1995); Cole Taylor Bank v. Corrigan, 595 N.E.2d 177 (Ill. App. Ct. 1992); State v. Ward, 510 N.W.2d 320 (Neb. Ct. App. 1993); Grant v. Forgash, 1995 WL 765154 (Ohio Ct. App. Dec. 26, 1995).

83 Cole Taylor Bank v. Corrigan, 595 N.E.2d 177 (Ill. App. Ct. 1992); Luke v. Unifund CCR Partners, 2007 WL 2460327 (Tex. App. Aug. 31, 2007). *But see* Citibank v. Kessler, 2004 WL 795689 (Ohio Ct. App. Apr. 15, 2004) (recovery allowed even though affidavit did not attach billing statements).

84 Powers v. Hudon & Keyse, L.L.C., 656 S.E.2d 578 (Ga. Ct. App. 2008).

85 *See* § 4.3.4.2.2, *infra*.

4.2.3.5 Inconsistent, Sloppy, and False Information

When documents are attached to the affidavit, look for inconsistencies between the documents and the affidavit itself, which will call into question the evidence being proffered both by the affidavit and by the documents.[86] Similarly, look for inconsistencies between the affidavit, the complaint, a collector's summary judgment motion, and other affidavits and documents in the case. For example, in one case the debt buyer's affidavit specified a date of assignment over three months after the date specified in the alleged "Bill of Sale."[87] In another case, the affidavit provided that the consumer owed an amount on one particular account while the attached business records referred to a different account number.[88]

See if the affidavit also contains false statements. Look for statements that the affiant is employed by the plaintiff, when in fact the affiant is employed by a collection agency hired by the plaintiff. Does an affiant employed by a debt buyer claim to have personal knowledge of the practices of the original creditor, when it would be impossible for that affiant to have that knowledge? In one case, the court cited with disapproval a debt buyer's affidavits and other documents that included three different interest rates and which referred to the debt buyer as being the original owner and the entity from whom goods or services were purchased.[89]

4.2.3.6 Notarizations and Signatures

Look for deficiencies in the affidavit's signature and notarization. Is the name of the individual signing the affidavit disclosed on the affidavit? Is the affidavit properly signed and notarized? Some states require that an affidavit disclose the affiant's employer. Has the affiant met this requirement? Is the notarization made and the affiant's signature affixed on the same date? And are the two supposedly signed at the same location?

A number of state laws require that sworn pleadings from other states be accompanied by a certificate authenticating the oath giver's authority,[90] and courts may reject sworn pleadings submitted without that certificate,[91] particularly if the con-

86 *See* § 4.2.4.2, *infra*.

87 Unifund CCR Assignee of Providian v. Ayhan, 2008 WL 2974639 (Wash. Ct. App. Aug. 5, 2008). *See also* Recovery Mgmt. Sys., Ltd. v. Coburn, 2008 WL 4801641 (Ohio Ct. App. Nov. 4, 2008).

88 Ezeoke v. FIA Card Servs., N.A., 320 Ga. App. 73 (Ga. Ct. App. 2013).

89 Barajas v. Harvest Credit Mgmt., VI-B, L.L.C., 2008 WL 4308334 (Tex. App. Aug. 28, 2008).

90 *See, e.g.*, Ind. Code § 34-37-1-7; Minn. Stat. § 600.09; N.Y. C.P.L.R. 2309(c) (McKinney).

91 *See* First Nat'l Bank of Dillsboro v. Mulford, 95 N.E. 432 (Ind. Ct. App. 1911); Citibank v. Suen, 814 N.Y.S.2d 889 (N.Y. App. Term 2005); Discover Bank v. Kagan, 803 N.Y.S.2d 18 (N.Y. App. Term 2005); Citibank v. Martin, 807 N.Y.S.2d 284 (N.Y. Civ. Ct. 2005). *See also* Centurion Capital Corp. v. Guarino, 951 N.Y.S.2d 85 (table), 2012 WL 1543286 (N.Y. Civ. Ct. Apr. 30, 2012). *But cf.* Raynor v. Raynor, 108 N.Y.S.2d 20 (N.Y. App. Div. 1951) ("the lack of an authenticating certificate was a defect or irregularity which could be corrected *nunc pro tunc*").

sumer objects.[92] Indiana's law, which is typical of such statutes, requires out-of-state affidavits sworn before judges and notaries to be certified under the seal of the clerk of court in the county where such judge or notary practices.[93] Other states may be more liberal in accepting out-of-state affidavits when they are properly notarized in that state,[94] or even when the witness just affirms under the penalties of perjury.

Also look for the sufficiency of the notarization. Robo-signing operations often can be sloppy on that score. For example, it is not uncommon for an affidavit to state that it is signed by the affiant in one state and the notary states that the affiant appeared before the notary in a different state.[95] This, in fact, is a felony in a number of states. Look also to see what type of documentation the notary keeps of its notarizations, whether this comports with state requirements, and what information is derived from such documentation, if kept.

4.2.3.7 Consumer Use of a Counter-Affidavit

The consumer should consider submitting an affidavit to counter facts alleged in the collector's affidavit, thus placing those facts in dispute. This response should be enough to defeat the collector's summary judgment motion.[96] If the court finds the consumer's affidavit conclusory or lacking in personal knowledge, the court should apply the same standard to the collector's affidavit.

4.2.4 Proof Using Documents

4.2.4.1 The Business Records Exception

4.2.4.1.1 General

Business records used to prove a collector's causes of action constitute hearsay.[97] Records to be introduced into evidence must fit within the business records exception to the rules prohibiting hearsay evidence. Of course, the business records exception is only relevant in courts that prohibit hearsay. In some state small claims courts—for example, California—hearsay is admissible, but the court determines its weight.[98]

In most courts, however, hearsay is inadmissible, and most state rules of evidence are similar to Federal Rule of Evidence 803(6), which establishes that a business record is exempt from the hearsay rule only if it is:

> . . . A record of an act, event, condition, opinion, or diagnosis if:
> (A) the record was made at or near the time by—or from information transmitted by—someone with knowledge;
> (B) the record was kept in the course of a regularly conducted activity of a business, organization, occupation, or calling, whether or not for profit;
> (C) making the record was a regular practice of that activity;
> (D) all these conditions are shown by the testimony of the custodian or another qualified witness, or by a certification that complies with Rule 902(11) or (12) or with a statute permitting certification; and
> (E) neither the source of information nor the method or circumstances of preparation indicate a lack of trustworthiness.[99]

4.2.4.1.2 Documents generated only for the litigation

Documents created for the litigation are not business records and the hearsay rule thus prevents their introduction.[100] There are two reasons for this. One is that the records are not contemporaneous, that is, they were not created at the same time as the occurrence of the event that the record is documenting. The records are not admissible if they were created years later, either by the original creditor or a debt buyer. The record must be created shortly after the event that it records, not a year later.[101]

Business records also must be kept in the regular course of a business activity, as part of a regular practice of conducting that activity. This is another reason that documents created for use in litigation do not qualify as business records.[102] The same is even the case when the records are produced by the originating creditor.[103] The records must have been created as

---

92 *See* MBNA Am. Bank v. Stehly, 855 N.Y.S.2d 814 (N.Y. App. Term 2008).

93 Ind. Code § 34-37-1-7.

94 *See, e.g.*, Fla. Stat. § 92.50; Ga. Code Ann. § 9-10-113; 5 Ill. Comp. Stat. § 255/6; La. Rev. Stat. Ann. § 13:3719; Mich. Comp. Laws § 565.262; N.J. Stat. Ann. § 41:2-17 (West); Wis. Stat. § 887.01; W. Va. Code § 57-5-9. *Cf.* Haston v. Gen. Motors Corp., 678 So. 2d 1164 (Ala. Civ. App. 1996) (witness affidavit was void and could not be considered in connection with manufacturer's motion for summary judgment in products liability action when Michigan notary public who had signed affidavit had failed to affix seal of office).

95 HSBC Bank v. Thompson, 2010 WL 3451130 (Ohio Ct. App. Sept. 3, 2010).

96 *See, e.g.*, Bozeman v. CACV of Colorado, L.L.C., 282 Ga. App. 256 (Ga. Ct. App. 2006); Colonial Credit Corp v. Dana, 2007 WL 446033 (Ohio Ct. App. Feb. 12, 2007).

97 Federal Rule of Evidence 801(c) provides that: "Hearsay is a statement, other than one made by the declarant while testifying at the trial or hearing, offered in evidence to prove the truth of the matter asserted."

98 *See also* GE Money Bank v. Morales, 773 N.W.2d 533 (Iowa 2009).

99 *See also* Great Seneca Fin. v. Felty, 869 N.E.2d 30 (Ohio Ct. App. 2006); Citibank v. Cramer, 139 Wash. App. 1089 (Wash. Ct. App. 2007).

100 *See, e.g.*, ANJ Corp. v. Ross, 2014 WL 721389 (Mass. App. Div. Feb. 20, 2014); Cach, L.L.C. v. Trevisano (Mo. Cir. Ct. Mar. 18, 2010), *available at* www.nclc.org/unreported.

101 *See* Ortega v. Cach, L.L.C., 396 S.W.3d 622 (Tex. App. 2013).

102 Rae v. State, 638 So. 2d 597 (Fla. Dist. Ct. App. 1994); Chase Bank v. Fekete (Fla. Cnty. Ct. Feb. 1, 2011), *available at* www.nclc.org/unreported; Reach Out, Inc. v. Capital Assocs., Inc., 336 S.E.2d 847 (Ga. Ct. App. 1985); Cach, L.L.C. v. Trevisano (Mo. Cir. Ct. Mar. 18, 2010), *available at* www.nclc.org/unreported; LVNV Funding, L.L.C. v. Mastaw (Tenn. Ct. App. Apr. 30, 2012), *available at* www.nclc.org/unreported; Ortega v. Cach, L.L.C., 396 S.W.3d 622 (Tex. App. 2013). *See also* LVNV Funding, L.L.C. v. Colvell, 22 A.3d 125 (N.J. Super. Ct. App. Div. 2011); Chase Bank v. Hershkovits, 28 Misc. 3d 1202(A) (N.Y. Civ. Ct. 2010).

103 Chase Bank v. Fekete (Fla. Cnty. Ct. Feb. 1, 2011), *available at* www.nclc.org/unreported.

part of the creditor's regular business of extending credit and receiving payments.[104]

Documents purporting to be business records often are created for purposes of litigation, and it is thus important to be able to identify this practice. Creditors rarely will keep copies of statements but instead will generate for the litigation a document similar to the original monthly statement. But this document will, in fact, have many differences from the original, and these differences can show that the record does not meet the requirement of contemporaneousness.

Look to see if the new document has the consumer's current address (instead of the address at which the consumer was residing at the time of the original record) or contains other discrepancies that are apparent on the face of the duplicate. Moreover, a careful cross-examination or deposition of the affiant introducing the record will generally show that the document is not the original but was produced in anticipation of the litigation.

That a record refers to the parties as "plaintiff" and "defendant" constitutes good evidence that a record was created for purposes of litigation.[105] The record's date in relation to the litigation is also a good clue.[106] Thus, a record of assignment created a year after an assignment and only a few months before litigation indicates that the record was created in anticipation of litigation.

4.2.4.1.3 Trustworthiness

Business records exempt from the hearsay rule also cannot lack trustworthiness. Inconsistencies between the records and the collector's affidavits, pleadings, or other documents can suggest a lack of trustworthiness in the records themselves. If the documents are introduced as true copies of what was sent to the consumer, they should not contain handwritten notes that were added after the document was sent to the consumer. Of course, an affidavit cannot be used to introduce into evidence business records if the records are not attached to the affidavit but merely referenced in the affidavit.[107]

4.2.4.1.4 No exception for self-generated computer records and operative documents

There is a line of cases finding that certain self-generated computer records are not hearsay, as when an electronic device is placed on a phone line and a computer automatically records the telephone numbers of calls made to the phone. There is no human involvement in the recording.

This exception to the hearsay rule does not apply to computerized consumer credit records. Human beings make entries into the computer system, turning those entries into computer-stored information (not computer-generated information).[108] Humans also specify the nature of the print-out from the computer. As a result, computer records are hearsay and must fall within the business records exception to be admissible.[109]

There is another line of cases finding that operative documents are not hearsay—documents that define the rights or liabilities of the parties in the case, such as contracts between the parties. But the definition of "operative documents" is narrow and does not apply to assignments of the debt from one party to another, computer spreadsheets, or affidavits of one of the parties.[110]

4.2.4.2 Affidavits Must Certify Business Records

When business records are introduced at trial, they are introduced by the testimony of the custodian of those records or some other qualified witness.[111] When they are utilized as attachments to a summary judgment motion, they also must be certified by a custodian of the records or other qualified person.[112] Business records cannot be the basis for the collector's summary judgment motion if they are unaccompanied by an affidavit swearing to or certifying the records.[113]

The witness or affiant must be familiar not just with the records but with how the business records were *created*. The federal rule concerning this certification states that the business record should be:

> [A]ccompanied by a written declaration of its custodian or other qualified person . . . certifying that the record—
> (A) was made at or near the time of the occurrence of the matters set forth by, or from information transmitted by, a person with knowledge of those matters;
> (B) was kept in the course of the regularly conducted activity; and
> (C) was made by the regularly conducted activity as a regular practice.[114]

Documents must be accompanied by an affidavit that is made on personal knowledge, sets forth facts as would be admissible in evidence, and shows that the affiant is competent to testify

104 *See* Ortega v. Cach, L.L.C., 396 S.W.3d 622 (Tex. App. 2013) (debt buyer's record dated prior to debt buyer obtaining the account shows record is untrustworthy).

105 *See* Ortega v. Cach, L.L.C., 396 S.W.3d 622 (Tex. App. 2013).

106 *Id.*

107 Midland Funding, L.L.C. v. Howell, 2013 WL 6008724 (Ariz. Ct. App. Nov. 12, 2013).

108 GE Money Bank v. Morales, 773 N.W.2d 533 (Iowa 2009).

109 *Id.*

110 Delaware Acceptance Corp. v. Swain, 2012 WL 1066357 (Del. Ct. Com. Pl. Mar. 9, 2012), *aff'd*, 2012 WL 6042644 (Del. Super. Ct. Nov.30, 2012).

111 Fed. R. Evid. 803(6).

112 *Id.*

113 *See* Unifund CCR Partners v. Harrell (Conn. Super. Ct. Aug. 3, 2005), *available at* www.nclc.org/unreported; Suggs v. Sherman Acquisition, L.P., 13 Fla. L. Weekly Supp. 301a (Fla. Cir. Ct. Sept. 28, 2005); Unifund CCR Partners v. Perkins 2013 WL 5350941 (La. Ct. App. Sept. 25, 2013). *See also* Discover Bank v. Jankowski, 2012 WL 4358190 (Ariz. Ct. App. Sept. 25, 2012).

114 Fed. R. Evid. 902(11). *See also* Beneficial Maine Inc. v. Carter, 25 A.3d 96 (Me. 2011).

to the matters stated in the affidavit.[115] This is the case even for an affidavit from the originating creditor.[116]

If the affidavit does not explicitly state that the affiant has personal knowledge of the *creation* of the records, then the records cannot be introduced.[117] It is not enough that an affiant is familiar with the business records; the affiant must be familiar with how the records were created near the time of the charges being incurred.[118]

Thus, when cross-examining a witness seeking to authenticate records, ask the witness what they did the prior day, the prior week, the prior month, and so forth. These are often professional witnesses who travel from trial to trial. Their recent activities will not include involvement in the creation, filing, maintenance, or correction of records, and they will only very recently have become aware of the records in this case.

Even though the witness may describe himself or herself as a records custodian, this will clearly not be the case. A conclusory claim as to familiarity with the mode of production is insufficient; the basis for such a representation must be provided.[119]

In one case, the court refused to accept as sufficient an affidavit from the creditor's servicing affiliate.[120] The court noted that the affiant worked for an affiliate that was involved not with creating account records but with collection efforts on defaulted accounts. The court also noted that the affiliate was physically located in a different state than the one in which the creditor did business and to which payments were sent. The affiant provided no details as to the affiant's involvement with the creditor's day-to-day business operations or record keeping practices. Claims of personal knowledge in this context are suspect, even more so when the affidavit has the look and feel of a robo-signed document and when it is virtually identical to the affidavit of others working for the same servicing affiliate.[121]

Similarly, an affidavit cannot certify documents if the substance of the affidavit conflicts with the documents themselves.[122] For example, an affidavit may state a total dollar amount owed, while component numbers in the attached business records may add up to a different number. In one case, the court cited with disapproval a debt buyer's affidavits and other documents that included three different interest rates and which referred to the debt buyer as being the original owner and the entity from whom goods or services were purchased.[123]

4.2.4.3 Can a Debt Buyer Authenticate a Creditor's Business Records?

4.2.4.3.1 The general rule

The affidavit authenticating the records of the original creditor must be sworn to by an employee of the original creditor and not by an employee of the debt buyer.[124] The employee of the debt buyer has no knowledge of how the records were created by the originating creditor and cannot testify to it.[125]

115 *See* Great Seneca Fin. v. Felty, 869 N.E.2d 30 (Ohio Ct. App. 2006); Palisades Collection, L.L.C. v. Kalal, 781 N.W.2d 503 (Wis. Ct. App. 2010). *See also* Unifund CCR Partners v. Lett (Ala. Cir. Ct. May 6, 2009), *available at* www.nclc.org/unreported; Cach, L.L.C. v. Kulas, 21 A.3d 1015 (Me. 2011).

116 *See, e.g.*, Midland Funding, L.L.C. v. Edwards (Cal. App. Dep't Super Ct. Dec. 13, 2013), *available at* www.nclc.org/unreported; HSBC Bank v. Griswold, 795 N.W.2d 64 (Wis. Ct. App. 2010). *See also* Citibank v. Austin (Cal. Super. Ct. Feb. 10, 2012), *available at* www.nclc.org/unreported.

117 Midland Funding, L.L.C. v. Edwards (Cal. App. Dep't Super Ct. Dec. 13, 2013), *available at* www.nclc.org/unreported; Chase Bank v. Curren, 946 N.E.2d 810 (Ohio Ct. App. Dec. 21, 2010).

118 Midland Funding, L.L.C. v. Edwards (Cal. App. Dep't Super Ct. Dec. 13, 2013), *available at* www.nclc.org/unreported; Citibank v. Austin (Cal. Super. Ct. Feb. 10, 2012), *available at* www.nclc.org/unreported; HSBC Bank v. Griswold, 795 N.W.2d 64 (Wis. Ct. App. 2010). *See also* Discover Bank v. Jankowski, 2012 WL 4358190 (Ariz. Ct. App. Sept. 25, 2012); Chase Bank v. Hershkovits, 28 Misc. 3d 1202(A) (N.Y. Civ. Ct. 2010).

119 Midland Funding, L.L.C. v. Edwards (Cal. App. Dep't Super Ct. Dec. 13, 2013), *available at* www.nclc.org/unreported.

120 *See* Discover Bank v. Shimer, 957 N.Y.S.2d 263 (table), 2012 WL 2912492 (N.Y. Dist. Ct. July 17, 2012).

121 *Id.*

122 Palisades Collection, L.L.C. v. Gonzalez, 809 N.Y.S.2d 482 (table), 2005 WL 3372971 (N.Y. Civ. Ct. Dec. 12, 2005); Barajas v. Harvest Credit Mgmt., VI-B, L.L.C., 2008 WL 4308334 (Tex. App. Aug. 28, 2008).

123 Barajas v. Harvest Credit Mgmt., VI-B, L.L.C., 2008 WL 4308334 (Tex. App. Aug. 28, 2008).

124 Webb v. Midland Credit Mgmt., Inc., 2012 WL 2022013 (N.D. Ill. May 31, 2012); LHR, Inc. v. Ayree (Md. Cir. Ct. July 26, 2010), *available at* www.nclc.org/unreported; Cach, L.L.C. v. Askew, 358 SW 3d 58 (Mo. 2012); Asset Acceptance v. Lodge, 325 S.W.3d 525 (Mo. Ct. App. 2010); DNS Equity Group Inc. v. Lavallee, 907 N.Y.S.2d 436 (table), 2010 WL 682466 (N.Y. Dist. Ct. Feb. 22, 2010); Palisades Collection, L.L.C. v. Haque, 2006 N.Y. Misc. LEXIS 4036 (N.Y. Civ. Ct. Apr. 13, 2006); Commonwealth Fin. Sys., Inc. v. Smith, 15 A.3d 492 (Pa. Super. Ct. 2011). *See also* Powell v. Vavro, McDonald & Assocs., 136 S.W.3d 762 (Tex. App. 2004); Matrix Computing, Inc. v. Davis, 554 S.W.2d 288 (Tex. App. 1997); Unifund CCR Partners v. Bonfigli, 2010 Vt. Super. LEXIS 24 (Vt. Super. Ct. May 5, 2010).

125 Webb v. Midland Credit Mgmt., Inc., 2012 WL 2022013 (N.D. Ill. May 31, 2012); Unifund CCR Partners v. Lett (Ala. Cir. Ct. May 6, 2009), *available at* www.nclc.org/unreported; Midland Funding, L.L.C. v. Edwards (Cal. App. Dep't Super Ct. Dec. 13, 2013), *available at* www.nclc.org/unreported; Seth v. Midland Funding, L.L.C., 997 N.E.2d 1139 (Ind. Ct. App. 2013); LHR, Inc. v. Ayree (Md. Cir. Ct. July 26, 2010), *available at* www.nclc.org/unreported; Asset Acceptance v. Lodge, 325 S.W.3d 525 (Mo. Ct. App. 2010); Zundel v. Bommarito, 778 S.W.2d 954 (Mo. Ct. App. 1989); Unifund CCR Partners v. Youngman, 932 N.Y.S.2d 609 (N.Y. Sup. Ct. 2011); Rushmore Recoveries X, L.L.C. v. Skolnick, 841 N.Y.S.2d 823 (N.Y. Dist. Ct. 2007); PRA III, L.L.C. v. MacDowell, 841 N.Y.S.2d 822 (N.Y. Civ. Ct. 2007); Palisades Collection, L.L.C. v. Haque, 2006 N.Y. Misc. LEXIS 4036 (N.Y. Civ. Ct. Apr. 13, 2006); Palisades Collection, L.L.C. v. Gonzalez, 809 N.Y.S.2d 482 (table), 2005 WL 3372971 (N.Y. Civ. Ct. Dec. 12, 2005); Ohio Receivables L.L.C. v. Williams, 2013 WL 1092258 (Ohio Ct. App. Mar. 15, 2013); Commonwealth Fin. Sys., Inc. v. Smith, 15 A.3d 492 (Pa. Super. Ct. 2011); Riddle v. Unifund CCR Partners, 298 S.W.3d 780 (Tex. App. 2009); Martinez v. Midland Credit Mgmt., Inc., 250 S.W.3d 481 (Tex. App. 2008); Powell v. Vavro, McDonald & Assocs.,

To certify business records the affiant must be familiar with the original creditor's record keeping practices—the habits and customary practices and procedures utilized in making the documents.[126] The affiant must be able to certify that the documents were made in the original creditor's regular course of business, that it was the original creditor's regular practice to make the documents, and that the original creditor created the documents contemporaneously with the facts that were recorded.[127]

Similarly, there can be little question that an employee of a third-party debt buyer in a chain of transfers cannot authenticate a document memorializing the assignment from the first to the second debt buyer in that chain of transfers.[128] The collector's employee has no first-hand knowledge as to the assignment or the creation of the assignment document.

When the affiant is not an employee of the company generating the original records, then the affiant has a burden of showing an understanding of the daily operation and first-hand knowledge of the recordkeeping by the other entity.[129] An employee of a third party must show personal knowledge as to the creation, maintenance, and transmission of the records by the entity generating the original records and how the third party obtains those records and integrates those records into its own business records.[130] It is not enough that an assignee received and kept documents in the ordinary course of business; the affiant must affirm with knowledge that the documents were created in the ordinary course of business.[131] Otherwise, courts will not allow business records into evidence.[132] A debt buyer's affidavit has no probative value when the affiant's claimed familiarity with the assignor's business records is derived solely from the affiant's review of those records after they came into the debt buyer's possession.[133]

4.2.4.3.2 *The minority rule of incorporation*

A minority of courts recognize a "rule of incorporation," which provides that records taken into custody by a business are considered "made" by that business if that business integrates the documents into its business records and relies upon them.[134]

136 S.W.3d 762 (Tex. App. 2004); Matrix Computing, Inc. v. Davis, 554 S.W.2d 288 (Tex. App. 1997); Unifund CCR Partners v. Bonfigli, 2010 Vt. Super. LEXIS 24 (Vt. Super. Ct. May 5, 2010); Palisades Collection, L.L.C. v. Kalal, 781 N.W.2d 503 (Wis. Ct. App. 2010). *See also* LVNV Funding, L.L.C. v. Mastaw, 2012 WL 1534785 (Tenn. Ct. App. Apr. 30, 2012), *available at* www.nclc.org/unreported. *But see* § 4.2.4.3.2, *infra* (citing a minority rule accepted by more recent Texas courts and certain federal courts).

126 Webb v. Midland Credit Mgmt., Inc., 2012 WL 2022013 (N.D. Ill. May 31, 2012); LHR, Inc. v. Ayree (Md. Cir. Ct. July 26, 2010), *available at* www.nclc.org/unreported; Asset Acceptance v. Lodge, 325 S.W.3d 525 (Mo. Ct. App. 2010); C & W Asset Acquisition, L.L.C. v. Somogyi, 136 S.W.3d 134 (Mo. Ct. App. 2004); Unifund CCR Partners v. Youngman, 932 N.Y.S.2d 609 (N.Y. Sup. Ct. 2011); Rushmore Recoveries X, L.L.C. v. Skolnick, 841 N.Y.S.2d 823 (N.Y. Dist. Ct. 2007); Palisades Collection, L.L.C. v. Gonzalez, 809 N.Y.S.2d 482 (table), 2005 WL 3372971 (N.Y. Civ. Ct. Dec. 12, 2005); Riddle v. Unifund CCR Partners, 298 S.W.3d 780 (Tex. App. 2009); Martinez v. Midland Credit Mgmt., Inc., 250 S.W.3d 481 (Tex. App. 2008); Unifund CCR Partners v. Bonfigli, 2010 Vt. Super. LEXIS 24 (Vt. Super. Ct. May 5, 2010); Palisades Collection, L.L.C. v. Kalal, 781 N.W.2d 503 (Wis. Ct. App. 2010). *See also* Dan Med., P.C. v. N.Y. Cent. Mut. Fire Ins. Co., 829 N.Y.S.2d 404 (N.Y. App. Div. 2006).

127 Webb v. Midland Credit Mgmt., Inc., 2012 WL 2022013 (N.D. Ill. May 31, 2012); C & W Asset Acquisition, L.L.C. v. Somogyi, 136 S.W.3d 134 (Mo. Ct. App. 2004); Rushmore Recoveries X, L.L.C. v. Skolnick, 841 N.Y.S.2d 823 (N.Y. Dist. Ct. 2007); Palisades Collection, L.L.C. v. Haque, 2006 N.Y. Misc. LEXIS 4036 (N.Y. Civ. Ct. Apr. 13, 2006); Commonwealth Fin. Sys., Inc. v. Smith, 15 A.3d 492 (Pa. Super. Ct. 2011); Banc One Asset Solution Corp. v. Thomas, 2001 WL 259140 (Tex. App. Mar. 16, 2001).

128 Wright v. Asset Acceptance Corp., 2000 WL 33216031 (S.D. Ohio Jan. 3, 2000); Norfolk Fin. Corp. v. Mazard, 2009 WL 3844481 (Mass. App. Div. Nov. 12, 2009); Colorado Capital Investments, Inc. v. Villar (N.Y. Civ. Ct. June 4, 2009), *available at* www.nclc.org/unreported; Unifund CCR Assignee of Providian v. Ayhan, 2008 WL 297439 (Wash. Ct. App. Aug. 5, 2008). *See* § 4.2.4.2, *supra*. *See also* Gigli v. Palisades Collection, L.L.C., 2008 WL 3853295 (M.D. Pa. Aug. 14, 2008); Persolve v. Uribe (Cal. Super. Ct. Dec. 9, 2010), *available at* www.nclc.org/unreported. *But see* Monroe v. Unifund CCR Partners, 2010 WL 1948332 (Tex. App. May 13, 2010) (court could believe collector's testimony on prior assignment, particularly when consumer did not offer contrary evidence).

129 Beneficial Maine Inc. v. Carter, 25 A.3d 96 (2011).

130 *Id.*

131 *See* White Indus., Inc. v. Cessna Aircraft Co., 611 F. Supp. 1049 (W.D. Mo. 1985); River Dock and Pile, Inc. v. O & G Indus., Inc., 595 A.2d 839 (Conn. 1991); Cuda & Assoc., L.L.P. v. Lumkin, 2011 WL 6413674 (Conn. Super. Ct. Nov. 29, 2011).

132 Webb v. Midland Credit Mgmt., Inc., 2012 WL 2022013 (N.D. Ill. May 31, 2012). *See, e.g.*, C & W Asset Acquisition, L.L.C. v. Somogyi, 136 S.W.3d 134 (Mo. Ct. App. 2004); Unifund CCR Partners v. Youngman, 932 N.Y.S.2d 609 (N.Y. Sup. Ct. 2011); Palisades Collection, L.L.C. v. Haque, 2006 N.Y. Misc. LEXIS 4036 (N.Y. Civ. Ct. Apr. 13, 2006); Palisades Collection, L.L.C. v. Gonzalez, 809 N.Y.S.2d 482 (table), 2005 WL 3372971 (N.Y. Civ. Ct. Dec. 12, 2005); Commonwealth Fin. Sys., Inc. v. Smith, 15 A.3d 492 (Pa. Super. Ct. 2011); Riddle v. Unifund CCR Partners, 298 S.W.3d 780 (Tex. App. 2009); Banc One Asset Solution Corp. v. Thomas, 2001 WL 259140 (Tex. App. Mar. 16, 2001); Unifund CCR Partners v. Bonfigli, 2010 Vt. Super. LEXIS 24 (Vt. Super. Ct. May 5, 2010). *But cf.* Bozeman v. CACV of Colorado, L.L.C., 638 S.E.2d 387 (Ga. Ct. App. 2006) (affirming summary judgment for creditor and rejecting consumer's hearsay argument because consumer failed to present evidence contradicting creditor's affidavit); Cockrell v. Republic Mortgage Ins. Co., 817 S.W.2d 106 (Tex. App. 1991) (assignee's affidavit comprises business records of the assignor if the assignee verifies the accuracy of the information generated by the assignee; receipt of records in the regular course of business sufficed to show the accuracy and trustworthiness of the loan histories).

133 LHR, Inc. v. Ayree (Md. Cir. Ct. July 26, 2010), *available at* www.nclc.org/unreported; Asset Acceptance v. Lodge, 325 S.W.3d 525 (Mo. Ct. App. 2010); C & W Asset Acquisition, L.L.C. v. Somogyi, 136 S.W.3d 134 (Mo. Ct. App. 2004); Unifund CCR Partners v. Youngman, 932 N.Y.S.2d 609 (N.Y. Sup. Ct. 2011); Rushmore Recoveries X, L.L.C. v. Skolnick, 841 N.Y.S.2d 823 (Dist. Ct. 2007); Palisades Collection, L.L.C. v. Kalal, 781 N.W.2d 503 (Wis. Ct. App. 2010). *See also* Riddle v. Unifund CCR Partners, 298 S.W.3d 780 (Tex. App. 2009).

134 *See* United States v. Adefehinti, 510 F.3d 319 (D.C. Cir. 2007); Midland Funding, L.L.C. v. Howell, 2013 WL 6008724 (Ariz. Ct. App. Nov. 12, 2013); Ainsworth v. CACH, L.L.C., 2012 WL 1205525 (Tex. App. Apr. 10, 2012); Dodeka, L.L.C. v. Campos, 377 S.W.3d 726 (Tex. App. 2012); Simien v. Unifund CCR Partners, 321 S.W.3d 235 (Tex. App. 2010); Wood v. Pharia, L.L.C., 2010 WL 5060621 (Tex. App. Dec. 9, 2010). *See also* Grant-Hall v. Cavalry Portfolio Serv., L.L.C., 2013 WL 855962

But most state courts reject this extension of the basic rules of evidence.[135] In any event, as described below, the rule of incorporation should not apply even to the typical case in which a debt buyer introduces the originating creditor's business records.

4.2.4.3.3 *Minority rule inapplicable to debt buyers who fail to incorporate records*

If a court accepts the rule of incorporation, this applies only to the originating creditor's records that are incorporated into the debt buyer's records. Records created by the debt buyer for litigation would be not be admissible. The records would not be contemporaneous to the activities being described.[136]

As for the creditor's original records, debt buyers rarely if ever integrate such documents into their records. When the debt buyer purchases an account, it will have only minimal information about the account on a spreadsheet, such as name, address, social security number, account number, and amount owed. The debt buyer will not possess any of the creditor's actual account records and thus will not have received or incorporated into its records account applications, the original credit agreement, amendments to the agreement, billing statements, additional communications from the creditor and any change of terms, a running account diary, or written communications between the creditor and consumer. The debt buyer will receive none of these documents when it purchases a debt.

While the debt buyer's affidavit may claim personal knowledge of the creditor's business records, the affiant in fact will have seen none of these records because, among other reasons, the debt buyer has not received copies of these records. The FTC has found that, "[f]or most portfolios, buyers did not receive any documents at the time of purchase."[137] The records will not in fact have been incorporated into the debt buyer's records. This is even more the case when an account has been sold from one debt buyer to another.

The forward flow agreements between creditor and debt buyer will specify what additional documentation—often limited and which may take weeks to obtain—that the debt buyer can request. When one debt buyer sells a debt to another, the agreement may even provide that the seller need not provide any business records about the account to the new debt buyer.

Assuming a debt buyer does request certain records from the creditor as part of its litigation, such records are not really incorporated into the debt buyer's records. Similar records will not be kept for other accounts. The debt buyer is likely not to maintain an itemized list of what records it has for an account and may not have information about when it received the records or from whom, making it impossible to know what records were in fact available at the debt buyer when the affiant claimed to review them. The ad hoc nature in which a debt buyer obtains such additional records also belies that they are obtained as part of a regular practice otherwise typical of business records-keeping. No document is routinely provided to the debt buyer from the creditor, and the debt buyer only obtains a particular type of record upon a special request to the creditor. The debt buyer bears the burden of proving that the records have in fact been incorporated into debt buyer's records and relied upon.[138]

4.2.4.3.4 *Minority rule inapplicable to records that are not trustworthy*

Even if a court were to accept the minority rule of incorporation, critical to the operation of this rule is that other circumstances indicate the trustworthiness of the document.[139] The debt buyer must incorporate the creditor's records in a manner that establishes reliability. This is far from the case for the typical debt buyer. The debt buyer will only have a few business records at most, not the complete set that the creditor kept, so the debt buyer's records will be incomplete at best. That the debt buyer may have the right to request additional records does not mean that the debt buyer has such records. Nor will the debt buyer take any steps to confirm the accuracy of the records it may in fact obtain. The affiant will typically not even state which specific account documents he or she has reviewed. It is often the case that there were few if any account documents to review.

When the creditor does provide a record to the debt buyer, the forward flow agreements generally disclaim any accuracy as to the records. The creditor certainly does not certify to the accuracy or otherwise make assurances as to the accuracy of the records provided to the debt buyer. Instead, the first attempt to certify the documents as business records will be made in the context of litigation.

Scrutinize all "forward flow" and other agreements between the creditor and its debt buyer. What remains relevant are the particular agreements that were in effect at the time of the assignment of the consumer's debt, not the cleaned-up and revised version now in effect.

Agreements between creditors and their debt buyers often include language stating that the creditor makes no representations whatsoever about the accuracy or completeness of the records, that the creditor may have failed to credit borrowers for some payments, that accuracy of account balances are

(N.D. Ill. Mar. 6, 2013); Beneficial Maine Inc. v. Carter, 25 A.3d 96 (Me. 2011); Ohio Receivables, L.L.C. v. Dallariva, 2012 WL 2859923 (Ohio Ct. App. July 12, 2012) (adopting the same rule under Ohio law).

135 Commonwealth Fin. Sys., Inc. v. Smith, 15 A.3d 492 (Pa. Super. Ct. 2011). *See also* LHR, Inc. v. Ayree (Md. Cir. Ct. July 26, 2010), *available at* www.nclc.org/unreported; Asset Acceptance v. Lodge, 325 S.W.3d 525 (Mo. Ct. App. 2010); Zundel v. Bommarito, 778 S.W.2d 954 (Mo. Ct. App. 1989); Powell v. Vavro, McDonald & Assocs., 136 S.W.3d 762 (Tex. App. 2004); Matrix Computing, Inc. v. Davis 554 S.W.2d 288 (Tex. App. 1977); Unifund CCR Partners v. Bonfigli, 2010 Vt. Super. LEXIS 24 (Vt. Super. Ct. May 5, 2010).

136 *See* §§ 4.2.4.1.1–4.2.4.1.3, *supra*.

137 Fed. Trade Comm'n, The Structure and Practices of the Debt Buying Industry, at iii (Jan. 2013).

138 *See* ANJ Corp. v. Ross, 2014 WL 721389 (Mass. App. Div. Feb. 20, 2014).

139 United States v. Adefehinti, 510 F.3d 319 (D.C. Cir. 2007); Simien v. Unifund CCR Partners, 321 S.W.3d 235 (Tex. App. 2010); Wood v. Pharia, L.L.C., 2010 WL 5060621 (Tex. App. Dec. 9, 2010). *See also* Portfolio Recovery Assoc., L.L.C. v. Strifler (Vt. Super. Ct. Sept. 2, 2011), *available at* www.nclc.org/unreported.

within a 10% margin of error, or that documentation to back up the data is available for only a certain percentage of the charged-off accounts.

For example, the April 14, 2010, Loan Sale Agreement between FIA Card Services and CACH, L.L.C., states that "it is possible that the figure provided in the Current Balance for any Loan may not reflect credits for payments made by or on behalf of any Obligor prior to the Cut-Off Date." [140] The same agreement states, in all-capital letters, that the evidence of indebtedness does not imply the debt is enforceable; the agreement also states, in all-capital letters, that the creditor does not represent that the loans are valid, the loans comply with the law, the current balance is accurate, or the accrued interest is accurate.[141] In reference to accounts, other agreements will use terms such as "sold as is" or "sold with all faults" or will otherwise limit the warranties as to whether the amount stated is actually the amount owed. The creditor will even disclaim any warranty that the debt is enforceable. These statements indicate that the creditor itself does not represent the underlying records as reliable, so it is hard to see how the debt buyer can rely upon them either.

Recent publicity has centered around the inaccuracy of bank records. Federal agencies have questioned the accuracy of bank records relating to the origination and servicing of mortgage loans.[142] If these are prone to error, one would expect even greater errors on smaller debts, such as credit card debt. For example, Chase Bank, one of the nation's largest credit card issuers, is the subject of an action by the Office of the Comptroller of the Currency because of Chase Bank's collection of credit card debt without having accurate records.[143] Numerous other news articles have also described problems with Chase Bank's credit card records while collecting on the debt or selling the debt to debt buyers.

Thus, in one case, a debt buyer's employee introduced Chase's business records, and the court found the records to be insufficiently reliable to allow the debt buyer to prevail.[144] Even if the debt buyer's employee were able to introduce business records whose reliability was uncontested, when the reliability of the records is in question the debt buyer's employee is in no position to address or be cross-examined about the originating creditor's record-keeping practices.[145]

Trustworthiness also can often be attacked by finding inconsistencies in the collector's presentation of the business records,[146] for example, when the supposed credit agreement was not in existence at the time the consumer opened an account, when account numbers are inaccurate, or when interest rates and attorney fee claims are not consistent with the contract introduced.[147] Moreover, it is likely that the person authenticating the business records will be an employee of the debt buyer with little, if any, knowledge of how the original business developed the records and passed them on to the debt buyer or even how they were used by the debt buyer.[148]

4.2.4.3.5 When affiant is not an employee of the debt buyer

Sometimes the individual testifying to the creditor's business records is not an employee of the debt buyer but an employee of another entity hired by the debt buyer. For example, in one case the affiant was an employee of Midland Credit Management, which serviced accounts for the debt buyer, Midland Funding, L.L.C. The affiant's affidavit regarding the debt buyer's incorporation of the creditor's business records was not adequate because the affidavit did not provide information as to the relationship between Midland Credit Management and Midland Funding, L.L.C., or provide trustworthy information as to whether Midland Credit Management relied on the records of either the original creditor or debt buyer.[149]

4.2.4.3.6 The New Jersey rule

The rule in New Jersey is that a witness who is not an employee of the entity creating business records can still lay the foundation for the records if a number of conditions are met. The witness must demonstrate that the record is what the witness claims it to be, that the witness is sufficiently familiar with the record system used, and the witness can establish that it was the regular practice of the business to make the record. Finally, the witness must show that the source of information and the method, purposes, and circumstances of preparation indicate that the record is trustworthy.[150]

4.2.4.4 Electronic Records

Business records must also be authentic. Ordinarily, the same proof as required to qualify for the exception from the hearsay rule is sufficient to show authenticity.[151] But electronic records create special authentication issues. Has the record been preserved during the time it was in the electronic file so as to ensure that the document being proffered is the

140 *Available online as companion material to this treatise.*

141 *Available online as companion material to this treatise.*

142 U.S. Gov't Accountability Office, Mortgage Foreclosures: Documentation Problems Reveal Need for Ongoing Regulatory Oversight, GAO-11-433 (May 2011); Federal Reserve System, Interagency Review of Foreclosure Policies and Practices (Apr. 2011).

143 *See OCC Probing JP Morgan Chase Credit Card Collections*, Am. Banker, Mar. 12, 2012.

144 Midland Funding, L.L.C. v. Snow (Md. Dist. Ct. Dec. 18, 2013), *available at* www.nclc.org/unreported.

145 *Id.*

146 *See* Commonwealth Fin. Sys., Inc. v. Smith, 15 A.3d 492 (Pa. Super. Ct. 2011).

147 *Id.*

148 Webb v. Midland Credit Mgmt., Inc., 2012 WL 2022013 (N.D. Ill. May 31, 2012); Commonwealth Fin. Sys., Inc. v. Smith, 15 A.3d 492 (Pa. Super. Ct. 2011).

149 Midland Funding, L.L.C. v. Howell, 2013 WL 6008724 (Ariz. Ct. App. Nov. 12, 2013). *See also* Seth v. Midland Funding, L.L.C., 997 N.E.2d 1139 (Ind. Ct. App. 2013).

150 Cavalry Portfolio Serv., L.L.C. v. Kumbaris, 2011 WL 6057861 (N.J. Super. Ct. App. Div. Dec. 7, 2011).

151 5 Jack B. Weinstein & Margaret A. Berger, Weinstein's Fed. Evidence § 900.06[2][a] (Joseph M. McLaughlin ed., 2d. ed. 1997).

same as the document that was originally created? This issue raises questions not only about the computer equipment and programs used but policies for use of the equipment, database and programs, how access is controlled, how changes are recorded, what the audit system is, and the like.[152] Thus, the affiant must have special knowledge of the computer system, database, access, and related issues before electronic records can be admitted.[153]

Courts have viewed with favor[154] an eleven-step foundation for computer records suggested by E. Imwinkelried's *Evidentiary Foundations*:

1. The business uses a computer.
2. The computer is reliable.
3. The business has developed a procedure for inserting data into the computer.
4. The procedure has built-in safeguards to ensure accuracy and identify errors.[155]
5. The business keeps the computer in a good state of repair.
6. The witness had the computer readout certain data.
7. The witness used the proper procedures to obtain the readout.
8. The computer was in working order at the time the witness obtained the readout.
9. The witness recognizes the exhibit as the readout.
10. The witness explains how he or she recognizes the readout.
11. If the readout contains strange symbols or terms, the witness explains the meaning of the symbols or terms for the trier of fact.[156]

An employee for the debt buyer will have no direct knowledge of almost any of these eleven items, and so a debt buyer's affidavit should not be able to introduce into evidence electronic records from the originating creditor.

Possible questions to ask a witness introducing records into evidence include questions in the following areas: the identity of the witness' employer (that is, the name found on the witness' paystub), job title and description, training and computer experience, training on the computer generating the records, and the identity of other records custodians in the company relating to that computer. Also establish that no paper records exist which are contemporaneous with the credit and that all documents in the case were generated recently by a computer. Identify the computer that generated the documents—its manufacturer, its age, whether data was moved from one computer software to another, what the software is, what training and support the individual receives for the computer and software in question.

What is the procedure for inserting data into the computer? What safeguards exist? Who printed out the documents? How does the witness know that the printout was done correctly? How do you know that the printout and the document being submitted are the same? Also ask the witness to describe all abbreviations, symbols, and other information on the documents.

Sometimes collectors argue that computer records do not need to be authenticated because the information "did not pass through a human mind" and thus is not hearsay. This ignores the fact that humans initiated the information that was entered into the computer, humans programmed the computer, and humans delivered the information from the computer.

New York statutes set out standards for the admission of paper printouts from electronic records. The record cannot permit additions, deletions or changes, and the affidavit accompanying the record must include the manner or method by which tampering or degradation of the reproduction is prevented.[157] Thus an attorney's affirmation of fact cannot be admitted when it was based upon "financial electronic records," when copies of the records were not attached, and when none of the requirements of the New York statutes were met.[158]

4.2.4.5 Developing Evidence to Challenge the Affidavit

When the collector brings a summary judgment motion and appends business records and an affidavit to authenticate them, the consumer may wish to question whether the affiant has sufficient knowledge as to how those records were created and kept. Federal Rule of Civil Procedure 56(d) and comparable state rules allow the consumer to ask the court to allow discovery of these facts. Nevertheless, the court has discretion whether to allow such discovery and, in any event, deposing an out-of-state affiant may be expensive.

If the court allows discovery as to the affiant's knowledge, there may be discovery requests that are less expensive than an out-of-state deposition but are still effective. A request for admissions can be sent to the collector concerning the affiant's knowledge. Interrogatories can also be sent to the collector seeking information about the affiant's activities both signing affidavits and reviewing files.

Of course, to the extent possible, it is preferable to conduct this discovery at the beginning of a case, before the collector moves for summary judgment, as the court may not allow discovery later. In many cases, though, the consumer will have to rely on the face of the affidavit to argue that it should not be admitted or should be given little credibility.

152 *In re* Vee Vinhnee, 336 B.R. 437 (B.A.P. 9th Cir. 2005). *See also* Lorraine v. Markel Am. Ins. Co., 241 F.R.D. 534 (D. Md. 2007).

153 *Id.*

154 *See, e.g.*, *In re* Vee Vinhnee, 336 B.R. 437 (B.A.P. 9th Cir. 2005). *See also* Lorraine v. Markel Am. Ins. Co., 241 F.R.D. 534 (D. Md. 2007); *In re* Vargas, 396 B.R. 511 (Bankr. C.D. Cal. 2008).

155 One court has elaborated on this element by mentioning details regarding computer policy and system control procedures, including control of access to the database, control of access to the program, recording and logging changes, backup practices, and audit procedures, to assure the continuing integrity of the records. *See In re* Vee Vinhnee, 336 B.R. 437 (B.A.P. 9th Cir. 2005).

156 E. Imwinkelried, Evidentiary Foundations § 4.03[2] (7th ed. 2008).

157 N.Y. C.P.L.R. Law § 4539 (McKinney), *as referenced by* N.Y. State Tech. Law § 306 (McKinney).

158 American Express Bank, FSB v. Dalbis, 2011 WL 873512 (N.Y. City Civ. Ct. Mar. 14, 2011).

4.2.4.6 Consumer Authentication of Creditor's Business Records

At trial, the collector may seek to avoid bringing in a witness to authenticate business records by trying to have the consumer do so. This can be avoided if the consumer is not in court and has not been timely subpoenaed to attend. Even if they are in court, consumers should state that they are not familiar with how the records were created, do not have their own copies of records in their possession, and do not recall whether any copies they did receive are exact copies of the records the collector is asking them to authenticate.

4.3 Collector as Real Party in Interest, Owner of the Debt

4.3.1 Introduction

Chapter 3, *supra*, examines situations in which the entity collecting the debt does not have authority to use the state's courts—such as when the entity is not properly licensed to collect on a debt or has not properly registered with the state as an out-of-state corporation.[159] This section examines whether the entity suing on the debt has standing to bring the action—is it the real party in interest?

There are at least five different scenarios in which a collector is bringing a lawsuit:

1. The collector is the originating creditor and has never assigned the account, even to a securitization trust.
2. The collector is a bank or other entity that is usually an originating creditor, but in this case is not the originating creditor, and instead has merged with or purchased the originating creditor or its portfolio of loans.
3. The collector is the originating creditor but has sold the receivables to a securitization trust and is either servicing the account or purchased the receivables back pursuant to a recourse agreement.
4. The collector is a debt collection agency that has been assigned the debt solely for collection purposes, and the debt collection agency is not the real owner of the debt. Sometimes this is described as the legal title—but not the equitable title—being transferred to the collector.
5. The collector is a debt buyer who either purchased the debt from the originating creditor or from another debt buyer. In this case, both legal and equitable titles have transferred.

Section 4.3.2, *infra*, considers the first three scenarios, in which a creditor is bringing the collection action. Section 4.3.3, *infra*, examines a collection agency's ability to bring an action in its name but on behalf of another. Finally, § 4.3.4, *infra*, treats in some detail a debt buyer's proof that it owns the debt and thus has a right to sue upon it.

159 *See* § 3.6, *supra*.

4.3.2 When a Bank or Other Creditor Is the Plaintiff

4.3.2.1 General

Even when a collection action is brought by a bank or other creditor, issues of real party in interest and proving ownership often arise. The first step is to determine if the entity suing on the debt has the exact same name as the entity that originated the credit. Often, this is not the case.

Increasingly today, the entity collecting the debt has merged with or purchased the lender who originally extended the credit, purchased the originating creditor's loan portfolio, or has simply changed its name. For example, MBNA Corporation merged with and into Bank of America Corporation, with MBNA America Bank becoming a subsidiary of Bank of America. Shortly thereafter, MBNA changed its name to FIA Card Services. When an action is brought in the name of FIA Card Services, the collector must provide admissible evidence that FIA Card Services has the right to sue on a debt originally owed to MBNA.[160]

Similarly, a case was dismissed when the collector never proved how a Household Bank account became a Bank of America account.[161] Similar problems may arise when a bank seeks to collect on a Providian credit card account, since it will have to show that Providian was sold to Washington Mutual, which then ceased to exist, and the account was then sold to the plaintiff.[162] Similarly, Bank One accounts are now being collected by Chase Bank.[163]

In proving the transfer of accounts from one bank to another, the records must meet all evidentiary standards. An appellate court had little trouble rejecting a collector's evidence of JP Morgan's purchase of credit card portfolios from other banks by reference to a *New York Times* article and to Wikipedia.[164] The collector failed to prove that First U.S.A., a division of Bank One, purchased the credit card operations of Chevy Chase Bank and that Bank One was purchased by J.P. Morgan & Co.[165]

Other confusion is created when the originating creditor brings the collection action but uses the name of a different subsidiary than the entity that originated the loan. Thus, a court questioned the standing of American Express Travel Related Services Company to bring a collection action when the monthly statements were sent by American Express and the agreement was with American Express Centurion Bank.[166]

160 *See* FIA Card Servs. v. Thompson, 859 N.Y.S.2d 894 (N.Y. Dist. Ct. 2008) (case dismissed when MBNA obtained arbitration award but sought confirmation under the name FIA Card Services).

161 Norfolk Fin. Corp. v. Mazard, 2009 WL 3844481 (Mass. Dist. Ct. Nov. 12, 2009).

162 *Cf.* Wirth v. Cach, L.L.C., 685 S.E.2d 433 (Ga. Ct. App. 2009).

163 *Cf.* Nat'l Check Bur., Inc. v. Ruth, 2009 WL 2516123 (Ohio Ct. App. Aug. 19, 2009).

164 Palisades Collection, L.L.C. v. Graubard, 2009 WL 1025176 (N.J. Super. Ct. App. Div. Apr. 17, 2009).

165 *Id.*

166 Am. Express Travel Related Servs. Co. v. Assih, 893 N.Y.S.2d 438 (N.Y. Civ. Ct. 2009).

If American Express is an assumed name, the company must comply with any applicable state law requiring corporations to file a certificate of doing business under an assumed name.[167]

An appellate court has also overturned a judgment when there was not sufficient proof that Citibank (South Dakota) owned two different accounts involving the consumer.[168] The first account was a Choice Visa account that Citibank claimed was now and always owned by Citibank, but Citibank offered no evidence of that fact. The second account originated as a Sears MasterCard account. Although Citibank claimed Citibank USA had purchased the assets of Sears National Bank, the court found insufficient as evidence of the purchase an Office of the Comptroller of the Currency (OCC) letter giving Citibank permission, with certain conditions, to purchase Sears National Bank. Permission to make a purchase does not prove that a purchase was made. Moreover, this would only show that Citibank USA, and not Citibank (South Dakota), made the purchase. Another OCC letter giving Citibank permission to move its credit card operations from Citibank USA to Citibank (South Dakota) was not evidence that the transfer was actually made.[169]

Even when a credit card issuer brings a collection action in its own exact name, questions can still arise as to whether the obligation was sold to a securitization trust and what that implies for the card issuer still remaining the real party in interest. That topic is briefly discussed in § 4.3.2.2, *infra*.

4.3.2.2 Securitization of Credit Card Obligations

It is common for a credit card issuer to securitize its credit card receivables—for example apparently all Citibank credit card accounts are securitized. There are a number of complex ways in which this is accomplished. To further complicate matters, a credit card securitization is different in many ways than a mortgage loan securitization. To oversimplify, a card issuer will sell the right to receivables from a portfolio of credit card accounts. After changing hands a number of times, ownership of those receivables will reside in a trust that can issue securities in the assets held by the trust.

The card issuer continues to "own" the account less the right to the receivables and thus remains the party with the contractual relationship with the cardholder and the card issuer services the account.[170] Thus, the card issuer can change interest rates and amend the contract, and it also receives payments and collects from the consumer when there is a delinquency. The trust owns the receivables on the card accounts—the right to payment. Since the amount owed and paid on a credit card account changes every month, the receivables held by the trust are constantly fluctuating.

The rights of the card issuer and the trust typically are spelled out in a pooling and servicing agreement (PSA). The PSA may provide that upon the occurrence of a default as defined in that agreement, the receivable is either automatically transferred back to the card issuer or the trust has the right to transfer the receivable back at its election. The PSA may also delegate to the card issuer, on behalf of the trust, the right to bring a lawsuit in its own name to collect delinquent accounts.

This means that, when a card issuer is collecting on a debt in its own name, any one of a number of different scenarios could be at play. The card issuer may have never securitized the loan, and there will be little question as to its right to bring a collection action in its own name. Alternatively, the card issuer may be suing in its own name as a servicer for the trust.[171] The trust's trustee is the real party in interest, and the servicer's right to bring the action in its own name will be determined by state law.[172] Or the trust has sold the receivables back to the card issuer, and the card issuer is bringing the action as a debt buyer.

When the creditor is acting as a servicer for the securitization trust, and when it is faced with a challenge to such a servicer's right to bring the action, the servicer will have to identify the owner of the receivables (the trust) and produce evidence that it has been delegated the right to bring the action on behalf of the trust (usually the evidence will be found in the PSA). Without this evidence, the servicer has no right to proceed. Even with this evidence, some states place additional restrictions on a servicer's right to do so. For example, Pennsylvania rules of procedure require that a plaintiff acting in a fiduciary or representative capacity disclose the capacity in the caption and in the plaintiff's initial pleading.[173]

Alternatively, the card issuer may be suing as a debt buyer after the rights to the receivables on the account have been transferred back to the card issuer from the trust. Then, for the card issuer to bring an action, it will have to prove that assignment from the trust back to the card issuer.[174]

When the PSA provides that the transfer back to the card issuer is automatic on the occurrence of certain events, it is unclear whether proof of this provision in the PSA will be enough or whether the card issuer must also produce a written transfer back to the card issuer.[175] If the PSA alone is deemed sufficient, then the card issuer will have to show that the events specified in the PSA as triggering the transfer have occurred.

Another scenario arises when the card issuer claims that it can bring the action, not as the servicer or the owner of the right to receivables, but based upon its remaining interest in the account after the right to receivables have been transferred to the trust. While at least one court has apparently accepted

167 Miller v. Wolpoff & Abramson, L.L.P., 2007 WL 2694607 (N.D. Ind. Sept. 7, 2007), *aff'd*, 309 Fed. Appx. 40 (7th Cir. 2009).
168 Citibank v. Rowe, 2013 WL 601600 (Ohio Ct. App. Feb. 19, 2013).
169 *Id.*
170 *See* Tostado v. Citibank, 2010 WL 55976 (W.D. Tex. Jan. 4, 2010).
171 *See* Capps v. FIA Card Servs., 240 P.3d 583 (Idaho 2010).
172 *See* National Consumer Law Center, Foreclosures § 4.5 (4th ed. 2012), *updated at* www.nclc.org/library.
173 Pa. Rules Civ. Proc. 2002(b).
174 *See* § 4.3.4, *infra*.
175 *Cf.* Citibank v. Carroll, 220 P.3d 1073 (Idaho 2009) (originating card issuer has standing to sue, although court did not consider whether there must be a separate document evidencing the assignment back to the creditor).

this basis to bring an action,[176] this is open to question since two different entities cannot both have the right to the same receivable—the consumer should not have to pay the amount owed twice.

In an odd twist, if there is no proof of a valid transfer of receivables from the card issuer to the trust, then the court may treat the case as properly brought by the card issuer because there is no proof that the issuer ever relinquished the right to payment. Thus, in order to dispute a card issuer's right to bring suit, the consumer might first prove that the right to receivables has been sold to a trust. This can be most effectively done by sending the card issuer a request to admit this fact. If the consumer introduces the PSA instead, the consumer will have then introduced the very evidence that the card issuer can use to help show its right to bring the action.[177]

The exact structure of a particular securitization can be both complex and unique, and there is little case law as to the right of a card issuer to bring a collection action after an account has been involved in a securitization. Suffice it to say that it may be difficult to unravel the rights of the parties and consumer attorneys may soon feel out of their depth. On the other hand, the collection attorney may not want to devote the resources to investigating and explaining to the court how the securitization works in the case of an individual consumer and why the card issuer has the right to pursue the case in its own name. It may be that a collection attorney facing consumer discovery or legal challenges concerning the securitization will opt to dismiss the case.

4.3.3 Collection Agency's Ability to Bring Action in Own Name on Behalf of Another

It is important to distinguish between a case brought by a debt buyer to collect a debt it claims to own and that brought by a debt collection agency suing on behalf of another, such as the originating creditor. In that latter case, the debt collection agency does not own the debt and will turn over at least a portion of what it collects on the debt to the account's owner.

Whether the action is brought on behalf of another or by a debt buyer in its own right, there must be a written assignment to the plaintiff giving it the right to sue on the debt. When challenged, the collector must produce such a written assignment. An affidavit stating there is such an assignment is not sufficient.[178] And of course there must be proof that the entity that is assigning those rights has the right to pursue the collection action.[179]

When a collection agency is suing not on behalf of itself but of another, additional requirements may apply. When an entity is in the business of collecting debts for another, there can be little question that the entity is covered by the state debt collection statute.[180] In turn, the state debt collection statute may place various limits on a debt collector who is suing on the debt. It may prohibit outright the collection agency from bringing legal actions to collect on the debt of another.[181] It may prohibit an unlicensed collection agency from bringing suit.[182] In other states, the debt collector will have to disclose in the pleadings on whose behalf it is suing. For example, Pennsylvania rules of procedure require that a plaintiff acting in a fiduciary or representative capacity disclose the capacity in the caption and in the plaintiff's initial pleading.[183]

Typically, the collector's authority to sue on behalf of another is based upon a written assignment, and state debt collection statutes may specify the nature of that assignment from the debt owner to the collection agency. In Ohio, for example, there must be a writing authorizing the collection agency to refer the matter to an attorney, the writing must specify the consideration to be received by the collection agency, the matter can only be brought in the county where the consumer resides, and the matter must be brought by an attorney admitted to practice in the state.[184] Illinois requires that the assignment to the debt collector be manifested in a written agreement, stating among other items the effective date of the assignment and the consideration for the assignment.[185] Delaware Justice of the Peace Directive 14 requires a collection agency to obtain a power of attorney from the creditor to bring suit on behalf of the creditor.[186] Florida has a requirement that the consumer be notified within thirty days of when a debt is assigned to another,[187] and this would seem to apply to an assignment for collection purposes only.

Because these requirements may apply only to a debt collector suing on behalf of another, and not to a debt buyer, it is important to carefully read the assignment document to determine the exact relationship between assignor and assignee—is the assignment transferring ownership or only the right to sue on the debt for another? The need to review the assignment document is another reason why the collector must produce the actual assignment and not an affidavit stating that the debt

176 *See* Tostado v. Citibank, 2010 WL 55976 (W.D. Tex. Jan. 4, 2010).

177 *See* Capps v. FIA Card Servs., 240 P.3d 583 (Idaho 2010).

178 Unifund CCR Partners v. Shah, 946 N.E.2d 885 (Ill. App. Ct. 2011).

179 *See* § 4.3.4, *infra*.

180 *See* National Consumer Law Center, Fair Debt Collection Appx. D (8th ed. 2014), *updated at* www.nclc.org/library (listing of state debt collection statutes).

181 *See, e.g.*, Conn. Gen. Stat. § 36a805(1). *See also* National Consumer Law Center, Fair Debt Collection § 10.5.2 (8th ed. 2011). *But see* Unifund CCR Partners v. Shah, 946 N.E.2d 885 (Ill. App. Ct. 2011) (assignee for collection only has authority to bring suit in its own name).

182 *See* 225 Ill. Comp. Stat. § 425/8(b). *See also* § 3.3.4, *supra*.

183 Pa. Rules Civ. Proc. 2002(b).

184 Ohio Rev. Code Ann. § 1319.12 (West); Recovery Mgmt. Sys., Ltd. v. Coburn, 2008 WL 4801641 (Ohio Ct. App. Nov. 4, 2008).

185 810 Ill. Comp. Stat. § 425/8b. *See also* Unifund CCR Partners v. Shah, 993 N.E.2d 518 (Ill. App. Ct. 2013) (discussing the requirements when there are multiple assignments for collection that follow multiple sales of the account to debt buyers); Mutual Mgmt. Serv., Inc. v. Swalve, 956 N.E.2d 594 (Ill. App. Ct. 2011) (assignment improper when disclosed date of assignment was many months before the date the assignment document was signed).

186 Hsu v. Great Seneca Fin. Corp., 2010 WL 2635771 (Del. Super. Ct. June 29, 2010), *aff'd*, 9 A.3d 476 (Del. 2010).

187 Fla. Stat. § 559.715 (notice of assignment within thirty days).

has been assigned, particularly when that affidavit is vague as to whether the assignment is for collection purposes only. An internet search or contacting the state debt collection licensing agency can also provide some rough indication of whether the collector is primarily in the business of purchasing debts or collecting debts on behalf of creditors.

4.3.4 Debt Buyer's Proof of Ownership of the Debt

4.3.4.1 Ownership Is a Precondition to a Collection Suit

A debt buyer's business model is to purchase debt for pennies on the dollar and then seek payments with a minimal investment of effort. The debt buyer is unlikely to put much effort into establishing proper documentation of an assignment when it is suing the consumer on one relatively small debt and, if challenged by the consumer, will often have difficulty meeting its burden of proving that it owns the debt.

A debt buyer seeking to sue on a debt it alleges it owns has the burden of proof that it does own the consumer's obligation.[188] The consumer's partial payment on the debt buyer does not waive the consumer's right to challenge the debt buyer's ownership.[189]

Some states have a rule requiring the defendant to specifically request that the plaintiff prove that it has the capacity to sue before the plaintiff must meet its burden of proof, but "capacity to sue" is very different than ownership of the debt allowing standing to sue. The burden of proving standing is on the plaintiff, and the defendant need not make a specific request that the plaintiff prove standing.[190]

A consumer defendant should always put the debt buyer to its proof that it owns the debt—debt buyers often cannot meet this burden. The consumer should not have to pay a debt to one party, only to find out later that another party is the true owner and that the consumer must now pay the same debt again to this second party.[191]

Debt buyers purchase large portfolios of accounts from creditors and then subdivide the portfolios into smaller segments and sell off those segments to different debt buyers. The same segment of a portfolio may be sold to multiple buyers, or the seller may not actually own a portfolio put up for sale.[192]

For example, debt buyers may purchase accounts with the debt buyer's payment to the assignor due in the future, and the assignor may take back the account if the debt buyer fails to make payments when due. But there is little to prevent the defaulting debt buyer from selling the accounts to another debt buyer, even though the original assignor takes back the same accounts.[193] The sale to a debt buyer may be evidenced by no more than a computer tape that can be easily duplicated and sold to additional buyers without the authority to do so.

The difficulty of the collector's proof that it owns the debt, and the risk that more than one debt buyer will seek payment from the consumer on the same debt, both increase as the debt is transferred from debt buyer to debt buyer. In one case, the successor company to Providian assigned a debt to Vision Management Services, which then assigned it three days later to Great Seneca Financial Corporation, which a month later assigned it to Account Management Services. Four months later, Account Management Services (which shortly thereafter changed its name) assigned the account to Madison Street Investments, which then assigned the account five months later to Jackson Capital, which on that same day assigned the account to Centurion Capital. Three weeks later Centurion hired Wolpoff and Abramson as their attorneys to collect on the debt. After the transfer to Jackson Capital, but before the transfer to Centurion Capital, the consumer was sued on the account by Melville Acquisitions Group (which appears nowhere in the above chain of ownership).[194]

188 Platinum Funding Serv., L.L.C. v. Petco Insulation Co., 2011 WL 1743417 (D. Conn. May 2, 2011); Great Seneca Fin. Corp. v. LeAnna, 2006 WL 2536275 (Conn. Super. Ct. Aug. 15, 2006); LVNV Funding, L.L.C. v. Shecter (Fla. Palm Beach Cnty. Ct. June 5, 2009), *available at* www.nclc.org/unreported; Midland Funding, L.L.C. v. Shines (Ga. Super. Ct. Oct. 18, 2012), *available at* www.nclc.org/unreported; Pasadena Receivables, Inc. v. Parker (Md. Cir. Ct. Oct. 13, 2011), *available at* www.nclc.org/unreported; Ray Klein, Inc. v. Kerr, 272 S.W.3d 896 (Mo. Ct. App. 2008); Midwestern Health Mgmt., Inc. v. Walker, 208 S.W.3d 295 (Mo. Ct. App. 2006); Midwestern Health Mgmt., Inc. v. Walker, 208 S.W.3d 295 (Mo. Ct. App. 2006); C & W Asset Acquisition, L.L.C. v. Somogyi, 136 S.W.3d 134 (Mo. Ct. App. 2004); New Century Fin. Serv. v. Sanchez (N.J. Super. Ct. Law Div. Apr. 12, 2002), *available at* www.nclc.org/unreported; Palisades Collection, L.L.C. v. Haque, 2006 N.Y. Misc. LEXIS 4036 (N.Y. Civ. Ct. Apr. 13, 2006); Palisades Collection, L.L.C. v. Gonzalez, 809 N.Y.S.2d 482 (table), 2005 WL 3372971 (N.Y. Civ. Ct. Dec. 12, 2005); Citibank v. Martin, 807 N.Y.S.2d 284 (N.Y. Civ. Ct. 2005); Recovery Mgmt. Sys., Ltd. v. Bethea, 2009 WL 321282 (Ohio Ct. App. Feb. 9, 2009); Unifund CCR Partners v. Laco, 2009 WL 4879348 (Tex. App. Dec. 17, 2009); Unifund CCR v. Ayhan, 2008 WL 2974639 (Wash Ct. App. Aug. 5, 2008). *See also* Henggeler v. Brumbaugh & Quandahl, P.C., 894 F. Supp. 2d 1180 (D. Neb. 2012); LVNV Funding, L.L.C. v. Mastaw (Tenn. Ct. App. Apr. 30, 2012), *available at* www.nclc.org/unreported.

189 Cach, L.L.C. v. Askew, 358 S.W.3d 58 (Mo. 2012).

190 Pasadena Receivables, Inc. v. Parker (Md. Cir. Ct. Oct. 13, 2011), *available at* www.nclc.org/unreported.

191 *See* Miller v. Wolpoff & Abramson, L.L.P., 2007 WL 2694607 (N.D. Ind. Sept. 7, 2007), *aff'd*, 309 Fed. Appx. 40 (7th Cir. 2009).

192 *See* United States v. Goldberg (S.D. Fla. Mar. 5, 2009), *available at* www.nclc.org/unreported (debt buyer obtained accounts without paying for them and then resold them, even though original seller had voided sale because of nonpayment); Wood v. M & J Recovery, L.L.C., 2007 U.S. Dist. LEXIS 24157 (E.D.N.Y. Apr. 2, 2007) (at least three different entities claim ownership of a consumer debt). *See also* Miller v. Wolpoff & Abramson, L.L.P., 2008 U.S. Dist. LEXIS 12283 (N.D. Ind. Feb. 19, 2008) (consumer obligated on debt even though another debt buyer is suing consumer on same debt), *aff'd*, 309 Fed. Appx. 40 (7th Cir. 2009).

193 *See* United States v. Goldberg (S.D. Fla. Mar. 5, 2009), *available at* www.nclc.org/unreported; Wood v. M & J Recovery, L.L.C., 2007 U.S. Dist. LEXIS 24157 (E.D.N.Y. Apr. 2, 2007).

194 *See* Miller v. Wolpoff & Abramson, L.L.P., 2007 WL 2694607 (N.D. Ind. Sept. 7, 2007), *aff'd*, 309 Fed. Appx. 40 (7th Cir. 2009).

4.3.4.2 Adequate Proof of Transfer of Ownership to a Debt Buyer

4.3.4.2.1 Collector must produce the actual document assigning ownership

A debt buyer must prove that it has been assigned an account through tender of proper documentation specifically relating to the particular account at issue.[195] It is insufficient to introduce a notice from the assignor to the consumer that it is assigning the debt to the assignee.[196] The actual assignment document should be introduced into evidence.[197]

A memorandum or other statement from the debt buyer stating that it has received assignment of the account at issue is insufficient.[198] Mere affirmation of the assignment in an affidavit is also insufficient; the debt buyer must submit actual contracts of assignment identifying the accounts at issue.[199] This is the case even if the creditor provides the affidavit that the account has been assigned to the plaintiff. In any event, such an affidavit as to the assignment prepared in anticipation of litigation is not a business record.[200]

In the typical debt buyer case, the actual assignment of ownership will be accomplished by the creation of three separate documents. First is a signed "forward flow" agreement, that is a lengthy document that will set out the terms of sale of debt in general between the creditor and debt buyer. When a particular portfolio of debt (typically thousands of accounts) are sold between those parties, the parties execute a bill or sale or other short assignment document. That document will reference the portfolio and the forward flow agreement for the terms of the sale. That short assignment document will be accompanied by a "sale data file" or "final data file" which is an electronic spreadsheet that lists the specific consumer accounts being transferred, which will typically be numbered in the thousands.

4.3.4.2.2 Assignment document must reference the account at issue

Debt buyers usually can produce a quite detailed contract or bill of sale delineating the relationship between the debt buyer's assignor and the debt buyer, but the document will make reference only generally to thousands of accounts being purchased at the same time and will not identify the consumer's account. Such evidence is not enough. An assignment document must indicate that one of the thousands of accounts the collector has purchased is the account at issue in the lawsuit. The debt buyer's documentation of an assignment must reference the specific account at issue.[201]

---

195 New Century Fin. Serv. v. Sanchez (N.J. Super. Ct. Law Div. Apr. 12, 2002), *available at* www.nclc.org/unreported; Citibank v. Martin, 11 Misc. 3d 219 (N.Y. Civ. Ct. 2005); Palisades Collections, L.L.C. v. Gonzalez, 809 N.Y.S.2d 482 (table), 2005 WL 3372971 (N.Y. Civ. Ct. Dec. 12, 2005); Zwick & Zwick v. Suburban Constr. Co., 134 N.E.2d 733 (Ohio Ct. App. 1956); Asset Acceptance, L.L.C. v. Jones (Pa. Ct. Com. Pl. June 10, 2011), *available at* www.nclc.org/unreported; Unifund CCR Assignee of Providian v. Ayhan, 2008 WL 2974639 (Wash. Ct. App. Aug. 5, 2008). *See also* LVNV Funding, L.L.C. v. Delgado, 899 N.Y.S.2d 60 (table), 2009 WL 2370987 (N.Y. Dist. Ct. Aug. 3, 2009); Unifund CCR Partners v. Hawthorne, 2009 WL 4879017 (Tex. App. Dec. 17, 2009); Unifund CCR Partners v. Perkins, 2009 WL 4202635 (Tex. App. Nov. 25, 2009).

196 Wright v. Asset Acceptance Corp., 2000 WL 33216031 (S.D. Ohio Jan. 3, 2000).

197 Cach, L.L.C. v. Kulas, 21 A.3d 1015 (Me. 2011). *See also* FIA Card Servs. v. Saintonge, 2013 WL 3441560 (Me. July 9, 2013).

198 *Id.*; New Century Fin. Serv. v. Sanchez (N.J. Super. Ct. Law Div. Apr. 12, 2002), *available at* www.nclc.org/unreported; Asset Acceptance, L.L.C. v. Jones (Pa. Ct. Com. Pl. June 10, 2011), *available at* www.nclc.org/unreported. *See also* Unifund CCR Partners v. Youngman, 932 N.Y.S.2d 609 (N.Y. Sup. Ct. 2011); LVNV Funding, L.L.C. v. Mastaw (Tenn. Ct. App. Apr. 30, 2012), *available at* www.nclc.org/unreported.

199 LVNV Funding, L.L.C. v. Shecter (Fla. Palm Beach Cnty. Ct. June 8, 2009), *available at* www.nclc.org/unreported; Palisades Collection, L.L.C. v. Thomas (Fla. Broward Cnty. Ct. Apr. 15, 2009), *available at* www.nclc.org/unreported; Powers v. Hudson & Keyse, L.L.C., 656 S.E.2d 578 (Ga. Ct. App. 2008); Unifund CCR Partners v. Shah, 946 N.E.2d 885 (Ill. App. Ct. 2011); FIA Card Servs. v. Saintonge, 2013 WL 3441560 (Me. July 9, 2013); Cach, L.L.C. v. Kulas, 21 A.3d 1015 (Me. 2011); Gemini Capital Group v. Tripp, 2013 WL 5872742 (Mo. Ct. App. Nov. 1, 2013); New Century Fin. Serv. v. Sanchez (N.J. Super. Ct. Law Div. Apr. 12, 2002), *available at* www.nclc.org/unreported;DNS Equity Group Inc. v. Lavallee, 907 N.Y.S.2d 436 (N.Y. Dist. Ct. Feb. 22, 2010); PRA III, L.L.C. v. MacDowell, 841 N.Y.S.2d 822 (table), 2007 WL 1429026 (N.Y. Civ. Ct. Mar. 16, 2007); Palisades Collection, L.L.C. v. Gonzalez, 809 N.Y.S.2d 482 (table), 2005 WL 3372971 (N.Y. Civ. Ct. Dec. 12, 2005); Citibank v. Martin, 807 N.Y.S.2d 284 (N.Y. Civ. Ct. 2005); Unifund Partners v. Hemm, 2009 WL 2106289 (Ohio Ct. App. July 17, 2001); Remit Corp. v. Potter (Pa. Ct. Com. Pl. June 2, 2008), *available at* www.nclc.org/unreported; Unifund CCR Assignee of Providian v. Ayhan, 2008 WL 2974639 (Wash. Ct. App. Aug. 5, 2008). *See also* Arrow Fin. Serv., L.L.C. v. Wright, 715 S.E.2d 725 (Ga. Ct. App. 2011); LVNV Funding, L.L.C. v. Mastaw, 2012 WL 1534785 (Tenn. Ct. App. Apr. 30, 2012), *available at* www.nclc.org/unreported.

200 *See* Ortega v. Cach, L.L.C., 396 S.W.3d 622 (Tex. App. 2013).

201 *In re* Kendall, 380 B.R. 37 (Bankr. N.D. Okla. 2007); Persolve v. Uribe (Cal. Super. Ct. Dec. 9, 2010), *available at* www.nclc.org/unreported; Cuda & Assocs., L.L.C. v. Lumpkin, 2011 Conn. Super. LEXIS 3025 (Conn. Super. Ct. Nov. 29, 2011); Velocity Invs. v. Bailey, 2007 WL 1828037 (Conn. Super. Ct. June 5, 2007); Cach, L.L.C. v. Taylor (Del. Ct. Com. Pl. Feb. 19, 2013), *available at* www.nclc.org/unreported; Nyankojo v. North Star Capital Acquisition, 679 S.E.2d 57 (Ga. Ct. App. 2009); Unifund CCR Partners v. Shah, 993 N.E.2d 518 (Ill. App. Ct. 2013); Arrow Fin. Serv., L.L.C. v. Guiliani, 32 A.3d 1055 (Me. 2011); Unifund CCR Partners v. Riley, 2010 WL 571829 (Mich. Ct. App. Feb. 18, 2010); Palisades Collection, L.L.C. v. Olosunde, 2008 WL 5233566 (N.J. Super. Ct. App. Div. Dec. 17, 2008); Midland Funding, L.L.C. v. Loreto, 950 N.Y.S.2d 492, 34 Misc. 3d 1232(A) (N.Y. Civ. Ct. 2012); CACH, L.L.C. v. Fatima, 936 N.Y.S.2d 58 (N.Y. Dist. Ct. 2011); Palisades Collection, L.L.C. v. Haque, 2006 N.Y. Misc. LEXIS 4036 (N.Y. Civ. Ct. Apr. 13, 2006); Midland Funding, L.L.C. v. Biehl, 2013 WL 5407593 (Ohio Ct. App Sept. 23, 2013); Liberty Credit Servs. v. Yonker, 2013 WL 5221219 (Ohio Ct. App. Sept. 16, 2013); Arrow Fin. Servs., L.L.C. v. Witmer (Pa. Ct. Com. Pl. May 13, 2010), *available at* www.nclc.org/unreported; Unifund CCR Partners v. Vo (Pa. Ct. Com. Pl. Feb. 17, 2009), *available at* www.nclc.org/unreported; Palisades Collection, L.L.C v. Grassmyer (Pa. Ct. Com. Pl. Jan. 15, 2008), *available at* www.nclc.org/unreported; Unifund CCR Assignee of Providian v. Ayhan, 2008 WL 2974639 (Wash. Ct. App. Aug. 5, 2008). *See also* LVNV Funding, L.L.C. v. Guest, 953 N.Y.S.2d 550 (table), 2012 WL 1957715 (N.Y. City Ct. May 29, 2012); Premier Capital, L.L.C. v. Baker, 972 N.E.2d 1125 (Ohio Ct. App. 2012); Portfolio Recovery Assoc., L.L.C. v. Strifler (Vt. Super. Ct. Sept. 2,

Debt buyers may seek to rectify this failing by saying that they are attaching the actual computer tape or spreadsheet listing all the assigned accounts, including the consumer's account. Nevertheless, in a surprising number of cases, the debt buyer will not attach the computer tape or offer any evidence that the particular consumer's account being sued on is on that computer tape. This lack of an attachment means that the evidence is not sufficient to prove assignment of a particular account.[202]

In one case the debt buyer introduced a bill of sale that referenced an electronic file listing a large number of accounts assigned pursuant to that bill of sale and also introduced a "screen capture" of an electronic file that showed the consumer's information. But this was found insufficient when the debt buyer neither introduced the complete file of all the accounts assigned nor provided evidence that the screen capture that showed the consumer's information was derived from the electronic file referenced in the bill of sale as listing the assigned accounts.[203]

Other times, an affidavit or documentation will refer to a schedule or appendix that allegedly will identify the account but no schedule or appendix will be attached.[204] Similarly, an affidavit cannot refer to an appendix that lists accounts (in the plural), but then only attach the consumer's account number and not other accounts, or even indicate that the consumer's information is part of that list of multiple accounts.[205] Even when an attachment includes the name of the consumer, the attachment has to be more than the consumer's name and a series of numerical codes, none of which matches the account number.[206]

When a specific account number is mentioned in the assignment documents, it should not conflict with the consumer's account number with the originating creditor. Unless the debt buyer can provide competent evidence explaining how the two account numbers relate to the same account, the assignment document is defective.[207]

4.3.4.2.3 Other defects in the assignment document

Carefully review all documents of assignment, because they are often incomplete or illegible. In one case the court found an assignment to be improper when the debt buyer submitted only four pages of a twenty-plus page loan sale agreement.[208] The court observed: "The first page, entitled "Loan Sale Agreement" merely identifies the parties and states the effective date of the transaction. The second page contains a pair of signatures, third page contains a redacted table of four accounts. These three pages do not appear to have any relationship to one another given that they were respectively numbered "i," "7," and "19 of 28."[209] Similarly, the bill of sale can reference a sales agreement (sometimes called a forward flow agreement) but the sales agreement is not attached.[210]

2011), *available at* www.nclc.org/unreported. *But see* New Century Fin. Servs., Inc. v. Oughla, 2014 WL 839180 (N.J. Super. Ct. App. Div. Mar. 5, 2014); Wood v. Pharia, L.L.C., 2010 WL 5060621 (Tex. App. Dec. 9, 2010) (even though no evidence that consumer's account was in the list of assigned accounts from card issuer, subsequent evidence was sufficient to establish proper transfer of the account).

202 Wright v. Asset Acceptance Corp., 2000 WL 33216031 (S.D. Ohio Jan. 3, 2000); Bullock v. Worldwide Asset Purchasing, L.L.C., 2008 WL 3159921 (Ky. Ct. App. Sept. 5, 2008); New Century Fin. Serv. v. Sanchez (N.J. Super. Law Div. Apr. 15, 2009), *available at* www.nclc.org/unreported; Nat'l Check Bureau, Inc. v. Cody, 2005 WL 174762 (Ohio Ct. App. Jan. 27, 2005) (dissent); Palisades Collection, L.L.C. v. Grassmyer (Pa. Ct. Com. Pl. Jan. 15, 2008), *available at* www.nclc.org/unreported. *But see* Mitchell v. Am. Acceptance Co., L.L.C., 968 N.E.2d 868 (Ind. Ct. App. 2012) (unpublished) (evidence sufficient when consumer did not present contrary evidence); Nat'l Check Bureau, Inc. v. Cody, 2005 WL 174762 (Ohio Ct. App. Jan. 27, 2005).

203 Portfolio Recovery Assocs. v. Gilbert (Pa. Ct. Com. Pl. Sept. 10, 2013), *available at* www.nclc.org/unreported.

204 Henggeler v. Brumbaugh & Quandahl, P.C., 894 F. Supp. 2d 1180 (D. Neb. 2012); Gigli v. Palisades Collection, L.L.C., 2008 WL 3853295 (M.D. Pa. Aug. 14, 2008); Velocity Invs. v. Bailey, 2007 WL 1828037 (Conn. Super. Ct. June 5, 2007); Hutto v. CACV of Colo., L.L.C., 707 S.E.2d 872 (Ga. Ct. App. 2011); Wirth v. Cach, L.L.C., 685 S.E.2d 433 (Ga. Ct. App. 2009); Powers v. Hudon & Keyse, L.L.C., 656 S.E.2d 578 (Ga. Ct. App. 2008); Unifund CCT Partners v. Shah, 946 N.E.2d 885 (Ill. App. Ct. 2011); Bullock v. Worldwide Asset Purchasing, L.L.C., 2008 WL 3159921 (Ky. Ct. App. Sept. 5, 2008); Arrow Fin. Serv., L.L.C. v. Guiliani, 32 A.3d 1055 (Me. 2011); Norfolk Fin. Corp. v. Mazard, 2009 WL 3844481 (Mass. Dist. Ct. App. Div. Nov. 12, 2009); Unifund CCR Partners v. Riley, 2010 WL 571829 (Mich. Ct. App. Feb. 18, 2010); Gemini Capital Group v. Tripp, 2013 WL 5872742 (Mo. Ct. App. Nov. 1, 2013); Colorado Capital Invs. Inc. v. Villar (N.Y. Civ. Ct. June 4, 2009), *available at* www.nclc.org/unreported (schedule does not include the consumer's account); Palisades Collection, L.L.C. v. Haque, 2006 N.Y. Misc. LEXIS 4036 (N.Y. Civ. Ct. Apr. 13, 2006); Midland Funding, L.L.C. v. Biehl, 2013 WL 5407593 (Ohio Ct. App Sept. 23, 2013; Unifund CCR Partners v. Hemm, 2009 WL 2106289 (Ohio Ct. App. July 17, 2009); Arrow Fin. Servs., L.L.C. v. Witmer (Pa. Ct. Com. Pl. May 13, 2010), *available at* www.nclc.org/unreported; Unifund CCR Partners v. Vo (Pa. Ct. Com. Pl. Feb. 17, 2009), *available at* www.nclc.org/unreported; Belmont Fin. Servs. Group, Inc. v. Hawkins (Pa. Ct. Com. Pl. July 24, 2008), *available at* www.nclc.org/unreported; Remit Corp. v. Potter (Pa. Ct. Com. Pl. June 2, 2008), *available at* www.nclc.org/unreported; Unifund CCR Partners v. Laco, 2009 WL 4879348 (Tex. App. Dec. 17, 2009); Unifund CCR Assignee of Providian v. Ayhan, 2008 WL 2974639 (Wash. Ct. App. Aug. 5, 2008). *See also* Ohlson v. The Cadle Co., 2008 US Dist. LEXIS 77328 (E.D.N.Y. Sept. 30, 2008). *But see* Jaramillo v. Portfolio Acquisitions, L.L.C., 2010 WL 1197669 (Tex. App. Mar. 30, 2010) (even though appendix was not attached, there was sufficient evidence when a spreadsheet identified the account at issue and an employee of the plaintiff-debt buyer testified at trial concerning the account). *But cf.* Eaves v. Unifund CCR Partners, 301 S.W.3d 402 (Tex. App. 2009) (exhibit not attached but sufficient other evidence proved account was assigned).

205 Unifund CCR Partners v. Shah, 993 N.E.2d 518 (Ill. App. Ct. 2013); Colo. Capital Invs. Inc. v. Villar (N.Y. Civ. Ct. June 4, 2009), *available at* www.nclc.org/unreported.

206 Premier Capital, L.L.C. v. Baker, 972 N.E.2d 1125 (Ohio Ct. App. 2012). *See also* Unifund CCR Partners v. Shah, 993 N.E.2d 518 (Ill. App. Ct. 2013).

207 *See* Cach, L.L.C. v. Trevisano (Mo. Cir. Ct. Mar. 18, 2010), *available at* www.nclc.org/unreported.

208 C & W Asset Acquisition, L.L.C. v. Somogyi, 136 S.W.3d 134, 140 (Mo. Ct. App. 2004).

209 *Id. See also* Henggeler v. Brumbaugh & Quandahl, P.C., 894 F. Supp. 2d 1180 (D. Neb. 2012).

210 Henggeler v. Brumbaugh & Quandahl, P.C., 894 F. Supp. 2d 1180 (D. Neb. 2012).

In another case, the debt buyer produced a series of exhibits that showed the defendant's name, address, and account number on a blackened-out photocopy that purported to evidence several transfers of the debt. The court found this evidence inadequate without a supporting affidavit.[211]

A bill of sale was also found to be defective when it purported to transfer ownership of a Bank of America account but identified the seller as FIA Card Services, and there was no evidence of the relationship of Bank of America to FIA Card Services.[212] Similarly, an appellate court refused to give credence to an assignment document that did not identify the assignee or the account being assigned.[213]

Also carefully review whether the documents that are proffered are consistent with each other. In one case, the bill of sale showed the assignee as Sherman Originator III, L.L.C., while the affidavit specified that the assignment was to Sherman Originator, L.L.C.—an entirely different entity.[214]

Attorneys report a surprising pattern when an assignment is dated *before* the loan goes into default. A request for admissions, deposition, or cross-examination can usually produce an admission that the debut buyer did not purchase the debt until after it was in default, thus placing in doubt the validity of the assignment. Debt buyers can also get into trouble by dating the listing of assigned accounts well after the bill of sale and after the date referenced by the bill of sale for the attachment.[215] In addition, the document assigning rights from the creditor to the debt buyer cannot be signed by a party related to the debt buyer but must be a representative of the creditor.[216]

4.3.4.2.4 Statutory requirements as to the assignment document

Some states have statutory requirements that apply to the assignment document. Florida law requires that an assignee must give a debtor written notice of the assignment within thirty days after the assignment.[217] If the collector cannot produce evidence of this notice, the case should be dismissed.[218]

Illinois has a statute providing that an assignee cannot institute suit unless there is an assignment showing the effective date of the assignment, the consideration of the assignment, and other information.[219] Illinois courts have found implicit in this requirement that the assignment identify the account being assigned.[220] And Illinois courts apply this requirement not only to debt collectors suing in their name for the creditor but also to debt buyers.[221] When any of the assignments in a chain of title are missing any of this information, the debt buyer presently holding the account does not have standing to sue.[222]

4.3.4.2.5 Affidavit authenticating document assigning ownership

The assignment document is a business record that needs authentication through a proper affidavit.[223] If the debt buyer's employee is the affiant attesting to a document assigning the debt to that collector, the affidavit must meet all the requirements necessary to satisfy the business records exception to the hearsay rule.[224] Most courts find that an employee of the debt buyer cannot authenticate the records of the debt buyer's assignor that created the assignment.[225] In any event, the business records cannot be authenticated when the debt buyer's employee fails to demonstrate sufficient knowledge of the assignment documents to that debt buyer.[226] There can be little question that an employee of a third debt buyer in a chain of transfers cannot authenticate a document memorializing the assignment from the first to the second debt buyer in a chain of transfers.[227] The collector's employee has no knowledge of the nature of the assignment or of the business records of those entities.

211 Great Seneca Fin. Corp. v. LeAnna, 2006 WL 2536275 (Conn. Super. Ct. Aug. 15, 2006). *See also* Great Seneca Fin. v. Felty, 869 N.E.2d 30 (Ohio Ct. App. 2006).

212 Cach, L.L.C. v. Fatima, 936 N.Y.S.2d 58 (N.Y. Dist. Ct. Aug. 3, 2011).

213 Nyankojo v. North Star Capital Acquisition, 679 S.E.2d 57 (Ga. Ct. App. 2009).

214 LVNV Funding, L.L.C. v. Guest, 953 N.Y.S.2d 550 (table), 2012 WL 1957715 (N.Y. City Ct. May 29, 2012).

215 Cach, L.L.C. v. Taylor (Del. Ct. Com. Pl. Feb. 19, 2013), *available at* www.nclc.org/unreported.

216 Brown Bark, II, L.P. v. Bay Area Floorcovering & Design, Inc., 2011 WL 2140368 (Mich. Ct. App. May 31, 2011).

217 Fla. Stat. § 559.715.

218 LVNV Funding, L.L.C. v. Harris (Fla. Miami-Dade Cnty. Ct. June 24, 2009), *available at* www.nclc.org/unreported.

219 225 Ill. Comp. Stat. § 425/8(b).

220 Unifund CCR Partners v. Shah, 946 N.E.2d 885 (Ill. App. Ct. 2011). *See also* Cavalry Portfolio Serv. v. Rocha, 979 N.E.2d 930 (Ill. App. Ct. 2012).

221 Cavalry Portfolio Serv. v. Rocha, 979 N.E.2d 930 (Ill. App. Ct. 2012).

222 *Id.*

223 *See* § 4.2.4.2, *supra*. *See also* Hutto v. CACV of Colo., L.L.C., 707 S.E.2d 872 (Ga. Ct. App. 2011); Gemini Capital Group v. Tripp, 2013 WL 5872742 (Mo. Ct. App. Nov. 1, 2013); Midland Funding, L.L.C. v. Berry (N.J. Super. Ct. July 25, 2013), *available at* www.nclc.org/unreported; Midland Funding, L.L.C. v. Loreto, 950 N.Y.S.2d 492, 34 Misc. 3d 1232(A) (N.Y. Civ. Ct. 2012); Premier Capital, L.L.C. v. Baker, 972 N.E.2d 1125 (Ohio Ct. App. 2012).

224 *See id. See also* Gemini Capital Group v. Tripp, 2013 WL 5872742 (Mo. Ct. App. Nov. 1, 2013); Premier Capital, L.L.C. v. Baker, 972 N.E.2d 1125 (Ohio Ct. App. 2012).

225 *See* § 4.2.4.3.1, *supra*. *See also* Webb v. Midland Credit Mgmt., Inc., 2012 WL 2022013 (N.D. Ill. May 31, 2012).

226 *See* Midland Funding, L.L.C. v. Berry (N.J. Super. Ct. July 25, 2013), *available at* www.nclc.org/unreported.

227 Webb v. Midland Credit Mgmt., Inc., 2012 WL 2022013 (N.D. Ill. May 31, 2012); Wright v. Asset Acceptance Corp., 2000 WL 33216031 (S.D. Ohio Jan. 3, 2000); Norfolk Fin. Corp. v. Mazard, 2009 WL 3844481 (Mass. Dist. Ct. Nov. 12, 2009); Cach, L.L.C. v. Askew, 358 S.W.3d 58 (Mo. 2012); Midland Funding, L.L.C. v. Berry (N.J. Super. Ct. July 25, 2013), *available at* www.nclc.org/unreported; Colorado Capital Invs., Inc. v. Villar (N.Y. Civ. Ct. June 4, 2009), *available at* www.nclc.org/unreported; Rushmore Recoveries X, L.L.C. v. Skolnick, 841 N.Y.S.2d 823 (N.Y. Dist. Ct. 2007); Unifund CCR Assignee of Providian v. Ayhan, 2008 WL 297439 (Wash. Ct. App. Aug. 5, 2008). *See* § 4.2.4.2, *supra*. *See also* Gigli v. Palisades Collection, L.L.C., 2008 WL 3853295 (M.D. Pa. Aug. 14, 2008); Persolve v. Uribe (Cal. Super. Ct. Dec. 9, 2010), *available at* www.nclc.org/unreported. *But see* Monroe v. Unifund CCR Partners, 2010 WL 1948332 (Tex. App. May 13, 2010) (court could believe collector's testimony on prior assignment, particularly when consumer did not offer contrary evidence).

In one case, the debt buyer submitted an affidavit from its agent with a printed copy of several pages from an electronic spreadsheet listing the consumer's account as one of the accounts sold to the debt buyer. The appellate court found this insufficient when the affidavit was not a proper foundation for the spreadsheet as a business record.[228] The agent did not establish that he was familiar with the debt buyer's business practices and procedures or when, how, or by whom the electronic spreadsheet submitted in paper form was made.[229] Furthermore, the agent failed to establish that the printed spreadsheet was a true and accurate representation of the electronic record.[230]

Even an affidavit from the assignor may not be sufficient. A court has found an affidavit to be inadequate because it did not indicate the date of the assignment, it was made on information and belief, and the assignment was not attached or even described.[231] The affidavit of the assignment cannot be prepared well after the assignment and just before litigation.[232] Nor can the assignee produce an affidavit that is dated well prior to the assignment.[233]

4.3.4.3 Debt Buyer Must Prove a Complete Chain of Ownership

4.3.4.3.1 General

A debt buyer cannot merely show that it received an assignment of the obligation from its immediate assignor (unless the assignor was the original creditor).[234] The debt buyer also must show a continuous, unbroken chain of assignments from the original creditor to the entity collecting on the debt.[235]

It is no excuse that the prior entities in the chain do not make their assignment documents available.[236] There must be proof that the plaintiff in fact owns the debt. It is not enough to list each entity in the chain of title—there must be adequate proof as to each assignment.[237]

An earlier debt buyer can assign to the current debt buyer only the rights it itself acquired from its assignor.[238] If an assignor is not proven to own the debt, then its assignment to another has no value. In fact, the language of the typical bill of sale assigning rights will specify that the assignor is assigning only those rights that it has in the account. Such language does not prove that it has rights in the account and instead states that it is only assigning rights it has.

4.3.4.3.2 Assignor in one link must have exact same name as assignee in prior link

At each link in the chain of ownership, the entity that has been assigned a debt must be identical to the entity that subsequently assigns it to the next buyer in the chain. For example, there is a break in the chain when evidence is offered of a transfer from Discover Bank to Vision Nevada, Inc. followed by a transfer from Vision Management Services to the current debt buyer.[239] The current debt buyer must provide evidence

228 Palisades Collection, L.L.C. v. Kedik, 890 N.Y.S.2d 230 (N.Y. App. Div. 2009). *See also* LVNV Funding, L.L.C. v. Guest, 953 N.Y.S.2d 550 (table), 2012 WL 1957715 (N.Y. City Ct. May 29, 2012); CACH, L.L.C. v. Fatima, 936 N.Y.S.2d 58 (N.Y. Dist. Ct. Aug. 3, 2011) (no proper foundation for excerpts from electronic spreadsheet allegedly referring to consumer's account).

229 Palisades Collection, L.L.C. v. Kedik, 890 N.Y.S.2d 230 (N.Y. App. Div. 2009); LVNV Funding, L.L.C. v. Guest, 953 N.Y.S.2d 550 (table), 2012 WL 1957715 (N.Y. City Ct. May 29, 2012).

230 Palisades Collection, L.L.C. v. Kedik, 890 N.Y.S.2d 230 (N.Y. App. Div. 2009); LVNV Funding, L.L.C. v. Guest, 953 N.Y.S.2d 550 (table), 2012 WL 1957715 (N.Y. City Ct. May 29, 2012).

231 DNS Equity Group Inc. v. Lavallee, 907 N.Y.S.2d 436 (table), 2010 WL 682466 (N.Y. Dist. Ct. 2010).

232 *Id. See also* Recovery Mgmt. Sys. Ltd. v. Coburn, 2008 WL 4801641 (Ohio Ct. App. Nov. 4, 2008); Unifund CCR Assignee of Providian v. Ayhan, 2008 WL 2974639 (Wash. Ct. App. Aug. 5, 2008).

233 DNS Equity Group Inc. v. Lavallee, 907 N.Y.S.2d 436 (table), 2010 WL 682466 (N.Y. Dist. Ct. 2010).

234 Palisades Collection, L.L.C. v. Graubard, 2009 WL 1025176 (N.J. Super. Ct. App. Div. Apr. 17, 2009).

235 *In re* Leverett, 378 B.R. 793 (E.D. Tex. 2007); Wright v. Asset Acceptance Corp., 200 WL 33216031 (S.D. Ohio Jan. 3, 2000); *In re* Kendall, 380 B.R. 37 (Bankr. N.D. Okla. 2007); Persolve v. Uribe (Cal. Super. Ct. Dec. 9, 2010), *available at* www.nclc.org/unreported; Midland Funding, L.L.C. v. Copes, 2012 WL 3006644 (Conn. Super. Ct. June 22, 2012); Palisades Collection, L.L.C. v. Thomas (Fla. Broward Cnty. Ct. June 8, 2009), *available at* www.nclc.org/unreported; LVNV Funding, L.L.C., Shecter (Fla. Palm Beach Cnty. Ct. June 8, 2009), *available at* www.nclc.org/unreported; Green v. Cavalry Portfolio Serv., L.L.C., 700 S.E.2d 741 (Ga. Ct. App. 2010); Wirth v. Cach, L.L.C., 685 S.E.2d 433 (Ga. Ct. App. 2009); Norfolk Fin. Corp. v. Mazard, 2009 WL 3844481 (Mass. Dist. Ct. Nov. 12, 2009); Cach, L.L.C. v. Askew, 358 S.W.3d 58 (Mo. 2012); Gemini Capital Group v. Tripp, 2013 WL 5872742 (Mo. Ct. App. Nov. 1, 2013); New Century Fin. Servs., Inc. v. Oughla, 2014 WL 839180 (N.J. Super. Ct. App. Div. Mar. 5, 2014); Rushmore Recoveries X, L.L.C. v. Skolnick, 841 N.Y.S.2d 823 (N.Y. Dist. Ct. 2007); N.Y. City Civ. Ct. Directives and Procedures DRP-182 (May 13, 2009); Premier Capital, L.L.C. v. Baker, 972 N.E.2d 1125 (Ohio Ct. App. 2012); Nat'l Check Bur. Inc. v. Ruth, 2009 WL 2516123 (Ohio Ct. App. Aug. 19, 2009); Nat'l Check Bur. v. Cody, 2005 WL 174762 (Ohio Ct. App. Jan. 27, 2005) (dissent); Four Seasons Invs., L.L.C. v. Petrucci (Pa. Ct. Com. Pl. May 10, 2011), *available at* www.nclc.org/unreported; Unifund CCR Partners v. Perkins, 2009 WL 4202635 (Tex. App. Nov. 25, 2009). *See also* PRA III, L.L.C. v. MacDowell, 841 N.Y.S.2d 822 (table), 2007 WL 1429026 (N.Y. Civ. Ct. 2007); Unifund CCR Partners v. Vo (Pa. Ct. Com. Pl. Feb. 17, 2009), *available at* www.nclc.org/unreported; Remit Corp. v. Miller, 5 Pa. D & C.5h 42 (Pa. Ct. Com. Pl. 2008); Unifund CCR Partners v. Hawthorne, 2009 WL 4879017 (Tex. App. Dec. 17, 2009). *But cf.* Nat'l Check Bur. Inc. v. Cody, 2005 WL 174762 (Ohio Ct. App. Jan. 27, 2005) (majority opinion) (finding sufficient evidence of the chain of title).

236 Four Seasons Invs., L.L.C. v. Petrucci (Pa. Ct. Com. Pl. May 10, 2011), *available at* www.nclc.org/unreported.

237 Arrow Fin. Serv., L.L.C. v. Wright, 715 S.E.2d 725 (Ga. Ct. App. 2011); Gemini Capital Group v. Tripp, 2013 WL 5872742 (Mo. Ct. App. Nov. 1, 2013).

238 Munoz v. Pipestone Fin., L.L.C., 397 F. Supp. 2d 1129 (D. Minn. 2005); Wright v. Asset Acceptance Corp., 2000 WL 33216031 (S.D. Ohio Jan. 3, 2000); LVNV Funding, L.L.C. v. Shecter (Fla. Palm Beach Cnty. Ct. June 8, 2009), *available at* www.nclc.org/unreported; Palisades Collection, L.L.C. v. Thomas (Fla. Broward Cnty. Ct. Apr. 15, 2009), *available at* www.nclc.org/unreported; Rushmore Recoveries X, L.L.C. v. Skolnick, 841 N.Y.S.2d 823 (N.Y. Dist. Ct. 2007); Premier Capital, L.L.C. v. Baker, 972 N.E.2d 1125 (Ohio Ct. App. 2012).

239 *Cf.* Great Seneca Fin. Corp. v. LeAnna, 2006 WL 2536275 (Conn. Super. Ct. Aug. 15, 2006) (not reaching the issue but implying this proof is inadequate).

that the two Vision entities are the same or that Vision Nevada, Inc. assigned the debt to Vision Management Services.

Similarly, a chain of title was broken when Atlantic sold a debt to Ameristar Financial Servicing Company and Ameristar Financial then sold the debt to the plaintiff in an action. There was no evidence of an assignment from Ameristar Financial Servicing Company to Ameristar Financial.[240] Similarly, an appellate court found no standing to bring a collection action when the chain of ownership was broken because the chain included a sale to Union Acceptance Corporation and then a sale from Union Acceptance Co., L.L.C., with no transfer from Union Acceptance Corporation to Union Acceptance Co., L.L.C.[241]

Also look for inconsistencies in the debt buyer's pleadings, affidavits, and documents as to the identity of an entity in the chain of ownership. For example, in one case the entity was first described as a Delaware limited liability company and later described as a New Jersey corporation.[242]

4.3.4.3.3 The assignment dates at each link in the chain must line up

An assignment from Debt Buyer B to Debt Buyer C is not valid if it is dated before the assignment from Debt Buyer A to Debt Buyer B. At the time of the assignment to Debt Buyer C, Debt Buyer B had nothing to assign.[243]

Also watch for assignments that are either back-dated or dated well after the actual assignment. Consider a case in which Debt Buyer A assigns a debt to Debt Buyer B in 2012. Debt Buyer B assigns it without proper documentation to Debt Buyer C in 2013. Debt Buyer C cannot rectify this mistake by obtaining a new assignment in 2014 directly from Debt Buyer A. In 2014, Debt Buyer A no longer had any ownership interest in the account, having assigned it to Debt Buyer B in 2012. In addition, always be skeptical of assignment documents dated after the collector began seeking payment on the debt.

4.3.4.3.4 Debt buyers may trip up in showing proper links at beginning of the chain

In a number of situations involving credit cards, the debt buyer's proof becomes even more complicated because the chain of ownership not only includes multiple debt buyers but also multiple card issuers. The proof may have to include evidence of transfers of blocks of accounts from one card issuer to another. Thus, in one case, ten bills of sale showing a chain of assignments was insufficient because the chain never indicated at its beginning how a Household Bank account became a Bank of America account.[244] In yet another case, Washington Mutual purchased accounts from Providian. A debt buyer in some documents claimed to have purchased an account from Providian and, in other documents, that it purchased the account from Washington Mutual. It not only failed to show an assignment to it but also provided no evidence of the assignment from Providian to Washington Mutual.[245]

In one case, the debt buyer tried to show a complete chain of ownership from Chevy Chase Bank. First U.S.A., a division of Bank One, purchased the credit card operations of Chevy Chase Bank, and Bank One was purchased by J.P. Morgan & Co. The debt buyer attempted to prove these transfers by reference to a *New York Times* article and to Wikipedia. The appellate court had little trouble rejecting this evidence.[246]

Another court found a chain of title insufficient when the chain that was proven began at GE Money Bank but the original creditor was Monogram Credit Card Bank, and even when the collector produced a certificate of merger between the two entities.[247] This was particularly the case since the alleged transfer from Monogram was to GE Capital Consumer Card Company and no evidence was produced as to the relationship of GE Capital Consumer Card Company and GE Money Bank.[248] And when a card issuer securitizes a group of accounts, the chain of ownership may even have to include transfers of accounts receivables to a trust and then back to the card issuer.[249]

4.3.4.4 Determining What Rights Have Been Assigned

Check at each transfer of ownership what rights were assigned to the assignee. An assignment should describe the rights assigned with sufficient particularity to identify the rights assigned, and the assignment should not be construed to assign additional rights not expressly described.[250] Rights assigned can be account receivables, rights under a contract, or choses in action. If owner A assigns only receivables to owner B, and owner B assigns only rights under the contract to owner

240 Jordan v. John Soliday Fin. Grp., L.L.C., 2010 WL 1462345 (N.D. Ohio Apr. 12, 2010). *See also* Centurion Capital Corp. v. Guarino, 951 N.Y.S.2d 85 (table), 2012 WL 1543286 (N.Y. Civ. Ct. Apr. 30, 2012).

241 Green v. Cavalry Portfolio Serv., L.L.C., 700 S.E.2d 741 (Ga. Ct. App. 2010). *See also* Benson v. Asset Acceptance, L.L.C., 712 S.E.2d 83 (Ga. Ct. App. 2011) (credit card with Citibank (S.D.), N.A., but assignment from Citibank USA to debt buyer and no evidence of transfer from Citibank (South Dakota), N.A., to Citibank USA); Hutto v. CACV of Colo., L.L.C., 707 S.E.2d 872 (Ga. Ct. App. 2011) (affidavit provides that JP Morgan Chase & Co. assigned debt to debt buyer, but debt was with Chase Manhattan Bank).

242 Palisades Collection, L.L.C. v. Haque, 2006 N.Y. Misc. LEXIS 4036 (N.Y. Civ. Ct. Apr. 13, 2006).

243 Persolve v. Uribe (Cal. Super. Ct. Dec. 9, 2010), *available at* www.nclc.org/unreported.

244 Norfolk Fin. Corp. v. Mazard, 2009 WL 3844481 (Mass. Dist. Ct. Nov. 12, 2009).

245 Wirth v. Cach, L.L.C., 685 S.E.2d 433 (Ga. Ct. App. 2009).

246 Palisades Collection, L.L.C. v. Graubard, 2009 WL 1025176 (N.J. Super. Ct. App. Div. Apr. 17, 2009). *See also* Nat'l Check Bureau, Inc. v. Ruth, 2009 WL 2516123 (Ohio Ct. App. Aug. 19, 2009); Portfolio Recovery Assoc., L.L.C. v. Strifler (Vt. Super. Ct. Sept. 2, 2011), *available at* www.nclc.org/unreported.

247 LVNV Funding, L.L.C. v. Guest, 953 N.Y.S.2d 550 (table), 2012 WL 1957715 (N.Y. City Ct. May 29, 2012).

248 *Id.*

249 *See* § 4.3.4.3.1, *supra*.

250 DC3 Entm't, L.L.C. v. John Galt Entm't, Inc., 412 F. Supp. 2d 1125 (W.D. Wash. 2006).

C, then owner C should not have either rights under the contract or rights to receivables. Owner B assigned rights that it did not have.

Assignment of a "receivable" has been interpreted as an assignment to collect what was owed at the time of assignment but not interest accruing after the assignment or the right to seek contractual attorney fees incurred after the assignment.[251] Conversely, if only rights under the contract are assigned, the collector will have difficulty recovering on a theory not based upon the contract, such as *quantum meruit*.

A collector suing on a promissory note or other negotiable instrument cannot base its rights on an assignment of an "account."[252] The Uniform Commercial Code does not treat a promissory note or other negotiable instrument as an account,[253] so the assignment of an account does not include a promissory note or other negotiable instrument. Most consumer debt collection cases do not involve promissory notes or other negotiable instruments, but there are exceptions, such as claims for mortgage deficiencies, certain car loans made directly with a lender (not installment sales), and check collections. In those cases, the assignment must be of the negotiable instrument and not just the "account."[254]

It is important to distinguish between an assignment of a debt for collection purposes (sometimes described as assignment of only legal title) from assignment of ownership of a debt (sometimes described as assignment of legal and equitable title). For example, an assignment from Unifund CCR Partners to Unifund Portfolio A may be for collection purposes only and Unifund Portfolio A continues to own the debt. When one of the entities in a chain of ownership states that the "assignor shall retain title and ownership of said receivables," the assignee or any subsequent entity in the chain of ownership from that assignee cannot claim or pass on ownership.[255]

4.3.4.5 Is Notice of Assignment a Precondition to Suing on the Debt?

State law may require that the consumer be notified when a debt is assigned to another.[256] When a collector can produce no evidence that notice of the assignment was provided, courts have dismissed the collection action because the notice is a precondition to a collection action based upon the assigned debt.[257]

4.4 Collector's Legal Theory in Its Pleadings Controls the Case

The collector's complaint or amended complaint establishes the collector's legal theory to collect on the debt. A court should rule only on the theory delineated in those pleadings and should not find for the collector on a different theory.[258] For example, if a collector seeks recovery on an "open account" theory, and the court finds the collector has not proven the elements of that claim, the court should not rule for the collector on an "account stated" theory,[259] when the consumer has not been given an opportunity to present evidence and law opposing an account stated claim.

The collector should not be able to amend its complaint informally. The collector must seek permission from the court. The amended complaint must be in writing and state its legal theory of recovery with specificity. If there is any ambiguity as to the collector's legal theory in its complaint, the consumer should obtain, under a state's rules of procedure, a more definite statement, a bill of particulars, or some similar specification of the causes of action.

For example, a collector's pleadings may be vague as to whether the collector is pleading based upon an "open account," "statement of account," contract theory, or money lent theory. Each of these causes of action may have different elements of proof.[260] Other times the complaint will allege facts relating to nonpayment but not specify any theory of the case.

A state's rules of procedure may require that the complaint attach documents supporting the cause of action, such as the credit contract or a statement of the account.[261] If these documents, which will help the consumer understand the collector's legal theory, are not attached, the consumer should move for either a more definite statement or for dismissal of the case.[262]

Some states' rules of civil procedure may allow the legal theory to be amended, even after trial, if this does not prejudice the other party. In these states, the consumer's attorney, at the start and throughout the case, should clarify with the court the collector's causes of action, object to evidence or argument relating to a different theory, and clarify the consumer's

251 Munoz v. Pipestone Fin., L.L.C., 397 F. Supp. 2d 1129 (D. Minn. 2005).
252 Harrington v. Asset Acceptance, L.L.C., 270 S.W.3d 405 (Ky. Ct. App. 2008).
253 U.C.C. § 9-102(a)(2).
254 Harrington v. Asset Acceptance, L.L.C., 270 S.W.3d 405 (Ky. Ct. App. 2008).
255 Palisades Collection, L.L.C. v. Thomas (Fla. Broward Cnty. Ct. Apr. 15, 2009), *available at* www.nclc.org/unreported; Shipley v. Unifund CCR Partners, 331 S.W.3d 27 (Tex. App. 2010).
256 *See* Fla. Stat. § 559.715 (notice of assignment within thirty days).
257 LVNV Funding, L.L.C. v. Harris (Fla. Miami-Dade Cnty. Ct. June 24, 2009), *available at* www.nclc.org/unreported; DNS Equity Group Inc. v. Lavallee, 907 N.Y.S.2d 436 (table), 2010 WL 682466 (N.Y. Dist. Ct. 2010). New Jersey law does not have this requirement. *See* New Century Fin. Servs., Inc. v. Oughla, 2014 WL 839180 (N.J. Super Ct. App. Div. Mar. 5, 2014).
258 *See* Wiltel Commc'ns, L.L.C. v. Sunrise Int'l Leasing Corp., 2005 WL 354030 (Minn. Ct. App. Feb. 15, 2005); Citibank v. Miller, 222 S.W.3d 318 (Mo. Ct. App. 2007); Palisades Collection, L.L.C. v. Gonzalez, 809 N.Y.S.2d 482 (table), 2005 WL 3372971 (N.Y. Civ. Ct. Dec. 12, 2005); Dodeka, L.L.C. v. Campos, 377 S.W.3d 726 (Tex. App. 2012); Effel v. McGarry, 339 S.W.3d 789 (Tex. App. 2011); Wynne v. Citibank, 2008 WL 1848286 (Tex. App. Apr. 25, 2008). *See also* Atlantic Credit Fin. v. Caro, 2010 WL 4516654 (Conn. Super. Ct. Oct. 21, 2010) (no summary judgment for collector when complaint did not clearly specify a legal theory); Hudson & Keyse, L.L.C. v. Carson, 2008 WL 2221968 (Ohio Ct. App. May 29, 2008) (collector cannot recover on summary judgment on different theory than used in summary judgment motion).
259 Citibank v. Miller, 222 S.W.3d 318 (Mo. Ct. App. 2007).
260 *See* §§ 4.5–4.7, *infra*.
261 *See* § 3.4, *supra*.
262 *See* § 3.5.1, *supra*.

prejudice if the court were to rule based upon a different cause of action than the one pleaded.

Not having an opportunity to defend a cause of action causes significant prejudice to the consumer. The legal theory specified in the complaint does more than just establish what elements the collector must prove. It can also determine which state's law controls, what statute of limitations applies, and whether and how interest and attorney fees are to be computed.

Credit contracts will often specify a choice of law—for example, Delaware law. Collector claims often are *not* based on the contract—debt buyers may have little evidence of the contract between the original creditor and the consumer. In that case the collector cannot argue for the contractual choice of law. The forum state's law will apply, since there is no proof of a contract or a contractual choice of law provision. Thus, the cause of action being pleaded may determine not only the elements that must be proven but also which state's laws apply.

The theory pleaded will also determine the statute of limitations.[263] A collection action based on the contract may have a longer limitations period than one based upon an account stated. The applicable statute of limitations can only be determined once the collector's legal theory is clearly established. Changing the collector's claim late in the case, or even after trial, may deprive the consumer of the opportunity to raise a statute of limitations defense that was not applicable under the original cause of action.

An interest rate and the right to attorney fees may be specified in the contract. But if the collector's claim is not based on the contract, and the collector does not provide a contract, then the contract is not a valid basis for the award of attorney fees and interest.[264] The collector may have to rely on state law regarding prejudgment interest and the collection of attorney fees. The same is the case for state laws allowing postjudgment interest to be based upon the contract rate.

Collectors, in an attempt to avoid these restrictions, may plead multiple theories in the alternative. This approach should *not* prevent a careful analysis of each theory to determine the required elements for that individual cause of action, the applicable statute of limitations, and the applicable theories for the collector to recover interest and fees. When these alternatives conflict with each other, the court cannot award a recovery under both theories but instead must select one theory and determine if the collector has met all the elements of that legal theory.

For example, a court should not issue an award for a collector on a breach of contract and a *quantum meruit* theory. *Quantum meruit*, in most states, is only available when there is no contract.[265] If the court adopts a *quantum meruit* theory, it must hold there was no binding contract, and then the consumer should not be liable for interest and attorney fees based upon the contract.

4.5 Proof of a Written Contract

4.5.1 Introduction

A common collector cause of action is breach of contract. The consumer entered into a credit agreement and defaulted, and the creditor has incurred damages. In a closed-end credit obligation—when the total obligation is spelled out in the contract—this claim is relatively straightforward. The collector, after establishing its standing, must prove the existence of a binding contract, the consumer's default, and how much of the original obligation is unpaid.

Matters are more complex in an open-end credit obligation, when the contract establishes the terms of the relationship but the consumer's indebtedness varies over time as obligations are incurred and payments are made. Moreover, the contract itself may have been amended over time, interest added at differing rates, and various fees and charges added on to the obligation. A credit card is the most common example of an open-end credit obligation, but there are many other examples, including obligations for cell phone, cable television, landline telephone, water, gas, and electric service. In such open-ended arrangements the collector must prove the balance owed on the open-ended account.

Proof that a credit card account was opened is not proof of the balance due upon default. Conversely, if the collector provides detail showing the charges and credits that resulted in the balance due, this is not proof of a contract, which is a necessary element of a breach of contract action.

This section focuses on proof of the existence of a contract. Proof of the balance due in an open-end transaction is examined in § 4.6, *infra*. Proof of the balance due is relevant not only to recovery on a breach-of-contract claim, but it may also be an important issue even when the collector does not prove a written contract but still seeks to recover the account balance under some other theory of liability.

4.5.2 What State Law Applies?

Many consumer credit contracts specify what state's law applies to the contract, which often is not the law of the consumer's residence or of the state where the consumer entered into the contract. In any case based upon breach of contract, litigants must be aware that the court may utilize the contractually chosen state's law and not the forum state's law.

Courts typically apply the contractually chosen state's laws to interpret the contract instead of the forum state's law, as long as the issue is viewed neither as purely procedural nor as

263 *See* § 3.6.6, *supra*.

264 *See, e.g.*, NetJets Aviation, Inc. v. LHC Commc'ns, L.L.C., 537 F.3d 168 (2d Cir. 2008); Capital One Bank v. Heidebrink, 2009 WL 1741515 (Ohio Ct. App. June 19, 2009). *Cf.* Jaramillo v. Portfolio Acquisitions, L.L.C., 2010 WL 1197669 (Tex. App. Mar. 30, 2010) (attorney fees not available under the contract, but available under a state statute providing for such fees when a collector recovers on a *quantum meruit* basis).

265 *See* § 4.8, *infra*.

impinging on a fundamental state interest.[266] An exception is that courts typically apply the forum state's statute of limitations, if shorter than that of the contractually chosen state, and may even select it when it is the longer of the two.[267]

An interesting question is which state's law applies to determine whether a contract was ever consummated—if the contract is not in effect, then the contractually chosen state's law should not be applied. At least some courts rule that, when the contract would be consummated under the law of the state selected in the contract, then the contract is enforceable, even if it would not be found to be consummated under the forum state's laws.[268]

4.5.3 Proof of the Contract

4.5.3.1 Introduction

To recover on a breach of contract claim, the collector must prove not only that the consumer has assented to a contract but the terms of that contract. Invariably, this means that the collector must produce into evidence the actual contract that the consumer has agreed to, with some evidence that the consumer has, in fact, agreed to it.

Surprisingly, this will often be difficult for the collector. Debt buyers will usually not possess this documentation when they purchase the debt and may be unable or unwilling to obtain the required documentation from the original creditor. For example, one debt buyer's contract to purchase accounts from a creditor states "No Media Requests: Buyer understands that Seller will not provide Buyer with any documentation relating to an Account, including applications, agreements, billing statements, correspondence, etc."[269]

Even more surprising, the original creditor may not retain this documentation.[270] Card issuers often destroy the originals of applications and other documents that indicate the credit card agreement and may have difficulty recovering electronic copies. Although practice varies from creditor to creditor, it appears that applications and other documents are destroyed after five to seven years.

4.5.3.2 Contract's Unavailability No Excuse for Non-Production

A collector unable to produce the applicable contract cannot excuse this lapse by pointing to federal Truth in Lending and Equal Credit Opportunity Act regulations that require creditors to retain documentation of a credit agreement and credit application for at least twenty-five months.[271] These regulations do not condone destruction of the documents after twenty-five months, and they certainly do not state that a debt can be collected without proof of a contract.[272]

The regulations require that creditors retain documents for a minimum number of months so that regulators can inspect the records for Truth in Lending and Equal Credit Opportunity Act compliance. After that, the creditor must use its own judgment as to how long it seeks to collect on a contract and how long to retain the contract. Minimum retention requirements do not excuse a creditor from providing proof that a contract exists. If the creditor wishes to prove the contract, it merely retains the documents for a longer period of time.[273]

In fact, other federal regulations require financial institutions to retain contracts and related evidence as long as a claim might be brought against the consumer. A federally regulated financial institution "should establish and maintain loan document practices that . . . ensure that any claim against a borrower is legally enforceable."[274] In addition, card issuers must post on the Internet their card agreements[275] and, even more significantly, must post and maintain each individual cardholder's agreement on its website or promptly provide the consumer with a copy upon request.[276]

California law provides that, when a creditor intentionally destroys or materially alters a written contract, that action extinguishes all contractual obligations that the consumer has to the creditor, unless the consumer consented to the destruction or alteration.[277] Other courts find that, when one party destroys documents, the presumption is that the destroyed documents will bolster the case of the other party,[278] although this presumption can be overcome.[279] Evidence that the creditor has destroyed the original may be found in other court dockets when the applicable creditor, in obtaining a default judgment, has submitted affidavits that it is submitting a copy of the contract because it destroyed the original.

4.5.3.3 Production of the Contract Applicable to the Particular Consumer

To prove breach of contract, collectors must produce a written agreement that is binding on the parties.[280] Collectors must

266 *See* Restatement (Second) of Conflict of Laws § 187 (1988).
267 *See* §§ 3.6.3.2.2, 3.6.3.2.3, *supra*.
268 *See* Jackson v. Pasadena Receivables, Inc., 921 A.2d 799 (Md. 2007).
269 Account Sale Agreement Between Capital One and Centurion Capital Corp. (Dec. 8, 2005).
270 Johnson v. MBNA Am. Bank, 357 F.3d 426 (4th Cir. 2004) (card issuer only retained documents for five years).
271 12 C.F.R. §§ 202.12, 1026.25 [§ 226.25].
272 Johnson v. MBNA Am. Bank, 357 F.3d 426 (4th Cir. 2004).
273 *See* Fla. Credit Research Inc. v. Felicien (Fla. Duval Cnty. Ct. Apr. 15, 2008), *available at* www.nclc.org/unreported.
274 12 C.F.R. pt. 30, app. A(C), Interagency Guidelines Establishing Standards for Safety and Soundness, Loan Documentation.
275 12 C.F.R. § 1026.58(c).
276 12 C.F.R. § 1026.58(e)(1).
277 Cal. Civil Code § 1700.
278 *See* Favors v. Fisher, 13 F.3d 1235 (8th Cir. 1994); Hicks v. The Gates Rubber Co., 833 F.2d 406 (11th Cir. 1987).
279 *See* Favors v. Fisher, 13 F.3d 1235 (8th Cir. 1994).
280 *See* Fla. Credit Research Inc. v. Felicien (Fla. Duval Cnty. Ct. Apr. 15, 2008), *available at* www.nclc.org/unreported.; Fla. Credit Research, Inc. v. Stromberg (Fla. Duval Cnty. Ct. June 22, 2007), *available at* www.nclc.org/unreported; LVNV Funding, L.L.C. v. Moehrlin (Fla. Volusia Cnty. Ct. Aug. 2006) (Green, J.; count dismissed when no contract proven and affidavit was not proper), *available at* www.nclc.org/unreported; Discover Bank v. Sea, 2010 WL 1404594 (Ky. Ct. App. Apr. 9, 2010); Citibank v. Martin, 807 N.Y.S.2d 284 (N.Y. Civ. Ct. 2005); Commonwealth Fin. Sys., Inc. v. Smith, 15 A.3d 492 (Pa. Super. Ct.

produce not just a standard form contract but the version of the contract that the particular consumer agreed to.[281] Courts have dismissed cases when the collector submits a generic, undated, and unsigned "customer agreement" that does not even contain the consumer's name or any indicia relating the document to the consumer.[282] Of course, the collector has offered insufficient evidence when, as sometimes happens, the collector offers a credit card agreement from the wrong creditor, or when the agreement produced is labeled under MasterCard and the consumer had a Visa card (or vice versa).

Similarly, evidence of a contract has been found insufficient when the contract contained blanks for several important terms and failed to include referenced attachments, even when the collector's employee testified at trial that the contract was applicable to the consumer's account.[283] Of course, production is similarly inadequate when the collector introduces only part of a contract or two different contracts. A New York statute provides that the portion of any printed contract involving a consumer transaction may not be received in evidence if the print is not clear and legible or is less than eight points in depth.[284]

The collector should produce the version of its standard form contract that was in effect when the consumer allegedly breached the contract. It is not sufficient to attach an unsigned standard form agreement from 2007 when the consumer first obtained credit in 2011.[285] Similarly, appending the creditor's current contract should not suffice if the consumer's account has been closed since well before that form of the standard form contract was ever used.

If the initial contract has been superseded before default by an entirely new contract, then that new contract must be produced[286]—the original contract, however, need not be produced if superseded by the new one.[287] On the other hand, the collector must produce not only the original contract, but all applicable amendments, if the amendments add or subtract to the original contract but do not replace it.[288]

Card issuers not only draft different standard form contracts from one year to the next, but at any given time may offer different standard form contracts to different categories of card holders. In addition, when Bank A purchases or merges with Bank B, Bank A's agreement with its preexisting card holders will certainly be different from Bank B's agreement with its preexisting card holders.[289] A collector cannot introduce Bank B's contract when the governing contract for a particular consumer is that offered by Bank A.

Certainly the requirement that the contract itself be introduced cannot be met merely by a report and affidavit purporting to describe the contract.[290] An affidavit certainly is not sufficient if it does not identify the account number.[291] Nor is it sufficient to state that a copy of the contract has been requested and will be provided upon receipt.[292]

A billing statement is not proof of a contract.[293] Even if a billing statement is evidence for an account stated claim, it does not indicate the nature of the underlying contract or even if there is such a contract.

Not only must the collector introduce the correct contract but must supply some linkage between the form contract and the particular consumer account to indicate that this contract does in fact apply to the consumer. This may require an affidavit from someone familiar with the card issuer's computers

2011); Palisades Collection, L.L.C v. Grassmyer (Pa. Ct. Com. Pl. Jan. 15, 2008), *available at* www.nclc.org/unreported; Barajas v. Harvest Credit Mgmt., VI-B, L.L.C., 2008 WL 4308334 (Tex. App. Aug. 28, 2008); Williams v. Unifund CCR Partners, 264 S.W.3d 231 (Tex. App. 2008). *See also* Jones v. Citibank, 2008 WL 442627 (Ark. Ct. App. Feb. 20, 2008); Citibank v. Razvi, 2008 WL 2521082 (N.J. Super. Ct. App. Div. June 26, 2008) (bank keeps original credit agreements for seven years and relies instead on consumer's use of the card as assent to new card terms sent in the mail); Remit Corp. v. Potter (Pa. Ct. Com. Pl. June 2, 2008), *available at* www.nclc.org/unreported. *Cf.* Roberson v. Ocwen Fed. Bank, 553 S.E.2d 162 (Ga. Ct. App. 2001) (describing an acceptable substitute for production of the contract when the contract was over ten years old and had been destroyed). *But see* Discover Bank v. Poling, 2005 WL 737404 (Ohio Ct. App. Mar. 31, 2005).

281 *See* Henggeler v. Brumbaugh & Quandahl, P.C., 894 F. Supp. 2d 1180 (D. Neb. 2012); Remit Corp. v. Miller, 5 Pa. D. & C.5th 43 (Pa. Ct. Com. Pl. 2008). *See also* American Express Bank, FSB v. Dalbis, 2011 WL 873512 (N.Y. Civ. Ct. Mar. 14, 2011).

282 Capital One Bank v. Mullis, 15 Fla. L. Weekly Supp. 370a (Fla. Cnty. Ct. Feb. 13, 2008); N. Star Capital Acquisition, L.L.C. v. Lewis, 15 Fla. L. Weekly Supp. 72a (Fla. Duval Cnty. Ct. Oct. 23, 2007), *available at* www.nclc.org/unreported; Discover Bank v. Sura, 951 N.Y.S.2d 85 (table), 2012 WL 1450028 (N.Y. City Ct. Apr. 26, 2012). *See also* Remit Corp. v. Miller, 5 Pa. D. & C.5th 43 (Pa. Ct. Com. Pl. 2008). *Cf.* Citibank v. Mahmoud, 866 N.Y.S.2d 90 (N.Y. Civ. Ct. 2008). *But cf.* Capitol One Bank v. Hardin, 178 S.W.3d 565 (Mo. Ct. App. 2005) (when original contract not produced, sufficient to produce signed application, revised agreement, two years of billing statements, and telephone log of calls between consumer and card issuer).

283 Jaramillo v. Portfolio Acquisitions, L.L.C., 2010 WL 1197669 (Tex. App. Mar. 30, 2010).

284 N.Y. C.P.L.R. Law § 4544 (McKinney). *See also* American Express Bank, FSB v. Dalbis, 2011 WL 873512 (N.Y. Civ. Ct. Mar. 14, 2011).

285 Capital One Bank v. Clevenstine, 7 Pa. D. & C. 153 (Pa. Ct. Com. Pl. 2009). *See also* American Express Bank, FSB v. Dalbis, 2011 WL 873512 (N.Y. City Civ. Ct. Mar. 14, 2011); Target Nat'l Bank v. Kilbride (Pa. Ct. Com. Pl. Feb. 5, 2010), *available at* www.nclc.org/unreported.

286 *See* Chase Bank v. Rader, 8 Pa. D. & C.5th 297 (Pa. Ct. Com. Pl. 2009), *aff'd*, 15 A.3d 537 (Pa. Super. Ct. 2010); Northstar Capital Acquisitions v. Haring (Utah Dist. Ct. Mar. 4, 2010), *available at* www.nclc.org/unreported.

287 Wood v. Pharia, L.L.C., 2010 WL 5060621 (Tex. App. Dec. 9, 2010).

288 Target Nat'l Bank v. Greiner (Pa. Commw. Ct. Sept. 30, 2009), *available at* www.nclc.org/unreported; Remit Corp. v. Miller, 5 Pa. D. & C.5th 43 (Pa. Ct. Com. Pl. 2008); FIA Card Servs. v. Kirasic (Pa. Ct. Com. Pl. Nov. 7, 2007), *available at* www.nclc.org/unreported; Worldwide Asset Purchasing, L.L.C. v. Stern (Pa. Ct. Com. Pl. May 13, 2005), *available at* www.nclc.org/unreported. *See also* Midland Funding v. Snyder (Pa. Commw. Ct. Jan. 11, 2008), *available at* www.nclc.org/unreported (date of contract is unstated).

289 *But see* Wynne v. Citibank, 2008 WL 1848286 (Tex. App. Apr. 25, 2008) (2003 contract version sufficient evidence of agreement entered into in 1996).

290 Velocity Invs., L.L.C. v. Alston, 922 N.E.2d 538 (Ill. App. Ct. 2010); PRA III, L.L.C. v. MacDowell, 841 N.Y.S.2d 822 (N.Y. Civ. Ct. 2007).

291 Hudson & Keyse, L.L.C. v. Carson, 2008 WL 2221968 (Ohio Ct. App. May 29, 2008).

292 *See* LVNV Funding, L.L.C. v. Theurer (Pa. Ct. Com. Pl. Feb. 2, 2009), *available at* www.nclc.org/unreported.

293 *See* Dodeka v. Keith, 2012 WL 6738479 (Ohio Ct. App. Dec. 31, 2012).

and record-keeping.[294] A debt buyer will have difficulty providing such proof.[295]

4.5.3.4 Providing Consumer Assent to the Contract

To prove breach of contract, the collector must not just introduce the applicable contract but must prove that the consumer has agreed to that contract. Ordinarily, proving that the consumer has agreed to a contract requires little more than producing the consumer's signature on a contract. For credit card agreements in particular, this may not be possible, because the consumer may never have signed the contract.

Nevertheless, for credit card accounts, in most states the collector need not produce a document containing the consumer's signature in order for the contract to be binding.[296] Most courts find that the consumer's use of the card is treated as the consumer's agreement to the terms of the card contract, particularly when the contract states that use of the card is treated as assent to the contract.[297] But the collector may have to prove the consumer's use of the card, such as by producing copies of the consumer's check payments or documentation of specific consumer usage and not just by submitting general, non-itemized monthly statements generated by the creditor.[298]

Some courts require more, such as that the collector provide a copy of the signed application.[299] If a forum state's laws would appear to require a signature,[300] the court may apply the law of the state chosen in the credit card agreement,[301] and that state's law may not require a signature.[302] But under any state's laws, the collector's burden is increased when the consumer disputes that an unsigned and undated form contract was ever received or used.[303]

The collector should offer evidence that the contract and any amendments were actually mailed to the consumer.[304] But employees of the debt buyer will have no idea what contract was sent to which card holders. Even the original creditor may be unable to rely on an affidavit of its own employee when the contract was sent out by a third-party mailing service.

The collector also may not be able to show consumer assent to an amendment to the contract or a replacement contract unilaterally sent to the consumer *after* the consumer stopped using the card. Use of the card as acceptance of a contract does not apply when the consumer no longer uses the card.[305] When an account is seriously delinquent, the consumer will either voluntarily stop using the account or the creditor will cut the consumer off. The collector thus must produce the version of the creditor's contract originally assented to and as subsequently amended up until the time the account stopped being used.

4.5.4 *Proof of Contractually Established Finance Charges and Other Fees*

4.5.4.1 Establishing the Rate Provided for in the Contract

A collector who proves the existence of a contract has additional proof requirements if it is to obtain finance charges and other fees, as allegedly specified by that contract. The creditor's

---

294 *See* Wincheck v. American Express Travel Related Servs. Co., 232 S.W.3d 197 (Tex. App. 2007). *See also* American Express Bank, FSB v. Dalbis, 2011 WL 873512 (N.Y. Civ. Ct. Mar. 14, 2011).

295 *See* Rushmore Recoveries X, L.L.C. v. Skolnick, 841 N.Y.S.2d 823 (N.Y. Dist. Ct. 2007); Palisades Collection, L.L.C. v. Gonzalez, 809 N.Y.S.2d 482 (table), 2005 WL 3372971 (N.Y. Civ. Ct. Dec. 12, 2005).

296 Davis v. Discover Bank, 627 S.E.2d 819 (Ga. Ct. App. 2006) (consumer's use of credit card constituted his acceptance of card member agreement); Jackson v. Pasadena Receivables, Inc., 921 A.2d 799 (Md. 2007); Am. Express Travel Related Servs. v. Redner, 2006 WL 664698 (Mich. Ct. App. Mar. 16, 2006) (corporate officer could be found to be individually liable on corporate credit card, even though he never signed an application or other document for the card, because his use of the card manifested an intent to be bound by the card member agreement, which imposed individual liability on him); Citibank v. Santoro, 150 P.3d 429 (Or. Ct. App. 2006) (following *Davis v. Discover Bank*); MBNA Am. Bank v. Goodman, 140 P.3d 589 (Utah Ct. App. 2006) (noting Utah Statute of Fraud specifically provides that a credit card agreement is binding without a signature of the consumer when it states that use of the card constitutes acceptance); Citibank v. Machleid, 154 Wash. App. 1033 (Wash. Ct. App. 2010).

297 *See* Davis v. Discover Bank, 627 S.E.2d 819 (Ga. Ct. App. 2006) (consumer's use of credit card constituted his acceptance of card member agreement); Meyer v. Nat'l City Bank, 903 N.E.2d 974 (Ind. Ct. App. 2009); Jackson v. Pasadena Receivables, Inc., 921 A.2d 799 (Md. 2007); Am. Express Travel Related Servs. v. Redner, 2006 WL 664698 (Mich. Ct. App. Mar. 16, 2006) (corporate officer could be found to be individually liable on corporate credit card, even though he never signed an application or other document for the card, because his use of the card manifested an intent to be bound by the card member agreement, which imposed individual liability on him); Bank One v. Palmer, 579 N.E.2d 284 (Ohio Ct. App. 1989); Citibank v. Kovach, 930 N.E.2d 394 (Ohio. Com. Pl. 2010); Citibank v. Santoro, 150 P.3d 429 (Or. Ct. App. 2006) (following *Davis v. Discover Bank*); Wood v. Pharia, L.L.C., 2010 WL 5060621 (Tex. App. Dec. 9, 2010); Wincheck v. Am. Express Travel Related Servs. Co., 232 S.W.3d 197 (Tex. App. 2007); Capital One Bank v. Wilkerson, 2009 WL 3792434 (Utah Ct. App. Nov. 13, 2009); MBNA Am. Bank v. Goodman, 140 P.3d 589 (Utah Ct. App. 2006) (noting Utah Statute of Fraud specifically provides that a credit card agreement is binding without a signature of the consumer when it states that use of the card constitutes acceptance); Discovery Bank v. Ray, 162 P.3d 1131 (Wash. Ct. App. 2007).

298 Citibank v. Ryan, 47 P.3d 778 (Wash. Ct. App. 2011); Discover Bank v. Bridges, 226 P. 191 (Wash. Ct. App. 2007). *See also* American Express Bank, FSB v. Dalbis, 2011 WL 873512 (N.Y. Civ. Ct. Mar. 14, 2011).

299 Target Nat'l Bank v. Greiner (Pa. Ct. Com. Pl. Sept. 30, 2009), *available at* www.nclc.org/unreported.

300 *See, e.g.*, Md. Code Ann., Com. Law § 12-503(e) (West).

301 *See* Jackson v. Pasadena Receivables, Inc., 921 A.2d 799 (Md. 2007).

302 *See* S.D. Codified Laws § 54-11-9 (South Dakota law, chosen in many credit card contracts, provides that use of a credit card and failure to cancel the card creates acceptance). *See also* Jackson v. Pasadena Receivables, Inc., 921 A.2d 799 (Md. 2007).

303 Palisades Collection, L.L.C. v. Haque, 2006 N.Y. Misc. LEXIS 4036 (N.Y. Civ. Ct. Apr. 13, 2006).

304 Chase Bank v. Hershkovits, 28 Misc. 3d 1202(A) (N.Y. Civ. Ct. 2010).

305 *See* Remit Corp. v. Potter (Pa. Ct. Com. Pl. June 2, 2008), *available at* www.nclc.org/unreported; Effel v. McGarry, 339 S.W.3d 789 (Tex. App. 2011). *See also* American Express Bank, FSB v. Dalbis, 2011 WL 873512 (N.Y. Civ. Ct. Mar. 14, 2011). *But see* Del. Code Ann. tit. 5, § 952(b)(2) (allowing unilateral changes in card agreement even after consumer stops using card; note that card issuers may attempt to apply this statute to consumers in other states when contract selects Delaware law).

proof of the terms of a contract must include those provisions that entitle the creditor to interest in a specified amount.[306] It is not enough just to point to some monthly statements with an interest rate disclosure.[307] For example, a contract may reference another document on which the interest rate and schedule of fees and charges are listed. If the collector does not produce this other document, the collector cannot collect the interest or charges on a breach of contract action.[308]

Of course, the collector will have to produce additional evidence if it seeks an interest rate different than that found in the credit agreement produced at trial. Look to the interest rate specified in monthly statements, and compare that interest rate with the rate authorized in the change-in-terms notices or other contracts. Any discrepancy will complicate the collector's proof.[309]

Moreover, credit card interest rates sometimes are disclosed as a certain number of points over a published index that varies over time. In such cases, since the interest rate is not disclosed, proof will require a demonstration of both the agreed-upon variable rate formula and the published index in effect at the appropriate times.[310]

4.5.4.2 Proof the Interest Rate Is Legal

National banks by federal law are subject to the interest limits and fee restrictions of the law of their home state, not the law of the state where the consumer resides.[311] State-chartered, federally insured banks can choose between the interest and fee restrictions found in their home state or those in the state where the loan was made.[312] Other lenders are generally subject to the interest and fee limits of the law of the state where the loan is made.

When a lender seeks to charge an interest rate or fees greater than that allowed by the state where the consumer resides, the lender must present evidence that another state's law is applicable.[313] Then the lender must prove that the interest rate and fees that the lender is charging are allowed by that other state. One court has stated:

> In credit card cases, the first concern of any court is whether the amount at issue is a lawful claim, which brings up for consideration whether the credit card's interest rate and related charges are subject to this State's usury limits. [footnote omitted] The information upon which a court may make that determination generally requires no more than (1) an identification of the organizational character of the credit card issuer, and (2) a statement and description of the law which governs the interest rate and related charges.[314]

To seek interest in excess of a state's usury limit, the collector must prove that the originating creditor was either a national bank, federal savings association, federal credit union, or a state-chartered, federally insured bank, savings association or credit union. The burden must be on the collector to explain why a state's law does not apply.

Another issue is whether an assignee of a national bank that itself is not a national bank is entitled to assess finance charges in excess of a state maximum during the time when the assignee owns the obligation. Several courts have held the assignee may do so.[315]

4.5.4.3 Finance Charges for the Period After Default

When a card issuer considers the consumer in default, card issuers often seek a higher interest rate. But to recover on this interest rate, the collector must comply with federal law as to interest rate changes[316] and also establish a contractual right to the higher rate. This requires either proof of a change in terms notice sent to the consumer specifying the higher interest rate being sought or a credit agreement that specifies that, upon certain facts, the interest rate will be increased to the amount requested in the case.[317]

---

306 Bevington v. Cavalry Portfolio Servs., L.L.C., 319 Ga. App. 746 (Ga. Ct. App. 2013); Barajas v. Harvest Credit Mgmt., VI-B, L.L.C., 2008 WL 4308334 (Tex. App. Aug. 28, 2008); Williams v. Unifund CCR Partners, 264 S.W.3d 231 (Tex. App. 2008); Citibank v. Cooper (Vt. Super. Ct. July 10, 2009), *available at* www.nclc.org/unreported. *See also* Gigli v. Palisades Collection, L.L.C., 2008 WL 3853295 (M.D. Pa. Aug. 14, 2008); McElroy v. Unifund CCR Partners, 2008 WL 4355276 (Tex. App. Aug. 26, 2008). *But see* Simien v. Unifund CCR Partners, 321 S.W.3d 235 (Tex. App. 2010) (affidavits submitted at trial were sufficient evidence of interest rate).

307 Tully v. Citibank, 173 S.W.3d 212 (Tex. App. 2005). *See also* McElroy v. Unifund CCR Partners, 2008 WL 4355276 (Tex. App. Aug. 26, 2008). *But see* Wynne v. Citibank, 2008 WL 1848286 (Tex. App. Apr. 25, 2008) (sufficient to put into evidence the credit card agreement that indicates finance charges are established on billing statements and then to put into evidence those billing statements).

308 *See* Cach, L.L.C. v. Trevisano (Mo. Cir. Ct. Mar. 18, 2010), *available at* www.nclc.org/unreported.

309 *See* Unifund CCR Partners v. Hemm, 2009 WL 2106289 (Ohio Ct. App. July 17, 2009).

310 Hay v. Citibank, 2006 WL 2620089 (Tex. App. Sept. 14, 2006).

311 12 U.S.C. § 85. If certain activities involve branch banks within the state where the loan is made, then that state's law may also apply.

312 *See* National Consumer Law Center, Consumer Credit Regulation § 3.4 (2012), *updated at* www/nclc.org/library.

313 Citibank v. Hansen, 902 N.Y.S.2d 299 (N.Y. Dist. Ct. 2010); Citibank v. Mahmoud, 866 N.Y.S.2d 90 (N.Y. Civ. Ct. 2008); Citibank v. Martin, 807 N.Y.S.2d 284 (N.Y. Civ. Ct. 2005). *See* National Consumer Law Center, Consumer Credit Regulation Ch. 3 (2012), *updated at* www .nclc.org/library (discussing the conditions for a national bank to avoid a state's usury limits).

314 Citibank v. Martin, 807 N.Y.S.2d 284 (N.Y. Civ. Ct. 2005).

315 *See* Munoz v. Pipestone Fin., L.L.C., 513 F. Supp. 2d 1076 (D. Minn. 2007). *See also* Olvera v. Blitt & Gaines, P.C., 431 F.3d 285 (7th Cir. 2005) (assignee debt buyer permitted to collect same interest as original creditor under Illinois Interest Act); PRA III, L.L.C. v. Hund, 846 N.E.2d 965 (Ill. App. Ct. 2006) (same). *But see* Citibank v. Martin, 807 N.Y.S.2d 284 (N.Y. Civ. Ct. 2005) (holding that non-national bank assignee cannot charge interest in excess of state law cap).

316 *See* National Consumer Law Center, Truth in Lending Ch. 7 (8th ed. 2012), *updated at* www.nclc.org/library.

317 *See* American Express Travel Related Servs. Co. v. Assih, 893 N.Y.S.2d 438 (N.Y. Civ. Ct. 2009). *See also* Resurgence Fin., L.L.C. v. Taylor, 295 S.W.3d 429 (Tex. App. 2009); Citibank v. Cooper (Vt. Super. Ct. July 10, 2009), *available at* www.nclc.org/unreported.

If the collector produces a new agreement delineating the higher interest rate, the collector must also show that the consumer has consented to that agreement. The consent cannot be based upon the consumer's use the card when the change in rate notice has been sent after the consumer stopped using the card.[318] Instead, the collector must rely upon a provision in the original agreement that allows for a higher interest rate upon certain conditions being met. Then, the collector must prove that the conditions have been met to allow for the higher rate. As one court put it, the collector "must prove that the fluctuating interest rates, fees, and changing credit limit complied with the Cardmember Agreement. . . ."[319]

Assuming a collector establishes its right to include finance charges and other fees of a certain amount, the question arises whether it is entitled to finance charges and fees based upon the contract for the period *after* the account is closed, or only for the period while the account is open. This question is one of contractual interpretation, whose answer will depend solely upon the contract language and state law.[320]

4.5.4.4 Debt Buyer Cannot Assess Finance Charges That Creditor Has Waived

A debt buyer has only the rights assigned to it. If a creditor waives interest charges for a period of time prior to the sale of the account to a debt buyer, it is evident that the debt buyer cannot retroactively seek finance charges for that period.

This principle has important practical implications in the case of credit card debt that is charged off and then at a later date sold to a debt buyer. Truth in Lending Act disclosure requirements often lead credit card issuers to stop charging interest and fees after they charge off a debt (an accounting device usually taking place six months after default), because it allows the card issuers to stop sending periodic notices to the consumer.[321] Despite this, there are reports that debt buyers add additional interest charges—computed not from the date of their purchase of the debt but from the earlier charge-off date—to the amount the card issuer claims is due.

A recent federal court decision in *McDonald* has found that, when the card issuer stopped charging interest as of the charge-off date, the debt buyer has no authority to compute interest starting from the charge-off date instead of the date on which the debt buyer purchased the account.[322] The card issuer waived that interest starting with the charge off date, and the debt buyer cannot undo what its assignor has done.[323] Instead, the debt buyer, at best, can only charge additional interest from the date it purchased the debt and only if it has a basis for so charging.

Not only is the interest charged between the charge-off date and the purchase date unauthorized, it may also be a Fair Debt Collection Practices Act (FDCPA) violation. The federal court in *McDonald* certified a class and granted summary judgment for the class on its FDCPA claim as to liability.[324]

This ruling may have particular applicability to a credit card account that is sold and resold a number of times—a common occurrence with credit card debt buyers. The last debt buyer in the chain bringing suit will have to justify any interest charge it seeks for the period after the account has been charged off. Does it have evidence that a prior debt buyer in the chain of title demanded interest from the consumer? Does it know when the prior debt buyer obtained the account? And does it know from what date the prior debt buyer computed interest?

The implication of the *McDonald* ruling is that the debt buyer bringing suit can only assess interest for those periods during which the owners of the debt had the right to, and in fact did, assess interest. It will be very tempting for the last debt buyer in the chain of title to avoid all these complications by using the charge-off date to trigger interest charges. *McDonald* indicates that this would clearly improper and may lead to an FDCPA cause of action.

4.5.5 Impact on the Collector's Cause of Action When a Contract Is Not Proven

The existence of a contract is an essential element in a cause of action for breach of contract. Failure to prove the existence of a contract will result in the claim being denied. The collector may be able to prevail on alternative claims not based upon the contract (for example, account stated or open account), but these alternative claims must have been clearly pleaded. The collector cannot change directions and switch theories, unless the court gives it leave to amend its pleadings.[325] The court should not deny the breach of contract claim but render judgment for the collector on a different theory not pleaded.[326]

In pursuing alternative theories of recovery, because no contract has been proven, the collector may find itself in a much less advantageous position. The statute of limitations for the alternate claims should not be based upon the statute of limitations for a written contract, because the recovery is not based upon breach of a written contract. The contract also cannot be the basis for the collector to seek attorney fees. There

318 *See* Remit Corp. v. Potter (Pa. Ct. Com. Pl. June 2, 2008), *available at* www.nclc.org/unreported; Effel v. McGarry, 339 S.W.3d 789 (Tex. App. 2011); First Select Corp. v. Grimes, 2003 WL 151940 (Tex. App. Jan. 23, 2003). *See also* American Express Bank, FSB v. Dalbis, 2011 WL 873512 (N.Y. Civ. Ct. Mar. 14, 2011). *But see* Del. Code Ann. tit. 5, § 952(b)(2) (allowing unilateral changes in card agreement even after consumer stops using card; note that card issuers may attempt to apply this statute to consumers in other states when contract selects Delaware law).

319 *See also* Citibank v. Cooper (Vt. Super. Ct. July 10, 2009), *available at* www.nclc.org/unreported.

320 Citibank v. Martin, 807 N.Y.S.2d 284 (N.Y. Civ. Ct. 2005) (cannot charge contract rate after the account is closed unless the contract so specifies).

321 *See* 12 C.F.R. § 1026.5(b)(2)(i).

322 *See* McDonald v. Asset Acceptance L.L.C., 2013 WL 4028947 (E.D. Mich. Aug. 7, 2013).

323 *Id.*

324 *Id.*

325 *See* § 4.4, *supra*.

326 *Id.*

may be a statutory entitlement to recover attorney fees,[327] but there can be no contractual recovery of attorney fees without a contract.[328]

If there is no contract, then there is no entitlement to contractual finance charges or other fees. It is not enough just to point to some monthly statements containing an interest rate disclosure.[329] This poses a difficult problem for a collector, depending on the alternative theory selected. If the collector uses an account stated claim and proves that the consumer has consented to a statement of account, it can recover interest and other fees that are included in that account stated but cannot recover contractual interest charges for the period after that statement of account.[330]

If the collector instead uses an "open account," "on account," or "money lent" cause of action, it may not be able to recover contract interest at all. In delineating past amounts lent to the consumer, the collector will have to exclude finance charges and other fees, because there is no contractual basis for them. The collector can only recover for cash advances or purchases but not for finance charges and fees.[331] But a debt buyer not entitled to finance charges or other fees is in a particularly difficult position, because the debt buyer will have records of the alleged total dollar amount owed by the consumer but no information on how the total amount is broken down between principal and interest and fees.

Any prejudgment or postjudgment interest must be based upon the state's statutory "legal" rate, and not upon the contract rate, because there is no proven contract.[332] Moreover, state statutes providing for prejudgment interest generally are interpreted as providing for interest when claims are liquidated or are for a readily ascertainable amount[333] but are not interpreted as providing for interest when the amount is not readily ascertainable.[334] For example, claims based upon *quantum meruit* may not be entitled to prejudgment interest.[335] Nevertheless, some courts award interest on claims that are not liquidated, if the damages are roughly ascertainable.[336] Other statutes do not allow prejudgment interest on the finance charge portion of an obligation, whether or not that charge is ascertainable.[337]

4.6 Seeking the Balance Due on Open-End Accounts

4.6.1 On Account, Open Account, and Breach of Contract

Proof of a written contract is not enough and may not even by necessary for a collector to recover on an open-end account, such as one involving a credit card, or cell phone, cable, water, gas, or electricity service. The collector must prove its damages—that is, the unpaid credit balance. Causes of action for the unpaid balance of an open account often are termed "on account" or "open account," but may use different terminology in other states. The cause of action may not even require

327 *See* § 6.2, *infra*.

328 *See, e.g.*, NetJets Aviation, Inc. v. LHC Commc'ns, L.L.C., 537 F.3d 18 (2d Cir. 2008); Rental Co., L.L.C. v. Carter Group, Inc., 399 SW 3d 63 (Mo. Ct. App. 2013); Citibank v. Martin, 807 N.Y.S.2d 284 (N.Y. Civ. Ct. 2005); Capital One Bank v. Heidebrink, 2009 WL 1741515 (Ohio Ct. App. June 19, 2009); Jaramillo v. Portfolio Acquisitions, L.L.C., 2010 WL 1197669 (Tex. App. Mar. 30, 2010) (attorney fees not available under the contract, but available under a state statute providing for such fees when a collector recovers on a *quantum meruit* basis).

329 Tully v. Citibank, 173 S.W.3d 212 (Tex. App. 2005). *See also* Citibank v. Majka (N.Y. Sup. Ct. July 18, 2012), *available at* www.nclc.org/unreported.

330 *See* § 4.7.1, *infra*.

331 *See* FIA Card Servs. v. Kirasic (Pa. Ct. Com. Pl. Nov. 7, 2007) (Wettick, J.), *available at* www.nclc.org/unreported.

332 *See* Jarvis v. First Resolution Mgmt. Corp., 983 N.E.2d 380 (Ohio Ct. App. 2012) (postjudgment interest only allowed at statutory rate when no contract proved).

333 Weaver v. Caldwell Tanks, Inc., 190 Fed. Appx. 404 (6th Cir. 2006) (prejudgment interest should have been awarded because damages were liquidated, as amount of sales commissions could be calculated when contract fixed the rate and due date); Egge v. Healthspan Servs., 2002 WL 31426190 (D. Minn. Oct. 28, 2002) (prejudgment interest allowed on "any legal indebtedness" if "liquidated or readily ascertainable"; when amount of overdue medical bill was not challenged, it was "readily ascertainable" even though conciliation court awarded less than hospital demanded); Heaven v. Timber Hill, L.L.C., 2004 WL 2547440 (Conn. Super. Ct. Oct. 21, 2004) (in contract action for liquidated sum, court has discretion to award up to 10% interest if "equitable considerations warrant" the payment of interest), *aff'd on other grounds*, 900 A.2d 560 (Conn. App. Ct. 2006); Cain v. Cain, 967 So. 2d 654 (Miss. Ct. App. 2007) (allowing prejudgment interest when amount due is certain, but liability is in doubt); State *ex rel.* Key W. Retaining Sys., Inc. v. Holm II, Inc., 59 P.3d 1280 (Or. Ct. App. 2002) (amount due was liquidated, and prejudgment interest should be awarded, when there was no "complicated series of transactions" even though there was dispute over amount; defendant owed a sum certain on a date certain); Crowley v. Black, 167 P.3d 1087 (Utah Ct. App. 2007) (allowing prejudgment interest "when both the amount due and the due date may be ascertained"; both lost rent and repair charges were readily ascertainable, even though repair charges reduced for normal wear and tear).

334 Champion Produce, Inc. v. Ruby Robinson Co., 342 F.3d 1016 (9th Cir. 2003) (Idaho law; amount due not "readily ascertainable" when it was key issue of "close and difficult" case with no prevailing party); Orion Fin. Corp. v. Am. Foods Group, Inc., 281 F.3d 733 (8th Cir. 2002) (prejudgment interest only available when damages known or reasonably ascertainable); Opportunity, L.L.C. v. Ossewarde, 38 P.3d 1258 (Idaho 2002) (when amount due not "capable of mathematical calculation" because it depended on contested market value of property, prejudgment interest denied); Structure & Design Unlimited, Inc. v. Contemporary Concepts, Bldg. & Design, Inc., 151 S.W.3d 904 (Mo. Ct. App. 2004) (prejudgment interest only available on liquidated claims; merely denying claim does not make it unliquidated; here, prejudgment interest allowed for cost of materials, which was clear, but not for labor costs, which were indefinite and sharply disputed).

335 *See* § 4.8, *infra*.

336 Dan B. Dobbs, Handbook on the Law of Remedies § 3.6 (2d ed. 1993). *See also* Scotts Co. v. Cent. Garden & Pet Co., 256 F. Supp. 2d 734 (S.D. Ohio 2003) (Ohio allows prejudgment interest whether or not claim is liquidated, or capable of ascertainment before court's determination; question is when claim became "due and payable" and which legal rate of interest applies); 11 Joseph M. Perillo, Corbin on Contracts § 57.18 (rev. ed. 2005).

337 D.A.N. Joint Venture III, L.P. v. Turk, 138 P.3d 1253 (Kan. Ct. App. 2006) (Kansas law allows prejudgment interest only on "the unpaid principal balance"; collection of interest on prejudgment interest violated the U.C.C.C.).

proof of a written contract but only proof of entitlement to the unpaid balance of the open-end account.[338]

The action for "on account" or "open account" allows the collector to prove in one action a series of charges and payments, resulting in a balance due, instead of having to bring a separate action for each individual charge.[339] As described in § 4.6.3, *infra*, though, there must still be some proof of each charge.

The consumer admitting to being in default (at trial, in responsive pleadings, or in an admission) is consistent with the consumer still disputing the size of the balance owing. The collector must still prove the exact amount due and how that amount was derived.[340] The fact that the consumer did not exercise rights under the Fair Credit Billing Act to dispute charges does not mean that the consumer has admitted to the amount due claimed by the collector.[341]

"Account stated" (examined in § 4.7, *infra*) is an entirely different cause of action than "on account," with different elements of proof.[342] It is easy to confuse the two, as both seek to prove a statement of account, and proof of the elements of "on account" sometimes involve proof of an account stated. Nevertheless, these are two separate causes of action and will be examined in two different sections of this chapter. Neither the collector nor the court should mix up the elements of these two causes of action or allow recovery on one when the collector only pleads the other.[343]

Historically, the causes of action for "on account" and "open account" involved a merchant and a consumer engaging in a series of purchases and payments, with no involvement of a third-party lender. Some courts question whether these common law causes of action even apply to a credit card debt, in which a lender finances a series of purchases from different merchants.[344] In other states "on account" or "open account" may not apply when there is a written contract. For example, California courts hold that an "open account" is "an unsettled debt, arising from items of work and labor, goods sold and delivered, and other open transactions, not reduced to writing," the sole record of which is usually the account books of the owner of the demand. The cause of action does not include express contracts or obligations reduced to writing.[345] In these states, a collector seeking to recover on credit card debt or other open-end debt based upon a written contract will have to utilize a different cause of action.

Of course, the collector can bring a breach of contract claim. In that case, the collector must prove a written contract, as examined in § 4.5, *supra*, breach of that contract, and the damages resulting from that breach. The breach is non-payment and the damages are the current amount due on the open-end account. Thus, this requires similar proof as an action for "on account" or "open account" as to establishing the amount due.

However a state or the collector labels the cause of action, this section examines the proof a collector must produce to recover the balance on an open-end account. The proof will be similar whatever the cause of action pleaded, with the exception of an account stated claim, which is based upon the consumer's agreement as to the amount due and the promise to pay that amount.[346] While the proof of the amount due on a breach of contract, "on account," or "open account" claim may be similar, § 4.6.2, *infra*, sets out how the collector's proof and the consequences of a collector's recovery will be very different depending upon whether the collector proves a binding written contract in conjunction with proof of the balance owed.

4.6.2 *Implications of Failure to Prove a Written Contract*

Even if a collector recovers on an open-end account or on account theory without proof of a written contract, the failure to prove that contract has a dramatic effect on the collector's recovery, as set out in more detail at § 4.5.5, *supra*. The collector's entitlement to finance charges and other fees are established by written contract. Without proof of such a contract, the collector is not entitled to recover finance charges or other fees as part of the balance due.[347] The collector's proof of the account balance should include only charges for cash advances and for goods and services purchased but should *not* include charges for finance charges, late fees, over-the-limit fees, and other fees.[348] A debt buyer not entitled to finance charges or other fees is in a particularly difficult position because the debt buyer will have to identify, for each billing statement, which portion of the statement is for credit charges and which is for finance charges and other fees.[349]

338 *See, e.g.*, Berlin v. Pickett, 221 S.W.3d 406 (Mo. Ct. App. 2006). On the other hand, if characterization of an account as open-ended is spurious, then the collector must prove a written contract in the closed-end transaction. Hurley State Bank v. Pickens, 861 So. 2d 846 (La. Ct. App. 2003).

339 *See* Capital One Bank v. Toney, 2007 WL 969420 (Ohio Ct. App. Mar. 28, 2007); Great Seneca Fin. v. Felty, 869 N.E.2d 30 (Ohio Ct. App. 2006).

340 Asset Acceptance Corp. v. Proctor, 804 N.E.2d 975 (Ohio Ct. App. 2004).

341 This Fair Credit Billing Act defense is described in more detail in § 4.7.6, *infra*.

342 Moreover, an action in Texas on a sworn account has different elements than either an action on an "account stated" or "on account." *See* § 4.9, *infra*.

343 *See* § 4.4, *supra*.

344 *Cf.* Citibank v. Whiteley, 149 S.W.3d 599 (Mo. Ct. App. 2004) (recognizing but not reaching the issue).

345 *See* Los Angeles Cnty. v. Continental Corp., 248 P.2d 157 (Cal. Ct. App. 1952) (quoting People v. Magee, 41 Cal. App. 727 (Cal. Ct. App. 1919)).

346 *See* § 4.7, *infra*.

347 *See* § 4.5.5, *supra*. *See also* FIA Card Servs. v. Kirasic (Pa. Ct. Com. Pl. Nov. 7, 2007) (Wettick, J.), *available at* www.nclc.org/unreported; Target Nat'l Bank v. Samanez (Pa. Ct. Com. Pl. Dec. 19, 2007) (Wettick, J.), *available at* www.nclc.org/unreported.

348 *See* FIA Card Servs. v. Kirasic (Pa. Ct. Com. Pl. Nov. 7, 2007) (Wettick, J.), *available at* www.nclc.org/unreported. *See also* Target Nat'l Bank v. Samanez (Pa. Ct. Com. Pl. Dec. 19, 2007) (Wettick, J.), *available at* www.nclc.org/unreported.

349 *See* FIA Card Servs. v. Kirasic (Pa. Ct. Com. Pl. Nov. 7, 2007) (Wettick, J.), *available at* www.nclc.org/unreported. *See also* Target Nat'l Bank v. Samanez (Pa. Ct. Com. Pl. Dec. 19, 2007) (Wettick, J.), *available at* www.nclc.org/unreported.

If the collector offers no proof of a written contract, it cannot recover attorney fees based upon that contract,[350] and it cannot seek to use another state's law based upon a contractual choice of law.[351] Similarly, the statute of limitations cannot be one based upon a written contract but must be some other applicable limitations period established by state law.[352]

4.6.3 Required Proof As to the Balance Due

One court has described how to prove the balance due:

> [A]n account must show the name of the party charged. It begins with a balance, preferably at zero, or with a sum recited that can qualify as [a specified amount that the consumer has previously agreed to pay], but at least the balance should be a provable sum. Following the balance, the item or items, dated and identifiable by number or otherwise, representing charges, or debits, and credits, should appear. Summarization is necessary showing a running or developing balance or an arrangement which permits the calculation of the balance claimed to be due.[353]

Courts require the collector to prove the amount of the charges for goods and services that are part of the claim, the dates of the charges, credits for payments, dates and amounts of interest charges, and dates and amounts of other charges (assuming there is proof of contractual entitlement to such interest and related charges).[354] The collector must produce not just the most recent statement but all monthly statements going back to a zero balance or a dollar amount to which the consumer has previously agreed.[355]

The collector does not meet its burden by showing a series of monthly statements, when those statements already start with a substantial balance.[356] Nevertheless, there are limits to how far back a collector need go. One court indicated that the collector need not go back thirty years to show each monthly statement, but it was sufficient to provide more than four years of statements.[357] The rule in Iowa is that the collector need not go back to a zero balance, but, if the evidence starts with an original amount due (for example, $1000) and shows a final balance of a higher number (for example, $3000), then the collector can recover only the difference between the two (example, $2000) and not the final balance.[358]

The collector need not prove each individual charge with signed sales slips or the like (unless the consumer disputes that charge),[359] but the collector must provide an itemized, running balance. Courts, for example, may accept as evidence a series of monthly statements relating to the charges at issue but should not accept just the most recent monthly statement,[360] unless the statement starts with a zero balance. When the terms of the written contract are not proven, the collector should specify as charges only cash advances and purchases of goods and services but not finance charges or other fees.[361]

New Jersey courts require that the collector produce the transactions for which payment has not been made, any payments that have been paid, the annual percentage and finance charge percentage rates, and the billing cycle information.[362] Wisconsin's Consumer Act provides that, upon the consumer's written request, the collector must submit copies of writing

350 Of course, state law can still provide for such fees. *See, e.g.*, Miss. Code Ann. § 11-53-81 (establishing the right to attorney fees if the collector first sends written demand correctly setting forth the amount owed with an itemized statement of the account in support of that demand).

351 *See* § 4.5.5, *supra*.

352 *See* § 3.6.6.1, *supra*.

353 Asset Acceptance Corp. v. Proctor, 804 N.E.2d 975, 977 (Ohio Ct. App. 2004) (quoting Brown v. Columbus Stamping & Mfg. Co., 223 N.E.2d 373 (Ohio Ct. App. 1967)); Capital Fin. Credit, L.L.C. v. Mays, 944 N.E.2d 1184 (Ohio Ct. App. 2010). *See also In re* Leverett, 378 B.R. 793 (E.D. Tex. 2007); CACV of Colorado, L.L.C. v. Spiehler, 11 So. 3d 673 (La. Ct. App. 2009); Premier Capital, L.L.C. v. Baker, 972 N.E.2d 1125 (Ohio Ct. App. 2012); Citibank v. Ogunduyile, 2007 WL 2812969 (Ohio Ct. App. Sept. 28, 2007); Capital One Bank v. Toney, 2007 WL 969420 (Ohio Ct. App. Mar. 28, 2007); Great Seneca Fin. v. Felty, 869 N.E.2d 30 (Ohio Ct. App. 2006). *But cf.* Ohio Receivables, L.L.C. v. Dallariva, 2012 WL 2859923 (Ohio Ct. App. July 12, 2012) (five years of billing statements sufficient even though statements do not start at zero balance).

354 Arrow Fin. Serv., L.L.C. v. Guiliani, 32 A.3d 1055 (Me. 2011). *See* LVNV Funding, L.L.C. v. Matthews, 15 Fla. L. Weekly Supp. 65a (Fla. Duval Cnty. Ct. Oct. 4, 2007), *available at* www.nclc.org/unreported (citing Fla. R. Civ. P. Form 1.932); CACV of Colorado, L.L.C. v. Spiehler, 11 So. 3d 673 (La. Ct. App. 2009); FIA Card Servs. v. Kirasic (Pa. Ct. Com. Pl. Nov. 7, 2007) (Wettick, J.), *available at* www.nclc.org/unreported. *See also* Portfolio Recovery Assocs., L.L.C. v. Ginn, 897 N.Y.S.2d 672 (N.Y. App. Term 2009); Unifund CCR Partners v. Hemm, 2009 WL 2106289 (Ohio Ct. App. July 17, 2009); Remit Corp. v. Potter (Pa. Ct. Com. Pl. June 2, 2008), *available at* www.nclc.org/unreported; Palisades Collection, L.L.C v. Grassmyer (Pa. Ct. Com. Pl. Jan. 15, 2008), *available at* www.nclc.org/unreported; Target Nat'l Bank v. Samanez (Pa. Ct. Com. Pl. Dec. 19, 2007) (Wettick, J.), *available at* www.nclc.org/unreported; 1 Am. Jur. 2d *Accounts and Accounting* § 17 (2007).

355 H & H Design Builders, Inc. v. Travelers' Indem. Co., 639 So. 2d 697 (Fla. Dist. Ct. App. 1994); Chase Bank v. Rader, 8 Pa. D. & C.5th 297 (Pa. Ct. Com. Pl. 2009), *aff'd*, 15 A.3d 537 (Pa. Super. Ct. 2010); Target Nat'l Bank v. Greiner (Pa. Commw. Ct. Sept. 30, 2009), *available at* www.nclc.org/unreported.

356 Great Seneca Fin. v. Felty, 869 N.E.2d 30 (Ohio Ct. App. 2006); Chase Bank v. Rader, 8 Pa. D. & C.5th 297 (Pa. Ct. Com. Pl. 2009), *aff'd*, 15 A.3d 537 (Pa. Super. Ct. 2010).

357 Am. Express Travel Related Servs. v. Silverman, 2006 WL 3491741 (Ohio Ct. App. Dec. 5, 2006).

358 Capital One Bank v. Denboer, 791 N.W.2d 264 (Iowa Ct. App. 2010).

359 *See* Cavalry SPV, L.L.C. v. Anderson, 260 S.W.3d 331 (Ark. Ct. App. 2007); 1 Am. Jur. 2d *Accounts and Accounting* § 17 (2007).

360 *See* FIA Card Servs. v. Kirasic (Pa. Ct. Com. Pl. Nov. 7, 2007) (Wettick, J.), *available at* www.nclc.org/unreported. *See also* Target Nat'l Bank v. Samanez (Pa. Ct. Com. Pl. Dec. 19, 2007) (Wettick, J.), *available at* www.nclc.org/unreported. *But cf.* Meyers v. Nat'l City Bank, 903 N.E.2d 974 (Ind. Ct. App. 2009) (one year of billing statements, an affidavit from an employee of the card issuer with access and control over the account, and the consumer's failure to produce contrary evidence was sufficient for summary judgment for card issuer). On the other hand, an action for "account stated" may rely only on the most recent account statement. But do not confuse the elements of "account stated" with "on account."

361 *See* § 4.6.2, *supra*.

362 LVNV Funding, L.L.C. v. Colvell, 22 A.3d 125 (N.J. Super. Ct. App. Div. 2011).

evidencing any transaction in an open-end credit account, and no recovery can be had if the collector does not do so.[363] This provision is interpreted as requiring the collector to provide writings evidencing each and every transaction in the account.[364]

Of course, the statement of charges must be a statement sent to the consumer by the creditor. A debt buyer cannot mimic the look of a card issuer's statement of account and introduce this in court as the statement that was sent to the consumer.[365]

Even as to evidence of the balance due, collectors often present far less evidence than is required. It should not be enough for a debt buyer to obtain summary judgment by producing an affidavit from one of its employees and a computer printout with a dollar amount owed.[366] The printout does not qualify as an admissible business record,[367] and it lacks sufficient detail as to the individual charges. The printout is usually created well after the consumer's default, on a computer system not belonging to the original creditor.[368] Moreover, an affidavit from an employee of the debt buyer is hardly sufficient evidence as to the nature of the original creditor's bookkeeping.

In addition, no affidavit or summary sheet can satisfy the requirement that, to prevail on an open account claim, the collector must produce the actual statements or some other itemization of individual charges and payments.[369] Summary sheets do not itemize each charge and each payment.

When the consumer contests the amount owed, the collector should not be able to prevail on a summary judgment motion merely by submitting an affidavit attesting to the amount owed.[370] The collector will instead have to produce business records proving the amount owed, properly authenticated by affidavit.[371] The proper authentication of business records is examined in § 4.2.4.2, *supra*.

Proof of the balance due on an open-end account may require proof of the reasonableness of each separate charge.[372] For example, if there is no proof as to an agreed price for a medical service, the collector may have to show that the charges were reasonable.[373]

Courts have even suggested that a collector suing on an open-end account must prove the reasonableness of charges found on a credit card statement.[374] On the other hand, because a third-party credit card statement is just a list of credit extensions made to various merchants on the consumer's behalf, a court may find that the consumer requested extensions in those amounts and that they are thus reasonable. Of course, this rationale does *not* apply to charges assessed by the card issuer, such as finance charges, late fees, over the limit fees, and the like. If it cannot be proved that the consumer agreed to these charges, then the collector will have to show some basis for its right to charge for those fees and that the amount of each is reasonable.

The Truth in Lending Act requires that for a credit card obligation "the burden of proof is upon the card issuer to show the use was authorized."[375] This federal requirement implies that a collector in proving an account balance on a credit card debt must present some evidence that the consumer applied for the card and that card charges were authorized by the consumer.[376] The consumer's failure to dispute the charges earlier does not shift the burden of proof from the collector.[377]

4.7 Account Stated

4.7.1 General

Collectors suing on credit card or other open account debts may allege a cause of action for an "account stated" to avoid showing how the amount due was computed and to avoid having to prove the terms of a written contract. Avoiding such proof is especially attractive for a debt buyer that may have little documentation of the credit contract or of individual charges. Nevertheless, there are a number of difficulties a collector will encounter using the account stated theory, as will be detailed in this section.

A claim for account stated is *not* based upon the various individual transactions contributing to a current balance owing on a debt and is not based upon breach of a written contract. Instead, it is based upon an agreement that the consumer has been extended credit and the consumer's agreement, either explicit or implicit, to pay the amount provided for in an

363 Wis. Stat. § 425.109(2).

364 Newgard *ex rel.* Newgard v. Bank of Am., 735 N.W.2d 578 (Wis. Ct. App. 2007).

365 *See* LVNV Funding, L.L.C. v. Colvell, 22 A.3d 125 (N.J. Super. Ct. App. Div. 2011). *See also* Premier Capital, L.L.C. v. Baker, 972 N.E.2d 1125 (Ohio Ct. App. 2012). *Cf.* Hartman v. Great Seneca Fin. Corp., 569 F.3d. 606 (6th Cir. 2009) (consumer's FDCPA case against debt buyer, for deceptive introduction of its imitation of an account statement, could go to trial).

366 New Century Fin. Serv. v. Sanchez (N.J. Super. Ct. Law Div. Apr. 12, 2002), *available at* www.nclc.org/unreported. *See also* LVNV Funding, L.L.C. v. Colvell, 22 A.3d 125 (N.J. Super. Ct. App. Div. 2011).

367 *See* § 4.2.4, *supra.*

368 *See id.*

369 Capital One Bank v. Toney, 2007 WL 969420 (Ohio Ct. App. Mar. 28, 2007).

370 Capital Fin. Credit, L.L.C. v. Mays, 944 N.E.2d 1184 (Ohio Ct. App. 2010).

371 Unifund CCR Partners v. Harrell, 2005 WL 2082731 (Conn. Super. Ct. Aug. 3, 2005); Asset Acceptance, L.L.C. v. Lemon, 2007 WL 3408304 (Ohio Ct. App. Nov. 5, 2007); Great Seneca Fin. v. Felty, 869 N.E.2d 30 (Ohio Ct. App. 2006). *Cf.* American Express Travel Related Servs. v. Silverman, 2006 WL 3491741 (Ohio Ct. App. Dec. 5, 2006) (affidavits found adequate to authenticate the records); Citibank v. Ogunduyile, 2007 WL 2812969 (Ohio Ct. App. Sept. 28, 2007) (same).

372 Citibank v. Whiteley, 149 S.W.3d 599 (Mo. Ct. App. 2004). *See also* Midwestern Health Mgmt., Inc. v. Walker, 208 S.W.3d 295 (Mo. Ct. App. 2006); 1 Am. Jur. 2d *Accounts and Accounting* § 8 (2007).

373 *See* § 9.5.5, *infra*.

374 *See* Citibank v. Miller, 222 S.W.3d 318 (Mo. Ct. App. 2007).

375 15 U.S.C. § 1643(b).

376 *See* Jones v. Citibank, 2008 WL 651689 (Ark. Ct. App. Mar. 12, 2008); Jones v. Citibank, 2008 WL 442627 (Ark. Ct. App. Feb. 20, 2008); Danner v. Discover Bank, 257 S.W.3d 113 (Ark. Ct. App. 2007); Unifund CCR Assignee of Providian v. Ayhan, 2008 WL 2974639 (Wash. Ct. App. Aug. 5, 2008). *See also* Bank of New York–Delaware v. Santarelli, 491 N.Y.S.2d 980 (N.Y. Greene Cnty. Ct. 1985). *See generally* National Consumer Law Center, Truth in Lending § 7.1.1.1 (8th ed. 2012), *updated at* www.nclc.org/library.

377 *See* § 4.7.6, *infra*.

account statement.[378] Instead of presenting to the court a series of monthly statements leading to the amount owed, the collector shows that the consumer is obligated on an account, that the consumer has been presented with an accounting of the amount owing, and that the consumer has explicitly or implicitly agreed to pay that amount. Some courts find this implicit agreement based upon little more than the consumer's silence upon receiving the account statement.

An account stated is an independent cause of action, superseding a cause of action based upon the credit agreement and the individual charges. In effect, the cause of action states that the parties have come to a new agreement that the consumer will pay a certain amount. The action then seeks to enforce this later agreement and is not based upon the original contract or charges.

There are several important limitations to the account stated cause of action because it is not based upon the original written contract. A contractual choice of law provision is not applicable to a claim for account stated, because the new agreement between the parties does not contain such a provision and the preexisting contract has not been proven.

Because an account stated claim typically is not founded upon a written contract between the parties but rather is based upon the consumer's implicit assent, the applicable statute of limitations is not one based upon a written contract. Instead, the applicable limitations period may be one for non-written contracts or one that is explicitly applicable to claims based upon account stated. In many states such limitations periods are shorter than for a written contract.[379]

An important implication of the account stated cause of action not being based upon the original written contract is that the collector is not entitled to contractual attorney fees.[380] The collector can only recover attorney fees based upon a statute, if one is applicable.

If the collector can prove that the consumer agreed to a statement of account, the amount in that statement might include finance charges and various fees. The collector can recover those amounts if it can show that the consumer consented to pay those amounts. But the collector has no right to recover finance charges or other fees pursuant to the contract *in addition* to those listed in the statement of account that may accrue during the period after the account statement has been presented.[381] The agreed-upon statement of account sets out a balance owed at that point in time and does not include the right to future amounts. If the collector seeks interest after that date, it can only do so based upon an applicable "legal" right of prejudgment or postjudgment interest provided for by state statute.

4.7.2 Does State Law Recognize the Account Stated Cause of Action?

The account stated claim developed historically when a consumer entered into a series of transactions with a merchant, and the merchant kept an accounting of those transactions. The cause of action was not developed with credit card transactions in mind and may be difficult to use for this type of debt, particularly in certain states.

Examine state law as to the availability of an account stated cause of action and note any limits on that cause of action for the type of debt at issue.

Pennsylvania courts, in particular, are skeptical of the account stated cause as it applies to credit card transactions. Thus, a Pennsylvania court has found that:

> [A]n account stated theory is not appropriate in a credit card account case. . . . An account stated theory may have been appropriate when credit card issuers gave cardholders fixed interest rates and charged very few fees. With the proliferation of credit cards over the past two decades, however, interest rates have varied and fees have increased in numbers and severity. It is unreasonable to expect the average debtor to understand the changing terms of a Customer Agreement such that he or she can object to any invoice received in a timely manner. For many, the first and only time they will consider what is in the "fine print" is when they fall behind on payments and find themselves in a position like the one in which Defendant now finds herself.[382]

Other Pennsylvania courts significantly limit the cause of action by finding that the consumer's silence is not assent to a credit card statement of account.[383]

A Vermont court has pointed out that there have been no account stated cases in that state since 1940 and has also raised doubts as to whether the doctrine applies to credit card debt when computations of payments and shifts in interest rates are not clear on the face of the account.[384]

---

378 Univ. of S. Ala. v. Bracy, 466 So. 2d 148 (Ala. Civ. App. 1985); Ahlbin v. Crescent Commercial Corp., 224 P.2d 131 (Cal. Ct. App. 1950); LVNV Funding, L.L.C. v. Moehrlin (Fla. Volusia Cnty. Ct. 2006) (Green, J.), *available at* www.nclc.org/unreported; Bank of New York–Delaware v. Santarelli, 491 N.Y.S.2d 980 (N.Y. Greene Cnty. Ct. 1985); Morrison v. Citibank, 2008 WL 553284 (Tex. App. Feb. 28, 2008); Restatement (Second) of Contracts § 282 (1981).

379 *See* § 3.6.4.1, *supra*. *See also* Richburg v. Palisades Collection, L.L.C., 247 F.R.D. 457 (E.D. Pa. 2008).

380 *See, e.g.*, NetJets Aviation, Inc. v. LHC Commc'ns, L.L.C., 537 F.3d 168 (2d Cir. 2008).

381 Citibank v. Martin, 807 N.Y.S.2d 284 (N.Y. Civ. Ct. 2005); Capital One Bank v. Heidebrink, 2009 WL 1741515 (Ohio Ct. App. June 19, 2009). *See also* WC Milling, L.L.C. v. Grooms, 841 N.E.2d 324 (Ohio Ct. App. 2005) (Ohio statute allows parties to set own interest rate for, *inter alia*, accounts stated, but requires a written agreement; not shown here, when no advance agreement as to interest and monthly statements disclosing interest rate never signed by buyers); Citibank v. Majka (N.Y. Sup. Ct. July 18, 2012), *available at* www.nclc.org/unreported.

382 Capital One Bank v. Clevenstine, 7 Pa. D. & C. 153 (Pa. Ct. Com. Pl. 2009). *See also* JMMM PC Corp. v. Stillwagon (Pa. Ct. Com. Pl. Mar. 31, 2011), *available at* www.nclc.org/unreported.

383 *See* Target Nat'l Bank v. Samanez (Pa. Ct. Com. Pl. Dec. 19, 2007), *available at* www.nclc.org;unreported. *See also* Target Nat'l Bank v. Greiner (Pa. Commw. Ct. Sept. 30, 2009), *available at* www.nclc.org;unreported.

384 Citibank v. Cooper (Vt. Super. Ct. July 10, 2009), *available at* www.nclc.org/unreported.

Wisconsin, by statute, has sharply limited the account stated cause of action in consumer credit transactions. Wisconsin's Consumer Act provides that, upon the consumer's written request, the collector must submit copies of writings evidencing any transaction in an open-end credit account, and no recovery can be had for the collector if it does not do so.[385] This provision has been interpreted as requiring the collector to provide written evidence of each and every transaction in the account,[386] and applies even to claims based upon an account stated.[387] In other words, even when the collector presents a statement of account and the consumer consents to that account, the consumer, when sued, can still demand evidence of each and every charge, and the collector cannot recover on any charges if it does not produce that evidence.[388]

New York law states that: "No agreement between the issuer and the holder shall contain any provision that a statement sent by the issuer to the holder shall be deemed correct unless objected to within a specified period of time. Any such provision is against public policy and shall be of no force or effect."[389] While not explicitly prohibiting account stated causes of action for credit card debt, it does indicate a legislative intent that liability should not be built upon the consumer's silence upon receiving an account. At least one New York court has rejected an account stated claim on this basis.[390] But New York appellate cases have ruled otherwise, without mentioning the New York statute.[391]

Connecticut at one point had a statute specifying the elements of a claim for account stated but has since repealed that statute.[392] Nevertheless, courts in Connecticut apparently allow a common law claim for account stated.[393]

Iowa's version of the 1974 Uniform Commercial Credit Code requires "an indication of how that amount was determined."[394] An appellate court has found that this does not preclude a claim based upon an account stated.[395]

There has been some confusion about Texas law. In Texas a "sworn account" (sometimes called "on account") claim cannot be used to collect on a credit card debt,[396] but an account stated claim *can* be pursued on a credit card debt.[397]

4.7.3 Requirement of an Underlying Obligation

For an account stated cause of action, there must be proof of an underlying obligation. The collector should offer proof that the consumer agreed to the relationship between the parties.[398] There must be an independent basis for liability—the accounting merely establishes the amount of the debt, not that there is a debt.[399] Thus, providing a copy of the credit agreement may be a precondition to an account stated cause of action.[400] Even an unsigned contract may not be enough if there is no evidence that a consumer has assented to the contract.[401] Other courts are satisfied with evidence of an implied agreement and do not require proof of a written agreement.[402]

If there is no existing relationship between the parties, the account stated cause of action does not apply.[403] An entity with no preexisting relationship with the consumer cannot send to the consumer a statement of an amount owed and then use the consumer's silence or other conduct to claim that the consumer has assented to the amount. For example, the consumer is not required to object to a debt buyer's dunning letter made to look like a statement and sent years after the account was closed. Merely receiving statements regarding an account that the consumer believes does not belong to the consumer cannot show assent to a statement of account.[404]

385 Wis. Stat. § 425.109(2).

386 Newgard *ex rel.* Newgard v. Bank of Am., 735 N.W.2d 578 (Wis. Ct. App. 2007).

387 *Id.*

388 *Id.*

389 N.Y. Gen. Bus. Law § 517 (McKinney).

390 Bank of New York–Delaware v. Santarelli, 491 N.Y.S.2d 980 (N.Y. Greene Cnty. Ct. 1985).

391 *See* Citibank v. Jones, 708 N.Y.S.2d 517 (N.Y. App. Div. 2000).

392 Conn. Gen. Stat. § 52-113 was repealed in 1978, by 1978 Conn. Pub. Acts 379, §§ 26, 27.

393 *See* Credit One, L.L.C. v. Head, 977 A.2d 767 (Conn. App. Ct. 2009); Palisades Collection, L.L.C. v. Wright, 2009 WL 416187 (Conn. Super. Ct. Jan. 27, 2009); Citibank v. Moniz, 2008 WL 714134 (Conn. Super. Ct. Feb. 27, 2008); Citibank v. Strumpf, 2006 WL 2773540 (Conn. Super. Ct. Sept. 13, 2006); Citibank v. Morgan, 2006 WL 574211 (Conn. Super. Ct. Feb. 27, 2006). *Contra* American Express Centurion Bank v. LaRose (Conn. Super. Ct. Dec. 12, 2013), *available at* www .nclc.org/unreported (account stated is merely a form of proving damages for breach of contract).

394 Iowa Code § 537.5114.

395 Capital One Bank v. Denboer, 791 N.W.2d 264 (Iowa Ct. App. 2010).

396 *See* Williams v. Unifund CCR Partners Assignee of Citibank, 264 S.W.3d 231 (Tex. App. 2008); Tully v. Citibank, 173 S.W.3d 212 (Tex. App. 2005).

397 *See* Busch v. Hudson & Keyse, L.L.C., 312 S.W.3d 294 (Tex. App. 2010); Jaramillo v. Portfolio Acquisitions, L.L.C., 2010 WL 1197669 (Tex. App. Mar. 30, 2010); Dulong v. Citibank, 261 S.W.3d 890 (Tex. App. 2008).

398 Cach, L.L.C. v. Stupack, 2010 WL 1225029 (Conn. Super. Ct. Mar. 1, 2010); Nelson v. First Nat'l Bank of Omaha, 2004 WL 2711032 (Minn. Ct. App. Nov. 30, 2004).

399 Trafton v. Youngblood, 442 P.2d 648 (Cal. 1968); Cach, L.L.C. v. Stupack, 2010 WL 1225029 (Conn. Super. Ct. Mar. 1, 2010); Dreyer Med. Clinic v. Corral, 591 N.E.2d 111 (Ill. App. Ct. 1992) (account stated is method of proving damages; creditor must first prove liability; creditor failed to prove several essential elements); Gen. Elec. Capital Corp. v. MHPG, Inc., 2006 WL 2560314 (Mass. Super. Ct. July 27, 2006); Nelson v. First Nat'l Bank of Omaha, 2004 WL 2711032 (Minn. Ct. App. Nov. 30, 2004); Citibank v. Martin, 807 N.Y.S.2d 284 (N.Y. Civ. Ct. 2005) (account stated cannot create a liability when none existed); Unifund CCR Partners v. Dover, 681 S.E.2d 565 (N.C. Ct. App. 2009).

400 Capital One Bank v. Denboer, 791 N.E.2d 264 (Iowa Ct. App. 2010).

401 Nelson v. First Nat'l Bank of Omaha, 2004 WL 2711032 (Minn. Ct. App. Nov. 30, 2004).

402 Busch v. Hudson & Keyse, L.L.C., 312 S.W.3d 294 (Tex. App. 2010).

403 Trafton v. Youngblood, 442 P.2d 648 (Cal. 1968); Cach, L.L.C. v. Stupack, 2010 WL 1225029 (Conn. Super. Ct. Mar. 1, 2010); Nelson v. First Nat'l Bank of Omaha, 2004 WL 2711032 (Minn. Ct. App. Nov. 30, 2004); Dodeka v. Keith, 2012 WL 6738479 (Ohio Ct. App. Dec. 31, 2012).

404 Nelson v. First Nat'l Bank of Omaha, 2004 WL 2711032 (Minn. Ct. App. Nov. 30, 2004).

4.7.4 Collector Must Introduce Into Evidence an Adequate Statement of Account

The collector must present into evidence the statement upon which the cause of action depends; in some states, the statement must be appended to the complaint.[405] Failure to produce a statement of account is grounds to dismiss the action.[406]

The statement must be more than just a memorandum and must indicate that it is intended to be a final settlement of an account up to date.[407] It should include more than a mere summary number but should indicate individual items, the accrual of each item, and the amount of each item.

A North Carolina statute requires "a verified itemized statement of such account."[408] A North Carolina appellate court has found a statement of account inadequate when it shows a previous balance and a separate listing for finance charges and fees but does not itemize the credit charges.[409]

Connecticut courts also appear to require that, in the context of a credit card case, the collector produce each and every monthly statement sent to the consumer. A court found inadequate the most recent two years of monthly account statements and found that the account stated claim required copies of all statements going back to when the account was opened.[410]

A debt buyer's letter indicating a balance due without more is certainly not a statement of account, even if it has been made to look like a billing statement.[411] The collector has shown no preexisting relationship between the parties. Without demonstration of an underlying obligation of the consumer to the collector, there can be no recovery on an account stated.[412]

Debt buyers sometimes submit as an account stated a copy of the collector's demand for payment and notice to the consumer of the right to seek verification of the debt. Such a statement cannot act as the basis for an account stated cause of action. The federal Fair Debt Collection Practices Act explicitly states that "the failure of a consumer to dispute the validity of a debt under this section may not be construed by any court as an admission of liability by the consumer."[413] A Pennsylvania court has also required more than just one billing statement to be an adequate statement of an account upon which to base a collection action.[414]

Any account statement must also be introduced properly as a business record.[415] When the collector seeks summary judgment, the affidavit describing the statement of account must be consistent with the document it is authenticating. In one case the affiant described the items as purchases when they were monthly charges for cell phone usage, negating the affidavit's credibility.[416] The affidavit must also be based upon personal knowledge and must meet the other requirements for an affidavit introducing a business record.[417] An employee of the debt buyer is also not qualified to produce an affidavit authenticating the originating creditor's statement of account.[418]

Debt buyers and even creditors have a tendency to produce statements of account prepared for the litigation and which, by their very terms, cannot have been sent to the consumer at the time alleged in the statement. For example, the document will reference websites, addresses, or other information that would never have been included in a document as of the alleged date.

The collector cannot seek more under an account stated theory than the amount that the account demands in payment. The consumer cannot have agreed to pay more than is requested by the account statement.[419] Thus when a credit card statement with a large balance only requests a minimum payment of a far lower amount, a court has found that the collector's account stated cause of action should be based solely on the minimum payment requested.[420]

---

405 *See* § 3.4, *supra*.

406 Ayers v. Cavalry SVP, L.L.C., 876 So. 2d 474 (Ala. Civ. App. 2003). *See* Fla. Credit Research Inc. v. Felicien (Fla. Duval Cnty. Ct. Apr. 15, 2008), *available at* www.nclc.org/unreported; Capital One Bank v. Mullis, 15 Fla. L. Weekly Supp. 370a (Fla. Cnty. Ct. Feb. 13, 2008); North Star Capital Acquisition, L.L.C. v. Lewis, 15 Fla. L. Weekly Supp. 72a (Fla. Duval Cnty. Ct. Oct. 23, 2007), *available at* www.nclc.org/unreported; Capital One Bank v. Gelsey, 15 Fla. L. Weekly Supp. 64a (Fla. Duval Cnty. Ct. July 3, 2007), *available at* www.nclc.org/unreported; LVNV Funding, L.L.C. v. Moehrlin (Fla. Volusia Cnty. Ct. 2006) (Green, J.), *available at* www.nclc.org/unreported; Wiltel Commc'ns, L.L.C. v. Sunrise Int'l Leasing Corp., 2005 WL 354030 (Minn. Ct. App. Feb. 15, 2005); Grandell Rehab. & Nursing Home v. Devlin, 809 N.Y.S.2d 481 (N.Y. Sup. Ct. 2005); Citibank v. Lesnick, 2006 WL 1670257 (Ohio Ct. App. May 18, 2006); Asset Acceptance Corp. v. Proctor, 804 N.E.2d 975 (Ohio Ct. App. 2004) (setting forth type of accounting required for account stated action); Mercy Franciscan Hosp. v. Willis, 2004 WL 2244809 (Ohio Ct. App. Sept. 24, 2004). *See also* Palisades Collection, L.L.C. v. Wright, 2009 WL 416187 (Conn. Super. Ct. Jan. 27, 2009); Citibank v. Goldberg, 901 N.Y.S.2d 898 (N.Y. App. Term 2009). *But see* Citibank v. Kessler, 2004 WL 795689 (Ohio Ct. App. Apr. 15, 2004) (lender entitled to summary judgment against *pro se* defendant on account stated claim based on affidavit of its keeper of records; no indication that an accounting or billing statements were provided).

407 Ahlbin v. Crescent Commercial Corp., 224 P.2d 131 (Cal. Ct. App. 1950).

408 N.C. Gen. Stat. § 8-45. *See also* Unifund CCR Partners v. Dover, 681 S.E.2d 565 (N.C. Ct. App. 2009).

409 Unifund CCR Partners v. Dover, 681 S.E.2d 565 (N.C. Ct. App. 2009).

410 Citibank v. Filip, 2010 WL 3039603 (Conn. Super. Ct. July 12, 2010). *See also* Discover Bank v. Sura, 951 N.Y.S.2d 85 (table), 2012 WL 1450028 (N.Y. City Ct. Apr. 26, 2012).

411 *Cf.* Hartman v. Great Seneca Fin. Corp., 569 F.3d 606 (6th Cir. 2009) (consumer's FDCPA case against debt buyer for deceptive introduction of its imitation of an account statement could go to trial).

412 *See* § 4.7.3, *supra*.

413 *See* 15 U.S.C. § 1692g(c). *See also* National Consumer Law Center, Fair Debt Collection § 5.7.4 (8th ed. 2014), *updated at* www.nclc.org/library.

414 Citibank v. Wadas (Pa. Ct. Com. Pl. June 14, 2012), *available at* www.nclc.org/unreported.

415 *See* § 4.2.4.2, *supra*.

416 Palisades Collection, L.L.C. v. Gonzalez, 809 N.Y.S.2d 482 (table), 2005 WL 3372971 (N.Y. Civ. Ct. Dec. 12, 2005).

417 *See* Discover Bank v. Sura, 951 N.Y.S.2d 85 (table), 2012 WL 1450028 (N.Y. City Ct. 2012).

418 Velocity Invs., L.L.C. v. Cocina, 909 N.Y.S.2d 853 (N.Y. App. Div. 2010); Unifund CCR Partners v. Dover, 681 S.E.2d 565 (N.C. Ct. App. 2009).

419 *See* Patrick Eng'g, Inc. v. City of Naperville, 976 N.E.2d 318 (Ill. 2012); Discover Bank v. Sura, 951 N.Y.S.2d 85 (table), 2012 WL 1450028 (N.Y. City Ct. Apr. 26, 2012).

420 Citibank v. Wadas (Pa. Ct. Com. Pl. June 14, 2012), *available at* www.nclc.org/unreported.

A collector's evidence of a statement of account is also weakened when the collector seeks an amount different than what is found on the alleged statement of account.[421] If a collector submits actual statements from the creditor, look to see if any of the statements reflect a zero balance because the account has been charged off. While charging off an account may not end the consumer's obligation,[422] an account stated cause of action will be significantly weakened if an account states the consumer has a zero balance.[423]

4.7.5 Has the Account Statement Been Reviewed by the Consumer?

For the consumer to assent to a statement of account, the consumer must receive it. "An account stated has been defined as an account in writing, examined and expressly or impliedly accepted by both parties thereto, as distinguished from a simple claim or a mere summary of accounts."[424]

At a minimum, the collector must prove that the statement was sent to the consumer.[425] Debt buyers can get into trouble trying to prove that the creditor mailed the account statement when the debt buyer produces an affidavit to the effect from an employee of the debt buyer, not from the original creditor that sent the statement.[426] For example, the employee of the debt buyer may have started employment after the account statement was alleged to have been mailed.[427] Also examine the mailing address listed on the document that the collector produces as the statement of account. It is likely to be found inadequate when the address is inaccurate as of the date when the document was purportedly mailed[428] or if the statement is just a sample and does not have a real address for the consumer.[429] Such problems are surprisingly common, because the collector often brings in a document generated for the litigation and not a copy of the original statement.

But merely sending the statement is not enough. This cause of action is not one in which a party is just showing compliance with a notice requirement. The collector must show that the consumer assented to the account, at least implicitly. If the consumer has not seen a statement, the consumer cannot have either explicitly or implicitly agreed to it.[430]

Consequently there must be evidence not only that the account statement was sent to the consumer but that it was received by the consumer.[431] The collector cannot recover on summary judgment when the consumer claims the account statement was never sent to the consumer and the consumer alleges that the statement produced by the collector does not pertain to the consumer.[432]

When there are joint owners of an account, no implied consent should be found if it can be shown that the joint owner being sued did not see the statements and was not knowledgeable about the charges and payments. Such a joint owner can hardly be found to assent in that situation.[433] In one case, the statements were sent to the husband's business address and the wife did not use the card and had no knowledge of the charges and payments. The account stated claim against the wife could not survive.[434]

4.7.6 Consumer's Implied Consent

4.7.6.1 General

Consumers rarely explicitly agree to pay a specified amount after reviewing a statement of account. The collector's action for account stated usually must rely on the consumer's implied consent to pay the amount found in the statement. The law is far from clear as to what actions by the consumer sufficiently imply consent, and the law may be different for transactions between businesses than for consumer obligations.

Implied consent will be found when there are discussions between the parties or other back and forth communications as to the amount that is due, resulting in agreement as to the amount due.[435] A communication from the consumer accept-

---

421 *See* Patrick Eng'g, Inc. v. City of Naperville, 976 N.E.2d 318 (Ill. 2012); Discover Bank v. Sura, 951 N.Y.S.2d 85 (table), 2012 WL 1450028 (N.Y. City Ct. Apr. 26, 2012).

422 *See* § 5.2.3.4, *infra*.

423 *See* Discover Bank v. Shimer, 957 N.Y.S. 263 (table), 2012 WL 2912492 (N.Y. Dist. Ct. Apr. 26, 2012).

424 13 Pa. Law Encyclopedia (Second) Contracts § 512.

425 Ayers v. Cavalry SVP I, L.L.C., 876 So. 2d 474 (Ala. Civ. App. 2004); LVNV Funding, L.L.C. v. Moehrlin (Fla. Volusia Cnty. Ct. Aug. 2006) (Green, J.), *available at* www.nclc.org/unreported; Nelson v. First Nat'l Bank Omaha, 2004 WL 2711032 (Minn. Ct. App. Nov. 30, 2004); Morrison, Cohen, Singer & Weinstein, L.L.P. v. Brophy, 798 N.Y.S.2d 379 (N.Y. App. Div. 2005); Capital One Bank USA NA v. Joseph, 2013 WL 5663260 (N.Y. Dist. Ct. Oct. 7, 2013); Chase Bank v. Hershkovits, 28 Misc. 3d 1202(A) (N.Y. Civ. Ct. 2010); Rushmore Recoveries X, L.L.C. v. Skolnick, 841 N.Y.S.2d 823 (N.Y. Dist. Ct. 2007); Citibank v. Martin, 807 N.Y.S.2d 284 (N.Y. Civ. Ct. 2005); Unifund CCR Partners v. Dover, 681 S.E.2d 565 (N.C. Ct. App. 2009). *See also* Erickson v. Johnson, 2006 WL 453201 (D. Minn. Feb. 22, 2006); Chase Bank v. Fekete (Fla. Cnty. Ct. Feb. 1, 2011), *available at* www.nclc.org/unreported.

426 *See* Capital One Bank USA NA v. Joseph, 2013 WL 5663260 (N.Y. Dist. Ct. Oct. 7, 2013); Palisades Collection, L.L.C. v. Gonzalez, 809 N.Y.S.2d 482 (table), 2005 WL 3372971 (N.Y. Civ. Ct. Dec. 12, 2005).

427 Capital One Bank USA NA v. Joseph, 2013 WL 5663260 (N.Y. Dist. Ct. Oct. 7, 2013).

428 *See* Chase Bank v. Fekete (Fla. Cnty. Ct. Feb. 1, 2011), *available at* www.nclc.org/unreported.

429 *See id.*

430 Ayers v. Cavalry SVP I, L.L.C., 876 So. 2d 474 (Ala. Civ. App. 2004); Nelson v. First Nat'l Bank Omaha, 2004 WL 2711032 (Minn. Ct. App. Nov. 30, 2004). *See also* First Merit Bank v. Wilson, 2007 WL 1827589 (Ohio Ct. App. June 27, 2007).

431 Cach, L.L.C. v. Stupack, 2010 WL 1225029 (Conn. Super. Ct. Mar. 1, 2010); Unifund CCR Partners v. Dover, 681 S.E.2d 565 (N.C. Ct. App. 2009); Morrison v. Citibank, 2008 WL 553284 (Tex. App. Feb. 28, 2008). *But see* Am. Express Centurion Bank v. Williams, 807 N.Y.S.2d 612 (N.Y. App. Div. 2005).

432 Palisades Collection, L.L.C. v. Olosunde, 2008 WL 5233566 (N.J. Super. Ct. App. Div. Dec. 17, 2008).

433 First Merit Bank v. Wilson, 2007 WL 1827589 (Ohio Ct. App. June 27, 2007).

434 First Merit Bank v. Wilson, 2007 WL 1827589 (Ohio Ct. App. June 27, 2007). *See also* Erickson v. Johnson, 2006 WL 453201 (D. Minn. Feb. 22, 2006).

435 *Cf.* Target Nat'l Bank v. Samanez (Pa. Ct. Com. Pl. Dec. 19, 2007), *available at* www.nclc.org/unreported.

ing responsibility for payment, but professing an inability to make that payment, might be found to be enough to show implied consent.[436] Similarly, in one case the defendant did not object to periodic invoices and acknowledged the existence of the outstanding debt.[437] Consent can also be found implicit in other affirmative actions by the consumer.[438] The consumer's failure to deny the account balance in the litigation itself can be seen as implying consent.[439]

On the other hand, certain consumer conduct refutes implied consent to the statement of account. Clearly this includes the consumer objecting to a statement of account.[440] Excellent evidence of a dispute is if the consumer has disputed a charge with a consumer reporting agency[441]—the reporting agency must forward the dispute to the creditor.

A consumer's dispute to the collector should qualify even if made over the telephone.[442] Companies routinely indicate that a call may be recorded, so consumers should be able to reasonably rely on a phone call as a means of documenting their dispute.[443] A consumer's objection is sufficient even when it is made over the phone and the consumer never completes a form (provided by the card issuer) intended to document the consumer's objection.[444]

The consumer's silence does not signify consent when the context of the submission of the statement of account to the consumer fails to suggest that the consumer should object. For example, the consumer would not be expected to object to a debt buyer's dunning letter made to look like a statement and sent years after the account was closed. If there is no existing relationship between the parties, assent should not be implied from silence.[445]

4.7.6.2 Consumer's Inaction and Silence After Receiving Regular Monthly Statements

The most common situation occurs when the consumer has taken no overt action to either consent or object to a statement of account, and the court must decide whether silence in the face of a series of monthly statements implies consent. Some courts require that there be more than just silence on the part of the consumer to indicate consent.[446] "Something more than mere acquiescence by failing to take exception to a series of statements of account received in the mail is required to create an account stated."[447] A New York statute prohibits credit card agreements from requiring that a credit card account be deemed correct just because the consumer fails to object within a specified period of time.[448]

The collector is the one with the burden of proving all elements of its cause of action, so the collector has the burden of showing the consumer's agreement to pay the charges and thus has the burden of showing that silence upon receiving the statement shows consent.[449] In addition, federal law places the burden on the collector to prove that credit card charges are authorized.[450] This burden is not met merely by referencing a statement of account and the consumer's silence.[451]

Some courts apply this federally created burden of proof only to claims for breach of contract and not to a claim for account stated.[452] But that approach does not comport with the actual language of the federal statute that applies the burden to "*any* action by a card issuer to enforce liability for use of a credit card."[453]

Silence does not indicate assent when the consumer never agreed to the credit arrangement in the first place.[454] There must be evidence that the consumer agreed to be liable on an account and the only issue is the amount that is owed. If there is no existing relationship between creditor and consumer, then the consumer cannot be blamed for remaining silent despite receipt of documents showing an amount owed.[455]

Nevertheless, some courts find silence is enough for implied consent.[456] Particularly for transactions between

436 Obermayer, Rebmann, Maxwell & Hippel v. Banta, 28 Pa. D. & C.4th 225 (Pa. Ct. Com. Pl. 1996), *aff'd in part, vacated in part*, 687 A.2d 866 (Pa. Super. Ct. 1996).

437 Residential Servs. Validated Publications v. Carus, 2006 WL 1026669 (E.D.N.Y. Apr. 19, 2006).

438 *See* 29 Richard A. Lord, Williston on Contracts, § 73:58 (4th ed. 2003); 13 Pa. Law Encyclopedia (Second) Contracts, §§ 512, 513.

439 Citibank v. Jones, 708 N.Y.S.2d 517 (N.Y. App. Div. 2000).

440 *See* Corby v. American Express Co., 2011 WL 4625719 (C.D. Cal. Oct. 5, 2011); Robinson v. Citibank, 2008 WL 2946005 (E.D.N.Y. July 29, 2008), *aff'd*, 368 Fed. Appx. 185 (2d Cir. 2010); Discover Bank v. Walker, 787 N.Y.S.2d 677 (N.Y. Sup. Ct. 2004); Palisades Collection, L.L.C. v. Haque, 2006 N.Y. Misc. LEXIS 4036 (N.Y. Civ. Ct. Apr. 13, 2006).

441 Unifund CCR Partners v. Riley, 2010 WL 571829 (Mich. Ct. App. Feb. 18, 2010).

442 Palisades Collection, L.L.C. v. Haque, 2006 N.Y. Misc. LEXIS 4036 (N.Y. Civ. Ct. Apr. 13, 2006).

443 *See id.*

444 *See* Robinson v. Citibank, 2008 WL 2946005 (E.D.N.Y. July 29, 2008), *aff'd*, 368 Fed. Appx. 185 (2d Cir. 2010.

445 Nelson v. First Nat'l Bank Omaha, 2004 WL 2711032 (Minn. Ct. App. Nov. 30, 2004).

446 Velocity Invs., L.L.C. v. Kahanic (Pa. Ct. Com. Pl. May 1, 2012), *available at* www.nclc.org/unreported. *See, e.g.*, Braude & Margulies, P.C. v. Fireman's Fund Ins. Co., 468 F. Supp. 2d 190 (D.D.C. 2007); Dreyer Med. Clinic v. Corral, 591 N.E.2d 111 (Ill. App. Ct. 1992); Citibank v. Wadas (Pa. Ct. Com. Pl. June 14, 2012), *available at* www.nclc.org/unreported; Target Nat'l Bank v. Samanez (Pa. Ct. Com. Pl. Dec. 19, 2007), *available at* www.nclc.org/unreported; Morrison v. Citibank, 2008 WL 553284 (Tex. App. Feb. 28, 2008). *See also* LVNV Funding, L.L.C. v. Moehrlin (Fla. Volusia Cnty. Ct. 2006) (Green, J.), *available at* www.nclc.org/unreported; C-E Glass v. Ryan, 70 Pa. D. & C.2d 251 (Pa. Ct. Com. Pl. 1975); Ryon v. Andershonis, 42 Pa. D.& C.2d 86 (Pa. Ct. Com. Pl. 1967); Sarah Howard Jenkins, 13 Corbin on Contracts, § 72.1(4) (rev. ed. 2003); 13 Pa. Law Encyclopedia (Second) Contracts § 513.

447 13 Pa. Law Encyclopedia (Second) Contracts § 513.

448 *See* N.Y. Gen. Bus. Law § 517 (McKinney).

449 Citibank v. Goldberg, 901 N.Y.S.2d 898 (N.Y. App. Term 2009).

450 15 U.S.C. § 1643(b).

451 *See* § 4.7.6.3, *infra*.

452 Citibank v. Poynton, 723 N.Y.S.2d 327 (N.Y. Sup. Ct. 2000).

453 15 U.S.C. § 1643(b) (emphasis added). *See also* Bank of N.Y. v. Santarelli, 491 N.Y.S.2d 980 (N.Y. Greene Cnty. Ct. 1985).

454 *See* § 4.7.3, *supra*.

455 *Id.*

456 *See* Univ. of S. Ala. v. Bracy, 466 So. 2d 148 (Ala. Civ. App. 1985); Zinn v. Fred R. Bright Co, 271 Cal. App. 2d 597 (Cal. Ct. App. 1969); Credit One, L.L.C. v. Head, 977 A.2d 767 (Conn. App. Ct. 2009); Citibank v. Durazzo, 2007 WL 1600049 (Conn. Super. Ct. May 22, 2007); Capital One Bank v. Denboer, 791 N.W.2d 264 (Iowa Ct. App. 2010); Jaramillo v.

two businesses, the courts find an obligation on the defendant to inspect a statement of account when presented to the defendant—agreement is implied if the defendant does not object within a reasonable time, unless fraud, mistake, or other equitable considerations are shown.[457] Of course, there must be competent evidence that the regular monthly statements were in fact sent to the consumer at the address provided by the consumer and that the final account statement is an accurate reflection of these monthly statements.[458]

4.7.6.3 Special Considerations for Credit Card Obligations

Whatever the merits of a court finding silence to imply consent, special considerations make such a ruling in a credit card case particularly suspect. The prior subsection mentions the federal Truth in Lending requirement, shifting the burden in credit card collections onto the collector to prove that a charge is authorized.[459] In addition, a perceptive Pennsylvania court opinion examines why a consumer's silence is insufficient to show implied consent in the credit card context, when the consumer cannot be expected to understand, and thus does not assent to, the computation of finance charges and other fees shown on the statement.[460] Its analysis will be excerpted at length:

> Credit cardholders who do not pay the full amount of the new balance usually do not know whether any charges, other than the charges for purchases and cash withdrawals, are correct. It is reasonable to assume that most credit cardholders have never attempted to read the entire initial cardholder agreement. Furthermore, even if they attempted to do so, it is unlikely that they would fully understand what they have read. Also, most agreements provide that they can be amended upon fifteen days' notice, and frequently the monthly statements are accompanied by amendments to the initial agreement that cannot be understood unless the credit cardholder has access to and does review the initial agreement, subsequent amendments, and the newest amendment. This does not occur.
>
> In the present case, for example, the annual percentage rates in the monthly statements from October 25, 2005 through September 25, 2007 frequently differed from month-to-month. In January 2006, the annual percentage rate for purchases was 20.99%; in May 2006, the annual percentage rate for purchases was 21.74%; in August 2006, the annual percentage rate for purchases was 22.24%; in December 2006, the annual percentage rate for purchases was 22.24%; and in March 2007, the annual percentage rate for purchases was 28.24%.
>
> For several months, there was a late payment fee charge of $35.00.
>
> While the credit cardholder, looking at the statement, can see the amount of the charges that were imposed, he or she is unlikely to know whether the charges are consistent with the writings governing the cardholder's obligations. Consequently, he or she is not in a position to either agree or disagree with the amount of the balance in any monthly statement that does not begin with a $0.00 balance.
>
> The above description of the cardholder and issuer relationship is consistent with the findings in a September 2006 108-page report prepared by the United States Government Accountability Office titled *Credit Cards—Increased Complexity in Rates and Fees Heightens Need for More Effective Disclosures to Consumers*, www.gao.gov, Document GAO-06-929 (912006) (the "Report").
>
> The portion of the Report titled *Results in Brief*, states that disclosures are too complicated for many consumers to understand. *Id.* at 4–6. In addition, the disclosures are often poorly organized, burying important information in the text, and scattering information about a single topic in numerous places. *Id.* at 6. The design of the disclosures often makes the disclosures hard to read with large amounts of the text in small, condensed typefaces and poor, ineffective headings. *Id.* at 6. The cardholder is not in a position to agree or disagree with the charges on a monthly statement that are unrelated to the cash withdrawals and purchases shown on the monthly statement because the obligations imposed on the cardholder are not easily understood.
>
> Prior to 1990, most issuers charged a fixed interest rate and imposed few other charges. Thus, furnishing an adequate disclosure was relatively easy. Today, credit cards feature complex pricing structures. *Id.* at 13. Most cards now assess one interest rate on balances from the purchase of goods, another on balances that are transferred from another credit card, and a third on balances that result from using the card to obtain cash. Also, the cards usually provide for payments to be allocated first to the balance assessed at the lowest interest rate. *Id.* at 14–15, 27.
>
> In addition to having separate rates for the different transactions, the cards increasingly impose interest rates that vary periodically as market interest rates change. Issuers typically establish these variable rates by taking the

---

Portfolio Acquisitions, L.L.C., 2010 WL 1197669 (Tex. App. Mar. 30, 2010); Butler v. Hudson & Keyse, L.L.C. 2009 WL 402329 (Tex. App. Feb. 19, 2009). *See also* CACV of Colo., L.L.C. v. Bair, 2007 WL 2080993 (Conn. Super. Ct. Apr. 5, 2007).

457 *See* Ayers v. Cavalry SVP I, L.L.C., 876 So. 2d 474 (Ala. Civ. App. 2003); Wiltel Commc'ns, L.L.C. v. Sunrise Int'l Leasing Corp., 2005 WL 354030 (Minn. Ct. App. Feb. 15, 2005); Nelson v. First Nat'l Bank Omaha, 2004 WL 2711032 (Minn. Ct. App. Nov. 30, 2004); Gross v. Empire Healthchoice Assur., Inc., 819 N.Y.S.2d 210 (N.Y. Sup. Ct. 2006). *See also* Citibank v. Otto, 2008 WL 5335823 (Minn. Ct. App. Dec. 23, 2008); Dulong v. Citibank, 261 S.W.3d 890 (Tex. App. 2008).

458 Capital One Bank v. Denboer, 791 N.W.2d 264 (Iowa Ct. App. 2010).

459 *See* § 4.7.6.2, *supra*.

460 Target Nat'l Bank v. Samanez (Pa. Ct. Com. Pl. Dec. 19, 2007), *available at* www.nclc.org/unreported. *See also* Target Nat'l Bank v. Greiner (Pa. Commw. Ct. Sept. 30, 2009), *available at* www.nclc.org/unreported; Citibank v. Cooper (Vt. Super. Ct. July 10, 2009), *available at* www.nclc.org/unreported. *Cf.* Capital One Bank v. Heidebring, 2009 WL 1741515 (Ohio Ct. App. June 19, 2009) (refusing to allow over-the-limit fees found on the last statement of account).

prevailing level of a base rate, such as the prime rate, and adding a fixed percentage amount. They frequently reset the interest rates on a monthly basis. *Id.* at 15.

Most credit cards provide for a penalty fee, described as a late fee, which issuers assess when they do not receive at least a minimum required payment by the due date. Most of the cards have a tiered fee structure depending upon the amount of the balance held by the cardholder (e.g., $15.00 late fee when the balances are between $100.00 and $250.00; $25.00 to $29.00 fee on accounts with balances up to $1,000.00; and $34.00 to $39.00 fee when the balance exceeds $1,000.00). *Id.* at 19–20.

Most issuers also assess cardholders a penalty fee for exceeding the credit limit, with the over limit fee also involving the use of a tiered structure. *Id.* at 20–21. Cards frequently have total credit limits at a lesser limit for cash. *Id.* at 22. Also, issuers do not reject purchases during the sale authorization even though the transaction puts the cardholder over the card's credit limits, thereby exposing the cardholder to an over limit fee and a higher interest rate. *Id.* at 30.

Many cards provide for higher interest rates to be assessed if cardholders make late payments or exceed the credit limit. *Id.* at 24. Many cards also provide for increased rates when cardholders fail to make payments to other creditors. *Id.* at 24–25.

Most of the cards also provide for the cardholder to pay fees for certain services (e.g., 3% of cash advance amounts, 3% of transfer of a balance from another creditor, 3% of purchases made in a foreign country). *Id.* at 23.

The Report concluded that the disclosures which provide information about the costs and terms of using credit cards "had serious weaknesses that likely reduce their usefulness to consumers; . . . The disclosures . . . [were] written at a level too difficult for the average consumer to understand, and [had] design features, such as text placement and font sizes, that did not conform to guidance for creating easily readable documents. When attempting to use these disclosures, cardholders were often unable to identify key rates or terms and often failed to understand the information in [the] documents." *Id.* at 33.

The pricing structures depend upon the circumstances of the cardholder, and credit card disclosures are inadequate to inform cardholders as to the interest rates, fees, penalties, and other costs that may be imposed. The Report stated that the "disclosure documents were written such that understanding them required a higher reading level than that attained by many U.S. cardholders; . . . nearly half of the adult population in the United States reads at or below the eighth-grade level." *Id.* at 38. Accordingly, the Securities and Exchange Commission recommends that disclosure materials be written at a sixth-to eighth-grade level. *Id.* Disclosures of credit card issuers on average were written "at a reading level commensurate with about a tenth-to twelfth-grade education." *Id.* at 37. An understanding of the disclosures in the solicitation letters would require "an eleventh-grade level of reading comprehension, while understanding the cardmember agreements would require about a twelfth-grade education. *Id.* In addition, certain portions of the typical disclosure documents required even higher reading levels to be understandable. For example, information about annual percentage rates, grace periods, balance computation, and payment allocation methods required "a minimum of a fifteenth-grade education, which is the equivalent of 3 years of college education." *Id.* at 38.

The Report described additional problems that also prevented cardholders from understanding the transactions, even assuming that the relevant documents were available. The disclosure documents do not use effective organizational structures and formatting. *Id.* at 38. The typical credit card disclosure lacks effective organization. *Id.* at 39. Many of the disclosure documents use font sizes that are difficult to read and thus hinder the consumer's ability to find information. *Id.* at 41. The typical disclosure documents are overly complex and present the relevant information in too much detail, "such as by using unfamiliar or complex terms to describe simple concepts." *Id.* at 46.

4.7.6.4 No Implied Consent from Consumer's Failure to Use Federal Dispute Rights

4.7.6.4.1 General

Federal law provides consumers with various dispute rights, and collectors may argue that failure to utilize these dispute rights implies consent to charges as indicated on a statement of account. One such dispute right involves a consumer's ability to ask a collector to verify a debt, but the Fair Debt Collection Practices Act explicitly states that "the failure of a consumer to dispute the validity of a debt under this section may not be construed by any court as an admission of liability by the consumer."[461]

The same result applies when the consumer fails to send a dispute in writing within sixty days of a billing error on an open-end account, pursuant to rights provided by Truth in Lending Act (TILA) Part D, commonly referred to as the Fair Credit Billing Act (FCBA).[462] Failure to utilize a statutory protection does not act as an admission as to the accuracy of the open-end account charges.[463] The FCBA's congressional intent is to protect consumers, not collectors.[464]

461 *See* 15 U.S.C. § 1692g(c). *See also* National Consumer Law Center, Fair Debt Collection § 5.7.4 (8th ed. 2014), *updated at* www.nclc.org/library.

462 15 U.S.C. § 1666. *See also* National Consumer Law Center, Truth in Lending § 7.9 (8th ed. 2012), *updated at* www.nclc.org/library.

463 DBI Architects, P.C. v. Am. Express Travel-Related Servs. Co., 388 F.3d 886 (D.C. Cir. 2004); Danner v. Discover Bank, 257 S.W.3d 113 (Ark. Ct. App. 2007); People's Bank v. Scarpetti, 1998 WL 61925 (Conn. Super. Ct. Feb. 5, 1998); Crestar Bank v. Cheevers, 744 A.2d 1043 (D.C. 2000) (need not bring FCBA dispute to claim charges are unauthorized); Citibank v. Mincks, 135 S.W.3d 545 (Mo. Ct. App. 2004).

464 *See* McSherry v. Capital One, 236 F.R.D. 516 (W.D. Wash. 2006); Thomas D. Mangelsen, Inc. v. Heartland Payment Sys., Inc., 2005 WL 2076421 (D. Neb. Aug. 26, 2005); Symeonidis v. Paxton Capital Group, Inc., 220 F. Supp. 2d 478, 480 n.3 (D. Md. 2002).

A number of TILA statutory and regulatory provisions all point to the clear result that failure to dispute a billing error under the FCBA within sixty days has no effect on a consumer's ability to later dispute a debt. Consumer Financial Protection Bureau TILA staff interpretations explicitly state that the consumer can raise claims and defenses on a debt pursuant to 15 U.S.C. §§ 1666i and 1643, even though the consumer does not send a written notice of dispute under the FCBA.[465]

TILA also provides that a credit card issuer has the burden of proof to show that use was authorized[466] (unauthorized use is one of the billing errors to which the FCBA explicitly relates).[467] If the card issuer has the burden of proof, then a consumer's failure to send a written notice within sixty days cannot be treated as consent to the unauthorized use.

TILA states that "this subchapter [that is, TILA including Part D, the FCBA[468]] and the regulations issued thereunder do not affect the validity or enforceability of any contract or obligation under State or Federal law."[469] That is, the FCBA does not affect the consumer's right to challenge the enforceability of an obligation.

4.7.6.4.2 *Incorrect minority view that FCBA creates affirmative duty on consumers*

A series of Connecticut trial court decisions and one Ohio appellate court take the unfounded and wrongheaded position that failure to send an FCBA billing error dispute within sixty days admits the accuracy of the charges.[470] These courts turn a consumer protection statute on its head into a debt buyer's protection statute by taking the strange position that the FCBA creates an affirmative obligation for consumers, if they believe a credit card statement is inaccurate, to send a written dispute letter within sixty days. This approach has no basis in the statutory language, congressional history, the TILA regulations, or TILA staff interpretations.

Not one sentence in the FCBA requires a consumer to take any action. The FCBA instead details actions the *creditor* can and cannot take if a consumer sends a particular written notice of dispute. Nor is there any legislative history that would indicate any congressional intent to limit the rights of a consumer who does not send written notice within sixty days.

Collectors often refer to a sentence in the Act that states: "Nothing in this section shall be construed to prohibit any action by a creditor to collect any amount which has not been indicated by the obligor to contain a billing error."[471] Even taken out of context, this sentence merely states that the FCBA does not prohibit the creditor from filing a suit to collect on a debt when the consumer has not raised a billing error dispute. The sentence does not prevent the consumer from raising defenses and counterclaims in such an action. In fact, the Consumer Financial Protection Bureau's staff interpretations to the Truth in Lending Act explicitly state that the consumer can raise claims and defenses on a debt pursuant to 15 U.S.C. §§ 1666i and 1643, even though the consumer does not send a written notice of dispute under the FCBA.[472]

Moreover, when this sentence is taken *in context*, its meaning is even clearer. The FCBA requires a creditor, in response to the consumer's written notice about a billing error, to refrain from taking any action to collect the amount until certain steps are taken.[473] The "nothing in this section" sentence simply means that this prohibition on taking action to collect on that portion of a debt under dispute does not apply to portions of a debt not in dispute.

The FCBA dispute procedures do not even apply to many areas in which a consumer may dispute a statement of account. The billing errors covered by the Act are set out in Regulation Z.[474] Not defined as a billing error, for example, are certain disputes relating to the goods or services purchased, such as disputes as to the quality of property or services that the consumer accepts.[475] How can the failure to send a billing dispute notice be treated as consent to certain charges, when the FCBA does not even apply to a consumer's dispute of those charges?

The FCBA allows the creditor to specify the procedure for sending in written disputes, and, if the consumer fails to follow that procedure, the creditor need not comply with the creditor's FCBA obligations.[476] Taken to its extreme, then, the collector's argument suggests that a consumer is treated as consenting to an account stated when the consumer objects to the account but fails to follow the creditor-specified procedures. If the creditor requires a separate written statement, then the collector is arguing that a consumer is deemed to have admitted to charges when the consumer strenuously objects orally or disputes in writing, but does so on the payment stub or on the statement itself sent back to the creditor.

465 Consumer Fin. Prot. Bureau, Official Interpretations of Reg. Z, 12 C.F.R. pt. 1026, Supp. I, §§ 1026.12(c)-1, 1026.12(b)(3)-3.

466 15 U.S.C. § 1643(c).

467 *See* 12 C.F.R. § 1026.13(a)(1).

468 Subchapter in this context means the Truth in Lending Act, including the Fair Credit Billing Act.

469 15 U.S.C. § 1610(d).

470 Citibank v. Strumpf, 2006 WL 2773540 (Conn. Super. Ct. Sept. 13, 2006); Citibank v. Lovell, 2006 WL 1229922 (Conn. Super. Ct. Apr. 13, 2006); Citibank v. Currea, 2006 WL 1229919 (Conn. Super. Ct. Apr. 13, 2006); Citibank v. Babuscio, 2005 WL 3667343 (Conn. Super. Ct. Dec. 21, 2005); Citibank v. Todd, 2005 WL 3666353 (Conn. Super. Ct. Dec. 21, 2005); Citibank v. Kilberg, 2005 WL 3665805 (Conn. Super. Ct. Dec. 21, 2005); Citibank v. Forcinelli, 2005 WL 3665635 (Conn. Super. Ct. Dec. 21, 2005); Citibank v. Gemske, 2005 WL 3665083 (Conn. Super. Ct. Dec. 21, 2005); Citibank v. Kessler, 2004 WL 795689 (Ohio Ct. App. Apr. 15, 2004). *See also* Jones v. Citibank, 2008 WL 651689 (Ark. Ct. App. Mar. 12, 2008); Jones v. Citibank S.D., 2008 WL 442627 (Ark. Ct. App. Feb. 20, 2008); Citibank v. Durazzo, 2007 WL 1600049 (Conn. Super. Ct. May 22, 2007). *Cf.* Asset Acceptance Corp. v. Proctor, 804 N.E.2d 975 (Ohio Ct. App. 2004) (finding no consent, because consumer never received statements).

471 15 U.S.C. § 1666(c).

472 Consumer Fin. Prot. Bureau, Official Interpretations of Reg. Z, 12 C.F.R. pt. 1026, Supp. I, §§ 1026.12(c)-1, 1026.12(b)(3)-3.

473 15 U.S.C. § 1666(a).

474 12 C.F.R. § 1026.13(a).

475 Consumer Fin. Prot. Bureau, Official Interpretations of Reg. Z, 12 C.F.R. pt. 1026, Supp. I, §§ 1026.13(a)(3)-1.

476 15 U.S.C. § 1666(a).

4.8 *Quantum Meruit* or Unjust Enrichment

Some collectors routinely add a *quantum meruit* or unjust enrichment claim to their collection action, perhaps in recognition that they will have difficulty proving either a contract or an account stated claim. The first question is whether the state recognizes the cause of action pleaded by the collector. For example, California does not recognize the cause of action for unjust enrichment.[477]

Quantum meruit and unjust enrichment claims are based upon an implied contract, and most courts find a claim upon an implied contract is *not* available when there is an existing contract.[478] Often the collector's own pleadings, affidavits, or submitted documents will allege an explicit contract, so that the collector's own case will be inconsistent with the cause of action for *quantum meruit* or unjust enrichment.[479]

Even if the collector does not allege a contract, federal law requires a written contract for any credit card account. Federal law requires, before a credit card account is opened, that the creditor send the consumer extensive written disclosures as to the terms of relationship[480] and also requires, with each monthly statement, additional statements as to the terms of the transaction.[481] Clearly, a credit card transaction involves an explicit contract. The fact that the collector cannot prove the terms of the contract does not alter the fact that a contract exists, and thus an action cannot be brought on such debts for *quantum meruit* or unjust enrichment.

When there is no contract between the collector and consumer (for example, when an authorized user on a credit card was provided only a card and no terms of use), there are certain logical limits to an action on *quantum meruit* or unjust enrichment. By definition there is no contract, and thus there can be no recovery for finance charges, late fees, and the like. A contractual choice of law cannot exist. There can be no recovery for contractual attorney fees.[482] In many states, prejudgment interest is not even allowed because there is no liquidated amount in an implied contract.[483]

Also carefully examine any assignment to a debt buyer. Is the assignment only of the contractual rights, or is there an assignment of any chose in action the original creditor possesses? If the former, than the assignee has no right to bring a *quantum meruit* or unjust enrichment claim, as its rights are based solely on contract, and there can be no *quantum meruit* action when there is a contract.

Moreover, the collector will have to prove what money, goods, or services were received by the consumer that form the basis of its claim and prove the value of those items received. In the credit card context, when a *quantum meruit* action is brought against an authorized user or someone else not obligated by contract, the collector will have to show which charges were for the benefit of that party and not for the benefit of the principal card holder. A debt buyer who has paid pennies on the dollar should not be able to claim unjust enrichment as a means of collecting the entire amount of the account. In some states, a claim for unjust enrichment also requires a showing that the consumer wrongfully secured a benefit that would be unconscionable to retain.[484]

The *quantum meruit* cause of action is also examined in Chapter 9, *infra*, in the context of medical debt. The price of medical services is often not established beforehand, and the *quantum meruit* claim will thus have to establish the reasonable value of those services.

---

477 *See* Corby v. American Express Co., 2011 WL 4625719 (C.D. Cal. Oct. 5, 2011).

478 Banner Iron Works, Inc. v. Amaz Zinc Co., 621 F.2d 883 (8th Cir. 1980); Owen v. Gen. Motors Corp., 2006 WL 2808632 (W.D. Mo. Sept. 28, 2006); May v. Sessums & Mason, P.A., 700 So. 2d 22 (Fla. Dist. Ct. App. 1994); N. Star Capital Acquisition, L.L.C. v. Lewis, 15 Fla. L. Weekly Supp. 72a (Fla. Duval Cnty. Ct. Oct. 23, 2007), *available at* www.nclc.org/unreported; Capital One Bank v. Gelsey, 15 Fla. L. Weekly Supp. 64a (Fla. Duval Cnty. Ct. July 3, 2007), *available at* www.nclc.org/unreported; American Express Travel Related Servs. Co. v. Seidenfeld, 781 N.Y.S.2d 622 (N.Y. Sup. Ct. 2003); Portfolio Recovery Assocs. v. Gilbert (Pa. C.P. Venango Cnty. Sept. 10, 2013), *available at* www.nclc.org/unreported; Truly v. Austin, 744 S.W.2d 934 (Tex. 1988); Pepi Corp. v. Galliford, 254 S.W.3d 457 (Tex. App. 2007); Tully v. Citibank, 173 S.W.3d 212 (Tex. App. 2005); Pioneer Roofing, Inc. v. Westra/Const., Inc., 622 N.W.2d 770 (Wis. Ct. App. 2000) (unreported). *See also* § 9.5.4, *infra* (additional supporting cases).

479 *See* N. Star Capital Acquisition, L.L.C. v. Lewis, 15 Fla. L. Weekly Supp. 72a (Fla. Duval Cnty. Ct. Oct. 23, 2007), *available at* www.nclc.org/unreported; Capital One Bank v. Gelsey, 15 Fla. L. Weekly Supp. 64a (Fla. Duval Cnty. Ct. July 3, 2007), *available at* www.nclc.org/unreported. *But see* Target Nat'l Bank v. Kilbride (Pa. Ct. Com. Pl. Feb. 5, 2010) (*quantum meruit* can be pleaded as an alternative claim to breach of contract), *available at* www.nclc.org/unreported; Jaramillo v. Portfolio Acquisitions, L.L.C., 2010 WL 1197669 (Tex. App. Mar. 30, 2010) (when collector failed to prove a contract, *quantum meruit* was an available claim); McElroy v. Unifund CCR Partners, 2008 WL 4355276 (Tex. App. Aug. 26, 2008).

480 15 U.S.C. § 1637(a). *See also* National Consumer Law Center, Truth in Lending Ch. 6 (8th ed. 2012), *updated at* www.nclc.org/library.

481 15 U.S.C. § 1637(b). *See also* National Consumer Law Center, Truth in Lending Ch. 6 (8th ed. 2012), *updated at* www.nclc.org/library.

482 *See* McLain v. W. Side Bone & Joint Ctr., 656 So. 2d 119 (Miss. 1995); Rental Co., L.L.C. v. Carter Group, Inc., 399 SW 3d 63 (Mo. Ct. App. 2013). *Cf.* McElroy v. Unifund CCR Partners, 2008 WL 4355276 (Tex. App. Aug. 26, 2008) (attorney fees can be awarded by statute in Texas when the collector prevails under a *quantum meruit* theory, even if the fees cannot be based upon the contract).

483 *See* 22 Am. Jur. 2d *Damages* § 468 (2003). *See also* George v. Double-D Food, Inc., 155 Cal. App. 3d 36 (Cal. Ct. App. 1984); *In re* Estate of Boyd, 8 P.3d 664 (Idaho Ct. App. 2000) (interest could not run from date of service when recovery was in *quantum meruit* rather than on open account); Falkner v. Stubbs, 121 So. 3d 899 (Miss. 2013); Southland Enters., Inc. v. Newton Cnty., 838 So. 2d 286 (Miss. 2003); Mclain v. W. Side Bone & Joint Ctr., 656 So. 2d 119 (Miss. 1995); Farmah v. Farmah, 348 N.C. 586 (N.C. 1998); Mobil Producing Tex. & N.M., Inc. v. Cantor, 93 S.W.3d 916 (Tex. App. 2002) (Texas law provides for attorney fees and prejudgment interest in contract actions; but denied when plaintiff prevailed on unjust enrichment, not contract, claim); Lockhard v. City of Salem, 43 S.E.2d 239 (W. Va. 1947) (*quantum meruit* claim is unliquidated).

484 Portfolio Recovery Assocs. v. Gilbert (Pa. Ct. Com. Pl. Sept. 10, 2013), *available at* www.nclc.org/unreported.

4.9 Other Causes of Action

Depending on state law, collectors may have available to them other causes of action to collect on a debt. Often these claims will be in lieu of a claim for breach of contract, because the collector is concerned that it cannot prove a contract. In selecting alternative claims, the collector will look to those that provide statutory attorney fees, allow for recovery of interest, or have other benefits to maximize the collector's recovery. When shoe-horning the facts into such a claim, the collector may be more concerned with the potential amount it can ask the court to award than whether such claims are legally viable. Most actions end in a default judgment, and the fact that the claim does not fit the facts may never be raised.

In defending against such causes of action, the consumer should first ascertain if the collector's complaint clearly states what causes of action are being alleged. For example, a claim for "credit card" may be meaningless under a state's jurisprudence. If the cause of action is not clearly stated, request a more definite statement or move to dismiss the count.

If the cause of action has a statutory basis, carefully parse the statutory language to determine its application and elements of proof. If a cause of action does not have a statutory basis, carefully consider the nature of the cause of action under the state's common law to see if it even applies to the debt. For example, does a claim for "materials and services supplied" apply to an action on a third-party credit card debt, when the lender did not supply materials and services but an extension of credit?

Consider the applicable limitations period for such a cause of action[485] and whether the cause of action is consistent with recovery of finance charges, prejudgment interest, fees, and attorney fees. For example, in a claim for materials and services supplied, it is unlikely that state law allows for finance charges and other fees, other than possibly prejudgment interest at the legal rate, and state law would only allow attorney fees if explicitly stated in a statute.[486]

485 *See, e.g.*, Slayter v. Slayer, L.L.C. v. Ryland, 953 So. 2d 1000 (La. Ct. App. 2007) (La. Civ. Code art. 3494(3) establishes a three-year limitations period for the cause of action of money lent).

486 *See* Neb. Rev. Stat. § 25-1801 (providing for limited attorney fees for actions under $4000 for materials and services supplied).

In some jurisdictions, money lent is a cause of action to recover funds. The creditor must show that money was delivered to the defendant, intended as a loan, and not repaid.[487] In some states the cause of action for money lent contemplates a loan of a definite amount, not an indefinite open-end agreement under which the amount lent could increase and decrease with time, such as a credit card obligation. In addition, in many states, to recover on a money lent claim, the plaintiff must show either a contractual relationship or an account proving the amount lent.[488]

In California, the common count of "money had and received" is generally not available when there is a contract between the parties.[489] Even if the claim is available when there is also a contract, an essential element is a fraudulent statement by the consumer.[490]

In Texas collectors may attempt to recover credit card debts using a "sworn account" theory, which is distinct from an action on an "account stated."[491] Collectors favor a "sworn account" cause of action because the collector need not provide a particularization or description of the nature of the component parts of an open account or claim, unless the trial court sustains special exceptions to the pleadings. The collector just files an affidavit, which is prima facie evidence unless the consumer files a written denial under oath. If the denial is not timely, the consumer cannot later deny the claim.[492]

Nevertheless, the action on a "sworn account" is founded on an open account or other claim for goods, wares, and merchandise, or for personal services furnished. Because of this, Texas courts find that the cause of action for "sworn account" does not apply to credit card debt owed to a third-party lender.[493]

487 *See* McIntyre v. Nice, 786 A.2d 620 (Me. 2001).

488 *See* LVNV Funding, L.L.C. v. Moehrlin (Fla. Volusia Cnty. Ct. Aug. 2006) (Green, J.), *available at* www.nclc.org/unreported.

489 Mathy v. Chase Manhatten Bank, 2009 WL 3489398 (C.D. Cal. Oct. 26, 2009).

490 *Id.*

491 Jaramillo v. Portfolio Acquisitions, L.L.C., 2010 WL 1197669 (Tex. App. Mar. 30, 2010).

492 Tex. R. Civ. P. 185.

493 Jaramillo v. Portfolio Acquisitions, L.L.C., 2010 WL 1197669 (Tex. App. Mar. 30, 2010); Gentry v. Great Seneca Fin. Corp., 2009 WL 3444936 (Tex. App. Oct. 27, 2009); Williams v. Unifund CCR Partners, 264 S.W.3d 231 (Tex. App. 2008); Sherman Acquisition II, L.P. v. Garcia, 229 S.W.3d 802 (Tex. App. 2007); Sherman Acquisition II Ltd. P'ship v. Graham, 2006 WL 2978570 (Tex. App. Oct. 18, 2006); Tully v. Citibank, 173 S.W.3d 212 (Tex. App. 2005). *But cf.* McManus v. Sears, Roebuck & Co., 2003 WL 22024238 (Tex. App. Aug. 28, 2003) (sworn account applies when merchant issues the credit card).

Chapter 5 Defenses and Counterclaims

5.1 About This Chapter

5.1.1 What This Chapter Covers

This chapter analyzes a number of basic defenses that apply to actions to collect credit card and other consumer debts. Depending on a state's procedures, some of these issues must be raised as affirmative defenses in the consumer's answer or they will be waived. For others, a simple denial of allegations in the collector's complaint will suffice. The defenses considered in this chapter include:

- Collector error in determining the amount owed;
- Payments have been misapplied, or the debt was settled or discharged in bankruptcy;
- The collector is suing the wrong consumer in a case of mistaken identity;
- Identity theft or other unauthorized use has occurred;
- The consumer is only an authorized user and not an account holder;
- The consumer is not liable for debts of a spouse;
- The consumer is not liable for the debts of a deceased family member;
- A credit protection product should pay off the debt;
- The consumer was incapacitated because of minority, mental incompetence, or intoxication;
- The debt was obtained through duress; and
- A collector seeking a deficiency judgment after selling the collateral has failed to meet its burden of proving that all aspects of the sale were commercially reasonable.

The chapter also examines consumer counterclaims in a collection action. The first question is whether to raise those counterclaims in the collection action, or whether it is better to raise them in a separate proceeding or even to abandon the claims. Special considerations apply when the counterclaims relate to the collector's own conduct in the collection litigation or when the consumer seeks to bring a class counterclaim.

This chapter also briefly reviews some possible counterclaims. These include Truth in Lending claims in a credit card collection case, counterclaims relating to pre-litigation collection contacts, and counterclaims relating to the collector's litigation conduct in the collection case itself. Finally, the chapter considers the ability to raise seller-related counterclaims when the FTC Holder Notice is found in the credit agreement.

5.1.2 Defenses and Counterclaims Analyzed Elsewhere

Other chapters in this treatise consider a number of other consumer defenses and counterclaims. The statute of limitations is an important defense in many collection actions, particularly those brought by debt buyers, and is examined in § 3.6, *supra*. Chapter 3, *supra*, also considers defenses related to jurisdiction, venue, an agreement that disputes will be resolved by arbitration, defects in the complaint, and the plaintiff's qualifications to use the state's courts. Chapter 4, *supra*, considers the collector's burden of proof to show it owns the debt and that its proof meets the elements of its causes of action. Chapter 4, *supra*, also considers the collector's right to finance charges and related fees and to postjudgment interest. A significant part of a collector's case is usually a request for attorney fees, and the consumer's defenses to that request are considered in Chapter 6, *infra*.

Those on active duty military have certain special defenses, examined in Chapter 7, *infra*. Collection actions for dishonored checks and for medical debt also provide special defenses which are examined in Chapters 8 and 9, *infra*, respectively. Collections by federal agencies of debt owed to the United States implicate special government collection remedies and special consumer defenses and are analyzed in Chapter 10, *infra*.

Nevertheless, a full discussion of all consumer defenses and counterclaims is beyond the scope of this treatise. Other NCLC treatises consider other important consumer defenses and counterclaims:

- Defenses and counterclaims to deficiency actions on automobile and other secured personal property loans are analyzed in NCLC's *Repossessions* treatise.
- Defenses and counterclaims to deficiency actions relating to home foreclosures are analyzed in NCLC's *Foreclosures* and also in NCLC's *Mortgage Lending*.
- Defenses related to student loan debt are comprehensively treated in NCLC's *Student Loans*.
- Defenses and counterclaims related to utility debt are analyzed in NCLC's *Access to Utility Service*.
- Counterclaims relating to abusive debt collection practices are more thoroughly treated in NCLC's *Fair Debt Collection*.
- Fair Credit Reporting Act counterclaims relating to an entity's impermissible use of a consumer report or inaccurate furnishing of information to a reporting agency are covered in NCLC's *Fair Credit Reporting*.
- Truth in Lending Act claims relating to credit card disclosures and practices and other credit transactions are analyzed in NCLC's *Truth in Lending*.
- Consumer Leasing Act claims relating to automobile lease disclosures and early termination charges are also analyzed in NCLC's *Truth in Lending*.
- Counterclaims regarding credit charges and terms are analyzed in NCLC's *Consumer Credit Regulation*.

- Counterclaims regarding credit discrimination, notice of credit denials, co-signers, and other violations of the Equal Credit Opportunity Act are found in NCLC's *Credit Discrimination*.
- Defenses and counterclaims regarding electronic transfers, checks, money orders, and other payment devices are analyzed in NCLC's *Consumer Banking and Payments Law*.
- Counterclaims under a state's unfair and deceptive practices (UDAP) statute can relate to almost any aspect of the transaction: pre-sale representations, sales techniques, product defects, credit terms, collection practices, and more. Unfair and deceptive practices are analyzed in NCLC's *Unfair and Deceptive Acts and Practices*.
- RICO counterclaims, counterclaims under the Telephone Consumer Protections Act, and other federal deception statutes are examined in NCLC's *Federal Deception Law*.
- Defenses and counterclaims can also relate to defective products or the consumer's revocation of acceptance of a product, as examined in NCLC's *Consumer Warranty Law*.
- Deficiency actions on car loans can also involve counterclaims relating to odometer rollbacks, undisclosed adverse prior history of a vehicle, or other fraudulent practices, as described in NCLC's *Automobile Fraud*.

An important issue affecting the raising of counterclaims in a collection action is the collector's derivative liability for the misconduct of others. For example, can the consumer raise counterclaims in a debt buyer's collection action based upon the conduct of the original creditor or a seller related to that creditor? While these issues are touched upon in § 5.5.6, *infra*, they are more thoroughly treated in other NCLC treatises, particularly in Chapter 4 of NCLC's *Federal Deception Law*.

5.2 Collector Error; Misapplication of Payments; Debt Settled or Discharged in Bankruptcy

5.2.1 Collector Error in Determining Amount Due

While the illusion of accurate computer records argues in favor of the accuracy of the amount due sought by a collector, what actually happens with credit records as they are passed along from creditor to debt buyer to collection attorney paints a very different picture. An Office of the Comptroller of the Currency probe found startling errors in the amount that JP Morgan Chase sued on consumer credit card debt. One whistleblower working for Chase stated that nearly a quarter of the files that were sampled showed incorrect amounts owed.[1] According to some reports, in almost 20% of the cases, the amount owed as shown in the files at collection law firms hired by Chase differed from Chase's own computer records.[2] Chase apparently had three different computer systems to handle accounts—one for active accounts, one for accounts in collection and litigation, and one for charge-offs. There were incompatibilities between systems and each might generate a different amount owed for the same account.[3] Compounding these errors was evidence of sloppy record-keeping at the collection law firms.[4]

The consumer attorney's task of proving such errors to a court will be difficult. Many judges will assume that a major bank's records as to the amount owed will be accurate—and in many cases they will be. But the JP Morgan Chase example also shows that in some cases they will not be accurate.

One approach is to obtain through discovery as many different statements as possible of the amount due and look for inconsistencies. Thus, seek the records being used by the collection law firm, the records held by the debt buyer, and the records as shown by each of the original creditor's computer systems. This may require an understanding of the process by which account information is originally generated by the creditor, what happens to the account information when put into collection or charged off, and what happens to the information when passed on to various debt buyers and then to the collection law firm.

In many of these steps, no exchange of paper is involved, simply one computer passing information on to another. Even the law firm suing on the debt may not have received paper records but have electronic access to a computer system residing at the creditor or the debt buyer.

5.2.2 Misapplication of Payments

Particularly when a debt is sold and resold, or when a creditor has hired multiple collection agencies to collect the same debt, consumer payments may not be properly credited resulting in the collector claiming an excessive amount owed or seeking collection on a debt already paid in full.[5] For example, Debt Buyer C may purchase a consumer's account as part of a bulk purchase from Debt Buyer B shortly after B purchased the consumer's account as part of another bulk purchase from Debt Buyer A. Consumers, having been dunned until recently by Collection Agency D, hired by Debt Buyer A, may make payments to D even after ownership of the account has been transferred to C, in part because the consumer was never notified that the account had been transferred from A to B or from B to C.[6]

1 *OCC Probing JPMorgan Chase Credit Card Collections*, Am. Banker (Mar. 12, 2012).

2 *Id.*

3 *Id.*

4 *Id.*

5 *See* Grimsley v. Messerli & Kramer, P.A., 2009 WL 928319 (D. Minn. Mar. 31, 2009) (collecting on already paid debt); McCammon v. Bibler, Newman & Reynolds, P.A., 493 F. Supp. 2d 1166 (D. Kan. 2007) (collection agency obtained judgment despite knowing that consumer had paid original creditor); Sweatt v. Sunkidd Venture, Inc., 2006 WL 1418652 (W.D. Wash. May 18, 2006) (collecting on already paid debt); Hooper v. Capital Credit & Collection Servs., Inc., 2004 WL 825619 (D. Or. Apr. 13, 2004) (attempted collection on debt already paid to original creditor); McHugh v. Check Investors, Inc., 2003 WL 21283288 (W.D. Va. May 21, 2003) (consumer had paid debt before collection agency ever began collection attempts).

6 *See* Smith v. Mallick, 514 F.3d 48, 50 (D.C. Cir. 2008). *See also* Assocs. Fin. Servs. Co. v. Bowman, Heintz, Boscia, & Vician, P.C., 2004 U.S.

The record of payments can become lost if Collection Agency D does not forward the payment to Debt Buyer A, if Debt Buyer A does not properly forward payment information to Debt Buyer B, or if Debt Buyer B does not properly forward this information to Debt Buyer C. Moreover, it is very likely that Collection Agency D and none of the three debt buyers have accounting systems to track consumer payments that are as reliable as the system in place with the original creditor.[7]

The consumer's problem will be one of proof, as the collector will deny that the payments were ever made. Ask the client how payment was made—by check, electronic fund transfer from the consumer's bank account, a money order, or by refinancing or consolidation whereby another entity was to pay off the debt as part of a new loan. Then try to obtain a record of the payment. See what evidence of the payment can be obtained from the consumer's bank or the entity providing the money order. If the consumer's bank or entity providing the money order does not cooperate, a subpoena can be issued. When payment to the collector came from another creditor as part of a refinancing or balance transfer, that third-party creditor can be brought into the case if it did not make the payment or refuses to verify that it made the payment.

Examine the consumer's credit report from one or more of the major credit reporting agencies. Details on how to obtain and decipher that report are found in NCLC's *Fair Credit Reporting*.[8] Entries indicating payment or showing an account balance lower than that claimed by the collector are support for the consumer's position. On the other hand, the report's failure to reflect the payment should *not* be taken adversely. It is no surprise when a debt buyer who refuses to acknowledge a payment does not report that payment to a reporting agency. While the original creditor will regularly furnish information about its accounts to reporting agencies, debt buyers and collection agencies are less likely to do so. Moreover, even the original creditor may stop furnishing data about an account after the account has been sold or charged off.

In the final analysis, when the consumer states that a payment has been made and the collector states the contrary, the question will be one for the fact finder. Sometimes just putting the question in controversy with admissible evidence, and thereby defeating the collector's summary judgment motion, is a victory, as many collectors have a business model that relies on default and summary judgments and will not pursue the matter at trial.

At trial, the burden to show the balance due will be on the collector. The reliability of a collector's denial that a payment was made is certainly weakened when the collector has no way of knowing whether that payment in fact was made, since payment was made to the original creditor, a prior debt buyer in the chain of ownership, or a collection agency hired by one of those entities. When the entity suing on the debt purchased the consumer's account, that entity received very sparse information about the debt and certainly did not receive a payment history.

5.2.3 *Proving Debt Already Settled*

5.2.3.1 General

Often consumers make a payment on a debt in reliance on the creditor's or debt buyer's representation that the partial payment will be in full settlement of the amount owed, or that agreement to a payment schedule will reduce the total obligation. Customer service agents are often authorized to waive or reduce fees and interest rates in response to customer requests. Nevertheless, it is possible that a collector refuses to honor the settlement, or the debt is sold to a new debt buyer and the new debt buyer pursues collection for the full amount.[9]

The effectiveness of this defense—that the debt has already been settled or reduced—may depend on what evidence of the settlement agreement the consumer has retained or can find and the court's view of the credibility of the parties. The consumer who states that there was a creditor or collector representation that the debt is settled in full or in part and that the consumer relied on that representation, is raising a factual dispute over whether the debt is still due. This evidence should be enough to defeat the collector's summary judgment motion and create a question of fact for trial. For example, a collector should not be able to recover through a summary judgment motion when the collector seeks fees and finance charges as part of the amount due, and the consumer alleges that a customer service representative waived all or some of those fees or finance charges.

That representation of the customer service representative need not be in writing and need not meet all the requirements of the original contract formation. The essential elements of equitable estoppel are: conduct by which one induces another to believe in certain material facts, resulting in justifiable reliance, causing injury to the consumer. Similarly, waiver of a right is enforceable when the consumer relies on that waiver.

The common law theory of accord and satisfaction is based upon the creditor's acceptance of payment with the agreement (which can be oral) that it constitutes full payment.[10] These

---

Dist. LEXIS 6520 (S.D. Ind. Mar. 31, 2004) (debts placed for collection were paid or already assigned to another collector).

7 *See* Overcash v. United Abstract Grp., Inc., 549 F. Supp. 2d 193 (N.D.N.Y. 2008) (consumer paid collection agency, but debt was subsequently resold multiple times and another agency presented the former debtor with a bill roughly $40,000 larger than the paid, settled amount); Chiverton v. Fed. Fin. Grp., Inc., 399 F. Supp. 2d 96 (D. Conn. 2005) (determining that former debtor paid one collection agency, but another firm later claimed they bought the debt and made multiple threatening and harassing phone calls to the former debtor); Fontana v. C. Barry & Assocs., L.L.C., 2007 WL 2580490 (W.D.N.Y. Sept. 4, 2007).

8 (8th ed. 2013), *updated at* www.nclc.org/library.

9 *See* Burke v. Messerli & Kramer P.A., 2010 WL 3167403 (D. Minn. Aug. 9, 2010); Overcash v. United Abstract Group, Inc., 549 F. Supp. 2d 193 (N.D.N.Y. 2008); Chiverton v. Federal Financial Group, Inc., 399 F. Supp. 2d 96 (D. Conn. 2005); Capital Credit & Collection Serv., Inc. v. Armani, 206 P.3d 1114 (Or. Ct. App. 2009) (debt collector settled a debt and then instituted litigation on the same debt).

10 *See* § 5.2.4, *infra*.

types of oral modifications and waivers are enforceable even if the underlying contract purports to require that all changes be made in writing.[11] The issue thus becomes whether there was, in fact, a representation that the debt would be canceled upon partial payment and whether the consumer relied upon this promise.

5.2.3.2 Developing the Consumer's Evidence

Any documentation beyond just the consumer's testimony will clearly strengthen the consumer's case. The consumer should provide any paperwork in his or her possession. Also try to obtain a copy of the canceled check to see if the consumer noted on the check "payment in full" or the like and look for other contemporaneous writings that may prove helpful. The consumer may also seek to discover from the creditor or collector any telephone recordings or other collector notations reflecting the settlement conversation.

The consumer's case will be bolstered by proof of a large payment made well after the account became delinquent. While such payment need not have been in full satisfaction of the debt, the fact of the payment is consistent with the consumer's version of events. Note also to whom the payment was made, because the current debt owner will have no evidence that a payment to a prior owner was not made in full satisfaction of the debt.

The consumer should not only develop the consumer's evidence for the settlement but also question whether the collector has any knowledge whether or not the amount was settled by a prior owner of a debt. For example, a debt buyer may only have an electronic spreadsheet with very limited information about the debt and thus has received no information from the original creditor or a prior debt buyer as to any possible settlement.

5.2.3.3 IRS Form 1099-C as Evidence of Debt Cancellation

An IRS Form 1099-C as evidence of discharge of an indebtedness (discussed in this subsection) must be distinguished from charging off a debt (discussed in § 5.2.3.4, *infra*). Creditors and debt buyers that discharge an indebtedness of at least $600 must file an information Form 1099-C with the IRS by March 31st of the following year and must also send a copy to the consumer.[12] The entity should also have a copy in its own records.

IRS regulations provide eight situations wherein a Form 1099-C must be sent; seven of these situations are triggered when the debt is discharged or the debt is uncollectible because the statute of limitations has run.[13] The eighth situation allows a creditor, but not a debt buyer,[14] to send out a Form 1099-C if no payment has been made and no collection has been undertaken for thirty-six months.[15]

Consequently, if the debt buyer sends Form 1099-C, then the debt buyer should only do so after discharging the obligation, and this should be near conclusive evidence that the debt is discharged. Far more typical is for the original creditor to send the Form 1099-C, and then it can have discharged the debt either because the obligation was discharged or because no payment was made and no collection undertaken for thirty-six months. For the collector to claim that the 1099-C Form does not discharge the debt, it should produce evidence that the original creditor who sent out the Form 1099-C did not receive payment for thirty-six months, with the thirty-six months being calculated as ending on December 31 of the year prior to the year the form was actually sent. For example, if a Form 1099-C is sent in February of 2014 for the 2013 tax year, no payments should have been made at least as of January 1, 2011.

The Fourth Circuit in *FDIC v. Cashion* dealt with an unusual case in which the only evidence of the balance on a $2 million debt being discharged was the sending of a Form 1099-C by a failed bank later taken over by the FDIC.[16] The Fourth Circuit, citing IRS letters that a Form 1099-C does not always mean a debt is discharged, found that this could not be the only evidence because the form could have been sent as a result of the debt being unpaid for three years. But the Fourth Circuit did state that, "[i]n another case, where a properly authenticated Form 1099-C is introduced into evidence along with other circumstantial evidence of cancellation of the debt, the Form 1099-C could be properly considered by the trier of fact under the totality of circumstances on the ultimate issue of whether the debt in question was, in fact, cancelled."[17]

Thus, even when it is the creditor that is sending out the Form 1099-C, the very fact of the form being sent is powerful evidence that the debt has been discharged,[18] particularly if other evidence also suggests the same thing. This evidence will be particularly hard to rebut for a debt buyer collecting on a debt. The debt buyer will have to show that there was at least a three-year period between when the creditor last received a payment and the debt being first sold to a debt buyer.

---

11 *See In re* R & D Contracting, L.L.C., 383 B.R. 890 (Bankr. E.D. Mich. 2008); Henley v. MacDonald, 971 So. 2d 998 (Fla. Dist. Ct. App. 2008); Fleming v. JE Merit Constr., Inc., 985 So. 2d 141 (La. Ct. App. 2008).

12 26 C.F.R. § 1.6050P-1(a).

13 26 C.F.R. § 1.6050P-1(b)(2)(i).

14 26 C.F.R. § 1.6050P-1(b)(2)(i)(H) (referencing entities described at 26 U.S.C. §§ 6050P(c)(2)(A) through (C)).

15 26 C.F.R. § 1.6050P-1(b)(2)(i)(H). There are some complications in computing this time period. *See* 26 C.F.R. § 1.6050P-1(b)(2)(iv).

16 720 F.3d 169 (4th Cir. 2013).

17 *Id.*

18 *See In re* Welsh, 2006 WL 3859233 (Bankr. E.D. Pa. Oct. 27, 2006); *In re* Crosby, 261 B.R. 470 (Bankr. D. Kan. 2001); Amtrust Bank v. Fossett, 224 P.3d 935 (Ariz. Ct. App. 2009) (issuance of 1099-C is prima facie evidence that debt discharged, but creditor's affidavit to the contrary created a genuine issue of material fact); Franklin Credit Mgmt. Corp. v. Nicholas, 812 A.2d 51 (Conn. App. Ct. 2002) (Form 1099-C sufficient evidence to determine if debt discharged when lender argued that form was issued by mistake but presented no evidence of the mistake). *But see* Atchison v. Hiway Fed. Credit Union, 2013 WL 1175020 (D. Minn. Mar. 20, 2013); *In re* Zilka, 407 B.R. 684 (W.D. Penn. 2009); Chivaho Credit Union v. McGuire, 2012 WL 6212706 (Ohio Ct. App. Nov. 28, 2012).

Creditors or debt buyers may also argue that the Form 1099-C was sent out by mistake. There is a much stronger argument for this if a corrected Form 1099-C had been sent out before the consumer raised it as evidence that the debt was discharged.[19] Moreover, a debt buyer is unlikely to have knowledge as to whether the original creditor or a prior debt buyer in the chain of assignments sent the Form 1099-C out by mistake.

5.2.3.4 Charging Off a Debt Does Not Cancel the Debt

Distinguish a debt being discharged or settled from a debt being charged off or written off. Charging off or writing off a debt is merely an accounting procedure whereby the debt is moved from one category of receivables to another. The purpose of this accounting procedure is to allow investors evaluating a company's balance sheet to have an accurate assessment as to the chances of payment on that debt.[20] For example, the United States has a "Uniform Retail Credit Classification and Account Management Policy" that states that retail loans past due for 180 days should be classified as losses and charged off.[21] This policy is a required accounting practice and not a requirement that the debt be canceled after 180 days.

Charging off or writing off a debt does not mean that the creditor has agreed to cancel the debt.[22] Similarly, the fact that the collector has not pursued a debt for some time does not mean that the creditor has canceled the debt, although at some point the statute of limitations will have run, making the debt uncollectible. A consumer arguing settlement of the debt should not allege that the debt was charged off, written off, or left dormant for years, but instead should point to a representation that a partial payment would be accepted as full satisfaction of the debt.

5.2.3.5 Impropriety of Charging Interest After Charge-Off

While charging off a debt will not extinguish the consumer's obligation, creditors often have a *voluntary policy* of not charging interest on the debt for the period after the charge-off.[23] Not assessing interest or other fees after charge-off is one of the grounds under the Truth in Lending Act for the card issuer not to have to send out a periodic statement,[24] so a card issuer may decide not to charge interest or fees after that date as a way of cutting down on its disclosures.

When a debt buyer purchases a debt in a situation in which the creditor had waived its right to interest after the charge-off period, the debt buyer cannot compute interest during the period from the date of charge-off until the date of the debt purchase because the creditor has waived that interest and the debt buyer cannot undo what its assignor has done.[25] Instead, the debt buyer can only charge additional interest from the date it purchases the debt and only if it has a basis for so charging.

5.2.4 Discharging the Debt by Accord and Satisfaction

When a consumer has made a partial payment of the amount the collector seeks, and notifies the collector that the payment is in full accord and satisfaction of the debt, then the debt is discharged if certain conditions are met. For payments made by check, these conditions are set out in UCC § 3-311.[26]

The consumer will have to prove that the check was tendered in good faith in satisfaction of the debt, the amount was subject to a bona fide dispute, and the creditor cashed the check. The check or accompanying written communication must contain a conspicuous statement that the check is being tendered as full satisfaction of the claim. The Comments to UCC § 3-311 state "almost any statement on the check should be noticed and therefore conspicuous."[27]

UCC § 3-311(c)(1) allows a creditor or collector to notify the consumer that such checks must be sent to a designated address; checks sent to another address will not be in full accord and satisfaction of the debt even if cashed. After the account is sold to a debt buyer, the consumer does not send the check to this address but to the debt buyer's address. Again, that debt buyer can specify an address to mail checks when a debt is disputed. But if it fails to specify a special address, or if the consumer sends the check to that address, a check indicating it is in full accord and satisfaction should satisfy a debt if cashed by the debt buyer.

If a creditor or collector does not provide notice of such a special address, the creditor or collector has an alternative way to avoid full accord and satisfaction after cashing the check. It can return the full amount of the consumer's payment within ninety days and avoid satisfaction of the debt.[28] This cure is not available to those providing a special address to which to send checks in full accord and satisfaction.[29]

---

19 *Cf.* Franklin Credit Mgmt. Corp. v. Nicholas, 812 A.2d 51 (Conn. App. Ct. 2002) (Form 1099-C sufficient evidence to determine if debt discharged when lender argued that form was issued by mistake but presented no evidence of the mistake).

20 The charge-off date also starts the clock running as to when information in a credit report is obsolete and must be deleted. *See* National Consumer Law Center, Fair Credit Reporting § 5.2.3.3 (8th ed. 2013), *updated at* www.nclc.org/library.

21 65 Fed. Reg. 36,903 (June 12, 2000).

22 *In re* Zilka, 407 B.R. 684 (W.D. Penn. 2009); Kelly v. Wolpoff & Abramson, L.L.P., 634 F Supp. 2d 1202 (D. Colo. 2008); Maresh v. Borenstein, 2008 WL 2797037 (D. Colo. July 18, 2008); CACV of Colo., L.L.C. v. Gangaway (Pa. Ct. Com. Pl. Feb. 1, 2010), *available at* www.nclc.org/unreported. *See also* Debt Buyers' Ass'n v. Snow, 481 F. Supp. 2d 1 (D.D.C. 2006).

23 *See* McDonald v. Asset Acceptance, L.L.C., 2013 WL 4028947 (E.D. Mich. Aug. 7, 2013).

24 *See* National Consumer Law Center, Truth in Lending § 6.7.2.1 (8th ed. 2012), *updated at* www.nclc.org/library.

25 McDonald v. Asset Acceptance, L.L.C., 2013 WL 4028947 (E.D. Mich. Aug. 7, 2013).

26 *See* Citibank v. Maniaci, 881 N.Y.S.2d 362 (N.Y. Dist. Ct. 2009).

27 Comment 8.

28 U.C.C. § 3-311(c)(2).

29 *Id.*

Even if a business specifies an address, and the consumer does not send the check to that address, or even if the business returns the payment within ninety days, the check is still in full accord and satisfaction if the consumer proves that the business or the business' agent knew that the check was tendered in full satisfaction of the debt.[30] For example, if the consumer hands to the debt buyer's lawyer a check that says it is in full satisfaction, then the debt should be discharged no matter what address is specified and whether or not the collector tries to later return payment. The lawyer should be charged with reading the check handed to him or her in person.

Some creditors may place in the credit agreement that its acceptance of a partial payment does not waive its rights under the agreement.[31] But this contract language should not prevent the consumer's payment from being in full accord and satisfaction of the debt. The consumer's payment in full satisfaction of the debt is not a "partial" payment because it is payment in full of a disputed debt, so the contractual language has no effect. Moreover, the acceptance of the check that states it is in full accord and satisfaction waives the contracts anti-waiver provision.

Some creditors now go one step further and state that they can accept payments that reflect "paid in full" or other restrictive endorsements without losing any rights under the agreement.[32] But even this language may not be sufficient to immunize the creditor. What rights is the creditor losing when the consumer proposes that the payment be in full satisfaction and the creditor accepts that offer by cashing the check?

One case found that a creditor whose contract included such language could cash a $110 check labeled in full satisfaction of the debt but could still seek the $6700 balance.[33] However, the court in that case should have found instead that the check was not tendered in good faith.

There is also an issue as to whether language in the fine print of the creditor's standard form contract concerning partial payments can supersede the scheme set out in U.C.C. § 3-311.[34] Even if the clause were to be found to supersede section 3-311 as to payments to the original creditor, it should not be found enforceable as to payments to a debt buyer, particularly if the debt buyer cannot produce that contract and produce evidence that the specific consumer assented to that specific contract.

5.2.5 Prior Collection Action on the Same Debt

An increasingly common practice is for the consumer to be sued twice on the same debt.[35] For example, a debt buyer may sell an account after the debt buyer's collection lawsuit has been dismissed with prejudice. Alternatively, a consumer can be sued on a debt, pay it off in full, and be sued on the same debt again. The same consumer debt is often sold and resold to multiple debt buyers, often as part of a portfolio of thousands of accounts that may be evidenced by nothing more than an Excel file. Debt buyers often are not careful about the status of any one account in the portfolio. It is even possible for two debt buyers to purchase the same account.

Always ask the consumer whether there has been a prior suit on the same debt and also check the consumer's credit report for any evidence of such a suit. When that prior suit was dismissed without prejudice, the collector can bring a second suit if within the statute of limitations but cannot if the prior suit was dismissed with prejudice. Similarly, when a prior suit has resulted in a judgment for the collector and the consumer has paid off that judgment, a collector cannot bring a second suit on the same debt. Under state law, a second collection suit most likely cannot be brought on the same debt even when the first suit resulted in a judgment for a collector and the judgment has not been fully satisfied. The judgment in the first suit will likely be treated under state law as extinguishing a debt outside of the judgment.

5.2.6 Debts Discharged in Bankruptcy

The discharge of a debt in bankruptcy is a complete defense to that debt. Nevertheless, some collectors continue to sue on debt discharged in bankruptcy. For example, in one case a U.S. trustee alleged that Capital One filed 5600 bankruptcy proofs of claim for debts previously discharged in bankruptcy. The parties reached a settlement in 2008 in which Capital One would refund amounts improperly collected.[36] This apparently did not stop Capital One from continuing the practice, and a court-appointed auditor in 2011 concluded that Capital One pursued 15,500 "erroneous claims" seeking recover of debts previously discharged in bankruptcy.[37]

In an individual case, it will not be difficult to show that a debt has been discharged in bankruptcy and is not subject to further collection. The typical bankruptcy is a no-asset chapter 7 case, and all that need be shown in such a case is that the debt was incurred before the bankruptcy filing and there was a

30 U.C.C. § 3-311(d).

31 *See, e.g.*, Citibank v. Maniaci, 881 N.Y.S.2d 362 (N.Y. Dist. Ct. 2009).

32 *See, e.g.*, Eaton v. Citibank, 73 U.C.C. Rep. Serv. 2d 107 (M.D. Penn. 2010).

33 *See, e.g.*, Eaton v. Citibank, 73 U.C.C. Rep. Serv. 2d 107 (M.D. Penn. 2010).

34 *But see* Eaton v. Citibank, 73 UCC Rep. Serv. 2d 107 (M.D. Penn. 2010). *But cf.* Citibank v. Maniaci, 881 N.Y.S.2d 362 (N.Y. Dist. Ct. 2009) (New York has a different treatment of accord and satisfaction than that under the current U.C.C., and the court found the contract language to control).

35 Chase Bank v. Cardello, 896 N.Y.S.2d 856 (N.Y. Civ. Ct. 2010) ("[O]n a regular basis this court encounters defendants being sued on the same debt by more than one creditor alleging they are the assignee of the original credit card obligation. Often these consumers have already entered into stipulations to pay off the outstanding balance due the credit card issuer and find themselves filing an order to show cause to vacate a default judgment from an unknown debt purchaser for the same obligation"). *See also* Grimsley v. Messerli & Kramer, P.A., 2009 WL 928319 (D. Minn. Mar. 31, 2009); McCammon v. Bibler, Newman & Reynolds, P.A., 493 F. Supp. 2d 1166 (D. Kan. 2007); Sweatt v. Sunkidd Venture, Inc., 2006 WL 1418652 (W.D. Wash. May 18, 2006); Hooper v. Capital Credit & Collection Serv., Inc., 2004 WL 825619 (D. Or. Apr. 13, 2004); McHugh v. Check Investors, Inc., 2003 WL 21283288 (W.D. Va. May 21, 2003).

36 Joint Motion for Entry of Stipulated Judgment, *In re* Gallery & Morse v. Capital One Bank (filed Bankr. D. Mass. Oct. 2, 2008), *reported in* 5 No. 12 Andrews Bankr. Litig. Rep. 4 (Oct. 17, 2008).

37 *Debts Go Bad, Then It Gets Worse*, Wall St. J., Dec. 23, 2011.

bankruptcy discharge.[38] The consumer will often have a copy of the discharge, and the consumer may also have a copy of the initial notice showing the date the bankruptcy was filed. If not, the consumer's complete bankruptcy file is accessible electronically over the Internet through a system called PACER,[39] including the discharge and the date the bankruptcy was filed. Finding the consumer's file on PACER is simplified with the bankruptcy file number, but the case can also be found using the consumer's name and the district where the bankruptcy case was filed.

In a no-asset chapter 7 case, most courts hold that the consumer need not have listed the individual debt in the bankruptcy schedules, and there is no problem if the debt is listed in a different amount than the collector claims or if the account number or other description in the bankruptcy schedules differs from the actual debt.[40] The debt is still discharged. On the other hand, for a bankruptcy discharge to be effective in a chapter 13 case or a chapter 7 case involving assets, the consumer must list the account in the bankruptcy schedules. Even in a no-asset chapter 7 case, it is safest to show that the debt was listed on the consumer's bankruptcy schedules. The consumer may have retained a copy of the schedules, and they are also available on PACER.

Check whether a consumer filing under chapter 13 eventually received a discharge. The consumer may have been making payments under a chapter 13 plan for several years but may never have completed the plan and thus never received a discharge. In that case the debt is not discharged, but payments under the plan should be credited on the account. If there is a dispute, the chapter 13 trustee will have records of the payments.

If the collector alleges that the individual debt was not discharged, because of fraud or some other reason, this allegation can be easily undermined by looking at the bankruptcy case records on PACER. Exceptions from discharge must be raised as an adversary proceeding. Whether an adversary proceeding was ever filed and brought to a conclusion will be apparent in the file. No adversary proceedings need be filed for certain exceptions to discharge, such as for student loans, but these exceptions will not apply to credit card debt or most other consumer debt.[41] In any event the burden is on the collector to show why a debt was not discharged in bankruptcy.

Similarly, if the collector claims that a debt has been reaffirmed, a reaffirmation is only enforceable if the reaffirmation agreement was filed with the court.[42] A review of the file on PACER will indicate whether a reaffirmation agreement was filed with the court and whether that agreement was disapproved by the court. In any event, the burden should be on the collector to produce a valid reaffirmation agreement.

38 *See* National Consumer Law Center, Consumer Bankruptcy Law and Practice § 3.6 (10th ed. 2012), *updated at* www.nclc.org/library.

39 Located at http://pacer.psc.uscourts.gov.

40 *See* National Consumer Law Center, Consumer Bankruptcy Law and Practice § 15.4.3.3 (10th ed. 2012), *updated at* www.nclc.org/library.

41 *Id.* Ch. 15.

42 *Id.* § 15.5.2.

5.3 Someone Else Owes the Debt

5.3.1 When Collector Mistakenly Identifies the Consumer As the Debtor

Sometimes a collector will sue the consumer on a debt about which the consumer has no knowledge. One explanation, discussed in the next subsection, is that an identity thief opened up an account in the consumer's name. Another possibility is that the collector mixed up the consumer's identity with that of the real debtor. This latter explanation is far more common than many realize, particularly with the explosive growth in accounts purchased by debt buyers. Not only do the debt buyers have minimal information on the account holder, but they are seeking to collect very old debt, when the debtor often has moved one or more times since the original creditor last received a valid mailing address.

Debt buyers who cannot find a consumer's present address often use a skip tracing service or reporting agency to locate the consumer, and some of these services only have minimal information on each individual in its data base, and the information they do have is not always accurate. For example, the skip tracing service will try to match a name to a new address without verifying that the social security numbers match; it is very easy for a service to try to find John A. Smith for example and provide the collector with the address of John B. Smith.

A consumer caught up in a case of mistaken identity will have no notion why it is happening and will either ignore collection contacts or simply tell the collector they have the wrong person.[43] The collector's next action might be a lawsuit filed against the wrong person for the debt.

When consumers are sued on a debt with which they have no connection, it is useful to distinguish between identity theft and a skip tracing error, as they look the same from the consumer's perspective but should be handled differently. For example, an attempt to collect on a credit account opened within the last year may involve identity theft; an attempt to collect on an account opened several years ago will more likely involve skip tracing.

A consumer who is the victim of identity theft typically learns of the scam when contacted by the creditor collecting the debt once the identity thief disappears, which usually happens soon after the account is opened. Nevertheless, about 20% of identity theft victims learn of the problem only after at least a year.[44] On the other hand, in the case of a skip tracing error, the real account owner is likely to have paid on the account for some time and, even after that owner's default, there will be a period of time before assignment to a debt buyer. So the account will likely have been opened some time ago.

43 The inquiry as to the consumer's credit report will be recorded with the reporting agency and can be seen if a consumer report is requested.

44 *See* Fed. Trade Comm'n, Identity Theft Victim Complaint Data, Figures and Trends Jan. 1 through Dec. 31, 2002, *available at* www.ftc.gov.

In defending a case of a mistaken identity, an obvious first step is to look at the way the defendant is identified in the complaint and accompanying documents. If the defendant is listed as James McOwen, then James McKeown has a good case that he should not have been served with the complaint and is not liable on the account. Also, seek through informal or formal discovery from the original creditor and the collector all identifying information about the account owner—previous addresses, Social Security number, age, employment, and so forth. This information may show that the individual owning the account is not the same one as the individual being sued.

Another step is to try to discover the source of the skip tracing error. One possible source is a report from a credit reporting agency. One can order consumer reports from the three major reporting agencies.[45] The inquiries section on each report will indicate who has pulled the report, and this information will allow the consumer to identify whether the collector utilized a report to locate the consumer. Look to see if the same debt is found in the consumer's report at the other two reporting agencies. Because the three major reporting agencies receive almost identical information from creditors but may have differing systems to match credit data to a particular individual, a debt found in the files of only one agency is a good indicator that the error in the agency's files is what caused the mix-up (typically, this happens when one consumer's debt is placed in the file of another consumer with a similar name, called mismerging).

Also look for an indication that the account has only recently been added to the consumer's file. Information on an account having been inserted into the consumer's file for many months can sometimes be explained by consistent mismerging over that period of time, but the sudden appearance of an account in the report with no history of payments often indicates a recent instance of mismerging.

Beside defending the collection action, the consumer, in the case of a mismerged file, should also send a dispute letter to the reporting agency with copies sent to the original creditor. Include the consumer's identifying information and state that the account does not belong to the consumer. Failure to properly reinvestigate may give the consumer a claim under the Fair Credit Reporting Act against the creditor and the reporting agency.[46]

5.3.2 Identity Theft and Other Unauthorized Charges

5.3.2.1 General

There are a number of situations in which a consumer can be wrongfully sued on charges that the consumer did not authorize. An identity thief can open an account in the consumer's name or make charges on an account opened by the consumer. Someone finding a lost credit card or gaining access to a credit card number can use it without authorization. There are also situations involving marital separation or other family discord when one family member uses another family member's account without proper authorization, or obtains or renews a credit card on the consumer's account without authorization.[47]

Federal law states that consumers are not liable for unauthorized use of credit cards.[48] Even when federal credit card protections do not apply, a consumer is not liable for the debt which the consumer has not agreed to. When the consumer provides credible testimony that he or she never took out a credit account, it will be up to the collector to offer convincing evidence to the contrary, and the consumer should not be found liable when the collector fails to do so.[49] In any event, when the consumer disputes that charges are correct or authorized, it will be difficult for a collector to prevail on a summary judgment motion.[50]

5.3.2.2 Federal Protections Against Unauthorized Use

The federal Truth in Lending Act contains strong consumer protections against unauthorized use of a credit card. These protections are examined in more detail in NCLC's *Truth in Lending*.[51] In brief, consumers are not liable for unauthorized charges on their own accounts but under some circumstances may be liable for up to $50.[52] Even $50 cannot be assessed for unauthorized transactions when the consumer did not request the credit card or when the card issuer promised not to assess the $50 charge.[53]

Federal law specifies that the creditor has the burden of proof to show that a credit card charge is authorized.[54] Thus, when the consumer claims that charges are unauthorized, the burden shifts to the collector to prove that they are.[55] "Unauthorized use" means the use of the credit card by a person other than the card holder who does not have actual, implied, or apparent

45 *See* National Consumer Law Center, Fair Credit Reporting Ch. 3 (8th ed. 2013), *updated at* www.nclc.org/library.

46 *Id.* §§ 10.2.1.3, 10.2.3.2, *infra*.

47 *See* Citibank v. Hauff, 668 N.W.2d 528 (S.D. 2003); Dillard Dep't Stores, Inc. v. Owens, 951 S.W.2d 915 (Tex. App. 1997) (card holder's estranged spouse obtained credit card on card holder's account after separation).

48 15 U.S.C. § 1643.

49 See Cach, L.L.C. v. Stupack, 2010 WL 1225029 (Conn. Super. Ct. Mar. 1, 2010).

50 *See* Discover Bank v. Stanley, 757 N.W.2d 756 (S.D. 2008); Unifund CCR Assignee of Providian v. Ayhan, 146 Wash. App. 1026 (Wash. Ct. App. 2008).

51 (8th ed. 2012), *updated at* www.nclc.org/library.

52 15 U.S.C. § 1643.

53 *See* National Consumer Law Center, Truth in Lending § 7.10.4 (8th ed. 2012), *updated at* www.nclc.org/library.

54 15 U.S.C. § 1643(b). *See also* Minskoff v. Am. Express Travel Related Servs. Co., 98 F.3d 703 (2d Cir. 1996); Citibank v. Gifesman, 773 A.2d 993 (Conn. App. Ct. 2001); Crestar Bank v. Cheevers, 744 A.2d 1043 (D.C. Ct. App. 2000).

55 *See* Jones v. CitiBank, 2008 WL 651689 (Ark. Ct. App. Mar. 12, 2008); Unifund CCR Assignee of Providian v. Ayhan, 146 Wash. App. 1026 (Wash. Ct. App. 2008).

authority for such use and from which the card holder receives no benefit.[56]

The consumer need not have notified the card issuer at the time of the unauthorized use in order for unauthorized use to be a defense in a collection action.[57] The consumer also need not have first complied with the Fair Credit Billing Act's notice requirements before raising unauthorized use as a defense in a collection action.[58]

These protections for unauthorized use apply only to credit cards, defined as "any card, plate, coupon book, or other credit device existing for the purpose of obtaining money, property, labor, or services on credit."[59] The protections apply to all types of credit cards, including store credit cards and telephone calling cards, and not just third-party cards, such as those with the VISA or MasterCard logos.

When an identity thief opens an account in the consumer's name, the consumer is not in fact the card holder and will not owe anything, whether for purchases, finance charges, or fees. Matters are more complicated when certain charges on the consumer's actual account are authorized and others are unauthorized. The consumer should not be liable for unauthorized charges or any finance charges or other fees flowing from those unauthorized charges.

5.3.2.3 Right to Obtain Information About an Account Opened by an Identity Thief

When an identity thief, rather than the consumer, opened an account, the consumer has a right to obtain information about that application and related business records to help demonstrate that the consumer did not open the account. The consumer, as an identity theft victim, has the right under federal law to obtain from the original creditor a copy of the application and business transaction records in control of that creditor, whether maintained by that entity or by another for that entity.[60] The request must be in writing,[61] and the creditor must first obtain proof of positive identification of the identity theft victim.[62] The creditor cannot charge for this information[63] and must respond within thirty days after receiving the consumer's request.[64]

56 15 U.S.C. § 1602(o). *Cf.* New Century Fin. Servs., Inc. v. Dennegar, 928 A.2d 48 (N.J. Super. Ct. App. Div. 2007) (roommate's use found to be authorized).

57 Danner v. Discover Bank, 257 S.W.3d 113 (Ark. Ct. App. 2007); People's Bank v. Scarpetti, 1998 WL 61925 (Conn. Super. Ct. Feb. 5, 1998); Crestar Bank v. Cheevers, 744 A.2d 1043 (D.C. Ct. App. 2000); Universal Bank v. McCafferty, 624 N.E.2d 358 (Ohio Ct. App. 1993); Fifth Third Bank/Visa v. Gilbert, 478 N.E.2d 1324 (Ohio Mun. Ct. 1984); Mich. Nat'l Bank v. Olson, 723 P.2d 438 (Wash. Ct. App. 1986). *See also* 15 U.S.C. § 1643(b) (burden on creditor to show use was authorized in a collection action).

58 *See* § 4.7.6.4.2, *supra*.

59 15 U.S.C. § 1602(k).

60 15 U.S.C. § 1681g(e)(1).

61 15 U.S.C. § 1681g(e)(3).

62 15 U.S.C. § 1681g(e)(2).

63 15 U.S.C. § 1681g(e)(4).

64 15 U.S.C. § 1681g(e)(1).

5.3.2.4 Consumer Actions After Discovering Identity Theft

Both to protect the consumer from future unauthorized charges and to bolster the consumer's defense in a collection action, the consumer should report the identity theft to local law enforcement and also to at least one reporting agency to put the account on a fraud alert. That agency is obligated to inform others of the identity theft.[65]

Federal and state law provide other protections for identity theft victims. Most states have security freeze laws that allow consumers to freeze access to their consumer reports.[66] This freeze prevents identity thieves from opening accounts in the consumer's name, because there is no access to a consumer report. Under the Fair Credit Reporting Act, consumers can also have a credit reporting agency block fraudulent information from their reports, and the credit reporting agency must notify the furnisher of that information, who must take steps so as not to furnish the same information again.[67]

5.3.3 Liability of Authorized Users

5.3.3.1 Distinguishing Authorized Users from Joint Account Holders

Those using open-end credit can be put into two different categories—account holders and authorized users. A credit account is in the name of one or more account holders, who applied for and agreed to be obligated on that account. The account holder can authorize others, who are called authorized users, to use the account. This distinction is important because account holders are liable on a debt, while authorized users generally are not.

Federal law clarifies the distinction between an account holder and an authorized user. A credit card can only be issued to someone who requests the card from the card issuer. If the account holder requests cards for anyone else, those individuals are authorized users.[68] Thus the distinction is that an account holder applies for the card from the card issuer. Anyone else is an authorized user.

In theory, it should be straightforward to determine who is an account holder and who is an authorized user. But a credit card issuer's electronic record-keeping should not be the determinative factor to resolve this inquiry. If a card issuer mistakenly (or deliberately) codes an authorized user as an account holder, that card issuer and all subsequent debt buyers will

65 *See* National Consumer Law Center, Fair Credit Reporting § 9.2 (8th ed. 2013), *updated at* www.nclc.org/library.

66 *See* National Consumer Law Center, Fair Credit Reporting Appx. H (8th ed. 2013), *updated at* www.nclc.org/library.

67 *Id.* § 9.2.1.

68 Official Interpretations of Regulation Z, 12 C.F.R. pt. 1026, Supp. I, §§ 1026.12(a)(1)-6. *See also* Cleveland Trust Co. v. Snyder, 380 N.E.2d 354 (Ohio Ct. App. 1978); Citibank v. Hauff, 668 N.W.2d 528 (S.D. 2003) (authorized user cannot apply for a renewal card); National Consumer Law Center, Truth in Lending § 7.10.2 (8th ed. 2012), *updated at* www.nclc.org/library.

treat that person as an account holder, but the fact remains that person is not an account holder. The card issuer's designation should not be enough—there must be evidence of the consumer requesting to be an account holder, not evidence that the card issuer decided to treat the individual as an account holder.

Surprisingly, the card issuer may have little or no documentation to support its designation of an individual as an account holder instead of an authorized user. In *Johnson v. MBNA America Bank*,[69] the card issuer was unable to show whether the consumer, the wife of the card holder, was an authorized user or joint account holder, because it did not have the original account agreement, having destroyed it pursuant to its document retention policy. The mere fact that the card issuer mailed statements jointly to the account holder and the wife did not prove that the wife was a joint account holder.[70]

Do not take at face value a document signed by the consumer that has a check box ticked off to identify the consumer as an account holder. In one case, the court found that the consumer could have signed the document for a different reason, and the card issuer had then checked a box marking the consumer as a joint account holder.[71]

Federal law requires that a credit card be issued only in response to a request or application for a card.[72] This means that, in order to prove a consumer is an account holder, the collector must show that the consumer in fact applied for the card.[73] Evidence from the real account holder that he or she requested the card for the consumer indicates that the consumer is an authorized user. If the collector has not retained a contemporaneous record of the credit card request that shows the consumer's application as an account owner, the collector may not be able to refute the consumer's evidence that the consumer is an authorized user. Certainly a debt buyer will have difficulty doing so when its only evidence is a printout from a prior debt buyer or creditor listing the consumer as an account owner, and the debt buyer has no firsthand knowledge how that designation came about.

The collector, in alleging that the consumer is an account holder, is claiming that the consumer has agreed to be responsible for all charges on the card. The consumer, by claiming to be only an authorized user, is saying that the consumer did not agree to be responsible for such charges. Federal law states that "[i]n any action by a card issuer to enforce liability for the use of a credit card, the burden of proof is upon the card issuer to show the use was authorized."[74] The collector thus has the burden of proof to show that the consumer authorized the card issuer to make the consumer liable on the account.

69 357 F.3d 426 (4th Cir. 2004).

70 *Id. See also* Wells Fargo Bank v. Blackburn, 2011 WL 346951 (Tex. App. Feb. 3, 2011).

71 Wells Fargo Bank v. Blackburn, 2011 WL 346951 (Tex. App. Feb. 3, 2011).

72 15 U.S.C. § 1642. *See also* National Consumer Law Center, Truth in Lending § 7.12 (8th ed. 2012), *updated at* www.nclc.org/library.

73 *Cf.* Wells Fargo Bank v. Blackburn, 2011 WL 346951 (Tex. App. Feb. 3, 2011) (finding consumer only an authorized user).

74 15 U.S.C. § 1643(b).

5.3.3.2 Liability of Authorized User for Account Owner's Obligations

The staff interpretations to Regulation Z (Truth in Lending) indicate that whether authorized users are liable for their own charges or on the account generally is a matter of state law.[75] State law generally limits the liability of authorized users, holding that an authorized user is not liable for debts incurred by the account holder or others.[76] Authorized users can be viewed as agents using the card for the principal, who is the cardholder. Under common law, agents purchasing for a principal are not obligated on the account.

The collector has the burden of proving that an agreement exists by which an authorized user consents to be liable for the charges of others on the account. Typically, there will be no provision making an authorized user liable for the debts of others, and some standard contracts explicitly provide that the authorized user is liable only for that user's own charges but not for charges incurred by the account holder or others. If there is an agreement that arguably makes the authorized user directly liable on the account, any ambiguity is construed against the creditor. Silence certainly does not create liability.[77]

If a provision in a standard form contract creates liability for the user,[78] then the collector still must prove that the authorized user agreed to that provision. It is not sufficient to have sent that contract to the account holder. There must be proof that the version of the standard form contract which contains the liability provision was sent to the authorized user who agreed to be bound by its terms.

Even if it can be shown that the authorized user was sent a contract containing such a provision, this may not be enough to create a binding contract providing for such liability. Can such liability be created by the fine print buried in the boilerplate of a standard form contract when an authorized user's

75 Official Interpretations of Reg. Z, 12 C.F.R. pt. 1026, Supp. I, §§ 1026.12(a)(1)-6. *See also* National Consumer Law Center, Truth in Lending § 7.10.8 (8th ed. 2012), *updated at* www.nclc.org/library.

76 Sears Roebuck & Co. v. Ragucci, 495 A.2d 923 (N.J. Super. Ct. Law Div. 1985); Bank One, Columbus v. Palmer, 579 N.E.2d 284 (Ohio Ct. App. 1989); First Nat'l Bank of Findlay v. Fulk, 566 N.E.2d 1270 (Ohio Ct. App. 1989); Cleveland Trust Co. v. Snyder, 380 N.E.2d 354 (Ohio Ct. App. 1978); State Home Sav. Card Ctr. v. Pinks, 540 N.E.2d 338 (Ohio Mun. Ct. 1988); Sears Roebuck & Co. v. Stover, 513 N.E.2d 361 (Ohio Mun. Ct. 1987); Wells Fargo Bank v. Blackburn, 2011 WL 346951 (Tex. App. Feb. 3, 2011); Chevy Chase Sav. Bank v. Strong, 46 Va. Cir. 422 (Va. Cir. Ct. 1998). *See also* Barrer v. Chase Bank USA, Inc., 566 F.3d 883, 885 n.1 (9th Cir. 2009) ("Cherly Barrer was an 'Authorized User' and therefore not legally responsible for the account"); Llames v. JP Morgan Chase & Co., 2012 WL 1032910 (N.D. Ill. Mar. 23, 2012). *Cf. In re* Laursen, 214 B.R. 378 (Bankr. D. Neb. 1997) (noting that there would have been no contractual liability even if husband had been an authorized user).

77 *See* Citibank v. Hauff, 668 N.W.2d 528 (S.D. 2003). *See also* Llames v. JP Morgan Chase & Co., 2012 WL 1032910 (N.D. Ill. Mar. 23, 2012).

78 *See In re* Garberg, 2006 WL 1997415 (Bankr. E.D. Pa. June 7, 2006); Am. Express Travel Related Servs. Co. v. Seidenfeld, 781 N.Y.S.2d 622 (table), 2003 WL 23148835 (N.Y. Sup. Ct. 2003). Sears's contracts also provide that the authorized user has the same liability as the account holder.

expectation is so different and the authorized user has not explicitly assented to those terms? In effect, the card issuer is sending not the requested authorized user card but an unsolicited joint owner card. The federal Truth in Lending Act prohibits issuance of a credit card other than in response to a request or application.[79] Neither the consumer nor the account holder requested or applied for a card that in effect converts the account into joint ownership.

5.3.3.3 Authorized User's Liability for Own Charges

Collectors who seek to hold an authorized user liable for that user's own charges (as opposed to charges by others on the account) create an immediate practical problem for themselves. Some credit cards have separate numbers for each user, allowing segregation of charges by user (however a debt buyer may not have access to that information). But other credit card accounts keep the same number for all users and it may be impossible for the card issuer to then segregate charges relating to one particular user from other charges on the account. Federal law puts on the card issuer the burden of proving that the use was authorized.[80] In addition, the authorized user should not be liable for finance charges and other fees, because these are computed based upon all charges on the account, not just upon the authorized user's charges.

If the collector does succeed in segregating only the authorized user's charges, then the collector must establish a basis for liability. *Quantum meruit* should not be applicable because there is an explicit contract covering the charges.[81] Because federal law requires that there be a request or application for the card and disclosure of the terms of the card,[82] there should always be an explicit contract covering the charges, making *quantum meruit* inapplicable.

For that reason, liability instead must be based upon an agreement sent to the authorized user, usually with the card, making the authorized user liable for his or her own charges. Some agreements with authorized users do not specify that the authorized user is liable for the user's own charges,[83] and any ambiguity is to be construed against the drafter.[84] Even if the creditor's standard form agreement specifies that the authorized user is liable for that user's own charges, the collector will have to produce this contract and prove that this contract was sent to the authorized user.[85] The collector alternatively may be able to produce a charge slip signed by the user that includes an agreement to pay for the charges. But the collector may not have that slip, the slip may not be signed, or it may not include that agreement.

5.3.4 Liability of Spouses

5.3.4.1 General

The default rule is that, absent an agreement or state law that makes spouses liable, consumers are not liable for their spouses' debts.[86] Nevertheless state law does make spouses liable in certain situations, particularly in community property states. Other states also have necessaries laws making spouses liable in discrete contexts. Thus, even if a consumer is only an authorized user, a consumer may still be liable in some states and in some situations for their spouse's debts.

Since a spouse's liability is so dependent upon state law, an important question is which state's law applies—the forum state's law, the law of a state specified in the credit agreement, or some other state, such as the one where the debts were incurred or where the parties lived at the time the debts were incurred. Because spousal liability is not based upon the contract, a choice of law clause in the contract should be of no effect and the forum state's choice of law rules should apply.

Using a contractually chosen choice of law would have very odd results in this context. A state's community property law would not apply to contracts consummated in that state if the law selected in the contract was that of a non-community property state. The result would be even odder if the law selected in the contract was that of a community property state when the forum was not a community property state.

5.3.4.2 Community Property States

In community property states, debts incurred after marriage and before separation are generally treated as community debts, even if only one spouse is obligated on the contract. If a credit card is issued in one spouse's name only, a collector can reach community property to pay for charges incurred during the marriage.[87]

Two exceptions are worth noting. The married partners can enter into an agreement that they are not responsible for

---

79 15 U.S.C. § 1642.

80 15 U.S.C. § 1643(b).

81 *See* § 4.8, *supra*. *See also* Sears, Roebuck & Co. v. Stover, 513 N.E.2d 361 (Ohio Mun. Ct. 1987).

82 *See* § 4.8, *supra*.

83 *See* Alabran v. Capital One Bank, 2005 WL 3338663 (E.D. Va. Dec. 8, 2005). *Cf.* First Nat'l Bank of Findlay v. Fulk, 566 N.E.2d 1270 (Ohio Ct. App. 1989) (authorized user not liable for own charges when no agreement that user would be liable).

84 Because many credit card agreements are to be interpreted using South Dakota law, a significant case for the proposition that ambiguities are to be interpreted against the drafter is the South Dakota Supreme Court's decision in *Citibank v. Hauff*, 668 N.W.2d 528 (S.D. 2003).

85 *See* § 4.5, *supra*. *See also* Am. Express Travel Related Servs. Co. v. Seidenfeld, 781 N.Y.S.2d 622 (table), 2003 WL 23148835 (N.Y. Sup. Ct. Dec. 8, 2003). *Cf. In re* Garberg, 2006 WL 1997415 (Bankr. E.D. Pa. June 7, 2006) (sufficient evidence that American Express agreement holding authorized user liable for own charges was accepted by the user); Am. Express Travel Related Servs. v. Redner, 2006 WL 664698 (Mich. Ct. App. Mar. 16, 2006) (card use manifested user's intent to be bound by agreement which imposed liability).

86 *See* Palisades Collection Co. v. Velazquez, 910 N.Y.S.2d 406 (N.Y. Sup. Ct. App. Term 2010).

87 *See, e.g.*, Bourdier v. Dermatology & Aesthetic Institute, L.L.C., 2013 WL 486971 (M.D. La. Feb. 6, 2013).

each other's debts.[88] A creditor also can only reach community property in recovering on the obligated spouse's account, not property belonging to the other spouse individually. Property separately held by the other spouse cannot be seized to pay the community debt.[89] Non-community property typically includes property brought into the marriage or received during marriage by bequest or gift, as long as those assets are not commingled with community property.

5.3.4.3 Necessaries Statutes and Liability for Spouses' Debts in Non-Community Property States

In non-community property states, one spouse's property cannot generally be taken to pay the other spouse's debts. However, many non-community property states have necessaries statutes that make spouses liable for certain of the other's debts. These statutes are examined in more detail in § 9.6, *infra*, in the context of medical debt, to which they are most applicable.

A necessaries statute typically will *not* provide a basis for holding a consumer liable on the other spouse's credit card, cell phone, or most other consumer debts. Necessaries statutes apply only to the purchase of necessaries—usually considered to be medical services, food, and shelter.[90] Not only will most credit card charges not be for necessaries, but the collector will have difficulty isolating individual charges that are in fact necessaries. The burden is on the collector to show what portion of the indebtedness is incurred for necessaries.[91]

Moreover, any finance charges, late charges, attorney fees, collection costs, and other fees the account holder may have incurred are certainly not necessaries, and the other spouse should not be obligated for those charges.[92] There is even a question whether a credit card issuer, as a lender, can take advantage of these necessaries statutes, as the card issuer is not supplying a necessary but a loan, which is not a necessary.[93]

State law may provide additional defenses for the non-account holder spouse. Separation may be a defense.[94] Some states require the collector to prove that the secondarily liable spouse had failed to support the primarily liable spouse.[95] It may be a defense that the financial resources of the spouse who incurred the expenses were sufficient;[96] that the creditor did not rely on the non-debtor spouse's credit to furnish the necessaries;[97] or that, as at common law, the non-debtor spouse's inability to pay the spouse's debts limits his or her responsibility to do so.[98] The secondarily liable spouse may also raise any defenses available to the other spouse.[99]

Furthermore, only certain states currently recognize the necessaries doctrine. Necessaries statutes evolved from Married Woman Acts that many states passed at the turn of the century. As originally written, these statutes imposed liability on husbands for wives' bills but not *vice versa*. Some states have abolished this doctrine or ruled the necessaries statute unconstitutional.[100] In states that have not yet ruled on extending the

---

88 *E.g.*, Schlaefer v. Fin. Mgmt. Serv., Inc., 996 P.2d 745 (Ariz. Ct. App. 2000) (debts for necessary medical care presumed to be community debts, but presumption rebutted by proof of valid premarital agreement that each spouse would be responsible for own debts).

89 *See* Samaritan Health Sys. v. Caldwell, 957 P.2d 1373 (Ariz. Ct. App. 1998) (health care debts are community debts, which may be satisfied from community property but not from separate property of non-debtor spouse).

90 *See* Nelson v. First Nat'l Bank Omaha, 2004 WL 2711032 (Minn. Ct. App. Nov. 30, 2004); Fifth Third Bank/Visa v. Gilbert, 478 N.E.2d 1324 (Ohio Mun. Ct. 1984) (father not liable for his minor daughter's unauthorized charges under necessaries doctrine, because none of purchases were for "necessaries").

91 *See* Walter v. Palisades Collection, L.L.C., 2011 WL 1666869 (E.D. Pa. May 2, 2011); Nelson v. First Nat'l Bank Omaha, 2004 WL 2711032 (Minn. Ct. App. Nov. 30, 2004) (credit card lender failed to show that items purchased on account were household necessaries, and thus lender not entitled to summary judgment on spouse's liability).

92 *See* N.A.R., Inc. v. Elmer, 141 P.3d 606 (Utah Ct. App. 2006) (interest and attorney fees, provided for in contract for medical services, are not necessaries within the meaning of the Utah Family Expense statute).

93 *See* N. Shore Cmty. Bank & Trust Co. v. Kollar, 710 N.E.2d 106 (Ill. App. Ct. 1999) (bank loan, even if the proceeds are spent for household needs, was not a "family expense" within the meaning of the Illinois family expense statute; widow not liable on loan taken by deceased husband; attorney fees to the widow).

94 Yale Univ. Sch. of Med. v. Scianna, 701 A.2d 65 (Conn. Super. Ct. 1997); Allen v. Keating, 517 N.W.2d 830 (Mich. Ct. App. 1994); Balyeat Collection Prof'ls v. Garland, 51 P.3d 1127 (Mont. 2002) (Montana statute provides exception if non-debtor has been abandoned by debtor); Doctors Laves, Sarewitz & Walko v. Briggs, 613 A.2d 506 (N.J. Super. Ct. Law Div. 1992); Roach v. Mamakos, 764 N.Y.S.2d 539 (N.Y. Sup. Ct. 2003). *But cf.* Bartrom v. Adjustment Bureau, 618 N.E.2d 1 (Ind. 1993); Forsyth Mem'l Hosp., Inc. v. Chisholm, 467 S.E.2d 88 (N.C. 1996); Mercy Health Sys. Corp. v. Gauss, 639 N.W.2d 803, 2001 WL 1632549 (Wis. Ct. App. Dec. 20, 2001); St. Mary's Hosp. Med. Ctr. v. Brody, 519 N.W.2d 706 (Wis. Ct. App. 1994).

95 Allen v. Keating, 517 N.W.2d 830 (Mich. Ct. App. 1994) (spouses were separated); Smith v. Hernandez, 794 P.2d 772 (Okla. Civ. App. 1990).

96 *In re* O'Lexa, 476 F.3d 177 (3d Cir. 2007) (Pennsylvania necessaries statute); Foster v. D.B.S. Collection Agency, 463 F. Supp. 2d 783 (S.D. Ohio 2006); St. Francis Reg'l Med. Ctr., Inc. v. Bowles, 836 P.2d 1123 (Kan. 1992); Bethany Med. Ctr. v. Niyazi, 890 P.2d 349 (Kan. Ct. App. 1995); Hawley v. Hawley, 904 S.W.2d 584 (Mo. Ct. App. 1995); Promenade Nursing Home, Inc. v. Lacey, 814 N.Y.S.2d 564 (table), 2005 WL 3592001 (N.Y. Civ. Ct. Nov. 29, 2005); Roach v. Mamakos, 764 N.Y.S.2d 539 (N.Y. Sup. Ct. 2003); Med. Bus. Assocs. Inc. v. Steiner, 183 A.D.2d 86 (N.Y. Sup. Ct. 1992); Landmark Med. Ctr. v. Gauthier, 635 A.2d 1145 (R.I. 1994).

97 Kent Gen. Hosp., Inc. v. Russell, 1997 WL 524079 (Del. Super. Ct. July 14, 1997), *aff'd*, 705 A.2d 244 (Del. 1998); Med. Bus. Assocs. Inc. v. Steiner, 183 A.D.2d 86 (N.Y. Sup. Ct. 1992) (citing Our Lady of Lourdes Mem. Hosp., Inc. v. Frey, 152 A.D.2d 73, 75 (N.Y. Sup. Ct. 1989); Promenade Nursing Home, Inc. v. Lacey, 814 N.Y.S.2d 564 (table), 2005 WL 3592001 (N.Y. Civ. Ct. Nov. 29, 2005).

98 *In re* O'Lexa, 476 F.3d 177 (3d Cir. 2007); Med. Bus. Assocs. Inc. v. Steiner, 183 A.D.2d 86 (N.Y. Sup. Ct. 1992) (citing Our Lady of Lourdes Mem. Hosp., Inc. v. Frey, 152 A.D.2d 73, 75 (N.Y. Sup. Ct. 1989)); Promenade Nursing Home, Inc. v. Lacey, 814 N.Y.S.2d 564 (table), 2005 WL 3592001 (N.Y. Civ. Ct. Nov. 29, 2005). *See also* Porter Mem'l Hosp. v. Wozniak, 680 N.E.2d 13 (Ind. Ct. App. 1997) (remanded to trial court to determine husband's ability to pay); MRI Co-op. v. Berlin, 1993 WL 257078 (Ohio Ct. App. June 30, 1993); Ohio State Univ. Med. Ctr. v. Calovini, 2002 WL 31953905 (Ohio Ct. Cl. Oct. 8, 2002).

99 St. Francis Reg'l Med. Ctr., Inc. v. Bowles, 836 P.2d 1123 (Kan. 1992).

100 *See* § 9.6, *infra*.

statute to wives, the non-debtor wife can argue that extending the doctrine to her is a task for the legislature, not the court.[101]

But in other states, the legislature or courts have rewritten the necessaries statutes in gender-neutral terms.[102] In addition, some courts enforce spousal liability not under a statute but under a common law theory.[103] Even when a state recognizes the doctrine under a gender-neutral statute, that statute may be subject to challenge under the Equal Credit Opportunity Act, which prohibits creditors from requiring that both spouses obligate themselves for one spouse's transaction.[104]

5.3.5 *Liability of Family Members for Decedent's Debts*

A decedent's estate is liable for the decedent's debts, and those debts may have to be paid ahead of distributions to those inheriting from the estate. But family members, even those who inherit from an estate, do not become liable for the debts of an individual just because that individual is deceased. Nevertheless, some creditors contact family members after the debtor's death and then, without a written agreement, create a new account in that family member's name, transferring the decedent's account obligation to the new account. The creditor then begins dunning the family member and even suing on the debt. Other times the creditor may sell the debt, and a debt buyer, having no knowledge of the "account's" origin, will sue on the debt.

The family member's defense is clear—the family member was never obligated on the decedent's debt and there is no written agreement under which the family member agreed to pay that debt. Even if a creditor sent a contract to the family member, the family member never signed the contract. Because the family member never used the account, the collector cannot imply assent on that basis.

When the collector seeks payment from a family member, and the debt is from a credit card account, the amount sought on the "account" should be considered an unauthorized charge, and the collector has the burden of proving it was authorized.[105] In addition, if the collector alleges the new account is a credit card account, then there is a Truth in Lending violation because the card was issued without the family member's request.[106]

5.3.6 *Should the Creditor's Protection Product Pay the Balance Due?*

Credit card issuers and other creditors aggressively market products that pay off an account balance if the consumer becomes unemployed, disabled, or dies. The collector should not seek a credit balance from the consumer if the creditor's protection product should pay off the balance due in the case of illness, unemployment, or the like.[107] If this product is purchased and a covered event occurs, the consumer should seek payment from the creditor.[108]

If the collector argues that the consumer does not qualify for the product benefits (because of age, disability, or employment status upon applying for the product, and so forth), then the consumer should not have been paying for the product and should receive a rebate of all charges and related finance charges.[109] Moreover, if the consumer's non-qualification was evident from information submitted to the creditor, then the creditor should be estopped from refusing to pay benefits.[110]

5.4 Debt Not Legal or Not Owed

5.4.1 *The Consumer's Incapacity—Minority, Mental Incompetence, or Intoxication*

5.4.1.1 General

An otherwise valid contract may be voidable because the consumer does not have the capacity to make the contract.[111] Parties must be capable of intelligent assent in order to make a valid contract, and there can be no contract when there is no capacity to understand or agree.[112] There are three conditions which give rise to questions about a person's capacity to contract: minority, mental disability, and intoxication. When the party with the defective capacity seeks to cancel the contract, that individual is entitled to have the creditor return whatever the individual gave under the contract and must usually restore to the creditor what it received under the contract.[113]

In a credit card situation, this principle would imply that the consumer's obligation on the account is canceled and all past payments for purchases, finance charges, and fees must be returned to the consumer. The consumer in turn must return to the card issuer the purchase price for all, but not any finance charges or fees. The result of this cancellation of obligation because of incapacity is that the individual with the defective capacity is no longer liable for finance charges and other fees.

5.4.1.2 Minority

The legal age of minority or infancy is determined by the law of the state in which the contract is made. A minor may void a contract whether or not the other party knew of the

101 *See id.*

102 *See id.*

103 *See id.*

104 15 U.S.C. § 1691(a)(1); 12 C.F.R. §§ 1002.7(d)(1), 1002.11(b)(1)(ii). *See* Edwards v. McCormick, 136 F. Supp. 2d 795, 803 n.9 (S.D. Ohio 2001) (stating in dicta that imposition of liability upon spouse probably violates Equal Credit Opportunity Act). *See generally* National Consumer Law Center, Credit Discrimination § 9.3 (6th ed. 2013), *updated at* www.nclc.org/library.

105 15 U.S.C. § 1643. *See also* § 5.3.2, *supra*.

106 15 U.S.C. § 1642.

107 *See* Portfolio Recovery Assocs., L.L.C. v. Lawrence, 907 N.Y.S.2d 103 (N.Y. Sup. Ct. App. Term 2010).

108 *Cf.* Discover Bank v. Owens, 822 N.E.2d 869 (Ohio Mun. Ct. 2004).

109 *See* National Consumer Law Center, Consumer Credit Regulation § 6.8.3 (2012), *updated at* www.nclc.org/library.

110 *Id.*

111 Dan B. Dobbs, Dobbs Law of Remedies § 13.4.1 (2d ed. 1993).

112 17A Am. Jur. 2d *Contracts* § 28 (2004).

113 *Id.* §§ 28, 580.

minority and whether or not the minor understood the nature of the contract.[114] Among other things, this rule protects the minor from being bound by contracts he or she may not understand, or may have entered into at the insistence of an overzealous or intimidating creditor.

One notable exception is that federal law states that the United States and guaranty agencies are not subject to a claim of minority for Federal Family Education Loans and Federal Direct Loans.[115] It appears that this exception does not apply to Perkins Loans, and it certainly does not apply to private student loans.

Other than this exception for federal student loans, a contract may be disaffirmed by the minor during his or her minority. It also may be disaffirmed within a reasonable period after the minor reaches majority, unless ratified when of legal age.[116] The minor disaffirms by giving the seller notice of his age or by offering to return to the seller any goods the minor may still have. A disaffirming minor need only return the goods in their present condition. If the goods have been damaged or dissipated, the seller must bear the loss.[117] Some states have modified this result by statute, requiring the minor to restore the value received.[118]

Despite the general rule about contracts entered into by minors, a minor may be liable for the fair market value of goods that are necessaries.[119] The disaffirming minor is not liable for the contract price of these goods but only for their fair market value. Whether goods are necessaries is determined by the facts of each case, depending upon the person and the circumstances, being relative to the minor's actual needs and status in life.[120]

Courts generally limit necessaries to food or clothing of a reasonable kind purchased for the minor or the minor's family and to medical and dental services. It has generally been held that an automobile is not a necessary.[121] If goods are not necessaries, then the general rule applies and the contract can be disaffirmed, as per the general rule for minors.

5.4.1.3 Mental Incompetence

The general rule is that a mentally incompetent person may avoid a contract upon proof of mental incapacity at the time of contracting, provided the incompetent can fully restore the other party to its position before the contract.[122] If the incompetent no longer has the consideration received, the incompetent cannot rescind the contract.[123] However the result would be different if the person was under guardianship when the contract was made, as such a contract is totally void.[124] In addition, if the seller is aware of the incompetency, the incompetent person may rescind the contract upon returning whatever is left of the consideration.[125]

The *Restatement (Second) of Contracts* finds a person mentally incompetent if that person is unable to understand in a reasonable manner the nature and consequence of a transaction *or* if the person is unable to act in a reasonable manner in relation to the transaction and the other party has reason to know of the condition.[126] An important difference between incapacity due to mental incompetence and incapacity due to minority is that the mental incompetence defense requires a showing that the party did not have the capacity to understand the nature and consequences of the contract.[127] As with minors, though, a person deemed mentally incompetent is still liable for the fair market value of necessaries.[128]

One who is no longer deemed incompetent because of mental illness or other disability may ratify a contract by indicating assent to it.[129] In addition, if the person, upon regaining legal competence, is aware of the contract made while legally incompetent and delays in disaffirming, this delay may constitute ratification.[130]

5.4.1.4 Intoxication

Persons who make contracts when they are so intoxicated that they cannot understand the nature and consequences of their act may be treated in the same manner as mentally

114 *See* Keser v. Chagnon, 410 P.2d 637 (Colo. 1966) (minor's absolute right to disaffirm is not diminished by minor's false representation of age); Gillis v. Whitley's Discount Auto Sales, Inc., 319 S.E.2d 661 (N.C. Ct. App. 1984) (fraudulent misrepresentation would not be valid defense to minor's action to disaffirm). There seems to be some move away from this rule in some jurisdictions. *See, e.g.*, A. D. Kaufman, Annotation, *Infant's Misrepresentation as to His Age as Estopping Him from Disaffirming His Voidable Transaction*, 29 A.L.R.3d 1270 (1970).

115 20 U.S.C. § 1091a(b)(2).

116 Keser v. Chagnon, 410 P.2d 637 (Colo. 1966). *See also* Gillis v. Whitley's Discount Auto Sales, Inc., 319 S.E.2d 661 (N.C. Ct. App. 1984).

117 Restatement (Second) of Contracts § 14 cmt. (c) (1981).

118 *Id.*

119 Webster Street P'ship, Ltd. v. Sheridan, 368 N.W.2d 439 (Neb. 1985) (liability based not on contractual but on quasi-contract theory). *See also* Joseph M. Perillo, Calamari and Perillo on Contracts §§ 8-7, 8-8 (6th ed. 2009).

120 Webster Street P'ship, Ltd. v. Sheridan, 368 N.W.2d 439 (Neb. 1985).

121 Star Chevrolet Co. v. Green, 473 So. 2d 157 (Miss. 1985) (car usually not a necessary for a minor).

122 Dan B. Dobbs, Dobbs Law of Remedies § 13.4(3) (2d ed. 1993).

123 *Id. See, e.g.*, Young v. Lujan, 461 P.2d 691 (Ariz. Ct. App. 1969); Davis v. Colo. Kenworth Corp., 396 P.2d 958 (Colo. 1964); Sjulin v. Clifton Furniture Co., 41 N.W.2d 721 (Iowa 1950); Lawson v. Bennett, 81 S.E.2d 162 (N.C. 1954).

124 Restatement (Second) of Contracts § 13 (1981).

125 Dan B. Dobbs, Dobbs Law of Remedies § 13.4(3) (2d ed. 1993); Sjulin v. Clifton Furniture Co., 41 N.W.2d 721 (Iowa 1950).

126 Restatement (Second) of Contracts § 15 (1981).

127 *In re* Estate of Hendrickson, 805 P.2d 20 (Kan. 1991) (courts will apply presumption in favor of mental capacity to contract and place burden of proof on those claiming incapacity to rebut that presumption); Restatement (Second) of Contracts § 15 (1981). *See also* 17A Am. Jur. 2d *Contracts* § 28 (2004); 53 Am. Jur. 2d *Mentally Impaired Persons* §§ 145/–/154 (2006).

128 Samuel Williston, Treatise on the Law of Contracts § 10.7 (Richard A. Lord ed., 4th ed. 2009).

129 Joseph M. Perillo, Calamari and Perillo on Contracts §§ 8.11, 8.4 (6th ed. 2009).

130 Samuel Williston, Treatise on the Law of Contracts §§ 10.5, 10.12 (Richard A. Lord ed., 4th ed. 2009).

incompetent persons.[131] Disaffirmance and ratification would occur in the manner described in § 5.4.1.3, *supra*. Presumably, drug abusers will be treated similarly to intoxicated persons and, in jurisdictions following the *Restatement* view, contracts they make when incompetent by reason of drug use will be voidable.

5.4.2 *Duress*

A defense to a contractual obligation is that the consumer was under duress in agreeing to the contract. The creditor must have exercised coercion and the consumer must have lost volition because of the coercion, resulting in the execution of a contract or note.[132] Duress as a defense is most common in the medical setting, when necessary medical treatment is conditioned upon agreement to a contract for payment, and thus this defense is examined in the chapter on medical debt at § 9.5.3.1, *infra*.

5.4.3 *No Deficiency When Insufficient Proof of Commercially Reasonable Sale*

A common type of collection action seeks a "deficiency" on an auto loan or other secured debt after the creditor has sold the collateral. The amount due on the loan plus certain expenses to prepare and sell the collateral is offset by the collateral's sale price, and the difference is called a deficiency.

This subsection focuses on one simple but very effective defense to a deficiency action, particularly when a debt buyer has purchased the right to bring the deficiency action. If the consumer denies that a repossession sale was conducted in a commercially reasonable manner,[133] the collector has the burden of proving the reasonableness of all aspects of the collateral's sale before the court will award a deficiency.[134]

The original secured party will have some difficulty proving that all aspects of a repossession sale were commercially reasonable, including the notice provided to the consumer, the advertising made to the public, the sale's timing, and the method of disposition. A debt buyer without knowledge of any of these facts will have great difficulty meeting its burden of proof.[135]

This requirement that the collector prove that all aspects of the sale were commercially reasonable makes perfect sense. Repossession and repossession sales are extraordinary remedies, allowing seizure and sale of the consumer's property with no court supervision and few judicial standards. The collector need not even show that the purchase price at the repossession sale was a good one. One of the few standards regulating this process is that, if the collector seeks to recover a deficiency after selling the consumer's property, it must show that the sale price resulted from a commercially reasonable sale of the property.

The collector must produce more evidence than just the resale price.[136] The issue is not whether the car or other property was in fact sold for the price used in the deficiency computation. The issue is whether that sale price was the result of a commercially reasonable sale that would produce a reasonable price to use in that deficiency computation. A conclusory affidavit from the secured party that it sold the collateral for the best possible price is insufficient.[137]

It is certainly insufficient for a debt buyer (who will have little if any knowledge of the actual sale) to produce an affidavit from one of its employees that the secured party sold the collateral for the best possible price. The collector's burden is not met by evidence that the price obtained at the sale was reasonable, if the collector cannot prove that the sale itself was conducted in a commercially reasonable manner.[138] The Uniform Commercial Code does not look to whether the sale price is reasonable, but whether the method of disposition was reasonable. States differ as to the remedy if a sale is not proven to be commercially reasonable. Some states bar the deficiency absolutely. Others put the burden of proof on the collector to prove the collateral's value by some measure other than the sale price.[139]

The consumer also has numerous other possible defenses and counterclaims to a collection action for a deficiency. Was there a valid security interest? Was there a default? Did the repossession breach the peace? Was other property seized with the collateral? Were notices proper? Was the consumer offered the required opportunity to cure or reinstate? Were the secured party's expenses reasonable, and was the deficiency correctly computed? Other counterclaims relate to deception in the original sale of the property to the consumer, defects in the product's subsequent performance, the terms of the financing, and the creditor's debt collection conduct. These defenses and counterclaims are examined in another NCLC treatise, *Repossessions*.[140]

5.5 Counterclaims

5.5.1 *Tactical Considerations in Raising Counterclaims*

5.5.1.1 General

There are significant advantages for a consumer in raising counterclaims in a collection action, but there may be situations in which it is better to wait and bring a separate action

131 *Id.* § 16.

132 *See* § 9.5.3.1, *infra*.

133 In at least California, the District of Columbia, and Maine, the consumer may not even have to deny that the sale was commercially reasonable; the collector still has the burden to show that it was conducted in such a manner. *See* National Consumer Law Center, Repossessions § 12.6.1.1 (8th ed. 2013), *updated at* www.nclc.org/library.

134 *See* National Consumer Law Center, Repossessions § 12.6.1.1 (8th ed. 2013), *updated at* www.nclc.org/library.

135 *See, e.g.*, Harrington v. Asset Acceptance, L.L.C., 270 S.W.3d 405 (Ky. Ct. App. 2008).

136 *See* National Consumer Law Center, Repossessions § 12.6.1.1 (8th ed. 2013), *updated at* www.nclc.org/library.

137 Boles v. Tex. Nat'l Bank, 750 S.W.2d 879 (Tex. App. 1988).

138 Hall v. Owen Cnty. State Bank, 370 N.E.2d 918 (Ind. Ct. App. 1977).

139 *See* National Consumer Law Center, Repossessions § 12.6 (8th ed. 2013), *updated at* www.nclc.org/library.

140 (8th ed. 2013), *updated at* www.nclc.org/library.

or even abandon the counterclaims. This subsection considers general factors concerning whether and when to raise counterclaims, and the next two subsections consider the same factors for two specific types of counterclaims—counterclaims concerning litigation misconduct and class counterclaims.

Failing to raise certain counterclaims in the collection action may forfeit these claims entirely, preventing the consumer from raising them later in affirmative lawsuits. Some counterclaims are so closely related to the collection action that they are compulsory and therefore will be lost if not brought as counterclaims in that action.[141] In such cases, the consumer's attorney will have to determine if counterclaims are tactically better abandoned or brought in the action. Other counterclaims are permissive, in which case the issue will be whether it is better to bring a separate affirmative action or bring the claim as a counterclaim in the collection action.

Bringing counterclaims tips off the collector that the matter will be aggressively contested, and the collector may then put more effort into its offers of proof. Without this advance warning, the collector's case preparation may not be sufficient to prevail when the consumer later challenges the proffered evidence. The consumer who then prevails when the collection action is dismissed with prejudice can still bring an affirmative new case, so long as that new claim was not a compulsory counterclaim. The collector will also be less willing to dismiss its complaint when there are counterclaims, because the counterclaims will remain even after the affirmative collection action is dismissed.

On the other hand, raising counterclaims in a collection action may encourage the collector to settle—many collectors sue to obtain a default judgment, have no interest in pursuing a case through trial, and may not even answer the counterclaim. In one case, a collector, faced with a counterclaim and discovery requests, dismissed its complaint and ignored the discovery requests. Eventually, the collector was sanctioned and a judgment was entered on the counterclaim for the consumer because the collector refused to respond to the discovery request.[142] In another case, the collector did not respond to the consumer's counterclaims or to the consumer's motion for a default judgment, and the court awarded the consumer $125,000 and then trebled this amount under the state deceptive practices statute.[143] The trial court and appellate court refused to set aside the judgment, although the appellate court eventually ordered a new trial to determine damages only.[144]

In addition, raising counterclaims limits a common collector tactic of dismissing cases without prejudice when the consumer appears in the case to contest the merits. The dismissal may be short-lived, as the collector may later bring a new action or sell the debt to a new buyer who later may bring a new action. Raising counterclaims will prevent the case from being dismissed without prejudice, because the consumer's counterclaims will survive the collector's voluntary dismissal.[145]

One advantage of raising certain counterclaims in the collection action is to provide a basis for an attorney fee award to the successful consumer. Although in about twenty states there will be a statutory basis for attorney fees for a prevailing consumer even if counterclaims are not added,[146] in the other states this will not be the case. In those remaining states, the best way for a prevailing consumer to recover fees is to bring a counterclaim for violation of a statute that awards fees to a successful consumer. Examples include the state deceptive practices (UDAP) statute, the federal Fair Debt Collection Practices Act, an installment sales act, and the Truth in Lending Act.

Another advantage of a counterclaim rather than bringing a new affirmative case is that certain counterclaims may be raised by way of a recoupment defense to offset the debt, even when the statute of limitations on an affirmative claim would otherwise have expired.[147] Often collection actions are brought years after a debt goes into default, while consumer statutes often have short statutes of limitations—Truth in Lending Act and Fair Debt Collection Practices Act claims, for example, both have one-year limitations periods. If a claim is not brought in the collection action by way of recoupment, it may not be available at all. Moreover, waiting until after the collection case is completed further risks the statute of limitations expiring on the consumer's claim.

A counterclaim in a collection action is also more likely to avoid an arbitration requirement than if the action were brought as a separate case. The collector may waive its ability to require arbitration when it proceeds with the litigation after the counterclaim is raised.[148] A court also may find it unconscionable that the collector can proceed in court but the consumer must bring counterclaims separately in arbitration.

In addition, the American Arbitration Association (AAA) has posted on its website that it refuses to hear claims "in which

141 *See, e.g.*, Ziolkowski v. Johnson, Rodenburg & Lauinger, P.L.L.P., 2013 WL 1291615 (D. Mont. Mar. 27, 2013); Lintz v. Credit Adjustments, Inc., 2008 WL 835824 (E.D. Mich. 2008). *But see* Unifund CCR Partners v. Young, 2013 WL 5447666 (Ohio Ct. App. Sept. 27, 2013) (FDCPA counterclaim is permissive, not compulsory); Estrada v. Mendoza, 275 P.3d 1024 (Utah Ct. App. 2012) (state deceptive practices claim not foreclosed even though not raised in collection action). *See generally* § 13.4.2.2, *infra*.

142 Palisades Collection L.L.C. v. Coleman, 2009 WL 2882940 (Tex. App. Sept. 9, 2009).

143 *See* Discover Bank v. Morgan, 2010 WL 1998765 (Tenn. Ct. App. May 19, 2010).

144 *Id.*

145 *See* Midland Funding, L.L.C. v. Buhr, 820 N.W.2d 160 (table), 2012 WL 2409671 (Iowa Ct. App. 2012).

146 *See* § 13.1, *infra*.

147 *See* Bull v. U.S., 295 U.S. 247 (1935) (recoupment arises "from some feature of the transaction upon which the plaintiff's action is grounded"); Mohawk Indus., Inc. v. U.S. (*In re* Mohawk Indus., Inc.), 82 B.R. 174 (Bankr. D. Mass. 1987) (common law recoupment applies when arising under the same transaction); Tex. Civ. Code § 16.069 (West); National Consumer Law Center, Truth in Lending § 12.2.5 (8th ed. 2012), *updated at* www.nclc.org/library.

148 *See* Liberty Credit Servs. v. Yonker, 2013 WL 5221219 (Ohio Ct. App. Sept. 16, 2013). *See generally* National Consumer Law Center, Consumer Arbitration Agreements Ch. 8 (6th ed. 2011), *updated at* www.nclc.org/library.

the company is the filing party and the case involves a credit card bill or the case involves a telecom bill or the case involves a consumer finance matter."[149] At least one appellate court has found that the company is the filing party when it initiated the collection action and seeks to require the consumer's counterclaim be moved to arbitration, and the AAA will therefore not hear the arbitration.[150] Since the forum designated by the arbitration agreement is unavailable, many courts find that the arbitration requirement cannot be enforced.[151]

Whether to bring a claim as a counterclaim or in separate litigation may also be determined by whether the consumer wishes to litigate a federal claim in federal or state court. Federal jurisdiction is based upon a federal claim in the complaint, not in the counterclaims.[152] As a result, if the consumer prefers to bring a federal claim in the state court system, bringing it as a counterclaim to a state law collection action ensures that the federal claim remains in state court. The case cannot be removed to federal court based upon a federal law counterclaim.[153] Conversely, the consumer who wishes to adjudicate a federal claim in federal court cannot raise it as a counterclaim in a state court collection action, because there will be no basis for the consumer to remove the case to federal court.[154]

5.5.1.2 Special Tactical Considerations for Litigation Misconduct Counterclaims

The collector's conduct in bringing the collection action may be so egregious as to merit consumer claims just for that litigation misconduct.[155] Special considerations in addition to those discussed in § 5.5.1.1, *supra*, help determine whether to bring such claims as counterclaims in the same collection action involving the misconduct or in a separate lawsuit at the conclusion of the collection action.

The main reason to bring such claims as counterclaims in the collection action is to increase the potential to recover the consumer's attorney fees, such as a statutory fee under the FDCPA or as actual damages for having to defend a groundless claim. This attraction for a counterclaim will not apply when state law already provides attorney fees to a prevailing consumer in a collection action.[156]

The counterclaim is not likely to produce other significant damages, since dismissal of the collection case may eliminate the consumer's injury (other than the consumer's attorney fees). Statutory damages under the FDCPA are capped at $1000. A separate affirmative claim for litigation misconduct after the collection case is dismissed may also be able to recover attorney fees for work expended in the first case as actual damages,[157] and then recover attorney fees in the second case as well, pursuant to the FDCPA's statutory fee-shifting provision. So the advantage of bringing counterclaims in the collection case is less than what it might at first appear.

There are a number of reasons why it may be better to wait to raise collector misconduct in a separate action *after* prevailing in the underlying collection case. Raising counterclaims in the collection case will alert the collector to weaknesses in its case, and may result in the collector making unusual efforts to prove its case, when it otherwise would not do so. While it is true the collector may drop the case in the face of this resistance, it may have done so anyway in the face of any other counterclaim or serious defense, or even merely an appearance for the consumer by counsel. And collectors may work up a case far more when an FDCPA claim for litigation misconduct is involved, particularly when the collector's attorneys are concerned about their own exposure.

Waiting until after the collection action is concluded to bring a separate FDCPA action for litigation misconduct will generally strengthen the case. This is true even when the FDCPA violation is manifest at the time the collector first files the collection suit, such as suing on a known time-barred debt[158] and suing without standing[159] or proper authorization under state law.[160] Such FDCPA claims can only become more appealing as the collection case proceeds, and the collector's persistence will help eliminate any defense of good faith.[161]

Some of the core false representation violations do not occur upon filing of the collection complaint, or even if they appear to, may initially be of marginal quality. However those deceptive, unsubstantiated, and sham allegations in the collection complaint are almost always repeated or ratified at a later point in the proceedings under circumstances that strengthen the resulting FDCPA claim.

For example, the Sixth Circuit has held that a debt buyer's routine practice of filing a collection suit without having immediate means of proving the collector's allegations is not unfair or an unlawful deception in violation of the FDCPA.[162] However, the same court later held that a collector who submitted an affidavit with the complaint which falsely stated that

149 www.adr.org/sp.asp?id=36427.

150 QuickClick Loans, L.L.C. v. Russell, 943 N.E.2d 166 (Ill. App. Ct. 2011).

151 National Consumer Law Center, Consumer Arbitration Agreements § 5.8 (6th ed. 2011), *updated at* www.nclc.org/library.

152 *See, e.g.*, Shamrock Oil & Gas Corp. v. Sheets, 313 U.S. 100, 61 S. Ct. 868, 85 L. Ed. 1214 (1941) (applying rule that the absence or presence of a federal claim in the complaint, and not in a counterclaim, determines whether there is federal court removal jurisdiction); Chase Manhattan Mortgage Corp. v. Smith, 507 F.3d 910 (6th Cir. 2007) (same). *Accord* Commonwealth Fin. Sys., Inc. v. Zemcik, 2009 WL 1911039 (W.D. Pa. July 1, 2009).

153 *Id.*

154 *See* Commonwealth Fin. Sys., Inc. v. Zemcik, 2009 WL 1911039 (W.D. Pa. July 1, 2009).

155 National Consumer Law Center, Fair Debt Collection § 5.5.2.13.4 (8th ed. 2014), *updated at* www.nclc.org/library.

156 *See* § 13.1, *infra*.

157 National Consumer Law Center, Fair Debt Collection § 2.5.2.2.3 (8th ed. 2014), *updated at* www.nclc.org/library.

158 *See, e.g.*, Freyermouth v. Credit Bureau Servs., 248 F.3d 787 (8th Cir. 2001).

159 *See, e.g.*, Wallace v. Washington Mut. Bank, F.A., 683 F.3d 323 (6th Cir. 2012).

160 *See, e.g.*, LeBlanc v. Unifund CCR Partners, 601 F.3d 1185 (11th Cir. 2011).

161 *See, e.g.*, McCollough v. Johnson, Rodenberg & Lauinger, 637 F.3d 939 (9th Cir. 2011).

162 Harvey v. Great Seneca Fin. Corp., 453 F.3d 324 (6th Cir. 2006).

the plaintiff was entitled to the relief sought did violate the FDCPA.[163] The federal courts appear to be more receptive to FDCPA violations based, for example, on false verifications attached to a pleading or false affidavits submitted in support of summary judgment, default judgment, or postjudgment proceedings, than they are to finding FDCPA violations based on essentially the same misrepresentation when merely recited in the pleading itself.

Moreover, suing immediately gives the collector the contemporaneous opportunity to try to undermine the federal claim by attempting to show that the falsehood was misunderstood, a mistake, or never intended to be acted upon. In addition, the consumer's proof in the second case may be simplified by the results of the first case. Res judicata and issue preclusion flowing from a final judgment in the state case are potentially dispositive in some derivative cases. In that event, knowing the outcome of the state case before filing the federal claim is a powerful advantage available to the consumer/federal plaintiff.

An FDCPA violation based on the litigating collector's bad faith strategy of filing suit only to obtain a default judgment or force settlement when it never had the intent or capability to prove its case necessarily requires completion of the collection suit.[164] Asserting such a counterclaim or filing a new action before the collection suit is dismissed will simply motivate the collector to persist in the collection litigation merely to disprove its original intentions.

One possible advantage of bringing the FDCPA action as a counterclaim is that, pursuant to the well-pleaded complaint doctrine,[165] the case cannot be removed to federal court and must stay in state court. In addition, the consumer can bring additional parties into the case and bring FDCPA and other federal claims against that additional party, and that new party cannot still remove the action to federal court.[166]

But the consumer also can stay in state court by limiting the consumer's claims in a subsequent affirmative action to those under state law. In many states, almost any conduct violating the FDCPA is also unfair and deceptive in violation of a state UDAP statute, leading in some of these states to multiple or punitive damages.[167] State tort claims can lead to punitive damages for unreasonable collection practices,[168] including such litigation abuses as suing or continuing to sue the wrong person once put on notice.[169] Nevertheless, when the consumer needs to utilize the FDCPA, the only way to insure that federal court jurisdiction is avoided is to bring the counterclaim in the state court collection action.

Bringing FDCPA violations as counterclaims in the collection action also has the advantage of avoiding the FDCPA's short one-year limitations period. On the other hand, when the FDCPA claims relate to current litigation misconduct and the collection case may be completed within one year, there should be sufficient time to bring the FDCPA claim as part of a separate affirmative action. In addition, that one-year period can be extended in federal and many state courts by filing the FDCPA action within the one-year period but delaying service of the complaint on the collector for up to four months.[170] At least for those additional months, the collector may not be aware of its exposure and may continue to pursue its collection action under its normal procedures. Another option is to bring a subsequent action using state law UDAP, tort, or other theories that have longer limitations periods.

5.5.1.3 Class Counterclaims

There are advantages to a consumer bringing a class counterclaim in the individual collection lawsuit as opposed to filing a separate affirmative class action. The class counterclaim stays in state court and cannot be removed to federal court—which may be a significant advantage in some jurisdictions. The Class Action Fairness Act (CAFA) significantly expands the grounds to remove a state court class action to federal court. A class counterclaim has the advantage of staying in state court, even when federal causes of action are raised,[171] and even when CAFA would otherwise allow removal of an original class action to federal court on diversity grounds.

CAFA substantially broadens the diversity grounds to remove a state court class action to federal court as long as there are more than 100 class members and the amount in controversy exceeds \$5 million.[172] CAFA is drafted, however, to allow only a "defendant" to remove a class action,[173] and courts find that CAFA does not provide a basis for a plaintiff to remove a class counterclaim to federal court.[174] The rule applies even

163 Gionis v. Javitch Block, Rathbone, L.L.P., 238 Fed. Appx. 24 (6th Cir. 2007) (unpublished), *cert. denied*, 552 U.S. 1185, 128 S. Ct. 1259, 170 L. Ed. 2d 68 (2008).

164 *See, e.g.*, Kuria v. Palisades Acquisition XVI, L.L.C., 752 F. Supp. 2d 1293, 1301–03 (N.D. Ga. 2010).

165 *See, e.g.*, Caterpillar Inc. v. Williams, 482 U.S. 386 (1987); Shamrock Oil & Gas Corp. v. Sheets, 313 U.S. 100, 61 S. Ct. 868, 85 L. Ed. 1214 (1941); Chase Manhattan Mortgage Corp. v. Smith, 507 F.3d 910 (6th Cir. 2007); Barkwell v. Portfolio Recovery Assocs., L.L.C., 2010 WL 2012149 (M.D. Ga. May 20, 2010).

166 Palisades Collections L.L.C. v. Shorts, 552 F.3d 327 (4th Cir. 2008).

167 *See* Russey v. Rankin, 911 F. Supp. 1449, 1461–62 (D.N.M. 1995). *See also* National Consumer Law Center, Unfair and Deceptive Acts and Practices § 6.10.1, Ch. 12 (8th ed. 2012), *updated at* www.nclc.org/library.

168 *See* Billsie v. Brooksbank, 525 F. Supp. 2d 1290, 1297 (D.N.M. 2007).

169 *See* Montgomery Ward v. Larragoite, 467 P.2d 399 (N.M. 1970).

170 *See* Fed. R. Civ. P. 4(m).

171 *See* § 5.5.1.1, *supra*.

172 *See* 28 U.S.C. § 1332(d); National Consumer Law Center, Consumer Class Actions Ch. 2 (8th ed. 2013), *updated at* www.nclc.org/library.

173 28 U.S.C. § 1453(b).

174 *See* Westwood Apex v. Contreras, 644 F.3d 799, 807 (9th Cir. 2011); First Bank v. DJL Props., L.L.C., 598 F.3d 915(7th Cir. 2010); Palisades Collections L.L.C. v. Shorts, 552 F.3d 327 (4th Cir. 2008); Progressive W. Ins. Co. v. Preciado, 479 F.3d 1014 (9th Cir. 2007); Resurgent Capital Servs. LP v. Thomason, 2012 WL 5398189 (W.D. Mo. Nov. 5, 2012); Deutsche Bank Nat'l Trust Co. v. Collins, 2012 WL 768206 (W.D. Ark. Mar. 7, 2012); HSBC Bank USA, Nat'l Ass'n v. Arnett, 767 F. Supp. 2d 827 (N.D. Ohio 2011); U.S. Bank v. Adams, 727 F. Supp. 2d 640 (N.D. Ohio 2010); Liberty Credit Servs. v. Yonker, 2010 WL 2639903 (N.D. Ohio June 29, 2010); Am. Gen. Fin. Servs. v. Griffin, 685 F. Supp. 2d 729 (N.D. Ohio 2010); Capital One Bank (USA) v. Reese, 2010 WL 2491008 (N.D. Ohio June 18, 2010) (citing an order

when the consumer brings additional counterclaim defendants into the case and then brings class counterclaims against those defendants. These additional counterclaim defendants cannot remove the class counterclaim to federal court.[175]

For example, in one case a debt buyer brought a collection action to recover on an unpaid cell phone obligation. The consumer added the cell phone carrier as an additional counterclaim defendant and brought a class counterclaim against the carrier for its early termination charge policy. The class counterclaim otherwise met the standards for CAFA removal. But, when the carrier removed the case to federal court, the federal court remanded the case to state court because CAFA did not authorize additional counterclaim defendants to remove cases to federal court.[176]

Another advantage of a class counterclaim over an affirmative class action in court is that there are additional grounds to challenge an arbitration requirement. The collector may have waived the arbitration requirement by initiating court litigation or waiting too long to respond to the class counterclaim. Alternatively, it may be unconscionable to prevent the consumer from bringing counterclaims in the same proceeding as the collector's action.

In addition, the American Arbitration Association (AAA) has posted on its website that it refuses to hear claims "in which the company is the filing party and the case involves a credit card bill or, the case involves a telecom bill or the case involves a consumer finance matter."[177] At least one appellate court has found that the company is the filing party when it initiated the collection action and seeks to require the consumer's class counterclaim be moved to arbitration, so that the AAA will not hear the arbitration.[178] Since the forum designated by the arbitration agreement is unavailable, the class counterclaim cannot be removed to arbitration.[179]

Nevertheless, a class counterclaim may run into problems with statutes of limitations. For example, when an FDCPA counterclaim is raised on behalf of a class, it must be brought within the FDCPA's limitations period if the claim is considered a permissive counterclaim, and not compulsory.[180] If compulsory, it may be that the counterclaim can relate back to the date the collection complaint in the case was brought, not the date of the filing of the class counterclaim.

5.5.2 Credit Card Related Truth in Lending Counterclaims

This subsection focuses on practical issues concerning TIL counterclaims to credit card collection cases. For details on TIL disclosure and substantive requirements, see NCLC's *Truth in Lending*.[181]

The Truth in Lending Act and Regulation Z set out disclosure requirements for advertisements, credit card applications and solicitations, account openings, periodic statements, and certain subsequent disclosures.[182] Substantive credit card requirements relate to protections against price increases and other account changes; protections against double cycle billing, penalty fees, and improvident lending; protections regarding payments; and limits on first year fees.[183] In addition, there are other TIL credit card protections relating to rights to dispute billing errors, protections against unauthorized use, the right to raise merchant-related claims and defenses, restrictions on issuing credit cards, limits on offsets of deposit accounts to pay for credit cards, restrictions on the creditor-merchant relationship, and other substantive protections.[184]

Violations of many, but not all, of these provisions lead to actual damages, statutory damages of twice the finance charge, and attorney fees.[185] Statutory damages are a minimum of $500 and a maximum of $5000,[186] but the maximum can be even greater in the case of an established pattern or practice violating TIL.[187] Because there is not a pre-computed finance charge in open-end credit, there is some uncertainty as to what finance charge to use in calculating statutory damages of twice the finance charge.[188] But there is no doubt that, when TIL statutory damages are available for a credit card violation, the smallest possible recovery would be $500 and attorney fees, no matter the size or nature of the violation.

TIL has a one year statute of limitations, but claims can be brought by way of recoupment beyond one year.[189] Thus, when a collection action is brought years after the TIL violation, that violation can be used to offset, but not exceed, the amount the collector recovers. In addition, the consumer recovers TIL attorney fees even if this exceeds the amount the collector recovers.[190]

The ability to bring a TIL counterclaim is fairly straightforward when the entity bringing the collection case is the

---

of the Sixth Circuit Court of Appeals denying a counterclaim defendant's petition for leave to appeal an order of remand in *In re* Morgan & Pottinger, P.S.C., No. 10-0309 (6th Cir. June 16, 2010)); CitiFinancial, Inc. v. Lightner, 2007 WL 1655225 (N.D. W. Va. June 6, 2007). *See also* Unifund CCR Partners v. Wallis, 2006 WL 908755 (D.S.C. Apr. 7, 2006).

175 Palisades Collections L.L.C. v. Shorts, 552 F.3d 327 (4th Cir. 2008); Deutsche Bank Nat'l Trust Co. v. Baxter, 2013 WL 5229994 (N.D. Ala. Sept. 18, 2013); Citibank v. Duncan, 2010 WL 379869 (M.D. Ala. Jan. 25, 2010); Wells Fargo Bank v. Gilleland, 621 F. Supp. 2d 545 (N.D. Ohio 2009); Ford Motor Credit Co. v. Jones, 2007 WL 2236618 (N.D. Ohio July 31, 2007).

176 Palisades Collections L.L.C. v. Shorts, 552 F.3d 327 (4th Cir. 2008).

177 www.adr.org/sp.asp?id=36427.

178 QuickClick Loans, L.L.C. v. Russell, 943 N.E.2d 166 (Ill. App. Ct. 2011) (Ill. App. Ct. Feb. 1, 2011).

179 National Consumer Law Center, Consumer Arbitration Agreements § 5.8 (6th ed. 2011), *updated at* www.nclc.org/library.

180 Unifund CCR Partners v. Young, 2013 WL 5447666 (Ohio Ct. App. Sept. 27, 2013).

181 (8th ed. 2012), *updated at* www.nclc.org/library.

182 *Id.* Ch. 6.

183 *Id.* §§ 7.2–7.8.

184 *Id.* §§ 7.9–7.15.

185 15 U.S.C. § 1640(a).

186 *Id.* § 1640(a)(2)(A)(iii).

187 *Id.*

188 *See* National Consumer Law Center, Truth in Lending § 11.6.3.4.2 (8th ed. 2012), *updated at* www.nclc.org/library.

189 *Id.* § 12.2.5.

190 *Id.* § 11.9.2.2.

card issuer. More complicated is when a debt buyer brings the action. TILA provides that civil actions that may be brought against the creditor may be brought against an assignee only if the violation is apparent on the face of the disclosure.[191] Since there is no requirement that the assignee review the disclosure, only that it be apparent on the face of the disclosure, TIL counterclaims for disclosure violations can be brought by way of recoupment against debt buyers even if the debt buyer never receives the disclosure statement, as long as the violation is apparent on the statement.

But what about substantive TIL violations that do not involve disclosure requirements, and thus by definition are never apparent on the face of the disclosure? Does the limitation apply even when it would be impossible for the violation to be apparent on the face of the disclosure, or does the limitation only apply to disclosure violations and not to substantive violations?[192]

In addition, TIL's limit on assignee liability refers to a civil action or proceeding which "may be maintained against any assignee." Does this limitation on an action "maintained against any assignee" apply only to a consumer's affirmative claim against an assignee and not to a recoupment claim when the action is maintained against *the consumer*?[193] That is, when a card issuer has violated TIL, can the consumer raise this violation by recoupment as a defense against the assignee's collection action?

If the TIL limitation on assignee liability does not apply to substantive violations, assignees step into the shoes of their assignors and are subject to all defenses that could be raised against the assignors. Then the consumer should be able to raise as a defense against a debt buyer's collection action anything the consumer could raise against a card issuer's collection action, including the card issuer's TIL substantive violations.

In bringing TIL counterclaims to credit card collection actions, practitioners should be aware that debt elimination companies and other scams encourage consumers to bring various frivolous counterclaims and defenses to collection actions, including those involving TIL. Many courts will be initially dismissive of a TIL counterclaim, and the consumer practitioner must be ready from the beginning of a case to clearly and forcefully show the merit of the TIL counterclaim with reference to Regulation Z provisions and documents to support the counterclaim.

5.5.3 Counterclaims Regarding Credit Card Add-Ons and Other Goods or Services

Credit card statements often include charges for payment protection products, credit rating monitoring, lost card protection, and other questionable products. Cell phone bills and other debts may also include suspect charges. While it may not be practical to do extensive discovery in an individual collection action concerning these charges, simple Internet searches may discover pending or recent law enforcement or class action cases against the same creditor for one of these practices. This may be enough to proceed to raise counterclaims relating to deception or non-payment and to defeat the collector's motion to dismiss a counterclaim or the collector's summary judgment motion.

5.5.4 Counterclaims Relating to Pre-Litigation Collection Contacts

Debt buyers may contact the consumer before initiating litigation, and the federal Fair Debt Collection Practices Act (FDCPA) regulates those collection contacts. Debt buyers who purchase debt after it is in default are defined as debt collectors and thus are covered by the FDCPA and must comply with the Act's requirements. Debt buyers should also be liable in tort and under state debt collection and deceptive practices act statutes for their collection misconduct.

Even collection contact by the originating creditor may be actionable. If the contact is done by an independent collection agency, the FDCPA still applies. If the contact is done by the creditor itself, state law may provide remedies. FDCPA and state claims and remedies under these claims are examined in another NCLC treatise, *Fair Debt Collection*.[194]

When a counterclaim relates to the debt buyer's own conduct and not the conduct of the originating creditor, there is no cap for the debt buyer's liability for its collection misconduct (unless it is that of an assignee for claims relating to the assignor). Liability in tort or under the FDCPA can exceed the amount sought in the collection action. Care must be taken though in bringing FDCPA claims, because of the short one year limitations period. It is possible that the FDCPA counterclaim can be raised after the one year limitations period by way of recoupment, but this will depend on whether state law treats the collection contacts as arising out of the same transaction as the debt.

5.5.5 Counterclaims Relating to Collector's Litigation Conduct

The consumer can bring an FDCPA, tort, or state statutory counterclaim[195] based upon a collector's current litigation misconduct in the collection case itself, particularly when the collector's unlawful action is egregious, such as when it knowingly filed the action outside the statute of limitations, knowingly sued on a debt discharged in bankruptcy, or was not licensed to bring collection actions in the state. Too often debt buyers abuse the court system by bringing inadequate

191 15 U.S.C. § 1641(a).

192 *See* National Consumer Law Center, Truth in Lending § 12.3 (8th ed. 2012), *updated at* www.nclc.org/library.

193 *See* National Consumer Law Center, Truth in Lending § 12.3.4 (8th ed. 2012), *updated at* www.nclc.org/library.

194 (8th ed. 2014), *updated at* www.nclc.org/library.

195 *See* Midland Funding, L.L.C. v. Giraldo, 961 N.Y.S.2d 743 (N.Y. Dist. Ct. 2013) (state deceptive practices act claim actionable).

claims, knowing they will prevail by default and so do not need to present a viable case.[196] Another possible improper collector litigation tactic is publicly disclosing the consumer's Social Security number in litigation documents.[197] For example, California has a statute specifically prohibiting the practice and providing $2500 statutory damages.[198]

Section 5.5.1.2, *supra*, considers whether such a counterclaim should be brought as a counterclaim or as a separate action, and § 13.4, *infra*, examines such a separate action. Even more detail is found in NCLC's *Fair Debt Collection*.[199] This subsection merely raises a few practical issues concerning such counterclaims.

Attorneys who regularly collect consumer debts, including through litigation, are covered by the FDCPA, as are debt buyers who purchase debt after default.[200] It is also clear that the FDCPA applies to the collector's conduct in the litigation and not just to contacts prior to litigation.[201]

An FDCPA counterclaim for litigation misconduct is unlikely to recover damages beyond the FDCPA's $1000 maximum statutory damages plus the consumer's attorney fees. Dismissal of the collection case will often eliminate many of the consumer's potential actual damages. Of course, the ability to obtain attorney fees from the collector may be key to an attorney's ability to represent the consumer, and the FDCPA will provide two theories for such a recovery of attorney fees: first, the FDCPA provides statutory attorney fees to any prevailing consumer and, second, the consumer's attorney fees to successfully defend the collection action may be treated as actual damages when the FDCPA violation results from the litigation itself.[202] The FDCPA has a one year statute of limitations, but tort, deceptive practices act, or state debt collection statutory claims will have longer limitations periods.

196 *Id.*

197 *See* Fowler v. First Fed. Sav. and Loan Ass'n (Bankr. D.S.C. Oct. 14, 2008), *available at* www.nclc.org/unreported. *Contra* Pittenger v. John Solday Fin. Grp., L.L.C., 2010 WL 1856224 (N.D. Ohio May 10, 2010); Feltman v. Blatt, Hasenmiller, Leibsker & Moore, L.L.C., 2008 WL1 5211024 (N.D. Ill. Dec. 11, 2008).

198 Cal. Fin. Code § 4507 (West).

199 (8th ed. 2014).

200 *See* National Consumer Law Center, Fair Debt Collection § 4.2.8 (8th ed. 2014).

201 Heinz v. Jenkins, 514 U.S. 291, 115 S. Ct. 1489, 131 L. Ed. 2d 395 (1995). *See also* National Consumer Law Center, Fair Debt Collection § 2.4.8 (8th ed. 2014); § 13.4.3.1, *infra*.

202 *See* National Consumer Law Center, Fair Debt Collection § 2.5.2.2.3 (8th ed. 2014), *updated at* www.nclc.org/library.

5.5.6 *When the FTC Holder Notice Is in the Credit Agreement*

An important issue in a collection case not involving credit card or cell phone debt will be whether the credit agreement includes or is required to include the "FTC Holder Notice." This notice requires that the holder of the credit agreement is subject to all claims and defenses that the consumer could have raised against the seller, up to the amount of the debt.[203]

As a matter of the terms of the agreement, the consumer can raise as counterclaims against the collector all claims that the consumer could have raised against the seller. For example, consider a debt buyer's collection action for a $4000 deficiency after a consumer had defaulted on a $15,000 car loan, the creditor had repossessed and sold the car, and the creditor then sold the right to the deficiency to the debt buyer. Assume the consumer has a $10,000 claim against the car dealer. The consumer can raise this $10,000 claim as a counterclaim in the collection action and come away from the case with a positive recovery.[204]

If the statute of limitations on the $10,000 claim has expired, it can be raised by way of recoupment even after the limitations period has expired, since this claim arose out of the same transaction as the car loan. The recoupment claim can offset the $4000 debt but cannot result in a positive recovery for the consumer after the statute of limitations for the consumer's claim has expired.

The FTC Holder Notice contract language makes holders liable for the consumer's claims against a "seller" and thus allows consumers to bring counterclaims in the collection action relating to the conduct of car dealers, home improvement contractors, and other credit sellers—as to both their conduct in the sales transaction and their conduct in extending credit. But the notice does not provide a basis to bring claims against banks and other lenders as to their conduct in extending loans, since they are not "sellers." On the other hand, the notice allows for seller-related counterclaims to be brought against the lender or the lender's assignee, even when the seller did not assign the loan to that lender but only referred the consumer to the lender. More on the operation of the FTC Holder Notice is found in NCLC's *Federal Deception Law*.[205]

203 16 C.F.R. § 433.

204 A number of courts have misinterpreted Federal Trade Commission language and limited recoveries under the FTC Holder Rule to the amount required to offset the amount owed on the debt. *See* National Consumer Law Center, Federal Deception Law § 4.3.4.3 (2012), *updated at* www.nclc.org/library.

205 National Consumer Law Center, Federal Deception Law Ch. 4 (2012), *updated at* www.nclc.org/library.

Chapter 6 State Restrictions on the Recovery of Attorney Fees and Other Collection Expenses

6.1 Overview

When a debtor fails to make timely payment of a debt, the common law strictly limits the damages a creditor may recover to the interest provided in the contract or by statute.[1] This general rule of damages law is justified by two considerations. Creditors set interest rates at levels that take into account that a certain portion of debtors necessarily default. Thus, the rate of interest already compensates the creditor for collection expenses and losses, so any separate recovery of collection expenses would be duplicative. The other consideration is that almost all consumer credit defaults result from the debtor's financial distress, and the imposition of collection fees would only exacerbate this financial distress and hinder the debtor's financial recovery.

Dissatisfied with this limitation on their profits, creditors and collectors have, through adhesion contracts and legislation, sought additional charges from consumers allegedly as compensation for their collection expenses. The most common inroad on the common law rule prohibiting recovery of more than interest for the failure of a consumer to pay a debt on time is the allowance by some courts of an attorney fee award for a creditor if it is authorized by the contract. In addition, some states have adopted statutes that authorize creditors to recover attorney fees from debtors. States tend to be considerably more restrictive with respect to collection agency fees.

This chapter first examines the award of attorney fees to the prevailing party pursuant to a contract term. The chapter analyzes whether states allow this method of fee-shifting, the creditor's need to establish that the consumer has in fact agreed to the contract containing the clause, and the interpretation of such clauses.

The chapter then turns to the question of whether a state has overridden the "American rule" (that attorney fees are not recoverable as damages) by statute for certain types of actions, whether the creditor is a prevailing party and therefore entitled to a fee award under such a statute or a contractual clause, and courts' varying approaches for determining the amount of attorney fees to award. The chapter concludes with an analysis of whether collection agency fees can be passed on to debtors. Dishonored check charges are addressed in a different chapter,[2] and late charges and judgment interest are discussed in a different treatise.[3]

The implications of these issues go beyond defeating a creditor's claim for attorney fees or a collector's claim for collection expenses. Collecting or attempting to collect attorney fees[4] or

---

1 Loudon v. Taxing Dist., 104 U.S. 771, 774, 26 L. Ed. 923 (1881); Union Mut. Life Ins. Co. v. Chrysler Corp. 793 F.2d 1 (1st Cir. 1986).

2 *See* Ch. 8, *infra*.

3 National Consumer Law Center, Consumer Credit Regulation Ch. 4 (2012), *updated at* www.nclc.org/library.

4 *See, e.g.*, McCollough v. Johnson, Rodenberg, & Lauinger, L.L.C., 637 F.3d 939 (9th Cir. 2011) (demand for attorney fees violated FDCPA in absence, at summary judgment stage, of admissible evidence that collector was entitled to them; generic testimony that all credit card agreements provide fee-shifting was insufficient to raise issue of fact); Reichert v. Nat'l Credit Sys., Inc., 531 F.3d 1002 (9th Cir. 2008) (when contract authorized prevailing party fees "in the event of legal action," only fees "incurred in successful litigation" could be recovered; demanding attorney fees when all attorney did was write a letter violated FDCPA); Moxley v. Pfundstein, 801 F. Supp. 2d 598 (N.D. Ohio 2011) (demand in payday loan collection suit for attorney fees that were not allowable under Ohio law is actionable as FDCPA violation); Kline v. Mortgage Elec. Sec. Systems, 2010 WL 6298271 (S.D. Ohio Dec. 30, 2010) (allowing consumer to proceed with claim that creditor's demand for unauthorized attorney fees violated UDAP statute), *report and recommendation adopted by* 2011 WL 1125346 (S.D. Ohio Mar. 25, 2011); Kirk v. Gobel, 622 F. Supp. 2d 1039 (E.D. Wash. 2009) (claim for statutory attorney fees in motion for default judgment violated FDCPA, but fact issue as to bona fide error); McCollough v. Johnson, Rodenberg & Lauinger, 587 F. Supp. 2d 1170 (D. Mont. 2008) (demand for attorney fees in complaint violated FDCPA when no statute provided for fees and no evidence of valid fee-shifting provision in contract); Som v. Daniels Law Offices, P.C., 573 F. Supp. 2d 349 (D. Mass. 2008) (fact question whether percentage-based fee, and fee for sums not yet collected, were "expressly authorized" by contract allowing attorney fees "incurred by us"); Barrows v. Chase Manhattan Mortgage Co., 465 F. Supp. 2d 347 (D.N.J. 2006) (FDCPA claim against lender's law firm; fact issue whether legal fees demanded for mortgage reinstatement complied with New Jersey court rule limiting costs and fees in foreclosure actions); Stolicker v. Muller, Muller, Richmond, Harms, Myers & Sgroi, 2005 WL 2180481 (W.D. Mich. Sept. 9, 2005) (law firm's affidavit in support of default judgment violated FDCPA by claiming 25% attorney fee when state law required judicial determination of reasonable fee); Brooks v. Auto Sales & Servs., Inc., 2001 WL 686950 (S.D. Ind. June 15, 2001) (allowing consumer to go forward with FDCPA action against attorney who routinely added 33.33% attorney fee to amount claimed in small claims actions for deficiency on repossessed cars, when contract clause allowed "reasonable" fees but did not specify a percentage); Padilla v. Payco Gen. Am. Credits, Inc., 161 F. Supp. 2d 264 (S.D.N.Y. 2001) (collector violated FDCPA by seeking to collect more than the 18% collection fee permitted by federal regulations; no defense that collector relied on figures given to it by creditor guarantee agency); *In re* Machnic, 271 B.R. 789 (Bankr. S.D. W. Va. 2002) (credit card issuer violated West Virginia Consumer Credit and Protection Act when it sought to collect fees authorized by contract but not explicitly permitted by Act); Ai v. Frank Huff Agency, Ltd., 607 P.2d 1304 (Haw. 1980) (placing clause allowing 33.33% attorney fees in note, when statute only allowed 25%, was a misrepresentation and violated state UDAP statute); Payday Today, Inc. v. Hamilton, 911 N.E.2d 26 (Ind. Ct. App. 2009) (collection letter that seeks attorney fees for collection of payday loan, contrary to statute, violates FDCPA); Davis Lake Cmty. Ass'n v. Feldman, 530 S.E.2d 865 (N.C. Ct. App. 2000) (UDAP violation to attempt to collect attorney fees in excess of 15% allowed by law); Green v. Morgan Props., 73 A.3d 478 (N.J. 2013) (allowing tenants to proceed with UDAP claim alleging that attorney fee clause in lease was unreasonable). *See also* Mund v. EMCC, Inc., 259 F.R.D. 180 (D. Minn. 2009) (certifying class in FDCPA class action alleging that collector's "one size fits all" percentage collection fee was not expressly provided for in members' contracts with vacation club). *But cf.* Newman v. Ormond, 396 Fed. Appx. 636 (11th Cir. 2010) (request

collection agency fees[5] beyond those allowed by law can subject the party to liability under the Fair Debt Collection Practices Act (FDCPA), the state deceptive practices (UDAP) statute, or a state debt collection statute. Even when a contract or statute allows fees, it may be a violation to seek them before they are actually incurred.[6]

for specific amount of attorney fees did not violate FDCPA even though amount of fees discretionary with court; contract allowed for reasonable fees, and fee request complied with Florida procedure); Singer v. Pierce & Assocs., P.C., 383 F.3d 596 (7th Cir. 2004) (when mortgage provided for "reasonable attorney fees," servicer could include $2250 attorney fees in pay-off amount, even though court in foreclosure action, dismissed when borrower arranged to sell to third party, had awarded half that amount); Sayyed v. Wolpoff & Abramson, L.L.P., 733 F. Supp. 2d 635 (D. Md. 2010) (request for arguably excessive fees not FDCPA violation, when made in pleadings addressed to court, not in correspondence with debtor); Riermersma v. Messerli & Kramer, P.A., 2008 WL 2390729 (D. Minn. June 9, 2008) (not an FDCPA violation to send complaint for debt "due and owing" that included specific sum for attorney fees); Hall v. Leone, Halpin & Konopinski, L.L.P., 2008 WL 608609 (N.D. Ind. Feb. 28, 2008) (demand for specific amount of attorney fees in complaint not an FDCPA violation); Cisneros v. Neuheisel Law Firm, 2008 WL 65608 (D. Ariz. Jan. 3, 2008) (request for specific amount of attorney fees, here set as a percentage of the debt, in state court complaint not an FDCPA violation); *In re* Tate, 253 B.R. 653 (Bankr. W.D.N.C. 2000) (state UDAP and debt collection statutes preempted by bankruptcy law when creditor charged improper "bankruptcy fee" to evade rules for claiming attorney fees in bankruptcy); Bowman Plumbing, Heating & Elec. v. Logan, 59 Va. Cir. 446 (Va. Cir. Ct. 2002) (violation of statute limiting late fees not per se UDAP violation; when late fee provision not part of contract, no violation of UDAP provision forbidding certain penalties). *See generally* § 8.4, *infra* (FDCPA and other claims against collectors who seek penalties for returned checks beyond those authorized by law); National Consumer Law Center, Fair Debt Collection §§ 5.5.4.3.1–5.5.4.3.3, 5.6.3, 5.7.2.6.4, 10.2.4.4.1–10.2.4.4.7, 10.3.5, 10.3.6 (8th ed. 2014), *updated at* www.nclc.org/library.

5 *See, e.g.*, Acik v. I.C. Sys., Inc., 640 F. Supp. 2d 1019 (N.D. Ill. 2009) (collector's addition of percentage fee to medical bill violated FDCPA; fee not "expressly authorized" by patient agreement or Illinois statute); Richard v. Oak Tree Group, Inc., 614 F. Supp. 2d 814 (W.D. Mich. 2008) (when contract did not obligate consumers to pay maximum possible commission to collector, demand for this sum violated FDCPA); Fields v. W. Mass. Credit Corp., 479 F. Supp. 2d 287 (D. Conn. 2007) (FDCPA violation to add collection agency fee to deficiency after motor vehicle repossession; Connecticut motor vehicle loan law allows fees only for attorney, not collection agency); Adams v. A. & S. Collection Assocs., Inc., 2007 WL 2206936 (D. Conn. July 30, 2007) (recommending award of punitive damages against collector that required creditor to add 49% collection fee and 18% interest to claims before forwarding them to agency when state law forbids agency to add such fees); Hansen v. Ticket Track, Inc. 280 F. Supp. 2d 1196 (W.D. Wash. 2003) (Washington collection agency statute forbade collector, but not creditor, to add collection fee to debt; fee here was added by collector, and thus unlawful, when collector's contract with creditor-parking lot operator required it to include fee provision in its contract with customers); Adair v. Sabharwal, 2002 WL 31243019 (S.D. Ind. Aug. 16, 2002) (patients stated claim under Indiana deception statute against doctor whose collector demanded 50% collection fee under contract making patient liable for sums "paid or incurred" when there was no evidence of amounts actually incurred); Evergreen Collectors v. Holt, 803 P.2d 10 (Wash. Ct. App. 1991) (attempt to collect fees to which collector is not entitled violates state debt collection law). *See also* Massa v. I.C. Sys. Inc., 2008 WL 504329 (S.D. Ind. Feb. 21, 2008) (attempt to collect unauthorized fifty percent collection fee violates FDCPA, but bona fide error shown when fee added by previous collector, and current collector reasonably relied on creditor as to amount of debt).

6 *See, e.g.*, Munoz v. Pipestone Fin., L.L.C., 513 F. Supp. 2d 1076 (D. Minn. 2007) (creditor liable under FDCPA for seeking fees at outset of collection suit, before they had been incurred); Meriweather v. Taylor, 2004 WL 1146495 (S.D. Ind. May 13, 2004) (refusing to dismiss FDCPA claim; when mortgage agreement provided for "foreclosure costs" and attorney fees "properly associated with the foreclosure proceeding," fees could not be charged for reinstatement prior to suit); Gostony v. Diem Corp., 320 F. Supp. 2d 932 (D. Ariz. 2003) (judicial proceeding was prerequisite for award under lease provision allowing "prevailing party" to recover attorney fees and collection costs; inclusion of fees in initial demand letter was unlawful); McDowall v. Leschack & Grodensky, P.C. 279 F. Supp. 2d 197 (S.D.N.Y. 2003) (demand for attorney fees in dunning letter violated FDCPA; fees could be awarded only after court proceeding); *In re* WCS Enters., 381 B.R. 206 (Bankr. E.D. Va. 2007) (entire 10% attorney fee did not become due when matter referred to attorney). *See also* Stolicker v. Muller, Muller, Richmond, Harms, Myers & Sgroi, 2005 WL 2180481 (W.D. Mich. Sept. 9, 2005) (when state law required a court to award attorney fees, prejudgment claim for a percentage fee violated FDCPA). *But see* Fields v. Wilber Law Firm, P.C. 383 F.3d 562 (7th Cir. 2004) (inclusion of pre-suit attorney fees in dunning letter proper when credit contract allowed "any and all collection costs and attorney fees," but demand for lump sum without breaking out attorney fee amount was misleading); Riermersma v. Messerli & Kramer, P.A., 2008 WL 2390729 (D. Minn. June 9, 2008) (not an FDCPA violation to send complaint for debt "due and owing" that included specific sum for attorney fees); Hall v. Leone, Halpin & Konopinski, L.L.P., 2008 WL 608609 (N.D. Ind. Feb. 28, 2008) (demand for specific amount of attorney fees in complaint not an FDCPA violation); Cisneros v. Neuheisel Law Firm, 2008 WL 65608 (D. Ariz. Jan. 3, 2008) (request for specific amount of attorney fees in state court complaint, here set as a percentage of the debt, not an FDCPA violation). *But cf.* Reyes v. Kenosian & Miele, L.L.P., 619 F. Supp. 2d 796 (N.D. Cal. 2008) (request for attorney fees in state court complaint, which cited two legal theories, one of which may have been inapplicable, not a false representation within meaning of FDCPA); Gonzalez v. Codilis & Assocs., 2004 WL 719264 (N.D. Ill. Mar. 31, 2004) (inclusion of attorney fees in pay-off amount for reinstatement of mortgage proper when fees authorized by contract and already incurred; distinguishing cases forbidding demand for future fees or those that can only be awarded by court); Hage v. Gen. Serv. Bureau, 306 F. Supp. 2d 883 (D. Neb. 2003) (Nebraska statute allows attorney fees in suits for $2000 or less for debts for necessaries if claimant establishes the claim and secures judgment; no statutory authorization for fees without a judgment, but fact question whether there is "a recognized and accepted uniform course of procedure" that allows attorney fees when consumers settle before judgment); Whaley v. Shapiro & Kreisman, L.L.C., 2003 WL 22232911 (N.D. Ill. Sept. 16, 2003) (mortgage provided for reasonable attorney fees and costs; attorney fees may be included in pay-off amount when house sold before foreclosure completed, even though court had not approved them; distinguishing case of statutory attorney fees that must be awarded by court).

6.2 Is the Creditor Entitled to Recover Attorney Fees?

6.2.1 *American Rule Denies Fees*

The "American rule" is that attorney fees are not recoverable as damages, and attorney fees will not be awarded in the absence of a statutory or contractual authorization, except for vexatious, frivolous litigation.[7] The common justification for the rule is that it discourages litigation.

Some states go beyond the American rule and codify a prohibition against or restrictions on fee-shifting regardless of the parties' contract. Other states, however, provide by statute for fee awards, or allow the parties to agree to fee-shifting. These variations are discussed in the following subsections.

6.2.2 *Whether a Contractual Attorney Fee Is Permissible*

The primary means by which a creditor may seek to create a right to recover attorney fees is by inserting a clause to this effect in the contract.[8] In some states, courts hold that such clauses are permissible, even in the absence of a specific authorizing statute, on a freedom of contract theory.[9]

Other states, however, limit or prohibit a creditor's recovery or attempted recovery of its attorney fees from the debtor regardless of the terms of any contract. These restrictions may be contained in statutes that apply only to specific creditors (for example, small loan companies or debt collection agencies) or only to certain types of credit (for example, small loans or retail installment sales).[10]

For example, West Virginia allows only those fees explicitly permitted by the state Consumer Credit and Protection Act.[11] Alabama prohibits attorney fee clauses in consumer credit contracts when the amount financed is $300 or less and restricts the amount of fees that can be charged when the amount financed exceeds $300.[12] Iowa prohibits attorney fee clauses altogether in consumer credit transactions.[13] South Dakota prohibits contractual attorney fees unless specifically authorized

7 Alyeska Pipeline Serv. Co. v. Wilderness Soc'y, 421 U.S. 240, 95 S. Ct. 1612, 44 L. Ed. 2d 141 (1975); Total Recycling Servs. of Conn., Inc. v. Conn. Oil Recycling Servs., L.L.C., 63 A.3d 896, 904 (Conn. 2013) (Connecticut follows American rule); *In re* Estate of Vayda, 875 A.2d 925 (N.J. 2005) (explaining rationale for American rule and reiterating New Jersey's "strong public policy against the shifting of costs"; no fee-shifting in action to remove executor); Wilborn v. Bank One Corp., 906 N.E.2d 396 (Ohio 2009); Eagle Ridge Estate Homeowners Ass'n, Inc. v. Anderson, 827 N.W.2d 859 (S.D. 2013) (South Dakota follows American rule); Cracker Barrel Old Country Store v. Epperson, 284 S.W.3d 303 (Tenn. 2009) (explaining public policy basis for American rule; provision for "costs" and "expenses" not explicit enough to override rule); Dave v. Valdez, 275 P.3d 485 (Wyo. 2012) (statutory exception to the American rule arises only if statute "explicitly makes available an award of attorney fees"; statute's authorization of "damages" is insufficient). *But see* O'Connell v. Will, 263 P.3d 41 (Alaska 2011) (Alaska rejects American rule). *See generally* Dan B. Dobbs, Dobbs Law of Remedies § 3.10 (2d ed. 1993).

8 *See generally* 17A Am. Jur. 2d *Contracts* §§ 288–290, 402–404, 489–490 (2014); Joan Kirshberg Davis, Annotation, *When may federal court decline to award to prevailing party attorneys' fees authorized by contract*, 56 A.L.R. Fed. 871 (1982); A. Della Porta, Annotation, *Validity of provision in promissory note or other evidences of indebtedness for payment as attorneys' fees, expenses and costs of collection, of specified percentage of note*, 17 A.L.R.2d 288 (1951); 11 Decennial Digest, *Bills and Notes* §§ 471, 529, 533, 534.

9 *See, e.g.*, Leamon v. Krajkiewcz, 132 Cal. Rptr. 2d 362 (Cal. Ct. App. 2003) (parties are free to define conditions for fee-shifting; provision denying fees to party who sues without first seeking mediation applied to buyer who had contract declared voidable on grounds of duress); Morris v. Belfor U.S.A. Group, Inc., 201 P.3d 1253 (Colo. App. 2008) (Colorado will enforce one-way fee-shifting provision); Butler v. Lembeck, 182 P.3d 1185 (Colo. App. 2007) (one-sided attorney fee provision enforceable as written; not against public policy and not unenforceable as a penalty); Roberts v. Row, 743 So. 2d 1145 (Fla. Dist. Ct. App. 1999) (trial court had no discretion to refuse to enforce attorney fee provision in contract); Himebaugh v. Weber Inv. Corp., 700 So. 2d 19 (Fla. Dist. Ct. App. 1997) (court had no discretion to refuse to enforce clause in subdivision covenant which provided for award of attorney fees incurred in collecting assessments); Losee v. Idaho Co., 220 P.3d 575 (Idaho 2009) (fee-shifting clauses generally enforceable); Mirar Dev. Inc. v. Kroner, 720 N.E.2d 270 (Ill. App. Ct. 1999) (attorney fee provision in construction contract is enforceable in mechanic's lien action, even though mechanic's lien statute is silent as to attorney fees); First Sec. Sav. Bank v. Aitken, 573 N.W.2d 307, 320 (Mich. Ct. App. 1997) ("contractual provisions for the payment of reasonable attorney fees are judicially enforceable"); Garner v. Hubbs, 17 S.W.3d 922 (Mo. Ct. App. 2000) (court must enforce attorney fee clause in separation agreement which is treated as a contract); Parkert v. Lindquist, 693 N.W.2d 529 (Neb. 2005) (citing freedom of contract in declining to extend its policy against fee-shifting in the courts to non-judicial foreclosures); Sophie F. Bronwiski Mulligan Irrevocable Trust v. Bridges, 44 A.3d 116 (R.I. 2012) (when fee-shifting clause of residential lease is unambiguous, and tenant offers no evidence of duress, provision enforced as written); Fletcher Hill, Inc. v. Crosbie, 872 A.2d 292 (Vt. 2005) (when contract specifically provides for attorney fees, Vermont courts are loathe to revise the agreement and deny the parties the benefit of their bargain); Schlesinger v. Woodcock, 35 P.3d 1232 (Wyo. 2001) (commercial loan; contractual attorney fee clauses will be enforced, but court will determine reasonableness using federal lodestar test).

10 *See, e.g.*, Payday Today, Inc. v. Hamilton, 911 N.E.2d 26 (Ind. Ct. App. 2009) (collection letter that seeks attorney fees for collection of payday loan, contrary to statute, violates FDCPA); Santa Rosa KM Assocs., P.C. v. Principal Life Ins. Co., 206 P.3d 40 (Kan. Ct. App. 2009) (Kan. Stat. Ann. § 58-2313 has been amended to eliminate ban on fee-shifting provisions in credit agreements but still forbids inclusion of costs incurred by salaried employee of creditor or assignee and the inclusion of both attorney fees and collection agency fees); Cheshire Academy v. Lee, 448 N.Y.S.2d 112 (N.Y. Civ. Ct. 1982) (denying attorney fees when statute governing retail installment obligations specifically voids any provision for payment of attorney fees). *See generally* National Consumer Law Center, Consumer Credit Regulation (2012), *updated at* www.nclc.org/library.

11 W. Va. Code §§ 46A-2-128(d) (prohibiting collection agencies from attempting to collect charge, fee, or expense unless it is expressly authorized by the agreement and by statute), 46A-3-101 (listing charges that may be included in consumer credit sale). *See In re* Machnic, 271 B.R. 789 (Bankr. S.D. W. Va. 2002) (credit card issuer violated West Virginia Consumer Credit and Protection Act when it sought attorney fees for collection when not explicitly permitted by Act, even though authorized by contract).

12 *See, e.g.*, Ala. Code § 5-19-10 (attorney fees forbidden on debts of $300 or less; permitted, with certain limitations, on larger debts).

13 Iowa Code § 537.2507.

by statute.[14] A District of Columbia municipal regulation forbids the inclusion of fee-shifting clauses in residential leases.[15] Texas law regulating home equity loans forbids the imposition on borrowers of personal liability for attorney fees but allows fees to be recovered from foreclosure proceeds.[16]

Even in the absence of an explicit statutory prohibition, some courts hold that contract clauses providing for the recovery of collection attorney fees are invalid unless there is specific statutory authorization of such fees. These courts look to a variety of legal theories to justify that conclusion. The most straightforward approach is that of the Nebraska courts, which hold such clauses to be contrary to public policy and invalid in the absence of statutory authorization.[17] Under North Carolina law, contractual clauses for attorney fees can be enforced only to the extent expressly allowed by a state statute.[18] The statute applicable to notes, conditional sales, and other evidence of indebtedness caps fees at 15% and requires an advance notice.[19]

In Ohio, a 1987 state supreme court decision upheld a clause in a residential condominium agreement that provided for attorney fees for any foreclosure action or action to collect homeowners' assessments, as long as the amount of the fee is fair, just, and reasonable.[20] A 2009 state supreme court decision, however, appears to narrow this ruling significantly.[21] There, the court reaffirmed its general commitment to the American rule and the rule that the agreement to pay attorney fees in a contract of adhesion is not enforceable, a position also expressed by the 1987 decision.[22] The court went on, however, to state a blanket rule that a contract to pay attorney fees upon the default of a debt obligation is void and unenforceable, as it operates as a penalty and encourages litigation.[23] Applying these principles to mortgage foreclosure actions, the court held that a standard contract clause prescribed by Fannie Mae that required the home owner to pay the creditor's attorney fees to reinstate a mortgage loan that was in foreclosure was valid and enforceable. On the other hand, a borrower who avoided foreclosure by paying off the outstanding principal, interest, and court costs in full rather than seeking reinstatement had a right to dismissal of the foreclosure action, and the mortgage holder could not condition dismissal on the borrower's payment of its attorney fees. A number of pre-2009 decisions had also invalidated attorney fee clauses, either in general,[24]

14 *See, e.g.*, S.D. Codified Laws § 15-17-39 (prohibiting contractual attorney fees in note, bond, mortgage, or other evidence of debt except as authorized by specific statute); Vanderwerff Implement, Inc. v. McCance, 561 N.W.2d 24 (S.D. 1997) (construing South Dakota statute that makes attorney fee clauses in certain contracts void). *Cf.* Kimball Inv. Land, Ltd. v. Chmela, 604 N.W.2d 289 (S.D. 2000) (specific South Dakota statute allowing attorney fees for mortgage foreclosure is exception to general prohibition of contractual fees). *But cf.* Orion Fin. Corp. v. Am. Foods Group, Inc., 281 F.3d 733 (8th Cir. 2002) (contract for services not covered by South Dakota statute forbidding fee-shifting clauses in "evidence of debt"); Citibank v. C & S Wholesale Grocers, Inc., 2009 WL 688991 (D. Vt. Mar. 9, 2009) (prohibition against contractual fees does not apply to credit card agreement); Credit Collection Servs., Inc. v. Pesicka, 721 N.W.2d 474 (S.D. 2006) (prohibition against contractual fees inapplicable to hospital's patient consent form, as it is not "evidence of debt").

15 14 D.C. Mun. Reg. § 304.4. *See* Pajic v. Foote Props., 72 A.3d 140 (D.C. 2013) (lease provision is void and unenforceable; noting that fee-shifting would "dramatically up the ante" for tenants seeking relief and would "threaten to chill" such litigation).

16 Huston v. U.S. Bank, N.A., ___ F. Supp. 2d ___, 2013 WL 6731988 (S.D. Tex. Dec. 19, 2013).

17 Mutual Concepts, Inc. v. First Nat'l Bank of Omaha, 495 Fed. Appx. 514 (5th Cir. 2012) (Nebraska's strong public policy against fee-shifting bars enforcement of choice-of-law provision choosing state, here Texas, with statute providing fee-shifting in contract actions); Stewart v. Bennett, 727 N.W.2d 424 (Neb. 2007) (attorney fee clause in lease void as against public policy as embodied in legislation that explicitly allows attorney fees for frivolous action but is silent as to other litigation); Chambers-Dobson, Inc. v. Squier, 472 N.W.2d 391 (Neb. 1991) (contractual fee-shifting contrary to public policy and void); First Nat'l Bank v. Schroeder, 355 N.W.2d 780 (Neb. 1984). *But cf.* Parkert v. Lindquist, 693 N.W.2d 529 (Neb. 2005) (contractual provision for fee-shifting in litigation would be void, but citing freedom of contract in declining to extend public policy against fee-shifting to non-judicial foreclosures).

18 Stillwell Enters., Inc. v. Interstate Equip. Co., 266 S.E.2d 812 (N.C. 1980). *See also* Sunbelt Rentals v. Corbridge, 171 F. Supp. 2d 14 (D. Me. 2001) (N.C. law).

19 N.C. Gen. Stat. § 6-21.2.

20 Nottingdale Homeowners Ass'n v. Darby, 514 N.E.2d 702 (Ohio 1987).

21 Wilborn v. Bank One Corp., 906 N.E.2d 396 (Ohio 2009).

22 *Id.* at 401. *See also* Moxley v. Pfundstein, 801 F. Supp. 2d 598 (N.D. Ohio 2011) (one-sided attorney fee clauses in contracts of adhesion are unenforceable; seeking fees pursuant to payday loan contract is actionable as FDCPA violation). *Cf.* Morgan Woods Homeowners' Ass'n v. Wills, 2012 WL 195409 (Ohio Ct. App. Jan. 23, 2012) (stating that fee-shifting clauses are enforceable, provided that fees awarded are fair, just, and reasonable; enforcing clause in homeowners' association agreement).

23 Wilborn v. Bank One Corp., 906 N.E.2d 396 (Ohio 2009).

24 *See, e.g.*, Clarklift, Inc. v. Clark Equip. Co., 869 F. Supp. 533 (N.D. Ohio 1994) (Ohio will not enforce attorney fee clauses in promissory notes as being against public policy; refusing to award attorney fees when the collateral was located in Ohio and the creditor relied on Ohio law in its action, despite a Michigan choice of law clause in a commercial contract), *aff'd*, 117 F.3d 1420 (6th Cir. 1997); Worth v. Aetna Cas. & Sur. Co., 513 N.E.2d 253 (Ohio 1987) (attorney fee clause inserted by creditor into ordinary contract or lease is contrary to public policy, but this agreement between company and its executives for indemnification of their legal expenses is enforceable); Glouster Cmty. Bank v. Winchell, 659 N.E.2d 330 (Ohio Ct. App. 1995) (inclusion of attorney fees and court costs provision in contract violated Ohio retail installment sales act and was a "willing violation" invalidating both the contract and the security interest); Telmark, Inc. v. Schierloh, 658 N.E.2d 43 (Ohio Ct. App. 1995) (denying enforcement of attorney fee clause in commercial lease on Ohio public policy grounds, despite New York choice of law clause; attorney fee clause generally disapproved but may be allowed in agreements between "competent parties with equal bargaining positions" who engage in "free and understanding negotiations"). *See also* Barany-Snyder v. Weiner, 539 F.3d 327 (6th Cir. 2008) ("Ohio law prohibits the collection of attorney fees in connection with a 'personal, family or household debt' "; but merely attaching a copy of contract with forbidden provision to a complaint, which did not demand attorney fees, not a threat to enforce the provision); Scotts Co. v. Cent. Garden & Pet Co., 256 F. Supp. 2d 734 (S.D. Ohio 2003) (clause preprinted on back of non-consumer invoice not enforceable).

or as contracts of adhesion,[25] but others upheld them.[26]

A few courts have held that a contract clause providing for attorney fees is a penalty prohibited by general contract law.[27] In distinguishing a forbidden penalty from an enforceable liquidated damages clause, courts will consider the difficulty of determining actual damages, the disparity between the actual and predicted damages, and any indicia of unconscionability, such as disparity of bargaining power and provisions highly unfavorable to the weaker party.[28]

Other fee provisions have been found to be a cloak for usury,[29] unconscionable,[30] or against equity under the particular facts

25 *See, e.g.*, Columbus Check Cashers, Inc. v. Rodgers, 2008 WL 4684781 (Ohio Ct. App. Oct. 23, 2008) (refusing to enforce one-way fee-shifting provision in payday loan contract; contract of adhesion, and unequal bargaining power); K & A Cleaning, Inc. v. Materni, 2006 WL 1047477 (Ohio Ct. App. Apr. 21, 2006) (unpublished) (attorney fee provision unenforceable if parties have unequal bargaining positions, or terms of provision not freely negotiable, or provision promotes litigation or illegal acts *or* acts as a penalty; unilateral attorney fee clause in cleaning woman's employment contract was so one-sided that it encouraged litigation and acted as penalty). *See also* Vermeer, Inc. v. Argo Constr. Co., 760 N.E.2d 1 (Ohio Ct. App. 2001) (fee-shifting clauses enforceable only if the product of "free and understanding negotiation" between "parties of equal bargaining power and similar sophistication"; not shown when provision of commercial equipment lease was part of two-page "unaltered form agreement provided by the advantaged party," presented and signed at the worksite when machine was delivered).

26 Crown Food Serv. Group, Inc. v. Hughes, 1999 U.S. Dist. LEXIS 21701 (S.D. Ohio July 12, 1999) (contractual attorney fees are now enforceable under Ohio law); Buckeye Check Cashing, Inc. v. Madison, 2008 WL 4436484 (Ohio Ct. App. Oct. 2, 2008) (enforcing fee-shifting provision of payday loan contract); Hagans v. Habitat Condo. Owners Ass'n, 851 N.E.2d 544, 551 (Ohio Ct. App. 2006) (Ohio permits fee-shifting provisions in condominium declarations); Furnier & Thomas, L.L.P. v. Bus. Info. Solutions, Inc., 2002 WL 31094472 (Ohio Ct. App. Sept. 20, 2002) (fee-shifting clause in unaltered form contract was enforceable when party attacking it was a law firm "of some sophistication in the interpretation of business contracts" and no evidence that it "did not or could not participate in a free and understanding negotiation if it chose"); Kitchen v. Lake Lorelei Homeowners' Ass'n, 2002 WL 1274256 (Ohio Ct. App. June 10, 2002) (provision enforceable if fees are "fair, just and reasonable"; allowing fees to homeowners' association in action to collect fine for violation of association rule); First Capital Corp. v. G. & J. Industries, Inc., 721 N.E.2d 1084 (Ohio Ct. App. 1999) (contractual attorney fee clause enforced between commercial parties, but result may be different if parties lack equal sophistication and bargaining power); Stults & Assocs., Inc. v. United Mobile Homes, Inc., 1998 Ohio App. LEXIS 5097 (Ohio Ct. App. Oct. 14, 1998) (commercial case; contractual attorney fee provisions are enforceable absent a showing of unequal bargaining positions, misunderstanding, deception or duress; strong freedom of contract language). *See also* Taylor v. Luper, Sheriff & Niedenthal Co., 74 F. Supp. 2d 761 (S.D. Ohio 1999) (collection attorney who demanded attorney fees protected by FDCPA bona fide error defense in light of changing Ohio law).

27 *See, e.g.*, El Escorial Owners' Ass'n v. DLC Plastering, Inc., 65 Cal. Rptr. 3d 524 (Cal. Ct. App. 2007) ("inadequately documented or overbilled" fees were "penalties disguised as attorney fees"); Corvee, Inc. v. French, 943 N.E.2d 844 (Ind. Ct. App. 2011) (40% attorney fee is unenforceable liquidated damages clause; collection attorney is entitled only to reasonable fees); Wasserbauer v. Marine Midland Bank-Rochester, 400 N.Y.S.2d 979 (N.Y. Sup. Ct. 1977) (refusing to dismiss claim that percentage attorney fees were illegal as a penalty); Exch. Bank v. Appalachian Land & Lumber Co., 38 S.E. 813 (N.C. 1901) (provision for 10% attorney fee if suit is necessary is void as a penalty and as a cover for usury); K & A Cleaning, Inc. v. Materni, 2006 WL 1047477 (Ohio Ct. App. Apr. 21, 2006) (unpublished) (unilateral attorney fee clause in cleaning woman's employment contract so one-sided that it acted as a penalty and encouraged litigation). *See also* Zenner v. Holcomb, 210 P.3d 552 (Idaho 2009) (although contract for actual attorney fees will be enforced as written, prevailing party does not have "unqualified right to unlimited attorney fees"; non-prevailing party may argue that fee is unconscionable penalty). *But see* Butler v. Lembeck, 182 P.3d 1185 (Colo. App. 2007) (provision requiring tenants to reimburse landlord for "reasonable attorney fees if legal action is required due to [tenant's] actions" was enforceable and not a penalty); Austin v. Bank of Am., 743 S.E.2d 399 (Ga. 2013) (percentage-based attorney fees, allowed by since-amended statute without consideration of reasonableness or actual amount incurred, not an unconstitutional penalty even though they grossly exceeded fees actually incurred); McIntire v. Cagley, 37 Iowa 676 (Iowa 1873) (10% attorney fee reasonable and not a penalty as it was not disproportionate to expected injuries). *But cf.* Equitable Lumber Co. v. IPA Land Dev. Co., 344 N.E.2d 391 (N.Y. 1976) (30% fee not unconscionable between commercial parties; remanding for determination whether 30% was reasonable forecast of actual collection costs or commensurate with actual fees and whether it was unreasonably large).

28 *See, e.g.*, Auto. Fin. Corp. v. Ridge Chrysler Plymouth L.L.C., 219 F. Supp. 2d 945 (N.D. Ill. 2002) (penalty unenforceable even if negotiated by sophisticated parties); Easton Telecomm Servs., L.L.C. v. CoreComm Internet Group, Inc., 216 F. Supp. 2d 695 (N.D. Ohio 2002) (liquidated damages clauses enforceable if reasonable compensation for actual damages is the legitimate objective, but not when "manifestly inequitable and unrealistic" and "one-sided boilerplate provision" not the subject of bargaining); Dist. Cablevision L.P. v. Bassin, 828 A.2d 714 (D.C. 2003) (disparity of bargaining power significant, also disproportion between fee and actual cost of collection and fact that same fee applied to all breaches regardless of whether additional collection effort required); Grunwald v. Quad City Quality Serv., Inc., 662 N.W.2d 370 (Iowa Ct. App. 2003) (liquidated damages clause in employment contract was penalty); Green v. Morgan Props., 73 A.3d 478 (N.J. 2013) (refusing to dismiss UDAP claim against residential landlords alleging that attorney fee clause in lease was unreasonable; not a true liquidated damages clause when it made tenant liable for higher amount if costs of representation exceeded amount stated in clause); Truck Rent-A-Center, Inc. v. Puritan Farms 2d, Inc., 361 N.E.2d 1015 (N.Y. 1977) (contractual penalties and forfeitures are against public policy, but enforcing early termination provisions of commercial lease when actual damages unpredictable, contractual provision a reasonable estimate, and no evidence of disparity of bargaining power or unconscionability); Lake Ridge Academy v. Carney, 613 N.E.2d 183 (Ohio 1993) (provision requiring payment of full tuition for withdrawal after Aug. 1 would be enforced when actual damages difficult to calculate but estimate reasonable, no evidence of duress or unconscionability, and parties' intention clear); Phillips v. Phillips, 820 S.W.2d 785 (Tex. 1991) (measure of damages in contract is just compensation; liquidated damages enforced only if actual damages unpredictable and contract amount is "reasonable forecast").

29 Merchants Nat'l Bank v. Sevier, 14 F. 662, 663 (E.D. Ark. Cir. Ct. 1882) (refusing to enforce 10% attorney fee provision as a penalty, usurious, and at the time beyond the power of a national bank); Exchange Bank v. Appalachian Land & Lumber Co., 38 S.E. 813 (N.C. 1901) (provision for 10% attorney fee in case suit is necessary is void as a penalty and as a cover for usury); Campen Bros. v. Stewart, 145 S.E. 381, 382 (W. Va. 1928). *See also* A. Della Porta, Annotation, *Validity of provision in promissory note or other evidences of indebtedness for payment as attorneys' fees, expenses and costs of collection, of specified percentage of note*, 17 A.L.R.2d 288, 313 (1951); National Consumer Law Center, Consumer Credit Regulation § 4.8.6.3 (2012), *updated at* www.nclc.org/library.

30 *See, e.g.*, Consumers Time Credit, Inc. v. Remark Corp., 259 F. Supp. 135 (E.D. Pa. 1966) (reducing attorney fee to 5%; 15% provision in

of a case.[31] Unauthorized practice of law statutes may also be construed to prohibit recovery of attorney fees from a debtor when the creditor represents itself or acts through individuals not licensed to practice law in the jurisdiction.[32]

Some state statutes can also be construed to prohibit collection attorney fees by implication. For example, the fees and charges permitted by state small loan or consumer credit statutes are construed by some courts to be the exclusive listing of permitted charges, and thus attorney fees or other collection charges are prohibited if they are not listed.[33]

contract was an unconscionable penalty), *aff'd*, 377 F.2d 553 (3d Cir. 1967); Arfa v. Zamir, 869 N.Y.S.2d 390 (N.Y. App. Div. 2008) (one-way fee-shifting provision in attorney's retainer agreement was "fundamentally unfair and unreasonable" and against public policy). *See also* Zenner v. Holcomb, 210 P.3d 552 (Idaho 2009) (although contract for actual attorney fees will be enforced as written, prevailing party does not have "unqualified right to unlimited attorney fees"; non-prevailing party may argue that fee is unconscionable penalty). *But see* Morris v. Belfor U.S.A. Group, Inc., 201 P.3d 1253 (Colo. App. 2008) (one-way fee-shifting provision not unconscionable). *But cf.* Helm Fin. Corp. v. Iowa N. Ry. Co., 214 F. Supp. 2d 934 (N.D. Iowa 2002) (one-sided attorney fee provision not unconscionable when commercial lease was product of "tedious" negotiations, lessee's principals were experienced businessmen, and lessee failed to present evidence of alleged market shortage that made lessor only source of necessary equipment). *See generally* § 6.5.2, *infra* (requirement that attorney fees be reasonable in amount).

31 *See* Healy v. Carlson Travel Network Ass'n, Inc., 227 F. Supp. 2d 1080 (D. Minn. 2002) (boilerplate provision in franchising contract is enforceable, but denying attorney fees "in consideration of the equities and of the nature of the contract" because of franchisor's superior bargaining power and failure to adhere strictly to the contract, and fact that franchise "never got off the ground"); Alpert, Goldberg, Butler, Norton & Weiss, P.C. v. Quinn, 983 A.2d 604 (N.J. Super. Ct. App. Div. 2009) (fee-shifting provisions of law firm's retainer agreement, hidden in "master retainer agreement" that was neither provided nor explained to clients, were unenforceable); Costas v. First Fed. Sav. & Loan Ass'n, 321 S.E.2d 51 (S.C. 1984) (declining to enforce contractual attorney fee clause in light of creditor's failure to timely discover that its loan file was incomplete and in view of parties' conduct).

32 *See* § 6.2.4, *infra*.

33 *See In re* Machnic, 271 B.R. 789 (Bankr. S.D. W. Va. 2002) (only fees explicitly permitted by West Virginia Consumer and Credit Protection Act may be charged, so collection agency's attempt to collect attorney fees and costs in addition to credit card debt violates state debt collection statute); New Fin., Ltd. v. Ellis, 225 So. 2d 784 (Ala. 1969); Harbour v. Arelco, Inc., 678 N.E.2d 381 (Ind. 1997) (attorney fee provision in car rental contract is unenforceable because such fees are not on statutory list of permitted fees); Columbus Check Cashers, Inc. v. Rodgers, 2008 WL 4684781 (Ohio Ct. App. Oct. 23, 2008) (statute regulating payday lenders does not list attorney fees among permitted charges; refusing to enforce fee-shifting provision); Elsea, Inc. v. Stapleton, 1998 WL 391943 (Ohio Ct. App. July 2, 1998) (when attorney fees are not among permitted fees enumerated in retail installment sales act, inclusion of attorney fee clause in contract is violation and also violates UDAP statute); Missouri Dep't of Consumer Affairs, Regulation & Licensing, Ruling No. 31 (Dec. 5, 1974). *Cf.* Keokuk State Bank v. Eckley, 354 N.W.2d 785 (Iowa Ct. App. 1984) (attorney fees not allowed when statute makes no express mention of attorney fees). *But cf. In re* Walters, 17 B.R. 644 (Bankr. S.D. Ohio 1982) (retail installment sales act prohibition of other charges does not prohibit a provision for collection attorney fees, because statute's focus is charges imposed at time of contracting).

6.2.3 Is There a Contract with the Consumer?

When the creditor claims a right to attorney fees based on a contract, a key initial question—assuming that such a clause is valid under state law—is whether the consumer has actually entered into a contract with the creditor. For example, the creditor may be asserting a claim based on *quantum meruit* that is not based on the existence of a contract. In that case, the creditor will not need to prove the existence of a contract—and in fact may have chosen the *quantum meruit* claim because it cannot prove that a contract existed.[34]

Contractual attorney fees cannot be awarded on a *quantum meruit* claim when the creditor has not proven that the consumer entered into a contract.[35] (In addition, even if the creditor proves the existence of a contract, the clause may not apply to claims that are not based on that contract.)[36] Likewise, if a debt buyer relies on a claim such as account stated or open account[37] without proving the existence of a written contract, it will not be able to hold the consumer liable for attorney fees under a clause in that contract.[38]

34 *See* § 4.5, *supra*.

35 Uncle Henry's, Inc. v. Plaut Consulting, Inc., 270 F. Supp. 2d 67 (D. Me. 2003) (denying contractual attorney fees for company that recovered in *quantum meruit*; did not "recover under the contract"); American Prop. Maint. v. Monia, 59 S.W.3d 640 (Mo. Ct. App. 2001) (reversing award of fees pursuant to contract clause when creditor prevailed on mechanic's lien and *quantum meruit* claims but lost on contract claim). *See also* Douglas E. Barnhart, Inc. v. CMC Fabricators, Inc., 149 Cal. Rptr. 3d 440 (Cal. Ct. App. 2012) (California's reciprocal fees statute does not cover promissory estoppel, which is a substitute for a contract and which occurs without parties' consent); Sheppard v. M. & R. Plumbing, Inc., 82 So. 3d 950 (Fla. Dist. Ct. App. 2011) (plumber who recovered in *quantum meruit* not entitled to fees pursuant to construction lien state, which requires showing of a contract); Lubkey v. Compuvac Sys., Inc., 857 So. 2d 966 (Fla. Dist. Ct. App. 2003) (party who claims fees pursuant to written agreement entitled to fees only on claims based on that agreement; claimant failed to show that successful claims arose under settlement agreement with fee-shifting clause); Rental Co., L.L.C. v. Carter Group, Inc., 399 S.W.3d 63 (Mo. Ct. App. 2013) (denying fees to lender who prevailed on unjust enrichment claim but not on claims arising from notes containing fee-shifting clauses); Waters Edge Builders v. Longa, 715 S.E.2d 193 (N.C. Ct. App. 2011) (fee-shifting pursuant to construction lien statute requires showing of express or implied-in-fact contract; *quantum meruit* or implied-at-law contract not enough). *See generally* § 4.6.2, *supra*.

36 *See* § 6.2.4, *infra*.

37 *See* § 4.6, 4.7, *supra*.

38 Norfolk Fin. Corp. v. MacDonald, 2003 Mass. App. Div. 153 (Mass. Dist. Ct. 2003) (denying summary judgment for attorney fees; no evidence that consumer received credit card agreement providing for fees); Citibank v. Martin, 807 N.Y.S.2d 284 (N.Y. Civ. Ct. 2005) (debt buyer must prove an agreement to pay fees). *But cf.* Christy v. Smith Mountain, Inc., 855 So. 2d 1103 (Ala. Civ. App. 2003) (allowing creditor to go forward with claim for late charges and attorney fees disclosed in credit application and charge account agreement); Stan's Lumber, Inc. v. Fleming, 538 N.W.2d 849 (Wis. Ct. App. 1995) (fee-shifting clause in application for open account became contractual obligation once seller/creditor approved the account and debtor began making purchases). *See generally* § 4.5.5, *supra*.

Even if the creditor can show that the consumer agreed to a contract, it may not be able to establish that the consumer agreed to the fee-shifting provision.[39] For example, a clause printed on the back of an invoice or a sign posted at a store may be insufficient to create a contract.[40]

An attorney fee clause in a contract with one party may not bind a different party.[41] For example, an attorney fee clause in a lease may not apply to a non-tenant occupant or a subtenant.[42] An attorney fee clause in the principal obligor's contract may not apply to a guarantor or surety.[43]

An attorney fee clause may not survive the termination or rescission of the contract that included it.[44] However, courts

39 McCollough v. Johnson, Rodenberg & Lauinger, 587 F. Supp. 2d 1170 (D. Mont. 2008) (unauthenticated card member agreement, dated two years after consumer's last payment and eight years after opening of account, was insufficient to show consumer's assent to fee-shifting provision); Dolben Co. v. Friedmann, 2008 WL 81549 (Mass. Dist. Ct. Jan. 2, 2008) (when landlord failed to provide tenant with required signed copy of lease, fee-shifting clause was unenforceable). *See also* Roberts v. Adams, 47 P.3d 690 (Colo. App. 2001) (real estate sale contract included attorney fee clause for "litigation arising out of this contract"; promissory note silent as to attorney fees, but when note existed only as result of payment terms of sales contract, attorney fees available in suit on note); Lazy Flamingo, U.S.A., Inc. v. Greenfield, 834 So. 2d 413 (Fla. Dist. Ct. App. 2003) (in action to enforce mediated settlement agreement, failure to include fees in agreement barred attorney fees, despite fee-shifting clause in underlying contract; fees could, however, be awarded as sanction for violating settlement agreement). *But see* Lake Pointe Townhomes Owners' Ass'n v. Bruce, 900 N.E.2d 636 (Ohio Ct. App. 2008) (condominium owner bound by rules, including fee-shifting provision, even though he did not receive copy at closing; evidence showed that he knew of rules).

40 Blackie's Rental Tool & Supply Co. v. Paladin Petroleum III, L.L.C., 2013 WL 705894 (M.D. La. Feb. 26, 2013) (fact issue whether small print on delivery ticket, signed by lessee, was sufficient); Scotts Co. v. Cent. Garden & Pet Co., 256 F. Supp. 2d 734 (S.D. Ohio 2003) (non-consumer contract; fee-shifting clause preprinted on back of invoice not enforceable); Ballard v. Equifax Check Serv., 27 F. Supp. 2d 1201 (E.D. Cal. 1998) (no contract for $20 bad check charge when holder failed to show that merchant had posted signs; note that statute has since been amended to authorize $25 to $35 charges); *In re* Dixie Produce & Packaging, L.L.C., 368 B.R. 533 (Bankr. E.D. La. 2007) (attorney fee provision printed at bottom of delivery ticket does not constitute a written agreement to pay, absent showing that buyer knew or should have known of it); Whorton v. Bruce, 17 So. 3d 661 (Ala. Civ. App. 2009) (mutual assent to attorney fee and late fee provisions not shown when they were first disclosed in invoice sent after completion of work); Braylor Corp. v. MTES Operations, Inc., 2002 WL 1614115 (Cal. Ct. App. July 23, 2002) (fee-shifting clause printed on packing slips unenforceable); Ricci Drain-Laying Co. v. Baskin, 744 A.2d 406 (R.I. 1999) (homeowner never agreed to provision which was preprinted in small type at the bottom of blank form on which parties' contract was typewritten); Agway Inc. v. Brooks, 790 A.2d 438 (Vt. 2001) (attorney fee provisions not binding when they were written on back of tallies or receipts, not intended as contracts). *But see* Monsanto Co. v. David, 516 F.3d 1009 (Fed. Cir. 2008) (attorney fee provision on back of contract between farmer and manufacturer of genetically modified seed is valid, in absence of showing of fraud).

41 Register v. Gabriel, 2011 WL 6145105 (Cal. Ct. App. Dec. 12, 2011) (unpublished) (deed of trust trustee not a party to condominium agreement that allowed fee-shifting); Hyduke's Valley Motors v. Lobel Fin. Corp, 117 Cal. Rptr. 3d 19 (Cal. Ct. App. 2010) (car wholesaler who successfully sued assignee of car dealer's installment contracts not entitled to fees pursuant to fee-shifting clauses in the contracts, to which it was neither party nor third-party beneficiary); Whiteside v. Tenet Healthcare Corp., 124 Cal. Rptr. 2d 580 (Cal. Ct. App. 2002) (attorney fee clause in contract between hospital and Blue Shield did not authorize award of attorney fees against patient); Estate of Raleigh v. Mitchell, 947 A.2d 464 (D.C. 2008) (fee-shifting clause in mortgage not binding on guarantor who signed only the promissory note); Civix Sunrise GC, L.L.C. v. Sunrise Road Maint. Ass'n, Inc., 997 So. 2d 433 (Fla. Dist. Ct. App. 2008) (reference in commercial lease's fee-shifting clause to "party" meant party to the lease; denying attorney fees to third-party beneficiaries who sued to enforce lease); Fielder v. Weinstein Design Group, Inc., 842 So. 2d 879 (Fla. Dist. Ct. App. 2003) (buyer's spouse, who did not sign contract, could neither claim nor be held liable for contractual attorney fees); Snedeker v. Lighthouse Realty Group, Inc., 773 So. 2d 109 (Fla. Dist. Ct. App. 2000) (reversing fee award as to developer when contract for sale of realty provided for prevailing party fees for buyer, seller, and brokers); Harris v. Bank of Commerce, 298 P.3d 1060 (Idaho 2013) (sellers of real property unsuccessfully sued bank that purchased in good faith from buyers who had never paid purchase price; no contractual fee-shifting because bank was not party to contract with sellers); Green Harbour Homeowners' Ass'n, Inc. v. G.H. Dev. & Constr., Inc., 763 N.Y.S.2d 114 (N.Y. App. Div. 2003) (fee-shifting clause in homeowners' association covenant did not apply in litigation between owners and developer); Haynes v. Adair Homes, Inc., 206 P.3d 1062 (Or. Ct. App. 2009) (homeowners and children sued builder in tort for physical injuries resulting from breach of contract; fees awarded to homeowners but not children, who were not parties to the contract); Prairie Hills Water & Dev. Co. v. Gross, 653 N.W.2d 745 (S.D. 2002) (action to enforce subdivision covenants that included fee-shifting clause; fees allowed against lot owners but not non-owner co-defendants); Fericks v. Lucy Ann Soffe Trust, 100 P.3d 1200 (Utah 2004) (fee-shifting clause in real estate contract to which realtors were not parties did not entitle them to fees; their agency relationship with party to contract did not confer right to enforce clause for their own benefit); Agway Inc. v. Brooks, 790 A.2d 438 (Vt. 2001) (attorney fee provisions in personal account not binding on corporation); Sixty-01 Ass'n of Apartment Owners v. Parsons, 314 P.3d 1121 (Wash. Ct. App. 2013) (provisions of condominium declaration and condominium statutes allowing fee-shifting in foreclosure actions applied only to actions against defaulting owners, not against foreclosure purchaser who sought to back out of sale).

42 *See, e.g.*, Brewster Park, L.L.C. v. Berger, 14 A.3d 334 (Conn. App. Ct. 2011) (fee-shifting clause in residential lease did not apply to occupant who was explicitly permitted to occupy the unit but did not sign the lease); White v. Marshall, 83 S.W.3d 57 (Mo. Ct. App. 2002) (roommate who never signed lease not bound by fee-shifting provision); Windsor Park Nursing Home, 850 N.Y.S.2d 342 (N.Y. Sup. Ct. Jan. 10, 2008) (fee-shifting provision in contract between cooperative and members not part of contract between cooperative member and his subtenant).

43 *See, e.g.*, McCarthy Bros. Co. v. Tilbury Constr., Inc., 849 So. 2d 7 (Fla. Dist. Ct. App. 2003) (surety not liable for attorney fees pursuant to fee-shifting clause in contract between general contractor and subcontractor); MSI Fin. Group v. Veterans Constr., 645 So. 2d 178 (Fla. Dist. Ct. App. 1994) (contract provision for "all court costs and reasonable attorneys fees" covered an action for a deficiency judgment against debtor's estate but not an action against guarantor). *But cf.* Jefferson Door Co. v. Lago Dev., L.L.C., 848 So. 2d 101 (La. Ct. App. 2003) (credit application and guarantee contract, read together, made guarantor liable for attorney fees).

44 Farrell v. Whiteman, 200 P.3d 1153 (Idaho 2009) (if contract is illegal, here because architect not licensed in Idaho, neither party may recover fees pursuant to fee-shifting provision); Brown & Brown, Inc. v. Mudron, 887 N.E.2d 437 (Ill. App. Ct. 2008) (contract unenforceable because of inadequate consideration, applied to whole contract, including fee-shifting provision; denying fees to party who prevailed by

distinguish between cases in which a contract is formed, then rescinded or found unenforceable, and cases in which no contract is ever formed—for example, because of the failure of a condition precedent.[45] In addition, some states have reciprocal fee statutes that provide that, when a contract makes fees available to one party, they must also be available to the other party.[46] In these states, some courts reason that a party who prevails on a claim that a contract is unenforceable is entitled to fees because the other party, had it prevailed, would have been entitled to a fee award.[47]

6.2.4 *Interpreting Contractual Provisions for Collection Attorney Fees*

6.2.4.1 Strict Construction of Attorney Fee Clauses

Because contractual attorney fee clauses are an exception to the generally applicable American rule and are harsh in effect, most courts construe them strictly.[48] In addition, as a

---

proving contract unenforceable); Overton v. Kingsbrooke Dev., Inc., 788 N.E.2d 1212 (Ill. App. Ct. 2003) (no attorney fees when consumers successfully disaffirmed entire contract that contained fee-shifting clause). *But see* Young v. Vlahos, 929 A.2d 362 (Conn. App. Ct. 2007) (fee-shifting clause for actions based upon default survived landlord's termination of lease for tenant's default); Bauchman-Kingston P'ship v. Haroldsen, 233 P.3d 18 (Idaho 2008) (party may be awarded contractual attorney fees even if contract found unenforceable, here because property description inadequate); O'Connor v. Harger Constr., Inc., 188 P.3d 846 (Idaho 2008) (allowing fees to party who prevailed by rescinding contract; "[e]ven though the contract was unenforceable, it was a contract and had a severability clause, so the attorney fee provision is capable of enforcement"); Castleberry v. Phelan, 101 P.3d 460 (Wyo. 2004) (attorney fee clause in contract for deed continued in force after contract terminated by buyer's default, when seller did not rescind but used the remedies provided in the contract).

45 High Bid, L.L.C. v. Everett, 522 Fed. Appx. 688 (11th Cir. 2013) (fee-shifting allowed; contract not enforceable because plaintiff lacked required license; distinguishing cases in which contract never formed); Carter v. Cline, ___ S.W.3d ___, 2013 WL 5570948 (Ark. Oct. 10, 2013) (denying fee-shifting because no contract formed; condition precedent to real estate sale never occurred); Surgical Partners, L.L.C. v. Choi, 100 So. 3d 1267 (Fla. Dist. Ct. App. 2012) (denying fee-shifting when defendant prevailed in breach-of-contract action by proving that condition precedent never occurred); Tarr v. Honea, 959 So. 2d 780 (Fla. Dist. Ct. App. 2007) (prospective purchaser terminated real estate contract, as permitted by provision for inspection period, then changed mind and sought to enforce it; contractual attorney fees proper when contract had existed and litigation "arose out of" it; distinguishing cases in which no contract formed); Fabing v. Eaton, 941 So. 2d 415 (Fla. Dist. Ct. App. 2006) (fee-shifting clause survives if contract found unenforceable, but not if contract never existed, for example because of mutual mistake); Dess Props. L.L.C. v. Sheridan Truck & Heavy Equip., L.L.C., 185 P.3d 1113 (Or. Ct. App. 2008) (Or. Rev. Stat. § 20.083, which allows contractual attorney fees even if party "prevails by reason of a claim or defense asserting that the contract is in whole or in part void or unenforceable," does not apply if no contract ever formed, here because parties did not intend draft agreement to become binding). *See also* Fici v. Koon, 642 S.E.2d 602 (S.C. 2007) (party who prevailed on statute of frauds defense to real estate contract entitled to contractual attorney fees; statute barred enforcement but did not void the contract).

46 *See* § 13.1, *infra*; National Consumer Law Center, Consumer Warranty Law § 13.9 (4th ed. 2010), *updated at* www.nclc.org/library.

47 Eden Twp. Healthcare Dist. v. Eden Med. Ctr., 162 Cal. Rptr. 3d 932 (Cal. Ct. App. 2013) (counterclaim alleging that contract is invalid is an action on a contract, covered by California's reciprocal fees statute); PM Group, Inc. v. Stewart, 64 Cal. Rptr. 3d 227 (Cal. Ct. App. 2007) (party who successfully claimed that no contract had been formed entitled to fees under provision of purported contract; reciprocal fees law provides that party is entitled to fees if other party, had it prevailed, would have been entitled); MBNA Am. Bank v. Gorman, 54 Cal. Rptr. 3d 724 (Cal. Ct. App. 2006) (California's reciprocal fees law requires attorney fees for party who prevails on the ground that contract is unenforceable if other party, had it prevailed, would have been entitled to fee award); Aaron Manor, Inc. v. Irving, 57 A.3d 342 (Conn. 2013) (awarding fees to daughter who successfully defended against nursing home's claim that she was liable for mother's bills; if home had prevailed, it would have been entitled to fees); Intermountain Real Props., L.L.C. v. Draw, L.L.C., 311 P.3d 734 (Idaho 2013) (awarding fees to landowner who defeated materialman's lien by showing that he did not own the parcel to which lien attached; if plaintiff alleges the existence of a contract, defendant who shows no contract exists is entitled to fees); A. & E. Sec. & Elec. Systems v. Fortalesa Incorporation, 290 P.3d 861 (Or. Ct. App. 2012) (Oregon reciprocal fees statute explicitly applies to contracts found void; if plaintiff sues on a contract, and can recover fees if it prevails, then prevailing defendant will be entitled to fees); Bilanzich v. Lonetti, 160 P.3d 1041 (Utah 2007) (contractual attorney fees for party who invalidated contract; reciprocal fees statute requires fee award if other party, had it prevailed, would have been entitled to fees); Fairway Estates Ass'n of Apartment Owners v. Unknown Heirs, Devisees of Young, 289 P.3d 675 (Wash. Ct. App. 2012) (statute provides for mutuality of remedy; when losing party, here a condo association, would have been entitled to fees if it prevailed, prevailing party is entitled to fees). *See also* Hooban v. Unicity Int'l, Inc., 285 P.3d 766 (Utah 2010) (defendant that defeated contract claim on ground that plaintiff was not a party to the contract may seek fees under statute that authorizes fees to prevailing party in action on a contract that allows fees to "at least one party").

48 U.S. Fid. & Guar. Co. v. Baspetro Oil Servs. Co., 369 F.3d 34, 74–78 (2d Cir. 2004) (N.Y. law) (contract clause allowing attorney fees must be strictly construed; construing contractual clause allowing "legal costs" not to include attorney fees); Coastal Power Int'l, Ltd. v. Transcontinental Capital Corp., 182 F.3d 163 (2d Cir. 1999) (N.Y. law) (contractual attorney fee clause must be "unmistakably clear"); R.R. Donnelley & Sons Co. v. Vanguard Transp. Sys. Inc., 641 F. Supp. 2d 707 (N.D. Ill. 2009) (attorney fee clauses strictly construed); *In re* Parker, 269 B.R. 522 (D. Vt. 2001) (construing fee-shifting clause strictly against the writer; no attorney fees when residential lease ambiguous and adhesive); Civix Sunrise GC, L.L.C. v. Sunrise Road Maint. Ass'n, Inc., 997 So. 2d 433 (Fla. Dist. Ct. App. 2008) (fee-shifting clause must "unambiguously state" intention); Islander Beach Club Condo. v. Skylark Sports, L.L.C., 975 So. 2d 1208 (Fla. Dist. Ct. App. 2008) (fee-shifting clause in commercial lease unenforceable; when clause as written was "incomprehensible," attempt to salvage it was error; "the right to contractual attorney fees is limited by the terms of the provision, and should be strictly construed"); Chapman v. Engel, 865 N.E.2d 330 (Ill. App. Ct. 2007) (fee-shifting clauses strictly construed; when contract required fee-shifting "in the event of default by seller or buyer," court's finding that neither party to failed real estate sale had breached contract meant fee-shifting clause was never triggered); Powers v. Rockford Stop'n'Go, Inc., 761 N.E.2d 237 (Ill. App. Ct. 2001) (contractual fee-shifting clauses enforceable but will be "strictly construed and enforced at the discretion of the trial court"); Thomas v. Capital Med. Mgmt. Assocs., L.L.C., 985 A.2d 51 (Md. Ct. Spec. App. 2009) (fee-shifting clauses strictly construed); N. Bergen Rex Transp., Inc. v. Trailer Leasing Co., 730 A.2d 843 (N.J. 1999) (New Jersey law disfavors shifting of attorney fees; shifting may be authorized by contract, but provision will be strictly construed and court

general rule, any ambiguity in a contract is construed against the drafter, and it is strictly construed against the drafter if a contract of adhesion is involved.[49] Even courts that reject a general rule of strict construction require attorney fee clauses to be unambiguous and to clearly identify the matter in which fees are recoverable.[50]

6.2.4.2 Interpreting the Scope of an Attorney Fee Clause

Questions may also arise as to the scope of an attorney fee clause. A clause allowing fees for "any litigation" between the parties will be given a broad scope.[51] A clause allowing fees for any litigation "arising out of" the contract is somewhat narrower but may still apply to tort claims that relate to the contract.[52]

On the other hand, if the clause allows fees for "enforcement" of the contract, it may not apply to a successful defense of a suit or to litigation of issues that are collateral to enforcement of the contract.[53] For example, it may only apply to

will evaluate reasonableness of claimed fees); Gotham Partners v. High River L.P., 906 N.Y.S.2d 205 (N.Y. App. Div. 2010) (American rule requires that fee-shifting clause be "unmistakably clear"); Green Harbour Homeowners' Ass'n, Inc. v. G.H. Dev. & Constr., Inc., 763 N.Y.S.2d 114 (N.Y. App. Div. 2003) (reiterating American rule and narrowly construing fee-shifting clauses in agreements between homeowners and developer); IHC Health Servs., Inc. v. D. & K. Mgmt., Inc., 196 P.3d 588 (Utah 2008) (fees only "in strict accordance" with contract); Westhaven Assocs., Ltd. v. C.C. of Madison, Inc., 652 N.W.2d 819 (Wis. Ct. App. 2002) (Wisconsin follows American rule; attorney fees only if contract "clearly and unambiguously provides"); Cowardin v. Finnerty, 994 P.2d 335 (Wyo. 1999) (contractual provision for attorney fees must be explicit). *See also* Metroplex Corp. v. Thompson Indus., Inc., 2002 WL 27295 (10th Cir. Jan. 10, 2002) (Pa. law) (denying attorney fees; American rule requires contractual fee-shifting clause to be unambiguous). *But see* O'Connell v. Will, 263 P.3d 41 (Alaska 2011) (Alaska rejects American rule; fee-shifting clauses broadly construed).

49 Adkins v. Chrysler Fin. Corp., 344 Fed. Appx. 144 (6th Cir. 2009) (construing provision strictly against drafter; fee-shifting "in connection with [creditor's] rights and remedies under this agreement" did not cover common-law conversion action against secured creditor); Gray v. Am. Express Co., 743 F.2d 10 (D.C. Cir. 1984); *In re* Cmty. Med. Ctr., 623 F.2d 864 (3d Cir. 1980); R.R. Donnelley & Sons Co. v. Vanguard Transp. Sys. Inc., 641 F. Supp. 2d 707 (N.D. Ill. 2009) (construing ambiguous clause against drafter; fee-shifting provision of commercial contract was indemnity clause that did not apply in litigation between the contracting parties); *In re* Woodham, 174 B.R. 346 (Bankr. M.D. Fla. 1994) (ambiguous clauses are to be construed against the drafter, especially in contracts of adhesion; denying fees when mortgage clause was ambiguous on whether it covered bank's attorney fees in debtor's bankruptcy). *See also* Pioneer Peat, Inc. v. Quality Grassing & Servs., Inc., 653 N.W.2d 469 (Minn. Ct. App. 2002) (commercial contract; construing ambiguous provision allowing "any/all attorney fees and collection agency fees in amount of 25% or $500 whichever was applicable" against drafter; seller gets $500 after trial).

50 *See, e.g.*, Sholkoff v. Boca Raton Cmty. Hosp., 693 So. 2d 1114 (Fla. Dist. Ct. App. 1997).

51 *See, e.g.*, Ozbakir v. Scotti, 906 F. Supp. 2d 188 (W.D.N.Y. 2013) (fee-shifting clause in real estate purchase contract covering "any litigation, arbitration, or other legal proceeding that may arise between any of the parties . . ." covered fraud and RICO claims alleging misrepresentations about the value of the property); Chinn v. KMR Prop. Mgmt., 82 Cal. Rptr. 3d 586 (Cal. Ct. App. 2008) (lease provision for fee-shifting in "any legal action or proceeding brought by either party to this agreement" was broad enough to cover tort action by tenant alleging failure to protect her against foreseeable crime); Sheppard v. East, 192 S.W.3d 518 (Mo. Ct. App. 2006) (attorney fee provisions for "litigation between the parties" applied to tort and contract claims by buyers against sellers). *See also* Fitzgerald v. Schroeder Ventures II, L.L.C., 345 S.W.3d 624 (Tex. App. 2011) (fee-shifting clause that applied to "any legal proceeding . . . with relation to . . . this transaction" covered tort action alleging failure to disclose information relevant to transaction).

52 *See, e.g.*, Cruz v. Ayromloo, 66 Cal. Rptr. 3d 725 (Cal. Ct. App. 2007) (fee award proper in tort action by group of tenants, some with leases providing fee-shifting in "any civil action in connection with the lease," others with no lease; provision broad enough to include tort claims, and "incidental" benefit to no-lease tenants did not require reduction when issues were identical); Thompson v. Miller, 4 Cal. Rptr. 3d 905 (Cal. Ct. App. 2003) (whether contractual fee-shifting agreement applies to buyer's fraud and elder abuse claims depends on specific language of provision; "any dispute under this agreement" is sufficient); *In re* Estate of Gattis, 318 P.3d 549 (Colo. App. 2013) (clause requiring fee-shifting for litigation "relating to" purchase agreement covered tort action alleging failure to disclose defects); Morris v. Edmonds, 2002 WL 31631005 (Cal. Ct. App. Nov. 22, 2002) (clause in purchase agreement providing for fee-shifting "in any action, proceeding or arbitration between [sellers] and [buyers] arising out of this agreement" was broad enough to apply to tort actions, here a dispute over removal of a monument); Caufield v. Cantele, 837 So. 2d 371 (Fla. 2002) (fee-shifting clause for litigation "arising out of" contract broad enough to cover claim of fraud in the inducement); Stratakos v. Parcells, 915 A.2d 1022 (Md. Ct. Spec. App. 2007) (real estate contract provided fee-shifting for "actions arising out of this contract"; fees properly awarded when buyers unsuccessfully sued sellers alleging misrepresentations in disclosure statement, as claim would not exist in the absence of the contract); Ft. Knox Self-Storage, Inc. v. Western Technologies, Inc., 142 P.3d 1 (N.M. Ct. App. 2006) (fee-shifting for "any action in connection with" contract covered negligence claim, even though contract not breached); Rigney v. McCabe, 842 N.Y.S.2d 34 (N.Y. App. Div. 2007) (real estate contract allowed fees for action or proceeding "arising out of the contract"; fees properly awarded in fraud action alleging misrepresentations about flood risk); Posner v. Equity Title Ins. Agency, Inc., 222 P.3d 775 (Utah Ct. App. 2009) (fee-shifting "in case of the employment of an attorney in any matter arising out of this listing agreement" authorized fees in tort action for breach of fiduciary duty that related directly to sale of the listed property). *See also* Erlenbush v. Largent, 819 N.E.2d 1186 (Ill. App. Ct. 2004) (consumer who sued in tort for fraud in the inducement was entitled to fees when real estate contract provided for attorney fees in "an action . . . with respect to this contract").

53 *See, e.g.*, Holiday Org., Inc. v. Builder MT, Inc., 334 Fed. Appx. 370 (2d Cir. 2009) (provision for fees "in the event that suit or action is instituted to enforce any of [plaintiff's] obligations under this agreement" did not cover defendant's contractual counterclaims); Ocean Reef Developers, II, L.L.C. v. Maddox, 96 So. 3d 870 (Ala. Civ. App. 2012) (clause allowing fee-shifting in action "to enforce" agreement does not allow fees for builder's successful defense of action to enjoin it from drawing on letter of credit after it had breached agreement to build condo); Hous. Auth. v. Lyles, 918 N.E.2d 1276 (Ill. App. Ct. 2009) (tenant who successfully resisted eviction not entitled to fees pursuant to provision allowing fees to non-defaulting party "incurred in enforcing this lease"); McQueen v. Jordan Pines Townhomes Owners' Ass'n, Inc., 298 P.3d 666 (Utah Ct. App. 2013) (condo declaration authorized fee-shifting in actions to enforce the declaration; denying fee-shifting in quite title action, alleging that foreclosure proceeding violated state statute). *Cf.* Gibson v. Decatur Fed. Sav. & Loan Ass'n, 508 S.E.2d 788 (Ga. Ct. App. 1998) (fee-shifting clause in mortgage note, which allowed lender to shift fees in case of

contract claims, not to tort claims.[54] Some courts allow fees under such a clause for tort claims that are inextricably intertwined with contract claims.[55] Defense of the debtor's Truth in Lending Act counterclaims was not compensable under a credit card clause allowing "collection" expenses, because successful defense of such counterclaims does not entitle a creditor to collect the underlying debt.[56]

Contracts often require a party who "defaults" to pay the other party's attorney fees. Such a clause could not support a fee award when a party paid all amounts claimed, and then unsuccessfully sued for its money back, as the party had not defaulted.[57]

If the clause specifies certain types of proceedings or remedies, a court may refuse to award fees when the creditor pursues a different type.[58] The clause may not apply when

borrower's default or a step such as bankruptcy that might affect lender's interest in the property, did not allow fees for lender's declaratory judgment action to correct its mistake in marking loan "paid in full"). *But cf.* PNC Bank v. Colonial Bank, 451 Fed. Appx. 835 (11th Cir. 2012) (contract provision allowing fee-shifting in actions to enforce the contract covered defendant's successful assertion that plaintiff suffered no damages, since damages are a required element of Florida contract claim); Garrett Invs., L.L.C. v. SE Prop. Holdings, L.L.C., 2013 WL 3441768 (S.D. Ala. 2012) (provision of mortgage guarantee authorizing fee-shifting for "enforcing or protecting" lender's rights in mortgage applied to action to set aside foreclosure); Smith v. National City Mortgage, 2010 WL 5477688 (E.D. Cal. Dec. 30, 2010) (provision for fee-shifting in action to enforce a contract applies in action challenging the validity of the contract); Ellipso Inc. v. Mann, 594 F. Supp. 2d 40 (D.D.C. 2009) (attorney fee clause providing for fees if lender successfully enforced contract by suit "or otherwise" allowed recovery when lender, after foreclosure, successfully defended against borrower's lawsuit challenging its right to foreclose); *In re* Patchell, 344 B.R. 8 (Bankr. D. Mass. 2006) (mortgage provided fees for "enforcing the note"; when adversary proceeding put validity of note and mortgage in question, defending it was necessary to enforcement, so fees properly awarded); Windsor Pac., L.L.C. v. Samwood Co., 152 Cal. Rptr. 3d 518 (Cal. Ct. App. 2013) (clause allowing fee-shifting "in any action or proceeding to enforce or interpret" the contract was broad enough to cover affirmative defenses); Escambia Cnty. v. U.I.L. Family L.P., 977 So. 2d 716 (Fla. 2008) (provision for fee-shifting in "judicial action to enforce this guarantee" covered action seeking declaratory judgment as to party's rights under the agreement).

54 Adkins v. Chrysler Fin. Corp., 344 Fed. Appx. 144 (6th Cir. 2009) (fee-shifting "in connection with [creditor's] rights and remedies under this agreement" did not cover common-law conversion action against secured creditor); *In re* Chen, 345 B.R. 197 (N.D. Cal. 2006) (narrow fee-shifting clause did not apply to "independent" fraud claims raised in nondischargeability proceeding; distinguishing tort claims "closely associated" with contract); Binns v. Westminster Mem'l Park, 89 Cal. Rptr. 3d 890 (Cal. Ct. App. 2009) ("a tort claim does not enforce a contract"; denying fee-shifting in action for negligent infliction of emotional distress by son of purchaser of burial plot, alleging distress from breach of the contract); El Escorial Owners' Ass'n v. DLC Plastering, Inc., 65 Cal. Rptr. 3d 524 (Cal. Ct. App. 2007) (provision for attorney fees "in any action or proceeding brought to construe or enforce the terms of this subcontract" did not apply to tort claims); Walters v. Luloff, 176 P.3d 1034 (Mont. 2008) (fee-shifting clause in contract for deed did not authorize fees in non-contract action, here tort claim alleging misrepresentations by sellers); Ulloa v. QSP, Inc., 624 S.E.2d 43 (Va. 2006) (fee-shifting clause for "action relating to this agreement" applied to contract claim but not statutory trade secrets claim, which was independent of contract); N. Coast Elec. Co. v. Selig, 151 P.3d 211 (Wash. Ct. App. 2007) (provisions for fee-shifting "if it becomes necessary to refer any account to an attorney" not applicable to tort counterclaims alleging that creditor had filed lien on wrong building; counterclaims were independent of contract and not a defense to contract liability); Norris v. Church & Co., 63 P.3d 153 (Wash. Ct. App. 2002) (contractual attorney fees not available when consumers sued builder for fraudulent concealment of defects, a tort, not breach of contract). *See also* Am. Int'l Dev. Corp. v. Valenza Dev. Corp., 2009 WL 1682145 (Ariz. Ct. App. June 16, 2009) (unpublished) (denying fees for negligence claim that could stand alone; duty of due care existed independent of the contract). *But see* MRW, Inc. v. Big O Tires, L.L.C., 684 F. Supp. 2d 1197 (E.D. Cal. Jan. 14, 2010) (defense of tort claim, for fraud in the inducement, was necessary to enforcement of the contract); Maynard v. BTI Group, Inc., 157 Cal. Rptr. 3d 148 (Cal. Ct. App. 2013) (provision for fee-shifting in "any dispute" allowed fees to party who prevailed on negligence claim and received net judgment); Haynes v. Adair Homes, Inc., 206 P.3d 1062 (Or. Ct. App. 2009) (provision for fee-shifting if "any legal proceeding is brought under this contract" is broad enough to cover homeowners' negligence action, alleging injuries resulting from builder's breach of contract). *But cf.* Copeland-Turner v. Wells Fargo Bank, 2011 WL 5117877 (D. Or. Oct. 25, 2011) (fee-shifting clause in deed of trust, covering actions that "may significantly affect lender's rights," applied to tort claims brought by borrower after foreclosure was complete).

55 *See, e.g.*, Dolphin L.L.C. v. WCI Communities, Inc., 715 F.3d 1243, 1250–51 (11th Cir. 2013) (Florida law) (claims for UDAP and violation of Interstate Land Sales Full Disclosure Act "arose out of" sales contract because they were "inextricably intertwined" with it, so prevailing party could claim fees under contract clause even though it did not seek fees under those statutes); Au v. Funding Group, Inc., 933 F. Supp. 2d 1264 (D. Haw. 2013) (awarding fees for tort claims inextricably entwined with contract and quasi-contract claims alleging mishandling of mortgage). *See also* Total Recycling Servs. of Conn., Inc. v. Conn. Oil Recycling Servs., L.L.C., 63 A.3d 896 (Conn. 2013) (party may recover fees for all work if apportionment is impractical because the claims arise from a common nucleus and are intertwined). *But see* Tony Gullo Motors I, L.P. v. Chapa, 212 S.W.3d 299 (Tex. 2006) (stating general rule that "inextricably intertwined" facts are not sufficient for recovery of fees on claim for which fees are not otherwise available; must show that specific legal services would have been required for the fee-generating claim, even if other claim not present).

56 Langenfeld v. Bank of Am., 2009 WL 1227650 (N.D. Okla. Apr. 29, 2009).

57 P.C. Crane Serv., L.L.C. v. McQueen Masonry, Inc., 273 P.3d 396 (Utah Ct. App. 2012). *See also* Canton Plaza, Inc. v. Regions Bank, Inc., 732 S.E.2d 449 (Ga. Ct. App. 2012) (contract allowed shifting of fees "incurred in connection with the enforcement of this agreement"; denying fees for lender's successful defense of claims brought by borrowers after loan had been paid off); Chapman v. Engel, 865 N.E.2d 330 (Ill. App. Ct. 2007) (when contract required fee-shifting "in the event of default by seller or buyer," court's finding that neither party to failed real estate sale had breached contract meant fee-shifting clause was never triggered); Ledbetter v. Homes by Paige, L.L.C., 110 So. 3d 141 (La. Ct. App. 2012) (provision of purchase and sale agreement allowing fee-shifting in case of default by seller did not apply to action, after title had been transferred, alleging defects in the property); Giusti v. Sterling-Wentworth Corp., 201 P.3d 966 (Utah 2009) (provision allowing fees "in the event of default" never triggered when former employee, who unsuccessfully sued in tort and contract alleging wrongful termination, was not a defaulting party).

58 *See, e.g.*, NetJets Aviation, Inc. v. LHC Commc'ns, L.L.C., 537 F.3d 168 (2d Cir. 2008) (attorney fees recoverable in case based on contract containing valid fee-shifting provisions, but not on account stated); *In re* Hatala, 295 B.R. 62 (Bankr. D.N.J. 2003) (contract provision allowing for fees in foreclosure action did not cover fees incurred in bankruptcy case after foreclosure); *In re* I-Mind Educ. Sys., Inc., 269 B.R. 47 (Bankr. N.D. Cal. 2001) (clause in commercial lease allowing attorney fees to prevailing party in any "suit or arbitration" did not entitle lessor to attorney fees for its motion to lift the automatic stay); Estate

the debtor sues the creditor.[59] (Note, however, that some states have reciprocal fee statutes that apply one-way attorney fee clauses equally to both parties.[60]) The exact language of the clause will be critical in making these distinctions.

of Raleigh v. Mitchell, 947 A.2d 464 (D.C. 2008) (clause reading "if this note is placed in the hands of an attorney for collection after a declaration of default" is narrow; not applicable in action by shareholder's estate, challenging foreclosure of property titled in his corporation); Pici v. First Union Nat'l Bank of Fla., 705 So. 2d 50 (Fla. Dist. Ct. App. 1997) ("If you hire an attorney to collect what I owe, I agree to pay our reasonable fees" did not authorize fees for a replevin action based on a non-monetary default); Louisville Mall Assocs., L.P. v. Wood Ctr. Props., Inc., 361 S.W.3d 323 (Ky. Ct. App. Jan. 27, 2012) (provision of commercial real estate sale contract authorizing fee-shifting in action "to interpret or enforce this agreement" did not apply to action to declare parties' rights under vendor's letter of credit); Jedon Corp. v. Indus. Paint Servs., 811 N.Y.S.2d 195 (N.Y. App. Div. 2006) (provision allowing attorney fees for repossession does not authorize fees for collection action); Bauman v. Long Cove Club Owners' Ass'n, 668 S.E.2d 420 (S.C. Ct. App. 2008) (provision allowing condominium association to recover fees from "violators" did not apply to owners who unsuccessfully sought declaratory judgment but did not violate association's rules). *See also* Jancewicz v. 1721, L.L.C., 39 A.3d 782 (Conn. App. Ct. 2012) (provision authorizing fee-shifting in matter "affecting the value of the property or [lender's] rights therein" did not apply to borrower's UDAP and good faith and fair dealing claims in controversy over division of insurance proceeds for damage to the building). *But cf.* O'Malia v. Regency Builders, Inc., 662 N.W.2d 373 (table), 2003 WL 289412 (Iowa Ct. App. Feb. 12, 2003) (when contract with fee-shifting provision also referred to warranties implied by law or specifically tendered by contractor, consumers entitled to attorney fees in action for breach of express and implied warranties), *aff'd*, 668 N.W.2d 568 (Iowa 2003); Chase v. Bearpaw Ranch Ass'n, 133 P.3d 190 (Mont. 2006) (provision for fee-shifting in action "for the enforcement of these covenants" broad enough to require fees in proceeding seeking attorney fees); Weter v. Archambault, 61 P.3d 771 (Mont. 2002) (fee-shifting clause in contract for deed broad enough to allow attorney fees to seller regardless of which remedy for default chosen); Kellam Assocs., Inc. v. Angel Projects, L.L.C., 814 A.2d 642 (N.J. Super. Ct. App. Div. 2003) (clause allowed fees incurred to collect past-due rent or enforce other term breached by tenant; attorney fees allowed in dispute over construction of rent escalator clause); FLCT Loans, L.P. v. Estate of Bracher, 93 S.W.3d 469 (Tex. App. 2002) (fee-shifting if suit is filed to collect on a default; fees awarded in action against borrowers' executors challenging certain transfers of estate funds); Harsch Properties, Inc. v. Nicholas, 932 A.2d 1045 (Vt. 2007) (fees properly awarded in action alleging breach of implied covenant of good faith and fair dealing when contract's fee-shifting clause applied to actions to enforce the "terms and conditions" of contract).

59 Holiday Org., Inc. v. Builder MT, Inc., 334 Fed. Appx. 370 (2d Cir. 2009) (provision for fees "in the event that suit or action is instituted to enforce any of [plaintiff's] obligations under this agreement" did not cover defendant's contractual counterclaims); Kellogg Co. v. Sabhlok, 471 F.3d 629 (6th Cir. 2006) (employee separation agreement required attorney fees if "employee files charges"; no fee-shifting when employee filed counterclaim in employer's declaratory judgment action); Swearingen v. Haas Automation, Inc., 2010 WL 1495204 (S.D. Cal. Apr. 14, 2010) (lease provided fees "in exercising any of lessor's rights and remedies"; no fees when lessee sued lessor, even though lessor's successful defense was grounded on contractual rights); Vill. 45 Partners, L.L.C. v. Racetrac Petroleum, Inc., 831 So. 2d 758 (Fla. Dist. Ct. App. 2002) (fee-shifting clause must identify matters to which it applies; no attorney fees when contract specified "in case of any violation or attempted violation" and buyer sought declaratory judgment on question whether its proposed use of property was lawful); Greenway, Inc. v. Lynn, 2004 WL 1635881 (Ky. Ct. App. July 23, 2004) (interpreting attorney fee clause not to allow fees to party who prevailed on counterclaim rather than on complaint); Hamilton v. Hopkins, 834 So. 2d 695 (Miss. 2003) (real estate contract provided attorney fees if buyer initiated litigation; no fee-shifting when seller sued); Dobron v. Bunch, 215 P.3d 35 (Nev. 2009) (provision in guarantee agreement for fees incurred in "collecting" the loan did not authorize fees for successful defense against borrowers' usury claim); Rossman v. Windermere Owners, L.L.C., 974 N.Y.S.2d 395 (N.Y. App. Div. 2013) (no fee-shifting in tenant's action alleging rent overcharges and seeking injunction; lease allowed fee-shifting only for tenant's breach or action to regain possession); Adams v. Wash. Group, L.L.C., 855 N.Y.S.2d 569 (N.Y. App. Div. 2008) (lease provision for fees for tenant's default in connection with its performance of its lease obligations did not authorize fees when landlord successfully defended against claim of breach of implied covenant of good faith); Dupuis v. 424 E. 77th Owners' Corp., 821 N.Y.S.2d 173 (N.Y. App. Div. 2006) (lease provided for fee-shifting in case of lessee's default; no fees when co-op member sued board alleging failure to abate nuisance); Conley v. KCA Fin. Servs., Inc., 931 P.2d 808 (Or. Ct. App. 1997) (attorney fee clause in consumer contract which imposed fees "if we start a collection action" did not entitle collector to attorney fees when debtors sued it for improper collection practices and their action was dismissed for failure to state a claim). *See also* Madden v. Alaska Mortgage Group, 54 P.3d 265 (Alaska 2002) (provision in deed of trust for "costs, fees and expenses of the trustee" did not entitle beneficiary to attorney fees in action to determine amount owed). *But see* Mortensen v. Mortgage Elec. Registration Servs., Inc., 2011 WL 1675269 (S.D. Ala. May 3, 2011) (Alabama construes fee-shifting provisions in mortgages to apply whether the lender sues the borrower or defends against challenge to validity or enforceability of the mortgage); Smith v. National City Mortgage, 2010 WL 5477688 (E.D. Cal. Dec. 30, 2010) (provision for fee-shifting in action to enforce a contract applies in action challenging the validity of the contract); Whittle v. Wells Fargo Bank, 2010 WL 1854110 (E.D. Cal. May 6, 2010) (mortgage and deed of trust provided for attorney fees if lender accelerated; borrower's unsuccessful efforts to enjoin foreclosure were sufficiently intertwined with contract to support attorney fees); Ellipso Inc. v. Mann, 594 F. Supp. 2d 40 (D.D.C. 2009) (attorney fee clause providing for fees if lender successfully enforced contract by suit "or otherwise" allowed recovery when lender, after foreclosure, successfully defended against borrower's lawsuit challenging its right to foreclose); *In re* Patchell, 344 B.R. 8 (Bankr. D. Mass. 2006) (mortgage provided fees for "enforcing the note"; when adversary proceeding put validity of note and mortgage in question, defending it was necessary to enforcement, so fees properly awarded); Esposito v. Riviera at Freehold Homeowners' Ass'n, 2011 WL 2566171 (N.J. Super. Ct. App. Div. June 30, 2011) (upholding fee award to homeowners' association that prevailed in declaratory judgment action that homeowners filed in response to association's threat to sue, even though contract allowed fees only if homeowners' association "institutes any action"); Hahnel v. Duchesne Land, L.L.C., 305 P.3d 208 (Utah Ct. App. 2013) (seller that successfully defended against buyer's breach-of-contract claim is entitled to fees under clause allowing fees for enforcement of the contract); Rappaport v. Four Lakes Vill. Homeowners' Ass'n, 300 P.3d 327 (Utah Ct. App. 2013) (clause allowing fee-shifting if condominium association "takes judicial action to enforce compliance" covered association's successful defense against homeowner's action). *But cf.* Rand v. Porsche Fin. Servs., 167 P.3d 111 (Ariz. Ct. App. 2007) (automobile lease provided attorney fees if lessor hires lawyer "to collect what you owe"; fees properly awarded on lessor's counterclaim for deficiency in lessee's tort and civil rights action alleging repossession misconduct).

60 *See* § 13.1, *infra*; National Consumer Law Center, Consumer Warranty Law § 13.9 (4th ed. 2010), *updated at* www.nclc.org/library.

A number of courts have held that the creditor is not entitled to fees for work that its attorney anticipates having to perform but has not yet performed, and to demand such fees may violate the Fair Debt Collection Practices Act (FDCPA).[61] An advance award of fees to take into account possible difficulties in collecting the judgment is error when the contract makes the debtor liable for fees that are "paid or incurred" by the creditor.[62]

Creditors may not be allowed to recover expenses of non-attorneys working for the collection attorney[63] or dunning activities by an attorney.[64] Some courts refuse to award fees when a creditor represents itself, either *pro se* or through in-house counsel, rather than hiring an outside attorney,[65] or when the creditor's attorney is not licensed in the jurisdiction.[66] A federal district court refused to dismiss a claim that a debt buyer was not entitled to attorney fees under a credit card agreement that allowed fees if the account was referred to an independent attorney, when the debt buyer was a limited liability company owned by the same seven attorneys to whose law firm the account was referred.[67] A clause that allows fees for "enforcement" of an obligation may not entitle a party to fees for attempts to negotiate a settlement of a collection action.[68]

61 *See* § 6.1, *supra*.

62 NCEF, L.L.C. v. Hendricks Bldg. Supply L.L.C., 2010 WL 4677772 (S.D. Ala. Nov. 8, 2010) (when lease provided for "lessor's costs of enforcing lessor's rights," award of future collection expenses would be "sheer speculation"; awarding attorney fees only in amount shown to have been already incurred); Akula v. Airbee Wireless, 2009 WL 122795 (E.D. Va. Jan. 14, 2009) (denying fees for "reasonably anticipated" costs of collection after default judgment because fees too speculative; creditor may apply again if fees actually incurred), *adopted by* 2009 WL 1248116 (E.D. Va. Apr. 30, 2009); Agri Credit Corp. v. Liedman, 337 N.W.2d 384 (Minn. 1983) (interpreting contract to allow creditor to recover fees only after they have been incurred); Naugatuck Sav. Bank v. Gross, 625 N.Y.S.2d 572 (N.Y. App. Div. 1995) (should not include fees "for anticipated future services which may be performed in enforcing the judgment").

63 *See* Walton v. Franklin Collection Agency, Inc., 1999 WL 33537147 (N.D. Miss. May 5, 1999) (consumers stated FDCPA claim with allegation that collector demanded and obtained judgments for attorney fees when in fact most of the work was done by collector's non-lawyer employees, who prepared and filed complaints that retained attorney signed; no discussion of whether fee claim was based on statute or contract). *But cf.* Blair v. Ing, 31 P.3d 184 (Haw. 2001) (attorney fees may include hours for law clerks' or paralegals' legal work, such as research and cite checking, but not their secretarial work, such as phone calls and document preparation); Med. Recovery Servs. v. Jones, 175 P.3d 795 (Idaho Ct. App. 2007) (fees may be awarded for paralegal's services); All Seasons Window & Door Mfg., Inc. v. Red Dot Constr., 181 S.W.3d 490 (Tex. App. 2005) (to recover for paralegals' and legal assistants' work, must show "substantive legal work" under supervision of attorney, hours worked, and hourly rate); North Coast Elec. Co. v. Selig, 151 P.3d 211 (Wash. Ct. App. 2007) (fees recoverable for legal work by legal assistants working under supervision of lawyer but not for "purely clerical" secretarial services). *See generally* § 6.6, *infra*.

64 Reichert v. Nat'l Credit Sys., Inc., 531 F.3d 1002 (9th Cir. 2008) (when contract authorized prevailing party fees "in the event of legal action," only fees "incurred in successful litigation" could be recovered; demanding attorney fees, when all attorney did was write a letter, violated FDCPA); Wetherbee v. Kusterer, 41 Mich. 359, 360 (Mich. 1879) ("the clause in the contract relative to costs and expenses does not apply to ordinary dunning"). *See also* Mechanics'-American Nat'l Bank v. Coleman, 204 F. 24 (8th Cir. 1913) (contractual attorney fees would not be awarded when the attorney only provided advice to the creditor and there was no suit; note, however, that the Eighth Circuit held in *In re* Morris, 602 F.2d 826 (8th Cir. 1979) that this decision wrongly relied on federal common law instead of Arkansas law); Myer v. Hart, 40 Mich. 517 (1879) (refusing to enforce such a clause for an attorney's expenses incurred prior to a power of sale foreclosure). *But see* Shapiro v. Riddle & Assocs., P.C., 351 F.3d 63 (2d Cir. 2003) (no FDCPA violation for attorney collector to demand $98 for collection letter when contract allowed the reasonable costs of collection); Monroe v. Staser, 33 N.E. 665 (Ind. Ct. App. 1893) (requiring reimbursement for attorney's efforts short of suit). *But cf.* Dole v. Wade, 510 S.W.2d 909 (Tenn. 1974) (assuming that fees for pre-suit work can be allowed when note provides for fees if placed in hands of attorney for collection, but rejecting claim for fees based on percentage of debt).

65 Fed. Deposit Ins. Corp. v. Bender, 182 F.3d 1 (D.C. Cir. 1999) (fees not available for in-house counsels' service as liaison with Justice Department attorneys who actually tried case); D'Elia v. First Capital, L.L.C., 2008 WL 4344571 (N.D. Ill. Mar. 19, 2008) (refusing to dismiss FDCPA claim; when same person was sole manager and equity owner of debt buyer and law firm it employed to collect, fact question whether attorney fees, owed arguably to itself, were "incurred"; issue whether observance of corporate forms would sanction a fraud or promote injustice); Bank of Woodland v. Treadwell, 55 Cal. 379 (Cal. 1880) (creditor not entitled to $100 counsel fees provided in contract when it used an employee attorney and the cost of the attorney's services could not be apportioned to this suit); Santa Rosa KM Assocs., P.C. v. Principal Life Ins. Co., 206 P.3d 40 (Kan. Ct. App. 2009) (Kan. Stat. Ann. § 58-2313, amended to eliminate ban on fee-shifting provisions in credit agreements, still forbids inclusion of costs incurred by salaried employee of creditor or assignee); Lambert v. Byron, 650 So. 2d 1201 (La. Ct. App. 1995) (note provided for attorney fees only if "placed in the hands of" or "referred to" an attorney); Thomas & Thomas Court Reporters, L.L.C. v. Switzer, 810 N.W.2d 677 (Neb. 2012) (*pro se* litigant cannot obtain fees, even if he is a licensed attorney); Stream v. CBK Agronomics, 48 A.D.2d 637 (N.Y. 1975); Thompson v. Chem. Bank, 375 N.Y.S.2d 729 (N.Y. Civ. Ct. 1975) (statute prohibiting all additional charges except "actual expenditures" for attorney fees did not allow attorney fee award to bank using in-house counsel). *See also* Seeger v. AFNI, Inc., 548 F.3d 1107 (7th Cir. 2008) (neither contract nor Wisconsin law entitled new owner of debt to collection fee that would be payable to itself, not third-party collector); Tenn. Att'y Gen. Op. No. 14, Pov. L. Rep. ¶ 25,494 (Sept. 7, 1977); *In re* Thompson, 174 N.Y. L.J. No. 52, p.8, Clearinghouse No. 16,597 (N.Y. Civ. Ct. 1975) (bank could not recover and retain attorney fees on default judgments obtained by its staff attorneys without engaging in the unauthorized practice of law). *But see* Vaughters v. Outlaw, 668 S.E.2d 13 (Ga. Ct. App. 2008) (allowing attorney fees when lawyer brought collection action *pro se*); Lockard v. Newman, 984 N.E.2d 259 (Ind. Ct. App. Feb. 20, 2012) (unpublished) (lawyer who represented self entitled to fees pursuant to retainer agreement that authorized collection costs, including attorney fees); Main St. Bldg. P'ship v. Hernandez, 844 N.Y.S.2d 617 (N.Y. Dist. Ct. 2007) (fee-shifting proper when landlord, a general partnership, was represented by attorney-partner); AMX Enters. L.L.P. v. Master Realty Corp., 283 S.W.3d 506 (Tex. App. 2009) (allowing recovery of fees for services of in-house counsel, but noting paucity of case law on method of calculation; choosing market rate and rejecting cost-plus).

66 Cheshire Academy v. Lee, 448 N.Y.S.2d 112 (N.Y. Civ. Ct. 1982) (refusing to award attorney fees pursuant to contract clause when creditor's attorney, although licensed in New York, did not maintain an office there and thus was not allowed to practice law there).

67 Ketchem v. Am. Acceptance Co., 641 F. Supp. 2d 782 (N.D. Ind. 2008).

68 Banca Della Svizzera Italiana v. Cohen, 756 F. Supp. 805 (S.D.N.Y. 1991) (commercial case).

6.2.4.3 Fees for Postjudgment Legal Work

Another question is whether attorney fees are available for an appeal or other postjudgment legal work. After a judgment is rendered, the cause of action on the contract may be considered to have merged with the judgment, so that the creditor can no longer avail itself of an attorney fee clause in the contract but instead is limited to the postjudgment remedies, such as postjudgment interest, that are provided by statute.[69] However, a number of courts have awarded fees for appeals[70] or for postjudgment enforcement[71] under a contract clause, usually without considering this theory.

6.2.4.4 References to "Costs"

Many courts refuse to award attorney fees when the contract only allows "costs and expenses" or "costs of collection" and does not specifically mention attorney fees.[72] This position is consistent with the general rule that attorney fee clauses must be entirely unambiguous and that they must be strictly construed.[73]

---

69 *See, e.g.*, Accubid Excavation, Inc. v. Kennedy Contractors, Inc., 981 A.2d 727 (Md. Ct. Spec. App. 2009) (contract provision cannot authorize fees after judgment, at which time contract has merged with judgment); Monarc Constr., Inc. v. Aris Corp., 981 A.2d 822 (Md. Ct. Spec. App. 2009) (same); Citizens Bank v. Landers, 570 S.W.2d 756, 765 (Mo. Ct. App. 1978) (bank's cause of action on note was merged with the judgment). *But see* Jaffe v. Pacelli, 82 Cal. Rptr. 3d 423 (Cal. Ct. App. 2008) (if a judgment includes contractual attorney fees, creditor is entitled to reasonable attorney fees incurred to collect the judgment, here by successfully seeking dismissal of debtor's bankruptcy case).

70 *See, e.g.*, Butler-Rupp v. Lourdeaux, 65 Cal. Rptr. 3d 242 (Cal. Ct. App. 2007) (appellate attorney fees permitted by California law and contractual fee-shifting clause); Indian Springs, L.L.C. v. Indian Springs Land Inv., L.L.C., 215 P.3d 457 (Idaho 2009) (assignee of mortgage and note, which contained fee-shifting provisions, entitled to attorney fees on appeal); First State Bank of St. Charles, Mo. v. Frankel, 86 S.W.3d 161 (Mo. Ct. App. 2002) (remanding to determine amount of attorney fees on appeal when contract provided for reasonable attorney fees incurred in enforcement); Bechtle v. Tandy Corp., 77 S.W.3d 689 (Mo. Ct. App. 2002) (commercial lease provision for attorney fees "incurred in enforcing this lease" required award of fees for post-trial motions and appeal); R.C. Hobbs Enters., L.L.C. v. J.G.L. Distrib., Inc., 104 P.3d 503 (Mont. 2004) (if contract provided for attorney fees, prevailing party entitled to appellate attorney fees if attorney fees awarded below); Prof'l Credit Collections v. Smith, 933 P.2d 307 (Okla. 1997) (consumer who prevailed on appeal is entitled to appellate fees under fee-shifting statute); Pannos v. Olson & Assocs. Constr., Inc., 123 P.3d 816 (Utah Ct. App. 2005) (real estate contract that provided for costs and reasonable attorney fees in "litigation to enforce this contract" included attorney fees on appeal); Thompson v. Lennox, 212 P.3d 597 (Wash. Ct. App. 2009) (fee-shifting clause in contract, here a restrictive covenant in a deed, entitles prevailing party to fees on appeal). *Cf.* LINC Fin. Corp. v. Onwuteaka, 129 F.3d 917 (7th Cir. 1997) (Ill. Law) (fee-shifting clause in commercial lease covering "all commercially reasonable costs and expenses incurred by [lessor] in enforcing [its] rights under this lease . . . including reasonable attorney's fees" enforced to allow costs and attorney fees at trial and on appeal).

71 *See, e.g.*, Limbright v. Hofmeister, 2012 WL 984276 (E.D. Ky. Mar. 22, 2012) (attorney fee clause in guarantee agreement covered fees incurred in collecting judgment against guarantors); O'Connell v. Will, 263 P.3d 41 (Alaska 2011) (provision authorizing attorney fees incurred in "a suit or action" covered postjudgment enforcement action; note that Alaska liberally construes fee-shifting provisions).

72 U.S. Fid. & Guar. Co. v. Baspetro Oil Servs. Co., 369 F.3d 34, 74–78 (2d Cir. 2004) (N.Y. law) (construing contractual clause allowing "legal costs" not to include attorney fees); Lockett v. Freedman, 2004 WL 856516 (N.D. Ill. Apr. 21, 2004) ("costs" does not include attorney fees; FDCPA violation to demand attorney fees under clause that referred to costs but was silent as to attorney fees); Benderson-Wainberg, L.P. v. Atlantic Toys, Inc., 228 F. Supp. 2d 584 (E.D. Pa. 2002) ("all costs . . . incurred . . . in the collection of any amounts owed" does not include attorney fees); Zosman v. Schiffer/Taxis, Inc., 697 So. 2d 1018 (Fla. Dist. Ct. App. 1997) (clause in contract providing for "all costs actually incurred in collecting overdue accounts," did not provide for attorney fees); Doss & Assocs. v. First Am. Title Ins. Co., ___ S.E.2d ___, 2013 WL 6511566 (Ga. Ct. App. Dec. 13, 2013) (provision requiring payment for "loss, cost and damage" is not an express provision for fee-shifting); Arbor Station Homeowners' Servs., Inc. v. Dorman, 567 S.E.2d 102 (Ga. Ct. App. 2002) (attorney fees not recoverable under provision allowing "costs of collection"); Negro Nest L.L.C. v. Mid-Northern Mgmt., Inc., 839 N.E.2d 1083 (Ill. App. Ct. 2005) (contract provision for "all collection costs incurred" does not allow attorney fees); Midland Prop. Partners, L.L.C. v. Watkins, 2013 WL 5904617 (Mo. Ct. App. Nov. 5, 2013) (provision for "all reasonable costs" incurred in collection or enforcing payment does not authorize fee-shifting); Watertown Sav. Bank v. Delaney, 876 N.Y.S.2d 603 (N.Y. Sup. Ct. 2009) (general term "costs" does not include attorney fees); Hagans v. Habitat Condo. Owners Ass'n, 851 N.E.2d 544, 552 (Ohio Ct. App. 2006); Arrowhead Ridge I, L.L.C. v. Cold Stone Creamery, Inc., 800 N.W.2d 730 (S.D. 2011) (clause that referred to "all taxes, charges, costs and expenses" and "all damages, costs, expenses and sums . . . that landlord may incur by reason of tenants' default" but did not use the words "attorney fees" did not authorize fee-shifting); Cracker Barrel Old Country Store v. Epperson, 284 S.W.3d 303 (Tenn. 2009) (provision for "costs" or "expenses" not explicit enough to override American rule; fee-shifting clause must specify "reasonable attorney fees"); Cowardin v. Finnerty, 994 P.2d 335 (Wyo. 1999) (clauses in purchase and sale agreement allowing non-defaulting party to "recover such damages as may be proper," and requiring return of earnest money "less costs incurred by sellers" if sale fell through, not specific enough to support award of attorney fees). *See also* M.D. Mark, Inc. v. Kerr-McGee Corp., 565 F.3d 753 (10th Cir. 2009) (Colo. law) ("any loss . . . resulting from or relating to any breach" does not encompass attorney fees); Fontana v. TLD Builders, 840 N.E.2d 767 (Ill. App. Ct. 2005) (contract authorizing party to "retain an attorney to assist in the enforcement" and authorizing recovery from "the party at fault" of "any and all reasonable expenses related to enforcement" did not authorize attorney fees); Thomas v. Capitol Med. Mgmt. Assocs., L.L.C., 985 A.2d 51 (Md. Ct. Spec. App. 2009) (contract must "specifically authorize" attorney fees; not shown when fees not mentioned in paragraph dealing with default). *But see* Sloan & Co. v. Liberty Mut. Ins. Co., 653 F.3d 175 (3d Cir. 2011) (Pa. law) (phrase "expenses and costs" in contract provision dealing with lawsuits and dispute resolution included attorney fees); Vaughters v. Outlaw, 668 S.E.2d 13 (Ga. Ct. App. 2008) (provision for "any and all reasonable costs for expenses and costs related to any collection efforts made necessary by delinquencies" is sufficient to authorize attorney fees). *But cf.* Peace River Seed Co-op, Ltd. v. Proseeds Mktg., 293 P.3d 1058 (Or. Ct. App. 2012) (words "costs of collection" in contract for sale of seeds are ambiguous; remanding to determine intent of parties as to fee-shifting), *rev. granted*, 300 P.3d 1222 (Or. 2013). *See generally* § 6.3.1, *infra* (interpretation of authorization of "costs" in statutes).

73 *See* § 6.2.4.1, *supra*.

If the contract provides for both attorney fees and costs, some courts hold that "costs" must be construed to be consistent with a state statute that specifies what court costs the losing party must bear.[74] Thus, such clauses cannot shift costs, such as expert witness fees and mailing, faxing, and photocopying expenses, which the statute does not require the losing party to pay.

6.3 State Statutes Allowing Recovery of Attorney Fees Regardless of Contract Terms

6.3.1 Construction of State Fee-Shifting Statutes

Several states permit recovery of collection attorney fees in certain circumstances, even when such fees are not authorized by the consumer credit contract. Some of these states provide that the debtor may avoid fees by paying the amount demanded in a pre-suit notice within a certain number of days. These statutes do not depend on the existence of a fee-shifting clause in the contract, and their requirements may be inapplicable to contractual fees.[75]

Because statutes allowing attorney fees are in derogation of the common law rule, courts may construe them strictly.[76] Courts construe statutes that assess "costs" or "damages" against the losing party not to encompass attorney fees.[77]

6.3.2 Statutes Allowing Fees for Suit on "Account Stated" or Open Account

A few states allow an attorney fee award in a suit on an "account stated" or "open account." The elements of these causes of action are discussed in §§ 4.6 and 4.7, *supra*. Some of these statutes also include attorney fee provisions, discussed in § 6.3.3, *infra*, that apply more broadly to contracts.

Arkansas provides that the prevailing party is entitled to fees in any civil action to recover on, *inter alia*, an open account, statement of account, or account stated.[78]

Idaho allows attorney fees to the prevailing party in any civil action to recover on an open account or account stated.[79]

Louisiana allows reasonable fees when a debtor fails to pay an open account within thirty days after the claimant sends a written demand correctly setting forth the amount owed.[80]

---

74 Toll Bros., Inc. v. Chang Su-O Lin, 2009 WL 1816993 (N.D. Cal. June 25, 2009) (applying federal statute to determine what costs recoverable; disallowing courier, mail, phone, and fax costs; allowing copying costs only if used in court or provided to opposing counsel); Kirk v. Gobel, 622 F. Supp. 2d 1039 (E.D. Wash. 2009) (even if contract allows for costs, demand for fee for unregistered process server was improper). *See also* Ripley v. Pappadopoulos, 28 Cal. Rptr. 2d 878 (Cal. Ct. App. 1994) (courts award of costs can only include items allowed by statute, regardless of parties' agreement). *Cf.* Ahwatukee Custom Estates Mgmt. v. Bach, 973 P.2d 106 (Ariz. 1999) (construing fee-shifting statute to allow award only of attorney fees and taxable costs, not other litigation expenses); First Nationwide Bank v. Mountain Cascade, Inc., 92 Cal. Rptr. 2d 145 (Cal. Ct. App. 2000) (court's cost award can only include items authorized by statute; if agreement allows recovery of other expenses, parties must plead and prove them). *But see* Monsanto Co. v. David, 516 F.3d 1009 (Fed. Cir. 2008) ("costs" in attorney fee clause may exceed those allowed as costs under federal statute); Bernhard-Thomas Bldg. Sys. L.L.C. v. Weitz Co., 2011 WL 5222682 (D. Conn. Oct. 31, 2011) (when contract allows shifting of "all attorney fees, expert fees, court costs, and all other third-party costs of litigation," federal rule specifying what costs are recoverable does not apply); Armada Bulk Carriers v. ConocoPhillips Co., 505 F. Supp. 2d 621 (N.D. Cal. 2007) ("all costs and expenses (including reasonable attorney fees)" was broad enough to include expert witness fees); Chase v. Scott, 38 P.3d 1001 (Utah Ct. App. 2001) (when contract included provision for costs and attorney fees, costs are not limited to those available under court rules; otherwise contractual provision would be superfluous).

75 Jesperson v. Sweetwater Ranch Apartments, 390 S.W.3d 644 (Tex. App. 2012) (attorney fee clause in residential lease allows lessor to receive attorney fees, despite lack of thirty-day pre-suit notice required for statutory fee-shifting).

76 Specialty Beverages L.L.C. v. Pabst Brewing Co., 537 F.3d 1165 (10th Cir. 2008) (Okla. Law) (narrowly interpreting statutory authorization for attorney fees); Saltzman v. Hadlock, 112 So. 3d 772 (Fla. Dist. Ct. App. 2013); Negro Nest, L.L.C. v. Mid-Northern Mgmt., Inc., 839 N.E.2d 1083, 1085, 1090 (Ill. App. Ct. 2005); Savant Ins. Servs., Inc. v. Central Oil & Supply Corp., 821 So. 2d 623 (La. Ct. App. 2002) (statute allowing attorney fees for open account is penal and must be strictly construed). *But see* O'Connell v. Will, 263 P.3d 41 (Alaska 2011) (Alaska rejects American rule; statutory or contractual fee-shifting provisions broadly construed); Turner v. Schultz, 96 Cal. Rptr. 3d 659 (Cal. Ct. App. 2009) (California liberally construes statute authorizing fee-shifting in action on contract; allowing fee-shifting in declaratory judgment action brought to determine meaning of contract clause, even though no prevailing party yet in underlying contract action); Discover Bank v. Barnes, 294 P.3d 453 (Okla. Civ. App. 2012) ("[e]xceptions to the American Rule are narrowly defined, because attorney fee awards against the non-prevailing party have a chilling effect on access to the courts," but noting that fee-shifting statutes may promote settlement; garnishee was prevailing party entitled to recover fees under garnishment statute when judgment creditor sued it but then abandoned the garnishment).

77 Linebarger v. Owenby, 83 S.W.3d 435 (Ark. Ct. App. 2002) (statutory provision for "costs" does not include attorney fees); People v. United States Fire Ins. Co., 149 Cal. Rptr. 3d 196 (Cal. Ct. App. 2012); Scion Breckenridge Managing Member, L.L.C. v. ASB Allegiance Real Estate Fund, 68 A.3d 665 (Del. 2013); Dessart v. Burak, 678 N.W.2d 615 (Mich. 2004) (term "costs" or "assessable costs" in a statute or court rule does not include attorney fees unless the term is explicitly defined to include them); Nemeth v. Abonmarche Dev. Co., 576 N.W.2d 641 (Mich. 1998) (environmental protection statute allowing court to apportion "costs" does not authorize shifting of attorney fees); Columbus Check Cashers, Inc. v. Rodgers, 2008 WL 4684781 (Ohio Ct. App. Oct. 23, 2008) ("damages, costs or disbursements" in statute prescribing permitted charges for payday loans not specific enough to authorize attorney fees in derogation of common law American rule). *See also* Dave v. Valdez, 275 P.3d 485 (Wyo. 2012) (statutory exception to American rule arises only if statute is explicit; statutory provision for "damages" is insufficient). *But see* Schweitzer v. Salamatof Air Park Subdivision Owners, Inc., 308 P.3d 1142, 1150 (Alaska 2013) (in Alaska statutes, the word "costs" generally includes attorney fees). *See generally* § 6.2.4.4, *supra* (interpretation of "costs" in attorney fee clauses).

78 Ark. Code Ann. § 16-22-308.

79 Idaho Code Ann. § 12-120(3). *See* Bingham Mem'l Hosp. v. Boyd, 8 P.3d 664 (Idaho Ct. App. 2000) (reversing award of attorney fees because hospital won judgment on *quantum meruit* rather than on open account). *See also* § 6.3.3, *infra* (discussion of this statute's more general provision of fees for contract claims).

80 La. Rev. Stat. Ann. § 9:2781(A). *See* Gold, Weems, Bruser, Sues & Rundell v. Metal Sales Mfg. Corp., 236 F.3d 214 (5th Cir. 2000) (La.

If, however, the claimant and the claimant's attorney have agreed on a fixed or determinable amount of attorney fees, the claimant is entitled to that amount, and no written demand is required.[81]

A *Mississippi* statute provides that a person who fails to pay an open account within thirty days of a written demand setting forth the correct amount with an itemized statement is liable for reasonable attorney fees.[82] An alleged debtor who prevails is also entitled to fees.[83]

New Mexico allows a reasonable attorney fee to the prevailing party in any civil action in district court, small claims court, or magistrate court on an open account.[84]

Oklahoma allows a reasonable attorney fee to the prevailing party in a civil action to recover on an open account, statement of account, or account stated.[85]

Texas allows recovery of attorney fees for a valid claim for rendered services, performed labor, furnished materials, or a sworn account.[86]

Many of these statutes specifically provide that fees are available only if the creditor sends a pre-suit demand. The creditor may lose its right to fees altogether if its demand for payment of the open account includes any charges that are not in fact owed.[87]

---

law) (attorney fees allowed for appeals and for representation by lawyer-employees under state open account statute); Tri-Parish Elec. Supply, Inc. v. Cypress Bend Inv., L.L.C., 105 So. 3d 1036 (La. Ct. App. 2012) (allowing fee-shifting; contract for building materials was open account, when materials ordered as needed, and amount needed was uncertain at time of contracting); Spectrum Auto. Finishers, Inc. v. Westbank Body Works, Inc., 27 So. 3d 875 (La. Ct. App. 2009) (open account sufficiently shown when series of numbered invoices showed "running dealings"); *In re* Troth Corp. v. Deutsch, Kerrigan & Stiles, L.L.P., 951 So. 2d 1162 (La. Ct. App. 2007) (when amount owed correctly stated and supported by invoices, creditor entitled to fees; amount discretionary with court; criteria include liable party's ability to pay); Wright & Moreno L.L.C. v. Clement, 891 So. 2d 704 (La. Ct. App. 2004) (Louisiana allows attorney fees for account stated thirty days after demand or fifteen days after filing petition, before which debtor may pay without incurring fees); Paddison Builders, Inc. v. Newpark Square One Condo. Ass'n, 848 So. 2d 750 (La. Ct. App. 2003) (contract for single project not open account; Louisiana requires "running or current" dealings or expectation of future work); Acadian Servs., Inc. v. Durand, 813 So. 2d 1142 (La. Ct. App. 2002) (transactions were open account when demolition contractor performed two jobs for homeowner, sent invoices but did not expect immediate payment, and anticipated further work on the same ongoing project); Hayes v. Taylor, 812 So. 2d 874 (La. Ct. App. 2002) ($1000 collection attorney fee for default judgment on an open account); Sears, Roebuck & Co. v. Richardson, 759 So. 2d 190 (La. Ct. App. 2000) (credit card account was open account, so 25% attorney fees allowed); Broussard v. Guilbeaux, 640 So. 2d 509 (La. Ct. App. 1994).

81 La. Rev. Stat. Ann. § 9:2781(A).

82 Miss. Code Ann. § 11-53-81. *See* T. Jackson Lyons & Assocs., P.A. v. Precious T. Martin, Sr., & Assocs. P.L.L.C., 87 So. 3d 444 (Miss. 2012) (allowing fees; agreement for provision of legal services was open account); Franklin Collection Serv., Inc. v. Stewart, 863 So. 2d 925 (Miss. 2003) (medical bill was open account for which statute allowed attorney fee; one-third contingent fee presumptively reasonable); Par Indus. v. Target Container Co., 708 So. 2d 44 (Miss. 1998) (fees must be reasonable; one-third of the amount of a non-consumer debt was reasonable); Hickman v. Citibank, 89 So. 2d 691 (Miss. Ct. App. 2012) (allowing fee-shifting; credit card is open account).

83 Miss. Code Ann. § 11-53-81.

84 N.M. Stat. Ann. § 39-2-2.1.

85 Okla. Stat. tit. 12, § 936. *See also* § 6.3.3, *infra* (discussion of this statute's provision of fees for contract claims).

86 Tex. Civ. Prac. & Rem. Code Ann. § 38.001 (West). *See* Citibank (South Dakota), NA v. Durden, 2012 WL 6096569 (Tex. App. Dec. 7, 2012) (credit card is open account; awarding fees to creditor); Busch v. Hudson & Keyse, L.L.C., 312 S.W.3d 294 (Tex. App. May 11, 2010) (open account proper cause of action for credit card debt; consumer's admission that she received demand letter sufficient to show presentment); Williams v. Unifund Partners, 264 S.W.3d 231 (Tex. App. 2008) (action on "sworn account" will lie only for sales of personal property, not "special contracts," here a bank credit card, when no personal property passed from bank to consumer); Pennwell Corp. v. Ken Assocs., Inc., 123 S.W.3d 756 (Tex. App. 2003) (elements of account stated are goods or services provided, price is either agreed upon or "usual, customary and reasonable," and account unpaid); Elhamed v. Quality Oil Trucking Serv., Inc., 2003 WL 22211543 (Tex. App. Sept. 25, 2003) (open account; burden on creditor to show reasonable charges; sufficient if it charged same amount to others for same services and materials at same time and place); Andrews v. E. Tex. Med. Ctr., 885 S.W.2d 264 (Tex. App. 1994) (open account shown when hospital provided itemized bill and testimony that charges were customary). *See also* § 6.3.3, *infra* (discussion of this statute's provision of fees for contract claims).

87 Dixie Produce & Packaging, L.L.C., 368 B.R. 533 (Bankr. E.D. La. 2007) (attorney fees under open account statute only if demand "strictly and exactly" states amount due; denying fee-shifting when seller demanded interest to which it was not entitled); Salley & Salley v. Stoll, 864 So. 2d 698 (La. Ct. App. 2003) (denying attorney fees when statute required demand for correct amount and creditor demanded late charges and interest not provided for in contract); Heck v. LaFourche Parish Council, 860 So. 2d 595 (La. Ct. App. 2003) (denying attorney fees because invoice and demand letter included work done in another parish); Contractors' Supply v. Caldarera & Co., 734 So. 2d 755 (La. Ct. App. 1999) (no attorney fees pursuant to open account statute when amount specified in demand letter was not correct); Heritage Worldwide, Inc. v. Jimmy Swaggart Ministries, 665 So. 2d 523 (La. Ct. App. 1995) (denying fee-shifting when demand included a sum which was not owed); Wayne v. A.V.A. Vending, Inc., 52 S.W.3d 412 (Tex. App. 2001) (unreasonable demand may bar statutory or contractual attorney fees and prejudgment interest; "if the claiming party makes an unreasonable demand, the other party should not be forced to pay the demand or else risk suffering the opposing party's attorney's fees"); Pennington v. Gurkoff, 899 S.W.2d 767 (Tex. App. 1995) (statute which allowed award of attorney fees in action on contract did not justify fees when creditor made demand of more than twice the actual recovery). *See also* Savant Ins. Servs., Inc. v. Central Oil & Supply Corp., 821 So. 2d 623 (La. Ct. App. 2002) (no attorney fees permitted when creditor demanded more than court found to be due). *But cf.* Indus. Screw & Supply Co. v. WPS, Inc., 926 So. 2d 134 (La. Ct. App. 2006) (when amount due was correctly stated in petition, though not in original demand letter, and not timely paid, attorney fees properly awarded for open account); Southern Nights, Inc. v. Barnett, 881 So. 2d 1225 (La. Ct. App. 2004) (attorney fees properly awarded for open account, even though judgment was for $1400 less than creditor demanded); Guidry's Seafood Distributors, Inc. v. Farmers Seafood Co., 759 So. 2d 806 (La. Ct. App. 1999) (attorney fees properly awarded in default judgment on open account even though amount awarded not same as amount demanded, when changes made to reflect payments made in the meantime, and amount was correct at various stages of the proceedings); Jefferson Door Co. v. Lewis, 713 So. 2d 835 (La. Ct. App. 1998) (seller's compliance was adequate when seller sent demand by certified mail to address given in credit application); Hernandez v. Lautensack, 201 S.W.3d 771 (Tex. App. 2006) (merely requesting more than jury determines is due is insufficient to deny fees, unless demand was made in bad faith).

6.3.3 *Statutes Allowing Fees for Suit on a Contract*

In addition, some states have statutorily overruled the American rule on attorney fees more broadly by permitting courts to award attorney fees to prevailing parties in civil suits generally or in contract actions.

An *Alaska* statute authorizes the state supreme court to adopt fee-shifting rules in certain civil actions.[88] A court rule implements this statute by providing that the prevailing party in a civil action is entitled to an attorney fee award, except as otherwise provided by law or agreed upon by the parties, and sets a fee schedule.[89] In general, the state rejects the American Rule and allows fee-shifting in a variety of circumstances.[90]

Under an *Arizona* statute, the court may award reasonable attorney fees to the successful party in any contested action arising out of contract.[91] Courts interpret this statute as permitting but not requiring a fee award.[92] The fee award need not equal or relate to the attorney fees the successful party actually paid or agreed to pay but may not exceed that amount.[93] The fee award may include tort claims that were intertwined with the contract claim.[94]

Under an *Arkansas* statute, the prevailing party is entitled to fees in any civil action to recover on an open account, statement of account, account stated, promissory note, bill, negotiable instrument, or contract relating to the purchase or sale of goods, wares, or merchandise, or for labor or services, or breach of contract, unless otherwise provided by law or the contract.[95] The state supreme court has held that an award of fees under this statute is discretionary, not mandatory.[96]

California requires an award of reasonable attorney fees to the prevailing party in any action on a contract or installment account, whether instituted by the seller, holder, or buyer.[97]

---

88 Alaska Stat. § 09.60.010.

89 Alaska R. Civ. P. 82. *See* O'Connell v. Will, 263 P.3d 41 (Alaska 2011) (fee-shifting provisions broadly construed; provision authorizing fees incurred in a "suit or action" covered postjudgment enforcement actions); Alaska Constr. & Eng'g, Inc. v. Balzer, 130 P.3d 932 (Alaska 2006) (Alaska rules authorize prevailing party fees in civil actions; commercial lessor who prevailed on claim and all but one counterclaim was prevailing party).

90 *See* O'Connell v. Will, 263 P.3d 41 (Alaska 2011).

91 Ariz. Rev. Stat. Ann. § 12-341.01. *See* Ahwatukee Custom Estates Mgmt. v. Bach, 973 P.2d 106 (Ariz. 1999) (construing fee-shifting statute to allow award only of attorney fees and taxable costs, not other litigation expenses); Arizona Tile, L.L.C. v. Berger, 224 P.3d 988 (Ariz. Ct. App. 2010) (claims against corporate officers for violation of statute requiring contractor to hold certain payments in trust for materials supplier arose from statute, not contract); Keystone Floors & More L.L.C. v. Arizona Registrar of Contractors, 219 P.3d 237 (Ariz. Ct. App. 2009) (homeowner not entitled to fees for contractor's unsuccessful appeal of administrative agency's orders regarding contractor's substandard work, as matter did not "arise out of a contract"); Hanley v. Pearson, 61 P.3d 29 (Ariz. Ct. App. 2003) (statute allowing fee-shifting in contract case does not apply when contract is "factual predicate," but not "essential basis," of claim; no fee-shifting in dispute between foreclosure purchaser and junior lienholder over payment of real estate taxes); Pelletier v. Johnson, 937 P.2d 668 (Ariz. Ct. App. 1996) (statute allows fees for contested contract actions; allowing fees when vinyl siding seller prevailed in *quantum meruit*, after its contract was held invalid for failure to comply with door-to-door sales law). *But cf.* Sitton v. DeutscheBank Nat'l Trust Co., 311 P.3d 237 (Ariz. Ct. App. 2013) (denying fee-shifting; consumers' unsuccessful claims alleged violation of statutes, not contract).

92 Ariz. Rev. Stat. § 12-341.01. *See* Motzer v. Escalante, 265 P.3d 1094 (Ariz. Ct. App. 2011) (Arizona court permitted but not required to award fees to prevailing party in contract action; not abuse of discretion to deny fees when plaintiff's recovery reduced by defendant's successful counterclaim and plaintiff had refused a reasonable settlement offer); Ad Hoc Comm. of Parishioners of Our Lady of Sun Catholic Church, Inc. v. Reiss, 224 P.3d 1002 (Ariz. Ct. App. 2010) (listing criteria for fee award, including whether unsuccessful party's claim or defense was meritorious, whether litigation could have been avoided or settled, hardship, and whether fee award would deter litigation of tenable claims or defenses).

93 Ariz. Rev. Stat. § 12-341.01(B).

94 Silver Springs Oasis, L.L.C. v. Lawyers Title of Ariz., Inc., 2014 WL 47342 (Ariz. Ct. App. Jan. 7, 2014) (tort claim "arises from" contract if claim could not exist but for the breach or avoidance of contract or is interwoven with contract claim; here allowing fee-shifting for misrepresentation and breach-of-fiduciary-duty claims alleging mishandling of real estate escrow); Law Offices of Ethan Frey v. Peck, 2013 WL 3326210 (Ariz. Ct. App. June 27, 2013) (awarding fees; clients' unsuccessful counterclaim for malpractice was inextricably entwined with law firm's action to enforce fee agreement); Bennet v. Baxter Group, Inc., 224 P.3d 230 (Ariz. Ct. App. 2010) (statutory fees allowable for tort claims that could not exist but for the contract or that are highly intertwined with contract); Modular Mining Sys., Inc. v. Jigsaw Technologies, 212 P.3d 853 (Ariz. Ct. App. 2009) (whether claim "arises out of" contract within meaning of Arizona statute may be difficult question; not reached here because statutory claims inextricably intertwined with contract claims on which fees available). *But cf.* Am. Int'l Dev. Corp. v. Valenza Dev. Corp., 2009 WL 1682145 (Ariz. Ct. App. June 16, 2009) (unpublished) (denying fees for negligence claim that could stand alone; duty of due care existed independent of the contract); Robert E. Mann Constr. Co. v. Liebert Corp., 60 P.3d 708 (Ariz. Ct. App. 2003) (Arizona statute allowing fee-shifting in contract case applies only in suit to enforce duty that would not exist but for contract; no fee-shifting in common law product liability action).

95 Ark. Code Ann. § 16-22-308. *See* Southern Wine & Spirits of Nev. v. Mountain Valley Spring Co., L.L.C., 712 F.3d 397 (8th Cir. 2013) (claim of breach of implied covenant of good faith and fair dealing is contract claim to which fee-shifting statute applies); Curry v. Thornsberry, 128 S.W.3d 438 (Ark. 2003) (attorney fees properly awarded against consumers who unsuccessfully sued builder for breach of implied warranty of habitability); Stephens Prod. Co. v. Blackard, 2013 WL 5424822 (Ark. Ct. App. Sept. 25, 2013) (declaratory judgment action seeking to interpret terms of lease and action to enforce settlement agreement are both contract actions within meaning of Arkansas statute).

96 Southern Bank of Commerce v. Union Planters Nat'l Bank, 289 S.W.3d 414 (Ark. 2008) (affirming denial of fee-shifting; award to prevailing party under this statute is discretionary as to whether to award any fees and as to amount).

97 Cal. Civ. Code § 1811.1 (West). *See* Barrientos v. 1801–1825 Morton L.L.C., 583 F.3d 1197 (9th Cir. 2009) (tenants' declaratory judgment action, concerning interaction between state rent control and federal regulations, was an action on a contract, because the complaint was one to enforce tenants' rights under the lease); Cussler v. Crusader Entm't, 150 Cal. Rptr. 895 (Cal. Ct. App. 2012) (declaratory judgment action seeking interpretation of contract is contract action); Douglas E. Barnhart, Inc. v. CMC Fabricators, Inc., 149 Cal. Rptr. 3d 440 (Cal. Ct. App. 2012) (fees awarded to party who prevails on contract claim, not on overall litigation; no fee-shifting for party who prevailed on claim of promissory estoppel, which is a substitute for a contract and

Hawaii requires attorney fees, in an amount determined by the court but capped at 25%, to be taxed to the losing party in actions in the nature of *assumpsit* and in all actions on a promissory note or other contract in writing that provides for attorney fees.[98] Most courts refuse to apply this statute to tort and statutory claims, even if they arise from a contractual relationship.[99]

Under an *Idaho* statute, the prevailing party is entitled to attorney fees in any civil action to recover on an open account, account stated, note, bill, negotiable instrument, guaranty, or contract relating to sale of goods or services, and in any commercial transaction unless otherwise prohibited by law.[100] The final portion of the statute, allowing fees in any "commercial transaction," is limited to non-consumer transactions.[101]

Nebraska provides that a creditor that prevails on a claim for $4000 or less for, *inter alia*, services rendered, labor performed, material furnished, or necessaries of life, is entitled to recover attorney fees.[102] The fee award is subject to a cap of $10 plus 10% of the judgment in excess of $50.[103] The plaintiff must present the claim to the defendant for payment ninety days before filing suit.[104]

Oklahoma allows a reasonable attorney fee to the prevailing party in a civil action to recover on an open account, statement of account, account stated, note, bill, negotiable instrument, or contract relating to purchase or sale of goods or services.[105]

---

occurs without parties' consent); Garcia v. Santana, 94 Cal. Rptr. 3d 299 (Cal. Ct. App. 2009) (statutory fee award must consider financial condition of non-prevailing party); Turner v. Schultz, 96 Cal. Rptr. 3d 659 (Cal. Ct. App. 2009) (declaratory judgment action is "on a contract" if it results in enforcement or denial of enforcement of contract clause; here, allowing fee-shifting, even though no prevailing party yet in underlying contract action).

98 Haw. Rev. Stat. § 607-14. *See* Courter v. Karolle, 2013 WL 5532831 (D. Haw. Oct. 4, 2013) (Hawaii's 25% cap inapplicable in case in which it would be impossible to determine what award would have been if plaintiff prevailed; calculating lodestar fees); Northern Trust N.A. v. Wolfe, 2013 WL 1856060 (D. Haw. Apr. 30, 2013) (allowing fee-shifting on counterclaim alleging false oral promises), *adopted by* 2013 WL 2147973 (D. Haw. May 16, 2013); Blair v. Ing, 31 P.3d 184 (Haw. 2001) (judgment of dismissal is sufficient for fees; paralegal time may be included in appropriate cases); Waikoloa Dev. Co. v. Waikoloa Heights Land Investors, L.P., 303 P.3d 1227 (Haw. Ct. App. 2013) (table) (declaratory judgment or specific performance action, seeking to interpret contract, will be *assumpsit* only if money damages are sought).

99 Valencia v. Carrington Mortgage Servs., L.L.C., 2013 WL 3223628 (D. Haw. June 25, 2013) (claim against mortgage broker based on verbal agreement is *assumpsit* claim for which fees are available, but not tort and statutory claims even though they arise from the same relationship); Paik-Apau v. Deutsche Bank Nat'l Trust Co., 2013 WL 1187039 (D. Haw. Feb. 22, 2013) (denying fee-shifting for consumer's unsuccessful challenge to foreclosure; claim that assignment was invalid did not attack validity of mortgage, and fraud claim was tort), *adopted by* 2013 WL 1187013 (D. Haw. Mar. 21, 2013); Benoist v. U.S. Bank, N.A., 2013 WL 704865 (D. Haw. Jan. 28, 2013) (denying fee-shifting for unsuccessful challenge to foreclosure; claims for statutory violations, fraud, and misrepresentation), *adopted by* 2013 WL 705100 (D. Haw. Feb. 25, 2013); Kam Ctr. Specialty Corp. v. LWC IV Corp., ___ P.3d ___, 2013 WL 376079 (Haw. Ct. App. Jan. 31, 2013) (table) (denying fee-shifting in tenant's unsuccessful UDAP action; duty alleged to be breached arose from statute, not lease). *But see* Au v. Funding Group, Inc., 933 F. Supp. 2d 1264 (D. Haw. 2013) (statute authorizing fees for "*assumpsit*" broad enough to cover contract and quasi-contract claims, and tort claims inextricably entwined with them, arising from alleged mishandling or residential mortgage); Young v. Geico Indemnity Co., 2009 WL 3049640 (D. Haw. Sept. 23, 2009) (statute authorizing fee-shifting for actions "in the nature of *assumpsit*" covers all possible contract claims, express or implied, oral or written, and quasi-contract; here applied also to tort claims "inextricably interwoven" with contract).

100 Idaho Code Ann. § 12-120(3). *See* Champion Produce, Inc. v. Ruby Robinson Co., 342 F.3d 1016 (9th Cir. 2003) (fees may be awarded to prevailing party in contract action under Idaho Code Ann. § 12-120(3), but here neither party prevailed); Med. Recovery Servs. v. Jones, 175 P.3d 795 (Idaho Ct. App. 2007) (listing criteria for calculating statutory fees; time and labor are important but fee must still be reasonable); Haight v. Dale's Used Cars, Inc., 87 P.3d 962 (Idaho Ct. App. 2003) (Idaho statute provides fee-shifting in action to recover on contract for sale of goods; consumer who unsuccessfully sued to revoke acceptance of vehicle was liable for attorney fees at trial and on appeal).

101 *See* Goodspeed v. Shippen, 303 P.3d 225 (Idaho 2013) (statute allowing fee-shifting in any commercial transaction does not apply to sale of home in which purchasers will reside); Stapleton v. Jack Cushing Drilling & Pump Co., 291 P.3d 418 (Idaho 2013) (denying fee-shifting; transaction involving well drilled on residential lot where consumer planned to build his home was consumer, not commercial); Troupis v. Summer, 218 P.3d 1138 (Idaho 2009) (sale of jointly owned real property was commercial transaction within meaning of fee-shifting statute; owners used property "to conduct business together"); Bajrektarevic v. Lighthouse Home Loans, Inc., 155 P.3d 691 (Idaho 2007) (borrower's action for breach of lock-in agreement in refinance of home loan does not involve commercial transaction); Karterman v. Jameson, 980 P.2d 574 (Idaho Ct. App. 1999) (no attorney fees under this provision in case arising from sale of personal residential property).

102 Neb. Rev. Stat. § 25-1801. *See* Powers v. Credit Mgmt. Servs., Inc., 2013 WL 1189114 (D. Neb. Mar. 14, 2013) (recommending that classes be certified in FDCPA and UDAP actions alleging that collector falsely alleged compliance with pre-suit notice requirements of Nebraska statute), *adopted by* 2013 WL 3716412 (D. Neb. July 12, 2013); Hage v. Gen. Serv. Bureau, 2002 WL 1796575 (D. Neb. Aug. 5, 2002) (Nebraska statute allows costs and attorney fees if contract is for services or necessities, but consumers stated claim for UDAP violation when collection letter demanded costs and attorney fees in absence of judgment); Thomas & Thomas Court Reporters, L.L.C. v. Switzer, 810 N.W.2d 677 (Neb. 2012) (denying statutory fees because statute applies only to claims of $4000 or less, and amount sought and awarded here exceeded that limit).

103 Neb. Rev. Stat. § 25-1801.

104 *Id.*

105 Okla. Stat. tit. 12, § 936. *See* Specialty Beverages L.L.C. v. Pabst Brewing Co., 537 F.3d 1165 (10th Cir. 2008) (provision for attorney fees in contract "relating to" the sale of goods is narrowly interpreted to apply only to suits to collect money promised as payment for goods; no fee-shifting in action for lost profits resulting from distributor's breach); C. & L. Enters. v. Citizen Band Potawatomi Tribe of Okla., 72 P.3d 1 (Okla. 2002) (provision for attorney fees in action on contract for services applies only if services provided; no fee-shifting when contract was repudiated before contractor started work); Prof'l Credit Collections v. Smith, 933 P.2d 307 (Okla. 1997) (consumer was prevailing party entitled to fees when creditor dismissed collection action after consumer won motion to vacate default judgment); Usrey v. Wilson, 66 P.2d 1000 (Okla. Civ. App. 2002) (provision for fee-shifting in action relating to purchase or sale of goods applied in negligence action against contractor who built defective wall, because contractor furnished the stone); Meredith v. Smith, 35 P.3d 1002 (Okla. Civ. App. 2001) (Oklahoma statute allows fee-shifting in suit for compensation

Rhode Island allows the court to award attorney fees in a contract action when a default judgment is entered or when there is "a complete absence of a justiciable issue of either fact or law raised by the losing party." [106]

Texas allows recovery of attorney fees for a valid claim for, *inter alia*, any oral or written contract.[107] In order to obtain a fee award under this statute, the claimant must show that (1) the claimant was represented by an attorney; (2) the claimant presented the claim to the opposing party or its authorized agent; and (3) payment for the just amount owed was not tendered within thirty days.[108] The Fifth Circuit has held that this statute makes an award of fees mandatory to a party who prevails, but the amount of the fee award is discretionary with the trial judge.[109] Fees are available only if the party recovers damages on the contract claim.[110] When a tort claim is joined with a contract claim, it is not sufficient to show that the facts of the two claims are inextricably intertwined; the claimant can recover only for specific legal services that would have been required for the contract claim, even if the tort claim had not been present.[111]

6.3.4 *Other State Fee-Shifting Statutes*

Some states also have statutes or court rules allowing attorney fee awards for enforcement of liens[112] or other particular types of actions.[113] State laws regarding fee-shifting when a creditor seeks a deficiency judgment after repossessing collateral are discussed in National Consumer Law Center, *Repossessions*.[114] In some states, statutes similar to Rule 68 of

for personal services; capped at 10% of judgment in uncontested small claims court case; cap did not apply when case contested).

106 R.I. Gen. Laws § 9-1-45.

107 Tex. Civ. Prac. & Rem. Code Ann. § 38.001 (West). *See* Guardian Life Ins. Co. v. Kinder, 663 F. Supp. 2d 544 (S.D. Tex. 2009) (to recover statutory fees, party must prevail and recover damages on contract claim); Med. City Dallas v. Carlisle Corp., 251 S.W.3d 55 (Tex. 2008) (action for breach of express warranty is action on a contract for purposes of fee-shifting statute); Crisp Analytical Labs v. Jakalam Props., ___ S.W.3d ___, 2014 WL 117415 (Tex. App. Jan. 13, 2014) (oral contract sufficient to allow statutory fee-shifting; recovery of any amount is sufficient to make prevailing party); Zorilla v. AYPCO Constr. II, ___ S.W.3d ___, 2013 WL 5506697 (Tex. App. Oct. 3, 2013) (fraud claim arising from breach of contract; plaintiff who elected to receive punitive damages on fraud count not entitled to attorney fees for breach of contract); Sewing v. Bowman, 371 S.W.3d 321 (Tex. App. 2012) (Texas statute applies to written or oral agreement; awarding fees to party who lost on contract claim but prevailed on claim based on oral partnership agreement); Gordon v. Leasman, 365 S.W.3d 109 (Tex. App. 2011) (attorney fees for breach of contract only if plaintiff presented claim and defendant did not pay within thirty days; shown here when plaintiff carpenter testified that he gave written invoice to customer); Charette v. Fitzgerald, 213 S.W.3d 505 (Tex. App. 2006) (comparing various provisions of Texas law allowing attorney fees; for open account, court may take judicial notice of customary and usual fees; for violation of property code, reasonableness must be shown); Time Out Grocery v. The Vanguard Group, 187 S.W.3d 41 (Tex. App. 2005) (plaintiff store sought attorney fees, pursuant to Texas statute allowing fees in contract action, against check writer who stopped payment; payee was third party who cashed check in plaintiff store; fees denied because no contract between store and check writer); G.R.A.V.I.T.Y. Enters., Inc. v. Reese Supply Co., 177 S.W.3d 537 (Tex. App. 2005) (fees available to party who prevails and recovers damages; no fees for party who successfully defends against contract claim); Cordova v. S. Bell Yellow Pages, Inc., 148 S.W.3d 441 (Tex. App. 2004) (Texas statute allows prevailing party attorney fees in certain contract actions; when claims are "inter-related," here collection of commercial debt and various counterclaims arising from same facts, fees may be awarded on all claims); Mobil Producing Tex. & N.M., Inc. v. Cantor, 93 S.W.3d 916 (Tex. App. 2002) (denying fees when plaintiff prevailed on unjust enrichment, not contract claim).

108 Tex. Civ. Prac. & Rem. Code Ann. § 38.002 (West). *See* Helping Hands Home Care v. Home Health of Tarrant Cnty., Inc., 393 S.W.3d 492 (Tex. App. 2013) (denying fees because notice not sufficient); Goodin v. Jolliff, 257 S.W.3d 341 (Tex. App. 2008) (denying fees because of failure to show presentment of claim to the other party and failure to pay within thirty days).

109 DP Solutions, Inc. v. Rollins, 353 F.3d 421, 433 (5th Cir. 2003) (Texas law).

110 MBM Fin. Corp. v. Woodlands Operating Co., 292 S.W.3d 660, 666–67 (Tex. 2009).

111 Tony Gullo Motors I, L.P. v. Chapa, 212 S.W.3d 299 (Tex. 2006).

112 *See, e.g.*, Magleby v. Garn, 296 P.3d 400 (Idaho 2013) (holding homebuyers liable for attorney fees incurred in lien foreclosure action resulting from defaulting builder's failure to pay construction manager, including fees incurred by bank in seeking to enjoin foreclosure); Solution Source, Inc. v. LPR Assocs. L.P., 652 N.W.2d 474 (Mich. Ct. App. 2002); Waters Edge Builders v. Longa, 715 S.E.2d 193 (N.C. Ct. App. 2011) (fee-shifting pursuant to construction lien statute requires showing of express or implied-in-fact contract; *quantum meruit* or implied-at-law contract not enough); Spriggs Group, P.C. v. Slivka, 738 S.E.2d 495 (S.C. Ct. App. 2013) (architects' off-site supervision services were labor within the meaning of South Carolina statute, which allows fees for enforcement mechanics' lien); A.K. & R. Whipple Plumbing & Heating v. Guy, 94 P.3d 270 (Utah 2004) (mechanics' lien statute authorizes fees for "successful party," construed as synonymous with "prevailing party"; fee-shifting denied when case was "a draw"). *Cf.* Caterpillar Fin. Servs. Corp. v. Burroughs Diesel, Inc., 125 So. 3d 659 (Miss. Ct. App. 2013) (neither mechanics' lien statute nor storage lien statute provides for attorney fees). *But cf.* Sheppard v. M. & R. Plumbing, Inc., 82 So. 3d 950 (Fla. Dist. Ct. App. 2011) (plumber who recovered in *quantum meruit* not entitled to fees pursuant to construction lien state, which requires showing of a contract); ParkWest Homes L.L.C. v. Barnson, 302 P.3d 18 (Idaho 2013) (state statute allowing attorney fees for foreclosure of mechanics' lien does not authorize appellate attorney fees).

113 *See, e.g.*, Chase Bank v. Staffenberg, 2011 WL 1445096 (N.J. Super. Ct. App. Div. Apr. 11, 2011) (interpreting statute that automatically taxes percentage-based counsel fees against judgment debtors in state small-claims-type court; this fee can be taxed even if judgment creditor was represented by in-house counsel); Stewart Title Guar. Title Co. v. Lewis, 788 A.2d 941 (N.J. Super. Ct. App. Div. 2001) (New Jersey court rules permit a small collection attorney fee in mortgage foreclosure cases, for example, 1% of debts exceeding $7500, and provide for downward, but not upward, adjustment); Horwitz v. Doubenskaia, 264 P.3d 744 (Okla. Civ. App. 2011) (garnishment statute authorizing fee-shifting "in case of the trial of any issue" applied when judgment creditor prevailed on summary judgment); First Quality Carpets, Inc. v. Kirschbaum, 54 A.3d 465 (Vt. 2012) (affirming attorney fee award under Prompt Pay Act against homeowners who did not have good faith basis to withhold payment for carpet installation). *Cf.* Register v. Gabriel, 2011 WL 6145105 (Cal. Ct. App. Dec. 12, 2101) (unpublished) (California statutes governing homeowners' associations and trustee sales did not authorize trustee to withhold surplus and apply it to fees incurred in homeowners' attempt to set aside foreclosure).

114 National Consumer Law Center, Repossessions § 11.3.6.4.3 (8th ed. 2013), *updated at* www.nclc.org/library.

the Federal Rules of Civil Procedure allow fee-shifting when a party rejects a settlement offer, goes to trial, and recovers less than the offer.[115]

Many states have statutes or court rules that allow fees to be awarded as a sanction for vexatious or frivolous litigation.[116] These provisions should be applied sparingly so that the purpose of deterring baseless claims is promoted without deterring colorable claims.[117]

6.4 Is the Creditor the Prevailing Party?

Whether allowed by statute or by contract, attorney fees are generally available only to the prevailing party.[118] A favorable decision on liability may be insufficient if no damages are awarded.[119] Voluntary dismissal of a collection action may bar the collector from recovering the costs associated with that action,[120] and in fact a collector who dismisses the action may be liable for fees.[121] A defendant who obtains a ruling dismissing

115 *See, e.g.*, Wash. Rev. Stat. §§ 4.84.250 to 4.84.330 (prevailing party attorney fees in actions for damages of $10,000 or less; plaintiff prevails if damages awarded exceed amount of settlement offer); Kirk v. Gobel, 622 F. Supp. 2d 1039 (E.D. Wash. 2009) (not FDCPA violation to request fees in complaint, but unfair and misleading to request them in motion for default judgment, as debtor had not rejected a settlement offer).

116 *See* § 13.1.8.4, *infra* (state-by-state list of state statutes and rules providing for attorney fees for groundless or frivolous litigation).

117 Swan Landing Dev. L.L.C. v. First Tenn. Bank, 97 So. 3d 326 (Fla. Dist. Ct. App. 2012) (statute allowing recovery of attorney fees as sanction for frivolous action must be applied "to ensure that it serves the purpose for which it was intended . . . to discourage baseless claims . . . and not to cast a chilling effect on the use of the courts"; award of fees was error when non-prevailing consumers had raised "colorable" claim). *See also* Albrecht v. Alaska Tr., L.L.C., 286 P.3d 1059 (Alaska 2012) (claim not sanctionably frivolous when two lower court decisions supported consumer's position).

118 *See In re* Hoopai, 581 F.3d 1090 (9th Cir. 2009) (Hawaii law; creditor who unsuccessfully argued that foreclosure sale extinguished debtor's private sale of home was not prevailing party despite recovering debt from debtor's sale of home, so not entitled to statutory fees); Ritter & Ritter, Inc. v. Churchill Condo. Ass'n, 82 Cal. Rptr. 3d 389 (Cal. Ct. App. 2008) (unit owners were prevailing parties in litigation against condominium association and individual directors; even though individuals were protected from liability by business judgment rule, unit owners attained their litigation objectives); Port-a-Weld, Inc. v. Padula & Wadsworth Constr., Inc., 984 So. 2d 564 (Fla. Dist. Ct. App. 2008) (Florida Supreme Court's definition of "prevailing party" as the one who prevailed on the significant issues cannot be contractually modified; subcontractor that won 60% of its claim is prevailing party, even though attorney fee clause required 75% recovery); Blair v. Ing, 31 P.3d 184 (Haw. 2001) (defendant who wins judgment of dismissal is prevailing party); Tasaki v. Moriarty, 225 P.3d 68 (Or. Ct. App. 2009) (prospective purchasers who received return of their earnest money were prevailing party even though their first choice remedy, specific performance, was denied); Fletcher Hill, Inc. v. Crosbie, 872 A.2d 292 (Vt. 2005) (manufactured-home installer could not recover fees pursuant to contract it had breached; no statutory fees because neither party clearly prevailed); Torgerson v. One Lincoln Tower, L.L.C., 210 P.3d 318 (Wash. 2009) (sellers, who had admittedly breached contract, were prevailing parties when only issue was enforceability of limitation of remedies clause). *But see* Trull v. Central Carolina Bank & Trust, 478 S.E.2d 39 (N.C. Ct. App. 1996) (adopting strained interpretation of statute to allow contractual fees even if creditor does not prevail; failing to give weight to statutory provision allowing fees only if the debt is "*collected* by or through an attorney"), *aff'd*, 490 S.E.2d 238 (N.C. 1997); Jones v. Riche, 216 P.3d 357 (Utah Ct. App. 2009) (if contract imposes fees on "defaulting party," no need to show that non-defaulting party was "successful" or "prevailing").

119 Hinz v. Neuroscience, Inc., 538 F.3d 979 (8th Cir. 2008) (Minnesota law) (plaintiff prevails under fee-shifting clause only if damages are awarded); Advanced Med. Diagnostics, L.L.C. v. Imaging Ctr. of Idaho, L.L.C., 303 P.3d 171 (Idaho 2013) (awarding fees to defendant when jury found liability but awarded no damages; defendant "came out ahead" on "primary issue," which was whether defendant owed damages for breach of contract); Trilogy Network Sys., Inc. v. Johnson, 172 P.3d 1119 (Idaho 2007) (denying statutory fee-shifting; when plaintiff proved liability, but failed to prove damages, no one prevailed); Scherer v. Angell, 253 S.W.3d 777 (Tex. App. 2007) (award of statutory attorney fees in contract action requires showing of damages; fee-shifting was error when jury awarded no damages on contract count, in case alleging tort and contract claims). *But see* Total Recycling Servs. of Conn., Inc. v. Connecticut Oil Recycling Servs., L.L.C., 970 A.2d 807 (Conn. App. Ct. 2009) (showing of breach is sufficient, damages need not be shown); Cornell Holdings, L.L.C. v. Woodland Creek Assocs., L.L.C., 882 N.Y.S.2d 586 (N.Y. App. Div. 2009) (allowing award of attorney fees to stand, despite reversal of judgment for damages, when seller was found to have breached contract). *But cf.* Benchmark Builders, Inc. v. Schultz, 751 S.E.2d 45 (Ga. 2013) (homeowners who successfully defended against builder's claim, but received zero damages on their counterclaim, were prevailing parties).

120 Glencoe v. Neue Sentimental Film AG, 85 Cal. Rptr. 3d 800 (Cal. Ct. App. 2008) (California reciprocal fees statute provides that there is no prevailing party, and thus no fee-shifting, if an action is voluntarily dismissed or dismissed pursuant to a settlement, regardless of the stage at which dismissal occurs). *See also* Pope v. Man-Data, Inc., 209 F.3d 1161 (9th Cir. 2000) (collection agency sued in small claims court but failed to pursue action and was defaulted; when debtor made partial payment, collector deducted the amount of its filing fee, etc., in the small claims action; because collector was not a prevailing party, it was not permitted to charge debtor for costs).

121 Fulton Homes Corp. v. BPP Concrete, 155 P.3d 1090 (Ariz. Ct. App. 2007) (affirming fee award; party was "successful" as required by statute when opponent stipulated to dismissal of its claim); Morris v. Edmonds, 2002 WL 31631005 (Cal. Ct. App. Nov. 22, 2002) (allowing contractual attorney fees against parties who voluntarily dismissed; California statute would forbid this result in contract action, but here fee-shifting clause applied in tort case arising from land sale); Trugreen Landcare, L.L.C. v. Elm City Dev. & Constr. Servs., Inc., 919 A.2d 1077 (Conn. App. Ct. 2007) (landlord whose eviction action was non-suited is liable for tenant's attorney fees under contract clause requiring "nonprevailing party" to pay fees); Bardon Trimount, Inc. v. Guyott, 732 N.E.2d 916 (Mass. App. Ct. 2000) (defendant who won dismissal on procedural grounds is prevailing party); Prof'l Credit Collections v. Smith, 933 P.2d 307 (Okla. 1997) (consumer was prevailing party entitled to fees when creditor dismissed collection action after consumer won motion to vacate default judgment); Epps v. Fowler, 351 S.W.3d 862 (Tex. 2011) (if plaintiff nonsuits with prejudice, defendant automatically prevails; if plaintiff nonsuits without prejudice, defendant prevails if court concludes nonsuit was taken to avoid unfavorable outcome). *See also* Raza v. Deutsche Bank Nat'l Trust Co., 100 So. 3d 121 (Fla. Dist. Ct. App. 2012) (consumer prevailed, and was entitled to fees, when foreclosure was involuntarily dismissed without prejudice because of bank's failure to comply with court order); Aquapower, L.C. v. Yurth, 2011 WL 2173793 (Utah June 2, 2011) (defendants prevailed when case dismissed after plaintiffs failed to file amended complaint; voluntary dismissal makes defendant prevailing party); Sterrett Props., L.L.C. v. Big-D Signature Corp., 314 P.3d 1155 (Wyo. 2013) (courts

a case without prejudice also may be a prevailing party entitled to statutory fees.[122] A creditor that obtains a favorable settlement of its claim but not a judgment may not be entitled to fees.[123]

Further, the collector may not be considered the prevailing party if it receives substantially less relief than it sought.[124] Simply demanding an excessive amount before suit may preclude a fee award altogether. As one court has reasoned, "if the claiming party makes an unreasonable demand, the other party should not be forced to pay the demand or else risk suffering the opposing party's attorney's fees."[125]

Determining whether a creditor has prevailed is complex when there are several claims and counterclaims and the debtor prevails on some of them.[126] Some courts simply define

---

have discretion to award attorney fees in case of voluntary dismissal but should do so only under "extraordinary circumstances," such as a party that makes a practice of dismissing claims after inflicting heavy litigation costs on the opposing party and the judicial system). *But see* Kraffert v. Shea Homes, 2002 WL 44262 (Cal. Ct. App. Jan. 14, 2002) (consumer sued seller of home for UDAP violations and fraud, but voluntarily dismissed before seller answered; no attorney fees for seller under provision allowing fees to "the party in whose favor the award or final judgment shall be entered"); Wachovia SBA Lending v. Kraft, 158 P.3d 1271 (Wash. Ct. App. 2007) (for Washington's reciprocal fees statute, prevailing party is one in whose favor "final judgment" is entered; when lender voluntarily dismissed after losing summary judgment motion, no final judgment and no reciprocal fees), *aff'd*, 200 P.3d 683 (Wash. 2009).

122 Balestieri v. Balestieri, 300 P.3d 560 (Ariz. Ct. App. 2013) (party that obtains dismissal for lack of personal jurisdiction entitled to fees, but only if fee request included in motion); Southwest Fertility Ctr., Ltd. v. Medscan Diagnostic Systems, Inc., 2013 WL 440640 (Ariz. Ct. App. Feb. 5, 2013) (defendant who obtained dismissal by enforcing forum selection clause was prevailing party); Landry v. Countrywide Home Loans, Inc. 731 So. 2d 137 (Fla. Dist. Ct. App. 1999) (when lender initiated and then voluntarily terminated foreclosure proceeding, homeowners were prevailing party entitled to attorney fees).

123 Reuille v. E.E. Brandenberger Constr. Co., 888 N.E.2d 770 (Ind. 2008) (when contract did not define prevailing party, only one who obtains judgment is included; mediated settlement not sufficient; noting that provision could be drafted to cover compromise, settlement, and so forth); Delgado v. Boyles, 922 N.E.2d 1267 (Ind. Ct. App. 2010) (to prevail, party must go to trial and successfully recover on or defend against a claim). *See also* Gostony v. Diem Corp., 320 F. Supp. 2d 932 (D. Ariz. 2003) (judicial proceeding was prerequisite for award under lease provision allowing "prevailing party" to recover attorney fees and collection costs; inclusion of fees in initial demand letter was unlawful). *But see* Medical Protective Co. v. Pang, 740 F.3d 1279 (9th Cir. 2013) (Arizona law) (fee award permissible when parties dismissed pursuant to settlement; court should consider "the totality of the circumstances and the relative success of the litigants"); Martha's Hands, L.L.C. v. Rothman, 328 S.W.3d 474 (Mo. Ct. App. 2010) (provision for fees if debt collected by an attorney "by suit or otherwise" applied when debtor paid after being sued but before judgment).

124 *See* Bowen Inv., Inc. v. Carneiro Donuts, Inc., 490 F.3d 27 (1st Cir. 2007) (Mass. law) (denying contractual fee-shifting when franchisor who demanded $120,000 got $12,000 on one claim and $1 on another); United States *ex rel.* Silva's Excavation, Inc. v. Jim Cooley Constr., Inc., 572 F. Supp. 2d 1276 (D.N.M. 2008) (defendant was prevailing party, even though plaintiff recovered half the amount it sought, when defendant had admitted from outset that it owed that much); Chinn v. KMR Prop. Mgmt., 82 Cal. Rptr. 3d 586 (Cal. Ct. App. 2008) (remanding for "pragmatic assessment" of each party's litigation success when tenant settled for less than she claimed but more than landlord initially offered); Flamingo Pools, Spas, Sunrooms & More Store v. Penrod, 993 S.W.2d 588 (Mo. Ct. App. 1999) (when seller was awarded barely one-third of the amount it demanded and amount due was key issue, seller did not prevail and was not entitled to fees); Kellam Assocs., Inc. v. Angel Projects, L.L.C., 814 A.2d 642 (N.J. Super. Ct. App. Div. 2003) (landlord who got 75% of amount requested in dispute over construction of rent escalator clause was prevailing party, but fee should be adjusted to reflect partial success); Smith v. Patrick W.Y. Tam Trust, 296 S.W.3d 545 (Tex. 2009) (commercial landlord received one-third of sum demanded and defeated tenant's counterclaims; award of full fees unreasonable in light of limited success, but refusal to award any fees unsupported by evidence); Shadley v. Lloyds of London, 776 N.W.2d 838 (Wis. Ct. App. 2009) (plaintiff who demanded $100,000 and was awarded $15,000 did not prevail; fees should be proportional to success, e.g., if plaintiff receives 20% of its demand, plaintiff should pay 80% of defendant's attorney fees and defendant should pay 20% of plaintiff's). *But see* Extreme Constr. Co. v. RCG Glenwood, L.L.C., 310 P.3d 246 (Colo. App. 2012) (if contract contains fee-shifting clause, party found liable for breach is liable for fees, even if amount recovered is much smaller than amount sought); King v. Brock, 646 S.E.2d 206 (Ga. 2007) (recovery of nominal damages sufficient to confer prevailing party status pursuant to contractual fee-shifting clause); Barcat, L.L.C. v. Nail, 15 So. 3d 1246 (La. Ct. App. 2009) (homeowners liable for fees even though contractor received less than half the sum he demanded); Twin Creek Estates, L.L.C. v. Tipps, 251 P.3d 756 (Okla. Civ. App. 2011) (party prevails if party wins some relief on the merits of the claim); Allco Enters., Inc. v. Goldstein Family Living Trust, 51 P.3d 1275 (Or. Ct. App. 2002) (equipment lessor was prevailing party even though it received only half of amount claimed); Crisp Analytical Labs v. Jakalam Props., ___ S.W.3d ___, 2014 WL 117415 (Tex. App. Jan. 13, 2014) (recovery of any amount is sufficient to make prevailing party; affirming $49,000 in attorney fees for party who recovered $513, which was less than 5% of amount demanded); Crowley v. Black, 167 P.3d 1087 (Utah Ct. App. 2007) (landlord's recovery of less than amount claimed not significant victory for tenant when landlord recovered something on all claims, and tenant consistently denied all liability). *But cf.* Oakes v. Boise Heart Clinic Physicians, P.L.L.C., 272 P.3d 512 (Idaho 2012) (plaintiff who received much less than he sought but successfully defended against substantial counterclaim was prevailing party); Bates v. Seldin, 203 P.3d 702 (Idaho 2009) (not abuse of discretion to award fees to party that received substantially less than it claimed but successfully defended against counterclaims).

125 Wayne v. A.V.A. Vending, Inc., 52 S.W.3d 412, 418 (Tex. App. 2001) (unreasonable demand may bar statutory or contractual attorney fees).

126 *See* Southern Wine & Spirits of Nev. v. Mountain Valley Spring Co., L.L.C., 712 F.3d 397 (8th Cir. 2013) (Arkansas law) (affirming finding of no prevailing party when one party prevailed on contract, one on covenant of good faith and fair dealing); Baptist Health v. Smith, 536 F.3d 869 (8th Cir. 2008) (Arkansas Law) (prevailing party is one who comes out "on top" at end of litigation; party who prevailed on count that did not authorize fees, and successfully defended against breach of contract counterclaim, is entitled to fees for the latter under statute allowing fees in contract claims); Brooks v. Hollaar, 297 P.3d 125 (Alaska 2013) (lender was prevailing party, even though deed of trust was found void, because it prevailed on claim on promissory note); Fielder v. Weinstein Design Group, Inc., 842 So. 2d 879 (Fla. Dist. Ct. App. 2003) (buyer who lost on counterclaims was nonetheless prevailing party when seller who sought $25,000 was required to pay buyer $5600 and accept return of goods); Hobson Fabricating Corp. v. SE/Z Constr., L.L.C., 294 P.3d 171 (Idaho 2012) (prevailing party should be determined by "over-all results," not claim by claim; should compare what each party sought with what it actually received); Grenfell v. Anderson, 56 P.3d 326 (Mont. 2002) (commercial tenant prevailed when landlord received small amount of back rent, which was uncontested, and tenant prevailed on other contested claims);

the prevailing party as the one that obtained a net recovery.[127] Other courts base the decision on an evaluation of whether one of the parties achieved the main objectives of the case.[128] Occasionally a court will declare the litigation a draw and deny attorney fees to both parties.[129] A prevailing party's extent of success is also a factor in determining the amount of the fee award.[130] In the alternative, if the creditor prevails on only one of several claims, it may be entitled to fees only for work on

---

Wilkes v. Zurlinden, 984 P.2d 261 (Or. 1999) (when plaintiff prevailed on claim and defendant on counterclaim and no damages awarded for either, both were prevailing parties and owed one another attorney fees); Villeneuve v. Beane, 933 A.2d 1139 (Vt. 2007) (although both lease and landlord-tenant statute provided for fee-shifting, denial of fees proper when net result of claims and counterclaims was "a wash"). *See also* First Sec. Sav. Bank v. Aitken, 573 N.W.2d 307 (Mich. Ct. App. 1997) (when commercial loan contract allowed attorney fees "in connection with the loan agreement," lender was entitled to fees both for its claim and for successful defense against borrowers' counterclaim when defeating counterclaim was necessary in order to prevail on complaint). *Cf.* Barbara Parmenter Living Trust v. Lemon, 194 P.3d 796 (Or. 2008) (tenants may be prevailing parties when they won on some fee-generating claims but lost on others).

127 *See, e.g.*, Weitz Co. v. MH Washington, 631 F.3d 510 (8th Cir. 2011) (when Missouri statute regarding prompt payment on construction contracts requires fees to "the" prevailing party, there can be only one; fees properly awarded to plaintiff whose recovery on claim exceeded defendant's recovery on counterclaim); Carrol v. UV Props., L.L.C. 2009 WL 2958646 (Ark. Ct. App. Sept. 16 2009) (multiple claims and counterclaims; sellers who received net recovery were prevailing party, even though they did not receive their first choice of remedy); Wheeler v. T.L. Roofing, Inc., 74 P.3d 499 (Colo. App. 2003) (multiple claims and counterclaims; applying net judgment rule to award fees to party with substantial recovery); Mantia v. Hansen, 77 P.3d 1143 (Or. Ct. App. 2003) (employee who lost on tort and retaliatory discharge claims was prevailing party when he received substantial net monetary recovery on his wage claims and defeated employer's counterclaims); Jakab v. Gran Villa Townhomes Ass'n, Inc., 149 S.W.3d 863 (Tex. App. 2004) (homeowners' association not prevailing party, because no net recovery as amount awarded on counterclaim for improper dues increase exceeded amount of homeowner's missed payments). *See also* Sampson v. DCI of Alexandria, 970 So. 2d 55 (La. Ct. App. 2007) (claims and counterclaims between homeowners and building contractor; fee award to homeowners when contractor found to owe money to them); R.T. Nielson Co. v. Cook, 40 P.3d 1119 (Utah 2002) (when recovery on claim greatly exceeded recovery on counterclaim, plaintiff was prevailing party). *But see* Robert Camel Contr., Inc. v. Krautschied, 134 P.3d 1065 (Or. Ct. App. 2006) (Or. Rev. Stat. § 20.077 requires that prevailing party be determined, and fees assessed, on a claim-by-claim basis—net judgment not proper standard).

128 *See, e.g.*, PNC Bank v. Colonial Bank, 451 Fed. Appx. 835 (11th Cir. 2012) (Fla. law) (defendant who prevailed on some defenses, but not on others, was prevailing party when it achieved "the overarching objective" of its defense); Alaska Constr. & Eng'g, Inc. v. Balzer, 130 P.3d 932 (Alaska 2006) (commercial lessor who prevailed on claim and all but one counterclaim was prevailing party; party who wins on "main issue" prevails; usually, as here, party who receives larger monetary award, but may be party who defeats potentially costly claim); Silver Creek L.L.C. v. Blackrock Realty Advisers, Inc., 93 Cal. Rptr. 3d 864 (Cal. Ct. App. 2009) (to determine prevailing party, compare relief awarded with parties' demands and litigation objectives; fees should have been awarded to seller that achieved its objective); Anglia Jacs & Co. v. Dubin, 830 So. 2d 169 (Fla. Dist. Ct. App. 2002) (discussion of prevailing party; question is who in fact prevailed on "significant issues"); Chang v. Soldier Summit Dev., 82 P.3d 203 (Utah Ct. App. 2003) (prevailing party is one who prevails on major issues and most expensive aspects; party who prevailed on two-thirds of matters was entitled to two-thirds of fees reasonably incurred); Garrison v. CC Builders, Inc., 179 P.3d 867 (Wyo. 2008) (homeowners who prevailed on some, but not all, claims were prevailing parties when "central issue" was whether they were overcharged on contract and they received significant financial recovery). *See also* Silver Creek L.L.C. v. Blackrock Realty Advisors, Inc., 93 Cal. Rptr. 3d 864 (Cal. Ct. App. 2009) (if neither party achieves complete victory, court has discretion to decide there was no prevailing party; here, however, vendor who obtained declaratory judgment approving its refusal to go through with real estate sale achieved its litigation objective; requirement to return prospective buyer's deposit was secondary).

129 *See, e.g.*, Cussler v. Crusader Entm't, 150 Cal. Rptr. 895 (Cal. Ct. App. 2012) (affirming finding of no prevailing party when each side defeated other's claims, but no affirmative relief awarded); M.A. Hajianpour, M.D., P.A. v. Khosrow Maleki, M.D., P.A., 975 So. 2d 1288 (Fla. Dist. Ct. App. 2008) (prevailing party fees properly denied when parties "battled to a draw"); Lasco Enters., Inc. v. Kohlbrand, 819 So. 2d 821 (Fla. Dist. Ct. App. 2002) (neither party was prevailing party and neither was entitled to fees when jury rejected both the claims and the counterclaims); Hobson Fabricating Corp. v. SE/Z Constr., L.L.C., 294 P.3d 171 (Idaho 2012) (affirming finding of no prevailing party when party who received net award settled for much less than it would have received if court had accepted its contention that contract was cost-plus); Powers v. Rockford Stop'n'Go, Inc., 761 N.E.2d 237 (Ill. App. Ct. 2001) (party may prevail even if it receives less than amount claimed, but reversing fee award when result was "essentially a draw"); Whipps L.L.C. v. Kaufman, Vidal, Hileman & Remilow, P.C., 156 P.3d 11 (Mont. 2007) (no prevailing party, so no contractual fee-shifting, when tenant gave up counterclaim and landlord accepted offer of 20% of the amount demanded); Stanley v. Lemire, 148 P.3d 643 (Mont. 2006) (no prevailing party when landlord prevailed on claim for possession and tenant on claim for back rent); Neff v. Neff, 247 P.3d 380 (Utah 2011) (in case with multiple claims, or in which each party receives mixed results, court may find that no party prevailed, even if statute requires award of fees to prevailing party); A.K. & R. Whipple Plumbing & Heating v. Guy, 94 P.3d 270 (Utah 2004) (mechanics' lien statute authorizes fees for "successful party," construed as synonymous with "prevailing party"; no fee-shifting when case was "a draw"); Fletcher Hill, Inc. v. Crosbie, 872 A.2d 292 (Vt. 2005) (modular home installer could not recover fees pursuant to contract it had breached; no statutory fees because neither party clearly prevailed); Stafford v. JHL, Inc., 194 P.3d 315 (Wyo. 2008) (affirming denial of fee-shifting when both parties had breached contract and had "unclean hands"); McGuire v. Lowery, 2 P.3d 527 (Wyo. 2000) (fees properly denied when no party clearly prevailed on all issues). *See also* Motzer v. Escalante, 265 P.3d 1094 (Ariz. Ct. App. 2011) (award of statutory attorney fees discretionary; no abuse of discretion to deny fees when plaintiff's recovery was substantially reduced by defendant's recovery on counterclaim and plaintiff had refused a reasonable settlement offer). *But see* Beggs v. Hart, 191 P.3d 747 (Or. Ct. App. 2008) (if contract provides for prevailing party fees, court has no discretion to decide there was no prevailing party; for multiple claims, must determine prevailing party on each claim).

130 *See, e.g.*, RFF Family P'ship, L.P. v. Link Dev., L.L.C., ___ F. Supp. 2d ___, 2013 WL 3282915 (D. Mass. June 26, 2013) (reduction of fees for limited success; lender prevailed on breach of contract but was denied deficiency), *order clarified by* 2013 WL 3990776 (D. Mass. Aug. 2, 2013); Eckhardt v. 424 Hitnze Mgmt., L.L.C., 969 So. 2d 1219 (Fla. Dist. Ct. App. 2007) (fees should be substantially reduced for limited success; landlord demanded $17,000, awarded only $4250 because of failure to mitigate); Litton Industries, Inc. v. IMO Industries, Inc., 982 A.2d 420 (N.J. 2009) (reducing lodestar when prevailing party received substantially less than demanded and fee was high in relation to amount awarded). *But see* Stuart v. North Shore Water & Sanitation Dist., 211 P.3d 59 (Colo. App. 2009) (lodestar need not be reduced for

that claim.[131] If a party prevails both on claims for which fee-shifting is available and on claims for which it is not available, some courts allow fees only for the time spent on the former.[132] However, a party who wins at trial is the prevailing party and may be entitled to fees even for unsuccessful pre-trial motions such as an unsuccessful summary judgment motion.[133] Time spent defeating defenses that would have prevented recovery is also likely to be compensable.[134]

Some fee-shifting statutes providing that a court "may award" fees have been construed to grant broad discretion: a court may decline to award fees even if one party is shown to have prevailed.[135] Arizona courts have articulated these criteria for awards of discretionary fees: (1) the merits of the claim or defense presented by the unsuccessful party; (2) whether the litigation could have been avoided or settled and the successful party's efforts were completely superfluous to achieving the result; (3) whether assessing fees against the unsuccessful party would cause an extreme hardship; (4) whether the successful party prevailed as to all the relief sought; (5) the novelty of the legal question presented and whether such claim or defense had previously been adjudicated in this jurisdiction; and (6) whether the award in any particular case would discourage other parties with tenable claims or defenses from litigating or defending legitimate contract issues for fear of incurring liability for substantial amounts of attorney fees.[136] A contract clause that the prevailing party "may recover" fees may be interpreted to give the court similar discretion.[137]

6.5 Determining the Amount of Attorney Fees a Creditor May Recover

6.5.1 Statutory Caps on Fees

In cases in which the creditor is entitled to recover attorney fees, the next question is the amount the creditor may recover. Some states cap the amount of a fee award by statute. Hawaii, for example, forbids collection agencies from recovering any collection expenses, except for attorney fees after filing suit, and it caps those fees at 25% of the debt.[138] North Carolina limits contractual attorney fees to 15%, if a note is collected by an attorney after maturity,[139] and requires that the debtor be

---

limited success; prevailing water district got half what it asked for, but homeowner had claimed he owed nothing).

131 Ellipso Inc. v. Mann, 594 F. Supp. 2d 40 (D.D.C. 2009) (allowing fees for lender's successful defense against borrower's action but not for lender's unsuccessful counterclaims); Planning Partners Int'l, L.L.C. v. QED, Inc., 304 P.3d 562 (Colo. 2013) (apportionment permitted but not required); Carroll Indep. Fuel Co. v. Washington Real Estate Inv. Trust, 32 A.3d 128 (Md. Ct. Spec. App. 2011) (eliminating fees attributable to claims on which party did not prevail); Indus. & Mech. Contractors of Memphis, Inc. v. Tim Mote Plumbing, L.L.C., 962 So. 2d 632 (Miss. Ct. App. 2007) (party who prevailed on only one of four claims entitled to fees only on that claim); Gullett v. VanDyke Constr. Co, 111 P.3d 220 (Mont. 2005) (proper to deny fees for claims on which party did not prevail and to reduce fees because of party's "shared responsibility for this dispute"); Ulloa v. QSP, Inc., 624 S.E.2d 43 (Va. 2006) (remanding to allow "marginally successful" plaintiff to show "with specificity" which fees attributable to claim on which it prevailed). *See also* Leon F. Cohn, M.D., P.A. v. Visual Health & Surgical Ctr., Inc., 125 So. 3d 860 (Fla. Dist. Ct. App. 2013) (when there are multiple claims or theories, there may be two prevailing parties; not shown here when all claims arose from same "aggregate of operative facts"). *But see* Greenstar, L.L.C. v. Heller, 934 F. Supp. 2d 672 (D. Del. 2013) (contractual fee-shifting provisions must be applied in an all or nothing manner, not claim by claim).

132 Douglas E. Barnhart, Inc. v. CMC Fabricators, Inc., 149 Cal. Rptr. 3d 440 (Cal. Ct. App. 2012) (fees awarded to party who prevails on contract claim, not on overall litigation; Fed. Deposit Ins. Corp. v. Dintino, 84 Cal. Rptr. 3d 38 (Cal. Ct. App. 2008) (for purposes of California's reciprocal fees statute, prevailing party is one who prevails on contract claim; even though bank achieved litigation objectives by prevailing on unjust enrichment claim, fees must be awarded to homeowners who prevailed on contract claim); A.J.P. Contractors, Inc. v. Hoch, 2008 WL 4448184 (Mass. Dist. Ct. Sept. 24, 2008) (homeowners who received net financial recovery were liable for landscaper's attorney fees, when homeowners prevailed on statutory claim that did not authorize fee-shifting, but landscaper prevailed on contract claim that did). *See also* Varner v. Cardenas, 218 S.W.3d 68 (Tex. 2007) (attorney fees are available for work necessary to recover on note, including defeat of defenses or counterclaims that would otherwise prevent recovery, but not for claims "intertwined with that claim). *See generally* §§ 6.2.4.2 (scope of fee-shifting clauses; claims intertwined with claims for which fees are available), 6.3.2, 6.3.3 (scope of statutes that make fees available for open account and contract claims), *supra*.

133 Ulrich v. Mercedes-Benz U.S.A., L.L.C., 931 N.E.2d 599 (Ohio Ct. App. 2010) (party prevails on claim if, at the end of the case, he successfully maintains it; party who won at trial entitled to fees on unsuccessful summary judgment motion). *But see* Specialty Retailers, Inc. v. Main St. NA Parkade L.L.C., 804 F. Supp. 2d 68 (D. Mass. 2011) (reducing fees to eliminate hours spent on certain unsuccessful motions). *But cf.* Magin v. Solitude Homeowner's, Inc., 255 P.3d 920 (Wyo. 2011) (homeowners' association not entitled to fees for portion of case that dealt with defendant homeowner's motion to disqualify its counsel when agreement allowed fees only for enforcing covenants).

134 Varner v. Cardenas, 218 S.W.3d 68 (Tex. 2007); Republic Bank v. Shook, 653 S.W.2d 278 (Tex. 1983) (fee award can be based not only on time necessary to prosecute collection action but also on time to overcome debtor's defenses).

135 Southern Wine & Spirits of Nev. v. Mountain Valley Spring Co., L.L.C., 712 F.3d 397 (8th Cir. 2013) (Arkansas fee-shifting statute gives broad discretion; court may refuse fees even if one party clearly prevailed, or find no prevailing party); Associated Indemnity Corp. v. Warner, 694 P.2d 1181 (Ariz. 1985); Saltzman v. Hadlock, 112 So. 3d 772 (Fla. Dist. Ct. App. 2013).

136 Associated Indemnity Corp. v. Warner, 694 P.2d 1181 (Ariz. 1985) (award of statutory fees discretionary; articulating criteria).

137 J. & M. Sec., L.L.C. v. Brown, 388 S.W.2d 566 (Mo. Ct. App. 2012) (provision of residential lease that prevailing party "may recover" fees does not require fee award; not abuse of discretion to deny fee-shifting here).

138 Haw. Rev. Stat. § 443B-9 (collection agency may not collect or attempt to collect any collection fee, except attorney fee up to 25% after filing suit). *See, e.g.,* Ai v. Frank Huff Agency, Ltd., 607 P.2d 1304 (Haw. 1980) (deceptive practice for a collection agency to attempt to collect attorney fees of one-third of the debt once matter was referred to attorney when attorney fees were limited by statute to 25% and allowed only after suit filed).

139 N.C. Gen. Stat. § 6-21.2. *See* Sunbelt Rentals v. Corbridge, 171 F. Supp. 2d 14 (D. Me. 2001) (N.C. law) (attorney fees only as permitted by statute; allowed for collection by attorney after maturity, capped at 15%; debtor must be given final five-day notice to pay without incurring

given a final five-day notice to pay without incurring fees.[140] Contractual fee clauses can be enforced in North Carolina only in compliance with this statute, and the 15% limit applies even when the parties' contract provides that attorney fees may be recovered.[141]

Georgia places a percentage cap on contractual attorney fees and allows them only if the obligor fails to pay the principal and interest within ten days of receipt of a final demand notice that meets certain statutory requirements.[142] The former version of this statute was construed to allow fees up to 15% of the amount owed, regardless of reasonableness or the amount of fees actually incurred by the creditor.[143] It has since been amended to provide that, if fees exceed $20,000, the debtor may demand proof of reasonableness.

Alabama's Mini-Code caps attorney fees at 15% of the unpaid debt for the transactions it covers.[144] Under the law of the District of Columbia, the agreement for a consumer credit sale or a direct installment loan may provide for reasonable attorney fees not in excess of 15% of the unpaid balance.[145] New Jersey court rules regulating the fees that may be charged in foreclosure actions override contractual provisions allowing for larger fees; courts have discretion to reduce, but not increase, fees calculated by the formula in the rules.[146]

6.5.2 *Requirement That Contractual Fees be Reasonable in Amount*

If there is no statutory guidance, some courts, taking a rigid freedom of contract approach, enforce attorney fee clauses that set a particular amount or formula for fees without regard to the reasonableness of the fees.[147] However some of these courts, though enforcing the clause in the particular case, qualify their opinions by indicating that a different result may be reached if there is proof that the clause is oppressive, unconscionable, or so disproportionate to foreseeable expenses as to be penal (violating the general contract law prohibition of penalty clauses in contracts).[148]

---

fees); Telerent Leasing Corp. v. Boaziz, 686 S.E.2d 520 (N.C. Ct. App. 2009) (applying statute capping attorney fees at 15%; when proceedings in state court and bankruptcy court were both necessary to recover on lease, total amount collected in the two proceedings could be used in calculating 15%); Reid v. Ayers, 531 S.E.2d 231 (N.C. Ct. App. 2000) (North Carolina statute limits attorney fees in debt collection matter to 15%). *See also In re* Jones, 2000 Bankr. LEXIS 1741 (Bankr. E.D.N.C. Dec. 22, 2000) (statutory cap on attorney fees, as applied to alternative mortgage, not preempted by federal law); N.C. Indus. Capital v. Clayton, 649 S.E.2d 14 (N.C. Ct. App. 2007) (North Carolina statute allowing attorney fees of 15% of "the outstanding balance" applies to lease; "outstanding balance" is amount actually awarded, not larger sum demanded by landlord); FNB Southeast v. Lane, 586 S.E.2d 530 (N.C. Ct. App. 2003) (guarantee contract is evidence of indebtedness covered by this statute). *Cf.* Trull v. Central Carolina Bank & Trust, 478 S.E.2d 39 (N.C. Ct. App. 1996) (adopting strained interpretation of statute to allow contractual fees even if creditor does not prevail; failing to give weight to statutory provision allowing fees only if the debt "be *collected* by or through an attorney"), *aff'd per curiam*, 490 S.E.2d 238 (N.C. 1997).

140 *See* Branch Banking & Trust Co. v. Price, 520 Fed. Appx. 262 (5th Cir. 2013) (N.C. law) (notice to guarantor was sufficient; when statute provides for 15% fees, showing of reasonableness not required); Davis Lake Cmty. Ass'n v. Feldman, 530 S.E.2d 865 (N.C. Ct. App. 2000) (North Carolina statute requires that before creditor could claim attorney fees it must notify consumer and provide a five-day grace period; statute also limits fees to 15% of debt). *But cf.* Finch v. Campus Habitat, L.L.C., 724 S.E.2d 174 (N.C. Ct. App. 2012) (notice and opportunity to pay not required when landlord counterclaimed for rent, in action brought by tenant).

141 Stillwell Enters., Inc. v. Interstate Equip. Co., 266 S.E.2d 812 (N.C. 1980); Lee Cycle Ctr. v. Wilson Cycle Ctr., 545 S.E.2d 745 (N.C. Ct. App. 2001), *aff'd per curiam*, 556 S.E.2d 293 (N.C. 2001). *See also* Sunbelt Rentals v. Corbridge, 171 F. Supp. 2d 14, 18 (D. Me. 2001) (N.C. law).

142 Ga. Code Ann. § 13-1-11(a)(3). *See* RadioShack Corp. v. Cascade Crossing II, L.L.C., 653 S.E.2d 680 (Ga. 2007) (state law placing 10% to 15% cap on percentage attorney fees provided for in "a note or other evidence of indebtedness" applies to real estate lease); Trust Assocs. v. Snead, 559 S.E.2d 502 (Ga. Ct. App. 2002) (demand letter inadequate when it failed to specify that grace period ran from date of receipt and failed to specifically identify the note and holder; reversing award of attorney fees).

143 Austin v. Bank of Am., 743 S.E.2d 399 (Ga. 2013).

144 Ala. Code § 5-19-10. *See Ex parte* Davis, 401 So. 2d 52 (Ala. 1980) (cap on attorney fees applies to federal credit unions and is not preempted by Federal Credit Union Act).

145 D.C. Code § 28-3806.

146 N.J. Rule of Court 4:42-9 (restricting amount of attorney fees that may be awarded in foreclosure action). *See* Barrows v. Chase Manhattan Mortgage Co., 465 F. Supp. 2d 347 (D.N.J. 2006) (FDCPA claim against lender's lawyer; fact issue whether legal fee demanded for mortgage reinstatement complied with New Jersey rule); *In re* Hatala, 295 B.R. 62 (Bankr. D.N.J. 2003) (discussion of New Jersey law concerning fee-shifting). *But cf.* Shinn v. Champion Mortgage Co., 2010 WL 500410 (D.N.J. Feb. 5, 2010) (Fair Foreclosure Act and regulations apply only to actual foreclosure, not to negotiated forbearance agreement).

147 Layfield v. Southeastern Constr. Coordinators, Inc., 492 S.E.2d 921 (Ga. Ct. App. 1997) (proof of reasonableness not required when clause made party liable for legal fees "incurred" and contractor presented evidence of amount of fees incurred); W.K. Henderson Iron Works & Supply Co. v. Meriwether Supply Co., 152 So. 69 (La. 1934) (enforcing 10% attorney fee clause; clause represents liquidated damages and is due regardless of extent or value of attorney's services); West v. Gladney, 533 S.E.2d 334 (S.C. Ct. App. 2000) (when contract specifies attorney fees as a percentage of the debt, court has no discretion to consider reasonableness; non-consumer case); Waller, Lansden, Dortch, Davis v. Hansey, 851 S.W.2d 131 (Tenn. 1992) (note's provision for 15% attorney fee if suit brought is an explicit and unconditional commitment to pay this amount, therefore is due even though attorneys represented themselves); Sturgis Nat'l Bank v. Smyth, 30 S.W. 678 (Tex. App. 1895) (clause for 10% attorney fee enforceable despite no charge for attorney services). *See also* Educ. Credit Mgmt. Corp. v. Cent. Equip. Co., 477 F. Supp. 2d 788 (E.D. Ky. 2007) (refusing to read requirement of reasonableness into fee-shifting statute).

148 *See, e.g.*, Zenner v. Holcomb, 210 P.3d 552 (Idaho 2009) (contract for actual attorney fees will be enforced as written, without determining reasonableness, but non-prevailing party may argue that fee is unconscionable penalty); McIntire v. Cagley, 37 Iowa 676 (Iowa 1873) (10% attorney fee reasonable and not a penalty as it was not disproportionate to expected injuries); Leventhall v. Krinsky, 90 N.E.2d 545 (Mass. 1950) (clause in note for percentage attorney fee is valid unless it is so unconscionable and oppressive as to amount to a penalty or a usurious device); Equitable Lumber Co. v. IPA Land Dev. Co., 344 N.E.2d 391 (N.Y. 1976) (30% fee not unconscionable between commercial parties, but remanding for determination whether 30% was unenforceable as a penalty because it was unreasonably large, not a reasonable

On the other hand, most courts read a requirement of reasonableness into any fee-shifting clause, regardless of its terms.[149] This position is consistent with the traditional authority of the courts to supervise the charging of fees for legal services under the courts' inherent and statutory power to regulate the practice of law.[150] Some of these courts explicitly adopt an indemnification theory, limiting the enforcement of the clause "only as indemnity for reasonable fees necessarily and properly paid or incurred." [151]

forecast of actual collection costs, or not commensurate with actual fees); Red Cliffs Corner, L.L.C. v. J.J. Hunan, Inc., 219 P.3d 619 (Utah Ct. App. 2009) (court has discretion to deny fees, notwithstanding an enforceable fee-shifting clause, under "extraordinary circumstances"; not shown here when statute explicitly permitted both treble damages and attorney fees for breach of commercial lease). *See generally* § 6.2.2, *supra* (whether contractual fee clauses are unenforceable as a penalty or invalid for other reasons).

149 *See, e.g.*, Fed. Deposit Ins. Corp. v. Bender, 127 F.3d 58, 63 (D.C. Cir. 1997) (under District of Columbia law, attorney fee provisions enforced "only as indemnity for reasonable fees necessarily and properly paid or incurred"); Regan v. Conway, 768 F. Supp. 2d 412 (E.D.N.Y. 2011) (court must determine reasonableness of contractual fees; here eliminating fees for which no contemporaneous time records provided and for hours spent on unsuccessfully resisting counterclaim, and further reducing fees to amount of plaintiff's recovery); Armada Bulk Carriers v. ConocoPhillips Co., 505 F. Supp. 2d 621 (N.D. Cal. 2007) (N.Y. law) (court awarding contractual fees must make its own determination whether the request is justified by the time and labor expended); Comi v. D.S.C. Fin., 994 F. Supp. 121 (N.D.N.Y. 1998) (Texas law) (contractual attorney fees must be reasonable in amount and in their relationship to amount in controversy, even if contract clause does not require reasonableness); Coop. Fin. Ass'n v. Garst, 927 F. Supp. 1179 (N.D. Iowa 1996) (fee-shifting provision will be enforced, but court will determine reasonableness of attorney fees); Consumers Time Credit, Inc. v. Remark Corp., 259 F. Supp. 135 (E.D. Pa. 1966) (amount specified in contract may not be reasonable; court may use its equitable powers to protect the borrower and deny or reduce fees), *aff'd*, 377 F.2d 553 (3d Cir. 1967); *In re* Coates, 292 B.R. 894 (Bankr. C.D. Ill. 2003) (standard of reasonableness implied in all contractual fee-shifting clauses; setting forth requirements for proof, which include terms of creditors' contract with their lawyers); Mahani v. Essex Media Group, 935 A.2d 242 (Del. Super. Ct. 2007) (when awarding contractual attorney fees, court should apply criteria of rules of professional conduct to determine reasonableness); Powers v. Rockford Stop'n'Go, Inc., 761 N.E.2d 237 (Ill. App. Ct. 2001) (fee-shifting clauses enforceable but will be "strictly construed and enforced at the discretion of the trial court"; criteria similar to federal lodestar test), Stewart v. TT Commercial One, L.L.C., 911 N.E.2d 51 (Ind. Ct. App. 2009) (contractual fees must be reasonable; if not inconsequential, must provide objective evidence of nature of services and reasonableness of fee); Bruno v. Wells Fargo Bank, 850 N.E.2d 940 (Ind. Ct. App. 2006) (fee-shifting clauses enforceable, but amount must be reasonable); Franklin College v. Turner, 844 N.E.2d 99, 105 (Ind. Ct. App. 2006) (awarding $420 to collection attorney who requested $4375; question is not how much creditor paid to its counsel, but what is a reasonable attorney fee); Berkemeier v. Rushville Nat'l Bank, 459 N.E.2d 1194 (Ind. Ct. App. 1984) (contingent fee contract between obligee and his attorney not binding upon debtor; obligee is limited to reasonable fee based on other factors); Leenerts Farms, Inc. v. Rogers, 421 So. 2d 216 (La. 1982) (courts may inquire into reasonableness of claimed attorney fee regardless of provisions of note); St. Hilaire & Assocs. v. Harbor Corp., 607 A.2d 905 (Me. 1992) (contract clause for attorney fees will be enforced, but fees must be reasonable); Myers v. Kayhoe, 892 A.2d 520 (Md. 2006) (interpreting fee-shifting provisions to allow reasonable fees; party claiming fees must provide court with information necessary to determine reasonableness; court has broad discretion, but abuse of discretion here as fees wholly denied); Carroll Indep. Fuel Co. v. Wash. Real Estate Inv. Trust, 32 A.3d 128 (Md. Ct. Spec. App. 2011) (whether or not contract specifies reasonable fees, trial court must determine reasonableness, applying criteria of Maryland Lawyers' Rule of Professional Conduct 1.5); Zeeland Farms v. JBL Enters., 555 N.W.2d 733, 736 (Mich. Ct. App. 1996) (recovery of contractual attorney fees limited to a reasonable amount); Sheppard v. East, 192 S.W.3d 518 (Mo. Ct. App. 2006) (enforcement of attorney fee clause not discretionary, but court must "hear from the parties" and apply its expertise to determine reasonable fees); Green v. Morgan Props., 73 A.3d 478 (N.J. 2013) (fee awards, regardless of their basis, must be reasonable); McMullen v. Kutz, 985 A.2d 769 (Pa. 2009) (even if contract specifies fees "incurred," court has discretion to determine reasonableness); Graystone Bank v. Grove Estates, L.P., 58 A.3d 1277 (Pa. Super. Ct. 2012) (percentage attorney fee provision, here in cognovit clause of non-consumer contract, "must work a reasonable result under the circumstances"), *appeals granted*, 70 A.3d 1242, 1243–44, 71 A.3d 271, 272–73 (Pa. 2013); Dole v. Wade, 510 S.W.2d 909 (Tenn. 1974) (court is not bound by contractual provision for particular amount of fees and will only enforce reasonable amount); Republic Bank v. Shook, 653 S.W.2d 278 (Tex. 1983); R.T. Nielson Co. v. Cook, 40 P.3d 1119 (Utah 2002) (contractual attorney fees provisions enforced, but court has discretion to determine reasonable fee; detailed documentation required); Kealamakia, Inc. v. Kealamakia, 213 P.3d 13 (Utah Ct. App. 2009) (contingent fee based on contract between prevailing party and its attorney is cap on fee amount; court must still determine reasonableness); Stafford v. JHL, Inc., 194 P.3d 315 (Wyo. 2008) (affirming denial of fees; even if contract has fee-shifting clause, court has discretion as to amount and may deny fees if award would be inequitable); McGuire v. Lowery, 2 P.3d 527 (Wyo. 2000) (although contract provision for attorney fees is valid, court must exercise discretion to award only reasonable fees and may disallow if award would be inequitable; fees properly refused when neither party clearly prevailed on all issues); McLain v. Anderson, 933 P.2d 468 (Wyo. 1997) (requiring showing that attorney fees were reasonable even though contract clause did not require reasonableness; attorney fees are a form of punitive damages which must be proven to have been incurred and reasonable).

150 *See, e.g.*, Leenerts Farms, Inc. v. Rogers, 421 So. 2d 216 (La. 1982) (courts may inquire into reasonableness of attorney fees as part of their inherent authority to regulate the practice of law); *In re* First Nat'l Bank of E. Islip v. Brower, 368 N.E.2d 1240, 1242 (N.Y. 1977).

151 Fed. Deposit Ins. Corp. v. Bender, 127 F.3d 58, 63 (D.C. Cir. 1997). *See also* Ozbnakir v. Scotti, 906 F. Supp. 2d 188, (W.D.N.Y. 2012) (contract provided for reasonable fees; court will limit award to fees actually incurred, if reasonable, based on what reasonable client would pay); *In re* Gebhard, 140 F. 571 (M.D. Pa. 1905) (clause in note providing for 5% collection fee merely allows indemnification for reasonable attorney fees up to 5%; when creditor-attorney pursued confession of judgment *pro se*, there were no out-of-pocket expenditures to indemnify); *In re* Mathews, 208 B.R. 506, 514 (Bankr. N.D. Ala. 1997) (Alabama treats contractual attorney fee clauses as intended to indemnify the creditor against any necessity for employing an attorney, but not to secure the payment of a fee for unnecessary services or services required because of some wrongful act by the creditor; party claiming contractual attorney fee must have acted reasonably in employing counsel, and services must be reasonable under the circumstances); Corvee, Inc. v. French, 943 N.E.2d 844 (Ind. Ct. App. 2011) (contractual fees are allowed only if reasonably and necessarily incurred; refusing to enforce 40% fee clause, and reducing fees from $3400 to $1000 for default judgment on medical bill); F.R. Hernandez Constr. v. Nat'l Bank of Commerce, 578 S.W.2d 675 (Tex. 1979) (agreement to pay attorney fees based on percentage of unpaid balance and interest on a promissory note was a contract to indemnify the holder of the note for attorney's expenses actually incurred in collection, not a promise to pay contractual

Courts that read a requirement of reasonableness into attorney fee clauses allow reimbursement only for fees actually incurred[152] and refuse to indemnify unnecessary expenses.[153] While the lodestar approach—multiplying the reasonable number of hours expended by a reasonable hourly rate—may be appropriate under certain fee-shifting statutes because of the public purposes they promote, it is not necessarily the correct approach for contractual fees, and courts may give significant weight to other factors such as the amount of the debt.[154]

When reasonableness is required (whether by case law, by statute, or by the terms of the contract), some courts do not require proof of actual expenditures by the plaintiff but hold that the amount stated in the contract is prima facie recoverable, subject to the defendant's proof of unreasonableness[155] or a finding by the court of excessiveness.[156] A Mississippi statute provides that, when a court is authorized to award reasonable

amount); Island Block Corp. v. Webster, 17 V.I. 29 (V.I. 1980) (attorney fee clause is a contract of indemnity and will be enforced only to the extent it reflects the cost of services actually rendered).

152 County of Oswego Indus. Dev. Agency v. Fulton Cogeneration Assocs., L.P., 636 F. Supp. 2d 159 (N.D.N.Y. 2009), *aff'd*, 91 Fed. Appx. 3 (2d Cir. 2010) (amount of fee actually incurred, so long as not unreasonable); *In re* WCS Enters., 381 B.R. 206 (Bankr. E.D. Va. 2007) ("an attorney's fee provision in a contract, even though measured as a percentage of the amount due, entitles the creditor only to reasonable fees based on the work performed"); Mix v. Tumanjan Dev. Corp., 126 Cal. Rptr. 2d 267 (Cal. Ct. App. 2002) (fees not "incurred" unless litigant liable to pay out of pocket; attorney who represented self not entitled to fees for own time but could claim fees for other attorney who assisted him); Cardo v. Bd. of Managers, Jefferson Vill. Condo 3, 891 N.Y.S.2d 97 (N.Y. App. Div. 2009) (condo board did not "incur" fees within meaning of by-laws, when attorney was paid by board's insurance company); Kamco Supply Corp. v. Annex Contracting, Inc., 261 A.D.2d 363 (N.Y. 1999) (contractual provision setting attorney fees as a percentage of the debt should be enforced only if the amount is reasonable and warranted for services actually rendered). *See also* Spencer v. Hendersen-Webb, Inc. 81 F. Supp. 2d 582 (D. Md. 1999) (lease that allowed legal costs and expenses does not allow collection of fees when none have been incurred); Mullins v. Richlands Nat'l Bank, 403 S.E.2d 334 (Va. 1991) (when contract provided for attorney fees but did not fix the amount, court's award must be based on time consumed, effort expended, nature of services, or other circumstance; expert testimony is usually necessary). *But cf.* Menasha Forest Prods. Corp. v. Curry Cnty. Title, Inc., 249 P.3d 126 (Or. 2011) (escrow agent "incurred" attorney fees, even though they were paid by title insurer; party incurs fees when it becomes obligated for them; here escrow agent would have owed fees if title insurer did not pay).

153 *See, e.g.*, Hog Slat, Inc. v. Ebert, 2002 WL 535061 (8th Cir. Apr. 11, 2002) (reducing fees from $62,000 to $38,000; court has discretion to determine reasonable amount); Cable Marine, Inc. v. M/V Trust Me II, 632 F.2d 1344 (5th Cir. 1980) (no recovery of contractual collection fees needlessly incurred by pursuing suit after generous settlement offer); First Nat'l Bank v. Union Tavern Corp., 794 P.2d 261 (Colo. App. 1990) (collection attorney fees may not be awarded for pursuing an erroneous claim); B. & P. Enters. v. Overland Equip. Co., 758 A.2d 1026 (Md. Ct. Spec. App. 2000) (detailed discussion of criteria for reasonable attorney fees; burden on party seeking fees); TAL Fin. Corp. v. CSC Consulting, Inc., 844 N.E.2d 1085 (Mass. 2006) (when case should have been resolved "long before [lessor] hired counsel," any fee award would be unreasonable; lessor, relying on unenforceable penalty provision, had sought $86,000 damages and received $9500, which was less than pre-trial settlement offer).

154 Electrical Wholesalers, Inc. v. V.P. Elec., Inc., 33 A.3d 828 (Conn. App. Ct. 2012) (guidelines for civil rights and UDAP cases not relevant in contract dispute between two similarly situated businesses); Monmouth Meadows Homeowners' Ass'n. v. Hamilton, 7 A.3d 1 (Md. 2010) (lodestar method is appropriate under fee-shifting statutes because of underlying public policies, but for contract claims fees should be based on factors listed in professional rules).

155 Fed. Deposit Ins. Corp. v. Bender, 127 F.3d 58 (D.C. Cir. 1997) (attorney fee clause may be enforced as written if debtors do not challenge reasonableness, but, when issue is properly raised, trial court determines reasonable fee); Webster Drilling Co. v. Walker, 286 F.2d 114 (10th Cir. 1961); Sherman St. Assocs., L.L.C. v. JTH Tax, Inc. 2011 WL 5925063 (D. Conn. Nov. 21, 2011) (when contract allows fee-shifting and does not require reasonableness, court should award amount billed unless it is unreasonable on its face or shown by other party to be unreasonable); *In re* Hathaway, 364 B.R. 220, 249 (Bankr. E.D. Va. 2007) (percentage attorney fee presumed reasonable); *In re* Bowden, 326 B.R. 62 (Bankr. E.D. Va. 2005) (20% attorney fee in note presumed reasonable when neither side introduced evidence of amount and value of attorney services); McDowell Mtn. Ranch Cmty. Ass'n v. Simons, 165 P.3d 667 (Ariz. Ct. App. 2007) (homeowners' association covenant provides for "all attorney fees and costs"; reasonableness of contractual fees presumed; burden on homeowner to show unreasonableness); Theobald v. Nosser, 752 So. 2d 1036 (Miss. 1999) (when commercial promissory note allowed reasonable attorney fees and non-prevailing party did not contest reasonableness of amount, court should allow attorney fees in amount claimed); F.R. Hernandez Constr. v. Nat'l Bank of Commerce, 578 S.W.2d 675 (Tex. 1979) (obligor must plead and prove that contractual fee was unreasonable and lesser amount was reasonable under the circumstances); O'Kehie v. Harris Leasing Co., 80 S.W.3d 316 (Tex. App. 2002) (25% fee provided by lease is prima facie reasonable, and losing party has burden of showing the contrary). *Cf.* A & E Int'l Enters., Inc. v. Gold Credit Co., 450 So. 2d 1166 (Fla. Dist. Ct. App. 1984) (statute creates conclusive presumption that attorney fee award is reasonable if amount stated in the instrument does not exceed 10% of principal). *But see* Coastal Cmty. Bank v. Jones, 23 So. 3d 757 (Fla. Dist. Ct. App. 2009) (Fla. Stat. § 687.06, which establishes a presumption of reasonableness of fee of 10% of remaining mortgage principal, does not excuse lender from showing that fee was actually incurred). *See generally* A. Della Porta, Annotation, *Validity of provision in promissory note or other evidences of indebtedness for payment as attorneys' fees, expenses and costs of collection, of specified percentage of note*, 17 A.L.R.2d 288, 303–04 (1951).

156 *See, e.g.*, S.N.A., Inc. v. Array, 173 F. Supp. 2d 347 (E.D. Pa. 2001) (discussion of reasonableness of counsel's hourly rate and number of hours; reducing claimed fees as excessive), *aff'd*, 2002 WL 1900053 (3d Cir. Aug. 19, 2002); Cooperative Fin. Ass'n v. Garst, 927 F. Supp. 1179 (N.D. Iowa 1996) (although prevailing creditor opted for "Rolls Royce class" representation, awarding fees only for "Chevrolet class," because contractual fee-shifting provisions "should not be used to justify gouging losers with the excuse that the losers agreed to them"); First Union Bank v. Kaskel, 847 F. Supp. 961 (S.D. Fla. 1994) (Fla. Stat. § 687.06 provided that it was unnecessary for a court to "adjudge an attorney's fee to be reasonable and just" if it did not exceed 10% of the amount due; court may review the reasonableness of any attorney fees; fees actually incurred, which totaled less than 10%, were reasonable); McKeever v. Fiore, 829 A.2d 846 (Conn. App. Ct. 2003) (court may reduce fees in foreclosure case *sua sponte* or after a hearing if opponent objects; sharply reducing attorney fees when delay resulted from "outrageous" lack of diligence by lender); Brandner v. New Orleans Office Supply, 654 So. 2d 858 (La. Ct. App. 1995) (court had discretion to reduce excessive attorney fees set by contract; approving 10% fees); Marine Midland Bank v. Scallen, 161 A.D.2d 103 (N.Y. 1990) (court not bound to award contractual 15% as attorney fees if court determines it not reasonable); Meredith v. Smith, 35 P.3d 1002 (Okla. Civ. App. 2001) (fee-shifting permitted but $3300 attorney fee for $458 default judgment in small claims court appears unreasonable; remanding to determine reasonable fee); Dole v. Wade, 510 S.W.2d 909 (Tenn.

attorney fees, it "shall not require the party seeking such fees to put on proof of reasonableness of the amount sought, but shall make the award based on the information already before it and the court's own opinion based on experience and observation." [157] But other courts require the creditor to submit evidence showing the expenditure of time reasonably necessary to collect the debt,[158] often including detailed affidavits of time and activity by attorneys seeking fees in collection actions.[159]

1974) (amount stated in contract is prima facie recoverable, subject to reduction by the court if sum is unreasonable).

157 Miss. Code Ann. § 9-1-41. *But cf.* Speights v. Speights, 126 So. 3d 7 (Miss. Ct. App. 2013) (evidence of reasonableness required when there are "many billable hours that the court is unable to observe or lacks knowledge of").

158 Kansas Penn Gaming, L.L.C. v. HV Props. of Kan., L.L.C., 790 F. Supp. 2d 1307 (D. Kan. 2011) (burden on claimant to show reasonableness), *aff'd*, 662 F.3d 1275 (10th Cir. 2011); Garden State Auto Park Pontiac GMC Truck, Inc. v. Elec. Data Sys. Corp., 31 F. Supp. 2d 378 (D.N.J. 1998) (Texas law) (burden is on party seeking fees); El Escorial Owners' Ass'n v. DLC Plastering, Inc., 65 Cal. Rptr. 3d 524 (Cal. Ct. App. 2007) ("inadequately documented or overbilled" fees sharply reduced); Greeley Nat'l Bank v. Sloan, 677 P.2d 409 (Colo. App. 1983) (plaintiff had burden to show reasonableness of attorney fees); Smith v. Snyder, 839 A.2d 589 (Conn. 2004) (party claiming statutory fee must state amount claimed and present evidence of hours worked, and court may apply its general knowledge in determining whether claim excessive); Gagne v. Vaccaro, 984 A.2d 1084 (Conn. App. 2009) (burden of showing reasonableness on claimant; more than "trial court's general knowledge" required: judgment debtor entitled to hearing to examine under oath the billing attorney); Murray v. Barrett, 571 S.E.2d 448 (Ga. Ct. App. 2002) (award of attorney fees not supported by evidence when party did not present evidence of actual amount and reasonableness, but only estimated fees as "about $6000," and judge noted that attorney was in good standing and "experienced"); Decatur Imaging Ctr. v. Ames, 608 N.E.2d 1198, 1202 (Ill. App. Ct. 1992) (dicta) (collection attorney who seeks fees must show that the fees sought are reasonable); Holliday v. Crooked Creek Villages Homeowners' Ass'n, 759 N.E.2d 1088 (Ind. Ct. App. 2001) (amount within trial court's discretion, but must be supported by evidence; counsel's representations to court regarding his hours and rate sufficient); Silwad Two, L.L.C. v. Zenith I, Inc., 111 So. 3d 405 (La. Ct. App. 2012) (drastically reducing claimed fees when prevailing party, who provided no evidence of hours, had just filed a motion and a petition and participated in a very short hearing); Rauch v. McCall, 761 A.2d 76 (Md. Ct. Spec. App. 2000) (court must evaluate reasonableness; evidence required; similar to federal lodestar); Zeeland Farms v. JBL Enters., 555 N.W.2d 733, 736 (Mich. Ct. App. 1996) (party seeking contractual fees has burden of introducing evidence of reasonableness; testimony of creditor's credit manager was probative when manager's duties included hiring lawyers and approving their invoices); Indus. & Mech. Contractors of Memphis, Inc. v. Tim Mote Plumbing, L.L.C., 962 So. 2d 632 (Miss. Ct. App. 2007) (entitlement to fees depends on specific proof; fees properly denied when party failed to allocate fees between successful and unsuccessful claims); Green v. Morgan Props., 73 A.3d 478, 492 (N.J. 2013) (party seeking contractual fees has burden of proving their reasonableness); Citibank v. Martin, 807 N.Y.S.2d 284 (N.Y. Civ. Ct. 2005) (debt buyer must show fee arrangement, services actually rendered, time spent, nature of issues, and other "relevant factors"); Chang v. Soldier Summit Dev., 82 P.3d 203 (Utah Ct. App. 2003) (criteria include hours worked and whether work was necessary; remanding for determination of reasonable fee); Anderson v. Meier, 641 P.2d 187 (Wyo. 1982) (proof of reasonableness of attorney fee must be introduced). *See also In re* Hight, 393 B.R. 484 (Bankr. S.D. Tex. 2008) (flat fee may be appropriate for attorney to conduct a foreclosure sale, but, when debtor established that foreclosure sale had not occurred, burden was on creditor to show reasonable number of hours); Charette v. Fitzgerald, 213 S.W.3d 505 (Tex. App. 2006) (for open account, court may take judicial notice of customary and usual fees; for violation of property code, reasonableness must be shown; reversing award of fees to tenants because evidence of reasonableness not presented); Lee v. Mulford, 611 S.E.2d 349 (Va. 2005) (upholding jury's determination that parties to a promissory note should bear their own attorney fees despite fee-shifting clause in the note in the absence of proof of attorney fees incurred). *Cf.* Allfirst Bank v. Dep't of Health & Mental Hygiene, 780 A.2d 440 (Md. Ct. Spec. App. 2001) (when percentage fee not specified, burden on party claiming fees to show reasonableness). *But cf.* Layfield v. Southeastern Constr. Coordinators, Inc., 492 S.E.2d 921 (Ga. Ct. App. 1997) (proof of reasonableness not required when contractor, in residential construction agreement containing attorney fee clause, proved actual amount of attorney fees).

159 *See, e.g.*, Au v. Funding Group, Inc., 933 F. Supp. 2d 1264 (D. Haw. 2013) (disapproving block billing); Regan v. Conway, 768 F. Supp. 2d 412 (E.D.N.Y. 2011) (denying portion of fee request that was not supported by contemporaneous time records); Student Loan Mktg. Ass'n v. Hanes, 181 F.R.D. 629 (S.D. Cal. 1998) (must provide evidence of reasonableness, including billing rates, hourly rate, and proof that this rate was reasonable for lawyer of counsel's skill and experience); Fleet Bank v. Steeves, 793 F. Supp. 18 (D. Me. 1992); *In re* Coates, 292 B.R. 894 (Bankr. C.D. Ill. 2003) (Illinois standard similar to federal lodestar); First Midwest Bank v. Sparks, 682 N.E.2d 373, 382 (Ill. App. Ct. 1997) (fee petition must specify services performed, by whom, amount of time, and hourly rate); Heller Fin. Inc. v. Johns-Byrne Co., 637 N.E.2d 1085 (Ill. App. Ct. 1994) (must document the hours, services performed, skill, and difficulty of the case, and show "reasonable connection between the fees and the amount involved in the litigation"); Bruno v. Wells Fargo Bank, 850 N.E.2d 940 (Ind. Ct. App. 2006) (fee affidavit insufficient when it showed only total hours and range of hourly rates and did not break down hours and rates for each attorney); B. & P. Enters. v. Overland Equip. Co., 758 A.2d 1026 (Md. Ct. Spec. App. 2000) (number of hours multiplied by hourly rate insufficient; detailed time records required); Riverview Muir Doran, L.L.C. v. JADT Dev. Group, L.L.C., 776 N.W.2d 172 (Minn. Ct. App. 2009) (Minn. Gen. R. Pract. §§ 119.01 to 119.05 prescribe contents of fee application: description of each item of work, date, time spent, identity of lawyer, and lawyer's billing rate); SO/Bluestar v. Canarsie Hotel Corp., 825 N.Y.S.2d 80 (N.Y. App. Div. 2006) (affidavit "wholly insufficient"; must provide breakdown of rates and hours); ACT South, L.L.C. v. Reco Elec. Co., 299 P.3d 505 (Okla. Civ. App. 2012) (fee requests must include detailed time records); Hardaway Concrete Co. v. Hall Contracting Corp., 647 S.E.2d 488 (S.C. Ct. App. 2007) (award of contractual or statutory attorney fees requires specific findings of fact regarding (1) nature, extent, and difficulty of legal services; (2) time and labor; (3) professional standing of counsel; (4) contingency of compensation; (5) fee customarily charged in the area for similar services; (6) beneficial results obtained); McLain v. Anderson, 933 P.2d 468 (Wyo. 1997) (party claiming contractual attorney fees must provide itemized billing plus proof of reasonableness). *See also* Troth Corp. v. Deutsch, Kerrigan & Stiles, L.L.P., 951 So. 2d 1162 (La. Ct. App. 2007) (fee request adequately supported when lawyer provided billing records, and court had opportunity to observe amount and quality of work); Usrey v. Wilson, 66 P.2d 1000 (Okla. Civ. App. 2002) (detailed time records preferred but not mandatory; may be possible to reconstruct basis for fees, but general estimate of hours is insufficient); Burnside Air Conditioning & Heating, Inc. v. T.S. Young Corp., 113 S.W.3d 889 (Tex. App. 2003) (court need not receive evidence on all factors; reasonableness shown when lawyer testified to hours worked, work done, and hourly rate); R.T. Nielson Co. v. Cook, 40 P.3d 1119 (Utah 2002) (attorney's affidavit acceptable when it provided legal

A California decision holds that equitable factors may be considered in determining the amount of a statutory or contractual attorney fee award.[160] It also holds, however, that the ability of the losing party to pay an attorney fee award should not be taken into account in determining the amount of contractual fees.[161]

6.5.3 Percentage-Based Fees

An important issue underlying the indemnification approach is whether a fee must be reasonable in relation to the efforts expended to collect the particular debt, or whether the fee is reasonable if it is set as a percentage of the debt. Courts are divided on this question.[162] The latter approach results in

basis for award, nature of work performed, hours worked by attorneys and non-attorneys, hourly rates, and affirmation that rates comparable to those for similar services; submission not ideal because did not include contemporary billing records). *Cf.* Sterling Homes, Ltd. v. Rasberry, 759 N.E.2d 163 (Ill. App. Ct. 2001) (lawyer's affidavit sufficient to show fees were "reasonable and warranted by existing law").

160 Walker v. Ticor Title Co., 138 Cal. Rptr. 3d 820 (Cal. Ct. App. 2012).

161 *Id.*

162 *Percentage fee permitted:* Taylor v. Luper, Sheriff, & Niedenthal, 74 F. Supp. 2d 761 (S.D. Ohio 1999) (collection attorney fee of one-third of debt not excessive when this was the amount the creditor would have to pay the collection attorney); BDG Int'l v. Bowers, 303 P.3d 140 (Colo. App. 2013) (Cal. law) (affirming judgment for attorney fees of 40% of amount due, rather than using lodestar method, when commercial contract made debtor liable for all costs incurred by creditor in event of default, and creditor's attorney charged 40% contingency fee); McIntire v. Cagley, 37 Iowa 676 (Iowa 1873) (10% attorney fee reasonable and not a penalty as it was not disproportionate to expected injuries); Indus. Screw & Supply Co. v. WPS, Inc., 926 So. 2d 134 (La. Ct. App. 2006) (enforcing contractual 25% attorney fee in open account claim; statute provides that if claimant and its attorney have agreed on fixed or determinable amount of attorney fees, the claimant is entitled to that amount); Leventhall v. Krinsky, 90 N.E.2d 545 (Mass. 1950) (clause in note for percentage attorney fee is valid unless it is so unconscionable and oppressive as to amount to a penalty or a usurious device); West v. Club at Spanish Peaks, L.L.C., 186 P.3d 1228 (Mont. 2008) (awarding 40% contingent fee when contract allowed fees "actually incurred"; noting that, when both contingent and hourly fees are "appropriate methods of billing," court is permitted but not required to award percentage fee and that sum here met statutory criteria for reasonableness); West v. Gladney, 533 S.E.2d 334 (S.C. Ct. App. 2000) (reversing refusal to award fees of 15% as specified by note; when contract specifies amount of attorney fee, court has no discretion to consider reasonableness; nonconsumer case); NationsBank v. Scott Farm, 465 S.E.2d 98 (S.C. Ct. App. 1995) (enforcing 10% attorney fee clause in non-consumer contract; when clause provides for specific rate, it governs and no finding of reasonableness is required); Waller, Lansden, Dortch, Davis v. Hansey, 851 S.W.2d 131 (Tenn. 1992) (note's provision for 15% attorney fee if suit brought is an explicit and unconditional commitment to pay this amount and is due even though attorneys represented themselves). *See also* Som v. Daniels Law Offices, P.C., 573 F. Supp. 2d 349 (D. Mass. 2008) (fact question whether percentage-based fee, and fee for sums not yet collected, were "expressly authorized" by contract allowing attorney fees "incurred by us"); Brandner v. New Orleans Office Supply, 654 So. 2d 858 (La. Ct. App. 1995) (La. Civil Code makes agreement to pay attorney fees in a fixed or determinable amount enforceable, but court still may deny "clearly excessive" fees; upholding 10% fee); Franklin Collection Serv., Inc. v. Stewart, 863 So. 2d 925 (Miss. 2003) (medical bill was open account for which statute allowed attorney fee; one-third contingent fee presumptively reasonable); Trull v. Central Carolina Bank & Trust, 478 S.E.2d 39 (N.C. Ct. App. 1996) (upholding contractual 15% attorney fee, even though it exceeded actual fees incurred, and creditor bank was only partially successful), *aff'd*, 490 S.E.2d 238 (N.C. 1997); Stewart v. Indus. Nat'l Bank, 458 A.2d 675 (R.I. 1983) (approving of entry of default judgments for amount due plus one-third attorney fee pursuant to contract clause for reasonable attorney fees when creditor submitted affidavit in each case).

Percentage fee forbidden: Fed. Deposit Ins. Corp. v. Bender, 127 F.3d 58, 63 (D.C. Cir. 1997) (District of Columbia law; contract clause for fixed percentage fees will not be enforced according to its terms; party only entitled to indemnity for reasonable fees necessarily and properly paid or incurred); Munoz v. Pipestone Fin., L.L.C., 513 F. Supp. 2d 1076 (D. Minn. 2007) (contingent fee agreement between creditor and collection firm not binding on debtor, who agreed in contract only to pay reasonable fees; creditor liable under FDCPA for seeking fees at outset of collection suit, before they had been incurred); Marine Midland Bank v. Kilbane, 573 F. Supp. 469 (D. Md. 1983) (New York law) (creditor only entitled to reasonable fees, even if note specifies a percentage); *In re* WCS Enters., 381 B.R. 206 (Bankr. E.D. Va. 2007) (entire 10% attorney fee did not become due when matter referred to attorney; "an attorney's fee provision in a contract, even though measured as a percentage of the amount due, entitles the creditor only to reasonable fees based on the work performed"); Corvee, Inc. v. French, 943 N.E.2d 844 (Ind. Ct. App. 2011) (refusing to enforce 40% fee for default judgment on medical debt; attorney fees should compensate for fees reasonably and actually incurred and not be "a cloak for speculation and profit"); Spears v. Brennan, 745 N.E.2d 862 (Ind. Ct. App. 2001) (contingency fee agreed to between creditor and its attorney cannot be added to a judgment against the debtor under a "reasonable attorney fee" clause without other objective evidence of reasonableness); Berkemeier v. Rushville Nat'l Bank, 459 N.E.2d 1194 (Ind. Ct. App. 1984) (contingent fee contract between obligee and his attorney not binding upon debtor; obligee is limited to reasonable fee based on other factors); Leenerts Farms, Inc. v. Rogers, 421 So. 2d 216 (La. 1982) (provision of note fixing attorney fee at 20% is not binding on court; court may inquire into reasonableness); Brecheen v. News Group, L.P., 105 So. 3d 1011 (La. Ct. App. 2012) (refusing to award amount of contingency fee that prevailing party paid its attorney; fee award must be based on usual criteria for reasonableness); Ford Motor Credit Co. v. Blanchard, 620 So. 2d 286 (La. Ct. App. 1992) (prohibition against attorney's acceptance of clearly excessive fee cannot be abrogated by provision in note; remanding for evidentiary hearing when there was insufficient evidence that 25% fee required by note was reasonable); Trustees of Tufts College v. Ramsdell, 554 N.E.2d 34 (Mass. App. Ct. 1990) (attorney fees are limited to reasonable amount, and court is not bound by creditor's one-third contingent fee contract with collection attorney); Alcoa Edgewater No. 1 Fed. Credit Union v. Carroll, 210 A.2d 68 (N.J. 1965) (percentage recovery fixed by note is allowable only if it is reasonable); Kamco Supply Corp. v. Annex Contracting, Inc., 261 A.D.2d 363 (N.Y. 1999) (contractual provision setting attorney fees as percentage of the debt should be enforced only if the amount is reasonable and warranted for services actually rendered); Cheshire Academy v. Lee, 448 N.Y.S.2d 112 (N.Y. Civ. Ct. 1982) (even if statute allowing 20% attorney fee were applicable, it would merely set a maximum); F.R. Hernandez Constr. v. Nat'l Bank of Commerce, 578 S.W.2d 675 (Tex. 1979) (agreement to pay attorney fees based on percentage of unpaid balance and interest on a promissory note was a contract to indemnify the holder of the note for reasonable attorney's expenses actually incurred in collection, not a promise to pay contractual amount). *See also* Stolicker v. Muller, Muller, Richmond, Harms, Myers & Sgroi, 2005 WL 2180481 (W.D. Mich. Sept. 9, 2005) (when state law required a court to award attorney fees, prejudgment claim for a percentage fee violated FDCPA); Richmond v. Malad, 2001 U.S. Dist. LEXIS 10505 (S.D. Ind. July 6, 2001) (denying motion to dismiss claim that seeking percentage-based attorney fee was deceptive and breach of statutory and contractual provisions allowing "reasonable" fee); Brooks v. Auto Sales & Servs., Inc., 2001 WL 686950 (S.D. Ind. June 15, 2001) (allowing consumer to go forward with FDCPA action against attorney who routinely added 33.33% attorney fee to amount claimed in small claims actions for deficiency on repossessed cars when contract clause allowed "reasonable" fees but did not specify a percentage); Kojetin v. C.U. Recovery, Inc., 1999 WL 33916416 (D. Minn. Feb. 17, 1999) (stating in dicta that Minnesota prohibits percentage attorney fee clauses and allows fees only to extent of reasonable value of services actually performed), *adopted by* 1999 WL 1847329 (D. Minn. Mar. 29, 1999), *aff'd*, 212 F.3d 1318 (8th Cir. 2000) (per curiam); Raza v. Deutsche Bank Nat'l Trust Co., 100 So. 3d 121 (Fla. Dist. Ct. App. 2012) (refusing fees when prevailing consumer, who had paid his attorney a flat fee, did not present evidence of hours worked or hourly rate); Discover Bank v. Rusher, 53 So. 3d 651 (La. Ct. App. 2010) (percentage fee not per se unreasonable, but 20% fee unreasonable and an abuse of discretion in credit card collection case in which creditor won on summary judgment; simplicity of the issues, amount of work actually done, and consumer's poverty require reduction); Harrison Cnty. Bd. of Supervisors v. Carlo Corp. Inc., 833 So. 2d 582 (Miss. 2002) (statute allows attorney fee not to exceed 25%; county board acted arbitrarily and capriciously in imposing attorney fee of 25% of corporate tax debt when this resulted in $79,000 fee for writing one letter; fee violated both common sense and rule of professional responsibility that required fees to be reasonable); Graystone Bank v. Grove Estates, L.P., 58 A.3d 1277 (Pa. Super. Ct. 2012) (percentage attorney fee provision, here in cognovit clause of non-consumer contract, "must work a reasonable result under the circumstances;" unconscionable provision, or one working unconscionable results, will not be enforced), *appeals granted*, 70 A.3d 1243–44, 71 A.3d 271–73 (Pa. 2013). *Cf. In re* First Nat'l Bank of E. Islip v. Brower, 368 N.E.2d 1240, 1242 (N.Y. 1977) (trial court properly awarded fees on *quantum meruit* basis rather than 15% provided by contract, even though statute allows contracts to provide for fees up to 15%; "the reasonable value of legal services rendered incident to the recovery of a default judgment will not automatically and always be equal to a particular percentage of the debt being collected"); Equitable Lumber Co. v. IPA Land Dev. Co., 344 N.E.2d 391 (N.Y. 1976) (30% fee not unconscionable between commercial parties, but remanding for determination whether 30% was unenforceable as a penalty because it was unreasonably large, not a reasonable forecast of actual collection costs, or not commensurate with actual fees); Best Bldg. Supply & Lumber Corp. v. Mastercraft Homes & Renovations, Inc., 835 N.Y.S.2d 355 (N.Y. App. Div. 2007) (error to award attorney fees as percentage of debt without evaluation of reasonableness); Coniglio v. Regan, 588 N.Y.S.2d 887 (N.Y. App. Div. 1992) (error to award fees based solely on fixed rate set forth in promissory note; remanding for evidence of reasonableness); Citizens & Southern Nat'l Bank v. Easton, 427 S.E.2d 640 (S.C. 1993) (stating that, when contracts provided for attorney fees at a specific rate—that is, 15% of principal and interest—"it was error to deny such fees," but also remanding for a "determination of attorney's fees incurred"); Cox v. Hagan, 100 S.E. 666 (Va. 1919) (construing contract providing that the "makers . . . pay costs of collection or ten per cent attorney's fee" to allow only a reasonable attorney fee for collection actually incurred); HCA Health Servs. of Va., Inc. v. Peters, 16 Va. Cir. 76 (1989) (refusing to enforce 25% collection attorney fee clause in medical services adhesion contract; awarding reasonable fee based on hours worked); Island Block Corp. v. Webster, 17 V.I. 29 (V.I. Terr. Ct. 1980) ("[S]uch a provision is a contract of indemnity . . . [and] should be enforced only to the extent that it reflects the cost of services actually rendered, whether by an attorney or by another legal representative. The 25% stipulation here has absolutely no relation to the services actually rendered."). *See generally* A. Della Porta, Annotation, *Validity of provision in promissory note or other evidences of indebtedness for payment as attorneys' fees, expenses and costs of collection, of specified percentage of note*, 17 A.L.R.2d 288, 304–05 (1951).

awards higher than justified by the actual value of collection efforts on average, particularly when the debt is large and recovery occurs with little effort.[163] As one court has pointed out, if percentage fees were allowed without regard to actual expenditure of time, the creditor and its attorney "would have a tremendous incentive to negotiate an extremely large contingency fee, since that fee would simply be collected from the debtor, in addition to the underlying debt."[164]

Creditors often argue that a percentage of debt recovery is necessary and appropriate because they do not unduly profit from these awards. This is because high fees in successful or simple collection cases pay for the expenses of unsuccessful or complex cases. The few cases that examine the extent of actual collection efforts reject the percentage of debt calculation. But in most cases there is no such examination, and the court may accept a percentage figure if it is reasonable in relation to customary charges. Consequently, consumer attorneys may be well served to present evidence of the minimal amount of the collection attorney's actual efforts, to draw the court's attention to the issue. Decisions examining the excessiveness of other fees of financial institutions as unconscionable[165] or in breach of the duty of good faith and fair dealing[166] may also provide support. There is no reason that one consumer should pay for the attorney expenses incurred against other consumers.[167]

6.6 Collection Agency Fees

While there is a fair amount of case law on the limitations applicable to the recovery of attorney fees for collection, there is little case law regarding collection agency fees. The traditional rule is that collection agencies are compensated by their contingent or flat-fee arrangements with creditors. Creditors, in turn, are compensated for losses due to a debtor's default by state laws that allow them to charge interest, and sometimes

163 Harrison Cnty. Bd. of Supervisors v. Carlo Corp. Inc., 833 So. 2d 582 (Miss. 2002) (county board acted arbitrarily and capriciously in imposing attorney fee of 25% of corporate tax debt when this resulted in $79,000 fee for writing one letter; fee violated both common sense and rule of professional responsibility that required fees to be reasonable).

164 Marine Midland Bank v. Kilbane, 573 F. Supp. 469, 471 (D. Md. 1983) (New York law).

165 *See* Perdue v. Crocker Nat'l Bank, 702 P.2d 503 (Cal. 1985); National Consumer Law Center, Consumer Credit Regulation § 2.4.7 (2012), *updated at* www.nclc.org/library; National Consumer Law Center, Unfair and Deceptive Acts and Practices § 4.4.9 (8th ed. 2012), *updated at* www.nclc.org/library.

166 *See* National Consumer Law Center, Consumer Credit Regulation § 2.4.10 (2012), *updated at* www.nclc.org/library.

167 Discover Bank v. Rusher, 53 So. 3d 651 (La. Ct. App. 2010) (rejecting argument that fees in some cases should make up for losses in other cases; denying 20% attorney fee for simple credit card collection when creditor won on summary judgment). *See* Bondanza v. Peninsula Hosp., 590 P.2d 22 (Cal. 1979) (unfair business practice to allocate all collection costs to the subset of accounts that collection agency successfully collects); Beasley v. Wells Fargo Bank, 1 Cal. Rptr. 2d 446, 458–59 (Cal. Ct. App. 1991) (upholding challenge to amount of insufficient funds fee; bank not allowed to spread costs of collection across all late debtors).

late charges as well, on overdue debts. Such interest rates are established by consumer credit legislation or more general statutes setting a "legal" interest rate that may be charged in the absence of a contractual agreement for post-maturity, prejudgment interest.[168]

As collection agencies are hired and paid by creditors, they do not have any contractual relationship with the debtors they pursue. Thus, collectors do not have any independent basis for claiming collection fees from the debtor. The only possible basis they might have for such a claim is a statute or the consumer's contract with the creditor.

Outside of the context of debts owed to governmental entities,[169] most decisions have held collection agencies not entitled to recover fees from consumers for their collection efforts, regardless of any clause in the contract.[170] Of the few decisions that might be construed as assuming that collection fees are allowable, most deny fees on grounds other than their illegality or treat some question as a fact issue for trial.[171]

Restrictions on collection fees may be found in state statutes regulating collection agencies.[172] Hawaii, for example,

168 *See* National Consumer Law Center, Consumer Credit Regulation § 2.3 (2012), *updated at* www.nclc.org/library.

169 Black v. Educ. Credit Mgmt. Corp., 459 F.3d 796 (7th Cir. 2006) (upholding Dep't of Education regulations permitting assessment of collection costs as percentage of debt); City of New Haven v. Bonner, 863 A.2d 680 (Conn. 2005) (collection agency fees that statute authorizes municipality to add to tax debt may be based on percentage of debt regardless of actual work performed). *See also* Lawrence Mall of New Haven, Inc. v. W. Haven, 37 Conn. L. Rptr. 903 (Conn. Super. Ct. 2004) (percentage of debt is reasonable as fee to private collector of municipal tax debts, regardless of amount of work done in individual case, because it compensates agency for risk that many stale tax debts were uncollectible and places cost of unsuccessful collections on delinquent rather than timely taxpayers), *later decision at* 2006 WL 853211 (Conn. Super. Ct. Mar. 20, 2006) (due process did not require that landowners be given advance notice that 15% collection fee would be imposed on late payments).

170 *Refusing to allow recovery of collection fees:* Seeger v. AFNI, Inc., 548 F.3d 1107 (7th Cir. 2008) (neither contract nor Wisconsin law entitled new owner of debt to collection fee, that would be payable to itself, not third-party collector); Fields v. W. Mass. Credit Corp., 479 F. Supp. 2d 287 (D. Conn. 2007) (collector not entitled to fee when debt arose from retail installment sale, as governing statute prohibits collection fees); Ozkaya v. Telecheck Servs., Inc., 982 F. Supp. 578 (N.D. Ill. 1997) (state collection agency law prohibits fees unless "expressly authorized by law"; collection agency not entitled to fee for check on which consumer stopped payment when state law allows fees for certain dishonored checks but is silent as to stop-payments); Patzka v. Viterbo College, 917 F. Supp. 654 (W.D. Wis. 1996) (Wisconsin prohibits collection fees, even if separately negotiated; even in absence of statutory prohibition, fees here would be impermissible because not disclosed on face of consumer's contract with creditor); Teemogonwuno v. Todd, Bremer & Larsen, Inc., Clearinghouse No. 45,946B (N.D. Ga. 1991) (under Georgia law non-legal expenses are not recoverable as collection costs); Bolden v. G.H. Perkins Assoc., Inc., Clearinghouse No. 31,470 (D. Conn. 1981) (finding collection agency's claims for collection expenses excessive; no challenge as to recoverability of a more reasonable claim for collection expenses); Bondanza v. Peninsula Hosp., 590 P.2d 22 (Cal. 1979) (enjoining collection agency's addition of one-third collection fee to hospital debt; finding fee to be a penalty unrelated to the actual anticipated expense of collection when the contract provided for reasonable attorney fees and collection expenses); Beasley v. Wells Fargo Bank, 1 Cal. Rptr. 2d 446 (Cal. Ct. App. 1992) (illegal for bank to charge customers the fixed percentage fee it pays debt collectors). *See also* Kojetin v. C.U. Recovery, Inc., 1999 WL 33916416 (D. Minn. Feb. 17, 1999) (creditor could not pass on to consumer the percentage fee that the collection agency charged it when percentage was not related to actual costs of collection effort and contract made debtor liable for "costs of collection"), *adopted by* 1999 WL 1847329 (D. Minn. Mar. 29, 1999), *aff'd*, 212 F.3d 1318 (8th Cir. 2000) (per curiam); Y-12 Credit Union v. Wiseman, 1986 WL 5240 (Tenn. Ct. App. May 6, 1986) (contract allowed reasonable fee of attorney or collection agency; refusing to award 40% collection fee when creditor did not prove that it was reasonable). *Cf.* Massa v. I.C. Sys., Inc., 2008 WL 504329 (S.D. Ind. Feb. 21, 2008) (attempt to collect unauthorized 50% collection fee violates FDCPA, but bona fide error shown when fee added by previous collector and current collector reasonably relied on creditor as to amount of debt).

Allowing recovery of collection fees: Talbott v. G.C. Servs., L.P., 53 F. Supp. 2d 846 (W.D. Va. 1999) (telephone company's tariff filed with FCC authorizes reasonable collection costs, so consumer can be required to pay collector's 35% fee); Grant Road Lumber Co. v. Wystrach, 682 P.2d 1146 (Ariz. Ct. App. 1984) (rejecting argument that collector committed unauthorized practice of law by filing suit and seeking collection fee; enforcing contractual clause requiring defendant to pay 20% collection fee); Decatur Imaging Ctr. v. Ames, 608 N.E.2d 1198 (Ill. App. Ct. 1992) (interpreting debt collection statute to allow collection fee if expressly authorized by contract; statement in contract here was sufficient, but creditor must prove not only that fees were incurred but also that they were reasonable).

171 *See, e.g.*, Durham v. Continental Cent. Credit, 600 F. Supp. 2d 1124 (S.D. Cal. 2008) (fact question whether percentage collection fee is liquidated damages); King's Choice Neckwear, Inc. v. Fedex Corp., 2007 WL 4554220 (D.N.J. Dec. 21, 2007) (unpublished) (when contract allowed "reasonable costs incurred . . . including collection agency fees," automatic 40% collection agency fee was "exorbitant and unenforceable"; customer stated claims for civil conspiracy and UDAP violation); Akalwadi v. Risk Mgmt. Alternatives, 336 F. Supp. 2d 492 (D. Md. 2004) (refusing to grant summary judgment for collection fee under lease that required renter to pay collection expenses incurred by owner; fact question whether owner actually incurred expenses); Gostony v. Diem Corp., 320 F. Supp. 2d 932 (D. Ariz. 2003) (interpreting lease clause allowing "prevailing party" to recover "collection agency fees" to allow recovery only when party prevails in judicial proceeding; collection agency violated FDCPA by seeking fee without having filed suit); Adair v. Sabharwal, 2002 WL 31243019 (S.D. Ind. Aug. 16, 2002) (refusing to dismiss claim that creditor added illegal collection fee, in absence of evidence that creditor actually paid or incurred fee, when contract obligated debtor to pay collection fees "paid or incurred" by creditor); Y-12 Credit Union v. Wiseman, 1986 WL 5240 (Tenn. Ct. App. May 6, 1986) (refusing to award 40% collection fee when creditor did not prove that it was reasonable).

172 *See, e.g.*, Mich. Comp. Laws § 339.915a(e) (prohibiting licensees from demanding or obtaining a share of the compensation for services performed by an attorney in collecting a claim or demand or collecting or receiving a fee or other compensation from a consumer for collecting a claim, other than a claim owing the creditor pursuant to the provisions of the original agreement between the creditor and debtor); N.H. Rev. Stat. Ann. § 358-C:3 (prohibiting collection agencies from adding charges to debt, other than court costs, unless charge is expressly authorized by the agreement creating the obligation and legally chargeable to the debtor); N.C. Gen. Stat. § 75-55(2) (prohibiting debt collectors from attempting to collect charges to which they are not legally entitled); W. Va. Code §§ 46A-2-128(d) (prohibiting collection agencies from attempting to collect charge, fee, or expense unless it is expressly authorized by the agreement and by statute), 46A-3-101 (listing charges that may be included in consumer credit sale). *See also* Adams v. A. & S. Collection Assocs., Inc., 2007 WL 2206936 (D. Conn. July 30,

forbids collection agencies to recover any collection expenses, except for attorney fees after filing suit.[173] Kansas forbids the inclusion of collection agency fees in a credit agreement that also includes attorney fees.[174] However, Iowa allows a collection agency to collect a fee from the debtor if the fee is reasonably related to the actions taken by the collector and the collector is legally authorized to collect it,[175] and a New Jersey statute allows a credit card lender to contract for a reasonable collection agency fee.[176]

In many cases, the debt will arise from a transaction that is governed by a statute that lists the charges that may be imposed on the debtor. If collection agency fees are not specifically listed, courts consider them forbidden.[177]

While a number of states recognize attorney fee clauses by statute, or impose fee-shifting for certain types of litigation even in the absence of a contractual clause,[178] it is rare for a state to have specific statutory authority for collection agency fees. Even if there is no prohibition against imposing the fee, the creditor must show that the consumer actually agreed to it,[179] and courts usually require the collector or creditor to show that the fee was actually incurred and is reasonable.[180]

When there is little case law, the law limiting recovery in other contexts (for example, contractually authorized attorney fees) may provide the rule of decision either directly or by analogy.[181] As with attorney fees clauses,[182] a collection fee clause may be unenforceable as a penalty[183] or may be held unconscionable.[184]

By analogy to attorney fee clauses, collection fee clauses should be strictly construed.[185] Indeed, courts should look on collection fee clauses with even greater disfavor, as attorneys must be licensed, must complete extensive professional training, are governed by rules of professional responsibility, and are subject to the inherent authority of courts to regulate the practice of law. Collection agencies are not subject to equivalent checks and balances and in many states need not even be licensed, so any purported authority to impose collection fees on the debtor should be even more strictly construed than in the case of attorney fees.

2007) (collector's requirement that creditor add 49% collection fee and 18% interest to claims before forwarding them to agency violates Connecticut Creditors' Collection Practices Law); Hansen v. Ticket Track, Inc. 280 F. Supp. 2d 1196 (W.D. Wash. 2003) (Washington collection agency statute, Wash. Rev. Code § 19.16.250(18), forbade collector, but not creditor, from adding collection fee to debt; fee here was added by collector, and thus unlawful, when collector's contract with creditor-parking lot operator required creditor to include fee provision in its contract with customers); Ozkaya v. Telecheck Servs., Inc., 982 F. Supp. 578 (N.D. Ill. 1997) (state collection agency law prohibits fees unless "expressly authorized by law"; collection agency not entitled to fee for check on which consumer stopped payment when state law allows fees for certain dishonored checks but is silent as to stop-payments). *But cf.* Bottoni v. Sallie Mae, Inc., 2011 WL 2293226 (N.D. Cal. June 8, 2011) (state restriction on liquidated damages applies only to sales of goods or services, not loans of money, so does not restrict student loan collection fee).

173 Haw. Rev. Stat. § 443B-9 (collection agency may not collect or attempt to collect any collection fee, except attorney fee up to 25% after filing suit). *See* Wiginton v. Pac. Credit Corp., 634 P.2d 111 (Haw. Ct. App. 1981) (claim for $1000 by a collection agency as the "probable expense of legal process" was deceptive as it was not due when the dunning letter was sent). *Cf.* Ai v. Frank Huff Agency, Ltd., 607 P.2d 1304 (Haw. 1980) (it was a deceptive practice for a collection agency to attempt to collect attorney fees of one-third of the debt when attorney fees were limited by statute to 25%).

174 Kan. Stat. Ann. § 58-2312.

175 Iowa Code § 537.7103(5)(c).

176 N.J. Stat. Ann. § 17:3B-40 (West). *See also* N.J. Stat. Ann. § 17:3B-14 (West).

177 *See, e.g.*, Fields v. W. Mass. Credit Corp., 479 F. Supp. 2d 287 (D. Conn. 2007) (collector not entitled to fee when debt arose from retail installment sale, as governing statute prohibits collection fees); Ozkaya v. Telecheck Servs., Inc., 982 F. Supp. 578 (N.D. Ill. 1997) (state collection agency law prohibits fees unless "expressly authorized by law"; collection agency not entitled to fee for check on which consumer stopped payment when state law allows fees for certain dishonored checks but is silent as to stop-payments); Patzka v. Viterbo Coll., 917 F. Supp. 654, 659 (W.D. Wis. 1996) (when collection fees are not among list of charges permitted by state consumer credit statute, they are forbidden). *See generally* § 6.2.2, *supra* (similar issue regarding attorney fee clauses).

178 *See* §§ 6.2.2, 6.3, *supra*.

179 Acik v. I.C. Sys., Inc., 640 F. Supp. 2d 1019 (N.D. Ill. 2009) (collector's addition of percentage fee to medical bill violated FDCPA; fee not "expressly authorized" by patient agreement or Illinois statute); King's Choice Neckwear, Inc. v. Fedex Corp., 2007 WL 4554220 (D.N.J. Dec. 21, 2007) (unpublished) (provision for "reasonable costs incurred . . . including collection agency fees" did not authorize "exorbitant and unenforceable" automatic 40% collection agency fee). *See also* Mund v. EMCC, Inc., 259 F.R.D. 180 (D. Minn. 2009) (certifying class in FDCPA class action alleging that collector's "one size fits all" percentage collection fee was not expressly provided for in members' contracts with vacation club). *Cf.* Alexson v. Hudson Valley Cmty. College, 125 F. Supp. 2d 27 (N.D.N.Y. 2000) (denying creditor's motion for summary judgment; fact question whether college violated state UDAP statute by seeking collection fee without having disclosed it fully in college catalog).

180 Richard v. Oak Tree Group, Inc., 614 F. Supp. 2d 814 (W.D. Mich. 2008) (consumers never agreed to liquidated damages provision); Bolden v. G.H. Perkins Assoc., Inc., Clearinghouse No. 31,470 (D. Conn. 1981) (finding collection agency's claims for collection expenses excessive); Decatur Imaging Ctr. v. Ames, 608 N.E.2d 1198, 1202 (Ill. App. Ct. 1992); Y-12 Credit Union v. Wiseman, 1986 WL 5240 (Tenn. Ct. App. May 6, 1986). *But see* Bradley v. Franklin Collection Serv., Inc., 2013 WL 1346714 (N.D. Ala. Mar. 28, 2013) (refusing to consider reasonableness of 40% fee added when medical bill was sent to collection, when contract authorized all collection expenses and creditor actually incurred the fee).

181 *See* Y-12 Credit Union v. Wiseman, 1986 WL 5240 (Tenn. Ct. App. May 6, 1986) (relying on attorney fee decisions by analogy; refusing to award 40% collection fee when creditor did not prove that it was reasonable).

182 *See* § 6.2.2, *supra*.

183 Durham v. Continental Cent. Credit, 600 F. Supp. 2d 1124 (S.D. Cal. 2008) (fact question whether percentage collection fee is liquidated damages); King's Choice Neckwear, Inc. v. Fedex Corp., 2007 WL 4554220 (D.N.J. Dec. 21, 2007) (unpublished) ("exorbitant" 40% collection agency fee was unenforceable penalty); Bondanza v. Peninsula Hosp., 23 Cal. 3d 260, 590 P.2d 22, 152 Cal. Rptr. 446 (1979) (enjoining collection agency's addition of one-third collection fee to hospital debt; finding fee to be a penalty unrelated to the actual anticipated expense of collection when the contract provided for reasonable attorney fees and collection expenses); Beasley v. Wells Fargo Bank, 1 Cal. Rptr. 2d 446 (Cal. Ct. App. 1992) (illegal for bank to charge customers the fixed percentage fee it pays debt collectors).

184 *See* § 6.2.2, *supra*.

185 *See* § 6.2.4, *supra*.

Chapter 7 Defending Military Personnel in Collection Actions

7.1 Introduction

The Servicemembers Civil Relief Act (SCRA)[1] was established to temporarily suspend judicial and administrative proceedings and transactions that affect servicemembers, thereby allowing them to focus on the national defense.[2] The provisions of the SCRA apply to all judicial or administrative proceedings commenced in any court or agency.[3] The Act primarily limits judicial collection tactics and enforcement of claims against active duty military personnel. It should be reviewed in detail whenever a current or former member of the military, or a dependent, is represented in a debt collection matter.

The SCRA provides both procedural and substantive protections and has been interpreted to be a strict liability statute, at least in part.[4] Among the Act's most significant procedural features are protections against default judgments,[5] the ability to vacate default judgments, stays, and the tolling of statutes of limitations.[6] The SCRA's substantive protections include reducing the interest rate on obligations entered into prior to military duty,[7] prohibitions against self-help repossession and non-judicial foreclosure,[8] restrictions on eviction from residential premises,[9] and the right to terminate residential or vehicle leases.[10] The Act also contains a variety of protections relating to matters such as taxes, life and health insurance, professional liability insurance, and powers of attorney that are beyond the scope of this chapter.

Each provision of the act must be liberally construed to protect members of the armed forces.[11] Although some SCRA provisions specifically extend their protections for a period after active duty military service, in general, SCRA protections begin with a servicemember's entry into military service and end upon his or her release from service.[12] An excellent and detailed Judge Advocate General (JAG) Corps manual analyzing the Act as amended in 2006 may be found online.[13] The American Bar Association also has an online collection of materials on the Act,[14] including a judge's guide with sample stay motions.[15]

Additional assistance with the SCRA or other civil matters affecting military clients can be obtained by contacting a local legal assistance attorney.[16] Each branch of the service and the Coast Guard has a legal assistance office that provides

---

1 50 U.S.C. app. §§ 501–596.

2 50 U.S.C. app. § 502.

3 50 U.S.C. app. § 512.

4 Roberts v. Chips Express Inc., 2012 WL 4866495 (E.D. Wis. Oct. 12, 2012) (strict liability applies under § 537 to storage facility owner for foreclosing on servicemember's property without judicial order); *see* United States v. B.C. Enters., 667 F. Supp. 2d 650, 663–64 (E.D. Va. 2009) (holding that defendant violated § 537(a)(1) under a strict liability analysis). *But see* Frazier v. HSBC Mortgage Servs., Inc. 2009 WL 4015574 (M.D. Fla. 2009) (citing to 50 U.S.C. §§ 527(a)(2), (3) as support for the idea that the SCRA is not a strict liability statute because creditors who overcharge a servicemember can forgive or reduce the obligation as a remedy), *aff'd*, 401 Fed. Appx. 436 (11th Cir. Oct. 26, 2010).

5 50 U.S.C. app. §§ 521, 522. *See* § 7.4.2, *infra*.

6 50 U.S.C. app. § 526. *See* §§ 7.4.2, 7.4.3, 7.4.5, 7.4.6, *infra*.

7 50 U.S.C. app. § 527. *See* § 7.5, *infra*.

8 50 U.S.C. app. § 532. *See* §§ 7.5.3, 7.5.4, *infra*.

9 50 U.S.C. app. § 531. *See* § 7.5.5, *infra*.

10 50 U.S.C. app. § 535. *See* §§ 7.5.7, 7.5.9, *infra*.

11 Boone v. Lightner, 319 U.S. 561, 63 S. Ct. 1223, 87 L. Ed. 1587 (1943); Gordon v. Pete's Auto Serv. of Denbigh, Inc., 637 F.3d. 454 (4th Cir. 2011) (SCRA "must be read with an eye friendly to those who dropped their affairs to answer their country's call"); Engstrom v. First Nat'l Bank, 47 F.3d 1459, 1462 (5th Cir. 1995); Bank of Nova Scotia v. George, 2008 WL 501263 (D. V.I. Feb. 15, 2008); Johnson v. City of Philadelphia, 2007 WL 3342413 (E.D. Pa. Nov. 6, 2007) (in evaluating whether to grant a stay, a servicemember's absence when his rights or liabilities are being adjudged is usually prima facie prejudicial); Merrill v. Beard, 2007 WL 461469 (N.D. Ohio Feb. 7, 2007) (in setting aside default judgments, courts strictly construe requirements of Act in favor of servicemembers); Sprinkle v. S B & C Ltd., 472 F. Supp. 2d 1235 (W.D. Wash. 2006) (acknowledging expansive purpose of protections under Act; construing requirement for affidavit of nonmilitary service to apply to garnishment proceeding); Atkins v. County of Alameda, 2004 WL 444105 (N.D. Cal. Mar. 8, 2004) ("Courts have long construed the 'stay' provisions of the Act liberally, retaining broad discretion to consider any and all stay-related factors."); Antioch Co. v. Scrapbook Borders, Inc., 210 F.R.D. 645 (D. Minn. 2002); Cathey v. First Republic Bank, 2001 U.S. Dist. LEXIS 13150, at *12 (W.D. La. July 6, 2001) ("Any doubts that arise as to the scope and application of the Act should be resolved in favor of the military person."); *In re* Burrell, 230 B.R. 309 (Bankr. E.D. Tex. 1999); Lenser v. McGowan, 191 S.W.3d 506 (Ark. 2004); State *ex rel.* Estate of Perry, 168 S.W.3d 577 (Mo. Ct. App. 2005) (Act's provisions on tolling of statutes of limitations are to be liberally construed); Bernhardt v. Alden Café, 864 A.2d 421 (N.J. Super. Ct. App. Div. 2005) (Act liberally construed to mandate appointment of counsel before default or default judgment may be entered against absent servicemember); Murdock v. Murdock, 526 S.E.2d 241 (S.C. Ct. App. 1999). *See also* Roberts v. Chips Express Inc., 2012 WL 4866495, at *4 (E.D. Wis. Oct. 12, 2012) (SCRA is "a very servicemember-friendly statute"). *But see In re* Marriage of Bradley, 137 P.3d 1030 (Kan. 2006) (recognizing rule of liberal construction of Act but denying stay when servicemember did not provide documentation required by section 522(b)(2) in support of request for stay). *But cf.* Chace v. Lopez, 89 S.W.3d 788 (Tex. App. 2002) (Act to be liberally construed but cannot be stretched to prohibit prejudgment interest on tort claim when nothing in Act addresses this topic).

12 50 U.S.C. app. § 511(3).

13 *Available at* www.justice.gov/crt/military/documents/jag_article.pdf (Mar. 2006) (Publication JA 260). NCLC understands this publication is currently being updated to reflect amendments to the SCRA after 2006.

14 *Available at* www.americanbar.org/portals/public_resources/aba_home_front/information_center/servicemembers_civil_relief_act.html.

15 Mark E. Sullivan, A Judge's Guide to the Servicemembers Civil Relief Act, *available at* http://apps.americanbar.org/family/military/scrajudgesguidecklist.pdf.

16 The Air Force maintains a website for locating military legal assistance offices at www.legalassistance.law.af.mil.

assistance and representation for servicemembers and their families in civil matters. Frequently the representation will not include litigation, which may instead be taken up by private practitioners. However, the military attorneys are very familiar with state law and federal law affecting the military, such as the SCRA, and are experts on the overlay and conflict between military life and civil contract expectations. For example, a legal assistance attorney may be able to help with understanding military orders, base locations, causes for a client's absence, and military effect on ability to perform, to name a few topics.

A number of states have laws similar to the SCRA.[17] These statutes are summarized on a state-by-state basis in the note below.[18] In comparing the SCRA to similar state

---

17 *See* Douglas W. Buchanan, *Complying with the Federal Servicemembers Civil Relief Act and Similar State Laws*, 60 Consumer Fin. L.Q. Rep. 286 (2006) (describing current and pending legislation in several states).

18 *Alabama:* Ala. Code §§ 31-12-1 to 31-12-10 preserve many servicemember rights and benefits during military service. They apply to National Guard and reserves called up to serve in armed conflict or a state of emergency for thirty days or more. They incorporate federal law into state law, preserve educational status, and require state and local governmental employers to pay their employees who are called into active duty the difference between military pay and the salary the employee would have received in the governmental job.

Alaska: Alaska Stat. § 26.05.135 extends the protections of the federal act to National Guard and naval militia on active duty.

Arizona: Ariz. Rev. Stat. Ann. § 6-1260(L) restricts payday lending ("deferred presentment transactions") to servicemembers and spouses. It applies primarily to collection methods. Ariz. Rev. Stat. Ann. § 20-1057(P) allows a reservist ordered to active military duty to reinstate health care coverage upon release from active duty. Ariz. Rev. Stat. Ann. § 23-1390(B) tolls the six-month limitation period for filing unfair labor practice complaint for agricultural worker if service in the armed forces prevented the worker from filing the charge. Ariz. Rev. Stat. Ann. § 33-1413(F) excuses a manufactured housing community tenant who is a member of the armed forces from the requirement to give two weeks' notice before terminating a rental agreement if he or she receives reassignment orders that do not allow such prior notification. Ariz. Rev. Stat. Ann. § 44-1793(G) allows suspension or cancellation of health spa contracts. Ariz. Rev. Stat. Ann. §§ 20-1377(L), 20-1408(L), (M), specify disability insurance policy rights.

Arkansas: Ark. Code Ann. §§ 12-62-701 to 12-62-718 apply to National Guard members called into active military service for the state by the governor for more than 180 continuous days. The state act provides extensive protections including prohibition against termination of installment contracts for the purchase of real or personal property for any breach that occurs during military service, prohibition against self-help repossession, extension of the statute of limitations, reduction of the interest rate on pre-active duty obligations to 6%, restriction on eviction, and prohibition of non-judicial foreclosure. Ark. Code Ann. §§ 12-62-801 to 12-62-808 (§ 12-62-805) prohibits discrimination based on military service in property, credit, or other contractual transactions.

California: Cal. Mil. & Vet. Code §§ 400 to 409.14 (West) apply to National Guard members ordered into active state service by the governor or into active federal service by the President, and to reservists called into active federal duty. The law provides extensive protections including stay of court actions; restrictions on eviction; deferral of financial obligations, foreclosure, and repossession; reduction of the interest rate on pre-active duty obligations to 6%; prohibition against non-judicial foreclosure; extension of redemption periods after foreclosure or tax sale; and tax deferral. Cal. Mil. & Vet. Code §§ 800 to 812 allows members of the U.S. Military Reserve or the California National Guard called to active duty as a part of the Iraq and Afghanistan conflicts to defer payments on mortgages, credit cards, and other debts and obligations. Cal. Mil. & Vet. Code §§ 820 to 829 provides for termination of cell phone contracts, motor vehicle lease termination, and utility shutoff protection. Cal. Civ. Code § 2923.55 (West) requires mortgage servicers to provide notice of protections and counseling services available to servicemembers or dependents prior to filing notice of default.

Colorado: Colo. Rev. Stat. §§ 28-3-1401 to 28-3-1407 provide protections for reservists and National Guard members when called to active duty in excess of thirty days. Protections include: stay of civil proceedings and enforcement of security interests; court intervention in eviction, distress, and rent payments; and modification of installment contracts. Additionally, Colo. Rev. Stat. §§ 28-3-1501 to 28-3-1504 create the Military Family Relief Fund to help families defray costs when a family member leaves for active military duty or is on active military duty in a hostile fire zone. Colo. Rev. Stat. §§ 10-4-628, 10-16-201, provide insurance policy protections.

Connecticut: Conn. Gen. Stat. § 12-146c prohibits municipalities from charging or collecting interest for one year on any property tax or installment payable by any member of the armed forces who is on active duty and was called to active service for military action against Iraq and is serving in the Middle East. Conn. Gen. Stat. § 27-100a establishes the Military Family Relief Fund, which makes grants to immediate family members of eligible members of the armed forces for essential personal or household goods or services if the payment for such goods or services would be a hardship because of the military service of the eligible member. Conn. Gen. Stat. § 21-82 allows members of the armed forces to terminate mobile home park rental agreements with less than thirty days' notice if they receive reassignment orders that do not allow prior notification. Conn. Gen. Stat. § 36a-737 provides a procedure to freeze the terms and conditions of pending mortgage applications from reservists and the National Guard during service.

Delaware: Del. Code Ann. tit. 25, § 7006(b)(9) prohibits rental agreements in manufactured home communities from containing a provision prohibiting a tenant from providing less than thirty days' notice to terminate a rental agreement when the tenant is a member of the armed forces and receives reassignment orders that do not allow prior notification. Del Code Ann. Tit. 26, § 118 prohibits termination of electric, gas, water, sewer, telephone, cable, and satellite television service when the customer has reduced income due to military service. Del. Code Ann. tit. 20, § 179 provides that National Guard or reservists should not be charged late fees related to license renewal when late renewal was due to active duty. Del. Code Ann. tit. 25, § 5314(b)(5) provides for tenant's right to early termination of lease upon entering active duty.

Florida: Fla. Stat. §§ 250.5201 to 250.5205 prohibit termination of installment contracts for the purchase of real or personal property for any breach that occurs during military service, allow a court to order a stay of proceedings, restrict eviction, and prohibit non-judicial foreclosure. These protections apply to persons called into state active duty by the governor for more than seventeen days. Additionally, Fla. Stat. § 250.5206 establishes the Family Readiness Program, which provides need-based financial assistance to eligible servicemembers of the Florida National Guard and United States Reserve Forces. Fla. Stat. § 83.682 gives servicemembers a right to terminate rental agreements. Fla. Stat. § 250.4815 provides that professional licenses will not expire for servicemembers during the period of service and ninety days thereafter. Fla. Stat. § 320.07 provides that a servicemember's manufactured home registration that expires during active duty shall not constitute a violation of vehicle registration laws. Fla. Stat. § 501.2077 provides UDAP penalties for violations involving service members and families. Fla. Stat. § 520.14 allows service member assigned overseas to terminate automobile leasing installment contract. Fla. Stat. § 627.6692 tolls the insurance cover period due to active duty.

Georgia: Ga. Code Ann. § 16-17-9 makes it a high and aggravated misdemeanor for payday lenders to violate collection limitations against members of the military services and their spouses. Ga. Code Ann. § 38-2-280 provides for rehire rights for persons who left their employment to serve in the military. Ga. Code Ann. § 46-5-8 provides the procedure for servicemembers to terminate their wireless telecommunication service contracts prior to the contract's expiration, when, for example, they are transferred or released from service. Ga. Code Ann. § 44-7-22 provides for the termination of residential leases for military personnel with terms that are more liberal than the federal act. This 2007 statute relates back to leases entered into on or after July 1, 2005. Similarly, Ga. Code Ann. § 44-7-37 limits the liability for rent of persons on active duty who receive change of station or temporary duty orders for a period in excess of three months.

Hawaii: Haw. Rev. Stat. §§ 657D-1 to 657D-63 constitute a comprehensive law similar to the federal act, including a prohibition against non-judicial foreclosures and a reduction of pre-active duty interest rates to 6%. It applies to persons called to active state duty. Haw. Rev. Stat. § 436B-14.5 provides that any license held by a servicemember that expires during active duty shall be restored. Haw. Rev. Stat. § 486N-7.5 allows suspension or cancellation of health club contracts.

Idaho: Idaho Code Ann. § 46-409 applies the provisions of the federal act and the Uniform Services Employment and Reemployment Rights Act (USERRA) to the air and army National Guard when called to active duty for thirty or more days. Idaho Code Ann. § 46-407 specifies reemployment rights.

Illinois: 330 Ill Comp. Stat. §§ 62/5-1 through 62-5/30 provide lease termination rights. 815 Ill. Comp. Stat. §§ 633/1 to 633/15 provides cellular phone contract termination rights. 815 Ill. Comp. Stat. § 636/37 provides motor vehicle lease termination rights. 35 Ill. Comp. Stat. §§ 200/21-15, 200/21-20, and 200/21-25 prohibit classifying active duty servicemembers as delinquent when they are late in paying their property taxes. 220 Ill. Comp. Stat. § 5/8-201.5 prohibits gas or electricity shutoffs for servicemembers on active duty. 330 Ill. Comp. Stat. § 60/5.1 allows a court to order a stay of proceedings if state or federal military service directly results in failure to meet pre-service obligations. Similarly, 735 Ill. Comp. Stat. § 5/9-107.10 provides for up to a ninety day stay of proceedings in eviction cases concerning servicemembers or their families. 815 Ill. Comp. Stat. § 122/2-50 requires payday lenders to suspend and defer collection activity against members of the military who have been deployed to a combat or combat support posting for the duration of the deployment. 330 Ill. Comp. Stat §§ 63/1 to 63/80 (Ill. Service Civil Relief Act) apply various statutory protections to servicemembers in several areas, including phone services, utilities, foreclosures, interest rates, insurance, installment sales, and tuition charges.

Indiana: Ind. Code § 10-16-7-23 extends the SCRA and USERRA to members of the National Guard. Ind. Code §§ 10-17-12-0.5 through 10-17-12-12 provide for the Military Family Relief Fund, which provides short term financial assistance to families of qualified servicemembers. Ind. Code § 25-1-12-6 provides for an extension of time for renewal of professional licenses.

Iowa: Iowa Code §§ 29A.90 through 29A.105 are similar to the federal act. Among other things, they bar a creditor from self-help repossession for breach, before or during military service, of an installment contract to buy real or personal property entered into before entry into service; reduce interest rates to 6%; and prohibit non-judicial foreclosure. They also provide for stays and reopening of default judgments. They apply to state military and reserve on full-time active duty and their dependents. Iowa Code § 654.17C limits mortgage foreclosure actions. Iowa Code § 29A.43 provides for continuous insurance coverage.

Kansas: Kan. Stat. Ann. § 16a-2-405 restricts collection activities of payday lenders against military borrowers. Kan. Stat. Ann. §§ 58-2504 and 58-2570 provide that not more than fifteen days' notice to terminate tenancy is required for persons when military orders necessitated the termination of tenancy. Kansas Stat. Ann. § 44-706 protects unemployment benefits for an individual who quits due to a spouse's military transfer or for an individual who left to enlist but was rejected or delayed. Kansas Stat. Ann. § 44-1126 prohibits employment discrimination against military members.

Kentucky: Ky. Rev. Stat. Ann. §§ 36.470 through 36.476 (West) provide for the Military Family Assistance Trust Fund, which provides for need-based grants to active duty servicemembers and their spouses to cover necessary expenses. Ky. Rev. Stat. Ann. § 38.510 (West) extends the benefits of the SCRA to active duty National Guard members. Ky. Rev. Stat. Ann. § 141.175 (West) provides for an extension to pay income taxes for active duty National Guard members or reservists serving in combat zones. Ky. Rev. Stat. Ann § 12.355 (West) deals with renewal of professional licensure or certification.

Louisiana: La. Rev. Stat. Ann. § 9:3261 provides that servicemembers may terminate residential leases (in case of transfer, for example). La. Rev. Stat. Ann. §§ 29:311 through 29:319 are similar to the federal act. Among other things, they reduce interest rates to 6%; provide for termination of motor vehicle, cell phone, and residential lease agreements in manufactured home communities; and prohibit utility shutoffs. La. Rev. Stat. Ann. §§ 29:401 through 29:426 incorporate the SCRA and USERRA into Louisiana law (§ 29:422) and provide, among other things, extensive provisions regarding servicemember health insurance, re-employment, and occupational licenses. La. Rev. Stat. Ann. § 22:1482 allows a 25% discount on automobile insurance premiums, and § 22:1482.1 allows a 10% discount for home insurance. Title 37 contains relevant provisions regarding annual recertification and fees for various professions to be waived for active duty members, for example, § 37:1208 (pharmacists).

Maine: Me. Rev. Stat. tit. 37-B, § 387 provides servicemember protections against evictions. Me. Rev. Stat. tit. 37-B, § 389-A provides servicemembers with the opportunity for stays of court proceedings, electronic testimony and evidence, and expedited hearings, among other provisions. Me. Rev. Stat. tit. 37-B, § 390 defers motor vehicle insurance coverage. Me. Rev. Stat. tit. 37-B, § 390-A provides extensions of professional licenses.

Maryland: Md. Code Ann., Pub. Safety § 13-704 (West) applies the protections of the federal act to members of the National Guard or Maryland Defense when ordered into military duty under state law for fourteen consecutive days or more. In addition, Md. Code Ann., Pub. Safety §§ 14-201 through 14-219 (West) apply many protections similar to those provided by the federal act to emergency management personnel during emergency periods and to people who suffer serious personal injury, family injury, or property damage during a declared emergency. These protections include stays of proceedings and provisions concerning installment contracts, mortgages, evictions, and taxes. Md. Code Ann., Ins. § 27-501(o) (West) protects rights to automobile and home insurance coverage. Md. Code Ann., Tax-General § 10-208 (West) provides for an income tax deduction for active duty national guard members.

Massachusetts: Mass. Gen. Laws ch. 59, § 5L provides for the deferral of local taxes assessed against active duty National Guard members and reservists on active duty. Similarly, Mass. Gen. Laws ch. 60A, § 9 provides for the deferral of excise taxes on motor vehicles for active duty National Guard members and reservists on active duty. Mass. Gen. Laws ch. 62C, § 81 provides for an extended deadline for paying taxes for individuals serving in the armed forces in combat zones. Mass. Gen. Laws ch. 10, § 35CC provides for a military family relief fund.

Michigan: Mich. Comp. Laws § 32.517 applies to those in active state service. It exempts the servicemember's property from execution, seizure, or attachment for debts incurred prior to or during state service; provides for stays of proceedings; and restricts termination of heat, water, electricity, or gas for unpaid bills for the servicemember or his or her household during the first ninety days of service. Mich. Comp. Laws §§ 460.9c, 484.2314a provide protection from disconnection of electric, gas, and telephone service due to a customer's reduced income from military service. Additionally, Mich. Comp. Laws § 484.1903 gives servicemembers a right to terminate wireless phone service, and Mich. Comp. Laws § 445.1013 gives them a right to terminate motor vehicle leases. Mich. Comp. Laws §§ 35.1211 through 35.1216 create the Military Family Relief Fund which provides assistance to individuals who are or were members of a reserve component of the United States armed forces. Mich. Comp. Laws § 339.411(11) waives for active duty members annual registration renewal requirements and fees for various professions.

Minnesota: Minn. Stat. § 190.055 incorporates the SCRA into state law. Minn. Stat. §§ 72A.20(8)(b) and (c), the state's Unfair Insurance Practices (UNIP) statute, provides protections regarding denial of life insurance and health insurance (or reinstatement after period of service) to servicemembers and their families (including the National Guard). Minn. Stat. § 325E.028 prohibits termination of utility service for certain servicemembers, and Minn. Stat. §§ 325G.54 and 325G.55 allow servicemembers to cancel wireless service contracts, rental contracts, club contracts, service contracts, and membership travel contracts without penalty.

Mississippi: Miss. Code Ann. § 37-103-19 provides in-state tuition for the spouse and child of the servicemember while on active duty if stationed in the state. Miss. Code Ann. § 75-24-5(2)(m) provides protections regarding reinstatement of motor vehicle insurance for returning servicemembers. Miss. Code Ann. § 33-1-39 provides that a servicemember's professional licenses shall not expire while on active duty. Miss. Code Ann. § 83-5-91 has insurance coverage protections.

Missouri: Mo. Rev. Stat. §§ 41.216 and 41.218 provide for the Military Family Relief Fund, which provides grants to families of persons who are members of the National Guard or members of the reserves of the armed forces of the United States and who have been called to active duty as a result of the Sept. 11, 2001, terrorist attacks. Mo. Rev. Stat. § 41.944 allows active duty servicemembers to terminate residential leases when transferred, released, or similar situations; Mo. Rev. Stat. § 41.950 relieves active duty servicemembers from several responsibilities, including insuring a motor vehicle, renewing a driver's license or car registration, filing certain corporate reports, and paying taxes on time. Mo. Rev. Stat. § 430.140 protects servicemembers from chattel liens for small repair bills. Mo. Rev. Stat. § 340.390 provides that veterinary students' service on active duty makes them eligible for a loan repayment deferral of up to four years. Mo. Rev. Stat. § 288.050 protects unemployment benefits for spouses. Title 22 contains exemptions for professional license renewal, for example, § 327.351.

Montana: Mont. Code Ann. § 10-1-903 allows a court to stay proceedings related to a servicemember's nonpayment on a lease or mortgage for their primary residence or to adjust payments due. Mont. Code Ann. §§ 10-1-1301 through 10-1-1310 provide for the Montana Family Relief Fund, which aids members of the Montana National Guard or reserve component who have been activated for federal service and the families of members. Mont. Code Ann. § 15-30-2632 defers the collection of taxes imposed on persons in the military service, and Mont. Code Ann. § 15-30-2633 allows courts to grant stays of enforcement against military personnel for tax obligations. Mont. Admin. R. 6.6.906 restricts the activities insurance salespeople may use on military bases, and Mont. Admin. R. 6.6.907 restricts the types of products and payment methods that insurance salespeople may offer to servicemembers. Section 33-18-605 of the Montana Code requires insurers to provide reasonable underwriting or rating exceptions for consumers whose credit report has been directly affected by military service overseas.

Nebraska: 210 Neb. Admin. Code ch. 82, § 006 restricts the sale of insurance on military installations. 210 Neb. Admin. Code ch. 82, § 007 restricts the products and payment methods that insurance salespeople may offer to servicemembers. Neb. Rev. Stat. § 60-4,121 concerns driver license validity while on active duty.

Nevada: Nev. Rev. Stat. § 604A.420 restricts the collection actions of lenders offering deferred deposit loans, high-interest loans, deferred deposit loans, title loans, and check-cashing services against members of the military. Nev. Rev. Stat. § 412.1435 provides for a military relief fund to assist Nevada National Guard members with economic hardship and insurance premium payment. Nev. Rev. Stat. §§ 412.139 to 412.1395 provide employment protection. Nev. Rev. Stat. §§ 372.7281, 374.7285 provide tax exemptions for Guard members and families. Title 54 provides exemptions for some professional license renewals, for example, § 637.121.

New Hampshire: N.H. Rev. Stat. Ann. § 110-C:2 incorporates the SCRA into state law. N.H. Rev. Stat. Ann. § 540:11-a provides protections regarding the termination of a residential lease when the servicemember is transferred, called up, or similar situations.

New Jersey: N.J. Stat. Ann. §§ 38:23C-1 through 38:23C-26 (West) constitute a comprehensive law similar to the federal act. Among other things it prohibits non-judicial foreclosure and provides that the period of military service is not included in any redemption period. It applies to those on active federal duty or in state military service pursuant to an order of the governor. N.J. Stat. Ann. § 45:1-15.2 provides that a servicemember's professional licenses shall not expire while on active duty.

New Mexico: N.M. Stat. Ann. § 20-4-7.1 extends the protection of the SCRA and USERRA to members of the National Guard ordered to active duty for a period of thirty or more consecutive days. N.M. Stat. Ann. § 28-15-1 specifies reemployment rights. N.M. Stat. Ann. § 61-1-34 provides for expedited occupational professional licensure for members or spouses. Chapter 61 contains exemptions for some professional license renewals, for example, § 61-3-24. N.M. Stat. Ann. § 66-12-6.1 provides for an excise tax exemption.

New York: N.Y. Mil. Law §§ 300 through 328 (McKinney) constitute a comprehensive law similar to the federal act. It applies to those on federal active duty or those in the military service of the state pursuant to an order of the governor. Among other things, it prohibits non-judicial foreclosure and provides that the period of military service is not included in any redemption period. N.Y. Ins. Law §§ 3216(c)(13), 3221(n), 4304(i) provide for a right to suspend, receive a refund for, and resume insurance coverage.

North Carolina: N.C. Gen. Stat. § 42-45 provides protections for members of the armed forces when they terminate residential leases due to deployment, change of station, or premature discharge from active duty. N.C. Gen. Stat. § 58-58-340 restricts the sale of insurance on military installations. N.C. Gen. Stat. §§ 58-58-320 through 58-58-350 restricts the products, payment methods, and sales tactics that insurance salespeople may offer to and use with servicemembers. N.C. Gen. Stat. § 127A-41.1 allows courts to stay legal proceedings when a person involved is called into service of the state. N.C. Gen. Stat. § 127A-119 provides that, when a servicemember is absent on active duty and his family are unable to support themselves during his absence, the board of commissioners of his county, on application, shall make towards their maintenance such allowance as may be deemed reasonable. N.C. Gen. Stat. § 45-21.12A bars, with certain exceptions, mortgage sales for debtors in military service. N.C. Gen. Stat. § 53-180.1 places restrictions on small loans. N.C. Gen. Stat. § 90-18.1 is an example of exemptions for some professional license renewals.

North Dakota: N.D. Cent. Code § 37-01-43 incorporates the SCRA into North Dakota law. N.D. Cent. Code § 43-51-11 authorizes licensing boards to address hardships due to active duty with regard to renewals for various occupations. N.D. Cent. Code § 57-55-10(1)(a) provides a mobile home tax exemption.

Ohio: Ohio Rev. Code Ann. §§ 5919.29, 5923.12 (West) extend the protections of the federal act to those ordered by the governor into National Guard active duty or training. Ohio Rev. Code Ann. § 317.322 (West) exempts servicemembers from paying for a recording fee for a power of attorney. Ohio Rev. Code Ann. § 125.021 (West) provides that the office of information technology may purchase bulk phone service for the use of active duty servicemembers and families. Ohio Rev. Code Ann. § 1343.031 (West) addresses interest rates. Ohio Rev.

Code Ann. § 1349.02 (West) addresses motor vehicle leases. Ohio Rev. Code Ann. § 1349.03 (West) addresses cell phone contracts. Ohio Rev. Code Ann. § 1923.062 (West) addresses residential evictions, including manufactured homes. Ohio Rev. Code Ann. § 4933.12(F) (West) addresses gas utility shutoffs. Ohio Rev. Code Ann. § 4933.121 (West) addresses electrical utility shutoffs. Ohio Rev. Code Ann. § 323.122 (West) extends the amount of time to pay property taxes. Ohio Rev. Code Ann. § 3770.07 (West) provides that certain active duty personnel may make delayed claims for lottery prizes. Ohio Rev. Code Ann. § 3915.053 (West) addresses insurance policies, providing that there is no lapse for nonpayment during active duty. Ohio Rev. Code Ann. § 5747.026 (West) extends the period of time for filing income tax returns or paying taxes for National Guard members and reservists called into active duty. Ohio Rev. Code Ann. § 5321.04(10) (West) requires landlords to comply with rights provided by the SCRA.

Oklahoma: Okla. Stat. tit. 44, § 208.1 provides civil relief for National Guard members and adopts SCRA and USERRA as state law and makes them applicable to National Guard members. Okla. Stat. tit. 44, § 237 establishes the Oklahoma National Guard Relief Program which provides financial relief for approved expenses to qualified members of the National Guard. Okla. Stat. tit. 51, § 25.6 provides that returning servicemembers who were employed by a city or incorporated town be returned to a position of similar seniority, status, and pay after military service; Okla. Stat. tit. 72, § 47 makes a similar provision for private employers. Okla. Stat. tit. 36, § 1164 protects insurance coverage. Okla. Stat. tit. 40, § 2-210 preserves spousal unemployment benefits. Okla. Stat. tit. 59, Professions and Occupations, contains provisions exempting active duty members from certain license renewal requirements or fees; there are also provisions providing for expedited or automatic endorsement for certification or licensing of members and spouses (§§ 4100.5, 4100.6).

Oregon: Or. Rev. Stat. § 90.472 provides that state servicemembers may terminate rental agreements without penalty when called into active service by the governor for ninety days or more; Or. Rev. Stat. § 90.475 provides for similar protections for members of the U.S. armed forces or members of the National Guard. Or. Rev. Stat. § 105.111 allows a court to stay eviction proceedings when the defendant is a state servicemember, the agreed-upon rent does not exceed $1200 per month, and the premises are occupied chiefly for dwelling purposes by the spouse, children, or other dependents of the defendant. Or. Rev. Stat. § 408.440 prohibits foreclosure or judicial sale of land owned by a servicemember called into active service during war. Additionally, Oregon's UDAP statute makes it unlawful to violate the SCRA and makes it an "unconscionable tactic" to knowingly take advantage of a customer or is a disabled veteran or servicemember, or a servicemember in active service. Or. Rev. St. § 646.605, 646.608(LLL). Or. Rev. St. §§ 30.136, 30.138 provides damages and attorney fees for violations of the federal SCRA and provides an exception to otherwise mandatory court-ordered arbitrations. Or. Rev. Stat. § 307.286 provides a property tax exemption, for up to $60,000 of assessed value. Or. Rev. Stat. § 314.091 provides for income tax liabilities being held in abeyance until six months after end of active duty. Or. Rev. Stat. §§ 659A.086, 659A.093 protect member and spousal rights to leave employment without loss of benefits. Or. Rev. Stat. ch. 423 (2013 enactment to be codified) allows termination, suspension, and reinstatement of various specified services without extra charges.

Pennsylvania: 51 Pa. Cons. Stat. § 4105 makes National Guard members on active state service exempt from civil process and suspends all presumptions arising from the lapse of time. 51 Pa. Cons. Stat. §§ 7301 through 7319 provide employment protections and allows courts to stay proceedings, extend the redemption period after a tax sale, provide for the maximum interest rates and rescheduling of debt payments to account for reduced income during service period for National Guard on active federal or state duty of thirty or more consecutive days, restricts eviction, and provides other protections.

Rhode Island: R.I. Gen. Laws § 30-7-10 extends the protections of the SCRA to all National Guard members on active duty for a continuous period exceeding ninety days. R.I. Gen. Laws § 44-5-10 provides that no unpaid property taxes bear interest for a period of six months after a resident's active service in the military. R.I. Gen. Laws § 30-3-41 establishes a military family relief fund. R.I. Gen. Laws § 30-11-3 protects Guard members' employment, including extension of federal rights under 38 U.S.C. § 4301 *et seq.* R.I. Gen. Laws § 34-27-4 provides for foreclosure protections and rights.

South Carolina: S.C. Code Ann. §§ 40-1-610, 40-1-620 provide for fee and education exemptions for recertification under its "Professions and Occupation" title.

South Dakota: S.D. Codified Laws § 33A-2-9 extends the protections of the SCRA and USERRA to any member of the National Guard ordered to active duty service. S.D. Codified Laws §§ 58-33-122 through 58-33-123 limit the sale of insurance on military installations. S.D. Codified Laws §§ 58-33-124 to 130 restrict the products, payment methods, and sales tactics that insurance salespeople may offer to and use with servicemembers.

Tennessee: Tenn. Code Ann. § 26-1-111 addresses foreclosure of home mortgages and motor vehicle retail installment sales contracts. Tenn. Code. Ann. § 58-1-701 through 58-1-706 provide for the Military Family Assistance Trust Fund which provides need-based assistance to servicemembers and their families. Tenn. Code Ann. § 67-6-303 provides exemption from vehicle sales tax.

Texas: Tex. Civ. Prac. & Rem. Code Ann. § 16.022 (West) tolls statute of limitations for actions to recover or defend title to real property for servicemembers on active duty in time of war. Tex. Fin. Code Ann. §§ 342.601 to 342.605 (West) addresses payday loans. Tex. Gov't Code Ann. § 466.408 (West) addresses claiming lottery prizes. Tex. Labor Code Ann. § 101.116 (West) addresses union dues. Tex. Prop. Code Ann. § 51.015 (West) provides for stays of foreclosure proceedings for active duty servicemembers. Tex. Prop. Code Ann. § 92.017 (West) addresses residential leases and a tenant's right to terminate. Tex. Tax Code Ann. § 31.02(b) (West) addresses extension of time to pay property taxes. Tex. Occ. Code Ann. §§ 55.002, 55.003 (West) provide for an exemption from penalties for failure to renew license and an extension of deadlines. Tex. Prop. Code Ann. §§ 24.0051, 209.006 (West) state that owners seeking recovery of unpaid rents or fees or seeking to evict must provide notice of protections under the SCRA or state law. Tex. Tax Code Ann. § 31.02 (West) states that delinquent property tax may be paid without penalties within specified times.

Utah: Utah Code Ann. §§ 39-7-101 through 39-7-119 (West), which are similar to the federal act, apply to National Guard members called into active full-time service by the governor for at least thirty days. The provisions of this law include suspension of the statute of limitations, restrictions on termination of contracts and self-help repossession, and prohibition of non-judicial foreclosure. Utah Code Ann. § 31A-22-717 (West) protects insurance coverage. Utah Code Ann § 35A-4-405(1)(e) (West) preserves a spouse's unemployment benefits.

Vermont: Vt. Stat. Ann. tit. 12, § 553 suspends the statute of limitations. Vt. Stat. Ann. tit. 21, §§ 491 to 493 provide for various employment protections. Vt. Stat. Ann. tit. 32, § 5830d authorizes an income tax deferral.

Virginia: Va. Code Ann. § 8.01-15.2 addresses default judgments and non-military affidavits. Va. Code Ann. § 38.2-508.1 addresses life insurance. Va. Code Ann. § 38.2-2205.1 addresses car insurance. Va. Code Ann. §§ 43-34 and 46.2-1200.2 require the state Department of Motor Vehicles to notify lien holders of the military status of vehicle owners and require those disposing of abandoned vehicles to comply with the federal act. Va. Code Ann. §§ 44-93 through 44-102.2 include provisions for continuances up to three weeks, employment rights, and a family relief fund. Va. Code Ann. § 55-248.21:1 addresses early termination of residential leases. Va. Code Ann. § 58.1-3916 provides for automatic extensions on real property, personal property, and vehicle taxes. Va. Code Ann. § 58.1-4020 addresses claiming lottery prizes.

Washington: Wash. Rev. Code § 4.16.220 suspends the statute of limitations. Wash. Rev. Code § 31.45.210 addresses payday lending.

statutes, or analyzing SCRA terms incorporated into contracts, it is important to understand military terms of art. The Department of Defense publishes a dictionary of such terms and acronyms.[19]

7.2 History of the Act and Amendments

The SCRA was originally adopted in 1940 as the Soldiers' and Sailors' Civil Relief Act providing expanded rights, benefits, and protections for the servicemember.[20] In 1991 Congress amended the Act to provide extra protections for military personnel called to active duty during the Desert Storm campaign.[21]

In 2003 Congress rewrote the law completely and renamed it the Servicemembers Civil Relief Act.[22] The 2003 law preserved most of the features of the previous Act, so decisions under the former law remain relevant. In addition, it expanded some protections, modernized the language, updated the caps on coverage of certain types of obligations, and applied existing protections to new situations. It also added a requirement that the military services give written notice to servicemembers of the protections provided by the Act.[23] The relevant portions of both the pre-2003 and post-2003 versions of the law are reproduced on the companion material to this treatise.

Since 2003, the Act has been amended a number of times for clarification as well as to enhance protections for servicemembers.[24] An explicit private right of action was added in 2010. Through the Veterans' Benefits Act of 2010, Congress added Title VIII on Civil Liability to the SCRA. Along with clarifying the attorney general's ability to commence a civil action, Title VIII gives servicemembers and any other person aggrieved by a violation of the SCRA a basis upon which to claim declaratory or equitable relief, along with monetary damages or other appropriate relief.[25] Some courts held that there was no private cause of action under the predecessor to the SCRA, the Soldiers' and Sailors' Civil Relief Act,[26] while others found an implied cause of action under the SCRA, thus causing confusion.[27] The Veterans' Benefits Act of 2010 alleviates the confusion that previously existed regarding whether a private right of action should be allowed under the SCRA, providing a broad basis for "any person aggrieved" by a violation of the SCRA to bring a civil action to obtain "any" and "all" appropriate relief.[28] It also provides for litigation costs and attorney fees.[29] One court found that the express private cause of action and damage provisions of Title VIII could be applied retroactively, allowing an earlier SCRA claim to proceed.[30]

Wash. Rev. Code §§ 38.42.010 through 38.42.904 provide protections similar to the federal act, addressing waivers, default judgments, stays, fines, and penalties under contracts, as well as business loan interest rates. Wash. Rev. Code §§ 59.18.200, 59.18.220, and 59.20.090 address early termination of rental agreements.

West Virginia: W. Va. Code § 15-1F-11 incorporates the SCRA into state law. W. Va. Code § 15-1F-1b tolls the running of any licensure or registration requirement for any active duty servicemember. W. Va. Code § 21-1A-6 extends the time allowed for filing unfair labor practice complaints. W. Va. Code § 33-4-21 prohibits dishonest or predatory insurance sales practices on federal land and facilities. W. Va. Code § 30-1-6b specifies waivers and extensions for professional and occupation licenses and certification.

Wisconsin: Wis. Stat. § 321.61 suspends the enforcement of certain tax liabilities, waives interest and penalties on some taxes, and terminates mobile telephone service for servicemembers in federal service. Wis. Stat. § 321.62 is a comprehensive law similar to the federal act. It applies to members of the National Guard or a state defense force who are called into active state service by order of the governor. It limits interest rates similarly to the federal act, provides for stays of proceedings, and restricts foreclosure, actions to resume possession of personal property and enforcement of storage liens.

Wyoming: Wyo. Stat. Ann. §§ 19-11-101 through 19-11-124 address employment and re-employment, benefits, insurance, and professional licenses, among other issues. The SCRA and USERRA are made applicable to certain National Guard members

19 *Available at* www.dtic.mil/doctrine/dod_dictionary.

20 Act of Oct. 17, 1940, ch. 888, 54 Stat. 1178.

21 Soldiers' and Sailors' Civil Relief Act Amendments of 1991, Pub. L. No. 102-12, 105 Stat. 34 (1991).

22 Pub. L. No. 108-189, 117 Stat. 2835 (2003).

23 50 U.S.C. app. § 515 (compare to former 50 U.S.C. app. § 515). *See also* 50 U.S.C. app. § 515a (effective Jan. 6, 2006; establishing general requirement for notifying servicemembers of rights under the Act during orientation and trainings and authorizing outreach to adult dependents of servicemembers).

24 Enacted as Pub. L. No. 108-189, effective Dec. 19, 2003, SCRA has been amended as follows: Pub. L. No. 108-454 (adding 50 U.S.C. § 511 (9) and amending § 517), Pub. L. No. 109-163 (adding § 515a), Pub. L. No. 110-181 (amending 50 U.S.C. app. §§ 521 and 522), Pub. L. No. 110-289 (amending 50 U.S.C. §§ 527 and 533), Pub. L. No. 109-233 (amending 50 U.S.C. app. § 594); Pub. L. No. 110-389 (amending §§ 527 and 535 and adding § 535a), Pub. L. No. 111-97 (amending 50 U.S.C. app. §§ 568, 571), Pub. L. No. 111-275 (amending §§ 535 and 535a and adding §§ 597, 597a and 597b), effective Oct. 13, 2010, Pub. L. No. 111-346 (amending Pub. L. No. 111-289 by extending the "sunset" provision of section 533(b) to Dec. 31, 2012), and Pub. L. No. 112-154, 126 Stat. 1165 (2012) (strengthening protections against sale, foreclosure, or seizure of property for limited time). *See* U.S. Dep't of Justice, www.justice.gov/crt/spec_topics/military/scratext.pdf (noting various amendments to SCRA).

Highlights of the amendments include defining "judgment" in 50 U.S.C. app. § 511, strengthening the safeguards against waiver in 50 U.S.C. app. § 517, clarifying that 50 U.S.C. app. § 522 allows both plaintiffs and defendants to obtain stays of civil actions and proceedings, and adding clarification and definitions to 50 U.S.C. app. § 535 regarding the servicemember's right to terminate a residential or motor vehicle lease.

25 Veterans' Benefits Act of 2010, P.L. 111-275 (section 303); 50 App. U.S.C.A. § 597a; 124 Stat. 2864.

26 *See* Huftstelter v. Davies, 309 F. Supp. 1372 (N.D. Ga. 1970).

27 *See* Gordon v. Pete's Auto Serv. of Denbigh, Inc., 637 F.3d. 454 (4th Cir. 2011) (applying the Veterans' Benefit Act of 2010 to permit plaintiff-servicemember to proceed with his damages claim), *rev'g* 670 F. Supp. 2d 453 (E.D. Va. 2009) (finding no cause of action for damages under SCRA); Batie v. Subway Real Estate Corp., 2008 WL 413627 (N.D. Tex. Feb. 15, 2008) (finding no implied private right of action under SCRA), *vacated,* 2008 WL 5136636 (N.D. Tex. Mar. 12, 2008).

28 50 U.S.C. app. § 597a.

29 *Id. See* Gordon v. Pete's Auto Serv. of Denbigh, Inc., 838 F. Supp. 2d 436 (E.D. Va. 2012) (SCRA's attorney fee provision applies to legal work performed after enactment date even though violations occurred before enactment; fees may also be awarded for legal work performed before enactment, as court had equitable authority to award fees even then).

30 *See* Gordon v. Pete's Auto Serv. of Denbigh, Inc., 670 F. Supp. 2d 453 (E.D. Va. 2009) (finding no cause of action for damages under SCRA), *rev'd*, 637 F.3d. 454 (4th Cir. 2011) (retroactively applying the Veterans'

Another court, rather than applying the private right of action provision (section 597a) retroactively, found that an implied private right of action already existed under section 522.[31] The permissibility of retroactive application under section 597a of SCRA has also been interpreted to depend upon whether a plaintiff could already assert the right on other grounds, such as state law.[32]

Aside from the changes brought under the Veterans' Benefits Act of 2010, Congress at the end of 2012 passed a bill that lengthened the period of SCRA protection against foreclosures from nine months to one year after the end of military service.[33] Congress is currently investigating alleged violations of the SCRA by financial institutions and whether the SCRA is effective in its current form. A number of bills proposing to amend the SCRA have been proposed in Congress, which incorporated recommendations from military attorneys and others involved in SCRA actions related to the investigations.[34] One Senate bill proposes to extend the existing one year period of SCRA protection against foreclosures to twenty-four months, increase criminal penalties for violations of SCRA foreclosure protections from misdemeanors to felonies, and double the civil penalties allowed in a civil action by the attorney general under section 597(b)(3) of the Act. Another bill proposes to eliminate pre-dispute waivers and arbitration provisions in contracts with servicemembers and to allow class action suits.[35]

7.3 Who Is Protected by the Act?

The Act applies to those in military service, defined to include the armed forces and the commissioned corps of the National Oceanic and Atmospheric Administration and the Public Health Service.[36] To be entitled to the Act's protections, the servicemember must either be in or recently released from "military service." Military service is defined in part as active duty.[37]

All servicemembers on active duty are entitled to the benefits of the Act, even if they are not stationed in a war zone or have not been mobilized. Active duty includes full-time training duty, annual training duty, and attendance at a military school while in active military service.[38] Mere enlistment or participation in a delayed entry/enlistment program does not constitute "active duty" under the SCRA.[39]

Active duty does not include full-time National Guard members or Reservists on active duty for fewer than thirty days.[40] However, the 2003 revisions to the Act recognized the importance of the application of the SCRA prior to reporting for duty in the case of National Guard servicemembers and Reservists. Although two weeks of local National Guard training conducted by the state did not constitute active duty under the SCRA's tolling provision,[41] SCRA protections have been deemed to apply to Reserve members upon receipt of orders to report for military service.[42]

"Military service" also includes periods of time that a servicemember is absent from duty on account of sickness, wounds, leave, or other lawful cause,[43] but not periods of time the servicemember is absent without leave (AWOL).[44] Military service in the case of the National Guard includes service responding to a national emergency under a call to active service authorized by the President or Secretary of Defense for over thirty consecutive days.[45]

Benefit Act of 2010 to permit plaintiff-servicemember to proceed with his damages claim). *See also* United States v. B.C. Enter., Inc., 696 F. Supp. 2d 593 (E.D. Va. 2010) (federal government has non-statutory right to sue under SCRA), *aff'd*, 447 Fed. Appx. 468 (4th Cir. 2011).

31 Jimenez v. Miami-Dade Cnty., 2013 WL 214673 (S.D. Fla. Jan. 18, 2013).

32 *See* Williams v. U.S. Bank, 2013 WL 571844, at *4 (C.D. Cal. Feb. 13, 2013).

33 The one year period expires on December 31, 2014. After the expiration date, the duration of the protection will revert to nine months from the end of active duty. *See* Pub. L. No. 112-154, 126 Stat. 1165 (Aug. 6, 2012) (sunset provisions).

34 *See* S. 486, 112th Cong. (as introduced Mar. 3, 2011) (hearings held by Committee on Veteran's Affairs).

35 *See* S. 1999, 113th Cong. (as introduced Feb,. 6, 2014).

36 50 U.S.C. app. § 511(1) (cross-referencing 10 U.S.C. § 101(a)(5)). *But cf. In re* Gaddy, 2004 WL 2044107 (Bankr. D. Kan. Apr. 12, 2004) (SCRA protections do not apply to civilian employees of private contractor engaged in support of uniformed servicemembers in Iraq).

37 50 U.S.C. app. § 511(2)(i)) (cross-referencing 10 U.S.C. § 101(d)(1)).

38 10 U.S.C. § 101(d)(1). *But cf.* Donahou v. Presidential Limousine & Auto Sales, Inc., 2007 WL 1229342 (W.D. Ark. Apr. 24, 2007) (active duty does not include eight-month "Delayed Entry" period between time servicemember enlisted and time he reported for duty; he had no military duties during this time and was able to maintain civilian employment).

39 Donahou v. Presidential Limousine & Auto Sales, Inc., 2007 WL 1229342 (W.D. Ark. 2007) (unpublished).

40 *Id.*

41 *See* Bowen v. United States, 49 Fed. Cl. 673 (Fed. Cl. 2001), *aff'd*, 292 F.3d 1383 (Fed. Cir. 2002).

42 50 U.S.C. app. § 516. *Cf.* Marin v. U.S. Postal Serv., 2003 WL 22427938 (2d Cir. Oct. 23, 2003) (reservist entitled to Act's benefits only when ordered to report for active duty); *In re* Marriage of Brazas, 662 N.E.2d 559 (Ill. App. Ct. 1996) (Soldiers and Sailors Civil Relief Act applies to reservists while on reserve duty; vacating default judgment entered on day when trial court and opposing counsel had actual notice that reservist was out of state on reserve duty); Sung Man Min v. Avila, 991 S.W.2d 495 (Tex. App. 1999) (statute of limitations is tolled only during active duty; annual two-week reserve duty is active duty but weekend reserve duty is not).

43 50 U.S.C. app. § 511(2)(C); Cronin v. United States, 98 Fed. Cl. 268 (Fed. Cl. 2011) (time spent on Temporary Disability Retirement List (TDRL) is military service). *See* Sec'y of Hous. & Urban Dev. v. McClenan, 4 Misc. 3d 1027(A) (table), 2004 WL 2187568 (N.Y. Civ. Ct. Sept. 22, 2004) (active duty servicemember receiving medical treatment pending deployment is protected by Act).

44 *In re* Marriage of Hampshire, 934 P.2d 58 (Kan. 1997) (interpreting pre-2003 version of Act not to protect soldier who was absent without leave or in military prison at the time of proceedings which led to default judgment for child support).

45 The Act was amended in 2002 to cover National Guard members who have been called up. *See* Pub. L. No. 107-330, § 305, 116 Stat. 2821 (2002), 50 U.S.C. app. § 511(2)(A)(ii). *But cf.* Gutridge v. Suburban Steel Supply Co., 2008 WL 2953662 (Ohio Ct. App. July 30, 2008) (unpublished) (active duty does not include fourteen-day National Guard training); Bowen v. United States, 292 F.3d 1383 (Fed. Cir. 2002) (two weeks of National Guard training, ordered by state but

In some cases, confinement in a military prison may be considered active duty to which the SCRA applies to toll the statute of limitations, if the confinement occurs before discharge.[46] In other cases, such confinement has been ruled to be outside SCRA's definition of active service.[47]

United States citizens serving with allied forces are also entitled to the protections of the Act during their service.[48]

Some protections of the SCRA explicitly cover the dependents or co-obligors of servicemembers.[49] A dependent is defined as the servicemember's spouse, child, or any individual for whom the servicemember provided more than one-half of the individual's support for the 180 days preceding the application for relief under the Act.[50] The definition of "child" incorporates the Internal Revenue Service's definition.[51] In many cases, however, the dependent or co-obligor must obtain a court order for protections that are automatic for servicemembers, and protection under the SCRA for dependents or co-obligors may be contingent upon whether the same protection has been granted to the servicemember.[52] State law, though, may explicitly allow dependents the same protection as servicemembers.[53]

While co-obligors may be protected under the SCRA, they are not entitled to protections greater than those afforded to the servicemember.[54] However, whenever a court enters a stay or vacates a judgment, it has discretion to grant the same relief to any surety, guarantor, endorser, accommodation maker, co-maker, or other person who may be primarily or secondarily liable.[55] Any waiver of these protections is invalid if it is made by a dependent of an individual who enters active duty after the dependent's execution of the waiver.[56]

Rights under the Act may be enforced by the servicemember directly[57] or by a lawyer or an individual with a power of attorney who is acting for the servicemember.[58] When there is a pattern of practice or significant public policy importance, the attorney general can also commence a civil action which can result in penalties of up to $55,000 for a first violation and up to $110,000 for each subsequent violation of the Act.[59] Additionally, under the 2010 SCRA Title VIII language that explicitly provides for a private right of action, "any person aggrieved by a violation of this Act" can bring a civil action to obtain "any" and "all" appropriate relief.[60] However, it remains to be seen to what extent courts interpret this new language to apply to dependents and other family members of servicemembers or civilians who may be affected by a violation of the SCRA. Courts have yet to determine whether persons other than servicemembers qualify as "person[s] aggrieved" under every provision of the SCRA, or only some provisions, such as those in which dependents and other non-military persons are explicitly mentioned.

In a number of cases, courts have extended SCRA protections from a servicemember to the servicemember's corporation.[61] The courts have supported their reasoning in these cases by liberally construing the SCRA and resolving any doubts of its application in favor of the servicemember. When

---

paid for with federal paycheck, is not "federal service on active duty" under pre-2003 version of the Act, so statute of limitations not tolled).

46 *See* Lowe v. United States, 79 Fed. Cl. 218 (Fed. Cl. 2007) (finding that confinement was "service-connected," the test for "active duty" that has been equated with "military service"), *appeal dismissed*, 333 Fed. Appx. 523 (Fed. Cir. 2009).

47 Reed v. Albaaj, 723 N.W.2d 50 (Minn. Ct. App. 2006) (Act does not apply to servicemember while incarcerated in military prison for crime committed while on active duty).

48 50 U.S.C. app. § 514.

49 *See* 50 U.S.C. app. § 538 (allowing court to grant dependents the protections of "this title," that is, Title, III, "Rent, Installment Contracts, Mortgages, Liens, Assignments, Leases, Telephone Service Contracts"); 50 U.S.C. app. § 513 (court has discretion to extend SCRA protection to persons who are primarily or secondarily liable with the servicemember). *See also* Flagstar Bank, FSB v. Pemberton, 2010 WL 924253 (D. V.I. 2010) (co-debtor, along with servicemember, protected against foreclosure action, but co-debtor did not receive servicemember's protection under SCRA from a judgment of default on the underlying debt obligation), *amended on reconsideration*, 2010 WL 2643378 (D. V.I. June 30, 2010); Tucson Telco Fed. Credit Union v. Bowser, 451 P.2d 322 (Ariz. Ct. App. 1969) (spouse protected).

50 50 U.S.C. app. § 511(4).

51 38 U.S.C. § 101(4).

52 50 U.S.C. app. § 513 (stay, postponement, suspension, vacation of judgments, and bail bonds), § 531(a)(1)(A) (evictions), § 535(b) (termination of real property and vehicle leases), § 538 (general extension to dependents), § 561 (tax sales); Umstead v. Chase Manhattan Mortgage Group, 2005 WL 2233554 (W.D. Va. Sept. 13, 2005) (servicemember's mother qualified as dependent under the Act and could proceed with her own action to seek stay and modification of mortgage obligation on grounds that her ability to pay was materially impaired by son's active duty); *In re* Cockerham, 336 B.R. 592 (Bankr. S.D. Ga. 2005) (co-debtor wife who was separated from servicemember husband was not entitled to SCRA stay when husband received no SCRA protection). *See* Tucson Telco Fed. Credit Union v. Bowser, 451 P.2d 322 (Ariz. Ct. App. 1969) (extending protections of former version of law to serviceman's wife with respect to premarriage debt incurred solely in her name when her ability to pay was impaired by serviceman's induction). *See also* § 7.5, *infra* (interest rate reduction).

53 *See, e.g.*, Cal. Mil. & Vet. Code § 409.5 (West) (extending service member benefits under sections 405 through 409.4 of the California Military and Veterans Code to dependents).

54 *See In re* Cockerham, 336 B.R. 592 (Bankr. S.D. Ga. 2005).

55 50 U.S.C. app. § 513.

56 50 U.S.C. app. § 513(d)(2). *See also* § 7.6, *infra* (general discussion of waivers).

57 50 U.S.C. app. § 519a.

58 50 U.S.C. app. § 519.

59 50 U.S.C. app. § 597; Veterans' Benefits Act of 2010, P.L. 111-275 (section 801).

60 50 U.S.C. app. 597a; Veterans' Benefits Act of 2010, P.L. 111-275 (section 802).

61 *See* Fifth Third Bank v. Schoessler's Supply Room, L.L.C., 940 N.E.2d 608 (Ohio Ct. App. 2010) (extending SCRA protection when servicemember was personally obligated to pay note owed by corporation that he owned and managed, and his presence was necessary to run the business); Linscott v. Vector Aerospace, 2006 WL 1310511 (D. Or. May 12, 2006) (unpublished) (citing Cathey v. First Republic Bank, 2001 U.S. Dist. LEXIS 13150 (W.D. La. July 6, 2001) (servicemember's protections extended to servicemember's family corporation when corporation depended upon servicemember's presence for profitability and servicemember personally guaranteed corporation's obligations)).

a servicemember personally and individually guarantees the loan issued to his corporation, the courts may consider the loan to be incurred by the servicemember.[62] The courts also found significant the fact that the profitability of the corporations depended upon the servicemembers' own labor and expertise.[63] In these cases, the courts applied the SCRA's protections against default judgments and the SCRA's limitation on interest rates to the servicemembers' corporations.

7.4 Procedural Protections in Court Proceedings

7.4.1 Introduction

The SCRA gives servicemembers important procedural protections in civil judicial and administrative proceedings.[64] It divides these protections into two main categories: cases in which the servicemember has been notified of the proceeding and/or makes an appearance,[65] and cases in which the servicemember has not been notified or does not make an appearance.[66] When the servicemember has received notice of a proceeding, the SCRA provides a mechanism by which the servicemember can stay the proceeding, when his or her current military duty materially affects the servicemember's ability to appear.[67] In instances in which the servicemember does not make an appearance, the SCRA effectively gives the servicemember the benefit of a presumption that military service impacted the servicemember's ability to appear and protects the servicemember in the event a court enters a default judgment.[68]

Types of administrative proceedings potentially affected include driver's license revocation hearings, proceedings to revoke business or professional licenses, zoning hearings, unemployment compensation and Social Security claims, and administrative child support proceedings. All of these proceedings are subject to the same rules about stays and defaults as judicial proceedings. The Act also restricts execution upon assets of the servicemember.[69]

7.4.2 Cases in Which the Servicemember, As Defendant, Has Not Been Notified or Has Not Made an Appearance

Special protections apply to servicemembers against default judgments in any civil action or proceeding wherein a defendant servicemember does not make an appearance. Except in limited situations,[70] the SCRA prohibits courts from entering default judgments in cases in which the defendant has not appeared, unless the plaintiff files an acceptable affidavit.[71] An affidavit of non-military service must also accompany a creditor's request for entry of judgment in an attachment proceeding, even though the defendant may not have been an active duty servicemember when the initial judgment was entered.[72]

The affidavit must either state whether the defendant is in military service and show facts in support of the statement,[73] or state that the plaintiff is unable to determine whether the defendant is in military service.[74] With ongoing deployment

62 Fifth Third Bank v. Schoessler's Supply Room, L.L.C., 940 N.E.2d 608, 613–14 (Ohio. Ct. App. 2010) (quoting Cathey v. First Republic Bank, 2001 U.S. Dist. LEXIS 13150, *12 (W.D. La. July 6, 2001) and Linscott v. Vector Aerospace, 2006 U.S. Dist. LEXIS 30023, *11 (D. Or. May 12, 2006) (unpublished)). *But cf.* Newton v. Bank of McKenney, 2012 WL 1752407 (E.D. Va. May 16, 2012) (stating SCRA does not apply to protect corporation of a defendant servicemember who personally guaranteed her business's loan).

63 Fifth Third Bank v. Schoessler's Supply Room, L.L.C., 940 N.E.2d 608, 613–14 (Ohio. Ct. App. 2010); Cathey v. First Republic Bank, 2001 U.S. Dist. LEXIS 13150, *12 (W.D. La. July 6, 2001); Linscott v. Vector Aerospace, 2006 U.S. Dist. LEXIS 30023, *11 (D. Or. May 12, 2006) (unpublished).

64 The 2003 revisions made SCRA protections applicable to administrative as well as judicial proceedings. 50 U.S.C. app. §§ 511(5) (defining "court" to include state and federal administrative agencies), 512(b) (Act applies to any judicial or administrative proceeding commenced in any court or agency), 521 (default judgments), 522 (stays).

65 *See* 50 U.S.C. app. § 522; § 7.4.3, *infra*.

66 *See* 50 U.S.C. app. § 521; § 7.4.2, *infra*.

67 50 U.S.C. app. § 522.

68 50 U.S.C. app. § 521(g).

69 *See* § 7.4.4, *infra*.

70 50 U.S.C. app. § 522(e) (when servicemember's application for the stay under section 522 is unsuccessful, servicemember cannot then claim protection under section 521).

71 *See* Premier Fin. Servs., L.L.C. v. Morris, 2010 WL 3342002 (D. Ariz. Aug. 25, 2010); Chanel, Inc. v. Adeymi, 2009 WL 2590640 (D. Ariz. Aug. 21, 2009) (plaintiff's filing an SCRA affidavit is a prerequisite before entry of judgment for the plaintiff); Merrill v. Beard, 2007 WL 461469 (N.D. Ohio Feb. 7, 2007) (because Act requires a written affidavit, a verbal statement on the record in open court upon request for default judgment cannot be substituted). *See also* Maredia v. Philip Morris USA Inc., 2007 WL 2462093 (E.D. Cal. Aug. 27, 2007) (affidavit requirement applies only if defendant has not appeared).

72 *See* Smith v. Lafrinere, 2011 WL 4575143 (D. Kan. Sept. 20, 2011) (granting defendant servicemember's motion to set aside default judgment that was entered despite plaintiff's failure to supply the affidavit, required under SCRA, stating whether defendant was in military service); Sprinkle v. S B & C Ltd., 472 F. Supp. 2d 1235 (W.D. Wash. 2006) (entry of judgment to garnish servicemember's bank account without submitting affidavit of non-military service violated SCRA, the Fair Debt Collection Practices Act, and state consumer protection statutes); Palisades Acquisitions, L.L.C. v. Ibrahim, 812 N.Y.S.2d 866 (N.Y. Civ. Ct. 2006) (in proceeding to garnish a joint bank account, creditor must submit affidavit for joint tenant who is not a judgment debtor as well as an affidavit for judgment debtor).

73 *See* Bank of Nova Scotia v. James, 2009 WL 902101 (D. V.I. Mar. 31, 2009) (denying motion for default judgment when creditor submitted printout from Department of Manpower Data Center showing defendant was not in military service without any affidavit or certification of authenticity); Bank of Nova Scotia v. George, 2008 WL 501263 (D. V.I. Feb. 15, 2008) (affidavit that defendant is not in military service must state facts in support; mere review of creditors' records insufficient).

74 50 U.S.C. app. § 521(b)(1) (former 50 U.S.C. app. § 520).

As the 2003 revision did not make any substantive changes to this requirement, courts are likely to continue to follow decisions under the former version of the law. United States v. Nicholson, 2000 U.S. Dist. LEXIS 11028 (E.D. Cal. July 11, 2000) (denying application for default judgment for unpaid taxes because of numerous faults in application, including failure to file required affidavit stating that defendant is not serving in the military), *adopted by* 2000 U.S. Dist. LEXIS of servicemembers in distant areas of conflict, several courts have articulated specific standards for the preparation of affidavits of non-military service under section 521 of the Act.[75] Counsel who submit inaccurate affidavits may be subject to sanctions or other forms of reprimand.[76] The Act authorizes criminal sanctions, including fines and imprisonment, against a person who knowingly makes or uses a false affidavit of non-military service or supporting document.[77]

A certificate of military service can satisfy the affidavit requirement, if declared to be true under penalty of perjury.[78] Certificates may be obtained from the Defense Manpower Data Center (DMDC).[79] One court has held that obtaining the report provided in response to a query to the DMDC satisfies the plaintiff's duty to investigate for an affidavit of non-military service.[80] However in some instances courts have noted that the DMDC reports were inaccurate.[81] If it appears that the defendant is in military service, the special protections apply. First, the court cannot enter a judgment until it appoints an attorney to represent the defendant.[82] However, the SCRA does not address how an attorney should be appointed, the specific procedures or duties that such appointment entails, or how an appointed attorney should be paid.[83] The provisions for appointment of an attorney to represent the servicemember apply only when the servicemember has been served with the complaint. If service cannot be made, the case cannot proceed. It must be stayed until service can be made or the servicemember leaves active duty.[84]

Second, the court is obligated to grant a stay of at least ninety days upon counsel's application or upon its own motion if it finds that the defendant is necessary to present a defense, or if counsel has been unable to contact the defendant or unable to determine if a meritorious defense exists.[85] If the court cannot determine whether the defendant is in military service, the court may require the plaintiff to post a bond.[86]

A default judgment that is entered without complying with the requirements of section 521 is voidable.[87] Additionally, the

---

13630 (E.D. Cal. Aug. 14, 2000); Murdock v. Murdock, 526 S.E.2d 241 (S.C. Ct. App. 1999) (failure to comply with Act's protections against default judgment renders judgment voidable). *See also In re* Paternity of T.M.Y., 725 N.E.2d 997 (Ind. Ct. App. 2000) (failure to comply with Act renders judgment voidable but defendant must show prejudice and a meritorious defense); U.S. Bank v. Coaxum, 2003 WL 22518107 (N.Y. Sup. Ct. Oct. 31, 2003) (affidavit must establish that respondent is not in United States or ally's military service and that the investigation was done after default occurred and shortly before affidavit submitted, and must set forth facts in a manner sufficient for court to evaluate). *Cf.* MNF Bank v. Thompson, 1999 Ohio App. LEXIS 5072 (Ohio Ct. App. Oct. 29, 1999) (judgment not voidable when it was entered more than thirty days after defendant left military service, even though suit was filed during the period of service; note that the 2003 revisions extended these protections to judgments entered up to sixty days after termination or release from active duty).

75 *See, e.g., In re* Templehoff, 339 B.R. 49 (Bankr. S.D.N.Y. 2005) (as an "essential step" in preparing affidavit of non-military service in relief from stay proceeding, creditor must examine the bankruptcy debtor's schedules to check for any information related to military employment); Water Pollution Control Auth. v. Mendes, 2004 WL 2165866 (Conn. Super. Ct. Sept. 1, 2004) (affidavit of non-military service must contain statement of personal knowledge and specify sources of information); New Century Fin. Servs., Inc. v. Sanchez, No. CD-2747-98 (N.J. Super. Ct. Law Div. Apr. 12, 2002), *available at* www.nclc.org/unreported (affidavit must be based on personal knowledge; if creditor cannot do so, it must either post a bond or show good cause for not being required to do so); Bergani v. Desena, 50 A.D.3d 716 (N.Y. App. Div. 2008) (portion of affidavit by process server stating that he asked the person to whom he delivered the complaint whether the defendant was in military service, and was told no, is sufficient); Sunset 3 Realty v. Booth, 824 N.Y.S.2d 766 (N.Y. Sup. Ct. 2006) (under local practice, affidavit will be rejected if it does not set forth facts supporting conclusions, and facts must have been ascertained within thirty to sixty days of submission of affidavit); Heritage East-West, L.L.C. v. Chung & Choi, 785 N.Y.S.2d 317 (N.Y. Civ. Ct. 2004) (affidavits must be based on communication with defendant or Department of Defense database search and may not rely solely on recent physical observation of defendant). *See also* Merrill v. Beard, 2007 WL 461469 (N.D. Ohio Feb. 7, 2007) (because Act requires a written affidavit, a verbal statement on the record in open court upon request for default judgment cannot be substituted).

76 *See* Heritage East-West, L.L.C. v. Chung & Choi, 785 N.Y.S.2d 317 (N.Y. Civ. Ct. 2004) (plaintiffs' counsel in eviction cases fined $1000 for each of six cases in which he sought default judgments without conducting investigations to support non-military affidavits); Sec'y of Hous. & Urban Dev. v. McClenan, 4 Misc. 3d 1027(A) (table), 2004 WL 2187568 (N.Y. Civ. Ct. Sept. 22, 2004) (finding counsel in eviction case acted in bad faith by ignoring ample evidence of defendant's active military service).

77 50 U.S.C. app. § 521(c).

78 50 U.S.C. app. § 521(b)(4). *See* Bank of Nova Scotia v. James, 2009 WL 902101 (D. V.I. Mar. 31, 2009) (denying motion for default judgment when creditor submitted printout from Department of Manpower Data Center showing defendant was not in military service without any affidavit or certification of authenticity).

79 Active duty status information for compliance with the SCRA is free from the DMDC and can be obtained at www.dmdc.osd.mil/scra/owa/home or by writing to Defense Manpower Data Center, Military Verification, 1600 Wilson Blvd., Suite 400, Arlington, VA, 22209.

80 363 Assocs., L.L.C. v. Sharhan, 774 N.Y.S.2d 907 (N.Y. Civ. Ct. 2003).

81 *See In re* Templehoff, 339 B.R. 49 (Bankr. S.D.N.Y. 2005) (counsel's good faith but mistaken reliance on DMDC record mitigated against imposition of Rule 9011 sanctions); Sec'y of Hous. & Urban Dev. v. McClenan, 4 Misc. 3d 1027(A) (table), 2004 WL 2187568 (N.Y. Civ. Ct. Sept. 22, 2004) (counsel acted in bad faith in claiming to rely on DMDC report when counsel was aware of other substantial evidence of defendant's active military service).

82 50 U.S.C. app. § 521(b)(2).

83 *See In re* Langen, 2010 Bankr. LEXIS 4375 (Bankr. S.D. Tex. Nov. 1, 2010) (denying bankruptcy defendant's petition asking court to appoint counsel for creditor who was covered by the SCRA when defendant did not offer to pay for the appointed counsel. *Cf.* 50 U.S.C. app. § 597a(b) (specifying fee-shifting, but only when a person aggrieved by an SCRA violation prevails in an affirmative suit).

84 Bryant v. Kinnamon, 2008 WL 4467803 (E.D. La. Sept. 30, 2008).

85 50 U.S.C. app. § 521(d).

86 50 U.S.C. app. § 521(b)(3).

87 Davidson v. Gen. Fin. Corp., 295 F. Supp. 878 (D. Ga. 1968). *Cf.* Shatswell v. Shatswell, 758 F. Supp. 662 (D. Kan. 1991) (Act does not give federal court authority to order state court case stayed; judgment must be attacked in the court that rendered it); Scheidegg v. Dep't of Air Force, 715 F. Supp. 11 (D.N.H. 1989) (federal court lacks authority to vacate or impede order or judgment of state court; judgment must be attached in court that rendered it), *aff'd*, 915 F.2d 1558 (1st Cir. 1990) (mem.); Goshorn v. Brown, 2003 WL 22176976 (Tex. App. Sept. 23, 2003). *But cf.* Pellegrini v. Silva, 2005 WL 3036321 (Mass. Land Ct. Nov. 14, 2005) (party's failure to comply with Act's affidavit requirement will not invalidate a foreclosure action when objecting

Act gives courts authority to vacate any default judgment that is entered while a servicemember is on active duty, or within sixty days of release from active duty.[88] The servicemember must apply to have the judgment vacated within ninety days after termination of or release from military service,[89] and must show a meritorious or legal defense and that military service materially affected the servicemember's ability to make a defense.[90] State law limits on vacating judgments are inapplicable.[91]

7.4.3 *Cases in Which the Servicemember, as Plaintiff or Defendant, Has Been Notified of the Proceeding*

7.4.3.1 Automatic Stay of at Least Ninety Days

The Act gives a servicemember who has received actual notice of a civil action or proceeding other than an eviction[92] the right to an automatic, non-discretionary stay of at least ninety days upon request.[93] The stay under section 522 is applicable whether the servicemember is the defendant or plaintiff.[94]

The stay request must: (1) set forth facts explaining why current military duty requirements materially affect the servicemember's ability to appear; (2) state a date when the servicemember will be able to appear; and (3) include a letter or other communication from the servicemember's commanding officer stating that the servicemember's current military duty prevents appearance and that military leave is not authorized.[95] The application does not constitute an appearance for jurisdictional purposes and is not a waiver of any substantive or procedural defenses.[96] The Act does not specify any formal requirements for the stay request, so it should not have to be in the form of an affidavit or motion.

One of the first courts to consider the scope of the stay under the amended Act held that it did not prevent a trial court from issuing a temporary child custody order in a divorce suit that a servicemember had commenced while he was on leave.[97] The child had been with the servicemember's mother prior to the temporary order, and the servicemember argued that the stay prevented the court from restoring custody to the child's mother. The appellate court held that the stay could only be used to shield a servicemember from the adverse effects of judicial proceedings, not to be used as a sword for tactical advantage. Other courts have expressed similar concerns about the calculated use of the stay as a tactic in contested child custody litigation.[98] However, the Act was amended in 2008 to make it explicit that the rules about stays apply to child custody proceedings.[99]

When the servicemember requests a stay, but has not provided the documentation required by section 522(b)(2), the court has the discretion to respond in several ways. The court may deny the motion.[100] The court may allow the servicemember an opportunity to cure the deficiency and then consider the request.[101] The court may grant the stay on its own motion under section 522 without the documentation as long as the

individuals never alleged they had been in military service); PNC Bank v. Kemenash, 761 A.2d 118 (N.J. Super. Ct. App. Div. 2000) (incarcerated servicemember who was not protected by Act could not challenge default judgment entered without affidavit of non-military service); Dep't of Hous. Preservation & Dev. v. W. 129th St. Realty Group, 802 N.Y.S.2d 826 (N.Y. Civ. Ct. 2005) (irregularity in non-military affidavit is not jurisdictional defect, so defaulting party who makes no claim of active military duty cannot proceed under Act to challenge judgment).

88 50 U.S.C. app. § 521(g). *But cf. In re* Gregory B., 2008 WL 684550 (Cal. Ct. App. Mar. 14, 2008) (unpublished) (bare assertion of unavailability is insufficient).

89 50 U.S.C. app. § 521(g)(2). *See* Collins v. Collins, 805 N.E.2d 410 (Ind. Ct. App. 2006) (under former 50 U.S.C. app. § 520(4) (current 50 U.S.C. app. § 521(g)(2)), servicemember precluded from moving under the Act to set aside default judgment because he did not do so within ninety days of termination of military service); Kenck v. State, 373 Mont. 168 (Mont. 2013).

90 50 U.S.C. app. § 521(g)(1). *See* Bernhardt v. Alden Café, 864 A.2d 421 (N.J. Super. Ct. App. Div. 2005) (although trial court's decision to vacate default judgment under 50 U.S.C. app. § 521(g) is discretionary, it abused that discretion when it refused to set aside default for servicemember whose military status was undisputed and who alleged a meritorious defense).

91 *In re* Marriage of Thompson, 666 N.W.2d 616 (Iowa Ct. App. 2003); *In re* B.T.T., 156 S.W.3d 612 (Tex. App. 2004).

92 50 U.S.C. app. § 522(f).
See § 7.5.9, *infra*, for protections in eviction actions.

93 50 U.S.C. app. § 522. *See* Hernandez v. Hernandez, 906 A.2d 429 (Md. Ct. Spec. App. 2006) (when servicemember has complied with documentation requirements of 50 U.S.C. app. § 522(b)(2), statute leaves no room for judicial discretion and court must grant initial ninety-day stay). Section 533(c) of the SCRA was amended in 2012 to allow for a stay of a foreclosure proceeding for any action filed within one year after the end of active duty. This extension will expire on December 31, 2014, and the previous nine months post-active-duty protection period will be reinstated. *See* Pub. L. No. 112-154, 126 Stat. 1165 (Aug. 6, 2012) (sunset provisions).

94 Veterans Benefits Improvement Act, Pub. L. No. 108-454, § 703, 118 Stat. 3598 (2004) (codified at 50 U.S.C. app. § 522(a)).

95 50 U.S.C. app. § 522(b). *See* Black v. Camon, 2008 WL 2119914 (M.D. Ga. May 19, 2008) (denying stay when servicemember presented only active duty order and did not document that he was currently deployed overseas); *In re* Walter, 234 S.W.3d 836 (Tex. App. 2007) (no abuse of discretion to deny stay when application for stay did not include letter from commanding officer).

96 50 U.S.C. app. § 522(c).

97 Lenser v. McGowan, 191 S.W.3d 506 (Ark. 2004).

98 *See* George P. v. Super. Ct., 24 Cal. Rptr. 3d 919 (Cal. Ct. App. 2005) (dependency action); *In re* Marriage of Grantham, 698 N.W.2d 140 (Iowa 2005); *In re* Marriage of Bradley, 137 P.3d 1030 (Kan. 2006).

99 Nat'l Defense Authorization Act for Fiscal Year 2008, Pub. L. No. 110-181, § 584, 122 Stat. 3 (2008).

100 Rodriguez v. Am. Express, 2006 WL 908613 (E.D. Cal. Apr. 7, 2006) (unpublished). *See* King v. Irvin, 614 S.E.2d 190 (Ga. Ct. App. 2005); *In re* Marriage of Bradley, 137 P.3d 1030 (Kan. 2006); Mirisoloff v. Monroe, 791 N.Y.S.2d 255 (N.Y. App. Div. 2005). *See also* City of Pendergrass v. Skelton, 628 S.E.2d 136 (Ga. Ct. App. 2006) (trial court abused its discretion in granting indefinite stay when servicemember had not provided documentation of deployment dates and unavailability of leave).

101 *See* Davenport v. Richards, 2006 WL 3791369 (W.D. Wash. Dec. 21, 2006) (granting stay after allowing servicemember thirty days to provide documents from commanding officer showing that current military duty prevents appearance).

party is a servicemember.[102] Finally, in exercising control over its own docket or acting in accordance with other procedural rules, the court may grant a stay without regard to the SCRA requirements.[103]

A request for stay under section 522 should be liberally construed. A servicemember's application for stay was granted when it did not technically meet all of the SCRA requirements but substantially complied with them.[104] The court granting the stay declared, "[a]n overly technical reading of the SCRA, in a manner that would disadvantage a servicemember on deployment overseas in defending his or her interests in pending litigation, would be contrary to its purpose. When, as here, a servicemember provides evidence sufficient to show that he or she is actually unavailable to appear in the proceedings, and the continuance of the proceedings would adversely affect his or her rights, a stay application should be granted."[105]

7.4.3.2 Discretionary Additional Stay

Either along with or after the initial nondiscretionary stay of not less than ninety days, the servicemember may seek an additional stay. This additional stay is not automatic. The court is to grant it if military duty continues to have a material effect on the servicemember's ability to appear. The court may grant it if the court determines that military duty continues to have a material effect on the servicemember's ability to appear.[106] This "material effect" standard is identical to the standard for all stays under the previous version of the statute, and the legislative history endorses the decisions that interpreted it.[107] Cases interpreting the standard under the old law are therefore relevant when the court rules on an application for an additional stay.[108] Relevant factors to consider when evaluating such requests as identified by courts under the former version of the law include whether the party seeking the stay and that party's counsel have acted with diligence, whether the servicemember is represented by competent counsel who has had sufficient time to prepare the case, and whether there are alternate ways to accommodate the servicemember's schedule.[109]

If the court denies an application for an additional stay, it must appoint counsel for the servicemember.[110] Leave of court is required for a plaintiff to proceed against co-defendants who are not in military service.[111]

---

102 Advanced Litig., L.L.C. v. Herzka, 2004 WL 1949292 (Del. Ch. Aug. 20, 2004).

103 Sottoriva v. Claps, 2006 WL 3775945 (C.D. Ill. Dec. 21, 2006) (granting stay for servicemember under court's general authority to set schedule for summary judgment proceedings under Fed. R. Civ. P. 56(f)); United States v. Smith, 2006 WL 2338267 (W.D. Okla. Aug. 10, 2006) (granting stay under discretionary power to control docket when defendant servicemember mistakenly applied for stay under wrong statutory section).

104 *In re* Amber M., 110 Cal. Rptr. 3d 25 (Cal. Ct. App. 2010) (concluding, in juvenile dependency proceeding, that servicemember's application for stay met the requirements of section 522 of SCRA, even though it did not specifically detail how military service would prevent him from appearing, when he would be able to appear, or provide an explicit statement from his commanding officer that military leave is not allowed).

105 *In re* Amber M., 110 Cal. Rptr. 3d 25, 30 (Cal. Ct. App. 2010).

106 50 U.S.C. app. § 522(d). *See* KCF v. TLSF, 839 N.Y.S.2d 433 (N.Y. Sup. Ct. Apr. 12, 2007) (balancing factors and denying stay when servicemember stationed overseas was able to take leave if necessary to attend custody hearing in New York).

107 H.R. Rep. No. 108-81 (2003), at 36 (explaining why the committee decided not to add a definition of "materially affected" to the Act).

108 Former 50 U.S.C. app. §§ 521, 522, 532. *See* Comer v. City of Palm Bay, 265 F.3d 1186 (11th Cir. 2001) (no abuse of discretion to deny stay when serviceman had nearly a year to do discovery before being called up and had entered the service while case was pending); White v. Black, 190 F.3d 366 (5th Cir. 1999) (court may stay proceedings on its own motion and has broad discretion); Dalenberg v. City of Waynesboro, 221 F. Supp. 2d 1380 (S.D. Ga. 2002) (burden of proving need for stay is imposed on neither party, but court is to use its sound sense; no stay of discovery when defendant was stationed near court and discovery could be accommodated to his schedule); Antioch Co. v. Scrapbook Borders, Inc., 210 F.R.D. 645 (D. Minn. 2002) (ordering accommodation of servicemember's schedule rather than stay; no stay for servicemember's co-defendant, at least for pretrial proceedings); Branch v. Stukes, 2001 U.S. Dist. LEXIS 19985 (S.D.N.Y. Nov. 30, 2001) (motion for stay denied without prejudice; servicemember must provide affidavit and memorandum of law showing how service will materially interfere with ability to participate in case); *In re* Lewis, 257 B.R. 431 (Bankr. D. Md. 2001) (adversary proceedings regarding dischargeability of debt stayed while debtor-husband serving abroad, but additional stay denied after his return to United States because no showing that military service would interfere with ability to defend); *In re* Burrell, 230 B.R. 309 (Bankr. E.D. Tex. 1999) (not granting stay *sua sponte* when absent serviceman neither moved for stay nor presented evidence on the question; allowing secured creditor to foreclose on collateral); *Ex parte* K.N.L., 2003 WL 21848949 (Ala. Civ. App. Aug. 8, 2003) (no abuse of discretion in denying stay of temporary custody order; specific findings unnecessary); Harris v. J.B. Hunt Transp., Inc., 2003 WL 22300305 (Ark. Ct. App. Oct. 8, 2003) (affirming denial of motion for stay); *In re* Brianna L., 2003 WL 220559 (Cal. Ct. App. Feb. 3, 2002) (denial of stay in neglected child case not error when soldier was represented by counsel throughout the proceedings); King-Coleman v. Geathers, 795 So. 2d 1092 (Fla. Dist. Ct. App. 2001) (court that denies a stay pursuant to SSCRA must make explicit findings, supported by the record, as to why servicemember's ability to defend will not be materially affected by military service); Ensley v. Carter, 538 S.E.2d 98 (Ga. Ct. App. 2000) (affirming trial court's discretion in denying stay); Greco v. Renegades, Inc., 761 N.Y.S.2d 426 (N.Y. App. Div. 2003) (proper to stay action unless plaintiff proves that servicemember defendant is assigned to location that will not materially affect ability to defend); *In re* Day, 2003 WL 1194244 (Ohio Ct. App. Mar.12, 2003) (trial court can deny stay only if it makes findings of fact that ability to defend is not materially affected by military service).

109 Dalenberg v. City of Waynesboro, 221 F. Supp. 2d 1380 (S.D. Ga. 2002); Antioch Co. v. Scrapbook Borders, Inc., 210 F.R.D. 645 (D. Minn. 2002). *See, e.g.*, George P. v. Super. Ct., 24 Cal. Rptr. 3d 919 (Cal. Ct. App. 2005) (affirming denial of additional stay in dependency action in which servicemember was represented and had testified on pertinent issues before deployment); *In re* Marriage of Grantham 698 N.W.2d 140 (Iowa 2005) (affirming denial of stay in custody modification action when servicemember was represented by counsel, witnesses were available, and servicemember failed to present evidence as to why his personal appearance was needed).

110 50 U.S.C. app. § 522(d)(2).

111 50 U.S.C. app. § 525(b) (former 50 U.S.C. app. § 524).

7.4.4 Other Stays Under the SCRA

The SCRA allows the court to stay execution of any judgment against a servicemember and to vacate or stay any prejudgment or postjudgment attachment or garnishment of property.[112] It also allows a court to stay a variety of other actions against servicemembers, including evictions,[113] foreclosures,[114] and enforcement of storage liens.[115] A stay applied for the benefit of a servicemember, however, does not necessarily apply to codefendants in the same proceeding.[116]

While the mandatory stay of civil actions or proceedings under section 522 must be for at least ninety days, the provision is inapplicable to stays under other provisions of the SCRA. Stays granted under provisions of the SCRA other than Sections 522 and 591 can extend for all or some portion of the entire period of military service, plus ninety days.[117]

7.4.5 Deferring Enforcement of Obligations During Active Duty

Servicemembers have the right to apply to a court to stay enforcement of an obligation for the period of active duty, plus a period of time after the servicemember is released from military service.[118] In the case of a contract to purchase real estate or a contract secured by a mortgage on real estate, the post-military service stay may last for a period equal to the remaining loan term plus the length of the military service period, and the balance must be paid in equal installments at the contract interest rate during this combined period.[119] For any other obligation, a servicemember leaving military service may be granted a period equal to the period of active duty to make up the deferred payments plus any accumulated interest.[120] These protections are substantively unchanged from the pre-2003 version of the law.[121] Courts may look closely at the material effect of military service before awarding the extreme relief granted in section 591.[122]

The obligee is not allowed to impose any penalties because of failure to comply with an obligation that has been stayed.[123] Nor can the obligee make an adverse credit report, deny additional credit, or change the terms of an existing credit arrangement solely on the basis of the stay.[124]

This option is particularly attractive for vehicle leases. Because vehicle leases do not bear interest, the person's obligation would be just to pay the deferred payments upon leaving military service.[125] For example, a person who had a $600 vehicle lease payment and was called to active duty for eight months, could stop making payments while on active duty. Upon leaving the military, the person would have eight months to catch up on the eight deferred payments, in equal installments.

Additionally, when an action for compliance with the terms of a contract is stayed under the SCRA, the law does not allow a penalty to accrue for failure to comply with the terms of the contract during the period of the stay.[126] If there is a failure to perform an obligation under a contract and a penalty is incurred, the court may, upon motion and showing of material effect on the servicemember's ability to comply, waive, or reduce the fine or penalty.[127]

Unlike the 6% interest cap that the SCRA requires for interest charged to servicemembers, payment deferments are neither automatic nor self-executing. Servicemembers must apply to a court for this relief,[128] and the statute only says that the court "may" grant it if the ability of the servicemember to pay is materially affected by his or her military service.[129] The application for a stay or modification of an obligation must be made to the court during or within 180 days of the termination of military service.[130] The court has discretion to stay enforce-

112 50 U.S.C. app. § 524 (former 50 U.S.C. app. § 513). *See* Sprinkle v. SB & C Ltd., 472 F. Supp. 2d 1235 (W.D. Wash. 2006) (requirement of 50 U.S.C. app. § 521 that creditor file affidavit of non-military service "before entry of judgment for plaintiff" applies to creditor's postjudgment entry of garnishment order against a bank); Palisades Acquisitions, L.L.C. v. Ibrahim, 812 N.Y.S.2d 866 (N.Y. Civ. Ct. 2006) (before creditor may execute against joint bank account, it must file affidavit of non-military service applicable to non-judgment debtor who has interest in account). *But cf.* World Tire Corp. v. Webb, 2007 WL 2812946 (Ohio Ct. App. Sept. 17, 2007) (unpublished) (not abuse of discretion to deny stay of execution under 50 U.S.C. app. § 524 when servicemember did not provide evidence, such as affidavits from his superiors, that he was in military and was deployed).

113 50 U.S.C. app. § 531(b). *See* § 7.5.9, *infra*.

114 50 U.S.C. app. § 533(b). *See* § 7.5.4, *infra*.

115 50 U.S.C. app. § 537(b). *See* § 7.5.5, *infra*.

116 50 U.S.C. app. § 525(b).

117 *See* 50 U.S.C. app. § 525(a) (section 525 stay does not apply to section 202 of 108 P.L. 189, that is, 50 U.S.C. app. § 522); Davenport v. Richards, 2006 WL 3791369 (W.D. Wash. Dec. 21, 2006) (granting stay for duration of active duty as indicated by commanding officer in statement provided to court); Mawer v. DaimlerChrysler Corp., 2006 WL 2253119 (S.D. Tex. Aug. 7, 2006); Hunt v. U.A.W. Local 1762, 2006 WL 572805 (E.D. Ark. Mar. 7, 2006) (administratively closing plaintiff servicemember's lawsuit pursuant to 50 U.S.C. app. § 522(a) and 50 U.S.C. app. § 525(a), with permission to reopen case within ninety days of return from active duty).

118 50 U.S.C. app. § 591 (former 50 U.S.C. app. § 590).

119 50 U.S.C. app. § 591(b)(1)(B).

120 50 U.S.C. app. § 591(b)(2)(B).

121 Former 50 U.S.C. app. § 590(2).

122 Santana-Archivald v. Banco Popular de P.R., 2012 WL 2359432 (D. P.R. June 19, 2012).

123 50 U.S.C. app. § 591(c).

124 50 U.S.C. app. § 518.

125 Of course, an implicit rate of return for the lessor is built into a vehicle lease. If the lessor argues that this rate of return is analogous to an interest rate and should accumulate while the servicemember is on active duty, the rejoinder is that if it is analogous to an interest rate it should be automatically reduced to 6%.

126 50 U.S.C. app. § 523(a).

127 50 U.S.C. app. § 523(b).

128 50 U.S.C. app. § 591(a) ("servicemember may . . . apply to a court"). *See* Koenig v. Waukesha State Bank, 2006 WL 2334841 (E.D. Wis. Aug. 10, 2006) (in absence of application by servicemember to court, 50 U.S.C. app. § 591 does not impose any enforceable duty upon creditor to negotiate a modification of obligation).

129 50 U.S.C. app. § 591(b).

130 50 U.S.C. app. § 591(a). *See* Rodriguez v. Am. Express, 2006 WL 908613 (E.D. Cal. Apr. 7, 2006) (servicemember must not only file a

ment of the lease not only for the person in military service but also for any co-signers.[131]

Student loans may also be deferred during active military duty under laws applying to student loans.[132]

7.4.6 Tolling of Statutes of Limitations

Section 526 of the SCRA prohibits counting the period of active duty toward any time limit for bringing any action or proceeding in a court, board, bureau, commission, department, or other agency of a state, a political subdivision of a state, or the federal government.[133] Thus, the statute of limitations is tolled not only for lawsuits but also for zoning appeals, unemployment compensation appeals, and similar administrative matters while the servicemember is on active duty.[134]

The period of active duty is also not to be included in computing any period for redeeming real property sold or forfeited to enforce any obligation, tax, or assessment.[135] The statute of limitations is tolled beginning on the date of a servicemember's entry into military service, which has been construed as the date upon which orders are received.[136] Limitations periods prescribed by the Internal Revenue Code are not, however, subject to tolling under the Act.[137]

Tolling applies to servicemembers, their heirs, executors, administrators, or assigns.[138] It is unconditional and automatic.[139] Tolling applies to federal statutes of limitations regardless of whether they expressly refer to the Act.[140] Courts' liberal construction of section 526(a) of the SCRA has also resulted in the tolling of statutory time periods under state law that have not been specifically designated as statutes of limitation.[141] The statute of limitations is tolled even if the defendant is stationed in the judicial district where the suit would be filed.[142] The Act has no provision allowing for servicemembers to waive the tolling of limitation periods.[143] On the other hand, although the tolling of statutes of limitations has been called mandatory,[144] it is not self-executing; if it is not raised by a non-servicemember and if not properly brought to the attention of the court, this protection may be forfeited, or waived, by a plaintiff asserting a claim against a servicemember.[145]

---

complaint with court within the statutory time frame but must also file separate motion for stay before end of 180-day post-discharge period).

131 50 U.S.C. app. § 513(a). *See* Umstead v. Chase Manhattan Mortgage Group, 2005 WL 2233554 (W.D. Va. Sept. 13, 2005) (servicemember's mother qualified as a dependent under Act and could bring her own application for modification of mortgage payments under 50 U.S.C. app. § 591). *But see In re* Cockerham, 336 B.R. 592 (Bankr. S.D. Ga. 2005) (when servicemember had agreed in chapter 13 plan to surrender collateral, court would not grant request of non-servicemember codebtor for a stay under the Act).

132 *See* 34 C.F.R. §§ 682.210(i), 674.34(c); National Consumer Law Center, Student Loan Law §§ 3.2.5, 3.2.6 (4th ed. 2010), *updated at* www.nclc.org/library.

133 50 U.S.C. app. § 526(a). *See, e.g.*, Remmie v. Mabus, 846 F. Supp. 2d 91 (D.D.C. 2012); State *ex rel.* Estate of Perry, 168 S.W.3d 577 (Mo. Ct. App. 2005) (50 U.S.C. app. § 526 tolls one-year statute of limitations for servicemember to file petition for presentment and application for letters testamentary in county probate court); *In re* Adoption of J.D.P., 198 P.3d 905 (Okla. Civ. App. 2008) (statute allows adoption of child without consent of parent who has failed to support child or maintain relationship for specified time period; active duty does not count toward this period); Walters v. Nadell, 751 N.W.2d 431 (Mich. 2008) (tolling of statute of limitations during active duty is mandatory, not discretionary, even though statute now uses term "may not"). *But see* Kegley v. City of Fayetteville, 613 S.E.2d 696 (N.C. Ct. App. 2005) (Act does not extend time for servicemember/property owner to challenge municipal annexation plan when his objection was to entire municipal plan and not specifically to treatment of his own property). *But see also* Lowe v. United States, 79 Fed. Cl. 218 (Fed. Cl. 2007) (statute of limitations is tolled during period servicemember was confined in military prison while still in the service); Lazarski v. Archdiocese of Philadelphia, 926 A.2d 459 (Pa. Super. Ct. 2007) (statutes of limitations are tolled only during active duty, not entire period of enlistment). *But cf.* Gutridge v. Suburban Steel Supply Co., 2008 WL 2953662 (Ohio Ct. App. July 30, 2008) (unpublished) (active duty does not include fourteen-day National Guard training).

134 Giel v. Winter, 503 F. Supp. 2d 208 (D.D.C. 2007) (SCRA tolls Administrative Procedure Act's time period for appealing administrative decision).

135 50 U.S.C. app. § 526(b). *See* Conroy v. Aniskoff, 507 U.S. 511, 113 S. Ct. 1562, 123 L. Ed. 2d 229 (1993) (under prior version of Act, soldier is entitled to extension of redemption period without need to show that military service caused hardship that should excuse the failure to act within the normal time). *See also* Small v. Kulesa, 204 S.W.3d 99 (Ark. Ct. App. 2005) (two-year limitation period for payment of overdue property taxes to prevent tax sale began with date servicemember left military service); Farran v. Wayne Cnty., 2005 WL 2219417 (Mich. Ct. App. Sept. 13, 2005) (50 U.S.C. app. § 526(b), unlike 50 U.S.C. app. § 561(a), tolls period for servicemember to redeem non-residential property from tax sale).

136 *See* DeTemple v. Leica Geosystems, Inc., 2013 WL 750461, at *4 (N.D. Ga. Feb. 27, 2013).

137 50 U.S.C. app. § 526(c).

138 50 U.S.C. app. § 526(a).

139 Cronin v. United States, 98 Fed. Cl. 268, 273 (Fed. Cl. 2011) (tolling provision language is unqualified); *In re* Brandt, 437 B.R. 294 (Bankr. M.D. Tenn. 2010) (holding that "may not" in section 526(a) of the SCRA indicates that tolling is mandatory, not permissive); Lowe v. United States, 79 Fed. Cl. 218 (Fed. Cl. 2007) (statute of limitations is tolled even when servicemember is in military prison, up until the time of his dishonorable discharge); Walters v. Nadell, 751 N.W.2d 431 (Mich. 2008) (civilian plaintiff can waive the SCRA's "mandatory" tolling of the statute of limitations period by failing to raise it against defendant-servicemember in trial court).

140 Bretherick v. Crittenden Cnty., 2007 WL 890200 (E.D. Ark. Mar. 21, 2007).

141 *In re* Adoption of W.C., 938 N.E.2d 1052, 1057 (Ohio Ct. App. 2010) (adoption/custody case).

142 *Id.*

143 Sedler v. Select Properties, Inc., 2004 WL 3392897 (Va. Cir. Ct. June 18, 2004) (servicemember's prior filing of suit on same cause of action against wrong defendant did not deprive servicemember of Act's tolling benefit when he filed second action).

144 *In re* Brandt, 437 B.R. 294 (Bankr. M.D. Tenn. 2010) (holding that "may not" in section 526(a) of the SCRA indicates that tolling is mandatory, not permissive); *In re* Adoption of W.C., 938 N.E.2d 1052, 1057 (Ohio Ct. App. 2010) (since the SCRA's tolling provision is mandatory, a servicemember may raise it for the first time on appeal).

145 *See* Walters v. Nadell, 751 N.W.2d 431 (Mich. 2008) (holding that the SCRA tolling protection may be waived by a plaintiff suing a servicemember, if not properly raised, just as a statute of limitations defense may be waived). *See also* Smith v. Washington Mut. Bank, 308 Fed. Appx. 707 (4th Cir. 2009) (when plaintiffs failed to timely file specific objections, they waived appellate review of their SCRA claims); Miller v. Lincoln Heights, 967 N.E.2d 255 (Ohio 2011) (holding that

The tolling of the statute of limitation preserves claims both by[146] and against[147] the servicemember.[148] However one court has held that an attorney's period of active duty military service does not toll time periods in a case he was handling for a non-servicemember.[149]

As the pre-2003 and post-2003 statutory language is similar, courts are likely to continue to follow decisions under the former version of the statute.[150]

7.5 Substantive Protections

7.5.1 Interest Rate Reduction to 6% for Pre-Active Duty Obligations

One of the most powerful provisions of the Act is the requirement that creditors limit the interest rate to 6% on any obligation or liability incurred by a servicemember before active duty.[151] The 6% interest rate is applied as of the date of entry into active duty.[152] The interest rate must be reduced unless a court decides, upon application by the lender, that the servicemember's ability to pay the higher interest rate is not materially affected by military service.[153] The rate reduction lasts during the period of military service and, in addition, for mortgages, trust deeds, or other security instrument in the nature of a mortgage, it continues for the year after active duty ends.[154] For other obligations, it lasts during the period of military service.[155]

The application of the interest rate reduction to any "obligation or liability"[156] means that it applies to all types of debt, including car loans, mortgages,[157] credit cards, federally insured student loans,[158] and business debts.[159] It even applies to debts when a corporation is the primary obligor, as long as the servicemember is personally liable.[160]

Because the interest rate reduction applies to "liabilities" as well as "obligations," postjudgment interest on a judgment debt must also be reduced to 6%.[161] The rate reduction even applies to the interest paid on obligations under a confirmed chapter 13 bankruptcy plan.[162]

The interest rate reduction only covers debts incurred *before* the servicemember entered active duty.[163] A different statute, discussed in § 7.5.2, *infra*, limits the interest rate on certain obligations that servicemembers incur after entering active duty.

The term "interest" includes service charges and late payment fees related to the obligation.[164] In the 2003 revision, Congress codified case law[165] holding that the interest must be forgiven, not just deferred.[166] Congress also added an explicit

---

servicemember failed to file complaint within the applicable statute of limitations when he failed to meet his burden to show that he was on active duty within the meaning of SCRA). *But cf. In re* Adoption of W.C., 938 N.E.2d 1052 (Ohio Ct. App. 2010) (since SCRA's tolling provision is mandatory, a servicemember may raise it for the first time on appeal).

146 *See, e.g.*, Baker v. England, 397 F. Supp. 2d 18 (D.D.C. 2005) (tolling extended limitations period for member's action to amend military record). *See also* Murphree v. Communication Technologies, Inc., 460 F. Supp. 2d 702 (E.D. La. 2006) (tolling allows servicemember to file state law tort claim in employment case).

147 *See, e.g.*, Beaver v. Fountain, 701 S.E.2d 384 (N.C. Ct. App. 2010) (three year statute of limitations for plaintiff to file cause of action against servicemember in a motor vehicle injury case was tolled by SCRA); Vincent v. Longwater, 538 S.E.2d 164 (Ga. Ct. App. 2000) (limitations tolled in personal injury action against member).

148 *See* Mouradian v. John Hancock Companies, 751 F. Supp. 272, 275 (D. Mass. 1990), *aff'd*, 930 F.2d 972 (1st Cir. 1991).

149 Kethley v. Jack & Kethley, 961 So. 2d 559 (La. Ct. App. 2007).

150 Former 50 U.S.C. app. § 525. *See In re* Brandt, 437 B.R. 294 (Bankr. M.D. Tenn. 2010); Walters v. Nadell, 751 N.W.2d 431 (Mich. 2008) (change in phrasing from "shall not be included" to "may not be included" did not make tolling discretionary).

151 50 U.S.C. app. § 527; Housing and Economic Recovery Act of 2008, Pub. L. No. 110-289, § 2203, 122 Stat. 2849 (2008) (amending SCRA section 207 to extend period to which prohibition on interest rates exceeding 6% is applied).

152 *See* Wallace Capital, L.L.C. v. Santiago, 2010 WL 3011315 (Mass. Land Ct. Aug. 2, 2010).

153 50 U.S.C. app. § 527(c). *See* Linscott v. Vector Aerospace, 2006 WL 1310511 (D. Or. May 12, 2006) (when lump-sum judgment against servicemember could not be broken down into principal, permissible interest, and excess interest, entire judgment was tainted by 18% interest rate; enforcement must be enjoined), *later op. at* 2007 WL 2220357 (D. Or. July 27, 2007) (denying SCRA relief because servicemember failed to send creditor a copy of his military orders).

154 50 U.S.C. app. § 527(a)(1)(A); Pub. L. No. 110-289, 122 Stat. 2849 (2008) (amending the SCRA with addition of provision specifying its application to a "mortgage, trust deed, or other security in the nature of a mortgage").

155 50 U.S.C. app. § 527a(1)(B).

156 50 U.S.C. app. § 527(a)(1).

157 A 2008 amendment makes the coverage of mortgage obligations explicit. 50 U.S.C. app. § 527(d)(2).

158 Higher Education Opportunity Act, Pub. L. 110-315 (Aug. 14, 2008) (amending 20 U.S.C. § 1078(d) to subject federally insured student loans to SCRA's interest rate cap).

159 *See* Cathey v. First Republic Bank, 2001 U.S. Dist. LEXIS 13150 (W.D. La. July 6, 2001) (business debt); Moll v. Ford Consumer Fin. Co., 1998 U.S. Dist. LEXIS 3638 (N.D. Ill. Mar. 23, 1998) (mortgage debt).

160 *See* Linscott v. Vector Aerospace, 2006 WL 1310511 (D. Or. May 12, 2006) (granting preliminary injunction against enforcing foreign judgment against corporation, which included interest in excess of the 6% allowed by Act, when corporation's obligations were personally guaranteed by servicemember), *later op. at* 2007 WL 2220357 (D. Or. July 27, 2007) (denying relief under SCRA because servicemember failed to send creditor a copy of his military orders). *See also* Cathey v. First Republic Bank, 2001 U.S. Dist. LEXIS 13150 (W.D. La. July 6, 2001) (decided under comparable language of pre-2003 version of Act).

161 Linscott v. Vector Aerospace, 2006 WL 1310511 (D. Or. May 12, 2006) (granting preliminary injunction against enforcing foreign judgment against corporation, which included interest in excess of the 6% allowed by Act, when corporation's obligations were personally guaranteed by servicemember), *later op. at* 2007 WL 2220357 (D. Or. July 27, 2007) (denying relief under SCRA because servicemember failed to send creditor a copy of his military orders).

162 *E.g.*, *In re* Watson, 292 B.R. 441 (Bankr. S.D. Ga. 2003).

163 50 U.S.C. app. § 527(a)(1).

164 50 U.S.C. app. § 527(d)(1). *See* Koenig v. Waukesha State Bank, 2006 WL 2334841, at *4 (E.D. Wis. Aug. 10, 2006).

165 Moll v. Ford Consumer Fin. Co., 1998 U.S. Dist. LEXIS 3638, at *4 (N.D. Ill. Mar. 23, 1998).

166 50 U.S.C. app. § 527(a)(2).

requirement that the periodic payment due from the servicemember must be reduced by the amount of the forgiven interest, thus foreclosing creditors from requiring the same payment amount but just applying a greater portion of the payment to principal.[167] Continuing the regular monthly payment, but applying a greater portion of the payment to principal, would be inconsistent with the statute's goal of providing short-term relief to servicemembers.[168] The legislative history indicates that Congress intended to allow lenders to reamortize the loan using a 6% interest rate so that the monthly payment is consistent from month to month.[169]

For high-rate loans, lowering the interest rate can save thousands of dollars. Consider a servicemember who entered into a thirty-year, $80,000 mortgage at 16% just before being called to active duty for a year. A 6% interest rate lowers monthly payments from $1075 to $479, while paying off $864 *more* in principal, with $8018 in interest savings for that one year. Paying off more principal provides additional benefits when the interest rate returns to 16%, saving $3171 more in interest over the remainder of the loan. The total savings in interest paid over the life of the loan is $11,189.

When the servicemember and his or her spouse are jointly liable on an obligation, the statute explicitly requires the interest rate to be reduced for both of them.[170] The same result should be reached when there are other co-obligors, as the statute requires the interest rate on the "obligation or liability," not the interest rate paid by the servicemember, to be reduced. As a court interpreting the former law noted, forcing co-obligors to pay the contract rate would place pressure on the servicemember to pay the contract rate.[171]

To take advantage of the interest rate reduction, the Act as revised in 2003 requires the servicemember to give written notice to the creditor and a copy of the military orders calling the servicemember to military service and any orders further extending military service.[172] This notice must be given no later than 180 days after the servicemember leaves active duty.[173] Once this requirement is met, the interest rate reduction is self-executing and is effective, retroactive to the date the servicemember was called to military service.[174] The Act does not require the servicemember to go to court to obtain this relief.

There is only one exception to the rate reduction. If the creditor proves to a court that the ability of the servicemember to pay interest on the debt at a rate over 6% is not materially affected by reason of the debtor's military service, the court may allow a higher rate.[175] The debtor does not have to prove a material effect, but the duty is on the creditor to go to court to seek a ruling allowing it a higher rate and, if it does not do so, it must reduce the interest rate.[176]

The Act prohibits creditors from cutting off credit, changing the terms of credit, denying credit, or making an adverse credit report because a servicemember exercises rights under the Act.[177] Even without this specific prohibition, it would be clear that adverse actions such as acceleration, repossession, or a negative credit report were wrongful as a matter of contract law; because the obligation now bears interest at 6%, a servicemember who pays 6% is simply not in default.

7.5.2 Thirty-Six Percent Cap on Certain Obligations Incurred During Active Duty

As part of the 2007 defense authorization legislation, Congress enacted new restrictions on credit extended to active duty servicemembers and their dependents.[178] This legislation was effective October 1, 2007. As implemented by regulations of the Department of Defense, it prohibits payday lenders, automobile title lenders, and refund anticipation loan (RAL) lenders from charging more than 36% (including fees) on loans to servicemembers and their families. It is not part of the SCRA, and unlike the SCRA it applies to credit extended *after* rather than *before* the servicemember has entered active duty. This law is discussed in detail in another NCLC treatise.[179]

7.5.3 Repossession

Section 532 of the Act forbids self-help repossession if a servicemember made a payment under a purchase contract prior to entering active duty.[180] This prohibition applies regardless of whether there are cosigners and whether the servicemember

167 50 U.S.C. app. § 527(a)(3).

168 Office of the Comptroller of the Currency, Bulletin 2008-30 (June 18, 2004).

169 Cong. Rec. H12,877 (Dec. 8, 2003) (statement of Rep. Smith of New Jersey); Cong. Rec. H12,876 (Dec. 8, 2003) (statement of Rep. Evans).

170 50 U.S.C. app. § 527(a)(1).

171 Cathey v. First Republic Bank, 2001 U.S. Dist. LEXIS 13150, at *14 (W.D. La. July 6, 2001).

172 50 U.S.C. app. § 527(b)(1).

173 50 U.S.C. app. § 527(b)(1).

174 50 U.S.C. app. § 527(b)(2). *See* Rodriguez v. Am. Express, 2006 WL 908613 (E.D. Cal. Apr. 7, 2006) (lender does not comply with 50 U.S.C. app. § 527 by making offer to servicemember to adjust interest rates; upon notice of debtor's military service creditor must proceed to adjust account and credit any sums overpaid since date of entry into active duty).

175 50 U.S.C. app. § 527(c); Santana-Archivald v. Banco Popular de P.R., 2012 WL 2359432 (D. P.R. June 19, 2012).

176 50 U.S.C. app. § 527(c).
The phrasing of the revised version of the Act is even clearer than the former version in this regard, in that it separates the creditor's right to seek relief from a court into a separate subsection, 50 U.S.C. app. § 207(c).

177 50 U.S.C. app. § 518 (former 50 U.S.C. app. § 518). *See* Marin v. Armstrong, 1998 U.S. Dist. LEXIS 22792 (N.D. Tex. Sept. 1, 1998) (recognizing private cause of action for violations); Office of the Comptroller of the Currency, Bulletin 2008-30 (June 18, 2004).

178 10 U.S.C. § 987.

179 National Consumer Law Center, Consumer Credit Regulation § 2.2.5 (2012), *updated at* www.nclc.org/library.

180 50 U.S.C. app. § 532 (former 50 U.S.C. app. § 531(1)). *See* Donahou v. Presidential Limousine & Auto Sales, Inc., 2007 WL 1229342 (W.D. Ark. Apr. 24, 2007) (Act prohibits self-help repossession of car servicemember bought during eight-month "Delayed Entry" period between time of enlistment and reporting for duty).

is the principal obligor, and it applies whether the delinquency arose prior to or during the servicemember's active duty.

If the creditor files a replevin or similar action to regain possession of the property, the court may, as a condition of allowing repossession, order the creditor to return the servicemember's payments. The court may also stay the proceedings if it finds that the servicemember's ability to comply with the contract is materially affected by military service and may make other dispositions as are equitable to preserve the interests of all parties.[181]

These protections apply to all contracts for the purchase, lease, or bailment of real or personal property, including motor vehicles.[182] All leases are included in this protection, whether or not the lease includes a purchase option.[183]

The Act's protections against repossession are discussed in more detail in another treatise in this series.[184]

7.5.4 Foreclosure

Similar protections apply in the case of foreclosure. The Act forbids non-judicial foreclosure on a servicemember's real or personal property for an obligation that originated prior to active duty, except upon court order or by an agreement made during or after the period of active duty.[185] In essence, for servicemember mortgages protected by the SCRA, no foreclosure may proceed (even in non-judicial foreclosure states) except by judicial order.[186] The exception to the SCRA's prohibition against non-judicial foreclosure arises when a servicemember has, pursuant to a written agreement executed during or after the servicemember's military service, agreed to waive this SCRA protection.[187]

By virtue of an amendment effective February 2, 2013, this prohibition lasts not only during active duty, but also for one year after the servicemember leaves active duty, an extension from the previous nine month period that was itself an extension of a ninety-day period.[188] This provision has been renewed or amended several times, each time extending the sunset date. It now expires on December 31, 2014.[189] After that date, the old provision from 2010 revives so that the prohibition lasts for nine months from the end of active duty service.[190]

If a foreclosure action is filed, the court may stay the proceedings or adjust the obligations to preserve the interests of all parties.[191] Such an order is mandatory if the servicemember applies for the stay and the servicemember's ability to comply with the obligation is materially affected by military service.[192] This provision applies not only during active duty but also for one year after the servicemember leaves active duty.[193]

The provision allowing the court to adjust the obligation gives the court sweeping authority to order a wide range of workouts and loan modifications, such as reducing payments, reducing the interest rate even below the 6% required by the Act, reducing the principal, reamortizing the loan, and waiving late charges and other default fees.[194] Additionally, the general protections that servicemembers have under the SCRA against the entry of default judgments are not superseded by the SCRA's specific mortgage provisions.[195] Therefore, even if the mortgage in question originated during the period of military service, in contrast to originating prior to military service as required by section 533(a)(1), a court may still refuse to order a sale or foreclosure under section 521 if the servicemember has not put in an appearance.[196]

Even if a foreclosure action is not filed, the servicemember may go to court to seek a stay of the enforcement of a mortgage obligation.[197] The stay can extend past the period of military service. The court must require payments in a specified amount during the post-service portion of the stay and can make the stay subject to other terms that are equitable.[198] The servicemember may make such a request to a

181 50 U.S.C. app. § 532(c)(2), (3) (former 50 U.S.C. app. § 531(3)).

182 50 U.S.C. app. § 532(a)(1). *See* § 7.5.7, *infra* (discussing automobile leases).

183 H.R. Rep. No. 108-81 (2003), at 40, 47.

184 National Consumer Law Center, Repossessions §§ 4.2.2, 6.3.5, 14.2.3.5, 14.2.9.7 (8th ed. 2013), *updated at* www.nclc.org/library.

185 50 U.S.C. app. §§ 533(a), 533(c), 517. *See* Brewster v. SunTrust Mortgage, 2014 WL 486187 (9th Cir. Feb. 7, 2014) (servicer violated SCRA by attempting to collect fees wrongfully imposed when mortgage lender, before transferring servicing rights, attempted foreclosure in violation of the Act). *But cf.* Williams v. U.S. Bank, 2013 WL 571844 (C.D. Cal. Feb. 13, 2013) (dismissing claim under section 533 of SCRA because the loan at issue did not originate before the period of military service); Newton v. Bank of McKenney, 2012 WL 1752407 (E.D. Va. May 16, 2012) (finding bank foreclosure on personal and real assets of defendant servicemember's corporation to be proper because corporations are not "servicemembers" under SCRA).

186 *See* Alleged Violations of the Servicemembers Civil Relief Act (SCRA), Statement of Colonel John S. Odom, Jr., USAF (Ret.) Esq. (Feb. 9, 2011 full House Committee on Veterans' Affairs hearing).

187 50 U.S.C. app. § 533(c) (referencing 50 U.S.C. § 517).

188 Honoring American's Veterans and Caring for Camp Lejeune Families Act of 2012, Pub L. 112-154, 126 Stat. 1165 (Aug. 6, 2012); Office of the Comptroller of the Currency, Bulletin regarding Servicemembers Civil Relief Act (Nov. 19, 2012), *available at* www.occ.gov/news-issuances/bulletings/2012/bulleting02912.37-html#ft1.

189 Pub. L. No. 112-154 (section 710(d)).

190 *See* Pub. L. No. 112-154, 126 Stat. 1165 (Aug. 6, 2012) (sunset provisions).

191 50 U.S.C. app. § 533(b).

192 50 U.S.C. app. § 533(b).

193 50 U.S.C. app. § 533(b).

194 *See* National Consumer Law Center, Foreclosures Ch. 5 (5th ed. 2014), *updated at* www.nclc.org/library (detailed discussion of mortgage workouts and loan modifications).

195 *See* HSBC Mortgage Corp. v. Cohen, 913 N.Y.S.2d 876 (N.Y. Sup. Ct. 2010). *But see* Wallace Capital, L.L.C. v. Santiago, 2010 WL 3011315 (Mass. Land Ct. Aug. 2, 2010) (finding that SCRA protection applied to defendant in proceeding when court appointed military attorney for defendant but, as the mortgage was clearly in default for several years, failure of defendant to immediately make monthly payments within sixty days would constitute just cause for plaintiff to move for judgment authorizing foreclosure).

196 HSBC Mortgage Corp. v. Cohen, 913 N.Y.S.2d (N.Y. Sup. Ct. 2010) (extending stay of foreclosure to protect absent servicemember based on SCRA's general protections against default judgments, even though specific mortgage-related protection under section 533 may have allowed the foreclosure to proceed).

197 50 U.S.C. app. § 591. *See* § 7.4.5, *supra*.

198 50 U.S.C. app. § 591(b)(1)(B)(ii).

court at any time during active duty or within 180 days after leaving active duty and must show that his or her ability to pay the obligation has been materially affected by military service.[199]

In addition, if the property is sold at foreclosure sale, the period of active duty cannot be counted toward any redemption period provided by state law.[200] This extension is automatic and does not require an application to a court for approval or any showing that military service impaired the servicemember's financial ability. The Act's protections against foreclosure are discussed in more detail in another treatise in this series.[201]

The Act also prohibits non-judicial tax sales of personal property and certain real property and extends the servicemember's period for redemption until 180 days after the end of active duty.[202] The restrictions on self-help repossession and non-judicial foreclosure are especially important because a creditor or debt collector who threatens such action is likely to be in violation of the Fair Debt Collection Practices Act or a state debt collection or deceptive practices (UDAP) statute.

Despite the existence of these SCRA protections, it is important that servicemembers and their advocates be informed, especially as financial institutions may not be fully educated on applying the protections of the SCRA.[203] For example, the Justice Department investigated possible violations of the SCRA by Morgan Stanley regarding twenty-three mortgage foreclosures.[204] In one case that settled, a Morgan Stanley subsidiary seized and sold a National Guard sergeant's home.[205] The sergeant returned from his service in Iraq to find that his home had been foreclosed upon and sold to another owner.[206] In another case Morgan Stanley's Saxon Mortgage Services, Inc., unit agreed to pay $2.35 million to settle a lawsuit alleging that it foreclosed on seventeen service members from 2006 to 2009 without court orders and without consistently or accurately checking on the military status of borrowers on whom it was foreclosing.[207] Additionally, JPMorgan Chase & Co. ("Chase") admitted to overcharging at least 4500 servicemembers with interest rates and fees above the SCRA's 6% cap and improperly foreclosing on servicemembers' home in eighteen cases.[208] Chase offered reductions in mortgage rates to 4% for borrowers during, and for the year following, active duty. The 4% interest rate is lower than the 6% interest rate cap established by the SCRA.[209] Chase also created a Military Modification Program, which promised to exceed what the borrower might obtain under the federal Home Affordable Modification Program.[210]

Additionally, to prevent a recurrence of these mistakes, Chase also centralized SCRA loans in a single unit and location where employees received enhanced training on interpreting military orders and where denials of eligibility for SCRA protection are reviewed and signed off by a manager.[211] Additionally, Chase implemented a daily review of all SCRA-protected loans to ensure that they remain protected and that interest rates on the loans are limited to 6%.[212] Chase has also implemented a policy of checking the DMDC website, which provides the active duty status of servicemembers, three times before a foreclosure sale.[213]

7.5.5 Enforcement of Liens

The 2003 revisions also broadened the protections against the enforcement of liens. The former law prohibited enforcement of liens for storage of a servicemember's household goods, furniture, or personal effects during any period of active duty or for ninety days thereafter, except by court order.[214] The revised law covers any and all liens on the property or effects of a servicemember, so it prohibits enforcement of landlords' liens, mechanics' liens, repair liens, dry cleaners' liens, and materialmen's liens in addition to storage liens.[215]

199 50 U.S.C. app. §§ 591(a), (b).

200 50 U.S.C. app. § 526(b).

201 National Consumer Law Center, Foreclosures § 8.11 (5th ed. 2014), *updated at* www.nclc.org/library.

202 50 U.S.C. app. § 561.

203 *See* Alleged Violations of the Servicemembers Civil Relief Act (SCRA), Statement of Colonel John S. Odom, Jr., USAF (Ret.) Esq. (Feb. 9, 2011, full House Committee on Veterans' Affairs Hearing) (counsel for Hurley v. Deutsche Bank Trust Co. Americas, 2009 WL 701006 (W.D. Mich. Mar. 13, 2009) noting that after handling hundreds of SCRA issues related to financial institutions, he is convinced that many of the financial institutions in the United States have a fundamental misunderstanding of the SCRA; bank compliance officers offered as experts were incompetent in interpreting the SCRA).

204 Diana B. Henriques, U.S. Inquiry of Military Family Foreclosures, *The New York Times*, Mar. 12, 2011, at B1 and B4.

205 *Id.* at B4.

206 *Id.* at B4.

207 *See* Press Release, U.S. Dep't of Justice, Justice Department Settles with Bank of America and Saxon Mortgage for Illegally Foreclosing on Servicemembers (May 26, 2011), *available at* www.justice.gov/usao/txn/PressRel11/SCRA_Settlement_pr.html.

208 *See* Alleged Violations of the Servicemembers Civil Relief Act (SCRA), Statement of Stephanie B. Mudick (Feb. 9, 2011, full House Committee on Veterans' Affairs hearing).

209 *See* 50 U.S.C. app. § 527(a) (1)(A); Pub. L. No. 110-289, 122 Stat. 2849.

210 The Associated Press, JPMorgan Offers Military Families Mortgage Help, Feb. 15, 2011, *available at* www.npr.org/2011/02/15/133781116/jpmorgan-offers-military-families-mortgage-help?sc=emaf (last visited Mar. 6, 2011).

211 *Id.*

212 *Id.*

213 *Id.*

214 Former 50 U.S.C. app. § 535.

215 50 U.S.C. app. § 537. *See* United States v. B.C. Enters., 667 F. Supp. 2d 650 (E.D. Va. 2009) (finding that (1) section 537(a)(1) applies strict liability to lienholders who foreclose or enforce any lien on a servicemember's property during the time prescribed by statute without a court order; and (2) section 537(c) applies criminal liability to anyone who knowingly enforces a storage lien against a servicemember without a court order). *See also* Roberts v. Chips Express Inc., 2012 WL 4866495 (E.D. Wis. Oct. 12, 2012) (holding that SCRA provides strict liability for storage facility owner that forecloses on servicemember's property without judicial order, even when Navy erroneously failed to pay storage bill, but giving storage facility an opportunity to defend by showing negligence on part of servicemember). *But see* Whigham v. Chase Auto Fin. Corp., 826 F. Supp. 2d 914 (E.D. Va. 2011) (concluding that "for any other reason" in 50 U.S.C. app. § 537 "should be read more restrictively to only encompass liens similar in nature to the ones specifically mentioned, namely liens for storage, repair, and cleaning. Enforcement of other types of liens are governed by other sections of the statute").

The language is also broad enough to cover water and sewer liens and the like, although those liens may also be governed by the similar protections that the law affords against sale of property to enforce a tax or assessment.[216] Liens may also be governed by the similar protections that the law affords against sale of property to enforce a tax or assessment.[217]

Under the SCRA, non-judicial enforcement by the lienholder of any storage lien on the property or effects of a servicemember, if knowingly performed during the period of military service or an additional ninety days thereafter, is a crime.[218] However, one court has held that, since the prohibition applies only to the person "holding the lien," the manager of a company that wrongfully enforced a lien was not liable for the violation when the lien was held by the company.[219]

7.5.6 *Protections Against Execution Upon Judgments*

The SCRA gives courts the authority to stay execution of any judgment against a servicemember and to vacate or stay any prejudgment or postjudgment attachment or garnishment of property.[220] In addition, the personal assets of a servicemember are not available for satisfaction of a trade or business debt for which the servicemember is personally liable.[221]

7.5.7 *Automobile Leases*

Section 535 of the SCRA gives the servicemember the option of terminating a vehicle lease, without penalty, upon entering active duty.[222] This right also applies if, after executing the lease, the lessee enters active duty under a call or order for 180 days or more.[223] Termination of a lease under section 535 also terminates the obligations of a servicemember's dependent under the lease.[224]

To terminate a vehicle lease, the servicemember must give the lessor written notice with a copy of the military orders and then return the vehicle within fifteen days.[225] Termination of the lease is effective once these two steps are accomplished. The lessor is prohibited from imposing an early termination charge but may charge for taxes, summonses, title and registration fees, and excess wear, use, or mileage.[226] Unpaid amounts for the period preceding the effective date of termination must be paid on a prorated basis.[227] The lessor must refund any lease payments that the servicemember paid in advance.[228] Upon application by the lessor to the court before the termination date, however, a court may modify the relief granted the servicemember as justice and equity require.[229] The court's equity analysis can be a general balancing of equities among the parties, and the lessor need not raise a specific equitable claim to receive relief.[230]

A particularly significant protection added in 2003 is the right to cancel vehicle leases executed during active duty if the lessee receives military orders for a permanent change of station outside the continental United States or to deploy with a military unit for 180 days or more.[231] The continental United States is defined as the forty-eight contiguous states and the District of Columbia.[232] The servicemember then has the same right to terminate the lease without penalty as if the lease had been signed before active duty began. For servicemembers who anticipate being posted overseas and do not have family members back home who will need the vehicle, this provision makes vehicle leasing a more attractive option than buying.

As an alternative, if the servicemember does not want to return the car, the servicemember can ask a court to stay enforcement of the payment obligation under the lease during the period of active duty, under a general provision of the law applicable to all obligations.[233] Then, upon leaving the service,

---

Even under the old law, the Fifth Circuit gave a broad interpretation to "personal effects," finding that it included a car. United States v. Bomar, 8 F.3d 226 (5th Cir. 1993). *See* Linscott v. Vector Aerospace, 2006 WL 240529 (D. Or. Jan. 31, 2006) (servicemember has private right of action for damages under 50 U.S.C. app. § 537 against creditor who enforced mechanic's lien against servicemember's property despite notice of servicemember's active duty status).

216 50 U.S.C. app. § 561.

217 *See* 50 U.S.C. app. § 561.

218 50 U.S.C. app. § 537(b).

219 United States v. B.C. Enters., Inc., 667 F. Supp. 2d 650, 658–59 (E.D. Va. 2009).

220 50 U.S.C. app. § 524 (former 50 U.S.C. app. § 513). *See* Sprinkle v. S B & C Ltd., 472 F. Supp. 2d 1235 (W.D. Wash. 2006) (requirement of 50 U.S.C. app. § 521 that creditor file affidavit of non-military service "before entry of judgment for plaintiff" applies to creditor's postjudgment entry of garnishment order against a bank); Palisades Acquisitions, L.L.C. v. Ibrahim, 812 N.Y.S.2d 866 (N.Y. Civ. Ct. 2006) (before creditor may execute against joint bank account, it must file affidavit of non-military service applicable to non-judgment debtor who has interest in account). *But cf.* World Tire Corp. v. Webb, 2007 WL 2812946 (Ohio Ct. App. Sept. 17, 2007) (unpublished) (not abuse of discretion to deny stay of execution under 50 U.S.C. app. § 524 when servicemember did not provide evidence, such as affidavits from his superiors, that he was in military and was deployed).

221 50 U.S.C. app. § 596. *See, e.g.*, Linscott v. Vector Aerospace, 2006 WL 1310511 (D. Or. May 12, 2006).

222 50 U.S.C. app. § 535(a). *See also* 50 U.S.C. app. § 511(2) (defining "military service").

The vehicle must be used or intended to be used by the servicemember or dependents for personal or business transportation.

223 50 U.S.C. app. § 535(b)(2)(A). *See also* Mich. Comp. Laws §§ 445.1011 through 445.1016 (allowing servicemember or his/her spouse to terminate a motor vehicle lease if the servicemember was deployed for active duty for at least 180 days and the lease was executed by or on behalf of the servicemember before deployment).

224 50 U.S.C. app. § 535(a)(2).

225 50 U.S.C. app. § 535(c).

The notice must be delivered by hand delivery, private business carrier, or U.S. mail return receipt requested.

226 50 U.S.C. app. § 535(e).

227 50 U.S.C. app. § 535(e).

228 50 U.S.C. app. § 535(f).

229 50 U.S.C. app. § 535(g).

230 *See* Climax, L.L.C. v. Snake River Oncology of E. Idaho, P.L.L.C., 241 P.2d 964 (Idaho 2010) (noting that, when servicemember opportunistically uses his or her deployment for personal gain at lessor's expense, the court may create equity under 50 U.S.C. app. § 535(g), that is, section 305(g) of Pub. L. No. 189).

231 50 U.S.C. app. § 535(b)(2).

232 50 U.S.C. app. § 535(i)(2).

233 50 U.S.C. app. § 591 (former 50 U.S.C. app. § 590).

the servicemember will have a period equal to the period of active duty to make up the deferred payments, with no interest or penalties. This option is discussed § 7.4.5, *supra*.

7.5.8 Termination of Telephone Service Contracts

Servicemembers may request the termination of telephone service contracts, including those for cellular service, any time after they receive orders that require relocation for a period of ninety days or more, if the new location does not support the contract.[234] This right applies to contracts entered into prior to receiving military orders to relocate. The servicemember's written or electronic request to terminate must include a copy of the orders.[235]

The cellular service provider may not charge an early termination fee. If the servicemember reinstates service by the ninetieth day following the end of the relocation period, no fees for reinstating can apply, except charges for normal installation or equipment fees that would apply to any subscriber.[236] The service provider must refund the servicemember any paid amounts beyond the billing period in which the termination occurred.[237]

7.5.9 Residential and Other Leases

7.5.9.1 Eviction

The pre-2003 version of the Act prohibited non-judicial eviction of servicemembers or their dependents from rental property if the rent did not exceed $1200 per month and allowed the court to stay such an eviction up to ninety days.[238] As revised in 2003, the law covered leases up to $2400 per month and includes an annual inflation adjustment.[239] It also allows the court to "adjust the obligation under the lease to preserve the interests of all parties," presumably meaning that the court can order rent to be deferred, order that a security deposit be applied to rent, allow subletting despite a prohibition in the lease, or make other orders that will preserve the tenancy.[240] The reference to "equity" in this provision may also allow the court to weigh the equities and make adjustments in favor of the lessor.[241]

7.5.9.2 Right to Break a Lease

Servicemembers also have the right to break a lease of premises that they or their dependents occupy or intend to occupy for residential, professional, business, agricultural, or similar purposes.[242] This right applies to leases signed before the servicemember enters active duty.[243] In addition it applies to leases signed after entering active duty if the servicemember receives military orders for a permanent change of station or to deploy with a military unit for ninety days or more.[244] "Military orders," as defined by the 2004 amendments, means official military orders or any notification, certification, or verification from the servicemember's commanding officer.[245] The servicemember is entitled to a refund of the unused portion of any rent that was paid in advance.[246]

After the 2003 and 2004 amendments to the SCRA, servicemembers were confronted with early termination fees, liquidated damages charges, and concession fees by landlords attempting to avoid the termination conditions of the SCRA. Amendments to the SCRA in 2010 clarified that the lessor cannot impose an early termination charge. However, the 2010 amendments left the door open for charges for taxes, summonses, and other obligations and liabilities of the lease, including excess wear.[247]

7.6 Prohibitions Against Retaliation and Waivers

The Act prohibits issuing an adverse credit report, denying, revoking, or changing the terms of a credit transaction, or taking certain other specified adverse actions because of the assertion of rights under the Act.[248] While the SCRA allows

234 50 U.S.C. app. § 535a.

235 50 U.S.C. app. § 535a(a)(3).

236 50 U.S.C. app. § 535a(e).

237 50 U.S.C. app. § 535a(f).

238 Former 50 U.S.C. app. § 530. *See* Mill Rock Plaza Assocs. v. Lively, 580 N.Y.S.2d 815 (N.Y. Civ. Ct. 1990) (in response to Desert Storm, court would look seriously at "non-military" affidavits in eviction cases: must show sufficient facts to support a trustworthy conclusion that the tenants involved were neither in the military, nor dependents of military personnel). *Cf.* Taylor v. Raabe-Manupule, 2003 WL 21782681 (Haw. Ct. App. July 29, 2003) (no right to stay when servicemember was the son and dependent of the tenant and had not signed lease).

239 50 U.S.C. app. § 531(a).

The maximum rent level effective January 1, 2014, is $3217.81, as set by the Department of Defense housing price inflation adjustment. 79 Fed. Reg. 115-01 (Jan. 1, 2014).

240 50 U.S.C. app. § 531(b)(1)(B). *See also* 50 U.S.C. app. § 591 (allowing court to defer servicemember's liability on any obligation during the period of active duty).

241 *See* Climax, L.L.C. v. Snake River Oncology of E. Idaho, P.L.L.C., 241 P.3d 964 (Idaho 2010) (noting SCRA provision allowing for the balancing of equities; SCRA may be used for lessor's benefit when servicemember opportunistically uses his or her deployment for personal gain at lessor's expense.

242 50 U.S.C. app. § 535.

243 50 U.S.C. app. § 535(b)(1)(A).

244 50 U.S.C. app. § 535(b)(1)(B). *See* United States v. Williams, 2013 WL 596473, at *3 (E.D. Va. 2013) (awarding summary judgment against landlord and landlord corporation that refused to acquiesce in early termination of lease and imposed fabricated charges for damage to the premises).

245 Veterans Benefits Improvement Act, Pub. L. No. 108-454, § 704, 118 Stat. 3598 (2004), *codified at* 50 U.S.C. app. § 535(i)(1).

246 50 U.S.C. app. § 535(f).

247 50 U.S.C. app. § 535(e)(1).

248 50 U.S.C. app. § 518. *See* Cathey v. First Republic Bank, 2001 U.S. Dist. LEXIS 13150 (W.D. La. July 6, 2001) (provision of former version of Act barring changes in credit terms does not forbid new loan to cover cost overruns that occur while commercial borrower is serving abroad). *But cf.* Murphy v. Bank of Am., 2012 WL 5954144 (N.D. Ala. Nov. 28, 2012) (section 518 does not prohibit adverse credit report unless solely in response to servicemember's receipt of a stay, postponement, or suspension pursuant to SCRA).

servicemembers to waive any and all rights provided under the Act,[249] it restricts waivers of the protections relating to modification, termination, or cancellation of contracts, leases, bailments, or mortgage debts, or to repossession, retention, foreclosure, sale, or forfeiture of property. A waiver of any of these protections is ineffective unless the waiver is evidenced by a clear, written agreement demonstrating an understanding of the waiver and is signed during or after active duty.[250] However, waiver may also be inadvertent, due to procedural deficiencies such as failure to preserve an issue for appeal.[251] A person who files an untimely suit against a servicemember, but fails to raise the SCRA's provision that tolls statutes of limitations during the servicemember's period of active duty, waives that provision.[252]

Beware of the prospective use of the waiver at the inception of a contract in an attempt to circumvent the application and rights of the servicemember under the SCRA. Rights under the SCRA cannot be waived until they accrue, and the servicemember has the ability to exercise the right or to voluntarily waive that right.[253]

7.7 Remedies for Violations

The 2010 amendments to the SCRA clarified the private cause of action, provided explicit authority for the attorney general to prosecute civil cases, and established a fee-shifting provision for self-enforcement.[254]

The ability of a court to award attorney fees to a prevailing plaintiff does not necessarily depend on whether a right to a private action exists under the 2010 amendments. Fees may be awarded for work performed before the 2010 amendments.[255] The debtor is not confined to raising the violation of the Act defensively, in response to a foreclosure or collection suit but can sue affirmatively.[256]

The Act also expressly preserves the servicemember's right to pursue conversion or wrongful eviction claims that are available for a violation of a number of its prohibitions.[257] A class action may be appropriate if a creditor follows a general practice of enforcing credit obligations in violation of the Act.[258] However, the SCRA does not guarantee a court trial, and servicemembers may be bound by an arbitration clause unless the clause is unconscionable.[259] One court has held that punitive damages may be available for SCRA violations.[260]

To receive injunctive relief for violations of the SCRA, plaintiffs should show a likelihood of the violation continuing in the future.[261] One court noted that it would not issue an order for injunctive relief to punish past offenses.[262] Additionally, courts may grant permanent injunctions only after plaintiffs succeed on the merits and also demonstrate that there is a real and immediate threat that the plaintiffs will again suffer the same injury complained of.[263]

Violations of the SCRA may also lead to Fair Debt Collection Practices Act (FDCPA) violations.[264] For example, a debt collector violated the SCRA, the FDCPA, and state consumer protection statutes when it entered judgment against a garnishee bank and seized a servicemember's military pay without the filing of an affidavit of non-military service.[265] The

249 50 U.S.C. app § 517(a).

250 50 U.S.C. app. § 517. *See* United States v. 4.3 Acres of Land, 2013 WL 433002 (D. Me. 2013) (declining to accept waiver that would allow proceeding to progress in servicemember's absence, when written waiver failed to demonstrate servicemember's understanding of rights she was being asked to waive).

251 *See* Smith v. Washington Mut. Bank, 308 Fed. Appx. 707 (4th Cir. 2009) (finding waiver of appellate review of plaintiffs' claims, challenging foreclosure under SCRA and state law, when plaintiffs failed to file specific and timely objections to magistrate judge's report and recommendation).

252 Walters v. Nadell, 751 N.W.2d 431 (Mich. 2008) (plaintiff who sued servicemember waived tolling of statute of limitations by failing to raise it in litigation).

253 Lapine v. Town of Wellesley, 304 F.3d 90, 105 (1st Cir. 2002) (addressing a similar provision under the Veterans Employment Rights Act: "It is considerably less clear that an individual at the threshold of entry upon military service can, at that time, prospectively waive his future right to reemployment. . . . [T]here are strong reasons of policy for ruling out such prospective waivers in all but the most exceptional circumstances"); Leonard v. United Airlines, 972 F.2d 155, 159 (7th Cir. 1992).

254 *See* 50 U.S.C. app. § 597a; Gordon v. Pete's Auto Serv. of Denbigh, Inc., 637 F.3d. 454 (4th Cir. 2011) (applying new, explicit private cause of action retroactively to suit initiated before the SCRA amendment clearly establishing the right).

255 Gordon v. Pete's Auto Serv. of Denbigh, Inc., 838 F. Supp. 2d 436, 443–48 (E.D. Va. 2012).

256 *Id.*; Hurley v. Deutche Bank Trust Co. Americas, 2009 WL 701006 (W.D. Mich. Mar. 13, 2009); Moll v. Ford Consumer Fin. Co., 1998 U.S. Dist. LEXIS 3638 (N.D. Ill. Mar. 23, 1998).

257 50 U.S.C. app. §§ 531(c)(2) (evictions and distress), 532(b)(2) (installment contracts), 533(d)(2) (mortgages and trust deeds), 535(h)(2) (vehicle leases), 536(e)(2) (life insurance), 537(c)(2) (foreclosure on storage liens). *See* Hurley v. Deutsche Bank Trust Co. Americas, 2008 WL 4539478 (W.D. Mich. Sept. 30, 2008) (allowing conversion claim based on violation of SCRA's foreclosure and eviction protections to go forward), *reconsideration granted in part on other grounds*, 2009 WL 701006 (W.D. Mich. Mar. 13, 2009) (servicemember has private cause of action under SCRA).

258 *See, e.g.*, Rowles v. Chase Home Fin., L.L.C., 2012 WL 80570 (D.S.C. 2012) (finding class properly certified for settlement purposes when issue was whether Chase systematically failed to implement SCRA); Moll v. Ford Consumer Fin. Co., 1998 U.S. Dist. LEXIS 3638 (N.D. Ill. Mar. 23, 1998). *See also* Alleged Violations of the Servicemembers Civil Relief Act (SCRA), Statement of Richard "Dick" Harpootlian (Feb. 9, 2001, full House Committee on Veterens' Affairs hearing) (testimony on facts underlying *Rowles v. Chase Home Fin., L.L.C.*, a class action lawsuit in the District of South Carolina).

259 *See* Beard v. Santander Consumer USA, Inc., 2012 WL 1292576 (E.D. Cal. Apr. 16, 2012), *adopted by*, 2012 WL 1576103 (E.D. Cal. May 3, 2012). *See generally* National Consumer Law Center, Consumer Arbitration Agreements (6th ed. 2011), *updated at* www.nclc.org/library.

260 Hurley v. Deutsche Bank Trust Co. Americas, 2009 WL 701006 (W.D. Mich. Mar. 13, 2009).

261 United States v. B.C. Enter., 667 F. Supp. 2d 650, 660 (E.D. Va. 2009).

262 *Id.*

263 *See* Fourte v. Countrywide Home Loans, Inc., 2009 WL 2998110 (D.N.J. Sept. 15, 2009).

264 *See* Owings v. Hunt & Henriques, 2010 WL 3489342 (S.D. Cal. Sept. 3, 2010) (law firm violated SCRA and FDCPA when it falsely declared in an affidavit supporting default judgment under SCRA that debtor was not in military service).

265 15 U.S.C. § 1692e(5), (10).

court held that by doing so the collector was proceeding with an action it had no lawful right to take and using false representations and deceptive means to collect a debt in violation of the FDCPA.[266] In addition, the FDCPA prohibits debt collectors from misrepresenting the amount of a debt and requires affirmative disclosure of the amount as part of the validation notice.[267] Dunning the servicemember or a co-obligor for a pre-active duty debt without having reduced the interest rate to 6% as required by the SCRA[268] is likely to violate this prohibition. Unauthorized contact with a servicemember's commanding officer regarding the servicemember's debt may also be an FDCPA violation.[269] As another example, using self-help repossession to recover property in violation of the SCRA[270] may violate the FDCPA prohibition against taking nonjudicial action to effect dispossession of property when there is no present right to possession.[271] If the creditor itself rather than an independent debt collector is collecting the debt, the FDCPA does not apply, but in many jurisdictions a state debt collection law will impose similar requirements.[272]

If a creditor violates the prohibition against making an adverse credit report because of the failure to pay the interest that should have been forgiven,[273] the debtor may also have a claim under the Fair Credit Reporting Act (FCRA). Before a consumer can sue a creditor under the FCRA for making an inaccurate report, the consumer must dispute the report with the credit reporting agency. The credit reporting agency is then required to ask the creditor who made the report to reinvestigate the debt. The creditor can be sued under the FCRA if it does not conduct a reasonable reinvestigation of the disputed item.[274] However, these preliminary steps are unnecessary when the consumer sues under the Civil Relief Act itself.[275]

In addition, a creditor or debt collector who threatens to foreclose or take other actions in violation of the Act is not only likely to be in violation of the FDCPA but also a state debt collection or UDAP statute.[276]

The attorney general also has authority to bring a civil action against any person who engages in a pattern or practice of violating the SCRA or engages in a violation that raises an issue of significant public importance.[277] The court may award equitable or declaratory relief, may award appropriate relief—including monetary damages—to any person aggrieved by the violation, and may assess a civil penalty.[278] A person aggrieved by the violation has a right to intervene in the attorney general's action.[279] A court awarded injunctive and monetary relief requested by the U.S. Attorney in Virginia, finding that a landlord and landlord corporation who wrongfully withheld a servicemember's security deposit may each be held liable under SCRA.[280]

The Civil Rights Division of the Department of Justice (DOJ) will consider taking action on a violation of the SCRA. However the servicemember must first seek the assistance of his or her military legal assistance office. If that office cannot resolve the complaint, it may choose to forward the complaint to the DOJ. The DOJ then will review the matter to determine whether DOJ action is appropriate.[281]

Lastly, the Dodd Frank Wall Street Reform and Consumer Protection Act has created a new Bureau of Consumer Financial Protection which includes an Office of Servicemember Affairs.[282] While the new agency may not be involved in SCRA issues to the extent of the DOJ, over time its responsibilities may be expected to increase in this area as the primary place for servicemembers, along with the public, to bring complaints about consumer financial products and services.[283]

---

266 Sprinkle v. S B & C Ltd., 472 F. Supp. 2d 1235 (W.D. Wash. 2006).

267 15 U.S.C. §§ 1692(e)(2)(a), 1692g(a)(1). *See* National Consumer Law Center, Fair Debt Collection §§ 5.5.4, 5.7.2.6.5 (8th ed. 2014), *updated at* www.nclc.org/library.

268 *See* § 7.5, *supra*.

269 *See* Weakley v. Redline Recovery Servs., 723 F. Supp. 2d 1341 (S.D. Cal. 2010) (denying motion to dismiss FDCPA claim), *clarified on denial of reconsideration by* 2010 WL 3033801 (S.D. Cal. Aug. 2, 2010).

270 *See* § 7.5, *supra*.

271 15 U.S.C. § 1692f(6).

272 *See* National Consumer Law Center, Fair Debt Collection § 10.2, Appx. D (8th ed. 2014), *updated at* www.nclc.org/library.

273 50 U.S.C. app. § 518.

274 15 U.S.C. § 1681s-2(b). *See* National Consumer Law Center, Fair Debt Collection §§ 8.6.2.1 (8th ed. 2014), *updated at* www.nclc.org/library; National Consumer Law Center, Fair Credit Reporting § 6.10.4 (8th ed. 2013), *updated at* www.nclc.org/library.

The 2003 amendments to the Fair Credit Reporting Act place some additional duties upon creditors, but communicating the dispute to the credit reporting agency is still a precondition of a private cause of action.

275 *See* Koenig v. Waukesha State Bank, 2006 WL 2334841 (E.D. Wis. Aug. 10, 2006) (50 U.S.C. app. § 518(3) prohibits negative reporting of a request for a stay or modification of an obligation, but creditors may make adverse reports of failure to make payments lawfully due during a stay period). *Cf.* Rodriguez v. Am. Express, 2006 WL 908613 (E.D. Cal. Apr. 7, 2006) (50 U.S.C. app. § 518(3) does not prohibit negative credit reporting that is based on actual credit problems unrelated to the servicemember's exercise of rights under the SCRA).

276 *See, e.g.*, Sprinkle v. S B & C Ltd., 472 F. Supp. 2d 1235 (W.D. Wash. 2006) (debt collector violated FDCPA and state UDAP statute by garnishing servicemember's bank account without filing affidavit of nonmilitary service required by Act).

277 50 U.S.C. app. § 597(a).

278 50 U.S.C. app. § 597(b).

279 50 U.S.C. app. § 597(c).

280 United States v. Williams, 2013 WL 596473 (E.D. Va. 2013).

281 *See* United States v. B.C. Enters., 667 F. Supp. 2d 650 (E.D. Va. 2009) (extraordinary writ of injunction will not issue to punish past offense, but only when necessary to prevent future violations); www.usdoj.gov/crt/military.

282 Pub. L. No. 111-203.

283 *See* Alleged Violations of the Servicemembers Civil Relief Act (SCRA), Testimony of Holly Petraus (Feb. 9, 2011, full House Committee on Veterans' Affairs hearing).

Chapter 8 Criminal and Civil Collection of Dishonored Checks

8.1 Introduction

A troublesome debt collection tactic is to threaten consumers with prosecution under criminal dishonored check statutes. When a consumer writes a check which is dishonored (bounced) because the consumer's account has insufficient funds (NSF) or credit to cover the check, or was closed, the person holding the check may threaten to initiate a dishonored check criminal prosecution against the consumer.

Civil dishonored check statutes, discussed in § 8.3, *infra*, give collectors additional leverage. These statutes reward bounty hunters by making consumers whose checks are dishonored liable for statutory or multiple damages, attorney fees, and other changes.

Even though these statutes evidence a public policy to discourage people from writing checks that will be dishonored, many creditors and collectors encourage consumers to do just that. Some debt collectors solicit post-dated checks from financially distressed consumers, knowing that the possibility of a dishonored check prosecution provides the collector with powerful leverage.[1] Payday lenders, who provide small, short-term loans at three-digit interest rates, commonly use this method of coercion.[2] Even banks have entered the high-cost loan business by offering "overdraft loans," the availability of which encourages consumers to write checks without money in the bank.[3]

There are many situations in which dishonored checks are written. The great growth in electronic deposits, electronic transfers, and debit card and ATM transactions makes it increasingly difficult for consumers to have accurate knowledge of their bank account balances, and overdrafts are widespread.[4]

In some states with legalized gambling, casino markers, which authorize the casino to access any present or future bank account of the debtor, are treated as checks and can lead to dishonored check prosecution if the account contains insufficient funds.[5]

There is an active debt buyer industry in the purchase of dishonored checks. Some companies guarantee to merchants that the checks customers write will be paid, and then these companies purchase and try to collect any checks that are dishonored. Some collection agencies specialize in collecting dishonored checks for merchants.

Another volume in this series, *Consumer Banking and Payments Law*,[6] addresses other issues regarding dishonored checks, including wrongful dishonor, the circumstances in which checks are and are not payable, electronic re-presentment of dishonored checks, and the consumer's right to stop payment on a check.

8.2 Criminal Dishonored Check Laws

8.2.1 Introduction

This section discusses the scope, limitations, and validity of criminal dishonored check laws as well as defenses to prosecution under those laws. This summary should aid the civil

1 *See, e.g.*, United States v. Cent. Adjustment Bur., Inc., 667 F. Supp. 370 (N.D. Tex. 1986) (collector violated 15 U.S.C. § 1692f(3) by soliciting post-dated checks with the purpose of threatening criminal prosecution), *aff'd*, 823 F.2d 880 (5th Cir. 1987) (per curiam); *In re* G.C. Servs. Corp., 83 F.T.C. 1521, 1525 (FTC 1974) (complaint alleged that collection agency solicited post-dated checks and later threatened criminal prosecution if the check was dishonored); National Consumer Law Center, Fair Debt Collection § 5.6.4 (8th ed. 2014), *updated at* www.nclc.org/library.

2 *See, e.g.*, Turner v. E-Z Check Cashing of Cookeville, Tenn., Inc., 35 F. Supp. 2d 1042 (M.D. Tenn. 1999) (payday lender violated deceptive practices statute by threatening groundless criminal dishonored check prosecution as means of collecting debt); Hamilton v. York, 987 F. Supp. 953 (E.D. Ky. 1997); *In re* Dorsey, 373 B.R. 528 (Bankr. N.D. Ohio 2007) (automatic stay did not bar criminal prosecution arising from check to payday lender); Watson v. State, 509 S.E.2d 87 (Ga. Ct. App. 1998) (payday lenders who used criminal dishonored check prosecutions to collect violated state criminal RICO statute; predicate offenses were multiple perjuries in swearing out dishonored check complaints stating that checks were given for merchandise when lender had no merchandise to sell).

3 *See* Gutierrez v. Wells Fargo Bank, 730 F. Supp. 2d 1080 (N.D. Cal. 2010) (documenting bank's unfair and deceptive acts to increase number of overdrafts), *aff'd in part, rev'd in part, remanded*, 704 F.3d 712 (9th Cir. 2012) (finding some claims preempted by federal law but affirming finding that bank made misleading statements in violation of state UDAP statute and remanding for determination of relief to be granted). *See generally* National Consumer Law Center, Consumer Credit Regulation Ch. 9 (2012), *updated at* www.nclc.org/library; National Consumer Law Center, Consumer Banking and Payments Law § 2.6.3 (5th ed. 2013), *updated at* www.nclc.org/library.

4 Fed. Deposit Ins. Corp., FDIC Study of Bank Overdraft Programs at 75–6, 79 (Nov. 2008), *available at* www.fdic.gov/bank/analytical/overdraft (over 25% of all accounts recorded at least one NSF fee and 12.1% of adult accounts recorded more than ten NSF transactions during the study year; 32.9% of accounts had average balances of less than $100).

5 Fleeger v. Bell, 95 F. Supp. 2d 1126 (D. Nev. 2000) (casino marker fits definition of "check or draft" in Nevada's criminal dishonored check statute), *aff'd*, 23 Fed. Appx. 741 (9th Cir. 2001); Shamburger v. Grand Casino of Miss., Inc., 84 F. Supp. 2d 794 (S.D. Miss. 1998) (treating marker as check); Strong v. El Dorado Casino Shreveport Joint Venture, 73 So. 3d 967 (La. Ct. App. 2011) (casino that strictly complied with procedures of civil bad check statute was entitled to multiple damages, costs, and attorney fees); TeleRecovery of La., Inc. v. Rayborn, 814 So. 2d 688 (La. Ct. App. 2002) (casino markers were checks and covered by NSF check law, but denying multiple damages when collector failed to comply with notice requirements). *See also In re* Park, 492 B.R. 668 (Bankr. S.D.N.Y. 2013) (debt for markers dischargeable; detailed description of how casino lured gambling addict to continue gambling); *In re* D'Amico, 2013 WL 6045732 (Bankr. S.D. Tex. Nov. 13, 2013) (finding debt for markers dischargeable).

6 National Consumer Law Center, Consumer Banking and Payments Law §§ 3.7, 3.8 (5th ed. 2013), *updated at* www.nclc.org/library.

practitioner in counseling clients who have written or endorsed checks not covered by sufficient funds. Familiarity with the limitations of criminal dishonored check laws should ease the fear of prosecution in many instances and may provide a basis for a civil claim against the collector who threatens prosecution. This discussion is intended, however, only as a general guide to issues that should be researched under applicable state laws in the event of a prosecution or threat of prosecution. Because the dishonored check criminal statutes are frequently changed by state legislatures, counsel should be particularly careful in determining which decisions apply to the current statute.

8.2.2 Defenses Based on Constitutional Rights

Most state constitutions contain a prohibition against imprisonment for debt,[7] although this is not a protection explicitly provided by the United States Constitution. Some state dishonored check laws have been declared facially unconstitutional under such provisions.[8] Other courts have construed dishonored check statutes to require proof of fraudulent intent in order to save them from unconstitutionality.[9]

Even when such a statute is facially constitutional, it may be applied in an unconstitutional manner in a particular collection case.[10] For example, the practice of not processing dishonored check cases in return for a $500 payment was held to deny equal protection to an indigent defendant who was unable to pay, went to trial, and was sentenced to jail. The court rejected an argument that this practice was a legitimate form of plea bargaining.[11]

8.2.3 Post-Dated Checks

Many courts have held that dishonored check laws do not apply to post-dated checks.[12] In some states, the statute is

7 *See* Comment, *Imprisonment for Debt and the Constitution*, 1970 Law & Social Order 658. *See generally* § 12.12, *infra*.

8 Burnam v. Commonwealth, 15 S.W.2d 256 (Ky. 1929) (dishonored check law unconstitutional when element of fraud deleted and debtor not permitted indigency defense required by state constitution); State v. Nelson, 237 N.W. 766 (S.D. 1931) (dishonored check law unconstitutional when punishment was for failing to pay post-dated check). *See also* People v. Vinnola, 494 P.2d 826 (Colo. 1972) (modified dishonored check law was unconstitutionally vague, violated protections against imprisonment for debt, and offended equal protection requirements); State v. Fisher, 349 N.W.2d 16 (N.D. 1984) (dishonored check statute was unconstitutional in that it discriminated on basis of wealth by making payment a defense). *But see* State v. Avery, 111 Kan. 588 (Kan. 1922); State v. Taylor, 73 S.W.2d 378 (Mo. 1934). *See generally* Wanda Ellen Wakefield, Annotation, *Constitutionality of "Bad Check" Statute*, 16 A.L.R.4th 631 (1982).

9 People v. Felgar, 58 P.3d 1122 (Colo. App. 2002) (check fraud statute must be construed to allow only permissive inference, not mandatory presumption, which would be unconstitutional; reversing check fraud conviction when jury was given mandatory presumption instruction); Neidlinger v. State, 88 S.E. 687 (Ga. Ct. App. 1916) (implying fraud as element of offense to avoid unconstitutional construction; no fraud when a post-dated check was given, as postdating implies insufficient present funds). *See also* State v. Owen, 935 P.2d 183 (Idaho Ct. App. 1997) (Idaho's theft by deception and theft by false promise statutes, which did not require proof of all elements of common law fraud, did not violate state constitutional prohibition of "imprisonment for debt except in case of fraud," when each included some deception); Walker v. State, 467 N.E.2d 1248 (Ind. Ct. App. 1984) (statutory provision that dishonor of check creates rebuttable presumption that defendant knew that check would not be paid is not unconstitutional); State v. Wilkens, 95 P.3d 135 (table), 2004 WL 1784607 (Kan. Ct. App. 2004) (rebuttable presumption of intent to defraud not unconstitutional); Semones v. Southern Bell Tel. & Tel. Co., 416 S.E.2d 909, 913 (N.C. Ct. App. 1992) (constitutionality would be doubtful if knowledge were not an element of the offense); State v. Robinson, 602 N.W.2d 730 (S.D. 1999) (both statute and due process required that jury be instructed that presumption of knowledge of insufficient funds is rebuttable and state still bears burden of proof beyond reasonable doubt); Colin v. State, 168 S.W.2d 500 (Tex. Crim. App. 1943) (dishonored check prosecution not imprisonment for debt because fraudulent intent required); State v. Tsoi, 2002 WL 662884 (Wash. Ct. App. 2002) (instruction that jury was permitted, but not required, to infer knowledge from writing NSF check was not unconstitutional "so long as the proven facts support the instruction"; affirming conviction when defendant business owner wrote fifteen NSF checks after being notified by bank of overdrawn account). *Cf.* State v. Allison, 607 N.W.2d 1 (S.D. 2000) (statute criminalizing failure to return military property not unconstitutional imprisonment for debt, as intent requirement is implied, accidental loss or destruction not a crime; also state's entrustment of property to militia members is not a debtor-creditor relationship). *But see* Dirk v. State, 305 So. 2d 187 (Fla. 1974) (upholding constitutionality of criminal NSF statute against challenges based on vagueness and existence of presumption); Carter v. Lowry, 151 S.E. 23 (Ga. 1929) (presumption of fraud established by dishonored check law does not offend due process).

10 *See* Knight v. Constantino, 2006 WL 1529567 (S.D. Ind. May 31, 2006) (consumer stated Fourth and Fourteenth Amendment claims arising from dishonored check prosecution when she alleged that check was post-dated and had been paid within ten days of notice of dishonor, either of which excluded it from Indiana's criminal dishonored check statute, and that investigator's affidavit knowingly misstated these facts); Helton v. Dixon, 2006 WL 751239 (E.D. Ky. Mar. 21, 2006) (fact issues in section 1983 action alleging malicious prosecution arising from NSF check charges); Durham v. State, 74 So. 3d 908 (Miss. Ct. App. 2011) (reversing conviction on due process grounds because jury instructions stated that failure to pay within fifteen days of notice was prima facie evidence of intent, without explaining that this presumption was rebuttable). *See generally* J. Potuto, *And Mussolini Had the Trains Running on Time: A Review of the Bad Check Offense and the Law Enforcement Debt Collector*, 65 Neb. L. Rev. 242 (1986) (critique of Neb. law and dishonored check criminal diversion plan).

11 Watson v. State, 509 S.E.2d 87 (Ga. Ct. App. 1998) (separate concurrence argued that majority did not go far enough: "the root of the problem lies in our statutory framework that subjects one who 'bounces' a check to criminal penalties"). *See also In re* Flatt-Moore, 959 N.E.2d 241 (Ind. 2010) (reprimanding prosecutor who allowed victim to set the amount of restitution in bad check case; "substantial and meaningful input" from victim is appropriate but "unfettered veto power" is not).

12 *See, e.g.*, Jones v. Kunin, 2000 WL 34402107, at *1 (S.D. Ill. May 1, 2000) (no intent to defraud when payee agrees not to present check until later time; transaction is in essence an extension of credit); Gibbs v. Commonwealth, 273 S.W.2d 583 (Ky. Ct. App. 1954); State v. Papillon, 389 N.W.2d 553 (Neb. 1986) (conviction cannot be based on post-dated check when both check writer and payee were aware that check was post-dated, even though check writer closed account shortly before the post-dated date). *See also* Conte v. County of Nassau, 2010 WL 3924677 (E.D.N.Y. Sept. 30, 2010) (section 1983 and state tort actions; fact question whether officials ignored exculpatory evidence; here, letter stating that post-dated check should not be cashed, because

explicit in excluding post-dated checks.[13] There are a number of reasons for this position. First, a post-dated check implicitly represents that the check writer lacks sufficient present funds to cover the check.[14] Second, a post-dated check is not payable on demand, a commercial law requirement for checks.[15] In addition, a post-dated check is little different from a promissory note for which nonpayment may not be prosecuted under dishonored check laws.[16] Other states hold that a post-dated check becomes a check on the date the check specifies,[17] allow conviction if the state shows that the check writer knew that funds would be insufficient on the date of the check,[18] or allow the defense only if the payee is made aware of the current lack of funds.[19] Giving two checks to the same person, one post-

services for which it was given could not be performed); Raine v. State, 57 So. 3d 669 (Miss. Ct. App. 2011) (fraudulent intent not shown if payee agreed to hold post-dated check, then altered date and cashed it early). *But see* People v. Vancamp, 2009 WL 691897 (Mich. Ct. App. Mar. 17, 2009) (unpublished) (affirming conviction of borrower who gave post-dated check to secure loan; statute allows conviction if intent to defraud shown); State v. Kelm, 672 A.2d 1261 (N.J. Super. Ct. App. Div. 1996) (state must show knowledge that funds would be insufficient on date of check; when account had negative balances for a month, knowledge was shown); State v. Brotzman, 108 Wash. App. 1042 (Wash. Ct. App. 2001) (post-dated check may support conviction for larceny by check if check writer had no assurance that funds would be available on its date). *But cf.* State v. Hammond, 498 N.W.2d 126 (N.D. 1993) (postdating no defense unless post-dated check is "knowingly received as such"); State v. Harris, 977 S.W.2d 127 (Tenn. Ct. App. 1998) (affirming conviction; although dishonored check statute does not apply to post-dated checks, it does apply to check that defendant signed but left blank as to date and all other respects). *See generally* John D. Perovich, Annotation, *Application of "Bad Check" Statute with Respect to Postdated Checks*, 52 A.L.R.3d 464 (1973); 32 Am. Jur. 2d *False Pretenses* § 70 (2007).

13 *See* Knight v. Constantino, 2006 WL 1529567 (S.D. Ind. May 31, 2006) (post-dated check explicitly excluded from coverage of Indiana criminal dishonored check statute; consumer stated Fourth Amendment claim with allegation that investigator's affidavit knowingly misrepresented that check was not post-dated); Banderas v. State, 372 So. 2d 489 (Fla. Dist. Ct. App. 1979); State v. Stooksberry, 872 S.W.2d 906 (Tenn. 1994) (post-dated check was not a check or a sight draft within the meaning of the worthless check statute); State v. Braham, 567 S.E.2d 624 (W. Va. 2002) (West Virginia dishonored check statute explicitly excludes post-dated checks; post-dated check may support larceny by fraudulent scheme conviction, but fraudulent intent not shown merely by NSF check).

14 People v. Abbott, 638 P.2d 781 (Colo. 1981); People v. Meller, 524 P.2d 1366 (Colo. 1974) (in absence of a representation that check is good, a payee who knows that a check is post-dated has notice of the check writer's lack of funds); People v. Cundiff, 305 N.E.2d 735 (Ill. App. Ct. 1973); State v. Mucci, 594 S.E.2d 411 (N.C. Ct. App. 2004) (check writer telling payee to hold check for a few days is proof that payee knew balance insufficient); State v. Boyd, 2003 WL 21060863 (Ohio Ct. App. May 9, 2003) (evidence insufficient to support larceny by check when defendant handed over undated check and told payee's employee to call him before cashing; "poor business practices" not sufficient); Commonwealth v. Kelinson, 184 A.2d 374 (Pa. Super. Ct. 1964); State v. Barnhart, 164 Wash. App. 1041 (Wash. Ct. App. 2011) (garage owner solicited post-dated check from customer who stated he could not pay immediately; defendant credibly testified that he expected to receive certain funds to cover check). *See also In re* Greer, 2002 WL 1558544 (Bankr. D. Colo. July 12, 2002) (NSF check not fraudulent misrepresentation when tenant told landlord check would bounce, but would be covered later; landlord presented check immediately); Young v. State, 594 S.E.2d 667 (Ga. Ct. App. 2004) (post-dated NSF check inadequate to support theft by deception charge when payee knowingly accepts it); Harmon v. State, 2005 WL 1743744 (Tex. App. July 25, 2005) ("taking without effective consent" element of theft not shown when buyer of cattle, who was allowed to take them before writing check, informed seller that he would need time to raise funds to cover post-dated check, apparently a usual practice). *Cf.* People v. Pugh, 127 Cal. Rptr. 2d 770 (Cal. Ct. App. 2002) (giving post-dated check not larceny when seller was informed of insufficient funds, and buyer believed he could cover, but larceny shown when buyer took possession of property and told seller to resubmit check, knowing that bank balance was insufficient). *But see* State v. Spitko, 195 A.2d 577 (Conn. Cir. Ct. 1963); Neese v. State, 994 N.E.2d 336 (Ind. Ct. App. 2013) (payee's knowledge is affirmative defense, on which defendant bears burden; must show that check dishonored for reason stated by defendant; affirming conviction when defendant told payee that funds were temporarily insufficient, but account was actually closed); State v. McWilliams, 178 P.3d 121 (Mont. 2008) (drawee's consent to take post-dated checks not a defense to criminal prosecution of check writer; while drawee may have consented to take the checks and refrain from depositing them immediately, this was not consent to nonpayment).

15 People v. Kubitz, 235 N.Y.S.2d 971 (N.Y. Monroe Cnty. Ct. 1963); State v. Stooksberry, 872 S.W.2d 906 (Tenn. 1994). *But see* State v. Taylor, 73 S.W.2d 378 (Mo. 1934) (even if post-dated check is not a check, it is a draft, for which statute allowed prosecution); State v. McWilliams, 178 P.3d 121 (Mont. 2008) (post-dated check is payable on demand and meets Uniform Commercial Code definition of check).

16 State v. Stout, 448 P.2d 115 (Ariz. Ct. App. 1968); Bivens v. State, 153 Ga. App. 631 (Ga. Ct. App. 1980); State v. Eikelberger, 239 P.2d 1069 (Idaho 1951); Gibbs v. Commonwealth, 273 S.W.2d 583 (Ky. Ct. App. 1954). *But see* People v. Vancamp, 2009 WL 691897 (Mich. Ct. App. Mar. 17, 2009) (affirming conviction of borrower who gave post-dated check to secure loan); State v. Wyman, 945 S.W.2d 74 (Mo. Ct. App. 1997) (intent to defraud shown, not merely failure to perform future promise to deposit money into account, when car buyer who gave seller post-dated check falsely stated that she already had financing).

17 State v. Fitanides, 683 A.2d 534 (N.H. 1996) (New Hampshire treats post-dated check as having been written on the day of its date; check writer was guilty if he or she knew check would not be paid; when bank balance was insufficient for two months after date, evidence was sufficient). *See also* Thompson v. Adcox, 63 S.W.3d 783 (Tenn. Ct. App. 2001) (post-dated check becomes check, for purposes of civil dishonored check statute, on post-dated date, even though criminal prosecution would not be allowed).

18 State v. Hogrefe, 557 N.W.2d 871 (Iowa 1996) (holding that theft by deception or theft by check conviction can be based on post-dated check if check writer never intended to pay or knew he or she would be unable to pay, but reversing conviction on other grounds); Belmonte v. State, 2011 WL 5966365 (Tex. App. Nov. 30, 2011) (knowledge sufficiently shown when business owner continued to write checks when she knew she had cash-flow problems).

19 Brown v. Smith, 342 Fed. Appx. 449 (11th Cir. 2009) (knowingly post-dating a check, without sufficient funds to cover it and without calling payee's attention to this fact, is sufficient for conviction of deposit account fraud); Albertson v. State, 69 A.3d 1186 (Md. Ct. Spec. App. 2013) (reversing conviction for failure to instruct jury that hold-check agreement negates intent element of bad-check offense); People v. Gerber, 453 N.Y.S.2d 998 (N.Y. Crim. Ct. 1982); State v. Wamsley, 2003 WL 1869927 (Ohio Ct. App. Apr. 14, 2003) (affirming conviction even though check writer told payee to wait a day before cashing checks, when account almost never had a positive balance and checks were never paid). *See also* People v. Pugh, 127 Cal. Rptr. 2d 770 (Cal. Ct. App. 2002) (giving post-dated check not larceny when seller was informed of insufficient funds and buyer believed he could cover, but larceny shown when buyer took possession of property and told seller

dated and one not, creates the inference that there were sufficient funds to cover the check that was not post-dated.[20]

8.2.4 Checks Given for Preexisting Debts

Courts may exclude checks given for preexisting debts from the application of dishonored check laws.[21] A payee who accepts a check for a preexisting debt gives up nothing of value in return—an express requirement of some dishonored check statutes.[22] In addition, no intent to defraud can be implied from giving such a check,[23] and a payee who solicits such a check may not in fact have been defrauded.[24]

Other courts, however, have held that if the check writer seeks a respite from collection efforts, this is sufficient return to support a dishonored check conviction.[25] If the payment of an arrearage is a condition for the continuing provision of goods or services, it will generally be sufficient to support a conviction.[26]

8.2.5 Other Limitations and Defenses

Other exceptions or defenses may be available under certain statutes or circumstances.[27] The advocate should always

to resubmit check, knowing that bank balance was insufficient); Lyles v. State, 12 So. 3d 532 (Miss. Ct. App. 2009) (distinguishing defendant's inadvertently dating check with wrong year from parties' mutual agreement to postdating); State v. Stewart, 921 A.2d 933 (N.H. 2007) (reversing conviction because of improper jury instructions; state must show that check writer knew or believed that check would not be paid when presented to bank, not just that funds were insufficient at time check was written). *Cf.* State v. Jones, 2008 WL 564723 (Ohio Ct. App. Mar. 3, 2008) (affirming conviction even though check writer asked payee to wait a day before depositing two $50,000 checks, when he did not reveal his financial condition and account had never had more than a $1000 balance).

20 People v. Abbott, 638 P.2d 781 (Colo. 1981).

21 *See* State v. Ripley, 889 So. 2d 1214 (La. Ct. App. 2004) (NSF check for antecedent debt will support conviction for theft by deception only if it is precondition for provision of future services; not shown here); Johnson v. State, 2005 WL 3387763 (Tex. App. Dec. 13, 2005) (reversing theft of services conviction when NSF check for day care was written at time when there was large arrearage and after the services were terminated). *See also* Commonwealth v. Goren, 893 N.E.2d 786 (Mass. App. Ct. 2008) (reducing larceny conviction to attempted larceny when defendant's delivery of checks drawn on closed account to pay past-due rent gained him nothing). *Cf.* Wenger v. Aceto, 883 N.E.2d 262 (Mass. 2008) (noting open question of Massachusetts law whether larceny by check requires showing that payee parted with something of value or whether check for past services is sufficient). *But see* Brown v. Smith, 342 Fed. Appx. 449 (11th Cir. 2009) (conviction was proper based on checks written in April and May for goods purchased in March and April, as time between purchase and check was so slight that exchange "can be characterized as a single contemporaneous transaction"); Land v. Helmer, 843 F. Supp. 2d 547 (D.N.J. 2012) (New Jersey now requires only issuance of check while knowing that it will not clear, not intent to defraud, so prosecution can be based on check for antecedent debt); People v. Gutierrez, 1 P.3d 241 (Colo. App. 1999) (NSF check written to pay preexisting debt violates Colorado dishonored check statute); Durham v. State, 74 So. 3d 908 (Miss. Ct. App. 2011) (Mississippi bad check statute explicitly applies to checks for preexisting debts); State v. Cruz, 263 P.3d 890 (N.M. 2011) (checks for antecedent debts covered; here, paychecks written after end of workers' pay period; noting that any other reading would exclude nearly all payroll checks); Merchant v. State, 4 P.3d 184 (Wyo. 2000) (writing NSF check to pay preexisting debt violates Wyoming dishonored check statute, which specifically refers to check "to pay a debt"). *But cf.* Gibson v. State, 727 S.E.2d 251 (Ga. Ct. App. 2012) (check was "present consideration," as required by Georgia statute, rather than payment of a preexisting debt when it was presented as soon as transaction was complete and bill had been calculated). *See generally* F. M. English, Annotation, *Construction and Effect of "Bad Check" Statute with Respect to Check in Payment of Pre-existing Debt*, 59 A.L.R.2d 1159 (1958); 32 Am. Jur. 2d *False Pretenses* § 68 (2007).

22 Holder v. State, 529 S.E.2d 907 (Ga. Ct. App. 2000) (NSF check given to independent contractor at end of week for that week's work was for "present consideration" when interval between work and payment was short, but check for payee's share of business's earnings was not when payee had not parted with anything of value in return for check). *See also In re* Mack, 2013 WL 3822075 (Bankr. N.D. Ohio July 23, 2013) (refraining from filing eviction action would be sufficient but, here, landlord knew that tenants were in process of moving out); Ellerbee v. State, 569 S.E.2d 902 (Ga. Ct. App. 2002) (reversing theft by deception conviction; wholesaler did not part with cars in reliance on false statement when failing used car business already possessed cars at time check was written; later promises to pay did not misrepresent any past or present fact); Daugherty v. State, 387 S.W.3d 654, 661, n. 23 (Tex. Crim. App. 2013) (theft of services statute requires showing that deception affected "the judgment of another in the transaction"; not shown when bad check was written after services already provided).

23 Phillips v. State, 136 So. 480 (Ala. Ct. App. 1931); Berry v. State, 111 S.E. 669 (Ga. Ct. App. 1922) ("evident purpose was to escape the importunate duns of his creditor, and to get temporary respite therefrom," not to take anything of value); State v. Blasi, 312 A.2d 135 (N.J. 1973); State v. Davis, 194 P. 882 (N.M. 1921). *See also* Lowery v. City of Boaz, 393 So. 2d 534 (Ala. Crim. App. 1981); State v. Durbin, 614 N.E.2d 799 (Ohio Ct. App. 1992) (limiting situations in which intent to defraud can be found when check is given for preexisting debt). *Cf.* State v. Campbell, 543 P.2d 1171 (Idaho 1975) (state may not rely on presumption of fraud but must prove it when dishonored check was given for preexisting debt).

24 Driskell v. State, 171 S.E. 389 (Ga. Ct. App. 1933).

25 *See* State v. Madani, 910 S.W.2d 362 (Mo. Ct. App. 1995) (statute does not require proof that defendant received anything of value; when dishonored check written to cover debt for two previous dishonored checks served to "stall creditor and frustrate prosecution," intent to defraud was sufficiently shown); Silverberg v. Mirenberg, 746 N.Y.S.2d 742 (N.Y. Civ. Ct. 2001) (check written for third party's antecedent debt is given for value; temporary cessation of legal action against third party was sufficient); State v. Bergsmark, 2004 WL 2426236 (Ohio Ct. App. Oct. 29, 2004) (need not show that "monetary benefit" was obtained; "any type of advantage," including creditor's belief that debt is paid, is sufficient); State v. Suber, 798 N.E.2d 684 (Ohio Ct. App. 2003) (temporary respite from collection action sufficient to show detriment from dishonored check written to cover previous dishonored checks); State v. Brotzman, 108 Wash. App. 1042 (Wash. Ct. App. 2001) (post-dated check written for preexisting debt will support larceny conviction; "brief reprieve" from collection efforts is sufficient); State v. Alams, 970 P.2d 367 (Wash. Ct. App. 1999).

26 *See* State v. Wamsley, 2003 WL 1869927 (Ohio Ct. App. Apr. 14, 2003) (affirming conviction when company issued check for preexisting debt to entice employee to continue working for it); Huse v. State, 180 S.W.3d 847 (Tex. App. 2005) (upholding theft of services conviction when NSF check for antecedent services induced payee to continue to provide services). *See also* Prince Hotel, S.A. v. Blake Marine Group, 2012 WL 4711897 (S.D. Ala. Oct. 12, 2012) (civil bad-check action; fact issue as to intent to defraud when defendant sought to receive continuing services from payee).

27 *See* 32 Am. Jur. 2d *False Pretenses* §§ 62–74 (2007).

investigate whether the payment method in question meets the statutory definition of a check.[28] The state's dishonored check law may not, for example, cover certain types of electronic payment methods. The use of electronic media may, however, support charges of wire fraud.[29]

There can be no fraud, an essential element in most states, when the payee of the check was informed of the check writer's financial distress or insufficient funds balance.[30] However, some courts affirm convictions when the check writer made additional false statements or took other steps to defraud the payee.[31] It may be a defense that the check writer reasonably expected the check to be paid when it was written or presented,[32] but courts have often found that such a belief was unreasonable or that the defense's evidence was insufficient to rebut a statutory presumption of intent.[33] Courts often cite a history

28 Rodgers v. State, 265 P.3d 235 (Wyo. 2011) (reversing check fraud conviction; money-order-type instrument that could be cashed only after calling issuer and verifying authorization number was not a check).

29 United States v. Schwartz, 2005 WL 834869 (E.D. Pa. Apr. 11, 2005) (bank fraud and wire fraud convictions were supported by NSF electronic payments to credit card company), *aff'd*, 315 Fed. Appx. 412 (3d Cir. 2009).

30 Turner v. E-Z Check Cashing of Cookeville, Tenn., Inc., 35 F. Supp. 2d 1042 (M.D. Tenn. 1999) (dishonored check prosecution not allowed; payday lender's knowledge that borrower's bank account lacked funds to cover checked is presumed); People v. Poyet, 492 P.2d 1150 (Cal. 1972) (fact that check was post-dated is a defense if check writer also told payee that account had insufficient funds); People v. Meller, 524 P.2d 1366 (Colo. 1974); White v. State, 110 S.E. 40 (Ga. Ct. App. 1921). *See also In re* Greer, 2002 WL 1558544 (Bankr. D. Colo. July 12, 2002) (NSF check not fraudulent misrepresentation when tenant told landlord check would bounce but would be covered later, yet landlord presented check immediately); People v. Nilbur, 264 N.Y.S. 148 (N.Y. App. Div. 1933) (reversing conviction when check writer told payee that account had insufficient funds and made reasonable efforts to obtain funds to deposit before check was presented). *Cf.* People v. McLaughlin, 462 N.E.2d 875 (Ill. App. Ct. 1984) (intent to defraud not shown when defendant told payee that check would be good when presented and requested that presentment be delayed); State v. Sneed, 908 S.W.2d 408 (Tenn. Ct. App. 1995) (dishonored check statute does not apply if payee or holder "knows or has good and sufficient reason to believe" that check writer had insufficient funds, but finding that payee here did not know). *But see* Neese v. State, 994 N.E.2d 336 (Ind. Ct. App. 2013) (payee's knowledge is affirmative defense, on which defendant bears burden; must show that check dishonored for reason stated by defendant; affirming conviction when defendant told payee that funds were temporarily insufficient, but account was actually closed); Heffernan v. State, 58 A.3d 547 (Md. Ct. App. 2012) (affirming conviction, even though defendant told landlord that she would not have funds to cover checks, written on the first of the month, until the 15th); State v. Kirkland, 249 P.3d 554 (Or. Ct. App. 2011) (informing payee that defendant did not have funds to cover was sufficient to support knowledge element of bad-check offense under statute that did not require fraudulent intent; court does not discuss fact that payee was not deceived); State v. Wallace, 138 P.3d 599 (Utah Ct. App. 2006) (not a defense to dishonored check charge that check writer told payee funds were insufficient or that there was an agreement to delay cashing). *But cf.* State v. Kelm, 672 A.2d 1261 (N.J. Super. Ct. App. Div. 1996) (upholding conviction even though check writer told payee she would have to wait "a few days" when account had negative balances for entire month). *See generally* § 8.2.3, *supra* (post-dated checks).

31 *See, e.g.*, People v. Weathington, 2003 WL 23003363 (Cal. Ct. App. Dec. 22, 2003) (unpublished) (if payee knows of insufficient funds, conviction barred no matter how fraudulent the promise to cover, but simply postdating check insufficient to show payee's knowledge; affirming conviction when payee checked with bank and was told balance sufficient, after which check writer withdrew funds); People v. Chrysler, 639 N.Y.S.2d 213 (N.Y. App. Div. 1996) (intent element of dishonored check offense may be negated by "an understanding" that a "check is not to be cashed until the check writer advises the payee that the check is good," but finding criminal intent when check writer said check would be good in a day or two, but it was written on closed account); State v. Fletcher, 2008 WL 5196523 (Ohio Ct. App. Dec. 12, 2008) (unpublished) (contractor told materials supplier that funds were insufficient but added, incorrectly, that funds were "in transit" from a loan draw; reasonable trier of fact could conclude that defendant knew, and payee did not, that statement about draw was not true).

32 Harmon v. RAR Enters., Inc., 2011 WL 5978483 (D. Ariz. Nov. 30, 2011) (fact issue as to intent to defraud, when corporate officer checked with staff and was misinformed that funds were available before he wrote checks); Parrot Heads, Inc. v. Dep't of Bus. & Prof'l Regulation, 741 So. 2d 1231 (Fla. Dist. Ct. App. 1999) (state must show that check writer knew that funds were insufficient); State v. Miller, 814 N.W.2d 623 (Iowa Ct. App. 2010) (negligent handling of checking account not sufficient to show intent); State v. Harris, 2005 WL 757584 (Minn. Ct. App. Apr. 5, 2005) (intent must be shown as of time check written; reversing conviction when check presented six weeks after it was written, at which time account was closed, and there was no evidence of time or circumstances of closure); Durham v. State, 74 So. 3d 908 (Miss. Ct. App. 2011) (reversing conviction of small business owner who wrote checks relying on bank's practice of paying overdrafts and charging a fee; bank stopped honoring checks when large creditor unexpectedly executed on the account); State v. Stewart, 921 A.2d 933 (N.H. 2007) (reversing conviction; state must show that check writer knew or believed that check would not be paid when presented to bank, not just that funds were insufficient at time check was written); State v. Barnhart, 164 Wash. App. 1041 (Wash. Ct. App. 2011) (at time when garage owner solicited post-dated check from customer who could not pay immediately, customer believed he would receive certain funds to cover check). *See also* State v. Collins, 81 So. 3d 135 (La. Ct. App. 2011) (knowledge of insufficient funds not shown when funds were sufficient at time defendant wrote check and for weeks thereafter, but check writer withdrew funds upon learning that payee had not done the work for which the check was payment). *Cf.* State v. Russell, 382 S.W.3d 312 (Tenn. 2012) (bad check statute does not criminalize an honest mistake; because it includes an element of dishonesty or false statement, a bad check conviction is admissible to impeach witness's credibility). *But see* State v. Mathisen, 356 N.W.2d 129 (N.D. 1984) (no "good faith" defense to violation of dishonored check statute; innocent impression that there were sufficient funds on deposit is not a defense). *See generally* 32 Am. Jur. 2d *False Pretenses* §§ 66–67 (2007); W. L. Heyman, Annotation, *Reasonable Expectation of Payment as Affecting Offenses Under "Worthless Check" Statutes*, 9 A.L.R.3d 719 (1966).

33 *E.g.*, Wells v. State, 807 So. 2d 132 (Fla. Dist. Ct. App. 2002) (affirming conviction of concert promoter who wrote dishonored checks for performers' travel, intending to cover checks from concert revenue, which failed to materialize); Baber v. Commonwealth, 2004 WL 1364283 (Ky. June 17, 2004) (fraudulent intent shown even though balance sufficient to pay check in question, when bank followed usual procedure of cashing largest item first, leaving no funds to pay this check, and defendant could have honored the check to avoid prosecution); Crawley v. Commonwealth, 2003 WL 22149310 (Ky. Sept. 19, 2003) (affirming theft by deception conviction; failure to cover within ten days created rebuttable presumption of intent; defendant used credit card "courtesy checks" and testified that he had checked with credit card issuer before doing so); State v. Mosby, 956 So. 2d 843 (La. Ct. App. 2007) (knowledge of insufficiency shown when bank statement showed sufficient funds on day check written, but insufficient funds next day and negative balance for two weeks thereafter); State v. Washington, 700 So.

of negative balances or bounced checks as evidence of intent or knowledge.[34] False statements or evidence suggesting check kiting are also probative.[35] Reckless disregard for the state of the account may be sufficient to support a conviction.[36]

Some statutes make it a defense that the check is paid within a statutory period after notice of dishonor.[37] Failure to pay within that time will, however, create a presumption of fraud that is difficult to overcome.[38] Some courts have even

2d 1068 (La. Ct. App. 1997) (finding intent to defraud, notwithstanding defendant's testimony that she intended to cover check, when she wrote $5000 NSF check as down payment for car and returned car six months later with 19,000 miles on it); Penn v. State, 684 P.2d 562 (Okla. Crim. App. 1984) (defendant's testimony that he thought there were sufficient funds to cover checks merely created jury questions); Dickews v. State, 2009 WL 3109881 (Tex. App. Sept. 7, 2009) (defendant's testimony that he never received notice of account closure or of dishonor of checks deposited in account, insufficient to overcome presumption of intent to deceive); State v. Hunter, 158 Wash. App. 1002 (Wash. Ct. App. 2010) (evidence of prior problems with account, and notices sent by bank, sufficient to show knowledge that account had been closed); State v. Brotzman, 108 Wash. App. 1042 (Wash. Ct. App. 2001) (affirming conviction when defendant wrote post-dated check believing she would receive income from pending business transaction, which fell through; future deal was "a mere expectancy"); State v. Alams, 970 P.2d 367 (Wash. Ct. App. 1997) (debtor's testimony not persuasive when check was written on account closed because of numerous overdrafts, debtor's testimony).

34 *See, e.g.*, Weathington v. Wong, 2008 WL 718477 (N.D. Cal. Mar. 14, 2008) (evidence of intent and knowledge sufficient: several bounced checks, withdrawal of funds after check was written, and prior incidents when defendant withdrew funds after checks written); Delay-Wilson v. State, 264 P.3d 375 (Alaska Ct. App. Oct. 28, 2011) (reasonable jury could disbelieve defense of mistake when funds in account were nowhere near sufficient, and defendant deposited check proceeds in another account and made substantial withdrawals before bank realized checks were bad); People v. Holt, 2011 WL 468853 (Cal. Ct. App. Oct. 7, 2011) (numerous NSF checks, and consistently low bank balance, sufficient to show that defendant could not have believed that checks would be paid); State v. Whiteside, 2012 WL 602417 (La. Ct. App. Feb. 10, 2012) (evidence of insufficient funds from one week before check was written, until several weeks thereafter); Lyles v. State, 12 So. 3d 532 (Miss. Ct. App. 2009) (bank statements showing prior bad checks and large negative balances sufficient to negate innocent mathematical error); State v. Carroll, 2000 WL 1128876 (Mo. Ct. App. Aug. 10, 2000) (intent to pay negated by negative balances over several month period), *aff'd in part, rev'd in part on other grounds*, 41 S.W.3d 878 (Mo. 2001); State v. Harris, 913 S.W.2d 348 (Mo. Ct. App. 1995) (check writer's testimony that she intended to pay on date of post-dated check disbelieved when balances were very low at all relevant times, and check writer had ceased to communicate with bank); State v. Cruz, 2012 WL 387235 (N.M. Ct. App. Jan. 25, 2012) (evidence sufficient to show that small-business owner, who received bank statements and ceased forwarding them to contract bookkeepers who printed workers' paychecks, knew bank balance was insufficient to cover the paychecks she signed); State v. Mucci, 594 S.E.2d 411 (N.C. Ct. App. 2004) (evidence that other checks bounced during same time period is probative of knowledge; check writer's request that payee hold check for a few days is proof that she knew balance insufficient); State v. Zeune, 2011 WL 198986 (Ohio Ct. App. Jan. 10, 2011) (affirming conviction; fact that another check was dishonored shortly before the subject checks were written was probative of knowledge); State v. Jones, 2008 WL 564723 (Ohio Ct. App. Mar. 3, 2008) (evidence of other bounced checks admissible to show intent, knowledge, plan, or absence of mistake or accident); State v. Bound, 2004 WL 2806430 (Ohio Ct. App. Dec. 1, 2004) (evidence sufficient for dishonored check and theft by deception convictions when owner of failing business wrote eleven dishonored checks and was able to cover only seven of them during statutory period); State v. Cline, 2008 WL 4915873 (Tenn. Crim. App. Nov. 17, 2008) (knowledge sufficiently shown; evidence of prior bad checks, written shortly before subject check, properly admitted); Womack v. State 2001 WL 1383179 (Tex. App. Nov. 8, 2001) (bank records showing negative balances and other NSF checks properly admitted to show intent, knowledge, and absence of mistake); Hartman v. Commonwealth, 2004 WL 237715 (Va. Ct. App. Feb. 10, 2004) (presumption of knowledge not rebutted by defendant's testimony that he was poor bookkeeper but did not intend to steal; evidence of other overdrafts was probative); State v. Lundy, 256 P.3d 466 (Wash. Ct. App. 2011) (evidence of prior overdrafts and NSF checks is relevant to show knowledge and the absence of mistake).

35 *See, e.g.*, State v. Mosby, 763 N.W.2d 277 (Iowa Ct. App. 2009) (evidence "overwhelmingly suggested" knowledge; classic check kite: deposited large bad check, then withdrew entire amount at first opportunity); State v. Weller, 2007 WL 4305884 (Ohio Ct. App. Dec. 11, 2007) (bounced paychecks of start-up business; when funds moved around between bank accounts in manner suggestive of check kiting, evidence showed more than a failed business venture); State v. Dickinson, 528 S.E.2d 675 (S.C. Ct. App. 2000) (defendant's testimony of intent to pay disbelieved when check was for $20,000 and bank officer testified that balance in account never exceeded $1000; defendant also gave false address).

36 Blackford v. Wal-Mart Stores, Inc., 912 F. Supp. 537 (S.D. Ga. 1996) (reckless disregard sufficient to meet knowledge element; distinguishing between "Russian roulette" approach and "an occasional arithmetic mistake"). *But cf.* State v. Miller, 814 N.W.2d 623 (Iowa Ct. App. 2010) (failure to file paperwork needed to continue receipt of direct-deposited unemployment compensation, and continuing to write checks without noticing that direct deposits had ceased, not sufficient to show intent).

37 *See, e.g.*, Knight v. Constantino, 2006 WL 1529567 (S.D. Ind. May 31, 2006) (defense to Indiana dishonored check charge that check was paid within ten days of notice; consumer stated Fourth Amendment claim with allegation that investigator's affidavit knowingly misrepresented that check was not paid); Lapp v. State, 100 P.3d 862 (Wyo. 2004) (reversing conviction when court properly instructed jury that failure to cover check within five days of demand was evidence of intent to defraud, but prosecution failed to prove whether defendant's payment was within or outside the five-day period). *See also* Commonwealth v. Goren, 893 N.E.2d 786 (Mass. App. Ct. 2008) (two days).

38 State v. Mason, 2011 WL 317070 (Ariz. Ct. App. Feb. 1, 2011) (testimony of owner of failing business that he expected to cover check, but was not paid for certain projects, insufficient to overcome presumption of fraud created by failure to pay within twelve days of notice); State v. Miller, 814 N.W.2d 623 (Iowa Ct. App. 2010) (negligent handling of checking account not sufficient to show intent; but proof of failure to make good after receipt of demand letter would be sufficient); State v. Mosby, 956 So. 2d 843 (La. Ct. App. 2007) (intent to defraud shown in light of evidence of statutory notice and nonpayment); People v. Thompson, 2003 WL 22928739 (Mich. Ct. App. Dec. 11, 2003) (failure to cover within statutory five-day period sufficient to support conviction, even though negative balance arose because another person's check bounced when deposited into check writer's account); State v. Napper, 2012 WL 850716 (Ohio Ct. App. Mar. 13, 2012) (defendant's testimony that NSF check was result of mistake, and that he informed payee as soon as mistake was discovered, was insufficient to overcome presumption of intent raised by failure to pay after receipt of demand letter); Glaze v. State, 230 S.W.3d 258 (Tex. App. 2007) (probable cause to arrest sufficiently alleged when notice was given and check not covered within statutory period); Leon v. State, 102 S.W.3d 776, 783–84 (Tex. App. 2003) (affirming conviction on theft by deception charge; presumption of intent can arise when defendant had actual notice, even if language of notice letters did not exactly conform to statute and even if others in office signed the certified mail receipts); Charles v. Commonwealth, 2011 WL 1466067 (Va. Ct. App. Apr. 19, 2011) (defendant who testified that she believed checks would be covered by bank's overdraft protection, but failed to provide details

given effect to this presumption when the notice of dishonor was sent but not received.[39]

The manner in which the dishonoring of the check occurs is also relevant. Some courts hold that the necessary element of fraud is lacking when the dishonored check was cashed at the bank at which the checking account was maintained, as the bank holding the account is charged with knowledge of the account balance.[40] Different rules may apply to checks drawn on closed or nonexistent accounts, or to stop payments.[41] Endorsing a third-party check that proves to be bad will not support a bad-check conviction, because the defendant is not the drawer of the check.[42]

When the check is in fact paid by the drawee bank, the consumer cannot be prosecuted under a dishonored check statute. For example, in one case a consumer wrote checks that she did not have funds to cover. However, her credit union had issued her a card by which it guaranteed payment of any checks she wrote, and it in fact paid her checks. The court held that, because the checks had been paid, the consumer could not be prosecuted under a dishonored check statute.[43]

8.2.6 *Prosecution for Larceny*

Some states, in addition to larceny by check statutes, have statutes forbidding "larceny by deception" or by "false promise,"[44]

---

about that program, failed to rebut presumption of intent created by failure to pay within set time after demand); Huff v. State, 992 P.2d 1071 (Wyo. 1999) (insufficient funds and failure to make good within five days after statutory notice is evidence of intent to deceive); Cox v. State, 964 P.2d 1235 (Wyo. 1998) (intent to defraud was sufficient to support dishonored check conviction when debtor failed to repay within five days of notice of dishonor, even though he paid within ten days and account on which $1500 check was written contained over $1200). *But cf.* Durham v. State, 74 So. 3d 908 (Miss. Ct. App. 2011) (reversing conviction on due process grounds because jury instructions stated that failure to pay within fifteen days of notice was prima facie evidence of intent, without explaining that this presumption was rebuttable). *See generally* 2 Manual of Credit and Commercial Laws, § 7-2 (2012).

39 State v. Wilkens, 95 P.3d 135 (table), 2004 WL 1784607 (Kan. Ct. App. Aug. 6, 2004) (unpublished) (rebuttable presumption of intent to defraud if not repaid within seven days of proper notice; mailing sufficient even though defendant testified to non-receipt; rejecting constitutional challenge to jury instruction regarding presumption); State v. Whiteside, 2012 WL 602417 (La. Ct. App. Feb. 10, 2012) (rebuttable presumption arises even though demand letter returned unclaimed); Cox v. Commonwealth, 2011 WL 3667526 (Va. Ct. App. Aug. 23, 2011) (failure to pay after receipt of demand letter sufficient to support conviction, even though defendant, who had moved, never received the letter); Charles v. Commonwealth, 2011 WL 1466067 (Va. Ct. App. Apr. 19, 2011) (presumption arose even though defendant, who had been evicted from her apartment, never received demand letter); Vance v. Commonwealth, 2007 WL 737557 (Va. Ct. App. Mar. 13, 2007) (nonpayment after notice creates presumption of intent to defraud; notice sent to address on check is sufficient, even if returned undelivered). *But cf.* State v. Collins, 81 So. 3d 135 (La. Ct. App. 2011) (when presumption did not arise because demand letter delivered to wrong address, intent must be proven beyond a reasonable doubt).

40 *See* Bruce I. McDaniel, Annotation, *Cashing Check at Bank at Which Account Is Maintained as a Violation of Bad Check Statutes*, 75 A.L.R.3d 1080 (1977). *But see* State v. Suber, 798 N.E.2d 684 (Ohio Ct. App. 2003) (check tendered to bank, drawn on account at that same bank, sufficient to support larceny by check when there was "a chain of instruments sure to be dishonored," that is, a classic check kite).

41 Albertson v. State, 69 A.3d 1186 (Md. Ct. Spec. App. 2013) (reversing conviction for NSF checks, but affirming as to checks on which defendant stopped payment); State v. Thomas, 2011 WL 2582728 (N.J. Super. Ct. App. Div. July 1, 2011) (reversing NSF check conviction, because trial court erroneously refused to admit evidence that defendant stopped payment on check upon discovering that car repairs were defective). *See also* Neese v. State, 994 N.E.2d 336 (Ind. Ct. App. 2013) (payee's knowledge is affirmative defense, but defendant must show that check was dishonored for reason stated by defendant; affirming conviction when defendant told payee that funds were temporarily insufficient, but account was actually closed); State v. Collins, 81 So. 3d 135 (La. Ct. App. 2011) (knowledge of insufficient funds not shown when funds were sufficient at time when defendant wrote check and for weeks thereafter, but check writer withdrew funds upon learning that payee had not done the work for which the check was payment). *But cf.* Sykes v. Commonwealth, 593 S.E.2d 545 (Va. Ct. App. 2004) (rebuttable statutory presumption of intent to defraud, which arises from check drawn on nonexistent account without need to send five-day notice, also applies to closed account).

42 Delay-Wilson v. State, 264 P.3d 375 (Alaska Ct. App. 2011).

43 Goldyn v. Hayes, 444 F.3d 1062 (9th Cir. 2006) (granting federal habeas corpus relief). *See also* State v. Terry, 929 N.E.2d 1111 (Ohio Ct. App. 2010) (defendant who negotiated stolen and altered check guilty of grand theft, forgery, and receiving stolen property, but not bad check offense, which requires knowledge that check will not be honored; entire scheme here turned on fact that it would be).

44 *See* State v. Martinez, 2011 WL 590427 (Ariz. Ct. App. Feb. 15, 2011) (upholding conviction for fraudulent scheme or artifice when defendant opened bank account with false Social Security number, deposited check drawn on overdrawn account, and made numerous misstatements); State v. Mason, 2011 WL 317070 (Ariz. Ct. App. Feb. 1, 2011) (upholding conviction for theft by misrepresentation when owner of failing business wrote check believing it would be covered but failed to make good after notice of dishonor); State v. Hogrefe, 557 N.W.2d 871 (Iowa 1996) (post-dated check which check writer told payee was not presently cashable may be promise with present intent not to perform, supporting larceny by deception conviction when check writer was in financial trouble, but reversing conviction on other grounds); Tanner v. Commonwealth, 2013 WL 658123 (Ky. Feb. 21, 2013) (theft by deception conviction supported by evidence that defendant wrote check on closed account) Crawley v. Commonwealth, 2003 WL 22149310 (Ky. Sept. 19, 2003) (affirming theft by deception conviction; failure to cover within ten days was sufficient; defendant used credit card "courtesy checks" and testified that he had checked with credit card issuer before doing so); Commonwealth v. Kaplan, 877 N.E.2d 642 (Mass. App. Ct. 2007) (criminal intent, required for larceny, was sufficiently shown when retailer stopped payment on check to wholesaler, sold the goods to innocent purchasers, and promised to cover but did not); State v. Holbruck, 410 S.W.3d 239 (Mo. Ct. App. 2013) (larceny by deceit; present intention not to perform shown by writing checks greatly exceeding bank balance, then falsely claiming that checkbook was stolen and stopping payment); State v. Widener, 2007 WL 293133 (Ohio Ct. App. Feb. 2, 2007) (affirming larceny by deception conviction arising from nonpayment of payday loan; when consumer realized she could not pay, she stopped payment in order to avoid NSF check charges and so informed payday lender); State v. Farah, 2003 WL 22511079 (Ohio Ct. App. Nov. 6, 2003) (defendant could be convicted of misdemeanor theft even after acquittal for larceny by check; gave blank check on closed account as security for loan of gaming chips and left owing money); Leon v. State, 102 S.W.3d 776 (Tex. App. 2003) (affirming conviction of chief executive officer of small company for theft by deception on basis of NSF company checks he allowed to be signed by another while he was ill; intent to deprive shown by fact that checks dishonored within thirty days and not paid within ten days after notice). *But see* Young v. State, 594 S.E.2d 667 (Ga. Ct. App. 2004) (post-dated NSF check insufficient

or obtaining property by false pretenses,[45] which may be applied to NSF checks. The requirements of these statutes may be more flexible than those of dishonored check statutes but generally require some evidence of a promise made with the present intent not to perform.[46] The prosecution will also be required to prove that the payee performed services or parted with property in reliance upon the false promise.[47] Federal bank fraud or mail and wire fraud statutes may also be applicable,[48] but at least one court has concluded that Congress did not intend that a bank fraud indictment be available for routine NSF checks.[49]

8.2.7 *Dishonored Checks and Bankruptcy*

A creditor may seek to use a dishonored check prosecution to gain an advantage in a consumer's bankruptcy. The bankruptcy automatic stay, which prohibits the commencement or continuation of any action or proceeding to collect a prepetition debt,[50] generally does not affect a criminal prosecution.[51] Some courts hold that this is an absolute exception to the automatic stay, regardless of bad faith or the purposes of the prosecution.[52] Other courts, however, hold that the exception does not apply when the primary motivation for the prosecution is collection of a debt, so a creditor may violate the automatic stay by pursuing a bad check prosecution against the debtor.[53]

---

to support theft by deception; distinguishing case in which check writer does not tell payee check is post-dated and lies about current state of bank account); Mizioler v. State, 2003 WL 22023915 (Tex. App. Aug. 27, 2003) (reversing theft by deception conviction, because matter was "contractual dispute": during heated confrontation after business hours, on lot which also contained car dealer's home, dealer gave angry customer a check for his money back, then stopped payment the next morning); State v. Braham, 567 S.E.2d 624 (W. Va. 2002) (post-dated NSF check alone insufficient for larceny by fraudulent scheme; must show fraudulent intent at time check written; defendant should have been allowed to present evidence of his reasons for stopping payment). *But cf.* Brady v. State, 599 S.E.2d 313 (Ga. Ct. App. 2004) (conviction for theft by deception not supported by evidence when defendant told car dealer he would have funds in a few days and took truck, but later wrote an NSF check, because at time dealer parted with truck all the misrepresentations concerned future events); State v. Miller, 814 N.W.2d 623 (Iowa Ct. App. 2010) (must show promise that defendant does not intend to perform or knows that she will be unable to perform; negligent handling of checking account not enough).

45 Creed v. Wilson, 2009 WL 211701 (M.D.N.C. Jan. 29, 2009) (passing of a worthless check for value is grounds for false pretense charge without further evidence of misrepresentation, fraud, notice or knowledge); State v. Rogers, 485 S.E.2d 619 (N.C. 1997) (writing of worthless check on closed account in exchange for property is sufficient without more to support conviction for obtaining property by false pretenses); Middleton v. State, 2009 WL 196063 (Tex. App. Jan. 29, 2009) (NSF checks are "false tokens" within meaning of Texas theft of services statute; affirming conviction when checks written on closed account or on account with grossly insufficient funds). *But see* Shropshire v. Commonwealth, 577 S.E.2d 521 (Va. Ct. App. 2003) (reversing larceny by false pretenses conviction when defendant took possession of car before he paid with dishonored check and returned car at some point after check dishonored; seller did not part with title, and mere possession was not sufficient). *But cf.* Wells v. Commonwealth, 2011 WL 3276194 (Va. Ct. App. Aug. 2, 2011) (reversing conviction for failure to pay wages; intent to defraud is key issue; here, insufficient funds resulted from bankrupt developer's failure to pay defendant subcontractor; fact issue as to what defendant told workers before they returned to work in reliance on post-dated paychecks).

46 State v. DeGennaro, 46 A.3d 1147 (Me. 2012) (key issue is whether, at time of contracting, defendant had no intention of performing; shown here when general contractor accepted money from homeowner, paid subcontractor with bad check, offered false and conflicting explanations, and refused to make refund); State v. Holbruck, 410 S.W.3d 239 (Mo. Ct. App. 2013) (larceny by deceit; present intention not to perform shown by writing checks greatly exceeding bank balance, then falsely claiming that checkbook was stolen and stopping payment); Wirth v. State, 361 S.W.3d 694 (Tex. Crim. App. 2012) (theft by deception shown by promise made with knowledge that it will not be performed; shown here when owner of failing car leasing business caused employee to issue sight drafts to car dealers, knowing that they could not be covered). *But cf.* Daugherty v. State, 387 S.W.3d 654 (Tex. Crim. App. 2013) (present intent not shown where customers' business failed after contractor agreed to perform work; upon completion they paid with bad check).

47 Levitan v. State, 100 So. 3d 776 (Fla. Dist. Ct. App. 2012) (reversing grand theft conviction of owner of failing business who wrote check to payroll service, then stopped payment; at time when check was written, payroll service had already sent checks to employees, so it lost no additional money as result of check); Ellerbee v. State, 569 S.E.2d 902 (Ga. Ct. App. 2002) (reversing theft by deception conviction; wholesaler did not part with cars in reliance on false statement when failing used car business already possessed cars at time check was written, and later promises to pay did not misrepresent any past or present fact); Daugherty v. State, 387 S.W.3d 654 (Tex. Crim. App. 2013) (must show that services were performed in reliance on promise that was false when made). *See also* Kiet Hoang Nguyen v. State, 299 P.3d 683 (Wyo. 2013) (if bank parted with property in reliance on false statements—that is, that deposited checks were good—then false pretenses would be shown).

48 *See* U.S. v. Stergios, 659 F.3d 127 (1st Cir. 2011) (affirming mail fraud conviction arising from check kite; defendant's use of debit cards, which bank mailed to customer, was sufficient to support mail fraud); United States v. Bistrian, 2005 WL 477998 (E.D. Pa. Mar. 1, 2005) (knowingly passing NSF check was "scheme to defraud" sufficient to sustain wire fraud conviction when checks were for entire purchase price of new luxury vehicle).

49 United States v. Repella, 359 Fed. Appx. 294 (3d Cir. 2009).

50 11 U.S.C. § 362(a)(1).

51 11 U.S.C. § 362(b)(1).

52 *See In re* Simonini, 69 Fed. Appx. 169 (4th Cir. 2003) (automatic stay inapplicable regardless of motive, and district court did not have power to enjoin prosecution); Dovell v. Guernsey Bank, 373 B.R. 533 (S.D. Ohio 2007) (vacating injunction against criminal prosecution; exception of criminal prosecutions from automatic stay is absolute); *In re* Dennison, 321 B.R. 378 (Bankr. D. Conn. 2005) (automatic stay does not bar criminal prosecution for NSF check, even if intended to collect a debt; rejecting motivation test of earlier cases); *In re* Pickett, 321 B.R. 663 (Bankr. D. Vt. 2005) (criminal prosecution for NSF check does not violate automatic stay or discharge injunction; provision of Bankruptcy Code making exception for criminal prosecution does not include exception for bad faith); *In re* Bibbs, 282 B.R. 876 (Bankr. E.D. Ark. 2002) (bankruptcy automatic stay does not bar criminal proceeding even if underlying purpose was debt collection).

53 *In re* Shepard, 2000 WL 33743081 (Bankr. M.D. Ga. Jan. 6, 2000) (finding creditor in contempt for initiating prosecution on bad check charges while automatic stay was in effect; prosecution may be enjoined if brought in bad faith unless state recognizes a defense that prosecution was brought for the purpose of collecting a debt). *See also In re* Dorsey, 373 B.R. 528 (Bankr. N.D. Ohio 2007) (criminal prosecution did not violate automatic stay; creditor's motive is relevant, but debtor here did not meet burden of showing that payday lender's primary

Another exception to the automatic stay allows negotiation of checks which were delivered prepetition.[54] Thus, if a creditor has received a post-dated check before the check writer's bankruptcy filing, presenting it for payment after the debtor has filed a bankruptcy petition may not violate the automatic stay.[55] But even if the postpetition presentment of a check and the creditor's receipt of funds from the debtor's account fall within this exception to the automatic stay, the debtor should be able to recover the funds, as the postpetition transfer is avoidable under section 549 of the Bankruptcy Code.[56]

Creditors may also argue that an NSF check is a fraudulent misrepresentation, which makes a debt nondischargeable if the creditor proves fraud in a timely action brought in the bankruptcy case.[57] Many decisions hold that the mere presentment of an NSF check, without more, is not a fraudulent misrepresentation sufficient to invoke this section.[58] A finding of liability under a state civil bad check law may, however, be sufficient to prove fraud.[59]

---

motive was debt collection, as it routinely prosecuted NSF checks to deter this conduct); *In re* Batt, 322 B.R. 776 (Bankr. N.D. Ohio 2005) (reluctantly recognizing "motivation test" but noting strong presumption in favor of criminal prosecution; improper motive not shown when creditor testified that its usual practice was to prosecute those who gave NSF checks); *In re* Reisen, 2004 WL 764628 (Bankr. N.D. Iowa Mar. 4, 2004) (dishonored check prosecution may be enjoined if "principal motivation" is collection of prepetition debt, but no automatic stay violation here when retailer's clerical error prevented collector from learning of bankruptcy). *Cf. In re* Michalski, 452 Fed. Appx. 656 (6th Cir. 2011) (declining to reach question, still open in the Sixth Circuit, whether there is a debt collection exception to the criminal prosecution exception; police refusal to dismiss case upon debtor's offer to cover the checks was sufficient to show that motive for prosecution was not debt collection).

54 11 U.S.C. § 362(b)(11). *See In re* Roete, 936 F.2d 963 (7th Cir. 1991).

55 *In re* Thomas, 428 F.3d 735 (8th Cir. 2005) (automatic stay makes exception for presentment of negotiable instrument); *In re* Blasco, 352 B.R. 888 (Bankr. N.D. Ala. 2006) (payday lender's attempt to cash check after petition date not stay violation; check was negotiable instrument); *In re* Mehaffey, 2005 WL 831805 (Bankr. N.D. Iowa Apr. 8, 2005) (same). *But see* Walton v. Clark & Washington, P.C., 454 B.R. 537 (Bankr. M.D. Fla. 2011) (postpetition deposit of prepetition post-dated check violates automatic stay or discharge injunction; disapproving practice of bankruptcy law firm that solicited post-dated checks for its fees); *In re* Wolfe, 2005 WL 579690 (Bankr. N.D. Iowa Feb. 2, 2005) (willful violation of stay). *But cf. In re* Hagood, 2007 WL 772556 (Bankr. N.D. Ala. Mar. 9, 2007) (payday lender violated discharge injunction by cashing check given prepetition to secure debt that was discharged in bankruptcy). *See generally* National Consumer Law Center, Consumer Bankruptcy Law and Practice § 9.4.6.9 (10th ed. 2012), *updated at* www.nclc.org/library.

56 *See In re* Thomas, 311 B.R. 75 (Bankr. W.D. Mo. 2004), *aff'd*, 428 F.3d 735 (8th Cir. 2005); *In re* Franklin, 254 B.R. 718 (Bankr. W.D. Tenn. 2000). *See generally* National Consumer Law Center, Consumer Bankruptcy Law and Practice § 10.4.2.6.6 (10th ed. 2012), *updated at* www.nclc.org/library.

57 11 U.S.C. § 523(a)(2). *See* National Consumer Law Center, Consumer Bankruptcy Law and Practice § 15.4.3.2 (10th ed. 2012), *updated at* www.nclc.org/library.

58 *See In re* Mack, 2013 WL 3822075 (Bankr. N.D. Ohio July 23, 2013) (presentation of NSF check not sufficient); *In re* Lamanna, 2012 WL 909652 (Bankr. E.D.N.C. Mar. 15, 2012) (issuance of check is not false representation in itself); *In re* Jacobs, 448 B.R. 453 (Bankr. N.D. Ill. 2011) (simply issuing NSF check does not make debt nondischargeable, but further misrepresentations shown here when employees continued to work in reliance on employer's promise that NSF paychecks would be made good, at time when employer knew that business's accounts had been frozen by IRS); *In re* Peel, 2010 WL 670026 (Bankr. E.D.N.C. Feb. 19, 2010) (NSF check not sufficient to show actual fraud; creditor failed to show "specific misrepresentations" by debtor); *In re* Alexander, 427 B.R. 183 (Bankr. D. Mass. 2010) (allowing discharge in close case; mother who had check-signing authority over untrustworthy daughter's small business enabled or failed to prevent daughter's writing bad checks); *In re* Cooper, 2009 WL 4729123 (Bankr. E.D.N.C. Dec. 3, 2009) (noting majority view that NSF check insufficient to support nondischargeability claim, but finding affirmative misrepresentations when debtor falsely told payee that funds were "pending" to cover it; also check was offered as recompense to victim of debtor's fraud); *In re* Hatley, 2009 WL 5205385 (Bankr. E.D. Tenn. Dec. 23, 2009) (must show "affirmative misrepresentation" in addition to issuance of check to support nondischargeability claim); *In re* Jackson, 2009 WL 348476 (Bankr. E.D. Ky. Jan. 29, 2009) (NSF check not sufficient to show intent to defraud when writers of post-dated check "subjectively believed" they would be able to cover it); *In re* McArthur, 391 B.R. 453 (Bankr. D. Kan. 2008) (nondischargeability proceeding; must show that debtor received something of value in contemporary exchange; not shown when principal of failing small business wrote check for antecedent debt); *In re* Hermes, 340 B.R. 369 (Bankr. C.D. Ill. 2006) (presumption of fraud under Illinois law rebutted by farmer's testimony that he expected check to be covered by his line of credit; debt was dischargeable); *In re* Bullock, 317 B.R. 885 (Bankr. M.D. Ala. 2004) (debtor gave automobile dealer two checks and told him to hold them for two weeks; dishonor of one check was not sufficient to show "intentional misrepresentation of past or existing fact" sufficient to deny discharge; promissory fraud was not shown either as it requires the lack of intent to pay at time); *In re* Barsamian, 318 B.R. 508 (Bankr. W.D. Wis. 2004) (writing NSF check is not, without more, a false representation); *In re* Sanchez, 277 B.R. 904 (Bankr. N.D. Ill. 2002) (NSF check written by small business and failure to cover upon demand not sufficient to make out prima facie case that debt resulted from false representation; nonpayment may have been "the unexpected result of the financial difficulties that drove the debtor to bankruptcy"); *In re* Greer, 2002 WL 1558544 (Bankr. D. Colo. July 12, 2002) (landlord's nondischargeability complaint not substantially justified when tenant told landlord that check would bounce but that he would be able to cover it later, yet landlord presented it immediately). *See also In re* Park, 492 B.R. 668 (Bankr. S.D.N.Y. 2013) (debt for casino marker dischargeable; neither false statement nor reliance shown when funds were sufficient when gambler signed marker, and casino based its decision on gambler's past performance); *In re* D'Amico, 2013 WL 6045732 (Bankr. S.D. Tex. Nov. 13, 2013) (finding debt for markers dischargeable; reliance not shown when casino relied on third party data sources; willful injury not shown, when casino repeatedly increased credit line); *In re* Salzillo, 2013 WL 4525199 (Bankr. W.D. Tex. Aug. 27, 2013) ("honest but unreasonable" belief in ability to pay not sufficient to show fraud; allowing discharge of debt for series of post-dated checks given for payments on promissory note); *In re* Bell, 2006 WL 3082110 (Bankr. D. Kan. Oct. 30, 2006) (state default judgment for treble damages on NSF check, which included finding of fraud, is nondischargeable). *But see In re* Callahan, 457 B.R. 25 (Bankr. E.D. Mo. 2011) (writing a check at a time when bank balance is insufficient is a misrepresentation about debtor's financial condition, sufficient to make debt non-dischargeable).

59 *In re* White, 444 B.R. 887 (Bankr. S.D. Ind. 2010) (finding of liability under Indiana's civil bad check law collaterally estops debtor from denying that debt was result of actual fraud); *In re* Howell, 2010 WL 4315042 (Bankr. N.D. Ohio Oct. 26, 2010) (municipal court

Restitution ordered in a criminal case is likely to be non-dischargeable.[60]

A bankruptcy discharge operates as an injunction against the commencement or continuation of an action to collect a discharged debt.[61] Initiation of a criminal prosecution to collect a debt for an NSF check that was discharged in bankruptcy may be a violation of the discharge injunction.[62]

8.2.8 Diversion Programs

The use of taxpayers' resources and the state's criminal powers to collect civil debts has been criticized on public policy and constitutional grounds.[63] As one court noted, "the justice of the peace . . . is not a collection bureau. If he acts as a collection bureau, or if he utilizes the criminal processes of the court to collect a civil debt, he is perverting the functions of this small claims court and bringing disrespect upon the entire judicial process."[64]

A particularly questionable practice is the use of privately operated diversion programs to process dishonored checks for prosecutors' offices. One program sent out letters saying that a criminal complaint had been received—even though no complaint had issued and the prosecutor had not evaluated the case—and informing the consumer that payment of the check, a fee, and a program fee for an educational class would prevent prosecution.[65] A court found the operator of such a program to be a debt collector within the meaning of the Fair Debt Collection Practices Act (FDCPA) and found the use of sheriff's letterhead to be a violation of the FDCPA and state law.[66]

In another case, the Eleventh Circuit reversed a trial court's holding that this type of program was an arm of the state and thus immune to FDCPA claims. The court noted that (1) the state's attorney's office exercised very little control over the program's operations and did not screen cases before letters were sent, (2) the program was not paid for by state funds, and (3) the state would not be liable for judgments against the program.[67]

Amendments made to the FDCPA in 2006 provide an exemption for check diversion debt collectors who meet its

judgment, awarding multiple damages under civil bad check law, is non-dischargeable). *But cf. In re* Duhon, 2013 WL 4510701 (Bankr. W.D. La. Aug. 26, 2013) (finding of liability under state bad check law not conclusive on dischargeability; when loan, secured by undated check, was obtained by deceit, denying discharge for loan amount, but discharging multiple damages and attorney fees for bad check); *In re* Mack, 2013 WL 3822075 (Bankr. N.D. Ohio July 23, 2013) (issue of actual fraud not litigated in civil bad check action, so no collateral estoppel); *In re* Turner, 2012 WL 6680363 (Bankr. D. Kan. Dec. 21, 2012) (default judgment for violation of Kansas civil theft statute arising from NSF check is not basis for collateral estoppel, as issue of intent to deceive was not litigated).

60 Kelly v. Robinson, 479 U.S. 36, 107 S. Ct. 353, 93 L. Ed. 2d 216 (1986) (non-dischargeable if (1) imposed as part of criminal sentence; (2) payable to a government unit; (3) not compensation for direct pecuniary loss); United Bldg. Ctrs. v. Ochs, 781 N.W.2d 79 (S.D. 2010) (applying *Kelly* test: bad check restitution was ordered in criminal proceeding; was payable to government unit, that is, probation office, even if probation then disbursed it to victim; and was not compensation for direct pecuniary loss when this was only one of several criteria prescribed by state restitution law). *See generally* National Consumer Law Center, Consumer Bankruptcy Law and Practice § 15.4.3.7 (10th ed. 2012), *updated at* www.nclc.org/library.

61 11 U.S.C. § 524(a)(2).

62 *In re* Fidler, 442 B.R. 763 (Bankr. D. Nev. 2010) (bankruptcy court cannot enjoin bad check prosecution but may be able to hold check holders in contempt for pursing prosecution as end run around discharge injunction). *See also In re* Byrd, 256 B.R. 246 (Bankr. E.D.N.C. 2000) (discharge injunction does not prevent state from initiating or continuing criminal prosecution, but it prevents creditor from doing so if its primary purpose is recovery of a debt). *But cf. In re* Swain, 325 B.R. 264 (B.A.P. 8th Cir. 2005) (merely delivering copy of bankruptcy paper to prosecuting attorney's office was not an attempt to collect the debt when prosecutor made independent decision to prosecute, so creditor did not violate discharge injunction); *In re* Michalski, 2009 WL 2256697 (Bankr. N.D. Ohio July 23, 2009) (criminal prosecution did not violate discharge injunction when prosecutor testified he would have gone forward to punish crime even if restitution could not be ordered).

63 *See, e.g.*, State v. Henninger, 945 P.2d 864 (Idaho Ct. App. 1997) (strong public policy against using criminal court to collect civil debt). *See also* Victory Distributors, Inc. v. Ayer Div. of the Dist. Ct. Dep't, 755 N.E.2d 273 (Mass. 2001) (upholding small town district court's refusal to issue criminal complaints for large retailer's NSF checks, citing lack of resources and the inappropriateness of using criminal court to collect civil debts). *See generally* J. Potuto, *And Mussolini Had the Trains Running on Time: A Review of the Bad Check Offense and the Law Enforcement Debt Collector*, 65 Neb. L. Rev. 242 (1986).

64 State *ex rel.* Richardson v. Edgeworth, 214 So. 2d 579, 588 (Miss. 1968) (wrongful death claim alleging that gross abuse of criminal process to collect very small checks was proximate cause of consumer's suicide). *See also In re* Frederic-Braud, 973 So. 2d 712 (La. 2008) (suspending justice of the peace for, *inter alia*, allowing constable to use her signature stamp on dishonored check notices, demand unauthorized fees, and misrepresent existence of arrest warrants); *In re* Fusilier, 837 So. 2d 1257 (La. 2003) (suspending judge for, *inter alia*, his dishonored check program in which he worked for complainant merchants).

65 Liles v. American Corrective Counseling Servs., 131 F. Supp. 2d 1114 (S.D. Iowa 2001). *See also* National Consumer Law Center, Fair Debt Collection § 1.5.2 (8th ed. 2014), *updated at* www.nclc.org/library.

66 Gradisher v. Check Enforcement Unit, 210 F. Supp. 2d 907 (W.D. Mich. 2002) (partial summary judgment for consumer class). *See also* Del Campo v. American Corrective Counseling Servs., Inc., 718 F. Supp. 2d 1116 (N.D. Cal. 2010) (private contractor that administered diversion program was debt collector; letters that sought unauthorized fees, gave false impression that they were from district attorney, falsely threatened prosecution, and did not include FDCPA disclosures violated FDCPA and state UDAP statute); Liles v. American Corrective Counseling Servs., 131 F. Supp. 2d 1114 (S.D. Iowa 2001) (denying summary judgment; issue of material fact whether program was a collector under FDCPA or Iowa debt collection statute); *In re* Reisen, 2004 WL 764628 (Bankr. N.D. Iowa Mar. 4, 2004) (diversion program was private collector, not instrumentality of government). *But see* Passa v. City of Columbus, 748 F. Supp. 2d 804 (S.D. Ohio Sept. 28, 2010) (use of bad check diversion program to collect payday loans did not violate FDCPA; city not a debt collector, and letters on city attorney's letterhead did not directly threaten criminal prosecution).

67 Rosario v. American Corrective Counseling Servs., 506 F.3d 1039 (11th Cir. 2007). *See also* DelCampo v. Mealing, 2013 WL 4764975 (N.D. Cal. Sept. 5, 2012) (independent contractor diversion program was neither a government employee nor a fiduciary for district attorney's office). *But cf.* Rush v. Lloyd, 2012 WL 4356802 (W.D. Mich. Sept. 24, 2012) (absolute immunity bars FDCPA claim against assistant prosecutor arising from letter about diversion program).

requirements.[68] Courts have rejected due process challenges to these programs, usually holding that diversion programs must meet due process requirements but that their notice and hearing procedures are constitutionally adequate.[69]

8.3 Civil Collection of Dishonored Checks

8.3.1 Civil Dishonored Check Statutes

Many states have enacted civil dishonored check laws, which encourage bounty hunters by providing for attorney fees and multiple or inflated damages.[70] Many of these statutes

68 15 U.S.C. § 1692p. *See* National Consumer Law Center, Fair Debt Collection § 4.3.12 (8th ed. 2014), *updated at* www.nclc.org/library. *Cf.* Del Campo v. American Corrective Counseling Servs., Inc., 718 F. Supp. 2d 1116 (N.D. Cal. 2010) (amendments not retroactive); Schwarm v. Craighead, 552 F. Supp. 2d 1056 (E.D. Cal. 2008) (amendments not retroactive; letters here violated former version of statute).

69 Del Campo v. Kennedy, 517 F.3d 1070 (9th Cir. 2008) (diversion program provided sufficient notice and opportunity to be heard to satisfy due process; also denying substantive due process and equal protection claims); Silvernail v. County of Kent, 385 F.3d 601 (6th Cir. 2004) (diversion program's notice and hearing procedures sufficient to satisfy due process); Landfried v. Spokane Cnty., 2011 WL 1584328, at *8–9 (E.D. Wash. Apr. 27, 2011) (diversion program did not deprive defendant of due process by threatening prosecution); Schwarm v. Craighead, 552 F. Supp. 2d 1056 (E.D. Cal. 2008) (no due process violation when letters not actually false, even if deceptive, and consumers who refused to pay would receive due process in criminal case); Hamilton v. American Corrective Counseling Servs., 2006 WL 3332828 (N.D. Ind. Nov. 14, 2006); Gradisher v. County of Muskegon, 255 F. Supp. 2d 720 (W.D. Mich. 2003) (no deprivation of property when writers of NSF checks voluntarily paid amounts demanded by diversion program; notices met due process standards in any event, even if they contained false statements), *aff'd*, 108 Fed. Appx. 388 (6th Cir. 2004).

70 The following is a list of civil dishonored check laws. Practitioners should use this list only as a starting point in researching the legality of a claim for a civil dishonored check penalty. Authority for a charge is sometimes hidden in a criminal statute or in the state's commercial code.

ALABAMA: Ala. Code § 6-5-285.

ALASKA: Alaska Stat. § 09.68.115. *See also* Alaska Stat. §§ 06.50.510, 06.50.550 (allowing payday lenders to recover costs and penalties (up to $700) under civil bad check law).

ARIZONA: Ariz. Rev. Stat. Ann. § 12-671.

ARKANSAS: Ark. Code Ann. § 21-6-411 (fees collected by prosecuting attorneys), § 4-60-103 (civil dishonored check remedies). *See also* Ark. Code Ann. §§ 5-37-302 (criminal offense), 5-37-303 (notice requirements), 5-37-305 (penalties), § 5-37-306 (criminal offense).

CALIFORNIA: Cal. Civil Code § 1719 (West) (requires notice to check writer); Cal. Fin. Code §§ 23035(b), 23035(c)(6), 23036(d) (West) (forbidding use of criminal process or Cal. Civ. Code § 1719 (West) for payday loans). *See also* Cal. Penal Code § 476a(a) (restitution), §§ 1001.60 through 1001.67 (West) (diversion program); Imperial Merch. Servs., Inc. v. Hunt, 580 F.3d 893 (9th Cir. 2009) (following California Supreme Court ruling that collector recovering service charge may not recover prejudgment interest under both Cal. Civ. Code §§ 1719 and 3287 (West)); Palmer v. Stassinos, 348 F. Supp. 2d 1070, 1077–83 (N.D. Cal. 2004), *as clarified on reconsideration by* 419 F. Supp. 2d 1151 (N.D. Cal. 2005) (debt collector cannot recover both interest and statutory treble damages on dishonored check).

COLORADO: Colo. Rev. Stat. § 13-21-109.

CONNECTICUT: Conn. Gen. Stat. § 52-565a.

DELAWARE: Del. Code Ann. tit. 6, § 1301A.

DISTRICT OF COLUMBIA: D.C. Code § 28-3152.

FLORIDA: Fla. Stat. § 68.065 (amended in 2013 to add a definition of "payment instrument," which explicitly includes debit card orders and electronic fund transfers). *See* F & A Dairy Products, Inc. v. Imperial Food Distributors, Inc., 798 So. 2d 803 (Fla. Dist. Ct. App. 2001) (when check writer presented no evidence that nonpayment resulted from economic hardship, nor that treble damages would result in economic hardship, court must award treble damages pursuant to civil dishonored check statute). *See also* Fla. Stat. §§ 832.08 (diversion program), 560.309 (allows check cashers to obtain relief pursuant to civil bad-check statute); 560.406 (allows payday lenders all relief except treble damages and requires them to disclose that they cannot seek treble damages).

GEORGIA: Ga. Code Ann. §§ 13-6-15 (damages for writing dishonored checks), 16-9-20(i), (j) (service charges; part of criminal statute). *See also* Ga. Code Ann. § 16-9-21 (criminal statute).

GUAM: Guam Code Ann. tit. 20, § 6104.

HAWAII: Haw. Rev. Stat. §§ 490:3-506, 490:3-506.5. *See also* Haw. Rev. Stat. § 480F-4 (payday lender not allowed to use this procedure).

IDAHO: Idaho Code Ann. §§ 1-2301A, 28-22-105, 28-22-107.

ILLINOIS: 720 Ill. Comp. Stat. § 5/17-1; 810 Ill. Comp. Stat. § 5/3-806. *See also* Ozkaya v. Telecheck Servs., Inc., 982 F. Supp. 578 (N.D. Ill. 1997) (Illinois statutes do not permit debt collector to tack on service charge when debtor has stopped payment); Int'l Bur. of Fraud Control, Ltd. v. Clayton, 544 N.E.2d 416 (Ill. App. Ct. 1989) (collector of NSF checks can recover only statutory fee; may recover "costs and expenses" only if it litigates).

INDIANA: Ind. Code §§ 34-24-3-1, 26-2-7-5, 26-2-7-6. *See also* Ind. Code §§ 35-43-5-5 (criminal statute; provides for service charges), 26-1-3.1-502.5 (surcharge after dishonor), 24-4.5-3-202(f) (U.C.C.C. provision limiting charges); Marion T, L.L.C. v. Northwest Metals Processors, Inc., 67 U.C.C. Rep. Serv. 2d 379 (N.D. Ind. 2008) (corporate officer who signed NSF company check cannot be found liable under Indiana's civil bad check statute, even though he can be convicted of criminal check deception).

IOWA: Iowa Code §§ 554.3512, 554.3513. *See also* Iowa Code § 625.22 (costs and attorney fees in action to recover for dishonored check).

KANSAS: Kan. Stat. Ann. §§ 60-2610, 60-2611. *See also* Kan. Stat. Ann. §§ 16a-2-501 (certain NSF charges permitted by U.C.C.C.), 21-5821 (criminal statute, but provides that payment of service charges after notice will prevent prosecution).

KENTUCKY: Ky. Rev. Stat. Ann. § 514.040(1)(e) (West). *See also* Ky. Rev. Stat. Ann. § 514.040 (4) through (8) (West) (criminal statute).

LOUISIANA: La. Rev. Stat. Ann. §§ 9:2782 through 9:2782.2. *See also* La. Rev. Stat. Ann. § 14:71 (criminal statute providing for mandatory restitution); Winn Fuel Serv., Inc. v. Booth, 34 So. 3d 515 (La. Ct. App. 2010) (because bad check statute is penal, it must be strictly construed; corporate employee who was neither owner nor officer, nor guarantor of corporate debts, not personally liable for corporate checks she signed); Cole Builders L.L.C. v. JJ Properties of W. Monroe, L.L.C., 961 So. 2d 569 (La. Ct. App. 2007) (award of double damages, costs, and attorney fees is mandatory when requirements of civil dishonored check statute are met).

MAINE: Me. Rev. Stat. tit. 14, §§ 6071 through 6073. *See* LaRocque *ex rel.* Spang v. TRS Recovery Serv., Inc., 185 F.R.D. 139 (D. Me. 2012) (certifying class action alleging that check processor and its affiliate violated Maine UDAP statute by demanding dishonored check fees without giving statutorily-required ten-day advance notice and opportunity to pay).

MARYLAND: Md. Code Ann., Com. Law §§ 15-802 through 15-804 (West).

MASSACHUSETTS: Mass. Gen. Laws ch. 93, § 40A.

MICHIGAN: Mich. Comp. Laws § 600.2952. *See also* Mich. Comp. Laws § 600.2953 (retail fraud), §§ 750.131 through 750.134 (criminal NSF check statutes).

provide for a flat fee even in the absence of a contractual basis for the charge.[71] In addition, a few states have statutes allowing damages for criminal acts, often without the requirement of a criminal conviction.[72]

Civil dishonored check statutes are strictly construed.[73] Often they allow penalties only if the payee sends the check

MINNESOTA: Minn. Stat. § 604.113. *See also* Minn. Stat. § 609.535 (criminal statute, but provides notice and opportunity to pay to avoid prosecution), § 628.69 (diversion program).

MISSISSIPPI: Miss. Code Ann. § 11-7-12. *See also* Miss. Code Ann. §§ 97-19-55 through 97-19-81 (criminal NSF check statutes).

MISSOURI: Mo. Rev. Stat. § 570.123. *See also* Mo. Rev. Stat. § 408.505(8) (check for payday loan not subject to criminal prosecution unless written on account closed by consumer before check was written, or consumer stops payment), § 570.120 (criminal statute, but also provides that recipient may, without seeking criminal charges, collect a service fee).

MONTANA: Mont. Code Ann. § 27-1-717. *See* Collection Bureau Servs., Inc. v. Morrow, 87 P.3d 1024 (Mont. 2004) (collector cannot seek penalties under civil dishonored check statute after debtor has defaulted on payment plan without sending new demand letter). *See also* Mont. Code Ann. § 31-1-722 (payday lender may not seek damages under § 27-1-717).

NEBRASKA: Neb. Rev. Stat. § 28-611 (criminal statute; provides for fees and requires notice to check writer).

NEVADA: Nev. Rev. Stat. §§ 205.0832(1)(i), 205.132 through 205.134, 205.380 (criminal statutes; provides for notice to check writer), 205.466 (restitution/diversion program).

NEW HAMPSHIRE: N.H. Rev. Stat. Ann. §§ 544-B:1 through 544-B:3, 358-C:5 (allows a $25 check collection charge in consumer credit transactions). *See also* N.H. Rev. Stat. Ann. §§ 507:7, 638:4 (criminal statute providing for mandatory restitution, including costs and protest fee).

NEW JERSEY: N.J. Stat. Ann. § 2A:32A-1 (West). *See also* N.J. Stat. Ann. § 17:16C-42(e) (retail installment contract may provide for return check fee not to exceed $20).

NEW MEXICO: N.M. Stat. Ann. § 56-14-1.

NEW YORK: N.Y. Gen. Oblig. Law §§ 11-104, 11-105, 5-328 (McKinney) (processing fee by holder of dishonored check). *See also* N.Y. Penal Law §§ 190.00 through 190.15 (McKinney) (criminal statute); Larsen v. JBC Legal Group, 533 F. Supp. 2d 290, 304 (E.D.N.Y. 2008) (N.Y. Gen. Oblig. Law § 11-104 (McKinney) allows recovery of twice the amount of each check or $400, whichever is less, but does not allow recovery of $20 service charge in addition; Fair Debt Collection Practices Act violation to demand both); Kissane v. Digitalville, Inc., 944 N.Y.S.2d 819 (N.Y. App. Div. 2012) (General Obligations Law permits statutory damages in excess of the face amount of dishonored only after drawer is sent two written demands in form specified by statute).

NORTH CAROLINA: N.C. Gen. Stat. § 6-21.3. *See also* N.C. Gen. Stat. §§ 14-107.2 (worthless check diversion program), 25-3-505 (evidence of dishonor), 25-3-506 (collection of processing fee for returned checks).

NORTH DAKOTA: N.D. Cent. Code §§ 6-08-16 through 6-08-16.4 (includes both criminal penalties and provisions for civil action and penalties).

OHIO: Ohio Rev. Code Ann. §§ 2307.60, 2307.61 (West) (civil action for "anyone injured in person or property by a criminal act," including a theft offense); Roseman Bldg. Sys., Inc. v. Vision Power Sys., Inc., 2010 WL 310586 (Ohio Ct. App. Jan. 15, 2010) (allowing civil treble damages for criminal act; when check dishonored within thirty days and not satisfied within ten days after notice of dishonor, no genuine issue of fact as to defendant's commission of crime). *See also* § 1321.41(D) (forbidding payday lender to claim treble damages pursuant to civil bad check statute).

OKLAHOMA: Okla. Stat. tit. 12, § 937 (attorney fees in actions to collect on NSF checks).

OREGON: Or. Rev. Stat. § 30.701. *See also* Or. Rev. Stat. § 725A.060 (forbidding payday lender to recover penalty or seek statutory damages pursuant to civil bad check statute).

PENNSYLVANIA: 42 Pa. Cons. Stat. § 8304.

RHODE ISLAND: R.I. Gen. Laws §§ 6-42-3, 6-42-4 (defenses).

SOUTH CAROLINA: S.C. Code Ann. § 34-11-75. *See also* S.C. Code Ann. §§ 17-22-710 (diversion program); 34-11-60, 34-11-70, 34-11-80 through 34-11-100 (criminal statutes).

SOUTH DAKOTA: S.D. Codified Laws §§ 21-57-1 through 21-57-7. *See also* S.D. Codified Laws § 21-1-14. Note that § 21-57-2 prohibits holder or assignee from asserting liability under § 21-57-1, unless a court has so ruled, and that § 21-57-3 includes significant defenses.

TENNESSEE: Tenn. Code Ann. §§ 47-29-101 through 47-29-103.

TEXAS: Tex. Bus. & Com. Code Ann. § 3.506 (West) (processing fee by holder of dishonored check); Tex. Crim. Proc. Code Ann. §§ 102.007 (fee for collecting and processing sight order), 102.0071 (justice court dishonored check collection fee) (West). *See also* Tex. Penal Code Ann. § 31.06 (West) (presumption for theft by check).

UTAH: Utah Code Ann. §§ 7-15-1, 7-15-2, 7-23-401 (West) (treble damages not available to payday lender; other § 7-15-1 remedies are). *See* Checkrite Recovery Servs. v. King, 52 P.3d 1265 (Utah 2002) (construing Utah statute to allow check collector to recover costs of collection including attorney fees, not just court costs, after filing suit on dishonored check).

VERMONT: Vt. Stat. Ann. tit. 9, §§ 2311 and 2312.

VIRGINIA: Va. Code Ann. §§ 8.01-27.1 (additional recovery in certain civil actions concerning checks; electronic funds transfers explicitly included), 8.01-27.2 (civil recovery). *See also* Va. Code Ann. §§ 6.2-1818, 6.2-2216 (payday lenders and auto title lenders not permitted to recover pursuant to § 8.01-27.2), 18.2-181 through 18.2-185 (criminal statutes).

WASHINGTON: Wash. Rev. Code §§ 62A.3-515, 31.45.082 (payday lender may recover collection costs, pursuant to § 62A.3-515, but not attorney fees or other interest or damages). *See also* Harper v. Collection Bureau of Walla Walla, Inc., 2007 WL 4287293 (W.D. Wash. Dec. 4, 2007) (Wash. Rev. Code § 62A.3-515 allows "reasonable handling fee" at any stage of the collection process, including suit).

WEST VIRGINIA: W. Va. Code §§ 55-16-1, 61-3-39 through 61-3-39q (criminal statute and diversion program).

WISCONSIN: Wis. Stat. § 943.245. *See* Lakeside Oil, Inc. v. Vernier, 2009 WL 4666486 (E.D. Wis. Dec. 1, 2009) (civil bad check count fails; required pre-suit notice not provided), *later decision*, 2010 WL 684995 (E.D. Wis. Feb. 22, 2010) (seller presented sufficient evidence of pre-suit notice; corporate officer with actual knowledge of insufficient funds personally liable for check amount and exemplary damages). *See also* Wis. Stat. § 895.446 (action for property damage or loss caused by crime; victim who has a cause of action under both this section and § 943.245 must elect which cause of action to bring).

WYOMING: Wyo. Stat. Ann. § 1-1-115.

71 *See, e.g.*, N.H. Rev. Stat. Ann. § 358-C:5 ($25 check collection charge by a creditor or debt collector permitted "unless otherwise expressly authorized by written agreement with the consumer"); Ohio Rev. Code Ann. § 1319.16 (West) (permitting collection agency to impose check collection charge of $30 or 10% of amount of the check, whichever is greater, plus the amount of any charge imposed by the financial institution on the holder of the check).

72 *See* Ind. Code § 34-24-3-1; Ohio Rev. Code Ann. §§ 2307.60 through 2307.61 (West); R.I. Gen. Laws § 9-1-2; Wis. Stat. § 895.446. *Cf.* Payday Today, Inc. v. McCullough, 841 N.E.2d 638 (Ind. Ct. App. 2006) (to recover multiple damages and attorney fees under dishonored check or civil theft statute, payday lender must show either fraudulent intent at the time check was written, or common law fraud; fraud not shown as customer stopped payment on checks given as security for loan). *But cf.* Rocano v. Harris, 2007 WL 1827955 (Conn. Super. Ct. June 1, 2007) (denying multiple damages under civil theft statute because issuing dishonored check does not amount to larceny). *See generally* National Consumer Law Center, Federal Deception Law § 8.8 (2012), *updated at* www.nclc.org/library.

73 The Group, Inc. v. Spanier, 940 P.2d 1120 (Colo. App. 1997) (collector must comply strictly with civil dishonored check statute); Stadler

writer a notice and waits a specified period of time.[74] Minor or technical errors in fulfilling the notice requirement may suffice to defeat recovery.[75] The statutes may apply only to NSF checks,[76] not checks on which the consumer stops payment, or the statute may impose additional preconditions to recovery for a stop payment.[77] The debtor's attorney should also investigate whether the payment method the debtor used is covered by the statute, as some civil dishonored check statutes may not be written to encompass certain electronic payment methods. Courts have rejected collector attempts to apply shoplifting[78] statutes to NSF check cases.

The relationship between the civil dishonored check law and criminal law remedies varies from state to state. The statute may bar a civil dishonored check claim if the check writer has already paid the face amount of the check plus any penalties required by the criminal dishonored check statute.[79]

Some civil dishonored check statutes exclude post-dated checks.[80] In addition, states that specifically regulate payday lending often restrict the use of criminal or civil dishonored check laws by lenders and may require that borrowers be informed of this restriction.[81] Regardless of the existence of a

---

v. Devito, 931 P.2d 573 (Colo. App. 1996) (strictly construing notice requirements of Colorado statute; notice insufficient when creditor did not make further efforts to find correct address after certified mail sent to incorrect address was returned "unknown"; creditor acted unlawfully in proceeding with treble damages claim); Commercial Med. Accounts v. Mackintosh, 662 N.E.2d 659 (Ind. Ct. App. 1996) (multiple damages and attorney fees were properly denied under civil dishonored check claim when plaintiff failed to prove it sent notice of dishonor, a statutory requirement); Winn Fuel Serv., Inc. v. Booth, 34 So. 3d 515 (La. Ct. App. 2010) (because bad check statute is penal, it must be strictly construed; corporate employee who was neither owner or officer, nor guarantor of corporate debts, not personally liable for corporate checks she signed); Royal Air, Inc. v. Pronto Delivery Serv., Inc., 917 So. 2d 1197 (La. Ct. App. 2005) (statute providing double damages for wrongful stop payment is penal and must be strictly construed; intent to defraud or absence of "justifiable dispute" not shown when customer stopped payment after repaired airplane malfunctioned during test flight); Wright & Moreno L.L.C. v. Clement, 891 So. 2d 704 (La. Ct. App. 2004) (strictly construing statute providing multiple damages for wrongful stop payment to be inapplicable to NSF check); Redden v. Ripley, 862 So. 2d 469 (La. Ct. App. 2003) (civil dishonored check law is narrowly construed and does not apply to checks drawn on "uncollected" rather than "insufficient" funds; bank negligently failed to credit cashier's check deposited by check writer before writing check); TeleRecovery of La., Inc. v. Rayborn, 814 So. 2d 688 (La. Ct. App. 2002) (denying multiple damages because creditor failed to comply with notice requirements); Sanders v. Mitchell, 810 So. 2d 1276 (La. Ct. App. 2002) (requiring strict compliance with dishonored check statute; denying multiple damages and attorney fees when notice letter gave debtor fifteen days instead of fifteen business days and failed to state statutory penalties); F. Christiana & Co. v. Matt's Grocery, Inc., 674 So. 2d 419 (La. Ct. App. 1996) (statute is penal and must be strictly construed; failure to comply exactly with statute bars award). *See also* Strong v. El Dorado Casino Shreveport Joint Venture, 73 So. 3d 967 (La. Ct. App. 2011) (statute must be strictly construed, but construed here to apply to casino markers).

74 Collection Bureau Servs., Inc. v. Morrow, 87 P.3d 1024 (Mont. 2004) (collector cannot seek penalties under civil dishonored check statute after debtor has defaulted on payment plan without sending new demand letter; FDCPA violation to demand statutory damages without new notice); Kissane v. Digitalville, Inc., 944 N.Y.S.2d 819 (N.Y. App. Term. 2012) (denying double damages to former employee whose paychecks were dishonored when employee failed to send the required demand letter).

75 *See, e.g.*, The Group, Inc. v. Spanier, 940 P.2d 1120 (Colo. App. 1997) (notice was defective when it sought attorney fees when statute only allowed "costs of collection" if check "assigned for collection to a person licensed as a collection agency"); Sanders v. Mitchell, 810 So. 2d 1276 (La. Ct. App. 2002) (denying multiple damages and attorney fees when notice letter gave debtor fifteen days instead of fifteen business days and failed to set forth statutory penalties); Rufener v. Lunau, 2004 WL 639851 (Ohio Ct. App. Mar. 19, 2004) (denying statutory damages and attorney fees when notice provision of demand letter was not conspicuous, but used same typeface as rest of letter). *But cf.* Charles v. Check Rite, Ltd., 1998 U.S. Dist. LEXIS 22512 (D. Ariz. Dec. 14, 1998) (adopting strained interpretation of state dishonored check law to allow collector to demand penalty before complying with statutory notice requirements).

76 Francis v. Snyder, 389 F. Supp. 2d 1034 (N.D. Ill. 2005) (collector's threat to use Illinois statute that did not apply to stop payments was threat of action that could not legally be taken); Jenkins v. Union Corp., 999 F. Supp. 1120 (N.D. Ill. 1998) (when Illinois law permitted imposition of fee for NSF check but not for stop payment, collector's attempt to collect $25 fee for stop payment check was unauthorized).

77 Ozkaya v. Telecheck Servs., Inc., 982 F. Supp. 578 (N.D. Ill. 1997); Uribe v. Correa, 862 So. 2d 883 (Fla. Dist. Ct. App. 2003) (civil dishonored check statute applies to checks on which check writer stops payment only if intent to defraud shown); Red Oak Diesel Clinic v. Teague, 814 N.W.2d 622 (Iowa Ct. App. Feb. 29, 2012) (denying bad-check damages; consumer stopped payment when repaired vehicle malfunctioned shortly after being picked up); Pro Car Care, Inc. v. Johnson, 118 P.3d 815 (Or. Ct. App. 2005) (civil dishonored check statute applies only if payment stopped "without reasonable cause"; not shown when vehicle failed to start shortly after leaving repair shop, even though problem turned out not to be repair shop's fault).

78 *See* Johnson v. Riddle, 305 F.3d 1107 (10th Cir. 2002) (FDCPA case; Utah courts will not apply civil shoplifting statute to NSF checks, because specific Utah statute dealing with dishonored checks limits penalty to $15).

79 *See* Dobbs v. State, 229 S.W.3d 651 (Mo. Ct. App. 2007) (payee of dishonored check may recover under either civil or criminal statute but not both).

80 *See, e.g.*, Nance v. Ulferts, 282 F. Supp. 2d 912 (N.D. Ind. 2003) (Indiana's civil dishonored check statute explicitly excludes post-dated checks; FDCPA violation when payday lender sought treble damages under that statute).

81 *See, e.g.*, Cal. Fin. Code §§ 23035(b), (c)(6), 23036 (West) (forbidding both criminal prosecution and application of civil multiple damages law to check for payday loan; borrower must be informed of this restriction); Haw. Rev. Stat. § 480F-4 (may not recover under civil multiple damages provision); Ind. Code § 24-4.5-7-406; Mont. Code Ann. § 31-1-722 (may recover $30 fee for NSF check but may not recover under civil multiple damages provision); Credit Serv. Co. v. Crasco, 264 P.3d 1061 (Mont. 2011) (assignee of payday lender cannot collect civil penalty authorized by bad-check law; payday loan law forbade assignor-lender from collecting penalty, and assignee stands in the shoes of assignor; statute has since been amended to make clear that restriction applies to assignees). *See also* Payday Today, Inc. v. Indiana Dep't of Fin. Institutions, 2006 WL 148943 (N.D. Ind. Jan. 17, 2006) (upholding constitutionality of small loan law that forbids payday lenders to threaten or bring criminal charges or contract for attorney fees and limits the fees they can charge for dishonored checks); Neidow v. Cash in a Flash/Merrillville, 841 N.E.2d 649 (Ind. Ct. App. 2006) (payday lender can recover civil penalties for NSF check only if it proves fraud); Payday Today, Inc. v. McCullough, 841 N.E.2d 638 (Ind. Ct. App. 2006) (to recover multiple damages and attorney fees under dishonored check or civil theft statute, payday lender must show either

specific statutory exemption, a debtor who gives a post-dated check to a payday lender does not have intent to defraud, which many civil dishonored check statutes require.[82]

8.3.2 *Other Authority for Imposition of Fees*

It is common for check collectors to demand fees that are not authorized by any statute. Some courts have found authority for service charges on returned checks in a provision of Article 2 of the Uniform Commercial Code (UCC)[83] that allows a person in the position of the seller to recover incidental damages for nonpayment of the price of goods.[84] Better-reasoned decisions hold that UCC Article 3, not Article 2, applies to collection of dishonored checks that have been sold to a third party.[85] Another justification for dishonored check charges that some courts have accepted is that signs posted at the merchant's place of business can create an implied contract to pay a fee for a dishonored check.[86]

8.3.3 *Statute of Limitations for Suit on Dishonored Check*

Because of the growth of the debt buying industry, collection attempts may continue on a dishonored check many years after the check was written. UCC Article 3 requires suit to be brought on a check within three years after its dishonor or ten years after the date on the check, whichever occurs first.[87] State statutes may set a shorter period. For example, the Ohio civil theft statute is a penalty statute, for which Ohio law provides a one year statute of limitations.[88]

8.4 Affirmative Remedies for Abuse of Dishonored Check Laws

The Third, Sixth, Seventh, Eighth, and Ninth Circuits,[89] a number of lower courts in other circuits,[90] and the

---

fraudulent intent at the time check was written, or common law fraud; fraud not shown as customer stopped payment on checks given as security for loan); Mich. Deferred Presentment Servs. Ass'n v. Comm'r of Office of Fin. & Ins. Regulation, 788 N.W.2d 842 (Mich. Ct. App. 2010) (upholding administrative order requiring payday lenders to abide by law prohibiting them from seeking statutory damages for NSF checks). *But see* Montclair v. L.O.I., Inc., 246 Fed. Appx. 535 (9th Cir. 2007) (Montana law) (collection agency-assignee of payday loan check can seek $500 penalty under civil dishonored check law; provisions denying penalty to payday lender licensees not applicable, because agency not a licensee). *But cf.* Smith v. Cash Store Mgmt., Inc., 195 F.3d 325 (7th Cir. 1999) (opining, in context of Truth in Lending issue, that payday lender could seek remedies under civil dishonored check statute that allows interest, costs and collection expenses).

82 Jones v. Kunin, 2000 WL 34402017 (S.D. Ill. May 1, 2000). *See generally* § 8.2.3, *supra*.

83 U.C.C. § 2-710.

84 *See* Freyermuth v. Credit Bureau Servs., 248 F.3d 767 (8th Cir. 2001); Tuttle v. Equifax Check Servs., 190 F.3d 9 (2d Cir. 1999) ($20 service charge); Martsolf v. JBC Legal Group, 2008 WL 275719 (M.D. Pa. Jan. 30, 2008) (U.C.C. permits assignee to demand $30 incidental damages); Abels v. JBC Legal Group, 434 F. Supp. 2d 763 (N.D. Cal. 2006) (if assignee acquired all payee's rights in check, it can seek U.C.C. Article 2 incidental damages in an amount that would be reasonable if imposed by original seller, as well as U.C.C. Article 3 damages); Lee v. Sec. Check, L.L.C., 203 F. Supp. 2d 657 (N.D. Miss. 2000) ($30 service charge permitted as incidental damages under U.C.C. when collector put itself in position of seller); Charles v. Check Rite, Ltd., 1998 U.S. Dist. LEXIS 22512 (D. Ariz. Dec. 14, 1998) ($25 fee was incidental damages under U.C.C. Article 2).

85 U.C.C. § 3-310(b)(3); U.C.C. § 3-310 cmt. 3 (a person other than the original seller who holds the check can only use U.C.C. Article 3 remedies). *See* Semper v. JBC Legal Group, 2005 WL 2172377 (W.D. Wash. Sept. 6, 2005) (law firm that purchased dishonored check debts for purpose of collection was not "seller" under U.C.C. Article 2, so its demand for incidental damages violated FDCPA); Ballard v. Equifax Check Serv., 27 F. Supp. 2d 1201 (E.D. Cal. 1998) (only seller, not check guarantee service, can claim U.C.C. Article 2 incidental damages; note that California has since enacted statutory authority for $25 to $35 charges); People *ex rel.* Spitzer v. Boyajian Law Offices, P.C., 851 N.Y.S.2d 72 (table), 2007 WL 3118767 (N.Y. Sup. Ct. Sept. 18, 2007) (debt buyers could not claim U.C.C. damages, as they did not sell goods nor incur the kind of incidental damages, such as stopping delivery or caring for goods, contemplated by U.C.C. Article 2).

86 *See* Merrel v. Research & Data Inc., 589 P.2d 120 (Kan. Ct. App. 1979) (merchant and consumer may contract for NSF check fee higher than that imposed by state dishonored check criminal statute; signs disclosing fee created valid contract); CybrCollect, Inc. v. North Dakota Dep't of Fin. Institutions, 703 N.W.2d 285 (N.D. 2005) (posting of sign allowed electronic collector of NSF checks to debit consumers' accounts for statutory fee without written authorization). *But cf.* Irwin v. Mascott, 96 F. Supp. 2d 968 (N.D. Cal. 1999) (even if collector could show that consumers were properly notified of service charge, charge would be a penalty, not liquidated damages, and thus forbidden by California law); Ballard v. Equifax Check Servs., 27 F. Supp. 2d 1201 (E.D. Cal. 1998) (rejecting argument that consumer had entered into contract for a dishonored check charge when there was no evidence of an oral agreement, a customary practice, or a sign posted).

87 U.C.C. § 3-118. *See also* Martsolf v. JBC Legal Group, 2008 WL 275719 (M.D. Pa. Jan. 30, 2008) (threatening suit on dishonored check after statute of limitations has expired is FDCPA violation); Dunaway v. JBC & Assocs., Inc., 2005 WL 1529574 (E.D. Mich. June 20, 2005) (threatening time-barred suit or criminal prosecution on check is FDCPA violation).

88 Duffey v. Pope, 2012 WL 4442753 (S.D. Ohio Sept. 25, 2012).

89 Fed. Trade Comm'n v. Check Investors, Inc., 502 F.3d 159 (3d Cir. 2007) (checks are FDCPA debts, check writers are consumers, and collectors to whom NSF checks are assigned meet FDCPA definition of debt collector); Volden v. Innovative Fin. Sys., Inc., 440 F.3d 947 (8th Cir. 2006); Snow v. Jesse L. Riddle, P.C., 143 F.3d 1350 (10th Cir. 1998) (dishonored check meets FDCPA definition of debt); Duffy v. Landberg, 133 F.3d 1120 (8th Cir. 1998) (dishonored check is FDCPA debt; check guarantee company is debt collector); Charles v. Lundgren & Assocs., P.C., 119 F.3d 739 (9th Cir. 1997) (dishonored check is FDCPA debt; Ryan v. Wexler & Wexler, 113 F.3d 91 (7th Cir. 1997) (dishonored check is FDCPA debt); Bass v. Stolper, Koritzinsky, Brewster & Neider, S.C., 111 F.3d 1322 (7th Cir. 1997) (check written to purchase consumer goods is FDCPA debt, even though check is later dishonored); Broadnax v. Greene Credit Serv., 106 F.3d 400 (table), 1997 WL 14777 (6th Cir. Jan. 15, 1997) (FDCPA applies to collection activity on check issued to pay commercial obligation when payee altered it and cashed it at supermarket to buy groceries).

90 Ernst v. Jesse L. Riddle, P.C., 964 F. Supp. 213 (M.D. La. 1997) (dishonored check for consumer goods is FDCPA debt); Byes v. Telecheck Recovery Serv., Inc., 1997 WL 736692 (E.D. La. Nov. 24, 1997) (claim on dishonored, allegedly forged check is FDCPA debt even though the person from whom the collector sought payment may not have been a consumer); Rosales v. Nat'l City Corp., 1997 U.S. Dist. LEXIS 23923 (D. Mass. Aug. 31, 1997); Fulcher v. Wexler, 1997 U.S. Dist. LEXIS 4229 (D. Conn. Feb. 24, 1997) (dishonored check for consumer goods is FDCPA debt); *In re* Schrimpsher, 17 B.R. 999 (Bankr. N.D.N.Y. 1982). *But see* Goodman v. Southern Credit Recovery, Inc., 1998 WL 240403 (E.D. La. May 12, 1998) (check is not FDCPA debt).

FTC[91] have concluded that dishonored checks are "debts" as defined by the Fair Debt Collection Practices Act (FDCPA), that consumers who write such checks meet the FDCPA's definition of "consumer," and that collectors of such checks—including check guarantee companies[92]—meet its definition of "collector." These courts have rightly concluded that the FDCPA is not limited to debts that arise from credit transactions.[93] They have also recognized that the FDCPA does not contain a fraud or tort exception that would exclude dishonored checks from the definition of "debt."[94]

The following acts by check collectors violate the Fair Debt Collection Practices Act (FDCPA) and state deceptive practices (UDAP)[95] statutes:

- Falsely threatening to initiate a criminal prosecution on a dishonored check;[96]
- Threatening to impose civil dishonored check penalties when the statute does not allow it or in an amount greater than allowed by the statute;[97]

91 Fed. Trade Comm'n, Staff Commentary on the Fair Debt Collection Practices Act § 803, 53 Fed. Reg. 50097, 50102 (Dec. 13, 1988) (listing dishonored check that was tendered in payment for goods or services acquired or used primarily for personal, family, or household purpose as an example of "debt"); John F. LeFevre, Att'y, Fed. Trade Comm'n, Informal Staff Letter to James A. Cathcart, Chief, California Bur. of Collection & Investigative Servs. (Aug. 24, 1981); John F. LeFevre, Att'y, Fed. Trade Comm'n, Informal Staff Letter to E.A. Fleming, Check-It Servs. (Apr. 1, 1982); John F. LeFevre, Att'y, Fed. Trade Comm'n, Informal Staff Letter to Paul H. Green, Chief Executive Officer, Cross Check, Inc. (Sept. 17, 1996); Laureen France, Investigative Specialist, Fed. Trade Comm'n, Informal Staff Letter to Judith Klayman, Evergreen Legal Servs. (Nov. 22, 1988) (check guarantee service covered).

92 Volden v. Innovative Fin. Sys., Inc., 440 F.3d 947 (8th Cir. 2006) (check guarantee service is debt collector covered by FDCPA); Duffy v. Landberg, 133 F.3d 1120 (8th Cir. 1998) Winterstein v. CrossCheck, Inc., 149 F. Supp. 2d 466, 470 (N.D. Ill. 2001); Ballard v. Equifax Check Servs., 27 F. Supp. 2d 1201 (E.D. Cal. 1998) (check authorization/guarantee company is debt collector under FDCPA); Laureen France, Investigative Specialist, Fed. Trade Comm'n, Informal Staff Letter to Judith Klayman, Evergreen Legal Servs. (Nov. 22, 1988) (check guarantee service covered). *But see* Alexander v. Moore & Assocs., Inc., 553 F. Supp. 948 (D. Haw. 1982) (finding check guarantee service for landlords and other creditors not to be debt collector; service did not collect on debts owed to another as it collected on the amount it had paid to the landlord).

93 Kelly v. Montgomery Lynch & Assocs., Inc., 2008 WL 1775251 (N.D. Ohio Apr. 15, 2008) (underlying monetary obligation is debt; efforts to collect NSF checks covered by FDCPA); Caron v. Charles E. Maxwell, P.C., 48 F. Supp. 2d 932 (D. Ariz. 1999) (FDCPA is not limited to debts arising out of an offer or extension of credit and applies to collection of dishonored checks). *See also* Pollice v. Nat'l Tax Funding, L.P., 225 F.3d 379 (3d Cir. 2000) (rejecting *dicta* in Zimmerman v. HBO Affiliate Group, 834 F.2d 1163 (3d Cir. 1987) that FDCPA covers a debt only if the obligation involves a credit agreement or the deferral of payment); Rogers v. Simmons, 2002 U.S. Dist. LEXIS 5457 (N.D. Ill. Mar. 28, 2002) (dishonored check written to casino was issued for purposes of entertainment and was a "debt" within FDCPA).

94 Armstrong v. Rose Law Firm, P.A., 2002 U.S. Dist. LEXIS 4039 (D. Minn. Mar. 7, 2002); Connor v. Automated Accounts, Inc., 202 F.R.D. 265 (E.D. Wash. 2001) (FDCPA has no "fraud exception"; it is irrelevant whether class members might have intended their checks to be dishonored); Irwin v. Mascott, 96 F. Supp. 2d 968 (N.D. Cal. 1999) (FDCPA covers dishonored checks, regardless of consumers' intent or knowledge).

95 *See generally* National Consumer Law Center, Fair Debt Collection § 10.3 (8th ed. 2014), *updated at* www.nclc.org/library (UDAP claims against debt collectors).

96 *Finding FDCPA violations:* Fed. Trade Comm'n v. Check Investors, Inc., 502 F.3d 159 (3d Cir. 2007) (false threats of criminal prosecution and civil suit violate FDCPA); Richardson v. William Sneider & Assocs., L.L.C., 2012 WL 3525625 (E.D. Va. July 24, 2012) (misrepresentations about Virginia bad-check law; threat of imminent arrest when collector could not bring charges itself and had not complained to law enforcement); Lensch v. Armada Corp., 795 F. Supp. 2d 1180 (W.D. Wash. 2011) (collector violated FDCPA by threatening prosecution for $25 dishonored check, when prosecution was time-barred and collector had no intention of prosecuting; FDCPA ban on false threats preempts Washington law, which allows notice of dishonor to include warning that check may be referred to law enforcement); *In re* Accelerated Recovery Systems, Inc., 431 B.R. 138 (W.D. Va. 2010) (statement that "if we file warrants it will be felony" could deceive least sophisticated consumer, when there were questions re knowledge and intent elements of bad check offense, and check collector could not "file warrants" but only seek them from magistrate); Kelly v. Montgomery Lynch & Assocs., Inc., 2008 WL 1775251 (N.D. Ohio Apr. 15, 2008) (collector violated FDCPA and UDAP statute by soliciting post-dated checks and, when one was dishonored apparently as a result of collector's clerical error, falsely implying that debtor had committed a crime, and threatening prosecution); Dunaway v. JBC & Assocs., Inc., 2005 WL 1529574 (E.D. Mich. June 20, 2005) (threatening to file criminal charges when statute of limitations has run or when collector does not intend to take this action is FDCPA violation); McHugh v. Check Investors Inc., 2003 WL 21283288 (W.D. Va. May 21, 2003) (collector threatened immediate arrest for dishonored check debt not owed); Gradisher v. Check Enforcement Unit, 210 F. Supp. 2d 907 (W.D. Mich. 2002) (diversion program's letter on sheriff's letterhead misrepresented collector's relationship with sheriff and likelihood of prosecution); Davis v. Commercial Check Control, Inc., 1999 U.S. Dist. LEXIS 1682 (N.D. Ill. Feb. 12, 1999) (threats of criminal prosecution violated FDCPA when, out of 20,000 checks, not one had been referred for criminal prosecution). *But see* Passa v. City of Columbus, 748 F. Supp. 2d 804 (S.D. Ohio 2010) (use of bad check diversion program to collect payday loans did not violate FDCPA; city not a debt collector, and letters on city attorney's letterhead did not directly threaten criminal prosecution); Guidry v. Clare, 442 F. Supp. 2d 282 (E.D. Va. 2006) (imposing Rule 11 sanctions against consumer who brought FDCPA and state tort claims after criminal dishonored check case *nolle prossed*; creditor had legal and factual basis for dishonored check claim). *See generally* National Consumer Law Center, Fair Debt Collection §§ 5.5.2, 5.5.7, 5.5.8, 5.5.10, 5.5.13, 9.2, 9.6.3, 10.2, 10.3 (8th ed. 2014), *updated at* www.nclc.org/library.

Finding UDAP violations: Turner v. E-Z Check Cashing of Cookeville, Tenn., Inc., 35 F. Supp. 2d 1042 (M.D. Tenn. 1999) (payday lender's threat of criminal dishonored check prosecution was UDAP violation; no basis for prosecution as lender knew borrowers did not have enough funds on deposit to cover checks); Hamilton v. York, 987 F. Supp. 953 (E.D. Ky. 1997) (payday lender's threat of criminal dishonored check prosecution was UDAP violation because debt was usurious and unenforceable). *See also* Fed. Trade Comm'n v. Check Investors, Inc., 502 F.3d 159 (3d Cir. 2007) (false threats of criminal prosecution and civil suit violate Federal Trade Commission Act).

97 Cruz v. Int'l Collection Corp., 673 F.3d 991 (9th Cir. 2012) (FDCPA violation to demand penalties allowed only by California law for check written in Nevada and governed by Nevada law); Veach v. Sheeks, 316 F.3d 690, 693 (7th Cir. 2003) (demanding treble damages, court costs, and attorney fees before suit violates FDCPA); Johnson v. Riddle, 305 F.3d 1107 (10th Cir. 2002) (collector violated FDCPA by seeking civil penalties for

- Threatening suit on a dishonored check after the statute of limitations has expired.[98]

Consumers may also have claims under state debt collection statutes for these acts.[99] Initiation of a dishonored check prosecution without probable cause may be actionable as a tort such as malicious prosecution,[100] intentional infliction of emotional

---

NSF checks under inapplicable shoplifting law); Picht v. Jon R. Hawks, Ltd., 236 F.3d 446 (8th Cir. 2001) (penalty under dishonored check statute discretionary with court; violation of Minnesota law and thus FDCPA when collector used garnishment procedure intended only for collection of definite sum); Gearing v. Check Brokerage Corp., 233 F.3d 469 (7th Cir. 2000) (check broker was not subrogee, so could not take advantage of damage provisions of Illinois dishonored check law when it bought dishonored checks with proviso that it could sell them back after sixty days, because this escape clause meant that it would not bear the loss if the check could not be collected; its attempt to collect damages under Illinois dishonored check law violated FDCPA); Duffy v. Landberg, 215 F.3d 871 (8th Cir. 2000) (collector violated FDCPA by referring to $100 penalty, when Minnesota dishonored check statute made amount of penalty discretionary with court, and by threatening attorney fees, which were available only for larger checks); Puglisi v. Debt Recovery Solutions, L.L.C., 822 F. Supp. 2d 218 (E.D.N.Y. 2012) (fact question whether debt collector violated FDCPA by attempting to collect bounced check fee in excess of maximum permitted by New York law); Ozkaya v. Telecheck Servs., Inc., 982 F. Supp. 578 (N.D. Ill. 1997); Hunt v. Check Recovery Servs., Inc., 478 F. Supp. 2d 1157 (N.D. Cal. 2007) (remedies of California civil dishonored check statute are exclusive; collector violated FDCPA when it also demanded prejudgment interest); Abels v. JBC Legal Group, 434 F. Supp. 2d 763 (N.D. Cal. 2006) (denying debt buyer's motion to dismiss FDCPA claim; California statute allowing $25 dishonored check charge not retroactive; fact issues whether assignee could recover under U.C.C.); Francis v. Snyder, 389 F. Supp. 2d 1034 (N.D. Ill. 2005) (payday loan collector violated FDCPA by threatening suit under statute that applied only to checks that are returned because of no account or insufficient funds, not when check writer stops payment); Semper v. JBC Legal Group, 2005 WL 2172377 (W.D. Wash. Sept. 6, 2005) (law firm that purchased dishonored check debts for purpose of collection was not "seller" within meaning of Washington dishonored check law and not entitled to statutory damages meant to reimburse merchants for incidental damages); Brumbelow v. Law Offices of Bennett & Deloney, P.C., 2005 WL 1566689 (D. Utah June 21, 2005) (FDCPA claim stated when law firm demanded sum for "settlement" and "covenant not to sue" in excess of sum permitted by state civil dishonored check law); Palmer v. Stassinos, 348 F. Supp. 2d 1070 (N.D. Cal. 2004) (denial of motion to dismiss; seeking interest on dishonored check, not allowed by California NSF check law, is FDCPA violation), *summary judgment on liability granted by* 2009 WL 86705 (N.D. Cal. Jan. 9, 2009) (collector violated FDCPA by demanding treble damages from check-writer's wife, as civil dishonored check statute imposes liability only on person who passes the check, and by demanding both treble damages and prejudgment interest; latter also amounts to UDAP violation if debtor paid interest); Nance v. Ulferts, 282 F. Supp. 2d 912 (N.D. Ind. 2003) (FDCPA violation when payday lender sought treble damages under Indiana's civil dishonored check statute, which explicitly excludes post-dated checks); Sonmore v. CheckRite Recovery Servs., 187 F. Supp. 2d 1128 (D. Minn. 2001) (FDCPA violations when collector referred to $100 penalty but amount of penalty was discretionary and defenses were available); Jones v. Kunin, 2000 WL 34402017 (S.D. Ill. May 1, 2000) (consumer stated FDCPA claim against payday lender that threatened liability for post-dated checks under Illinois civil dishonored check law, as it requires "intent to defraud"); Ballard v. Equifax Check Servs., Inc., 27 F. Supp. 2d 1201 (E.D. Cal. 1998) (collector's incorrect statement that dishonored check service charge was allowed by California law was false representation); Jenkins v. Union Corp., 999 F. Supp. 1120 (N.D. Ill. 1998) (when Illinois law permitted imposition of fee for NSF check but not for stop payment, collector's attempt to collect $25 fee for stopped check was unauthorized); Collection Bureau Servs., Inc. v. Morrow, 87 P.3d 1024 (Mont. 2004) (FDCPA violation to demand statutory damages without new notice after consumer defaulted on payment plan negotiated with NSF check collector). *See also* Del Campo v. American Corrective Counseling Servs., Inc., 718 F. Supp. 2d 1116 (N.D. Cal. 2010) (private contractor, operating diversion program, violated FDCPA and state UDAP statute by charging unauthorized "program fee" in addition to authorized fee). *Cf.* Armstrong v. Rose Law Firm, 2002 WL 461705 (D. Minn. Mar. 22, 2002) (letter violated FDCPA by not clearly stating amount of debt when it lumped together check amount and statutory service charge and called it "amount referred," but reference to additional penalty of "up to" $100 not a violation when this correctly stated Minnesota law); Irwin v. Mascott, 96 F. Supp. 2d 968 (N.D. Cal. 1999) (certifying class; even if collector could show that consumers were properly notified of service charge, charge would be a penalty, not liquidated damages, and thus forbidden by California law); Havens-Tobias v. Eagle, 2003 WL 1601461 (Ohio Ct. App. Mar. 28, 2003) (UDAP claim would lie against creditor who referred claim to collector while blocking consumer's attempts to cover NSF check, but no tort or UDAP claim against attorney who reasonably relied on incomplete information from creditor). *But see* Havens-Tobias v. Eagle, 127 F. Supp. 2d 889 (S.D. Ohio 2001) (no violation of FDCPA by seller's collection attorney when seller refused to accept face amount of NSF check and instead chose to sue, because Ohio statute provided for civil recovery from one who commits theft offense including passing dishonored checks); Charles v. Check Rite, Ltd., 1998 U.S. Dist. LEXIS 22512 (D. Ariz. Dec. 14, 1998) (collector did not violate FDCPA by demanding penalty before complying with statutory notice requirements). *But cf.* Volden v. Innovative Fin. Sys., Inc., 440 F.3d 947 (8th Cir. 2006) (electronically debiting statutory dishonored check fee without written permission of account holder not FDCPA violation; although it violated automated clearing house rules and breached contract between clearing house and check guarantee service, it was permitted by state law so long as sign conspicuously disclosed the fee).

98 Duffey v. Pope, 2012 WL 4442753 (S.D. Ohio Sept. 25, 2012) (Ohio's civil theft statute is penalty statute with one-year statute of limitations; mistake of law not a defense to FDCPA claim alleging knowingly filing a time-barred claim); Larsen v. JBC Legal Group, 533 F. Supp. 2d 290, 303 (E.D.N.Y. 2008); Martsolf v. JBC Legal Group, 2008 WL 275719 (M.D. Pa. Jan. 30, 2008); Dunaway v. JBC & Assocs., Inc., 2005 WL 1529574 (E.D. Mich. June 20, 2005). *See also* Lensch v. Armada Corp., 795 F. Supp. 2d 1180 (W.D. Wash. 2011) (collector violated FDCPA by threatening prosecution, when prosecution was time-barred and collector had no intention of prosecuting).

99 *See, e.g.*, Gradisher v. Check Enforcement Unit, 210 F. Supp. 2d 907 (W.D. Mich. 2002) (diversion program's letter on sheriff's letterhead misrepresented collector's relationship with sheriff and the likelihood of prosecution, in violation of FDCPA and state collection law); People *ex rel.* Spitzer v. Boyajian Law Offices, P.C., 851 N.Y.S.2d 72 (table), 2007 WL 3118767 (N.Y. Sup. Ct. Sept. 18, 2007) (violations of state debt collection law by collector of NSF checks include misstating provisions of New York dishonored check law and demanding damages to which it was not entitled). *But cf.* Webb v. Envision Payment Solutions, Inc., 2011 WL 2160789 (W.D. Pa. May 31, 2011) (questionable whether Pennsylvania debt collection statute applies to collection of NSF checks; UDAP statute does not apply to collection of checks written for cash).

100 Hayfield v. Home Depot, U.S.A., Inc., 168 F. Supp. 2d 436 (E.D. Pa. 2001) (allowing consumer to go to trial on malicious prosecution claim against retailer that vigorously prosecuted criminal dishonored check charges although customer had shown that check was refused not for insufficient funds but because of negligent misprint by check printing company); *In re* BFW Liquidation, L.L.C., 471 B.R. 652 (Bankr. N.D. Ala. 2012) (victim stated claim for malicious prosecution against store that cashed check for thief despite obvious problems with identification, then prosecuted victim); Wal-Mart Stores v. Patterson, 816 So. 2d 1 (Ala. 2001) (checking account owner who was arrested and charged after his

distress,[101] abuse of process,[102] or defamation.[103] A consumer who is arrested may have a cause of action for false imprisonment, but note that, if the arrest is pursuant to a warrant, the consumer must show that the creditor knowingly lied to law enforcement.[104] Some states have statutes that immunize creditors from malicious prosecution claims if they follow certain procedures before initiating a dishonored check prosecution.[105] If law enforcement officials are involved, or a private creditor has acted under color of state law, a civil rights claim pursuant to 42 U.S.C. § 1983 may be available.[106]

It may be unethical in some states for a lawyer to threaten or initiate criminal dishonored check proceedings solely to collect a civil debt for fees.[107] In extreme cases a collector may be criminally liable for threatening criminal prosecution on a dishonored check charge.[108]

A payday lender who used dishonored check prosecutions as a collection device was convicted of violating Georgia's criminal RICO statute. The predicate offenses were perjuries and swearing that the checks had been written for "merchandise," when the lender had no merchandise to sell.[109]

---

ex-wife forged his signature stated claim for negligence and malicious prosecution); Papadopoulos v. Josem, 2002 WL 194494 (Conn. Super. Ct. Jan. 11, 2002) (allowing plaintiff to go forward with malicious prosecution claim against her former attorney who allowed a criminal dishonored check prosecution to go forward, even though she had covered the check); Gooch v. Tudor, 674 S.E.2d 331 (Ga. Ct. App. 2009) (affirming malicious prosecution judgment and punitive damages against contractor who initiated theft by deception prosecution by swearing falsely that consumer, who offered to pay undisputed portion of bill and negotiate about the rest, had refused to pay). *But see* Guidry v. Clare, 442 F. Supp. 2d 282 (E.D. Va. 2006) (imposing Rule 11 sanctions against consumer who brought state tort claims after criminal dishonored check case *nolle prossed*; creditor had legal and factual basis for dishonored check claim); Wenger v. Aceto, 883 N.E.2d 262 (Mass. 2008) (allowing anti-SLAPP motion to dismiss malicious prosecution and abuse of process claims; creditor's action had "reasonable basis in law" when law unclear whether check for antecedent debt could support larceny charge). *See generally* National Consumer Law Center, Fair Debt Collection § 9.6.2 (8th ed. 2014), *updated at* www.nclc.org/library.

101 McHugh v. Check Investors Inc., 2003 WL 21283288 (W.D. Va. May 21, 2003) (awarding actual and punitive damages for intentional infliction of emotional distress when collector threatened immediate arrest for dishonored check debt not owed). *But see* Ross v. Creel Printing & Publ'g Co., 122 Cal. Rptr. 2d 787 (Cal. Ct. App. 2002) (creditor's conduct not outrageous enough to support claim of intentional infliction of emotional distress for prosecution for NSF check written by debtor in his official capacity as chief executive officer of corporation). *See generally* National Consumer Law Center, Fair Debt Collection § 9.6.2 (8th ed. 2014), *updated at* www.nclc.org/library.

102 Alexander v. Manheim Serv. Corp., 2007 WL 2026455 (S.D. Miss. July 9, 2007) (car dealer stated claims for abuse of process, malicious prosecution, wrongful repossession, negligence, defamation, and civil conspiracy against auto auction that agreed to hold check but cashed it prematurely and swore out criminal complaint when it bounced). *But see* Semones v. Southern Bell Tel. & Tel. Co., 416 S.E.2d 909 (N.C. Ct. App. 1992) (bringing dishonored check prosecution without reasonable grounds to believe that company president had knowledge that check would not clear is malicious prosecution but not abuse of process, which requires wrongful act *after* proceeding is initiated). *See generally* National Consumer Law Center, Fair Debt Collection § 9.6.3 (8th ed. 2014), *updated at* www.nclc.org/library.

103 *In re* BFW Liquidation, L.L.C., 471 B.R. 652 (Bankr. N.D. Ala. 2012) (store cashed check for thief despite obvious problems with ID, then prosecuted theft victim; libel claim raises fact issues whether malice sufficiently shown to defeat conditional privilege for complaint to law enforcement). *But see* Kastner v. Kroger Co., 2012 WL 4757290 (Tex. App. Oct. 4, 2012) (store cashed check for thief, sent bad check notices to wrong address, and swore out criminal complaint against theft victim, who was arrested; libel claim fails because complaint to police is absolutely privileged). *See generally* National Consumer Law Center, Fair Debt Collection §§ 9.5.1, 9.5.4–9.5.6 (8th ed. 2014), *updated at* www.nclc.org/library.

104 *In re* BFW Liquidation, L.L.C., 471 B.R. 652 (Bankr. N.D. Ala. 2012) (store cashed check for thief despite obvious problems with ID, then prosecuted theft victim; false arrest claim fails because arrest was pursuant to a warrant). *But see* Kastner v. Kroger Co., 2012 WL 4757290 (Tex. App. Oct. 4, 2012) (store cashed check for thief, sent bad check notices to wrong address, and swore out criminal complaint against theft victim, who was arrested; libel claim fails because complaint to police is absolutely privileged, and false arrest claim fails because arrest was pursuant to a warrant). *See generally* National Consumer Law Center, Fair Debt Collection § 9.7.1–9.7.5 (8th ed. 2014), *updated at* www.nclc.org/library.

105 *See* McLean v. B.J.'s Wholesale Club, Inc., 605 F. Supp. 2d 1357 (N.D. Ga. 2009) (merchant's substantial compliance with bad check procedure sufficient to immunize it from tort liability for bad check arrest); Blue Moon Cycle v. Jenkins, 642 S.E.2d 637 (Ga. 2007) (reversing false arrest and malicious prosecution judgments arising from criminal prosecution of agent who physically delivered NSF company check, signed by company president; Georgia dishonored check law provides immunity to holder who sends proper notices, also criminalizes "delivery" of NSF check). *Cf.* West v. Bruno's, Inc., 837 So. 2d 303 (Ala. Civ. App. 2002) (Alabama dishonored check statute grants civil and criminal immunity only to holder of "worthless" negotiable instrument who follows statutory procedure; fact question here whether check was worthless when consumer's bank records showed that her bank had paid it).

106 Conte v. County of Nassau, 2010 WL 3924677 (E.D.N.Y. Sept. 30, 2010) (§ 1983 and state tort actions; fact question whether officials ignored exculpatory evidence; here, letter stating that post-dated check should not be cashed, because services for which it was given could not be performed); Van Buren v. Cave, 2008 WL 4664227 (M.D. La. Oct. 21, 2008) (fact issue whether creditor acting under color of state law; "symbiotic relationship" and "close nexus" sufficiently alleged when district attorney's office benefited financially from dishonored check prosecutions); Greenberg v. Pryszlak, 46 A.3d 591 (N.J. Super. Ct. App. Div. 2012). *See also* Del Campo v. Kennedy, 517 F.3d 1070 (9th Cir. 2008) (private check diversion company that contracted with district attorney's office is not entitled to sovereign immunity from section 1983 suit). *But cf.* Brown v. Smith, 342 Fed. Appx. 449 (11th Cir. 2009) (sheriff had probable cause to arrest for writing of payday loan checks that were returned NSF); Creed v. Wilson, 2009 WL 211701 (M.D.N.C. Jan. 29, 2009) (dismissing § 1983 claim against arresting officer; probable cause to arrest shown). *See generally* National Consumer Law Center, Fair Debt Collection §§ 8.12.1, 8.12.2, 8.12.2.1, 8.12.2.3, 8.12.2.5, 8.12.3, 8.12.4 (8th ed. 2014), *updated at* www.nclc.org/library.

107 *See* Papadopoulos v. Josem, 2002 WL 194494 (Conn. Super. Ct. Jan. 11, 2002) (allowing plaintiff to go forward with claims of negligence, malicious prosecution, and UDAP violation against her former attorney who allowed her to be arrested for bouncing a check for his fees, even though she had covered the NSF check). *See generally* Gregory G. Sarno, Annotation, *Initiating, or threatening to initiate, criminal prosecution as a ground for disciplining counsel*, 42 A.L.R.4th 1000 (1985); National Consumer Law Center, Fair Debt Collection § 9.6 (8th ed. 2014), *updated at* www.nclc.org/library.

108 State v. Ross, 573 N.W.2d 906 (Iowa 1998) (fraudulent telemarketer's conviction for extortion supported by evidence that he threatened criminal prosecution and public humiliation of older victim who stopped payment on her check when she realized she was being defrauded).

109 Watson v. State, 509 S.E.2d 87 (Ga. Ct. App. 1998).

Chapter 9 Medical Debt

9.1 Introduction

9.1.1 *The Problem of Medical Debt*

Medical debt has been, and continues to be, an enormous problem for both low-income and middle-class American consumers. About 48 million Americans, or nearly 15.4% of the United States' population, lack health insurance.[1] When consumers are uninsured or their insurance coverage is inadequate, the result is medical debt.

The amount of medical debt burdening consumers is enormous. According to one study, nearly 75 million working-age adults (or about 41%) experienced problems with medical bills.[2] In addition, 41 million adults (or about 22%) were contacted by a collection agency for unpaid medical bills.[3] There may be racial disparities in the distribution of medical debt, as people of color make up a disproportionate share of the uninsured.[4]

A landmark study of bankruptcies found that 27% of filings involved medical bills of over $1000, and about half of all bankruptcies are caused in part by medical reasons, such as illness or injury, medical debt, or lost work due to medical reasons.[5] Out of pocket medical costs for "medical bankruptcy" debtors averaged nearly $12,000.[6] Most startling, this study found that 75% of medical bankruptcy debtors had health insurance coverage at the onset of illness.[7] In fact, having health insurance is no guarantee against medical debt, especially for the "underinsured," that is, patients with inadequate insurance coverage or with high co-payment or deductibles.[8] Thus, even with the passage of the Affordable Care Act,[9] medical debt will remain a problem for tens of millions of American consumers.

Medical debt is especially onerous because it is often sudden, unplanned, and unavoidable, and debtors may be vulnerable due to illness or infirmity.[10] The problem is further exacerbated by the fact that not only is medical care extremely expensive, but uninsured consumers are often charged several times more for the same medical services as private insurers or Medicaid, thus adding to their debt burden.[11]

Low-income consumers may have a variety of health law and consumer law defenses to debt collection efforts by doctors, hospitals, and their collection agencies. This chapter focuses on the consumer law defenses that may be available. Other resources should be consulted regarding health law defenses.[12]

9.1.2 *Aggressive Debt Collection*

Many hospitals and health care providers are quick to send unpaid medical bills to collection agencies. Hospitals vary greatly in how long they wait before sending unpaid bills to collection agencies, from 150 to 210 days to as little as 30 to 60 days.[13]

---

1 Carmen DeNavas-Walt, Bernadette D. Proctor, Jessica Smith, U.S. Census Bur., Income, Poverty, and Health Insurance Coverage in the United States: 2012 (Sept. 2013), at 22, *available at* www.census.gov/prod/2013pubs/p60-245.pdf.

2 Sara R. Collins et al., The Commonwealth Fund, Insuring the Future: Current Trends in Health Coverage and the Effects of Implementing the Affordable Care Act 6 (Apr. 2013), *available at* www.commonwealthfund.org/~/media/Files/Publications/Fund%20Report/2013/Apr/1681_Collins_insuring_future_biennial_survey_2012_FINAL.pdf).

3 *Id. See also* Robert W. Seifert, Access Project, Home Sick: How Medical Debt Undermines Housing Security (Nov. 2005) (finding that 46% of low-income clients of Volunteer Income Tax Assistance sites had medical debt); Dennis Andrulis, Lisa Duchon, Carol Pryor & Nanette Goodman, Access Project, Paying for Health Care When You're Uninsured (Jan. 2003) (46% of uninsured consumers have outstanding medical debts).

4 *See* Michelle M. Doty, Jennifer Edwards, & Alyssa Holmgren, Commonwealth Fund, Seeing Red: Americans Driven Into Debt by Medical Bills (Aug. 2005) (52% of African Americans reported difficulties paying medical bills versus 34% of Hispanics and 28% of whites); SEIU Hosp. Accountability Project, Why the Working Poor Pay More (Mar. 2003) (finding the greatest number of "self-pay" or uninsured patients who were discharged from hospitals in Cook County, Illinois, came from high minority areas).

5 David U. Himmelstein, Elizabeth Warren, Deborah Thorne & Steffie Woolhandler, *Illness and Injury as Contributors to Bankruptcy*, Health Affairs—Web Exclusive (Feb. 2, 2005), *available at* http://content.healthaffairs.org/cgi/reprint/hlthaff.w5.63v1.

6 *Id.*

7 *Id.*

8 Cathy Schoen, Michelle M. Doty, Sara R. Collins & Alyssa L. Holmgren, *Insured But Not Protected: How Many Adults Are Underinsured?*, Health Affairs—Web Exclusive (June 2005), *available at* http://content.healthaffairs.org/content/early/2005/06/14/hlthaff.w5.289.short. *See also* Sara R. Collins, Commonwealth Fund, Gaps in Health Insurance: An All-American Problem: Findings from the Commonwealth Fund Biennial Health Insurance Survey (Apr. 2006) (18% of consumers who had health insurance owed medical debt they could not pay); Robert W. Seifert, Access Project, Home Sick: How Medical Debt Undermines Housing Security (Nov. 2005) (41% of medical debtors surveyed had insurance at the time bills were incurred).

9 *See* § 9.3.1, *infra*.

10 *See* Mark A. Hall & Carl E. Schneider, *Patients As Consumers: Courts, Contracts, and the New Medical Marketplace*, 106 Mich. L. Rev. 642 (Feb. 2008) (discussing special vulnerability of patients as consumers due to illness and reliance upon advice of doctors).

11 *See* § 9.1.3, *infra*.

12 Alan Alop, Defending Hospital Collection Cases (rev. ed. 2005), *available at* www.illinoislegaladvocate.org/index.cfm?fuseaction=home.dsp_content&contentID=728; Nat'l Health Law Program, An Advocate's Guide to the Medicaid Program (2012), *available at* www.medicaidguide.org.

13 Access Project, The Consequences of Medical Debt: Evidence from Three Communities (Feb. 2003). *See, e.g.*, Credit Bureau Servs. v. Lundberg, 10 So. 3d 883 (La. Ct. App. 2009) (hospital referred bill to debt collector ninety days after patient's discharge from emergency room visit; debt collector filed lawsuit the following day).

In 2012, 41 million adults (or 22% of the adult working-age population) were contacted by a collection agency for unpaid medical bills.[14]

Medical debt collection agencies can be very aggressive.[15] Documented tactics include liens on homes,[16] wage garnishments,[17] and bank account attachments.[18] Medical collectors in Minnesota used that state's unusual provision permitting debt collectors to seize bank accounts without seeking a judgment or even court authorization.[19] In New York, state collection agencies collected decades-old hospital collection judgments using electronic service of garnishment orders.[20]

Some hospitals have been known to use the tactic of a *capias* or body attachment.[21] One hospital that engaged in aggressive debt collection techniques lost its tax-exempt status as a result.[22] Health care providers have also been known to agree to payment plans, only to sue the patients months or years later for the amount of the debt.[23]

The Minnesota attorney general documented an outrageous pattern of aggressive debt collection by a large debt collection agency, Accretive L.L.C., under its contract with Fairview Health Services.[24] Some of the notable tactics included planting debt collectors within hospital staff; demanding payment for past bills from patients seeking emergency room services; dunning patients for past-due bills at their bedside (with a special emphasis on pregnant women in delivery); and using confidential medical information to maximize debt collection recoveries.[25] The Minnesota attorney general characterized

---

14 Sara R. Collins et al., The Commonwealth Fund, Insuring the Future: Current Trends in Health Coverage and the Effects of Implementing the Affordable Care Act 6 (Apr. 2013), *available at* www.commonwealthfund.org/~/media/Files/Publications/Fund%20 Report/2013/Apr/1681_Collins_insuring_future_biennial_survey_2012 _FINAL.pdf).

15 This aggressiveness drew the attention of Congress in the mid-2000s. Internal Revenue Serv., Hospital Compliance Project—Interim Report (July 2007), *available at* www.irs.gov/pub/irs-tege/eo_interim_hospital _report_072007.pdf; Minority Staff, Senate Fin. Comm., Tax-Exempt Hospitals: Discussion Draft (July 18, 2007), *available at* http://grassley .senate.gov/releases/2007/07182007.pdf.

16 Fred Schulte & James Drew, *In Their Debt*, Balt. Sun, Dec. 21, 2008 (study by *Baltimore Sun* found that Maryland hospitals filed 132,000 lawsuits and placed liens on 8000 homes in the past five years); Fred Schulte & James Drew, *Their Day in Court*, Balt. Sun, Dec. 22, 2008 (finding that 29 of 47 Maryland hospitals used liens on patients' homes as a collection tactic in the past five years); Elisabeth Benjamin, Amy Chung & Renee Philips, Health Law Unit—Legal Aid Soc'y of N.Y., State Secret 2005: How Government Statutes and Hospitals' Voluntary Efforts Fail to Protect Uninsured Patients (Jan. 2005) (finding that 15 out of 31 New York City not-for-profit hospitals use liens on patients' homes as a collection tactic); Conn. Ctr. for a New Economy, Yale, Don't Lien on Me (Sept. 2003) (finding that Yale-New Haven Hospital placed liens on an estimated 7.5% of owner-occupied homes in New Haven during the past nine years).

One government program has been known to place a lien on the patient's home if the patient receives payment assistance from the program. *In re* Hendricks, 2010 WL 744259 (Bankr. D. Idaho Mar. 1, 2010) (describing Idaho's statutory lien on homes of patients who receive assistance from County Medical Indigency Care Program).

17 Elisabeth Benjamin, Amy Chung & Renee Philips, Health Law Unit—Legal Aid Soc'y of N.Y., State Secret 2005: How Government Statutes and Hospitals' Voluntary Efforts Fail to Protect Uninsured Patients (Jan. 2005) (finding that 27 out of 31 New York City not-for-profit hospitals use wage garnishments as a collection tactic); Steve Tripoli & Chi Chi Wu, National Consumer Law Center, Unhealthy Pursuits: How the Sick and Vulnerable Are Harmed by Abusive Medical Debt Collection Tactics (Dec. 2005), *available online as companion material to this treatise. See, e.g.*, Meyer v. Debt Recovery Solutions of Ohio, Inc., 2010 WL 3515663 (N.D. Ohio Sept. 2, 2010) (hospital garnished wages for bill despite fact that patient had already paid debt collector for bill); Credit Bur. of E. Idaho v. Lecheminant, 235 P.3d 1188 (Idaho 2010) (particularly egregious case, second wife's wages were garnished for debt that husband owed for first wife's medical bill); Laffitte v. S. Fin. Systems, Inc., 30 So. 3d 1236 (Miss. Ct. App. 2009) (upholding wage garnishment for medical bill after default judgment, despite allegations of failure of service); Hillcrest Med. Ctr. v. Monroy, 38 P.3d 931 (Okla. Civ. App. 2001) (upholding stay on hospital's garnishment of patient's wages due to hardship and ordering lower court to determine whether already garnished wages should be refunded).

18 Elisabeth Benjamin, Amy Chung & Renee Philips, Health Law Unit—Legal Aid Soc'y of N.Y., State Secret 2005: How Government Statutes and Hospitals' Voluntary Efforts Fail to Protect Uninsured Patients (Jan. 2005) (finding that 24 out of 31 New York City not-for-profit hospitals use bank account attachments as a collection tactic).

19 Office of the Minn. Att'y Gen., Compliance Review of Fairview Health Servs. (Jan. 31, 2005).

20 Lucette Lagnado, *Cold Case Files: Dunned for Old Bills, Poor Find Some Hospitals Never Forget*, Wall St. J., June 8, 2004, at A1.

21 A *capias* or body attachment is an arrest warrant that creditors or collection agencies obtain when a debtor fails to show up for a court hearing.

22 Lucette Lagnado, *Hospital Found "Not Charitable" Loses Its Status as Tax Exempt*, Wall St. J., Feb. 19, 2004 (describing how the Illinois Department of Revenue revoked the tax exempt status of Provena Covenant Medical Center, in part because of Provena's aggressive use of lawsuits and other debt collection methods to collect from uninsured patients); Lucette Lagnado, *Hospitals Try Extreme Measures to Collect Their Overdue Debts*, Wall St. J., Oct. 30, 2003, at A1 (documenting that Provena sought 164 arrest warrants for medical debtors since 1995). The Department of Revenue's decision to revoke Provena's tax-exempt status was upheld in Provena Covenant Medical Ctr. v. Dep't of Revenue, 925 N.E.2d 1131 (Ill. 2010).

23 *See, e.g.*, Valley Hosp. v. Laubshire, 2007 WL 1342187 (N.J. Super. Ct. App. Div. May 9, 2007) (hospital sued patient despite the fact patient had made monthly payments on the debt for seven years pursuant to statements sent by the hospital); Univ. Ortho & Sports v. Pleasant, 2007 WL 867625 (Ohio Ct. App. Mar. 23, 2007) (provider's agreement to accept payment plan did not bar provider from suing patient later). *Cf.* Marino v. Hoganwillig, P.L.L.C., 910 F. Supp. 2d 492 (W.D.N.Y. 2012) (collector continued to dun patient, despite patient's assertion that provider agreed to accept partial payment in satisfaction of debt); Scott v. Associated Credit Servs., Inc., 2012 WL 4856060 (D. Mass. Oct. 10, 2012) (collector continued dun patient even though patient had entered into payment plan with provider and was current).

24 The details of the attorney general's investigation are set forth in a six-volume report entitled "Compliance Review of Fairview Health Services' Management Contracts with Accretive Health, Inc.," which is available at www.ag.state.mn.us/Consumer/Health. *See also* Marvin H. Morris Revocable Trust v. Bronfman, 2013 WL 5348357 (N.D. Ill. Sept. 24, 2013) (shareholder action detailing knowing violations of state and federal healthcare, debt collection, privacy, and consumer laws by Accretive); Complaint, State v. Accretive Health, Inc., No. 21-cv-000145 (D. Minn. Jan. 19, 2012), *available at* www.ag.state.mn.us/ PDF/Consumer/AccretiveHealth20120119.pdf.

25 Office of the Minn. Att'y Gen., Violations of Federal and State Debt Collection Laws, 5 Compliance Review of Fairview Health Services' Management Contracts with Accretive Health, Inc.

the atmosphere created by Accretive as "[t]he Emergency Room meets Glengarry Glen Ross."[26] Unfortunately, some of the tactics used by Accretive may become more common, as hospitals are encouraged to become more aggressive in collections and move toward "front-end" or "point-of-service" collections, that is, demanding payment from patients upfront in the hospital instead of waiting until after treatment.[27]

The American Hospital Association (AHA), a private trade association, has issued guidance to hospitals on billing and collection practices.[28] The AHA recommends that hospitals establish and widely publicize written financial assistance policies, provide financial counseling to patients, limit charges for patients who qualify for financial assistance to no more than the amounts generally billed to insured patients, and define standards for third-party debt collectors acting on their behalf.[29] Many of these recommendations are actually required by the debt collection provisions of the Affordable Care Act.[30]

The American Healthcare Financial Management Association and ACA International, the trade association for debt collectors, have issued draft guidelines on medical debt collection. Among other things, these draft guideline recommend that collectors allow patients 120 days to pay a medical bill before reporting the account to a credit reporting agency, remove paid medical debts from credit reports within forty-five days, and comply with the provider's collection policies and procedures.[31]

9.1.3 Discriminatory or "Chargemaster" Pricing: How the Poor Pay More

One of the most bizarre and ironic aspects of medical debt is that the poorest, most vulnerable patients—the uninsured—are often charged significantly higher prices than third-party payers such as health maintenance organizations (HMOs), private insurers, and Medicare/Medicaid. This disparity results from "discriminatory" or "chargemaster" pricing, a phenomenon described as follows by the hospitals' own trade group, the American Hospital Association:

> While a hospital charges all patients receiving the same service the same price, what varies dramatically is how much a hospital is actually paid for the care it provides. The Medicare and Medicaid programs set payments that are not only less than charges, but also often less than the actual cost of caring for these patients. Private insurers negotiate discounts from charges on behalf of the enrollees they cover. As pressure increases from private insurers and managed care companies for deeper discounts, charges have increased, as hospitals struggle to balance government under-funding and find the resources to care for those without insurance. But in the absence of health care coverage for all in America, people without insurance face bills reflecting these higher charges, with no one to negotiate on their behalf. They are victims of America's fragmented and inconsistent health care payment system.[32]

The result is that uninsured patients pay several times more than HMOs, insurance companies, and the government. It also results in uninsured individuals paying several times more than the hospital's actual cost of services.[33] These uninsured

(Apr. 2012), *available at* www.ag.state.mn.us/PDF/PressReleases/ComplianceReview/Vol. 5.pdf.

26 Office of the Minn. Att'y Gen., Culture Wars, 2 Compliance Review of Fairview Health Services' Management Contracts with Accretive Health, Inc. (Apr. 2012), *available at* www.ag.state.mn.us/PDF/PressReleases/ComplianceReview/Vol.2.pdf. *Glengarry Glen Ross* refers to a David Mamet play depicting a boiler room real estate sales office in which managers use abuses and profanity to motivate the sales agents.

27 *See, e.g.*, Press Release, TransUnion "Pulse Poll" Reveals Untapped Opportunity in Hospital Point-of-Service Collections (Aug. 17, 2011).

28 Bd. of Trustees of the Am. Hosp. Ass'n, Hospital Billing and Collection Practices—Statement of Principles and Guidelines (rev. May 5, 2012), *available at* www.aha.org/content/12/120505-bill-collec-prac-statement.pdf.

29 *Id.* A list of hospitals that have confirmed their commitment to these guidelines is available at www.aha.org/content/00-10/cocweblist.pdf.

30 *See* § 9.3.1, *infra*.

31 American Healthcare Fin. Mgmt. Ass'n & ACA Int'l, Medical Debt Resolution Overview (June 2013). *See also* American Healthcare Fin. Mgmt. Ass'n & ACA Int'l, Draft Guidelines for Medical Debt Resolution (Aug. 2013).

32 Am. Hosp. Ass'n, Alert—Four Related Issues Drawing Media and Congressional Attention—Know Your Organization's Policies (June 10, 2003). *See also* Steven Brill, *Bitter Pill: Why Medical Bills are Killing Us*, Time, Feb. 20, 2013, *available at* www.time.com/time/magazine/article/0,9171,2136864,00.html (visited Mar. 2014; paid subscription required) (extensive and comprehensive discussion of the problems posed by use of chargemaster pricing and the abuses that discriminatory pricing perpetrates on uninsured and underinsured consumers); Mark A. Hall & Carl E. Schneider, *Patients as Consumers: Courts, Contracts, and the New Medical Marketplace*, 106 Mich. L. Rev. 642 (Feb. 2008); Uwe E. Reinhardt, *The Pricing Of U.S. Hospital Services: Chaos Behind A Veil Of Secrecy*, 25:1 Health Affairs 57–69 (2006).

Discriminatory pricing also occurs with respect to prescription medications. Lindsey Johnson, U.S. Pub. Interest Research Group, Paying the Price: The High Cost of Prescription Drugs for Uninsured Americans (Oct. 2004) (finding that uninsured consumers pay 78% more on average for twelve common prescription drugs than the federal government pays for the same medications).

33 Gerard F. Anderson, *From "Soak the Rich" to "Soak the Poor": Recent Trends In Hospital Pricing*, 26:3 Health Affairs 780–89 (2007) (giving examples of markups and noting that rates charged to many uninsured patients are often two-and-a-half times what most insurers actually paid and more than three times costs allowed by Medicare); Marilyn Weber Serafini, *Sticker Shock*, Nat'l J., Oct. 18, 2003, at 3180 (chart of average markup of gross charges—what the uninsured pay—from hospitals' cost, showing in some states, hospital charges were 200% over costs).

For a history of how discriminatory pricing developed see *A Review of Hospital Billing and Collection Practices Before the Subcomm. on Oversight and Investigations of the H. Comm. on Energy and Commerce*, 108th Cong. (2004) (statement of Gerard Anderson, Professor, Bloomberg Sch. of Pub. Health, Johns Hopkins Univ.).

Dr. Anderson testified how in the mid-1980s, hospital "list charges" were typically only 25% above costs, but now it is common for list charges to be two to four times higher than costs. List charges are also two to four times what most insurers pay, and most insurers pay costs plus or minus 15%. *Id.*

individuals are charged prices from the hospital's "chargemaster," which are "gross" or list rates. One commentator has called chargemaster pricing "the source of poison coursing through the health care ecosystem."[34]

Discriminatory pricing has been documented in a number of reported cases:

- The chief executive officer (CEO) of a regional health care system testified that the average markup of hospital services was 2.3 or 2.4 times the cost of providing such services. The defendant hospital in this case used such a markup, yet only received about 39% of its total "chargemaster" (or list price) charges, yielding an actual net profit of 3%. In other words, the hospital had to charge nearly two and a half times its cost in order to receive payments slightly above its costs from most of its payers (insurers). This CEO opined that the chargemaster charges would not be a reasonable amount for a patient who had insurance but were a reasonable charge for an uninsured patient.[35]
- In a legal dispute between a hospital and an HMO, the chief financial officer (CFO) of a hospital admitted that his hospital received 80% or more of its chargemaster rates no more than 6% of the time.[36] The opposing counsel's expert economist testified that the hospital received the full amount of chargemaster rates only about 1% to 3% of the time and that these rates had risen from 172% of actual costs in 1994 to 300% in 1996. He also noted that private insurers typically paid only 112% of costs in 1996, and Medicaid and Medicare paid even less. The hospital's CFO admitted that none of the twelve private insurers who had contracts with the hospital paid the chargemaster rates.[37]
- An expert witness provided evidence showing that the range of cost-to-charge ratios for hospitals in one state was an astounding 10%–15%.[38] In other words, the cost for the hospitals to provide service was just 10% to 15% of the amount of the hospitals' chargemaster rates.
- A hospital admitted it generally had a markup of 221%, had marked up a band-aid by 1000%, and charged $9 for a 10-cent sleeping pill, yet testified that it believed its charges to be reasonable.[39]
- A court upheld judgment against patients for full chargemaster rates despite evidence that these charges were 400% of the hospital's costs, only 2% of patients were ever charged full price, and the hospital usually accepted about one-third of its listed prices.[40]
- In a dispute between a surgery center and a worker's compensation insurer, a court noted that one center accepted 30% or less of its chargemaster rates from 82% of insurers and another accepted less than 24% of its billed charges from 89% of insurers.[41]
- In a personal injury case, a hospital billed over $70,000 for a back surgery but accepted $5310 from the patient's insurer plus co-pays and deductibles.[42]
- For purposes of personal injury damages, the California Supreme Court held that price negotiated by an insurer—about $60,000—was a better indication of reasonable value of services than the chargemaster rate of $190,000.[43]
- In an especially egregious case, a hospital obtained a judgment against a low-income patient for over $6000 out of a $9400 bill, even after the consumer's insurance already paid the hospital $2500.[44] Moreover, Medicare would have paid only a few hundred dollars for the same service.[45]

Hospitals had previously defended their discriminatory pricing policies by arguing that the Medicaid and Medicare programs require them to charge "uniform rates" and to make reasonable collection efforts of Medicare co-payments and deductibles. This argument was laid to rest when the U.S. Department of Health and Human Services issued guidance permitting hospitals and other providers to "provide discounts to uninsured and underinsured patients who cannot afford their hospital bills and to Medicare beneficiaries who cannot afford their Medicare cost-sharing obligations."[46] This guidance provides support for practitioners who are negotiating with providers to seek to reduce the amount of a medical debt.[47]

Litigation challenging discriminatory pricing has met with mixed success.[48] Discriminatory pricing can also be used defensively when the client is faced with a collections lawsuit.[49]

Discriminatory pricing is also an issue for insured patients who are billed for a co-payment based on a percentage (for example, 20%) of the full chargemaster rate, not the discounted

34 Steven Brill, *Bitter Pill: Why Medical Bills are Killing Us*, Time, Feb. 20, 2013, *available at* www.time.com/time/magazine/article/0,9171,2136864,00.html.

35 Howard v. Willis-Knighton Med. Ctr., 924 So. 2d 1245 (La. Ct. App. 2006).

36 Temple Univ. Hosp., Inc. v. Healthcare Mgmt. Alternatives, Inc., 832 A.2d 501 (Pa. Super. Ct. 2003).

37 *Id.*

38 El Paso Healthcare Sys., Ltd. v. Molina Healthcare of New Mexico, Inc., 683 F. Supp. 2d 454 (W.D. Tex. 2010).

39 Univ. of S. Alabama Hosps. v. Blackmon, 42 So. 3d 1258 (Ala. Civ. App. 2009).

40 Banner Health v. Med. Sav. Ins. Co., 163 P.3d 1096 (Ariz. Ct. App. 2007).

41 Canyon Ambulatory Surgery Centers v. SCF Arizona, 239 P.3d 733 (Ariz. Ct. App. 2010).

42 Martinez v. Milburn Enters., Inc., 233 P.3d 205 (Kan. 2010).

43 Howell v. Hamilton Meats & Provisions, Inc., 257 P.3d 1130 (Cal. 2011) (in depth discussion of hospital pricing and what constitutes a reasonable value).

44 Steven Brill, *Bitter Pill: Why Medical Bills are Killing Us*, Time, Feb. 20, 2013, *available at* www.time.com/time/magazine/article/0,9171,2136864,00.html.

45 *Id.* The bulk of the hospital's bill consisted of $6538 in charges for three CT scans. In addition to the fact that three CT scans were probably overkill for a slip and fall nosebleed, Medicare would have paid only $825 for these scans.

46 Letter from Tommy G. Thompson, Sec'y of United States Dep't of Health & Human Servs., to Richard J. Davidson, President, Am. Hosp. Ass'n (Feb. 19, 2004).

47 *See, e.g.*, Vince Galloro, *Tenet to Offer Discounts*, Modern Healthcare, Mar. 8, 2004, at 8 (for-profit hospital chain announces implementation of discount rate plan for the uninsured; plan had been on hold for one year pending Department of Health and Human Services guidance).

48 *See* § 9.4.2.2, *infra*.

49 *See* § 9.5.5.2, *infra*.

price. Insured patients can also be affected by discriminatory pricing when providers "balance bill" them for amounts in excess of what insurers pay,[50] or if their insurers do not have a contract with the provider establishing negotiated prices, and the insurer refuses to pay the full list or "chargemaster" prices for services, leaving patients liable for the balance.[51]

Another form of inflated pricing occurs when patients receive care at medical clinics considered to be hospital-based. These clinics may charge significant additional "facility" fees, which can double or triple a bill from what patients would pay for the exact same service provided at a non-hospital-based medical practice.[52] Failure to disclose these facility fees could be challenged as deceptive under state UDAP law.[53]

9.1.4 Practical Solutions for Medical Debt

A very effective method to deal with medical debt is to find someone else to pay for it. Advocates should make sure that their clients have applied for any assistance programs to which they are entitled. This may include government or private programs, such as Medicaid,[54] Medicare Savings Programs,[55] an overlooked insurance source,[56] pharmacy assistance programs,[57] church or social service assistance programs, or low-cost dental care from dental school programs.

If a client has low or moderate income, make sure to inquire about charity or "free care" eligibility. These programs arise from the implicit duty of not-for-profit hospitals, because of their charitable status, to provide a certain amount of free care to low-income patients. In some states this obligation is already explicit.[58] The Affordable Care Act will require non-profit hospitals to establish financial assistance programs and to inform patients of their availability.[59] Ironically, many hospitals count an unpaid medical debt as "charity care" despite the fact the hospital or a debt collector continues to attempt to collect the debt.[60] One limitation of charity care programs is that they may only cover hospital bills, leaving the patient still owing significant debts to a physician or other health care provider.

Informal negotiation over medical debt can be especially effective. Hospitals and other medical providers may be more willing to reduce bills because of the fact that these bills are often several times more than both what the hospital's actual costs are, as well as what the hospital would receive from Medicaid or Medicare.[61] Any settlement to pay medical bills should of course be documented in writing.[62] If medicals bills have adversely affected the consumer's credit report,[63] any settlement should require the provider or collector to remove or correct this negative information. Sample language is available in another treatise in this series.[64]

Medical debt is generally unsecured debt and less of a priority than essential expenses such as food, housing costs (rent or mortgage), utilities, or other secured debt (for example, car payments).[65] Clients should be advised to pay the higher priority bills first. Clients should be advised to be very careful about converting medical debt into secured debt, for example, by taking out a second mortgage to pay for medical bills.[66] They should also be careful not to use credit cards to pay medical bills, which has become a common practice.[67] Credit card lenders are notorious for abusive practices, such as charging extraordinarily high penalty interest rates and fees.[68] Moreover, unlike a health care provider, patients will not be able to negotiate with a credit card lender to reduce a bill because of discriminatory pricing.

---

50 *See* § 9.3.7, *supra*.

51 *Id.*

52 Julie Appleby, *"Hospital-Based" Clinics Can Charge More*, USA Today, Nov. 16, 2006.

53 *See, e.g.*, Virginia Mason Med. Ctr. v. Executive Risk Indem., Inc., 2007 WL 3473683 (W.D. Wash. Nov. 14, 2007) (discussing prior settlement of UDAP lawsuit over facility charges), *aff'd*, 331 Fed. Appx. 473 (9th Cir. 2009). *See* § 9.4.2, *infra*.

54 Note that individuals who qualify for Medicaid can get retroactive benefits to cover medical expenses incurred up to three months before the date of application. 42 U.S.C. § 1396a(a)(34); 42 C.F.R. § 435.914.

55 These programs help low-income Medicare recipients pay for Medicare premiums. Some programs may also cover co-insurance and deductibles for certain people. To learn more, see Medicare and You 2014, at 108–09, *available at* www.medicare.gov/publications/pubs/pdf/10050.pdf.

56 Overlooked insurance sources can include workers' compensation, home owner's insurance, automobile insurance, or insurance from a current or former employer or spouse.

57 One example is the Partnership for Prescription Assistance, whose website is located at www.pparx.org.

58 The Community Catalyst website has a guide to free care programs in each state at www.communitycatalyst.org/initiatives-and-issues/initiatives/hospital-accountability-project/free-care.

59 *See* § 9.3.1, *infra*.

60 *See* Internal Revenue Serv., Hospital Compliance Project—Interim Report (July 2007), *available at* www.irs.gov/pub/irs-tege/eo_interim_hospital_report_072007.pdf (in survey of 487 tax-exempt hospitals, 44% admitted they included some bad debt as "uncompensated care" for the purposes of reporting community benefits expenditures).

61 *See* § 9.1.3, *supra*.

62 A payment plan, especially if it is not written, may not be an adequate defense if the provider decides to later sue on the debt. *See, e.g.*, Univ. Ortho & Sports v. Pleasant, 2007 WL 867625 (Ohio Ct. App. Mar. 23, 2007) (provider's agreement to accept payment plan not binding because no additional consideration provided).

63 *See* § 9.3.5, *infra*.

64 National Consumer Law Center, Fair Credit Reporting Appx. J.9 (8th ed. 2013), *updated at* www.nclc.org/library. *See also id.* § 12.6.4.

65 These considerations are discussed in more detail in NCLC Guide to Surviving Debt (2013). This publication is available from NCLC at www.nclc.org.

66 A study of bankruptcy filers found that 15% of home owners in the group who had taken out a second or third mortgage cited medical bills as a reason for doing so. Even worse, follow up interviews revealed that among home owners with high cost home loans (interest rates greater than 12% or points and fees 8% or greater), nearly 14% cited a medical reason for taking out the loan. David U. Himmelstein, Elizabeth Warren, Deborah Thorne & Steffie Woolhandler, Illness and Injury as Contributors to Bankruptcy, Health Affairs—Web Exclusive (Feb. 2, 2005), *available at* http://content.healthaffairs.org/cgi/reprint/hlthaff.w5.63v1.

67 *See* § 9.4.5, *infra*.

68 *See* National Consumer Law Center, Consumer Credit Regulation Ch. 8 (2012), *updated at* www.nclc.org/library.

A non-monetary consideration that is unique to medical debt is whether the debtor will be able to continue to get care from the particular facility. In non-emergency situations, hospitals and other providers are usually allowed to turn away a patient because of prior debt.[69] They may also require that the patient pay a deposit before services will be provided.[70] However, there may be "safety net" facilities nearby, such as a public hospital or a community health center. In emergency situations, the debtor should be able to obtain care from a hospital regardless of past debt under the Emergency Medical Treatment and Active Labor Act (EMTALA), an "anti-dumping" statute.[71] Also, Medicaid prohibits providers from denying services to Medicaid recipients on the basis of outstanding debts for co-payments or deductibles.[72]

9.1.5 Finding Out the Extent of the Debt

A single medical incident will often create debts owed to a variety of actors. For example, a single hospital visit can result in bills from the ambulance service, the hospital itself, the surgeon, the anesthesiologist, and medical equipment providers. Medical debt is often owed to hospitals, but significant numbers of debtors report owing amounts to doctors, ambulances services, pharmacies, and others.[73] Thus, even if a patient has insurance coverage, is able to obtain charity care, or can negotiate a settlement to cover a hospital bill, she may still owe significant debts to a physician or other healthcare provider.[74]

A practical issue for some medical debtors is that they may not be aware of owing debt to all these creditors. Previously, attorneys could obtain a fairly complete inventory of medical debt by pulling the debtor's credit report. However a provision added in 2003 to the Fair Credit Reporting Act prohibited credit reporting agencies from including the identity of medical creditors/collectors unless the information does not disclose either the specific provider or nature of the medical services.[75]

One way to find out more information about a debtor's medical bill is to request the full invoice that itemizes individual charges from the hospital. Federal health care privacy regulations require that hospitals provide a copy of medical records and other health information to patients at their request.[76] Practitioners may want to specifically ask for "Form CMS-1450," which is a form used by hospitals and other institutions to complete a Medicare claim.

Practitioners may attempt to obtain more information by requesting verification under the Fair Debt Collection Practices Act (FDCPA). However, collection agencies are not required to give itemized billing statements pursuant to a request for verification under the FDCPA.[77] If the debtor has insurance but owes medical debt due to co-payments or deductibles, another way to obtain more information is to obtain the Explanation of Benefits (EOB) from the debtor's insurance company. Once a debtor has a copy of his or her bill, the next big hurdle is deciphering it. Medical bills are notorious for being incomprehensible.[78] Patients sometimes refuse to pay bills because they fail to itemize the amounts sought or explain what the charges were for.[79]

---

69 Access Project, The Consequences of Medical Debt: Evidence from Three Communities (Feb. 2003) (one-third of medical debtors in study reported that providers refused or delayed care due to prior medical bills). For an especially egregious example, see Marsala v. Yale New Haven Hosp., Inc., 2013 WL 6171307 (Conn. Super. Ct. Oct. 30, 2013) (hospital removed patient from respirator and life support because patient was unable to pay for treatment, despite family members clear objections that removal was against patient's wishes).

70 *See, e.g.*, Office of the Minn. Att'y Gen., Violations of Federal and State Debt Collection Laws, 5 Compliance Review of Fairview Health Services' Management Contracts with Accretive Health, Inc. (Apr. 2012), *available at* www.ag.state.mn.us/PDF/PressReleases/ComplianceReview/Vol. 5.pdf (Accretive demanded payment for past bills from patients seeking emergency room services); Access Project, The Consequences of Medical Debt: Evidence from Three Communities (Feb. 2003) (30% of medical debtors surveyed were asked to pay prior medical bills upfront).

71 42 U.S.C. § 1395dd. *See* § 9.3.3, *infra*.

72 Beeker v. Olzewski, 415 F. Supp. 2d 734 (E.D. Mich. 2006). The court did note that recently enacted amendments to Medicaid may have an impact on this prohibition. *Id.*

73 In a study of bankruptcy filers, among those who reported owing medical debt, hospital bills were the biggest expense for 42.5%, while doctors' bills were the biggest for 20%. David U. Himmelstein, Elizabeth Warren, Deborah Thorne & Steffie Woolhandler, Illness and Injury as Contributors to Bankruptcy, Health Affairs—Web Exclusive (Feb. 2, 2005), *available at* http://content.healthaffairs.org/cgi/reprint/hlthaff.w5.63v1; Robert W. Seifert, Access Project, Home Sick: How Medical Debt Undermines Housing Security (Nov. 2005) (70% of medical debtors owed debt to hospitals, 44% owed debt to physicians, 20% owed debt to a lab, and 13% owed debt to an ambulance service).

74 *See, e.g.*, Shields v. Merchants & Med. Credit Corp., 2010 WL 2613086 (E.D. Mich. June 28, 2010) (patient dunned for $85 bill for anesthesia, despite fact that hospital records showed he owed no balance; unclear whether bill was from hospital or physician group within hospital); Princeton Surgical Assoc. v. Aziz, 2010 WL 1425112 (N.J. Super. Ct. App. Div. Apr. 8, 2010) (patient's HMO paid hospital's bill, but not surgeon's bill, because surgeon was out-of-network; patient liable despite hospital's failure to ensure that surgeon was in-network).

75 15 U.S.C. § 1681c(a)(6). *See* § 9.3.5, *infra*.

76 45 C.F.R. § 164.502(a)(2). *See* § 9.3.4, *infra*.

77 Recker v. Cent. Collections Bur., Inc., 2005 WL 2654222 (S.D. Ind. Oct. 17, 2005) (computer printout setting forth amount of debts, medical services provided, and dates that debts were incurred were sufficient for verification under FDCPA); Zaborac v. Mutual Hosp. Serv., Inc., 2004 WL 2538643 (S.D. Ind. Oct. 7, 2004). *See also* McNall v. Credit Bur. of Josephine Cnty., 689 F. Supp. 2d 1265 (D. Or. 2010) (itemized invoice sufficient; debt collector not required to investigate or provide documentation substantiating hospital debt).

78 *See* Tara Siegel Bernard, Decoding Your Medical Bill, N.Y. Times, June 22, 2012, *available at* http://bucks.blogs.nytimes.com/2012/06/22/decoding-your-medical-bill/?_php=true&_type=blogs&_r=0 (tips on how to read a hospital bill).

79 *See, e.g.*, Shields v. Merchants & Med. Credit Corp., 2010 WL 2613086 (E.D. Mich. June 28, 2010) (patient dunned for $85 bill for anesthesia, which he refused to pay, as hospital records showed he owed no balance to hospital; unclear whether bill was from hospital or physician group within hospital); McNall v. Credit Bur. of Josephine Cnty., 689 F. Supp. 2d 1265 (D. Or. 2010) (collector reported hospital debts as delinquent to credit reporting agency despite consumer's dispute over bills due to lack of documentation); Univ. of Wis. Med. Found., Inc. v. Turner, 735 N.W.2d 195 (Wis. Ct. App. 2007) (*pro se* patient held liable for bill

9.2 Federal Fair Debt Collection Practices Act Claims Over Medical Debt

9.2.1 Applicability of FDCPA to Medical Debt

The full panoply of laws that protect consumers from abusive debt collection tactics, including the Fair Debt Collection Practices Act (FDCPA), are available to patients who have been subject to such tactics by health care providers and their collectors. The FDCPA clearly applies to medical debt.[80] It applies to third-party debt collectors collecting medical debt but may not apply to collection by medical providers' staff.[81] In addition to the FDCPA, consumers may have claims under the Telephone Consumer Protection Act, which provides for certain restrictions on automated and prerecorded telephone calls.[82] These claims are sometimes brought along with FDCPA claims.[83]

The FDCPA, other debt collection laws, and other consumer protection laws applicable to medical debt are discussed in detail in other treatises in this series.[84]

9.2.2 FDCPA Coverage of Various Actors in Medical Debt Collection

9.2.2.1 General

The fact that the FDCPA applies primarily to collection agencies and collection lawyers, and usually not to creditors, is not so significant in the health care field because hospitals and doctors are major users of collection agencies.[85] In addition, health care providers sell debts to debt buyers,[86] who are also covered under the FDCPA.[87] Some providers are also transferring

---

despite his confusion over the bill and questions as to whether services were actually provided for all of the charges).

80 Anderson v. DiDonato, 2012 WL 6553675 (E.D. Va. Nov. 19, 2012) ("debt incurred for medical services is the type of debt contemplated by the FDCPA"), *adopted by* 2012 WL 6561259 (E.D. Va. Dec. 14, 2012); Frazier v. Absolute Collection Serv., Inc., 767 F. Supp. 2d 1354 (N.D. Ga. 2011) ("plaintiff's obligation to pay a hospital bill that arose for personal purposes is a consumer debt"); Kelly v. Montgomery Lynch & Assocs., Inc., 2008 WL 1775251, at *3 (N.D. Ohio Apr. 15, 2008) (debt for medical services is "classic transaction out of which debts arise under the FDCPA"); Campion v. Credit Bureau Servs., Inc., 2000 U.S. Dist. LEXIS 20233 (E.D. Wash. Sept. 19, 2000); Finnegan v. Univ. of Rochester Med. Ctr., 21 F. Supp. 2d 223 (W.D.N.Y. 1998); Creighton v. Emporia Credit Servs., 981 F. Supp. 411 (E.D. Va. 1997); Adams v. Law Offices of Stuckert & Yates, 926 F. Supp. 521 (E.D. Pa. 1996) (even though consumer and physician expected consumer's insurer to pay the bill, still considered consumer's debt because consumer was ultimately responsible for paying); Bingham v. Collection Bureau, Inc., 505 F. Supp. 864 (D.N.D. 1981); Roger J. Fitzpatrick, Att'y, Div. of Credit Practices, Fed. Trade Comm'n, Informal Staff Letter to Thomas Isgrigg, Vice President, U.S. Credit Bureau Inc. (Dec. 22, 1992); Fed. Trade Comm'n, Official Staff Commentary to FDCPA § 803(5), 53 Fed. Reg. 50,097 (Dec. 13, 1988). *But see* Eades v. Kennedy, P.C. Law Offices, 2013 WL 6241272 (W.D.N.Y. Dec. 3, 2013) (nursing home debt owed pursuant to state necessaries statute or doctrine was not debt within meaning of FDCPA because it was a statutory obligation of support); Dokumaci v. MAF Collection Serv., 2010 WL 2560024 (M.D. Fla. June 17, 2010) (plaintiff failed to adequately plead that debt was a consumer debt; insufficient to simply allege that debt was owed to a hospital). *See generally* National Consumer Law Center, Fair Debt Collection § 4.4.2.2 (8th ed. 2014), *updated at* www.nclc.org/library.

81 *See* § 9.2.2, *infra*.

82 47 U.S.C. § 227. *See generally* National Consumer Law Center, Fair Debt Collection § 8.3.2 (8th ed. 2014), *updated at* www.nclc.org/library.

83 *See, e.g.*, Mais v. Gulf Coast Collection Bureau, 944 F. Supp. 2d 1226 (S.D. Fla. 2013) (patient did not provide consent for collector to call his cell phone when wife listed cell number on hospital admissions form; FCC ruling that consumer provides consent under TCPA by listing cell number on credit application form not entitled to Chevron deference or, in the alternative, does not apply to healthcare setting), *interlocutory appeal certified*; Whatley v. CreditWatch Serv., Ltd., 2012 WL 2885640 (E.D. Tex. July 13, 2012) (FDCPA and TCPA claims against medical debt collector for "robo-calls" that also failed to disclose collector's identity), *adopted by* 2012 WL 3151261 (E.D. Tex. Aug. 2, 2012); Yarbrough v. Credit Control Servs., Inc., 2011 WL 860435 (S.D. Fla. Feb. 12, 2011), *report and recommendation adopted by* 2011 WL 860431 (S.D. Fla. Mar. 9, 2011).

84 National Consumer Law Center, Fair Debt Collection (8th ed. 2014), *updated at* www.nclc.org/library; National Consumer Law Center, Fair Credit Reporting (8th ed. 2013), *updated at* www.nclc.org/library; National Consumer Law Center, Unfair and Deceptive Acts and Practices (8th ed. 2012), *updated at* www.nclc.org/library.

85 *See* Our View on Bill Collectors: Firms Employ Questionable Techniques to Collect Debts, USA Today, Sept. 13, 2010 (sidebar showing that health care bills constitute 42% of collections market and "health care companies are the biggest customers of third party debt collectors"); Robert M. Hunt, Fed. Reserve Bank of Philadelphia, *Collecting Consumer Debt in America*, Bus. Rev., at 13 (2d Qtr. 2007), *available at* www.philadelphiafed.org/research-and-data/publications/business-review/2007/q2/hunt_collecting-consumer-debt.pdf ("health-care providers represented the most important group of customers [for debt collectors], accounting for more than a quarter of all revenues"); Ass'n of Credit & Collection Prof'ls, White Paper—Healthcare Billing and Collections: The Industry Perspective (May 2004) (three-fifths of ACA members engaged in billing and collections for healthcare providers).

86 *See* Fed. Trade Comm'n, *Structure and Practices of the Debt Buying Industry*, at , T-4, T-7 (Jan. 2013), *available at* http://ftc.gov/os/2013/01/debtbuyingreport.pdf (finding that 17% of debt portfolios sold to debt buyers consists of medical debt; for debt that is sold from the original creditor—that is, not a resale by another debt buyer, that figure jumps to 33%); Cynthia Wilson, *Medical Debt Sellers Looking for Buyers in Weak Financial Market*, InsideARM, Jan. 23, 2009, www.insidearm.com/go/arm-news/medical-debt-sellers-looking-for-buyers-in-weak-financial-market (debt buyer stating it planned to buy $20 billion in medical debt receivables in 2009). *See also* Hosp. & Doctors Serv. Bureau v. Mitchell, 2007 WL 1136080 (N.J. Super. Ct. App. Div. Apr. 18, 2007) (hospital's nonprofit status did not bar it from assigning medical bills to debt buyer).

There are debt buyers that specialize in the purchase of medical debt. See, for example, www.medclr.com (debt buyer specializing in purchase of medical debt).

Interestingly, debt buyers appear to pay much less for medical debt than other types of debt, such as credit card accounts. *See* Fed. Trade Comm'n, Structure and Practices of the Debt Buying Industry 4, 24 (Jan. 2013) (prices for medical debt tend to be lower, and the average price for sold debts is four cents on the dollar); Kaulkin Ginsberg Co., Kaulkin Ginsberg Healthcare ARM Report 33 (2006) (hospital executive stated that his institution received a mere two to three cents for every dollar of medical debt sold).

87 *See* National Consumer Law Center, Fair Debt Collection § 4.2 (8th ed. 2014), *updated at* www.nclc.org/library. For more on debt buyers, see *id.*, at § 1.4.

medical debt to lenders, such as banks or finance companies.[88] These debts may be in default and, if so, the lenders should be covered by the FDCPA.[89] Yet it is unclear that these lenders are giving the notices required under the FDCPA.

9.2.2.2 Coverage of Debt Collectors Acting As Billing Service Providers

Debt collectors sometimes provide services to hospitals in addition to collection activities, such as providing admission and registration support, collecting financial information from patients to support a Medicaid or charity care application, providing customer support on billing questions, and conducting follow up with insurance companies.[90] Courts often find that these activities are not covered under the FDCPA,[91] because there is an exemption in the FDCPA for debts not in default.[92]

Unfortunately, the line between a debt that is in "default" and one that is not can be blurry in the context of medical debt.[93] In one case, a court extended the exemption into a legal gray area by holding that a medial bill was not in "default" even though it was overdue because the creditor's "state of mind" determined whether the debt was in default.[94] This approach is flawed as it depends on the subjective vagaries of the creditors, rather than examining the objective tri-party relationships between the creditor, the collection agency, and the consumer. However medical billing companies may be subject to state laws[95] or other regulatory schemes.[96] There are even state agencies that act as medical debt collectors;[97] they would not be subject to the FDCPA.[98]

Debt collectors that provide medical billing services to hospitals may cross the line into FDCPA-covered activities. A stark example is the arrangement between one of the nation's largest debt collectors, Accretive, L.L.C., and the Minnesota hospital chain Fairview Health Services. According to an investigation by the Minnesota attorney general, Fairview contracted with Accretive for the latter to take over the entire "revenue cycle" management for Fairview.[99] Accretive provided both admissions and billing services but, at the same time, also made an aggressive effort to collect past medical bills, an activity that would be covered under the FDCPA.[100] These aggressive debt collection tactics included requiring hospital employees to demand payment for past bills from patients seeking emergency room services; dunning patients for past-due bills at their bedside (with a special emphasis on pregnant women in delivery); and using confidential medical information to maximize debt collection recoveries.[101]

9.2.2.3 Coverage of Providers' In-House Collection Entities

While hospitals and doctors are generally "creditors" not subject to the FDCPA,[102] there are a number of instances in

88 Brian Grow & Robert Berner, Fresh Pain for the Uninsured, Bus. Week, Nov. 21, 2007. *See, e.g.*, Katiuzhinsky v. Perry, 62 Cal. Rptr. 3d 309 (Cal. Ct. App. 2007) (example of a specialized medical financing company to which hospitals sell accident victims' debts at a 50% discount; finance company then waits until tort recovery to collect full amount of debt).

89 *See* National Consumer Law Center, Fair Debt Collection § 4.2 (8th ed. 2014), *updated at* www.nclc.org/library.

90 Ass'n of Credit & Collection Prof'ls, White Paper—Healthcare Billing and Collections: The Industry Perspective (May 2004). *See, e.g.*, Gould v. ClaimAssist, 876 F. Supp. 2d 1018 (S.D. Ill. 2012) (company that helped hospitals process medical insurance claims was not a debt collector); Williams v. Emergency Groups Office, 2012 WL 1032700 (Cal. Ct. App. Mar. 28, 2012) (unpublished) (collector that provided both back office support for provider and engaged in debt collection activities).

91 Gould v. ClaimAssist, 876 F. Supp. 2d 1018 (S.D. Ill. 2012) (company that helps hospitals others process medical insurance claims was not a debt collector); Dickard v. Okla. Mgmt. Servs. for Physicians, L.L.C., 2007 WL 3025020 (W.D. Ark. Oct. 15, 2007) (company that provided billing service was not debt collector under FDCPA because debt was not in default when bill was sent); Healy v. Jzanus, Inc., 2006 WL 898067 (E.D.N.Y. Apr. 4, 2006) (FDCPA did not apply when service that both engaged in debt collection and processed Medicaid claims sent letter to debtor, because letter sought information for Medicaid application and debt was not in default). *Cf.* Williams v. Emergency Groups Office, 2012 WL 1032700 (Cal. Ct. App. Mar. 28, 2012) (unpublished) (upholding denial of class certification because class would have been overly broad given that collector also provided back office support for provider and thus not all communications for purpose of debt collection).

92 15 U.S.C. § 1692a(6)(F)(iii). *See generally* National Consumer Law Center, Fair Debt Collection § 4.3.10.1–4.3.10.3 (8th ed. 2014), *updated at* www.nclc.org/library.

93 *See, e.g.*, Whatley v. AHF Fin. Servs., L.L.C., 2012 WL 7159707 (E.D. Tex. Dec. 17, 2012) (court unable to determine on summary judgment whether defendant was a "debt collector" under FDCPA; arrangement between provider and company consisted of a "handshake agreement").

94 Roberts v. NRA Group, L.L.C., 2012 WL 3288076 (M.D. Pa. Aug. 10, 2012). For more discussion of this case, see National Consumer Law Center, Fair Debt Collection § 4.3.10.1–4.3.10.3 (8th ed. 2014), *updated at* www.nclc.org/library.

95 *See, e.g.*, Whatley v. AHF Fin. Servs., L.L.C., 2012 WL 7159707 (E.D. Tex. Dec. 17, 2012) (court unable to determine whether defendant was "debt collector" under FDCPA, but clearly covered under Texas debt collection law; debtor failed to allege damages under Texas act); Flores v. Rawlings Co., 177 P.3d 341 (Haw. 2008) (provider of "claims recovery services" was a collection agency under Hawaii law even though it asserted that it did not collect "debts"; Hawaii statute covers entity that collects "claims or money due on accounts" for another).

96 *See, e.g.*, Office of Inspector General, United States Dep't of Health & Human Servs., Compliance Program Guidance for Third-Party Medical Billing Companies, 63 Fed. Reg. 70,138 (Dec. 18, 1998).

97 Mike Bevel, *State Passes Bill Enabling It to Act As Debt Collector for Medical Bills* (May 14, 2007), *at* www.insidearm.com/2007/05/page/16 (scroll down webpage to find article).

98 *See* National Consumer Law Center, Fair Debt Collection § 4.3.4 (8th ed. 2014), *updated at* www.nclc.org/library.

99 Office of Minn. Att'y Gen., The Accretive Management Contracts, 1 Compliance Review of Fairview Health Services' Management Contracts with Accretive Health, Inc. (Apr. 2012), *available at* www.ag.state.mn.us.

100 Office of the Minn. Att'y Gen., Violations of Federal and State Debt Collection Laws, 5 Compliance Review of Fairview Health Services' Management Contracts with Accretive Health, Inc. (Apr. 2012), *available at* www.ag.state.mn.us/PDF/PressReleases/ComplianceReview/Vol. 5.pdf.

101 *Id.*

102 Sabeta v. Baptist Hosp. of Miami, Inc., 410 F. Supp. 2d 1224 (S.D. Fla. 2005) (FDCPA does not apply to hospital collecting its own debts in its own name); Kolari v. N.Y. Presbyterian Hosp., 382 F. Supp. 2d 562 (S.D.N.Y. 2005) (same), *vacated in part on other grounds*, 455 F.3d 118

which they have formed in-house or affiliated collection entities. These entities may be subject to the FDCPA. An example of one such entity was described in detail in *Orenbuch v. North Shore Health Systems*.[103] In *Orenbuch*, a group of hospitals formed Regional Claims Recovery Service (RCRS), a debt collection agency that was an unincorporated subdivision of a corporation that provided the hospitals' administrative support. RCRS had its own employees and computer system at a separate location. RCRS also actively marketed its services to hospitals outside the North Shore family and used its own letterhead. It was undisputed that RCRS was subject to the FDCPA.[104]

Other examples of similar entities have been described in Federal Trade Commission (FTC) informal staff letters.[105] For example, the FTC discussed the example of a nonprofit hospital that created a separate collection organization to collect debts for itself and other health care providers.[106] The FTC has stated that if a hospital and a debt collection agency do share common ownership, the agency should indicate its affiliation with the hospital when collecting the hospital's debts unless the agency is functionally independent of the hospital.[107] However, if an affiliated collection agency is actually staffed and run by another collection agency, it should operate under the name of the collection agency, as it controls the employees.[108]

Even if a health care provider does not use a separate entity or affiliate to collect its debts, the provider's own conduct might subject it to the FDCPA. For example, if a hospital's internal bill collector misrepresents that he or she is calling from a collection agency or a private law firm, both the employee and the hospital are covered by the FDCPA.[109] An FTC informal staff letter indicated that a hospital staff attorney's plan to send collection letters on letterhead, implying that he was a private practitioner without disclosing his hospital employment, would violate the FDCPA and subject both the hospital and the attorney to FDCPA liability.[110] A hospital that operated its collection division under a separate name instead of its true name was found to be a debt collector under the FDCPA and to have violated section 1692a(6) by sending a dunning letter using the fictitious name.[111] A provider that actively controlled the actions of a debt collector, including instructing the collector when to file suit and providing a copy of the applicable contract despite confidentiality provisions, was found to have violated the FDCPA.[112]

(2d Cir. 2006); Burton v. William Beaumont Hosp., 373 F. Supp. 2d 707 (E.D. Mich. 2005) (FDCPA does not apply to hospital collecting its own debts in its own name); Corely v. John D. Archibold Mem'l Hosp., Inc., 2005 WL 4732727 (M.D. Ga. Mar. 31, 2005). *See also* Mitchell v. Kaiser Found. Health Plan, Inc., 2010 WL 5387712 (N.D. Cal. Dec. 22, 2010) (health insurer is not "debt collector" under FDCPA). *But see* Umoh v. Marks, 2010 WL 2651939 (N.D.N.Y. June 25, 2010) (medical facility that sent bills to patients on behalf of doctor could be debt collector under FDCPA, although court was "deeply skeptical" of the allegations); Blanford v. St. Vincent Hosp. & Health Care Ctr., Inc., 2009 WL 500527 (S.D. Ind. Feb. 27, 2009) (hospital could be a debt collector under the "false name" exception if third-party debt collector acted at the hospital's direction and did not exercise independent judgment); Pickering v. Coast Ctr. for Orthopedic Arthroscopic Surgery & Treatment, 2009 WL 932629 (Cal. Ct. App. Apr. 8, 2009) (unpublished) (provider could be liable under FDCPA because of its significant control and active involvement in debt collector's unlawful and fraudulent collector efforts). *See generally* National Consumer Law Center, Fair Debt Collection § 4.3.2 (8th ed. 2014), *updated at* www.nclc.org/library.

103 250 F. Supp. 2d 145 (E.D.N.Y. 2003).

104 *Id.* (finding no violation of the FDCPA for failure to disclose the relationship between RCRS and affiliated hospitals). *See* Carlson v. Long Island Jewish Med. Ctr., 378 F. Supp. 2d 128 (E.D.N.Y. 2005) (case also involving Regional Claims Recovery Service). *See also* Healy v. Jzanus, Ltd., 2002 WL 31654571 (E.D.N.Y. Nov. 20, 2002) (FDCPA applied to unincorporated association called "Medicaid Recovery Services" that sought information for Medicaid application but also included in its letters a "balance due" and statement that "this is an attempt to collect a debt").

105 *See* National Consumer Law Center, Fair Debt Collection § 3.2.5 (8th ed. 2014), *updated at* www.nclc.org/library (discussing legal status of FTC informal staff letters).

106 Informal Staff Letter from Norman E. Oliver, Att'y, Div. of Credit Practices, Fed. Trade Comm'n, to Joan M. Healy, Att'y (Dec. 2, 1981) (noting that use of an attorney letterhead by collector's staff attorney without indicating attorney's employment by collector would violate FDCPA subjecting collector and attorney to liability).

107 Informal Staff Letter from Jonathan D. Jerison, Att'y, Div. of Credit Practices, Fed. Trade Comm'n, to William E. Roach, Jr., Att'y, Gardner, Carton & Douglas (Nov. 8, 1983).

108 *Id.*; Orenbuch v. North Shore Health Sys., 250 F. Supp. 2d 145 (E.D.N.Y. 2003) (not deceptive to use name under which affiliated but functionally separate collector was licensed; disclosure of corporate affiliation not required).

109 Lester E. Cox Med. Ctr. v. Huntsman, 408 F.3d 989 (8th Cir. 2005) (use of fictitious name violated FDCPA); Hartley v. Suburban Radiologic Consultants, Ltd., 2013 WL Y5467300 (D. Minn. Sept. 30, 2013) (patient stated claim for provider's use of "flat rating," that is, use of letterhead creating false impression that a collection agency is dunning the patient); Alarcon v. TransUnion Mktg., 2007 WL 1201624 (N.D. Ohio Apr. 20, 2007) (claim for flat rating); Sabeta v. Baptist Hosp. of Miami, Inc., 410 F. Supp. 2d 1224 (S.D. Fla. 2005) (granting leave to amend to allege use of fictitious name); Carlson v. Long Island Jewish Med. Ctr., 378 F. Supp. 2d 128 (E.D.N.Y. 2005) (denying hospital's motion to dismiss FDCPA claim when plaintiff alleged use of fictitious name); Cargile v. Baylor Health Care Sys., 2005 WL 2445482 (N.D. Tex. Aug. 10, 2005) (granting leave to amend to allege use of fictitious name with respect to collection of debts against plaintiffs). *But see* Medica Self-Insured v. Tenet Healthcare Corp., 2007 WL 1385589 (D. Minn. May 4, 2007) (hospital entity that used fictitious name to collect debts, but disclosed that it was hospital's collection department, was not debt collector under FDCPA). *See generally* National Consumer Law Center, Fair Debt Collection § 4.2.5 (8th ed. 2014), *updated at* www.nclc.org/library.

110 Informal Staff Letter from Alan D. Reffkin, Att'y, Div. of Credit Practices, Fed. Trade Comm'n, to James E. McDonald, Esq. (Apr. 10, 1980).

111 Lester E. Cox Med. Ctr. v. Huntsman, 408 F.3d 989 (8th Cir. 2005). *See also* Blanford v. St. Vincent Hosp. & Health Care Ctr., Inc., 2009 WL 500527 (S.D. Ind. Feb. 27, 2009) (hospital could be a debt collector under the "false name" exception if third-party debt collector acted at the hospital's direction and did not exercise independent judgment). *But see* Mahan v. Laboratory Corp. of Am., 2011 WL 836674 (S.D. Ala. Mar. 9, 2011) (medical laboratory did not deceptively use separate name and was not a debt collector under FDCPA when it sent bills using name "LCA Collections, a division of Laboratory Corp. of America").

112 Pickering v. Coast Ctr. for Orthopedic Arthroscopic Surgery & Treatment, 2009 WL 932629 (Cal. Ct. App. Apr. 8, 2009) (unpublished).

9.2.2.4 Limited CFPB Supervision over Medical Debt Collectors

One significant difference between medical debt and other consumer debt is that collectors who exclusively or predominately collect medical debt are not likely to be supervised by the Consumer Financial Protection Bureau (CFPB). Under the Dodd-Frank Wall Street Reform and Consumer Protection Act, the CFPB has supervisory and enforcement authority over "larger participants" in a market for consumer financial products and services.[113] The CFPB has defined "larger participants" as any debt collector with receipts over $10 million.[114] However, medical debts are not included in the calculation of this $10 million threshold.[115] Thus, if a debt collector exclusively or predominately collects medical debts (and does not have $10 million in receipts from other types of consumer debt), they will not be considered a "larger participant" for purposes of CFPB authority.

9.2.3 Examples of FDCPA Violations by Medical Bill Collectors

There have been many instances of medical collection agencies, and even providers, violating the FDCPA. Collectors and providers have violated the FDCPA's general prohibitions against:

- Harassment;[116]
- Deception;[117] and
- Unfair debt collection practices.[118]

There have also been examples of when medical bill collectors:

- Failed to provide consumers with appropriate notices under the FDCPA;[119]

---

113 12 U.S.C. § 5514(a)(1)(B).

114 12 C.F.R. § 1090.105.

115 12 C.F.R. § 1090.105(a)(3)(v).

116 *See, e.g.*, White v. Emergency Billing & Coding Co., 2013 WL 4551919 (E.D. Mich. Aug. 28, 2013) (collector sent text message to mother of disabled debtor stating, "B**ch will coming to your f**king house and blow your to [sic] stupid ass up you dumb ad [sic] B**CH"); Summers v. Merchants and Medical Credit Corp., 2013 WL 1507529 (E.D. Mich. Apr. 12, 2013) (collector called consumer a liar and threatened to refer account for lawsuit if consumer did not obtain a credit card to pay off debt); Douyon v. N.Y. Med. Healthcare, P.C., 894 F. Supp. 2d 24 (E.D.N.Y. 2012) (debt collector retained by hospital threatened, "I'm gonna see about coming with the sheriff and have you arrested"), *later proceeding at* 2013 WL 5423800 (E.D.N.Y. Sept. 25, 2013) (granting summary judgment to consumer on FDCPA claim); Smyth v. Merchants' Credit Corp., 2012 WL 588744 (W.D. Wash. Feb. 22, 2012) (collector of hospital bill "vilified, threatened, embarrassed, humiliated and overwhelmed" consumer); Smith v. ProCollect, Inc., 2011 WL 1375667 (E.D. Tex. Apr. 12, 2011) (collector for dentist's bill allegedly called consumer as much as six times per day and called her an obscene name); Klemen v. Prof'l Collection Systems, 2011 WL 31396 (M.D. Fla. Jan. 4, 2011) (collector stated to debtor: "pay your damn bills" and called three or four times per day to harass debtor); Dokumaci v. MAF Collection Serv., 2010 WL 2560024 (M.D. Fla. June 17, 2010) (collector called debtor constantly and continuously five times every Sunday for several weeks); Herber v. Prof'l Adjustment Corp., 2010 WL 2103025 (M.D. Fla. May 25, 2010) (collector made constant and continuous calls over hospital bill, used abusive language, and told consumer he should "give up 'luxuries' and pay the bill"); McNall v. Credit Bureau of Josephine Cnty., 689 F. Supp. 2d 1265 (D. Or. 2010) (process server for medical debt collector went to consumer's house and repeatedly yelled in a loud voice for consumer to "come out"); Majeski v. I.C. Sys., Inc., 2010 WL 145861 (N.D. Ill. Jan. 8, 2010) (collector for doctor called sixty-seven times in six months, sometimes in two- to five-hour intervals); Baruch v. Healthcare Receivable Mgmt., Inc., 2007 WL 3232090 (E.D.N.Y. Oct. 30, 2007) (aggressive dunning by medical debt collector, including repeated letters, calls, and threats, over debt for which provider had agreed to not to bill patient and accept whatever Medicaid paid); Flamm v. Sarner & Assoc., P.C., 2006 WL 43770 (E.D. Pa. Jan. 3, 2006) (process server hired by collection attorney repeatedly showed up to debtor's workplace, informed debtor's supervisor that debtor owed large debt to doctor, and made accusations in loud and aggressive tone to administrative assistant that plaintiff was "sneaky little thief" who "stole thousands of dollars from a doctor"); Joseph v. J.J. Mac Intyre Companies, 238 F. Supp. 2d 1158 (N.D. Cal. 2002) (barrage of phone calls to disabled senior citizen, despite requests to stop). *See generally* Steve Tripoli & Chi Chi Wu, National Consumer Law Center, Unhealthy Pursuits: How the Sick and Vulnerable Are Harmed by Abusive Medical Debt Collection Tactics (Dec. 2005), *available online as companion material to this treatise*.

117 *See, e.g.*, Kelley v. Med-1 Solutions, L.L.C., 548 F.3d 600 (7th Cir. 2008) (debt collector sued in its own name in state court, despite fact that hospital continued to own the debt and did not assign it to debt collector; *Rooker-Feldman* doctrine barred FDCPA claim); Lester E. Cox Med. Ctr. v. Huntsman, 408 F.3d 989 (8th Cir. 2005) (FDCPA violation to use letterhead bearing name that appeared to be third-party collection agency, when agency was owned by hospital); Shields v. Merchants & Med. Credit Corp., 2010 WL 2613086 (E.D. Mich. June 28, 2010) (granting summary judgment to plaintiff on claim that collector violated FDCPA by telling consumer that only way to remove disputed medical debt from credit report was to pay it); Blanford v. St. Vincent Hosp. & Health Care Ctr., Inc., 2009 WL 500527 (S.D. Ind. Feb. 27, 2009) (following *Kelley v. Med-1 Solutions*); *In re* Cambron, 2007 WL 4287376 (M.D. Ala. Dec. 5, 2007) (medical collector violated FDCPA by implying potential garnishment or attachment over time-barred debt with letter stating it would be seeking information about consumer's assets and income); Carlson v. Long Island Jewish Med. Ctr., 378 F. Supp. 2d 128 (E.D.N.Y. 2005) (use of fictitious name may violate FDCPA); Weiss v. Collection Ctr., Inc., 667 N.W.2d 567 (N.D. 2003) (consumers stated FDCPA claim against clinic's collector for sending letter informing consumers that collector had obtained information from DMV about consumer's vehicle; letter could be read by unsophisticated consumer as threat to seize vehicle).

118 Mikula v. Great Lakes Fin. Servs., Inc., 2004 WL 1656556 (N.D. Ill. July 22, 2004) (FDCPA claim against hospital for balance billing in violation of hospital's preferred provider agreement with insurer); Carroll v. Butterfield Health Care, Inc., 2003 WL 22462604 (N.D. Ill. Oct. 29, 2003) (nursing home violated Medicaid law by requiring personal guarantee of patient's son-in-law; son-in-law stated FDCPA claim against attorney-collector for suing on illegal guarantee); Edwards v. McCormick, 136 F. Supp. 2d 795 (S.D. Ohio 2001) (demanding payment of medical bill from non-debtor spouse and threatening forced sale of home contrary to state exemption law violated FDCPA); Finnegan v. Univ. of Rochester Med. Ctr., 21 F. Supp. 2d 223 (W.D.N.Y. 1998) (denying motion to dismiss when collector continued to attempt to collect debt it knew was disputed and reported the debt to credit reporting agency).

119 Summers v. Merchants & Med. Credit Corp., 2013 WL 1507529 (E.D. Mich. Apr. 12, 2013) (collector failed to send validation notice required by FDCPA); Anderson v. DiDonato, 2012 WL 6553675 (E.D. Va. Nov. 19, 2012) (medical collector failed to provide validation notice and mini-Miranda warnings within five days of initial communication), *adopted by* 2012 WL 6561259 (E.D. Va. Dec. 14, 2012); Searle v. Credit

- Failed to disclose their identities in telephone calls and disclose that the calls were from a debt collector;[120]
- Sued consumers in an inappropriate forum;[121]
- Failed to abide by a cease communications request;[122]
- Failed to verify debts and respond to requests for validation as required by the FDCPA;[123]
- Contacted debtors represented by counsel;[124]
- Contacted third parties for information beyond location information;[125]
- Engaged in "flat-rating," that is, the practice of a creditor collecting its own debts by using a debt collector's letterhead to add intimidation value;[126]
- Sent debt verification notices that instructed debtors to direct questions regarding insurance filings with insurers, which could mislead debtors into believing that they should resolve debt collection issues by pursuing claim with insurers;[127]
- Attempted to collect against consumers who had filed for bankruptcy protection, in violation of the automatic stay or discharge injunction;[128]
- Sued[129] or threatened to sue[130] consumers on debts past the expiration of the statute of limitations;
- Misstated the amount of a debt as more than legally owed;[131]

Adjustments, Inc., 2012 WL 1079328 (M.D. Pa. Mar. 30, 2012) (medical collector's letter, allegedly first, failed to include validation notice and mini-Miranda warnings); Smith v. ProCollect, Inc., 2011 WL 1375667 (E.D. Tex. Apr. 12, 2011) (collector for dentist's bill allegedly failed to provide FDCPA-required validation language); Stair *ex rel.* Smith v. Thomas & Cook, 254 F.R.D. 191 (D.N.J. 2008) (medical debt collector sent letters with language that contradicted notice of validation rights); Santoro v. Aargon Agency, Inc., 252 F.R.D. 675 (D. Nev. 2008) (medical debt buyer failed to include right to validation notice, itemize additional charges, and list creditor's name in its collection letters; granting class certification); Cinelli v. MCS Claims Servs., Inc., 236 F.R.D. 118 (E.D.N.Y. 2006) (class action settlement of FDCPA claim that verification letter from hospital's debt collector that failed to inform debtors that disputes over validity of the debt must be in writing); Williams v. Emergency Groups' Office, 2012 WL 1032700 (Cal. Ct. App. Mar. 28, 2012) (unpublished) (collector for medical center failed to provide validation notice and to disclose that communications were from a debt collector; class certification denied).

120 Whatley v. CreditWatch Serv., Ltd., 2012 WL 2885640 (E.D. Tex. July 13, 2012), *adopted by* 2012 WL 3151261 (E.D. Tex. Aug. 2, 2012); Frazier v. Absolute Collection Serv., Inc., 767 F. Supp. 2d 1354 (N.D. Ga. 2011).

121 Tedrow v. Cowles, 2007 WL 2688276 (S.D. Ohio Sept. 12, 2007) (class certification of FDCPA and UDAP action alleging that attorney for hospital filed collection actions in Ohio county where patients neither resided nor received services); Jones v. Ginn, Clearinghouse No. 48,160 (N.D. Ohio 1992) (consent judgment) (in case settlement hospital's debt collectors enjoined from bringing civil suit against consumers in a distant forum, that is, a state court located in state other than that in which consumer resides); Jack Mailman & Leonard Flug, D.D.S. v. Whaley, 2002 WL 31988623 (N.Y. Civ. Ct. Nov. 25, 2002) (venue improper under state or federal statute when Brooklyn consumers were sued in Staten Island court; court expresses disapproval of attorney-collector's practice of bringing large volume of collection cases there and orders collector to bring future suits in the county where the debtor resides).

122 Marino v. Hoganwillig, P.L.L.C., 910 F. Supp. 2d 492 (W.D.N.Y. 2012); Bishop v. I.C. Sys., Inc., 713 F. Supp. 2d 1361 (M.D. Fla. 2010) (granting summary judgment to consumer); Barton v. Revenue Corp., 2007 WL 892994 (N.D. Ohio Mar. 21, 2007); Clark v. Capital Credit & Collection Servs., Inc., 2004 WL 1305326 (D. Or. Jan. 23, 2004), *aff'd in relevant part, rev'd in part*, 460 F.3d 1162 (9th Cir. 2006), *aff'd in part*, 198 Fed. Appx. 623 (9th Cir. 2006).

123 Moscona v. California Bus. Bur., Inc., 2011 WL 5085522 (S.D. Cal. Oct. 25, 2011) (medical bill collector violated FDCPA by reporting debt to credit reporting agencies before validating it in response to validation request; summary judgment for consumer); Smith v. ProCollect, Inc., 2011 WL 1375667 (E.D. Tex. Apr. 12, 2011) (collector of dentist's bill allegedly failed to provide verification when consumer requested it); Wielicki v. HMC Group, 2009 WL 2496642 (N.D. Ohio Aug. 13, 2009).

124 Echlin v. Asset Systems, Inc., 2013 WL 308984 (W.D. Wash. Juan. 25, 2013); Walch v. Columbia Collection Serv., Inc., 2012 WL 4093826 (D. Or. June 19, 2012), *adopted by* 2012 WL 4092651 (D. Or. Sept. 17, 2012); Klemen v. Prof'l Collection Systems, 2011 WL 31396 (M.D. Fla. Jan. 4, 2011); Zaborac v. Mutual Hosp. Serv., Inc., 2004 WL 2538643 (S.D. Ind. Oct. 7, 2004) (debt collector violated FDCPA's prohibition against communicating with consumer known to be represented by counsel; bona fide error defense allowed).

125 Anderson v. DiDonato, 2012 WL 6553675 (E.D. Va. Nov. 19, 2012) (medical collector contacted debtor's daughter and left her message that civil warrant would be served on debtor unless payment made), *adopted by* 2012 WL 6561259 (E.D. Va. Dec. 14, 2012); Douyon v. N.Y. Med. Healthcare, P.C., 894 F. Supp. 2d 245 (E.D.N.Y. 2012)(freelance debt collector frequently retained by hospital showed up at consumer's workplace and discussed debt in presence of consumer's coworkers); Shand-Pistilli v. Prof'l Account Servs., Inc., 2010 WL 2978029 (E.D. Pa. July 26, 2010).

126 Lester E. Cox Med. Ctr. v. Huntsman, 408 F.3d 989 (8th Cir. 2005); Hartley v. Suburban Radiologic Consultants, Ltd., 2013 WL 5467300 (D. Minn. Sept. 30, 2013) (certifying FDCPA class); Alarcon v. TransUnion Mktg., 2007 WL 1201624 (N.D. Ohio Apr. 20, 2007) (patient stated claim for provider's use of "flat rating").

127 Smith v. Paramount Recovery Sys., 2008 WL 4951227 (D.N.J. Nov. 18, 2008).

128 Yu v. Kevin B. Wilson Law Offices, 919 F. Supp. 2d 661 (D. Md. 2013) (collector dunned debtor for hospital debt after debtor filed for bankruptcy; bona fide error defense allowed); Eide v. Colltech, Inc., 2013 WL 6499413 (D. Minn. Dec. 11, 2013) (collector dunned debtor for hospital debt discharged in bankruptcy); Walch v. Columbia Collection Serv., Inc., 2012 WL 4093826 (D. Or. June 19, 2012) (collector dunned debtor for hospital debt discharged in bankruptcy, including obtaining default collection judgment, garnishing debtor's wages, and illegally contacting employer), *adopted by* 2012 WL 4092651 (D. Or. Sept. 17, 2012); Bacelli v. MFP, Inc., 729 F. Supp. 2d 1328 (M.D. Fla. 2010) (debt collection attempts in violation of automatic stay and discharge injunction; hospital placed account with debt collector despite receiving notices of patient's bankruptcy filing and discharge); *In re* Wingard, 382 B.R. 892 (Bankr. W.D. Pa. 2008) (characterizing medical debt collector's actions as "repugnant of our bankruptcy process").

129 *New Jersey Settles with Medical Collection Agency*, Inside ARM, June 16, 2009, *available at* www.insidearm.com/go/arm-news/new-jersey-settles-with-medical-collection-agency (New Jersey attorney general's settlement with medical debt buyer that attempted to collect debts that were very old and past the statute of limitations); Fred Schulte & James Drew, *Their Day in Court*, Balt. Sun, Dec. 22, 2008 (study by *Baltimore Sun* found 132,000 lawsuits filed by hospitals in the last five years, some of which were for debts more than three years old; Maryland statute of limitations is three and a half years; at least one instance of time-barred lawsuit documented).

130 Fallon v. Quality Asset Recovery, L.L.C., 2013 WL 3770684 (E.D. Pa. July 17, 2013) (patient stated FDCPA claim for threat of lawsuit over debt past the statute of limitation).

131 Pipiles v. Credit Bur. of Lockport, Inc., 886 F.2d 22 (2d. Cir. 1989) (attempt to collect debt which included amount incurred by

- Dunned or sued consumers who were not liable for the debt;[132]
- Agreed to take a post-dated check, then threatened or sought criminal prosecution when it was returned unpaid;[133]
- Collected debts already paid by insurance, government programs, or the debtor;[134]
- Attempted to collect debts that were disputed by the consumer while failing to provide the validation required by the FDCPA;[135]
- Sued consumers for debts that had been forgiven under a charity care program;[136]
- Falsely threatened imminent legal action;[137]
- Sued consumers for debts that the provider had not assigned to the collector;[138]
- Demanded repayment of illegal and excessive collection fees not authorized by contract or state law;[139]
- Made unauthorized withdrawals from consumer's bank account;[140]
- Dunned consumers who clearly did not receive the services allegedly incurred;[141] and

---

ex-husband's new wife, for which consumer was not legally liable); Anderson v. Good Shepard Hosp., Inc., 2011 WL 846091 (E.D. Tex. Mar. 8, 2011) (collector dunned Medicare patient for hospital charges in excess of liability insurance proceeds, in violation of Medicare rules); Grden v. Leiken, Ingber & Winters, P.C., 2010 WL 199947 (E.D. Mich. Jan. 19, 2010) (collection firm misstated amount of debt, but dismissing FDCPA case on basis that misstatement was not in connection with collection of a debt).

132 Mellinger v. Midwest Audit Serv., 2012 WL 405008 (E.D. Mich. Feb. 8, 2012) (collector dunned husband for wife's medical bills); Robinson v. Credit Serv. Co., 1991 WL 186665 (D.N.J. Sept. 16, 1991) (dunning a parent of a twenty-year-old child for the child's medical bill may misrepresent a parent's liability, in violation of FDCPA); CMRE Fin. Serv., Inc. v. Parton, 109 Cal. Rptr. 3d 139 (Cal. Ct. App. 2010) (consumer stated FDCPA claim against collector for lawsuit against her over medical bills owed by ex-husband for which she did not have liability).

133 Van Buren v. Cave, 2008 WL 4664227 (M.D. La. Oct. 21, 2008); Kelly v. Montgomery Lynch & Assocs., Inc., 2008 WL 1775251 (N.D. Ohio Apr. 15, 2008).

134 *New Jersey Settles with Medical Collection Agency*, Inside ARM, June 16, 2009, *available at* www.insidearm.com/go/arm-news/new-jersey-settles-with-medical-collection-agency (New Jersey attorney general's settlement with medical debt buyer that attempted to collect debts which patients claimed had already been paid by insurers). *See also* Smyth v. Merchants Credit Corp., 2012 WL 588744 (W.D. Wash. Feb. 22, 2012) (FDCPA claim arising from collection of hospital bill already paid by insurance); Meyer v. Debt Recovery Solutions of Ohio, Inc., 2010 WL 3515663 (N.D. Ohio Sept. 2, 2010) (garnishment for hospital bill despite fact that patient had already paid debt collector for bill); Loggins v. Diagnostic Radiology of Nacogdoches, 2010 WL 3783382 (E.D. Tex. Aug. 30, 2010) (collector dunned consumer for bill already paid by third party), *report and recommendation adopted by* 2010 WL 3783147 (E.D. Tex. Sept. 17, 2010); Trunzo v. Debt Recovery Solutions of Ohio, Inc., 2012 WL 6680359 (Ohio Ct. App. Dec. 19, 2012) (consumers sued for several bills, two of which they paid already; dismissal of FDCPA claims by *pro se* consumers who only alleged failure to give FDCPA notices); Joseph Neff, *Persistent Collections Not Unique to Charlotte Area*, Charlotte Observer, Apr. 23, 2012 (jury award of $37,501 in FDCPA case against medical debt collector demanding payment of $501 bill that patient had already paid). *Cf.* Evans v. Trans Union, L.L.C., 2011 WL 672061 (S.D. Va. Feb. 14, 2011) (medical center wrongfully reported bill already paid by insurance on plaintiff's credit report).

135 Leeb v. Nationwide Credit Corp., 2013 WL 6169408 (N.D. Ill. Nov. 21, 2013) (consumer disputed debt, alleging insurer should have paid it but provider failed to provide required documentation).

136 Mansour-White v. Grant & Weber, 2013 WL 5616960 (Cal. Ct. App. Oct. 15, 2013) (unpublished) (reversing malicious prosecution and Rosenthal Act judgments for consumer because malice not shown and violation of Rosenthal Act was due to bona fide error).

137 Summers v. Merchants & Med. Credit Corp., 2013 WL 1507529 (E.D. Mich. Apr. 12, 2013) (threatening to refer account for lawsuit if consumer did not obtain a credit card to pay off debt); Anderson v. DiDonato, 2012 WL 6553675 (E.D. Va. Nov. 19, 2012) (medical collector made several threats to serve civil warrant on consumer but never filed legal action), *adopted by* 2012 WL 6561259 (E.D. Va. Dec. 14, 2012); Searle v. Credit Adjustments, Inc., 2012 WL 1079328 (M.D. Pa. Mar. 30, 2012) (medical collector's letter threatened garnishment and loss of patient's home but allegedly could not take such actions); Kelly v. Montgomery Lynch & Assocs., Inc., 2008 WL 1775251 (N.D. Ohio Apr. 15, 2008) (soliciting post-dated checks and then threatening criminal prosecution when patient could not be prosecuted for passing bad check); *In re* Cambron, 2007 WL 4287376 (M.D. Ala. Dec. 5, 2007) (deceptive to imply that medical debt collector could garnish wages or seize assets to recover time-barred debts); Bankston v. Phycom Corp., 2007 WL 4170627 (N.D. Cal. Nov. 19, 2007); Kreek v. Phycom Corp., 2007 WL 1229315 (N.D. Cal. Apr. 25, 2007).

138 Wayne Hosp. Co. v. Palmer, 2013 WL 5724506 (S.D. Ohio Oct. 21, 2013) (provider alleged that collector violated the FDCPA when he kept trying to collect provider's debts after provider had fired him; dismissed for lack of standing); Eager v. Credit Bureau Collection Servs., Inc., 2013 WL 5719224 (W.D. Mich. Oct. 18, 2013) (collector sued consumers for debts owed to multiple providers, including providers that had not assigned their debts to the collector; dismissing UDAP and some but not all FDCPA claims on the basis of res judicata/collateral estoppel).

139 Shula v. Lawent, 359 F.3d 489 (7th Cir. 2004) (agency collecting doctor's bill; deceptive to demand specific amount of court costs in absence of court order when Illinois law made award of costs discretionary); Moscona v. California Bus. Bureau, Inc., 2011 WL 5085522 (S.D. Cal. Oct. 25, 2011) (medical debt collector attempted to collect interest on bill from date of service, not when bill became delinquent a year later; not authorized by contract, summary judgment for consumer); Agostino v. Quest Diagnostics, 2011 WL 5410667 (D.N.J. Nov. 3, 2011) (summary judgment for consumer on FDCPA claim that collector added fee not permitted by provider's contract with insurer); Quesenberry v. Alliant Law Group, P.C., 2010 WL 1189457 (E.D. Tex. Mar. 5, 2010) (medical bill collector charged interest not authorized by Texas law), *report and recommendation adopted by* 2010 WL 1189481 (E.D. Tex. Mar. 24, 2010); Majeski v. I.C. Sys., Inc., 2010 WL 145861 (N.D. Ill. Jan. 8, 2010) (collector sought 19% collection fee when allegedly not entitled to fee under the contract); Kelly v. Montgomery Lynch & Assocs., Inc., 2008 WL 1775251, at *3 (N.D. Ohio Apr. 15, 2008) (medical debt collector charged $5 fee per check not authorized by contract); Adams v. A & S Collection Assocs., Inc., 2007 WL 2206935 (D. Conn. July 23, 2007) (doctor's bill added a 49% collection fee and 18% interest in violation of state law), *subsequent proceeding at* 2007 WL 2206936 (D. Conn. July 30, 2007); Foster v. D.B.S. Collection Agency, 463 F. Supp. 2d 783 (S.D. Ohio 2006) (debt collector filed improperly filed lawsuits without legal capacity, sought attorney fees in violation of state law and sued spouses of medical debtors without showing necessaries doctrine applied). *But see* Bradley v. Franklin Collection Serv., Inc., 2013 WL 1346714 (N.D. Ala. Mar. 28, 2013) (addition of 33% collection fee to medical debts did not violate FDCPA or RICO; fee permitted when provider's agreement allowed for "reasonable" collection fees).

140 Anderson v. DiDonato, 2012 WL 6553675 (E.D. Va. Nov. 19, 2012), *adopted by* 2012 WL 6561259 (E.D. Va. Dec. 14, 2012).

141 Mavilla v. Absolute Collection Serv., Inc., ___ Fed. Appx. ___, 2013 WL 4799313 (4th Cir. Sept. 10, 2013) (consumer dunned for obstetrical services despite fact that she was incapable of bearing children).

- Sued victims of identity theft for medical bills incurred by the thief.[142]

Violations of other laws could violate the FDCPA. In particular, a violation of the prohibition against a provider "balance billing" a consumer—that is, seeking to collect more from a consumer than what Medicare, Medicaid, or other insurers would pay[143]—could violate the FDCPA or state debt collection laws.[144]

FDCPA claims may be asserted in individual suits against the collection agency, as one of several counts in a broader health services class action, or as a counterclaim or third-party complaint in a collection suit filed by a collection agency or a health care provider.

9.3 Federal Statutes Applicable to Medical Debt

9.3.1 The Patient Protection and Affordable Care Act of 2010

9.3.1.1 Introduction

The enactment of the Patient Protection and Affordable Care Act of 2010 (Affordable Care Act),[145] that is, the health care reform law, brought significant changes to the health care and health insurance landscape in the United States. Among its many provisions, there are a number of consumer protections, such as:

- Prohibitions against insurance companies refusing to provide coverage or renew policies because of a consumer's preexisting medical conditions;[146]
- Prohibitions against insurance companies revoking or "rescinding" coverage from patients when they become ill;[147] and
- Provisions that eliminate lifetime caps on insurance coverage and restrict annual limits on coverage.[148]

There are a number of resources on these and other protections of the Affordable Care Act.[149] With respect to the issue of medical debt, the Act added a provision to the Internal Revenue Code governing charity care and debt collection by not-for-profit hospitals.[150] This provision established four requirements that hospitals must meet in order to qualify for tax-exempt status under section 501(c)(3) of the Internal Revenue Code. Tax-exempt hospitals:

- Must develop written financial assistance policies;[151]
- Are prohibited from imposing chargemaster rates[152] and must provide discounts for patients eligible for financial assistance;[153]
- Are prohibited from engaging in "extraordinary" collection actions until after they make a reasonable effort to determine eligibility for assistance;[154] and
- Must conduct regular community needs assessments.[155]

The first three requirements are discussed below. The IRS is charged with the enforcement of these requirements and has authority to issue further guidance and regulations.[156] The IRS issued proposed regulations in June 2012.[157] Final regulations have not yet been promulgated but, in December 2013, the IRS issued guidance advising non-profit hospitals that they may rely on the proposed regulations until final ones are issued.[158]

---

142 Howard v. Reid Hosp., 2012 WL 3269690 (S.D. Ohio Aug. 10, 2012) (FDCPA barred by Rooker-Feldman because victim lost small claims action), *adopted by* 2012 WL 3731689 (S.D. Ohio Aug. 28, 2012).

143 *See* § 9.3.7, *infra*.

144 *See, e.g.*, Marshall v. Bonded Adjustment Co., 2012 WL 6190616 (E.D. Wash. Dec. 12, 2012) (provider balance billed consumer and sued for bill that was covered by worker's compensation insurance; no FDCPA or UDAP violation because insurer did not confirm it would "accept" bill and make payment until after lawsuit was filed); Weathers v. Gem City Account Serv., Inc., 2010 WL 3210985 (C.D. Ill. Aug. 13, 2010) (patient stated FDCPA claim for misrepresentation of legal status of debt when collector dunned patient for doctor's bill that had been submitted to Medicaid and had been denied reimbursement); Pickering v. Coast Ctr. for Orthopedic Arthroscopic Surgery & Treatment, 2009 WL 932629 (Cal. Ct. App. Apr. 8, 2009) (unpublished) (provider violated FDCPA and state fair debt law by suing patient even after provider had received payment from insurer, in violation of contractual prohibition against balance billing); Mikula v. Great Lakes Fin. Servs., Inc., 2004 WL 1656556 (N.D. Ill. July 22, 2004) (FDCPA claim against hospital for balance billing in violation of hospital's preferred provider agreement with insurer). *Cf.* Agostino v. Quest Diagnostics, Inc., 2011 WL 5410667 (D.N.J. Nov. 3, 2011) (summary judgment for consumer on FDCPA claim that collector added fee not permitted by provider's contract with insurer); Fla. Health Sciences Ctr., Inc. v. Elsenheimer, 952 So. 2d 575 (Fla. Dist. Ct. App. 2007) (challenge to Medicaid balance billing under state debt collection statute; class action status denied for lack of commonality or typicality). *But see* Richmond v. Higgins, 435 F.3d 825 (8th Cir. 2006) (no FDCPA violation for debt collection activities that may have violated Medicaid balance billing provisions, because plaintiff's attorney failed to raise issue until six months after first debt collection attempt); Nelson-McGourty v. L & P Fin. Adjusters, Inc., 2010 WL 3190711 (N.D. Ill. Aug. 12, 2010) (no FDCPA violation because collector ceased demanding payment once it learned that debt was subject of worker's compensation claim).

145 Pub. L. 111-148 (2010), *as amended by* the Health Care and Education Reconciliation Act of 2010, Pub. L. 111-152 (2010).

146 42 U.S.C. § 300gg-3.

147 42 U.S.C. § 300gg-12.

148 42 U.S.C. § 300gg-11.

149 The Department of Health and Human Services has a webpage explaining the Affordable Care Act at www.healthcare.gov/law/introduction/index.html. *See also* The Commonwealth Fund, Health Reform Res. Ctr., *at* www.commonwealthfund.org/Health-Reform/Health-Reform-Resource.aspx; Kaiser Family Found., Summary of the Affordable Care Act (Apr. 25, 2013), *available at* http://kff.org/health-reform/fact-sheet/summary-of-new-health-reform-law.

150 26 U.S.C. § 501(r).

151 *See* § 9.3.1.2, *infra*.

152 *See* § 9.1.3,*supra* (discussing discriminatory pricing and the difference between chargemaster rates versus what insurers pay).

153 *See* § 9.3.1.3, *infra*.

154 See § 9.3.1.4, *infra*.

155 The Affordable Care Act imposes a $50,000 per year penalty for failure to comply with the community needs assessment requirements. 26 U.S.C. § 4959.

156 26 U.S.C. § 501(r)(7).

157 77 Fed. Reg. 38,148 (June 26, 2012).

158 Internal Revenue Serv., Reliance on Proposed Regulations for Tax-exempt Hospitals, Notice 2014-2 (Dec. 30, 2013), *available at* www.irs.gov/pub/irs-drop/n-14-02.pdf.

There is likely not to be an affirmative private right of action for violation of these requirements,[159] but they could be raised defensively in a collections lawsuit.

9.3.1.2 Written Financial Assistance Policies

The Affordable Care Act requires hospitals to develop written financial assistance policies, which must include:[160]

- The eligibility criteria established by the hospital for receiving financial assistance and whether such assistance includes free or discounted care;
- The basis used to calculate how much patients are charged for care;
- A description of the methods for applying for financial assistance;
- If the hospital does not have a separate billing and debt collection policy, a description of the actions that the hospital might take to collect payment, including collection lawsuits and reporting to credit reporting agencies; and
- The measures used by the hospital to publicize the financial assistance policy widely in the community it serves.

In addition to a written financial assistance policy, hospitals must a written policy requiring the provision of care for emergency medical conditions without discrimination and regardless of ability to pay.[161]

Note that the Affordable Care Act does not actually require hospitals to provide any sort of financial assistance; it merely requires them to disclose what their policies are. It does not establish any minimum eligibility criteria or recommended application procedures.

The IRS issued proposed regulations setting forth what steps nonprofit hospitals must take to widely publicize their financial assistance policies in June 2012.[162] The proposed regulations do not establish minimum eligibility criteria.

9.3.1.3 Limited Protections Against Discriminatory Pricing

If a patient is eligible for financial assistance under the hospital's policy, hospitals cannot charge that patient for emergency or other "medically necessary" care more than the amount generally billed to individuals who have insurance covering such care.[163] This provision appears to restrict discriminatory pricing against uninsured or underinsured patients,[164] if they are eligible for assistance under the hospital's policy. The legislative history of the Affordable Care Act states "[i]t is intended that amounts billed to those who qualify for financial assistance may be based on either the best, or an average of the three best, negotiated commercial rates, or Medicare rates." [165]

A separate provision of the Affordable Care Act also prohibits hospitals from using "gross charges," [166] that is, chargemaster rates. The plain language of this provision appears to ban the use of chargemaster rates for all patients.[167] However, the legislative history suggests that the ban only applies to patients eligible for financial assistance.[168] The IRS proposed regulations implementing this provision similarly provide that the ban only applies to patients eligible for financial assistance.[169] Even if the ban were to have been interpreted to apply to all patients, there is no standard in place as to what a hospital must bill in place of its chargemaster rates.

The restrictions against discriminatory pricing were effective for taxable years after March 23, 2010.[170]

9.3.1.4 Restrictions on "Extraordinary" Debt Collection

The Affordable Care Act prohibits non-profit hospitals from engaging in "extraordinary collection actions" before they make a "reasonable" effort to determine whether a person qualifies for the hospital's financial assistance policy.[171] The Act does not define what constitutes a "reasonable" effort, but the legislative history states that "[i]t is intended that for this purpose, "reasonable efforts" includes notification by the hospital of its financial assistance policy upon admission and in written and oral communications . . . before collection action or reporting to credit rating agencies is initiated." [172] The IRS proposed regulations implementing this provision impose a number of requirements for hospitals to notify patients of their financial assistance policies.[173]

The term "extraordinary collection action" is also undefined in the Act, but the legislative history suggests it includes lawsuits, liens on residences, arrests, and body attachments.[174]

159 *See* § 9.4.6.2, *infra* (string of cases rejecting claims for breach of contract or charitable trust based on hospital's obligations under § 501(c)(3) of the Internal Revenue Code).

160 26 U.S.C. § 501(r)(4).

161 *Id.* at § 501(r)(4)(A).

162 77 Fed. Reg. 38,148 (June 26, 2012).

163 26 U.S.C. § 501(r)(5)(A).

164 *See* § 9.1.3, *supra* (discussing discriminatory pricing and the difference between chargemaster rates versus what insurers pay).

165 Joint Comm. on Taxation, *Technical Explanation of the Revenue Provisions of the "Reconciliation Act of 2010," as amended, in combination with the "Patient Protection and Affordable Care Act,"* JCX-18-10, at 82 (Mar. 21, 2010).

166 26 U.S.C. § 501(r)(5)(B).

167 *See* § 9.1.3, *supra* (discussing discriminatory pricing and the difference between chargemaster rates versus what insurers pay).

168 Joint Comm. on Taxation, *Technical Explanation of the Revenue Provisions of the "Reconciliation Act of 2010," as amended, in combination with the "Patient Protection and Affordable Care Act,"* JCX-18-10, at 82 (Mar. 21, 2010).

169 77 Fed. Reg. 38,148 (June 26, 2012) (proposed 26 C.F.R. § 1.501(r)-5(a)).

170 Pub. L. 111-148, § 9007(f)(1) (2010), *as amended by* Pub. L. 111-152 (2010).

171 26 U.S.C. § 501(r)(6).

172 Joint Comm. on Taxation, *Technical Explanation of the Revenue Provisions of the "Reconciliation Act of 2010," as amended, in combination with the "Patient Protection and Affordable Care Act,"* JCX-18-10, at 82 (Mar. 21, 2010).

173 77 Fed. Reg. 38,148 (June 26, 2012) (proposed 26 C.F.R. § 1.501(r)-6(b)).

174 Joint Comm. on Taxation, Technical Explanation of the Revenue Provisions of the "Reconciliation Act of 2010," as amended, in combination with the "Patient Protection and Affordable Care Act," JCX-18-10, at 82 (Mar. 21, 2010).

The proposed regulations by the IRS define extraordinary collection actions as any action that requires a legal or judicial process (including wage garnishment, liens, and lawsuits), reporting adverse information to credit reporting agencies, and selling a debt.[175] The proposal would require hospitals to provide patients with a 120-day time period to apply for financial assistance.[176] Furthermore, if the patient applies for financial assistance after that, up to 240 days after the first bill, the hospital must suspend any extraordinary collection actions.[177]

The restriction against extraordinary debt collection became effective for taxable years after March 23, 2010.[178]

9.3.1.5 Other IRS Rules

Prior to the Affordable Care Act's passage, the IRS had already begun requiring hospitals to describe their financial assistance policies in Schedule H of IRS Form 990, as well as to report on the amount of charity care they provided, their debt collection policies, and the amount of bad debt that is estimated to be attributable to patients eligible for financial assistance.[179] Schedule H and Form 990s are publicly available and could be useful to practitioners.

9.3.2 Truth in Lending

Many hospitals offer payment plans to consumers who owe large amounts of medical debt. Under certain circumstances, these plans will be covered by the federal Truth in Lending Act (TILA).[180] A non-credit transaction, such as the typical medical bill, can be converted to a credit transaction subject to TILA if several requirements are met.

First, the creditor and the consumer must enter into an agreement that gives the consumer the right to defer payment of the debt.[181] Second, the agreement must provide for the imposition of a finance charge or payment of the debt in more than four installments.[182] Note that the imposition of late charges cannot be equated with finance charges to bring the agreement under TILA; if the debt is still structured as an account receivable that is due in full, the imposition of late charges will not make it a credit transaction subject to TILA.[183] If there is a payment plan, there must be a written agreement reflecting payment terms, not simply "an informal workout arrangement," to bring it within the scope of TILA.[184]

Finally, the consumer must be able to show that the creditor "regularly" extends consumer credit. Regulation Z defines "regularly" to mean that the creditor must have extended credit more than twenty-five times in the preceding calendar year (or more than five times for transactions secured by a dwelling).[185]

In addition to the above factors to establish TILA coverage, the credit arrangement must be "consummated," that is offered by the creditor and accepted by the consumer.[186] The hospital's mere offer of an installment plan is insufficient to establish TILA coverage.[187]

If TILA does cover the a medical bill payment plan, the creditor will be required to clearly disclose certain terms of that credit to the consumer prior to consummation.[188] When the TILA applies to a payment plan for a medical debt and the creditor fails to make key TILA disclosures, the creditor will be liable to the consumer for actual damages, statutory

175 77 Fed. Reg. 38,148 (June 26, 2012) (proposed 26 C.F.R. § 1.501(r)-6(b)).

176 *Id.* (proposed 26 C.F.R. § 1.501(r)-1(b)(18)).

177 *Id.* (proposed 26 C.F.R. § 1.501(r)-1(b)(3)).

178 Pub. L. No. 111-148, § 9007(f)(1) (2010), *as amended by* Pub. L. No. 111-152 (2010).

179 Some of this information is now required by 26 U.S.C. § 6033(b)(15). *See also* Internal Revenue Serv., New Requirements for 501(c)(3) Hospitals Under the Affordable Care Act (Mar. 4, 2014), *available at* www.irs.gov/Charities-&-Non-Profits/Charitable-Organizations/New-Requirements-for-501%28c%29%283%29-Hospitals-Under-the-Affordable-Care-Act.

180 15 U.S.C. §§ 1601–1640. *See* National Consumer Law Center, Truth in Lending Ch. 2 (8th ed. 2012), *updated at* www.nclc.org/library. *Cf.* Jack Mailman & Leonard Flug, D.D.S. v. Whaley, 2002 WL 31988623 (N.Y. Civ. Ct. Nov. 25, 2002) (consumer credit transaction within meaning of state consumer credit statute; imposition of service charge showed that time payments were contemplated).

181 15 U.S.C. § 1602(e); Regulation Z, 12 C.F.R. § 1026.2(a)(14) (definition of "credit"). *See* Pollice v. Nat'l Tax Funding, L.P., 225 F.3d 379 (3d Cir. 2000) (installment payment agreement entered into between consumer and collection agency to repay delinquent water bills was credit transaction subject to TILA). *See generally* National Consumer Law Center, Truth in Lending § 2.2.4.1.1, 2.2.4.1.2 (8th ed. 2012), *updated at* www.nclc.org/library.

182 15 U.S.C. § 1602(f)(1); Regulation Z, 12 C.F.R. § 1026.(a)(17)(i). *See* National Consumer Law Center, Truth in Lending § 2.3.4 (8th ed. 2012), *updated at* www.nclc.org/library.

183 Regulation Z, 12 C.F.R. § 1026.4(c)(2); Consumer Fin. Prot. Bureau, Official Interpretations, 12 C.F.R. pt. 1026, Supp. I, § 1026.4(c)(2)-1, *reprinted in* National Consumer Law Center, Truth in Lending Appx. C (8th ed. 2012), *updated at* www.nclc.org/library. *See* Bright v. Ball Mem'l Hosp. Ass'n, 616 F.2d 328 (7th Cir. 1980) (because the entire lump sum was due, and there was no new formal written arrangement for time payments, a .75% per month charge was a "late charge."). *See generally* National Consumer Law Center, Truth in Lending § 3.9.3.4 (8th ed. 2012), *updated at* www.nclc.org/library.

184 Bright v. Ball Mem'l Hosp. Ass'n, 616 F.2d 328 (7th Cir. 1980); Finnegan v. Univ. of Rochester Med. Ctr., 21 F. Supp. 2d 223 (W.D.N.Y. 1998) (arrangement with hospital to hold off on collection while debtor pursued Social Security appeal was an "informal workout agreement," not an extension of credit for purposes of TILA). *See* National Consumer Law Center, Truth in Lending § 2.3.4.3 (8th ed. 2012), *updated at* www.nclc.org/library.

185 Regulation Z, 12 C.F.R. § 1026.(a)(17)(i). *See* National Consumer Law Center, Truth in Lending § 2.3.3 (8th ed. 2012), *updated at* www.nclc.org/library.

186 Regulation Z, 12 C.F.R. § 1026.2(a)(13); Consumer Fin. Prot. Bureau, Official Interpretations, 12 C.F.R. pt. 1026, Supp. I, § 1026.2(a)(13), *reprinted in* National Consumer Law Center, Truth in Lending Appx. C (8th ed. 2012), *updated at* www.nclc.org/library. *See* National Consumer Law Center, Truth in Lending § 4.4.4 (8th ed. 2012), *updated at* www.nclc.org/library.

187 *E.g.*, Bright v. Ball Mem'l Hosp. Ass'n, 616 F.2d 328 (7th Cir. 1980) (no evidence that consumer accepted hospital's payment plan offer, so TILA did not apply).

188 *See* National Consumer Law Center, Truth in Lending Chs. 4, 5 (8th ed. 2012), *updated at* www.nclc.org/library, for a description of disclosures required for closed-end credit. Disclosures for open-end credit are discussed in Chapter 10 of the same treatise.

damages,[189] and attorney fees.[190] Suit may be brought to recover TILA damages within one year of the violation,[191] or, in most states, TILA violations may be raised at any time as a recoupment or counterclaim to the provider's collection suit.[192] In addition to TILA, state laws may govern the terms of medical credit. A few states limit the amount of interest or late charges that a hospital may impose for medical bills.[193]

Some healthcare providers offer loans or lines of credit to pay for medical services. Many times this credit is extended by a separate lender, not the provider—although the provider may be acting as a loan broker and subject to state laws governing that activity.[194] These credit arrangements would clearly be subject to TILA, and practitioners should examine whether proper disclosures were made.[195] In some cases lenders may characterize the credit as "open-end" credit, that is, a reusable credit line, when it is really closed-end credit, because the disclosure requirements for open-end credit are much weaker. Practitioners may want to challenge such spurious open-end credit arrangements.[196] On the other hand, if the credit is truly open-end but is accessed using a card or other device, it may constitute a "credit card" under TILA.[197]

Certain insurers may pay for a patient's medical bills under the theory that the payments are a "loan" to the patient.[198] This arrangement is a form of subrogation so that the insurer can recover the payments should the patient receive funds in, for example, a tort lawsuit.[199] If these loans involve a finance charge or a written agreement to repay in four or more installments, TILA should apply.

189 Statutory damages are twice the finance charge but minimum and maximums of (1) $400 and $4000 for home-secured, closed-end credit; (2) $500 and $5000 for open-end, non-home-secured credit, and (3) $200 and $2000 for all other forms of credit.

190 *See* National Consumer Law Center, Truth in Lending Ch. 11 (8th ed. 2012), *updated at* www.nclc.org/library.

191 *See id.* § 12.2.

192 15 U.S.C. § 1640(e). *See also* National Consumer Law Center, Truth in Lending § 12.2.5 (8th ed. 2012), *updated at* www.nclc.org/library.

193 *See, e.g.*, N.D. Cent. Code § 13-01-14.1(5)(b) (limiting interest on hospital bills to 12% per year, not to exceed $25 per month).

Several states have medical debtor protection laws that, among other things, limit the amount of interest hospitals may impose for payment plans with income-eligible patients. *See* § 9.4.3.2 (California), § 9.4.3.3 (Connecticut), § 9.4.3.6 (Massachusetts), § 9.4.3.7 (Nevada), § 9.4.3.9 (New York), *infra*.

194 *See* § 9.4.5, *infra*.

195 *See, e.g.*, Jones v. People's Heritage Bank, 433 F. Supp. 2d 1328 (S.D. Ga. 2006) (dental credit plan charged hidden administrative fee withheld from amount paid to dentist; holding that hidden fee was not a finance charge because plaintiff did not pay more because she paid by credit, but rather because she did not pay at inception of work; court ignores fact that only a patient paying in cash could pay at inception and that therefore the additional amount owed is related to use of credit).

196 See National Consumer Law Center, Truth in Lending § 6.2.3 (8th ed. 2012), *updated at* www.nclc.org/library, for a discussion of challenging spurious open-end credit.

197 15 U.S.C. § 1602(k). *See* National Consumer Law Center, Truth in Lending § 6.2.4.1 (8th ed. 2012), *updated at* www.nclc.org/library.

198 *See, e.g.*, Flores v. Rawlings Co., 177 P.3d 341 (Haw. 2008).

199 *See* § 9.7.3, *infra*.

9.3.3 EMTALA

If a debtor was refused treatment at an emergency room because of medical debt, a counterclaim may exist pursuant to the Emergency Medical Treatment and Active Labor Act (EMTALA).[200] EMTALA is a federal statute that prohibits hospitals from turning away a patient in need of emergency medical treatment because, among other things, the patient may not be able to pay for the care.[201] EMTALA should prohibit a hospital from turning away a patient in need of emergency care because of prior bills owed to that hospital.[202]

EMTALA prohibits delay in providing medical screening or care in order to inquire about payment for care.[203] However, one court has held that that EMTALA only prohibits a delay in screening, not treatment, in order to ask about payment,[204] despite the fact that the provision mentions both screening and treatment to at least stabilize the patient. The U.S. Department of Health and Human Services has issued a regulation under EMTALA permitting hospitals to employ "reasonable registration processes," which include asking about payment, so long as the inquiry does not delay treatment or screening.[205] A number of courts have interpreted this regulation to allow hospitals to seek the signature of patients on consent forms that include a provision (usually hidden) requiring patients' agreement to pay for the medical care provided.[206]

200 42 U.S.C. § 1395dd.

201 *See* St. Anthony Hosp. v. United States Dep't of Health & Human Servs., 309 F.3d 680 (10th Cir. 2002) (Congress enacted the EMTALA to address the problem of hospital emergency rooms "refusing to accept or treat patients with emergency conditions if the patient does not have medical insurance"; citing H.R. Rep. No. 99-241, pt. 1, at 27 (1985)); Battle *ex rel.* Battle v. Mem'l Hosp., 228 F.3d 544 (5th Cir. 2000) (EMTALA's purpose "to prevent 'patient dumping,' which is the practice of refusing to treat patients who are unable to pay").

202 *See* Marvin H. Morris Revocable Trust v. Bronfman, 2013 WL 5348357 (N.D. Ill. Sept. 24, 2013) (debt collector Accretive Health, which also acted as billing services provider to hospital, violated EMTALA by using scripts to collect past debts from patients by implying that patient would not be treated until payment was made); Ziegler v. Elmore Cnty. Health Care Auth., 56 F. Supp. 2d 1324 (M.D. Ala. 1999) (denying hospital's motion for summary judgment on EMTALA claim of child whose recovery was delayed and suffering prolonged after being turned away from emergency room because mother owed bill).

203 42 U.S.C. § 1395dd(h).

204 Rosado-Gonzelez v. Alejandro Otero Lopez Hosp., 836 F. Supp. 2d 48 (D. P.R. 2011).

205 42 C.F.R. § 489.24(d)(4)(iv).

One problem with this regulation is that such an inquiry could deter some uninsured patients from seeking services. For instance, a debt collection industry advisor recommends to hospitals that they conduct "review of payment expectations before a patient is admitted for additional services" in an emergency room. Kaulkin Ginsberg Co., Kaulkin Ginsberg Healthcare ARM Report 12 (2006).

206 Parker v. Salina Reg'l Health Ctr., Inc., 463 F. Supp. 2d 1263 (D. Kan. 2006); Jellison v. Fla. Hosp. Healthcare Sys., Inc., 2005 WL 4732730 (M.D. Fla. Mar. 15, 2005); Sabeta v. Baptist Hosp. of Miami, Inc., 410 F. Supp. 2d 1224 (S.D. Fla. 2005); Grant v. Trinity Health Mich., 390 F. Supp. 2d 643 (E.D. Mich. 2005); Kolari v. N.Y. Presbyterian Hosp., 382 F. Supp. 2d 562 (S.D.N.Y. 2005), *vacated in part on other grounds*, 455 F.3d 118 (2d Cir. 2006); Burton v. William Beaumont Hosp., 373 F. Supp. 2d 707 (E.D. Mich. 2005); Amato v. UPMC, 371 F. Supp. 2d 752

EMTALA applies to private hospitals which accept Medicare or Medicaid and to certain public hospitals.[207] EMTALA provides for a private cause of action against hospitals,[208] but not physicians,[209] who violate its provisions.[210]

The Act also does not apply to ambulance service providers.[211] The patient may obtain any remedies available under applicable tort law in the state where the hospital is located, such as actual damages, attorney fees, and in some states punitive damages.[212] However, the patient must allege "personal harm" from the EMTALA violation that would be compensable under that state's personal injury law. Thus a number of courts have held that economic injury due to debt collection or discriminatory pricing is not actionable under EMTALA.[213] Violation of EMTALA might be challenged using a state deceptive practices (UDAP) statute.[214]

Some states may have emergency admission requirements that are more detailed or stricter than the federal statute.[215] Note that EMTALA does not provide for *free care*—if an uninsured patient does receive treatment, the patient may be held liable for medical bills.[216] Indeed, in several dozen cases challenging uninsured patients' medical bills as excessive, the courts have dismissed EMTALA claims.[217]

9.3.4 Debt Collection and Privacy of Medical Information

Practitioners should look out for potential violations of medical privacy rules by providers when they send medical information to debt collectors. The United States Department of Health and Human Services (HHS) has issued rules governing the privacy of medical information pursuant to the Health Insurance Portability and Accountability Act (HIPAA) of 1996.[218] The HIPAA privacy rule applies to health care

---

(W.D. Pa. 2005); Hutt v. Albert Einstein Med. Ctr., 2005 WL 2396313 (E.D. Pa. Sept. 28, 2005); Feliciana v. Thomas Jefferson Univ. Hosp., 2005 WL 2397047 (E.D. Pa. Sept. 28, 2005).

207 EMTALA applies to public hospitals operated by subdivisions of the state, such as counties and municipalities, but not to hospitals operated by the state itself, which have Eleventh Amendment immunity. *See* Root v. New Liberty Hosp. Dist., 209 F.3d 1068 (8th Cir. 2000) (public hospital operated by local hospital district may be sued under EMTALA, which preempts state sovereign immunity statute); Drew v. Univ. of Tenn. Reg'l Med. Ctr. Hosp., 2000 U.S. App. LEXIS 8936 (6th Cir. May 1, 2000) (Eleventh Amendment barred EMTALA suit against the state university hospital, which is an arm of the state); Lebron v. Ashford Presbyterian Cmty. Hosp., 975 F. Supp. 407 (D. P.R. 1997) (University of Puerto Rico is a state entity protected from EMTALA liability by Eleventh Amendment).

208 42 U.S.C. § 1395dd(a).

209 *See* Eberhardt v. City of Los Angeles, 62 F.3d 1253 (9th Cir. 1995); King v. Ahrens, 16 F.3d 265 (8th Cir. 1994) (no cause of action against individual physician); Delaney v. Cade, 986 F.2d 387 (10th Cir. 1993) (plain language of statute indicates actions may be brought against hospitals but not doctors); Baber v. Hosp. Corp. of Am., 977 F.2d 872 (4th Cir. 1992) (no cause of action against individual physician); Gatewood v. Wash. Healthcare Corp., 933 F.2d 1037 (D.C. Cir. 1991).

210 42 U.S.C. § 1395dd(d)(2).

211 Kenyon v. Hospital San Antonio, Inc., 2013 WL 3243557 (D. P.R. June 28, 2013) (EMTALA did not apply to ambulance service's refusal to transfer seriously ill child without upfront payment, because ambulance service is not a covered hospital).

212 42 U.S.C. § 1395dd(d)(2).

213 Harrison v. Christus St. Patrick Hosp., 430 F. Supp. 2d 591 (W.D. La. 2006); Feliciana v. Thomas Jefferson Univ. Hosp., 2005 WL 2397047 (E.D. Pa. Sept. 28, 2005); Nash v. Lee Mem'l Health Sys., 2005 WL 2043642 (M.D. Fla. Aug. 25, 2005); Cargile v. Baylor Health Care Sys., 2005 WL 2445482 (N.D. Tex. Aug. 10, 2005); Gardner v. North Miss. Health Servs., Inc., 2005 WL 1312753 (N.D. Miss. May 31, 2005); Jakubiec v. Sacred Heart Health Sys., Inc., 2005 WL 1261443 (N.D. Fla. May 27, 2005); Ellis v. Phoebe Putney Health Sys., Inc., 2005 WL 4732728 (M.D. Ga. Apr. 8, 2005); Peterson v. Fairview Health Servs., 2005 WL 226168 (D. Minn. Feb. 1, 2005); Sabeta v. Baptist Hosp. of Miami, Inc., 410 F. Supp. 2d 1224 (S.D. Fla. 2005); Grant v. Trinity Health Mich., 390 F. Supp. 2d 643 (E.D. Mich. 2005) (EMTALA claim dismissed because damages for "personal harm" only encompass mental distress and bodily harm); Kolari v. N.Y. Presbyterian Hosp., 382 F. Supp. 2d 562 (S.D.N.Y. 2005); Burton v. William Beaumont Hosp., 373 F. Supp. 2d 707 (E.D. Mich. 2005); Amato v. UPMC, 371 F. Supp. 2d 752 (W.D. Pa. 2005); Quinn v. BJC Health Sys., 364 F. Supp. 2d 1046 (E.D. Mo. 2005); Valencia v. Miss. Baptist Med. Ctr., 363 F. Supp. 2d 867 (S.D. Miss. 2005); Kizzire v. Baptist Health Systems, Inc., 343 F. Supp. 2d 1074 (N.D. Ala. 2004), *aff'd on other grounds*, 441 F.3d 1306 (11th Cir. 2006). *But see* Fotia v. Palmetto Behavioral Health, 317 F. Supp. 2d 638 (D.S.C. 2004) (plaintiff sufficiently alleged "personal harm" to sustain claim for retaliatory firing for revealing hospital's EMTALA violation; only his damages were limited to those damages available in personal injury claims).

A number of courts subsequently held that the analysis of "personal harm" in *Fotia* is limited to cases brought under the "whistleblower" provisions of EMTALA. Burton v. William Beaumont Hosp., 373 F. Supp. 2d 707 (E.D. Mich. 2005); Jakubiec v. Sacred Heart Health Sys., Inc., 2005 WL 1261443 (N.D. Fla. May 27, 2005).

214 Coast Plaza Doctors Hosp. v. UHP Healthcare, 129 Cal. Rptr. 2d 650 (Cal. Ct. App. 2002) (hospital stated a claim for violation of California UDAP law with allegation that health maintenance organization caused patients to be transferred in violation of EMTALA).

215 *See, e.g.*, Mass. Gen. Laws ch. 111, § 70E (detailed requirements for safe and comfortable transfer); N.Y. Pub. Health Law § 2805-b (McKinney) (certain general hospitals may not transfer for inability to pay; violation of this section, or preventing access to required services, is a misdemeanor).

216 El Paso Healthcare Sys., Ltd. v. Molina Healthcare of New Mexico, Inc., 683 F. Supp. 2d 454 (W.D. Tex. 2010) (EMTALA does not extinguish an emergency patient's obligation to pay for treatment under state law); Emergency Physicians Integrated Care v. Salt Lake Cnty., 167 P.3d 1080 (Utah 2007) (EMTALA requires provision of emergency care but does not prevent the provider from seeking payment from patient or, in this case, county that had statutory duty to care for inmates).

217 *See, e.g.*, Harrison v. Christus St. Patrick Hosp., 430 F. Supp. 2d 591 (W.D. La. 2006); Sabeta v. Baptist Hosp. of Miami, Inc., 410 F. Supp. 2d 1224 (S.D. Fla. 2005); Grant v. Trinity Health Mich., 390 F. Supp. 2d 643 (E.D. Mich. 2005).

One of these cases noted that EMTALA does not prohibit discriminatory pricing. Quinn v. BJC Health Sys., 364 F. Supp. 2d 1046 (E.D. Mo. 2005).

218 Pub. L. No. 104-191, 110 Stat. 1936 (1996).

The HIPAA privacy rule may be found in 45 C.F.R. parts 160 and 164. A summary of the HIPAA privacy rule is available from the HHS Office of Civil Rights, which is responsible for its implementation. United States Dep't of Health & Human Servs., Office of Civil Rights, Summary of the HIPAA Privacy Rule (May 2003), *available at* www.hhs.gov/ocr/privacy/hipaa/understanding/summary/privacysummary.pdf.

providers, as well as health plans and clearinghouses.[219] In general, the HIPAA privacy rule permits health care providers to disclose individually identifiable health information only in certain circumstances, unless the individual's written consent is obtained.[220] These circumstances include, among others, treatment, payment, and health care operations activities.[221]

The HIPAA privacy rule does generally permit the disclosure of medical information without the consumer's consent in order to collect payment for services.[222] The disclosure is limited to certain parties, including the provider's "business associates," which presumably would include third-party collection agencies.[223] However, the health care provider must make reasonable efforts to disclose only the minimum amount of protected health information needed to accomplish the intended purpose of the disclosure.[224] Thus, the provider should not disclose the consumer's entire medical record to the debt collector, unless it can specifically justify why the entire record is reasonably needed for debt collection. Furthermore, the HIPAA privacy rule permits the debt collector to disclose protected health information in order to obtain payment, but the collector may only disclose the minimum information necessary to do so.[225] One interesting issue is whether the collector can attach a list of medical expenses to a complaint in a collection action without violating the HIPAA rules.

Note that the HIPAA rules do not provide for a private right of action, but patients might be able to seek relief under some state UDAP statutes.[226] Some states may have health information privacy laws that are more protective than the HIPAA privacy rules.[227] Conduct that violates HIPAA might also violate state laws protecting patient-physician confidentiality or constitute common law torts, such as invasion of privacy.[228] Finally, patients can seek relief for a HIPAA violation with the HHS's Office of Civil Rights.[229]

Medical information is sometimes the object of data security breaches.[230] An especially egregious example of a security breach that was also a HIPAA violation involved Accretive, L.L.C., a debt collector that also acted as a medical billing services provider to Fairview Health Services in Minnesota. Accretive had access to the confidential medical information of Fairview's patients and used it to collect past-due debts from patients, a practice that in itself was allegedly a violation of HIPAA.[231] This confidential medical information was stored in

219 45 C.F.R. § 160.102.

220 45 C.F.R. § 164.502.

221 45 C.F.R. §§ 164.502, 164.506.

222 45 C.F.R. §§ 164.502, 164.506; Zaborac v. Mutual Hosp. Serv., Inc., 2004 WL 2538643 (S.D. Ind. Oct. 7, 2004) (permissible disclosure under HIPAA to obtain "payment" includes debt collection activities).
An exception to this rule is psychotherapy notes, which may not be disclosed without the patient's authorization for payment purposes. 45 C.F.R. § 164.508(a)(2).

223 The HHS's Office of Civil Rights has stated that the HIPAA privacy rule does not prevent health care providers from using third-party collection agencies. *See* United States Dep't of Health & Human Servs., Does the HIPAA Privacy Rule Prevent Health Plans and Providers from Using Debt Collection Agencies?, *available at* www.hhs.gov/hipaafaq/providers/smaller/268.html. Note that the provider must include certain provisions in its contract with a business associate such as a debt collection agency, including safeguards for the health information used or disclosed by that business associate. In addition, the provider may not contractually authorize its business associate to make any use or disclosure of protected health information that would violate the HIPAA privacy rule. 45 C.F.R. § 164.504(e).

224 45 C.F.R. §§ 164.502(b), 164.514(d).

225 Zaborac v. Mutual Hosp. Servs., 2004 WL 2538643 (S.D. Ind. Oct. 7, 2004) (discussing interaction between HIPAA and FDCPA's debt verification requirement).

226 Acara v. Banks, 470 F.3d 569 (5th Cir. 2006). *See generally* National Consumer Law Center, Unfair and Deceptive Acts and Practices § 3.2.7 (8th ed. 2012), *updated at* www.nclc.org/library. But see Maxwell v. Barney, 2009 WL 1707959 (D. Utah June 17, 2009) (dismissing FDCPA claim over debt collector's attachment of sensitive medical information to complaint, potentially in violation of HIPAA).

227 For a summary of state health information privacy laws, see Joy Pritts, Angela Choy, Leigh Emmart, and Joanne Hustead, The State of Health Privacy, Volumes 1 and 2 (2d ed. 2002), *available at* www.cdt.org/files/pdfs/The%20State%20of%20Health%20Privacy%20(Volume%201).pdf.

228 *See, e.g.*, Ortiz v. Aurora Health Care (*In re* Ortiz), 477 B.R. 714 (E.D. Wis. 2012) (hospital violated Wisconsin medical confidentiality law by filing proof of claims with bankruptcy court containing information about debtors' medical conditions; disclosures were in excess of that required for collection purposes); Brown v. Mortensen, 253 P.3d 522 (Cal. 2011) (claim existed under state privacy law against collector that disclosed confidential medical information to credit reporting agencies; claim not preempted by Fair Credit Reporting Act); Franklin Collection Serv., Inc. v. Kyle, 955 So. 2d 284 (Miss. 2007) (collection agency disclosed patient's medical information in lawsuit pleading; no claim for violation of patient-physician confidentiality, but invasion of privacy claim survived summary judgment "by barest thread"). *But see, e.g.*, *In re* Carter, 411 B.R. 730 (Bankr. M.D. Fla. 2009) (hospital that filed proof of claim with bankruptcy court containing debtor's medical information did not commit invasion of privacy under Florida law; declining to sanction hospital for violation of bankruptcy rule providing for privacy protection). *But cf.* OhioHealth Corp. v. Ryan, 2012 WL 68733 (Ohio Ct. App. Jan. 10, 2012) (because disclosure for purposes of payment permitted under HIPAA, hospital did not commit tort of unauthorized disclosure of nonpublic information). *See generally* National Consumer Law Center, Fair Credit Reporting § 10.5 (8th ed. 2013), *updated at* www.nclc.org/library.

229 United States Dep't of Health & Human Servs., Office of Civil Rights, How to File A Health Information Privacy Complaint With The Office For Civil Rights, *available at* www.hhs.gov/ocr/privacy/hipaa/complaints/index.html.

230 *See, e.g.*, Garnett v. Millennium Med. Mgmt., 2010 5140055 (N.D. Ill. Dec. 9, 2010) (unencrypted portable hard drive containing plaintiff's medical information stolen; plaintiff's Fair Credit Reporting Act claim dismissed; plaintiff did not bring HIPAA claim); Cooney v. Chicago Pub. Schools, 943 N.E.2d 23 (Ill. App. Ct. 2010) (data security breach involving medical information of 1700 teachers; no private remedy to enforce HIPAA violation; state data breach security law applied but defendant had complied with law's remedial requirements); Paul v. Providence Health Systems-Oregon, 273 P.3d 106 (Or. 2012) (computer disks and tapes containing personal information from estimated 365,000 patients stolen from the car of one of provider's employees). *See generally* National Consumer Law Center, Fair Credit Reporting § 9.6 (8th ed. 2013), *updated at* www.nclc.org/library.

231 Office of the Minn. Att'y Gen., Privacy Violations, 4 Compliance Review of Fairview Health Services' Management Contracts with Accretive Health, Inc. (Apr. 2012), *available at* www.ag.state.mn.us/PDF/PressReleases/ComplianceReview/Vol.%204.pdf.

an unsecured manner (unencrypted) on an Accretive employee's laptop, which was subsequently stolen.[232] The Minnesota attorney general alleged that this data breach violated HIPAA.[233]

9.3.5 *Credit Reporting Issues and Medical Debt*

9.3.5.1 Impact of Medical Debt on Credit Reports

Medical debt can have a significant impact on a consumer's credit history. Providers will often send a medical debt to a collection agency, which, in turn, will report the debt to a consumer reporting agency (CRA). This, in turn, will result in a derogatory item on the consumer's credit report[234] and a resulting decrease of the consumer's credit score.[235] A study by Federal Reserve Board researchers found that 52% of all accounts reported by collection agencies to a CRA consisted of medical debt.[236] A 2010 study by Ernst & Young similarly found that medical debts constituted more than half (52.2%) of the debt collected by debt collection agencies in 2010—more than twice as much as credit card and other financial debt.[237] A study of medical debtors found that, of those surveyed who knew the answer, three out of five reported that their medical debts had shown up in their credit reports.[238] Some of these black marks were for small dollar amounts: 16% of the medical debts showing up on credit reports were for under $500.[239]

A unique and troubling aspect of medical debt in credit reports is that in many cases, the consumer is never contacted by a collector or even sent a bill by the original provider. Instead, the first time that some consumers learn about medical debts is when they examine their credit reports and learn of a damaging collection account, sometimes in the midst of seeking a mortgage or other credit.[240]

Medical debt is sometimes also reported on the credit reports of spouses or other relatives.[241] Medical debt has even appeared on credit reports as a result of "medical identity theft," in which a thief incurs medical bills in the name of the victim.[242]

The impact of medical debt on a consumer's credit report is especially egregious when the medical debt is one which an insurer arguably should have paid. Disputes between health insurers, providers, and consumers occur frequently and can be of extended duration. Many medical bills are referred to collection agencies during these disputes but are ultimately paid by insurers.[243] A consumer's credit history and credit score may be damaged as a result of a debt being sent to collections during a dispute, or even if the insurer is simply slow in paying the bill.[244] This is true even after the bill is paid, as

232 Complaint, State v. Accretive Health, Inc., No. 21-cv-000145 (D. Minn. Jan. 19, 2012), *available at* www.ag.state.mn.us/PDF/Consumer/AccretiveHealth20120119.pdf (extremely sensitive and personal medical data of 23,500 patients stored on stolen laptop).

233 *Id.*

234 *See* National Consumer Law Center, Fair Credit Reporting § 3.3.3.8 (8th ed. 2013), *updated at* www.nclc.org/library.

235 *See id.* § 14.5.2.1.

236 Robert Avery, Paul Calem, Glenn Canner & Raphael Bostic, An Overview of Consumer Data and Credit Reporting 69, Fed. Reserve Bull. (Feb. 2003).

237 Ernst & Young, The Impact of Third-Party Debt Collection on the National and State Economies 18 (Feb. 2012), *available at* www.acainternational.org/files.aspx?p=/images/21594/2011acaeconomicimpactreport.pdf.

238 Robert W. Seifert, Access Project, Home Sick: How Medical Debt Undermines Housing Security (Nov. 2005).

239 *Id.*

For examples of the impact of credit reporting of medical debt, see generally Steve Tripoli & Chi Chi Wu, National Consumer Law Center, Unhealthy Pursuits: How the Sick and Vulnerable Are Harmed by Abusive Medical Debt Collection Tactics (Dec. 2005), *available online as companion material to this treatise*.

240 *See* Walecia Konrad, Protecting Your Credit Score from the Medical Bill Maze, New York Times, Dec. 18, 2010, at B7 (examples of consumers who first learn of medical debts when they review their credit reports).

241 *See, e.g.*, Mellinger v. Midwest Audit Serv., 2012 WL 405008 (E.D. Mich. Feb. 8, 2012) (collector dunned husband for wife's medical bills and reported debt on husband's credit report); Dunn v. Lehigh Valley Ctr. for Sight, P.C., 2003 WL 22299275 (E.D. Pa. Sept. 30, 2003) (provider entitled to report delinquent medical debt on credit report of spouse because spouse also liable for debt under Pennsylvania necessaries statute); Bickford v. Onslow Mem'l Hosp. Found., Inc., 855 A.2d 1150 (Me. 2004) (alleging claims for intentional infliction of emotional distress, as well as for defamation and tortuous interference with an economic advantage, over hospital wrongfully reporting to CRA that plaintiff owed bills for services to ex-wife's daughter, to whom plaintiff had no legal relationship).

242 Pam Dixon, World Privacy Forum, Medical Identity Theft: The Information Crime That Can Kill You (May 3, 2006).

243 *See, e.g.*, Chamberlain v. Farm Bureau Mut. Ins. Co., 137 P.3d 1081 (Kan. Ct. App. 2006) (accident victim's insurer refused to pay full amount of provider's charges because insurer believed they exceeded customary and usual charges, resulting in harm to victim's credit record). *See also* Examining the Uses of Consumer Credit Data: Hearing Before the Subcomm. on Fin. Inst. and Consumer Credit Hearing of the H. Comm. on Fin. Serv., 112th Cong. (2012) (statement of Chi Chi Wu) (examples of harm to credit reports of consumers due to insurer or provider error); Pamela Yip and Jason Robertson, *Consumer Advocate Say Medical Debt's Hit on Credit Is Unfair*, Dallas Morning News, Oct. 24, 2009; Consumer Fed'n of Am. & Nat'l Credit Reporting Ass'n, Credit Score Accuracy and Implications for Consumers 31 (Dec. 17, 2002), *available at* http://consumerfed.org/elements/www.consumerfed.org/file/finance/121702CFA_NCRA_Credit_Score_Report_Final.pdf.

244 *E.g.*, Carvalho v. Equifax Info. Servs., L.L.C., 629 F.3d 876 (9th Cir. 2010) (negative credit reporting due to $118 bill not paid by insurer); Lockett v. Advocate Ill. Masonic Hosp., 2010 WL 5135909 (N.D. Ill. Dec. 10, 2010) (patient received charity care letter covering all hospital bills, but full amount of bills reported on TransUnion credit report); McNall v. Credit Bur. of Josephine Cnty., 689 F. Supp. 2d 1265 (D. Or. 2010) (collector reported hospital debts as delinquent to CRA despite consumer's dispute over bills due to lack of documentation); Nelson-McGourty v. L & P Fin. Adjusters, Inc., 2010 WL 3190711 (N.D. Ill. Aug. 12, 2010) (patient complained that her credit report had been "trashed" because of failure of worker's compensation to pay medical bills, despite Illinois law prohibiting providers from demanding payment from patient in that circumstance); Shields v. Merchants & Med. Credit Corp., 2010 WL 2613086 (E.D. Mich. June 28, 2010) (patient ended up with negative entry on credit report for $85 bill for anesthesia, despite fact that hospital records showed he owed no balance; unclear whether bill was from hospital or physician group within hospital); Majeski v. I.C. Sys., Inc., 2010 WL 145861 (N.D. Ill. Jan. 8, 2010) (provider referred debt to collector, resulting in negative credit report, only two months after insurance paid everything but co-pay, and only one month

an account reported as a collection matter will remain on a credit report even after the balance is paid off.[245] At least one credit scoring developer appears to have recognized the issues presented by medical and other collection items that are paid and has changed its scoring models to exclude consideration of these items.[246]

9.3.5.2 Right to Dispute Erroneous Medical Debt Reporting Under the Fair Credit Reporting Act

Consumers facing wrongful credit reporting damage relating to medical debt may want to file a written dispute with the consumer reporting agencies (CRAs).[247] Filing written disputes with the CRAs provides a cause of action under the Fair Credit Reporting Act (FCRA) against the furnisher of the information, if the furnisher fails to undertake a reasonable investigation of the dispute.[248] However, in some cases, courts will decline to find an FCRA violation because, while a patient's insurer should have paid the bill, the patient is technically liable as well.[249]

A patient can also file an FCRA dispute directly with the furnisher of the information; however, there is no private right of action for violation of these "furnisher direct disputes" if the furnisher fails to undertake a reasonable investigation.[250] There is also no private right for violation of the FCRA's accuracy requirements for furnishers; thus, any inaccurate reporting by a provider prior to a dispute is not actionable under the FCRA.[251] However, a credit reporting inaccuracy by a debt collector might be actionable under the FDCPA.[252] There may also be common law claims available,[253] but such claims face the daunting and complex issue of preemption of state law claims under the FCRA.[254]

Whenever reaching a settlement over medical bills that have adversely affected the consumer's credit record, practitioners should obtain the agreement of the provider or collector to remove or correct this negative information. Sample language to do so is available in another treatise in this series.[255]

9.3.5.3 Fair Credit Reporting Act Protections for Medical Privacy

The FCRA contains several restrictions on medical information contained in credit reports. The FCRA prohibits consumer reporting agencies (CRAs) from furnishing for employment purposes, or in connection with a credit or insurance transaction, a credit report that contains medical information, unless the consumer consents.[256] The consent for employment and credit purposes (but not for insurance) must be written, must be specific, and must describe the use of the information.[257] In addition, the medical information must be relevant to the employment or credit transaction at issue.[258]

---

after provider billed patient for co-pay); Witherwax v. Transcare, Inc., 801 N.Y.S.2d 782 (table), 2005 WL 1458061 (N.Y. Sup. Ct. Apr. 22, 2005) (provider failed to bill insurer and instead sent bill to collection agency, resulting in negative items on patient's credit report); Angelucci v. Fairmont Gen. Hosp., Inc., 618 S.E.2d 373 (W. Va. 2005) (hospital failed to submit bills to insurer and then sent bill to collection agency, resulting in negative items on patient's credit report).

245 *See* National Consumer Law Center, Fair Credit Reporting § 14.6.2.5 (8th ed. 2013), *updated at* www.nclc.org/library. *See, e.g.*, Pettway v. Equifax Info. Servs., L.L.C., 2010 WL 653708 (S.D. Ala. Feb. 17, 2010) (medical debts appeared as collection items on patient's credit report even after she had paid providers directly); White v. Global Payments, Inc., 2010 WL 320480 (S.D. Ala. Jan. 21, 2010) (not only continuing to report debt once paid off but repeatedly and erroneously reporting account as "open").

246 Kevin Wack, *Credit Scoring Model Bucks the Industry Line on Paid Debts*, Am. Banker, Mar. 11, 2013 (VantageScore removing paid collection accounts from its latest scoring model).

247 *See* Bickford v. Onslow Mem'l Hosp. Found., Inc., 855 A.2d 1150 (Me. 2004) (noting that medical billing dispute reflected in credit report could have been addressed through FCRA's dispute resolution procedures). For more information on submitting an FCRA dispute, *see* National Consumer Law Center, Fair Credit Reporting § 4.5.2 (8th ed. 2013), *updated at* www.nclc.org/library.

248 *See* National Consumer Law Center, Fair Credit Reporting § 6.10 (8th ed. 2013), *updated at* www.nclc.org/library.

249 *See* Carvalho v. Equifax Info. Servs., L.L.C., 629 F.3d 876 (9th Cir. 2010) (negative credit reporting due to $118 bill not paid by insurer; FCRA claim dismissed because patient legally liable for bill despite plaintiff's allegation that hospital failed to properly bill insurer); Witherwax v. Transcare, Inc., 801 N.Y.S.2d 782 (table), 2005 WL 1458061 (N.Y. Sup. Ct. Apr. 22, 2005) (dismissing state law claim for defamation of credit because patient was liable on debt); Angelucci v. Fairmont Gen. Hosp., Inc., 618 S.E.2d 373 (W. Va. 2005) (dismissing state law claim for wrongful and malicious credit reporting because patient liable for debt).

250 *See* National Consumer Law Center, Fair Credit Reporting §§ 6.1.2, 6.5.2.1 (8th ed. 2013), *updated at* www.nclc.org/library.

251 *See id. See, e.g.*, Lockett v. Advocate Ill. Masonic Hosp., 2010 WL 5135909 (N.D. Ill. Dec. 10, 2010) (patient received charity care letter covering all hospital bills, but full amount of bills reported on TransUnion credit report; no FCRA violation for error because patient never filed dispute with CRAs).

Thus, if the furnisher does correct the consumer's credit report after a dispute, there is no cause of action under the FCRA. *See, e.g.*, Krieg v. U.M.C. Hosp., 217 Fed. Appx. 604 (9th Cir. 2007) (no FCRA violation when hospital took back account from collection agency, resulting in correction to patient's credit report, after it received information that patient's medical bills would be paid by federal and state government agencies).

252 *See, e.g.*, Moscona v. California Bus. Bureau, Inc., 2011 WL 5085522 (S.D. Cal. Oct. 25, 2011) (medical bill collector violated FDCPA by failing to report consumer's dispute to CRAs; summary judgment for consumer). *See* National Consumer Law Center, Fair Credit Reporting § 6.13 (8th ed. 2013), *updated at* www.nclc.org/library.

253 *See, e.g.*, Evans v. Trans Union, L.L.C., 2011 WL 672061 (S.D. Va. Feb. 14, 2011) (permitting negligence claim against medical center that wrongfully reported bill already paid by insurance on plaintiff's credit report; FCRA did not preempt claim).

254 *See generally* National Consumer Law Center, Fair Credit Reporting § 10.7.4 (8th ed. 2013), *updated at* www.nclc.org/library.

255 National Consumer Law Center, Fair Credit Reporting § 12.6.4, Appx. J.9 (8th ed. 2013), *updated at* www.nclc.org/library.

256 15 U.S.C. § 1681b(g). *See* National Consumer Law Center, Fair Credit Reporting § 5.4.1.2 (8th ed. 2013), *updated at* www.nclc.org/library.

257 15 U.S.C. § 1681b(g)(1)(B)(ii).

258 15 U.S.C. § 1681b(g)(1)(B)(i).

The FCRA also prohibits CRAs from including the name, address, or telephone number of medical information furnishers unless the CRA formats the information so that it does not disclose either the specific provider or the nature of the medical services.[259] In order to help CRAs comply with this requirement, health care providers and medical information furnishers must notify CRAs of their status as such.[260]

The FCRA also prohibits creditors from obtaining or using a consumer's medical information in connection with evaluating creditworthiness, unless permitted by regulation.[261] The regulations generally permit the use of financial information related to a medical condition (in other words, medical debts) so long as the creditor does not treat the consumer less favorably on the basis of the medical condition.[262] Another treatise in this series provides more information on the FCRA's provisions regarding medical information.[263]

State laws may also provide protections against reporting of certain medical debts on credit reports. For example, California law prohibits hospitals from reporting negative information about uninsured or underinsured patients to a CRA during the first 150 days after sending the initial bill to the patient.[264] Florida law prohibits a health care provider from reporting a debt to a CRA if the provider in good faith knows that an HMO is liable for the debt.[265]

9.3.5.4 Healthcare Providers As Users of Credit Reports

In addition to being furnishers of information to consumer reporting agencies (CRAs), health care providers may be users of credit reports. Hospitals sometimes order the credit reports of patients, including patients who apply for or are eligible for charity care,[266] claiming that they do so in order to verify income and thus their eligibility for charity care. However, credit reports do not contain information about a consumer's income,[267] causing concern that these hospitals were instead looking for lines of credit that the applicants could use to pay hospital bills.[268] In addition, consumer reporting agencies have developed specialized health care credit scores that rely on hospital payment records.[269] One question is whether hospitals that are using credit reports or credit scores to determine charity care eligibility are complying with the FCRA's notice requirements when they reject patients.[270]

A provider must have a permissible purpose under the FCRA in order to access a patient's credit report.[271] One court held that a dentist had a permissible purpose in ordering the credit report of a potential patient as a "legitimate business need" under the FCRA.[272]

9.3.6 *Nursing Home Law*

If the medical debt is owed to a nursing home facility, regulations governing that industry may provide a defense or cause of action. The federal Nursing Home Reform Law (NHRL) prohibits a facility from requiring a resident's family or friends to become financially responsible for expenses.[273] The NHRL regulations also require that nursing facilities inform consumers of all charges, including (for Medicaid recipients) those charges not covered by Medicaid.[274]

While the NHRL prohibits a facility from requiring relatives to accept responsibility for expenses, the NHRL does not prohibit the facility from asking relatives to *voluntarily* agree to be financially responsible.[275] The tricky issue is, of course, whether such agreement is truly voluntary or whether it is obtained by using a form contract that includes a boilerplate

---

259 15 U.S.C. § 1681c(a)(6).
There is an exception to this prohibition for insurance companies other than property and casualty insurers. 15 U.S.C. § 1681c(a)(6).

260 15 U.S.C. § 1681s-2(a)(9).

261 15 U.S.C. § 1681b(g)(2)(5).

262 *See* National Consumer Law Center, Fair Credit Reporting § 5.4.1.5 (8th ed. 2013), *updated at* www.nclc.org/library.

263 *Id.* § 5.4.1.

264 Cal. Health & Safety Code § 127425(d) (West).

265 Fla. Stat. § 641.3154(4).

266 *See* Sarah Bernstein, *Why Hospitals Want Your Credit Report*, Wall St. J., Mar. 18, 2008; Phuong Cat Le, *Harborview Checks On Charity Patients' Credit: Hospital Quietly Tests Need For Financial Help*, Seattle Post-Intelligencer, Feb. 27, 2007.

267 *See* National Consumer Law Center, Fair Credit Reporting § 3.2.3 (8th ed. 2013), *updated at* www.nclc.org/library.

268 *See, e.g.*, *Overdose of Debt*, Consumer Reports, July 2008, at 14 (hospital bill collector convinced patient to charge $13,000 in medical bills to credit card that collector discovered by ordering patient's credit report). *Cf.* Robert Berner & Chad Terhune, *Hospitals X-Ray Patient Credit Scores*, BusinessWeek, Nov. 20, 2008 (example of a hospital that denies charity care if the patient's credit score is too high because high scorers are "likely to pay").

269 Robert Berner & Chad Terhune, *Hospitals X-Ray Patient Credit Scores*, BusinessWeek, Nov. 20, 2008 (specialty scoring systems from SearchAmerica and Passport Health Communications); Michelle Andrews, *Worries About Healthcare Credit Scores*, On Health & Money—U.S. News and World Report On-Line (Apr. 10, 2008), *available at* www.usnews.com/blogs/on-health-and-money/2008/4/10/worries-about-healthcare-credit-scores.html; Sarah Bernstein, *Why Hospitals Want Your Credit Report*, Wall St. J., Mar. 18, 2008.

270 *See* National Consumer Law Center, Fair Credit Reporting Act § 8.2.6 (8th ed. 2013), *updated at* www.nclc.org/library.

271 *See* National Consumer Law Center, Fair Credit Reporting Ch. 7 (8th ed. 2013), *updated at* www.nclc.org/library.

272 Wallace v. Finkel, 2006 WL 1731149 (M.D. Ala. June 22, 2006).
Note that the court did not engage in an analysis of what exactly was the dentist's business need, as the court appeared to place the burden on the consumer to show that the defendant's reason for obtaining the report was impermissible. *See* National Consumer Law Center, Fair Credit Reporting § 7.2.8 (8th ed. 2013), *updated at* www.nclc.org/library (discussing legitimate business need permissible purpose for obtaining a credit report).

273 42 U.S.C. § 1395i-3(c)(5)(A)(ii); 42 U.S.C. § 1396r(c)(5)(A)(ii) (Medicaid Act); Carroll v. Butterfield Health Care, Inc., 2003 WL 22462604 (N.D. Ill. Oct. 29, 2003) (nursing home violated NHRL by requiring personal guarantee from patient's son-in-law; son-in-law stated FDCPA claim against attorney-collector for suing on illegal guarantee). *See* National Consumer Law Center, Unfair and Deceptive Acts and Practices § 9.3.3 (8th ed. 2012), *updated at* www.nclc.org/library.

274 42 C.F.R. § 483.10(b)(5), (6).

275 Podolsky v. First Healthcare Corp., 58 Cal. Rptr. 2d 89 (Cal. Ct. App. 1996).

financial responsibility provision that the relative does not read or comprehend.[276]

In addition, the NHRL does not prohibit a resident's representative who has legal access to the resident's income or assets from agreeing to use those funds to pay for care.[277] Many nursing home contracts have language that require the resident's representative to use the resident's income and assets to pay for care and that also hold the representative personally liable for failing to do so.[278] Courts have differed as to the extent of that personal liability.[279] Also, such "responsible party" provisions do not render liable persons who do not have control or power of attorney over the patient's assets.[280]

The NHRL may not provide for a private right of action,[281] but violation of this law may be actionable under a state UDAP statute.[282] Violation may also render a contract void and unenforceable as to the third-party guarantor.[283] State laws may provide additional protections, such as requirements for financial disclosure and restrictions on transfer or discharge for non-payment.[284] State statutes vary widely as to the existence and scope of a private remedy for violations.[285] One court has held

276 *See* Katherine C. Pearson, *The Responsible Thing to Do About "Responsible Party" Provisions in Nursing Home Agreements: A Proposal for Change on Three Fronts*, 37 U. Mich. J.L. Reform 757 (2004). For a disturbing example, see *In re* State *ex rel.* Martin, 2010 WL 5479899 (La. Ct. App. Dec. 22, 2010) (son did not sign contract under duress or mistake, even though sheriff's deputies came to his house to forcibly remove his mother, who had been found to be neglected, and nursing home employee represented that he was only signing forms authorizing admission; court noted that there had been no threats or coercion and he was informed that his mother would be admitted regardless of whether he signed agreement).

277 42 U.S.C. § 1395i-3(c)(5)(B)(ii); 42 U.S.C. § 1396r(c)(5)(B)(ii) (Medicaid Act).

278 *See, e.g.*, White v. Jewish Ass'n on Aging, 2013 WL 5963128 (W.D. Pa. Nov. 7, 2013) (responsible party provision did not require personal guarantee in violation of NHRL); Cook Willow Health Ctr. v. Andrien, 2012 WL 5200369 (Conn. Super. Ct. Sept. 28, 2012) ("responsible party" provision did not require personal guarantee in violation of NHRL); Bishop Wicke Health Ctr. v. Gorel, 2007 WL 2318097 (Conn. Super. Ct. July 27, 2007) (nursing home could sue representative for breach of contract for failing to maintain resident's eligibility for Medicaid, but NHRL barred *quantum meruit* and unjust enrichment claims against third party); Sunshine Care Corp. v. Warrick, 957 N.Y.S.2d 122 (N.Y. App. Div. 2012) (NHRL did not prevent home from seeking to hold wife personally liable for breaching agreement to use resident' funds to pay home, to the extent she had access to funds); Troy Nursing and Rehabilitation Ctr., L.L.C. v. Naylor, 944 N.Y.S.2d 323 (N.Y. App. Div. 2012) (not a violation of NHRL for nursing home to sue daughter for breach of contract when she had agreed to use resident's funds to pay debts to home, but damages limited to amount of resident's assets available to daughter); Liberty Nursing Ctr. of Englewood, Inc. v. Valentine, 2012 WL 928249 (Ohio Ct. App. Mar. 16, 2012).

279 Athena Holdings, L.L.C. v. Marcus, 2013 WL 2132060 (Conn. Super. Ct. Apr. 22, 2013) (son who signed "responsible party" provision liable for amount of mother's funds he failed to turn over, but not the losses resulting from denial of Medicaid); Lexington Healthcare Ctr. v. Graves, 2013 WL 1279487 (Ill. App. Ct. Mar. 27, 2013) (provision did not render patient's daughter personally liable, as she signed agreement only as agent for her father); New Vanderbilt Rehabilitation & Care Ctr., Inc. v. Brown, 934 N.Y.S.2d 35 (N.Y. Sup. Ct. 2011) (holding representative liable and voiding transfer of resident's house to representative).

280 *See* Aaron Manor, Inc. v. Irving, 12 A.3d 584 (Conn. App. Ct.2011) (daughter who signed "responsible party" provision not liable for father's bill when another sibling had power of attorney and access to father's resources), *rev'd in part on other grounds*, 57 A.3d 342 (Conn. 2013) (attorney fees issue); Northgate Healthcare Corp. v. Moores, 2012 WL 6212792 (Mass. Super. Ct. Nov. 23, 2012) (provision was signed by patient's daughter, but daughter was not liable for breach given that she did not have control over patient's assets).

281 White v. Jewish Ass'n on Aging, 2013 WL 5963128 (W.D. Pa. Nov. 7, 2013) (discussing cases and noting split of authority on question whether NHRL is privately enforceable).

282 *See* Podolsky v. First Healthcare Corp., 58 Cal. Rptr. 2d 89 (Cal. Ct. App. 1996) (while nursing home was not prohibited from asking relatives to voluntarily agree to be financially responsible, lack of consideration for voluntary agreement and failure to inform relatives of their rights under NHRL was deceptive in violation of California UDAP law); National Consumer Law Center, Unfair and Deceptive Acts and Practices § 9.3.3 (8th ed. 2012), *updated at* www.nclc.org/library. *Cf.* Altman v. Lifespace Cmtys., Inc., 2012 WL 414826 (S.D. Fla. Feb. 8, 2012) (Florida law incorporates NHRL's prohibition against requiring a third-party guarantee and provides for private remedy); Mary Elizabeth Nursing Ctr., Inc. v. Lyon, 2012 WL 6924420 (Conn. Super. Ct. Dec. 24, 2012) (UDAP claim not preempted by NHRL provision allowing "responsible party" provision requiring family member to pay from patient's resources); Haven Health Ctr. of Lichfield Hills v. Parente, 2007 WL 123602 (Conn. Super. Ct. Jan. 8, 2007) (son of nursing home patient, who alleged that he signed only as his mother's power of attorney and that he was never given a copy of preprinted contract, could bring UDAP claim against nursing home). *But see* Carroll v. Butterfield Health Care, Inc., 2003 WL 22462604 (N.D. Ill. Oct. 29, 2003) (no UDAP claim under Illinois law against nursing home that unlawfully required guarantee; guarantor failed to show substantial injury because he did not allege that he was coerced into admitting patient to that home or that he had no choice of alternative facilities).

283 *See* Knight v. John Knox Manor, Inc., 92 So. 3d 111 (Ala. Civ. App. 2012) (violation of NHRL rendered unenforceable nursing home admission contract that imposed personal liability on resident's son); Manor of Lake City, Inc. v. Hinners, 548 N.W.2d 573 (Iowa 1996) (same). *Cf.* Guest House of Slidell v. Hills, 76 So. 3d 497 (La. Ct. App. 2011) (construing ambiguous nursing home admission contract to hold that resident—not his stepson who signed as agent—was responsible for bills).

284 *See, e.g.*, Fla. Stat. § 400.022 (financial disclosures and billing); La. Rev. Stat. Ann. § 40:2010.8 (financial disclosures; discharge or transfer); Minn. Stat. § 144.6501 (may not require co-signer to assume personal liability; must disclose this requirement in bold capitals); Carlton at the Lake, Inc. v. Barber, 928 N.E.2d 1266 (Ill. App. Ct. 2010) (Illinois Nursing Home Care Act requires that contract be signed by patient; tender of care to patient and acceptance of services not sufficient); Oak Crest Vill., Inc. v. Murphy, 841 A.2d 816 (Md. 2004) (provision of continuing care retirement community contract that prohibited resident from divesting assets below certain amount violated Maryland Nursing Home Patient's Bill of Rights); Northfield Care Ctr., Inc. v. Anderson, 707 N.W.2d 731 (Minn. Ct. App. 2006) (state law permits nursing home to solicit voluntary agreement for relative to be financially responsible, but only to the extent that the patient's income or assets are misapplied or relative acted in bad faith). *Cf.* Home for Armenian Aged v. Symeonidis, 2012 WL 5834373 (N.J. Super. Ct. App. Div. Sept. 11, 2012) (agreement signed by unrelated caregiver, which purported to make her personally liable for patient's expenses, was unconscionable and unenforceable when caregiver had limited English literacy, had been misled by home's staff, and felt compelled to sign in order to ensure patient received care).

285 *See* Mass. Gen. Laws ch. 111, § 70E ("in addition to any other action allowed by law or regulation" civil cause of action for malpractice); Mich. Comp. Laws § 333.20203 (guidelines only; do not expand or limit rights under other law; no civil or criminal liability for non-compliance); Minn. Stat. § 144.6501 (nursing home contracts are consumer contracts within meaning of consumer protection statutes). *But see* Darviris v.

that a state necessaries statute,[286] which imposed liability on adult children of patients, was not preempted by the Nursing Home Reform Law.[287]

9.3.7 Protections Against Balance Billing

Medicaid programs often reimburse providers at rates less than what private insurers pay and far less than "chargemaster" or "list" charges."[288] State Medicaid programs prohibit health care providers from engaging in the practice of "balance billing," or collecting additional amounts from Medicaid patients to make up for the difference in rates, when the service in question is a covered benefit.[289]

Despite the clear protections against balance billing, hospitals have been known to make collection efforts and obtain judgments against patients who are covered by Medicaid.[290] Unfortunately, at least one federal court of appeals has held that the Medicaid Act does not provide for a private remedy to enforce the balance billing prohibition.[291]

The Medicare Act contains a similar protection against balance billing.[292] There is also no private right of action to bring an affirmative suit under this provision of the Medicare Act.[293] However, a patient might be able to assert a claim for violation of the Medicare or Medicaid prohibitions against balance billing under the FDCPA,[294] a state UDAP law,[295] or as a defense to a collection action.

The prohibition against balance billing applies when the provider submits a claim for Medicaid payment, even if Medicaid denies the claim.[296] Some cases have barred providers from recovering against a patient when the provider fails to timely bill Medicaid,[297] or even for failing to assist the patient in applying for Medicaid.[298] However, a provider may be permitted to bill at full chargemaster rates once the patient's Medicare benefits have been exhausted.[299] The Medicaid balance billing prohibitions may prevent providers and insurers from placing a lien on the tort recoveries of Medicaid beneficiaries and attempting to collect amounts greater than what Medicaid pays.[300]

Petros, 812 N.E.2d 1188 (Mass. 2004) (violation of Mass. Gen. Laws ch. 111, § 70E, not addressable under UDAP statute, despite regulation making violations of certain statutes per se UDAP violations).

286 *See* § 9.6, *infra* (description of state necessaries doctrines and statutes).

287 Eades v. Kennedy, P.C. Law Offices, 2013 WL 6241272 (W.D.N.Y. Dec. 3, 2013) (NHRL does not preempt Pennsylvania statute requiring adult children of indigent parent to be responsible for necessaries).

288 *See* § 9.1.3, *supra* (explaining the differing rates paid by Medicaid and private insurers and how they are far less than the "chargemaster" or "list" charges assessed against uninsured patients).

289 42 U.S.C. § 1396a(a)(25)(c); 42 C.F.R. § 447.15; Spectrum Health Continuing Care Group v. Anna Marie Bowling Irrevocable Trust, 410 F.3d 304 (6th Cir. 2005) (nursing home violated Medicaid's balance billing prohibition by seeking recovery from patient's tort settlement after accepting Medicaid funds for care of patient); Evanston Hosp. v. Hauck, 1 F.3d 540 (7th Cir. 1993) (once hospital accepts Medicaid or Medicare payment, it is barred from pursuing the patient for any balance, and it cannot avoid this prohibition by returning the payment to the government); Olszewski v. Scripps Health, 135 Cal. Rptr. 2d 1 (Cal. 2003) (federal Medicaid law preempted state hospital lien law that permitted lien for customary charges); West v. Shelby Cnty. Healthcare Corp., 2013 WL 500777 (Tenn. Ct. App. Feb. 11, 2013) (once hospital accepts payment from Medicaid, patient no longer owes debt to hospital and hospital cannot seek lien against tort recovery).

For more on Medicaid law and the prohibition against balance billing (also called the "payment in full" defense), see National Health Law Program, An Advocate's Guide to the Medicaid Program (2012), *available at* www.medicaidguide.org.

290 *See, e.g.*, Fred Schulte & James Drew, *Their Day in Court*, Balt. Sun, Dec. 22, 2008 (noting that "[s]ome hospitals have won judgments against patients covered by Medicaid for bills the giant government health plans didn't pay, despite a Maryland law outlawing [the practice]").

291 Martes v. Chief Executive Officer of S. Broward Hosp. Dist., 683 F.3d 1323 (11th Cir. 2012). Specifically, the court held that a section 1983 claim will not lie against officials of a government hospital for violation of the Medicaid balance billing prohibition.

292 42 U.S.C. § 1395cc(a)(1)(A).

293 Wentz v. Kindred Hosps. E., L.L.C., 333 F. Supp. 2d 1298 (S.D. Fla. 2004) (no private right of action to enforce Medicare's balance billing prohibition, but patient could proceed with breach of contract claim that charges were "unlawful" and thus violated the provider's contract); Wogan v. Kunze, 666 S.E.2d 901 (S.C. 2008) (no private right of action under Medicare Act for physician's failure to file Medicare claim).

294 *See* § 9.2.3, *supra*.

295 *See* § 9.4.2.4, *infra*.

296 Banks v. Sec'y of Indiana Family & Soc. Servs. Admin., 997 F.2d 231 (7th Cir. 1993) (provider is precluded from seeking payment from patient after submitting claim to Medicaid, whether Medicaid pays the claim or denies it); Serafini v. Blake, 213 Cal. Rptr. 207 (Cal. Ct. App. 1985) (provider cannot bill Medicaid patient for claims denied by Medicaid due to provider error).

297 Layton Physical Therapy Co. v. Palozzi, 777 N.E.2d 306 (Ohio Ct. App. 2002) (when patient was eligible for Medicaid, and Medicaid approved the treatments, provider could not sue patient or parents for covered services; failure to timely bill Medicaid did not make services "uncovered" for billing purposes). *Cf.* Evanston Hosp. v. Hauck, 1 F.3d 540 (7th Cir. 1993) (once hospital accepts Medicaid or Medicare payment, it is barred from pursuing the patient for any balance, and it cannot avoid this by returning the payment to the government); Picker v. Castro, 776 N.Y.S.2d 433 (N.Y. App. Term 2003) (provider's refusal to fill out insurance paperwork violated duty of good faith and fair dealing; provider precluded from recovering fees from patient). *But see* Wentz v. Kindred Hosps. E., L.L.C., 333 F. Supp. 2d 1298 (S.D. Fla. 2004) (provider returned Medicare payment so it could seek recovery against patient's personal injury settlement).

At least one state (Texas) similarly prohibits providers from recovering from a patient the amount that would have been paid by an insurer, if the reason for non-coverage is that the provider failed to bill the insurer in a timely manner. Tex. Civ. Prac. & Rem. Code Ann. §§ 146.002, 146.003 (West) (provider must submit bill within either eleven months or the time specified in any contract with insurer).

298 Mount Sinai Hosp. v. Kornegay, 347 N.Y.S.2d 807 (N.Y. Civ. Ct. 1973) (when hospital failed to submit Medicaid application it was barred from seeking payment from the patient). *See* Alan Alop, Defending Hospital Collection Cases (rev. ed. 2005), *available at* www.illinoislegaladvocate.org/index.cfm?fuseaction=home.dsp_content&contentID=728.

299 Froedtert Mem'l Lutheran Hosp., Inc. v. Nat'l States Ins. Co., 765 N.W.2d 251 (Wis. 2009) (in case involving Medigap insurance, hospital permitted to bill Medigap insurer at full chargemaster rates; hospital not limited to Medicare rates).

300 Manjusha P. Kulkarni, Nat'l Health L. Program, Fact Sheet: State and Provider Liens Asserted Against the Recoveries of Medicaid and Medicare Beneficiaries (June 2004), *available at* www.healthlaw.org/publications/browse-all-publications/factsheet-state-and-provider-liens#.UziHh8f7ofE.

Thus, one tactic used by providers is to decline billing Medicaid/Medicare, or a private insurer, to avoid balance billing prohibitions.[301] Unfortunately, several courts have allowed this tactic, holding that if a hospital never bills Medicare or Medicaid at all, it is permitted to seek recovery from the patient's tort settlement.[302] Indeed, guidelines issued by the Centers for Medicare & Medicaid not only permit this practice, they allow the provider to charge full chargemaster rates instead of Medicare rates.[303] However, if a Medicare patient does have a potential recovery from liability insurance, Medicare rules may prohibit the hospital from charging more than the amount of the proceeds of the insurance, minus "applicable procurement" costs.[304]

The flip side of the Medicaid and Medicare balance billing protections is that beneficiaries must assign their right to payment from any liable third party to the Medicaid or Medicare program so that the program will have a lien against beneficiaries' tort recoveries.[305] However, the amount of this lien may not exceed the portion of the tort recovery allocated to medical expenses.[306]

There are similar protections against balance billing for services covered by worker's compensation and other government programs.[307] Providers may also be precluded from balance billing patients with private insurance under state law[308]

A provision in the Medicare regulations that similarly prohibited liens against beneficiaries' tort recoveries was eliminated in 2003; thus it appears such liens are permissible with respect to Medicare beneficiaries under certain conditions. *Id. See* § 9.7, *infra* (discussing provider and insurer liens on tort recoveries).

301 See § 9.7.2, *infra*, for a discussion of provider liens on tort settlements after receiving insurance payments. *See, e.g.*, Whittaker v. Lee Mem'l Health Sys., 177 Fed. Appx. 892 (11th Cir. 2006) (patient had viable third-party beneficiary contract claim against hospital that declined insurance payments in order to seek lien against patient's automobile insurance policy); Wentz v. Kindred Hosps. E., L.L.C., 333 F. Supp. 2d 1298 (S.D. Fla. 2004) (provider returned Medicare payment so it could seek recovery against patient's personal injury settlement); Constantine v. MCG Health, Inc., 619 S.E.2d 718 (Ga. Ct. App. 2005) (hospital that was paid by insurer attempted to return payment and then claim lien on patient's tort recovery), *overruled on other grounds by* MCG Health, Inc. v. Owners Ins. Co., 707 S.E.2d 349 (Ga. 2011).

302 Miller v. Gorski Wladyslaw Estate, 547 F.3d 273 (5th Cir. 2008) (since hospital never billed Medicaid, protections were never triggered); Bogolia v. Danielson, 978 N.E.2d 756 (Ind. Ct. App. 2012) (since patient may have had tort recovery, provider did not violate balance billing prohibition as a matter of law, even when Medicare was billed and provider simply refused to accept payment check; citing Medicare's status as secondary payer); Speegle v. Harris Methodist Health Sys., 303 S.W.3d. 32 (Tex. App. 2009) (because Medicare requires hospital to bill other payers first, hospital could seek lien against patient's tort recovery and refrain from billing Medicare; Texas statute requiring that hospital bill Medicare first was preempted); Gister v. Am. Family Mut. Ins. Co., 818 N.W.2d 880 (Wis. 2012) (Wisconsin statute implementing Medicaid balance billing prohibition did not bar hospital lien against recipients' tort recoveries, following Miller v. Gorski Wladyslaw Estate, 547 F.3d 273 (5th Cir. 2008)).

303 Bogolia v. Danielson, 978 N.E.2d 756 (Ind. Ct. App. 2012) (concurrence; citing Medicare Secondary Payer (MSP) Manual, Ch. 2, § 40.2(D)).

304 Anderson v. Good Shepard Hosp., Inc., 2011 WL 846091 (E.D. Tex. Mar. 8, 2011) (permitting FDCPA claim against collector that dunned Medicare patient for hospital charges in excess of liability insurance proceeds).

305 42 U.S.C. §§ 1395y(b)(2)(Medicare), 1396a(a)(25)(H)(Medicaid). *See generally* Manjusha P. Kulkarni, Nat'l Health Law Program, Fact Sheet: State and Provider Liens Asserted Against the Recoveries of Medicaid and Medicare Beneficiaries (June 2004), *available at* www.healthlaw.org/publications/browse-all-publications/factsheet-state-and-provider-liens#.UziHh8f7ofE.

306 Arkansas Dep't of Health & Social Servs. v. Ahlborn, 547 U.S. 268, 126 S. Ct. 1752, 164 L. Ed. 2d 459 (2006). *See also* Wos v. E.M.A. *ex rel.* Johnson, 133 S. Ct. 1391 (2013) (state law allocating one-third of tort recoveries of Medicaid beneficiaries to medical expenses, upon which state could impose lien, violated federal Medicaid law).

307 *See* Haw. Rev. Stat. § 386-27(b)(2); Va. Code Ann. § 65.2-601.1; Marshall v. Bonded Adjustment Co., 2012 WL 6190616 (E.D. Wash. Dec. 12, 2012) (Washington state prohibits provider from balance billing patient covered by worker's compensation insurance, but only after insurer confirm it will "accept" a claim); Greene v. Life Care Centers of Am., Inc., 2008 WL 5378259 (D.S.C. Dec. 23, 2008) (regulations implementing TRICARE insurance program for military veterans prohibits providers from balance billing covered veterans); Nelson-McGourty v. L & P Fin. Adjusters, Inc., 2010 WL 3190711 (N.D. Ill. Aug. 12, 2010) (Illinois Worker's Compensation Act prohibits any collection attempts over services that are the subject of a worker's compensation claim); Rutherford v. Ralph Hutton & Assocs., 2004 WL 1119676 (Cal. Ct. App. May 20, 2004) (unpublished) (hospital's balance billing by attempting to enforce lien against personal injury recovery was forbidden by hospital's contract with county government program to provide medical care to indigent and uninsured patients); Am. Family Mut. Ins. Co. v. Centura Health-St. Anthony Centura Hosp., 46 P.3d 490 (Colo. App. 2002) (workers' compensation statute prescribes amount hospital may charge); Rivera v. Veterans Mem'l Med. Ctr., 818 A.2d 731 (Conn. 2003) (class action alleging violations of Connecticut UDAP law, abuse of process, and breach of the implied covenant of good faith and fair dealing over hospital's collection activities for medical services that were covered by workers' compensation); Pub. Health Trust v. Dade Cnty. Sch. Bd., 693 So. 2d 562 (Fla. Dist. Ct. App. 1996); MCG Health, Inc. v. Owners Ins. Co., 707 S.E.2d 349 (Ga. 2011) (TRICARE program prohibited hospital from balance billing); Valley Rehab. & Med. Servs. v. Cash, 789 N.Y.S.2d 869 (N.Y. Dist. Ct. 2004) (New York worker's compensation law permits provider to recover against patient only if patient fails to prosecute claim for worker's compensation or board determines patient's condition is not covered by program; otherwise provider must collect fees from the carrier); Grey v. Walgreen Co., 2011 WL5999029 (Ohio Ct. App. Dec. 1, 2011) (Ohio law limits amount that healthcare providers are permitted to charge worker's compensation recipients, but no private right of action against pharmacy that overcharged recipients); Daughters of Charity Health Servs. v. Linnstaedter, 226 S.W.3d 409 (Tex. 2007) (when workers' compensation insurer reimbursed hospital, labor code limits on charges barred hospital from filing property code lien against tort recovery from at-fault driver). *But see* Alaska Native Tribal Health Consortium v. Settlement Funds Held for or to Be Paid on Behalf of E.R. *ex rel.* Ridley, 84 P.3d 418 (Alaska 2004) (hospital that provided free care to Alaska natives could place lien on tort recoveries; federal statute that forbade Indian Health Service facilities to charge patients did not prohibit them from recovering under Alaska lien law); Allen & Norman, L.L.C. v. Chauvin, 916 So. 2d 1071 (La. Ct. App. 2005) (provider not prohibited by Louisiana workers' compensation law from balance billing by placing lien on tort recovery of patient).

308 N.C. Gen. Stat. § 131E-91(a) (prohibiting hospitals from billing insured patients for charges that would have been covered by insurance if a claim had been timely submitted); Tex. Civ. Prac. & Rem. Code Ann. §§ 146.002, 146.003 (West) (prohibiting providers from recovering from a patient the amount that would have been paid by an insurer, if the reason for non-coverage is that the provider failed to bill the insurer in a timely manner); Families USA, Medical Debt: What States

or under their contracts with insurers.[309] Some insurers have even filed lawsuits against providers who balanced billed their members.[310] On the other hand, patients have sued their insurers for providers' balance billing, based on the insurers' guarantees that they would not be billed for amounts other than co-payments and deductibles.[311] A particularly difficult issue is

Are Doing to Protect Consumers (Nov. 2009) (summary of state law protections against balance billing). *See* Peoria Tazewell Pathology Group, S.C. v. Messmore, 2011 WL 4498937 (N.D. Ill. Sept. 23, 2011) (dismissing constitutional challenge to Illinois law prohibiting balance billing of insured patients by out-of-network providers); Agostino v. Quest Diagnostics, Inc., 256 F.R.D. 437 (D.N.J. 2009) (discussing various state law prohibitions against balance billing but denying class certification); Prospect Med. Group, Inc. v. Northridge Emergency Med. Group, 198 P.3d 86 (Cal. 2009) (California law prohibits providers from balance billing HMO members, even when provider did not have contract with HMO, but HMO obligated to pay bill under Cal. law requiring payment for emergency care); Gianetti v. Siglinger, 900 A.2d 520 (Conn. 2006) (health plan agreement and Conn. law forbade balance billing; affirming trial court's award of $26,000 and attorney fees of $40,000 under Connecticut UDAP statute for physician's repeated violation of both agreement and law); Gianetti v. Rutkin, 70 A.3d 104 (Conn. App. Ct. 2013) (Connecticut law prohibits balance billing of enrollees in health insurance plan but only extends to in-network providers); Joseph L. Riley Anesthesia Assocs. v. Stein, 27 So. 3d 140 (Fla. Dist. Ct. App. 2010) (hospital-based anesthesiologists prohibited by Fla. law from balance billing HMO subscribers, despite fact that only hospital and not anesthesiologists had contract with HMO); Scull v. Groover, Christie & Merrit, P.C., 76 A.3d 1186 (M.D. 2013) (Maryland HMO Act prohibits providers from balance billing patients for any services covered by the HMO; no private remedy under HMO Act but allowing UDAP claim to go forward); Valley Hosp. v. Kroll, 847 A.2d 636 (N.J. Super. Ct. Law Div. 2003) (New Jersey law prohibited hospital from balance billing difference between "list charges" and amount covered by private Medigap insurance); McArthur v. Randall, 852 N.E.2d 198 (Ohio Ct. App. 2006) (Ohio law requires providers to seek compensation for services covered by insurance solely from insurer; if provider was under contract with patient's insurer, he could not recover against patient); Grandview/Southview Hosps. v. Monie, 2005 WL 737393 (Ohio Ct. App. Apr. 1, 2005) (noting that Ohio law requires providers to seek compensation for covered services solely from insurer except for co-pays and deductibles); Seminole Family Med. Clinic v. Southern, 116 P.3d 191 (Okla. Civ. App. 2005) (noting Okla. State Board of Health rule requiring contracts between HMOs and providers to hold patients harmless if HMO does not pay claim; in this case, patient failed to show she was covered by HMO during relevant time period of services). *Cf.* Richmond *ex rel.* Richmond v. Caban, 754 N.E.2d 871 (Ill. App. Ct. 2001) (hospital could choose whether to bill HMO or place lien on tort recovery; but lien may be invalid under provision of HMO statute that forbids provider to have recourse against plan members for anything except co-pays, deductibles, and non-covered services; open question regarding interaction between HMO statute and lien statute).

309 Mikula v. Great Lakes Fin. Servs., Inc., 2004 WL 1656556 (N.D. Ill. July 22, 2004) (FDCPA claim alleged against hospital for balance billing in violation of hospital's preferred provider agreement with insurer); Lutheran Gen. Hosp., Inc. v. Printing Indus. of Illinois/Indiana Employee Benefit Trust, 24 F. Supp. 2d 846 (N.D. Ill. 1998) (when hospital's agreement with employee benefit plan forbade it to dun patients for services covered by plan, and patient had properly authorized hospital to bill plan, hospital was forbidden to bill patient for covered services; remanded on issue of whether all services were covered); Pickering v. Coast Ctr. for Orthopedic Arthroscopic Surgery & Treatment, 2009 WL 932629 (Cal. Ct. App. Apr. 8, 2009) (unpublished) (upholding jury's finding of fraud and FDCPA violations when provider accepted partial payment from insurer, then balance billed remainder at chargemaster rates, and initiated collection lawsuit in violation of contract with insurer and provider's representations to patient that insurer would cover bill for surgery); Parnell v. Adventist Health Sys./West, 109 P.3d 69 (Cal. 2005) (provider who agreed to accept insurer's reimbursement as "payment in full" for medical services could not assert lien on patient's tort recovery, despite state law permitting lien, because patient did not owe debt to provider); Constantine v. MCG Health, Inc., 619 S.E.2d 718 (Ga. Ct. App. 2005) (contract between hospital and insurer forbade billing patient), *overruled on other grounds by* MCG Health, Inc. v. Owners Ins. Co., 707 S.E.2d 349 (Ga. 2011); Lopez v. Morley, 817 N.E.2d 592 (Ill. App. Ct. 2004) (lien not permitted but court notes that hospital's contract could have provided that insurance payment would not extinguish debt); N.C. *ex rel.* L.C. v. A.W. *ex rel.* R.W, 713 N.E.2d 775 (Ill. App. Ct. 1999) (HMO contract forbade balance billing; acceptance of HMO payment canceled debt; lien not permitted); Morgan v. St. Luke's Hosp. of Kansas City, 403 S.W.3d 115 (Mo. Ct. App. 2013) (when hospital had contract with patient's insurer and had been paid contract amount, contract prohibited hospital from placing lien seeking additional amounts); Midwest Neurosurgery, P.C. v. State Farm Ins. Companies, 686 N.W.2d 572 (Neb. 2004) (when provider had agreed with HMO to accept specific amount, this was the "amount due"; provider could not place lien on personal injury recovery for its undiscounted bill; note that this depended on precise wording of the contract provisions); Dorr v. Sacred Heart Hosp., 597 N.W.2d 462 (Wis. Ct. App. 1999) (lien was void when auto accident victim was covered by HMO, contract between the hospital and the HMO, as well as a provision of state statute, forbade the hospital to bill the patient for services covered by HMO; allegation that hospital refused to present claim to HMO and sought lien instead sufficient to state a claim for breach of contract, UDAP, and racketeering). *See also* Rutherford v. Ralph Hutton & Assocs., 2004 WL 1119676 (Cal. Ct. App. May 20, 2004) (unpublished) (hospital's balance billing by attempting to enforce lien against personal injury recovery was forbidden by hospital's contract with county government program to provide medical care to indigent and uninsured patients). *But see* Watts v. Promina Gwinnett Health Sys., Inc., 530 S.E.2d 14 (Ga. Ct. App. 2000) (patient's payment of bill waived claim that charge violated hospital's contract with HMO); Rogalla v. Christie Clinic, 794 N.E.2d 384 (Ill. App. Ct. 2003) (subrogation clause in plan's contract with hospital did not conflict with ban on balance billing; hospital's claim was against a fund, that is, the personal injury recovery, not the plan member); Valley Hosp. v. Spunt, 2010 WL 363828 (N.J. Super. Ct. App. Div. Feb. 3, 2010) (contractual provision against balance billing only applies when health care service is covered by HMO policy; hospital permitted to bill patiently directly for uncovered service).

See § 9.7.2, *infra*, for other cases in which providers have sought liens against patients' tort recoveries even after payment of medical bills by insurers.

310 *See, e.g.*, Prospect Med. Group, Inc. v. Northridge Emergency Med. Group, 39 Cal. Rptr. 3d 456 (Cal. Ct. App. 2006) (managed care insurer had standing to litigate reasonableness of balanced billed charges to its subscribers), *rev'd on other grounds*, 198 P.3d 86 (Cal. 2009) (California law prohibits providers from balance billing HMO members, even when provider did not have contract with HMO, but HMO obligated to pay bill under Cal. law requiring payment for emergency care); Joseph L. Riley Anesthesia Assocs. v. Stein, 27 So. 2d 140 (Fla. Dist. Ct. App. 2010) (HMO, along with class of patients/subscribers, filed lawsuit seeking declaration that Fla. law prohibited providers from balance billing subscribers). *See also* Press Release, Horizon Blue Cross Blue Shield of New Jersey Granted Preliminary Injunctive Relief Against Vanguard Anesthesia Associations (Jan. 2007) (HMO obtained injunction against providers over balance billing of its members).

311 Hill v. Senenet, Inc. Employee Health Care Plan, 2012 WL 5199605 (D.S.C. Oct. 22, 2012) (insurer paid discounted amount and patient was

balance billing by providers, especially emergency room physicians, who do not have contracts with managed care organizations.[312] Some states have passed laws protecting patients from this form of balance billing.[313]

9.4 State Laws Applicable to Medical Debt Collection

9.4.1 State Remedies for Medical Debt Collection Abuses

9.4.1.1 Introduction

The most suitable remedies to address medical debt collection might be a state debt collection statute, state unfair and deceptive acts and practices (UDAP) statute, a common law theory such as the tort of intentional infliction of emotional distress, or other state remedies.[314] These remedies may allow suit directly against the health care provider as well as against a collection agency for abusive collection tactics. In addition to private remedies, state regulators can take action against financial misconduct by regulated professionals.[315]

9.4.1.2 State Debt Collection Statutes

State debt collection statutes were passed mostly in the 1960s and 1970s to protect consumers against abusive debt collection practices.[316] The statutes often apply to both creditors and collection agencies.[317] They may have a broader definition of collection agency than the FDCPA, covering other entities such as medical billing providers.[318] They often provide for private actions, attorney fees, and actual damages (and sometimes statutory damages).[319]

9.4.1.3 State Tort Law

In some cases of medical debt collection, state tort law may provide a cause of action. The tort of intentional infliction of emotional distress has widespread recognition and is often

balance billed for remainder; default judgment against insurer under ERISA for failure to pay remainder); Cohen v. Health Net of Cal., Inc., 29 Cal. Rptr. 3d 46 (Cal. Ct. App. 2005) (suit preempted by ERISA). *See also* Franco v. Conn. Gen. Life Ins. Co., 818 F. Supp. 2d 792 (D.N.J. 2011) (permitting ERISA and RICO claims, but dismissing antitrust claim, by consumers against their insurers for failing to pay usual and customary charges to out-of-network providers and leaving consumers exposed to balance billing), *later proceeding at* 289 F.R.D. 121 (D.N.J. 2012) (denying class certification); Clark v. Group Hospitalization & Med. Serv., Inc., 2010 WL 5093629 (S.D. Cal. Dec. 7, 2010) (permitting ERISA and UDAP claims against insurer for failing to pay usual and customary charges to out-of-network providers and leaving consumers exposed to balance billing; UDAP claims not preempted by ERISA).

312 Jack Hoadley, Kevin Lucia, & Sonya Schwartz, California HealthCare Found., Unexpected Charges: What States Are Doing About Balance Billing (Apr. 2009), *available at* www.chcf.org/~/media/MEDIA%20LIBRARY%20Files/PDF/U/PDF%20UnexpectedChargesStatesAndBalanceBilling.pdf. *See, e.g.*, Gianetti v. Rutkin, 70 A.3d 104 (Conn. App. Ct. 2013) (state law prohibition against balance billing did not extend to out-of-network surgeon); Chamberlain v. Farm Bur. Mut. Ins. Co., 137 P.3d 1080 (Kan. Ct. App. 2006) (accident victim's insurer refused to pay full amount of provider's charges because insurer believed they exceeded customary and usual charges, resulting in harm to victim's credit record); Froedtert Mem'l Lutheran Hosp., Inc. v. Nat'l States Ins. Co., 765 N.W.2d 251 (Wis. 2009) (Medigap insurer refused to pay $130,000 difference between full chargemaster and what Medicare would have paid; court required insurer to pay full chargemaster rate).

313 Jack Hoadley, Kevin Lucia, & Sonya Schwartz, California HealthCare Found., Unexpected Charges: What States Are Doing About Balance Billing (Apr. 2009) at 6–91, *available at* www.chcf.org/documents/insurance/UnexpectedChargesStatesAndBalanceBilling.pdf (listing several state law approaches addressing balance billing by out-of-network providers). *See, e.g.*, Peoria Tazewell Pathology Group, S.C. v. Messmore, 2011 WL 4498937 (N.D. Ill. Sept. 23, 2011) (dismissing constitutional challenge to Illinois law prohibiting balance billing of insured patients by out-of-network providers); Prospect Med. Group, Inc. v. Northridge Emergency Med. Group, 198 P.3d 86 (Cal. 2009) (California law prohibits providers from balance billing HMO members, even when provider did not have contract with HMO but HMO obligated to pay bill); Joseph L. Riley Anesthesia Assocs. v. Stein, 27 So. 3d 140 (Fla. Dist. Ct. App. Jan. 29, 2010) (Florida law prohibits providers from balance billing HMO subscribers, even if providers do not have contract with HMO). *But see* Princeton Surgical Assoc. v. Aziz, 2010 WL 1425112 (N.J. Super. Ct. App. Div. Apr. 8, 2010) (patient's HMO paid hospital's bill, but not surgeon's bill, because surgeon was out-of-network; patient liable despite hospital's failure to ensure surgeon was in-network).

314 *See, e.g.*, Joseph v. J.J. Mac Intyre Companies, 238 F. Supp. 2d 1158 (N.D. Cal. 2002) (claims for state and federal debt collection violations, UDAP, and common law torts; barrage of phone calls to disabled senior citizen, despite requests to stop), *later op. at* 281 F. Supp. 2d 1156 (N.D. Cal. 2003) (collector's motion for summary judgment denied); Cal. Shock Trauma Air Rescue v. Holland, 2010 WL 3442212 (Tex. App. Aug. 31, 2010) (upholding default judgment for patient under Texas debt collection and UDAP statutes against air rescue company for violation of agreement to forbear dunning in exchange for patient's partial payment and filing of insurance appeal).

315 *See, e.g.*, Havsy v. Washington State Dep't of Health, 123 Wash. App. 1030 (Wash. Ct. App. 2004) (state board sanctioned doctor in part for misleading patients about the price of treatment, failing to inform patient of the high cost of a certain procedure and that insurance would not cover that procedure, and using a "small-print" form to obtain patient's agreement to be liable for charges; doctor's conduct breached fiduciary duty to patient).

316 *See* National Consumer Law Center, Fair Debt Collection § 10.2 (8th ed. 2014), *updated at* www.nclc.org/library.

317 *Id.* § 10.2.3, Appx. E; Pickering v. Coast Ctr. for Orthopedic Arthroscopic Surgery & Treatment, 2009 WL 932629 (Cal. Ct. App. Apr. 8, 2009) (unpublished) (healthcare provider covered as debt collector under California Rosenthal Act); Mary Elizabeth Nursing Ctr., Inc. v. Lyon, 2012 WL 6924420 (Conn. Super. Ct. Dec. 24, 2012) (state debt collection claim allowed to proceed against original creditor, that is, the nursing home; not preempted by federal nursing home law or Medicaid Act).

318 *See, e.g.*, Whatley v. AHF Fin. Servs., L.L.C., 2012 WL 7159707 (E.D. Tex. Dec. 17, 2012) (court unable to determine whether defendant was "debt collector" under FDCPA, but clearly covered under Texas debt collection law); Flores v. Rawlings Co., 177 P.3d 341 (Haw. 2008) (provider of "claims recovery services" was a collection agency under Hawaii law even though it asserted that it was not covered under FDCPA because it did not collect "debts"; Hawaii statute covers entity that collects "claims or money due on accounts" for another).

319 *See* National Consumer Law Center, Fair Debt Collection § 10.2.5 (8th ed. 2014), *updated at* www.nclc.org/library.

applied in the debt collection context.[320] The advantage of this tort is the likelihood of recovery of punitive damages in an egregious case in which the collector's malice is readily apparent. Some courts permit large punitive damage awards against tortfeasors who make large profits in hopes of deterring similar misconduct by others.[321] The difficulty with this tort is that it is available in many states only for clearly outrageous conduct resulting in very severe distress.[322] The courts often impose a greater duty of care upon debt collectors who are dealing with people known to be disabled or convalescing.[323]

9.4.2 State UDAP Statutes

9.4.2.1 General

State UDAP statutes often proscribe unfair or deceptive debt collection tactics.[324] In some states, UDAP statutes provide for recovery of double or treble actual damages as well as attorney fees. Thus, a harassed consumer with substantial actual damages might recover more under the UDAP statute than the FDCPA.[325]

A UDAP claim may be available for unfair or deceptive practices by providers beyond collection issues.[326] For example, Connecticut courts have held that failure to inform indigent patients of the availability of free care under Hill-Burton or the state free care statute may constitute a violation of the Connecticut Unfair Trade Practices Act.[327]

9.4.2.2 Using UDAP Statutes to Challenge Discriminatory Pricing

UDAP actions have been brought to challenge hospital discriminatory pricing practices when hospitals have charged uninsured patients several times the amounts that are paid by private insurers, Medicaid, or Medicare for the same procedures.[328] There have been several cases which have met with some success,[329]

---

320 *See, e.g.*, Bickford v. Onslow Mem'l Hosp. Found., Inc., 855 A.2d 1150 (Me. 2004) (alleging claims for intentional infliction of emotional distress, as well as for defamation and tortuous interference with an economic advantage, over hospital wrongfully reporting to credit reporting agency that plaintiff owed bills for services to ex-wife's daughter, to whom plaintiff had no legal relationship).

321 *See* National Consumer Law Center, Fair Debt Collection § 6.5 (8th ed. 2014), *updated at* www.nclc.org/library.

322 *See, e.g.*, Ziegler v. Elmore Cnty. Health Care Auth., 56 F. Supp. 2d 1324 (M.D. Ala. 1999) (mother whose sick child was denied treatment at hospital because she owed past-due bill failed to state claim for outrage when child recovered fully and mother alleged no ill effects from her emotional distress); Weiss v. Collection Ctr., Inc., 667 N.W.2d 567 (N.D. 2003) (consumer stated claim for FDCPA violation but not intentional infliction of emotional distress; letter which could be read by unsophisticated consumer as threat to seize vehicle for $255 clinic bill not extreme and outrageous); Froemming v. Perez, 2006 WL 704479 (Tex. App. Mar. 22, 2006) (plaintiff could recover under state UDAP statute, but not for tort of mental anguish, when orthodontist agreed to give plaintiff a discounted price for braces, then reneged on agreement and attempted to extract more money by refusing to complete treatment for plaintiff's daughter).

323 *See* National Consumer Law Center, Fair Debt Collection § 9.2 (8th ed. 2014), *updated at* www.nclc.org/library.

324 *See id.* § 10.3.4. *See also* National Consumer Law Center, Unfair and Deceptive Acts and Practices §§ 2.2.2, 2.3.10, 6.10 (8th ed. 2012), *updated at* www.nclc.org/library.

325 For examples of UDAP cases involving medical debt collection, see Joseph v. J.J. Mac Intyre Companies, 238 F. Supp. 2d 1158 (N.D. Cal. 2002) (state debt collection, UDAP and tort claims for barrage of phone calls to disabled senior citizen), *later op. at* 281 F. Supp. 2d 1156 (N.D. Cal. 2003) (collector's motion for summary judgment denied) and Ahmad v. Yale New Haven Hosp., 38 Conn. L. Rptr. 238 (Conn. Super. Ct. 2004) (use of aggressive debt collection against patients who were eligible for—but never informed of—free or discounted care is actionable under UDAP statute), *later proceeding at* 933 A.2d 1208 (Conn. App. Ct. 2007) (affirming denial of class certification because individualized inquiry required); Cal. Shock Trauma Air Rescue v. Holland, 2010 WL 3442212 (Tex. App. Aug. 31, 2010) (upholding default judgment for patient under Texas debt collection and UDAP statutes against air rescue company for violation of agreement to forbear dunning in exchange for patient's partial payment and filing of insurance appeal).

326 *See, e.g.*, Mary Elizabeth Nursing Ctr., Inc. v. Lyon, 2012 WL 6924420 (Conn. Super. Ct. Dec. 24, 2012) (nursing home sued daughter for services provided to her father; UDAP counterclaim not preempted by Medicaid Act or federal nursing home law); Palmer v. St. Joseph Healthcare, P.S.O., Inc., 77 P.3d 560 (N.M. Ct. App. 2003) (Medicare law did not preempt UDAP and common law claims against HMO that raised premiums and cut back services shortly after promising that these would not change for a year; detailed discussion of Medicare preemption); Froemming v. Perez, 2006 WL 704479 (Tex. App. Mar. 22, 2006) (upholding trial court's decision in favor of plaintiff in UDAP action; patient alleged that orthodontist agreed to a discounted price for braces, then reneged on agreement and attempted to extract more money by refusing to complete treatment). *But see* SWA, Inc. v. Straka, 2003 WL 21434637 (Ohio Ct. App. June 19, 2003) (daughter who did not sign nursing home admission agreement not a consumer within meaning of UDAP, because no transaction with home; when home sued daughter for mother's care, remedy for baseless suit was motion for sanctions, not UDAP counterclaim); Trevino v. Christus Santa Rosa Healthcare Corp., 2002 WL 31423711 (Tex. App. Oct. 30, 2002) (improperly triaged patient gave birth in the bathroom, hospital billed her for labor and delivery; billing for services not performed not a UDAP violation when that section of statute applies only to repairs of goods).

327 Yale New Haven Hosp., Inc. v. Mitchell, 683 A.2d 1362 (Conn. Super. Ct. 1995) (correcting opinion at 662 A.2d 178). *See also* Ahmad v. Yale New Haven Hosp., 38 Conn. L. Rptr. 238 (Conn. Super. Ct. 2004) (finding private right of action under Connecticut free care statute; failure to inform eligible patients of free care availability may violate both free care statute and UDAP statute), *later proceeding at* 933 A.2d 1208 (Conn. App. Ct. 2007) (affirming denial of class certification because individualized inquiry required). *But see* Martinez v. Yale New Haven Hosp., 2005 WL 2364901 (Conn. Super. Ct. Sept. 1, 2005) (striking UDAP claims because plaintiffs failed to allege how violation of charity care statute related to entrepreneurial or business aspect of hospital services).

328 *See* § 9.1.3, *supra*.

329 *See* Hill v. Sisters of St. Francis Health Servs., Inc., 2006 WL 3783415 (N.D. Ill. Dec. 20, 2006) (denying dismissal of UDAP and unconscionability claims for discriminatory pricing); Hale v. Sharp Healthcare, 108 Cal. Rptr. 3d 669 (Cal. Ct. App. 2010) (patient stated claim for violation of Cal. Unfair Competition law and Cal. Legal Remedies Act for discriminatory pricing); *In re* Sutter Health Uninsured Pricing Cases, 2005 WL 1842582 (Cal. Super. Ct. July 16, 2005) (denying dismissal of UDAP and unconscionability claims for discriminatory pricing); Greenfield v. Manor Care, Inc., 705 So. 2d 926 (Fla. Dist. Ct. App. 1997) (reversing dismissal of several claims against nursing home that inflated billing price of pharmaceuticals and other supplies it provided to patients), *overruled on other grounds by* Knowles v. Beverly Enters., 898 So. 2d 1 (Fla. 2004); Servedio v. Our Lady of the Resurrection Med. Ctr., Clearinghouse No. 55,626 (Ill. Cir. Ct. Cook Cnty. Jan. 6,

including settlements of class actions.[330] On the other hand, many courts have found discriminatory pricing not actionable under UDAP statutes,[331] and some have expressed a judicial reluctance or even hostility to the concept that discriminatory pricing is an unfair practice.[332]

2005); Turner v. Legacy Health Sys., 2006 WL 657176 (Or. Cir. Ct. Oct. 4, 2005) (granting class certification in case challenging discriminatory pricing under Oregon UDAP statute). *See also* Press Release, Court Rules That Advocate Health Care Network May Be Liable for Price Gouging, Hospital Accountability Project—SEIU, Jan. 27, 2006; Mary Jo Feldstein, *BJC Overpayment Case is Class-Action*, St. Louis Post-Dispatch, Mar. 7, 2007 (class action certification granted in discriminatory pricing case against St. Louis area hospital). *Cf.* Urquhart v. Manatee Mem'l Hosp., 2007 WL 781738 (M.D. Fla. Mar. 13, 2007) (while breach of contract and UDAP claim challenging discriminatory pricing were viable, failure to allege actual injury from practice required dismissal); Colomar v. Mercy Hosp., Inc., 461 F. Supp. 2d 1265 (S.D. Fla. 2006) (while fact that uninsured patients paid more than insurers for same services alone would not give rise to UDAP clam, allegations that hospital's prices were excessive in comparison to other hospitals and in comparison to actual cost of services would support viable UDAP claim), *later decision at* 2007 WL 2083562 (S.D. Fla. July 20, 2007) (dismissing claim because patients failed to show hospital's prices were unreasonable by providing evidence of what other hospitals in the same market charged or substantiate what services cost hospital to provide versus what hospital charged); Howard v. Willis-Knighton Med. Ctr. 924 So. 2d 1245 (La. Ct. App. 2006) (discriminatory pricing not sufficient to prove chargemaster rates were not per se unreasonable for the uninsured but might be unreasonable in certain cases, depending upon patient's financial circumstances; need for individual consideration defeated class action certification).

330 *In re* Tenet Healthcare Cases II, 2005 WL 1949562 (Cal. Super. Ct. Aug. 8, 2005); Class Action Settlement and Release, Christiani v. Advocate Health Sys. Care, No. 03 L 014635 (Fla. Cir. Ct. Aug. 15, 2008), *available online as companion material to this treatise*; Order Preliminarily Approving Class Action Settlement, Quintana v. Health Mgmt. Assocs., Case No.: 04-16944 CA-31 (Fla. Cir. Ct. Oct. 31, 2006), *available online as companion material to this treatise. See also* Steven Carter, *Providence Health System Will Offer Refunds To Uninsured*, Portland Oregonian, June 24, 2006; Keith Darcé, *Scripps To Settle Uninsured Billing Suit*, San Diego Union-Tribune, Feb. 1, 2008; Bob Egelko, *Hospital Chain Agrees To Settlement: Catholic Healthcare West Says It Will Pay $423 Million Refund*, San Francisco Chron., Jan. 12, 2007; David Phelps, *Uninsured Patients May Get Discounts: Allina and Fairview Settled a Class-Action Suit Claiming That People Without Health Coverage Paid Too Much For Medical Care*, Minneapolis Star-Tribune, Mar. 17, 2007; Judith Graham, *Hospital Lawsuit Settlement May Help Tens of Thousands of Uninsured Patients*, Chi. Tribune, Jan. 14, 2009 (settlements with Resurrection Health Care and Advocate Health Care).

The *Sutter Health*, *Turner v. Legacy Health*, and *Resurrection Medical* cases all settled as well. *In re* Sutter Health Uninsured Pricing Cases, 89 Cal. Rptr. 3d 615 (Cal. Ct. App. 2009) (approving proposed settlement); *Legacy Uninsured Lawsuit Settlement Approved*, Portland Bus. J., Mar. 6, 2007; Mark Taylor, *Legal Harbinger? Consumer Fraud Settlement May Lead To More*, Modern Healthcare, June 20, 2005 (*Servedio* case). *Cf.* Class Settlement Agreement and Release, *In re* Columbia HCA Healthcare Corp. Billing Practices Litig., No. 3-98-MDL-1227 (M.D. Tenn. Apr. 2003) (settlement of class action alleging ERISA and UDAP violations for billing for medical services not rendered, for exaggerated patient illness, for unnecessary treatment, as well as excessive, unreasonable, or impermissibly high amounts).

331 Geico Indem. Ins. Co. v. Kannaday, 2007 WL 2990552 (D. Kan. Oct. 11, 2007) (discriminatory pricing not unconscionable under Kansas UDAP statute because no evidence of deceptive, oppressive or overreaching actions; uninsured consumer was not "similar consumer in a similar transaction" compared with insured consumer); Harrison v. Christus St. Patrick Hosp., 430 F. Supp. 2d 591 (W.D. La. 2006) (dismissing breach of contract and fiduciary duty claims, as well as unjust enrichment for discriminatory pricing claim); Banner Health v. Med. Sav. Ins. Co., 163 P.3d 1096 (Ariz. Ct. App. 2007) (discriminatory pricing was not unconscionable or unreasonable because hospital was required to file its rates with state agency); Nunes v. The Hosp. Comm. for Livermore-Pleasanton Areas, 2012 WL 1925537 (Cal. Ct. App. May 29, 2012) (no UDAP violation for discriminatory pricing when hospital informed consumer of availability of financial assistance); Williams v. Mission Viejo Emergency Med. Assoc., 2011 WL 5025932 (Cal. Ct. App. Oct. 21, 2011) (unpublished) (discriminatory pricing not actionable under UDAP statute because plaintiff failed to establish that lower negotiated fees for insurers should be deemed "usual, customary and reasonable" rates); Durell v. Sharp Healthcare, 108 Cal. Rptr. 3d 682 (Cal Ct. App. 2010)(discriminatory pricing not an "unfair business practice" under California Unfair Competition Law; relying on narrower construction of "unfairness" prong); Hillsborough Cnty. Hosp. Auth. v. Fernandez, 664 So. 2d 1071 (Fla. Dist. Ct. App. 1995) (evidence that hospital entered into contracts with managed care providers for certain discounts was not sufficient to prove that rates charged to uninsured individuals were excessive); Satterfield v. S. Reg'l Health Sys., Inc., 634 S.E.2d 530 (Ga. Ct. App. 2006) (discriminatory pricing was not deceptive or confusing in violation of Georgia UDAP statute); Morrell v. Wellstar Health Sys., Inc., 633 S.E.2d 68 (Ga. Ct. App. 2006) (discriminatory pricing was not deceptive or confusing in violation of Georgia UDAP statute); Cox v. Athens Reg'l Med. Ctr., Inc., 631 S.E.2d 792 (Ga. Ct. App. 2006) (same); Galvan v. Northwestern Mem'l Hosp., 888 N.E.2d 529 (Ill. App. Ct. 2008) (discriminatory pricing not unfair because insured and uninsured patients are not similarly situated); Rockford Mem'l Hosp. v. Havrilesko, 858 N.E.2d 56 (Ill. App. Ct. 2006) (excessive charges were not unfair under Illinois UDAP statute; plaintiffs failed to sufficiently plead claim that hospital deceptively concealed facts about billing practices); Thorne v. Doe, 724 So. 2d 242 (La. Ct. App. 1998) (price of certain blood products administered in the hospital was 400% to 500% higher than price for same products for home administration; overcharging not shown, when no showing that plaintiff was billed more than "hospital's established price"); Shelton v. Duke Univ. Health Sys., Inc., 633 S.E.2d 113 (N.C. Ct. App. 2006) (no breach of contract or fiduciary duty claims for discriminatory pricing); Firelands Reg'l Med. Ctr. v. Jeavons, 2008 WL 4408600 (Ohio Ct. App. Sept. 30, 2008) (following *Galvan* to hold that discriminatory pricing not unfair because insured and uninsured patients are not similarly situated); Mercy Health Partners of Southwest Ohio v. Miller, 2005 WL 2592674 (Ohio Ct. Ct. Com. Pl. Sept. 30, 2005) (discriminatory pricing not unfair practice under Ohio UDAP statute and plaintiff failed to allege any statements about hospital pricing that were misleading); Nygaard v. Sioux Valley Hosp. & Health Sys., 731 N.W.2d 184 (S.D. 2007) (discriminatory pricing not deceptive practice; note that South Dakota UDAP statute does not prohibit "unfair" practices).

332 DiCarlo v. St. Mary's Hosp., 2006 WL 2038498 (D.N.J. July 19, 2006) ("For a court to presume to address [the problems of discriminatory pricing] would be rushing in where angels fear to tread"; relying on *Kolari* even after reversal), *aff'd*, 530 F.3d 255 (3d Cir. 2008) (adopting district court decision); Kolari v. N.Y. Presbyterian Hosp., 382 F. Supp. 2d 562 (S.D.N.Y. 2005) ("This orchestrated assault on scores of nonprofit hospitals, necessitating the expenditure of those hospitals' scarce resources to beat back meritless legal claims, is undoubtedly part of the litigation explosion that has been so well-documented in the media."), *vacated in relevant part*, 455 F.3d 118 (2d Cir. 2006) (trial court abused its discretion in exercising supplemental jurisdiction over state law claims after dismissing federal claims).

Some courts have dismissed UDAP claims citing state statutes that require hospitals to disclose their charges to consumers or file them with state agencies. For example, the court in *Cox v. Athens Regional Medical Center*[333] based its decision, in part, on the fact that Georgia law provided patients with the right to request a copy of hospital charges, and Georgia policy was to encourage market forces to control health care costs by providing information so that consumers could make cost-effective decisions by comparison shopping.

The problem with this reasoning is that comparison shopping is often difficult when medical decisions are involved, especially in emergency situations. Note that two of the plaintiffs in *Cox* received treatment, respectively, for a burned hand and in the emergency room. Would it have been realistic for them to go "comparison shopping"?

Other courts have held that UDAP claims for discriminatory pricing failed because the patients never paid the charges and thus did not suffer actual damages.[334] However some UDAP statutes permit patients to seek injunctive relief.[335] In addition, patients could claim they suffered damages in the form of collection activity against them, negative credit reports showing the inflated hospital bills as delinquent debts, or even health consequences from being deterred from seeking additional care due to the inflated debts.[336] One problem with requiring patients to first pay the inflated bill before bringing a UDAP action is that defendants might then argue that patients are foreclosed from bringing a claim because of the voluntary payment doctrine.[337]

A few state attorneys general have challenged discriminatory pricing as an unfair practice.[338] A hospital seeking inflated charges when placing liens against tort settlements[339] might be subject to a UDAP claim.[340]

9.4.2.3 UDAP Claims for "Double Dipping"

UDAP statutes might be used to challenge the practices of hospitals who sell their debts to debt buyers[341] after the hospitals have received some sort of payment, reimbursement, or "credit" for such debt. For example, hospitals often receive federal government reimbursements for unpaid deductibles and co-pays owed by Medicare beneficiaries. A condition for such reimbursements is that there is "no likelihood of recovery at any time in the future" of such debts.[342] Medicare beneficiaries could challenge as an unfair practice the selling and

---

333 631 S.E.2d 792 (Ga. Ct. App. 2006). *See also* Satterfield v. S. Reg'l Health Sys., Inc., 634 S.E.2d 530 (Ga. Ct. App. 2006) (discriminatory pricing was not deceptive or confusing in violation of Georgia UDAP statute); Morrell v. Wellstar Health Sys., Inc., 633 S.E.2d 68 (Ga. Ct. App. 2006) (discriminatory pricing was not deceptive or confusing in violation of Georgia UDAP statute). *Cf.* Banner Health v. Med. Sav. Ins. Co., 163 P.3d 1096 (Ariz. Ct. App. 2007) (because hospital was required to file its rates with state agency, the rates could not be challenged as unconscionable or unreasonable, despite the fact that rates were 400% of hospital's costs and hospital only charged full rates to 2% of patients).

334 Urquhart v. Manatee Mem'l Hosp., 2007 WL 781738 (M.D. Fla. Mar. 13, 2007) (while breach of contract and UDAP claim challenging discriminatory pricing were viable, failure to allege actual injury from practice required dismissal); Freeman Health Sys. v. Wass, 124 S.W.3d 504 (Mo. Ct. App. 2004) (discriminatory pricing claim failed to allege ascertainable loss required as element under Missouri UDAP statute, because patients had not paid the amount hospital charged). *Cf.* Woodrum v. Integris Health, Inc., 2007 WL 201045 (W.D. Okla. Jan. 24, 2007) (breach of contract action dismissed because patients would not be able to show damages because they had not paid amount charged by hospital); Lester E. Cox Med. Ctr. v. Huntsman, 2003 WL 22004998 (W.D. Mo. Aug. 5, 2003) (UDAP claim for overcharging; ascertainable damages not shown, as amount of alleged overcharge was much less than amount owing on bill and litigation expenses in contesting the bill not recoverable as damages), *aff'd*, 408 F.3d 989 (8th Cir. 2005); Hoover v. Mercy Health, ___ S.W.2d. ___, 2012 WL 2549485 (Mo. Ct. App. July 3, 2012), *transferred to Missouri Supreme Court*, 408 S.W.3d 140 (Mo. 2013) (UDAP claim over discriminatory pricing failed because plaintiff paid $5300 out of $17,337 bill and failed to show that $5300 exceeded reasonable value; following *Freeman*).

335 Smallwood v. Cent. Peninsula Gen. Hosp., 151 P.3d 319 (Alaska 2006) (patient did not suffer actual damages from hospital's balance billing but could seek injunctive relief under state UDAP statute). *See generally* National Consumer Law Center, Unfair and Deceptive Acts and Practices § 13.6.2 (8th ed. 2012), *updated at* www.nclc.org/library.

336 *See* Woodrum v. Integris Health, Inc., 2007 WL 201045 (W.D. Okla. Jan. 24, 2007) (patients could potentially show damages from being charged too much, even though they had not paid the bill; however, in this case, plaintiffs failed to offer evidence that they had actually suffered such damages); Hale v. Sharp Healthcare, 108 Cal. Rptr. 3d 669 (Cal. Ct. App. 2010) (patient adequately pleaded injury in fact from discriminatory pricing, despite having not paid entire bill, as she faced an imminent invasion or injury to a legally protected interest).

337 *See* Hall v. Humana Hosp. Daytona Beach, 686 So. 2d 653 (Fla. Dist. Ct. App. 1996) (granting summary judgment against class of patients who had already paid their bills in class action seeking to recover alleged overcharges for pharmaceuticals, medical supplies, and laboratory services); Watts v. Promina Gwinnett Health Sys., Inc., 530 S.E.2d 14 (Ga. Ct. App. 2000) (patient's voluntary payment of hospital bill out of proceeds of tort judgment barred claim that charges were unreasonable and not authorized by hospital's agreement with health maintenance organization or patient's assignment of benefits). *But see* Ramirez v. Smart Corp., 863 N.E.2d 800 (Ill. App. Ct. 2007) (voluntary payment doctrine did not apply to UDAP claims). *See generally* National Consumer Law Center, Unfair and Deceptive Acts and Practices § 4.2.19.5 (8th ed. 2012), *updated at* www.nclc.org/library.

338 Press Release, Office of the Wis. Att'y Gen., Actions Against Hospitals for Overcharging the Uninsured (Nov. 7, 2005) (lawsuits against St. Joseph's Regional Medical Center and Wisconsin Heart Hospital by Wisconsin attorney general alleging discriminatory pricing constitute unfair trade practice); Agreement, *In re* Allina Health Sys., No. C1-05-4576 (May 2005) (settlement between Minnesota attorney general and Allina Health System that requires Allina to charge uninsured consumers no more than the rate for "most favored insurer" and to reform debt collection practices).

339 *See* § 9.7, *infra* (discussing hospital liens on tort settlements).

340 Via Christi Reg'l Med. Ctr., Inc. v. Reed, 314 P.3d 852 (Kan. 2013) (permitting UDAP claim against hospital for inflated pricing and duplicate charges in asserting lien). *But see* Baker v. Baptist Hosp., 115 So. 3d 1123 (Fla. Dist. Ct. App. 2013) (filing a hospital lien not an act in trade or commerce and thus is not covered under UDAP statute).

341 *See* National Consumer Law Center, Fair Debt Collection § 9.2.3 (8th ed. 2014), *updated at* www.nclc.org/library (discussion of debt buyers).

342 42 C.F.R. § 413.89(e).

The Department of Health and Human Services has denied reimbursement to hospitals for claimed bad debts that are in possession of an outside collection agency. *See, e.g.*, Battle Creek Health Sys. v. Leavitt, 498 F.3d 401 (6th Cir. 2007); Mesquite Cmty. Hosp. v. Levitt, 2008 WL 4148970 (N.D. Tex. Sept. 5, 2008).

collection of debt for which a hospital has already received a payment from the federal government,[343] especially given that the hospital has represented to the government that there was no likelihood of recovery of that debt.

Another example of such "double dipping" would be the sale of medical debts for which hospitals have received reimbursement as part of a state charity care or rate-setting program. For example, a media investigation revealed that hospitals in Maryland routinely collected debts that they have already factored into the hospitals' rate requests to the state agency that sets their rates.[344] The rates set by the state agency were supposed to compensate the hospitals for bad debts. If such debts had been sold to a debt buyer, one could argue that the hospitals unfairly "double dipped" by collecting additional sums after their rates have been set to allow for bad debt recovery. Other states may have programs that compensate hospitals for charity or uncompensated care.[345]

9.4.2.4 Other UDAP Claims for Medical Debt

Other unfair or deceptive practices by health care providers can be challenged under UDAP statutes. Some UDAP statutes provide that a violation of a federal or another state law is a per se UDAP violation.[346] Thus, UDAP actions have been brought against health care providers that violate prohibitions against the balance billing[347] of patients who are covered by Medicare, Medicaid, workers compensation, or private insurance.[348] However UDAP actions against insurers over balance billing may be preempted by ERISA.[349]

A UDAP claim might be brought against a provider who misrepresents that the patient's insurance will pay all charges and who then subsequently bills the patient.[350] UDAP actions may lie against providers who pressure non-responsible relatives to accept liability for medical bills.[351] A UDAP counterclaim may be raised when the provider's actions prevent the patient

343 Ironically, hospitals appear to believe that selling the debt actually relieves them from noncompliance with these Medicare rules. Cynthia Wilson, *Medical Debt Sellers Looking for Buyers in Weak Financial Market*, www.insideARM.com (Jan. 23, 2009) (noting that "some hospitals are selling the self-pay portion of the Medicare receivables . . . to ensure the hospital stays in compliance with the Centers for Medicare and Medicaid Services rules for not benefiting from future collection efforts").

344 Fred Schulte & James Drew, *In Their Debt*, Balt. Sun, Dec. 21, 2008.

345 For an overview of state charity or free care programs, *see* www.communitycatalyst.org/initiatives-and-issues/initiatives/hospital-accountability-project/free-care.

346 *See* National Consumer Law Center, Unfair and Deceptive Acts and Practices § 3.2.7 (8th ed. 2012), *updated at* www.nclc.org/library.

347 *See* § 9.3.7, *supra*.

348 *See, e.g.*, Greene v. Life Care Centers of Am., Inc., 2008 WL 5378259 (D.S.C. Dec. 23, 2008) (patient could bring claim for "false representation" when provider billed patient in violation of regulations against balance billing); Wentz v. Kindred Hosps. E., L.L.C., 333 F. Supp. 2d 1298 (S.D. Fla. 1298 (S.D. Fla. 2004) (no private right of action to enforce Medicare's balance billing prohibition, but patient could proceed with breach of contract claim that charges were "unlawful" and thus violated provider's contract); Smallwood v. Cent. Peninsula Gen. Hosp., 151 P.3d 319 (Alaska 2006) (patients could challenge hospital's balance billing in violation of Medicaid regulations as UDAP violation and as third-party beneficiary of agreement between state and hospital); Pickering v. Coast Ctr. for Orthopedic Arthroscopic Surgery & Treatment, 2009 WL 932629 (Cal. Ct. App. Apr. 8, 2009) (unpublished) (upholding jury's finding of common law fraud and FDCPA violations when provider accepted partial payment from insurer, then balance billed remainder at chargemaster prices and initiated collection lawsuit in violation of contract with insurer); Gianetti v. Siglinger, 900 A.2d 520 (Conn. 2006) (affirming trial court's award of $26,000 and attorney fees of $40,000 under UDAP statute for physician's repeated violation of health plan agreement and Connecticut law prohibiting balance billing); Rivera v. Veterans Mem'l Med. Ctr., 818 A.2d 731 (Conn. 2003) (class action alleging violations of Connecticut UDAP law, abuse of process, and breach of the implied covenant of good faith and fair dealing over hospital's balance billing and collection efforts when workers' compensation covered medical services); Scull v. Groover, Christie & Merrit, P.C., 76 A.3d 1186 (M.D. 2013) (Maryland HMO Act prohibits providers from balance billing patients for any services covered by the HMO; no private remedy under HMO Act but allowing UDAP claim to go forward); Morgan v. St. Luke's Hosp. of Kansas City, 403 S.W.3d 115 (Mo. Ct. App. 2013) (allowing UDAP claim when hospital violated contract with patient's insurer by balance billing). *Cf.* Agostino v. Quest Diagnostics, Inc., 2011 WL 5410667 (D.N.J. Nov. 3, 2011) (summary judgment for consumer on FDCPA claim that collector added fee not permitted by provider's contract with insurer). *But see* Olszewski v. Scripps Health, 135 Cal. Rptr. 2d 1 (Cal. 2003) (no UDAP claim against provider that filed lien for customary charges pursuant to Cal. law; court held that Cal. lien law was preempted by federal Medicaid law but provided safe harbor defense against UDAP claim); Williams v. Mission Viejo Emergency Med. Assoc., 2011 WL 5025932 (Cal. Ct. App. Oct. 21, 2011) (unpublished) (balance billing not actionable under UDAP statute because economic injury resulted from deductible, not from balance billing); Wogan v. Kunze, 623 S.E.2d 107 (S.C. Ct. App. 2005) (patient's widow failed to state UDAP claim for balance billing in violation of Medicare Act because statute did not permit her to sue in representative capacity; in this case, patient paid for prescription drug out of pocket). *Cf.* Ruggiero v. Kavlich, 2010 WL 3351429 (Ohio Ct. App. Aug. 26, 2010) (reversing judgment in favor of patient for abuse of process claim for balance billing; provider's staff mistakenly billed Medicare, but court noted provider returned payments).

349 *See* Cohen v. Health Net of Cal., Inc., 29 Cal. Rptr. 3d 46 (Cal. Ct. App. 2005). *See* National Consumer Law Center, Unfair and Deceptive Acts and Practices § 10.3.7 (8th ed. 2012), *updated at* www.nclc.org/library. *But see generally* Clark v. Group Hospitalization & Med. Serv., Inc., 2010 WL 5093629 (S.D. Cal. Dec. 7, 2010) (UDAP claim not preempted by ERISA because did not seek to enforce the terms of plan; instead it sought to injunction to enforce California law's prohibitions against balance billing).

A claim might be available under ERISA itself for balance billing. *See* Franco v. Conn. Gen. Life Ins. Co., 818 F. Supp. 2d 792 (D.N.J. 2011) (permitting ERISA and RICO claims by consumers against their insurers for failing to pay usual and customary charges to out-of-network providers and leaving consumers exposed to balance billing), *later proceeding at* 289 F.R.D. 121 (D.N.J. 2012) (denying class certification).

350 Pickering v. Coast Ctr. for Orthopedic Arthroscopic Surgery & Treatment, 2009 WL 932629 (Cal. Ct. App. Apr. 8, 2009) (unpublished) (upholding jury's finding of common law fraud when provider initiated collection lawsuit despite its representations to patient that insurer would cover bill for surgery).

351 Podolsky v. First Healthcare Corp., 58 Cal. Rptr. 2d 89 (Cal. Ct. App. 1996) (nursing home violated UDAP law by soliciting relatives for voluntary agreement to be financially responsible for patient, due to lack of consideration for voluntary agreement and failure to inform relatives of their rights under federal law to refuse agreement). *But see* Carroll v. Butterfield Health Care, Inc., 2003 WL 22462604 (N.D.

from obtaining insurance coverage,[352] or when the provider uses unfair or deceptive tactics in soliciting patients to apply for a medical credit card.[353]

One court held it was not a deceptive practice under a state UDAP law for a hospital to have a hidden policy of granting discounts to patients who asked for them but not disclosing this policy to all patients.[354]

9.4.2.5 Exemptions for Health Care Providers in State UDAP Statutes

Some state UDAP statutes exempt transactions between consumers and physicians, or members of learned professions in general.[355] These exemptions have defeated several challenges to discriminatory pricing.[356] These exemptions may not, however, apply to a transaction with a service provider such as an HMO.[357] These exemptions also should not apply to debt collectors working on behalf of medical professionals.[358]

In other states there is an exemption for the professional aspects of medical care, but not the entrepreneurial aspects, so misrepresentations about billing would probably not be exempt.[359] Health care providers might also be excluded from UDAP coverage under state laws that exempt businesses governed by a regulatory body[360] or nonprofits.[361]

9.4.3 Comprehensive Medical Debtor Protection Laws

9.4.3.1 Introduction

Several states, recognizing the special burden created by health care debts and the problem of discriminatory pricing, have enacted medical debtor protection laws. These states include California, Connecticut, Illinois, Maryland, Nevada, New Jersey, New York, and North Carolina. Massachusetts has established medical debtor protections by regulation. In addition, the Minnesota and Wisconsin Attorney Generals' Offices have reached agreements with hospitals in their states, providing for similar protections.[362]

Most of these medical debtor protection laws limit what hospitals can charge uninsured and under-insured patients who are low- or moderate-income, often to the amount paid by government or private insurers. They require hospitals to establish charity care policies and to notify patients of these polices. Some of these laws include debt collection protections and limits on interest. Many of these laws are similar to, but sometimes stronger than, the financial assistance debt collection protections of the Affordable Care Act.[363]

Unfortunately, compliance with these medical debtor laws has been spotty at best. A study by the Community Service Society of New York (CSS) found that the majority of New York hospitals studied by CSS were violating the New York medical debtor law.[364] The Minnesota attorney general's office found significant noncompliance by one hospital chain,

---

Ill. Oct. 29, 2003) (no state UDAP claim against nursing home that required guarantee in violation of federal law).

For examples of pressuring non-responsible relatives, see § 9.5.3.2, *infra*. For a discussion of the prohibition in the Nursing Home Reform Law against requiring a resident's family or friends to become financially responsible for expenses, see § 9.3.6, *supra*.

352 *See, e.g.*, Cambridge Manor of Fairfield, L.L.C. v. Myers, 2012 WL 6582542 (Conn. Super. Ct. Nov. 26, 2012) (in defense of collection lawsuit against her, patient's daughter could bring UDAP counterclaim against nursing home that failed to provide monthly statements as promised in contract, which prevented patient from qualifying for Medicaid benefits to pay for bills).

353 *See, e.g.*, St. John v. Wagner, 302 P.3d 906 (Wyo. 2013) (alleging that dental office violated UDAP statute by compelling patient to obtain medical credit card).

354 Buller v. Sutter Health, 74 Cal. Rptr. 3d 47 (Cal. Ct. App. 2008).

355 *See, e.g.*, Ohio Rev. Code Ann. § 1345.01 (West) (transactions between attorneys, physicians, or dentists and their clients or patients). *See generally* National Consumer Law Center, Unfair and Deceptive Acts and Practices § 2.3.10 (8th ed. 2012), *updated at* www.nclc.org/library.

356 DiCarlo v. St. Mary's Hosp., 2006 WL 2038498 (D.N.J. July 19, 2006) (no UDAP claim for discriminatory pricing, because state UDAP statute exempts medical professionals), *aff'd*, 530 F.3d 255 (3d Cir. 2008) (adopting district court decision); Shelton v. Duke Univ. Health Sys., Inc., 633 S.E.2d 113 (N.C. Ct. App. 2006) (no UDAP claim for discriminatory pricing because state UDAP statute exempts medical professionals).

357 Summa Health Sys. v. Viningre, 749 N.E.2d 344 (Ohio Ct. App. 2000) (HMO made misrepresentations about financial aspects of patient's care).

358 Foster v. D.B.S. Collection Agency, 463 F. Supp. 2d 783 (S.D. Ohio 2006) (also noting in dicta that Ohio UDAP exemption for medical professionals does not apply to hospitals). *Cf.* Freeman Health Sys. v. Wass, 124 S.W.3d 504 (Mo. Ct. App. 2004) (medical goods and services are merchandise within meaning of UDAP statute).

359 *See, e.g.*, Scull v. Groover, Christie & Merrit, P.C., 76 A.3d 1186 (M.D. 2013) (medical billing is not a "professional service" within the meaning of UDAP exemption, which only exempts professional services and not "commercial" aspects such as billing). *See generally* National Consumer Law Center, Unfair and Deceptive Acts and Practices § 2.3.10 (8th ed. 2012), *updated at* www.nclc.org/library.

360 Burton v. William Beaumont Hosp., 373 F. Supp. 2d 707 (E.D. Mich. 2005) (hospital's discriminatory pricing practices exempted from Michigan UDAP law under regulated industries exception). *But see* Smallwood v. Cent. Peninsula Gen. Hosp., 151 P.3d 319 (Alaska 2006) (UDAP claim against hospital for balance billing was not barred because hospital was governed by Medicaid regulations). *See generally* National Consumer Law Center, Unfair and Deceptive Acts and Practices § 2.3.3 (8th ed. 2012), *updated at* www.nclc.org/library.

361 *See* National Consumer Law Center, Unfair and Deceptive Acts and Practices § 2.3.5.1 (8th ed. 2012), *updated at* www.nclc.org/library.

362 Press Release, Office of the Minn. Att'y Gen., Attorney General Lori Swanson and Minnesota Hospitals Announce Continuation of Medical Billing Agreement (Apr. 4, 2007), *available online as companion material to this treatise*; Agreement, *In the Matter of* Wheaton Franciscan Servs., d/b/a Covenant Healthcare Systems, Inc. & All Saints Healthcare System, Inc. (May 1, 2006); Agreement, *In the Matter of* Mercy Health Sys. Corp. (Dec. 21, 2006).

363 *See* § 9.3.1, *supra*.

364 Elisabeth R. Benjamin, Arianne Slagle, & Carrie Tracy, Cmty. Serv. Soc'y of N.Y., Incentivizing Patient Financial Assistance: How to Fix New York's Hospital Indigent Care Program (Feb. 2012), *available at* www.cssny.org/publications/entry/incentivizing-patient-financial-assistanceFeb2012.

For example, of the 181 hospital financial aid applications reviewed by CSS, 120 (66%) violated the law. *Id.* at 2. An additional twenty hospitals (10% of the sample size) refused to even provide their financial aid applications to CSS for review. *Id.*

Fairview Health Services, in that chain's agreement with the attorney general.[365]

9.4.3.2 California

California prohibits discriminatory pricing for uninsured or underinsured patients whose income is under 350% of the federal poverty level ("financially qualified patients").[366] Hospitals cannot charge financially qualified patients more than what they receive from Medicare, Medicaid, or another government program.[367] California's law also requires hospitals to have a written financial assistance policy, which must be based on income and must cover all financially qualified patients.[368] Hospitals are required to provide payment plans for financially qualified patients who receive a discount, and the payment plan must be interest free.[369]

California's law provides debt collection protections for medical debt. Hospitals cannot sue uninsured or underinsured patients within the first 150 days after sending them the initial bill, and such time periods are extended during appeals.[370] They also cannot report negative information to a credit reporting agency during that time frame.[371] Hospitals cannot use wage garnishments or home liens against financially qualified patients or foreclose on the patient's home.[372] They cannot send a bill to collections while a patient is applying for financial assistance, negotiating over a bill, or in a payment plan unless the collector agrees to comply with the law's requirements for providing discounts, financial assistance, and payment plans.[373]

California's law requires hospitals to have written policies defining when a debt is forwarded for collection, who has authority to send a debt into collections, and standards for debt collection and to obtain the agreement of debt collectors to adhere to these standards.[374] Finally, the law provides for a number of mandatory notices regarding the hospital's financial assistance policies, as well as advising patients about Medicaid availability and their debt collection rights under federal and California law.[375] California has also enacted a statute imposing substantially similar requirements on physicians who contract with hospitals to provide emergency room services.[376]

Other California laws also address medical debt. California prohibits health facilities from detaining a patient for nonpayment of a medical debt.[377] It also requires hospitals to make a copy of their retail "chargemaster" rates publicly available.[378] The intent of the disclosure was both to enable consumers to comparison shop and to provide an impetus for hospitals to limit their markups. Finally, California prohibits county hospitals from adding interest to a medical debt and from enforcing liens against the family home while the debtor or his dependent children reside there.[379]

9.4.3.3 Connecticut

Connecticut passed the first medical debtor protection law, in part in response to reports of aggressive debt collection by Yale New Haven Hospital. This law prohibits a hospital that receives "free bed funds," that is, charity care funds, from suing a medical debtor unless it determines that the debtor is not eligible for the free bed funds.[380] The law also requires hospitals to include information about free bed funds and other free care programs in all bills and collection notices.[381] A Connecticut court has held there is a private right of action to enforce this section under the pre-2003 version of this statute.[382]

Hospitals are prohibited from collecting from certain uninsured patients more than the actual cost of services and thus cannot collect "chargemaster" rates.[383] Patients are eligible for this "uninsured patient discount" if they have an income at or below 250% of the poverty level and have been turned down for state-administered assistance or Medicare.[384] A hospital does not violate this section if it bills for, but does not actually collect, more than the uninsured patient discount; however, the statute might be raised as defense to debt collection, as grounds for injunctive relief, and possibly to define public

---

365 The details of the attorney general's investigation are set forth in a six-volume report, *Compliance Review of Fairview Health Services' Management Contracts with Accretive Health, Inc., available at* www.ag.state.mn.us. *See also* Complaint, State v. Accretive Health, Inc., No. 21-cv-000145 (D. Minn. Jan. 19, 2012), *available at* www.ag.state.mn.us/PDF/Consumer/AccretiveHealth20120119.pdf. See § 9.1.2, *supra*, for more details.

366 Cal. Health & Safety Code §§ 127400–127446 (West).

367 Cal. Health & Safety Code § 127405(d) (West).
A hospital's reduction of a bill pursuant to this section is not considered "support" or assistance for purposes of eligibility for certain benefits that California law requires counties to provide to indigent residents. Brown v. Crandall, 132 Cal. Rptr. 388 (Cal. Ct. App. 2011).

368 Cal. Health & Safety Code § 127405(a) (West).

369 Cal. Health & Safety Code §§ 127405(b), 127425(g) (West).

370 Cal. Health & Safety Code § 127425(d) (West).

371 Cal. Health & Safety Code § 127425(d) (West).

372 Cal. Health & Safety Code § 127425(f)(1) (West).
However, a debt collector is permitted to use wage garnishments upon court order, as well as home liens. Cal. Health & Safety Code § 127425(f)(2) (West). The collector cannot foreclose upon a home lien while the debtor, debtor's spouse, or debtor's minor child resides in the home.

373 Cal. Health & Safety Code § 127425(e) (West).

374 Cal. Health & Safety Code § 127425(a), (b) (West).

375 Cal. Health & Safety Code §§ 127410, 127420, 127430 (West).

376 Emergency Physicians Fair Pricing Policies, Cal. Health & Safety §§ 127450 through 127462.

377 Cal. Health & Safety Code § 1285 (West).

378 Cal. Health & Safety Code § 1339.51(a)(1) (West).

379 Cal. Welf. & Inst. Code § 17401 (West).
This protection has been limited to medical debts incurred by indigent patients. Joseph v. J.J. Mac Intyre Companies, 238 F. Supp. 2d 1158 (N.D. Cal. 2002).

380 Conn. Gen. Stat. § 19a-673b.

381 Conn. Gen. Stat. § 19a-509b.

382 Ahmad v. Yale New Haven Hosp., Inc., 38 Conn. L. Rptr. 238 (Conn. Super. Ct. 2004), *later proceeding at* 933 A.2d 1208 (Conn. App. Ct. 2007) (affirming denial of class certification because individualized inquiry required).

383 Conn. Gen. Stat. § 19a-673. *See* § 9.1.3, *supra* (discussion of chargemaster rates and discriminatory pricing).

384 Conn. Gen Stat. § 19a-673(a)(4).

policy for UDAP claim.[385] Furthermore, a hospital cannot sue a debtor unless it has determined whether the debtor qualifies for this uninsured patient discount.[386]

If a hospital has information that a debtor qualifies for free beds funds, the uninsured patient discount, or any other program that could reduce a medical debt, the hospital's debt collectors must cease collection, even if there is a judgment against the debtor, until a determination is made regarding eligibility for these programs.[387] Finally, the law provides an increased homestead exemption for hospital debts, limits the amount of prejudgment and postjudgment interest, and prohibits wage garnishment, bank account executions, and lien foreclosures if a medical debtor is complying with a court-ordered installment payment plan.[388]

9.4.3.4 Illinois

Illinois has two laws addressing medical debt. The "Hospital Uninsured Discount Act" caps rates charged to uninsured Illinois patients by hospitals.[389] Uninsured patients qualify for this discount if they are Illinois residents and their family income is under 600% of the federal poverty level, unless a rural or critical access hospital is involved.[390] For rural and critical access hospitals, uninsured patients qualify only if their family income is under 300% of the federal poverty level.[391]

The Illinois law prohibits hospitals from collecting more than 35% over their cost of services for any one inpatient or outpatient visit costing more than $300.[392] In addition, the maximum amount that hospitals can collect in one year from any patient is 25% of the patient's household income.[393] However, if a patient has assets (other than a primary residence, pensions or retirement benefits, or exempt assets) that exceed 600% of the federal poverty level (300% for rural hospitals), this maximum 25% limit does not apply.[394]

Hospitals must disclose the availability of this discount in their bills and invoices to patients.[395] Patients must apply for the discount within sixty days of the date they were discharged or received treatment, and patients may be required to prove their income, assets, and Illinois residency.[396] Hospitals may require patients to apply for Medicare, Medicaid, or other public insurance programs in order to receive the discount.[397] The hospital is not obligated to provide a discount if the patient fails to provide documentation upon request or to apply for a public insurance program within thirty days of the hospital's request.[398]

The Illinois Hospital Uninsured Discount Act does not require hospitals to provide any particular treatment or service to an uninsured patient.[399] The Illinois law authorizes the state attorney general to enforce its provisions, and hospitals are required to file their Medicare Cost Reports with the state attorney general.[400] The Act preempts any inconsistent municipal laws.[401]

Illinois also has a Fair Patient Billing Act that provides protections for medical debtors in billing and collections. This law is separate and apart from the requirements of the Illinois Hospital Uninsured Discount Act.[402]

The Fair Patient Billing Act requires that hospitals include certain information in their bills, such as a brief description of the services provided, the dates of service, the amount owed for such services, contact information for billing inquiries, a description of how an uninsured patient can apply for financial assistance, and a notice that the patient can obtain an itemized bill.[403] The Illinois law also requires hospitals to establish procedures for billing inquiries and disputes, including providing a telephone number for inquiries and disputes, and requires that hospitals return telephone calls about bills within two business days.[404] The law does not set forth what kind of investigation or action the hospital must undertake in order to resolve a billing dispute.

The Illinois law prohibits hospitals from suing uninsured patients who have "clearly demonstrated" insufficient income and assets to pay.[405] Furthermore, hospitals can only institute a collection lawsuit after the hospital has provided the patient with opportunities to: (1) apply for financial assistance; (2) avail themselves of a payment plan; and (3) assess the accuracy of a bill.[406] If the circumstances suggest the patient is eligible for charity care, the hospital must provide sixty days for the patient to apply before instituting a lawsuit.[407] If the patient is already in a payment plan, the hospital can only sue if the patient has failed to make payments.[408]

385 Ahmad v. Yale New Haven Hosp., Inc., 38 Conn. L. Rptr. 238 (Conn. Super. Ct. 2004), *later proceeding at* 933 A.2d 1208 (Conn. App. Ct. 2007) (affirming denial of class certification because individualized inquiry required).

386 Conn. Gen. Stat. § 19a-673b.

387 Conn. Gen. Stat. § 19a-673d.

388 Conn. Gen. Stat. §§ 37-3a(b), 52-352b(t), 52-356a, 52-356d.

389 210 Ill. Comp. Stat. §§ 89/1 to 89/30.

390 210 Ill. Comp. Stat. § 89/10(a)(1).

391 210 Ill. Comp. Stat. § 89/10(a)(3).

392 210 Ill. Comp. Stat. §§ 89/5 and 89/10(b). *See* Illinois Dep't of Pub. Health, Hospital Uninsured Patient Discount Act, at www.healthcarereportcard.illinois.gov/contents/view/Hospital_Uninsured_Patient_Discount_Act.

393 210 Ill. Comp. Stat. § 89/10(c)(1).

394 210 Ill. Comp. Stat. § 89/10(c)(4).

395 210 Ill. Comp. Stat. § 89/10(d).

396 210 Ill. Comp. Stat. § 89/15(b).

397 210 Ill. Comp. Stat. § 89/15(a).

398 210 Ill. Comp. Stat. § 89/15(c). *See* Collection Prof'ls, Inc. v. Schlosser, 977 N.E.2d 315 (Ill. App. Ct. 2012) (hospital not required to provide discount when patient failed to provide requested income verification, despite fact that patient claimed she could not provide verification because she was unemployed).

399 210 Ill. Comp. Stat. § 89/20(c).

400 210 Ill. Comp. Stat. § 89/25.

401 210 Ill. Comp. Stat. § 89/30.

402 210 Ill. Comp. Stat. § 89/20(d).

403 210 Ill. Comp. Stat. § 88/20.

404 210 Ill. Comp. Stat. § 88/25.

405 210 Ill. Comp. Stat. § 88/35.

406 210 Ill. Comp. Stat. § 88/30(a)(1).

407 210 Ill. Comp. Stat. § 88/30(a)(3).

408 210 Ill. Comp. Stat. § 88/30(a)(4).

Under the Fair Patient Billing Act, hospitals cannot sue patients who have applied for Medicaid until the application is denied.[409] Debt collectors cannot sue a patient without the approval of an authorized hospital employee.[410] Hospitals cannot refer a bill to a debt collector without providing an opportunity for the patient to request a reasonable payment plan with the first thirty days after the initial bill.[411] An Illinois appellate court has held that, once the provider met the procedural requirements of the Fair Patient Billing Act, a patient could liable for full chargemaster prices even though she was indigent and had applied for financial assistance but failed to provide requested income verification[412]

Finally, a separate Illinois law restricts the percentage of a personal injury recovery that may be subject to a lien by certain health care providers.[413]

9.4.3.5 Maryland

Maryland's comprehensive medical debtor protection law requires hospitals to develop financial assistance policies for providing free and reduced-cost care to uninsured and underinsured patients.[414] These financial assistance policies must provide for:

- Free medically necessary care to patients with family incomes at or below 150% of the federal poverty level.
- Reduced-cost medically necessary care to low-income patients with family incomes above 150% of federal poverty.[415]

In addition, the Maryland Health Services Cost Review Commission (Commission) has the authority to establish higher income thresholds by regulation.[416]

The Maryland law requires hospitals to develop and distribute an information sheet that describes the hospital's financial assistance policy. The information sheet must include contact information for the hospital department that assists patients with applying for charity care, contact information for the state Medicaid program, and an explanation that physician charges are billed separately.[417] The hospital must post its financial assistance policy throughout the hospital and ensure the availability of staff who are trained to assist patients on billing issues and applying for charity care.[418] The Maryland law also requires the Commission to develop a uniform financial assistance application to be used by hospitals.[419]

The Maryland law requires hospitals to develop a debt collection policy and submit to the policy to the Commission.[420] Most critically, the debt collection policy must prohibit the hospital from selling its debt.[421] Thus, Maryland prohibits debt buying of hospital bills. In addition, the debt collection policy must prohibit the hospital from charging interest to "self-pay" patients before a court judgment is obtained.[422] Finally, a hospital's debt collection policy must describe the hospital's collection procedures, including when the hospital will initiate a collection lawsuit, and must require active oversight by the hospital of debt collection contracts.[423]

The Maryland law also requires hospitals to provide a review process for denials of free care,[424] requires refunds and correction of any adverse credit reporting for patients and guarantors if patients are found to be eligible for free care,[425] forbids foreclosure on a patient's primary residence for a hospital debt (although a lien is permitted),[426] forbids adverse credit reports for 120 days after the issuance of a bill,[427] and sets standards for hospitals' oversight of their collection agencies.[428]

9.4.3.6 Massachusetts

Massachusetts has a set of regulations issued by its Executive Office of Health and Human Services governing the debt collection practices of hospitals and community health centers participating in the Health Safety Net program.[429] These regulations prohibit Health Safety Net hospitals from billing certain patients, including patients receiving Medicaid, state welfare, and Healthy Start services,[430] as well as participants in the Children's Medical Security plan whose family income is under 400% of the federal poverty level.[431] The regulations also prohibit billing "low income patients" for services eligible to be covered under the Health Safety Net program.[432] Low-income patients are defined as Massachusetts residents whose "modified adjusted gross income" is less than 400% of federal poverty level and who are not eligible or are terminated from the state's Medicaid program.[433] To qualify

409 210 Ill. Comp. Stat. § 88/30(a)(5).
410 210 Ill. Comp. Stat. § 88/30(c).
411 210 Ill. Comp. Stat. § 88/30(b).
412 Collection Prof'ls, Inc. v. Schlosser, 977 N.E.2d 315 (Ill. App. Ct. 2012).
413 770 Ill. Comp. Stat. § 23/10(a) (limiting the total amount of all provider liens to 40% of the patients' recovery).
For more on the ability of medical providers to seek liens on personal injury recovery, see § 9.7, *infra*.
414 Md. Code Ann., Health-Gen. § 19-214.1(b)(1) (West).
415 Md. Code Ann., Health-Gen. § 19-214.1(b)(2) (West).
416 Md. Code Ann., Health-Gen. § 19-214.1(b)(3) (West).
417 Md. Code Ann., Health-Gen. § 19-214.1(f) (West).
418 Md. Code Ann., Health-Gen. §§ 19-214.1(c), (g) (West).
419 Md. Code Ann., Health-Gen. § 19-214.1(d) (West).
420 Md. Code Ann., Health-Gen. § 19-214.2(a) (West).
421 Md. Code Ann., Health-Gen. § 19-214.2(b)(2) (West).
422 Md. Code Ann., Health-Gen. § 19-214.2(b)(3) (West).
423 Md. Code Ann., Health-Gen. §§ 19-214.2(b)(1), (5), (6) (West).
424 Md. Code Ann., Health-Gen. § 19-214.2(b)(9) (West).
425 Md. Code Ann., Health-Gen. §§ 19-214.2(b)(7), (b)(8), (c) (West).
426 Md. Code Ann., Health-Gen. § 19-214.2(e) (West).
427 Md. Code Ann., Health-Gen. § 19-214.2(d)(1) (West).
428 Md. Code Ann., Health-Gen. § 19-214.2(f) (West).
429 101 Mass. Code Regs. pt. 613. *Cf.* Health Law Advocates & Volunteer Lawyers Project, Medical Debt: A Guide for Massachusetts Advocates (Feb. 2006) (handbook on dealing with medical debt in Massachusetts), *available at* www.healthlawadvocates.org/tools/publications/files/0001.pdf.
430 101 Mass. Code Regs. § 613.08(3)(a).
431 101 Mass. Code Regs. § 613.08(3)(b).
432 101 Mass. Code Regs. § 613.08(3)(c).
433 101 Mass. Code Regs. § 613.04(1).

for low-income patient status, patients must apply to the state's Medicaid agency for a determination.[434] Finally, the regulations prohibit billing patients who have qualified for "medical hardship" status above their required contribution.[435] Medical hardship status requires patients to apply to the Health Safety Net Office for a determination.[436]

The Massachusetts regulations require hospitals to offer deposit and payment plans. Deposits for low-income and medical hardship patients are prohibited for emergency care and otherwise limited by the regulations.[437] Patients with a bill under $1000 must be offered at least a one-year payment plan, interest free, with a minimum monthly payment of $25.[438] Patients with higher bills must be offered at least a two-year payment plan.[439]

The Massachusetts regulations require each hospital to establish a credit and collections policy, which must be filed with the Health Safety Net Office.[440] This policy must include provisions regarding standard collection policies, financial information collection procedures, deposit and payment plan policies, and a description of any discount policies for the insured.[441]

A hospital may not execute a lien against the residence or automobile of a low-income patient without the express permission of the hospital's board of trustees.[442] Note that the regulations do require hospitals to take collection actions, including sending bills and making subsequent contacts, against uninsured patients for 120 days before sending the bill of an uninsured patient to the Health Safety Net Office.[443]

9.4.3.7 Nevada

Nevada has a medical debtor protection law that prohibits hospitals from collecting a bill from a consumer who has or is eligible for insurance benefits or a public program that may pay all or part of the bill, until the hospital has billed the insurer or program and a determination has been made about payment of the claim.[444] This prohibition does not apply to copayments or deductibles.[445]

A hospital may not begin collection efforts until thirty days after the patient is sent a bill for the amount that he or she is responsible for, and this amount is to be determined after the insurer or public program has made a determination about payment of the claim.[446] Interest may accrue on the bill but not exceed the prime rate at the largest bank in Nevada, plus 2%.

The Nevada law requires hospitals, when collecting their own debts, to act in a "professional, fair and lawful manner."[447] The law applies the Fair Debt Collection Practices Act to hospitals collecting their own debts.[448] It prohibits hospitals from imposing collection costs, attorney fees, and costs except as awarded by a court, or any other fees.[449] It establishes a four-year statute of limitations for hospital debt, which is tolled during any period in which the hospital is awaiting a determination of payment or eligibility for benefits.[450]

Nevada law also forbids execution on the primary residence for medical debts during the lifetime of the debtor and certain specified dependents.[451] A lien may be created which may be foreclosed only after the residence ceases to be occupied by the protected persons.

Previously under Nevada law, unpaid charges from a county or district hospital automatically created a lien on the patient's real property.[452] Nevada revised its law to prohibit a county or district hospital from assigning, selling, or transferring the hospital's interest in that lien.[453]

9.4.3.8 New Jersey

New Jersey requires hospitals to notify patients about charity care and sets up a mandatory screening process for charity care eligibility.[454] If a patient qualifies for charity care and family income is below 200% of poverty, the patient is eligible for medically necessary services without cost.[455] Charity care patients with incomes between 200 to 300% of poverty are billed according to a sliding scale.[456] Furthermore, if medical expenses exceed 30% of a family's income, any excess is eligible for 100% coverage as charity care.[457] New Jersey also prohibits collection activities for hospital bills that are covered by charity care.[458]

New Jersey limits hospital charges for low-income uninsured patients. Uninsured patients with family incomes less than 500% of the federal poverty level cannot be charged more than 15% above the Medicare payment rate.[459] The New Jersey Department of Health and Senior Services must establish a sliding scale for such patients setting forth what percentage of the hospital charge an uninsured patient is required to pay.[460]

434 101 Mass. Code Regs. § 613.04(2).
435 101 Mass. Code Regs. § 613.08(3)(g).
436 101 Mass. Code Regs. § 613.05(2).
437 101 Mass. Code Regs. § 613.08(1)(f).
438 101 Mass. Code Regs. § 613.08(1)(f)-4.
439 *Id.*
440 101 Mass. Code Regs. § 613.08(1)(c)-1.
441 101 Mass. Code Regs. § 613.08(1)(c)-2.
442 101 Mass. Code Regs. § 613.08(1)(b).
443 101 Mass. Code Regs. § 613.06(1)(a).
444 Nev. Rev. Stat. § 449.757(1).
445 Nev. Rev. Stat. § 449.757(1).
446 Nev. Rev. Stat. § 449.757(2).
447 Nev. Rev. Stat. § 449.759.
448 Nev. Rev. Stat. § 449.759.
449 Nev. Rev. Stat. § 449.757(3).
450 Nev. Rev. Stat. § 11.2095.
451 Nev. Rev. Stat. § 21.095 provides that the primary dwelling (including a manufactured home) and land may not be executed upon for a medical bill during the lifetime of the debtor, the debtor's spouse, a joint tenant who was a joint tenant at the time judgment was entered, or the debtor's dependent disabled adult child, or during the minority of any child of the debtor.
452 Nev. Rev. Stat. § 108.662.
453 Nev. Rev. Stat. § 108.662(5).
454 N.J. Admin. Code § 10:52-11.5.
455 N.J. Admin. Code § 10:52-11.8(b).
456 N.J. Admin. Code § 10:52-11.8(c).
457 N.J. Admin. Code § 10:52-11.8(d).
458 N.J. Admin. Code § 10:52-11.14.
459 N.J. Stat. Ann. § 26:2H-12.52 (West).
460 N.J. Stat. Ann. § 26:2H-12.53 (West).

In addition, New Jersey has established a Hospital Care Payment Commission to which hospitals can voluntarily assign medical debts.[461] The commission has the power to set off state tax refunds and other state refunds to collect medical debts,[462] but the hospital must agree to first determine whether patients are eligible for charity care.[463]

9.4.3.9 New York

New York's medical debtor protection law prohibits discriminatory pricing by hospitals that receive state charity care funding.[464] Hospitals cannot charge uninsured patients whose income is under 300% of the federal poverty level more than what the hospitals receive from Medicare, Medicaid, or the highest volume payer for that hospital.[465] New York's law requires that hospitals have a written financial assistance policy and sets forth the actual sliding scale and discount rates that hospitals must provide.[466] Patients with income under the federal poverty threshold can only be required to pay a nominal amount, while those with incomes of 100% to 150% of poverty can be required to pay up to 20% of the amount paid by insurers.[467] In addition, hospitals are required to provide for payment plans, for which the monthly payment cannot exceed 10% of the patient's gross monthly income and for which interest is limited to the rate on a ninety-day Treasury bill plus 0.5%.[468]

New York's law also provides debt collection protections for medical debt. If a patient is eligible for Medicaid or is applying for financial assistance, the hospital cannot send the bill to collections during the application process.[469] Hospitals must provide a thirty-day notice to patients before referring a bill to a debt collector.[470] The New York law does not prohibit home liens for medical debt, but it does prohibit foreclosures on the patient's home.[471] Debt collectors must obtain the consent of the hospital to institute a lawsuit over medical bills.[472] In addition, collectors must follow the hospital's financial assistance policies and provide information on such policies.[473] Finally, the New York law requires hospitals to provide notices of their financial assistance policies.[474]

Unfortunately, compliance with the New York law has been spotty at best. A study by the Community Service Society of New York (CSS) found that the majority of New York hospitals studied by CSS were violating the law.[475] For example, of the 181 hospital financial aid applications reviewed by CSS, 120 (66%) violated the law.[476] An additional twenty hospitals (10% of the sample size) refused to even provide their financial aid applications to CSS for review.[477]

9.4.3.10 North Carolina

North Carolina has a limited medical debtor protection law. The law requires hospitals to publicize their financial assistance policies.[478] Hospital must also require their debt collection contractors or debt buyers to inform patients of such policies when engaging in collection activities.[479]

If a patient has applied for financial assistance, the law prohibits them from referring the debt to a collection agency while the application is pending.[480] Hospitals must give patients thirty days' written notice before referring a debt to a collection agency.[481] Hospitals must require collection agencies to obtain their written consent before filing a lawsuit to collect the debt.[482]

The law does not provide for reduced pricing for low-income uninsured or underinsured patients or otherwise address discriminatory pricing. However, it requires hospitals to disclose prices for the 100 most frequent medical procedures by admission, including for each procedure: (1) the chargemaster price; (2) averaged negotiated settlement price for uninsured patients; (3) the amount reimbursed by Medicaid; (4) the amount reimbursed by Medicare; and (5) the prices paid by the five largest health insurers that pay the hospital for the procedure.[483]

The North Carolina law requires hospitals to either provide itemized bills or disclose the right to obtain such a bill.[484] It prohibits foreclosures on the homes of parents over hospital debts incurred for the care of their minor children until the child becomes an adult.[485]

9.4.3.11 Washington State

Washington State does not have a comprehensive medical debtor law. However, it does have a law mandating that hospitals must develop charity care policies that provide for a sliding

461 N.J. Stat. Ann. § 17B:30-41 through 17B:30-57 (West). In return, hospitals let the state keep 50% of the amount collected, plus administrative and collection costs. N.J. Stat. Ann. § 17B:30-44 (West).

462 N.J. Stat. Ann. § 17B:30-45 (West).

463 N.J. Stat. Ann. § 17B:30-47 (West).

464 N.Y. Pub. Health Law § 2807-k(9-a) (McKinney). *See generally* Legal Aid Soc'y Health Law Unit, How to Prevent and Fix Medical Debt (Feb. 2010) (handbook on how to utilize protections of New York state's Hospital Financial Assistance Law), *available at* www.legal-aid.org/media/131295/medical%20debt%20guide%20final%202_5_10.pdf.

465 N.Y. Pub. Health Law § 2807-k(9-a)(a) (McKinney).

466 N.Y. Pub. Health Law § 2807-k(9-a)(b) (McKinney).

467 N.Y. Pub. Health Law § 2807-k(9-a)(b) (McKinney).

468 N.Y. Pub. Health Law § 2807-k(9-a)(d) (McKinney).

469 N.Y. Pub. Health Law § 2807-k(9-a)(h) (McKinney).

470 N.Y. Pub. Health Law § 2807-k(9-a)(h) (McKinney).

471 N.Y. Pub. Health Law § 2807-k(9-a)(h) (McKinney).

472 N.Y. Pub. Health Law § 2807-k(9-a)(h) (McKinney).

473 N.Y. Pub. Health Law § 2807-k(9-a)(h) (McKinney).

474 N.Y. Pub. Health Law § 2807-k(9-a)(c) (McKinney).

475 Elisabeth R. Benjamin, Arianne Slagle, & Carrie Tracy, Cmty. Serv. Soc'y of N.Y., Incentivizing Patient Financial Assistance: How to Fix New York's Hospital Indigent Care Program (Feb. 2012), *available at* www.cssny.org/userimages/downloads/IncentivizingPatientFinancialAssistanceFeb2012.pdf.

476 *Id.* at 2.

477 *Id.*

478 N.C. Gen. Stat. § 131E-214.8(a).

479 N.C. Gen. Stat. § 131E-91(d)(3).

480 N.C. Gen. Stat. § 131E-91(d)(1).

481 N.C. Gen. Stat. § 131E-91(d)(2).

482 N.C. Gen. Stat. § 131E-91(d)(4).

483 N.C. Gen. Stat. § 131E-214.7(b).

484 N.C. Gen. Stat. § 131E-91(a).

485 N.C. Gen. Stat. § 131E-91(d)(6).

scale of discounts for low-income patients.[486] The charity care policies must provide that patients whose incomes are less than 100% of the federal poverty level qualify for charity care for the full amount of charges, and patients whose incomes are between 100% and 200% of the federal poverty level must be given discounts.[487] The Washington State Department of Health is authorized to review charity care policies and to reject them if they do not meet the requirements of the law.[488] The regulations provide acceptable examples of policies, such as:[489]

- Patients between 100% and 200% of the federal poverty level not covered by another payment source will have their bill reduced to 40% of that portion of their household income which is over 100% of the federal poverty level. The bill can be paid in monthly installments over a reasonable period of time, without interest or late fees.
- Patients between 100% and 200% of federal poverty level will have their bill reduced according to the following schedule:

Income as a Percentage of Federal Poverty	*Discount*
100% to 133%	75%
134% to 166%	50%
167% to 200%	25%

- The bill can be paid in monthly installments over a reasonable period of time, without interest or late fees.

The regulations also require hospitals to have policies that govern procedures with respect to bad debt, including reasonable and uniform standards for collections.[490] Hospitals may not initiate collections until they have determined whether the patient qualifies for public or private insurance or charity care.[491] While the regulations only provide for civil penalties to be imposed by the Department of Health for violations,[492] a failure to provide charity care discounts could be raised as a defense in a collection action.[493]

9.4.4 *Special Medical Debt Exemption Statutes*

States sometimes have special provisions in their exemption or other statutes that protect medical debtors.

Kansas forbids wage garnishments for two months after the return to employment of a debtor after an illness of the debtor or of a family member which has kept the debtor out of work for two or more weeks.[494] Virginia prohibits health care providers from collecting any debts arising from medical treatment, or referring those debts to a collector, if a claim has been made for workers' compensation[495] or compensation for crime victims.[496]

Ohio forbids execution on the primary residence for health care debts during the lifetime of the debtor and certain specified dependents.[497] A lien may be created which may be foreclosed only after the residence ceases to be occupied by the protected persons. Louisiana provides a homestead exemption for the full value of the home for debts arising from catastrophic or terminal illness or injury.[498] West Virginia provides a larger homestead exemption for debts resulting from "catastrophic illness or injury."[499]

Ohio has a special provision protecting children and former spouses for whom a family court has ordered the other ex-spouse to provide health insurance. If the required health insurance is not provided, Ohio law prohibits any provider or collection agency from seeking to collect medical bills that should have been covered by such health insurance, if the former spouse or children provides a copy of the relevant court order and reasonable help in locating the responsible party.[500]

North Dakota law governs a healthcare provider's ability to impose late payment charges on medical bills.[501] A bill is not considered delinquent until ninety days after services have been rendered and forty-five days after a bill has been issued.[502] North Dakota also limits the late charge to 1% per month and, for hospitals, the late charge must not to exceed twenty-five dollars per month.[503] The provider must also send monthly or periodic statements in order to impose a late charge.[504]

486 Wash. Rev. Code § 70.170.060(5).

487 Wash. Admin. Code § 246-453-040.

488 Wash. Admin. Code § 246-453-070(3).

489 Wash. Admin. Code § 246-453-050(2).

490 Wash. Admin. Code § 246-453-070(2).

491 Wash. Admin. Code § 246-453-020(1).

492 Wash. Admin. Code § 246-453-090.

493 *See* Audit & Adjustment Co. v. Earl, 267 P.3d 441 (Wash. Ct. App. 2011) (consumer able to raise denial of charity care as defense, but holding that he failed to establish eligibility).

494 Kan. Stat. Ann. § 60-2310(c).

495 Va. Code Ann. § 65.2-601.1.

496 Va. Code Ann. § 19.2-368.5:2.

497 Ohio Rev. Code Ann. §§ 2329.66(A)(1)(a), 2329.661 (West) provide that, for debts for health care services or supplies, the homestead exemption has no dollar limitation. *See* Edwards v. McCormick, 136 F. Supp. 2d 795 (S.D. Ohio 2001) (threatening forced sale of home contrary to state exemption is FDCPA violation); Wickliffe Country Place v. Kovacs, 765 N.E.2d 975 (Ohio Ct. App. 2001) (remanding for determination whether services provided by nursing home were "health care services and supplies," in which case lien would be precluded).

498 La. Rev. Stat. Ann. § 20:1. *See In re* Collet, 351 B.R. 395 (Bankr. W.D. La. 2006) (debtors not entitled to unlimited homestead exemption for catastrophic illness, because not all of the credit card cash advances they borrowed were used to pay medical expenses).

499 W. Va. Code § 38-9-3 provides a blanket $5000 exemption which increases to $7500 for hospital or medical expenses for catastrophic illness or injury.

500 Ohio Rev. Code Ann. § 1349.01 (West).

Also, the provider or collection agency may not report to any credit reporting agency, and the credit reporting agency may not report, any information about the nonpayment in the file of the former spouse.

501 N.D. Cent. Code § 13-01-14.1.

502 N.D. Cent. Code § 13-01-14.1(2).

503 N.D. Cent. Code § 13-01-14.1(4).

504 N.D. Cent. Code § 13-01-15.

However, failure to send periodic statements does not prevent a provider from obtaining prejudgment interest under North Dakota's general law permitting prejudgment interest. Weeks v. Geiermann, 814 N.W.2d 792 (N.D. 2012).

Many states have statutes detailing the rights of health care patients, often called patients' bills of rights. Although these statutes generally focus on issues such as privacy and informed consent, they may also be useful in a debt collection case. Massachusetts, for example, requires providers to provide itemized bills and explanations of charges and, upon request, information about financial aid and free care.[505] Florida's HMO Act prohibits unfair or deceptive trade practices but is not privately enforceable.[506] New York has a Prompt Pay Law, which provides that, when an insurer is clearly liable to pay a health care claim, the provider or patient must be paid with thirty days of receipt of the claim.[507] One court has held that there is a private right of action under this law.[508]

9.4.5 *Health Care Providers As Brokers*

9.4.5.1 Pitfalls of Medical Debt Converted to Credit Card or Other Debt

A common debt collection tactic by health care providers is to take on the role of loan brokers, steering patients toward lenders to borrow money to pay off medical bills.[509] As commentators have noted, health care providers who steer patients to specific lenders have an inherent conflict of interest.[510] Medical bills are a significant source of credit card and home-secured debt.[511] One study estimated that Americans charge $45 billion in medical expenses to credit cards.[512] Another study found that medical bills contribute to the credit card debt of 29% of low-income and middle-income borrowers.[513]

For providers, the advantages of getting patients to pay their medical bills with credit cards are obvious: providers get their money right away, while offloading the burden of pursuing payments to third parties. In addition, some credit card lenders pay "rebates" to the providers when the providers steer patients to those credit cards.[514] Patients, however, may become burdened by the high interest rates charged by some lenders, as well as by losing the ability to negotiate a reduction in the bill on the basis of discriminatory pricing.[515] They have also noted that patients tend to trust their healthcare providers and may follow their recommendation to opt for financial products with unfavorable terms.[516]

Medical credit cards sometimes offer deceptive deferred interest programs, which promote "no interest" until a certain date, but then retroactively assess interest starting from the purchase date if the consumer does not pay off the entire balance by the specified date.[517] Many consumers do not understand that they could be charged interest retroactively for the entire deferred interest period if they do not pay off the balance at the end of the period. These cards are frequently offered for dental treatment,[518] vision care, and cosmetic surgery.

---

505 Mass. Gen. Laws ch. 111, § 70E.

506 Electrostim Med. Servs., Inc. v. Aetna Life Ins. Co., 2007 WL 470481 (M.D. Fla. Feb. 13, 2007).
However patients could bring claims under common law or other theories based on the same allegations. *Id.*

507 N.Y. Ins. Law § 3224-a(a).

508 Maimonides Med. Ctr. v. First United Am. Life Ins. Co., 941 N.Y.S.2d 447 (N.Y. Sup. Ct 2012).

509 For examples of health care providers acting as loan brokers, see Jim Hawkins, *Doctors As Bankers: Evidence from Fertility Markets*, 84 Tulane L. Rev. 841 (Mar. 2010); Sarah Rubenstein, *Facing a Choice Between Home and Health Care*, Wall St. J., Nov. 25, 2008 (describing how debt collectors pressured one patient to take out a second mortgage to pay $60,000 in medical bills); *Overdose of Debt*, Consumer Reports, July 2008, at 14 (discussing healthcare "credit cards"); Brian Grow and Robert Berner, *Fresh Pain for the Uninsured*, Bus. Week, Nov. 21, 2007; Steve Tripoli & Chi Chi Wu, National Consumer Law Center, Unhealthy Pursuits: How the Sick and Vulnerable are Harmed by Abusive Medical Debt Collection Tactics (Dec. 2005), *available online as companion material to this treatise. See also* Summers v. Merchants & Med. Credit Corp., 2013 WL 1507529 (E.D. Mich. Apr. 12, 2013) (threatening to refer account for lawsuit if consumer did not obtain a credit card to pay off medical debt); Jones v. People's Heritage Bank, 433 F. Supp. 2d 1328 (S.D. Ga. 2006) (dentist arranged financing with lender offering credit program specially designed for dental bills); St. John v. Wagner, 302 P.3d 906 (Wyo. 2013) (alleging that dental office violated UDAP statute by compelling patient to obtain medical credit card).

510 Jim Hawkins, *Doctors As Bankers: Evidence from Fertility Markets*, 84 Tulane L. Rev. 841 (Mar. 2010).

511 See § 9.1.4, *supra*, regarding the use of home loans to pay down medical debt.

512 Jessica Bennett, *The Other Credit Crunch*, Newsweek Web, Nov. 24, 2008, www.newsweek.com/id/170701.

513 Cindy Zeldin & Mark Rukavina, Demos & Access Project, Borrowing to Stay Healthy: How Credit Card Debt is Related to Medical Expenses (Jan. 2007). This same study also found that consumers with medical debt had a higher level of credit card debt than those without ($11,623 versus $7964). Patients have had to resort to even more abusive forms of lending to pay medical bills. A survey of households using an emergency food pantry found that 25% had borrowed from a payday lender to pay medical bills. James Thalman, *Utah's Poor Feeling Crunch of Rising Costs*, Deseret News, May 28, 2008.

514 Press Release, Attorney General Cuomo Launches Industry-Wide Investigation Into Predatory Health Care Lending That Is Pushing Consumers Nationwide Into Debt (Aug. 4, 2010) (announcing investigation of medical credit cards, including allegations of payments or "kickbacks" by GE CareCredit to providers). The CFPB's Consent Order against GE Capital prohibits the bank from paying rebates to providers).

515 *See* § 9.1.3, *supra* (discussing discriminatory pricing).

516 John Kiernan, *Are Doctors Moonlighting as Creditors?* CardHub, Jan. 9, 2013, *available at* www.cardhub.com/edu/financing-medical-care. *See, e.g.*, St. John v. Wagner, 302 P.3d 906 (Wyo. 2013) (alleging that dental office violated UDAP statute by compelling patient to obtain medical credit card).

517 *See* Consent Order, In the Matter of GE Capital Retail Bank, CareCredit L.L.C., No. 2013-CFPB-0009, ¶¶ 14–16 (Consumer Fin. Prot. Bureau Dec. 10, 2013), *available at* http://files.consumerfinance.gov/f/201312_cfpb_consent-order_ge-carecredit.pdf (describing deferred interest credit card offered by GE Capital, which 85% of cardholders opted for); National Consumer Law Center, Consumer Credit Regulation § 8.8.1 (2012), *updated at* www.nclc.org/library; National Consumer Law Center, Truth in Lending § 6.4.6 (8th ed. 2012), *updated at* www.nclc.org/library.

518 *See* Consent Order, In the Matter of GE Capital Retail Bank, CareCredit L.L.C., No. 2013-CFPB-0009, ¶ 12 (Consumer Fin. Prot. Bureau Dec. 10, 2013), *available at* http://files.consumerfinance.gov/f/201312_cfpb_consent-order_ge-carecredit.pdf (55% of providers offering CareCredit card are dentists); Frontline, *Transcript—Dollars and Dentist* (June 27, 2012), *available at* www.pbs.org/wgbh/pages/frontline/health-science-technology/dollars-and-dentists/transcript-23 (discussing

In December 2013, the Consumer Financial Protection Bureau (CFPB) brought an enforcement action against one issuer of medical credit cards, GE Capital Retail Bank, which offers the CareCredit card.[519] The CFPB alleged that some providers had misled patients by not clearly explaining the terms of the deferred interest program when the patients signed up and by not giving patients the legally required credit card disclosures.[520] Furthermore, the CFPB alleged it was GE Capital's lack of oversight and monitoring that allowed this deception.[521]

GE Capital settled the case by agreeing to provide enhanced disclosures to consumers and to implement a training program for providers who offer the CareCredit Card.[522] Furthermore, the bank agreed to contact new applicants within seventy-two hours to explain the product over the phone, and to require any consumer submitting an application for dental services over $1000 to apply directly with CareCredit instead of with the provider's staff.[523] GE Capital also promised in its contracts with providers to prohibit charges for services not yet rendered, with limited exception.[524] The bank agreed to pay up to $34.1 million in restitution to injured consumers.[525]

Another problem with using credit to pay for medical care is that patients end up saddled with enormous debts for shoddy or incomplete treatment.[526] Patients who have credit card debts caused by shoddy treatment may want to consider invoking their rights under the Fair Credit Billing Act to withhold payment to a credit card lender based upon claims that they have against a merchant (that is, the provider).[527]

9.4.5.2 Legal Challenges Under State Loan Broker and Other Laws

Hospitals that steer patients toward lenders may be violating state laws that regulate loan brokers. Some of these laws require loan brokers to obtain a license from state banking departments, which presumably many health care providers have not done.[528] A few states also cap the loan rates that can be charged.[529] Doctors, dentists, or for-profit hospitals that act as loan brokers may also violate state credit services organizations laws.[530]

California has enacted a special statute regulating dentists and their employees who broker or arrange for credit from a third party. The statute requires dentists or their employees to provide special disclosures and a written treatment plan before arranging for credit.[531] It prohibits dentist or their employees from arranging for credit while the patient is under the influence of nitrous oxide, general anesthesia, or conscious sedation, and requires the dentist or their employees to make refunds within fifteen days of a request for any payments that are for treatments not yet rendered.[532]

In some cases, patients may not be aware that their medical bills have been transferred to a third-party lender. The "authorization" for such a transfer may be buried in the fine print of the hospital's admissions form.[533] Such lenders often charge

case of eighty-seven-year-old consumer who was signed up for a deferred interest credit card without her knowledge).

519 Press Release, Consumer Fin. Prot. Bureau, CFPB Orders GE CareCredit to Refund $34.1 Million for Deceptive Health-Care Credit Card Enrollment (Dec. 10, 2013), *available at* www.consumerfinance.gov/newsroom/cfpb-orders-ge-carecredit-to-refund-34-1-million-for-deceptive-health-care-credit-card-enrollment.

520 *Id.*

521 *Id.*

522 Consent Order, In the Matter of GE Capital Retail Bank, CareCredit L.L.C., No. 2013-CFPB-0009 (Consumer Fin. Prot. Bureau Dec. 10, 2013), *available at* http://files.consumerfinance.gov/f/201312_cfpb_consent-order_ge-carecredit.pdf.

523 *Id.* at ¶¶ 32, 36.

524 *Id.* at ¶ 31.

525 *Id.* at 7.

526 *See, e.g.*, Press Release, Attorney General Cuomo Launches Industry-Wide Investigation Into Predatory Health Care Lending That Is Pushing Consumers Nationwide Into Debt (Aug. 4, 2010) (several examples of patients who were charged full amount for procedures despite receiving no services, incomplete services, or treatments that failed); Press Release, Office of Attorney General Martha Coakley, AG Announces JP Morgan Chase and Capital One Have Agreed to Implement Enhanced Dispute Resolution Process for Victims of Spectrum Dental, Coast Dental and Sierra Dental (Sept. 11, 2009) (dentist whose licensed had been revoked signed up patients for financing for dental treatments; treatments were unfinished or mismanaged).

527 *See* National Consumer Law Center, Truth in Lending § 7.11 (8th ed. 2012), *updated at* www.nclc.org/library (explaining right to withhold payment under 15 U.S.C. § 1666*i* for claims and defenses against a merchant). *But see* GE Money Bank v. Caccioti, 2012 WL 1139065 (Conn. Super. Ct. Mar. 8, 2012) (summary judgment for bank despite patient's argument that credit card debt was for dental services that were unsatisfactory). Note that the patient asserted a billing error claim under 15 U.S.C. § 1666 in this case, but failed to assert a claim for the right to withhold payment under 15 U.S.C. § 1666*i*.

528 Ala. Code §§ 5-19-1 through 5-19-31 (requiring loan brokers to obtain a license); Ariz. Rev. Stat. Ann. §§ 6-601 through 6-615 (requiring loan brokers to obtain a license); Iowa Code §§ 535C.1 through 535C.14 (prohibiting loan brokers from collecting advance fees and requiring written loan brokerage agreements); Neb. Rev. Stat. §§ 45-189 through 45-191.11 (requiring loan brokers to file disclosure and brokerage agreements with the state and to pay a filing fee to the state; prohibiting loan brokers from collecting advance fees; and requiring brokers to provide borrowers with disclosures and written agreements); N.J. Stat. Ann. §§ 17:11C-1 through 17:11C-49 (West) (requiring loan brokers to obtain a license); N.D. Cent. Code § 13-04.1-02 (requiring loans brokers to obtain a license).

529 For example, Massachusetts requires small loan brokers to obtain a license from the state Division of Banks and prohibits them from brokering loans that charge over 23% annual interest. Mass. Gen. Laws ch. 140, § 96; 209 Mass. Code Regs. § 26.01.

Pennsylvania requires brokers of loans under $25,000 to be licensed and caps rates at 24% per year. 7 Pa. Stat. Ann. §§ 6201–6219 (§ 6213) (West). *See also* Ga. Code Ann. §§ 7-3-1 through 7-3-29 (requiring brokers of loans of $3000 or less to obtain a license and capping interest rates); R.I. Gen. Laws §§ 19-14-2, 19-14.1-2 (requiring loan brokers to obtain a license and capping interest rates); Tex. Fin. Code Ann. § 342.051 (West) (requiring persons who engage in the business of negotiating loans to obtain a license and capping interest on those loans as specified under Tex. Fin. Code Ann. § 342.201 (West)).

530 *See* National Consumer Law Center, Fair Credit Reporting § 15.3 (8th ed. 2013), *updated at* www.nclc.org/library (describing state credit services organization laws). These laws generally exempt nonprofit entities. *Id.* at § 15.3.3.

531 Cal. Bus & Prof. Code § 654.3(c) and (d) (West).

532 *Id.* § 654.3(b) and (f).

533 *See, e.g.*, Brian Grow & Robert Berner, *Fresh Pain for the Uninsured*, Bus. Week, Nov. 21, 2007.

high interest rates, and the contractual basis to charge such rates is questionable.

Some credit programs designed for medical bills also entail automatic deductions from a patient's wages and thus involve employers offering the programs.[534] This practice may also expose the employers to loan brokering issues. If the wage assignments are not cancelable at the option of the employee, they might also violate the Federal Trade Commission's Credit Practices Rule.[535]

9.4.6 Claims Based on Hospital's Charitable Status

9.4.6.1 General

Many hospitals are organized as not-for-profit corporations and have tax-exempt status under state law and the Internal Revenue Code. As such, they have an implicit duty to provide a certain amount of free care to low-income patients; in some states this obligation is explicit.[536] Engaging in collection activities against low-income patients while failing to inform them of their eligibility to apply for charity care may be actionable under state laws prohibiting unfair and deceptive acts and practices.[537] Such conduct might also constitute a breach of the hospital's charitable duty under state tax law.[538] However, several dozen federal courts have rejected the theory that such conduct violates a charitable trust based upon the tax-exempt status of the hospital under section 501(c)(3) of the Internal Revenue Code.[539] The IRS did impose certain reporting requirements after these lawsuits.[540] Also, the Affordable Care Act (ACA) imposes new obligations on nonprofit hospitals based on their tax status, which the IRS is in the process of issuing regulations to implement.[541] It remains to be seen whether any private actions are possible for violations of these ACA obligations.

A few hospitals still have obligations under the Hill-Burton Act,[542] a federal law that provided hospitals with construction and renovation grant funds. In return, hospitals were obligated to provide a certain amount of uncompensated care for twenty years. While most hospitals are no longer bound by this obligation, a few still are.[543] Failure to comply with the Hill-Burton Act may give rise to a claim.[544] In addition, some states may provide special tax-exempt bonds, financing, or other benefits for hospital construction. At least one plaintiff has unsuccessfully sought to bring a claim as a third-party beneficiary of such arrangements.[545]

---

534 Sarah Bernstein, *In New Health Plan, Patients Pay Their Share—Or Else*, Wall St. J., Mar. 13, 2006 (describing UnitedHealth Group's OnePay plan, which uses automatic wage deduction and imposes 7.5% interest rate to repay loans used to pay deductibles and co-payments; notes that UnitedHealth chartered its own bank for OnePay).

535 16 C.F.R. § 444. *See* National Consumer Law Center, Federal Deception Law § 2.3 (2012), *updated at* www.nclc.org/library.

The FTC rule does not apply to banks, but many banks are governed by comparable rules. *Id.*

536 The website of Community Catalyst has a guide to free care programs in each state, *see* www.communitycatalyst.org/initiatives-and-issues/initiatives/hospital-accountability-project/free-care

537 *See* Martinez v. Yale New Haven Hosp., 2005 WL 2364901 (Conn. Super. Ct. Sept. 1, 2005) (informing patients that their only option was to pay charges, despite availability of charity care funds, may be actionable as negligent misrepresentation); Ahmad v. Yale New Haven Hosp., 38 Conn. L. Rptr. 238 (Conn. Super. Ct. 2004) (finding private right of action under Connecticut free care statute; failure to inform eligible patients of free care availability may violate both free care statute and UDAP statute), *later proceeding at* 933 A.2d 1208 (Conn. App. Ct. 2007) (affirming denial of class certification because individualized inquiry required). *See* § 9.4.2, *supra* (UDAP section).

538 Alan Alop, Defending Hospital Collection Cases (rev. ed. 2005), *available at* www.illinoislegaladvocate.org/index.cfm?fuseaction=home.dsp_content&contentID=728. *Cf.* Hill v. Sisters of St. Francis Health Servs., Inc., 2006 WL 3783415 (N.D. Ill. Dec. 20, 2006) (allegation that discriminatory pricing violated state's charitable organization exemption supported claim that hospital violated UDAP statute); Ahmad v. Yale New Haven Hosp., 38 Conn. L. Rptr. 238 (Conn. Super. Ct. 2004) (action alleging violations of free care statute did not violate rule that beneficiaries may not sue to enforce charitable trust), *later proceeding at* 933 A.2d 1208 (Conn. App. Ct. 2007) (affirming denial of class certification because individualized inquiry required). *But see* Servedio v. Our Lady of the Resurrection Med. Ctr., Clearinghouse No. 55,626 (Ill. Cir. Ct. Cook Cnty. Jan. 6, 2005) (dismissing plaintiff's claim that hospital's discriminatory pricing violated charitable obligation under Illinois revenue code; no private right of action under revenue code).

New York law specifically prohibits patients from using the fact that a hospital receives state charity care funds as a legal defense in a hospital collection action. N.Y. Pub. Health Law § 2807-k(14) (McKinney).

539 *See* § 9.4.6.2, *infra*.

540 *See* § 9.3.1.5, *supra*.

541 *See* § 9.3.1, *supra*.

542 42 U.S.C. § 291c.

543 Hospitals that have Hill-Burton obligations are identified online at www.hrsa.gov/gethealthcare/affordable/hillburton/facilities.html.

544 Yale New Haven Hosp., Inc. v. Gargiulo, 1999 WL 989422 (Conn. Super. Ct. Oct. 18, 1999) (special defense of failure to mitigate sufficiently alleged; hospital failed to advise patient of Hill-Burton or other aid programs, or to assist her in applying). *See also* Flagstaff Med. Ctr., Inc. v. Sullivan, 962 F.2d 879 (9th. Cir. 1992) (applying state contract law to hold that indigent patients are third-party beneficiaries of contract between HHS and hospital that accepted Hill-Burton funds; eligible patients who were denied such care may be granted relief from debt to hospital); Davis v. Ball Mem'l Hosp. Ass'n., 640 F.2d 30 (7th Cir. 1980) (regulation created an entitlement to uncompensated care); Creditor's Serv. Inc. v. Shaffer, 659 P.2d 694 (Colo. 1982); Yale New Haven Hosp., Inc. v. Mitchell, 683 A.2d 1362 (Conn. Super. Ct. 1995) (correcting opinion at 662 A.2d 178) (failure to notify indigent patients of the availability of free care under Hill-Burton or the Connecticut Hospital Bed fund is a defense to a hospital debt collection suit; case remanded to trial court for factual findings on issue whether failure to notify was also unfair trade practice); Hosp. Ctr. at Orange v. Cook, 426 A.2d 526 (N.J. Super. Ct. App. Div. 1981) (hospital's failure to comply with Hill-Burton a bar to suit for services rendered). *But see* White v. Moses Taylor Hosp., 841 F. Supp. 629 (M.D. Pa. 1992) (*Flagstaff* decision considered and rejected; private right of action only to compel future compliance by hospital).

545 Davis v. Phoebe Putney Health Sys., Inc., 634 S.E.2d 452 (Ga. Ct. App. 2006) (uninsured patients were not third-party beneficiaries of lease agreement between hospital and county hospital authority, even though lease required hospital to provide indigent care).

9.4.6.2 Not-for-Profit Hospital Litigation Cases

In the early 2000s, several dozen class action lawsuits challenging hospital billing practices were filed in an orchestrated campaign. The suits were based on a number of legal claims but primarily focused on the theory that the hospitals had violated contracts with the federal government, to which the plaintiffs were third-party beneficiaries, to provide charitable care in exchange for federal tax-exempt status.[546] The suits also included claims under the Emergency Medical Treatment and Active Labor Act (EMTALA), the Fair Debt Collection Practices Act (FDCPA), as well as state claims for UDAP violations, breach of the duty of good faith and fair dealing, and breach of contract.

Most of the federal claims in these lawsuits were dismissed on the pleadings. The courts uniformly dismissed claims for breach of contract or charitable trust based upon a theory of the hospital's obligations under section 501(c)(3) of the Internal Revenue Code.[547] The courts held that tax-exempt status does not create a contract between the hospital and the Internal Revenue Service and that, even if it did, the plaintiffs could not enforce that contract because they were at most incidental beneficiaries. Furthermore, these courts held that there is no private right of action to enforce section 501(c)(3).[548]

Several courts distinguished cases finding a private right of action for patients to enforce the Hill-Burton Act.[549] These courts noted that in the Hill-Burton cases, the hospitals did actually enter into a written agreement with the government and received funds under that agreement. Furthermore, the courts noted that Hill-Burton provided a private right of action to litigants.

The courts also uniformly dismissed claims for violation of a charitable trust, holding that there was no intent to establish a charitable trust and, even if there were, the plaintiffs would have no right to enforce it.[550] The courts similarly uniformly

546 Harrison v. Christus St. Patrick Hosp., 430 F. Supp. 2d 591 (W.D. La. 2006); Nash v. Lee Mem'l Health Sys., 2005 WL 2043642 (M.D. Fla. Aug. 25, 2005); Kabeller v. Orlando Reg'l Healthcare Sys., Inc., 2005 WL 1925717 (M.D. Fla. Aug. 11, 2005); Cargile v. Baylor Health Care Sys., 2005 WL 2445482 (N.D. Tex. Aug. 10, 2005); Gardner v. North Miss. Health Servs., Inc., 2005 WL 1312753 (N.D. Miss. May 31, 2005); Jakubiec v. Sacred Heart Health Sys., Inc., 2005 WL 1261443 (N.D. Fla. May 27, 2005); Ellis v. Phoebe Putney Health Sys., Inc., 2005 WL 4732728 (M.D. Ga. Apr. 8, 2005); Corely v. John D. Archibold Mem'l Hosp., Inc., 2005 WL 4732727 (M.D. Ga. Mar. 31, 2005); Fields v. Banner Health, 2005 WL 4806305 (D. Ariz. Mar. 24, 2005); Jellison v. Fla. Hosp. Healthcare Sys., Inc., 2005 WL 4732730 (M.D. Fla. Mar. 15, 2005); Wright v. St. Dominic Health Servs., Inc., 2005 WL 743339 (S.D. Miss. Mar. 1, 2005); Schmitt v. Protestant Mem'l Med. Ctr., 2005 WL 4157466 (S.D. Ill. Feb. 23, 2005); Peterson v. Fairview Health Servs., 2005 WL 226168 (D. Minn. Feb. 1, 2005); Daly v. Baptist Health, 2005 WL 4386003 (E.D. Ark. Jan. 31, 2005); Washington *ex rel.* Washington v. Med. Ctr. of Cent. Ga., Inc., 2005 WL 4157465 (M.D. Ga. Jan. 21, 2005); Hudson v. Cent. Ga. Health Servs., 2005 WL 4145745 (M.D. Ga. Jan. 13, 2005); Sabeta v. Baptist Hosp. of Miami, Inc., 410 F. Supp. 2d 1224 (S.D. Fla. 2005); Grant v. Trinity Health Mich., 390 F. Supp. 2d 643 (E.D. Mich. 2005); McCoy v. East Tex. Med. Ctr., 388 F. Supp. 2d 760 (E.D. Tex. 2005); Bobo v. Christus Health, 227 F.R.D. 479 (E.D. Tex. 2005); Kolari v. N.Y. Presbyterian Hosp., 382 F. Supp. 2d 562 (S.D.N.Y. 2005), *vacated in part on other grounds*, 455 F.3d 118 (2d Cir. 2006); Quinn v. BJC Health Sys., 364 F. Supp. 2d 1046 (E.D. Mo. 2005); Valencia v. Miss. Baptist Med. Ctr., 363 F. Supp. 2d 867 (S.D. Miss. 2005); Ferguson v. Centura Health Corp., 358 F. Supp. 2d 1014 (D. Colo. 2004); Burton v. William Beaumont Hosp., 347 F. Supp. 2d 486 (E.D. Mich. 2004); Kizzire v. Baptist Health Systems, Inc., 343 F. Supp. 2d 1074 (N.D. Ala. 2004), *aff'd on other grounds*, 441 F.3d 1306 (11th Cir. 2006); Darr v. Sutter Health, 2004 WL 2873068 (N.D. Cal. Nov. 20, 2004).

547 Harrison v. Christus St. Patrick Hosp., 430 F. Supp. 2d 591 (W.D. La. 2006); Nash v. Lee Mem'l Health Sys., 2005 WL 2043642 (M.D. Fla. Aug. 25, 2005); Kabeller v. Orlando Reg'l Healthcare Sys., Inc., 2005 WL 1925717 (M.D. Fla. Aug. 11, 2005); Cargile v. Baylor Health Care Sys., 2005 WL 2445482 (N.D. Tex. Aug. 10, 2005); Gardner v. North Miss. Health Servs., Inc., 2005 WL 1312753 (N.D. Miss. May 31, 2005); Jakubiec v. Sacred Heart Health Sys., Inc., 2005 WL 1261443 (N.D. Fla. May 27, 2005); Ellis v. Phoebe Putney Health Sys., Inc., 2005 WL 4732728 (M.D. Ga. Apr. 8, 2005); Corely v. John D. Archibold Mem'l Hosp., Inc., 2005 WL 4732727 (M.D. Ga. Mar. 31, 2005); Fields v. Banner Health, 2005 WL 4806305 (D. Ariz. Mar. 24, 2005); Jellison v. Fla. Hosp. Healthcare Sys., Inc., 2005 WL 4732730 (M.D. Fla. Mar. 15, 2005); Wright v. St. Dominic Health Servs., Inc., 2005 WL 743339 (S.D. Miss. Mar. 1, 2005); Schmitt v. Protestant Mem'l Med. Ctr., 2005 WL 4157466 (S.D. Ill. Feb. 23, 2005); Peterson v. Fairview Health Servs., 2005 WL 226168 (D. Minn. Feb. 1, 2005); Daly v. Baptist Health, 2005 WL 4386003 (E.D. Ark. Jan. 31, 2005); Washington *ex rel.* Washington v. Med. Ctr. of Cent. Ga., Inc., 2005 WL 4157465 (M.D. Ga. Jan. 21, 2005); Hudson v. Cent. Ga. Health Servs., 2005 WL 4145745 (M.D. Ga. Jan. 13, 2005); Sabeta v. Baptist Hosp. of Miami, Inc., 410 F. Supp. 2d 1224 (S.D. Fla. 2005); Grant v. Trinity Health Mich., 390 F. Supp. 2d 643 (E.D. Mich. 2005); McCoy v. East Tex. Med. Ctr., 388 F. Supp. 2d 760 (E.D. Tex. 2005); Bobo v. Christus Health, 227 F.R.D. 479 (E.D. Tex. 2005); Kolari v. N.Y. Presbyterian Hosp., 382 F. Supp. 2d 562 (S.D.N.Y. 2005), *vacated in part on other grounds*, 455 F.3d 118 (2d Cir. 2006); Quinn v. BJC Health Sys., 364 F. Supp. 2d 1046 (E.D. Mo. 2005); Valencia v. Miss. Baptist Med. Ctr., 363 F. Supp. 2d 867 (S.D. Miss. 2005); Ferguson v. Centura Health Corp., 358 F. Supp. 2d 1014 (D. Colo. 2004); Burton v. William Beaumont Hosp., 347 F. Supp. 2d 486 (E.D. Mich. 2004); Kizzire v. Baptist Health Systems, Inc., 343 F. Supp. 2d 1074 (N.D. Ala. 2004), *aff'd on other grounds*, 441 F.3d 1306 (11th Cir. 2006); Darr v. Sutter Health, 2004 WL 2873068 (N.D. Cal. Nov. 20, 2004).

548 While claims based on a theory that a hospital violated its tax-exempt status have almost uniformly failed, one court has held that such a violation could be used to show that the hospital's practices violated public policy, which was an issue under that state's UDAP statute. *See* Hill v. Sisters of St. Francis Health Servs., Inc., 2006 WL 3783415 (N.D. Ill. Dec. 20, 2006).

549 Feliciana v. Thomas Jefferson Univ. Hosp., 2005 WL 2397047 (E.D. Pa. Sept. 28, 2005); Hutt v. Albert Einstein Med. Ctr., 2005 WL 2396313 (E.D. Pa. Sept. 28, 2005); Corely v. John D. Archibold Mem'l Hosp., Inc., 2005 WL 4732727 (M.D. Ga. Mar. 31, 2005); Fields v. Banner Health, 2005 WL 4806305 (D. Ariz. Mar. 24, 2005); Jellison v. Fla. Hosp. Healthcare Sys., Inc., 2005 WL 4732730 (M.D. Fla. Mar. 15, 2005); Schmitt v. Protestant Mem'l Med. Ctr., 2005 WL 4157466 (S.D. Ill. Feb. 23, 2005); Washington *ex rel.* Washington v. Med. Ctr. of Cent. Ga., Inc., 2005 WL 4157465 (M.D. Ga. Jan. 21, 2005); Sabeta v. Baptist Hosp. of Miami, Inc., 410 F. Supp. 2d 1224 (S.D. Fla. 2005); Grant v. Trinity Health Mich., 390 F. Supp. 2d 643 (E.D. Mich. 2005); McCoy v. East Tex. Med. Ctr., 388 F. Supp. 2d 760 (E.D. Tex. 2005); Kolari v. N.Y. Presbyterian Hosp., 382 F. Supp. 2d 562 (S.D.N.Y. 2005), *vacated in part on other grounds*, 455 F.3d 118 (2d Cir. 2006); Quinn v. BJC Health Sys., 364 F. Supp. 2d 1046 (E.D. Mo. 2005); Valencia v. Miss. Baptist Med. Ctr., 363 F. Supp. 2d 867 (S.D. Miss. 2005); Ferguson v. Centura Health Corp., 358 F. Supp. 2d 1014 (D. Colo. 2004).

550 Harrison v. Christus St. Patrick Hosp., 430 F. Supp. 2d 591 (W.D. La. 2006); Nash v. Lee Mem'l Health Sys., 2005 WL 2043642 (M.D. Fla. Aug. 25, 2005); Kabeller v. Orlando Reg'l Healthcare Sys., Inc., 2005

dismissed EMTALA claims.[551] Claims under the FDCPA met with mixed success. While these claims were dismissed in most cases,[552] courts in other cases denied dismissal or dismissed without prejudice, permitting plaintiffs to amend their claims.[553] Civil rights claims under 42 U.S.C. § 1983 were dismissed because there had been no action committed under color of state law.[554] The Fifth Circuit upheld a denial of class certification in a case that primarily sought injunctive relief under Federal Rule of Civil Procedure 23(b)(2), holding that individual issues predominated.[555]

After dismissal of the federal claims, most of the district courts declined to exercise supplemental jurisdiction over the remaining state law claims. A few courts did rule substantively on the state law claims, dismissing counts for UDAP violations, fraud, breach of contract, and unjust enrichment.[556] However, the Second Circuit rebuked one district court for abusing its discretion in exercising supplemental jurisdiction and dismissing the state law claims.[557] Some of the cases were refiled in state court, where a few met with more success.[558]

An initial settlement of one of these cases was eventually undone. A tentative settlement of unfiled claims against North Mississippi Medical Center unraveled when news of the settlement resulted in a dramatic increase in that hospital's charity care volume, as uninsured patients from both the hospital's area and across the state bypassed other hospitals to seek care at North Mississippi, and workers allegedly dropped their health insurance coverage to take advantage of the settlement.[559] After North Mississippi backed out of the settlement it successfully moved to dismiss the plaintiff's case in federal court.[560]

9.4.7 *Other State Common Law Claims*

Other state common law claims may be applicable in particular instances of medical debt collection. These claims may include:

- Breach of contract;[561]

WL 1925717 (M.D. Fla. Aug. 11, 2005); Cargile v. Baylor Health Care Sys., 2005 WL 2445482 (N.D. Tex. Aug. 10, 2005); Gardner v. North Miss. Health Servs., Inc., 2005 WL 1312753 (N.D. Miss. May 31, 2005); Jakubiec v. Sacred Heart Health Sys., Inc., 2005 WL 1261443 (N.D. Fla. May 27, 2005); Corely v. John D. Archibold Mem'l Hosp., Inc., 2005 WL 4732727 (M.D. Ga. Mar. 31, 2005); Fields v. Banner Health, 2005 WL 4806305 (D. Ariz. Mar. 24, 2005); Jellison v. Fla. Hosp. Healthcare Sys., Inc., 2005 WL 4732730 (M.D. Fla. Mar. 15, 2005); Wright v. St. Dominic Health Servs., Inc., 2005 WL 743339 (S.D. Miss. Mar. 1, 2005); Schmitt v. Protestant Mem'l Med. Ctr., 2005 WL 4157466 (S.D. Ill. Feb. 23, 2005); Peterson v. Fairview Health Servs., 2005 WL 226168 (D. Minn. Feb. 1, 2005); Daly v. Baptist Health, 2005 WL 4386003 (E.D. Ark. Jan. 31, 2005); Washington *ex rel.* Washington v. Med. Ctr. of Cent. Ga., Inc., 2005 WL 4157465 (M.D. Ga. Jan. 21, 2005); Hudson v. Cent. Ga. Health Servs., 2005 WL 4145745 (M.D. Ga. Jan. 13, 2005); Sabeta v. Baptist Hosp. of Miami, Inc., 410 F. Supp. 2d 1224 (S.D. Fla. 2005); Grant v. Trinity Health Mich., 390 F. Supp. 2d 643 (E.D. Mich. 2005); McCoy v. East Tex. Med. Ctr., 388 F. Supp. 2d 760 (E.D. Tex. 2005); Bobo v. Christus Health, 227 F.R.D. 479 (E.D. Tex. 2005); Kolari v. N.Y. Presbyterian Hosp., 382 F. Supp. 2d 562 (S.D.N.Y. 2005), *vacated in part on other grounds*, 455 F.3d 118 (2d Cir. 2006); Quinn v. BJC Health Sys., 364 F. Supp. 2d 1046 (E.D. Mo. 2005); Valencia v. Miss. Baptist Med. Ctr., 363 F. Supp. 2d 867 (S.D. Miss. 2005); Ferguson v. Centura Health Corp., 358 F. Supp. 2d 1014 (D. Colo. 2004); Burton v. William Beaumont Hosp., 347 F. Supp. 2d 486 (E.D. Mich. 2004); Kizzire v. Baptist Health Systems, Inc., 343 F. Supp. 2d 1074 (N.D. Ala. 2004), *aff'd on other grounds*, 441 F.3d 1306 (11th Cir. 2006); Darr v. Sutter Health, 2004 WL 2873068 (N.D. Cal. Nov. 20, 2004).

551 *See* § 9.3.3, *supra*.

552 Hutt v. Albert Einstein Med. Ctr., 2005 WL 2396313 (E.D. Pa. Sept. 28, 2005); Corely v. John D. Archibold Mem'l Hosp., Inc., 2005 WL 4732727 (M.D. Ga. Mar. 31, 2005); Washington *ex rel.* Washington v. Med. Ctr. of Cent. Ga., Inc., 2005 WL 4157465 (M.D. Ga. Jan. 21, 2005); Kolari v. N.Y. Presbyterian Hosp., 382 F. Supp. 2d 562 (S.D.N.Y. 2005).

553 Sabeta v. Baptist Hosp. of Miami, Inc., 410 F. Supp. 2d 1224 (S.D. Fla. 2005); Cargile v. Baylor Health Care Sys., 2005 WL 2445482 (N.D. Tex. Aug. 10, 2005).

554 Corely v. John D. Archibold Mem'l Hosp., Inc., 2005 WL 4732727 (M.D. Ga. Mar. 31, 2005); Washington *ex rel.* Washington v. Med. Ctr. of Cent. Ga., Inc., 2005 WL 4157465 (M.D. Ga. Jan. 21, 2005).

555 Maldonado v. Ochsner Clinic Found., 493 F.3d 521 (5th Cir. 2007).

556 Carlson v. Long Island Jewish Med. Ctr., 378 F. Supp. 2d 128 (E.D.N.Y. 2005); Burton v. William Beaumont Hosp., 373 F. Supp. 2d 707 (E.D. Mich. 2005).

557 Kolari v. N.Y. Presbyterian Hosp., 455 F.3d 118 (2d Cir. 2006).

558 *See In re* Sutter Health Uninsured Pricing Cases, 2005 WL 1842582 (Cal. Super. Ct. July 16, 2005) (denying dismissal of UDAP and unconscionability claims for discriminatory pricing); Turner v. Legacy Health Sys., 2006 WL 657176 (Or. Cir. Ct. Oct. 4, 2005) (granting class certification in case challenging discriminatory pricing under breach of contract and UDAP theory). *See also* Press Release, Statement from Dick Scruggs Nonprofit Hospital Litig., Oct. 11, 2005 (stating that motions to dismiss were denied in eleven state court cases); Steven Carter, *Providence Health System Will Offer Refunds To Uninsured*, Portland Oregonian, June 24, 2006; Bob Egelko, *Hospital Chain Agrees To Settlement: Catholic Healthcare West Says It Will Pay $423 Million Refund*, San Francisco Chron., Jan. 12, 2007; David Phelps, *Uninsured Patients May Get Discounts: Allina and Fairview Settled a Class-Action Suit Claiming That People Without Health Coverage Paid Too Much For Medical Care*, Minneapolis Star-Tribune, Mar. 17, 2007.

559 Ceci Connolly, *Tax-Exempt Hospitals' Practices Challenged, 46 Lawsuits Allege That Uninsured Pay the Most*, Wash. Post, Jan. 29, 2005, at A1.

560 Gardner v. North Miss. Health Servs., Inc., 2005 WL 1312753 (N.D. Miss. May 31, 2005).

561 Greene v. Life Care Centers of Am., Inc., 2008 WL 5378259 (D.S.C. Dec. 23, 2008) (patient could bring breach of contract claim over provider's collection efforts in violation of balance billing prohibitions); Urquhart v. Manatee Mem'l Hosp., 2007 WL 781738 (M.D. Fla. Mar. 13, 2007) (hospital's excessive charges could be challenged as breach of contract); Colomar v. Mercy Hosp., Inc., 461 F. Supp. 2d 1265 (S.D. Fla. 2006) (same); Wentz v. Kindred Hosps. E., L.L.C., 333 F. Supp. 2d 1298 (S.D. Fla. 2004) (when provider returned Medicare payment so it could seek recovery against patient's personal injury settlement, patient could proceed with breach of contract claim that charges were "unlawful" and thus violated the provider's contract); Cambridge Manor of Fairfield, L.L.C. v. Myers, 2012 WL 6582542 (Conn. Super. Ct. Nov. 26, 2012) (in defense of collection lawsuit against her, patient's daughter could bring breach of contract counterclaim against nursing home that failed to provide monthly statements as promised in contract, which prevented patient from qualifying for Medicaid benefits to pay for bills); Servedio v. Our Lady of the Resurrection Med. Ctr., Clearinghouse No. 55,626 (Ill. Cir. Ct. Cook Cnty. Jan. 6, 2005) (consumer permitted to proceed on breach of contract claim for hospital's discriminatory pricing charging uninsured patients several times more

- Breach of the covenant of good faith and fair dealing, which is incorporated into health care contracts[562]—this duty may require that charges not set forth specifically in an agreement be reasonable;[563]
- Breach of fiduciary duty;[564]
- Unconscionability;[565]
- Unjust enrichment;[566]
- Fraud;[567]

---

than private and public insurers); Turner v. Legacy Health Systems, 2006 WL 657176 (Or. Cir. Ct. Oct. 4, 2005) (granting class certification in case challenging discriminatory pricing as breach of contract); California Shock Trauma Air Rescue v. Holland, 2010 WL 3442212 (Tex. App. Aug. 31, 2010) (upholding default judgment for patient for breach of contract claim against air rescue company for violation of agreement to forbear dunning in exchange for patient's partial payment and filing of insurance appeal). *But see* Agostino v. Quest Diagnostics, 2011 WL 5410667 (D.N.J. Nov. 3, 2011) (no third-party beneficiary breach-of-contract claim for balance billing); Harrison v. Christus St. Patrick Hosp., 430 F. Supp. 2d 591 (W.D. La. 2006) (no breach of contract or fiduciary duty claim, or unjust enrichment claim, for discriminatory pricing); DiCarlo v. St. Mary's Hosp., 2006 WL 2038498 (D.N.J. July 19, 2006) (same), *aff'd*, 530 F.3d 255 (3d Cir. 2008) (adopting district court decision); Burton v. William Beaumont Hosp., 373 F. Supp. 2d 707 (E.D. Mich. 2005) (same); Nunes v. The Hosp. Comm. for Livermore-Pleasanton Areas, 2012 WL 1925537 (Cal. Ct. App. May 29, 2012) (no breach of contract claim for discriminatory pricing when contact and hospital provided availability of financial assistance); Hale v. Sharp Healthcare, 108 Cal. Rptr. 3d 669 (Cal. Ct. App. 2010) (no breach of contract or fiduciary duty claim for discriminatory pricing); Durell v. Sharp Healthcare, 108 Cal. Rptr. 3d 682 (Cal Ct. App. 2010) (same); Morrell v. Wellstar Health Sys., Inc., 633 S.E.2d 68 (Ga. Ct. App. 2006) (same); Cox v. Athens Reg'l Med. Ctr., Inc., 631 S.E.2d 792 (Ga. Ct. App. 2006) (same); Allen v. Clarian Health Partners, Inc. 980 N.E.2d 306 (Ind. 2012) (dismissing breach of contract claim for discriminatory pricing, following *DiCarlo v. St. Mary Hospital*); Morgan v. State, 787 N.Y.S.2d 356 (N.Y. App. Div. 2004) (dismissing breach of contract claim for discriminatory pricing); Shelton v. Duke Univ. Health Sys., Inc., 633 S.E.2d 113 (N.C. Ct. App. 2006) (no breach of contract or fiduciary duty claim for discriminatory pricing); Firelands Reg'l Med. Ctr. v. Jeavons, 2008 WL 4408600 (Ohio Ct. App. Sept. 30, 2008) (discriminatory pricing did not constitute anticipatory breach of contract); Knoop v. Orthopaedic Consultants of Cincinnati, Inc., 2008 WL 2955393 (Ohio Ct. App. Aug. 4, 2008) (dismissing patient's claim that provider's "Self Pay Policy" document amounted to contract that was breached when provider charged more than policy represented); Nygaard v. Sioux Valley Hosp. & Health Sys., 731 N.W.2d 184 (S.D. 2007) (no breach of contract or fiduciary duty claim for discriminatory pricing).

562 Greene v. Life Care Centers of Am., Inc., 2008 WL 5378259 (D.S.C. Dec. 23, 2008) (patient could bring claim for breach of the covenant of good faith and fair dealing over provider's collection efforts in violation of balance billing prohibitions); Rivera v. Veterans Mem'l Med. Ctr., 818 A.2d 731 (Conn. 2003) (class action alleging violations of state UDAP law, abuse of process, and breach of the implied covenant of good faith and fair dealing over hospital's balance billing and collection efforts when workers' compensation covered medical services); Cambridge Manor of Fairfield, L.L.C. v. Myers, 2012 WL 6582542 (Conn. Super. Ct. Nov. 26, 2012) (in defense of collection lawsuit against her, patient's daughter could bring counterclaim for breach of implied covenant of good faith and fair dealing against nursing home that failed to provide monthly statements as promised in contract, which prevented patient from qualifying for Medicaid benefits to pay for bills); Picker v. Castro, 776 N.Y.S.2d 433 (N.Y. App. Term 2003) (provider's refusal to fill out insurance paperwork violated duty of good faith and fair dealing; provider precluded from recovering fees from patient).

563 Greenfield v. Manor Care, Inc., 705 So. 2d 926 (Fla. Dist. Ct. App. 1997) (contract with nursing home included duty of good faith and fair dealing, which required that, when no price term specified, only reasonable price could be charged), *overruled on other grounds by* Knowles v. Beverly Enters., 898 So. 2d 1 (Fla. 2004). *But see* Kizzire v. Baptist Health Systems, Inc., 441 F.3d 1306 (11th Cir. 2006) (claim of breach of duty of good faith and fair dealing dismissed on res judicata grounds; all claims relating to price of care were compulsory counterclaims in hospital's collection action); Urquhart v. Manatee Mem'l Hosp., 2007 WL 781738 (M.D. Fla. Mar. 13, 2007) (no breach of duty of good faith and fair dealing over discriminatory pricing); Hale v. Sharp Healthcare, 108 Cal. Rptr. 3d 669 (Cal. Ct. App. 2010) (same); Durell v. Sharp Healthcare, 108 Cal. Rptr. 3d 682 (Cal Ct. App. 2010) (same).

564 Havsy v. Washington State Dep't of Health, 123 Wash. App. 1030 (Wash. Ct. App. 2004) (licensing board sanctions affirmed in case in which doctor breached fiduciary duty to patient by misleading patient about the price of treatment, failing to inform patient of the high cost of a certain procedure and that insurance would not cover that procedure, and using a "small-print" form to obtain patient's agreement to be liable for charges). *But see* Harrison v. Christus St. Patrick Hosp., 430 F. Supp. 2d 591 (W.D. La. 2006) (no breach of contract or fiduciary duty claim, or unjust enrichment claim, for discriminatory pricing); DiCarlo v. St. Mary's Hosp., 2006 WL 2038498 (D.N.J. July 19, 2006), *aff'd*, 530 F.3d 255 (3d Cir. 2008) (adopting district court decision); Morrell v. Wellstar Health Sys., Inc., 633 S.E.2d 68 (Ga. Ct. App. 2006); Cox v. Athens Reg'l Med. Ctr., Inc., 631 S.E.2d 792 (Ga. Ct. App. 2006); Shelton v. Duke Univ. Health Sys., Inc., 633 S.E.2d 113 (N.C. Ct. App. 2006); North Ohio Med. Specialists, L.L.C. v. Huston, 2009 WL 3683632 (Ohio Ct. App. Nov. 6, 2009) (doctor did not have a fiduciary duty to the patient beyond the duty to diagnose and treat diseases and injuries); Nygaard v. Sioux Valley Hosp. & Health Sys., 731 N.W.2d 184 (S.D. 2007) (no breach of contract or fiduciary duty claim for discriminatory pricing). *See generally* Mark A. Hall & Carl E. Schneider, *Patients as Consumers: Courts, Contracts, and The New Medical Marketplace*, 106 Mich. L. Rev. 642 (Feb. 2008).

565 *See* Hill v. Sisters of St. Francis Health Servs., Inc., 2006 WL 3783415 (N.D. Ill. Dec. 20, 2006) (denying dismissal of UDAP and unconscionability claims for discriminatory pricing); Phoenix Baptist Hosp. & Med. Ctr. v. Aiken, 877 P.2d 1345 (Ariz. Ct. App. 1994) (permitting unconscionability when husband signed contract when wife had just had heart attack, husband was distraught and could not read contract due to absence of reading glasses); *In re* Sutter Health Uninsured Pricing Cases, 2005 WL 1842582 (Cal. Super. Ct. July 16, 2005) (denying dismissal of UDAP and unconscionability claims for discriminatory pricing); Via Christi Reg'l Med. Ctr., Inc. v. Reed, 314 P.3d 852 (Kan. 2013) (permitting unconscionability claim against hospital for inflated pricing and duplicate charges in asserting lien on patient's tort settlement). *See generally* National Consumer Law Center, Unfair and Deceptive Acts and Practices §§ 4.3, 4.4 (8th ed. 2012), *updated at* www.nclc.org/library; Mark A. Hall & Carl E. Schneider, *Patients as Consumers: Courts, Contracts, and The New Medical Marketplace*, 106 Mich. L. Rev. 642 (Feb. 2008); George A. Nation, *Obscene Contracts: The Doctrine of Unconscionability and Hospital Billing of the Uninsured*, 94 Ky. L.J. 101–137 (2005–2006). *But see* Geico Indem. Ins. Co. v. Kannaday, 2007 WL 2990552 (D. Kan. Oct. 11, 2007) (discriminatory pricing not unconscionable under Kansas UDAP statute because no evidence of deceptive, oppressive, or overreaching actions).

566 Agostino v. Quest Diagnostics, 2011 WL 5410667 (D.N.J. Nov. 3, 2011) (summary judgment for consumer on unjust enrichment claim that collector added fee not permitted by provider's contract with insurer).

567 Pickering v. Coast Ctr. for Orthopedic Arthroscopic Surgery & Treatment, 2009 WL 932629 (Cal. Ct. App. Apr. 8, 2009) (unpublished) (upholding jury's finding of fraud when provider accepted partial payment from insurer, then balance billed remainder at chargemaster rates and initiated collection lawsuit in violation of contract with insurer and provider's representations to patient that insurer would cover surgery); Martinez v. Yale New Haven Hosp., 2005 WL 2364901 (Conn. Super. Ct. Sept. 1, 2005)

- Limitations on collection fees;[568]
- Usury;[569]
- Malicious prosecution;[570] and
- Other common law claims.[571]

9.5 Defenses to a Medical Debt Collection Action

9.5.1 General

Practitioners defending consumers sued over medical debt have a number of viable defenses. Aggressive advocacy can often result in very favorable outcomes. Medical debt collectors are accustomed to obtaining default judgments and are not used to being forced to put on a case.[572] Defending a consumer against a collection action is also important because once a default judgment has entered, res judicata may preclude the consumer from bringing a separate action to challenge the abuses or unfair practices of medical creditors.[573]

As few medical debt collection suits go to trial, collectors may overlook a necessary element of proof. Practitioners may prevail because of such a failure of proof, as well as by establishing the consumer's defenses and counterclaims. Practitioners are advised to review the defenses discussed in Chapters 3 through 5, *supra*, of this treatise that generally apply when defending collection lawsuits, such as statutes of limitations, lack of proof that a debt buyer owns the debt, or an amount already paid.

A medical debt collector may sue under various theories, each with different elements and different burdens of proof. The burdens of proof may also differ from state to state. For example, a medical debt collection suit may be an action for breach of contract, on a promissory note, on an open account or an account stated theory, for breach of an implied contract, or for *quantum meruit*. Practitioners should pay attention to the differences in proof required. In particular, if a medical debt collection action is based on an implied contract, on *quantum meruit*, on an account stated, or on a contract without a definite, agreed price, the collector may be required to prove the ordinary and reasonable value of the service provided in order to recover.[574] Proof of the health provider's license may be a necessary element to recover under any theory,[575] as may be proof that the collector is licensed.[576]

9.5.2 Account Stated Actions

Health providers' collection suits frequently are based on an account stated theory. For a general discussion of defending a collection action based on this theory, see § 4.7, *supra*.

(informing patients that only option was to pay charges, despite availability of charity care funds, not actionable as fraud but actionable as negligent misrepresentation); Summa Health Sys. v. Viningre, 749 N.E.2d 344 (Ohio Ct. App. 2000) (fraud judgment affirmed when HMO told patient who had been injured by HMO's misreading of test that she would not be required to pay for further testing and surgery, but then negotiated malpractice settlement making no mention of bills and billed her for the surgery); Cal. Shock Trauma Rescue v. Holland, 2010 WL 3442212 (Tex. App. Aug. 31, 2010) (upholding default judgment for patient for fraud claim against air rescue company for violation of agreement to forbear dunning in exchange for patient's partial payment and filing of insurance appeal). *But see* SWA, Inc. v. Straka, 2003 WL 21434637 (Ohio Ct. App. June 19, 2003) (misrepresentations in nursing home admission materials not actionable when incorrect statement caused no damage to patient or family); Mercy Health Partners of Southwest Ohio v. Miller, 2005 WL 2592674 (Ohio Ct. Ct. Com. Pl. Sept. 30, 2005) (discriminatory pricing not actionable as fraud under Ohio law).

568 *E.g.*, HCA Health Servs., Inc. v. Peters, Clearinghouse No. 44,663 (D. Va. 1989) (when parent assumed financial responsibility for emergency care for child and signed contract before admittance which was open-ended, speculative, and under the complete control of health care provider, court held unenforceable as unreasonable provision for 25% collection attorney fees). *See* National Consumer Law Center, Fair Debt Collection § 10.8 (8th ed. 2014), *updated at* www.nclc.org/library.

569 Press Release, Office of the Minn. Att'y Gen., Attorney General Lori Swanson Files Suit Against Allina Health System for Charging Usurious 18% Interest on Medical Debts (Jan. 22, 2009). *Cf.* Egge v. Healthspan Servs. Co., 115 F. Supp. 2d 1126 (D. Minn. 2000) (usury not shown when consumer never paid debt; illegal interest was never collected, an essential element under Minnesota statute).

570 *See, e.g.*, Rutherford v. Ralph Hutton & Assocs., 2004 WL 1119676 (Cal. Ct. App. May 20, 2004) (unpublished) (malicious prosecution action brought against hospital over its attempt to enforce lien against personal injury recovery when balance billing was forbidden by hospital's contract with county aid program). *See generally* National Consumer Law Center, Fair Debt Collection § 9.6 (8th ed. 2014), *updated at* www.nclc.org/library.

571 Joseph v. J.J. Mac Intyre Companies, 238 F. Supp. 2d 1158 (N.D. Cal. 2002) (barrage of phone calls to disabled senior citizen; consumer stated claims for intrusion on seclusion and "tort-in-se"), *later op. at* 281 F. Supp. 2d 1156 (N.D. Cal. 2003) (collector's motion for summary judgment denied); Bickford v. Onslow Mem'l Hosp. Found., Inc., 855 A.2d 1150 (Me. 2004) (alleging claims for defamation and tortuous interference with economic advantage, over hospital's wrongful credit reporting). *Cf.* Muse v. Charter Hosp., Inc., 452 S.E.2d 589 (N.C. Ct. App. 1995) (malpractice judgment proper when hospital's policy of requiring patients to be discharged when their insurance was used up "interfered with" treating physician's medical judgment), *aff'd*, 342 N.C. 403 (1995) (per curiam).

572 An analysis of collection actions filed by a Connecticut hospital revealed that 70% of the debtors never filed an appearance with the court. Only 9% of debtors were represented by counsel. Connecticut Ctr. for a New Economy, Uncharitable Care: Yale-New Haven Hospital's Charity Care and Collection Practices (Jan. 2003).

573 *See* Kizzire v. Baptist Health Systems, Inc., 441 F.3d 1306 (11th Cir. 2006) (discriminatory pricing and other claims dismissed on res judicata grounds; court held claims should have been raised as compulsory counterclaims in hospital's collection suit); Franklin Collection Serv., Inc. v. Stewart, 863 So. 2d 925 (Miss. 2003) (res judicata barred challenge by patients that open account theory was not applicable to recover unpaid medical debt).

574 *See* § 9.5.5, *infra*.

575 *See, e.g.*, Diagnostic Servs. of S. Fla. v. State Farm Mut. Auto Ins. Co., 877 So. 2d 1 (Fla. Dist. Ct. App. 2004) (Florida statute provides that charges by unlicensed "clinics" are unenforceable, but mobile diagnostic service did not violate law in that it was not "clinic" within the meaning of licensing statute); Reddix v. Chatham County Hosp. Auth., 216 S.E.2d 680 (Ga. Ct. App. 1975) (hospital required to show licensing; while hospital testified it was licensed, it failed to introduce the license, the best evidence of that fact), *overruled by* Merrill Lynch, Pierce, Fenner & Smith v. Zimmerman, 285 S.E.2d 181 (Ga. 1981) (testimony of license is sufficient).

576 *See generally* § 3.3.5, *supra*.

This theory is often inappropriate for medical debt cases because there was no prior agreement on the price or value of the services.[577] Furthermore, there is an argument that the account stated theory should be impermissible with respect to consumer debts covered by the Fair Debt Collection Practices Act (FDCPA), because it deprives the consumer of the FDCPA's right to dispute a debt.[578] If the consumer does dispute a debt, that may be enough to defeat the account stated claim.[579]

Collection suits based on the theory of account stated frequently fail to allege the necessary elements of such an action, subjecting the complaint to dismissal.[580] In some cases, the medical debt will arise from a one-time transaction, which does not give rise to an account stated claim because there was no expectation of ongoing transactions.[581] Another common failing in collection actions alleging an account stated claim is the omission of documentation of the account itself.[582]

---

577 *See* Braude & Margulies, P.C. v. Fireman's Fund Ins. Co., 468 F. Supp. 2d 190 (D.D.C. 2007) (claim for account stated requires express or implied agreement as to the amount due; "mere mailing of a bill and the recipient's silence do not reflect an agreement to pay"); Merkle v. Health Options, Inc., 940 So. 2d 1190 (Fla. Dist. Ct. App. 2006) (physician could not recover against insurer of patients that he treated under an account stated claim, because there was no agreement as to the amount due, nor was there an express or implicit promise to pay); *In re* Estate of Boyd, 8 P.3d 664 (Idaho Ct. App. 2000) (when critically ill patient never signed contract, cause of action was quasi-contract, not open account, and attorney fees could not be awarded under open account statute); Dreyer Med. Clinic v. Corral, 591 N.E.2d 111 (Ill. App. Ct. 1992) (sending of bill and lack of objection by recipient insufficient to prove account stated; here provider failed to prove several essential elements); Baca Chiropractic, P.C. v. Cobb, 317 S.W.3d 674 (Mo. Ct. App. 2010) (reversing summary judgment for chiropractor on open account claim; genuine issue of fact as to whether charges were reasonable); N.Y. Ctr. for Neuropsychology & Forensic Behavioral Science v. Rubenstein, 2007 WL 3391601 (N.Y. Civ. Ct. Nov. 14, 2007) (prima facie case of account stated requires that debtor agree upon the amount owed and to pay the debt); Parsell v. Martinez, 2008 WL 623864 (Ohio Ct. App. Mar. 10, 2008) (affirming judgment for patient because provider failed to prove that patient consented to services and the reasonable cost of the services). *See also* Protestant Hosp. Builders Club, Inc. v. Goedde, 424 N.E.2d 1302 (Ill. App. Ct. 1981). *But see* La. Rev. Stat. Ann. § 9:2781(D) (explicitly applies account stated cause of action to medical bills, whether or not the parties contemplate a series of transactions); Touro Infirmary v. American Maritime Officer, 34 So. 3d 878 (La. Ct. App. 2010) (three year limitations period for open account claim, not ten year period for contract claim); Franklin Collection Serv., Inc. v. Stewart, 863 So. 2d 925 (Miss. 2003) (medical bills were open accounts under Mississippi statute); Huntington Hosp. v. Abrandt, 779 N.Y.S.2d 891 (N.Y. App. Term 2004) (acceptance of medical services created implied contract to pay; summary judgment for hospital on account stated).

578 15 U.S.C. § 1692g. *See* National Consumer Law Center, Fair Debt Collection § 5.7 (8th ed. 2014), *updated at* www.nclc.org/library.

Section 1692g(c) provides that a court may not treat a consumer's failure to dispute a debt under that section as an admission of liability. Thus, to the extent that an account stated action would require the court to construe the consumer's silence as acceptance of a bill, one could argue that section 1692g(c) prohibits such an assumption.

579 *See, e.g.*, Jackson v. Trancik, 953 N.E.2d 1087 (Ind. Ct. App. 2011) (reversing judgment for doctor on account stated claim; affidavit of medical billing expert should have been permitted and raised genuine issue whether doctor overcharged consumer for services); Ochsner Clinic Found. v. Arguello, 80 So. 3d 622 (La. Ct. App. 2011) (affirming dismissal of clinic's action; patient's disputes regarding accuracy of bills and whether she was given credit for payments were sufficient to establish inaccuracy and defeat open account claim); Baca Chiropractic, P.C. v. Cobb, 317 S.W.3d 674 (Mo. Ct. App. 2010) (reversing summary judgment for chiropractor on open account claim, patients' challenge of reasonableness of charges raised genuine issue of material fact; Baptist Home of Brooklyn v. Schott, 902 N.Y.S.2d 368 (N.Y. App. Div. 2010) (claim for account stated may not be utilized as another means to collect under a disputed contract); Good Samaritan Hosp. v. Parim, 906 N.Y.S.2d 772 (N.Y. App. Term 2009) (patient's dispute over whether he actually received hospital room for which he was billed defeated summary judgment). *Cf.* Orthopedic Spine Care of Long Island, P.C. v. Ingardia, 2011 WL 3841439 (E.D.N.Y. Aug. 11, 2011) (while account stated claim fails if there was dispute as to amount of bill, *pro se* defendant's statement that treatment was substandard without supporting evidence did not create issue of fact; failure to object to bill within reasonable time after receipt and partial payment established implicit assent). *See generally* § 4.7.6, *supra*.

580 Alan Alop, Defending Hospital Collection Cases (rev. ed. 2005), *available at* www.illinoislegaladvocate.org/index.cfm?fuseaction=home.dsp_content&contentID=728. *See* Dreyer Med. Clinic v. Corral, 591 N.E.2d 111 (Ill. App. Ct. 1992) (account stated is method of proving damages; creditor must first prove liability; creditor failed to prove several essential elements); UAB Hosp. v. Herman, 2007 WL 4248513 (La. Ct. App. Dec. 5, 2007) (reversing summary judgment for hospital on open account claim because statements, which had a series of confusing credits and debits, showed a balance of zero, contrary to hospital affiant's claim that patient owed over $28,000); St. Tammany Parish Hosp. v. Burris, 804 So. 2d 960 (La. Ct. App. 2001) (reversing summary judgment for hospital on open account claim when hospital failed to properly identify the patient, named only as "the minor child of" alleged debtor, or to allege that debtor was responsible for child's bill; hospital also failed to prove notice, essential to its claim for attorney fees); XL Care Agency v. Johns, 2013 WL 5877305 (N.Y. Sup. Ct. Oct. 17, 2013) (denying summary judgment on account stated claim; home health care agency failed to establish it sent regular invoices, since invoices submitted to support motion were all dated with the same date); Epakchi v. Araghi, 960 N.Y.S.2d 53 (N.Y. Cnty. Ct. 2012) (dentist failed to meet necessary elements for account stated claim, because he did not provide an accounting or regular bills); Ellenville Reg'l Hosp. v. Mendez, 873 N.Y.S.2d 511 (table) (N.Y. Poughkeepsie City Ct. 2008) (provider not entitled to summary judgment on account stated claim when it failed to establish that statements were properly sent to patient; affidavit did not establish that affiant had personal knowledge of provider's billing practices). *See also* Reddix v. Chatham Cnty. Hosp. Auth., 216 S.E.2d 680 (Ga. Ct. App. 1975), *overruled on other grounds by* Merrill Lynch, Pierce, Fenner & Smith v. Zimmerman, 285 S.E.2d 181 (Ga. 1981). *But see* Women's Care Specialists v. Troupin, 408 S.W.3d 310 (Mo. Ct. App. 2013) (provider entitled to judgment on account stated claim, including for amounts that should have been paid by insurer, even though provider failed to bill insurer).

581 Morse L.L.C. v. United Wis. Life Ins. Co., 356 F. Supp. 2d 1296 (S.D. Fla. 2005) (provider failed to state claim for account stated against insurer because provider did not allege expectation of future transactions, and instead the facts reflected a one-time claim that was objected to); Reigelsperger v. Siller, 23 Cal. Rptr. 3d 249 (Cal. Ct. App. 2005) (no open book account existed between patient and chiropractor when there was no ongoing doctor-patient relationship or expectation of future transactions), *rev'd on other grounds*, 150 P.3d 764 (Cal. 2007).

582 Reigelsperger v. Siller, 23 Cal. Rptr. 3d 249 (Cal. Ct. App. 2005) (dismissing open book account claim in part because there was no evidence of a permanent record showing an open account with debits and credits), *rev'd on other grounds*, 150 P.3d 764 (Cal. 2007); Grandell Rehab. & Nursing Home, Inc. v. Devlin, 809 N.Y.S.2d 481 (table), 2005 WL 3240554 (N.Y. Sup. Ct. Nov. 29, 2005) (dismissing action

Note that, in some states, an "account stated" claim actually differs from an "open account claim."[583] Some states require an independent basis for liability in an account stated claim and consider the accounting to merely establish the amount of the debt.[584] In addition the provider may be required to prove the ordinary and reasonable price of its services.[585] A debt buyer using an account stated theory should be required to provide proof of assignment.[586]

9.5.3 Defenses to Contract Claims

9.5.3.1 Duress As a Defense

A potential defense to a hospital collection action based on breach of contract is duress. A hospital's requirement that a debtor agree to pay the patient's medical bills in order for the patient to be admitted or discharged may give rise to the complete contractual defense of duress, especially if the debtor is not the patient, but a relative or friend.[587]

Duress consists of the following three elements:[588]

- *The creditor's exercise of coercion.* Coercion is any form of constraint or compulsion improperly exercised upon the debtor. One form of compulsion may be refusal to admit a patient unless a relative or friend agrees to give a third-party guarantee. Mandatory emergency admittance statutes such as EMTALA may be critical in these situations, showing that the refusal to admit the patient was unlawful.[589] Another form of constraint may be the act or threat of a hospital detaining a patient by refusing to discharge the patient until a bill is paid.[590] Although coercion directed at one other than

---

for failure to describe or attach any statement of account and because defendant—the adult son of the patient—disputed liability for his mother's bills); Parsell v. Martinez, 2008 WL 623864 (Ohio Ct. App. Mar. 10, 2008) (affirming judgment for patient when provider failed to prove that patient consented to services and the reasonable cost of services); Mercy Franciscan Hosp. v. Willis, 2004 WL 2244809 (Ohio Ct. App. Sept. 24, 2004) (upholding trial court's removal of default when the complaint had failed to attach a copy of an accounting; debtor had moved for relief from default alleging he did "not know what this bill is for").

583 *See, e.g.*, SunDance Rehabilitation Corp. v. Hermitage Healthcare of Manokin Manor, L.L.C., 2012 WL 2190749 (D. Md. June 13, 2012) (distinguishing "account stated" cause of action from one for a "running account"; provider stated claim for latter but not former); Ayers v. Cavalry SVP, L.L.C., 876 So. 2d 474 (Ala. Civ. App. 2003) (different statute of limitations under Alabama law for account stated versus open account claim).

584 *See* Dreyer Med. Clinic v. Corral, 591 N.E.2d 111 (Ill. App. Ct. 1992) (account stated is method of proving damages; creditor must first prove liability; creditor failed to prove several essential elements); Citibank v. Martin, 807 N.Y.S.2d 284 (N.Y. Civ. Ct. 2005) (account stated cannot create a liability when none existed). *Cf.* Baptist Home of Brooklyn v. Schott, 902 N.Y.S.2d 368 (N.Y. App. Div. 2010) (claim for account stated may not be utilized as another means to collect under a disputed contract). *But see* Berlin v. Pickett, 221 S.W.3d 406 (Mo. Ct. App. 2006) (no express agreement needed for open account claim).

585 Midwestern Health Mgt., Inc. v. Walker, 208 S.W.3d 295 (Mo. Ct. App. 2006) (elements of an action on an open account include: "the charges were reasonable"); Irvington Phys. Therapy v. Shapiro & Berezin, P.C., 2010 WL 1658039 (N.J. Super. Ct. App. Div. Apr. 26, 2010) (office manager's testimony sufficient to establish entitlement for recovery, but patient could challenge reasonable value of services); Parsell v. Martinez, 2008 WL 623864 (Ohio Ct. App. Mar. 10, 2008) (affirming judgment for patient when provider failed to prove that patient consented to services and the reasonable cost of services); St. Luke's Episcopal-Presbyterian Hosp. v. Underwood, 957 S.W.2d 496 (Mo. Ct. App. 1997) (in action on account, hospital must prove reasonableness of charges; testimony of "credit assistant" that charges were in line with those of other hospitals in the area was relevant and should have been admitted). *See also* 1 Am. Jur. 2d *Accounts and Accounting* § 8 (2005); 1 C.J.S. *Account, Action On* §§ 21, 26 (2005). *Cf.* Jackson v. Trancik, 953 N.E.2d 1087 (Ind. Ct. App. 2011) (in account stated claim, unlike tort case, issue is not reasonable value of services but whether amounts charged were usual, customary, and reasonable).

For more on reasonable value, see generally § 9.5.5, *infra*.

586 *See, e.g.*, Midwestern Health Mgt., Inc. v. Walker, 208 S.W.3d 295 (Mo. Ct. App. 2006) (reversing judgment for debt buyer due to lack of proof of assignment). *See* § 4.3, *supra*.

587 *See, e.g.*, Greenfield v. Manor Care, Inc., 705 So. 2d 926 (Fla. Dist. Ct. App. 1997) (surviving spouse allowed to raise defense of imposition when contract provision allowing immediate eviction of resident for nonpayment prevented her from challenging alleged overcharges at time of payment), *overruled on other grounds by* Knowles v. Beverly Enters., 898 So. 2d 1 (Fla. 2004); Home for Armenian Aged v. Symeonidis, 2012 WL 5834373 (N.J. Super. Ct. App. Div. Sept. 11, 2012) (agreement signed by unrelated caregiver, which purported to make her personally liable for patient's expenses, was unconscionable and unenforceable when caregiver had limited English literacy, had been misled by home's staff, and felt compelled to sign in order to ensure patient received care). *But see In re* State *ex rel.* Martin, 2010 WL 5479899 (La. Ct. App. Dec. 22, 2010) (son did not sign contract under duress, at time when sheriff's deputies came to his house to forcibly remove his mother, who had been found to be neglected; court noted that there had been no threats or coercion and he was informed that his mother would be admitted regardless of whether he signed agreement); Heartland Health Systems, Inc. v. Chamberlin, 871 S.W.2d 8 (Mo. Ct. App. 1993) (mother of a patient had not signed contract under duress when she believed guarantee was needed to provide treatment to her eighteen-year-old son who was bleeding out his ears and mouth and had a bone sticking out through the skin).

An unreported case exemplifies how the duress defense can be successfully utilized. A hospital had brought a $56,000 suit against the patient's widow who had signed an agreement believing it was necessary to gain admittance for her husband, who was in great pain and vomiting, while waiting for emergency treatment. He later died in the hospital of cancer. The jury voided the bill. *Jury Voids Dead Man's Hospital Bill*, Wash. Post, May 8, 1979, at C1.

588 The elements may differ by state. *See, e.g.*, Eden Park Mgmt., Inc. v. Schrull, 2007 WL 706583 (Conn. Super. Ct. Feb. 14, 2007) (elements of duress are (1) a wrongful act or threat, (2) that left the victim with no reasonable alternative, (3) to which the victim acceded, and (4) the resulting transaction was unfair to the victim; patient failed to demonstrate duress).

589 *Cf.* Heartland Health Systems, Inc. v. Chamberlin, 871 S.W.2d 8, 11 (Mo. Ct. App. 1993) (no duress because the hospital could have withheld its services unless and until mother of patient agreed to pay for services; EMTALA not raised). *See* § 9.3.3, *supra* (discussing EMTALA).

590 *See* Gadsden Gen. Hosp. v. Hamilton, 103 So. 553 (Ala. 1925) (hospital's threat not to release plaintiff until she paid her bill combined with her resultant stay in the hospital eleven hours after she was medically capable of release amounted to false imprisonment, even though she was *not* physically restrained). *See also* Williams v. Rentz Banking Co., 145 S.E.2d 256 (Ga. Ct. App. 1965) (a debtor's signing a note only after bank officials refused to allow debtor to leave the bank can be duress), *rev'd on other grounds*, 114 Ga. App. 718 (Ga. Ct. App. 1966).

the debtor usually does not constitute actionable duress, an exception is often made when the other person is the debtor's close relative.[591]

- *The debtor's loss of volition as a result of the coercion.* A hospital's resort to a threat not to admit or discharge a patient may go a long way toward meeting this subjective test, particularly when the patient or the relative or friend refused to sign a note prior to the threat but did so afterwards.
- *A promissory note or contract must be executed as a result of the wrongful coercion.* When a hospital sues on a contract for health care, practitioners should probe their client about the circumstances surrounding the signing of the contract to determine if coercion was applied. Because of the power of hospitals over people's lives, the possibilities for coercion in signing such contracts abound. However, some hospitals do not rely on contracts when suing on hospital bills, and the duress defense is available only against a suit on a contract or note.

This defense of duress may be lost if the consumer pays voluntarily after the coercion has ceased.[592] However, the voluntary payment doctrine may not apply if the payment was made out of necessity and the patient had no reasonable alternative, or if deception was involved.[593] Even if a contract is voided for duress, the consumer may be liable in *quantum meruit*.[594]

9.5.3.2 Other Defenses to a Contract Action

Hospitals often base their contract claims on agreements contained in admission forms, which often state no more than "I am financially responsible for services that are not covered by my health insurance plan."[595] A few courts have held that these forms are not specific enough to constitute valid contracts, especially concerning the price of services.[596] Debt buyers might even lack this simple document to produce as evidence of an actual contract for a contract claim.[597]

When a relative or friend of the patient signs an admission form containing a clause making him or her financially responsible for the patient's bills, the court may find that there was no actual intent to accept financial responsibility.[598] Alternatively,

591 *See* Greenfield v. Manor Care, Inc. 705 So. 2d 926 (Fla. Dist. Ct. App. 1997) (surviving spouse allowed to raise defense of "imposition" when contract provision allowing immediate eviction of resident for nonpayment prevented her from challenging alleged overcharges at time of payment), *overruled on other grounds by* Knowles v. Beverly Enters., 898 So. 2d 1 (Fla. 2004); Bedard v. Notre Dame Hosp., 151 A.2d 690 (R.I. 1959) (action for trespass on the case upheld when hospital detained son until bill for son's treatment paid); Robertson v. Shinn Grocery Co., 34 S.W.2d 367 (Tex. App. 1930) (threat of arrest of son coerced signing of deed of trust).

592 Greene v. Alachua Gen. Hosp., Inc., 705 So. 2d 953 (Fla. Dist. Ct. App. 1998) (when hospital sent bill after patient was out of hospital, and not under pressure greater than that felt by any debtor, defense of imposition not proven); Hall v. Humana Hosp. Daytona Beach, 686 So. 2d 653 (Fla. Dist. Ct. App. 1996) (granting summary judgment against class of patients who had already paid their bills in class action seeking to recover alleged overcharges for pharmaceuticals, medical supplies, laboratory services; patients alleged "imposition," that is, that they had been coerced into signing contract which included price list). *Cf.* Watts v. Promina Gwinnett Health Sys., Inc., 530 S.E.2d 14 (Ga. Ct. App. 2000) (patient's voluntary payment of hospital bill out of proceeds of tort judgment barred claim that charges were unreasonable and not authorized by hospital's agreement with HMO or patient's assignment of benefits).

593 Ramirez v. Smart Corp., 863 N.E.2d 800 (Ill. App. Ct. Feb. 16, 2007). The voluntary payment doctrine also does not apply to UDAP claims. *Id.*

594 Milford Hosp. v. Champeau, 2001 Conn. Super. LEXIS 1166 (Conn. Super. Ct. Apr. 27, 2001) (duress not shown although wife alleged she was told she "had to" sign contract before admission of her seriously ill husband; even if duress defense made out, couple was liable in *quantum meruit*, and wife was liable under necessaries statute); Galloway v. Methodist Hosps., Inc., 658 N.E.2d 611 (Ind. Ct. App. 1995) (consumers alleged there was no contract because of "extreme duress" when husband, a lawyer, signed for wife's admission for an obstetrical emergency but did not sign for financial responsibility; however, court found both spouses liable in *quantum meruit*). *See generally* § 9.5.4, *infra*.

595 *See, e.g.*, Carvalho v. Equifax Info. Servs., L.L.C., 629 F.3d 876 (9th Cir. 2010) (patient was liable for bill based on statement that "I hereby authorize my insurance company to pay benefits directly to Bayside Medical Group, Inc., and I am financially responsible for non-covered services"); Doe v. HCA Health Servs. of Tenn., Inc., 46 S.W.3d 191 (Tenn. 2001) (agreement simply stated "I understand I am financially responsible to the hospital for charges not covered by this authorization").

596 *See* Joseph M. Still Burn Centers, Inc. v. Liberty Mut. Ins. Co., 2010 WL 55471 (S.D. Ga. Jan. 6, 2010) (under Georgia law, price is essential element of contract and "an alleged contract on which there is no firm agreement as to the price is unenforceable"); Doe v. HCA Health Servs. of Tenn., Inc., 46 S.W.3d 191 (Tenn. 2001) (express contract voided because of the lack of specificity in determining the amount of charges, holding that only an implied-in-law contract existed requiring patient to pay reasonable value of services). *But see* Portercare Adventist Health Sys., 286 P.3d 525 (Colo. 2012) (hospital lawsuit over medical bill was a suit for a contract containing a fixed amount or "liquidated debt" even though it did not contain set forth the actual charges; a liquidated debt could refer to extrinsic evidence of the hospital's charges); Martinez v. Yale New Haven Hosp., 2005 WL 2364901 (Conn. Super. Ct. Sept. 1, 2005) (despite fact that contract did not specify price in dollars, court held that contract contained a definite and enforceable standard to determine a liquidated price); Holland v. Trinity Health Care Corp., 791 N.W.2d 724 (Mich. Ct. App. 2010) (term "usual and customary charges" was unambiguous and referred to hospital's chargemaster list prices); Shelton v. Duke Univ. Health Sys., Inc., 633 S.E.2d 113 (N.C. Ct. App. 2006) (when contract specified that patient would be charged hospital's "regular" rates, contract was sufficiently definite); Woodruff v. Ft. Sanders Sevier Med. Ctr., 2008 WL 148951 (Tenn. Ct. App. Jan. 16, 2008) (pricing in contract was not indefinite when it obligated patient to pay "facility's rates and terms"; distinguishing *Doe* on basis that "facility's rates and terms" were nouns compared to verb "charges" in the *Doe* contract; citing *Shelton* with approval).

597 National Consumer Law Center, Fair Debt Collection § 4.5 (8th ed. 2014), *updated at* www.nclc.org/library.

598 *See* Carroll v. Butterfield Health Care, Inc., 2003 WL 22462604 (N.D. Ill. Oct. 29, 2003) (nursing home's violation of Medicaid law by requiring personal guarantee of patient's son-in-law; son-in-law stated FDCPA but not UDAP claim against attorney-collector for suing on illegal guarantee); Phoenix Baptist Hosp. & Med. Ctr. v. Aiken, 877 P.2d 1345 (Ariz. 1994) (permitting unconscionability defense when husband signed contract when wife had just had heart attack, was distraught, and could not read contract due to absence of reading glasses); Samaritan Health Sys. v. Caldwell, 957 P.2d 1373 (Ariz. Ct. App. 1998) (when wife signed admission agreement only as attorney in fact pursuant to husband's durable power of attorney, debt not enforceable against her separate property); Haven Health Ctr. of Lichfield Hills

the court may conclude that the contract documents simply do not impose personal liability on the relative.[599] A patient who signs a contract in an impaired state may be able to argue that she lacked capacity to enter into a contract at the time of execution.[600] See § 4.5 and Chapter 5, *supra*, for more on defenses to a breach of contract claim.

9.5.4 Quantum Meruit

Quantum meruit or implied contract is especially important in the health care context. For a general discussion on this cause of action, see § 4.8, *supra*.

In the health care context, *quantum meruit* may be asserted as a basis for liability after a contract has been invalidated for duress or on other grounds,[601] when consent could not be

v. Parente, 2007 WL 123602 (Conn. Super. Ct. Jan. 8, 2007) (son of nursing home patient, who alleged that he signed only as his mother's power of attorney and that he was never given a copy of the preprinted contract, could bring UDAP claim against nursing home); Walton v. Mariner Health of Md., Inc., 894 A.2d 584 (Md. 2006) (daughter did not agree to be personally liable for mother's nursing home bills by signing admission contract as her mother's agent); Home for Armenian Aged v. Symeonidis, 2012 WL 5834373 (N.J. Super. Ct. App. Div. Sept. 11, 2012) (agreement signed by unrelated caregiver, which purported to make her personally liable for patient's expenses, was unconscionable and unenforceable when caregiver had limited English literacy, had been misled by home's staff, and felt compelled to sign in order to ensure patient received care); Pediatric Surgical Assocs. v. Brennan, 2012 WL 652484 (N.J. Super. Ct. App. Div. Mar. 1, 2012) (vacating default judgment; provider failed to show that consumer had contracted to pay for services of minor patient, who was the child of consumer's ex-wife but not consumer; only role of consumer was that child was covered by consumer's health insurance); Valley Hosp. v. Kroll, 847 A.2d 636 (N.J. Super. Ct. Law Div. 2003) (agreement signed by patient's wife that would require her to pay balance of hospital bill not paid by Medigap insurance was unenforceable as a contract of adhesion); XL Care Agency v. Johns, 2013 WL 5877305 (N.Y. Sup. Ct. Oct. 17, 2013) (consumer raised triable issue of fraudulent inducement to enter contract for care of aunt when home health care agency led consumer to believe that it would submit invoices to Medicaid after aunt's resources ran out—but agency was not licensed to provide services to Medicaid recipients); St. John's Episcopal Hosp. v. McAdoo, 405 N.Y.S.2d 935 (N.Y. Civ. Ct. 1978) (refusing to enforce liability provision that was buried in assignment of insurance benefits form; contract of adhesion; hospital should know contracts will be signed under circumstances when reasonable person too distraught to read whole document); Columbia Hosp. v. Hraska, 338 N.Y.S.2d 527 (N.Y. Civ. Ct. 1972). *See also* Wright v. Polk Gen. Hosp., 99 S.E.2d 162 (Ga. Ct. App. 1957) (no consideration); Baton Rouge Gen. Hosp. v. Superior Cleaners, 93 So. 2d (1957) (Louisiana; no intent). *Cf.* Podolsky v. First Healthcare Corp., 58 Cal. Rptr. 2d 89 (Cal. Ct. App. 1996) (nursing home violated California UDAP law by soliciting relatives for voluntary agreement to be financially responsible for patient, home failed to show consideration for voluntary agreement and failed to inform relatives of their rights under federal law); JML Care Ctr. v. Bishop, 2004 Mass. App. Div. 63 (Mass. Dist. Ct. 2004) (longtime friend and assistance signed admission agreement merely to facilitate admission; in this case, nursing home did not attempt to impose liability on friend); Epakchi v. Araghi, 960 N.Y.S.2d 53 (N.Y. Co. Ct. 2012) (dentist failed to establish elements for breach of contract because there was no meeting of the minds; patients were family friends who denied they had agreed to make monthly payments). *But see* Cho v. Santa Clara, 2009 WL 925332 (Cal. Ct. App. Apr. 7, 2009) (unpublished) (widow was liable for husband's hospital bill because she signed contract despite her inability to read English); Care Ctr. of Kansas City v. Horton, 173 S.W.3d 353 (Mo. Ct. App. 2005) (daughter was personally liable when she signed admission contract as agent for father, because contract imposed liability on agents); Trocki Plastic Surgery Ctr. v. Bartkowski, 782 A.2d 447 (N.J. Super. Ct. App. Div. 2001) (wife's alleged inability to understand agreement no defense when no allegation of duress, fraud or coercion).

599 *See, e.g.*, Slovik v. Prime Healthcare Corp., 838 So. 2d 1054 (Ala. Civ. App. 2002) (nursing home's dealings with patient's stepson/personal representative did not amount to contract by which he agreed to be personally liable); Aaron Manor, Inc. v. Irving, 12 A.3d 584 (Conn. App. 2011) (daughter who signed "responsible party" agreement for her father's admission to nursing home not liable for father's bill when another sibling had power of attorney and access to father's resources), *rev'd in part on other grounds*, 57 A.3d 342 (Conn. 2013) (attorney fees issue); Lexington Healthcare Ctr. v. Graves, 2013 WL 1279487 (Ill. App. Ct. Mar. 27, 2013) (construing agreement and "responsible party" provision as not rendering patient's daughter personally liable, because daughter signed agreement only as agent for her father); Rainbolt v. Guha, 260 P.3d 1249 (Kan. Ct. App. Oct. 7, 2011) (unpublished) (consent form contract signed by patient was ambiguous; under covenant of good faith fair dealing and court's interpretation, contract did not require patient to pay for services he did not request); Guest House of Slidell v. Hills, 76 So. 3d 497 (La. Ct. App. 2011) (construing ambiguous nursing home admission contract to hold that stepson who signed contract was signing as agent for resident and not as responsible party liable for bills; Grandell Rehab. & Nursing Home, Inc. v. Devlin, 809 N.Y.S.2d 481 (table), 2005 WL 3240554 (N.Y. Sup. Ct. Nov. 29, 2005) (dismissing nursing home's action against adult son of patient when son had never contracted with home and ordering hearing on sanctions against collection attorney). *Cf.* Northfield Care Ctr., Inc. v. Anderson, 707 N.W.2d 731 (Minn. Ct. App. 2006) (Minnesota law provides that son who signed admission contract was personally liable, but only to the extent that mother's assets were misapplied).

600 *See* Daughters of Charity Health Sys. v. Simoncini, 2012 WL 2948597 (Cal. Ct. App. July 20, 2012) (unpublished) (consumer did not assent by conduct to all of the terms of the written contract given that he was an incapacitated patient brought by ambulance to emergency room; his later conduct could evidence an agreement to pay for medical services but not attorney fee provision); Eden Park Mgmt., Inc. v. Schrull, 2007 WL 706583 (Conn. Super. Ct. Feb. 14, 2007) (patient alleged she was confused at the time of signing; allegations sufficient to plead lack of capacity, that is, that patient may not have understood the nature, extent, and consequences of signing the contract). *See generally* § 5.4.1, *supra*.

601 *See In re* Estate of Reed, 201 P.3d 1264 (Colo. App. 2008) (provider's lien signed by mother was not enforceable against child's estate, but provider could recover under *quantum meruit*); Yale Diagnostic Radiology v. Estate of Harun Fountain, 838 A.2d 179 (Conn. 2004) (minor is liable in *quantum meruit* for necessaries such as medical care; parent is primarily liable but, if parent cannot or will not pay, minor is liable); Milford Hosp. v. Champeau, 2001 Conn. Super. LEXIS 1166 (Conn. Super. Ct. Apr. 27, 2001) (even if contract signed by wife were invalid, couple was liable in *quantum meruit* for husband's treatment); Yale New Haven Hosp., Inc. v. Gargiulo, 1999 WL 989422 (Conn. Super. Ct. Oct. 18, 1999) (if no express contract between patient and hospital, implied contract to pay reasonable value of the services rendered); Galloway v. Methodist Hosp., Inc., 658 N.E.2d 611 (Ind. Ct. App. 1995) (even if contract, signed by husband at time of wife's admission for obstetrical emergency, was invalid, both spouses were liable in *quantum meruit*); Valley Hosp. v. Kroll, 847 A.2d 636 (N.J. Super. Ct. Law Div. 2003) (agreement signed by patient's wife was unenforceable as a contract of adhesion, but hospital could recover against her in *quantum meruit*; wife not liable because reasonable value of services already paid

obtained,[602] or even if consent has been refused.[603] However, if a valid express contract is in effect, the theory might not be valid in some states, since *quantum meruit* is based on a theory of implied contract which is inapplicable when there is an express contract.[604]

The elements of *quantum meruit* are that a benefit was conferred and accepted, under circumstances such that the recipient should know the provider expected to be paid, and it would be unjust to accept the benefit without paying.[605] The provider

by insurer); Comm'r of the Dep't of Social Servs. v. Fishman, 720 N.Y.S.2d 493 (N.Y. App. Div. 2001) (New York statute provides that furnishing medical benefits by Department of Social Services creates implied contract with responsible relative, here the spouse of nursing home patient); Layton Physical Therapy Co. v. Palozzi, 777 N.E.2d 306 (Ohio Ct. App. 2002) (if parents do not pay for necessaries, here medical care, minor child secondarily liable in quasi-contract); Dallas Cnty. Hosp. Dist. v. Wiley *ex rel.* Wiley, 2002 WL 1286515 (Tex. App. June 12, 2002) (lien invalid, but *quantum meruit* claim may go forward). *See also* JML Care Ctr. v. Bishop, 2004 Mass. App. Div. 63 (Mass. Dist. Ct. 2004) (*quantum meruit* not available when valid contract in effect but would be available as equitable remedy if contract were unenforceable); Parmatown Spinal & Rehab. Ctr., Inc. v. Lewis, 2003 WL 22208786 (Ohio Ct. App. Sept. 25, 2003) (provider could recover against patient in *quantum meruit* despite the fact that provider had express contract with insurer).

602 *See* Gianetti v. Rutkin, 2011 WL 5531376 (Conn. Super. Ct. Oct. 27, 2011) (patient's consent to contract applied only to services rendered on or after date of agreement, but liable in *quantum meruit* for services rendered before contract was signed), *aff'd*, 70 A.3d 104 (Conn. App. Ct. 2013); *In re* Estate of Boyd, 8 P.3d 664 (Idaho Ct. App. 2000) (patient's estate was liable in implied contract even though critically ill patient did not sign any papers); Carlton at the Lake, Inc. v. Barber, 928 N.E.2d 1266 (Ill. App. Ct. 2010) (unsigned contract was not enforceable, but patient could be liable in *quantum meruit*); Novak v. Credit Bureau Collection Serv., 2007 WL 4339450 (Ind. Ct. App. Dec. 13, 2007) (unpublished) (hospital entitled to recover in *quantum meruit* for services provided to unconscious patient who never requested or agreed to services); Tufts Univ. Cummings Sch. of Veterinary Medicine v. Safran, 2011 WL 1744223 (Mass. App. Div. May 4, 2011) (even if consumer could prove lack of consent to contract, provider could still recover under *quantum meruit*); Mercy Flight Ctr., Inc. v. Kondolf, 973 N.Y.S.2d 521 (N.Y. City Ct. 2013) (air ambulance company could recover in *quantum meruit* claim for transporting patient who never gave consent because of head injury; denying summary judgment because question of fact whether services were medically necessary).

603 Crane v. Native Am. Air Ambulance, Inc., 2007 WL 625917 (D. Ariz. Feb. 23, 2007) (patient was liable for air ambulance service bill of $12,825 even though he did not request service and claimed he did not need service); *Ex parte* Univ. of S. Ala., 737 So. 2d 1049 (Ala. 1999) (patient was liable for her share of bill at hospital, which paramedics chose because it had helicopter landing pad, when she accepted treatment there willingly, even though she requested a different hospital when her insurance would have paid 100% of bill); Yale New Haven Hosp. v. Alsever, 2000 Conn. Super. LEXIS 3612 (Conn. Super. Ct. Dec. 22, 2000) (granting summary judgment on quasi-contract liability but reserving amount of damages for trial when some services allegedly performed over patient's objection); Credit Bureau Enters., Inc. v. Pelo, 608 N.W.2d 20 (Iowa 2000) (patient liable in *quantum meruit* for expenses of involuntary commitment, when treatment was necessary to prevent serious bodily harm or pain, provider reasonably believed that patient would consent if able to do so, and refusal of consent not binding as patient was incompetent), *partially superseded by statute*, Tama Cnty. v. Grundy Cnty., 648 N.W.2d 83 (Iowa 2002) (amendments to Iowa law made county of patient's residence liable for involuntary commitment expenses to private hospital). *Cf.* Baptist Mem'l Hosp. N. Miss. v. Parks, 2013 WL 4458738 (N.D. Miss. Aug. 19, 2013) (patient liable for hospital charges even though she refused consent for treatment based on her signing of admission agreement with boilerplate accepting financial responsibility for services). *But see* Rainbolt v. Guha, 260 P.3d 1249 (Kan. Ct. App. Oct. 7, 2011) (unpublished) (*quantum meruit* is an equitable doctrine that does not compel a patient to pay for services that he did not request and specifically expressed he did not want).

604 Joseph M. Still Burn Centers, Inc. v. AmFed Nat'l Ins. Co., 702 F. Supp. 2d 1371 (S.D. Ga. 2010) (under Georgia law, "[q]uantum meruit is not available when there is an express contract," citing Watson v. Sierra Contracting Corp., 485 S.E.2d 563 (Ga. Ct. App. 1997)); Ctr. for Special Procedures v. Conn. Gen. Life Ins. Co., 2010 WL 5068164 (D.N.J. Dec. 6, 2010) ("recovery under an unjust enrichment or a *quantum meruit* theory is unavailable where an express agreement exists"); Burton v. William Beaumont Hosp., 373 F. Supp. 2d 707 (E.D. Mich. 2005) (unjust enrichment claim not viable when an express contract governs); Morse L.L.C. v. United Wis. Life Ins. Co., 356 F. Supp. 2d 1296 (S.D. Fla. 2005) (dismissing *quantum meruit* claim because provider had alleged existence of an express contract; *quantum meruit* claim is a "fiction [that] can not be maintained, however, when the rights of the parties are described in an express contract"); Plantation Gen. Hosp. v. Cayman Islands, 2012 WL 913246 (S.D. Fla. Mar. 16, 2012) (hospital could not bring claim for *quantum meruit* when express written contract existed); HCR-Manor Care v. Fugee, 2010 WL 780020 (Del. Super. Ct. Jan. 26, 2010) (when patient's son had signed Admission Agreement as responsible party, *quantum meruit* not applicable); Maimonides Med. Ctr. v. First United Am. Life Ins. Co., 941 N.Y.S.2d 447 (N.Y. Sup. Ct 2012) (provider cannot bring alternative claims for breach of contract and unjust enrichment unless there is a bona fide dispute as to the existence of the contract or the contract does not cover the dispute in issue); Promenade Nursing Home, Inc. v. Lacey, 814 N.Y.S.2d 564 (table), 2005 WL 3592001 (N.Y. Civ. Ct. Nov. 29, 2005) (existence of written contract precluded claim for *quantum meruit* or other quasi-contract claims). *But see* SunDance Rehabilitation Corp. v. Hermitage Healthcare of Manokin Manor, L.L.C., 2012 WL 2190749 (D. Md. June 13, 2012) (contract and unjust enrichment may be pleaded in the alternative, even though plaintiff cannot recover under both theories).

605 Plantation Gen. Hosp. v. Cayman Islands, 2012 WL 913246 (S.D. Fla. Mar. 16, 2012) (in lawsuit against Cayman Islands government for costs of Cayman resident's care, hospital failed to allege sufficient facts for *quantum meruit* claim, that is, what benefits the hospital conferred to the government and the government accepted); Joseph M. Still Burn Centers, Inc. v. Liberty Mut. Ins. Co., 2010 WL 55471 (S.D. Ga. Jan. 6, 2010) (under Georgia law, elements of claim are: "(1) the performance of valuable services; (2) accepted by the recipient or at his request; (3) the failure to compensate the provider would be unjust; and (4) the provider expected compensation at the time services were rendered); Cardiology Assocs. v. Sussman, 2000 Conn. Super. LEXIS 1544 (Conn. Super. Ct. June 16, 2000) (patient liable in implied contract when provider showed that it provided services under circumstances such that it could expect to be paid and billed for the fair, reasonable and customary amount); *In re* Estate of Boyd, 8 P.3d 664 (Idaho Ct. App. 2000); Pediatric Surgical Assocs. v. Brennan, 2012 WL 652484 (N.J. Super. Ct. App. Div. Mar. 1, 2012) (provider failed to establish *quantum meruit* claim because it failed to show that services conferred benefit to consumer; services were rendered to ex-wife's child, who was not offspring of consumer; only role of consumer was that child was covered by consumer's health insurer); Princeton Surgical Assocs. v. Aziz, 2010 WL 1425112 (N.J. Super. Ct. App. Div. Apr. 8, 2010) (elements of claim are: (1) the performance of services in good faith; (2) the acceptance of services; (3) an expectation of compensation therefore; and (4) the reasonable value of the services); Parmatown Spinal

may also be required to show the reasonable value of the services rendered.[606]

This is especially true because *quantum meruit* is an equitable doctrine, and courts may frown upon providers seeking full chargemaster rates[607] when they accept much lower amounts from insurers.[608]

9.5.5 *Reasonable Value*

9.5.5.1 Proof of Reasonable Value

A critical issue in many medical debt collection cases will be the reasonable value of the medical services rendered. Medical service providers often do not discuss the price of services in advance, so the consumer has not already assented to the actual amount of the charges. An inquiry into the reasonable value may be required even when there is an express contract.[609] This inquiry has been rejected in some states in

---

& Rehab. Ctr., Inc. v. Lewis, 2003 WL 22208786 (Ohio Ct. App. Sept. 25, 2003) (elements of claim are that: (1) a benefit was conferred on the recipient, (2) the recipient had knowledge of that benefit, and (3) it would unjust or inequitable to permit the recipient to retain the benefit without compensating the party that conferred the benefit).

606 Joseph M. Still Burn Centers, Inc. v. AmFed Nat'l Ins. Co., 702 F. Supp. 2d 1371 (S.D. Ga. 2010) (under Georgia law, provider must show reasonable value of services for *quantum meruit* claim); Canyon Ambulatory Surgery Centers v. SCF Arizona, 239 P.3d 733 (Ariz. Ct. App. 2010) (providers could recover from insurer under *quantum meruit* theory but are required to provide reasonable value of services); McMeans v. Med. Liabilities Recoveries, Inc., 2002 WL 31835746 (Cal. Ct. App. Dec. 19, 2002) (unpublished) (hospital lien limited to reasonable value of necessary services, testimony of chief executive officer as to customary rates not probative when she had no personal knowledge of care provided); Gianetti v. Riether, 2011 WL 4347211 (Conn. Super. Ct. Aug. 24, 2011) (patient not liable in *quantum meruit* for amount not paid by insurance, because doctor failed to show that reasonable value of services was greater than the sum paid by insurer), *aff'd*, 56 A.3d 474 (Conn. App. Ct. 2012); Milford Hosp. v. Champeau, 2001 Conn. Super. LEXIS 1166 (Conn. Super. Ct. Apr. 27, 2001) (question of reasonableness relevant only to damages, not liability, when hospital asserted claims for *quantum meruit*, unjust enrichment, and spousal liability for necessaries); Yale New Haven Hosp. v. Alsever, 2000 Conn. Super. LEXIS 3612 (Conn. Super. Ct. Dec. 22, 2000) (granting summary judgment to hospital on quasi-contract claim, but only as to liability; amount of damages required trial due to question whether services were necessary or were competently performed; some services apparently provided over patient's objection); William H. Stoll, L.L.C. v. Scarber, 652 S.E.2d 834 (Ga. Ct. App. 2007) (plaintiff in *quantum meruit*—in this case, an attorney—was required to prove the reasonable value of services); Carlton at the Lake, Inc. v. Barber, 928 N.E.2d 1266 (Ill. App. Ct. 2010) (provider had burden of demonstrating both the services it provided and the reasonable value of those services); Estate of Bonner, 954 S.W.2d 356 (Mo. Ct. App. 1997) (medical provider must prove that services were rendered, were medically necessary, and price was reasonable, but need not present expert evidence on medical necessity unless patient/debtor raised that issue); Pediatric Surgical Assocs. v. Brennan, 2012 WL 652484 (N.J. Super. Ct. App. Div. Mar. 1, 2012) (one element of *quantum meruit* claim is to show "the value of the services is reasonable"); Valley Hosp. v. Kroll, 847 A.2d 636 (N.J. Super. Ct. Law Div. 2003) (*quantum meruit* claim limited to reasonable value of services by hospital; payments made by Medigap insurer presumed reasonable; patient's wife not liable for additional amounts); Charlotte-Mecklenberg Hosp. Auth. v. Talford, 727 S.E.2d 866 (N.C. 2012) (hospital was required to demonstrate the reasonable value of its services, but affidavits of hospital's Director of Revenue Management and Vice President of Medical Education were sufficient); Hailey v. MedCorp., 2006 WL 2640238 (Ohio Ct. App. Sept. 15, 2006) (ambulance service entitled to recover only reasonable value of services under *quantum meruit* theory); Temple Univ. Hosp., Inc. v. Healthcare Mgmt. Alternatives, Inc., 832 A.2d 501 (Pa. Super. Ct. 2003) (hospital that treated Medicaid-HMO members at a time when it had no contract entitled to recover in *quantum meruit*; must show reasonable value of its services; posted rates not probative when posted rates were 300% of costs and hospital received this amount in only 1–3% of cases); Doe v. HCA Health Servs. of Tenn., Inc., 46 S.W.3d 191 (Tenn. 2001) (patient only liable for reasonable charges when hospital charges were set forth only in a confidential, changing, internal price list); H.E. Butt Grocery Co. v. Rencare, Ltd., 2004 WL 199272 (Tex. App. Feb. 4, 2004) (reasonable value an essential element for *quantum meruit* claim; jury entitled to weigh evidence beyond provider's charges to determine reasonable value); Emergency Physicians Integrated Care v. Salt Lake Cnty., 167 P.3d 1080 (Utah 2007) (if physicians could prove *quantum meruit* claim, they were entitled to the reasonable value of service). *See* Alan Alop, Defending Hospital Collection Cases (rev. ed. 2005), *available at* www.illinoislegaladvocate.org/index.cfm?fuseaction=home.dsp_content&contentID=728. *But see* Portercare Adventist Health Sys. v. Lego, 286 P.3d 525 (Colo. 2012) (hospital lawsuit over medical bill was a suit for a "liquidated debt" even though it did not contain set forth the actual charges; a liquidated debt could refer to extrinsic evidence of the hospital's charges); Huntington Hosp. v. Abrandt, 779 N.Y.S.2d 891 (N.Y. App. Term 2004) (summary judgment for hospital on implied contract claim; patient's challenge to hospital's charges based on fact that patient was charged more than other payers not sufficient to create triable issue of fact as to reasonableness of charges).

607 *See* § 9.1.3, *supra* (discussing discriminatory pricing and the difference between chargemaster rates versus what insurers pay).

608 *See, e.g.*, Joseph M. Still Burn Centers, Inc. v. AmFed Nat'l Ins. Co., 702 F. Supp. 2d 1371 (S.D. Ga. 2010) (chastising provider for seeking full chargemaster rates in *quantum meruit* action when worker's compensation insurer had already paid rates mandated by law).

609 *See* Urquhart v. Manatee Mem'l Hosp., 2007 WL 781738 (M.D. Fla. Mar. 13, 2007) (Florida requires amount of open pricing contract to be reasonable; hospital's excessive charges could be challenged as breach of contract); Colomar v. Mercy Hosp., Inc., 461 F. Supp. 2d 1265 (S.D. Fla. 2006) (same); Hutchinson Hosp. Corp. v. Neal, 154 P.3d 521 (Kan. Ct. App. 2007) (if contract does not contain explicit price term, court required to establish reasonable price); Howard v. Willis-Knighton Med. Ctr., 924 So. 2d 1245 (La. Ct. App. 2006) (whether express or implied contract, charges must be reasonable unless fixed in contract); Estate of Bonner, 954 S.W.2d 356 (Mo. Ct. App. 1997) (medical provider must prove that services were rendered, were medically necessary, and price was reasonable); Castro v. E. End Plastic, Reconstructive & Hand Surgery, P.C., 850 N.Y.S.2d 483 (N.Y. App. Div. 2008) (provider not entitled to judgment for difference between insurance payment and provider's charges, absent evidence of the reasonable value of services); Hailey v. MedCorp., 2006 WL 2640238 (Ohio Ct. App. Sept. 15, 2006) (ambulance service entitled to recover only reasonable value of services); Turner v. Legacy Health Sys., 2006 WL 657176 (Or. Cir. Ct. Oct. 4, 2005) (when contracts for medical services did not specify price for services, such fees must be reasonable under the circumstances); Doe v. HCA Health Servs. of Tenn., Inc., 46 S.W.3d 191 (Tenn. 2001) (express contract voided because of the lack of specificity in determining the amount of charges, holding that only an implied-in-law contract existed requiring patient to pay reasonable value of services). *Cf.* Ramirez v. Smart Corp., 863 N.E.2d 800 (Ill. App. Ct. 2007) (when patients had statutory right to obtain their medical records, hospitals must charge a reasonable amount for

which hospitals are statutorily required to disclose or file their charges.[610] However, the Affordable Care Act of 2010 amends the Internal Revenue Code to prohibit not-for-profit hospitals from imposing their "gross" or chargemaster list prices.[611]

The provider should bear the burden of proving reasonable value,[612] although some courts have placed the burden on the debtor or held the provider to a very minimal level of prima

copying services). *But see* Martinez v. Yale New Haven Hosp., 2005 WL 2364901 (Conn. Super. Ct. Sept. 1, 2005) (despite fact that contract did not specify price in dollars, court held that contract contained a definite and enforceable standard to determine a liquidated price); Portercare Adventist Health Sys., 286 P.3d 525 (Colo. 2012) (hospital lawsuit over medical bill was a suit over a contract for a fixed amount or "liquidated debt" even though it did not contain set forth the actual charges; a liquidated debt could refer to extrinsic evidence of the hospital's charges); Allen v. Clarian Health Partners, Inc. 980 N.E.2d 306 (Ind. 2012) (contracts under which patients guaranteed "payment of the account" referred to hospital's chargemaster rates, and thus contracts were not indefinite as to price); Holland v. Trinity Health Care Corp., 791 N.W.2d 724 (Mich. Ct. App. 2010) (term "usual and customary charges" was unambiguous and referred to hospital's chargemaster list prices); Shelton v. Duke Univ. Health Sys., Inc., 633 S.E.2d 113 (N.C. Ct. App. 2006) (when contract specified that patient would be charged hospital's "regular" rates, contract was sufficiently definite for hospital to impose chargemaster list prices on the uninsured, despite charging reduced rates to third-party payers); Nygaard v. Sioux Valley Hosp. & Health Sys., 731 N.W.2d 184 (S.D. 2007) (when complaint pleaded that contract stated prices were "fixed," no implied term in contract that prices would be fair and reasonable, despite charging reduced rates to third-party payers); Woodruff v. Ft. Sanders Sevier Med. Ctr., 2008 WL 148951 (Tenn. Ct. App. Jan. 16, 2008) (pricing in contract was not indefinite when it obligated patient to pay "facility's rates and terms"; distinguishing *Doe* on basis that "facility's rates and terms" were nouns compared to verb "charges" in the *Doe* contract; citing *Shelton* with approval).

610 Banner Health v. Med. Sav. Ins. Co., 163 P.3d 1096 (Ariz. Ct. App. 2007) (because hospital was required to file its rates with state agency, the rates could not be challenged as unconscionable or unreasonable, despite the fact that rates were 400% of hospital's costs and hospital only charged full rates to 2% of patients); Portercare Adventist Health Sys., 286 P.3d 525 (Colo. 2012) (hospital lawsuit over medical bill was a suit for contract for a fixed amount; court relied on state statute giving consumers right to disclosure of "average facility charges" prior to receiving care); Satterfield v. S. Reg'l Health Sys., Inc., 634 S.E.2d 530 (Ga. Ct. App. 2006) (rates need not be reasonable); Morrell v. Wellstar Health Sys., Inc., 633 S.E.2d 68 (Ga. Ct. App. 2006) (rates need not be reasonable; noting that Georgia law provided right for patient to request copy of hospital charges and that Georgia policy was to encourage market forces to control health care costs by providing information so that consumers could make cost-effective decisions by comparison shopping); Cox v. Athens Reg'l Med. Ctr., Inc., 631 S.E.2d 792 (Ga. Ct. App. 2006) (same).

611 *See* § 9.3.1, *supra*.

612 Canyon Ambulatory Surgery Centers v. SCF Arizona, 239 P.3d 733 (Ariz. Ct. App. 2010) (in challenging amounts paid by worker's compensation insurer, providers required to provide reasonable value of services); *In re* Estate of Reed, 201 P.3d 1264 (Colo. App. 2008); Mercy Hosp., Inc. v. Carr, 297 So. 2d 598 (Fla. Dist. Ct. App. 1974) (patient may not be bound by charges in the contract because he was entitled to question the reasonableness thereof); Greenfield v. Manor Care, Inc. 705 So. 2d 926 (Fla. Dist. Ct. App. 1997) (when no price specified, only a reasonable price may be charged), *overruled on other grounds by* Knowles v. Beverly Enters., 898 So. 2d 1 (Fla. 2004); Payne v. Humana Hosp. Orange Park, 661 So. 2d 1239 (Fla. Dist. Ct. App. 1995) (when contract allegedly did not specify the price for medical services, patient not bound to pay "unreasonable" charges and stated a claim in a class complaint); Reddix v. Chatham Cnty. Hosp. Auth., 216 S.E.2d 680 (Ga. Ct. App. 1975) (hospital failed to prove reasonableness and value of services), *overruled on other grounds by* Merrill Lynch, Pierce, Fenner & Smith v. Zimmerman, 285 S.E.2d 181 (Ga. 1981); Culverhouse v. Jackson, 127 Ga. App. 635 (Ga. Ct. App. 1972) (physician failed to prove ordinary and reasonable value of services); Victory Mem'l Hosp. v. Rice, 493 N.E.2d 117 (Ill. 1986); Collection Prof'ls, Inc. v. Schlosser, 977 N.E.2d 315 (Ill. App. Ct. 2012) (hospital must establish that its charges are reasonable); Fowle v. Parsons, 141 N.W. 1049 (Iowa 1913); Hutchinson Hosp. Corp. v. Neal, 154 P.3d 521 (Kan. Ct. App. 2007) (entry of judgment at pre-trial conference improper without copy of bill, affidavit as to reasonableness of bill, or further findings of fact because the reasonableness of the bills remained in dispute); Freeman Health Sys. v. Wass, 124 S.W.3d 504 (Mo. Ct. App. 2004) (hospital cannot prevail in collection lawsuit without showing reasonable value of services); St. Luke's Episcopal-Presbyterian Hosp. v. Underwood, 957 S.W.2d 496 (Mo. Ct. App. 1997) (in action on account, hospital must prove reasonableness of charges; testimony of "credit assistant" that charges were in line with those of other hospitals in the area was relevant); Estate of Bonner, 954 S.W.2d 356 (Mo. Ct. App. 1997) (medical provider must prove that services were rendered, were medically necessary, and price was reasonable); Valley Hosp. v. Kroll, 847 A.2d 636 (N.J. Super. Ct. Law Div. 2003) (*quantum meruit* claim limited to reasonable value of services by hospital; payments made by Medigap insurer presumed reasonable; patient's wife not liable for additional amounts); Charlotte-Mecklenberg Hosp. Auth. v. Talford, 727 S.E.2d 866 (N.C. 2012) (hospital was required to demonstrate the reasonable value of its services, but affidavits of hospital's Director of Revenue Management and Vice President of Medical Education were sufficient); Hailey v. MedCorp., 2006 WL 2640238 (Ohio Ct. App. Sept. 15, 2006) (in order to recover against patient, ambulance service required to demonstrate reasonable value of services at trial by competent, credible evidence); Piggee v. Mercy Hosp., 186 P.2d 817 (Okla. 1947) (summary judgment inappropriate); Turner v. Legacy Health Sys., 2006 WL 657176 (Or. Cir. Ct. Oct. 4, 2005) (when contracts for medical services did not specify price for services, such fees must be reasonable under the circumstances); Temple Univ. Hosp., Inc. v. Healthcare Mgmt. Alternatives, Inc., 832 A.2d 501 (Pa. Super. Ct. 2003) (hospital that treated Medicaid-HMO members at a time when it had no contract entitled to recover in *quantum meruit*; must show reasonable value of its services; posted rates not probative when posted rates were 300% of costs and hospital received this amount in only 1–3% of cases); River Park Hosp. v. BlueCross BlueShield of Tenn., Inc., 173 S.W.3d 43 (Tenn. 2002) (in action for unjust enrichment, both hospital's standard rate and HMO's reimbursement rate were relevant to the determination of a reasonable rate, but not conclusive; case remanded for a determination of a reasonable rate); Doe v. HCA Health Servs. of Tenn., Inc., 46 S.W.3d 191 (Tenn. 2001) (when price not specified in contract, hospital can only require patient to pay "fair value" of goods and services); H.E. Butt Grocery Co. v. Rencare, Ltd., 2004 WL 199272 (Tex. App. Feb. 4, 2004) (reasonable value an essential element for *quantum meruit* claim; jury entitled to weigh evidence beyond provider's charges to determine reasonable value). *See* Alan Alop, Defending Hospital Collection Cases (rev. ed. 2005), *available at* www.illinoislegaladvocate.org/index.cfm?fuseaction=home.dsp_content&contentID=728. *Cf.* Select Med. Corp. v. Allen, 2012 WL 5879821 (M.D. Ga. Nov. 21, 2012) (even for default judgment, hospital must adequately prove damages); Prospect Med. Group, Inc. v. Northridge Emergency Med. Group, 39 Cal. Rptr. 3d 456 (Cal. Ct. App. 2006) (following *Bell* and noting that hospital's chargemaster prices are not determinative of the reasonable value; insurer permitted to challenge such prices), *rev'd on other grounds*, 198 P.3d 86 (Cal. 2009); Bell v. Blue Cross, 31 Cal. Rptr. 3d 688 (Cal. Ct. App. 2005) (under California law that requires HMOs to pay out-of-network emergency room physicians for services rendered to insureds, physicians were entitled to "reasonable and customary value" for such services).

facie proof.[613] The question of reasonable value is a pure question of fact for a jury and thus should allow the debtor to defeat the collector's motion for summary judgment or directed verdict.[614]

Two factors that courts look at to determine reasonable value are: (1) internal factors of the hospital, including the hospital's cost of operations and its budgetary needs, and (2) charges for comparable services by similar hospitals.[615] The Fifth Circuit has stated that a "reasonable charge" is an individualized inquiry which depends on the individual circumstances of the patient, the time frame in which the services were provided, and the costs of the hospital and its peers at that time.[616] The Fifth Circuit noted that there is no set charge

613 Sholkoff v. Boca Raton Cmty. Hosp., Inc., 693 So. 2d 1114 (Fla. Dist. Ct. App. 1997); Wash. Cnty. Mem'l Hosp. v. Hattabaugh, 717 N.E.2d 929 (Ind. Ct. App. 1999) (burden of proof was on consumers who claimed services were not worth what hospital charged; amount billed was prima facie evidence of value of services); Galloway v. Methodist Hosps., Inc., 658 N.E.2d 611 (Ind. Ct. App. 1995) (amount of bill was prima facie evidence of amount owed in *quantum meruit*; charges were reasonable when they were comparable to other facilities in the area and based upon hospital's budgetary needs); Dawson v. Prager, 76 P.3d 1036 (Kan. 2003) (provider's affidavit that amounts owed constituted co-payments after insurance coverage sufficient to grant summary judgment for provider, despite objection of patient that she paid "regularly" paid co-payments); Trocki Plastic Surgery Ctr. v. Bartkowski, 782 A.2d 447 (N.J. Super. Ct. App. Div. 2001) (reasonableness shown when consumers received bill and did not complain about the charges, nor about the quality of the service); Hahnemann Univ. Hosp. v. Dudnick, 678 A.2d 266 (N.J. Super. Ct. App. Div. 1996) (burden is on patient to show that charges are not "usual, customary and reasonable"; charges were in accord with other teaching institutions in the area and had been approved by state Insurance Commission); Albany Med. Ctr. Hosp. v. Huberty, 428 N.Y.S.2d 746 (N.Y. App. Div. 1980) (affidavit from hospital's associate director of business affairs was sufficient to establish reasonable rate when affidavit stated that posted rates were commensurate with those of other hospitals, based on operating expenses of hospital and included no element of profit); Fulton Cnty. Health Ctr. v. Jones, 2007 WL 4277583 (Ohio Ct. App. Dec. 7, 2007) (summary judgment for provider on issue of reasonable value when debtor failed to submit evidence contesting it); Dickey v. Burick, 829 N.E.2d 1242 (Ohio Ct. App. 2005) (provider's bill was prima facie evidence of amount owed; provider not required to lay foundation that charges were reasonable and necessary unless challenged by debtor). *See also* Martinez v. Yale New Haven Hosp., 2005 WL 2364901 (Conn. Super. Ct. Sept. 1, 2005) (despite fact that contract did not specify price in dollars, court held that contract contained a definite and enforceable standard to determine a liquidated price; in this case, patients had brought a breach of contract claim alleging unreasonable price).

614 Joseph M. Still Burn Centers, Inc. v. AmFed Nat'l Ins. Co., 702 F. Supp. 2d 1371 (S.D. Ga. 2010) (under Georgia law, "the question of reasonable value of services rendered generally lies with the jury when such value is disputed") (citing Synergy Worldwide, Inc. v. Long, Haymes, Carr, Inc., 44 F. Supp. 2d 1348, 1358 (N.D. Ga. 1998)); Shellnut v. Randolph Cnty. Hosp., 469 So. 2d 632 (Ala. Civ. App. 1985); Reyher v. State Farm Mut. Ins. Co., 171 P.3d 1263 (Colo. App. 2007) (reasonableness of charges was issue of fact for jury); Collection Prof'ls, Inc. v. Schlosser, 977 N.E.2d 315 (Ill. App. Ct. 2012) (assessment of reasonableness of charges "strictly a question of fact"); Fowle v. Parsons, 141 N.W. 1049 (Iowa 1913); Baca Chiropractic, P.C. v. Cobb, 317 S.W.3d 674 (Mo. Ct. App. 2010) (reversing summary judgment for chiropractor on open account claim; genuine issue of fact as to whether charges were reasonable); Piggee v. Mercy Hosp., 186 P.2d 817 (Okla. 1947) (summary judgment inappropriate); Turner v. Legacy Health Sys., 2006 WL 657176 (Or. Cir. Ct. Oct. 4, 2005) (whether highest rates were "reasonable fees" is fact question for jury); H.E. Butt Grocery Co. v. Rencare, Ltd., 2004 WL 199272 (Tex. App. Feb. 4, 2004) (jury entitled to weigh evidence beyond provider's charges to determine reasonable value; entitled to weigh credibility of employee's testimony regarding specific items, including why provider charged $150 for box of gloves that cost $25; could also consider center's contracts with third-party payers). *Cf.* Sisters of Third Order of Notre Dame v. Summerson, 577 N.E.2d 177 (Ill. App. Ct. 1991). *But see* Dawson v. Prager, 76 P.3d 1036 (Kan. 2003) (provider's affidavit that amounts owed constituted co-payments after insurance coverage sufficient to grant summary judgment for provider, despite objection of patient that she paid "regularly" paid co-payments); Huntington Hosp. v. Abrandt, 779 N.Y.S.2d 891 (N.Y. App. Term 2004) (summary judgment for hospital; patient's challenge to hospital's charges based on fact that patient was charged more than other payers not sufficient to create triable issue of fact as to reasonableness of charges); Charlotte-Mecklenberg Hosp. Auth. v. Talford, 727 S.E.2d 866 (N.C. 2012) (upholding summary judgment; affidavits of hospital's Director of Revenue Management and Vice President of Medical Education were sufficient to show that rates billed by hospital were reasonable value of services; patient's affidavits as to price differences in drug charges insufficient to create issue of fact).

615 Lifespan Physicians Prof'l Serv. Org. v. Healthcare Value Mgmt., Inc., 2006 WL 1549054 (D.R.I. June 5, 2006) ("reasonable and customary" prices are determined by what other hospitals in the area charge); Canyon Ambulatory Surgery Centers v. SCF Arizona, 239 P.3d 733 (Ariz. Ct. App. 2010) (reasonable value demonstrated by either (1) fair market value of services or (2) cost of services plus reasonable rate of return); Bell v. Blue Cross, 31 Cal. Rptr. 3d 688 (Cal. Ct. App. 2005) (the "reasonable and customary value" for medical services should be based upon the physician's qualifications, nature of services, provider's usual charges, and prevailing provider rates charged in the area); Collection Prof'ls, Inc. v. Schlosser, 977 N.E.2d 315 (Ill. App. Ct. 2012) (provider need only show that charges are customary and usual as compared to other area hospitals); Victory Mem'l Hosp. v. Rice, 493 N.E.2d 117 (Ill. App. Ct. 1986); Howard v. Willis-Knighton Med. Ctr., 924 So. 2d 1245 (La. Ct. App. 2006) (following *Victory Memorial Hospital* and *Ellis Hospital*); Ellis Hosp. v. Little, 409 N.Y.S.2d 459 (N.Y. App. Div. 1978) (price shown to be fair and reasonable when hospital itemized the services provided, treasurer testified as to relationship of prices to hospital's costs, and officer of another hospital testified as to customary charges in the community); Charlotte-Mecklenberg Hosp. Auth. v. Talford, 727 S.E.2d 866 (N.C. 2012) ("reasonable value of a service is ascertained by examining the market for that service"; court will look to "time and labor expanded, skill, knowledge and experience involved" as well as "rates charged by other similar market participants"); Doe v. HCA Health Servs. of Tenn., Inc., 46 S.W.3d 191 (Tenn. 2001). *Cf.* Majid v. Stubblefield, 589 N.E.2d 1045 (Ill. App. Ct. 1992) (doctor's evidence of rates charged by the only two other practitioners of his specialty in a rural three-county area was sufficient despite patient's evidence of lower rates over a larger, more diverse area).

One court has cautioned that a market analysis comparing prices of other hospitals is not determinative as to whether prices are reasonable. Colomar v. Mercy Hosp., Inc., 461 F. Supp. 2d 1265 (S.D. Fla. 2006) ("if other hospitals grossly overcharge for services relative to their costs, then a mere side-by-side comparison of hospitals' unreasonable charges would make them appear reasonable"). However, this court later dismissed the plaintiff's claim because she failed to provide evidence of what other hospitals in the same market charged for the same services and also failed to substantiate her claim that the cost to the hospital for those services were one-sixth of what the hospital charged. Colomar v. Mercy Hosp., Inc., 2007 WL 2083562 (S.D. Fla. July 20, 2007).

616 Maldonado v. Ochsner Clinic Found., 493 F.3d 521, 524 (5th Cir. 2007). *See also* Eufala Hosp. Corp. v. Lawrence, 32 So. 3d 30 (Ala. 2009)

which constitutes a reasonable fee.[617] However, other courts, including the California Supreme Court, have held that the rates paid by insurers and other third-party payers are better indicators of reasonable value than chargemaster rates.[618]

A hospital or medical provider often attempts to meet its burden by having a staff member testify as to the above factors. Courts have allowed such testimony and held it sufficient to establish reasonable value.[619]

Some courts have even held that conclusory statements by a hospital employee that the charges were fair and reasonable were sufficient, so long as such statements were uncontroverted.[620] Thus, it is critical for the patient's counsel to challenge such statements by attacking them on cross-examination and by presenting evidence supporting any of the theories discussed in this section.[621]

Practitioners should be aware of medical industry reference guides such as MediCode and the RedBook (for pharmaceuticals and supplies).[622] Note that a challenge to the reasonable

---

(following *Maldonado*).

617 Maldonado v. Ochsner Clinic Found., 493 F.3d 521, 524 n.3 (5th Cir. 2007).

618 Howell v. Hamilton Meats & Provisions, Inc., 257 P.3d 1130 (Cal. 2011) (in depth discussion of hospital pricing and what constitutes a reasonable value); Nassau Anesthesia Assocs. P.C. v. Chin, 924 N.Y.S.2d 252 (N.Y. Dist. Ct. 2011) (reasonable value awarded to provider was the average amount that provider would accept from insurers or government programs, rather than chargemaster price).

619 Galloway v. Methodist Hosp., 658 N.E.2d 611, 613 (Ind. Ct. App. 1995); St. Francis Med. Ctr. v. Reeves, 356 S.W.3d 813, 814, n.1 (Mo. Ct. App. 2012) (error to exclude testimony of hospital's business manager as to whether medical bills were "reasonable and necessary"); St. Luke's Episcopal-Presbyterian Hosp. v. Underwood, 957 S.W.2d 496, 498–99 (Mo. Ct. App. 1997); Irvington Phys. Therapy v. Shapiro & Berezin, P.C., 2010 WL 1658039 (N.J. Super. Ct. App. Div. Apr. 26, 2010) (office manager's testimony sufficient to establish entitlement for recovery, but patient could challenge reasonable value of services); Ellis Hosp. v. Little, 409 N.Y.S.2s 459, 461 (N.Y. App. Div. 1978); Charlotte-Mecklenberg Hosp. Auth. v. Talford, 727 S.E.2d 866 (N.C. 2012) (affidavits of hospital's Director of Revenue Management and Vice President of Medical Education were sufficient to show that rates billed by hospital were reasonable value of services, but bill for services standing alone would not be); OhioHealth Corp. v. Ryan, 2012 WL 68733 (Ohio Ct. App. Jan. 10, 2012) (*pro se* litigant; affidavit of keeper of records was admissible to establish amount owed as either based on personal knowledge or under business records exception); Med. College of Wis. v. Missimer, 769 N.W.2d 878 (Wis. Ct. App. 2009). *But see* McMeans v. Med. Liabilities Recoveries, Inc., 2002 WL 31835746 (Cal. Ct. App. Dec. 19, 2002) (unpublished) (hospital lien limited to reasonable value of necessary services; testimony of chief executive officer as to customary rates not probative when she had no personal knowledge of care provided); Majid v. Stubblefield, 589 N.E.2d 1045 (Ill. App. Ct. 1992) (allowing office manager to testify that physician's charges were similar to other physician charges in the region but suggesting that such hearsay testimony was only permissible because it was a small claims court proceeding); Advocacy Org. for Patients & Providers v. Auto Club Ins. Ass'n, 670 N.W.2d 569 (Mich. Ct. App. 2003) (providers' customary charges do not define "reasonable charges" for purposes of no-fault automobile insurance), *aff'd*, 693 N.W.2d 358 (Mich. 2005).

620 *See Ex parte* Univ. of S. Ala., 737 So. 2d 1049, 1053 (Ala. 1999); Dawson v. Prager, 76 P.3d 1036 (Kan. 2003) (provider's affidavit that amounts owed constituted co-payments after insurance coverage sufficient to grant summary judgment for provider, despite objection of patient that she paid "regularly" paid co-payments); Women's Care Specialists v. Troupin, 408 S.W.3d 310 (Mo. Ct. App. 2013) (office coordinator's testimony that charges were reasonable was sufficient for judgment when *pro se* patient conceded reasonableness); Heartland Health Systems, Inc. v. Chamberlin, 871 S.W.2d 8, 11 (Mo. Ct. App. 1993) (hospital employee's assertion that charges were reasonable and customary sufficient to shift burden to patient to challenge necessity and reasonableness of particular items); St. Joseph Hosp. v. Blake, 1989 Ohio App. LEXIS 2838 (Ohio Ct. App. July 19, 1989). *Cf.* Univ. of Wis. Med. Found., Inc. v. Turner, 735 N.W.2d 195 (Wis. Ct. App. 2007) (*pro se* patient; testimony of accounts manager was sufficient to prove bills were for medical services that were reasonable and necessary).

621 *See* Victory Mem'l Hosp. v. Rice, 493 N.E.2d 117, 120 (Ill. App. Ct. 1986) (patient is "free to attack the reasonableness of the charges through cross-examination and presentation of this case"); Irvington Phys. Therapy v. Shapiro & Berezin, P.C., 2010 WL 1658039 (N.J. Super. Ct. App. Div. Apr. 26, 2010) (in new trial, patient could challenge reasonable value of services, but court noted failure to cross-examine office manager in first trial). *Compare* Jackson v. Trancik, 953 N.E.2d 1087 (Ind. Ct. App. 2011) (reversing judgment for doctor; affidavit of medical billing expert should have been permitted and raised genuine issue whether amount doctor overcharged consumer for services), Estate of Bonner, 954 S.W.2d 356 (Mo. Ct. App. 1997) (because patient's estate put accuracy of records at issue by cross-examination, trial court acted within discretion in disallowing certain charges), Baca Chiropractic, P.C. v. Cobb, 317 S.W.3d 674 (Mo. Ct. App. 2010) (reversing summary judgment for chiropractor on open account claim; patients' affidavits challenging reasonableness of charges raised genuine issue of material fact), *and* H.E. Butt Grocery Co. v. Rencare, Ltd., 2004 WL 199272 (Tex. App. Feb. 4, 2004) (employee cross-examined regarding method of calculating line items, that is, why dialysis center charged $150 for box of gloves that cost $25; also evidence of center's contracts with other payers, payment structure of other plans, fact that center charged Blue Cross a lump sum charge for same services; take-nothing judgment affirmed), *with* Lewis, Miller & Co. v. Carrick, 2013 WL 6529314 (Cal. Ct. App. Dec. 13, 2012) (patient failed to adequately challenge reasonableness of helicopter transport service charges by only relying on brochure from commercial helicopter tour operator), *In re* Estate of Boyd, 8 P.3d 664, 669 (Idaho Ct. App. 2000) (appellate court declined to examine reasonableness of award to hospital given failure by patient's estate to challenge amount of charges), Lester E. Cox Med. Centers v. Richards, 252 S.W.3d 236 (Mo. Ct. App. 2008) (judgment for hospital upheld when patient failed to properly preserve for appeal his hearsay objections to collection supervisor's affidavit that hospital's charges were reasonable and customary), Southern N.H. Med. Ctr. v. Hayes, 992 A.2d 596 (N.H. 2010) (patient failed to produce any facts or affidavit supporting allegations that hospital's charges were not reasonable), Charlotte-Mecklenberg Hosp. Auth. v. Talford, 727 S.E.2d 866 (N.C. 2012) (upholding summary judgment; affidavits of hospital's Director of Revenue Management and Vice President of Medical Education were sufficient to show that rates billed by hospital were reasonable value of services; patient's affidavits as to price differences in drug charges insufficient to create issue of fact), Brezeale v. Hensley, 2009 WL 196026 (Tenn. Ct. App. Jan. 28, 2009) (when hospital asserted that its charges were reasonable, patient's failure to produce evidence refuting assertion resulted in affirmance of award), *and* Med. College of Wis. v. Missimer, 769 N.W.2d 878 (Wis. Ct. App. 2009) (collection representative's affidavit sufficient to establish that charges were reasonable and customary in the absence of factual submission by patient disputing it).

622 Catholic Healthcare West-Bay Area v. Seafarers' Health & Benefits Plan, 2007 WL 160995 (N.D. Cal. Jan. 18, 2007) (upholding insurer's use of MediCode and RedBook to determine reasonable prices to pay hospital), *rev'd on other grounds*, 321 Fed. Appx. 563 (9th Cir. 2008) (unpublished).

value of air transportation ambulance services may be preempted by the Airline Deregulation Act.[623] An insurer's failure to pay reasonable value to a provider, leaving patients exposed to balance billing, could be a violation of ERISA.[624]

9.5.5.2 Reasonable Value and Discriminatory Pricing

One of the most potentially powerful ways to prove that a hospital bill is unreasonable is to show discriminatory pricing. Discriminatory pricing is explained in detail at § 9.1.3, *supra*.

Discriminatory pricing has been challenged under state laws that prohibit unfair and deceptive acts and practices.[625] These affirmative legal challenges have met with limited success.[626] Discriminatory pricing has also been unsuccessfully challenged in one state as a violation of that state's "Discount Statute."[627]

However, the most effective use of this phenomenon may be as evidentiary proof to establish that the hospital's bill is unreasonably high. The patient can also argue that the hospital's charges to the uninsured are not reasonable in that they are not the "usual and customary" charges, because most patients pay less.[628] (Conversely, one court has held that an insurer's payment of the full price charged by the hospital was sufficient to establish that the price was reasonable.)[629]

Note that the hospital may "charge" every payer the same amount but accept as full payment from third-party payers amounts *less* than the full charges. Unfortunately, several courts have accepted this semantic legerdemain.[630]

Other courts have rejected challenges to discriminatory pricing, based on a belief that it is reasonable for hospitals to give insurers (or insured patients) a discount due to the certainty of payment from the insurer or the volume of transactions with the insurer.[631] However, this argument fails to recognize the

623 Crane v. Native Am. Air Ambulance, Inc., 2007 WL 625917 (D. Ariz. Feb. 23, 2007).

624 Franco v. Conn. Gen. Life Ins. Co., 818 F. Supp. 2d 792 (D.N.J. 2011) (permitting ERISA and RICO claims but dismissing antitrust claim, by consumers against their insurers for failing to pay usual and customary charges to out-of-network providers and leaving consumers exposed to balance billing), *later proceeding at* 289 F.R.D. 121 (D.N.J. 2012) (denying class certification); Clark v. Group Hospitalization & Med. Serv., Inc., 2010 WL 5093629 (S.D. Cal. Dec. 7, 2010) (permitting ERISA and UDAP claims against insurer for failing to pay usual and customary charges to out-of-network providers and leaving consumers exposed to balance billing; UDAP claims not preempted by ERISA).

625 *See* § 9.4.2, *supra*.

626 *Id.*

627 *In re* Hosp. Pricing Litig., King v. AnMed Health, 659 S.E.2d 131 (S.C. 2008) (S.C. Code Ann. § 38-71-120 did not require hospitals to provide all insured patients with a uniform discount, as it only applied to "service contracts" which insurers no longer offered; statute did not require hospitals to offer same discounts to uninsured patients that were offered to insured patients).

Another court held that discriminatory pricing did not violate the Social Security Act, the equal protection and due process clauses of the state and federal constitutions, or public policy. Methodist Med. Ctr. of Ill. v. Taylor, 489 N.E.2d 351 (Ill. App. Ct. 1986).

628 Colomar v. Mercy Hosp., Inc., 461 F. Supp. 2d 1265 (S.D. Fla. 2006) (while discriminatory pricing alone would not give rise to UDAP clam, allegations that hospital's prices were excessive in comparison to other hospitals and in comparison to actual cost of services would support viable UDAP claim); Canyon Ambulatory Surgery Centers v. SCF Arizona, 239 P.3d 733 (Ariz. Ct. App. 2010) (in determining reasonable value of services, the correct standard was not list price but what the seller accepts from a willing buyer; in case of medical services, what hospital accepts from insurers is true measure); Valley Hosp. v. Kroll, 847 A.2d 636 (N.J. Super. Ct. Law Div. 2003) (*quantum meruit* claim limited to reasonable value of services by hospital; payments made by Medigap insurer presumed reasonable; patient's wife not liable for additional amounts); Nassau Anesthesia Assocs. P.C. v. Chin, 924 N.Y.S.2d 252 (N.Y. Dist. Ct. 2011) (discussing phenomenon of discriminatory pricing in holding that reasonable value was the average amount that provider would accept from insurers or government programs, rather than chargemaster price); H.E. Butt Grocery Co. v. Rencare, Ltd., 2004 WL 199272 (Tex. App. Feb. 4, 2004) (jury entitled to consider evidence of contracts with other payers, payment structure of other plans, fact that dialysis center charged Blue Cross lump sum charge for same services; evidence supported jury's award of damages in amount lesser than provider's charges). *Cf.* Synergy Worldwide, Inc. v. Long, Haymes, Carr, Inc., 44 F. Supp. 2d 1348, 1358 (N.D. Ga. 1998) (summary judgment denying provider's claims against worker's compensation insurer for full chargemaster rates; fact that insurer paid amounts required by worker's compensation schedules meant that provider had already been compensated for reasonable value of those services). *But see* Univ. of S. Ala. Hosps. v. Blackmon, 42 So. 3d 1258 (Ala. Civ. App. 2009) (trial court erred in reducing hospital's award based on rates paid by Medicaid, Medicare, and Blue Cross); Huntington Hosp. v. Abrandt, 779 N.Y.S.2d 891 (N.Y. App. Term 2004) (discriminatory pricing not sufficient to create triable issue of fact as to reasonableness of charges; summary judgment for hospital); Charlotte-Mecklenberg Hosp. Auth. v. Talford, 727 S.E.2d 866 (N.C. 2012) (upholding summary judgment; patient's affidavits as to price differences in drug charges insufficient to create issue of fact).

629 Crane v. Native Am. Air Ambulance, Inc., 2007 WL 625917 (D. Ariz. Feb. 23, 2007). *See also* Colomar v. Mercy Hosp., Inc., 2007 WL 2083562 (S.D. Fla. July 20, 2007) (plaintiff failed to show that price charged by hospital was unreasonable when she was charged 155% more than what Medicare paid but her expert opined that charging 150% of the Medicare rate would be per se reasonable).

630 Collection Prof'ls, Inc. v. Schlosser, 977 N.E.2d 315 (Ill. App. Ct. 2012) (upholding trial court's decision to exclude evidence of discounts provided to insurers, relying on collateral source rule to hold that amounts paid by others not relevant); Parnell v. Madonna Rehab. Hosp., Inc., 602 N.W.2d 461 (Neb. 1999) (phrase "usual and customary charges" means the amount typically billed, not the amount typically received, by medical providers). *See also* Burton v. William Beaumont Hosp., 373 F. Supp. 2d 707 (E.D. Mich. 2005) (no breach of contract claim for discriminatory pricing; noting that hospital's charges for certain services were uniform regardless of insurance status, but failing to note whether the hospital accepted lower payments for insured); Univ. of S. Alabama Hosps. v. Blackmon, 42 So. 3d 1258 (Ala. Civ. App. 2009) (following *Parnell*); Roberts v. Univ. of Ala. Hosp., 27 So. 2d 512 (Ala. Civ. App. 2008) (same). *Cf.* Maldonado v. Ochsner Clinic Found., 493 F.3d 521, 526 n.7 (5th Cir. 2007) (noting that all patients are charged the same rate but hospitals offer varying discounts from that rate; Fifth Circuit held that reasonable price was an individual inquiry foreclosing class treatment but did not explicitly accept that chargemaster rates were per se reasonable).

631 *See* Geico Indem. Ins. Co. v. Kannaday, 2007 WL 2990552 (D. Kan. Oct. 11, 2007) (discriminatory pricing not unconscionable under Kansas UDAP statute because no evidence of deceptive, oppressive, or overreaching actions; uninsured consumer was not "similar consumer in a similar transaction" with insured consumer); Galvan v. Northwestern Mem'l Hosp., 888 N.E.2d 529 (Ill. App. Ct. 2008) (discriminatory pricing not unfair because insured and uninsured patients

difference between hospitals (at least not-for-profit ones) and other merchants. Nonprofit hospitals have a charitable mission that should be considered in determining whether it is fair to charge uninsured, generally low-income patients prices that are 200% to 400% more than what insurance companies and government programs pay.[632] Furthermore, it fails to recognize the special nature of medical services versus other goods and services, such as the fact that they are often involuntarily incurred. Finally, the Affordable Care Act contains a provision that prohibit the imposition of "gross charges," although this has been interpreted to be limited to only patients eligible for financial assistance.[633]

Several courts have held that a "reasonable charge" is an individualized inquiry which precludes class certification.[634] By implication, these courts have not accepted the argument that chargemaster rates are reasonable, but they have effectively precluded litigation that could result in systemic changes to a hospital's pricing policies.

Discriminatory pricing can also be used as a defense for patients who had health insurance at the time of the hospitalization but are being dunned for a co-payment based on a percentage (for example, 20%) of the bill. It is critical to learn what the insurance company has actually paid the hospital. If the hospital discounted the bill in calculating the amount that the insurance company had to pay, it can be argued that the patient should be responsible only for paying 20% of the discounted bill—not 20% of the full charges.[635]

9.5.5.3 Overbilling, Error, and Hospital Negligence

Another way to attack the reasonableness of the hospital's charges is to show an error in them. The American Medical Association has estimated that one in five claims is processed inaccurately.[636] Another expert has estimated that 30% to 40% of all medical bills contain errors.[637]

Obtaining the medical records and the pharmacy ledger or record and comparing them to an itemized list of the goods and services allegedly provided to the patient may reveal that some goods and services were not actually provided or were inadvertently billed for twice. Sometimes double-billing occurs because a separately billed service is already included in the charge for another procedure.[638]

Overbilling can also result from the hospital's use of the wrong diagnostic related grouping (DRG) code to label, and therefore bill for, a procedure. Practitioners will need to investigate the DRG coding through discovery or obtain expert assistance in this regard.[639]

---

are not similarly situated); Flushing Hosp. & Med. Ctr. v. Woytisek, 41 N.Y.2d 1081 (N.Y. 1977) (patient was not entitled to economic benefit of discount that insurer had obtained from hospital, because discount could have been based on volume of payments or assurance of payment); Firelands Reg'l Med. Ctr. v. Jeavons, 2008 WL 4408600 (Ohio Ct. App. Sept. 30, 2008) (following *Galvan* to hold that discriminatory pricing did not violate Ohio UDAP statute prohibition against excessive price because insured and uninsured patients are not similarly situated).

632 *See* Hill v. Sisters of St. Francis Health Servs., Inc., 2006 WL 3783415 (N.D. Ill. Dec. 20, 2006) (allegation that discriminatory pricing violated state's charitable organization exemption supported claim that hospital violated UDAP statute).

633 *See* § 9.3.1.3, *supra*.

634 Maldonado v. Ochsner Clinic Found., 493 F.3d 521, 526, n.7 (5th Cir. 2006); Colomar v. Mercy Hosp., Inc., 242 F.R.D. 671 (S.D. Fla. 2007); Eufala Hosp. Corp. v. Lawrence, 32 So. 3d 30 (Ala. 2009) (following *Maldonado*); Howard v. Willis-Knighton Med. Ctr., 924 So. 2d 1245 (La. Ct. App. 2006) (need for individual consideration defeated class action certification).

635 *See* McConocha v. Blue Cross & Blue Shield of Ohio, 898 F. Supp. 545 (N.D. Ohio 1995) (in a suit against the *insurer* on this theory, the court ruled that it was reasonable for the patient to expect to have to pay only 20% of the amount the hospital would actually receive as opposed to 20% of full, undiscounted charges). *See also* Corsini v. United HealthCare Servs., Inc., 145 F. Supp. 2d 184 (D.R.I. 2001) (holding that an HMO's method of calculating 20% co-payments as a percentage of charges as opposed to discounted fees actually paid, violated the terms of coverage); Everson v. Blue Cross & Blue Shield of Ohio, 898 F. Supp. 532 (N.D. Ohio 1994) (terms of coverage ambiguous as to whether the "reasonable charge" from which co-payments calculated reflected agreed upon discounts; construing the ambiguity against the insurer). *But see* Hoover v. Blue Cross & Blue Shield of Ala., 855 F.2d 1538, 1543 (11th Cir. 1988) (health insurer did not breach its fiduciary duty by requiring members to pay 20% of undiscounted hospital charges); Lefler v. United HealthCare of Utah, Inc., 162 F. Supp. 2d 1310 (D. Utah 2001) (HMO acted reasonably by pegging co-pay percentage to full, undiscounted amounts), *aff'd*, 72 Fed. Appx. 818 (10th Cir. 2003); Crosse v. BCBSD, Inc., 836 A.2d 492 (Del. Super. Ct. 2003) (Blue Cross did not owe fiduciary duty to insureds to pass on discounts and rebates received from providers); Flushing Hosp. & Med. Ctr. v. Woytisek, 41 N.Y.2d 1081 (N.Y. 1977) (patient was not entitled same discount that insurer had obtained from hospital, because discount could have been based on volume of payments or assurance of payment). *But cf.* Ries v. Humana Health Plan, Inc., 1995 WL 669583 (N.D. Ill. Nov. 8, 1995) (breach of fiduciary duty when an HMO put $8947 lien on member's settlement award for treatment of her injuries from a car accident although it settled her medical bills for just $600).

A similar discounting agreement was the subject of the United States Supreme Court's decision in Humana v. Forsyth, 525 U.S. 299, 119 S. Ct. 710, 142 L. Ed. 2d 753 (1999). Nevada hospital gave discounts of 40% to 96% to an insurance company that owned it, yet the hospital billed patients for co-payments calculated as a percentage of the undiscounted bill.

636 American Med. Ass'n, *2010 National Health Insurer Report Card, available at* www.ama-assn.org/ama/pub/news/news/2010-report-card.page.

637 Jessica Silver-Greenberg, *Medical Billing Errors Surge*, Wall St. J., Feb. 11, 2011 ("Stephen Parente, a professor of health finance at the University of Minnesota who has studied medical billing extensively, estimates that 30% to 40% of bills contain errors").

638 *See, e.g.*, Lester E. Cox Med. Centers v. Huntsman, 2003 WL 22004998 (W.D. Mo. Aug. 5, 2003) (bill for $1800 "bundle" of supplies resulted in patient being charged for items that were unnecessary for her surgery), *aff'd on other grounds*, 408 F.3d 989 (8th Cir. 2005). *See also* Tara Siegel Bernard, *Decoding Your Medical Bill*, N.Y. Times, June 22, 2012, *available at* http://bucks.blogs.nytimes.com/2012/06/22/decoding-your-medical-bill/?_php=true&_type=blogs&_r=0; Jeanne Lee, *8 Things You Must Do to Prevent Hospital Overcharges*, www.Health.com (Jan. 10, 2011), *at* www.health.com/health/article/0,,20456472,00.html.

639 There are some companies that conduct "mini-audits," which consist of expert review of the itemized hospital bill. Some of these companies may be found at http://billadvocates.com.

Delays caused by the hospital and infections acquired during hospitalization[640] may also result in a longer stay and a higher bill than are reasonable.

9.5.6 *Other Defenses or Counterclaims in Medical Debt Collection Suits*

9.5.6.1 Using Affirmative Claims Defensively

Many of the affirmative claims discussed in § 9.4, *supra*, can be asserted as defenses in a medical debt collection suit, including:

- Failure to comply with Hill-Burton Act requirements or other laws creating a duty to provide free or reduced cost care;[641]
- Breach of the hospital's charitable duty under state tax law;[642]
- The provider's acceptance, or even application for, a Medicaid or Medicare payment that by statute or regulation must be considered payment in full;[643]
- Failure of the provider to process public aid applications or to bill Medicaid or Medicare,[644] or to properly bill the patient's insurer;[645]
- Provisions of the provider's contract with an HMO or a state health insurance statute that bar the provider from billing an HMO member for services covered by the HMO;[646]
- Breach of the duty of good faith and fair dealing;[647]
- Breach of a fiduciary duty;[648] and
- Misrepresentation or other UDAP violation.[649]

9.5.6.2 Other Defenses

Defenses that may be available against a medical debt collection suit include:

- The provider negligently misinformed patient as to extent of insurance coverage;[650]
- The provider's failure to provide a translation of the contract for a non-English speaking consumer;[651] and
- The provider's malpractice, which may be raised as a defense to a debt, even if the consumer did not sue for malpractice.[652]

9.6 Liability for Familial Medical Care Under Necessaries Statutes

Necessaries statutes, which evolved from Married Woman Acts passed by many states at the turn of the century, make spouses liable for each other's medical bills. The typical necessaries statute, as written, imposed liability on husbands for wives' medical bills, but not *vice versa*. Some states have abolished this doctrine or ruled the necessaries statute

---

Patients have been able to successfully use medical billing experts in challenging bills in collection lawsuits. *See, e.g.*, Jackson v. Trancik, 953 N.E.2d 1087 (Ind. Ct. App. 2011) (reversing judgment for doctor; affidavit of medical billing expert should have been permitted and raised genuine issue whether doctor overcharged consumer for services by using wrong billing methodology).

640 *See, e.g.*, Walter F. Roche, Jr., *Meningitis Outbreak: Bills Mount as Victims Still Suffer*, The Tennessean, Apr. 3, 2012 (hospitals dunning patients for treatment of meningitis infection that was caused by tainted injections that hospitals administered). *See* Duke Univ. Med. Ctr., Hospital-Acquired Antibiotic-Resistant Infections Triple Costs and Lengths of Hospitalizations (Sept. 28, 1997).

641 *See* §§ 9.1.4, 9.4.2.1, 9.4.6.1, *supra*.

642 *See* § 9.4.6.2, *supra*.

643 *See* § 9.3.7, *supra*.

644 *Id.*

645 Grandview/Southview Hosps. v. Monie, 2005 WL 737393 (Ohio Ct. App. Apr. 1, 2005) (upholding trial court's judgment denying recovery to hospital that billed wrong insurance company).

At least one state requires that health care providers bill insurers or patients in a timely manner. Tex. Civ. Prac. & Rem. Code Ann. § 146.002 (West) (provider must submit bill within either eleven months or the time specified in any contract with insurer).

646 *See* § 9.3.7, *supra*.

647 *See* § 9.4.7, *supra*.

648 *Id.*

649 *See, e.g.*, Cambridge Manor of Fairfield, L.L.C. v. Myers, 2012 WL 6582542 (Conn. Super. Ct. Nov. 26, 2012) (in defense of collection lawsuit against her, patient's daughter could bring UDAP counterclaim against nursing home that failed to provide monthly statements as promised in contract, which prevented patient from qualifying for Medicaid benefits to pay for bills); Baptist Home of Brooklyn v. Schott, 902 N.Y.S.2d 368 (N.Y. App. Div. 2010) (reversal of judgment for nursing home, failure to show absence of triable issue of fact as to whether consumer was induced to execute Admissions Agreement by misrepresentation of home's representative). *See generally* § 9.4.2, *supra*.

650 *See, e.g.*, Yale New Haven Hosp. v. Vignola, 2002 WL 377675 (Conn. Super. Ct. Feb. 15, 2002) (at time of admission, patient asked whether treatment was covered by her insurance, and hospital employee stated, incorrectly, that it was; hospital had no duty to ascertain insurance coverage but, when it undertook to advise patient, duty of due care arose); Havsy v. Wash. State Dep't of Health, Bd. of Osteopathic Medicine & Surgery, 123 Wash. App. 1030 (Wash. Ct. App. 2004) (licensing board sanctions affirmed doctor breached fiduciary duty to patient by misleading patient about the price of treatment, failing to inform patient of the high cost of a certain procedure and that insurance would not cover that procedure). *But see* MRI Co-op. v. Berlin, 1993 WL 257078 (Ohio Ct. App. June 30, 1993) (assignment of insurance benefits, which provided that patient would be liable if insurance did not pay, enforced as written, even though provider's employee told patient that his insurance would cover the cost).

651 *See* Alan Alop, Defending Hospital Collection Cases (rev. ed. 2005), *available at* www.illinoislegaladvocate.org/index.cfm?fuseaction=home.dsp_content&contentID=728; National Consumer Law Center, Unfair and Deceptive Acts and Practices § 5.6.1 (8th ed. 2012), *updated at* www.nclc.org/library. *But see* Cho v. Santa Clara, 2009 WL 925332 (Cal. Ct. App. Apr. 7, 2009) (unpublished) (widow was liable for husband's hospital bill because she signed contract despite her lack of ability to read English).

A failure to provide a translation of the contract may also violate Title VI of the Civil Rights Act of 1964, 42 U.S.C. §§ 2000d to 2000d-7, and its implementing regulations. Title VI prohibits discrimination on the basis of race, ethnicity, or national origin by any healthcare provider that receives federal funds (including Medicare and Medicaid). Consumers can file complaints for violation of Title VI with their regional office of the Department of Health & Human Service's Office for Civil Rights. There is, however, no private right of action under Title VI for this type of violation. Alexander v. Sandoval, 532 U.S. 275, 121 S. Ct. 1511, 149 L. Ed. 2d 517 (2001).

652 Wash. Cnty. Mem'l Hosp. v. Hattabaugh, 717 N.E.2d 929 (Ind. Ct. App. 1999) (consumers, who did not sue for malpractice, allowed to introduce evidence that surgery had resulted in permanent damage, as defense to collection suit).

unconstitutional.[653] But other states have rewritten the necessaries statutes in gender-neutral terms, often believing its historical form violated the Equal Protection Clause, and extended it to impose liability on a wife for her husband's medical expenses.[654] In addition to necessaries statutes, state Medicaid law imposes liability on a responsible relative, generally the spouse, for payment of nursing home expenses.[655] In community property states, the non-debtor spouse is liable for the patient's debts but, in some cases, only to the extent of their community property.[656]

Liability for a spouse's medical care becomes a major problem if a prolonged last illness threatens the surviving spouse with impoverishment.[657] There are several arguments that the spouse may use to avoid liability. Imposition of liability upon a spouse even under a gender-neutral statute may violate the Equal Credit Opportunity Act, which prohibits creditors from requiring that both spouses obligate themselves for one spouse's

653 *See* Egge v. Healthspan Servs. Co., 115 F. Supp. 2d 1126 (D. Minn. 2000) (Minnesota's elimination of spousal liability for necessaries in 1997 was not retroactive); Emanuel v. McGriff, 596 So. 2d 578 (Ala. 1992) (striking down doctrine of necessaries as unconstitutional gender discrimination, refusing to extend the doctrine to include wives' liability for husbands' necessaries, and deferring to legislature); Connor v. Southwest Fla. Reg'l Med. Ctr., Inc., 668 So. 2d 175 (Fla. 1995) (common law doctrine of necessaries abolished on equal protection grounds); Condore v. Prince George's Cnty., 425 A.2d 1011 (Md. 1981) (based on Maryland's Equal Rights Amendment, court invalidated necessaries statute; extension of statute best determined by legislature); North Ottawa Cmty. Hosp. v. Kieft, 578 N.W.2d 267 (Mich. 1998) (Married Woman's Property Act and provisions of state constitution which protect married women's separate property were constitutional and prevented the expansion of the common law doctrine of necessaries to make wife liable for husband's medical bills; doctrine of necessaries was abrogated; deferring to the legislature); Account Specialists & Credit Collections, Inc. v. Jackman, 970 P.2d 202 (Okla. Civ. App. 1998) (statute which codified common law doctrine of husband's liability for wife's necessaries was unconstitutional; legislature, not court, should now decide whether to impose liability on both spouses, or on neither); Medical Ctr. Hosp. v. Lorain, 675 A.2d 1326 (Vt. 1996) (choosing to abolish rather than expand the doctrine; it was not very effective in protecting needy spouses, and the complex social issues involved should be addressed by the legislature). *See also* Govan v. Med. Credit Servs., Inc., 621 So. 2d 928 (Miss. 1993) (absent express consent, spouse not responsible to health care provider for other spouse's debts).

654 *E.g.*, Conn. Gen. Stat. § 46b-37 (both spouses jointly liable for family expenses, including reasonable and necessary medical care); 750 Ill. Comp. Stat. § 65/15 (both spouses jointly liable for family expenses, including reasonable and necessary medical care); Mass. Gen. Laws ch. 209, § 1; N.C. Gen. Stat. § 131E-91(d)(5); N.D. Cent. Code § 14-07-08(3) (spouses jointly liable for any debts incurred for necessary medical care while living together); 23 Pa. Cons. Stat. § 4102; Tex. Fam. Code Ann. § 2.501 (West); Va. Code Ann. §§ 8.01-220.2, 55-37; Wis. Stat. § 765.001(2). *See* Lester E. Cox Med. Centers v. Huntsman, 2003 WL 22004998 (W.D. Mo. Aug. 5, 2003) (husband was liable for wife's medical bill; not FDCPA violation to dun him for bill), *aff'd on other grounds*, 408 F.3d 989 (8th Cir. 2005); *In re* Balthrop, 2005 WL 3691335 (Bankr. E.D. Va. Nov. 28, 2008) (discussing two Virginia necessaries statutes: one applicable to all necessaries, Va. Code Ann. § 55-37, and one specifically applicable to emergency medical care, Va. Code Ann. § 8.01-220.2; only latter statute permits recovery against the marital home); Queen's Med. Ctr. v. Kagawa, 967 P.2d 686 (Haw. 1998) (under gender-neutral spousal liability statute, wife was liable for husband's hospital bill); Memorial Hosp. v. Hahaj, 430 N.E.2d 412 (Ind. 1992) (necessaries statute extended to impose liability on both spouses); St. Francis Reg'l Med. Ctr., Inc. v. Bowles, 836 P.2d 1123 (Kan. 1992) (necessaries statute violates Equal Protection Clause of Fourteenth Amendment; statute expanded to apply to husbands and wives equally); Pioneer Valley Postal Fed. Credit Union v. Soja, 2002 Mass. App. Div. 193 (Mass. Dist. Ct. 2002) (necessaries statute, Mass. Gen. Laws ch. 209, § 1, applies to all spouses' property, not just that held in tenancy by entireties); Hulse v. Warren, 777 S.W.2d 319 (Mo. 1989) (necessaries statute extended to impose liability on both spouses); St. Joseph Hosp. v. Rizzo, 676 A.2d 98 (N.H. 1996) (doctrine of necessaries extended to create liability for a wife for her husband's medical treatment); Jersey Shore Med. Center-Fitkin Hosp. v. Estate of Baum, 417 A.2d 1003, 1010 (N.J. 1980) (necessaries statute should be expanded to apply to both spouses; joint and several approach); Medical Bus. Assocs. Inc. v. Steiner, 588 N.Y.S.2d 890 (N.Y. App. Div. 1992) (necessaries statute violated the Equal Protection Clause; unconstitutionality to be remedied by extending common law rule to both spouses); Forsyth Mem'l Hosp., Inc. v. Chisholm, 467 S.E.2d 88 (N.C. 1996); N.C. Baptist Hosps., Inc. v. Harris, 354 S.E.2d 471 (N.C. 1987) (necessaries statute expanded to apply to both husbands and wives); MRI Cooperative v. Berlin, 1993 WL 257078 (Ohio Ct. App. June 30, 1993) (wife liable under family expense statute if able to pay); Landmark Med. Ctr. v. Gauthier, 635 A.2d 1145 (R.I. 1994); Richland Mem'l Hosp. v. Burton, 318 S.E.2d 12 (S.C. 1984) (necessaries statute extended to impose liability on both spouses); Accounts Mgmt., Inc. v. Lichfield, 576 N.W.2d 233 (S.D. 1998) (widow was liable for late husband's medical bills; medical care was a "necessary" within meaning of statute, making each spouse liable for "all necessaries of life" of the other); Outpatient Diagnostic Ctr. v. Christian, 1997 Tenn. App. LEXIS 305 (Tenn. Ct. App. Apr. 30, 1997) (either spouse is liable for the other's medical bills under common law doctrine of necessaries). *See also In re* Olexa, 317 B.R. 290 (Bankr. W.D. Pa. 2004) (detailed analysis of Pennsylvania necessaries statute, 23 Pa. Cons. Stat. § 4102, and cases construing it; statute was amended after enactment of state equal rights amendment), *aff'd*, 476 F.3d 177 (3d Cir. 2007).

Ohio, which recognized common law marriage, made common law spouses liable for each other's necessaries, including last illness expenses. Warren Gen. Hosp. v. Brink, 610 N.E.2d 1128 (Ohio Ct. App. 1992).

655 *See* Robbins *ex rel.* Robbins v. DeBuono, 218 F.3d 197 (2d Cir. 2000) (New York's practice of attributing income of institutionalized spouse to non-institutionalized spouse required her to deplete her resources so as to be impoverished when spouse died; as to Social Security benefits, practice was forbidden by anti-assignment statute, as to ERISA benefits it was permissible); Comm'r of the Dep't of Soc. Servs. v. Fishman, 720 N.Y.S.2d 493 (N.Y. App. Div. 2001) (widow who had assets and income liable in implied contract for husband's nursing home expenses); *In re* Estate of Bergman, 688 N.W.2d 187 (N.D. 2004) (construes impoverished spouse provisions of Medicaid law).

656 Samaritan Health Sys. v. Caldwell, 957 P.2d 1373 (Ariz. Ct. App. 1998) (health care debts are community debts, which may be satisfied from community property but not from separate property of non-debtor spouse); Cho v. Santa Clara, 2009 WL 925332 (Cal. Ct. App. Apr. 7, 2009) (unpublished) (Cal. Fam. Code § 914 (West) permits creditor to recover against spouse's separate property for "necessaries of life" but because hospital failed to plead claim under that section, widow was only liable for husband's medical bills as community debt to extent of the community property).

657 For examples of the harsh impact of the necessaries doctrine on surviving spouses, see Steve Tripoli & Chi Chi Wu, National Consumer Law Center, Unhealthy Pursuits: How the Sick and Vulnerable Are Harmed by Abusive Medical Debt Collection Tactics (Dec. 2005), *available online as companion material to this treatise*. One court has held that the necessaries doctrine even permits a provider to report medical debt on the credit report of a spouse, despite the fact that the spouse's liability had not been reduced to judgment. Dunn v. Lehigh Valley Ctr. for Sight, P.C., 2003 WL 22299275 (E.D. Pa. Sept. 30, 2003).

transaction.[658] In states that have not yet ruled on extending the statute to wives, the non-debtor wife can argue that extending the doctrine to her is a task for the legislature, not the court.[659]

In addition, courts in states that continue to recognize the necessaries doctrine may limit the circumstances in which they will impose liability on the non-debtor spouse.[660] Some state statutes apply the doctrine only to emergency care.[661] The creditor may be required to prove that the services provided were actually a "necessary,"[662] although that may be an easier burden in a medical debt case.[663] Also, the creditor's recovery against the spouse may be limited to the amount owed for medical services and may not extend to liability for attorney fees, interest, or collection costs.[664] The spouse who incurred the debt may remain primarily liable, and the other spouse may only be secondarily liable.[665] Failure to make a timely claim against the estate of the primary debtor wife may defeat an attempt to collect from the secondarily liable spouse.[666] The creditor may not have to sue the primarily liable

658 15 U.S.C. § 1691(a)(1); 12 C.F.R. §§ 1002.7(d)(1), 1002.11(b)(1)(ii). *See* Edwards v. McCormick, 136 F. Supp. 2d 795, 803 n.9 (S.D. Ohio 2001) (stating in dicta that imposition of liability upon spouse probably violates Equal Credit Opportunity Act). *See generally* National Consumer Law Center, Credit Discrimination § 9.3 (6th ed. 2013), *updated at* www.nclc.org/library.

659 *See* Davis v. Baxter Cnty. Reg'l Hosp., 855 S.W.2d 303 (Ark. 1993) (common law doctrine of necessaries not superseded or amended and remains in effect; equal protection violation not argued or considered); Medlock v. Ft. Smith Serv. Fin. Corp., 803 S.W.2d 930 (Ark. 1991); Connor v. Southwest Fla. Reg'l Med. Ctr., Inc., 668 So. 2d 175 (Fla. 1995); Rydstrom v. Bayfront Med. Ctr., 632 So. 2d 143 (Fla. Dist. Ct. App. 1994); Account Specialists & Credit Collections, Inc. v. Jackman, 970 P.2d 202 (Okla. Civ. App. 1998) (statute which codified common law doctrine of husband's liability for wife's necessaries was unconstitutional; legislature, not court, should now decide whether to impose liability on both spouses, or on neither); Medical Ctr. Hosp. v. Lorain, 675 A.2d 1326 (Vt. 1996); Hitchcock Clinic, Inc. v. Mackie, 648 A.2d 817 (Vt. 1993). *Cf.* Adams v. Riddle, 2010 WL 668762 (Ky. Ct. App. Feb. 26, 2010) (declining to address constitutional challenge to Kentucky necessaries statute because of failure to notify attorney general's office as required by Kentucky law).

660 *E.g.*, Schlaefer v. Fin. Mgmt. Serv., Inc., 996 P.2d 745 (Ariz. Ct. App. 2000) (debts for necessary medical care presumed to be community debts, but presumption rebutted by proof of valid premarital agreement that each spouse would be responsible for own debts); Wilton Meadows L.P. v. Coratolo, 14 A.3d 982 (Conn. 2011) (nursing home expenses are not included in the scope of the spousal liability statute, Conn. Gen. Stat. § 46b-37; wife not liable for husband's nursing home bill); N. Shore Cmty. Bank & Trust Co. v. Kollar, 710 N.E.2d 106 (Ill. App. Ct. 1999) (bank loan, even if the proceeds are spent for household needs, was not a "family expense" within the meaning of the Illinois family expense statute; widow not liable on loan taken by deceased husband; attorney fees to the widow); Bartrom v. Adjustment Bureau, Inc., 618 N.E.2d 1 (Ind. 1993); Ohio State Univ. Med. Ctr. v. Calovini, 2002 WL 31953905 (Ohio Ct. Cl. Oct. 8, 2002) (wife not liable for husband's medical care; fulltime housewife with no independent means had no ability to pay); Doctors Laves, Sarewitz & Walko v. Briggs, 613 A.2d 506 (N.J. Super. Ct. Law Div. 1992) (when wife separated from husband for five years with no financial interdependence, wife not liable for husband's medical expenses as wife but liable in *quantum meruit* up to the amount of insurance proceeds paid to her husband's estate for those medical expenses); Ellis Hosp. v. Little, 409 N.Y.S.2d 459 (N.Y. App. Div. 1978) (social service law that imposes spousal liability provides exemption for homestead "essential and appropriate to the needs of the household" (N.Y. Soc. Serv. Law § 336 (McKinney)); fact question as to widow's ability to pay depends on value of her non-exempt real estate); Roach v. Mamakos, 764 N.Y.S.2d 539 (N.Y. Sup. Ct. 2003) (ex-husband not liable because alleged creditor, who was wife's father, failed to show that he expected to be paid, had sought payment from wife and that she was unable to pay; also doctrine of necessaries inapplicable when support order defined husband's duty to support, or when separation was fault of debtor spouse); Raleigh Gen. Hosp. v. Caudill, 591 S.E.2d 315 (W. Va. 2003) (former W. Va. Code § 48-3-22 [now § 48-29-303] made spouses liable for "the reasonable and necessary services of a physician rendered to either spouse while residing together as husband and wife;" court construed this narrowly; widow not liable for hospital costs other than physician's services).

661 Sentara Va. Beach Gen. Hosp. v. LeBeau, 188 F. Supp. 2d 623 (E.D. Va. 2002) (emergency not shown when cancer patient underwent testing to determine results of chemotherapy and was scheduled for surgery two weeks later).

662 Walter v. Palisades Collection, L.L.C., 2011 WL 1666869 (E.D. Pa. May 2, 2011) (credit card debt; rejecting argument that any debt that qualifies for FDCPA coverage because it is "primarily for personal, family, or household purposes" is a debt for necessaries; debt buyer's failure to obtain copies of statements or receipts precluded examination to determine whether charges were for necessaries); Nelson v. First Nat'l Bank of Omaha, 2004 WL 2711032 (Minn. Ct. App. Nov. 30, 2004) (credit card lender failed to show that items purchased on account were household necessities, and thus lender not entitled to summary judgment on liability of spouse); Rienzo v. Parisi, 2008 WL 190488 (N.J. Super. Ct. App. Div. Jan. 24, 2008) (creditor must show that it was the direct provider of necessaries to recover from spouse; loan of money used to pay necessaries does not qualify).

663 *But see* Emerson Vill., L.L.C. v. Jode, 2012 WL 6928123 (Mass. Super. Ct. Dec. 15, 2012) (nursing home seeking to recover from widow for late husband's expenses; widow liable for necessaries, but fact issue as to what goods and services were necessaries); St. Francis Med. Ctr. v. Watkins, 413 S.W.3d 354 (Mo. Ct. App. 2013) (hospital failed to show that services provided to wife were medically necessary; judgment for husband on hospital's necessaries claim).

664 *E.g.*, N.A.R., Inc. v. Elmer, 141 P.3d 606 (Utah Ct. App. 2006) (interest and attorney fees, provided for in contract for medical services, are not necessaries within the meaning of the Utah Family Expense statute).

665 *E.g.*, *In re* Olexa, 476 F.3d 177 (3d Cir. 2007) (contracting spouse primarily liable under Pennsylvania necessaries statute); Bartrom v. Adjustment Bureau, Inc., 618 N.E.2d 1 (Ind. 1993) (absent express contractual liability or authorization under the laws of agency, husband not responsible to health care provider for wife's debts; however, when a shortfall between dependent spouse's necessary expenses and separate funds exists, financially superior spouse becomes secondarily liable through doctrine); Mem'l Hosp. v. Hahaj, 430 N.E.2d 412 (Ind. 1992); St. Francis Reg'l Med. Ctr., Inc. v. Bowles, 836 P.2d 1123 (Kan. 1992); Bethany Med. Ctr. v. Niyazi, 890 P.2d 349 (Kan. Ct. App. 1995); Hulse v. Warren, 777 S.W.2d 319 (Mo. 1989); Hawley by Cordell v. Hawley, 904 S.W.2d 584 (Mo. Ct. App. 1995); Cheshire Med. Ctr. v. Holbrook, 663 A.2d 1344 (N.H. 1995); Rienzo v. Parisi, 2008 WL 190488 (N.J. Super. Ct. App. Div. Jan. 24, 2008) (creditor must seek satisfaction from the primarily liable spouse in order to seek recourse under necessaries doctrine); Medical Bus. Assocs. Inc. v. Steiner, 588 N.Y.S.2d 890 (N.Y. App. Div. 1992); Roach v. Mamakos, 764 N.Y.S.2d 539 (N.Y. Sup. Ct. 2003) (failure to sue primarily liable spouse is fatal to necessaries claim); THC Piketon v. Edwards, 2007 WL 4305719 (Ohio Ct. App. Dec. 11, 2007) (in order to hold spouse liable for medical bills creditor must show that patient is unable to pay the medical bills); Landmark Med. Ctr. v. Gauthier, 635 A.2d 1145 (R.I. 1994); Trident Reg'l Med. Ctr. v. Evans, 454 S.E.2d 343 (S.C. Ct. App. 1995); Anderson Mem'l Hosp., Inc. v. Hagen, 443 S.E.2d 399 (S.C. Ct. App. 1994).

666 Collection Bureau of San Jose v. Rumsey, 99 Cal. Rptr. 2d 792 (Cal. Ct. App. 2000) (one-year statute of limitations for claims against an estate barred a claim against a widow, under necessaries statute, for husband's last illness expenses); Hickory Creek at Connersville v. Estate

debtor spouse separately, however, as long as it has demanded payment unsuccessfully from the primarily liable spouse.[667] Other states hold that the creditor must prove that the secondarily liable spouse had failed to support the primarily liable spouse.[668] A creditor may be required to prove that not only were the patient and spouse legally married,[669] but that there was a mutual expectation that the spouses would share assets, expenses, and debt.[670]

It may be a defense that the financial resources of the spouse who incurred the expenses were sufficient;[671] that the creditor did not rely on the non-debtor spouse's credit to furnish the necessaries;[672] or that, as at common law, the non-debtor spouse's inability to pay the spouse's debts limits his or her responsibility to do so.[673] The secondarily liable spouse may also raise any defenses available to the other spouse.[674]

---

of Combs, 992 N.E.2d 209 (Ind. Ct. App. 2013) (nursing home's failure to seek reimbursement from patient's estate barred it from seeking recovery from patient's widower pursuant to necessaries statute; liability for necessaries is secondary); Anderson Mem'l Hosp., Inc. v. Hagen, 443 S.E.2d 399 (S.C. Ct. App. 1994); Accounts Mgmt., Inc. v. Nelson, 663 N.W.2d 237 (S.D. 2003) (hospital that failed to make timely claim on father's estate could not sue adult children for necessaries). *But see* Samaritan Health Sys. v. Caldwell, 957 P.2d 1373 (Ariz. Ct. App. 1998) (limitation on claims against estate did not bar suit on community debt against community property in hands of surviving spouse); Aker v. Ft. Wayne Urology Corp., 562 N.E.2d 751 (Ind. Ct. App. 1990); Wesley Long Nursing Ctr. v. Harper, 653 S.E.2d 256 (N.C. Ct. App. 2007) (provider need not seek payment for nursing home expenses from wife's estate first; surviving spouse liable for debt); Fulton Cnty. Health Ctr. v. Jones, 2007 WL 4277583 (Ohio Ct. App. Dec. 7, 2007) (summary judgment for provider, despite surviving spouse's argument that provider failed to establish that patient's estate unable to pay bill).

667 Bethany Med. Ctr. v. Niyazi, 890 P.2d 349 (Kan. Ct. App. 1995); Cheshire Med. Ctr. v. Holbrook, 663 A.2d 1344 (N.H. 1995); Trident Reg'l Med. Ctr. v. Evans, 454 S.E.2d 343 (S.C. Ct. App. 1995).

668 Allen v. Keating, 517 N.W.2d 830 (Mich. Ct. App. 1994) (spouses were separated); Smith v. Hernandez, 794 P.2d 772 (Okla. Civ. App. 1990). *Cf.* Aharoni v. Michael, 598 N.E.2d 1215 (Ohio Ct. App. 1991) (Ohio law requires creditors to give notice and show that parent refused or neglected to provide for minor's necessaries before charging parent for such).

669 North Ohio Med. Specialists, L.L.C. v. Huston, 2009 WL 3683632 (Ohio Ct. App. Nov. 6, 2009) (husband was not liable for patient's medical bills when provider failed to properly allege in the pleadings that patient and husband were married).

670 Southern N.H. Med. Ctr. v. Hayes, 992 A.2d 596 (N.H. 2010). *But see* Dignity Care Home v. Montgomery Ryan, 246 P.3d 413 (Kan. Ct. App. 2011) (post-nuptial agreement requiring spouses to handle their financial affairs separately did not bar application of necessaries doctrine).

671 *In re* Olexa, 476 F.3d 177 (3d Cir. 2007) (creditor may go after other spouse under Pennsylvania necessaries statute only if contracting spouse's assets insufficient); Foster v. D.B.S. Collection Agency, 463 F. Supp. 2d 783 (S.D. Ohio 2006) (debt collector not entitled to sue spouse under Ohio necessaries doctrine when collector failed to establish that the primary debtor was unable to pay debt); St. Francis Reg'l Med. Ctr., Inc. v. Bowles, 836 P.2d 1123 (Kan. 1992); Bethany Med. Ctr. v. Niyazi, 890 P.2d 349 (Kan. Ct. App. 1995); Hawley by Cordell v. Hawley, 904 S.W.2d 584 (Mo. Ct. App. 1995); Medical Bus. Assocs. Inc. v. Steiner, 588 N.Y.S.2d 890, 897 (N.Y. App. Div. 1992); Roach v. Mamakos, 764 N.Y.S.2d 539 (N.Y. Sup. Ct. 2003) (must show that primarily liable spouse is unable to pay); Promenade Nursing Home, Inc. v. Lacey, 814 N.Y.S.2d 564 (table), 2005 WL 3592001 (N.Y. Civ. Ct. Nov. 29, 2005) (claim for medical necessaries must show that the primary debtor is unable to pay for the debt out of his own resources; that the creditor relied on the credit of non-patient spouse in deciding to extend credit; and that the non-patient spouse has the means to pay the debt); Home Helpers/Direct Link v. St. Pierre, 964 N.E.2d 41 (Ohio Ct. App. 2011) (Ohio necessaries statute requires that married person be unable to support himself or herself before the spouse is liable); THC Piketon v. Edwards, 2007 WL 4305719 (Ohio Ct. App. Dec. 11, 2007) (in order to hold spouse liable for medical bills creditor must show that patient is unable to pay the medical bills); Landmark Med. Ctr. v. Gauthier, 635 A.2d 1145 (R.I. 1994) ("Only if the spouse who received the benefit has insufficient resources to satisfy the debt may the other spouse be liable.").

672 Kent Gen. Hosp., Inc. v. Russell, 1997 Del. Super. LEXIS 336 (Del. Super. Ct. July 14, 1997) (doctrine of necessaries did not apply when hospital relied on wife's individual credit), *aff'd*, 705 A.2d 244 (table), 1998 WL 15010 (Del. Jan. 12, 1998); Ellenville Reg'l Hosp. v. Mendez, 873 N.Y.S.2d 511 (N.Y. Poughkeepsie City Ct. 2008) (creditor must demonstrate that the necessaries were furnished on the non-debtor spouse's credit in order to recover under the doctrine); Medical Bus. Assocs. Inc. v. Steiner, 588 N.Y.S.2d 890, 897 (N.Y. App. Div. 1992); Promenade Nursing Home, Inc. v. Lacey, 814 N.Y.S.2d 564 (table); 2005 WL 3592001 (N.Y. Civ. Ct. 2005) (claim for medical necessaries must show that the primary debtor is unable to pay for the debt out of his own resources, that the creditor relied on the credit of non-patient spouse in deciding to extend credit, and that the non-patient spouse has the means to pay the debt); Prof'l Orthopedic & Sports P.T.P.C. v. Pittore, 959 N.Y.2d 92 (N.Y. City Ct. 2012) (creditor seeking to recover debt against spouse bears the burden of demonstrating that the necessaries were furnished on the spouse's credit and that the spouse has the ability to satisfy the debt).

673 *In re* Olexa, 317 B.R. 290 (Bankr. W.D. Pa. 2004) (pecuniary circumstances of the non-contracting spouse are relevant under Pennsylvania necessaries statute), *aff'd*, 476 F.3d 177 (3d Cir. 2007); Kent Gen. Hosp., Inc. v. Russell, 1997 Del. Super. LEXIS 336 (Del. Super. Ct. July 14, 1997) (doctrine of necessaries did not apply when hospital relied on wife's individual credit), *aff'd*, 705 A.2d 244 (table), 1998 WL 15010) (Del. Jan. 12, 1998); Ellenville Reg'l Hosp. v. Mendez, 873 N.Y.S.2d 511 (N.Y. Poughkeepsie City Ct. 2008) (creditor must demonstrate that the non-debtor spouse has the ability to satisfy the debt); Medical Bus. Assocs. Inc. v. Steiner, 588 N.Y.S.2d 890, 897 (N.Y. App. Div. 1992); Promenade Nursing Home, Inc. v. Lacey, 814 N.Y.S.2d 564 (table), 2005 WL 3592001 (N.Y. Civ. Ct. Nov. 29, 2005) (claim for medical necessaries must show that the primary debtor is unable to pay for the debt out of his own resources; that the creditor relied on the credit of non-patient spouse in deciding to extend credit; and that the non-patient spouse has the means to pay the debt); Prof'l Orthopedic & Sports P.T.P.C. v. Pittore, 959 N.Y.2d 92 (N.Y. City Ct. 2012) (creditor seeking to recover debt against spouse bears the burden of demonstrating that the necessaries were furnished on the spouse's credit and that the spouse has the ability to satisfy the debt). *See also* Porter Mem'l Hosp. v. Wozniak, 680 N.E.2d 13 (Ind. Ct. App. 1997) (when medical care was necessary, and debtor-wife's resources insufficient, remanded to trial court to determine husband's ability to pay); Ellis Hosp. v. Little, 409 N.Y.S.2d 459 (N.Y. App. Div. 1978) (social service law that imposes spousal liability provides exemption for homestead "essential and appropriate to the needs of the household" (N.Y. Soc. Serv. Law § 336 (McKinney)); fact question as to widow's ability to pay depends on value of her non-exempt real estate); MRI Coop. v. Berlin, 1993 WL 257078 (Ohio Ct. App. June 30, 1993) (wife liable under family expense statute if able to pay; remanded to determine ability to pay); Ohio State Univ. Med. Ctr. v. Calovini, 2002 WL 31953905 (Ohio Ct. Cl. Oct. 8, 2002) (wife not liable for husband's medical care; fulltime housewife with no independent means had no ability to pay).

674 St. Francis Reg'l Med. Ctr., Inc. v. Bowles, 251 Kan. 334, 836 P.2d 1123 (1992); Carlton at the Lake, Inc. v. Barber, 928 N.E.2d 1266 (Ill. App. Ct. 2010) (spouse's liability under necessaries statute is clearly dependent and reliant on patient's underlying liability; when contract was unenforceable as to patient, no liability for spouse). *But see* Porter Mem'l Hosp. v. Wozniak, 680 N.E.2d 13 (Ind. Ct. App. 1997)

Difficult problems may be created by divorce or separation.[675] In some states, separation is a defense,[676] but in others it is not.[677]

Divorce decrees often require one spouse to provide health insurance for the other and for the children. A spouse who fails to comply may be found to be a self-insurer for expenses which should have been covered.[678] Courts are divided on the question whether a spouse who provides the required level of coverage may nonetheless be liable for expenses not covered.[679]

In some states, there is familial duty of support that extends beyond spouses. This duty may impose joint and several liability on both parents of a minor child[680] or even secondary

(debtor-wife's discharge in bankruptcy did not eliminate husband's liability under doctrine of necessaries).

675 *See* CMRE Fin. Serv., Inc. v. Parton, 109 Cal. Rptr. 3d 139 (Cal. Ct. App. 2010) (California law provides that ex-spouse is not liable after divorce for individual debt of other spouse incurred during the marriage); Proctor Hosp. v. Taylor, 665 N.E.2d 872 (Ill. App. Ct. 1996) (Illinois's family support statute, 750 Ill. Comp. Stat. § 65/15(a)(3), imposed liability on non-custodial divorced parent for hospital bill of unemancipated minor child); Allen v. Keating, 517 N.W.2d 830 (Mich. Ct. App. 1994) (if spouses separated, burden on creditor to prove that non-debtor husband has failed to support wife; husband not liable if there is an adequate support order, or he has "otherwise provided adequate support"); Roach v. Mamakos, 764 N.Y.S.2d 539 (N.Y. Sup. Ct. 2003) (ex-husband not liable because alleged creditor, who was wife's father, failed to show that he expected to be paid, had sought payment from wife, and that she was unable to pay; also doctrine of necessaries inapplicable when support order defined husband's duty to support, or when separation was fault of debtor spouse); Prof'l Orthopedic & Sports P.T.P.C. v. Pittore, 959 N.Y.2d 92 (N.Y. City Ct. 2012) (ex-husband not liable for ex-wife's medical bill incurred three years after divorce, given that divorce decree absolved ex-husband from any obligations for ex-wife's medical care); Recovery Res. L.L.C. v. Cupido, 818 N.W.2d 787 (N.D. 2012) (ex-wife was jointly liable for ex-husband's medical debt incurred prior to their divorce, despite divorce judgment making ex-husband liable for the debt); Potter v. Karivalis, 718 A.2d 823 (Pa. Super. Ct. 1998) (gender-neutral statute upheld against constitutional challenge; incarcerated husband liable for wife's medical expenses under Pennsylvania necessaries statute); St. Mary's Hosp. Med. Ctr. v. Brody, 519 N.W.2d 706 (Wis. Ct. App. 1994) (ex-wife liable for husband's medical expenses incurred during the marriage, despite provision in divorce decree that husband should be responsible for those expenses).

676 *E.g.*, CMRE Fin. Serv., Inc. v. Parton, 109 Cal. Rptr. 3d 139 (Cal. Ct. App. 2010)(spouse is not liable for necessaries under California law if she was living apart from husband by agreement unless support is stipulated in that agreement); Yale Univ. Sch. of Med. v. Scianna, 701 A.2d 65 (Conn. Super. Ct. 1997) (when couple was separated and husband was paying support to wife, wife was not liable for husband's medical bills; Connecticut's poorly drafted necessaries statute construed to allow "separation defense" to all recipient spouses, that is, those who are receiving or entitled to receive support from "provider spouse"); Balyeat Collection Prof'ls v. Garland, 51 P.3d 1127 (Mont. 2002) (Montana statute provides exception if non-debtor has been abandoned by debtor, or if couple living separately by agreement; remanded for fact finding on abandonment when couple were going through divorce); Southern N.H. Med. Ctr. v. Hayes, 992 A.2d 596 (N.H. 2010) (if marriage has broken down to extent that spouses are no longer sharing assets or debts, spouse is not be liable for medical expenses); Roach v. Mamakos, 764 N.Y.S.2d 539 (Sup. Ct. 2003) (doctrine of necessaries inapplicable if support order defined husband's duty to support, or if separation was fault of debtor spouse); THC Piketon v. Edwards, 2007 WL 4305719 (Ohio Ct. App. Dec. 11, 2007) (no liability for spouse of patient if patient has abandoned spouse without cause).

677 *E.g.*, Queen's Med. Ctr. v. Kagawa, 967 P.2d 686 (Haw. 1998) (under gender-neutral spousal liability statute, wife was liable for husband's hospital bill, even though couple was in process of getting a divorce; case remanded to trial court to determine if each charge was necessary and reasonable); Bartrom v. Adjustment Bureau, 618 N.E.2d 1 (Ind. 1993) (non-debtor spouse has limited liability for necessaries, which continues regardless of separation, as long as a duty to support continues to exist; misconduct by the debtor spouse may eliminate non-debtor spouse's duty); Dignity Care Home v. Montgomery Ryan, 246 P.3d 413 (Kan. Ct. App. 2011)(spouse liable even after eight-year separation and post-nuptial agreement requiring spouses to handle their financial affairs separately); Forsyth Mem'l Hosp., Inc. v. Chisholm, 467 S.E.2d 88 (N.C. 1996) (separation not a defense when health care provider had no actual notice that spouses were separated; wife transported seriously ill husband to hospital and "admitted" him, without informing hospital of the separation); Home Helpers/Direct Link v. St. Pierre, 964 N.E.2d 41 (Ohio Ct. App. 2011) (spouse liable even though he had moved out of marital home and filed complaint for legal separation); Med. College of Wis. v. Missimer, 769 N.W.2d 878 (Wis. Ct. App. 2009) (spouse was liable for medical bills even though she was separated from patient and a divorce action was pending); Mercy Health Sys. Corp. v. Gauss, 639 N.W.2d 803 (Wis. Ct. App. 2001) (table) (text available at 2001 WL 1632549) (separation not a defense to medical debt of ex-wife incurred during marriage).

678 Ohio Rev. Code Ann. § 1349.01 (West) (ex-spouse who fails to provide court-ordered health insurance liable for uncovered medical bills); Blair v. Blair, 527 S.E.2d 177 (Ga. 2000); Tietjens v. Tietjens, 744 N.E.2d 1064 (Ind. Ct. App. 2001) (separation agreement, which became part of divorce decree, required husband to provide health insurance until couple mutually agreed it was no longer necessary; husband was liable for insurance premiums and for bills incurred while wife was uninsured).

679 *Compare In re* Dixon, 245 B.R. 367 (Bankr. W.D. Mo. 2000) (support order in divorce decree replaced husband's common law duty to support); Tietjens v. Tietjens, 744 N.E.2d 1064 (Ind. Ct. App. 2001) (when couple deleted from draft separation agreement the requirement that husband pay medical bills not covered by insurance, husband was not liable), *and* Roach v. Mamakos, 764 N.Y.S.2d 539 (N.Y. Sup. Ct. 2003) (doctrine of necessaries inapplicable if support order defined husband's duty to support, or if separation was fault of debtor spouse), *with* Sheppard Pratt Physicians, P.A. v. Sakwa, 725 So. 2d 755 (Miss. 1998) (common law duty to provide necessary medical care survived the divorce decree), *and* McLain v. W. Side Bone & Joint Ctr., 656 So. 2d 119 (Miss. 1995) (provider could recover from father even though he had complied with all medical insurance obligations of divorce decree; father's remedy was to seek divorce court order for reimbursement from mother).

680 Phillips v. Dodds, 867 N.E.2d 1122 (Ill. App. Ct. 2007) (aunt could liable for medical bills of niece under Illinois family expense statute when she accepted niece into her household and stood *in loco parentis*, even though aunt was not niece's legal guardian); Proctor Hosp. v. Taylor, 665 N.E.2d 872 (Ill. App. Ct. 1996) (Illinois family expense statute imposed liability on non-custodial divorced parent of unemancipated minor child); Schmidt v. Mut. Hosp. Servs., Inc., 832 N.E.2d 977 (Ind. Ct. App. 2005) (parents' duty to support child makes them liable for the child's medical bills even when parents had explicitly refused consent to treatment); Sheppard Pratt Physicians, Prof'l Ass'n v. Sakwa, 725 So. 2d 755 (Miss. 1998) (common law duty to support made non-custodial father, who had provided health insurance as required by divorce decree, liable for minor daughter's medical expenses not covered by insurance); McLain v. W. Side Bone & Joint Ctr., 656 So. 2d 119 (Miss. 1995) (non-custodial father who had complied with support order by providing health insurance for child liable for expenses not covered by insurance); Estate of Bonner, 954 S.W.2d 356 (Mo. Ct. App.

liability on adult children of an indigent parent.[681] One court has held that a necessaries statute imposing liability on adult children of patients is not preempted by the Nursing Home Reform Law,[682] which prohibits homes from requiring family or friends to become financially responsible for a patient's expenses.[683] A minor may be held liable for necessaries, and may be sued after reaching the age of majority, if the parents are shown to be unwilling or unable to provide them.[684]

9.7 Health Care Providers' Lien on Personal Injury Recoveries

9.7.1 General

Health care providers may be able to place a lien on a patient's tort recovery from the entity that caused the patient's injuries.[685] The amount of the lien may be regulated by statute.[686] State law will also prescribe substantive and procedural

1997) (conservatorship estate of incompetent mother was liable, under the doctrine of necessaries, for care provided to infant son); Brookdale Hosp. Med. Ctr. v. Lewis, 803 N.Y.S.2d 17 (table), 2005 WL 1792593 (N.Y. Civ. Ct. July 28, 2005) (non-custodial parent may be held liable for child's medical bills, even if the parent did not request the services, if parent has the financial ability and fails to support child).

681 *In re* Marriage of Leni, 50 Cal. Rptr. 3d 886 (Cal. Ct. App. 2006) (California imposes statutory duty to support indigent older parent, and such obligation becomes a community debt); Boe v. Dep't of Human Servs., 844 A.2d 531 (N.J. Super. Ct. App. Div. 2004) (even without statutory lien, which defeated patient's son's right of survivorship in jointly owned house, son was responsible relative who would be liable for mother's state hospital care), *vacated on other grounds*, 873 A.2d 500 (N.J. 2005) (statute adopted extinguishing liens against persons treated at psychiatric facility); Four Seasons Healthcare Ctr. v. Linderkamp, 837 N.W.2d 147 (N.D. 2013) (adult children liable for parents' necessaries, here nursing home care); Presbyterian Med. Ctr. v. Budd, 832 A.2d 1066 (Pa. Super. Ct. 2003) (nursing home stated claim against adult daughter under Pennsylvania statute that requires adult children "of sufficient ability" to support "indigent" parents); Landmark Med. Ctr. v. Gauthier, 635 A.2d 1145 (R.I. 1994); Accounts Mgmt., Inc. v. Nelson, 663 N.W.2d 237 (S.D. 2003) (deceased father not indigent within meaning of family support statute when estate contained sufficient funds to pay bill; hospital that failed to make timely claim on estate could not sue adult children); Prairie Lakes Healthcare Sys., Inc. v. Wookey, 583 N.W.2d 405 (S.D. 1998) (South Dakota statute makes adult child responsible for support of indigent parent, if adult child is financially able). *Cf.* Vencor, Inc. v. Gray, 66 P.3d 323 (table), 2003 WL 329248 (Mont. Feb. 14, 2003) (healthcare provider had no standing to sue under statute requiring adult child to support indigent parent; only the county or the parent could sue; but note that statute makes promise to pay for parents' necessaries binding).

682 Eades v. Kennedy, P.C. Law Offices, 2013 WL 6241272 (W.D.N.Y. Dec. 3, 2013) (NHRL does not preempt Pennsylvania statute requiring adult children of indigent parent to be responsible for necessaries).

683 *See* § 9.3.6, *supra*.

684 Williams v. Baptist Health Sys., Inc., 857 So. 2d 149 (Ala. Civ. App. 2003) (parents primarily liable, child secondarily liable; when mother's bankruptcy showed inability to pay, daughter's wages could be garnished after majority); *In re* Estate of Reed, 201 P.3d 1264 (Colo. App. 2008) (if parent cannot or will not pay for necessaries, including medical care, the provider can seek to recover against child in *quantum meruit*); Yale Diagnostic Radiology v. Estate of Harun Fountain, 838 A.2d 179 (Conn. 2004) (minor is liable in *quantum meruit* for necessaries such as medical care; parent is primarily liable but, if parent cannot or will not pay, minor is liable; when parent's debts discharged in bankruptcy, hospital could reach estate created by minor's personal injury recovery); Woodberry v. Hammond Lumber Co., 2003 WL 1665251 (Me. Super. Ct. Mar. 10, 2003) (child will be liable for cost of medical care if parents unable or unwilling to provide it); Schmidt v. Prince George's Hosp., 784 A.2d 1112 (Md. 2001) (eighteen-year-old could be sued for emergency treatment provided when she was sixteen; parents' unwillingness to pay shown by father's receiving and spending Blue Cross check, instead of forwarding it to provider); Layton Physical Therapy Co. v. Palozzi, 777 N.E.2d 306 (Ohio Ct. App. 2002) (if parents do not pay for necessaries, here medical care, minor child secondarily liable in quasi-contract); Dallas Cnty. Hosp. Dist. v. Wiley *ex rel.* Wiley, 2002 WL 1286515 (Tex. App. June 12, 2002) (hospital could sue minor "by and through" his parent for minor's medical expenses). *Cf. In re* Marshall, 634 N.W.2d 300 (Neb. Ct. App. 2001) (hospital's necessaries claim against child not decided on merits because time-barred); State *ex rel.* Packard v. Perry, 655 S.E.2d 548 (W. Va. 2007) (minor may be responsible for his or her own medical expenses under West Virginia doctrine of necessaries).

685 Mercado v. Allstate Ins. Co., 340 F.3d 824 (9th Cir. 2003) (not a UDAP violation for insurer to require that county and lawyer be co-payees of settlement check, when county that provided medical care entitled to a lien, and lawyer had already filed one); *Ex parte* Univ. of S. Ala., 761 So. 2d 240 (Ala. Civ. App. 1999) (analyzing Alabama's hospital lien statute); Alaska Native Tribal Health Consortium v. Settlement Funds Held for or to Be Paid on Behalf of E.R. *ex rel.* Ridley, 84 P.3d 418 (Alaska 2004) (hospital that provided free care to Alaska natives could place lien on tort recoveries); McMeans v. Med. Liabilities Recoveries, Inc., 2002 WL 31835746 (Cal. Ct. App. Dec. 19, 2002) (unpublished) (detailed discussion of California lien law); Kenneth F. White, Chartered v. St. Alphonsus Reg'l Med. Ctr., 31 P.3d 926 (Idaho Ct. App. 2001) (hospital lien took priority over attorney fees); Marquez v. Progressive Ins. Co., 944 So. 2d 876 (La. Ct. App. 2006) (Louisiana law entitles hospital to entirety of insurance proceeds, leaving nothing for accident victim); Marvin's Midtown Chiropractic Clinic, Inc. v. State Farm Mut. Auto. Ins. Co., 142 S.W.3d 751 (Mo. Ct. App. 2004) (enforcing lien agreement that chiropractor required of accident victims); Wyant v. Kenda, 102 P.3d 1260 (Mont. 2004) (tortfeasor's insurer acted permissibly when it named lienor-chiropractor as co-payee of settlement check); Bergan Mercy Health Sys. v. Haven, 620 N.W.2d 339 (Neb. 2000) (hospital lien statute not unconstitutional "special legislation," and is not overridden by more general statute providing exemption for personal injury recoveries); Broadway Clinic v. Liberty Mut. Ins. Co., 139 P.3d 873 (Okla. 2006) (Oklahoma physician's lien statute allows recovery from both patient's own automobile insurance policy as well as tortfeasor's insurance); Hermann Hosp. v. Martinez, 990 S.W.2d 476 (Tex. App. 1999) (hospital lien is valid against recovery on any claim brought by injured person "which is attributed to the negligence of another"); Riegleman v. Krieg, 679 N.W.2d 857 (Wis. Ct. App. 2004) ("doctor's lien" document signed by patient and attorney was valid contract). *But cf.* Holeton v. Crouse Cartage Co., 748 N.E.2d 1111 (Ohio 2001) (workers' compensation subrogation statute was unconstitutional when it allowed fund to reach personal injury recovery even if victim was not made whole and allowed the fund to reach recoveries of third parties, that is, parents and adult children in death cases). *See generally* Daniel L. Saar, *Blindsided (Again): Iowa Hospitals' Abuse of the Hospital Lien Statute and What Has Been Done To Correct It*, 56 Drake L. Rev. 463 (2008); C. Crocca, Annotation, *Construction, Operation, and Effect of Statutes Giving Hospital Lien Against Recovery from Tortfeasor Causing Patient's Injuries*, 16 A.L.R.5th 262 (1993).

686 *See* 770 Ill. Comp. Stat. § 23/10(a) (limiting the total amount of all provider liens to 40% of the patient's recovery); HealthOne, Inc. v. Columbia Wesley Med. Ctr., 93 F. Supp. 2d 1152 (D. Kan. 2000) (Kansas hospital lien act allows lien for up to $5000; any additional amounts are subject to "equitable distribution" of settlement amount);

requirements, and a provider's failure to comply will invalidate the lien.[687] In some cases, a provider's claim will not fall within the scope of the state law.[688]

The lien may be reduced if the patient can show unreasonableness.[689] Other courts, however, have held that liens for full "chargemaster" prices[690] did not violate state UDAP laws.[691] Other issues likely to arise are the scope of the trial court's power to apportion the recovery, or limit further collection action by the health care creditor, and whether the provider's share of a common fund should be reduced by the pro-rated share of attorney fees and other costs.[692]

Cullimore v. St. Anthony Med. Ctr., Inc., 718 N.E.2d 1221 (Ind. Ct. App. 1999) (Indiana hospital lien statute provides that if recovery not sufficient to pay all liens, amount will be proportioned pro rata, leaving enough for patient to get 20%; court held that underlying debt is not extinguished and hospital may sue patient for the balance); King Cnty. Rehab, L.L.C. v. Clackamas Cnty., 164 P.3d 1190 (Or. Ct. App. 2007) (long term care provider's lien limited to cost of care under statute and did not extend to attorney fees for collection); Daughters of Charity Health Servs. v. Linnstaedter, 226 S.W.3d 409 (Tex. 2007) (worker's compensation insurer reimbursed hospital; labor code barred hospital from filing property code lien against tort recovery from at-fault driver). *See also* Shelter Mut. Ins. Co. v. Kennedy, 60 S.W.3d 458 (Ark. 2001) (insurance company not entitled to subrogation when accident victim not made whole by tort settlement; victim had continuing medical problems and would require future treatment).

687 *E.g.*, *In re* Pratt, 2000 Bankr. LEXIS 94 (B.A.P. 10th Cir. Feb. 15, 2000) (lien filed by physician for certain itemized amounts "up to the final balance" was good only as to the itemized amounts); *In re* Norton, 248 B.R. 131 (Bankr. W.D. Wis. 2000) (financial responsibility form, which required patient to pay provider out of proceeds of any settlement, was merely a promise to pay, not an explicit assignment, and thus did not create lien); *In re* Woodward, 234 B.R. 519 (Bankr. N.D. Okla. 1999) (hospital liens not perfected at time of bankruptcy filing; detailed discussion of Oklahoma procedural requirements for hospital liens); *Ex parte* Infinity S. Ins. Co., 737 So. 2d 463 (Ala. 1999) (failure to strictly comply with statute invalidated hospital lien, but hospital was free to sue patient); San Bernardino v. Calderon, 56 Cal. Rptr. 3d 333 (Cal. Ct. App. 2007) (hospital's lien did not become effective until it gave notice as required under statute); Mares v. Baughman, 112 Cal. Rptr. 2d 264 (Cal. Ct. App. 2001) (California statute allowing county that provided medical services a lien against "judgments" does not authorize a lien on a settlement); Wilson v. F.B. McAfoos & Co., 800 N.E.2d 177 (Ill. App. Ct. 2003) (physician's lien not assignable; statutory creation, unknown to common law, must be narrowly construed); Anderson v. Dep't of Mental Health & Developmental Disabilities, 711 N.E.2d 1170 (Ill. App. Ct. 1999) (no lien for Department of Mental Health, when it failed to prove causal connection between treatment it gave and injuries for which patient sued tortfeasor); Via Christi Reg'l Med. Ctr., Inc. v. Reed, 314 P.3d 852 (Kan. 2013) (strict compliance with Kansas hospital lien statute necessary for effective and enforceable lien); Sam v. Direct Gen. Ins. Co., 951 So. 2d 482 (La. Ct. App. 2007) (providers who failed to comply with procedural requirements of Louisiana lien statute were not entitled to a share of the tort recovery); Neb. Health Sys. v. Bear (*In re* Marshall), 634 N.W.2d 300 (Neb. Ct. App. 2001) ("substantial compliance" required; not shown when hospital failed to provide required notices to tortfeasor and court, so lien never perfected). *But see In re* Brown, 2007 WL 2029498 (Bankr. D. Kan. July 10, 2007) (hospital's lien attached to settlement funds, notwithstanding the failure of the lien statements to name (and the failure to serve) all of the parties identified); Andrews v. Samaritan Health Sys., 36 P.3d 57 (Ariz. Ct. App. 2001) (untimely recording did not invalidate lien); Stephens v. Parkview Hosp., Inc., 745 N.E.2d 262 (Ind. Ct. App. 2001) (hospital lien valid even though required notice sent to wrong attorney; victim's attorney had actual notice, so no prejudice); Baker v. Iowa Methodist Med. Ctr., 542 N.W.2d 847 (Iowa 1996) (hospital's failure to comply with notice requirement did not hamper ability to enforce lien); St. Francis Hosp. v. Vaughn, 971 P.2d 401 (Okla. Civ. App. 1998) (hospital lien was timely and valid when attorney received notice of lien after insurance company mailed settlement check but before attorney received and deposited check).

688 *In re* Pratt, 2000 Bankr. LEXIS 94 (B.A.P. 10th Cir. Feb. 15, 2000) (Oklahoma physicians' lien statute strictly construed; does not allow medical corporation to file physician's lien); Weston Reid, L.L.C. v. Am. Ins. Group, Inc., 94 Cal. Rptr. 3d 748 (Cal. Ct. App. 2009) (hospital lien statute did not apply to proceeds from patient's own insurance for uninsured motorist coverage; only allows lien encumbering third-party coverage); *In re* Estate of Reed, 201 P.3d 1264 (Colo. App. 2008) (provider obtained lien against parents, but lien did not encumber child's estate, in this case child's tort recovery); St. Anthony's Med. Ctr. v. Metze, 23 S.W.3d 692 (Mo. Ct. App. 2000) (Missouri hospital lien statute did not allow lien against proceeds of wrongful death action, which benefited the survivors, not the estate); Quality Chiropractic, P.C. v. Farmers Ins. Co., 51 P.3d 1172 (N.M. Ct. App. 2002) (New Mexico statute allows lien by hospital but not individual providers, so court refuses to enforce "irrevocable lien and assignment" signed by patient as condition of receiving treatment); Dallas Cnty. Hosp. Dist. v. Wiley *ex rel.* Wiley, 2002 WL 1286515 (Tex. App. June 12, 2002) (hospital lien statute does not apply to proceeds of "an insurance policy in favor of the injured individual or the injured individual's beneficiary"; no lien against proceeds of action against minor patient's father's uninsured motorist insurance carrier, but *quantum meruit* claim allowed to go forward).

689 McMeans v. Med. Liabilities Recoveries, Inc., 2002 WL 31835746 (Cal. Ct. App. Dec. 19, 2002) (unpublished) (when hospital permitted to place lien despite payment by insurer, amount of lien limited to reasonable value of necessary services); Phillips v. DeCarlo, 705 N.E.2d 113 (Ill. App. Ct. 1998) (trial court should have allowed patient to present evidence of unreasonableness; remanded for evidentiary hearing); Temesvary v. Houdek, 703 N.E.2d 613 (Ill. App. Ct. 1998) (unreasonableness not proven when patient's expert not familiar with the differences between freestanding nuclear medicine center and hospital and when lienor sufficiently explained basis for calculation of fees); Via Christi Reg'l Med. Ctr., Inc. v. Reed, 314 P.3d 852 (Kan. 2013) (hospital only entitled to lien on reasonable and necessary charges; permitting UDAP claim against hospital for inflated charges and duplicate charges in asserting lien); Riegleman v. Krieg, 679 N.W.2d 857 (Wis. Ct. App. 2004) (treatment was necessary and charges reasonable; independent medical examination concluded that it was not, but court, which heard evidence from provider and patient, found otherwise).

690 *See* § 9.1.3, *supra* (discussion of discriminatory pricing and difference between chargemaster prices versus prices paid by most insurers).

691 *See, e.g.*, Geico Indem. Ins. Co. v. Kannaday, 2007 WL 2990552 (D. Kan. Oct. 11, 2007); Univ. of S. Ala. Hosps. v. Blackmon, 42 So. 3d 1258 (Ala. Civ. App. 2009) (patient failed to establish that hospital's charges were unreasonable; reversing decision of trial court in reducing hospital's award); Roberts v. Univ. of Ala. Hosp., 27 So. 2d 512 (Ala. Civ. App. 2008); Galvan v. Northwestern Mem'l Hosp., 888 N.E.2d 529 (Ill. App. Ct. 2008).

692 *See* Howe *ex rel.* Howe v. Scottsdale Ins. Co., 204 F.3d 624 (5th Cir. 2000) (hospital which claimed statutory lien on tort recovery not required to contribute to attorney fees and costs of tort action); Iron Workers Locals 40, 361 and 417 Health Fund v. Dinnigan, 911 F. Supp. 2d 243 (S.D.N.Y. 2012) (enforcing subrogation clause under ERISA but reducing payment by 25% to account for attorney fees); Mitchell v. Kaiser Found. Health Plan, Inc., 2010 WL 5387712 (N.D. Cal. Dec. 22, 2010) (California law provides for common fund rule, but failure to reduce medical bill to account for rule did not give rise to RICO claim); IBEW-NECA Southwestern Health & Benefit Fund v. Gurule, 337 F. Supp. 2d 845 (N.D.

9.7.2 *Hospitals' Ability to Seek a Lien After Receipt of Insurance Payment*

Some providers may seek to place a lien on a tort recovery, even though the services provided were covered by the patient's HMO or insurance plan (which will pay substantially less than the gross charges or list price).[693] Some courts have disapproved this practice, reasoning that once the patient authorizes payment from the HMO, he or she owes no debt to the provider.[694] Other courts, however, have allowed a hospital a lien for the difference between the HMO reimbursement and its customary charges.[695]

Tex. 2004) (ERISA preempted New Mexico statute requiring liens to be reduced by pro rata share of attorney fees); Fairfield Mfg. Co. v. Hartman, 132 F. Supp. 2d 1142 (N.D. Ind. 2001) (provision of ERISA agreement allowing subrogation, and making beneficiary responsible for all expenses of recovery including attorney fees, not unconscionable; plan not required to pay share of attorney fees); HealthOne, Inc. v. Columbia Wesley Med. Ctr., 93 F. Supp. 2d 1152 (D. Kan. 2000) (hospital lien is junior to attorney's lien, and priority cannot be defeated by prior assignment); Alaska Native Tribal Health Consortium v. Settlement Funds Held for or to Be Paid on Behalf of E.R. *ex rel.* Ridley, 84 P.3d 418 (Alaska 2004) (hospital that provided free care to Alaska natives could place lien on tort recoveries; amount must be reduced by pro rata share of attorney fees); Gilman v. Dolby, 98 Cal. Rptr. 3d 231 (Cal. Ct. App. 2009) (attorney lien for costs would have priority over an earlier medical lien); Trevino v. HHL Fin. Servs., Inc., 945 P.2d 1345 (Colo. 1997) (assignee of health care debt could file lien against tort settlement; no reduction for its share of fees and costs); Holland v. State Farm Mut. Auto. Ins. Co., 513 S.E.2d 48 (Ga. Ct. App. 1999) (lien for accident victim's attorney fees took priority over hospital and Medicaid reimbursement liens; except for this exception, hospital and welfare department took entire amount of plaintiff's recovery); Kenneth F. White, Chartered v. St. Alphonsus Reg'l Med. Ctr., 31 P.3d 926 (Idaho Ct. App. 2001) (hospital lien took priority over attorney fees; no attorney's lien when attorney negotiated settlement without filing suit; common fund doctrine did not apply); Wendling v. Southern Illinois Hosp. Servs., 950 N.E.2d 646 (Ill. 2011) (hospital's statutory lien was not subject to reduction for prorated share of patients' attorney fees pursuant to common fund doctrine); Cullimore v. St. Anthony Med. Ctr., Inc., 718 N.E.2d 1221 (Ind. Ct. App. 1999) (Indiana hospital lien statute provides that if recovery not sufficient to pay all liens, amount will be proportioned pro rata, leaving enough for patient to get 20%; court held that underlying debt is not extinguished and hospital may sue patient for the balance); Marquez v. Progressive Ins. Co., 944 So. 2d 876 (La. Ct. App. 2006) (under Louisiana law, attorney's lien has precedence over hospital's lien); Wyant v. Kenda, 102 P.3d 1260 (Mont. 2004) (under Montana law, healthcare lien may not be reduced by amount of attorney fees; note however that attorney's lien takes priority over healthcare lien); Eaton Martinez & Hart v. Univ. Hosp., 934 P.2d 270 (N.M. 1997) (public hospital's lien would not be reduced by its share of costs; court noted that result might be different for private hospital); Martino v. Dyer, 2000 Tenn. App. LEXIS 764 (Tenn. Ct. App. Nov. 22, 2000) (when personal injury judgment sufficient to pay both hospital and attorney, hospital liens should not be reduced by its share of attorney fees; statute giving priority to attorney's lien applied only when proceeds insufficient to go around).

693 *See* § 9.1.3, *supra*.

694 Satsky v. United States, 993 F. Supp. 1027 (S.D. Tex. 1998) (no debt, no lien; hospital that had accepted discounted payment from insurer as "payment in full" could not place lien on personal injury recovery); Parnell v. Adventist Health Sys./West, 109 P.3d 69 (Cal. 2005) (provider who agreed to accept insurer's reimbursement as "payment in full" for medical services could not assert lien on patient's tort recovery, despite state law permitting lien, because patient did not owe debt to provider); Rutherford v. Ralph Hutton & Assocs., 2004 WL 1119676 (Cal. Ct. App. May 20, 2004) (unpublished) (hospital's balance billing by attempting to enforce lien against personal injury recovery was forbidden by hospital's contract with county government program to provide medical care to indigent and uninsured patients); Gianetti v. Siglinger, 900 A.2d 520 (Conn. 2006) (health plan agreement and Connecticut law forbade balance billing; affirming trial court's award of $26,000 and attorney fees of $40,000 under Connecticut UDAP statute for physician's repeated violation of both agreement and law) Lopez v. Morley, 817 N.E.2d 592 (Ill. App. Ct. 2004) (lien not permitted but court notes that hospital's contract could have provided that insurance payment would not extinguish debt); N.C. by L.C. v. A.W. by R.W., 713 N.E.2d 775 (Ill. App. Ct. 1999) (lien was void when automobile accident victim was covered by HMO, which paid hospital the sum agreed upon in contract between hospital and HMO; no lien can exist when there is no underlying debt and patient's debt was extinguished by HMO's payment to hospital); Howard v. Willis-Knighton Med. Ctr., 924 So. 2d 1245 (La. Ct. App. 2006) (certifying classes of insured patients who were charged full list prices instead of discount prices negotiated by their insurers when hospital placed lien on their tort recoveries); Morgan v. St. Luke's Hosp. of Kansas City, 403 S.W.3d 115 (Mo. Ct. App. 2013) (prohibiting lien against tort recovery when hospital had contract with patient's insurer and had been paid contract amount; patient no longer owed debt to hospital); Midwest Neurosurgery, P.C. v. State Farm Ins. Companies, 686 N.W.2d 572 (Neb. 2004) (when provider had agreed with HMO to accept specific amount, this was the "amount due"; provider could not place lien on personal injury recovery for its undiscounted bill; note that this depended on precise wording of the contract provisions); West v. Shelby Cnty. Healthcare Corp., 2013 WL 500777 (Tenn. Ct. App. Feb. 11, 2013) (hospital that accepted payment from Medicaid and private insurers for treatment of accident victims could not place lien on victim's recovery from tortfeasor, because victim no longer owed debt to hospital); Dorr v. Sacred Heart Hosp., 597 N.W.2d 462 (Wis. Ct. App. 1999) (lien was void when auto accident victim was covered by HMO, and contract between the hospital and the HMO, as well as a provision of state statute, forbade the hospital to bill the patient for services covered by HMO; patient who alleged this practice had stated sufficient facts to support state UDAP and racketeering claims). *See also* MCG Health, Inc. v. Owners Ins. Co., 707 S.E.2d 349 (Ga. 2011) (hospital permitted to seek lien even if insurer paid medical bill; absence of debt did not preclude lien but patient's insurer—-U.S. Department of Defense TRICARE program—prohibited hospital from seeking to collect on lien); Daughters of Charity Health Servs. v. Linnstaedter, 226 S.W.3d 409 (Tex. 2007) (when workers' compensation insurer reimbursed hospital, labor code limits on charges barred hospital from filing property code lien against tort recovery from at-fault driver).

695 Samsel v. Allstate Ins. Co., 59 P.3d 281 (Ariz. 2002) (medical expenses paid by HMO are "actually incurred" within meaning of automobile insurance policy when, although hospital cannot bill patient, it has lien on tort recovery for its full charges); Andrews v. Samaritan Health Sys., 36 P.3d 57 (Ariz. Ct. App. 2001) (allowing lien despite "paid in full" language in the HMO contract, when the hospital contract reserved the right of recourse against third parties and a state statute allowed a hospital lien for customary charges); Whiteside v. Tenet Healthcare Corp., 124 Cal. Rptr. 2d 580 (Cal. Ct. App. 2002) (hospital that was reimbursed by one insurance company at preferred provider rate could recover from patient's second insurance policy for difference between that and regular rate; contract forbade billing the patient but specifically permitted billing third-party payers); MCG Health, Inc. v. Knight, 750 S.E.2d 813 (Ga. Ct. App. 2013) (hospital had valid lien on patient's tort recovery, despite insurer's payment, because state law did not require an underlying debt for effective lien, and insurer's contract did not prohibit balance billing); Rogalla v. Christie Clinic, P.C., 794 N.E.2d 384 (Ill. App. Ct. 2003) (disagreeing with N.C. by L.C. v. A.W. by R.W., 713 N.E.2d 775 (Ill. App. Ct. 1999)); provider entitled to seek lien against patient's tort recovery under Illinois Physician Lien Act despite agreement with insurer that provider could not seek payment from patients other than co-payments and deductibles); Richmond *ex rel.* Richmond v. Caban, 754 N.E.2d 871 (Ill. App. Ct. 2001) (hospital could choose whether to bill HMO or place lien on

The outcome of these cases may turn on the precise wording of the contract between the provider and the insurer. State laws that prohibit providers from balance billing patients with private insurance may also limit the ability of a hospital to assert claims against a tort recovery.[696] However, Medicare balance billing prohibitions no longer appear to prohibit provider liens; and in fact, guidelines issued by the Centers for Medicare & Medicaid not only permit this practice, they allow the provider to charge full chargemaster rates instead of Medicare rates.[697]

9.7.3 *Liens by Insurers or Third-Party Payers*

Many HMOs or employee benefit plans include subrogation clauses allowing them to reach a member's tort recovery,[698] even if the recovery is grossly insufficient to compensate the victim—as in the familiar case in which the costs of a lawsuit and the tortfeasor's lack of non-exempt assets mandate a settlement for insurance policy limits.[699] Similarly, Medicaid and Medicare have the right to place a lien on the tort recoveries of their beneficiaries.[700] Some clauses even allow the plan to recover more than it spent, for example by placing a lien for the chargemaster rate, even though it pays the provider a discounted rate.[701] Other subrogation arrangements consist of insurers who characterize their payments of a patient's medical bills as a "loan" to the patient.[702] State laws that forbid or limit subrogation[703] may not apply to employee benefit plans, because of preemption by the Employee Retirement Income Security Act (ERISA),[704] or Medicaid and Medicare statutes giving those programs lien rights.[705] ERISA in fact provides employee benefit plans with a cause of action to enforce subrogation provisions.[706]

---

tort recovery; note however that lien may be invalid under provision of HMO statute that forbids provider to have recourse against plan members for anything except co-pays, deductibles and non-covered services; open question regarding interaction between HMO statute and lien statute).

696 *See* § 9.3.7, *supra*.

697 Bogolia v. Danielson, 978 N.E.2d 756 (Ind. Ct. App. 2012) (concurrence; citing Medicare Secondary Payer (MSP) Manual, ch. 2, § 40.2(D)).

698 A claim for subrogation under one of these clauses may be considered a "debt" under the Fair Debt Collection Practices Act. Hamilton v. United Health Care of La., Inc., 310 F.3d 385 (5th Cir. 2002), *later op. at* Hamilton v. Trover Solutions, Inc., 2003 WL 21105100 (E.D. La. May 13, 2003) (subrogation collection company not a debt collector, because debts not delinquent when it obtains them), *aff'd*, 104 Fed. Appx. 942 (5th Cir. 2004). *But see* Mitchell v. Kaiser Found. Health Plan, Inc., 2010 WL 5387712 (N.D. Cal. Dec. 22, 2010) (medical bills sent by insurer claiming lien was not debt under FDCPA because plaintiff failed to allege that amount was in default).

699 *See, e.g.*, Iron Workers Locals 40, 361 and 417 Health Fund v. Dinnigan, 911 F. Supp. 2d 243 (S.D.N.Y. 2012) (enforcing subrogation clause that provided plan would be paid first, whether or not victim was made whole, but reducing payment by 25% to account for attorney fees); Administrative Comm. for Wal-Mart Stores, Inc. Associates' Welfare Plan v. Salazar, 525 F. Supp. 2d 1103 (D. Ariz. 2007) (ERISA permitted plan to recover from personal injury recovery, even though result was that plan was made whole and accident victim was not); IBEW-NECA Southwestern Health & Benefit Fund v. Gurule, 337 F. Supp. 2d 845 (N.D. Tex. 2004) (subrogation clause provided that plan would be paid first, whether or not victim was made whole, and without regard to any allocation of funds by court); Franks v. Prudential Health Care Plan, 164 F. Supp. 2d 865 (W.D. Tex. 2001); *In re* Carpenter, 252 B.R. 905 (E.D. Va. 2000), *aff'd*, 2002 WL 1162277 (4th Cir. June 3, 2002).

However, if the subrogation clause in an ERISA plan does not give the insurer the right of first reimbursement, the insurer's recovery may be limited by the common law make-whole rule. Barnes v. Indep. Automobile Dealers Ass'n, 64 F.3d 1389 (9th Cir. 1995).

700 *See* § 9.3.7, *supra*.

701 *See, e.g.*, Reinhart Cos. Employee Benefit Plan v. Vial, 2011 WL 976505 (W.D. Mich. Mar. 17, 2011) (subrogation provision provided that payment for medical services constitutes an advancement of health plan's assets, and plan had priority to receive repayment out of tort recovery); Franks v. Prudential Health Care Plan, 164 F. Supp. 2d 865 (W.D. Tex. 2001) (consumer failed to state cause of action in complaint alleging this practice); Rogalla v. Christie Clinic, Prof'l Corp., 794 N.E.2d 384 (Ill. App. Ct. 2003) (HMO entitled to lien on patient's personal injury recovery for more than it paid for patient's share of monthly capitation, that is, flat fee, that HMO paid to provider). *But see* Swanson v. St. John's Reg'l Med. Ctr., 118 Cal. Rptr. 2d 325 (Cal. Ct. App. 2002) (California statute limits HMO liens to the amount actually paid to the provider), *overruled on other grounds by* Parnell v. Adventist Health Sys./West, 109 P.3d 69 (Cal. 2005).

702 *See, e.g.*, Flores v. Rawlings Co., 117 Haw. 153 (Haw. 2008).

703 *See, e.g.*, N.Y. Gen. Oblig. L. § 5-335(a) (limiting subrogation); 75 Pa. Cons. Stat. § 1720 (prohibiting insurer subrogation in tort recoveries involving motor vehicles); Va. Code Ann. § 38.2-3405; Shelter Mut. Ins. Co. v. Kennedy, 347 Ark. 184, 60 S.W.3d 458 (Ark. 2001) (insurance company not entitled to subrogation when accident victim not made whole by tort settlement); Wheat v. Blue Cross of Cal., 2002 Cal. App. Unpub. LEXIS 448 (Cal. Ct. App. Apr. 29, 2002) (insurer not entitled to subrogation when accident victim not made whole, and its suit seeking reimbursement may amount to malicious prosecution); Martinez v. Milburn Enters., Inc., 233 P.3d 205 (Kan. 2010) (K.A.R 40-1-20 provides that insurer shall not issue contracts of insurance containing a subrogation clause).

Note that state law on this subject varies widely; when the Maryland supreme court in Riemer v. Columbia Med. Plan, 747 A.2d 677 (Md. 2000), construed a state statute to forbid subrogation, the legislature immediately amended the statute to permit it.

704 29 U.S.C. § 1144(a); FMC Corp. v. Holliday, 498 U.S. 52, 111 S. Ct. 403, 112 L. Ed. 2d 356 (1990); Wirth v. Aetna U.S. Healthcare, 469 F.3d 305 (3d Cir. 2006); Iron Workers Locals 40, 361 and 417 Health Fund v. Dinnigan, 911 F. Supp. 2d 243 (S.D.N.Y. 2012) (ERISA preempts N.Y. statute limiting subrogation); State Farm Mut. Auto Ins. Co. v. Smith, 342 F. Supp. 2d 541 (W.D. Va. 2004) (ERISA preempts Virginia anti-subrogation statute but only for health insurance plans that are self-funded); Franks v. Prudential Health Care Plan, 164 F. Supp. 2d 865 (W.D. Tex. 2001); *In re* Carpenter, 252 B.R. 905 (E.D. Va. 2000), *aff'd*, 2002 WL 1162277 (4th Cir. June 3, 2002) (unpublished). *But see* Singh v. Prudential Health Care Plan, Inc., 335 F.3d 278 (4th Cir. 2003) (Maryland law prohibiting subrogation was saved from preemption as regulation on insurance; Maryland law subsequently amended to permit subrogation); Bishop v. Burgard, 764 N.E.2d 24 (Ill. 2002) (ERISA does not preempt Illinois's common fund doctrine when ERISA plan seeks to enforce lien on personal injury proceeds, pursuant to subrogation clause in plan; lien reduced by plan's share of attorney fees).

705 *See, e.g.*, Meek-Horton v. Trover Solutions, Inc., 915 F. Supp. 2d 486 (S.D.N.Y. 2013) (New York statute limiting subrogation preempted by Medicare Secondary Payer Act).

706 Sereboff v. Mid Atl. Med. Serv., 547 U.S. 356, 126 S. Ct. 1869 (2006); Iron Workers Locals 40, 361 and 417 Health Fund v. Dinnigan, 911 F. Supp. 2d 243 (S.D.N.Y. 2012) (self-insured plan could recover against tort recoveries of beneficiaries pursuant to ERISA provision permitting equitable relief); Trustees of Teamsters Local 443 Health Servs. & Ins. Plan v. Papero, 485 F. Supp. 2d 67 (D. Conn. 2007) (employee benefit plan could proceed with ERISA claim against patient's personal injury attorney, because attorney may be a fiduciary under ERISA and thus liable to the plan for retaining tort recovery funds).

Chapter 10 Defending Consumers Against Collection by Federal Administrative Agencies

10.1 Debt Collection Powers of the Federal Government

10.1.1 The Federal Government's Administrative and Judicial Debt Collection Powers

In recent decades, Congress has passed numerous laws to strengthen the tools available to the United States when it has a claim against a person. Many in Congress believed that this would help reduce the large budget deficits facing the federal government. Unfortunately much of the increased federal debt collection effort hit financially distressed and low-income households who had been the intended beneficiaries of federal student loan and housing programs and who did not have the resources to repay the claims of the United States, much less balance the federal budget.

Federal agencies have extensive extrajudicial collection powers, governed primarily by the Federal Claims Collection Act, as amended by the Debt Collection Improvement Act,[1] and a host of regulations. Pursuant to these statutes and regulations, the Treasury Department administers a centralized program, the Treasury Offset Program or TOP, to offset claims against tax refunds and other government payments. It also coordinates centralized collection efforts for debts referred to its "cross-servicing" program by creditor agencies. The statute also authorizes imposition of interest, administrative charges, and penalties, reporting the debt to credit reporting agencies, administratively garnishing wages, offsetting the debt against a federal employee's salary, and hiring private collection agencies and collection attorneys. These non-judicial collection powers are discussed in § 10.2, *infra*.

Given the breadth of the government's non-litigation debt collection powers, many claims never proceed to litigation. When the government does litigate a claim, the suit is governed by the Federal Debt Collection Procedures Act (the "Procedures Act").[2] Litigation under the Procedures Act is discussed in § 10.3, *infra*.

10.1.2 The Federal Government's Collection of State Debts

By statute, the federal government makes its non-judicial collection powers available to collect delinquent debts of certain types owed to states. It makes offset of federal tax refunds available to states as a means of collecting delinquent state income tax and child support obligations as well as unemployment compensation debts incurred through fraud or failure to report earnings.[3] The Treasury Department will also offset child support debts against other types of federal payments.[4] In addition, statute allows the Secretary of the Treasury to enter into reciprocal agreements with states to collect debts owed to states by offsetting them against federal payments.[5] The Treasury Department publishes an annual report showing the amounts collected for the states under each of these programs.[6]

States may also have non-judicial collection powers pursuant to state statutes. Advocates should be alert for attempts by state agencies to go beyond the scope of these statutes or to ignore other restrictions—such as the federal restrictions on the amount of a person's wages that can be garnished[7]—when they use these collection powers.

10.2 Federal Agencies' Non-Litigation Collection Methods

10.2.1 Overview of Federal Collection Laws and Regulations

10.2.1.1 Federal Collection Statutes

The extrajudicial collection of debts by United States administrative agencies is governed primarily by the Federal Claims Collection Act.[8] The Act requires federal agencies to attempt to collect overdue obligations. It also permits those agencies to settle, suspend, terminate collection activity on, or discharge claims when appropriate.

The Claims Collection Act was amended in October 1982 by the Debt Collection Act of 1982.[9] The Debt Collection Act toughened the debt collection and debt prevention procedures available to federal agencies. In particular, it permitted the release to commercial credit reporting agencies of obligors' names, addresses, and amounts owing.[10] It also made IRS information about debtors' addresses available to agencies for collection purposes.[11] Later amendments allowed agencies to

1 31 U.S.C. §§ 3701–3720E. *See* § 10.2.1.1, *infra*.
2 28 U.S.C. §§ 3001–3308. *See generally* § 10.3, *infra*.

3 *See* § 10.2.7, *infra*.
4 31 C.F.R. § 285.1.
5 31 U.S.C. § 3716(h)(1).
6 U.S. Dep't of the Treasury, Bureau of the Fiscal Serv., Fiscal Year 2012: Annual Report to the States (June 2013), *available at* www.fms.treas.gov/debt/TOP_annual_report_to_states_fy12.pdf.
7 *See* § 12.4.1, *infra*.
8 31 U.S.C. §§ 3711–3719. *See* Red River Farms v. United States, 2009 WL 2983195, at *3 (D. Ariz. Sept. 17, 2009) (government may use Claims Collection Act procedure without bringing suit).
9 Pub. L. No. 97-365, 96 Stat. 1749 (1982).
10 5 U.S.C. §§ 552a(b)(12), (m)(2); 31 U.S.C. § 3711(e). *See* § 10.2.3, *infra*.
11 5 U.S.C. §§ 552a(b)(12), (m)(2); 26 U.S.C. §§ 6103(*l*)(3), (*l*)(6), (*l*)(8), (m)(2), (p)(4).

hire collection agencies and private collection attorneys,[12] and intercept consumers' federal tax refunds and other sums owed by the government to consumers.[13]

In 1996 Congress again strengthened the debt collection powers of federal agencies, in ways that weigh heavily on some low-income households, by passing the Debt Collection Improvement Act of 1996.[14] This law amended the Claims Collection Act and other federal statutes to:

- Permit administrative offset against formerly exempt Social Security, Black Lung, and Railroad Retirement benefits.[15]
- Allow administrative wage garnishment of up to 15% of disposable pay, "notwithstanding state law."[16] This procedure and its relation to federal wage garnishment limits are discussed in § 12.4.2.1, *infra.*
- Allow creditor agencies to disclose the identity of debtors and the existence of the debt and require the Treasury Department to adopt regulations concerning the dissemination of information about delinquent debts owed to the government.[17] The Treasury Department initially published notices that it planned to issue proposed regulations on this topic,[18] but withdrew the matter from its docket in 2005.[19] The existing regulations do, however, require creditor agencies to implement procedures to report delinquent debts to credit bureaus.[20] They also allow delinquent debtors' addresses to be reported to other agencies and to collection agencies.[21]
- Deny federal loans, loan insurance, or guarantees, other than disaster loans, to debtors delinquent on federal non-tax claims.[22]
- Mandate a computer match to locate federal employees who owe debts to federal agencies so the debts can be offset against their earnings. The amendments also expanded the salary offset program to reach salaries of employees of all federal agencies.[23]
- Allow federal agencies to sell delinquent non-tax debts to debt buyers.[24]
- Increase oversight of agencies' debt collection performance and provide incentives for more active pursuit of collections.[25]

The statute with these various amendments will be referred to in this chapter as the Claims Collection Act. Its key provisions are reproduced in Appendix B, *infra.*

In addition to these general statutes authorizing federal collection efforts, there are often special statutes governing particular agencies' collections. Neither the Claims Collection Act nor the regulations under it supersede any other applicable statute, the common law, or contract term relating to collection procedure.[26]

10.2.1.2 Regulations Under the Claims Collection Act

The Claims Collection Act calls for the collection of debts to be carried out under guidelines promulgated jointly by the attorney general and the Secretary of the Treasury.[27] These regulations (the "joint regulations")[28] detail the procedures that all agencies must follow in their collection efforts. A second set of regulations sets requirements for administrative wage garnishment and specifies the steps the Treasury Department takes when agencies refer claims to it for centralized offset.[29] In addition, the Treasury Department has posted manuals and guides online for agencies to use when referring cases to the Department.[30]

The Claims Collection Act also requires individual creditor agencies to have their own regulations about collecting claims.[31] Virtually all agencies that offer direct consumer loans, guarantee or insure consumer loans, or administer benefit programs collect debts under the authority of the Federal Claims Collection Act and have regulations parallel to the joint regulations.[32]

10.2.1.3 Scope

The Claims Collection Act is applicable to "claims" and "debts," which are defined as any amount of funds or property that has been determined by an appropriate official of the federal government to be owed to the United States.[33] The statute includes a non-exhaustive list of examples, including funds owed on loans made, insured, or guaranteed by the government, deficiency judgments, overpayments, fines, and penalties.[34] A criminal restitution order meets the definition of "claim."[35]

---

12 31 U.S.C. § 3718. *See* § 10.2.4, *infra.*
13 31 U.S.C. § 3720A. *See* § 10.2.7, *infra.*
14 Pub. L. No. 104-134, 110 Stat. 1321.
15 31 U.S.C. § 3716(c)(3)(A)(i). *See* § 10.2.8, *infra.*
16 31 U.S.C. § 3720D.
17 31 U.S.C. § 3720E.
18 66 Fed. Reg. 62,091 (Dec. 3, 2001).
19 70 Fed. Reg. 27,364 (May 16, 2005).
20 31 C.F.R. § 901.4. *See* § 10.2.3, *infra.*
21 31 C.F.R. § 901.11(b).
22 *See* § 10.2.9, *infra.*
23 5 U.S.C. § 5514(a)(1). *See* § 10.2.6, *infra.*
24 31 U.S.C. § 3711(i).
25 31 U.S.C. §§ 3719, 3720C.
26 31 C.F.R. §§ 900.1(c), 901.9(i). *See* McBride Cotton & Cattle Corp. v. Veneman, 296 F. Supp. 2d 1125 (D. Ariz. 2003) (upholding broader Agriculture Department offset regulations as permissible under separate statute). *See also* § 10.2.8.1, *infra* (government's retention of common law right of offset).
27 31 U.S.C. §§ 3711(d)(2). *See also* 31 U.S.C. §§ 3711(g)(10), 3716(b), 3716(c)(5), 3717(h), 3720A(d), 3720B(a) (other authority to adopt regulations).
28 31 C.F.R. pts. 900–904.
These rules replace a set of rules formerly found at 4 C.F.R. pts. 101–105. *See* 65 Fed. Reg. 70,390 (Nov. 22, 2000).
29 31 C.F.R. pt. 285.
30 These items may be found at www.fiscal.treasury.gov.
31 5 U.S.C. § 5514(b)(1); 31 U.S.C. § 3716(b). *See also* 31 C.F.R. § 285.5(d)(4).
32 *See* § 10.2.12, *infra* (review of selected agencies' rules).
33 31 U.S.C. § 3701(b)(1).
34 31 U.S.C. §§ 3701(b)(1)(A), (C), (F).
35 United States v. Harrison, 2007 WL 2332662 (N.D. Tex. Aug. 16, 2007).

Most provisions of the Act do not apply to debts arising under the Internal Revenue Code or the tariff laws,[36] or (with some significant exceptions) to debts arising under the Social Security Act.[37]

10.2.2 The Federal Agency Must Make Proper Written Demand for Payment

Until 2000, the joint regulations required federal agencies, in most cases, to make three written demands for payment before taking further action against the debtor, other than charging interest.[38] That requirement has now been reduced to a single demand letter.[39] The demand letter must inform the debtor of the basis for the indebtedness, the debtor's right to seek review within the agency, the standards for imposing interest, penalties, or administrative costs, the date by which payment should be made to avoid late charges and enforced collection (usually no more than thirty days from mailing), and the name, address, and phone number of a contact person or office within the agency.[40]

The joint regulations specify that agencies should take steps to ensure that all demand letters are mailed on the same day they are dated,[41] thus insuring the debtor the maximum time to respond before the deadline. In addition, agencies are directed to respond promptly to communications from the debtor.[42] The agency can sue or take other action before sending a written demand when a statute of limitations is about to run or prompt action is necessary to protect the government's interest for other reasons.[43] Courts have held that the agency need not prove that the debtor actually received the notice as long as it was properly sent.[44]

Agencies must give debtors advance notice that litigation may be initiated.[45] Notice to the debtor is also required if the agency or the Treasury Department is going to report the debt to a credit reporting agency[46] or offset the debt against a payment owed to the debtor.[47] These notices can be combined with the initial demand letter.[48]

If the agency's demand letter provides insufficient detail, the debtor may want to make a Freedom of Information Act request to obtain information about the claimed debt.[49]

10.2.3 Release of Information to Credit Reporting Agencies

The Claims Collection Act authorizes federal agencies to disclose debtor information to credit reporting agencies.[50] This authority does not apply to tax debts, debts arising under the Social Security Act (other than certain overpayments), or debts for tariffs.[51] Information that may be released is limited to the name, address, and Social Security number of the obligor, the amount, status, and history of the claim, and the agency involved.[52]

The agency must verify the validity of the claim prior to releasing information.[53] In addition, at least sixty days before

---

36 31 U.S.C. §§ 3701(d)(1) and (3) (making sections 3711(e) and 3716 to 3719 inapplicable to tax and tariff debts), 3720B(a) (making provisions for denial of federal loans inapplicable to tax debts), 3720D(a) (making administrative wage garnishment applicable only to nontax debts), 3720E(a) (making provisions regarding dissemination of information about identity of delinquent debtors applicable only to nontax debts). *See also* 31 C.F.R. § 901.12(a) (making all the collection methods set forth by pt. 901 inapplicable to tax and tariff debts).

37 31 U.S.C. § 3701(d)(2) makes §§ 3711(e) and 3716 to 3719 inapplicable to debts arising under the Social Security Act, except as provided in 42 U.S.C. §§ 404(f) and 1383(b)(4).

Those sections make 31 U.S.C. §§ 3711(f) (probably intended to refer to credit reporting under 31 U.S.C. § 3711(e), see section 31001(k) of Pub. L. No. 104-134, 110 Stat. 1341 (1996)), 3716 (administrative offset), 3717 (interest and penalties on claims), and 3718 (contracts for collection services), plus 5 U.S.C. § 5514 (offset against federal employee's salary) applicable to certain Social Security and SSI overpayments (those which were made after the beneficiary became eighteen years old and are not recoverable by other methods after the debtor stops receiving benefits).

In addition, section 3720A (tax intercept) applies to OASDI overpayments if the overpaid individual is not currently receiving Title II benefits (see section 3720A(f)(1)).

Sections 3720B (denial of federal loans), 3720D (administrative wage garnishment), and 3720E (dissemination of information regarding identity of debtors) are silent as to their application to debts arising under the Social Security Act. *See also* 31 C.F.R. § 901.12(a).

38 4 C.F.R. § 102.2(a), *superseded by* 31 C.F.R. pts. 900–904, *as announced by* 65 Fed. Reg. 70,390 (Nov. 22, 2000)).

39 31 C.F.R. § 901.2(a), *as adopted by* 65 Fed. Reg. 70,390 (Nov. 22, 2000) ("[g]enerally, one demand letter should suffice," although agencies have discretion to determine the number of demand letters).

40 31 C.F.R. § 901.2(b). *See also* 31 C.F.R. § 285.5(d)(6).

41 31 C.F.R. § 901.2(c).

42 31 C.F.R. § 901.2(e).

43 31 C.F.R. § 901.2(a). *See also* United States v. Golden Elevator, Inc., 868 F. Supp. 1063 (C.D. Ill. 1994) (due process did not require Small Bus. Admin. to give debtor notice of possible administrative remedies or opportunity to exhaust administrative remedies before acceleration and foreclosure; debtor knew of right to accelerate from original contact and had been given deferments, seasonal payments, etc.).

44 Shabtai v. United States Dep't of Educ., 2003 WL 21983025 (S.D.N.Y. Aug. 20, 2003); Roth v. United States, 2003 WL 21730094 (D. Minn. July 22, 2003); Setlech v. United States, 816 F. Supp. 161 (E.D.N.Y. 1993) (for tax refund intercept, notice mailed to last address known to IRS was sufficient, even though it was not received by the debtor), *aff'd*, 17 F.3d 390 (2d Cir. 1993).

45 31 C.F.R. § 901.2(g).

46 31 U.S.C. § 3711(d)(1)(C). *See also* 31 C.F.R. § 901.4(a)(2).

47 31 C.F.R. §§ 285.5(d)(6), 901.3(b)(4)(ii). *See* §§ 10.2.6, 10.2.8.4, *infra*.

48 31 C.F.R. §§ 901.2(g), 901.3(b)(4)(iv).

49 5 U.S.C. § 552.

50 31 U.S.C. § 3711(e). *See also* 31 C.F.R. § 901.4.

51 *Taxes and tariffs*: 31 U.S.C. §§ 3701(d)(1) and (3) make section 3711(e) inapplicable to these debts. *See also* 31 C.F.R. § 901.12(a).

Debts arising under Social Security Act: 31 U.S.C. § 3701(d)(2) makes section 3711(e) inapplicable to debts arising under the Social Security Act, except as provided in 42 U.S.C. §§ 404(f) and 1383(b)(4). Those sections make 31 U.S.C. §§ 3711(f) (probably intended to refer to credit reporting under 31 U.S.C. § 3711(e), see section 31001(k) of Pub. L. No. 104-134, 110 Stat. 1341 (1996)) applicable to certain Social Security and SSI overpayments (those which were made after the beneficiary became eighteen years old and are not recoverable by other methods after the debtor stops receiving benefits). *See also* 31 C.F.R. § 901.12(a); 45 C.F.R. § 30.13 (Department of Health and Human Services regulation concerning credit reporting); § 10.2.12.3, *infra*.

52 31 U.S.C. § 3711(e)(1)(F).

53 31 U.S.C. § 3711(e)(1)(B).

information is actually released to a credit reporting agency, the government agency must notify the affected individual both that a report will be made and that the individual has a right to administrative review of that action.[54] The federal agency cannot contact a credit reporting agency at all if a repayment plan has been agreed upon or administrative review requested.[55]

An agency planning to release information to a credit reporting agency must establish procedures to update the reported information and to respond to requests from the consumer reporting agency for verification.[56] It must also get satisfactory assurances from the credit reporting agency that the agency is complying with the Fair Credit Reporting Act (FCRA)[57] and other applicable statutes concerning consumer credit information.[58]

If the debtor disputes the debt with the credit reporting agency, the credit reporting agency is required to ask the government agency to reinvestigate the claim.[59] If the government agency does not conduct a reasonable investigation and report back to the credit reporting agency,[60] the alleged debtor may be able to bring an FCRA claim against the government agency.[61]

Prior to the 1982 amendments, agencies were required to comply with the Privacy Act of 1974[62] in making reports to credit reporting agencies. The 1982 amendments specifically excluded reports to credit reporting agencies from compliance with the Privacy Act requirement to obtain the consent of the individual to whom the record pertains.[63] However, a provision of the joint regulations generally requires agencies to comply with the Privacy Act when reporting delinquent consumer debts to credit bureaus.[64]

10.2.4 Contracts with Private Debt Collection Agencies and Collection Lawyers

The Claims Collection Act authorizes agencies to contract with private collection agencies and attorneys to collect debts,[65] except those arising under the Internal Revenue Code and the tariff laws and certain claims arising under the Social Security Act.[66] When contracting with a private collection agency, the federal agency must retain authority to resolve disputes, compromise claims, end collection actions, and refer claims to the attorney general for suit.[67] The private collection service is bound by the Privacy Act and the Fair Debt Collection Practices Act and all other applicable federal and state laws and regulations relating to debt collection practices.[68] The former use of private collection agencies to collect tax debts is discussed in another treatise in this series.[69]

The attorney general is also authorized to hire private lawyers to collect government debts (for example, student loans and FHA loans).[70] The government agency to which the debt is owed must retain full authority to resolve disputes about claims, compromise claims, and terminate collection actions.[71] The Act provides that private collection attorneys retained to collect government debts are debt collectors as defined by the Fair Debt Collection Practices Act, notwithstanding the exemption in 15 U.S.C. § 1692a(6) for, among other things, officers and employees of the United States.[72] If a consumer asserts a counterclaim in a collection action brought by a private attorney for the government, it must be served on the attorney general or the local United States attorney as well as on the private attorney.[73] Regulations for the program have been adopted, largely tracking the statute.[74]

10.2.5 Interest, Administrative Charges, and Penalties

The Claims Collection Act requires federal agencies to charge interest on overdue claims of at least the annual average rate the Treasury Department earns on bank accounts into which it deposits taxes and loan repayments that it collects.[75] The interest rate is to be a fixed rate, determined when the agency first notifies the debtor of the amount due.[76] If the contract, a repayment agreement, or another statute establishes a different rate, however, that rate should be imposed instead.[77]

---

54 31 U.S.C. § 3711(e)(1)(C).
55 31 U.S.C. § 3711(e)(1)(D).
56 31 U.S.C. § 3711(e)(1)(E).
57 15 U.S.C. § 1681. *See* National Consumer Law Center, Fair Credit Reporting (8th ed. 2013), *updated at* www.nclc.org/library.
58 31 U.S.C. § 3711(e)(1)(E)(iii).
59 15 U.S.C. § 1681i(a)(2).
60 15 U.S.C. § 1681s-2(b). *See also* 31 U.S.C. § 3711(e)(1)(E)(ii).
61 *See* § 10.2.13.8, *infra*. *See generally* National Consumer Law Center, Fair Credit Reporting §§ 2.3.5.6, 6.2.1, 6.10 (8th ed. 2013), *updated at* www.nclc.org/library.
62 5 U.S.C. § 552a.
63 5 U.S.C. § 552a(b)(12), *as amended by* Pub. L. No. 97-365, § 2, 96 Stat. 1749 (1982).
64 31 C.F.R. § 901.4(a)(1).
65 31 U.S.C. § 3718.
66 31 U.S.C. § 3701(d). *See* U.S. Dep't of the Treasury, Fiscal Year 2011 Report to the Congress: U.S. Government Receivables and Debt Collection Activities of Federal Agencies 7–8 (June 2012), *available at* www.fms.treas.gov/news/reports/debt11.pdf (reporting on volume of referrals to private collectors).
67 31 U.S.C. § 3718(a)(1). *See also* 31 C.F.R. §§ 901.5(a)(1), (2).
68 31 U.S.C. § 3718(a)(2). *See also* 31 C.F.R. § 901.5(a)(3).
69 National Consumer Law Center, Fair Debt Collection § 8.10 (8th ed. 2014, *updated at* www.nclc.org/library.
70 31 U.S.C. § 3718(b).
71 31 U.S.C. § 3718(b)(5).
72 31 U.S.C. § 3718(b)(6).
73 31 U.S.C. § 3718(b)(7).
74 28 C.F.R. §§ 11.1–11.3.
75 31 U.S.C. § 3717(a)(1). *See* 31 C.F.R. § 901.9.
76 31 U.S.C. § 3717(c). *See* Precision Pine & Timber, Inc. v. United States, 75 Fed. Cl. 80 (Fed. Cl. 2006), *aff'd*, 257 Fed. Appx. 268 (Fed. Cir. 2007).
77 31 U.S.C. § 3717(g)(1); 31 C.F.R. § 901.9(b)(2). *See* United States v. Hyundai Merchant Marine Co., 172 F.3d 1187, 1192 (9th Cir. 1999) (Claims Collection Act's interest and penalty provisions do not apply when other statute sets interest rate); United States v. Spann, 797 F. Supp. 980 (S.D. Fla. 1992) (government could not recover 6% interest on student loan because contract set rate at 3%); Westchester Fire Ins. Co. v. United States, 52 Fed. Cl. 567 (Fed. Cl. 2002) (awarding interest based on contractual clause rather than section 3717).

Agencies are also directed to assess charges to cover certain administrative costs of handling overdue claims[78] and penalties of up to 6% per year on claims more than ninety days late.[79] Penalties accrue from the date of the delinquency,[80] while interest accrues from the date the agency sends a notice.[81]

Interest and administrative charges may not be imposed if a claim is paid within thirty days after the interest first accrues, and this period may be extended by the agency.[82] Agencies must have regulations setting forth the circumstances under which they will suspend the imposition of interest and administrative charges while a review request is pending.[83]

The statute allows agencies to adopt regulations setting forth circumstances in which it is appropriate to waive collection of interest and charges.[84] The joint regulations allow waiver of interest, penalties, and administrative costs, in whole or in part, under the general standards for the compromise of claims[85] or if it is determined that collection of the charges "is against equity and good conscience or is not in the best interest of the United States."[86]

Interest cannot be calculated on interest, penalties, or administrative costs.[87] Interest is allowed only when the underlying claim is a contractual obligation to pay money.[88] The creditor agency must give the debtor a written notice explaining the charges.[89]

The requirements of the Claims Collection Act regarding interest, penalties, and administrative charges do not apply to claims arising under the Social Security Act (with the exception of certain overpayments),[90] the Internal Revenue Code, or the tariff laws,[91] or to claims under contracts executed before October 25, 1982.[92] This latter exception may help debtors with very old student loans.[93] For debts not governed by the statute, the government may have a common law right to claim interest, however.[94]

10.2.6 *Offset Against Federal Employee's Salary*

Federal agencies can collect on debts owed them by a federal employee through an offset against the employee's pay or other compensation.[95] Agencies are required to refer debts to the Treasury Department, which conducts a centralized computer match to identify federal employees who owe debts to the federal government for the purpose of offsetting the debts against their earnings.[96]

Salary offset is limited to 15% of the employee's disposable income unless the employee agrees otherwise in writing.[97] Until 2009, debts could be referred to the Treasury Department for centralized salary offset only within ten years after the agency's right of action accrued, except for judgment debts and as otherwise authorized by law.[98] In 2008, Congress deleted the ten-year limit,[99] and in 2009 the Treasury Department issued an

78 31 U.S.C. § 3711(g)(6); 31 C.F.R. §§ 901.1(f), 901.9(c); 31 C.F.R. § 285.2(h) (adding fees for tax refund intercept to the debt). *See* United States v. A.R.A.Z., Inc., 2007 WL 2693668 (E.D.N.Y. Sept. 10, 2007) (finding authority for "debt management service" charge, but denying claim for it because government failed to justify amount).

79 31 C.F.R. § 901.9(d).

80 31 C.F.R. § 901.9(d). *See* Am. Airlines, Inc. v. United States, 77 Fed. Cl. 672 (Fed. Cl. 2007), *aff'd on other grounds*, 551 F.3d 1294 (Fed. Cir. 2008), *reh'g granted*, 319 Fed. Appx. 914 (Fed. Cir. 2009).

81 31 U.S.C. § 3717(b). *See* Am. Airlines, Inc. v. United States, 77 Fed. Cl. 672 (Fed. Cl. 2007), *aff'd on other grounds*, 551 F.3d 1294 (Fed. Cir. 2008), *reh'g granted*, 319 Fed. Appx. 914 (Fed. Cir. 2009). *Cf.* 31 C.F.R. § 901.9(b)(1) (interest accrues from date of delinquency "or as otherwise provided by law").

82 31 C.F.R. § 901.9(g).

83 31 C.F.R. § 901.9(h). *See also* § 10.2.11, *infra* (rules regarding suspension of collection activity).

84 31 U.S.C. § 3717(h).

85 *See* 31 C.F.R. pt. 902.

86 31 C.F.R. § 901.9(g). *See* Titan Wheel Corp. v. United States Envtl. Prot. Agency, 291 F. Supp. 2d 899, 933 (S.D. Iowa 2003) (upholding agency's discretion not to waive interest), *aff'd*, 113 Fed. Appx. 734 (table) (8th Cir. 2004).

87 31 U.S.C. § 3717(f) (interest does not accrue on administrative costs and penalties); 31 C.F.R. § 901.9(b)(3) (interest may not be charged on interest, penalties, or administrative costs, but accrued charges can be added to new repayment agreement if debtor defaults).

88 Thermalon Indus., Ltd. v. United States, 51 Fed. Cl. 464 (Fed. Cl. 2002).

89 31 C.F.R. § 901.9(a).

90 31 U.S.C. § 3701(d)(2) makes section 3717 inapplicable to debts arising under the Social Security Act, except as provided in 42 U.S.C. §§ 404(f) and 1383(b)(4). Those sections make section 3717 (interest and penalties on claims) applicable to certain Social Security and SSI overpayments (those which were made after the beneficiary became eighteen years old and are not recoverable by other methods after the debtor stops receiving benefits).

91 31 U.S.C. §§ 3701(d)(1), 3701(d)(3); 31 C.F.R. § 901.12(a).

92 31 U.S.C. § 3717(g)(2). *See* United States v. S. Cal. Edison Co., 300 F. Supp. 2d 964, 992 (E.D. Cal. 2004) (because case involved contract executed before Oct. 25, 1982, no costs are allowed).

93 *See* United States v. Burns, 1992 WL 247438 (S.D. Fla. Sept. 14, 1992) (declining to award costs because student loan debts arose in 1975 and 1977).

94 31 C.F.R. § 901.9(i). *See* Seaboard Lumber Co. v. United States, 48 Fed. Cl. 814 (Fed. Cl. 2001), *aff'd on other grounds*, 308 F.3d 1283 (Fed. Cir. 2002).

95 5 U.S.C. § 5514.

The regulations may be found at 31 C.F.R. § 285.7 and 5 C.F.R. §§ 550.1101 to 550.1110. The joint regulations are inapplicable to salary offset to the extent that they are inconsistent with these regulations. *See* 31 C.F.R. § 901.3(a)(2)(iv).

96 5 U.S.C. § 5514(a)(1). *See* Dep't of the Treasury, Fin. Mgmt. Serv., Red to Black: Improving Collection of Delinquent Debt Owed to the Government, Testimony of Comm'r David A. Lebryk before House Oversight and Gov't Reform Subcomm. on Gov't Org., Efficiency, and Financial Mgmt. (Mar. 11, 2011) at 3, *available at* www.fiscal.treasury.gov (reporting that $85.4 million was collected through salary offset in fiscal year 2010); Dep't of the Treasury, Fact Sheet, Delinquent Debt Collection, Fiscal Year 2006 (Mar. 7, 2007), *available at* www.fiscal.treasury.gov (noting that, as of fiscal year 2006, Treasury was processing offsets against salaries paid by Agriculture, Defense, and Interior Departments, the GSA, and the Postal Service). *See also* 41 C.F.R. §§ 105-56.024–105-56.033 (GSA regulation for offsets against its employees' salaries).

97 5 U.S.C. § 5514(a)(1).

98 31 C.F.R. § 285.7(d)(3)(ii) (prior to amendment effective June 10, 2009).

99 31 U.S.C. § 3716(e) (as amended by Pub. L. No. 110-275, 122 Stat. 2494 (2008)).

interim rule and then a final rule removing the ten-year limit from its regulations.[100]

Agency employees subject to salary offset are entitled to notice and hearing.[101] The agency that holds the debt must give the employee at least a thirty-day advance written notice.[102] The notice must state the nature and amount of the debt; that the agency plans to use salary offset; that the employee may inspect and copy the agency's record of the debt; that the employee may enter into a written contract with the agency to repay the debt; and that the agency will provide the employee an opportunity for a hearing on the existence or amount of the debt or the terms of a repayment schedule established other than by written agreement.[103] A timely request for a hearing stays collection proceedings.[104]

In addition, the agency that employs the debtor must give the debtor advance written notice of the amount of the salary deductions and the date they will commence.[105] Another notice, stating the amount of the offset and the identity of the creditor agency, and providing a contact within the creditor agency, is required when the offset occurs, unless this information is included in the first notice.[106]

When the debtor's federal employment ends before repayment is completed, the debt may be offset against any payments of any nature that are due the individual.[107] The statute is not clear whether the 15% limit still applies. The regulation takes the position that the 15% limitation on salary offset does not apply to final and lump-sum payments made to employees leaving federal service.[108]

One decision holds that the entire payment due to an independent contractor from a government contract could be set off to collect a government debt.[109] The court held that the cap on the amount that could be offset from a person's salary did not apply, because the debtor was an independent contractor and did not receive a "salary." The court failed to consider whether the statutory cap on administrative wage garnishment[110] or the statutory cap on installment deductions from a person's pay[111] might apply. Although both of those statutes use the term "employer" or "employee" from time to time, neither cap is limited to "salary," but refers to "pay," a term that is clearly broad enough to encompass payments to independent contractors.

10.2.7 Tax Refund Interception

The federal government may intercept federal income tax refunds to offset a federal agency's claim against a taxpayer.[112] For example, a consumer entitled to a federal income tax refund because of over-withholding of taxes may have that refund intercepted and applied to an old student loan claim by the Department of Education or to an old manufactured-home loan claim by HUD.[113] Tax refunds may also be intercepted for past-due state income tax, past-due child support debts, and state unemployment compensation debts that arise due to fraud or failure to report earnings that are reported to the Treasury Department by the states.[114] Intercept is not allowed as a means of collecting Social Security and SSI overpayments from people who are still receiving Social Security benefits.[115]

Tax refund interception is governed not by the general administrative offset regulations[116] but by a separate set of tax intercept regulations.[117] Agencies participating in the tax intercept program must also adopt their own regulations.[118]

Until 2009, intercept was allowed only for debts that were referred to the Treasury Department for offset within ten years after the agency's right of action accrued, except for judgment debts or as otherwise allowed by law.[119] At the end of 2008, however, Congress amended the general administrative offset statute to delete the ten-year limit.[120] The Treasury Department deleted this limitation from its regulations effective December 28,

100 74 Fed. Reg. 27,707 (June 11, 2009) (adopting interim rule); 74 Fed. Reg. 68,149 (Dec. 23, 2009) (adopting final rule; amending 31 C.F.R. § 285.7).

101 5 U.S.C. § 5514(a)(2).

102 5 U.S.C. § 5514(a)(2).

103 5 U.S.C. § 5514(a)(2); 31 C.F.R. § 285.7(d)(3); 5 C.F.R. § 550.1104(d) (specifying details that agencies must include in their notices).

104 5 U.S.C. § 5514(a)(2). *See* Ramirez v. Dep't of the Army, 86 M.S.P.B. 211 (Merit Sys. Prot. Bd. 2000) (creditor agency cannot deduct debt from retirement pay until it has completed hearing requested by debtor).

105 31 C.F.R. § 285.7(i).

106 31 C.F.R. § 285.7(i)(2).

107 5 U.S.C. § 5514(a)(1).

108 31 C.F.R. § 285.7(a)(6).

109 Miller v. D. Smith, ___ F. Supp. 2d ___, 2013 WL 3463259 (D.D.C. July 10, 2013).

110 31 U.S.C. § 3720D(b) (15%).

111 5 U.S.C. § 5514 (15%).

112 Authority to intercept tax refunds as a means of collecting debts owed to the federal government was added to the Federal Claims Collection Act, 31 U.S.C. § 3720A, and the Internal Revenue Code, 26 U.S.C. § 6402(d), by the Deficit Reduction Act, Pub. L. No. 98-369, § 2653, 98 Stat. 1153 (1984). *See also* 42 U.S.C. § 664 (directing the Department of Health and Human Services to notify the Department of the Treasury to intercept tax refund payments for past due support).

113 *See, e.g.*, Ingram v. Cuomo, 51 F. Supp. 2d 667 (M.D.N.C. 1999) (manufactured-home loan).

114 26 U.S.C. § 6402(c), (e), (f); 31 C.F.R. § 285.8. *See* U.S. Dep't of the Treasury, Fiscal Year 2012 Report to the Congress, U.S. Government Receivables and Debt Collection Activities of Federal Agencies 11 (Mar. 2013), *available at* www.fms.treas.gov/news/reports/debt12.pdf (reporting that, in fiscal year 2012, federal tax intercepts collected $561.8 million in state income taxes, and that forty states and the District of Columbia were participating in the offset program for collection of certain unemployment compensation debts).

115 31 U.S.C. § 3720A(f). *See also* 31 U.S.C. § 3701(d)(2) (exempting Social Security benefits from other provisions of the Claims Collections Act); 31 C.F.R. §§ 285.2(b)(4), (d)(1)(iv). Additional restrictions imposed by Social Security statutes are that the overpayment must have occurred after the beneficiary reached age eighteen and the debt must not be recoverable by other means. 42 U.S.C. §§ 404(f), 1383(b).

116 *See* 31 C.F.R. § 901.3(a)(iii) (general administrative offset regulation inapplicable to debts arising under or payments made under Internal Revenue Code).

117 31 C.F.R. §§ 285.2, 285.3, 285.8.

118 31 C.F.R. § 285.2(c); 26 C.F.R. § 301.6402-6(b). *See In re* Huff, 343 B.R. 136, 142 (W.D. Pa. 2006).

119 31 C.F.R. § 285.2(d)(1)(ii).

120 *See* § 10.2.8.1, *infra*.

2009.[121] The revised rule allows the government not only to continue to intercept tax refunds after the ten-year period expires but also to intercept tax refunds for debts that had gone past the ten-year limit before the rule was amended.[122]

The statute[123] provides that, before referring a debt to the Treasury Department for tax intercept, the creditor agency must:

- Notify the borrower that the agency intends to take such action;[124]
- Give the consumer at least sixty days to present evidence that the debt is not past due or legally enforceable;[125]
- Consider any evidence and determine that an amount is past due and legally enforceable;[126]
- Satisfy relevant Treasury Department regulations;[127] and
- Certify to the Treasury Department that the agency has made reasonable efforts to obtain payment of the debt.[128]

Treasury Department regulations also require that, prior to intercept, the debtor be given the opportunity to enter into a repayment agreement.[129] In most cases, the creditor agency must also disclose the debt to a credit reporting agency before referring the debt to the IRS for interception.[130]

A parallel section of the Internal Revenue Code requires the IRS to intercept the tax refund check upon notice from any federal agency.[131] The IRS is required to remit the intercepted amount to the creditor agency and to send notification of the offset to the taxpayer.[132] Unlike the notice sent by the creditor agency, this notice must be sent at the time of each intercept.[133] The notice must advise any non-debtor spouse who filed a joint tax return with the debtor of the steps to take to secure his or her proper share of the tax refund.[134]

If the taxpayer owes more than one debt, the tax refund will be applied against the debts in the order in which they accrued.[135] Courts have disagreed about whether the government can proceed with an offset to collect a dischargeable debt when the debtor files bankruptcy and claims the tax refund as exempt.[136]

A taxpayer whose refund has been intercepted for a child support, state income tax, or federal agency debt is prohibited from suing the IRS over the tax intercept; recourse is limited to action against the federal agency requesting the offset.[137]

In *Sorenson v. Secretary of the Treasury*,[138] the United States Supreme Court held that the earned income credit portion

---

121 74 Fed. Reg. 68,537 (Dec. 28, 2009).

122 31 C.F.R. § 285.2(d)(6)(ii) (allowing revival of collection efforts upon notice to debtor).

123 31 U.S.C. § 3720A(b).

124 *See* 31 C.F.R. § 285.2(d)(1)(ii)(B) (requiring "reasonable attempt" to give notice). *See also* Kipple v. United States, 102 Fed. Cl. 773 (Fed. Cl. 2012) (finding agency's computer records and affidavit insufficient to establish that it mailed notices; entertaining suit challenging tax refund offset); *In re* Shortt, 277 B.R. 683 (Bankr. N.D. Tex. 2002) (notice of intent to set off tax refund, sent to debtors' last known address, sufficient even though never received; debtors had not notified creditor of address change). *Cf. In re* Huff, 343 B.R. 136 (W.D. Pa. 2006) (creditor agency need only give notice once, before initial submission of debt to Treasury Department, not every year before taxes are intercepted).

125 31 C.F.R. § 285.2(d)(1)(ii)(C).

126 *See, e.g.*, Ingram v. Cuomo, 51 F. Supp. 2d 667 (M.D.N.C. 1999) (deficiency due after manufactured-home repossession and sale was "past due and legally enforceable" even though it had not been reduced to judgment); Abbe v. Bochert, 2001 WL 651557 (Ohio Ct. App. June 13, 2001) (if obligor is up-to-date on payments of current support and court-ordered installments toward arrearage, and no amount is past due, then tax refund offset is not authorized despite the existence of the debt, but *pro se* litigant failed to preserve issue for review).

127 26 C.F.R. § 301.6402-6.

128 31 U.S.C. § 3720A(b)(5); 31 C.F.R. § 285.2(d)(1)(ii). *See* Kipple v. United States, ___ Fed. Cl. ___, 2012 WL 92096 (Fed. Cl. Jan. 12, 2012) (entertaining suit alleging that tax offset was illegal because agency failed to provide notice, consider evidence that the debtor does not owe debt, and certify that it made reasonable attempts to collect it).

129 31 C.F.R. § 285.2(d)(1)(ii)(D).

130 26 C.F.R § 301.6402-6(c)(6).

131 26 U.S.C. § 6402(d) (interception of non-child support claims); 26 U.S.C. § 6402(c) (offset of past-due support).

132 26 U.S.C. § 6402(d)(1)(C); 26 C.F.R. § 301.6402-6(h); 31 C.F.R. § 285.2(f).

133 26 C.F.R. § 301.6402-6(h)(1) (requiring notice of amount and date of offset). *See In re* Huff, 343 B.R. 136 (W.D. Pa. 2006).

134 31 C.F.R. § 285.2(f). *See* Ingram v. Cuomo, 51 F. Supp. 2d 667 (M.D.N.C. 1999) (spouse's claim to portion of refund is not defense to creditor agency's claim but should be asserted through IRS procedures).

135 26 U.S.C. § 6402(d)(2).

136 Beaucage v. United States Internal Revenue Serv., 342 B.R. 408 (D. Mass. 2006) (allowing offset); *In re* Killen, 249 B.R. 585 (Bankr. D. Conn. 2000) (no offset of tax refund for Department of Housing and Urban Development loan when tax refund claimed exempt); *In re* Pigott, 330 B.R. 797 (Bankr. S.D. Ala. 2005) (allowing offset); *In re* Lyle, 324 B.R. 128 (Bankr. N.D. Cal. 2005) (tax refund never became part of child support obligor's bankruptcy estate; obligor had no right to receive refund because statute required IRS to reduce it by amount of support debt before sending it out); *In re* Bourne, 262 B.R. 745 (Bankr. E.D. Tenn. 2001) (allowing offset). *See also In re* Luongo, 259 F.3d 323 (5th Cir. 2001) (IRS may set off tax refund against earlier tax liability, even though old debt has been discharged in bankruptcy and debtor claimed refund as exempt). *Cf. In re* Stewart, 253 B.R. 51 (Bankr. E.D. Ark. 2000) (no violation of automatic stay to hold tax refund pending determination of right to offset). *See generally* National Consumer Law Center, Consumer Bankruptcy Law and Practice § 10.4.2.6.7 (10th ed. 2012), *updated at* www.nclc.org/library.

137 26 U.S.C. § 6402(f), (g); 26 C.F.R. § 301.6402-6(*l*); 31 C.F.R. § 285.2(*i*). *See* Dasisa v. Dep't of Treasury, 951 F. Supp. 2d 45 (D.D.C. 2013); Johnson v. United States, 469 Fed. Appx. 79 (3d Cir. 2012); Greenland v. Van Ru Credit Corp., 2006 WL 2884458 (W.D. Mich. Oct. 10, 2006) (granting Treasury Department's motion to dismiss); *In re* Cannon, 2005 WL 3278003 (Bankr. E.D. Ark. Oct. 31, 2005) (dismissing claim based on interception of tax refund against Internal Revenue Service, but allowing debtor to amend to state claim against creditor agency). *Cf.* Hall-Ditchfield v. United States, 2008 WL 2381533 (E.D. Pa. June 10, 2008), *aff'd*, 366 Fed. Appx. 391 (3d Cir. 2010) (section 6402(f) bars suit to recover tax refund that was applied to child support, state taxes, or federal agency debt, but not one that was applied to federal taxes).

138 475 U.S. 851, 106 S. Ct. 1600, 89 L. Ed. 2d 855 (1986). *See also* Bosarge v. United States Dep't of Educ., 5 F.3d 1414 (11th Cir. 1993) (refusing to create a "public policy exception" to bar intercept of refunds consisting of earned income credit to repay student loan); *In re* Allen, 266 B.R. 713 (Bankr. N.D. Iowa 2001) (earned income credit may be intercepted for debts owed to HUD and U.S. Department of Agriculture, even though exempt public benefit under Iowa law; state exemptions not applicable to tax refund intercepts).

of a federal tax refund is subject to interception for overdue child support, along with the rest of the refund. The Court allowed the interception despite the argument that the earned income tax credit was more like a government benefit than a tax overpayment. Consumers can avoid offset of the earned income tax credit, however, by using it to decrease the amount of federal income tax withheld from earnings by the employer so that it will not form part of a tax refund that would be subject to intercept.[139]

Agencies can continue to use other collection methods, such as wage garnishment, even while the Treasury Department is intercepting a tax refund.[140] The best way for consumers to avoid a tax intercept is to adjust their income tax withholding so there is no refund to intercept.

10.2.8 Administrative Offset Against Federal Benefits and Other Payments

10.2.8.1 General

The Debt Collection Improvement Act significantly expanded federal agencies' ability to offset non-tax debts against federal benefits and other payments due the debtor.[141] Most administrative offsets are handled centrally by the Treasury Department, but individual agencies also have authority to make offsets,[142] including *ad hoc* non-centralized offsets.[143] In addition, a number of decisions recognize a common law right of offset on the part of federal agencies.[144]

The six-year statute of limitations for suits by the federal government[145] is inapplicable to administrative offset.[146] Until 2008, the statute allowed offset only for claims that had been outstanding for ten years or less.[147] In 2008, the statute was amended to repeal this restriction.[148] The Treasury Department did not, however, delete the ten-year limitation from its regulations until June 11, 2009, when an interim rule became effective.[149] It adopted the interim rule as a final rule on December 23, 2009, effective that day.[150] The amended rule not only allows the government to continue collection after the ten-year period expires but also purports to allow the government to revive collection for debts that had gone past the ten-year limit before the rule was amended.[151]

The Treasury Department may charge a fee for the cost of the offset procedure, which may be added to the debt.[152] The statute allows the Secretary of the Treasury to enter into reciprocal agreements with states so that debts owed to states can also be offset against federal payments.[153]

A debtor can check whether there is a debt that would qualify for offset by calling an automated Treasury Department toll-free number at (800) 304-3107.

10.2.8.2 Benefits and Other Federal Payments Against Which Debts Can Be Offset

Debts can be offset against any type of federal payment,[154] such as payments under federal contracts.[155] Debts cannot be offset against federally insured student loan payments and other payments made by the Department of Education under Title

139 *See* Internal Revenue Service, Employer's Tax Guide, Circular E, *available at* http://irs.gov/pub/irs-pdf/p15.pdf.

140 31 C.F.R. § 285.2(b)(5).

141 31 U.S.C. § 3716.

142 31 C.F.R. §§ 901.3(b)(4)(iii)(C), (c).

143 31 C.F.R. § 901.3(c). *See* § 10.2.8.4, *infra*.

144 Johnson v. All-State Constr., Inc., 329 F.3d 848 (Fed. Cir. 2003) (government retains common law right of offset); Amoco Production Co. v. Fry, 118 F.3d 812 (D.C. Cir. 1997) (government has common law offset rights); McCall Stock Farms, Inc. v. United States, 14 F.3d 1562 (Fed. Cir. 1993) (common law offset rights supplement statutory provisions); United States v. York, 909 F. Supp. 4 (D.D.C. 1995), *rev'd on other grounds*, 112 F.3d 1218 (D.C. Cir. 1997); Brumley v. United States, 55 Fed. Cl. 431 (Fed. Cl. 2003); Boers v. United States, 44 Fed. Cl. 725 (Fed. Cl. 1999) (offset of dairy indemnity payments against Farmer's Home Admin. loan was available under either common law or Debt Collection Improvement Act), *aff'd*, 243 F.3d 561 (Fed. Cir. 2000). *See also* Briggs v. United States, 2008 WL 4667117 (N.D. Cal. Oct. 22, 2008) (United States has the right to set off amounts in litigation, although existence and amount of debt must be determined before offset can be implemented).

145 28 U.S.C. § 2415.

146 28 U.S.C. § 2415(i).

147 31 U.S.C. § 3716(e)(1) (prior to amendment effective July 15, 2008). *See* Lewis v. United States Dep't of Agric., 245 Fed. Appx. 330 (5th Cir. 2007) (when agency has not accelerated debt, ten-year period runs from date each unpaid installment became due); Seward v. United States Dep't of Agric., 229 F. Supp. 2d 557, 569–70 (S.D. Miss. 2002) (interpreting debt as "outstanding" at least from the point it became delinquent). *See also* Brumley v. United States, 55 Fed. Cl. 431 (Fed. Cl. 2003) (discussing government's argument that partial payment extends the ten-year period, but deciding case on other grounds because a separate statute allowed offset without regard to length of time debt was outstanding); § 10.2.12.2, *infra* (discussion of ten-year limitation in context of student loan collections).

148 31 U.S.C. § 3716(e) (as amended by Pub. L. No. 110-275, 122 Stat. 2494 (2008)). *See* Red River Farms v. United States, 2009 WL 2983195 (D. Ariz. Sept. 17, 2009) (government may pursue offset even though suit on debt is barred by statute of limitations); Briggs v. United States, 2008 WL 4667117 (N.D. Cal. Oct. 22, 2008) (noting amendment).

149 74 Fed. Reg. 27,707 (June 11, 2009).

150 74 Fed. Reg. 68,149 (Dec. 23, 2009) (amending 31 C.F.R. §§ 285.5, 285.7). *See also* 74 Fed. Reg. 68,537 (Dec. 28, 2009); 75 Fed. Reg. 745 (Jan. 6, 2010) (correcting an effective date).

151 31 C.F.R. § 285.5(d)(6).

152 31 C.F.R. § 285.4(g); 31 C.F.R. § 285.5(j).

153 31 U.S.C. § 3716(h)(1). *See also* 31 C.F.R. § 285.6; U.S. Dep't of the Treasury, Fiscal Year 2012 Report to the Congress, U.S. Government Receivables and Debt Collection Activities of Federal Agencies 26, *available at* www.fms.treas.gov/news/reports/debt12.pdf (Mar. 2013) (noting that Kentucky, Maryland, Minnesota, New Jersey, New York, and Wisconsin are participating).

154 *See, e.g.*, United States v. Approximately $3174.00 in U.S. Currency, 928 F. Supp. 2d 1040 (E.D. Wis. Mar. 8, 2013) (federal debts can be offset against assets that are seized as part of a criminal case and then returned); Crenshaw v. Alabama Dep't of Human Res., 2008 WL 4416434 (D. Md. Sept. 23, 2008) (federal employee's travel reimbursement can be offset for delinquent child support even though travel reimbursements are exempt from garnishment, as offset is not garnishment). *But cf. In re* Return of Seized Prop., 2011 WL 3759702 (S.D. Cal. Aug. 23, 2011) (mag.) (government's return of cash seized as suspected drug proceeds is not a federal payment so is not subject to offset).

155 Miller v. D. Smith, ___ F. Supp. 2d ___, 2013 WL 3463259 (D.D.C. July 10, 2013).

IV of the Higher Education Assistance Act,[156] veterans benefits,[157] benefits under Part C of the Black Lung Act, or "tier 2" Railroad Retirement benefits.[158] The Secretary of the Treasury also has general authority to exempt any means-tested payments from offset, when so requested by the agency administering the program, and may also exempt other benefits if offset would substantially interfere with or defeat the purposes of the program.[159] When the Secretary had not exercised this discretion, a court refused to protect benefits under a Department of Energy disability program, even though they were are similar in purpose to protected Black Lung Act benefits.[160]

Administrative offset is allowed against Social Security benefits, benefits under Part B of the Black Lung Act, and some Railroad Retirement benefits, notwithstanding the general protection from assignment and execution that these benefits enjoy.[161] Although the statute, as opposed to the regulation,[162] does not explicitly exempt SSI benefits from offset, at current benefit levels SSI benefits will always fall below the statutory $9000 threshold for offset. Veterans' benefits are protected from offset by 38 U.S.C. §§ 5301 and 5314 except for debts arising from veterans' benefit overpayments.

The Supreme Court has held that the government may set off a debt owed by a Social Security disability benefit claimant against an attorney fee granted under the Equal Access to Justice Act (EAJA) for the debtor's attorney's work on the benefits case.[163] The Court held that the EAJA fee award belongs to the debtor, not the attorney, and was not explicitly exempted from the reach of the administrative offset statute.

10.2.8.3 Offset Calculations for Social Security, Black Lung Act, and Railroad Retirement Benefits

Offset against Social Security benefits, benefits under Part B of the Black Lung Act, and some Railroad Retirement benefits is limited to 15% of the "monthly covered benefit payment."[164] Furthermore, $9000 per year ($750 per month) is exempt.[165]

In computing whether any portion of benefits is available for offset, amounts already being deducted to repay overpayments are not counted as received by the debtor.[166] The amount of Social Security benefits available for offset is also reduced by any Medicare insurance premiums that are deducted from the debtor's Social Security check.[167] Thus, if a debtor's $850 monthly Social Security benefit amount is reduced by a $45 monthly Medicare premium and a $50 monthly deduction to repay an overpayment, leaving the debtor with a $755 monthly check, only the amount in excess of $750—in this example, $5—will be available for offset.

Under the statute, the $9000 annual exemption figure is to be reduced by the amount of any federal benefits the debtor receives during the same year that are not subject to offset.[168] Thus, if a debtor received $5000 in veterans' benefits, which are not subject to offset, plus $7000 in Social Security benefits, the $5000 in veterans' benefits would be subtracted from the $9000 exemption, leaving only a $4000 exemption to be applied to the Social Security benefits. The Treasury Department has, however, deferred implementation of this provision because of its complexity.[169]

10.2.8.4 Offset Procedures

There are a number of regulations regarding standards and procedures for administrative offset. The most extensive are the joint regulations,[170] which focus on the steps creditor agencies must take prior to offset, and a set of Treasury Department regulations that govern its implementation of centralized administrative offset.[171] In addition, agencies are required to adopt their own regulations before they collect claims by administrative offset.[172]

Federal agencies are required to refer debts over 180 days delinquent to the Secretary of the Treasury in order to pursue centralized administrative offset.[173] Before submitting the debt to the Treasury Department for offset, the creditor agency must give the debtor notice of the claim, an opportunity to inspect and copy the relevant records, an opportunity for administrative review, and an opportunity to enter into a payment agreement.[174] If a debtor requests a review of the debt and a question

156 31 U.S.C. § 3716(c)(1)(C).

157 38 U.S.C. §§ 5301, 5314.

158 See 63 Fed. Reg. 44,986 (Aug. 21, 1998) (listing these benefit programs as not subject to offset). *Cf.* 31 U.S.C. § 3716(c)(3)(A)(i) (allowing offset against payments due under Part B of Black Lung Benefits Act and Railroad Retirement benefits other than tier 2 benefits).

159 31 U.S.C. § 3716(c)(3)(B); 31 C.F.R. § 901.3(b)(6).

160 State *ex rel.* Dep't of Human Servs. v. Palmer, 212 P.3d 491 (Okla. Civ. App. 2009) (benefits under Energy Employees Occupational Illness Compensation Program are subject to offset).

161 31 U.S.C. § 3716(c)(3)(A).

162 31 C.F.R. § 285.4(b) (defining "covered benefit" to include "a Federal benefit payment payable to an individual under the Social Security Act (other than SSI payments)").

163 Astrue v. Ratliff, 130 S. Ct. 2521, 177 L. Ed. 2d 91 (2010).

164 31 C.F.R. § 285.4(e)(1)(ii). *See also* 31 C.F.R. § 285.4(b) (defining "monthly covered benefit payment" as a "covered benefit payment payable to a payee on a recurring basis at monthly intervals that is not expressly limited in duration, at the time the first payment is made, to a period of less than 12 months").

165 31 U.S.C. § 3716(c)(3)(A)(ii). *See* Yagman v. Whittlesey, 2013 WL 4760968 (C.D. Cal. Aug. 9, 2013) (rejecting debtor's argument that offset is limited to 15% of debtor's benefits after $9000 is first subtracted; interpreting this provision only to require that debtor be left with at least $9000 after the offset).

166 31 U.S.C. § 3716(c)(3)(A)(ii).

167 31 C.F.R. § 285.4(b) (definition of "covered benefit payment"). *See also* Section Analysis (b), 63 Fed. Reg. 44,986, 44,987 (Aug. 21, 1998).

168 31 U.S.C. § 3716(c)(3)(A)(ii)(I).

169 63 Fed. Reg. 44,986, 44,987 (Aug. 21, 1998).

170 31 C.F.R. § 901.3.

171 31 C.F.R. §§ 285.1–285.8.

172 31 U.S.C. § 3716(b); 31 C.F.R. § 901.3(b)(4)(i).

173 31 U.S.C. § 3716(c)(6); 31 C.F.R. §§ 285.12(c), (d), 901.3(b)(1).

174 31 U.S.C. § 3716(a); 31 C.F.R. § 901.3(b)(4)(ii), (e). *See* Sec. & Exch. Comm'n v. Fonecash, Inc., 795 F. Supp. 2d 73 (D.D.C. 2011) (requiring agency to cease collection and return the funds it had collected though Social Security offset when it sent notice to wrong address); Frew v. Van Ru Credit Corp., 2006 WL 2261624 (E.D. Pa. Aug. 7, 2006)

of credibility or veracity is raised, the joint regulations provide for an oral hearing.[175] When an oral hearing is not required, the agency must allow the debtor a "paper hearing," that is, a review of the written record.[176]

Once the claim has been submitted to the Treasury Department, but before offset occurs, the disbursing official must give the debtor a second notice stating the date the offset will begin and other information.[177] A third notice, with similar information, is required at the time of the offset.[178] A debtor who is unsure about how to contact the creditor agency can get contact information by calling the Treasury Offset Program Call Center at (800) 304-3107.

Administrative offsets must be implemented in a manner that meets due process requirements.[179] Agencies are required to establish procedures for providing the debtor with appropriate procedural protections.[180] However, agencies can also conduct their own *ad hoc* offsets, without going through the Treasury Department,[181] and in exigent circumstances can do so without giving notice or providing a prior opportunity for a review hearing.[182]

10.2.8.5 Defenses to Offsets

A consumer may be able to attack a tax intercept or other administrative offset when the statutory and regulatory preconditions to intercept have not been met. The joint regulations provide that "[t]he standards in this chapter do not create any right or benefit, substantive or procedural, enforceable at law or in equity by a party against the United States, its agencies, its officers, or any other person, nor shall the failure of an agency to comply with [these provisions] be available to any debtor as a defense."[183] However, this regulation can be interpreted to mean that failure to comply with the regulations is not a defense to the underlying debt but can still be a basis for quashing the particular collection method.[184] Even if the regulation is interpreted to bar raising noncompliance with the joint regulations as a defense to the offset itself, it should be remembered that many agencies have their own regulations about offset procedures. Failure of the creditor agency to follow its own regulations may be a defense.[185] In addition, many of the steps required by the joint

---

(remanding case to agency because of failure to give debtor hearing she requested); Christensen v. United States, 2006 WL 744296 (W.D. Mo. Mar. 23, 2006) (denying government's motion for summary judgment when notice was deficient in that it did not say that debt would be collected by way of administrative offset); § 10.2.2, *supra*.

175 31 C.F.R. § 901.3(e).

176 31 C.F.R. § 901.3(e).

177 31 C.F.R. § 285.4(f)(1).

178 31 C.F.R. § 285.4(f)(2). *See also* 31 C.F.R. § 901.3(b)(3).

179 *See* Allison v. Madigan, 951 F.2d 869 (8th Cir. 1991) (upholding Farmer's Home Admin.'s 1990 regulations for administrative offset of farmer loans against due process challenge); Old Republic Ins. Co. v. Fed. Crop Ins. Corp., 947 F.2d 269 (7th Cir. 1991) (agency's informal hearing procedures afforded debtor due process); Moseanko v. Yeutter, 944 F.2d 418 (8th Cir. 1991) (describing history of due process litigation regarding offset against farmer subsidies and allowances); Shlikas v. U.S. Dep't of Educ., 2012 WL 1999302 (D. Md. June 1, 2012) (allowing debtor to proceed with claim that he was deprived of due process when he was given only post-offset notice and opportunity for review); Shlikas v. SLM Corp., 2010 WL 3385473 (D. Md. Aug. 25, 2010) (compliance with offset regulations satisfies due process, but government must show that it ruled on debtor's objections and informed him of decision); McBride Cotton & Cattle Corp. v. Veneman, 296 F. Supp. 2d 1125 (D. Ariz. 2003) (upholding offset procedures even though only individual debtors, not corporate debtors, received notice and opportunity to object); United States v. Golden Elevator, Inc., 868 F. Supp. 1063 (C.D. Ill. 1994) (due process did not require Small Bus. Admin. to give debtor notice of possible administrative remedies or opportunity to exhaust administrative remedies before acceleration and foreclosure; debtor knew of right to accelerate from original contact and had been given deferments, seasonal payments, and so forth); Glover v. Brady, 1994 U.S. Dist. LEXIS 13211 (S.D.N.Y. Sept. 13, 1994) (manner of giving notice of offset meets due process requirements if it is reasonably calculated to provide actual notice); Setlech v. United States, 816 F. Supp. 161 (E.D.N.Y. 1993) (reasonable efforts to give pre-offset notice satisfy due process requirements), *aff'd*, 17 F.3d 390 (table) (2d Cir. 1993); Atwater v. Roudebush, 452 F. Supp. 622 (N.D. Ill. 1976) (government's informal conference with debtor before setting off FHA debt against his final salary check did not meet due process requirements). *See also* Omegbu v. United States Dep't of Treasury, 118 Fed. Appx. 989 (7th Cir. 2004) (procedure for offsetting Social Security disability benefits for student loan satisfied due process; one letter to last known address, stating that debt would be referred for offset and disclosing right to hearing; six years later, debtor was approved for SSDI and informed that 15% would be offset); McCarty v. Astrue, 505 F. Supp. 2d 624 (N.D. Cal. 2007) (agency's offset notice satisfied due process); Sibley v. Diversified Collection Servs., Inc., 1997 U.S. Dist. LEXIS 23583 (N.D. Tex. June 10, 1997) (failure to offer borrowers an in-person hearing and failure to notify them of several possible defenses to administrative wage garnishment did not deny them due process); Wagner v. Duffy, 700 F. Supp. 935 (N.D. Ill. 1988) (state procedure for intercept of state and federal income tax refunds to enforce support orders violated due process notice requirements by failing to give unsophisticated defendants notice of common defenses); Knisky v. Bowman, 656 F. Supp. 1540 (W.D. Mich. 1987) (state tax intercept procedure not violative of due process); § 12.3, *infra*.

180 31 C.F.R. § 901.3(b)(4), (5). *See also* Johnson v. United States Dep't of Treasury, 300 Fed. Appx. 860 (11th Cir. 2008) (unpublished) (it is duty of creditor agency, not Treasury, to provide due process protections to debtor); United States v. Beukle, 892 F. Supp. 2d 1176, 1186–87 (D.S.D. 2012) (debtor can seek redress in court only after exhausting administrative remedies); Lepelletier v. United States Dep't of Educ., 2009 WL 4840153 (D.D.C. Dec. 14, 2009) (it is duty of creditor agency, not Treasury, to provide due process protections to debtor).

181 31 C.F.R. § 901.3(c).

182 31 C.F.R. § 901.3(b)(4)(iii)(C).

183 31 C.F.R. § 900.8. *See In re* Zandford, 2006 WL 3533230 (Bankr. D. Del. Nov. 27, 2006) (agency's failure to refer debt to Treasury Department is not a defense to the debt).

184 *See* Ramirez v. Dep't of the Army, 86 M.S.P.B. 211 (Merit Sys. Prot. Bd. 2000) (creditor agency cannot deduct debt from retirement pay until it has complied with its own regulations by completing hearing requested by debtor). *Cf. In re* Zandford, 2006 WL 2036990 (Bankr. D. Del. July 18, 2006) (agency's failure to refer debt to Treasury Department within 180 days was not defense to claim), *reconsideration denied*, 2006 WL 3533230 (Bankr. D. Del. Nov. 27, 2006) (elaborating on reasons).

185 *See* Ramirez v. Dep't of the Army, 86 M.S.P.B. 211 (Merit Sys. Prot. Bd. 2000). *But cf.* Brannum v. Gaddy, 2003 WL 252135 (D.C. Cir. Feb. 3, 2003) (agency's failure to follow statutory notice requirements exactly not a defense, when debtor received actual notice); Lewis v. Glickman, 104 F. Supp. 2d 1311 (D. Kan. 2000) (flawed preliminary hearing not prejudicial when debtor subsequently had full evidentiary hearing and

regulations are duplicated in the statute, and failure to follow the steps that the statute requires before offset should be a defense to the offset.

The regulations state that the failure of a benefits recipient to receive the notices required before and at the time of the offset does not affect the validity of the offset of benefits.[186] The regulations also take the position that a disbursing agency's failure to give notice of offset against a recurring payment does not affect the validity of the offset.[187] These positions seem to conflict with due process and may be attacked on those grounds. Furthermore, to the extent that the regulations set forth due process requirements, failure to comply with them or to follow other procedures that would afford due process would be a defense to the offset.[188]

Another potential defense is that the debt is not in fact past due[189] or legally enforceable.[190] For example, the debtor might be current on payments, the debt may have been discharged in bankruptcy, the government may be estopped by its conduct from enforcing the debt, the agency may have failed to credit the debtor's payments, or the debt may not have been properly assigned from a private party to the government. Under the statutory scheme, these claims should be raised through the creditor agency's appeal system when the creditor agency notifies the debtor that it intends to implement an offset or refer the claim to the Treasury Department for centralized offset.[191]

10.2.9 Denial of Federal Loans, Loan Insurance, and Guarantees

The Claims Collection Act prohibits federal loans, loan insurance, or guarantees, other than disaster loans, to debtors delinquent on federal non-tax claims.[192] This restriction may be waived by an agency head as to an individual debtor or a class of claims.[193] It does not apply if the debt has been discharged in bankruptcy or is being challenged by a timely appeal.[194] It does apply, however, to debts for which the creditor agency has suspended or terminated collection.[195] The debtor can regain eligibility for federal loans, insurance, and guarantees by curing the delinquency or entering into a written repayment agreement that is acceptable to the creditor agency.[196]

10.2.10 Installment Plans and Other Compromises

Installment repayment plans are specifically authorized if the debtor documents an inability to pay in a lump sum.[197] The regulation provides that the amounts and schedule of payments should bear a reasonable relation to the size of the debt and the debtor's ability to pay.[198] The regulations require that installment agreements provide for payment in full within three years or less when possible.[199]

In addition, the joint regulations establish specific procedures for federal agencies to compromise claims.[200] A compromise of a debt in excess of $100,000 must be approved by the Justice Department.[201] Any compromise reached must have some relationship to anticipated possible recovery through further administrative or judicial proceedings.[202]

An agency may compromise a debt if the debtor is unable to pay the full amount in a reasonable time or the government is unable to collect the debt in full within a reasonable time by enforced collection proceedings.[203] In determining whether the debtor is unable to pay, the agency must verify the debtor's financial circumstances through a sworn financial statement and a credit report and must consider the debtor's health, age, present and potential income, assets, and prospects.[204]

Claims may be also be compromised when the cost of collection does not justify the enforced collection of the full

---

administrative appeal; agency's violation of own rule concerning stay not prejudicial when its right to offset was ultimately upheld), *aff'd*, 2002 U.S. App. LEXIS 13269 (10th Cir. July 3, 2002).

186 31 C.F.R. § 285.4(f)(3).

187 31 C.F.R. § 285.5(g)(1).

188 *See* § 10.2.8.4, *supra*.

189 31 U.S.C. § 3716(c)(6); 31 C.F.R. § 901.3(b). *See* Abbe v. Bochert, 2001 Ohio App. LEXIS 2618 (Ohio Ct. App. June 13, 2001) (if obligor is up-to-date on payments of current support and court-ordered installments toward arrearage, and no amount is past due, then despite existence of debt tax refund offset cannot be authorized, but *pro se* litigant failed to preserve issue for review). *See also* Davis v. North Carolina Dep't of Human Res., 505 S.E.2d 77 (N.C. 1998) (interception of federal tax refund was improper when father was current on court-ordered payments; intercept would be allowed if department obtained opinion of attorney general that court-ordered support plan was inadequate for collection of arrears).

190 Seward v. United States Dep't of Agric., 229 F. Supp. 2d 557 (S.D. Miss. 2002) (Department of Agriculture equitably estopped from using offset to collect on farm loan); *In re* Norton, Clearinghouse No. 51,290 (United States Dep't of Hous. & Urban Dev. Bd. of Contract Appeals 1996) (HUDBCA No. 94-A-NY-S732) (lender's failure to give notice of private sale of manufactured home to debtor at last known address barred deficiency claim and thus tax intercept and entitled consumer to U.C.C. § 9-507 damages from HUD). *But cf.* Ingram v. Cuomo, 51 F. Supp. 2d 667 (M.D.N.C. 1999) (deficiency owed after manufactured-home repossession and sale was "past due and legally enforceable" even though it had not been reduced to judgment); Blake v. Cisneros, 837 F. Supp. 834 (S.D. Tex. 1993) (divorce court order did not release debtor, as divorce courts do not have jurisdiction to interfere with creditor's right to collect from either divorcing party).

191 United States v. Harrison, 2007 WL 2332662 (N.D. Tex. Aug. 16, 2007) (declining to hear challenge to amount claimed when debtor had not presented objection to creditor agency).

192 31 U.S.C. § 3720B.

193 31 U.S.C. § 3720B.

194 31 C.F.R. §§ 285.13(d)(2)(ii), (iii).

195 31 C.F.R. § 285.13(d)(3).

196 31 C.F.R. §§ 285.13(e)(1)(iii), (iv).

197 31 C.F.R. § 901.8(a).

198 31 C.F.R. § 901.8(b).

199 31 C.F.R. § 901.8(b).

200 31 C.F.R. pt. 902. *See also* 31 U.S.C. § 3711(a)(2).

201 31 C.F.R. § 902.1.

202 31 C.F.R. § 902.2(c).

203 31 C.F.R. §§ 902.2(a)(1), (2).

204 31 C.F.R. §§ 902.2(b), (c), (g).

amount of the debt,[205] or if there are significant doubts about the agency's chances of winning a lawsuit.[206] Statutory penalties, forfeitures, or claims normally imposed as an aid to enforcement and to compel compliance may also be compromised if the ends of enforcement and compliance are served by the compromise.[207] The statute gives the Secretaries of Defense, Homeland Security, and Veterans Affairs special authority to suspend or terminate collection of claims against the estates of debtors who died while serving on active military duty.[208]

10.2.11 Suspension, Termination, and Discharge of Claims

The former joint regulations allowed agencies to forego offset in light of the debtor's circumstances, or if offset would substantially interfere with or defeat the purposes of the program authorizing the payments against which offset was contemplated.[209] The revised regulations adopted in 2000 do not contain this provision. The statute and the revised regulations do, however, allow for suspension or termination of collection activity or discharge of the indebtedness in certain circumstances.[210]

An agency has authority to suspend collection activity on a debt when it cannot locate the debtor, the debtor's financial condition is expected to improve, or the debtor has requested waiver or review of the debt.[211] In determining whether to suspend collection activity based on the debtor's financial condition, the agency is to take a debtor's future prospects into account and determine whether the applicable statute of limitations is close, whether the debt can be collected in the future by administrative offset, and whether the debtor will pay interest.[212]

Of more benefit to low-income debtors is the authority of agencies to terminate collection activity. Termination is allowed when:

- The agency is unable to collect any substantial amount through its own efforts or the efforts of others;
- The agency is unable to locate the debtor;
- Costs of collection are anticipated to exceed the amount recoverable;
- The debt is legally without merit or cannot be substantiated or enforcement is barred by the applicable statute of limitations; or
- The debt has been discharged in bankruptcy.[213]

After terminating collection activity on a debt, an agency may still sell the debt, offset it against future income or assets that the debtor acquires, or resume collection if the debtor's status changes or a new collection tool becomes available.[214] The agency can also screen future applicants for prior indebtedness[215] and can deny loans, licenses, and other federal benefits and privileges.[216]

If a creditor agency has taken all appropriate steps to collect a debt, it may discharge the debt.[217] Before discharging a debt, the creditor agency must try to sell it if the Treasury Department determines that sale is in the best interests of the United States.[218] Once discharged, however, a debt cannot be sold, and further collection action is precluded.[219]

10.2.12 Federal Agencies' Implementation of Collection Requirements

10.2.12.1 Survey of Selected Agencies

This section briefly describes the actions of selected federal agencies to implement the debt collection authority and requirements already described. Additional limitations or defenses provided by those agencies' enabling statutes and regulations are beyond the scope of this discussion.

10.2.12.2 Department of Education: Student Loans

One of the most pervasive debt collection programs run by the federal government involves student loans. Through the last two decades, Congress kept increasing the Department of Education's arsenal of collection tools to deal with delinquent federal student loans. Department of Education student loan collection efforts are analyzed in detail in NCLC's *Student Loan Law*.[220]

Congress has granted the Department of Education debt collection powers, including administrative wage garnishment, tax refund offset,[221] exemption from statutes of limitations,[222] and authority to collect reasonable collection fees.[223] The Treasury Department allows the Department of Education to handle collection of student loan debts, instead of requiring it to refer claims to it for cross-servicing.[224]

205 31 C.F.R. §§ 902.2(a)(3), (e).
206 31 C.F.R. §§ 902.2(a)(4), (d).
207 31 C.F.R. § 902.3. *See also* 31 C.F.R. § 901.9(g).
208 31 U.S.C. § 3711(f).
209 4 C.F.R. § 102.3(a)(2), *superseded by* 31 C.F.R. pts. 900–904 (as adopted by 65 Fed. Reg. 70,390 (Nov. 22, 2000)).
210 31 U.S.C. § 3711(a)(3); 31 C.F.R. pt. 903. *See* § 10.2.11, *infra*.
211 31 C.F.R. §§ 903.2(a), (b). *See also* 31 U.S.C. § 3711(a)(3).
212 31 C.F.R. § 903.2(b).
213 31 C.F.R. § 903.3(a). *See also* 31 U.S.C. § 3711(a)(3).

214 31 C.F.R. § 903.3(b). *See also* 31 U.S.C. § 3711(i)(1) (authority to sell debts).
215 31 C.F.R. § 903.3(b)(4).
216 31 U.S.C. § 3720B; 31 C.F.R. § 285.13(d)(3). *See* § 10.2.9, *supra*.
217 31 C.F.R. § 903.5.
218 31 U.S.C. § 3711(i)(2); 31 C.F.R. § 903.5(b).
219 31 C.F.R. § 903.5.
220 (4th ed. 2010), *updated at* www.nclc.org/library.
221 *See* National Consumer Law Center, Student Loan Law Ch. 8 (4th ed. 2010), *updated at* www.nclc.org/library.
222 20 U.S.C. § 1091a, *as amended by* Pub. L. No. 102-26, 105 Stat. 123 (1991).
223 *See generally* National Consumer Law Center, Student Loan Law § 7.3 (4th ed. 2010), *updated at* www.nclc.org/library.
224 Dep't of the Treasury, Fin. Mgmt. Serv., Fiscal Year 2009 Report to the Congress: U.S. Government Receivables and Debt Collection

Administrative wage garnishments to collect student loans may be initiated by the Department of Education or by guaranty agencies, depending on the type of loan. Separate statutory authority applies depending on which entity is garnishing. The Higher Education Act (HEA) garnishment authority applies when guaranty agencies are garnishing.[225] The Debt Collection Improvement Act applies to Department of Education garnishments.[226] Although there are some differences between the two statutes, the most significant is no longer relevant. Prior to Congressional changes in 2005, the Higher Education Act administrative wage garnishment statute and regulations allowed garnishment "only" up to 10% of "disposable pay" compared to a 15% limit in the Debt Collection Improvement Act. As of July 1, 2006, the HEA limit was increased to 15%.[227]

15 U.S.C. § 1673 also limits total garnishments to 25% of disposable income, so that a student loan garnishment plus other garnishments should not exceed 25% of income.[228]

Since nearly all federal loans are now originated through the government Direct Loan Program, and many guaranteed loans have been assigned to the Department, over time the vast majority of garnishments will be through the Department and DCIA authority.

Student loans are also denied discharge in bankruptcy except upon a showing of undue hardship.[229] There are, however, a number of grounds on which debtors can seek forgiveness or restructuring of student loan debts under the Higher Education Act and Department of Education regulations.[230]

The Department of Education also has authority to offset Social Security benefits (except SSI benefits) and many other federal benefits to collect student loan debts.[231] The Supreme Court, in *Lockhart v. United States*,[232] held that there was no statute of limitations on the offset of Social Security benefits to pay a student loan.

When collection agencies or attorneys are collecting a student loan, the student is protected by the Fair Debt Collection Practices Act (FDCPA).[233] A private guaranty agency is also defined as a debt collector under the FDCPA unless it obtained the debt before it went into default or falls into the exemption for fiduciaries because of their relationship to the government.[234] State guaranty agencies will likely be exempted under the FDCPA's exclusion for state employees.[235] The Department of Education and the student loan lender itself are exempt from the FDCPA.[236] Private collectors of student loans may also be subject to claims under state debt collection laws.[237]

10.2.12.3 Department of Health and Human Services

The debt collection regulations of the Department of Health and Human Services (HHS) are similar to the joint regulations.[238] They authorize administrative offset, credit bureau reports, installment payment agreements, tax intercepts, administrative wage garnishment, transfer to the Treasury Department for centralized collection, offset against federal employees' salaries, compromise of debts, suspension and termination of collection activities, and referral to collection agencies.

Interest is not charged on debts arising from payments to beneficiaries under Titles II, XVI, and XVIII of the Social Security Act, except for certain overpayments.[239] The Secretary may waive collection of interest, administrative costs, and penalties in certain circumstances.[240]

Debts arising from payments to beneficiaries under Titles II, XVI, and XVIII of the Social Security Act are not to be reported to credit reporting agencies or referred to collection agencies except for certain overpayments.[241] For debts of less than $20,000, the Secretary has authority to compromise the debt or terminate or suspend collection if the debtor is unable

Activities of Federal Agencies 15, *available at* www.fms.treas.gov/news/reports/debt09.pdf.

225 20 U.S.C. § 1095a.

226 31 U.S.C. § 3720(D).

227 20 U.S.C. § 1095a(a)(1); 34 C.F.R. § 682.410(b)(9)(i)(A). *See generally* National Consumer Law Center, Student Loan Law § 5.3 (4th ed. 2010), *updated at* www.nclc.org/library.

228 *See* § 12.4, *infra*.

229 11 U.S.C. § 523(a)(8). *See* National Consumer Law Center, Consumer Bankruptcy Law and Practice § 15.4.3.8 (10th ed. 2012), *updated at* www.nclc.org/library.

230 *See, e.g.*, National Consumer Law Center, Student Loan Law § 6.2 (closed school discharge), § 6.3 (false certification discharge), § 6.4 (unpaid refund discharge), § 6.6 (disability discharge), § 8.2 (loan consolidation), Ch. 9 (borrower's claims against the school) (4th ed. 2010), *updated at* www.nclc.org/library.

231 *See* National Consumer Law Center, Student Loan Law § 8.4 (4th ed. 2010), *updated at* www.nclc.org/library.

232 546 U.S. 142, 126 S. Ct. 699, 163 L. Ed. 2d 557 (2005).

233 31 U.S.C. § 3718(a)(2). *See generally* National Consumer Law Center, Student Loan Law § 7.4.3 (4th ed. 2010), *updated at* www.nclc.org/library; National Consumer Law Center, Fair Debt Collection §§ 4.2.3.1–4.2.3.4, 4.3.8, 4.4.2.2 (8th ed. 2014), *updated at* www.nclc.org/library.

234 *See generally* National Consumer Law Center, Student Loan Law § 7.4.3.5 (4th ed. 2010), *updated at* www.nclc.org/library.

235 15 U.S.C. § 1692a(6)(C). *See* National Consumer Law Center, Fair Debt Collection §§ 4.2.3.1–4.2.3.4, 4.3.8 (8th ed. 2014), *updated at* www.nclc.org/library.

236 15 U.S.C. §§ 1692a(6)(A), 1692a(6)(C).

237 *See* National Consumer Law Center, Fair Debt Collection § 11.2.2 (8th ed. 2014), *updated at* www.nclc.org/library; National Consumer Law Center, Student Loan Law § 7.4.4 (4th ed. 2010), *updated at* www.nclc.org/library.

238 45 C.F.R. pts. 30–33.

239 31 U.S.C. § 3701(d)(2) (making section 3717 inapplicable); 31 C.F.R. § 901.12(a). *Cf.* 20 C.F.R. § 422.303 (Social Security Admin. will charge interest, penalties, and collection costs when authorized by the joint regulations); 45 C.F.R. § 30.18.

Title II refers to Old Age, Survivors, and Disability insurance benefits; Title XVI refers to Supplemental Security Income for Aged, Blind, and Disabled (SSI); Title XVIII refers to Health Insurance for Aged and Disabled (Medicare).

240 45 C.F.R. § 30.18.

241 31 U.S.C. § 3701(d)(2) (making section 3711(e) inapplicable); 45 C.F.R. § 30.13(a); 20 C.F.R. §§ 422.305, 422.301(a)(2), 404.527(a), 416.590(a). *See also* 42 U.S.C. § 404(f) (referring to 31 U.S.C. § 3711(f) but probably means 31 U.S.C. § 3711(e)).

to pay, or if collection would not be cost-effective.[242] Larger debts can also be compromised, but only with Department of Justice approval.

The Social Security Administration has a separate set of rules that allow it to use credit reports, administrative offsets, and administrative wage garnishment to recover Title II[243] and Supplemental Security Income[244] overpayments. In addition, Social Security Administration regulations allow it to reduce Title II benefits by up to 10% a month to recover Title II or SSI overpayments.[245] The recipient may request that less be withheld from the monthly benefit.[246] The entire amount of a retroactive award may be offset to recover an overpayment.[247] The agency has extensive regulations about waiver of overpayments and the procedure for seeking a waiver.[248]

10.2.12.4 Department of Housing and Urban Development

The debt collection regulations of the Department of Housing and Urban Development (HUD) authorize administrative offset, administrative wage garnishment, and salary offset.[249] In 2011, HUD revised these regulations to eliminate provisions that simply repeated requirements of the joint regulations.[250]

10.2.12.5 Department of Veterans Affairs

The debt collection regulations of the Department of Veterans Affairs (VA)[251] permit disclosure to a credit reporting agency that an individual owes an obligation to the United States.[252] The VA regulations regarding administrative offset set forth additional standards for collection efforts.[253] They explicitly state, however, that the Department's failure to comply with the standards shall not be available as a defense to any debtor.[254] The VA has statutory authority to offset benefit overpayments, but not other debts, against veterans' benefits.[255]

Waiver of benefit overpayments and loan debts is authorized when recovery would be against equity and good conscience as defined by VA regulations.[256] In deciding whether to waive all or part of a debt, the agency must weigh the relative fault of the veteran and the agency and consider whether full repayment would result in undue hardship, whether waiver would result in unjust enrichment, whether collection would defeat the purpose of the benefit program, and whether the veteran detrimentally relied on an agency error.[257] Waiver is not permitted if there is fraud, misrepresentation, or bad faith.[258]

The veteran has the right to dispute the existence or the amount of the debt, request waiver of collection, and have a hearing on the waiver request.[259] The veteran also has the right to appeal the VA's decision on either the existence or amount of the debt.[260] Judicial review is, however, deferential: an agency decision will be reversed only if arbitrary and capricious.[261]

There is no deadline for disputing the existence or amount of the debt, but the veteran has only 180 days from the notice of the debt to request waiver of collection.[262] If, within thirty days after the date of notification of the debt, the debtor submits a written dispute of the existence or amount of the debt or requests waiver, offset against current benefits is stayed until the matter is resolved.[263] Offset is limited to 15% of the net monthly payment of veterans' benefits.[264]

With respect to debts arising from VA-guaranteed home loans, the VA does not attempt to collect deficiency judgments after foreclosure from veterans except in cases involving fraud, misrepresentation, or bad faith.[265] When a veteran sells

242 45 C.F.R. §§ 30.22, 30.24, 30.26, 30.31, 30.32.

243 20 C.F.R. §§ 404.501–404.545, 422.301–422.445 (reporting to credit bureaus, administrative offset, administrative wage garnishment; note that according to 20 C.F.R. §§ 404.527 and 415.590(a) these steps are allowed only if the overpayment occurred after the beneficiary became eighteen, the beneficiary is no longer entitled to benefits, and the Social Security Administration has determined that the overpayment is not otherwise recoverable).

244 20 C.F.R. §§ 416.581–416.590.

245 42 U.S.C. § 1320b-17(b)(1); 20 C.F.R. §§ 416.571, 416.573(b)(1).
The 10% cap does not apply if the debt involved fraud, willful misrepresentation, or concealment of information. 42 U.S.C. § 1320b-17(b)(2); 20 C.F.R. § 416.571.

246 20 C.F.R. § 416.571.

247 20 C.F.R. § 416.573(a).

248 20 C.F.R. §§ 404.506–404.512.

249 24 C.F.R. §§ 17.61–17.113.

250 76 Fed. Reg. 69,044 (Nov. 7, 2011).

251 38 C.F.R. §§ 1.901–1.995.

252 38 C.F.R. § 1.916.

253 38 C.F.R. §§ 1.911, 1.912, 1.912a. *See also* 38 C.F.R. §§ 1.980–1.995 (offset against federal employees' salaries).

254 38 C.F.R. § 1.901.

255 38 U.S.C. §§ 5301, 5314.

256 38 C.F.R. §§ 1.962–1.965.

257 38 C.F.R. § 1.965(a).

258 38 C.F.R. § 1.965(b).

259 38 C.F.R. § 1.911(c).

260 38 C.F.R. § 1.911(c). *See, e.g.*, Steward v. Nicholson, 20 Vet. App. 227 (table), 2005 WL 3028821 (Vet. App. Oct. 13, 2005) (vacating and remanding denial of waiver of mortgage guarantee debt; agency should make findings regarding circumstances of foreclosure); King v. Principi, 19 Vet. App. 160 (table), 2004 WL 3111063 (Vet. App. Dec. 17, 2004) (vacating denial of waiver); Cullen v. Brown, 5 Vet. App. 510 (Vet. App. 1993) (vacating and remanding denial of waiver when agency failed to consider key factors).

261 Mueller v. Nicholson, 20 Vet. App. 510 (table), 2006 WL 176517 (Vet. App. Jan. 11, 2006); Kinslow v. Nicholson, 20 Vet. App. 132 (table), 2005 WL 1545135 (Vet. App. June 20, 2005) (not arbitrary and capricious); Zyglewicz v. Nicholson, 20 Vet. App. 127 (table), 2005 WL 1239147 (Vet. App. May 19, 2005) ("plausible basis" for finding).

262 38 U.S.C. § 5302.

263 38 C.F.R. § 1.912a(c). *See* Ginish v. Prinicipi, 2003 WL 21191195 (Vet. App. May 16, 2003) (finding that VA wrongfully offset VA benefits while veteran's dispute of the debt was pending).
The length of the stay depends on various factors listed in the regulation. The VA has the authority to begin offset immediately if deferring offset would jeopardize collection.

264 38 C.F.R. § 1.912a(e)(3).

265 38 U.S.C. § 3703(e)(1).
This protection applies to loans secured on or after Jan. 1, 1990. *See also* 38 C.F.R. §§ 1.964, 1.965.

a VA-financed home, the VA has special rules for releasing the veteran from further liability on the mortgage debt.[266]

The National Veterans Legal Services Project has published a manual to assist veterans and their representatives in dealing with VA benefit and debt issues.[267]

10.2.12.6 Department of Agriculture

The collection of loans owed to the Department of Agriculture is governed by rules reflecting the provisions of the Claims Collection Act.[268] In early 2008, the Department overhauled these rules.[269] The agency must give the debtor written notice thirty days before exercising administrative offset, explaining the proposed action and the method of obtaining review.[270] The debtor may request, in writing, a review of the agency's determination that the debt exists and the propriety of the administrative offset.[271] The debtor may avoid offset by submitting a repayment plan acceptable to the agency.[272] There are similar provisions for advance notice, hearings, and written repayment agreements when salary offset is proposed.[273] The Department has also adopted separate offset regulations for some of its programs under the authority of certain agriculture statutes.[274]

The Department's rules do not apply to collection of Food Stamp debts owed by individual recipients.[275] Collection of those debts is the obligation of states when administering their Food Stamp programs.[276]

10.2.13 Debtor Remedies for Illegal Agency Collection Practices

10.2.13.1 Overview

The joint regulations expressly prohibit raising agency misconduct as a defense to a claim: "[T]he failure of an agency to comply with the provisions of this chapter shall not be available as a defense to any debtor."[277] In addition, the joint regulations state that they do "not create any right or benefit, substantive or procedural, enforceable at law or in equity by a party against the United States, its agencies, its officers, or any other person."[278] Nonetheless, there are a number of judicial remedies available to those illegally harassed for debts they owe to federal agencies. These are discussed in the subsections that follow.

If the debtor seeks review of the interception of a tax refund to pay a child support, state tax, or federal agency debt, federal tax law prevents federal courts from exercising jurisdiction over the Treasury Department.[279] That statute, however, does not preclude federal court jurisdiction over the agency to which the offset was paid.[280]

There is a six-year statute of limitations for actions against the government.[281] Some courts hold that this statute of limitations is jurisdictional and that the usual exceptions to statutes of limitations, such as equitable tolling, do not apply.[282]

If the government is using procedures under the Claims Collection Act to collect a judgment, the court that issued the judgment might provide a forum to resolve collection disputes—even disputes that relate to administrative offset and other non-judicial collection efforts.[283]

266 38 U.S.C. § 3713. *See also* 38 C.F.R. § 1.964.

267 Veterans Benefits Manual (2013).

For information about ordering this manual, visit the website of the National Veterans Legal Services Program, www.nvlsp.org, or the website of LexisNexis, which publishes the manual, http://bookstore.lexis.com.

268 7 C.F.R. pt. 3. *See In re* Huff, 343 B.R. 136 (W.D. Pa. 2006) (discussing notice requirements for tax intercept to repay Rural Housing Service loan); Lewis v. Glickman, 104 F. Supp. 2d 1311 (D. Kan. 2000) (upholding agency's offset decision despite its dilatoriness and multiple procedural violations when debtor failed to show prejudice), *aff'd*, 2002 U.S. App. LEXIS 13269 (10th Cir. July 3, 2002).

269 73 Fed. Reg. 1 (Jan. 2, 2008).

270 7 C.F.R. § 3.41.

271 7 C.F.R. § 3.42.

272 7 C.F.R. § 3.42.

273 7 C.F.R. §§ 3.70–3.87.

274 7 C.F.R. pt. 792 (Farm Services Agency), pt. 1403 (Commodity Credit Corp. and, by cross-reference, Farm Services Agency). *See* 60 Fed. Reg. 43,705 (Aug. 23, 1995) (citing statutory authority for these regulations). *See also* McBride Cotton & Cattle Corp. v. Veneman, 296 F. Supp. 2d 1125 (D. Ariz. 2003) (upholding scope of offset authority of 7 C.F.R. § 1403.7 as permissible under agriculture statute).

275 7 C.F.R. § 3.1(c)(1). *See also* 73 Fed. Reg. 1, 1 (Jan. 2, 2008).

276 *See* 7 C.F.R. § 273.18 (setting forth requirements for states' Food Stamp debt collections).

277 31 C.F.R. § 900.8. *See* § 10.2.8.5, *supra*.

278 31 C.F.R. § 900.8.

279 26 U.S.C. § 6402(f). *See* United States v. Hunter, 2007 WL 2122052 (E.D.N.Y. July 23, 2007); Albert v. OSI Educ. Servs., Inc., 2004 WL 483166 (D. Minn. Mar. 11, 2004). *Cf.* Hall-Ditchfield v. United States, 2008 WL 2381533 (E.D. Pa. June 10, 2008), *aff'd*, 366 Fed. Appx. 391 (3d Cir. 2010) (§ 6402(f) bars suit to recover tax refund that was applied to child support, state taxes, or federal agency debt, but not to federal taxes).

280 26 U.S.C. § 6402(f).

281 28 U.S.C. § 2401(a).

282 Kim v. United States, 707 F.3d 335 (D.C. Cir. 2013) (statute of limitations for 26 U.S.C. § 7433 claim for improper tax collection practices is jurisdictional and non-waivable); Stocker v. United States, 705 F.3d 225 (6th Cir. 2013) (affirming dismissal when taxpayer presented evidence that claim had been mailed on last day of limitations period, but postmark date is only acceptable proof of timely mailing; here refusing to order adverse inference against IRS, which had destroyed post-marked envelope); Adams v. I.R.S., 2014 WL 457915 (C.D. Cal. Feb. 3, 2014) (claims for return of overpaid taxes; equitable tolling not available, but may be tolled if taxpayer can prove disability); Terry v. United States Small Bus. Admin., 699 F. Supp. 2d 49 (D.D.C. 2010) (refusing to toll statute of limitations in action seeking review of defendant's determination that loans were in default). *But see* Santos *ex rel.* Beato v. United States, 559 F.3d 189 (3d Cir. 2009) (equitably tolling statute of limitations for filing administrative claim, a prerequisite for FTCA claim, when, despite counsel's diligence, claimant failed to learn that doctor at federally funded, apparently private, clinic, was federal employee for FTCA purposes; claim here brought within Pennsylvania statute for claims by minors but outside FTCA limitations period).

283 *See, e.g.*, Sec. & Exch. Comm'n v. Fonecash, Inc., 795 F. Supp. 2d 73 (D.D.C. 2011) (requiring agency to cease collection and return the funds it had collected though Social Security offset when it sent notice to wrong address), *motion for reconsideration dismissed and opinion vacated in light of parties' resolution of the debt*, 2012 WL 3656482 (D.D.C. Mar. 21, 2012).

10.2.13.2 *Bivens* Suit

Individual federal employees may be found liable for violation of constitutional rights when their conduct "violates clearly established statutory or constitutional rights of which a reasonable person would have known."[284] In *Bivens v. Six Unknown Named Agents of the Federal Bureau of Narcotics*,[285] the United States Supreme Court determined that a federal employee otherwise entitled to qualified immunity from suit loses this defense in the face of unreasonable conduct. "Reasonableness" is to be measured objectively by reference to law clearly established at the time of the incident in question.[286] *Bivens* effectively creates a private cause of action for damages for constitutional violations.[287] The Supreme Court has refused, however, to extend *Bivens* to permit suits against federal agencies (as opposed to federal employees).[288]

A *Bivens* remedy does not lie when (1) Congress has provided an equally effective alternative remedy and declared it to be a substitute for recovery under the Constitution, or (2) "special factors counsel hesitation."[289] A *Bivens* suit is not allowed even when the remedy Congress has created offers the plaintiff significantly less protection.[290] A number of courts applying these criteria have concluded that a *Bivens* remedy is not available against the IRS, because the remedies in the Internal Revenue Code are adequate.[291] Judicial immunity will shield many government attorneys from liability.[292]

A *Bivens* complaint must allege facts that tie a specific federal employee to a specific wrongful act.[293] A *Bivens* claim will not lie for vicarious or supervisory liability.[294]

Regardless of *Bivens*, consumers may be able to seek injunctive relief against federal actors when their due process rights under specific federal laws have been violated.[295] In addition, sovereign immunity can be expressly waived by statute, giving a consumer a right to seek money damages in circumstances in which a *Bivens* suit would be unavailable.[296]

284 Harlow v. Fitzgerald, 457 U.S. 800, 818, 102 S. Ct. 2727, 73 L. Ed. 2d 396 (1982).

285 Bivens v. Six Unknown Named Agents of the Fed. Bureau of Narcotics, 403 U.S. 388, 91 S. Ct. 1999, 29 L. Ed. 2d 619 (1971), *on remand*, 456 F.2d 1339 (2d Cir. 1972).

286 Harlow v. Fitzgerald, 457 U.S. 800, 818, 102 S. Ct. 2727, 73 L. Ed. 2d 396 (1982). *See also* Hanlon v. Berger, 526 U.S. 808, 119 S. Ct. 1706, 143 L. Ed. 2d 978 (1999); Lopez v. United States, 2013 WL 5526422 (M.D. Fla. Aug. 27, 2013) (violation of clearly established right not shown; prison officials who garnished debtor's account were acting within scope of their discretionary authority).

287 *See* Hernandez v. Lattimore, 612 F.2d 61, 65 (2d Cir. 1979); Adams v. United States, 2009 WL 395192 (E.D. Cal. Feb. 17, 2009), *report and recommendations adopted by* 2009 WL 959962 (E.D. Cal. Apr. 6, 2009) (farmers alleged sufficient facts for *Bivens* claim: that individual Farm Service Agency credit manager failed to provide information and forms necessary for workout option, made misrepresentations, and concealed wrongful acts); Shiraishi v. United States, 2007 WL 2263071 (D. Haw. Aug. 3, 2007) (borrower stated *Bivens* claim for denial of due process against Farm Service employee whose delay in processing homestead application caused farmer to lose opportunity to lease back farm, but claim barred by res judicata because same issues raised in foreclosure proceeding), *aff'd*, 316 Fed. Appx. 587 (9th Cir. 2009); Wahad v. Fed. Bureau of Investigation, 994 F. Supp. 237, 239 (S.D.N.Y. 1998); Taylor v. United States Internal Revenue Serv., 915 F. Supp. 1015, 1019 (N.D. Iowa 1996), *aff'd*, 106 F.3d 833 (8th Cir. 1997).

288 Fed. Deposit Ins. Corp. v. Meyer, 510 U.S. 471, 114 S. Ct. 996, 127 L. Ed. 2d 308 (1994). *See also* Ashcroft v. Iqbal, 129 S. Ct. 1937, 1948, 173 L. Ed. 2d 868, 556 U.S. 662 (2009) (noting reluctance to extend *Bivens* to new contexts or new categories of defendants); Dye v. United States, 516 F. Supp. 2d 61 (D.D.C. 2007) (*Bivens* allows actions against individual agents but not the government itself).

289 Carlson v. Green, 446 U.S. 14, 18–19, 100 S. Ct. 1468, 64 L. Ed. 2d 15 (1980). *See also* Yowell v. Abbey, 532 Fed. Appx. 708 (9th Cir. 2013) (no *Bivens* claim against Bureau of Land Management officials enforcing trespass and grazing permit rule), *on remand*, 2013 WL 5278772 (D. Nev. Sept. 16, 2013) (dismissing claims); Doe v. Rumsfeld, 683 F.3d 390 (D.C. Cir. 2012) (dismissing *Bivens* claim; special factors, here national security, and lack of private remedy in Detainee Treatment Act, counsel hesitation in extending *Bivens* remedy); Taylor v. Defense Finance & Accounting Serv., 2014 WL 28820 (E.D. Cal. Jan. 2, 2014) (Board of Correction of Military Records provides adequate remedy for misconduct in collection of disputed salary overpayment); Hopper v. United States, 2013 WL 1908333 (D. Nev. May 7, 2013) (18 U.S.C. § 3664(p), part of criminal restitution statute, which provides that the statute cannot be construed to create a cause of action, bars *Bivens* claim against federal officer who allegedly misapplied restitution payments).

290 Bush v. Lucas, 462 U.S. 367, 388–90, 103 S. Ct. 2404, 76 L. Ed. 2d 648 (1983). *See also* Schweicker v. Chilicky, 487 U.S. 412, 425, 108 S. Ct. 2460, 101 L. Ed. 2d 370 (1988) (plaintiffs complaining of wrongful acts by Social Security administrators must confine their complaints to the procedures provided by the Social Security Act); Wilson v. Astrue, 333 Fed. Appx. 179 (9th Cir. 2009) (*Bivens* action will not lie for offsetting of disability benefits for student loan debt); Hudson Valley Black Press v. Internal Revenue Serv., 409 F.3d 106 (2d Cir. 2005) (comprehensiveness of statutory scheme, not adequacy of remedies, is determinative); Murrhee v. Principi, 364 F. Supp. 2d 782 (C.D. Ill. 2005) (no *Bivens* claim for due process violations in veterans' pension matter; remedial scheme provided by statute). *But cf.* Hardesty v. Sacramento Metro. Air Quality Mgmt. Dist., 2012 WL 1131387 (E.D. Cal. Mar. 29, 2012) (APA does not provide adequate mechanism to challenge warrantless entry on plaintiff's property, because this was not "final agency action"; allowing *Bivens* action to go forward for "straightforward Fourth Amendment claim"); Reagan v. Peterson, 2011 WL 6433701 (N.D. Tex. Nov. 15, 2011) (Civil Asset Forfeiture statute did not provide remedy when agents turned seized cars over to lender without bringing any forfeiture action; former owner could state *Bivens* claim), *report and recommendation adopted by* 2011 WL 6592372 (N.D. Tex. Dec. 22, 2011).

291 *See* § 10.2.13.10, *infra*.

292 Uptergrove v. United States, 2009 WL 2244185 (E.D. Cal. July 27, 2009) (U.S. attorney and trial attorney from Tax Division of Department of Justice).

293 Nuclear Transp. & Storage, Inc. v. United States, 890 F.2d 1348 (6th Cir. 1989); Allen v. Dep't of Educ., 2009 WL 649578 (N.D. Tex. Mar. 12, 2009) (must show that individual defendant was personally involved in the intentional deprivation of a constitutional right); Bateman v. United States, 2009 WL 2043871 (M.D. Tenn. July 9, 2009).

294 Ashcroft v. Iqbal, 129 S. Ct. 1937, 173 L. Ed. 2d 868, 556 U.S. 662 (2009).

295 *See, e.g.*, Atwater v. Roudebush, 452 F. Supp. 622 (N.D. Ill. 1976) (denying government's motion for summary judgment on due process claim for injunctive relief regarding offset of Federal Housing Admin. debt against salary).

296 Irwin v. Dep't of Veterans Affairs, 498 U.S. 89, 111 S. Ct. 453, 112 L. Ed. 2d 435 (1990); United States v. Mitchell, 445 U.S. 535, 538, 100 S. Ct. 1349, 63 L. Ed. 2d 607 (1980) (waiver of sovereign immunity must be unequivocally expressed). *See also* Donovan v. Gober, 5 F. Supp. 2d 142 (W.D.N.Y. 1998) (Department of Veterans Affairs has waived

10.2.13.3 Suit Under Privacy Act

A debtor might consider a claim under the Privacy Act[297] if, for example, the government wrongfully discloses information about the debt. A Privacy Act claim will lie only against a federal agency or "government-controlled corporation," not against individual federal employees[298] or private collectors, private colleges, or other non-federal entities involved in collecting a debt.[299]

If a violation of the Privacy Act is intentional or willful, the remedy is an award of at least $1000 or any greater sum which represents actual damages, plus costs and attorney fees.[300] The plaintiff must prove some actual damages in order to qualify for the $1000 award.[301] Emotional distress damages are not available.[302] The statute also makes injunctions available in some circumstances.[303] The plaintiff may need to exhaust administrative remedies before filing suit.[304] Some courts hold that, since the Privacy Act provides a comprehensive remedial scheme, it precludes a *Bivens* action for damages.[305]

sovereign immunity, so suit for money damages caused by unconstitutional administrative offset may be filed against it even though such a suit could not be brought under *Bivens*).

297 5 U.S.C. § 552a.

298 Huene v. U.S. Dep't of the Treasury, 2012 WL 1197564 (E.D. Cal. Apr. 10, 2011) (dismissing claim against employee; agency is only proper defendant), *adopted by* 2012 WL 22610007 (E.D. Cal. June 15, 2012); Lim v. United States, 2011 WL 2650889 (D. Md. July 5, 2011) (same).

299 Lengerich v. Columbia College, 633 F. Supp. 2d 599 (N.D. Ill. 2009) (private college, to which DOE delegated significant authority to process student loan applications, not a "government-controlled corporation"); Huertas v. Dep't of Educ., 2009 WL 3165442 (D.N.J. Sept. 28, 2009) (no claim against private collector hired by defendant).

300 5 U.S.C. § 552a(g)(4). *See, e.g.*, Taylor v. Defense Finance & Accounting Serv., 2014 WL 28820 (E.D. Cal. Jan. 2, 2014) (intentional or willful act not shown; failed to show that premature reporting of disputed salary overpayment was intentional, and not, as agency claimed, a computer programming error); Beattie v. Astrue, 845 F. Supp. 2d 184 (D.D.C. 2012) (construing "intentional or willful" to mean "so patently egregious and unlawful that anyone undertaking the conduct should have known it unlawful"; not shown here when requester seeking records to support privacy claim was told he could obtain records from local SSA office and information from a manual); Grant v. United States, 2012 WL 5289309 (E.D. Cal. Oct. 23, 2012) (negligence not sufficient; claim fails when Veterans Administration had procedure for redacting sensitive information from claim packet sent to insurers, but employee who prepared claim did not realize that names of certain drugs would reveal "sensitive medical condition"), *adopted by* 2011 WL 2967323 (E.D. Cal. July 19, 2011).

301 Doe v. Chao, 540 U.S. 614, 124 S. Ct. 1204, 157 L. Ed. 2d 1122 (2004) (actual damages must be shown).

302 F.A.A. v. Cooper, 132 S. Ct. 1441 (2012).

303 5 U.S.C. § 552a(g)(2), (3).

304 Reitz v. United States Dep't of Agriculture, 2010 WL 786586 (D. Kan. Mar. 4, 2009) (exhaustion not shown; farmers seeking correction of their files failed to respond to agency's request for more detailed information).

305 Wilson v. Libby, 535 F.3d 697 (D.C. Cir. 2008); Lim v. United States, 2011 WL 2650889 (D. Md. July 5, 2011) (no *Bivens* action for conduct actionable under Privacy Act); Sullivan v. United States Postal Serv., 944 F. Supp. 191 (W.D.N.Y. 1996); Williams v. Dep't of Veterans' Affairs 879 F. Supp. 578 (E.D. Va. 1995).

10.2.13.4 Administrative Procedures Act

The Administrative Procedures Act (APA) provides that "final agency actions for which there is no other adequate remedy in a court are subject to judicial review."[306] This language might be broadly construed to cover a case of agency misconduct in debt collection.[307] An APA action is also available to review an agency's determination to offset a debt against a tax refund or other government payment.[308] The agency decision must be final, that is, it must be the culmination of agency action, and legal consequences must flow from it.[309]

APA review is also available if an agency fails to take "a discrete agency action that it is required to take" and is not

306 5 U.S.C. § 704.

307 *See* Reitz v. United States Dep't of Agriculture, 2010 WL 786586 (D. Kan. Mar. 4, 2010) (Farm Serv. Administration decision to accelerate farm loan was not in accordance with the law when it violated statute and agency policy applying moratorium on acceleration of loans when farmer had discrimination claim pending; remanding to agency); Sanon v. Dep't of Higher Educ., 2010 WL 1049264 (E.D.N.Y. Mar. 18, 2010) (APA review available for Department of Education's decision to garnish wages, but highly deferential "arbitrary and capricious" standard), *aff'd*, 453 Fed. Appx. 28 (2d Cir. 2011); Standifer v. Sec. Exch. Comm'n, 542 F. Supp. 2d 1312 (N.D. Ga. 2008).

308 *See* Anand v. United States Nat'l Sec. Agency, 2006 WL 3257430 (N.D.N.Y. Nov. 9, 2006) (APA action may lie for agency's failure to comply with Debt Collection Improvement Act, but debtor here failed to exhaust administrative remedies, and agency's threats to use collection methods were not final actions); Lewis v. Glickman, 104 F. Supp. 2d 1311 (D. Kan. 2000), *aff'd*, 2002 U.S. App. LEXIS 13269 (10th Cir. July 3, 2002); Ingram v. Cuomo, 51 F. Supp. 2d 667 (M.D.N.C. 1999). *Cf.* Sheehy v. Johanns, 2007 WL 656429 (W.D.N.Y. Feb. 27, 2007) (review is available only of agency's determination to accelerate loans, which debtor appealed within agency, not unappealed agency decision to institute administrative offsets). *But cf.* Shabtai v. United States Dep't of Educ., 2003 WL 21983025 (S.D.N.Y. Aug. 20, 2003) (injunction against offset not available unless Sec. of Educ. acted outside authority).

309 Sackett v. U.S. Envtl. Prot. Agency, 132 S. Ct. 1367 (2012) (EPA compliance order is final agency action; consequences include financial liability that increases with time; enforcement action not adequate remedy when timing is up to agency and penalties will continue to increase); Cohen v. United States, 650 F.3d 717 (D.C. Cir. 2011) (IRS notice setting forth procedure for claiming refund of wrongfully collected telephone taxes was final agency action, reviewable under APA; action for refund pursuant to Internal Revenue Code not an adequate remedy at law); Furie Operating Alaska v. U.S. Dep't of Homeland Sec., 2013 WL 1628639 (D. Alaska Apr. 15, 2013) (agency's penalty determination was final determination for which there was no adequate remedy in court; decision created obligation, which would increase if not timely paid; collection action brought by government was not adequate remedy because it would not provide de novo review of the correctness of the penalty and because obligee's business would suffer from continuing existence of the penalty); Yagman v. Whittlesey, 2012 WL 5831169 (C.D. Cal. Nov. 2, 2012) (agency's failure to honor debtor's request that Social Security offset be reduced by $100 per month not final agency action, so court lacks jurisdiction); Bituminous Cas. Corp. v. Walden Res., L.L.C., 672 F. Supp. 2d 835 (E.D. Tenn. 2009) (Coast Guard's demand for specific sum from polluter was consummation of agency action, but "legal consequences" did not result because failure to pay would lead to referral to other agency, which would make own decisions about collection tactics).

discretionary.[310] APA review is not, however, the proper cause of action on a claim for money damages.[311]

An APA action is not available if another statute grants permission to sue, or expressly or impliedly forbids the relief sought,[312] or if a decision is committed to the agency's sole discretion.[313] The APA applies only to agency decisions that must be determined on the record after hearing; if less formality is permitted, APA review is not available.[314]

The standard of review is a highly deferential "arbitrary and capricious" standard, and decisions will be reversed only if the agency ignores non-frivolous arguments or makes a decision unsupported by evidence or inconsistent with its precedents.[315] Generally, administrative remedies must be exhausted before judicial review is sought.[316] When the exhaustion requirement is not mandated by the underlying statute itself, it may be waivable in some circumstances, such as when the appellant shows that exhaustion would be futile.[317]

10.2.13.5 Federal Tort Claims Act

The Federal Tort Claims Act (FTCA)[318] may provide an avenue for redress against a federal agency for negligence or certain intentional torts committed by its employees. The FTCA acts as a statutory waiver of the United States' sovereign immunity for tortious conduct, but the numerous exceptions to this waiver work to bar claims against federal employees

310 Sheldon v. Vilsack, 538 Fed. Appx. 644 (6th Cir. 2013) (no APA review when statute provides that agency "may" provide various forms of relief to rural homeowner borrowers); Kostenko v. U.S. Dep't of Health and Human Serv., 916 F. Supp. 2d 661 (S.D.W.V. 2013)(no jurisdiction when agency had not yet issued a decision on claim for waiver of scholarship repayment, despite long delay after last communication from agency).

311 O'Connell v. Mills, 2014 WL 354696 (E.D. Mich. Jan. 31, 2014); Howard v. United States, 949 F. Supp. 2d 54 (D.D.C. 2013) (APA does not waive sovereign immunity for claim for money damages); Houseal v. McHugh, 2013 WL 4517178 (D.D.C. Aug. 27, 2013) (claim for equitable relief from agency's refusal to forgive a debt, here ROTC scholarship, not claim for money damages; noting distinction between cases seeking declaration that funds need not be paid in future and cases seeking refund of funds already paid out).

312 Sackett v. U.S. Envtl. Prot. Agency, 132 S. Ct. 1367 (2012) (noting strong presumption in favor of reviewability; Clean Water Act does not forbid APA review of EPA compliance order); Junior v. New York Hous., Preservation and Dev. Corp., 2013 WL 646464 (S.D.N.Y. Jan. 18, 2013) (claim that HUD negligently supervised the agency that administered a subsidized housing program was tort claim covered by FTCA; when claim barred by failure to exhaust administrative remedies, FTCA forbade APA relief); Faison v. Duncan, 2012 WL 1231890 (N.D. Ga. Apr. 12, 2012) (APA review available, because Department of Education provides no appeals process or dispute resolution mechanism to challenge reinstatement of student loan after disability discharge); Russell v. United States, 2009 WL 4050938 (N.D. Cal. Nov. 20, 2009) (equitable relief unavailable under APA for government's collection of charges forbidden by its contract with debtors, as Little Tucker Act, which gives courts jurisdiction to hear contract claims, impliedly prohibits injunctive relief). *See also* Young v. U.S. Dep't of Agric., 2011 WL 4543083 (W.D. Ky. Sept. 28, 2011) (review unavailable if alternative remedy was available, even if it no longer is).

313 Molina v. BBCN Bank, 2013 WL 4590793 (C.D. Cal. Aug. 26, 2013) (Small Business Administration's decision whether to purchase loan from bank is committed to agency's sole discretion; APA review not available).

314 Young v. U.S. Dep't of Agric., 2011 WL 4543083 (W.D. Ky. Sept. 28, 2011) (decision to foreclose or accelerate Farm Service loans not required to be made on the record; APA review not available).

315 Crow Tribal Hous. Auth. v. U.S. Dep't of Hous. & Urban Dev., 924 F. Supp. 2d 1217 (D. Mont. 2013) (review is deferential, but court must determine whether agency has "examined the relevant data and articulated a satisfactory explanation for its action, including a rational connection between the facts found and the choice made"; agency action was arbitrary and capricious when it failed to provide required hearing to housing authority from which it sought to recoup overpayment); Lubow v. U.S. Dep't of State, 923 F. Supp. 2d 28 (D.D.C. 2013) (court should "determine whether or not as a matter of law the evidence in the administrative record permitted the agency to make the decision it did"; agency must "articulate a rational connection between the facts found and the choice made"; here affirming agency's decision that employees had been overpaid and repayment should not be waived); Turner v. Vilsack, 2013 WL 6074114 (D. Or. Nov. 18, 2013) (agency's failure to comply with its handbook raises "serious questions going to the merits" sufficient to support preliminary injunction against foreclosure on subsidized housing complex); Foster v. Mabus, 895 F. Supp. 2d 135 (D.D.C. 2012) (must show a rational connection between facts found and decision made); Wilhelmus v. Geren, 796 F. Supp. 2d 157 (D.D.C. 2011); Buckingham v. Mabus, 772 F. Supp. 2d 295 (D.D.C. 2011) (review especially deferential when agency given broad discretion; record shows that Board of Correction of Naval Records weighed mitigating factors before ordering former probationary officer to pay back ROTC scholarship); Norasteh v. U.S. Dep't of Educ., 2011 WL 2473457 (S.D.N.Y. Mar. 18, 2011) (agency's review of documents was sufficient to support decision to garnish wages and offset tax refunds), *report and recommendation adopted by* 2011 WL 2493968 (S.D.N.Y. June 22, 2011).

316 O'Connell v. Mills, 2014 WL 354696 (E.D. Mich. Jan. 31, 2014) (denying preliminary judgment against offset; no likelihood of success because of, *inter alia*, failure to exhaust administrative remedies); Boyce v. NCO Fin. Sys. Inc., 2013 WL 364721 (W.D. Wash. Jan. 30, 2013) (dismissing debtor's challenge to administrative wage garnishment because he failed to seek administrative review); Beattie v. Astrue, 845 F. Supp. 2d 184 (D.D.C. Feb. 28, 2012) (notwithstanding extensive efforts to challenge overpayment determination, Social Security recipient failed to either exhaust administrative remedies or show that exhaustion would be futile); United States v. Margolis, 2009 WL 2255336 (D.N.J. July 28, 2009) (exhaustion of remedies shown; neither statute nor IRS rule required administrative procedure before judicial review of decision to terminate installment agreement); Anand v. United States Nat'l Sec. Agency, 2006 WL 3257430 (N.D.N.Y. Nov. 9, 2006) (dismissing challenge to federal collection efforts due to failure to exhaust agency remedies).

317 Bartlett v. U.S. Dep't of Agric., 716 F.3d 464 (8th Cir. 2013) (setting forth narrow exceptions to exhaustion requirement: futility, legal question, and equitable estoppel; here denying equitable estoppel even though Department of Agriculture employees misinformed farmers about exhaustion requirement); Avocados Plus, Inc. v. Veneman, 370 F.3d 1243 (D.C. Cir. 2004); Marine Mammal Conservancy, Inc. v. Dep't of Agriculture, 134 F.3d 409 (D.C. Cir. 1998). *See also* McCarthy v. Madigan, 503 U.S. 140, 146, 112 S. Ct. 1081, 117 L. Ed. 2d 291 (1992).

318 28 U.S.C. §§ 2671–2680, *as amended by* the Federal Employees Liability Reform and Tort Compensation Act of 1988 (FELRTCA, or the *Westfall* Act), Pub. L. No. 100-694, 102 Stat. 4564 (1988). *See generally* Lester Jayson & Robert Longstreth, Handling Federal Tort Claims Administrative and Judicial Remedies (2001 with annual updates).

for certain torts.[319] A judgment on a claim under the FTCA bars any action, including a *Bivens* claim against the federal employee.[320] Nonetheless, an FTCA claim and a *Bivens* claim can be joined in a single action.[321]

The basic elements of a cause of action under the FTCA are set forth in 28 U.S.C. § 1346(b). That section specifies six conditions which must be met in order to impose liability on the United States under the Act: (1) the claim must be for money damages; (2) the damage claim must be for injury or loss of property, or for personal injury or death; (3) the damage must have been caused by a negligent or wrongful act or omission; (4) the wrongful actor must have been a federal employee; (5) the employee must have been acting within the scope of his employment; and (6) the circumstances must be such that, if the United States were a private person, liability would be imposed under the law of the place of where the wrongful act or omission occurred.[322]

Although many exceptions to governmental liability for intentional torts are enumerated in the Act,[323] intentional infliction of emotional distress is not among them and is therefore actionable.[324] Furthermore, negligent infliction of emotional harm may be asserted as a claim if such a cause of action is available under state law.[325] The statute likewise does not enumerate an exception for invasion of privacy claims,[326] so such a claim is actionable as long as it is recognized under local law.[327]

Several exceptions to the FTCA are likely to be significant in debt collection matters. The waiver of sovereign immunity does not apply to the assessment or collection of any tax,[328] leaving taxpayers with only the limited remedies found in the Internal Revenue Code.[329] The Act does not waive sovereign immunity for a list of torts—assault, battery, false imprisonment, false arrest, malicious prosecution, abuse of process, libel, slander, misrepresentation, deceit, and interference with contract rights.[330] However, sovereign immunity *is* waived

319 28 U.S.C. § 2680(h).

320 28 U.S.C. § 2676. *See* Williams v. Fleming, 597 F.3d 820 (7th Cir. 2010) (dismissal of FTCA claim on sovereign immunity grounds bars *Bivens* Fifth Amendment claim against bank examiner). *But cf.* Kreider v. Breault, 2012 WL 3518470 (E.D. Pa. Aug. 15, 2012) (grant of summary judgment on FTCA claim for intentional infliction of emotional distress did not bar Fourth Amendment *Bivens* claim, raised in the same action, alleging excessive force).

321 *See* Ortiz v. Pearson, 1999 U.S. Dist. LEXIS 22450 (S.D.N.Y. Nov. 5, 1999), *adopted by* 88 F. Supp. 2d 151 (S.D.N.Y. 2000).

322 *See* Fed. Deposit Ins. Corp. v. Meyer, 510 U.S. 471, 114 S. Ct. 996, 127 L. Ed. 2d 308 (1994).

323 28 U.S.C. § 2680(h).

324 *See* Truman v. United States, 26 F.3d 592 (5th Cir. 1994); Sheehan v. United States, 896 F.2d 1168 (9th Cir. 1990) (California law), *as amended by* 917 F.2d 424 (9th Cir. 1990); Hart v. United States, 894 F.2d 1539, 1548 (11th Cir. 1990) (Florida law); DeFord v. Sec'y of Labor, 700 F.2d 281, 290 (6th Cir. 1983); Gross v. United States, 676 F.2d 295 (8th Cir. 1982), *after remand*, 723 F.2d 609 (8th Cir. 1983); Wilkinson v. United States, 2007 WL 3544062 (D.N.D. Nov. 9, 2007) (awarding damages for intentional infliction of emotional distress, also trespass and conversion, against Bur. of Indian Affairs, which wrongfully leased out Indians' land, at request of Farm Serv. Agency, after default on farm loans), *aff'd in relevant part, rev'd in part*, 564 F.3d 927 (8th Cir. 2009) (affirming damage award on intentional infliction of emotional distress claim, but reversing liability finding as to other torts); Daigle v. United States, 2011 WL 4479517 (D. Nev. Sep. 26, 2011) (allowing IIED claim to go forward; outrageous conduct included assault and battery). *But cf.* Ruddy v. United States, 2011 WL 5834953 (M.D. Pa. Nov. 21, 2011) (no FTCA claim for emotional distress that arises from one of the excepted torts; here, allowing claim to go forward for workplace harassment that included other misconduct in addition to defamation); Vandemyle v. United States, 2011 WL 2461249 (D. Utah June 17, 2011) (FTCA exception for slander bars claim for emotional distress arising from false accusation); Harris v. Taxpayer Advocate Serv., 2006 WL 536194 (N.D. Tex. Feb. 24, 2006) (mag.) (no waiver of immunity for IRS for intentional infliction of emotional distress), *adopted sub nom.* Harris v. United States, 2006 WL 1305285 (N.D. Tex. Mar. 31, 2006).

325 D'Ambra v. United States, 354 F. Supp. 810 (D.R.I. 1973), *aff'd in part, vacated in part on other grounds*, 481 F.2d 14 (1st Cir. 1973). *See also* Olivas v. United States, 506 F.2d 1158 (9th Cir. 1974); Ginaitt v. Haronian, 806 F. Supp. 311 (D.R.I. 1992); Ellington v. United States, 404 F. Supp. 1165 (M.D. Fla. 1975). *See generally* National Consumer Law Center, Fair Debt Collection § 9.2 (8th ed. 2014), *updated at* www.nclc.org/library (state recognition of tort of negligent infliction of emotional distress).

326 28 U.S.C. § 2680(h). *See* Mundy v. United States, 983 F.2d 950, 953 (9th Cir. 1993); O'Donnell v. United States, 891 F.2d 1079 (3d Cir. 1989) (Pennsylvania law); Doe v. DiGenova, 779 F.2d 74, 87 (D.C. Cir. 1985), *on remand*, 642 F. Supp. 624 (D.D.C. 1986), *later proceedings at* 851 F.2d 1457 (D.C. Cir. 1988); Black v. Sheraton Corp. of Am., 564 F.2d 531 (D.C. Cir. 1977); Flowers v. United States, 348 F.2d 910 (10th Cir. 1965); Lopez-Pacheco v. United States, 627 F. Supp. 1224 (D. P.R. 1986), *aff'd*, 815 F.2d 692 (1st Cir. 1987) (mem.); Fagot v. Fed. Deposit Ins. Corp., 584 F. Supp. 1168, 1176 (D. P.R. 1984). *But see* Ruddy v. United States, 2011 WL 5834953 (M.D. Pa. Nov. 21, 2011) (no FTCA claim for invasion of privacy that arises from one of the excepted torts); Dolan v. United States, 2008 WL 362556 (D. Or. Feb. 8, 2008) (invasion of privacy claim that arose from physical attack barred by assault and battery exception; must "look beyond the labels").

327 Hurwitz v. United States, 884 F.2d 684 (2d Cir. 1989) (plaintiff could not assert invasion of privacy claim under FTCA when New York did not recognize this cause of action, as a private person would not be liable on this claim in New York). *See generally* National Consumer Law Center, Fair Debt Collection § 9.3 (8th ed. 2014), *updated at* www.nclc.org/library (state recognition of tort of invasion of privacy).

328 28 U.S.C. § 2680(c). *See* § 10.2.13.10, *infra*.

329 26 U.S.C. §§ 6330, 7422, 7432, 7433. *See* § 10.2.13.10, *infra*.

330 28 U.S.C. § 2680(h). *See* Tatum v. United States, 465 Fed. Appx. 313 (5th Cir. 2012) (holding that claim that agency manipulated billing process to create default and impose unauthorized fees arose from fraud or misrepresentation, so is barred, but remanding to determine if borrower states breach-of-contract claim); Conard v. Evans, 193 Fed. Appx. 945 (11th Cir. 2006) (affirming dismissal of claims for false arrest, libel, and slander based on student loan collection tactics); Pauly v. United States Dep't of Agric., 348 F.3d 1143 (9th Cir. 2003); Lawrence v. United States, 340 F.3d 952 (9th Cir. 2003); Howard v. United States, 949 F. Supp. 2d 54 (D.D.C. 2013) (dismissing negligent interference with contract claim); 1200 Sixth St. L.L.C. v. United States *ex rel.* Gen. Serv. Admin., 848 F. Supp. 2d 767 (E.D. Mich. 2012) (promissory estoppel claim, arising from alleged misstatements by agency, barred by intentional tort exception); Richards v. Great W. Ins. Co., 2012 WL 718715 (D. Minn. Mar. 5, 2012) (claim that agency published wrong address for its consumer assistance program was barred by misrepresentation exception); Ard v. FDIC, 770 F. Supp. 2d 1029 (C.D. Cal. Feb. 11, 2011) (misrepresentation exception bars negligence claim alleging that FDIC provided inaccurate information about failing bank); Omegbu v. United States, 2011 WL 2912703 (E.D.

for the first six of these torts if committed by a United States investigative or law enforcement officer.[331] Note, however, that absolute or qualified immunity is often available to officers acting in the scope of their employment.[332]

The waiver of sovereign immunity also does not apply to federal employees' discretionary acts.[333] A discretionary act is defined as one that includes an element of choice, grounded in considerations of public policy.[334] Because the waiver of sovereign immunity applies only to actions which would be tortious if done by a private actor, it does not allow due process or equal protection claims, which concern government action.[335]

Suits brought under the FTCA must be brought against the United States itself, rather than against specific agencies or employees.[336] In addition, any claim asserted under the Act must first be brought before the agency in question,[337] unless it is asserted as a cross-claim, counterclaim, or third-party complaint.[338]

Wis. July 18, 2011) (claim alleging mishandling of records is claim for intentional or negligent misrepresentation, both barred by FTCA exception), *aff'd on other grounds*, 475 Fed. Appx. 628 (7th Cir. 2012); Vandemyle v. United States, 2011 WL 2461249 (D. Utah June 17, 2011) (FTCA exception for slander bars claim for emotional distress arising from false accusation); Trusted Integration, Inc. v. United States, 679 F. Supp. 2d 70 (D.D.C. 2010) (FTCA exception for misrepresentation applies if "government misstatements or misinformation are essential to a plaintiff's claim"); Andrews v. United States, 2009 WL 5210129 (D. Colo. Dec. 23, 2009) (misrepresentation exception to FTCA bars claims alleging that misstatements by SBA stymied borrowers' efforts to modify loan or cure default); Standifer v. Sec. Exch. Comm'n, 542 F. Supp. 2d 1312 (N.D. Ga. 2008) (FTCA claims arising from SEC receivership barred by exception for claims of interference with contract rights); Dolan v. United States, 2008 WL 362556 (D. Or. Feb. 8, 2008) (invasion of privacy claim that arose from physical attack barred by assault and battery exception); Avery v. United States, 534 F. Supp. 2d 40 (D.D.C. 2008) (defamation claim alleging false reporting of student loan information barred by intentional torts exception); Gayton v. United States, 2006 WL 408562 (N.D. Cal. Feb. 17, 2006) (neither employee nor United States liable for assault by non-law enforcement employee); Nogueras-Cartagena v. United States, 172 F. Supp. 2d 296 (D. P.R. 2001), *aff'd*, 75 Fed. Appx. 795 (1st Cir. 2003); Bickley v. U.S. Dep't of the Treasury, 2000 WL 637345 (W.D. Va. Jan. 18, 2000), *aff'd*, 225 F.3d 653 (table) (4th Cir. 2000). *But cf.* Daigle v. United States, 2011 WL 4479517 (D. Nev. Sep. 26, 2011) (allowing IIED claim to go forward; outrageous conduct included assault and battery).

331 28 U.S.C. § 2680(h).

332 *See, e.g.*, Schmidt v. United States, 2013 WL 5492311 (E.D. Cal. Oct. 2, 2013) (absolute quasi-judicial immunity for marshals serving facially valid bench warrant; actions in besieging but entering home in which subject was staying not unreasonable).

333 28 U.S.C. § 2680(a).

334 Dichter-Mad Family Partners, L.L.P. v. United States, ___ F.3d ___, 2013 WL 310284 (9th Cir. Jan. 28, 2013) (discretionary function exception bars claims by victims of Ponzi scheme, alleging that agency missed numerous opportunities to detect and shut down scam); Lawrence v. United States, 340 F.3d 952 (9th Cir. 2003); FDIC v. Mahajan, 2013 WL 505167 (N.D. Ill. Feb. 12, 2013) (discretionary function exception may be used to bar affirmative defenses, as well as tort claims; here applied to defenses of waiver, estoppel, and contributory negligence, raised by bank officers being sued by receiver FDIC); Burroughs v. Abrahamson, 2913 WL 3964065 (D. Or. July 31, 2013) (discretionary function exception bars FTCA claim alleging failure to train or supervise IRS auditor who coerced sexual favors from taxpayer); Pearson v. United States, 831 F. Supp. 2d 514 (D. Mass. 2011) (discretionary function exception bars claim that agency negligently supervised employees who conducted foreclosure sale), *clarified by* 905 F. Supp. 2d 400 (D. Mass. 2012); Am. State Bank & Trust Co. of Williston v. Anderson, 2011 WL 6217046 (D. Mont. Dec. 14, 2011) (decisions whether to restructure farm service loan or provide interest assistance were discretionary). *But cf.* Estate of Redd v. United States, 2012 WL 2417610 (D. Utah. June 26, 2012) (discretionary function exception does not protect constitutional violations such as use of knowingly false evidence to secure a search warrant, or excessive force when making arrest).

335 Lewis v. Glickman, 104 F. Supp. 2d 1311 (D. Kan. 2000), *aff'd*, 2002 U.S. App. LEXIS 13269 (10th Cir. July 3, 2002). *See also* Am. State Bank & Trust Co. of Williston v. Anderson, 2011 WL 6217046 (D. Mont. Dec. 14, 2011) (no FTCA claim for violation of Agricultural Credit Act and regulations, which place no duty on private actor); Deutsche Bank Nat'l Trust Co. v. F.D.I.C., 784 F. Supp. 2d 1142 (C.D. Cal. Jan. 7, 2011) (claim alleging violation of FIRREA provisions that do not impose duties on private actors not a FTCA claim), *reconsideration granted on other grounds*, 854 F. Supp. 2d 756 (C.D. Cal. 2011) (dismissing additional claim). *But cf.* Liranzo v. United States, 690 F.3d 78 (2d Cir. 2012) (refusing to dismiss claim that citizen was mistakenly detained as illegal immigrant; although only government may detain illegal immigrant, there is a "private analog"—a New York state claim for false imprisonment).

336 28 U.S.C. § 2679(a).

337 28 U.S.C. § 2675(a). *See, e.g.*, Palay v. United States, 349 F.3d 418 (7th Cir. 2003) (dismissing one of plaintiff's two claims because it was not sufficiently stated in his administrative claim); Hogan v. Northwest Airlines, 2013 WL 607852 (E.D. Mich. Feb. 19, 2013) (dismissing FTCA claim for failure to exhaust administrative remedies; plaintiff filed report with airport police and was falsely assured that it would be forwarded to defendant Transportation Security Administration); Donnely v. Sibelius, 851 F. Supp. 2d 109 (D.D.C. 2012) (administrative claim requirement not satisfied; older consumer made lengthy and unsuccessful efforts to obtain prescription drug payment but did not file correct form with HHS); Wilson v. U.S. Dep't of Educ., 2012 WL 1443274 (D. Or. Apr. 24, 2012)(administrative claim requirement not satisfied by letter asserting that student loan had been paid in full but not making demand for sum certain), *adopted by* 2012 WL 3065270 (D. Or. July 27, 2012); Schneider Elec., Inc. v. Courtney, 2011 WL 6217116 (E.D. Ky. Dec. 14, 2011) (bringing state court suit and serving complaint on attorney general does not satisfy claim presentation requirement); Smith v. Business Dev. Corp., 2010 WL 3724736 (D.S.C. Aug. 24, 2010) (numerous attempts to contact SBA and orally discuss loan problems insufficient; allegation of written complaint insufficient when agency denied receipt), *adopted by* 2010 WL 3724734 (D.S.C. Sept. 16, 2010); Lowery v. United States Dep't of Educ., 499 F. Supp. 2d 928 (N.D. Ohio 2007) (plaintiff bears burden of proof on presentation issue; allegation that letters were sent at unspecified time to unnamed employees of Department of Education telling them they were dunning wrong person not sufficient); Ortiz-Romany v. United States, 497 F. Supp. 2d 285 (D. P.R. 2007) (filing suit just fifteen days after filing administrative claim and before agency ruled does not constitute exhaustion of administrative remedies); Curtis v. Treasury Dep't, 2007 WL 2854274 (N.D. Cal. Sept. 27, 2007) (faxing draft complaint to employees of agency not sufficient presentation, because doing so would not "trigger an administrative process"), *aff'd*, 324 Fed. Appx. 629 (9th Cir. 2009).

338 Chaney v. Chaney, 2010 WL 320324 (W.D Ark. Jan. 20, 2010) (claim by defendants alleging that Department of Agriculture official was complicit in allowing plaintiff to encumber land owned by defendants not a counterclaim because not against plaintiff; not a third-party complaint because it does not allege that official is liable for any sum owed to plaintiff; claim barred by failure to exhaust administrative remedies). *But see* U.S. v. Kotterman Law Firm. P.L.L.C., 2013 WL 3866525

Apart from the exclusions set forth in the statute, applicable state law defines the elements of torts[339] and affirmative defenses[340] under the FTCA. However, the statutes of limitations are fixed by federal law, which also determines whether or not the period of limitations may be tolled.[341]

In 1988, the Supreme Court held in *Westfall v. Ervin*[342] that a federal employee was *not* immune from personal liability for state common law torts unless his conduct was not only within the scope of his employment but also was in exercise of governmental discretion. Congress worked swiftly to overturn this decision by enacting amendments to the FTCA known collectively as the Federal Employees Liability Reform and Tort Compensation Act (FELRTCA) or the "*Westfall* amendments."[343] This legislation specifically immunizes employees from personal liability for damages resulting from common law torts committed within the ambit of their federal jobs.[344] The exclusive remedy for such torts is an action against the United States itself under the FTCA.[345] The *Westfall* amendments also permit the United States to use any defenses available to it independently, including the numerous exceptions to liability set forth in the FTCA, even though the defenses would not have been available to the employee.[346]

10.2.13.6 Tucker Acts

The Little Tucker Act[347] and the Big Tucker Act[348] provide a means of enforcing claims against the government based on contract. These statutes may be of use as a way of enforcing limits—such as a limit on interest or penalties—that are set forth in the underlying contract with the government.[349]

The Little Tucker Act gives United States District Courts and the United States Court of Federal Claims concurrent jurisdiction, with certain exceptions, over civil actions or claims against the United States that do not exceed $10,000 in amount and that are founded upon, *inter alia*, an express or implied contract with the United States or any act of Congress.[350] The Big Tucker Act does not contain a monetary limit on the amount of the claim,[351] so provides jurisdiction over claims that exceed the Little Tucker Act's $10,000 cap.

The Big Tucker Act gives the United States Court of Federal Claims jurisdiction over claims against the federal government based on an express or implied contract, the Constitution, or a federal statute or regulation, and over other claims that do not sound in tort[352] and are for liquidated or unliquidated damages.[353]

(N.D. Fla. July 25, 2013) (counterclaims barred by failure to exhaust administrative remedy). *But cf.* United States v. Andre, 2012 WL 728737 (N.D. Cal. Mar. 6, 2012) (exception for counterclaims applies only to compulsory counterclaims; not shown when borrower asserted tort counterclaims in contract action).

339 *See, e.g.*, Regatta Bay Ltd. v. United States, 506 Fed. Appx. 617 (9th Cir.2013) (claims fail because plaintiff fails to show "special relationship" with agency, a necessary element of Nevada claim of breach of fiduciary duty or breach of duty of good faith and fair dealing); Wilkinson v. United States, 564 F.3d 927 (8th Cir. 2009) (applying North Dakota definitions of conversion and trespass to chattels); Howard v. United States, 949 F. Supp. 2d 54 (D.D.C. 2013) (dismissing claims alleging that Department of Education wrongfully denied disability discharge; borrower failed to allege any local law that would make private actor liable); Pearson v. United States, 831 F. Supp. 2d 514 (D. Mass. 2011) (Massachusetts recognizes tort claim for breach of fiduciary duty; developer stated claim with allegations that FDIC was grossly uncooperative in efforts to liquidate foreclosed property), *clarified by* 905 F. Supp. 2d 400 (D. Mass. 2012); Holland v. United States, 2009 WL 3241680 (W.D. Tenn. Sept. 30, 2009) (Tennessee law; prison officials who debited inmate's account for expired obligation were negligent).

340 *See, e.g.*, Banks v. City of New Orleans, 628 F. Supp. 2d 686 (E.D. La. 2009).

341 28 U.S.C. § 2401. *See* Santos *ex rel.* Beato v. United States, 559 F.3d 189 (3d Cir. 2009) (equitably tolling statute of limitations for filing administrative claim, a prerequisite for FTCA claim, when, despite counsel's diligence, claimant failed to learn that doctor at federally funded, apparently private, clinic, was federal employee for FTCA purposes; claim here brought within Pennsylvania statute for claims by minors but outside FTCA limitations period); Hogan v. Northwest Airlines, 2013 WL 607852 (E.D. Mich. Feb. 19, 2013) (even if equitable tolling is available for failure to timely present FTCA claim to agency, it requires more than ordinary excusable neglect; here, plaintiff made report to airport police and was falsely informed that it would be forwarded to defendant Transportation Security Agency).

342 484 U.S. 292, 108 S. Ct. 580, 98 L. Ed. 2d 619 (1988).

343 Pub. L. No. 100-694, 102 Stat. 4564 (1988); 28 U.S.C. § 2679.

344 Note that FELCRTA does not prevent injunctive or equitable relief or suit for constitutional violations against individuals.

345 *See* United States v. Smith, 499 U.S. 160, 111 S. Ct. 1180, 113 L. Ed. 2d 134 (1991); Rivera v. United States, 928 F.2d 592 (2d Cir. 1991).

346 28 U.S.C. §§ 2674, 2680(h). *See* Haber v. United States, 2010 WL 92499 (E.D.N.Y Jan. 10, 2010) (neither agency nor employee is liable for assault and battery committed by postal employee acting in the course of her duties); Fair v. Swenson, 753 F. Supp. 875 (D. Colo. 1991), *aff'd*, 947 F.2d 953 (table), 1991 WL 225805 (10th Cir. 1991).

347 28 U.S.C. § 1346(a)(2).

348 28 U.S.C. § 1491.

349 *See, e.g.*, Russell v. United States, 2009 WL 4050938 (N.D. Cal. Nov. 20, 2009) (Little Tucker Act provides jurisdiction over claim that Treasury Department, in collecting delinquent debts on credit cards issued by military exchange service, imposed collection fees that were not authorized by the contracts), *later decision*, 661 F.3d 1371 (Fed. Cir. 2011) (claim mooted by payment to named plaintiff of amount owed to him; remanding to determine whether class action may go forward). *See also* Tatum v. United States, 465 Fed. Appx. 313 (5th Cir. 2012) (claim that Small Business Administration was misdating monthly statements and sending them late, so as to maximize late fees and interest, alleged breach of contract, which could be brought pursuant to Little Tucker Act).

350 28 U.S.C. § 1346(a)(2).

351 28 U.S.C. § 1491.

352 *See, e.g.*, Johnson v. United States, 105 Fed. Cl. 85 (Fed. Cl. 2012) (dismissing negligence claim arising from mishandling of student loan payments). *See also* Bafford v. United States, 2012 WL 1197139 (Fed. Cl. Apr. 5, 2012) (dismissing claim for emotional distress arising from mishandling of HUD loan resulting in foreclosure). *But cf.* Road & Highway Builders L.L.C. v. United States, 102 Fed. Cl. 89 (Fed. Cl. 2012) (claim alleging failure of consideration was contract claim, not tort claim for misrepresentation).

353 28 U.S.C. § 1491. *See* Houseal v. McHugh, 2013 WL 4517178 (D.D.C. Aug. 27, 2013) (claim for equitable relief from agency's refusal to forgive a debt, here ROTC scholarship, not claim for money damages; APA review available; Tucker Act did not require action to be brought in federal claims court).

It permits injunctive relief only if incidental to a claim for damages.[354] The Big Tucker Act operates as a waiver of sovereign immunity for the claims to which it applies.[355]

The Big Tucker Act allows claims based on contracts,[356] including implied-in-fact contracts.[357] A claim of an implied-in-fact contract requires a showing of conduct, not merely silence, indicating acceptance of the contract, by a person authorized to bind the government to a contract.[358] The Big Tucker Act does not, however, allow claims based on contracts implied-at-law.[359]

The Big Tucker Act also gives courts jurisdiction over illegal exaction claims if the exaction is based on an asserted statutory power.[360] To assert an illegal exaction claim, the claimant must show that the government possesses "money that was improperly paid, exacted or taken from the complainant in contravention of the Constitution, a statute or regulation."[361] One type of illegal exaction is the offset of wages or a federal benefit for a tax or student loan debt that the claimant does not owe.[362] The Big Tucker Act does not apply to offsets for the collection of criminal fines, penalties and restitution, however, because the statute governing collection of these debts gives exclusive jurisdiction to District Courts.[363]

The Big Tucker Act does not create any right to money damages but merely gives the Court of Federal Claims jurisdiction to award damages if they are required by some other provision of law.[364] If the other law does not explicitly authorize money damages, the claimant must show that it "establishes specific duties, that the government has failed to faithfully perform them, and that the law can be fairly interpreted as mandating compensation for damages sustained as a result of breaching those duties."[365]

10.2.13.7 Violation of Bankruptcy Stay

If the debtor has filed bankruptcy, a government creditor may violate bankruptcy law by, for example, freezing a bank account in violation of the automatic stay or attempting to collect a discharged debt. Available relief includes compensatory damages, including damages for mental anguish, the return of improperly intercepted funds, and, if the misconduct is willful or in bad faith, attorney fees.[366]

---

354 Wilburn v. United States, 103 Fed. Cl. 495 (Fed. Cl. 2011) (Court of Federal Claims has no jurisdiction to enjoin offset of retirement benefits for student loan when borrower did not seek money recovery).

355 United States v. Mitchell, 463 U.S. 206, 103 S. Ct. 2961, 77 L. Ed. 580 (1983).

356 Bafford v. United States, 2012 WL 1197139 (Fed. Cl. Apr. 5, 2012) (must show contract with United States; dismissing claim that HUD, as insurer, mishandled its insurance of contract with private lender).

357 28 U.S.C. § 1491(a)(1) ("any express or implied contract").

358 *See, e.g.*, Martin v. United States, 102 Fed. Cl. 779 (Fed. Cl. 2012) (rejecting taxpayer's attempt to bind IRS to contract by letter stating that failure to respond within set period was acceptance, because silence is not sufficient, and addressee of letter not shown to have authority to bind government).

359 United States v. Mitchell, 463 U.S. 206, 103 S. Ct. 2961, 77 L. Ed. 580 (1983).

360 Norman v. United States, 429 F.3d 1081, 1905 (Fed. Cir. 2005).

361 *See, e.g.*, Ibrahim v. United States, 112 Fed. Cl. 333 (Fed. Cl. 2013) (taxpayer stated illegal exaction claim against Department of Education; offset of tax refund for debt of person who used taxpayer's Social Security number but had totally different name); Kipple v. United States, 102 Fed. Cl. 773 (Fed. Cl. 2012). *See also* Ontario Power Generation, Inc. v. United States, 369 F.3d 1298 (Fed. Cir. 2004).

362 Ibrahim v. United States, 112 Fed. Cl. 333 (Fed. Cl. 2013) (taxpayer stated illegal exaction claim against Department of Education for wrongful offset of tax refund); Kipple v. United States, 102 Fed. Cl. 773 (Fed. Cl. 2012); Wagstaff v. United States, 105 Fed. Cl. 99 (Fed. Cl. 2012) (claimant can proceed with illegal exaction claim based on administrative wage garnishment in violation of Debt Collection Improvement Act); Greene v. Dep't of Justice Financial Litig. Unit, 2013 WL 5707873 (N.D. Okla. Oct. 18, 2013) (taxpayer stated claim for illegal exaction: funds from settlement with IRS offset to pay criminal fine).

363 Eliot v. United States, 96 Fed. Cl. 666 (Fed. Cl. 2011), *later decision*, 111 Fed. Cl. 754 (Fed. Cl. 2013) (granting summary judgment to United States; borrower failed to show that debt was not owed or due process not provided). *But cf.* Greene v. Dep't of Justice Financial Litig. Unit, 2013 WL 5707873 (N.D. Okla. Oct. 18, 2013) (taxpayer stated claim for illegal exaction: funds from settlement with IRS offset to pay criminal fine).

364 United States v. Navajo Nation, 556 U.S. 287, 290, 129 S. Ct. 1547, 173 L. Ed. 429 (2009); United States v. Mitchell, 463 U.S. 206, 103 S. Ct. 2961, 77 L. Ed. 580 (1983); United States v. Testan, 424 U.S. 392, at 400, 96 S. Ct. 948, 47 L. Ed. 2d 114 (1976). *See also* Wagstaff v. United States, 105 Fed. Cl. 99 (Fed. Cl. 2012) (Tucker Act does not give Court of Federal Claims jurisdiction over due process, equal protection, and First Amendment claims because those constitutional amendments do not mandate compensation for their breach, but claimant can proceed with illegal exaction claim based on government's violation of Debt Collection Improvement Act); Kortlander v. United States, 107 Fed. Cl. 357 (Fed. Cl. 2012).

365 United States v. Navajo Nation, 556 U.S. 287, 290, 129 S. Ct. 1547, 173 L. Ed. 429 (2009). *See also* United States v. Testan, 424 U.S. 392, at 400, 96 S. Ct. 948, 47 L. Ed. 2d 114 (1976) (Civil Service Classification Act and Back Pay Act do not provide right to back pay for misclassified employees); Dustin v. United States, 113 Fed. Cl. 366 (Fed. Cl. 2013) (Tucker Act provides jurisdiction to hear claim alleging that VA reneged on promise to make student loan payments for employee, as statute authorizing loan repayment provides that agency "shall" make payments in accordance with agreements); Johnson v. United States, 105 Fed. Cl. 85 (Fed. Cl. 2012) (APA is limited to actions seeking relief other than money damages; provisions of Higher Education Act authorizing agency to discharge loans if borrower becomes disabled do not mandate compensation, but provisions requiring repayment of certain overpayments by borrower do); Wilburn v. United States, 103 Fed. Cl. 495 (Fed. Cl. 2011) (violation of Debt Collection Improvement Act's notice requirements does not entitle debtor to money damages, so no Tucker Act claim).

366 United States v. Harchar, 371 B.R. 254 (N.D. Ohio 2007) (chapter 13 debtors stated claim for violation of automatic stay when IRS froze their accounts); *In re* Bryant, 340 B.R. 569 (Bankr. N.D. Tex. 2006) (IRS's post-discharge attempt to collect interest on tax debt paid in chapter 13); *In re* Atkins, 279 B.R. 639 (Bankr. N.D.N.Y. 2002) (awarding $30,000 compensatory damages when government dunned consumer for fourteen years and intercepted three tax refunds, although debt discharged in bankruptcy and mortgaged home voluntarily surrendered to Farmer's Home Administration). *But see In re* Rivera Torres, 432 F.3d 20 (1st Cir. 2005) (sovereign immunity not waived as to emotional distress damages; reversing award of emotional distress damages for IRS attempts to collect discharged debt), *on remand*, *In re* Torres, 377 B.R. 428 (Bankr. D. P.R. 2007) ("money recovery" in the section of bankruptcy law waiving sovereign immunity not as broad as "money damages" and does not include pecuniary loss awarded here). *See generally* National

10.2.13.8 Fair Debt Collection Practices Act and Fair Credit Reporting Act

Debt collection by United States officers and employees is excluded from the provisions of the Fair Debt Collection Practices Act (FDCPA).[367] However, private collection agencies and collection attorneys hired by the government are bound by the FDCPA and all other applicable legislation regulating debt collection practices.[368] Claims under that statute may be appropriate if a collector has, for example, misrepresented the government's rights in connection with collection of a claim.

There are strong arguments that the Fair Credit Reporting Act, which defines "person" to include government and governmental subdivisions or agencies,[369] waives sovereign immunity on the part of the federal government.[370] There is not yet a definitive resolution of the question, however. The Supreme Court has explicitly declined to decide whether the FCRA waives sovereign immunity and remanded a case raising that issue back to the Seventh Circuit for further proceedings.[371]

10.2.13.9 State Agencies

A state agency, such as a state welfare department, that is engaged in a joint federal-state program may be subject to state restrictions on its collection processes.[372] In addition, state actors are subject to suit under 42 U.S.C. § 1983.[373] Federal employees also may be sued under 42 U.S.C. § 1983 if they have conspired with state officials to violate a debtor's constitutional rights.[374]

10.2.13.10 Remedies for Abuses by IRS

Tax practice is a highly complex subject, beyond the scope of this treatise, but practitioners should be aware of the special problems presented by IRS debt collection. Most of the remedies for abusive collection conduct by the federal government do not apply to federal tax collection. The Federal Tort Claims Act explicitly exempts from its waiver of sovereign immunity the assessment or collection of any tax.[375] The Anti-Injunction Act and the Declaratory Judgment Act generally forbid injunctions and declaratory judgments against the IRS.[376] The Administrative Procedure Act does not authorize review of agency action if another statute that provides consent to suit expressly or impliedly forbids the relief sought.[377] Actions under 42 U.S.C. § 1983 will not lie for deprivation of rights under color of federal law.[378]

All circuits that have considered *Bivens* actions against IRS agents have concluded that the remedies provided in the Internal Revenue Code are usually adequate, despite their

---

Consumer Law Center, Consumer Bankruptcy Law and Practice § 9.6 (10th ed. 2012), *updated at* www.nclc.org/library.

367 15 U.S.C. § 1692a(6)(C). *See* National Consumer Law Center, Fair Debt Collection § 4.3.4 (8th ed. 2014), *updated at* www.nclc.org/library. *See also* Dep't of the Treasury, Managing Federal Receivables, Ch. 6, pp. 6–14, app. 7, *available at* http://tfm.fiscal.treasury.gov/v1/supplements.html (guidelines for employee collection efforts based on FDCPA).

368 31 U.S.C. §§ 3718(a)(2)(B), 3718(b)(6). *See also* 31 C.F.R. § 901.5(a)(3). *See generally* § 10.2.4, *supra*.

369 15 U.S.C. § 1681a(b). *See also* 15 U.S.C. § 1681s-2(b) (imposing duties on any "person" that provides information to a credit reporting agency).

370 *See also* Wilson v. U.S. Dep't of Educ., 2012 WL 1443274 (D. Or. Apr. 24, 2012) (tort claims alleging improper credit reporting, which were dismissed for failure to exhaust administrative remedies, could be pleaded as FCRA claim), *adopted by* 2012 WL 3065270 (D. Or. July 27, 2012); Talley v. United States Dep't of Agriculture, 2009 WL 303134 (N.D. Ill. Feb. 4, 2009) (awarding FCRA damages against USDA), *aff'd*, 595 F.3d 754 (7th Cir. 2010) (sovereign immunity waived by FCRA definition of person), *affirmance vacated on rehearing en banc* (June 10, 2010), *district court opinion aff'd without opinion on rehearing en banc by equally divided court*, 2010 WL 5887796 (7th Cir. Oct. 1, 2010); Johnson v. United States Dep't of Defense, 2000 WL 33956225 (D. Minn. Oct. 17, 2000) (dismissing tort claims for failure to exhaust administrative remedies, but allowing FCRA claims to go forward). *But see* Stellick v. U.S. Dep't of Educ., 2013 WL 673856 (D. Minn. Feb. 25, 2013) (FCRA, even though it defines person to include governmental entities, does not waive sovereign immunity as to sections allowing money damages). *See generally* National Consumer Law Center, Fair Credit Reporting § 11.2.2.2 (8th ed. 2013), *updated at* www.nclc.org/library.

371 United States v. Bormes, 133 S. Ct. 12 (2012).

372 *See, e.g.*, Wyatt v. Commonwealth, 463 A.2d 64 (Pa. Commw. Ct. 1983) (state welfare worker's false implication to client that welfare would be repaid from exempt Social Security lump-sum payment violates state law principle that agency may only use "fair means" of debt collection).

373 *See* National Consumer Law Center, Fair Debt Collection § 8.2 (8th ed. 2014), *updated at* www.nclc.org/library.

374 Melo v. Hafer, 912 F.2d 628, 638 (3d Cir. 1990), *aff'd*, 502 U.S. 21, 112 S. Ct. 358, 116 L. Ed. 2d 301 (1991), *on appeal after remand* 13 F.3d 736 (3d Cir. 1994). *See* National Consumer Law Center, Fair Debt Collection §§ 8.12.1, 8.12.2, 8.12.2.1, 8.12.2.3, 8.12.3, 8.12.4, 8.12.2.5 (8th ed. 2014), *updated at* www.nclc.org/library; § 12.3, *infra*.

375 8 U.S.C. § 2680(c).

376 26 U.S.C. § 7421; 28 U.S.C. § 2201. *See* Godt v. Internal Revenue Serv., 268 Fed. Appx. 474 (7th Cir. 2008) (unpublished) (Anti-Injunction Act bars action in which taxpayer is "trying to evade collection"); Bateman v. United States, 2009 WL 2043871 (M.D. Tenn. July 9, 2009) (tax exceptions broad enough to cover investigative activities that are intended to or may culminate in the assessment or collection of taxes, including tax penalties); United States v. Berk, 374 B.R. 385 (D. Mass. 2007) (claims for injunctive or declaratory relief, here seeking to enjoin real estate foreclosure, barred by Anti-Injunction Act); Sterner v. United States Drug Enforcement Agency, 467 F. Supp. 2d 1017 (S.D. Cal. 2006) (Anti-Injunction Act protects actions "that may culminate in the assessment or collection of taxes"; refusing to enjoin IRS seizure of doctor's confidential patient records, but would consider injunction against dissemination for non-tax purposes). *But cf.* Cohen v. United States, 650 F.3d 717 (D.C. Cir. 2011) (Anti-Injunction Act does not bar action challenging IRS procedure for claiming refund of wrongfully collected telephone tax because these taxes have already been collected, and decision will not affect future assessment or collection); United States v. Margolis, 2009 WL 2255336 (D.N.J. July 28, 2009) (sections barring claim to restrain "assessment or collection" did not bar claim alleging wrongful termination of installment payment agreement).

377 5 U.S.C. § 702(2). *See* Neilson v. United States, 674 F. Supp. 2d 248 (D.D.C. 2009) (no right to bring APA suit challenging issuance of third-party summonses by IRS, since specific provisions of tax code provide limited consent to suit). *But see* Cohen v. United States, 650 F.3d 717 (D.C. Cir. 2011) (allowing APA review of IRS notice setting forth procedure for claiming refund of wrongfully collected telephone taxes; action for refund pursuant to Internal Revenue Code not an adequate remedy at law).

378 Rogers v. Vicuna, 264 F.3d 1 (1st Cir. 2001).

limitations.[379] *Bivens* suits are thus barred, with a possible exception for extreme cases: a "lawless and arbitrary vendetta" for which the statute provides no adequate remedy[380] or violations of the First or Fourth Amendments.[381]

In most cases, the only remedies available to aggrieved taxpayers are those found in the Internal Revenue Code. Taxpayers may seek a refund of an incorrectly assessed tax, but must first pay the disputed amount and pursue an administrative claim for refund, and may recover only the amount of the tax, not expenses incurred in, for example, mortgaging one's house to pay the tax or pursuing administrative and judicial remedies.[382] Taxpayers may sue for actual damages resulting from reckless, intentional, or negligent disregard of Internal Revenue statutes or regulations in the collection[383]—but not the assessment[384]—of taxes or for failure to release a lien.[385] Note, however, that many of the standards governing IRS agents' conduct are found in agency rulings or an agency manual, which are neither statutes nor regulations within the meaning of this section.[386] However, the tax code does include restrictions on collection calls at inconvenient times and places, contacts with taxpayers represented by attorneys, contacts at the taxpayer's place of employment, and harassment and abuse.[387]

If liability is shown, the United States is liable for the plaintiff's "actual, direct economic damages" plus "the costs of the action," except that, in suits alleging negligent disregard

379 Kenny v. United States, 489 Fed. Appx. 628 (3d Cir. 2012) (dismissing *Bivens* claim alleging that IRS misused practitioner misconduct claims to retaliate against tax lawyer who filed administrative claims against IRS officer; tax code remedies are adequate); Kim v. United States, 632 F.3d 713 (D.C. Cir. 2011) (no *Bivens* remedy is available because of tax code's comprehensive remedial scheme); Godt v. Internal Revenue Serv., 268 Fed. Appx. 474 (7th Cir. 2008) (unpublished) (no *Bivens* action for "relatively trivial" misconduct by individual IRS agents); Hudson Valley Black Press v. Internal Revenue Serv., 409 F.3d 106 (2d Cir. 2005); Adams v. Johnson, 355 F.3d 1179 (9th Cir. 2004); Shreiber v. Mastrogiovanni, 214 F.3d 148 (3d Cir. 2000) (no *Bivens* remedy if statute provides "some mechanism of relief"; *Bivens* claim will not lie for any allegedly unconstitutional actions by IRS); Dahn v. United States, 127 F.3d 1249 (10th Cir. 1997) (IRS agents not subject to *Bivens* actions); Fishburn v. Brown, 125 F.3d 979 (6th Cir. 1997); Vennes v. An Unknown Number of Unidentified Agents, 26 F.3d 1448 (8th Cir. 1994) (no *Bivens* remedy for overzealous tax assessment or collection); Wages v. Internal Revenue Serv., 915 F.2d 1230 (9th Cir. 1990) (even if taxpayer stated claim for constitutional violation, *Bivens* action not available because statutory remedies adequate); Baddour, Inc. v. United States, 802 F.2d 801 (5th Cir. 1986) (no *Bivens* remedy, when tax code provides adequate remedies for improper levy).

380 Cameron v. Internal Revenue Serv., 773 F.2d 126 (7th Cir. 1985) (tax code remedies generally adequate, but *Bivens* action might lie if agents "ransacked a home" or engaged in a "lawless vendetta"); Rutherford v. United States, 702 F.2d 580 (5th Cir. 1983) (*Bivens* action would be appropriate if taxpayer showed a "vendetta" which required lengthy and expensive litigation to undo); Meredith v. Erath, 182 F. Supp. 2d 964 (C.D. Cal. 2001) (allowing *Bivens* action to go forward with claims of excessive force and improper detention, arising from IRS's early morning armed raid on residence and business premises), *rev'd in part on other grounds*, 342 F.3d 1057 (9th Cir. 2003).

381 Nat'l Commodity & Barter Ass'n v. Gibbs, 886 F.2d 1240 (10th Cir. 1989) (*Bivens* available for First or Fourth Amendment violations by IRS). *But see* Hudson Valley Black Press v. Internal Revenue Serv., 409 F.3d 106 (2d Cir. 2005) (*Bivens* action will not lie for First and Fourth Amendment claims alleging IRS attack on publication that criticized its treatment of minority taxpayers); Adams v. Johnson, 355 F.3d 1179 (9th Cir. 2004) (*Bivens* claim will not lie for any allegedly unconstitutional actions by IRS in assessment or collection of taxes).

382 26 U.S.C. § 7422; 28 U.S.C. § 1346. *See* Kimball v. Internal Revenue Serv., 351 Fed. Appx. 170 (9th Cir. 2009) (unpublished) (district court has no jurisdiction over tax claims when claimant has neither paid the disputed tax nor exhausted administrative remedies); McMillen v. United States Dep't of the Treasury, 960 F.2d 187 (1st Cir. 1991) (payment of disputed amount a prerequisite to challenge to tax assessment).

383 26 U.S.C. § 7433. *See* Kim v. United States, 632 F.3d 713 (D.C. Cir. 2011) (IRS levies, liens, and provision of notice of assessment are related to collection, but these plaintiffs lack standing), *aff'd after remand*, 707 F.3d 335 (D.C. Cir. 2013) (no standing because claims were untimely; SOL is jurisdictional and non-waivable); Foley v. Comm'r, 2007 WL 806521 (N.D. Cal. Mar. 15, 2007) (section 7433 is exclusive remedy when, because of misreading of Social Security number, one taxpayer was accused of earning—and not reporting—income earned by another); Ross v. United States, 460 F. Supp. 2d 139 (D.D.C. 2006) (section 7433 is exclusive remedy for misconduct in collection of taxes; replevin action will not lie for property seized by IRS); Sepp v. United States, 2006 WL 213995 (D. Ariz. Jan. 25, 2006) (sections 7432 and 7433 are waivers of sovereign immunity, which must be narrowly construed).

384 *See* Buchanan v. United States, 2014 WL 202746 (D. Minn. Jan. 17, 2014) (dismissing section 7433 claim alleging attempt to collect from individual taxes owed only by business entities; claim alleged improper assessment, not collection); Marsoun v. United States, 880 F. Supp. 2d 59 (D.D.C. July 30, 2012) (dismissing section 7433 claim; alleged failures to develop process for levies, or confirm supervisory approval of penalty determination related to assessment, not collection); Noret v. Dep't of the Treasury, 2012 WL 345920 (E.D. Cal. Feb. 1, 2012) (denying claim that IRS refused to provide refund after VA redefined certain taxable benefits as non-taxable disability benefits; IRS action related to assessment, not collection); Telford v. United States, 2011 WL 6942303 (E.D. Tex. Nov. 30, 2011) (claim will not lie for wrongful refusal of refund), *report and recommendation adopted by* 2012 WL 12880 (E.D. Tex. Jan. 3, 2012); Gust v. United States, 789 F. Supp. 2d 58 (D.D.C. June 6, 2011) (claim that IRS used incorrect procedures to prepare substitute return or maintained inaccurate records arose from assessment, not collection), *aff'd*, 462 Fed. Appx. 8 (D.C. Cir. 2012); Richard v. United States, 746 F. Supp. 2d 778 (E.D. Va. 2010) (no section 7433 claim for collection activities arising from allegedly wrongful assessment), *aff'd without op.*, 425 Fed. Appx. 264 (4th Cir. 2011); Brewer v. Comm'r, 430 F. Supp. 2d 1254 (S.D. Ala. 2006). *See also* Jones v. United States, 2012 WL 1424170 (D.D.C. Feb. 13, 2012) (after tax court awarded substantial refund, IRS used it to pay student loan arising from attendance at closed trade school; no section 7433 claim because this was not tax collection).

385 26 U.S.C. § 7432. *Cf.* Richard v. United States, 746 F. Supp. 2d 778 (E.D. Va. 2010) (no claim for failure to release lien when lien self-released after four years), *aff'd without op.*, 425 Fed. Appx. 264 (4th Cir. 2011); Kabakjian v. United States, 92 F. Supp. 2d 435 (E.D. Pa. Apr. 12, 2000) (burden on taxpayers to show actual economic damages from delayed release of lien; not shown when taxpayers alleged one denial of a credit card application; emotional distress damages not recoverable), *aff'd*, 267 F.3d 208 (3d Cir. 2001).

386 Shwarz v. United States, 234 F.3d 428 (9th Cir. 2000) (IRS manual and policy statement not statutes or regulations within meaning of section 7433; no cause of action for violation); United States v. Meisner, 2007 WL 1290088 (D. Neb. May 2, 2007) (IRS manual does not have force of law; no private right of action for failure to follow its procedures); Sachs v. United States, 2001 WL 1203281 (E.D. Mich. Aug. 20, 2001) (no cause of action for violation of IRS manual or revenue rulings), *aff'd*, 59 Fed. Appx. 116 (6th Cir. 2003).

387 26 U.S.C. § 6304.

of a provision of the Internal Revenue Code, damages may not exceed $100,000.[388] In a suit alleging disregard of a provision of the Internal Revenue Code, if the taxpayer's position is found to be frivolous or groundless, the taxpayer may be required to pay a penalty of up to $10,000.[389] The taxpayer may also be found liable for attorney fees.[390]

The Internal Revenue Code also provides for notice and an administrative hearing, with an appeal to the Tax Court, for taxpayers threatened with a levy.[391] These sections contain strict procedural requirements—often including short time limits.[392] Failure to exhaust administrative remedies will bar any subsequent judicial review,[393] although it is probably an affirmative defense, rather than a jurisdictional requirement.[394]

10.2.13.11 Government Counterclaim for the Debt

The government may seek to nullify a suit challenging its collection methods by counterclaiming for the underlying debt or arguing that the underlying debt should operate as an offset against any amount owed to the plaintiff. One court has rejected this approach in a case involving illegal administrative offsets by the government. It held that the government's claim for the debt did not arise out of the same transaction or occurrence as the illegal offset, and so did not fall within an exception to the six-year statute of limitations for the government to sue on a debt.[395] The court did not completely reject the government's argument that it ought to be able to set off the underlying debt against the plaintiff's claim but held that the government's offset rights could not be determined until the existence and amount of the plaintiff's claim was determined. In a later order, the court concluded that the government could set off the class members' unpaid debts against any recovery they won, but only if it could prove the amount of those debts. The court also held that the government could not set off the class members' debts against the processing fees it charged for its illegal administrative offsets.[396]

10.3 Federal Debt Collection Procedures Act

10.3.1 Civil Procedure and Exemptions for Collection of Federal Government's Claims

In 1990 Congress passed the Federal Debt Collection Procedures Act ("Procedures Act").[397] Congress intended the Act to create a new statutory framework for the judicial enforcement of most debts owed to the U.S. government. The sponsors believed this would facilitate the collection of U.S. government debts and reduce the federal budget deficit.[398]

Rather than defer to state judicial remedies, as does Rule 64 of the Federal Rules of Civil Procedure, the Procedures Act establishes a federal judicial collection scheme that in large part preempts and replaces state law when the United States

---

388 26 U.S.C. § 7433(b). *See* Kovacs v. United States, 2011 WL 4625637 (E.D. Wis. Sept. 30, 2011) (construing damages provision of section 7433; attorney fees not actual damages but may be awarded pursuant to section 7430 if taxpayer was prevailing party and U.S. litigating position not substantially justified), *aff'g decision after remand*, *In re* Kovacs, 2012 WL 3234818 (E.D. Wis. Aug. 6, 2012) (taxpayer was prevailing party when key issue was whether IRS violated discharge injunction; U.S. litigating position not substantially justified when IRS failed to reasonably investigate whether debt it tried to collect was discharged).

389 26 U.S.C. § 6673(b).

390 *See, e.g.*, Heger v. United States, 2014 WL 172549 (Fed. Cl. Jan. 16, 2014) (assessing attorney fees pursuant to Equal Access to Justice Act against taxpayer who lost, at summary judgment stage, action seeking a refund; also finding that action was pursued in bad faith).

391 26 U.S.C. § 6330. *See* Zapara v. C.I.R., 652 F.3d 1042 (9th Cir. 2011) (in section 6330 proceeding, Tax Court may address failure of IRS to comply with statute, here refusal to sell levied stock when requested by taxpayer, and "apply the full range of equitable principles"); Beeler v. C.I.R., 434 Fed. Appx. 41 (2d Cir. 2011) (Tax Court decisions reviewed with deferential "clear error" standard; here remanding to give Tax Court opportunity to explain factual basis of its decision); Barry v. United States, 215 Fed. Appx. 933 (11th Cir. 2007) (district court lacked subject matter jurisdiction over due process challenge to IRS administrative hearing; even for constitutional issues, appeal to Tax Court is only remedy); United States v. LeBeau, 2012 WL 835160 (S.D. Cal. Mar. 12, 2012) (innocent spouse claim may be raised only by administrative claim with review by Tax Court); Weber v. United States Internal Revenue Serv., 2007 WL 316460 (W.D. Wis. Jan. 8, 2007) (district court lacks subject matter jurisdiction over due process claim alleging IRS refusal of face-to-face hearing to hearing-impaired taxpayer); Bartschi v. Tracy, 2001 U.S. Dist. LEXIS 16333 (D. Ariz. Sept. 5, 2001) (claim of improper levy procedure may be brought only under 26 U.S.C. § 6330); Skillo v. United States, 68 Fed. Cl. 734 (Fed. Cl. 2005) (dismissing due process claim; petition to Tax Court, with ninety-day limitations period, is only remedy for taxpayer who disagrees with deficiency assessment).

392 *See, e.g.*, Gray v. CIR, 723 F.3d 790 (7th Cir. 2013) (applying thirty-day time limit to bar claims arising from notice of determination following collection due process hearing; noting that limitations period varies, depending on what issues raised at hearing); Stocker v. United States, 705 F.3d 225 (6th Cir. 2013) (affirming dismissal; postmark date is only acceptable proof of timely mailing).

393 *See, e.g.*, Nogueras-Cartagena v. United States, 125 Fed. Appx. 323 (1st Cir. 2005) (section 7433 requires a showing of exhaustion of administrative remedies); Munaco v. United States, 522 F.3d 651 (6th Cir. 2008) (exhaustion requirements apply to third party who seeks refund of sum paid to release improper lien and clear title to property); Grey v. United States, 723 F.3d 795 (7th Cir. 2013) (IRS properly construed section 7433 to require exhaustion of remedies).

394 Hoogherheide v. I.R.S., 637 F.3d 634 (6th Cir. 2011) (section 7433 exhaustion requirement not jurisdictional, but claim fails for failure to exhaust, and exhaustion requirement is non-waivable). *See* Kim v. United States, 632 F.3d 713 (D.C. Cir. 2011) (failure to exhaust is an affirmative defense rather than a jurisdictional requirement that must be pleaded).

395 Briggs v. United States, 2008 WL 4667117 (N.D. Cal. Oct. 22, 2008).

396 Briggs v. United States, 2009 WL 1176297 (N.D. Cal. Apr. 30, 2009).

397 Pub. L. No. 101-647, tit. XXXVI, 104 Stat. 4933 (codified at 28 U.S.C. §§ 3001–3308). *See also* Schueler v. Rayjas Enters., Inc., 847 F. Supp. 1147 (S.D.N.Y. 1994) (appendix contains government's statement and section by section analysis of the bill which became the Federal Debt Collections Procedures Act).

398 H.R. Rep. No. 101-736, at 23, *reprinted in* 1990 U.S.C.C.A.N. 6630, 6631. *See* Export-Import Bank v. Asia Pulp & Paper Co., 609 F.3d 111, 116 (2d Cir. 2010); United States v. Bongiorno, 106 F.3d 1027 (1st Cir. 1997) (goal of statute was reduction of U.S. deficit).

is collecting a debt it originated or guaranteed.[399] Nonetheless, the Procedures Act allows alleged debtors in such actions to choose between federal bankruptcy exemptions or the exemptions provided by other federal law and the law of the debtor's home state.[400]

The Procedures Act only governs debts owed to the United States.[401] It does not govern debts that arise from contracts to which the government was not an original party.[402] However, several courts have held that the Mandatory Victim Restitution Act gives the government the authority to use the Procedures Act to collect restitution awards owed to third parties.[403]

The Procedures Act does not apply to or affect the offset programs discussed earlier in this chapter.[404] It does not curtail the government's rights under other federal and state laws to collect certain types of debts, including fines, penalties, assessments, restitution, or forfeitures arising in a criminal case, and taxes and other amounts that can be collected in the same manner as taxes.[405] For those debts, the government is not required to proceed under the Procedures Act but may choose instead to proceed under state law.[406] Some courts have allowed the government to use the Procedures Act to collect a larger amount than the debtor was paying under the payment schedule set forth in a criminal restitution order.[407]

Most of the provisions of the Procedures Act can be invoked only by the United States or "counsel for the United States." The "United States" is defined as a federal corporation, an agency, department, commission, board, or other entity of the United States or an instrumentality of the United States.[408] "Counsel for the United States" is defined as a U.S. Attorney, an Assistant U.S. Attorney designated to act on behalf of the U.S. Attorney, an attorney with the U.S. Justice Department or with a federal agency who has litigation authority, or a private attorney authorized by contract under the Debt Collection Improvement Act[409] to conduct litigation for collection of debts on behalf of the United States.[410] Since an entity that buys a debt from the United States will then own the debt, a suit on the debt will have to be brought in the debt buyer's name and will not be on behalf of the United States. The attorney for the debt buyer is unlikely to meet the definition of counsel for the United States, so the Procedures Act should be inapplicable.[411] In addition, a debt that has been sold to a private party will no longer meet the definition of "debt" in the Procedures Act, which encompasses only amounts that are owing to the United States.[412] The section of the Debt Collection Improvement Act that allows the government to sell debts[413] does not authorize the debt buyer to use the Procedures Act in collecting debts.

---

399 28 U.S.C. §§ 3001(a), (b), 3003(d). *See* Export-Import Bank v. Asia Pulp & Paper Co., 609 F.3d 111, 117 (2d Cir. 2010) (Procedures Act preempts inconsistent state law but adopts state law as to whether asset is the debtor's property); Markham v. Fay, 74 F.3d 1347 (1st Cir. 1996); Mahler v. United States Dep't of Justice, 2001 U.S. Dist. LEXIS 19266 (S.D. Fla. Oct. 5, 2001) (procedural requirements of Florida's Enforcement of Foreign Judgments Act are explicitly preempted).

400 28 U.S.C. § 3014. *See* § 10.3.5, *infra*.

401 *See* Fed. Trade Comm'n v. Nat'l Bus. Consultants, Inc., 376 F.3d 317 (5th Cir. 2004) (Procedures Act applies to judgment in favor of FTC even though recovery will be used in part for consumer redress); United States v. Veal, 2005 WL 1532748 (W.D. Mo. June 28, 2005) (debt was owed "to the U.S." under Procedures Act even though only a small fraction of damages were payable to the government in discrimination action brought by government on behalf of aggrieved women). *See also* Kelley v. College of St. Benedict, 901 F. Supp. 2d 1123 (D. Minn. 2012) (only the U.S., not court-appointed receiver of Ponzi scheme's assets, can use Procedures Act).

402 28 U.S.C. § 3002(3)(B). *See* Sobranes Recovery Pool I, L.L.C. v. Todd & Hughes Constr. Corp., 509 F.3d 216 (5th Cir. 2007) (Procedures Act does not apply to judgment obtained by FDIC on note between private party and failed bank); United States *ex rel.* Small Bus. Admin. v. Commercial Tech., Inc., 354 F.3d 378, 382 n.4 (5th Cir. 2003); Office of Thrift Supervision v. Felt, 748 F. Supp. 2d 710 (S.D. Tex. 2010) (Procedures Act does not apply to judgment that OTS won as agent for investors).

403 United States v. Witham, 648 F.3d 40 (1st Cir. 2011); United States v. Mays, 430 F.3d 963 (9th Cir. 2005); United States v. Phillips, 303 F.3d 548 (5th Cir. 2002).

404 28 U.S.C. § 3003(c)(6). *See* Bosarge v. United States Dep't of Educ., 5 F.3d 1414 (11th Cir. 1993) (student loan debtor could not take advantage of state exemptions incorporated by Procedures Act to protect income tax refund from offset); United States v. Beukle, 892 F. Supp. 2d 1176, 1187–88 (D.S.D. 2012) (even when matters regarding the claim are being litigated, government may refer debt to Treasury offset program, and court order is unnecessary).

405 28 U.S.C. § 3003(b). *See* Sequoia Prop. & Equip. L.P. v. United States, 100 Fed. Appx. 638 (9th Cir. 2004) (government can collect tax debts either under Procedures Act or Internal Revenue Code); United States v. Grant, 2013 WL 1729380 (S.D. Fla. Apr. 22, 2013) (government can proceed under Internal Revenue Code rather than Procedures Act to collect tax debt); United States v. Patiwana, 267 F. Supp. 2d 301 (E.D.N.Y. 2003). *See also* 18 U.S.C. § 3613(a) (allowing government the option of proceeding under the Procedures Act to collect criminal fines). *Cf.* McKean v. United States, 563 F. Supp. 2d 182 (D.D.C. 2008) (rejecting defendant's argument that government had to follow Procedures Act in collecting tax debt; stating that tax laws provide exclusive procedure).

406 United States v. Clayton, 613 F.3d 592 (5th Cir. 2010) (federal government has option of using Procedures Act to collect criminal restitution debt); United States v. Carney, 796 F. Supp. 700 (E.D.N.Y. 1992) (Procedures Act left IRS free to choose whether to use it or state law—here, the New York Debtor-Creditor Law's broader definition of "fraudulent transfer"—to collect taxes). *See also* United States v. Golden Elevator, Inc., 868 F. Supp. 1063 (C.D. Ill. 1994) (allowing government the option of proceeding under state law even for a debt not listed in 28 U.S.C. § 3003(b); having chosen state law to foreclose on mortgage, government could not seek the 10% surcharge allowed by the Procedures Act).

407 United States v. Ekong, 518 F.3d 285 (5th Cir. 2007); United States v. Clayton, 646 F. Supp. 2d 827 (E.D. La. 2009), *aff'd*, 613 F.3d 592 (5th Cir. 2010); United States v. Miller, 588 F. Supp. 2d 789 (W.D. Mich. 2008). *See also* United States v. Hawkins, 392 F. Supp. 2d 757 (W.D. Va. 2005) (that defendant was current on the monthly installments due pursuant to her Mandatory Victims Restitution Act payment schedule did not prevent government from obtaining a debtor's examination pursuant to the Procedures Act to independently enforce the restitution order).

408 28 U.S.C. § 3002(15).

409 31 U.S.C. § 3718. *See* § 10.2.4, *supra*.

410 28 U.S.C. § 3002(1).

411 *But cf.* Buckeye Retirement Co. v. Ruotolo, 2013 WL 4777192 (D. Me. Sept. 5, 2013) (mag. dec.) (applying Procedures Act to suit brought in name of debt buyer without discussion of these issues).

412 28 U.S.C. § 3002(3).

413 31 U.S.C. § 3711(i).

The federal government often uses the Procedures Act to collect fines and restitution from criminal defendants and monetary awards won by the FTC against fraudulent companies. It also uses the Act to collect student loans and other debts from ordinary consumers, but advocates are more likely to encounter the administrative collection methods discussed in § 10.2, *supra*.

10.3.2 Six-Year Statute of Limitations

In general, with a number of exceptions, suits by the United States for money damages based on an express or implied contract are subject to a six-year statute of limitations.[414] The same limitations period applies to suits to recover money erroneously paid to a civilian employee of a federal agency or a member or dependent of the uniformed services.[415] The limitations period for most tort suits by the United States is three years.[416] These limitations periods are inapplicable to actions that are brought by the IRS or that are incidental to the collection of federal taxes.[417] They are also inapplicable to administrative offset.[418]

10.3.3 Prejudgment Remedies

The Procedures Act establishes both prejudgment and postjudgment remedies. The prejudgment remedies are attachment, receivership,[419] garnishment (of non-earnings), and sequestration of income from property.[420] These remedies are only available upon a showing of extraordinary circumstances—for example, that the debtor is about to leave the United States or dispose of property.[421] The debtor is entitled to notice of the right to a prompt post-seizure hearing to assert the absence of grounds for the remedy, the lack of a valid claim, a defense, or an exemption.[422]

10.3.4 Postjudgment Remedies

10.3.4.1 Overview

The Procedures Act's postjudgment remedies[423] provide for judgment liens, notice of exempt property rights, execution of judgments,[424] installment payment orders against self-employed persons or persons concealing substantial earnings,[425] and garnishment, including garnishment of earnings. The definition of "earnings"[426] is identical to that in the Consumer Credit Protection Act's wage garnishment restrictions.[427] Another provision of the Act provides for setting aside fraudulent conveyances.[428] The Act has only limited provisions for postjudgment receivership.[429] The Act may override state time limits on execution upon judgments.[430]

10.3.4.2 Judgment Liens

Judgment liens are effective for twenty years, unless satisfied, and may be renewed for another twenty years.[431] Until the judgment lien is satisfied, the debtor is ineligible for grants or loans made, insured, guaranteed, or financed directly or indirectly by the federal government, although agencies have authority to promulgate regulations for waiver of this provision.[432]

10.3.4.3 Garnishment and Installment Payments

The Procedures Act specifies procedures the government must follow to obtain a wage garnishment.[433] The government must make demand on the debtor for payment of the debt at

414 28 U.S.C. § 2415(a).

415 28 U.S.C. § 2415(c).

416 28 U.S.C. § 2415(b).

417 18 U.S.C. § 2415(h).

418 28 U.S.C. § 2415(i). *See also* Red River Farms v. United States, 2009 WL 2983195 (D. Ariz. Sept. 17, 2009) (government may use Claims Collection Act procedures to collect debt on which Oil Spill Act's statute of limitations bars suit).

419 United States v. Brosseau, 2005 WL 94550 (N.D. Tex. Jan. 14, 2005) (under Procedures Act, court may appoint a receiver only at government's request, not at request of judgment debtor).

420 28 U.S.C. §§ 3102–3105. *But cf.* United States v. Cap Quality Care, Inc., 400 F. Supp. 2d 295 (D. Me. 2005) (prejudgment remedies of receivership or sequestration under Procedures Act not available when government was not seeking to enforce an existing debt but had merely filed suit seeking penalties and fines).

421 28 U.S.C. § 3101(b).

422 28 U.S.C. §§ 3101(d). *See also* Nat'l Labor Relations Bd. v. E.D.P. Med. Computer Sys., Inc., 6 F.3d 951 (2d Cir. 1993) (prejudgment garnishment warranted when property at risk of disappearing; Procedures Act complies with due process); United States v. Teeven, 862 F. Supp. 1200 (D. Del. 1992) (detailed and fact-specific discussion of what government must show "with particularity" to demonstrate probable validity of debt and "compelling circumstances" to justify prejudgment remedies; debtors have burden of going forward at post-seizure hearing).

423 28 U.S.C. §§ 3201–3205.

424 *See, e.g.*, United States v. Santee Sioux Tribe, 254 F.3d 728 (8th Cir. 2001) (allowing execution upon bank accounts bearing defendant's federal tax identification number).

425 *See* Davis v. United States, 2011 WL 4712077 (W.D. La. Oct. 6, 2011) (detailing calculation methods for determining amount of installment payments), *aff'd*, 479 Fed. Appx. 601 (5th Cir. 2012); United States v. Runnells, 335 F. Supp. 2d 724 (E.D. Va. 2004) (ordering document production so that court can decide whether to order installment payments from self-employment earnings).

426 28 U.S.C. § 3205(b)(1).

427 28 U.S.C. § 1672(a). *See* § 12.4.1.4, *infra*.

428 28 U.S.C. §§ 3301–3308. *Cf.* United States v. Goforth, 465 F.3d 730 (6th Cir. 2006) (husband's monthly transfers to wife for household expenses not fraudulent transfers).

429 28 U.S.C. § 3103(c) (prejudgment receivership may not extend past judgment unless court orders it continued under section 3203(e) or unless court otherwise directs its continuance), section 3203(e) (allowing postjudgment receivership pending levy of execution). *See also* United States v. Bradley, 644 F.3d 1213, 1310–11 (11th Cir. 2011) (appointment of receiver is inappropriate when government has other adequate methods of collecting the judgment).

430 United States v. Gianelli, 543 F.3d 1178 (9th Cir. 2008).

431 28 U.S.C. § 3201(c).

432 28 U.S.C. § 3201(e).

433 28 U.S.C. § 3205(c). *See* United States v. Flores, 2012 WL 4832815 (S.D.N.Y. Oct. 4, 2012).

least thirty days before applying for a writ of garnishment.[434] Wage and bank account garnishments may be continuous.[435] One court held that the Procedures Act overrides state limits on wage garnishment,[436] but it relied for this statement on a House report that discussed an earlier version of the bill before it was amended to allow debtors to choose state exemptions.[437] Support orders take priority over government garnishments.[438] While the Procedures Act allows garnishment of up to 25% of the debtor's disposable earnings,[439] several courts have held that this is a maximum, and the court has discretion to reduce the amount in light of the debtor's circumstances.[440]

If the government shows that the judgment debtor is receiving or will receive substantial non-exempt disposable earnings from self-employment that are not subject to garnishment, or is diverting or concealing earnings, the court may order the judgment debtor to make specified installment payments.[441] Installment payments cannot be ordered, however, if there is a writ of garnishment of earnings in effect, issued under the Procedures Act and based on the same debt.[442]

10.3.4.4 Debtor's Ability to Challenge Postjudgment Remedy

A judgment debtor who disputes the government's right to a particular postjudgment remedy may file a motion to quash.[443] The District Court must conduct a hearing on the motion as soon as practicable, but the issues are limited to the validity of any claim of exemption and the government's compliance with the Procedures Act's requirements.[444] The issues may be somewhat broader if the judgment is a default judgment, however.[445] A judgment debtor objecting to a writ of garnishment must also meet certain procedural requirements.[446] The court has the authority, on its own initiative or the motion of any person, to deny, limit, condition, regulate, extend, or modify the use of any of the Procedures Act's enforcement procedures,[447] but the debtor does not have the right to a hearing on such a motion.[448]

10.3.5 Property Exempt from Seizure

The law provides debtors with a choice between the federal exemptions provided in the Bankruptcy Code[449] or the combination of state exemptions and non-Bankruptcy Act federal exemptions.[450] The level of exemptions was one of the greatest contrasts between the House and Senate bills leading to the Procedures Act. The Senate had chosen a list of exemptions similar to, but even slightly more limited than, those in the Bankruptcy Code.[451] The House bill was more generous, providing, for example, a homestead exemption of $70,000 to $99,999.99.[452]

The compromise allows the debtor to choose between the Bankruptcy Act exemptions or the state exemptions plus federal non-bankruptcy exemptions.[453] In addition, the remedies

---

434 28 U.S.C. § 3205(b)(1)(B). *See* United States v. Tisdale, 2013 WL 4804286 (N.D. Tex. Sept. 9, 2013) (mailing of demand letter satisfies section 3205 even if defendant did not receive it).

435 28 U.S.C. §§ 3104, 3205(a).

436 Pierce v. United States, 232 B.R. 333 (E.D.N.C. 1999) (government can continue to garnish debtor's wages despite state law prohibiting enforcement of judgment against personal property more than ten years after date of judgment).

437 H.R. Rep. 101–736 p. 38 (Sept. 21, 1990).

438 28 U.S.C. § 3205(c)(8).

439 28 U.S.C. §§ 3003(c)(4), 3205; 15 U.S.C. 1673(a). *See generally* § 12.4, *infra* (interpretation of section 1673).

440 28 U.S.C. § 3013. *See* United States v. Woods, 2010 WL 4386900 (S.D. Ala. Oct. 29, 2010); United States v. Ernst, 2010 WL 3746950 (M.D. Fla. Sept. 21, 2010); United States v. Picklesimer, 2010 WL 2572850 (W.D.N.C. June 24, 2010); United States v. Ogburn, 499 F. Supp. 2d 28 (D.D.C. 2007); United States v. Crowther, 473 F. Supp. 2d 729, 731 (N.D. Tex. 2007); United States v. George, 144 F. Supp. 2d 161 (E.D.N.Y. 2001); United States v. Kaye, 93 F. Supp. 2d 196, 199 (D. Conn. 2000). *But see* United States v. Miller, 588 F. Supp. 2d 789 (W.D. Mich. 2008) (wage garnishment is limited to 25%, but debtor's financial circumstances are irrelevant); United States v. Hanhardt, 353 F. Supp. 2d 957 (N.D. Ill. 2004) (court does not have authority to reduce garnishment of pension below 25%).

441 28 U.S.C. § 3204.

442 28 U.S.C. § 3204(c).

443 28 U.S.C. § 3202(d).

444 28 U.S.C. § 3202(d). *See* United States v. Pugh, 75 Fed. Appx. 546 (8th Cir. 2003) (requiring hearing on exemptions, government's compliance with Procedures Act, and debtor's claim that balance of debt had already been reduced); United States v. Manuel, 2013 WL 5530679 (D. Ariz. Oct. 7, 2013) (denying hearing on garnishment when only ground stated was that debtor was already making payments and needed the money to support dependents); United States v. Hubbard, 2010 WL 2169073 (N.D. Iowa May 28, 2010) (hearing not required on claim that wage garnishment would cause hardship), *report and recommendation adopted by* 2010 WL 2540106 (N.D. Iowa June 21, 2010); United States v. Poitra, 2009 WL 3063013 (D.N.D. Sept. 18, 2009) (listing issues that defendant may raise); United States v. Miller, 588 F. Supp. 2d 789 (W.D. Mich. 2008) (no right to hearing if debtor does not raise one of the enumerated objections); United States v. Young, 2008 WL 427942 (D.N.D. Feb. 14, 2008) (granting government's motion to limit issues at garnishment hearing to those listed in section 3202), *aff'd*, 593 F.3d 773 (8th Cir. 2010); United States v. Greenberg, 2006 WL 3791373 (D. Vt. Dec. 22, 2006).

445 28 U.S.C. § 3202(d)(3).

446 28 U.S.C. § 3205(c)(5). *See* United States v. Crowther, 473 F. Supp. 2d 729 (N.D. Tex. 2007) (judgment debtor failed to meet procedural requirements imposed by section 3205(c)(5) when he filed blank exemption form and separate request for hearing and did not disclose substance of his objection until hearing).

447 28 U.S.C. § 3013.

448 *See, e.g.*, United States v. Hubbard, 2010 WL 2169073 (N.D. Iowa May 28, 2010) (hearing not required on claim that wage garnishment would cause hardship), *report and recommendation adopted by* 2010 WL 2540106 (N.D. Iowa June 21, 2010).

449 11 U.S.C. § 522(d). *See* National Consumer Law Center, Consumer Bankruptcy Law and Practice Ch. 10 (10th ed. 2012), *updated at* www.nclc.org/library.

450 28 U.S.C. § 3014. *See* Connell v. United States, 69 Fed. Appx. 867 (9th Cir. 2003) (debtor may use state exemptions, but his insurance settlement is still not exempt); United States v. Neff, 2007 WL 776532 (D.N.D. Mar. 12, 2007) (debtors may claim state homestead exemption).

451 *See* S. 84, 101st Cong. § 3401 (1989), *reprinted in* 135 Cong. Rec. S14,685–S14,697 (daily ed. Nov. 3, 1989).

452 H.R. 5640, 101st Cong. § 3014 (1989).

453 28 U.S.C. § 3014(a). *But cf.* Sec. Exch. Comm'n v. AMX Int'l, Inc., 7 F.3d 71 (5th Cir. 1993) (Procedures Act's exemptions not available to debtor who is subject to disgorgement order entered by consent in

available to the United States can be enforced against property co-owned by the debtor and another person only to the extent allowed by the law of the state where the property is located.[454] The statute appears to allow debtors to exempt entireties property in states that recognize that doctrine even if they choose the bankruptcy exemptions.[455]

A non-debtor has the right to move for an order denying, limiting, conditioning, regulating, extending, or modifying the use of any enforcement procedure.[456] The government can also join third parties and pursue fraudulent transfers of assets.[457]

The Procedures Act does not supersede or modify the federal garnishment protections of 75% of earnings or thirty times the minimum wage, whichever is greater.[458] In addition, the federal Bankruptcy Code[459] or state personal property exemptions[460] may provide an additional protection for earnings and savings.

The exemptions provided by the Procedures Act do not restrict the government's ability to collect fines or criminal restitution debts.[461] Instead, a separate statute incorporates certain of the exemptions that apply to tax collection, and the wage garnishment limits set by the Consumer Credit Protection Act.[462]

10.3.6 Government's Right to Impose a Surcharge

The Procedures Act allows the government to recover a surcharge of up to 10% of the debt to cover the costs of processing and handling the litigation and enforcement of the claim.[463] This surcharge can only be recovered, however, in proceedings seeking prejudgment or postjudgment remedies, not in a suit on the underlying debt.[464] The government is not entitled to a surcharge when it is awarded attorney fees, or the law on which the claim is based provides any other amount to cover such costs.[465]

10.3.7 Distant Filing of Collection Suits Possible

Perhaps the most draconian measure in the Procedures Act is the establishment of nationwide service of process,[466] with the resulting specter that the federal government could

---

securities fraud action, as such an order does not meet statute's definition of "debt"); United States v. Udoh, 2013 WL 956943 (W.D. La. Mar. 12, 2013) (Mandatory Victim Restitution Act preempts state exemptions, so Procedures Act does not give defendant a choice of state law exemptions when government is collecting restitution debt); Pierce v. United States, 232 B.R. 333 (E.D.N.C. 1999) (government can continue to garnish debtor's wages despite state law prohibiting enforcement of judgment against personal property more than ten years after date of judgment; erroneously relying on House report that discusses a significantly different earlier version of the bill). *See generally* Ch. 12, *infra* (discussion of state exemption law); Appx. G, *infra* (summaries of state exemption laws).

454 28 U.S.C. §§ 3010(a), 3014(a)(2)(B) (debtors who choose the state exemptions plus federal nonbankruptcy exemptions can also exempt their interest in entireties or community property if allowed by state law). *See* United States v. Duran, 701 F.3d 912 (11th Cir. 2012) (district court has jurisdiction to resolve third party's claim of ownership); United States v. Yielding, 657 F.3d 722 (8th Cir. 2011) (ownership interest is defined by state law); United States v. Loftis, 607 F.3d 173 (5th Cir. 2010) (applying Texas law and allowing garnishment of wife's interest in certain community property); United States v. Sprint Equities NY, Inc., 92 Fed. Appx. 841 (2d Cir. 2004); Nat'l Labor Relations Bd. v. J & D Masonry, Inc., 2008 WL 4960157 (W.D. Mich. Nov. 19, 2008) (section 3010 protects funds that state law requires to be held in trust); Fischre v. United States, 852 F. Supp. 628 (W.D. Mich. 1994) (federal lien can only attach to debtor's contingent survivorship interest in entireties property). *See also* United States v. Rogan, 639 F.3d 1106 (7th Cir. 2011) (fact that writ issued by government has priority over other writs does not enable government to attach a third party's interest in the property); United States v. Sowada, 2003 WL 22902613 (E.D. La. Dec. 8, 2003) (requiring government to give notice and opportunity for hearing to spouse before garnishing community property; government can reach property co-owned by debtor and spouse because state law allows it).

455 28 U.S.C. § 3010(a).

456 28 U.S.C. § 3013. *See* United States v. Yielding, 657 F.3d 722 (8th Cir. 2011) (third party who claims ownership has due process right to adjudication of this claim); United States v. Kollintzas, 501 F.3d 796 (7th Cir. 2007) (non-party who has interest in the target property may participate in case without formally intervening); United States v. Tedder, 2004 WL 415270 (W.D. Wis. Feb. 26, 2004).

457 28 U.S.C. § 3304. *See, e.g.*, Fed. Trade Comm'n v. Nat'l Bus. Consultants, Inc., 376 F.3d 317 (5th Cir. 2004); *In re* Phillips & Hornsby Litig., 306 F. Supp. 2d 631 (M.D. La. 2004), *aff'd*, 204 Fed. Appx. 398 (5th Cir. 2006).

458 28 U.S.C. § 3003(c)(4); 15 U.S.C. § 1673(a). *See also* United States v. Hanhardt, 353 F. Supp. 2d 957 (N.D. Ill. 2004) (government's legal claim to garnishment of 25% of defendant's annuity payments to satisfy restitution order was superior to defendant's other financial obligations). *See generally* §§ 12.2.8.2, 12.4.1.2, 12.4.1.3, *infra*.

459 11 U.S.C. § 522(d)(5).

460 *See* § 12.8, *infra*.

461 18 U.S.C. §§ 3613(a)(2), 3613(f). *See* § 12.2.8.2, *infra*.

462 18 U.S.C. § 3613(a)(1), (3).

463 28 U.S.C. § 3011. *See* United States v. Goyette, 446 Fed. Appx. 718 (5th Cir. 2011) (unpublished) (upholding imposition of surcharge); Bd. of Governors of the Fed. Reserve Sys. v. Pharaon, 169 F.3d 110 (2d Cir. 1999) (government entitled to 10% surcharge, and interest on surcharge, after it sought a prejudgment restraining order against dissipation of assets); United States v. Jean-Baptiste, 2007 WL 3197390 (E.D.N.Y. Oct. 26, 2007); United States v. Goo, 2002 WL 31934169 (Haw. Nov. 18, 2002) (allowing surcharge in addition to foreclosure expenses).

464 Gonzalez v. Dep't of Labor, 609 F.3d 451 (D.C. Cir. 2010) (10% surcharge cannot be assessed when debtor loses suit challenging the debt); United States v. Rostoff, 164 F.3d 63 (1st Cir. 1999) (government cannot assess surcharge in an action to determine the amount of the debt); United States v. Sackett, 114 F.3d 1050 (10th Cir. 1997) (surcharge is available only for prejudgment or postjudgment proceedings); United States v. Lyon, 2011 WL 2226308 (E.D. Cal. June 7, 2011), *adopted by* 2011 WL 2909936 (E.D. Cal. July 14, 2011); United States v. George, 144 F. Supp. 2d 161 (E.D.N.Y. 2001) (government entitled to surcharge based on postjudgment enforcement proceedings only once it brings such proceedings, and interest on surcharge runs from date it is imposed, not from date of judgment); United States v. Mauldin, 805 F. Supp. 35 (N.D. Ala. 1992) (surcharge cannot be assessed against debtor in suit on student loan debt when government did not use any of Procedures Act's prejudgment or postjudgment remedies).

465 28 U.S.C. § 3011(b). *But cf.* United States v. Ensminger, 2013 WL 1800330 (E.D. Cal. Apr. 29, 2013) (government is entitled to surcharge despite having been awarded attorney fee on underlying claim when it was not awarded fees for the enforcement proceeding).

466 28 U.S.C. § 3004(b).

sue in a forum thousands of miles from the alleged debtor's current residence. Federal courts have interpreted this part of the Procedures Act to mean that a court can acquire personal jurisdiction over a debtor even if the debtor does not have the "minimum contacts" with the forum state that *International Shoe Company v. Washington*[467] requires. Instead, the court can exercise personal jurisdiction as long as the debtor has minimum contacts anywhere within the United States.[468]

One court has held, however, that an additional inquiry—an analysis of personal jurisdiction under the five-factor "reasonableness" test enunciated in *Asahi Metal Industries Company v. Superior Court*[469]—is necessary after establishing that the debtor has minimum contacts with the United States.[470] This test requires analysis of: (1) the burden that the exercise of jurisdiction will impose on the defendant; (2) the interests of the forum state in adjudicating the case; (3) the plaintiff's interest in obtaining convenient and effective relief; (4) the interstate judicial system's interest in obtaining the most efficient resolution of the controversy; and (5) the shared interest of the states in furthering substantive social policies.[471]

The nationwide service provision is somewhat ameliorated by the defendant's right to transfer the case to the district where he or she resides[472] and the requirement that the debtor be given notice of the right to transfer.[473] However the defendant has only twenty days after receiving the notice to request the transfer.[474]

The statute expresses the requirement to transfer venue upon the defendant's request as mandatory,[475] and the Sixth Circuit has held that it is in fact mandatory.[476] However, some courts hold that a sentencing court's continuing jurisdiction over criminal restitution overrides a defendant's right under the Procedures Act to transfer a case to his or her home district.[477] This position finds some support in a provision that the Procedures Act shall not be construed as curtailing or limiting the right of the United States to collect any fine, penalty, assessment, restitution, or forfeiture arising in a criminal case.[478] One court,[479] however, bases this view on the court's authority to make orders "denying, limiting, conditioning, regulating, extending, or modifying the use of any enforcement procedure" under the Procedures Act.[480] This interpretation would apply to any type of federal debt, not just those arising from criminal cases. It improperly treats venue as an "enforcement procedure" and reads the "shall" out of the venue transfer statute. Another court even extends the reasoning of these cases to suits involving debts other than criminal restitution.[481]

Several courts have held the Procedures Act transfer provision inapplicable to a fraudulent conveyance action commenced under subchapter D of the Procedures Act.[482] They base this conclusion on the fact that the right to request a transfer arises under the statute only after the government sends the debtor a notice that it is seeking a prejudgment or postjudgment remedy,[483] and no such notice is required in the case of a fraudulent transfer action.

467 326 U.S. 310, 66 S. Ct. 154, 90 L. Ed. 95 (U.S. 1945).

468 United States v. Coker, 2010 WL 4286380 (E.D. Cal. Oct. 22, 2010); United States v. Rogan, 2008 WL 4853478 (N.D. Ill. Nov. 3, 2008); Reese Bros., Inc. v. United States Postal Serv., 477 F. Supp. 2d 31, 40 (D.D.C. 2007); United States v. Sutton, 2005 WL 281162, at *1 (D. Conn. Jan. 10, 2005).

469 480 U.S. 102, 113–14, 107 S. Ct. 1026, 94 L. Ed. 2d 92 (1987).

470 2005 WL 281162 (D. Conn. Jan. 10, 2005).

471 *Id.*

472 28 U.S.C. § 3004(b)(2). *See* United States v. Allison, 2007 WL 2491192 (W.D.N.C. Aug. 29, 2007) (ordering transfer). *But cf.* United States v. Nash, 175 F.3d 440 (6th Cir. 1999) (failure to grant transfer was harmless error).

473 28 U.S.C. § 3101(d).

474 28 U.S.C. § 3004(b)(2).

475 28 U.S.C. § 3004(c) ("If the debtor so requests, . . . the action or proceeding . . . shall be transferred . . .").

476 United States v. Nash, 175 F.3d 440, 442 (6th Cir. 1999).

477 United States v. Furkin, 165 F.3d 33 (table), 1998 WL 846873 (7th Cir. Nov. 24, 1998) (upholding denial of transfer request for collection proceedings brought to enforce the criminal judgment entered by trial court); United States v. Mathews, 793 F. Supp. 2d 72 (D.D.C. 2011) (finding transfer provision not to be mandatory); United States v. Poulson, 2010 WL 1849294 (S.D. Ohio May 3, 2010); United States v. Jeburk, 2008 WL 4499982 (S.D. Ga. Oct. 6, 2008); United States v. Tedder, 2004 WL 415270 (W.D. Wis. Feb. 26, 2004). *But cf.* United States v. Vieira, 2009 WL 3678098 (D.R.I. Nov. 4, 2009) (when defendant was sentenced before Mandatory Victims Restitution Act was adopted, its procedures do not override Collection Act's mandatory transfer right).

478 28 U.S.C. § 3003(b)(2).

479 United States v. Gipson, 714 F. Supp. 2d 571, 579 (E.D. Va. 2010).

480 28 U.S.C. § 3013.

481 Equal Employment Opportunity Comm'n v. 5042 Holding Ltd., 2013 WL 1636577 (N.D. W. Va. Apr. 16, 2013). *See also* United States v. Hobson, 2013 WL 4545687 (D. Idaho Aug. 27, 2013) (holding, in non-criminal case, that debtor does not have a right to transfer postjudgment enforcement proceedings to his new state of residence, without discussing the mandatory language of section 3004; applying general venue factors and denying transfer).

482 United States v. Preston, ___ F. Supp. 2d ___, 2013 WL 4401818 (D.D.C. Aug. 16, 2013) (interpreting statutory language to hold that venue transfer provision applies to prejudgment remedies and the post-judgment remedies set forth in Subchapter C but not to fraudulent conveyance actions); United States v. Sutton, 2005 WL 281162 (D. Conn. Jan. 10, 2005). *See also* United States v. Klearman, 1998 WL 122250 (E.D. Pa. Mar. 10, 1998).

483 28 U.S.C. § 3004(b)(B)(2).

Chapter 11 Challenging a Collection Judgment

11.1 Introduction

After a collector obtains a judgment on a debt, consumers have a number of steps they can take to set aside the judgment or minimize its effect. Most collection actions end in either a default judgment or a stipulation for judgment. This chapter considers how the consumer can set aside such judgments (even a litigated judgment), allowing a fresh trial on the merits. Also reviewed briefly are consumer steps after an arbitration award for the collector.

Another option to deal with a judgment in favor of the collector is filing bankruptcy, because a bankruptcy discharge will eliminate many of the adverse consequences that a judgment holds for the consumer. Section 11.5, *infra*, briefly examines consumer bankruptcy rights to deal with a judgment and whether bankruptcy is a good option for a particular consumer, while making reference to other NCLC publications that more thoroughly treat the subject.

Section 11.6, *infra*, considers the advisability of another option—bringing a separate court action challenging the collector's litigation misconduct. Chapter 13, *infra*, offers a more detailed discussion of such separate court actions, in the context of a litigation brought after the consumer *prevails* in the collection action. Section 11.6, *infra*, examines the advisability of such an action after a judgment for the collector.

If the judgment cannot be set aside or otherwise avoided, Chapter 12, *supra*, examines consumer defenses to the collector's attempts at wage garnishment, seizure of funds from the consumer's bank account, placement of liens on the consumer's property, and other creditor postjudgment remedies. Such consumer defenses largely rest on the consumer being able to claim certain income or assets as exempt under federal or state law.

One approach will not be covered in this chapter—if the consumer has answered the suit and lost on the merits, the consumer can appeal the decision, arguing that the court made an error in law or allowed the collector to recover without an adequate evidentiary showing. With certain exceptions,[1] the consumer cannot appeal if the consumer did not answer the complaint and did not present the issue on appeal to the trial court.

While this treatise does not include a discussion of the procedure and standards to review a court's decision in a collection case, earlier chapters examine the applicable law and the collector's evidentiary burden,[2] all of which will be relevant to such an appeal. For guidance on appellate procedures, advocates should consult other resources at the state level, because these procedures vary from state to state and from court to court within a state.

1 For example, when a default judgment does not comport with legal requirements, the consumer should be able to appeal the default judgment even when the consumer had not previously appeared in the case.

2 *See* Chs. 3, 4, *supra*.

11.2 Servicemembers' Federal Right to Vacate Default Judgment

The federal Servicemembers Civil Relief Act (SCRA) provides servicemembers with the right to set aside a judgment in which the servicemember did not make an appearance when the judgment was entered while the servicemember was on active duty or within sixty days after release from active duty.[3] An application to set aside such a judgment must be made within ninety days after the termination of or release from military service.[4]

Upon the servicemember's application, the court entering the judgment "shall" reopen a default judgment for the purpose of allowing the servicemember to defend the action.[5] To qualify, the servicemember must show a meritorious or legal defense and that military service materially affected the servicemember's ability to make a defense.[6] State law limits on vacating judgments are inapplicable to this right.[7] The court may also set aside the default judgment as to any person who is or may be primarily or secondarily liable on the debt, including co-signers and guarantors.[8]

The SCRA is examined in more detail at Chapter 7, *supra*. Section 7.1, *supra*, also lists a number of state laws that provide similar protections to servicemembers.

11.3 Setting Aside a Default, Stipulated, or Litigated Judgment

11.3.1 Setting Aside a Judgment May Be Uncontested

The first step in setting aside a default or stipulated judgment should be to contact the collector's attorney and ask the attorney to voluntarily set aside the judgment. Practitioners

3 50 U.S.C. app. § 521(g). *See* § 7.3,*supra* (a more detailed discussion of what individuals are covered by the Act).

4 50 U.S.C. app. § 521(g)(2). *See also* Collins v. Collins, 805 N.E.2d 410 (Ind. Ct. App. 2004) (servicemember precluded from moving under the Act to set aside default judgment because he did not do so within ninety days after termination of military service).

5 50 U.S.C. app. § 521(g)(1).

6 *Id. See also* Bernhardt v. Alden Café, 864 A.2d 421 (N.J. Super. Ct. App. Div. 2005) (although trial court's decision to vacate default judgment under section 521(g) is discretionary, it abused that discretion when it refused to set aside default for servicemember whose military status was undisputed and who alleged a meritorious defense).

7 *In re* Marriage of Thompson, 666 N.W.2d 616 (Iowa Ct. App. 2003); *In re* B.T.T., 156 S.W.3d 612 (Tex. App. 2004).

8 50 U.S.C. app. § 513(b).

report surprising success with this request. If this fails, the consumer attorney should proceed to ask the court to set aside the judgment pursuant to the state court's rules of procedure.

Surprisingly, even though the consumer may send notice to the collection attorney of record concerning the motion to set aside the judgment, the collector may not appear to oppose the action. In some cases the attorney of record no longer represents the collector but the collector's new attorney was never substituted in the court files. Some of the most active attorneys of record in collection cases prior to 2011, such as Wolpoff & Abramson or Mann Bracken, no longer exist as entities. Thus, the consumer acts properly in providing notice to the attorney of record, but negligence by the collector's attorney results in the notice being sent to the old law firm, such that the collector may not appear to contest the action.[9] Of course, the consumer should make reasonable efforts to notify the collector's current attorney of the motion to set aside the judgment, or the collector may be able later to attack a successful motion based upon the lack of notice.[10]

11.3.2 The Law Favors Setting Aside a Default Judgment

Certain trial judges have little sympathy for even unsophisticated *pro se* defendants who fail to properly answer and contest a collection action, and these judges are loathe to set aside default judgments. But state law is generally favorable to allowing a default judgment to be set aside. A state's procedure to set aside a judgment is remedial and should be liberally construed so that justice is served.[11] For example, the New Jersey Supreme Court has stated that a "court should view the opening of default judgments . . . with great liberality," and should tolerate "every reasonable ground for indulgence . . . to the end that a just result is reached." [12] Doubts should be resolved in favor of the consumer who is seeking to reopen the default judgment.[13] The Illinois Supreme Court has stated that a default judgment should not be enforced "when it would be unfair, unjust, or unconscionable." [14]

Washington's Supreme Court has stated that it "is the policy of the law that controversies be determined on the merits rather than by default." [15] A New York appellate court also has stated that a default should be re-opened in view of a showing of a potentially meritorious defense, the absence of legal prejudice to the plaintiff as a result of the delay, and the strong public policy of resolving disputes on the merits.[16]

A number of other state supreme courts also have stated that default judgments are disfavored and the trial court is vested with broad discretion to set them aside.[17] The trial judge's decision to set aside a judgment will not be disturbed on appeal absent an abuse of discretion.[18]

11.3.3 Stipulated Judgments Described

While many consumer collection actions result in default judgments, others result in stipulated judgments of various forms. Stipulated judgments consented to in advance by provisions in the original credit documents, known as cognovits or confessions of judgment, are generally illegal[19] and are examined in another NCLC treatise.[20] Nor will this section discuss settlements reached at arm's length when the consumer is represented by an attorney. Such settlements are examined elsewhere in this treatise.[21]

When an unrepresented consumer attends a court hearing on the debt, a favorite collector technique, sometimes encouraged by judges or other court personnel, is to take the consumer out into the corridor and resolve the matter without appearing before the judge. This procedure has clear potential for abuse as unrepresented consumers go up against sophisticated collection attorneys and then sign documents they do not fully understand, often without being fully informed about their options to contest the matter in court.

9 *See* Centurion Capital Corp. v. Guarino, 951 N.Y.S.2d 85 (table), 2012 WL 1543286 (N.Y. Civ. Ct. Apr. 30, 2012).

10 *See* Midland Funding, L.L.C. v. Cady, 110 So. 3d 656 (La. Ct. App. 2013).

11 Kay v. Marc Glassman, Inc., 665 N.E.2d 1102 (Ohio 1996).

12 Mancini v. EDS *ex rel.* N.J. Auto. Full Ins. Underwriting Ass'n, 625 A.2d 484, 486 (N.J. 1993) (citation omitted). *See also* Geer v. Jacobsen, 880 So. 2d 717 (Fla. Dist. Ct. App. 2004); Midland Funding, L.L.C. v. Angwenyi, 2013 WL 4710620 (N.J. Super. Ct. App. Div. Sept. 3, 2013); LVNV Funding, L.L.C. v. DiCicco, 2010 WL 4107856 (N.J. Super Ct. App. Div. June 22, 2010); NCO Portfolio Mgmt. v. Lorenzo, 2010 WL 3516751 (N.J. Super. Ct. App. Div. Sept. 10, 2010); Columbia Recovery Corp. v. Menchaca, 2008 WL 961037 (N.J. Super. Ct. App. Div. Mar. 12, 2008); Asset Acceptance, L.L.C. v. Scott, 2007 WL 3145360 (N.J. Super. Ct. App. Div. Oct. 30, 2007).

13 Mancini v. EDS *ex rel.* N.J. Auto. Full Ins. Underwriting Ass'n, 625 A.2d 484 (N.J. 1993); Midland Funding, L.L.C. v. Angwenyi, 2013 WL 4710620 (N.J. Super. Ct. App. Div. Sept. 3, 2013); Portfolio Recovery Assocs., L.L.C. v. Thacker, 2009 WL 2675665 (Ohio Ct. App. Aug. 28, 2009).

14 Smith v. Airoom, Inc., 499 N.E.2d 1381 (Ill. 1986).

15 Griggs v. Averbeck Realty, Inc., 599 P.2d 1289, 1292 (Wash. 1979) (quoting Dlouhy v. Dlouhy, 55 Wash. 2d 718 (Wash. 1960)).

16 Capital One Bank v. Roman, 841 N.Y.S.2d 825 (N.Y. Sup. Ct. 2007).

17 *See, e.g.*, Idaho State Police *ex rel.* Russell v. Real Prop. Situated in Cnty. of Cassia, 156 P.3d 561 (Idaho 2007); Asset Acceptance, L.L.C. v. Moberly, 241 S.W.3d 329 (Ky. 2007); Kennedy v. Black, 424 A.2d 1250 (Pa. 1981). *See also* Asset Acceptance, L.L.C. v. Moberly, 2009 WL 1347164 (Ky. Ct. App. May 15, 2009); Atlantic Credit & Fin., Inc. v. Guiliana, 829 A.2d 340 (Pa. Super. Ct. 2003). *But see* Bland v. Hammond, 935 A.2d 457 (Md. Ct. Spec. App. 2007).

18 *See* Atlantic Credit & Fin. v. Dustrude, 2008 WL 570791 (Minn. Ct. App. Mar. 4, 2008); Mancini v. EDS *ex rel.* N.J. Auto. Full Ins. Underwriting Ass'n, 625 A.2d 484 (N.J. 1993).

19 *See* 16 C.F.R. § 444.2(a)(1). *See also* Ala. Code § 8-9-11; Cal. Civ. Proc. Code § 1132 (West); 735 Ill. Comp. Stat. § 5/2-1301(c); Md. Rules (Dist. Ct.), R. 3.611; Mass. Gen. Laws ch. 231, § 13A; Minn. Stat. § 53C.08(b) (motor vehicle installment sales); N.J. Stat. Ann. § 2A:16-9 (West); N.J. R. of Ct. 4:45-1; N.Y. C.P.L.R. § 3201 (McKinney); Ohio Rev. Code Ann. § 2323.13(E) (West); Or. R. Civ. P. 73A(2); Tenn. Code Ann. § 25-2-101.

20 National Consumer Law Center, Federal Deception Law § 2.3.4 (2012), *updated at* www.nclc.org/library.

21 *See* § 2.9, *supra*.

Even though the consumer may have valid defenses, collectors may succeed in obtaining more than they could have obtained from the court just by persuading the consumer to sign a stipulation for judgment drafted by the collector's attorney. The stipulation may be one-sided and include inflated amounts as to the balance due, future interest charges, and attorney fees. As a result, the ability to set aside a stipulated judgment will be considered in this section along with the ability to set aside a default judgment. In general, the procedure for setting aside both types of judgment is the same.

11.3.4 General State Standards for Setting Aside a Judgment

11.3.4.1 State Standards Based Upon the Federal Rules

Standards to set aside a default judgment are found in a state's statutes or rules of procedure. Procedures differ for different level courts within the same state and from state to state. A good starting point is the Federal Rules of Civil Procedure, because many states pattern their procedures after these rules.

Under the federal rules, the same standards for setting aside a default judgment apply to setting aside a stipulation for judgment or a litigated judgment. Fed. R. Civ. Pro. 60 states that, "on motion and just terms, the court may relieve a party or its legal representative from a final judgment, order, or proceeding for the following reasons."[22] By its own language, this rule applies to any type of judgment and not just to default judgments.

Federal Rule of Civil Procedure 55(c) states that a default judgment can be set aside pursuant to Rule 60(b), and most states have a parallel rule.[23] The federal version of Rule 60(b) states that a final judgment can be set aside for the following reasons:

(1) Mistake, inadvertence, surprise, or excusable neglect;
(2) Certain newly discovered evidence;
(3) Fraud, misrepresentation, or misconduct by an opposing party;
(4) The judgment is void;
(5) The judgment has been satisfied, released or discharged; it is based on an earlier judgment that has been reversed or vacated; or applying it prospectively is no longer equitable; or
(6) Any other reason that justifies relief.

Rule 60(d) states that Rule 60(b) does not limit a court's power to entertain an independent action to set aside a judgment for fraud on the court.

11.3.4.2 State Standards Not Following the Federal Rules

Most states enumerate similar grounds to those found in Rule 60, but there are variations.[24] One estimate is that thirty-five states have adopted language substantially the same as the federal rules, eight states have reserved equity or broad powers to revise a final judgment, and the remainder limit the grounds to set aside a judgment to certain specific situations.[25]

Some states also allow a judgment to be set aside within thirty days without requiring any special reasons for the action.[26] Maine has a special standard applicable specifically to collection actions on consumer debt, allowing either the court on its own motion or the consumer to seek, while the

22 Fed. R. Civ. P. 60(b).

23 *See* Ala. R. Civ. P. 55(c) (motion to set aside default judgment must be made within thirty days after judgment entered, and such motions are thereafter subject to Ala. R. Civ. P. 60); Alaska R. Civ. P. 55(e) (default judgment may be set aside in accordance with Alaska R. Civ. P. 60(b)); Ariz. R. Civ. P. 55(c) (default judgment may be set aside under Ariz. R. Civ. P. 60(c)); Colo. R. Civ. P. 55(c) (default judgment may be set aside under Colo. R. Civ. P. 60(c)); Conn. Gen. Stat. § 52-212 (motion must be made within four months); Del. Sup. Ct. R. Civ. P. 55(c) (default judgment may be set aside under Del. Sup. Ct. R. Civ. P. 60(b)); D.C. Sup. Ct. R. Civ. P. 55(c) (motion to set aside judgment); Fla. R. Civ. P. 1.500(d) (default judgment set aside in accordance with Fla. R. Civ. P. 1.540(b)); Haw. R. Civ. P. 55(c) (default judgment set aside in accordance with Haw. R. Civ. P. 60(b)); Idaho Ct. R. Civ. P. 55(c) (default judgment set aside in accordance with Idaho Ct. R. Civ. P. 60(b)); Ind. Trial P. Rule 55(c) (default judgment set aside in accordance with Ind. R. Civ. P. 60(b)); Kan. Stat. Ann. § 60-255(b) (default judgment set aside in accordance with Kan. Stat. Ann. § 60-260(b)); Ky. R. Civ. P. 55.02 (default judgment set aside in accordance with Ky. R. Civ. P. 60.02); Me. R. Civ. P. 55 (court may set aside default judgment under Me. R. Civ. P. 60(b)); Mass. R. Civ. P. 55 (court may set aside default judgment under Mass. R. Civ. P. 60(b)); Minn. R. Civ. P. 60.02; Miss. R. Civ. P. 55(c) (court may set aside default judgment under Miss. R. Civ. P. 60(b)); Mont. R. Civ. P. 55(c) (court may set aside default judgment under Mont. R. Civ. P. 60(b)); Nev. R. Civ. P. 55(c) (court may set aside default judgment under Nev. R. Civ. P. 60(b)); N.J. R. of Ct. 4:43-3 (default judgment may be set aside in accordance with N.J. R. of Ct. 4:50); N.M. R. 1-055(C) (default judgment may be set aside under N.M. R. 1-060); N.C. Gen Stat. § 1A-1, Rule 55(d) (default judgment set aside in accordance with N.C. Gen Stat. § 1A-1, Rule 60(b)); N.D. R. Civ. P. 60(b); Ohio Civ. R. 55(B) (default judgment may be set aside under Ohio Civ. R. 60(B)); Or. R. Civ. P. 69(c) (default judgment may be set aside under Or. R. Civ. P. 71); S.C. R. Civ. P. 55(c) (default judgment may be set aside under S.C. R. Civ. P. 60); S.D. Codified Laws § 15-6-55(c) (default judgment set aside in accordance with S.D. Codified Laws § 15-6-60(b)); Tenn. R. Civ. P. 55.02 (default judgment set aside under Tenn. R. Civ. P. 60.02); Utah R. Civ. P. 55(c) (default judgment set aside under Utah R. Civ. P. 60(b)); Vt. R. Civ. P. 55(c) (default judgment set aside under Vt. R. Civ. P. 60(b)); Wash. Sup. Ct. Civ. R. 55(c) (default judgment set aside under Wash. Sup. Ct. Civ. R. 60(b)); W. Va. R. Civ. P. 55(c) (default judgment set aside under W. Va. R. Civ. P. 60(6)); Wyo. R. Civ. P. 55(c) (default judgment set aside under Wyo. R. Civ. P. 60(b)).

24 The amount of variation differs by state. *See, e.g.*, Ariz. R. Civ. P. 60(c) (largely following the federal rule but shortening the one-year period to six months); Ky. R. Civ. P. 60.02 (little variation); Minn. R. Civ. P. 60.02 (interpreting "any other reason that justifies relief" to be limited to a reason that is extraordinary in nature); N.J. R. of Ct. 4:50-1, 4:50-2 (little variation); N.Y. C.P.L.R. 5015 (McKinney) (time periods are different, lack of jurisdiction is a ground instead of "judgment is void," and "other reason that justifies relief" is not included); Ohio Civ. R. 60(B) (deletes "judgment is void" as a ground); W. Va. R. Civ. P. 60(b), (c) (little variation).

25 *See* Andresen v. Andresen, 564 A.2d 399 (Md. 1989).

26 *See, e.g.*, Ala. R. Civ. P. 55 (c).

court retains jurisdiction, to modify or revoke the order "as the interest of justice may require."[27]

Maryland's rules allow for a default judgment to be revised only for fraud, mistake, or irregularity; newly discovered evidence; or clerical mistakes,[28] and these terms are strictly applied.[29] Georgia, Connecticut, and Iowa are other examples of states that are far more restrictive than the federal rules as to the grounds to set aside a judgment.

Georgia limits the grounds to lack of jurisdiction; fraud, accident, or mistake, as the acts of the adverse party unmixed with the negligence or fault of the movant; or a non-amendable defect which appears upon the face of the record or pleadings, showing that no claim in fact existed.[30] Connecticut sets a strict four-month time limit on reopening a default judgment and requires a showing of reasonable cause, or that a good cause of action or defense in whole or in part existed, and that the plaintiff or defendant was prevented by mistake, accident, or other reasonable cause from making the defense.[31] Iowa has a similar provision, with a sixty-day deadline.[32] But even in these states, the consumer should be able to set aside the judgment after that period if the court lacked jurisdiction to award the judgment, such as when the consumer was never properly served with process.[33]

11.3.5 Timing Considerations

Federal Rule of Civil Procedure 60(c) requires that a motion under Rule 60(b) be made within a reasonable time and, if based on any of the following, no more than one year after the entry of judgment: (1) mistake, inadvertence, surprise, or excusable neglect; (2) newly discovered evidence; and (3) fraud, misrepresentation, or misconduct by an opposing party.[34] Some state rules provide only four or six months[35] to make such a motion, instead of one year, while others appear to have no time limit.[36]

Rule 60(c) does not set a time limit (other than within a reasonable time) for the other three grounds to set aside a judgment: (4) the judgment is void; (5) the judgment has been satisfied, released, or discharged, it is based on an earlier judgment that has been reversed or vacated, or applying it prospectively is no longer equitable; or (6) any other reason that justifies relief. In addition, Rule 60(d) states that Rule 60(c) on timing does not limit a court's power to entertain an independent action to set aside a judgment for fraud on the court, so there is no time limit on such an action.

Whether or not there is a one year limit, an action under Rule 60(b) must be brought within a reasonable time, which will depend on the totality of circumstances.[37] When a consumer moves to set aside the default shortly after learning of the judgment, the motion will generally be considered to have been made within a reasonable time.[38]

The sooner the motion is brought, the stronger will be the consumer's position. Courts will look for the consumer's diligence in bringing the motion to set aside judgment *after* the consumer realizes action is necessary.[39] While the consumer should act promptly when the consumer becomes aware of the need to set aside the judgment, this does not mean the consumer needs to immediately file a motion but can instead enter into discussions with the other party.[40] Moreover, courts have stated that it is only a secondary factor whether the consumer showed due diligence in seeking to set aside the default after realizing that such action is necessary.[41]

Counting from when a judgment is issued, there is no fixed time frame when the motion to set aside the judgment must be brought, as long as the action is brought within any maximum time period (for example, one year for certain grounds) as set out in a state rule or statute. Certainly one month is a reasonable timeframe.[42] An appellate court has found an eight month delay to be reasonable when the consumer retained legal counsel after the default but that counsel failed to take action for six months. The consumer then had to retain other counsel, explaining the eight month delay.[43]

In cases in which the consumer seeks to set aside a default for "any other reason that justifies relief," courts have also allowed the consumer to bring the action years after the judgment—four and a half years in one case, when the individual had no reason to believe the action was related to that individual, and the individual's mental and physical condition was impaired at the time.[44] In another case, it was allowed nine years after the judgment.[45] Moreover, when a judgment is void there should be no limit at all for the consumer's right to bring an action to set aside the judgment.

---

27 Me. Rev. Stat. Ann. tit. 9A, § 5-114.

28 Md. Rules 2-535 (circuit court), 3-535 (district court, whose jurisdiction is limited to $15,000).
Md. Rule 2-613(g) limits the ability to revise a circuit court judgment only as to relief obtained but does not so limit a district court judgment.

29 Bland v. Hammond, 935 A.2d 457 (Md. Ct. Spec. App. 2007).

30 Ga. Code Ann. § 9-11-60(d).

31 Conn. Gen. Stat. §§ 52-212, 52-212a.

32 Iowa Rule 1.977.

33 *See* § 11.3.11.1.1, *infra*.

34 *See, e.g.*, First Resolution Inv. Corp. v. Coffey, 2007 WL 4441576 (Ohio Ct. App. Dec. 19, 2007).

35 *See, e.g.*, Ala. R. Civ. P. 60(b) (four months); Ariz. R. Civ. P. 60(c) (six months); Cal. Civ. Proc. Code § 473(b) (West) (six months); Conn. Gen. Stat. § 52-212 (four months).

36 *See, e.g.*, Ark. R. Civ. P. 55(c).

37 *See* Great Seneca Fin. Corp. v. Dwek, 2008 WL 960453 (N.J. Super. Ct. App. Div. Apr. 10, 2008).

38 Dottore v. Feathers, 2007 WL 1461320 (Ohio Ct. App. May 18, 2007).

39 *See* Atlantic Credit & Fin. v. Dustrude, 2008 WL 570791 (Minn. Ct. App. Mar. 4, 2008); Little v. King, 161 P.3d 345 (Wash. 2007).

40 Webb v. Erickson, 655 P.2d 6 (Ariz. 1982).

41 Little v. King, 161 P.3d 345 (Wash. 2007).

42 Columbia Recovery Corp. v. Menchaca, 2008 WL 961037 (N.J. Super. Ct. App. Div. Mar. 12, 2008). *See also* Gen. Motors Acceptance Corp. v. Deskins, 474 N.E.2d 1207 (Ohio Ct. App. 1984) (motion timely when filed three months after judgment entered and one month after defendant learned of judgment).

43 Capital One Bank v. Largent, 314 S.W.3d 364 (Mo. Ct. App. 2010).

44 Webb v. Erickson, 655 P.2d 6 (Ariz. 1982).

45 *See* N.Y. Hosp. v. Robinson, 1999 WL 34876247 (N.J. Super. Ct. App. Div. May 28, 1999).

11.3.6 Meritorious Defense

Before setting aside a judgment, courts typically want to be satisfied that the consumer has a meritorious defense.[46] The court may not want to expend resources deciding whether to set aside a judgment and then retry the case if the consumer has no defense to the action. The meritorious defense should be pleaded with some particularity, more so than in responding to the original complaint.[47] A conclusory statement that the consumer does not owe the debt may not be sufficient.[48] Nonetheless, the consumer need only allege a meritorious defense, not prove that the consumer will prevail on that defense.[49] "A proffered defense is meritorious when it is not a sham and when, if true, it states a defense in part, or in whole, to the claims for relief set forth in the complaint."[50]

The consumer's allegation of a meritorious defense certainly can be made by affidavit; there need not be a mini-trial of the facts.[51] Courts may not even require that evidence supporting the defense be presented as part of the motion.[52]

Although a meritorious defense can be almost any valid defense, courts may look more kindly on the consumer's motion when the consumer's defense is apparent on the face of the collector's pleadings, as when the form of the complaint fails to meet state requirements[53] or when insufficient evidence was presented to support a prima facie case.[54] Similarly, when the consumer claims never to have opened an account, a meritorious defense is established when the collector offers little evidence that the individual opened the account or was otherwise obligated on the account.[55]

11.3.7 Prejudice to the Prevailing Party

A few courts consider, as one factor in determining whether to set aside a judgment, whether setting aside the judgment will cause substantial prejudice to the opposing party.[56] But this has been called a secondary factor,[57] just one factor to be weighed among others.[58] Prejudice also is more than that the collector may not win on the merits if the judgment is set aside. The prejudice is not that the case may have a different outcome but that the other party is no longer able to present its case because of the passage of time. An example of a factor that may be relevant as to prejudice is the plaintiff's death, when the plaintiff's estate would be without a witness if the case had to be re-litigated.[59]

11.3.8 Mistake, Inadvertence, Surprise, or Excusable Neglect

The most common ground to set aside a default judgment is "mistake, inadvertence, surprise, or excusable neglect." Most cases focus on whether the consumer's neglect in responding to a case was excusable, but the federal rule and similar state rules also allow a judgment to be set aside because of mistake, inadvertence, or surprise. For example, consider when a consumer was under the impression that a settlement with the collector would result in the case's dismissal, but the collector obtained a default even though the consumer was meeting the terms of the settlement. The consumer's failure to participate could be termed mistake or surprise as easily as excusable neglect. Mistake may also apply to an unrepresented and unsophisticated consumer's confusion as to what legal rights are available and how to contest a proceeding.

Courts generally find that excusable neglect means that the consumer has a reasonable excuse for failing to respond to the complaint. The Ohio Supreme Court has defined excusable neglect in the negative by stating that "the inaction of the defendant is not 'excusable neglect' if it can be labeled as a 'complete disregard for the judicial system.' "[60]

The excuse need not be something beyond the consumer's control. The United States Supreme Court distinguished "excusable neglect" from another ground listed in Rule 60 to set aside a judgment—"any other reason that justifies relief."

46 *See* Geer v. Jacobson, 880 So. 2d 717 (Fla. Dist. Ct. App. 2004); Idaho State Police *ex rel.* Russell v. Real Prop. Situated in Cnty. of Cassia, 156 P.3d 561 (Idaho 2007); Asset Acceptance, L.L.C. v. Moberly, 241 S.W.3d 329 (Ky. 2007); Atlantic Credit & Fin. v. Dustrude, 2008 WL 570791 (Minn. Ct. App. Mar. 4, 2008); Capital One Bank v. Largent, 314 S.W.3d 364 (Mo. Ct. App. 2010); Asset Acceptance L.L.C. v. Scott, 2007 WL 3145360 (N.J. Super. Ct. App. Div. Oct. 30, 2007); Capital One Bank v. Bostinto, 906 N.Y.S.2d 771 (N.Y. Sup. Ct. 2009); Capital One Bank v. Erhabor, 867 N.Y.S.2d 373 (N.Y. Sup. Ct. 2008); Nat'l City Bank v. Poling, 2005 WL 351765 (Ohio Ct. App. Feb. 15, 2005); Little v. King, 161 P.3d 345 (Wash. 2007).

47 Idaho State Police *ex rel.* Russell v. Real Prop. Situated in Cnty. of Cassia, 156 P.3d 561 (Idaho 2007); Meglan, Meglan & Co. v. Bostic, 2006 WL 1230687 (Ohio Ct. App. May 9, 2006).

48 Unifund CCR Partners v. Balisok, 2013 WL 2096002 (N.Y. Sup. Ct. App. Term May 6, 2013).

49 Meglan, Meglan & Co. v. Bostic, 2006 WL 1230687 (Ohio Ct. App. May 9, 2006); Gen. Motors Acceptance Corp. v. Deskins, 474 N.E.2d 1207 (Ohio Ct. App. 1984). *See also* Portfolio Recovery Assocs., L.L.C. v. Thacker, 2009 WL 2675665 (Ohio Ct. App. Aug. 28, 2009).

50 Meglan, Meglan & Co. v. Bostic, 2006 WL 1230687, at *3 (Ohio Ct. App. May 9, 2006).

51 Webb v. Erickson, 655 P.2d 6 (Ariz. 1982); Meglan, Meglan & Co. v. Bostic, 2006 WL 1230687 (Ohio Ct. App. May 9, 2006). *See also* Capital One Bank v. Largent, 314 S.W.3d 364 (Mo. Ct. App. 2010).

52 Idaho State Police *ex rel.* Russell v. Real Prop. Situated in Cnty. of Cassia, 156 P.3d 561 (Idaho 2007).

53 *See, e.g.*, Cavalry Portfolio Serv. v. Rocha, 979 N.E.2d 930 (Ill. App. Ct. 2012); Atlantic Credit & Fin., Inc. v. Guiliana, 829 A.2d 340 (Pa. Super. Ct. 2003).

54 Morales v. Santiago, 526 A.2d 266 (N.J. Super. Ct. App. Div. 1987).

55 Columbia Recovery Corp. v. Menchaca, 2008 WL 961037 (N.J. Super. Ct. App. Div. Mar. 12, 2008).

56 *See* Rule v. Capital One Bank, 2007 WL 779135 (Ky. Ct. App. Mar. 16, 2007); Atlantic Credit & Fin. v. Dustrude, 2008 WL 570791 (Minn. Ct. App. Mar. 4, 2008); Little v. King, 161 P.3d 345 (Wash. 2007).

57 Little v. King, 161 P.3d 345 (Wash. 2007).

58 Top Value Homes, Inc. v. Harden, 460 S.E.2d 427 (S.C. Ct. App. 1995).

59 Grunke v. Kloskin, 355 N.W.2d 207 (Minn. Ct. App. 1984).

60 Kay v. Marc Glassman, Inc., 665 N.E.2d 1102, 1105 (Ohio 1996) (citations omitted). *See also* Asset Acceptance, L.L.C. v. Allen, 2009 WL 3119490 (Ohio Ct. App. Sept. 30, 2009) (consumer has burden of showing excusable neglect).

The Court found that, unlike excusable neglect, "any other reason that justifies relief" only applies to factors over which the consumer has no control.[61] Thus, excusable neglect by implication can relate to a situation in which the consumer has control over the factors but still does not act.

Excusable neglect has been found when:

- The consumer was out of town for several weeks without checking his mail;[62]
- A *pro se* defendant was confused as to court procedure or ignorant concerning the consequences of a default;[63]
- The consumer, after receiving a complaint, was told to "forget it" by the creditor's attorney;[64]
- The consumer promptly asked an attorney for advice, subsequent court notices went to the attorney, and the attorney never informed the consumer that the attorney was not taking the case;[65]
- A *pro se* litigant failed to inform the court of his new address;[66]
- The consumer requested a continuance, but never received notice of the new court date, so did not attend—the collector sent the notice to the wrong address;[67]
- The consumer is incarcerated and did not receive notice of the action;[68]
- The consumer's husband appeared for the third time on behalf of the consumer and the collector suddenly objected to the non-attorney husband representing the consumer, which led to a default judgment.[69]

An important issue is whether failure to understand English can be the basis for excusable neglect. Two Delaware cases show some possible distinctions. In one case, the court found excusable neglect when the defendant could not speak or write English and depended on friends for translations and when this language problem led to actual confusion.[70] The court found excusable neglect even though the defendant spoke some minimal English and ran a successful business.[71] On the other hand, another court found no excusable neglect when English was the defendant's second language, and the defendant was somewhat difficult to understand, but spoke and understood English and did not need a translator.[72]

11.3.9 Newly Discovered Evidence

Federal Rule of Civil Procedure 60(b)(2) lists as grounds to set aside a judgment "newly discovered evidence that, with reasonable diligence, could not have been discovered in time to move for a new trial under Rule 59(b)."[73] Under Rule 59(b), a party has twenty-eight days to seek a new trial. As a result, if evidence is discovered within twenty-eight days of a judgment, the proper procedure under the federal rules is to seek a new trial. After twenty-eight days, the proper practice is to seek to set aside the judgment.

An example of newly discovered evidence might be that a second collector is suing the consumer on the same debt, raising new issues as to whether the collector with the judgment in fact owned the debt. Another example might be if it is discovered that a particular collector was systematically misrepresenting facts in its affidavits or improperly signing or notarizing the affidavits.

11.3.10 Fraud, Misrepresentation, or Misconduct by an Opposing Party

11.3.10.1 General

The federal rules establish two different standards for setting aside a default judgment based upon the collector's misconduct. A collector's fraud, misrepresentation, or misconduct relating *to the consumer* is grounds for setting aside a default judgment, if the consumer acts within one year to set aside the judgment.[74] On the other hand, when there is fraud *on the court*, and not just misconduct affecting the consumer, the judgment can be set aside even after the one-year period.[75]

In arguing for an expansive reading of both collector misconduct and fraud upon the court, remember that the consumer is not seeking damages and need not prove all the elements of fraud. Instead, the consumer is seeking equity, so the consumer can be heard upon the merits when the collector's misrepresentation prevented that from occurring.

61 Pioneer Inv. Servs. Co. v. Brunswick Assocs., L.P., 507 U.S. 380, 113 S. Ct. 1489, 123 L. Ed. 2d 74 (1993). *See also* Asset Acceptance, L.L.C. v. Moberly, 241 S.W.3d 329 (Ky. 2007).

62 Grunke v. Kloskin, 355 N.W.2d 207 (Minn. Ct. App. 1984).

63 *See* TCI Group Life Ins. Plan v. Knoebber, 244 F.3d 691 (9th Cir. 2001) (lack of familiarity with the legal system, while not sufficient in itself to demonstrate excusable neglect, is a relevant consideration; so is depression following spouse's death); Canfield v. Van Atta Buick/GMC Truck, Inc., 127 F.3d 248 (2d Cir. 1997) (lack of familiarity with court rules may constitute excusable neglect); Briones v. Riviera Hotel & Casino, 116 F.3d 379 (9th Cir. 1997) (omissions of a *pro se* defendant may constitute excusable neglect); Enron Oil Corp. v. Diakuhara, 10 F.3d 90 (2d Cir. 1993) (error not to consider defendant's *pro se* status in considering whether to set aside a default); Stirm v. Puckett, 695 P.2d 431 (Idaho 1985) (mental illness).

64 Gen. Motors Acceptance Corp. v. Deskins, 474 N.E.2d 1207 (Ohio Ct. App. 1984).

65 Idaho State Police *ex rel.* Russell v. Real Prop. Situated in Cnty. of Cassia, 156 P.3d 561 (Idaho 2007).

66 *In re* Beekman, 1991 WL 179580 (Ohio Ct. App. Sept. 10, 1991).

67 Unifund CCR Partners v. Rodgers, 281 S.W.3d 881 (Mo. Ct. App. 2009).

68 Dottore v. Feathers, 2007 WL 1461320 (Ohio Ct. App. May 18, 2007).

69 Capital One Bank v. Largent, 314 S.W.3d 364 (Mo. Ct. App. 2010).

70 Canton Inn, Inc. v. Sec. Ins. Co., 1986 WL 2258 (Del. Super. Ct. Jan. 31, 1986).

71 *Id.*

72 Palisades Collection, L.L.C. v. Yu, 2008 WL 4694586 (Del. Ct. Com. Pl. Oct. 9, 2008).

73 *See also* Cavalry Portfolio Servs., L.L.C. v. Laufgas, 2010 WL 909133 (N.J. Super. Ct. App. Div. Mar. 15, 2010).

74 Fed. R. Civ. P. 60(b), 60(c).

75 Fed. R. Civ. P. 60(d).

11.3.10.2 Fraud on the Consumer

A good example of collector misconduct affecting the consumer would be a collector's attorney telling the consumer to "forget about" the complaint served by that attorney.[76] Another good example of collector misconduct involves a collector representing to the consumer that it will dismiss the case if the consumer enters into a repayment program. Instead, the collector pursues the case and obtains a default judgment, even though the consumer makes payments as agreed.

Misrepresentation or misconduct can also occur when the collector convinces the consumer to agree to a stipulated judgment, including misrepresentations as to the nature of the document the consumer is signing or the implications of signing that document. Also grounds to set aside the judgment should be any misrepresentation made by the collector or its attorney as to the validity of the consumer's defenses.

Look not only for collector misrepresentations but also for unethical behavior by the collector's attorney, which should be considered misconduct sufficient to set aside a judgment. A state's code of legal ethics will have provisions concerning contacts with unrepresented individuals. For example, commentary to the Florida Bar Rules states that the other side's lawyer "should not give advice to an unrepresented person other than the advice to obtain counsel."[77]

One court explained why it was particularly concerned about a stipulated settlement between a debt buyer and a *pro se* consumer:

> The circumstances at hand presented a classic case for granting such judicial relief. The defendant, in this case, ignorant of her rights, signed an imprudent settlement, agreeing to pay plaintiff, a debt buyer, monthly sums otherwise needed for food and rent. The settlement agreement obligated her to make payments to plaintiff, monthly, for more than four years. Although settlements like this often benefit both debtors and creditors, the defendant told the Court, in no uncertain terms, that she had been "intimidated" into the signing of the settlement, and that plaintiff had convinced her that she had no choice but to capitulate to plaintiff's demands.
>
> Under the circumstances presented, it was painfully obvious to the Court that plaintiff obtained the settlement outside of court by taking undue advantage of the defendant. The judges of this Court, and the lawyers practicing before them, know all too well that debt buyers rarely have readily available proof to establish an assigned debt claim. The pennies paid by debt buyers for the right to pursue stale and questionable claims certainly do not justify misleading and heavy-handed collection tactics outside of Court. When such matters actually come on for trial, they are typically abandoned, dismissed, or compromised for a small fraction of their hypothetical value.[78]

Typically, the question of the collector's misconduct will be one of credibility between the consumer and the collector's attorney as to what was said in the corridor. Trying such a dispute may be inconvenient for the collector because ethical rules may require the collector to find a new attorney to handle the motion to set aside the stipulated judgment, because the collector's first attorney will be a witness in the matter.

11.3.10.3 A Special Case: Mailing Stipulations with the Complaint

A number of Florida cases have dealt with a collector's practice of including a stipulated judgment with the initial service of process of the summons and complaint. In those cases, the process server delivered the summons, complaint, and a cover letter from the collector's attorney and a "stipulation for entry of final judgment execution withheld." The cover letter asked the consumer to contact the law firm to negotiate a payment amount that would be included in the stipulated judgment, on which the judgment amount was preprinted. The letter stated that, if an agreed amount is reached, the consumer would not have to go to court. The stipulation called for postjudgment interest of 20.4%, almost double the statutory rate, and for the consumer to waive garnishment defenses. A number of consumers contacted the law firm, were told what amount to include in the stipulation, and signed the stipulation.

Florida courts have had little trouble setting aside such stipulated judgments. The courts pointed to the fact that the stipulations were illegally included with the court summons and that this misled the consumer as to the consequences of signing the stipulation, providing grounds to set aside the stipulated judgment.[79] The consumer "was misled as to [the stipulation's] nature, her options and was not informed of important legal rights she was forfeiting by signing same."[80] "Serving the Stipulation and cover letter with the initial process simulates legal process and gives the document an air of authority and importance even though it is not a true legal pleading."[81] Another ground for setting aside the stipulated

76 *See* Gen Motors Acceptance Corp. v. Deskins, 474 N.E.2d 1207 (Ohio Ct. App. 1984).

77 Commentary to Rules Regulating the Florida Bar, Rule 4-4.3.

78 LR Credit 21 L.L.C. v. Paryshkura, 914 N.Y.S.2d 614 (N.Y. Dist. Ct. 2010).

79 Capital One Bank v. Mullis, 15 Fla. L. Weekly Supp. 262a (Fla. Duval Cnty. Ct. Nov. 28, 2007), *available at* www.nclc.org/unreported; Capital One Bank v. Brannon, 15 Fla. L. Weekly Supp. 84a (Fla. Duval Cnty. Ct. Aug. 17, 2007), *available at* www.nclc.org/unreported.

80 Capital One Bank v. Brannon, 15 Fla. L. Weekly Supp. 84a (Fla. Duval Cnty. Ct. Aug. 17, 2007), *available at* www.nclc.org/unreported. *See* Capital One Bank v. Mullis, 15 Fla. L. Weekly Supp. 262a (Fla. Duval Cnty. Ct. Nov. 28, 2007), *available at* www.nclc.org/unreported.

81 Capital One Bank v. Mullis, 15 Fla. L. Weekly Supp. 262a (Fla. Duval Cnty. Ct. Nov. 28, 2007), *available at* www.nclc.org/unreported. *See also* Capital One Bank v. Miller, 14 Fla. L. Weekly Supp. 585 (Fla. Duval Cnty. Ct. Oct. 24, 2006); North Star Capital Acquisitions, L.L.C. v. Krig, 14 Fla. L. Weekly Supp. 166a (Fla. Duval Cnty. Ct. Sept. 13, 2006); Capital One Bank v. Livingston, 13 Fla. L. Weekly Supp. 1203a (Fla. Duval Cnty. Ct. Aug. 10, 2006).

judgment was that the stipulation is unconscionable and thus unenforceable.[82]

11.3.10.4 Fraud on the Court

A collector's filing false affidavits with the court should be not just misconduct affecting the consumer but also fraud upon the court. State rules may require that certain documentation be presented to the court before a default judgment will be issued. False statements in that documentation should also be fraud upon the court. An example might be when an affidavit states certain facts upon the affiant's personal knowledge, when the affiant cannot possibly have that personal knowledge. Another is when the collector signs affidavits in bulk in one location and then sends them to another to be notarized in bulk.

11.3.11 The Judgment Is Void

11.3.11.1 Improper Service of the Complaint or Notice of the Default Hearing

11.3.11.1.1 General

The most common example of a void judgment is when the defendant has never been properly served with the complaint and thus has had no notice that a legal proceeding is taking place. Another example is when the collector fails to provide the required notice to the consumer that a hearing for a default judgment is to take place. Default judgments have also been vacated even when service of the complaint was made and the collector did not file an affidavit of service.[83]

On the other hand, an affidavit of service may constitute prima facie evidence that the defendant was validly served.[84] But if the consumer can show that service or notice is defective, then the court issuing the judgment does not have personal jurisdiction over the consumer, and the judgment is void.[85] Some state rules explicitly provide that lack of jurisdiction is grounds to set aside a judgment.[86] Federal Rule 60(b) and other state rules provide for setting the judgment aside if the judgment is void, and lack of personal jurisdiction makes the judgment void.[87] Inadequate service should suffice to set aside a judgment even if a state's rules do not list lack of jurisdiction or a judgment being void as grounds to set aside a judgment.[88]

Lack of jurisdiction can be raised at any time to attack a judgment.[89] As a result, there is no time limit to challenge a void judgment.[90] For example, in one case the default judgment was set aside six years after it was issued because of defective service.[91] The consumer did not have to show that the delay was reasonable.[92] While it is prudent to do so, the consumer need not even show a meritorious defense.[93] Once the lack of personal jurisdiction is established, the court has no discretion but to set aside the judgment.[94]

---

82 Capital One Bank v. Mullis, 15 Fla. L. Weekly Supp. 262a (Fla. Duval Cnty. Ct. Nov. 28, 2007), *available at* www.nclc.org/unreported; Capital One Bank v. Brannon, 15 Fla. L. Weekly Supp. 84a (Fla. Duval Cnty. Ct. Aug. 17, 2007), *available at* www.nclc.org/unreported.

83 Moore v. Hall, 2013 WL 5657698 (N.Y. Sup. Ct. Oct. 8, 2013).

84 *See* Cavalry Portfolio Servs., L.L.C. v. Reisman, 55 A.D. 3d 524 (N.Y. App. Div. 2008). *See also* Unifund CCR Partners v. Balisok, 2013 WL 2096002 (N.Y. App. Term May 6, 2013).

85 Midland Funding, L.L.C. v. Dixon, 2013 WL 6054606 (Ohio Ct. App. Nov. 15, 2013).

86 *See* Unifund CCR Partners v. Dale, 801 N.Y.S.2d 782 (N.Y. City Ct. 2005).

87 *See* Wolfe v. Stevens, 965 So. 2d 1257 (Fla. Dist. Ct. App. 2007); First Select Co. v. Mastromattei, 2007 Mass. App. Div. 77 (Mass. Dist. Ct. 2007); Dombrowski v. Chute, 2000 Mass. App. Div. 127 (Mass. Dist. Ct. 2000); Gassett v. Snappy Car Rental, 906 P.2d 258 (Nev. 1995); Unifund CCR Partners v. Kelley, 245 P.3d 694 (Or. Ct. App. 2010); B B & T v. Taylor, 633 S.E.2d 501 (S.C. 2006). *See also* Unifund CCR Partners v. Rodgers, 281 S.W.3d 881 (Mo. Ct. App. 2009) (even after proper service, there was good cause to set aside default when notice of hearing date was sent to the wrong address).

88 Peralta v. Heights Med. Ctr., Inc., 485 U.S. 80, 108 S. Ct. 896, 99 L. Ed. 2d 75 (1988) (due process requires the judgment to be set aside); Vasquez v. Dreyfus, 34 Ariz. 184 (Ariz. 1928); Hilgeman v. American Mortgage Sec., Inc., 196 Ariz. 215 (Ariz. Ct. App. 1979); Dobbs v. Discover Bank, ___ S.W.3d ___, 2012 Ark. App. 678 (Ark. 2012); Midland Funding, L.L.C. v. Dixon, 2013 WL 6054606 (Ohio Ct. App. Nov. 15, 2013); TCC Mgmt., Inc. v. Clapp, 2005 WL 2008677 (Ohio Ct. App. Aug. 23, 2005); Ameritrust Co. v. Spigutz, 2004 WL 2578898 (Ohio Ct. App. Nov. 10, 2004).

89 Fort Trumbull Conservancy, L.L.C. v. Alves, 815 A.2d 1188 (Conn. 2003); Capital One Bank v. Czekala, 884 N.E.2d 1205 (Ill. App. Ct. 2008); Young v. Progressive Cas. Ins. Co., 671 A.2d 515 (Md. Ct. Spec. App. 1996); First Select Co. v. Mastromattei, 2007 Mass. App. Div. 77 (Mass. Dist. Ct. 2007); Dombrowski v. Chute, 2000 Mass. App. Div. 127 (Mass. Dist. Ct. 2000); Palisades Collection, L.L.C. v. Brown, 2010 WL 5104824 (N.J. Super. Ct. App. Div. Dec. 15, 2010); Portfolio Recovery Assocs., L.L.C. v. Thacker, 2009 WL 2675665 (Ohio Ct. App. Aug. 28, 2009). *Cf.* Wellington v. Asset Acceptance, L.L.C., 881 N.E.2d 101 (table), 2008 WL 442490 (Ind. Ct. App. Feb. 20, 2008) (unpublished) (indicating improper service can always be attacked on jurisdictional grounds, but finding service in this case proper). *But see* N.Y. C.P.L.R. 317 (McKinney) (motion must be made within five years and meritorious defense must be presented).

90 *See, e.g.*, Master Fin., Inc. v. Woodburn, 90 P.3d 1236 (Ariz. Ct. App. 2004); United Bank of Boulder v. Buchanan, 836 P.2d 473 (Colo. App. 1992); Falkner v. Ameritrust Fed. Sav. & Loan Ass'n, 489 So. 2d 758 (Fla. Dist. Ct. App. 1986); Sarkissian v. Chicago Bd. of Educ., 776 N.E.2d 195 (Ill. 2002); Galbreath v. Coleman, 596 N.W.2d 689 (Minn. Ct. App. 1999); Midland Funding, L.L.C. v. Dixon, 2013 WL 6054606 (Ohio Ct. App. Nov. 15, 2013). *But see* McDaniel v. U.S. Fid. Guar. Co., 478 S.E.2d 868 (S.C. Ct. App. 1996) (motion to set aside default judgment on basis that judgment is void must be brought within reasonable time); Ind. R. of Trial Proc. 60(B)(6) (motion on basis that judgment is void must be filed within a reasonable time). *But cf.* Plaza Hollister, L.P. v. Cnty. of San Benito, 84 Cal. Rptr. 2d 715 (Cal. Ct. App. 1999) (judgment which is void on its face may be set aside at any time, but motion to set aside judgment not void on the record must be brought within statutory time period).

91 *See* First Select Co. v. Mastromattei, 2007 Mass. App. Div. 77 (Mass. Dist. Ct. 2007).

92 Capital One Bank v. Czekala, 884 N.E.2d 1205 (Ill. App. Ct. 2008); Midland Funding, L.L.C. v. Dixon, 2013 WL 6054606 (Ohio Ct. App. Nov. 15, 2013).

93 Peralta v. Heights Med. Ctr., Inc., 485 U.S. 80, 108 S. Ct. 896, 99 L. Ed. 2d 75 (1988). *See also* Ark. R. Civ. P. 55; D.C. R. Civ. P. 55; Master Fin., Inc. v. Woodburn, 90 P.3d 1236 (Ariz. Ct. App. 2004); NCO Portfolio Mgmt. v. Lorenzo, 2010 WL 3516751 (N.J. Super. Ct. App. Div. Sept. 10, 2010); Palisades Collection L.L.C. v. Lieber, 2007 WL 2262851 (N.J. Super. Ct. App. Div. Aug. 9, 2007); Midland Funding, L.L.C. v. Dixon, 2013 WL 6054606 (Ohio Ct. App. Nov. 15, 2013).

94 *See* First Select Co. v. Mastromattei, 2007 Mass. App. Div. 77 (Mass. Dist. Ct. 2007); Enterprise Rent-A-Car, Inc. v. Bigelow, 2004 Mass.

11.3.11.1.2 Sewer service

When state rules require that a summons be delivered by hand to the consumer's residence, a common cause of defective service is "sewer service." The individual tasked with visiting the consumer's residence and serving the summons fails to serve the summons but then claims to have done so. For example, the New York attorney general's office in 2009 alleged that Americal Legal Process failed to properly serve consumers across New York State, and the attorney general sought to throw out an estimated 100,000 default judgments. In addition, the Administrative Judge of the New York Unified Court System commenced a special proceeding against several law firms using Americal Legal Process, seeking to vacate all default judgments entered in cases in which service was made by Americal Legal Process servers. The action was settled by consent order.[95]

The consumer will have to present evidence that service was not made even though the process server claims to have made service. Seek through discovery or a subpoena information to determine the actual route the process server used that day, during which the consumer was allegedly served. It may be possible to show that the process server could not physically travel to all the locations claimed in the time period specified. Even the sheer number of locations served in a day may create doubt in the court's mind and lead the court to place more credibility on the consumer's testimony.

Similarly, the minimal amount the server is paid per summons might indicate pressure on the server to engage in sewer service just to earn a living wage. So would the fact that the collector only paid the process service company for attempts at service that were reported as completed and paid nothing for service attempts that were not reported as completed.[96] Also persuasive would be testimony from other consumers denying receipt of process who were allegedly served by the same process server.

Sometimes defects as to proper service of process are apparent on the face of the documents. In New York, if the summons is affixed to a door, a copy must also be mailed within twenty days. When the collector's own documents indicate that the summons was mailed twenty-eight days later, service is defective.[97] In California, *both* the process server and the process serving company must be listed on the proof of service, and this must include both of their names, addresses, phone numbers, and process serving license numbers. Check to see if the phone numbers and addresses are legitimate, or purely fictitious.

App. Div. 165 (Mass. Dist. Ct. 2004); Dombrowski v. Chute, 2000 Mass. App. Div. 127 (Mass. Dist. Ct. 2000).

95 *See* Matter of Pfau v. Forster & Garbus (N.Y. Sup. Ct. 2009). *See also* Velocity Invs., L.L.C. v. McCaffrey, 921 N.Y.S.2d 799 (N.Y. Dist. Ct. 2011); Palisades Collection, L.L.C. v. Cerrito, 906 N.Y.S.2d 774 (N.Y. Poughkeepsie City Ct. 2009).

96 *See* Sykes v. Mel Harris & Assocs., L.L.C., 757 F. Supp. 2d 413 (S.D.N.Y. 2010).

97 Velocity Invs., L.L.C. v. McCaffrey, 921 N.Y.S.2d 799 (N.Y. Dist. Ct. 2011).

New York courts also allow default judgments to be set aside when the process server does not show sufficient diligence in seeking to contact the consumer. Visiting the consumer's home three times, all during working hours, does not demonstrate due diligence.[98] Neither does failing to attempt to serve the consumer by locating the consumer's work address.[99]

11.3.11.1.3 Mail service to the wrong address

More common than personal service are state rules that allow service by some combination of certified and First Class mail. A common failing with such service is that it will be sent to the wrong address. The frequency of this problem is magnified when debt buyers send service years after the consumer last had contact with the original creditor, and the debt buyer relies solely on address information the original creditor provided.

The general rule is that, when First Class mail is not returned, service is presumed received if sent to the consumer's last and usual place of residence, even if the consumer is not at that location at the time.[100] If certified mail is returned unclaimed, regular mail still constitutes adequate service unless it too is returned.[101]

Of course, the rule is different if mail service is returned with an indication that the consumer is not at the address. For example, when a certified mailing was returned with the notation "in jail," this was sufficient to show that mail service was inadequate.[102]

When First Class mail is sent and not returned, the consumer's mere denial of receipt without any evidence is usually considered inadequate to defeat service.[103] However, mailing the summons is no more than a rebuttable presumption that service has been made.[104] The mere fact that the collector sent a number of letters to the address that were not returned does not prove that service was proper.[105] This presumption disappears when there is conflicting evidence. This is the case even when someone signs for a certified letter—the consumer can

98 LVNV Funding, L.L.C. v. Stasi, 950 N.Y.S.2d 723 (table), 2012 WL 1556569 (N.Y. Sup. Ct. Apr. 25, 2012).

99 *Id.*

100 *See* Sears, Roebuck & Co. v. Ford, 2006 Mass. App. Div. 172 (Mass. Dist. Ct. 2006); Atlantic Credit & Fin. v. Dustrude, 2008 WL 570791 (Minn. Ct. App. Mar. 4, 2008); Asset Acceptance, L.L.C. v. Allen, 2009 WL 3119490 (Ohio Ct. App. Sept. 30, 2009). *See also* Portfolio Recovery Assocs., L.L.C. v. Rohan, 901 N.Y.S.2d 910 (N.Y. Sup. Ct. 2009).

101 *See* N.J. R. of Ct. 6:2-3(d)(1). *See also* Asset Acceptance, L.L.C. v. Allen, 2009 WL 3119490 (Ohio Ct. App. Sept. 30, 2009).

102 Palisades Collection L.L.C. v. Brown, 2010 WL 5104824 (N.J. Super. Ct. App. Div. Dec. 15, 2010).

103 *See* Atlantic Credit & Fin. v. Dustrude, 2008 WL 570791 (Minn. Ct. App. Mar. 4, 2008).

104 Asset Acceptance L.L.C. v. Scott, 2007 WL 3145360 (N.J. Super. Ct. App. Div. Oct. 30, 2007) (due process requires the judgment to be set aside); TCC Mgmt., Inc. v. Clapp, 2005 WL 2008677 (Ohio Ct. App. Aug. 23, 2005).

105 *See* First Select Co. v. Mastromattei, 2007 Mass. App. Div. 77 (Mass. Dist. Ct. 2007).

still provide evidence that the consumer did not reside at that address at the time.[106]

When the consumer advances proof that rebuts the presumption of effective service, the burden may shift to the collector to establish that service was made.[107] The consumer is entitled to a hearing on the factual issue.[108] This is particularly the case when the consumer offers an affidavit to prove that the consumer did not reside at the location served at the time of service,[109] or did not see the service.[110] An affidavit from the present occupant of the address denying the consumer resided there should also be sufficient to provide a hearing on the issue.[111] The consumer can also overcome the presumption as to proper service by showing that the consumer was incarcerated at the time of service.[112]

Particularly powerful is the consumer's affidavit that the consumer has never lived at the address listed in the summons.[113] This can happen in any number of ways. Sloppy record-keeping can result in small errors that send the service to the wrong address. For example, the presumption was rebutted when the consumer lived on 211 Keats Drive and the summons and complaint were mailed to 211 Keats Court.[114]

Other times, the collector will rely on credit reports or skip tracing to locate the consumer's new address, and errors will occur in that process. Thus, in one case, a skip tracing service's information that someone with the consumer's name lived at the address at the time of the summons was not determinative, since the tracing service also listed the consumer as residing at a different address at the same point in time.[115]

Additional errors as to mailing addresses can occur when the consumer is married. In one case, service to the consumer's ex-husband's address was improper because the consumer never resided at that address.[116] Other times husband and wife will both be sued but service will be received by only one spouse. For example, consider when husband and wife lived at the same address, the husband opened the mail service but never informed the wife about the service. A hearing should be held on whether service on the wife was proper when both husband and wife submit affidavits that the wife never saw or knew about the summons.[117]

11.3.11.1.4 Improper notice of the default hearing

Obtaining a default judgment is a two-step process in many states. The consumer is summoned with a complaint, and failure to respond within a specified time period leads to a default. The collector then files a motion to turn that default into a default judgment. State rules patterned after Federal Rule of Civil Procedure 55(b)(2) require that the collector serve the consumer with written notice of its application for a default judgment, if the consumer has filed an appearance in the case.[118] When the consumer is not sent this second notice, the resulting default judgment can later be set aside.[119] Just as the consumer must be properly served the lawsuit itself, the consumer must also be properly served the motion for a default judgment.

The federal rule and many state rules limit the right to this additional notice to situations in which the consumer has filed an appearance. In a surprising number of default judgments the consumer has in fact filed an appearance, even though the consumer has defaulted. For example, when states require the consumer to file both an appearance and an answer, unrepresented consumers may mistakenly believe that filing an appearance is enough. Merely filing the appearance may not stop a default, but it entitles the consumer to the second notice.

Moreover, some courts have construed "appearance" broadly to include conduct and communications prior to the filing of an action, even when the defendant does not make an appearance after the case is commenced.[120] In Texas, notice of the motion for a default judgment must be sent if the consumer answers, and a verified letter from the consumer was found to be such an answer, even though not in proper form as an answer.[121]

106 Liberty Credit Servs., Inc. v. Walsh, 2005 WL 488395 (Ohio Ct. App. Mar. 3, 2005).

107 Asset Acceptance L.L.C. v. Scott, 2007 WL 3145360 (N.J. Super. Ct. App. Div. Oct. 30, 2007).

108 Portfolio Recovery Assocs., L.L.C. v. Thacker, 2009 WL 2675665 (Ohio Ct. App. Aug. 28, 2009); TCC Mgmt., Inc. v. Clapp, 2005 WL 2008677 (Ohio Ct. App. Aug. 23, 2005); Ameritrust Co. v. Spigutz, 2004 WL 2578898 (Ohio Ct. App. Nov. 10, 2004).

109 Unifund CCR Partners v. Dale, 801 N.Y.S.2d 782 (N.Y. Mt. Vernon City Ct. 2005); Liberty Credit Servs., Inc. v. Walsh, 2005 WL 488395 (Ohio Ct. App. Mar. 3, 2005).

110 TCC Mgmt., Inc. v. Clapp, 2005 WL 2008677 (Ohio Ct. App. Aug. 23, 2005).

111 First Select Co. v. Mastromattei, 2007 Mass. App. Div. 77 (Mass. Dist. Ct. 2007).

112 *See* NCO Portfolio Mgmt. v. Lorenzo, 2010 WL 3516751 (N.J. Super. Ct. App. Div. Sept. 10, 2010).

113 *See* First Select Co. v. Mastromattei, 2007 Mass. App. Div. 77 (Mass. Dist. Ct. 2007); Dombrowski v. Chute, 2000 Mass. App. Div. 127 (Mass. Dist. Ct. 2000). *See also* NCO Portfolio Mgmt. v. Lorenzo, 2010 WL 3516751 (N.J. Super. Ct. App. Div. Sept. 10, 2010).

114 Asset Acceptance L.L.C. v. Scott, 2007 WL 3145360 (N.J. Super. Ct. App. Div. Oct. 30, 2007).

115 *See* First Select Co. v. Mastromattei, 2007 Mass. App. Div. 77 (Mass. Dist. Ct. 2007).

116 Palisades Collection L.L.C. v. Lieber, 2007 WL 2262851 (N.J. Super. Ct. App. Div. Aug. 9, 2007).

117 TCC Mgmt., Inc. v. Clapp, 2005 WL 2008677 (Ohio Ct. App. Aug. 23, 2005).

118 The federal rule specifies three days' notice, but state rules may require more time. *See, e.g.*, N.Y. C.P.L.R. § 3215(g) (McKinney) (five days); La. Code Civ. P. art. 1702 (seven days); Mass. R. Civ. P. 55 (b)(2) (seven days); Ohio Civ. R. 55 (seven days).

119 *See* Nat'l City Bank of Michigan/Illinois v. Hayden, 2003 WL 193510 (Mich. Ct. App. Jan. 28, 2003); Lindblom v. Prime Hospitality Corp., 90 P.3d 1283 (Nev. 2004); Midland Funding, L.L.C. v. Angwenyi, 2013 WL 4710620 (N.J. Super. Ct. App. Div. Sept. 3, 2013); Meglan, Meglan & Co. v. Bostic, 2006 WL 1230687 (Ohio Ct. App. May 9, 2006); Asset Acceptance L.L.C. v. Springer, 2004 WL 2526369 (Ohio Ct. App. Nov. 5, 2004); Unifund CCR Partners v. Kelley, 245 P.3d 694 (Or. Ct. App. 2010). *See also* Webb v. Erickson, 655 P.2d 6 (Ariz. 1982); Reid v. Asset Acceptance, L.L.C., 2006 WL 3028072 (Tex. App. Oct. 25, 2006).

120 *See, e.g.*, Lindblom v. Prime Hospitality Corp., 90 P.3d 1283 (Nev. 2004) (pre-suit interactions evinced a clear intent to appear and defend). *But see* Morin v. Burris, 161 P.3d 956 (Wash. 2007).

121 Reid v. Asset Acceptance, L.L.C., 2006 WL 3028072 (Tex. App. Oct. 25, 2006).

Some states require that the collector serve notice of the hearing on the default judgment on the consumer, even when the consumer does not file an appearance. In New York, if more than one year has elapsed since the entry of default, a defendant (even one who has not filed an appearance) must still be given notice of the hearing for a default judgment.[122] Even if one year has not elapsed, notice must be sent if the action is based upon the nonpayment of a contractual obligation and is not filed in small claims court. If the notice is returned as undeliverable or if the residence is unknown, then it must be mailed to the party's place of employment, if known. If that is unknown, it must be mailed to the last known address.[123]

Notice of the motion for a default judgment is just as important when the parties stipulate to a default judgment if the consumer does not make promised payments. For example, in one case the stipulation provided that a default judgment would be entered if the consumer did not make specified payments but that the consumer would receive ten days' notice before judgment would be entered. The judgment could be vacated because the ten days' notice was not provided.[124]

11.3.11.2 Other Jurisdictional Challenges

In addition to lack of proper service, judgment can also be set aside based on any other jurisdictional failure or when the judgment is void for any other reason. This principle is explicit in the federal rules—that a void judgment can be set aside and that the one-year time limit does not apply to this rationale.[125]

Of course, void means more than just that the judgment was erroneous as to the law or the facts.[126] It must be void ab initio. If the judgment is void ab initio, then the consumer need not show that the consumer is likely to prevail on the merits or that the consumer exercised due diligence.[127]

A judgment is void if the court has no jurisdiction over the matter.[128] Lack of subject matter jurisdiction can be shown when the type of case or the amount awarded is beyond the powers of a court—for example, when a small claims court has authority only to issue judgments up to $10,000 and yet issues an award for $11,000. When state law views proper venue as jurisdictional, filing the action in an improper venue should also provide a basis to set aside the default judgment.

Lack of subject matter jurisdiction, in at least some states, also occurs when the collector does not own the debt and thus has no standing to sue on the debt.[129] A consumer should thus be able to obtain a hearing to set aside a judgment with evidence that the collector does not own the debt. In some states an assignment of the debt in question must be attached to the complaint if someone other than the original creditor brings the action.[130] If that assignment is not attached, is not signed, is not a proper assignment, or does not show a continuous chain of assignments from the original creditor,[131] then this deficiency should be enough for the consumer to obtain a hearing on the motion to set aside a judgment. The same should be the case when the consumer, after the judgment, is contacted by another collector claiming ownership of the same debt. This should be sufficient evidence to place the first collector's ownership of the debt in doubt. In Pennsylvania, a default can be re-opened when the complaint does not allege that the plaintiff owns the debt but only references the originating creditor.[132]

In some states, a debt buyer must register with the state in order to use the state's courts.[133] If an unregistered debt buyer obtains a default judgment, the judgment may be void ab initio and thus can be set aside even if the consumer's motion is not timely.[134] Similarly, certain state statutes limit a party's access to the courts when that party lacks a license or because certain entities (such as debt collection agencies) cannot collect debts in the state's courts.[135] If such an entity obtains a judgment, and the state treats this as void ab initio, then the judgment should be set aside.

Fundamental due process requires that a court in a default judgment not award an amount in excess of the amount sought in the complaint. When a court does issue such an award, it is an abuse of discretion for a trial court not to reopen the default judgment.[136] A New York case has found that a default judgment can be collaterally attacked if the attorney fees awarded in the judgment were entered without authority of law and were thus null and void.[137]

122 N.Y. C.P.L.R. § 3215(g)(1) (McKinney).

123 N.Y. C.P.L.R. § 3215(g)(3) (McKinney).

124 Capital One Bank v. Hembrick, 851 N.Y.S.2d 68 (N.Y. Civ. Ct. 2007).

125 Fed. R. Civ. P. 60(b)(4), 60(c). *See also* Wasserbauer v. Marine Midland Bank—Rochester, 400 N.Y.S.2d 979 (N.Y. Sup. Ct. 1977).

126 Coleman v. First Star, Inc., 646 S.E.2d 443 (N.C. Ct. App. 2007). *See also* New Century Fin. Servs., Inc. v. Carrero, 2008 WL 199729 (N.J. Super. Ct. App. Div. Jan. 25, 2008).

127 *See* LVNV Funding, L.L.C. v. Trice, 952 N.E.2d 1232 (Ill. App. Ct. 2011).

128 *See* Capital One Bank v. Czekala, 884 N.E.2d 1205 (Ill. App. Ct. 2008).

129 Virtually all cases find no subject matter jurisdiction when the plaintiff lacks standing. *See, e.g.*, Stalley *ex rel.* United States v. Orlando Reg'l Healthcare Sys., Inc., 524 F.3d 1229 (11th Cir. 2008); Morrison v. Bd. of Educ., 521 F.3d 602 (6th Cir. 2008); Faibisch v. Univ. of Minn., 304 F.3d 797 (8th Cir. 2002); Swafford v. Norton, 992 So. 2d 20 (Ala. Civ. App. 2008); Fort Trumbull Conservancy, L.L.C. v. Alves, 943 A.2d 420 (Conn. 2008); Planning Bd. v. Zoning Bd. of Appeals, 695 N.E.2d 650 (Mass. 1998); *In re* H.G., 267 S.W.3d 120 (Tex. App. 2008). *But see* Mid-State Trust IX v. Davis, 2008 WL 1838350 (Ohio Ct. App. Apr. 25, 2008).

130 *See* § 3.4, *supra*.

131 *See* § 4.3, *supra*.

132 North Star Capital Acquisition, L.L.C. v. Smith (Pa. Ct. Com. Pl. July 21, 2011), *available at* www.nclc.org/unreported. *See also* Kim v. Westmoore Partners, Inc., 201 Cal. App. 4th 267 (Cal. Ct. App. 2011).

133 *See* § 3.3.5, *supra*.

134 LVNV Funding, L.L.C. v. Trice, 2011 WL 2623304 (Ill. App. Ct. June 30, 2011).

135 *See* § 3.3, *supra*.

136 Masny v. Vallo, 2005 Ohio App. LEXIS 2098 (Ohio Ct. App. May 5, 2005).

137 Wasserbauer v. Marine Midland Bank—Rochester, 400 N.Y.S.2d 979 (N.Y. Sup. Ct. 1977).

11.3.12 *"Any Other Reason That Justifies Relief"*

Federal Rule of Civil Procedure 60(b)(6) provides that a default judgment can be reopened for "any other reason that justifies relief." There is no one-year limit on the consumer's ability to raise this reason as ground for relief, as long as the motion is brought within a reasonable time.[138] This approach is an attractive alternative for a consumer when more than a year has elapsed and when it is thus no longer possible to set aside the judgment for excusable neglect.

The United States Supreme Court, in interpreting the federal rule, finds that "any other reason that justifies relief" is limited to "extraordinary circumstances" beyond the movant's control and not just to excusable neglect.[139] The circumstances must suggest that the party is faultless in the delay.[140]

State courts and state rules[141] may also limit this basis for relief to "extraordinary circumstances" [142] or "exceptional situations," [143] and use this basis sparingly.[144] It should not be used to undermine the time constraints applicable to Rule 60(b)'s other subsections.[145] As the rule states "any other reason," this section does not include grounds mentioned in the prior sections,[146] such as excusable neglect.

The standard, though, is not an impossible one to meet. The Arizona Supreme Court has quoted the United States Supreme Court approvingly regarding this ground to set aside a judgment: it "vests power in courts adequate to enable them to vacate judgments whenever such action is appropriate to accomplish justice." [147]

The United States Supreme Court found "any other reason that justifies relief" present when an individual's incarceration, ill health, and other factors beyond his reasonable control prevented him from seeking to reopen a default judgment for four years.[148] The Arizona Supreme Court has found exceptional circumstances to set aside a default judgment after four-and-a-half years when the individual had no reason to believe the action was related to that individual, the summons and writ were confusing, and the individual's mental and physical condition was impaired at the time.[149] Another factor was the lack of notice of the default judgment.[150]

In another case, a default judgment was reopened for exceptional circumstances after nine years had passed.[151] The consumer contacted Medicaid about a hospital bill (hospitals may not sue Medicaid recipients) and was told it would be taken care of. Then, on receipt of the default judgment, the consumer contacted the collector's law firm to explain that Medicaid said it would take care of the matter. Nine years later, immediately after the first garnishment of the consumer's wages, the consumer sought to reopen the default. Upon denial, she sought legal assistance. The court in these circumstances found the failure to respond to the complaint to be justified and allowed the default judgment to be set aside.[152]

Reopening a judgment was also proper when the consumer's representative had deceived the consumer into believing the representative was a licensed attorney.[153] An Ohio appellate court has even approved reopening a default for exceptional circumstances primarily because the collector's complaint was defective and the consumer denied owing the debt.[154]

Similarly, a trial court found exceptional circumstances to reopen a default judgment after two years when the consumer's alcoholism made her incapable of managing her affairs.[155] After various appellate decisions, the trial court was eventually overruled because the consumer had failed to present medical evidence of the consumer's incapacity or to show that the consumer was incapacitated over much of the intervening period.[156] Another court refused to reopen a default judgment for exceptional circumstances when the consumer was incapacitated for eighteen months but waited over three years to move to reopen the default.[157]

11.3.13 *Mass* Vacatur

New York has a statute that allows for a large number of defaults in consumer credit transactions to be vacated in one action:

> An administrative judge, upon a showing that default judgments were obtained by fraud, misrepresentation, illegality, unconscionability, lack of due service, violations of

138 *Cf.* First Resolution Inv. Corp. v. Coffey, 2007 WL 4441576 (Ohio Ct. App. Dec. 19, 2007).

139 Pioneer Inv. Servs. Co. v. Brunswick Assocs., L.P., 507 U.S. 380, 113 S. Ct. 1489, 123 L. Ed. 2d 74 (1993).

140 *Id.*

141 *See, e.g.*, Ky. R. Civ. P. 60.02.

142 Pioneer Inv. Servs. Co. v. Brunswick Assocs., L.P., 507 U.S. 380, 113 S. Ct. 1489, 123 L. Ed. 2d 74 (1993); Webb v. Erickson, 655 P.2d 6 (Ariz. 1982); First Resolution Inv. Corp. v. Coffey, 2007 WL 4441576 (Ohio Ct. App. Dec. 19, 2007).

143 *See* N.Y. Hosp. v. Robinson, 1999 WL 34876247 (N.J. Super. Ct. App. Div. May 28, 1999).

144 *See* Asset Acceptance, L.L.C. v. Moberly, 241 S.W.3d 329 (Ky. 2007); Great Seneca Fin. Corp. v. Dwek, 2008 WL 960453 (N.J. Super. Ct. App. Div. Apr. 10, 2008).

145 Asset Acceptance, L.L.C. v. Moberly, 241 S.W.3d 329 (Ky. 2007); First Resolution Inv. Corp. v. Coffey, 2007 WL 4441576 (Ohio Ct. App. Dec. 19, 2007).

146 Webb v. Erickson, 655 P.2d 6 (Ariz. 1982).

147 Webb v. Erickson, 655 P.2d 6, 10 (Ariz. 1982) (quoting Klapprott v. United States, 335 U.S. 601, 69 S. Ct. 384, 93 L. Ed. 266 (1949)).

148 Klapprott v. United States, 335 U.S. 601, 69 S. Ct. 384, 93 L. Ed. 266 (1949).

149 Webb v. Erickson, 655 P.2d 6 (Ariz. 1982).

150 *Id.*

151 *See* N.Y. Hosp. v. Robinson, 1999 WL 34876247 (N.J. Super. Ct. App. Div. May 28, 1999).

152 *Id.*

153 MBNA Am. Bank v. Garcia, 205 P.3d 53 (Or. Ct. App. 2009).

154 Mercy Franciscan Hosp. v. Willis, 2004 Ohio App. LEXIS 4595 (Ohio Ct. App. Sept. 24, 2004).

155 *See* Asset Acceptance, L.L.C. v. Moberly, 241 S.W.3d 329 (Ky. 2007) (discussing trial court's decision on consumer's motion).

156 Asset Acceptance, L.L.C. v. Moberly, 2009 WL 1347164 (Ky. Ct. App. May 15, 2009).

157 Great Seneca Fin. Corp. v. Dwek, 2008 WL 960453 (N.J. Super. Ct. App. Div. Apr. 10, 2008).

law, or other illegalities or when such default judgments were obtained in cases in which those defendants would be uniformly entitled to interpose a defense predicated upon but not limited to the foregoing defenses, and when such default judgments have been obtained in a number deemed sufficient by him to justify such action as set forth herein, and upon appropriate notice to counsel for the respective parties, or to the parties themselves, may bring a proceeding to relieve a party or parties from them upon such terms as may be just. The disposition of any proceeding so instituted shall be determined by a judge other than the administrative judge.[158]

For example, when there was evidence of widespread "sewer service" by Americal Legal Process, the Administrative Judge of the New York Unified Court System, seeking to vacate all default judgments entered in cases in which service was made by Americal Legal Process servers, commenced a special proceeding against several law firms using Americal Legal Process. The action was settled by consent order.[159]

In addition, state enforcement actions or even class actions can result in court orders or settlements by which large numbers of default judgments are re-opened or when the consumers receive restitution. This was the case in a 2012 settlement between a Maryland state agency and LVNV Funding and Resurgent Capital Services.[160]

11.4 Resisting or Setting Aside Confirmation of an Arbitration Award

At one point, hundreds of thousands of arbitration proceedings a year were initiated to collect consumer debts. Creditors and debt buyers took advantage of arbitration provisions in credit agreements to bring collection actions not in court but before arbitrators. The forum used almost exclusively was the National Arbitration Forum (NAF), and there were widespread allegations that the NAF was biased in favor of the collectors.

Often, the arbitration was concluded solely on paperwork that the collector submitted electronically without anyone physically appearing before an arbitrator. The arbitrator would issue an award, invariably for the collector. When that award was confirmed by a court, it had the same force and effect as a court judgment. The corollary to this is that an arbitration award not yet confirmed does not have the force of a judgment and cannot form the basis for garnishment or other postjudgment remedies.

For all practical purposes, new collection actions via arbitration ceased in July 2009 when the NAF agreed in a law enforcement action to stop consumer collection arbitrations (in part because of interlocking ownership between the NAF and the major collection law firm appearing before it), and the American Arbitration Association stated that it would not conduct such arbitration proceedings until standards were put in place.[161] As a result, collection via arbitration is rarely if ever used today, and this treatise will not consider this form of litigation or resisting or setting aside confirmation of an arbitration award. Instead the topic is treated in chapter 11 of NCLC's *Consumer Arbitration Agreements*.[162]

11.5 Bankruptcy Filing's Ability to Limit the Effect of a Judgment

Bankruptcy offers prompt and permanent relief from a court judgment and is often the simplest way to deal with a collector's judgment. With only a few narrow exceptions, the merits of the collector's claim that led to the judgment are irrelevant. Unless the collector has already obtained a lien on the consumer's property, the bankruptcy discharge wipes out the judgment's effect without the need for any additional motion filings either in the court in which the judgment was entered or in the bankruptcy court. If the collector has already obtained a judgment lien on the consumer's property, the consumer can ask the bankruptcy court to void the lien if it affects exempt property or for certain other reasons.

The filing of the consumer's initial bankruptcy petition puts into effect the automatic stay. The stay operates as a federal court injunction against a wide range of collection activities and specifically prohibits any collector action to enforce a judgment entered against the debtor prior to the date of the bankruptcy filing.[163] This prohibition clearly encompasses a stay of attachments, garnishments, and execution sales by judicial officers. It also bars the judgment creditor or its agents from seeking to collect on the judgment by use of dunning letters, phone calls, or any other form of coercion or harassment.

Exceptions to the applicability of the automatic stay are very limited, pertaining mostly to debts that arose out of criminal or family court proceedings.[164] For example, in a chapter 7 bankruptcy, the stay does not apply to collection of child support from the debtor's wages earned after the bankruptcy was filed.

Once notified of a bankruptcy filing, the judgment creditor must take prompt action to terminate any ongoing activities being carried out to collect upon a judgment. The creditor must release attachments of bank accounts and cease garnishing wages. Continuation of any of these collection actions, or initiation of any new actions, can subject the creditor to an action for damages, costs, and attorney fees.[165] Bankruptcy

158 N.Y. C.P.L.R. 5015(c) (McKinney).

159 *See* Matter of Pfau v. Forster & Garbus (N.Y. Sup. Ct. 2009). *See also* Velocity Invs., L.L.C. v. McCaffrey, 921 N.Y.S.2d 799 (N.Y. Nassau Cnty. Dist. Ct. 2011); Palisades Collection, L.L.C. v. Cerrito, 906 N.Y.S.2d 774 (N.Y. Poughkeepsie City Ct. 2009).

160 *See* In the Matter of LVNV (Office of Commissioner of Financial Regulation June 28, 2012) (settlement agreement), *available at* www.nclc.org/unreported.

161 *See* National Consumer Law Center, Consumer Arbitration Agreements § 11.1 (6th ed. 2011), *updated at* www.nclc.org/library.

162 (6th ed. 2011), *updated at* www.nclc.org/library.

163 11 U.S.C. § 362(a).

164 *See* National Consumer Law Center, Consumer Bankruptcy Law and Practice § 9.4.6 (10th ed. 2012), *updated at* www.nclc.org/library.

165 11 U.S.C. § 362(k).

also has the advantage of allowing the debtor to recover wages and other property claimed as exempt and seized in execution of a judgment within the ninety-day preference period preceding the commencement of the bankruptcy case.

There are drawbacks to filing a bankruptcy, but generally not the ones consumers fear. For example, concern over a consumer's credit rating or ability to obtain future loans is often misplaced. Also misplaced are concerns that the consumer will lose most of his or her personal property, that bankruptcy will substantially harm the consumer's reputation in the community, or that bankruptcy will lead to other forms of discrimination.

One drawback to a bankruptcy filing may be its cost. A chapter 7 filing costs $306 and a chapter 13 filing costs $281, although these amounts can be paid in installments, and certain low-income households can request a waiver of the chapter 7 fee. The consumer will also have to pay for an attorney, unless such representation is offered by a pro bono panel or a neighborhood legal services office. Mandatory credit counseling before a bankruptcy filing will also cost roughly $25 (depending on the provider).

Another consideration is deciding *when* to file bankruptcy. Filing too soon will prevent the discharge of debts incurred after the date of filing. A first bankruptcy filing limits the consumer's ability to file a second bankruptcy to discharge debts incurred after the first bankruptcy filing. A consumer can only obtain one chapter 7 bankruptcy discharge every eight years, although a subsequent chapter 13 plan can be filed sooner. It is generally best to wait for all debts to ripen before filing for bankruptcy.

Chapter 20 of*NCLC Guide to Surviving Debt*[166] is a good resource for consumers explaining how bankruptcy works and the pros and cons of filing bankruptcy. Attorneys considering filing their first bankruptcy case should consider utilizing NCLC's *Bankruptcy Basics*,[167] which leads the attorney step-by-step through every stage of the bankruptcy process and also provides samples to complete the official forms. For the most complete discussion of all consumer bankruptcy issues, see NCLC's *Consumer Bankruptcy Law and Practice*.[168]

11.6 Consumer's Separate Suit Challenging Litigation Misconduct

One option for consumers after the collector has obtained a default or stipulated judgment is for the consumer to bring a separate action, in state or federal court, challenging the collector's litigation misconduct. The substance of such a claim is considered in Chapter 13, *infra*. This section focuses only on whether it is advisable to bring those claims after the collector has obtained a judgment.

In general it is best, and may even be required, to bring those claims only after setting aside a default or stipulated judgment in the underlying action.[169] Filing a motion to set aside the default judgment gives the collector an opportunity to commit the same or additional violations through its response. Conversely, as in any other derivative suit, the consumer's hasty FDCPA case will guarantee that the collector gives its underlying collection case extra attention and makes an effort to undo some of the consequences of its litigation misconduct. It may be better to set aside the judgment, obtain a dismissal of the collection action with prejudice, and then decide whether it is in the consumer's best interest to bring the affirmative case for the collector's litigation misconduct.

In addition, questions of claim preclusion may prevent a separate litigation without first setting aside a default or stipulated judgment. The default or stipulated judgment has adjudicated, or should have adjudicated, the issue being raised in the subsequent litigation, and judicial economy requires that it not be raised again.

Nevertheless, in some situations, res judicata may not prevent a separate suit challenging litigation misconduct. In some states res judicata does not apply to a default judgment.[170] There is also a question of whether res judicata prevents an action against the collector's attorney, even when an action against the collector is barred.

In addition, the applicability of res judicata will depend on the litigation misconduct at issue. For example, a collector who induces the consumer to default by making a false representation that it would not pursue the suit if the consumer starts making payments presents a different issue than was before the court in the default judgment. More on the preclusive effect of a judgment for the collector on the consumer's subsequent affirmative action is found in other NCLC treatises.[171]

A default or stipulated judgment that is set aside no longer has preclusive effect on a separate consumer action against the collector. After the judgment is set aside, the consumer must then decide whether to bring claims regarding collection misconduct as a separate action or as a counterclaim in a newly revived collection action. Certain factors in making this decision are examined in § 5.5, *supra*. But an additional factor is that the collector, once it knows that the consumer has obtained legal representation and intends to litigate vigorously, may not pursue the collection action. There may be no case in which the consumer can raise a counterclaim, and the consumer will be forced instead to decide whether to bring an affirmative action.

---

166 NCLC Guide to Surviving Debt (2013 ed.) ($25, 528 pages, with significant discounts if purchased in bulk). *See* www.nclc.org/shop.

167 (2d ed. 2013), *updated at* www.nclc.org/library.

168 (10th ed. 2012), *updated at* www.nclc.org/library (two volumes).

169 *See, e.g.*, Harrington v. CACV of Colo., L.L.C., 508 F. Supp. 2d 128 (D. Mass. 2007).

170 Anderson v. Gamache & Myers, P.C., 2007 WL 1577610 (E.D. Mo. May 31, 2007) (state court default judgment against plaintiff did not address the issues or claims in plaintiff's case, which was also not the same as plaintiff's FDCPA cause of action); Flores v. Quick Collect, Inc., 2007 WL 433239 (D. Or. Jan. 31, 2007) (issue preclusion does not attach by virtue of a judgment taken by default).

171 *See* National Consumer Law Center, Fair Debt Collection § 7.4.2 (8th ed. 2014), *updated at* www.nclc.org/library; National Consumer Law Center, Truth in Lending § 12.6.5 (8th ed. 2012), *updated at* www.nclc.org/library; National Consumer Law Center, Foreclosures § 10.6.5 (5th ed. 2014), *updated at* www.nclc.org/library.

In any action in federal court, such as one raising the Fair Debt Collection Practices Act (FDCPA), the implications of the *Rooker-Feldman* doctrine must be considered. The doctrine is a narrow one that bars "cases brought by state-court losers complaining of injuries caused by state-court judgments rendered before the district court proceedings commenced and inviting district court review and rejection of those judgments."[172] Courts employ subtle distinctions between *Rooker-Feldman* and claim and issue preclusion. In addition, certain types of actual damages are barred as a result of the prior adjudication while other damage theories and components are not. It is unclear whether the doctrine, in the context of an FDCPA claim filed after a default judgment for the collector, poses any additional issues not raised by res judicata. The doctrine may not apply at all when the consumer's subsequent action is against the collector's attorney, rather than the client who was a party in the state collection suit. These issues are examined in more detail in other NCLC treatises.[173]

172 Exxon Mobil Corp. v. Saudi Basic Industries Corp., 544 U.S. 280, 125 S. Ct. 1517, 161 L. Ed. 2d 454 (2005). *Accord* Lance v. Dennis, 546 U.S. 459, 126 S. Ct. 1198, 163 L. Ed. 2d 1059 (2006).

173 *See* National Consumer Law Center, Fair Debt Collection § 7.4.4 (8th ed. 2014), *updated at* www.nclc.org/library; National Consumer Law Center, Foreclosures § 10.6.5 (5th ed. 2014), *updated at* www.nclc.org/library.

Chapter 12 Protecting Debtors from Creditors' Postjudgment Remedies

12.1 Introduction

State and federal exemption laws provide fundamental protections for low-income debtors and their families. Every state has a general exemption law that protects a variety of income and property from judgment creditors.[1] In addition, many federal and state statutes that deal with a particular type of income or asset, such as Social Security benefits or state employees' pensions, include their own exemption provisions. Special exemption rules are also sometimes found in statutes dealing with a certain types of debt, such as tax debts. The Bankruptcy Code provides a federal exemption scheme in bankruptcy for states that do not provide their own bankruptcy exemptions.[2]

Exemption statutes provide protection against general or unsecured creditors, such as most bank credit cards, most retailers who issue their own credit cards,[3] tort creditors, landlords, utilities, and medical providers. State exemption statutes usually do not protect property from seizure by a creditor who has a security interest in it through a security agreement, mortgage, or deed of trust.[4] Such creditors are referred to as secured creditors. Typical secured transactions are car loans and mortgage loans to purchase homes. Secured creditors usually pursue repossession or replevin of any valuable collateral as their first collection option.[5] Even with secured debts, however, exemption statutes often come into play if a creditor tries to collect a deficiency judgment after having sold the collateral.

A debtor who possesses *only* exempt assets is referred to as "judgment proof" or "collection proof." While a judgment may be taken against such a person, there is no way for the creditor to compel collection of the judgment from the debtor's income or assets unless the debtor's circumstances change. Evaluating whether a debtor has income or assets that a creditor can reach is important, both at the outset of a collection defense case and at the point when a creditor is attempting to execute upon a judgment.[6]

This chapter examines collection devices that are available to a creditor that has recovered a judgment against a debtor. The chapter focuses upon asserting state and federal restrictions to protect the debtor's essential property and income. It starts by examining basic principles of interpretation of exemption laws, the due process limitations on garnishment, and other general issues. It then analyzes the federal and state laws that protect a debtor's wages, benefit payments, bank accounts, home, tangible personal property, and other property such as pensions, insurance, annuities, and causes of action. The discussion of bank accounts and wages includes analysis of the question whether these exempt funds retain their exempt character when deposited in a bank account. The chapter concludes by examining several special issues: waiver of exemptions by debtors, interstate enforcement of judgments, imprisonment for debt, debtor's examinations, assignment of judgments, and the statute of limitations for enforcement of judgments. The right of a bank to set off a debt against a debtor's deposit account is discussed in another treatise in this series.[7]

Each state's exemption laws are cited and summarized in Appendix G, *infra*. The full text of most of these statutes is reprinted in volumes 12 and 13 of *Collier on Bankruptcy* (16th ed. revised). A thorough analysis of exemptions provided under the Bankruptcy Code for debtors filing bankruptcy is found in Chapter 10 of NCLC's *Consumer Bankruptcy Law and Practice*.[8] NCLC's 2013 report, *No Fresh Start: How States Allow Debt Collectors to Push Families into Poverty* (October 2013),[9] which accompanies its Model Family Financial Protection Act,[10] includes state-by-state comparisons of state exemption laws.

This chapter cites extensively to decisions interpreting state and federal exemption laws. However, exemption laws vary greatly from state to state. Decisions from one state may be based on specific language that is absent from another state's statute. In addition, some states have a pattern of amending their exemption statutes frequently, so a decision from that state may be based on language that is no longer in the statute. For all of these reasons, practitioners should review out-of-state and even in-state decisions carefully before citing them as precedent.

---

1 *See* Appx. G, *infra*.

2 11 U.S.C. § 522. *See* National Consumer Law Center, Consumer Bankruptcy Law and Practice Ch. 10 (10th ed. 2012), *updated at* www.nclc.org/library.

3 Some retailers, however, purport to take a security interest in items purchased with their own credit card. *See* National Consumer Law Center, Repossessions § 3.9 (8th ed. 2013), *updated at* www.nclc.org/library.

4 *See In re* Johnson, 439 B.R. 416, 443–45 (Bankr. E.D. Mich. Oct. 14, 2010) (debtor waived exemption for disability benefits under employer's long-term disability plan by giving creditor a security interest in them), *aff'd on other grounds*, 2011 WL 1983339 (E.D. Mich. May 23, 2011); *In re* Cabrera, 2009 WL 4666460 (Bankr. S.D. Fla. Dec. 8, 2009) (bank account containing exempt funds, here wages, may be pledged as security for a loan). *See generally* § 12.7.7, *infra* (mortgages and consensual liens on home).

5 *See* National Consumer Law Center, Repossessions (8th ed. 2013), *updated at* www.nclc.org/library (comprehensive analysis of repossession law).

6 *See* §§ 2.1, 2.3.7, *supra* (case acceptance and strategy considerations).

7 National Consumer Law Center, Consumer Banking and Payments Law Ch. 5 (5th ed. 2013), *updated at* www.nclc.org/library.

8 National Consumer Law Center, Consumer Bankruptcy Law and Practice (10th ed. 2012), *updated at* www.nclc.org/library.

9 *Available at* www.nclc.org/issues/no-fresh-start.html.

10 *Available at* www.nclc.org/images/pdf/debt_collection/model_family_financial_protection_act.pdf.

12.2 General Principles

12.2.1 Constitutionality and Validity of Exemption Statutes

12.2.1.1 Impairment of Contracts

Whether an amendment to an exemption law applies to preexisting debts is first a question of statutory construction.[11] Assuming that an amendment increasing an exemption applies to preexisting debts, the question may arise whether this application is constitutional.

Exemption laws do not unconstitutionally impair the obligation of contracts, even when an increase in the exemption amount applies to debts incurred before the change.[12] The Contract Clause does not bar every state law that affects a contractual relationship. The reservation of certain essential attributes of sovereign power,[13] such as the right to declare exemptions and to modify them in response to economic changes, must be read into every contract. As one court noted, "[i]nflation is an economic reality; as long as it continues, the legislature has a legitimate interest in making corresponding reforms to outdated and unrealistic state laws." [14]

To balance the legitimate expectations of contracting parties with the reserved police power of the state, the Supreme Court has articulated a three-part test for impairment of contract claims. First, does the statute substantially impair the contract? If so, does it serve a "significant and legitimate" public purpose, such as "remedying a broad and general social or economic problem"? Finally, does it adjust "the rights and responsibilities of the contracting parties" based upon "reasonable conditions . . . appropriate to the public purpose"?[15]

On the first criterion—whether the statute substantially impairs the contract—severity of impact is a key question. "Minimal alteration" of contract rights will end the inquiry at step one; "severe impairment" will require a "careful examination of the nature and purpose" of the state legislation.[16] Courts distinguish between statutes that affect the "core purpose" of a contract and those that merely modify the remedy, such as increased exemptions that place more of an asset off limits.[17] The latter will not be a substantial impairment, unless

---

11 *See* § 12.7.8, *infra.*

12 CFCU Cmty. Credit Union v. Hayward, 552 F.3d 253 (2d Cir. 2009) (retroactive application of New York's increased homestead not impairment of contract); *In re* Selzer, 104 F.3d 234 (9th Cir. 1996) (retroactive application of statute exempting individual retirement accounts does not impair contracts); *In re* Little, 2007 WL 2791122 (N.D.N.Y. Sept. 24, 2007) (application of New York's increased homestead exemption to preexisting debt not unconstitutional impairment of contract); *In re* Brown, 2007 WL 2120380 (Bankr. N.D.N.Y. July 23, 2007) (application of increased homestead amount not impairment of contract), *aff'd*, 2007 WL 4560671 (N.D.N.Y. Dec. 18, 2007); *In re* Evans, 362 B.R. 275 (Bankr. D.S.C. 2006); *In re* Betz, 273 B.R. 313 (Bankr. D. Mass. 2002); *In re* Larson, 260 B.R. 174 (Bankr. D. Colo. 2001) (impairment of contract not substantial when change affected only the remedy, and creditors could reasonably expect exemption amounts to change with time); *In re* Johnson, 69 B.R. 988 (Bankr. D. Minn. 1987) (application of increased homestead exemption to existing unsecured debt not impairment of contract; bank could not reasonably expect that exemption laws would remain unchanged); *In re* Punke, 68 B.R. 936 (Bankr. N.D. Iowa 1987) (application of new exemption amounts to preexisting debts, not impairment of contract); *In re* Hockinson, 60 B.R. 250 (Bankr. N.D. Ill. 1986) (increased exemption amount is "minimal alteration" of contractual relationship; no substantial impairment); *In re* Barnhart, 47 B.R. 277 (Bankr. N.D. Tex. 1985) (Texas's increased homestead exemption applies to existing judgment liens; sovereign's power to change laws is read into all contracts); Homeside Lending, Inc. v. Miller, 31 P.3d 607 (Utah Ct. App. 2001) (allowing application of increased exemption and noting that Supreme Court has rejected Contract Clause challenge); Macumber v. Shafer, 637 P.2d 645 (Wash. 1981) (increasing exemption only modified remedy; reasonable exercise of police power in response to cost of living increases). *See also In re* Stewart, 246 B.R. 134 (Bankr. D.N.H. 2000) (application of federal bankruptcy law to exempt individual retirement account that was created before state exemption was adopted does not violate contract clause, which only limits states, not federal government); *In re* Bartlett, 168 B.R. 488 (Bankr. D.N.H. 1994) (New Hampshire's constitutional prohibition against retroactive statutes applies only to substantive rights, not remedies; creditor has no "vested substantive right" in lower exemption amount). *But see In re* Fossum, 59 B.R. 820 (Bankr. D. Minn. 1986) (applying new amounts to preexisting debt would violate contract clause); Builders Supply Co. v. Pine Belt Sav. & Loan Ass'n, 369 So. 2d 743, 745 (Miss. 1979).

13 El Paso v. Simmons, 379 U.S. 497, 85 S. Ct. 577, 13 L. Ed. 2d 496 (1965); Home Bldg. & Loan Ass'n v. Blaisdell, 290 U.S. 398, 54 S. Ct. 231, 78 L. Ed. 413 (1934) (upholding Depression-era statute that extended period for redemption from foreclosure); *In re* Barnhart, 47 B.R. 277 (Bankr. N.D. Tex. 1985); Macumber v. Shafer, 637 P.2d 645 (Wash. 1981) ("it is presumed that parties contract with knowledge that reservation of essential attributes of sovereign power is written into all contracts").

14 *In re* Punke, 68 B.R. 936, 941 (Bankr. N.D. Iowa 1987). *See also* CFCU Cmty. Credit Union v. Hayward, 552 F.3d 253 (2d Cir. 2009) (adjustment of homestead amount because inflation had made old amount "tantamount to no exemption at all"); *In re* Little, 2007 WL 2791122 (N.D.N.Y. Sept. 24, 2007) (when homestead exemption so unreasonably low as to be "tantamount to no exemption," legislature recognized need to "review and update"; application of new amount to preexisting debt not unconstitutional); *In re* Brown, 2007 WL 2120380 (Bankr. N.D.N.Y. July 23, 2007) (amendment to take account of "economic reality"), *aff'd*, 2007 WL 4560671 (N.D.N.Y. Dec. 18, 2007).

15 Energy Reserves Group, Inc. v. Kan. Light & Power Co., 459 U.S. 400, 103 S. Ct. 697, 74 L. Ed. 2d 569 (1983). *See also* Allied Structural Steel Co. v. Spanaus, 438 U.S. 234, 98 S. Ct. 2716, 57 L. Ed. 2d 727 (1979); Home Bldg. & Loan Ass'n v. Blaisdell, 290 U.S. 398, 54 S. Ct. 231, 78 L. Ed. 413 (1934).

16 Allied Structural Steel Co. v. Spanaus, 438 U.S. 234, 98 S. Ct. 2716, 57 L. Ed. 2d 727 (1979) (severity of impact on contract rights defines "height of the hurdle" that state legislation must clear; when law regarding employee pension rights had severe impact on employer's rights, public purpose was insufficient to save it).

17 CFCU Cmty. Credit Union v. Hayward, 552 F.3d 253 (2d Cir. 2009) (impairment not substantial when homestead adjusted for inflation); *In re* Larson, 260 B.R. 174 (Bankr. D. Colo. 2001) (impairment of contract not substantial when change in exemption amount affected only the remedy); *In re* Bartlett, 168 B.R. 488 (Bankr. D.N.H. 1994) (state constitutional prohibition against retroactive statutes does not apply to remedies such as exemption amount); *In re* Hockinson, 60 B.R. 250 (Bankr. N.D. Ill. 1986) (increased exemption amount is "minimal alteration" of contractual relationship; no substantial impairment); Macumber v. Shafer, 637 P.2d 645 (Wash. 1981) (increased exemption amounts merely modified remedy). *See also In re* Bartlett, 168 B.R. 488 (Bankr. D.N.H. 1994) (New Hampshire's constitutional prohibition against retroactive statutes applies only to substantive rights, not remedies; creditor has no "vested substantive right" in lower exemption

a very large or unexpected change "destroy[s] the value of the contract by destroying any meaningful remedy."[18]

The other two criteria closely resemble the familiar "rational relationship to a proper public purpose" balancing test applied in due process and equal protection cases. Courts have generally held that state legislatures may properly shield debtors from total destitution, respond to economic crises, or amend unrealistic statutes to allow for changed prices and that reasonable exemption statutes are a rational means to these ends.[19]

The reasonable expectations of the parties are highly significant.[20] "State regulation that restricts a party to the gains that it reasonably expected from a contract does not necessarily constitute a substantial impairment."[21] If, for example, exemption amounts are updated to account for inflation, "the reasonable expectations of creditors are realized, not disturbed, by the increased statutory exemption."[22]

One important factor in determining reasonableness is the extent of regulation of the subject matter at the time the contract is formed.[23] Because exemption laws have been in existence for many decades and have changed periodically to accommodate increased prices, a creditor may not reasonably rely upon their remaining frozen.

12.2.1.2 Due Process and the Taking of Property

Most courts agree that application of increased exemption amounts is not a taking of property without just compensation in violation of due process.[24] A statutory "program adjusting the benefits and burdens of economic life to promote the common good" will be more deferentially reviewed than a physical taking.[25] Courts will first decide whether an economic expectancy is solid enough to be treated as a property right protected by the takings clause and, if so, whether a statute's impact is sufficiently serious to constitute a taking. As with impairment of contract claims, reasonable expectations are a key issue.[26]

---

amount). *Cf.* W. Des Moines State Bank v. Mills, 482 N.W.2d 432 (Iowa 1992) (rejecting homeowners' claim that retroactive application of statute eliminating special notice requirement for homestead waivers was an unconstitutional impairment of contract; they had raised failure to include this notice in their mortgage documents as a defense to foreclosure).

18 *In re* Echevarren, 2 B.R. 215 (Bankr. D. Idaho 1980) (increased exemption amount may be used if "reasonable" and "does not destroy the value of the contract by destroying any meaningful remedy," but retroactive application of increase in homestead from $10,000 to $25,000 would unconstitutionally impair contract).

19 Home Bldg. & Loan Ass'n v. Blaisdell, 290 U.S. 398, 54 S. Ct. 231, 78 L. Ed. 413 (1934) (upholding Depression-era statute that extended period for redemption from foreclosure); CFCU Cmty. Credit Union, 552 F.3d 253 (2d Cir. 2009) (even if increased homestead substantially impaired contracts, adjustment for inflation served "significant and legitimate public purpose"); *In re* Johnson, 69 B.R. 988 (Bankr. D. Minn. 1987) (changes in homestead exemption were reasonable response to "catastrophic" situation in agriculture); *In re* Barnhart, 47 B.R. 277 (Bankr. N.D. Tex. 1985); Macumber v. Shafer, 637 P.2d 645 (Wash. 1981) (reasonable response to increased cost of living).

20 CFCU Cmty. Credit Union v. Hayward, 552 F.3d 253 (2d Cir. 2009) (creditors could reasonably expect homestead to be adjusted for inflation); *In re* Little, 2007 WL 2791122 (N.D.N.Y. Sept. 24, 2007) (no substantial impairment; amendment of unreasonably low homestead exemption to account for inflation was foreseeable when creditor made loan); *In re* Brown, 2007 WL 2120380 (Bankr. N.D.N.Y. July 23, 2007) (change in unreasonably low homestead exemption foreseeable), *aff'd*, 2007 WL 4560671 (N.D.N.Y. Dec. 18, 2007); *In re* Evans, 362 B.R. 275 (Bankr. D.S.C. 2006) (considering the choice of law provisions of the bankruptcy law and the mobility of the population, no reasonable creditor could assume that a certain set of exemptions would apply); *In re* Larson, 260 B.R. 174 (Bankr. D. Colo. 2001) (creditors could reasonably expect exemption amounts to change with time); *In re* Johnson, 69 B.R. 988 (Bankr. D. Minn. 1987) (bank could not reasonably expect exemption statutes to remain unchanged and did not rely on this assumption when, at time of loan, it appeared to be fully secured); *In re* Punke, 68 B.R. 936 (Bankr. N.D. Iowa 1987) (when inflation is an economic reality, legislation that adjusts for it will realize, rather than disturb, creditors' expectations). *See also In re* Varanasi, 394 B.R. 430 (Bankr. S.D. Ohio 2008) (in today's mobile society, creditor cannot reasonably rely on debtor's being entitled to a specific state's exemptions; here Bankruptcy Code required application of New Hampshire's homestead exemption, which is ten times Ohio's exemption, to Ohio property).

21 Energy Reserves Group, Inc. v. Kan. Light & Power Co., 459 U.S. 400, 103 S. Ct. 697, 74 L. Ed. 2d 569 (1983) (quoting El Paso v. Simmons, 379 U.S. 497, 85 S. Ct. 577, 13 L. Ed. 2d 496 (1965)).

22 *In re* Punke, 68 B.R. 936, 941 (Bankr. N.D. Iowa 1987). *See also In re* Little, 2006 WL 1524594 (Bankr. N.D.N.Y. Apr. 24, 2006) (application of new amount to preexisting debt not impairment of contract); Macumber v. Shafer, 637 P.2d 645 (Wash. 1981).

23 Energy Reserves Group, Inc. v. Kan. Light & Power Co., 459 U.S. 400, 103 S. Ct. 697, 74 L. Ed. 2d 569 (1983) (natural gas highly regulated); *In re* Evans, 362 B.R. 275 (Bankr. D.S.C. 2006) (noting heavily regulated nature of debt collection and bankruptcy; not unconstitutional impairment of contract to apply increased homestead exemption that was in effect on petition date to preexisting debt); *In re* Johnson, 69 B.R. 988 (Bankr. D. Minn. 1987) (exemption laws had long history); *In re* Punke, 68 B.R. 936 (Bankr. N.D. Iowa 1987); *In re* Barnhart, 47 B.R. 277 (Bankr. N.D. Tex. 1985). *See also* Allstate Ins. Co. v. Kim, 829 A.2d 611 (Md. 2003) (heavy regulation of insurance industry).

24 *In re* McDole, 2008 WL 4330777 (W.D. Wash. Sept. 18, 2008) (increased homestead amount not a taking; creditor's rights were subject to changes in state law); *In re* Trudell, 381 B.R. 441 (Bankr. W.D.N.Y. 2008) (application of increased homestead to avoid preexisting judgment lien not a taking; lien not a "vested right" under New York law); *In re* Brown, 2007 WL 2120380 (Bankr. N.D.N.Y. July 23, 2007) (increase of homestead amount made unrealistic by inflation simply adjusted economic benefits and burdens and served important public purpose; no unconstitutional taking); *In re* Larson, 260 B.R. 174 (Bankr. D. Colo. 2001) (security interest is property, but impairment, which resulted from "adjustment of benefits and burdens," not severe enough to equal taking); *In re* Bartlett, 168 B.R. 488 (Bankr. D.N.H. 1994) (judicial liens; impairment was reasonable in light of public policy of bankruptcy and exemption laws; creditor did not have property right in assumption that collateral would be sufficient to pay off loan); *In re* Punke, 68 B.R. 936 (Bankr. N.D. Iowa 1987) (application of new exemption amounts to preexisting debts not a taking; statute adjusted benefits and burdens; change was within reasonable expectations of creditors). *But see In re* Sticha, 60 B.R. 717 (Bankr. D. Minn. 1986) (security interest in specific property); *In re* Fossum, 59 B.R. 820 (Bankr. D. Minn. 1986) (same).

25 Pa. Cent. Transp. Co. v. City of New York, 438 U.S. 104, 98 S. Ct. 2646, 57 L. Ed. 2d 631 (1978).

26 *In re* McDole, 2008 WL 4330777 (W.D. Wash. Sept. 18, 2008) (increased homestead amount not a surprise); *In re* Trudell, 381 B.R. 441 (Bankr. W.D.N.Y. 2008) (application of predictably increased homestead to avoid preexisting judgment lien not a taking); *In re* Betz, 273 B.R. 313

An unsecured creditor's hope that a debtor's non-exempt property will be sufficient to cover the debt is generally not a property right.[27] Even a judgment lien that has attached to specific property may not be protected.[28] A security interest is more likely to be protected.[29] Even if a property right is found, courts will weigh the severity of the impact against the public purpose served by the statute and may find a permissible adjustment of economic benefits and burdens, rather than a taking.[30]

Application of a new exemption statute to cases pending on the date of enactment is not a violation of due process.[31] Whether garnishment and execution procedures comply with due process requirements is discussed in § 12.3, *infra*.

12.2.1.3 Equal Protection

Exemption statutes' distinctions among different types of creditors and among debtors in different circumstances have generally been upheld against equal protection challenges.[32] The Supreme Court has adopted a balancing test for equal protection claims. If the statutes involves a suspect classification, such as race, gender, or national origin, or a fundamental right, such as the right to vote, or the freedom of speech or religion, then it will be subject to strict (or at least intermediate level) scrutiny; if it does not, then it need only have a rational relationship to a proper legislative purpose.[33] No court has held that creditors are a suspect class or that there is a fundamental right to a specific collection method.[34] Courts have generally recognized exemption statutes as rational means to achieve proper legislative purposes.[35]

12.2.1.4 Validity of Bifurcated Exemption Schemes

Some states provide two exemption schemes, one in bankruptcy and another for execution upon judgments.[36] The differences may be significant. Courts have generally upheld

---

(Bankr. D. Mass. 2002); *In re* Johnson, 69 B.R. 988 (Bankr. D. Minn. 1987) (bank could not reasonably expect that exemption laws would remain unchanged).

27 *In re* Varanasi, 394 B.R. 430 (Bankr. S.D. Ohio 2008); *In re* Johnson, 69 B.R. 988 (Bankr. D. Minn. 1987).

28 *In re* McDole, 2008 WL 4330777 (W.D. Wash. Sept. 18, 2008) (judgment lien not vested right); *In re* Calloway, 423 B.R. 627 (Bankr. W.D.N.Y. 2010) (judgment lien not a vested property right under New York law; application of increased homestead limit to judgment lien perfected before effective date of amendment not unconstitutional taking); *In re* Trudell, 381 B.R. 441 (Bankr. W.D.N.Y. 2008) (judgment lien not a vested right under New York law); *In re* Longey, 2008 WL 2074041 (Bankr. W.D. Wash. May 14, 2008) (judgment lien not a vested right; allowing retroactive application of increased homestead, but distinguishing cases in which lien was completely eliminated). *But cf.* State *ex rel.* Six v. Mike W. Graham & Assocs., 220 P.3d 1105 (Kan. Ct. App. Dec. 4, 2009) (statute that retroactively invalidated judgment liens on cemeteries is unconstitutional).

29 *In re* Larson, 260 B.R. 174 (Bankr. D. Colo. 2001) (security interest is property); *In re* Sticha, 60 B.R. 717 (Bankr. D. Minn. 1986) (security interest in specific property); *In re* Fossum, 59 B.R. 820 (Bankr. D. Minn. 1986) (same). *But see In re* Bartlett, 168 B.R. 488 (Bankr. D.N.H. 1994) (judicial liens; creditor did not have property right in assumption that collateral would be sufficient to pay off loan).

30 *See, e.g., In re* Brown, 2007 WL 2120380 (Bankr. N.D.N.Y. July 23, 2007) (adjustment of homestead amount made unrealistic by inflation served important public purpose), *aff'd*, 2007 WL 4560671 (N.D.N.Y. Dec. 18, 2007); *In re* Larson, 260 B.R. 174 (Bankr. D. Colo. 2001) (security interests were property but impairment here, which resulted from an adjustment of economic benefits and burdens, did not have sufficient impact to be a taking).

31 Reliance Ins. Co. v. Ziegler, 938 F.2d 781 (7th Cir. 1991). *See also In re* Starns, 52 B.R. 405 (S.D. Tex. 1985) (rejecting debtor's due process challenge to amendment to Texas exemption statute that protected more property for most debtors but, as applied, disadvantaged this debtor).

32 St. Ann's Hosp. v. Arnold, 672 N.E.2d 743 (Ohio Ct. App. 1996) (greater restrictions on garnishment for health care debts reasonable in light of public policy of encouraging people to seek needed medical care); Wooster Cmty. Hosp. v. Anderson, 670 N.E.2d 563 (Ohio Ct. App. 1996) (greater protection of health care debtors was reasonable because of life or death necessity of health care and the extra burdens imposed by paying back a debt while also suffering health problems); *In re* Davis, 681 N.W.2d 452 (S.D. 2004) (increased homestead exemption for persons age seventy or over not arbitrary, nor denial of equal protection, but unlimited exemption violated state constitutional requirement that exemptions be reasonable). *See also In re* Patterson, 216 B.R. 413 (C.D. Ill. 1998) (exception of wages from wildcard exemption does not violation state constitution's prohibition of special laws); Accounts Mgmt., Inc. v. Williams, 484 N.W.2d 297 (S.D. 1992) (state wage garnishment exemption did not violate privileges and immunities clause of state constitution by favoring wage earners over others); § 12.2.1.4, *infra* (constitutionality of bifurcated exemption schemes). *But see* Credit Bur. of E. Idaho, Inc. v. Lecheminant, 235 P.3d 1188 (Idaho 2010) (statute making wife's property exempt from execution against husband, but not vice versa, denies equal protection); Community Physical Therapy v. Wayt, 639 N.E.2d 515 (Ohio Ct. App. 1994) (statute placing greater restrictions on garnishment for health care debts was unconstitutional because it had no rational relationship to any governmental purpose).

33 Central State Univ. v. Am. Ass'n of Univ. Professors, Central State Univ. Chapter, 526 U.S. 124, 127, 119 S. Ct. 1162 (1999); Vacco v. Quill, 521 U.S. 793, 799, 117 S. Ct. 2293 (1997).

34 *See* Sharp v. Park 'N Fly of Tex., 969 S.W.2d 572 (Tex. App. 1998) ("in examining classifications of economic or property interests, the court employs a rational basis test"); *In re* Honeycutt, 908 P.2d 976 (Wyo. 1995) (construing state constitution; using rational relationship standard to uphold statute denying exemption to privately funded individual retirement account but exempting employer-sponsored plans).

35 *See* §§ 12.2.1.1, 12.2.1.2, *supra*.

36 *See In re* Watts, 298 F.3d 1077 (9th Cir. 2002) (briefly discussing California's complex bankruptcy/non-bankruptcy, automatic/non-automatic exemptions); *In re* Reaves, 285 F.3d 1152 (9th Cir. 2002) (bankruptcy debtor using California bankruptcy exemptions could exempt her car even though, before she filed bankruptcy, state court had denied her the California non-bankruptcy exemption for the vehicle); *In re* Sassak, 426 B.R. 680 (E.D. Mich. 2010) (bankruptcy-specific exemptions not exclusive; debtor may claim exemptions from Michigan's general exemptions also); *In re* Dean, 470 B.R. 643 (Bankr. M.D. Ga. 2012) (Georgia's bankruptcy-only exemptions, which cap the amount of insurance exemption, are exclusive; unlimited exemption found in Insurance Code not applicable in bankruptcy); *In re* Petrozelli, 139 B.R. 241 (Bankr. E.D. Cal. 1992) (discussing California's dual exemption scheme). *But cf.* MPM Fin. Group, Inc. v. Morton, 2007 WL 1452536 (Ky. Ct. App. May 18, 2007) (Kentucky exemption statute that incorporates federal bankruptcy exemptions applies to all debtors whether in bankruptcy or not; it and another Kentucky statute provide complementary exemption schemes, one a floor and the other a ceiling).

bifurcated exemption schemes against constitutional and preemption challenges.[37]

12.2.1.5 Validity Under State Constitutions

In many states certain exemptions, most commonly the homestead exemption, are found in the state constitution. A constitutional exemption will be less subject to waiver or loss than a statutory exemption, and a statute that limits a constitutional exemption is likely to be found invalid.[38] Some courts have also struck down statutory exemptions that were more generous than those in the state constitution.[39] An unlimited exemption may violate a state constitutional provision for "reasonable" exemptions but can usually be saved by reading in a requirement that the amount exempted be reasonably necessary for the support of the debtor and dependents.[40]

12.2.2 Exemption Laws Must Be Liberally Construed in Favor of the Debtor

State and federal exemption laws, which exclude a wide variety of income and property from seizure by creditors, are a fundamental safeguard for the protection of low-income persons. Exemption laws are designed to protect debtors and their families from destitution and to afford debtors a means of financial rehabilitation.

Exemption laws were established to protect a limited amount of a debtor's property from forced sale for the payment of debts. The courts have enumerated the following purposes of exemption laws: (1) to provide the debtor with enough money to survive; (2) to protect the debtor's dignity; (3) to afford a means of financial rehabilitation; (4) to protect the family unit from impoverishment; and (5) to spread the burden of a debtor's support from society to his creditors.[41]

Exemptions are to be liberally construed in favor of the debtor and the debtor's family.[42] Courts recognize the strong

37 *In re* Schafer, 689 F.3d 601 (6th Cir. 2012) (Michigan's bifurcated exemption scheme not preempted); Sheehan v. Peveich, 574 F.3d 248 (4th Cir. 2009) (West Virginia exemptions not preempted; opt-out provision does not require that state's exemptions be uniform in and out of bankruptcy); *In re* Murray, 506 B.R. 129 (B.A.P. 10th Cir. 2014) (Kansas' bankruptcy-only exemption for tax refunds attributable to earned income credit is constitutional; overruling trustee's objection to exemption); *In re* Westby, 486 B.R. 509 (B.A.P. 10th Cir. 2013) (same); *In re* Applebaum, 422 B.R. 684 (B.A.P. 9th Cir. 2009); *In re* McFarland, 481 B.R. 242 (Bankr. S.D. Ga. 2012) (upholding Georgia's bifurcated exemption scheme); *In re* Earned Income Tax Credit Exemption Constitutional Challenge Cases, 477 B.R. 791 (Bankr. D. Kan. 2012) (Kansas' bankruptcy-only exemption for tax refunds attributable to earned income credit is constitutional); *In re* Morrell, 394 B.R. 405 (Bankr. N.D. W. Va. 2008); *In re* Brown, 2007 WL 2120380 (Bankr. N.D.N.Y. July 23, 2007), *aff'd*, 2007 WL 4560671 (N.D.N.Y. Dec. 18, 2007).

38 Gonzales v. Ameriquest Mortgage, 2005 WL 3333259 (W.D. Tex. Dec. 8, 2005) (borrower entitled to claim homestead exemption despite disclaimer that property was not his homestead when borrower owned only one piece of residential property and lived there); *In re* Hendricks, 237 B.R. 821 (Bankr. M.D. Fla. 1999) (homestead exemption in constitution is not affected by change in fraudulent conveyance statute); Havoco of Am., Ltd. v. Hill, 790 So. 2d 1018 (Fla. 2001) (legislature is powerless to subject constitutional homestead exemption to fraudulent transfer statute); Torgelson v. 17138 88th Ave., 749 N.W.2d 24 (Minn. 2008) (Minnesota's constitutional homestead exemption, which protects against "debts or liabilities of every kind or description without exception," bars state drug law forfeiture of homestead); Household Fin. Corp. v. Ellis, 419 S.E.2d 592 (N.C. Ct. App. 1992) (statute unconstitutional to extent it limits the claiming of constitutional exemptions to twenty days after service of notice), *aff'd*, 429 S.E.2d 716 (N.C. 1993) (per curiam); State v. One 1965 Red Chevrolet Pickup, 37 P.3d 815 (Okla. 2001) (home but not vehicle exempt from state criminal law forfeiture; homestead exemption found in state constitution, motor vehicle exemption and forfeiture provisions are statutory). *See also* Chames v. DeMayo, 972 So. 2d 850 (Fla. 2007) (waiver of homestead requires mortgage formalities; waiver in unsecured, adhesive contract was unenforceable because against public policy). *But cf.* Dominguez v. Castaneda, 163 S.W.3d 318 (Tex. App. 2005) (debtor owning two residential properties bound by warranty that parcel not homestead).

39 *In re* Holt, 894 F.2d 1005 (8th Cir. 1990) (statutory exemptions are contrary to, and therefore limited by, the lower ceilings in the Arkansas Constitution). *But see* Clinical Study Ctrs., Inc. v. Boellner, ___ S.W.3d ___, 2012 WL 2150718 (Ark. June 14, 2012) (Arkansas exemption for IRAs did not violate state constitutional limit on personal property exemptions; exemption for specified type of fund, as opposed to unlimited exemption of personal property, is permissible).

40 *In re* Cross, 255 B.R. 25 (Bankr. N.D. Ind. 2000) (unlimited exemptions violate state constitution unless debtor shows exemption is needed for necessities of life); Citizens' Nat'l Bank v. Foster, 668 N.E.2d 1236 (Ind. 1996) (exemption for individual retirement accounts, which were limited by federal tax law, satisfied state constitutional provision for "reasonable" exemptions, but unlimited exemption for life insurance was questionable; debtor must show "reasonable necessity" of amount claimed); Estate of Jones by Blume v. Kvamme, 529 N.W.2d 335 (Minn. 1995) (exemption for individual retirement accounts and certain employee benefits that had no limit on amount and no reference to needs of debtor and family violated Minnesota constitutional provision requiring "reasonable exemptions"); *In re* Davis, 681 N.W.2d 452 (S.D. 2004) (increased homestead exemption for persons seventy or over permissible, but unlimited exemption violated state constitutional requirement of reasonable exemptions; legislature must provide cap). *See also In re* Bannourah, 201 B.R. 954 (Bankr. S.D. Ind. 1996) (state insurance policy exemption, construed so as to avoid state constitutional problem, exempted amount required to afford the necessities of life). *But see In re* Reiland, 377 B.R. 232 (Bankr. D. Minn. 2007) (unlimited exemption for disability insurance cannot be saved; reasonable exemption must prescribe dollar amount, objective criteria, or reference to other statute creating limits), *vacated as moot*, 2008 WL 4876758 (D. Minn. Nov. 12, 2008); *In re* Craig, 545 N.W.2d 764 (N.D. 1996) (limitation of $100,000 per item, $200,000 total for life insurance policies and certain retirement funds was reasonable within meaning of state constitution, which would bar an unlimited exemption).

41 *See, e.g., In re* Johnson, 880 F.2d 78, 83 (8th Cir. 1989) (Minnesota law); *In re* Kester, 339 B.R. 749 (B.A.P. 10th Cir. 2006) (Kansas law) (homesteads protected "for the benefit of society and of the family—to protect the family from destitution and society from the danger of her citizens becoming paupers"), *aff'd*, 493 F.3d 1208 (10th Cir. 2007); *In re* Longey, 2008 WL 2074041 (Bankr. W.D. Wash. May 14, 2008) (intention of homestead laws "is to ensure shelter for families, not to protect the rights of creditors"); *In re* Dwyer, 305 B.R. 582, 585 (Bankr. M.D. Fla. 2004) (protect families from destitution and relieve state of support burden); North Side Bank v. Gentile, 385 N.W.2d. 133 (Wis. 1986); W. Vukowich, *Debtors Exemption Rights*, 62 Geo. L.J. 779 (1974).

42 *STATES*: Wilder v. Inter-Island Stream Navigation Co., 211 U.S. 239, 29 S. Ct. 58, 53 L. Ed. 164 (1908).

ALABAMA: In re Rutland, 318 B.R. 588 (Bankr. M.D. Ala. 2004); *In re* Hughes, 306 B.R. 683, 686 (Bankr. M.D. Ala. 2004); *In re* Avery, 514 So. 2d 1380 (Ala. 1987).

ALASKA: Gutterman v. First Nat'l Bank of Anchorage, 597 P.2d 969 (Alaska 1979).

ARIZONA: In re Thiem, 443 B.R. 832 (Bankr. D. Ariz. 2011); *In re* Buchberger, 311 B.R. 794 (Bankr. D. Ariz. 2004) (liberally construing motor vehicle exemption to include all-terrain vehicle).

ARKANSAS: In re Kelley, 455 B.R. 710 (Bankr. E.D. Ark. 2011); *In re* Evans, 190 B.R. 1015 (Bankr. E.D. Ark. 1995), *aff'd*, 108 F.3d 1381 (8th Cir. 1997) (table).

CALIFORNIA: In re Kelley, 2012 WL 5878240 (C.D. Cal. Nov. 20, 2012); *In re* Morse, 237 F. Supp. 579 (S.D. Cal. 1964); Wells Fargo Fin. Leasing, Inc. v. D & M Cabinets, 99 Cal. Rptr. 3d 97 (Cal. Ct. App. Aug. 28, 2009) (construing homestead exemption liberally; refusing to allow creditor to enforce clause allowing appointment of receiver to sell home as a way of bypassing judicial procedure for foreclosure of judgment lien on homestead).

COLORADO: In re Elliot, 448 B.R. 843 (Bankr. D. Colo. 2011) (Colorado homestead exempts proceeds of voluntary sale or sheriff's sale but is silent as to non-judicial foreclosure; principle of liberal interpretation requires exemption of surplus from non-judicial foreclosure); Fleet v. Zwick, 994 P.2d 480 (Colo. App. 1999); *In re* Marriage of Gedgaudas, 978 P.2d 677 (Colo. App. 1999).

CONNECTICUT: In re Clifford, 222 B.R. 8 (Bankr. D. Conn. 1998).

DELAWARE: Wilmington Trust Co. v. Barry, 338 A.2d 575 (Del. Super. Ct. 1975), *aff'd*, 359 A.2d 664 (Del. 1976) (mem.).

DISTRICT OF COLUMBIA: Hollywood Credit Clothing Co. v. Jones, 117 A.2d 226 (D.C. App. 1955).

FLORIDA: In re Colwell, 196 F.3d 1225 (11th Cir. 1999); *In re* Prestwood, 322 B.R. 463 (Bankr. S.D. Fla. 2005) (liberally construing Florida homestead exemption to apply when debtor maintained extensive ties to California but sufficiently demonstrated intent to live in Florida); *In re* Yettaw, 316 B.R. 560 (Bankr. M.D. Fla. 2004) (recreational vehicle occupied as residence was exempt); *In re* Dwyer, 305 B.R. 582, 585 (Bankr. M.D. Fla. 2004); *In re* Lazin, 217 B.R. 332 (Bankr. M.D. Fla. 1998) (liberally construing Florida exemption for annuity contracts); Osborne v. Dumoulin, 55 So. 3d 577, 582 (Fla. 2011) (applying rule of liberal construction to statutory personal property exemption that depends on not claiming homestead exemption); Goldenberg. v. Sawczak, 791 So. 2d 1078 (Fla. 2001) (Florida law); Havoco of Am., Ltd. v. Hill, 790 So. 2d 1018 (Fla. 2001) (constitutional homestead exemption is liberally construed); Broward v. Jacksonville Med. Ctr., 690 So. 2d 589 (Fla. 1997).

GEORGIA: *In re* McFarland, 500 B.R. 279, 283 (Bankr. S.D. Ga. 2013).

HAWAII: Schuler v. Wallace, 61 Haw. 590, 607 P.2d 411 (Haw. 1980).

IDAHO: Novas v. Russ Dean Ford, Inc., 2009 WL 721549 (D. Idaho Mar. 17, 2009); *In re* Moore, 269 B.R. 864 (Bankr. D. Idaho 2001); *In re* Marples, 266 B.R. 202 (Bankr. D. Idaho 2001); *In re* Atkinson, 258 B.R. 769 (Bankr. D. Idaho 2001); *In re* Gallegos, 226 B.R. 111 (Bankr. D. Idaho 1998).

ILLINOIS: In re Simpson, 238 B.R. 776 (Bankr. S.D. Ill. 1999); *In re* Brockhouse, 220 B.R. 623 (Bankr. C.D. Ill. 1998).

INDIANA: Levin v. Dare, 203 B.R. 137 (S.D. Ind. 1996) (liberally construing ambiguous statute to hold property exempt); *In re* Robertson, 227 B.R. 844 (Bankr. S.D. Ind. 1998) (Indiana courts have a longstanding practice of construing exemption statutes liberally in favor of debtors). *Cf. In re* Oakley, 344 F.3d 709, 712 (7th Cir. 2003) (Indiana law) (noting rule of liberal construction but rejecting debtor's interpretation of exemption statute).

IOWA: In re Wilson, 305 B.R. 4 (Bankr. N.D. Iowa 2004); *In re* Longstreet, 246 B.R. 611 (Bankr. S.D. Iowa 2000); LPP Mortgage, Ltd. v. Meurer, 2004 WL 57585 (Iowa Ct. App. Jan. 14, 2004). *See also* Iowa State Bank & Trust Co. v. Michel, 683 N.W.2d 95 (Iowa 2004) (homestead rights are jealously guarded by the law).

KANSAS: In re Thexton, 39 B.R. 367 (Bankr. D. Kan. 1984); Redmond v. Kester, 159 P.3d 1004 (Kan. 2007); Bohl v. Bohl, 234 Kan. 227, 670 P.2d 1344 (1983); Celco, Inc. v. Davis Van Lines, 226 Kan. 366, 598 P.2d 188 (1979).

KENTUCKY: In re Powell, 173 B.R. 338 (Bankr. E.D. Ky. 1994).

LOUISIANA: In re Black, 225 B.R. 610 (Bankr. M.D. La. 1998); Grantham v. Johnson, 134 So. 3d 164 (La. Ct. App. 2014) (homestead exemption liberally construed; statute denying homestead for judgments resulting from criminal conviction is penal and strictly construed; allowing homestead for defendant found civilly liable, but not criminally convicted, for attempted murder for which co-defendant was convicted).

MAINE: In re Maylin, 155 B.R. 605 (Bankr. D. Me. 1993).

MARYLAND: Rosemann v. Salsbury, Clements, Bekman, Marder & Adkins, L.L.C., 987 A.2d 48 (Md. 2010).

MASSACHUSETTS: In re Perry, 357 B.R. 175 (B.A.P. 1st Cir. 2006); *In re* Gray, 378 B.R. 728 (Bankr. D. Mass. 2007) (applying rule of liberal construction to exempt manufactured home on leased land); Dwyer v. Cempellin, 673 N.E.2d 863 (Mass. 1996).

MICHIGAN: Blow v. Blow, 350 N.W.2d 890 (Mich. Ct. App. 1984).

MINNESOTA: In re Irish, 403 F.3d 611 (8th Cir. 2005); *In re* Drenttel, 403 F.3d 611 (8th Cir. 2005); *In re* Johnson, 880 F.2d 78, 83 (8th Cir. 1989). *But cf.* Lang v. Dorosh, 2010 WL 5292607 (Minn. Ct. App. Dec. 28, 2010) (debtor must strictly comply with procedure for claiming exemptions; denying exemption for retirement account because debtor failed to enclose required account statements).

MISSISSIPPI: In re Cobbins, 227 F.3d 302 (5th Cir. 2000) (liberal construction required, but mobile home not exempt unless debtor also owns land).

MISSOURI: In re Moore, 251 B.R. 380 (Bankr. W.D. Mo. 2000) (liberally construing motor vehicle exemption to include recreational all-terrain vehicles when statute did not specifically exclude them); *In re* Galvin, 158 B.R. 806 (Bankr. W.D. Mo. 1993).

MONTANA: In re Siegle, 2000 Bankr. LEXIS 1627 (Bankr. D. Mont. Dec. 6, 2000), *amended by* 257 B.R. 591 (Bankr. D. Mont. 2001); *In re* Rhines, 227 B.R. 308 (Bankr. D. Mont. 1998).

NEBRASKA: In re Bailey, 172 F. Supp. 925 (D. Neb. 1959).

NEVADA: In re Christensen, 149 P.3d 40 (Nev. 2006); Besnilian v. Wilkinson, 25 P.3d 187 (Nev. 2001).

NEW HAMPSHIRE: Deyeso v. Cavadi, 66 A.3d 1236 (N.H. 2013); Landry v. Landry, 917 A.2d 1262 (N.H. 2007).

NEW MEXICO: Morgan Keegan Mortgage Co. v. Candelaria, 951 P.2d 1066 (N.M. Ct. App. 1997).

NEW YORK: In re Miller, 103 B.R. 65 (Bankr. N.D.N.Y. 1989).

NORTH CAROLINA: In re Cain, 235 B.R. 812 (Bankr. M.D.N.C. 1998); Household Fin. Corp. v. Ellis, 107 N.C. App. 262, 419 S.E.2d 592 (1992), *aff'd*, 429 S.E.2d 716 (N.C. 1993) (per curiam).

NORTH DAKOTA: In re Danduran, 657 F.3d 749 (8th Cir. 2011) (homestead exemption); *In re* Hankel, 223 B.R. 728 (Bankr. D.N.D. 1998).

OHIO: In re Gaydos, 441 B.R. 102 (Bankr. N.D. Ohio 2010) (liberally construing Ohio's provision of specific exemption for motor vehicle not to bar use of tools-of-trade exemption for truck used to earn living); *In re* Jones, 318 B.R. 841 (Bankr. S.D. Ohio 2005); *In re* Shaffer, 228 B.R. 892 (Bankr. N.D. Ohio 1998); Meadow Wind Healthcare Ctr. v. McInnes, 2000 Ohio App. LEXIS 3415 (Ohio Ct. App. July 24, 2000).

OKLAHOMA: In re Anderson, 932 P.2d 1110 (Okla. 1996).

OREGON: In re Casserino, 379 F.3d 1069 (9th Cir. 2004); *In re* Stratton, 269 B.R. 716 (Bankr. D. Or. 2001).

PENNSYLVANIA: Marine Midland Bank v. Surfbelt, Inc., 532 F. Supp. 728 (W.D. Pa. 1982).

PUERTO RICO: *In re* Rivera, 499 B.R. 175 (Bankr. D. P.R. 2013) (noting rule of liberal construction); *In re* Soto, 2013 WL 3779382 (Bankr. D. P.R. July 18, 2013) (noting rule of liberal construction and finding sufficient compliance with procedure for claiming homestead).

public policy in favor of the preservation of the home,[43] "the necessary shelter and personal property required for [families'] welfare in difficult economic circumstances,"[44] and the assurance of "the basic necessities."[45] If it is possible to construe an exemption statute in ways that are both favorable and unfavorable to the debtor, the favorable method should be chosen.[46] Courts have the equitable power to stay executions upon terms and conditions that are just, such as installment payments.[47]

Conversely, as garnishment is a harsh remedy, created by statute in derogation of common law, garnishment statutes are strictly construed. A creditor's failure to comply strictly with all procedural requirements of the statute will result in

SOUTH DAKOTA: In re Lind, 10 B.R. 611 (Bankr. D.S.D. 1981); Beck v. Lapsley, 593 S.W.2d 410, 413 (S.D. 1999).

TENNESSEE: In re Hogue, 286 S.W.3d 890 (Tenn. 2009).

TEXAS: In re Perry, 345 F.3d 303 (5th Cir. 2003) (Texas homestead law); *In re* Crockett, 158 F.3d 332 (5th Cir. 1998); *In re* McDaniel, 70 F.3d 841 (5th Cir. 1995); *In re* Bading, 376 B.R. 143 (Bankr. W.D. Tex. 2007) (homesteads are "a favorite of the law"; liberal construction required); Pierce v. Wash. Mut. Bank, 226 S.W.3d 711 (Tex. App. 2007) (history of homestead laws; principle of liberal construction).

UTAH: In re Carlson, 303 B.R. 478 (B.A.P. 10th Cir. 2004); P.I.E. Employees Fed. Credit Union v. Bass, 759 P.2d 1144 (Utah 1988); Homeside Lending, Inc. v. Miller, 31 P.3d 607 (Utah Ct. App. 2001).

VERMONT: In re Roberge, 307 B.R. 442 (Bankr. D. Vt. 2004); Mercier v. Partlow, 149 Vt. 523, 546 A.2d 787 (1988).

VIRGINIA: Tignor v. Parkinson, 729 F.2d 977, 981 (4th Cir. 1984); *In re* Webb, 214 B.R. 553 (E.D. Va. 1997); *In re* Hasse, 246 B.R. 247 (Bankr. E.D. Va. 2000); *In re* Ward, 210 B.R. 531 (Bankr. E.D. Va. 1997). *But see In re* McWilliams, 296 B.R. 424 (Bankr. E.D. Va. 2002) (strictly construing recording requirements of Virginia homestead exemption statute). *But cf. In re* Stoney, 445 B.R. 543, 546–47 (Bankr. E.D. Va. 2011) (substantive provisions are construed liberally but procedural requirements strictly); *In re* Jackson, 2001 Bankr. LEXIS 525 (Bankr. E.D. Va. Mar. 30, 2001) (homestead exemption statute is liberally construed, but its procedural requirements are construed strictly, so homestead deed untimely).

WASHINGTON: In re Longey, 2008 WL 2074041 (Bankr. W.D. Wash. May 14, 2008) (applying rule of liberal construction when state law unclear as to retroactive application of increased homestead amount); Macumber v. Shafer, 637 P.2d 645 (Wash. 1981); *In re* Elliott, 74 Wash. 2d 600, 446 P.2d 347 (Wash. 1968); Cowart v. Pan Am. Bank, 2000 Wash. App. LEXIS 2132 (Wash. Ct. App. Nov. 3, 2000).

WEST VIRGINIA: ACF Industries, Inc. v. Credithrift of Am., Inc., 312 S.E.2d 746 (W. Va. 1983).

WISCONSIN: In re Bogue, 240 B.R. 742 (Bankr. E.D. Wis. 1999); Schwanz v. Teper, 66 Wis. 2d 157, 223 N.W.2d 896 (Wis. 1974).

WYOMING: In re Vigil, 2003 WL 22024830 (10th Cir. Aug. 26, 2003); *In re* Kwiecinski, 245 B.R. 672 (B.A.P. 10th Cir. 2000); *In re* Winters, 251 B.R. 441 (table), 2000 WL 914181 (B.A.P. 10th Cir. June 26, 2000); *In re* Bechtoldt, 210 B.R. 599 (B.A.P. 10th Cir. 1997).

43 *See, e.g., In re* Perry, 357 B.R. 175 (B.A.P. 1st Cir. 2006) (noting important public policy of protecting home and allowing exemption when it was impossible to tell whether homestead declaration or bankruptcy petition filed first); *In re* Kester, 339 B.R. 749 (B.A.P. 10th Cir. 2006) (Kansas law) (homesteads protected "for the benefit of society and of the family—to protect the family from destitution and society from the danger of her citizens becoming paupers"), *aff'd*, 493 F.3d 1208 (10th Cir. 2007); *In re* Kelley, 2012 WL 5878240 (C.D. Cal. Nov. 20, 2012) ("[T]he purpose of the homestead law is not . . . to protect creditors, but protects the home against creditors . . . preserving the home for the family . . . this strong public policy requires courts to adopt a liberal construction"); *In re* McCollum, 363 B.R. 789 (E.D. La. 2007); United States v. Neff, 2007 WL 776532 (D.N.D. Mar. 12, 2007) (history of North Dakota homestead law; noting important public policy served by homestead; ambiguous language in loan documents does not waive homestead exemption); Fix v. First State Bank of Roscoe, 359 B.R. 755 (D.S.D. 2007) (strong public policy in favor of South Dakota homesteads; waivers permitted but must be very clear; invalid here as against public policy); *In re* McDaniel, 2012 WL 174370 (Bankr. N.D. Ala. Jan. 20, 2012) (homestead exemption protects spouse and family as well as declarant, and they should not be punished for his wrongdoing); *In re* Ritter, 2009 WL 1024656 (Bankr. E.D. Tex. Mar. 26, 2009) (Texas homestead law "can neutralize the ignorance and improvidence of affected borrowers . . . penalize the complicity of colluding lenders . . . no means of evasion—no means of execution—are free from scrutiny or exempt from reversal"); *In re* Walsh, 359 B.R. 389 (Bankr. D. Mass. 2007) (Massachusetts homestead declaration protects entire family, not just individual who files); *In re* Hughes, 306 B.R. 683, 686 (Bankr. M.D. Ala. 2004) (rule of liberal construction applies especially to laws protecting homestead); First Ala. Bank v. Renfro, 452 So. 2d 464 (Ala. 1984); Wells Fargo Fin. Leasing, Inc. v. D & M Cabinets, 99 Cal. Rptr. 3d 97 (Cal. Ct. App. 2009); Fleet v. Zwick, 994 P.2d 480 (Colo. App. 1999) ("it has long been the policy of this state to preserve the home for the family, even at the sacrifice of just demands"); Havoco of Am., Ltd. v. Hill, 790 So. 2d 1018 (Fla. 2001); Citimortgage, Inc. v. Danielson, 771 N.W.2d 653 (table) (Iowa Ct. App. 2009); *In re* Bly, 456 N.W.2d 195 (Iowa 1990) (homestead exemption "not for the benefit of the husband or wife alone, but for the family of which they are a part"; exemption protected against drug forfeiture); Dwyer v. Cempellin, 673 N.E.2d 863 (Mass. 1996) ("the value of securing to householders a home for the family regardless of the householder's financial condition"); Deyeso v. Cavadi, 66 A.3d 1236 (N.H. 2013) (New Hampshire homestead statute "expresses the legislature's intent to place the security of families in their homes before the interests of unsecured creditors"); *In re* Martin, 875 P.2d 417 (Okla. 1994) ("the beneficent spirit of protecting the family home"); Pierce v. Wash. Mut. Bank, 226 S.W.3d 711 (Tex. App. 2007) (history of homestead laws). *See also* Ash-Will Farms, L.C. v. Leachman Cattle Co., 2006 WL 3827453 (D. Mont. Dec. 27, 2006) (refusing on equitable grounds to order marshalling, which would have required government creditor to enforce debt against homestead and leave non-exempt property for other creditors; causing farmers to lose their homestead would be "an injustice"); *In re* Gardner, 2013 WL 3804594 (Bankr. D. Colo. June 19, 2013) (special position of homesteads).

44 *In re* Brockhouse, 220 B.R. 623 (Bankr. C.D. Ill. 1998).

45 *In re* Hazelhurst, 228 B.R. 199 (Bankr. E.D. Tenn. 1998).

46 *In re* Perry, 357 B.R. 175 (B.A.P. 1st Cir. 2006) (allowing exemption when it was impossible to tell whether homestead declaration or bankruptcy petition filed first, because clerks' time stamps indicated same minute); *In re* Kimble, 344 B.R. 546 (Bankr. S.D. Ohio 2006) (liberally construing Ohio exemption of "an interest" to include future interest, here a remainder interest); *In re* Brockhouse, 220 B.R. 623 (Bankr. C.D. Ill. 1998); *In re* Snyder, 149 P.3d 26 (Mont. 2006) (liberally construing homestead to include sale proceeds, even if no homestead declaration filed before sale; noting inconsistency in statutes that exempt proceeds but require that declaration include statement that owner resides on property).

47 *See, e.g.*, Quality Carpets v. Carter, 587 A.2d 254 (N.H. 1991); Keystone Sav. Ass'n v. Kitsock, 633 A.2d 165 (Pa. Super. Ct. 1993) (court in which execution proceedings are pending has inherent right to stay proceedings when it is necessary to protect the rights of the parties). *See also* Gerber v. Holcomb, 2006 WL 3019731 (Tenn. Ct. App. Oct. 25, 2006) (courts have authority to order wage garnishment in amount lower than statutory maximum). *See generally* § 12.4.3.3, *infra*.

quashing the garnishment.[48] Exceptions to exemption laws are narrowly construed.[49]

12.2.3 Exempt Property Purchased with Non-Exempt Funds or Proceeds of Wrongdoing

Even though exemption laws are entitled to a liberal construction, exemptions may not be construed to aid wrongdoing.[50] Thus, property purchased or improved with the proceeds of wrongdoing is generally non-exempt, and some courts enable a creditor to execute on the property by recognizing an equitable lien in favor of the creditor, at least up to the amount of the traceable funds.[51] For example, courts hold a home non-exempt to the extent it was purchased or a mortgage

48 Patino v. El Rey del Chivito Corp., 2013 WL 6670428 (S.D. Fla. Dec. 18, 2013) (quashing garnishment because bank's answer disclosed joint account and creditor failed to show service on co-owner; describing strict notice requirements for bank account garnishment); Crop Productions Servs., Inc. v. Baxter, 2010 WL 5621323 (N.D. Fla. Dec. 16, 2010) (dissolving writ of garnishment for failure to comply with Florida requirement for sworn statement to support creditor's opposition to defendant's claim of exemption), *adopted by* 2011 WL 194618 (N.D. Fla. Jan. 18, 2011); Dinh v. Motorcars of Distinction, Inc., 2009 WL 3096459 (S.D. Fla. Sept. 23, 2009) (creditor who misses short deadline for response to debtor's head of household wage exemption claim is deemed to have admitted facts in claim; dissolving garnishment and barring new filing); Great Am. Ins. Co. v. Gen. Contractors & Constr. Mgmt., Inc., 2008 WL 5056526 (S.D. Fla. Nov. 21, 2008) (dissolving writs because creditor's response to claims of exemption was untimely and unsworn); Moory v. Quadras, Inc., 970 S.W.2d 275 (Ark. 1998) (garnishment is a purely statutory remedy, and the statute must be strictly construed; writ of garnishment may be issued only by the county court which rendered the judgment); *In re* Marriage of Hankins, 2008 WL 4615967 (Cal. Ct. App. Oct. 20, 2008) (unpublished) (if creditor failed to comply with statutory procedure for contesting hardship exemption, garnished funds must be returned to debtor; remanding to determine whether creditor had good cause for missed deadline); Pineiro v. Am. Express Card Serv. Co., 105 So. 3d 614 (Fla. Dist. Ct. App. 2013) (garnishment statute strictly construed; postjudgment garnishment cannot be for amounts such as postjudgment attorney fees that have not been incorporated into a final judgment); Caproc Third Ave., L.L.C. v. Donisi Ins. Inc., 67 So. 3d 312 (Fla. Dist. Ct. App. 2011) (dissolution of writ of garnishment required; attorney's hearsay affidavit insufficient because statute requires affidavit of person who sued out the writ); Daluisio v. Daluisio, 894 N.E.2d 1112 (Ind. Ct. App. 2008) (unpublished) (income withholding order, arising from California judgment, failed to comply with California law); Requena v. Salomon, Smith, Barney, Inc., 2002 WL 356696 (Tex. App. Mar. 7, 2002) (writ of garnishment properly dissolved when service on debtor not made "as soon as practicable" after service on garnishee; statutory requirements must be strictly complied with); Watkins v. Peterson Enters., 973 P.2d 1037 (Wash. 1999) (garnishment is a harsh remedy and creditor must strictly follow statutory procedure); Bartel v. Zucktriegal, 47 P.3d 581 (Wash. Ct. App. 2002); Layne v. West Virginia Child Support Enforcement Div., 518 S.E.2d 357 (W. Va. 1998) (garnishment of disability benefits to collect child support arrearage allowed only if exact statutory procedure is followed). *But see* ML Manager, L.L.C. v. Jensen, 842 N.W.2d 566 (Neb. 2014) (although garnishment statutes are in derogation of the common law, they are to be interpreted, like other parts of the code of civil procedure, using ordinary rules of statutory construction; overruling line of cases calling for strict construction). *But cf.* De la Cerda Cabrera v. Chase Manhattan Bank, U.S.A., N.A., 2013 WL 4634843 (Tex. App. Aug. 27, 2013) (garnishment judgment not void if debtor had actual notice of proceeding; technical defects in service do not void judgment if they do not deprive a party of meaningful opportunity to appear and answer).

49 *In re* Skinner, 2001 WL 1699660 (Bankr. M.D.N.C. Aug. 7, 2001); Havoco of Am., Ltd. v. Hill, 790 So. 2d 1018, 1021 (Fla. 2001); Carrel v. Carrel, 791 S.W.2d 831 (Mo. Ct. App. 1990) (exceptions to maximum garnishment restrictions must be narrowly construed).

50 *In re* Pickard, 2012 WL 4919791 (Bankr. N.D. Iowa Oct. 15, 2012) (debtors sold old home and purchased new without paying off mortgage on old home; allowing bank an equitable lien on new homestead); *In re* Brown, 427 B.R. 715 (D. Minn. 2010) (exemptions not "a safe harbor for ill-gotten gains"; here, traceable proceeds of fraud used to purchase homestead and IRA); Coppler & Mannick v. Wakeland, 117 P.3d 914 (N.M. 2005) (owner's tortious conduct—tearing out fixtures and vandalizing home when faced with imminent foreclosure—constituted "extraordinary circumstances" sufficient to warrant equitable lien on homestead).

51 Janvey v. Alguire, 2013 WL 2451738 (N.D. Tex. Jan. 22, 2013) (denying exemption for IRA funded with proceeds of Ponzi scheme; "net winners" had no right to possess the funds); *In re* Huie, 2007 WL 2317152 (Bankr. E.D. Tex. Aug. 8, 2007) (homestead purchased with fraudulently obtained funds non-exempt up to the amount of those funds); *In re* Hecker, 316 B.R. 375 (Bankr. S.D. Fla. 2004), *aff'd*, 264 Fed. Appx. 786 (11th Cir. 2008); *In re* Linsey, 296 B.R. 582 (Bankr. D. Mass. 2003) (lien on homestead for amount of traceable stolen funds spent on improvements); Randazzo v. Randazzo, 980 So. 2d 1210 (Fla. Dist. Ct. App. 2008) (ex-wife's misconduct sufficiently egregious to support lien on homestead; after agreeing to make court-ordered payment out of sales proceeds of house, she filed bankruptcy, sold the house while divorce action was stayed, and invested the proceeds in Florida homestead); Havoco of Am., Ltd. v. Hill, 790 So. 2d 1018 (Fla. 2001) (expressing willingness to impose equitable lien when proceeds of fraud are invested in homestead, but not otherwise); Hirchert Family Trust v. Hirchert, 65 So. 3d 548 (Fla. Dist. Ct. App. 2011) (breach of fiduciary duty sufficient to trigger fraud exception to Florida homestead); Lackey v. Lackey, 691 So. 2d 990 (Miss. 1997) (exemption for insurance proceeds would not protect beneficiaries of policy purchased with funds stolen by fiduciary); Casterline v. Roberts, 284 P.3d 743 (Wash. Ct. App. 2012) (equitable lien may be placed on home purchased with proceeds of fraud, here, a trustee's misuse of trust property to benefit self). *See also In re* Pickard, 2012 WL 4919791 (Bankr. N.D. Iowa Oct. 15, 2012) (allowing equitable mortgage on new homestead purchased with proceeds of former homestead when debtors contrived to sell former homestead without paying off the mortgage); *In re* Keck, 363 B.R. 193 (Bankr. D. Kan. 2007) (allowing equitable lien on homestead when debtor's large credit card cash advances could be traced to homestead); Sell v. Sell, 949 So. 2d 1108 (Fla. Dist. Ct. App. 2007) (ex-husband's conduct in evading court orders, for which he was jailed for contempt, sufficiently reprehensible to support equitable lien on homestead). *Cf. In re* Mazon, 368 B.R. 906 (Bankr. M.D. Fla. 2007) (debtors concealed and dissipated non-exempt property; trustee could surcharge exempt retirement accounts but not homestead, when dissipated property could not be traced to homestead). *But see* Bank of Nashville v. Chipman, 201 WL 3433012 (Tenn. Ct. App. Aug. 5, 2011) (Tennessee exemption for retirement funds bars imposition of constructive trust on IRA even though proceeds of fraud contributed to account). *But cf. In re* Deerey, 371 B.R. 525 (Bankr. M.D. Fla. 2007) (purchase of homestead with illegally obtained funds not sufficient to support equitable lien; must be proceeds of fraud or egregious conduct, narrowly defined); Partridge v. Partridge, 790 So. 2d 1280 (Fla. Dist. Ct. App. 2001) (ex-husband's failure to sell homestead to pay alimony not the sort of conduct that justifies foreclosure of equitable lien); Grygorwicz v. Trujillo, 203 P.3d 865 (N.M. 2009) (homestead exemption available in tort action, even if judgment is punitive; equitable lien available only if misconduct involves the homestead itself).

on it paid down with the proceeds of a Ponzi scheme, embezzlement, or other fraud.[52] The exemption may be denied even as to a co-owner who is innocent of the wrongdoing by which the proceeds were obtained.[53] The creditor has the burden of proving that the proceeds were so obtained and that they can be traced.[54]

On the other hand, when exempt property was purchased with non-exempt but legitimately obtained funds, the usual rule is that the property is exempt unless the transaction qualifies as a fraudulent transfer under state law.[55] Conversion of

52 *In re* Fin. Federated Title & Trust, Inc., 347 F.3d 880 (11th Cir. 2003) (Florida law) (home purchased with traceable proceeds of Ponzi scheme not exempt); Crawford v. Silette, 608 F.3d 275 (5th Cir. June 3, 2010); *In re* Chew, 496 F.3d 11 (1st Cir. 2007) (Massachusetts law) (exempt property, purchased in part with proceeds of fraud or breach of fiduciary duty, is non-exempt up to amount of traceable proceeds of wrongdoing); *In re* Brown, 427 B.R. 715 (D. Minn. 2010) (exemptions not "a safe harbor for ill-gotten gains"; here, traceable proceeds of fraud used to purchase homestead and IRA); C & M Inv. Group, Ltd. v. Campbell, 2010 WL 1459735 (M.D. Fla. Apr. 12, 2010) (allegation that proceeds of fraud were given to wife, who used them to purchase homestead, sufficient to trigger fraud exception to Florida homestead); *In re* Gamble-Ledbetter, 419 B.R. 682 (Bankr. E.D. Tex. 2009) (allowing judicial lien on homestead for the amount of embezzled funds used to pay down mortgage); *In re* Beveridge, 416 B.R. 552 (Bankr. N.D. Tex. 2009) (constructive trust when down payment on homestead made with proceeds of fraud; tracing proceeds using lowest intermediate balance method); *In re* Mazon, 387 B.R. 641 (Bankr. M.D. Fla. 2008) (proceeds of fraud sufficiently traced into purchase of condominium), *rev'd in part on other grounds*, 395 B.R. 742 (M.D. Fla. 2008); Synod of S. Atl. Presbyterian Church v. Magpusao (*In re* Magpusao), 265 B.R. 492 (Bankr. M.D. Fla. 2001) (allowing equitable lien on home bought with funds stolen by wife when husband knowingly benefited from her fraud); Maki v. Chong, 75 P.3d 376 (Nev. 2003) (home purchased with traceable proceeds of fraud subject to equitable lien for benefit of victim); *In re* Estate of Byrom, 2013 WL 3967432 (Tex. App. July 32, 2013) (homestead exemption does not protect funds misappropriated by a fiduciary; affirming grant of constructive trust on homestead); Paulman v. Pemberton (*In re* Paulman), 633 N.W.2d 715 (Wis. Ct. App. 2001) (homestead exemption does not protect home purchased with funds converted from judgment creditor). *But cf.* *In re* Morgan, 2010 WL 4922581 (Bankr. E.D. Tenn. Nov. 29, 2010) (allowing debtor to exempt home purchased by her child's father with proceeds of massive Ponzi scheme; although exemption may not be good against certain creditors—that is, the victims—it is good against creditors in general); *In re* Laing, 329 B.R. 761 (Bankr. M.D. Fla. 2005) (denying equitable lien when debtor was, at most, a "net recipient" and not an "active participant" in Ponzi scheme); *In re* McClung, 327 B.R. 690 (Bankr. M.D. Fla. 2005) (repairs to homestead with funds removed, without creditor permission, from account pledged as collateral did not constitute fraudulent or egregious conduct sufficient to justify lien on homestead).

53 Crawford v. Silette, 608 F.3d 275 (5th Cir. 2010) (Texas law; imposing equitable lien on home of Ponzi-schemer's girlfriend, who did not know that gift used to pay down mortgage was proceeds of scheme); *In re* Thiel, 275 B.R. 633 (Bankr. M.D. Fla. 2001) ("fraudulent or egregious act" shown when mortgage paid down with proceeds of debtor-husband's fraud; equitable lien on homestead property could be imposed even if joint-owner wife was innocent); Hirchert Family Trust v. Hirchert, 65 So. 3d 548 (Fla. Dist. Ct. App. June 17, 2011) (proceeds of breach of fiduciary duty invested in homestead; equitable lien trumps innocent spouse's homestead right in order to prevent unjust enrichment). *But see* Williams v. Aloisi, 271 B.R. 676 (M.D. Fla. 2002) (home purchased with proceeds of sale of condominium may be protected if ex-wife did not know that funds ex-husband used to pay off condominium mortgage were derived from theft).

54 *EXEMPT: In re* Boykin, 465 B.R. 665 (Bankr S.D. Ala. 2012) (granting exemption for insurance policy when creditor failed to show how much, if any, of proceeds of husband's fraud were used to purchase it); *In re* Levasseur, 482 B.R. 15 (Bankr. D. Mass. 2012) (creditor failed to show that home was purchased or mortgage paid down with proceeds of fraud); *In re* Landry, 2009 WL 5110670 (Bankr. D. Mass. Dec. 16, 2009) (burden on creditor to show home purchased with proceeds of wrongdoing; not shown here when debtor bought house with funds owned before the date of the fraud); *In re* Romano, 353 B.R. 738 (Bankr. D. Mass. 2006) (creditor failed to prove homestead purchased with proceeds of embezzlement; constructive trust denied); Kyle v. Tuttle, 2012 WL 6097232 (Minn. Ct. App. Dec. 10, 2012) (traceability must be shown by clear and convincing evidence; burden not carried here, issue whether legitimate funds were deposited in account along with fraud proceeds). *But cf.* Henry v. Rizzolo, 2012 WL 4092604 (D. Nev. Sept. 17, 2012) (tracing need not be "dollar for dollar," creditor need only identify "the relevant pathways"; denying exemption for annuities when fraudulently transferred funds were placed in account from which funds were drawn to buy the annuities, and defendant did not show what other funds were in account).

55 *In re* Addison, 540 F.3d 805 (8th Cir. 2008) (applying Minn. Stat. § 513.44(b); fraud not shown in pay down of mortgage or purchase of individual retirement accounts, so they are exempt); *In re* Chauncey, 454 F.3d 1292 (11th Cir. 2006) (Florida law) (refusing to impose equitable lien on homestead when debtor, after large judgment entered against her, used non-exempt personal injury settlement to pay down mortgage on homestead); Shaia v. Meyer (*In re* Meyer), 244 F.3d 352 (4th Cir. 2001) (Virginia law) (debtor-husband's use of non-exempt funds, an inheritance, to pay off mortgages on home owned with non-debtor wife in tenancy by entireties not fraudulent transfer; home was exempt); *In re* Bradley, 294 B.R. 64 (B.A.P. 8th Cir. 2003) (Arkansas law) (home purchased during period of financial distress with proceeds of fair, arms-length sale of non-exempt property was exempt); *In re* Danduran, 438 B.R. 658 (B.A.P. 8th Cir. 2010) (North Dakota law), *aff'd*, 657 F.3d 749 (8th Cir. 2011); *In re* Hodes, 287 B.R. 561 (D. Kan. 2002) (investing proceeds of non-exempt assets in improvements to homestead did not defeat exemption of homestead or of funds prepaid to builder); *In re* Halinga, 2013 WL 6191952 (Bankr. D. Idaho Nov. 27, 2013) (close call, but intent to hinder creditors not shown; couple whose business was failing paid off home mortgage with proceeds of sale of non-exempt liquor license; no evidence that debtors knew about exemption, also wife testified that she feared husband would waste license proceeds in effort to save business); *In re* Love-Baker, 2013 WL 6898920 (Bankr. S.D. Tex. Dec, 31, 2013) (large payment on mortgage, using proceeds of non-exempt stock, at time when debtor faced large judgment, not fraudulent; legitimate business reasons shown when debtor had been advised that stock market was likely to become unstable during government shutdown); *In re* Thomas, 477 B.R. 778 (Bankr. D. Idaho 2012) (use of non-exempt cash value of insurance policy to purchase retirement accounts did not exceed the limits of proper exemption planning; more than timing must be shown); *In re* Koehler, 2012 WL 719744 (Bankr. E.D.N.C. Mar. 5, 2012) (debtors caused furniture from unprofitable rental properties to be auctioned, and used proceeds to buy retirement funds; fraudulent intent not shown when debtors were in their fifties, rental properties had been bought as an investment for retirement, and sale was carried out openly, by impartial third party, for full value); *In re* Woller, 483 B.R. 886 (Bankr. W.D. Wis. 2012) (exemption planning that involves no concealment or subterfuge is permissible); *In re* Hall, 464 B.R. 896 (Bankr. D. Idaho 2012) (applying Idaho fraudulent transfer criteria to conclude that purchase of exempt annuity not an attempt to hinder creditors); *In re* Cook, 460 B.R. 911 (Bankr. N.D. Fla. 2011) (use of non-exempt tax refund to purchase home not fraud on creditors because "reasonable in light of the circumstances"; new home was substantially less expensive than home debtors had been forced to sell, and

debtors needed a "stable, permanent place to live" which is the purpose of the homestead exemption); *In re* Bronk, 444 B.R. 902 (Bankr. W.D. Wis. 2011) (intent to hinder not shown when widower of modest means, faced with overwhelming bills for wife's last illness, purchased exempt annuity with non-exempt funds); *In re* Beaudin, 2010 WL 3748735 (Bankr. D. Colo. Sept. 21, 2010) (purchase of IRA with tax refund, debtor's only asset, not fraudulent when amount was modest and transfer was not concealed); *In re* Champalanne, 425 B.R. 707 (Bankr. S.D. Fla. 2010) (use of non-exempt funds to purchase Florida homestead not sufficient to justify equitable lien); *In* re Cassell, 443 B.R. 200 (Bankr. N.D. Ga. 2010) (Georgia law) (conversion of non-exempt to exempt property not fraudulent in absence of intent to hinder creditors; allowing exemption for annuity purchased by sixty-five-year-old debtor, whose irregular work history prevented her from receiving employer pension); *In re* Channon, 424 B.R. 895 (Bankr. D. N.M. 2010) (thirty-two-year-old debtor's use of non-exempt funds to purchase IRA not fraudulent; transfers made openly, in only tax-qualified amounts, and saving for retirement was prudent); *In re* Whatley, 2010 WL 1379690 (Bankr. W.D. Tex. Mar. 31, 2010) (sale on eve of bankruptcy of investment account that was declining in value, and use of proceeds to pay down mortgage, make needed home repairs, and assist financially distressed daughter not fraudulent); *In re* Booth, 417 B.R. 820 (Bankr. M.D. Fla. 2009) (intent to hinder creditors not shown when debtor who needed to move out of home she could no longer afford purchased new home using non-exempt funds); *In re* Montanaro, 398 B.R. 688 (Bankr. W.D. Mo 2008) (allowing exemption to debtor who sold mutual funds and purchased individual retirement account when amount involved was modest and extrinsic evidence of fraud not present); *In re* Hawkins, 377 B.R. 761, 767 (Bankr. S.D. Fla. 2007) (no grounds for equitable lien if debtor merely borrowed money, used it to buy home, and failed to repay it); *In re* Gosman, 362 B.R. 549 (Bankr. S.D. Fla. 2007) (encumbering homestead without creditor's permission, although breach of contract, not "fraud or egregious conduct" sufficient to justify lien on homestead); *In re* Peres, 2007 WL 2766776 (Bankr. N.D. Tex. Sept. 18, 2007) (conversion of non-exempt property to exempt property not fraudulent absent actual intent to defraud creditors); *In re* Agnew, 355 B.R. 276 (Bankr. D. Kan. 2006) (trustee failed to show fraudulent transfer; land swap involving family farmland was part of elderly mother's estate planning); *In re* Moreno, 352 B.R. 455 (Bankr. N.D. Ill. 2006) (transfer to tenancy by entireties not fraudulent; move to "gang free" neighborhood was legitimate family purpose); *In re* Tolson, 338 B.R. 359 (Bankr. C.D. Ill. 2005) (transfer of property to tenancy by entireties not fraudulent if legitimate family purpose shown, here, estate planning); *In re* Vangen, 334 B.R. 241 (Bankr. W.D. Wis. 2005) (Wisconsin law) (retirement-related annuities purchased with non-exempt funds considered exempt given no extrinsic evidence of fraud); *In re* McGinnis, 306 B.R. 279 (Bankr. W.D. Mo. 2004) (debtors with "some legitimate reasons" for moving to Kansas could claim exemption in house purchased with sales proceeds of Missouri home and various non-exempt assets, despite evidence of intent to hinder creditors); *In re* Burghart, 2004 WL 2026805 (Bankr. D. Kan. Jan. 15, 2004) (investing non-exempt funds in exempt asset not fraud on creditor unless creditor has constructive trust on specific non-exempt asset; not fraudulent transfer to use year-end bonus to pay down debt on family truck); *In re* Rodriguez, 282 B.R. 194 (Bankr. N.D. Tex. 2002) (not fraud within meaning of exception to Texas homestead exemption when transfers—from mortgagor to ex-wife to debtor—arguably violated due on sale clause of mortgage); *In re* McCabe, 280 B.R. 841 (Bankr. N.D. Iowa 2002) (conversion of non-exempt to exempt property not per se fraudulent, even if done to put property beyond reach of creditors); *In re* Lowery, 262 B.R. 875 (Bankr. M.D. Fla. 2001) (addition of parcels to their citrus farm and transfer of parcels from trust to joint tenancy by financially distressed married couple were not fraudulent); *In re* Simms, 243 B.R. 156 (Bankr. S.D. Fla. 2000) (use of non-exempt proceeds of sale of homestead to purchase exempt annuity not fraudulent when debtors bought it because of advancing age and ill health, did not conceal the transaction, and though in debt were not subject to collection pressure); *In re* Young, 235 B.R. 666 (Bankr. M.D. Fla. 1999) (sale of non-exempt property in Illinois and purchase of Florida homestead not sufficient to show fraud); Havoco of Am., Ltd. v. Hill, 790 So. 2d 1018 (Fla. 2001) (homestead purchased to protect assets from creditors is exempt); Conseco Servs. L.L.C. v. Cuneo, 904 So. 2d 438 (Fla. Dist. Ct. App. 2005) (purchase of homestead with non-exempt funds at time when litigation imminent not sufficient to justify lien on homestead); Robles v. Robles, 860 So. 2d 1014 (Fla. Dist. Ct. App. 2003) (equitable lien on homestead for delinquent alimony improper when failure of husband's law practice impaired ability to pay and there was no showing of affirmative fraudulent or reprehensible conduct); Smith v. Smith, 761 So. 2d 370 (Fla. Dist. Ct. App. 2000) (homestead could not be sold to foreclose lien awarded to ex-wife to compensate for injuries inflicted by abusive husband, because homestead was not purchased with proceeds of fraud, nor was purchase part of financial manipulations to avoid support obligation); Russell v. Black, 2000 Mass. Super. LEXIS 350 (Mass. Super. Ct. July 28, 2000) (filing a declaration of homestead at time when homeowner is threatened with lawsuit not a fraudulent transfer); Deyeso v. Cavadi, 66 A.3d 1236 (N.H. 2013) (allowing exemption for homestead purchased with funds provided by third-party who was trying to avoid judgment debt; homestead is exempt so long as neither homeowner nor third party engaged in fraud or illegality to obtain the funds). *See also* Cadle Co. v. Newhouse, 20 Fed. Appx. 69 (2d Cir. 2001) (transfer of husband's earnings to non-debtor wife was fraudulent, but New York earnings exemption continued to protect them, if needed for reasonable living expenses); *In re* Ventura, 2011 WL 1979864 (Bankr. E.D.N.Y. May 20, 2011) (adding wife's name to title of car previously titled in husband alone was permissible exemption planning, not fraudulent transfer); *In re* Williams, 2011 WL 883922 (Bankr. N.D. Ill. Mar. 11, 2011) (intent to hinder not shown; property transferred into tenancy by entireties at time when debtor was in default on business debt but no showing of misrepresentation, concealment, purchase of exempt property on credit, or transfer that resulted in insolvency).

NON-EXEMPT: In re Eilbert, 162 F.3d 523 (8th Cir. 1998) (when elderly widow purchased annuity with a single payment consisting of almost the entire proceeds of her husband's estate, at a time when a substantial personal injury suit was pending against estate, and chose a "retirement date" two months after her payment, this was not exempt under Iowa law as a "pension, annuity or similar plan" making payments "on account of age" because widow had unfettered discretion as to when payments would begin); *In re* Kelley, 2007 WL 2492732 (M.D. Fla. Aug. 30, 2007) (fraudulent transfer shown when debtor repaid sum borrowed against exempt life insurance when bankruptcy imminent and debtor insolvent); *In re* Wreyford, 505 B.R. 47 (Bankr. D. N.M. 2014) (conversion of non-exempt to exempt property not, without more, sufficient to show fraud, but transactions that placed all debtors' property beyond reach of creditors after they had been sued were fraudulent enough to result in loss of exemption for IRAs and denial of bankruptcy discharge); *In re* Lafferty, 469 B.R. 235 (Bankr. D.S.C. 2012) (homestead exemption lost because of unclean hands; at time when large judgment was imminent, divorcing couple sold their interests in home to their respective lovers for no consideration and later took it back); *In re* Stanton, 457 B.R. 80 (Bankr. D. Nev. 2011) (reducing homestead by amount of fraudulent transfer; just before a large judgment was awarded against debtor, she gave non-exempt funds to her son, with the understanding that he would pay down her mortgage); *In re* Osejo, 447 B.R. 352 (Bankr. S.D. Fla. 2011) (two months before filing bankruptcy, debtor sold non-exempt stock and bought and improved a home; giving heavy weight to debtor's non-disclosure of various transactions); *In re* Asumaa, 2010 WL 1379790 (Bankr. M.D. Fla. Mar. 31, 2010) (intent to hinder creditors shown; purchase of IRA with non-exempt funds ten days before bankruptcy); *In re* Sissom, 366 B.R. 677 (Bankr. S.D. Tex. 2007) (when "badges of fraud" present, homestead non-exempt up to amount of proceeds of sale of non-exempt stock used to purchase homestead); *In re* Orgeron, property from one exempt form to another is almost never a fraudulent transfer, however.[56]

Some exemption statutes that deal with specific types of assets such as annuities provide that they do not protect that asset to the extent that it was created by a transfer of other property in fraud of creditors.[57] In addition, many states have a general fraudulent transfer statute. However, Florida's fraudulent transfer statute does not override the homestead exemption that is found in the state constitution,[58] and the Texas fraudulent transfer statute applies only to personal property.[59]

In jurisdictions in which the homestead exemption is found in the state constitution, homesteads may be treated more favorably than other property in analyzing possibly fraudulent transfers.[60] Courts may apply estoppel or similar theories to deny an exemption if the debtor obtained the

---

2006 WL 335438 (Bankr. W.D. Mo. Feb. 2, 2006) (individual retirement account is exempt except for contributions made in contemplation of bankruptcy); *In re* Ziegler, 239 B.R. 375 (Bankr. C.D. Ill. 1999) ("sale" of homestead to close relative, while debtors continued to live there and pay mortgage, was fraudulent); *In re* Sholdan, 218 B.R. 475 (Bankr. D. Minn. 1998) (finding fraudulent transfer under Minnesota law when ninety-year-old in fragile health and faced with large personal injury judgment quietly invested life savings in a house, moved into it, and immediately filed for bankruptcy just before dying), *aff'd*, 217 F.3d 1006 (8th Cir. 2000); Gilchinsky v. Nat'l Westminster Bank, 732 A.2d 482 (N.J. 1999) (rollover of funds from New York employer's ERISA plan to New Jersey individual retirement account was fraudulent, and individual retirement account was non-exempt, when moving funds to New Jersey would help debtor avoid collection of New York judgment for funds embezzled from employer); Huntington Nat'l Bank v. Winter, 2011 WL 1378727 (Ohio Ct. App. Apr. 13, 2011) (debtor, who was in serious financial trouble, used large amount of non-exempt funds to pay premiums on existing life insurance policies; policies not exempt). *See also* Soza v. Hill (*In re* Soza), 542 F.3d 1060 (5th Cir. 2008) (Texas law) (even without intent to defraud, transfer of an inheritance into an annuity on eve of bankruptcy as way of preventing bankruptcy court from adjudicating its ownership is fraudulent). *Cf. In re* Jennings, 533 F.3d 1333 (11th Cir. 2008) (fraudulent transfer shown under bankruptcy law when debtor facing large judgment paid large sum to builder who was working on homestead; debtor's testimony about transaction "lacked candor").

56 Evans v. Wolinsky, 347 B.R. 9 (D. Vt. 2006) (transfer of entireties property to wife individually, at time when no joint debts, not fraudulent; no harm to creditors when property was already exempt before transfer); *In re* Arends, 506 B.R. 516 (Bankr. N.D. Iowa 2013) (debtors cashed in exempt insurance policy, deposited check in bank account until it cleared, and wired funds to mortgage company to pay down mortgage on exempt homestead; short period in non-exempt bank account did not destroy exemption, when this was only practical way to transfer funds from one exempt form to another); *In re* Ellis, 454 B.R. 404 (Bankr. S.D. Tex. 2011) (exempt annuity purchased with rollover of exempt IRA); *In re* Matthews, 360 B.R. 732 (Bankr. M.D. Fla. 2007) (transfer from one form of exempt property to another not fraudulent); *In re* Dismore, 2005 WL 419709 (Bankr. M.D. Fla. Jan. 4, 2005) (transfer of asset from exempt tenancy by entireties status into name of non-debtor spouse is not fraudulent transfer); Alamanza v. Salas, 2014 WL 554807 (Tex. App. Feb. 22, 2014) (transfer of homestead can never be fraudulent transfer; key issue is whether property was homestead at time of transfer); Martinek Grain and Bins, Inc. v. Bulldog Farms, Inc., 366 S.W.3d 800 (Tex. App. 2012) (transfer of exempt homestead to trust could not be fraudulent); Goebel v. Brandley, 174 S.W.3d 359 (Tex. App. 2005) (purchase of savings bonds for children by payroll deduction was transfer of exempt property, in this case unpaid wages, which could not be fraudulent transfer). *But see In re* Pringle, 495 B.R. 447 (B.A.P. 9th Cir. 2013) (Idaho law) (rejecting "no harm no foul" rule; transfer of property, here a homestead, may be fraudulent even if the property, if retained by the debtor, would be exempt); *In re* Panepinto, 487 B.R. 370 (Bankr. W.D.N.Y. 2013) (homestead exemption lost by transfer of half-interest to wife; under New York's Uniform Fraudulent Conveyance Act, transfer from one exempt form to another can be fraudulent; distinguishing cases from states that have enacted the more recent Uniform Fraudulent Transfer Act). *See generally* National Consumer Law Center, Consumer Bankruptcy Law and Practice § 10.2.3.4.3 (10th ed. 2012), *updated at* www.nclc.org/library (bankruptcy law restrictions when debtor converted non-exempt property into homestead with fraudulent intent).

57 *See, e.g.*, *In re* Duffin, 457 B.R. 820 (B.A.P. 10th Cir. 2011) (Utah insurance exemption makes exception for premiums paid within one year before "a creditor's levy or execution"; denying exemption for amount of premiums paid within one year before bankruptcy); Henry v. Rizzolo, 2012 WL 4092604 (D. Nev. Sept. 17, 2012) (Nevada annuity exemption has fraud exception; denying exemption for annuities purchased with check from account into which funds had been fraudulently transferred); *In re* Preuit, 2013 WL 2467976 (Bankr. D. Idaho June 7, 2013) (Iowa annuity exemption has fraud exception; fraud shown when debtors, facing large judgment for failed real estate deal, sold all their non-exempt properties and purchased a $120,000 annuity); *In re* Meredith, 2012 WL 1835516 (Bankr. C.D. Ill. May 18, 2012) (Illinois tenancy by entireties exemption has fraud exception; transfer was fraudulent when transfer into TBE occurred on same day large judgment was entered against husband); *In re* Hall, 464 B.R. 896 (Bankr. D. Idaho 2012) (Idaho annuity exemption excepts amounts paid with intent to hinder creditors; applying Idaho fraudulent transfer criteria to conclude that purchase of exempt annuity not shown to be attempt to hinder); *In re* Baker, 273 B.R. 892 (Bankr. D. Wyo. 2002) (Wyoming annuities exemption excepts transfers to hinder creditors; sale of non-exempt property and purchase of annuities on eve of bankruptcy, placing all assets beyond reach of creditors, went beyond "exemption planning" and was fraudulent); Tewhey v. Bodkins, 2012 WL 1390180 (Mass. Super. Ct. Jan. 6, 2012) (Massachusetts denies homestead exemption for judgment debts arising from "fraud, mistake, duress, undue influence or lack of capacity"; here for multiple-damages UDAP judgment); Leibman v. Grand, 981 S.W.2d 426 (Tex. App. 1998) (Texas exemption for annuities makes exception if premium payments were made in fraud of creditors; annuity not exempt when husband, who was grossly delinquent in various obligations resulting from divorce, sold non-exempt property and purchased annuity).

58 Havoco of Am., Ltd. v. Hill, 790 So. 2d 1018 (Fla. 2001) (homestead purchased to protect assets from creditors is exempt; fraudulent transfer laws do not apply; homestead is subject to sale only for the three reasons listed in the state constitution, that is, taxes, obligations to purchase or improve the homestead, and obligations for labor performed on the realty; expressing no opinion on whether a family support obligation is another exception).

59 Tex. Prop. Code Ann. § 42.004(a) (West). *See In re* Coates, 242 B.R. 901 (Bankr. N.D. Tex. 2000) (Texas fraudulent transfer statute applies only to personal property, so homestead purchased with proceeds of sale of non-exempt property in order to defeat creditors was exempt but motor vehicle was not).

60 *In re* Potter, 320 B.R. 753 (Bankr. M.D. Fla. 2005) (legislative acts may limit statutory exemptions but not constitutional exemptions); Torgelson v. Real Prop. Known As 17138 880th Ave., 749 N.W.2d 24 (Minn. 2008) (constitutional homestead exemption bars forfeiture for state offenses); State v. One 1965 Red Chevrolet Pickup, 37 P.3d 815 (Okla. 2001) (homestead exemption found in state constitution protects against state criminal law forfeiture, but statutory personal property exemption does not).

extension of credit by misrepresenting that the property in question was not exempt.[61]

In some circumstances, federal bankruptcy law may override state law that would protect exempt property that was purchased with non-exempt assets. Three provisions added to the Bankruptcy Code in 2005 limit debtors from taking full advantage of state exemptions: (1) section 522(o), which deals with prepetition conversion of non-exempt property with fraudulent intent; (2) section 522(p), which covers acquisitions of homestead property within 1215 days of the bankruptcy filing; and (3) section 522(q), which relates to the commission of certain bad acts by the debtor.[62]

12.2.4 Proceeds of Exempt Property

Many decisions hold that the proceeds of the sale of exempt property deposited in a bank account are exempt.[63] Commingling with non-exempt funds may present a problem of tracing for some courts, however.[64]

Some states also protect real and personal property that is purchased with exempt benefit payments.[65] This position is particularly common in the workers compensation context,[66] as

61 *See, e.g.*, Skelton v. Wash. Mut. Bank, 61 S.W.3d 56 (Tex. App. 2001) (widow had no claims on homestead, and mortgage not invalidated by lack of her signature, when couple agreed husband alone should apply for mortgage because of wife's bad credit record and husband falsely informed lender he was single); Denman v. Atlas Leasing, L.L.C., 285 S.W.3d 591 (Tex. App. 2009) (spousal signature requirement cannot be used to defraud creditor but, here, no evidence that wife who, while living apart from husband, bought house and contracted for repairs, deceived creditor about her marital status; mechanic's lien is void). *See also In re* Pich, 253 B.R. 562 (Bankr. D. Idaho 2000) (using building as residence in violation of zoning laws did not in itself preclude homestead exemption, but debtor was estopped by his rezoning application, which was an implicit representation that he would not live there); James v. Thaggard, 795 So. 2d 738 (Ala. Civ. App. 2001) (denying homestead exemption on grounds of equity and good conscience when borrower falsely represented he was unmarried but then defended foreclosure on grounds that wife had not signed mortgage).

62 *See* § 12.7.5.1–12.7.5.3, *infra*.

63 *In re* White, 2013 WL 1601667 (Bankr. D. Neb. Apr. 15, 2013) (fire insurance proceeds of destroyed homestead exempt in bank account); *In re* Elliot, 448 B.R. 843 (Bankr. D. Colo. 2011) (exempting bank account containing exempt proceeds of sale of homestead); *In re* Castro, 2006 WL 4005571 (Bankr. S.D. Fla. Oct. 24, 2006) (proceeds exempt in bank account; fact that bad credit would make new home purchase problematical not sufficient to negate intent to reinvest); *In re* Dezonia, 347 B.R. 920 (Bankr. M.D. Fla. 2006) (proceeds of voluntary or involuntary sale of homestead, here foreclosure surplus, are exempt if intended to be used for new homestead and not commingled with other funds); *In re* Alam, 336 B.R. 320 (Bankr. N.D. Ohio 2005) (settlement proceeds from lawsuit for disability benefits exempt, as are investment account funds traceable to settlement proceeds), *aff'd, remanded for factual findings*, 359 B.R. 142 (B.A.P. 6th Cir. 2006); McKernan Co. v. Gregory, 643 N.E.2d 1370 (Ill. App. Ct. 1994). *Cf. In re* Nye, 210 B.R. 857 (D. Colo. 1997) (proceeds from sale of exempt home could have been exempt if debtor had met burden of proof). *But see In re* Carelock, 2006 WL 3708688 (Bankr. S.D. Ga. Jan. 13, 2006) (Georgia law does not exempt proceeds of exempt property); *In re* Roberts, 2005 WL 1924180 (Bankr. M.D. La. Aug. 10, 2005) (annuity not exempt under Louisiana law even though purchased with distribution from exempt 401k plan); *In re* Simpson, 238 B.R. 776 (Bankr. S.D. Ill. 1999) (insurance payment for damage to vehicle did not fall within exemption for debtor's "interest in motor vehicle"). *See generally* W. Vukowich, Debtors Exemption Rights, 62 Geo. L.J. 779, 826 (1974); § 12.6.2.2, *infra* (protection of exempt benefits deposited in bank account).

64 *See, e.g., In re* Fouracre, 358 B.R. 384 (Bankr. D. Ariz. 2006) (refusing to trace; proceeds of homestead lost exemption when commingled with other funds in bank account). *But cf. In re* Lantz, 451 B.R. 843 (Bankr. N.D. Ill. 2011) (proceeds of homestead are exempt if traceable, even if comingled with other funds). *See generally* § 12.6.2.3, *infra*.

65 *See, e.g., In re* Meyer, 392 B.R. 416 (Bankr. N.D. Iowa 2008) (house purchased with personal injury settlement was exempt when proceeds were traceable and home was needed for support); Faro v. Porchester Holdings, Inc., 792 So. 2d 1262 (Fla. Dist. Ct. App. 2001) (holding that exemption extended to certificate of deposit purchased with insurance policy's cash surrender value, which is exempt under Florida law). *But see In re* Duemey, 347 B.R. 875 (Bankr. S.D. Ohio 2006) (vehicle purchased for debtor by ex-husband, to satisfy his debt for back child support, not exempt child support); *In re* Burchard, 214 B.R. 494 (Bankr. D. Neb. 1997) (proceeds of personal injury judgment remained exempt while they were "cash or cash equivalent," but exemption did not protect personal property bought with the proceeds); Asset Acceptance Corp. v. Hughes, 706 N.W.2d 446 (Mich. Ct. App. 2005) (once used to pay rent, Social Security benefits are no longer exempt, so homestead property tax credit based on rent payments could be garnished); *In re* Christensen, 149 P.3d 40 (Nev. 2006) (wage exemption does not protect property purchased with exempt wages); Canton Student Loan Found. v. Mayo, 2008 WL 1970023 (Ohio Ct. App. Apr. 28, 2008) (SSI funds remain exempt in bank account but lose exemption when spent; here, debtor paid SSI funds to contractor, who failed to perform, and recovered from his bond; recovery not exempt); Gray v. Gray, 922 P.2d 615 (Okla. 1996) (veterans disability funds lost quality of moneys when used to purchase property; specially adapted vehicle was jointly acquired property which could be divided up by divorce judgment); Fox v. Fox, 2001 Tenn. App. LEXIS 239 (Tenn. Ct. App. Apr. 11, 2001) (veterans' benefits lost "the quality of moneys" when used to purchase land). *See generally* § 12.5, *infra* (exemption of benefit payments).

66 *In re* Williams, 171 B.R. 451 (D.N.H. 1994) (car; noting that workers' compensation benefits were "meant to be put to useful purposes"); *In re* Stanley, 494 B.R. 287 (Bankr. E.D. Mich. Mar. 4, 2013) (workers' compensation funds lost exemption when used as down-payment on vehicle); *In re* Baker, 2006 WL 2079919 (Bankr. M.D. Ala. July 25, 2006) (purpose of workers' compensation is to rehabilitate worker, not to pay his antecedent debts; exemption survives in hands of worker and in motor vehicles purchased with traceable proceeds of workers' compensation settlement); *In re* Gardiner, 332 B.R. 891 (Bankr. S.D. Cal. 2005) (asset acquired, in part, with workers' compensation award retains exempt status, subject to tracing requirements); *In re* King, 208 B.R. 570 (Bankr. M.D. Fla. 1997) (Florida exemption for workers' compensation "due and payable" protects benefits that have been deposited in bank account; *In re* Nelson, 179 B.R. 811 (Bankr. W.D. Va. 1994) (manufactured home and lot purchased with workers compensation). *Cf. In re* Sills, 82 F.3d 111 (5th Cir. 1996) (declining to decide whether house purchased with workers' compensation lump-sum settlement was exempt from levy by Internal Revenue Service; even if it were exempt from levy, it remained subject to federal tax lien). *But see In re* Irwin, 371 B.R. 344 (Bankr. C.D. Ill. 2007) (workers' compensation settlement funds remained exempt in money market account used only for workers' compensation but lost exemption when used to pay down lien on motor vehicle); *In re* Rajkovic, 289 B.R. 197 (Bankr. M.D. Fla. 2002) (workers' compensation funds lost exemption when large lump sum was transferred to debtor's closely held corporation and used to purchase limousine; funds "invested in a business venture" were no longer used to rehabilitate worker or save him from poverty while disabled); Sullo v. Cinco Star, Inc., 755 So. 2d 822 (Fla. Dist. Ct. App. 2000) (exemption lost when worker received large

the benefits are "meant to be put to useful purposes."[67] Outside the workers compensation context, however, courts sometimes hold that the exemption is lost once the benefits are spent.[68]

A number of states have statutes that specifically protect the proceeds of the sale of a homestead or other exempt property.[69] Such a provision typically protects the proceeds not only of a voluntary sale but also of a foreclosure sale[70] or a sale ordered by a divorce court[71] or bankruptcy

lump sum, bought certificate of deposit, and pledged that certificate of deposit as security for a loan); Holsman v. Holsman, 49 S.W.3d 795 (Mo. Ct. App. 2001) (in absence of evidence that gift was not intended, depositing workers' compensation lump sum in couple's joint account made it marital property that could be divided up at divorce); Feliciano v. McClung, 556 S.E.2d 807 (W. Va. 2001) (lump-sum workers' compensation award would remain exempt in ordinary bank account, but purchase of certificate of deposit turns it into non-exempt investment).

67 *In re* Williams, 171 B.R. 451, 453 (D.N.H. 1994).

68 Hebert v. Royal (*In re* Hebert), 463 B.R. 142 (B.A.P. 10th Cir. 2011) (table, text at 2011 WL 1670898) (interpreting Wyoming law not to exempt funds withheld from exempt unemployment benefits and retirement plan payments when returned to debtor as a federal income tax refund); *In re* Kramer, 339 B.R. 761 (Bankr. D. Colo. 2006) (wages would remain exempt in bank account, but stock purchased by payroll deductions had undergone "change of character" and become non-exempt personal property); *In re* Duemey, 347 B.R. 875 (Bankr. S.D. Ohio 2006) (vehicle purchased for debtor by ex-husband, to satisfy his debt for back child support, not exempt; child support had lost "quality as monies"); Asset Acceptance Corp. v. Hughes, 706 N.W.2d 446 (Mich. Ct. App. 2005) (Social Security disability benefits lost exempt status when used to pay rent, therefore tax credit resulting from payment of rent not exempt); *In re* Christensen, 149 P.3d 40 (Nev. 2006) (wage exemption does not protect property purchased with exempt wages); Rolle v. A.T.M. Three, L.L.C., 856 N.Y.S.2d 502 (N.Y. Dist. Ct. 2008) (exemption lost when Social Security benefits used to pay rent); Canton Student Loan Found. v. Mayo, 2008 WL 1970023 (Ohio Ct. App. Apr. 28, 2008) (SSI funds remain exempt in bank account but lose exemption when spent; here, debtor paid SSI funds to contractor, who failed to perform, and recovered from his bond; recovery not exempt).

69 *In re* Cunningham, 513 F.3d 318 (1st Cir. 2008) (proceeds of voluntary postpetition sale of exempt Massachusetts homestead remain exempt); *In re* Danduran, 438 B.R. 658 (B.A.P. 8th Cir. 2010) (applying principle of liberal interpretation to exempt entire proceeds of sale of homestead plus appliances, rugs, and sound system; proceeds not allocated between real and personal property), *aff'd*, 657 F.3d 749 (8th Cir. 2011); *In re* Cerchione, 414 B.R. 540 (B.A.P. 9th Cir. 2009) (home under construction was exempt when debtors applied proceeds of old homestead to cost of construction, and bank provided loan for the balance); *In re* Roberts, 450 B.R. 159 (N.D. Iowa May 5, 2011) (because Iowa homestead continues in sales proceeds and home purchased with proceeds, debtor may exempt home that she must sell in order to relocate); *In re* McCollum, 363 B.R. 789 (E.D. La. 2007) (Louisiana homestead exemption protects proceeds of voluntary sale); *In re* Rich, 2013 WL 1628723 (Bankr. D. Kan. Apr. 16, 2013) (fully exempting homestead purchased with proceeds of old homestead, exempt IRA and other funds; trustee, who had burden of proof, failed to show what portion of funds was not homestead proceeds); *In re* Bading, 376 B.R. 143 (Bankr. W.D. Tex. 2007) (when homestead sold as two parcels, debtor could exempt proceeds of both sales); Battin v. Bayside Fin. Corp., 2004 WL 2307102 (Cal. Ct. App. Oct. 14, 2004) (proceeds of sale of homestead exempt, even for debt that was nondischargeable in bankruptcy for fraud); Kerzner v. Kerzner, 77 So. 3d 214 (Fla. Dist. Ct. App. 2011) (proceeds of sale of marital home are exempt); *In re* Estate of Hamel, 821 So. 2d 1276 (Fla. Dist. Ct. App. 2002) (deceased was in process of selling condominium at time of death, and executor closed sale shortly thereafter; proceeds exempt in hands of adult daughters); *In re* Snyder, 149 P.3d 26 (Mont. 2006) (proceeds exempt for eighteen months even though no homestead declaration filed at time of sale). *See also In re* Nork, 2012 WL 6027765 (Bankr. D. Or. Dec. 4, 2012) (allowing exemption of proceeds of lease of corner of rural homestead for cell phone tower; debtor was using proceeds to pay her mortgage); *In re* Patterson, 482 B.R. 755 (Bankr. D. Vt. 2012) (new home purchased with proceeds of old is exempt; when couple divorced, wife received marital home, husband received a package of other assets, including the IRA he used to pay for new home). *But see In re* Canto, 476 B.R. 370 (Bankr. D. Mass. 2012) (Massachusetts exempts only proceeds "received" by debtor; denying exemption to foreclosure surplus tied up in interpleader action). *But cf. In re* Fehmel, 372 Fed. Appx. 507 (5th Cir. 2010) (sale proceeds not exempt because debtors acquired new homestead before the sale; property then ceased to be homestead); *In re* Schlakman, 2007 WL 1482011 (Bankr. S.D. Fla. Jan. 16, 2007) (debtor could not exempt proceeds of former marital home, located in New York, despite intention to reinvest in Florida home; proceeds exempt only if property was located in Florida); *In re* Wiley, 352 B.R. 716 (Bankr. D. Idaho 2006) (debtors could not claim homestead exemption in both their remaining property and the proceeds of eminent domain taking of one corner); Dep't of Revenue *ex rel.* Vickers v. Pelsey, 779 So. 2d 629 (Fla. Dist. Ct. App. 2001) (intent to use funds to build and repair a homestead does not make funds exempt; department could levy on funds obtained as mortgage loan on vacant and presently uninhabitable property, which debtor intended to rehabilitate for use as his home); Beck v. Lapsley, 593 N.W.2d 410 (S.D. 1999) (if homeowners over the age of seventy, who are entitled to exempt entire value of homestead, sell home, they may claim only the standard $30,000 exemption in the proceeds).

70 *See, e.g.*, *In re* Elliot, 448 B.R. 843 (Bankr. D. Colo. 2011) (Colorado homestead exempts proceeds of voluntary sale or sheriff's sale but is silent as to non-judicial foreclosure; principle of liberal interpretation requires exemption of surplus from non-judicial foreclosure); *In re* Dezonia, 347 B.R. 920 (Bankr. M.D. Fla. 2006) (proceeds of voluntary or involuntary sale of homestead, here foreclosure surplus, exempt if intended to be used for new homestead and not commingled with other funds); *In re* Miller, 246 B.R. 564 (Bankr. E.D. Tenn. 2000) (Tennessee homestead exemption survives in proceeds of involuntary sale of residence); Morgan Keegan Mortgage Co. v. Candelaria, 951 P.2d 1066 (N.M. Ct. App. 1997) (homestead exemption protected $20,000 of proceeds of private sale conducted with court's permission before foreclosure judgment; exemption would have applied to proceeds of foreclosure sale and public policy favored voluntary sales during foreclosure to maximize debtor's return); Upton v. Household Fin. Indus. Loan Co., 6 P.3d 1231 (Wash. Ct. App. 2000) (homestead exemption protects surplus resulting from foreclosure sale, but holder of second mortgage has priority over homeowner's homestead rights); *In re* Sweet, 944 P.2d 414 (Wash. Ct. App. 1997) (Washington's homestead exemption protects surplus paid to homeowners after non-judicial foreclosure).

71 *In re* Westmeyer, 2010 WL 2103571 (Bankr. N.D. Iowa May 24, 2010) (house being sold by order of divorce court; debtor may exempt any proceeds left over after payment of debt to ex-wife); *In re* Strasser, 303 B.R. 841 (Bankr. D. Ariz. 2004); *In re* Willoughby, 2003 WL 22849766 (Bankr. C.D. Ill. Dec. 2, 2003) (wife's court-ordered payment to husband as compensation for award to her of former marital home was exempt when husband intended to invest it in new home). *See also In re* Hurt, 2009 WL 382631 (Bankr. D. Neb. Feb. 12, 2009) (divorcing couple sold former marital home and split the proceeds; when each spouse had undivided half interest in the house, this was sufficient to support a homestead exemption in the entire proceeds); *In re* Ballato, 318 B.R. 205 (Bankr. M.D. Fla. 2004) (ex-husband could claim homestead exemption in proceeds of marital home sold by court order during property division; non-occupancy not a bar when it was required by restraining order); *In re* Cumberbatch, 302 B.R. 675 (Bankr. C.D. Cal. 2003) (court-ordered sale of home during property division was "forced sale to satisfy a money judgment" within meaning

court.[72] However, a few states protect proceeds only in case of an involuntary sale.[73] Some courts have also held that the proceeds of refinancing of the home do not result from a sale and so are not exempt under these provisions.[74]

If a home is sold to buyers who will be making installment payments, the exemption will protect the stream of payments.[75] The buyer's deposit is also exempt as proceeds of the sale of a home.[76] Compensation for damage to or destruction of the homestead is also usually treated as proceeds.[77] The exemption may extend to damage award against an insurer that wrongfully denies an insurance claim for damage to the property[78] and to an award against the seller of the home on a warranty-like claim.[79]

---

of California statute allowing automatic exemption, for six months, for proceeds); *In re* Kalnynch, 284 B.R. 149 (Bankr. M.D. Fla. 2002) (ex-wife, who received house, ordered to pay $15,000 to husband when house sold or refinanced; husband could exempt this as proceeds of homestead). *But see In re* Jefferies, 468 B.R. 373 (B.A.P. 9th Cir. 2012) (Washington protects only proceeds of voluntary sale; sale pursuant to divorce decree not voluntary, even though it incorporated separation agreement voluntarily negotiated by couple); *In re* Herrell, 210 B.R. 386 (Bankr. N.D. Fla. 1997) (ex-wife's right to receive a sum from ex-husband, at a date more than one year after property division, secured by a lien on the former marital home, was not proceeds from sale of a homestead, within meaning of Minnesota homestead exemption). *But cf. In re* Schissler, 250 B.R. 697 (Bankr. W.D. Mo. 2000) (Missouri homestead exemption did not protect funds awarded to husband in lieu of specific marital property in divorce which granted house to wife).

72 *See, e.g.*, *In re* May, 329 B.R. 789 (Bankr. D.N.H. 2005) (when house sold during bankruptcy, debtor receives up to amount of homestead exemption from proceeds).

73 *See, e.g.*, *In re* Murdock, 2008 WL 728879 (Bankr. N.D.N.Y. Mar. 17, 2008) (no New York exemption for proceeds of voluntary sale; debtors who sold farm, intending to buy back farmhouse, not entitled to exemption in proceeds set aside for down payment); *In re* Kujan, 286 B.R. 216 (Bankr. D. Conn. 2002) (Connecticut exempts proceeds of forced sale but not voluntary sale; ex-wife who quitclaimed house to husband could not exempt husband's obligation to pay her when youngest child reached eighteen or house sold); Schalebaum v. Town of Wolfeboro (*In re* Schalebaum), 273 B.R. 1 (Bankr. D.N.H. 2001) (New Hampshire homestead exemption does not cover proceeds of voluntary sale of homestead). *See also In re* Lares, 188 F.3d 1166 (9th Cir. 1999) (Idaho exempts homestead and sale proceeds from "attachment, execution or forced sale," but not from bank's contractual setoff).

74 *In re* Polimino, 345 B.R. 708 (B.A.P. 10th Cir. 2006) (no homestead exemption in proceeds of refinancing; refinancing not a sale within meaning of Colorado statute exempting sales proceeds); Homeside Lending, Inc. v. Miller, 31 P.3d 607 (Utah Ct. App. 2001) (proceeds of refinancing not sale proceeds within meaning of Utah exemption statute).

75 *See, e.g.*, *In re* Greene, 451 B.R. 331 (Bankr. D. Vt. 2011) (debtor may exempt, as homestead proceeds, stream of payments from buyer's promissory note; no time limit and no need to prove intent to reinvest in new home); *In re* VanSickle, 350 B.R. 897 (Bankr. D. Idaho 2006) (Oregon homestead exemption, which protects proceeds of sale of homestead if reinvested in homestead within one year, will protect payments made by buyers pursuant to promissory note, when house sold ten months earlier, provided funds are timely reinvested).

76 Gen. R.A.C., Inc. v. Coldwell Banker Residential Real Estate, Inc., 876 So. 2d 606 (Fla. Dist. Ct. App. 2004) (buyer's deposit, held in escrow by realtor, was proceeds of seller's homestead, exempt for reasonable time). *See also In re* Takes, 334 B.R. 642 (N.D. Iowa 2005) (returned entrance deposit from retirement community was exempt as proceeds of homestead), *aff'd on other grounds*, 478 F.3d 902 (8th Cir. 2007). *But cf. In re* Stewart, 452 B.R. 726 (Bankr. C.D. Ill. 2011) (refund of amounts that had been held in their escrow account that sellers received when they sold their home is not homestead proceeds, because not traceable to buyers); *In re* Jones, 327 B.R. 297 (Bankr. S.D. Tex. 2005) (asset other than new homestead that is purchased with proceeds of homestead sale is not exempt under Texas law).

77 *In re* White, 2013 WL 1601667 (Bankr. D. Neb. Apr. 15, 2013) (fire insurance proceeds of destroyed homestead exempt in bank account); *In re* Lehman, 2009 WL 497125 (Bankr. W.D. Wash. Feb. 26, 2009) (insurance check for storm damage to homestead remains exempt for one year even if deposited in unsegregated bank account); *In re* Barbe, 2006 WL 2403826 (Bankr. E.D. La. Feb. 17, 2006) (insurance proceeds for exempt property destroyed by hurricane are exempt); *In re* Hoffpauir, 258 B.R. 447 (Bankr. D. Idaho 2001) (Idaho exemption statute protects fire insurance proceeds of destroyed property); Quiroga v. Citizens Prop. Ins. Corp., 34 So. 3d 101 (Fla. Dist. Ct. App. 2010) (insurance proceeds for hurricane damage to homestead exempt; contingent fee agreement with attorney who sued insurer to obtain payment not sufficient to waive homestead exemption in proceeds); *In re* Estate of Tolson, 690 N.W.2d 680 (Iowa 2005) (insurance proceeds for water damage to homestead are exempt for reasonable time if used to repair or replace). *See also In re* Carelock, 2006 WL 3708688 (Bankr. S.D. Ga. Jan. 13, 2006) (insurance proceeds, which debtor intended to use to replace totaled car, not exempt because Georgia law does not exempt proceeds of exempt property); *In re* Burns, 482 B.R. 164 (Bankr. E.D. La. 2012) (compensation for loss or destruction of exempt property is exempt; here, applying state exemption for disposable earnings to portion of personal injury judgment that compensated for lost wages); *In re* Guenther, 417 B.R. 685 (Bankr. W.D.N.Y. 2009) (New York $5000 exemption for household goods survives in insurance proceeds for destroyed goods; debtors may exempt a combined total of $5000 in insurance proceeds and surviving goods). *But see In re* Plant, 503 B.R. 224 (Bankr. D. Mass. 2013) (Massachusetts law explicitly exempts insurance proceeds of homestead but is silent as to personal property; denying exemption to fire insurance proceeds from damaged personal property); *In re* Foor, 259 B.R. 899 (Bankr. C.D. Ill. 2000) (cause of action for termite damage that occurred before debtors owned house not protected by homestead exemption); *In re* Simpson, 238 B.R. 776 (Bankr. S.D. Ill. 1999) (Illinois exemption for debtor's "interest in a motor vehicle" did not exempt insurance proceeds for "totaled" vehicle). *But cf. In re* MacNeal, 2007 WL 917255 (Bankr. S.D. Fla. Mar. 22, 2007) (TILA, HOEPA, and usury claims, arising from purchase of homestead, were personal property, not covered by Florida homestead exemption).

78 *See, e.g.*, West v. Carlew, 2012 WL 3002197 (S.D. Tex. July 23, 2012) (proceeds of action against insurer that wrongfully refused to pay for hurricane damage); *In re* Hill, 2011 WL 6936357 (Bankr. S.D. Tex. Dec. 30, 2011) (insurance proceeds take the place of exempt homestead; allowing exemption of proceeds of action against insurer who wrongfully failed to compensate insured for hurricane damage). *Cf. In re* Crooks, 351 B.R. 783 (Bankr. S.D. Fla. 2006) (Florida homestead exemption protects insurance proceeds that compensate for damage to or destruction of homestead; no homestead when debtors did not own and owner did not reside in house on date of storm, but proceeds exempt because received in trust for owner and mortgage lender, to be used only for repairs).

79 *In re* Murphy, 367 B.R. 711 (Bankr. D. Kan. 2007) (deceptive practices and breach of warranty causes of action, arising from sale of defective manufactured home, exempt under Kansas homestead law). *See also In re* Gilley, 236 B.R. 441 (Bankr. M.D. Fla. 1999) (settlement proceeds from lawsuit against pesticide manufacturer whose product contaminated homestead farmland exempt, because debtor planned to spend proceeds on efforts to clean up land), *aff'd*, 211 F.3d 131 (11th Cir. 2000) (table). *But cf. In re* Schubert, 218 B.R. 603 (Bankr. N.D. Okla.

Some jurisdictions protect the proceeds of the sale of the homestead without any requirement that they be reinvested in a new home.[80] Others, however, require proof of intent to purchase another homestead with the proceeds or require that the proceeds be so used within a certain period of time.[81] Courts may allow this period to be tolled if circumstances prevent the

1998) (Oklahoma homestead exemption exempts compensation for damage to homestead property but not homeowners' cause of action against sellers and inspector over undisclosed defects in the property); *In re* Bradley, 212 B.R. 998 (Bankr. M.D. Ala. 1997) (homestead exemption did not exempt homeowners' cause of action against sellers and realtor for concealment of termite damage before current owners owned home, as this was not analogous to fire insurance proceeds for damage to home).

80 *See, e.g., In re* Godfrey, 386 B.R. 339 (Bankr. D. Utah 2008) (Utah homestead proceeds exempt for one year; no requirement that they be kept separate or in their "original form"; here part of proceeds used for apartment, the rest spent for wedding ring and honeymoon); *In re* Simms, 243 B.R. 156 (Bankr. S.D. Fla. 2000) (proceeds of sale of home retain exemption if rolled over into exempt annuity without fraudulent intent); *In re* Duffy, 240 B.R. 60 (Bankr. D. Nev. 1999) (Nevada homestead exemption protects proceeds of sale of homestead, whether or not debtor intends to reinvest in new homestead).

81 *ARIZONA: In re* White, 389 B.R. 693 (B.A.P. 9th Cir. 2008) (proceeds in bank account lost exemption when used for stock trading and not reinvested in homestead within eighteen months); *In re* Konnoff, 356 B.R. 201 (B.A.P. 9th Cir. 2006) (Arizona law) (proceeds exempt on petition date lose exemption if not timely reinvested); *In re* Smith, 342 B.R. 801 (B.A.P. 9th Cir. 2006) (Arizona proceeds lose exemption if not invested in new homestead within eighteen months; when period expired during bankruptcy, proceeds became part of bankruptcy estate); *In re* Fouracre, 358 B.R. 384 (Bankr. D. Ariz. 2006) (proceeds lost exemption, even though debtors, whose bad credit prevented purchase in own name, used funds for earnest money and down payment on purchase of home by relatives, with whom debtors resided in both old and new home).

CALIFORNIA: In re Perpinan, 2007 WL 2345019 (Bankr. N.D. Cal. Aug. 15, 2007) (purported reinvestment was sham; homestead exemption lost and bankruptcy discharge denied).

COLORADO: Fleet v. Zwick, 994 P.2d 480 (Colo. App. 1999) (when proceeds of sale of homestead were placed in separate bank account, use of some funds for non-exempt purpose did not destroy exempt status of remaining funds). *See also In re* Bertola, 2012 WL 1945426 (Bankr. D. Colo. May 30, 2012) (funds must remain "separate and identifiable"; homestead proceeds placed in brokerage account, used to invest in stocks, but funded only with the proceeds, remained exempt), *aff'd*, 498 B.R. 391 (B.A.P. 10th Cir. 2013).

FLORIDA: In re Fling, 449 B.R. 580 (Bankr. N.D. Fla. 2011) (intent to reinvest sufficiently shown; debtor hired a realtor, viewed six properties, made unsuccessful offers on three, and ceased trying only after creditor froze bank account containing homestead proceeds); *In re* Gauthier, 2007 WL 1580100 (Bankr. S.D. Fla. May 30, 2007) (exemption lost when proceeds used for "living expenses"; note that here concealment of funds was sufficient to deny discharge); *In re* Castro, 2006 WL 4005571 (Bankr. S.D. Fla. Oct. 24, 2006) (proceeds exempt in bank account; fact that bad credit would make new home purchase problematical not sufficient to negate intent to reinvest, but funds lost exemption when dissipated postpetition for living expenses); *In re* Kalnynch, 284 B.R. 149 (Bankr. M.D. Fla. 2002) (delay in acquiring new homestead not fatal); *In re* Binko, 258 B.R. 515 (Bankr. S.D. Fla. 2001) (proceeds exempt when debtors showed good faith and due diligence in seeking less expensive home and proceeds not commingled with other funds, although debtors spent some on rental housing while house hunting); *In re* Delson, 247 B.R. 873 (Bankr. S.D. Fla. 2000) (Florida homestead proceeds exempt only if there is intention to purchase another homestead within reasonable time); Town of Lake Park v. Grimes, 963 So. 2d 940 (Fla. Dist. Ct. App. 2007) (burden on debtors to show good faith intent to reinvest; not shown here); Rossano v. Britesmile, Inc., 919 So. 2d 551 (Fla. Dist. Ct. App. 2005) (intent to reinvest shown when homestead proceeds were escrowed prior to closing on new homestead). *See also* Kerzner v. Kerzner, 77 So. 3d 214 (Fla. Dist. Ct. App. 2011) (separation agreement required husband to use part of proceeds to pay certain debts; remaining proceeds exempt when he credibly testified that he intended to use them to buy new home); Fong v. Town of Bay Harbor Islands, 864 So. 2d 76 (Fla. Dist. Ct. App. 2003) (no lien against homestead for code violations but, if homestead sold and proceeds not reinvested within six months, town may file lien against proceeds).

IDAHO: In re VanSickle, 350 B.R. 897 (Bankr. D. Idaho 2006) (Oregon homestead exemption, which protects proceeds if reinvested in homestead within one year, protects payments made by buyers pursuant to promissory note, when house sold ten months earlier, provided funds are timely reinvested).

ILLINOIS: U.S. v. Capital Tax, 2011 WL 2565690 (N.D. Ill. June 29, 2011) (no homestead exemption for stream of payments from reverse mortgage being used for day-to-day expenses; payments are sales proceeds which are exempt only if debtor intends to invest in new homestead); *In re* Stewart, 452 B.R. 726 (Bankr. C.D. Ill. 2011) (intent to reinvest need not be proven, but bankruptcy does not toll one-year period, and debtor can be ordered not to spend proceeds for non-homestead purpose); *In re* Snowden, 386 B.R. 730 (Bankr. C.D. Ill. 2008) (homestead proceeds exempt; intention to reinvest sufficiently shown when debtor testified that she would "explore her options" for new home, might use funds as entrance fee to retirement community); *In re* Ziegler, 239 B.R. 375 (Bankr. C.D. Ill. 1999) (homestead proceeds not exempt without showing of intent to buy another homestead). *But see In re* Lantz, 446 B.R. 850 (Bankr. N.D. Ill. 2011) (Illinois's one-year exemption for homestead proceeds does not require proof of intent to reinvest; proceeds that were exempt on petition date remain exempt).

IOWA: In re Roberts, 450 B.R. 159 (N.D. Iowa May 5, 2011) (because Iowa homestead continues in sales proceeds and home purchased with proceeds, debtor may exempt home which she must sell in order to relocate); *In re* Dittmer, 2011 WL 652759 (Bankr. S.D. Iowa Jan. 12, 2011) (homeowners are entitled to a reasonable time to reinvest proceeds in new homestead); *In re* Russow, 357 B.R. 133 (Bankr. N.D. Iowa 2007) (proceeds of old homestead rolled over into new one are exempt as to preexisting debts); Braunger v. Karber, 563 N.W.2d 1 (Iowa 1997) (proceeds of sale of homestead are exempt for reasonable time after sale if seller intends to use them to buy a new homestead; applying this rule when judgment creditor attempted to execute on portion of purchase price in hands of buyers before they paid it to debtors). *See also In re* White, 293 B.R. 1 (Bankr. N.D. Iowa 2003) (once established, homestead exemption may be transferred from one residence to another; no abandonment when debtors lived for short time in an apartment due to "timing problems" with sale of one house and purchase of next); *In re* Estate of Tolson, 690 N.W.2d 680 (Iowa 2005) (insurance proceeds for water damage to homestead exempt for reasonable time if used to repair or replace); John Deere Cmty. Credit Union v. Miller, 810 N.W.2d 896 (Iowa Ct. App. 2012) (unpublished) (when debtor agreed to use inherited homestead proceeds to reimburse estate for money improperly taken during testator's lifetime, this showed intention not to invest in new homestead; exemption lost).

KANSAS: In re Letterman, 356 B.R. 540 (Bankr. D. Kan. 2006) (no homestead exemption in house lot or fire insurance proceeds when debtor neither occupied homestead on petition date, nor testified to intention to use proceeds to rebuild); *In re* Ginther, 282 B.R. 16 (Bankr. D. Kan. 2002) (proceeds exempt only if used for purchase of Kansas homestead, not when debtors moved to Colorado).

MISSOURI: In re Seeley, 341 B.R. 277 (Bankr. W.D. Mo. 2006) (homestead not lost when property placed on market when debtor testified that proceeds would be used for new homestead).

debtor from using the funds to purchase a new homestead.[82]

12.2.5 Procedure for Claiming Exemptions

States differ in the procedures they specify for asserting exemptions. Some states require debtors to assert the protections provided by the exemption statutes affirmatively[83] and may even require strict compliance with these procedures.[84] This requirement is not universal, however,[85] and there is a

NEBRASKA: In re Roberts, 215 B.R. 197 (Bankr. D. Neb. 1997) (intention to sell the homestead property was not abandonment when Nebraska law made proceeds exempt for six months)

OKLAHOMA: In re Barnes, 307 B.R. 731 (B.A.P. 10th Cir. 2004) (Oklahoma law). *See also* Bowles v. Goss, 309 P.3d 150 (Okla. Civ. App. July 16, 2013) (funds voluntarily withdrawn from reverse mortgage line of credit are homestead proceeds, exempt only if held for reinvestment in new homestead).

OREGON: In re Wynn, 369 B.R. 605 (Bankr. D. Or. 2007) (money spent on rent was reinvested in homestead).

TEXAS: West v. Carlew, 2012 WL 3002197 (S.D. Tex. July 23, 2012) (requirement that proceeds be invested within six months applies only to sales proceeds, not insurance; insurance proceeds remain exempt). *See also* Zibman v. Tow (*In re* Zibman), 268 F.3d 298 (5th Cir. 2001) (Texas homestead exemption protects proceeds of sale only if reinvested in another Texas homestead within six months); *In re* D'Avila, 498 B.R. 150 (Bankr. W.D. Tex. 2013) (if homestead sold prepetition, proceeds lose exemption and become property of bankruptcy estate if not used to purchase new home, but when, as here, home is homestead—not proceeds—on petition date, exemption is final and debtor may use proceeds as she chooses); *In re* Mills, 2011 WL 1810487 (Bankr. S.D. Tex. May 11, 2011) (debtor sold part of homestead land to pay for repair of hurricane damage; note required buyer to make three annual payments; six-month period for reinvestment began to run with each payment); *In re* Presto, 376 B.R. 554 (Bankr. S.D. Tex. 2007) (exemption for homestead proceeds ends with purchase of new homestead; leftover funds not exempt); Cadle Co. v. Harvey, 46 S.W.3d 282 (Tex. App. 2001) (complicated series of transactions, including leasing home to another for two years, ending up with lease with option to buy, did not create gap in homestead exemption). *But cf. In re* Fehmel, 372 Fed. Appx. 507 (5th Cir. 2010) (sale proceeds not exempt because debtors acquired new homestead before the sale; property then ceased to be homestead).

See generally § 12.7.4.2, *infra* (abandonment of homestead).

82 *In re* Marriott, 427 B.R. 887 (Bankr. D. Idaho 2010) (allowing equitable tolling when divorce court had ordered homestead proceeds be held in attorney's trust account while other issues were resolved); London v. London, 342 S.W.3d 768 (Tex. App. 2011) (tolling the six-month period because trial court erroneously required payment of proceeds to receiver). *See also In re* Bading, 376 B.R. 143 (Bankr. W.D. Tex. 2007) (when debtor had to sell homestead as two parcels because creditor refused to release clearly invalid lien on second parcel, time began to run only upon second sale). *But cf. In re* Jacobson, 676 F.3d 1193 (9th Cir. 2012) (filing bankruptcy during six month period for investment of proceeds does not toll this limitation; proceeds lose exemption after six months); Hodes v. Diagnostic Experts of Austin, Inc., 2010 WL 2867344 (Tex. App. July 22, 2010) (exemption lost after six months, even though funds tied up in court-ordered trust fund; even if tolling permitted, an issue not reached here, debtor must request tolling before expiration of six months).

83 *See* Johns Hopkins Hosp. v. Post, 321 Fed. Appx. 259 (4th Cir. 2009) (Maryland law) (burden on debtor to assert and prove exemption; when there was no non-speculative way to allocate lump-sum personal injury settlement between exempt pain and suffering and loss of future wages and non-exempt past wages and property loss, entire fund was non-exempt); Mayer v. Quy Van Nguyen, 211 F.3d 105 (4th Cir. 2000) (Virginia law); Moore v. Branch Banking & Trust Co., 2010 WL 4962909 (W.D. Ky. Dec. 1, 2010) (burden on debtor to claim exemptions; *pro se* debtor's letter to garnishee bank insufficient); Silver v. Law Offices of Lee Schiff, P.C., 2010 WL 3000053 (D. Conn. July 28, 2010) (Connecticut wildcard exemption not self-executing; debtor must follow prescribed procedure to claim it); Chanel, Inc. v. Adamson, 2008 WL 249157 (W.D. Ark. Jan. 29, 2008) (method of claiming exemptions determined by state law; denying exemptions for failure to follow Arkansas procedure); Shrestha v. State Credit Adjustment Bur., 117 F. Supp. 2d 142 (D. Conn. 2000) (no violation of Fair Debt Collection Practices Act to garnish account when Connecticut wildcard exemption was not "self-executing" because debtor had to identify property to which it would apply); *In re* Khanh Viet Nguyen, 2011 WL 3889714 (Bankr. E.D. Va. Sept. 2, 2011) (procedural requirements of Virginia exemption statutes are strict; court has no power to excuse compliance with five-day deadline); *In re* Lamb, 409 B.R. 534 (Bankr. N.D. Fla. 2009) (burden is on debtor to claim exemptions; letter to creditor stating that she is "a single mother with kids" insufficient to claim head-of-household exemption; wrongful garnishment and FDCPA claims fail); Zivitz v. Zivitz, 16 So. 3d 841 (Fla. Dist. Ct. App. 2009) (exemption for proceeds of homestead was irretrievably lost by failure to claim it within twenty days of garnishment notice); Belden v. Belden, 389 S.W.3d 717 (Mo. Ct. App. 2012) (homestead exemption lost by failure to timely claim it); Citibank (S.D.) v. Masters, 2008 WL 754873 (Ohio Ct. App. Mar. 24, 2008) (burden is on debtor to show that funds exempt; denying exemption when debtor testified that bank account contained earnings but failed to produce financial records); Millen v. Shelby Ct. Sheriff's Office, 2010 WL 4515007 (Tenn. Ct. App. Nov. 10, 2010) (burden is on debtor to claim wildcard exemption and specify property to which it applies, or to request a hearing on a payment plan; when debtor did neither, seizure and sale of car were proper). *See also* Dish Network L.L.C. v. Sonicview U.S.A., Inc., 2012 WL 4848954 (S.D. Cal. Oct. 11, 2012) (allowing judgment debtor to claim veterans benefits in bank account as exempt even though he missed deadline for filing exemption claim, as creditor failed to cite any authority allowing waiver of this exemption, but other exemptions are waived by untimely filing); *In re* Neilson, 427 B.R. 581 (Bankr. W.D. Va. 2010) (letter from creditor describing creditor remedies, including garnishment, but not mentioning exemptions is not deceptive because Florida law places burden on debtor to claim exemptions); Lang v. Dorosh, 2010 WL 5292607 (Minn. Ct. App. Dec. 28, 2010) (procedure to claim exemption for account in financial institution is "very meticulous"; denying exemption for IRA because account statement not timely disclosed); CBI, Inc. v. McCrea, 285 P.3d 429 (Mont. 2012) (upholding denial of *pro se* debtor's request for hearing on claim that bank account contains exempt funds, for failure to make "particularized factual and legal showing" in her request for hearing).

84 *See, e.g.*, Hendricks & Lewis, P.L.L.C. v. Clinton, 2011 WL 4861855 (N.D. Fla. Aug. 9. 2011) (Mag. recommendation) (strictly construing procedural requirements for objecting to garnishment; exemption for bank account containing Social Security funds lost by failure to meet time limits of Florida statute), *adopted by* 2011 WL 4861844 (N.D. Fla. Oct. 13, 2011); *In re* Stoney, 445 B.R. 543, 546–47 (Bankr. E.D. Va. 2011); Lang v. Dorosh, 2010 WL 5292607 (Minn. Ct. App. Dec. 28, 2010) (debtor must strictly comply with procedure for claiming exemptions; denying exemption for retirement account because debtor failed to enclose required account statements).

85 *See, e.g.*, Novas v. Russ Dean Ford, Inc., 2009 WL 721549 (D. Idaho Mar. 17, 2009) (when annuity was clearly exempt debtor did not have to file an exemption claim, and insurer cannot be held in contempt for failing to turn over exempt portion of annuity in response to writ of execution); *In re* Mootosammy, 387 B.R. 291 (Bankr. M.D. Fla. 2008) (exemptions not waived by failure to follow Florida procedure for claiming exemptions within fifteen days after levy); Osborne v.

strong argument that depriving a debtor of a federal exemption because of failure to meet a state procedural requirement violates federal law.[86] A Treasury Department rule, effective in 2011, moots this issue to a large extent in cases involving Social Security and certain other exempt federal benefits, by placing the burden on depository institutions to identify and protect approximately two months of exempt benefits.[87]

Some states provide a method for a debtor to identify exempt property prior to its seizure. Whether a homestead exemption must be claimed in advance through a filing with the recorder of deeds is discussed in § 12.7.8, *infra*.

Whether state exemption procedures meet due process requirements is discussed in § 12.3, *infra*.

12.2.6 Marshalling of Assets

Marshalling of assets is an equitable doctrine by which a senior creditor, who has more than one fund or item of collateral available to satisfy a debt, may be ordered to proceed in a way that preserves the rights of junior creditors. For example, a court may require a senior creditor to proceed against an asset that it alone can reach, rather than against an asset that is a junior creditor's sole security. Marshalling cannot, however, be used to deprive a debtor of a state exemption such as a homestead exemption.[88] For example, a junior creditor cannot force a senior creditor to proceed against a homestead that the junior creditor could not reach.[89]

12.2.7 Wildcard Exemptions and Stacking

Some states provide a "wildcard" exemption that exempts any property specified by the debtor up to a certain amount.[90] Some states limit the wildcard exemption to personal property[91] or tangible personal property,[92] but in other states it can be applied to any property.[93] In some states the wildcard exemption may be used to exempt wages that are not otherwise protected.[94]

Dumoulin, 55 So. 3d 577, 583, 587 (Fla. 2011) (homestead exemption is self-executing; debtor need not interpose exemption claim at time of levy); DiGiorgio v. DiGiorgio, 48 So. 3d 968 (Fla. Dist. Ct. App. 2010) (actual residence, not filing of declaration, determines whether property is homestead); Balanof v. Niosi, 791 N.Y.S.2d 553 (N.Y. App. Div. 2005) (requirement that debtor assert exemptions does not apply when property is "easily identifiable" as exempt); Sears Roebuck & Co. v. Cosey, 44 P.3d 582 (Okla. Civ. App. 2002) (strict compliance with procedure for claiming exemption not required, especially for unrepresented debtor). *See also* Hillcrest Med. Ctr. v. Monroy, 38 P.3d 931 (Okla. Civ. App. 2001) (hardship exemption not lost by failure to timely claim it; allowing untimely claim and ordering return of previously garnished funds). *Cf.* Cal. Civ. Proc. Code § 704.080(e) (West) (first $1225 to $3650 of deposit account is exempt without making a claim; to execute upon excess over this amount, judgment creditor must make claim that it does not consist of exempt funds); Navistar Fin. Corp. v. Hrobuchak, 2009 WL 483123 (M.D. Pa. Feb. 25, 2009) (when garnishee responds and provides documentation that funds are exempt, here an IRA, burden is on creditor to show any exception, for example, that debtor contributed more than permissible amount).

86 *See* § 12.6.6, *infra*.

87 *See* §§ 12.6.3.1, 12.10.1, *infra*.

88 Meyer v. United States, 375 U.S. 233, 84 S. Ct. 318, 11 L. Ed. 2d 293 (1963).

89 *In re* Ferrari, 2006 WL 3247120 (Bankr. D. Alaska Oct. 25, 2006) (refusing to apply marshalling of assets to homestead; IRS, which could recover against exempt or non-exempt property, takes non-exempt property, leaving debtor with homestead and non-governmental creditor with nothing); Gaumer v. Hartford-Carlisle Sav. Bank, 451 N.W.2d 497 (Iowa 1990). *But see In re* Szywd, 444 B.R. 10 (Bankr. D. Mass. 2011) (IRS, which can reach homestead that is exempt as to other creditors, will be required to take homestead so that other creditors can collect from non-homestead property).

90 *See In re* Sueng Oh Cho, 2012 WL 1424508 (Bankr. E.D.N.Y. Apr. 24, 2012) (allowing New York wildcard exemption for check for surplus proceeds of repossession sale of car, which was not protected by cash in hand or motor vehicle exemptions); *In re* Sharp, 286 B.R. 627 (Bankr. E.D. Ky. 2002) (debtor may use wildcard to exempt part of tax refund; may also use exemption for public benefits to exempt portion attributable to earned income credit); Schalebaum v. Town of Wolfeboro (*In re* Schalebaum), 273 B.R. 1 (Bankr. D.N.H. 2001) (New Hampshire wildcard, which includes cash, protects proceeds of voluntary sale of homestead); *In re* Foor, 259 B.R. 899 (Bankr. C.D. Ill. 2000) (Illinois wildcard would exempt cause of action against sellers of house for undisclosed termite damage); *In re* Ball, 201 B.R. 204 (Bankr. N.D. Ill. 1996) (Illinois's $2000 wildcard exemption may be used to exempt debtor's share of Truth in Lending Act class action claim); *In re* Miller, 198 B.R. 500 (Bankr. N.D. Ohio 1996) (Ohio's wildcard exemption may be used to avoid liens on real property); *In re* Arnold, 193 B.R. 897 (Bankr. W.D. Mo. 1996) (wildcard exemption may be used to exempt bank accounts); *In re* Scrams, 172 B.R. 297 (Bankr. D. Neb. 1994) (Nebraska's wildcard "in lieu of homestead" exemption may be used to exempt a car, up to the $2500 limitation); ARL Credit Servs., Inc. v. Piper, 736 N.W.2d 771 (Neb. Ct. App. 2007) (debtor may use head of household's "in lieu of homestead" exemption to protect bank account). *But see In re* Siegle, 2000 Bankr. LEXIS 1627 (Bankr. D. Mont. Dec. 6, 2000), *amended by* 257 B.R. 591 (Bankr. D. Mont. 2001) (interpreting Montana's exemption statute to allow exemption only of property that falls within a listed category, without a wildcard).

91 *See, e.g.*, *In re* Anzalone, 318 B.R. 127 (Bankr. C.D. Ill. 2004) (real estate commissions, paid or to be paid to debtor, were "personal property" that could be exempted under Illinois wildcard exemption); *In re* Latham, 317 B.R. 733 (Bankr. E.D. Tenn. 2004) (enforceable contract for sale of real property turns seller's interest into personal property; debtor could claim personal property exemption for his share of sale proceeds when buyers had received warranty deed); *In re* Young, 297 B.R. 492 (Bankr. E.D. Tex. 2003) (interest in a trust fund, inherited from father, not personal property within meaning of Texas personal property exemption).

92 *See, e.g.*, *In re* Oakley, 344 F.3d 709 (7th Cir. 2003) (cash was not "tangible personal property" within meaning of Indiana exemption; protected only by $100 exemption for intangibles).

93 *See, e.g.*, *In re* Garcia, 709 F.3d 861 (9th Cir. 2013) (California wildcard for "any property" may be used to exempt car, which could also be exempted under tools of trade or motor vehicle exemptions); *In re* Neitzelt, 387 B.R. 649 (Bankr. D. Del. 2008) (Delaware wildcard, exempting "property," is broad enough to cover real as well as personal property, in this case non-homestead realty); *In re* Oglesby, 333 B.R. 788 (Bankr. S.D. Ohio 2005) (Ohio exemption for "any property" covers real or personal property; may be applied to one item or split among several).

94 *In re* Irish, 311 B.R. 63 (B.A.P. 8th Cir. 2004); *In re* Eutsler, 2010 WL 27499 (Bankr. W.D.N.C. Jan. 12, 2012) (wildcard available for year-end bonus, which was not protected by exemption for wages earned within sixty days); *In re* Robinson, 240 B.R. 70 (Bankr. N.D. Ala. 1999) (state constitutional wildcard exemption could be used to protect future wages not protected by statutory wildcard exemption); *In re* Johnson, 57 B.R. 635 (Bankr. N.D. Ill. 1986) (permitting wildcard exemption for "any other property" to be stacked with 85% exemption

The debtor may be required to act affirmatively to claim the wildcard.[95]

In some states, the wildcard exemption is available only if the debtor does not claim a homestead exemption or only in the amount of the unused portion of the homestead exemption.[96] The interpretation of Florida's $4000 wildcard exemption is particularly complex. It is available to a debtor who "does not claim or receive the benefits" of the constitutional homestead exemption.[97] In 2011, the Florida Supreme Court held, in *Osborne v. Dumoulin*, that a debtor who files bankruptcy but does not formally claim the homestead exemption does not "claim or receive the benefits of" the homestead exemption, so is entitled to the $4000 wildcard exemption.[98] The court held that merely being eligible for the exemption does not amount to claiming or receiving its benefits. It reasoned that, while the homestead exemption is self-executing and the debtor need do nothing to claim it, the situation is different in bankruptcy. In bankruptcy, if the debtor does not claim the homestead exemption, the home will be part of the bankruptcy estate and will be administered by the trustee. The court held that the debtor in the case before it had not claimed the homestead exemption within the meaning of the statute even though she had originally claimed it but then amended her bankruptcy papers to delete that claim.

The court further held that a debtor is entitled to the $4000 personal property exemption even if the bankruptcy trustee decides to abandon the home to the debtor and the debtor retains it[99] and even if the debtor has received the benefits of the homestead exemption in the past or will receive them in the future.[100] The debtor is entitled to the $4000 wildcard exemption as long as the homestead exemption "does not otherwise present an obstacle to the bankruptcy trustee's administration of the estate."[101]

The court suggested that the $4000 exemption would not be available if a non-debtor spouse's homestead exemption prevented the trustee from administering the home as part of the estate.[102] Some courts have applied this suggestion to hold that a debtor who owns a home in tenancy by the entireties with a non-debtor spouse is indirectly receiving the benefits of the exemption because the spouse can use the homestead exemption to prevent a forced sale, so the debtor cannot claim the wildcard exemption.[103] If, however, the property is

---

for wages to preserve all of debtor's wages from garnishment; statute was later amended to restrict use of wildcard to protect wages); *In re* Avery, 514 So. 2d 1380 (Ala. 1987) ($3000 state personal property exemption could be applied to future wages; note that this exemption was amended in 1988 so that it no longer applies to wages); Pruett v. Worldwide Asset Purchasing, L.L.C., 2013 WL 4290086 (Ala. Civ. App. Aug. 16, 2013) (Alabama's constitutional $1000 personal property exemption applies to 25% of wages that could be garnished); Bank of Am. v. Stine, 839 A.2d 727 (Md. 2003) (wage garnishment within ninety days of bankruptcy may be avoided as preferential transfer, and debtor can then use Maryland wildcard "cash or other property" exemption to exempt the funds thus recovered). *See also* Chrysler Fin. Servs., L.L.C. v. Provenzano, 2011 WL 4974672 (N.J. Super. Ct. App. Div. Oct. 20, 2011) (New Jersey's $1000 wildcard applies to wage execution, but this simply means that creditor must wait until debtor has received $1000 in wages, at which time garnishment goes into effect and continues until debt is paid). *But see In re* Cervantes, 503 B.R. 689 (Bankr. N.D. Ill. 2013) (Illinois wildcard explicitly excludes wages); *In re* Ealy, 2007 WL 1077792 (Bankr. N.D. Ill. Apr. 6, 2007) (state exemption inapplicable to garnished wages recovered by bankruptcy trustee as preferential transfer); *In re* Ealy, 355 B.R. 685 (Bankr. N.D. Ill. 2006) (sums deducted from wages pursuant to garnishment order not exempt; noting change in statute barring use of wildcard exemption for wages); *In re* Royer, 2006 WL 978878 (Bankr. C.D. Ill. 2006) (neither wildcard nor wage exemption protects accrued earnings, here commissions, in hands of employer from turnover in bankruptcy case); *In re* Patterson, 216 B.R. 413 (Bankr. C.D. Ill. 1998) (upholding amended statute as constitutional); *In re* Youngblood, 212 B.R. 593 (Bankr. N.D. Ill. 1997); *In re* Andres, 212 B.R. 306 (Bankr. N.D. Ill. 1997); *In re* Franklin, 210 B.R. 560 (Bankr. N.D. Ill. 1997); Chrysler Credit Corp. v. Parker, 2008 WL 4647881 (N.J. Super. Ct. App. Div. Oct. 17, 2008) (state personal property wildcard exemption does not cover wages, which are governed by a different statutory scheme).

95 Silver v. Law Offices of Lee Schiff, P.C., 2010 WL 3000053 (D. Conn. July 28, 2010) (Connecticut wildcard exemption not self-executing; debtor must follow prescribed procedure to claim it); Millen v. Shelby Ct. Sheriff's Office, 2010 WL 4515007 (Tenn. Ct. App. Nov. 10, 2010) (burden is on debtor to claim wildcard exemption and specify property to which it applies).

96 *See, e.g.*, Doeling v. Vranicar, 2012 WL 3135542 (D.N.D. Aug. 1, 2012) (North Dakota allows debtor to exempt manufactured home as part of homestead, or claim specific exemption for manufactured home; debtor who uses specific exemption may claim in-lieu-of-homestead wildcard); *In re* Wade, 466 B.R. 20 (Bankr. D. Colo. 2012) (debtors who exempted the entire equity of their home, in an amount exceeding the amount of the in-lieu-of-homestead wildcard, could not claim the wildcard); *In re* Porter, 2012 WL 1655813 (Bankr. D.N.D. May 10, 2012) (same); *In re* Leach, 2012 WL 1655831 (Bankr. D.N.D. May 10, 2012) (same); *In re* Payne, 2004 WL 2757907 (Bankr. M.D.N.C. Nov. 15, 2004) (property owned in tenancy by entireties fully exempt if no joint creditors; because couple claimed entireties exemption, not homestead exemption, each debtor entitled to "in lieu of homestead" wildcard to protect other property); *In re* McDonald, 279 B.R. 382 (Bankr. D.D.C. 2002) (District of Columbia "unused homestead" exemption exempts the difference between $8075 and the homestead amount claimed).

97 Fla. Stat. § 222.25(4).

98 Osborne v. Dumoulin, 55 So. 3d 577 (Fla. 2011). *See also In re* Iuliano, 2011 WL 1627172 (M.D. Fla. Apr. 29, 2011) (allowing enhanced exemption for debtor who opposed turnover of heavily encumbered property but did not claim a homestead exemption); *In re* Rodale, 452 B.R. 290 (Bankr. M.D. Fla. 2011) (allowing enhanced wildcard when debtors reaffirmed mortgage debt but neither spouse claimed homestead exemption; couple hoped to remain in home, but trustee was not prevented from administering it).

99 Osborne v. Dumoulin, 55 So. 3d 577, 588 (Fla. 2011).

100 *Id.* at 588–89.

101 *Id.* at 590.

102 *Id.* at 589–90.

103 *In re* Barandiaran, 477 B.R. 842 (Bankr. M.D. Fla. 2012) (debtor who owns home in TBE with non-debtor spouse is indirectly receiving benefits because spouse can use homestead exemption to prevent forced sale); *In re* Perez, 2012 WL 6027743 (Bankr. S.D. Fla. Dec. 4, 2012); *In re* Watford, 427 B.R. 552 (Bankr. S.D. Fla. 2010) (debtor who owned property in tenancy by entireties with non-debtor spouse could not claim exemption because she benefited indirectly from spouse's exemption); *In re* Franzese, 383 B.R. 197 (Bankr. M.D. Fla. 2008) (denying exemption; debtor who owned home in tenancy by entireties, lived there, and had not waived exemption was receiving benefits of the constitutional exemption). *But see In re* Kehoe, 2012 WL 1077171 (Bankr. M.D. Fla. Mar. 30, 2012) (question of whether debtor who

solely owned by the debtor's spouse—even if the spouses file jointly—the debtor will be entitled to the exemption, because, without a property interest in the home, the debtor could not claim the homestead exemption.[104]

One court has held that the holding of *Osborne* may be limited to chapter 7 bankruptcies.[105] The court's rationale is that, because chapter 13 is forward-looking, and the homestead exemption protects the property from forced sale during the term of the plan, a chapter 13 debtor receives the benefit of the exemption. However, this view is inconsistent with *Osborne*, which held that a debtor who might receive the benefit of the homestead exemption in the future could still claim the $4000 wildcard exemption. Some Florida courts have held that the statutory exemption for a manufactured or modular home on land not owned by the debtor is separate from, not a clarification of, the constitutional homestead exemption, and therefore have allowed the wildcard exemption to a debtor who made use of this exemption.[106]

Inside or outside of bankruptcy, the possibility of stacking a wildcard exemption with another exemption should be considered.[107] For example, a debtor was able to stack New Hampshire's wildcard exemption, which provides for a $1000 exemption for any property and up to $7000 in certain unused exemptions, with a $5000 exemption for tools of the trade, in order to exempt $13,000 in mechanic's tools.[108]

---

owns home in TBE is indirectly receiving the benefits is fact intensive; when spouse's exemption did not prevent trustee from doing anything he otherwise could do, debtor was not receiving benefit and could claim wildcard); *In re* Fyock, 391 B.R. 882 (Bankr. M.D. Fla. 2008) (allowing wildcard exemption; debtors who claimed common law tenancy by entireties exemption did not receive benefit of constitutional exemption). *But cf. In re* Orozco, 444 B.R. 472 (Bankr. S.D. Fla. Feb. 7, 2011) (debtor did not receive the benefit of ex-husband's exemption, because only current spouses can own property in tenancy by entireties).

104 *In re* Castillo, 2014 WL 843606 (Bankr. S.D. Fla. Mar. 3, 2014) (husband resided in home solely owned by wife; enhanced wildcard allowed because homestead protects only property owned by debtor); *In re* Walton, 503 B.R. 159 (Bankr. S.D. Fla. 2013) (joint-filing wife owned property before marriage and never transferred property to TBE or other form of joint ownership; future or indirect benefit not sufficient to bar enhanced exemption); *In re* Sanon, 403 B.R. 737 (Bankr. M.D. Fla. 2009) (debtor who resided in home owned by non-debtor wife, in which he had no present ownership interest but did have certain inheritance rights, could claim enhanced exemption). *But cf. In re* Im, 495 B.R. 46 (Bankr. M.D. Fla. 2013) (denying enhanced exemption because debtor, who was co-settlor, co-trustee, and co-beneficiary of trust that owned couple's home, had ownership interest sufficient to support claim of homestead).

105 *In re* Valone, 2014 WL 970024 (M.D. Fla. Mar. 12, 2014) (denying exemption to chapter 13 debtors who did not claim exemption in heavily encumbered home where they continued to reside).

106 *In re* Lisowski, 395 B.R. 771 (Bankr. M.D. Fla. 2008); *In re* Heckman, 395 B.R. 737 (Bankr. N.D. Fla. 2008); *In re* Munao, 2008 WL 4602352 (Bankr. M.D. Fla. Sept. 23, 2008).

107 *See, e.g., In re* Turpen, 482 B.R. 273 (B.A.P. 8th Cir. 2012) (Missouri law) (head of household wildcard applies only to children by birth or adoption; allowing head of household to claim wildcard for his own children, but not those of female co-habitant); *In re* Irish, 311 B.R. 63 (B.A.P. 8th Cir. 2004) (debtor school teacher may stack exemption for 75% of wages with exemption for "accrued wages or tax refund" to exempt July and August salary that accrued at end of school year in June); Little v. Reaves (*In re* Reaves), 256 B.R. 306 (B.A.P. 9th Cir. 2000) (motor vehicle exemption may be stacked with wildcard and unused portion of homestead exemptions), *aff'd on other grounds*, 285 F.3d 1152 (9th Cir. 2002); *In re* Feliciano, 487 B.R. 47 (Bankr. D. Mass. 2013) (allowing married debtors to stack federal wildcard exemptions to protect non-homestead real property); *In re* Winters, 2010 WL 1418337 (Bankr. D. Neb. Mar. 17, 2010) (when motor vehicle was tool of trade, debtors could stack tools of trade and wildcard exemption); *In re* Mootosammy, 387 B.R. 291 (Bankr. M.D. Fla. 2008) (debtor could stack statutory $4000 in-lieu-of-homestead wildcard with $1000 constitutional personal property exemption and $1000 motor vehicle exemption to exempt $6000 of value of truck); *In re* Hafner, 383 B.R. 350 (Bankr. N.D. Fla. 2008); *In re* Bezares, 383 B.R. 796 (Bankr. M.D. Fla. 2007) (Florida's statutory in-lieu-of-homestead wildcard can be stacked with constitutional personal property exemption); *In re* Urie, 2006 WL 533514 (Bankr. W.D. Mo. Jan. 31, 2006) (Missouri exemption for "any motor vehicle . . . in the aggregate" may be split between two vehicles and stacked with wildcard exemption; wedding ring exemption may be stacked with jewelry exemption); *In re* Gagnon, 2005 WL 1331142 (Bankr. D.N.H. June 1, 2005) (New Hampshire wildcard exemption of $1000 plus up to $7000 in unused exemptions may be applied to one piece of property or spread over several); Price v. Manufacturers & Traders Trust Co. (*In re* Price), 266 B.R. 572 (Bankr. W.D.N.Y. 2001) (New York law exempts 90% of wages and $2500 in cash in hand; cash exemption may be used to protect the 10% of wages not protected by the wage exemption); Vaillancourt v. Granite Group (*In re* Vaillancourt), 260 B.R. 66 (Bankr. D.N.H. 2001) (New Hampshire wildcard exemption for "any property" may be stacked with homestead or personal property exemptions); *In re* Rutter, 247 B.R. 334 (Bankr. M.D. Fla. 2000) (debtor may stack Florida's constitutional personal property exemption with its statutory motor vehicle exemption to exempt entire equity in his truck); *In re* Ambrose, 179 B.R. 982 (Bankr. S.D. Ga. 1995) (state wildcard exemption can be stacked with $200 per item household goods exemption to enable debtors to exempt entire value of appliances and living room set); Landry v. Landry, 917 A.2d 1262 (N.H. 2007) (wildcard and unused portion of certain other exemptions may be stacked with tools-of-trade exemption to fully exempt mechanic's tools); *In re* Anderson, 932 P.2d 1110 (Okla. 1996) (liberally construing Oklahoma law, which allows one $50,000 exemption for each interest in a claim for personal injury, death, or workers' compensation, to allow two exemptions when plaintiff's work injury resulted in a workers' compensation claim and a malpractice judgment against the doctor who performed "unauthorized surgery"). *But see In re* Thornton, 269 B.R. 682 (W.D. Mo. 2001) (debtors who resided in manufactured home not permitted to stack homestead exemption with exemption for "mobile home used as principal residence"; when home was permanently attached, homestead exemption applied); *In re* Dowactor, 2008 WL 4615040 (Bankr. C.D. Ill. Oct. 8, 2008) (personal property wildcard may be used for business property only if stacked with tools-of-trade exemption; not applicable to equipment and inventory of failed business, when retired debtors had ceased to practice trade); *In re* Jenks, 2008 WL 3005165 (Bankr. S.D. Ind. July 31, 2008) (wildcard for "*other* real or personal property" cannot be stacked with homestead exemption); *In re* Hughes, 244 B.R. 448 (Bankr. D.S.D. 1999) (refusing to allow stacking of "additional personal property" exemption to protect proceeds of sale of homestead that exceeded homestead limit). *But cf. In re* Runkle, 2008 WL 429197 (Bankr. N.D. Iowa Feb. 14, 2008) (Iowa exemption for "other personal property not otherwise specifically provided for" cannot be stacked with capped exemption); *In re* Struckhoff, 231 B.R. 69 (Bankr. E.D. Mo. 1999) (Missouri exemption for "any" motor vehicle allows exemption of only one vehicle per debtor, so, if debtor's interest in the car is worth less than the statutory $1000, the balance may not be applied to other vehicle or personal property).

108 Landry v. Landry, 917 A.2d 1262 (N.H. 2007).

In addition, many states allow married couples to claim two exemptions and to stack them to exempt a larger amount of personal property.[109] Courts may require each member of the couple to have an ownership interest in the item.[110] If the couple is living apart, some courts allow each partner a full complement of exemptions,[111] while others allow an exemption only for the former marital home or only one exemption per couple for other property.[112] States that recognize domestic

109 *In re* Lampe, 278 B.R. 205 (B.A.P. 10th Cir. 2002) (Kansas law) (spouses could stack exemptions in farm equipment purchased with funds from couple's joint account, when wife signed notes and state law presumes equal ownership by husband and wife), *aff'd*, 331 F.3d 750 (10th Cir. 2003); *In re* Halcomb, 2011 WL 2133560 (S.D. Ind. May 25, 2011) (allowing wife to exempt entire value of car owned in joint tenancy, leaving husband enough exemption to protect solely owned motorcycle); Planned Parenthood of Columbus/Willamette, Inc. v. American Coal. of Life Activists, 2007 WL 4118597 (S.D. Ohio Nov. 16, 2007) (debtor and non-debtor spouse may stack aggregate and per item household goods exemptions); Schilling v. Tran, 287 B.R. 887 (W.D. Ky. 2002) (allowing husband and wife to stack motor vehicle exemptions to exempt one vehicle; *In re* Watson, 2012 WL 8436264 (Bankr. E.D. Cal. Dec. 12, 2012) (couple could stack tools of trade exemption, even if each spouse did not personally use each tool, if both spouses substantially participated in business); *In re* Ventura, 2011 WL 1979864 (Bankr. E.D.N.Y. May 20, 2011) (adding wife's name to title of car previously titled in husband alone was permissible exemption planning, not fraudulent transfer; allowing couple to stack two exemptions); *In re* Tucker, 430 B.R. 499 (Bankr. N.D. Ill. 2010) (non-debtor wife may stack her $4000 wildcard with that of debtor husband, to exempt entire amount in joint bank account); *In re* Reisdorff, 2010 WL 4852457 (Bankr. D. Neb. Nov. 27, 2010) (spouses who each used jointly owned vehicle to commute to work could stack two tools of trade and two wildcard exemptions); *In re* Sullivan, 2008 WL 3914494 (Bankr. E.D. Tenn. Aug. 20, 2008) (married debtors who own property in tenancy by entireties may each exempt up to 50% of the value of each piece of property, up to the $4000 per person limit); *In re* Gatto, 380 B.R. 88 (Bankr. M.D. Fla. 2007) (married couple may stack $4000 statutory in-lieu-of-homestead and $1000 constitutional personal property exemptions for total of $10,000 per couple; when title listed both spouses in alternative, each had ownership interest); *In re* Bell, 333 B.R. 839 (Bankr. W.D. Mo. 2005) (married couple could stack head-of-household, two wildcard, one motor vehicle, and part of another motor vehicle exemption to exempt one vehicle and apply balance of second motor vehicle exemption to second vehicle); *In re* Hoffpauir, 258 B.R. 447 (Bankr. D. Idaho 2001) (when amended statute eliminated "per household" caps, each spouse could claim exemption in fire insurance proceeds of destroyed household goods); *In re* Guyot, 240 B.R. 326 (Bankr. D. Minn. 1999) (when Minnesota statute allowed exemption of one life insurance contract, each spouse could exempt one contract); *In re* Sherman, 237 B.R. 551 (Bankr. N.D.N.Y. 1999) (when New York's homestead and personal property exemptions refer to "an individual debtor," a married couple may stack two exemptions). *But see In re* Rivera, 499 B.R. 175 (Bankr. D. P.R. 2013) (spouses may stack Puerto Rico exemptions); *In re* Hedrick, 441 B.R. 601 (Bankr. S.D. Ill. 2010) (couple's household goods owned in tenancy in common; wife could exempt only her 50% share; when husband did not exempt his share, trustee could sell goods), *aff'd*, 2011 WL 2199371 (S.D. Ill. June 7, 2011) (if couple owns property in tenancy in common, one spouse may exempt only 50% of its value); *In re* Garvin, 262 B.R. 529 (Bankr. D. Mont. 2001) (married debtors could claim only one state exemption in jointly owned motor vehicle); *In re* Jackson, 194 B.R. 867 (Bankr. D. Ariz. 1995) (allowing married debtors to stack their $1500 motor vehicle exemptions to exempt $3000 in one car); *In re* Fox, 302 P.3d 1137 (Nev. 2013) (debtor may not claim or stack exemptions on behalf of non-debtor spouse; Nevada statute protects only property "of the judgment debtor"). *But cf. In re* Nye, 250 B.R. 46 (Bankr. W.D.N.Y. 2000) (each spouse can exempt only his or her own one-half interest in a particular item, even if exemption amount would cover its full value). *See generally* § 12.7.3.2, *infra* (stacking of homestead exemptions).

110 *In re* Stone, 504 B.R. 908 (Bankr. C.D. Ill. 2014) (when couple owned all property in common, wife could claim exemption for tools used by husband); *In re* Bippert, 311 B.R. 456 (Bankr. W.D. Tex. 2004) (both spouses sought to exempt cause of action for personal injury to wife alone; looking to state marital property law and allowing each to exempt their property in claim; claim was wife's separate property except for lost wages, which were community, and loss of consortium, which was husband's separate property); *In re* Perez, 302 B.R. 661 (Bankr. D. Ariz. 2003) (spouse who filed individual bankruptcy could stack own and non-filing spouse's motor vehicle exemptions to protect family car; community property was part of bankruptcy estate, and individual spouse could act on behalf of community); *In re* Hejmowski, 296 B.R. 645 (Bankr. W.D.N.Y. 2003) (couple who filed joint tax return may stack New York's $2500 cash exemptions to protect $5000 in tax return, even if only one spouse earned income that tax year); *In re* Kieffer, 279 B.R. 290 (Bankr. D. Kan. 2002) (spouses could stack exemptions for farm equipment, when wife was co-owner, because equipment purchased with joint funds and wife signed notes). *But see In re* Landsinger, 2012 WL 2994832 (Bankr. W.D. Wis. July 23, 2012) (when real property was titled in wife alone, but mortgage was being paid from joint account, husband could exempt one-half of the equity acquired by making the payments and stack it with wife's wildcard). *But cf. In re* Gazvoda, 2011 WL 2946171 (Bankr. N.D. Ohio July 21, 2011) (couple may not stack exemptions for tax refund attributable to earnings of only one spouse); *In re* Basler, 2011 WL 867131 (Bankr. D. Neb. Mar. 10, 2011) (when life insurance was owned by one spouse, only he could exempt it; no stacking); *In re* Toland, 346 B.R. 444 (Bankr. N.D. Ohio 2006) (husband could not claim exemption in car titled in wife's name; Ohio exemption law requires "an interest" in property; one spouse has no interest in other spouse's property); *In re* Horstman, 276 B.R. 80 (Bankr. E.D.N.C. 2002) (wife may not use her wildcard exemption to exempt husband's car; her ownership interest insufficient, even though car marital property under state domestic relations law); *In re* Miller, 255 B.R. 221 (Bankr. D. Neb. 2000) (if truck titled in husband's name, only husband may claim an exemption in it); *In re* Schapiro, 246 B.R. 751 (Bankr. W.D.N.Y. 2000) (New York exemption for cash protected a bequest but, when only husband was beneficiary, couple could claim only one exemption).

111 *In re* Colwell, 196 F.3d 1225 (11th Cir. 1999) (when couple are legitimately living apart, that is, not for purposes of fraud, each is entitled to a homestead exemption); *In re* Roberts, 219 B.R. 235 (B.A.P. 8th Cir. 1998); *In re* Hall, 395 B.R. 722 (Bankr. D. Kan. 2008) (married couple living apart may claim two homesteads, provided that each spouse has clearly established a homestead and arrangement is not for purpose of defrauding creditors), *aff'd*, 441 B.R. 680 (B.A.P. 10th Cir. 2009); *In re* Roberge, 307 B.R. 442 (Bankr. D. Vt. 2004) (exemptions intended to protect family group; married debtors living apart, each with a child, were two family groups, each entitled to full set of exemptions). *Cf.* Mayo v. Sikes, 2006 WL 1750882 (W.D. La. June 20, 2006) (Louisiana exempts one motor vehicle "per household"; only one exemption allowed when evidence insufficient to show that divorcing couple were living apart on bankruptcy petition date). *But see In re* Ruck, 451 B.R. 128 (Bankr. D. Kan. 2011) (divorcing couple who are still married on petition date may exempt only one homestead).

112 *In re* Thorpe, 251 B.R. 723 (Bankr. W.D. Mo. 2000) (when married couple was living apart without dependents, only one motor vehicle and one wildcard exemption allowed for motorcycle of which husband was sole owner). *See also In re* Meier, 2010 WL 4340814 (Bankr. D.S.D. Oct. 27, 2010) (when couple was separated, each spouse living with a child or children from prior marriage, there were two households

partnerships may treat the partners like married couples for exemption purposes.[113]

12.2.8 Special Exemption Schemes for Particular Types of Debt

12.2.8.1 Health Care Debts

A few states, recognizing the special burden created by health care debts, have enacted statutes limiting health care debt collection or otherwise assisting debtors facing health problems. Nevada[114] and Ohio[115] forbid execution on the primary residence for health care debts during the lifetime of the debtor and certain specified dependents; a lien may be created, which may be foreclosed only after the residence ceases to be occupied by the protected persons. West Virginia provides a larger homestead exemption for debts resulting from "catastrophic illness or injury."[116]

If an illness of the debtor or a family member has kept the debtor out of work for two or more weeks, Kansas forbids wage garnishments for two months after the debtor returns to employment.[117] Wyoming exempts from garnishment contributions to a qualified medical savings account (*except* for health care debts) to the extent the contributions are allowable under the Internal Revenue Code.[118]

A now-repealed Ohio statute, which limited the percentage of wage garnishment for health care debts, was upheld as a reasonable classification, in light of the public policy of encouraging people to seek needed medical care.[119] Medical debt is discussed in detail in Chapter 9, *supra*.

but only one family, so only one spouse—the one with the higher income—could claim "head of family" wildcard). *Cf.* § 12.7.3.2, *infra* (whether married couples may claim two homestead exemptions).

113 *See In re* Rabin, 359 B.R. 242 (B.A.P. 9th Cir. 2007) (intent of California domestic partnership act was to treat domestic partners as spouses; partners who had merged their finances entitled to only one exemption, same as married couple).

114 Nev. Rev. Stat. § 21.095.

115 Ohio Rev. Code Ann. §§ 2329.66(A)(1)(a), 2329.661 (West). *See* Edwards v. McCormack, 136 F. Supp. 2d 795 (S.D. Ohio 2001) (lawyer-collector violated Fair Debt Collection Practices Act and Ohio deceptive practices statute by threatening foreclosure on real property owned by Ohio health-care debtors); Wickliffe Country Place v. Kovacs, 765 N.E.2d 975 (Ohio Ct. App. 2001) (fact question whether nursing home provided health care services and supplies).

116 W. Va. Code § 38-9-3(b).

117 Kan. Stat. Ann. § 60-2310. *But see* State *ex rel.* Moeller v. White, 216 P.3d 727 (Kan. Ct. App. 2009) (statute does not apply to permanently disabled worker who is receiving regular disability benefits).

118 Wyo. Stat. Ann. § 1-20-111.

119 St. Ann's Hosp. v. Arnold, 672 N.E.2d 743 (Ohio Ct. App. 1996); Wooster Cmty. Hosp. v. Anderson, 670 N.E.2d 563 (Ohio Ct. App. 1996) (classification is rational: health care debtors are different from others because of the life or death necessity of health care and the extra burdens imposed by paying back a debt while also suffering health problems). *But see* Community Physical Therapy v. Wayt, 639 N.E.2d 515 (Ohio Ct. App. 1994) (statute is unconstitutional because it has no rational relationship to any governmental purpose).

12.2.8.2 IRS Debts, Federal Restitution Orders, and Other Federal Debts

The Internal Revenue Service (IRS) collects federal income taxes subject to wage and property exemptions provided in the Internal Revenue Code.[120] It provides exemptions for income that may be more generous for families and less generous for individuals[121] than the federal wage garnishment protections in the Consumer Credit Protection Act (CCPA).[122] It exempts other income, such as unemployment benefits, workers' compensation, and income to fulfill a child support obligation, from IRS seizure.[123] Wearing apparel, a family's personal effects and furniture, tools of the trade, and certain other personal property are also exempt.[124] The taxpayer's principal residence is exempt from levy unless a United States district court judge or magistrate approves the levy.[125] The statute authorizing tax levies specifically refers to Social Security, so the anti-alienation provision of the Social Security Act does not bar the IRS from taking Social Security benefits.[126] However, the statute also limits any levy to 15% of the monthly payment.[127] Other exemption laws are not applicable to the IRS.[128]

120 26 U.S.C. § 6334.

121 26 U.S.C. § 6334(d) provides for weekly exemption of the standard deduction provided by 26 U.S.C. § 63(c) and the deduction provided for personal exemptions in 26 U.S.C. § 151 divided by fifty-two.

122 15 U.S.C. § 1673(b)(1)(C) (making CCPA limits inapplicable to garnishment for tax debts). *See* United States v. Clayton, 613 F.3d 592 (5th Cir. 2010) (retirement-type benefits can be garnished for restitution order for unpaid taxes; CCPA makes 25% limit inapplicable to tax debts). *See generally* § 12.4, *infra*.

123 26 U.S.C. § 6334(a).

124 26 U.S.C. § 6334(a).

125 26 U.S.C. § 6334(a)(13) and (e). *Cf.* Sills v. Dep't of Treasury (*In re* Sills), 82 F.3d 111 (5th Cir. 1996) (distinguishing tax lien, which is merely a security interest, from a levy, which operates as a seizure; tax lien can be placed on home even if home is exempt from levy).

126 26 U.S.C. § 6334. *See* Blanchette v. Social Sec. Admin., 2014 WL 667514 (D. Mass. Feb. 21, 2014) (*pro se*).

127 26 U.S.C. § 6331(h).

128 26 U.S.C. § 6334(c). *See, e.g.* United States v. Craft, 535 U.S. 274, 122 S. Ct. 1414, 152 L. Ed. 2d 437 (2002) (tax lien can attach to debtor husband's interest despite Michigan's recognition of tenancy by entireties); United States v. Offiler, 336 Fed. Appx. 907 (11th Cir. 2009) (Florida homestead exemption will not protect property against foreclosure of federal tax lien); United States v. Sawaf, 74 F.3d 119 (6th Cir. 1996) (ERISA's anti-alienation provision does not bar garnishment of taxpayer's interest in an ERISA pension fund for unpaid taxes); United States v. Berk, 374 B.R. 385 (D. Mass. 2007) (state homestead exemption does not protect against federal tax lien); United States v. Hanson, 2005 WL 3116099 (D. Minn. Apr. 21, 2005) (Minnesota homestead exemption does not protect non-debtor wife against sale of homestead for husband's individual tax liability); *In re* Jones, 206 B.R. 614 (Bankr. D. Colo. 1997) (broad anti-alienation provision of federal statute governing thrift savings plans does not protect against federal tax lien and levy). *See also In re* Szwyd, 408 B.R. 547 (D. Mass. 2009) (IRS can reach homestead property, other creditors cannot; equities favor ordering IRS to take homestead and leave non-exempt property for other creditors when tax debt is large, non-exempt property is small, and debtor's conduct was reprehensible); Brown v. Ford Motor Co., 797 N.E.2d 546 (Ohio Ct. App. 2003) (state garnishment law does not apply to IRS garnishment, and employer who complies is immune from any liability to employee).

The statute which provides for fines and restitution in federal criminal cases has its own list of exemptions that includes some, but not all, of the property exempted from tax levy. Most non-governmental pension benefits and Social Security benefits, for example, may be garnished for criminal fines or restitution.[129] The wage garnishment restrictions of the CCPA apply to collection of criminal fines and restitution.[130] However, many courts hold that a lump-sum payment, as opposed to a stream of periodic payments, can be seized in its entirety.[131] One court held that exempt property can be reached to collect contempt sanctions imposed by a bankruptcy court, which are not "mere money judgments" but "orders imposed in the public interest."[132]

Federal agencies have special administrative powers when collecting debts.[133] These include the power of administrative offset of debts against Social Security and certain other otherwise exempt federal benefits.[134] Furthermore, there is a special statutory exemption scheme that applies when a federal agency litigates a debt in court.[135] These rules are discussed in Chapter 10, *supra*.

12.2.8.3 Alimony, Child Support, and Similar Claims

Many exempt funds may be reached for child support or alimony.[136] The Social Security Act[137] allows child support and

129 28 U.S.C. § 3613(a), (f) (allowing United States to enforce fines and restitution without regard to Social Security anti-alienation statute and providing closed list of exemptions); United States v. DeCay, 620 F.3d 534 (5th Cir. 2010) (pension that would be exempt under state law can be garnished to collect federal criminal restitution order, but CCPA 25% limit applies); United States v. Phillips, 303 F.3d 548 (5th Cir. 2002) (Mandatory Victim Restitution Act empowers government to use procedures of Federal Debt Collection Procedures Act to enforce an order; government could garnish retirement account); United States v. Cunningham, 866 F. Supp. 2d 1050, 1055–56 (S.D. Iowa June 11, 2012) (state law exemption for state employee pension is inapplicable when federal government is collecting criminal restitution; harsher rule for these debts is not unconstitutional); United States v. Golden, 2010 WL 5141706 (W.D. Okla. Dec. 13, 2010) (federal law preempts state exemption; retirement fund may be garnished for restitution). *See also* Fed. Trade Comm'n v. Neiswonger, 580 F.3d 769 (8th Cir. 2009) (court ordering disgorgement, here of profits from deceptive marketing scheme, not bound by state exemptions; may seize, *inter alia*, retirement account); United States v. Taylor, 2012 WL 1309863 (E.D. Mich. Mar. 16, 2012) (debtor entitled to take the entire amount in his profit-sharing account upon "separation," defined as one year without contributions; this will occur a few days after his release from prison; because garnishment is continuing, government can seize the funds when debtor becomes entitled to receive them), *adopted by* 2012 WL 1339081 (E.D. Mich. Apr. 17, 2012); United States v. Anderson, 2007 WL 2703160 (W.D. Okla. Sept. 13, 2007) (Oklahoma garnishment exemptions for "undue hardship" not applicable to federal garnishment for criminal restitution); United States v. Gaudet, 2004 WL 2367734 (E.D. La. Oct. 20, 2004) (husband's pension was being garnished for restitution of funds he stole from pension fund; because wife's rights were derivative of husband's, that is, qualified domestic relations order awarded her a percentage of pension, she could not claim exemption), *aff'd*, 187 Fed. Appx. 410 (5th Cir. 2006).

130 18 U.S.C. § 3613(a)(3), (f). *See* United States v. Lee, 659 F.3d 619 (7th Cir. 2011) (payments from retirement accounts are earnings within the meaning of CCPA; garnishment for criminal fine is limited to 25%); United States v. DeCay, 620 F.3d 534 (5th Cir. 2010) (pension that would be exempt under state law can be garnished to collect federal criminal restitution order, but CCPA 25% limit applies); U.S. v. Thomas, 2012 WL 147876 (E.D. Cal. Jan. 18, 2012) (CCPA garnishment limits apply to criminal court's restitution order), *adopted by* 2012 WL 869512 (E.D. Cal. Mar. 9, 2012). *But see* United States v. Belan, 2008 WL 2444496 (E.D. Mich. June 13, 2008) (CCPA 25% limits do not apply to garnishment of ERISA benefits for federal criminal restitution, because funds ceased to be earnings when deposited in retirement account). *But cf.* U.S. v. King, 2012 WL 1080297 (E.D. Pa. Apr. 2, 2012) (CCPA cap does not apply to garnishment of corpus of retirement account for criminal restitution).

131 *See, e.g.*, United States v. Hosking, 567 F.3d 329 (7th Cir. 2009) (affirming criminal court order that takes almost the entire principal of defendant's retirement account); United States v. Novak, 476 F.3d 1041 (9th Cir. 2007) (ERISA plan can be reached for criminal restitution, but cash-out can be required only if beneficiary could take entire amount in lump sum; barred if spousal consent required); United States v. Bollin, 264 F.3d 391 (4th Cir. 2001) (federal forfeiture law preempts state law garnishment limitations, so entire individual retirement account subject to forfeiture); United States v. McKnight, 2012 WL 5336165 (W.D. Tex. Oct. 26, 2012) (if debtor is permitted to withdraw retirement funds as lump sum, government may take the entire amount; if periodic payments are required, garnishment limited to the 25% allowed by CCPA); United States v. Greco, 2013 WL 101931 (N.D. Ohio Jan. 8, 2012) (government can seize entire lump-sum award of retroactive state employee's disability benefits, but garnishment of future payments is limited to 25%); United States v. Edward D. Jones & Co., L.P., 2011 WL 7025905 (E.D. Tex. Dec. 21, 2011) (CCPA limit does not apply if debtor can take funds as lump sum), *adopted by* 2012 WL 113605 (E.D. Tex. Jan. 13, 2012). *See generally* § 12.4.1.4.2, *infra* (application of CCPA to periodic payments from pension plan).

132 Faulkner v. Kornman, 2012 WL 864574 (Bankr. S.D. Tex. Mar. 13, 2012), *appeal certified*, 2012 WL 3071102 (Bankr. S.D. Tex. July 27, 2012).

133 *See* § 10.2, *supra*.

134 *See* § 10.2.8, *supra*.

135 *See* § 10.3.5, *supra*.

136 *See, e.g.*, Cameron v. Hughes, 825 P.2d 882 (Alaska 1992) (creditor may levy against otherwise exempt property, for example, workers' compensation and Social Security benefits, for past-due child support because of compelling public policy of enforcing child support obligations); Hamel v. Hamel, 2009 WL 888648 (Ariz. Ct. App. Apr. 2, 2009) (husband's share of homestead proceeds could be set off against arrears of family support; ex-spouse is not the kind of creditor the homestead protects against); Drachmeister v. Brassart, 93 P.3d 566 (Colo. App. 2004) (personal injury judgment may be reached for child support even though otherwise exempt); Reffalt v. Reffalt, 94 So. 3d 1222 (Miss. Ct. App. 2012) (Social Security may be counted in setting alimony but not divided in property settlement; agreement to give wife half of husband's retirement income "as alimony" could include Social Security as well as private income without violating anti-assignment provision); *In re* Flores Children v. Flores, 1987 WL 19752 (Ohio Ct. App. Nov. 6, 1987) (Railroad Retirement benefits, though sole source of income, are subject to garnishment under federal and state law and regulations when garnishment is to pay delinquent child support); State *ex rel.* Dep't of Human Servs., Child Support Enforcement Div. v. Palmer, 212 P.3d 491 (Okla. Civ. App. 2009) (benefits from Energy Employees Occupational Illness Compensation Program, awarded to son whose father was killed by occupational exposure to radiation, could be garnished for child support); Horton v. Horton, 335 S.W.3d 862 (Tex. App. 2011) (Social Security may be garnished for child support arrearages, even after child has reached majority). *See also* Russo v. Russo, 474 A.2d 473 (Conn. App. Ct. 1984) (divorce court may order ex-husband to pay certain debts, even if his income comes from exempt Social Security benefits,

alimony to be collected from Social Security benefits and other federal payments as long as the entitlement to the payment is based upon remuneration for employment. Accordingly, Social Security Disability (SSD)[138] payments can be garnished for child support and alimony.[139] Payments such as SSI benefits[140] and children's Social Security benefits[141] that are not based on remuneration for employment are still protected, however.[142]

Veterans benefits,[143] civil service retirement benefits,[144] military retirement,[145] and workers' compensation benefits[146] may

---

when he also had other potential sources of income available); State *ex rel.* Lisby v. Lisby, 890 P.2d 727 (Idaho 1995) (lump-sum workers' compensation could be garnished for family support, but amount for "future medical care" remained exempt); Refferty-Plunkett v. Plunkett, 910 N.E.2d 670 (Ill. App. Ct. 2009) (enforcing property settlement, which required husband to pay half his state university retirement benefits to wife, notwithstanding couple's failure to execute paperwork required by pension law); Young v. Young, 314 S.W.3d 306 (Ky. Ct. App. 2010) (even though firefighter's pension is protected by statute from execution, it is marital asset that can be divided at divorce). *But see* Rosemann v. Salsbury, Clements, Bekman, Marder & Adkins, L.L.C., 987 A.2d 48 (Md. 2010) (personal injury settlement exempt even from claims for child support; distinguishing wages and unemployment, which are meant to benefit the family, while personal injury recovery is meant to restore the injured person); Crawford v. Haddock, 621 S.E.2d 127 (Va. 2005) (general statute establishing state retirement system allows garnishment for family support debts, but specific statute dealing with group life insurance exempts the proceeds from "levy, garnishment, and other legal process"; insurance proceeds are exempt). *See generally* §§ 12.7.6, *supra* (family support claims and homestead exemption), 12.5.7, *infra* (whether exempt income may be counted in determining amount of family support payments).

137 42 U.S.C. § 659(a). *See* Knickerbocker v. Norman, 938 F.2d 891 (8th Cir. 1991) (Social Security disability benefits can be garnished for child support even after obligation is assigned to state agency); McPherson v. Social Sec. Admin., 2010 WL 1609975 (M.D. Tenn. Mar. 5, 2010) (Social Security Administration is not liable for implementing child support garnishment order that is regular on its face), *report and recommendation adopted by* 2010 WL 1609676 (M.D. Tenn. Apr. 20, 2010); Shepherd v. Shepherd, 467 N.W.2d 237 (Iowa 1991); Mariche v. Mariche, 758 P.2d 745 (Kan. 1988); Sharlot v. Sharlot, 494 N.Y.S.2d 238 (N.Y. App. Div. 1985); Hobson v. Hobson, 901 P.2d 914 (Or. Ct. App. 1995).

138 SSD is the non-means tested benefit program financed from payroll deductions. SSD is a substitute for earned income and represents money that an employee and his or her employer have paid for the employee's benefit into a common trust fund under the Social Security Act. *See* 42 U.S.C. § 405.

139 *See In re* Marriage of Truhlar, 935 N.E.2d 1199 (Ill. App. Ct. 2010) (obligation to pay for daughter's college education, required by divorce decree, is child support for which SSDI benefits may be reached); State *ex rel.* Moeller v. White, 216 P.3d 727 (Kan. Ct. App. 2009) (SSDI benefits may be garnished for child support arrearages).

140 Supplemental Security Income (SSI) benefits are means-tested and are available only when a disabled person's income is insufficient to provide for basic needs. In contrast to SSD payments, SSI benefits are not based on how much one paid into the system but rather how much one needs to maintain a minimum level of subsistence based on federal standards. *See* Schweiker v. Wilson, 450 U.S. 221, 101 S. Ct. 1074, 67 L. Ed. 2d 186 (1981).

141 State *ex rel.* Raybon v. McElrath, 2003 WL 22401276 (Tenn. Ct. App. Oct. 22, 2003) (child support obligation may not be imposed on disabled person whose only source of income is Social Security benefits for disabled adult child of deceased worker; "remuneration for employment" means that of recipient, not deceased parent).

142 42 U.S.C. §§ 407, 659, 1383(d)(1). *See* Sykes v. Bank of Am., 723 F.3d 399 (2d Cir. 2013) (SSI may not be reached for child support); Davis v. Office of Child Support Enforcement, 20 S.W.3d 273 (Ark. 2000) (SSI benefits not considered in determining child support); H.C.P. v. G.A.B., 2008 WL 2898419 (Del. Fam. Ct. Apr. 24, 2008) (SSI may not be considered in setting child support; parent whose only income is SSI may not be held in contempt for non-payment of arrearage); Dep't of Pub. Aid *ex rel.* Lozada v. Rivera, 755 N.E.2d 548 (Ill. App. Ct. 2001) (SSI benefits already paid to recipient exempt from child support order; when only source of income is SSI, order vacated); Fort-Hollstein v. Hollstein, 2011 WL 10123 (N.J. Super. Ct. App. Div. Apr. 9, 2011) (lump-sum retroactive SSI award cannot be reached for child support arrears); Crespo v. Crespo, 928 A.2d 833 (N.J. Super. Ct. App. Div. 2007) (reversing order requiring payment of child support arrearages by obligor whose only source of income was SSI); Green v. Redd, 2006 WL 2237700 (N.J. Super. Ct. App. Div. Aug. 7, 2006) (SSI income may not be considered in setting child support; when SSI is obligor's only source of income, collection of arrearage must be suspended until he has other income). *See also* Robinson v. Leonard, 2011 WL 2306859 (N.J. Super. Ct. App. Div. May 11, 2011) (suspending payments of child support for obligor whose only income was SSI, but refusing to eliminate arrearage accrued while he was a recipient); Moore v. Sharp, 532 N.Y.S.2d 811 (N.Y. App. Div. 1988); Langlois v. Langlois, 441 N.W.2d 286 (Wis. Ct. App. 1989). *But see* Chambliss v. Buckner, 804 F. Supp. 2d (M.D. Ala. 2011) (repeated contempt petitions, brought against child support obligor whose only income was SSI, not other legal process because they made no reference to SSI and did not seek to attach the benefits); Burns v. Copeland, 2011 WL 1217930 (M.D. Ala. Mar. 31, 2011) (dismissing individual-capacity section 1983 action against officials who vigorously attempted to coerce SSI recipient into using benefits to pay child support); Commonwealth Cabinet for Health & Family Servs. v. Ivy, 353 S.W.3d 324 (Ky. 2011) (child support order may be entered and contempt proceeding brought against obligor whose only income is SSI; SSI award not conclusive on issue of earning ability); Commonwealth *ex rel.* Hale v. Stovall, 2007 WL 1784081 (Ky. Ct. App. June 8, 2007) (unpublished) (obligor whose only income was SSI required to make payment on child support arrearages; ongoing payments suspended, but only because of "bare subsistence" situation—not receipt of benefits); Whitmore v. Kenney, 626 A.2d 1180 (Pa. Super. Ct. 1993). *But cf.* Burns v. Edwards, 842 A.2d 186 (N.J. Super. Ct. App. Div. 2004) (child support may not be ordered if obligor's only source of income is SSI); Tennessee Dep't of Human Servs. v. Young, 802 S.W.2d 594 (Tenn. 1990).

143 *See* Rose v. Rose, 481 U.S. 619, 107 S. Ct. 2029, 95 L. Ed. 2d 599 (1987) (state court may hold veteran in contempt for failing to pay child support even though his only source of payment is veterans benefits; one purpose of veterans benefits is support of family); Woods v. Nicholson, 2006 WL 3840220 (Vet. App. Dec. 16, 2006) (continuing garnishment of veterans disability benefits to satisfy Family Court order was mandatory, in absence of evidence that excessive amount garnished, or indebtedness discharged), *aff'd*, 245 Fed. Appx. 20 (Fed. Cir. 2007); *In re* Pope-Clifton, 823 N.E.2d 607 (Ill. App. Ct. 2005) (bank account containing only funds from veterans disability benefits may be garnished for child support, as benefits that have been paid are not protected by Illinois law, and federal law allows seizure for family support); *In re* Strong, 8 P.3d 763 (Mont. 2000) (custodial spouse's attorney fees incurred in seeking child support may not be assessed against veterans disability benefits).

144 5 U.S.C. §§ 8345(j), 8346; Harmand v. Harmand, 931 So. 2d 18 (Ala. Civ. App. 2005) (federal civil service retirement benefits may be divided at divorce, and Office of Personnel Management may be ordered to pay ex-spouse; here some of the benefits were separate property because were earned after marriage terminated, but couple had separation agreement, and party may bargain away separate property).

145 42 U.S.C. § 659(a), (h).

146 McNabb v. State *ex rel.* Rhodes, 890 So. 2d 1038 (Ala. Civ. App. 2003) (lump-sum workers' compensation may be garnished for child support,

also be reached for family support obligations. Unlike military retirement pay, veterans disability benefits cannot be divided as part of the property settlement in a divorce.[147] Some courts have allowed debtors to avoid paying family support obligations by waiving non-exempt military retirement pay in favor of exempt disability pay.[148] Whether exempt benefits can be considered in calculating a family support obligation is discussed at § 12.5.7, *infra*.

12.3 Due Process Protections from Garnishment or Execution on Exempt Property

12.3.1 Introduction

Garnishment is a frequently used debt collection technique in which the collector seizes money someone owes to the debtor. For example, a creditor may seize the debtor's wages directly from the employer or seize the debtor's bank account directly from the bank. Similarly, creditors may execute on property in the debtor's possession, such as a car or household goods, by obtaining an order for it to be seized and sold.

Until 1969, collectors often used these techniques even before obtaining judgments on the underlying debts. In 1969 the Supreme Court struck down a state prejudgment wage garnishment statute as unconstitutional on its face.[149] The practical result is that garnishments are commonly used today to enforce

---

up to CCPA limit, here 50% for obligor supporting other dependent); Cameron v. Hughes, 825 P.2d 882 (Alaska 1992) (exemption of workers' compensation is intended to protect workers and their families, not to protect workers from their families); Div. of Child Support Enforcement v. Colorado Indus. Claim Appeals Office, 109 P.3d 1042 (Colo. App. 2004) (workers' compensation lump-sum settlement subject to administrative lien for child support); State *ex rel.* Lisby v. Lisby, 890 P.2d 727 (Idaho 1995) (lump-sum workers' compensation can be garnished for child support, but only up to the 55% limit applicable to weekly earnings; sum for "future medical care" is exempt as "benefits payable for medical, surgical, or hospital care"); Illinois Dep't of Healthcare & Family Servs. *ex rel.* Black v. Bartholomew, 920 N.E.2d 542 (Ill. App. Ct. 2009) (workers' dependents are intended beneficiaries of workers' compensation; lump-sum settlement may be garnished for arrearages as well as current support); Shine v. Iowa Dep't of Human Servs., 592 N.W.2d 684 (Iowa 1999) (lump sum from workers' compensation fund can be set off for child support arrearages); Marriage of Carr & Parr, 591 N.W.2d 627 (Iowa 1999) (proper to calculate 50% garnishment amount before attorney fees and costs, even though this left injured worker with nothing); Siciliano v. State, 742 N.Y.S.2d 282 (N.Y. App. Div. 2002) (workers' compensation is income subject to attachment for family support; lump-sum settlement can be taken by income attachment to satisfy ex-wife's lien for support payments). *See also* Moyle v. Dir., Office of Workers' Compensation Programs, 147 F.3d 1116 (9th Cir. 1998) (disability benefits under Longshore and Harbor Workers' Compensation Act can be garnished for alimony or child support); Hanley v. Industrial Comm'n, 21 P.3d 850 (Ariz. Ct. App. 2001) (when workers' compensation payments suspended if claimant imprisoned, except when assigned for family support, family court could order state to pay entire amount of prisoner's benefits for child support); American Compensation Ins. Co. v. McBride, 107 P.3d 973 (Colo. App. 2004) (Colorado statute allowing garnishment of workers' compensation temporary or permanent total disability benefits for court-ordered child support applies to benefits arising from injuries that occurred before statute's effective date).

147 *In re* Marriage of Williamson, 205 P.3d 538 (Colo. App. 2009) (temporary disability retirement benefits, awarded to airman whose chronic illness would prevent him from completing the twenty years' service required for regular retirement, were not marital property and could not be divided at divorce); *In re* Marriage of Wojcik, 838 N.E.2d 282 (Ill. App. Ct. 2005) (veterans disability payments may not be considered in allocating marital property at divorce, but should be counted in setting amount of family support). *See also* Gillis v. Gillis, 15 A.3d 720 (Me. 2011) (veterans disability benefits cannot be divided at divorce, but the amount must be considered in determining ability to pay and setting support amount); Halstead v. Halstead, 596 S.E.2d 353 (N.C. Ct. App. 2004) (military disability pay, unlike military retirement pay, may not be treated—directly or indirectly—as a marital asset in division of property).

148 *See* Uniformed Services Former Spouses Protection Act, 10 U.S.C. § 1408 (allowing "disposable retirement pay" to be distributed as marital property, but excepting from the definition amounts that have been waived in favor of disability); Griffin v. Griffin, 872 N.E.2d 653 (Ind. Ct. App. 2007) (veterans disability benefits may not be divided or considered in property division; here, after being ordered to split military retirement with ex-wife, husband waived retirement benefits to receive disability); Brouillette v. Brouillette, 51 So. 3d 898 (La. Ct. App. 2010) (servicemember husband's post-decree waiver of non-exempt retirement pay in favor of exempt Combat Related Special Pay leaves wife with nothing); Mallard v. Burkart, 95 So. 3d 1264 (Miss. 2012) (husband's election of disability reduced payments to wife from $570/month to $120; state court powerless to allocate disability payments); Ghrist v. Ghrist, 2007 WL 1372690 (Tex. App. May 11, 2007) (ex-husband waived military retirement benefits to receive veterans disability; anti-alienation clause prevented any consideration of these benefits in property division; wife entitled only to half of remaining retirement benefits); Youngbluth v. Youngbluth, 6 A.3d 677 (Vt. 2010) (when military spouse, post-decree, waives non-exempt retirement pay in favor of exempt disability pay, divorce court may neither divide the disability pay nor alter original order to grant a larger percentage of the remaining retirement pay). *See also In re* Marriage of Poland, 264 P.3d 647 (Colo. App. 2011) (portion of retirement benefits that represents temporary disability retired list pay cannot be divided between divorcing spouses, but remainder of benefits can be). *But see* Bandini v. Bandini, 935 N.E.2d 253 (Ind. Ct. App. 2010) ("a military spouse may not, by a post-decree waiver of retirement pay in favor of disability benefits or CRSC, unilaterally and voluntarily reduce the benefits awarded to a spouse in a dissolution decree"). *But cf.* Nelms v. Nelms, 99 So. 3d 1228 (Ala. Civ. App. 2012) (spouse whose income includes veterans disability may be required to pay alimony, even if part of all of it must be paid from the disability benefits); Stone v. Stone, 26 So. 3d 1232 (Ala. Civ. App. 2009) (approving provision in divorce judgment forbidding husband to take any action to reduce wife's share of military disposable retirement pay, effectively forbidding him to waive non-exempt retirement pay and receive exempt veterans disability); Allen v. Allen, 941 A.2d 510 (Md. Ct. Spec. App. 2008) (husband who agreed to divide military pension with ex-wife, then voluntarily rejected regular retirement pay to collect exempt disability, breached a contract and can be ordered to pay ex-wife the promised sum); Scheidel v. Scheidel, 4 P.3d 670 (N.M. Ct. App. 2000) (veterans disability exempt from property division, but when husband voluntarily agreed to take disability benefits resulting in decrease in non-exempt retirement benefits, he could be required to compensate ex-wife, so long as disability benefits not required to be used); *In re* Marriage of Hayes, 208 P.3d 1046 (Or. Ct. App. 2009) (enforcing settlement agreement by which husband agreed to division of retirement pay, notwithstanding husband's later decision to waive retirement pay in favor of disability).

149 Sniadach v. Family Fin. Corp., 395 U.S. 337, 89 S. Ct. 1820, 23 L. Ed. 2d 349 (1969).

only postjudgment debts. Some states allow *ex parte* prejudgment property attachments, but these statutes have generally been held unconstitutional unless they are limited to exigent circumstances and include substantial procedural safeguards.[150]

Postjudgment garnishment and execution must still comply with federal due process standards. The major due process concern is to allow debtors to assert that certain of their assets are exempt from execution and thus may not be taken. In general, the due process clause requires notice of exemptions and the opportunity for a hearing on exemptions. It is also a due process violation to increase the judgment amount or the amount listed on a writ of execution without giving the debtor notice and an opportunity to be heard.[151]

Remedies for due process violations are discussed in more detail in other volumes in this series.[152]

12.3.2 The Constitutional Balancing of Interests

It is clear that a debtor has a significant property interest in assets which are exempt from garnishment,[153] and that garnishment involves state action sufficient to invoke Fourteenth Amendment protections.[154] Nevertheless, it is only since the late 1970s that courts have seriously considered the due process rights of judgment debtors. The relative dearth of earlier litigation and analysis was largely the result of a 1924 Supreme Court decision, *Endicott-Johnson v. Encyclopedia Press*,[155] which held that a judgment debtor has had his day in court and has, in effect, been given "notice of what will follow, no further notice being necessary to advance justice."[156] Thus the view of many courts was that the original service and proceedings in an action on a debt provided all the process the debtor was constitutionally due.[157]

---

150 Connecticut v. Doehr, 501 U.S. 1, 111 S. Ct. 2105, 115 L. Ed. 2d 1 (1991) (Connecticut statute allowing *ex parte* prejudgment attachment of realty in absence of exigent circumstances and without bond is unconstitutional); *In re* Foust, 310 F.3d 849 (5th Cir. 2002) (construing Mississippi prejudgment replevin statute to save its constitutionality; pre-seizure hearing required "where feasible"; denial of due process here, because complaint was "skeletal" and no showing that hearing not feasible); McLaughlin v. Weathers, 170 F.3d 577 (6th Cir. 1999) (Tennessee prejudgment attachment statute not unconstitutional on its face when attachment available only under "specified exigent circumstances" and procedure was available to challenge issuance of writ); Tri-State Dev. Ltd. v. Johnston, 160 F.3d 528 (9th Cir. 1998) (Washington's prejudgment attachment statute was unconstitutional on its face when attachment could be obtained *ex parte* without showing of exigent circumstances); Puerto Rican Am. Ins. v. Burgos-Diaz, 2005 WL 1643299 (D. P.R. June 30, 2005) (Puerto Rico's prejudgment remedy statute satisfies *Doehr* criteria, if construed to require either "extraordinary circumstances" or a prior interest in the subject property, and a likelihood of success on the merits); Gem Plumbing & Heating Co. v. Rossi, 867 A.2d 796 (R.I. 2005) (Rhode Island mechanics' lien statute, as amended to provide prompt hearing to challenge lien, satisfies due process); Shawmut Bank v. Costello, 643 A.2d 194 (R.I. 1994) (prejudgment remedy statute unconstitutional when *ex parte* writ issued with no showing of exigent circumstances and no requirement that creditor post bond); Van Blaricom v. Kronenberg, 50 P.3d 266 (Wash. Ct. App. 2002) (attorney may be liable for section 1983 violation for using Washington prejudgment statute that is unconstitutional as applied when no exigent circumstances). *See also* Frasher v. Fox Distrib. of S.W. Fla., Inc., 813 So. 2d 1017 (Fla. Dist. Ct. App. 2002) (affidavit insufficient to support prejudgment attachment, on both due process and state statutory grounds, when affiant failed to allege personal knowledge of removal, concealment, and so forth); State *ex rel.* Goldberg v. Mahoning Cnty. Probate Ct., 753 N.E.2d 192 (Ohio 2001) (judge's prejudgment order to seize property of attorney accused of stealing settlement proceeds was unconstitutional because no affidavit, bond, or ruling by independent magistrate). *But see* Quinata v. Nishimura, 2013 WL 5503108 (D. Haw. Oct. 2, 2013) (exigent circumstances need not be shown for *ex parte* writ of immediate possession when procedure included a sworn affidavit, a bond, issuance of the writ by a judge, opportunity for debtor to post counter-bond, and prompt post-deprivation hearing). *See generally* National Consumer Law Center, Repossessions § 5.3 (8th ed. 2013), *updated at* www.nclc.org/library (constitutionality of state replevin procedures).

151 Grillo v. BA Mortgage, L.L.C., 2004 WL 2250974 (E.D. Pa. Oct. 4, 2004); Union Nat'l Bank v. Ciongoli, 595 A.2d 179 (Pa. Super. Ct. 1991) (violation of due process to add late charges, escrow costs, attorney fees, and advances to amount of mortgage foreclosure judgment without giving debtor notice and opportunity to be heard).

152 National Consumer Law Center, Fair Debt Collection § 8.12 (8th ed. 2014); National Consumer Law Center, Repossessions § 13.7 (8th ed. 2013), *updated at* www.nclc.org/library.

153 Dionne v. Bouley, 757 F.2d 1344 (1st Cir. 1985); Mayers v. N.Y. Cmty. Bancorp, Inc., 2005 WL 2105810 (E.D.N.Y. Aug. 31, 2005) (exemption for Social Security benefits in bank account is property right protected by due process clause), *later decision at* 2006 WL 2013734 (E.D.N.Y. July 18, 2006) (denying defendants' motion for interlocutory appeal).

154 *See, e.g.*, Sniadach v. Family Fin. Corp., 395 U.S. 337, 89 S. Ct. 1820, 23 L. Ed. 2d 349 (1969); New v. Gemini Capital Group, 859 F. Supp. 2d 990 (S.D. Iowa 2012) (denying judgment creditor's motion for summary judgment; state action shown when judgment creditor jointly participated with state officials to seize disputed property under statute challenged as constitutional); Mayers v. N.Y. Cmty. Bancorp, Inc., 2005 WL 2105810 (E.D.N.Y. Aug. 31, 2005) (procedure for pre-garnishment bank account freeze was state action; state coercion present because bank that disregarded notice could be sanctioned for contempt), *later decision at* 2006 WL 2013734 (E.D.N.Y. July 18, 2006) (denying defendants' motion for interlocutory appeal); Doyle v. Schultz, 97 F. Supp. 2d 763 (W.D. La. 2000) (creditor and attorney were state actors when they set in motion state execution procedure that was unconstitutional as applied). *See also* Lugar v. Edmondson Oil Co., 457 U.S. 922, 932–33, 102 S. Ct. 2744, 73 L. Ed. 2d 482 (1982) ("the constitutional requirements of due process apply to garnishment and prejudgment attachment procedures whenever officers of the State act jointly with a creditor in securing the property in dispute"). *But cf.* Sykes v. Bank of Am., 723 F.3d 399 (2d Cir. 2013) (when judgment debtor is not challenging constitutionality of the procedure, garnishee bank is not acting under color of state law when it complies with state child support enforcement agency's improper garnishment order); McCarthy v. Wachovia Bank, 2008 WL 5145602 (E.D.N.Y. Dec. 4, 2008) (misuse of state procedure to garnish bank account would not be action under color of state law; fact question here); Christensen v. Arizona Cent. Credit Union, 2008 WL 4853414 (D. Ariz. Nov. 10, 2008) (misuse of state garnishment procedure to freeze account containing exempt Social Security not action under color of state law). *See generally* National Consumer Law Center, Fair Debt Collection § 8.12.2.1 (8th ed. 2014).

155 266 U.S. 285, 45 S. Ct. 61, 69 L. Ed. 288 (1924).

156 Endicott-Johnson v. Encyclopedia Press, 266 U.S. 285, 45 S. Ct. 61, 266 U.S. 288 (1924).

157 *See, e.g.*, Pitts v. Dallas Nurseries Garden Ctr., 545 S.W.2d 34 (Tex. App. 1976).

The blanket application of *Endicott* has, however, been seriously undermined by the influence of more recent Supreme Court due process decisions analyzing property deprivation in general and prejudgment garnishment in particular.[158] In addition, there is a growing judicial recognition that the garnishment involved in *Endicott*, which was decided before the legislative creation of most federal property exemptions and which did not refer to the possibility of exemptions, is facially distinguishable from modern garnishment cases involving potentially exempt property.[159]

Since the Third Circuit's 1980 decision in *Finberg v. Sullivan*,[160] the erosion of *Endicott* has proceeded rapidly. Although *Endicott* has not been expressly overruled, all circuits that have considered postjudgment garnishment or execution on potentially exempt property since 1976 have recognized the significant property interests of judgment debtors and have applied a balancing-of-interests analysis to determine the extent of debtors' due process rights to notice and hearing.[161] This approach has also been expressly adopted by virtually all federal district courts and state courts that have considered the issue after the *Finberg* decision.[162]

158 *See, e.g.*, North Ga. Finishing Inc. v. Di-Chem, Inc., 419 U.S. 601, 95 S. Ct. 719, 42 L. Ed. 2d 751 (1975); Mitchell v. W.T. Grant Co., 416 U.S. 600, 94 S. Ct. 1895, 40 L. Ed. 2d 406 (1974); Fuentes v. Shevin, 407 U.S. 67, 92 S. Ct. 1983, 32 L. Ed. 2d 556 (1972); Sniadach v. Family Fin. Corp., 395 U.S. 337, 89 S. Ct. 1820, 23 L. Ed. 2d 349 (1969).

159 Adkins v. Rumsfield, 464 F.3d 456 (4th Cir. 2006) (although *Endicott* not overruled, Supreme Court has "significantly revised" approach to due process in garnishment cases; applying *Matthews* balancing test and upholding procedure for enforcing state domestic relations orders); Dionne v. Bouley, 757 F.2d 1344 (1st Cir. 1985); New v. Gemini Capital Group, 859 F. Supp. 2d 990 (S.D. Iowa 2012); Dorwart v. Caraway, 966 P.2d 1121 (Mont. 1998) (distinguishing *Endicott* and questioning its continuing validity; Montana postjudgment procedure violates due process by failing to require prompt post-seizure notice of exemptions and procedure for claiming them).

160 634 F.2d 50 (3d Cir. 1980).

161 Aacen v. San Juan Cnty. Sheriff's Dep't, 944 F.2d 691 (10th Cir. 1991) (due process violation when notice failed to reveal existence of exemptions other than homestead exemption, or how to claim them); Reigh v. Schleigh, 784 F.2d 1191 (4th Cir. 1986) (new garnishment statute complied with due process); McCahey v. L.P. Investors, 774 F.2d 543 (2d Cir. 1985) (procedures satisfied due process); Dionne v. Bouley, 757 F.2d 1344 (1st Cir. 1985) (finding due process violation); Duranceau v. Wallace, 743 F.2d 709 (9th Cir. 1984) (procedures satisfied due process); Finberg v. Sullivan, 634 F.2d 50 (3d Cir. 1980) (finding due process violation); Brown v. Liberty Loan Corp. of Duval, 539 F.2d 1355 (5th Cir. 1976) (procedures satisfied due process). *See also* Revis v. Meldrum, 489 F.3d 273 (6th Cir. 2007) (*Endicott* inapplicable to postjudgment seizure of home; notice and opportunity for hearing necessary before removing debtor from home); Adkins v. Rumsfield, 464 F.3d 456 (4th Cir. 2006) (applying *Matthews* balancing test and concluding that Defense Department may implement state domestic relations garnishment orders without giving them more than facial scrutiny). *Cf.* Walsh v. Wal-Mart Stores, Inc., 836 F.2d 1152 (8th Cir. 1988) (no claim stated against employer for due process noncompliance in a garnishment proceeding; claim was against creditor).

162 *See, e.g.*, Mayers v. N.Y. Cmty. Bancorp, Inc., 2005 WL 2105810 (E.D.N.Y. Aug. 31, 2005) (plaintiffs sufficiently stated due process claim challenging New York's postjudgment garnishment procedure after rebalancing interests in light of technological changes), *later decision at* 2006 WL 2013734 (E.D.N.Y. July 18, 2006) (denying defendants' motion for interlocutory appeal); Hutchinson v. Cox, 784 F. Supp. 1339 (S.D. Ohio 1992) (due process requires that judgment debtor be informed, during postjudgment execution, of available exemptions and right to hearing); Jacobson v. Johnson, 798 F. Supp. 500 (C.D. Ill. 1991); Cristiano v. Courts of the Justice of the Peace, 669 F. Supp. 662 (D. Del. 1987) (Justice of the Peace courts' process for garnishment of wages invalid for failure to provide prompt post-deprivation hearing and sufficient notice of procedure for challenge); Follette v. Cooper, 658 F. Supp. 514 (N.D.N.Y. 1987); Follette v. Vitanza, 658 F. Supp. 492 (N.D.N.Y. 1987) (failure to give notice of federal wage garnishment exemptions and state procedures to assert them unconstitutional); Davis v. Paschall, 640 F. Supp. 198 (E.D. Ark. 1986); Fry's Food Stores v. CBM, Inc., 636 F. Supp. 168 (D. Ariz. 1986) (supplementary process statute unconstitutional); Green v. Harbin, 615 F. Supp. 719 (D. Ala. 1985); Neeley v. Century Fin. Co., 606 F. Supp. 1453 (D. Ariz. 1985) (garnishment statute unconstitutional; *Endicott* applies only when no exemptions possible); Clay v. Fisher, 584 F. Supp. 730 (S.D. Ohio 1984); Harris v. Bailey, 574 F. Supp. 966 (W.D. Va. 1983); Phillips v. Robinson Jewelers, Inc., Clearinghouse No. 31,761 (W.D. Okla. 1983); Deary v. Guardian Loan Co., 534 F. Supp. 1178 (S.D.N.Y. 1982); Betts v. Coltes, 467 F. Supp. 544 (D. Haw. 1979); Betts v. Tom, 431 F. Supp. 1369 (D. Haw. 1977); Dorwart v. Caraway, 966 P.2d 1121 (Mont. 1998) (Montana postjudgment procedure violates U.S. and Montana due process clauses by failing to require prompt post-seizure notice of exemptions, procedure for claiming them, and availability of hearing). *See also* Roy v. Smith, 735 F. Supp. 313 (C.D. Ill. 1990) (wages); Kirby v. Sprouls, 722 F. Supp. 516 (C.D. Ill. 1989) (state statute violated due process requirements when it failed to require notice of garnishment proceeding, notice of exemption rights under state and federal law, notice of debtor's right to exercise those rights and a prompt hearing); Burris v. Mahaney, 716 F. Supp. 1051 (M.D. Tenn. 1989); Jones v. Marion Cnty. Small Claims Ct., 701 F. Supp. 1414 (S.D. Ind. 1988) (state statute for garnishment of bank accounts violated due process requirements of prompt notice and hearing); Imperial Bank v. Pim Elec., Inc., 39 Cal. Rptr. 3d 432 (Cal. Ct. App. 1995); Cole v. Goldberger, Pederson & Hochron, 410 N.Y.S.2d 950 (N.Y. Sup. Ct.1978); Layne v. West Va. Child Support Enforcement Div., 518 S.E.2d 357 (W. Va. 1998) (due process requires notice and an opportunity for hearing before disability benefits can be garnished for child support arrearage). *Cf.* Bell v. Beightler, 2003 WL 116146 (Ohio Ct. App. Jan. 14, 2003) (upholding procedures for garnishment of prison inmate's account; administrative hearing on exemptions is sufficient). *But see* Aga v. Steele, 2009 WL 649914 (D. Haw. Mar. 12, 2009) (*Endicott* still good law; for judgment debt, right to prompt post-garnishment notice and hearing not "clearly established"); Haines v. Gen. Motors Corp., 603 F. Supp. 471 (S.D. Ohio 1983) (*Endicott* is controlling). *But cf.* Huggins v. Pataki, 2002 WL 1732804 (E.D.N.Y. July 11, 2002) (New York's bank account garnishment procedure, which requires creditor to send notice to debtor after account is frozen, is constitutional even though bank could have determined that account consisted entirely of directly-deposited Social Security funds, and even though creditor failed to send the required notice); *In re* Thelen, 156 B.R. 786 (Bankr. W.D. Mich. 1993) (*Endicott* still good law, no notice or hearing required for seizure of clearly non-exempt property; distinguishing cases requiring notice of possible exemptions).

Earlier decisions generally rejected due process challenges but had no uniform rationale for doing so. *See, e.g.*, First Nat'l Bank v. Hasty, 410 F. Supp. 482 (E.D. Mich. 1976) (rejecting pre-garnishment hearing under *Mitchell*); Phillips v. Bartolomie, 121 Cal. Rptr. 56 (Cal. Ct. App. 1975) (debtor may be required to file exemption claim); Raigoza v. Sperl, 110 Cal. Rptr. 296 (Cal. Ct. App. 1973) (statute contained sufficient due process protections); Warner/Elektra/Atlantic Corp. v. B. & B. Record & Tape Merchandisers, 570 P.2d 1320 (Colo. App. 1977) (no exemption issue); Wilson v. Grimes, 207 S.E.2d 5 (Ga. 1974); Bittner v. Butts, 514 S.W.2d 556 (Mo. 1974); Plaza Hotel Assocs. v. Wellington Assocs., 378 N.Y.S.2d 859 (N.Y. Sup. Ct. 1975); Hehr v. Tucker, 472 P.2d 797 (Or. 1970); Pitts v. Dallas Nurseries Garden Ctr., 545 S.W.2d

The due process analysis for postjudgment garnishment and execution procedures relating to exempt property incorporates the balancing test set out by the Supreme Court in 1976 in *Matthews v. Eldridge*.[163] Under this three-pronged approach, a court considering the process due when a person is deprived of property must weigh:

- The competing interests involved and the effect of state action on these interests;
- The risk of erroneous deprivation of property under the existing system and the probable value of additional or substitute procedures; and
- The cost and administrative burden of the new procedures in comparison to their probable value.

A creditor has a clear interest in the prompt and inexpensive satisfaction of judgments it has obtained,[164] and a state has a parallel interest in seeing that judgments that it issues are given effect. However, the creditor has no interest whatsoever in the debtor's exempt property, and depriving a debtor of exempt assets may both endanger the debtor's subsistence and frustrate the legislative policies upon which the exemptions are based.

The strength of creditor and debtor property interests may be modified, at least in part, by the facts of a particular case. For example, creditor interests appear to be stronger when garnishment is for child support than when it is for an ordinary civil judgment.[165] On the debtor's side of the equation, some courts have suggested that bank accounts containing exempt funds deserve even stronger protection than a debtor's wages because the garnishment of such an account may deprive the debtor of *all* money needed immediately for food and shelter, whereas a partial wage garnishment would still leave the debtor with most of his or her salary.[166]

Applying the *Matthews* tests, courts generally hold that postjudgment garnishment and execution must comply with four procedural requirements. These standards are discussed in the next four subsections. Section 12.3.7, *infra*, discusses the due process issues when a bank account containing exempt funds is frozen upon the bank's receipt of a garnishment order.

12.3.3 Prompt Post-Garnishment Notice Is Required

Courts applying the *Matthews* analysis have almost uniformly ruled that state laws violate due process when they allow garnishment without any notice (other than the actual notice the debtor gets upon, for example, receiving a smaller paycheck).[167] The reason for this is fairly clear: a notice require-

34 (Tex. App. 1976); Dep't of Social & Health Servs. v. Gerlack, 612 P.2d 382 (Wash. Ct. App. 1980). *See also* McCahey v. L.P. Investors, 774 F.2d 543, 547 n.5 (2d Cir. 1985).

163 424 U.S. 319, 96 S. Ct. 893, 47 L. Ed. 2d 18 (1976).

164 McCahey v. L.P. Investors, 774 F.2d 543, 549 (2d Cir. 1985) (creditor has interest in reaching bank accounts and other liquid assets because this is lowest-cost method of satisfying judgments).

165 This observation, while frequently not acknowledged by courts, seems to be borne out by the results in child support cases. *See, e.g.*, DeTienne v. DeTienne, 815 F. Supp. 394 (D. Kan. 1993) (Social Security disability benefits are subject to garnishment for child support and alimony). *See also* Levy v. San Joaquin Cnty. Dep't of Child Support Servs., 2013 WL 1891402 (N.D. Cal. May 6, 2013) (if debtor owed child support, he had no protectable property interest in licenses and garnished wages, because he had not entitlement to them); Green v. Harbin, 615 F. Supp. 719 (D. Ala. 1985) (adopting consent decree that imposed due process protections on garnishment but excluded garnishment for child and spousal support).

166 Reigh v. Schleigh, 595 F. Supp. 1535 (D. Md. 1984), *rev'd on other grounds*, 784 F.2d 1191 (4th Cir. 1986); Harris v. Bailey, 574 F. Supp. 966 (W.D. Va. 1983). *But cf.* Neeley v. Century Fin. Co., 606 F. Supp. 1453 (D. Ariz. 1985) (wages entitled to greater protection than other assets).

167 *See* Dionne v. Bouley, 757 F.2d 1344 (1st Cir. 1985); Jones v. Marion Cnty. Small Claims Ct., 701 F. Supp. 1414 (S.D. Ind. 1988) (state statute for garnishment of bank accounts violated due process requirements of prompt notice and hearing); Reigh v. Schleigh, 595 F. Supp. 1535 (D. Md. 1984), *rev'd on other grounds*, 784 F.2d 1191 (4th Cir. 1986); Clay v. Fisher, 584 F. Supp. 730 (S.D. Ohio 1984); Deary v. Guardian Loan Co., 534 F. Supp. 1178 (S.D.N.Y. 1982); E.J. McKernan Co. v. Gregory, 643 N.E.2d 1370 (Ill. App. Ct. 1994) (former version of Illinois non-wage garnishment law was unconstitutional because, prior to issuance of garnishment summons, it failed to provide notice and hearing regarding possible exemptions); Dorwart v. Caraway, 966 P.2d 1121 (Mont. 1998); Cole v. Goldberger, Pederson & Hochron, 410 N.Y.S.2d 950 (N.Y. Sup. Ct.). *See also* Doyle v. Schultz, 97 F. Supp. 2d 763 (W.D. La. 2000) (Louisiana procedure for executing on judgments was unconstitutional as applied when house was seized pursuant to Texas judgment without notice that judgment had been domesticated); CBM v. Sevier, 910 P.2d 654 (Ariz. Ct. App. 1996) (when creditor sought to garnish one spouse's wages for pre-marital debt, in a community property state non-debtor spouse should be joined in order to have notice and opportunity to be heard on what property each spouse contributed); Romero v. Star Mkts., 922 P.2d 1018 (Haw. Ct. App. 1996) (when procedure for collecting workers' compensation awards was to move for entry of court judgment, employer who had already participated in administrative hearing must be served with motion; employee's *ex parte* garnishment violated due process). *Cf.* Sheppard v. Welch, 2005 WL 1656873 (S.D. Ind. July 5, 2005) (child support obligor stated due process claim when prosecutor issued wage and bank account garnishment orders without the required notice to obligor), *later decision at* 2006 WL 3134869 (S.D. Ind. Oct. 3, 2006) (summary judgment for state; no section 1983 violation when lack of notice was "random and unauthorized" and state post-deprivation remedy was adequate); Savage v. Scales, 310 F. Supp. 2d 122 (D.D.C. 2004) (due process requires only reasonable effort to provide notice; sending notice of administrative garnishment for student loan to last known address is sufficient); First Resolution Inv. Corp. v. Seker, 795 A.2d 868 (N.J. 2002) (holding that notice procedure permitting ordinary mail if certified mail "unclaimed" satisfied due process, but recommending that rule be revised to require that creditor show how it obtained debtor's "last known address"). *But see* Brown v. Liberty Loan Corp., 539 F.2d 1355 (5th Cir. 1976) (primarily but not exclusively addressing pre-garnishment notice). *But cf.* Roush v. Basham, 1998 U.S. App. LEXIS 12903 (4th Cir. June 18, 1998) (no denial of due process when child support enforcement agency was simply negligent, and state court had already ordered return of improperly garnished wages); Farrar v. Glantz, 2000 U.S. Dist. LEXIS 6502 (N.D. Ill. Apr. 25, 2000) (no due process violation when computer error prevented consumer from receiving notice of small claims proceeding; simple negligence is not sufficient, and state court proceeding enabled consumer to prevent taking of any property); Price v. Sec'y of Revenue & Taxation, 664 So. 2d 802 (La. Ct. App. 1995) (under community property law,

ment places little burden on a creditor and gives the debtor an opportunity to challenge any improper garnishment.

Nevertheless, a number of courts have ruled that due process does not require notice *prior* to garnishment.[168] This position is based on the fear that, in cases involving the garnishment of bank accounts or moveable property, a debtor might remove the property to defeat a valid garnishment. However a prior notice requirement has also been rejected in some wage garnishment cases,[169] even though there can be no reason to fear that unpaid wages will be concealed or removed. In the case of wage garnishment, the only burden placed on the creditor by prior notice would be a minor delay in the commencement of the garnishment while the debtor is given an opportunity to defend his or her wages.

Instead of pre-garnishment notice, courts have required that notice be contemporaneous with, or immediately follow, the garnishment. Exactly what this means in practice is unclear. For example, a district court in Hawaii required notice *and a hearing* within two days of garnishment.[170] The Second Circuit upheld a rule allowing the mailing of notice within four days of garnishment.[171] Another court found twenty days between garnishment and notice to be clearly too long.[172] A district court in Idaho held that notice provided only when garnished funds were about to be turned over to the creditor was insufficient.[173] Because there will necessarily be a delay from when the debtor receives notice of a garnishment until the debtor can obtain a hearing, it is important for the debtor to receive notice as soon as possible.

A related procedural protection would be to require the creditor, in seeking a writ of garnishment, to file an affidavit with a judicial officer, stating that the assets to be garnished are not exempt. One court held, in the wage garnishment context, that the absence of such a requirement was a "substantial defect," although it found the garnishment procedure as a whole to meet due process requirements.[174]

---

wages of non-debtor wife could be garnished without notice for tax debt of husband's corporation).

168 *See, e.g.*, Lind v. Midland Funding, L.L.C., 688 F.3d 402 (8th Cir. 2012) (notice that allows assertion of exemptions is sufficient even if given after garnishment is issued; notice just to debtor sufficient when non-debtor co-owner of bank account had actual notice); Nat'l Labor Relations Bd. v. E.D.P. Med. Computer Sys., Inc., 6 F.3d 951 (2d Cir. 1993) (*ex parte* writ justified by extraordinary situation); McCahey v. L.P. Investors, 774 F.2d 543 (2d Cir. 1985) (bank account); Dionne v. Bouley, 757 F.2d 1344 (1st Cir. 1985) (bank account); Finberg v. Sullivan, 634 F.2d 50 (3d Cir. 1980) (bank account); Brown v. Liberty Loan Corp., 539 F.2d 1355 (5th Cir. 1976) (wages); Tift v. Snohomish Cnty., 764 F. Supp. 2d 1247 (W.D. Wash. 2011) (judgment debtor need not be provided opportunity to claim exemptions at the moment of seizure of personal property; providing notice of procedure to assert exemptions is sufficient); Hollowell v. Hosto, 2010 WL 1416519 (E.D. Ark. Apr. 8, 2010) (prompt post-garnishment hearing sufficient to protect rights in bank account containing Social Security funds; neither due process nor the Social Security Act forbid temporary freeze while debtor exercises exemption rights), *aff'd as modified*, 389 Fed. Appx. 583 (8th Cir. 2010) (unpublished); Carter v. Welch, 1999 U.S. Dist. LEXIS 6705 (S.D. Ala. Mar. 12, 1999) (due process requirements satisfied by offering a pre-deprivation hearing before taking funds from inmate account to satisfy court-ordered restitution), *adopted by* 1999 U.S. Dist. LEXIS 6771 (S.D. Ala. Apr. 27, 1999); Nelson v. Silverman, 888 F. Supp. 1041 (S.D. Cal. 1995) (Internal Revenue Service may levy on wages or real property without pre-seizure notice or hearing; post-seizure procedures satisfy due process); Roy v. Smith, 735 F. Supp. 313 (C.D. Ill. 1990) (wages); Ortiz v. Valdez, 971 P.2d 1076 (Colo. App. 1998) (following *Endicott*; Colorado's postjudgment garnishment scheme acceptable, even though it resulted in non-debtor's exempt Social Security funds being frozen for at least five weeks); First Union Nat'l Bank v. Knyal, 874 So. 2d 716 (Fla. Dist. Ct. App. 2004) (pre-garnishment notice not required for postjudgment garnishment); Collection Prof'ls, Inc. v. Logan, 695 N.E.2d 1344 (Ill. App. Ct. 1998) (amended Illinois postjudgment garnishment statute provided due process when it required debtors to be notified of garnishment, exemptions, procedure for claiming them, and hearing within two days of service of garnishment summons); Leger v. Comm'r of Revenue, 654 N.E.2d 927 (Mass. 1995) (tax collection an exception to rule that requires pre-seizure notice for liens on real estate). *See also* Huggins v. Pataki, 2002 WL 1732804 (E.D.N.Y. July 11, 2002) (New York's bank account garnishment procedure, which requires creditor to send notice to debtor after account is frozen, is constitutional even though bank could have determined that account consisted entirely of directly-deposited Social Security funds and even though creditor failed to send the required notice); United Presidential Life Ins. Co. v. King, 361 So. 2d 710 (Fla. 1978) (constitution does not require notice to judgment debtor and hearing before issuance of writ of garnishment); Harrel v. State, 286 S.W.3d 315 (Tex. 2009) (prisoner has property right in inmate trust account, but garnishment for court costs presents small risk of erroneous deprivation when costs set at time of conviction and defendant has opportunity to contest; notice at time of garnishment and post-garnishment hearing sufficient to handle claim that amount of garnishment does not accord with court order). *Cf.* Kennedy v. Comm'r of Social Sec., 1999 U.S. App. LEXIS 34031 (6th Cir. Dec. 21, 1999) (Social Security recipient failed to state due process claim for state's failure to follow state procedures in garnishing exempt funds when he did not allege that state failed to provide meaningful post-deprivation process). *But see* Doyle v. Schultz, 97 F. Supp. 2d 763 (W.D. La. 2000) (Louisiana procedure for executing on judgments unconstitutional as applied when it allowed seizure for out-of-state judgment before notifying debtors that judgment had been domesticated).

169 Brown v. Liberty Loan Corp., 539 F.2d 1355 (5th Cir. 1976); Roy v. Smith, 735 F. Supp. 313 (C.D. Ill. 1990); Betts v. Coltes, 467 F. Supp. 544 (D. Haw. 1979). *See also* Raigoza v. Sperl, 110 Cal. Rptr. 296 (Cal. Ct. App. 1973); Wilson v. Grimes, 207 S.E.2d 5 (Ga. 1974); Hehr v. Tucker, 472 P.2d 797 (Or. 1970).

170 Betts v. Tom, 431 F. Supp. 1369 (D. Haw. 1977). *But see* Aga v. Steele, 2009 WL 649914 (D. Haw. Mar. 12, 2009) (*Endicott* still good law; for judgment debt, right to prompt post-garnishment notice and hearing not "clearly established").

171 McCahey v. L.P. Investors, 593 F. Supp. 319 (E.D.N.Y. 1984), *aff'd*, 774 F.2d 543 (2d Cir. 1985). *But see* Mayers v. N.Y. Cmty. Bancorp, Inc., 2005 WL 2105810 (E.D.N.Y. Aug. 31, 2005) (suggesting *McCahey* should be re-evaluated in light of technological changes), *later decision at* 2006 WL 2013734 (E.D.N.Y. July 18, 2006) (denying defendants' motion for interlocutory appeal).

172 Neeley v. Century Fin. Co., 606 F. Supp. 1453 (D. Ariz. 1985).

173 New v. Gemini Capital Group, 859 F. Supp. 2d 990 (S.D. Iowa 2012) (denying judgment creditor's motion for summary judgment; notice also failed to disclose existence of exemptions or procedure for claiming them).

174 Brown v. Liberty Loan Corp., 539 F.2d 1355, 1369 (5th Cir. 1976). *See also* Betts v. Tom, 431 F. Supp. 1369 (D. Haw. 1977) (affidavit required for *ex parte* garnishments). *See generally* North Ga. Finishing Inc. v. Di-Chem, Inc., 419 U.S. 601, 95 S. Ct. 719, 42 L. Ed. 2d 751 (1975).

12.3.4 *Notice Must Inform Debtor of Exemptions*

Numerous cases have set out a consistent set of guidelines as to what a garnishment notice must state in order to satisfy due process. The notice must inform the debtor that garnishment has occurred, describe major legal exemptions from garnishment, and describe what procedures the debtor can follow to contest the garnishment.[175] Disclosing this information places little burden on creditors or the state, because the information can be included in a preprinted form. These disclosures, on the other hand, are very important to a debtor who often does not know of the existence of exemptions or how to contest improper garnishment.

The courts have not required garnishment notices to list exhaustively all the potential legal exemptions. Courts have reasoned that this would place an excessive burden on creditors who would have to change the notice whenever federal or state exemption law changed,[176] that the notice would be too complicated to be understood by most debtors,[177] and that composing notices is widely regarded as a legislative task.[178] However, notices violate due process if they do not at least include mention of some of the most important exemptions.[179] In particular, courts have required notices to list the potential availability of exemptions for Social Security,[180] TANF benefits,[181] and wage payments.[182] Other exemptions which may have to be listed include SSI, veterans benefits, unemployment compensation, workers' compensation, alimony and child support, pensions, personal property, and lump-sum state exemptions.[183] The list will vary from state to state.

12.3.5 *Notice Must Inform Debtor of Procedures to Contest Garnishment*

In a utility termination case, the Supreme Court held that notice of the customer's right to dispute a municipal utility's actions was not meaningful unless the notice included a statement of the procedure which the customer should use to challenge the deprivation of services.[184] Federal courts have applied this principle to garnishment and execution notices by requiring that the notice state what action a debtor may take to contest the procedure.[185]

---

175 Aacen v. San Juan Cnty. Sheriff's Dep't, 944 F.2d 691 (10th Cir. 1991); McCahey v. L.P. Investors, 774 F.2d 543 (2d Cir. 1985) (reference to exemptions and fact that procedures exist, and suggestion to contact legal aid society, is sufficient); Dionne v. Bouley, 757 F.2d 1344 (1st Cir. 1985); Finberg v. Sullivan, 634 F.2d 50 (3d Cir. 1980); New v. Gemini Capital Group, 859 F. Supp. 2d 990 (S.D. Iowa 2012) (denying judgment creditor's motion for summary judgment; notice that did not disclose exemptions or method for claiming them was inadequate); Montanez v. Beard, 2012 WL 6917775 (M.D. Pa. Aug. 10, 2012) (fact issue whether sentencing hearing and new inmate orientation materials provided constitutionally adequate notice of procedure for contesting the taking of funds from inmate account for fines, fees, or restitution); Jacobson v. Johnson, 798 F. Supp. 500 (C.D. Ill. 1991); Neeley v. Century Fin. Co., 606 F. Supp. 1453 (D. Ariz. 1985); Reigh v. Schleigh, 595 F. Supp. 1535 (D. Md. 1984), *rev'd on other grounds*, 784 F.2d 1191 (4th Cir. 1986); Clay v. Fisher, 584 F. Supp. 730 (S.D. Ohio 1984) (due process requires prompt and adequate notice and hearing on exemption claims); Harris v. Bailey, 574 F. Supp. 966 (W.D. Va. 1983); Deary v. Guardian Loan Co., 534 F. Supp. 1178 (S.D.N.Y. 1982); Betts v. Tom, 431 F. Supp. 1369 (D. Haw. 1977); Collection Prof'ls, Inc. v. Logan, 695 N.E.2d 1344 (Ill. App. Ct. 1998) (amended Illinois postjudgment garnishment statute provided due process of law when it required debtors to be notified of garnishment, exemptions, procedure for claiming them, and hearing within two days of service of garnishment summons); Dorwart v. Caraway, 966 P.2d 1121 (Mont. 1998). *See also* Zeppieri v. New Haven Provision Co., 163 F. Supp. 2d 126 (D. Conn. 2001) (Connecticut postjudgment bank execution statute meets due process standards by requiring bank to send exemption claim form to debtor promptly after receiving execution); Hutchinson v. Cox, 784 F. Supp. 1339 (S.D. Ohio 1992) (denial of due process not to inform judgment debtor of exemptions and right to hearing during postjudgment execution); Roy v. Smith, 735 F. Supp. 313 (C.D. Ill. 1990); Kirby v. Sprouls, 722 F. Supp. 516 (C.D. Ill. 1989); State of Washington v. Thompson, 6 S.W.3d 82 (Ark. 1999) (procedures for child support obligor to challenge out-of-state order, which require an affirmative request for a hearing by a deadline, meet due process, but it was error to deny hearing when obligor was sent inconsistent instructions about the procedure); Imperial Bank v. Pim Elec., Inc., 39 Cal. Rptr. 3d 432 (Cal. Ct. App. 1995) (due process satisfied when notice of possible exemptions given at time of seizure); First Resolution Inv. Corp. v. Seker, 795 A.2d 868 (N.J. 2002) (rejecting constitutional challenge to New Jersey notice procedure but recommending rule changes to give debtors more information about how to contest garnishment). *Cf. In re* Pontes, 310 F. Supp. 2d 447 (D.R.I. 2004) (tax sale notice must advise debtor of right of redemption); Resler v. Messerli & Kramer, Prof'l Ass'n, 2003 WL 193498 (D. Minn. Jan. 23, 2003) (allegation that garnishment notice failed to disclose certain state exemptions stated claims under Fair Debt Collection Procedures Act and state law).

176 *See* Dionne v. Bouley, 757 F.2d 1344 (1st Cir. 1985); Reigh v. Schleigh, 595 F. Supp. 1535 (D. Md. 1984), *rev'd on other grounds*, 784 F.2d 1191 (4th Cir. 1986).

177 Reigh v. Schleigh, 595 F. Supp. 1535 (D. Md. 1984), *rev'd on other grounds*, 784 F.2d 1191 (4th Cir. 1986).

178 Neeley v. Century Fin. Co., 606 F. Supp. 1453 (D. Ariz. 1985). *See also* Brown v. Liberty Loan Corp., 539 F.2d 1355 (5th Cir. 1976).

179 Aacen v. San Juan Cnty. Sheriff's Dep't, 944 F.2d 691 (10th Cir. 1991) (due process violation when notice failed to reveal existence of exemptions other than homestead exemption or how to claim them). *But see* Reigh v. Schleigh, 595 F. Supp. 1535 (D. Md. 1984) (mere notice that there are federal and state exemptions was sufficient), *rev'd on other grounds*, 784 F.2d 1191 (4th Cir. 1986).

180 Harris v. Bailey, 574 F. Supp. 966 (W.D. Va. 1983).

181 Betts v. Tom, 431 F. Supp. 1369 (D. Haw. 1977).

182 Neeley v. Century Fin. Co., 606 F. Supp. 1453 (D. Ariz. 1985). *See also* Roy v. Smith, 735 F. Supp. 313 (C.D. Ill. 1990).

183 Aacen v. San Juan Cnty. Sheriff's Dep't, 944 F.2d 691 (10th Cir. 1991) (due process violation when notice failed to reveal existence of exemptions other than homestead exemption or how to claim them); McCahey v. L.P. Investors, 774 F.2d 543 (2d Cir. 1985) (upholding New York statute); Hutchinson v. Cox, 784 F. Supp. 1339 (S.D. Ohio 1992) (denial of due process not to inform judgment debtor of personal property exemptions and that debtor could obtain a hearing to claim exemption); Green v. Harbin, 615 F. Supp. 719 (D. Ala. 1985) (consent decree).

184 Memphis Light, Gas & Water Div. v. Craft, 436 U.S. 1, 98 S. Ct. 1554, 56 L. Ed. 2d 30 (1978). *See also* Mullane v. Central Hanover Bank & Trust Co., 339 U.S. 306, 70 S. Ct. 652, 94 L. Ed. 865 (1950) (discussing notice requirements).

185 *See* § 12.3.4, *supra*. *See also* New v. Gemini Capital Group, 859 F. Supp. 2d 990 (S.D. Iowa 2012) (denying judgment creditor's motion

A few courts have held that a mere citation to the statute or court rule governing procedures to contest garnishment is a sufficient description of those procedures.[186] For example, the Second Circuit upheld a garnishment notice which told the debtor that procedures were available to challenge garnishment, cited the procedures without explanation, and told the debtor to contact either the creditor or an attorney, including legal aid. The court found no due process violation in that case even though the debtor had contacted the creditor, as the notice advised, and the creditor continued the garnishment process, denying receiving the welfare check stub which the debtor sent him to prove the exemption. A far more effective procedure to enable the debtor to protect exempt property is a garnishment notice that contains the form the state's courts use to claim an exemption, specifies the where and when to file an exemption claim, and advises the debtor to consult an attorney.[187]

12.3.6 Debtor Has a Right to a Prompt Hearing

Due process also requires that debtors have the right to obtain a hearing to contest a garnishment or execution within a reasonable period after it has occurred.[188] The courts have widely recognized that delays can impose severe hardship on debtors and that a statute allowing a significant delay prior to a hearing is unconstitutional. As with the timing of notice of garnishment or execution, however, no particular reasonable time before a hearing has been agreed upon. The Third Circuit held that a court rule allowing fifteen days before a hearing on a debtor's petition allowed too much time to elapse,[189] and cases rejecting longer periods are common.[190] One district court required a hearing within two days of garnishment.[191]

Several courts have strongly criticized statutory provisions which allow discretionary continuances or pre-hearing delays pending discovery.[192] At least one court has ruled that such provisions violate due process.[193] That court did not cite any evidence that the provisions were actually invoked, but other courts have required proof that the debtor was excessively delayed in his or her attempt to obtain a hearing to contest the garnishment or execution.[194] To be safe, the consumer's attorney should develop a full factual record before challenging the statute on this ground, such that the existence in actual practice of unconstitutional delays will be unquestioned.

---

for summary judgment; notice that did not disclose exemptions or method for claiming them was inadequate); Hutchinson v. Cox, 784 F. Supp. 1339 (S.D. Ohio 1992) (denial of due process not to inform judgment debtor of exemptions and right to hearing during postjudgment execution).

186 McCahey v. L.P. Investors, 774 F.2d 543 (2d Cir. 1985). *See also* Burris v. Mahaney, 716 F. Supp. 1051 (M.D. Tenn. 1989) (judgment debtor attributed with notice of contents of garnishment document, served on employer, that stated debtor had right to court hearing and directed her to clerk for forms but that debtor did not read in its entirety); Neeley v. Century Fin. Co., 606 F. Supp. 1453 (D. Ariz. 1985).

187 *See, e.g.*, First Resolution Inv. Corp. v. Seker, 795 A.2d 868 (N.J. 2002) (rejecting constitutional challenge but ordering Civil Practice Committee to revise form notice to provide further information to debtor about how to challenge garnishment).

188 *See, e.g.*, Dionne v. Bouley, 757 F.2d 1344 (1st Cir. 1985); Finberg v. Sullivan, 634 F.2d 50 (3d Cir. 1980); Brown v. Liberty Loan Corp., 539 F.2d 1355 (5th Cir. 1976); Kirby v. Sprouls, 722 F. Supp. 516 (C.D. Ill. 1989) (constitutional right to opportunity for hearing "within a meaningful time"); Jones v. Marion Cnty. Small Claims Ct., 701 F. Supp. 1414 (S.D. Ind. 1988) (state statute for garnishment of bank accounts violated due process requirements of prompt notice and hearing); Neeley v. Century Fin. Co., 606 F. Supp. 1453 (D. Ariz. 1985); Reigh v. Schleigh, 595 F. Supp. 1535 (D. Md. 1984), *rev'd on other grounds*, 784 F.2d 1191 (4th Cir. 1986); Dorwart v. Caraway, 966 P.2d 1121 (Mont. 1998). *See also* Jordan v. Fox, Rothschild, O'Brien & Frankel, 20 F.3d 1250 (3d Cir. 1994) (absent prejudgment waiver, obtaining execution on confessed judgment without providing any means of securing pre-deprivation hearing or prompt post-seizure relief deprives debtor of due process); Alaska Dep't of Revenue v. Maxwell, 6 P.3d 733 (Alaska 2000) (child support order void for denial of due process when obligor was given no opportunity to be heard on issue of paternity before issuance of administrative order); Highsmith v. Dep't of Pub. Aid, 803 N.E.2d 652 (Ill. App. Ct. 2004) (administrative hearing on attachment of investment account for child support arrears inadequate when departmental rule excluded non-documentary proof of ownership); Collection Prof'ls, Inc. v. Logan, 695 N.E.2d 1344 (Ill. App. Ct. 1998) (right to hearing on postjudgment garnishment within twenty-one to thirty days is sufficient); Flowers v. Flowers, 799 N.E.2d 1183 (Ind. Ct. App. 2003) (due process requires that child support obligor be allowed to attend hearing on income withholding). *Cf.* McCahey v. L.P. Investors, 774 F.2d 543 (2d Cir. 1985) (absence of mandatory time limit for hearing did not violate due process without evidence that debtor could not, in fact, receive prompt hearing); Montanez v. Beard, 2012 WL 6917775 (M.D. Pa. Aug. 10, 2012) (inmate grievance process was adequate opportunity to be heard as to removal of funds from inmate accounts for fines, fees, or restitution; pre-deprivation hearing not required); Tift v. Snohomish Cnty., 764 F. Supp. 2d 1247 (W.D. Wash. 2011) (judgment debtor need not be provided opportunity to claim exemptions at the moment of seizure of personal property; providing notice of procedure to assert exemptions is sufficient). *But see* Ortiz v. Valdez, 971 P.2d 1076 (Colo. App. 1998) (finding Colorado's postjudgment garnishment scheme acceptable, even though it resulted in freezing of non-debtor's exempt Social Security funds for at least five weeks). *But cf.* Sommer v. Maharaj, 854 N.E.2d 441 (Mass. 2006) (through his contumacious actions, facilitated by his wife, judgment debtor forfeited his right to hearing on wife's claims that assets were hers).

189 Finberg v. Sullivan, 634 F.2d 50 (3d Cir. 1980). *But see* Reigh v. Schleigh, 595 F. Supp. 1535 (D. Md. 1984) (court should not specify exact timetable), *rev'd on other grounds*, 784 F.2d 1191 (4th Cir. 1986).

190 Neeley v. Century Fin. Co., 606 F. Supp. 1453 (D. Ariz. 1985) (thirty-four days with possible continuance); Clay v. Fisher, 584 F. Supp. 730 (S.D. Ohio 1984) (five weeks); Harris v. Bailey, 574 F. Supp. 966 (W.D. Va. 1983) (two months). *But see* Green v. Harbin, 615 F. Supp. 719 (D. Ala. 1985) (consent decree apparently allowing up to three weeks before hearing a contested motion to dissolve garnishment).

191 Betts v. Tom, 431 F. Supp. 1369 (D. Haw. 1977).

192 Finberg v. Sullivan, 634 F.2d 50 (3d Cir. 1980); Neeley v. Century Fin. Co., 606 F. Supp. 1453 (D. Ariz. 1985). *See also* Green v. Harbin, 615 F. Supp. 719 (D. Ala. 1985).

193 Neeley v. Century Fin. Co., 606 F. Supp. 1453 (D. Ariz. 1985).

194 McCahey v. L.P. Investors, 774 F.2d 543 (2d Cir. 1985) (refusing to find statute that did not specify time for hearing unconstitutional on its face, when a prompt hearing was allowed and the debtor failed to use proper procedure to contest the garnishment); Reigh v. Schleigh, 595 F. Supp. 1535 (D. Md. 1984), *rev'd on other grounds*, 784 F.2d 1191 (4th Cir. 1986).

12.3.7 Due Process Issues When Account Is Frozen Upon Bank's Receipt of Garnishment Notice

In general, state bank account garnishment procedures contemplate that the bank will freeze the debtor's bank account upon its receipt of a garnishment order. Many state laws specifically authorize the bank to freeze only *non*-exempt funds.[195] However, some state laws may be interpreted to require a bank to freeze a debtor's bank account upon receipt of a garnishment notice, even if the account consists wholly or partially of exempt funds such as Social Security benefits. The account remains frozen until the debtor obtains a ruling or an acknowledgment by the creditor that the funds are exempt—a process that may take weeks.

Due process litigation in the 1970s focused on informing the borrower of the procedures to claim exemptions and the need for a prompt resolution of exemption claims but did not generally protect exempt funds from being frozen while those procedures took place. A 2005 district court decision, *Mayers v. New York Cmty. Bankcorp*,[196] takes a fresh look at the constitutionality of freezing the debtor's bank account in light of technological changes. In particular, the court noted that the Social Security Administration's requirement that beneficiaries receive payments electronically, unless they specifically opt out, has increased the risk and severity of erroneous deprivation and decreased the burden of determining whether bank accounts contain only exempt funds. Balancing these factors, along with the government's interest in avoiding clogging up the courts with exemption claims, the *Mayers* court held that the plaintiffs had the right to proceed on their claim that the New York bank account garnishment procedure denied debtors procedural due process by allowing accounts that contained only exempt electronically deposited Social Security funds to be frozen upon service of the garnishment order. A subsequent decision, *Granger v. Harris*, also finds that the constitutional balancing test may dictate a different result than previous cases because of the new realities.[197]

There is also an argument, not yet reached by the courts, that the Supremacy Clause requires that federal exemptions trump any state law procedures that would defeat the efficacy of the federal exemptions by allowing the benefits to be frozen in the consumer's bank account.[198] Even if it is proper for state procedures to apply to garnishment of funds exempt under state law, they should not apply to benefits that are exempt under federal law, when those state procedures affect federal substantive rights. Many state statutes were enacted long before direct deposit of federal benefits and even before the existence of exempt benefits under federal law. It would be odd if funds exempt under *federal* law could be forfeited when the consumer fails to follow a *state*-required procedure.

The New York garnishment law at issue in *Granger* and *Mayers* has subsequently been changed to protect exempt funds more effectively.[199] Pennsylvania has also changed its bank account garnishment procedures so that banks are now instructed to freeze only non-exempt funds, and service of the writ will not attach funds in an account in which funds are direct-deposited on a recurring basis and identified as exempt under state or federal law.[200] Connecticut[201] and California[202] provide that some amount of benefits are exempt without a claim being made. A debtor's failure to claim the exemption does not result in waiver.[203] In all four states, however, the debtor must file a claim to prevent the freezing and turnover of any additional exempt amount over and above the amount protected from an initial freeze.

---

195 Mo. Rev. Stat. § 525.080 (2); Vt. R. Civ. P. Forms 33 and 34 (execution is to be levied only against non-exempt property); Wash. Rev. Code § 6.27.060 (writ of garnishment must allege that plaintiff has reason to believe and does believe, *inter alia*, that garnishee "is indebted to the defendant in amounts exceeding those exempted from garnishment by any state or federal law"); Wyo. Stat. Ann. § 1-15-402 (writ of garnishment can be used to reach property not exempt under state or federal law).

196 2005 WL 2105810 (E.D.N.Y. Aug. 31, 2005), *later decision at* 2006 WL 2013734 (E.D.N.Y. July 18, 2006) (denying defendants' motion for interlocutory appeal). *See also* New v. Gemini Capital Group, 859 F. Supp. 2d 990 (S.D. Iowa 2012) (allowing judgment debtor to proceed on claim that state procedure, which requires notice only when judgment creditor seeks turnover of garnished funds, not when the funds are frozen, violates due process); McCarthy v. Wachovia Bank, 2008 WL 5145602 (E.D.N.Y. Dec. 4, 2008) (application of *Matthews* balancing test to New York's restraining notice procedure, which requires banks to freeze accounts pending determination of exemptions, is fact question). *But see* Hollowell v. Hosto, 2010 WL 1416519 (E.D. Ark. Apr. 8, 2010), *aff'd as modified*, 389 Fed. Appx. 583 (8th Cir. 2010) (unpublished) (prompt post-garnishment hearing sufficient to protect rights in bank account containing Social Security funds; neither due process nor the Social Security Act forbid temporary freeze while debtor exercises exemption rights); Henneberger v. Cohen & Slamowitz, L.L.P., 2010 WL 1405578 (W.D.N.Y. Mar. 31, 2010) (freezing accounts containing only exempt benefits did not violate due process or Social Security Act; creditor need not rely on debtor's claim of exemption but could use New York procedure to adjudicate the question).

197 Granger v. Harris, 2007 WL 1213416 (E.D.N.Y. Apr. 17, 2007) (recipient stated section 1983 claim against bank that disbursed funds to creditor despite knowledge that funds were Social Security; state statute imposing sanctions on bank that failed to comply with restraining order was state compulsion sufficient to allege action under color of state law).

198 *Cf.* Granger v. Harris, 2007 WL 1213416 (E.D.N.Y. Apr. 17, 2007) (appearing to recognize potential for this preemption); Mayers v. New York Cmty. Bancorp, Inc., 2005 WL 2105810 (E.D.N.Y. Aug. 31, 2005) (same).

199 N.Y. C.P.L.R. § 5222(h) (McKinney). *See* § 12.6.3.9, *infra* (this similar protections in other statutes).

200 Pa. R. Civ. P. 3111.1, 3123.

201 Conn. Gen. Stat. § 52-367b(n), (o).

202 Cal. Civ. Proc. Code § 704.080(b)(4), (d) (West) ("deposit account" into which Social Security benefits are directly deposited by the government or its agent is exempt up to specified amounts without filing a claim of exemption; any amounts in an account in excess of the specified amount must be placed by the financial institution in a suspense account or be otherwise prohibited from withdrawal, and a judgment creditor may then file a notice of opposition alleging that the excess funds are not exempt). *See* Shop Ironworkers Local 790 Pension Plan v. COFAB Steel Corp., 2008 WL 4790592 (N.D. Cal. Oct. 30, 2008).

203 Cal. Civ. Proc. Code § 704.080 (West); Conn. Gen. Stat. § 52-367b.

A 2011 rule adopted by the Treasury Department and other federal agencies resolves many of these concerns. It requires banks to protect approximately two months of electronically deposited exempt federal benefits. While the Treasury rule has some gaps, it goes a long way toward resolving the problems of freezing exempt federal benefits. It is discussed in detail in § 12.6.4.3, *infra*.

12.4 Protection of Debtors' Wages

12.4.1 Federal Wage Garnishment Protections

12.4.1.1 Purposes of Consumer Credit Protection Act Wage Garnishment Restrictions

The wage garnishment provisions of the federal Consumer Credit Protection Act (CCPA)[204] exempt a portion of a worker's earnings from garnishment and prohibit an employer from firing a worker due to garnishment resulting from a single indebtedness. Prior to these federal protections, state law provided debtors few protections from garnishment abuses.[205]

As a means to "relieve countless honest debtors driven by economic desperation from plunging into bankruptcy in order to preserve their employment and insure a continued means of support for themselves and their families,"[206] Congress enacted the CCPA garnishment provisions, effective in 1970. The statute lists three purposes for its garnishment restrictions:

- Reduction of predatory extensions of credit;
- Increased job stability; and
- Increased uniformity in bankruptcy laws and protections.[207]

The CCPA's wage garnishment protections are intended to be self-executing and need not be affirmatively asserted by the debtor.[208] The statute and regulations are reprinted in Appendix C, *infra*.

12.4.1.2 The Meaning of "Subject to Garnishment"

The CCPA protects earnings which are "subject to garnishment." The statute defines garnishment as any legal or equitable procedure through which the earnings of any individual are required to be withheld for payment of debt.[209] The term "subject to garnishment" has been interpreted broadly to relate to any seizure flowing from judicial action,[210] thus applying to proceedings in aid of execution and attachment proceedings.[211] Most wage garnishments are made by court order, with a creditor seeking to satisfy a claim against an employee by reaching an employee's earnings before they are paid.

The CCPA wage garnishment provisions do not apply to seizures pursuant to a contractual agreement, such as a wage assignment.[212] However, the Federal Trade Commission's Credit Practices Rule broadly prohibits contractual wage assignment provisions unless they are revocable.[213] The CCPA garnishment provisions do apply to wage assignments that result from a judicial order.[214]

---

204 15 U.S.C. §§ 1671–1677, *reprinted in* Appx. C.1, *infra*. *See* Annotation, *Validity, Construction and Application of Secs. 301–307 of Consumer Credit Protection Act (15 U.S.C.S. Secs. 1671–1677) Placing Restrictions on Garnishment of Individuals' Earnings*, 14 A.L.R. Fed. 447 (1973).

205 W. Douglas, Points of Rebellion 48 (1970) ("[T]oday's garnishment proceedings are as destructive and vicious as the debtors' dungeons. . . . In many states the percentage of wages garnished has been so high that a man and his family are often reduced to a starvation level.").

One proposal would have completely abolished garnishment. H.R. 1040, 90th Cong. (1968), *reprinted in* 1968 U.S.C.C.A.N. 1978. *See also* § 12.4.1.5, *infra* (some states ban wage garnishment).

206 H.R. Rep. No. 1040, 90th Cong. (1968), *reprinted in* 1968 U.S.C.C.A.N. 1979.

207 15 U.S.C. § 1671(a)(3). *See also* Brown v. Liberty Loan Corp., 392 F. Supp. 1023, 1032 (M.D. Fla. 1974) (federal garnishment restrictions were directed "towards abuses of garnishment procedures by consumer financial lenders, such as loan companies"), *rev'd on other grounds*, 539 F.2d 1355 (5th Cir. 1976).

208 United States Dep't of Labor, Wage & Hour. Div., Field Operations Handbook, ch. 16, § 16a06, *available at* www.dol.gov/whd/garnishment/index.htm.

209 15 U.S.C. § 1672(c).

210 Western v. Hodgson, 494 F.2d 379, 382 (4th Cir. 1974); Igbal v. Mucci, 852 A.2d 195 (N.J. Super. Ct. App. Div. 2004) (order requiring debtor to make installment payments to judgment creditor is same as garnishment and cannot exceed CCPA limits); Lough v. Robinson, 675 N.E.2d 1272 (Ohio Ct. App. 1996) (child support order was a garnishment within meaning of CCPA and Ohio law). *See also* Branham v. Varble, 952 N.E.2d 744 (Ind. 2011) (installment payment order against employed debtor is a garnishment subject to state wage garnishment limits); Caulley v. Caulley, 806 S.W.2d 795 (Tex. 1991) (reversing, on state law grounds, lower court's ruling that federal garnishment protections do not apply to order to turn future wages over to receiver who would pay 90% as alimony arrearages and 10% to former husband). *But see* United States v. Jaffe, 417 F.3d 259 (2d Cir. 2005) (criminal restitution order that directs restitution payments but does not restrain use of specific funds not covered by CCPA); Frankel v. Frankel, 886 A.2d 136 (Md. Ct. Spec. App. 2005) (CCPA does not limit amount of child support, only amount collectible by garnishment); Allstar Capital, Inc. v. Curry, 900 N.Y.S.2d 852 (N.Y. Sup. Ct. 2010) (debtor, here a pro basketball player, can be ordered to make installment payments on top of wage garnishment).

211 Hodgson v. Hamilton Mun. Court, 349 F. Supp. 1125, 1139 (S.D. Ohio 1972).

212 *See, e.g.*, Western v. Hodgson, 494 F.2d 379 (4th Cir. 1974); *In re* O'Neil, 992 A.2d 672 (N.H. 2010) (husband agreed to wage assignment during divorce proceedings; voluntary assignment not covered by CCPA); Liedka v. Liedka, 423 N.Y.S.2d 788 (N.Y. Fam. Ct. 1979). *See also* Sears, Roebuck & Co. v. A. T. & G. Co., 239 N.W.2d 614 (Mich. Ct. App. 1976) (federal law does not restrict employer's deduction from debtor's earnings to pay debt to employer).

213 16 C.F.R. § 444.2(a)(3). *See* § 12.4.5, *infra*. *See also* National Consumer Law Center, Federal Deception Laws § 2.3 (2012), *updated at* www.nclc.org/library.

214 Voss Products, Inc. v. Carlton, 147 F. Supp. 2d 892 (E.D. Tenn. 2001) (order of wage assignment entered in divorce case pursuant to defendant's agreement was garnishment); Donovan v. Hamilton Cnty. Mun. Court, 580 F. Supp. 554, 556 (S.D. Ohio 1984) (wage assignment for support issued pursuant to a decree of divorce or dissolution was a garnishment under 15 U.S.C. § 1672(c)); Koethe v. Johnson, 328 N.W.2d 293, 297 (Iowa 1982) (court-ordered wage assignment to satisfy child support obligation was "garnishment" and governed by CCPA); Carrel v. Carrel, 791 S.W.2d 831 (Mo. Ct. App. 1990) (involuntary wage assignment ordered by court as part of contempt order in marriage dissolution case is garnishment).

An early decision held that setoff against a federal employee's salary by a federal agency to collect a debt was not restricted by the CCPA.[215] However, statutes governing the collection of federal debts now incorporate the CCPA restrictions, or greater restrictions.[216] A 1977 amendment clarified that the CCPA applies not only to court-ordered garnishments but also when "any State (or officer or agency thereof) . . . make[s], execute[s], or enforce[s] any order or process,"[217] so setoffs by state agencies are covered by the CCPA restrictions.[218]

Some courts have held that the CCPA only protects against garnishment and does not operate as an exemption when the debtor files bankruptcy.[219] In practice this position means that a debtor who is owed accrued, unpaid wages at the time of filing bankruptcy cannot use the CCPA to exempt them. A state wage exemption[220] or a wildcard exemption[221] may apply, however.

12.4.1.3 Types of Debts to Which the Protections Apply

The CCPA protections apply to wage garnishment orders to collect fines and restitution awards in federal criminal prosecutions.[222] While they do not apply to actions to collect state or federal taxes,[223] the Internal Revenue Code itself exempts a portion of income from seizure that may be more generous than the CCPA for families and less generous for individuals without dependents.[224] One court has held that the job protection provision in the CCPA, protecting employees from job termination for their first garnishment, applies to an Internal Revenue Service levy on wages.[225]

The CCPA wage garnishment protections are not limited to consumer debts or debts incurred through credit transactions but apply to garnishment to collect "any debt."[226] Thus, they apply to debts incurred for business as well as consumer purposes.[227] One court held that the CCPA did not prevent or limit the amount of the attachment of the salary of a polluter to fund sewage treatment for his property, however. The court held that the order requiring him to pay for the cleanup was

215 Atwater v. Roudebush, 452 F. Supp. 622 (N.D. Ill. 1976).

216 *See* §§ 10.2.6, *supra*.

217 15 U.S.C. § 1673(c).

218 Shine v. Iowa Dep't of Human Servs., 592 N.W.2d 684 (Iowa 1999).

219 *See, e.g.*, *In re* Sinclair, 417 F.3d 527 (5th Cir. 2005) (Louisiana garnishment limitation not an exemption); Smith v. Frazier, 421 B.R. 513 (S.D. Ill. 2009) (garnishment cap of the CCPA is not an exemption and cannot be used in bankruptcy); *In re* Riendeau, 293 B.R. 832 (D. Vt. 2002), *aff'd on other grounds*, 336 F.3d 78 (2d Cir. 2003); *In re* Horton, 2011 WL 832946 (Bankr. E.D. Ky. Mar. 4, 2011); *In re* Bloomstein, 2010 WL 4607525 (Bankr. D. Mass. Nov. 5, 2010); *In re* Reinhart, 291 P.3d 228 (Utah 2012). *See also In re* Brissette, 561 F.2d 779, 786 (9th Cir. 1977) (contrasting CCPA with California wage garnishment statute); *In re* Lane, 2010 WL 148634 (Bankr. C.D. Ill. Jan. 12, 2010) (Illinois garnishment cap not an exemption; wages earned but unpaid on petition date not exempt but may be covered by wildcard exemption); *In re* Koeneman, 410 B.R. 820 (Bankr. C.D. Ill. 2009).

220 *In re* Brissette, 561 F.2d 779, 786 (9th Cir. 1977) (California wage garnishment protection); *In re* Robinson, 241 B.R. 447 (9th Cir. 1999) (interpreting Oregon's protection of wages as an exemption applicable in bankruptcy); *In re* Irish, 311 B.R. 63 (B.A.P. 8th Cir. 2004) (federal garnishment limits operate as a bankruptcy exemption because they are incorporated into Iowa exemption law; debtor can stack this exemption with another exemption for $1000 in wages or tax refunds); *In re* Hoetmer, 2011 WL 2893628 (Bankr. S.D. Ind. July 14, 2011); *In re* Lantz, 2009 WL 113729 (Bankr. E.D. Cal. Jan. 13, 2009) (California bankruptcy exemption applies to earned but unpaid wages); *In re* Haraughty, 403 B.R. 607 (Bankr. S.D. Ind. 2009) (Indiana garnishment limit, Ind. Code § 24-4.5-5-105, is an exemption that may be used in bankruptcy; earned but unpaid wages exempt up to statutory limit); *In re* Cole, 2009 WL 1616777 (Bankr. S.D. Ind. June 8, 2009) (same); *In re* Mayer, 388 B.R. 869, 872 n.1 (Bankr. N.D. Ill. 2008) (Illinois restriction on wage garnishment is an exemption that applies in bankruptcy); *In re* Jones, 318 B.R. 841 (Bankr. S.D. Ohio 2005) (federal garnishment limits operate as bankruptcy exemption because they are incorporated into Ohio's exemption statute). *See also In re* Randall, 2011 WL 5417092 (Bankr. N.D. Iowa 2011) (wages garnished prepetition and paid into court but not yet condemned, that is, ordered paid over to creditor, were exempt pursuant to Iowa's accrued wages exemption); *In re* Reinhart, 291 P.3d 228 (Utah 2012) (Utah statute limiting the amount of garnishment is not an exemption that can be used in bankruptcy). *But see In re* Kapusta, 2011 WL 2173675 (C.D. Ill. June 2, 2011) (noting that Illinois courts are divided on the question of whether the Illinois Wage Deduction Act, which does not protect wages after payment to debtor, is an exemption that may be used in bankruptcy; concluding that it is not); *In re* Radzilowsky, 448 B.R. 767 (N.D. Ill. 2011) (Illinois Wage Deduction Act, which protects wages only before payment to debtor, is not an exemption that can be used in bankruptcy); *In re* Lawrence, 219 B.R. 786 (E.D. Tenn. 1998); *In re* Thum, 329 B.R. 848 (C.D. Ill. 2005); *In re* Jokiel, 2012 WL 33246 (Bankr. N.D. Ill. Jan. 5, 2012) (Illinois Wage Deduction Act does not create an exemption usable in bankruptcy); *In re* Mordkin, 452 B.R. 311 (Bankr. D.D.C. 2011) (District of Columbia wage garnishment limit, which does not protect wages after payment to debtor, is not an exemption that can be claimed in bankruptcy); *In re* Parsons, 437 B.R. 854 (Bankr. E.D. Mo. 2010). *But cf. In re* Sikes, 2004 WL 2028021 (Bankr. W.D. Ky. Sept. 8, 2004) (stating that Kentucky statute protecting wages does not apply in bankruptcy; statement is *dicta* because issue was protection of tax refund, not wages). *See generally* §§ 12.4.3.1–12.4.3.3, Appx. G, *infra*.

221 *See* § 12.2.7, *supra*.

222 18 U.S.C. § 3613(a)(3). *See* United States v. Lee, 659 F.3d 619 (7th Cir. 2011) (payments from retirement accounts were earnings within the meaning of CCPA; garnishment for criminal fine was limited to 25%); U.S. v. Thomas, 2012 WL 147876 (E.D. Cal. Jan. 18, 2012) (CCPA garnishment limits apply to criminal court's restitution order), *adopted by* 2012 WL 869512 (E.D. Cal. Mar. 9, 2012); United States v. Johnson, 2009 WL 1033773 (E.D. La. Apr. 15, 2009). *See also* United States v. Otto, 2012 WL 2529406 (W.D.N.C. June 29, 2012) (applying 25% CCPA limit to garnishment of pension payments for criminal restitution). *But see* U.S. v. Cunningham, 866 F. Supp. 2d 1050 (S.D. Iowa 2012) (state employees' disability retirement payments are earnings, subject to the 25% cap of the CCPA, but court may issue order pursuant to the All Writs Act ordering state to pay the remaining 75% of the payments as restitution while defendant is incarcerated).

223 15 U.S.C. § 1673(b). *See* United States v. Clayton, 613 F.3d 592 (5th Cir. 2010) (CCPA limits inapplicable to order that defendant convicted of failing to file income tax returns make restitution to IRS).

224 26 U.S.C. § 6334(d) provides for weekly exemption of the standard deduction provided by 26 U.S.C. § 63(c) and the deduction provided for personal exemptions in 26 U.S.C. § 151 divided by 52. Other exemptions are provided by 26 U.S.C. § 6334, including exemption of many government benefits and specified personal property. *See generally* § 12.2.8.2, *supra*.

225 Martin v. Hawkeye Int'l Trucks, Inc., 782 F. Supp. 1320 (S.D. Iowa 1991).

226 15 U.S.C. § 1672(c).

227 Midlantic Nat'l Bank/North v. Reif, 732 F. Supp. 354 (E.D.N.Y. 1990).

not a judgment, so the CCPA did not apply.[228] Another court held that the CCPA garnishment provisions did not apply to a state's suit seeking reimbursement for the cost of incarceration from a prisoner's accumulated disability pension payments.[229] The court did not articulate a rationale, other than the belief that the CCPA was not intended to apply to garnishment for this purpose.

12.4.1.4 Earnings Subject to CCPA Garnishment Protections

12.4.1.4.1 Wages, vacation pay, sick pay

The CCPA garnishment provisions protect consumers from garnishment of "earnings," defined as "compensation paid or payable for personal services, whether denominated as wages, salary, commission, bonus, or otherwise, and includes periodic payments pursuant to a pension or retirement program."[230] The key question is whether payments are compensation "for personal services."[231] For example, accounts receivable may be protected under the CCPA and similar state statutes if they are owed to the debtor for personal services.[232] Disability benefit payments received through a former employer are compensation for personal services even though they are received at a time when the employee is no longer able to work.[233] On the other hand, compensation to a business owner that is based on profits or on others' work is unlikely to be protected.[234]

228 Friends of the Sakonnet v. Dutra, 125 B.R. 69 (D.R.I. 1991) (CCPA not meant to be used by polluters to avoid court orders to comply with federal and state environmental laws).

229 State Treasurer v. Gardner, 583 N.W.2d 687 (Mich. 1998).

230 15 U.S.C. § 1672(a).

231 United States v. Ashcraft, 732 F.3d 860 (8th Cir. 2013) (question is whether payments are compensation for personal services, not whether they are labeled as wages); Shearin v. Beaman, 323 B.R. 917 (E.D.N.C. 2004) (North Carolina exemption of earnings for personal services would exempt portion of year-end bonus but not interest in capital account of partnership), *aff'd*, 126 Fed. Appx. 640 (4th Cir. 2005) (per curiam); *In re* Im, 495 B.R. 46 (Bankr. M.D. Fla. 2013) (funds in bank account of president of small business not earnings; account contained fees received from clinic patients, but owner had no employment agreement with his clinic, and controlled its disbursements); Ighnat v. Ighnat, 1989 WL 34733 (Ohio Ct. App. Apr. 11, 1989) (profit-sharing proceeds were "earnings" protected by CCPA and Ohio law, even when garnishment was for child support and alimony). *See also* Bueno v. Pyle, 2001 WL 1544455 (10th Cir. Dec. 5, 2001) (Colorado garnishment limitation applies only to earnings; state tax authorities could garnish prison inmate's account, which contained gifts); Rooney v. Rooney, 669 N.W.2d 362 (Minn. Ct. App. 2003) (church was employer and payer within meaning of child support garnishment statute; it required members to give up all individual property and provided for their needs; obligor was doing work for the church). *Cf.* Cadle Co. v. G & G Assocs., 757 So. 2d 1278 (Fla. Dist. Ct. App. 2000) (evidentiary hearing required to determine if sums held by employer for "expense reimbursement," "reimbursement for investment," and "capital account" were earnings under Florida statute); Bartel v. Zucktriegal, 47 P.3d 581 (Wash. Ct. App. 2002) (judgment creditor could garnish employee's compensation that was disguised by collusive employer). *But see* Cusano v. Klein, 485 Fed. Appx. 175 (9th Cir. 2012) (song royalties—not specified whether debtor was composer or performer—not earnings for personal services covered by CCPA); United States v. Crawford, 2006 WL 2458710 (E.D. Cal. Aug. 22, 2006) (annuities funded by deductions from deceased father's salary not protected by CCPA; not personal earnings of debtor); Aetna Cas. & Surety Co. v. Rodco Auto Body, 965 F. Supp. 104 (D. Mass. 1996) (debtor's voluntary contributions to individual retirement account were not earnings protected by garnishment limitations of CCPA); John Hancock Mut. Life Ins. Co. v. Frost Nat'l Bank, 393 F. Supp. 204 (E.D. Tenn. 1974) (proceeds of life insurance policy were not "earnings," as term is used in 15 U.S.C. § 1672(a), because such proceeds were not payment for "personal services"), *aff'd*, 516 F.2d 901 (6th Cir. 1975) (table).

232 *See, e.g.*, *In re* Mayer, 388 B.R. 869, 872 n.1 (Bankr. N.D. Ill. 2008) (accounts receivable for professional services are protected by Illinois statute that applies to "wages, salary, commissions and bonuses"); *In re* Atkinson, 258 B.R. 769 (Bankr. D. Idaho 2001) (doctor's accounts receivables are compensation for personal services so are protected as earnings); Rhodes v. Sinclair, 2012 WL 5993806 (Ohio Ct. App. Nov. 30, 2012) (legal fees owed to solo practitioner are earnings for personal services, which can be reached only by garnishment, not by a creditors' bill, which would enable creditor to take the entire amount). *See also In re* Sheeran, 369 B.R. 910 (Bankr. E.D. Va. 2007) (earnings of solo law firm were result of personal services; debtor could claim wage exemption). *But see In re* Osworth, 234 B.R. 497 (B.A.P. 9th Cir. 1999) (despite broad language, Oregon statute did not protect the accounts receivable of self-employed real estate agent); *In re* Lawrence, 219 B.R. 786 (E.D. Tenn. 1998) (Tennessee garnishment statute did not protect accounts receivable of podiatrist; it is not an exemption statute but simply a restriction on use of a wage deduction order to reach earnings in hands of employer), *aff'g* 205 B.R. 115 (Bankr. E.D. Tenn. 1997); *In re* Siegel, 214 B.R. 329 (W.D. Tenn. 1997) (Tennessee statute limiting garnishment of wages does not provide exemption for lawyers' accounts receivable); *In re* Cerda, 2007 WL 4893451 (Bankr. D. Neb. Dec. 6, 2007) (Nebraska exemption does not protect accounts receivable of home health aide, an independent contractor; key issue is degree of control exercised by employer). *But cf. In re* Tobkin, 2013 WL 1292679 (Bankr. S.D. Fla. Mar. 26, 2013) (key issue is whether there is an arm's length agreement for payment or whether debtor controls amount of compensation; denying exemption for contingent fee owed to solo practice attorney); *In re* Smith, 284 B.R. 460 (Bankr. W.D. Mo. 2002) (accounts receivable from sales of old cars restored by debtors not exempt earnings; debtors were selling a product—that is, the cars—not a service, and sale price included purchase of cars and parts as well as debtors' labor); Mickler v. Mickler, 245 S.W.3d 809 (Ky. Ct. App. 2008) (fact question whether accounts receivable are earnings; here, physician failed to show that sums owed to his practice by insurers were for his services, not those of his employees).

233 United States v. Ashcraft, 732 F.3d 860 (8th Cir. 2013); Villano v. Villano, 414 N.Y.S.2d 625 (N.Y. Sup. Ct. 1979) (disability pension payments are "earnings" protected by CCPA).

234 *See, e.g.*, *In re* McDermott, 2011 WL 740727 (M.D. Fla. Feb. 24, 2011) (distinguishing between "a salaried job" and "running a business"; when debtors controlled timing and amount of payments from family-owned business, funds were non-exempt equity withdrawals, not exempt earnings); ASKM, L.L.C. v. Fry, 2009 WL 4642060 (D. Utah Dec. 1, 2009) (returns on investments paid to a corporate entity not "compensation for personal services" and thus not earnings); *In re* Adams, 506 B.R. 688 (Bankr. E.D. N.C. 2014) (rentals from ownership of mobile home park not earnings for personal services; they arose from ownership of the land, not any specific services performed by debtors); *In re* Oberdick, 490 B.R. 687 (Bankr. W.D. Pa. 2013) (draws owed to working partner, calculated based on partnership profits and partner's billable hours, are not protected earnings); *In re* Christy, 306 B.R. 611 (Bankr. C.D. Ill. 2004) (fact question as to what part of receivables of two-physician professional corporation was attributable to personal services of debtor-physician and therefore exempt as wages or salary under Illinois law); *In re* McDermott, 425 B.R. 848 (Bankr.

Vacation pay qualifies as "earnings" within the scope of the statute and is thus protected.[235] Sick pay is likewise protected.[236] A court held that "disposable earnings" in a state wage exemption statute encompasses the proceeds of a personal injury settlement that replaced wages that were lost due to an industrial disease.[237]

12.4.1.4.2 *Periodic pension plan payments*

The statute is explicit that "periodic payments pursuant to a pension or retirement program" constitute "earnings" protected by the CCPA garnishment limits.[238] The language "pursuant to" refers to payments *from* the pension plan to a retiree, rather than payments by the employer or employee into the pension plan.[239] However, wage garnishment protections may not prevent a creditor from reaching the fund itself, as opposed to the periodic payments it makes, to the extent the retiree is entitled to cash out the retirement fund.[240]

M.D. Fla. 2010) (earnings from business controlled by debtor not exempt), *aff'd*, 2011 WL 740727 (M.D. Fla. Feb. 24, 2011); *In re* Welty, 217 B.R. 907 (Bankr. D. Wyo. 1998) (earnings of business owner who paid himself what was left after settling expenses of the business were not exempt earnings under federal or Wyoming law); *In re* Harrison, 216 B.R. 451 (Bankr. S.D. Fla. 1997) ("deferred wages" due to dentist after dissolution of professional association, over which he exercised substantial control, were intended as return on his investment and were not exempt earnings for personal services); *In re* Zamora, 187 B.R. 783 (Bankr. S.D. Fla. 1995) (courts will look behind labels "employee" and "independent contractor" to determine whether debtor has an arrangement "like a job" or is in control of business, with power to decide how much to draw for salary; income from solo law practice and marina owned by debtor was not exempt); Corto v. Nat'l Scenery Studios, Inc., 705 A.2d 615 (D.C. 1997) (producer's share of box office receipts of theatrical production was not exempt "wages" for "personal services"); Brock v. Westport Recovery Corp., 832 So. 2d 209 (Fla. Dist. Ct. App. 2002) (key question is whether work is like "a salaried job" or "running a business"; "draws" taken by vice-president of family corporation from profits not "compensation for personal services or labor" within meaning of Florida statutes); Vining v. Siegal, 731 So. 2d 826 (Fla. Dist. Ct. App. 1999) (accounts holding proceeds of sole proprietorship's dental practice not earnings within meaning of Florida garnishment exemption); Gerry Elson Agency Inc. v. Muck, 509 S.W.2d 750, 753 (Mo. Ct. App. 1974) (debtor leased eight trucks from trucking company, hired drivers, and hauled loads for it; its payments to him are not "earnings" under CCPA); Swig v. Properties Asset Mgmt. Servs., L.L.C., 924 N.Y.S.2d 368 (N.Y. App. Div. 2011) ("base salary" not earnings when contract provided that it was earned if debtor's company provided the services of asset managers, who need not be debtor personally; incentive compensation not earnings when it depended on profits, and no showing that debtor's services were the cause of profits); Friedt v. Moseanko, 498 N.W.2d 129 (N.D. 1993) (earnings do not include "business profits"; milk distributor's payments to dairy farmer not exempt). *See also In re* Morley, 2013 WL 501681 (Bankr. D. Mont. Feb. 11, 2013) (state exemption law uses CCPA definitions; denying exemption to debtor who received fixed amount per month to perform services for one company but did business as sole proprietorship and reported earnings as profit and loss for business); *In re* Woller, 483 B.R. 886 (Bankr. W.D. Wis. 2012) (payments for trucking services, by independent owner-operator who drove the truck himself, were earnings for personal services, protected by Wisconsin wage garnishment limits); *In re* Cook, 454 B.R. 204 (Bankr. N.D. Fla. 2011) (base salary, paid at regular intervals to minority shareholder of closely-held corporation, who worked full-time in the business, was earnings; bonuses, paid at irregular intervals and dependent on the company's profits, were not).

235 *In re* Hidy, 364 B.R. 679 (Bankr. W.D. Mo. 2007) (payments for unused sick leave and vacation, required by employment contract, were for personal services); Bd. of Educ. of E. Hartford v. Booth, 654 A.2d 717 (Conn. 1995) (Connecticut definition of earnings covers accumulated sick leave and a deferred salary increase payable at termination); Riley v. Kessler, 441 N.E.2d 638 (Ohio 1982); United States Dep't of Labor, Wage & Hour Div., Field Operations Handbook ch. 16, § 16a11, *available at* www.dol.gov/whd/FOH/FOH_Ch16.pdf (sick and vacation pay are considered earnings under CCPA). *See also* Montgomery Ward Credit Corp. v. Brewer, Clearinghouse No. 44,517 (D. Minn. 1989) (state law intended to exempt severance pay from garnishment). *But see In re* Henrickson, 2007 WL 703620 (Bankr. D. Alaska Mar. 5, 2007) (exemption for property traceable to "weekly net wages" protects only amount accrued during one work week, not accrued vacation pay and tax refund). *But cf. In re* Marples, 266 B.R. 202 (Bankr. D. Idaho 2001) (questioning whether car awarded by random drawing among employees who met sales goal was "earnings").

236 United States Dep't of Labor, Wage & Hour Div., Field Operations Handbook ch. 16, § 16a11, *available at* www.dol.gov/whd/FOH/FOH_Ch16.pdf (sick and vacation pay are considered earnings under CCPA).

237 *In re* Burns, 482 B.R. 164 (Bankr. E.D. La. 2012). *But cf. In re* Nelson, 2003 WL 22331776 (Bankr. D. Colo. Oct. 1, 2003) (judgment for tortious interference with prospective economic relation, calculated as amount of earnings lost, was not earnings under Colorado exemption statute because plaintiff performed no personal services).

238 15 U.S.C. § 1672(a). *See* United States v. Lee, 659 F.3d 619 (7th Cir. 2011) ("earnings" within the meaning of CCPA include periodic payments from a pension or retirement program, here annual distributions; garnishment for criminal fine is limited to 25%); United States v. DeCay, 620 F.3d 534 (5th Cir. 2010); Sposato v. First Mariner Bank, 2013 WL 4049718 (D. Md. Aug. 8, 2013) (although payments from unfunded "top hat" retirement plan are not wages as defined by state garnishment law, they are earnings protected by CCPA); United States v. Cunningham, 866 F. Supp. 2d 1050 (S.D. Iowa 2012) (state employees' disability retirement payments are earnings subject to CCPA garnishment limits); United States v. Otto, 2012 WL 2529406 (W.D.N.C. June 29, 2012) (applying 25% CCPA limit to garnishment of pension payments for criminal restitution); United States v. Beukle, 892 F. Supp. 2d 1176 (D.S.D. 2012); Phillips v. Phillips, 2011 WL 487837 (N.J. Super. Ct. App. Div. Feb. 14, 2011); Ward v. Ward, 396 A.2d 365 (N.J. Super. Ct. Ch. Div. 1978) (protected earnings include pension benefits). *See also* AFLAC, Inc. v. Diaz-Verson, 2012 WL 1903904 (M.D. Ga. May 25, 2012) (applying state 25% garnishment limit to payments from "top hat" retirement plan); Farren v. Farren, 2011 WL 32311233 (Conn. Super. Ct. June 14, 2011) (Connecticut prejudgment remedy cannot reach "earnings," broadly defined to include compensation for personal services, including a pension based on length of service and pay rate). *But cf.* United States v. Blondeau, 2011 WL 6000499 (E.D.N.C. Nov. 1, 2011) (disagreeing that CCPA applies to periodic payments from pension fund, but case appears to involve garnishment of corpus of fund rather than periodic payments), *report and recommendation adopted by* 2011 WL 6001281 (E.D.N.C. Nov. 30, 2011).

239 United States v. DeCay, 620 F.3d 534 (5th Cir. 2010) (noting that lower court decisions to the contrary had misquoted the statutory language).

240 United States v. DeCay, 620 F.3d 534, 544–45 (5th Cir. 2010); United States v. Edward D. Jones & Co., 2011 WL 7025905 (E.D. Tex. Dec. 21, 2011) (CCPA does not protect retirement fund that debtor could cash out at any time), *report and recommendation adopted by* 2012 WL 113605 (E.D. Tex. Jan. 13, 2012); United States v. Whitt, 2011 WL 4062459 (E.D. Mich. Sept. 13, 2011); United States v. Tischendorf, 2011 WL 2413346 (N.D. Tex. May 17, 2011), *report and recommendation*

12.4.1.4.3 Tips

The wages of serving staff at restaurants are likely to amount to less than thirty times the minimum wage and thus be completely protected from garnishment, as long as tips are not considered part of their "earnings." A Department of Labor handbook states that tips paid directly to an employee by a customer are not considered earnings within the meaning of the CCPA.[241] The same rule applies to tips that are transferred free and clear to a worker at the direction of a credit customer who adds a tip to the bill. The handbook points out that garnishment is designed to reach earnings held by the employer and that such tips never pass to the employer. On the other hand, if a restaurant or other employer adds a fee to a bill and then pays this amount to the employee, the compensation passes from the employer to the employee and amounts to earnings under the CCPA.[242]

A Maryland decision reaches a different conclusion, holding that tips paid directly to a worker constitute wages for purposes of the state wage garnishment law and therefore must be added to the wages paid by the employer to determine whether the worker's earnings exceed the threshold protected from garnishment.[243] The opinion does not address the effect of the CCPA, which would likely have preempted this less protective provision of state law.[244] A New Jersey decision adopts the rationale of the Department of Labor and holds that, if tips are paid in cash to the worker or charged on a credit card and immediately remitted to the worker, the tips are not subject to wage garnishment.[245]

12.4.1.4.4 Payments to independent contractors

The CCPA explicitly includes "commissions" in its definition of earnings,[246] suggesting an intent to cover the typical earnings of independent contractors as long as the compensation is for personal services. Even a court that takes the view, not supported by the statutory language, that the CCPA applies only to compensation that is paid periodically,[247] may accept this position, since commissions are often paid biweekly or monthly.[248]

Nonetheless, many courts have found that payments to independent contractors are not protected by state statutes.[249]

adopted by 2011 WL 2327312 (N.D. Tex. June 13, 2011). *See also* United States v. Blondeau, 2011 WL 6000499 (E.D.N.C. Nov. 1, 2011) (earnings do not remain exempt after being passed into a retirement account or annuity in the hands of the employee, so government can reach corpus of retirement account regardless of CCPA; court does not indicate whether retiree had the right to cash out the fund), *report and recommendation adopted by* 2011 WL 6001281 (E.D.N.C. Nov. 30, 2011). *See generally* §§ 12.2.8.2, *supra* (garnishment of pension funds for debts to federal government), 12.9.1, *infra* (protection of pensions).

241 United States Dep't of Labor, Wage & Hour Div., Field Operations Handbook Ch. 16, § 16a07, *available at* www.dol.gov/whd/FOH/FOH_Ch16.pdf. *See* Erlanger Med. Ctr. v. Strong, 382 S.W.3d 349 (Tenn. Ct. App. 2012) (tips paid directly to employee, including those charged on customers' plastic, may not be counted in calculating disposable income for garnishment).

242 *See also In re* Holmes, 414 B.R. 868 (Bankr. S.D. Fla. 2009) (when bartender employer added a percentage "service charge" to customers' bills and passed it on to employee in paycheck, service charge was exempt earnings under Florida law).

243 Shanks v. Lowe, 774 A.2d 411 (Md. 2001).

244 *See* Big M, Inc. v. Texas Roadhouse Holding, L.L.C., 1 A.3d 718 (N.J. Super. Ct. App. Div. 2010) (CCPA preempts state law that might subject tips to wage garnishment). *See generally* § 12.4.4, *infra*.

245 Big M, Inc. v. Texas Roadhouse Holding, L.L.C., 1 A.3d 718 (N.J. Super. Ct. App. Div. 2010).

246 15 U.S.C. § 1672(a).

247 *See* § 12.4.1.4.5, *infra*.

248 *See* Indiana Surgical Specialists v. Griffin, 867 N.E.2d 260 (Ind. Ct. App. 2007) (commission-based earnings, paid to independent contractor on biweekly basis, are earnings under Indiana definition, which is identical to CCPA).

249 *See In re* New River Drydock, Inc., 2012 WL 5675911 (11th Cir. Nov. 16, 2012) (earnings of a business, even a sole proprietorship, not protected by Florida's head-of-household exemption, if proprietor does not pay self a set salary; here allowing garnishment of one-man real estate agency's funds); Global Money Mgmt. v. McDonnold, 2009 WL 3352574 (S.D. Cal. Oct. 15, 2009) (Cal. Civ. Pro. § 706.011 definition of earnings excludes independent contractor or self-employed professional, but section 708.510 requires that any attachment order against a natural person consider "the reasonable requirements of the judgment debtor"); Pellegrino v. Koeckriz Dev. of Boca Raton, Inc., 2009 WL 1437813 (S.D. Fla. May 15, 2008), *report and recommendations adopted,* 2009 WL 1798382 (S.D. Fla. June 24, 2009) (Florida statute does not protect earnings of independent contractor or business owner); Transportation Mgmt. & Consulting, Inc. v. Black Crystal Co., 2008 WL 205592 (N.D. Cal. Jan. 24, 2008) (earnings of solo practice lawyer not exempted by Cal. Civ. Proc. Code § 487.010 (West), which protects only those who work for an employer who controls both what should be done and how it should be done); Resolution Trust Corp. v. Texas Moline, Ltd., 96 F. Supp. 2d 644 (S.D. Tex. 2000) (management, accounting, and investment banking fees paid to independent contractor not protected by Texas wage exemption; debtor was principal of financial firm, had own office, and employed others to do much of the work); *In re* Bosack, 454 B.R. 625 (Bankr. W.D. Pa. 2011) (Pennsylvania garnishment statute does not protect earnings of independent contractor, here a salesman paid on commission); *In re* Domitrovich, 2008 WL 141904 (Bankr. D.N.D. Jan. 10, 2008) (North Dakota wage exemption does not protect earnings of self-employed person); *In re* Cerda, 2007 WL 4893451 (Bankr. D. Neb. Dec. 6, 2007) (Nebraska exemption does not protect accounts receivable of home health aide, an independent contractor; key issue is degree of control exercised by employer); Idaho Pac. Lumber Co. v. Celestial Land Co. Ltd., 2013 WL 5397427 (Colo. App. Sept. 26, 2013) (payments to independent contractor, even if for personal services, not protected by Colorado wage garnishment limitation); Coward v. Smith, 636 P.2d 793 (Kan. Ct. App. 1981) (payments to roofing contractor not earnings under state garnishment law); Campbell v. Stucki, 220 S.W.3d 562 (Tex. App. 2007) (Texas exemption for current wages does not protect earnings of independent contractor); DeVore v. Central Bank & Trust, 908 S.W.2d 605 (Tex. App. 1995) (earnings of attorney in private practice not exempt as "current wages" under Texas statute). *See also In re* Branscum, 229 B.R. 32 (Bankr. M.D. Fla. 1999) (Florida's earnings exemption does not protect earnings of private investigator, who was independent contractor); *In re* Segall, 1998 Bankr. LEXIS 209 (Bankr. S.D. Fla. Jan. 26, 1998) (realtor's commissions were not exempt earnings when realtor was paid only commissions, paid own self-employment taxes, had to pay "franchise fee" for use of office and equipment, and controlled his own schedule); *In re* Lee, 204 B.R. 78 (Bankr. M.D. Fla. 1996) (insurance agent who was free to make own business decisions and was responsible for all expenses was independent contractor, so earnings not exempt under Florida law); *In re* Galvez, 990 P.2d 187 (Nev. 1999) (real estate agent's lump-sum commissions paid at closing were not "earnings" within meaning of Nevada exception, which protects only periodic payments); Gentek Bldg. Products, Inc. v. Check, 590 N.W.2d 282 (Wis. Ct. App. 1999) (unpublished) (commissions earned by seller of building products who was described in contract as "independent contractor" and who received no other compensation not "earnings" protected by Wisconsin

In some cases, this interpretation may be explained by statutory language that is narrower than the CCPA, for example protecting just "wages" rather than "earnings." Other courts applying state wage exemption laws and the CCPA have held that the protections do extend to independent contractors.[250]

12.4.1.4.5 *Non-periodic payments*

Courts differ as to whether the protections of the CCPA and similar state statutes extend to non-periodic payments which result from employment, such as profit sharing,[251] incentive payments, deferred compensation, and tax refunds. Some courts simply conclude that tax refunds[252] and non-periodic

statute). *But cf.* Davidson Tex., Inc. v. Garcia, 664 S.W.2d 791 (Tex. App. 1984) (because of level of control exercised by employer, debtor was employee, not independent contractor, and therefore fully protected from garnishment under Texas exemption for "current wages").

250 *In re* Carter, 182 F.3d 1027 (9th Cir. 1999) (entertainer who was sole shareholder of corporation which arranged her contracts, paid business expenses, and so forth could claim California exemption for earnings; remanding to determine whether large lump sum paid to self on eve of bankruptcy was earnings); *In re* Pruss, 235 B.R. 430 (B.A.P. 8th Cir. 1999) (solo practice attorney's accounts receivable that were attributable to her personal services fall within Nebraska statute's protection for "compensation paid or payable for personal services, whether denominated as wages, salary, commission, bonus or otherwise"); Warfield v. Alaniz, 2008 WL 700160 (D. Ariz. Mar. 13, 2008) (commissions of independent contractor insurance agent are earnings; Arizona statutory definition explicitly includes commissions); Bargas v. Nye (*In re* Nye), 210 B.R. 857 (D. Colo. 1997) (Colorado exemption statute explicitly protects payments received by independent contractor for labor or services); Morrison v. Kobernusz (*In re* Kobernusz), 160 B.R. 844 (D. Colo. 1993) (payments to construction subcontractor are for labor and meet state garnishment law's definition of "earnings"); Mass. Mut. Life Ins. Co. v. Shoemaker, 849 F. Supp. 30 (S.D. Tex. 1994) (Texas amended its exemption statute to allow commissions to be treated more like wages); *In re* Woller, 483 B.R. 886 (Bankr. W.D. Wis. 2012) (payments for trucking services, by independent owner-operator who drove the truck himself, were earnings for personal services, protected by Wisconsin wage garnishment limits); *In re* Hoetmer, 2011 WL 2893628 (Bankr. S.D. Ind. July 14, 2011) (real estate broker's commissions); *In re* Graham, 2010 WL 3463720 (Bankr. M.D. La. Aug. 30, 2010) (Louisiana garnishment statute protects earnings of doctor, an independent contractor who provided services to clinics); *In re* Roetman, 405 B.R. 336 (Bankr. D. Ariz. 2009) (Arizona garnishment statute protects payments for personal services, here commissions of independent contractor realtor, whether or not recipient is in employer-employee relationship with payer); *In re* Sheeran, 369 B.R. 910 (Bankr. E.D. Va. 2007) (earnings of solo law firm were result of personal services; debtor could claim wage exemption); *In re* Jones, 318 B.R. 841 (Bankr. S.D. Ohio 2005) (CCPA, which Ohio incorporates into its state exemptions, protects earnings of independent contractor if attributable to personal services); *In re* Parsons, 252 B.R. 480 (Bankr. W.D. Mo. 2000) (Missouri wage exemption applies to earnings of real estate broker insofar as funds were compensation for her personal services), *aff'd*, 280 F.3d 1185 (8th Cir. 2002) (approving method of calculating percentage of income attributable to personal services); *In re* Pettit, 224 B.R. 834 (Bankr. M.D. Fla. 1998) (Florida exemption for head of household's earnings protects earnings of "independent contractor" salesman who received fixed amount of monthly compensation and did not own or control company); *In re* Price, 195 B.R. 775 (Bankr. D. Kan. 1996) (real estate agent's commissions were exempt earnings, even though contract described her as an independent contractor, when she had invested no capital in the business, performed all services personally, and worked for one broker, which exercised considerable control over her work); *In re* Sexton, 140 B.R. 742 (Bankr. S.D. Iowa 1992) (issue is not whether debtor is independent contractor or employee, but whether payments are for personal services); *In re* Duncan, 140 B.R. 210, 213 (Bankr. E.D. Tenn. 1992) (state garnishment exemption protected insurance salesman's commissions earned on renewals of policies he had originally sold); Harrington v. Dyer, 937 A.2d 77 (Conn. Super. Ct. 2007) (commissions of independent contractor real estate salesperson were earnings, exempt from prejudgment garnishment); Riggs Nat'l Bank v. Simplicio, 54 U.S.L.W. 2457 (D.C. Super. Ct. 1986) (D.C. statute modeled after CCPA protected commissions of real estate agent, an independent contractor); California-Peterson Currency Exch., Inc. v. Friedman, 736 N.E.2d 616 (Ill. App. Ct. 2000) (earnings of independent contractor, described by employer as "agent" or "outside contractor," protected by Illinois garnishment limitations); Indiana Surgical Specialists v. Griffin, 867 N.E.2d 260 (Ind. Ct. App. 2007) (commission-based earnings, paid to independent contractor on biweekly basis, are earnings under Indiana definition, which is identical to CCPA); Marian Health Ctr. v. Cooks, 451 N.W.2d 846 (Iowa Ct. App. 1989); Decision Point, Inc. v. Reece & Nichols Realtors, Inc., 144 P.3d 706 (Kan. 2006) (realtors' commissions were earnings, assignment of which was forbidden by UCCC); Smythe, Cramer Co. v. Guinta, 762 N.E.2d 1083 (Ohio Mun. Ct. 2001) (realtor's commissions were personal earnings within meaning of state and federal garnishment statutes). *See also* Allied Home Mortgage Capital v. Belli, 2012 WL 3059423 (D. Mass. July 25, 2012) (debtor must be treated as an employee for purposes of wage garnishment procedures in the absence of evidence that the debtor falls within the independent contractor exception to the state law definition of "employee"); Waitkus v. Pressler & Pressler, L.L.P., 2012 WL 686025 (D.N.J. Mar. 2, 2012) (allowing FDCPA claim to proceed against debt collectors who attempted to execute turnover order against 100% of plaintiff's commission-based earnings, in violation of CCPA and state law); Baker v. Storfer, 51 So. 3d 652 (Fla. Dist. Ct. App. 2011) (commissions are "wages or salary" within the meaning of the Florida statute authorizing writs of continuing garnishment).

251 *See, e.g.*, Genesee Cnty. Friend of the Court v. Gen. Motors Corp., 626 N.W.2d 395 (Mich. 2001) (profit-sharing payments, recognition awards, and signing bonuses are "earnings" under CCPA); Meyer Jewelry Co. v. Johnson, 581 N.W.2d 734 (Mich. Ct. App. 1998) (profit sharing payment was "payment for work and labor" within meaning of this section; plan was offered to employees and was part of their compensation package); Swig v. Properties Asset Mgmt. Servs., L.L.C., 924 N.Y.S.2d 368 (N.Y. App. Div. 2011) (incentive compensation not earnings when it depended on profits, and no showing that debtor's services were the cause of profits). *But see In re* Larkins, 2012 WL 1378470 (Bankr. N.D. Ohio Apr. 19, 2012) (profit-sharing bonus, paid when company made a profit, in amount determined by performance and length of service, not earnings under state law because both discretionary and non-periodic).

252 *In re* Annis, 229 B.R. 802 (B.A.P. 10th Cir. 1999) (tax refund is not "earnings for personal services" within meaning of Oklahoma hardship exemption), *aff'd*, 232 F.3d 749 (10th Cir. 2000); *In re* Dickerson, 227 B.R. 742 (B.A.P. 10th Cir. 1998) (earned income credit is not earnings within meaning of Oklahoma hardship exemption); Royster v. Dep't of Revenue, 2006 WL 1687834 (N.D. Fla. June 15, 2006) (income tax refund is not protected); *In re* Arthur, 2010 WL 4674450 (Bankr. S.D. Iowa Oct. 20, 2010) (tax refund not earnings; using CCPA precedent to construe substantially similar Iowa provision); *In re* Rivenbark, 2010 WL 2643323 (Bankr. E.D. Va. June 29, 2010) (tax refund not earnings under Virginia law); *In re* Arthur, 2010 WL 4674450 (Bankr. S.D. Iowa Oct. 20, 2010) (interpreting Iowa wage garnishment statutes not to protect tax refunds); *In re* Sebastian, 2008 WL 5063084 (Bankr. D. Mont. Nov. 5, 2008) (tax refund not earnings; following *Kokoszka* because Montana definition of earnings same as federal CCPA); *In re* Fandrich, 2008 WL 4610030 (Bankr. D.N.D. Oct. 16, 2008) (tax refund not earnings); *In re* Minton, 348 B.R. 467 (Bankr. S.D. Ohio 2006) (tax refund not earnings under federal or Ohio definition, because not periodic); *In re* Rangel, 317 B.R. 553 (Bankr. D. Kan. 2004) (tax refund not exempt as "earnings" under Kansas law; not periodic and has lost "direct connection" to wages); *In re* Demars, 279 B.R. 548 (Bankr. W.D. Mo. 2002) (tax refund not exempt

earnings are not protected.[253] Others consider whether the payments in question are the kind of regular, predictable compensation on which workers depend for day-to-day living.[254]

earnings); *In re* Sikes, 2004 WL 2028021 (Bankr. W.D. Ky. Sept. 8, 2004) (tax refund not exempt as "earnings" under Kentucky wage garnishment statute); *In re* Fishbein, 245 B.R. 36 (Bankr. D. Md. 2000) (tax refunds are not wages within meaning of Maryland's wage garnishment limitations); Funk v. Utah State Tax Comm'n, 839 P.2d 818 (Utah 1992) (because of their non-periodic nature, tax refunds do not constitute disposable earnings and are not protected). *See also In re* Benn, 491 F.3d 811 (8th Cir. 2007) (tax refunds not exempt under Missouri law; opt-out statute that allows exemptions pursuant to "the law of Missouri" refers only to statutes, not common law that denied attachment of tax refunds in the hands of taxing authorities); Brown v. Schwegmann, 990 So. 2d 1282 (La. Ct. App. 2008) (trust consisting of accumulated fringe benefits not protected by Louisiana wage garnishment restrictions because payments are not made weekly, biweekly, or monthly).

253 Pallante v. Int'l Venture Invs., Ltd., 622 F. Supp. 667 (N.D. Ohio 1985) (lump-sum severance payment under voluntary separation plan not earnings because not periodic); *In re* Cook, 454 B.R. 204 (Bankr. N.D. Fla. 2011) (bonuses, paid at irregular intervals to minority shareholder of closely-held corporation and dependent on the company's profits, are not earnings); *In re* Merrill, 431 B.R. 239 (Bankr. D. Idaho 2009) (early withdrawal of entire IRA was non-periodic payment, so exemption lost); *In re* Radez, 2009 WL 1404326 (Bankr. S.D. Ind. May 15, 2009) (end of year bonus not earnings; Indiana definition applies only to periodic payments); *In re* Petitt, 2009 WL 1012977 (Bankr. S.D. Ind. Apr. 15, 2009) ("separation bonus" paid to employees of closed plant, pursuant to agreement with union, not earnings); *In re* Galvez, 990 P.2d 187 (Nev. 1999) (Nevada wage exemption does not protect real estate agent's non-periodic lump-sum commission). *Cf. In re* Marples, 266 B.R. 202 (Bankr. D. Idaho 2001) (expressing doubt whether car, awarded by random drawing from pool of sales leaders, is exempt "earnings" under state law).

254 Shearin v. Beaman, 323 B.R. 917 (E.D.N.C. 2004) (North Carolina exemption of earnings for personal services exempts portion of year-end bonus but not interest in capital account of partnership), *aff'd*, 126 Fed. Appx. 640 (4th Cir. 2005) (per curiam); *In re* Dittmar, 2011 WL 1238914 (Bankr. D. Kan. Mar. 30, 2011) (cash bonus and shares of stock were earnings for personal services when they were provided by company in exchange for union's agreement to a pay reduction and were available only to employees who worked during specified time); *In re* Grauer, 2009 WL 4938497 (Bankr. D. Md. Dec. 10, 2009) (severance pay is earnings); Cadle Co. v. G & G Assocs., 757 So. 2d 1278 (Fla. Dist. Ct. App. 2000) (evidentiary hearing required to determine if various sums held by employer for "expense reimbursement," "reimbursement for investment," and "capital account" were earnings within meaning of Florida statute exempting head of household's earnings from garnishment). *See also In re* Eutsler, 2010 WL 27499 (Bankr. W.D.N.C. Jan. 12, 2012) (year-end bonus is earnings within meaning of North Carolina statute but, because it was earned over the previous year, it is not covered by exemption for personal services within sixty days preceding the order of execution); Bohrer v. DeHart, 969 P.2d 801 (Colo. App. 1999) ("distribution" from two-person corporation to "employee" who owned and controlled corporation was in fact earnings for personal services and thus could be reached by writ of continuing garnishment). *But see In re* Kramer, 339 B.R. 761 (Bankr. D. Colo. 2006) (stock purchased by payroll deductions as part of compensation package not exempt earnings under Colorado exemption statute; stock was personal property). *But cf. In re* Lawton, 261 B.R. 774 (Bankr. M.D. Fla. 2001) (stock options offered to employees not exempt wages because neither tied to individual performance nor provided in lieu of conventional compensation); *In re* Stroup, 221 B.R. 537 (Bankr. M.D. Fla. 1997) ("deferred compensation" paid to physician upon leaving medical group was not earnings within meaning of Florida exemption, when amount was determined by income of entire group, so was more like severance pay or a dividend on the physician part-owner's financial investment, rather than payment for personal services).

In *Kokoszka v. Belford*,[255] in holding that an income tax refund was not "earnings" under the CCPA, the United States Supreme Court stated that it agreed with a court of appeals opinion that earnings are limited to periodic payment of compensation. However the statute itself defines earnings to include any "bonus,"[256] which would not be a periodic payment.[257] In addition, the statute defines payments from a pension plan as earnings only if they are periodic,[258] without so limiting other parts of the definition of earnings, thereby implying that the protections apply to non-pension compensation, whether or not it is periodic. The Supreme Court's statement has been characterized as *dictum*, in that the issue before the Court was not the scope of the earnings exemption but whether Congress intended the wage garnishment protections to override the bankruptcy laws.[259]

The Michigan Supreme Court has concluded that the only question under the CCPA is whether a payment is compensation for personal services, and it is irrelevant whether it is periodic, predictable, or non-discretionary.[260] Thus profit-sharing payments, a "signing bonus" awarded to each employee as a result of union wage negotiations, and "recognition awards" made to certain salaried employees who were not eligible for regular pay increases, were all protected as "earnings." Other courts have held that lump-sum severance payments are protected as "earnings."[261]

12.4.1.5 Calculating the Amount of Wages Protected

12.4.1.5.1 Calculation rules

The CCPA garnishment provisions set a ceiling on the amount of a debtor's disposable earnings that may be garnished. This subsection discusses these rules. State restrictions on garnishment, discussed in § 12.4.3, *infra*, should be also checked in every case, as they may provide greater protection for the debtor.

255 417 U.S. 642, 651, 94 S. Ct. 2431, 41 L. Ed. 2d 374 (1974).

256 15 U.S.C. § 1672(a).

257 *See* United States v. Ashcraft, 732 F.3d 860, 863 n.4 (8th Cir. 2013) (noting that bonuses are frequently not periodic, that the Supreme Court's discussion was in an analysis of legislative history, and that the statute is not limited to periodic payments).

258 *Id.*

259 Genesee Cnty. Friend of the Court v. Gen. Motors Corp., 626 N.W.2d 395, 401 n.7 (Mich. 2001).

260 *Id.*

261 *In re* Grauer, 2009 WL 4938497 (Bankr. D. Md. Dec. 10, 2009) (severance pay is earnings); Shah v. City of Farmington Hills, 748 N.W.2d 592 (Mich. Ct. App. 2008); Gen. Elec. Capital Corp. v. ICO, Inc., 230 S.W.3d 702 (Tex. App. 2007) (severance pay in hands of employer is exempt current wages, but exemption lost when paid over to employee). *But see* Pallante v. Int'l Venture Invs., Ltd., 622 F. Supp. 667 (N.D. Ohio 1985) (lump-sum severance payment under voluntary separation plan not earnings because not periodic); *In re* A'Hearn, 2011 WL 4704235 (Bankr. N.D. Iowa Oct. 4, 2011) (monthly installments of severance pay to downsized executive were not earnings within the meaning of the CCPA or the Iowa statute, which uses CCPA definitions); *In re* Johnson, 199 B.R. 155 (Bankr. W.D. Ky. 1995) (severance pay not earnings within meaning of Kentucky exemption statute).

The "disposable earnings" protected by the CCPA are that part of the employee's earnings remaining after the deduction of any amount required by law to be withheld. These deductions include federal, state, and local taxes, Social Security, and other governmental retirement programs required by law.[262] Deductions such as those for union dues, health and life insurance, charitable contributions, voluntary wage assignments, and savings bonds are usually not considered required by law to be withheld when calculating the exemption.[263] One court has held, however, that payments into a 401(k) retirement plan should be deducted from gross wages to determine disposable income, because these payments are not considered earnings in the first place, at least for federal income tax purposes.[264]

A Department of Labor fact sheet states that deductions employers make to repay themselves for salary advances extended to workers or merchandise purchased by workers are not required by law to be withheld.[265] Such a deduction may be treated as a garnishment entitled to priority under state law, however.[266] It can also be argued that an amount withheld by the employer to repay itself does not meet the federal definition of "earnings,"[267] because it is neither "paid" nor "payable."

An existing garnishment for child support should not be treated as a deduction from income. Instead, after the disposable earnings are calculated, the court should treat the child support garnishment as a preexisting garnishment. If it consumes 25% or more of the debtor's disposable earnings, there are no earnings available for creditors' garnishments.[268]

The maximum amount of disposable earnings that may be garnished (for debts other than court-ordered child support and alimony[269]) is the lesser of:

- Twenty-five percent of the disposable earnings for that workweek; or
- The amount by which disposable earnings for that week exceed thirty times the federal minimum hourly wage.

As of July 24, 2009, the federal minimum wage is $7.25 per hour.[270]

12.4.1.5.2 Wage garnishment calculations

After July 23, 2009, with a minimum wage of $7.25 per hour in effect, no garnishment can be made if an employee's disposable earnings are $217.50 or less for the week in question. When an employee's disposable earnings exceed $217.50 but are less than $290.00, only the amount over $217.50 can be garnished. For example, assume that an employee's gross earnings in a particular week are $250.00. After deductions required by law, the disposable earnings are $220.00. Because only the amount over $217.50 may be garnished when the disposable earnings are less than $290.00, only $2.50 may be garnished and $217.50 must be paid to the employee.

An employee is entitled to a full exemption even if the employee does not work the full pay period. For example, if an employee with a weekly pay period works only 10 hours at $10.00 per hour after the allowable deductions, all $100.00 of the earnings are exempt for that week.[271]

When an employee's disposable earnings are $290.00 or more in a given week, up to 25% of those earnings can be

262 15 U.S.C. § 1672(b). *See also* Marshall v. Dist. Ct., 444 F. Supp. 1110 (E.D. Mich. 1978); First Nat'l Bank v. Hasty, 415 F. Supp. 170 (E.D. Mich. 1976), *aff'd*, 573 F.2d 1310 (6th Cir. 1977) (table); DiZazzo v. DiZazzo, 1992 WL 98124 (Conn. Super. Ct. Apr. 23, 1992) (voluntary 401(k) contributions and health insurance premiums were not required to be withheld so were "disposable earnings"; those amounts may be deducted from "earnings" under state exemption law but only to extent reasonable in light of support needs of beneficiaries under support order); Sears, Roebuck & Co. v. A. T. & G. Co., 239 N.W.2d 614 (Mich. Ct. App. 1976) (deduction from debtor's earnings to pay debt to employer was not a deduction required by law to be withheld, but employer's deduction has priority under state law).

263 Dep't of Labor, Fact Sheet #30, *available at* www.dol.gov/esa/regs/compliance/whd/whdfs30.htm. *See* U.S. v. Thomas, 2012 WL 147876 (E.D. Cal. Jan. 18, 2012) (voluntary contributions to retirement fund should not be deducted in calculating disposable income), *adopted by*, 2012 WL 869512 (E.D. Cal. Mar. 9, 2012); Nichols v. Weston, 2011 WL 1630336 (Ariz. Ct. App. Apr. 26, 2011) ("voluntary" payments to IRS, by wage assignment to which debtors agreed to avoid a levy, do not count towards 25% cap; private creditor may garnish 25% of wages).

264 *In re* Robinson, 240 B.R. 70 (Bankr. N.D. Ala. 1999).

265 *Id.*

266 Sears, Roebuck & Co. v. A. T. & G. Co., 239 N.W.2d 614 (Mich. Ct. App. 1976) (deduction from debtor's earnings to pay debt to employer takes priority over judgment creditor's garnishment).

267 15 U.S.C. § 1672(a).

268 Comptroller v. First Ala. Bank, 642 So. 2d 1349 (Ala. Civ. App. 1993) (child support order against debtor is considered a prior garnishment and is to be deducted from income available for garnishment rather than from gross income to determine disposable earnings); *In re* Marriage of Herrick, 640 N.E.2d 969, 973 (Ill. App. Ct. 1994); Koethe v. Carmel Heights Apartments, 328 N.W.2d 293 (Iowa 1982) (court-ordered assignment of wages to meet child support obligation must be treated as a prior garnishment, not as a deduction from gross income, when determining disposable income); *In re* Rummel, 954 N.E.2d 207 (Ohio Ct. App. 2011) (child support orders should not be deducted from income in determining amount available for garnishment); Union Pac. R.R. v. Trona Valley Fed. Credit Union, 57 P.3d 1203 (Wyo. 2002).

269 *See* § 12.4.1.5.4, *infra*.

The minimum wage had been $4.25 per hour from 1991 (Pub. L. No. 101-157, § 2, 103 Stat. 938) until Oct. 1, 1996, when it increased to $4.75 per hour by virtue of the Small Business Protection Act, Pub. L. No. 104-188, § 2104, 110 Stat. 1755, which amended the Fair Labor Standards Act, 29 U.S.C. § 206. The same Act also enacted an increase, effective October 1, 1997, to $5.15 per hour. In 2007, Congress adopted Pub. L. No. 110-28, §§ 8101–8104, 121 Stat. 112 (2007), increasing the federal minimum wage from $5.15 to $5.85 per hour as of July 24, 2007, from $5.85 to $6.55 per hour as of July 24, 2008, and from $6.55 to $7.25 per hour as of July 24, 2009. The Washington, D.C. and regional offices of the Wage and Hour Division of the United States Department of Labor may be phoned for information on the current minimum wage. This information is also available on the Department of Labor's website at www.dol.gov/dol/topic/wages/index.htm. The Department of Labor regulations, 29 C.F.R. Part 870, which are reprinted in Appendix C.2, *infra*, still refer to the pre-1997 minimum wage levels. Calculations using the 2007 minimum wage level may be found in the Department of Labor's Fact Sheet #30, available at www.dol.gov/esa/regs/compliance/whd/whdfs30.htm.

270 Pub. L. No. 110-28, §§ 8101–8104, 121 Stat. 112 (2007).

271 *See, e.g.*, First Nat'l Bank v. Columbia Credit Corp., 499 P.2d 1163 (Colo. 1972).

garnished. For example, assume that an employee's gross earnings in a particular week are $350.00. After deductions required by law, the disposable earnings are $320.00. In this week, 25% of disposable earnings, that is, $80.00, could be garnished. $240.00 must be paid to the employee.

12.4.1.5.3 Calculations when worker is not paid weekly

Some additional calculations are necessary when a worker is not paid weekly but instead is paid bi-weekly, semi-monthly, or monthly. Department of Labor regulations specify how to perform these calculations for these irregular pay periods:

- Assume a calendar month consists of four and one-third workweeks;
- Multiply the number of workweeks or fractions thereof in the irregular pay period times 30 times the minimum hourly wage (as of July 24, 2009, this comes to $217.50).[272]

Consequently, as of July 24, 2009, the maximum amount allowed to be garnished is the lesser of:

(1) 25% of disposable earnings for the pay period, or
(2) the amount by which disposable earnings for the pay period exceed $435.00 for a bi-weekly pay period, $471.25 for a semi-monthly period and $942.50 for a monthly period.

12.4.1.5.4 Child support and alimony

The CCPA garnishment provisions offer debtors fewer protections when the debt involves a court order for child support or alimony.[273] The maximum amount of disposable income that may be garnished for child support or alimony payments may not exceed:

- 50% for a debtor also supporting another spouse or child;[274]
- 55% for such a debtor if support is twelve weeks or more in arrears;
- 60% for a debtor not supporting another spouse or child;
- 65% for such a debtor if support is twelve weeks or more in arrears.[275]

Some courts have held that they have the authority to order the obligor to make periodic support payments over and above the amounts withheld from earnings.[276]

12.4.1.5.5 Multiple garnishments; multiple jobs

When there is more than one garnishment, the priority among them is determined by state law.[277] Some states give

---

272 29 C.F.R. § 870.10(c), *reprinted in* Appendix C.2, *infra*; Dep't of Labor Fact Sheet #30 (includes examples based on 2009 increase to minimum wage), *available at* www.dol.gov/whd/garnishment/index.htm. *See also* Koethe v. Johnson, 328 N.W.2d 293 (Iowa 1982) (describing formula for bi-weekly pay period; decision also holds that, when garnishment order arrives in middle of pay period, before entire period's pay is earned, full pay for entire period should be used in CCPA calculations); Eaton Family Credit Union v. Brier, 2012 WL 171089 (Ohio Ct. App. Jan. 19, 2012) (when debtor received a paycheck every two weeks, but one check each month included that month's commissions, the proper formula for calculating the garnishment amount was that for bi-weekly, not monthly, pay).

273 Marriage of Eklofe, 586 N.W.2d 357 (Iowa 1998) (Iowa's $800 per year limitation on garnishment of certain low income debtors' wages applied to wage garnishment for alimony, but not child support; discussion of complicated interrelationship of garnishment and family support law, which has changed since case was decided); Albrecht v. Albrecht, 1999 Ohio App. LEXIS 622 (Ohio Ct. App. Feb. 23, 1999) (garnishment of 30% of income was permitted as "child support" when obligor was liquidating arrears, after children were emancipated); Gest v. Gest, 1998 Ohio App. LEXIS 1798 (Ohio Ct. App. Apr. 29, 1998) (federal and state limitations on garnishment for family support apply only to garnishment; court could order spousal and child support and provision of medical insurance for children, which added up to more than 60% of obligor's income, provided wage assignment did not exceed 60%); Laws v. Laws, 758 A.2d 1226 (Pa. Super. Ct. 2000) (maximum child support garnishment under CCPA could be based on obligor's earning capacity rather than lower actual earnings). *Cf.* Naedel v. Naedel, 693 A.2d 60 (Md. Ct. Spec. App. 1997) (narrowly construing family support exception to CCPA garnishment limitation: alimony obligation that arose from a voluntary agreement, which was then "incorporated but not merged in[to]" the divorce decree and was non-modifiable by the court, was neither "ordered by a court" nor "subject to judicial review," so 25% limitation would apply); Carrel v. Carrel, 791 S.W.2d 831 (Mo. Ct. App. 1990) (family support exception to CCPA garnishment limits did not apply to court-ordered wage assignment to satisfy obligation to pay spouse's attorney fees in marriage dissolution case); Cashin v. Cashin, 451 A.2d 1331 (N.J. Super. Ct. Ch. Div. 1982) (construing award of counsel fees in divorce action as support, so allowing higher percentage of wages to be garnished). *But cf.* Heller v. Heller, 359 S.W.3d 902 (Tex. App. 2012) (alimony order resulting from agreement between spouses is ordinary debt, for which current wages may not be garnished, absent evidence that wife is unable to support self).

274 Bitzer v. Bitzer, 986 S.W.2d 122 (Ark. Ct. App. 1999) (husband was supporting second wife, within meaning of CCPA, when he earned slightly larger income and was obligated on mortgage of her house, and she was supporting a child from her previous marriage, so garnishment by first wife was limited to 55% of disposable income); Rios v. Mireles, 937 P.2d 840 (Colo. App. 1996) (when debtor owed a support judgment to his second ex-wife but had not paid, he was not "supporting another spouse" within meaning of the CCPA, so first ex-wife could garnish up to 50%); Ctr. for Gastrointestinal Med., Inc. v. Willitts, 623 A.2d 752 (N.H. 1993) (no more than 50% of father's wages could be garnished to satisfy a child support order, due to his obligation to support minor child in his custody, even though he was found to have intentionally restricted his income).

275 15 U.S.C. § 1673(b)(2). *See also* Champion Int'l Corp. v. Ayars, 587 F. Supp. 1274 (D. Conn. 1984); DiZazzo v. DiZazzo, 1992 WL 98124 (Conn. Super. Ct. Apr. 23, 1992) (65% of disposable earnings, not 60%, may be garnished when child support or alimony in arrears); Turkette v. Turkette, 2010 WL 624335 (Mich. Ct. App. Feb. 23, 2010) (awarding ex-wife 50% of Navy pension as property division and an additional 15% as alimony did not violate CCPA, which allows garnishment of up to 65% of disposable income for family support).

276 Hamilton v. Hamilton, 914 N.E.2d 747 (Ind. 2009) (CCPA does not limit amount of family support order, only amount that can be collected by garnishment; obligor may be held in contempt for failure to pay additional amount but, here, affirming refusal to hold struggling obligor in contempt); Frankel v. Frankel, 886 A.2d 136 (Md. Ct. Spec. App. 2005); Zollar v. Zollar, 2009 WL 580798 (Ohio Ct. App. Mar. 9, 2009) (unpublished); *In re* Prade, 734 N.E.2d 430 (Ohio Ct. App. 1999) (court has power to order family support in amount greater than that which may be collected by garnishment).

277 Long Island Trust Co. v. United States Postal Serv., 647 F.2d 336 (2d Cir. 1981); Voss Products, Inc. v. Carlton, 147 F. Supp. 2d 892 (E.D. Tenn. 2001); Koethe v. Carmel Heights Apartments, 328 N.W.2d 293 (Iowa 1982). *See also* Sears, Roebuck & Co. v. A. T. & G. Co., 239 N.W.2d 614 (Mich. Ct. App. 1976) (deduction from debtor's earnings to pay debt to employer takes priority over judgment creditor's garnishment).

priority to the garnishment that is prior in time.[278] Other states require creditors to take turns garnishing a debtor's earnings, so a later garnishment may take priority over an earlier one.[279] Between creditor garnishments and garnishments for support, however, states often give priority to those for support, regardless of their timing, so a debtor who is subject to a support garnishment that consumes 25% or more of his or her disposable earnings will be immune from creditor garnishment.[280]

The Department of Labor takes the position that when a worker has more than one job the CCPA restrictions are separately applicable to each employer, assuming that the employers are completely separate and distinct and act independently of each other. Thus, a worker who works two jobs and receives disposable earnings from each job that fall below thirty times the minimum wage is completely protected from garnishment, even if the earnings would exceed thirty times the minimum wage if added together.[281]

12.4.1.6 Remedies for Excessive Wage Garnishment

There are no specified penalties for court orders allowing excessive wage garnishments. Congress intended the court issuing the garnishment to abide by the provisions of the Act, by stating that "no court of the United States . . . may make, execute or enforce any order or process in violation of this section."[282] The debtor, and probably the debtor's employer, can litigate the propriety of the garnishment in the court that issued it and appeal from that court's decision.[283]

While the Wage and Hour Division of the Department of Labor has authority to interpret and enforce the wage garnishment restrictions,[284] the CCPA does not give debtors an explicit private right of action under the CCPA for excessive wage garnishment orders.[285] Nonetheless, it may be possible for an employee to recover monies erroneously paid over to a judgment creditor, and a misuse of process or a failure to correct an erroneous garnishment may entitle an employee to damages from the creditor, the debtor's employer, or both.[286]

---

278 *See, e.g.*, Long Island Trust Co. v. United States Postal Serv., 647 F.2d 336 (2d Cir. 1981); Koethe v. Carmel Heights Apartments, 328 N.W.2d 293 (Iowa 1982).

279 *See, e.g.*, Bohrer v. DeHart, 969 P.2d 801 (Colo. App. 1999).

280 Long Island Trust Co. v. United States Postal Serv., 647 F.2d 336 (2d Cir. 1981); Voss Products, Inc. v. Carlton, 147 F. Supp. 2d 892 (E.D. Tenn. 2001); *In re* Borochov, 2008 WL 2559433 (Bankr. D. Haw. June 23, 2008); Gen. Motors Acceptance Corp. v. Metro. Opera Ass'n, 413 N.Y.S.2d 818 (N.Y. App. Term 1978); Lough v. Robinson, 675 N.E.2d 1272 (Ohio Ct. App. 1996) (if child support garnishment exceeds 25% of disposable earnings, creditor garnishments forbidden); Union Pac. R.R. v. Trona Valley Fed. Credit Union, 57 P.3d 1203 (Wyo. 2002). *See also* Igbal v. Mucci, 852 A.2d 195 (N.J. Super. Ct. App. Div. 2004) (when more than 25% of judgment debtor's income was being garnished for child support, court could not order installment payments on ordinary creditor's judgment, because this could lead to wage execution).

281 United States Dep't of Labor, Wage & Hour Div., Field Operations Handbook ch. 16, § 16b11, *available at* www.dol.gov/whd/garnishment/index.htm.

282 15 U.S.C. § 1673(c). *See also* Dyche v. Dyche, 570 S.W.2d 293 (Mo. 1978) (courts have the responsibility to enforce the garnishment protections created by the federal statute and any state statute supplementing it).

283 Union Pac. R.R. v. Trona Valley Fed. Credit Union, 57 P.3d 1203 (Wyo. 2002). *See also* Prof'l Credit Collections v. Smith, 933 P.2d 307 (Okla. 1997) (ex-wife who opened default judgment and quashed wage garnishment for ex-husband's debt on grounds of improper service, at which point creditor voluntarily dismissed action, was prevailing party entitled to attorney fees at trial and appellate levels). *Cf.* Guidry v. Sheet Metal Workers Nat'l Pension Fund, 856 F.2d 1457 (10th Cir. 1988) (debtor who failed to raise objections to state court garnishment in accord with state procedure cannot raise them in federal suit), *rev'd on other grounds*, 493 U.S. 365 (1990).

284 15 U.S.C. § 1676.

285 Sheils v. Bucks Cnty. Domestic Relations Section, 921 F. Supp. 2d 396 (E.D. Pa. 2013) (no private right of action under CCPA or federal statutes and regulations requiring states to provide certain due process protections to child support obligors); Steele v. Steele, 2011 WL 2413400 (E.D. Ky. June 10, 2011); Evans v. Social Sec. Admin., 2009 WL 2596647 (D. Col. Aug. 20, 2009) (section 1673 does not create private right of action, but debtor may have state cause of action for improper garnishment); Colbert v. Roling, 2005 WL 3302212 (W.D. Mo. Dec. 5, 2005) (no private right of action under CCPA and therefore no federal right to assert claim under 42 U.S.C. § 1983), *aff'd*, 233 Fed. Appx. 587 (8th Cir. 2007); Pressman v. Neubardt, 2002 WL 31780183 (S.D.N.Y. Dec. 12, 2002) (no federal private cause of action for violation of 15 U.S.C. § 1673); Perkins v. Metro. Water Reclamation Dist., 1990 U.S. Dist. LEXIS 12594 (N.D. Ill. Sept. 24, 1990) (no private cause of action against employer for garnishing more than allowed by CCPA); Burris v. Mahaney, 716 F. Supp. 1051 (M.D. Tenn. 1989) (no private cause of action under 15 U.S.C. § 1673 or 42 U.S.C. § 1983 for excessive wage garnishment); Whitney v. Chicago Transit Auth., 1987 U.S. Dist. LEXIS 4564 (N.D. Ill. June 2, 1987) (no private cause of action against employer for violating CCPA); Follette v. Vitanza, 658 F. Supp. 492 (N.D.N.Y. 1983) (debtor cannot bring section 1983 claim to enforce federal limits on wage garnishment); Western v. Hodgson, 359 F. Supp. 194 (S.D. W. Va. 1973), *aff'd on other grounds*, 494 F.2d 379 (4th Cir. 1973); Oldham v. Oldham, 337 F. Supp. 1039 (N.D. Iowa 1972) (granting unopposed motion to dismiss cause of action alleging wage garnishment in violation of CCPA). *See also* Williams v. M.R.C. Polymers, 2000 U.S. Dist. LEXIS 2726 (N.D. Ill. Feb. 23, 2000) (suggesting that there is no private right of action); Winslow v. Bauer, 585 F. Supp. 1048 (D. Colo. 1984) (private cause of action cannot be founded on section 1671, which merely sets forth Congressional purposes); *In re* O'Neil, 992 A.2d 672 (N.H. 2010) (no private right of action to recover for allegedly excessive garnishment during divorce).

286 Cowart v. David J. Axelrod & Assocs., 2004 WL 1013352 (N.D. Ill. Apr. 27, 2004) (allowing employee—who was not the judgment debtor—to amend complaint to add common law wrongful garnishment and conversion claims against employer who withheld wages without court order, based on garnishment notice with wrong name); Betts v. Coltes, 467 F. Supp. 544 (D. Haw. 1979); Giles v. Gen. Motors Corp., 802 N.E.2d 858 (Ill. App. Ct. 2003) (employee stated claims for gross negligence or wanton and willful misconduct against employer who continued to withhold wages for two-and-a-half years after expiration of court order; court order not a defense when it included termination date). *See also* Zaleski v. Collection Bureau, 664 N.W.2d 32 (Neb. Ct. App. 2003) (reversing dismissal of claim asserting statutory private cause of action against creditor and custodians of bank account for wrongful garnishment of exempt wages on deposit). *Cf.* Evans v. Social Sec. Admin., 2009 WL 2596647 (D. Colo. Aug. 20, 2009) (section 1673 does not create private right of action, but debtor may have state cause of action for improper garnishment); First Va. Bank v. Randolph, 110 F.3d 75 (D.C. Cir. 1997) (sovereign immunity protects government from any liability to judgment creditor for refusing, mistakenly or otherwise, to withhold federal employee's wages after employee moved

Garnishing excess wages may also violate other federal or state debt collection laws.[287] In addition, wrongful garnishment or attachment may give rise to a claim for malicious prosecution or abuse of process,[288] in which case punitive damages may be available.[289] Remedies under bankruptcy law will be available if a creditor violates the automatic stay by garnishing the wages of a debtor who has filed bankruptcy[290] or by seeking turnover of funds garnished prepetition.[291] If the employer

to quash garnishment order). *But see In re* O'Neil, 992 A.2d 672 (N.H. 2010) (no private right of action to recover for allegedly excessive garnishment during divorce). *But cf.* Broughton v. Magnetic Ticket & Label Corp., 2006 WL 181669 (M.D. Tenn. Jan. 24, 2006) (employer owed no duty to child support obligor; even if delay in remitting funds withheld from wages caused obligor to be jailed for contempt, obligor failed to state a claim for negligent or intentional infliction of emotional distress). *See generally* § 12.6.2, *infra* (remedies for wrongful garnishment of exempt funds in bank account).

287 *See, e.g.*, Backlund v. Messerli & Kramer, P.A., 2012 WL 3582963 (D. Minn. Aug. 17, 2012) (if collection law firm violated state statute prescribing notice requirements for garnishment, it violated FDCPA provision forbidding collection of amounts not permitted by law); Waitkus v. Pressler & Pressler, L.L.P., 2012 WL 686025 (D.N.J. Mar. 2, 2012) (allowing FDCPA claim to proceed against debt collectors who attempted to execute turnover order against 100% of plaintiff's commission-based earnings, in violation of CCPA and state law, and violated New Jersey rules regarding notice to debtor); Adkins v. Weltman, Weinberg & Reis Co., L.P.A., 2012 WL 604249 (S.D. Ohio Feb. 24, 2012) (garnishment action directed to debtor's employer is an action "against" debtor, within the meaning of the FDCPA; FDCPA venue provision applies to postjudgment enforcement actions, including the garnishment action here); Gruen v. EdFund, 2009 WL 2136785 (N.D. Cal. July 15, 2009) (borrower stated FDCPA and California UDAP claims against collector of student loans; allegations included improper wage garnishment); Sial v. Unifund CCR Partners, 2008 WL 4079281 (S.D. Cal. Aug. 28, 2008) (*Noerr-Pennington* doctrine did not bar FDCPA action alleging litigation misconduct, here obtaining default judgment without proper service on time-barred debt, then garnishing wages; state litigation privilege did not bar Rosenthal Act claim). *See also* Todd v. Weltman, Weinberg & Reis. Co. L.P.A., 434 F.3d 432 (6th Cir. 2006) (consumer stated FDCPA claim against collection firm that regularly filed affidavits alleging reasonable belief that bank accounts contained non-exempt funds, with no knowledge whether this was true; here, account contained only exempt Social Security and disability payments); Lewis v. Asset Acceptance, L.L.C., 2012 WL 1801987 (D. Or. Apr. 6, 2012) (sending garnishment notices, required by state law, to an address that collector knew or should have known was obsolete, was unfair or unconscionable in violation of FDCPA). *But cf.* Engelen v. Erin Capital Mgmt., 2012 WL 12680 (S.D. Cal. Jan. 3, 2012) (bona fide error defense applies when second garnishment for debt already paid resulted from clerical error); Reeves v. Messerli & Kramer, P.A., 2012 WL 926063 (D. Minn. Mar. 16, 2012) (not FDCPA violation for collection firm to continue with wage garnishment while verifying debtor's claim that his wages were protected by state law exemption for recipients of need-based public benefits). *See generally* Joel E. Smith, Annotation, *Recovery of damages for mental anguish, distress, suffering, or the like, in action for wrongful attachment, garnishment, sequestration, or execution*, 83 A.L.R.3d 598 (1978); National Consumer Law Center, Fair Debt Collection §§ 5.6.1–5.6.3 (8th ed. 2014); § 12.6.2 *infra*.

288 *See* Todd v. Weltman, Weinberg & Reis. Co. L.P.A., 434 F.3d 432 (6th Cir. 2006) (action for wrongful garnishment may lie even if underlying debt is valid); Pinsky v. Duncan, 79 F.3d 306 (2d Cir. 1996) (wrongful attachment may give rise to cause of action for malicious prosecution or abuse of process, but not without evidence of malice and lack of probable cause); Cordero v. Calvary SpVI L.L.C., 2004 WL 1244107 (N.D. Ill. June 3, 2004) (consumer stated claim against creditor's lawyers and process servers, who caused wages to be garnished based on false affidavit of service); Ky. Farm Bureau Mut. Ins. Co. v. Burton, 922 S.W.2d 385 (Ky. Ct. App. 1996) (recognizing cause of action for wrongful garnishment; if plaintiff also proves malice and lack of probable cause, common law malicious prosecution claim is available, but judgment creditor's defense of good faith reliance on advice of counsel prevails here). *But cf.* Brown v. Kennard, 113 Cal. Rptr. 2d 891 (Cal. Ct. App. 2001) (litigation privilege prevents abuse of process claim based on wrongful postjudgment execution proceeding unless it is repeated). *See generally* National Consumer Law Center, Fair Debt Collection § 9.6 (8th ed. 2014).

289 Addair v. Huffman, 195 S.E.2d 739 (Va. 1973) (assessing compensatory and punitive damages against owner of collection agency in tort action arising from wrongful wage garnishment). *See also* Johnson v. JP Morgan Chase Bank, 395 B.R. 442 (E.D. Cal. 2008) (consumer stated claim for nondischargeability of bankrupt collector's debt to her when collector garnished her wages and engaged in other collection activity after being informed by original creditor bank that debt was result of identity theft); Thomas J. Goger, Annotation, *What Constitutes Malice Sufficient To Justify An Award of Punitive Damages In Action for Wrongful Attachment or Garnishment*, 61 A.L.R.3d 984 (1975).

290 *In re* Rose, 2012 WL 4511342 (Bankr. N.D. Ill. Oct. 2, 2012) (collection attorney violated automatic stay by serving citation to discover assets, which resulted in hold on bank account, and refusing to release hold upon being notified of bankruptcy); *In re* Tuecke, 2006 WL 3000028 (Bankr. N.D. Iowa Oct. 10, 2006) (awarding punitive damages for postpetition wage garnishment after actual notice of bankruptcy; disregard for rights was "blatant" and creditor was "a sophisticated player in the credit industry"); *In re* See, 301 B.R. 549 (Bankr. N.D. Iowa 2003) (sanctions, including punitive damages, for bank's violation of automatic stay in continuing to garnish exempt wages despite knowledge of bankruptcy and exempt status of funds). *See also In re* Culley, 347 B.R. 115 (B.A.P. 10th Cir. 2006) (table) (affirming $10,000 punitive damages award for garnishment in violation of bankruptcy discharge; evidence of actual intent to harass and intimidate debtor, who was creditor's ex-spouse); *In re* Johnson, 479 B.R. 159, 178 (Bankr. N.D. Ga. 2012) (bank violated automatic stay by proceeding against debtor's employer for failing to respond to prepetition wage garnishment).

291 Great Am. Ins. Co. v. Gen. Contractors & Constr. Mgmt., Inc., 2008 WL 5056526 (S.D. Fla. Nov. 21, 2008) (sanctioning creditor who, with actual notice of bankruptcy, went to state court and obtained turnover of funds garnished prepetition, which debtor had properly claimed as exempt); *In re* Trujillo, 485 B.R. 238 (Bankr. D. Colo. 2012) (collection lawyer violated automatic stay by refusing to return funds garnished prepetition when state law gave debtor right to contest the garnishment); *In re* Brugueras, 2012 WL 605603 (Bankr. E.D. Va. Dec. 6, 2012) (creditor violated automatic stay when, with actual knowledge of bankruptcy filing, it went to state court and demanded that funds garnished prepetition be paid over to it); *In re* Forkner, 2010 WL 5462543 (Bankr. N.D. Iowa Dec. 22, 2010) (debt buyer violated automatic stay by, after receiving notice of bankruptcy, accepting and depositing check for funds that had been garnished prepetition; creditor who is notified of bankruptcy has affirmative duty to stop garnishment and return funds); *In re* Myers, 402 B.R. 370 (Bankr. M.D. Ala. 2009) (upon being notified of bankruptcy, creditor must "take all necessary affirmative steps" to terminate garnishment; creditor who received and held garnished funds after notice of bankruptcy willfully violated automatic stay); *In re* Terrell, 2008 WL 4401398 (Bankr. E.D. Va. Sept. 23, 2008) (sanctioning creditor who, with actual notice of bankruptcy, went to state court and obtained payment of garnished funds, which had been properly claimed as exempt in bankruptcy case). *See also In re* Iwan, 2008 WL 321507 (Bankr. M.D. Fla. Jan. 16, 2008) (creditor, who had prepetition writ of garnishment, violated stay when it took funds garnished from paycheck issued postpetition).

prevails in litigation with the creditor about whether it properly complied with a garnishment order, it may be an entitled to an attorney fee award from the creditor.[292]

An employer who pays more to a creditor than the CCPA allows may be liable to the employee under the federal minimum wage laws. The excess amount garnished does not count toward the federal minimum wage requirement.[293] If the excess amount of the garnishment brings the worker's wages below the minimum wage, the worker has a private cause of action against the employer.[294] The worker may also have a cause of action against the employer under a state wage law, which may apply to any failure to pay wages that are legally due, regardless of whether there is a minimum wage violation.[295] One court awarded costs and attorney fees to an employer as a sanction against an attorney who persistently tried to garnish the wages of an employee against whom no judgment had been taken.[296]

12.4.1.7 Federal Protections Against Employee Discharge for Wage Garnishment

12.4.1.7.1 CCPA discharge prohibition

The preservation of an employee's job is one of the dominant purposes of the CCPA garnishment protections, which provide that no employer may discharge an employee whose earnings have been subject to garnishment for any one indebtedness.[297] The Department of Labor interprets this protection as applying even if the garnishment is not the only factor motivating the employer: "[O]nly where garnishment for a single indebtedness plays no real part in the discharge is it beyond the prohibition of the Act."[298] The term "one indebtedness" refers to a single debt. Thus an employee may not be discharged regardless of the number of levies or proceedings brought to collect a single debt.[299]

The CCPA restrictions do not protect an employee whose salary has been garnished for more than one debt.[300] That is, the CCPA allows an employer to discharge an employee because there are multiple garnishment orders for different debts. However, if a creditor joins several debts in a court action and obtains one judgment, that one judgment is considered a single indebtedness.[301]

Even in cases of multiple garnishments for multiple debts, the earnings must first be actually "withheld" pursuant to a garnishment order before the employee can be legally discharged. If the employee obtains a release from the creditor after the employer receives a garnishment notice, but before the actual garnishment takes place, then the earnings have not been "withheld," and a discharge would violate the Act.[302] Similarly, if a prior garnishment renders the second garnishment order unenforceable, then a discharge on the basis of the second order would violate the CCPA.[303]

12.4.1.7.2 Criminal and administrative enforcement

The CCPA provides criminal sanctions for wrongful discharge of an employee.[304] The CCPA also provides that its garnishment restrictions are to be enforced by the Secretary of Labor acting through the Wage and Hour Division of the Department of Labor.[305] The Secretary of Labor has the authority to seek injunctive and declaratory relief,[306] and reinstatement of a wrongfully discharged employee.[307] However, enforcement by the Secretary of Labor is discretionary.[308]

12.4.1.7.3 Is there a federal private cause of action?

The Fifth, Eighth, and Ninth Circuits and a number of district courts have held that there is no federal private right of action to enforce the CCPA garnishment protections against employee discharges.[309] These decisions are based on the

292 *See* Discover Bank v. Barnes, 294 P.3d 453 (Okla. Civ. App. 2012) (requiring creditor to pay employer's attorney fees; creditor wrote employer that consumer's account was closed and employer need not garnish any more funds, then a year later sued employer for failing to comply with garnishment order).

293 29 C.F.R. § 531.39.

294 29 U.S.C. § 216(b) (authorizing suit for unpaid minimum wages plus additional equal amount as liquidated damages, equitable relief, and attorney fees).

295 *See, e.g.*, Marshall v. Safeway, Inc., 2014 WL 1227629 (Md. 2014) (excessive wage garnishment violates state Wage Payment Act provision forbidding unauthorized deductions; but claim moot because employer has refunded improperly garnished funds and agreed to use correct formula in future).

296 Neubauer v. Ohio Remcon, Inc., 2006 WL 772020 (Ohio Ct. App. Mar. 28, 2006).

297 15 U.S.C. § 1674(a).

298 United States Dep't of Labor, Wage & Hour Div., Field Operations Handbook ch. 16, § 16c07, *available at* www.dol.gov/whd/garnishment/index.htm.

299 *See* United States Dep't of Labor, Wage & Hour Div., Field Operations Handbook ch. 16, § 16c03, *available at* www.dol.gov/whd/garnishment/index.htm.

300 Cheatham v. Va. Alcoholic Beverage Control Bd., 501 F.2d 1346 (4th Cir. 1974).

301 *See* United States Dep't of Labor, Fact Sheet No. ESA-1078 (1982). *See also* United States Dep't of Labor, Wage & Hour Div., Field Operations Handbook ch. 16, § 16c03(b) ("Ordinarily, a separate debt may be identified as the full amount of the debt represented by a single judgment"), *available at* www.dol.gov/whd/garnishment/index.htm.

302 Donovan v. S. Calif. Gas Co., 715 F.2d 1405 (9th Cir. 1983).

303 Brennan v. Kroger Co., 513 F.2d 961 (7th Cir. 1975).

304 "Whoever willfully violates [the discharge provision] shall be fined not more than $1,000 or imprisoned not more than one year or both." 15 U.S.C. § 1674(b).

305 15 U.S.C. § 1676. *See also* Hodgson v. Consol. Freightways, Inc., 503 F.2d 797, 799 (9th Cir. 1974).

306 *See, e.g.*, Donovan v. Hamilton Cnty. Mun. Ct., 580 F. Supp. 554 (S.D. Ohio 1984); Hodgson v. Hamilton Mun. Ct., 349 F. Supp. 1125 (S.D. Ohio 1972).

307 Hodgson v. Consol. Freightways, Inc., 503 F.2d 797 (9th Cir. 1974). *See also* Martin v. Hawkeye Int'l Trucks, Inc., 782 F. Supp. 1320 (S.D. Iowa 1991) (awarding damages for wrongful termination in suit brought by Secretary on behalf of employee who was discharged because of Internal Revenue Service wage levy).

308 McCabe v. City of Eureka, 664 F.2d 680, 684 n.1 (8th Cir. 1981).

309 LeVick v. Skaggs Companies, Inc., 701 F.2d 777 (9th Cir. 1983); McCabe v. City of Eureka, 664 F.2d 680 (8th Cir. 1981) (noting that a different subchapter of the Act enacted on the same day as part of same law as 15 U.S.C. § 1676 contained a detailed provision for a private right of action); Smith v. Cotton Bros. Baking Co., 609 F.2d 738

availability of alternative remedies. Some note the mandate in 15 U.S.C. § 1676 that the Secretary of Labor "shall enforce the provisions of this subchapter," while others rely on the view that state statutes provide adequate private remedies. For example, the Uniform Consumer Credit Code (UCCC) expressly provides for a private civil action for a wrongful discharge based upon a wage garnishment.[310] While a few other courts have found that a private right of action must be implied under the CCPA in order to effectively carry out the purposes of the federal legislation,[311] they pre-date the Supreme Court's reworking of the test for implying such actions.[312]

When the employer is a state or municipal governmental entity, another approach may be used. At least one court has held that an employee discharged because of garnishment proceedings may maintain a private action under 42 U.S.C. § 1983 for deprivation without due process of his or her property interest in continued employment.[313] In this situation a state's Tort Claims Act will not afford immunity to either the governmental entity or its officials.[314]

12.4.1.7.4 *Title VII claims*

When the CCPA garnishment provisions do not provide an employee with protection from dismissal, or when the CCPA remedies are inadequate, another approach to challenging an employee discharge for garnishment is one based on Title VII of the Civil Rights Act of 1964, which prohibits discrimination in employment based on race or certain other characteristics.[315] This statute may also be used to challenge disciplinary action short of discharge.[316]

Three U.S. circuit courts of appeal[317] and the U.S. Equal Employment Opportunity Commission (EEOC)[318] have recognized that Title VII can be used to challenge the discharge or disciplining of minority employees for wage garnishments. An employment practice, such as discharging employees whose wages are garnished, which is facially neutral and evenhandedly applied, with no employer intention to discriminate, may still violate Title VII if the practice has a significantly greater adverse impact on one class (defined by race, color, religion, sex, or national origin) than on another class.[319] These are commonly known as "disparate impact" cases under Title VII.

The seminal Title VII garnishment case, *Johnson v. Pike*,[320] found that a policy of discharge for multiple garnishments had a disparate impact on black workers based on the court's examination of garnishment statistics for the general population.[321] The EEOC has explicitly adopted the reasoning in *Johnson*.[322]

The Fifth Circuit has adopted a different approach, requiring a showing of a statistically significant disparity between the garnishment policy's impact on black and on white employees of the particular employer, not of the general population.[323] Indeed, the trend in disparate impact litigation has

---

(5th Cir. 1980); Stouch v. Williamson Hospitality Corp., 22 F. Supp. 2d 431 (W.D. Pa. 1998); Western v. Hodgson, 359 F. Supp. 194 (S.D. W. Va. 1973), *aff'd on other grounds*, 494 F.2d 379 (4th Cir. 1974); Simpson v. Sperry Rand Corp., 350 F. Supp. 1057 (W.D. La. 1972), *vacated on other grounds*, 488 F.2d 450 (5th Cir. 1973); Oldham v. Oldham, 337 F. Supp. 1039 (N.D. Iowa 1972); Higgins v. Wilkerson, 63 Lab. Cas. (CCH) ¶ 32,379 (D. Kan. 1970). *Accord* Dole v. Hopple Plastics, Inc., 902 F.2d 33, n.1 (6th Cir. 1990) (dicta). *See also* Flax v. Delaware Div. of Family Servs., 2008 WL 1758857 (D. Del. Apr. 16, 2008) (no private cause of action for unspecified violation of CCPA garnishment protections), *aff'd*, 329 Fed. Appx. 360 (3d Cir. 2009); Mobile Cnty. Personnel Bd. v. City of Satsuma, 513 So. 2d 2 (Ala. Civ. App. 1987) (city employee had no private right to assert 15 U.S.C. § 1674(a) as a bar to his discharge for wage garnishment).

310 U.C.C.C. § 5.202(6) (providing for up to six weeks lost wages and reinstatement).

311 Ellis v. Glover & Gardner Constr. Co., 562 F. Supp. 1054 (M.D. Tenn. 1983); Maple v. Citizens Nat'l Bank & Trust Co., 437 F. Supp. 66 (W.D. Okla. 1977); Nunn v. City of Paducah, 367 F. Supp. 957 (W.D. Ky. 1973). *See also* Note, *The Implication of a Private Cause of Action Under Title III of the Consumer Credit Protection Act*, 47 S. Cal. L. Rev. 383, 398–400 (1974).

312 *See* Wisniewski v. Rodale, Inc., 510 F.3d 294, 297–301 (3d Cir. 2007) (summarizing Supreme Court decisions).

313 Johnson v. Town of Trail Creek, 771 F. Supp. 271 (N.D. Ind. 1991). *See also* Gonzaga Univ. v. Doe, 536 U.S. 273, 280 n.8, 122 S. Ct. 2268, 153 L. Ed. 2d 309 (2002); Middlesex Cnty. Sewerage Auth. v. Nat'l Sea Clammers Ass'n, 453 U.S. 1, 101 S. Ct. 2615, 69 L. Ed. 2d 435 (1981) (section 1983 is presumed to provide a remedy unless defendants can show that the statute contains a comprehensive enforcement mechanism whose breadth or scope suggests that Congress viewed that mechanism as the sole means for statutory enforcement).

314 Johnson v. Town of Trail Creek, 771 F. Supp. 271, 275 (N.D. Ind. 1991).

315 Civil Rights Act of 1964, 42 U.S.C. §§ 2000e–2000e-17 (as amended by Equal Employment Opportunity Act of 1972, § 703).

316 Keenen v. American Cast Iron Pipe Co., 707 F.2d 1274 (11th Cir. 1983) (reprimand, loss of fringe benefits); Robinson v. City of Dallas, 514 F.2d 1271 (5th Cir. 1975) (suspension).

317 Keenen v. American Cast Iron Pipe Co., 707 F.2d 1274 (11th Cir. 1983) (reprimand, loss of fringe benefits); Robinson v. City of Dallas, 514 F.2d 1271 (5th Cir. 1975) (suspension); Wallace v. Debron Corp., 494 F.2d 674 (8th Cir. 1974). *See also* Allan L. Schwartz, Annotation, *Garnishment Discharge Policy of Employer As Unlawful Employment Practice Violative of Title VII of Civil Rights Act of 1964 (42 U.S.C.A. §§ 2000e et seq.)*, 26 A.L.R. Fed. 394 (1976).

318 Equal Employment Opportunity Comm'n, Dec. No. 74-27, Empl. Prac. Guide (CCH) ¶ 6396 (1983); Equal Employment Opportunity Comm'n, Dec. No. 74-34, Empl. Prac. Guide (CCH) ¶ 6407 (1973); Equal Employment Opportunity Comm'n, EEOC Guide to Pre-Employment Inquiries (Aug. 1981), *reproduced in* Fair Empl. Prac. Cas (BNA) ¶ 443:65.

319 Griggs v. Duke Power, 401 U.S. 424, 91 S. Ct. 849, 28 L. Ed. 2d 158 (1971) (requirement of high school diploma for hiring or transfer not shown significantly related to job performance). *See also* 42 U.S.C. § 2000e-2k.

320 332 F. Supp. 490 (C.D. Cal. 1971).

321 *Id.* at 494.

322 Equal Employment Opportunity Comm'n, Dec. No. 74-27, Empl. Prac. Guide (CCH) ¶ 6396 (1983); Equal Employment Opportunity Comm'n, Dec. No. 74-34, Empl. Prac. Guide (CCH) ¶ 6407 (1973).

323 Robinson v. City of Dallas, 514 F.2d 1271, 1273–74 (5th Cir. 1975). *See also* Keenen v. American Cast Iron Pipe Co., 707 F.2d 1274 (11th Cir. 1983).

been toward very demanding, and difficult to acquire, proof of racially disparate impact.[324]

In addition to challenging plaintiffs' proof of disparate impact, the major employer defense to a Title VII discrimination litigation is "business necessity"—that the practice is necessary to the safe and efficient operation of the business, and that no alternative practice of lesser differential impact would be feasible.[325] Mere employer inconvenience or minor expense is not sufficient justification for discharge of the employee whose wages are garnished if such a practice has a disproportionate impact on a protected class of employees. Employers must show a negative relationship between garnishments and job performance and/or safety and efficiency. Conclusory statements are not sufficient evidence of lowered work efficiency.[326] Because Title VII litigation is a complex and fast changing area of the law, an attorney bringing a Title VII action should very carefully analyze the latest case developments.[327]

Because disparate impact litigation is extremely complex and costly, pursuing a Title VII claim before the EEOC is likely to be an attractive alternative. Indeed, plaintiffs are required to exhaust their administrative remedies by filing a claim with the EEOC before suing. The statute of limitations for filing a claim with the EEOC is either 180 or 300 days, depending on whether the state has a work-sharing agreement with the EEOC.[328] The EEOC may be willing to assume that a disparate impact exists, rather than requiring the plaintiff to prove disparate impact. Because the EEOC does not often receive claims based on wage garnishment, the claim should include a cover letter explaining the employee's disparate impact theory.

12.4.1.7.5 State law wrongful discharge claims

Even if federal causes of action cannot be maintained, an employee discharged because of a single wage garnishment will probably have a state law tort claim for wrongful discharge. Most states place tort liability on an employer who discharges an employee in violation of specific public policy interests of the state.[329] In some states this tort has been specifically recognized in the context of discharge because of wage garnishment.[330]

Many courts have held that a public policy embodied in federal as well as state statutes can form the basis for this tort.[331] An important advantage of a state law tort claim is that punitive damages as well as compensatory damages may be available.[332]

12.4.2 Special Federal Wage Garnishment Provisions for Particular Categories of Creditors or Debtors

12.4.2.1 Wage Garnishment Restrictions When Federal Agency or Student Loan Guaranty Agency Is Creditor

The federal Debt Collection Improvement Act,[333] enacted April 26, 1996, empowers federal agencies to which delinquent debts are owed to issue administrative orders requiring debtors' wages to be withheld "notwithstanding any provision of state law."[334] The amount deducted is limited to 15% of disposable wages.[335] The statute does not mention the CCPA exemption of thirty times the minimum wage,[336] but the statute's specific preemption of state law, compared to its silence about other

324 *See, e.g.*, Equal Employment Opportunity Comm'n v. Kaplan Higher Educ. Corp., 748 F.3d 749 (6th Cir. 2014) (rejecting testimony of EEOC's statistical expert in litigation alleging that credit checks had racially disparate impact in employment).

325 Barbara Lindemann, Paul Grossman, et al, Employment Discrimination Law 191–93 (4th ed. 2007).

326 *See* Wallace v. Debron Corp., 494 F.2d 674 (8th Cir. 1974); Johnson v. Pike, 332 F. Supp. 490 (C.D. Cal. 1971); Equal Employment Opportunity Comm'n, Dec. No. 74-27, Empl. Prac. Guide (CCH) ¶ 6396 (1983); Equal Employment Opportunity Comm'n, Dec. No. 74-34, Empl. Prac. Guide (CCH) ¶ 6407 (1973).

327 *See, e.g.*, Lex K. Larson, Employment Discrimination (2d ed. 2010), *updated at* www.nclc.org/library; Barbara Lindemann, Paul Grossman, et al, Employment Discrimination Law (4th ed. 2007).

328 Advocates should check with their regional EEOC office or check the EEOC's website, www.eeoc.gov.

329 Henry H. Perritt, Employee Dismissal Law and Practice §§ 7.01 to 7.12 (5th ed. 2006 looseleaf with annual updates).

330 Greeley v. Miami Valley Maint. Contractors, 551 N.E.2d 981 (Ohio 1990) (state statute that prohibited discharge because of wage garnishment order but did not provide a private cause of action set forth the state's public policy, so worker who was discharged because his employer was ordered to withhold a portion of his wages for child support could bring wrongful discharge claim).

331 *See, e.g.*, Faulkner v. United Technologies Corp., 240 Conn. 576, 693 A.2d 293 (1997) (recognizing tort claim for discharging employee who refused to violate federal fraud standards); Wheeler v. Caterpillar Tractor Co., 108 Ill. 2d 502, 485 N.E.2d 372 (1985) (public policy embodied in federal standards for handling of radioactive materials can be basis for wrongful discharge tort); Kulch v. Structural Fibers, Inc., 677 N.E.2d 308 (Ohio 1997); Thompson v. St. Regis Paper Co., 102 Wash. 2d 219, 685 P.2d 1081 (1984) (recognizing public policy exception to employment at will doctrine; federal Foreign Corrupt Practices Act can be basis of public policy). *But see* Griffin v. Mullinix, 947 P.2d 177 (Okla. 1997) (only state statute, not federal, can be basis for public policy underlying wrongful discharge claim).

332 Wheeler v. Caterpillar Tractor Co., 108 Ill. 2d 502, 485 N.E.2d 372 (1985).

333 Pub. L. No. 104-134, § 31001(o)(1), 110 Stat. 1321 (1996). *See* § 10.2.1.1, *supra*.

334 31 U.S.C. § 3720D; 31 C.F.R. pt. 285 (implementing regulations). *See* Bennett v. Premiere Credit of N. Am., L.L.C., 2013 WL 310066 (11th Cir. Jan. 28, 2013) (Georgia statute forbidding prejudgment garnishment is preempted by Higher Education Act's provision for administrative wage garnishment); Frew v. Van Ru Credit Corp., 2006 WL 2261624 (E.D. Pa. Aug. 7, 2006) (Debt Collection Improvement Act overrides Pennsylvania restrictions on wage garnishment). *See generally* § 10.2.1.1, *supra*.

335 31 U.S.C. § 3720D(b)(1). *See* Christensen v. United States, 2006 WL 744296 (W.D. Mo. Mar. 23, 2006) (declining to decide whether retirement payments are subject to this limit).

336 *See* § 12.4.1, *supra*.

This limitation would be relevant for part-time employees, as reducing a part-time employee's wages by 15% could leave the employee with less than thirty times the minimum wage.

federal law, indicates an intention that the CCPA limitation should apply in addition to the 15% limit. Most of the CCPA limitations are incorporated in the Treasury Department's implementing regulations.[337] The creditor agency may reduce the amount garnished upon request by the debtor and a showing of financial hardship.[338]

Agencies have the authority to institute the garnishment administratively, without ever suing the debtor. The creditor agency must give the debtor notice thirty days in advance and an opportunity to request a hearing or negotiate a payment plan.[339] If a debtor has been involuntarily separated from employment, no garnishment may take place until the debtor has been reemployed continuously for twelve months.[340]

The Act forbids the dismissal, refusal to employ, or discipline of an employee whose wages are garnished pursuant to the Act.[341] A private right of action is available, with mandatory attorney fees to a prevailing worker and, in the discretion of the court, reinstatement, back pay, and punitive damages.[342]

A separate statute, the Higher Education Act,[343] governs wage garnishments to collect student loan debts owed to the Department of Education or a federal student loan guaranty agency. This statute is discussed in detail in another treatise in this series.[344] The amount garnished is limited to 15% of disposable pay unless the debtor consents to a larger garnishment.[345] Department of Education regulations in addition specify that the amount that can be garnished is the *lesser* of 15% of disposable income or the amount that exceeds thirty times the prevailing minimum wage.[346] One court has held that this statute does not abrogate the state's sovereign immunity, so wages owed by state governmental employers cannot be garnished.[347]

12.4.2.2 Garnishment of Federal Employees' Wages

Sovereign immunity protected federal government employees from garnishment[348] until 1994, when Congress authorized garnishment of the paychecks of civilian and military federal employees.[349] That law provides that the CCPA protections, and any more protective state exemptions, are available to federal employees.[350] This statute does not, however, authorize the garnishment of federal pension benefits.[351]

Federal agencies must honor wage garnishment orders in the same manner and to the same extent as if the agency were a private employer. However, the agency may deduct an administrative fee from the amount it sends the creditor, even if the fee would not be allowed by state law.[352]

Offset of a federal employee's salary to repay a federal debt is discussed in § 10.2.6, *supra*.

12.4.2.3 Debt Collection Against Military Personnel

The military has adopted regulations placing special restrictions on garnishment. No garnishment will be allowed if "the exigencies of military service" prevented the servicemember from being present at the judicial proceeding at which judgment was rendered, or if the Servicemembers Civil Relief Act[353] has not been complied with.[354] Garnishment is limited to the lesser of 25% of the servicemember's pay subject to involuntary allotment,[355] or the amount permitted by a more protective state statute.[356] Another federal statute forbids the garnishment of civilian seafarers' wages, except for family support.[357]

Historically, the payment by military personnel of just, personal debts in a timely fashion was considered a military concern.[358] Consequently, creditors were generally successful in

337 31 C.F.R. § 285.11(i).

338 31 C.F.R. § 285.11(k).

339 31 U.S.C. § 3720D(b)(2), (4), (5). *See* Christensen v. United States, 2006 WL 744296 (W.D. Mo. Mar. 23, 2006) (fact issues preclude summary judgment for government on claim that agency instituted garnishment without opportunity for hearing).

340 *See* Kort v. Diversified Collection Servs., Inc., 2001 WL 881449 (N.D. Ill. July 31, 2001) (denial of motion to dismiss; collection agency's letter was misleading in stating that debtor had to submit written documentation of exemption).

341 31 U.S.C. § 3720D(e).

342 31 U.S.C. § 3720D(e)(2).

343 20 U.S.C. § 1091a. *See also* Savage v. Scales, 310 F. Supp. 2d 122 (D.D.C. 2004) (Higher Education Act (HEA) preempts Dist. of Columbia garnishment statute, which requires pre-garnishment notice; HEA post-garnishment procedure adequate to provide due process); Nelson v. Diversified Collection Servs., Inc., 961 F. Supp. 863 (D. Md. 1997) (upholding constitutionality of administrative wage garnishment procedures).

344 National Consumer Law Center, Student Loan Law (4th ed. 2010), *updated at* www.nclc.org/library.

345 20 U.S.C. § 1095a(a)(1).

346 34 C.F.R. § 682.410(b)(9)(i)(A).

347 U.S. Student Aid Funds, Inc. v. South Carolina Dep't of Health & Envtl. Control, 588 S.E.2d 599 (S.C. 2003).

348 *See, e.g.*, May Dep't Stores v. Walton, 572 F.2d 1275 (8th Cir. 1978) (Veterans Admin. employees may not be garnished).

349 Hatch Act Reform Amendments of 1993, Pub. L. No. 103-94, § 9, 110 Stat. 1321 (codified at 5 U.S.C. § 5520a) (allowing garnishment of federal employees' wages, including employees of executive, judicial and legislative agencies, members of congress and military personnel). *See* § 10.2.6, *supra*.

350 5 U.S.C. § 5520a(b). *See* S. Rep. No. 103-57 at 6, *reprinted in* 1993 U.S.C.C.A.N. 1802, 1807.

351 *See* 5 U.S.C. § 5520a(a)(4)(A).

352 5 U.S.C. § 5520a. *See* Hadley Mem. Hosp. v. Kynard, 981 F. Supp. 690 (D.D.C. 1997) (upholding $75 fee).

353 50 U.S.C. app. §§ 501–596 (discussed in Ch. 7, *supra*).

354 32 C.F.R. § 112.6. *See also* 32 C.F.R. § 113.6 (prescribing procedure for determining whether exigencies of military service prevented the debtor's presence in court).

355 *See* 32 C.F.R. § 113.3(c) (defining the calculation to determine the "pay subject to involuntary allotment").

356 32 C.F.R. § 113.4.

357 46 U.S.C. § 11109. *See* Beneficial La., Inc. v. Wilson, 862 So. 2d 1049 (La. Ct. App. 2003) (debtor, a welder, worked 78% of the time on derrick barges, the rest in employer's fabrication yard on land; seaman status not lost by doing some work on land).

358 Cabell, Fed. Trade Comm'n, Report Of The Presiding Officer On The Proposed Trade Regulation Rule On Credit Practices 316 (1978). *See*

obtaining the assistance of commanding officers in collecting delinquent debts owed by subordinate military personnel.[359] Federal regulations, however, place restrictions on when the military will assist debt collectors.[360] These regulations adopt some of the protections provided to consumers by other laws. For example, the regulations incorporate the Fair Debt Collection Practices Act's prohibition of third-party contacts by debt collection agencies.[361] Thus, debt collectors cannot contact commanding officers about the debts of military personnel without a court order or the debtor's consent, and any violation is actionable under the FDCPA. The regulations also incorporate any state law restrictions on debt collection in the state where the military facility is located.[362] State debt collection restrictions often apply not just to debt collectors but also to creditors collecting their own debts, and many allow a private cause of action for violations.[363]

In addition, creditors seeking the assistance of the military in collecting debts must submit documentation that the transaction complied with the Truth in Lending Act.[364] They must also certify that they have complied with standards of fairness prescribed by the regulations, which include limitations on interest rates and late charges, and a general right to cancel contracts for personal goods or services.[365] Protections under the Servicemembers Civil Relief Act are discussed in Chapter 7, *supra*.

12.4.3 State Restrictions on Wage Garnishment

12.4.3.1 Overview

Every state has a statute that limits the amount of wages that a creditor can garnish. Some of these statutes simply duplicate the protections of the Consumer Credit Protection Act, which limits most creditors to the lesser of 25% of weekly wages or the amount by which the debtor's disposable earnings exceed thirty times the minimum wage per week.[366] However, many states set higher amounts that may not be garnished by creditors, thus offering more protection for the debtor. The state statute may also exempt more types of income than the federal statute.[367]

A model for a higher exemption is section 5.105 of the Uniform Consumer Credit Code (UCCC), which provides for a weekly exemption of forty instead of thirty times the minimum hourly wage. The Uniform Law Commission (formerly the National Conference of Commissioners on Uniform State Laws or NCCUSL), which drafted the UCCC, believed that the federal exemption "scarcely leave[s] enough for a family to subsist on, much less any disposable income which might encourage a debtor to accommodate his creditors without resorting to bankruptcy."[368] NCLC's Model Family Financial Protection Law[369] is a more updated model, protecting eighty times the state or federal minimum wage and allowing garnishment of only 10% to 15%, depending on the debtor's income, of wages above that amount.

Some states have allowed debtors to use a separate exemption, usually a wildcard exemption, to protect the portion of wages that is subject to garnishment.[370] State domestic relations law defining marital or community property will determine when, if at all, one spouse's wages may be garnished for an individual debt of the other.[371] Whether state wage exemptions follow wages after deposit is discussed in § 12.6.2, *infra*.

---

32 C.F.R. § 112.4 (1995).

359 Williams, Fed. Trade Comm'n, Staff Report On The Proposed Trade Regulation Rule On Credit Practices 395–96 (1980).

360 32 C.F.R. §§ 112–113.

361 15 U.S.C. § 1692c(b) (discussed in National Consumer Law Center, Fair Debt Collection §§ 5.3.5, 5.3.6, 5.3.8 (8th ed. 2014); 32 C.F.R. § 112.5(c)(3) ("Pursuant to . . . 15 U.S.C. §§ 1962–1692o ("Fair Debt Collection Practices Act"), contact by a debt collector with third parties, such as commanding officers, for aiding debt collection is prohibited without a court order or the debtor's prior consent given directly to the debt collector").

362 32 C.F.R. § 112.5(c)(1).

363 *See* National Consumer Law Center, Fair Debt Collection §§ 10.2.3.3.1, 10.2.5 (8th ed. 2014).

364 32 C.F.R. § 113.6(a)(1).

365 32 C.F.R. § 113.6.
Standards of fairness are set forth in appendix B to 32 C.F.R. § 113.

366 15 U.S.C. §§ 1671–1677. *See* § 12.4.1, *supra*.

367 *See* § 12.4.1.4, *supra*.

368 Note, *State Variations of the UCCC*, 48 Denver L.J. 239, 258 (1971).

369 National Consumer Law Center, Model Family Financial Protection Act (Oct. 2013), *available at* www.nclc.org/issues/debt-collection.html.

370 *See* § 12.2.7, *supra* (discussion of wildcard exemptions).

371 *See, e.g.*, U.S. v. Banks, 2013 WL 359369 (N.D. Tex. Jan. 13, 2012) (applying Texas community property law to conclude that United States may garnish non-debtor wife's wages and retirement account, which are sole management community property, for restitution owed by now-imprisoned husband); *In re* Dietz, 2013 WL 2393790 (Bankr. E.D. Cal. Feb. 22, 2013) (California judgment may be satisfied out of community property, including non-debtor spouse's wages, but separation decree here made wife's wages separate property); State *ex rel.* Indus. Comm'n. v. Wright, 43 P.3d 203 (Ariz. Ct. App. 2002) (spouse's wages are community property, which cannot be reached for individual debt; may be made individual property by pre-nuptial agreement; when couple amended agreement after husband incurred a debt, change was fraudulent transfer and husband's wages could be garnished); M.P. Allen Gen. Contractors, Inc. v. Kervin, 2002 WL 265060 (Cal. Ct. App. Feb. 26, 2002) (when married couple separated, wife's wages her separate property; may not be garnished for debt incurred by husband alone during marriage); Trost v. Aesthetic Lifetouch, 2012 WL 2877605 (Wash. Ct. App. July 16, 2012) (applying Washington marital property law to approve garnishment of husband's wages for judgment against his now-estranged wife, arising from wife's theft of trade secrets, which occurred partly before and partly after marriage); Schultz v. Sykes, 638 N.W.2d 76 (Wis. Ct. App. 2001) (non-debtor spouse's wages were marital property and could be garnished). *See also* Action Collection Serv., Inc. v. Seele, 69 P.3d 173 (Idaho Ct. App. 2003) (wages are community property; when each spouse has equal right to manage property, wife's wages can be garnished for pre-marital debt). *Cf.* United States v. Wahlen, 459 F. Supp. 2d 800 (E.D. Wis. 2006) (court may order criminal forfeiture of marital property, including innocent spouse's individual retirement account and gifts and inheritance she received that were commingled with other marital property).

12.4.3.2 States That Protect More Than the Federal Minimum From Garnishment

Many states protect a higher multiple of either the federal or state minimum wage.[372] For example, New Hampshire[373] protects fifty times the federal minimum wage. Massachusetts protects fifty times the federal or state minimum wage, or 85% of the debtor's gross wages, whichever is greater.[374] Although this section has not yet been interpreted by the courts, under its plain meaning a debtor is entitled to receive this amount even if it means that his or her *net* wages are entirely protected. A number of other states protect forty times the state or federal minimum wage.[375]

Always examine whether a state law protects a multiple of the federal or the state minimum wage, because state minimums are often significantly higher. For example, Connecticut[376] and Maine[377] protect forty times the state minimum wage. Illinois protects forty-five times the state minimum wage or the federal minimum wage, whichever is greater, and in addition restricts garnishment to 15% of the debtor's gross wages.[378] State minimum wage levels are collected on a Department of Labor website.[379]

Alaska exempts $473 of weekly net earnings, increased to $743 if the debtor's wages are the sole support of the household.[380] Missouri allows only 10% of the wages of the head of the household to be garnished.[381] Florida protects a head of family's earnings up to $750 per week and allows garnishment of greater amounts only by written permission of the debtor.[382] Iowa has three overlapping statutes that protect wages.[383] One adopts the CCPA limits and places yearly limits on garnishment,[384] the second limits garnishment to the lesser of 25% of disposable earnings or the amount by which those earnings exceed forty times the federal minimum wage,[385] and the third provides an additional exemption of $1000 in bankruptcy.[386] A former Ohio statute[387] put greater limits on garnishment for health care debts than for other types of debts, but courts split on its constitutionality and it has now been repealed.[388]

A few states prohibit garnishment for most consumer debts. For example, Texas exempts current wages for personal services, except for court-ordered child support payments.[389] Pennsylvania allows wage garnishment only in very limited circumstances.[390] North Carolina completely exempts the wages of the head of the household to the extent needed for family support.[391]

---

372 *See, e.g.*, Conn. Gen. Stat. § 52-361a; Me. Rev. Stat. tit. 9-A, § 5-105; Minn. Stat. §§ 571.922, 550.136; N.M. Stat. Ann. § 35-12-7; N.D. Cent. Code § 32-09.1-03; S.D. Codified Laws § 21-18-51; Vt. Stat. Ann. tit. 12, § 3170. *See generally* Appx. G, *infra*; National Consumer Law Center, No Fresh Start: How States Allow Debt Collectors to Push Families into Poverty (Oct. 2013), *available at* www.nclc.org/issues/no-fresh-start.html (state-by-state comparison of amount of wages protected from garnishment).

373 N.H. Rev. Stat. Ann. § 512:21(II).

374 Mass. Gen. Laws. ch. 246, § 28.

375 *See* National Consumer Law Center, No Fresh Start: How States Allow Debt Collectors to Push Families into Poverty (Oct. 2013), *available at* www.nclc.org/issues/no-fresh-start.html (state-by-state comparisons of amount protected from garnishment).

376 Conn. Gen. Stat. §§ 31-58, 52-361a.

377 Me. Rev. Stat. tit. 9-A, § 5-105; Me. Rev. Stat. tit. 26, § 664.

378 735 Ill. Comp. Stat. § 5/12-803; 820 Ill. Comp. Stat. § 105/4(a). *But see* Wienco v. Scene Three, Inc., 29 F.3d 329 (7th Cir. 1994) (interpreting separate statute, 735 Ill. Comp. Stat. § 5/2-1402(c)(1), as allowing order requiring debtor himself to turn over 25% of earnings to creditor; court fails to mention amendment to section 5/2-1402(c)(2) effective seven months before decision that explicitly exempts amounts protected by garnishment statute).

379 www.dol.gov/whd/minwage/america.htm.

380 Alaska Stat. §§ 09.38.030, 09.38.050, 09.38.115; Alaska Admin. Code tit. 8, § 95.030.

381 Mo. Rev. Stat. § 525.030. *See* Anani v. Griep, 406 S.W.3d 479 (Mo. Ct. App. 2013) (employer acted properly in garnishing 10%, not 25%, of earnings when employee verbally informed employer that he was head of household; written confirmation not required). *But cf.* United States v. Webster, 2008 WL 5191460 (W.D. Mo. Dec. 11, 2008) (debtor does not qualify for head-of-household exemption because unemployed but able-bodied adult son not a dependent).

382 Fla. Stat. § 222.11(2). *See* Brandt v. Magnificent Quality Florals Corp., 2013 WL 1289259 (S.D. Fla. Mar. 28, 2013) (debtor not head of household because wife's earnings exceeded his in period before garnishment); USAmeribank v. Kelpal, 100 So. 3d 56 (Fla. Dist. Ct. App. 2011) (finding vague language in promissory note to be agreement to garnish otherwise exempt wages; persuasive dissent; statute now has specific requirements for waiver).

383 *See In re* A'Hearn, 2011 WL 4704325 (Bankr. N.D. Iowa Oct. 4, 2011) (concluding that Iowa's double adoption of the CCPA 75% limit allows debtor in bankruptcy to exempt 75% of already-garnished wages).

384 Iowa Code § 642.21.

385 Iowa Code § 537.5105.

386 Iowa Code § 627.6(10). *See In re* Randall, 2011 WL 5417092 (Bankr. N.D. Iowa Nov. 8, 2011) (accrued-wages exemption protected funds that were garnished prepetition and turned over to sheriff but not condemned or paid to creditor).

387 Ohio Rev. Code Ann. § 2716.051 (West) (repealed in 1995).

388 *Compare* St. Ann's Hosp. v. Arnold, 672 N.E.2d 743 (Ohio Ct. App. 1996) (classification was reasonable, in light of public policy of encouraging people to seek needed medical care), *and* Wooster Cmty. Hosp. v. Anderson, 670 N.E.2d 563 (Ohio Ct. App. 1996) (classification was rational: health care debtors are different from others because of the life or death necessity of health care and of the extra burdens imposed by paying back a debt while also suffering health problems), *with* Community Physical Therapy v. Wayt, 639 N.E.2d 515 (Ohio Ct. App. 1994) (statute was unconstitutional because it had no rational relationship to any governmental purpose).

389 Tex. Prop. Code Ann. § 42.001(b) (West). *See* Heller v. Heller, 359 S.W.3d 902 (Tex. App. 2012) (alimony order resulting from agreement between spouses is ordinary debt, for which current wages may not be garnished, absent evidence that wife is unable to support self).

390 42 Pa. Cons. Stat. § 8127. *See* Tenuto v. Transworld Sys., Inc., 2000 U.S. Dist. LEXIS 14344 (E.D. Pa. Sept. 29, 2000) (certifying Fair Debt Collection Practices Act class action for Pennsylvania consumer debtors who received a dunning notice referring to wage garnishment). *But see* West v. Ford Motor Credit Co., 2013 WL 497159 (E.D. Pa. Feb. 11, 2013) (allowing garnishment of Pennsylvania wages in response to Maryland court order, enforcing Maryland judgment, served on Maryland office of employer).

391 N.C. Gen. Stat. § 1-362. *See also In re* Morris, 2013 WL 2595936 (Bankr. W.D. N.C. June 11, 2013) (construing "necessary" to mean bare subsistence, and allowing court to evaluate need only on petition date, not looking to future; denying exemption for wages of wealthy debtor deposited in money market account); *In re* Ray, 2011 WL 9043 (Bankr. W.D.N.C. Jan. 3, 2011) (earnings of debtor who was supporting

12.4.3.3 Hardship Exceptions

Courts may have discretion to limit garnishment, especially in cases of hardship.[392] Kansas forbids wage garnishment for two months after recovery of the debtor or a family member from an illness which has prevented the debtor from working at his or her usual employment for two weeks.[393]

California exempts "the portion of the judgment debtor's earnings which the judgment debtor proves is necessary for the support of the judgment debtor or the judgment debtor's family supported in whole or in part by the judgment debtor."[394] Even if the funds are not earnings within the narrow California definition, every attachment order against a natural person must consider "the reasonable requirements of the judgment debtor."[395]

Oklahoma provides a hardship exemption for heads of families with monthly incomes below 120 times the federal minimum wage who can show that garnishment would reduce their income below a minimum level of subsistence.[396] Arizona allows a garnishment to be reduced to 15% in case of "extreme economic hardship" and forbids garnishment if the debt is "subject to an effective agreement for debt scheduling between the judgment debtor and a qualified debt counseling organization."[397]

Vermont allows an increased exemption if the debtor shows that weekly expenditures "reasonably incurred" for the maintenance of the debtor or his or her dependents exceed the statutorily exempt amount.[398] Connecticut allows garnishment only after a judgment debtor has failed to comply with an installment payment order and allows for modification of the amount upon motion by the debtor.[399] Some states provide additional protection for certain present or former recipients of needs-tested benefits.[400]

12.4.4 Relation Between Federal and State Wage Garnishment Protections

The federal Consumer Credit Protection Act explicitly provides that its garnishment restrictions do not limit the operation of state laws that exempt a larger share of a debtor's wages from garnishment.[401] Nor does the CCPA limit the operation

his fiancée and her child were exempt; actual dependency is sufficient; legal obligation need not be shown); Livingston v. Naylor, 920 A.2d 34 (Md. Ct. Spec. App. 2007) (wages exempt under North Carolina law but not Maryland law; when North Carolina judgment was domesticated in Maryland and employer did business in both states, Maryland court could order garnishment only of portion of wages debtor earned while working in Maryland). *Cf. In re* Connelly, 276 B.R. 421 (Bankr. W.D.N.C. 2002) (unmarried debtor with no dependents could not exempt earnings as necessary for support of family). *But cf. In re* Eutsler, 2010 WL 27499 (Bankr. W.D.N.C. Jan. 12, 2012) (statute exempts wages earned within sixty days; year-end bonus, earned over the course of a year, not exempt).

392 Warner Bros. Records, Inc. v. Patnode, 2010 WL 431908 (W.D. Mich. Feb. 5, 2010) (under Michigan procedure, court has discretion to set installment payments "in such amounts . . . as the defendant is able to pay"; here, about one-half of CCPA maximum); Midlantic Nat'l Bank/North v. Reif, 732 F. Supp. 354 (E.D.N.Y. 1990) (ordering reduction of wage garnishment due to hardship, as allowed by N.Y. C.P.L.R. § 5231 (McKinney)); Creditmax, Inc. v. Jones, 988 N.E.2d 402 (Ind. Ct. App. May 20, 2013) (unpublished) (UCCC provision setting maximum amount of wage garnishment does not require this amount; court has discretion to order lesser amount or none, but abuse of discretion not shown here); LaFreniere-Nietz v. Nietz, 547 N.W.2d 895 (Minn. Ct. App. 1996) (statute permits garnishments of less than statutory maximum; court which allowed garnishment for child support arrearage and forbade further garnishments properly exercised its equitable powers when larger garnishment might cause father to lose car or apartment, which would likely result in losing job, and father's financial problems were adversely affecting his visitation with child); Hillcrest Med. Ctr. v. Monroy, 38 P.3d 931 (Okla. Civ. App. 2001) (judgment debtor may file motion for statutory hardship exemption at any time until continuing garnishment terminates; trial court had power to order refund of sums already garnished); Gerber v. Holcomb, 2006 WL 3019731 (Tenn. Ct. App. Oct. 25, 2006) (garnishment statute sets maximum; creditor has no "statutory entitlement" to that sum; trial court did not abuse discretion in ordering lesser amount). *See also* American Contractors' Indemnity Co. v. Bill Whorff, Inc., 2012 WL 104986 (D. Me. Jan. 11, 2012) (describing Maine procedure for setting installment payments on judgment; must consider the reasonable requirements of debtor and dependents), *adopted by*, 2012 WL 315639 (D. Me. Feb. 1, 2012). *But see* Hartford Postal Employees Credit Union v. Rosemond, 635 A.2d 876 (Conn. App. Ct. 1994) (power to "modify" wage execution does not include power to vacate it; issuance of wage execution was "mandatory" if judgment debtor did not keep up installment payments); Master Fin. Co. v. Pollard, 283 P.3d 817 (Kan. Ct. App. 2012) (Kansas court has no discretion to reduce amount of garnishment to account for individual circumstances; must order full 25%). *But cf.* United States v. Anderson, 2007 WL 2703160 (W.D. Okla. Sept. 13, 2007) (Oklahoma garnishment exemptions for "undue hardship" not applicable to federal garnishment for criminal restitution).

393 Kan. Stat. Ann. § 60-2310.

394 Cal. Civ. Proc. Code § 706.051 (West). *See* United States v. Arevalo, 2007 WL 2220969 (N.D. Cal. Aug. 1, 2007) ("necessary for support" does not mean "bare subsistence," but includes "the conveniences of refined society," here cable television and cell phone); Smedberg v. Toste, 2012 WL 695643 (Cal. Ct. App. Mar. 6, 2012) (unpublished) (burden is on debtor to show necessity; exemption denied when debtor failed to present evidence of spouse's assets); *In re* Marriage of Hankins, 2008 WL 4615967 (Cal. Ct. App. Oct. 20, 2008) (debtor failed to show hardship but, if creditor failed to comply with statutory procedure for contesting exemption, garnished funds must be returned to debtor), *aff'd*, 2009 WL 806853 (Cal. Ct. App. Mar. 30, 2009). *See also* Kelly v. Barela, 2009 WL 449637 (Cal. Ct. App. Feb. 24, 2009) (describing procedure for claiming and contesting hardship exemption).

395 Global Money Mgmt. v. McDonnold, 2009 WL 3352574 (S.D. Cal. Oct. 15, 2009) (requirement applies to income of independent contractor, excluded from earnings definition by Cal. Civ. Pro. § 706.011).

396 Okla. Stat. tit. 31, §§ 1.1, 1.3. *See* Hillcrest Med. Ctr. v. Monroy, 38 P.3d 931 (Okla. Civ. App. 2001) (hardship exemption not lost by failure to timely claim it; allowing untimely claim and ordering return of previously garnished funds).

397 Ariz. Stat. Ann. § 12-1598.10(B)(5), (C), (F).

398 Vt. Stat. Ann. tit. 12, § 3170(b)(3).

399 Conn. Gen. Stat. § 52-361a. *See* Chase Bank v. Arborio, 2011 WL 1734448 (Conn. Super. Ct. Apr. 7, 2011) (if debtor fails to abide by installment payment order, judgment creditor may seek property execution, not just wage garnishment).

400 *See* § 12.5.1, *infra*.

401 15 U.S.C. § 1677. *See, e.g., In re* Irish, 311 B.R. 63, 65 n.2 (B.A.P. 8th Cir. 2004); *In re* Duncan, 140 B.R. 210, 213 n.2 (Bankr. E.D. Tenn.

of any state laws that prohibit employee discharge in cases in which the CCPA does not prohibit discharge.[402] Congress enacted the CCPA to maximize debtor protections,[403] only preempting state law that is less protective of debtors.[404]

Even if portions of a state law conflict with the federal provisions, the federal law will only preempt those portions that are less protective than the CCPA.[405] For example, a court held that New York wage garnishments must comply both with a state law that limited garnishment to 10% of gross wages and with the CCPA's limit of 25% of disposable income.[406] If the state law and the CCPA use different formulas to calculate the maximum amount that can be garnished, the formula that protects the most wages in the particular case must be used.[407]

State limits on wage garnishment that do not directly conflict with the CCPA will be applied in addition to the federal protections.[408] Combining state and federal restrictions can result in "stacking" of restrictions and significantly greater protections. For example, in Ohio a former state law allowed garnishment of 17.5% of the month's earnings and prohibited more than one wage garnishment every thirty days. Federal courts held that these restrictions had to be applied in combination with the CCPA, which limits garnishments to 25% of the disposable earnings for the pay period.[409] Thus, if the debtor was paid on a weekly basis, only 25% of his or her disposable earnings for that week could be garnished, plus there could be only one wage garnishment every thirty days.

The Secretary of Labor has the authority to exempt from the CCPA provisions any state that provides garnishment restrictions which are "substantially similar" to those provided under the federal statute.[410] Virginia is the only jurisdiction currently exempted.[411]

12.4.5 Wage Assignments

Wage assignments can affect debtors in ways similar to wage garnishments. The Federal Trade Commission's Credit Practices Rule prohibits wage assignments in connection with the extension of credit to consumers in or affecting commerce.[412] There are three exceptions:

- The assignment by its terms is revocable at the will of the debtor;
- The assignment is a payroll deduction plan or preauthorized payment plan of the sort used in credit unions; or
- The assignment applies only to wages already earned at the time of the assignment. (This last exception allows a borrower to assign the portion of his or her monthly salary that has already been earned at the time credit is extended.[413])

The restrictions apply to all types of compensation paid or payable to an individual for personal services—whether denominated wages, salary, commissions, bonuses, or otherwise—and also apply to periodic payments under pension, retirement, and disability programs.[414] A contract term that violates the Credit Practices Rule is unenforceable.[415] These restrictions apply only to consumer credit debts, however, and states may require wage assignments in other contexts such as family support.[416] Many states also have statutes that restrict wage assignments.[417]

1992) (section 1677 "allows states to enact statutes that would prohibit garnishments altogether or place a greater limit on garnishments than required under the Act"); *In re* Sanders, 69 B.R. 569 (Bankr. E.D. Mo. 1987) (Missouri's 10% limitations applied to prepetition income); Benson v. Richardson, 537 N.W.2d 748 (Iowa 1995) (federal CCPA did not preempt Iowa's more protective treatment of wages, which remained exempt for ninety days in checking or savings account, so long as reasonably traceable); Marshall v. Safeway, Inc., 2014 WL 1227629, at *2 (Md. 2014); Liedka v. Liedka, 423 N.Y.S.2d 788 (N.Y. Fam. Ct. 1979).

402 15 U.S.C. § 1677.

403 *See, e.g.*, *In re* Kokoszka, 479 F.2d 990 (2d Cir. 1973), *aff'd sub nom.* Kokoszka v. Belford, 417 U.S. 642 (1974); Anderson v. Anderson, 404 A.2d 275, 280 (Md. 1979).

404 *See, e.g.*, Evans v. Evans, 429 F. Supp. 580 (W.D. Okla. 1976); Crane v. Crane, 417 F. Supp. 38 (E.D. Okla. 1976); Hodgson v. Hamilton Mun. Ct., 349 F. Supp. 1125 (S.D. Ohio 1972); Knight v. Knight, 658 So. 2d 478 (Ala. Civ. App. 1994) (federal law allowing up to 65% of wages to be garnished for alimony or child support did not preempt Alabama law which limited such garnishments to 25%); *In re* Marriage of Herrick, 640 N.E.2d 969 (Ill. App. Ct. 1994) (when garnishment for attorney fees, on top of existing garnishment for support, would exceed statutory limit of 25% of debtor's wages, second garnishment must be abated; federal law preempted state law which would have allowed this second garnishment); Benson v. Richardson, 537 N.W.2d 748 (Iowa 1995) (federal CCPA did not preempt Iowa's more protective treatment of wages, which remained exempt for ninety days in checking or savings account, so long as reasonably traceable); Big M, Inc. v. Texas Roadhouse Holding, L.L.C., 1 A.3d 718 (N.J. Super. Ct. App. Div. 2010).

405 Hodgson v. Hamilton Mun. Ct., 349 F. Supp. 1125 (S.D. Ohio 1972); Hodgson v. Cleveland Mun. Ct., 326 F. Supp. 419 (N.D. Ohio 1971); Phillips v. Gen. Fin. Corp., 297 So. 2d 6 (Fla. 1974); *In re* Marriage of Herrick, 640 N.E.2d 969 (Ill. App. Ct. 1994); Kropf v. Kropf, 538 N.W.2d 496 (Neb. 1995) (when Nebraska law did not limit amount of Social Security benefits which could be garnished for support of ex-wife, CCPA limits applied).

406 Midlantic Nat'l Bank/North v. Reif, 732 F. Supp. 354 (E.D.N.Y. 1990).

407 Midlantic Nat'l Bank/North v. Reif, 732 F. Supp. 354 (E.D.N.Y. 1990); Evans v. Evans, 429 F. Supp. 580 (W.D. Okla. 1976).

408 *Id.*; Hodgson v. Hamilton Mun. Ct., 349 F. Supp. 1125 (S.D. Ohio 1972); Hodgson v. Cleveland Mun. Ct., 326 F. Supp. 419 (N.D. Ohio 1971); Marshall v. Safeway, Inc., 2014 WL 1227629, at *2 (Md. 2014).

409 Hodgson v. Hamilton Mun. Ct., 349 F. Supp. 1125 (S.D. Ohio 1972); Hodgson v. Cleveland Mun. Ct., 326 F. Supp. 419 (N.D. Ohio 1971).

410 15 U.S.C. § 1675; 29 C.F.R. § 870.51.

411 29 C.F.R. § 870.57.

412 16 C.F.R. § 444.2(a)(3). *See generally* National Consumer Law Center, Federal Deception Laws § 2.3 (2012), *updated at* www.nclc.org/library.

413 16 C.F.R. § 444.2(a)(3). *See* Scott, Fed. Trade Comm'n, Informal Staff Opinion Letter (Mar. 1, 1985).

414 16 C.F.R. § 444.1(h).

415 *In re* Raymond, 103 B.R. 846 (Bankr. W.D. Ky. 1989) (security interest that violates credit practices rule is unenforceable); *In re* Boyer, 63 B.R. 153 (Bankr. E.D. Mo. 1986) (same); Free Bridge Auto Sales v. Fitzgerald, 48 Va. Cir. 1 (1999) (waiver of exemptions that violates credit practices rule is unenforceable).

416 *See, e.g.*, *In re* Marriage of Mease, 92 P.3d 1148 (Mont. 2004) (court may order wage assignment for family support).

417 *See, e.g.*, Decision Point, Inc. v. Reece & Nichols Realtors, Inc., 144 P.3d 706 (Kan. 2006) (state U.C.C.C. forbids assignment of wages, here realtors' commissions).

The FTC has proceeded against an online payday lender that required borrowers to agree to a clause stating the following: "Should you default on this Agreement, you hereby consent and agree to the potential garnishment of wages by us or our assigns or service agents to ensure repayment of this Agreement, fees and costs associated in the collection of outstanding principal and interest."[418] When debtors became delinquent, the defendants, without obtaining court orders permitting garnishment, mailed the debtor's employer a "garnishment packet" and a copy of the clause, and instructed the employer to withhold a portion of the employee's wages.[419] The FTC characterized the clause as a wage assignment and charged that it violated the credit practices rule because it was not revocable at the will of the debtor, was not a payment plan that commenced at the time of the transaction but took effect only upon delinquency, and applied to future earnings, not just to wages already earned.[420] In a stipulated permanent injunction, the defendants agreed to stop taking wage assignments in violation of the rule.[421]

In addition, federal law prohibits enlisted members of the Army, Navy, Air Force, or Marine Corps from assigning their pay, defined to include retirement pay, and provides that any assignment is void.[422] The law allows commissioned officers to assign their pay accounts when due and payable pursuant to regulations prescribed by the secretary of the military service in question,[423] but no such regulations have been adopted.

12.4.6 Do Federal Wage Protections Apply to Paid or Deposited Earnings?

A paycheck that the employer has drawn but has not yet delivered to an employee is protected by the federal CCPA.[424] Ignoring the CCPA's remedial purpose, however, several decisions have held that the CCPA does not protect earnings of a wage earner after the time that they are paid over to the employee, so the exemption is lost once the earnings are deposited in a financial institution.[425] However, even these courts may recognize a distinction between direct deposit—an increasingly common way for employees to pay wages—and the situation in which a worker cashes a paycheck and then deposits some or all of the money. At the very least, they should hold that a compulsory direct deposit as a condition of employment renders the earnings subject to the restrictions of the CCPA even after they are deposited in a bank.[426]

In many but not all states, state wage exemptions apply to wages after deposit,[427] sometimes because of explicit statutory

---

418 Complaint, Fed. Trade Comm'n v. Payday Fin., L.L.C., No. 3:11-cv-03017-RAL, ¶ 22 (D.S.D, complaint dated Mar. 1, 2012), *available at* www.ftc.gov/enforcement/cases-proceedings/112-3023/payday-financial-llc-et-al.

419 *Id.* at ¶¶ 28–30.

420 *Id.* at ¶ 23.

421 Stipulated Order for Permanent Injunction and Civil Penalties, Fed. Trade Comm'n v. Payday Fin., L.L.C., No. 3:11-cv-03017-RAL (D.S.D filed Apr. 4, 2014), *available at* www.ftc.gov/enforcement/cases-proceedings/112-3023/payday-financial-llc-et-al.

422 37 U.S.C. §§ 701(c) (prohibiting assignment of pay of enlisted members of Army, Navy, Air Force, or Marine Corps; any assignment is void), 101 (defining "pay" to include retirement pay); 38 U.S.C. § 5301(a)(1), (3) (prohibiting assignment of payment of benefits due or to become due under any law administered by Secretary of Veterans Affairs).

423 37 U.S.C. § 701(a).

424 Hodgson v. Christopher, 365 F. Supp. 583 (D.N.D. 1973).

425 Usery v. First Nat'l Bank, 586 F.2d 107 (9th Cir. 1978) (unrealistic to ask bank to determine which deposits are traceable to employee pay check, so bank not responsible for determining exemptions under the CCPA); United States v. Tisdale, 2013 WL 4804286 (N.D. Tex. Sept. 9, 2013); United States v. Crawford, 2006 WL 2458710 (E.D. Cal. Aug. 22, 2006) (CCPA protects earnings only in hands of employer); Dunlop v. First Nat'l Bank, 399 F. Supp. 855 (D. Ariz. 1975) (wage protections do not apply after deposit into bank); John O. Melby & Co. Bank v. Anderson, 88 Wis. 2d 252, 276 N.W.2d 274 (Wis. 1979) (even when money in checking account was directly traceable to payroll earnings, CCPA garnishments restrictions did not apply). *See also* United States v. Gaddis, 2010 WL 908666 (W.D. Okla. Mar. 9, 2010) (CCPA garnishment limit does not protect funds in retirement account; wages were transformed into investment); Triple J Saipan, Inc. v. Norita, 2007 WL 4124477 (N. Mar. I. Nov. 16, 2007) (garnishment limitations cease to protect funds upon payment to debtor).

426 Household Fin. Corp. v. Kinder, 3 Ohio Misc. 2d 3, 444 N.E.2d 99 (Mun. Ct. 1982); Horace E. Menasco, United States Dep't of Labor, CCPA Letter No. 303 (Aug. 3, 1972) (stating, in response to letter from employer that paid all its employees by direct deposit, that CCPA protections apply to wages after deposit), *available online as companion material to this treatise. See also* § 12.7, *infra*.

427 *ALASKA: See* Miller v. Monrean, 507 P.2d 771 (Alaska 1973) (state exemption law protects earnings after they are received and deposited into bank account).

ARIZONA: But see In re Palidora, 310 B.R. 164 (Bankr. D. Ariz. 2004) (Arizona exemption does not protect wages deposited directly into bank account); Frazer, Ryan, Goldberg, Keyt & Lawless v. Smith, 907 P.2d 1384 (Ariz. Ct. App. 1995) (Arizona statute modeled on CCPA distinguished between exempt wages and non-exempt "monies"; wages became "monies" when deposited in bank account). *But cf. In re* Mulvihill, 326 B.R. 459 (Bankr. D. Ariz. 2005) (debtors permitted to exempt 75% of actual damage award for unpaid wages; exemption would have been lost if amounts had actually been paid to debtor).

CALIFORNIA: See Ford Motor Credit Co. v. Waters, 83 Cal. Rptr. 3d 826 (Cal. Super. Ct. 2008) (debtor may exempt 75% of the paid earnings that remain in the account on day of levy). *See also* Sourcecorp, Inc. v. Shill, 142 Cal. Rptr. 3d 414 (Cal. Ct. App. 2012) (wages protected for thirty days after payment, but lose exemption after that time).

COLORADO: See In re Nye, 210 B.R. 857 (D. Colo. 1997) (Colorado's garnishment limitation explicitly protects earnings after deposit in checking account; debtor, however, fails to carry burden of proof as to origin of funds); Morrison v. Kobernusz (*In re* Kobernusz), 160 B.R. 844 (D. Colo. 1993); Rutter v. Shumway, 26 P. 321 (Colo. 1891) (state exemption continues to protect wages after their deposit into bank account).

CONNECTICUT: See Discover Bank v. Marchetti, 2012 WL 3064665 (Conn. Super. Ct. June 21, 2012) (wages do not lose Connecticut wage garnishment statute's protection by being electronically direct-deposited in a bank account; creditor must follow that statute's procedures in order to reach the funds). *But see* Cadle Co. v. Fletcher, 2013 WL 6092515 (D. Conn. Nov. 19, 2013) (wages left over after garnishment lose exemption when deposited in wife's bank account).

DISTRICT OF COLUMBIA: But see In re Mordkin, 452 B.R. 311 (Bankr. D.D.C. 2011) (District of Columbia wage garnishment limit does not protect wages after payment to debtor).

FLORIDA: See Brandt v. Magnificent Quality Florals Corp., 2013 WL 1289259 (S.D. Fla. Mar. 28, 2013) (Florida's exemption for 25% of wages survives in bank account); *In re* Shaw, 2013 WL 1282403 (Bankr.

language. The Ohio Supreme Court has held that wages that are immune from execution, garnishment, or attachment

M.D. Fla. Mar. 29, 2013) (exemption continues even after wages are deposited in third party's bank account as long as they are traceable; here, debtor used wages to pay refundable retainer that attorney deposited in trust account); Dinh v. Motorcars of Distinction, Inc., 2009 WL 3096459 (S.D. Fla. Sept. 23, 2009) (exemption survives payment to debtor and deposit in debtor-car dealer's corporate bank account); *In re* Holmes, 414 B.R. 868 (Bankr. S.D. Fla. 2009) (Florida earnings exempt in bank account); *In re* Weinshank, 406 B.R. 413 (Bankr. S.D. Fla. 2009) (Fla. Stat. § 222.11 exemption for bank account traceable to exempt earnings applies whether or not debtor is head of family); *In re* Stevenson, 374 B.R. 891 (Bankr. M.D. Fla. 2007) (Florida exemption for head of family's wages explicitly covers traceable funds in bank account, but debtor failed to prove he was head of family).

IDAHO: See In re Santillannes, 2005 WL 4704994 (D. Idaho Nov. 5, 2005) (debtor could exempt 75% of wages directly deposited in shared savings account; funds directly traceable to wages retained quality as monies even though pledged as collateral for credit union loan). *But cf. In re* Merrill, 431 B.R. 239 (Bankr. D. Idaho 2009) (wages accumulated in a pension plan may retain their exemption when distributions are taken periodically but not when debtor cashed out entire IRA and deposited it in checking account).

ILLINOIS: But see Wienco, Inc. v. Scene Three, Inc., 29 F.3d 329 (7th Cir. 1994) (approving order requiring recalcitrant judgment debtor to turn over 75% of wages, even though Illinois limits garnishment to 15%; rejecting argument that wage garnishment act continues to protect wages after payment to wage earner); *In re* Radzilowsky, 448 B.R. 767 (N.D. Ill. 2011) (Illinois Wage Deduction Act protects wages only before payment to debtor); *In re* Kapusta, 2011 WL 2173675 (C.D. Ill. June 2, 2011) (Illinois Wage Deduction Act does not protect wages after payment to debtor).

INDIANA: But see In re Stewart, 2006 WL 2666153 (Bankr. S.D. Ind. Sept. 6, 2006) (exemption for wages does not apply to wages that teacher had employer place in escrow account, to be paid out during summer vacation).

IOWA: See E.J. Benson v. Richardson, 537 N.W.2d 748 (Iowa 1995) (Iowa statute providing that exempt wages remain so for ninety days in checking or savings account, if reasonably traceable, applies when debtor husband deposited earnings in account of non-debtor wife; property purchased by wife during ninety days was exempt); Midamerica Sav. Bank v. Miehe, 438 N.W.2d 837 (Iowa 1989).

KANSAS: See In re Urban, 262 B.R. 865 (Bankr. D. Kan. 2001) (Kansas wage exemption protects wages directly deposited in a bank account). *But see In re* Adcock, 264 B.R. 708 (D. Kan. 2000) (wages electronically deposited in debtors' bank account not protected by Kansas wage exemption, which protects wages only in hands of employer); Dillon Companies, Inc. v. Davis, 181 P.3d 570 (Kan. Ct. App. 2008) (Kansas exemption does not protect wages in bank account; prison inmate's "incentive pay" may be reached by non-wage garnishment of prison bank account).

KENTUCKY: But see Shafizadeh v. Shafizadeh, ___ S.W.3d ___, 2012 WL 6213707 (Ky. Ct. App. Dec. 14, 2012) (Kentucky wage garnishment statute does not protect wages after payment to employee or deposit on bank account); Brown v. Kentucky Natural Res. & Env't Cabinet, 40 S.W.3d 873 (Ky. Ct. App. 1999) (Kentucky wage garnishment statute, which tracks CCPA, does not protect wages deposited in bank account).

LOUISIANA: But see In re Sinclair, 417 F.3d 527 (5th Cir. 2005) (Louisiana garnishment limitation not an exemption and does not protect wages deposited directly into bank account).

MICHIGAN: But see United States v. Thomas, 2009 WL 4638862 (E.D. Mich. Dec. 1, 2009) (Michigan wage garnishment limit does not protect wages after deposit in bank account).

MINNESOTA: See Montgomery Ward Credit Corp. v. Brewer, Clearinghouse No. 44,517 (D. Minn. 1989) (75% of earnings and all severance pay deposited in joint bank account exempt from garnishment).

MISSOURI: See In re Arnold, 193 B.R. 897 (Bankr. W.D. Mo. 1996) (under Missouri law exempt wages do not lose their exemption by being commingled with other funds in bank account).

NEBRASKA: See Zaleski v. Collection Bureau of Grand Island, 664 N.W.2d 32 (Neb. Ct. App. 2003) (Nebraska forbids garnishment of wages earned within sixty days before date of garnishment; inmate stated claim against collector who garnished "release savings account" into which wages were compulsorily deposited).

NEVADA: See In re Norris, 203 B.R. 463 (Bankr. D. Nev. 1996) (interpreting "disposable income" exemption to protect earnings commingled with other funds in checking account so long as funds remain traceable and easily withdrawable); *In re* Christensen, 149 P.3d 40 (Nev. 2006) (Nevada statute recently amended to specify that exemption protects earnings deposited in bank account; even before amendment, statute protected deposited earnings).

NEW YORK: See Cadle Co. v. Newhouse, 20 Fed. Appx. 69 (2d Cir. 2001) (New York earnings exemption continued to protect husband's earnings, if needed for reasonable living expenses, even after fraudulent transfer to account in name of non-debtor wife); *In re* Coolbaugh, 250 B.R. 162 (Bankr. W.D.N.Y. 2000) (New York earnings exemption protects earnings in checking account if earned for personal services within past sixty days and necessary to debtor's support).

NORTH DAKOTA: See In re Fandrich, 2008 WL 4610030 (Bankr. D.N.D. Oct. 16, 2008) (earnings do not lose exemption by deposit into bank account, but these funds are not traceable to earnings when balance in account was less than amount of most recent deposit of non-exempt funds).

OHIO: See also Grant Hosp. v. O'Nail, 1997 WL 101657 (Ohio Ct. App. Mar. 4, 1997) (exempt earnings deposited into joint checking account of debtor and spouse would remain exempt, if traceable, but exempt earnings deposited in savings account were not exempt).

OREGON: See In re Drescher, 2013 WL 4525232 (Bankr. D. Or. Aug. 27, 2013) (debtor deposited earnings in bank and withdrew cash; Oregon exemption for earnings "paid or payable" survives if debtor can show traceability); *In re* Platt, 270 B.R. 773 (Bankr. D. Or. 2001) (Oregon garnishment statute protected bank account containing funds traceable to debtor-husband's earnings so long as funds remained identifiable and accumulation did not exceed $7500).

TENNESSEE: But see In re Lawrence, 205 B.R. 115 (Bankr. E.D. Tenn. 1997) (Tennessee garnishment statute, substantially identical to CCPA, did not protect wages in the hands of the debtor), *aff'd*, 219 B.R. 786 (E.D. Tenn. 1998).

TEXAS: But see Mass. Mut. Life Ins. Co. v. Shoemaker, 849 F. Supp. 30 (S.D. Tex. 1994) (Texas exemption for "current wages" does not survive deposit); Stephens v. Dyck O'Neal, Inc., 2012 WL 524432 (Tex. App. Feb. 16, 2012) (wages lose their exemption when electronically direct-deposited in debtor's bank account); Gen. Elec. Capital Corp. v. ICO, Inc., 230 S.W.3d 702 (Tex. App. 2007) (Texas exemption for current wages lost upon payment to employee); Am. Express Travel Related Servs. v. Harris, 831 S.W.2d 531 (Tex. App. 1992) (bank account containing wages can be garnished).

VERMONT: But see Allen v. Moorcroft, 2012 WL 1293691 (Vt. Mar. 15, 2012) (unpublished) (Vermont exemption applies to earnings, not to funds held by a debtor that derive from earnings).

WASHINGTON: But see Thatcher v. Dep't of Social & Health Servs., 908 P.2d 920 (Wash. Ct. App. 1996) (earnings which were 50% exempt under child support statute lost their exemption as soon as deposited in bank account; same rule as under general garnishment statute).

WYOMING: But see In re Walsh, 96 P.3d 1 (Wyo. 2004) (Wyoming garnishment statute protects only accrued and unpaid wages).

See generally Annotation, *Deposit of exempt funds as affecting debtor's exemption*, 67 A.L.R. 1203 (1930); 31 Am. Jur. 2d *Exemptions* § 45 (2002); W. Vukowich, *Debtors' Exemptions Rights*, 62 Geo. L.J. 779, 836–37 (1974); § 12.6.2.2, *infra* (general discussion of protection of exempt income after deposit).

under state law retain their exempt character when deposited in a checking account, so long as the source of the funds is known or reasonably traceable.[428] In so holding, the court recognized that the purpose of exemption statutes is to "protect funds intended primarily for maintenance and support of the debtor's family."[429] That purpose would be frustrated if wages lost their exempt character upon deposit in an account maintained to pay those expenses.[430]

In an age when cash is no longer the common method of paying bills, and wages are commonly paid by direct deposit, such a conclusion is the only sensible one. As one court noted more than half a century ago, "[i]t would be an unreasonable construction to hold that by deposit of the earnings in the bank . . . and [acquiring] in lieu thereof, a credit due him from the bank . . . the exempt character of the funds should be lost."[431] It is also the rule as to veterans' benefits,[432] Social Security benefits,[433] welfare benefits,[434] and workers' compensation.[435]

The reasoning in the CCPA decisions is strained. The context in which they arose may explain why the courts failed to follow the usual rule. In apparently the earliest case to rule on the issue, the Secretary of Labor brought an action against the bank when the paycheck was deposited and would have required the bank to identify the exempt amount and assert the exemptions.[436] The Ninth Circuit was clearly uncomfortable with the notion of placing this kind of burden on the bank and stressed the novelty of the question as well as the difficulty of calculating the exempt amount.[437] Laboring under the mistaken notion that there was no guidance on "whether . . . compensation retains its character as 'earnings' after it has been deposited in the employee's bank account,"[438] the court then strained to find a difference between the congressional purpose in exempting Social Security and veterans benefits (to provide maintenance and support) and the congressional purpose for exempting a portion of wages.

The Ninth Circuit focused on the legislative concern with preserving the stability of the employer-employee relationship, a purpose not directly furthered by extending the exemption to deposited wages. That rationale, of course, ignored the more fundamental purpose of "insuring a continued means of support [of the debtors] and their families," also a specified congressional purpose,[439] and the fundamental historical purpose behind exemptions.[440] It further tortured the plain language of the federal statute, which specifically defines earnings as "compensation *paid* or payable for personal services."[441] The use of the past tense "paid" has been interpreted to mean there is no distinction between exempt funds in the hands of the payer and in the hands of the debtor.[442] To the contrary, the absence of the word "paid" in a former version of a state exemption statute was critical in another court's refusal to hold wages exempt upon deposit.[443]

The burden on the banks postulated by the Ninth Circuit is a phantom one. If the identity of the deposits as wages is not clear from the bank's records, the debtor can be required to come forward to establish the exemption. Any accounting difficulties can be overcome by simple tracing rules such as the first in, first out rule (FIFO). Concerning arguments about tracing difficulties, the Colorado Supreme Court said "[t]his reasoning is altogether too subtle and refined to be applied to a statute requiring a liberal construction," and suggested adopting a FIFO approach.[444] In other situations when tracing of funds is important, courts have felt free to adopt tracing rules which will accomplish the necessary purpose.[445]

As the CCPA was the first federal wage garnishment act, the logical place for those courts to have looked for precedent on whether wages retained their exempt earnings would have been to state wage exemption law, in which precedent did in fact exist.[446] In fact, the similar argument that wages

428 Daugherty v. Central Trust Co. of N. Ohio, 504 N.E.2d 1100 (Ohio 1986).

429 *Id.* at 1103.

430 *Id.*

431 Staton v. Vernon, 229 N.W. 763, 764, 67 A.L.R. 1200 (Iowa 1931).

432 *See* § 12.5, *infra*.

433 Philpott v. Essex Cnty. Welfare Bd., 409 U.S. 413, 93 S. Ct. 590, 34 L. Ed. 2d 608 (1973). *See* § 12.5, *infra*.

434 *See* § 12.5, *infra*.

435 *See* § 12.5.6, *infra*.

436 Usery v. First Nat'l Bank, 586 F.2d 107 (9th Cir. 1978). *See also* Horace E. Menasco, United States Dep't of Labor, CCPA Letter No. 303 (Aug. 3, 1972) (stating that CCPA protections apply to wages after deposit), *available online as companion material to this treatise*.

437 Usery v. First Nat'l Bank, 586 F.2d 107, 109–10 n.8 (9th Cir. 1978).

438 *Id.* at 110.

439 H.R. 1040, 90th Cong. (1968), *reprinted in* 1968 U.S.C.C.A.N. 1966, 1979.

440 W. Vukowich, *Debtors' Exemptions Rights*, 62 Geo. L.J. 779, 784–86 (1974).

441 15 U.S.C. § 1672(a).

442 Consumer Credit Corp. v. Lewis, 313 N.Y.S.2d 879 (N.Y. Dist. Ct. 1970).

443 Holmes v. Blazer Fin. Servs., Inc., 369 So. 2d 987, 989 (Fla. Dist. Ct. App. 1979) (statute exempted funds "due for personal labor or services"). *But cf.* Brown v. Kentucky Natural Res. & Env't Cabinet, 40 S.W.3d 873 (Ky. Ct. App. 1999) (Kentucky wage garnishment statute, which tracks the CCPA, does not protect wages deposited in bank account).

The Florida statute which *Holmes* construed was later amended to make it clear that wages remained exempt six months after deposit. Further, the Florida Supreme Court has declined to apply the *Holmes* court's reasoning to workers' compensation funds on deposit, holding these benefits exempt even though the statute only covered benefits "due or payable." Broward v. Jacksonville Med. Ctr., 690 So. 2d 589 (Fla. 1997).

444 *Id.* "It certainly is quite as reasonable to presume that the money first earned was first expended as to suppose the contrary." *Id. See also In re* Coolbaugh, 250 B.R. 162 (Bankr. W.D.N.Y. 2000) (setting forth rules for tracing New York earnings deposited in bank account); Unif. Exemptions Act, 13 U.L.A. § 9(c) (suggesting alternative tracing rules).

445 *See, e.g., In re* Drescher, 2013 WL 4525232 (Bankr. D. Or. Aug. 27, 2013) (FIFO tracing for earnings deposited in and withdrawn from bank account); *In re* Linklater, 48 B.R. 916 (Bankr. D. Nev. 1985); *In re* Conn, 16 B.R. 454 (Bankr. E.D. Tenn. 1982) (using first-in, first-out rule to determine extent of purchase money security interest).

446 *See, e.g.*, Rutter v. Shumway, 26 P. 321 (Colo. 1891); Staton v. Vernon, 229 N.W. 763 (Iowa 1931); Annotation, *Deposit of exempt funds as affecting debtor's exemption*, 67 A.L.R. 1203 (1930). *See generally* § 12.6.2.3, *infra*.

were exempt only while in the employer's hands had been presented—and rejected—before:

> Such a construction would practically frustrate the beneficent objects of the statute . . . think of the court [saying to a debtor]: "Yes, the money was your wages before you received it, and was exempt; but, having received it, it is no longer wages, but capital, and is not exempt. You were entitled to enjoy it before you received it, but not afterwards."[447]

Kokoszka v. Belford,[448] cited by the courts that have denied exempt status for deposited wages, is not to the contrary. It held that an income tax refund traceable to wages was not exempt under the CCPA. More on point is *Porter v. Aetna Casualty & Surety Company*,[449] in which the Supreme Court recognized that the Veterans Administration exemption would not be lost as long as the benefits on deposit "are readily available as needed for support and maintenance, retain the quality of moneys, and have not been converted into permanent investments."

Given the weaknesses in their reasoning, the cases denying the exempt status of deposited wages under the CCPA should not be considered dispositive. It is to be hoped that in the future some court will take a more rational look at this question under the CCPA. At the very least, these decisions should not be inappropriately used to justify expanding their rule to state wage garnishment exemptions. The federal act does not preempt any state law providing for *greater* protection from garnishment than allowed under the CCPA.[450]

12.5 Protection of Benefit Payments

12.5.1 General

Most government benefit payments are exempt under the laws governing the assistance program. In addition, many state exemption laws repeat some or all of the federal exemptions for types of benefits.[451]

In general, government benefits continue to be exempt after payment to the beneficiary.[452] Some states also extend the exemption to real or personal property purchased with workers compensation or other exempt payments.[453] The protection of exempt benefits that have been deposited into a bank account is discussed in § 12.6.2, *infra*. Even though benefits are exempt, however, the recipient can agree to pay them voluntarily for goods or services.[454]

447 Rutter v. Shumway, 26 P. 321, 322 (Colo. 1891).

448 417 U.S. 642, 94 S. Ct. 2431, 41 L. Ed. 2d 374 (1974).

449 370 U.S. 159, 162, 82 S. Ct. 1231, 8 L. Ed. 2d 407 (1962).

450 15 U.S.C. § 1677(1). *See* § 12.4.4, *supra*.

451 *See* Appx. G, *infra*.

452 *See* § 12.6.2, *infra*.

453 *See* § 12.2.4, *supra*.

454 *In re* Guardianship of Huseman, 831 N.E.2d 1147 (Ill. App. Ct. 2005) (recipient can pay for legal representation from exempt benefits); Tookes v. N.Y.C. Parking Violations Bureau, 663 N.Y.S.2d 28 (N.Y. App. Div. 1997) (garnishment of benefits forbidden, but voluntary payment plan to recover seized car was permissible, even though only income was exempt benefits).

Some courts hold that a judgment may not be taken against a person whose only income is exempt benefits.[455] Others allow a judgment to be taken but hold that it cannot be satisfied against the benefits.[456] In addition, the exemption may not protect accumulated Social Security and VA benefits after the beneficiary's death.[457]

12.5.2 Public Assistance Benefits

Generally, public assistance grants are exempt under state statutes.[458] Several courts have found that economic stimulus payments are not exempt public assistance, however.[459] Courts have also declined to hold that benefits such as educational tax credits that are not based on need are exempt as public assistance.[460]

455 Provident Life & Cas. Co. v. Crean, 804 So. 2d 236 (Ala. Civ. App. 2001) (insurer seeking judgment for overpayment must prove that beneficiary has non-exempt income); Continental Cas. Co. v. Hunt, 913 P.2d 292 (Okla. 1996) (no judgment to recover insurance overpayments from retroactive Social Security disability; lawsuit, threat of lawsuit or judgment is "other legal process").

456 Bressmer v. Fed. Express Corp. Long Term Disability Plan, 2000 U.S. App. LEXIS 11024 (2d Cir. May 16, 2000) (insurer could have judgment for overpayments resulting from delayed SSDI application but could not satisfy it from exempt benefits); Commonwealth Cabinet for Health & Family Servs. v. Ivy, 353 S.W.3d 324 (Ky. 2011) (child support order may be entered and contempt proceeding brought against obligor whose only income is SSI; SSI award not conclusive on issue of earning ability); State Cent. Collection Unit v. Stewart, 438 A.2d 1311 (Md. 1981) (state suing for mental hospital reimbursement; could have judgment, in case state discovered or debtor acquired non-exempt income, but could not satisfy it from exempt benefits); Park Hope Nursing Home v. Eckelberger, 713 N.Y.S.2d 918 (N.Y. Sup. Ct. 2000) (Medicaid and Social Security recipient refused to pay patient-paid amount; nursing home entitled to judgment but not to order requiring turnover of future checks).

457 Estate of McPherson, 382 P.3d 1135 (Wash. Ct. App. 2012).

458 *See, e.g., In re* Wilson, 305 B.R. 4 (Bankr. N.D. Iowa 2004) (Iowa exemption for public assistance benefits covers "safety net" farm payments based on amount of crops grown, limited to farmers with gross income less than $2.5 million); MacQuarrie v. Balch, 285 N.E.2d 103 (Mass. 1972); Guardian Loan Co. v. Baylis, 270 A.2d 304 (N.J. Dist. Ct. 1970); Consumer Credit Corp. v. Lewis, 313 N.Y.S.2d 879 (N.Y. Dist. Ct. 1970). *But see In re* Reshetov, 2011 WL 4102770 (Bankr. N.D. Okla. Sept. 14, 2010) (tax refund attributable to additional child tax credit not exempt when Oklahoma neither specifically exempts it nor has broad public assistance exemption that has been construed to include it); *In re* Boyett, 250 B.R. 822 (Bankr. S.D. Ga. 2000) (federal crop loss disaster relief payment not covered by Georgia's "local public assistance benefits" exemption); Asset Acceptance Corp. v. Hughes, 706 N.W.2d 446 (Mich. Ct. App. 2005) (state homestead property tax credit not a public assistance benefit).

459 *In re* Wooldridge, 393 B.R. 721 (Bankr. D. Idaho 2008); *In re* Sebastian, 2008 WL 5063084 (Bankr. D. Mont. Nov. 5, 2008); *In re* Schwenke, 2008 WL 4381822 (Bankr. D. Mont. Sept. 25, 2008); *In re* Campillo, 2008 WL 2338316 (Bankr. D. Ariz. June 6, 2008). *See also In re* Arthur, 2010 WL 4674450 (Bankr. S.D. Iowa Oct. 20, 2010) (Making Work Pay tax credit, available to individuals with income up to $95,000, not exempt public assistance).

460 *In re* Briley, 2013 WL 3146901 (Bankr. S.D. Ind. June 19, 2013) (American Opportunity tax credit not exempt public assistance, because available to wider range of incomes than the earned income tax credit; Indiana exemption for EITC very specific and cannot be construed to cover American Opportunity tax credit); *In re* Crampton,

At least six states exempt the wages, as well as the benefits, of certain present or former recipients of means-tested benefits. Rhode Island exempts all wages of a debtor who is, or within one year was, "an object of relief from any state, federal, or municipal corporation or agency."[461] Minnesota forbids all wage garnishments for six months after a return to employment and termination of public benefits if the debtor has been a recipient of needs-based assistance or an inmate in a correctional institution.[462] Vermont forbids wage garnishments if a debtor was, within two months of the garnishment hearing, a welfare recipient.[463] New York forbids garnishment of the wages of a debtor who receives public assistance or would qualify for public assistance if the amount of the garnishment were subtracted from his or her wages.[464] Connecticut exempts wages earned by recipients under an incentive earnings or similar program.[465] Wisconsin completely exempts the wages of a debtor whose income is below the poverty line or who is (or within the past six months was found eligible to be) a recipient of needs-based public assistance.[466]

12.5.3 Social Security and SSI Benefits

12.5.3.1 Nature of the protection

The Social Security Act provides that Social Security and Supplemental Security Income (SSI) benefits are not transferable or assignable,[467] and forbids "execution, levy, attachment, garnishment or other legal process" to reach benefits paid or payable to recipients.[468] These benefits are exempt both before and after payment to the beneficiary,[469] and regardless of whether the creditor is a state or a private entity.[470] Because of the Supremacy Clause, these protections override contrary state laws.[471] There is no exception for debts that arise when a state provides for the Social Security recipient's care and maintenance.[472]

The anti-alienation clause further provides that benefits, "paid or payable," are not "subject to . . . the operation of any bankruptcy or insolvency law."[473] The Eighth Circuit has construed this provision to exclude from the bankruptcy estate funds traceable to Social Security benefits.[474]

Nonetheless, Social Security and certain other federal benefits may, within limits, be administratively offset for debts, including student loans, owed to the federal government.[475] In the discretion of the Secretary, debts owed to state governments can also be set off against these benefits.[476] Additionally, child support and alimony may be collected from certain types of Social Security benefits.[477]

12.5.3.2 "Other legal process"

The Social Security Act's prohibition of execution, levy, attachment, and garnishment needs little interpretation. This prohibition encompasses, for example, a divorce court's apportionment of property between divorcing spouses.[478]

On the other hand, the meaning of "other legal process" is less clear. In *State of Washington Department of Social & Health Services v. Guardianship Estate of Keffeler*, the Supreme Court interpreted this term to refer to "process much like the processes of execution, levy, attachment, and garnishment."[479] It stated that the term, "at a minimum, would seem to require utilization of some judicial or quasi-judicial mechanism, though not necessarily an elaborate one, by which

249 B.R. 215 (Bankr. D. Idaho 2000) (federal tax credit for education benefits a wide range of taxpayers, including the affluent, so is not exempt as public assistance benefit). *See also* § 12.5.6, *infra*.

461 R.I. Gen. Laws § 9-26-4(8).

462 Minn. Stat. § 550.37(14). *See* Burns v. Einess, 2011 WL 5829323 (Minn. Ct. App. Nov. 21, 2011) (statutory list of assistance programs is non-exclusive, but being allowed to litigate in forma pauperis is not sufficient; although IFP status is based on need, the criteria are less rigorous than those of the listed programs, and it does not provide a direct payment or subsidy). *Cf.* Bar-Meir v. North Am. Die Casting Ass'n, 2003 WL 22015444 (Minn. Ct. App. Aug. 26, 2003) (debtor failed to show that funds in account were either exempt benefits or earnings of a benefit recipient).

463 Vt. Stat. Ann. tit. 12, § 3170.

464 N.Y. Soc. Serv. Law § 137-a (McKinney).

465 Conn. Gen. Stat. § 52-352b(d).

466 Wis. Stat. § 812.34(2)(b).

467 *See, e.g.*, Tidwell v. Schweiker, 677 F.2d 560 (7th Cir. 1982) (state violated anti-assignment provision by asking patients entering state mental hospitals to sign form allowing state to accumulate patient's Social Security benefits in a trust fund and use any amount over $400 to pay costs of the patient's care); Odell v. Wallingford Mun. Fed. Credit Union, 2012 WL 4466339 (Conn. Super. Ct. Sept. 10, 2012) (prohibition of assignment or transfer of benefits means that credit union cannot use contractual security agreement in borrower's deposit account as basis for setting off debt against borrower's Social Security payments).

468 42 U.S.C. §§ 407(a), 1383(d)(1).

469 Philpott v. Essex Cnty. Welfare Bd., 409 U.S. 413, 93 S. Ct. 590, 34 L. Ed. 2d 608 (1973); Hall v. Liberty Life Assurance Co., 595 F.3d 270 (6th Cir. 2010) (disability insurer cannot obtain equitable lien on insured's future Social Security benefits to recover overpayment); Fahringer v. Paul Revere Ins. Co., 317 F. Supp. 2d 504 (D.N.J. 2003) (insurer cannot obtain equitable lien on future Social Security benefits to recover overpayment); Hambrick v. First Sec. Bank, 336 F. Supp. 2d 890 (E.D. Ark. 2004) (protects all benefits, lump sum as well as periodic payments); Binder & Binder, Prof'l Corp. v. Barnhart, 281 F. Supp. 2d 574 (E.D.N.Y. 2003) (anti-alienation clause prevented attachment of attorney's charging lien to SSI benefits recovered in proceeding when attorney represented claimant), *vacated on other grounds*, 399 F.3d 128 (2d Cir. 2005) (jurisdictional grounds). *See generally* § 12.6.2.2, *infra* (protection of exempt benefits in bank account).

470 Bennett v. Arkansas, 485 U.S. 395, 108 S. Ct. 1204, 99 L. Ed. 2d 455 (1988); Philpott v. Essex Cnty. Welfare Bd., 409 U.S. 41, 93 S. Ct. 590, 34 L. Ed. 2d 608 (1973).

471 Bennett v. Arkansas, 485 U.S. 395, 108 S. Ct. 1204, 99 L. Ed. 2d 455 (1988).

472 *Id.* (state cannot attach Social Security benefits to repay costs of imprisoning recipient).

473 42 U.S.C. § 407.

474 *In re* Carpenter, 614 F.3d 930 (8th Cir. 2010) (cashier's check traceable to lump-sum award of back SSDI benefits was not part of bankruptcy estate).

475 *See* § 10.2.8, *supra*.

476 37 U.S.C. § 3716(h).

477 *See* § 12.2.8.3, *supra*.

478 *See* § 12.5.7, *infra*.

479 537 U.S. 371, 385, 123 S. Ct. 1017, 154 L. Ed. 2d 972 (2003).

control over property passes from one person to another in order to discharge or secure discharge of an allegedly existing or anticipated liability."[480] The Court concluded that it is not "other legal process" for a state official to obtain an appointment as representative payee for a foster child who was receiving state services and use the benefits to reimburse the state.[481] The Court noted that the state did not have a claim of debt against the foster child, so was not using its representative payee status to obtain repayment of a debt.[482] Furthermore, the court reasoned that the state's actions were explicitly permitted by Social Security regulations, and the process of becoming a representative payee is not similar enough to execution, levy, attachment, and garnishment, the acts specified in section 407, to qualify as "other legal process."[483]

The implications of *Keffeler* outside the context of the appointment of representative payees are not yet clear. Cases holding that recipients may not be ordered to turn over future checks or income from future checks to creditors clearly satisfy *Keffeler*'s requirements, because they bar a judicial remedy that accomplishes the same result as garnishment or attachment.[484] The state's seizure of exempt funds from inmate accounts for prison or mental hospital expenses should also still be considered "other legal process," especially when the state requires that the inmate deposit the funds in that account.[485] This type of seizure is a means of collecting a debt owed by the inmate, and it involves using a state statute or regulation to transfer the beneficiary's funds to the state.

480 State of Washington Dep't of Social & Health Servs. v. Guardianship Estate of Keffeler, 537 U.S. 371, 385, 123 S. Ct. 1017, 154 L. Ed. 2d 972 (2003).

481 *See also* Gossett v. Czech, 581 F.3d 891 (9th Cir. 2009) (anti-alienability statute does not bar state hospital trust officer's use of incompetent veteran's benefits to pay for hospital care); Gean v. Hattaway, 330 F.3d 758 (6th Cir. 2003); Mason v. Sybinski, 280 F.3d 788 (7th Cir. 2002) (state hospital, as representative payee for SSI recipient, used funds to pay hospital; no deprivation of due process when procedure for appointing representative payee met due process standards; no taking when patient received food, shelter, and medical care in return; use of funds complied with Social Security Admin. regulations); King v. Shafer, 940 F.2d 1182 (8th Cir. 1991) (Social Security regulations specifically permitted appointment of hospital official as representative payee and use of benefits for hospital expenses); Nau v. State, 183 P.3d 626 (Colo. App. 2007) (state hospital superintendent appointed fiduciary for incompetent beneficiaries; use of Veterans Admin. benefits and state old age benefits for current charges not violation of anti-alienation provisions of statutes, nor taking without due process); Weaver v. State, 999 N.Y.S.2d 64 (N.Y. App. Div. 2012) (dismissing claims by former state hospital patients alleging that hospital officials, as representative payees, had conflict of interest, violated a fiduciary duty, and violated various New York statutes by taking patients' Social Security to pay hospital expenses); Kolbeson v. State of Washington Dep't of Social & Health Servs., 118 P.3d 901 (Wash. Ct. App. 2005) (state hospital as representative payee could take involuntary patient's benefits to pay for hospitalization; procedure for determining amount due was not "other legal process"). *Cf. In re* J.G., 652 S.E.2d 266 (N.C. Ct. App. 2007) (anti-alienability statute does not prevent state court from ordering state agency that has custody of minor child to use child's Social Security benefits in certain way for benefit of child).

482 State of Washington Dep't of Social & Health Servs. v. Guardianship Estate of Keffeler, 537 U.S. 371, 386, 123 S. Ct. 1017, 154 L. Ed. 2d 972 (2003).

483 *Id.*

484 Branham v. Varble, 952 N.E.2d 744 (Ind. 2011) (installment payment order may not be entered against judgment debtor who has only exempt income, here exempt benefits and wages so low as to be totally exempt under Indiana garnishment law); Becker Cnty. Human Servs. v. Peppel, 493 N.W.2d 573 (Minn. Ct. App. 1992) (enforcing payment by threatening to hold obligor in contempt is "other legal process"); Park Hope Nursing Home v. Eckelberger, 713 N.Y.S.2d 918 (N.Y. Sup. Ct. 2000) (Medicaid and Social Security recipient refused to pay patient-paid amount; nursing home entitled to judgment but not to order requiring turnover of future checks); First Nat'l Bank & Trust Co. v. Arles, 816 P.2d 537 (Okla. 1991) (trial court's order requiring installment payments, and its use of contempt to enforce this order, were impermissible "other legal process" when debtor's only income was exempt benefits); Silver v. Pinsky, 981 A.2d 284 (Pa. Super. Ct. 2009) (ordering father who received Social Security checks for children to split checks with wife who shared custody "verged on" other legal process; proper procedure was to set a child support amount, counting the benefits as other income in the father's household). *Cf.* Hoult v. Hoult, 373 F.3d 47 (1st Cir. 2004) (close question whether it was "other legal process" for court to order judgment debtor to deposit all his income, including exempt benefits, in one bank account, from which he could withdraw only court-approved sum for living expenses; not reached because parties agreed to omit Social Security benefits from order); Burns v. Buckner, 2010 WL 1994927 (M.D. Ala. May 18, 2010) (qualified immunity for state child support collection officials who brought contempt petition against obligor whose only income was SSI, requiring numerous court appearances; not well established that this was other legal process). *But see* Chambliss v. Buckner, 804 F. Supp. 2d (M.D. Ala. 2011) (repeated contempt petitions, brought against child support obligor whose only income was SSI, not other legal process because they made no reference to SSI and did not seek to attach the benefits).

485 Bennett v. Arkansas, 485 U.S. 395, 108 S. Ct. 1204, 99 L. Ed. 2d 455 (1988) (statute that permitted state to seize exempt benefits to pay for cost of imprisonment was preempted by anti-alienation clause); Crawford v. Gould, 56 F.3d 1162 (9th Cir. 1995) (withdrawal of Social Security funds from mental patient's trust accounts, in which they were required to deposit all funds received, was "other legal process" in violation of anti-assignment clause; authorization form, even if signed, was not meaningful consent when it did not explain that benefits were exempt); Brinkman v. Rahm, 878 F.2d 263 (9th Cir. 1989) (deducting exempt benefit funds from patient's hospital accounts to pay for care was other legal process; court specifically did not reach question of whether benefits could be counted in determining ability to pay); Tidwell v. Schweiker, 677 F.2d 560 (7th Cir. 1982) (mental patients asked to sign agreement placing benefits in account from which they would be seized for hospital expenses; not told that funds were exempt or agreement was voluntary; even if agreement was revocable and voluntary, this was forbidden "transfer or assignment"). *See also* Nelson v. Heiss, 271 F.3d 891 (9th Cir. 2001) (anti-alienation clause violated when prison allowed inmate, whose account was funded with veterans benefits, to draw against insufficient funds and then put a hold on his account to cover overdraft); State *ex rel.* Nixon v. McClure, 969 S.W.2d 801 (Mo. Ct. App. 1998) (federal civil service pension could not be seized for prison reimbursement). *But cf.* Lopez v. Wash. Mut. Bank, 302 F.3d 900 (9th Cir.), *as amended by* 311 F.3d 928 (9th Cir. 2002) (bank's collection of amounts owed under overdraft checking account plan from direct-deposited Social Security benefits was equivalent to voluntary payment because plaintiffs continued direct deposits after incurring overdrafts, so not barred by section 407; distinguishing *Nelson*, because rules for prison account not voluntarily accepted).

A number of courts have held that "other legal process" includes setoff of exempt funds in bank accounts.[486] These holdings are also consistent with the Supreme Court's definition in *Keffeler*, because a bank when making a setoff is transferring funds from the debtor to itself to repay a debt. Unlike the representative payee procedure in *Keffeler*, a setoff is almost identical to "execution, levy, attachment, [or] garnishment" on a bank account.[487] The bank is able to use the right of set off as an alternative to the judicial process only because it is wearing two hats—one as the creditor and the other as the holder of the consumer's deposit. But that dual status should not enable the bank to avoid the protections of the anti-alienability clause. The only reason a court is not involved is because of the bank's dual status.

In *Lopez v. Washington Mutual Bank*, however, the Ninth Circuit held that when a bank covered checks for which a depositor had insufficient funds, it could set off the overdraft fees against the consumer's Social Security benefits that were subsequently deposited into the account.[488] The court stressed that the fees were not a separate, preexisting debt but were related to the operation of the depositor's checking account. Because the depositor could have directed the Social Security Administration to deposit the benefits elsewhere, the court treated each deposit to the account after the overdraft as a voluntary payment of the debt.

There are critical distinctions between *Lopez* and the usual bank setoff. In *Lopez*, the debt was incurred in the same account, so the bank could be said to have been simply balancing the account: the debit created by the overdraft was simply balanced by the credit of the deposit. In the more traditional bank setoff, the bank is setting off an unrelated debt against a deposit account. The protection of exempt funds in bank accounts is discussed in more detail in § 12.6.2, *infra*.

The account agreement, to the extent it authorizes setoff against exempt funds, might also violate the prohibition against assignment of future benefits. One court rejected this argument on the theory that an account agreement cannot amount to an assignment of future benefits because offset can occur only once the benefits are paid.[489] However, this circular reasoning would strip the prohibition of meaning, as no agreement to assign future benefits will ever result in an actual loss of benefits until the benefits are actually paid out. Several decisions take a better-reasoned view, concluding that the anti-assignment provision prevents a creditor from setting a debt off against social security benefits on the basis of an agreement giving the creditor a security interest in a deposit account.[490]

Exempt benefits may be protected by state law as well as federal law. If a court interprets federal law not to protect benefits from a particular type of seizure, the advocate should investigate whether state law does. The California Supreme Court has held, however, that California law allows a bank to debit an account containing exempt benefits as a way of recouping fees or overdrafts on other accounts in the same bank.[491]

An express or implied threat to use a judicial or quasi-judicial process to seize exempt funds is also "other legal process." Thus, while a state may bill beneficiaries or their representative payees for state hospital expenses,[492] it may not threaten a lawsuit, a tax refund intercept, or other collection methods to compel the turnover of exempt benefits.[493] Remedies for garnishment or threats to garnish exempt funds are discussed in § 12.6.6, *infra*.

Applications for Social Security disability or SSI benefits often result in long delays, followed by the award of a large lump sum of retroactive benefits. If a disability insurer or the state has paid benefits to enable the disabled person to survive the delay, an overpayment often results. The Social Security Act allows the Social Security Administration to withhold

486 Tom v. First Am. Credit Union, 151 F.3d 1289 (10th Cir. 1998); Marengo v. First Am. Bank, 152 F. Supp. 2d 92 (D. Mass. 2001); *In re* Capps, 251 B.R. 73 (Bankr. D. Neb. 2000). *See* § 12.6.2, *infra*. *Cf.* Hambrick v. First Sec. Bank, 336 F. Supp. 2d 890 (E.D. Ark. 2004) (open question of whether setoff is "other legal process"; court does not reach question because fact question whether account was closed at time Social Security funds direct deposited). *But see* Odell v. Wallingford Mun. Credit Union, 2012 WL 4466339 (Conn. Super. Ct. Sept. 10, 2012) (common law setoff is not other legal process because it is extra-judicial, but contractual security agreement in deposit account is an improper assignment or transfer when used as a basis for seizing exempt benefits), *later decision* 2013 WL 4734783 (Conn. Super. Aug. 8, 2013) (awarding damages for civil theft, and punitive damages, when credit union diverted exempt funds mistakenly sent by Social Security Administration to closed account into another account that it then set off).

487 *See* Tom v. First Am. Credit Union, 151 F.3d 1289 (10th Cir. 1998) (noting that there is no relevant difference between setoff and garnishment).

488 Lopez v. Wash. Mut. Bank, 302 F.3d 900, 905 (9th Cir.), *as amended by* 311 F.3d 928 (9th Cir. 2002). *See also* Wilson v. Harris, 2007 WL 2608521 (N.D. Ill. Sept. 4, 2007) (not "other legal process" for bank to debit overdraft fees against direct-deposited Social Security benefits).

489 Wilson v. Harris, 2007 WL 2608521 (N.D. Ill. Sept. 4, 2007).

490 Hambrick v. First Sec. Bank, 336 F. Supp. 2d 890 (E.D. Ark. 2004) (denying creditor's motion for summary judgment on claim that provision in loan agreement allowing setoff against deposit account was illegal transfer or assignment of future Social Security payments); *In re* Brewer, 2002 WL 32917680 (Bankr. S.D. Ill. 2002); Odell v. Wallingford Mun. Fed. Credit Union, 2012 WL 4466339 (Conn. Super. Ct. Sept. 10, 2012) (prohibition of assignment or transfer of benefits means that credit union cannot use contractual security agreement in borrower's deposit account as basis for setting off debt against borrower's Social Security payments).

491 Miller v. Bank of Am., 207 P.3d 531 (Cal. 2009) (rejecting claim that bank's practice of debiting overdrafts against depositors' Social Security benefits violated public policy and state statute limiting setoff).

492 Kriegbaum v. Katz, 909 F.2d 70 (2d Cir. 1990) (repeated billings permitted); Fetterusso v. State of New York, 898 F.2d 322 (2d Cir. 1990) (billing procedure not "other legal process" because no express or implied threat of legal sanctions).

493 King v. Shafer, 940 F.2d 1182 (8th Cir. 1991) (threat of legal action is "other legal process"; what the state may not do, it may not threaten to do); Moore v. Colautti, 483 F. Supp. 357 (E.D. Pa. 1979) ("other legal process" includes implied or express threats of formal sanctions; violation for caseworkers to admonish welfare recipients, who had signed reimbursement agreements, not to cash their lump-sum SSI checks). *See also* Kriegbaum v. Katz, 909 F.2d 70 (2d Cir. 1990) ("special proceeding" to remove conservator who refused to turn over funds is "other legal process").

a recipient's retroactive SSI award to reimburse the state for public assistance benefits it provided while the recipient's SSI application was pending.[494] On the other hand, courts have refused to allow disability insurers to recoup overpayments from the lump-sum award, regardless of any agreement with the beneficiary.[495] Courts have, however, allowed the insurer to set off this overpayment against future benefits, that is, to reduce or discontinue benefits until the overpayment is made up.[496] This is not "other legal process," because the insurer or the state does not take control of the benefits.

12.5.4 Unemployment Compensation and Workers Compensation

The purpose of the unemployment compensation and workers' compensation laws is to provide a substitute for wages lost during a period of unemployment. State statutes generally exempt this income,[497] including lump-sum payments[498]

494 42 U.S.C. § 1383(g).

495 Bilyeu v. Morgan Stanley Long-Term Disability Plan, 683 F.3d 1083 (9th Cir. 2012) (private disability overpayment resulting from receipt of SSDI; Social Security Act anti-assignment provision forbids reimbursement agreement that authorizes recovery from Social Security); Mote v. Aetna Life Ins. Co., 435 F. Supp. 2d 827 (N.D. Ill. 2006) (insurer seeking to recover disability overpayment may not have constructive trust on account containing Social Security disability payments; anti-alienation clause of Social Security Act trumps statute allowing recovery of overpayments); Continental Cas. Co. v. Hunt, 913 P.2d 292 (Okla. 1996) (no money judgment to recover private insurance overpayments from lump-sum retroactive Social Security disability; question is not whether agreement mentioned exempt funds but whether recovery would come from exempt funds). *But cf.* Smithson v. Aetna Life Ins. Co., 2014 WL 340392 (E.D. Ky. Jan. 30, 2014) (allowing counterclaim for amount of benefits; insurer was seeking recovery from specific fund—the overpaid insurance—not the benefits); O'Brien-Shure v. U.S. Labs., Inc. Health & Welfare Benefit Plan, 2013 WL 3321569 (N.D. Ill. July 1, 2013) (allowing insurer to counterclaim for amount of exempt benefits lump sum; insurer was seeking overpaid insurance funds, not exempt benefits); Smith v. Accenture U.S. Group Long-Term Disability Ins. Plan, 2006 WL 2644957 (N.D. Ill. Sept. 13, 2006) (insurer seeking to recover disability overpayment arising from receipt of Social Security disability benefits may reach bank account in which SSDI benefits are commingled with non-exempt funds; because this is a "lien by agreement," tracing is not necessary); Williams v. Blue Cross of Idaho, 260 P.3d 1186 (Idaho 2011) (anti-alienation provision of workers' compensation statute did not prevent private health insurer from claiming subrogation of workers' lump-sum workers' compensation award; noting distinction between subrogees and creditors and finding that statute only applied to creditors).

496 *In re* Terry, 687 F.3d 961 (8th Cir. 2012) (applying a recoupment theory to allow private insurer to reduce its payments to recover amount of lump-sum SSDI award; although recoupment is an equitable remedy, court not permitted to balance the equities); Weitzenkamp v. Unum Life Ins. Co. of Am., 661 F.3d 323 (7th Cir. 2011) (anti-alienation clause does not prevent long-term disability insurer from recouping payments made while awaiting Social Security decision; insurer's lien attached to its overpayments, not the benefits); Mayhew v. Hartford Life and Accident Ins. Co., 822 F. Supp. 2d 1028 (N.D. Cal. 2011) (anti-alienation clause did not forbid insurer's setting off of long term disability benefits to recover overpayments resulting from receipt of SSDI by insured's child); Hawk v. Century Tel. Enters., 2009 WL 775394 (W.D. La. Mar. 23, 2009) (plan may set off ERISA benefits in the amount of SSDI received by participant; ERISA anti-alienation clause applies only to pension benefits, not welfare benefits, such as disability plans); Revells v. Metropolitan Life Ins. Co., 261 F. Supp. 2d 1359 (M.D. Ala. 2003); Stuart v. Metropolitan Life Ins. Co., 664 F. Supp. 619 (D. Me. 1987) (recoupment agreement allowing this practice does not violate section 407(a)), *aff'd*, 849 F.2d 1534 (1st Cir. 1988); *In re* Zimmerman, 2013 WL 3380170 (Bankr. S.D. Ill. July 8, 2013) (allowing setoff of future benefits to recoup overpayment resulting from lump-sum workers' compensation award, even though overpayment debt was discharged in bankruptcy; insurer could treat lump-sum benefits as equivalent to stream of future payments and reduce insurance payments accordingly); *In re* Morin, 2006 WL 2085224 (Bankr. D.N.J. July 11, 2006) (erroneously paid disability retirement payments could be set off against retirement benefits when debtor becomes eligible for retirement, notwithstanding ERISA anti-alienation clause; here, however, benefits were exempted by N.J. exemption for certain trusts). *See also* Eubanks v. Prudential Ins. of Am., 336 F. Supp. 2d 521 (M.D.N.C. 2004) (ERISA's anti-alienation provision does not forbid insurer from setting off present benefits to recoup previous overpayment); Hurd v. Ill. Bell Tel. Co., 136 F. Supp. 125 (D. Ill. 1955) (provision in private pension plan to reduce benefits when Social Security increased not transfer or assignment), *aff'd*, 234 F.2d 942 (7th Cir. 1955); Yustin v. Dep't of Pub. Safety, 19 A.2d 611 (Vt. 2011) (self-insured employer permitted to set off Workers' Comp. benefits to recoup sick pay paid during appeal of initial denial; treating the sick pay as an advance on the Workers' Comp. and noting policy against double recovery).

497 *See, e.g.*, Iowa Code § 96.15(3) (unemployment compensation, so long as not commingled with other funds, remains exempt from any remedy whatsoever for the collection of all debts); Strong v. Laubach, 371 F.3d 1242 (10th Cir. 2004) (Oklahoma law) (workers' compensation settlement, including bi-weekly payments, lump sum and annuity, is fully exempt); *In re* Nielsen, 401 B.R. 149 (Bankr. M.D. Pa. 2009) (unliquidated workers' compensation claim was "right to receive . . . income on account of disability"; lump sum awarded postpetition and allocated between medical expenses and future lost wages was fully exempt); *In re* Herald, 294 B.R. 440 (Bankr. W.D.N.Y. 2003) (proceeds of workers' compensation settlement covered by state exemption for disability benefits); *In re* Meyer, 211 B.R. 203 (Bankr. E.D. Va. 1997) (noting statutory protection for unemployment benefits and workers' compensation benefits even if deposited and commingled); *In re* Ladomer, 215 B.R. 265 (Bankr. S.D. Fla. 1997) (a contingent and unliquidated workers compensation claim is exempt); *In re* Nelson, 179 B.R. 811 (Bankr. W.D. Va. 1994) (manufactured home and lot purchased with workers' compensation funds). *See also In re* Jokiel, 453 B.R. 743 (Bankr. N.D. Ill. 2011) (Illinois exemption for plan "intended in good faith to qualify as a retirement plan under applicable provisions of the Internal Revenue Code" did not protect "top hat" plan, which debtor knew from the start could not be tax-qualified; exemption was meant to protect employees if employer bungled in setting up or operating plan, or misinformed employee as to tax qualification), *later decision*, 2012 WL 33246 (Bankr. N.D. Ill. Jan. 5, 2012) (fact issue whether severance payment to executive whose job was lost in a merger was an exempt unemployment benefit); *In re* Gonsalves, 2010 WL 5342084 (Bankr. D. Mass. Dec. 21, 2010) (finding debtor's severance pay to be "in the nature of an unemployment benefit," so exempt under federal bankruptcy law); *In re* Arnold, 2010 WL 1416031 (Bankr. C.D. Ill. Mar. 31, 2010) (investment account not exempt under Illinois law; intent to save for retirement not sufficient when account not tax-qualified); *In re* Lindsay, 261 B.R. 209 (Bankr. S.D. Ohio 2001) (annuity purchased to fund structured settlement of workers' compensation claim fully exempt under Ohio law); Kaliner v. Murphy (*In re* Murphy), 2000 Bankr. LEXIS 59 (Bankr. E.D. Pa. Jan. 19, 2000) (annuity purchased to fund monthly workers' compensation payments to totally disabled worker was a disability benefit, exempt under federal bankruptcy exemptions); *In re* Anderson, 932 P.2d 1110 (Okla. 1996) (Oklahoma law allows one $50,000 exemption for each interest in a claim for personal injury, death, or workers' compensation; two exemptions permissible when plaintiff's work injury resulted in a workers' compensation

and payments deposited into bank accounts.[499] As with other exempt benefits, garnishment may be permitted for child support or alimony.[500]

12.5.5 FEMA Disaster Relief Assistance

One of the primary federal programs available to help individual victims of disaster is the Individuals and Households Program (IHP), administered by the Federal Emergency Management Agency (FEMA).[501] One component of IHP is housing assistance,[502] which may be used to pay for rent, repair, or housing construction. Another component is other needs assistance,[503] which may be provided to replace personal property (clothing, furnishings, appliances, and so forth) or to meet other disaster-related necessary expenses such as medical, dental, funeral, or transportation costs.

The implementing federal regulation makes all assistance provided through the IHP "exempt from garnishment, seizure, encumbrance, levy, execution, pledge, attachment, release or waiver."[504] The regulation also prohibits recipients from transferring or assigning their rights under the program. However these limitations do not apply to FEMA's recovery of assistance fraudulently obtained or misapplied.

12.5.6 Other Benefits and Payments

Veterans benefits administered by the Department of Veterans Affairs are generally exempt[505] even after deposit in a checking account.[506] A number of types of tribal benefits are protected from creditors.[507] Student loan proceeds are exempt.[508]

In some states, tax refunds consisting of the earned income tax credit (EITC) may be exempt as earnings, as support, or as public assistance benefits.[509] A few states also exempt tax

claim and a malpractice judgment against the doctor who performed unauthorized surgery).

498 Strong v. Laubach, 371 F.3d 1242 (10th Cir. 2004) (Oklahoma law); Johnson v. Iannacone, 314 B.R. 779 (D. Minn. 2004) (Minnesota exemption for "any claim for [workers' compensation] covered lump sum as well as periodic payments) Gagne v. Christians, 172 B.R. 50 (D. Minn. 1994) (lump-sum workers' compensation settlement, which served the same purpose as periodic payments, exempt under Minnesota law); *In re* Stanley, 494 B.R. 287 (Bankr. E.D. Mich. Mar. 4, 2013) (Michigan exemption for "money or other benefits, paid, provided . . . by a . . . life, health or casualty insurance company because of the disability due to injury or sickness of an insured person . . ." is broad enough to cover lump-sum workers' compensation award; funds remained exempt in bank account); *In re* Nielsen, 401 B.R. 149 (Bankr. M.D. Pa. 2009) (lump-sum workers compensation payment). *But see In re* Lebourdais, 2014 WL 1165803 (Bankr. E.D. Mich. Mar. 19, 2014) ("accrued" workers' compensation not exempt but debtor here allowed to exempt entire lump sum as funds traceable to compensation for loss of future earnings).

499 *In re* Arsenault, 318 B.R. 616 (Bankr. D.N.H. 2004) (New Hampshire protects workers' compensation "regardless of the form" into which benefits converted, so long as traceable; lump-sum workers' compensation remained exempt in bank account held as "Totten trust" for worker's son, when worker controlled funds and son's rights accrued only on father's death); *In re* Harrelson, 311 B.R. 618 (Bankr. M.D. Fla. 2004) (large lump-sum workers' compensation settlement invested in money market account, treasury bonds, and mutual fund shares remained exempt, because still could be drawn upon to provide for living expenses or medical care), *aff'd*, 143 Fed. Appx. 238 (11th Cir. 2005); Kruger v. Wells Fargo Bank, 521 P.2d 441 (Cal. 1974) (unemployment compensation and disability benefits deposited into bank account retain their exemption). *Cf. In re* Bonuchi, 322 B.R. 868 (Bankr. W.D. Mo. 2005) (workers' compensation loses exemption upon payment to worker, but annuity that funds structured settlement of tort and workers' compensation claims is exempt as annuity "payable upon disability"). *But see In re* Wydner, 454 B.R. 565 (Bankr. W.D.N.Y. 2011) (New York exempts only the right to receive workers compensation; bank account containing benefits not exempt); Fla. Asset Fin. Corp. v. Utah Labor Comm'n, 147 P.3d 1189 (Utah 2006) (Utah statute does not protect benefits after payment to worker; worker may assign benefits after receipt but may not order commission to pay directly to creditor). *See generally* §§ 12.2.4, *supra*, 12.6.2, *infra*.

500 *See* Gunhammer v. Bowen, 2007 WL 2123786 (D.S.D. July 20, 2007) (allowing income withholding for child support from unemployment compensation).

501 The IHP is statutorily authorized under the Robert T. Stafford Disaster Relief and Emergency Assistance Act. 42 U.S.C. §§ 5121–5207. The Stafford Act authorizes the President to issue major disaster declarations thereby triggering the assistance available through the Act. Through executive orders the President has delegated responsibility for administering the major provisions of the Act to FEMA. *See* Exec. Order No. 12673, 54 Fed. Reg. 12,571 (Mar. 23, 1989).

502 42 U.S.C. § 5174(c); 44 C.F.R. § 206.117(b).

503 42 U.S.C. § 5174(e); 44 C.F.R. § 206.119(a), (b).

504 44 C.F.R. § 206.110(g).

505 38 U.S.C. § 5301. *See* Funeral Fin. Servs., Inc. v. United States, 234 F.3d 1015 (7th Cir. 2000) (anti-alienation provisions of statutes governing National Service Insurance and veterans benefits violated when beneficiaries assigned benefits to funeral home, which assigned them to lender, for advance to pay for funeral); Angell v. Angell, 791 N.W.2d 530 (Minn. 2010) (death gratuity paid to servicemember's survivor is exempt under section 5301 and cannot be apportioned by divorce court). *But cf.* Lawson v. Clarke, 2007 WL 2778259 (W.D. Wash. Sept. 21, 2007) (military retirement pay is not paid by the VA and is not protected by 38 U.S.C. § 3801); New York State Crime Victims' Bd. *ex rel.* K.A.S. v. Wendell, 815 N.Y.S.2d 438 (N.Y. Sup. Ct. 2006) (military retirement pay not exempt veterans' benefits).

506 Porter v. Aetna Cas. & Surety Co., 370 U.S. 159, 82 S. Ct. 1231, 8 L. Ed. 2d 407 (1962) (deposited VA benefits remain exempt so long as they remain subject to demand and use for needs of recipient for maintenance and support and are not converted to permanent investment); *In re* Cook, 406 B.R. 770 (Bankr. S.D. Ohio 2009) (veteran's disability benefits, and tax refund resulting from overpayment of tax on such benefits, remain exempt in a bank account, so long as traceable). *See generally* § 12.6.2, *infra*.

507 *See, e.g.*, 25 U.S.C. § 117b (trust funds distributed by Secretary of Interior are not liable for payment of previously contracted obligations except as provided for by tribe's governing body), § 410 (money from sale or lease of lands held in trust is not liable for certain debts).

508 20 U.S.C. § 1095a(d).

509 *See In re* James, 406 F.3d 1340 (11th Cir. 2005) (tax refund attributable to EITC was "paid or payable as public assistance to needy persons" within meaning of Alabama exemption statute); *In re* Murray, 506 B.R. 129 (B.A.P. 10th Cir. 2014) (Kansas's bankruptcy-only exemption for tax refunds attributable to EITC is constitutional); *In re* Westby, 486 B.R. 509 (B.A.P. 10th Cir. 2013) (same); Flanery v. Mathison, 289 B.R. 624 (W.D. Ky. 2003) (Kentucky exemption for "all public benefits" covers tax refund attributable to EITC); *In re* Brasher, 253 B.R. 484 (M.D. Ala. 2000) (EITC falls within Alabama exemption for "all amounts paid or payable as public assistance to needy persons"); *In re* Marve, 484 B.R. 735 (Bankr. N.D. Ind. 2013)

refunds attributable to the additional child tax credit.[510] A number of decisions, however, have been unable to find a basis for exempting tax credits for tuition payments.[511] In addition, the Supreme Court has held that income tax refunds are not protected by the CCPA even though they derive from earnings.[512]

Many states exempt crime victims' compensation.[513] The Tennessee exemption for certain benefits on account of disability, or for lost earning power, has been construed to enable a widow to exempt payments received as the surviving spouse of a federal nuclear weapons worker who died of occupational disease.[514] Alimony and child support are generally exempt in the hands of the recipient, at least so far as necessary for support.[515]

(exempting bank account containing tax refunds traceable to state and federal EITCs); *In re* Matsuura, 2013 WL 6577389 (Bankr. D. Idaho Dec. 16, 2013) (commingling of exempt EITC funds in account with proceeds of non-exempt child tax credit does not bar public assistance exemption, but burden is on debtor to trace; here allowing exemption); *In re* Cook, 2013 WL 5574978 (Bankr. N.D. Ala. Oct. 10, 2013) (Alabama exemption for "all amounts paid or payable as public assistance to needy persons" covers tax refund attributable to EITC); *In re* Corbett, 2013 WL 1344717 (Bankr. W.D. Mo. Apr. 2, 2013) (2012 amendment to Missouri statute, which deleted "local" from public assistance exemption, exempts tax refunds attributable to the EITC); *In re* Maine, 461 B.R. 723 (Bankr. S.D. Ohio 2011) (Ohio exemption for tax refund attributable to EITC survives in bank account so long as traceable); *In re* Glanville, 2011 WL 4830027 (Bankr. D. Or. Oct. 12, 2011) (Oregon exempts funds traceable to the EITC; when half of tax refund was attributable to the EITC, and that sum was deposited in separate bank account, account was exempt); *In re* Patterson, 2010 WL 3606893 (Bankr. N.D. Ohio Sept. 10, 2010) (Ohio has specific exemption for EITC and child tax credit; exemption survives in traceable funds in bank account); *In re* Tomczyk, 295 B.R. 894 (Bankr. D. Minn. 2003) (tax refund attributable to EITC covered by Minnesota exemption for "all relief based on need"); *In re* Sharp, 286 B.R. 627 (Bankr. E.D. Ky. 2002) (Kentucky exemption for "all public benefits" covers tax refund attributable to EITC); *In re* Sanderson, 283 B.R. 595 (Bankr. M.D. Fla. 2002) (recently amended Fla. Stat. § 222.25 exempts tax refunds attributable to EITC, even after deposit and commingling, but not ordinary tax refunds); *In re* Longstreet, 246 B.R. 611 (Bankr. S.D. Iowa 2000) (EITC is exempt as "public assistance benefit"); *In re* Brockhouse, 220 B.R. 623 (Bankr. C.D. Ill. 1998) (EITC is exempt as "public assistance benefit"). *See also In re* Walsh, 298 B.R. 894 (Bankr. D. Colo. 2003) (Colorado exemption for "earned income credit" applies to specific program that enables low-income taxpayers to get back sum that may exceed tax refund and not to various other tax credits, here the adoption credit, that are available to taxpayers with incomes below specific level). *Cf. In re* Barnett, 214 B.R. 632 (Bankr. W.D. Okla. 1997) (EITC was "earnings from personal services" which qualify for state hardship exemption). *But see In re* Collins, 170 F.3d 512 (5th Cir. 1999) (EITC was not exempt under Louisiana law exempting benefits "under this title," that is, Louisiana public assistance law); *In re* Colbert, 385 B.R. 799 (B.A.P. 6th Cir. 2007) (EITC not personal earnings; not exempt under Ohio law; statute was amended the next year to provide a specific exemption); *In re* Trudeau, 237 B.R. 803 (B.A.P. 10th Cir. 1999) (EITC was neither earnings nor public assistance within meaning of Wyoming exemption statutes); *In re* Egorov, 2013 WL 6185401 (Bankr. S.D. Cal. Nov. 22, 2013) (tax refunds attributable to EITC and child tax credit not exempt public assistance; list of exempt benefits in California statute is exhaustive); *In re* Fasarakis, 423 B.R. 34 (Bankr. E.D.N.Y. 2010) (tax refunds attributable to EITC or child tax credit not exempt as local public assistance); *In re* Builder, 368 B.R. 10 (Bankr. D. Ariz. 2007) (Arizona exemption for "assistance granted under this title" and "money paid or payable under this title" did not exempt federal EITC; distinguishing cases from states with broader public assistance exemptions); *In re* Demars, 279 B.R. 548 (Bankr. W.D. Mo. 2002) (EITC not exempt "local public assistance"); *In re* Garrett, 225 B.R. 301 (Bankr. W.D.N.Y. 1998) (tax refunds consisting of state and federal EITC, and state child care and real property tax credits, were not protected by exemption for Social Security, unemployment, or local public assistance, but first $2500 could be exempted under New York exemption for "cash"); *In re* Rutter, 204 B.R. 57 (Bankr. D. Or. 1997) (EITC is not exempt under Oregon exemptions for "general" or "public" assistance, which refer to specific Oregon welfare programs, or for "spousal support, child support or separate maintenance"); *In re* Goertz, 202 B.R. 614 (Bankr. W.D. Mo. 1996) (EITC is not exempt under Missouri exemption for "local public assistance benefits"). *But cf. In re* Benn, 491 F.3d 811 (8th Cir. 2007) (anticipated tax refunds not exempt under Missouri law; no discussion of EITC issue); *In re* Hardy, 503 B.R. 722 (B.A.P. 8th Cir., 2013) (additional child tax not public assistance because available to persons whose income made them ineligible for welfare; distinguishing EITC, which is exempt pursuant to amended Missouri statute); *In re* George, 1997 U.S. Dist. LEXIS 22829 (N.D. Okla. Aug. 7, 1997), *adopting* 1997 U.S. Dist. LEXIS 22830 (N.D. Okla. May 28, 1997) (EITC is not "support" exempt under Oklahoma law); *In re* Sohn, 300 B.R. 332 (Bankr. D. Minn. 2003) (EITC must be counted in calculating disposable income for chapter 13 bankruptcy). *See generally* § 12.4.1.4.5, *supra*.

510 *In re* Reshetov, 2011 WL 4102770 (Bankr. N.D. Okla. Sept. 14, 2010) (listing states which exempt this tax credit; no exemption in Oklahoma).

511 *In re* Likins, 505 B.R. 319 (Bankr. D. Kan. 2014) (federal exemption for student loan funds did not protect American Opportunity tax credit; "traceable to" student aid funds means that the asset was once student aid funds, for example, a bank account in which aid funds are deposited); *In re* Briley, 2013 WL 3146901 (Bankr. S.D. Ind. June 19, 2013) (American Opportunity tax credit not exempt public assistance because available to wider range of incomes than the earned income tax credit; Indiana exemption for EITC very specific and cannot be construed to cover American Opportunity tax credit); *In re* Crampton, 249 B.R. 215 (Bankr. D. Idaho 2000) (federal tax credit for education benefits a wide range of taxpayers, including the affluent, so is not exempt as public assistance benefit). *See also In re* Arthur, 2010 WL 4674450 (Bankr. S.D. Iowa Oct. 20, 2010) (tax credits under Making Work Pay and Hope Scholarship programs not exempt under Iowa law because they do not provide ongoing support and are not aimed at the poor).

512 Kokoszka v. Belford, 417 U.S. 642, 94 S. Ct. 2413, 41 L. Ed. 2d 374 (1974).

513 *See* Appx. G, *infra*. *See also In re* Soares, 471 B.R. 20 (Bankr. D. Mass. 2012) (federal bankruptcy exemption for award pursuant to crime victims' law covers court-ordered restitution for pecuniary loss, here embezzlement by financial advisor, not just personal injury or lost earning power). *But cf. In re* Ortega, 2013 WL 1084499 (Bankr. S.D. Fla. Mar. 14, 2013) (Florida exemption for crime victims' compensation applies only to crimes resulting in physical injury or death; restitution for grand larceny not exempt); *In re* Seymour, 285 B.R. 57 (Bankr. N.D. Ga. 2002) (interpreting Georgia exemption for crime victim reparation to cover only payments for bodily injury or loss of earning power, not restitution for financial loss).

514 *In re* Luttrell, 313 B.R. 751 (Bankr. E.D. Tenn. 2004).

515 Harbaugh v. Sweet (*In re* Harbaugh), 257 B.R. 485 (E.D. Mich. 2001) (installment payments ordered by court in return for certain marital property that were necessary for ex-wife's support were exempt alimony, not property settlement, under federal exemptions); *In re* Neff, 2012 WL 3063141 (Bankr. N.D. Ohio July 27, 2012) (child and spousal support payments remain exempt if deposited in bank accounts separate from other funds); *In re* Kleinsmith, 361 B.R. 504 (Bankr.

12.5.7 Whether Exempt Benefits Can Be Treated As Income or Divided in Divorce

Some courts hold that exempt benefits may be considered as income for various purposes,[516] such as setting the amount of family support payments[517] or determining eligibility or benefit levels for Medicaid or other public assistance.[518] Courts have

S.D. Iowa 2006) (credit union forbidden to set off accounts containing only exempt child support); *In re* Palidora, 310 B.R. 164 (Bankr. D. Ariz. 2004) (court-ordered child support from former spouse exempt in hands of recipient and remains exempt in bank account); Holmes v. Wooley, 792 A.2d 1018 (Del. Super. Ct. 2001) (child support funds being garnished from husband's wages and routed to wife via state agency could not be attached for debt owed by wife to husband; Delaware does not exempt child support but provides that recipient is fiduciary for children); *In re* Marriage of Comley, 32 P.3d 1128 (Kan. 2001) (funds paid into court by ex-husband's employer to satisfy support order may not be garnished for ex-wife's attorney fees); Balanof v. Niosi, 791 N.Y.S.2d 553 (N.Y. App. Div. 2005) (holding alimony exempt so far as needed for support and limiting attempt by wife's lawyer to garnish alimony payments for attorney fees). *See also In re* Edwards, 255 B.R. 726 (Bankr. S.D. Ohio 2000) (Ohio exemption for right to receive child support applies to arrearage, but only so far as necessary for support of debtor and dependents). *But see In re* Diener, 483 B.R. 196 (B.A.P. 9th Cir. 2012) (California law) (retirement account awarded to wife at divorce was not exempt as alimony, support or separate maintenance; giving effect to separation agreement in which wife waived support; refusing to admit testimony that wife sought to "buy out" support rights because of husband's irregular payments and bad checks for periodic alimony); *In re* Hageman, 260 B.R. 852 (Bankr. S.D. Ohio 2001) (lump-sum distribution from ex-husband's retirement plan was non-exempt property settlement, not exempt alimony, when separation agreement provided that neither spouse would owe support to the other). *But cf. In re* Evert, 342 F.3d 358 (5th Cir. 2003) (promissory note executed by ex-husband during property division not exempt "alimony, support or separate maintenance under bankruptcy code"; for exemption claim court will not look beyond the labels to distinguish support from property division); *In re* Delmoe, 365 B.R. 124 (Bankr. S.D. Ohio 2007) (Ohio exemption for "an allowance or other maintenance to the extent reasonably necessary for the support of the person or any of the person's dependents" refers only to legally required support; no exemption for trust voluntarily created by late father's will to pay allowance to adult daughter); *In re* Duemey, 347 B.R. 875 (Bankr. S.D. Ohio 2006) (vehicle purchased for debtor by ex-husband, to satisfy his debt for back child support, not exempt child support); Schwartz v. Haas, 739 A.2d 1188 (Vt. 1999) (family court properly set off sum owed by ex-wife as part of property division against ex-husband's alimony obligation; alimony is exempt under Vermont law, but ex-wife here is not a "debtor" within meaning of the exemption statute).

516 Pettaway v. U.S. Dep't of Educ., 2013 WL 4052130 (E.D. Va. Aug. 9, 2013) (exempt SSDI and personal injury recovery considered in denying hardship discharge of student loans; only issue is whether debtor's financial condition prevents repayment); Slupkowski v. Terrell, 2008 WL 3911386 (D. Minn. Aug. 18, 2008) (veterans disability benefits may be counted in determining whether litigant is entitled to proceed *in forma pauperis*). *But see* State v. Eaton, 99 P.3d 661 (Mont. 2004) (Social Security benefits may not be counted in calculating income for purposes of state criminal restitution order set at 20% of "net income").

517 Norman v. Norman, 50 So. 3d 1107 (Ala. Civ. App. 2010) (military allowances for housing, among other things, which are exempt from taxation and garnishment, may be considered part of servicemember's gross income when calculating family support amount at divorce); Leathers v. Leathers, 166 P.3d 929 (Ariz. Ct. App. 2007) (ordering husband to pay "one half the value" of his Social Security as spousal maintenance did not violate anti-alienation clause); Loving v. Sterling, 680 A.2d 1030 (D.C. 1996) (state may consider veteran's disability benefits as income for purposes of setting amount of child support); Lanier v. Lanier, 608 S.E.2d 213 (Ga. 2005) (exempt Railroad Retirement income, which may not be divided in marital property division, should nonetheless be counted in determining spousal support obligation); Ballou v. Ballou, 2012 WL 2946138 (Ky. Ct. App. July 20, 2012) (veterans disability may be counted in calculating gross income for application of child support guidelines); Gillis v. Gillis, 15 A.3d 720 (Me. 2011) (although veterans disability benefits cannot be divided at divorce, the amount must be considered in determining ability to pay and setting support amount); Barnes v. Dep't of Human Servs., 42 So. 3d 10 (Miss. 2010) (although SSI benefits cannot be reached by an income withholding order, courts may consider them when calculating the amount of child support); Reffalt v. Reffalt, 94 So. 3d 1222 (Miss. Ct. App. 2012) (Social Security may be counted in setting alimony but not divided in property settlement); *In re* Strong, 8 P.3d 763 (Mont. 2000) (veterans disability benefits may be considered as part of veteran's earning power when setting child support, but custodial spouse's attorney fees incurred in seeking child support may not be assessed against these exempt benefits); Urbaniak v. Urbaniak, 807 N.W.2d 621 (S.D. 2011) (veterans disability benefits must be considered in setting amount of family support, even if they are the main source of income; here, husband's income from SSDI and veterans disability benefits was more than twice wife's income from minimum wage job); LaMothe v. LeBlanc, 70 A.3d 977 (Vt. 2013) (court may not divide derivative SSDI benefits paid to custodial mother because of non-custodial father's disability, but benefits must be credited to father in calculating his child support obligation). *See also* Silver v. Pinsky, 981 A.2d 284 (Pa. Super. Ct. 2009) (ordering father who received Social Security checks for children to split checks with wife who shared custody "verged on" other legal process; proper procedure was to set a child support amount, counting the benefits as other income in the father's household); *In re* Marriage of Triggs, 163 Wash. App. 1016 (Wash. Ct. App. 2011) (anti-alienation clause does not bar provision of divorce judgment requiring husband, who had other sources of income in addition to Social Security, to pay maintenance including one half the difference between his social security and that of ex-wife who had stayed home to care for children). *Cf.* Metz v. Metz, 101 P.3d 779 (Nev. 2004) (SSI benefits may not be counted in calculating child support, but Social Security benefits may be). *But see Ex parte* Billeck, 777 So. 2d 105 (Ala. 2000) (amount of veterans disability benefits cannot be considered in setting alimony obligation when retiree became disabled and non-exempt retirement benefits decreased because of disability benefits); H.C.P. v. G.A.B., 2008 WL 2898419 (Del. Fam. Ct. Apr. 24, 2008) (SSI may not be considered in setting child support; parent whose only income is SSI may not be held in contempt for non-payment of arrearage); *In re* Marriage of Wojcik, 838 N.E.2d 282 (Ill. App. Ct. 2005) (although veterans disability payments may not be considered in allocating marital property at divorce, they should be counted in setting amount of family support); Green v. Redd, 2006 WL 2237700 (N.J. Super. Ct. App. Div. Aug. 7, 2006) (SSI income may not be considered in setting child support; when SSI is obligor's only source of income, collection of arrearage must be suspended until he has other income); Burns v. Edwards, 842 A.2d 186 (N.J. Super. Ct. App. Div. 2004) (SSI payments may not be considered in calculating child support obligation); Cote v. Cote, 30 A.3d 1279 (Vt. 2011) (exempt veterans disability benefits may not be counted in calculating the amount of disposable income that may be garnished for family support). *See generally* § 12.2.8.3, *supra* (whether exempt benefits can be reached for support obligations).

518 Wojchowski v. Daines, 498 F.3d 99 (2d Cir. 2007) (allocation of institutionalized spouse's Social Security income to community spouse does

held that to do so is not "other legal process," so does not violate the Social Security Act's anti-alienation clause, even if it requires recipients to spend benefits. Thus, a threat of eviction from a homeless shelter was not other legal process, when the agreement to pay rent, in an amount based on exempt benefits income, was treated as voluntary.[519]

Some exempt benefits may be counted in determining a chapter 13 debtor's disposable income and whether a plan is proposed in good faith,[520] but Social Security and SSI may not be considered.[521] Most courts, however, hold that exempt benefits cannot be divided between the parties as part of the property division in a divorce case.[522]

---

not violate anti-alienation clause; Johnson v. Wing, 12 F. Supp. 2d 311 (S.D.N.Y. 1998) (calculating resident's share of payments for homeless shelter), *aff'd*, 178 F.3d 611 (2d Cir. 1999); Estate of Palmer v. Dep't of Pub. Aid, 760 N.E.2d 80 (Ill. App. Ct. 2001) (Social Security and veterans benefits may be considered in setting amount of Medicaid, but state may not seek to recoup overpayments from estate which contains only exempt public benefits); State Cent. Collection Unit v. Stewart, 438 A.2d 1311 (Md. 1981) (ability to pay for mental hospital services); Fish v. Comm'r of Minnesota Dep't of Human Servs., 748 N.W.2d 360 (Minn. Ct. App. 2008) (fact that debtor sustained the disabling injury while working in disaster area did not bring Social Security disability benefits within Disaster Relief and Emergency Assistance Act provision which excludes from countable income "assistance provided pursuant to a Federal statute on account of [a declared disaster]," so they must be counted in calculating spend-down for medical assistance); *In re* Estate of Tomeck, 872 N.E.2d 236 (N.Y. 2007) (allocation of institutionalized spouse's Social Security income to community spouse does not violate anti-alienation clause). *But see* Robbins v. DeBuono, 218 F.3d 197 (2d Cir. 2000) (New York Medicaid program's practice of attributing institutionalized person's Social Security income to non-institutionalized spouse was "other legal process"; note that *Ruck v. Novello*, 295 F. Supp. 2d 258 (W.D.N.Y. 2003) holds that this decision has no continuing validity in light of *Keffeler*).

519 Johnson v. Wing, 12 F. Supp. 2d 311 (S.D.N.Y. 1998), *aff'd*, 178 F.3d 611 (2d Cir. 1999).

520 *In re* Scholz, 699 F.3d 1167 (9th Cir. 2012) (Railroad Retirement benefits can be counted toward projected disposable income); *In re* Royal, 397 B.R. 88 (Bankr. N.D. Ill. 2008) (earned income credit, which is exempt public benefit under Illinois law, must be included in disposable income for chapter 13 plan); *In re* Waters, 384 B.R. 432 (Bankr. N.D. W. Va. 2008) (exempt veterans' benefits are disposable income for chapter 13 purposes); *In re* Wyatt, 2008 WL 4572506 (Bankr. E.D. Va. Oct. 10, 2008) (Veterans Admin. disability must be counted as disposable income for chapter 13 purposes); *In re* Sohn, 300 B.R. 332 (Bankr. D. Minn. 2003) (income from exempt sources, here the earned income credit, must be counted in calculating disposable income for chapter 13 bankruptcy). *See generally* National Consumer Law Center, Consumer Bankruptcy Law and Practice § 12.3.4.4 (10th ed. 2012), *updated at* www.nclc.org/library.

521 *See, e.g.*, Mort Ranta v. Gorman, 721 F.3d 241 (4th Cir. 2013) (Social Security not included in projected disposable income but may be considered on issue of feasibility, if debtor chooses to commit it to plan); *In re* Welsh, 711 F.3d 1120 (9th Cir. 2013) (Social Security may not be considered); *In re* Ragos, 700 F.3d 220 (5th Cir. 2012) (Social Security anti-alienation clause protects funds from the operation of any bankruptcy or insolvency law; debtors who did only what the law permits have not acted in bad faith); *In re* Cranmer, 697 F.3d 1314 (10th Cir. 2012) (SSI may not be counted in determining projected disposable income; failure to include it not bad faith).

522 *In re* Marriage of Anderson, 252 P.3d 490 (Colo. App. 2011) (provision of separation agreement requiring division of Social Security benefits was unenforceable); *In re* Marriage of Crook, 813 N.E.2d 198 (Ill. 2004) (court may not consider one spouse's Social Security in determining division of community property); *In re* Marriage of Hulstrom, 794 N.E.2d 980 (Ill. App. Ct. 2003) (anti-alienation clause bars provision of marital property division that would pool and divide in half the spouses' Social Security benefits); Luttrell v. Luttrell, 994 N.E.2d 298 (Ind. Ct. App. 2013) (lump-sum SSDI award not marital asset; cannot be divided at divorce, but not reaching question of whether it may be considered in making equitable division); Severs v. Severs, 837 N.E.2d 498 (Ind. 2005) (SSDI benefits are not a marital asset and may not be divided at divorce); Williams v. Williams, 104 So. 3d 760 (La. Ct. App. 2012) (anti-alienation clause forbids any attempt to equalize property division based on Social Security; affirming award of part of wife's civil service pension to husband who received Social Security); Young v. Young, 931 So. 2d 541 (La. Ct. App. 2006) (SSDI benefits are not community property); Dapp v. Dapp, 65 A.3d 214 (Md. Ct. Spec. App. 2013) (anti-alienation clause bars enforcement of negotiated separation agreement in which husband agreed to share exempt benefits with wife); Biondo v. Biondo, 809 N.W.2d. 397 (Mich. Ct. App. 2011) (anti-alienation clause bars provision of agreement for division of property requiring husband who worked full-time to make payments to equalize Social Security to wife who dropped out of labor force to keep house; on remand, court may consider Social Security "among all other factors" in making equitable division of marital property); Reffalt v. Reffalt, 94 So. 3d 1222 (Miss. Ct. App. 2012) (Social Security may be counted in setting alimony but not divided in property settlement; agreement to give wife half of husband's retirement income "as alimony" could include Social Security as well as private income without violating anti-assignment provision); Webster v. Webster, 716 N.W.2d 47 (Neb. 2006) (court may neither directly divide Social Security benefits nor adjust property division to compensate for unequal Social Security); Simmons v. Simmons, 634 S.E.2d 1 (S.C. 2006) (family court erred in approving property settlement that called for division of husband's Social Security benefits); *In re* Marriage of Everse, 2013 WL 3362054 (Tex. App. June 18, 2013) (investment accounts funded with exempt benefits may not be divided or even considered at divorce); LaMothe v. LeBlanc, 70 A.3d 977 (Vt. 2013) (although court may not divide derivative SSDI benefits paid to custodial mother because of non-custodial father's disability, benefits must be credited to father in calculating his child support obligation). *See also In re* Marriage of Hammond and Abrams-Hamond, 2014 WL 1004169 (Wash. Ct. App. Mar. 13, 2014) (anti-alienation clause does not require court to deduct from husband's state pension the amount that replaces Social Security before dividing pension at divorce). *But see* Williams v. Williams, 996 N.E.2d 533 (Ohio Ct. App. 2013) (must consider wife's Social Security benefits when determining equitable division of husband's state employee's retirement benefits). *But cf.* Depot v. Depot, 893 A.2d 995 (Me. 2006) (Social Security benefits, or their present value, are not marital property and may not be divided, nor may marital property be transferred to offset Social Security benefits; in determining a fair distribution of property, however, court must consider "all relevant factors" including expected receipt of benefits); Neville v. Neville, 791 N.E.2d 434 (Ohio 2003) (although Social Security benefits cannot be divided as marital property, parties' future Social Security may be considered, along with all other assets, in making equitable division of marital property); Hochstetler v. Hochstetler, 2012 WL 2196306 (Ohio Ct. App. June 13, 2012) (court dividing property at divorce may take into account present value of each party's Social Security and public pension without violating anti-assignment provision); *In re* Marriage of Herald and Steadman, 322 P.3d 546 (Or. 2014) (retreating from blanket rule forbidding any consideration of Social Security; trial court properly refused to award half of wife's teacher's pension to husband who had Social Security; considering wife's lack of Social Security in dividing up her own pension was not assignment of husband's Social Security). *See generally* § 12.2.8.3, *supra* (treatment of veterans disability benefits).

12.6 Protection of Bank Accounts

12.6.1 *Specific State Statutory Exemptions for Bank Accounts*

Some states provide for a small amount of money held in a bank account to be exempt, ranging from $100 up to $7500.[523] State statutes that allow families to create prepaid college tuition trust funds also often exempt all or part of the funds from creditors of the donor, the prospective student, or both.[524]

Some states also exempt tax-qualified health care savings accounts,[525] but some courts have rejected attempts to exempt these accounts under more general exemptions for health insurance, retirement plans, or disability benefits.[526] Also, some states codify the rule that exempt property, for example, Social Security income, that is deposited in a bank account continues to be exempt, at least so long as it is not so commingled with non-exempt funds as to be untraceable.[527]

Wildcard exemptions are also often available to protect some amount of cash. Attempts to treat cash as an exempt household good or tangible personal property have failed, however.[528]

Sometimes an electronic fund transfer goes through an intermediary bank on its way from the transferor's bank to the transferee's bank. The Second Circuit, relying on UCC provisions,[529] has held that the funds are not the property of either the transferor or the transferee while in the hands of the intermediary bank.[530] To garnish the money to pay a judgment against the transferee, the judgment creditor must wait until the electronic fund transfer reaches the judgment debtor's bank, and the garnishment order must be issued to that bank. Likewise, to enforce a judgment against the transferor, a garnishment must be issued to the transferor's bank before the transfer occurs.[531] Thus, if a court does not have jurisdiction to issue a garnishment order against the judgment debtor's bank, it will not be

523 *See* Appx. G, *infra*. *See also In re* Sutherland, 495 B.R. 134 (Bankr. D. Mass. 2013) (Massachusetts has two exemptions that apply to bank accounts; debtor may claim both and stack them); *In re* Schapiro, 246 B.R. 751 (Bankr. W.D.N.Y. 2000) (when will left a specific sum of money, this amount was currency within meaning of New York exemption and beneficiary could exempt $2500). *Cf.* Calton v. Pressler and Pressler, L.L.P., 2011 WL 3423971 (S.D.N.Y. Aug. 3, 2011) (holding that, if amount in account exceeds protected amount, then garnishee bank can restrain entire amount; failing to apply first sentence of N.Y. C.P.L.R. § 5222(i), which states that restraining order "shall not apply" to the protected amount; also holding, without support in statutory language, that protected amount is applied to cumulative total of all accounts, not account-by-account). *But cf. In re* Lark, 438 B.R. 652 (Bankr. W.D. Wis. 2010) (Wisconsin exemption for "depository account" does not encompass federal tax refund even though overwithholding of federal taxes is a savings device); *In re* Cordy, 254 B.R. 413 (Bankr. N.D. Ohio 2000) (Ohio exemption for "money on deposit in a bank, savings and loan institution, credit union, public utility, landlord or other person" covers only bank accounts and security deposits; U.S. savings bonds and cash surrender value of life insurance policy not exempt).

524 *See, e.g.*, Fla. Stat. § 222.22; N.Y. C.P.L.R. 5205(j) (McKinney); Ohio Rev. Code Ann. § 2329.66(A)(16) (West); Tex. Prop. Code Ann. § 42.0022 (West); Wis. Stat. § 815.18(3)(o). *See also In re* Cheatham, 309 B.R. 631 (Bankr. M.D. Ala. 2004) (prepaid affordable college tuition contract, pursuant to Ala. Code §§ 16-33C-1 to 16-33C-13, belongs to children and is not part of parent's bankruptcy estate). *But cf. In re* Addison, 540 F.3d 805 (8th Cir. 2008) (prepaid tuition accounts not protected by federal bankruptcy exemptions prior to 2005 amendments); *In re* Bronk, 444 B.R. 902 (Bankr. W.D. Wis. 2011) (Wisconsin distinguishes between prepaid tuition accounts, which are exempt as to debts of creditor and beneficiary, and educational savings accounts, exempt only as to debts of beneficiary; account here was educational savings account); *In re* Bourguignon, 416 B.R. 745 (Bankr. D. Idaho 2009) (college tuition savings account failed to meet criteria for Bankruptcy Act exemption or uniform gifts to minors act and was not spendthrift trust; entire fund non-exempt, including sums contributed by non-debtor relatives); *In re* Quackenbush, 339 B.R. 845 (Bankr. S.D.N.Y. 2006) (funds placed by father in trust for daughter's education several years before enactment of tuition savings account statute not protected by this statute and, under gifts to minors law, ceased to be held in trust when beneficiary reached majority, so were non-exempt property of daughter); *In re* Darby, 212 B.R. 382 (Bankr. M.D. Ala. 1997) (Alabama exemption for spendthrift trusts did not protect prepaid college tuition contracts purchased from state agency when parent could cancel at any time and get refund), *later op. at* 226 B.R. 126 (Bankr. M.D. Ala. 1998) (father held tuition contracts in trust, so funds were not available to father's creditors).

525 *See, e.g.*, Fla. Stat. § 222.22 (money paid in to or out of health care savings account); Ind. Code § 34-55-10-2; Miss. Code Ann. § 85-3-1; Tenn. Code Ann. § 26-2-105 (Archer medical savings account or tax-qualified health savings account); Tex. Prop. Code Ann. § 42.0021 (West); Wyo. Stat. Ann. § 1-20-111 (contributions to a qualified medical savings account, except for debts for medical expenses, to the extent that contributions are allowable under the Internal Revenue Code).

526 *In re* Leitch, 494 B.R. 918 (B.A.P. 8th Cir. 2013) (Minnesota law; HSA not health insurance; noting also that, by paying a tax penalty, debtor could access funds for any purpose); *In re* Mooney, 503 B.R. 916 (Bankr. M.D. Ga. 2014) (HSA not exempt disability or illness benefit, nor right to receive funds on account of illness, nor substitute for wages); *In re* Gardner, 2013 WL 3804594 (Bankr. D. Colo. June 19, 2013) (not exempt; not a retirement plan nor earnings); *In re* Lombardy, 2012 WL 435816 (Bankr. N.D. Ohio Feb. 9, 2012) (health savings account not exempt; no specific exemption, and not retirement plan because could be accessed regardless of age or employment status); *In re* Stanger, 385 B.R. 758 (Bankr. D. Idaho 2008) (funds in health care savings account not exempt; no explicit Idaho exemption, and does not fit any existing exemption); Commercial Research, L.L.C. v. Roup, 2013 WL 6354558 (Colo. App. Dec. 5, 2013) (HSA not a retirement plan, because not replacement for lost income).

527 *See* § 12.6.2, Appx. G, *infra*.

528 *In re* Oakley, 344 F.3d 709 (7th Cir. 2003) (cash was not "tangible personal property" within meaning of Indiana exemption, so was protected only by $100 exemption for intangibles); *In re* Moss, 258 B.R. 427 (Bankr. W.D. Mo. 2001) ($1000 cash could not be exempted as household good but $400 could be exempted under wildcard exemption), *aff'd on other grounds*, 266 B.R. 697 (B.A.P. 8th Cir. 2001), *aff'd*, 289 F.3d 540 (8th Cir. 2002); Bank of Am. v. Ivey, 234 P.3d 867 (Mont. 2010) (money in checking account, here an economic stimulus payment, not a household good). *See also In re* Young, 297 B.R. 492 (Bankr. E.D. Tex. 2003) (interest in a trust fund, inherited from father, not protected by Texas personal property exemption); Cartwright v. Deposit Guar. Nat'l Bank, 675 So. 2d 847 (Miss. 1996) (exemption for "tangible" personal property did not protect funds in bank account).

529 U.C.C. § 4A-503; U.C.C. § 4A-502 cmt. 1; U.C.C. § 4A-503 cmt. 1.

530 Shipping Corp. v. Jaldhi Overseas PTE Ltd., 585 F.3d 58 (2d Cir. 2009).

531 *Id.*

able to reach the funds by issuing a garnishment order against an intermediary bank through which the electronic fund transfer happens to pass.

12.6.2 Protection of Exempt Funds That Have Been Paid or Deposited into Bank Accounts

12.6.2.1 Key Issues

The continuing protection of exempt funds deposited in bank accounts is especially critical today, as paper checks are being replaced by direct deposit and electronic benefit transfer.[532] The key issues are:

- Whether funds remain exempt when paid to the debtor or deposited in a checking, savings, certificate of deposit, or similar account.
- Whether the exemption is lost by commingling with non-exempt funds of the beneficiary or another.
- The impact of the 2011 Treasury rule creating a self-enforcing mechanism to protect certain exempt federal benefits when they are electronically deposited into a bank account.
- The special protections that apply to the Direct Express card and Electronic Transfer Accounts.

These issues are addressed in the subsections that follow, concluding with a subsection analyzing consumer remedies for garnishment of exempt funds. The applicability to wages of the general rule that exemptions continue after payment or deposit is discussed in § 12.4.6, *supra*. Whether exempt funds on deposit in a bank account are protected against the bank's self-help remedy of set off for debts owed to the bank is addressed in another treatise in this series.[533]

12.6.2.2 Are Benefits Exempt Once Deposited in Bank Account?

In *Porter v. Aetna Casualty & Surety Company*,[534] the Supreme Court held that veterans disability benefits deposited in a bank account remain exempt so long as they are readily traceable and "retain the qualities of moneys," that is, they are readily available for the day-to-day needs of the recipient and have not been converted into a "permanent investment."

The statutes creating other federal and state benefit programs, such as Social Security benefits,[535] SSI,[536] workers' compensation benefits,[537] and welfare benefits,[538] have likewise

532 *See* National Consumer Law Center, Consumer Banking and Payments Law Chs. 5, 6 (5th ed. 2013), *updated at* www.nclc.org/library (discussion of electronic benefits payments and electronic fund transfers).

533 National Consumer Law Center, Consumer Banking and Payments Law § 5.3 (5th ed. 2013), *updated at* www.nclc.org/library.

534 370 U.S. 159, 162, 82 S. Ct. 1231, 8 L. Ed. 2d 407 (1962).

535 42 U.S.C. § 407(a). *See* Philpott v. Essex Cnty. Welfare Bd., 409 U.S. 413, 93 S. Ct. 590, 34 L. Ed. 2d 608 (1973); United States v. West, 2009 WL 1654573 (E.D. Mich. June 11, 2009) (*pro se* defendant's assertion that all his income comes from exempt Social Security is sufficient to allege a meritorious defense, in action to open default judgment allowing garnishment); Granger v. Harris, 2007 WL 1213416 (E.D.N.Y. Apr. 17, 2007) (recipient stated section 1983 claim against bank that disbursed funds to creditor, despite knowledge that funds were Social Security funds); S & S Diversified Servs. L.L.C. v. Taylor, 897 F. Supp. 549 (D. Wyo. 1995) (warning creditors of sanctions if they attempt to garnish exempt funds); NCNB Fin. Servs. v. Shumate, 829 F. Supp. 178 (W.D. Va. 1993) (applying first-in first-out accounting rule to exempt old age Social Security benefits), *aff'd*, 45 F.3d 427 (4th Cir. 1994) (table); *In re* Franklin, 506 B.R. 765 (Bankr. C.D. Ill. 2014) (anti-alienation clause of Social Security Act protects benefits in bank account; funds never become part of bankruptcy estate); *In re* McFarland, 481 B.R. 242 (Bankr. S.D. Ga. 2012) (Social Security benefits retain exemption when deposited in bank account); *In re* Hensley, 393 B.R. 186 (Bankr. E.D. Tenn. 2008) (traceable proceeds of lump-sum Social Security disability benefits remain exempt, under federal and Tennessee law, after deposit in savings account of debtor's mother); *In re* Radford, 265 B.R. 827 (Bankr. W.D. Mo. 2000) (lump-sum Social Security disability payment, received by debtor and deposited in bank account, exempted by "paid or payable" language; no need to determine whether funds necessary for support); Anderson Boneless Beef v. Sunshine Ctr., 852 P.2d 1340 (Colo. App. 1993) (creditor not entitled to garnish Social Security and supplemental security income checks deposited by debtor for care and maintenance of beneficiaries); Collins, Webster & Rouse v. Coleman, 776 S.W.2d 930 (Mo. Ct. App. 1989) (Social Security benefits exempt); People v. Douglas, 2009 WL 32677 (N.Y. Mt. Vernon City Ct. Jan. 5, 2009) (remanding to determine whether bank account, seized for judgment and civil penalties for criminal violations of building code, contained exempt Social Security funds); Gen. Motors Acceptance Corp. v. Deskins, 474 N.E.2d 1207 (Ohio Ct. App. 1984); Ultra Thin, Inc. v. Lane, 210 P.3d 872 (Okla. Civ. App. 2009) (if funds in account were Social Security payments to minor grandson, for whom debtor was representative, account was exempt). *See also In re* Carpenter, 614 F.3d 930 (8th Cir. 2010) (Social Security benefits not subject to "the operation of any bankruptcy or insolvency law"; cashier's check traceable to lump-sum award of back SSDI benefits was not part of bankruptcy estate); *In re* Capps, 251 B.R. 73 (Bankr. D. Neb. 2000) (bank cannot set off debt against account which contains only Social Security benefits). *See generally* § 12.5.3.2, *supra* (meaning of "other legal process").

536 42 U.S.C. § 1383(d)(1).

537 *In re* Stanley, 494 B.R. 287 (Bankr. E.D. Mich. Mar. 4, 2013) (lump-sum workers' compensation award remains exempt in bank account); *In re* Baker, 2006 WL 2079919 (Bankr. M.D. Ala. July 25, 2006) (exemption survives in hands of worker); *In re* Arsenault, 318 B.R. 616 (Bankr. D.N.H. 2004) (New Hampshire protects workers' compensation "regardless of the form" into which benefits converted; so long as traceable, lump-sum workers' compensation remained exempt in bank account held as "Totten trust" for worker's son); *In re* Harrelson, 311 B.R. 618 (Bankr. M.D. Fla. 2004) (large lump-sum workers' compensation settlement invested in money market account, treasury bonds and mutual fund shares remained exempt, because still could be drawn upon to provide for living expenses or medical care), *aff'd*, 143 Fed. Appx. 238 (11th Cir. 2005); *In re* Mix, 244 B.R. 877 (Bankr. S.D. Fla. 2000) (workers' compensation settlement remains exempt when deposited in checking account, even if commingled with non-exempt funds, so long as traceable); *In re* Ladomer, 215 B.R. 265 (Bankr. S.D. Fla. 1997) (Florida exemption for workers' compensation benefits protects workers' compensation claim which had been filed but not yet decided, as well

been interpreted to exempt those benefits from attachment by creditors after deposit into a bank account, as long as the funds are available on demand or for the support of the beneficiary. The same reasoning holds that exemptions for personal injury tort recoveries[539] and payments from retirement funds,[540] private disability insurance policies,[541] or annuities[542] continue after payment or deposit.

The position that benefits retain their exemption after deposit is particularly clear when the statute, like those governing Social Security Act benefits[543] and SSI,[544] explicitly protects both the "right to receive" benefits and funds "paid or payable."[545] But the less explicit language governing veterans

as at all later stages, including deposit in a bank account); Broward v. Jacksonville Med. Ctr., 690 So. 2d 589 (Fla. 1997) (exemption for workers' compensation benefits "due or payable" continued to protect benefits deposited in bank account, so long as traceable); Decker & Mattison Co. v. Wilson, 44 P.3d 341 (Kan. 2002) (proceeds of workers' compensation settlement, deposited in couple's joint account, then used to purchase certificate of deposit remained exempt when funds were traceable and certificate of deposit a usual means of safekeeping). *See also In re* Sanchez, 362 B.R. 342 (Bankr. W.D. Mich. 2007) (bank account containing traceable proceeds of workers' compensation settlement not exempt under federal bankruptcy law as "right to receive" workers' compensation but exempt so far as needed for support as traceable proceeds of compensation for loss of future earnings). *Cf.* Fla. Asset Fin. Corp. v. Utah Labor Comm'n, 147 P.3d 1189 (Utah 2006) (Utah is one of a few states that permits assignment of workers' compensation benefits; if worker who has assigned benefits to creditor reneges and orders Labor Commission to pay him, assignee may sue worker but may not compel Labor Commission to pay benefits to assignee). *But see In re* Holstine, 2012 WL 2891220 (E.D. Mich. July 15, 2012) (lump-sum workers' compensation award; federal exemption for right to receive disability, illness, or unemployment benefits terminates upon payment to debtor, but exemption for right to receive or property traceable to compensation for loss of future earnings survives payment to worker and deposit in joint account with spouse); Mier v. Andrus, 2006 WL 1228892 (W.D. La. May 3, 2006) (Louisiana workers' compensation funds lose exemption upon payment to worker); *In re* Wydner, 454 B.R. 565 (Bankr. W.D.N.Y. 2011) (New York exempts only the right to receive workers compensation; bank account containing benefits not exempt); *In re* Moore, 203 B.R. 802 (Bankr. S.D. Fla. 1997), *questioned by In re* Ladoner, 215 B.R. 265 (Bankr. S.D. Fla. 1997) (revising interpretation in light of intervening Florida Supreme Court decision); Borrayo v. Lefever, 159 P.3d 657 (Colo. App. 2006) (Colorado workers' compensation payments lose exemption when paid to worker); SSM Health Care Sys. v. Bartel, 914 S.W.2d 8 (Mo. Ct. App. 1995) (exemption for workers' compensation "payable to" worker did not exempt funds in the hands of the beneficiary); Nat'l Check Bureau v. Carter, 2005 WL 1714200 (Ohio Ct. App. July 22, 2005) (under Ohio law workers' compensation not exempt once paid, but compensation paid by United States to disabled former federal employee was exempt pursuant to federal statute). *But cf. In re* Bonuchi, 322 B.R. 868 (Bankr. W.D. Mo. 2005) (workers' compensation award paid into annuity not exempt because no longer "payable," however, annuity itself may be exempt under separate statutory provision). *See generally* Jay M. Zitter, Annotation, *Validity, Construction, and Effect of Statutory Exemptions of Proceeds of Workers' Compensation Awards*, 48 A.L.R.5th 473 (1997).

538 *See, e.g.*, MacQuarrie v. Balch, 285 N.E.2d 103 (Mass. 1972); Guardian Loan Co. v. Baylis, 270 A.2d 304 (N.J. Dist. Ct. 1970); Consumer Credit Corp. v. Lewis, 313 N.Y.S.2d 879 (N.Y. Dist. Ct. 1970); First Nat'l Master Charge v. Gilardi, 324 N.E.2d 576 (Ohio Ct. App. 1975) (poor relief funds retain exemption after deposit into checking account).

539 *In re* Meyer, 392 B.R. 416 (Bankr. N.D. Iowa 2008) (house purchased with proceeds of personal injury settlement was exempt). *But see* Midland Credit Mgmt. v. Chatman, 796 N.W.2d 534 (Minn. Ct. App. 2011) (personal injury proceeds not exempt in bank account; Minnesota exempts only "rights of action for injuries to the person," and statute protecting funds in bank account, which lists specific types of exempt property, does not include personal injury proceeds).

540 *In re* Sunstrom, 2012 WL 5305807 (Bankr. D. Md. Oct. 26, 2012) (bank account contained proceeds of tax-qualified retirement account, that had not been rolled over; funds remained exempt); *In re* Anderson, 410 B.R. 289 (Bankr. W.D. Mo. 2009) (although exemptions are usually lost when exempt funds deposited in bank account, exemption for federal civil service retirement survives); *In re* Cook, 406 B.R. 770 (Bankr. S.D. Ohio 2009) (Ohio public employees' disability benefits, and tax refund resulting from overpayment of tax on such benefits, remain exempt in a bank account, so long as traceable); *In re* Hunt, 250 B.R. 482 (Bankr. E.D.N.Y. 2000) (state employees' pensions); Beardsley v. Admiral Ins. Co., 647 So. 2d 327 (Fla. Dist. Ct. App. 1994) (commingling exempt federal retirement funds and non-exempt funds did not destroy exemption; funds should be allocated or traced, if possible). *But see In re* Pink, 2012 WL 1655972 (N.D. Ill. May 10, 2012) (funds withdrawn from self-directed retirement account and deposited in lawyers' trust account lost exemption when withdrawn); *In re* Banks, 2014 WL 180693 (Bankr. C.D. Ill. Jan. 16, 2014) (lump sum withdrawn from retirement account and deposited in bank lost exemption; note that result would be different in case of periodic payments); *In re* McFarland, 481 B.R. 242 (Bankr. S.D. Ga. 2012) (Georgia exemption for "right to receive" various benefits, here teacher's retirement, terminates upon payment to debtor); *In re* Kemp, 2011 WL 4434996 (Bankr. D.D.C. Sept. 22, 2011) (bank account containing pension money not exempt because D.C. exempts only the right to receive pension); *In re* Garcia, 2011 WL 482838 (Bankr. D. Kan. Feb. 7, 2011) (Kansas exempts retirement funds only when "payable"); State *ex rel.* Nixon v. Mahmud, 11 S.W.3d 718 (Mo. Ct. App. 1999) (Missouri exemption for funds "payable to" a participant or beneficiary of a retirement account did not protect funds once disbursed to the beneficiary and deposited in bank account); Anthis v. Copland, 270 P.3d 574 (Wash. 2012) (exemption for police and firefighters' pensions is lost upon payment to retiree; exemptions survive in hands of beneficiary only if statute explicitly states "paid or payable" or "in the hands of the beneficiary").

541 *In re* Alam, 336 B.R. 320 (Bankr. N.D. Ohio 2005) (settlement proceeds from lawsuit for disability benefits exempt as benefits paid under sickness and accident insurance; investment account funds traceable to settlement proceeds also exempt), *aff'd*, 359 B.R. 142 (B.A.P. 6th Cir. 2006); Parl v. Parl, 699 So. 2d 765 (Fla. Dist. Ct. App. 1997).

542 *In re* Lazin, 217 B.R. 332 (M.D. Fla. 1998).

543 42 U.S.C. § 407(a).

544 42 U.S.C. § 1383(d)(1).

545 Granger v. Harris, 2007 WL 1213416 (E.D.N.Y. Apr. 17, 2007) (recipient stated section 1983 claim against bank that disbursed funds to creditor, despite knowledge that funds were Social Security funds); Midwest Checkwrite, Inc. v. Law, 255 P.3d 1228 (Kan. Ct. App. 2011) (SSI remains exempt, so long as traceable, in prison inmate's account, but burden on debtor to trace; funds not exempt when debtor failed to present account history—that is, other deposits, withdrawals, and so forth). *See also* Bennett v. Arkansas, 485 U.S. 395, 108 S. Ct. 1204, 99 L. Ed. 2d 455 (1988); Philpott v. Essex Cnty. Welfare Bd., 409 U.S. 413, 93 S. Ct. 590, 34 L. Ed. 2d 608 (1973); Tom v. First Am. Credit Union, 151 F.3d 1289 (10th Cir. 1998); Crawford v. Gould, 56 F.3d 1162 (9th Cir. 1995); Brinkman v. Rahm, 878 F.2d 263 (9th Cir. 1989); S & S Diversified Servs. L.L.C. v. Taylor, 897 F. Supp. 549 (D. Wyo. 1995); *In re* Lazin, 217 B.R. 332 (Bankr. M.D. Fla. 1998); Hatfield v. Christopher, 841 S.W.2d 761 (Mo. Ct. App. 1992); Collins, Webster & Rouse v. Coleman, 776 S.W.2d 930 (Mo. Ct. App. 1989); Sears, Roebuck & Co. v. Harris, 854 P.2d 921 (Okla. Civ. App. 1993). *But see* Fraser v. Deppe, 770 S.W.2d 479 (Mo. Ct. App. 1989) (repudiated

disability[546] and civil service retirement[547] benefits has also been construed to exempt funds paid to the recipient.

By virtue of explicit statutory language, federally insured student loans, federal educational grants, federal student work assistance, and property traceable to such assistance are exempt from garnishment or attachment, except for educational debts owing to the Department of Education.[548] Similarly, most states apply state exemptions to wages,[549] unemployment compensation,[550] or other exempt funds[551] that have been paid to the debtor or deposited in a bank account. Some courts apply this same rule to retirement and pension payments.[552] The increasing use of direct deposit to pay benefits makes this conclusion all the more compelling, as the debtor cannot be said to have even received the payment until it has been deposited.

---

by later decision in *Collins, Webster & Rouse v. Coleman*); Ponath v. Hedrick, 126 N.W.2d 28 (Wis. 1964).

546 38 U.S.C. § 5301 (benefits "due or to become due" and payments "made to, or on account of, a beneficiary"); Porter v. Aetna Cas. & Surety Co., 370 U.S. 159, 82 S. Ct. 1231, 8 L. Ed. 2d 407 (1962); *In re* McFarland, 481 B.R. 242 (Bankr. S.D. Ga. 2012) (Veterans' Benefits retain exemption when deposited in bank account); *In re* Cook, 406 B.R. 770 (Bankr. S.D. Ohio 2009) (veteran's disability benefits, and tax refund resulting from overpayment of tax on such benefits, remain exempt in a bank account, so long as traceable); Sears, Roebuck & Co. v. Harris, 854 P.2d 921 (Okla. Civ. App. 1993). *See also* Dish Network L.L.C. v. Sonicview U.S.A., Inc., 2012 WL 4848954 (S.D. Cal. Oct. 11, 2012) (exemption for veterans benefits in bank account cannot be waived by missing a deadline, but debtor has burden of showing that funds are traceable to benefits).

547 5 U.S.C. § 8346 ("money mentioned by this subchapter is not . . . subject to execution, levy, attachment, garnishment, or other legal process"). *See* Tom v. First Am. Credit Union, 151 F.3d 1289 (10th Cir. 1998); Waggoner v. Game Sales Co., 702 S.W.2d 808 (Ark. 1986); Missouri *ex rel.* Nixon v. McClure, 969 S.W.2d 801 (Mo. Ct. App. 1998); Joseph v. Giacalone, 637 N.Y.S.2d 771 (N.Y. App. Div. 1996). *See also* Sears, Roebuck & Co. v. Harris, 854 P.2d 921 (Okla. Civ. App. 1993) (exemption clearly applies to future payments, and court "not particularly impressed" with argument that it does not apply to payments already made).

548 20 U.S.C. § 1095a(d). *See, e.g.*, Brindle v. Arata, 940 N.E.2d 320 (Ind. Ct. App. 2010) (exemption survives deposit in bank account; "we cannot imagine that Congress wishes those who receive student loans to stuff their mattresses with their rent money").

549 *See* § 12.4.3, *infra*.

550 *See, e.g.*, Kruger v. Wells Fargo Bank, 521 P.2d 441 (Cal. 1974) (unemployment compensation and disability benefits deposited into bank account retain their exemption). *But see In re* Swetic, 493 B.R. 635 (Bankr. M.D. Fla. 2013) (Florida exempts only the right to receive unemployment compensation; exemption lost upon payment to worker or deposit in bank); *In re* Wyman, 437 B.R. 478 (Bankr. D. Mass. 2010) (federal bankruptcy exemption, which protects only right to receive benefits, does not protect unemployment compensation not exempt after payment; distinguishing cases exempting Social Security, which is covered by explicit anti-alienation provision of SSA).

551 *In re* Cook, 406 B.R. 770 (Bankr. S.D. Ohio 2009) (Ohio public employees' disability benefits and tax refund resulting from overpayment of tax on such benefits remain exempt in bank account, so long as traceable); *In re* Sparks, 410 B.R. 602 (Bankr. S.D. Ohio 2009) (tax refunds attributable to overpayment of taxes on clearly exempt funds—here, Social Security, unemployment, and public employees' disability benefits—remain exempt in bank account; noting that Ohio exemptions generally survive in traceable funds); Kruger v. Wells Fargo Bank, 521 P.2d 441 (Cal. 1974) (unemployment compensation and disability benefits deposited into bank account retain their exemption); McKernan Co. v. Gregory, 643 N.E.2d 1370 (Ill. App. Ct. 1994) (traceable proceeds of exempt property, the cash value of an insurance policy, remained exempt so long as they were held "for the support of debtor and his family"; exemption would be lost if funds were "transformed into an investment"). *But see In re* Leitch, 494 B.R. 918 (B.A.P. 8th Cir. 2013) (Minnesota law; exemptions for "right to receive" various benefits lost when funds deposited in debtor's account); *In re* McQuaid, 492 B.R. 514 (Bankr. N.D. Ill. 2013) (special needs trust funded with proceeds of disability insurance not exempt; Illinois exempts only right to receive disability payment, so funds lost exemption when paid to insured); *In re* Russell, 2013 WL 4591985 (Bankr. C.D. Ill. Aug. 28, 2013) (bank accounts containing tax refunds attributable to EITC not exempt; Illinois exempts only the right to receive public assistance); *In re* McFarland, 481 B.R. 242 (Bankr. S.D. Ga. 2012) (Georgia exemption for "right to receive" certain benefits terminates upon payment); Behavior Mgmt. Assocs. v. Bucilli, 726 N.E.2d 592 (Ohio Ct. App. 1999) (lottery winnings deposited in checking account were not exempt when statute provided that "no right of any person to prize award shall be assignable, or subject to garnishment"); Anthis v. Copland, 270 P.3d 574 (Wash. 2012) (loss of exemption upon distribution is the norm; exemption survives only if statute explicitly provides "paid or payable" or "in the hands of the beneficiary").

552 *See, e.g., In re* Sunstrom, 2012 WL 5305807 (Bankr. D. Md. Oct. 26, 2012) ("payable" confers broader exemption that "right to receive"; exempting proceeds of tax-qualified retirement account that were deposited in bank account and not rolled over into another account); *In re* Cornett, 332 B.R. 289 (Bankr. E.D. Ky. 2005) (funds distributed from teacher's retirement fund do not lose exemption when deposited in checking account); *In re* Hunt, 250 B.R. 482 (Bankr. E.D.N.Y. 2000) (state employees' pensions retain exemption when paid to employee and deposited in bank account); Dowling v. Chicago Options Assocs., Inc., 847 N.E.2d 741 (Ill. App. Ct. 2006) (401(k) funds remain exempt after payout if "periodic payments for support" but not if "lump sum available for investment"); J.M. v. Hobbs, 797 N.W.2d 227 (Neb. 2011) (statute authorizing state police retirement benefits makes them exempt after payment to debtor; no equitable exception for tort judgment arising from serious crime). *Cf. In re* Meyer, 211 B.R. 203 (Bankr. E.D. Va. 1997) (military retirement pay was exempt under federal law and retained exempt status under Virginia law when directly deposited in Navy Federal Credit Union, but lost exempt status when transferred to debtor's checking account in another institution that had not been opened especially for deposit of these funds). *But see In re* Gordon, 2013 WL 5763314 (Bankr. D. Colo. Oct. 24, 2013) (Colorado exemption for funds "held in or payable from . . ." retirement account lost when funds withdrawn and placed in savings account); *In re* Stokesberry, 2013 WL 4806426 (Bankr. S.D. Tex. Sept. 5, 2013) (funds in retirement plan lose exemption when paid to retiree and deposited in bank); Bartz v. Washington State Dep't of Corrections, 2013 WL 1812590 (E.D. Wash. Feb. 5, 2013), *adopted by* 2013 WL 1435145 (E.D. Wash. Apr. 9, 2013) (military retirement pay, deposited in personal bank account, then withdrawn and deposited in prisoner's inmate account, could be taken for costs of incarceration); *In re* Schena, 439 B.R. 776 (Bankr. D.N.M. 2010) (federal bankruptcy exemption for "right to receive" retirement benefits did not protect military retirement benefits already received and deposited in segregated account); Forys v. Forys, 2010 WL 199695 (Ariz. Ct. App. Jan. 21, 2010) (ERISA benefits lose exemption when deposited in bank account); Community Bank v. Noble, 552 N.W.2d 37 (Minn. Ct. App. 1996) (Employee Retirement Income Security Act (ERISA) preempted state statute which exempted pension funds; under ERISA, funds lose their exempt status as soon as disbursed; creditor could seize uncashed pension check). *But cf. In re* Miller, 435 B.R. 561 (Bankr. N.D. Ind. 2010) (exemption survives only if a statute, such as the anti-alienation provision of the Social Security Act, explicitly so provides; no exemption for proceeds of loan from retirement plan).

Some general state exemption statutes also specifically protect exempt funds in bank accounts.[553]

Interpreting exemption statutes to protect paid or deposited funds is a straightforward construction that accomplishes their purpose of protecting funds necessary for the support of the debtor and the debtor's family.[554] It is also consistent with the general principle that exemption statutes are to be liberally construed.[555] A notable exception to this rule, however, is the holding of several courts that the federal limitations on wage garnishment do not protect earnings once they are deposited in an account.[556] Some decisions also hold that an exemption may be lost if the funds are accumulated beyond the amount needed for daily care and maintenance.[557]

Once it is established that the benefit remains exempt after payment, the rule applies whether the benefits are deposited in a checking account,[558] a savings account,[559] a certificate of deposit,[560] or some other form of readily accessible

553 *See, e.g.*, Minn. Stat. § 550.37(14), (20) (needs-based assistance is explicitly protected from setoff or security interest by bank); Or. Rev. Stat. § 18.348 (exempt funds in bank accounts); Vt. Stat. Ann. tit. 12, § 2740(19) (property traceable to debtor's right to receive a long list of exempt funds, including insurance, crime victims benefits, family support, personal injury recoveries as well as government benefits); Dinh v. Motorcars of Distinction, Inc., 2009 WL 3096459 (S.D. Fla. Sept. 23, 2009) (exemption survives payment to debtor and deposit in debtor-car dealer's corporate bank account); *In re* Weinshank, 406 B.R. 413 (Bankr. S.D. Fla. 2009) (exemption for bank account traceable to exempt earnings applies whether or not debtor is head of family); *In re* Holmes, 414 B.R. 868 (Bankr. S.D. Fla. 2009) (Florida earnings exempt in bank account); *In re* Merrill, 431 B.R. 239 (Bankr. D. Idaho 2009) (exemption protects bank account containing payments of wages or pension, but exemption lost when entire IRA cashed out and deposited in checking account). *Cf. In re* Watts, 2006 WL 3899996 (Bankr. S.D. W. Va. Aug. 17, 2006) (interpreting West Virginia statute to allow weekly exemption of funds on deposit in a financial institution, wages or salary, up to the greater of $1000 or 125% of the federal poverty line divided by the number of pay periods per year); *In re* Sanderson, 283 B.R. 595 (Bankr. M.D. Fla. 2002) (recently amended Fla. Stat. § 222.25 exempts tax refunds attributable to earned income credit, even after deposit and commingling). *See generally* § 12.6.1, *supra*.

554 Porter v. Aetna Cas. & Surety Co., 370 U.S. 159, 162, 82 S. Ct. 1231, 8 L. Ed. 2d 407 (1962).

555 *See* § 12.2, *supra*.

556 *See* § 12.4.6, *supra*.

557 *In re* Schoonover, 331 F.3d 575 (7th Cir. 2003) (Illinois exemption and federal anti-alienation clause meant to protect "minimum monthly income of beneficiaries," not "hoards of cash"—here over $75,000 in various accounts); *In re* Lazin, 217 B.R. 332 (Bankr. M.D. Fla. 1998) (if funds accumulate, court must address question of necessity); *In re* Crandall, 200 B.R. 243 (Bankr. M.D. Fla. 1995) (11th Circuit gives narrow interpretation to "ability to meet basic needs"; allowing disabled SSI recipient whose income barely covered day to day needs to keep only $5000 of $10,000 lump-sum retroactive benefit payment). *See also* Citronelle-Mobile Gathering, Inc. v. Watkins, 934 F.2d 1180 (11th Cir. 1991) (refusing to allow multimillionaire who fled to Switzerland to exempt $2300 Social Security commingled in account with $63,000 balance); *In re* Treadwell, 699 F.2d 1050 (11th Cir. 1983) (debtor gave away money to family members). *But see In re* Franklin, 506 B.R. 765 (Bankr. C.D. Ill. 2014) (no "equitable exception" for accumulated funds; bank accounts containing only Social Security funds are never part of bankruptcy estate); *In re* Radford, 265 B.R. 827 (Bankr. W.D. Mo. 2000) (lump-sum Social Security disability payment, received by debtor and deposited in his bank account, exempted by "paid or payable" language; no need to determine whether funds necessary for support); E.W. v. Hall, 917 P.2d 854 (Kan. 1996) (prison inmate's Social Security funds in savings account and certificate of deposit were exempt even though prison was meeting all his daily living needs).

558 Porter v. Aetna Cas. & Surety Co., 370 U.S. 159, 82 S. Ct. 1231, 8 L. Ed. 2d 407 (1962); Granger v. Harris, 2007 WL 1213416 (E.D.N.Y. Apr. 17, 2007) (recipient stated section 1983 claim against bank that disbursed funds to creditor, despite knowledge that funds were Social Security funds); Neilson v. McGuire, 2006 WL 1875383 (D. Neb. July 5, 2006) (Social Security and certain other exempt funds remained exempt when commingled with non-exempt funds in bank account); S & S Diversified Servs. L.L.C. v. Taylor, 897 F. Supp. 549 (D. Wyo. 1995); *In re* Patterson, 2010 WL 3606893 (Bankr. N.D. Ohio Sept. 10, 2010) (Ohio exemption for earned income credit and child tax credit survives in traceable funds in bank account; FIFO tracing); *In re* Lichtenberger, 337 B.R. 322 (Bankr. C.D. Ill. 2006) (Social Security benefits remain exempt when commingled with other funds in checking account, so long as traceable); *In re* Cornett, 332 B.R. 289 (Bankr. E.D. Ky. 2005) (funds distributed from teacher's retirement account do not lose exemption when deposited in checking account); United Home Foods Dist., Inc. v. Villegas, 724 P.2d 265 (Okla. Civ. App. 1986) (veterans disability benefits deposited in bank account did not lose their exempt status merely by being deposited in account).

559 Porter v. Aetna Cas. & Surety Co., 370 U.S. 159, 82 S. Ct. 1231, 8 L. Ed. 2d 407 (1962) (benefits paid by the Veterans' Administration were not "investments," but retained their exempt status after being deposited in an account in a federal savings and loan association subject to withdrawal only after a thirty-day demand, when withdrawal could in fact be made as quickly as a withdrawal from a checking account, and funds were only ones available to meet veteran's needs); *In re* Santillannes, 2005 WL 4704994 (D. Idaho Nov. 5, 2005) (debtor could exempt 75% of wages directly deposited in shared savings account; funds were directly traceable to wages and retained quality as monies even though pledged as collateral for credit union loan); *In re* Franklin, 506 B.R. 765 (Bankr. C.D. Ill. 2014) (Social Security funds in bank account containing only benefits); *In re* Hensley, 393 B.R. 186 (Bankr. E.D. Tenn. 2008) (traceable proceeds of lump-sum Social Security disability benefits remained exempt, under federal and Tennessee law, after deposit in savings account of debtor's mother); Younger v. Mitchell, 777 P.2d 789 (Kan. 1989)(debtor's Veterans' Administration disability benefits were exempt from garnishment, regardless of whether benefits were deposited in savings account). *But see In re* Stewart, 2006 WL 2666153 (Bankr. S.D. Ind. Sept. 6, 2006) (portion of teacher's salary escrowed for summer vacation was converted into savings account and was non-exempt).

560 *In re* Tessendorf, 449 B.R. 793 (Bankr. D. Kan. June 21, 2011) (distinguishing between simply depositing funds in financial institution and "investing in equity"—that is, stock—and property; CD is usual means of safekeeping and retains the quality of moneys); *In re* Smith, 242 B.R. 427 (Bankr. E.D. Tenn. 1999) (proceeds of veteran's life insurance policy remained exempt when widow used them to purchase certificate of deposit and funds were not commingled with other funds); Jones v. Goodson, 772 S.W.2d 609 (Ark. 1989) (key issue was accessibility: depositor could obtain funds at will, although he would be penalized by loss of some interest); Decker & Mattison Co. v. Wilson, 44 P.3d 341 (Kan. 2002) (proceeds of workers' compensation settlement, deposited in couple's joint account and then used to purchase certificate of deposit remained exempt, when funds were traceable and certificate of deposit a usual means of safekeeping); E.W. v. Hall, 917 P.2d 854 (Kan. 1996). *But see* Feliciano v. McClung, 556 S.E.2d 807 (W. Va. 2001) (lump-sum workers' compensation award would remain exempt in ordinary bank account, but purchase of certificate of deposit turns it into non-exempt investment). *But cf.* Sullo v. Cinco Star, Inc., 755 So. 2d 822 (Fla. Dist. Ct. App. 2000) (exemption lost when worker received large lump sum, bought certificate of deposit, and pledged that certificate of deposit as security for a loan).

deposit,[561] so long as these are "usual means of safekeeping" money used for daily living expenses. Traceable proceeds of the benefits and items purchased with the benefits may also be exempt, particularly in the context of workers compensation.[562]

12.6.2.3 Commingling of Exempt and Non-Exempt Funds

Commingling of exempt funds with non-exempt funds or funds of another raises the problem of traceability. Most courts will continue to protect such funds,[563] generally applying a first-in first-out accounting method.[564] Others, a minority,

561 *In re* Harrelson, 311 B.R. 618 (Bankr. M.D. Fla. 2004) (large lump-sum workers' compensation settlement invested in money market account, treasury bonds, and mutual fund shares remained exempt, because still could be drawn upon to provide for living expenses or medical care), *aff'd*, 143 Fed. Appx. 238 (11th Cir. 2005).

562 *See* § 12.2.6, *supra*.

563 *See, e.g.*, Tom v. First Am. Credit Union, 151 F.3d 1289 (10th Cir. 1998); U.S. v. $72,050.00 in U.S. Currency, 2013 WL 4042859 (E.D. Ky. Aug. 8, 2013) (mingling of tainted—and forfeitable—funds with exempt funds does not destroy exemption; here, son sought to launder proceeds of fraudulent investment scheme by depositing them in account containing father's Black Lung benefits; father's benefits remained exempt); Dish Network L.L.C. v. Sonicview U.S.A., Inc., 2012 WL 4848954 (S.D. Cal. Oct. 11, 2012) (veterans benefits in bank account exempt if debtor can show traceability); Neilson v. McGuire, 2006 WL 1875383 (D. Neb. July 5, 2006) (Social Security and certain exempt funds remained exempt when commingled with non-exempt funds in bank account; calculating from bank statements that 75% of account was Social Security funds); *In re* Nye, 210 B.R. 857 (D. Colo. 1997); S & S Diversified Servs. L.L.C. v. Taylor, 897 F. Supp. 549 (D. Wyo. 1995) (Social Security old age benefits remain exempt when commingled with other funds in joint account, so long as they are reasonably traceable; warning creditors of sanctions if they attempt to garnish exempt funds); *In re* Williams, 171 B.R. 451 (D.N.H. 1994); NCNB Fin. Servs. v. Shumate, 829 F. Supp. 178 (W.D. Va. 1993), *aff'd*, 45 F.3d 427 (4th Cir. 1994); *In re* Smith, 2011 WL 722401 (Bankr. W.D. Mich. Feb. 18, 2011) (liberally construing Colorado statute which exempts unemployment funds if not "commingled" to hold that funds lose exemption only when no longer traceable); *In re* Dunkin, 2011 WL 4905588 (Bankr. S.D. Iowa Sept. 14, 2011) (wages do not lose exemption by deposit in bank account, but non-exempt here because debtor failed to trace); *In re* Glanville, 2011 WL 4830027 (Bankr. D. Or. Oct. 12, 2011) (discussing methods of tracing funds that are commingled upon receipt, here tax refund partly attributable to earned income credit); *In re* Lehman, 2009 WL 497125 (Bankr. W.D. Wash. Feb. 26, 2009) (insurance check for storm damage to homestead, deposited in unsegregated bank account, is exempt for one year; statute does not require traceability or segregation); *In re* Hensley, 393 B.R. 186 (Bankr. E.D. Tenn. 2008) (traceable proceeds of lump-sum Social Security disability benefits remained exempt, under federal and Tennessee law, after deposit in savings account of debtor's mother); *In re* Lichtenberger, 337 B.R. 322 (Bankr. C.D. Ill. 2006) (Social Security benefits remain exempt when commingled with other funds in checking account, so long as traceable); *In re* Gardiner, 332 B.R. 891 (Bankr. S.D. Cal. 2005) (asset acquired, in part, with workers' compensation award retained exempt status, subject to tracing requirements); *In re* Sanderson, 283 B.R. 595 (Bankr. M.D. Fla. 2002) (recently amended Fla. Stat. § 222.25 exempts tax refunds attributable to earned income credit, even after deposit and commingling); *In re* Mix, 244 B.R. 877 (Bankr. S.D. Fla. 2000) (workers' compensation settlement remains exempt in checking account, even if commingled with non-exempt funds, so long as traceable); *In re* Lazin, 217 B.R. 332 (Bankr. M.D. Fla. 1998); *In re* Ryzner, 208 B.R. 568 (Bankr. M.D. Fla. 1997); *In re* Norris, 203 B.R. 463 (Bankr. D. Nev. 1996); Waggoner v. Game Sales Co., 702 S.W.2d 808 (Ark. 1986); Orlyn v. Novastar Mortgage, Inc., 2006 WL 1102688 (Cal. Ct. App. Apr. 27, 2006) (Social Security and wages commingled in bank account; Social Security automatically exempt; wages not exempt when debtor failed to prove they had been earned with thirty days); Am. Express v. Locicero, 2008 WL 2895850 (Conn. Super. Ct. July 7, 2008) (non-debtor's Social Security benefits, commingled in joint account with debtor, remained exempt); Broward v. Jacksonville Med. Ctr., 690 So. 2d 589 (Fla. 1997); Bennett v. Soc'y of Lloyd's, 51 So. 3d 568 (Fla. Dist. Ct. App. 2010) (commingling of exempt Social Security with other funds does not destroy exemption; court must attempt to allocate); Parl v. Parl, 699 So. 2d 765 (Fla. Dist. Ct. App. 1997); Beardsley v. Admiral Ins. Co., 647 So. 2d 327 (Fla. Dist. Ct. App. 1994); Decker & Mattison Co. v. Wilson, 44 P.3d 341 (Kan. 2002) (proceeds of workers' compensation settlement, deposited in couple's joint account, then used to purchase certificate of deposit remained exempt, when funds were traceable and certificate of deposit a usual means of safekeeping); Midwest Checkwrite, Inc. v. Law, 255 P.3d 1228 (Kan. Ct. App. 2011) (SSI remains exempt, so long as traceable, in prison inmate's account, but burden on debtor to trace; funds not exempt when debtor failed to present account history—that is, other deposits, withdrawals, and so forth); Hatfield v. Christopher, 841 S.W.2d 761 (Mo. Ct. App. 1992); Collins, Webster & Rouse v. Coleman, 776 S.W.2d 930 (Mo. Ct. App. 1989); Dean v. Fred's Towing, 801 P.2d 579 (Mont. 1990); *In re* Christensen, 149 P.3d 40 (Nev. 2006) (commingling does not destroy exemption, so long as funds remain available for day-to-day use and reasonably traceable). *See also In re* Danduran, 657 F.3d 749 (8th Cir. 2011) (North Dakota law) (home was sold for $225,000 along with $7700 for personal property contents, and the mortgage was paid off from this comment pool of proceeds and the remainder placed in a bank account; entire bank account must be treated as exempt proceeds of homestead because creditor was unable to prove that it contained any part of the payment for the non-exempt personal property); *In re* Meyer, 211 B.R. 203 (Bankr. E.D. Va. 1997) (noting statutory protection for unemployment benefits and workers' compensation benefits even if deposited and commingled). *But cf.* States Res. Corp. v. McColum, 2008 WL 4549974 (W.D. Okla. Oct. 7, 2008) (debtor failed to trace funds in account to Social Security); Citibank (S.D.) v. Five Star Bank, 824 N.Y.S.2d 761 (N.Y. Sup. Ct. 2006) (exempt funds deposited in joint account several months before were no longer traceable when there were numerous deposits and withdrawals thereafter); Bless v. Aguilera, 2010 WL 5238658 (Utah Ct. App. Dec. 28, 2010) (currently employed debtor failed to show that funds in account were traceable to earlier unemployment benefits).

564 *See, e.g.*, S & S Diversified Servs., L.L.C. v. Taylor, 897 F. Supp. 549 (D. Wyo. 1995); NCNB Fin. Servs. v. Shumate, 829 F. Supp. 178 (W.D. Va. 1993), *aff'd*, 45 F.3d 427 (4th Cir. 1994) (table); *In re* Marve, 484 B.R. 735 (Bankr. N.D. Ind. 2013) (using FIFO to trace tax returns attributable to earned income tax credit, commingled with non-exempt funds in bank account); *In re* Matsuura, 2013 WL 6577389 (Bankr. D. Idaho Dec. 16, 2013) (commingling of exempt and non-exempt funds does not destroy public assistance exemption, but burden is on debtor to trace; here allowing exemption of funds attributable to earned income credit, commingled in accounts with proceeds of non-exempt child tax credit); *In re* Wiltsie, 463 B.R. 223 (Bankr. N.D.N.Y. 2011) (FIFO tracing for exempt wages direct-deposited into account containing non-exempt funds); *In re* Patterson, 2010 WL 3606893 (Bankr. N.D. Ohio Sept. 10, 2010) (FIFO tracing for earned income credit and child tax credit in bank account); *In re* Fandrich, 2008 WL 4610030 (Bankr. D.N.D. Oct. 16, 2008) (funds not traceable to earnings when balance in account was less than amount of most recent deposit of non-exempt funds); *In re* Lichtenberger, 337 B.R. 322 (Bankr. C.D. Ill. 2006) (using first-in, first-out method to trace Social Security funds commingled in joint checking account); Dean v. Fred's Towing, 801 P.2d 579 (Mont.

simply refuse to trace, finding that the exemption is lost when the funds are commingled.[565] The use of an account which is limited to exempt funds should offer protection in such states. The 2011 Treasury rule, discussed in § 12.6.3, *infra*, will protect two months of electronically-deposited federal benefits, regardless of commingling.

12.6.3 Treasury Rule Protects Electronically Deposited Exempt Federal Benefits from Garnishment

12.6.3.1 Introduction

A federal rule, effective May 1, 2011, vastly strengthens protections for exempt federal benefits deposited into bank accounts.[566] The rule, announced by the Treasury Department and several benefits-paying agencies, limits creditors' ability to garnish bank accounts that contain Social Security, Supplemental Security Income (SSI), VA, and certain other federal benefits.

Federal law makes these funds immune from seizure by creditors. But in practice, when a bank receives a garnishment order, it typically freezes the entire bank account up to the amount of the debt, even when the account contains protected funds. A beneficiary may be unable to access urgently needed funds for weeks or months. Often, the paperwork and procedures needed to end an illegal freeze prove too daunting for a recipient, such that the bank turns over supposedly "untouchable" funds to the creditor.

There are strong arguments that, even before the adoption of the Treasury rule, freezing or garnishing exempt funds violated federal law. State statutes cannot abrogate a federal right, and the federal law establishing that the funds are exempt is clear. It would seem improper to interpret a state statute to mean that funds which are exempt under federal law can lose that protected status just because the consumer fails to follow a state-required procedure.[567] However, decisions on this question have been inconsistent.[568]

The rule prohibits the practice of denying beneficiaries access to these essential funds in bank accounts. It requires all banks to determine whether certain exempt federal benefits have been electronically deposited within the preceding two months. If they have, the bank must protect whatever amount was deposited during that period. To protect funds deposited before the two-month window, or funds which have been transferred between accounts, the recipient will have to use state procedures.

The rule protects Social Security, SSI, VA benefits, federal Railroad Retirement, federal Railroad Unemployment and Sickness, federal Civil Service Retirement System, and federal Employee Retirement System benefits.[569] The rule does not protect military retirement payments or other military benefits but, when they announced the rule, the agencies stated that its framework could be expanded in the future to protect these and other federal payments that are intended to

---

1990); *In re* Christensen, 149 P.3d 40 (Nev. 2006) (choosing first-in, first-out after comparing four tracing methods); Lincoln Fin. Servs., Inc. v. Miceli, 17 Misc. 3d 1109(A) (Dist. Ct. 2007) (table) (text available at 2007 WL 2917242) (first-in, first-out tracing for Social Security benefits in bank account). *Cf. In re* Stokesberry, 2013 WL 4806426 (Bankr. S.D. Tex. Sept. 5, 2013) (choosing lowest intermediate balance method to trace Social Security mingled in account with non-exempt funds); *In re* Maine, 461 B.R. 723 (Bankr. S.D. Ohio 2011) (choosing lowest intermediate balance method to trace tax refund attributable to earned income credit); *In re* Perkins, 2011 WL 4458961 (Bankr. N.D. Ohio Sept. 23, 2011) (choosing lowest intermediate balance method to trace student loan funds, but citing other cases choosing FIFO); *In re* Lantz, 451 B.R. 843 (Bankr. N.D. Ill. 2011) (choosing lowest intermediate balance tracing method when proceeds of homestead were first deposited in account with other non-exempt funds, then moved to segregated account).

565 *See, e.g.*, Colo. Rev. Stat. § 13-54-102.5 (child support payment loses exemption if intermingled with any other money); Idaho Code Ann. § 11-604 (exemptions for insurance, disability and family support are "lost immediately upon the commingling of any of the funds . . . with any other funds"); Pellegrino v. Koeckriz Dev. of Boca Raton, Inc., 2009 WL 1437813 (S.D. Fla. May 15, 2008) (even if funds were exempt earnings, exemption lost when funds commingled in joint account), *report and recommendation adopted*, 2009 WL 1798382 (S.D. Fla. Jan. 24, 2009); *In re* Cauley, 374 B.R. 311 (Bankr. M.D. Fla. 2007) (Alabama law) (wages lose exemption when commingled with other funds in bank account); *In re* Fouracre, 358 B.R. 384 (Bankr. D. Ariz. 2006) (proceeds of homestead lose exemption when commingled with other funds in bank account); Bernardini v. Central Bank, 290 S.E.2d 863 (Va. 1982); Rue & Assocs., Inc. v. White, 2006 WL 2022184 (Va. Cir. Ct. July 18, 2006) (Social Security benefits lose exemption when commingled with non-exempt funds in joint bank account).

566 76 Fed. Reg. 9939 (Feb. 23, 2011), *to be codified at* 31 C.F.R. §§ 212.1 through 212.12. *See* Margot Saunders & Johnson M. Tyler, *Past, Present, and Future Threats to Federal Safety Net Benefits in Bank Accounts*, 16 N.C. Banking Inst. 43 (2012) (describing background and history of Treasury rule). *See also* Comptroller's Handbook CC-GA, Consumer Compliance (CC), Garnishment of Accounts Containing Federal Benefit Payments (Apr. 2014), *available at* www.occ.gov/publications/publications-by-type/comptrollers-handbook/pub-ch-garnishment-of-accounts.pdf (containing background information for banks and examination guidelines regarding the new rule).

567 *See, e.g.*, Dish Network L.L.C. v. Sonicview U.S.A., Inc., 2012 WL 4848954 (S.D. Cal. Oct. 11, 2012) (exemption for veterans benefits in bank account cannot be waived by missing a deadline). *See also* §§ 12.3.7, *supra*, 12.10.1, *infra*.

568 *See, e.g.*, Hendricks & Lewis, P.L.L.C. v. Clinton, 2011 WL 4861855 (N.D. Fla. Aug. 9, 2011) (mag.) (exemption for bank account containing Social Security funds lost by failure to meet time limits of Florida statute), *adopted by* 2011 WL 4861844 (N.D. Fla. Oct. 13, 2011); Hollowell v. Hosto, 2010 WL 1416519 (E.D. Ark. Apr. 8, 2010) (no FDCPA claim against law firm that froze account containing exempt Social Security when debtor did not allege that he asserted exemption; state may place reasonable burden on debtor to claim exemptions), *aff'd as modified*, 389 Fed. Appx. 583 (8th Cir. 2010) (modifying district court order to dismiss all claims with prejudice); Chappell v. Friedman, 2009 WL 2246575 (D. Md. July 24, 2009) (bank had no duty to exert exemption or disburse exempt direct-deposited Social Security funds to debtor; burden is on debtor to claim exemptions); Zeppieri v. New Haven Provision Co., 163 F. Supp. 2d 126 (D. Conn. 2001) (exemption of Social Security funds in bank account is not self-executing).

569 76 Fed. Reg. 9939, n.1 (Feb. 23, 2011). *See* § 12.5, *supra*.

be immune from garnishment.[570] The rule does not protect state benefit payments, such as state employee retirement benefits, workers compensation benefits, and unemployment compensation.

Prior to adoption of the rule, a few states adopted statutes or rules of court that achieve approximately the same result.[571]

12.6.3.2 How the Rule Operates

The rule applies to state and federal banks, credit unions, and any other entity chartered under federal or state law to engage in the business of banking.[572] Upon receipt of a garnishment order against an account holder, the bank must review all accounts owned by that individual to determine whether any of the specified federal benefits were electronically deposited during the preceding two months (the "look-back period"). (The benefits-paying agencies are adding electronic markers that banks will be permitted to rely on to determine whether an electronic deposit is an exempt benefit.) If exempt benefits have been deposited during the look-back period, then the bank must calculate the "protected amount." The "protected amount" is the lesser of the sum of all exempt benefits electronically deposited into the debtor's account during the look-back period, or the balance of the account on the day the review is conducted.[573]

If the account contains a protected amount, the bank cannot freeze or otherwise restrict the account holder's "full and customary" access to that amount.[574] The bank must give the beneficiary the same degree of access that was provided before the bank received the garnishment order.[575]

Upon determining that the account contains a protected amount, the bank must send the account holder a notice describing what the bank has done and giving some basic information about how to protect exempt benefits that exceed the protected amount.[576] The rule protects the bank from contempt citations or similar penalties and from any liability to the creditor for preserving the debtor's access to the protected amount.[577]

12.6.3.3 Exceptions for Debts Owed to the Federal Government or a State Child Support Agency

The account review is not required, and there is no automatic protection of any amount, if either the federal government or a state IV-D child support agency issued the garnishment order. These orders must contain a special notice.[578] The rationale is that different exemption regimes apply in these cases. In these cases, the debtor can still assert exemptions but must do so through the usual state procedures.[579] Unfortunately, this exemption is too broad, as some benefits—such as SSI benefits—are not subject to the collection of child support.[580]

12.6.3.4 A Self-Executing Protection; Debtor No Longer Has Burden of Asserting Exemption at Any Stage

The primary problem that the rule is designed to address is the temporary freeze of a debtor's bank account while the bank, the parties, and the court system sort out the question of whether funds are exempt. But the effect of the rule is much more sweeping.

The rule nullifies any requirement that the debtor take any affirmative step to assert an exemption for the protected amount. The bank has an unconditional obligation to make the protected amount available to the debtor. In addition, the bank is prohibited from complying with any court order to pay the protected amount to the creditor—even if, for example, the debtor fails to comply with a state law requirement to assert the exemption or the state court concludes that the exemption was improper.

This conclusion is clear from three parts of the rule. The rule provides: "An account holder shall have no requirement to assert any right of garnishment exemption prior to accessing the protected amount in the account."[581] Second, "[a] protected amount calculated and established by a financial institution pursuant to this section shall be conclusively considered to be exempt from garnishment under law."[582] Third, the notice that the bank is required to send to the account holder says "You may use the 'protected amount' of money in your account as you normally would. There is nothing else that you need to do to make sure that the 'protected amount' is safe."[583]

12.6.3.5 Commingled Funds, Co-Owners, Lump-Sum Payments

In some states, courts have held that exempt funds lose their protected status if they are commingled with non-exempt funds.[584] The rule's protections apply whether or not

570 75 Fed. Reg. 9939, 9941 (Feb. 23, 2011).

571 *See* § 12.6.4.3, *infra*. *See also* London v. RBS Citizens, 600 F.3d 742 (7th Cir. 2010) (interpreting Illinois garnishment statutes and forms as prohibiting even temporary freeze of exempt funds).

572 31 C.F.R. § 212.3 (definition of "financial institution"). This section will refer to all of these institutions as "banks."

573 31 C.F.R. § 212.3.

574 31 C.F.R. § 212.6(a).

575 76 Fed. Reg. 9939, 9945 (Feb. 23, 2011).

576 31 C.F.R. § 212.7. A notice is required only if the account had a positive balance on the review date. *See also* 31 C.F.R. pt. 212, app. A, Model Notice to Account Holder.

577 31 C.F.R. § 212.10. *See* Tillimon v. Wheeler, 2012 WL 6096574 (Ohio Ct. App. Dec. 7, 2012) (unpublished) (affirming denial of contempt charge against bank that followed Treasury rule and refused to turn over protected amount). *See, e.g.*, Tillimon v. Wheeler, 2012 WL 6096574 (Ohio Ct. App. Dec. 7, 2012) (denying creditor's motion for contempt citation against garnishee bank that complied with Treasury rule).

578 31 C.F.R. § 212.4(a).

579 31 C.F.R. § 212.4(a).

580 *See* § 12.2.8, *supra*.

581 31 C.F.R. § 212.6(a).

582 31 C.F.R. § 212.6(c).

583 31 C.F.R. pt. 212, app. A, Model Notice to Account Holder (emphasis in original).

584 *See* § 12.6.2.3, *supra*.

the protected funds have been commingled with other funds: as long as the specified federal benefits were electronically deposited into the account during the look-back period, they are protected regardless of what other funds might be in the account.[585]

Nor does it make any difference if there is a co-owner on the account. Whatever amount of benefits was deposited during the look-back period is exempt, even if it was deposited in the name of the non-debtor co-owner.[586]

The rule does not contain any cap on the amount of benefits that are protected. If the beneficiary received a lump-sum payment by electronic deposit within the two-month look-back period, it is protected regardless of its amount. However, a lump-sum payment that remains unspent in an account will lose the rule's automatic protection after two months. In that case, if a garnishment order arrives, the beneficiary will need to invoke whatever state procedures are available to protect the unspent portion of the lump-sum payment.

Also, if the exempt funds were electronically deposited into one account and then transferred into another account, the funds are not protected. The "protected amount" under the rule is limited to funds that were electronically deposited into each account the bank holds in the name of the debtor.[587]

12.6.3.6 Continuing Garnishments and Repeat Garnishments

According to the Treasury Department, in a few states creditors can obtain continuing garnishments of bank accounts, requiring the bank to monitor the account and garnish funds as new deposits come in.[588] The rule prohibits a bank that is served with a continuing garnishment order from complying with that order's ongoing requirements.[589]

Likewise, if the same garnishment order is served on a bank a second time, the bank is prohibited from taking any action on it.[590] If the creditor obtains and serves a new garnishment order,[591] however, the bank must go through the account review procedure again and determine if there is a protected amount.

Banks may perceive it as a burden to perform repeat account reviews in response to multiple garnishment orders, particularly since they are not allowed to deduct any garnishment fees from the protected amount.[592] For these reasons, banks may want to close a beneficiary's bank account if repeat garnishment orders come in. While the supplementary material to the rule indicates that the rule does not address this issue,[593] the language of the rule requiring the bank to provide "full and customary access to the protected amount"[594] would appear to prohibit banks from closing accounts. Closing the account and sending a check for the remaining amount is not "full and customary access."

Additionally, it may be a violation of the FDCPA, a state debt collection statute, or a state UDAP statute if a creditor or collector threatens or issues repeat garnishments as a means of harassing a debtor who is known to have only exempt funds in the account.[595]

12.6.3.7 What If the Debtor Wants to Pay the Debt?

Occasionally a debtor may want to allow a garnishment to be implemented in whole or in part as a way of paying the debt. For example, the debtor may want to protect other non-exempt assets and may be able to work out a release of the entire debt in exchange for allowing the bank to pay some part of the protected amount to the creditor. The rule allows this, but only if the bank receives an express written instruction that is both dated and provided by the account holder to the bank after the date the garnishment order was served on the bank.[596] These requirements are designed to ensure that an account holder cannot instruct a financial institution in advance or in a standing agreement to use exempt funds to satisfy a garnishment order.[597] Other than this exception, "[t]he requirements of the rule may not be changed by agreement."[598]

12.6.3.8 Advising Clients: How to Make the Most of the Treasury Rule's Protections

Exempt funds delivered by paper checks are not protected under the Treasury rule and can only be protected through the applicable state process.[599] Beneficiaries who are receiving paper checks should consider switching to electronic deposit or to the Direct Express card.[600]

---

585 31 C.F.R. § 212.5(d)(1).

586 31 C.F.R. § 212.5(d)(2); 76 Fed. Reg. 9939, 9950 (Feb. 23, 2011).

587 31 C.F.R. § 212.6(b).

588 76 Fed. Reg. 9939, 9951 (Feb. 23, 2011). *See* Ala. Unified Judicial System, Form C-21 Rev. 11/06; Ga. Code Ann. § 18-4-111; 735 Ill. Comp. Stat. § 5/2-1402(f)(1); Iowa Code § 642.22; N.Y. C.P.L.R. § 5222(b) (McKinney); Pa. R. Civ. P. No. 3111.

589 31 C.F.R. § 212.6(g).

590 31 C.F.R. § 212.6(f).

591 *See* Comptroller's Handbook CC-GA, Consumer Compliance (CC), Garnishment of Accounts Containing Federal Benefit Payments 7, n.10 (Apr. 2014), *available at* www.occ.gov/publications/publications-by-type/comptrollers-handbook/pub-ch-garnishment-of-accounts.pdf (stating that a "new" garnishment order means that the creditor has gone back to court and obtained a new order, as opposed to refiling an order previously served, and that a garnishment order re-issued after the return date under a new number does not qualify as "new").

592 31 C.F.R. § 212.6(h). *See* § 12.6.4.3, *infra*.

593 76 Fed. Reg. 9939, 9946 (Feb. 23, 2011).

594 31 C.F.R. § 212.6(a).

595 *See* § 12.6.6, *infra*.

596 31 C.F.R. § 212.10(d)(3).

597 76 Fed. Reg. 9939, 9949 (Feb. 23, 2011).

598 76 Fed. Reg. 9939, 9949 (Feb. 23, 2011). *See also* 31 C.F.R. § 212.8(b) (rule does not invalidate terms or conditions of bank account agreements that are not inconsistent with the rule).

599 As of May 1, 2011, paper checks were no longer available—with few limited exceptions—for delivery of federal benefits to new recipients. As of March 1, 2013, the same rule applied to existing recipients. 31 C.F.R. pt. 208; 75 Fed Reg. 80,315 (Dec. 22, 2010).

600 *See* § 12.6.4.2, *infra*.

The rule will not provide full protection for benefit recipients who accumulate more than two months of benefits in their accounts, or who have not yet spent down a lump-sum payment. These beneficiaries are vulnerable to garnishment of whatever amount exceeds the "protected amount." For example, if an account contains $5000, but only two $2000 federal benefit payments were deposited within the last two months, the remaining $1000 is vulnerable. Although already-paid benefits cannot be transferred onto the card, switching to the Direct Express card will protect the full amount of future benefits. Otherwise, the beneficiary will have to rely on asserting the exemption through state court procedures. In the alternative, the beneficiary can withdraw cash or spend down the bank account to protect the full amount. However, any non-exempt items the beneficiary purchases may be vulnerable to execution and, although it is logistically difficult, the creditor may also be able to execute upon cash.

Beneficiaries should not transfer funds from one account to another, as the protections of the rule will not follow the transferred funds. For example, if a beneficiary receives a $1500 electronic deposit of federal benefits and transfers $1000 to a different account, leaving $500 in the first account, only the remaining $500 in the first account is protected by the rule. The $1000 transferred to the second account is vulnerable, although state law may protect this sum if it can be traced to the exempt benefits.

If there is any chance that a beneficiary will need to rely on state exemption procedures, the account should include just exempt benefits, not any other amounts, as some courts have denied state exemptions when the exempt funds were commingled with non-exempt funds.[601]

12.6.3.9 The Role of State Protections; Preemption and the Safe Harbor

The Treasury rule fills a significant gap. Federal law has long provided an absolute exemption for Social Security and other benefits but did not specify any effective mechanism for implementing this protection. State laws have also generally recognized the exemptions, but their procedures placed burdens on the beneficiary that often resulted in freezing or even loss of the protected funds.

While the rule fills this gap, there is still room for additional state protections. The Treasury rule protects only two months of benefits, and it applies only to certain federal benefits. States could enhance the Treasury rule's protections by adopting procedures similar to those required by the Treasury rule but applying them to a larger amount or additional types of benefits. One approach, which would also simplify compliance for banks, would be to create a flat, automatic exemption for a certain dollar amount in any bank account. Then, banks would only have to analyze accounts that exceeded that amount.

Even before the Treasury rule was adopted, some state exemption statutes and rules provided automatic protections along these lines. Pennsylvania court rules protect the first $10,000 of any account into which recurring exempt benefit payments are electronically deposited.[602] A California statute provides an automatic exemption for up to $2425 of directly deposited Social Security benefits,[603] which for some recipients may be more than the two months of benefits protected under the federal rule. Connecticut has a similar provision and specifically confers immunity on a bank that attempts in good faith to comply with the statute.[604] It also allows the serving officer to serve an execution on only one bank at a time and wait until the bank responds before serving the execution on another bank. New York protects a flat $2500 (adjusted periodically for inflation) if any reasonably identifiable exempt funds have been electronically deposited within forty-five days preceding service of a garnishment order.[605] However, the state's highest court has held that there is no private right of action for a bank's violation of this statute, and the debtor's only remedy is a special proceeding against the judgment creditor.[606]

The federal rule preempts state laws only to the extent that the state law prevents banks from complying with the rule.[607] A state law that protects a higher amount than the federal rule is not preempted if the bank can comply with both requirements.[608] Likewise, a state law prohibiting a bank from freezing exempt funds deposited by check is not preempted.[609]

601 *See* § 12.6.2.3, *supra*.

602 Pa. R. Civ. P. 3111.1.

603 Cal. Civ. Proc. Code § 704.080 (West). *See In re* Hernandez, 483 B.R. 713 (B.A.P. 9th Cir. 2012) (the automatic exemption protects Social Security benefits, and creditor that garnished benefits before debtor filed bankruptcy must surrender them); Shop Ironworkers Local 790 Pension Plan v. Cofab Steel Corp., 2008 WL 4790592 (N.D. Call. Oct. 30, 2008) (statutory amount automatically exempt; awarding balance to creditor because debtor failed to present evidence of exemption).

604 Conn. Gen. Stat. § 52-367b.

605 N.Y. C.P.L.R. § 5205 (McKinney). *See* LR Credit 22, L.L.C. v. Eggleston, 951 N.Y.S.2d 658 (N.Y. Sup. Ct. 2012) (detailed explanation of C.P.L.R. § 5222-1 procedures; here sanctioning creditor for non-compliance with rule requiring release of prejudgment freezes on accounts containing exempt funds); Midland Funding L.L.C. v. Roberts, 950 N.Y.S.2d 867 (N.Y. Sup. Ct. 2012) (exemption claim form filed by debtor need not be supported by documentation; it is prima facie evidence that funds are exempt, and shifts burden to creditor to demonstrate that they are not); LR Credit 21, L.L.C. v. Burnett, 967 N.Y.S. 2d 916 (N.Y. Dist. Ct. 2013) (creditor must plead and prove strict compliance with Exempt Income Protection Act; here ordering account unfrozen and denying bank fees when debt buyer failed to follow procedures; account here was joint and contained Social Security funds). *But see* Stephens v. Capitol One Fin. Corp., 2012 WL 2458173 (E.D.N.Y. June 22, 2012) (Exempt Income Protection Act does not apply when the creditor is the state—here for a tax debt); Distressed Holdings, L.L.C. v. Ehrler, 976 N.Y.S.2d 517 (N.Y. App. Div. Dec. 4, 2013) (restraining account without providing required notice denies due process; but refusing to lift restraint when creditor filed all proper forms and could not prevent bank's failure to forward them to debtor).

606 Cruz v. T.D. Bank, 2 N.E.3d 221 (N.Y. 2013).

607 31 C.F.R. § 212.9.

608 31 C.F.R. § 212.9(b). *See also* 31 C.F.R. § 212.5(d)(6) (bank must perform account review without consideration for any instructions to the contrary in the garnishment order).

609 *See* 76 Fed. Reg. 9939, 9941 (Feb. 23, 2011) ("The fact that the rule does not address Treasury checks in no way affects an individual's right

State laws are preempted if they would stand in the way of the automatic, self-executing protection of federal benefits that the Treasury rule requires.[610] For example, state laws that require banks to freeze the "protected amount" or that require the benefit recipient to take affirmative steps to assert the exemption are preempted.

The rule includes a safe harbor for banks that comply with it in good faith.[611] This safe harbor is intended primarily to prevent creditors from using state law remedies to force garnishee banks to freeze and turn over exempt funds.[612] The safe harbor also protects the bank from any claim by an account holder for freezing exempt funds in the limited circumstance under which a garnishment order from the federal government or a state child support enforcement agency results in the freezing of funds.

Any argument that that the safe harbor provides cover for a bank's violation of a more protective state law is rebutted by the explicit language in the preemption provision: "(b) Consistent law not preempted. This regulation does not annul, alter, affect, or exempt any financial institution from complying with the laws of any State with respect to garnishment practices, except to the extent of an inconsistency."[613] There is no inconsistency between the Treasury rule and a state's higher standard providing protection for exempt funds deposited by check, for example.

12.6.3.10 Bank Setoff and Bank Fees

The rule prohibits banks from debiting fees for processing the garnishment against the protected amount.[614] In addition, the bank may collect such a fee only on the day the account is reviewed, so the bank cannot collect a fee at all if an account contains only the protected amount on that day.[615] Except for these provisions, the rule is intentionally silent about bank setoff rights, including the key question of whether a bank can use setoff against exempt funds as a means of collecting a debt owed to the bank.[616] However, the prohibition against banks taking fees from the protected amount supports the idea that banks do not have unfettered access to exempt amounts.[617]

to assert or receive an exemption from garnishment by following the procedures specified under the applicable law").

610 31 C.F.R. § 212.9(a).

611 31 C.F.R. § 212.10(b).

612 76 Fed. Reg. 9939, 9952 (Feb. 23, 2011).

613 31 C.F.R. § 212.9(b).

614 31 C.F.R. § 212.6(h).

615 *Id.* Garnishment fees may be deducted from funds on deposit which are not included in the protected amounts. 76 Fed. Reg. 9939, 9947 (Feb. 23, 2011).

616 76 Fed. Reg. 9939, 9947 (Feb. 23, 2011).

617 *See* National Consumer Law Center, Consumer Banking and Payments Law § 10.2 (5th ed. 2013), *updated at* www.nclc.org/library (legality of banks' use of setoff against exempt funds).

12.6.4 Practical Ways of Protecting Exempt Funds After Payment

12.6.4.1 Separate Accounts or Special Purpose Accounts

There are a number of steps that recipients can take to protect exempt funds in a bank account. They should avoid placing the funds in a joint account, where the funds may be vulnerable to the other account holder's creditors. If someone else needs to have access to the funds because of the beneficiary's illness or absence, a power of attorney is a better approach. It is also best to avoid commingling the exempt benefits with non-exempt funds.

If the exempt benefits belong to someone else—for example, if the account holder is the representative payee for another person's Social Security benefits—the account should be unambiguously labeled, for example as an account held in trust for the other person.

If a debtor receives exempt benefits, but also has some non-exempt income or savings, the protection for the exempt benefits can be maximized by setting up two bank accounts, one to receive the exempt benefits and the other for the non-exempt funds. The debtor should then spend the non-exempt funds first.

12.6.4.2 Direct Express Card

The Direct Express card is a MasterCard-branded prepaid (stored value) debit card that the federal government uses as an alternative to direct deposit for most federal benefits payments, including Social Security, SSI funds, and VA benefits. It provides a way of protecting the full amount of these benefits from most garnishment orders.

The Treasury Department has entered into a contract with Comerica Bank to automatically disburse Treasury payments onto each card on the payment date.[618] The funds are loaded electronically and remotely, so beneficiaries need not go into a financial institution, government office, or check cashing outlet to obtain access to their benefits each month.

Benefits paid through the Direct Express Card cannot be frozen or garnished, except to the extent that the funds are not exempt under federal law, such as seizure of benefits to pay child support or alimony. In addition, Social Security (but not SSI) payments may be administratively offset, within limits, to satisfy debts owed to the federal government (such as taxes or student loans),[619] but administrative offsets are deducted from the payment before it is even made, whether that is by direct deposit, a paper check, or disbursement to the Direct Express card.

618 The terms of the Direct Express card are *not* set out by regulation, but only by Treasury's contract with Comerica, and this contract is not public. Thus this section is based on Treasury's statements found on its website.

619 *See* §§ 10.2.8.2, 10.2.8.3, 12.5.3, *supra*.

The Direct Express card can be used to withdraw cash from ATMs, make purchases at stores that accept MasterCard debit cards, get cash back when purchases are made, or make payments over the telephone or the Internet. It can be used to purchase money orders from the U.S. Post Office but cannot be used to write personal checks. Unlike some bank accounts, there are no overdraft fees. The card carries some fees, but they are relatively modest and recipients can avoid most of them.[620] Signing up is easy.[621]

The Direct Express card is discussed in more detail in another treatise in this series.[622]

12.6.4.3 Electronic Transfer Accounts (ETAs)

In 1996, in conjunction with an effort to replace paper checks with direct deposit as a means of disbursing federal benefits, salaries, and retirement pay,[623] the Treasury Department established a program for low-cost electronic transfer accounts (ETAs) for federal benefit recipients. These accounts can be a way to receive and protect exempt benefits. They are described in more detail in NCLC's *Consumer Banking and Payments Law*.[624]

Financial institutions are permitted, but not required, to offer low-cost ETAs to recipients for the direct deposit of federal benefits.[625] Once an institution decides to offer ETAs, however, it must make them available to any federal benefit recipient who requests one, regardless of credit history and without any minimum balance requirement.[626] There are limits on the fees that can be charged and minimum requirements for other terms and conditions for ETAs.

The Treasury requirements for ETA accounts specifically address the protection of exempt funds from attachment and set off.[627] Federal benefits may not be attached. A bank may choose to allow the deposit of funds other than federal benefits in an ETA, however, and these other funds are subject to attachment in the usual way. If the bank allows the deposit of non-exempt funds it must, at the time when the account is opened, explain to the customer that these funds may be attached. If the funds are attached the bank must promptly notify the customer.

12.6.5 *Judgment Creditor's Right to Garnish Funds in a Joint Bank Account May Be Limited to Debtor's Contribution*

12.6.5.1 Introduction

It is not unusual for an individual to list another person, perhaps a relative or friend, jointly on a bank account even though only one of them deposits funds into the account. The reason may be to facilitate care for an aging parent, hold money in trust for a child, or facilitate management of an account while a member of the armed forces is serving overseas. While listing another person on an account may be simpler than setting up a power of attorney or a trust account, the owner of the funds runs that risk that the other person's creditors will seek to garnish the funds.[628]

Some protection is provided for members of the armed forces by the Servicemembers Civil Relief Act, which one court has interpreted to require a judgment creditor to file a non-military affidavit for each joint tenant before executing on a joint account.[629] This ruling would mean that, when one owner of a joint account is in active military service, the court cannot enter a judgment or order[630] without appointing an attorney to represent the servicemember.[631]

Most jurisdictions are in agreement that joint accounts are subject to legal process by the creditor of a single co-depositor,[632] but only to the extent of the debtor-depositor's equitable interest in the funds.[633] In determining what portion

---

620 *See* http://fms.treas.gov/directexpresscard/questions.html (series of questions and answers about the card); National Consumer Law Center, Consumer Banking and Payments Law § 7.10.2, Appx. I.5 (5th ed. 2013), *updated at* www.nclc.org/library.

621 Social Security, SSI, and VA benefit recipients can sign up for the Direct Express Card by contacting Comerica Bank, at 1-877-212-9991 (toll-free) or by visiting www.USDirectExpress.com. For faster service, have available a copy of a Treasury check.

622 National Consumer Law Center, Consumer Banking and Payments Law § 7.10.2 (5th ed. 2013), *updated at* www.nclc.org/library.

623 31 U.S.C. § 3332(f)(1) (commonly known as "EFT-99").

624 National Consumer Law Center, Consumer Banking and Payments Law § 6.2.10 (5th ed. 2013), *updated at* www.nclc.org/library.

625 31 C.F.R. § 208.5; 64 Fed. Reg. 38,510 (July 16, 1999).

626 64 Fed. Reg. 38,510 (July 16, 1999).
The financial institution can, however, deny a recipient an account to someone who has committed fraud or abuse of an ETA account. *Id.*

627 64 Fed. Reg. 38,510, 38,512–38,514 (July 16, 1999).

628 *See, e.g., In re* Simkins, 2013 WL 6010496 (Bankr. D. Wyo. Nov. 13, 2013) (bank advised daughter that adding her name to account was only way to "monitor" account of elderly father who had been victimized by telemarketers; burden was on daughter, now a bankruptcy debtor, to prove her lack of "equitable interest" in the account; shown here when she neither deposited nor withdrew funds); Buehner v. Evansville Teachers Federal Credit Union, 999 N.E.2d 470 (Ind. Ct. App. 2013) (unpublished; not citable) (allowing garnishment of son's savings account for father's business debt; account opened "for [son] by [mother}" without the words "as custodian for" or cite to gifts to minors statute; even if addition of father's name to membership agreement was a mistake, son ratified it by using account after he attained majority); Branch Banking Trust Co. v. Bartley, 2006 WL 1113632 (Ky. Ct. App. Apr. 28, 2006) (father sued bank that allowed creditor to garnish non-custodial account containing minor son's funds; bank raised fact question on counterclaim that father breached fiduciary duty by setting up ordinary joint account and failing to respond to creditor's garnishment notice); Olbres v. Hampton Co-Op. Bank, 698 A.2d 1239 (N.H. 1997) (certificate of deposit held in trust for debtors' daughter could be set off by parents' creditor when trust was tentative trust—that is, statute allowed parents to use the money—and daughter had right of survivorship).

629 Palisades Acquisition, L.L.C. v. Ibrahim, 812 N.Y.S.2d 866 (N.Y. Civ. Ct. 2006).

630 *See* 50 U.S.C. app. § 511(9) (broad definition of "judgment" to include orders and rulings).

631 50 U.S.C. app. § 521(b)(2).

632 *See generally* L.C. Di Stasi, Jr., Annotation, *Attachment-Joint Bank Account*, 11 A.L.R.3d 1465, 1468 (1967).

633 *See, e.g., In re* Magness, 276 B.R. 167 (Bankr. N.D. Miss. 2002) (certificates of deposit held in names of debtor and his parents; bank may not set off funds held in trust for another; nature of funds, not name of account, is controlling, but key question is whether bank knew of trust

of the account represents the debtor's interest, some courts find the agreement between the bank and the depositors to be dispositive and irrebuttable.[634] More commonly, courts evaluate the realities of ownership and allow the non-debtor account holder to prove ownership of the funds in a joint account.[635]

Some jurisdictions, including Colorado,[636] Minnesota,[637] Nebraska,[638] New Mexico,[639] and South Dakota,[640] have a statute specifying how joint accounts are treated, usually adopting the rule that the parties own the funds in proportion to their net contributions.[641] Even a statute stating that funds in a joint account may be paid to either party does not establish the rights of the account holders against each other, however.[642]

In some circumstances there may be ambiguities about whether an account is a joint account or is just in the name of one person.[643] Only if the account is a joint account do these questions arise.

Some states allow married couples to own personal property, including bank accounts, as tenants by the entireties, which shields marital property from attachment for individual debts.[644] In community property states, a creditor can reach assets held in the name of a non-debtor spouse in some circumstances.[645]

The Eighth Circuit has held that due process is satisfied by giving a non-debtor depositor a post-garnishment opportunity to contest the seizure of funds in a joint account with the debtor.[646] It also rejected the non-debtor's claim that the failure to send her a separate notice denied her due process, when she had received actual notice of the garnishment.

12.6.5.2 The Contract Approach

A few courts have held that the agreement between the bank and the depositors is determinative and irrebuttable.[647] These agreements (and the laws which regulate them) usually provide that, in the absence of customers' instructions to the contrary, each co-depositor has a right to withdraw any or all of the funds at any time. If, it is reasoned, a single co-depositor has an absolute right to withdraw funds without notice to co-depositors and is able to use those funds for any purpose (including payment of the debt in question), a creditor should

---

or fiduciary relationship). *See also* LSF Franchise REO I, L.L.C. v. Emporia Restaurants, Inc., 152 P.3d 34, 41 (Kan. 2007) (garnishment is limited to "the actual, and not apparent, property of the defendant"; must be actual ownership, but this debtor failed to establish that funds in accounts were for payroll and taxes or were held in trust for taxing authorities). *See generally* 10 Am. Jur. 2d *Banks* §§ 662–674 (2009); L.C. Di Stasi, Jr., Annotation, *Attachment-Joint Bank Account*, 11 A.L.R.3d 1465, 1469 (1967).

634 *See* § 12.6.5.2, *infra*.

635 *See* § 12.6.5.3, *infra*.

636 Colo. Rev. Stat. § 15-15-211(2).

637 Minn. Stat. § 524.6-203(a). *See* Savig v. First Nat'l Bank of Omaha, 781 N.W.2d 335 (Minn. 2010) (statute does not prevent creditor from serving garnishment on joint account even when only one account holder is judgment debtor; debtor is rebuttably presumed to own entire account; burden is on account holders to show net contributions).

638 Neb. Rev. Stat. § 30-2722. *See* Craig v. Hasting State Bank, 380 N.W.2d 618 (Neb. 1986); LaBenz v. LaBenz, 575 N.W.2d 161 (Neb. Ct. App. 1998) (funds in joint account belong to parties in proportion to their net contributions unless there is clear and convincing evidence of contributing tenant's intent to make gift to non-contributor; husband's placement of funds, which he owned at time of marriage, in joint account with wife did not create a presumption of a gift). *Cf. In re* Overton, 169 B.R. 196 (Bankr D. Neb. 1994) (contract and security agreement allowed bank to set off account for debt of non-contributing account holder, but what was left after setoff belonged to sole depositor, not non-contributor's bankruptcy estate; contract governed relations of account holders with bank but not with one another).

639 N.M. Stat. Ann. § 58-1-7 (prescribing procedure for protection of non-debtor joint depositors). *But see* Alcantar v. Sanchez, 257 P.3d 966 (N.M. Ct. App. Apr. 22, 2011) (requirements of statute may be overridden by account agreement allowing garnishee bank to treat all funds in account as those of debtor; fact issue whether consumers here were bound by this agreement).

640 S.D. Codified Laws § 29A-6-103.

641 *See also* Wis. Stat. § 700.20 (tenants in common are presumed to own equal undivided interests if no intent is expressed in document of title, instrument of transfer, or bill of sale).

642 State v. Lavigne, 57 A.3d 332 (Conn. 2012) (affirming niece's larceny conviction for withdrawing and spending funds belonging to her aunt, even though they were in joint account).

643 *See, e.g.*, Grass v. Grass, 706 A.2d 1369 (Conn. App. Ct. 1998) (no joint account created when contract required signatures of both co-tenants but only one signed).

644 *See* § 12.8.5, *infra*.

645 United States v. Stallons, 2014 WL 1663074 (5th Cir. Apr. 28, 2014) (Texas law allows garnishment of joint management community property for debts of one spouse contracted before or during the marriage; garnishing joint accounts containing property of innocent husband for restitution for wife's crime); Nat'l Union Fire Ins. Co. v. Greene, 985 P.2d 590 (Ariz. 1999) (judgment creditor, who obtained judgment in a non-community property state, could garnish bank account of debtor and non-debtor spouse, who had moved to Arizona, a community property state, but non-debtor spouse must be given notice and an opportunity to be heard); Grover v. Bay View Bank, 104 Cal. Rptr. 2d 677 (Cal. Ct. App. 2001) (under California law creditor may levy on account of non-debtor spouse but must submit affidavit regarding marital relationship; when prescribed procedure not followed, bank could not freeze account and was not liable to creditor when spouse withdrew funds); *In re* Diafos, 37 P.3d 304 (Wash. Ct. App. 2001) (if debtor's individual property not sufficient, creditor may be able to reach half of community property for premarital debt; creditor allowed to challenge premarital agreement). *Cf.* Nat'l Bank of Ariz. v. Moore, 122 P.3d 1265 (N.M. Ct. App. 2005) (comparing Arizona and New Mexico garnishment law related to community property bank accounts; Arizona forbids collection of individual debt from community property, New Mexico allows debt to be satisfied from debtor-spouse's half interest; applying New Mexico law to New Mexico bank account owned by Arizona couple).

646 Lind v. Midland Funding, L.L.C., 688 F.3d 402 (8th Cir. 2012).

647 Fleet Bank v. Carillo, 691 A.2d 1068 (Conn. 1997) (by putting her money in joint account, non-debtor wife took risk that husband might use account to pay his individual debts, as either spouse could withdraw entire balance; husband's judgment creditor can reach entire account, and non-debtor has no right to establish actual ownership of the funds); Park Enters., Inc. v. Track, 47 N.W.2d 194 (Minn. 1951) (since deposit agreement gives debtor right to access entire account, it can be garnished in its entirety, and non-debtor co-owner has no right to establish ownership; now superseded by statute); Univ. of Mont. v. Coe, 704 P.2d 1029 (Mont. 1985) (right of third-party creditor to garnish joint account depends on terms of account agreement, regardless of evidence presented by account holders regarding actual ownership).

be able to "stand in the depositor's shoes," and attach the entire account.[648] Put more succinctly, an "unqualified contractual right to receive property is itself a property right subject to seizure by levy."[649]

Cases involving the banker's right of setoff should be distinguished from third-party garnishment cases. When a bank exercises the right of setoff, it is collecting its own debt by taking money from a bank account that the depositors established with it, so it is a party to the account agreement. Courts are less likely to find the account agreement binding and incontestable when a third party who is a stranger to the contract is seeking to garnish the account.[650] Cases holding the account agreement binding in disputes between the two holders of a joint account are also distinguishable, because both holders are parties to the account agreement.

One of the few decisions to hold the account agreement binding in a third-party garnishment situation is *University of Montana v. Coe*.[651] There, the Montana Supreme Court held that a creditor's right to garnish a joint account depends entirely on the terms of the deposit agreement, regardless of extrinsic evidence presented by the account holders regarding actual ownership of the funds. If the deposit agreement creates a joint tenancy, a creditor can reach the entire account. If it creates a tenancy in common, each account holder has an equal share in the account, and a creditor can reach only the debtor's share. The dissent characterized the court's rationale as "bewildering."

Some decisions stating that the account agreement is binding and incontestable arise in the context of a suit by the non-debtor account holder against the bank for having released the funds in response to the garnishment. These decisions usually go on to state that the non-debtor account holder could have raised the claim of ownership of the funds by intervening in the garnishment proceeding itself.[652] Thus, these decisions do not stand for the proposition that the account agreement is binding in the sense that it prevents the non-debtor from asserting a claim to the funds in the garnishment proceeding.

648 United States v. Nat'l Bank of Commerce, 472 U.S. 713, 105 S. Ct. 2919, 86 L. Ed. 2d 565 (1985) (IRS had right to levy on taxpayer's joint accounts since delinquent taxpayer had absolute right under Arkansas law to withdraw from joint accounts, but other owner can assert an ownership claim through IRS administrative procedure after levy).

649 St. Louis Union Trust Co. v. United States, 617 F.2d 1293, 1302 (1980) (IRS levy).

650 *See* Sears Roebuck & Co. v. Cosey, 44 P.3d 582, 584 (Okla. Civ. App. 2002) (distinguishing between right of bank that holds the deposit and right of third-party creditors). *But see* Fleet Bank v. Carillo, 691 A.2d 1068 (Conn. 1997) (refusing to make distinction between garnishment and setoff).

651 Univ. of Mont. v. Coe, 704 P.2d 1029 (Mont. 1985).

652 *See, e.g.*, Triplett v. Brunt-Ward Chevrolet, Oldsmobile, Pontiac, Cadillac, GMC Trucks, Inc., 812 So. 2d 1061 (Miss. Ct. App. 2001); Ingram v. Hocking Valley Bank, 708 N.E.2d 232 (Ohio Ct. App. 1997). *Cf.* Alcantar v. Sanchez, 257 P.3d 966 (N.M. Ct. App. 2011) (suggesting, in context of conversion and negligence claims against bank, that account agreement might be binding if non-debtor account holder had agreed to it, but also stating that, by statute, funds in joint account belong to the parties in proportion to their contributions).

12.6.5.3 The Net Contribution Approach

Other courts do not rely woodenly on the account agreement but hold that a third-party creditor can reach funds in a joint account only to the extent of the judgment debtor's actual ownership interest.[653] Courts generally place the burden on the account holders to establish their respective interests in the account and do not require the garnishee bank to investigate ownership.[654] (However, the bank does have a duty to abide by the terms of the account. For example, a bank will be liable to the depositors for paying over the funds in response to a garnishment if the account is not structured as a joint account—for example, if it requires the signatures of both account holders to withdraw funds.[655]

Often courts start with a presumption of one sort or another in determining whether funds in a joint account can be reached by a creditor that holds a judgment against one of the cotenants. Sometimes the presumption is established by statute. In some jurisdictions, a judgment debtor presumptively holds the entire account and, unless he or she is able to establish otherwise, all monies in the account may be reached.[656] In other

653 *See, e.g.*, *In re* Simkins, 2013 WL 6010496 (Bankr. D. Wyo. Nov. 13, 2013) (creditor can execute on joint account only to extent of debtor's equitable interest in it); Watlow Elec. Mfg. Co. v. Wrob, 881 S.W.2d 650 (Mo. Ct. App. 1994) (right of creditor to garnish joint account depends on actual ownership of funds in the account).

654 Triplett v. Brunt-Ward Chevrolet, Oldsmobile, Pontiac, Cadillac, GMC Trucks, Inc., 812 So. 2d 1061 (Miss. Ct. App. 2001) (bank has duty to implement garnishment of joint account, since account agreement gives either party right to withdraw the funds; bank has no duty to notify non-debtor joint account holder of garnishment; either holder could, however, intervene and assert non-debtor's ownership of the funds); Ingram v. Hocking Valley Bank, 708 N.E.2d 232 (Ohio Ct. App. 1997) (upholding summary judgment against consumer on claim against bank, creditor, and collector based on garnishment of joint account; under Ohio law, either party to joint account may withdraw entire amount, so bank properly turned over entire balance of joint account in response to garnishment, without inquiring into ownership, but opinion suggests that non-debtor co-owner can obtain release of the funds by requesting a hearing and presenting evidence of net contributions in court that issued the garnishment).

655 Ross v. Thrift Sav. & Loan Co., 573 N.E.2d 788 (Ohio Ct. App. 1989) (when account was established by spouses to freeze assets pending their divorce and required two signatures for withdrawal, equal ownership not presumed; bank wrongfully paid husband's creditor on a garnishment order when husband could not withdraw funds on his own signature).

656 Lind v. Midland Funding, L.L.C., 688 F.3d 402 (8th Cir. 2012) (Minnesota law) (all funds presumed to belong to debtor; burden on non-debtor to prove they do not); United States v. Seymour, 275 Fed. Appx. 278 (5th Cir. 2008) (reversing decision allowing garnishment of only half of joint account funded by debtor-husband; non-debtor wife failed to carry burden of proof as to her ownership rights; equitable division principles applicable at divorce not relevant here); Soc'y of Lloyd's v. Collins, 284 F.3d 727 (7th Cir. 2002) (non-debtor wife rebutted presumption of joint ownership when funds came from her rental property and account was used to pay her debts or joint debts; husband's use of account to pay credit card bill on which wife was jointly liable did not make it subject to garnishment); Ackley State Bank v. Thielke, 920 F.2d 521 (8th Cir. 1990) (Iowa law); Harp's Food Stores, Inc. v. Res. Group Servs., L.L.C., 2006 WL 2056648 (E.D. Okla. July 21, 2006) (non-debtor ex-wife rebutted presumption of debtor's

jurisdictions, it is presumed that co-depositors share equally in the ownership of the account.[657] Some decisions require clear and convincing evidence to rebut one of these presumptions.[658]

ownership; only funds in account were deposited by husband to satisfy court order requiring payment to wife upon refinancing of marital home); Puerto Rican Am. Ins. v. Burgos-Diaz, 2005 WL 1643299 (D. P.R. June 30, 2005) (mag.) (lifting attachment of joint bank account after father rebutted presumption of ownership by establishing that funds were his and that debtor son's name had been added for convenience); S & S Diversified Servs. L.L.C. v. Taylor, 897 F. Supp. 549 (D. Wyo. 1995) (when non-debtor claimed that funds in account came from her annuity, she must prove both ownership of the annuity and her intent in depositing funds in joint account); *In re* Grodetzky, 2012 WL 714349 (Bankr. E.D.N.Y. Mar. 5, 2012) (rebuttable presumption that debtor owns entire account; here debtors failed to show convenience account, but creditor allowed to attach only 50% of funds when both owners contributed); *In re* Tucker, 430 B.R. 499 (Bankr. N.D. Ill. 2010) (evidence that non-debtor deposited large sum not sufficient to rebut presumption); *In re* Johnson, 232 B.R. 735 (Bankr. C.D. Ill. 1999) (placing another's name on a bank account creates a presumption that a gift was intended, rebuttable only by clear and convincing evidence); *In re* Nunley, 19 B.R. 785 (Bankr. E.D. Tenn. 1982) (presumption of joint ownership created by bank account agreement can be rebutted by clear and convincing evidence); Maloy v. Stuttgart Mem'l Hosp., 872 S.W.2d 401 (Ark. 1994) (non-debtor, who contributed all funds to account, failed to rebut presumption with testimony that she intended to avoid probate, enable her children to write checks in an emergency, and shield funds from possible nursing home bills); Traders Travel Int'l, Inc. v. Howser, 753 P.2d 244 (Haw. 1988) (judgment debtor presumptively holds all of joint account and has burden of showing otherwise); Highsmith v. Dep't of Pub. Aid, 803 N.E.2d 652 (Ill. App. Ct. 2004) (burden on non-debtor to show ownership of funds); Brown v. Kentucky Natural Res. & Env't Cabinet, 40 S.W.3d 873 (Ky. Ct. App. 1999) (rebuttable presumption that debtor owned the whole account; trial court should consider net contributions of each spouse, whether non-debtor spouse was sufficiently removed from other spouse's indebtedness, and spouses' expectations about use of the funds); Delta Fertilizer, Inc. v. Weaver, 547 So. 2d 800 (Miss. 1989) (judgment debtor is rebuttably presumed to hold entire account, but rebutted when debtor's mother showed that she deposited all the funds); *In re* Estate of Johnson, 777 N.Y.S.2d 212 (N.Y. App. Div. 2004) (presumption of joint tenancy rebutted here by clear and convincing evidence of convenience account); Tayar v. Tayar, 618 N.Y.S.2d 35 (N.Y. App. Div. 1994) (opening of joint account creates presumption that each tenant is possessed of whole account; burden of proof on party seeking to rebut); Jiminez v. Brown, 509 S.E.2d 241 (N.C. 1998) (funds in joint account with minor son were available to creditors "to the extent of debtor's contribution to the account"; funds presumed to be those of debtor, burden on debtor and co-tenants to prove ownership); Sears Roebuck & Co. v. Cosey, 44 P.3d 582 (Okla. Civ. App. 2002) (presumption that joint account holder is entitled to use entire account may be rebutted even if account agreement allows single signature withdrawal; rebutted here by evidence that non-debtor mother deposited all the funds); Mitchell v. Mitchell, 756 A.2d 179 (R.I. 2000) (rebuttable presumption that putting name on joint account shows intent to make a gift, but convenience accounts still recognized); Russ *ex rel.* Schwartz v. Russ, 734 N.W.2d 874 (Wis. 2007) (depositor to joint account presumed to make gift to co-tenants, absent clear and convincing evidence of other intent). *See also* Dobbs v. Dobbs, 2008 WL 3843528 (S.D.N.Y. Aug. 14, 2008) (presumption that depositor into joint account intends a gift is rebuttable, regardless of account agreement's language; fact issue here whether deceased depositor intended convenience account); RPS, Inc. v. Travel-Max Int'l, Inc., 823 So. 2d 243 (Fla. Dist. Ct. App. 2002) (judgment creditor entitled to jury trial on question of whether funds in bank account belonged to debtor or to third-party claimant); Savig v. First Nat'l Bank of Omaha, 781 N.W.2d 335 (Minn. 2010) (there is a statutory presumption that co-depositors own the funds in proportion to their net contributions but, in garnishment proceeding, depositors have burden of proving their net contribution; without such a showing, the judgment debtor is presumed to have contributed all the funds); Food Servs. Corp. v. Rheam, 145 S.W.3d 484 (Mo. Ct. App. 2004) (non-debtor tenants may show that debtor contributed nothing and that they did not intend a gift; L. C. Di Stasi, Jr., Annotation, *Joint bank account as subject to attachment, garnishment, or execution by creditor of one of the joint depositors*, 11 A.L.R.3d 1465, 1476 (1967).

657 *See* Kieffer v. New Century Fin. Servs., Inc., 2011 WL 2489901 (D.N.J. June 21, 2011) (rebuttable presumption of 50/50 ownership); Blue Cross Blue Shield v. Askanzi, 2007 WL 2874012 (E.D. Mich. Sept. 25, 2007) (rebuttable presumption that each owner of joint account owns half the funds; rebutted here by tracing origin of funds); Fed. Deposit Ins. Corp. v. Koffman, 849 F. Supp. 176 (N.D.N.Y. 1994); *In re* Rochester, 2008 WL 1782350 (Bankr. D.N.M. Apr. 16, 2008) (rebuttable presumption that married joint owners made equal contributions; rebutted here when funds in account were wife's separate property and debtor-husband, whose name was added for estate planning purposes, never wrote checks on account); *In re* Kondora, 194 B.R. 202 (Bankr. N.D. Iowa 1996) (joint accounts presumed to be owned in equal shares, rebuttable by clear and convincing evidence; funds may be garnished only to the extent of the debtor's interest in the property); *In re* Baugh, 60 B.R. 102 (Bankr. E.D. Ark. 1986) (in absence of evidence of different contributions to an account jointly held by spouses, presumed that one-half of account was a gift to each other, making one-half of the account available to the creditor of one of them); Danielson v. Lazoski, 531 N.W.2d 799 (Mich. Ct. App. 1995); Univ. of Mont. v. Coe, 704 P.2d 1029 (Mont. 1985); Sicari v. First Fid. Bank, 668 N.Y.S.2d 406 (N.Y. App. Div. 1998) (parties to joint checking account are presumed to be entitled to equal shares); Velocity Invs., L.L.C. v. Kawski, 864 N.Y.S.2d 734 (N.Y. Dunkirk City Ct. 2008) (limiting creditor to half of joint account even though non-judgment debtor joint tenant did not respond after being served with garnishment petition); Velocity Invs. L.L.C./Citibank v. Astoria Fed. Sav. & Loan, 824 N.Y.S.2d 767 (N.Y. Dist. Ct. 2006) (presumption of fifty-fifty ownership, but fact question when non-debtor father testified that debtor daughter's name was on account only so she could write checks for invalid mother if he was "not around"); Vetter v. Hampton, 375 N.E.2d 804 (Ohio 1978); Citizens Fed. Sav. Bank v. Zierolf, 694 N.E.2d 496 (Ohio Ct. App. 1997) (presumption of equal ownership is rebuttable). *See also* LR Credit 10, L.L.C. v. Welsh, 851 N.Y.S.2d 70 (N.Y. Auburn City Ct. 2007) (if both debtor and non-debtor joint tenants default after service of garnishment petition, creditor is entitled to turnover of entire account); Ford Motor Credit Co. v. Astoria Fed., 189 Misc. 2d 475, 733 N.Y.S.2d 583 (N.Y. Dist. Ct. 2001) (non-debtor co-tenant's failure to respond to notice of garnishment of account was sufficient to rebut presumption that non-debtor owned 50% of account, so creditor could seize entire account). *Cf.* Kieffer v. New Century Fin. Servs., Inc., 2012 WL 1853895 (D.N.J. May 21, 2012) (not wrongful for creditor to issue garnishment against entire joint bank account despite statutory presumption that it was owned in equal shares by debtor and non-debtor spouse; account owners must follow statutory procedures to release funds). *See generally* L. C. Di Stasi, Jr., Annotation, *Joint bank account as subject to attachment, garnishment, or execution by creditor of one of the joint depositors*, 11 A.L.R.3d 1465, 1477 (1967).

658 *See, e.g.*, *In re* Johnson, 232 B.R. 735 (Bankr. C.D. Ill. 1999) (placing another's name on a bank account creates a presumption that a gift was intended, rebuttable by "clear and convincing" evidence, but hearing allowed on mother's claim that convenience account was intended, even though there was no written agreement as provided for by Illinois statute regarding trust and payable on death accounts); *In re* Kondora, 194 B.R. 202 (Bankr. N.D. Iowa 1996); *In re* Nunley, 19 B.R. 785 (Bankr. E.D. Tenn. 1982) (presumption of joint ownership created by bank account agreement can be rebutted by clear and convincing evidence);

Courts often find evidence of the net contribution of the joint depositors sufficient to establish each depositor's proportional ownership rights and to rebut any contrary presumption.[659] However, it may also be necessary for the non-debtor to establish that his or her contributions were not a gift to the debtor.[660] (Or, conversely, the debtor may seek to establish that his or her contributions to the account were a gift to the non-debtor, thereby placing them beyond the reach of the judgment creditor.[661])

12.6.6 *Liability for Wrongful Seizure of Bank Account Funds*

Judgment creditors and banks may be liable for wrongfully seizing funds from the debtor's bank account. For example, in *Cruthis v. Firstar Bank*,[662] the court upheld a jury determination that the bank had illegally converted funds from a debtor's checking account. Acting on a letter from the debtor's employer requesting the return of payroll deposits, the bank withdrew funds from the debtor's account without notice. While acknowledging that banks generally have a right of setoff, the court stated that the bank could not "offset" debts owed by the depositor to third parties. However, the court also found that the bank's lack of good judgment did not rise to the level of willful and wanton conduct such that it would support the jury's punitive damages award.

The more difficult question arises when a bank takes exempt funds from a depositor's account pursuant to writ of execution or other court order served by the judgment creditor. A number of courts have declined to impose liability on banks, holding that they have no duty to determine independently whether funds in an account are exempt.[663] However, given the

Craig v. Hasting State Bank, 380 N.W.2d 618, 623 (Neb. 1986); LaBenz v. LaBenz, 575 N.W.2d 161 (Neb. Ct. App. 1998); Fireman's Fund Ins. Co. v. Northwest Paving & Constr. Co., 891 P.2d 747 (Wash. Ct. App. 1995); Russ *ex rel.* Schwartz v. Russ, 734 N.W.2d 874 (Wis. 2007).

659 Coiro v. Wachovia Bank, 2011 WL 5196725 (D.N.J. Oct. 31, 2011) (denying bank's motion to dismiss action challenging its practice of freezing joint accounts if one owner files bankruptcy; applying New Jersey's net contribution rule to determine ownership of account and decide whether it is included in bankruptcy estate); *In re* Estate of Delaney, 819 A.2d 968 (D.C. 2003) (inheritance case; Dist. of Columbia law presumes convenience account, notwithstanding language of signature cards, when one party deposits all the funds); *In re* Kolodziejczyk & Rotella v. Wing, 689 N.Y.S.2d 825 (N.Y. App. Div. 1999) (testimony of mother that she owned money in joint account and had put her son's name on account only to confer right of survivorship was sufficient to rebut statutory presumption of joint ownership; money was not "available to" son so as to disqualify him for food stamps); Blanton v. Clark, 2002 WL 709958 (Ohio Ct. App. Apr. 19, 2002) (court will "look to the realities of ownership," but funds here were traceable to debtor); Fireman's Fund Ins. Co. v. Northwest Paving & Constr. Co., 891 P.2d 747 (Wash. Ct. App. 1995) (presumption that funds belong to co-tenants in proportion to amounts deposited by each may be rebutted by clear and convincing evidence of a contrary intent at the time the account was opened). *See also* Biliar v. Atl. Credit & Fin., Inc., 2011 WL 3418196 (D. Minn. Aug. 4, 2011) (freezing of non-debtor's funds in joint accounts was deprivation of property sufficient to invoke Due Process clause, but plaintiffs failed to state a claim when collector's cover letter instructed bank to freeze only debtor's funds); *In re* Estate of Mayer, 664 N.E.2d 583 (Ohio Ct. App. 1995) (when contributing co-tenant died, non-contributor owed the estate the sums she had withdrawn for her own use during his lifetime). *But see* Alcantar v. Sanchez, 257 P.3d 966 (N.M. Ct. App. 2011) (New Mexico follows net contribution rule but may be overridden by contract provision allowing garnishee bank to treat entire account as property of debtor). *But cf. In re* Houston, 2012 WL 4490890 (E.D. Mich. Sept. 26, 2012) (statute giving credit union the right to set off debt against entire account to which debtor is a party is more specific so is an exception to general multi-party account statute).

660 Hayden v. Gardner, 381 S.W.2d 752 (Ark. 1964) (garnishment allowed only to extent of debtor's ownership, which can be established by parol evidence of contributions and intent to make a gift); *In re* Estate of Shea, 848 N.E.2d 185 (Ill. App. Ct. 2006) (estate rebutted presumption that adding joint tenant was a gift when account owner had discussed, with lawyer and others, need for someone to pay bills and so forth if he became disabled); Highsmith v. Dep't of Pub. Aid, 803 N.E.2d 652 (Ill. App. Ct. 2004) (burden on non-debtor to show ownership of funds and lack of donative intent; when father funded account for son's education and son did not choose to be educated, this was at most a conditional gift and could not be reached for son's child support obligation); Enright v. Lehmann, 735 N.W.2d 326 (Minn. 2007) (by statute, funds belong to depositors in proportion to contribution; no garnishment of funds contributed by non-debtor, unless creditor can show intent to make gift to debtor); Craig v. Hasting State Bank, 380 N.W.2d 618, 623 (Neb. 1986) (Nebraska presumes that there is no intent to make a gift without clear and convincing evidence). *See also In re* Sciarra, 175 B.R. 2 (Bankr. D. Conn. 1994) (depositor told bank he wanted funds in certificate of deposit to pass to his brother upon depositor's death; brother's name, but not signature, on the signature card; no intent to make *inter vivos* gift, so certificate of deposit could not be set off for brother's debt); Food Servs. Corp. v. Rheam, 145 S.W.3d 484 (Mo. Ct. App. 2004) (non-debtors may show that debtor contributed nothing and that they did not intend a gift). *But cf.* Vitacco v. Eckberg, 648 N.E.2d 1010 (Ill. App. Ct. 1995) (Illinois presumes that depositor intends a gift to non-contributing co-tenants, but presumption overcome here by clear and convincing evidence of convenience account when elderly depositor sued his co-tenant after he learned she was writing checks to herself instead of paying his bills).

661 *See, e.g.*, Giove v. Stanko, 882 F.2d 1316 (8th Cir. 1989) (Nebraska law) (allowing creditor to garnish certificates of deposit held jointly by debtor and children; rejecting claim that debtor made a gift of the funds to the children which would have shielded the funds from garnishment); Gen. Elec. Capital Corp. v. Bunker Aircraft Mgmt., Inc., 2013 WL 6000018 (N.D. Ind. Nov. 12, 2013) (allowing garnishment of entire joint account for husband's debt when non-debtor wife, who did not contribute any of the funds, failed to establish that husband made a gift to the funds to her).

662 822 N.E.2d 454 (Ill. App. Ct. 2005). *See also* Odell v. Wallingford Mun. Fed. Credit Union, 2012 WL 4466339 (Conn. Super. Ct. Sept. 10, 2012) (credit union's use of setoff to seize Social Security funds was UDAP violation).

663 *See, e.g.*, Gorstein v. World Sav. Bank, 110 Fed. Appx. 9 (9th Cir. 2004) (bank has no duty to determine whether portion of funds in account were exempt); Kieffer v. New Century Fin. Servs., Inc., 2012 WL 1853895 (D.N.J. May 21, 2012) (garnishee bank has no duty to determine judgment debtor's share of funds in joint account); McCarthy v. Wachovia Bank, 759 F. Supp. 2d 265, 277–78 (E.D.N.Y. 2011); Chappell v. Friedman, 2009 WL 2246575 (D. Md. July 24, 2009) (bank has no duty to assert exemption or disburse exempt direct-deposited Social Security funds to debtor; burden is on debtor to claim exemptions). *See also* Alexander v. Bank of Am., 2007 WL 3046637 (W.D. Mo. Oct. 17, 2007) (bank not liable for six-week freeze of SSDI benefits; only remedy for violation of anti-alienation clause is release of garnishment, no intentional infliction of emotional distress when bank acted "promptly" to release garnishment; court assumes that bank could not

relative ease with which banks can now determine the source of electronic deposits and whether the accounts contain only exempt funds, courts are beginning to require them to exercise more diligence.[664] Indeed, a California statute requires the garnishee bank to do exactly that.[665] The 2011 rule adopted by the United States Treasury Department, discussed in § 12.6.3, *supra*, also requires banks to determine whether an account contains electronically deposited exempt federal benefits and to protect two months of benefits from garnishment.

Creditors and creditors' attorneys who wrongfully seize or freeze exempt funds in bank accounts may be subject to common law claims such as conversion,[666] negligence,[667] abuse of process,[668] civil conspiracy,[669] or intentional infliction of emotional distress.[670] They may also be subject to statutory claims for violations of the Fair Debt Collection Practices Act (FDCPA)[671] or state debt collection or deceptive practices

know funds were exempt until debtor formally claimed exemption); Parker v. Wetch & Abbot, P.L.C., 2006 WL 4846042 (S.D. Iowa July 11, 2006) (freeze of account containing exempt benefits did not violate anti-alienation clause of Social Security Act, state or federal fair debt collection acts, or state consumer protection law). *Cf.* Sykes v. Bank of Am., 723 F.3d 399 (2d Cir. 2013) (bank not a state actor when it obeyed wrongful garnishment notice from state child support agency, when plaintiffs did not allege that garnishment procedure itself was unconstitutional); London v. RBS Citizens, 600 F.3d 742 (7th Cir. 2010) (bank not acting under color of state law when it violated state law by freezing exempt funds in response to garnishment order clearly limited to non-exempt funds); Moore v. Branch Banking and Trust Co., 2010 WL 4962909 (W.D. Ky. Dec. 1, 2010) (bank that froze and disbursed non-debtor joint owner's SSDI funds not a state actor); Walton v. U.S. Bank, 2010 WL 3928507 (D. Utah Oct. 4, 2010) (bank not acting under color of state law when it responded to garnishment order by freezing account containing Social Security and veterans' benefits of debtor's non-debtor father; anti-alienation clause of Social Security Act does not confer private right of action against third-party garnishee).

664 *See* Granger v. Harris, 2007 WL 1213416 (E.D.N.Y. Apr. 17, 2007) (recipient stated section 1983 claim against bank that disbursed funds to creditor, despite knowledge that funds were Social Security funds; state statute imposing sanctions on bank that failed to comply with restraining order was state compulsion sufficient to allege action under color of state law); Mayers v. N.Y. Cmty. Bancorp, Inc., 2005 WL 2105810 (E.D.N.Y. Aug. 31, 2005) (recent changes in technology, for example, electronic direct deposit of Social Security benefits and ease of identifying deposits as exempt funds, require a re-evaluation of New York procedure allowing prejudgment freeze of bank accounts), *later decision at* 2006 WL 2013734 (E.D.N.Y. July 18, 2006) (denying defendants' motion for interlocutory appeal). *See also* Lincoln Fin. Servs., Inc. v. Miceli, 17 Misc. 3d 1109(A) (Dist. Ct. 2007) (table) (text available at 2007 WL 2917242) (ordering return of garnished Social Security funds and ordering creditor to include instructions and form in future restraining notices, allowing bank to report and not restrain Social Security funds). *But see* Christensen v. Ariz. Cent. Credit Union, 2008 WL 4853414 (D. Ariz. Nov. 10, 2008) (42 U.S.C. § 407(a) provides cause of action against creditor's lawyers but not garnishee bank).

665 Cal. Civ. Proc. Code § 704.080 (West). *See* Chung v. Bank of Am., 2004 WL 1938272 (Cal. Ct. App. 2004) (bank garnishee had duty to verify whether funds were exempt).

666 Phillips v. Messerli & Kramer, 2008 WL 5050127 (D. Minn. Nov. 20, 2008) (allowing negligence claim to go forward against law firm that levied on third party's funds that were in joint account with judgment debtor; litigation privilege does not protect the firm); Rahaman v. Weber, 2005 WL 89413 (Minn. Ct. App. Jan. 18, 2005) (procedure for claiming exemption, including damages if creditor seized exempt property, did not preclude common law causes of action for conversion against creditor and its attorneys). *But cf.* Cruz v. T.D. Bank, 2 N.E.3d 221 (N.Y. 2013) (no private right of action for bank's violation of state Exempt Income Protection Act, and debtor's only remedy is a special proceeding against judgment creditor).

667 Phillips v. Messerli & Kramer, 2008 WL 5050127 (D. Minn. Nov. 20, 2008) (allowing negligence claim to go forward against law firm that levied on third party's funds that were in joint account with judgment debtor; litigation privilege does not protect the firm); Alcantar v. Sanchez, 257 P.3d 966 (N.M. Ct. App. 2011) (allowing negligence claim to go forward against bank that failed to notify non-debtor depositors of garnishment of joint account for debt of one depositor).

668 Davis v. Nebraska Furniture Mart, Inc., 2012 WL 1252633 (D. Kan. Apr. 13, 2012) (knowingly garnishing bank account containing only exempt funds is abuse of process; fact issues here as to knowledge, when account was in out-of-state bank used by Department of Employment Security for direct deposit of benefits and debtor was known to be unemployed); Hogue v. Palisades Collection, Inc., 494 F. Supp. 2d 1043 (S.D. Ohio 2007) (debtor stated abuse of process claim against creditor and its attorney who continued garnishment after being shown affidavit and bank statements showing that account contained only exempt Social Security benefits). *But see* Parker v. Wetch & Abbot, P.L.C., 2006 WL 4846042 (S.D. Iowa July 11, 2006) (garnishment of exempt funds in bank account not abuse of process, as procedure was used for its intended purpose). *But cf.* Smith v. Levine, 2006 WL 3704622 (Cal. Ct. App. Dec. 18, 2006) (unpublished) (litigation privilege barred abuse of process claim arising from levy on non-debtor's account and conversion claim arising from refusal to return improperly seized funds).

669 Estrada v. Mendoza, 275 P.3d 1024 (Utah Ct. App. 2012) (allowing consumer to proceed with civil conspiracy claim based on UDAP violation involving deception in obtaining writ to garnish more than the amount owed, but claim based on fraud is dependent on a determination that the underlying garnishment orders were illegal so is barred by collateral estoppel).

670 Albright v. Allied Int'l Credit Corp, 2003 WL 22350928 (C.D. Cal. Aug. 25, 2003) (refusing to dismiss claim that creditor committed tort of intentional infliction of emotional distress by threatening to garnish exempt benefits).

671 *See* Todd v. Weltman, 434 F.3d 432 (6th Cir. 2006), *on remand*, 2008 WL 419943 (S.D. Ohio Feb. 14, 2008) (fact question whether affidavits were deceptive or unconscionable in violation of FDCPA and, if so, whether bona fide error defense proven); Kieffer v. New Century Fin. Servs., Inc., 2011 WL 2489901 (D.N.J. June 21, 2011) (couple stated FDCPA claim; levy on joint account containing mostly non-debtor's earnings was unfair tactic to pressure husband to pay wife's pre-marital debt; fact issue whether creditor knew account was joint); Bray v. Cadle Co., 2010 WL 4053794 (S.D. Tex. Oct. 14, 2010) (FDCPA claim: garnishment of account knowing or having reason to know that it contained only exempt funds and refusal to release funds upon showing that they were exempt); Phillips v. Messerli & Kramer, 2008 WL 5050127 (D. Minn. Nov. 20, 2008) (allowing FDCPA claim to go forward against law firm that levied on third party's funds that were in joint account with judgment debtor; litigation privilege does not protect the firm); Lee v. Javitch, Block, & Rathbone, 522 F. Supp. 2d 945 (S.D. Ohio 2007) (fact question whether statutory requirement of "reasonable cause to believe" met when large-volume collection firm did crude screening, eliminating debtors aged over age sixty-five with no employer or trade lines listed on credit report; denying summary judgment on FDCPA and UDAP claims); Hogue v. Palisades Collection, Inc., 494 F. Supp. 2d 1043 (S.D. Ohio 2007) (debtor stated claim under federal and Iowa fair debt collection acts and Iowa Uniform Consumer Credit Code against creditor and its attorney who continued garnishment after being shown affidavit and bank statements showing that account contained only

statutes.[672] The debtor may also have a private cause of action directly under the anti-alienation provision of the Social Security Act.[673] If the state procedures are insufficient to satisfy due process requirements, the debtor may have a section 1983 claim against the state actors and any private parties who acted in concert with them.[674]

Cases have often turned on the question of whether the creditor or collector knew the funds were exempt, or falsely stated in court filings that it had reason to believe they were not exempt.[675] For example, in *Todd v. Weltman*,[676] a collection attorney had obtained a bank account garnishment order by submitting an affidavit stating that "the affiant has a reasonable basis to believe that the [bank] may have property, other than personal earnings, of the judgment debtor that is not exempt under the law of this state or the United States."[677] In fact, according to the complaint, the bank account contained solely Social Security benefits. The plaintiffs alleged that the collection attorney had not conducted a debtor's exam, undertaken discovery, or had any factual basis for believing that the bank account contained non-exempt funds. The Sixth Circuit denied the attorney's immunity claim, thereby allowing the plaintiff to proceed on his claim that the collection attorney

exempt Social Security benefits); Jordan v. Thomas & Thomas, 2007 WL 2838474 (S.D. Ohio Sept. 26, 2007) (FDCPA claim stated; frozen account contained only exempt Social Security funds; fact question whether collector's attorneys conducted investigation or had reasonable cause to believe account contained non-exempt funds); Estrada v. Mendoza, 275 P.3d 1024 (Utah Ct. App. 2012) (allowing consumer to proceed with UDAP claim based on creditor's deception in obtaining writs of garnishment for more than amount owed; collateral estoppel does not bar this claim because consumers are not seeking to have the writs withdrawn or the garnishments released). *See also* Biliar v. Atl. Credit & Fin., Inc., 2011 WL 3418196 (D. Minn. Aug. 4, 2011) (FDCPA violation if creditor's employee stated that creditor could seize non-debtor's funds from joint accounts); Strom v. Nat'l Enter. Sys., Inc., 2011 WL 1233118 (W.D.N.Y. Mar. 30, 2011) (threat to seize or freeze exempt Social Security violates FDCPA); Stewart v. Cheek & Zeehandelar, L.L.P., 252 F.R.D. 387 (S.D. Ohio 2008) (granting class certification on claim that law firm and collector violated FDCPA and state consumer protection law by bringing garnishment actions and freezing bank accounts without investigating whether bank accounts contained non-exempt funds). *Cf.* Henneberger v. Cohen & Slamowitz, L.L.P., 2010 WL 1405578 (W.D.N.Y. Mar. 31, 2010) (freezing account containing only exempt benefits did not violate FDCPA because collector had right to use New York procedure to determine whether debtor's claim of exemption was valid, but threatening to take exempt funds did violate provisions forbidding harassing conduct or threat to take action that could not legally be taken). *But see* Beler v. Blatt, Hasenmiller, Liebsker, Moore, L.L.C., 480 F.3d 470 (7th Cir. 2007) (law firm's service of citation on bank that resulted in three-week freeze on account containing only exempt SSI funds not unfair or unconscionable under FDCPA when procedure complied with state law); Riordan v. Jaburg & Wilk, P.C., 2010 WL 3023292 (D. Ariz. July 30, 2010) (no FDCPA claim against law firm that repeatedly froze account containing only exempt Social Security); Lange v. CIR. Law Offices, 2010 WL 2524089 (S.D. Cal. June 22, 2010) (FDCPA and state debt collection act claims fail; must show knowing garnishment of exempt funds; creditor has no duty to investigate source of funds when California law places that duty on garnishee financial institution); Hollowell v. Hosto, 2010 WL 1416519 (E.D. Ark. Apr. 8, 2010) (no FDCPA claim against law firm that froze account containing exempt Social Security when debtor did not allege that he asserted exemption; state may place reasonable burden on debtor to claim exemptions), *aff'd as modified*, 389 Fed. Appx. 583 (8th Cir. 2010) (modifying district court order to dismiss all claims with prejudice); Wetherelt v. Larsen Law Firm, P.L.L.C., 577 F. Supp. 2d 1128 (D. Mont. 2008) (dismissing FDCPA claim; not unfair or unconscionable to freeze account containing only Social Security funds; debtor's statement to creditor was unsworn and Montana provides no alternative ways to find out if account contains non-exempt funds).

672 Lee v. Javitch, Block, & Rathbone, 522 F. Supp. 2d 945 (S.D. Ohio 2007) (fact question whether statutory requirement of "reasonable cause to believe" met when large-volume collection firm did crude screening, eliminating debtors aged over age sixty-five with no employer or trade lines listed on credit report; denying summary judgment on FDCPA and UDAP claims); Estrada v. Mendoza, 275 P.3d 1024 (Utah Ct. App. 2012) (allowing consumer to proceed with UDAP claim based on creditor's deception in obtaining writs of garnishment for more than amount owed; collateral estoppel does not bar this claim because consumers are not seeking to have the writs withdrawn or the garnishments released). *But see* Lange v. CIR. Law Offices, 2010 WL 2524089 (S.D. Cal. June 22, 2010) (FDCPA and state debt collection act claims fail; must show knowing garnishment of exempt funds; creditor has no duty to investigate source of funds when California law places that duty on garnishee financial institution); Parker v. Wetch & Abbot, P.L.C., 2006 WL 4846042 (S.D. Iowa July 11, 2006) (freeze of account containing exempt benefits did not violate anti-alienation clause of Social Security Act, state or federal fair debt collection acts, or state consumer protection law).

673 Christensen v. Ariz. Cent. Credit Union, 2008 WL 4853414 (D. Ariz. Nov. 10, 2008) (anti-alienation provision of the Social Security Act provides a cause of action against creditor's lawyers but not garnishee bank), *later op. at* 2008 WL 5054562 (D. Ariz. Nov. 24, 2008) (allowing claim under anti-alienation provision to go forward against debt buyer); Albright v. Allied Int'l Credit Corp., 2003 WL 22350928 (C.D. Cal. Aug. 25, 2003) (denying motion to dismiss claim that collector violated anti-alienation provision by threatening to garnish exempt benefits). *But see* Strine v. Gennessee Valley Credit Union, 2013 WL 636469 (W.D. N.Y. Jan. 29, 2013), *adopted by* 2013 WL 636714 (W.D.N.Y. Feb. 20, 2013) (no private right of action for violation of anti-alienation provision); Alexander v. Bank of Am., 2007 WL 3046637 (W.D. Mo. Oct. 17, 2007) (unpublished) (no private right of action for violation, by creditor, creditor's attorney, or bank, of the anti-alienation provision; only remedy is release of the garnishment); Zeppieri v. New Haven Provision Co., 163 F. Supp. 2d 126 (D. Conn. 2001) (anti-alienation provision's exemption of Social Security funds in bank account is not self-executing, so sheriff not liable under section 1983 for role in executing upon exempt funds). *But cf.* Parker v. Wetch & Abbot, P.L.C., 2006 WL 4846042 (S.D. Iowa July 11, 2006) (freeze of account containing exempt benefits did not violate anti-alienation clause of Social Security Act, as state law provided adequate procedural mechanism for debtor to assert exemption).

674 *See* § 12.3, *supra*.

675 *See, e.g.*, Lange v. CIR. Law Offices, 2010 WL 2524089 (S.D. Cal. June 22, 2010) (collection firm not liable under federal and state debt collection statutes without evidence that it knew funds were exempt); Hogue v. Palisades Collection, Inc., 494 F. Supp. 2d 1043 (S.D. Iowa 2007) (debtor stated abuse of process claim against creditor and its attorney who continued garnishment after being shown affidavit and bank statements showing that bank account contained only exempt funds).

676 434 F.3d 432 (6th Cir. 2006).

677 Todd v. Weltman, 434 F.3d 432, 435 (6th Cir. 2006). *See also* Rahaman v. Weber, 2005 WL 89413 (Minn. Ct. App. Jan. 19, 2005); Contact Res. Servs., L.L.C. v. Gregory, 806 N.Y.S.2d 407 (N.Y. City Ct. 2005) (protective order requires creditor to include in prejudgment restraining notice statement that notice ineffective as to accounts containing only exempt SSI and SSD benefits).

violated the FDCPA by using unfair methods and false, deceptive, and misleading representations to collect the debt.

Standing to sue various defendants can be an issue when bringing suit because of the wrongful seizure of exempt funds, especially if the suit names defendants who have control over, and ability to change, the statewide procedures that allow such seizures. To establish standing, a plaintiff must show that: (1) he or she has suffered an injury in fact; (2) the injury is "fairly traceable" to the defendant's action; and (3) the injury can likely be redressed by the cause of action.[678] One decision held that a debtor did not have standing to sue the chief justice of the state supreme court who had approved or issued the garnishment forms, or the court clerks who issued the writs of garnishment, when the debtor's complaint alleged that the wrongful temporary seizure of her exempt funds resulted from misuse of the forms.[679] If the complaint had alleged that the injury resulted from state's procedure itself, the result might have been different. By contrast, although it did not address standing, another decision allowed a suit that challenged the state bank account garnishment procedures to go forward against the state's chief judge and chief administrative judge, who had general administrative authority over the state courts that issued garnishment orders.[680] The court also allowed the suit to go forward against the state superintendent of banks, who supervised and regulated the banks that process garnishment orders.

12.7 Homestead Exemptions

12.7.1 *Introduction*

Homestead exemptions are designed to protect the home for the debtor and the debtor's family. The only states that do not provide homestead exemptions for debtors outside of bankruptcy are Maryland, New Jersey, and Pennsylvania.[681] However, the states that have homestead exemptions vary widely in the amount and nature of the exemption.[682]

12.7.2 *What Homesteads Are Protected?*

12.7.2.1 Dollar Amounts or Acreage Protected

The amount of the homestead exemption varies significantly from state to state. For example, Alabama allows $5000 and Massachusetts allows up to $500,000.[683] Florida does not set a dollar amount but allows up to 160 acres outside a municipal area and a half acre within a municipal area.[684] Some states provide a larger homestead exemption for older or disabled persons.[685] Tennessee provides an enhanced exemption for persons having legal custody of a minor child.[686] When a statute caps the value of an exempt parcel of land, but not its acreage, there is no limit on the size of the parcel.[687]

The dollar amount of the homestead exemption generally refers to the debtor's equity in the property. For example, if a $200,000 property is encumbered by a $190,000 mortgage, then a $10,000 homestead exemption will make it completely exempt.[688] California's automatic homestead exemption bars a

678 Lujan v. Defenders of Wildlife, 504 U.S. 555, 560–61, 112 S. Ct. 2130, 119 L. Ed. 2d 351 (1992).

679 Christensen v. Ariz. Cent. Credit Union, 2008 WL 4853414 (D. Ariz. Nov. 10, 2008).

680 Mayers v. N.Y. Cmty. Bancorp, Inc., 2005 WL 2105810 (E.D.N.Y. Aug. 31, 2005).

681 *See* Appx. G, *infra*.

682 *See* Appx. G, *infra*; National Consumer Law Center, No Fresh Start: How States Allow Debt Collectors to Push Families into Poverty (Oct. 2013), *available at* www.nclc.org/issues/no-fresh-start.html (state-by-state comparison of homestead exemptions).

683 Ala. Code § 6-10-2; Mass. Gen. L. Ann. Ch. 188, § 1.

684 Braswell v. Braswell, 890 So. 2d 379 (Fla. Dist. Ct. App. 2004) (discussing method of calculating half acre, here considering rights in common areas of condo complex).

685 *See, e.g.*, *In re* Bush, 346 B.R. 207 (Bankr. S.D. Cal. 2006) (explaining method of calculating income, for California statute granting enhanced homestead exemption to low-income debtors age 55 and older: sole proprietor of small business may deduct cost of goods and any legitimate business expenses but not "investment losses"); *In re* Sweitzer, 332 B.R. 614 (Bankr. C.D. Cal. 2005) (investment losses may be deducted in calculating gross income to determine eligibility for enhanced homestead exemption available to debtors age fifty-five or over with gross annual income below $15,000); *In re* Rolland, 317 B.R. 402 (Bankr. C.D. Cal. 2004) (debtors not entitled to increased exemption for "physically or mentally disabled," when wife, although diagnosed with depression, claimed monthly income from self-employment and monthly expense for self-employment tax); *In re* LaHaye, 2003 WL 22764771 (Bankr. N.D. Cal. Sept. 10, 2003) (standard for disability same as for Social Security disability; burden of proof on objector; when evidence inconclusive, enhanced exemption allowed); *In re* Davis, 681 N.W.2d 452 (S.D. 2004) (increased homestead for the elderly permissible, but unlimited exemption violates state constitutional requirement of reasonableness); Tarlesson v. Broadway Foreclosure Invs., L.L.C., 109 Cal. Rptr. 3d 319 (Cal. Ct. App. 2010) (debtor who swore she was over fifty-five, unmarried, and had an income less than $15,000 was entitled to enhanced $150,000 homestead; burden was on creditor to show she was not entitled); Shamban v. Masidlover, 705 N.E.2d 1136 (Mass. 1999) (disabled person who filed declaration of homestead claiming $200,000 exemption, but failed to include statutorily required evidence of disability, could claim only standard $100,000 exemption). *But cf. In re* Collet, 351 B.R. 395 (Bankr. W.D. La. 2006) (Louisiana's enhanced homestead exemption for debts "arising directly" from "catastrophic or terminal illness or injury" did not apply when part of borrowed money used for family living expenses while debtor recovered from surgery).

686 *In re* Allman, 2011 WL 4053129 (Bankr. E.D. Tenn. Sept. 12, 2011) (in case of non-parent, court order must be shown; couple who cared for minor child of their incarcerated daughter, pursuant to revocable power of attorney, not entitled to exemption).

687 *In re* Gregory, 229 B.R. 168 (Bankr. N.D. Ohio 1999).

688 *See, e.g.*, KLC, Inc. v. Trayner, 426 F.3d 172 (2d Cir. 2005) (after payment of consensual and statutory liens, but not judgment liens, debtor entitled to foreclosure sale proceeds up to amount of exemption); *In re* Cox, 315 B.R. 850, 858 (B.A.P. 8th Cir. 2004) (Iowa law) (homestead exemption applies to equity in the residence, that is, value of home minus amount of consensual liens); Martone-Rosato v. Guardiano-Neizwanger, 2001 Conn. Super. LEXIS 1294 (Conn. Super. Ct. Apr. 11, 2001) (lien may be placed against property if owner's equity exceeds statutory exemption), *aff'd*, 802 A.2d 927 (Conn. App. Ct. 2002) (table); Kipp v. Sweno, 629 N.W.2d 468 (Minn. Ct. App. 2001) (remanding to determine if equity exceeded cap); Baumann v. Chaska Bldg. Ctr., Inc., 621 N.W.2d 795 (Minn. Ct. App. 2001) (cap on homestead exemption applies to owner's equity, not fair market value); State *ex*

forced sale, unless a court finds that the proposed sale will bring in more than the amount of existing encumbrances plus the homestead exemption amount.[689]

If the area or value of the homestead exceeds the statutory cap, the court may divide the land into exempt and non-exempt parcels.[690] If division is not feasible, for example, a quarter acre homestead in a suburb with one acre zoning, the homestead may be sold and the debtor will receive the exempt amount.[691]

12.7.2.2 Distinctions Between Rural and Urban Homesteads

Many states distinguish between rural and urban homesteads, exempting much more land,[692] and sometimes allowing much higher value,[693] for rural homesteads. The enhanced exemption may be available only if the land is used for agricultural purposes.[694] Some states also provide a separate exemption for personal property used in agriculture.[695]

The urban/rural distinction presents difficult problems when land uses are changing, municipalities are expanding into formerly unincorporated areas, and farmers turn to non-agricultural work to sustain themselves. Courts will generally consider first the character of the area, then whether the individual parcel is used for traditionally rural activities that support the family.[696] The availability of municipal services is often determinative. A parcel that lacks sewer or fire protection service, or that is protected by the county sheriff rather

rel. Koster v. Quick, 332 S.W.3d 199 (Mo. Ct. App. 2010) (homestead amount in Missouri Incarceration Reimbursement Act refers to debtor's equity in property); Miller Constr. Co. v. Coltran, 43 P.3d 67 (Wash. Ct. App. 2002) (in determining whether equity is available to satisfy judgment lien, only liens senior to the judgment lien may be considered). *See also In re* Anderson, 378 B.R. 296 (Bankr. W.D. Wash. 2007) (judgment lien can attach to homestead only if there is equity in excess of homestead amount); *In re* DeLavern, 337 B.R. 239 (Bankr. W.D. Wash. 2005) (filing a judgment creates lien on value of homestead in excess of exemption; when debtors' equity was less than exemption amount, judgment creditor was unsecured); *In re* Contrevo, 153 P.3d 652 (Nev. 2007) (judgment lien cannot attach to fully exempt property). *But cf. In re* Watts, 298 F.3d 1077 (9th Cir. 2002) (California law; creditor may file lien on property in which debtor has no non-exempt equity and may execute once equity is created by appreciation of home and pay down of mortgage).

689 Fidelity Nat'l Title Ins. v. Schroeder, 179 Cal. App. 4th 834 (Cal. Ct. App. 2009) (creditor could not show injury in fact, a prerequisite for setting aside a fraudulent transfer, when prior encumbrances plus homestead exemption exceeded the value of the transferred property).

690 *In re* Bradley, 294 B.R. 64 (B.A.P. 8th Cir. 2003) (Arkansas law) (allowing debtors to select which quarter acre was homestead, the value of which would be paid to them out of proceeds); *In re* Wait, 2009 WL 3151184 (Bankr. N.D. Iowa Sept. 1, 2009) (choosing between debtor's and trustee's proposals for division; allowing debtor to keep house and certain out-buildings, leaving two square parcels for sale). *See also In re* Hartley, 483 B.R. 700 (Bankr. W.D. Wis. 2012) (large parcel could be divided into homestead and non-homestead parcels).

691 Siewak v. AmSouth Bank, 2007 WL 141186 (M.D. Fla. Jan. 16, 2007) (fact issue whether property could be divided, or must be sold and proceeds apportioned); *In re* Quraeshi, 289 B.R. 240 (S.D. Fla. 2002) (when half acre was 19% of total acreage, debtor allowed to exempt 19% of net proceeds of sale); *In re* Bradley, 301 B.R. 546 (Bankr. W.D. Ark. 2003) (formula for allocating sales proceeds if zoning or subdivision covenant prevents division). *See also In re* McCabe, 299 B.R. 564 (Bankr. N.D. Iowa 2003) (no "equitable exception" to Iowa's half acre limit for urban homestead; partition will result in parcels of low value); Jackson v. Halls, 314 P.3d 1065 (Utah Ct. App. 2013) (after sale debtor must receive homestead amount in cash, not as credit against judgment; other interpretation would nullify provision making proceeds exempt for one year). *But cf. In re* Weathers, 423 B.R. 530 (Bankr. W.D. Ark. 2009) (when home located on 0.3 acre parcel, which could not be subdivided, debtors allowed to keep their home and buy back the 0.05 acres by which the lot exceeded the 0.25 acre limit, at a price calculated by the court).

692 *See, e.g.*, Ark. Code Ann. § 16-66-210 (quarter acre or eighty acres); La. Rev. Stat. Ann. § 20:1 (five acres or 200 acres); Tex. Prop. Code Ann. § 41.002 (West) (ten acres or 100 acres for individual, 200 acres for family).

693 *See, e.g.*, Minn. Stat. § 510.02 ($975,000 agricultural; otherwise $300,000). These amounts are adjusted on July 1 of even-numbered years, for changes in the Consumer Price Index. Minn. Stat. 550.37(4a).

694 *See, e.g.*, *In re* Grimlie, 439 B.R. 710 (B.A.P. 8th Cir. 2010) (Minnesota law) (denying enhanced agricultural exemption; debtors not principally engaged in farming when property was used to raise horses and hay but most income came from manufacture and sale of equipment); *In re* Baker, 307 B.R. 860 (Bankr. N.D. Tex. 2003) (cattle grazing and hunting on non-contiguous parcels is sufficient; placing land in conservation reserve does not eliminate homestead).

695 *See* § 12.8, *infra*.

696 *In re* Perry, 345 F.3d 303, 315–19 (5th Cir. 2003) (rural homestead may be exempt under former version of statute even if used for non-agricultural purposes, here a campground); Painewebber Inc. v. Murray, 260 B.R. 815 (E.D. Tex. 2001) (factors include municipal services, location of the land, presence of platted streets; rural homestead was exempt when contiguous and non-contiguous tracts used for residence, recreation, gardening, hunting, woodcutting, and fishing); *In re* Schott, 449 B.R. 697 (Bankr. W.D. Tex. 2011) (operation of non-agricultural business, here a golf course, on rural parcel does not eliminate homestead); *In re* Engstrom, 370 B.R. 205 (Bankr. D. Minn. 2007) ("rural" not synonymous with "agricultural"; low-density use and lack of subdivisions were sufficiently rural to permit exemption of five-acre lot not used for farming); *In re* McLachlan, 266 B.R. 220 (Bankr. M.D. Fla. 2001) (homeowner in rural area could exempt contiguous lot with palm grove from which he occasionally sold palm trees; land can be part of rural homestead even though it is income producing); *In re* Kyllonen, 264 B.R. 17 (Bankr. D. Minn. 2001) (homestead not rural, despite debtors' small-scale ginseng crop, when both debtors had full-time non-agricultural jobs, neighborhood was suburban and zoned "rural residential," main land use was houses, and any farming was hobby; if character of the area is unclear, court will look at parcel's use); *In re* Webb, 263 B.R. 788 (Bankr. W.D. Tex. 2001) (non-contiguous parcels rented to tenants unrelated to debtor not rural homestead; distinguishing farmland rented for share of crops); *In re* Cole, 205 B.R. 382 (Bankr. E.D. Tex. 1997) (when land not occupied by residence was pasture land, homestead was rural under former version of statute even though located within city limits); Davis v. Davis, 864 So. 2d 458 (Fla. Dist. Ct. App. 2003) (rural homestead may include non-agricultural income-producing property, here a manufactured-home park); Baumann v. Chaska Bldg. Ctr., Inc., 621 N.W.2d 795 (Minn. Ct. App. 2001) (court should look first to character of area, then to use of parcel). *See also* Iowa State Bank & Trust Co. v. Michel, 683 N.W.2d 95 (Iowa 2004) (land was agricultural within meaning of statute regulating waiver of homestead exemption when landowners pastured horses and grew feed for them there, even though neither worked the land themselves nor received income from agriculture; key question is whether land is "suitable for farming"). *Cf.* Marketic v. U.S. Bank, 436 F. Supp. 2d 842 (N.D. Tex. 2006) (Texas statute forbids foreclosure of home equity loan against property designated as agricultural for tax purposes as of date of foreclosure, even though not so designated at time of loan).

than municipal police, is likely to be rural.[697] In Texas the availability of municipal services is a statutory criterion.[698]

12.7.2.3 Multiple Parcels

Subject to area and value limitations, a landowner may be able to exempt more than one parcel, if used for homestead purposes.[699] Even non-contiguous parcels may be exempt if they are used for homestead purposes.[700]

697 *In re* Kelley, 455 B.R. 710 (Bankr. E.D. Ark. 2011) (urban/rural distinction highly fact-specific; when property had some municipal services, not including sewer and police, and debtor had a barn and some animals, factors were evenly balanced; applying principle of liberal construction to find property rural).

698 Tex. Prop. Code Ann. § 41.002 (West). *See, e.g.*, *In re* Bouchie, 324 F.3d 780 (5th Cir. 2003) (detailed history of Texas' recently amended rural homestead definition; land was rural when it was within jurisdiction of a municipality but did not receive specified municipal services); Smith v. Hennington, 249 S.W.3d 600 (Tex. App. 2008) (property within city limits and served by municipal services was urban).

699 *In re* Stenzel, 301 F.3d 945 (8th Cir. 2002) (Minnesota law; fact question whether contiguous parcel sporadically used for agriculture was "used and occupied" as homestead); *In re* Fiffy, 293 B.R. 550 (B.A.P. 1st Cir. 2003) (later-purchased contiguous parcels homestead if "used and occupied" for residence; family recreation is sufficient); *In re* Kwiecinski, 245 B.R. 672 (B.A.P. 10th Cir. 2000) (Wyoming homestead exemption protected both of two contiguous parcels, one of which included owner's farmhouse, when owner used both parcels); *In re* McDonald, 471 B.R. 194 (E.D. Mich. 2012) (allowing exemption for parcel lying between home and the road, when debtors fed deer, walked nature trails, and cut firewood); Painewebber, Inc. v. Murray, 260 B.R. 815 (E.D. Tex. 2001) (land claimed as "rural homestead of a family" must be used to support family; tracts used for residence, agriculture, and family recreation were exempt; when parcels non-contiguous, more than aesthetic enjoyment must be shown, but activity need not make a profit); *In re* Johns, 504 B.R. 657 (Bankr. D. Idaho 2014) (exempting parcels containing barns, riding areas, and gardens; presence of rental home did not eliminate exemption); *In re* Soles, 497 B.R. 601 (Bankr. D. Colo. 2013) (exemption for "lot or lots" covers contiguous vacant lot); *In re* Mead, 489 B.R. 363 (Bankr. D. Vt. 2013) (homestead is not limited to single parcel under Vermont law; allowing homestead exemption when two parcels were treated as one); *In re* Huff, 2012 WL 710146 (Bankr. S.D. Ala. Mar. 5, 2012) (subdivision into separate parcels does not impair homestead when second parcel actually used for family recreation); *In re* Stox, 2011 WL 5902882 (Bankr. E.D.N.C. May 27, 2011) (allowing homestead claim for three contiguous lots with manufactured homes occupied by debtors and various relatives, vegetable garden, fruit orchard, and storage sheds); *In re* Ford, 415 B.R. 51 (Bankr. N.D.N.Y. 2009) (allowing homestead claim for contiguous parcels; Parcel A contained manufactured home with no running water and would be uninhabitable without Parcel B, which contained building with bathroom and laundry facilities used by debtor); *In re* Marcus, 2009 WL 262762 (Bankr. M.D. Ala. Feb. 4, 2009) (ownership and homestead use sufficiently shown when debtor owned one-eighth interest in lot contiguous to home and used it for gardening, parking, and recreation); *In re* Mohammed, 376 B.R. 38 (Bankr. S.D. Fla. 2007) (contiguous lot may be exempt, if within the area limitations and not used for business purposes); *In re* Irene, 359 B.R. 435 (Bankr. W.D.N.Y. 2007) (condominium owner's deeded parking space exempt; applying New York Real Property Law definition of condominium unit); *In re* Goff, 2007 WL 1434895 (Bankr. W.D. La. May 11, 2007) (homestead exemption for three contiguous lots: debtors' home, garage apartment, and vacant lot); *In re* McManus, 2006 WL 2846861 (Bankr. W.D. La. Mar. 29, 2006) (Louisiana homestead exemption protects contiguous parcels up to statutory size limit); *In re* Hughes, 306 B.R. 683 (Bankr. M.D. Ala. 2004) (homestead exemption protected tract of land that debtors used for parking and as children's playground and that was adjacent to leased land on which their manufactured home stood); *In re* Hunter, 295 B.R. 882 (Bankr. W.D. Ark. 2003) (later-purchased, contiguous land was homestead when area limitations not exceeded but here homestead was lost by abandonment); *In re* Allman, 286 B.R. 402 (Bankr. D. Ariz. 2002) (contiguous parcel exempt, if within dollar limit and not used for non-homestead purpose); *In re* Carey, 282 B.R. 118 (Bankr. D. Mass. 2002) (Massachusetts homestead exemption covers entire property, including home business, storage space and rental property, subject only to dollar limitation; debtors could exempt entire owner-occupied three-decker; rent used to pay mortgage is "as necessary as the furnace"); *In re* Edwards, 281 B.R. 439 (Bankr. D. Mass. 2002) (burden of proof on objector; homestead use shown when contiguous lot was bought "for privacy," had some landscaping and a dog run, and children played there; possibility of future development or sale did not destroy exemption); *In re* Kyllonen, 264 B.R. 17 (Bankr. D. Minn. 2001) (contiguous parcels could be exempted but, when land was urban, area limit applied); *In re* Zantman, 261 B.R. 41 (Bankr. D. Idaho 2001) (contiguous parcels, acquired at different times, were exempt when debtors raised farm animals and planned to plant oats; so long as land used as one parcel it is homestead, even if zoning law permitted division); Davis v. Davis, 864 So. 2d 458 (Fla. Dist. Ct. App. 2003) (rural homestead not limited to debtor's residence; if it comprises not more than 160 acres of contiguous land it may include income-producing property, here a manufactured home park); Baker v. Baker, 202 P.3d 983 (Wash. Ct. App. 2009) (homestead includes residence and land by which it is surrounded; allowing homestead claim for five contiguous parcels, only one of which included house). *See also In re* Olson, 2009 WL 1241294 (Bankr. D. Neb. May 4, 2009) (couple owned two contiguous lots, with a house on each; one house occupied by debtors and children, the other by husband's frail elderly father; wife who moved into second house to care for father-in-law could claim homestead for that lot); *In re* Jones, 397 B.R. 765 (Bankr. D.S.C. 2008) (debtors could exempt house in which they lived and lot needed for access to it). *But see In re* Wilson, 347 B.R. 880 (E.D. Tenn. 2006) (Tennessee exemption for property owned and used as "principal place of residence" did not protect contiguous parcel used for family purposes; debtors "resided" only on parcel with house); *In re* Yonkin, 2013 WL 100416 (Bankr. M.D. Fla. Jan. 8, 2013) (Florida homestead will not cover land which, although within acreage limitations, is clearly not debtor's home, here, a separately platted parcel with a manufactured home rented to unrelated third parties); *In re* Beck, 471 B.R. 187 (Bankr. W.D. Ky. 2012) (denying exemption to property separated from home by a road and having a separate address); *In re* Williams, 345 B.R. 853 (Bankr. N.D. Ohio 2006) (Ohio exemption for "one parcel" will not protect non-contiguous land). *But cf.* Lanier v. Beaman, 394 B.R. 382 (E.D.N.C. 2008) (homestead exemption did not cover adjacent nine-acre lot used to care for rescued horses; distinguishing cases of use for storage, parking, or other "family purposes"); *In re* Kology, 499 B.R. 20 (Bankr. D. Mass. 2013) (homestead exemption did not extend to contiguous lots that debtors had created by subdividing the land on which their home stands); *In re* Issacs, 491 B.R. 893 (Bankr. W.D. Wis. 2013) (occasional hunting or fruit and firewood gathering not sufficient to exempt vacant contiguous parcel); *In re* Whitney, 459 B.R. 712 (Bankr. N.D. Ohio 2011) (debtors failed to show homestead use of contiguous vacant lot); *In re* McComber, 422 B.R. 334 (Bankr. D. Mass. 2010) (debtor owned contiguous parcels, purchased from same grantor at same time but, when homestead declaration used only the street address of the parcel on which debtor resided and referenced only that deed, second lot not exempt because homestead declaration gave no notice that second parcel was included); *In re* Majorins, 2010 WL 1418366 (Bankr. D. Neb. Feb. 22, 2010) (debtor sought to exempt two townhomes, physically joined but on separate lots with separate addresses; because second home could be sold without displacing

The exemption is likely to protect subsidiary structures on the land, not just the home.[701] Colorado's exemption, which includes a farm, has been construed to protect water rights, if necessary to farming.[702] One court, however, held that the homestead exemption does not protect subsurface oil and gas rights and allowed a bankruptcy trustee to enter into an oil and gas lease permitting fracking for natural gas development on the debtor's homestead.[703] The homestead exemption may also protect materials bought, but not yet installed, to repair or improve the homestead.[704]

12.7.2.4 Non-Traditional Homesteads, Cooperatives, and Manufactured Homes

Homestead exemptions should be construed to extend beyond the traditional single-family home owned in fee simple, because these non-traditional dwellings serve the same purpose as traditional homesteads.[705] A number of state homestead statutes make specific provision for mobile or manufactured homes, and other courts construe their exemptions liberally to include these dwellings.[706] When the debtor owns

---

debtor and family from the first, it was not a dwelling in which claimant resided); *In re* Olsen, 322 B.R. 400 (Bankr. E.D. Wis. 2005) (homestead exemption not applicable to contiguous parcel that was not "reasonably necessary" for homestead purposes); *In re* Webb, 263 B.R. 788 (Bankr. W.D. Tex. 2001) (separate parcels on which rental houses were located not part of homestead; distinguishing case of rental for share of crops). *But cf. In re* Welty, 217 B.R. 907 (Bankr. D. Wyo. 1998) (Wyoming homestead exemption did not protect lots where debtor did not reside and which debtor owned individually, while contiguous lot with residence was owned jointly with spouse).

700 *In re* Schott, 449 B.R. 697 (Bankr. W.D. Tex. 697 Mar. 16, 2011) (to exempt non-contiguous parcel, must show homestead use; occasional recreational use not sufficient); *In re* Dietz, 2011 WL 671959 (Bankr. E.D. Tex. Feb. 16, 2011) (only rural homestead may exempt non-contiguous lot; raising vegetables, cutting firewood, and storing personal property were sufficient homestead use); *In re* Haseltine, 2007 WL 2932807 (Bankr. D.N.H. Oct. 25, 2007) (second lot used for "homestead purposes" need not be contiguous, key issue is use; here, contiguous lot with barn and horses was homestead); *In re* Baker, 307 B.R. 860 (Bankr. N.D. Tex. 2003) (non-contiguous land must be used for "comfort, convenience or support" of the family; cattle grazing and hunting sufficient; placing land in conservation reserve does not eliminate homestead). *See also* United States v. Neff, 2007 WL 776532 (D.N.D. Mar. 12, 2007) (two parcels exempt; separated by rough country road and farmed together); *In re* Norra, 421 B.R. 782 (Bankr. S.D. Tex. 2009) (debtor owned two non-contiguous manufactured home communities and resided in a unit in one; homestead allowed in entire community where she resided but not in second community). *Cf. In re* Palmer, 391 B.R. 386 (Bankr. E.D. Tex. 2008) (non-contiguous parcel can be homestead, but debtor must show use "for the purpose of a home"; not shown here when debtors planned to use land for hay and cattle business but had not yet done so). *But see In re* Keena, 2011 WL 6293219 (Bankr. W.D. Wis. 2011) (contiguous wooded lot, used for gathering firewood and hunting, not homestead); Michels v. Kozitza, 610 N.W.2d 368 (Minn. Ct. App. 2000) (Minnesota exemption protects only land contiguous to land on which residence is located, even if non-contiguous land is "agricultural homestead" for tax purposes). *But cf. In re* Mazon, 387 B.R. 641 (M.D. Fla. 2008) (cabana not part of homestead condo; purchased at different time, located eight floors below homestead, and used as dressing room for pool not as residential).

701 *See, e.g., In re* Young, 471 B.R. 715 (Bankr. E.D. Tenn. 2012) (allowing exemption of entire parcel, containing debtors' home and an unoccupied house); *In re* Sadler, 327 B.R. 654 (Bankr. N.D. Iowa 2005) (farm buildings, here a machine shed, fall within Iowa statutory exemption for "appurtenances" to homestead).

702 Shigo, L.L.C. v. Hocker, 2014 WL 785478 (Colo. App. Feb. 27, 2014).

703 *In re* Cassetto, 475 B.R. 874 (Bankr. N.D. Ohio 2012). *But see In re* Graff, 457 B.R. 429 (Bankr. W.D. Pa. 2011) (homestead exemption under federal bankruptcy law extends to the land on which debtors' manufactured home sits, and the oil and gas rights, not just to the manufactured home).

704 Cal. Civ. Pro. § 704.030 (exempting $2425 in material purchased in good faith for use in the repair or improvement of judgment debtor's principal residence); *In re* Grucza, 413 B.R. 96 (Bankr. W.D.N.Y. 2009) (cement blocks, delivered to property but not yet assembled into retaining wall that was needed to protect house from serious hazard, are exempt).

705 *In re* Carlson, 303 B.R. 478 (B.A.P. 10th Cir. 2004) (Utah law) (liberally construing homestead exemption to include manufactured home on land not owned by debtor); *In re* Bernhardt, 2008 WL 2484582 (Bankr. D. Neb. June 17, 2008) (leased manufactured home connected to water and propane was a "dwelling"; citing old case holding that anything down to "a tent of cloth" can be a homestead); *In re* Yettaw, 316 B.R. 560 (Bankr. M.D. Fla. 2004) (debtor could claim homestead in inoperable, but possibly repairable, recreational vehicle (RV) in space rented month-to-month in RV park). *See also In re* Hamilton, 461 B.R. 878 (Bankr. D.N.M. 2011) (finding that homestead use predominated over commercial; debtor lived in warehouse and used it only incidentally for business, here seasonal sale of fireworks). *See generally* W. Vukowich, *Debtors Exemption Rights*, 62 Geo. L.J. 779, 798 (1974).

706 *In re* Carlson, 303 B.R. 478 (B.A.P. 10th Cir. 2004) (Utah law) (liberally construing homestead exemption to include manufactured home on land not owned by debtor); *In re* Thornton, 269 B.R. 682 (W.D. Mo. 2001) (manufactured home placed on foundation and connected to well and septic system was real property entitled to homestead exemption instead of smaller statutory exemption for manufactured home); *In re* Ashton, 2013 WL 211243 (Bankr. D. Idaho Jan. 18, 2013) (fifth-wheel trailer may be homestead, but must show it is principal residence; not shown when debtor oil-driller resided in trailer near job sites but used address of apartment where wife and family resided for mail, voting, licensing, among other things); *In re* Gray, 378 B.R. 728 (Bankr. D. Mass. 2007) (Massachusetts homestead statute, which covers owners who "rightfully possess the premises . . . by lease or otherwise," exempts manufactured home owned by debtors and resting on leased land); *In re* MacLeod, 295 B.R. 1 (Bankr. D. Me. 2003) (manufactured home is exempt personal property under Maine law, which exempts real or personal property used as a residence); Gold v. Schwartz, 774 So. 2d 879 (Fla. Dist. Ct. App. 2001) (constitutional homestead exemption, which protects "land and improvements thereon," covered manufactured home that was permanently affixed to land); Capitol Aggregates, Inc. v. Walker, 448 S.W.2d 830 (Tex. App. 1969) (debtor whose manufactured home was on land rented month-to-month entitled to homestead exemption). *Cf. In re* Heckman, 395 B.R. 737 (Bankr. N.D. Fla. 2008) (statutory exemption for manufactured or modular home on land not owned by debtor is separate from, not a clarification of, constitutional homestead; allowing in-lieu-of-homestead wildcard to debtor who exempted modular home on land he did not own); *In re* Rogers, 225 B.R. 755 (Bankr. D. Idaho 1998) (a manufactured home is not a "household good" for purposes of avoiding a non-possessory, non-purchase money security interest, when Idaho law allows claim of homestead in manufactured home). *But see In re* Cobbins, 227 F.3d 302 (5th Cir. 2000) (manufactured home on land not owned by debtor was not exempt under Mississippi law as "land and buildings," nor as personal property, when statute enumerated types of property exempted and manufactured homes were not listed); *In re* Kelly, 334 B.R. 772 (Bankr. D. Mass. 2005) (debtor who was neither elderly nor disabled could not claim homestead in manufactured home

the land on which a manufactured home sits, the land should be considered part of the homestead even though the home is, at least in theory, more easily removed than a site-built home.[707]

A resident of a cooperative should similarly be protected, even though the resident actually owns a share in the cooperative association and then leases the unit.[708] New York's homestead exemption explicitly protects shares in a cooperative.[709]

Some courts allow homestead exemptions in non-traditional homesteads such as recreational vehicles,[710] watercraft,[711] and office space.[712] Even a truck may be a homestead if it has living facilities and is used as a residence.[713]

---

when term "manufactured homes" had been added to elderly and disabled exemption but not to general homestead provision). *But cf. In re* Hurd, 441 B.R. 116 (B.A.P. 8th Cir. 2010) (Missouri law) (manufactured home statute sets minimum size; denying exemption to camping trailer that was too small and was not dwelling house within meaning of general homestead statute).

707 *In re* Graff, 457 B.R. 429 (Bankr. W.D. Pa. 2011) (need not show that every acre of large rural lot is used for homestead purposes; allowing exemption of manufactured home, nineteen-acre lot, and oil and gas rights). *See also In re* Greene, 346 B.R. 835 (Bankr. D. Nev. 2006) (if debtor actually owns and occupies land, "mode of occupation" is irrelevant under Nevada homestead exemption; here, debtor lived on the land in a travel trailer and then a tent and had signed contracts to improve land and build house), *rev'd on other grounds*, 583 F.3d 614 (9th Cir. 2009) (reversing application of federal bankruptcy law's 1215-day look-back period to this homestead). *But see In re* White, 287 B.R. 232 (Bankr. E.D. Mo. 2002) (debtor who lives in manufactured home on land owned by another may claim only personal property exemption in home).

708 *In re* Dougan, 2013 85146 (Bankr. D. Mass. Jan. 8, 2013) (applying principle of liberal construction to exempt a co-op; new Massachusetts statute does not exempt leases, or mention co-ops in definition of homeowner, but co-ops are included in definition of a home); Southern Walls, Inc. v. Stilwell Corp., 810 So. 2d 566 (Fla. Dist. Ct. App. 2002). *Cf.* Maher v. Harris Trust & Sav. Bank, 506 F.3d 560 (7th Cir. 2007) (shares in cooperative where couple resided can be owned in tenancy by entireties).

709 N.Y. C.P.L.R. 5206 (McKinney). *See* Travis v. 29–33 Convent Ave. HDFC, 859 N.Y.S.2d 336 (N.Y. Sup. Ct. 2008) (landlord may not enforce judgment by selling shareholder-tenant's shares, which would have the effect of evicting shareholder-tenant).

710 *In re* Fisher, 2012 WL 240652 (Bankr. D. Kan. Jan. 22, 2012) (allowing exemption when debtor was residing in camper, despite lack of basic sanitation); *In re* Bernhardt, 2008 WL 2484582 (Bankr. D. Neb. June 17, 2008) (leased motor home connected to water and propane was a "dwelling"; anything down to "a tent of cloth" can be a homestead); *In re* Greene, 346 B.R. 835 (Bankr. D. Nev. 2006) (allowing homestead exemption for land where debtor lived in travel trailer when he had signed contracts to improve land and build house), *rev'd on other grounds*, 583 F.3d 614 (9th Cir. 2009) (reversing application of federal bankruptcy law's 1215-day look-back period to this homestead); *In re* Yettaw, 316 B.R. 560 (Bankr. M.D. Fla. 2004) (debtor, who had sold home and purchased inoperable recreational vehicle, set up in month-to-month rental space in park, could claim homestead); *In re* Irwin, 293 B.R. 28 (Bankr. D. Ariz. 2003) ("mobile home" in Arizona exemption includes self-propelled motor home, when debtors were Arizona residents and occupied it as their only residence); *In re* Bubnak, 176 B.R. 601 (Bankr. M.D. Fla. 1994) (motor home in park, with permanent utility hookups, had sufficient permanency to qualify as Florida homestead). *Cf. In re* Scott, 233 B.R. 32 (Bankr. N.D.N.Y. 1998) (New York homestead may be established in land with a motor home on it if debtor can show actual physical presence and intent to reside there permanently, but not shown here). *But see In re* Andiorio, 237 B.R. 851 (Bankr. M.D. Fla. 1999) (no homestead exemption for recreational vehicle that stood on land rented month-to-month in park, but hookups were easily removable, RV had tires, and was maintained and insured for highway travel; physical permanency essential characteristic for Florida homestead); *In re* Kirby, 223 B.R. 825 (Bankr. M.D. Fla. 1998) (Florida homestead exemption did not protect motor home used as principal residence when there was no "permanency"; motor coach was not attached to land, and debtors neither owned nor leased land in Florida). *But cf. In re* Hurd, 441 B.R. 116 (B.A.P. 8th Cir. 2010) (Missouri law) (denying exemption to camping trailer, which was too small for size requirement of mobile home definition).

711 *In re* Mead, 255 B.R. 80 (Bankr. S.D. Fla. 2000) (allowing debtors to claim homestead in motorboat, which was their only home, when boat was tied up in leased space and equipped with living space and debtors used marina address for driver's license and voter registration); *In re* Ross, 210 B.R. 320 (Bankr. N.D. Ill. 1997) (allowing homestead exemption in charter fishing boat on which owner lived during fishing season); Miami Cnty. Day Sch. v. Bakst, 641 So. 2d 467 (Fla. Dist. Ct. App. 1994) (houseboat moored in rented marina slip was exempt; analogous to manufactured home in park). *But see In re* Hacker, 260 B.R. 542 (Bankr. M.D. Fla. 2000) (motorboat can never be homestead, because it is self-propelled and designed for transportation, not residence); *In re* Brissont, 250 B.R. 413 (Bankr. M.D. Fla. 2000) (cabin cruiser cannot qualify for homestead exemption); *In re* Walter, 230 B.R. 200 (Bankr. S.D. Fla. 1999) (no homestead exemption for motor boat, although it was debtors' primary residence, when it was a recreational vehicle capable of travel and not designed as a permanent residence); Norris v. Thomas, 215 S.W.3d 851 (Tex. 2007) (houseboat can never be Texas homestead; law requires land or a structure that can be affixed to land), *followed by In re* Norris, 499 F.3d 443 (5th Cir. 2007).

712 *In re* Villareal, 401 B.R. 823 (Bankr. S.D. Tex. 2009) (actual homestead use, even if secret, is sufficient to make property homestead; here, family ashamed of having lost home to foreclosure was living behind a curtain in their place of business), *later decision*, 402 Fed. Appx. 28 (5th Cir. 2010) (certifying question to Texas Supreme Court: are debtors equitably estopped from claiming homestead when homestead use was secret and debtors stated, when they obtained loan, that property was not homestead); *In re* Wilson, 393 B.R. 778 (Bankr. S.D. Fla. 2008) (nightclub owner's apartment in club building, where he actually resided, could be homestead, even though it lacked kitchen and bathroom; club kitchen and bathroom, although used by owner, not part of homestead because not used exclusively for living space); *In re* Hageman, 388 B.R. 896 (Bankr. C.D. Ill. 2008) (living space in debtor's business premises was homestead when debtor lived there and used address for voting, driver's license, and Social Security, even though it lacked bathroom or kitchen); *In re* Turner, 2005 WL 1397150 (Bankr. W.D. Mo. June 1, 2005) (zoning violation not bar to homestead claim in commercial storage facility which debtor owned and occupied as his principal residence). *See also In re* Pich, 253 B.R. 562 (Bankr. D. Idaho 2000) (debtor living in office at site of failed business could have claimed homestead, even though residential use forbidden, but was estopped by having applied for light industrial zoning). *But see* Mitchell v. Stringfellow, 2010 WL 4850736 (E.D. Tex. Nov. 23, 2010) (debtor's move, part of a pattern of evading creditors, into trailer on site of gravel pit he leased to his corporation did not make this industrialized land a homestead).

713 *In re* Tullar, 434 B.R. 69 (Bankr. W.D.N.Y. 2010) (long-haul trucker living in his truck, which included bed, lavatory, heat, refrigeration, and minimal cooking facilities; when he used truck two-thirds of the time as residence and one-third to earn a living, homestead exemption allowed as to two-thirds of truck's value; tools-of-trade exemption applied to remaining third); *In re* Laube, 152 B.R. 260 (Bankr. W.D. Wis. 1993) (tractor trailer cab, in which trucker slept, received visitors, completed trucking forms, and ate some meals, was "dwelling" within

One court has articulated these criteria for a non-traditional homestead: (1) the debtor's intent to make the non-traditional abode his homestead; (2) whether the debtor has no other residence; (3) whether the evidence establishes a continuous habitation; (4) whether the debtor maintains at least a possessory right associated with the land establishing a physical presence; (5) whether the non-traditional abode has been physically maintained to allow long-term habitation versus mobility; (6) whether the physical configuration of the abode permits habitation (the physical characteristics of the home are otherwise immaterial).[714]

12.7.3 Who May Claim Homestead Exemption

12.7.3.1 Head of Household Requirements; Surviving Family Members

Frequently homestead exemptions are available only to heads of households, but not to individuals. "Head of household" is generally defined as a married person or anyone supporting a dependent.[715]

the meaning of Wisconsin homestead exemption, even though it did not have a bathroom or cooking facilities).

714 *In re* Yettaw, 316 B.R. 560, 562–63 (Bankr. M.D. Fla. 2004). *See also In re* Hamilton, 461 B.R. 878 (Bankr. D.N.M. 2011) (metal warehouse that lacked heat and running water was homestead when debtor had bedroom set and a microwave, and an adjoining trailer with a bathroom, and actually lived there).

715 *ARKANSAS:* Richardson v. Klaesson, 210 F.3d 811 (8th Cir. 2000) (debtor-family trust which owned house and rented it to debtor-couple could not claim homestead exemption because it was neither married nor head of household; couple could exempt only their interest, here a tenancy at will); *In re* Purvis, 427 B.R. 6 (Bankr. W.D. Ark. 2010) (single person may be head of household if she has moral obligation to support dependent members of household; exemption established when terminally ill brother resided in home remained valid after his death); *In re* Morris, 340 B.R. 78 (Bankr. W.D. Ark. 2006) (allowing head-of-household exemption when debtor's frail, low-income mother was a dependent; criteria are duty to support, which need not be legal, dependency, which need not be total, and position of authority; exemption, once established, continued after mother's death); *In re* Warnock, 323 B.R. 249 (Bankr. W.D. Ark. 2005) (debtor qualified as head of household when she lived in and co-owned home with seventy-nine-year-old mother and had assumed duty of supporting mother); *In re* Kimball, 270 B.R. 471 (Bankr. W.D. Ark. 2001) (divorced debtor with no dependents not entitled to "married or head of household" exemption amount); Tri-State Delta Chems., Inc. v. Wilson, 55 S.W.3d 304 (Ark. Ct. App. 2001) (house became homestead when owner married and lived there with wife; exemption survived divorce).

CALIFORNIA: In re Billings, 262 B.R. 88 (Bankr. N.D. Cal. 2001) (California allows larger homestead exemption for one who is part of "family unit," which may include adult relative unable to support self, here debtor's epileptic daughter who could not drive and was irregularly employed at low-paying jobs).

FLORIDA: In re Plaster, 271 B.R. 202 (Bankr. M.D. Fla. 2001) (debtor-niece not head of household when, although she assisted her aunt and paid some household bills, "continuing personal authority, responsibility and obligation" not shown).

GEORGIA: In re Holt, 357 B.R. 917 (Bankr. M.D. Ga. 2006) (debtors could claim homestead exemption in manufactured home occupied by twenty-two-year-old daughter and minor grandson, as daughter was dependent).

MISSOURI: In re Turpen, 482 B.R. 273 (B.A.P. 8th Cir. 2012) (head of household wildcard applies only to children by birth or adoption; allowing head of household to claim wildcard for his own children, but not those of female co-habitant); *In re* Townsend, 344 B.R. 915 (Bankr. W.D. Mo. 2006) (Missouri head-of-household wildcard exemption, which refers to "family," is available to debtor living with same-sex partner and partner's two children when partners had changed last names to indicate commitment, shared parenting, and household duties, and debtor was economic support of household and made financial decisions); *In re* White, 287 B.R. 232 (Bankr. E.D. Mo. 2002) (widow with no dependents may not claim head-of-household exemption); *In re* Thorpe, 251 B.R. 723 (Bankr. W.D. Mo. 2000) (no head-of-household exemption when couple was separated and had no dependents). *See also* United States v. Webster, 2008 WL 5191460 (W.D. Mo. Dec. 11, 2008) (debtor not head of household within meaning of Missouri wage exemption provision, because unemployed but able-bodied adult son not a dependent).

NEBRASKA: In re Roberts, 219 B.R. 235 (B.A.P. 8th Cir. 1998) (any married person, whether or not supporting a dependent and even if separated from spouse, may claim the Nebraska homestead exemption); *In re* Saythongphet, 2010 WL 3259363 (Bankr. D. Neb. Aug. 17, 2010) (debtor sufficiently alleged that adult daughter who lived with her was unable to support self; exemption allowed); *In re* Keller, 2008 WL 361126 (Bankr. D. Neb. Feb. 8, 2008) (allowing head-of-household exemption for home where unmarried debtor had resided with elderly mother, providing financial support and hands-on care; exemption survived after mother ceased to reside there); *In re* Deines, 2007 WL 4892122 (Bankr. D. Neb. Dec. 19, 2007) (unmarried person not head of household unless dependent is residing there on petition date, or resided there when home was purchased; denying exemption to debtor who provided home for her disabled brother during some winters); *In re* Allison, 209 B.R. 494 (D. Neb. 1997) (Nebraska homestead exemption, which defined head of family to include anyone living with an adult son or daughter "unable to support themselves," applied to debtor whose adult daughter had less than a high school education, could not find work nearer than forty miles away, had no reliable transportation, and needed to spend part of her time caring for ill family members); *In re* Uhrich, 355 B.R. 783 (Bankr. D. Neb. 2006) (two single persons resided in jointly owned house with their minor child and the minor niece of one of them; partner who had an income was head of house; niece did not qualify other partner as head of second household, because not the child of a deceased sibling as required by Nebraska definition); *In re* Roush, 215 B.R. 592 (Bankr. D. Neb. 1997) (two single adults, who both had minor children and lived together in a house they occupied as joint tenants, qualified as heads of households and could each claim a homestead exemption for his or her interest in the property). *See also In re* Stewart, 2013 WL 5793441 (Bankr. D. Neb. Oct. 28, 2013) (denying exemption to single debtor who had no dependent living with her on petition date); *In re* Olson, 2009 WL 1241294 (Bankr. D. Neb. May 4, 2009) (couple owned two contiguous lots, with a house on each; one house occupied by debtors and children, the other by husband's frail elderly father; wife who moved into second house to care for father-in-law could claim homestead for that lot).

NORTH DAKOTA: In re Sandvik, 2004 WL 3383656 (Bankr. D.N.D. Dec. 1, 2004) (debtor not head of household; sister, who lived rent-free with debtor, not dependent when capable of self-support); *In re* Hankel, 223 B.R. 728 (Bankr. D.N.D. 1998) (son was not head of household when mother was not financially dependent on him and he provided only minimal physical assistance).

SOUTH DAKOTA: In re Davis, 228 B.R. 242 (Bankr. D.S.D. 1999) (wife could not claim head of household $6000 personal property exemption when husband earned slightly more than she did, even though she handled most of day-to-day management of household because husband's work required frequent absences from home).

TEXAS: Duran v. Henderson, 71 S.W.3d 833 (Tex. App. 2002) (father, adult daughter, and her child were family for purpose of increased Texas

A homestead exemption may survive the death of the homeowner, to protect the home from his or her debts in the hands of a surviving spouse or other close relative or dependent.[716]

12.7.3.2 Effect of Divorce, Joint Tenancy, Co-Ownership by Spouses

Courts vary widely in their treatment of interests created by property division in divorce. In some states, a spouse who has left the home, but whose name is still on the title, is entitled to a homestead exemption.[717] In other states, occupancy is required.[718] When a spouse no longer has title to a home, but is entitled to a share of the proceeds when the home is sold or to a "buy-out" payment from the other spouse, some courts allow a homestead exemption,[719] but this rule is not universal.[720]

---

homestead exemption when all three relied on father's Social Security check and daughter cared for incapacitated father; father had "at least a moral obligation" to provide for daughter and granddaughter). *See also In re* Fink, 2009 WL 3015340 (Bankr. S.D. Tex. Sept. 17, 2009) (father who paid child support for child of prior marriage was head of household, entitled to $60,000 personal property exemption).

716 *In re* Cutignola, 450 B.R. 445 (Bankr. S.D.N.Y. 2011) (home titled in wife alone; when she died shortly after petition date, her homestead exemption continued to protect surviving husband); *In re* Collins, 2005 WL 3506356 (Bankr. C.D. Ill. Nov. 30, 2005) (widow who inherited marital home could stack her exemption, as owner, with deceased husband's exemption, which protected surviving spouse and minor child); *In re* Spann, 2005 WL 3200400 (Bankr. C.D. Ill. Nov. 29, 2005) (surviving spouse who continues to reside in marital home may stack own homestead exemption with that of deceased spouse; right not terminated by remarriage); Traeger v. Credit First Nat'l Ass'n, 864 So. 2d 1188 (Fla. Dist. Ct. App. 2004) (protection applies to all heirs, even those who would not inherit under intestacy laws); Estate of Shefner v. Shefner-Holden, 2 So. 3d 1076 (Fla. Dist. Ct. App. 2009) (homestead devised to qualified heir, here testator's son, is exempt from creditors' claims against estate); *In re* Estate of Hamel, 821 So. 2d 1276 (Fla. Dist. Ct. App. 2002) (debtor was in process of selling condo at time of death, and executor closed sale shortly thereafter; proceeds exempt in hands of adult daughters); Thompson v. Laney, 766 So. 2d 1087 (Fla. Dist. Ct. App. 2000) (homestead exemption survives owner's death if property passes to spouse or lineal descendent); *In re* Estate of Tolson, 690 N.W.2d 680 (Iowa 2005) (homestead exemption survived when property left to adult children); John Deere Cmty. Credit Union v. Miller, 810 N.W.2d 896 (Iowa Ct. App. 2012) (unpublished) (Iowa homestead passes to owner's child free of debts of owner or preexisting debts of child; inherited proceeds must be used within a reasonable time to purchase or repair a homestead); Estate of Darby v. Stinson, 68 So. 3d 702 (Miss. Ct. App. 2011) (exempt property, including homestead, passes to spouse, children or grandchildren free of debts of deceased; Medicaid contract that allowed claim against the estate not a waiver of statutory homestead, because it did not make clear that recipient was waiving homestead); Parker v. Gates, 2000 Tex. App. LEXIS 8485 (Tex. App. Dec. 21, 2000) (Texas law allows homestead to descend free and clear of decedent's debts, if surviving spouse, minor child, or unmarried adult child resides there; not shown when adult daughter rented apartment and owned business in another city even though she moved in after mother's death). *But cf. In re* Joseph, 262 B.R. 33 (Bankr. W.D.N.Y. 2001) (widow not permitted to claim both her own homestead exemption and that of husband who had died in 1980; New York statute which allows survival of homestead exemption for protection of spouse and children applies only to decedent's debts, not individual debts of the survivor).

717 *In re* Tofani, 365 B.R. 338 (Bankr. D. Mass. 2007) (debtor could claim homestead in home co-owned with ex-wife, who resided there with children when debtor paid for upkeep, visited his children there, and intended to buy and live in house after child support obligations terminated); Beltram v. Kalb, 63 So. 3d 783 (Fla. Dist. Ct. App. 2011) (jointly-owned home is still protected against ex-husband's debts even after he has moved out, as long as wife and daughter reside there).

718 *In re* Sacharko, 356 B.R. 786 (table), 2007 WL 128775 (B.A.P. 1st Cir. 2007) (no homestead exemption for 40% interest in former marital home, now occupied by ex-wife and couple's minor daughter; Rhode Island homestead requires occupancy); Clark v. Guttman, 2013 WL 812017 (D. Md. Mar. 4, 2013) (denying California exemption to debtor who owned former marital home in joint tenancy with ex-wife, with informal agreement that she could live there until child turned 21); *In re* Simmons, 308 B.R. 559 (Bankr. M.D. Ala. 2004) (husband could not exempt his half-interest in marital home when couple were separated and husband lived in apartment); *In re* Roberts, 280 B.R. 450 (Bankr. D. Mass. 2001) (intent to occupy not shown when, at time of filing, debtor had left marital home); Chase Home Fin. L.L.C. v. Davis, 1 So. 3d 643 (La. Ct. App. 2008) (division of surplus after foreclosure sale; ex-wife who resided in former marital home entitled to entire homestead exemption; ex-husband gets none because occupancy required); *In re* Nilsson, 315 P.3d 966 (Nev. 2013) (denying exemption for home occupied by ex-wife and minor children; Nevada homestead requires occupancy by debtor). *See also In re* Wilson, 341 B.R. 21 (B.A.P. 9th Cir. 2006) (Washington homestead generally requires occupancy, or failing that at least an equitable interest; denying exemption when husband was barred from house by court order prepetition and declared homestead was filed after divorce decree had already divested husband of interest in property); *In re* Parr, 2009 WL 3517602 (Bankr. D. Mont. Oct. 26, 2009) (when divorcing couple were living apart on petition date, husband had no exemption because he did not reside on property), *aff'd*, 2010 WL 6259974 (B.A.P. 9th Cir. July 19, 2010) (unpublished). *See generally* § 12.7.4.1, *infra*.

719 *See, e.g., In re* Wenstrom, 2013 WL 321678 (Bankr. D.N.D. Jan. 28, 2013) (allowing exemption of buy-out payment awarded to wife, who was required to quitclaim her share of marital home to husband); *In re* Patterson, 482 B.R. 755 (Bankr. D. Vt. 2012) (homestead exemption continues in new home purchased with proceeds of old; when couple divorced, wife received marital home, husband received a package of other assets, including the IRA he used to pay for new home); *In re* Dubravsky, 374 B.R. 467 (Bankr. D.N.H. 2007) (allowing homestead exemption for former marital home, although debtor was excluded by divorce decree, when home to be sold at later date and proceeds divided); *In re* Willoughby, 2003 WL 22849766 (Bankr. C.D. Ill. Dec. 2, 2003) (wife's court-ordered payment to husband as compensation for award of former marital home was exempt as proceeds of homestead); *In re* Marriage of Christodolou, 383 S.W.3d 718 (Tex. App. 2012) (exempting promissory note executed by ex-husband to guarantee payment of wife's share of value of marital home). *See also In re* Ballato, 318 B.R. 205 (Bankr. M.D. Fla. 2004) (ex-husband could claim homestead exemption for his share of proceeds of marital home, sold by court order during property division); *In re* Cumberbatch, 302 B.R. 675 (Bankr. C.D. Cal. 2003) (court-ordered sale of home during property division was "forced sale to satisfy a money judgment" within meaning of California statute allowing automatic exemption for six months in proceeds). *But cf. In re* Jefferies, 468 B.R. 373 (B.A.P. 9th Cir. 2012) (Washington protects only proceeds of voluntary sale; sale pursuant to divorce decree not voluntary, even though it incorporated separation agreement voluntarily negotiated by couple).

720 *In re* Johnson, 375 F.3d 668 (8th Cir. 2004) (lien on former marital home, to assure ex-wife's payment of husband's share of value, not an interest in land within meaning of Minnesota homestead exemption); *In re* Gourdin, 431 B.R. 885 (B.A.P. 1st Cir. 2010) (debtor's interest in former marital home ended when probate court ordered him to deed it to wife, even though he had not complied; only remaining interest was right to payment of money, which cannot be exempted under Massachusetts homestead); *In re* Majors, 2008 WL 5330002 (Bankr.

Joint tenancies also raise problems. While there is little disagreement that a debtor can exempt a fractional interest[721] in a home, courts differ as to whether the debtor may apply the full exemption[722] or only a proportional amount of the exemption.[723] Some states allow each member of a married couple to claim a homestead exemption and allow them to stack their exemptions.[724] Courts sometimes extend this benefit to unmarried co-owners as well.[725] Stacking may be allowed even if one

---

N.D. Ala. Dec. 18, 2008) (ownership interest required for Alabama homestead; not shown when house titled in ex-wife, but separation agreement allowed debtor husband to live there while renovating it for sale and entitled him to half the sales proceeds); *In re* Toppi, 378 B.R. 9 (Bankr. D. Me. 2007) (denying exemption for ex-husband's right to receive $50,000 from wife, to whom he quitclaimed home, when home was sold or in seven years); *In re* Kujan, 286 B.R. 216 (Bankr. D. Conn. 2002) (ex-wife who had quitclaimed her share of house to husband at divorce could not claim homestead exemption in her right to receive payment when youngest child reached eighteen or house was sold; she had no right to occupy or buy property and sum might be paid without selling house). *Cf. In re* Dixon, 327 B.R. 421 (Bankr. E.D. Mo. 2005) (husband could not claim homestead exemption for $15,000 ex-wife owed him pursuant to divorce decree when no evidence linked lump sum specifically to debtor's equity in marital home).

721 *In re* Stenzel, 301 F.3d 945 (8th Cir. 2002) (Minnesota law) (one-third remainder interest in property was sufficient to support exemption); *In re* Marcus, 2009 WL 262762 (Bankr. M.D. Ala. Feb. 4, 2009) (one-eighth interest is sufficient ownership for Alabama homestead statute, which applies to a "fee or less estate" held "in common or in severalty").

722 *In re* Moore, 495 B.R. 1 (B.A.P. 8th Cir. 2013) (Missouri law allows one co-owner to claim entire exemption, provided other owners do not claim exemption); Abernathy v. LaBarge (*In re* Abernathy), 259 B.R. 330 (B.A.P. 8th Cir. 2001) (debtor who owned one-third interest in property, in joint tenancy with non-debtor sisters, could claim entire amount of Missouri homestead exemption), *aff'd*, 2001 WL 1104482 (8th Cir. Sept. 20, 2001); *In re* Nguyen, 332 B.R. 393 (Bankr. W.D. Mo. 2005) (debtor could claim whole $15,000 exemption in her half interest in home owned in joint tenancy with non-debtor domestic partner); *In re* LaHaye, 2003 WL 22764771 (Bankr. N.D. Cal. Sept. 10, 2003) (debtor could claim entire exemption for her half-interest in property); *In re* Cunningham, 276 B.R. 314 (Bankr. D. Mass. 2002) (debtor may claim a homestead interest in all of a triple-decker, occupied by her and her two sisters, in which she owns a two-thirds interest). *See also In re* Gatrost, 2008 WL 545002 (Bankr. D. Neb. Feb. 22, 2008) (rejecting interpretation that would have applied homestead exemption only to husband's undivided one-half interest in the property, leaving wife's interest unprotected). *But see* Vinson v. Dakmak, 347 B.R. 620 (E.D. Mich. 2006) (Michigan homestead amount is aggregate maximum; co-owners may not stack).

723 *In re* Strobbe, 2007 WL 2562611 (Bankr. D. Mont. Aug. 31, 2007) (owner of undivided one-sixth entitled to exempt one-sixth of statutory exemption amount); *In re* Kleinfeldt, 2007 WL 2138748 (Bankr. D. Vt. July 23, 2007) (part owner entitled to proportionate share of homestead exemption); *In re* Norton, 327 B.R. 193 (Bankr. D. Vt. 2005) (joint tenant, not married to co-tenant, who owned one-half interest in property could claim one-half of Vermont homestead amount); *In re* Smith, 254 B.R. 751 (Bankr. W.D. Mo. 2000) (debtor who co-owned home with his sister could not claim entire statutory homestead exemption when sister had also filed bankruptcy and claimed the exemption). *See also In re* Bradigan, 501 B.R. 151 (W.D.N.Y. Oct. 29, 2013) (valuing husband's interest in tenancy by entireties property as 50% in absence of actuarial evidence to the contrary). *Cf. In re* Wynn, 369 B.R. 605 (Bankr. D. Or. 2007) (separated couple who sold marital home could allocate exemption between themselves as they chose, so long as total did not exceed cap).

724 *See, e.g., In re* Butturini, 411 B.R. 553 (E.D. Tenn. 2009) (Tennessee allows $25,000 homestead for individual with custody of minor child; married couple with one child could claim an exemption apiece and stack them); *In re* Rich, 2013 WL 1628723 (Bankr. D. Kan. Apr. 16, 2013) (allowing couple to stack federal exemptions even though Kansas exemptions cannot be stacked); *In re* Young, 471 B.R. 715 (Bankr. E.D. Tenn. 2012) (allowing stacking); *In re* Staggs, 381 B.R. 230 (Bankr. M.D. Tenn. 2008) (Tennessee allows $25,000 homestead for individual with custody of minor child; married couple with one child could claim an exemption apiece and stack them); *In re* Limperis, 370 B.R. 859 (Bankr. S.D. Fla. 2007) (married couple, subject to $125,000 Bankruptcy Code cap for homestead acquired within 1215 days, could claim an exemption apiece and stack them for total exemption of $250,000); *In re* Rasmussen, 349 B.R. 747 (Bankr. M.D. Fla. Sept. 8, 2006) (each spouse is entitled to $125,000 homestead allowed by bankruptcy law for property acquired during 1215-day look-back period; couple may stack exemptions); *In re* Burnett, 303 B.R. 684 (Bankr. M.D. Ga. 2003) (applying Georgia law that allows double exemption in bankruptcy when couple's home is owned by individual debtor); *In re* Dawson, 266 B.R. 355 (Bankr. N.D. Tex. 2001) (until divorce is final, husband can only claim marital home as homestead, as family is entitled to just one homestead). *Cf. In re* Duncan, 294 B.R. 339 (B.A.P. 10th Cir. 2003) (applying Wyoming state law exemptions; spouses may stack their homestead exemptions, but wife who had no ownership interest on petition date had no exemption). *But see* U.S. v. Fincher, 593 F.3d 702 (8th Cir. 2010) (Arkansas law allows only one homestead per married couple); *In re* Garran, 338 F.3d 1 (1st Cir. 2003) (Massachusetts law) (couple could not stack exemptions; wife's filing of homestead declaration, which protected entire household, superseded husband's earlier homestead declaration); *In re* Rowe, 236 B.R. 11 (B.A.P. 9th Cir. 1999) (Nevada law allows a married couple, even if living apart, to claim only one homestead exemption); *In re* Wilson, 2012 WL 46959 (Bankr. E.D. Wis. Jan. 9, 2012) (when co-habiting unmarried couple's agreement to keep property separate did not specify that it would terminate upon marriage, it survived marriage and barred wife from claiming homestead in marital home that was owned by husband before marriage); *In re* Drew, 2011 WL 4915006 (Bankr. D. Mass. Oct. 17, 2011) (debtor may not stack his Massachusetts elderly homestead exemption with that of his non-debtor wife); *In re* Arrendondo-Smith, 436 B.R. 412 (Bankr. W.D. Tex. 2010) (only one homestead per married couple; denying homestead to debtor estranged wife's new home because she had established homestead in former marital home, owned by husband); *In re* Gunnison, 397 B.R. 186 (Bankr. D. Mass. 2008) (separated but still married couple could claim only one homestead; husband's later-filed homestead declaration terminated wife's homestead in her solely owned property); *In re* Lindstrom, 331 B.R. 267 (Bankr. E.D. Mich. 2005) (married couple may claim only one homestead exemption); *In re* Arnold, 73 P.3d 861 (Okla. 2003) (married couple may claim only one 160-acre rural homestead). *But cf. In re* Ellis, 446 B.R. 22 (Bankr. D. Mass. 2011) (although Massachusetts homestead exemption protects owners' spouse, wife who has no property interest in property titled in husband cannot claim exemption); *In re* Scotti, 456 B.R. 760 (Bankr. D.S.C. 2011) (South Carolina homestead requires ownership interest; when property titled in wife, husband had at most a possessory interest and equitable distribution rights in case of divorce; allowing couple only one exemption); *In re* Taylor, 320 B.R. 214 (Bankr. N.D. Ga. 2005) (debtor who owned residence jointly with non-debtor husband limited to single $10,000 homestead exemption); *In re* Soper, 258 B.R. 748 (Bankr. W.D. Mo. 2001) (married couple living together may claim equity in only one home, even though combined equity in house and vacation cabin less than state homestead cap; statute exempts "a dwelling house"); Kipp v. Sweno, 683 N.W.2d 259 (Minn. 2004) (married couple entitled to only one exemption, but individual debtor can claim entire exemption to protect his survivorship interest).

725 *Cf. In re* Rabin, 359 B.R. 242 (B.A.P. 9th Cir. 2007) (California law) (treating registered domestic partners, living together in house they co-owned, same as married couple, so they are entitled to only one

spouse has died[726] or the spouses are separated.[727] The Seventh Circuit has ruled, however, that a spouse must have a title interest in the home, not merely the right to claim an interest in the home when the title holder dies, in order to claim a homestead exemption under Illinois law.[728]

Joint tenancy with right of survivorship is sometimes used as a form of do-it-yourself estate planning: an aging parent adds the name of a son or daughter to the title, instead of making a will. This can result in the parent's losing the home, if the son or daughter incurs debts.[729] The risk is especially serious if the son or daughter does not reside in the home and so cannot claim a homestead exemption.[730] Similar issues arise with respect to joint bank accounts.[731]

12.7.3.3 Holders of Remainder Interests and Other Interests Less Than Fee Simple

Homestead statutes generally require some form of legal ownership,[732] although it need not be fee simple. Sometimes the debtor will have only a remainder interest in the home, while a parent or some other relative holds a life estate. Many courts apply the rule of liberal construction to protect the holder of the remainder interest.[733]

---

homestead exemption); *In re* Ewbank, 359 B.R. 807 (Bankr. D.N.M. 2007) (New Mexico statute, permitting stacking of exemptions for "homestead owned jointly by two persons," did not require joint tenancy; tenancy in common was sufficient).

726 *In re* Collins, 2005 WL 3506356 (Bankr. C.D. Ill. Nov. 30, 2005) (widow who inherited marital home could stack her exemption, as owner, with deceased husband's exemption, which protected surviving spouse and minor child). *But cf. In re* Joseph, 262 B.R. 33 (Bankr. W.D.N.Y. 2001) (widow not permitted to claim both her own homestead exemption and that of husband who had died in 1980; N.Y. statute which allows survival of homestead exemption for protection of spouse and children applies only to debts of deceased spouse, not individual debts of survivor).

727 *In re* Green, 319 B.R. 913 (Bankr. M.D. Ga. 2004) (when residence titled in name of one spouse, Georgia statute allows double homestead exemption of $20,000; marital separation of debtor and spouse not relevant).

728 *In re* Belcher, 551 F.3d 688 (7th Cir. 2008). *See also In re* Cassity, 281 B.R. 365 (S.D. Ala. 2001) (homestead exemption cannot be based on dower interest); *In re* Martinez, 469 B.R. 74 (Bankr. D. N.M. 2012) (non-titled husband's rights in marital home not sufficient to support exemption; must show that property is "owned, leased, or being purchased"; no equitable lien because he failed to show that funds he spent for repairs were his separate property); *In re* Padilla Padilla, 2011 WL 5911243 (Bankr. D. P.R. Nov. 28, 2011) (non-titled spouse who invested substantial funds and labor in improving marital residence had no property interest to support homestead exemption). *But see In re* Wycuff, 332 B.R. 297 (Bankr. N.D. Ohio 2005) (husband's dower interest in wife's property was property interest within meaning of homestead statute, so he could assert exemption up to the value of this interest). *But cf. In re* Lindquist, 395 B.R. 707 (Bankr. D. Or. 2008) (husband's name not on title, but he lived in marital home and made the payments; his equitable interest was sufficient that couple could claim the larger exemption for joint owners).

729 *In re* Cario, 2012 WL 1122887 (Bankr. S.D. Fla. Apr. 3, 2012) (mother transferred half interest in home to daughter, for no consideration, noting on the deed "for estate purposes"; this was insufficient to put bona fide purchaser on notice, so daughter's bankruptcy trustee could sell the home). *But see* Wachter v. Lezdey (*In re* Lezdey), 373 B.R. 164 (Bankr. M.D. Fla. 2007) (deed for joint tenancy with rights of survivorship does not conclusively establish that joint tenants own equal shares; fact question whether brother's name was placed on deed merely as estate planning).

730 *In re* Santiago, 2012 WL 393405 (Bankr. S.D.N.Y. 2012) (non-contributing daughter's name was on title of home sold many months prepetition; daughter had no homestead exemption because she did not reside in home on petition date, and New York exempts only proceeds of involuntary sale; trustee could sue non-debtor mother for half the sales proceeds).

731 *See* § 12.6.3.5, *supra*. *See also* National Consumer Law Center, Consumer Banking and Payments Law § 10.2.7.3 (5th ed. 2013), *updated at* www.nclc.org/library (application of banker's right of setoff to joint bank accounts).

732 Bullard v. IndyMac Bank, FSB, 539 Fed. Appx. 665 (6th Cir. 2013) (unpublished) (Michigan homestead exemption available only to debtor who owns and occupies the property, not to husband when property was solely in wife's name); *In re* Varrone, 2012 WL 1079005 (E.D.N.Y. Mar. 30, 2012) (debtor whose ownership rights had been cut off by decree of partition and sale could not claim homestead, even though she could occupy home until it was sold; New York homestead requires both ownership and occupancy); *In re* Hampshire, 505 B.R. 668 (Bankr. E.D. Pa. Feb. 27, 2014) (debtor had no ownership interest in property inherited by wife; right to elective share if wife pre-deceased him was not sufficient); *In re* Martinez, 469 B.R. 74 (Bankr. D.N.M. 2012) (non-titled husband's rights in marital home not sufficient to support exemption; must show that property is "owned, leased, or being purchased"); *In re* Padilla Padilla, 2011 WL 5911243 (Bankr. D. P.R. Nov. 28, 2011) (non-titled spouse who invested substantial funds and labor in improving marital residence had no property interest to support homestead exemption). *But see In re* Mazoue, 240 B.R. 878 (E.D. La. 1999) (finding Louisiana homestead exemption inapplicable to debtor's one-quarter ownership interest in home where he lived with co-owner family members; erroneously applying a Louisiana statute that addresses rights of surviving spouses and minor children, not rights of co-owners); Marine Credit Union v. Detlefson-Delano, 830 N.W.2d 859 (Minn. 2013) (husband's deed quitclaiming all right, title, and interest in property to wife did not eliminate homestead rights; mortgage was void for lack of his signature).

733 *In re* Stenzel, 301 F.3d 945 (8th Cir. 2002) (Minnesota law) (one-third remainder interest in property, in which mother held life estate, was sufficient to support homestead exemption; remanding to resolve occupancy questions); *In re* Rasmussen, 456 B.R. 1 (E.D.N.Y. 2011) (debtors, who owned remainder interest and resided with life tenant, owned and occupied the property; vested remainder is ownership interest); *In re* Thomason, 2013 WL 625343 (Bankr. D. Idaho Feb. 19, 2013) (remainder interest plus clear showing of intent to reside sufficient; here, debtors had filed declaration of abandonment for current residence and declaration of homestead for remainder interest, and made arrangements to move in and care for frail life tenant); *In re* Hildebrandt, 432 B.R. 852 (Bankr. N.D. Fla. June 30, 2010) (debtor who owned remainder interest had present right to occupy sufficient to support Florida homestead; evidence showed that when elderly aunt, with whom debtor had resided for years, deeded her the property, she intended to grant right of occupancy); *In re* Williams, 427 B.R. 541 (Bankr. M.D. Fla. 2010) (debtor, who resided with life tenant, his mother, and assisted her with daily living and had vested remainder interest pursuant to both Florida probate law and contract with mother, had sufficient right to occupy to support Florida homestead); *In re* Kimble, 344 B.R. 546 (Bankr. S.D. Ohio 2006) (debtors who owned remainder interest, and resided in manufactured home on property with permission of life tenant, could claim exemption; "interest" in Ohio exemption statute includes future interests); *In re* Franklino, 329 B.R. 363 (Bankr. D.R.I. 2005) (homestead exemption may be applicable to remainder interest in out-of-state property if claimant shows intent to occupy property when it becomes available); *In re* Cain, 235 B.R. 812 (Bankr. M.D.N.C. 1998) (allowing remainderman to claim homestead exemption in home where he resided with mother, when

It may also be possible to exempt a life estate.[734]

Some courts allow homestead exemptions when the property is owned by a trust.[735] However, in one case a bankruptcy court held that the debtors' power to amend a trust into which they had transferred their home became property of the estate when they filed bankruptcy. The court allowed the bankruptcy trustee to exercise this power and appoint a substitute trustee to sell the property, paying the debtors the value of the life estate they had reserved.[736]

Courts have also applied homestead exemptions to homes tied up in probate,[737] homes being purchased under installment

mother is life tenant); *In re* Hankel, 223 B.R. 728 (Bankr. D.N.D. 1998) (North Dakota homestead exemption protects son's future interest in house where he resided with his elderly mother, who held a life estate). *See also In re* Vasques, 337 B.R. 255 (Bankr. D. Mass. 2006) (mother's homestead declaration sufficient to protect remainder interest of daughter who lived there). *Cf. In re* Plaster, 271 B.R. 202 (Bankr. M.D. Fla. 2001) (owner of remainder interest may not claim homestead unless head of household; not shown here although debtor assisted her aunt, the life tenant, and paid some household bills). *But see* Gordon v. Pappalardo (*In re* Gordon), ___ B.R. ___, 2013 WL 987768 (B.A.P. 1st Cir. Mar. 13, 2013) (Massachusetts homestead exemption does not protect a remainder interest, as it is not listed in definition of "owner"); *In re* Collymore, 2014 WL 184728 (Bankr. D. Mass. Jan. 15, 2014) (applying former version of Massachusetts statute; daughter's remainder interest not exempt; estate of homestead lost when mother, without explicitly reserving homestead, conveyed property to daughter reserving life interest for herself); *In re* Pettit, 231 B.R. 101 (Bankr. M.D. Fla. 1999) (Florida's homestead exemption did not protect future interest when debtor resided with mother, who had deeded property to debtor but reserved a life interest for herself). *But cf. In re* Corse, 486 B.R. 241 (Bankr. D. R.I. Jan. 18, 2013) (denying exemption for one-quarter remainder interest when no intent to reside on property; must show either current residence or intent to reside "as soon as legally possible"), *aff'd on other grounds*, 2014 WL 652268 (D.R.I. Feb. 19, 2014); *In re* Brunson, 498 B.R. 160 (Bankr. W.D. Tex. 2013) (remainder exempt only if present possessory interest shown; denying exemption although debtors resided in house and cared for life-tenant father, because life estate did not formally grant right to occupy).

734 *See, e.g.*, *In re* Peirce, 467 B.R. 260 (Bankr. D. Mass. 2012) (debtors owned life estate in property owned by trust of which they were trustees; allowing exemption of life estate).

735 *In re* Kester, 493 F.3d 1208 (10th Cir. 2007) (Kansas law) (allowing homestead exemption when property owned by self-settled, revocable trust); *In re* Vazquez, 2012 WL 601593 (W.D. Tex. Feb. 23, 2012) (Texas statute allowing exemption of homes owned by certain trusts is purely prospective but, even without statute, debtor who was sole trustee and sole beneficiary of trust that owned her home was owner who could claim exemption); *In re* Welch, 486 B.R. 1 (Bankr. D. Mass. 2013) (Massachusetts homestead law exempts property owned by a trust); *In re* Peake, 480 B.R. 367 (Bankr. D. Kan. 2012) (beneficiary of self-settled trust that owns his home can claim homestead for his equitable interest in the property); *In re* Starr, 485 B.R. 835 (Bankr. N.D. Ohio 2012) (exempting home owned by self-settled trust; noting lack of Ohio authority, and applying principle of liberal construction); *In re* Larsen, 2011 WL 4621556 (Bankr. S.D. Iowa Sept. 30, 2011) (Iowa explicitly permits homestead in property owned by certain types of trusts); *In re* Rodrigues, 2010 WL 716192 (Bankr. D. Mass. Feb. 23, 2010) (home owned by debtor's estate planning trust exempt under Massachusetts law allowing homestead for non-owner who possesses premises "by lease or otherwise" when debtor as trustee granted herself right to occupy); *In re* Cocke, 371 B.R. 554 (Bankr. M.D. Fla. 2007) (liberally construing homestead exemption to protect property owned by trust, when debtors resided on property, had right to exclude others, and all other rights of ownership except right to divide up property; key issue is whether debtors had legal or equitable right to use property as residence); Fitton v. Bank of Little Rock, 365 S.W.3d 888 (Ark. 2010) (allowing homestead in property owned by revocable trust, of which debtor was both trustee and beneficiary); Cutler v. Cutler *ex rel.* Estate of Cutler, 994 So. 2d 341 (Fla. Dist. Ct. App. 2008) (property was homestead even though long-time owner conveyed it to an irrevocable trust for estate planning purposes, reserving a life estate); Callava v. Feinberg, 864 So. 2d 429 (Fla. Dist. Ct. App. 2003) (judgment debtor may claim Florida homestead exemption in her residence, although property titled in trustee, as debtor has "beneficial interest"). *See also In re* Swyzd, 370 B.R. 882 (B.A.P. 1st Cir. 2007) (debtor may claim homestead exemption in house owned by a trust when, at time homestead filed, debtor had succeeded parents as trustee and was the only beneficiary, so debtor held both legal and equitable interests); *In re* Bogetti, 349 B.R. 14 (E.D. Cal. 2006) (when home was owned by self-settled revocable trust, it was property of the estate, but debtors could claim homestead exemption); *In re* Im, 495 B.R. 46 (Bankr. M.D. Fla. 2013) (debtor who, with his wife, was co-owner, co-settlor, and co-beneficiary of trust that owned their home had ownership interest sufficient to support homestead claim; denying enhanced personal property exemption for those who do not receive benefit of a homestead exemption); *In re* Bellingroehr, 403 B.R. 818 (Bankr. W.D. Mo. 2009) (tenancy by entireties exemption not lost by transfer to estate planning trust, which imposed same restrictions on alienation by one spouse as are imposed by tenancy by entireties); *In re* Alexander, 346 B.R. 546 (Bankr. M.D. Fla. 2006) (Florida statute requires occupancy and a legal or equitable interest that gives right to occupy; here debtor could claim homestead in property owned by revocable trust of which he was sole trustee and primary beneficiary). *Cf.* Duran v. Henderson, 71 S.W.3d 833 (Tex. App. 2002) (transfer of homestead to family trust did not make it vulnerable to creditors, when Texas fraudulent transfer law does not apply to transfer of exempt property). *But see In re* Betcher, 2009 WL 210677 (Bankr. S.D. Tex. Jan. 26, 2009) (couple who had transferred home to irrevocable living trust could exempt their possessory right but not fee ownership); *In re* Zmijewski, 390 B.R. 24 (Bankr. D. Mass. 2008) (couple who owned life interests in home, with remainder held by family trust of which they were trustees, could exempt life interests but not remainder; their interests in trust were personal, not real property); *In re* Estarellas, 338 B.R. 538 (Bankr. D. Conn. 2006) (no exemption for property owned by revocable, self-settled, spendthrift trust); *In re* Barnes, 275 B.R. 889 (Bankr. E.D. Cal. 2002) (motor home in which debtors resided not homestead because owned by an irrevocable trust); *In re* Bosonetto, 271 B.R. 403 (Bankr. M.D. Fla. 2001) (Florida homestead exemption does not apply to property owned by trust). *But cf.* Boyle v. Weiss, 962 N.E.2d 169 (Mass. 2012) (former version of Massachusetts homestead statute would not exempt home owned by trust of which debtor was beneficiary and 50% owner).

736 *In re* Peirce, 483 B.R. 368 (Bankr. D. Mass. 2012).

737 *In re* Tinsley, 2010 WL 4823208 (Bankr. N.D. Tex. Nov. 16, 2010) (possessory interest sufficiently shown when debtor was devisee under father's will and no evidence he would not receive title); *In re* Martinez, 392 B.R. 530 (Bankr. E.D.N.Y. 2008) (allowing homestead exemption to debtor who resided in home owned by her late father, who had died intestate and whose estate was being administered, as title vests in heir by operation of law upon decedent's death); *In re* Dougan, 350 B.R. 892 (Bankr. D. Idaho 2006) (mother's will, which was still in probate, left home to debtor daughter who resided there, with mother's permission, during mother's lifetime; possessory interest, plus equitable interest arising from will, were sufficient ownership and occupation to support homestead exemption); *In re* Robertson, 227 B.R. 844 (Bankr. S.D. Ind. 1998) (liberally construing Indiana exemptions to allow homestead exemption in house which had been left to debtor by his deceased landlord, even though landlord's estate was still

contracts,[738] and even rental homes.[739] Other equitable interests may also be protected.[740] Courts have been less willing to rec-

in probate); *In re* Tetreault, 11 A.3d 635 (R.I. 2011) (mother's will left property, including the home, to be divided equally between son and daughter; son's rights as devisee were sufficient ownership to support a homestead exemption, but he no longer met homestead exemption's occupancy requirement once executrix gave him notice of termination of his tenancy and began eviction action). *But cf. In re* Stoner, 487 B.R. 410 (Bankr. D. N.J. 2013) (denying exemption to interest of one-third contingent beneficiary who was occupying late father's home on petition date; father's will did not bequeath house but directed that property be evenly divided among children); *In re* Wisotzke, 2011 WL 445812 (Bankr. W.D.N.Y. Feb. 4, 2011) (decedent's son did not have sufficient ownership interest in home to claim homestead exemption when will did not direct transfer of home to him, but he would merely inherit any assets left after estate was administered, and he had not administered the estate or conducted himself as owner); *In re* Howlett, 440 B.R. 186 (Bankr. D. Idaho 2010) (denying homestead exemption for debtor's interest in deceased mother's estate planning trust, which owned house; no "current possessory interest" when debtor did not reside in house on petition date and had right only to a percentage of the sales price).

738 *In re* Stone, 329 B.R. 860 (Bankr. N.D. Iowa 2005) (house being purchased on contract for deed, occupied by debtor's fiancée and children); *In re* Hunter, 295 B.R. 882 (Bankr. W.D. Ark. July 29, 2003) (homestead established when married person or head of household occupies property as home; "contract for deed" sufficient); *In re* Sorrell, 292 B.R. 276 (Bankr. E.D. Tex. 2002) (buyers could claim homestead in house they were buying under contract for deed, under which seller retained title until payments completed); *In re* New, 2013 WL 4715685 (Bankr. E.D. Ky. 2013) (allowing exemption, despite failure to properly record contract for deed); Redmond v. Kester, 159 P.3d 1004 (Kan. 2007) (homestead exemption may be based on executory contract to purchase). *See also In re* Hodes, 402 F.3d 1005 (10th Cir. 2005) (homestead exemption for funds prepaid to builder pursuant to binding contract for addition to homestead); *In re* McKown, 2003 WL 22119193 (Bankr. C.D. Ill. Sept. 8, 2003) (debtor may claim homestead exemption in property purchased at sheriff's sale when she had paid the sale price and moved in and sale was confirmed, even though deed not yet issued). *But cf. In re* Page, 289 B.R. 484 (Bankr. S.D. Ga. 2003) (seller had no homestead exemption in property she was selling under contract for deed, when purchasers were living in house and making payments; seller's interest was security interest, which gave her no right to occupy property).

739 *In re* Casserino, 379 F.3d 1069 (9th Cir. 2004) (occupancy, not legal title, is basis for homestead; Oregon exemption protects prepaid rent and security deposits for leased premises, because loss would likely result in eviction); *In re* Cohen, 2012 WL 400719 (Bankr. D.N.M. Feb. 7, 2012) (leasehold with option to purchase; statute allows homestead in house on land owned by another if debtor is leasing or purchasing the dwelling); *In re* McCallister, 2008 WL 515508 (Bankr. S.D. Ill. Feb. 22, 2008) (Illinois homestead, which applies to "interest in land or buildings . . . rightfully possessed . . . by lease or otherwise" protects tenant's security deposit; purpose of homestead is to keep roof over debtor's head, and requirement to turn over security deposit would likely result in eviction); *In re* Coffey, 339 B.R. 689 (Bankr. N.D. Ind. 2006) ($7500 prepaid rent was exempt "leasehold"); *In re* Rutland, 318 B.R. 588 (Bankr. M.D. Ala. 2004) (Alabama homestead protects tenancy in rented apartment; prepaid rent is exempt); *In re* McAtee, 154 B.R. 346, 347 (Bankr. D. Fla. 1993) (debtors who had house on public land, which they rented on ninety-nine-year lease, may claim homestead exemption); *In re* Bartlett, 153 B.R. 881, 883 (Bankr. D. Neb. 1993) (allowing homestead in house situated on leased land); *In re* Buzzell, 110 B.R. 440 (Bankr. D. Neb. 1990) (life estate or leasehold interest sufficient; manufactured home on rented land is exempt); Geraci v. Sunstar EMS, 93 So. 3d 384 (Fla. Dist. Ct. App. 2012) (condo occupied pursuant to 100-year lease covered by Florida homestead exemption); Redmond v. Kester, 159 P.3d 1004 (Kan. 2007) (Kansas homestead may be based on leasehold). *See also In re* Takes, 478 F.3d 902 (8th Cir. 2007) (leasehold that can be sold, here created by paying entrance fee to assisted living community, is property right that will support a homestead exemption, but ordinary landlord-tenant relationship is not); *In re* Wynn, 369 B.R. 605 (Bankr. D. Or. 2007) (proceeds of former marital home spent on rent exempt). *But see In re* Eagle, 373 B.R. 609 (B.A.P. 8th Cir. 2007) (no homestead exemption in leased property; "ownership interest" required); *In re* LaVelle, 350 B.R. 505 (Bankr. D. Idaho 2005) (no homestead claim for land occupied under oral at-will sublease from company wholly owned by husband, which was tenant under lease from L.L.C. 70% owned by debtors; lease terminable at will was not "ownership interest"); *In re* Tenorio, 107 B.R. 787, 788 (Bankr. S.D. Fla. 1989); Savage v. Pierson, 157 P.3d 697 (Nev. 2007) (prepaid rent not exempt under homestead or dwelling exemptions that cover land, manufactured home, cooperative unit or condominium; right to possession not sufficient; equity must be shown). *See generally* § 12.7.2.4, *supra* (co-op units and manufactured homes on leased land).

740 *In re* Brown, 408 B.R. 262 (Bankr. D. Minn. 2009) ("any interest in the land whether legal or equitable" will support homestead exemption; here, domestic partner of record owner had "constructive trust and equitable ownership" because of financial contributions, continued residency and agreement with partner); *In re* Lindquist, 395 B.R. 707 (Bankr. D. Or. 2008) (husband's name not on title, but he lived in marital home and made the payments; his equitable interest was sufficient that couple could claim the larger exemption for joint owners); *In re* Cadengo, 370 B.R. 681 (Bankr. S.D. Tex. 2007) ("any sort of title, legal or equitable" will support homestead exemption; allowing homestead claim when parents' divorce decree required father to deed house to debtor, who resided there, when she reached majority, which he had not done); Coy v. Mango Bay Prop. & Invs., Inc., 963 So. 2d 873 (Fla. Dist. Ct. App. 2007) (right to occupy is sufficient; once acquired, homestead not lost by court order awarding possession to other spouse; ex-husband entitled to hearing on claim of homestead in former marital home, titled in wife alone); Redmond v. Kester, 159 P.3d 1004 (Kan. 2007) (debtors who occupy and intend to occupy property as homestead may base claim on many kinds of property interests, including co-tenancy, equitable title, executory contract to purchase, leasehold estate, and life estate; "equitable interest" is sufficient). *But see* Fix v. First State Bank of Roscoe, 559 F.3d 803 (8th Cir. 2009) (when mother gave up life estate to allow holder of remainder interest to refinance, lender's written promise to allow mother to reside in home for life was not an ownership interest that would support a homestead exemption); *In re* Belcher, 551 F.3d 688 (7th Cir. 2008) (Illinois law; husband, whose name was not on title of marital home, could not claim homestead; some kind of "formal title interest" required, though it need not be fee simple); *In re* Scotti, 456 B.R. 760 (Bankr. D.S.C. 2011) (South Carolina homestead requires ownership interest; when property titled in wife, husband had at most a possessory interest and equitable distribution rights in case of divorce; allowing couple only one exemption); *In re* Majors, 2008 WL 5330002 (Bankr. N.D. Ala. Dec. 18, 2008) (ownership interest required; not shown when house titled in ex-wife, but separation agreement allowed debtor husband to live there while renovating it for sale and entitled him to half the sales proceeds); *In re* Hendrix, 2008 WL 276576 (Bankr. M.D. Ala. Jan. 29, 2008) (wife could not claim homestead when she and husband lived in manufactured home affixed to land owned solely by husband; right to claim a share after husband's death insufficient); *In re* LaVelle, 350 B.R. 505 (Bankr. D. Idaho 2005) (no homestead claim for land occupied under oral at-will sublease from company wholly owned by husband, which was tenant under lease from L.L.C. 70% owned by debtors; lease terminable at will was not "ownership interest"; no homestead claim for interest in a legal entity, here the L.L.C.). *But cf. In re* Doubov, 423 B.R. 505 (N.D. Ohio Feb. 8, 2010) (wife who quitclaimed property to

ognize a homestead exemption in property owned by a partnership[741] or limited liability corporation.[742]

12.7.4 *Occupancy Requirements and Abandonment*

12.7.4.1 Occupancy

The establishment of a homestead generally requires actual occupancy, with intent to make the property one's home.[743] Nonetheless, the homestead exemption may apply to a home

husband without reserving dower interest may not claim homestead; Ohio requires a property interest); *In re* Hart, 332 B.R. 439 (D. Wyo. 2005) (occupancy plus some legal or equitable interest necessary for statutory homestead exemption; mere occupant not entitled to assert exemption over interests of owner or one with superior title); *In re* Gibson, 433 B.R. 868 (Bankr. N.D. Okla. 2010) (denying homestead exemption for home debtor had quitclaimed to wife; Oklahoma may allow homestead for bare right to possession, but not here when debtor voluntarily relinquished all rights in property); *In re* Perpinan, 2006 WL 3507943 (Bankr. N.D. Cal. Dec. 4, 2006) (California homestead requires both occupancy and ownership; no exemption when alleged ownership arose from sham transaction; debtor purchased interest from mother, with check she never cashed, and shortly thereafter deeded his interest back to her).

741 *In re* Steffen, 405 B.R. 486 (M.D. Fla. 2009) (denying homestead exemption to home owned by limited partnership); *In re* Hoggarth Bros., 2004 WL 903814 (D.N.D. Apr. 22, 2004) (farm couples resided on land owned by husbands' farm partnership; wives had no homestead rights); *In re* Bell, 2007 WL 4190686 (Bankr. N.D. Cal. Nov. 21, 2007) (debtor lived in unit in multiple-unit dwelling owned by partnership; California homestead protects only property of natural person, not a partnership); *In re* Shepard, 2007 WL 1385725 (Bankr. D.N.M. May 7, 2007) (partners may not claim homestead exemption in home owned by partnership); *In re* Lyle, 355 B.R. 161 (Bankr. D. Ariz. Dec. 13, 2006) (no homestead exemption for property owned by partnership owned by debtors; rights in partnership were personal, not real property); *In re* Monsivais, 274 B.R. 263 (Bankr. W.D. Tex. 2002) (no homestead exemption for home owned by family partnership); *In re* Cole, 205 B.R. 382 (Bankr. E.D. Tex. 1997) (homestead was abandoned when land was transferred from natural person to a "family limited partnership"); Siller v. LPP Mortgage, Ltd., 264 S.W.3d 324 (Tex. App. 2008) (partnership property cannot be homestead).

742 *In re* Breece, 2013 WL 197399 (B.A.P. 6th Cir. Jan. 18, 2013) (no homestead exemption for home owned by L.L.C.); *In re* Schmakel, 2013 WL 594317 (Bankr. N.D. Ohio Feb. 14, 2013) (member of LLC has no ownership interest in property titled to LLC; statute allowing exemptions in partnership property does not apply to LLC); *In re* Coenan, ___B.R. ___, 2012 WL 3960313 (Bankr. W.D. Wis. Sept. 10, 2012) (no exemption for property owned by L.L.C. or corporation); *In re* Kochman, 2011 WL 5325792 (Bankr. D. Conn. Nov. 3, 2011) (property owned by L.L.C. can never be homestead because homestead may be claimed only by natural person, and property must be owner-occupied); *In re* Arnhoelter, 431 B.R. 453 (Bankr. E.D. Wis. 2010) (denying Wisconsin homestead exemption because property was titled in debtor's LLC when creditor's judgment was docketed; title is key issue); *In re* Hecker, 414 B.R. 499 (Bankr. D. Minn. 2009) (denying homestead to home owned by LLC; Minnesota courts will pierce corporate veil for equitable reasons, generally for homes owned by family farm corporations; declining to do so for luxury home occupied by sophisticated businessman, who did not require the property for his livelihood); *In re* Moore, 2009 WL 1066135 (Bankr. S.D. Tex. Mar. 27, 2009) (transfer of homestead to LLC of which property owners were sole members eliminated homestead exemption); *In re* LaVelle, 350 B.R. 505 (Bankr. D. Idaho 2005) (no homestead claim for interest in LLC that owned land leased and occupied by debtors). *See also In re* Kane, 2011 WL 2119015 (Bankr. D. Mass. May 23, 2011) (property owned by debtor's L.L.C., which had been administratively dissolved, was not homestead; dissolved LLC still existed because it had not been properly wound up); Radosevich v. Allen, 2010 WL 1531427 (Cal. Ct. App. Apr. 19, 2010) (unpublished) (no homestead for property owned by corporation; distinguishing revocable trust cases). *But see In re* Basler, 2011 WL 867131 (Bankr. D. Neb. Mar. 10, 2011) (debtors' "tacit agreement" with their LLC that they could occupy home it owned was a sufficient "estate or interest in land which gives the right of occupancy or possession" to support Nebraska homestead).

743 *In re* Sacharko, 356 B.R. 786 (table), 2007 WL 128775 (B.A.P. 1st Cir. 2007) (Rhode Island homestead exemption requires occupancy; no homestead exemption for ex-husband's interest in former marital home that would not vest until child turned 19); *In re* Kelley, 300 B.R. 11 (B.A.P. 9th Cir. 2003) (California law) (automatic homestead requires intent to reside permanently; not shown when owner moved into apartment, visited home "occasionally" to repair damage, and rented it to cousin; declared homestead continued, because no new homestead established, but would not protect against forced sale); *In re* Antonie, 447 B.R. 610 (D. Idaho 2011) (debtor who jointly owned home occupied by her mother, but did not live there, could not exempt the home); *In re* Kology, 499 B.R. 20 (Bankr. D. Mass. 2013) (actual occupancy is key; absence of several years, living in trailer and "work camping" at campgrounds did not eliminate exemption when debtors were residing on property on petition date); *In re* Fling, 449 B.R. 580 (Bankr. N.D. Fla. 2011) (debtor re-established homestead in property that had been rented out to tenants, when he moved back in and stayed for eighteen months); *In re* Harris, 2010 WL 2595294 (Bankr. D. Idaho June 23, 2010) (denying Washington exemption for home located in Washington that was rented out to others when wife worked and attended school in Idaho and husband's job prospects in Washington were dubious); *In re* Harwood, 404 B.R. 366 (Bankr. E.D. Tex. 2009) (newly divorced debtor, who had moved onto his separate property after marital home awarded to wife, could claim homestead in the property where he resided), *aff'd on other grounds*, 427 B.R. 392 (E.D. Tex. 2010); *In re* Patterson, 487 B.R. 485 (Bankr. W.D. Tenn. 2013) (present right to occupy is sufficient; allowing exemption for property formerly rented to tenants; note that debtors, whose home had been foreclosed, had no right to occupy any other property); *In re* Crooks, 351 B.R. 783 (Bankr. S.D. Fla. 2006) (debtors living in house they did not yet own on date of hurricane; insurance proceeds not proceeds of homestead because debtors did not own, and owner did not occupy house; but proceeds exempt because received by debtors in trust for owner and mortgage lender, to be used for repairs); *In re* Greene, 346 B.R. 835 (Bankr. D. Nev. 2006) (if debtor actually owns and occupies land, "mode of occupation" is irrelevant; here, debtor lived in travel trailer and had signed contracts to improve land and build house), *rev'd on other grounds*, 583 F.3d 614 (9th Cir. 2009) (reversing application of federal bankruptcy law's 1215-day look-back period to this homestead); *In re* Tetreault, 11 A.3d 635 (R.I. 2011) (son whose interest in home derived from deceased mother's will no longer met homestead exemption's occupancy requirement once executrix gave him notice of termination of his tenancy and began eviction action against him); Gibson v. Fauber, 2004 WL 2002560 (Tex. App. Sept. 8, 2004) (debtor occupied home with mother, later with wife, lived elsewhere only when incarcerated or working at out of town jobs); Houghton v. Miller, 118 P.3d 293 (Utah Ct. App. 2005) (property not "primary personal residence" at time when judgment lien attached; debtor had filed homestead declaration and caused repairs to be begun but was living elsewhere). *See also In re* Jones, 397 B.R. 765 (Bankr. D.S.C. 2008) (debtors moved into smaller house they owned after former home became unaffordable; small house was homestead when it was equipped with "the appointments for comfortable living" and debtors actually lived there). *See generally* § 12.7.3.2, *supra*.

if the debtor is temporarily absent but intends to return.[744] In some states, occupancy by a family member of the debtor may be sufficient.[745] Immigrants who have the right to reside in the United States only temporarily may be unable to meet an occupancy requirement that requires an intent to reside in the home permanently.[746]

Occupancy of the entire property may not be necessary to exempt it.[747] For example, a debtor who owns a two-family house, occupies one unit, and rents out the other unit may be allowed to exempt the entire house.[748] Likewise, a property

744 *See, e.g.*, *In re* Schott, 449 B.R. 697 (Bankr. W.D. Tex. Mar. 16, 2011) (intent to stay away permanently not shown when debtor moved to city for business reasons, here to construct a "spec house"). *But cf.* Feucht v. Pierce, 2006 WL 3354507 (D.S.D. Nov. 15, 2006) (no homestead exemption for wife who had moved out of home jointly owned with estranged husband; intent to return that is "merely possible" or contingent on other event—here, husband's departure or couple's reconciliation—is insufficient); *In re* Schuster, 2006 WL 2711800 (D. Mont. Sept. 21, 2006) (residence required with some exceptions for temporary absence with intent to return; not shown here as debtor had not resided in condominium for ten years but intended to return when his dog died); *In re* Taliercio, 2012 WL 441421 (Bankr. D. Conn. Feb. 19, 2012) (denying exemption when, on petition date, property was rented to tenants on one-year lease; intent to return not sufficient); *In re* Cochran, 2009 WL 605298 (Bankr. S.D. Ala. Mar. 9, 2009) (Alabama residency requirement is strict; debtor who temporarily moved in with parents and rented out homestead, because this was the only way he could afford mortgage, lost homestead exemption). *See generally* § 12.7.4.2, *infra* (abandonment of homestead).

745 *In re* Hall, 441 B.R. 680 (B.A.P. 10th Cir. 2009) (Kansas law) (debtor may claim homestead exemption either in own residence or in residence occupied by family; when wife resided in house and husband in manufactured home, each spouse must choose which interest to exempt); Flynn v. Farmer Masonry, Inc., 2008 WL 346032 (N.D. Iowa Feb. 6, 2008) (continued occupancy by non-debtor wife prevented judgment lien from attaching even though judgment debtor husband had moved out); *In re* Goulakos, 456 B.R. 729 (Bankr. D. Mass. 2011) (even though married couple had been separated for ten years and did not intend to reconcile, wife remained a family member, covered by husband' homestead declaration); *In re* Nelson, 2010 WL 3911387 (Bankr. E.D.N.C. Oct. 1, 2010) (continued occupancy by dependent wife sufficient to preserve exemption of debtor husband who leaves marital home); *In re* Thompson, 2008 WL 1766592 (Bankr. D. Mass. Apr. 14, 2008) (occupancy by adult daughter of ex-husband who had filed homestead declaration was sufficient to maintain Massachusetts exemption); Beltram v. Kalb, 63 So. 3d 783 (Fla. Dist. Ct. App. 2011) (Florida homestead exemption continues in former marital home now occupied by debtor's ex-wife and couple's daughter); Grisolia v. Pfeffer, 77 So. 3d 732 (Fla. Dist. Ct. App. 2011) (homestead protected widow and son who resided in home); Garcia v. Andonie, 101 So. 3d 339 (Fla. 2012) (Florida's constitutional homestead protects property maintained as a permanent residence for owner's dependents; state tax statute allowing exemption only if owner personally resided on the premises was unconstitutional). *See also In re* Mixon, 2014 WL 28669 (Bankr. S.D. Ga. Jan. 2, 2014) (fact that non-dependent mother also lived in a mobile home on the tract on which debtor's mobile home stood did not eliminate exemption); *In re* Andris, 471 B.R. 761 (Bankr. D. Mass. 2012) (allowing estranged husband to claim homestead in home occupied by his wife and daughter; construing former Massachusetts statute as to effect of wife's filing of homestead declaration subsequent to husband's filing). *But see In re* Antonie, 447 B.R. 610 (D. Idaho 2011) (debtor who lived elsewhere could not assert her mother's homestead exemption to protect jointly-owned home where mother lived); *In re* Clark, 2012 WL 3597410 (Bankr. D. Md. Aug. 20, 2012) (debtor cannot claim California homestead for property owned in joint tenancy with former wife and occupied by former wife and children), *aff'd*, Clark v. Guttman, 2013 WL 812017 (D. Md. Mar. 4, 2013); *In re* Ramey, 2011 WL 1044584 (Bankr. D.N.M. Mar. 17, 2011) (contiguous parcel with house rented to relatives not homestead; occupancy not shown); Phillips v. Phillips, 2004 WL 503905 (Conn. Super. Ct. Feb. 25, 2004) (must be actually occupied by debtor as principal residence; not shown when debtor owned and paid bills for house occupied by relatives but ate and slept in another house he shared with wife and used that address on driver's license); *In re* Nilsson, 315 P.3d 966 (Nev. 2013) (denying exemption for home occupied by ex-wife and minor children; Nevada homestead requires occupancy by debtor).

746 *See, e.g.*, *In re* Fodor, 339 B.R. 519 (Bankr. M.D. Fla. 2006) (alien who did not obtain permanent resident status until after filing bankruptcy petition not entitled to exemption); *In re* Walter, 230 B.R. 200 (Bankr. S.D. Fla. 1999) (Canadian citizens who did not have permanent visas could not claim Florida homestead, because they could not intend to permanently reside there). *See also In re* Oulette, 2009 WL 1936896 (Bankr. M.D. Fla. Mar. 26, 2009) (limitation of homestead to residence of the owner does not apply to rural homestead; debtors who resided in one manufactured home and rented the other to unrelated third parties could claim homestead in land and both homes); De la Mora v. Andonie, 101 So. 3d 339 (Fla. 2012) (resident aliens, not qualified to become citizens, could not intend to permanently reside, but occupation of home by their American-born children sufficient to qualify it for homestead tax exemption). *But cf.* Grisolia v. Pfeffer, 77 So. 3d 732 (Fla. Dist. Ct. App. 2011) (intent to reside permanently shown; debtor's American citizen son resided on property; also deceased debtor and surviving wife had both applied for permanent residency).

747 *See, e.g.*, *In re* Navarro, 2014 B.R. 293247 (Bankr. D. P.R. Jan. 28, 2014) (disallowing exemption for part of house, here one room, rented to tenant); *In re* Prosser, 2013 WL 594312 (Bankr. D. V.I. Feb. 14, 2013) (debtors' occupation of guest house was sufficient to exempt entire parcel, including unfinished mansion).

748 *In re* Rupp, 415 B.R. 72 (Bankr. W.D.N.Y. 2008) (debtor who lived in one half of duplex and rented other half to tenants may exempt the entire property; noting that for many Buffalo residents, buying a duplex and renting one half is "the only way to attain homeownership"); *In re* Majewski, 362 B.R. 67 (Bankr. D. Conn. 2007) (Connecticut defines homestead as "owner-occupied real property . . . used as a primary residence," but entire property need not be so used; debtor may exempt three-unit building when he lives in one unit and rents out the other two); *In re* McBratney, 2007 WL 2684072 (Bankr. D. Kan. Sept. 7, 2007) (use of part of tract to provide income for family does not eliminate homestead; debtor who depended on tenants' rent to pay mortgage could exempt whole owner-occupied four-unit building); *In re* McCambry, 327 B.R. 469 (Bankr. D. Kan. 2005) (homeowners entitled to exempt entire duplex even though they rented out one unit); *In re* Shell, 295 B.R. 129 (Bankr. D. Alaska 2003) (allowing debtor to exempt entire owner-occupied six-unit building; rental income also exempt under Alaska Stat. § 9.38.030(b)); *In re* Carey, 282 B.R. 118 (Bankr. D. Mass. 2002) (debtors could exempt entire owner-occupied triple-decker; court notes that the rent used to pay mortgage is "as necessary as the furnace"); *In re* Trigonis, 224 B.R. 152 (Bankr. D. Nev. 1998) (allowing Nevada homestead exemption on entire four-unit building, when owner resided in one unit and rented out the other three); *In re* Ruggles, 210 B.R. 57 (Bankr. D. Vt. 1997) (debtor could exempt duplex as homestead when she resided in one-half and rented the other); Sifuentes v. Arriola, 2009 WL 1099253 (Tex. App. Apr. 22, 2009) (unpublished) (allowing homestead exemption of four-unit building; debtors lived in one unit and rented the others). *See also In re* Johns, 504 B.R. 657 (Bankr. D. Idaho 2014) (presence of rental house did not eliminate exemption for parcels used for horses and livestock, and garden); *In re* Springman, 328 B.R. 251 (Bankr. D.D.C.

may be the debtor's homestead even if part of it is used for business purposes.[749] At least one state, Texas, specifically exempts a "business homestead," that is, property used for both residential and business purposes.[750]

An occupancy requirement may be a problem for a debtor who seeks to claim a homestead in a less than full-time home.[751] Courts will consider the duration and the reason for the occupancy, the existence of another residence, and other indicia of residency such as the location of bank accounts, business, and voting or motor vehicle registration.[752] The analysis is similar

2005) (renting out two bedrooms of single-family home and "incidental" business use does not destroy homestead). *Cf. In re* Myers, 323 B.R. 11 (Bankr. D.N.H. 2005) (debtor entitled to homestead protection in both units of duplex when second unit occupied by dependent elderly mother and not used for production of income). *But see In re* MacLeod, 295 B.R. 1 (Bankr. D. Me. 2003) (manufactured-home park owned by debtor not homestead when nineteen lots were rented out and twentieth occupied by owner); *In re* Tsoupas, 250 B.R. 466 (Bankr. D.N.H. 2000) (debtors who resided in four-unit apartment building, in which husband owned a half interest, could claim homestead only in the part they occupied, as measured by percentage of floor space); Menard v. Univ. Radiation Oncology Assocs., L.L.P., 976 So. 2d 69 (Fla. Dist. Ct. App. 2008) (if part of property, here a triplex, is leased to others, exemption protects only the part occupied by debtor; if partition impossible, property must be sold, and debtor paid a pro rata share of proceeds).

749 *See, e.g., In re* Graff, 457 B.R. 429 (Bankr. W.D. Pa. 2011) (need not show that every acre of large rural lot used for homestead purposes; allowing exemption of manufactured home, nineteen-acre lot, and oil and gas rights); *In re* Giles, 443 B.R. 524 (Bankr. W.D. Ark. 2011) (entire property is homestead even though it includes small family-run business as well as debtors' home); *In re* McCarthy, 2011 WL 5833869 (Bankr. N.D.N.Y. Nov. 18, 2011) (allowing "indivisible homestead" in property that could not be lawfully subdivided; property included building in which debtors lived and carried on business, and two-family home rented out to unrelated tenants); *In re* Carey, 282 B.R. 118 (Bankr. D. Mass. 2002) (Massachusetts homestead exemption covers entire property, including home business, storage space and rental property, subject only to dollar limitation). *See also In re* Nork, 2012 WL 6027765 (Bankr. D. Or. Dec. 4, 2012) (exempting proceeds of lease of corner of rural homestead for cell phone tower; debtor was using proceeds to pay her mortgage). *But see In re* Radtke, 344 B.R. 690 (Bankr. S.D. Fla. 2006) (when debtor's home and rental recreational vehicle sites were both located on same parcel, and parcel could not be divided, it had to be sold and proceeds allocated between homestead and bankruptcy estate); *In re* Carpenter, 278 B.R. 102 (Bankr. N.D. Miss. 2001) (non-contiguous parcel used mainly for commercial purposes not homestead, even though debtor sometimes kept a few cows there); *In re* Bell, 252 B.R. 562 (Bankr. M.D. Fla. 2000) (homestead exemption did not protect commercial building on same parcel of land as residence; if land could not be subdivided, it must be sold and the proceeds apportioned); *In re* Sears, 246 B.R. 881 (Bankr. S.D. Iowa 2000) (debtors may claim as homestead their house and one garage of small value, but not buildings used for salvage and repair business), *aff'd*, 246 B.R. 341 (B.A.P. 8th Cir. 2000). *But cf. In re* Pich, 253 B.R. 562 (Bankr. D. Idaho 2000) (application for light industrial zoning, which barred residential use, estopped debtor from claiming homestead, although he was living in office at site).

750 *See In re* Jay, 432 F.3d 323 (5th Cir. 2005) (Texas law; property where debtors worked but did not reside was not homestead); *In re* Kang, 243 B.R. 666 (Bankr. N.D. Tex. 1999) (shopkeeper who owned strip mall could claim business homestead in his shop and adjacent parking but not rest of mall). *Cf. In re* Perry, 481 B.R. 862 (Bankr. N.D. Tex. 2012) (adjacent lots with residence and workshop; business homestead in workshop lost when debtor abandoned residence).

Prior to a statutory amendment in 2000, the Texas "business homestead" was applicable to property used for an occupation to support the household without regard to residential use. *See, e.g., In re* John Taylor Co., 935 F.2d 75 (5th Cir. 1991) (property used for manufacturing and selling of bedding supplies exempt).

751 *In re* Fisher, 486 B.R. 200 (Bankr. D. Kan. 2013) (allowing exemption of rural land where debtor lived in trailer; crediting debtor's testimony that he was separated from wife, even though he used marital home as mailing address); *In re* Demeter, 478 B.R. 281 (Bankr. E.D. Mich. 2012) (federal exemption allows debtor who owns and lives in two residences to choose which to exempt; here debtors allowed to exempt second home in which they resided for almost half the year; note that principal residence was "underwater" and debtors were seeing work in area of second home); *In re* Lawrence, 469 B.R. 140 (Bankr. D. Mass. May 2, 2012) (federal law, unlike Massachusetts, does not require showing that property is principal residence; if debtors own and use two residences, they may choose which to exempt; debtors allowed to claim homestead for Maine condominium when their Massachusetts home was being foreclosed on, and they had arranged to move their household goods to Maine); *In re* Kaplan, 468 B.R. 246 (Bankr. W.D Ky. 2012) (staying overnight occasionally on property that lacked refrigerator or cooking facilities insufficient for federal bankruptcy exemption that refers to state definition of residence); *In re* Belding, 2010 WL 5376295 (Bankr. D. Vt. Dec. 23, 2010) (debtors who resided more than half the year in Florida apartment allowed to claim homestead in family home in Vermont; debtors paid resident income taxes in Vermont, owned no real property in Florida, and had not registered to vote there); *In re* Brown, 299 B.R. 425 (Bankr. N.D. Tex. 2003) (vacation timeshare that debtors who resided on military base used for two weeks per year is not homestead under Florida law so is not exempt under federal bankruptcy exemptions); *In re* Marsico, 278 B.R. 1 (Bankr. D.N.H. 2002) (couple who lived and operated seasonal businesses in New Hampshire, but lived in New Jersey during off-season, not entitled to New Hampshire homestead exemption; "vacation or seasonal" occupancy not sufficient); *In re* Lowery, 262 B.R. 875 (Bankr. M.D. Fla. 2001) (use of part of qualified homestead for commercial purposes does not destroy homestead status; debtors could exempt home and citrus farm).

752 Smith v. Winnsboro Equip., Inc., 2011 WL 1655577 (S.D. Tex. May 1, 2011) (debtor's testimony that he lived in Louisiana "only for business purposes" was outweighed by evidence that he bought a house, lived there with his family, voted, maintained bank accounts and was active in community affairs in Louisiana); *In re* Harwell, 2008 WL 410590 (D. Colo. Feb. 13, 2008) (ranch was "hobby and tax shelter," not homestead, when debtor changed motor vehicle and voting registrations to ranch address but continued to pay bills for family home—occupied by wife and children, where he had resided up to time of bankruptcy—and to claim tax deduction for family home's mortgage); *In re* Ashton, 2013 WL 211243 (Bankr. D. Idaho Jan. 18, 2013) (denying homestead exemption for oil field worker's fifth-wheel trailer, which he would site in an RV park near each jobsite and in which he spent about two-thirds of his time; concluding that rented apartment in which his wife and children resided and which he used for mail, voting, licenses, among other things, was principal residence); *In re* Middleton, 462 B.R. 832 (Bankr. N.D. Fla. 2011) (denying homestead exemption when, shortly before defaulting on large debt, debtor bought Florida property and changed driver's license and voting registration, as "financial and social affairs" linked debtor to Georgia; debtor registered his company car, maintained bank accounts, received healthcare, and attended church in Georgia), *aff'd sub nom.* Middleton v. Phillips, 2012 WL 764196 (N.D. Fla. Feb. 29, 2012); *In re* Capps, 438 B.R. 668 (Bankr. D. Idaho 2010) (debtor who lived, worked, registered to vote, registered her car, and paid taxes in Idaho could not exempt Colorado property, occupied by her mother, to which debtor hoped to retire);

but not identical to the determination of residency for other legal purposes.[753]

Typically courts evaluate whether an occupancy requirement has been met as of the date of the bankruptcy filing or the levy on the home.[754] However, many courts allow a debtor to exempt a recently-acquired home if the debtor has taken concrete steps to move or to prepare it for occupancy.[755]

In re Tinsley, 2010 WL 4823208 (Bankr. N.D. Tex. Nov. 16, 2010) (when there is ambiguity as to debtor's residence, debtor may choose which parcel to exempt; allowing exemption when family home was occupied by debtor's son and grandchildren, debtor's business was located there, and debtor listed address on his tax filings, even though debtor slept and received mail on property owned by wife); *In re* Lloyd, 394 B.R. 605 (Bankr. S.D. Fla. 2008) (voter and motor vehicle registrations probative but not determinative; allowing exemption for Florida property of debtor who changed registrations while living in month-to-month rentals in California, but returned to Florida to care for property, and was prevented from living there by hurricane damage); *In re* Hageman, 388 B.R. 896 (Bankr. C.D. Ill. 2008) (crude accommodation added to debtor's business premises was homestead, when debtor lived there and used address for voting, driver's license, and Social Security); *In re* Dilbeck, 2008 WL 867897 (Bankr. E.D. Tenn. Mar. 28, 2008) (changing voter registrations three days before bankruptcy not sufficient to confer homestead status; debtors lived and worked elsewhere and listed other address on driver's licenses); *In re* Meltzer, 2007 WL 543922 (Bankr. S.D. Tex. Feb. 16, 2007) (property was homestead; debtor used address on bankruptcy forms, received homestead tax exemption, and family friend testified that debtor lived there); *In re* Siehler, 2006 WL 2034385 (Bankr. M.D. Fla. Apr. 27, 2006) (debtor could not claim homestead exemption in parent's house in which she owned one-third interest; intent to reside there permanently not shown when she had not changed driver's license and voter registration and admitted that she would return to marital home if she reconciled with husband); *In re* Wilson, 338 B.R. 315 (Bankr. W.D. Ky. 2006) (no homestead exemption in property not listed by debtors as their address for bankruptcy petition; offices of debtors' company located on property, and no evidence of permanent or continuous residence); *In re* Prestwood, 322 B.R. 463 (Bankr. S.D. Fla. 2005) (allowing Florida homestead exemption when debtor maintained extensive ties to California but sufficiently demonstrated intent to live in Florida); *In re* Whitehead, 278 B.R. 597 (Bankr. M.D. Fla. 2002) (debtor who bought home in Florida and eventually found work there but maintained various ties with former home in Indiana, including a temporary job, bank accounts, and physician, was entitled to Florida homestead exemption because evidence was equally balanced and party who challenged exemption bore burden of proof); Konover Constr. Co. v. Silberstein, 2003 WL 21805576 (Conn. Super. Ct. July 22, 2003) (house was homestead, even though debtor spent about half of her nights at assisted living facility she owned; she had bought house with husband, used address for driver's license and voter registration, and been served with process there); Antonello v. Reilly, 2012 WL 5381908 (Minn. Ct. App. Nov. 5, 2012) (debtors' testimony that they were living in second home not sufficient to outweigh their use of address of former home on drivers' license, tax returns and mailing, and their affirmation, when refinancing, that it was principal residence). *But see In re* Curry, 2009 WL 5198294 (Bankr. D. Kan. Dec. 22, 2009) (homestead exemption in old family home survived, even though debtors voted, worked, and received mail in another city where they lived for two and a half years in rented housing).

753 *In re* Marsico, 278 B.R. 1 (Bankr. D.N.H. 2002) (debtors established residency for purpose of bankruptcy filing but not for homestead exemption); Union Square Fed. Credit Union v. Clay, 2009 WL 1099434 (Tex. App. Apr. 23, 2009) (loss of homestead tax exemption, because debtors did not reside in house, did not result in loss of homestead exemption; debtors had not established homestead in new house, when they neither sold nor rented old house, maintained it and kept personal property there).

754 *In re* Holland, 474 B.R. 826 (Bankr. E.D. Mich. 2012) (denying exemption when debtors not living on property on petition date; moving there after postpetition foreclosure not sufficient); *In re* Anderson, 2012 WL 1110056 (Bankr. D. Mont. Apr. 2, 2012) (denying exemption when, on date homestead declaration was filed, debtor was working in California, living in an apartment for which rent was current, and had stopped making mortgage payments on subject property in Montana); *In re* Pendley, 2013 WL 141595 (Bankr. W.D. Tex. Jan. 11, 2013) (when debtor's wife and children were residing in old home on petition date, denying exemption for property where they planned to live after foreclosure); *In re* Dilbeck, 2008 WL 867897 (Bankr. E.D. Tenn. Mar. 28, 2008) (status of land determined as of petition date; no homestead for land where debtors planned to live after retirement; house was residence and therefore homestead); *In re* Maloney, 311 B.R. 525 (Bankr. W.D. Mo. 2004) (moving back into abandoned homestead after petition filed and creditors' meeting held was too late to establish new homestead); Gonzalez v. Toews, 4 Cal. Rptr. 3d 434 (Cal. Ct. App. 2003) (judgment debtor who moves into property after it has been levied upon cannot assert homestead exemption to defeat sale). *See also* Ramsey v. Davis, 261 S.W.3d 811 (Tex. App. 2008) (home buyers were residing on property on date when developer's creditor filed a lien; property was homestead, so lien could not attach). *But see In re* Voliva, 2011 WL 6301232 (Bankr. E.D.N.C. Dec. 16, 2011) (allowing exemption although, on petition date, debtors were living with their son because of medical problems; utilities were turned on in manufactured home on property where debtors had lived for ten years).

755 *In re* Robinson, 295 B.R. 147 (10th Cir. 2003) (Oklahoma law) (must show "overt acts of preparation followed within a reasonable time by actual occupancy or good faith attempt to occupy"; debtor's visit with small overnight bag on eve of bankruptcy filing not sufficient when house owned by debtor's late father was unoccupied and deteriorating or occupied by unsatisfactory tenants); Wechsler v. Carrington, 214 F. Supp. 2d 1348 (S.D. Fla. 2002) (Florida homestead requires actual occupation; when debtor had bought condominium but was still living in hotel on date judgment was recorded, condominium not exempt; burden of proof on objector); *In re* Whitney, 2014 WL 183821 (Bankr. E.D. N.C. Jan. 15, 2014) (recently inherited, badly run-down, home was "being used as a residence" for which debtor wife paid taxes and utilities, lived there ten days a month to see that it was maintained, and brought in furniture and personal property; note that couple's marital home was heavily encumbered); *In re* Issa, 501 B.R. 223 (Bankr. S.D.N.Y. 2013) (preparation to occupy not shown; debtor acquired rundown home in divorce a year prepetition but did not seek estimate for repairs until after the petition date); *In re* Thomason, 2013 WL 625343 (Bankr. D. Idaho Feb. 19, 2013) (allowing debtors to exempt remainder interest in home occupied by mother; debtors had filed paperwork to abandon former homestead and declare new homestead, and made plans to move in and care for mother); *In re* Ziccardi, 2011 WL 1770413 (Bankr. D. Kan. May 9, 2011) (Kansas occupancy requirement met by preparatory steps; allowing homestead in home that debtors were attempting to renovate; debtors were occupants even though problems with the renovation thwarted their physical occupancy); *In re* Knotts, 405 B.R. 322 (Bankr. E.D. Mo. 2009) (family member's offer of financial assistance with repair or replacement of uninhabitable house is insufficient to show intent to occupy; must show some overt acts); *In re* Bernhardt, 2008 WL 2484582 (Bankr. D. Neb. June 17, 2008) (debtors who were renovating old house could claim homestead because they were taking active steps to make the house habitable); *In re* Tofani, 365 B.R. 338 (Bankr. D. Mass. 2007) (debtor could claim homestead in home co-owned with ex-wife, who resided there with children; debtor paid for upkeep, spent significant time visiting his children there, and credibly testified that he intended to buy and live in house after child support

A homestead claim may also be possible in land where one plans to make a home, if substantial steps have been taken to prepare the land for occupancy.[756] A debtor who has sold a

obligations terminated); *In re* Lindsey, 2006 WL 4112666 (Bankr. M.D. Fla. Dec. 13, 2006) (allowing homestead exemption under Florida law for debtor who was entitled to exclusive possession of home acquired shortly before parties separated and who intended to live there, even though she had not yet moved in); *In re* Wipperling, 286 B.R. 106 (Bankr. N.D. Iowa 2002) (allowing debtor to claim homestead in newer manufactured home he was living in "as best he could" during set up and renovation, that is, he had to fetch water from uninhabitable older home, because plumbing in new one not yet functional); AgVantage FS v. Western Farming, Inc., 803 N.W.2d 672 (Iowa Ct. App. 2011) (debtors sold homestead and used proceeds to purchase land and a modular home; new parcel was homestead even though home was not yet ready for occupancy); Kendall Builders, Inc. v. Chesson, 149 S.W.3d 796 (Tex. App. 2004) (allowing Texas homestead even though wife and children remained in California while Texas home being remodeled, when husband began working in Texas, both spouses registered to vote, obtained drivers licenses and opened checking account in Texas, shipped their car there and registered it, and donated to local charities, and contractor knew that family intended to live in house). *But see In re* Banks, 2012 WL 3201569 (B.A.P. 9th Cir. July 31, 2012) (intent to occupy not sufficiently shown, despite filing of declaration of abandonment of current home and declaration of homestead for subject property, when debtors were paying mortgage on current home and had not indicated an intent to surrender it, subject property was not zoned for residential use and was leased to a tenant, and debtors had not applied for variance); *In re* Lehr, 479 B.R. 90 (Bankr. N.D. Cal. 2012) (actual occupancy required; denying exemption for newly purchased property being repaired to make it habitable); *In re* Felgner, 2011 WL 5056994 (Bankr. N.D. Ohio Oct. 24, 2011) (must show either current occupancy, or former occupancy and temporary absence; debtors who planned to surrender current home to lender and move into former summer home could not exempt summer home); Chas Roberts Air Conditioning, Inc. v. Pekrul, 2012 WL 1571400 (Ariz. Ct. App. May 3, 2012) (denying exemption for motor home parked in driveway of home being foreclosed on; debtors failed to show that they were actually living in the motor home); Walbridge v. Estate of Beaudoin, 48 A.3d 964 (N.H. 2012) (present physical occupancy required; no homestead claim on land where couple was building a house). *But cf. In re* Lynn, 2013 WL 6234511 (B.A.P. 9th Cir. Dec. 2, 2013) (unpublished) (denying exemption even though debtor had filed declaration of abandonment for old homestead and declaration of homestead for land; intent to occupy not shown when debtor had taken no steps to prepare the land and had listed it for sale as required by divorce decree); *In re* Pendley, 2013 WL 141595 (Bankr. W.D. Tex. Jan. 11, 2013) (denying exemption for new home in which debtor resided; old homestead not abandoned when debtor's wife and daughter remained in foreclosed home while daughter finished school year); *In re* Harle, 422 B.R. 310 (Bankr. M.D. Fla. 2010) (debtors in process of moving could claim homestead in new house when they resided there on petition date, even if they spent some nights at old home while clearing out the property, but exemption did not protect against judgment lien that attached before the move, as the property was not yet their homestead at that point); *In re* Campbell, 2009 WL 2762716 (Bankr. W.D. Mo. Aug. 25, 2009) (occupancy must be imminent or "reasonably close in time and neither indefinite nor incapable of measurement"; not shown when debtors planned to move in two years, but no evidence of how they would fund necessary repairs or find new jobs in the area).

756 AG Acceptance Corp. v. Veigel, 564 F.3d 695 (5th Cir. 2009) (Texas law) (to establish homestead in land one does not presently occupy, must show present intent to use the property as a home at a reasonable and definite future time and an unequivocal overt act in furtherance of this intent; commercial or recreational use, or a written declaration of intent are insufficient); *In re* Ramsey, 2012 WL 3205415 (B.A.P. 9th Cir. Aug. 3, 2012) (intent to occupy unimproved land sufficiently shown when debtors had filed declaration of abandonment for present home, which they intended to surrender in bankruptcy, filed declaration of homestead for the land, obtained necessary variances and drawn up plans for house, even though construction was delayed by inability to obtain financing); Graham v. Kleb, 2008 WL 243669 (S.D. Tex. Jan. 29, 2008) (homestead exemption for rural land on which debtor hunted, fished and raised vegetables for food, and planned to reside in future); Parks v. Buckeye Retirement Co., 2006 WL 1662945 (S.D. Tex. June 9, 2006) (adjoining parcels where debtors hoped to build home were still homestead, even though parcel with home where family formerly lived had been foreclosed upon and sold); *In re* Kincaide, 2010 WL 3745901 (Bankr. E.D.N.C. Sept. 20, 2010) (land on which hog barn stood, which debtor was renovating as residence, was homestead even though debtor was surrendering manufactured home in which he was living and the portion of the parcel on which it was located); *In re* Kleb, 2007 WL 1760925 (Bankr. S.D. Tex. June 19, 2007) (debtor, who lived in temporary housing, could claim homestead in inherited land where he maintained vegetable garden, hunted for food, and had drawn up plans for house; overt acts of homestead use plus intent to reside sufficiently shown); *In re* Greene, 346 B.R. 835 (Bankr. D. Nev. 2006) (if debtor actually owns and occupies land, "mode of occupation" is irrelevant; here debtor lived in travel trailer and had signed contracts to improve land and build house), *rev'd on other grounds*, 583 F.3d 614 (9th Cir. 2009) (reversing application of federal bankruptcy law's 1215-day look-back period to this homestead). *See also In re* Hodes, 287 B.R. 561 (D. Kan. 2002) (debtors could claim homestead in funds prepaid to builder who was constructing addition to home). *Cf. In re* Cerchione, 414 B.R. 540 (B.A.P. 9th Cir. 2009) (home under construction not exempt pursuant to Idaho Code Ann. § 55-1004 because required declaration not filed, but covered by Idaho Code Ann. § 55-1008 because paid for with proceeds of old homestead). *But see In re* Lozada Rivera, 470 B.R. 109 (Bankr. D. P.R. 2012) (denying exemption in property on which home was being built; must show that property is "owned and occupied as a residence"); *In re* Bace, 364 B.R. 166 (Bankr. S.D.N.Y. 2007) (property on which debtor was building home not homestead because not "principal residence" when debtor was living in apartment and listed that address on bankruptcy papers), *rev'd on other grounds*, 2008 WL 800672 (S.D.N.Y. Mar. 25, 2008); *In re* Gott, 2006 WL 2843008 (Bankr. W.D. La. Aug. 31, 2006) (no homestead exemption for vacant land; homestead lost when debtor stated intention to surrender manufactured home to lender, even though she intended to put other home on site); *In re* Gandy, 327 B.R. 807 (Bankr. S.D. Tex. 2005) (federal homestead exemption requires actual occupancy; denying homestead when debtor had cleared land, arranged for utilities and bought a trailer but not moved in); *In re* Estad, 295 B.R. 905 (Bankr. D. Minn. 2003) (exemption in newly built home only as of date family moved in; did not protect against lien that attached while house was under construction); Walbridge v. Estate of Beaudoin, 48 A.3d 964 (N.H. 2012) (present physical occupancy required; no homestead claim on land where couple was building a house). *But cf. In re* Gardner, 417 B.R. 616 (Bankr. D. Idaho 2009) (failure to file declaration of abandonment of homestead where debtors were currently living invalidated declaration of homestead on land where new home was being built), *aff'd*, 2010 WL 6259995 (B.A.P. 9th Cir. June 14, 2010); *In re* Taggart, 2009 WL 3571254 (Bankr. D. Idaho Oct. 27, 2009) (declaration of homestead was ineffective because it failed to state that claimants planned to occupy land as their homestead); Thorp v. Gugino, 2009 WL 2567399 (D. Idaho Aug. 12, 2009) (declaration of homestead on land where debtor plans to build home is invalid without declaration of abandonment of home where debtor currently resides); *In re* Ronk, 2006 WL 2385240 (Bankr. N.D. Tex. June 19, 2006) (property not homestead when it only contained a shed and two pads and nobody lived there); *In re* Brooks, 233 B.R. 696 (Bankr. N.D. Tex. 1999) (actual occupation or preparation to occupy are essential to Texas homestead; no exemption when debtor had "always intended" to build on parcel someday).

previous home to purchase a new home or land should also explore whether the homestead exemption applies to the proceeds of the sale.[757]

12.7.4.2 Abandonment

A homestead can be lost by abandonment, either by living elsewhere[758] or by using it for non-homestead purposes.[759] Merely

757 *See* § 12.2.4, *supra*.

758 *ABANDONMENT SHOWN: In re* Kelley, 300 B.R. 11 (B.A.P. 9th Cir. 2003) (California law) (automatic homestead requires intent to reside permanently; not shown when owner moved into apartment, visited home "occasionally" to repair damage, and rented it to cousin; declared homestead continued because no new homestead established, but would not protect against forced sale); Feucht v. Pierce, 2006 WL 3354507 (D.S.D. Nov. 15, 2006) (no homestead exemption for wife who had moved out of home jointly owned with estranged husband; intent to return that is "merely possible" or contingent on other event—here, husband's departure or couple's reconciliation—is insufficient); *In re* Schuster, 2006 WL 2711800 (D. Mont. Sept. 21, 2006) (residence required, with some exceptions for temporary absence with intent to return; not shown here when debtor had not resided in condominium for ten years but intended to return when his dog died); Huggins v. Pierce, 2000 WL 33348257 (W.D. Tex. June 21, 2000) (deceased parents' home not debtor's homestead when he was employed abroad, intended to continue that employment, had resided in home only for brief visits, had placed home on market, had agreed to split proceeds with siblings, and had changed his mailing address); *In re* Issa, 501 B.R. 223 (Bankr. S.D.N.Y. 2013) (debtor who had not resided in marital home for years was awarded it at divorce, but made no move for over a year to arrange for repairs; sought estimate only after this litigation was in progress); *In re* Kerrigan-Ronan-Prew, 2013 WL 1191241 (Bankr. D. Colo. Mar. 22, 2013) (intent to return not shown even though debtor, who lived in rental accommodation in Colorado had kept her California driver's and real estate licenses, was seeking work in California, and had not rented out California house, in which she kept personal property); *In re* Feliciano, 487 B.R. 47 (Bankr. D. Mass. 2013) (denying federal homestead exemption for Puerto Rico property where debtors had not lived for ten years; debtors had no immediate plans to return and structure on property was uninhabitable); *In re* Paul, 2012 WL 5828618 (Bankr. D.S.D. Nov. 16, 2012) (debtor who resided with family in house owned by wife failed to show present intent to occupy his former home, which was rented to tenants, "within a reasonable time"), *aff'd*, *In re* Paul, 488 B.R. 104 (B.A.P. 8th Cir. 2013); *In re* Taliercio, 2012 WL 441421 (Bankr. D. Conn. Feb. 19, 2012) (denying exemption when, on petition date, property was rented to tenants on one-year lease; intent to return not sufficient); *In re* Genzler, 426 B.R. 407 (Bankr. D. Mass. 2010) (estranged husband could not exempt marital home that he had left eleven years ago); *In re* Ormiston, 2010 WL 2746345 (Bankr. N.D. Okla. July 9, 2010) (denying Oklahoma exemption to debtor who lived in Switzerland when her testimony contradicted statements made in her tax filings); *In re* Fink, 417 B.R. 786 (Bankr. E.D. Wis. 2009) (homestead exemption unavailable when, eight years earlier, husband moved out of home and deeded it to wife as part of divorce settlement, retained a lien to secure payment of $25,000 owed to him within ten years, but had taken no steps to procure new homestead); *In re* Cochran, 2009 WL 605298 (Bankr. S.D. Ala. Mar. 9, 2009) (Alabama residency requirement is strict; debtor who temporarily moved in with parents and rented out homestead, because this was the only way he could afford mortgage, lost homestead exemption); *In re* Gaines, 2007 WL 1228157 (Bankr. M.D. Fla. Apr. 18, 2007) (intent to abandon shown; debtor stayed away five years, failed to maintain property so manufactured home was removed by city, and provided no support for assertion he left because of serious illness), *aff'd*, 2008 WL 3200276 (M.D. Fla. Aug. 5, 2008); *In re* Gott, 2006 WL 2843008 (Bankr. W.D. La. Aug. 31, 2006) (debtor lost homestead exemption in lot when she moved out of manufactured home located on it and indicated intent to surrender home to secured lender, even though she intended to put another home on site); *In re* Boward, 334 B.R. 350 (Bankr. D. Mass. 2005) (wife could not exempt her share of proceeds of marital home when she had moved out of state, found a job, and quitclaimed her share of house to husband); *In re* Maloney, 311 B.R. 525 (Bankr. W.D. Mo. 2004) (debtor moved out when she married, lived elsewhere for seventeen years; could not show intent to return, which must exist at time of leaving); *In re* Pierce, 2003 WL 22860034 (Bankr. D. Vt. Dec. 1, 2003) (wife abandoned her interest in former marital home when, after husband entered nursing home, she returned to parents, bought house as joint tenant with them, used that address for driver's license and bankruptcy petition, and claimed it as homestead); *In re* Hunter, 295 B.R. 882 (Bankr. W.D. Ark. July 29, 2003) (homestead abandoned when parcel containing house was sold and remaining parcel used to raise livestock; debtor resided elsewhere and spent night on parcel only when attending foalings); *In re* Holman, 286 B.R. 882 (Bankr. D. Minn. 2002) (ex-wife, who moved out and obtained divorce prepetition, lost any homestead right she might have had as result of husband's continued occupancy); *In re* Klaiber, 265 B.R. 290 (Bankr. M.D. Fla. 2001) (temporary absence for health, economic or family reasons not abandonment, but abandonment shown when debtor put house on market, took out-of-state job, and gave out-of-state address for tax and banking records); *In re* Weza, 248 B.R. 470 (Bankr. D.N.H. 2000) (New Hampshire resident could not claim homestead in Massachusetts property owned in tenancy by entireties with his estranged wife); Phillips v. Phillips, 2004 WL 503905 (Conn. Super. Ct. Feb. 25, 2004) (debtor owned and paid bills for house occupied by son and other relatives but ate and slept in another house he shared with wife and used that address on driver's license); Meadow Groves Mgt. v. McKnight, 689 So. 2d 315 (Fla. Dist. Ct. App. 1997) (homestead exemption in manufactured home lost when owner evicted from rental lot); Jones, Givens, Gotcher & Bogan, Prof'l Corp. v. Berger, 46 P.3d 698 (Okla. 2002) (abandonment shown by leaving with intent not to return; may consider reasons for and duration of absence, whether home put on market or new home purchased; establishing another homestead is sufficient); Barrera v. State, 2005 WL 1691037 (Tex. App. July 21, 2005) (intent not to return shown by acquisition of new homestead); Lares v. Garza, 153 S.W.3d 97 (Tex. App. 2004) (owner who had formerly lived and worked on property was living in mother's house and renting property to a business); *In re* Trustee's Sale of Real Prop. of Brown, 250 P.3d 134 (Wash. Ct. App. 2011) (failure to file declaration of non-abandonment raises presumption of abandonment; here, debtors caused water to be turned off, stopped making mortgage payments in order to afford rent in new location, moved into apartment with one-year lease, and changed drivers licenses to new address). *See also In re* Davis, 2012 WL 122577 (Bankr. D. Idaho Jan. 17, 2012) (detailed discussion of Idaho procedure for acquiring and abandoning homesteads).

ABANDONMENT NOT SHOWN: In re Karr, 278 Fed. Appx. 741 (9th Cir. 2008) (when California deleted "actually" from before "resides" in automatic homestead statute, it showed that temporary absence would not eliminate homestead; four-month absence not abandonment when personal property and dog remained on claimed locus and debtor used that address for motor vehicle and voting registration); *In re* Davila, 2014 WL 335393 (Bankr. N.D.N.C. Jan. 30, 2014) (allowing divorced debtor, who had resided in North Carolina during marriage, to claim homestead in house in Mexico; debtor had paid taxes on Mexico property, allowed family members to live there, and kept personal property there); *In re* McDonald, 486 B.R. 843 (Bankr. S.D. Tex. 2013) (debtor showed intent "to return as soon as she is able"; debtor, who lived in rented space and worked at low-paying job in Louisiana, had not rented out house or listed it for sale, had kept the utilities on, visited frequently, and was actively seeking better job in Texas); *In re* Kology, 499 B.R. 20 (Bankr. D. Mass. 2013) (actual occupancy is key; absence of several years, living in trailer and "work camping" at campgrounds, listing a home for sale or forming an intent to sell is not abandonment of the homestead if the debtor continues in occupancy.[760] On the other hand, moving out and putting a homestead

did not bar exemption, when debtors were in residence on petition date); *In re* Mead, 489 B.R. 363 (Bankr. D. Vt. 2013) (abandonment not shown; home was burnt down, and debtor resided sporadically in hunting cabin on contiguous parcel and credibly testified he intended to live in cabin); *In re* Schott, 449 B.R. 697 (Bankr. W.D. Tex. Mar. 16, 2011) (intent to stay away permanently not shown when debtor moved to city for business reasons, here to construct a "spec house"); *In re* Belding, 2010 WL 5376295 (Bankr. D. Vt. Dec. 23, 2010) (intent to return is critical issue; allowing debtors who resided more than half the year in Florida apartment to claim homestead in family home in Vermont; debtors paid resident income taxes in Vermont, owned no real property in Florida, and had not registered to vote there); *In re* Gedenk, 2010 WL 4257489 (Bankr. N.D. Ill. Oct. 20, 2010) (allowing debtors who resided with family member in Illinois and used Illinois address for voting and drivers' licenses to exempt Wisconsin home to which they planned to return when wife finished lengthy course of medical treatment in Illinois); *In re* Forshee, 2010 WL 3711918 (Bankr. D. Idaho Sept. 17, 2010) (debtor residing in short-term rental housing in Utah, working at job with three-month contract, who had not changed voter registration or drivers' license and believed she could reconcile with husband, could exempt former marital home in Idaho); *In re* Curry, 2009 WL 5198294 (Bankr. D. Kan. Dec. 22, 2009) (Kansas fiercely protects homestead once established; allowing homestead in old family home for debtors who worked, voted, and registered their cars in another city where they resided in apartment); *In re* Melito, 357 B.R. 684 (Bankr. D. Mass. 2007) (homestead statute requires a writing to terminate homestead; declining to consider whether abandonment also terminates it, as debtors here merely vacated home to accommodate prospective buyer whose financing then fell through); *In re* Ledzey, 2007 WL 295213 (Bankr. M.D. Fla. Jan. 30, 2007) (intent to discontinue homestead not shown when debtor lived on property but a scrivener's error, corrected as soon as discovered, caused deed to be recorded transferring property); Devine v. Devine, 2005 WL 1926038 (Bankr. N.D. Iowa Aug. 5, 2005) (farmers intending to return to farming could claim homestead in farmhouse even though living in rented apartment and working off-farm); *In re* Woodruff, 2005 WL 1139891 (Bankr. W.D. Mo. Apr. 28, 2005) (non-occupancy creates presumption of abandonment, rebuttable by evidence that, at the time debtor vacated residence, he intended to return); *In re* Marrama, 307 B.R. 332 (Bankr. D. Mass. 2004) (once homestead filed, creditor alleging abandonment must provide "unequivocal evidence"; not shown when owner was living in unheated summer cottage in Maine and leasing home to tenants; owner testified he intended to move back when lease expired), *aff'd on other grounds*, 316 B.R. 418 (B.A.P. 1st Cir. 2004); *In re* Murphy, 292 B.R. 403 (Bankr. D.N.D. 2003) (debtor rented home to tenants while attending graduate school out-of-state, but was on leave of absence and continued to receive medical benefits from North Dakota job and paid taxes and insurance on house in which she had left personal property); *In re* Patterson, 275 B.R. 578 (Bankr. D. Colo. 2002) (presumption of abandonment rebutted; family fled from vandalism and stalking, left belongings in the house, did significant renovations, kept up mortgage payments, and returned when stalker left the area); *In re* Kimball, 270 B.R. 471 (Bankr. W.D. Ark. 2001) (once homestead established, it survives divorce; abandonment not shown when debtor lived in homestead on date of petition, even though she had listed house for sale as required by divorce decree); *In re* Laing, 242 B.R. 538 (Bankr. S.D. Fla. 1999) (homestead may be lost by abandonment but no intent to abandon when debtor lived with girlfriend and rented out homestead, then returned to homestead); *In re* Anderson, 240 B.R. 254 (Bankr. W.D. Tex. 1999) (abandonment not shown under federal bankruptcy exemption when debtor in army rented out house but listed it as her home in military records and intended to return there); *In re* Sebio, 237 B.R. 1 (Bankr. D. Mass. 1999) (summer home was exempt when owner filed homestead declaration for it and subsequently moved there for year-round occupancy); *In re* Harrison, 236 B.R. 788 (Bankr. M.D. Fla. 1999) (homestead not abandoned when debtor co-owner was living elsewhere because of divorce but house was on market and debtor intended to invest her share of proceeds in new homestead); *In re* Lazin, 221 B.R. 982 (Bankr. M.D. Fla. 1998) (payment of year's rent on Pennsylvania apartment did not defeat claim of homestead in Florida condominium when debtor was living in condominium and had moved to Florida for health reasons); LPP Mortgage, Ltd. v. Meurer, 2004 WL 57585 (Iowa Ct. App. Jan. 14, 2004) (intent to return shown when debtor lost job and worked out-of-state after divorce, but home was occupied by relatives, debtor visited most weekends, and his employer planned to open facility in Iowa); Lamkin v. Flanagan, 865 So. 2d 916 (La. Ct. App. 2004) (paying taxes and making repairs sufficient to maintain homestead exemption when debtor testified he intended to return to home, even though because of health problems he spent only two or three nights there over seven years); Fairfield Fin. Group, Inc. v. Synnott, 300 S.W.3d 316 (Tex. App. 2009) (homestead protection not lost even if husband moved out, when property continued to be wife's homestead); Union Square Fed. Credit Union v. Clay, 2009 WL 1099434 (Tex. App. Apr. 23, 2009) (debtors had lived in new house for four years but did not lose homestead exemption for old house which they had neither sold nor rented, continued to maintain, and where they kept personal property); Pierce v. Wash. Mut. Bank, 226 S.W.3d 711 (Tex. App. 2007) (if new homestead not established, abandonment is fact question; must show voluntary departure and manifestation of intent not to return); Wilcox v. Marriott, 103 S.W.3d 469 (Tex. App. 2003) (factual question of owner's intent to use property as homestead precludes summary judgment); Estate of Montague v. Nat'l Loan Investors, Ltd. P'ship, 70 S.W.3d 242 (Tex. App. 2001) (debtors did not abandon homestead despite their declaration that it was not homestead when they continued to live there and never left it without returning). *See also In re* Newcomb, 2009 WL 961503 (Bankr. D. Mass. Apr. 8, 2008) (Massachusetts homestead may be terminated, during the life of the owner, only by a release, recorded in the registry of deeds, or by a deed, recorded or unrecorded, that does not reserve homestead).

759 *EXEMPTION LOST: In re* Pietrunti, 207 B.R. 18 (Bankr. M.D. Fla. 1997) (when debtors subdivided their property into four lots and rented out homes on three of them, Florida homestead exemption protected only the fourth lot occupied by debtors' home); Lares v. Garza, 153 S.W.3d 97 (Tex. App. 2004) (owner who had formerly lived and worked on property was living in mother's house and renting the property to a business).

PROPERTY EXEMPT: In re Patterson, 487 B.R. 485 (Bankr. W.D. Tenn. 2013) (allowing exemption for property formerly rented to tenants; debtor's present right to occupy was sufficient); *In re* Giles, 443 B.R. 524 (Bankr. W.D. Ark. 2011) (debtors did not abandon homestead by selling portion of land on which their home was located, where they built another home on the remainder, nor by establishing a small family-run business on it); *In re* Haning, 252 B.R. 799 (Bankr. M.D. Fla. 2000) (Florida homestead exemption protected garage, located on same parcel as residence, which owner used for a used car business, but would be lost if owner rented out part of property to another for business purposes); Owens v. Hawkins, 2012 WL 1366577 (Tex. App. Apr. 18, 2012) ("continuously" renting homestead will destroy exemption; not shown here when debtor had rented out a cabin on his property). *See also* Siewak v. AmSouth Bank, 2007 WL 141186 (M.D. Fla. Jan. 16, 2007) (question of fact whether business use eliminated homestead exemption). *See generally* § 12.7.4.1, *supra* (use of part of homestead for business purposes).

760 *In re* Wengerd, 453 B.R. 243 (B.A.P. 6th Cir. 2011) (when debtors owned and resided in property on petition date, it was homestead, even though they had entered into contract to sell it and sale closed four days later); *In re* Bellefiore, 492 B.R. 109) (Bankr. E.D.N.Y. 2013) (allowing homestead for debtor who resided in long-term home on petition date, even though it was subject to contract to sell; sale closed a few days later); *In*

on the market is probative on the issue of abandonment.[761]

Problems arise when a debtor who must relocate or seek a less expensive home must move out before a sale is completed. Some courts have held that it is the acquisition of a new homestead, not moving out of the old, that terminates the homestead.[762] Many of these cases turn on the jurisdiction's rules about whether the proceeds of the sale of the homestead are exempt.[763]

Courts usually find no abandonment when there are good reasons, such as health problems[764] or flood or hurricane damage

---

re Gentry, 459 B.R. 861 (Bankr. M.D. Fla. 2011) (abandonment shown only by moving away and taking up residence elsewhere; not shown when debtor who could not afford to reaffirm intended to remain in home until forced out by foreclosure); *In re* Caudill, 2007 WL 3171745 (Bankr. S.D. Tex. Oct. 25, 2007) (abandonment not shown when property was listed for sale, but debtor resided there at all relevant times); *In re* Baker, 307 B.R. 860 (Bankr. N.D. Tex. 2003) (intention to sell or even pending sale not abandonment). *See also In re* Mixon, 2014 WL 28669 (Bankr. S.D. Ga. Jan. 2, 2014) (drawing up subdivision plat that was never recorded did not eliminate exemption). *But see In re* Lynn, 2013 WL 6234511 (B.A.P. 9th Cir. Dec. 2, 2013) (unpublished) (denying exemption; listing property for sale, as required by divorce decree, and absence of efforts to make a home on unoccupied property); Carpenter v. Brown, 2013 WL 4047017 (S.D. Fla. 2013) (debtor was living on property on petition date, but property subject to contract for sale, with provision allowing buyer specific performance if seller defaulted; placing property on market was sufficient to show abandonment); *In re* Kology, 499 B.R. 20 (Bankr. D. Mass. 2013) (preparation of subdivision plat, which was approved by town, and construction of road showed abandonment of vacant lot contiguous to homestead parcel).

761 *In re* Perry, 481 B.R. 862 (Bankr. N.D. Tex. 2012) (moving out of residence, and stating intent to surrender it to creditor in bankruptcy, showed abandonment); *In re* Ellis, 456 B.R. 401 (Bankr. E.D. Ark. 2011) (homestead lost when debtors contracted to sell home, received large payment, and used it to buy new home; not reestablished when, after sale fell through, debtors planned to move back into former home); *In re* Vick, 2008 WL 2444526 (Bankr. S.D. Fla. June 16, 2008) (contract to sell did not extinguish homestead; exemption survives until debtor establishes new domicile or "alienates" old homestead); *In re* Troutman, 378 B.R. 331 (Bankr. W.D. Okla. 2007) (contract of sale does not eliminate homestead; exemption survives until property is formally handed over to buyer at closing); *In re* Martiny, 378 B.R. 52 (Bankr. W.D.N.Y. 2007) (debtors currently residing in home they have contracted to sell may claim homestead); Bovey v. Coffey, 2012 WL 1448530 (Tex. App. Apr. 26, 2012) (conveyance of the homestead to another, even if without consideration and with the belief that it would be conveyed back to grantor, was abandonment sufficient to end homestead exemption; note that debtor also lived elsewhere). *But cf. In re* Westmeyer, 2010 WL 2103571 (Bankr. N.D. Iowa May 24, 2010) (attempt to sell house in response to divorce court order not voluntary abandonment, even though debtor had moved out, when debtor intended to reinvest proceeds in new home).

762 *In re* Pendley, 2013 WL 141595 (Bankr. W.D. Tex. Jan. 11, 2013) (denying exemption for new home in which debtor resided; old homestead not abandoned when debtor's wife and daughter remained in foreclosed home while daughter finished school year); *In re* Younger, 373 B.R. 111 (Bankr. D. Idaho 2007) (property not shown to be abandoned before sale when debtor spent some nights on property and removed his belongings only when purchaser gave him one week to do so); *In re* Melito, 357 B.R. 684 (Bankr. D. Mass. 2007) (debtors who were living in apartment could claim homestead exemption in home vacated to accommodate prospective buyer whose financing had fallen through); *In re* Seeley, 341 B.R. 277 (Bankr. W.D. Mo. 2006) (presumption of abandonment rebutted when property put on market but debtor planned to use proceeds to acquire nearby homestead); *In re* Huddleston, 2005 WL 2271859 (Bankr. C.D. Ill. Sept. 7, 2005) (debtors who vacated two-story residence because of health problems and put home on the market able to claim homestead when they demonstrated good faith intent to sell home and invest proceeds in one-story homestead within a reasonable period of time); *In re* Wagenbach, 232 B.R. 112 (Bankr. C.D. Ill. 1999) (proceeds exempt even though debtors moved out of home before closing, when they continued to maintain old home and intended to use proceeds to buy new home); McMillan v. Aru, 773 So. 2d 355 (Miss. Ct. App. 2000) (sheriff's sale permanently enjoined when sellers had moved out and judgment creditor attached after closing but before deed recorded; homestead exemption survived until deed executed, after which sellers had no interest left); Union Square Fed. Credit Union v. Clay, 2009 WL 1099434 (Tex. App. Apr. 23, 2009) (buying and moving into new house did not establish new homestead; debtors could claim exemption for old house they continued to maintain, had neither sold nor rented, where they left personal property); Barrera v. State, 2005 WL 1691037 (Tex. App. July 21, 2005) (intent not to return shown by acquisition of new homestead; strong showing of abandonment when furniture moved to new house, new address used for business, taxes, mail, and driver's license). *Cf. In re* Johnson, 2009 WL 2848983 (Bankr. E.D. La. May 14, 2009) (homestead exemption was lost when owner moved out of damaged house and filed for homestead tax exemption for home she temporarily occupied).

763 *See* § 12.2.4, *supra*.

764 *See, e.g.*, United States v. Neff, 2007 WL 776532 (D.N.D. Mar. 12, 2007) (abandonment not shown when farmer moved to town to care for frail eighty-eight-year-old mother, leaving many belongings in farmhouse, which was neglected but needed only minor repairs); *In re* Voliva, 2011 WL 6301232 (Bankr. E.D.N.C. Dec. 16, 2011) (allowing exemption when debtors were living with their son on petition date because of medical problems but utilities were turned on in manufactured home on property where they had lived for ten years); *In re* McKeithan, 2011 WL 1331986 (Bankr. E.D. Tex. Apr. 7, 2011) (homestead not lost when frail elderly debtor was forced to move in with daughter; abandonment must be voluntary), *aff'd*, 486 Fed. Appx. 482 (5th Cir. 2012); *In re* Seeley, 341 B.R. 277 (Bankr. W.D. Mo. 2006) (presumption of abandonment rebutted when debtor intended, at time of removal, to return once health problems and children's problems with school system were resolved); *In re* Huddleston, 2005 WL 2271859 (Bankr. C.D. Ill. Sept. 7, 2005) (allowing homestead; debtors vacated two-story residence because of health problems but intended to sell it and invest proceeds in one-story homestead); *In re* Owens, 269 B.R. 794 (Bankr. N.D. Ill. 2001) (not abandonment when debtor left state to care for mother during long illness, but kept in touch with Illinois employer and hoped to resume her job upon return); Citizens State Bank v. Ruebel, 804 N.W.2d 314 (Iowa Ct. App. 2011) (sick elderly debtor moved in with daughter, leaving most of her belongings in her home of fifty years; abandonment not shown); Farstveet v. Rudolph, 630 N.W.2d 24 (N.D. 2000) (no abandonment when debtor went into hospital and nursing home, even though relatives lived in home and sold belongings to pay medical bills). *Cf.* Meadow Wind Health Care Ctr. v. McInnes, 2000 Ohio App. LEXIS 3415 (Ohio Ct. App. July 24, 2000) (question of fact whether homestead abandoned during nursing home stay when debtor used nursing home address for mail and voting but eventually returned home). *But see In re* Naputi, 2007 WL 1864075 (Bankr. D. Idaho June 28, 2007) (six-month absence without filing homestead declaration creates rebuttable presumption of abandonment; debtors left home to help sister care for terminally ill husband but remained for over a year after his death; claim that hiring freeze prevented return to former jobs not sufficient to rebut presumption); *In re* Burns, 218 B.R. 897 (Bankr. N.D. Ind. 1998) (actual residence, not legal domicile, determines availability of homestead exemption; ninety-eight-year-old debtor who resided with daughter because of his poor health could not claim homestead exemption in his former home).

to the home,[765] that force the debtor to live elsewhere temporarily. A debtor who travels extensively for business or other reasons can maintain a homestead despite only sporadic occupancy.[766] Most courts hold that a spouse who flees domestic conflict or is excluded by a restraining order does not abandon the homestead.[767] Except in the case of a life sentence,[768] a prisoner normally does not intend the prison to be a permanent residence and so may be able to claim a homestead exemption in his or her former home.[769]

12.7.5 Homestead Exemption Limits in Bankruptcy

12.7.5.1 Overview

The extreme variation in state homestead amounts, and the existence of states with high or unlimited homestead

765 *See, e.g., In re* Lloyd, 394 B.R. 605 (Bankr. S.D. Fla. 2008) (allowing Florida homestead to debtor who was living in month-to-month rental in California but frequently returned to Florida to maintain uninhabitable hurricane-damaged property and had not established new homestead); *In re* Foster, 348 B.R. 58 (Bankr. E.D.N.C. 2006) (debtor could claim homestead in property rendered uninhabitable by 1999 hurricane damage when she was living in camper, paying property taxes and storing personal belongings on property, and seeking financial help for repairs; intent to return is key). *See also In re* Gill, 2011 WL 4712087 (Bankr. M.D.N.C. Aug. 19, 2011) (debtor who moved out because of mold contamination he could not afford to remediate, but continued to pay mortgage and did not change address on drivers' license, did not abandon homestead).

766 *In re* Simpson, 206 B.R. 230 (Bankr. E.D. Okla. 1997) (Oklahoma property was exempt homestead when owner had lived there for a year, intended to retire there, and had never rented it out or turned off the utilities, even though owner worked in Texas during the work week and on some weekends); McCone Cnty. Fed. Credit Union v. Gribble, 216 P.3d 206 (Mont. 2009) (debtor who had a "traveling job" kept all his belongings in house; residence is "the place where a person remains when not called elsewhere for labor or other temporary purpose, and to which the person returns in seasons of repose"); *In re* Estate of Casida, 13 S.W.3d 519 (Tex. App. 2000) (abandonment not shown when homeowner traveled a lot but returned several times a year and did not remove furnishings from home or acquire other real estate). *See also In re* McDonald, 486 B.R. 843 (Bankr. S.D. Tex. 2013) (debtor showed intent "to return as soon as she is able"; she lived in rented space and worked at low-paying job in Louisiana but had not rented out house or listed it for sale, had kept the utilities on, visited frequently, and was actively seeking better job in Texas).

767 *In re* Roberts, 450 B.R. 159 (N.D. Iowa May 5, 2011) (homestead not lost when couple agreed to separation agreement that barred debtor from former marital home); *In re* Wenstrom, 2013 WL 321678 (Bankr. D.N.D. Jan. 28, 2013) (exempting buy-out payment awarded to wife who was required to quitclaim her share of marital home to husband; leaving home because of marital strife was not abandonment); *In re* Marcovitz, 2011 WL 5041507 (Bankr. D. Idaho Oct. 24, 2011) (failure to file declaration of non-abandonment created rebuttable presumption of abandonment; rebutted here when court order in divorce required debtor to move out); *In re* Moulterie, 398 B.R. 501 (Bankr. E.D.N.Y. 2008) (allowing homestead exemption to debtor-husband because family court granted exclusive occupancy to wife while property division being resolved; noting that danger might result if parties to acrimonious divorce were compelled to live together to avoid loss of property); *In re* Dubravsky, 374 B.R. 467 (Bankr. D.N.H. 2007) (leaving home when required by divorce decree not abandonment; home here to be sold at later date and proceeds divided); *In re* Lindsey, 2006 WL 4112666 (Bankr. M.D. Fla. Dec. 13, 2006) (allowing homestead exemption; debtor not residing on premises because she feared for safety of self and children while ex-husband lived nearby); *In re* MacFarlane, 325 B.R. 908 (Bankr. M.D. Fla. 2005) (intent to abandon not shown when domestic violence order barred debtor from home); *In re* Ballato, 318 B.R. 205 (Bankr. M.D. Fla. 2004) (ex-husband excluded by restraining order could claim homestead exemption in his share of sale proceeds of former marital home); *In re* Chase, 2003 WL 22454876 (Bankr. D.N.H. Oct. 14, 2003) (temporary and involuntary absence resulting from incarceration or restraining order not abandonment, but failure to return after restraining order ended showed establishment of new home); *In re* Detko, 290 B.R. 494 (Bankr. D. Vt. 2003) (living in Florida for six months, opening bank account and obtaining driver's license there, and putting house on market not abandonment when debtor was fleeing violent alcoholic ex-husband); *In re* Taylor, 280 B.R. 294 (Bankr. D. Mass. 2002) (debtor wife who left home because of marital problems could claim homestead); *In re* Webber, 278 B.R. 294 (Bankr. D. Mass. 2002) (debtor husband excluded by restraining order; continued occupation by wife and children sufficient to maintain homestead); Phillips v. Fuller, 814 So. 2d 885 (Ala. Civ. App. 2001) (homestead not abandoned by wife who fled abusive husband); Coy v. Mango Bay Prop. & Invs., Inc., 963 So. 2d 873 (Fla. Dist. Ct. App. 2007) (homestead, once acquired, not lost by court order awarding possession to other spouse; ex-husband entitled to hearing on claim of homestead in former marital home, titled in wife alone); Chrissikos v. Chrissikos, 2002 WL 342653 (Tex. App. Mar. 6, 2002) (wife moved out during divorce). *See also In re* Gott, 2006 WL 2843008 (Bankr. W.D. La. Aug. 31, 2006) (homestead exemption not lost when debtor fled abusive husband, who continued to harass her after leaving home; but lost when debtor surrendered manufactured home, leaving land vacant); *In re* Nguyen, 332 B.R. 393 (Bankr. W.D. Mo. 2005) (debtor did not abandon home by moving to mother's nearby home and staying there seven months after fight with domestic partner). *Cf. In re* McClamrock, 2004 WL 229521 (Bankr. M.D.N.C. Feb. 5, 2004) (leaving former home to escape abusive husband not abandonment, but failure to return for years after he left showed that absence not temporary). *But see In re* Wilson, 341 B.R. 21 (B.A.P. 9th Cir. 2006) (Washington law) (no automatic homestead when court order had barred husband from occupancy; declared homestead came too late when it was filed after divorce decree had divested husband of interest in property). *But cf. In re* Herding, 2007 WL 397276 (Bankr. D.S.D. Jan. 31, 2007) (debtor, originally excluded from home by family court order, showed intent not to return when he stopped making mortgage payments and, in settlement negotiations, offered house to wife).

768 Polk v. Polk, 2009 WL 2613930 (Cal. Ct. App. Aug. 26, 2009) (prisoner sentenced to life imprisonment, but appeal pending; could have claimed exemption while awaiting trial, but not after conviction and sentence); Stewart v. Bader, 907 A.2d 931 (N.H. 2006) (prison inmate serving life sentence without possibility of parole could not claim homestead, absence not temporary).

769 *In re* Gerholdt, 2011 WL 4352353 (Bankr. N.D. Iowa Sept. 16, 2011) (allowing prisoner starting fourteen-year sentence to claim homestead currently being leased to tenants); Holden v. Cribb, 561 S.E.2d 634 (S.C. Ct. App. 2002) (homestead not abandoned when homeowner in jail because no intent to make jail his permanent home); Alamanza v. Salas, 2014 WL 554807 (Tex. App. Feb. 22, 2014) (incarceration not abandonment, so home was homestead); Driver v. Conley, 320 S.W.3d 516 (Tex. App. 2010) (prisoner serving long sentence did not voluntarily abandon homestead). *See also* Gibson v. Fauber, 2004 WL 2002560 (Tex. App. Sept. 8, 2004) (debtor lived elsewhere only when incarcerated or working at out-of-town jobs). *But see* Old Republic Nat'l Title Ins. v. Kornegay, 292 P.3d 1111 (Colo. App. 2012) (prisoner's intent to return to former home not sufficient to support homestead exemption); *In re* Arrington, 167 Wash. App. 1019 (Wash. Ct. App. 2012) (unpublished) (incarceration for more than six months is voluntary abandonment, which terminates homestead exemption; this debtor did not file declaration of non-abandonment).

exemptions and narrow fraud exceptions, led to concern about the use of homestead exemptions to shelter unreasonable amounts from creditors. The 2005 amendments to the Bankruptcy Code limit debtors from taking full advantage of state homestead exemptions in several circumstances.[770]

Courts have held that these limits apply only to ordinary state exemptions, not to the immunity recognized by many states for property owned in tenancy by entireties.[771] In addition, the Bankruptcy Code's exceptions to exemptions—the look-back period, exceptions for specified types of fraud, among others—are exclusive and cannot be enlarged by the courts: the Supreme Court refused to allow a homestead exemption to be surcharged for attorney fees incurred in attacking debtor's egregiously fraudulent lien.[772]

The restrictions added by the 2005 amendments are outlined in the next two subsections. They are discussed in detail in National Consumer Law Center, *Consumer Bankruptcy Law and Practice*.[773]

12.7.5.2 Conversion of Non-Exempt Property Into Homestead Property; $125,000 Cap

Section 522(o) of the Code limits a debtor's state homestead exemption when the debtor converted non-exempt property into exempt homestead property within ten years before the filing of the petition with the intent to hinder, delay, or defraud a creditor.[774]

In addition, two new provisions cap state homestead exemptions at $125,000 (adjusted for inflation every three years) in certain circumstances. Section 522(p) of the Code applies this cap to homestead property acquired during a 1215-day "look-back" period before filing a petition for bankruptcy.[775] However the monetary cap does not apply to any interest transferred from a debtor's previous principal residence to the debtor's current principal residence if both are in the same state.[776] Section 522(q) of the Code applies this cap to a debtor's homestead exemption if the debtor has been convicted of felonies or owes debts arising from certain unlawful conduct.[777]

12.7.5.3 Extraterritoriality

Another issue created by the 2005 amendments to the Bankruptcy Code is the extraterritorial effect of state exemption laws. Section 522(b)(3)(A), enacted to close the "mansion loophole"—that is, to prevent wealthy debtors from immunizing their entire fortune by moving to a state with an unlimited homestead exemption and a narrow fraud exception and buying a mansion there with all funds available to them—has created serious problems for ordinary debtors who happen to have moved within 730 days before bankruptcy. They are required to apply the exemption law of the state where they were domiciled for the 730 days immediately preceding the bankruptcy filing. If the debtor's domicile was not located in a single state for this 730-day period, the debtor must use the exemption law of the state where the debtor was domiciled for the 180 days immediately preceding this 730-day period (or where the debtor was domiciled for the longest part of that 180-day period).

This requirement can force a debtor who owns a home in one state to apply the law of a former domiciliary state that does not extend its homestead exemption to real estate outside its borders. The problem is that some state homestead exemption statutes do not protect out-of-state real estate. Some state homestead exemption statutes are explicitly limited to in-state real estate.[778] If the statute is silent about its application to real estate located outside the state, some courts construe the statute to protect such property.[779] If the result of this analysis is that

770 *See* National Consumer Law Center, Consumer Bankruptcy Law and Practice § 10.2.3.4 (10th ed. 2012), *updated at* www.nclc.org/library.

771 *In re* Davis, 403 B.R. 914 (Bankr. M.D. Fla. 2009) (BAPCA provisions limiting homestead exemption do not apply to tenancy by entireties exemption; entireties property was exempt even though purchased with funds fraudulently transferred from non-exempt individual account); *In re* Hinton, 378 B.R. 371 (Bankr. M.D. Fla. 2007) (cap does not apply to property owned in tenancy by entireties); *In re* Buonopane, 359 B.R. 346 (Bankr. M.D. Fla. 2007) (cap for homesteads acquired within 1215 days of bankruptcy does not apply to property owned in tenancy by entireties); *In re* Schwarz, 362 B.R. 532 (Bankr. S.D. Fla. 2007) (debtor barred from using Florida homestead exemption could exempt tenancy by entireties property).

772 Law v. Siegal, 134 S. Ct. 1188 (2014) (statutory list of exceptions to exemptions is exclusive; noting other ways to punish debtor's fraud here).

773 National Consumer Law Center, Consumer Bankruptcy Law and Practice (10th ed. 2012), *updated at* www.nclc.org/library.

774 *See* National Consumer Law Center, Consumer Bankruptcy Law and Practice § 10.2.3.4.3 (10th ed. 2012), *updated at* www.nclc.org/library.

775 *See* National Consumer Law Center, Consumer Bankruptcy Law and Practice, § 10.2.3.4.4 (10th ed. 2012), *updated at* www.nclc.org/library.

776 11 U.S.C. § 522(p)(2)(b).

777 National Consumer Law Center, Consumer Bankruptcy Law and Practice, § 10.2.3.4.5 (10th ed. 2012), *updated at* www.nclc.org/library.

778 *See* Appx. G, *infra*.

779 *In re* Drenttel, 403 F.3d 611 (8th Cir. 2005) (debtor who had just moved to Arizona could claim Minnesota exemption for new home); *In re* Stephens, 402 B.R. 1 (B.A.P. 10th Cir. 2009) (when Iowa homestead statute is silent on extraterritoriality, Oklahoma debtor allowed to exempt sales proceeds of Iowa former home); *In re* Fernandez, 2011 WL 3423373 (W.D. Tex. Aug. 5, 2011) (Nevada constitution and statutes silent as to extraterritoriality of homestead exemption; Texas resident required by bankruptcy law to claim Nevada exemptions may claim $500,000 Nevada exemption for Texas home); *In re* Roberts, 450 B.R. 159 (N.D. Iowa 2011) (construing silence in favor of extraterritoriality; Iowa homestead available for California property); *In re* Arrendondo-Smith, 436 B.R. 412, 2010 WL 2950358 (Bankr. W.D. Tex. 2010) (California homestead exemption may be claimed for out-of-state property but denied here because only one homestead per married couple); *In re* Varanasi, 394 B.R. 430 (Bankr. S.D. Ohio 2008) (New Hampshire homestead applied to Ohio property; no unconstitutional taking, impairment of contract, or denial of equal protection, even though New Hampshire's homestead amount was ten times Ohio's); *In re* Jevne, 387 B.R. 301 (Bankr. S.D. Fla. 2008) (Rhode Island law is silent on extraterritoriality, so under principle of liberal interpretation it applies to Florida property); *In re* Dubravsky, 374 B.R. 467 (Bankr. D.N.H. 2007) (New Hampshire law allows claim of homestead in out-of-state property, here former marital home from which debtor was excluded by divorce decree); *In re* Williams, 369 B.R. 470 (Bankr. W.D. Ark. 2007) (Iowa law is silent concerning

the debtor is ineligible to take advantage of any state's exemptions, the debtor may use the federal bankruptcy exemptions.[780]

12.7.6 *Special Rules for Health Care, Family Support, Criminal Law Forfeitures, and Tax Debts*

Some states forbid execution on a primary dwelling for health care debts during the lifetime of the debtor, the debtor's spouse, or certain dependents; instead, a lien is created which may be enforced if the property is sold.[781]

---

extraterritoriality; debtors may claim Iowa exemption for Arkansas home); *In re* Stone, 329 B.R. 860 (Bankr. N.D. Iowa 2005) (Iowa debtor could claim homestead in Wisconsin house, in amount of Wisconsin exemption); *In re* Franklino, 329 B.R. 363 (Bankr. D.R.I. 2005) (homestead exemption may be applicable to remainder interest in out-of-state property if claimant shows intent to occupy property when it becomes available); *In re* Woodruff, 2005 WL 1139891 (Bankr. W.D. Mo. Apr. 28, 2005) (liberally construing Missouri statute, which is silent about extraterritorial application, to allow debtor to claim homestead in Mississippi house); *In re* Stratton, 269 B.R. 716 (Bankr. D. Or. 2001) (where Oregon law is silent, homestead exemption granted for debtor's California property). *See also In re* Camp, 396 B.R. 194 (Bankr. W.D. Tex. 2008) (debtors who moved from Florida to Texas barred from use of federal exemptions by Florida's opt-out, but federal bankruptcy law requires that Florida exemptions apply to Texas property as if it were in Florida); *In re* Jarski, 301 B.R. 342 (Bankr. D. Ariz. 2003) (debtor with residence in California may be able to claim Arizona homestead in Arizona house; issue discussed but not decided). *But see In re* Stephens, 2012 WL 3205362 (B.A.P. 9th Cir. Aug. 2, 2012) (Idaho statute silent, but cases hold that Idaho homestead may not be claimed for out-of-state property); *In re* Schlakman, 2007 WL 1482011 (Bankr. S.D. Fla. Jan. 16, 2007) (debtor could not exempt proceeds of former marital home, located in New York, despite intention to reinvest in Florida home; proceeds exempt only if property was located in Florida); *In re* Giffune, 343 B.R. 883 (Bankr. N.D. Ill. 2006) (Illinois allows tenancy by entireties only in homesteads, Michigan in all real property; Illinois debtor not entitled to tenancy by entireties exemption for non-homestead property in Michigan); *In re* Ginther, 282 B.R. 16 (Bankr. D. Kan. 2002) (proceeds exempt only if used for purchase of Kansas homestead; not exempt when debtors moved to Colorado). *But cf. In re* Nelms, 2005 WL 318802 (Bankr. E.D. Mich. Feb. 4, 2005) (status of real property determined by law of jurisdiction where property located; Michigan debtors cannot claim tenancy by entireties exemption in property in Louisiana, which does not recognize tenancy by entireties). *See generally* Appx. G, *infra* (summarizing extraterritoriality and other aspects of state exemption laws).

780 *In re* Stephens, 2012 WL 3205362 (B.A.P. 9th Cir. Aug. 2, 2012) (debtor who moved from Idaho must use Idaho exemptions, which cannot be applied to out-of-state property; cannot exempt new home in Alaska); Shell v. Yoon, 499 B.R. 610 (N.D. Ind. 2013) (debtors who moved from Illinois to Indiana may use federal exemptions; Illinois opt-out is limited to Illinois residents); *In re* Alcorn, 2013 WL 3353837 (Bankr. D.S.D. July 3, 2013) (debtors who moved from Nebraska may use federal exemptions; Nebraska opt-out is limited to residents); *In re* Rody, 468 B.R. 384 (Bankr. D. Ariz. 2012) (when Arizona law left debtors with no exemptions, they could use federal exemptions); *In re* Kelsey, 477 B.R. 870 (Bankr. M.D. Fla. 2012) (Colorado homestead does not apply extraterritorially, but personal property exemptions do; must use Colorado exemptions for personal property, but savings clause allows use of federal homestead exemption); *In re* Footen, 2012 WL 669849 (Bankr. D. Or. Feb. 29, 2012) (as non-residents, debtors who moved from Idaho were forbidden by Idaho law to use Idaho exemptions; since Idaho has opted out of federal exemptions, debtors are left with no exemptions and may thus use federal); *In re* Townsend, 2012 WL 112995 (Bankr. D. Kan. Jan. 12, 2012) (because Oklahoma opt-out applies only to residents of Oklahoma, Kansas debtors required by BAPCA to use Oklahoma law may claim federal exemptions); *In re* Cole, 2011 WL 3207369 (Bankr. S.D. Ind. July 26, 2011) (Georgia statute, making exemptions available only to "an individual whose domicile is in Georgia" not preempted by bankruptcy law; debtor may claim federal exemptions); *In re* Beckwith, 448 B.R. 757 (Bankr. S.D. Ohio 2011) (Florida opt-out is explicitly limited to Florida residents; debtor may claim federal exemptions); *In re* Connor, 419 B.R. 304 (Bankr. E.D.N.C. 2009) (wife who lived in Florida during relevant period, and could not claim Florida's residents-only exemptions, could use federal exemptions; husband, who had lived in North Carolina, barred by opt-out from claiming federal exemptions; spouses must use different exemption schemes); *In re* Karavias, 438 B.R. 86 (Bankr. W.D. Pa. 2010) (allowing federal exemptions for debtor who moved to Pennsylvania from Virginia, an opt-out state that denies exemptions to non-residents); *In re* Nickerson, 375 B.R. 869 (Bankr. W.D. Mo. 2007) (Kansas exemptions have no extraterritorial effect; Missouri debtors required to use Kansas exemption law may claim federal exemptions); *In re* Adams, 375 B.R. 532 (Bankr. W.D. Mo. 2007) (Florida exemptions have no extraterritorial effect; when bankruptcy law required Missouri debtors to use Florida exemption law, debtors could claim federal exemptions because no state exemptions available); *In re* Tate, 2007 WL 81835 (Bankr. D. Or. Jan. 8, 2007) (Texas homestead law has no extraterritorial effect; when use of Texas law resulted in no exemption for Oregon home, debtor could use federal exemptions). *See also In re* Stephens, 402 B.R. 1 (10th Cir. 2009) (bankruptcy law does not preempt state law provisions limiting exemptions to residents); *In re* Willis, 495 B.R. 856 (Bankr. W.D. Wis. 2013) (debtor who moved from Indiana may use federal exemptions; Illinois opt-out limited to residents); *In re* Garrett, 435 B.R. 434 (Bankr. S.D. Tex. 2010) (federal law requiring application of North Carolina law to Texas debtors preempts North Carolina provision barring exemption of out-of-state property). *Cf. In re* George, 440 B.R. 164 (Bankr. E.D. Wis. 2010) (Illinois personal property exemptions not applicable to debtor who has moved to Wisconsin; since Illinois opt-out statute is explicitly limited to Illinois residents, it does not apply to Wisconsin residents, and debtor may claim federal exemptions). *But cf. In re* Katseanes, 2007 WL 2962637 (Bankr. D. Idaho Oct. 9, 2007) (Utah exemptions have no extraterritorial effect; when Utah exemptions "available," even though they result in no exemption for Idaho home, debtor could not use federal exemptions). *See generally* § 12.7.2.1, *supra* (extraterritorial application of state exemption laws).

781 *See, e.g.*, Nev. Rev. Stat. § 21.095 (protecting debtor, spouse, joint tenant who was a joint tenant at the time judgment was entered, dependent disabled adult child, or minor child during minority); Ohio Rev. Code Ann. §§ 2329.66(A)(1)(a), 2329.661 (West) (protecting debtor, surviving spouse, or minor child). *See also* Edwards v. McCormack, 136 F. Supp. 2d 795 (S.D. Ohio 2001) (lawyer-collector violated Fair Debt Collection Practices Act and state UDAP statute by threatening health-care debtors with foreclosure on real property, because foreclosure forbidden by Ohio statute); Wickliffe Country Place v. Kovacs, 765 N.E.2d 975 (Ohio Ct. App. 2001) (remanding for factual development to determine whether nursing home provided health care services); Meadow Wind Healthcare Ctr. v. McInnes, 2000 Ohio App. LEXIS 3415 (Ohio Ct. App. July 24, 2000) (fact question whether services of nursing home were "health care services or supplies"; if debtor shows that home provided any health care service or supply, statute will apply). *But cf. In re* Collet, 351 B.R. 395 (Bankr. W.D. La. 2006) (Louisiana's enhanced homestead exemption for debts "arising directly" from "catastrophic or terminal illness or injury" did not apply when part of borrowed money used for family living expenses while debtor recovered from surgery).

Frequently debts for child support or alimony may be enforced against the homestead, and the sale of a home may be ordered as part of the property division during a divorce.[782] Nonetheless, some courts hold that proceeds of a homestead sale may not be used to satisfy an unsecured debt for attorney fees that arises from divorce or some other family law matter.[783]

In many states, the homestead exemption does not protect against criminal law forfeitures.[784] An Illinois statute which was construed to provide such protection[785] was amended to eliminate it.[786] The Florida exemption has, however, been construed to exempt the homestead against a lien for court-ordered restitution in a criminal case.[787] Federal criminal law preempts any state homestead or tenancy by entireties exemption that would protect the debtor's property against a federal restitution or forfeiture order, however.[788] State homestead or

782 *In re* Elmasri, 374 Fed. Appx. 75 (2d Cir. 2010) (New York law) (judicial liens for child support take priority over homestead exemption); Hamel v. Hamel, 2009 WL 888648 (Ariz. Ct. App. Apr. 2, 2009) (husband's share of homestead proceeds could be set off against arrears of family support; ex-spouse is not the kind of creditor the homestead protects against); Wallace v. Wallace, 922 So. 2d 1008 (Fla. Dist. Ct. App. 2006) (lien may be placed on homestead to secure ex-wife's "special equity" granted to compensate for funds she spent on renovation); Dep't of Revenue *ex rel.* Greene v. Bush, 838 So. 2d 653 (Fla. Dist. Ct. App. 2003) (homestead exemption does not protect against claim for child support); Hieke v. Hieke, 782 So. 2d 443 (Fla. Dist. Ct. App. 2001) (homestead exemption did not protect against ex-wife's equitable lien on home, because it was an ownership interest); Brose v. Brose, 750 So. 2d 717 (Fla. Dist. Ct. App. 2000) (homestead could be sold for alimony obligation, when it was purchased with proceeds of financial manipulations intended to put assets beyond reach of ex-wife); Kautzman v. Kautzman, 618 N.W.2d 500 (N.D. 2000) (homestead could be sold to foreclose equitable lien awarded to ex-wife in response to husband's wrongful financial manipulations); *In re* Marriage of Maresh, 78 P.3d 157 (Or. Ct. App. 2003) (homestead exemption did not bar sheriff's sale to foreclose lien imposed by divorce decree); Pearson v. Pearson, 169 Vt. 28, 726 A.2d 71 (1999) (homestead statute, which is intended to protect family home against creditors, does not prevent family court encumbrance to give effect to property division in divorce judgment); *In re* Marriage of Foley, 930 P.2d 929 (Wash. Ct. App. 1997) (homestead exemption did not apply when court ordered sale or refinancing of former marital home, to enable husband, who received home, to pay wife her share of community property). *But see* Cannon v. Cannon, 254 B.R. 773 (S.D. Fla. 2000) (lien created by divorce judgment cannot attach to homestead property; homestead exemption arises from state constitution, and support obligation not listed among exceptions); Smith v. Smith, 761 So. 2d 370 (Fla. Dist. Ct. App. 2000) (no forced sale of homestead when homestead not purchased with proceeds of fraud nor as part of financial juggling to avoid support obligation, even though wife's equitable lien was awarded to compensate for physical injuries inflicted by abusive husband); Solomon v. Lesay, 369 S.W.3d 540 (Tex. App. 2012) (lien for child support not an exception to Texas homestead exemption). *But cf.* Anderson v. Veblen Premium Pork, Inc., 2000 Minn. App. LEXIS 891 (Minn. Ct. App. Aug. 22, 2000) (creditor could not foreclose on husband's homestead based on ex-wife's assignment of lien created by divorce court to secure husband's obligations to her, as this would be attempt by creditor to evade the exemption); *In re* Children of Knight v. Lincoln, 317 P.3d 210 (Okla. Civ. App. 2013) (although Oklahoma homestead generally protects sales proceeds used to purchase new homestead, proceeds of voluntary sale are income that should be counted in setting amount of child support); Barras v. Barras, 396 S.W.3d 154 (Tex. App. 2013) (lien may not be imposed on homestead to ensure just property division at divorce, but lien here, for equalization payment to wife for her share of home awarded to husband, was purchase money lien, an exception to Texas homestead exemption). *See generally* Jane Massey Draper, Annotation, *Enforcement of a Claim for Alimony or Support, or for Attorney's Fees or Costs in Connection Therewith, Against Exemptions*, 52 A.L.R.5th 221 (1997).

783 Harleaux v. Harleaux, 154 S.W.3d 925 (Tex. App. 2005) (court may not order attorney fees, arising from dispute over sale of marital home, paid from proceeds of homestead); *In re* Marriage of Banks, 887 S.W.2d 160 (Tex. App. 1994) (ordering payment of unsecured creditors—including attorney fees—from proceeds of homestead would "circumvent the constitutional and statutory provisions" that protect the homestead from general creditors). *Cf.* Dyer v. Beverly & Tittle, P.A., 777 So. 2d 1055 (Fla. Dist. Ct. App. 2001) (ex-wife's attorney fees were connected to support obligation so as to create equitable lien on homestead, but homestead exemption barred forced sale when no showing of fraudulent or egregious conduct by husband). *But see In re* Bingham, 344 B.R. 648 (Bankr. W.D. Okla. 2006) (attorney's lien may attach to otherwise exempt property, including homestead, divided up in divorce); *In re* Jarski, 301 B.R. 342 (Bankr. D. Ariz. 2003) (attorney fees in child support matters were child support; lien could attach to homestead); Sell v. Sell, 949 So. 2d 1108 (Fla. Dist. Ct. App. 2007) (ex-husband's share of homestead proceeds could be reached for wife's attorney fees; husband's egregious evasion of court orders resulted in jailing for contempt).

784 *In re* Smith, 176 B.R. 221 (Bankr. N.D. Ala. 1995) (homestead exemption does not apply in state drug forfeiture proceeding); Nielsen v. 2003 Honda Accord, 2013 WL 6834501 (Minn. Dec. 26, 2013) (exemption statute generally does apply to criminal law forfeitures, but newer more specific DWI forfeiture law trumps older more general exemption statute); Lot 39, Sec. C, N. Hills Subdivision v. State, 85 S.W.3d 429 (Tex. App. 2002) (Texas constitutional homestead exemption does not protect against criminal law forfeiture); Tellevik v. Real Prop. in Pierce Cnty., 921 P.2d 1088 (Wash. Ct. App. 1996) (Washington's homestead exemption does not protect against drug forfeiture). *But see* Torgelson v. Real Prop. Known As 17138 880th Ave., 749 N.W.2d 24 (Minn. 2008) (constitutional homestead exemption bars forfeiture for state offenses; noting that Florida, Iowa, Kansas, and Oklahoma homestead exemptions also bar state law drug forfeitures); State v. One 1965 Red Chevrolet Pickup, 37 P.3d 815 (Okla. 2001) (homestead, but not personal property, is exempt, and personal property not exempt from state criminal forfeiture, when homestead exemption found in state constitution, but forfeiture provisions and personal property exemptions are statutory). *But cf.* Grantham v. Johnson, 134 So. 3d 164 (La. Ct. App. 2014) (statute denying homestead for judgment arising from felony conviction is penal, and strictly construed; allowing homestead for defendant who was found civilly liable but not criminal convicted of attempted murder for which co-defendant was convicted).

785 People v. One Residence, 621 N.E.2d 1026 (Ill. App. Ct. 1993) (homestead exemption applied to "involuntary taking of property for any purpose" including forfeiture pursuant to state controlled substances statute).

786 735 Ill. Comp. Stat. § 5/12-903.5.

787 Ergos v. State, 670 So. 2d 1079 (Fla. Dist. Ct. App. 1996). *See also* Matthieu v. City of Lauderdale Lakes, 961 So. 2d 363 (Fla. Dist. Ct. App. 2007) (liens for municipal code violations may not be foreclosed against homestead property); Fong v. Town of Bay Harbor Islands, 864 So. 2d 76 (Fla. Dist. Ct. App. 2003) (no lien against homestead for continuing code violations). *But cf.* United States v. Jaffe, 417 F.3d 259 (2d Cir. 2005) (Florida homestead preempted by federal law; federal court restitution order that may require sale of exempt homestead is valid).

788 United States v. Hyde, 497 F.3d 103 (1st Cir. 2007); United States v. Fleet, 498 F.3d 1225 (11th Cir. 2005); United States v. One Parcel of Real Prop. Known as 16614 Cayuga Rd., 2003 WL 21437207 (10th Cir. June 23, 2003) (Oklahoma homestead exemption does not bar federal forfeiture of homestead used as marijuana farm); United States v. Wagoner Real Estate, 278 F.3d 1091 (10th Cir. 2002) (federal forfeiture law preempts Oklahoma homestead exemption); United States v. Lampien, 89

tenancy by the entireties exemptions also will not prevent seizures for a federal tax debt.[789]

12.7.7 Mortgages and Other Consensual Liens on Home

Mortgages, deeds of trust, and mechanics liens based on contracts are usually considered waivers or exclusions from homestead protections.[790] In addition, some state homestead laws provide that they do not protect the home from debts for the purchase of the home.[791] However, if both

F.3d 1316 (7th Cir. 1996) (Wisconsin homestead exemption does not protect against federal government lien for restitution, and it would be preempted if it did); S.E.C. v. Solow, 682 F. Supp. 2d 1312 (S.D. Fla. 2010) (federal court ordering disgorgement, here of profits from securities fraud, may reach property covered by state homestead and tenancy by entireties exemptions), *aff'd*, 396 Fed. Appx. 635 (11th Cir. 2010); Wang v. Wang, 2007 WL 2460729 (M.D. Fla. Aug. 24, 2007); United States v. One Single Family Residence at 2200 S.W. 28th Ave., 204 F. Supp. 2d 1361 (S.D. Fla. 2002) (federal forfeiture law preempts state homestead exemptions); *In re* Hutchins, 306 B.R. 82 (Bankr. D. Vt. 2004) (lien for husband's federal criminal fines encumbered his interest in real property even though it would have been protected by state entireties doctrine). *But cf.* United States v. Lee, 232 F.3d 556 (7th Cir. 2000) (when property was neither used in the commission of a crime nor purchased with proceeds thereof, tenancy by entireties protects innocent spouse against forfeiture of even guilty spouse's share). *See generally* Ch. 10, *supra* (collection of government debts).

789 United States v. Craft, 535 U.S. 274, 122 S. Ct. 1414, 152 L. Ed. 2d 437 (2002); United States v. Rogers, 461 U.S. 677, 103 S. Ct. 2132, 76 L. Ed. 2d 236 (1983); United States v. Offiler, 336 Fed. Appx. 907 (11th Cir. 2009) (Florida homestead exemption will not protect property against foreclosure of federal tax lien); United States v. Kimmel, 2010 WL 1240579 (D. Colo. Mar. 22, 2010) (authorizing sale for husband's debt; Colorado homestead exemption does not apply); United States v. Barczyk, 697 F. Supp. 2d 789 (E.D. Mich. Mar. 24, 2010) (U.S. may foreclose on and sell tenancy by entireties homestead property for tax debt of one spouse; non-debtor spouse is entitled to 50% of proceeds), *aff'd*, 434 Fed. Appx. 488 (6th Cir. 2011); United States v. Boscaljon, 2010 WL 1053688 (D.S.D. Mar. 22, 2010) (homestead does not protect against seizure for tax debt of husband, but court has discretion to delay foreclosure until innocent seventy-four-year-old wife can find other housing); *In re* Szwyd, 408 B.R. 547 (D. Mass. 2009) (IRS can reach homestead property, but other creditors cannot; equities favor ordering IRS to take homestead and leave non-exempt property for other creditors when tax debt is large, non-exempt property is small, and debtor's conduct was reprehensible). *See generally* Ch. 10, *supra* (collection of government debts).

790 Vogel v. Veneman, 276 F.3d 729 (5th Cir. 2002) (homestead exemption does not apply to refinancing of original purchase money debt); *In re* Anderson, 308 B.R. 25 (B.A.P. 8th Cir. 2004) (Minnesota homestead exemption does not protect against voluntary liens); United States v. Berk, 374 B.R. 385 (D. Mass. 2007) (homestead exemption does not protect against mortgage); Cavazos v. Munoz, 305 B.R. 661 (S.D. Tex. 2004) (mechanics lien was good, as to homeowners, when contractor complied with all procedural requirements except the lien affidavit, which serves to protect third parties); *In re* Liberman, 244 B.R. 557 (E.D.N.Y. 2000) (New York homestead exemption does not protect against foreclosure of purchase money mortgage), *aff'd*, 225 F.3d 646 (2d Cir. 2000) (table); *In re* Laird, 2010 WL 1664079 (Bankr. M.D. Ala. Apr. 22, 2010) (homestead does not protect against validly executed second mortgage; if homestead mortgage formalities complied with, no need for waiver of homestead procedure provided by another statute); *In re* Wycuff, 332 B.R. 297 (Bankr. N.D. Ohio 2005); *In re* Evans, 2005 WL 3845700 (Bankr. N.D. Fla. Dec. 21, 2005) (Florida homestead exemption does not protect against mortgage, and bankruptcy discharge eliminates only personal liability; foreclosure permitted after discharge); *In re* St. Onge, 317 B.R. 39 (Bankr. D.N.H. 2004) (second mortgage will encumber homestead if signed by both spouses with formalities required for conveyance of land); *In re* Desroches, 314 B.R. 19 (Bankr. D. Mass. 2004) (homestead exemption subordinate to second mortgage signed by both spouses with words of grant and mortgage covenants, even though it did not explicitly release homestead); Homeside Lending, Inc. v. Miller, 31 P.3d 607 (Utah Ct. App. 2001); Upton v. Household Fin. Indus. Loan Co., 6 P.3d 1231 (Wash. Ct. App. 2000) (deed of trust beneficiary's interest in real property and its proceeds is superior to homestead exemption). *See also* Abir v. Stern, 2010 WL 1170060 (E.D.N.Y. Mar. 22, 2010) (no homestead exemption in proceeds of bankruptcy trustee's sale of homestead when proceeds used to pay off consensual mortgage); *In re* Stepka, 425 B.R. 820 (Bankr. D. Minn. 2010) (no homestead exemption after bankruptcy trustee invalidated mortgage because of defective property description; debtors intended to and voluntarily did, grant mortgage); *In re* Wade, 354 B.R. 876 (Bankr. N.D. Iowa 2006) (Iowa homestead real estate may be pledged but may be sold only if deficiency remains after all non-homestead collateral is sold); Knolls Condo. Ass'n v. Harms, 781 N.E.2d 261 (Ill. 2002) (homestead exemption not a defense against eviction action brought by condominium association for unpaid fees); *In re* Trustee's Sale of Real Prop. of Ervin, 134 Wash. App. 1047 (Wash. Ct. App. 2006) (second mortgage takes priority over homestead exemption in distribution of proceeds of first mortgage foreclosure). *But see* United States v. Neff, 2007 WL 776532 (D.N.D. Mar. 12, 2007) (North Dakota forbids waiver of homestead exemption for chattel debt); *In re* Rose, 2012 WL 1492338 (Bankr. D. Mont. Apr. 27, 2012) (mortgage exception does not extend to judgment lien on Property A resulting from deficiency after foreclosure on Property B). *But cf. In re* Sorrell, 292 B.R. 276 (Bankr. E.D. Tex. 2002) (falsified mechanic's lien documents did not override homestead exemption); Cross v. Strader Constr. Co., 768 So. 2d 465 (Fla. Dist. Ct. App. 2000) (contractor's judgment in *quantum meruit* not a mechanic's lien so does not fall within exception to homestead exemption); Iowa State Bank & Trust Co. v. Michel, 683 N.W.2d 95 (Iowa 2004) (applying Iowa restrictions against waiver of homestead exemption by consensual mortgage of agricultural land); U.S. Bank N.A. v. McConnell, 305 P.3d 1 (Kan. Ct. App. 2013) (wife validly waived homestead by signing mortgage, even though she did not sign note secured by mortgage); Earls v. Chase Bank of Tex., 59 P.3d 364 (Mont. 2002) (mortgage void when regulated lender failed to obtain written waiver of homestead rights required by former Montana statute); Brooks v. Northglen Ass'n, 141 S.W.3d 158 (Tex. 2004) (fees imposed by covenants running with land and in effect at time of purchase may be enforced by foreclosure on homestead, but increased fees allowed by statute may not); Chase Manhattan Mortgage Corp. v. Cook, 141 S.W.3d 709 (Tex. App. 2004) (bank failed to prove that loan used to pay off mechanic's lien, so lien on homestead not permitted by Texas law); Nat'l Loan Investors, L.P. v. Taylor, 79 S.W.3d 633 (Tex. App. 2002) (lender who financed finishing and set up of manufactured home failed to comply with requirements for lien on homestead, but homeowners judicially estopped from denying lien after they listed it on secured creditors schedule in bankruptcy). *See generally* §§ 12.1, *supra* (consensual liens on property other than home), 12.10, *infra* (waiver of exemptions).

791 *See, e.g.*, Mohn's Inc. v. Wilson, 475 B.R. 674 (E.D. Wis. July 11, 2012) (broadly construing Wisconsin homestead law's exception for debt for "purchase price" to include homebuilder's claim for work done in constructing house); Spikes v. OneWest Bank, 106 So. 3d 475 (Fla. Dist. Ct. App. 2012) (purchase money exception applies to equitable lien on interest of wife who had been present at closing but was "inadvertently" not asked to sign); Barras v. Barras, 396 S.W.3d 154 (Tex. App. 2013) (equalization payment to ex-wife for her share of home awarded

homestead and non-homestead property are pledged, the secured creditor may be required to proceed first against the non-homestead property.[792] In some states both spouses must sign when a married couple is involved,[793] although

to husband was purchase money debt, for which lien may be imposed on homestead). *See also In re* Rubino, 2004 WL 1701105 (Bankr. N.D. Iowa May 28, 2004) (Iowa homestead exemption does not protect against debt "incurred for work done or material furnished exclusively for the improvement of the homestead," here semi-permanent above-ground pool).

792 *See, e.g., In re* Hartley, 483 B.R. 700 (Bankr. W.D. Wis. 2012) (discussing allocation of equity and mortgage debt on parcels formed by splitting large mortgaged parcel into homestead and non-homestead parcels; giving decisive weight to Wisconsin requirement that debt be satisfied first from non-homestead property); *In re* Timmer, 423 B.R. 870 (Bankr. N.D. Iowa 2010).

793 Bullard v. IndyMac Bank, FSB, 539 Fed. Appx. 665 (6th Cir. 2013) (unpublished) (Michigan law) (spousal signature not needed when wife owned property before marriage and never granted it to husband; without ownership, husband had no ownership right); Avakian v. Citibank, N.A., 2014 WL 346861 (N.D. Miss. Jan. 30, 2014) (two-signature requirement strictly enforced; not satisfied when each spouse signed a deed of trust, but fact question here whether couple was separated on date mortgages were signed; Clark v. IndyMac Mortgage Servs., 2014 WL 122453 (N.D. Ala. Jan. 13, 2014) (Alabama's two-signature rule applies only if property occupied as homestead on day mortgage was signed); *In re* Doubov, 423 B.R. 505 (N.D. Ohio Feb. 8, 2010) (when wife's signature not properly notarized, mortgage valid only as to husband's half-interest); Wells Fargo Home Mortgage, Inc. v. Dietz, 2005 WL 758595 (D. Minn. Mar. 30, 2005) (purchase money mortgage signed by only one of two joint tenants, here a married couple, does not confer rights in non-signing spouse's interest; creditor entitled to only half of sales proceeds); *In re* Ramsey, 424 B.R. 217 (Bankr. N.D. Miss. 2009) (spousal signature requirement cannot be waived, and omission cannot be cured by later action; deed of trust void and equitable mortgage denied, even though signing spouse lied and forged a signature); *In re* Linne, 414 B.R. 536 (Bankr. D.N.D. 2008) (North Dakota strictly enforces requirement for notarized signatures of both spouses for sale or encumbrance of homestead; mortgage was unenforceable even though both spouses admitted genuineness of signatures); *In re* Miller, 352 B.R. 908 (Bankr. M.D. Fla. 2006) (under Alabama law purported conveyance of homestead property, signed by only one spouse, was entirely void, not just as to amount of homestead exemption); *In re* St. Onge, 317 B.R. 39 (Bankr. D.N.H. 2004) (second mortgage will encumber homestead if signed by both spouses with formalities required for conveyance of land); *In re* Melber, 315 B.R. 181 (Bankr. D. Mass. 2004) (husband who owned homestead property conveyed it to self and wife as tenants by entireties without reserving homestead and without wife's signature; two wrongs made a right; exemption survived); *In re* Desroches, 314 B.R. 19 (Bankr. D. Mass. 2004) (homestead exemption subordinate to second mortgage signed by both spouses with words of grant and mortgage covenants, even though it did not explicitly release homestead); *In re* Jakab, 293 B.R. 621 (Bankr. D. Vt. 2003) (mortgage of homestead void for lack of wife's signature); Phillips v. Fuller, 814 So. 2d 885 (Ala. Civ. App. 2001) (homestead not abandoned by wife who fled from abusive husband; mortgage invalid without her signature); Richardson v. Estate of Berthelot, 2013 WL 203271 (Alaska Jan. 16, 2012) (Alaska law gives non-signing non-titled spouse one year to challenge deed of trust; right survives signing spouse's death; allowing wife to invalidate deed of trust and claim her homestead allowance from estate); Nat'l Bank of Alaska v. Ketzler, 71 P.3d 333 (Alaska 2003) (if non-signing spouse's name is on title, one-signature deed is void on its face; otherwise non-signer must sue within one year); Taylor v. Maness, 941 So. 2d 559 (Fla. Dist. Ct. App. 2006) (contract of sale, signed by owner-husband but not non-owner wife, could not be enforced by specific performance; wife not tortuously interfering with contract because homestead law gave her "absolute legal right" to refuse); *In re* Estate of Battle, 778 N.W.2d 218, 2009 WL 4842477 (Iowa Ct. App. 2009) (refusing to reinstate original mortgage loan when cash-out refinance loan that paid it off was void for lack of spousal signature; giving weight to bank's negligence in failing to obtain wife's signature); Citimortgage, Inc. v. Danielson, 771 N.W.2d 653 (Iowa Ct. App. 2009) (mortgage void for lack of spousal signature; equitable mortgage not available because no proof of fraud); Martin v. Martin, 720 N.W.2d 732 (Iowa 2006) (one-signature deed void even though parties were in process of getting divorce, and home was owned by husband before marriage and was awarded to him in divorce); Beal Bank v. Siems, 670 N.W.2d 119 (Iowa 2003) (if at time mortgage is signed, married owner resides on property and claims homestead, both spouses must sign, even if other spouse neither resides nor claims homestead there); Marine Credit Union v. Detlefson-Delano, 830 N.W.2d 859 (Minn. 2013) (husband's deed granting "all title right and interest" to wife not sufficient to eliminate homestead; mortgage void for lack of husband's signature); Nat'l City Bank v. Engler, 777 N.W.2d 762 (Minn. Ct. App. 2010) (wife's signature as "non-borrower . . . for the purpose of waiving any and all homestead rights" sufficient to comply with two-signature rule for mortgage of homestead); Peterson v. Lenz, 2004 WL 2793331 (Minn. Ct. App. Dec. 7, 2004) (waiver of homestead filed while divorce pending, to enable wife's lawyer to file attorney's lien, was invalid without husband's signature); Wells Fargo Home Mortgage, Inc. v. Chojnacki, 668 N.W.2d 1 (Minn. Ct. App. 2003) (two signatures required on all except purchase money mortgages; loan secured by manufactured home, not purchase money, when part of proceeds paid off seller's lien; creditor failed to show ratification by non-signing wife; mortgage was void); Wells Fargo Home Mortgage, Inc. v. Newton, 646 N.W.2d 888 (Minn. Ct. App. 2002) (specific requirement for both spouses' signatures on mortgage of homestead trumps general provision of married women's act allowing wife to manage separate property; wife's attempt to mortgage homestead without husband's signature invalid, but wife liable on promissory note); Peterson v. Hinz, 605 N.W.2d 414 (Minn. Ct. App. 2000) (attempt to impose attorney's lien on homestead property, when wife had not signed the homestead waiver, was frivolous); Countrywide Home Loans, Inc. v. Parker, 975 So. 2d 233 (Miss. 2008) (couple resided in house owned by wife; she refinanced without husband's signature, falsely stating that they were separated; deed of trust was void, and lender not entitled to equitable mortgage); Snoddy v. Snoddy, 791 So. 2d 333 (Miss. Ct. App. 2001) (house became homestead when couple lived there during marriage, even though it was separate property of husband; husband's attempted conveyance was void when wife did not sign); Thurman v. Thurman, 770 So. 2d 1015 (Miss. Ct. App. 2000) (if couple are married and living together, valid deed of trust requires both signatures); Besnilian v. Wilkinson, 25 P.3d 187 (Nev. 2001) (one spouse may not alienate homestead property without consent of the other); Denman v. Atlas Leasing, L.L.C., 285 S.W.3d 591 (Tex. App. 2009) (mechanic's lien void for lack of husband's signature; couple were living apart but still married when wife bought house and negotiated for work in her own name, but no evidence she deceived creditor); Cadle Co. v. Ortiz, 227 S.W.3d 831 (Tex. App. 2007) (mechanic's lien on property titled in wife's name alone invalid when husband did not sign; homestead exemption waived if married person deliberately misrepresents self as single, but burden of proof on creditor; not shown here); Equitable Bank v. Chabron, 618 N.W.2d 262 (Wis. Ct. App. 2000). *See also* Wells Fargo Bank v. Hudson, 742 N.W.2d 605 (Iowa Ct. App. 2007) (Iowa strictly enforces two-signature rule). *But see In re* Muther, 479 B.R. 316 (Bankr. D. Vt. 2012) (rule applies only if non-signing spouse has homestead interest in property; here, non-signing wife had lost homestead as result of transfer between spouses); Gottstein v. Kraft, 274 P.3d 469 (Alaska 2012) (when couple were separated and neither was residing in former marital home, it was not a "family home or homestead" within the meaning of two-signature

both signatures may not be necessary for a purchase money mortgage.[794]

Some states forbid or restrict encumbrances of the homestead.[795] Texas, in particular, has strict constitutional limits, relaxed somewhat by 2003 amendments, that protect the homestead from encumbrances.[796]

statute); Spikes v. OneWest Bank, 106 So. 3d 475 (Fla. Dist. Ct. App. 2012) (allowing foreclosure of equitable mortgage when non-signing wife was present at closing and willing to sign but was inadvertently not asked to do so). *But cf.* GMAC Mortgage Co. v. Orcutt, 2014 WL 806171 (D. Vt. Feb. 28, 2014) (lack of signature by husband who was actually present at closing made mortgage voidable, not void; *Erie*-guessing that Vermont would allow equitable mortgage on these facts); *In re* Hoggarth Bros., 2004 WL 903814 (D.N.D. Apr. 22, 2004) (farm couples resided on land owned by farm partnership; because non-partner wives owned no interest in land, mortgage signed only by partner-husbands was valid); *In re* Cox, 408 B.R. 407 (Bankr. D. Kan. 2009) (allowing equitable lien; wife's statutorily required signature on mortgage was forged, but strong evidence that wife knew of, agreed to, and received the benefits of the refinancing); *In re* Clark, 384 B.R. 563 (Bankr. W.D. Mo. 2008) (when spouses were living apart, husband's signature not required; he had no homestead rights in property he neither owned nor occupied); James v. Thaggard, 795 So. 2d 738 (Ala. Civ. App. 2001) (husband could not avoid mortgage on grounds that wife had not signed, when she lived, worked, and claimed a homestead on a residence in another state and had never resided on the mortgaged property); Terminix Int'l, Inc. v. Rice, 904 So. 2d 1051 (Miss. 2004) (two-signature requirement did not apply to arbitration agreement in contract with exterminator, as contract did not affect wife's ownership interest in home); Walbridge v. Beaudoin, 48 A.3d 964 (N.H. 2012) (spousal signature not required for mortgage of property on which couple were building a house; statute applies only to homesteads, which require present physical occupancy); Skelton v. Wash. Mut. Bank, 61 S.W.3d 56 (Tex. App. 2001) (widow had no claims on homestead, and mortgage not invalidated by lack of her signature, when couple agreed husband alone should apply for mortgage because of wife's bad credit record and husband falsely informed lender he was single); Charter One Bank v. Estate of Spillane, 807 A.2d 452 (Vt. 2002) (lack of signature renders mortgage voidable, not void; when husband took out home equity line, then first wife died and husband and second wife divorced and remarried after date of last advances, wives' rights were extinguished by death or divorce); Jones v. Estate of Jones, 646 N.W.2d 280 (Wis. 2002) (broad language in premarital agreement allowing spouses to manage separate property waived homestead rights; when husband deeded house to wife and wife deeded it to another, second deed valid without husband's signature).

794 *See In re* Burks, 421 B.R. 762 (Bankr. N.D. Miss. 2009) (purchase money mortgage valid without wife's signature, but subordinate deed of trust for loan to cure mortgage delinquency not purchase money, and invalid); Wells Fargo Home Mortgage, Inc. v. Newton, 646 N.W.2d 888 (Minn. Ct. App. 2002) (when proceeds of refinancing used partly to pay off old mortgage and partly for other purposes, only the sum used to pay off mortgage will be treated as purchase money, excluded from homestead protection). *See also* Deutsche Bank Nat'l Trust Co. v. Roberts, 233 P.3d 805 (Okla. Civ. App. 2010) (extending Oklahoma purchase money exception to refinancing that paid off purchase money loan; granting equitable lien to lender when refinance loan was void due to forgery of wife's signature). *But cf. In re* Rhymes, 2008 WL 723975 (Bankr. S.D. Miss. Mar. 14, 2008) (deed of trust void for lack of wife's signature, even though she conveyed her interest in land to husband before he signed; purchase money exception not applicable, when loan to purchase manufactured home was secured by underlying land, already owned and occupied by borrowers).

795 United States v. Neff, 2007 WL 776532 (D.N.D. Mar. 12, 2007) (homestead exemption may not be waived for chattel debt; creditor also failed to show waiver was knowing and voluntary). *See generally* § 12.10, *infra* (waiver of exemptions).

796 Priester v. J.P. Morgan Chase Bank, N.A., 708 F.3d 667 (5th Cir. 2013) (violation of Texas home equity provisions makes mortgage voidable, not void ab initio; mortgage becomes valid if not challenged within four-year statute of limitations period); Smith v. JPMorgan Chase Bank, 825 F. Supp. 2d 859 (S.D. Tex. 2011) (lender has very limited right to cure; no statute of limitations for claim of violation of constitutional provisions regulating home equity loans); United States v. Candelario-Gomez, 2007 WL 1480658 (W.D.N.C. May 18, 2007) (Texas homestead exemption bars United States from executing on homestead for defaulted bail, even though relative who posted bail gave real estate note and deed of trust); Marketic v. U.S. Bank, 436 F. Supp. 2d 842 (N.D. Tex. 2006) (statute forbids foreclosure of home equity loan against property designated as agricultural for tax purposes as of date of foreclosure, even though not so designated at time of loan); Box v. State Bank, 340 B.R. 782 (S.D. Tex. 2006) (Texas forbids home equity loan that is conditioned upon paying off unsecured debt to same lender; shown here, despite disclaimer in loan documents); *In re* Quigley, 2011 WL 1045224 (Bankr. N.D. Tex. Mar. 16, 2011) (home equity loan was void, and lender forfeited interest and principal, when contract provided for non-judicial foreclosure and lender was not one of the kinds of persons permitted to make home-equity loans); *In re* Lovelace 443 B.R. 494 (Bankr. W.D. Tex. 2011) (construing constitutional provisions permitting certain home equity loans strictly against lender; loans permitted only when there is no prior encumbrance, with exception for purchase money mortgage; home equity loan that refinances purchase money mortgage not a purchase money mortgage, so second loan was void); *In re* Chambers, 419 B.R. 652 (Bankr. E.D. Tex. 2009) (refinancing loan fell within Texas Constitution's exception to ban on home equity lending; it met requirement of voluntariness even though bank was threatening foreclosure, when homeowners' financial distress was not caused by any misconduct of lender); *In re* Ritter, 2009 WL 1024656 (Bankr. E.D. Tex. Mar. 26, 2009) (bank advised farmers that they should incorporate their business and deed part of homestead, used to secure loan, to corporation; bank handled the paperwork and never told farmers that this would destroy homestead exemption; sale invalid because bank "initiated and actually facilitated" the evasion of homestead law); *In re* Cadengo, 370 B.R. 681 (Bankr. S.D. Tex. 2007) (homestead waiver ineffective when creditor had actual knowledge of homestead use); Patton v. Porterfield, 411 S.W.3d 147 (Tex. App. 2013) (extensive discussion of Texas home equity provisions; payment of home equity loan out of proceeds of foreclosure sale does not violate requirement that home equity loans be secured only by homestead); Thomas v. Graham Mortgage Corp., 408 S.W.3d 581 (Tex. App. 2013) (lender may rely on non-homestead affidavit, if there are not "visible circumstances" showing occupation as homestead); Ramsey v. Davis, 261 S.W.3d 811 (Tex. App. 2008) (home buyers were residing on property on date when developer's creditor filed a lien; because property was homestead, lien could not attach; creditor who refused to release purported lien was liable for slander of title); Robinson v. Saxon Mortgage Servs., Inc., 240 S.W.3d 311 (Tex. App. 2007) (waiver was valid, despite minor errors in paperwork, when documents showed permissible refinancing to pay mortgage and mechanics' liens); LaSalle Bank v. White, 217 S.W.3d 573 (Tex. App. 2006) (Texas constitution invalidates home equity loan secured by homestead property designated for agricultural use); Florey v. Estate of McConnell, 212 S.W.3d 439 (Tex. App. 2006) (lien to secure attorney fee not among exceptions to Texas's ban on loans secured by homestead). *Cf.* Sloan v. Owners Ass'n of Westfield, Inc., 167 S.W.3d 401 (Tex. App. 2005) (lien created by subdivision restrictions came into existence before homestead established; lien for subdivision fees, late fees, and attorney fees incurred in litigation over restrictions).

12.7.8 *Preexisting Debts and Advance Filing Requirements*

Some states do not protect a homestead against debts which pre-date the acquisition of the homestead.[797] The homestead exemption may, however, continue as to debts incurred during ownership of a former homestead, if the proceeds of its sale were used to purchase the debtor's current home.[798] In addition, a debt incurred after the effective date of a homestead exemption statute will be subject to the homestead law, even if it is incurred pursuant to a line of credit that pre-dated the statute.[799]

A few states make the homestead exemption inapplicable not only to debts that pre-date the acquisition of the homestead but also to debts that pre-date the debtor's formal filing of a homestead declaration with the recorder of deeds.[800] This was formerly the rule in Massachusetts for all homestead

797 *In re* Bassin, 637 F.2d 668 (9th Cir. 1980) (interpreting California law not to apply increase in homestead exemption to preexisting debts); *In re* Harle, 422 B.R. 310 (Bankr. M.D. Fla. 2010) (judgment lien that attached before debtors occupied new home took priority over homestead); *In re* Malatek, 2009 WL 3754234 (Bankr. N.D. Iowa Nov. 9, 2009) (fact issue whether land was homestead when debt incurred; exemption denied when, at time debt incurred, husband "temporarily staying" on property, doing repairs to make it habitable, while wife continued to reside in old home); *In re* Harwood, 404 B.R. 366 (Bankr. E.D. Tex. 2009) (homestead exemption does not protect against lien that attached before property became homestead), *aff'd on other grounds*, 427 B.R. 392 (E.D. Tex. 2010); *In re* Lewis, 400 B.R. 417 (Bankr. D. Vt. 2009) (bankruptcy law does not preempt provision of state homestead law that makes it inapplicable to preexisting debt); *In re* Whelan, 325 B.R. 462 (Bankr. M.D. Fla. 2005) (judgment lien, recorded against debtors who owned no real property, attached to homestead purchased four years later); *In re* Allen, 301 B.R. 55 (Bankr. S.D. Iowa 2003) (debtors owned and lived in House A, then bought and moved to House B while renting out House A, then sold House B and moved back to House A; homestead exemption did not protect House A against debt incurred while debtors lived in House B); *In re* Estad, 295 B.R. 905 (Bankr. D. Minn. 2003) (did not protect against lien that attached while new house under construction; not homestead until family actually moved in); *In re* Norkus, 256 B.R. 298 (Bankr. S.D. Iowa 2000) (Iowa homestead exemption does not protect against debts incurred before homestead acquired); Kamerick v. Marion Cnty. Bank, 2003 WL 23006949 (Iowa Ct. App. Dec. 24, 2003) (wife's guarantee of farm loan before she acquired homestead was a preexisting debt not protected by homestead exemption); Garcia v. Kentucky Employers Mut. Ins. Co., 2009 WL 3326807 (Ky. Ct. App. Oct. 16, 2009) (unpublished) (Ky. Rev. Stat. Ann. § 427.060 denies a homestead exemption if debt or liability existed before purchase of property or erection of improvements thereon). *But see In re* Rose, 2012 WL 1492338 (Bankr. D. Mont. Apr. 27, 2012) (no preexisting debt exception to Montana homestead exemption).

798 *See, e.g., In re* Takes, 478 F.3d 902 (8th Cir. 2007) (Iowa law) (new homestead exempt insofar as purchased with exempt proceeds of former homestead that pre-dated the debt but non-exempt as to balance of purchase price); *In re* Patterson, 482 B.R. 755 (Bankr. D. Vt. 2012) (new home that was purchased with proceeds of old home is exempt as to preexisting debt; when couple divorced, wife received marital home, husband received a package of other assets, which were the proceeds he used to pay for new home); *In re* Russow, 357 B.R. 133 (Bankr. N.D. Iowa 2007) (proceeds of old homestead rolled over into new homestead exempt as to preexisting debts); *In re* White 293 B.R. 1 (Bankr. N.D. Iowa 2003) (Iowa homestead exemption does not protect against preexisting debts but may be transferred from one residence to another; no interruption in homestead here, even though debtors lived briefly in an apartment between selling one house and purchasing the next). *See also In re* Larsen, 2011 WL 4621556 (Bankr. S.D. Iowa Sept. 30, 2011) (transfer of home from fee simple ownership to estate planning trust was mere change in form of ownership; debt that accrued between time of purchase of house and transfer to trust could not attach to homestead); *In re* Meyer, 392 B.R. 416 (Bankr. N.D. Iowa 2008) (new homestead remains exempt up to value of former homestead, even if proceeds of old homestead used to pay off business debt and new homestead purchased with proceeds of personal injury settlement); AgVantage FS v. Western Farming, Inc., 803 N.W.2d 672 (Iowa Ct. App. 2011) (homestead continued uninterrupted when debtors sold homestead and used proceeds to purchase land and a modular home in which they planned to reside; new parcel was homestead even though home was not ready for occupancy). *But cf. In re* Shirley, 472 B.R. 19 (B.A.P. 8th Cir. 2012) (Iowa law) (when divorcing debtor was ordered out of marital home and bought new home with funds provided by mother, new home could be sold for debt that preceded purchase); *In re* Walters, 2010 WL 3909230 (Bankr. S.D. Iowa, Oct. 1, 2010) (new Iowa homestead not exempt as to preexisting debt when debtors failed to show that new home purchased with proceeds of former homestead); SBAM Partners v. Cheng Min Wang, 79 Cal. Rptr. 3d 752 (Cal. Ct. App. 2008) (homestead does not protect against judgment lien recorded before purchase of homestead, when homestead not purchased with proceeds of former homestead). *See generally* § 12.2.3, *supra* (exemption for proceeds of sale of exempt property).

799 Alessandro v. People's Bank (*In re* Alessandro), 254 B.R. 521 (Bankr. D. Conn. 2000) (Connecticut's new homestead statute, which applies prospectively only, applies to credit extended after its effective date on preexisting line of credit that was terminable at will); *In re* Caraglior, 251 B.R. 778 (Bankr. D. Conn. 2000) (Connecticut homestead exemption protects against debts for balances accrued after its effective date on credit cards issued before that date).

800 *In re* Shepard, 2007 WL 1385725 (Bankr. D.N.M. May 7, 2007) (California automatic homestead not available; no homestead declaration filed, and debtors were living and working out-of-state); Title Trust Deed Serv. Co. v. Pearson, 33 Cal. Rptr. 3d 311 (Cal. Ct. App. 2005) (distinguishing between automatic and declared homestead under California law; the latter, but not former, may have priority over judgment lien); Kim v. First Fed. Bank, 2002 WL 1579602 (Cal. Ct. App. July 17, 2002) (no declared exemption when homestead declaration was recorded after judgment lien had already attached; automatic exemption does not protect from sale pursuant to mortgage or deed of trust; sale proceeds not exempt). *See also* Sanches v. Telles, 960 S.W.2d 762 (Tex. App. 1997) (property was not homestead, even though owner had lived there for eight years, when owner had not filed a homestead deed and had pledged property for bail bond, signing a statement that the property was not homestead). *But see* Siewak v. AmSouth Bank, 2007 WL 141186 (M.D. Fla. Jan. 16, 2007) (failure to file homestead notice not fatal to homestead claim; procedure is voluntary, not mandatory); *In re* Mariano, 311 B.R. 335 (Bankr. D. Mass. 2004) (homestead declaration filed after levy on home is valid, if property has not yet been sold); *In re* Allman, 286 B.R. 402 (Bankr. D. Ariz. 2002) (Arizona statute amended; filing of homestead declaration no longer required); Osborne v. Dumoulin, 55 So. 3d 577, 582–83 (Fla. 2011) (no action necessary to make property a homestead other than acquiring it and making it one's home); *In re* Snyder, 149 P.3d 26 (Mont. 2006) (liberally construing statute to allow debtor to claim homestead in sale proceeds, even if no homestead declaration filed before sale); Cowart v. Pan Am. Bank, 2000 Wash. App. LEXIS 2132 (Wash. Ct. App. Nov. 3, 2000) (Washington property automatically acquires homestead status if it is occupied as residence; judgment creditor may acquire a lien against the value in excess of the homestead exemption only by strictly complying with filing procedure).

exemptions,[801] but amendments effective in 2011 make the basic homestead exemption automatic. A filing is necessary only for an enhanced exemption for older or disabled homeowners.[802]

Virginia enforces a much less onerous filing requirement. In order to exempt a homestead or certain personal property, Virginia requires the debtor to file a homestead deed prior to the execution sale of the property or, in the case of bankruptcy, within five days after the first meeting of creditors.[803]

Some courts have construed statutes that increase the amount of the homestead exemption to apply to debts incurred before the change.[804] Other states, however, refuse to apply a homestead exemption, or an amended version of it, to debts that arose before its effective date.[805] The result may be different in bankruptcy.[806]

---

801 *In re* Garran, 338 F.3d 1 (1st Cir. 2003) (only one homestead declaration per parcel; wife's later filing superseded husband's "disabled person" filing; exemptions could not be stacked); *In re* Perry, 357 B.R. 175 (B.A.P. 1st Cir. 2006) (Massachusetts law) (homestead declaration must be filed before bankruptcy petition; when it was impossible to tell which filed first, because clerks' time stamps showed same minute, principle of liberal interpretation applied and exemption allowed); *In re* Hildebrandt, 320 B.R. 40 (B.A.P. 1st Cir. 2005) (homestead exemption lost when unmarried couple, who had purchased house as tenants in common and recorded homestead, then conveyed house to one tenant without reserving homestead); ClearOne Commc'ns, Inc. v. Chiang, 717 F. Supp. 2d 142 (D. Mass. 2010) (Massachusetts exception for preexisting debts applies only to judgment entered before homestead filed; homestead declaration filed after verdict but before entry of judgment protected property against judgment debt; note that as of 2011, filing is no longer necessary for a basic homestead amount of $125,000); *In re* Guido, 344 B.R. 193 (Bankr. D. Mass. 2006) (second mortgage took priority over homestead rights when it was executed before filing of homestead declaration but not recorded until after); *In re* Vizard, 327 B.R. 515 (Bankr. D. Mass. 2005) (homestead exemption lost when homestead conveyed to wife from husband and wife without reservation of homestead); *In re* Melber, 315 B.R. 181 (Bankr. D. Mass. 2004) (husband who owned homestead property conveyed it to self and wife as tenants by entireties without reserving homestead and without wife's signature; two wrongs made a right; exemption survived); *In re* Farrenkopf, 305 B.R. 382 (Bankr. D. Mass. 2004) (wife may claim homestead exemption in property for which husband has filed homestead declaration; only one owner may file, but exemption protects whole family); *In re* Govoni, 289 B.R. 500 (Bankr. D. Mass. 2002) (no homestead exemption for contiguous lot that contained home's septic system, because debtor failed to include that lot in homestead declaration); *In re* Cassesse, 286 B.R. 472 (Bankr. D. Mass. 2002) (ex-wife, who owned house jointly with ex-husband, not covered by his homestead declaration, because after divorce she was no longer family within meaning of statute; she should have filed her own homestead exemption); *In re* Swyzd, 346 B.R. 290, 291 n.1 (Bankr. D. Mass. 2006) (criticizing Massachusetts statute, which purports to protect debtors' homes, but protection "may be easily and inadvertently lost by statutory language and conditions that are hyper-technical and often counter-intuitive"), *aff'd*, 370 B.R. 882 (B.A.P. 1st Cir. 2007); *In re* Mariano, 311 B.R. 335 (Bankr. D. Mass. 2004) (homestead declaration filed after levy on home is valid, and judgment lien can be avoided under bankruptcy law, if property has not yet been sold); Shamban v. Masidlover, 705 N.E.2d 1136 (Mass. 1999) (disabled person who filed declaration of homestead claiming $200,000 exemption, but failed to include statutorily required evidence of disability, could claim only standard $100,000 exemption); Russell v. Black, 2000 Mass. Super. LEXIS 350 (Mass. Super. Ct. July 28, 2000) (unliquidated malpractice claim not a prior debt within meaning of Mass.'s prior debt exception to homestead). *Cf. In re* Gaudreault, 315 B.R. 1 (Bankr. D. Mass. 2004) (debtor in involuntary bankruptcy may obtain Massachusetts homestead by filing declaration after petition and before order for relief).

802 Mass. Gen. Laws ch. 188, §§ 1, 2, 4.

803 Va. Code Ann. §§ 34-6, 34-14, 34-17. *See In re* Cambre, 463 B.R. 340 (Bankr. W.D. Va. 2012) (homestead deed invalid as to real property because filed in the wrong county; invalid as to proceeds because it claimed only real property); *In re* Strickland, 2010 WL 1332657 (Bankr. E.D. Va. Mar. 30, 2010) (Virginia law does not provide for filing of revised homestead deed; when debtors exempted CD used to secure home loan, but not the heavily encumbered home, no exemption for surplus resulting from sale of CD and home); *In re* Neilson, 427 B.R. 581 (Bankr. W.D. Va. 2010) (to exempt earned but unpaid wages, debtor must file homestead deed on or before return date of garnishment summons); *In re* Connor, 408 B.R. 88 (Bankr. W.D. Va. 2009) (exemption lost when it was filed in wrong county and second attempt was untimely; five-day deadline includes weekends); *In re* Ahmed, 411 B.R. 537 (Bankr. E.D. Va. 2009) (exemption lost when paperwork was mailed within five-day deadline but received thereafter); *In re* Diab, 2008 WL 4588018 (Bankr. E.D. Va. Oct. 14, 2008) (failure to timely file Virginia homestead deed, which applies to personal as well as real property, results in loss of exemption); *In re* Cook, 2007 WL 2238397 (Bankr. E.D. Va. July 31, 2007) (debtor lost opportunity to exempt her tax refunds when she failed to file homestead deed within five days after meeting of creditors); *In re* Alley, 354 B.R. 783 (Bankr. W.D. Va. 2006) (Virginia statute allows homestead filing up to five days after meeting of creditors; filing was timely when forms and fee delivered to clerk within that time, even though sent back for noncompliance with local rule concerning form); *In re* Shelton, 343 B.R. 545 (Bankr. W.D. Va. 2006) (under new statute debtor has five days after rescheduled creditors' meeting actually takes place to file). *But cf. In re* Diaz, 2010 WL 2425960 (Bankr. E.D. Va. June 10, 2010) (debtor who missed short Virginia deadline to exempt IRAs could exempt them pursuant to section 522(b)(3)(C) of bankruptcy code).

804 *In re* Magee, 444 B.R. 254 (Bankr. S.D.N.Y. 2011) (New York's increased homestead exemption applies to preexisting debts, even if they have been reduced to judgment); *In re* Little, 2006 WL 1524594 (Bankr. N.D.N.Y. Apr. 24, 2006) (increased exemption applied to preexisting debt); Homeside Lending, Inc. v. Miller, 31 P.3d 607 (Utah Ct. App. 2001) (statute set amount debtor could claim as homestead exemption "at the time of sale"); Macumber v. Shafer, 637 P.2d 645 (Wash. 1981). *Cf.* First Nat'l Bank v. Jones, 6 N.E.3d 1231 (Ohio Ct. App. 2014) (homestead exemption amount in effect on date of issuance of execution, not on date creditor obtained judgment lien, applies). *See generally* § 12.2.1.1, *supra* (constitutionality of application of increased exemption to preexisting debts).

805 *In re* Tardugno, 262 B.R. 168 (Bankr. D. Mass. 2001) (Massachusetts statute which increased exemption does not apply retroactively; when statute became effective after debtor filed bankruptcy, lower exemption applied); *In re* Skjetne, 213 B.R. 274 (Bankr. D. Vt. 1997) (under Vermont law, increase in homestead exemption does not apply to preexisting debts, but result is different when debtor files bankruptcy); *In re* Corson, 206 B.R. 17 (Bankr. D. Conn. 1997) (Connecticut's homestead exemption, which applies prospectively only, did not protect home when debtor incurred debt before statute's effective date, even though creditor sued and obtained lien afterwards); Builders Supply Co. v. Pine Belt Sav. & Loan Ass'n, 369 So. 2d 743, 745 (Miss. 1979). *See generally* § 12.2.1.2, *supra* (constitutional issues in application of amended exemption statutes to preexisting debts).

806 *In re* Weinstein, 164 F.3d 677 (1st Cir. 1999); *In re* Mayer, 167 B.R. 186 (B.A.P. 9th Cir. 1994) (exemption amount in effect on date of bankruptcy filing applies); *In re* Noonan, 2014 WL 184776 (Bankr. D. Mass. Jan. 15, 2014) (Massachusetts preexisting debt exception is preempted by bankruptcy law); *In re* Depascale, 496 B.R. 860 (Bankr. N.D. Ohio Aug. 8, 2013) (using amount in effect on petition date); *In re* LaVictoire, 2011 WL 1168288 (Bankr. D. Vt. Mar. 29, 2011) (Vermont increased its

12.7.9 Entireties Property

The usual rule is that non-exempt real property that is jointly owned can be reached for the debts of either of the co-tenants.[807] However, although the rule is not universal,[808] many jurisdictions, either by statute or under common law, protect the marital home against seizure for the debts of one spouse.[809]

---

homestead amount between the date when creditor obtained judgment and the date when debtor filed bankruptcy; bankruptcy law requires use of the amount existing on petition date); *In re* Suelflow, 2008 WL 5157933 (Bankr. D.N.M. Oct. 10, 2008) (increased exemption amount, in effect on petition date, applied for lien avoidance); *In re* Dubois, 306 B.R. 423 (Bankr. D. Me. 2004) (Maine statute providing that increase in homestead exemption was prospective only was preempted by bankruptcy law that provided short list of debts that can be collected from exempt property; new exemption amount applied to preexisting debt); *In re* Betz, 273 B.R. 313 (Bankr. D. Mass. 2002) (debtor entitled to increased state exemption in effect on bankruptcy filing date, even as to preexisting debts that were specifically excepted by state statute); *In re* Homonoff, 261 B.R. 551 (Bankr. D.R.I. 2001) (bankruptcy law uses exemptions as of date of filing even though Rhode Island statute denies homestead protection against debts which pre-date either the enactment of the statute or the acquisition of the homestead). *But see In re* Lewis, 400 B.R. 417 (Bankr. D. Vt. 2009) (bankruptcy law does not preempt provision of state homestead law that makes it inapplicable to debt that pre-dated the acquisition of the homestead); *In re* Banner, 394 B.R. 292 (Bankr. D. Conn. 2008) (Connecticut's newly enacted homestead exemption, in effect on petition date, not applicable to judgment lien that attached before its effective date).

807 *See, e.g.*, *In re* Antonie, 447 B.R. 610 (D. Idaho 2011) (manufactured home owned in joint tenancy with non-debtor mother could be reached for daughter's debts); *In re* Risler, 443 B.R. 508 (Bankr. W.D. Wis. 2010) (refusing to receive extrinsic evidence that father was on deed only to assist ill son in managing the property when deed stated that property was owned in joint tenancy by father and non-debtor son; father's bankruptcy trustee could sell property).

808 *See, e.g.*, *In re* Prosser, 2008 WL 2677863 (D. V.I. July 1, 2008) (under New York law, real property held as tenancy by entireties is subject to execution for debt of individual spouse); Kaplan v. First Options of Chicago, 189 B.R. 882, 891 (E.D. Pa. 1995) (New Jersey law does not protect entireties real estate from claim by creditor of one spouse against that spouse's interest in the property); *In re* Watford, 427 B.R. 552 (Bankr. S.D. Fla. 2010) (Georgia does not recognize tenancy by entireties; property owned by spouses is tenancy in common, which is severable); *In re* Garrett, 435 B.R. 434 (Bankr. S.D. Tex. 2010) (Texas does not recognize tenancy by entireties; even when bankruptcy law required application of North Carolina law to Texas debtors, entireties claim was governed by law of state where property was located); *In re* Nelms, 2005 WL 318802 (Bankr. E.D. Mich. Feb. 4, 2005) (Michigan debtors cannot claim tenancy by entireties exemption for property located in Louisiana, which does not recognize tenancy by entireties); *In re* Arwood, 289 B.R. 889 (Bankr. E.D. Tenn. 2003); Lurie v. Sheriff of Gallatin Cnty., 999 P.2d 342 (Mont. 2000) (tenancy by entireties not recognized in Montana for personal or real property).

809 *ALASKA:* Smith v. Kofstad, 206 P.3d 441 (Alaska 2009) (judgment creditor of deceased husband could not execute on home that was owned by entireties before husband's death).

ARKANSAS: *In re* White, 460 B.R. 744 (B.A.P. 8th Cir. 2011), *aff'd*, 470 Fed. Appx. 538 (8th Cir. 2012).

DELAWARE: *In re* Kelly, 316 B.R. 629 (D. Del. 2004) (permitting debtor to exempt property held as tenants by the entirety with non-debtor spouse); *In re* Mintz, 2005 WL 758813 (Bankr. D. Del. Mar. 31, 2005) (allowing exemption of residence held as tenants by the entirety when trustee unable to show debtors had any joint debts).

FLORIDA: *In re* Sinnreich, 391 F.3d 1295 (11th Cir. 2004) (Florida law) (real and personal property held in tenancy by entireties with non-debtor spouse is exempt); United States v. Lee, 232 F.3d 556 (7th Cir. 2000) (Florida law) (when property was neither used in the commission of a crime nor purchased with proceeds thereof, tenancy by entireties protects innocent spouse against forfeiture of even guilty spouse's interest); *In re* Holland, 2009 WL 2971087 (Bankr. N.D. Ill. Sept. 8, 2009) (Florida entireties law applies to Florida land owned by Illinois debtors; land deeded to married couple presumed to be owned by entireties); *In re* Ramsurat, 361 B.R. 246 (Bankr. M.D. Fla. 2006) (to create Florida tenancy by entireties, couple must be married at time property conveyed; no tenancy by entireties when sale closed before marriage); *In re* Mitchell, 344 B.R. 171 (Bankr. M.D. Fla. 2006) (if property deeded to married couple, tenancy by entireties is presumed; when property was deeded to couple and son, one joint tenant was the entireties and the other was the son); *In re* Willoughby, 212 B.R. 1011 (Bankr. M.D. Fla. 1997) (tenancy by entireties protects homestead from individual debts of husband, even debt for child support from prior marriage). *But cf.* Republic Credit Corp. I v. Upshaw, 10 So. 3d 1103 (Fla. Dist. Ct. App. 2009) (proceeds of California homestead, used to purchase home in Florida, could not be owned by entireties, because California does not recognize that form of ownership).

ILLINOIS: 735 Ill. Comp. Stat. Ann. § 5/12-112. *See* Maher v. Harris Trust & Sav. Bank, 506 F.3d 560 (7th Cir. 2007) (by statute, Illinois allows tenancy by entirety in property maintained or intended as homestead by both husband and wife; rejecting creditor's argument that shares in cooperative where couple resided were personal property that could not be owned in tenancy by entireties); *In re* Berg, 387 B.R. 524 (Bankr. N.D. Ill. 2008) (only homestead property may be owned in tenancy by entireties; if property ceases to be, or never was, homestead, ownership becomes tenancy in common); *In re* Eichorn, 338 B.R. 793 (Bankr. S.D. Ill. 2006) (filing of joint bankruptcy neither severs tenancy by entireties, nor "merges" bankruptcy estates; tenancy by entireties property remains exempt as to debt of individual spouse); *In re* Moreno, 352 B.R. 455 (Bankr. N.D. Ill. Sept. 20, 2006) (home held in tenancy by entireties cannot be reached for debt of one spouse); *In re* Tolson, 338 B.R. 359 (Bankr. C.D. Ill. 2005) (property could not be reached for individual debts under Illinois statute that applies when property is transferred into tenancy by entireties with sole intent to avoid payment of existing debts when financially troubled couple engaged in estate planning and lawyer drafted husband's will at same time as deed). *But cf. In re* Meredith, 2012 WL 1835516 (Bankr. C.D. Ill. May 18, 2012) (Illinois TBE exemption has fraud exception; transfer that occurred on same day large judgment was entered against husband was fraudulent).

INDIANA: Rhodes v. Indiana Nat'l Bank, 544 N.E.2d 179 (Ind. Ct. App. 1989) (Indiana protects real property, but not personal property, that is held in tenancy by entireties, from debts of one spouse; rents received from real property are personal property).

IOWA: *In re* Powers, 286 B.R. 726 (Bankr. N.D. Iowa 2002) (homestead right of husband and wife cannot be split, so cannot be executed upon for non-joint debt).

KENTUCKY: *In re* Brinley, 403 F.3d 415 (6th Cir. 2005) (Kentucky law) (explaining how to apply Bankruptcy Code lien avoidance provisions to property owned in tenancy by entireties with non-debtor spouse).

MARYLAND: Schlossberg v. Barney, 380 F.3d 174 (4th Cir. 2004) (Maryland law) (spouse who files individual bankruptcy can exempt property held in tenancy by entireties with non-debtor spouse); *In re* Greathouse, 295 B.R. 562 (Bankr. D. Md. 2003) (if no joint debts and no tax debts, property owned in tenancy by entireties completely exempt).

MASSACHUSETTS: *In re* Snyder, 249 B.R. 40 (B.A.P. 1st Cir. 2000) (Massachusetts law) (husband has 100% interest in home owned as tenancy by entireties), *aff'd*, 248 F.3d 1127 (1st Cir. 2001) (table). *But cf.* *In re* Hidler, 192 B.R. 790 (Bankr. D. Me. 1996) (when Massachusetts tenancy by entireties was created before passage of tenancy by entireties statute, common law applied and property could be sold for individual debt of husband).

MICHIGAN: In re Raynard, 354 B.R. 834 (B.A.P. 6th Cir. Oct. 25, 2006) (Michigan law) (in or out of chapter 13, tenancy by entireties property exempt from creditors of individual spouse); *In re* Spears, 313 B.R. 212 (W.D. Mich. 2004) (filing of bankruptcy by one spouse does not sever tenancy by entireties; entireties property may be reached only for joint debts). *Cf.* United States v. Craft, 535 U.S. 274, 122 S. Ct. 1414, 152 L. Ed. 2d 437 (2002) (describing Michigan's recognition of tenancy by entireties; property tax lien can nonetheless attach to debtor husband's interest).

MISSOURI: Brown v. Eads (*In re* Eads), 271 B.R. 371 (Bankr. W.D. Mo. 2002); *In re* Brown, 234 B.R. 907 (Bankr. W.D. Mo. 1999) (under Missouri law, real and personal property of married couple is presumed to be owned in tenancy by entireties and thus exempt from claims of individual creditors).

NORTH CAROLINA: N.C. Gen. Stat. § 39-13.6; *In re* Payne, 2004 WL 2757907 (Bankr. M.D.N.C. Nov. 15, 2004) (property owned in tenancy by entireties fully exempt if no joint creditors; because couple did not claim homestead exemption, each debtor entitled to "in lieu of homestead" wildcard).

OHIO: First Fed. Sav. & Loan Ass'n v. Dus, 2003 WL 21545126 (Ohio Ct. App. July 10, 2003) (lien could not attach to real property owned in tenancy by entireties for husband's individual debt; divorce changed tenancy by entireties into joint tenancy, but lien still did not attach because it came into existence while parties were married).

PENNSYLVANIA: In re Olexa, 476 F.3d 177 (3d Cir. 2007) (entireties property cannot be reached even though debts were for necessaries, as necessaries statute refers only to spouse's separate property); Sterrett v. Sterrett, 166 A.2d 1 (Pa. 1960).

RHODE ISLAND: In re Pearlman, 2005 WL 1331256 (Bankr. D.R.I. Apr. 18, 2005) (commercial property exempt and bankruptcy estate's interest limited to value of contingent expectancy interest when property held as tenants by the entirety); *In re* Strandberg, 253 B.R. 584 (Bankr. D.R.I. 2000) (when property owned in tenancy by entireties, debtor-husband may claim entire homestead exemption; Rhode Island law allows only one owner to claim exemption, which cannot be divided).

VERMONT: Evans v. Wolinsky, 347 B.R. 9 (D. Vt. 2006) (entireties property cannot be reached by creditors, so transfer to wife individually, at time when no joint debts, not fraudulent); *In re* Hutchins, 306 B.R. 82 (Bankr. D. Vt. 2004) (Vermont recognizes entireties doctrine, but lien for federal criminal fine can attach to husband's interest); RBS Citizens v. Ouhrabka, 30 A.3d 1266 (Vt. 2011) (Rights of Married Women Act did not eliminate the basis for tenancy by entireties).

VIRGINIA: In re Thomas, 312 F.3d 145 (4th Cir. 2002) (Virginia law) (even in joint bankruptcy, entireties property may be reached only by joint creditors); *In re* Sampath, 314 B.R. 73 (Bankr. E.D. Va. 2004) (deed to married couple grants tenancy by entireties, even if deed silent as to marital status; adding daughter to deed did not sever tenancy by entireties; couple's share could not be reached for individual debt of husband); *In re* Zella, 196 B.R. 752 (Bankr. E.D. Va. 1996) (proceeds of sale of entireties real estate are, like the real estate, exempt from the claims of one spouse's creditors), *aff'd*, 202 B.R. 712 (E.D. Va. 1996); *In re* Scialdone, 197 B.R. 225 (Bankr. E.D. Va. 1995) (real property held in tenancy by entirety was exempt from attachment by creditor of only one spouse; tenancy by entirety can be created only by explicit language in the deed); Rogers v. Rogers, 512 S.E.2d 821 (Va. 1999) (when creditors had federal court judgment against husband and state judgment against wife, both apparently resulting from the same transactions, entireties property could not be attached; only a joint judgment against husband and wife could be satisfied from entireties property).

VIRGIN ISLANDS: In re Prosser, 2013 WL 594312 (Bankr. D. V.I. Feb. 14, 2013) (property owned in joint tenancy before marriage does not automatically become TBE upon marriage; conveyance must be shown).

While the scope of this protection varies from state to state, most states base the protection on the theory that the interests of both husband and wife extend to the whole of the property.[810] For as long as the marriage continues, this tenancy by the entireties cannot be severed, terminated, or partitioned by either spouse without the other's consent.[811] The estate is severed, however, by divorce or the death of one spouse,[812] or the transfer of the property by both spouses to some other form of ownership.[813] In the case of divorce, the tenancy by entireties becomes a tenancy in common.[814] If one spouse dies, the property passes to the other in its entirety.[815]

810 *In re* Thomas, 312 F.3d 145 (4th Cir. 2002); *In re* Raynard, 354 B.R. 834 (B.A.P. 6th Cir. Oct. 25, 2006) (Michigan law); *In re* Snyder, 249 B.R. 40 (B.A.P. 1st Cir. 2000) (Massachusetts law), *aff'd*, 248 F.3d 1127 (1st Cir. 2001) (table).

811 *In re* Brinley, 403 F.3d 415 (6th Cir. 2005) (explaining how to apply Bankruptcy Code lien avoidance provisions to property owned in tenancy by entireties with non-debtor spouse); *In re* Thomas, 312 F.3d 145 (4th Cir. 2002); *In re* Raynard, 354 B.R. 834 (B.A.P. 6th Cir. Oct. 25, 2006) (Michigan law); *In re* Snyder, 249 B.R. 40 (B.A.P. 1st Cir. 2000) (Massachusetts law), *aff'd*, 248 F.3d 1127 (1st Cir. 2001) (table); *In re* Spears, 313 B.R. 212 (W.D. Mich. 2004) (filing of bankruptcy by one spouse does not sever tenancy by entireties); *In re* Levinson, 372 B.R. 582 (Bankr. E.D.N.Y. 2007), *aff'd*, 395 B.R. 554 (E.D.N.Y. 2008); *In re* Eichorn, 338 B.R. 793 (Bankr. S.D. Ill. 2006) (filing of joint bankruptcy neither severs tenancy by entireties, nor "merges" bankruptcy estates; tenancy by entireties property remains exempt as to debt of individual spouse). *See also* § 12.7.6, *supra* (state requirements that both spouses sign mortgage).

812 *See* United States v. Craft, 535 U.S. 274, 122 S. Ct. 1414, 152 L. Ed. 2d 437 (2002) (describing theory and history of tenancy by entireties); *In re* Snyder, 249 B.R. 40 (B.A.P. 1st Cir. 2000) (Massachusetts law), *aff'd*, 248 F.3d 1127 (1st Cir. 2001); *In re* Ryan, 282 B.R. 742 (D.R.I. 2002); *In re* LaBorde, 231 B.R. 162 (Bankr. W.D.N.Y. 1999) (divorce severs tenancy by entireties; when husband, after divorce, deeded his half-interest in home to former wife, she took subject to judgment liens against him); *In re* Shannis, 229 B.R. 234 (Bankr. M.D. Fla. 1999) (under Florida law, tenancy by entireties is severed by divorce; property is then owned in tenancy in common and can be reached by creditors of individual spouse). *But cf.* First Fed. Sav. & Loan Ass'n v. Dus, 2003 WL 21545126 (Ohio Ct. App. July 10, 2003) (divorce turned tenancy by entireties into joint tenancy, but lien for husband's individual debt still would not attach, because debt incurred during marriage); *In re* Ballato, 318 B.R. 205 (Bankr. M.D. Fla. 2004) (divorce turned tenancy by entireties into tenancy in common but did not destroy homestead exemption, which protects any interest in land).

813 *See In re* Stanke, 234 B.R. 439 (Bankr. W.D. Mo. 1999) (tenancy by entireties severed, and protection lost, when couple transferred property to tax planning trust, with provisions inconsistent with tenancy by entireties). *But see In re* Bellingroehr, 403 B.R. 818 (Bankr. W.D. Mo. 2009) (entireties status not lost by transfer to estate planning trust, which imposed same restrictions on alienation by one spouse as are imposed by tenancy by entireties).

814 *In re* Snyder, 249 B.R. 40 (B.A.P. 1st Cir. 2000) (Massachusetts law), *aff'd*, 248 F.3d 1127 (1st Cir. 2001) (table); *In re* Hutchins, 306 B.R. 82 (Bankr. D. Vt. 2004); *In re* Shannis, 229 B.R. 234 (Bankr. M.D. Fla. 1999).

815 *In re* Thomas, 312 F.3d 145 (4th Cir. 2002); *In re* Snyder, 249 B.R. 40 (B.A.P. 1st Cir. 2000) (Massachusetts law), *aff'd*, 248 F.3d 1127 (1st Cir. 2001) (table); Smith v. Kofstad, 206 P.3d 441 (Alaska 2009) (judgment creditor of deceased husband cannot execute on home that was owned by entireties before husband's death, as husband's share was extinguished upon his death, and wife acquired full ownership).

Tenancy by the entireties will not protect against a lien that attached before the debtor married and transferred the property to entireties status.[816] In addition, the United States may foreclose on and sell entireties property for the tax debt of one spouse.[817]

Entireties property can be reached by a creditor if both husband and wife owe the debt.[818] In some states, a judgment creditor can place an attachment on the debtor spouse's interest in the property and enforce it if and when the debtor spouse survives the death of the other spouse.[819] In some states the judgment creditor can also sell or force the sale of this contingent future expectancy interest.[820] A significant benefit of tenancy by entireties is that some of the restrictions on the use of state exemptions, created by recent amendments to bankruptcy law, do not apply to the tenancy by entireties exemption.[821]

Tenancy by the entireties in personal property is discussed in § 12.8.5, *infra*.

12.8 Tangible Personal Property: Household Goods, Vehicles, Health Aids, Tools of the Trade; Tenancy By Entireties in Personal Property

12.8.1 Purpose

Every state protects at least some of a debtor's basic personal possessions from the reach of creditors. The purpose of these statutes is to allow debtors to retain basic necessities for living. The specific items exempted under each state statute differ, usually as a result of the antiquity of the statutes, geography, and the local economy. For example, states in the north frequently exempt a certain amount of products that are to be used as fuel. States with a strong agricultural community allow for a certain amount of crops and farm animals to be retained, in order to allow the debtor to continue to earn a living. Exemptions for personal property may not apply to purchase money debts[822] or criminal forfeitures.[823]

Many exemption statutes limit the number of items in certain categories that may be exempted. In these states, the debtor may have to itemize the exemption claim in order to show that the number of items in each category does not exceed the limit.[824]

12.8.2 Household Goods and Personal Items

Some exemption statutes list specific items or categories of household goods that are exempt. States frequently amend these statutes, so a decision that holds an item non-exempt may have been displaced by an amendment dealing with that item.

Other states exempt all necessary household goods or household furnishings, often subject to a dollar cap. Courts construe "necessary" to include not just what is needed for bare subsistence, but items generally found in the home and

816 *In re* Moore-Brown, 2009 WL 2868233 (Bankr. E.D.N.C. Sept. 1, 2009).

817 United States v. Craft, 535 U.S. 274, 122 S. Ct. 1414, 152 L. Ed. 2d 437 (2002); United States v. Barczyk, 697 F. Supp. 2d 789 (E.D. Mich. 2010) (non-debtor spouse entitled to 50% of proceeds), *aff'd*, 434 Fed. Appx. 488 (6th Cir. 2011) (entireties property may be sold for tax debt of one spouse; non-debtor spouse is entitled to one-half of sales proceeds). *See also* U.S. v. Cardaci, 2013 WL 5816823 (D. N.J. Oct. 29, 2013) (trial court has discretion to decline to order sale of entireties property for debt of one spouse when it would displace innocent family members); S.E.C. v. Solow, 682 F. Supp. 2d 1312 (S.D. Fla. 2010) (property may be reached to pay disgorgement order in SEC securities fraud enforcement action, notwithstanding state homestead and tenancy by entireties exemptions), *aff'd*, 396 Fed. Appx. 635 (11th Cir. 2010).

818 *In re* Kartman, 354 B.R. 70 (Bankr. W.D. Pa. 2006) (when creditor seeks to levy on entireties property key issue is whether both spouses liable); *In re* Kartman, 354 B.R. 70 (Bankr. W.D. Pa. 2006) (if creditor has claim for joint debt, tenancy by entireties property not exempt in individual spouse's bankruptcy); *In re* Guzior, 347 B.R. 237 (Bankr. E.D. Mich. 2006) (in bankruptcy, tenancy by entireties property is non-exempt to the amount of joint debt minus the homestead exemption). *But cf. In re* Holler, 463 B.R. 733 (Bankr. E.D. Pa. 2011) (spouses who owned home by entireties signed separate guarantees for loan to their jointly-owned company; guarantees could not be enforced against entireties property; joint debt means something more than liability for the same debt), *aff'd*, 2012 WL 3526466 (E.D. Pa. Aug. 14, 2012); *In re* Davis, 403 B.R. 914 (Bankr. M.D. Fla. 2009) (creditor who had judgment against the husband for a debt, and against the wife as recipient of fraudulent transfer, was not joint creditor; two debts, even to same creditor, not a joint debt); *In re* Olexa, 317 B.R. 290 (Bankr. W.D. Pa. 2004) (wife alone filed for bankruptcy, but debts were for necessaries within meaning of Pennsylvania law; because necessaries statute referred only to spouse's separate property, entireties property could not be reached), *aff'd*, 476 F.3d 177 (3d Cir. 2007); Rogers v. Rogers, 512 S.E.2d 821 (Va. 1999) (when creditors had federal court judgment against husband and state judgment against wife, both apparently resulting from the same transactions, entireties property could not be attached; only a joint judgment against husband and wife can be satisfied from entireties property).

819 *In re* Ryan, 282 B.R. 742 (D.R.I. 2002) (bankruptcy trustee may sell debtor's contingent future expectancy interest in entireties property).

820 *In re* Ryan, 282 B.R. 742 (D.R.I. 2002); *In re* Arwood, 289 B.R. 889 (Bankr. E.D. Tenn. 2003) (trustee can sell debtor-spouse's survivorship interest in property owned in tenancy by entireties with non-debtor spouse); Kipp v. Sweno, 683 N.W.2d 259 (Minn. 2004) (husband's survivorship interest can be sold, but he can claim entire $200,000 homestead exemption). *See also In re* Weza, 248 B.R. 470 (Bankr. D.N.H. 2000) (debtor-husband's interest in Massachusetts property held by common law tenancy by entireties could be sold by husband's creditor, and both husband and wife dispossessed, subject to survivorship rights of wife).

821 *See* §§ 12.7.5.1–12.7.5.3, *supra*.

822 *See* Coonts v. Potts, 316 F.3d 745 (8th Cir. 2003) (Missouri law); *In re* Johnson, 179 B.R. 800 (Bankr. E.D. Va. 1995) (when consumer borrowed money from credit union for stated purpose of buying car but never listed lien on title certificate, debt was purchase money and car was not exempt).

823 Nielson v. 2003 Honda Accord, 823 N.W.2d 347 (Minn. Ct. App. 2012) (state statutory and constitutional personal property exemptions do not bar criminal law forfeiture of motor vehicle; distinguishing homestead cases because of preferred position given to homesteads by Minnesota law); State v. One 1965 Red Chevrolet Pickup, 37 P.3d 815 (Okla. 2001) (exemption from "every other species of forced sale" not broad enough to shield personal property from criminal forfeiture).

824 *See, e.g., In re* Wade, 466 B.R. 20 (Bankr. D. Colo. 2012) (household goods exemption has per/item limit; denying exemption to all household goods of debtors who failed to itemize).

used to facilitate day-to-day living.[825] The question of what is necessary will depend on local usage and may change over time. For example, televisions and VCRs or DVD players have become so common that they are likely to be considered necessary.[826]

Some states have amended their exemption statutes to cover computers or other electronics.[827] One court, while declining to exempt a "relatively sophisticated" and "not inexpensive" computer system as "home furnishings," left the door ajar by comparing home computers today with televisions in the 1950s, which evolved from an "expensive curiosity" to "a virtual necessity which can be purchased for relatively little."[828] Shortly thereafter, that court exempted a computer system used by members of a debtor's family for schoolwork.[829] For some debtors, a computer may also qualify under an exemption for tools of the trade.[830]

Courts have varied widely in their treatment of small amenities such as entertainment, hobby, and sports equipment,[831]

825 *In re* Rivera, 499 B.R. 175 (Bankr. D. P.R. 2013) (exemption for "home use kitchens" covers stove, microwave, dishes, cookware, and utensils; exemptions for furniture with no cap must be for reasonable amount); *In re* Cintron, 499 B.R. 209 (Bankr. D. P.R. 2013) (stove may be exempted either as home use kitchen or household furniture); *In re* Robinson, 498 WL 207 (Bankr. S.D. Ill. Aug. 20, 2013) (200-year-old Book of Mormon, valued at $10,000, not covered by exemption for bibles and schoolbooks; exemption protected "an ordinary bible for daily devotional purposes" such as the paper and electronic copies owned and used by debtors here); *In re* Dunnaway, 466 B.R. 515 (Bankr. E.D. Cal. 2012) (local community standards must be considered in defining household goods; recreational items permitted; allowing exemption of firearms used for personal protection, food hunting, or recreation, but not for display); *In re* Harwood, 404 B.R. 366 (Bankr. E.D. Tex. 2009) (amendment replacing "household and kitchen furniture" with "home furnishings" broadened the exemption; reasonable necessity need not be shown; allowing exemption of home office and gym, but not hobby equipment), *aff'd on other grounds*, 427 B.R. 392 (E.D. Tex. 2010); *In re* Goss, 352 B.R. 309 (Bankr. E.D. Okla. 2006) (large commercial-type safe not a household good; even if family needed safe place for papers, this safe went beyond what was reasonably necessary; cow used for breeding not exempt under statute exempting "milk cow"); *In re* LaJuerrne, 2004 WL 2192515 (Bankr. D. Kan. July 9, 2004) (using broad definition of household goods, many items in collection of automotive memorabilia are exempt); *In re* Heath, 318 B.R. 115 (Bankr. W.D. Ky. 2004) ("functional nexus" test exempts items that foster or help enable daily existence in the household; rifle for deer hunting exempt but not tanning bed); *In re* Larson, 203 B.R. 176 (Bankr. W.D. Okla. 1996) (home furnishings exemption includes items "reasonably necessary to the maintenance of a home," not just bare necessities of survival); *In re* Latham, 182 B.R. 479 (Bankr. W.D. Va. 1995) (exempt furniture must be used for day to day living in debtors' home; furniture of beach house which was sometimes used for family vacations and sometimes rented out was not exempt). *See also In re* Glimcher, 458 B.R. 549 (Bankr. D. Ariz. 2011) (Arizona exemption for "food, fuel and provisions for six months" did not protect gift card from grocery chain that sold food and provisions; only actual existing goods were protected); New Century Fin. Servs., Inc. v. Arellano, 2006 WL 3344985 (N.J. Super. Ct. App. Div. Nov. 30, 2006) (safe deposit box not protected by exemption for "goods and chattels"; creditor entitled to court order to open box to see if it contained non-exempt property). *Cf.* Chasoudian v. Pate, 17 So. 3d 49 (La. Ct. App. 2009) (exemption for "all dogs, cats, and other domestic pets" covered only pet dogs and cats; purebred show dogs being boarded at a kennel were not exempt).

826 Planned Parenthood of Columbus/Willamette, Inc. v. Am. Coal. of Life Activists, 2007 WL 4118597 (S.D. Ohio Nov. 16, 2007) (personal computers, printers, software, VCR, stereo and at least one television are exempt); *In re* Caldero Padilla, 2014 WL 183669 (Bankr. D. P.R. Jan. 14, 2014) (allowing exemption of "trivial amount" for DVD and VCR players, even though statute specifies only television; mobile phones not exempt); *In re* Rivera, 499 B.R. 175 (Bankr. D. P.R. 2013) (exemption for "radio receiving set" covers sound system; DVD player, mobile phone, computer, and printer not exempt because not listed in statute and have no "intrinsic resemblance" to listed items); *In re* Yawn, 2010 WL 599392 (Bankr. S.D. Ga. Feb. 5, 2010) (television and laptop are household goods; second TV and second computer not exempt because statute specifies one of each; camera not a household good); *In re* Zieg, 409 B.R. 917 (Bankr. W.D. Mo. 2009) (construing statute's reference to "one VCR" "in light of changing technology" to exempt a DVD player); *In re* Biancavilla, 173 B.R. 930 (Bankr. D. Idaho 1994) (television and VCR were exempt; recreational equipment and computer system were not household goods). *See also In re* Doss, 298 B.R. 866 (Bankr. W.D. Tenn. 2003) (big screen television was household good within meaning of bankruptcy lien avoidance provision); *In re* Hicks, 276 B.R. 84 (Bankr. W.D. Va. 2001) (television and VCR exempt); *In re* Elst, 210 B.R. 790 (Bankr. E.D. Wis. 1997) (second television set falls within federal bankruptcy exemption for household goods, because it provided entertainment for family and guests in the house); *In re* Sydlowski, 186 B.R. 907 (Bankr. N.D. Ohio 1995) (television, VCR and, for debtor with custody of child, a video game); *In re* Kinnemore, 181 B.R. 516 (Bankr. D. Idaho 1995) (television and VCR); *In re* French, 177 B.R. 568 (Bankr. E.D. Tenn. 1995) (VCR).

827 *See* Appx. G, *infra*.

828 *In re* Larson, 203 B.R. 176 (Bankr. W.D. Okla. 1996).

829 *In re* Ratliff, 209 B.R. 534 (Bankr. W.D. Okla. 1997) (computer and printer used by children and one debtor who was a student, to do schoolwork, was exempt under "household and kitchen furniture" exemption). *Accord In re* Hicks, 276 B.R. 84 (Bankr. W.D. Va. 2001) (computer used for educational purposes was exempt); *In re* Andrews, 225 B.R. 485 (Bankr. D. Idaho 1998) (one computer is reasonably necessary to household, so is exempt under Idaho exemptions). *See* § 12.8.5, *infra*. *See also In re* Rhines, 227 B.R. 308 (Bankr. D. Mont. 1998) (computer exempt as household good under federal bankruptcy exemptions); *In re* Crawford, 226 B.R. 484 (Bankr. N.D. Ga. 1998) (computer used for educational purposes was household good under federal bankruptcy exemptions). *But see* CSC Holdings, Inc. v. Sam's Electronics, Inc., 2006 WL 1620242 (W.D. Okla. June 8, 2006) (computer is not household good; note that debtor provided no evidence of how computer would be used when moved from business premises to home); *In re* Irwin, 232 B.R. 151 (Bankr. D. Minn. 1999) (Minnesota exemption for household appliances did not cover computer, which is not usually thought of as an appliance and was not included in statute's list of entertainment and information items that were exempt). *But cf. In re* Liston, 206 B.R. 235 (Bankr. W.D. Okla. 1997) (computer not exempt as home furnishing).

830 *See* § 12.8.4, *infra*.

831 *EXEMPT: In re* Lucas, 77 B.R. 242 (B.A.P. 9th Cir. 1987) (golf clubs, camera equipment, and exercise bicycle fall within California household property exemption); *In re* Gallegos, 226 B.R. 111 (Bankr. D. Idaho 1998) (horse was household pet, within meaning of Idaho exemption, when it was kept as a companion, to be ridden by debtor's young daughter, even though it was kept outside rather than in house); *In re* Holzapfel, 262 P.3d 1114 (Mont. 2011) (four-wheel ATV not covered by "firearms and other sporting goods" exemption because it is covered by specific exemption for motor vehicles). *See also* Fraley v. Commercial Credit, 189 B.R. 398 (W.D. Ky. 1995) (goods need not be "essential for survival" to be household goods; stereo, aquarium and camcorder (the modern equivalent of a photo album) were household goods under federal bankruptcy exemption); *In re* Harwood, 404 B.R. 366 (Bankr. E.D. Tex. 2009) (golf equipment exempt; photography and other hobby

jewelry,[832] and decorative items such as knickknacks and art.[833] Virginia has a specific exemption for heirlooms, items of sentimental value that have been inherited at least once, which the debtor intends to leave to the next generation.[834] Nebraska exempts "immediate personal possessions."[835] Some states specifically list firearms as exempt,[836] and in other states courts have found them covered by more general exemptions.[837]

equipment non-exempt), *aff'd on other grounds*, 427 B.R. 392 (E.D. Tex. 2010); *In re* LaJuerrne, 2004 WL 2192515 (Bankr. D. Kan. July 9, 2004) (many but not all items in collection of automotive memorabilia exempt); *In re* Doss, 298 B.R. 866 (Bankr. W.D. Tenn. 2003) (big screen television was household good within meaning of bankruptcy lien avoidance provision); *In re* French, 177 B.R. 568 (Bankr. E.D. Tenn. 1995) (camera and accessories used to take family pictures and VCR used for personal entertainment were household goods under federal bankruptcy exemptions); *In re* Lynch, 139 B.R. 868 (Bankr. N.D. Ohio 1992) (household goods are "items of personal property reasonably necessary for the day-to-day existence of people in their homes"; sound system and recordings were household goods, but not cameras). *Cf. In re* Hirsch, 338 B.R. 193 (Bankr. W.D.N.Y. 2006) (coin collection exempt up to face value of coins under New York exemption for cash; to extent numismatic value exceeded face value, collection would be sold and exempt amount paid to debtors).

NON-EXEMPT: Crockett v. Lowe (*In re* Crockett), 158 F.3d 332 (5th Cir. 1998) (jet ski was not exempt under Texas exemption for "athletic and sporting equipment, including bicycles," which had been construed in other bankruptcy cases to exclude sailboats and motorboats); *In re* Schreiber, 231 B.R. 17 (Bankr. D. Me. 1999) (pop-up camper not household good within meaning of Maine law, because no nexus with "daily use, maintenance or upkeep of the debtor's household"). *See also In re* Elst, 210 B.R. 790 (Bankr. E.D. Wis. 1997) (under federal bankruptcy exemptions, bicycle was not a household good because it was not used in and around the house). *But see In re* Thomas, 2005 WL 2429963 (Bankr. C.D. Ill. Sept. 21, 2005) (pool table not household goods for purposes of lien avoidance under 11 U.S.C. § 522(f)); *In re* Hicks, 276 B.R. 84 (Bankr. W.D. Va. 2001) (movie and video cameras and pool table not exempt as household goods).

832 *In re* Cintron, 499 B.R. 209 (Bankr. D. P.R. 2013) (exemption for necessary wearing apparel protects wedding bands, here of low value); *In re* Rivera, 499 B.R. 175 (Bankr. D. P.R. 2013) (Puerto Rico exemption for "necessary and proper" wearing apparel protects jewelry if needed for debtor's "social, business or professional engagements" and was not purchased as an investment); *In re* Fink, 2009 WL 3015340 (Bankr. S.D. Tex. Sept. 17, 2009) (Texas jewelry exemption limited to 25% of total personal property exemption; debtor entitled to $60,000 head-of-household exemption could exempt up to $15,000 in jewelry); *In re* Urie, 2006 WL 533514 (Bankr. W.D. Mo. Jan. 31, 2006) (Missouri's $1500 exemption for "wedding ring" covers engagement ring and may be stacked with $500 jewelry exemption to fully exempt $2000 ring); *In re* Hazelhurst, 228 B.R. 199 (Bankr. E.D. Tenn. 1998) (some jewelry may be exempted as "necessary and proper wearing apparel," depending on value, how often it is worn, and for what occasions; diamond engagement ring from former husband, which debtor no longer wore, was not exempt, but amethyst ring inherited from grandmother and worn about once a week was exempt); *In re* Wilson, 213 B.R. 413 (Bankr. D.R.I. 1997) (championship football ring which player wore daily was "held primarily for personal use" and was exempt when ring had significant sentimental value and had not been bought as investment); *In re* Meyer, 211 B.R. 203 (Bankr. E.D. Va. 1997) (Virginia exemption for wearing apparel protected cuff links and inexpensive watch that had been bought for everyday wear rather than investment purposes). *But see In re* Weeden, 306 B.R. 449 (Bankr. W.D.N.Y. 2004) (diamond engagement ring not exempt); *In re* Tiberia, 227 B.R. 26 (Bankr. W.D.N.Y. 1998) (diamond engagement ring not used in wedding ceremony, was not "wedding ring" within meaning of New York exemption). *But cf. In re* Lebovitz, 360 B.R. 612 (B.A.P. 6th Cir. 2007) (Tennessee's unlimited exemption for "necessary and proper" wearing apparel protects "serviceable apparel appropriate to the work performed by the debtor," but even if some jewelry included, "luxury items," ranging in price from $1000 to $8000, were not necessary and proper); CSC Holdings, Inc. v. Sam's Electronics, Inc., 2006 WL 1620242 (W.D. Okla. June 8, 2006) (watch was exempt, ring was not; both worn regularly, but debtor provided evidence of small value only of watch); *In re* Prosser, 2008 WL 2677863 (Bankr. D. V.I. July 1, 2008) (Virgin Islands personal property exemption explicitly excludes jewelry); *In re* Stegall, 2007 WL 1125635 (Bankr. S.D. Iowa Apr. 3, 2007) (former Iowa exemption for ring "owned and received by the debtor . . . on or before the date of marriage" would not exempt replacement diamond, bought after original was lost; note that statute has been amended to delete the operative language); *In re* Peterson, 280 B.R. 886 (Bankr. S.D. Ala. 2001) (items bought to enhance prestige or display wealth, such as expensive jewelry, not exempt; mink coat not exempt because "monetary value clearly outweighs utility value"; less expensive of two watches exempt); *In re* Lynch, 139 B.R. 868 (Bankr. N.D. Ohio 1992) (watch and diamond and ruby jewelry not exempt as household goods); Merrill Lynch Interfunding, Inc. v. Argenti, 2001 Conn. Super. LEXIS 1992 (Conn. Super. Ct. July 20, 2001) (diamond ring given to wife on twelfth anniversary was neither wedding nor engagement ring and was not necessary apparel when it was large, expensive, and not worn regularly); *In re* Winters, 40 P.3d 1231 (Wyo. 2002) (mother's wedding ring that unmarried debtor inherited not exempt as wedding ring under Wyoming law).

833 *In re* Lucas, 77 B.R. 242 (B.A.P. 9th Cir. 1987) (applying California household property exemption; Hummel figurines exempt); *In re* LaJuerrne, 2004 WL 2192515 (Bankr. D. Kan. July 9, 2004) (many but not all items in collection of automotive memorabilia are exempt). *But see In re* Pullman, 317 B.R. 324 (Bankr. E.D. Va. 2004) (sports memorabilia that were not received from ancestor not heirlooms, and thus not exempt, despite intent to pass them on to children); Estate of Hersh v. Schwartz, 959 N.E.2d 1061 (Ohio Ct. App. 2011) (must show something more than sentimental value, but not absolute necessity; art, antiques and collectibles not exempt household goods).

834 *In re* Sempeles, 471 B.R. 178 (Bankr. W.D. Va. 2012) (may be used to exempt intangible property, here shares in a hunting preserve, inherited from father when debtor had hunted with father and now hunted with son, to whom he intended to leave the shares).

835 *In re* Anthony, 2012 WL 1207421 (Bankr. D. Neb. Apr. 11, 2012) (noting lack of authority construing this section; holding that items covered by other specific exemptions, here furniture, not covered; allowing exemption of athletic awards, photo albums and antique camera; foreign coins are non-exempt cash in hand if valuable but are exempt souvenirs if of "minimal" value).

836 *See In re* Wilkinson, 402 B.R. 756 (Bankr. W.D. Tex. 2009) (Texas specifically exempts two firearms, and additional firearms may not be exempted under other categories; criminal code definition, which excludes antiques, not applicable to exemption statute; mounting antique firearms on plaques for display does not turn them into home furnishings); *In re* McCabe, 280 B.R. 841 (Bankr. N.D. Iowa 2002) (when exemption for one firearm had no cap, debtor could exempt costly shotgun bought on eve of bankruptcy); *In re* Maynard, 139 P.3d 803 (Mont. 2006) (statute protects required military equipment plus one gun; debtor not in National Guard or militia may use wildcard to exempt second gun). *But see In re* Lawson, 2006 WL 2130650 (E.D. Okla. June 21, 2006) (Oklahoma firearms exemption applies only to guns for personal or household use, not to valuable collection held for investment or used in business as bail bondsman). *But cf. In re* Brown, 189 B.R. 653 (Bankr. M.D. La. 1995) (Louisiana exemption for arms and military accoutrements applies only to weapons kept for military purposes, not those kept for hunting or collectibles).

837 *In re* Dunnaway, 466 B.R. 515 (Bankr. E.D. Cal. 2012) (firearms are exempt household goods if used for self-protection, food hunting, or

Lawnmowers and other equipment for maintaining the property are often found to fall within an exemption for household appliances or furnishings.[838]

12.8.3 Motor Vehicles; Modified Vans and Other Health Aids

Many statutes provide an exemption for motor vehicles. These exemptions have often been construed to include motorcycles,[839] motor homes,[840] and other recreational vehicles,[841] but usually not powerboats.[842] Debtors may also be able to exempt trailers or other equipment that are subject to state vehicle registration requirements.[843] On the other hand, one court adopted a judicially-created definition that had originated in a criminal case and held that a motor vehicle was a "self-propelled vehicle with wheels that is designed to be used, or is ordinarily used, to transport people or property on roads." It applied this definition to conclude that a tractor was not exempt.[844] It may be possible to exempt a disassembled vehicle if all essential parts are present.[845] The availability of the exemption may depend on the use the debtor makes of the vehicle.[846]

Some jurisdictions allow a debtor to exempt more than one vehicle, if this can be done within the exemption's monetary limits.[847] Co-debtors may be able to stack their exemptions to

---

recreation, not merely for display); *In re* Heath, 318 B.R. 115 (Bankr. W.D. Ky. 2004) (in rural area where adult son hunted deer for family table, one rifle suitable for deer hunting was exempt household good); *In re* Karaus, 276 B.R. 227 (Bankr. D. Neb. 2002) (firearm kept for self-defense is household good, but gun collection acquired for historical or aesthetic interest is not exempt as "immediate personal possession"); *In re* Mason, 254 B.R. 764 (Bankr. D. Idaho 2000) (firearm may be exempt as household good, even though Idaho also has separate exemption for firearms; use of firearm for hunting or home defense favors exemption); *In re* Rhines, 227 B.R. 308 (Bankr. D. Mont. 1998) (rifle and shotgun were household goods under federal bankruptcy exemptions when debtor regularly hunted and game was main source of meat for family); *In re* Crawford, 226 B.R. 484 (Bankr. N.D. Ga. 1998) (rifle kept to defend home was household good under federal bankruptcy exemptions); *In re* Maynard, 139 P.3d 803 (Mont. 2006) (debtors may exempt one gun under firearms exemption and another under wildcard). *See also In re* Shell, 295 B.R. 129 (Bankr. D. Alaska 2003) (only one gun may be exempted under Alaska's household goods exemption); *In re* Raines, 161 B.R. 548 (Bankr. N.D. Ga. 1993) (handgun kept for defense had sufficiently strong "functional nexus" with the home to make it an exempt household good under federal bankruptcy exemptions), *aff'd*, 170 B.R. 187 (N.D. Ga. 1994). *But see In re* Debias, 1999 U.S. App. LEXIS 29860 (10th Cir. Nov. 15, 1999) (handgun not an exempt household good under Colorado law because it was "not akin" to any items on statutory list of exempt items). *But cf. In re* McGreevy, 955 F.2d 957 (4th Cir. 1992) (shotgun and rifle used primarily for sport away from home do not support and facilitate day-to-day living within the home so are not "household goods" for purposes of lien avoidance under bankruptcy law); *In re* French, 177 B.R. 568 (Bankr. E.D. Tenn. 1995) (revolver kept for self-defense was not a household good under federal bankruptcy exemptions when debtor lived with sister who already owned a handgun for that purpose, nor was shotgun when husband testified that wife needed it to protect home in his absence, but wife did not know how to load or fire it).

838 *In re* Yawn, 2010 WL 599392 (Bankr. S.D. Ga. Feb. 5, 2010) (lawnmower exempt as household goods); *In re* Irwin, 232 B.R. 151 (Bankr. D. Minn. 1999) (Minnesota exemption for household appliances covers lawn mower, which was necessary to maintain home); *In re* Andrews, 225 B.R. 485 (Bankr. D. Idaho 1998) (hand tools were reasonably necessary household goods); *In re* Payne, 215 B.R. 889 (Bankr. N.D. Okla. 1997) (both riding lawn mower and push lawn mower were exempt as "household and kitchen furniture," as both were reasonably necessary to keep lawn acceptable and avoid nuisance citation by municipality).

839 *See, e.g.*, *In re* Clemons, 441 B.R. 519 (Bankr. N.D. Miss. 2010) (motorcycle is motor vehicle); *In re* Lund, 2005 WL 3620335 (Bankr. W.D. Mo. Dec. 9, 2005) (motorcycle is exempt but not motorized bicycle). *See also In re* Sutherland, 495 B.R. 134 (Bankr. D. Mass. 2013) (Massachusetts general exemption for automobile does not cover motorcycle but enhanced exemption for "vehicle" of elderly or disabled debtor does). *But see In re* Drewes, 217 B.R. 978 (D.N.H. 1998) (motorcycle is not protected by exemption for "automobile").

840 *See, e.g.*, *In re* Sleeth, 300 B.R. 351 (Bankr. D. Ariz. 2003) (motor home is motor vehicle). *But cf. In re* Scott, 2012 WL 2576783 (Bankr. E.D. Va. July 3, 2012) (manufactured home not exempt motor vehicle; neither self-propelled, nor primarily designed to be attached to vehicle to provide mobile dwelling).

841 *See, e.g.*, *In re* Buchberger, 311 B.R. 794 (Bankr. D. Ariz. 2004) ("personal, family or household" purposes include recreation; applying rule of liberal construction and definition in transportation statute to exempt ATV); *In re* Moore, 251 B.R. 380 (Bankr. W.D. Mo. 2000) (when Missouri motor vehicle exemption did not explicitly exclude recreational ATVs, principle of liberal construction required inclusion); *In re* Holzapfel, 262 P.3d 1114 (Mont. 2011) (four-wheel ATV is a motor vehicle). *But see In re* Bosworth, 449 B.R. 104 (Bankr. D. Idaho 2011) (ATV with restricted license plate, which could not be lawfully operated on limited access highway, was not a motor vehicle).

842 *In re* Potter, 2009 WL 902415 (Bankr. E.D. Va. Mar. 24, 2009) (powerboat not a motor vehicle within meaning of Virginia exemption); *In re* Barbera, 285 B.R. 355 (Bankr. D.R.I. 2002) (Rhode Island motor vehicle exemption does not cover boat, when definition of vehicle in state transportation law includes operation on highway).

843 *In re* Alexander, 472 B.R. 815 (B.A.P. 9th Cir. 2012) (allowing motor vehicle exemption for mobile kitchen used in debtors' barbecue business when Nebraska law required that trailer be titled and registered as motor vehicle).

844 *In re* Matthews, 449 B.R. 833 (Bankr. M.D. Ga. 2011) (farm tractor, although it may be driven for short distances on public road, is not a motor vehicle).

845 *See, e.g.*, *In re* Bailey, 326 B.R. 750 (Bankr. S.D. Iowa 2004) (Iowa motor vehicle exemption would cover classic Ford, disassembled and currently inoperable, being rebuilt for investment; when essential parts were present, it was "self-propelled vehicle" within statutory definition). *But see In re* McMillin, 441 B.R. 348 (Bankr. D. Or. 2010) (denying vehicle exemption to parts that were sufficient to build a vehicle but had not yet been assembled).

846 *In re* Letizia, 2014 WL 184438 (Bankr. D. Ariz. Jan. 14, 2014) (Arizona motor vehicle exemption only protects car used for personal or household purposes; vehicles used by sole proprietorship may be exempted only as tools of trade); *In re* Hill, 310 B.R. 294 (Bankr. W.D. La. 2004) (Louisiana motor vehicle exemption applies only to vehicle used for work or commuting; retired or unemployed debtor may not exempt vehicle).

847 *See, e.g.*, *In re* Scott, 332 B.R. 377 (Bankr. E.D. Mo. 2005) (Missouri's amended motor vehicle exemption, "any vehicle in the aggregate," may be split to protect two vehicles). *See also In re* McLean, 505 B.R. 361 (Bankr. D. Me. 2014) (couple owned two vehicles in joint tenancy with right of survivor; each spouse could exempt full value of one vehicle); *In re* Bell, 333 B.R. 839 (Bankr. W.D. Mo. 2005) (amended Missouri statute covering "any motor vehicle in the aggregate" allows debtors to split the exemption between two vehicles; here, debtors stacked head-of-household, two wildcard, one motor vehicle, and part of another motor vehicle exemption to exempt one vehicle and applied balance

protect a more expensive vehicle.[848] Motor vehicle title laws may create a presumption as to ownership, but this may be rebutted by evidence that a non-titled spouse paid for or drives the vehicle.[849]

In some states the exempt amount for a motor vehicle is increased if the debtor or a family member is disabled.[850] Most states provide an exemption for health aids, and one court has allowed a mobility-impaired debtor to exempt a modified van, up to the value of the modifications, and stack that exemption with the motor vehicle exemption.[851] Another court allowed an exemption for the extensive improvements made to a debtor's condominium to accommodate her chemical sensitivity; this exemption could be stacked with her homestead exemption.[852]

Whether a motor vehicle can be exempted as a tool of the debtor's trade is discussed in § 12.8.4, *infra*.

of second motor vehicle exemption to second vehicle). *But see In re* Savoie, 351 B.R. 392 (Bankr. W.D. La. 2006) (former Louisiana statute, now amended, allowed exemption only for one vehicle per household used for work or commuting; debtors could exempt either pickup or family car); *In re* Struckhoff, 231 B.R. 69 (Bankr. E.D. Mo. 1999) (Missouri exemption for "any motor vehicle" covers exemption of only one motor vehicle when other exemptions refer to "one or more" or use the plural; statute has been amended).

848 *See, e.g.*, Schilling v. Tran, 287 B.R. 887 (W.D. Ky. 2002) (allowing husband and wife to stack motor vehicle exemptions to exempt one vehicle; when title listed both spouses in alternative each had ownership interest); *In re* Reisdorff, 2010 WL 4852457 (Bankr. D. Neb. Nov. 27, 2010) (spouses, who each used jointly owned vehicle to commute to work, could stack two tools of trade and two wildcard exemptions).

849 *In re* Jourdain, 2013 WL 944948 (Bankr. E.D.N.C. Mar. 8, 2013) (wife could exempt 50% interest in car titled in husband; car paid for with joint funds and driven by wife). *Cf. In re* Browning, 2010 WL 1541629 (Bankr. C.D. Ill. Apr. 19, 2010) (vehicles owned in joint tenancy with right of survivorship; one spouse may claim exemption, even if it exceeds half the value of vehicle).

850 *See In re* Sleeth, 300 B.R. 351 (Bankr. D. Ariz. 2003) (applying enhanced exemption for "physically disabled" when debtor had serious heart disease and qualified for Social Security disability payments). *But see In re* Coleman, 209 B.R. 739 (Bankr. D. Colo. 1997) (Colorado's $3000 "elderly or disabled" exemption for a motor vehicle did not protect a motor vehicle used by an able-bodied debtor to transport an arguably disabled dependent to medical treatment).

851 *In re* Hellen, 329 B.R. 678 (Bankr. N.D. Ill. 2005) (doctor-recommended modifications to van to enable patient to drive entitled to exemption as "professionally prescribed heath aids" even though no written prescription). *See also In re* Dowell, 456 B.R. 578 (Bankr. M.D. Fla. 2011) (car was equipped with device to enable debtor to steer with one hand; device was a health aid, but car was not, when device could be easily detached and used in other car). *But cf. In re* Khan, 375 B.R. 5 (Bankr. M.D. Fla. 2007) (unmodified van, approved for a handicapped parking permit, not an exempt health aid; must be "uniquely suited" to accommodate disability); *In re* McCashen, 339 B.R. 907 (Bankr. N.D. Ohio 2006) (even if unmodified van could be health aid—which is debatable—not exempt when neither professionally prescribed nor medically necessary; no health aid exemption for only model of van roomy enough for morbidly obese debtor).

852 *In re* Man, 428 B.R. 644 (Bankr. M.D.N.C. 2010) (encyclopedic collection of cases defining health aids).

12.8.4 Tools of the Trade

A useful exemption found in many state statutes protects "tools of a trade."[853] Some states also have an exemption for property used in agriculture.[854]

In defining tools of the trade, many states apply a use test, holding that an item is a tool of the trade if it is actually used by the debtor in his or her usual trade on a regular basis and

853 *But cf. In re* White, 234 B.R. 388 (Bankr. W.D. Tex. 1999) (custom software which debtor computer programmers had created and licensed to their employer was not a tool but a product of their trade and thus was not exempt).

854 Painewebber, Inc. v. Murray, 260 B.R. 815 (E.D. Tex. 2001) (when rural homestead used for agriculture debtor could exempt tractor, riding mower, and pick-up truck under agricultural exemption, in addition to vehicle allowed by motor vehicle exemption); *In re* Larson, 260 B.R. 174 (D. Colo. 2001) (livestock used for breeding is exempt); *In re* Schley, 2011 WL 1344595 (Bankr. N.D. Iowa Apr. 7, 2011) (farm wife, who had full-time job as school principal, was engaged in farming when she operated farm equipment, kept the books, and dealt with the bank, suppliers, and so forth, so could claim state law exemption in farm equipment); *In re* Miller, 370 B.R. 914 (Bankr. D. Minn. 2007) (farm wife who worked full-time off-farm was engaged in farming and therefore entitled to exemption for farm machines when she kept farm books, delivered meals to field, ran errands, drove tractor, and sometimes worked in fields); Devine v. Devine, 2005 WL 1926038 (Bankr. N.D. Iowa Aug. 5, 2005) (farming equipment exempt); *In re* Thompson, 311 B.R. 822 (Bankr. D. Kan. 2004) (allowing exemption for farm equipment when husband worked at least forty hours on farm, in addition to full-time off-farm employment, and wife, also employed off-farm, devoted "considerable energy and personal resources" to farming; intention to make a profit must be shown, but expectation need not be reasonable); *In re* Kieffer, 279 B.R. 290 (Bankr. D. Kan. 2002) (allowing husband and wife to stack their exemptions for farm equipment when wife shared work on farm in addition to her off-farm employment, couple made business decisions together, and wife had signed notes for purchase of farm equipment); *In re* Larson, 260 B.R. 174 (Bankr. D. Colo. 2001) (debtors were "engaged in agriculture as principal occupation" even though they were working in trucking business in attempt to save unprofitable family farm; husband and wife could each stack an agricultural exemption with a tools-of-trade exemption for farm implements and livestock). *See also In re* Stokesberry, 2013 WL 4806426 (Bankr. S.D. Tex. Sept. 5, 2013) (tractor used to clear brush on debtor's and neighbors' land is "farming or ranching implement" within meaning of Texas personal property exemption). *But cf. In re* Grimlie, 439 B.R. 710 (B.A.P. 8th Cir. 2010) (Minnesota law) (denying exemption for property used in agriculture; debtors not principally engaged in farming when property was used to raise horses and hay but most income came from manufacture and sale of equipment); *In re* Matthews, 449 B.R. 833 (Bankr. M.D. Ga. 2011) (wife who worked in garden and picked pecans not engaged in farming; denying her claim of exemption in a tractor she never drove); *In re* Skillen, 2009 WL 4823802 (Bankr. N.D. Iowa Dec. 14. 2009) (denying exemption when former farmers were not currently farming and did not show affirmative steps towards return); *In re* Taylor, 2008 WL 1805384 (Bankr. S.D. Ill. Apr. 18, 2008) (when Illinois does not have a specific exemption for livestock, animals used for breeding are capital assets, not tools of trade, so not exempt); *In re* Hintzman, 2007 WL 80964 (Bankr. D. Minn. Jan. 8, 2007) (debtors not principally engaged in farming, so not entitled to farm machinery exemption, when they had four-year history of unprofitable farming, and stated intent to return, but had no arrangements to resume).

is reasonably necessary to that trade.[855] Others, however, use a narrower definition and confine the exemption to personal items of modest value.[856] Some decisions hold that real estate cannot be a tool of the trade.[857] A computer system was found to be a tool of a trade, when the employer furnished software so the debtor could work at home, even though work at home was not mandatory.[858]

A "tools of the trade" exemption may be used in some jurisdictions to exempt a vehicle that is necessary to the debtor's livelihood. One question is whether the existence of a specific exemption for motor vehicles means that the "tools of the trade" exemption cannot also be applied to a vehicle. Courts differ on this question.[859] Extending the exemption to vehicles is more consistent with the rule that exemption laws are to be construed liberally,[860] especially since preservation of the debtor's earning capacity is of great importance in accomplishing the purposes of these laws.

To exempt a vehicle as a tool of the debtor's trade, something more than commuting must often be shown,[861] but it

---

855 *In re* Weimann, 2009 WL 383426 (Bankr. C.D. Ill. Feb. 13, 2009) (applying use test; boats and trailer of modest value were tools of trade for boat rental business, not capital assets, so are exempt under Illinois law); *In re* Giles, 340 B.R. 543 (Bankr. E.D. Pa. 2006) (applying use test for federal bankruptcy exemption; standard motor vehicle was tool of trade for artisan who made hats and sold at craft fairs; public transportation not a reasonable alternative for buying materials and attending shows); *In re* Gray, 303 B.R. 632 (Bankr. W.D. Mo. 2003) (applying use test; horses and cattle used to teach riding and roping are tools of trade of riding and rodeo skills instructor); *In re* Aurelio, 252 B.R. 102 (Bankr. N.D. Miss. 2000) (tools are exempt if reasonably necessary for the performance of debtor's occupation; restaurant equipment qualifies but not proceeds of its sale in absence of evidence of intent to resume the business). *See also In re* Gregory, 245 B.R. 171 (B.A.P. 10th Cir. 2000) (Wyoming law) (applying use test, but Air Force security officer's practice pistol was not a means of carrying on his trade, when he had another pistol which he actually carried while on duty and employer did not require practice pistol), *aff'd*, 246 F.3d 681 (10th Cir. 2000); *In re* Siegel, 214 B.R. 329 (W.D. Tenn. 1997) (lawyer in solo practice could exempt computer system as tool of trade; rejecting test whether item is "uniquely suited" to use in the trade, in favor of fact-based consideration of the role of computers in a modern law office); *In re* Mackey, 209 B.R. 251 (Bankr. E.D. Okla. 1997) (Oklahoma tools of the trade exemption should be broadly construed to include not only small, handheld things but also any other property which is "reasonably necessary, convenient or suitable for [the owner's] trade or profession"; allowing independent truck driver to exempt up to $5000 limit for value of Peterbilt truck). *Cf. In re* Nipper, 243 B.R. 33 (Bankr. E.D. Tenn. 1999) (reciting use test but holding that Tennessee tools-of-trade exemption is meant to apply to hand tools of small value, not capital assets or major pieces of machinery such as independent trucker's tractor-trailer). *But cf. In re* Rollins, 2007 WL 2428079 (Bankr. W.D. Mo. Aug. 17, 2007) (certificates of deposit, used to post security required by statute in order for debtor credit repair service to receive advance payments from customers, is not tool of trade, as the business may be conducted without it).

856 *In re* Hively, 358 B.R. 752 (Bankr. C.D. Ill. 2007) (limiting exemption to tools of modest value, but here cargo trailer, worth less than statutory cap, was exempt when it was used to haul food and cooking equipment by caterers who cooked at events was exempt); *In re* Gentry, 297 B.R. 553 (Bankr. C.D. Ill. 2003) (Illinois exemption is construed narrowly to cover only artisans' "tools of modest value"; self-employed contractor may not exempt Bobcat regardless of its use). *See also In re* Nickeas, 503 B.R. 453 (Bankr. W.D. Wis. 2013) (liquor license not a tool of trade; limiting definition to personal items of modest value such as "rakes and hand tools"). *Cf. In re* Baldowski, 191 B.R. 102 (Bankr. N.D. Tex. 1996) (property need not be "peculiarly adapted" to the trade but must be "tools" or "apparatus"; ordinary dishes, cutlery, tables, exempt as tools of the trade of a cafe owner).

857 *See, e.g., In re* Maestas, 497 B.R. 167 (B.A.P. 10th Cir. 2013) (table) (Colorado exemption applies only to personal property, not real estate); *In re* Montgomery, 2010 WL 3369829 (Bankr. N.D. Ohio Aug. 23, 2010) (denying exemption to building equipped for use in debtor's business; definition of "implement" cannot be stretched to cover real property).

858 *In re* Biancavilla, 173 B.R. 930 (Bankr. D. Idaho 1994). *See also In re* Siegel, 214 B.R. 329 (W.D. Tenn. 1997) (lawyer in solo practice could exempt computer system as tool of trade); *In re* Carson, 184 B.R. 587 (Bankr. N.D. Okla. 1995) (Oklahoma tools-of-trade exemption protects lawyer's computer system). *But see In re* Massey, 2009 WL 2848861 (Bankr. E.D. La. Apr. 23, 2009) (debtor who, on petition date, had separate business office not allowed to exempt home office equipment); *In re* Hoffpauir, 258 B.R. 447 (Bankr. D. Idaho 2001) (computer not tool of trade when debtor wife sometimes worked at home, but no evidence that this was required; evidence that employer supplied software or equipment would be probative).

859 *In re* Woller, 483 B.R. 886 (Bankr. W.D. Wis. 2012) (over-the-road truck driver could exempt semi-tractor despite existence of specific exemption for motor vehicle); *In re* Gaydos, 441 B.R. 102 (Bankr. N.D. Ohio 2010) (applying principle of liberal interpretation to conclude that Ohio's provision of specific exemption for motor vehicle does not bar use of tools-of-trade exemption for truck used to earn living); *In re* VanWinkle, 265 B.R. 247 (Bankr. D. Colo. 2001) (truck may be exempted as tool of the trade even though state also provides a specific motor vehicle exemption; independent truck driver may exempt truck). *See also In re* Letizia, 2014 WL 184438 (Bankr. D. Ariz. Jan. 14, 2014) (vehicles used by sole proprietorship may be exempted *only* as tools of trade; motor vehicle exemption applies only to vehicles for personal or household use). *But see In re* Belsome, 434 F.3d 774 (5th Cir. 2005) (Louisiana's specific exemption for motor vehicles trumps general tools-of-trade exemption; school bus exempt only up to amount of motor vehicle exemption); *In re* Cleavers, 407 B.R. 354 (B.A.P. 8th Cir. 2009) (under Iowa law, motor vehicle can be exempted only under specific motor vehicle exemption, not tools of trade, but may be tool of trade for purposes of lien avoidance under bankruptcy law).

860 *See* § 12.2.2, *supra*.

861 *In re* Sedillo, 476 B.R. 619 (Bankr. D. Colo. 2012) (car used to transport foster children to daily activities not a tool of trade; foster parenting not a "gainful occupation" covered by Colorado exemption); *In re* King, 451 B.R. 884 (Bankr. N.D. Iowa 2011) (car used only for commuting not tool of trade under federal bankruptcy definition, even if loss of car will cause loss of job); *In re* Taylor, 2005 WL 846222 (Bankr. D. V.I. Apr. 7, 2005) (motor vehicle not a tool of a trade unless it is itself used a tool, for example, as a taxi or a tow truck). *See also In re* Caldero Padilla, 2014 WL 183669 (Bankr. D. P.R. Jan. 14, 2014) (Social Security recipients' car not exempt because not used for work); *In re* White, 352 B.R. 633 (Bankr. E.D. La. 2006) (vehicle used for commuting not exempt tool of trade under federal bankruptcy exemptions). *Cf. In re* Rivera, 499 B.R. 175 (Bankr. D. P.R. 2013) (Puerto Rico exemption for horse and wagon used by professional covers motor vehicle if used in carrying out professional responsibilities). *But see* Neb. Rev. Stat. § 25-1556 (explicitly exempting motor vehicle required to get to work); *In re* Stewart, 2013 WL 5793441 (Bankr. D. Neb. Oct. 28, 2013) (overlooking explicit statutory language and holding that Nebraska does not exempt vehicle used only for commuting); *In re* Cardwell, 2013 WL 4874323 (Bankr. D. Neb. Sept. 2013) (Nebraska exempts car used for commuting, but federal law does not; applying federal definition to deny lien avoidance, even though debtor was required to use Nebraska exemptions); *In re* Reisdorff, 2010 WL

may be sufficient if the debtor's job requires visits to widespread job sites or transportation of equipment or products.[862] An independent owner-operator may be allowed to exempt a truck.[863] Courts have been less receptive to the argument that a vehicle is a tool of the debtor's trade when the debtor owns other vehicles or the vehicle in question has luxury features.[864]

Some states limit tools of the trade to the debtor's principal occupation.[865] Wyoming has construed this to limit only the number of exemptions: the debtor may exempt the tools of one part-time occupation or several, up to the $2000 cap, but may not claim an exemption for each trade.[866] A debtor who seeks to exempt the tools of a casual or part-time occupation may be required to prove that it is more than a hobby and that there is at least an expectation of profit.[867] A debtor who is

---

4852457 (Bankr. D. Neb. Nov. 27, 2010) (spouses who each used jointly owned vehicle to commute to work could stack two tools of trade and two wildcard exemptions).

862 *In re* Sackett, 394 B.R. 544 (Bankr. D. Colo. 2008) (allowing tools-of-trade exemption for nurse supervisor's sports utility vehicle; employer did not provide vehicle, and job required her to transport equipment and training materials to healthcare facilities and patients' homes); *In re* Black, 280 B.R. 258 (Bankr. D. Colo. 2002) (self-employed building contractor may exempt truck used to tow equipment and transport tools to worksites, as otherwise debtor could not practice his occupation); *In re* Clifford, 222 B.R. 8 (Bankr. D. Conn. 1998) (tools of trade of building contractor included pickup truck used to transport workers and materials to job sites, lift truck, crawler loader, and fax machine used for bidding, all of which were necessary to enable debtor to compete as contractor); *In re* Lyall, 193 B.R. 767 (Bankr. E.D. Va. 1996) (automobile is "necessary" within meaning of the Virginia "tools of a trade" exemption if debtor would be unable to compete effectively without it; when self-employed architect used car frequently to visit job sites and attend meetings with municipal officials, it was exempt); Charlie's Concrete Servs., Inc. v. Anthony, 2009 WL 2342523 (V.I. Super. Ct. July 24, 2009) (motor vehicle can be tool of trade if "reasonably necessary" to debtor's occupation; one truck or van is reasonably necessary to enable building contractor to move tools and equipment to worksites). *See also In re* Garcia, 709 F.3d 861 (9th Cir. 2013) (remanding to bankruptcy court to determine whether car was tool of trade of realtor); *In re* Giles, 340 B.R. 543 (Bankr. E.D. Pa. 2006) (standard motor vehicle was tool of trade under federal bankruptcy exemptions for artisan who made hats and sold at craft fairs; public transportation not a reasonable alternative for buying materials and attending shows). *Cf. In re* Rawn, 199 B.R. 733 (Bankr. E.D. Cal. 1996) (car would be "tool of the trade" only if debtor's occupation was "uniquely dependent on" its use, for example, a realtor who showed houses to prospective buyers). *But see In re* Robinson, 2010 WL 4053667 (C.D. Ill. Oct. 14, 2010) (car used occasionally to call on customers or make deliveries not exempt; tools of trade limited to artisans' tools of small value); *In re* Erwin, 199 B.R. 628 (Bankr. S.D. Tex. 1996) (more than "general value and use in business" was required to make a car a tool of the trade; when debtor was a constable who served process, but any four-door car, including a rental, would serve, car was not exempt).

863 *In re* VanWinkle, 265 B.R. 247 (Bankr. D. Colo. 2001) (independent truck driver may exempt truck). *See also In re* Woller, 483 B.R. 886 (Bankr. W.D. Wis. 2012) (taking narrow view of exemption; truck is "integral part" of trucking business, but noting that car is not a tool of trade for realtor, or van for plumber).

864 *In re* Balck, 2011 WL 6130418 (Bankr. D. Colo. Dec. 8, 2011) (refusing to exempt vehicles, including a motorcycle and an antique auto, when debtors had already exempted a pick-up truck and trailer, more suitable for use in their excavation business); *In re* Heimbouch, 246 B.R. 895 (Bankr. D. Neb. 2000) (Nebraska exemption for motor vehicle used in connection with business did not exempt farmer's classic Corvette, although sometimes used for farm business, when farmer also owned pickup trucks and jeep). *See also In re* Black, 225 B.R. 610 (Bankr. M.D. La. 1998) (tools-of-trade exemption would protect truck, which debtor did not personally drive, when debtor depended on income from truck for her living, but denying exemption because truck's size brought it within former statute's definition of non-exempt "luxury automobile"); *In re* Juhasz, 208 B.R. 32 (Bankr. S.D. Tex. 1997) (ordinary Porsche used to call on customers and deliver jewelry and collectibles was not a tool of the trade when there was no modification which adapted it for particular use as a delivery vehicle).

865 *In re* Lampe, 278 B.R. 205 (B.A.P. 10th Cir. 2002) (Kansas law) (spouses could exempt farm equipment when farming was principal occupation, even though both spouses also worked off-farm), *aff'd*, 331 F.3d 750 (10th Cir. 2003); Seel v. Wittman, 173 B.R. 734 (D. Kan. 1994) (lawn mower used in side business not exempt); *In re* Shoemaker, 2009 WL 3244750 (Bankr. D. Kan. 2009) (tools-of-trade exemption only for tools of principal occupation; when couple owned cows and were trying to build a herd, but wife worked as LPN in nursing home, cattle raising was not principal occupation); *In re* Matthews, 449 B.R. 833 (Bankr. M.D. Ga. 2011) (wife who worked in garden and picked pecans not engaged in farming; denying her claim of exemption in a tractor she never drove); *In re* Weddington, 457 B.R. 102 (Bankr. D. Kan. 2011) (denying exemption for equipment used by debtor as hunting guide for about four weeks per year; debtor had year-round job, from which he earned nearly all his income); *In re* Cordova, 394 B.R. 389 (Bankr. E.D. Va. July 28, 2008) (former contractor, who earned living at desk job, could not exempt tools and truck used for weekend and evening carpentry work); *In re* Kieffer, 279 B.R. 290 (Bankr. D. Kan. 2002) (wife's principal occupation was farming, even though she also worked off the farm); *In re* Zink, 177 B.R. 713 (Bankr. D. Kan. 1995) (construing Kansas "principal occupation" language to allow exemption for tools of only that occupation). *See also In re* Wilkinson, 2010 WL 821345 (Bankr. D. Kan. Mar. 5, 2010) (debtor estopped from exempting tools for his "side job," because he reported no income from it on tax returns). *Cf.* United States v. Neuzil, 2010 WL 4116853 (N.D. Iowa Oct. 1. 2010) (federal tools-of-trade exemption inapplicable to coin collection when debtor failed to show he was in business of buying and selling coins; kept no records and sold only occasionally), *report and recommendation adopted*, 2010 WL 4115392 (N.D. Iowa Oct. 19, 2010). *But see In re* Thompson, 311 B.R. 822 (Bankr. D. Kan. 2004) (may exempt tools of more than one occupation, as long as activity "has a legitimate business or profit motive," but one $7500 cap applies to total for all trades; even if principal occupation test applied, farm equipment was exempt when husband farmed at least forty hours a week and wife devoted "considerable energy and personal resources" to farm); Kono v. Meeker, 126 Cal. Rptr. 3d 208 (Cal. Ct. App. 2011) (denying exemption for antique dealers' inventory of antique tools, as they did not use items as tools in the exercise of their trade). *But cf. In re* McHugh, 2010 WL 2176298 (Bankr. D. Idaho May 27, 2010) (debtor can exempt tools for a second occupation, if necessary for financial support, but not shown here when debtors, a physician and an accountant, raised alfalfa and horses and were trying to establish vineyard, but most of their income came from their professions).

866 *In re* Bechtoldt, 210 B.R. 599 (B.A.P. 10th Cir. 1997) (Wyoming law) (allowing debtor who worked primarily as plumber but also as painter to exempt painting tools).

867 *In re* Sharp, 490 B.R. 592 (Bankr. D. Colo. 2013) (fact issues whether boats, ATV, firearms, fishing equipment, used in three-year-old guiding business, now running at substantial loss, were tools of a "gainful occupation"), *aff'd*, 2014 WL 1400073 (B.A.P. 10th Cir. Apr. 11, 2014). *See also In re* Stone, 504 B.R. 908 (Bankr. C.D. Ill. 2014) (ride-on lawn mower not tool of trade; debtor mowed neighbors' lawns for small fee and ball diamond for free, but most of his income came from other sources and he did not hold himself out to public as yard worker); *In*

not currently practicing a trade but intends to return to it may be able to claim a tools of the trade exemption, depending on the strength of the evidence.[868] A debtor who does business as a limited liability company or other corporate entity may be unable to claim an exemption for tools owned by that entity.[869]

12.8.5 Tenancy by the Entireties in Personal Property

Some states recognize tenancy by the entireties, which protects marital property from attachment for individual debts of one spouse, not just in real property but also in personal property.[870] A number of states hold that, when a married couple

re Goss, 352 B.R. 309 (Bankr. E.D. Okla. 2006) (farm equipment not exempt when farmer was retired or, at most, farming only as "hobby").

868 Planned Parenthood of Columbus/Willamette, Inc. v. American Coal. of Life Activists, 2007 WL 4118597 (S.D. Ohio Nov. 16, 2007) (minister not presently serving as pastor may claim books as tools of trade, when he writes and plans someday to return to preaching; considerations include time away and whether debtor has reasonable prospect of returning to trade); *In re* Quintero, 2012 WL 3638504 (Bankr. D. Neb. Aug. 22, 2012) (must show ability and intention to return; allowing exemption of car for debtor who had been unemployed because of illness but was recovered and using car in job hunt); *In re* Ferro, 2010 WL 310857 (Bankr. S.D. Tex. Jan. 21, 2010) (allowing debtor who had been boat builder for thirty-three years to exempt boat molds; two boat resellers testified that they would advance him money to build boats when market improved); *In re* Weimann, 2009 WL 383426 (Bankr. C.D. Ill. Feb. 13, 2009) (operator of boat rental business, who had suspended operations for one year, had reasonable prospect of return when he had already negotiated contract with city); *In re* Miller, 370 B.R. 914 (Bankr. D. Minn. 2007) (intent to return shown; thirty-five years of farming, and "definite arrangements" to resume); Devine v. Devine, 2005 WL 1926038 (Bankr. N.D. Iowa Aug. 5, 2005) (debtors who were living and working off farm could exempt farming equipment when intent to return to farming sufficiently shown); *In re* Thompson, 311 B.R. 822 (Bankr. D. Kan. 2004) (farmers who raised game birds sold entire stock "to make ends meet," but intended to resume as soon as they could raise the necessary money; equipment was exempt); *In re* Lund, 2003 WL 21673545 (Bankr. N.D. Iowa July 14, 2003) (farm equipment exempt even though couple who had farmed for decades did not plant crop because bank cut off credit; factors include intensity of past farming and sincerity and reasonableness of intent to resume; that profits are "speculative" is not fatal); Girgis v. Macaluso Realty Co., 778 So. 2d 1210 (La. Ct. App. 2001) (temporary non-use of tools does not eliminate exemption); Landry v. Landry, 917 A.2d 1262 (N.H. 2007) (incarcerated debtor could exempt mechanics' tools; had worked as mechanic before imprisonment and intended to do so upon release). *See also In re* Lampe, 278 B.R. 205 (B.A.P. 10th Cir. 2002) (farming remained debtors' principal occupation even though they were facing farm foreclosure and had taken outside jobs, when they continued to farm and would do so on other land even if foreclosure went through), *aff'd*, 331 F.3d 750 (10th Cir. 2003). *But see In re* Blackburn, 2011 WL 160608 (Bankr. D. Idaho Jan. 19, 2011) (Idaho exempts only tools needed to make a living; issue is whether tools are needed for support; when builder, whose company could not find work during economic downturn, was earning living as laborer, builders' tools were not exempt). *But cf. In re* Pickard, 2012 WL 4919791 (Bankr. N.D. Iowa Oct. 15, 2012) (shop and skid loader, used in now defunct business, not exempt); *In re* Skillen, 2009 WL 4823802 (Bankr. N.D. Iowa Dec. 14, 2009) (former farmers failed to show intent to return; statement of intent must be bolstered by reasonable prospects and objective fact; here, no showing of affirmative steps to resume farming); *In re* Cordova, 394 B.R. 389 (Bankr. E.D. Va. 2008) (former contractor, who earned living at desk job, could not show intention to return; return was contingent on improvement in housing market, which might take years); *In re* Massey, 2009 WL 2848861 (Bankr. E.D. La. Apr. 23, 2009) (must show that debtor is gainfully employed in a trade or profession and that tools are necessary to that work; debtor who had started writing a novel but never received income for writing not gainfully employed, so home office non-exempt); *In re* Tracy, 2008 WL 5225840 (Bankr. D. Neb. Dec. 12, 2008) (Nebraska allows tools-of-trade exemption for vehicle used for commuting; temporary interruption of employment does not bar exemption, but disabled debtor who had not worked for two years failed to show that he could return to former employment); *In re* Behnke, 2008 WL 4951975 (Bankr. D. Neb. Nov. 18, 2008) (debtors who were unemployed on petition date could not claim tools-of-trade exemption for car); *In re* Fehmel, 2008 WL 2151797 (Bankr. W.D. Tex. May 22, 2008) (denying exemption to debtor who reported no income from use of tools, formerly used in failed business), *aff'd on other grounds*, 372 Fed. Appx. 507 (5th Cir. 2010); *In re* Hintzman, 2007 WL 80964 (Bankr. D. Minn. Jan. 8, 2007) (intent to return not shown; four years of unprofitable farming, no arrangements to resume; simple statement of intent not enough); *In re* Banke, 275 B.R. 317 (Bankr. N.D. Iowa 2002) (considering intensity of past business, sincerity of intent to return, prospects for return, lapse of time, and other circumstances; boat not tool of trade of fishing guide when not used for twelve years, during which time debtor worked full time at other occupation); *In re* Aurelio, 252 B.R. 102 (Bankr. N.D. Miss. 2000) (tools-of-trade exemption did not cover proceeds of sale of equipment, when no intent to invest in new equipment and resume business); *In re* Mausser, 225 B.R. 667 (Bankr. N.D. Iowa 1998) (debtors not actively engaged in farming must establish objective facts that show reasonable prospects of resuming, not just subjective intent; not shown here).

869 *In re* Checiek, 492 B.R. 918 (Bankr. M.D. Fla. 2013) (denying reverse veil piercing for truck owned by debtor truck-driver's wholly owned corporation; distinguishing cases in which lenders have required debtors to incorporate to evade usury laws); *In re* Gardner, 2013 WL 3804594 (Bankr. D. Colo. June 19, 2013) (no exemption for assets of partnership, which is separate legal entity); *In re* Miller, 2011 WL 4018267 (Bankr. D. Colo. Sept. 8, 2011) (debtor cannot exempt property owned by corporation). *But see In re* Schwab, 378 B.R. 854 (Bankr. D. Minn. 2007) (allowing exemption when debtor did business as limited liability corporation but purchased tools in own name using personal credit line; also noting the possibility of "reverse veil piercing" for individual or family business). *But cf. In re* Calderon, 501 B.R. 726 (Bankr. D. Colo. 2013) (debtor who incorporated his small business as S Corporation could exempt tools he personally owned and used in the business; he had owned them long before he incorporated).

870 *DISTRICT OF COLUMBIA:* Morrison v. Potter, 764 A.2d 234 (D.C. 2000) (married couples' joint checking accounts presumed to be held in tenancy by entireties; standard joint tenancy language in account agreement does not rebut presumption); Roberts & Lloyd, Inc. v. Zyblut, 691 A.2d 635 (D.C. 1997) (property owned by married couple presumed to be owned in tenancy by entirety, even if words of conveyance would have created ordinary joint tenancy).

DELAWARE: In re Scioli, 2013 WL 318718 (Bankr. D. Del. Jan. 18, 2013) (Delaware recognizes TBE in personal property; household goods, property titled in both spouses' names, and property directly derivative of TBE property—for example, purchased with funds from joint account—are rebuttably presumed to be owned in TBE, but car titled in husband alone and purchased with funds from his business account not owned in TBE).

FLORIDA: In re Sinnreich, 391 F.3d 1295 (11th Cir. 2004) (Florida law) (real and personal property held in tenancy by entireties with non-debtor spouse is exempt); Branch Banking and Trust. Co. v. Maxwell, 2012 WL 4078407 (M.D. Fla. Aug. 4, 2012) (settlement check, for action arising from installation of defective materials in marital home, was owned in TBE, even after deposit in bank account that may not have been TBE), *adopted by* 2012 WL 4078155 (M.D. Fla. Sept. 17, 2012); *In re* Freeman, 387 B.R. 871 (Bankr. N.D. Fla. 2008) (allowing tenancy by entireties exemption for tax refund resulting from joint return; unities not destroyed by provision of tax law that would allow a spouse to revoke decision to file jointly); *In re* Kepley, 352 B.R. 526 (Bankr. M.D. Fla. 2006) (funds in bank account owned in tenancy by entireties cannot be reached for individual debts; here, no suggestion that funds belonged only to debtor or were placed in account for purpose of hindering creditors); *In re* Kossow, 325 B.R. 478 (Bankr. S.D. Fla. 2005) (noting disagreement among Florida courts as to breadth of *Beal Bank* presumption and concluding it applies to all personal property acquired in accordance with the unities of an entireties estate); Beal Bank v. Almand & Assocs., 780 So. 2d 45 (Fla. 2001) (couple with two names on account presumed to own it by entireties unless expressly disclaimed; signature card for joint tenancy not express disclaimer unless couple was offered entireties account and declined). *See also In re* Koesling, 210 B.R. 487 (Bankr. N.D. Fla. 1997) (Florida recognizes tenancy by entireties in personal property; couple met burden of proof of intent when ownership of promissory note was in both names and husband testified as to intent; note that *Beal Bank* removes the burden of proof from the debtors); Nunez v. Fernandez, 724 So. 2d 182 (Fla. Dist. Ct. App. 1999) (judgment debt of one spouse may not be set off against mortgage and promissory note owned by couple in tenancy by entireties). *Cf. In re* Hill, 197 F.3d 1135 (11th Cir. 1999) (transfer to tenancy by entireties may be attacked as fraudulent transfer, but due process requires that non-debtor spouse be made a party to this proceeding); *In re* Gorny, 2008 WL 5606583 (Bankr. M.D. Fla. Aug. 29, 2008) (allowing exemption for tax refund, but denying it for household furnishings, when debtors failed to show dates of marriage and of acquisition of property; denying exemption for car, which is governed by motor vehicle title law); Thomas J. Konrad & Assocs. v. McCoy, 705 So. 2d 948 (Fla. Dist. Ct. App. 1998) (creditor of husband sought to garnish couple's bank account owned by tenancy of entireties; remanding to decide whether husband's transfer of his separate funds into joint account, after judgment had been entered against him, was fraudulent). *But cf. In re* Pereau, 2007 WL 907545 (Bankr. M.D. Fla. Mar. 13, 2007) (listing six "unities" needed for tenancy by entireties; unity of interest not present when settlement check covered husband's injuries and wife's loss of consortium, two distinct claims), *aff'd*, 2008 WL 2074412 (M.D. Fla. May 15, 2008); Xayavong v. Sunny Gifts, Inc., 891 So. 2d 1075 (Fla. Dist. Ct. App. 2004) (*Beal Bank* presumption that married couple's property owned in tenancy by entireties does not apply to motor vehicles when title statute unambiguously prescribes how to create co-ownership interest).

HAWAII: Traders Travel Int'l, Inc. v. Howser, 753 P.2d 244 (Haw. 1988) (statute allows TBE in real or personal property, but bank account here was a joint account).

MARYLAND: Merrill Lynch Bus. Fin. Servs., Inc. v. Targan, 2008 WL 2858921 (D. Md. July 22, 2008) (Md. Code Ann., Cts. & Jud. Proc. § 11-603(1) (West) makes all married couples' accounts, in effect, tenancy by entireties, by forbidding garnishment for debt of one spouse, if the account was joint on date of judgment; but here transfer to joint ownership was fraudulent, because judgment imminent); Cruickshank-Wallace v. Cnty. Banking & Trust Co., 885 A.2d 403 (Md. Ct. Spec. App. 2005) (Maryland recognizes tenancy by entireties in personal property, but here tax refunds arising from husband's individual earnings not owned in tenancy by entireties, even though couple filed joint returns and had agreed that their property would be owned in tenancy by entireties).

MICHIGAN: Zavradinos v. JTRB, Inc., 753 N.W.2d 60 (Mich. 2008) (married couple's property—here, a securities account—is presumed owned in tenancy by entireties unless otherwise "expressly provided").

MISSOURI: *In re* Brown, 234 B.R. 907 (Bankr. W.D. Mo. 1999) (under Missouri law, real and personal property of married couple is presumed to be owned in tenancy by entireties and thus exempt from claims of individual creditors). *Cf. In re* Booth, 309 B.R. 568 (Bankr. W.D. Mo. 2004) (presumption of tenancy by entireties rebutted when vehicle purchased during marriage was titled in husband alone; no tenancy by entireties in vehicles purchased before marriage); *In re* Walker, 279 B.R. 544 (Bankr. W.D. Mo. 2002) (despite Missouri presumption that married couples own their property by entireties, tax refund of debtor and sole wage-earner wife was her individual property and could be garnished by her individual creditors); *In re* Thorpe, 251 B.R. 723 (Bankr. W.D. Mo. 2000) (Missouri permits ownership of personality by entireties, but requirements not satisfied even though motor vehicle was acquired during marriage); Scott v. Union Planters' Bank, 196 S.W.3d 574 (Mo. Ct. App. 2006) (bank not liable to wife for allowing husband to withdraw entire sum in bank account, but noting that this decision is not meant to "disturb settled law" that an execution for a judgment against one spouse cannot affect a bank account held in tenancy by entireties).

PENNSYLVANIA: 78 Arch St. Assocs. v. Blatstein (*In re* Blatstein), 192 F.3d 88, 96 (3d Cir. 1999) (in Pennsylvania, real or personal property of married couple is presumed to be owned in tenancy by entireties); DiFlorido v. DiFlorido, 459 Pa. 641, 331 A.2d 174 (1975) (household goods are presumed to be entireties property); Cohen v. Goldberg, 431 Pa. 192, 244 A.2d 763 (1968) (money held in joint bank account was entireties property).

RHODE ISLAND: *In re* Homonoff, 261 B.R. 551 (Bankr. D.R.I. 2001) (personal property may be owned by entireties, but only if that intent clearly appears in conveyance; not shown here).

TENNESSEE: *In re* Sullivan, 2008 WL 3914494 (Bankr. E.D. Tenn. Aug. 20, 2008) (married debtors who own personal property in tenancy by entireties may each exempt up to 50% of the value of each piece of property, up to the $4000 per person limit); *In re* Garretson, 6 B.R. 127 (Bankr. E.D. Tenn. 1980) (CD in name of "husband or wife" is held in tenancy by entireties and cannot be reached by trustee in husband's bankruptcy); Avenell v. Gibson, 2005 WL 458733 (Tenn. Ct. App. Feb. 28, 2005) (1988 change in bank account attachment procedure did not change long-standing rule that presumes that married couple's bank account is held in tenancy by entireties, notwithstanding account agreement describing joint tenancy).

VERMONT: Beacon Mill. Co. v. Larose, 418 A.2d 32 (Vt. 1980) (if bank account held as tenancy by entirety, it was not chargeable for husband's sole debts). *See also* McNeilly v. Geremia, 249 B.R. 576 (B.A.P. 1st Cir. 2000) (proceeds of entireties real estate in Rhode Island that were transferred to Vermont bank account owned in tenancy by entireties were exempt under Vermont law, which applied even though debtors were in Rhode Island).

VIRGINIA: *In re* Thomas, 312 F.3d 145 (4th Cir. 2002) (even in joint bankruptcy, entireties property may be reached only by joint creditors); *In re* McKain, 455 B.R. 674 (Bankr. E.D. Tenn. 2011) (Virginia law allows tenancy by entireties in personal property, but no presumption of this form of ownership; must show all the unities, plus intent to create tenancy by entireties); *In re* Massey, 225 B.R. 887 (Bankr. E.D. Va. 1998) (under Virginia law, personal property could be owned in tenancy by entirety, even if it was not proceeds of sale of entireties real estate; when brokerage account described shares as owned by couple "as tenants by entirety," this was sufficient). *But cf. In re* Cordova, 394 B.R. 389 (Bankr. E.D. Va. 2008) (Virginia generally permits tenancy by entireties for personal property, but specific statute governing motor vehicle titles explicitly forbids it); *In re* Potter, 274 B.R. 224 (Bankr. E.D. Va. 2002) (personal property in Virginia may be owned by entireties, but documents must either use the words "tenancy by entireties" or describe owners as husband and wife; not applicable when stock titled to couple's two names, in joint tenancy with right of survivorship, and no mention of marital status); Rue & Assocs., Inc. v. White, 2006 WL 2022184 (Va. Cir. Ct. July 18, 2006) (married couple's bank accounts were joint tenancy, not tenancy by entireties, when papers did not specify tenancy by entireties).

WYOMING: *In re* Welty, 217 B.R. 907 (Bankr. D. Wyo. 1998) (intangibles, here a business, could be held in tenancy by entirety, but documents must show clear intent to create this type of ownership).

jointly owns personal property, a presumption arises that it is owned by the entireties.[871] Documentation such as a bank signature card that states that the asset is held as a joint tenancy does not necessarily rebut this presumption.[872] Other jurisdictions do not recognize tenancy by the entireties in personal property.[873] The general rules governing entireties property are discussed in § 12.7.9, *supra*.

12.9 Pensions, Insurance, Annuities, Causes of Action, Debts Owed to Judgment Debtors

12.9.1 Exemptions for Pensions and Retirement Benefits

There is a strong public policy favoring protection of retirement plans, without which the state might have to support people made destitute by deprivation of their retirement income.[874] Federal law provides that civil service retirment benefits are not assignable or subject to execution, levy, attachment, garnishment, or other legal process.[875] Military retirement pay is also exempt under federal law, because it is not listed among the types of federal employee compensation made subject to garnishment by 5 U.S.C. § 5520, nor listed in regulations as subject to "involuntary allotment."[876] Pension plans governed by ERISA must provide that benefits cannot be assigned or alienated, with an exception for qualified domestic relations orders,[877] and this provision puts them beyond the reach of creditors.[878]

871 78 Arch St. Assocs. v. Blatstein (*In re* Blatstein), 192 F.3d 88, 96 (3d Cir. 1999); *In re* Hensley, 393 B.R. 186 (Bankr. E.D. Tenn. 2008) (presumption of tenancy by entireties for married couple's car, titled in husband but used by both spouses); *In re* Hinton, 378 B.R. 371 (Bankr. M.D. Fla. 2007) (property of married couple presumed to be held in tenancy by entireties; when individual tax refunds deposited in bank account or used to purchase certificate of deposit held in tenancy by entireties, refunds were exempt); *In re* Pereau, 2007 WL 907545 (Bankr. M.D. Fla. Mar. 13, 2007) (*Beal Bank* presumption applies to all property, not just bank accounts, but tenancy by entireties not shown here because no unity of interest), *aff'd*, 2008 WL 2074412 (M.D. Fla. May 15, 2008); *In re* Kossow, 325 B.R. 478 (Bankr. S.D. Fla. 2005) (presumption that all personal property of married couple is held as tenancy by entireties as long as acquired in accordance with unities of possession, interest, title, and time with right of survivorship); Beal Bank v. Almand & Assocs., 780 So. 2d 45 (Fla. 2001) (recognizing presumption; creditor has burden of rebutting it); Avenell v. Gibson, 2005 WL 458733 (Tenn. Ct. App. Feb. 28, 2005) (bank accounts of married couples presumed held as tenancy by entireties). *But see In re* McKain, 455 B.R. 674 (Bankr. E.D. Tenn. 2011) (must show all the unities, plus intent to create tenancy by entireties); *In re* Gorny, 2008 WL 5606583 (Bankr. M.D. Fla. Aug. 29, 2008) (burden on debtors to show the required unities: possession, interest, title, time, survivorship, and marriage; denying exemption for household furnishings because debtors failed to show date of marriage or of acquisition of property). *But cf. In re* Scioli, 2013 WL 318718 (Bankr. D. Del. Jan. 18, 2013) (purchase of car using funds from checking account of husband's business was sufficient to rebut the presumption).

872 Matthews v. Cohen, 382 B.R. 526 (M.D. Fla. 2007) (*Beal Bank* presumption not overcome; debtors checked "joint tenancy with survivorship" box on stock certificate; check box for "other" provided, but none for "tenancy by entireties"), *aff'd*, 307 Fed. Appx. 266 (11th Cir. 2009); *In re* Canovas, 2009 WL 2386062 (Bankr. S.D. Fla. July 31, 2009) (titling of married couple's account in "Mr. C or Mrs. C" not sufficient to rebut the presumption of entireties ownership); *In re* Hensley, 393 B.R. 186 (Bankr. E.D. Tenn. 2008) (certificate of title not determinative; married couple's car, titled in husband but used by both spouses, is owned in tenancy by entireties); Morrison v. Potter, 764 A.2d 234 (D.C. 2000) (married couples' joint checking accounts presumed to be held in tenancy by entireties; standard joint tenancy language in account agreement does not rebut presumption); Beal Bank v. Almand & Assocs., 780 So. 2d 45 (Fla. 2001); Zavradinos v. JTRB, Inc., 753 N.W.2d 60 (Mich. 2008) (married couple's property presumed owned in tenancy by entireties; checking "joint tenancy with right to survival" box on brokerage account paperwork not sufficient to rebut; must specify "and not in tenancy by entireties"); Avenell v. Gibson, 2005 WL 458733 (Tenn. Ct. App. Feb. 28, 2005) (1988 change in bank account attachment procedure did not change long-standing rule that presumes that married couple's bank account is held in tenancy by entireties, notwithstanding account agreement describing joint tenancy). *But see* O'Brien v. Bank of Am., N.A., 75 A.3d 964 (Md. Ct. Spec. App. 2013) (account not owned in TBE because account agreement specified joint tenancy with right of survivorship).

While *Beal Bank* dealt with a bank signature card, it probably overrules other Florida cases holding that the form of ownership stated on a title or other ownership document is conclusive, for example: *In re* Mastrofino, 247 B.R. 330 (Bankr. M.D. Fla. 2000) (no tenancy by entireties in car that was titled to "husband or wife" and could be sold by either co-owner, nor in bank account when signature card created joint tenancy and permitted withdrawal on one signature).

873 *See, e.g.*, 735 Ill. Comp. Stat. § 5/12-112 (TBE only in real property, beneficial interest in a land trust, or certain real property held in inter vivos trust); *In re* Adams, 506 B.R. 688 (Bankr. E.D. N.C. 2014) (no TBE for personal property, including sale proceeds of TBE real property); *In re* Prosser, 2012 WL 246279 (Bankr. D. V.I. Jan. 20, 2012) (Florida recognizes TBE in personal property but the Virgin Islands do not; Virgin Islands residents, who filed bankruptcy in the Virgin Islands, could not claim TBE for personal property located in Florida; debtors also failed to show the six unities); *In re* Gillette, 248 B.R. 845 (Bankr. M.D. Fla. 1999) (tenancies by entireties do not exist in Wisconsin; joint bank account may be reached); Whitlock v. Pub. Serv. Co., 159 N.E.2d 280 (Ind. 1959) (only real estate and certain crops can be owned in TBE); Lurie v. Sheriff of Gallatin Cnty., 999 P.2d 342 (Mont. 2000) (tenancy by entireties not recognized in Montana, for personal or real property); State v. Myndyllo, 542 A.2d 478 (N.J. Super. Ct. App. Div. 1988) (proceeds of the sale of realty are personalty and cannot be owned in TBE); Brown v. Havens, 85 A.2d 812 (N.J. Super. Ct. Ch. Div. 1952) (ninety-nine-year lease is personalty and cannot be owned in TBE).

874 *In re* Seltzer, 104 F.3d 234 (9th Cir. 1996).

875 5 U.S.C. § 8470. *See also In re* O'Neal, 462 B.R. 324 (Bankr. D. Mass. 2012) (funds in thrift savings plan, a tax-deferred retirement savings plan for civilian federal employees, were not part of bankruptcy estate because they subject to a restriction on transfer enforceable under non-bankruptcy law; even if they were part of the estate, they would be exempt as tax-qualified retirement plan).

876 *See In re* Meyer, 211 B.R. 203 (Bankr. E.D. Va. 1997) (military retirement pay retains exempt status when directly deposited in Navy Federal Credit Union but not when transferred to debtor's non-special purpose checking account in another institution). *See also* 29 U.S.C. § 1051 (exempting various types of plans from Subtitle B, Part 2, which includes the anti-alienation provision). *But see* New York State Crime Victims Bd. *ex rel.* K.A.S. v. Wendell, 815 N.Y.S.2d 438 (N.Y. Sup. Ct. 2006) (finding that military pay is not protected from garnishment by federal statute; ignoring the distinction between "pay" and "retired pay" or a "pension").

877 29 U.S.C. §§ 1056(d)(1), 1051(6) (excluding certain individual retirement accounts from ERISA's protection).

878 *See* Patterson v. Shumate, 504 U.S. 753, 112 S. Ct. 2242, 119 L. Ed. 2d 519 (1992) (ERISA-qualified pension plan funds are not available

Similarly, most states exempt at least a portion of benefits received under various employee retirement or pension plans. Sometimes a state's exemption is found in the statute creating or regulating the retirement or pension plan, rather than in a general exemption law. Generally the courts extend an exemption for employee pension plans to tax-qualified individual retirement accounts[879] and to Keogh

to creditors in or out of bankruptcy); Guidry v. Sheet Metal Workers Nat'l Pension Fund, 493 U.S. 365, 110 S. Ct. 680, 107 L. Ed. 2d 782 (1990) (ERISA's anti-alienation provisions for pension benefits prohibit their garnishment even when in form of constructive trust); *In re* Sandvik, 2004 WL 3383656 (Bankr. D.N.D. Dec. 1, 2004) (in determining whether individual retirement account exceeds state statutory exemption, court will not count ERISA plan which, under federal law, is not part of bankruptcy estate); *In re* Tomlin, 315 B.R. 439 (Bankr. E.D. Mich. 2004) (individual retirement account is exempt in bankruptcy; ERISA does not preempt Michigan law, enacted when state opted out of federal bankruptcy exemptions); *In re* Handel, 301 B.R. 421 (Bankr. S.D.N.Y. 2003) (anti-alienation clause sufficient to make plan exempt, even though debtor dealt with plan in way that caused it to lose favorable tax treatment); Ditto v. McCurdy, 978 P.2d 783 (Haw. 1999) (ERISA anti-alienation provision preempts Hawaii statute which would allow garnishment of retirement plan contributions made within three years before filing bankruptcy or becoming a defendant in a lawsuit). *Cf.* Mackey v. Lanier Collection Agency & Serv., Inc., 486 U.S. 825, 836, 108 S. Ct. 2182, 100 L. Ed. 2d 836 (1988) (ERISA prohibits assignment or alienation of benefits provided by ERISA pension plans but not ERISA welfare benefit plans). *But cf. In re* Radcliffe, 563 F.3d 627 (7th Cir. 2009) (debt that arises from criminal acts or fiduciary defalcation involving ERISA plan may be set off against ERISA benefits owed to the wrongdoer under the plan, but offset cannot be based on corporate officer's personal guarantee of company's obligation to make contributions to plan even though company breached this obligation); Lampkins v. Golden, 2002 U.S. App. LEXIS 900 (6th Cir. Jan. 17, 2002) (Simplified Employee Pension is not protected by ERISA's exemption provision, and ERISA preempts state exemption law that might have applied to it); AFLAC, Inc. v. Diaz-Verson, 2012 WL 1903904 (M.D. Ga. May 25, 2012) (ERISA's anti-alienation provision does not apply to "top hat" plan, but Georgia's 25% garnishment limit applies); Katzenberg v. Lazzari, 2007 WL 1017645 (E.D.N.Y. Mar. 12, 2007) (debt that arises from ERISA plan fiduciary's misappropriate of money from the plan or breach of other duties to the plan may be offset against ERISA benefits owed to the fiduciary). *But cf. In re* Lawrence, 235 B.R. 498 (Bankr. S.D. Fla. 1999) (plan not exempt when it did not meet ERISA's requirements because it benefited only the company owner), *rev'd on other grounds*, 244 B.R. 868 (S.D. Fla. 2000 (finding trustee's objection untimely).

879 Rousey v. Jacoway, 544 U.S. 320, 125 S. Ct. 1561, 161 L. Ed. 2d 563 (2005) (tax-qualified individual retirement accounts, funded by distributions from employer's pension plan, are covered by federal bankruptcy exemption for "similar plan . . . on account of . . . age" when tax penalty for withdrawal before age 59½ was "substantial barrier" to early withdrawal); *In re* Krebs, 527 F.3d 82 (3d Cir. 2008) (retirement account may be exempt even if debtor does not have present right to receive payments without penalty; remanding to determine whether individual retirement account needed for support); Sawczak v. Goldenberg, 218 F.3d 1264 (11th Cir. 2000) (individual retirement accounts exempt when they fit the Florida statutory definition, were not acquired with proceeds of fraud, and were not a transfer of non-exempt to exempt assets on the eve of bankruptcy); Premier Capital, Inc. v. Decarolis (*In re* Decarolis), 259 B.R. 467 (B.A.P. 1st Cir. 2001) (if IRA itself is part of tax-qualified retirement plan, it is exempt under New Hampshire law, even if certain contributions exceeded tax-exempt amount); State Farm Mut. Ins. Co. v. Lincow, 792 F. Supp. 2d 806 (E.D. Pa. 2011) (burden on debtor to prove tax-qualification); *In re* Sheeran, 369 B.R. 910 (Bankr. E.D. Va. 2007) (debtor could exempt individual retirement account, into which she had rolled over 401(k) from former employer, except for a sum mistakenly deposited by employer in the 401(k)); *In re* Bashara, 293 B.R. 216 (Bankr. D. Neb. 2003) (tax-qualified individual retirement accounts are "similar plans" under Nebraska statute that exempts pensions, profit sharing and similar plans; exempt insofar as needed for support); *In re* Buzza, 287 B.R. 417 (Bankr. S.D. Ohio 2002) (Ohio exemption for individual retirement accounts not preempted by ERISA because individual retirement accounts not "employee benefit plans"); *In re* McCabe, 280 B.R. 841, 846 (Bankr. N.D. Iowa 2002) (Iowa law) (older debtors allowed to keep entire individual retirement account, when annual contributions had never exceeded the $2000 permitted by tax code); *In re* Stewart, 246 B.R. 134 (Bankr. D.N.H. 2000) (tax-qualified individual retirement account fully exempt under New Hampshire law, but only as to debts incurred after effective date of statute; this limitation does not apply in bankruptcy); *In re* Bruski, 226 B.R. 422 (Bankr. W.D. Wis. 1998) (Wisconsin's exemption for annuities which comply with Internal Revenue Code covers tax-deferred annuity, which would begin paying out at age fifty-nine-and-a-half, even though there was no limit on contributions, but exemption could raise serious problems if used by wealthier debtors to shelter large sums); *In re* Luttge, 204 B.R. 259 (Bankr. S.D. Fla. 1997) (tax-qualified individual retirement account was exempt under Florida law, even though not covered by ERISA); *In re* McKown, 203 B.R. 722 (Bankr. E.D. Cal. 1996) (individual retirement account was sufficiently similar to "pension, profit-sharing, annuity" to be exempt under California law; result would be different if account were being used as "savings account" or to shelter funds from creditors), *aff'd*, 203 F.3d 1188 (B.A.P. 9th Cir. 1997); *In re* Ritter, 190 B.R. 323 (Bankr. N.D. Ill. 1995) (under Illinois statute which exempted private plans "intended in good faith" to provide for retirement, Keogh and individual retirement accounts were exempt—even though debtor had made early withdrawals during period of unemployment and might do so again—when there was no evidence of lack of good faith at the time the plans were established); *In re* Bates, 176 B.R. 104 (Bankr. D. Me. 1994) (when Maine law exempted pensions, annuities, and "any similar plan" on account of age, disability, an individual retirement account was a "similar plan" even though debtor could pay penalty and take early withdrawal); Schwartzman v. Wilshinsky, 57 Cal. Rptr. 2d 790 (Cal. Ct. App. 1996) (California law) (individual retirement accounts were exempt only to extent necessary to support debtor and dependents; plan funded by employer profit sharing and employee deferred compensation was wholly exempt); Russell's AmericInn v. Eagle Gen. Contractors, L.L.C., 772 N.W.2d 81 (Minn. Ct. App. 2009) (exempt retirement account need not be derived from employment; exempting IRA under Minnesota law when it was funded partly with an inheritance and partly with rollover from tax-qualified account); Kinlaw v. Harris, 702 S.E.2d 294 (N.C. 2010) (corpus of IRA remained exempt under North Carolina law, even though debtor had taken substantial withdrawal); C.P. v. Piscataway Twp. Bd. of Educ., 681 A.2d 105 (N.J. Super. Ct. App. Div. 1996) (New Jersey statute which exempted "pension funds" covered tax-qualified individual retirement accounts); Massey v. Casals, 2011 WL 1734066 (Tenn. Ct. App. May 3, 2011) (Tennessee law) (IRA accounts at issue in child support case are exempt from garnishment when withdrawal of funds possible but would involve substantial penalty); Lozano v. Lozano, 975 S.W.2d 63 (Tex. App. 1998) (Texas law) (individual retirement account was exempt, whether or not the source of funds, here a rollover from a former employer's plan, was exempt). *See also* Elias Bros. Restaurants v. Acorn Enters., 931 F. Supp. 930 (D. Mass. 1996) (Massachusetts law) (IRAs exempt only to extent deposits do not exceed statutory cap); *In re* Spradlin, 231 B.R. 254 (Bankr. E.D. Mich. 1999) (construing Michigan statutory exemption for "an" individual retirement account to allow debtor to exempt only one of his two individual retirement accounts); *In re* Outen, 220 B.R. 26 (Bankr. D.S.C. 1998) (South Carolina law) (individual retirement account was exempt, subject to

plans.[880] Some courts also extend this protection to other good faith private retirement plans, including annuities,[881]

"reasonable necessity" limitation, whether or not debtor had present right to payments); *In re* Francisco, 204 B.R. 799 (Bankr. M.D. Fla. 1996). *Cf.* Merrill Lynch Bus. Fin. Servs., Inc. v. Targan, 2008 WL 2858921 (D. Md. July 22, 2008) (Maryland law) (retirement account not SEP, because no employer contributions; individual retirement account exempt only up to amount of allowed contributions); *In re* Gurry, 253 B.R. 406 (Bankr. E.D. Va. 2000) (debtor who had both an ERISA plan and an individual retirement account was not entitled to Virginia's unlimited exemption for individual retirement account, and funds in exempt ERISA plan counted against individual retirement account exemption); *In re* Hasse, 246 B.R. 247 (Bankr. E.D. Va. 2000) (Virginia law allows unlimited exemption for individual retirement account only if debtor does not have employer-sponsored retirement plan established pursuant to certain sections of the Internal Revenue Code; plan that was similar but not identical to such plans did not bar exemption for individual retirement account). *But see* Schoonover v. Karr, 285 B.R. 695 (S.D. Ill. 2002) (Illinois law) (account not exempt because not tax-qualified), *aff'd*, 331 F.3d 575 (7th Cir. 2003); *In re* Sims, 241 B.R. 467 (Bankr. N.D. Okla. 1999) (Oklahoma law) (individual retirement account inherited from father was no longer a retirement planning tool so was not exempt). *But cf.* United States v. Infelise, 159 F.3d 300 (7th Cir. 1998) (individual retirement account governed by 26 U.S.C. § 408 could be subjected to forfeiture in criminal case); *In re* Malsch, 400 B.R. 584 (Bankr. N.D. Ohio 2008) (account into which widow placed life insurance proceeds did not restrict withdrawals so did not qualify for IRA exemption).

880 *See, e.g.*, *In re* Baker, 590 F.3d 1261 (11th Cir. 2009) (Keogh plan that complies with tax law is covered by Florida exemption); *In re* Ritter, 190 B.R. 323 (Bankr. N.D. Ill. 1995) (under Illinois statute, which exempted private plans "intended in good faith" to provide for retirement, Keogh and individual retirement accounts were exempt—even though debtor had made early withdrawals during period of unemployment and might do so again—when there was no evidence of lack of good faith at the time the plans were established). *But see In re* Sutton, 272 B.R. 802 (Bankr. M.D. Fla. 2002) (Keogh plan of solo practice realtor not exempt under Florida law); *In re* Kuraishi, 237 B.R. 172 (Bankr. C.D. Cal. 1999) (Keogh plan was "self-settled spendthrift trust" and thus not exempt under California law, when same person, a doctor, was employer, employee, and beneficiary).

881 *In re* Miller, 500 B.R. 578 (B.A.P. 8th Cir. 2013) (exempting annuity purchased with funds rolled over from tax-qualified IRA by debtor who was of retirement age); Warfield v. Alaniz, 2007 WL 4287838 (D. Ariz. Dec. 6, 2007) (annuity purchased with funds from debtor's individual retirement account was protected by Arizona exemption for individual retirement accounts); *In re* Pepmeyer, 273 B.R. 782 (N.D. Iowa 2002) ("individual retirement annuity" exempt under Iowa law); *In re* Delaney, 268 B.R. 57 (D. Vt. 2001) (remanding to determine whether annuity, payable at specific age or upon disability, is "payable on account of death, disability, retirement, or termination of employment" under Vermont law, and whether the funds are necessary for support of debtor); *In re* Kiceniuk, 2012 WL 4506597 (Bankr. D.N.J. Sept. 28, 2012) (plan exempt under 11 U.S.C. § 522(d)(10)(E) if it is a substitute for wages, which pays on account of age, and is needed for support; allowing exemption of variable annuity, purchased with funds rolled over from 401(k), with payout beginning at age 69; necessity shown when debtor was unable to work and only other income was Social Security); *In re* Woller, 483 B.R. 886 (Bankr. W.D. Wis. 2012) (annuity that qualified for tax deferral was exempt retirement plan); *In re* Vickers, 408 B.R. 131 (Bankr. E.D. Tenn. 2009) (annuity that was neither tax-qualified nor employment-related was exempted by Tenn. Code. Ann. § 26-2-111(1)(D); purchased with rollover from SEP-IRA variable annuity, and monthly payments would serve as "wage substitute" in retirement; underlying assets fully exempt, and monthly payments exempt to same extent as wages); *In re* Deem, 2007 WL 295437 (Bankr. N.D. Ohio Jan. 29, 2007) ("retirement annuity" offered by employer was exempt under Ohio provision for property exempt under nonbankruptcy federal law); *In re* Sforzo, 332 B.R. 294 (Bankr. N.D. Ohio 2005) (ERISA-qualified tax-sheltered annuity exempt under Ohio law); *In re* Vangen, 334 B.R. 241 (Bankr. W.D. Wis. 2005) (retirement-related annuities purchased with non-exempt funds exempt under Wisconsin law given no extrinsic evidence of fraud); *In re* Lynch, 321 B.R. 114 (Bankr. S.D.N.Y. 2005) (annuity exempt under New York law so far as needed for support); *In re* Bogue, 240 B.R. 742 (Bankr. E.D. Wis. 1999) (Wisconsin exemption for retirement plans protects annuities which comply with any section of the Internal Revenue Code); Goldenberg v. Sawczak, 791 So. 2d 1078 (Fla. 2001) (proceeds of annuity contract exempt under Florida law if there is a surrender penalty); Silliman v. Cassell, 738 S.E.2d 606 (Ga. 2013) (annuity was exempt substitute for wages; sixty-five-year-old debtor, who had been self-employed and had no access to employer plan, purchased annuity with single payment and chose stream of payments guaranteed for ten years); Cashio v. Tollin, 712 So. 2d 254 (La. Ct. App. 1998) (annuity was exempt under Louisiana law, whether or not purchased with tax-exempt funds). *See also In re* Henrickson, 277 B.R. 759 (B.A.P. 8th Cir. 2002) (annuities are exempt retirement plans only if contributions "tied to" employment, including self-employment, or come from exempt source). *But see In re* Simpson, 557 F.3d 1010 (9th Cir. 2009) (single-premium annuity was an investment, not a private retirement plan, under California law); Eilbert v. Pelican, 162 F.3d 523 (8th Cir. 1998) (annuity was not a "similar plan" within meaning of Iowa statute which exempted retirement plans when debtor had complete control over when and how payments would be made, plan was funded by single lump-sum payment by debtor when large personal injury judgment was imminent, and debtor chose to start receiving payments two months after purchase of the annuity), *aff'g* 212 B.R. 954 (B.A.P. 8th Cir. 1997); Huisinga v. Kemmerer (*In re* Kemmerer), 251 B.R. 50 (B.A.P. 8th Cir. 2000) (individual retirement annuity into which debtor rolled over 401(k) funds was not exempt under Iowa law that only covered individual retirement accounts); Ohio Farmers Ins. Co. v. Special Coatings, L.L.C., 2010 WL 4775630 (M.D. Tenn. Nov. 16, 2010) (annuity not a retirement plan; purchased with single payment, could be cashed out at will; no provisions re age, disability, among other things); Schoonover v. Karr, 285 B.R. 695 (S.D. Ill. 2002) (account not exempt because not tax-qualified), *aff'd*, 331 F.3d 575 (7th Cir. 2003); *In re* Watson, 2012 WL 8436264 (Bankr. E.D. Cal. Dec. 12, 2012) (California exemption protects only plans provided by employer or employee organization); *In re* Chen, 2011 WL 2358653 (Bankr. N.D. Cal. June 8, 2011) (California protects only plans provided by an employer or an employee organization; "independent retirement investments" such as the annuities here, are not exempt); *In re* Wolf, 2011 WL 1298277 (Bankr. N.D. Ill. Mar. 31, 2011) (subjective intent to use annuities for retirement not sufficient when annuities not tax-qualified); *In re* Hupton, 287 B.R. 438 (Bankr. N.D. Iowa 2002) (retirement annuity inherited from father not exempt; payments not on account of debtor's age, disability, or the like; Iowa does not exempt annuities; not a spendthrift trust because lump-sum distribution possible); *In re* Barnes, 275 B.R. 889 (Bankr. E.D. Cal. 2002) (annuity purchased with single lump sum not a retirement plan; plan requires gradual accumulation, also must either be provided by third party such as employer, or be tax-qualified self-employed plan); *In re* Collett, 253 B.R. 452 (Bankr. W.D. Mo. 2000) (Missouri exemption for annuity which pays out on account of illness, age, length of service, disability or death, did not protect annuity purchased to comply with testator's instructions that her nephew's inheritance should be paid out in increments); *In re* Bruce, 224 B.R. 505 (Bankr. M.D. Fla. 1998) (annual payments to lottery winner were not an exempt annuity under Florida law when state paid winnings from income from bonds purchased with income from ticket sales); *In re* Dunn, 215 B.R. 121 (Bankr. E.D. Mich. 1997), *supplemental op. at* 215 B.R. 848 (Bankr. E.D. Mich. 1997)

profit-sharing plans,[882] deferred compensation plans,[883] and other retirement funds.[884] States differ as to whether Roth IRAs are exempt.[885] One court has held that a "voluntary buy-out"

(annuity savings plan which was funded entirely by voluntary contributions of employee was not exempt under either federal or Michigan law). *But cf. In re* Martin, 297 B.R. 750 (8th Cir. 2003) (annuities exempted as "employee benefits" under Minnesota law, but only if funded with wages or other sums derived from employment, including self-employment, and payable on account of age, disability, illness, or length of service; not shown when annuity purchased with sale proceeds of farmland); *In re* Quinn, 327 B.R. 818 (W.D. Mich. 2005) (state university retirement plan was an exempt trust; strong anti-alienation language in both plan documents and state statute governing retirement system); *In re* LeClair, 461 B.R. 86 (Bankr. D. Mass. 2011) (tax-qualified retirement annuity not protected by Mass. Gen. Laws ch. 175, § 119A; statute requires that plan have anti-alienation clause that forbids "anticipation"; when debtor could access funds by paying a tax penalty, anticipation was allowed; noting that funds may be protected under another section of Massachusetts law protecting rollovers from qualified plans); *In re* Green, 2007 WL 1031677 (Bankr. E.D. Tenn. Apr. 2, 2007) (exemption for annuity payable on account of age, illness, length of service, and so forth, refers to product purchased over time to serve as substitute for wages upon retirement or disability; no exemption under Georgia law for annuity that funded structured settlement for wrongful death of debtor's minor son, upon whom debtor was never dependent, even though debtor was now disabled and annuity was only source of income); *In re* Thomas, 331 B.R. 798 (Bankr. W.D. Ark. 2005) (individual retirement account and annuity not exempt when they lacked requisite transfer restrictions); *In re* Ellis, 274 B.R. 782 (Bankr. S.D. Ill. 2002) (Illinois law; whole life insurance policy that provided for payment of annuity after age sixty-five was neither an annuity nor a retirement plan; annuity was one of several ways to cash in the policy, and plan was not tax-qualified); *In re* Rogers, 222 B.R. 348 (Bankr. S.D. Cal. 1998) ("life and health insurance annuity" that was not tax-qualified and was purchased with a single lump sum was not a retirement plan under California law).

882 *See, e.g., In re* Foellmi, 473 B.R. 905 (B.A.P. 8th Cir. 2012) (Minnesota exemption for employee benefit plans covered "limited partnership units" made available to long-term employees by employer's profit-sharing plan); *In re* Butler, 472 B.R. 786 (Bankr. W.D. Wis. 2012) (profit-sharing plan was a "similar plan or contract" covered by federal exemption; long-term employees could acquire "limited partnership units" and keep them upon retirement for age, disability or length of service; because debtor, a part-time cashier at a convenience store, was not an insider, plan need not be tax-qualified). *But see In re* Lowe, 252 B.R. 614 (W.D.N.Y. 2000) (profit sharing plan not exempt under New York law as pension or similar plan when the amount owed to employee did not depend on length of service, age, disability, or the like; not an exempt spendthrift trust, because employee could access funds as soon as employer declared it payable). *But cf.* Century Surety Co. v. 350 W.A., L.L.C., 2008 WL 2630959 (S.D. Cal. June 27, 2008) (to exempt profit-sharing plan under California law, must show both that plan was designed to comply with legal requirements for retirement plans and that funds were "treated in a manner consistent with use for retirement purposes"; not shown here).

883 *See, e.g., In re* Lawless, 2012 WL 2974759 (Bankr. E.D. Tenn. July 20, 2012) (deferred compensation plan, that paid on account of age, death, or disability not a retirement plan under Tennessee law, because it offered option of lump-sum payout); *In re* Maurer, 268 B.R. 335 (Bankr. W.D.N.Y. 2001) (state employees deferred compensation plan is a "similar plan" within meaning of New York exemption, if IRS has found the plan qualified under section 457), *aff'd*, 2002 WL 1012985 (W.D.N.Y. May 13, 2002); Dillabaugh v. Ellerton, 259 P.3d 550 (Colo. App. 2011) (Colorado's definition of retirement plan included executive's non-ERISA deferred compensation plan, which would make payments starting at age 65, in an amount based on salary and length of service). *But see In re* Madia, 294 B.R. 177 (Bankr. M.D. Fla. 2003) (Florida uses federal bankruptcy criteria for exempt retirement plans; deferred compensation pursuant to section 457 of Internal Revenue Code not exempt because this section not listed in bankruptcy exemption and compensation was not on account of age, disability, length of service, or the like). *But cf.* Segovia v. Schoenmann, 408 Fed. Appx. 61 (9th Cir. 2011) (long-term incentive compensation plan not exempt under federal or California law; compensation was received during employee's career, not deferred until retirement).

884 *In re* Spector, 2010 WL 4258260 (Bankr. E.D. Mo. Oct. 26, 2010) (gift annuity was exempt spendthrift trust; settlor donated money to university, on condition that it make monthly payments to settlor's long-term employee, beginning on her 60th birthday and continuing for life; former employee's rights were non-assignable); *In re* Gill, 2007 WL 2990564 (Bankr. D.D.C. Oct. 11, 2007) (thrift savings plan exempt under Dist. of Columbia law if tax-qualified); *In re* Reinhart, 267 P.3d 895 (Utah 2011) (Utah exemption for plans "described in" section 401(a) of the Internal Revenue Code protects a plan that substantially complies but is not tax-qualified; legislature did not intend for debtors to lose their entire retirement exemption because of technical defects). *Cf. In re* Ondrey, 1999 WL 409497 (W.D.N.Y. June 15, 1999) (American citizen who was employed in Canada could exempt employer-sponsored retirement plan under New York law, but retirement savings plan not exempt because debtor could withdraw funds at will). *But see In re* Rice, 478 B.R. 275 (E.D. Mich. 2012) (federal bankruptcy exemption did not protect cashier's check, purchased with lump-sum distribution from tax-qualified plan and kept in safe deposit box; exemption available only if funds in a tax-qualified account on petition date); *In re* Phillips, 218 B.R. 520 (N.D. Cal. 1998) (purported "private retirement plan" was not designed or used for retirement purposes within meaning of California exemption when it was informal, attempts to formalize it were made only when a large judgment was imminent, and owners retained control over the funds and used them for purposes not related to retirement); *In re* Bodeker, 2013 WL 2467975 (Bankr. D. Mont. June 2, 2013) (Montana retirement exemption did not cover buried gold and silver, alleged to be kept for retirement); *In re* Jokiel, 453 B.R. 743 (Bankr. N.D. Ill. 2011) (Illinois exemption for plan "intended in good faith to qualify as a retirement plan under applicable provisions of the Internal Revenue Code" did not protect "top hat" plan, which debtor knew from the start could not be tax-qualified; exemption was meant to protect employees if employer bungled in setting up or operating plan, or misinformed employee as to tax qualification); *In re* Arnold, 2010 WL 1416031 (Bankr. C.D. Ill. Mar. 31, 2010) (investment account not exempt under Illinois law; intent to save for retirement not sufficient when account not tax-qualified); *In re* Behnke, 2008 WL 4951975 (Bankr. D. Neb. Nov. 18, 2008) (Nebraska annuity exemption will not protect annuity purchased within three years before bankruptcy); *In re* Johnson, 274 B.R. 473 (Bankr. E.D. Mich. 2002) (brokerage account not exempt under Michigan law because not an individual retirement account); *In re* Selfe, 260 B.R. 463 (Bankr. E.D. Mo. 2001) (proceeds of Fed. Employees' Group Life Insurance policy are life insurance, not a "death benefit plan" exempt under Missouri law; life insurance not exempt); *In re* Handshaw, 198 B.R. 633 (Bankr. M.D. Fla. 1996) (debtor's interest in county retirement plan not exempt: state statute preempted by ERISA, and benefits were not within ERISA governmental unit exception, when benefits were provided by the National Association of Counties and not directly by the governmental unit; county's own deferred compensation plan was exempt). *But cf. In re* Davis, 2009 WL 982141 (Bankr. D. Kan. Mar. 23, 2009) (shares of stock, which employer allowed employee to purchase in exchange for unused vacation time, not exempt under 11 U.S.C. § 522(d)(10)(E) because not a "wage substitute").

885 *EXEMPT: In re* Vandeberg, 276 B.R. 581 (Bankr. E.D. Tenn. 2001) (Roth individual retirement account so similar to types of individual retirement accounts included in Tennessee statute that it was exempt

used by an employer to encourage early retirement was a "similar plan" within the meaning of a state exemption statute.[886]

If an exemption applies only to tax-qualified plans, the plan will become non-exempt if the funds are used in a transaction prohibited by tax law.[887] This issue may arise when a consumer, whose IRA is managed by an investment company, is required to sign a form agreement granting the company a lien on all the consumer's investments for any debt owed to the company. The Sixth Circuit has ruled that this agreement is not a prohibited transaction, so long as the consumer does not borrow from the company or engage in actions, such as trading on the margin, that create a risk of incurring debt.[888]

Inherited IRAs may also be exempt, at least if they meet the requirements for tax-qualification.[889] In bankruptcy, the

even before amendment to include Roths); Mexic v. Mexic, 808 So. 2d 685 (La. Ct. App. 2001) (Roth individual retirement account was a "tax-deferred arrangement" exempted by Louisiana statute even before amendment to specifically include Roths).

NON-EXEMPT: In re Razzano, 2010 WL 3075603 (Bankr. N.D. Cal. Aug. 4 2010) (Roth IRA not a retirement plan under California law; neither created by employer nor funded with taxable compensation).

886 *In re* Carlson, 192 B.R. 755 (Bankr. D. Idaho 1996) (exemption for pensions, profit sharing, "similar plans"). *See also In re* Murphy, 434 B.R. 67 (Bankr. W.D.N.Y. 2010) (voucher for purchase of new car, part of early retirement package offered when General Motors restructured, exempted as right to receive or property that is traceable to a payment in compensation for loss of future earnings); *In re* Gonsalves, 2010 WL 5342084 (Bankr. D. Mass. Dec. 21, 2010) (federal exemptions; severance package provided to downsized employees exempt as right to receive an unemployment benefit). *But see In re* Bartholomew, 214 B.R. 322 (Bankr. S.D. Ohio 1997) (severance pay, one year's salary paid to long-term employee whose job was being eliminated, was not a "pension, annuity or similar plan" within meaning of Ohio exemption when lump sum was offered on a one-time basis to small group of employees affected by downsizing).

887 *In re* Plunk, 481 F.3d 302 (5th Cir. 2007) (bankruptcy court could find plan non-exempt because no longer tax-qualified due to disqualifying events); *In re* Miller, 500 B.R. 578 (B.A.P. 8th Cir. 2013) (allowing exemption; yearly contribution limit does not apply to annuity purchased with funds rolled over from tax-qualified IRA by retirement-age debtor); Daniels v. Agin, 482 B.R. 1 (D. Mass. 2012) (profit sharing plan of one-man business not tax-qualified, notwithstanding IRS letter approving the form of the plan, because debtor engaged in prohibited transactions; denying exemption to IRAs into which plan funds were rolled over), *aff'd sub. nom.* Daniels v. Agin, 736 F.3d 70 (1st Cir. 2013); *In re* Bauman, 2014 WL 816407 (Bankr. N.D. Ill. Mar. 4, 2014) (Illinois exemption requires showing of "good faith attempt to comply with the Internal Revenue Code" in both establishment and operation of plan; not shown here when sole stockholder and sole employee did not pay self a regular salary and funded the plan with sums that were not "W-2" earnings); *In re* Gardner, 2013 WL 3804594 (Bankr. D. Colo. June 19, 2013) (plan not tax qualified because contributions exceeded statutory maximum and did not come from employer contributions); In *re* Rudd, 2013 WL 2684541 (Bankr. E.D.N.C. June 12, 2013) (debtor withdrew funds from IRA for living expenses but paid them back within sixty days; no prohibited transaction because tax law allows this transaction without consequences); *In re* Patrick, 411 B.R. 659 (Bankr. C.D. Cal. 2008) (individual retirement account lost tax qualification and federal exemption when funds rolled over more than once in one-year period); *In re* Hughes, 293 B.R. 528 (Bankr. M.D. Fla. 2003) (individual retirement account lost exempt status when debtor used funds for loan to his corporation; prompt repayment did not restore exemption); *In re* Marriage of LaMoure, 165 Cal. Rptr. 3d 417 (Cal. Ct. App. 2013) (plan lost California and federal exemptions when used for "secreting, shielding and illicitly funneling community property assets" during divorce; plan not being used for retirement purposes loses exemption); Aebig v. Cox, 2006 WL 1360504 (Mich. Ct. App. May 18, 2006) (debtor's self-directed individual retirement account lost status and exemption as a result of prohibited transaction, that is, lease of property to corporation owned by his wife); Nu-Way Energy Corp. v. Delp, 205 S.W.3d 667 (Tex. App. 2006) (tax qualification and exemption both lost because of complex commercial transaction involving release of personal guarantee of corporate debt). *See also In re* Jones, 2014 WL 1270093 (D. Neb. Mar. 26, 2014) (pension funds paid to estate and distributed to heirs not exempt; funds lost exemption when they lost tax-deferred status). *But see In re* Goldstein, 2011 WL 5909626 (Bankr. E.D.N.C. Sept. 23, 2011) (prohibited transaction not shown; debtor took large withdrawals from IRA to pay daily expenses but was old enough to do so without incurring tax penalty).

888 *In re* Daley, 717 F.3d 506 (6th Cir. 2013) (giving weight to IRS guidance that agreement is not prohibited transaction so long as client does not obtain extension of credit).

889 *EXEMPT: In re* Hamlin, 465 B.R. 863 (B.A.P. 9th Cir. 2012) (funds in IRA inherited from grandmother are "retirement funds," and new IRA into which funds were transferred is tax-qualified and exempt); *In re* Trawick, 497 B.R. 572 (Bankr. C.D. Cal. 2013) (inherited plan exempt under bankruptcy law if tax-qualified, but tax qualification not shown here; not exempt under California law because not payable on account of age, illness, among other factors); *In re* Seeling, 471 B.R. 320 (Bankr. D. Mass. 2012) (exempting IRA funded with proceeds of tax-deferred annuity inherited from relative); *In re* Thiem, 443 B.R. 832 (Bankr. D. Ariz. 2011) (IRA inherited from mother remains tax-qualified and is exempt under federal and Arizona exemptions for retirement funds; also exempt under Arizona provision for money payable upon the life of a deceased parent); *In re* LeClair, 2011 WL 5282605 (Bankr. D. Mass. Nov. 2, 2011) (widow inherited husband's IRA, placed it in rollover IRA, withdrew funds and purchased an annuity; annuity was exempt); *In re* Tabor, 433 B.R. 469 (Bankr. M.D. Pa. 2010) (tax-qualified inherited IRA exempt under both federal and Pennsylvania law), *aff'd*, 2010 WL 8914472 (M.D. Pa. Dec.2, 2010); *In re* Weilhammer, 2010 WL 3431465 (Bankr. S.D. Cal. Aug. 30, 2010) (IRA inherited from mother and tax qualification preserved); *In re* McClelland, 2008 WL 89901 (Bankr. D. Idaho Jan. 7, 2008) (broad language of Idaho retirement fund exemption—"any citizen of Idaho . . . any employee benefit plan"—exempted annuity purchased with proceeds of individual retirement account inherited from debtor's aunt).

NON-EXEMPT: In re Clark, 714 F.3d 559 (7th Cir. 2013) (inherited IRA not exempt retirement funds; noting differences in tax treatment of inherited IRAs and other IRAs), *cert. granted*, 134 S. Ct. 678 (2013); *In re* Jones, 2014 WL 1270093 (D. Neb. Mar. 26, 2014) (pension funds paid to estate and distributed to heirs not exempt; declining to reach issue, whether inherited IRAs exempt); *In re* Leonard, 2012 WL 1658294 (Bankr. N.D. Cal. May 11, 2012) (denying exemption for annuity inherited from mother; inherited plans may be exempt, but debtors who were not of retirement age could not show that purpose of plan was to accumulate income to provide for retirement); *In re* Klipsch, 435 B.R. 586 (Bankr. S.D. Ind. 2010) (inherited IRA, even if tax-qualified, not retirement plan under Indiana law); *In re* Ard, 435 B.R. 719 (Bankr. M.D. Fla. 2010) (Florida law; giving weight to the difference in tax consequences between inherited and personal IRAs); *In re* Chilton, 426 B.R. 612 (Bankr. E.D. Tex. 2010) (IRA inherited from mother and deposited in debtor's own IRA); *In re* Navarre, 332 B.R. 24 (Bankr. M.D. Ala. 2004) (Alabama law) (interest in individual retirement account inherited from mother not exempt because no longer tax-qualified; non-spouse beneficiary cannot roll over funds into own individual retirement account); *In re* Greenfield, 289 B.R. 146 (Bankr. S.D. Cal. 2003) (inherited retirement account from which federal exemption for tax-qualified inherited IRAs is available even in opt-out states.[890]

Pension and disability benefits awarded to the wage earner's former spouse or domestic partner may be protected the same as if paid to the wage earner.[891] But exemptions or anti-alienation provisions will generally not prevent an ex-spouse from claiming pension or retirement benefits pursuant to a divorce decree.[892]

State exemptions seek to balance the need for security in old age against the possible abuse of retirement accounts to shelter unreasonable amounts from creditors. Some statutes exempt retirement funds so far as "reasonably necessary" for the retiree's needs,[893] while others set a dollar cap on the

forty-one-year-old debtor was receiving payments not exempt under California law because not used for retirement purposes).

890 *In re* Stephenson, 2011 WL 6152960 (E.D. Mich. Dec. 12, 2011); Chilton v. Moser, 444 B.R. 548, 551 n.1 (E.D. Tex. 2011), *aff'd on other grounds*, 674 F.3d 486 (5th Cir. 2012); *In re* Kalso, 2011 WL 3678326 (Bankr. E.D. Mich. Aug. 19, 2011); *In re* Mathusa, 446 B.R. 601 (Bankr. M.D. Fla. 2011); *In re* Cutignola, 450 B.R. 445 (Bankr. S.D.N.Y. 2011); *In re* Johnson, 452 B.R. 804 (Bankr. W.D. Wash. 2011).

891 *In re* Metz, 225 B.R. 173 (B.A.P. 9th Cir. 1998) (former wife's share of husband's retirement plan, awarded to her at divorce, was exempt under both ERISA and California law); *In re* West, 507 B.R. 252 (Bankr. N.D. Ill. 2014) (debtor may exempt share of husband's retirement account, awarded but not yet transferred to her in divorce; transfer will be by qualified domestic relations order, enabling her to roll it over into another exempt form); *In re* Remia, 503 B.R. 6 (Bankr. D. Mass. 2013) (retirement funds transferred pursuant to separation agreement, which was not a qualified domestic relations order, exempt under 29 U.S.C. § 1056(d)(3)(H)(ii), (v), when law provides eighteen-month window to obtain qualified domestic relations order); *In re* Dzielak, 435 B.R. 538 (Bankr. N.D. Ill. 2010) (debtor whose divorce is pending may exempt share of husband's retirement account that may be awarded to her); *In re* Hartman, 345 B.R. 826 (Bankr. N.D. Ohio 2005) (Ohio individual retirement account exemption protects funds rolled over from ex-husband's plan as required by qualified domestic relations order because they are tax-qualified); *In re* Farmer, 295 B.R. 322 (Bankr. W.D. Wis. 2003) (retirement account awarded to wife by qualified domestic relations order was exempt under both ERISA's anti-alienation clause and Wisconsin exemption for retirement accounts); *In re* Seddon, 255 B.R. 815 (Bankr. W.D.N.C. 2000) (anti-alienation provision for federal civil service retirement benefits protects benefits granted to ex-wife by divorce decree); *In re* Lummer, 219 B.R. 510 (Bankr. S.D. Ill. 1998) (Illinois' broadly worded exemption for retirement benefits protects former wife's share of husband's military retirement pay); *In re* Cason, 211 B.R. 72 (Bankr. N.D. Fla. 1997) (anti-alienation provision of Florida's State Retirement System Act, which protects "benefits accrued to any person," exempts half-interest in benefits awarded to state employee's ex-spouse). *See also* Connor v. Seaside Nat'l Bank, 2014 WL 1255340 (Fla. Dist. Ct. App. Mar. 28, 2014) (Florida law; allowing exemption of annuities awarded to wife at divorce; although she was not yet the named annuitant, she was the beneficiary, because the divorce decree gave her the right to the proceeds). *But see* Deretich v. City of St. Francis, 128 F.3d 1209 (8th Cir. 1997) (Minnesota exemption for employee benefits does not protect disability insurance benefits which had been awarded to employee's ex-wife as part of divorce settlement); *In re* Wilbur, 126 F.3d 1218 (9th Cir. 1997) (Oregon exemption for retirement plans did not protect funds derived from exempt retirement plan, paid to former domestic partner pursuant to court judgment dividing property when partners separated); *In re* Anderson, 269 B.R. 27 (B.A.P. 8th Cir. 2001) (husband's interest in ex-wife's individual retirement account, awarded to him by divorce decree, not exempt retirement plan under Minnesota law, because his rights did not arise from employment); *In re* Ahmed, 2012 WL 4513771 (E.D. Mich. Sept. 29, 2012) (payment that divorce court ordered retirement fund administrator to pay to wife from husband's 401(k) plan as compensation for her equity in house after husband failed to pay was not exempt retirement funds); *In re* Yashura, 2012 WL 847752 (Bankr. N.D. Ohio Mar. 12, 2012) (no exemption for ex-wife's right to payment from husband as part of divorce, even though she intended to invest the money in an IRA and the award was intended to compensate her for a lack of retirement funds); *In re* Hageman, 260 B.R. 852 (Bankr. S.D. Ohio 2001) (Ohio's exemption for retirement plans protects only plan participant, not ex-spouse awarded interest in the plan); *In re* Thurman, 255 B.R. 730 (Bankr. M.D. Tenn. 2000) (retirement plans exempt under Tennessee law only if they are the debtor's plan, so proceeds of ex-husband's 401K, awarded to debtor in divorce, not exempt when plan was in husband's name only). *But cf. In re* Diener, 483 B.R. 196 (B.A.P. 9th Cir. 2012) (retirement account awarded to wife not exempt "alimony, support or separate maintenance" when separation agreement waived support rights; refusing to admit extrinsic evidence that wife chose to buy out support rights because of husband's unreliability with alimony).

892 Harmand v. Harmand, 931 So. 2d 18 (Ala. Civ. App. 2005) (federal civil service retirement benefits may be divided at divorce and Office of Personnel Management may be ordered to pay ex-spouse; here some of the benefits were separate property because were earned after marriage terminated, but couple had separation agreement, and party may bargain away separate property); *In re* Marriage of Drexler & Bruce, 315 P.3d 179 (Colo. App. 2013) (qualified domestic relations order exception to ERISA anti-alienation clause preempts any state statute that might have made retirement funds exempt from garnishment in divorce); Forrester v. Forrester, 953 A.2d 175 (Del. Super. Ct. 2008) (although Social Security benefits cannot be divided at divorce, police pension that substitutes for Social Security can be; anti-alienation clause of state pension statute narrower than that of Social Security Act); Erb v. Erb, 747 N.E.2d 230 (Ohio 2001) (anti-alienation provision in police and fire fighters' pension fund did not bar court-ordered payments directly to ex-wife, as divorce decree gave wife property interest in pension; statute has since been amended to expressly permit direct payments). *But see* Smith v. Mo. Local Employees Retirement Sys., 235 S.W.3d 578 (Mo. Ct. App. 2007) (specific statute creating state employees' pension system allowed garnishment for child support but did not mention spousal support; notwithstanding general statute providing that no property was exempt as to spousal maintenance, pension not garnishable for spousal maintenance). *See generally* § 12.2.8.3, *supra* (special exemption rules for domestic relations obligations).

893 *In re* Davis, 323 B.R. 732 (B.A.P. 9th Cir. 2005) (individual retirement account and Keogh not reasonably necessary for support within meaning of California exemption when debtor expected to receive distribution of at least $200,000 pursuant to divorce decree); Premier Capital, Inc. v. Decarolis (*In re* Decarolis), 259 B.R. 467 (B.A.P. 1st Cir. 2001) (if retirement plan itself is tax-qualified, it is exempt under New Hampshire law, even if certain contributions exceed tax exempt amounts); *In re* Hamo, 233 B.R. 718 (B.A.P. 6th Cir. 1999) (fifty-four-year-old debtor with heart condition allowed to exempt only $20,000 of $96,000 individual retirement account under Ohio law, when debtor was adequately supported by his wife); *In re* Spenler, 212 B.R. 625 (B.A.P. 9th Cir. 1997) (individual retirement account not reasonably necessary for fifty-five-year-old unmarried doctor's support within meaning of California exemption when other retirement funds would provide him over $5000/month after retirement and his current earnings were sufficient to build up significant retirement fund before retirement); Straitshot Commc'ns, Inc. v. Telekenex, Inc., 2012 WL 4105125 (N.D. Cal. Sept. 17, 2012) (IRAs exempt so far as needed for support; burden on debtor to show necessity; denying exemption because financial statement was inadequate); Doe v. Manson, 773 F. Supp. 2d 183 (D. Me. 2011) (Maine exempts retirement funds as

exemption.[894] These limits may create a hardship for long-term employees who lose their jobs and must roll over substantial sums from their former employer's pension fund into an individual retirement account. State courts have reached differing conclusions on the question of whether to treat rollovers as simply transfers from one exempt form to another[895]

needed for support; here approving increase in installment payments after judgment creditor showed that debtor was spending excessive amount to lease luxury car); Walsh v. McMurry, 2006 WL 2422583 (W.D. Pa. Aug. 18, 2006) (articulating criteria for determining whether individual retirement account needed for support of debtor or dependents and remanding for fact finding on that issue); *In re* Patrick, 411 B.R. 659 (Bankr. C.D. Cal. 2008) (must consider present and anticipated expenses, age, health, ability to work, other assets, ability to save for retirement, and life expectancy; debtor here allowed to exempt entire amount under federal bankruptcy law); *In re* Booth, 331 B.R. 233 (Bankr. W.D. Pa. 2005) (individual retirement account and annuity both needed for support when husband was disabled, wife's job was low-paying, and husband's disability payments would end when he qualified for Social Security); *In re* Guikema, 329 B.R. 607 (Bankr. S.D. Ohio 2005) (finding tax-sheltered annuity not necessary for support in light of present and future income); *In re* Lynch, 321 B.R. 114 (Bankr. S.D.N.Y. 2005) (New York exempts any annuity so far as needed for support; semi-retired lawyer who received large fee in the form of an annuity could exempt proceeds, which were a "significant part" of his monthly budget); *In re* Rosen, 318 B.R. 166 (Bankr. D. Neb. 2004) (tax-qualified individual retirement account, into which debtor never deposited more than the permitted $2000/year, exempt so far as needed for support); *In re* Bashara, 293 B.R. 216 (Bankr. D. Neb. 2003) (tax-qualified individual retirement accounts exempt so far as needed for support; when trustee failed to raise issue, individual retirement account fully exempt); *In re* Conkle, 275 B.R. 530 (Bankr. S.D. Ohio 2002) (denying exemption for tax-deferred annuity in light of debtors' expenses, ability to keep working until age sixty-five, and amount of Social Security and pensions to be received, even though sixty-year-old husband is unemployed and fifty-nine-year-old wife has health problems); *In re* Roselle, 274 B.R. 486 (Bankr. S.D. Ohio 2002) (benefits from private disability policy are exempt only as needed for support; court scrutinizes debtor's lifestyle, concludes that disabled debtor can move from house to apartment and does not need long-term care insurance); *In re* Cluckey, 221 B.R. 192 (Bankr. N.D. Ohio 1998) (entire $23,000 retirement account was "reasonably necessary" for fifty-four-year-old debtor of limited earning power, with no resources for retirement); *In re* Parker, 219 B.R. 972 (Bankr. S.D. Ohio 1998) ($20,000 retirement account was "reasonably necessary" for sixty-seven-year-old man with significant health problems, but $34,000 retirement account was not reasonably necessary for fifty-eight-year-old woman who was employed despite health problems, had an ERISA-qualified plan at work, and could continue contributing to that plan for a number of years); *In re* Hoppes, 202 B.R. 595 (Bankr. N.D. Ohio 1996) (allowing couple in mid-fifties to exempt $75,000 of a $150,000 individual retirement account when husband had substantial earnings but was close to retirement and had significant health problems, but some of their expenses were not "reasonably necessary"); *In re* Webb, 189 B.R. 144 (Bankr. S.D. Ohio 1995) (allowing fifty-two-year-old debtor to exempt all of individual retirement account as reasonably necessary for support in retirement, when her ability to save for retirement was limited and average Social Security payment would fall far short of her expenses); *In re* Bates, 176 B.R. 104 (Bankr. D. Me. 1994) (individual retirement account could be "necessary for debtor's support," even though debtor was still under fifty-nine-and-a-half years of age; allowing fifty-year-old unemployed debtor living in economically "unpromising" area to keep entire $18,000 individual retirement account); McMullan v. Haycock, 54 Cal. Rptr. 3d 660 (Cal. Ct. App. 2007) (private pension plans fully exempt; individual retirement accounts exempt so far as needed for support); Citizens' Nat'l Bank v. Foster, 668 N.E.2d 1236 (Ind. 1996) (exemption for individual retirement accounts, which were limited by federal tax law, met state constitutional requirement that exemptions be reasonable, but exemption for life insurance naming the insured's spouse as beneficiary, which was not limited in amount, was questionable; debtor must show "reasonable necessity" of amount claimed); Steelstone Indus. v. McCrum, 785 A.2d 1256 (Me. 2001) (to claim exemption, debtor must make prima facie case that individual retirement account necessary for support); Associated Bank v. Twaiten, 2007 WL 2245756 (Minn. Ct. App. Aug. 7, 2007) (disability insurance exempt so far as needed for support; "basic necessities" only, not accustomed standard of living). *See also* Estate of Jones by Blume v. Kvamme, 529 N.W.2d 335 (Minn. 1995) (exemption for individual retirement accounts and certain employee benefits that had no limit on the amount and no reference to the needs of the debtor and family violated Minnesota constitutional provision requiring "reasonable exemptions").

894 *See* Elliot & Callan, Inc. v. Crofton, 2009 WL 3297506 (D. Minn. Oct. 13, 2009) (funds in federally exempt ERISA account must be counted in applying Minnesota cap; if sum in ERISA account exceeds cap, no state exemption for other retirement funds); Abbate v. Spear, 289 B.R. 62 (E.D. Va. 2003) (IRAs exempt insofar as needed to provide $17,500 per year income; if debtor has both individual retirement account and ERISA pension, ERISA must be considered in determining amount of income available); *In re* Cathcart, 203 B.R. 599 (Bankr. E.D. Va. 1996) (holding most of debtor's individual retirement account exempt under Virginia exemption for retirement accounts sufficient to provide a benefit of $17,500 per year for life starting at age sixty-five). *See also In re* Bissell, 255 B.R. 402 (E.D. Va. 2000) (Virginia debtor had individual retirement account, simplified employee pension, and ERISA pension; Virginia cap cannot be applied to ERISA, and amount in ERISA plan may not be considered in applying cap to other plans); *In re* Malsch, 400 B.R. 584 (Bankr. N.D. Ohio 2008) (annuity purchased with lump sum from deceased husband's life insurance was exempt as an individual retirement annuity, but since it was funded with life insurance proceeds rather than through a rollover the exemption was capped at the amount of permitted annual contributions); *In re* Hawkinson, 222 B.R. 334 (Bankr. D. Minn. 1998) (only non-ERISA plans, not plans that are independently exempt due to ERISA, should be included in determining whether their value exceeds statutory cap); *In re* Craig, 545 N.W.2d 764 (N.D. 1996) (limitation of $100,000 per item, $200,000 total applied to life insurance policies, individual retirement accounts, Keoghs and simplified employee pensions; this was reasonable within meaning of the state constitution, which would bar an unlimited exemption).

895 State Farm Mut. Auto. Ins. Co. v. Lincow, 2010 WL 4909582 (E.D Pa. Nov. 30, 2010) (exemption survived when debtor could trace funds through complicated series of rollovers, and creditor could not show any prohibited transaction), *objections to magistrate's ruling overruled in part and sustained in part*, 792 F. Supp. 2d 806 (E.D. Pa. 2011) (burden of proof is on debtor to show tax qualification; affirming that one account was tax-qualified but remanding to allow trial court to apply correct burden of proof as to second account); Bayerische Hypo- und Vereinsbank AG v. DiGiorgio, 902 N.Y.S.2d 85 (N.Y. App. Div. 2010) (funds rolled over from employer-provided retirement account into IRA remained exempt; no evidence that second IRA funded from any non-exempt source). *See In re* Groff, 234 B.R. 153 (Bankr. M.D. Fla. 1999) (funds rolled over from one tax-exempt retirement plan to another are exempt); *In re* Allen, 228 B.R. 132 (Bankr. W.D. Pa. 1998) (transfer of retirement funds from one brokerage house to another was not a "contribution" when tax-exempt status of funds did not change); *In re* Hickox, 215 B.R. 257 (Bankr. M.D. Fla. 1997) (Florida law exempts individual retirement account, which was funded with money "traceable to" debtor's 401(k) plan, even though this rollover was circuitous); McMullan v. Haycock, 54 Cal. Rptr. 3d 660 (Cal. Ct. App. 2007) (funds rolled over from pension plan to individual retirement account retained full exemption so far as needed for support); Pauk

or as new contributions to the individual retirement account.[896] Many state legislatures have recently addressed the protection of retirement accounts, so practitioners should be certain that they have the latest version of their state statute.

One court held that an employee's cause of action against an employer who had mismanaged a Keogh plan so that it lost its exempt status, was itself exempt by analogy to the exemption for funds which compensate for the loss or destruction of other exempt property.[897] When a trial court erroneously ordered the turnover of a retirement account and the appellate court ordered the funds returned, the exemption survived in the lawyers' trust account in which the funds were being held.[898] As with other exempt property, retirement funds may be vulnerable to garnishment for family support obligations,[899] criminal fines or restitution,[900] and delinquent taxes.[901]

The Supreme Court has ruled that state laws that single out Employee Retirement Income Security Act (ERISA) benefits for special protections are preempted by ERISA.[902] While this decision dealt with an employee welfare plan, not an employee pension plan, it interpreted an ERISA preemption provision that is equally applicable to both. On the other hand, an exemption law that is generally applicable to both ERISA and non-ERISA benefits will not be preempted if the court concludes that it has only a tenuous, remote, or peripheral connection

---

v. Pauk, 648 N.Y.S.2d 134 (N.Y. App. Div. 1996) (statutory exemption for individual retirement accounts applies to all individual retirement accounts whether funded by rollover from employer's plan or by debtor's own money); 415 E. 52d St. Assocs. v. Oppenheimer & Co., 638 N.Y.S.2d 300 (N.Y. App. Div. 1996) (individual retirement account created by rollover from qualified profit sharing plan is exempt); Chapman v. Wells, 557 N.W.2d 725 (N.D. 1996) (when 401(k), which was exempted by ERISA without limitation on amount, was rolled over into an individual retirement account, blanket exemption was lost, but North Dakota law exempted up to $100,000, plus additional amounts necessary for the support of the North Dakota resident and resident's dependents). *See also In re* Richey, 2011 WL 4485900 (B.A.P. 9th Cir. Aug. 8, 2011) (profit-sharing plan from which funds were rolled over into IRA annuities was tax-qualified; declining to reach question of whether recent changes in Arizona law would make the annuities exempt even if it were not); Straitshot Commc'ns, Inc. v. Telekenex, Inc., 2012 WL 4105125 (N.D. Cal. Sept. 17, 2012) (401(k) funds fully exempt, IRAs exempt so far as needed for support; funds rolled over from 401(k) to IRA retain full exemption, but debtor here did not meet burden of showing traceability); Warfield v. Alaniz, 2007 WL 4287838 (D. Ariz. Dec. 6, 2007) (annuity purchased with funds from debtor's individual retirement account is protected by Arizona exemption for individual retirement accounts); *In re* Pepmeyer, 273 B.R. 782 (N.D. Iowa 2002) ("individual retirement annuity," funded with rollover from individual retirement account, a $2000 inheritance, and $2000 per year contributions from debtor, is exempt under Iowa law); *In re* Sunstrom, 2012 WL 5305807 (Bankr. D. Md. Oct. 26, 2012) (bank account contained proceeds of tax-qualified retirement account that had not been rolled over; funds remained exempt); *In re* LeClair, 2011 WL 5282605 (Bankr. D. Mass. Nov. 2, 2011) (widow inherited husband's IRA, placed it in rollover IRA, withdrew funds and purchased an annuity; annuity was exempt); *In re* Mooney, 248 B.R. 391 (Bankr. C.D. Cal. 2000) (when debtor rolled over funds from fully-exempt ERISA-qualified employer plan to private individual retirement account which is exempt only "to the extent necessary for the support of debtor and dependents," the lesser exemption applied). *But see In re* Roberts, 2005 WL 1924180 (Bankr. M.D. La. Aug. 10, 2005) (no exemption for annuity purchased with funds rolled over from 401(k); Louisiana exempts funds rolled over from one 401(k) to another, or one annuity to another, but not from 401(k) to annuity or vice versa).

896 *In re* Barshak, 106 F.3d 501 (3d Cir. 1997) (when debtor who lost job after fifteen years rolled over entire contents of ERISA pension into individual retirement account, Pennsylvania law required rollover to be treated as "contribution" subject to $15,000/year limitation); *In re* Goldman, 192 B.R. 1 (D. Mass. 1996) (Massachusetts statute limiting exemption for funds "deposited in" retirement accounts within five years before bankruptcy applied to funds rolled over into individual retirement account from exempt employee pension fund). *Cf.* Phillips v. Bottoms, 260 B.R. 393 (E.D. Va. 2000) (ERISA anti-alienation provision does not protect funds after rollover into individual retirement account, but Virginia exemption will protect as much as is needed to provide annual income of $17,500 at retirement).

897 State Farm Life Ins. Co. v. Swift (*In re* Swift), 129 F.3d 792 (5th Cir. 1997). *See also In re* Alam, 359 B.R. 142 (B.A.P. 6th Cir. 2006) (bank, money market and mutual fund accounts, traceable to settlement of ERISA action against insurer who wrongfully terminated disability benefits, were "benefits paid under a policy of sickness or accident insurance" within meaning of Ohio exemption). *But see In re* Pellegrini, 467 B.R. 117 (Bankr. W.D. Mich. 2012) (debtor rolled over funds from exempt retirement account into self-directed IRA, lost them to investment fraud, recovered a judgment against the fraudster and deposited the proceeds in a bank account; not exempt because funds were not in a tax-qualified account on petition date). *But cf.* Helfman v. GE Group Life Assurance Co., 489 Fed. Appx. 112 (6th Cir. 2012) (attorney fees awarded to insured who had successfully sued insurer who wrongfully denied disability benefits were not exempt benefits).

898 *In re* Davis, 403 B.R. 914 (Bankr. M.D. Fla. 2009). *See also In re* Sutton-Robinson, 472 B.R. 77 (Bankr. D. Ariz. 2012) (funds mistakenly transferred out of IRA, as result of bookkeeping error by brokerage firm, and returned to IRA when mistake discovered did not lose exemption). *But see In re* Pink, 2012 WL 1655972 (N.D. Ill. May 10, 2012) (funds withdrawn from self-directed retirement account and deposited in lawyers' trust account lost exemption when withdrawn; distinguishing cases involving Workers Compensation or similar benefits).

899 *See, e.g., In re* Crum, 414 B.R. 103 (Bankr. N.D. Tex. 2009) (tax-qualified retirement plans, unavailable to ordinary creditors, could be reached by ex-wife for family support arrears); Ventura Cnty. Dep't of Child Support Servs. v. Brown, 11 Cal. Rptr. 3d 489 (Cal. Ct. App. 2004) (spendthrift trust, exempt as to ordinary creditors, may be reached for delinquent family support); Siegal v. Siegal, 700 So. 2d 414 (Fla. Dist. Ct. App. 1997) (court could consider amount in ex-spouse's individual retirement account, generally exempt under Florida law, in determining whether ex-spouse could afford to pay sum required to purge contempt for non-payment of domestic relations obligation); Duke v. Duke, 675 A.2d 822 (R.I. 1996) (statute forbidding attachment of police and firefighters' pensions did not bar family court from ordering withdrawal of pension funds for child support arrearages).

900 *See generally* § 12.2.8.2, *supra* (inapplicability of exemptions to federal restitution).

901 *See* § 12.2.8.2, *supra* (Internal Revenue Service and other federal debts).

902 Mackey v. Lanier Collection Agency & Serv., Inc., 486 U.S. 825, 830, 108 S. Ct. 2182, 100 L. Ed. 2d 836 (1988). *See also* Dist. of Columbia v. Greater Wash. Bd. of Trade, 506 U.S. 125, 113 S. Ct. 580, 121 L. Ed. 2d 513 (1992) (state law that referred to ERISA plans, albeit without using word "ERISA," is preempted); *In re* DiGiulio, 303 B.R. 144 (Bankr. N.D. Ohio 2003) (simplified employee pension plan not exempted by ERISA anti-alienation clause, and Ohio law that would have exempted it is preempted by ERISA); Community Bank Henderson v. Noble, 552 N.W.2d 37 (Minn. Ct. App. 1996) (finding Minnesota exemption statute preempted even though it did not refer specifically to ERISA plans).

to ERISA plans.[903] In addition, if a state enacted an exemption for ERISA plans when it opted out of the federal bankruptcy exemptions, courts have held that the exemption is not preempted.[904]

Exemptions for pensions and retirement plans may continue after the benefits are paid out.[905] The federal cap on the amount of a wage garnishment applies to periodic payments from a pension fund, although possibly not to the corpus of the fund to the extent that the retiree has the right to cash out the fund.[906]

12.9.2 Insurance Benefits and Policies

Almost every state exempts a certain amount of insurance benefits from creditors.[907] States vary widely, however, as to

903 Dist. of Columbia v. Greater Wash. Bd. of Trade, 506 U.S. 125, 113 S. Ct. 580, 583 n.1, 121 L. Ed. 2d 513 (1992); Mackey v. Lanier Collection Agency & Serv., Inc., 486 U.S. 825, 830, 108 S. Ct. 2182, 100 L. Ed. 2d 836 (1988) (general law allowing garnishment not preempted; because ERISA itself does not prohibit garnishment of employee welfare benefits, they may be garnished). *See also* Standard Ins. Co. v. Saklad, 849 P.2d 1150 (Or. Ct. App. 1993) (state law of general applicability not preempted even though it exempted ERISA welfare plan benefits that ERISA itself did not exempt).

904 *In re* Schlein, 8 F.3d 745 (11th Cir. 1993) (Florida exemption statute, which refers to provisions of Internal Revenue Code that designate ERISA-qualified plans, would be preempted but is saved because it was enacted as part of state's opt-out of federal bankruptcy exemptions); *In re* Dyke, 943 F.2d 1435, 1446–50 (5th Cir. 1991) (state law exempting right to receive payments under any stock bonus, pension, profit sharing, or similar plan refers to ERISA plans by description, so would be preempted but is saved because state adopted it when it opted out of federal bankruptcy exemptions); *In re* Tomlin, 315 B.R. 439 (Bankr. E.D. Mich. 2004) (Michigan individual retirement account exemption not preempted because enacted as part of bankruptcy opt-out).

905 *In re* Anderson, 410 B.R. 289 (Bankr. W.D. Mo. 2009) (exemption for federal civil service retirement survives deposit into bank account); *In re* Cook, 406 B.R. 770 (Bankr. S.D. Ohio 2009) (veterans' benefits, Ohio public employees' disability benefits, and tax refund resulting from overpayment of tax on such benefits remain exempt in a bank account, so long as traceable); *In re* Meyer, 211 B.R. 203 (Bankr. E.D. Va. 1997) (exempt military retirement pay remains exempt when directly deposited in Navy Federal Credit Union but not when transferred to debtor's non-special purpose checking account in another institution); *In re* Ryzner, 208 B.R. 568 (Bankr. M.D. Fla. 1997) (former police officer's disability payments remain exempt when deposited in bank account, so long as they remain traceable); *In re* Bresnahan, 183 B.R. 506 (Bankr. S.D. Ohio 1995) (retirement pension, exempt under Ohio law so far as reasonably necessary for the support of debtor and dependents, remains exempt when deposited in checking account); Dowling v. Chicago Options Assocs., Inc., 847 N.E.2d 741 (Ill. App. Ct. 2006) (401(k) funds remain exempt after payout if "periodic payments for support" but not if "lump sum available for investment"); J.M. v. Hobbs, 797 N.W.2d 227 (Neb. 2011) (statute authorizing state police retirement benefits makes them exempt after payment to debtor; no equitable exception for tort judgment arising from serious crime). *But see* Hoult v. Hoult, 373 F.3d 47 (1st Cir. 2004) (ERISA does not exempt funds in hands of beneficiary; anti-alienation clause not violated by court order requiring judgment debtor to deposit all his income, including ERISA funds, in one bank account, from which he could withdraw only court-approved sum for monthly expenses); *In re* Carbaugh, 278 B.R. 512 (B.A.P. 10th Cir. 2002) (investment account containing only distribution from exempt ERISA account not exempt; benefits lost exempt status when distributed; state exemption for benefits "payable from" retirement account lost when benefits paid); *In re* Gordon, 2013 WL 5763314 (Bankr. D. Colo. Oct. 24, 2013) (Colorado exemption for funds "held in or payable from . . ." retirement account lost when funds withdrawn and placed in savings account); *In re* Bridges, 2013 WL 1344572 (Bankr. D. Colo. Apr. 2, 2013) (IRA funds lose exemption when withdrawn from IRA and placed in bank account); *In re* Driskell, 2008 WL 4670995 (Bankr. S.D. Ill. Oct. 17, 2008) (funds cashed out of individual retirement account lose exemption if not rolled over into another qualified plan); *In re* McDonald, 2003 WL 23211570 (Bankr. M.D.N.C. Sept. 27, 2003) (funds in ERISA plan lose exemption when paid to beneficiary; funds borrowed from plan and deposited in credit union not exempt, so credit union could set off account); *In re* McCollum, 287 B.R. 750 (Bankr. E.D. Mo. 2002) (Missouri exemption protects only "right to receive" retirement funds; exemption lost when debtor who lost job cashed in her retirement fund, paid off bills with part of proceeds, and then established individual retirement account with the remainder); Forys v. Forys, 2010 WL 199695 (Ariz. Ct. App. Jan. 21, 2010) (allowing garnishment of account containing state retirement funds; funds lost exemption when disbursed to retiree); Briceno v. Briceno, 2007 WL 4146280 (Tenn. Ct. App. Nov. 21, 2007) (ERISA exemption ends once funds are disbursed, so family court may impose constructive trust on pension payments after their payment). *But cf. In re* Johnson, 2009 WL 3763709 (Bankr. E.D. Va. Nov. 6, 2009) (Virginia law; funds cashed out from exempt federal Thrift Savings Plan, deposited first in regular checking account, then in "segregated" account, lost exemption because accounts lacked any restriction on alienation); *In re* Carlson, 2009 WL 2589161 (Bankr. D. Idaho Aug. 20, 2009) (funds withdrawn from 401k as "hardship withdrawal" and placed in bank account non-exempt; exemption survives only if funds rolled over into another tax-qualified plan or distributed on account of age, illness, or length of service); *In re* Crum, 414 B.R. 103 (Bankr. N.D. Tex. 2009) (funds rolled over from tax-qualified account into another account, which debtor had been advised—incorrectly—was also tax-qualified, lost exemption); *In re* Cobb, 231 B.R. 236 (Bankr. D.N.J. 1999) (funds from ERISA-qualified thrift plan lost exemption when withdrawn and deposited in regular checking account, when debtor had no intention of rolling them over into another exempt plan). *See generally* § 12.6.2, *supra*.

906 *See* § 12.4.1.4.2, *supra*.

907 *See, e.g., In re* Payne, 323 B.R. 723 (B.A.P. 9th Cir. 2005) (criteria for deciding whether an annuity is exempt life insurance or a non-exempt investment under California law); *In re* Kennedy, 336 B.R. 600 (B.A.P. 10th Cir. 2005) (table, text at 2005 WL 2662328) (Colo. Rev. Stat. § 10-7-106 exemption applicable only when life insurance policy or annuities contain anti-alienation provisions); *In re* Dean, 470 B.R. 643 (Bankr. M.D. Ga. 2012) (Georgia' bankruptcy-only exemptions, which cap amount of insurance exemption, are exclusive; unlimited exemption found in Insurance Code not applicable in bankruptcy); *In re* Miller, 370 B.R. 914 (Bankr. D. Minn. 2007) (when couple owned several insurance policies, Minnesota law allows exemption of only one policy per spouse, even though total amount of policies less than exemption cap); *In re* Ashley, 317 B.R. 352 (Bankr. C.D. Ill. 2004) (history of Illinois's "convoluted" insurance exemption provisions; allowing widow to exempt proceeds without showing of need); Angell v. Angell, 791 N.W.2d 530 (Minn. 2010) (Servicemembers' Group Life Insurance benefits are exempt under statute similar to Social Security Anti-Assignment provision and cannot be apportioned by divorce court). *But see In re* Valentine, 2009 WL 3336081 (Bankr. D.N.H. Oct. 14, 2009) (lump-sum disability insurance settlement not exempt; debtor sought exemption pursuant to N.H. Rev. Stat. Ann. § 167:75, which exempts only public assistance); *In re* Besser, 356 B.R. 531 (Bankr. D. Colo. 2006) (Colorado exempts life insurance but not annuities; statute forbidding beneficiaries to encumber, among other things, benefits in hands of issuer is not an exemption statute, and even if it were would not protect against debts of owner

both the amount and the scope of their insurance exemptions. Some cap the proceeds or the periodic payment that is exempt.[908] Indiana courts, construing the exemption in accordance with a state constitutional requirement of "reasonable" exemptions, hold that only the amount needed to afford the necessities of life is exempt.[909] Other state statutes explicitly impose this limitation.[910] Life insurance proceeds are *usually* exempt as to the insured's debts but may be non-exempt, or exempt only as needed for support, for debts of the beneficiary.[911]

---

of annuity); *In re* Selfe, 260 B.R. 463 (Bankr. E.D. Mo. 2001) (life insurance not exempt in Missouri). *But cf.* Milligan v. Trautmen, 496 F.3d 366 (5th Cir. 2007) (sum received for prepetition surrender and cancellation of insurance policy not exempt); *In re* Andrews, 301 B.R. 211 (Bankr. N.D. Ohio 2003) (annuities "upon the life of any person" are fully exempt under Ohio law, but they must serve same purpose as life insurance, that is, compensate the beneficiary for death of insured and be worth more in hands of beneficiary; not shown when, in case of retiree's early death, beneficiary received same payments as would have gone to retiree). *See generally* Appx. G, *infra* (summarizing each state's exemption laws).

908 Mass. Gen. Laws ch. 175, § 110A. *See* Liberty Mut. Ins. Co. v. Rosenthal, 204 F. Supp. 2d 140 (D. Mass. 2002) ($400/week cap on disability insurance benefits applies to aggregate amount, not to each policy; debtor with income from four disability policies could exempt $400 not $1600).

909 Citizens Nat'l Bank v. Foster, 668 N.E.2d 1236 (Ind. 1996) (insurance exemption, construed to avoid unconstitutionality, exempts only the amount needed to afford "the necessities of life"; creditor has burden of showing that claimed exemption is unreasonable). *See also In re* Stinnett, 465 F.3d 309 (7th Cir. 2006) (Indiana exemption for 100% of disability insurance benefits must be construed to exempt only enough to provide "the necessary comforts of life," as state constitution mandates reasonable exceptions); *In re* Bannourah, 201 B.R. 954 (Bankr. S.D. Ind. 1996) (state insurance policy exemption, construed so as to avoid state constitutional problem, exempts amount "required to afford the necessities of life"; allowing thirty-eight-year-old widow, with limited earning ability and a four-year-old son, to keep $200,000).

910 *See, e.g., In re* Morehead, 283 F.3d 199 (4th Cir. 2002) (West Virginia law) (payments from private disability insurance policy exempt only as needed for support of debtor); *In re* Walck, 459 B.R. 208 (Bankr. M.D. Pa. 2011) (insurance proceeds reasonably necessary for support of sixty-seven-year-old widow; giving weight to her age and fact that she earned her living by manual labor as a housekeeper; high mortgage payment not unreasonable, when trustee provided no evidence of appropriate alternative housing); *In re* Tooker, 174 B.R. 33 (Bankr. D. Vt. 1994) (allowing sixty-two-year-old widow to keep entire amount, about $130,000; factors include age, health, earning ability, special needs, other assets); Sanders v. Sanders, 711 A.2d 124 (Me. 1998) (income from disability policy is exempt only insofar as reasonably necessary for debtor's support); Associated Bank v. Twaiten, 2007 WL 2245756 (Minn. Ct. App. Aug. 7, 2007) (disability insurance exempt so far as needed for "basic necessities" only, not accustomed standard of living; must consider present and future needs, based on age, employment, and general health); J.P. Morgan Case Bank v. Saedi, 2011 WL 683886 (Ohio Ct. App. Feb. 24, 2011) (unpublished) (entire amount of lump-sum settlement with disability insurer exempt; debtor was totally disabled and presented evidence of expenses). *But see In re* Bird, 288 B.R. 546 (Bankr. C.D. Ill. 2002) (widow could fully exempt proceeds of late husband's life insurance, regardless of need for support).

911 Plastipak Packaging, Inc. v. DiPasquale, 75 Fed. Appx. 86 (3d Cir. 2003) (Pennsylvania law) (insurance policy naming spouse as beneficiary is exempt as to debts of insured even if purchased with intent to hinder creditors); Ohio Farmers Ins. Co. v. Special Coatings, L.L.C., 2010 WL 4775630 (M.D. Tenn. Nov. 16, 2010) (Florida law) (life insurance proceeds not exempt as to debts of beneficiary); *In re* Stilwell, 321 B.R. 471 (C.D. Ill. 2005) (applying principle of liberal construction and holding that proceeds of deceased spouse's life insurance are fully exempt in wife's bankruptcy); *In re* DeMarco, 491 B.R. 236 (Bankr. W.D. Tenn. 2013) (exempt only as to debts of the insured, and only if beneficiary is spouse, child, or dependent relative); *In re* Rudd, 483 B.R. 354 (Bankr. M.D. Ala. 2012) (construing together various sections of Alabama law: insurance on one's own life for the benefit of spouse is exempt as to debts of insured; insurance on one's spouse for one's own benefit is exempt as to debts of both insured and beneficiary; insurance on spouse's life for benefit of non-debtor third party is exempt as to debts of beneficiary and insured); *In re* Ladd, 448 B.R. 207 (Bankr. N.D. Ohio 2011) (Ohio insurance exemption protects only against creditors of the insured); *In re* Bordelon, 443 B.R. 725 (Bankr. M.D. La. 2011) (Louisiana exempts insurance proceeds for debts of beneficiary that exist at the time benefits received; debt here arose later, so proceeds not exempt); *In re* Sims, 421 B.R. 745 (Bankr. D.S.C. 2010) (under South Carolina law, proceeds and cash surrender value of an insurance policy payable to a beneficiary other than insured's estate and "for the primary benefit of insured's spouse . . ." are exempt as to debts of the insured, even if insured retains ability to change the beneficiary); *In re* Roberts, 2008 WL 4543038 (Bankr. D. Kan. Oct. 8, 2008) (life insurance benefits exempt under Kansas law in hands of "any person named as a beneficiary in a policy of insurance"; father, the debtor, was "named" when deceased son failed to choose beneficiary, as policy specified order in which family members would receive benefits if other beneficiary not chosen); *In re* McCall, 383 B.R. 419 (Bankr. N.D. Ohio 2007) (Ohio exemption for group insurance makes life insurance exempt as to debts of beneficiary, here surviving spouse); *In re* Fahey, 352 B.R. 288 (Bankr. D. Colo. 2006) (proceeds of group life insurance exempt as to debts of both insured and beneficiary; note that this is more favorable than Colorado's treatment of individual life insurance); *In re* Lewis, 327 B.R. 645 (Bankr. S.D. Ohio 2005) (proceeds of employee's group insurance policy, payable to beneficiary who is actually dependent on employee, exempt both before and after payment, as to debts of insured or beneficiary); *In re* Ashley, 317 B.R. 352 (Bankr. C.D. Ill. 2004) (allowing widow to exempt proceeds without showing of need); *In re* McWhorter, 312 B.R. 695 (Bankr. N.D. Ala. 2004) (proceeds of life insurance policy exempt as to debts of deceased but not those of beneficiary); *In re* Kleinman, 272 B.R. 339 (Bankr. D. Md. 2001) (proceeds of life insurance protected from creditors of deceased spouse and those of the beneficiary); *In re* Romp, 249 B.R. 853 (Bankr. E.D.N.C. 2000) (proceeds of insurance policy, exempt for deceased spouse's debts, not exempt for joint debts); Morey v. Everbank, 93 So. 3d 482 (Fla. 2012) (Florida's insurance exemption makes proceeds exempt as to creditors of estate but, when life insurance was payable to a trust, trust language, setting forth how assets were to be used upon settlor's death, overrode the exemption); Blanton v. Clark, 2002 WL 709958 (Ohio Ct. App. Apr. 19, 2002) (proceeds of deceased spouse's life insurance may be garnished for joint debts, or for debts of surviving spouse); Carts & Parts, Inc. v. Rosales, 225 P.3d 1 (Okla. Civ. App. 2009) (Oklahoma exemption broadly protects life insurance proceeds from any "legal or equitable process or operation of law to pay any debt or liability of the insured or the beneficiary"; here, an attempt by deceased wife's employer to obtain a constructive trust on property allegedly paid for by wife's embezzlement). *See also In re* Fick, 249 B.R. 108 (Bankr. W.D.N.C. 2000) (North Carolina exemption for group insurance protects proceeds against creditors of the insured but not against creditors of the beneficiary). *But see In re* Erickson, 463 B.R. 142 (B.A.P. 10th Cir. 2011) (Kansas exempts life insurance proceeds as to debts of beneficiary; here allowing widow to exempt proceeds when joint debtor husband died shortly after filing bankruptcy); *In re* Fadeley, 2011 WL 350508 (Bankr. W.D.N.C. Feb. 1, 2011) (proceeds of group life insurance exempt as to debts of insured or beneficiary; construing ambiguous language in uniform statute). *See generally* § 12.3, *supra*.

In some states, an exemption for accident, health, or disability benefits has been interpreted to protect uninsured motorist proceeds.[912] However, at least two courts have held that an exemption for accident or disability insurance is not broad enough to protect payments to a personal injury tort plaintiff from the tortfeasor's insurance.[913]

The Florida exemption for disability income benefits under any policy or contract of life, health, accident or other insurance has been construed to protect benefits deposited in a bank account, if traceable.[914] Minnesota and Wisconsin achieve the same result by a statutory exemption for funds traceable to certain insurance benefits.[915] Ohio exempts "an interest in" certain monthly or lump-sum disability benefits, and this provision has been construed to cover traceable proceeds.[916] Advocates may also argue that the "paid or payable"[917] or "proceeds of" language found in other statutes provides for a continuing exemption.[918]

Another question is whether the policy itself is exempt. Many states exempt the cash value of a life insurance policy.[919] A Texas court has held that the cash value of life insurance policies exempted by the state Insurance Code is not subject to the cap on exempt property in the Property Code.[920] Courts have

912 *See, e.g., In re* Thompkins, 263 B.R. 223 (Bankr. W.D. Tenn. 2001) (also holding that cap for personal injury judgments does not apply); *In re* Portal, 45 P.3d 891 (N.M. 2002) (uninsured motorist policy is "accident" policy within meaning of New Mexico exemption for "payments of every kind from any life, accident, or health insurance policy").

913 Kollar v. Miller, 176 F.3d 175 (3d Cir. 1999) (Pennsylvania law) (debtors had no "property or other rights" in tortfeasor's insurance); *In re* Jackson, 2007 WL 4179849 (Bankr. N.D. Iowa Nov. 21, 2007) (statute exempts indemnity or benefit only "as to the insured").

914 Parl v. Parl, 699 So. 2d 765 (Fla. Dist. Ct. App. 1997) (remanding to trial court to determine which funds in bank account were traceable to exempt disability benefits).

915 Minn. Stat. § 550.37; Wis. Stat. § 815.18(3)(i). *See* Associated Bank v. Twaiten, 2007 WL 2245756 (Minn. Ct. App. Aug. 7, 2007) (exemption for disability insurance, so far as needed for support, covers traceable proceeds in bank account).

916 *In re* Alam, 336 B.R. 320 (Bankr. N.D. Ohio 2005) (settlement proceeds from lawsuit for disability benefits exempt as benefits paid under sickness and accident insurance; investment account funds traceable to settlement proceeds also exempt), *aff'd*, 359 B.R. 142 (B.A.P. 6th Cir. 2006).

917 *See* Philpott v. Essex Cnty. Welfare Bd., 409 U.S. 413, 93 S. Ct. 590, 34 L. Ed. 2d 608 (1973) (interpreting this language to protect bank accounts traceable to exempt benefits). *See generally* § 12.6.2.2, *supra*.

918 *See generally* § 12.2.4, *supra* (protection of proceeds of sale of exempt property).

919 Milligan v. Trautmen, 496 F.3d 366 (5th Cir. 2007) (Texas law) (cash value of existing policy exempt, but not sum received for prepetition surrender and cancellation of policy); *In re* Vigil, 2003 WL 22024830 (10th Cir. Aug. 26, 2003) (insured may exempt cash surrender value of life insurance policy); *In re* Moosman, 2013 WL 4460001 (D. Colo. Aug. 30, 2013) (Colorado exemption for cash surrender value excepts increases in value attributable to payments made during forty-eight months before bankruptcy; Equal Emp't Opportunity Comm'n v. 5042 Holdings Ltd., 2013 WL 1636577 (N.D. W. Va. Apr. 16, 2013) (cash surrender value of life insurance policy is exempt under D.C. law); when borrowing had reduced cash surrender value of policy below the amount of increase attributable to these payments, entire amount was non-exempt); *In re* Sims, 421 B.R. 745 (Bankr. D.S.C. 2010) (cash surrender value exempt if statutory criteria are met); *In re* Shethi, 389 B.R. 588 (Bankr. N.D. Ill. 2008) (cash surrender value exempt, even if payable to insured, if the beneficiaries are within the class of family members listed in statute); *In re* Levesque, 2008 WL 3893705 (Bankr. D. Mass. Aug. 21, 2008) (if beneficiary is the one named when policy was purchased, cash surrender value is exempt; allowing exemption because beneficiary never changed); *In re* Rice, 2006 WL 2051842 (Bankr. M.D.N.C. June 21, 2006) (exemption for "money or other benefit" provided by fraternal benefit association protects cash surrender value of life insurance policy issued by such association); *In re* Johnson, 274 B.R. 473 (Bankr. E.D. Mich. 2002) (Michigan statute explicitly exempts cash surrender value of debtor's life insurance if spouse or children are beneficiaries); *In re* Davis, 275 B.R. 134 (Bankr. D.D.C. 2002) (District of Columbia law permits debtor to exempt cash surrender value of policy on his or her life if spouse, children, or dependents are beneficiaries; cash surrender value is an exempt "proceed or avail" of the policy); Technical Chems. & Products, Inc. v. Porchester Holdings, Inc., 785 So. 2d 636 (Fla. 2001) (cash surrender value of whole life or limited whole life insurance policies fully exempt under Florida statute). *See also* Soc'y of Lloyd's v. Collins, 284 F.3d 727 (7th Cir. 2002) (life insurance policy of which spouse was beneficiary exempt under Illinois law, even as to premium payments made after debt accrued, when no showing of fraudulent intent); *In re* Trautman, 296 B.R. 651 (Bankr. W.D.N.Y. 2003) (mother and daughter's reciprocal life insurance policies both wholly exempt when both filed bankruptcy; beneficiary had "mere expectancy" that was not part of estate); Faro v. Porchester Holdings, Inc., 792 So. 2d 1262 (Fla. Dist. Ct. App. 2001) (applying Florida exemption to certificate of deposit bought with proceeds of cash surrender value of insurance policy). *Cf. In re* Oxford, 274 B.R. 887 (Bankr. D. Idaho 2002) (unlimited exemption for unmatured life insurance policy merely allows debtor to keep the policy; limited exemption for loan value applies cap to the aggregate of all policies, not to each separate policy). *But see In re* McFarland, 481 B.R. 242 (Bankr. S.D. Ga. 2012) (Georgia insurance exemption does not protect the cash surrender value of whole life insurance policy); *In re* Sims, 421 B.R. 745 (Bankr. D. S.C. 2010) (surrender value not exempt); *In re* Lowery, 272 B.R. 317 (Bankr. M.D. Fla. 2001) (cash surrender value not exempt when policy insures one spouse but is owned by the other); *In re* Watkins, 267 B.R. 703 (Bankr. E.D. Va. 2001) (Virginia's unlimited exemption for life insurance proceeds, which protects beneficiary but not insured, does not protect cash surrender value, but homestead exemption may apply); *In re* Jacobs, 264 B.R. 274 (Bankr. W.D.N.Y. 2001) (married debtors could not exempt cash surrender value of life insurance policies on each other's lives); Flatau v. Waggoner (*In re* Waggoner), 244 B.R. 492 (Bankr. M.D. Ga. 2000) (debtor may exempt unmatured life insurance policy itself but may not exempt its cash value); Schenk Boncher & Prasher v. Vanderlaan, 2003 WL 22026405 (Mich. Ct. App. Aug. 28, 2003) (surrender value of policy not exempt; debtor may be ordered to surrender policy and pay proceeds to judgment creditor). *But cf.* Plastipak Packaging, Inc. v. DiPasquale, 75 Fed. Appx. 86 (3d Cir. 2003) (Pennsylvania law) (funds borrowed from policy by insured not exempt because not being held for benefit of beneficiary); *In re* Zerbi, 2011 WL 175923 (Bankr. W.D. Mich. Jan. 6, 2011) (under federal bankruptcy exemptions, debtor can be required to turn over non-exempt portion of cash value of insurance, even if this means he must surrender the policy); *In re* Sloss, 279 B.R. 6 (Bankr. D. Mass. 2002) (exemption for insurance policy lost when divorce decree made wife, formerly the beneficiary, trustee for the children); Marriage of Gedgaunas, 978 P.2d 677 (Colo. App. 1999) (creditor ex-wife could garnish so much of cash value of life insurance as was attributable to premium payments made during twenty-four months previous to attachment); Dowling v. Chicago Options Assocs., Inc., 847 N.E.2d 741 (Ill. App. Ct. 2006) (Illinois exemption for policy payable to spouse or dependents applies only if policy payable to natural person; no exemption for policy payable to trust which would distribute proceeds to minor children).

920 *In re* Borchers, 192 B.R. 698 (Bankr. W.D. Tex. 1996).

reached differing results—even when construing identical language—on the question of whether a debtor may exempt the cash value of an insurance policy that is payable to close relatives such as parents or adult children who are not dependent on the debtor.[921] One court that allowed the exemption noted society's interest in encouraging adult children to take care of their elderly parents and in alleviating the financial burdens that a parent's death may place on adult children.[922] A statute exempting the cash surrender value of insurance taken out "for the benefit of" any creditor applied only to those who were creditors at the time the policy was purchased.[923]

12.9.3 Annuities

Some states provide an exemption for annuities.[924] Georgia has interpreted its exemption to apply only to annuities that provide income that substitutes for wages.[925]

In states that do not provide a specific exemption for annuities, the issue arises of whether an annuity, or a similar product that may pay a beneficiary upon the owner's death, is exempt as life insurance. In general, courts will determine whether the payment serves the same purpose as life insurance and whether the beneficiary has an unconditional right to payment. Thus an annuity that will pay a beneficiary only if the owner happens to die before the owner has been paid a guaranteed amount will not be exempt.[926]

---

921 *DEPENDENCY MUST BE SHOWN: In re* Bunting, 322 B.R. 852 (Bankr. C.D. Ill. 2005) (proceeds of mother's insurance policy not exempt in hands of non-dependent adult son; only a spouse may exempt without showing of dependency); *In re* Maggard, 2013 WL 1337306 (Bankr. N.D. Iowa Apr. 1, 2013) (dependency must be shown, but allowing exemption of policy benefitting non-dependent parents when debtors and parents testified that proceeds were to be used for care of debtors' minor children); *In re* Bunnell, 322 B.R. 331 (Bankr. N.D. Ohio 2005) (life insurance policy not exempt under Ohio law when beneficiary not a dependent); *In re* Peacock, 292 B.R. 593 (Bankr. S.D. Ohio 2002) (Ohio exempts policy payable to "dependent" of debtor; not exempt when beneficiaries, debtor's elderly mother and aunt, neither lived with debtor nor depended on her for income or personal services); *In re* Grace, 273 B.R. 570 (Bankr. S.D. Ill. 2002) (dependents only, but twenty-year-old college student whose mother was subsidizing his education and some other expenses is a dependent); *In re* Sommer, 228 B.R. 674 (Bankr. C.D. Ill. 1998) (adult son may exempt insurance on his life, for which his parents are beneficiaries, only if parents are dependent on him); People *ex rel.* Dir. of Corrections v. Ruckman, 843 N.E.2d 882 (Ill. App. Ct. 2005) (prison inmate could not exempt proceeds of deceased mother's life insurance because he was not mother's dependent). *See also In re* Rief, 2008 WL 168951 (D. Md. Jan. 15, 2008) (exemption for insurance policy of which spouse, children, or dependents were beneficiaries did not cover policy payable to debtor's estate, of which spouse and children were beneficiaries, because they were not beneficiaries of policy; children's life insurance policies not exempt; debtor was neither insured nor dependent of insured); *In re* Glimcher, 458 B.R. 544 (Bankr. D. Ariz. 2011) (exemption for policy payable to, *inter alia*, a spouse, did not protect policy, mandated by divorce decree, payable to ex-spouse; even if it did, dependency must be shown).

DEPENDENCY NEED NOT BE SHOWN: In re Spears, 2014 WL 295172 (Bankr. N.D. Ind. Jan. 9, 2014) (dependency need not be shown if beneficiary is spouse or child of insured); *In re* Frederick, 495 B.R. 813 (Bankr. N.D. Ohio 2013) (dependency requirement does not apply to group policy; policy obtained as a group policy remained so when insured retired and took "portability option"); *In re* Wandrey, 334 B.R. 427 (Bankr. N.D. Ind. 2005) (dependency not required to claim life insurance policy as exempt); *In re* Bush, 253 B.R. 863 (Bankr. S.D. Ohio 2000) (to claim Ohio exemption, debtor need only show that beneficiaries were her children, not that they were dependent, but result might be different if this were an effort to shelter a substantial inheritance); *In re* Romp, 249 B.R. 853 (Bankr. E.D.N.C. 2000) (insurance policies, the beneficiaries of which are debtor's adult, non-dependent offspring, are exempt); *In re* Shaffer, 228 B.R. 892 (Bankr. N.D. Ohio 1998) (Ohio exemption for insurance policies payable to "the spouse or children, or any persons dependent on" debtor allowed debtor to exempt cash surrender value of policy when beneficiary was his adult, non-dependent, son).

922 *In re* Shaffer, 228 B.R. 892 (Bankr. N.D. Ohio 1998).

923 *In re* Falter, 2013 WL 211294 (Bankr. N.D. Ohio Jan. 18, 2013) (not exempt when policy, of which parents were beneficiaries, had been owned for many years, and debtor had only recently borrowed from parents).

924 *In re* Aden, 484 B.R. 379 (D. Idaho 2012) (Idaho exemption requires an obligation to pay "certain sums at stated times"; inclusion of lump-sum payout option does not bar exemption, when annuitants have not chosen it, and default option provides periodic payments); Neal v. First Alliance Bank, 2013 WL 5739701 (W.D. Tenn. Oct. 22, 2013) (Tennessee annuity exempt only if spouse, child, or dependent relative is beneficiary; no exemption when annuitant and beneficiary are same person); *In re* Baldwin, 2012 WL 5513347 (Bankr. D. Idaho Nov. 13, 2012) (exempting annuity that funds structured settlement for personal injuries to debtor's spouse); *In re* Abbott, 466 B.R. 118 (Bankr. S.D. Ohio 2012) (annuity owned by tortfeasor and used to fund payments of wrongful death settlement was exempt, but if annuity had been owned by victim's widow, it would probably be a non-exempt investment); *In re* Spuhler, 2012 WL 5193776 (Bankr. N.D. Ohio Oct. 19, 2012) (annuity that funded structured settlement for wrongful death of debtor's father, on whom she was dependent, exempt so far as needed for support); *In re* Crowl, 415 B.R. 849 (Bankr. N.D. Okla. 2009) (Oklahoma annuity exemption is not limited to annuities generated by insurance); Connor v. Seaside Nat'l Bank, 2014 WL 1255340 (Fla. Dist. Ct. App. Mar. 28, 2014) (allowing exemption of annuities awarded to wife at divorce; although she was not yet the named annuitant, she was the beneficiary, because the divorce decree gave her the right to the proceeds). *See also In re* Jadud, 2012 WL 4757870 (Bankr. N.D. Ohio Oct. 5, 2012) (interpreting Ohio exemption to protect annuity only if it is substitute for wages; inherited annuity exempt when needed for support). *But see In re* Messer, 2012 WL 762828 (B.A.P. 9th Cir. Mar. 9, 2012) (Arizona exemption protects only annuities owned by the insured; denying exemption for structured settlement annuity owned by tortfeasor's insurance company); *In re* Lesak, 2012 WL 1029313 (Bankr. N.D. Ill. Mar. 26, 2012) (exemption for annuity contracts payable to spouse of the insured applies only to benefits payable upon death; denying exemption to annuity funding structured settlement for loss of consortium). *See generally* § 12.9.1, *supra* (exemptions for annuities as part of retirement plans).

925 Silliman v. Cassell, 738 S.E.2d 606 (Ga. 2013) (annuity was exempt substitute for wages; sixty-five-year-old debtor, who had been self-employed and had no access to employer plan, purchased annuity with single payment and chose stream of payments guaranteed for 10 years). *See also In re* Sheffield, 507 B.R. 400 (Bankr. S.D. Ga. 2014) (annuity exempt if it pays out on account of age and illness, among other factors, and serves as a substitute for wages; not shown here when owner could freely withdraw funds); *In re* McFarland, 500 B.R. 279 (Bankr. S.D. Ga. 2013) (single-payment annuity not a substitute for wages; debtor could withdraw funds, subject to penalty, and on his death widow had choice of lump sum or stream of payments).

926 *In re* Bryan, 466 B.R. 460 (B.A.P. 8th Cir. 2012) (annuity was not exempt as insurance under Missouri law when it was funded only at

12.9.4 Personal Injury and Other Causes of Action and Judgments; Debts Owed to the Judgment Debtor

Some states exempt personal injury recoveries. In Maryland, personal injury compensation is exempt, even against claims for child support.[927] Oregon places a cap on its exemption but interprets it to apply to the sum left over after deduction of liens for medical care, public assistance, attorney services, and the like.[928] Some states exempt recoveries only so far as reasonably necessary for the support of the debtor.[929] One court read the District of Columbia's tortuously worded exemption to find a personal injury settlement non-exempt.[930] The North Carolina exemption for "compensation for personal injury" extends to the portion of the settlement allocated to attorney fees.[931]

Courts have reached varying results as to the status of annuities used to fund structured settlements. Courts in Florida,[932] Idaho,[933] Louisiana,[934] Missouri,[935] New York,[936] Ohio,[937] and Texas[938] have applied the annuities exemption,[939] but North Dakota[940] and Oklahoma[941] and apply their exemption for personal injury claims. A federal court held that the Kansas exemption for the right to receive payment under an annuity arising on account of illness, disability, death, age, or length of service only applied to workers' retirement-type annuities, not to an annuity purchased as part of a structured settlement of a claim for wrongful death of a child's parent.[942] The Eighth Circuit ruled that Minnesota's exemption for "rights of action" for personal injuries to the debtor did not exempt the proceeds of an annuity purchased by a tortfeasor to fund a structured settlement.[943] Another decision rejects a debtor's argument that the monthly benefit payable from an annuity arising from a settlement for the wrongful death of her husband fell within Arizona's exemption for trusts, as the debtor failed to establish that a trust had been created and she could transfer the

---

its inception rather than through payments at regular intervals and was payable at a pre-determined date rather than at death); *In re* Kukowski, 356 B.R. 712 (B.A.P. 8th Cir. 2006) (annuity that guaranteed payment for the longer of 360 months or debtor's lifetime not exempt as annuity, life insurance, and so forth payable to a spouse, children or dependent upon the insured's death; beneficiaries' right to payment not unconditional because debtor might live more than 360 months); *In re* Andrews, 301 B.R. 211 (Bankr. N.D. Ohio 2003) (Ohio exempts annuities to extent needed for support, but annuity "upon the life of any person" is fully exempt if it serves same purpose as life insurance of compensating beneficiary for death of insured and is worth more in hands of beneficiary). *See also In re* Simpson, 557 F.3d 1010 (9th Cir. 2009) (California law) (single premium annuity was an investment; inclusion of a death benefit not sufficient to turn it into exempt life insurance).

927 Rosemann v. Salsbury, Clements, Bekman, Marder & Adkins, L.L.C., 987 A.2d 48 (Md. 2010). *See also* Butcher, 189 B.R. 357 (Bankr. D. Md. 1995) (structured settlement with present value of $4 million exempt for debtor who was permanently disabled by his injuries; unlimited exemption was reasonable, facially and as applied), *aff'd*, 125 F.3d 238 (4th Cir. 1997). *But cf. In re* Short, 2010 WL 4736209 (Bankr. D. Md. Nov. 16, 2010) (exemption inapplicable to portions of personal injury award that represent lost wages and medical bills that debtor is discharging in bankruptcy).

928 Valley Credit Serv. v. Kelley, 994 P.2d 1229 (Or. Ct. App. 2000) (exemption is for "right to receive" payments for bodily injury; no right to receive sums required to be deducted before payment to victim).

929 *See In re* Gose, 308 B.R. 41 (B.A.P. 9th Cir. 2004) (California law); *In re* Spuhler, 2012 WL 5193776 (Bankr. N.D. Ohio Oct. 19, 2012) (annuity that funded structured settlement for wrongful death of debtor's father, on whom she was dependent, exempt so far as needed for support); *In re* Abbott, 466 B.R. 118 (Bankr. S.D. Ohio 2012) (exempting entire amount of wrongful death settlement; widow's need sufficiently shown); *In re* Wilcox, 2008 WL 450816 (Bankr. D. Idaho Feb. 15, 2008) (structured settlement not covered by personal injury exemption because no showing of necessity for support, but annuity exemption applied); *In re* Constantino, 274 B.R. 580 (Bankr. N.D.N.Y. 2002) (monthly payments under annuity that funded structured settlement were exempt, but not "singular" every-five-year payments).

930 Howell-Robinson v. Albert, 384 B.R. 19 (D.D.C. 2008).

931 *In re* Simmons, 2006 WL 3392943 (Bankr. M.D.N.C. Nov. 22, 2006).

932 *In re* Belue, 238 B.R. 218 (Bankr. S.D. Fla. 1999) (annuity purchased to fund structured settlement is exempt under Florida annuities exemption if debtor is beneficiary, even if tortfeasor's insurer is owner).

933 *In re* Wilcox, 2008 WL 450816 (Bankr. D. Idaho Feb. 15, 2008) (annuity exempt if purchased for valuable consideration; release of personal injury claim is sufficient). *But see In re* Baldwin, 2012 WL 5513347 (Bankr. D. Idaho Nov. 13, 2012) (annuity funding structured settlement for injury to debtor's spouse; personal injury exemption not applicable because debtor not shown to be dependent, but general exemption for annuities applies).

934 *In re* Orso, 283 F.3d 686 (5th Cir. 2002) (annuity purchased to fund personal injury settlement resulting from catastrophic accident, and structured to comply with tax code provisions for such annuities, falls within Louisiana exemption for annuities).

935 *In re* Bonuchi, 327 B.R. 428 (Bankr. W.D. Mo. 2005) (annuity "payable on account of disability" and used to fund children's college-related expenses partially exempt; not reasonable to pay all of children's college expenses to the detriment of unsecured creditors).

936 *In re* Lyons, 381 B.R. 444 (Bankr. S.D.N.Y. 2008) (annuity partly exempt; court may order "just and proper" payments to creditor; analysis is similar to "necessary for support" in federal exemptions); *In re* Tappan, 277 B.R. 491 (Bankr. W.D.N.Y. 2002) (New York exempts annuities if annuitant paid consideration for the contract; debtor's release of personal injury claim in return for structured settlement funded by annuity meets this requirement).

937 *In re* Jadud, 2012 WL 4757870 (Bankr. N.D. Ohio Oct. 5, 2012) (Ohio exemption for retirement plans, which covers substitutes for wages, will protect structured settlement annuity for person whose ability to earn was lost or damaged); *In re* Spuhler, 2012 WL 5193776 (Bankr. N.D. Ohio Oct. 19, 2012) (annuity that funded structured settlement for wrongful death of debtor's father, on whom she was dependent, exempt so far as needed for support); *In re* Abbott, 466 B.R. 118 (Bankr. S.D. Ohio 2012) (annuity owned by tortfeasor and used to fund payments of wrongful death settlement was exempt; noting that if annuity had been owned by victim's widow, it would probably be an non-exempt investment).

938 *In re* Alexander, 227 B.R. 658 (Bankr. N.D. Tex. 1998) (structured settlement of wrongful death case, funded by annuity purchased by tortfeasor's insurance carrier, falls within Texas exemption for annuities).

939 *See generally* § 12.9.3, *supra*.

940 *In re* Kukowski, 356 B.R. 712 (B.A.P. 8th Cir. 2006) (annuity that funded structured settlement is exempt as personal injury settlement).

941 *In re* Alexander, 980 P.2d 659 (Okla. 1999) (only structured settlement payments received after bankruptcy filing are property of bankruptcy estate, and those payments are exempt except to the extent they exceed $50,000 exemption).

942 Ortiz v. Rajala, 436 B.R. 133 (D. Kan. 2010).

943 Christians v. Dulas, 95 F.3d 703 (8th Cir. 1996).

payments with court approval.[944] One court held that, in a bankruptcy proceeding, a structured settlement law should be construed to promote the best interests of the bankruptcy estate, not the debtor.[945] The court approved the trustee's sale of the debtor's right to $130,000 in future payments for $64,800, out of which the debtor was to receive her $28,000 exemption.

Beneficiaries of structured settlements, who may be financially desperate or impaired by their injuries, are vulnerable to predatory transactions whereby they sell, assign, or pledge a large number of future payments for a much smaller amount in hand. Most annuities funding such settlements include an anti-assignment clause, and some states have enacted structured settlement protection laws. Unscrupulous lenders or asset purchasers devise elaborate schemes to circumvent these requirements, with varying degrees of success.[946]

Some states also exempt compensation for loss of future earnings.[947] This exemption may be stacked with the personal injury exemption if part of the award was for lost earning power.[948] Payments for loss of consortium may also be exempt.[949]

In some states the definition of "personal injury" is narrow and excludes physical damage resulting from a non-physical wrong.[950] Some state statutes track the federal bankruptcy

944 *In re* Messer, 2012 WL 762828 (B.A.P. 9th Cir. Mar. 9, 2012).

945 *In re* Jackus, 442 B.R. 365 (Bankr. D. N.J. 2011).

946 Liberty Life Assurance Co. v. Gilbert, 507 F.3d 952 (6th Cir. 2007) ("loan agreement" with payments of $159,840 for $51,000 loan; annuity payments sent to post office box and deposited in bank account controlled by lender; assignment was invalid, and this kind of factoring transaction was against Virginia public policy); Symetra Nat'l Life Ins. Co. v. Rapid Settlements, Ltd., 2009 WL 1057339 (Tex. App. Apr. 21, 2009) (disapproving of defendant's use of arbitration to circumvent structured settlement protection laws), *later decision*, 2011 WL 4807901 (S.D. Tex. Oct. 11, 2011) (granting summary judgment for insurer on tortious interference claim; provisions of statutes were so clear that settlement purchaser could not have had good faith belief in rights it asserted), *as amended by* 2012 WL 1553045 (S.D. Tex. May 1, 2012); Coffey v. Singer Asset Fin. Co., L.L.C., 223 S.W.3d 559 (Tex. App. 2007) (pledge of future payments as security for loans violated neither anti-assignment clause nor state legislation; public policy does not bar pledge or assignment of structured settlement proceeds). *See generally* National Consumer Law Center, Repossessions § 2.2.8.2 (8th ed. 2013), *updated at* www.nclc.org/library; National Consumer Law Center, Consumer Credit Regulation Ch. 13 (2012), *updated at* www.nclc.org/library.

947 *In re* John, 459 B.R. 684 (Bankr. E.D. Mich. 2011) (compensation for loss of future earnings, here an employer's buyout in return for early termination of employment, is exempt so far as needed for support); *In re* Jones, 446 B.R. 466 (Bankr. D. Kan. 2011) (lump-sum payment from annuity, received in settlement of FELA claim by severely injured railroad worker, was exempt either as disability compensation or as compensation for loss of future earnings; both of these federal exemptions are applicable in Kansas pursuant to Kan. Stat. Ann. § 60-2321). *See In re* McFarland, 481 B.R. 242 (Bankr. S.D. Ga. 2012) (Georgia exemption for payments in compensation for loss of future earnings would cover annuity if payable for illness, disability, death, age or length of service, so far as reasonably necessary for support); *In re* Whitson, 319 B.R. 614 (Bankr. E.D. Ark. 2005) (allowing debtor to claim federal exemption for loss of future earnings with respect to entire amount of proceeds from settlement of personal injury claim); *In re* Hanson, 226 B.R. 106 (Bankr. D. Idaho 1998) (any award for "loss of future earnings" in sexual harassment suit would be exempt only insofar as debtors could show that funds were reasonably necessary for their support); *In re* Gilbert, 213 B.R. 502 (Bankr. E.D. Ky. 1997) (Kentucky exemption for loss of future wages protected debtors' personal injury recovery, even though debtors were not employed and were receiving government benefits at time of injury; bankruptcy trustee failed to carry burden of proof that debtors had no earning capacity). *See also* Todd v. Whinery, 2013 WL 3285525 (D. Nev. June 26, 2013) (fact issue as to what portion of unallocated personal injury settlement was attributable to loss of future earnings; failure to allocate does not bar exemption); *In re* Burns, 482 B.R. 164 (Bankr. E.D. La. 2012) (state exemption for disposable earnings protects the portion of personal injury judgment that compensated for lost wages; compensation for loss or destruction of exempt property is exempt). *But cf. In re* Ballard, 238 B.R. 610 (Bankr. M.D. La. 1999) (Louisiana statutes provided no exemption for personal injury cause of action, and earnings exemption was not broad enough to cover tort recovery for loss of future earning capacity).

948 *In re* Bova, 205 B.R. 467 (Bankr. E.D. Pa. 1997) (debtor could stack state exemption for payments "on account of personal bodily injury" with exemption for "compensation of loss of future earnings" when part of personal injury damages was for loss of earning power and was "reasonably necessary" for support of debtor or dependents). *Cf. In re* Pless, 202 B.R. 664 (Bankr. N.D.N.Y. 1996) (New York allows exemption for $7500 of personal injury judgment; fact question whether debtor is entitled to additional state exemption for "compensation for future earnings . . . to the extent reasonably necessary" for debtor's support).

949 *In re* Shumac, 425 B.R. 139 (Bankr. M.D. Pa. Mar. 4, 2010) (exempting wife's claim for loss of consortium, because it is derivative from husband's claim for personal bodily injury); *In re* Bippert, 311 B.R. 456 (Bankr. W.D. Tex. 2004) (allowing husband to exempt loss of consortium claim); *In re* Tosti, 276 B.R. 204 (Bankr. S.D. Ohio 2001) (loss of consortium is personal injury within meaning of Ohio exemption; debtor wife who was named plaintiff in husband's tort case and signed release at settlement is entitled to exemption for her share of proceeds); *In re* Dealey, 204 B.R. 17 (Bankr. C.D. Ill. 1997) (state exemption for bodily injury judgment covers uninjured spouse's loss of consortium claim, thereby allowing two exemptions to married couple); *In re* Turner, 190 B.R. 836 (Bankr. S.D. Ohio 1996) (Ohio exemption of $5000 for payments "on account of personal bodily injury" exempts uninjured spouse's award for loss of consortium, so married co-debtors got one exemption for the injury and one for the loss of consortium). *But see In re* Marble, 2010 WL 3198901 (E.D. Mich. Aug. 12, 2010) (minor children's settlement with tortfeasor who injured their father compensated for loss of consortium, not loss of earnings; exemption denied); *In re* Chapman, 424 B.R. 823 (Bankr. E.D. Tenn. 2010) (denying exemption for loss of consortium); *In re* Patton, 200 B.R. 172 (Bankr. N.D. Ohio 1996) (allowing exemption for personal injury but not loss of consortium).

950 *In re* Cope, 280 B.R. 516 (D. Or. 2001) (remanding to determine whether the "unlawful employment practices" that gave rise to emotional distress damages included physical injury); *In re* Barner, 239 B.R. 139 (Bankr. W.D. Ky. 1999) (when physical injury is shown recovery will be exempt under Kentucky statute except insofar as it compensates for purely mental suffering without physical manifestations, or for actual pecuniary loss); *In re* Hanson, 226 B.R. 106 (Bankr. D. Idaho 1998) (proceeds of pending sexual harassment suit would be exempt under Oregon's "personal bodily injury" exemption only if plaintiff could show "appreciable" physical injury); *In re* Chapman, 223 B.R. 137 (Bankr. N.D. Ill. 1998) (cause of action for defamation, invasion of privacy, and breach of contract, which alleged only emotional injury, was not exempt under Illinois exemption for "personal bodily injury"); *In re* Langa, 222 B.R. 843 (Bankr. C.D. Ill. 1998) (cause of action for employment discrimination, which alleged sexual harassment by inappropriate touching, resulting in emotional suffering, was not exempt under Illinois exemption for "personal bodily injury" because there was no "physical injury or impairment of physical condition"); *In re* Ciotta, 222 B.R. 626 (Bankr. C.D. Cal. 1998) (California exemption

exemption for personal injury,[951] which excludes both pain and suffering and actual pecuniary loss.

Sometimes debtors have tried to fit causes of action into another exemption. One court held that a malpractice action against an attorney for mishandling a child support and alimony claim does not fall within the state exemption for child support and alimony.[952] Colorado's household goods exemption did not cover a cause of action against the tortfeasor who destroyed the goods, but another exemption for a "claim for the loss, destruction, or damage of exempt property" would apply.[953] The federal exemption for "a payment in compensation for loss of future earnings" was applied to the portion of the settlement of a wrongful termination claim attributable to postpetition loss of earnings.[954] A cause of action may also be exempt under a state wildcard exemption.[955] In at least some jurisdictions, an unliquidated claim for damages is not subject to garnishment.[956]

12.9.5 Debts Owed to the Judgment Debtor

Sometimes another person or entity owes a debt to the judgment debtor. The state's execution laws may have a special provision allowing the judgment debtor to garnish this obligation, or this asset may fall within some general category of property subject to execution. If it is subject to execution, then the creditor can obtain a garnishment order directing the person or entity that owes the debt to pay it to the judgment creditor rather than to the judgment debtor.

Garnishing debts owed to the judgment debtor is often useful when a judgment creditor is trying to collect a debt owed by a business, as businesses often have accounts receivable. Individual judgment debtors are less likely to have debts owing to them, so the issue of garnishment of such debts rarely arises. However, in one case a court allowed a creditor to garnish the stream of payments that an older judgment debtor was receiving through a reverse mortgage.[957] The court could find no state or federal statute protecting the proceeds of a reverse

---

for "personal bodily injury" required showing of "appreciable physical injury"; sexual harassment complainant's "discomfort" and "physical distress" resulting from inappropriate touching may be sufficient if proven); *In re* Marshall, 208 B.R. 690 (Bankr. D. Minn. 1997) (exemption for rights of action for "injuries to the person" did not exempt a sexual harassment claim, even if the harassment resulted in physical injury; in order for this exemption to apply "original trauma must be to the debtor's body"); *In re* Crawford, 208 B.R. 924 (Bankr. D. Minn. 1994) (discrimination and defamation claims do not fall within exemption for actions for injury to the person). *See also* Sylvester v. Hafif, 220 B.R. 89 (B.A.P. 9th Cir. 1998) (California's exemption of "personal injury" recoveries allows debtor to exempt portion of malpractice recovery against his former attorney that was attributable to claims for emotional distress, but not portion attributable to harassment and wrongful discharge claims; only amounts reasonably necessary for debtor's support are exempt); *In re* Graci, 394 B.R. 691 (Bankr. W.D.N.Y. Sept. 23, 2008) (denying exemption for Americans with Disabilities Act claim; injury alleged was employment discrimination, even though disability that was subject of discrimination was caused by personal injury); *In re* Nelson, 2003 WL 22331776 (Bankr. D. Colo. Oct. 1, 2003) (judgment for interference with prospective economic relation does not fall under exemption for damage to person or property when damages were based on lost profits); *In re* Barner, 239 B.R. 139 (Bankr. W.D. Ky. 1999) (when physical injury is shown, recovery is exempt under Kentucky law except insofar as it compensates for purely mental suffering without physical manifestations, or for actual pecuniary loss); Miller v. Accelerated Bureau of Collections, 932 P.2d 824 (Colo. App. 1996) (recovery for Fair Debt Collection Practices Act violations is not exempt; Colorado exemption for "proceeds of any claim for damages for personal injuries suffered by any debtor" did not exempt punitive damages). *But see In re* Walters, 339 B.R. 607 (Bankr. W.D. Va. 2006) (Virginia's exemption for "all causes of action for personal injury" and proceeds of court award or settlement thereof covers any "injury to personal rights," here libel and negligence); *In re* Dobbins, 249 B.R. 849 (Bankr. D. Md. 2000) (Maryland exemption for personal injury covers mental injury, so sexual harassment settlement which compensated for humiliation and depression is exempt); *In re* LoCurto, 239 B.R. 314 (Bankr. E.D.N.C. 1999) (North Carolina exemption for compensation for personal injury, not including pain and suffering or actual pecuniary loss, covered damages for physical results of stress due to wrongful discharge, but not compensation for lost wages); *In re* Webb, 210 B.R. 266 (Bankr. E.D. Va. 1997) (Virginia exemption for personal injury judgments protects settlement in federal gender discrimination lawsuit when hostile work environment resulted in severe depression), *aff'd*, 214 B.R. 553 (E.D. Va. 1997). *Cf. In re* Keenan, 443 B.R. 169 (Bankr. D. Minn. 2011) (severe psychological injury resulting from sexual molestation not "personal bodily injury," so not exempt under federal bankruptcy law); *In re* Key, 255 B.R. 217 (Bankr. D. Neb. 2000) (proceeds of cause of action for employment discrimination claim are exempt as "proceeds or benefits of personal injury claims" insofar as they compensate for psychological injury rather than back pay, but cause of action itself is not exempt).

951 11 U.S.C. § 522(d)(11)(D). *See* National Consumer Law Center, Consumer Bankruptcy Law and Practice § 10.2.2.12 (10th ed. 2012), *updated at* www.nclc.org/library.

952 *In re* Hice, 223 B.R. 155 (Bankr. N.D. Ill. 1998).

953 *In re* Fager, 274 B.R. 537 (Bankr. D. Colo. 2002). *See generally* § 12.2.4, *supra* (protection of proceeds of exempt property).

954 *In re* Jackson, 593 F.3d 171 (2d Cir. 2010).

955 Ball v. Nationscredit Fin. Servs. Corp., 207 B.R. 869 (N.D. Ill. 1997) (Illinois wildcard exception may be used to exempt a cause of action under Truth in Lending Act); *In re* Foor, 259 B.R. 899 (Bankr. C.D. Ill. 2000) (cause of action against sellers of house for undisclosed termite damage); *In re* Kelsey, 224 B.R. 495 (Bankr. M.D. Fla. 1998) (Florida's exemption for "personal property" protects debtor's interest in class action lawsuit, up to $1000 statutory cap); *In re* Ball, 201 B.R. 210 (Bankr. N.D. Ill. 1996) (discussing method of setting value of Truth in Lending claim for purposes of determining how much of it was exempt under $2000 wildcard exemption). *See also In re* Soares, 471 B.R. 20 (Bankr. D. Mass. 2012) (federal bankruptcy wildcard covers civil cause of action against financial advisor who embezzled from debtor); *In re* Reschick, 343 B.R. 151 (Bankr. W.D. Pa. 2006) (annuity purchased by insurer to fund structured settlement of personal injury action could be exempted under wildcard exemption, as well as personal injury exemption); *In re* Kelin, 341 B.R. 521 (Bankr. W.D. Pa. 2006) (personal injury settlement not covered by personal injury exemption because actual pecuniary loss was being compensated, but could be exempted under wildcard and unused homestead exemptions). *But see* Howe v. Richardson, 193 F.3d 60 (1st Cir. 1999) (Rhode Island law provides no exemption for causes of action, including personal injury or breach of contract).

956 *In re* Williams, 293 B.R. 769 (W.D. Mo. 2003) (unliquidated and unassignable potential personal injury claim is fully exempt); Keaton v. Ft. Wayne Neurosurgery, 780 N.E.2d 1183 (Ind. Ct. App. 2003). *But cf. In re* Mahony, 374 B.R. 717 (Bankr. W.D. Mo. 2007) (Missouri's common law protection of unliquidated personal injury claims from garnishment or assignment is not an exemption that is available in bankruptcy).

957 Cameron v. Ewing, 38 A.3d 611 (N.J. Super. Ct. App. Div. 2012).

mortgage and held that the anti-assignment provision in the reverse mortgage contract was merely an inter-party restriction that did not prevent the creditor from seizing the stream of payments. The court did not consider whether the reverse mortgage payments could be protect as proceeds of an exempt homestead.[958] The court did, however, remand to the trial court to apply a state statute limiting the percentage of a debtor's "wages, debts, earnings, salary, income from trust funds or profits due and owing" that could be garnished.[959]

12.10 Waiver of Exemptions

12.10.1 General

Many states prohibit waivers of personal exemptions, considering them to be void and against public policy.[960] The states that do allow waiver generally require that it be in writing, signed by the appropriate parties, and acknowledged.[961] Strict compliance with these requirements is necessary.[962] In addition, a Federal Trade Commission (FTC) rule prohibits executory waivers of exemptions in consumer credit contracts.[963]

Another way that otherwise exempt property can become subject to collection remedies is if it is collateral for the debt. Most exemption statutes provide exceptions for property given as collateral in a security agreement, making collateral subject to seizure by the secured creditors.[964] Likewise, the FTC prohibition on waivers of exemptions does not restrict the use of otherwise exempt property as collateral.[965]

Courts may also find that exemptions do not shelter income from claims that are related to the acquisition of that income. For example, one court held that an attorney who won a retroactive child support award for a client could execute upon the award to collect his fee, even though state statutes generally exempted child support from execution.[966]

958 *See* §§ 12.2.4, 12.7, *supra*.

959 N.J. Stat. Ann. § 2A:17-56.

960 *See, e.g.*, United States v. Neff, 2007 WL 776532 (D.N.D. Mar. 12, 2007) (North Dakota forbids waiver of homestead exemption for chattel debt); *In re* Box, 340 B.R. 782 (S.D. Tex. 2006) (lien against homestead invalid when home equity lender did not strictly comply with constitutional requirements, despite borrowers' acknowledgment that requirements were satisfied); Gonzalez v. Ameriquest Mortgage, 2005 WL 3333259 (W.D. Tex. Dec. 8, 2005) (debtor's statement that property not homestead insufficient to waive homestead protection when debtor owned only one residential property and lived there); Tuxis-Ohr's Fuel, Inc. v. Trio Marketers Inc., 2005 WL 3047266 (Conn. Super. Ct. Oct. 26, 2005) (waiver of homestead in contract, here personal guarantee of a business debt, void as against public policy); Osborne v. Dumoulin, 55 So. 3d 577, 583 (Fla. 2011) (homestead exemption not waivable; once established, homestead can be lost only by abandonment or alienation); Chames v. DeMayo, 972 So. 2d 850 (Fla. 2007) (waiver of homestead in an unsecured agreement is unenforceable); Estate of Montague v. Nat'l Loan Investors, Ltd. P'ship, 70 S.W.3d 242 (Tex. App. 2001) (invalidating debtor's statement that land was not homestead). *Cf. In re* Morris, 2007 WL 2120177 (Bankr. N.D. Ala. July 18, 2007) (Alabama statute forbidding waiver of exemptions refers to specific exemptions provided by statute; does not exempt entire value of truck when statute caps exemption at $3000). *But cf.* Dominguez v. Castaneda, 163 S.W.3d 318 (Tex. App. 2005) (borrower who owned two residential properties bound by warranty that one parcel not homestead).

961 Chelsea State Bank v. Wagner (*In re* Wagner), 259 B.R. 694 (B.A.P. 8th Cir. 2001) (mortgages unenforceable for noncompliance with Iowa requirement that waiver of homestead exemption for agricultural land or buildings be in ten-point boldface type and contain prescribed language); Fix v. First State Bank of Roscoe, 359 B.R. 755 (D.S.D. 2007) (waiver void as against public policy; waivers permitted but must be "so clear that there can be no question concerning the intended effect"; not shown here when settlement agreement for unrelated matter did not mention homestead); *In re* Cadengo, 370 B.R. 681 (Bankr. S.D. Tex. 2007) (homestead waivers strictly limited in Texas; waiver here was ineffective); *In re* Hebert, 301 B.R. 19 (Bankr. N.D. Iowa 2003) (statement in personal guarantee of corporate debt that guarantors "waive the benefit of all homestead laws" not sufficient to comply with Iowa law; homestead waiver must specifically describe piece of property to which it applies); Chames v. DeMayo, 972 So. 2d 850 (Fla. 2007) (waiver of homestead requires mortgage formalities; waiver in unsecured, adhesive contract was unenforceable because against public policy); Citizens State Bank v. Ruebel, 804 N.W.2d 314 (Iowa Ct. App. 2011) (when property included homestead and agricultural land, mortgage was void because lender failed to provide statutory notice and obtain signed waiver); Republic Leasing Corp. v. Farnes, 2000 Minn. App. LEXIS 390 (Minn. Ct. App. Apr. 25, 2000) (homestead exemption may be waived only by "an act which evidences an unequivocal intention to do so"; not shown when settlement agreement required defendants to provide "adequate security" for note but did not define adequate security); Midland Funding, L.L.C. v. Giambanco, 28 A.3d 831 (N.J. Super. Ct. App. Div. 2011) (waiver of right to notice of wage garnishment not against public policy if knowing and voluntary; not shown here when consent judgment does not make clear to debtor what rights are being given up); Red River State Bank v. Reierson, 533 N.W.2d 683 (N.D. 1995) (waiver of homestead rights invalid when it was no more conspicuous than rest of mortgage). *See also In re In re* Rhymes, 2008 WL 723975 (Bankr. S.D. Miss. Mar. 14, 2008) (deed of trust encumbering homestead void for lack of wife's signature, even though she conveyed her interest in land to husband before he signed); Estate of Darby v. Stinson, 68 So. 3d 702 (Miss. Ct. App. 2011) (Mississippi law provides that exempt property, including homestead, passes to spouse, children or grandchildren free of debts of deceased; Medicaid contract that allowed claim against the estate not a waiver of statutory homestead, because it did not make clear that recipient was waiving homestead). *Cf.* USAmeriBank v. Klepal, 100 So. 3d 56 (Fla. Dist. Ct. App. 2011) (paragraph in promissory note consenting to writ of continuing garnishment and attachment against disposable earnings to satisfy any judgment in favor of lender was sufficient to waive statutory head of family wages exemption).

962 Linne, 414 B.R. 536 (Bankr. D.N.D. 2008) (North Dakota strictly enforces requirement for notarized signatures of both spouses for sale or encumbrance of homestead; when signatures not notarized, mortgage was unenforceable, even though both spouses admitted genuineness of signatures); Red River State Bank v. Reierson, 533 N.W.2d 683 (N.D. 1995).

963 16 C.F.R. § 444.2(a)(2). *See* § 12.10.2, *infra*.

964 *See* § 12.7.4.2, *supra*.

965 *See* § 12.10.2, *infra*.

966 *In re* Wageman, 968 P.2d 1114 (Kan. Ct. App. 1998). *But see* Binder & Binder, Prof'l Corp. v. Barnhart, 281 F. Supp. 2d 574 (E.D.N.Y. 2003) (anti-alienation clause of Social Security Act prevents the attachment of attorney's charging lien to SSI benefits recovered in proceeding in which attorney represented claimant), *vacated on other grounds*, 399 F.3d 128 (2d Cir. 2005) (jurisdictional grounds). *But cf.* Quiroga v. Citizens Prop. Ins. Corp., 34 So. 3d 101 (Fla. Dist. Ct. App. 2010) (when Florida homestead waiver requires mortgage formalities, contingent fee agreement with attorney who sued insurer to obtain payment for hurricane damage not sufficient to waive exemption in the proceeds).

In some states the debtor may also waive exemptions by failing to assert them, or by failing to assert them properly.[967] Courts that adhere more closely to the rule that exemption statutes should be construed liberally in favor of the debtor[968] do not find a waiver when a debtor does not comply strictly with procedural requirements.[969]

12.10.2 FTC Prohibition of Waiver of Exemptions

The FTC's Credit Practices Rule prohibits lenders and retail installment sellers from including waiver of exemption clauses in their consumer contracts.[970] The rule prohibits a clause that: "[c]onstitutes or contains an executory waiver or a limitation of exemption from attachment, execution, or other process on real or personal property held, owned by, or due to the consumer." There is an exception that makes it clear that this provision does not prohibit security interests in exempt property, but the effect of this exception is limited by the separate prohibition in the Credit Practices Rule of most non-purchase money security interests in household goods.[971]

While there is no private cause of action for violation of an FTC Rule,[972] inclusion of a clause that the FTC has declared unfair will be a violation of most states' unfair and deceptive acts and practices (UDAP) statutes, as long as the creditor is covered by the statute.[973] Such a clause is also unenforceable.[974]

West Virginia's highest court found deceptive a contractual provision waiving the consumer's rights to exempt certain property from seizure. The waiver was only "to the extent permitted by law," and West Virginia prohibits such a waiver. The creditor argued that the contractual provision was not deceptive because the provision had no effect as it was not "permitted by law." But the court found the provision misleading and likely to cause confusion or misunderstanding.[975]

12.11 Interstate Enforcement of Judgments

12.11.1 General

In general, a court can execute upon assets only if they are located within the reach of its service of process.[976] The Restatement of Conflict of Laws provides that a state has the power to garnish a debtor's chattel if the court has jurisdiction over the garnishee and the chattel is located in the state.[977] Thus the first question to examine in any interstate execution is where the asset at issue is located.

It is easy to tell whether a tangible asset such as land or a vehicle is located within the jurisdiction of the court issuing the judgment or outside that court's jurisdiction. For those types of tangible assets, the creditor must go to the state where the asset is located and institute execution there. If the asset is located in a state other than the one that rendered the judgment, the creditor can use the procedures of the Uniform Enforcement of Foreign Judgments Act, discussed in § 12.11.2, *infra*.

The question becomes knotty, though, when an intangible asset such as a bank account or the right to payment of wages is at issue.[978] These two cases are examined in §§ 12.11.3 and 12.11.4, *infra*.

12.11.2 Use of One State's Courts to Enforce Another State's Judgment

As noted in the previous section, to reach out-of-state assets the creditor must apply to a court in that other state. The United States Constitution requires the court in that second

967 Chanel, Inc. v. Adamson, 2008 WL 249157 (W.D. Ark. Jan. 29, 2008) (denying exemptions for failure to follow Arkansas procedure); Hendricks & Lewis, P.L.L.C. v. Clinton, 2011 WL 4861855 (N.D. Fla. Aug. 9, 2011) (mag.) (exemption for bank account containing Social Security funds lost by failure to meet time limits of Florida statute), *adopted by* 2011 WL 4861844 (N.D. Fla. Oct. 13, 2011); *In re* Khanh Viet Nguyen, 2011 WL 3889714 (Bankr. E.D. Va. Sept. 2, 2011) (procedural requirements of Virginia exemption statutes are strict; court has no power to excuse compliance with five-day deadline); Lang v. Dorosh, 2010 WL 5292607 (Minn. Ct. App. Dec. 28, 2010) (procedure to claim exemption for account in financial institution is "very meticulous"; denying exemption for IRA because account statement not timely disclosed). *See also* § 12.6.3.1, *supra* (whether federal exemption can be waived by failure to follow state procedure).

968 *See* § 12.2.2, *supra*.

969 *In re* Mootosammy, 387 B.R. 291 (Bankr. M.D. Fla. 2008) (exemptions not waived by failure to follow Florida procedure for claiming exemptions within fifteen days after levy); *In re* Skinner, 2001 WL 1699660 (Bankr. M.D.N.C. Aug. 7, 2001) (minor procedural omission by debtor is not permanent waiver of exemptions). *See also* Household Fin. Corp. v. Ellis, 419 S.E.2d 592 (N.C. Ct. App. 1992) (waiver of exemptions by failing to assert them at time of first execution does not prevent debtor from asserting them against subsequent executions; statutory requirement that constitutional exemption be asserted prior to payment of proceeds of sale to creditor is unconstitutional), *aff'd*, 429 S.E.2d 716 (N.C. 1993) (per curiam). *See generally* § 12.6.3.1, *supra*.

970 16 C.F.R. § 444.2(a)(2), *adopted by* 49 Fed. Reg. 7740 (Mar. 1, 1984). *See generally* National Consumer Law Center, Federal Deception Law § 2.3.5 (2012), *updated at* www.nclc.org/library.

971 16 C.F.R. § 444.2(a)(4).

972 *See* National Consumer Law Center, Federal Deception Law § 2.2.3 (2012), *updated at* www.nclc.org/library.

973 *See* National Consumer Law Center, Federal Deception Law § 2.2.3.2 (2012), *updated at* www.nclc.org/library.

974 Free Bridge Auto Sales v. Fitzgerald, 48 Va. Cir. 1 (1999); F & S Fin. v. Jordan, 48 Va. Cir. 580 (1997).

975 Orlando v. Fin. One, 369 S.E.2d 882 (W. Va. 1988).

976 *See* Baker v. Bennett, 644 So. 2d 901 (Ala. 1994) (Alabama courts do not have jurisdiction to issue garnishment orders to reach assets outside its territorial jurisdiction); Desert Wide Cabling & Installation v. Wells Fargo & Co., 958 P.2d 457 (Ariz. Ct. App. 1998) (Arizona writ of garnishment cannot be served on California bank); Gryphon Domestic VI, L.L.C. v. APP Int'l Fin. Co., 836 N.Y.S.2d 4, 9 (N.Y. App. Div. 2007) (it would violate the sovereignty of another state if New York sheriff tried to attach property there, but New York court can direct a defendant over whom it has jurisdiction to bring property into New York). *See generally* Gary Clifford Korn, *Attachment of Bank Deposits in the Electronic Age: The Doctrine of Digitrex*, 100 Banking L.J. 607 (Aug.–Sept. 1983).

977 Restatement (Second) of Conflict of Laws § 67.

978 *Cf.* Koh v. Inno-Pacific Holdings, Ltd., 54 P.3d 1270 (Wash. Ct. App. 2002) (corporation's interest in a partnership is located where the partnership is formally organized).

state to give full faith and credit to the judgment issued by the first state.[979]

The full faith and credit requirement does not mean that the second state must adopt the practices of the first state regarding the time, manner, and mechanisms for enforcing judgments: "Enforcement measures do not travel with the sister state judgment . . . ; such effects remain subject to the even-handed control of forum law."[980] So, for example, a creditor that is enforcing a California judgment through the Indiana courts can make use of Indiana collection remedies, not those available in California. If Indiana disallows certain remedies that would be available in California, or gives debtors different protections, the creditor is bound by the Indiana rules.[981]

As a matter of constitutional law, a state's exercise of *in rem* or *in personam* jurisdiction must comport with fair play and substantial justice.[982] Courts have, however, held that this rule does not require a judgment creditor to obtain *in personam* jurisdiction over the debtor in order to enforce a judgment in a state other than the one that issued it. Instead, the presence of the debtor's asset in that second state is sufficient to support jurisdiction.[983]

To regulate enforcement of one state's judgment in a second state, most states have adopted the Uniform Enforcement of Foreign Judgments Act.[984] This Act provides a procedure for registering a judgment in another jurisdiction and initiating execution proceedings on assets located there. The creditor may also have the right to use older procedures such as filing a new suit on the judgment in the second state.[985]

Under the uniform act, the judgment creditor must first file an authenticated copy of the judgment with a court in the state where enforcement is sought.[986] The creditor must also file an affidavit setting forth the names and last known addresses of the judgment debtor and the judgment creditor.[987] The court is then required to send a prompt notice of the filing of the judgment to the judgment debtor at the address given.[988] However, the Act provides that if the creditor mails notice to the judgment debtor and files proof of mailing with the court, any failure of the court to mail the notice does not affect the enforcement proceedings.[989]

Upon accomplishment of these steps, the creditor can use the same enforcement procedures as would be available for a judgment entered by the courts in that state.[990] However, the uniform law allows the state to specify a limited time period during which the state's enforcement procedures would be available.[991]

If the debtor appeals the underlying judgment or obtains a stay from the court that issued it, the stay applies in the

979 U.S. Const., art. IV, § 1. *See also* Livingston v. Naylor, 920 A.2d 34 (Md. Ct. Spec. App. 2007).

980 Baker v. Gen. Motors Corp., 522 U.S. 222, 235, 118 S. Ct. 657, 139 L. Ed. 2d 580 (1998). *See also* Weiss v. Weiss, 100 So. 3d 1220 (Fla. Dist. Ct. App. 2012) (Florida property settlement cannot be enforced by use of contempt power, but Illinois property settlement can; Florida is required to give full faith and credit to Illinois judgment but is not bound to adopt Illinois's "practices regarding the time, manner and method of enforcing judgments" or to violate Florida public policy barring imprisonment for debt); Caddie Homes, Inc. v. Falic, 235 A.2d 437 (Pa. Super. Ct. 1967); Restatement (Second) of Conflict of Laws § 99 (1971) ("the local law of the forum determines the method by which a judgment of another state is enforced").

981 Mahl v. Aaron, 809 N.E.2d 953 (Ind. Ct. App. 2004).

982 Shaffer v. Heitner, 433 U.S. 186, 207, 97 S. Ct. 2569, 53 L. Ed. 2d 683 (1977); Livingston v. Naylor, 920 A.2d 34, 53 (Md. Ct. Spec. App. 2007). *See also* Goodyear Tire & Rubber Co. v. Ruby, 540 A.2d 482 (Md. 1988) (Maryland court can enforce its judgment by issuing order requiring out-of-state corporation that is doing business in Maryland to garnish Texas employee's wages only if the corporation has sufficient minimum contacts with Maryland); Bianco v. Concepts "100," Inc., 436 A.2d 206 (Pa. Super. Ct. 1981) (Pennsylvania court may issue garnishment against out-of-state insurance company only if company has sufficient minimum contacts with Pennsylvania to allow personal jurisdiction).

983 Huggins v. Deinhard, 654 P.2d 32 (Ariz. Ct. App. 1982) (Arizona court may enforce registered California judgment against debtor's Arizona bank account without acquiring personal jurisdiction over debtor); Bank of Babylon v. Quirk, 472 A.2d 21 (Conn. 1984); UMS Partners, Ltd. v. Jackson, 1995 WL 413395 (Del. Super. Ct. June 15, 1995) (Pennsylvania judgment is enforceable against assets located in Delaware regardless of whether judgment debtor is subject to personal jurisdiction in Delaware); Tabet v. Tabet, 644 So. 2d 557 (Fla. Dist. Ct. App. 1994); Williamson v. Williamson, 275 S.E.2d 42 (Ga. 1981) (personal jurisdiction over debtor unnecessary as long as debtor has property in the state that can be executed upon); Hexter v. Hexter, 386 N.E.2d 1006 (Ind. Ct. App. 1979); Ruiz v. Lloses, 559 A.2d 866 (N.J. Super. Ct. App. Div. 1989); Breezevale Ltd. v. Dickinson, 693 N.Y.S.2d 532 (N.Y. App. Div. 1999); Fine v. Spierer, 486 N.Y.S.2d 9 (N.Y. App. Div. 1985); Lenchyshyn v. Pelko Elec., Inc., 723 N.Y.S.2d 285 (N.Y. App. Div. 2001); Fraser v. Littlejohn, 386 S.E.2d 230, 233 (N.C. Ct. App. 1989); Berger v. Berger, 417 A.2d 921 (Vt. 1980); Koh v. Inno-Pacific Holdings, Ltd., 54 P.3d 1270, 1273 (Wash. Ct. App. 2002). *See also* Shaffer v. Heitner, 433 U.S. 186, 211 n.36, 97 S. Ct. 2569, 53 L. Ed. 2d 683 (1977) (dictum) ("Once it has been determined by a court of competent jurisdiction that the defendant is a debtor of the plaintiff, there would seem to be no unfairness in allowing an action to realize on that debt in a State where the defendant has property, whether or not that State would have jurisdiction to determine the existence of the debt as an original matter"); Restatement (Second) of Conflict of Laws § 60 (1971) (state has power to exercise judicial jurisdiction to affect interests in a chattel in the state even if owner is not within court's personal jurisdiction). *Cf.* Electrolines, Inc. v. Prudential Assurance Co., Ltd., 677 N.W.2d 874, 885 (Mich. Ct. App. 2003) (court cannot enforce foreign judgment unless it has jurisdiction over the defendant or the defendant's property).

984 According to the website of the Uniform Law Commission (formerly the National Conference of Commissioners on Uniform State Laws or NCCUSL), www.uniformlaws.org, all jurisdictions except California, Massachusetts, Puerto Rico, and Vermont have adopted the uniform law.

985 *See, e.g.*, Mori v. Mori, 931 P.2d 854 (Utah 1997) (judgment plaintiff may file an action on a foreign judgment; Uniform Enforcement of Foreign Judgments Act does not apply to judgments from other countries that are not subject to Full Faith and Credit Clause).

986 Unif. Enforcement of Foreign Judgments Act (UEFJA) § 2.

987 *Id.* § 3.

988 *Id.* § 3(b).

989 *Cf.* Doyle v. Schultz, 97 F. Supp. 2d 763 (W.D. La. 2000) (judgment creditor and collection firm may be liable under 42 U.S.C. § 1983 for invoking state procedures that allowed issuance of writ for constructive seizure of home without judicial approval or notice and opportunity for hearing based on out-of-state judgment that was not yet final).

990 Unif. Enforcement of Foreign Judgments Act (UEFJA) § 2.

991 *Id.* § 3(c).

enforcing state as well.[992] In addition, the debtor can seek a stay or an order reopening or vacating the judgment from the court in the enforcing state, following the same procedures that would apply to a judgment issued by that state's courts.[993]

12.11.3 Bank Accounts

While it is clear that to execute upon tangible property, such as land or a vehicle, the creditor must use the courts of the state where the property is located, the issue becomes more complicated with a bank account. Creditors may argue that the location of the branch bank where the debtor maintains the bank account is not dispositive. Instead, they may argue that execution can issue in any state where any branch or office of the debtor's bank is located, and that the bank then must restrain all the debtor's accounts even if they are located in other states (or countries).

A number of decisions reject this view and treat bank accounts as located in the specific branch bank where the debtor maintains the account. These courts require a creditor that seeks to garnish a debtor's bank account to serve the garnishment on the branch bank where the debtor maintains the account, not on a different office or branch of the bank, particularly one located in a different jurisdiction.[994] Thus, if a consumer maintains an account in a branch bank outside of the state where the court issued the judgment, the collector will have to go to that other state to enforce the judgment on that bank account. It cannot issue a garnishment order against a branch of the bank that is located in the state where the judgment was issued.

This position is consistent with Article 4 of the Uniform Commercial Code, which provides that "[a] branch or separate office of a bank is a separate bank for the purpose of computing the time within which and determining the place at or to which action may be taken or notices or orders shall be given under this Article and under Article 3."[995] A few jurisdictions also have statutes specifying the effect of service of an execution upon a branch bank.[996]

Not only debtors but also banks would be harmed by any other rule. If service of an execution order at one branch restrained any accounts at any other branches, the bank would be liable to the creditor if it cashed any checks or allowed any withdrawals from any accounts at any branches the moment after the execution was served. Even with computer networks, a bank branch cannot be expected to implement a real-time system-wide freeze on the debtor's accounts in all branches.[997]

In 2009 New York's highest court held that a garnishment order that was properly served upon a New York bank could order it to turn over stock certificates that were held by its parent bank in Bermuda.[998] Once the court acquired personal

992 *Id.* § 4.

993 *Id.* § 2.

994 Det Bergenske Dampskibsselskab v. Sabre Shipping Corp., 341 F.2d 50 (2d Cir. 1965) (each bank branch is a separate business entity, and service on a main office or branch does not restrain an account maintained at a separate branch; applying New York law); Shinto Shipping Co. v. Fibrex & Shipping Co., 425 F. Supp. 1088 (N.D. Cal. 1976) (enforcing California statute that garnishment is effective only as to accounts maintained in branch bank where garnishment order is served), *aff'd on other grounds*, 572 F.2d 1328 (9th Cir. 1978); Nat'l Shipping & Trading Corp. v. Weeks Stevedoring Co., 252 F. Supp. 275 (S.D.N.Y. 1966) (attachment must be served on branch where account is maintained); Baker v. Bennett, 644 So. 2d 901 (Ala. 1994) (Alabama court cannot reach judgment debtor's assets in New York brokerage account by serving brokerage's Alabama office; court cannot obtain jurisdiction of out-of-state property by issuing writ to bailee over whom the court has personal jurisdiction); McCloskey v. Chase Manhattan Bank, 183 N.E.2d 227 (N.Y. 1962) (levy upon bank in New York is ineffective to reach deposits maintained in Oregon branch); Nat'l Union Fire Ins. Co. v. Advanced Employment Concepts, Inc., 703 N.Y.S.2d 3 (N.Y. App. Div. 2000) (service of execution upon bank office in one jurisdiction is insufficient to reach account in branch bank in different jurisdiction). *See also* Macatawa Bank v. Wipperfurth, 822 N.W.2d 237 (Mich. Ct. App. 2011) (situs of intangible asset is domicile of owner, so Florida debtor's IRA cannot be reached by serving garnishment upon financial institution's Michigan branch). *Cf.* Yayasan Sabah Dua Shipping SDN BHD v. Scandinavian Liquid Carriers Ltd., 335 F. Supp. 2d 441 (S.D.N.Y. 2004) (finding that situs of bank account was New York when Cayman Island branch where account was listed appeared to be a paper bank entirely controlled and managed by New York branch); Ellis v. Barclays Bank PLC-Miami Agency, 594 So. 2d 826 (Fla. Dist. Ct. App. 1992) (garnishment served on Miami branch of international bank cannot reach deposits held in other countries; bank had responded as to all its domestic branches, but court does not comment on whether this was proper or required). *But see* Marisco, Ltd. v. American Samoa Gov't, 889 F. Supp. 2d 1244 (D. Hawaii 2012) (predicting that Hawaii courts will reject separate entity rule; serving garnishment on Hawaii bank is sufficient to reach account at its American Samoa branch); Digitrex, Inc. v. Johnson, 491 F. Supp. 66 (S.D.N.Y. 1980) (terming existing rule "obsolete" in light of banks' use of high-speed computers; service of postjudgment restraining notice on main bank office is effective to restrain an account maintained at a branch; note that Nat'l Union Fire Ins. Co. v. Advanced Employment Concepts, Inc., 703 N.Y.S.2d 3 (N.Y. App. Div. 2000) essentially limits this decision to its facts); Wilton Enter., Inc. v. Cook's Pantry, Inc., 552 A.2d 1031 (N.J. Super. Ct. App. Div. 1988) (levy served on bank branch is effective as to deposit maintained in another branch, when bank had practice of notifying appropriate branch by telephone, even though it did not follow that practice in this case).

995 U.C.C. § 4-107. *But see* Wilton Enter., Inc. v. Cook's Pantry, Inc., 552 A.2d 1031 (N.J. Super. Ct. Law Div. 1988) (inexplicably interpreting this language to mean that service on one branch of a bank is effective as service on other branches and requires the bank to act with due diligence to inform other branches).

996 Idaho Code Ann. § 8-507 (general rule is that service of execution on bank office only restrains account maintained in that office, but bank may designate a particular office to receive executions, in which case an execution served on that office restrains all accounts at any branches); Wash. Rev. Code § 6.27.080 (writ naming financial institution attaches deposits in that institution). *See also* Desert Wide Cabling & Installation, Inc. v. Wells Fargo & Co., N.A., 958 P.2d 457 (Ariz. Ct. App. 1998) (interpreting Arizona statute limiting effectiveness of levy to branch bank where service is made, or, upon payment of $25, to other branches in same county; Arizona court cannot serve garnishment order on out-of-state bank).

997 *See* Gary Clifford Korn, *Attachment of Bank Deposits in the Electronic Age: The Doctrine of Digitrex*, 100 Banking L.J. 607 (Aug.–Sept. 1983) (discussing problems that banks would face). *See also* Desert Wide Cabling & Installation, Inc. v. Wells Fargo & Co., N.A., 958 P.2d 457, 458 (Ariz. Ct. App. 1998) (noting problem of double payment).

998 Koehler v. Bank of Bermuda, Ltd., 911 N.E.2d 825 (N.Y. 2009). *See also* JW Oilfield Equip., L.L.C. v. Commerzbank AG, 764 F. Supp. 2d

jurisdiction over the New York bank by serving the order upon it, it could order it to bring the specified property into the state. The case did not involve consumer bank accounts, so the provisions of Article 4 of the UCC did not come into play, making the case distinguishable from the typical consumer collection case. Courts have differed as to whether this decision silently overruled previous New York decisions on the question, and the state's highest court has agreed to hear a case that may resolve the issue.[999]

12.11.4 Wages

Earned but unpaid wages, like bank accounts, are not clearly "located" in a specific state like tangible property is. The question then is whether a court can issue a wage garnishment order that affects wages the consumer earns in a different state.

A court in one state will not have jurisdiction over an employer in another state and therefore cannot issue a garnishment order to an out-of-state employer. However, the creditor may argue that the court can garnish wages earned out of state by serving a garnishment order on an in-state facility of the employer. This argument is based on the theory that the wages owed to the consumer reside wherever the employer has a presence and can be reached anywhere that the employer can be served. For example, a collector, after obtaining a judgment in Missouri, might seek to garnish the consumer's wages earned at an Indiana Walmart store by serving the order on a Walmart store in Missouri.

This view would dilute "fair play and substantial justice" to meaninglessness, as wages earned for a nationwide corporation in one state could be garnished in any of the forty-nine other states.[1000] For example, the Georgia Supreme Court rejected a judgment creditor's attempt to garnish a California debtor's Army pay in Georgia.[1001] The court rejected the creditor's argument that, because the employer had a presence in Georgia, Georgia courts could order it to turn over wages regardless of where they were earned.

Likewise, a Maryland court held that Maryland courts can enforce foreign judgments only against wages earned in Maryland. Thus a garnishment order issued against a corporation headquartered in Maryland is effective as to an employee's wages earned in Maryland but not as to wages earned in other states.[1002] A Pennsylvania Attorney General opinion similarly holds that, if a debtor works in Pennsylvania, a judgment creditor cannot obtain an out-of-state judgment, obtain a wage garnishment order in that state, and then serve the order on an office of the debtor's employer in that state.[1003] More recently, a federal court has held that wages are located in the state where they were earned, so the judgment creditor must domesticate its judgment there and follow that state's garnishment laws.[1004] A law review article points out that any other rule would invite creditors to forum shop to find the most remote jurisdiction with the most liberal garnishment laws and the most grudging exemption laws.[1005]

Allowing this sort of interstate garnishment would also subject employers to potential double liability, as they could be liable to the creditor for any wages paid out to the debtor at any location anywhere in the country—indeed, anywhere in the world—after service of the garnishment order. An employer that withheld a portion of an employee's wages in compliance with an out-of-state garnishment order could also face sanctions for violation of the wage and hour laws in the state where the employee worked.

---

587 (S.D.N.Y. 2011) (applying *Koehler*; if court has personal jurisdiction over garnishee bank, it can issue garnishment order to it and can reach assets that are outside the jurisdiction, even if it does not have *in rem* jurisdiction over those assets); *In re* Marriage of Kosmond, 830 N.E.2d 596 (Ill. App. Ct. 2005) (when court has *in personam* jurisdiction over all the parties, it can issue order to a bank to freeze a party's assets in another country; Illinois does not follow "separate entity" rule that treats each bank branch as a separate entity for purposes of seizing assets or deposits).

999 Tire Eng'g & Distrib., L.L.C. v. Bank of China, Ltd., 740 F.3d 108 (2d Cir. 2014) (summarizing different views and certifying question whether New York's "separate entity" rule prevents New York court from ordering bank, which has branches in New York, to turn over or restrain assets held in branches in other jurisdictions), *certified question accepted*, 5 N.E.3d 590 (N.Y. 2014), *withdrawal of certified questions in one of two companion cases noted*, 7 N.E.3d 506 (N.Y. 2014).

1000 *See* Robert Laurence, *Out of State Garnishments: Work-in-Progress, Offered in Tribute to Dr. Robert A. Leflar*, 50 Ark. L. Rev. 415, 418 (1997) ("this rule is an out-moded doctrine that does not survive modern constitutional analysis").

1001 Williamson v. Williamson, 275 S.E.2d 42 (Ga. 1981). *Accord* Polacke v. Superior Court, 823 P.2d 84 (Ariz. Ct. App. 1991) (military retirement pay that is not issued or received in Arizona is not constructively present there and cannot be attached by an Arizona court that lacks *in personam* jurisdiction over the debtor); Ferguson v. Ferguson, 634 N.E.2d 506 (Ind. Ct. App. 1994) (even though federal government has a presence in all fifty states, military benefits that were neither issued nor received in Indiana cannot be garnished there by court that lacks *in personam* jurisdiction over debtor).

1002 Livingston v. Naylor, 920 A.2d 34, 53 (Md. Ct. Spec. App. 2007). *Accord* Brown v. Arabian Am. Oil Co., 278 N.Y.S.2d 256 (N.Y. Sup. Ct. 1967) (interpreting New York's service rules not to allow enforcement of New York judgment by serving a garnishment order on New York employer, when debtor worked in Saudi Arabia).

1003 Pennsylvania Attorney Gen., Official Op. No. 67 (Oct. 5, 1973), *available at* www.nclc.org/unreported. *But see* West v. Ford Motor Credit Co., 2013 WL 497159 (E.D. Pa. Feb. 11, 2013) (allowing garnishment of Pennsylvania wages in response to Maryland court order, enforcing Maryland judgment, served on Maryland office of employer; Pennsylvania generally forbids wage garnishments, Maryland permits them). *But cf.* Morgan v. Neville, 74 Pa. 52 (Pa. 1873) (allowing Pennsylvania creditor to attach debtor's wages earned in Pennsylvania by serving his Pennsylvania employer in Maryland even though wages are protected from creditors in Pennsylvania; this ancient decision appears to be based on the *in rem* jurisdictional theory repudiated by Shaffer v. Heitner, 433 U.S. 186 (1977)).

1004 Memorial Hosp. of Martinsville v. D'Oro, 2011 WL 2679593 (W.D. Va. July 8, 2011) (creditor with Virginia judgment against debtor who now lives in Pennsylvania must domesticate judgment in Pennsylvania and follow that state's wage garnishment law; cannot garnish wages by issuing garnishment order to non-Pennsylvania branch of debtor's employer).

1005 Robert Laurence, *Out of State Garnishments: Work-in-Progress, Offered in Tribute to Dr. Robert A. Leflar*, 50 Ark. L. Rev. 415, 421 (1997).

Some cases, however, allow wages earned out of state to be garnished by serving a garnishment order on an in-state facility of the debtor's employer. These courts hold that such a step is permissible if the garnishment order is issued by the court that issued the original judgment and acquired personal jurisdiction over the debtor at that time.[1006] For example, a Texas court held that a Florida divorce court could enforce its alimony order by serving a wage garnishment order on a Florida office of the judgment debtor's employer, even though the debtor had moved to Texas and was working there.[1007] The court stressed that the judgment for alimony and the garnishment order were issued by the same court that had rendered the initial judgment against the debtor before he moved to Texas, and that the debtor conceded that the Florida judgment was valid and entitled to full faith and credit. The result might have been different if the Florida court had not acquired *in personam* jurisdiction over the debtor in the first instance.[1008]

The Illinois garnishment statute's limits, which are more protective of debtors than the federal limits,[1009] apply "irrespective of the place where the compensation was earned or payable and the state where the employee resides."[1010] The apparent effect of this provision is that, if the employer is served with a garnishment order in Illinois, then the Illinois garnishment limits apply regardless of whether the debtor works or lives in another state.

12.11.5 Application of the FDCPA's Venue Abuse Prohibition

The FDCPA may provide a remedy in some cases in which a creditor files a garnishment action in a judicial district other than where the consumer resides or entered into the contract. The FDCPA provides that, in the case of an action that does not involve enforcing a security interest in real property, "[a]ny debt collector who brings any legal action on a debt against any consumer shall . . . bring such action only in the judicial district or similar legal entity—(A) in which such consumer signed the contract sued upon; or (B) in which such consumer resides at the commencement of the action."[1011]

The Ninth Circuit allowed a consumer to go to trial on a claim that collectors violated this prohibition by obtaining a wage garnishment order in an improper county.[1012] The collector had originally brought suit on the debt against the debtor in Maricopa County, which was not the proper venue under state law. The suit was transferred to the debtor's county of residence, Pima County, and then dismissed. The creditor then sued the debtor again in Maricopa County, the case was transferred again to Pima County, and the consumer agreed to a judgment. Then the collector filed an application for a writ of garnishment against the consumer—again in Maricopa County. The Ninth Circuit held that the garnishment action was a "legal action," so was subject to the FDCPA's venue abuse provision.

A First Circuit decision takes a different view.[1013] In that case, the creditor obtained a judgment against a New Bedford consumer in a New Bedford court. However, the consumer's employer was located in the Attleboro judicial district, and Massachusetts law required the judgment creditor to obtain a wage garnishment in the district where the debtor's employer was located. The court held that such an action was an action against the employer, not a legal action against the consumer, so the FDCPA's venue abuse provisions were inapplicable. The court distinguished states that do not require applications for wage garnishment to be filed in the employer's venue. This issue is discussed in more detail in National Consumer Law Center's *Fair Debt Collection*.[1014]

1006 *See, e.g.*, Smith v. Lorillard, Inc., 945 F.2d 745 (4th Cir. 1991) (Kentucky court that rendered judgment against Kentucky debtor may serve garnishment order on debtor's employer, who does business in Kentucky, even though debtor has moved to North Carolina and now works there); Champion Int'l Corp. v. Ayars, 587 F. Supp. 1274 (D. Conn. 1984) (allowing child and spousal support to be collected by garnishment of wages earned out-of-state by service upon employer's in-state facility); Garrett v. Garrett, 490 P.2d 313 (Colo. App. 1971) (divorce judgment entered by Colorado court that obtained personal jurisdiction over debtor can be enforced by wage garnishment order against Colorado office of debtor's Washington employer; Colorado exemptions apply); State *ex rel.* Dep't of Revenue v. Control Data Corp., 713 P.2d 30 (Or. 1986) (debtor had enough contacts with Oregon to allow Oregon court to render judgment against him, and then it could issue a wage garnishment order to his employer's in-state office, even though he now worked for that employer in a different state); Jones v. U.S. Steel Corp., 4 Pa. D. & C.3d 552 (Pa. Ct. Com. Pl. 1977) (when Pennsylvania judgment debtor was employed at employer's New Jersey plant when New Jersey wage garnishment order was served on employer, employer must comply with order even after debtor transferred to plant in Pennsylvania, which does not allow wage garnishment); Austin v. Westinghouse Elec. Corp., 59 Pa. D. & C.2d 178 (Pa. Ct. Com. Pl. 1972) (Ohio judgment can be enforced against Pennsylvania debtor who is employed in Pennsylvania by serving wage garnishment order on employer's Ohio office, even though Pennsylvania does not allow wage garnishment). *See also* First v. Montana Dep't of Soc. & Rehab. Servs., 808 P.2d 467 (Mont. 1991) (Montana court can enforce child support order by using income withholding procedure against Montana unemployment compensation benefits, even though debtor lived on Native American reservation); Birl v. Birl, 24 Pa. D. & C.2d 421 (Pa. Ct. Com. Pl. 1961) (interpreting Pennsylvania law to allow alimony judgment to be collected through garnishment of wages earned out-of-state by service of garnishment order on employer's in-state office).

1007 Knighton v. Int'l Bus. Mach. Corp., 856 S.W.2d 206 (Tex. App. 1993).

1008 *But cf.* Sagona v. Doty, 1991 WL 835319 (Va. Cir. Ct. Nov. 21, 1991) (allowing garnishment order based on Illinois judgment to issue against Virginia agent of debtor's North Carolina employer even though debtor had no contacts with Virginia, and North Carolina does not allow wage garnishment; from court's opinion it appears that judgment debtor was notified of Virginia garnishment proceeding but not served with it).

1009 *See* § 12.4.3, *supra*.

1010 735 Ill. Comp. Stat. § 5/12-803.

1011 15 U.S.C. § 1692*i*.

1012 Fox v. Citicorp Credit Servs., Inc., 15 F.3d 1507 (9th Cir. 1994).

1013 Smith v. Solomon & Solomon, P.C., 714 F.3d 73 (1st Cir. 2013).

1014 National Consumer Law Center, Fair Debt Collection § 5.9.2 (8th ed. 2014).

12.12 Imprisonment for Debt

12.12.1 State Constitutional and Statutory Provisions

Imprisonment for debt is prohibited in all or nearly all the states and the District of Columbia.[1015] These prohibitions represent a break with the rule that had prevailed in England until 1838, which allowed body attachment or a writ of *capias ad satisfaciendum* as a means of enforcing a civil judgment for a debt.[1016]

Most states include a prohibition against imprisonment for debt in their state constitutions. In several states there is a statutory rather than a constitutional prohibition.[1017] In a few states, the prohibition is not found in any statute or constitutional provision but is recognized by judicial decisions, sometimes based on the repeal of a statute that formerly authorized the practice.[1018] The United States Constitution does not include a parallel provision, but a federal statute prohibits federal courts from ordering imprisonment for debt in states where it is prohibited.[1019] In interpreting a state constitutional prohibition against imprisonment for debt, every doubt must be resolved in favor of the citizen.[1020]

12.12.2 Exceptions to the Prohibition

Many of the state prohibitions make an exception for fraud[1021] or tort.[1022] Some states allow imprisonment for debt when the debtor is about to leave the jurisdiction,[1023] or when the debtor "refuses to deliver up his estate for the benefit of his cred-

---

1015 *ALABAMA:* Ala. Const. art. I, § 20.
ALASKA: Alaska Const. art. I, § 17.
ARIZONA: Ariz. Const. art. II, § 18.
ARKANSAS: Ark. Const. art. II, § 16.
CALIFORNIA: Cal. Const. art. I, § 10.
CONNECTICUT: It appears that Connecticut abolished imprisonment for debt by repealing a statute that had formerly provided for body attachment. *See* Lee v. BSB Greenwich Mortgage Ltd. P'ship, 2007 WL 2743435, at *5 (Conn. Super. Ct. Aug. 31, 2007).
COLORADO: Colo. Const. art. II, § 12.
DELAWARE: Del. Code Ann. tit. 10, § 5052.
DISTRICT OF COLUMBIA: D.C. Code § 15-320(c).
FLORIDA: Fla. Const. art I § 11.
GEORGIA: Ga. Const. art. I, § 1, ¶ XXIII.
HAWAII: Haw. Const. art. I, § 19.
IDAHO: Idaho Const. art. I, § 15.
ILLINOIS: Ill. Const. art. I, § 14.
INDIANA: Ind. Const. art. I, § 22.
IOWA: Iowa Const. art. I, § 19.
KANSAS: Kan. Const. Bill of Rights § 16.
KENTUCKY: Ky. Const. Bill of Rights § 18.
LOUISIANA: La. Rev. Stat. Ann. § 13:4281 (abolishing writ of *capias ad satisfaciendum*).
MAINE: Me. Rev. Stat. tit. 14, § 3701.
MARYLAND: Md. Const. art. III, § 38.
MASSACHUSETTS: Mass. Gen. Laws ch. 224, § 6 (prohibiting arrest on execution in civil action unless creditor proves that debtor intends to leave the state).
MICHIGAN: Mich. Const. art. I, § 21.
MINNESOTA: Minn. Const. art. I, § 12.
MISSISSIPPI: Miss. Const. art. III, § 30.
MISSOURI: Mo. Const. art. I, § 11.
MONTANA: Mont. Const. art. II, § 27.
NEBRASKA: Neb. Const. art. I, § 20.
NEVADA: Nev. Const. art. I, § 14.
NEW HAMPSHIRE: Vt. Nat'l Bank v. Taylor, 445 A.2d 1122 (N.H. 1982) (noting that New Hampshire repealed the last of its statutes authorizing imprisonment for debt in 1971, although writs of *capias* can still be used in some circumstances).
NEW JERSEY: N.J. Const. art. I, § 13
NEW MEXICO: N.M. Const. art. II, § 21.
NEW YORK: N.Y. Debt. & Cred. Law §§ 100 through 111 (McKinney) (providing procedure for insolvent debtor to petition for exemption from arrest and imprisonment).
NORTH CAROLINA: N.C. Const. art. I, § 28.
NORTH DAKOTA: N.D. Const. art. I, § 15.
OHIO: Ohio Const. art. I, § 15.
OKLAHOMA: Okla. Const. art. II, § 13.
OREGON: Or. Const. art. I, § 19.
PENNSYLVANIA: 42 Pa. Con. Stat. § 5108.
RHODE ISLAND: R.I. Const. art. I, § 11.
SOUTH CAROLINA: S.C. Const. art. I, § 19.
SOUTH DAKOTA: S.D. Const. art. VI, § 15.
TENNESSEE: Tenn. Const. art. I, § 18.
TEXAS: Tex. Const. art. I, § 18.
UTAH: Utah Const. art. I, § 16.
VERMONT: Vt. Const. ch. II, § 40.
VIRGINIA: Makarov v. Commonwealth, 228 S.E.2d 573 (Va. 1976) (although there is no state constitutional prohibition, "[I]t is nevertheless established in this state that a person may not be imprisoned, absent fraud, for mere failure to pay a debt arising from contract or for mere failure to pay a judgment for a debt founded on contract. . . . [I]mprisonment of poor debtors offends fundamental principles of justice in today's ordered society.").
WASHINGTON: Wash. Const. art. I, § 17.
WEST VIRGINIA: See Boarman v. Boarman, 556 S.E.2d 800, 804 (W. Va. 2001) ("West Virginia has abandoned the Dickensian notion of 'debtor's prison.' ").
WISCONSIN: Wis. Const. art. I, § 16.
WYOMING: Wyo. Const. art. I, § 5.

1016 Becky A Vogt, *State v. Allison: Imprisonment for Debt in South Dakota*, 46 S.D. L. Rev. 334, 343 (2001) (describing history of imprisonment for debt).

1017 *See, e.g.*, La. Rev. Stat. Ann. § 13:4281 (abolishing writ of *capias ad satisfaciendum*); 42 Pa. Cons. Stat. § 5108.

1018 *See, e.g.*, Lee v. BSB Greenwich Mortgage Ltd. P'ship, 2007 WL 2743435, at *5 (Conn. Super. Ct. Aug. 31, 2007) (noting that Connecticut abolished imprisonment for debt by repealing a statute that had formerly provided for body attachment); Makarov v. Commonwealth, 228 S.E.2d 573 (Va. 1976) (although there is no state constitutional prohibition, "[I]t is nevertheless established in this state that a person may not be imprisoned, absent fraud, for mere failure to pay a debt arising from contract or for mere failure to pay a judgment for a debt founded on contract. . . . [I]mprisonment of poor debtors offends fundamental principles of justice in today's ordered society."). *See also In re* Birchall, 913 N.E.2d 799 (Mass. 2009) (supplementary process, which requires debtor's exam and places burden on creditor to show ability to pay, replaced former procedure that allowed imprisonment for debt).

1019 28 U.S.C. § 2007. *See generally* Annotation, *Constitutionality, construction, and application of statutes empowering court to require judgment debtor to make payment out of income or by installments*, 111 A.L.R. 392 (1937).

1020 State v. Riggs, 807 S.W.2d 32 (Ark. 1991).

1021 *See, e.g.*, Ariz. Const. art. II, § 18; Ind. Const. art. I, § 22.

1022 *See, e.g.*, Colo. Const. art. II, § 12. *But see* Cal. Const. art. I, § 10 (explicitly including civil actions for tort in the prohibition).

1023 *See, e.g.*, Alaska Const. art. I, § 17; Mass. Gen. Laws ch. 224, § 6; Or. Const. art. I, § 19.

itors."[1024] A number of states restrict the protection to civil actions.[1025]

It is common for states to interpret their prohibitions not to prohibit imprisonment for non-payment of family support obligations[1026] and fines,[1027] and in some states these are explicit exceptions.[1028] States that allow imprisonment for non-payment of family support debts often distinguish between court-ordered alimony or child support, which may be enforced by imprisonment, and property division, which is treated like any other civil debt.[1029] Courts may also distinguish between an order to turn over specific marital property—which may include a specific sum in existence at the time of the order—and an order to pay with no identified source.[1030] Even for fines or restitution ordered in a criminal case, the defendant must be given an opportunity to demonstrate inability to pay.[1031]

Many states apply their prohibitions against imprisonment for debt to disallow incarceration on dishonored check charges unless there is a showing that the defendant acted with criminal intent.[1032] Only when criminal intent is established will the case fall within the exception for fraud,[1033] although intent may be presumed in some states by failure to pay the check after a notice period expires.[1034]

12.12.3 Can a Court Order a Judgment Debtor to Make Payments and Enforce the Order by Contempt?

Despite the near universal prohibition against imprisonment for ordinary civil debts, there are exceptions in some states that may amount to the same thing. A critical question

1024 Ill. Const. art. I, § 14. *Accord* Colo. Const. art. II, § 12; Ky. Const. Bill of Rights § 18; Mont. Const. art. II, § 27; N.D. Const. art. I, § 15; 42 Pa. Con. Stat. § 5108; R.I. Const. art. I, § 11.

1025 *See, e.g.*, Iowa Const. art. I, § 19; Ohio Const. art. I, § 15.

1026 *See, e.g.*, State *ex rel.* Dep't of Economic Sec. v. Cumming, 2013 WL 5775153 (Ariz. Ct. App. Oct. 24, 2013) (unpublished) (court-ordered child support not a debt within meaning of constitutional provision banning imprisonment for debt); Mitchell v. Mitchell, 871 N.E.2d 390 (Ind. Ct. App. 2007) (in some circumstances trial court may use contempt to enforce property settlement that is incorporated into divorce decree); Foley v. Mannor, 844 N.E.2d 494 (Ind. Ct. App. 2006) (imprisonment for contempt for failure to pay child support is constitutional, but only when the minor needs support, not after minor becomes emancipated or is adopted); Kokinda v. Commonwealth, 2013 WL 5676741 (Ky. Ct. App. Oct. 18, 2013) (criminal non-support statute not unconstitutional; it punishes "intentional financial abandonment," not debt; due process did not require hearing on ability to pay, when guilty plea admitted failure to pay despite ability to do so); Collette v. Baxter, 2012 WL 1059910 (Ohio Ct. App. Mar. 28, 2012) (family support obligations—including attorney and expert fees incurred in case seeking modification of child support—are not debts within the meaning of Ohio's constitutional prohibition of imprisonment for debt); Brooks-Lee v. Lee, 2012 WL 344985 (Ohio Ct. App. Feb. 2, 2012) (failure to follow court orders to pay share of children's uninsured medical expenses, to reimburse wife for penalties and interest on earlier tax returns); Stychno v. Stychno, 2009 WL 5064144 (Ohio Ct. App. Dec. 24, 2009) (thirty-day imprisonment for non-payment of alimony arrearage not imprisonment for debt when debtor given opportunity to show inability to pay); *Ex parte* Hall, 854 S.W.2d 656 (Tex. 1993) (order to pay child or spousal support that is authorized by family law is enforceable by contempt, but not shown here); *In re* Davis, 372 S.W.3d 253 (Tex. App. 2012) (order to use community funds to pay debts necessary to preserve community assets may be enforced by contempt; order to pay spouse's attorney fees may not). *See also* Hissa v. Hissa, 2014 WL 1407952 (Ohio Ct. App. Apr. 10, 2014) (contempt power may be used to enforce separation agreement that had not been reduced to judgment; "punishment for violation of divorce decree provisions does not impinge upon the constitutional prohibition of imprisonment for debt"); *In re* Skero, 253 S.W.3d 884 (Tex. App. 2008) (abuser may be found in contempt of court and jailed for failing to pay attorney fees in domestic violence case, as domestic violence order creates legal duty rather than contractual obligation). *But cf.* Simpson v. Simpson, 68 So. 3d 958 (Fla. Dist. Ct. App. 2011) (contempt power cannot be used to enforce order that ex-husband pay wife's car loan); Randall v. Randall, 948 So. 2d 71 (Fla. Dist. Ct. App. 2007) (using contempt to enforce equitable distribution order requiring ex-spouse to pay debts owed to third parties would be unconstitutional as imprisonment for debt); Sizemore v. Sizemore, 2010 WL 1270362 (Ohio Ct. App. Apr. 5, 2010) (once child support arrearage is reduced to lump-sum judgment, it is a debt and cannot be enforced by incarceration for contempt); *In re* Green, 221 S.W.3d 645 (Tex. 2007) (constitutional prohibition of imprisonment for debt means that contractual agreement to pay spousal support cannot be enforced by contempt).

1027 Lavender v. City of Tuscaloosa, 198 So. 459, 461 (Ala. 1940).

1028 *See, e.g.*, Md. Const. art. III, § 38 (explicit exception for spousal or child support); Mo. Const. art. 1, § 11 (explicit exception for fines and penalties imposed by law).

1029 Weiss v. Weiss, 100 So. 3d 1220 (Fla. Dist. Ct. App. 2012) (Florida property settlement cannot be enforced by use of contempt power, but Illinois property settlement can); Randall v. Randall, 948 So. 2d 71 (Fla. Dist. Ct. App. 2007) (using contempt to enforce equitable distribution order requiring ex-spouse to pay debts owed to third parties would be unconstitutional imprisonment for debt); Love v. Love, 33 A.3d 1268 (Pa. Super. Ct. 2011) (court-ordered family support may be enforced by incarceration, but only ordinary contract remedies are available to enforce separation agreement); *In re* Greene, 221 S.W.3d 645 (Tex. 2007) (constitutional prohibition of imprisonment for debt means that contractual agreement to pay spousal support cannot be enforced by contempt); Shumate v. Shumate, 310 S.W.3d 149 (Tex. App. 2010) (order requiring ex-husband to pay credit card debts not enforceable by contempt).

1030 *In re* Kinney, 2014 WL 1414280 (Tex. App. Mar. 25, 2014) (granting habeas corpus to ex-wife imprisoned for failure to timely make equalization payment ordered when she was awarded home; no evidence of specific fund from which she might make payment).

1031 Turner v. Rogers, 131 S. Ct. 2507, 2516, 180 L. Ed. 2d 452 (2011); Hicks v. Feiock, 485 U.S. 624, 631, 108 S. Ct. 1423, 99 L. Ed. 2d 721 (1988); Bearden v. Georgia, 461 U.S. 660 (1983) (revocation of probation for failure to pay fine or restitution violates due process if probationer was unable to pay despite reasonable bona fide efforts to do so, unless no alternative measures are inadequate to meet state's objectives of punishment or deterrence); DelValle v. State, 80 So. 3d 999 (Fla. 2011) (indigent probationer should not be imprisoned based on inability to pay a monetary obligation; state must show ability to pay, burden then shifts to probationer to show inability; statute that required heightened "clear and convincing" standard for proof of inability created unconstitutional risk of imprisonment for debt); State v. Lundy, 308 P.3d 755 (Wash. Ct. App. 2013) (Washington criminal restitution statute, which specifically forbids consideration of ability to pay when imposing restitution, is constitutional, provided there are adequate safeguards to prevent imprisonment of indigents for non-payment).

1032 *See* § 8.2.2, *supra.*

1033 *See, e.g.*, State v. Riggs, 807 S.W.2d 32 (Ark. 1991) (striking down statute because it allowed imprisonment upon showing of willful failure to pay rather than fraud).

1034 *See* § 8.2, *supra.*

is whether a court has the power to order a debtor to make payments on a debt and then hold the debtor in contempt for failing to do so.[1035] Some courts hold that this stratagem does not result in imprisonment for debt, reasoning that the debtor is not being punished for owing the debt but for violating the court order.[1036] Typically these courts allow punishment for contempt only if there is a showing that the debtor has the financial means to comply with the order, on the theory that the contempt order would be punishment for the mere act of owing the debt without such a showing.[1037] Some courts only allow a debtor to be held in civil contempt, which means that the debtor must be able to avoid imprisonment by making the payment.[1038]

Other jurisdictions, however, recognize that allowing courts to order debtors to pay debts, and then holding them in civil or criminal contempt if they do not, amounts to imprisonment for debt.[1039] For example, the highest court in the District of Columbia holds that "contempt in general, and imprisonment

---

1035 *See, e.g.*, 735 Ill. Comp. Stat. § 5/2-1402(c)(2) (allowing court to order a debtor to make installment payments out of non-exempt income); Mass. Gen. Laws ch. 224, § 16 (allowing court to order debtor to make payments if it finds that debtor is financially able and providing that noncompliance can be punished as contempt); N.J. Stat. Ann. § 2A:17-64 (West) (allowing court to order debtor to pay judgment in installments from non-exempt income); N.Y. C.P.L.R. § 5226 (allowing court to order debtor to make installment payments). *See generally* Annotation, *Constitutionality, construction, and application of statutes empowering court to require judgment debtor to make payment out of income or by installments*, 111 A.L.R. 392 (1937).

1036 *See* Albarran v. Liberty Healthcare Mgmt., 2013 WL 6493097 (Ark. Ct. App. Dec. 11, 2013) (imprisonment for civil contempt, for failure to obey court order to pay money judgment, does not violate state constitutional ban on imprisonment for debt when debtor presented no evidence of inability to pay); Mason Furniture Corp. v. George, 362 A.2d 188 (N.H. 1976) (court may, after considering a number of factors, imprison judgment debtor for failing to make installment payment under an existing order); Paulis v. Super. Ct., 2004 WL 3704007 (N. Mar. I. June 8, 2004) (denying writ of prohibition; even if prohibition against imprisonment for debt is part of Northern Mariana Islands common law, imprisonment of debtor for failing to comply with order to pay $25 per month would not be a violation). *Cf.* DeGeorge v. Warheit, 741 N.W.2d 384, 391 (Mich. Ct. App. 2007) (affirming finding of contempt when debtor violated stipulated order not to transfer personal assets without court approval; "the punishment was for [defendant's] violation of the court's order, and not for failure to pay appellees for debts owed on a private contract").

1037 State Farm Mut. Auto Ins. Co. v. American Rehab & Physical Therapy, Inc., 376 Fed. Appx. 182 (3d Cir. 2010) (affirming injunction ordering time payments in amount greater than could be garnished from wages; no imprisonment for debt because evidence of ability to pay was clear); Liberty Mut. Ins. Co. v. Aventura Eng'g & Constr. Co., 2009 WL 3190962 (S.D. Fla. Sept. 15, 2009) (inability to post collateral as ordered by court to secure payment of judgment is defense only when debtor did not "create" the inability; must make "in good faith all reasonable efforts" to comply, but not required to bankrupt self; reasonable efforts shown even though debtor did not cash out retirement accounts when this would leave debtor and family "destitute"); Ivy v. Keith, 92 S.W.3d 671 (Ark. 2002) (because of prohibition against imprisonment for debt, indigency is a defense to contempt finding for non-payment of Rule 11 sanctions); Jensen v. Estate of Gambidilla, 896 So. 2d 917 (Fla. Dist. Ct. App. 2005) (trial court may not use civil contempt to incarcerate former personal representative of estate for failing to return estate property without express finding that contemnor has present ability to comply); *In re* Birchall, 913 N.E.2d 799 (Mass. 2009) (burden on creditor to show, by clear and convincing evidence, that debtor has current ability to pay, in whole or in installments); Wells v. State, 474 A.2d 846 (Me. 1984) (debtors cannot be sentenced to fixed term of confinement for failing to comply with stipulated order that they make payments on a civil debt; court must find that they have the present ability to pay and must allow them to obtain release by making the payments); Yoder v. Cnty. of Cumberland, 278 A.2d 379 (Me. 1971) (due process violation to imprison person for noncompliance with order to pay wife's divorce attorney fees without a prior hearing on the reasons for non-payment); *Ex parte* Cannon, 685 S.E.2d 814 (S.C. Ct. App. 2009) (affirming six-month conditional sentence for civil contempt when clear and convincing evidence, including cash purchase of land in Honduras to place assets beyond reach of creditor, showed that debtor either had ability to pay or had created inability); Vt. Nat'l Bank v. Taylor, 445 A.2d 1122 (Vt. 1982) (court cannot issue *ex parte* writ of *capias* upon debtor's failure to make payments ordered by the court; debtor must first be given opportunity for hearing on reasons for non-payment and ability to pay); Britannia Holdings Ltd. v. Greer, 113 P.3d 1041 (Wash. Ct. App. 2005) (not imprisonment for debt to hold a party in contempt for failure to comply with an order entered in supplemental proceedings to deliver money or property to pay a civil debt, as long as it is shown that debtor has ability to pay).

1038 *See* Wells v. State, 474 A.2d 846 (Me. 1984).

1039 *See, e.g.*, Hill v. Paluzzi, 581 S.E.2d 730 (Ga. Ct. App. 2003) (money judgment can be enforced by execution, but not by contempt, even when consent decree requires specific payments); Rosenthal v. American Constr. & Realty Co., 247 N.W. 119, 120 (Mich. 1933); *In re* Estate of Downs, 300 S.W.3d 242 (Mo. Ct. App. 2009) (constitution and statute forbid confinement for failure to pay money judgment, even if debtor has financial ability to pay); Igbal v. Mucci, 852 A.2d 195 (N.J. Super. Ct. App. Div. 2004) (order requiring debtor to make installment payments to judgment creditor is same as garnishment and cannot exceed CCPA limits); Galluzo v. Galluzo, 2013 WL 4536836 (Ohio Ct. App. Aug. 23, 2013) (court costs are a civil debt, which may be collected only by methods allowed for civil debt—which do not include contempt; error to order indigent defendant to "work off" court costs by community service); Hirzel v. Ooten, 2008 WL 5456384 (Ohio Ct. App. Dec. 22, 2008) (unpublished) (contempt cannot be used to collect divorce court costs, as this is a civil debt); McCall v. Cunard, 2008 WL 307706 (Ohio Ct. App. Feb. 1, 2008) (unpublished) (reversing finding that tenant was in contempt for failing to pay rent as ordered by eviction court; contempt proceeding is not a proper method by which to collect a civil judgment); *Ex parte* Hall, 854 S.W.2d 656 (Tex. 1993) (failure to comply with an order to pay a debt is not contempt punishable by imprisonment); *In re* Byrom, 316 S.W.3d 787 (Tex. App. 2010) (order to former executor/sole beneficiary to pay funds into court registry; because sum was judgment against estate, confinement for disobedience was unconstitutional imprisonment for debt). *See also* Tillman v. Patton, 2012 WL 4510048 (S.D. Miss. Sept. 28, 2012) (imprisonment of delinquent judgment debtor was error, but judge protected from section 1983 or tort liability by judicial immunity); Pineiro v. Pineiro, 988 So. 2d 686 (Fla. Dist. Ct. App. 2008) (using contempt to enforce divorce court order prohibiting withdrawal of stock options would violate state constitutional prohibition against imprisonment for debt). *But cf.* Roth v. Roth, 973 So. 2d 580 (Fla. Dist. Ct. App. 2008) (divorce court order requiring signature on deed is enforceable by contempt, even though property division that involves payment of money is not); McKenna v. Gray, 438 S.E.2d 901 (Ga. 1994) (in the absence of statutory authority or other extraneous circumstances, contempt is not an available remedy to enforce a money judgment, even if debtor violates an order requiring payment); Bald, Fat, and Ugly v. Keane, 303 P.3d 166 (Idaho 2013) (contempt power may not be used to enforce contract or money judgment, here order confirming arbitration award that awarded money judgment).

in particular, are not appropriate means to enforce a money judgment."[1040] The Indiana Supreme Court holds that "refusal to discharge a money judgment is not contempt of court and cannot be punished as a contempt of court."[1041]

A related question is whether a court has authority to order installment payments or make other coercive orders in the first instance.[1042] In some states, a statute allows a court to enter an order *permitting* a judgment debtor to pay in installments.[1043] If a judgment debtor fails to make the installment payments contemplated by such an order, the creditor's remedy should not be contempt but simply the garnishment or property execution that would have been available in the absence of the order. The federal limitations on wage garnishment[1044] likely apply to payment orders.[1045]

12.12.4 Constitutional Limits on Punishment for Contempt

The Constitution places some limits on imprisoning a judgment debtor on a contempt charge for failing to abide by a payment order. In evaluating what the Constitution requires, the first question is whether the debtor is being imprisoned for civil contempt or criminal contempt, that is, whether it is remedial or punitive. According to the Supreme Court, a sentence of imprisonment is remedial if the defendant will be released upon performing the affirmative act required by the court's order, and it is punitive if it is for a definite period.[1046] A fine is remedial if it is paid to the injured party or if the defendant can avoid paying the fine by performing the affirmative act required by the court's order; it is punitive if it is payable to the court and unconditional.[1047] Contempt is civil when it seeks only to coerce the defendant to do what the court had previously ordered.[1048]

A judgment debtor who faces criminal contempt charges for failing to abide by a payment order is entitled to the protections the Constitution requires for criminal cases, including proof beyond a reasonable doubt and appointment of counsel.[1049] By contrast, a civil contempt case must meet due process requirements but need not afford the defendant the protections applicable in criminal cases.[1050]

The Supreme Court has held that a court may not impose punishment in a civil contempt proceeding when it is clearly established that the defendant is unable to comply with the terms of the order.[1051] Accordingly, when the underlying court order involves payment of money, a defendant who is unable to pay cannot be imprisoned on a civil contempt charge.[1052]

A judgment debtor who is facing imprisonment for civil rather than criminal contempt may have the right to appointed counsel, or at least to alternate procedural safeguards. The Supreme Court addressed this issue in 2011 in *Turner v. Rogers*,[1053] a case in which an obligor was held in civil contempt and imprisoned for a year for failure to pay child support. Noting the differences between civil contempt and criminal contempt, the Court held that the Sixth Amendment, which establishes a right to counsel in criminal cases, was inapplicable, as the defendant could have purged himself of contempt and obtained his release by paying the amount owed. Instead, the Court analyzed the case under the Due Process Clause.

Applying the familiar balancing test of *Mathews v. Eldridge*,[1054] the Court held that there is no categorical right to appointed counsel in cases in which the party seeking the contempt citation is also unrepresented, as long as the state provides alternate procedural safeguards. The Court held that, in these circumstances, the following set of alternate procedural safeguards would be sufficient to guarantee fundamental fairness: (1) notice to the defendant that ability to pay will be a critical issue; (2) the use of a form (or the equivalent) to elicit

1040 *In re* Estate of Bonham, 817 A.2d 192, 195 (D.C. 2003).

1041 Bahre v. Bahre, 230 N.E.2d 411, 414 (Ind. 1967). *Accord* Carter v. Grace Whitney Properties, 939 N.E.2d 630 (Ind. Ct. App. 2010) (contempt power cannot be used to enforce obligation to pay except for child support or fraud: "personal order of garnishment," requiring debtor to turn over portion of earnings, may have use for self-employed debtor but must be based on finding of ability to pay); Button v. James, 909 N.E.2d 1007 (Ind. Ct. App. 2009) (debtor may not be imprisoned for failure to pay judgment debt; in addition, any installment payment order must be based on evidence of ability to pay). *See also* Risk v. Thompson, 147 N.E.2d 540 (Ind. 1958) (court cannot decree installment payments in action for specific performance, because enforcement of such an order would result in imprisonment for debt in violation of Indiana Constitution).

1042 *See* Branham v. Varble, 952 N.E.2d 744 (Ind. 2011) (court lacks authority to order debtor to undertake job search); *In re* Estate of Preston, 346 S.W.3d 137, 166 (Tex. App. 2011) (court has no authority to order debtor to make installment payments on home mortgage; order is void). *See also* Burns v. Miller, Hiersche, Martens & Hayward, 948 S.W.2d 317 (Tex. App. 1997) (noting Texas statute that prohibits orders requiring debtors to turn over paychecks or proceeds of exempt property).

1043 *See, e.g.*, Mich. Comp. Laws § 600.6201. *See also* Conn. Gen. Stat. § 52-356d (court may order installment payments, but order may not be enforced by contempt; upon default, judgment creditor may apply for wage execution).

1044 *See* § 12.4, *supra*.

1045 *See* Igbal v. Mucci, 852 A.2d 195 (N.J. Super. Ct. App. Div. 2004) (order requiring debtor to make installment payments to judgment creditor is same as garnishment and cannot exceed CCPA limits). *See generally* § 12.4.1.2, 12.4.1.3, *supra*.

1046 Hicks v. Feiock, 485 U.S. 624, 638 n.9, 108 S. Ct. 1423, 99 L. Ed. 2d 721 (1988).

1047 *Id.*

1048 Turner v. Rogers, 131 S. Ct. 2507, 2516, 180 L. Ed. 2d 452 (2011). *See also* Home S. & L. Co. v. Midway Marine, 2012 WL 1971134 (Ohio Ct. App. May 25, 2012) (thirty day sentence imposed on debtor unless he revealed the location of collateral that was subject to replevin order was civil).

1049 Turner v. Rogers, 131 S. Ct. 2507, 2516, 180 L. Ed. 2d 452 (2011); Hicks v. Feiock, 485 U.S. 624, 631, 108 S. Ct. 1423, 99 L. Ed. 2d 721 (1988).

1050 Hicks v. Feiock, 485 U.S. 624, 638, 108 S. Ct. 1423, 99 L. Ed. 2d 721 (1988). *See also* Liming v. Damos, 979 N.E.2d 297 (Ohio 2012) (counsel not required for purge hearing, at which child support obligor, who had been found in contempt and ordered to make payments, was jailed for non-payment, as contempt was civil; applying *Matthews* balancing and concluding that possibility of error was "highly unlikely"; because inability to pay is a defense, obligor has burden of proof).

1051 Hicks v. Feiock, 485 U.S. 624, 638 n.9, 108 S. Ct. 1423, 99 L. Ed. 2d 721 (1988).

1052 Hicks v. Feiock, 485 U.S. 624, 638, 108 S. Ct. 1423, 99 L. Ed. 2d 721 (1988).

1053 Turner v. Rogers, 131 S. Ct. 2507, 180 L. Ed. 2d 452 (2011).

1054 424 U.S. 319, 96 S. Ct. 893, 47 L. Ed. 2d 18 (1976).

relevant financial information; (3) an opportunity at the hearing for the defendant to respond to questions about his or her financial circumstances; and (4) an express finding by the court that the defendant has the ability to pay. The Court also suggested that other protections, such as providing the assistance of a neutral social worker, might be sufficient in the alternative.

One of the reasons that the Court did not require appointed counsel in all cases was that the opposing party is often unrepresented when the civil contempt proceedings are brought by the custodial parent rather than the state. In this situation, appointing counsel for the defendant would create its own asymmetry. The Court stressed that appointed counsel might be constitutionally required if the state rather than the custodial parent seeks the contempt citation and is represented by counsel or if the issues are unusually complex.

Given the principles articulated by the Supreme Court, appointed counsel may be constitutionally necessary before an indigent judgment debtor can be imprisoned on civil contempt charges for failure to abide by a payment order if the judgment creditor is represented by counsel or if the issues are complex. When counsel is not appointed for the judgment debtor, alternative procedural safeguards must be in place, including clear notice that inability to pay is a defense, a procedure for eliciting financial information, an opportunity to respond and dispute relevant information, and court findings.

States have the authority to interpret their state constitutions more broadly. For example, the New Jersey Supreme Court held that both the state constitution and the Due Process Clause of the U.S. Constitution require appointment of counsel for indigent civil contempt defendants in child support proceedings.[1055] Even after *Turner v. Rogers*, state courts remain free to maintain their own interpretations of their state constitutions.

12.13 Debtor's Examinations

States generally make postjudgment discovery proceedings available to creditors to force debtors to answer questions about their assets. The creditor may have the right to issue interrogatories to the debtor, summon the debtor to a debtor's examination to answer questions in person, and issue a subpoena *duces tecum* requiring the debtor to produce assets or records. These proceedings are sometimes called supplementary proceedings.

There are limits on debtor's examinations. A Missouri court held that debtor's examinations are limited statutory creations, so courts do not have authority to compel the attendance of third parties not listed in the statute.[1056] In some states a creditor has the right to institute postjudgment supplementary proceedings only after unsuccessfully attempting to execute upon the judgment.[1057] The court may have discretion to prohibit repeat examinations in the absence of a showing of some reason to believe that the debtor's financial circumstances have changed.[1058] A debtor may assert the Fifth Amendment privilege against self-incrimination at a debtor's examination.[1059]

Debtor's examination procedures must comport with due process. A New Jersey court held that the procedural protections were adequate when the debtor could be arrested for failure to respond to postjudgment interrogatories only after a series of notices, and only if the debtor was found at the address where the notices were served, and the debtor was required to be released as soon as he or she answered the interrogatories.[1060] A federal court refused to dismiss a section 1983 claim against attorneys who allegedly conspired with a state court judge to use imprisonment of debtors who failed to appear for examinations as a way to coerce them to pay the underlying judgments.[1061]

Debtor's examinations create particular problems because in most if not all states the debtor can be held in contempt of court for failure to appear for a debtor's examination.[1062] Debtors frequently fail to appear at debtor's examinations because the notice is in obtuse legalese, they have no means of transportation to the examination site, or they are unable to miss work without risking job termination. A debtor who has failed to appear for a debtor's examination may feel compelled to pay the debt because of the fear of incarceration.

A debtor who fails to appear for a debtor's examination may face either criminal contempt or civil contempt. Criminal contempt is intended as punishment, while civil contempt is intended to coerce compliance. If the contemnor is sentenced to a fixed term of imprisonment, it is considered criminal contempt. With civil contempt, the contemnor can obtain release by complying with the original court order and so is said to have the keys to the prison in his pocket.[1063] A defendant may be

1055 Pasqua v. Council, 892 A.2d 663 (N.J. 2006).

1056 State *ex rel.* Long v. Askren, 874 S.W.2d 466 (Mo. Ct. App. 1994). *But cf.* Imperial Bank v. PIM Elec., Inc., 39 Cal. Rptr. 2d 432, 437 (Cal. Ct. App. 1995) (noting that California allows judgment creditor to examine third persons who have property of, or are indebted to, the judgment debtor).

1057 *See, e.g.*, Mo. Rev. Stat. § 513.380; N.H. Rev. Stat. Ann. § 498:8. *See also* Parker v. Wetch & Abbot, P.L.C., 2006 WL 4846042 (S.D. Iowa July 11, 2006) (interpreting Iowa law to allow debtor's examination only if a garnishment fails). *Cf.* Hogue v. Palisades Collection, L.L.C., 494 F. Supp. 2d 1043 (S.D. Iowa 2007) (noting that Nebraska law that formerly required execution to be returned unsatisfied before debtor's examination could be conducted has been amended to delete this requirement; interpreting Iowa law not to require unsuccessful garnishment before debtor's examination could be conducted).

1058 Carter v. Grace Whitney Properties, 939 N.E.2d 630, 637 (Ind. Ct. App. 2010).

1059 State *ex rel.* Nothum v. Kintz, 380 S.W.3d 557 (Mo. 2012); Redwine v. Starboard, L.L.C., 251 P.3d 192 (Or. Ct. App. 2011); Empire Wholesale Lumber Co. v. Meyers, 85 P.3d 339 (Or. Ct. App. 2004).

1060 New Century Fin. Servs., Inc. v. Nason, 842 A.2d 179 (N.J. Super. Ct. App. Div. 2004).

1061 Ballard v. Wall, 413 F.3d 510 (5th Cir. 2005) (concluding that plaintiffs adequately alleged that attorneys for judgment creditor were state actors, even though judge was immune).

1062 *In re* Weick, 127 P.3d 178 (Idaho 2005); Too Easy Entertainment, Inc. v. Seven Arts Pictures, Inc., 943 So. 2d 1194 (La. Ct. App. 2006); *In re* Birchall, 913 N.E.2d 799 (Mass. 2009) (debtor jailed for failure to attend debtor's exam; after exam, continued incarceration for civil contempt requires creditor to show, by clear and convincing evidence, debtor's ability to pay).

1063 *See, e.g.*, Ameritech Publishing, Inc. v. Mayo Bail Bonds & Surety, Inc., 2013 WL 872408 (Ohio Ct. App. Mar. 8, 2013) (unpublished) (defining different types of contempt; this was civil contempt since defendant could purge the contempt by supplying the information that entitled to greater constitutional safeguards in the case of criminal contempt than civil contempt. A debtor who does not have the ability to comply with the court's order cannot be found in civil[1064] or criminal contempt.[1065] The state may require special procedures before a debtor may be arrested for failing to appear for a debtor's examination and, if it does, the court must follow them and cannot rely on its inherent authority to enforce its orders.[1066] Some states follow a practice of allowing debtors to avoid contempt by rescheduling the examination. Failure to comply with a debtor's examination may also be grounds for dismissing the debtor's appeal of the underlying judgment.[1067]

A Virginia decision holds that arresting a debtor for failing to appear at a debtor's examination is not imprisonment for debt when the debtor could obtain his release by answering the creditor's questions and surrendering any assets to which the creditor was entitled.[1068] The court reached this conclusion even though the trial court's order also allowed the debtor to obtain his release by paying the underlying judgment.

Even if a debtor's examination is lawful, it can be used improperly and abusively. Scheduling a debtor's examination in a distant venue may violate the Fair Debt Collection Practices Act (FDCPA).[1069] It may also constitute abuse of process[1070] or lead to a claim of false imprisonment.[1071] Debt collectors may also violate the FDCPA by using the possibility of contempt for failure to appear at a debtor's examination as a basis for threatening or implying that non-payment of a debt will result in imprisonment.[1072] If the underlying judgment is not just voidable but void, the judgment debtor may challenge it in defending against a contempt citation for failure to answer questions at a debtor's examination.[1073]

12.14 Assignment of Judgments

State laws regarding assignment of judgments often require the assignment to be recorded on the docket of the court that entered the judgment.[1074] The statute may specify information that assignments must contain and requirements such as notarization that they must meet.[1075] Court rules may impose additional requirements on the form, content, acknowledgment, and filing of assignments.[1076] Although Article 9 of the Uniform Commercial Code has a number of provisions regarding sale and assignment of obligations, it does not apply to the assignment of judgments.[1077]

Some state laws explicitly require that the assignment of a judgment be signed by the owner of the judgment or the owner's attorney or agent,[1078] but even when this is not set forth explicitly it is likely an implicit requirement. A debt buyer that acquired a judgment from another party may be unable to show that that party owned the judgment. This is particularly

---

the debtor's examination had sought; when the contempt occurred in the presence of the court it was direct rather than indirect contempt and fewer procedural safeguards were necessary).

1064 Johnson & Placke v. Norris, 874 So. 2d 340 (La. Ct. App. 2004); *In re* Birchall, 913 N.E.2d 799 (Mass. 2009) (general discussion of Massachusetts law of civil and criminal contempt; non-payment is civil and requires creditor to prove debtor's ability to pay).

1065 Diaz v. Baca, 203 Fed. Appx. 884 (9th Cir. 2006) (inability to comply is affirmative defense to contempt charge; charge appears to have been criminal contempt because imprisonment was for fixed three-day period); *In re* Weick, 127 P.3d 178 (Idaho 2005) (for indirect criminal contempt for failure to appear at debtor's examination, complainant must prove elements beyond reasonable doubt, but defendant has burden of producing evidence that creates a reasonable doubt as to his ability to comply).

1066 Hiber v. Creditors Collection Serv., 961 P.2d 898 (Or. Ct. App. 1998).

1067 *See, e.g.*, Stoltenberg v. Ampton Invs., Inc., 155 Cal. Rptr. 3d. 228 (Cal. Ct. App. 2013), *as modified by* 159 Cal. Rptr. 3d 1 (Cal. Ct. App. 2013).

1068 Early Used Cars, Inc. v. Province, 239 S.E.2d 98 (Va. 1977).

1069 Flores v. Quick Collect, Inc., 2007 WL 433239 (D. Or. Jan. 31, 2007).

1070 *See, e.g.*, Dishaw v. Wadleigh, 44 N.Y.S. 207 (N.Y. App. Div. 1897) (claim for abuse of process stated when attorney filed collection suits in distant counties, took default judgments, and collected them by issuing subpoenas to debtors, who paid the debts rather than journeying to the cities where the subpoenas were issued. *But see* Porter v. Stormont-Vail Hosp., 621 P.2d 411 (Kan. 1980) (numerous orders to appear in aid of execution and two arrests of a judgment debtor residing 200 miles from the court over disputed debt not abuse of process). *But cf.* Davis v. Nebraska Furniture Mart, Inc., 2013 WL 3854462 (D. Kan. July 24, 2013) (not abuse of process to schedule repeated debtors examinations when debtor's financial circumstances were changing). *See generally* National Consumer Law Center, Fair Debt Collection § 9.6 (8th ed. 2014).

1071 *See* National Consumer Law Center, Fair Debt Collection §§ 9.7.1–9.7.8 (8th ed. 2014). *But cf.* Dahlz v. Cnty. of San Mateo, 2001 U.S. App. LEXIS 3541 (9th Cir. Mar. 2, 2001) (rejecting *pro se* debtor's § 1983 claim against creditor and creditor's attorney for having him arrested for failure to appear for debtor's examination, as they were not state actors; arresting officers were immune); Hiber v. Creditors Collection Serv., 961 P.2d 898 (Or. Ct. App. 1998) (attorney who obtained arrest warrant for judgment debtor's failure to appear at debtor's examination is not liable for false imprisonment in the absence of malice or bad faith, even though warrant was void because of failure to follow state procedure).

1072 *But see* Spinarski v. Credit Bureau, 1996 U.S. Dist. LEXIS 22547 (D.N.M. Sept. 19, 1999) (reference in pre-suit collection letter to possibility of arrest for failure to appear at debtor's examination not FDCPA violation; court accepts what appears to be extremely thin evidence that the collector ever employed this tactic or that judgment debtors were ever arrested).

1073 Moore v. Kaufman, 117 Cal. Rptr. 3d 196 (Cal. Ct. App. 2010).

1074 *See, e.g.*, N.C. Gen. Stat. § 1-246; Wis. Stat. § 806.18.

1075 *See, e.g.*, N.J. Stat. Ann. § 2A:16-41 (West) (assignment of judgment must be in writing and must be acknowledged or proved in same manner as real estate conveyances); Or. Rev. Stat. § 18.205 (must be signed by judgment creditor or its agent or attorney, signature must be acknowledged before a notary, and assignment must be filed with court that entered the judgment or in any county lien record where judgment was recorded); Wash. Rev. Code § 4.56.090 (assignment of judgment may not be filed unless it is properly acknowledged before an officer qualified to take acknowledgment of deeds); Wis. Stat. § 806.18 (assignment may be made by statement signed by owner of judgment, with date affixed and witnessed by court clerk).

1076 *See* Chase Bank v. Cardello, 896 N.Y.S.2d 856 (N.Y. Civ. Ct. 2010) (dismissing action because assignment of judgment was not acknowledged in same manner as deed, was not accompanied by certificate establishing notary's authority to take the acknowledgment, and did not indicate that judgment debtor had been notified of the assignment, all as required by Civil Practice Law and Rules).

1077 U.C.C. § 9-109(d)(9) (Art. 9 does not apply to assignment of a right represented by a judgment, other than a judgment taken on a right to payment that was collateral).

1078 *See, e.g.*, Or. Rev. Stat. § 18.205; Wis. Stat. § 806.18.

true if any of the previous owners of the judgment are out of business.[1079] A New York court refused to allow a debt buyer to enforce a judgment when it did not show a chain of assignments from the original judgment creditor to it.[1080]

A debt buyer that is a foreign corporation may be required to register to do business in the state before it can engage in the practice of bringing suit in the courts of that state to enforce assigned judgment debts.[1081]

12.15 Statutes of Limitations for Enforcement of Judgments

The question of statutes of limitation on judgments becomes increasingly important as debt buyers purchase and seek to collect very old debts. Limitations periods for enforcement of judgments vary widely, ranging from four to twenty years.[1082] Especially in states with relatively short periods, a debt buyer's

1079 *See, e.g.*, Centurion Capital Corp. v. Guarino, 951 N.Y.S.2d 85 (N.Y. City Civ. Ct. 2012) (finding evidence that assignor had authority to assign judgment insufficient when assignor had ceased business before date of assignment).

1080 *Id. See generally* § 4.3.4, *supra*.

1081 Centurion Capital Corp. v. Guarino, 951 N.Y.S.2d 85 (N.Y. City Civ. Ct. 2012) (third-party debt buyer must be registered to do business in state and licensed as debt collector before it can file suit on assigned judgments); Chase Bank v. Cardello, 896 N.Y.S.2d 856 (N.Y. Civ. Ct. 2010) (before it can enforce assigned judgments, debt buyer must show that it is registered to do business in state). *See generally* § 3.3, *supra*.

1082 *ALABAMA:* Ala. Code § 6-2-32 20.

ALASKA: Alaska Stat. § 09.10.040 (ten years, action on a judgment or decree of any federal or state court), §§ 09.10.200, 9.10.210 (may be restarted by written acknowledgment or promise, or by payment), § 09.10.220 (foreign judgment, between non-residents of Alaska, cannot be brought if it is time-barred by the SOL of the foreign state).

ARIZONA: Ann. §§ 12-544(3), 12-549 (four years for out-of-state judgments, except support judgments; foreign judgment that would be time-barred in home state also barred in Arizona). For in-state judgments, it appears that the applicable statute of limitations is the general catchall for actions for which no limitation is otherwise prescribed, Ann. § 12-550.

ARKANSAS: Ark. Code Ann. § 16-56-114 (ten years).

CALIFORNIA: Cal. Civ. Proc. Code § 337.6 (ten years, action upon the judgment of any federal or state court); § 355 (if a an action is commenced within the limitations period, and a judgment for the plaintiff is reversed on appeal other than on the merits, one year to bring a new action), § 360 (SOL can be restarted by written acknowledgment or by payment), § 360.5 (SOL may be extended by up to four years by written waiver during the limitations period; successive waivers permitted), § 661 (judgment from another state or country, that is time-barred by the laws of that jurisdiction, is barred unless it is in favor of one who has been a citizen of California and has held the cause of action from the time it accrued).

CONNECTICUT: Conn. Gen. Stat. Ann. § 52-598 (twenty years for execution to enforce state court judgment and twenty-five years for action based upon a state court judgment, but, for small claims court judgment, ten years for execution, fifteen years for action based on judgment).

DELAWARE: Del. Code Ann. tit. 10, §§ 5072, 5073 (five years for execution on judgment, measured from date when judgment or an installment fell due).

DISTRICT OF COLUMBIA: D.C. Stat. § 15-101 (twelve years for judgment of U.S. Dist. Ct. for D.C. or of D.C. Superior Ct.; revival permitted, if sought before expiration of the SOL), § 15-103 (order of revival extends SOL for twelve years).

FLORIDA: Fla. Stat. § 95.11(1), (2)(a) (twenty years for judgment of Florida court of record; five years for foreign judgment, or judgment of Florida court not of record).

GEORGIA: Ga. Code Ann. § 9-12-60 (judgment becomes dormant after seven years), § 9-12-61 (may be revived within three years after dormancy), § 9-3-20 (actions on judgments obtained outside the state, five years).

HAWAII: Haw. Rev. Stat. § 657-5 (ten years for judgment of any state court of record; extensions permitted if sought before dormancy; may not extend beyond twenty years from date of original judgment); § 657-1(2) (six years for state court not of record, or foreign judgments), § 657-9 (foreign judgment time-barred in its home state is also barred in Hawaii, except for judgment in favor of Hawaii resident, who has held the cause of action from the time it accrued).

IDAHO: Idaho Code Ann. § 5-215(1) (six years for judgment of any state or federal court), § 538 (may be extended by written acknowledgment or promise, or by payment), § 539 (foreign judgments time-barred in home state also time-barred in Idaho, except judgment in favor of one who has been Idaho resident and has held the cause of action from the time it accrued).

ILLINOIS: Either of two Illinois statutes might possibly apply to a judgment: 735 Ill. Comp. Stat. § 5/13-205 (five-year limitation for "civil actions not otherwise provided for") or 735 Ill. Comp. Stat. § 5/13-210 (foreign judgment time-barred in home state also time-barred in Illinois). *See also* 735 Ill. Comp. Stat. § 5/13-218 (may be revived any time within twenty years after entry of judgment).

INDIANA: Ind. Code § 34-11-2-12 (twenty years for judgments of all federal or state courts of record), § 34-11-2-13 (action to recognize foreign country judgment must be brought within the lesser of ten years or the foreign country's limitation period).

IOWA: Iowa Code §§ 614.1(5) and (6) (judgment of any court of record, twenty years; courts not of record, ten years), § 614.13 (may be revived by written acknowledgment or payment).

KANSAS: Kan. Stat. Ann. § 60-511(5) (five-year catchall statute), § 60-516 (if cause of action arose in another state, it is time-barred in Kansas if time-barred in that state, except if plaintiff is a resident of Kansas and has held the cause of action from the time it accrued).

KENTUCKY: § 413.090(1) (judgment of any state or federal court, fifteen years computed from last execution thereon).

LOUISIANA: La. Civ. Code Ann. § 3501 (judgment of any state or federal court, ten years from date judgment becomes final, may be revived within that time, unlimited number of ten-year revivals permitted; foreign judgment time-barred in its home state is time-barred in Louisiana).

MAINE: Maine Rev. Stat. Ann., tit. 14, § 854 (judgment of any state or federal court of record, or Maine justice of the peace court, twenty years).

MARYLAND: Md. Ct. & Jud. Pro. Code § 5-102(a)(3) (twelve years after accrual; payment will extend period for three years).

MICHIGAN: Mich. Comp. Laws § 600.5809(3) (judgment of court of record, ten years, except actions for support; court not of record, six years), § 600.5861 (foreign judgment time-barred in home state is time-barred in Michigan, except if cause of action in favor of Michigan resident), § 600.5866 (may be revived by written acknowledgment).

MINNESOTA: Minn. Stat. § 541.04 (judgment of any state or federal Court, ten years), § 541.17 (may be revived by written acknowledgment).

MISSISSIPPI: Miss. Code Ann. § 15-1-43 (judgment of state court of record seven years; may be renewed by application made before expiration), § 15-1-45 (foreign judgments of courts or record, seven years, except that if defendant was Mississippi resident at time action commenced, limitation is three years from date of judgment).

MISSOURI: Mo. Stat. Ann. § 516.350 (judgment of any court of record, except certain domestic relations judgment, ten years; ten year portfolio of old debts may include many on which a judgment was entered well outside the limitations period, giving the debtor a strong defense[1083] and possibly an FDCPA claim.[1084]

Some states have one limitations period for judgments of courts of record and a significantly shorter period for courts "not of record" such as small claims courts.[1085] States may also have a shorter limitations period for foreign judgments or provide that judgments time-barred in the foreign state are time-barred, even if within the state's own limitations period.[1086]

The running of a statute of limitations may be tolled by a payment, or by a written acknowledgment of the debt.[1087] As a result, collectors may pressure unsophisticated consumers to make a token payment or agree to a payment plan, in order to extend the statute. Many states also provide that the statute of limitations for enforcement of a judgment may be extended by an application to the court within the limitations period, or a prescribed period thereafter, often through a process called revival.[1088]

---

revivals permitted), § 516.190 (foreign judgment time-barred in home state also time-barred in Missouri).

MONTANA: Mont. Code Ann. § 27-2-201(1) and (2) (ten years, except for child support or criminal restitution).

NEBRASKA: Neb. Rev. Stat. § 25-205 (foreign judgments, five years.).

NEVADA: Nev. Rev. Stat. § 11.190(1)(a) (judgment of any state or federal court, six years), § 11.020 (foreign judgment time-barred in home state also time-barred in Nevada, except if in favor of Nevada resident who has held the cause of action from the time it accrued).

NEW HAMPSHIRE: N.H. Rev. Stat. Ann. § 508:5 (all judgments, twenty years).

NEW JERSEY: N.J. Stat. Ann. § 2A:14-5 (New Jersey court of record, twenty years; foreign judgment, lesser of twenty years or the home state's SOL).

NEW MEXICO: N.M. Stat. Ann. § 37-1-2 (state court of record, fourteen years; federal judgments or those of courts of record of other states, lesser of fourteen years or the foreign period of limitations), § 37-1-3 (judgment of court not of record, six years), § 37-1-16 (restarted by payment, or written acknowledgment or new promise).

NEW YORK: N.Y. C.P.L.R. § 211(b) (twenty years; judgment conclusively presumed to be satisfied, but time extended by written acknowledgment or part payment).

NORTH CAROLINA: N.C. Gen. Stat. § 1-47 (all judgments, ten years).

NORTH DAKOTA: N.D. Cent. Code § 28-01-15 (any state or federal judgment, ten years), § 28-01-36 (may be extended by written acknowledgment).

OHIO: Ohio Rev. Code Ann. § 2305.14 (West) (catchall SOL of ten years), 2305.03 (if cause of action accrued out of state, action barred if SOL of that state has run), § 2325.18 (judgment may be revived within ten years after time when it became dormant).

OKLAHOMA: Okla. Stat. tit. 12, § 95(A)(2), (12) (in-state judgments, five years (catchall statute), foreign judgments, three years), § 101 (may be extended by written acknowledgment or payment).

OREGON: Or. Rev. Stat. § 12.070 (judgment of any state or federal court, ten years).

PENNSYLVANIA: Pa. Con. Stat. Ann. tit. 42, § 5525(a)(5) (four years for an action upon a judgment or decree of any state or federal court), § 5521 (for claim originating outside Pennsylvania, the lesser of the Pennsylvania SOL or that of the foreign state).

RHODE ISLAND: R.I. Gen. Laws § 9-1-17 (judgments of any court of record, twenty years).

SOUTH CAROLINA: S.C. Code Ann. § 15-3-600 (catchall statute; ten years), § 15-3-120 (may be extended by written acknowledgment or part payment).

SOUTH DAKOTA: S.D. Codified Laws § 15-2-6 (twenty years for an action upon a judgment or decree of any court of this state, except when a different limitation is prescribed by statute), § 15-2-8 (ten years for judgment of federal or out-of-state court).

TENNESSEE: Tenn. Code Ann. § 28-3-110(2) (ten years, actions on judgments or decrees of courts of records of this or any other state or government), § 28-1-112 (if the SOL of another state has barred an action, which accrued there, while the party to be charged was a resident of that state, action also barred in Tennessee).

TEXAS: Tex. Civ. Prac. & Rem. Code § 16.066 (foreign judgments barred in Texas if barred by SOL in foreign state; action against person who has resided for ten years in Texas may not be brought on foreign judgment rendered more than ten years before commencement of action in Texas), § 31.006 (dormant judgment may be revived within two years of the date it became dormant).

UTAH: Utah Code Ann. § 78B-2-311 (judgment of any state or federal court, eight years).

VERMONT: Vt. Stat. Ann. tit. 12 § 506 (actions on judgments and actions for the renewal or revival of judgments shall be brought by filing a new and independent action on the judgment within eight years after the rendition of the judgment, and not after), § 511 (catchall statute for all civil actions; exempts actions on judgments of courts of record, so appears to apply to actions on judgments of courts not of record).

VIRGINIA: Va. Code Ann. § 8.01-251 (all judgments, twenty years, may be extended for an additional twenty years by a motion made before dormancy).

WASHINGTON: Rev. Code Wash. § 4.16.020(2) (all judgments, ten years), § 6.17.020 (ten-year extensions available).

WEST VIRGINIA: W.V. Code § 55-2-13 (foreign judgment time-barred in home state is barred in West Virginia; foreign judgment against person who resided in W. Va. for the ten years preceding that action, ten years after the commencement of the action).

WISCONSIN: Wis. Stat. § 893.40 (twenty years action upon judgment or decree of court of record of U.S. or any state).

WYOMING: Wyo. Stat. Ann. § 1-3-109 (catchall statute, ten years), § 1-3-105(a)(3) (action must be brought within five years after a debtor establishes residence in Wyoming on a foreign judgment incurred before the debtor resided in Wyoming).

1083 *See* § 3.6, *supra* (general discussion of statute of limitations defenses).

1084 *See* § 13.4.3.4, *infra*.

1085 *See, e.g.*, Conn. Gen. Stat. Ann. § 52-598; N.M. Stat. Ann. §§ 37-1-2, 37-1-3; Wis. Stat. §§ 893.40, 893.42.

1086 *See, e.g.*, Kan. Stat. Ann. § 60-516; Okla. Stat. tit. 12, § 95(A)(2), (12); Tenn. Code Ann. § 28-1-112; Tex. Civ. Prac. & Rem. Code § 16.066.

1087 *See, e.g.*, Cal. Civ. Proc. Code § 360 (can be restarted by written acknowledgment or by payment); N.M. Stat. Ann. § 37-1-16 (restarted by payment, or written acknowledgment or new promise); Wis. Stat. § 894.45 (can be extended by acknowledgment in writing).

1088 *See, e.g.*, Cal. Civ. Proc. Code § 360.5 (may be extended by up to four years by written waiver during the limitations period; successive waivers permitted); D.C. Code § 15-103 (order of revival extends SOL for twelve years); Ga. Code Ann. § 9-12-61 (may be revived within three years after dormancy); Ohio Rev. Code Ann. § 2325.18 (West) (judgment may be revived within ten years after time when it became dormant). *See also* FDIC v. SLE, Inc., 722 F.3d 264 (5th Cir. 2013) (*ex parte* grant of revival of dormant judgment did not violate due process).

Chapter 13 Prevailing Consumers' Postjudgment Actions

13.1 Attorney Fees for the Prevailing Consumer

13.1.1 Introduction

The American rule is that attorney fees are not recoverable absent contractual or statutory authority. This section enumerates seven ways in which a prevailing *consumer* can receive an attorney fee award. In twenty states, there is explicit statutory authority for attorney fees, at least in certain types of collection actions. In all states there are grounds for the award of fees to a prevailing consumer.

Other related topics, such as how to calculate that award and the proper procedure for seeking the award, are covered in other NCLC treatises. Because collection actions are usually brought in state court, state law will generally govern the attorney fee award, even when the award is based upon federal counterclaims. As a result, while good resources on attorney fees under federal fee-shifting statutes include NCLC's *Fair Debt Collection*[1] and *Truth in Lending*,[2] the most comprehensive discussion of fees under a *state* fee-shifting statute will be found in NCLC's *Unfair and Deceptive Acts and Practices*.[3] In addition, sample pleadings and other sample documentation concerning attorney fee applications will be found in NCLC's *Consumer Law Pleadings (Online with Index Guide)*,[4] in which most documents are available electronically in Microsoft Word format.

This section focuses solely on the theories by which a prevailing consumer defendant in a collection action can recover the attorney fees required to defend the case. It does not treat other attorney fee topics.

13.1.2 Right to Fees Based upon the Contract

Parse the attorney fee provision in the credit contract if the collector or consumer has produced this contract for the court. Credit contracts typically provide for attorney fees only for a prevailing collector, but occasionally such contracts provide for fees for the prevailing *party*, whether that party is the collector or the consumer. Any ambiguity as to whether an attorney fee provision applies only to a prevailing collector or to either prevailing party should be construed in the consumer's favor, as the creditor has drafted the standard form contract.

1 National Consumer Law Center, Fair Debt Collection § 6.8 (8th ed. 2014), *updated at* www.nclc.org/library.

2 National Consumer Law Center, Truth in Lending § 11.9 (8th ed. 2012), *updated at* www.nclc.org/library.

3 National Consumer Law Center, Unfair and Deceptive Acts and Practices § 12.8 (8th ed. 2012), *updated at* www.nclc.org/library.

4 (2013), *updated at* www.nclc.org/library.

13.1.3 Consumer's Statutory Right to Fees When Collector Has a Contractual Right to Fees

Ten states—California, Connecticut, Florida, Hawaii, Montana, New Hampshire, New York, Oregon, Utah, and Washington—have enacted statutes that provide for reciprocal attorney fees. If a credit agreement provides attorney fees for a prevailing creditor, then, under a reciprocal fee statute, a prevailing consumer has the right to recover fees.[5] Since a debt buyer has the right to recover fees when the contract provides fees for a prevailing creditor, the reciprocal statute provides fees to the consumer who prevails in a debt buyer's collection action.

The concept of reciprocal attorney fees may also apply in states other than the ten listed above. Consider a credit agreement that specifies that the contract will be governed by the laws of Utah (or one of the other nine states that has reciprocal fee statutes). Consumers can argue that the laws of Utah (or one of these other states) include the reciprocal fee statute and this statute should be given effect even when the contract was consummated in some other state.

The opposite is not the case. When a collection action is brought in a state with a reciprocal attorney fee provision, that provision applies even when the contract selects another state's law as applying to the contract—and when that other state's law does not provide for reciprocal attorney fees.[6] The forum state has a fundamental public policy in allowing both parties to a contract to recover fees if one can, in particular when the fee provision is found in an adhesion contract in which the creditor has far more bargaining power than the consumer.[7]

Further support for this conclusion can be found when the state statute provides that the reciprocal attorney fee provision cannot be waived.[8] The forum state also has a significant interest in the outcome of the case because it involves a consumer residing in the forum state being sued in the forum state.[9]

5 Cal. Civ. Code § 1717 (West); Conn. Gen. Stat. § 42-150bb; Fla. Stat. § 57.105(7); Haw. Rev. Stat. § 607-14; Mont. Code Ann. § 28-3-704; N.H. Rev. Stat. Ann. § 361-C:2; N.Y. Gen. Oblig. Law § 5-327 (McKinney); Or. Rev. Stat. § 20.096; Utah Code Ann. § 78B-5-826; Wash. Rev. Code § 4.84.330. *See also In re* Penrod, 493 B.R. 140 (N.D. Cal. 2013); Goray v. Unifund CCR Partners, 2007 WL 4260017 (D. Haw. Dec. 4, 2007); Douglas E. Barnhart, Inc. v. CMC Fabricators, Inc., 211 Cal. App. 4th 430 (Cal. Ct. App. 2012); Insight Assets, Inc. v. Farias, 2013 WL 3990783 (Utah Aug. 6, 2013); McQueen v. Jordan Pines Townhomes Owners Ass'n, Inc., 298 P.3d 666 (Utah App. 2013); Northstar Capital Acquisitions v. Haring (Utah Dist. Ct. Mar. 4, 2010), *available at* www.nclc.org/unreported; United Wholesale Supply, Inc. v. Wear, 106 Wash. App. 1042 (Wash. Ct. App. 2001).

6 Capital One Bank v. Fort, 255 P.3d. 508 (Or. Ct. App. 2011).

7 *Id.*

8 *Id.*

9 *Id.*

Often a consumer will prevail in a collection action because the collector failed to prove a binding contract, and the reciprocal fee statute depends on the existence of a contract providing for fees to a prevailing creditor. The Oregon statute provides for the consumer to recover fees even if the court rules that the contract—and therefore the fee provision for a prevailing creditor—is unenforceable.[10] California and Utah have the same rule, as developed by case law.[11] "The statute would fall short of its goal of full mutuality of remedy if its benefits were denied to parties who defeat contract claims by proving that they were not parties to the alleged contract or that it was never formed."[12] In addition, if the collector alleges that it is entitled to fees under its contract, it may be estopped from denying that later when the consumer prevails.[13] But when a collector sues on a buyer's order that does not contain an attorney fee clause, the consumer might be advised to introduce into evidence the installment sales agreement that does include such a clause.[14]

In California and other states where their statutes use terms such as "shall," the award of fees to the consumer is mandatory if it is clear that the consumer has prevailed.[15] The fees are still mandatory even where the consumer is not being charged by the consumer's attorney.[16]

But in some cases it may be unclear whether the consumer has prevailed sufficiently to trigger a reciprocal fee award. For example, does a consumer prevail by setting aside a default judgment or succeeding in dismissing a case but without prejudice? In Florida, the consumer is entitled to fees under such a provision if the collector dismisses the action with prejudice during the trial.[17] Florida courts have also awarded fees to a consumer after an action was dismissed for the failure to prosecute the claim.[18]

The California statute provides that the court determines which party is the prevailing party, whether or not the suit proceeds to final judgment, and that the prevailing party is the party that recovers the greater relief.[19] But when an action is voluntarily dismissed or dismissed pursuant to a settlement, neither party prevails.[20] Of course, even when an action is voluntarily dismissed, the consumer may still recover fees under some other theory.[21]

When a state has more than one statute providing for attorney fees, issues can arise to which statute applies. In California, when a bank brings an action based upon a credit card agreement, there can be no question that the reciprocal fee statute applies.[22] The other California statute (which limits fees to $800) does not apply to banks and explicitly does not apply when there is a contract providing for attorney fees.[23]

13.1.4 State Statutes Provide Fees for the Prevailing Party Under Certain Causes of Action

Notwithstanding whether there is an attorney fee provision in the credit contract, at least eleven states provide for attorney fees for the prevailing party in a collection action or provide fees for the party prevailing as to certain enumerated causes of action:

- *Alaska* provides that "except as otherwise provided by law or agreed to by the parties, the prevailing party in a civil case shall be awarded attorney's fees calculated under this rule."[24]
- *Arizona* provides that in a contested action "arising out of a contract, express or implied, the court may award the successful party reasonable attorney fees."[25] Since the statute mentions both express and implied contracts, this statute allows the consumer to recover even in cases in which the collector does not seek to prove a written contract.
- *Arkansas* provides fees to the prevailing party in most collection actions.[26]
- *California* legislation relating to retail sales states: "Reasonable attorney's fees and costs shall be awarded to the prevailing party in any action on a contract or installment account subject to the provisions of this chapter regardless of whether such action is instituted by the seller, holder or buyer."[27]
- *California* legislation provides for $800 attorney fees when the consumer prevails on an action on a "book account" for which the contract does not provide for attorney fees, as long as the collector is not a depository institution, a subsidiary or

10 Or. Rev. Stat. §§ 20.083, 20.096.

11 Hsu v. Abbara, 891 P.2d 804 (Cal. 1995). *See also* Diamond v. John Martin Co., 753 F.2d 1465 (9th Cir. 1985) (California law); Anmaco, Inc. v. Bohlken, 16 Cal. Rptr. 2d 675 (Cal. Ct. App. 1993); Jones v. Vincent Drain, 196 Cal. Rptr. 827 (Cal. Ct. App. 1983); Insight Assets, Inc. v. Farias, 2013 WL 3990783 (Utah Aug. 6, 2013).

12 Hsu v. Abbara, 891 P.2d 804 (Cal. 1995).

13 Credit Card Receivables Fund, Inc. v. Cleary, 2006 WL 3775899 (Fla. Cir. Ct. Dec. 19, 2006). *But see* Great Seneca Fin. Corp. v. Lisher, 196 P.3d 86 (Or. Ct. App. 2008); Unifund CCR Assignee of Providian v. Ayhan, 146 Wash. App. 1026 (Wash. Ct. App. 2008).

14 Tylinski v. Klein Automotive, Inc., 90 So. 3d 870 (Fla. Dist. Ct. App. 2012).

15 MHC Financing Ltd. P'ship v. City of San Rafael, 714 F.3d 1118 (9th Cir. 2013); Zintel Holdings, L.L.C. v. McLean, 209 Cal. App. 4th 431 (Cal. Ct. App. 2012).

16 Healdsburg Citizens for Sustainable Solutions v. City of Healdsburg, 206 Cal. App. 4th 988 (Cal. Ct. App. 2012).

17 Landry v. Countrywide Home Loans, Inc., 731 So. 2d 137 (Fla. Dist. Ct. App. 1999); Credit Card Receivables Fund, Inc. v. Cleary, 2006 WL 3775899 (Fla. Cir. Ct. Dec. 19, 2006). *But see* Wachovia SBA Lending, Inc. v. Kraft, 200 P.3d 683 (Wash. 2009).

18 Vivot v. Bank of Am., N.A., 115 So. 3d 428 (Fla. Dist. Ct. App. 2013).

19 Cal. Civ. Code § 1717(b)(1) (West). *See also In re* American Suzuki Motor Corp., 494 B.R. 466 (Bankr. C.D. Cal. 2013); *In re* Tobacco Cases I, 216 Cal. App. 4th 570 (Cal. Ct. App. 2013).

20 Cal. Civ. Code § 1717(b)(2) (West).

21 *See* Khavarian Enters., Inc. v. Commline Inc., 216 Cal. App. 4th 310 (2013).

22 *See* Discover Bank v. Scott (Cal. Super. Ct. Apr. 26, 2013), *available at* www.nclc.org/unreported.

23 Cal. Civ. Code § 1717.5 (West).

24 Alaska R. Civ. P. 82(a).

25 Ariz. Rev. Stat. Ann. § 12-341.01(A).

26 Ark. Code Ann. § 16-22-308.

27 Cal. Civ. Code § 1811.1 (West).

affiliate of a depository institution, an industrial loan company, or a licensed consumer finance lender.[28]

- *Colorado* legislation provides attorney fees to the prevailing party in a damages action based upon a bounced check or failure to pay a draft or order.[29]
- *Delaware* legislation provides that a prevailing party recovers fees in an action regarding an installment sales contract.[30]
- *Idaho* provides that "in any civil action to recover on an open account, account stated, note, bill, negotiable instrument, guaranty, or contract relating to the purchase or sale of goods, wares, merchandise, or services and in any commercial transaction unless otherwise provided by law, the prevailing party shall be allowed a reasonable attorney's fee to be set by the court, to be taxed and collected as costs."[31] Idaho also provides, when that provision does not apply, that the prevailing party still receives attorney fees if the amount the collector pleaded is less than $35,000.[32] A third fee-shifting provision applies to commercial transactions but excludes those for personal or household purposes.[33]
- *Illinois* legislation states that, when an action is brought on a credit card against a consumer and the consumer calls into question any transaction arising from use of such card, the burden of proof is on the collector. If the consumer prevails on such an issue, the court may award a reasonable attorney fee for the consumer.[34]
- *Mississippi* has a statute providing attorney fees for the prevailing party in an action on an open account.[35]
- *Nevada* provides that the court may award fees to the prevailing party when that party has not recovered more than $20,000.[36]
- *New Mexico* provides for attorney fees for the prevailing party on an action on an open account if the action is filed in the district court, small claims court, or magistrate court.[37]
- *Oklahoma* provides fees to the prevailing party "in any civil action to recover for labor or services rendered, or on an open account, a statement of account, account stated, note, bill, negotiable instrument, or contract relating to the purchase or sale of goods, wares, or merchandise."[38]
- *Wisconsin* has a statute[39] that is interpreted as allowing the court to award attorney fees when an action is voluntarily dismissed.[40] It is error for a court not to at least consider this as grounds for the consumer to recover after the collector voluntarily dismisses a case.[41]

With any of these statutes, an issue will be whether the consumer has sufficiently prevailed in the action to merit a fee award. Oklahoma's Supreme Court has upheld an award for the consumer under its statute when the consumer succeeded in setting aside a default judgment and the collector then voluntarily dismissed the case.[42] While a consumer might not be considered to prevail in a case if the collector dismisses the case before the consumer seeks affirmative relief,[43] the motion to vacate the default judgment is such an attempt at affirmative relief. The key is not whether the consumer obtained a judgment but whether the consumer had a successful result.[44]

13.1.5 Fee Awards Pursuant to Consumer Counterclaims

Statutes underlying certain consumer counterclaims provide for fees for a prevailing consumer, including the Fair Debt Collection Practices Act (FDCPA), the state unfair and deceptive acts and practices (UDAP) statute, a state debt collection statute, and state credit laws.[45] Section 5.5.1.1, *supra*, examines whether to bring various counterclaims, but one obvious benefit is when a counterclaim allows a prevailing consumer to recover statutory attorney fees. Such fees are awarded whether those statutory causes of action are brought affirmatively or as counterclaims. While the attorney fees may compensate only for time spent litigating the statutory counterclaim, that work is likely to be intertwined with, if not inseparable from, the collection case, allowing the consumer to recover a significant attorney fee award.[46]

In addition, a counterclaim for litigation misconduct may claim as actual damages the attorney fees the consumer must pay to defend the case. As discussed in the following subsection, the successful counterclaim may result in compensation for attorney time not only for prosecuting the counterclaim (as a statutory fee award) but also for the time spent defending the collector's inappropriate causes of actions (as actual damages).

28 Cal. Civ. Code § 1717.5 (West).
29 Colo. Rev. Stat. § 13-21-109(6).
30 Del. Code Ann. tit. 6 § 4344.
31 Idaho Code Ann. § 12-120(3).
32 Idaho Code Ann. § 12-120(1). *See* Mickelsen v. Broadway Ford, Inc., 280 P.3d 176, 183 (Idaho 2012) (pleading that sought both damages and rescission of a lease does not qualify for fees under this section).
33 Idaho Code Ann. § 12-120(3). *See* Mickelsen v. Broadway Ford, Inc., 280 P.3d 176, 183 (Idaho 2012) (fees not available when claim involved warranties on truck leased for personal use).
34 815 Ill. Comp. Stat. § 145/2(b).
35 Miss. Code Ann. § 11-53-81.
36 Nev. Rev. Stat. § 18.010(2)(a).
37 N.M. Stat. Ann. § 39-2-2.1.
38 Okla. Stat. tit. 12, § 936. *Cf.* Borst v. Bright Mortgage Co., 824 P.2d 1102 (Okla. 1991); Cadle Co. v. Bianco, 849 P.2d 437 (Okla. Civ. App. 1992).
39 Wis. Stat. § 805.04(2).
40 Arrow Fin. Servs., L.L.C. v. Lunemann, 771 N.W.2d 930 (Wis. Ct. App. 2009).
41 Arrow Fin. Servs., L.L.C. v. Lunemann, 771 N.W.2d 930 (Wis. Ct. App. 2009).
42 Prof'l Credit Collections, Inc. v. Smith, 933 P.2d 307 (Okla. 1997); Capital One Bank v. Parsons, 217 P.3d 636 (Okla. Civ. App. 2009). *But cf.* Velocity Invs., L.L.C. v. Cocina, 909 N.Y.S.2d 853 (N.Y. App. Div. 2010) (consumer had not prevailed when consumer had just defeated a summary judgment motion).
43 *See* Asset Acceptance, L.L.C. v. Smith, 229 P.3d 1287 (Okla. Civ. App. 2010).
44 Prof'l Credit Collections, Inc. v. Smith, 933 P.2d 307 (Okla. 1997).
45 *See* § 5.5, *supra*.
46 *See* National Consumer Law Center, Unfair and Deceptive Acts and Practices § 12.8.11.4 (8th ed. 2012), *updated at* www.nclc.org/library. *See generally* Hensley v. Eckerhart, 461 U.S. 424, 103 S. Ct. 1933, 76 L. Ed. 2d 40 (1983).

13.1.6 A Second Lawsuit to Recover the Consumer's Fees Incurred in the First Action

When the prevailing consumer cannot recover attorney fees in the collection action, the consumer can consider bringing a second action after conclusion of the first, seeking to recover for attorney time spent defending the collection action. Such a lawsuit seeking attorney fees as damages under the FDCPA, under a UDAP statute, or for malicious prosecution is examined at § 13.4, *infra*. The prevailing consumer in this second action should be able to recover statutory fees for attorney time spent on the second action (such as an FDCPA or UDAP cause of action) and also recover as actual damages in the second action the fees expended in the first case.[47]

To perfect the claim for actual damages, the consumer needs to be financially obligated to pay the attorney the fees resulting from the successful defense of the collection case, even if those fees have not been paid. To constitute recoverable actual damages the consumer's fee obligation should be for a sum certain and not for an unliquidated, contingent, or other inchoate amount. In some states these fees, as actual damages, might even be trebled under a UDAP statute or enhanced by punitive damages under a malicious prosecution claim.

13.1.7 Fees When Collector Denies the Consumer's Request for Admissions

Chapter 2, *supra*, discusses reasons why the consumer might (or might not) wish to send requests for admissions to a collector, and § 4.2.2.1, *supra*, examines the consequences of a party's denials of requests for admissions. Just as a consumer might be liable, the collector can be liable as well for the reasonable expenses of the consumer's proof when the collector denies facts propounded in the consumer's request for admissions. If the consumer later proves those facts to be true, and the collector did not have a reasonable basis for that denial, then the collector is liable for the reasonable expenses of the consumer's proof—which would include attorney fees and other expenses.[48]

47 *See* Lowe v. Elite Recovery Solutions L.P., 2008 WL 324777 (E.D. Cal. Feb. 5, 2008); Owens v. Howe, 365 F. Supp. 2d 942 (N.D. Ind. 2005); Venes v. Prof'l Serv. Bureau, Inc., 353 N.W.2d 671 (Minn. Ct. App. 1984). *See also* McKnight v. Benitez, 176 F. Supp. 2d 1301 (M.D. Fla. 2001); Evanauskas v. Strumpf, 2001 U.S. Dist. LEXIS 14326 (D. Conn. June 27, 2001). *But see* Goray v. Unifund CCR Partners, 2007 WL 4260017 (D. Haw. Dec. 4, 2007) (no additional attorney fees awarded as damages in second suit when attorney fees awarded to consumer in collection action, there was no showing that the consumer did not owe the debt, and collection action was dismissed only because collector was not registered).

48 *See* Fed. R. Civ. P. 37(c)(2).

13.1.8 Attorney Fees for Groundless Litigation

13.1.8.1 Introduction

A number of state statutes and court rules provide that the court can require a plaintiff to pay the prevailing defendant's attorney fees when the plaintiff's claim was groundless (or words of similar import). Thus a consumer defendant can recover attorney fees after prevailing in a collection action by asking the court that has just ruled for the consumer to also award the consumer an attorney fee award because the collector's action was groundless.

While historically courts rarely order such relief, debt buyer litigation is not typical of other forms of litigation in that the debt buyer will often sue with virtually no information about the case. Many debt buyer claims fall nicely within statutory standards for such relief, and consumers pushing this approach may find success, at least in certain courts.

The approach may be simpler than bringing a second FDCPA or UDAP action based upon the collector's litigation misconduct in the first case. The court deciding whether to provide the consumer with a fee award is already familiar with the facts and has already ruled for the consumer. The consumer need only ask the court not only to dismiss the collector's claim but to rule that the claim was groundless. A host of issues that might come up in a second case are avoided, as is a second filing fee and much time and effort.

Asking for this relief at the end of the case may also be preferable to a counterclaim in the same case alleging litigation misconduct. The counterclaim ups the stakes for the collector, leading the collector to do a more thorough job obtaining and presenting evidence. The collector will also be less likely to dismiss a case in which such a counterclaim is still pending.

13.1.8.2 Standards for Rule 11 Sanctions

State statutes and rules often are similar to Federal Rule of Civil Procedure 11, providing for sanctions which may include reasonable attorney fees and other expenses[49] if the litigation meets *any* of the following three standards:

- The litigation is being pursued for any improper purpose, such as to harass, cause unnecessary delay, or needlessly increase the cost of litigation.
- The claim is not warranted by existing law or by a non-frivolous argument for modifying existing law.
- The factual contentions do not have evidentiary support unless, if specifically so identified, they will likely have evidentiary support after a reasonable opportunity for further investigation or discovery.[50]

The third of these standards is the one most applicable to a debt buyer collection action, since debt buyers often do not have evidentiary support for their claims (but only a spreadsheet

49 Fed. R. Civ. P. 11(c)(4).

50 Fed. R. Civ. P. 11(b).

with basic data on the consumer) and do not specifically identify that they will likely have evidentiary support after a reasonable opportunity for further investigation.

Federal Rule of Civil Procedure 11(c)(2) requires that a motion for sanctions be made separately from any other motion and must describe the specific conduct that violated the Rule. The motion must be properly served upon the other party.[51]

13.1.8.3 State Statutory Standards

Like Rule 11, a number of state statutes or rules provide for attorney fees for a prevailing party when there is no evidentiary support for the other party's claims, when a claim is brought without "substantive justification," when there is "no justiciable issue of law or fact," or when the claim is "groundless."[52] For example, fees have been awarded under such a statute when the collector sued an identity theft victim without sufficient basis.[53] Such standards should also be met when a claim is clearly outside the statute of limitations or when the collector has no evidence on which to base its claim.[54]

The collector must make a reasonable inquiry into its own pleadings to see if it has evidentiary support for its own allegations.[55] For example, sanctions have been awarded when the collector received a copy of the consumer's credit report, which showed that the debt had been discharged in bankruptcy and thus was not owed, but the collector proceeded with the case anyway.[56] Confirming that a collector received a copy of the consumer's credit report is a simple matter. The consumer can obtain a copy of the report from the reporting agency,[57] and the inquiry section of the consumer's copy will show who has received a copy of the report during the previous year.[58]

A New York court also awarded attorney fees to the consumer as a sanction when the collector continued to press a case in which all the collector possessed to prove a debt was a document it had created that stated the name of a consumer, the name of the original creditor, a dollar amount due, and an APR, and the collector did not dismiss the case until it was clear that the represented consumer would pursue an aggressive defense.[59] Sanctions have also been awarded in New York when a collector brought two suits on the same debt, even though it sought to dismiss both suits.[60] In a New York *pro se* case, the court ordered sanctions to be paid to the Lawyer's Fund for Client Protection when the collection attorney on a number of occasions failed to comply with the court's order to produce proof that the debt buyer owned the account.[61]

Georgia has a statute that provides attorney fees if the other party lacked substantial justification or the action was interposed for delay or harassment or if the other party "unnecessarily expanded the proceeding by other improper conduct."[62] A Georgia court awarded fees to a consumer when the collector delayed an action for months and then dropped the case as soon as the consumer hired an attorney, since the collector's long delay before dismissing its own case was viewed as an unnecessary expansion of the proceeding.[63]

Other statutes are somewhat vaguer in their standards, providing fees when a claim is "frivolous"[64] or "unreasonable"[65] or "vexatious."[66] Even more difficult to prove is a standard that the claim is frivolous *and* brought in bad faith,[67] or that it is brought for harassment.[68]

In reviewing state statutes, look carefully whether the standards for attorney fees use "or" or "and." For example, Idaho allows for fees if the action is meant to harass *or* not supported in fact *or* not warranted by existing law.[69] Thus, all that need be shown is that the action is not supported in fact. On the other hand, Hawaii requires that the action not be supported by the facts *and* the law *and also* that the claim is frivolous.[70] The consumer would have to prove all three of these conditions.

Also look for any indication of legislative intent. Nevada's statutes state that they are to be liberally construed in favor of awarding fees.[71] Also examine the statute for any defenses or procedural requirements on the consumer. In some states, the consumer's request for fees must meet certain time

51 *See, e.g.*, Bourdier v. Dermatology & Aesthetic Inst., L.L.C., 2013 WL 486971 (M.D. La. Feb. 6, 2013).

52 *See* § 13.1.8.4, *infra*. *See also* Countrywide Home Loans, Inc. v. Rood, 784 N.E.2d 1050 (Ind. Ct. App. 2003).

53 Credigy Receivables, Inc. v. Whittington, 689 S.E.2d 889 (N.C. Ct. App. 2010).

54 *Cf.* Palisades Collection, L.L.C. v. Delaney, 29 So. 3d 885 (Ala. Civ. App. 2009) (award of fees reversed when consumer did not request fees in a timely manner).

55 Unifund CCR Partners v. Villa, 299 S.W.3d 92 (Tex. 2009).

56 Unifund CCR Partners v. Villa, 273 S.W.3d 385 (Tex. App. 2008), *rev'd*, 299 S.W.3d 92 (Tex. 2009) (consumer's testimony that debt buyer had reviewed credit report was hearsay and no other evidence supported the sanctions).

57 How to obtain a copy of the report is explained in National Consumer Law Center, Fair Credit Reporting Ch. 3 (8th ed. 2013), *updated at* www.nclc.org/library. *See also* § 13.2.4.1, *infra*.

58 *See* National Consumer Law Center, Fair Credit Reporting § 3.5.4.1 (8th ed. 2013), *updated at* www.nclc.org/library.

59 Worldwide Asset Purchasing, L.L.C. v. Akrofi, 884 N.Y.S.2d 631 (N.Y. Civ. Ct. 2009).

60 Palisades Collection, L.L.C. v. Sadowski, 884 N.Y.S.2d 843 (N.Y. Dist. Ct. 2009).

61 LVNV Funding L.L.C. v. Guest, 953 N.Y.S.2d 550 (table), 2012 WL 1543286 (N.Y. City Ct. May 29, 2012).

62 Ga. Code Ann. § 9-15-14(b).

63 *See* Portfolio Recovery Assoc., L.L.C. v. Carmichael (Ga. Cnty. Ct. July 12, 2012), *available at* www.nclc.org/unreported.

64 Haw. Rev. Stat. § 607-14.5; Neb. Rev. Stat. § 25-824; N.H. Super. Ct. R. 59L; N.H. Dist. Ct. R. 1.8; S.D. Codified Laws § 15-17-51; Wash. Rev. Code § 4.84.185.

65 N.H. Super. Ct. R. 59L; N.H. Dist. Ct. R. 1.8.

66 *See, e.g.*, 42 Pa. Cons. Stat. § 2503.

67 Mass. Gen. Laws ch. 231 § 6F; Mo. Rev. Stat. § 514.205. *See also* Ariz. Rev. Stat. Ann. § 12-341.01(C); N.D. Cent. Code § 28-26-31; Utah Code Ann. § 78B-5-825 (West).

68 Miss. Code Ann. § 11-55-5.

69 Idaho Code Ann. § 12-123.

70 Haw. Rev. Stat. § 607-14.5.

71 Nev. Rev. Stat. §§ 7.085, 18.010.

deadlines.[72] Other times, the provision does not apply in small claims court, or does not apply to the collector's attorney (but only the collector) if the attorney is acting in good faith based upon representations by the collector.[73]

A number of statutes provide a defense to the award of fees if the losing party voluntarily dismissed the case on a timely basis.[74] But absent such a statutory defense, attorney fees can still be assessed when the collector voluntarily dismisses a claim.[75] Debt buyers bring thousands of cases, counting on default judgments in virtually all of them. The collector's bad faith is not lessened when it brings many invalid cases and then drops the few in which a vigorous defense is offered.

13.1.8.4 State-by-State Listing of Standards for Groundless Litigation

What follows is a detailed but by no means complete listing of state statutes and rules that provide for attorney fees for a prevailing party when the other party's claims were groundless or involved vexatious litigation:

- *Ala. Code § 12-19-272:* attorney fees when action is brought without substantial justification, either in whole or part. No attorney fees or costs shall be assessed if a voluntary dismissal is filed as to any action, claim, or defense within ninety days after filing.
- *Ark. Code Ann. § 16-22-309:* attorney fees when there is complete absence of a justiciable issue of either law or fact, unless a voluntary dismissal is filed within a reasonable time. Lacking a justiciable issue of law or fact means, among other things, that the party's attorney knew, or should have known, that the action was without any reasonable basis. The fee is not to exceed 10% of the amount in controversy.
- *Cal. Civ. Proc. Code § 128.5:* attorney fees for tactics that are totally and completely without merit.
- *Colo. Rev. Stat. § 13-17-102:* reasonable attorney fees when action, either in whole or in part, lacks substantial justification, meaning substantially frivolous, substantially groundless, or substantially vexatious. No attorney fees shall be assessed if, after filing suit, a voluntary dismissal is filed within a reasonable time.
- *Fla. Stat. § 57.105:* reasonable attorney fees when claim is not supported by the material facts necessary to establish the claim or defense, or would not be supported by the application of then-existing law to those material facts.[76]
- *Fla. R. Civ. P. 1.420(d):* "costs" relating to defending a first action when the plaintiff voluntarily dismisses that action without prejudice and then brings a similar second action. When the credit contract itself defines "costs" to include attorney fees (for example, when the contract states that the creditor is entitled to "costs, including attorney fees"), the consumer can recover attorney fees as costs.[77]
- *Ga. Code Ann. § 9-15-14:* attorney fees when there is a complete absence of any justiciable issue of law or fact, such that it could not be reasonably believed that a court would accept the asserted claim, but must be sought not later than forty-five days after the final disposition of the action.
- *Haw. Rev. Stat. § 607-14.5:* attorney fees when all or a portion of the party's claim is frivolous and not reasonably supported by the facts and the law. If the plaintiff is requested to dismiss the frivolous claims, and does so within a reasonable length of time, no fees shall be awarded.
- *Idaho Code Ann. § 12-123:* when a claim is not supported in fact or warranted under existing law, attorney fees may be awarded within twenty-one days of entry of judgment.
- *Ind. Code § 34-52-1-1:* attorney fees when claim is frivolous, unreasonable, or groundless.[78]
- *Iowa Code § 652.22*: court may award fees when action to recover on a written contract is frivolous.
- *Kan. Stat. Ann. § 60-211(c)*: attorney fees for frivolous actions.
- *Md. R. 1-34:* attorney fees when claim is without substantial justification.
- *Mass. Gen. Laws ch. 231, § 6F:* attorney fees if claim is wholly insubstantial, frivolous, and not advanced in good faith. The court shall include in such finding the specific facts and reasons on which the finding is based.
- *Mich. Comp. Laws § 600.2591:* attorney fees when there is no reasonable basis to believe that the facts underlying that party's legal position are in fact true or the party's legal position is devoid of arguable legal merit.
- *Miss. Code Ann. § 11-55-5:* attorney fees if claim is for delay or harassment, or if the court finds that an attorney or party unnecessarily expanded the proceedings by other improper conduct; but no fees if a voluntary dismissal is filed within a reasonable time.
- *Mo. Ann. Stat. § 514.205:* attorney fees if claim is brought frivolously and in bad faith.
- *Neb. Rev. Stat. § 25-824:* attorney fees when claim is frivolous or made in bad faith, unless voluntarily dismissed within a reasonable period of time.

72 *See, e.g.*, Ga. Code Ann. § 9-15-14; Idaho Code Ann. § 121-123. *See also* Palisades Collection, L.L.C. v. Delaney, 29 So. 3d 885 (Ala. Civ. App. 2009) (award of fees reversed when consumer did not request fees in a timely manner).

73 *See, e.g.*, Fla. Stat. § 57.105.

74 *See, e.g.*, Ala. Code § 12-19-272; Ark. Code Ann. § 16-22-309; Colo. Rev. Stat. § 13-17-102; Fla. Stat. § 57.105; Haw. Rev. Stat. § 607-14.5; Miss. Code Ann. § 11-55-5; Neb. Rev. Stat. § 25-824.

75 Palisades Collection, L.L.C. v. Sadowski, 884 N.Y.S.2d 843 (N.Y. Dist. Ct. 2009); Unifund CCR Partners v. Villa, 273 S.W.3d 385 (Tex. App. 2008), *rev'd on other grounds*, 299 S.W.3d 92 (Tex. 2009).

76 *See also* Wilson v. Rose Printing Co., 624 So. 2d 257 (Fla. 1993); Commercial Serv. of Perry, Inc. v. Campbell, 861 So. 2d 1258 (Fla. Dist. Ct. App. 2003); Ensign Bank v. S. Fla. Warehousing II, 582 So. 2d 165 (Fla. Dist. Ct. App. 1991).

77 Credit Receivables Fund, Inc. v. Cleary, 2006 WL 3775899 (Fla. Cir. Ct. Dec. 19, 2006). *See also* Wilson v. Rose Printing Co., 624 So. 2d 257 (Fla. 1993). *But cf.* Commercial Serv. of Perry, Inc. v. Campbell, 861 So. 2d 1258 (Fla. Dist. Ct. App. 2003).

78 *See also* Countrywide Home Loans, Inc. v. Rood, 784 N.E.2d 1050 (Ind. Ct. App. 2003).

- *Nev. Rev. Stat. § 18.010:* attorney fees when claim is brought without reasonable ground, liberally construed in favor of awarding fees.
- *Nev. Rev. Stat. § 7.085:* attorney fees when action is not well-grounded in fact or is not warranted by existing law, liberally construed in favor of awarding fees.
- *N.H. Rev. Stat. Ann. § 507:15:* attorney fees when contract action is frivolous.
- *N.H. Super. Ct. R. 59L; N.H. Dist. Ct. R. 1.8:* attorney fees when there is frivolous or unreasonable conduct.
- *N.J. Stat. Ann. § 2A:15-59.1:* attorney fees when non-prevailing party knew, or should have known, that the complaint was without any reasonable basis in law or equity.
- *N.Y. R. of Ct. § 130-1.1:* attorney fees for claims that are completely without merit in law or that assert material factual statements that are false.[79]
- *N.C. Gen. Stat. § 6-21.5:* attorney fees when complete absence of a justiciable issue of either law or fact.[80]
- *N.D. Cent. Code § 28-26-01:* attorney fees when claim is frivolous—there is such a complete absence of actual facts or law that a reasonable person could not have thought a court would render judgment in that person's favor, providing that the prevailing party has, in responsive pleading, alleged the frivolous nature of the claim.
- *N.D. Cent. Code § 28-26-31:* attorney fees when allegations in pleadings are made without reasonable cause and not in good faith.
- *Or. Rev. Stat. § 20.105:* in a suit in circuit court, attorney fees shall be awarded when there is no objectively reasonable basis for asserting the claim.
- *42 Pa. Cons. Stat. § 2503:* attorney fees when conduct of collector is arbitrary, vexatious, or in bad faith.
- *R.I. Gen. Laws § 9-29-21*: attorney fees when proceeding is frivolous.
- *S.C. Code Ann. § 15-36-10(G)*: attorney fees when proceeding is frivolous.
- *S.D. Codified Laws § 15-17-51:* attorney fees when proceeding is frivolous.
- *Tex. Civ. Prac. & Rem. Code Ann. §§ 10.001, 10.004:* attorney fees where, when signing a complaint, the signatory falsely certifies that each claim is warranted by existing law, each allegation has evidentiary support.[81]
- *Utah Code Ann. § 78B-5-825:* attorney fees if action is without merit and not brought or asserted in good faith.
- *Wash. Rev. Code § 4.84.185:* attorney fees when claim is frivolous and advanced without reasonable cause, and fees are sought within thirty days after entry of the order.
- *Wis. Stat. § 802.05:* attorney fees when proceeding is frivolous.

13.2 Cleaning Up the Consumer's Credit Record

13.2.1 The Consumer's Credit Record

13.2.1.1 Background

Consumers have a strong interest in ensuring that accurate information is reflected in their credit reports, particularly after they prevail in a collection action. The reports and resulting credit scores determine, among other things, the consumer's access to and the cost of credit and insurance.[82] Credit reports can even affect whether the consumer is able to obtain or keep employment. The consumer's credit reports often will contain adverse public record information when a collection lawsuit is filed.

Surprisingly, winning the collection action by itself may do little or nothing to improve the prevailing consumer's credit report. Instead, consumers must take affirmative steps to update their credit report based upon the court judgment. Even that affirmative action may accomplish less than most consumers would expect.

Here are some "facts of life" about the credit reporting system. Credit bureaus are called consumer reporting agencies (CRAs) and their activities are regulated by the Fair Credit Reporting Act (FCRA).[83] The three major "nationwide CRAs"—Equifax, Experian, and TransUnion—each maintain records on well over 200 million Americans, and each *month* they receive from creditors and other furnishers about four billion pieces of information concerning approximately 1.5 billion credit accounts. The information about these credit accounts is called "tradelines."

A credit report is a snapshot in time. What a consumer sees one month will not be the same as what the consumer or a creditor sees when requesting the report at a different point in time. A credit report will contain identifying information about the consumer, an inquiries section showing what entities have requested a report on the consumer within the last year, and a public records section showing information on court actions and bankruptcies. A large portion of the report will be a listing of credit accounts (that is, tradelines).[84] For each tradeline, the report will list information about the account and the creditor, when the account was opened, the last update on the account, the highest amount ever owed, the current balance, the date and amount of the maximum delinquency, and the number of times the consumer has been thirty, sixty, or ninety days delinquent on the account.

79 Erin Servs. Co. v. Bohnet, 907 N.Y.S.2d 100 (N.Y. Dist. Ct. 2010); Palisades Collection, L.L.C. v. Sadowski, 884 N.Y.S.2d 843 (N.Y. Dist. Ct. 2009); Worldwide Asset Purchasing, L.L.C. v. Akrofi, 884 N.Y.S.2d 631 (N.Y. Civ. Ct. 2009).

80 N.C. Gen. Stat. § 6-21.5. *See also* Credigy Receivables, Inc. v. Whittington, 689 S.E.2d 889 (N.C. Ct. App. 2010).

81 *See also* Unifund CCR Partners v. Villa, 299 S.W.3d 92 (Tex. 2009).

82 *See generally* National Consumer Law Center, Fair Credit Reporting, Chs. 7, 12, 14 (8th ed. 2013), *updated at* www.nclc.org/library.

83 15 U.S.C. §§ 1681–1681x. *See also* National Consumer Law Center, Fair Credit Reporting (8th ed. 2013), *updated at* www.nclc.org/library.

84 *See* National Consumer Law Center, Fair Credit Reporting § 3.7 (8th ed. 2013), *updated at* www.nclc.org/library.

13.2.1.2 Reports Sometimes Fail to Include Court Outcomes Favorable to Consumers

The nationwide CRAs hire outside "public record vendors" who search, among other things, court records and furnish that information to the CRAs. The largest public records vendor is LexisNexis, which supplies information to all three nationwide CRAs.

Public records vendors routinely note and report the filing of collection lawsuits and entry of judgments for the collector. On the other hand, sometimes the nationwide CRAs fail to update this information, including failing to report that a lawsuit's outcome that is favorable to the consumer.[85] The public record vendor may not provide such information to the nationwide CRA, or the CRA might not purchase the information to update preexisting information in the consumer's file.[86] As a result, the pendency of a collection action often remains as the latest information that the CRAs claim to know, even when the case has concluded in the consumer's favor.

When the original creditor, who regularly furnishes information about the consumer's account, brought the collection action, it is possible that updated information which reflects the court judgment will be forwarded to the CRA as part of that creditor's regular reporting regarding its tradeline. Such updated reporting would ideally reflect that the consumer does not owe the debt. However, the updated information often may not be provided, and in any event it likely may not affect the reporting of the same debt in the public records portion of the file.

When a debt buyer brought the collection action, the original creditor will have long since stopped furnishing information about the account to the CRAs. The debt buyer is less likely to regularly update information on its accounts with the CRAs. As a result, new information may not be sent to the CRA from the original creditor or debt buyer after the debt buyer's collection action is dismissed.

Creditors and collectors establish systems to regularly report the status of payments on an account and its collection status, but the systems are not designed to report court cases in these tradelines. Court cases are reflected in the public records section, and, as has been indicated, these vendors may not report outcomes favorable to the consumer, or the CRAs might not purchase the updates.

Moreover, there is no private enforcement of the FCRA provision requiring furnishers, such as the original creditor, a subsequent debt buyer,[87] or the public records vendor, to affirmatively update the information that they provide to a CRA; nor is there private enforcement of the FCRA duty to furnish accurate and complete information in the first place.[88] Furnishers' only privately enforceable legal obligation to accurately report and to correct and update information is triggered by the consumer initiating an FCRA dispute with a CRA, thereby causing a reinvestigation.[89]

13.2.2 Correcting Inaccurate Information After Prevailing in Court

13.2.2.1 The Dispute Process

The best way to update and correct inaccurate or incomplete information in the consumer's report after prevailing in a collection action is for the consumer to lodge a dispute with the CRA. The consumer should dispute any inaccurate or incomplete information in the original creditor's tradeline, in any collection tradeline reflecting the same debt, and in any entry in the public records section of the report reflecting the collection action.

The CRA will then ask anyone furnishing disputed information (for example, the public record vendor, the original creditor, and/or the debt buyer) to reinvestigate that information. This process requires the public record vendor, creditor, or debt buyer to correct and update information previously supplied to the CRA, including acknowledging the judgment for the consumer in the collection case. The furnisher is liable for the full range of FCRA private remedies for any breach of its reinvestigation duties.[90]

13.2.2.2 Manner of Case's Resolution Determines Whether Report's Historical Data Will Be Corrected

The FCRA requires that a tradeline must accurately reflect the results of the court proceedings, which, after all, is a conclusive determinant of the accuracy of the information.[91] If the dispute process works the way it is supposed to (it often does not), then the consumer should be able to use the outcome of the court case to correct the *current* information in the report—the current status of the account. If the court dismisses a collection action with prejudice, then the current information on the account should reflect a zero balance. For example, when consumers prove that their account had been previously paid in full, the report should notate a zero balance.

While a prevailing consumer's dispute with the CRA thus should clean up a consumer's current information, the same is not always the case with historical information found in the

85 *See, e.g.*, Soutter v. Equifax Info Serv., 2011 WL 1226025 (E.D. Va. Mar. 30, 2011) (alleging that Equifax failed to obtain and update purchase status updates for public records from Virginia courts), *rev'd and remanded*, 498 Fed. Appx. 260 (4th Cir. 2012) (reversing grant of class certification for lack of commonality).

86 National Consumer Law Center, Fair Credit Reporting §§ 4.3.2.5, 4.4.6.10 (8th ed. 2013), *updated at* www.nclc.org/library.

87 However, there may be a claim against a debt buyer under the FDCPA. *See id.* § 6.13.

88 15 U.S.C. §§ 1681s-2(a)(1), (2). *See* National Consumer Law Center, Fair Credit Reporting § 6.1.2 (8th ed. 2013), *updated at* www.nclc.org/library.

89 15 U.S.C. § 1681s-2(b). *See* National Consumer Law Center, Fair Credit Reporting § 6.10 (8th ed. 2013), *updated at* www.nclc.org/library.

90 *See* National Consumer Law Center, Fair Credit Reporting § 6.10 (8th ed. 2013), *updated at* www.nclc.org/library.

91 Carvalho v. Equifax Info. Servs., L.L.C., 629 F.3d 876 (9th Cir. 2010).

consumer's report. Historical data includes such information as that the account was more than sixty days delinquent in the past or that the account involves a repossession or a charge-off. It may be difficult to eliminate adverse historical information when the favorable resolution of the collection case does not challenge that history. When that historical information is correct, it can remain on the report for seven years, notwithstanding the ultimate result in the collection case.

On the other hand, the historical information must be removed completely when consumers prevail in court because they prove that the account was not theirs. Thus, the exact manner in which a case is resolved in the consumer's favor is critical in determining the consumer's ability to eliminate adverse historical information.

The best way for a case to be resolved is for the court to not only rule in the consumer's favor but to order the creditor to inform the CRA that certain historical data in the consumer's file is inaccurate. For example, in a case of identity theft, the court can order the creditor to correct the fact that the consumer was ever delinquent in payments on the account. The court has found the consumer not to owe the debt now or in the past.

When a collection case is brought by a debt buyer, the CRA may not accept a debt buyer's correction of historical information on a debt because it was the originating creditor, not the debt buyer, who had originally reported the historical information. In that case, the court can issue a written decision finding that the consumer never owed the debt and so could not have been delinquent in the past. The consumer can send this court decision to the original creditor (or other entity furnishing the historical information to the CRA) and dispute the accuracy of the historical information with the CRA. The creditor will have to re-investigate this with knowledge of the court decision ruling that the consumer never owed the debt.

Settling a collection case, particularly when it is settled with the originating creditor, provides the consumer's attorney an opportunity to deal directly with the treatment of historical data in the consumer's file. Section 2.9.2, *supra*, provides model language that can be used in a settlement whereby the creditor agrees to take certain actions that should lead to the cleaning up of adverse information on the consumer's creditor report.

13.2.3 How to Dispute Information in the Consumer's File

13.2.3.1 Obtain a Consumer Report on the Consumer

Before disputing information in a consumer's credit report, obtain a copy of that report from at least one of the three major nationwide CRAs but preferably all three. Information in the three reports will be similar but not identical. For example, sometimes one report will not pick up a lawsuit or judgment, while reports from the other CRAs will do so. The consumer will have to make sure that the information in all three reports is updated. If the consumer gets only one report, the same dispute can be sent to the other two nationwide CRAs, resulting in a free copy from each CRA. At that point, a new dispute can be made as to the additional information.

The consumer is entitled to one free report a year from each of the three nationwide CRAs, using any of the three following methods:

- Online at www.annualcreditreport.com;
- By calling toll free (877) 322-8228; or
- By sending a letter to Annual Credit Report Request Service, P.O. Box 105281, Atlanta, GA 30374-5281.

The consumer may be asked detailed information about existing credit accounts and employment, as a form of identification, in addition to the usual forms of identification.

In addition to a free annual report from the three nationwide CRAs, consumers have a number of other rights to obtain an additional free consumer report.[92] The consumer is entitled to a free credit report after an identity theft incident,[93] after a consumer receives notice of an adverse credit action that resulted from the consumer's credit report,[94] if the consumer is unemployed or on public assistance,[95] or if state law so provides.[96] The consumer can also purchase a report relatively inexpensively, or purchase one of the many other more expensive (and largely unnecessary) products that the nationwide CRAs are now marketing. Going to the three CRAs' websites will provide easy access to all of these paid, but often useless, products.

Analyze the report carefully to see which entities supplied what information to the CRA, what information was inaccurate prior to the court judgment, and what information is now inaccurate because the consumer prevailed in the collection action. The consumer's next step is to dispute with the relevant CRA all inaccurate information in the report, as described below.

---

92 Although the CRAs change their phone numbers and addresses frequently, here is contact information for the three major CRAs when requesting a credit report other than the annual free report:

Equifax
P.O. Box 740241
Atlanta, GA 30374-0241
www.equifax.com
(800) 685-1111

Experian
P.O. Box 2002
Allen, TX 75013
www.experian.com
(888) EXPERIAN (397-3742)

TransUnion
P.O. Box 1000
Chester, PA 19022
www.transunion.com
(800) 888-4213

93 *See* National Consumer Law Center, Fair Credit Reporting § 3.3.5 (8th ed. 2013), *updated at* www.nclc.org/library.

94 *Id.* § 3.3.6.

95 *Id.* § 3.3.7.

96 *Id.* § 3.3.8.

13.2.3.2 Send a Dispute at Least to All Three Major Nationwide Consumer Reporting Agencies

The first and most important step to start the FCRA dispute process is to mail a dispute directly to the CRA that produced the inaccurate credit report.[97] Disputing the information in a report with the collector, original creditor, or any other furnisher of information—and not with the CRA—is not as effective in protecting the consumer's rights under the FCRA.[98] While the FCRA does give the consumer a right to dispute directly with a furnisher, there is no private remedy if the information furnisher fails to conduct a reasonable investigation.[99]

When a consumer sends a dispute to a CRA, the CRA must ask the information furnisher to reinvestigate the information. If the furnisher agrees with the consumer or fails to respond to the CRA within thirty days (in some cases, forty-five days), the CRA must delete that information. If the furnisher claims it has reinvestigated and informs the CRA that the information is correct, the report will remain unchanged. But if that reinvestigation is improper, the furnisher is subject to FCRA remedies.

It is not enough to dispute an error with one CRA. A creditor or debt collector furnishing incorrect information to one nationwide CRA will often furnish the same incorrect information to the other two. Moreover, contrary to expectations, correcting a consumer's file with one CRA often does not lead to correction at the other two.

13.2.3.3 Also Notify the Collector and Original Creditor of the Dispute

Consumers should directly notify the collector or original creditor furnishing the disputed information, at the same time they notify the CRAs. The critical dispute notice must be directed to the CRA, which will then ask the collector or creditor to reinvestigate. But consumers strengthen their position when they also notify the furnisher of the inaccurate information. It is also helpful to put the original creditor on notice of the judgment, if it is not on notice already.

Sending a detailed notice to the collector and original creditor prevents any argument from furnishers that they failed to receive adequate information to conduct an adequate investigation. Previously, the nationwide CRAs, in forwarding the consumer's dispute to the furnisher, often reduced the consumer's detailed dispute letter to an electronic message, with the underlying dispute translated to a generic two-digit dispute code (for example, "01 not his/hers") and perhaps a short, one-line paraphrase of some aspect of the dispute (for example, "Consumer states belongs to husband only"). While the nationwide CRAs have now begun forwarding the consumer's entire dispute to the furnisher,[100] supplying the furnisher directly with a copy of the consumer's detailed dispute letter that he or she is sending to the CRA thwarts any claim by the furnisher that it did not understand the consumer's dispute because of the abbreviated notice that it received from the CRA.

13.2.3.4 Form of the Request

Although not required by the FCRA, the consumer's dispute with the CRA should be in writing, and the consumer should keep copies of all correspondence. Telephone disputes do not allow for the presentation of copies of the judgment and other important documents. They do not create an adequate record in the event a consumer follows a failed dispute with litigation.

Sending the request by mail, return receipt requested, is highly advisable. This will prevent problems if the CRA loses all record of a consumer's dispute. Without a return receipt, a CRA might claim that it never received the dispute and will argue that it merely made a mistake, rather than that its procedures themselves are inadequate.

Previously, practitioners advised avoiding using the Internet to forward disputes because, until recently, consumers who made disputes through a CRA's website were limited to a "check-box" dispute form and could not forward the judgment or other documents that are essential to support their claim. The nationwide CRAs have now added the capability for consumers to upload documents to their website when disputing a report.[101] It remains to be seen whether this will result in more meaningful investigations by furnishers. Also, with Internet disputes, the consumer still might not be able to conveniently send a copy of the dispute to the creditor or debt buyer.

When consumers request copies of their credit reports from the three nationwide CRAs, they will receive a dispute form that they will be encouraged to use. These forms provide a list of "check box" dispute choices. Consumers using such a form for a dispute should supplement it with additional written details and documentary support.

Having the consumer sign the dispute under oath converts the letter into an affidavit, with potential benefits. The affidavit provides greater credibility to the consumer's complaint, especially in contrast to the furnisher's automated, unsworn response. Moreover, furnishers may have policies that give greater weight to consumer affidavits and may therefore more readily accept the consumer's version of the dispute and be more likely to resolve it favorably.

A request for reinvestigation is often just the beginning of a protracted battle with the CRA or furnisher, who may ignore correspondence or fail to follow up as promised. It is good practice for the consumer to establish a file of all correspondence sent and received and to keep proof that the CRA and furnisher have received the consumer's correspondence.

97 *See id.* § 4.5.2.
98 *Id.* § 6.10.
99 *Id.* § 6.5.2.
100 *Id.* §§ 4.5.6, 6.10.3.2.
101 Gail Hillebrand, Consumer Fin. Prot. Bureau, *Now you have better options to dispute a credit report error*, Consumer Fin. Prot. Bureau Blog (Feb. 27, 2014), *available at* www.consumerfinance.gov/blog/now-you-have-better-options-to-dispute-a-credit-report-error.

13.2.3.5 Content of the Dispute Letter

The dispute itself should be detailed and specific and should enclose a court-endorsed copy of the judgment resulting from the collection action. The dispute letter might also include the name and telephone numbers of the court clerk and of the attorney who represented the collector.

Particularly when a court order simply dismisses the case, the consumer might include other documentation prepared for trial—such as an affidavit stating the consumer never had an account with the creditor or a spouse was never liable for a credit account—that explains why not just the current balance, but also historical information in the consumer report, is inaccurate. Include all other documentary evidence and information that supports the dispute. A consumer's word alone is rarely sufficient. If the original creditor or collector has ever admitted that any of the disputed information is incorrect, include that admission.

The dispute notice should adequately identify the consumer, fully identify the account or other item being disputed, explain why it is disputed, and explain what the consumer wants the CRA to do. Dispute notices should be both very specific and also general enough to avoid technical interpretations that evade the thrust of the consumer's dispute. Otherwise, the CRAs may do nothing more than what is literally requested in the dispute notice.

For example, if the consumer states, "I have never had an MBNA credit card, so delete MBNA account #1234," the CRA may only delete an account with that number and not other MBNA accounts attributed to the consumer. Many creditors change account numbers after an initial dispute is made; correcting just the old account will not affect these new accounts. Other times, the account number the consumer finds on a periodic statement will be different from the number used in the consumer's file at the CRA.

To prevent these problems, a reinvestigation request should describe the full range of accounts the dispute covers. For example, "I have never had an MBNA credit card. Any MBNA account in my credit file is not mine and should be deleted. This includes account number 1234, as well as any other account you may be reporting, as well as any account that may be reported by any debt collector who is reporting a debt originating from an MBNA account." For First USA accounts, which became Bank One and then Chase accounts, a consumer could state, "I am disputing First USA account #2345. It may also be reported as a Bank One or a JPMorgan Chase account."

13.2.4 When Dispute Fails to Correct the Credit Report

If the CRA fails to correct the consumer's report, then the consumer has several additional steps to take. First, the consumer can repeat the dispute process, providing additional explanations or details, and see if that works the second time through. New information should be specifically included and referenced as new, because the CRA may refuse to investigate again on the basis that it has already done so. Submitting such additional disputes will always enhance the value of any subsequent litigation and sometimes may actually correct the inaccuracy.

Another option is to bring an FCRA action against the CRA and the furnisher that improperly reinvestigated the dispute. Such litigation is examined in another volume in this series.[102] The FCRA sets a thirty-day to forty-five-day timeframe to resolve a formal dispute. After that, the failure to correct a patent inaccuracy, particularly one that is irrefutably documented by a copy of the court judgment, constitutes a host of FCRA violations by the CRA and furnisher that failed in its reinvestigation. An FCRA action has a two-year statute of limitations and may be brought in state or federal court. The consumer can recover actual damages and attorney fees.[103] If the violation is willful, the consumer can also recover statutory and punitive damages.[104]

In addition, if the furnisher is a collection agency or a debt buyer subject to the Fair Debt Collection Practices Act (FDCPA) and communicates information that it knows or should know is false to the CRA, it may be liable for violating the FDCPA, which can result in an award of up to $1000 in statutory damages, actual damages, and attorney fees.[105] This FDCPA violation occurs any time the debt collector/furnisher knowingly communicates false information to a CRA and not just during the FCRA reinvestigation process.

13.2.5 Important Steps to Take After Cleaning Up a Credit Report

After the dispute is resolved to the consumer's satisfaction, look at the consumer's report again in three to six months to see if the disputed information has in fact been changed or whether it has been changed and then improperly reinserted.[106] At the same time, review the inquiries section of the report to see if the collector continues to obtain copies of the consumer's report even after the judgment, when the collector is no longer a creditor and no longer has a permissible purpose to request the report—a clear FCRA violation.[107]

13.3 Responding to Renewed Collection on the Same Debt

A debt buyer who loses a collection suit may improperly continue to seek collection on the debt itself.[108] Alternatively,

102 National Consumer Law Center, Fair Credit Reporting §§ 4.5, 6.1, Ch. 11 (8th ed. 2013), *updated at* www.nclc.org/library.

103 15 U.S.C. § 1681o.

104 15 U.S.C. § 1681n.

105 15 U.S.C. § 1692e(8). *See also* National Consumer Law Center, Fair Debt Collection § 5.5.11 (8th ed. 2014), *updated at* www.nclc.org/library.

106 National Consumer Law Center, Fair Credit Reporting § 4.7 (8th ed. 2013), *updated at* www.nclc.org/library (discussion of "reinsertion").

107 *See* § 13.3, *infra*.

108 *See* Centurion Capital Corp. v. Druce, 828 N.Y.S.2d 851 (N.Y. Civ. Ct. 2006).

the debt buyer may re-package the extinguished debt into one of its portfolios, which it then sells to another debt buyer who may pursue collection on the extinguished debt.

Of course, the consumer has a complete defense if sued a second time on the same debt after the first case was dismissed with prejudice. The consumer also has good legal claims even when there are only collection contacts on the same debt after the judgment for the consumer.

The same is the case even if a collector only pulls the consumer's credit report after a judgment for the consumer, because there is no longer any debt, and the collector thus has no permissible purpose to obtain the report. Requesting a credit report without a permissible purpose is a violation of the Fair Credit Reporting Act.[109] Consequently, it is prudent to review the inquiries section of the consumer's credit report obtained a number of months after the judgment. It is best to review a report from the same credit bureau that the collector has used in the past.

When a collector loses a collection suit with prejudice, the collector also engages in a clear FDCPA violation by continuing to seek collection or by reselling the debt without disclosure that the obligation has been extinguished. The debt collector who reports to a credit bureau that the debt is still owed after it loses a collection action also violates the FDCPA by communicating credit information that it knew or should have known was false.[110]

Any purchaser of that debt may also violate the FDCPA when it duns the consumer on an extinguished debt, though it will claim to be nothing more than an innocent victim of its assignor's deception. The best course of action when one collector lost the first collection lawsuit and another collector is continuing collection is to bring both collectors into the FDCPA action as defendants.

Magrin v. Unifund CCR Partners, Inc. is the leading case finding an FDCPA violation when a debt buyer sold the debt after its action on the debt had been dismissed.[111] The Ninth Circuit found that the essential ingredients of liability under the FDCPA for such a claim was that the debt seller sold the extinguished debt knowing that it was misrepresenting the debt's legal status (either by affirmative false representation or by omission of the material fact that the debt had been extinguished) and with the knowledge that the second debt buyer would undertake efforts to collect the debt. The FDCPA prohibits deceptive or misleading representations "in connection with the collection of any debt."[112] That the debt buyer selling the debt is not the one collecting on the debt is irrelevant, because the debt buyer's misrepresentation is in connection with the second debt buyer's collection of the debt.

The debt seller is also violating the FDCPA provision requiring a collector, whenever communicating "credit information," to disclose that a debt is known to be disputed.[113] The debt seller that lost the collection lawsuit can hardly deny that it knew that the consumer disputes the debt. Furthermore, the collector is communicating credit information when it completes the assignment documents selling the debt to the next buyer. Consequently, even if the collection suit was only dismissed without prejudice once the consumer filed an answer, the debt seller must disclose the fact that the debt is disputed when it assigns the account.[114]

In bringing FDCPA claims against the debt buyer, the consumer can recover up to $1000 in statutory damages, attorney fees to pursue the FDCPA action, plus actual damages.[115] Actual damages will depend on the facts of the case but should include the cost to the consumer of hiring an attorney to respond to the second debt buyer's collection contacts plus any aggravation and suffering caused by those contacts. Moreover, a state deceptive practices (UDAP) claim should be available to challenge the same conduct, leading in some states to punitive or treble damages.[116]

In *Magrin*, the second debt buyer's defense was that it too was an innocent victim of the first debt buyer.[117] The consumer may be able to convert that protestation into proof establishing the liability of the first debt buyer (the debt buyer that lost the collection action), since the first debt buyer did not disclose to the second that the debt was discharged. In the highly unlikely event that the first debt buyer actually disclosed to its assignee that the debt had been extinguished, the second debt buyer, rather than the assignor, would become the principal target of the FDCPA litigation. More likely, the second debt buyer will produce the assignment documentation proving the first debt buyer's misrepresentations and omissions. Either way, the consumer should be able to establish that one or the other debt buyer is culpable.

13.4 Consumer's Follow-Up Lawsuit Relating to Collector's Litigation Misconduct

13.4.1 Scope of This Section

After prevailing in the collection action, the consumer may wish to initiate a new case, bringing affirmative claims against the collector or the collector's attorney based upon their conduct in the collection action. Chapter 5, *supra*, examines the advisability of bringing such claims as counterclaims in the collection action itself. This section considers such claims brought separately after the successful conclusion of the litigation, with a focus on claims brought under the federal Fair

109 *See* National Consumer Law Center, Fair Credit Reporting Ch. 7 (8th ed. 2013), *updated at* www.nclc.org/library.

110 15 U.S.C. 1692e(8). *See also* National Consumer Law Center, Fair Debt Collection § 5.5.11 (8th ed. 2014), *updated at* www.nclc.org/library.

111 Magrin v. Unifund CCR Partners, Inc., 52 Fed. Appx. 938 (9th Cir. 2002). *But cf.* Kawa v. U.S. Bancorp, Inc., 2008 WL 4585432 (D. Neb. Oct. 14, 2008) (debtor sued the wrong entity for selling settled debt).

112 15 U.S.C. § 1692e.

113 15 U.S.C. § 1692e(8).

114 *See* National Consumer Law Center, Fair Debt Collection § 5.5.11 (8th ed. 2014), *updated at* www.nclc.org/library.

115 15 U.S.C. § 1692k(a).

116 *See* National Consumer Law Center, Unfair and Deceptive Acts and Practices Appx. A (8th ed. 2012), *updated at* www.nclc.org/library.

117 *See* Kawa v. U.S. Bancorp, Inc., 2008 WL 4585432 (D. Neb. Oct. 14, 2008).

Debt Collection Practices Act (FDCPA).[118] State deceptive practices act (UDAP), malicious prosecution, and abuse of process claims are also considered.

FDCPA litigation is the topic of another NCLC treatise, *Fair Debt Collection*.[119] This section provides a brief overview of some of the topics concerning a consumer's individual action. FDCPA class actions for litigation misconduct by collection attorneys or collectors will not be treated here at all, and the reader is referred to NCLC's *Fair Debt Collection* and also to another NCLC treatise, *Consumer Class Actions*.[120]

13.4.2 Factors to Consider When Initiating Follow-Up Litigation

13.4.2.1 Relief Sought

The relief the consumer seeks is central to any follow-up action suing the collector or the collector's attorney. Americans' sense of justice and the proper operation of the court system are often deeply offended by collector litigation misconduct. Collectors bring suits when they have no legal right to recover, when they have insufficient evidence that the consumer is liable, or when they seek attorney fees and other charges beyond all reason. The collectors are using the court system as a rubber stamp for default judgments, taking advantage of consumers' lack of legal sophistication and inability to afford legal representation.

No matter how offensive these practices are, they may not justify an individual action for litigation misconduct if the litigation is unlikely to lead to meaningful relief. The first consideration in bringing follow-up litigation should be what damages has the consumer suffered from having to defend an abusive and unsuccessful collection action. If the consumer recovered attorney fees by prevailing in the collection action,[121] then that action may have caused the consumer minimal or no out-of-pocket damages. On the other hand, consumers who have paid lawyers money to successfully defend them in collection actions, and have not been reimbursed for those attorney fees, may have incurred significant damages.[122]

Other consumer damages from the collector's unsuccessful collection action are likely to involve emotional injury, which is compensable as actual damages under the FDCPA.[123] There may be other out-of-pocket damages in addition to attorney fees, such as lost time from work and transportation costs.

The FDCPA provides for statutory damages up to $1000 in addition to actual damages and attorney fees to prosecute the FDCPA claim.[124] Other than their salutary deterrent effect, these statutory damages on their own might not be sufficiently large to justify an FDCPA action when actual damages are not proven, particularly considering the complexity of an FDCPA claim for collection litigation misconduct. A class action seeking actual and statutory damages may be more practical, unless there are individualized facts that preclude class treatment. In cases of egregious litigation misconduct, punitive damages are possible under a tort theory, such as malicious prosecution[125] and, in a few states, under the UDAP statute.[126]

13.4.2.2 Must the Consumer's Claim Have Been Brought As a Compulsory Counterclaim in the Collection Action?

States have different rules on compulsory counterclaims, and case law in this area is examined in section 7.4.2 of NCLC's *Fair Debt Collection*.[127] Whether an FDCPA claim for litigation misconduct is a compulsory counterclaim in the original collection action—and thus lost if not brought in that action—will often be determined by the facts. An FDCPA claim for litigation misconduct can be brought subsequently when the second case's defendant was not a party to the first case, as when the consumer sues the creditor's attorney in the second case rather than the creditor. Beware, though, that some judges have little sympathy for a prevailing consumer suing the other side's attorney.

A consumer's claim cannot be a compulsory counterclaim in the collection action when the collector's litigation misconduct did not occur until after the answer to the collection complaint was filed.[128] While some collection litigation misconduct arises upon the filing of the collection complaint, many violations accrue only later on, for example, as a result of misrepresentations made in the course of the litigation, such as false sworn statements submitted in support of summary judgment.

Malicious prosecution claims do not have to be brought as compulsory counterclaims. An element of the claim for malicious prosecution is that the consumer must have prevailed in the underlying litigation. Malicious prosecution cannot be raised as a counterclaim in the collection action, because the consumer has not yet prevailed.[129]

13.4.2.3 Choice of Federal or State Court

The consumer who wants to litigate FDCPA claims in federal court will have no choice but to bring a separate action for litigation misconduct. Except under very unusual circumstances,

118 National Consumer Law Center, Fair Debt Collection § 5.5.2.13.4 (8th ed. 2014), *updated at* www.nclc.org/library.

119 (8th ed. 2014), *updated at* www.nclc.org/library.

120 (8th ed. 2013), *updated at* www.nclc.org/library.

121 *See* § 13.1, *supra*.

122 *See* Midland Funding, L.L.C. v. Giraldo, 961 N.Y.S.2d 743 (Nassau Cnty. Dist. Ct. 2013) (attorney fees to defend collection case could be actual damages).

123 *See* National Consumer Law Center, Fair Debt Collection § 2.5.2.2 (8th ed. 2014), *updated at* www.nclc.org/library.

124 *See id.* §§ 6.4, 6.8.

125 *See id.* § 9.6.

126 *See* National Consumer Law Center, Unfair and Deceptive Acts and Practices Appx. A (8th ed. 2012), *updated at* www.nclc.org/library.

127 (8th ed. 2014).

128 *See* Fed. R. Civ. P. 13(a) (establishing as an element of a compulsory counterclaim "any claim which at the time of serving the pleading the pleader has against any opposing party").

129 *See* § 13.4.5, *infra*.

the consumer cannot remove a state court collection action to federal court, because the existence of a counterclaim based on federal law does not create federal jurisdiction.[130]

On the other hand, the consumer may wish to litigate the follow-up claims in state court. There are important reasons to do so. As described in § 13.4.2.5, *infra*, one consideration in any subsequent lawsuit is whether the consumer's case will be forced into arbitration. State courts in many states are more likely to find an arbitration requirement unenforceable than are federal courts. State courts may also be more concerned about litigation abuses in their own court system.

The consumer who wishes to stay in state court runs the risk, when bringing an affirmative state court FDCPA action, that the case will be removed to federal court. The safer course is either to bring the FDCPA violation as a counterclaim in the collection action or to bring an affirmative action based upon only state law. State UDAP, debt collection, and tort claims may be available.[131]

13.4.2.4 Timing Considerations

The FDCPA has a one-year limitations period,[132] so a consumer must act quickly in bringing any follow-up litigation, particularly when the one year period begins to run early in the collection action. On the other hand, it is dangerous to bring an affirmative FDCPA federal court action while the state court collection action is still pending. A natural response by the federal judge is to defer to the state court, and the state court may view with disfavor the consumer's end-around action in federal court.

As described in an earlier chapter,[133] there are also tactical reasons to not bring FDCPA claims while the state court collection action is pending, but instead to let the collector's suit run its normal course. The indiscriminate and routine nature of the misconduct and resulting violations committed by debt buyers helps establish a later-filed FDCPA case. Filing the separate federal action while the state case is continuing disrupts that flow. A pending derivative federal FDCPA suit imbues the state collection case with an exceptional significance that insures that the collector will give it very careful and special treatment that can only strengthen its collection suit and weaken the consumer's FDCPA case. This effect can be particularly dramatic when the federal court case defendant is the state court case collection attorney.

If the one-year limitations period makes a follow-up FDCPA claim impossible, then it may be possible to bring other claims that generally have longer limitations periods. UDAP statutes typically have limitation periods of two years or more,[134] as will most tort claims. Another approach is to file in federal court within the limitations period but not serve the complaint on the defendant until as many as four months afterwards.[135]

13.4.2.5 Arbitration Requirements

Credit contracts usually contain a requirement that disputes be settled by binding arbitration. When the consumer sues the collector or the collector's attorney, the defendant will typically seek to enforce the arbitration requirement.

Before enforcing the arbitration requirement, the collector must produce evidence of a binding arbitration agreement applying to the consumer.[136] If the court in the collection action ruled that there is no written agreement applying to the consumer, then the collector in the subsequent litigation is collaterally estopped from claiming the existence of an arbitration provision.

When, instead, the collector did not present sufficient evidence of the terms of the contract to prevail in its collection action, and this failure is not treated as collateral estoppel, the collector bears the same burden to prove the terms of the contract when it seeks to enforce that contract's arbitration provision in the consumer's affirmative action.[137] Similarly, if there is no evidence that the consumer's contract has been assigned to the collector, than the collector cannot take advantage of the arbitration clause in the contract.[138] Expect a debt buyer in a subsequent FDCPA action to go to greater efforts to offer proof of the terms of a contract applying to the consumer, and proof that the contract has been assigned to the debt buyer, than the debt buyer did in the initial collection action.

If an arbitration agreement applicable to the consumer is produced, then there are still a number of reasons why that arbitration provision may not be enforceable. These issues are examined in detail in NCLC's *Consumer Arbitration Agreements*,[139] and this subsection just suggests a few of the main themes.

Arbitration agreements are generally viewed as applying to disputes with both the original creditor and the creditor's assignees.[140] Thus, a debt buyer is likely to receive protection

130 *See, e.g.*, Chase Manhattan Mortgage Corp. v. Smith, 507 F.3d 910 (6th Cir. 2007) (case remanded after consumer improperly removed foreclosure action on basis of FDCPA counterclaim).

131 *See* National Consumer Law Center, Fair Debt Collection Chs. 9, 10 (8th ed. 2014), *updated at* www.nclc.org/library. *See also* Midland Funding, L.L.C. v. Giraldo, 961 N.Y.S.2d 743 (Nassau Cnty. Dist. Ct. 2013) (UDAP claim for deceptive collection litigation conduct).

132 *See* Fair Debt Collection § 6.10 (8th ed. 2014).

133 § 5.5.1.1, *supra*.

134 *See* National Consumer Law Center, Unfair and Deceptive Acts and Practices § 11.2 (8th ed. 2012), *updated at* www.nclc.org/library.

135 *See* Fed. R. Civ. P. 4(m).

136 *See* Gemini Capital Group v. Tripp, 2013 WL 5872742 (Mo. Ct. App. Nov. 1, 2013).

137 *See* Henggeler v. Brumbaugh & Quandahl, P.C., L.L.O., 894 F. Supp. 2d 1180 (D. Neb. 2012) (denying debt buyer's motion to compel arbitration of FDCPA claim: "On this record, the court finds there is a failure of proof with respect to a valid arbitration agreement. The court has not been provided any signed credit card application, credit card agreement or with the affidavit of any person with personal knowledge that Henggeler had signed such an agreement.").

138 Gemini Capital Group v. Tripp, 2013 WL 5872742 (Mo. Ct. App. Nov. 1, 2013); Liberty Credit Servs. v. Yonker, 2013 WL 5221219 (Ohio Ct. App. Sept. 16, 2013).

139 (6th ed. 2011), *updated at* www.nclc.org/library.

140 *See* National Consumer Law Center, Consumer Arbitration Agreements § 7.5.1 (6th ed. 2011), *updated at* www.nclc.org/library.

under the arbitration agreement if it has been assigned rights under the contract. On the other hand, if the debt buyer has been assigned only receivables or choses in action, then it has not been assigned the contract and cannot claim protection under the arbitration agreement.

The ability of a collection attorney to gain protection from the arbitration clause is more complicated. Carefully parse the arbitration agreement to see how it treats agents of the creditor or agents of assignees of the creditor. In addition, courts are divided as to whether a collection attorney is an agent of the collector.[141] The collector's attorney should not be able to invoke an arbitration agreement between the consumer and the creditor that, by its own terms, does not apply to a debt buyer's attorney.[142]

There is also a question as to whether an FDCPA claim for litigation misconduct is one of the types of disputes to which the arbitration requirement applies. Look to see if the language of the arbitration agreement would cover this type of dispute. Such disputes are certainly outside the parties' expectation as to the arbitration agreement's coverage. The expectation is that the arbitration requirement deals with disputes concerning the original transaction, not litigation abuse by the creditor's assignee. A number of courts have found similar practices to be outside the scope of an arbitration clause.[143]

There is also extensive case law addressing whether an arbitration clause is unconscionable and therefore unenforceable. Unconscionability may relate to the cost of the arbitration proceeding, to the arbitration agreement's limitation on consumer remedies, to the fact that the agreement only requires the consumer to litigate disputes and not the collector, and to the procedure by which the arbitration requirement was imposed.[144]

13.4.3 FDCPA's Applicability to Litigation Misconduct

13.4.3.1 FDCPA's Coverage of Litigation Practices

A wide range of state court collection activity is subject to the FDCPA. The Supreme Court in *Heintz v. Jenkins* confirmed that normal collection litigation is included among the collection activities regulated by the FDCPA.[145] Congress itself has since implicitly reaffirmed that principle twice by amending the FDCPA to exempt "a formal pleading" made in a "legal" or "civil action" from certain disclosure requirements.[146] These exceptions would be meaningless if inclusion of collection litigation were not already the rule.

FDCPA coverage is present whenever the state court plaintiff is a debt buyer or other debt collector pursuing a qualifying consumer debt.[147] The FDCPA cannot be used to sue an original creditor, but it can be used to sue that creditor's collection attorney, so long as collecting consumer debts is part of the attorney's "regular" business activities.[148]

A small minority of states recognize a litigation privilege or immunity that bars tort[149] or statutory[150] remedies to redress collection litigation abuse or misconduct. Nevertheless, no litigation privilege or immunity applies under the FDCPA to collection litigation misconduct.[151] Accordingly, FDCPA claims are always available to redress any qualifying litigation misconduct, whether brought as an affirmative suit in state or federal court or as a counterclaim in the collection action.

13.4.3.2 General Standards as to Actionable Litigation Misconduct

The FDCPA protects consumers from unlawful debt collection practices, regardless of whether a valid debt actually exists.[152] Consistent with the *Heintz* admonition that not every unsuccessful collection case is an FDCPA violation (discussed below), the resulting liability inquiry focuses on the method of collection and not the result.

The basis for some of the clearest FDCPA violations is the FDCPA section 1692e prohibition against "any" false or deceptive representations or means made in connection with the collection of a debt. Included among the recited statutory examples illustrating this broad proscription are the "false representation of the character, amount, or legal status of any debt"[153] and "the threat to take any action that cannot legally be taken."[154] At first blush, these violations describe much of the collection litigation initiated by the debt buyer industry.

Literally applied, section 1692e would establish automatic FDCPA violations whenever debt collectors file collection actions that are ultimately unsuccessful. However, the Supreme Court in *Heintz* imposed a restriction on the application of the FDCPA to collection litigation when, in response to this specific prospect, the Court stated that "we do not see how the fact that a lawsuit turns out ultimately to be unsuccessful could, by itself, make the bringing of it an 'action that cannot legally be taken.' "[155] One challenge for consumers in asserting FDCPA claims is determining what additional conditions

141 *See* National Consumer Law Center, Fair Debt Collection § 2.8 (8th ed. 2014), *updated at* www.nclc.org/library.

142 *See* National Consumer Law Center, Consumer Arbitration Agreements § 7.5 (6th ed. 2011), *updated at* www.nclc.org/library.

143 *Id.* § 7.3.

144 *Id.* Ch. 6.

145 514 U.S. 291, 115 S. Ct. 1489, 131 L. Ed. 2d 395 (1995).

146 15 U.S.C. §§ 1692e(11), 1692g(d).

147 15 U.S.C. § 1692a(5), (6).

148 *See* National Consumer Law Center, Fair Debt Collection § 4.2.8 (8th ed. 2014), *updated at* www.nclc.org/library.

149 *See* National Consumer Law Center, Fair Debt Collection § 9.1.3 (8th ed. 2014), *updated at* www.nclc.org/library.

150 *See id.* § 11.1.3.

151 Sayyed v. Wolpoff & Abramson, 485 F.3d 226 (4th Cir. 2007); Todd v. Weltman, Weinberg, Reis & Co., 434 F.3d 432 (6th Cir. 2006). *See* National Consumer Law Center, Fair Debt Collection § 7.4.6 (8th ed. 2014), *updated at* www.nclc.org/library.

152 *See* National Consumer Law Center, Fair Debt Collection § 4.4.1 (8th ed. 2014), *updated at* www.nclc.org/library.

153 15 U.S.C. § 1692e(2)(A).

154 15 U.S.C. § 1692e(5).

155 514 U.S. 291, 295–96, 115 S. Ct. 1489, 131 L. Ed. 2d 395 (1995). *See also* Hemmingsen v. Messerli & Kramer, P.A., 674 F.3d 814 (8th Cir. 2012).

will meet the Supreme Court's directive that something more than a losing collection case is necessary to establish a derivative FDCPA violation.

An FDCPA action in federal court is a poor vehicle through which to establish the rules or parameters of state law or to determine whether the consumer owes the debt. Much better is to bring the federal case after the state courts have ruled on state law issues (such as that the action was brought outside the state statute of limitations) or that the debt is not owed. Among the criteria for good case selection is not only the obvious need to prove that the defendant collector used a prohibited means to collect the debt but also, as a practical matter, the ability to show that the collector knew or should have known that the challenged conduct was wrongful.[156]

Although the FDCPA is a strict liability statute,[157] intent and knowledge can always be relevant. For example, one of the recited factors in setting statutory damages is the extent to which the collector's "noncompliance was intentional."[158] In addition, a few specific violations require establishing the collector's knowledge or intent.[159]

13.4.3.3 The Bona Fide Error Defense

Collectors may raise the affirmative bona fide error defense in which good intentions and the absence of culpable knowledge are two of the necessary elements.[160] The bona fide error defense was given added strength when the Supreme Court in *Heintz* cited it as an available mechanism to defeat the suggestion that litigation coverage "automatically would make liable any litigating lawyer who brought, and then lost, a claim against a debtor."[161]

On the other hand, the Supreme Court in 2010 ruled that the bona fide error defense does not apply to errors of law as to the FDCPA's requirements.[162] Although it did not reach the issue of whether errors of other law could fall within the bona fide error defense, the decision's reasoning indicates that such errors do not fall within that defense, at least when the state law the collector has disregarded is clear as to its meaning. Thus, when a case is brought outside a limitations period that is clearly defined by state law, a bona fide error defense should not apply to an FDCPA claim against the collector for bringing an action outside that limitations period.

13.4.3.4 Examples of Litigation Conduct As FDCPA Violations

State court collection litigation presents recurring examples of FDCPA noncompliance when collectors engage in objectively dishonest, false, and illegal collection methods.[163] These unlawful practices include collector misrepresentation as to its legal entitlement to fees, interest, or other additional charges that are prohibited by established state law,[164] and filing sworn declarations that state that the affiants reviewed certain documents when they in fact have not done so or that misrepresent the specific contents of those documents.[165]

On the other hand, an allegation made "on information and belief" or otherwise when applicable state law imposes no duty of inquiry or due diligence may not be a good basis for a successful FDCPA action, even when the statement turns out to be false. An especially poor candidate for a derivative FDCPA violation is an assertion in the collection proceedings of the collector's entitlement to relief, even if ultimately proven to be unfounded, when the falsity of the assertion was not settled when it was made.

Established FDCPA violations occur when the collection court plaintiff is not authorized to appear or sue under state law.[166] These violations typically result from the failure of the collection court plaintiff to be properly licensed or registered in accordance with state laws regulating who may file suit in the state.[167] In some states a plaintiff is not allowed to sue based on a contingent assignment of the debt[168] or when the plaintiff is not the real party in interest.[169] An FDCPA claim was also allowed to proceed when the collector brought an action multiple times against the consumer in the wrong court, resulting in the actions being dismissed without prejudice.[170]

---

156 *See* Hare v. Hosto & Buchan, P.L.L.C., 774 F. Supp. 2d 849 (S.D. Tex. 2011) (state law unclear as to deadline to bring action to confirm arbitration award).

157 *See* National Consumer Law Center, Fair Debt Collection § 5.2.3 (8th ed. 2014), *updated at* www.nclc.org/library.

158 15 U.S.C. § 1692k(b).

159 *See* 15 U.S.C. §§ 1692e(5) (the second clause prohibiting the threat to take any action "that is not intended to be taken"), 1692e(8) (communicating credit information "which is known or which should be known to be false"), 1692f(3) (solicitation of post-dated check "for the purpose of threatening or instituting criminal prosecution"), 1692f(6)(B) (threatening repossession of property without a "present intention" to do so), 1692c(a)(1) (communicating with a consumer at a "time or place known or which should be known to be inconvenient"), 1692c(a)(2) (communicating with a consumer "if the debt collector knows the consumer is represented by an attorney"), 1692c(a)(3) (communicating with a consumer at work "if the debt collector knows or has reason to know that the consumer's employer prohibits" such contacts), 1692d(5) (using the telephone "with the intent to annoy, abuse, or harass any person"), 1692j (furnishing forms "knowing that such forms would be used to create the false belief" of third-party participation).

160 15 U.S.C. § 1692k(c).

161 514 U.S. 291, 295, 115 S. Ct. 1489, 131 L. Ed. 2d 395 (1995).

162 Jerman v. Carlisle, McNellie, Rini, Kramer & Ulrich L.P.A., 130 S. Ct. 1605, 176 L. Ed. 2d 519 (2010).

163 *See* National Consumer Law Center, Fair Debt Collection § 5.5.2.13.4 (8th ed. 2014), *updated at* www.nclc.org/library.

164 *See* National Consumer Law Center, Fair Debt Collection §§ 5.5.4.3, 5.6.3 (8th ed. 2014), *updated at* www.nclc.org/library.

165 *See* National Consumer Law Center, Fair Debt Collection Appx. J.2.4.12 (8th ed. 2014), *updated at* www.nclc.org/library.

166 *See* LeBlanc v. Unifund CCR Partners, 601 F.3d 1185 (11th Cir. 2010); Wallace v. Washington Mut. Bank, F.A., 683 F.3d 323 (6th Cir. 2012); Chulsky v. Hudson Law Offices, P.C., 777 F. Supp. 2d 811 (D.N.J. 2011), *amended in part by* 777 F. Supp. 2d 823 (D.N.J. Mar. 22, 2011).

167 *See* National Consumer Law Center, Fair Debt Collection § 5.5.8.5 (8th ed. 2014), *updated at* www.nclc.org/library.

168 *See id.* § 5.5.8.6.

169 *See* § 4.2.3, *supra*.

170 Curto v. Palisades Collection, L.L.C., 2011 WL 5196708 (W.D.N.Y. Oct. 31, 2011).

Another recurring affirmative FDCPA claim arising from litigation abuse involves the collector suing on a known time-barred debt.[171] Some collectors "launder" these stale and worthless debts when they sue on time-barred debts, hoping the consumer will either default or not assert the statute of limitations as an affirmative defense in the consumer's answer. But even suing on a time-barred debt may not result in an FDCPA violation. In two recent cases,[172] no FDCPA violation was found when the applicable limitations period was not yet established under state law when the time-barred suits were filed. Both courts excused the resulting violations as bona fide errors because of the unsettled state of the state law when the violation occurred.[173]

On the other hand, a federal court has found FDCPA violations when a state court interprets the state statute of limitations as barring the case, distinguishing precedent relied upon by the collector in arguing for a longer limitations period.[174] Even though the state interpretation finding a shorter limitations period was issued after the collector brought the collection action, the bona fide error defense was found not applicable.[175] The rules surrounding this violation when the underlying law establishing the applicable statute of limitations is unsettled must be evaluated in view of the subsequent decision from the Supreme Court holding that the FDCPA bona fide error defense generally does not apply to errors of law.[176]

A growing body of law now establishes an FDCPA violation based on the litigating collector's bad faith strategy of filing a collection suit only to obtain a default judgment or force settlement when it never had an intent or capability to prove its case.[177] As in any developing area of the law, care must be taken when bringing such cases to not undermine the putative cause of action. Filing suit on behalf of consumers who objectively have no liability for the debt and waiting until the state court complaint is dismissed once the consumer appeared and defended are two criteria for informed case selection in this area.

Other possible FDCPA violations involve the collector bringing a complaint even though it had knowledge that the alleged account was invalid and not belonging to the consumer[178] or suing a non-liable spouse on a debt owed by the other spouse.[179] Suing on a debt when the collector misrepresented that it owned the debt can also be an FDCPA violation.[180] Similarly, knowingly filing false affidavits to support a collection action can be an FDCPA violation.[181] So is filing complaints without complying with state law requirements that the assignment of the debt to the collector be substantiated in the complaint.[182] Another recurring FDCPA violation arises when a collector seeks in its complaint attorney fees to which it is not entitled.[183]

13.4.4 *UDAP Claims for Litigation Misconduct*

State deceptive practices (UDAP) statutes are often available to challenge litigation misconduct.[184] Successful UDAP challenges have involved collection cases brought in inconvenient venues, filing actions after the limitations period has run, improper service of process, confusing summons, filing meritless collection actions, and deceptive settlement practices leading to default judgments.[185]

UDAP statutes generally do not require intent or knowledge, and usually there is no bona fide error defense.[186] UDAP statutes in most states are very broad in scope but in a few states will not apply to creditors, attorneys, or debt collectors.[187] UDAP remedies typically include actual damages, attorney fees, and either minimum, multiple, or punitive damages.

171 *See* National Consumer Law Center, Fair Debt Collection § 5.5.2.12.3 (8th ed. 2014), *updated at* www.nclc.org/library. *See also* Diaz v. Portfolio Recovery Assocs., L.L.C., 2012 WL 661456 (E.D.N.Y. Feb. 28, 2012), *report and recommendation adopted by* 2012 WL 1882976 (E.D.N.Y. May 24, 2012); Parkis v. Arrow Fin. Servs., L.L.S., 2008 WL 94798 (N.D. Ill. Jan. 8, 2008); Klewer v. Cavalry Invests., L.L.C., 2002 WL 2018830 (W.D. Wis. Jan. 30, 2002).

172 Pescatrice v. Orovitz, 539 F. Supp. 2d 1375 (S.D. Fla. 2008); McCorriston v. L.W.T., Inc., 536 F. Supp. 2d 1268 (M.D. Fla. 2008).

173 *But see* § 13.4.3.3, *supra*.

174 Herkert v. MRC Receivables Corp., 655 F. Supp. 2d 870 (N.D. Ill. 2009).

175 *Id.*

176 Jerman v. Carlisle, McNellie, Rini, Kramer & Ulrich, L.P.A., 130 S. Ct. 1605 (2010).

177 *E.g.*, Kuria v. Palisades Acquisition XVI, L.L.C., 752 F. Supp. 2d 1293 (N.D. Ga. 2010); Royal Financial Group, L.L.C. v. Perkins, 2013 WL 449343 (Mo. Ct. App. Aug. 20, 2013).

178 Moriarity v. Henriques, 2011 WL 4769270 (E.D. Cal. Oct. 7, 2011).

179 Walter v. Palisades Collection, L.L.C., 2011 WL 1666869 (E.D. Pa. May 2, 2011).

180 *See* Dicesari v. Asset Acceptance L.L.C., 2012 WL 4108944 (E.D. Pa. Sept. 18, 2012); Royal Financial Group, L.L.C. v. Perkins, 2013 WL 449343 (Mo. Ct. App. Aug. 20, 2013).

181 Winemiller v. Worldwide Asset Purchasing, L.L.C., 2011 WL 1457749 (D. Md. Apr. 15, 2011); Sykes v. Mel Harris & Assocs., L.L.C., 757 F. Supp. 2d 413 (S.D.N.Y. 2010).

182 Grant-Hall v. Cavalry Portfolio Servs., L.L.C., 856 F. Supp. 2d 929 (N.D. Ill. 2012).

183 McCollough v. Johnson, Rodenberg & Lauinger, 637 F.3d 939, 949–50 (9th Cir. 2011); Royal Financial Group, L.L.C. v. Perkins, 2013 WL 449343 (Mo. Ct. App. Aug. 20, 2013).

184 *See* Midland Funding, L.L.C. v. Giraldo, 961 N.Y.S.2d 743 (Nassau Cnty. Dist. Ct. 2013).

185 *See* National Consumer Law Center, Unfair and Deceptive Acts and Practices § 6.10 (8th ed. 2012), *updated at* www.nclc.org/library. *See also* Sykes v. Mel Harris & Assocs., L.L.C., 757 F. Supp. 2d 413 (S.D.N.Y. 2010); Harrington v. CACV of Colo., L.L.C., 508 F. Supp. 2d 128 (D. Mass. 2007).

186 National Consumer Law Center, Unfair and Deceptive Acts and Practices §§ 4.2.4–4.2.6 (8th ed. 2012), *updated at* www.nclc.org/library.

187 *Id.* §§ 2.2.1, 2.2.2, 2.3.9.

13.4.5 Malicious Prosecution and Abuse of Process

13.4.5.1 Introduction

Tort claims have the advantage of applying to any creditor, collector, or collector's attorney and of providing for punitive damages in appropriate cases. Malicious prosecution and abuse of process are both torts that apply to wrongful use of judicial processes. Malicious prosecution is the more widely accepted, highly developed, and difficult to establish of the two. Both apply to civil proceedings, with malicious prosecution sometimes labeled "wrongful civil prosecution" when applied to civil processes. Both torts are examined in detail in NCLC's *Fair Debt Collection*.[188]

13.4.5.2 Malicious Prosecution

Malicious prosecution occurs under the following circumstances:

- A proceeding is instituted;
- The proceeding is without probable cause or possible valid claim;
- The proceeding was instituted either maliciously or for an improper purpose; and
- The proceeding is terminated in favor of the defendant.[189]

Lack of probable cause can be found when an attorney would have found the action not tenable based upon the facts known by the collector at the time the action was instigated.[190] On the other hand, mere dismissal without prejudice may not be enough to show lack of probable cause,[191] and, when the collector prevails in the collection suit, there cannot be a malicious prosecution claim.[192]

Malice can be found when the collector is bringing an action to collect money even though the collector has no knowledge of the facts of the case.[193] Some states impose an additional requirement of "special injury" such as seizure of property.[194] A proceeding has been held to be terminated in favor of the defendant when the plaintiff voluntarily dismissed the claim after realizing the consumer will put up a strong defense.[195]

13.4.5.3 Abuse of Process

Abuse of process is often described as the use of "legal process against another in an improper manner to accomplish a purpose for which it was not designed."[196] In contrast to malicious prosecution, the tort of abuse of process is not based on the improper institution of legal proceedings but on the improper use of process *after* it has been issued to accomplish a purpose for which it was not designed.[197] While courts vary in their listings of the elements of the tort, one common statement is:

- The defendant made an illegal, improper, perverted use of the process, a use neither warranted nor authorized by the process;
- The defendant had an ulterior motive or purpose; and
- Damage resulted to the plaintiff from the irregularity.[198]

Some decisions require actual seizure of property as an element, or that the defendant act willfully, but malice usually is not a required element.[199]

The New Mexico Supreme Court has found that a claim for abuse of process can be based on actions taken in an arbitration proceeding and need not involve a court case.[200] Thus, a collector's use of arbitration to sue on a debt can involve abuse of process.

Query whether it is abuse of process for a collector to use admissions to trick an unrepresented consumer to admit to liability that the consumer disputes.[201] Suing in an improper venue has been found to be abuse of process,[202] as has obtaining and executing upon a default judgment after agreeing to dismiss the case,[203] falsifying an affidavit of service of process,[204] and continuing litigation known to be baseless.[205]

188 (8th ed. 2014), *updated at* www.nclc.org/library.

189 *See* National Consumer Law Center, Fair Debt Collection § 9.6.2 (8th ed. 2014), *updated at* www.nclc.org/library.

190 Turner v. Debt Buyers Inc., 2011 WL 287901 (Cal. Ct. App. Jan. 31, 2011) (unpublished).

191 Carr v. Asset Acceptance, L.L.C., 2011 WL 3568338 (E.D. Cal. Aug. 12, 2011).

192 Watson v. Auto Advisors, Inc., 822 N.E.2d 1017 (Ind. Ct. App. 2005).

193 Turner v. Debt Buyers Inc., 2011 WL 287901 (Cal. Ct. App. Jan. 31, 2011) (unpublished).

194 *See* National Consumer Law Center, Fair Debt Collection § 9.6.2 (8th ed. 2014).

195 Pasternak v. Trans Union, 2008 WL 928840 (N.D. Cal. Apr. 3, 2008); Turner v. Debt Buyers Inc., 2011 WL 287901 (Cal. Ct. App. Jan. 31, 2011) (unpublished). *But see* Carr v. Asset Acceptance, L.L.C., 2011 WL 3568338 (E.D. Cal. Aug. 12, 2011).

196 *See* National Consumer Law Center, Fair Debt Collection § 9.6.3 (8th ed. 2014), *updated at* www.nclc.org/library.

197 *Id.*

198 *Id.*

199 *Id.*

200 Durham v. Guest, 204 P.3d 19 (N.M. 2009).

201 *See* McCollough v. Johnson, Rodenberg & Lauinger, 637 F.3d 939 (9th Cir. 2011) (sending requests for admission to establish a known time-barred debt is an FDCPA violation and tortious under state law).

202 *See* National Consumer Law Center, Fair Debt Collection § 9.6.3 (8th ed. 2014), *updated at* www.nclc.org/library.

203 *See* Goodwin Agency, Inc. v. Chesser, 206 S.E.2d 568 (Ga. Ct. App. 1974).

204 Cordero v. Calvary SpIV L.L.C., 2004 WL 1244107 (N.D. Ill. June 3, 2004); Kappell v. Bartlett, 246 Cal. Rptr. 815 (Cal. Ct. App. 1988); Parks v. Neuf, 578 N.E.2d 282 (Ill. App. Ct. 1991).

205 Gen. Elec. Capital Corp. v. MHPG, Inc., 2006 WL 2560314 (Mass. Super. Ct. July 27, 2006).

Appendix A Selected Provisions of the Servicemembers Civil Relief Act

50 U.S.C. App. §§ 501–596

[*As enacted by* Pub. L. No. 108–189, 117 Stat. 2835 (2003), unless otherwise noted]

TITLE 50 APPENDIX— WAR AND NATIONAL DEFENSE

Servicemembers Civil Relief Act

50 U.S.C. App.

TITLE 50 APPENDIX— WAR AND NATIONAL DEFENSE

50 U.S.C. app. § 501. Short title

This Act [sections 501 to 596 of this Appendix] may be cited as the "Servicemembers Civil Relief Act."

50 U.S.C. app. § 502. Purpose

The purposes of this Act are—

(1) to provide for, strengthen, and expedite the national defense through protection extended by this Act to servicemembers of the United States to enable such persons to devote their entire energy to the defense needs of the Nation; and

(2) to provide for the temporary suspension of judicial and administrative proceedings and transactions that may adversely affect the civil rights of servicemembers during their military service.

Title I—General Provisions

50 U.S.C. app. § 511. Definitions

For the purposes of this Act:

(1) Servicemember

The term "servicemember" means a member of the uniformed services, as that term is defined in section 101(a)(5) of title 10, United States Code.

(2) Military service
The term "military service" means—
(A) in the case of a servicemember who is a member of the Army, Navy, Air Force, Marine Corps, or Coast Guard—
(i) active duty, as defined in section 101(d)(1) of title 10, United States Code, and
(ii) in the case of a member of the National Guard, includes service under a call to active service authorized by the President or the Secretary of Defense for a period of more than 30 consecutive days under section 502(f) of title 32, United States Code, for purposes of responding to a national emergency declared by the President and supported by Federal funds;
(B) in the case of a servicemember who is a commissioned officer of the Public Health Service or the National Oceanic and Atmospheric Administration, active service; and
(C) any period during which a servicemember is absent from duty on account of sickness, wounds, leave, or other lawful cause.

(3) Period of military service
The term "period of military service" means the period beginning on the date on which a servicemember enters military service and ending on the date on which the servicemember is released from military service or dies while in military service.

(4) Dependent
The term "dependent," with respect to a servicemember, means—
(A) the servicemember's spouse;
(B) the servicemember's child (as defined in section 101(4) of title 38, United States Code); or
(C) an individual for whom the servicemember provided more than one-half of the individual's support for 180 days immediately preceding an application for relief under this Act.

(5) Court
The term "court" means a court or an administrative agency of the United States or of any State (including any political subdivision of a State), whether or not a court or administrative agency of record.

(6) State
The term "State" includes—
(A) a commonwealth, territory, or possession of the United States; and
(B) the District of Columbia.

(7) Secretary concerned
The term "Secretary concerned"—
(A) with respect to a member of the armed forces, has the meaning given that term in section 101(a)(9) of title 10, United States Code;
(B) with respect to a commissioned officer of the Public Health Service, means the Secretary of Health and Human Services; and
(C) with respect to a commissioned officer of the National Oceanic and Atmospheric Administration, means the Secretary of Commerce.

(8) Motor vehicle
The term "motor vehicle" has the meaning given that term in section 30102(a)(6) of title 49, United States Code.

(9) Judgment
The term "judgment" means any judgment, decree, order, or ruling, final or temporary.

[*As amended by* Pub. L. No. 108–454, 118 Stat. 3624 (2004)]

50 U.S.C. app. § 512. Jurisdiction and applicability of Act

(a) Jurisdiction
This Act applies to—
(1) the United States;
(2) each of the States, including the political subdivisions thereof; and
(3) all territory subject to the jurisdiction of the United States.

(b) Applicability to proceedings
This Act applies to any judicial or administrative proceeding commenced in any court or agency in any jurisdiction subject to this Act. This Act does not apply to criminal proceedings.

(c) Court in which application may be made
When under this Act any application is required to be made to a court in which no proceeding has already been commenced with respect to the matter, such application may be made to any court which would otherwise have jurisdiction over the matter.

50 U.S.C. app. § 513. Protection of persons secondarily liable

(a) Extension of protection when actions stayed, postponed, or suspended
Whenever pursuant to this Act a court stays, postpones, or suspends (1) the enforcement of an obligation or liability, (2) the prosecution of a suit or proceeding, (3) the entry or enforcement of an order, writ, judgment, or decree, or (4) the performance of any other act, the court may likewise grant such a stay, postponement, or suspension to a surety, guarantor, endorser, accommodation maker, comaker, or other person who is or may be primarily or secondarily subject to the obligation or liability the performance or enforcement of which is stayed, postponed, or suspended.

(b) Vacation or set-aside of judgments
When a judgment or decree is vacated or set aside, in whole or in part, pursuant to this Act, the court may also set aside or vacate, as the case may be, the judgment or decree as to a surety, guarantor, endorser, accommodation maker, comaker, or other person who is or may be primarily or secondarily liable on the contract or liability for the enforcement of the judgment or decree.

(c) Bail bond not to be enforced during period of military service
A court may not enforce a bail bond during the period of military service of the principal on the bond when military service prevents the surety from obtaining the attendance of the principal. The court may discharge the surety and exonerate the bail, in accordance with principles of equity and justice, during or after the period of military service of the principal.

(d) Waiver of rights
(1) Waivers not precluded
This Act does not prevent a waiver in writing by a surety, guarantor, endorser, accommodation maker, comaker, or other person (whether primarily or secondarily liable on an obligation or liability) of the protections provided under subsections (a) and (b). Any such waiver is effective only if it is executed as an instrument separate from the obligation or liability with respect to which it applies.
(2) Waiver invalidated upon entrance to military service
If a waiver under paragraph (1) is executed by an individual who after the execution of the waiver enters military service, or by a dependent of an individual who after the execution of the waiver enters military service, the waiver is not valid after the beginning of the period of such military service unless the waiver was executed by such individual or dependent during the period specified in section 106 [section 516 of this Appendix].

50 U.S.C. app. § 514. Extension of protections to citizens serving with allied forces

A citizen of the United States who is serving with the forces of a nation with which the United States is allied in the prosecution of a war or military action is entitled to the relief and protections provided under this Act if that service with the allied force is similar to military service as defined in this Act. The relief and protections provided to such citizen shall terminate on the date of discharge or release from such service.

50 U.S.C. app. § 515. Notification of benefits

The Secretary concerned shall ensure that notice of the benefits accorded by this Act is provided in writing to persons in military service and to persons entering military service.

50 U.S.C. app. § 515a. Information for members of the armed forces and their dependents on rights and protections of the Servicemembers Civil Relief Act

(a) Outreach to members
The Secretary concerned shall provide to each member of the Armed Forces under the jurisdiction of the Secretary pertinent information on the rights and protections available to members and their dependents under the Servicemembers Civil Relief Act [50 U.S.C. app. §§ 501–596].

(b) Time of provision
The information required to be provided under subsection (a) of this section to a member shall be provided at the following times:

(1) During the initial orientation training of the member.

(2) In the case of a member of a reserve component, during the initial orientation training of the member and when the member is mobilized or otherwise individually called or ordered to active duty for a period of more than one year.

(3) At such other times as the Secretary concerned considers appropriate.

(c) Outreach to dependents
The Secretary concerned may provide to the adult dependents of members under the jurisdiction of the Secretary pertinent information on the rights and protections available to members and their dependents under the Servicemembers Civil Relief Act.

(d) Definitions
In this section, the terms "dependent" and "Secretary concerned" have the meanings given such terms in section 101 of the Servicemembers Civil Relief Act [50 U.S.C. app. § 511].

[*Added by* Pub. L. No. 109–163, 119 Stat. 3337 (2006)]

50 U.S.C. app. § 516. Extension of rights and protections to reserves ordered to report for military service and to persons ordered to report for induction

(a) Reserves ordered to report for military service
A member of a reserve component who is ordered to report for military service is entitled to the rights and protections of this title and titles II and III [of this Appendix] during the period beginning on the date of the member's receipt of the order and ending on the date on which the member reports for military service (or, if the order is revoked before the member so reports, or the date on which the order is revoked).

(b) Persons ordered to report for induction
A person who has been ordered to report for induction under the Military Selective Service Act (50 U.S.C. app. 451 et seq.) is entitled to the rights and protections provided a servicemember under this title and titles II and III [of this Appendix] during the period beginning on the date of receipt of the order for induction and ending on the date on which the person reports for induction (or, if the order to report for induction is revoked before the date on which the person reports for induction, on the date on which the order is revoked).

50 U.S.C. app. § 517. Waiver of rights pursuant to written agreement

(a) In general
A servicemember may waive any of the rights and protections provided by this Act. In the case of a waiver that permits an action described in subsection (b), the waiver is effective only if made pursuant to a written agreement of the parties that is executed during or after the servicemember's period of military service. The written agreement shall specify the legal instrument to which the waiver applies and, if the servicemember is not a party to that instrument, the servicemember concerned. Any such waiver that applies to an action listed in subsection (b) of this section is effective only if it is in writing and is executed as an instrument separate from the obligation or liability to which it applies.

(b) Actions requiring waivers in writing
The requirement in subsection (a) for a written waiver applies to the following:

(1) The modification, termination, or cancellation of—

(A) a contract, lease, or bailment; or

(B) an obligation secured by a mortgage, trust, deed, lien, or other security in the nature of a mortgage.

(2) The repossession, retention, foreclosure, sale, forfeiture, or taking possession of property that—

(A) is security for any obligation; or

(B) was purchased or received under a contract, lease, or bailment.

(c) Prominent display of certain contract rights waivers
Any waiver in writing of a right or protection provided by this Act [sections 501 to 596 of this Appendix] that applies to a contract, lease, or similar legal instrument must be in at least 12 point type.

(d) Coverage of periods after orders received
For the purposes of this section—

(1) a person to whom section 106 [section 516 of this Appendix] applies shall be considered to be a servicemember; and

(2) the period with respect to such a person specified in subsection (a) or (b), as the case may be, of section 106 [section 516 of this Appendix] shall be considered to be a period of military service.

[*As amended by* Pub. L. No. 108–454, 118 Stat. 3624 (2004)]

50 U.S.C. app. § 518. Exercise of rights under Act not to affect certain future financial transactions

Application by a servicemember for, or receipt by a servicemember of, a stay, postponement, or suspension pursuant to this Act in the payment of a tax, fine, penalty, insurance premium, or other civil obligation or liability of that servicemember shall not itself (without regard to other considerations) provide the basis for any of the following:

(1) A determination by a lender or other person that the servicemember is unable to pay the civil obligation or liability in accordance with its terms.

(2) With respect to a credit transaction between a creditor and the servicemember—

(A) a denial or revocation of credit by the creditor;

(B) a change by the creditor in the terms of an existing credit arrangement; or

(C) a refusal by the creditor to grant credit to the servicemember in substantially the amount or on substantially the terms requested.

(3) An adverse report relating to the creditworthiness of the servicemember by or to a person engaged in the practice of assembling or evaluating consumer credit information.

(4) A refusal by an insurer to insure the servicemember.

(5) An annotation in a servicemember's record by a creditor or a person engaged in the practice of assembling or evaluating consumer credit information, identifying the servicemember as a member of the National Guard or a reserve component.

(6) A change in the terms offered or conditions required for the issuance of insurance.

50 U.S.C. app. § 519. Legal representatives

(a) Representative

A legal representative of a servicemember for purposes of this Act [sections 501 to 596 of this Appendix] is either of the following:

(1) An attorney acting on the behalf of a servicemember.

(2) An individual possessing a power of attorney.

(b) Application

Whenever the term "servicemember" is used in this Act [sections 501 to 596 of this Appendix], such term shall be treated as including a reference to a legal representative of the servicemember.

Title II—General Relief

50 U.S.C. app. § 521. Protection of servicemembers against default judgments

(a) Applicability of section

This section applies to any civil action or proceeding, including any child custody proceeding, in which the defendant does not make an appearance.

(b) Affidavit requirement

(1) Plaintiff to file affidavit

In any action or proceeding covered by this section, the court, before entering judgment for the plaintiff, shall require the plaintiff to file with the court an affidavit—

(A) stating whether or not the defendant is in military service and showing necessary facts to support the affidavit; or

(B) if the plaintiff is unable to determine whether or not the defendant is in military service, stating that the plaintiff is unable to determine whether or not the defendant is in military service.

(2) Appointment of attorney to represent defendant in military service

If in an action covered by this section it appears that the defendant is in military service, the court may not enter a judgment until after the court appoints an attorney to represent the defendant. If an attorney appointed under this section to represent a servicemember cannot locate the servicemember, actions by the attorney in the case shall not waive any defense of the servicemember or otherwise bind the servicemember.

(3) Defendant's military status not ascertained by affidavit

If based upon the affidavits filed in such an action, the court is unable to determine whether the defendant is in military service, the court, before entering judgment, may require the plaintiff to file a bond in an amount approved by the court. If the defendant is later found to be in military service, the bond shall be available to indemnify the defendant against any loss or damage the defendant may suffer by reason of any judgment for the plaintiff against the defendant, should the judgment be set aside in whole or in part. The bond shall remain in effect until expiration of the time for appeal and setting aside of a judgment under applicable Federal or State law or regulation or under any applicable ordinance of a political subdivision of a State. The court may issue such orders or enter such judgments as the court determines necessary to protect the rights of the defendant under this Act.

(4) Satisfaction of requirement for affidavit

The requirement for an affidavit under paragraph (1) may be satisfied by a statement, declaration, verification, or certificate, in writing, subscribed and certified or declared to be true under penalty of perjury.

(c) Penalty for making or using false affidavit

A person who makes or uses an affidavit permitted under subsection (b) (or a statement, declaration, verification, or certificate as authorized under subsection (b)(4)) knowing it to be false, shall be fined as provided in title 18, United States Code, or imprisoned for not more than one year, or both.

(d) Stay of proceedings

In an action covered by this section in which the defendant is in military service, the court shall grant a stay of proceedings for a minimum period of 90 days under this subsection upon application of counsel, or on the court's own motion, if the court determines that—

(1) there may be a defense to the action and a defense cannot be presented without the presence of the defendant; or

(2) after due diligence, counsel has been unable to contact the defendant or otherwise determine if a meritorious defense exists.

(e) Inapplicability of section 202 procedures

A stay of proceedings under subsection (d) shall not be controlled by procedures or requirements under section 202 [section 522 of this Appendix].

(f) Section 202 protection

If a servicemember who is a defendant in an action covered by this section receives actual notice of the action, the servicemember may request a stay of proceeding under section 202 [section 522 of this Appendix].

(g) Vacation or setting aside of default judgments

(1) Authority for court to vacate or set aside judgment

If a default judgment is entered in an action covered by this section against a servicemember during the servicemember's period of military service (or within 60 days after termination of or release from such military service), the court entering the judgment shall, upon application by or on behalf of the servicemember, reopen the judgment for the purpose of allowing the servicemember to defend the action if it appears that—

(A) the servicemember was materially affected by reason of that military service in making a defense to the action; and

(B) the servicemember has a meritorious or legal defense to the action or some part of it.

(2) Time for filing application

An application under this subsection must be filed not later than 90 days after the date of the termination of or release from military service.

(h) Protection of bona fide purchaser

If a court vacates, sets aside, or reverses a default judgment against a servicemember and the vacating, setting aside, or reversing is because of a provision of this Act, that action shall not impair a right or title acquired by a bona fide purchaser for value under the default judgment.

[*As amended by* Pub. L. No. 110–181, 122 Stat. 128 (2008)]

50 U.S.C. app. § 522. Stay of proceedings when servicemember has notice

(a) Applicability of section
This section applies to any civil action or proceeding, including any child custody proceeding, in which the plaintiff or defendant at the time of filing an application under this section—

(1) is in military service or is within 90 days after termination of or release from military service; and
(2) has received notice of the action or proceeding.

(b) Stay of proceedings

(1) Authority for stay
At any stage before final judgment in a civil action or proceeding in which a servicemember described in subsection (a) is a party, the court may on its own motion and shall, upon application by the servicemember, stay the action for a period of not less than 90 days, if the conditions in paragraph (2) are met.

(2) Conditions for stay
An application for a stay under paragraph (1) shall include the following:

(A) A letter or other communication setting forth facts stating the manner in which current military duty requirements materially affect the servicemember's ability to appear and stating a date when the servicemember will be available to appear.
(B) A letter or other communication from the servicemember's commanding officer stating that the servicemember's current military duty prevents appearance and that military leave is not authorized for the servicemember at the time of the letter.

(c) Application not a waiver of defenses
An application for a stay under this section does not constitute an appearance for jurisdictional purposes and does not constitute a waiver of any substantive or procedural defense (including a defense relating to lack of personal jurisdiction).

(d) Additional stay

(1) Application
A servicemember who is granted a stay of a civil action or proceeding under subsection (b) may apply for an additional stay based on continuing material affect of military duty on the servicemember's ability to appear. Such an application may be made by the servicemember at the time of the initial application under subsection (b) or when it appears that the servicemember is unavailable to prosecute or defend the action. The same information required under subsection (b)(2) shall be included in an application under this subsection.

(2) Appointment of counsel when additional stay refused
If the court refuses to grant an additional stay of proceedings under paragraph (1), the court shall appoint counsel to represent the servicemember in the action or proceeding.

(e) Coordination with section 201 [section 521 of this Appendix]
A servicemember who applies for a stay under this section and is unsuccessful may not seek the protections afforded by section 201 [section 521 of this Appendix].

(f) Inapplicability to section 301 [section 531 of this Appendix]
The protections of this section do not apply to section 301 [section 531 of this Appendix].

[*As amended by* Pub. L. No. 108–454, 118 Stat. 3624 (2004); Pub. L. No. 110–181, 122 Stat. 128 (2008)]

50 U.S.C. app. § 523. Fines and penalties under contracts

(a) Prohibition of penalties
When an action for compliance with the terms of a contract is stayed pursuant to this Act, a penalty shall not accrue for failure to comply with the terms of the contract during the period of the stay.

(b) Reduction or waiver of fines or penalties
If a servicemember fails to perform an obligation arising under a contract and a penalty is incurred arising from that nonperformance, a court may reduce or waive the fine or penalty if—

(1) the servicemember was in military service at the time the fine or penalty was incurred; and
(2) the ability of the servicemember to perform the obligation was materially affected by such military service.

50 U.S.C. app. § 524. Stay or vacation of execution of judgments, attachments, and garnishments

(a) Court action upon material affect determination
If a servicemember, in the opinion of the court, is materially affected by reason of military service in complying with a court judgment or order, the court may on its own motion and shall on application by the servicemember—

(1) stay the execution of any judgment or order entered against the servicemember; and
(2) vacate or stay an attachment or garnishment of property, money, or debts in the possession of the servicemember or a third party, whether before or after judgment.

(b) Applicability
This section applies to an action or proceeding commenced in a court against a servicemember before or during the period of the servicemember's military service or within 90 days after such service terminates.

50 U.S.C. app. § 525. Duration and term of stays; codefendants not in service

(a) Period of stay
A stay of an action, proceeding, attachment, or execution made pursuant to the provisions of this Act by a court may be ordered for the period of military service and 90 days thereafter, or for any part of that period. The court may set the terms and amounts for such installment payments as is considered reasonable by the court.

(b) Codefendants
If the servicemember is a codefendant with others who are not in military service and who are not entitled to the relief and protections provided under this Act, the plaintiff may proceed against those other defendants with the approval of the court.

(c) Inapplicability of section
This section does not apply to sections 202 and 701 [sections 522 and 591 of this Appendix].

50 U.S.C. app. § 526. Statute of limitations

(a) Tolling of statutes of limitation during military service
The period of a servicemember's military service may not be included in computing any period limited by law, regulation, or order for the bringing of any action or proceeding in a court, or in any board, bureau, commission, department, or other agency of a State (or political subdivision of a

State) or the United States by or against the servicemember or the servicemember's heirs, executors, administrators, or assigns.

(b) Redemption of real property

A period of military service may not be included in computing any period provided by law for the redemption of real property sold or forfeited to enforce an obligation, tax, or assessment.

(c) Inapplicability to internal revenue laws

This section does not apply to any period of limitation prescribed by or under the internal revenue laws of the United States.

50 U.S.C. app. § 527. Maximum rate of interest on debts incurred before military service

(a) Interest rate limitation

(1) Limitation to 6 percent

An obligation or liability bearing interest at a rate in excess of 6 percent per year that is incurred by a servicemember, or the servicemember and the servicemember's spouse jointly, before the servicemember enters military service shall not bear interest at a rate in excess of 6 percent—

(A) during the period of military service and one year thereafter, in the case of an obligation or liability consisting of a mortgage, trust deed, or other security in the nature of a mortgage; or

(B) during the period of military service, in the case of any other obligation or liability.

(2) Forgiveness of interest in excess of 6 percent

Interest at a rate in excess of 6 percent per year that would otherwise be incurred but for the prohibition in paragraph (1) is forgiven.

(3) Prevention of acceleration of principal

The amount of any periodic payment due from a servicemember under the terms of the instrument that created an obligation or liability covered by this section shall be reduced by the amount of the interest forgiven under paragraph (2) that is allocable to the period for which such payment is made.

(b) Implementation of limitation

(1) Written notice to creditor

In order for an obligation or liability of a servicemember to be subject to the interest rate limitation in subsection (a), the servicemember shall provide to the creditor written notice and a copy of the military orders calling the servicemember to military service and any orders further extending military service, not later than 180 days after the date of the servicemember's termination or release from military service.

(2) Limitation effective as of date of order to active duty

Upon receipt of written notice and a copy of orders calling a servicemember to military service, the creditor shall treat the debt in accordance with subsection (a), effective as of the date on which the servicemember is called to military service.

(c) Creditor protection

A court may grant a creditor relief from the limitations of this section if, in the opinion of the court, the ability of the servicemember to pay interest upon the obligation or liability at a rate in excess of 6 percent per year is not materially affected by reason of the servicemember's military service.

(d) Definitions

In this section:

(1) Interest

The term "interest" includes service charges, renewal charges, fees, or any other charges (except bona fide insurance) with respect to an obligation or liability.

(2) Obligation or liability

The term "obligation or liability" includes an obligation or liability consisting of a mortgage, trust deed, or other security in the nature of a mortgage.

(e) Penalty

Whoever knowingly violates subsection (a) shall be fined as provided in title 18, United States Code, imprisoned for not more than one year, or both.

[*As amended by* Pub. L. No. 110–289, 122 Stat. 2849 (2008); Pub. L. No. 110–389, 122 Stat. 4189 (2008); Pub. L. No. 111–275, 124 Stat. 2877 (2010)]

Title III—Rent, Installment Contracts, Mortgages, Liens, Assignment, Leases, Telephone Service Contracts

50 U.S.C. app. § 531. Evictions and distress

(a) Court-ordered eviction

(1) In general

Except by court order, a landlord (or another person with paramount title) may not—

(A) evict a servicemember, or the dependents of a servicemember, during a period of military service of the servicemember, from premises—

(i) that are occupied or intended to be occupied primarily as a residence; and

(ii) for which the monthly rent does not exceed $2,400, as adjusted under paragraph (2) for years after 2003; or

(B) subject such premises to a distress during the period of military service.

(2) Housing price inflation adjustment

(A) For calendar years beginning with 2004, the amount in effect under paragraph (1)(A)(ii) shall be increased by the housing price inflation adjustment for the calendar year involved.

(B) For purposes of this paragraph—

(i) The housing price inflation adjustment for any calendar year is the percentage change (if any) by which—

(I) the CPI housing component for November of the preceding calendar year, exceeds

(II) the CPI housing component for November of 1984.

(ii) The term "CPI housing component" means the index published by the Bureau of Labor Statistics of the Department of Labor known as the Consumer Price Index, All Urban Consumers, Rent of Primary Residence, U.S. City Average.

(3) Publication of housing price inflation adjustment

The Secretary of Defense shall cause to be published in the Federal Register each year the amount in effect under paragraph (1)(A)(ii) for that year following the housing price inflation adjustment for that year pursuant to paragraph (2). Such publication shall be made for a year not later than 60 days after such adjustment is made for that year.

(b) Stay of execution

(1) Court authority

Upon an application for eviction or distress with respect to premises covered by this section, the court may on its own motion and shall, if a request is made by or on behalf of a servicemember whose ability to pay the agreed rent is materially affected by military service—

(A) stay the proceedings for a period of 90 days, unless in the opinion of the court, justice and equity require a longer or shorter period of time; or

(B) adjust the obligation under the lease to preserve the interests of all parties.

(2) Relief to landlord

If a stay is granted under paragraph (1), the court may grant to the landlord (or other person with paramount title) such relief as equity may require.

(c) Misdemeanor

Except as provided in subsection (a), a person who knowingly takes part in an eviction or distress described in subsection (a), or who knowingly attempts to do so, shall be fined as provided in title 18, United States Code, or imprisoned for not more than one year, or both.

(d) Rent allotment from pay of servicemember

To the extent required by a court order related to property which is the subject of a court action under this section, the Secretary concerned shall make an allotment from the pay of a servicemember to satisfy the terms of such order, except that any such allotment shall be subject to regulations prescribed by the Secretary concerned establishing the maximum amount of pay of servicemembers that may be allotted under this subsection.

(e) Limitation of applicability

Section 202 [section 522 of this Appendix] is not applicable to this section.

[*As amended by* Pub. L. No. 111–275, 124 Stat. 2877 (2010)]

50 U.S.C. app. § 532. Protection under installment contracts for purchase or lease

(a) Protection upon breach of contract

(1) Protection after entering military service

After a servicemember enters military service, a contract by the servicemember for—

(A) the purchase of real or personal property (including a motor vehicle); or

(B) the lease or bailment of such property,

may not be rescinded or terminated for a breach of terms of the contract occurring before or during that person's military service, nor may the property be repossessed for such breach without a court order.

(2) Applicability

This section applies only to a contract for which a deposit or installment has been paid by the servicemember before the servicemember enters military service.

(b) Misdemeanor

A person who knowingly resumes possession of property in violation of subsection (a), or in violation of section 107 of this Act [section 517 of this Appendix], or who knowingly attempts to do so, shall be fined as provided in title 18, United States Code, or imprisoned for not more than one year, or both.

(c) Authority of court

In a hearing based on this section, the court—

(1) may order repayment to the servicemember of all or part of the prior installments or deposits as a condition of terminating the contract and resuming possession of the property;

(2) may, on its own motion, and shall on application by a servicemember when the servicemember's ability to comply with the contract is materially affected by military service, stay the proceedings for a period of time as, in the opinion of the court, justice and equity require; or

(3) may make other disposition as is equitable to preserve the interests of all parties.

[*As amended by* Pub. L. No. 111–275, 124 Stat. 2877 (2010)]

50 U.S.C. app. § 533. Mortgages and trust deeds

(a) Mortgage as security

This section applies only to an obligation on real or personal property owned by a servicemember that—

(1) originated before the period of the servicemember's military service and for which the servicemember is still obligated; and

(2) is secured by a mortgage, trust deed, or other security in the nature of a mortgage.

(b) Stay of proceedings and adjustment of obligation

In an action filed during, or within one year[1] after, a servicemember's period of military service to enforce an obligation described in subsection (a), the court may after a hearing and on its own motion and shall upon application by a servicemember when the servicemember's ability to comply with the obligation is materially affected by military service—

(1) stay the proceedings for a period of time as justice and equity require, or

(2) adjust the obligation to preserve the interests of all parties.

(c) Sale or foreclosure

A sale, foreclosure, or seizure of property for a breach of an obligation described in subsection (a) shall not be valid if made during, or within one year[2] after, the period of the servicemember's military service except—

(1) upon a court order granted before such sale, foreclosure, or seizure with a return made and approved by the court; or

(2) if made pursuant to an agreement as provided in section 107 [section 517 of this Appendix].

(d) Misdemeanor

A person who knowingly makes or causes to be made a sale, foreclosure, or seizure of property that is prohibited by subsection (c), or who knowingly attempts to do so, shall be fined as provided in title 18, United States Code, or imprisoned for not more than one year, or both.

[*As amended by* Pub. L. No. 110–289, 122 Stat. 2849 (2008); Pub. L. No. 111–275, 124 Stat. 2877 (2010); Pub. L. No. 112–154, tit. VII, § 710(a), (b), 126 Stat. 1208 (Aug. 6, 2012)]

50 U.S.C. app. § 534. Settlement of stayed cases relating to personal property

(a) Appraisal of property

When a stay is granted pursuant to this Act in a proceeding to foreclose a mortgage on or to repossess personal property, or to rescind or terminate a contract for the purchase of personal property, the court may appoint three disinterested parties to appraise the property.

(b) Equity payment

Based on the appraisal, and if undue hardship to the servicemember's dependents will not result, the court may order that the amount of the servicemember's equity in the property be paid to the servicemember, or the servicemember's dependents, as a condition of foreclosing the mortgage, repossessing the property, or rescinding or terminating the contract.

---

1. *Editor's Note:* This amendment, made by Pub. Law No. 112–154 (2012), will expire on December 31, 2014. The period will return to 90 days on January 1, 2015.
2. *Editor's Note:* This amendment, made by Pub. Law No. 112–154 (2012), will expire on December 31, 2014. The period will return to 90 days on January 1, 2015.

50 U.S.C. app. § 535. Termination of residential or motor vehicle leases

(a) Termination by lessee

(1) In general

The lessee on a lease described in subsection (b) may, at the lessee's option, terminate the lease at any time after—

(A) the lessee's entry into military service; or

(B) the date of the lessee's military orders described in paragraph (1)(B) or (2)(B) of subsection (b), as the case may be.

(2) Joint leases

A lessee's termination of a lease pursuant to this subsection shall terminate any obligation a dependent of the lessee may have under the lease.

(b) Covered leases

This section applies to the following leases:

(1) Leases of premises

A lease of premises occupied, or intended to be occupied, by a servicemember or a servicemember's dependents for a residential, professional, business, agricultural, or similar purpose if—

(A) the lease is executed by or on behalf of a person who thereafter and during the term of the lease enters military service; or

(B) the servicemember, while in military service, executes the lease and thereafter receives military orders for a permanent change of station or to deploy with a military unit, or as an individual in support of a military operation, for a period of not less than 90 days.

(2) Leases of motor vehicles

A lease of a motor vehicle used, or intended to be used, by a servicemember or a servicemember's dependents for personal or business transportation if—

(A) the lease is executed by or on behalf of a person who thereafter and during the term of the lease enters military service under a call or order specifying a period of not less than 180 days (or who enters military service under a call or order specifying a period of 180 days or less and who, without a break in service, receives orders extending the period of military service to a period of not less than 180 days); or

(B) the servicemember, while in military service, executes the lease and thereafter receives military orders—

(i) for a change of permanent station—

(I) from a location in the continental United States to a location outside the continental United States; or

(II) from a location in a State outside the continental United States to any location outside that State; or

(ii) to deploy with a military unit, or as an individual in support of a military operation, for a period of not less than 180 days.

(c) Manner of termination

(1) In general

Termination of a lease under subsection (a) is made—

(A) by delivery by the lessee of written notice of such termination, and a copy of the servicemember's military orders, to the lessor (or the lessor's grantee), or to the lessor's agent (or the agent's grantee); and

(B) in the case of a lease of a motor vehicle, by return of the motor vehicle by the lessee to the lessor (or the lessor's grantee), or to the lessor's agent (or the agent's grantee), not later than 15 days after the date of the delivery of written notice under subparagraph (A).

(2) Delivery of notice

Delivery of notice under paragraph (1)(A) may be accomplished—

(A) by hand delivery;

(B) by private business carrier; or

(C) by placing the written notice in an envelope with sufficient postage and with return receipt requested, and addressed as designated by the lessor (or the lessor's grantee) or to the lessor's agent (or the agent's grantee), and depositing the written notice in the United States mails.

(d) Effective date of lease termination

(1) Lease of premises

In the case of a lease described in subsection (b)(1) that provides for monthly payment of rent, termination of the lease under subsection (a) is effective 30 days after the first date on which the next rental payment is due and payable after the date on which the notice under subsection (c) is delivered. In the case of any other lease described in subsection (b)(1), termination of the lease under subsection (a) is effective on the last day of the month following the month in which the notice is delivered.

(2) Lease of motor vehicles

In the case of a lease described in subsection (b)(2), termination of the lease under subsection (a) is effective on the day on which the requirements of subsection (c) are met for such termination.

(e) Arrearages and other obligations and liabilities (1) Leases of premises

Rent amounts for a lease described in subsection (b)(1) that are unpaid for the period preceding the effective date of the lease termination shall be paid on a prorated basis. The lessor may not impose an early termination charge, but any taxes, summonses, or other obligations and liabilities of the lessee in accordance with the terms of the lease, including reasonable charges to the lessee for excess wear, that are due and unpaid at the time of termination of the lease shall be paid by the lessee.

(2) Leases of motor vehicles

Lease amounts for a lease described in subsection (b)(2) that are unpaid for the period preceding the effective date of the lease termination shall be paid on a prorated basis. The lessor may not impose an early termination charge, but any taxes, summonses, and title and registration fees, or other obligations and liabilities of the lessee in accordance with the terms of the lease, including reasonable charges to the lessee for excess wear or use and mileage, that are due and unpaid at the time of termination of the lease shall be paid by the lessee.

(f) Rent paid in advance

Rents or lease amounts paid in advance for a period after the effective date of the termination of the lease shall be refunded to the lessee by the lessor (or the lessor's assignee or the assignee's agent) within 30 days of the effective date of the termination of the lease.

(g) Relief to lessor

Upon application by the lessor to a court before the termination date provided in the written notice, relief granted by this section to a servicemember may be modified as justice and equity require.

(h) Misdemeanor

Any person who knowingly seizes, holds, or detains the personal effects, security deposit, or other property of a servicemember or a servicemember's dependent who lawfully terminates a lease covered by this section, or who knowingly interferes with the removal of such property from premises covered by such lease, for the purpose of subjecting or attempting to subject any of such property to a claim for rent accruing subsequent to the date of termination of such lease, or attempts to do so, shall be fined as provided in title 18, United States Code, or imprisoned for not more than one year, or both.

(i) Definitions

(1) Military orders

The term "military orders", with respect to a servicemember, means official military orders, or any notification, certification, or verification from the servicemember's commanding officer, with respect to the servicemember's current or future military duty status.

(2) CONUS

The term "continental United States" means the 48 contiguous States and the District of Columbia.

[*As amended by* Pub. L. No. 108–454, 118 Stat. 3624 (2004); Pub. L. No. 111–275, 124 Stat. 2877 (2010)]

50 U.S.C. app. § 535a. Termination of telephone service contracts

(a) Termination by servicemember

(1) Termination

A servicemember may terminate a contract described in subsection (b) at any time after the date the servicemember receives military orders to relocate for a period of not less than 90 days to a location that does not support the contract.

(2) Notice

In the case that a servicemember terminates a contract as described in paragraph (1), the service provider under the contract shall provide such servicemember with written or electronic notice of the servicemember's rights under such paragraph.

(3) Manner of termination

Termination of a contract under paragraph (1) shall be made by delivery of a written or electronic notice of such termination and a copy of the servicemember's military orders to the service provider, delivered in accordance with industry standards for notification of terminations, together with the date on which the service is to be terminated.

(b) Covered contracts

A contract described in this subsection is a contract for cellular telephone service or telephone exchange service entered into by the servicemember before receiving the military orders referred to in subsection (a)(1).

(c) Retention of telephone number

In the case of a contract terminated under subsection (a) by a servicemember whose period of relocation is for a period of three years or less, the service provider under the contract shall, notwithstanding any other provision of law, allow the servicemember to keep the telephone number the servicemember has under the contract if the servicemember re-subscribes to the service during the 90-day period beginning on the last day of such period of relocation.

(d) Family plans

In the case of a contract for cellular telephone service entered into by any individual in which a servicemember is a designated beneficiary of the contract, the individual who entered into the contract may terminate the contract—

(1) with respect to the servicemember if the servicemember is eligible to terminate contracts pursuant to subsection (a); and

(2) with respect to all of the designated beneficiaries of such contract if all such beneficiaries accompany the servicemember during the servicemember's period of relocation.

(e) Other obligations and liabilities

For any contract terminated under this section, the service provider under the contract may not impose an early termination charge, but any tax or any other obligation or liability of the servicemember that, in accordance with the terms of the contract, is due and unpaid or unperformed at the time of termination of the contract shall be paid or performed by the servicemember. If the servicemember re-subscribes to the service provided under a covered contract during the 90-day period beginning on the last day of the servicemember's period of relocation, the service provider may not impose a charge for reinstating service, other than the usual and customary charges for the installation or acquisition of customer equipment imposed on any other subscriber.

(f) Return of Advance Payments

Not later than 60 days after the effective date of the termination of a contract under this section, the service provider under the contract shall refund to the servicemember any fee or other amount to the extent paid for a period extending until after such date, except for the remainder of the monthly or similar billing period in which the termination occurs.

(g) Definitions

For purposes of this section:

(1) The term "cellular telephone service" means commercial mobile service, as that term is defined in section 332(d) of the Communications Act of 1934 (47 U.S.C. 332(d)).

(2) The term "telephone exchange service" has the meaning given that term under section 3 of the Communications Act of 1934 (47 U.S.C. 153).

[*Added by* Pub. L. No. 110–389, 122 Stat. 4188 (2008), *and amended by* Pub. L. No. 111–275, 124 Stat. 2877 (2010)]

50 U.S.C. app. § 536. Protection of life insurance policy

(a) Assignment of policy protected

If a life insurance policy on the life of a servicemember is assigned before military service to secure the payment of an obligation, the assignee of the policy (except the insurer in connection with a policy loan) may not exercise, during a period of military service of the servicemember or within one year thereafter, any right or option obtained under the assignment without a court order.

(b) Exception

The prohibition in subsection (a) shall not apply—

(1) if the assignee has the written consent of the insured made during the period described in subsection (a);

(2) when the premiums on the policy are due and unpaid; or

(3) upon the death of the insured.

(c) Order refused because of material affect

A court which receives an application for an order required under subsection (a) may refuse to grant such order if the court determines the ability of the servicemember to comply with the terms of the obligation is materially affected by military service.

(d) Treatment of guaranteed premiums

For purposes of this subsection, premiums guaranteed under the provisions of title IV of this Act shall not be considered due and unpaid.

(e) Misdemeanor

A person who knowingly takes an action contrary to this section, or attempts to do so, shall be fined as provided in title 18, United States Code, or imprisoned for not more than one year, or both.

[*As amended by* Pub. L. No. 111–275, 124 Stat. 2877 (2010)]

50 U.S.C. app. § 537. Enforcement of storage liens

(a) Liens

(1) Limitation on foreclosure or enforcement

A person holding a lien on the property or effects of a servicemember may not, during any period of military service of the servicemember and for 90 days thereafter, foreclose or enforce any lien on such property or effects without a court order granted before foreclosure or enforcement.

(2) Lien defined

For the purposes of paragraph (1), the term "lien" includes a lien for storage, repair, or cleaning of the property or effects of a servicemember or a lien on such property or effects for any other reason.

(b) Stay of proceedings

In a proceeding to foreclose or enforce a lien subject to this section, the court may on its own motion, and shall if requested by a servicemember whose ability to comply with the obligation resulting in the proceeding is materially affected by military service—

(1) stay the proceeding for a period of time as justice and equity require; or

(2) adjust the obligation to preserve the interests of all parties.

The provisions of this subsection do not affect the scope of section 303 [section 533 of this Appendix].

(c) Misdemeanor

A person who knowingly takes an action contrary to this section, or attempts to do so, shall be fined as provided in title 18, United States Code, or imprisoned for not more than one year, or both.

[*As amended by* Pub. L. No. 111–275, 124 Stat. 2877 (2010)]

50 U.S.C. app. § 538. Extension of protections to dependents

Upon application to a court, a dependent of a servicemember is entitled to the protections of this title if the dependent's ability to comply with a lease, contract, bailment, or other obligation is materially affected by reason of the servicemember's military service.

* * *

Title V—Taxes and Public Lands

50 U.S.C. app. § 561. Taxes respecting personal property, money, credits, and real property

(a) Application

This section applies in any case in which a tax or assessment, whether general or special (other than a tax on personal income), falls due and remains unpaid before or during a period of military service with respect to a servicemember's—

(1) personal property (including motor vehicles); or

(2) real property occupied for dwelling, professional, business, or agricultural purposes by a servicemember or the servicemember's dependents or employees—

(A) before the servicemember's entry into military service; and

(B) during the time the tax or assessment remains unpaid.

(b) Sale of property

(1) Limitation on sale of property to enforce tax assessment

Property described in subsection (a) may not be sold to enforce the collection of such tax or assessment except by court order and upon the determination by the court that military service does not materially affect the servicemember's ability to pay the unpaid tax or assessment.

(2) Stay of court proceedings

A court may stay a proceeding to enforce the collection of such tax or assessment, or sale of such property, during a period of military service of the servicemember and for a period not more than 180 days after the termination of, or release of the servicemember from, military service.

(c) Redemption

When property described in subsection (a) is sold or forfeited to enforce the collection of a tax or assessment, a servicemember shall have the right to redeem or commence an action to redeem the servicemember's property during the period of military service or within 180 days after termination of or release from military service. This subsection may not be construed to shorten any period provided by the law of a State (including any political subdivision of a State) for redemption.

(d) Interest on tax or assessment

Whenever a servicemember does not pay a tax or assessment on property described in subsection (a) when due, the amount of the tax or assessment due and unpaid shall bear interest until paid at the rate of 6 percent per year. An additional penalty or interest shall not be incurred by reason of nonpayment. A lien for such unpaid tax or assessment may include interest under this subsection.

(e) Joint ownership application

This section applies to all forms of property described in subsection (a) owned individually by a servicemember or jointly by a servicemember and a dependent or dependents.

* * *

50 U.S.C. app. § 570. Income taxes

(a) Deferral of tax

Upon notice to the Internal Revenue Service or the tax authority of a State or a political subdivision of a State, the collection of income tax on the income of a servicemember falling due before or during military service shall be deferred for a period not more than 180 days after termination of or release from military service, if a servicemember's ability to pay such income tax is materially affected by military service.

(b) Accrual of interest or penalty

No interest or penalty shall accrue for the period of deferment by reason of nonpayment on any amount of tax deferred under this section.

(c) Statute of limitations

The running of a statute of limitations against the collection of tax deferred under this section, by seizure or otherwise, shall be suspended for the period of military service of the servicemember and for an additional period of 270 days thereafter.

(d) Application limitation

This section shall not apply to the tax imposed on employees by section 3101 of the Internal Revenue Code of 1986.

50 U.S.C. app. § 571. Residence for tax purposes

(a) Residence or domicile

(1) In general

A servicemember shall neither lose nor acquire a residence or domicile for purposes of taxation with respect to the person, personal property, or income of the servicemember by reason of being absent or present in any tax jurisdiction of the United States solely in compliance with military orders.

(2) Spouses

A spouse of a servicemember shall neither lose nor acquire a residence or domicile for purposes of taxation with respect to the person, personal property, or income of the spouse by reason of being absent or present in any tax jurisdiction of the United States solely to be with the servicemember in compliance with the servicemember's military orders if the residence or domicile, as the case may be, is the same for the servicemember and the spouse.

(b) Military service compensation

Compensation of a servicemember for military service shall not be deemed to be income for services performed or from sources within a tax jurisdiction of the United States if the servicemember is not a resident or domiciliary of the jurisdiction in which the servicemember is serving in compliance with military orders.

(c) Income of a military spouse

Income for services performed by the spouse of a servicemember shall not be deemed to be income for services performed or from sources within a tax jurisdiction of the United States if the spouse is not a resident or domiciliary of the jurisdiction in which the income is earned because the spouse is in the jurisdiction solely to be with the servicemember serving in compliance with military orders.

(d) Personal property

(1) Relief from personal property taxes

The personal property of a servicemember or the spouse of a servicemember shall not be deemed to be located or present in, or to have a situs for taxation in, the tax jurisdiction in which the servicemember is serving in compliance with military orders.

(2) Exception for property within member's domicile or residence

This subsection applies to personal property or its use within any tax jurisdiction other than the servicemember's or the spouse's domicile or residence.

(3) Exception for property used in trade or business

This section does not prevent taxation by a tax jurisdiction with respect to personal property used in or arising from a trade or business, if it has jurisdiction.

(4) Relationship to law of State of domicile

Eligibility for relief from personal property taxes under this subsection is not contingent on whether or not such taxes are paid to the State of domicile.

(e) Increase of tax liability

A tax jurisdiction may not use the military compensation of a nonresident servicemember to increase the tax liability imposed on other income earned by the nonresident servicemember or spouse subject to tax by the jurisdiction.

(f) Federal Indian reservations

An Indian servicemember whose legal residence or domicile is a Federal Indian reservation shall be taxed by the laws applicable to Federal Indian reservations and not the State where the reservation is located.

(g) Definitions

For purposes of this section:

(1) Personal property

The term "personal property" means intangible and tangible property (including motor vehicles).

(2) Taxation

The term "taxation" includes licenses, fees, or excises imposed with respect to motor vehicles and their use, if the license, fee, or excise is paid by the servicemember in the servicemember's State of domicile or residence.

(3) Tax jurisdiction

The term "tax jurisdiction" means a State or a political subdivision of a State.

[*As amended by* Pub. L. No. 111–97, 123 Stat. 3007 (2009)]

Title VI—Administrative Remedies

50 U.S.C. app. § 581. Inappropriate use of Act

If a court determines, in any proceeding to enforce a civil right, that any interest, property, or contract has been transferred or acquired with the intent to delay the just enforcement of such right by taking advantage of this Act, the court shall enter such judgment or make such order as might lawfully be entered or made concerning such transfer or acquisition.

50 U.S.C. app. § 582. Certificates of service; persons reported missing

(a) Prima facie evidence

In any proceeding under this Act, a certificate signed by the Secretary concerned is prima facie evidence as to any of the following facts stated in the certificate:

(1) That a person named is, is not, has been, or has not been in military service.

(2) The time and the place the person entered military service.

(3) The person's residence at the time the person entered military service.

(4) The rank, branch, and unit of military service of the person upon entry.

(5) The inclusive dates of the person's military service.

(6) The monthly pay received by the person at the date of the certificate's issuance.

(7) The time and place of the person's termination of or release from military service, or the person's death during military service.

(b) Certificates

The Secretary concerned shall furnish a certificate under subsection (a) upon receipt of an application for such a certificate. A certificate appearing to be signed by the Secretary concerned is prima facie evidence of its contents and of the signer's authority to issue it.

(c) Treatment of servicemembers in missing status

A servicemember who has been reported missing is presumed to continue in service until accounted for. A requirement under this Act that begins or ends with the death of a servicemember does not begin or end until the servicemember's death is reported to, or determined by, the Secretary concerned or by a court of competent jurisdiction.

50 U.S.C. app. § 583. Interlocutory orders

An interlocutory order issued by a court under this Act may be revoked, modified, or extended by that court upon its own motion or otherwise, upon notification to affected parties as required by the court.

Title VII—Further Relief

50 U.S.C. app. § 591. Anticipatory relief

(a) Application for relief

A servicemember may, during military service or within 180 days of termination of or release from military service, apply to a court for relief—

(1) from any obligation or liability incurred by the servicemember before the servicemember's military service; or

(2) from a tax or assessment falling due before or during the servicemember's military service.

(b) Tax liability or assessment

In a case covered by subsection (a), the court may, if the ability of the servicemember to comply with the terms of such obligation or liability or pay such tax or assessment has been materially affected by reason of military service, after appropriate notice and hearing, grant the following relief:

(1) Stay of enforcement of real estate contracts

(A) In the case of an obligation payable in installments under a contract for the purchase of real estate, or secured by a mortgage or other instrument in the nature of a mortgage upon real estate, the court may grant a stay of the enforcement of the obligation—

(i) during the servicemember's period of military service; and

(ii) from the date of termination of or release from military service, or from the date of application if made after termination of or release from military service.

(B) Any stay under this paragraph shall be—

(i) for a period equal to the remaining life of the installment contract or other instrument, plus a period of time equal to the period of military service of the servicemember, or any part of such combined period; and

(ii) subject to payment of the balance of the principal and accumulated interest due and unpaid at the date of termination or release from the applicant's military service or from the date of application in equal installments during the combined period at the rate of interest on the unpaid balance prescribed in the contract or other instrument evidencing the obligation, and subject to other terms as may be equitable.

(2) Stay of enforcement of other contracts

(A) In the case of any other obligation, liability, tax, or assessment, the court may grant a stay of enforcement—

(i) during the servicemember's military service; and

(ii) from the date of termination of or release from military service, or from the date of application if made after termination or release from military service.

(B) Any stay under this paragraph shall be—

(i) for a period of time equal to the period of the servicemember's military service or any part of such period; and

(ii) subject to payment of the balance of principal and accumulated interest due and unpaid at the date of termination or release from military service, or the date of application, in equal periodic installments during this extended period at the rate of interest as may be prescribed for this obligation, liability, tax, or assessment, if paid when due, and subject to other terms as may be equitable.

(c) Affect of stay on fine or penalty

When a court grants a stay under this section, a fine or penalty shall not accrue on the obligation, liability, tax, or assessment for the period of compliance with the terms and conditions of the stay.

50 U.S.C. app. § 592. Power of attorney

(a) Automatic extension

A power of attorney of a servicemember shall be automatically extended for the period the servicemember is in a missing status (as defined in section 551(2) of title 37, United States Code) if the power of attorney—

(1) was duly executed by the servicemember—

(A) while in military service; or

(B) before entry into military service but after the servicemember—

(i) received a call or order to report for military service; or

(ii) was notified by an official of the Department of Defense that the person could receive a call or order to report for military service;

(2) designates the servicemember's spouse, parent, or other named relative as the servicemember's attorney in fact for certain, specified, or all purposes; and

(3) expires by its terms after the servicemember entered a missing status.

(b) Limitation on power of attorney extension

A power of attorney executed by a servicemember may not be extended under subsection (a) if the document by its terms clearly indicates that the power granted expires on the date specified even though the servicemember, after the date of execution of the document, enters a missing status.

* * *

50 U.S.C. app. § 594. Health insurance reinstatement

(a) Reinstatement of health insurance

A servicemember who, by reason of military service as defined in section 703(a)(1) [section 593(a)(1) of this Appendix], is entitled to the rights and protections of this Act [sections 501 to 596 of this Appendix] shall also be entitled upon termination or release from such service to reinstatement of any health insurance that—

(1) was in effect on the day before such service commenced; and

(2) was terminated effective on a date during the period of such service.

(b) No exclusion or waiting period

The reinstatement of health care insurance coverage for the health or physical condition of a servicemember described in subsection (a), or any other person who is covered by the insurance by reason of the coverage of the servicemember, shall not be subject to an exclusion or a waiting period, if—

(1) the condition arose before or during the period of such service;

(2) an exclusion or a waiting period would not have been imposed for the condition during the period of coverage; and

(3) in a case in which the condition relates to the servicemember, the condition has not been determined by the Secretary of Veterans Affairs to be a disability incurred or aggravated in the line of duty (within the meaning of section 105 of title 38, United States Code).

(c) Exceptions

Subsection (a) does not apply to a servicemember entitled to participate in employer-offered insurance benefits pursuant to the provisions of chapter 43 of title 38, United States Code.

(d) Time for applying for reinstatement

An application under this section must be filed not later than 120 days after the date of the termination of or release from military service.

(e) Limitation on premium increases

(1) Premium protection

The amount of the premium for health insurance coverage that was terminated by a servicemember and required to be reinstated under subsection (a) may not be increased, for the balance of the period for which coverage would have been continued had the coverage not been terminated, to an amount greater than the amount chargeable for such coverage before the termination.

(2) Increases of general applicability not precluded

Paragraph (1) does not prevent an increase in premium to the extent of any general increase in the premiums charged by the carrier of the health care insurance for the same health insurance coverage for persons similarly covered by such insurance during the period between the termination and the reinstatement.

[*As amended by* Pub. L. No. 109–233, 120 Stat. 406 (2006)]

* * *

50 U.S.C. app. § 596. Business or trade obligations

(a) Availability of non-business assets to satisfy obligations
If the trade or business (without regard to the form in which such trade or business is carried out) of a servicemember has an obligation or liability for which the servicemember is personally liable, the assets of the servicemember not held in connection with the trade or business may not be available for satisfaction of the obligation or liability during the servicemember's military service.

(b) Relief to obligors
Upon application to a court by the holder of an obligation or liability covered by this section, relief granted by this section to a servicemember may be modified as justice and equity require.

Title VIII—Civil Liability

50 U.S.C. app. § 597. Enforcement by the Attorney General

(a) Civil action
The Attorney General may commence a civil action in any appropriate district court of the United States against any person who—

(1) engages in a pattern or practice of violating this Act; or

(2) engages in a violation of this Act that raises an issue of significant public importance.

(b) Relief
In a civil action commenced under subsection (a), the court may—

(1) grant any appropriate equitable or declaratory relief with respect to the violation of this Act;

(2) award all other appropriate relief, including monetary damages, to any person aggrieved by the violation; and

(3) may, to vindicate the public interest, assess a civil penalty—

(A) in an amount not exceeding $55,000 for a first violation; and

(B) in an amount not exceeding $110,000 for any subsequent violation.

(c) Intervention
Upon timely application, a person aggrieved by a violation of this Act with respect to which the civil action is commenced may intervene in such action, and may obtain such appropriate relief as the person could obtain in a civil action under section 802 with respect to that violation, along with costs and a reasonable attorney fee.

[*Added by* Pub. L. No. 111–275, 124 Stat. 2877 (2010)]

50 U.S.C. app. § 597a. Private right of action

(a) In general
Any person aggrieved by a violation of this Act may in a civil action—

(1) obtain any appropriate equitable or declaratory relief with respect to the violation; and

(2) recover all other appropriate relief, including monetary damages.

(b) Costs and attorney fees
The court may award to a person aggrieved by a violation of this Act who prevails in an action brought under subsection (a) the costs of the action, including a reasonable attorney fee.

[*Added by* Pub. L. No. 111–275, 124 Stat. 2877 (2010)]

50 U.S.C. app. § 597b. Preservation of remedies

Nothing in section 597 or 597a shall be construed to preclude or limit any remedy otherwise available under other law, including consequential and punitive damages.

[*Added by* Pub. L. No. 111–275, 124 Stat. 2877 (2010)]

Appendix B Selected Provisions Governing Collection of Debts Owed to Federal Government

B.1 Debt Collection Improvement Act

The Debt Collection Improvement Act of 1996 was enacted by Pub. L. No. 104–134, § 31001, 110 Stat. 1321. It is principally codified as part of the Claims Collection Act, 31 U.S.C. §§ 3701–3733, relevant portions of which are reprinted below.

TITLE 31—MONEY AND FINANCE

Chapter 37—Claims

31 U.S.C.

Subchapter I—General

Subchapter II—Claims of the United States Government

* * *

SUBCHAPTER I—GENERAL

31 U.S.C. § 3701. Definitions and application

(a) In this chapter—

(1) "administrative offset" means withholding funds payable by the United States (including funds payable by the United States on behalf of a State government) to, or held by the United States for, a person to satisfy a claim.

(2) "calendar quarter" means a 3-month period beginning on January 1, April 1, July 1, or October 1.

(3) "consumer reporting agency" means—

(A) a consumer reporting agency as that term is defined in section 603(f) of the Fair Credit Reporting Act (15 U.S.C. 1681a(f)); or

(B) a person that, for money or on a cooperative basis, regularly—

(i) gets information on consumers to give the information to a consumer reporting agency; or

(ii) serves as a marketing agent under an arrangement allowing a third party to get the information from a consumer reporting agency.

(4) "executive, judicial, or legislative agency" means a department, agency, court, court administrative office, or instrumentality in the executive, judicial, or legislative branch of Government, including government corporations.

(5) "military department" means the Departments of the Army, Navy, and Air Force.

(6) "system of records" has the same meaning given that term in section 552a(a)(5) of title 5.

(7) "uniformed services" means the Army, Navy, Air Force, Marine Corps, Coast Guard, Commissioned Corps of the National Oceanic and Atmospheric Administration, and Commissioned Corps of the Public Health Service.

(8) "nontax" means, with respect to any debt or claim, any debt or claim other than a debt or claim under the Internal Revenue Code of 1986.

(b) **(1)** In subchapter II of this chapter and subsection (a)(8) of this section, the term "claim" or "debt" means any amount of funds or property that has been determined by an appropriate official of the Federal Government to be owed to the United States by a person, organization, or entity other than another Federal agency. A claim includes, without limitation—

(A) funds owed on account of loans made, insured, or guaranteed by the Government, including any deficiency or any difference between the price obtained by the Government in the sale of a property and the amount owed to the Government on a mortgage on the property,

(B) expenditures of nonappropriated funds, including actual and administrative costs related to shoplifting, theft detection, and theft prevention,

(C) over-payments, including payments disallowed by audits performed by the Inspector General of the agency administering the program,

(D) any amount the United States is authorized by statute to collect for the benefit of any person,

(E) the unpaid share of any non-Federal partner in a program involving a Federal payment and a matching, or cost-sharing, payment by the non-Federal partner,

(F) any fines or penalties assessed by an agency; and

(G) other amounts of money or property owed to the Government.

(2) For purposes of section 3716 of this title, each of the terms "claim" and "debt" includes an amount of funds or property owed by a person to a State (including any past-due support being enforced by the State), the District of Columbia, American Samoa, Guam, the United States Virgin Islands, the Commonwealth of the Northern Mariana Islands, or the Commonwealth of Puerto Rico.

(c) In sections 3716 and 3717 of this title, the term "person" does not include an agency of the United States Government.

(d) Sections 3711(e) and 3716–3719 of this title do not apply to a claim or debt under, or to an amount payable under—

(1) the Internal Revenue Code of 1986 (26 U.S.C. 1 *et seq.*),

(2) the Social Security Act (42 U.S.C. 301 *et seq.*), except to the extent provided under sections 204(f) and 1631(b)(4) of such Act and section 3716(c) of this title, or

(3) the tariff laws of the United States.

(e) In section 3716 of this title—

(1) "creditor agency" means any agency owed a claim that seeks to collect that claim through administrative offset; and

(2) "payment certifying agency" means any agency that has transmitted a voucher to a disbursing official for disbursement.

(f) In section 3711 of this title, "private collection contractor" means private debt collectors under contract with an agency to collect a nontax debt or claim owed the United States. The term includes private debt collectors, collection agencies, and commercial attorneys.

[*As amended by* Pub. L. No. 97–258, 96 Stat. 970 (1982); Pub. L. No. 97–452, 96 Stat. 2469 (1983); Pub. L. No. 103–387, 108 Stat. 4077 (1994); Pub. L. No. 104–134, 110 Stat. 1321–359 (1996); Pub. L. No. 104–316, 110 Stat. 3835 (1996); Pub. L. No. 106–169, 113 Stat. 1832 (1999); Pub. L. No. 107–107, 115 Stat. 1060 (2001)]

31 U.S.C. § 3702. Authority to settle claims

(a) Except as provided in this chapter or another law, all claims of or against the United States Government shall be settled as follows:

(1) The Secretary of Defense shall settle—

(A) claims involving uniformed service members' pay, allowances, travel, transportation, payments for unused accrued leave, retired pay, and survivor benefits; and

(B) claims by transportation carriers involving amounts collected from them for loss or damage incurred to property incident to shipment at Government expense.

(2) The Director of the Office of Personnel Management shall settle claims involving Federal civilian employees' compensation and leave.

(3) The Administrator of General Services shall settle claims involving expenses incurred by Federal civilian employees for official travel and transportation, and for relocation expenses incident to transfers of official duty station.

(4) The Director of the Office of Management and Budget shall settle claims not otherwise provided for by this subsection or another provision of law.

(b) (1) A claim against the Government presented under this section must contain the signature and address of the claimant or an authorized representative. The claim must be received by the official responsible under subsection (a) for settling the claim or by the agency that conducts the activity from which the claim arises within 6 years after the claim accrues except—

(A) as provided in this chapter or another law; or

(B) a claim of a State, the District of Columbia, or a territory or possession of the United States.

(2) When the claim of a member of the armed forces accrues during war or within 5 years before war begins, the claim must be received within 5 years after peace is established or within the period provided in paragraph (1) of this subsection, whichever is later.

(3) A claim that is not received in the time required under this subsection shall be returned with a copy of this subsection, and no further communication is required.

(c) One-year limit for check claims.—

(1) Any claim on account of a Treasury check shall be barred unless it is presented to the agency that authorized the issuance of such check within 1 year after the date of issuance of the check or the effective date of this subsection, whichever is later.

(2) Nothing in this subsection affects the underlying obligation of the United States, or any agency thereof, for which a Treasury check was issued.

(d) The official responsible under subsection (a) for settling the claim shall report to Congress on a claim against the Government that is timely presented under this section that may not be adjusted by using an existing appropriation, and that the official believes Congress should consider for legal or equitable reasons. The report shall include recommendations of the official.

(e) (1) The Secretary of Defense may waive the time limitations set forth in subsection (b) or (c) in the case of a claim referred to in subsection (a)(1)(A). In the case of a claim by or with respect to a member of the uniformed services who is not under the jurisdiction of the Secretary of a military department, such a waiver may be made only upon the request of the Secretary concerned (as defined in section 101 of title 37).

(2) Payment of a claim settled under subsection (a)(1)(A) shall be made from an appropriation that is available, for the fiscal year in which the payment is made, for the same purpose as the appropriation to which the obligation claimed would have been charged if the obligation had been timely paid, except that in the case of a claim for retired pay or survivor benefits, if the obligation claimed would have been paid from a trust fund if timely paid, the payment of the claim shall be made from that trust fund.

(3) This subsection does not apply to a claim in excess of $25,000.

[*As amended by* Pub. L. No. 97–258, 96 Stat. 970 (1982); Pub. L. No. 97–452, 96 Stat. 2470 (1983); Pub. L. No. 100–86, 101 Stat. 659 (1987); Pub. L. No. 104–201, 110 Stat. 2542 (1996); Pub. L. No. 104–316, 110 Stat. 3843 (1996); Pub. L. No. 105–85, 111 Stat. 1874 (1997); Pub. L. No. 106–398, 114 Stat. 1654 (2000); Pub. L. No. 107–314, 116 Stat. 2574 (2002); Pub. L. No. 109–163, 119 Stat. 3440 (2006), *as amended by* Pub. L. No. 111–383, 124 Stat. 4377 (2011)]

SUBCHAPTER II—CLAIMS OF THE UNITED STATES GOVERNMENT

31 U.S.C. § 3711. Collection and compromise

(a) The head of an executive, judicial, or legislative agency—

(1) shall try to collect a claim of the United States Government for money or property arising out of the activities of, or referred to, the agency;

(2) may compromise a claim of the Government of not more than $100,000 (excluding interest) or such higher amount as the Attorney General may from time to time prescribe that has not been referred to another executive or legislative agency for further collection action, except that only the Comptroller General may compromise a claim arising out of an exception the Comptroller General makes in the account of an accountable official; and

(3) may suspend or end collection action on a claim referred to in clause (2) of this subsection when it appears that no person liable on the claim has the present or prospective ability to pay a significant amount of the claim or the cost of collecting the claim is likely to be more than the amount recovered.

(b) (1) The head of an executive, judicial, or legislative agency may not act under subsection (a)(2) or (3) of this section on a claim that appears to be fraudulent, false, or misrepresented by a party with an interest in the claim, or that is based on conduct in violation of the antitrust laws.

(2) The Secretary of Transportation may not compromise for less than $500 a penalty under section 21302 of title 49 for a violation of chapter 203, 205, or 207 of title 49 or a regulation or requirement prescribed or order issued under any of those chapters.

(c) A compromise under this section is final and conclusive unless gotten by fraud, misrepresentation, presenting a false claim, or mutual mistake of fact. An accountable official is not liable for an amount paid or for the value of property lost or damaged if the amount or value is not recovered because of a compromise under this section.

(d) The head of an executive, judicial, or legislative agency acts under—

(1) regulations prescribed by the head of the agency; and

(2) standards that the Attorney General, the Secretary of the Treasury, may prescribe.

(e) **(1)** When trying to collect a claim of the Government under a law except the Internal Revenue Code of 1986 (26 U.S.C. 1 *et seq.*), the head of an executive, judicial, or legislative agency shall disclose to a consumer reporting agency information from a system of records that a person is responsible for a claim if—

(A) notice required by section 552a(e)(4) of title 5 indicates that information in the system may be disclosed to a consumer reporting agency;

(B) the head of the agency has reviewed the claim and decided that the claim is valid and overdue;

(C) the head of the agency has notified the person in writing—

(i) that payment of the claim is overdue;

(ii) that, within not less than 60 days after sending the notice, the head of the agency intends to disclose to a consumer reporting agency that the person is responsible for the claim;

(iii) of the specific information to be disclosed to the consumer reporting agency; and

(iv) of the rights the person has to a complete explanation of the claim, to dispute information in the records of the agency about the claim, and to administrative repeal or review of the claim;

(D) the person has not—

(i) repaid or agreed to repay the claim under a written repayment plan that the person has signed and the head of the agency has agreed to; or

(ii) filed for review of the claim under paragraph (2) of this subsection;

(E) the head of the agency has established procedures to—

(i) disclose promptly, to each consumer reporting agency to which the original disclosure was made, a substantial change in the condition or amount of the claim;

(ii) verify or correct promptly information about the claim on request of a consumer reporting agency for verification of information disclosed; and

(iii) get satisfactory assurances from each consumer reporting agency that the agency is complying with all laws of the United States related to providing consumer credit information; and

(F) the information disclosed to the consumer reporting agency is limited to—

(i) information necessary to establish the identity of the person, including name, address, and taxpayer identification number;

(ii) the amount, status, and history of the claim; and

(iii) the agency or program under which the claim arose.

(2) Before disclosing information to a consumer reporting agency under paragraph (1) of this subsection and at other times allowed by law, the head of an executive, judicial, or legislative agency shall provide, on request of a person alleged by the agency to be responsible for the claim, for a review of the obligation of the person, including an opportunity for reconsideration of the initial decision on the claim.

(3) Before disclosing information to a consumer reporting agency under paragraph (1) of this subsection, the head of an executive, judicial, or legislative agency shall take reasonable action to locate a person for whom the head of the agency does not have a current address to send the notice under paragraph (1)(C).

(4) The head of each executive agency shall require, as a condition for insuring or guaranteeing any loan, financing, or other extension of credit under any law to a person, that the lender provide information relating to the extension of credit to consumer reporting agencies or commercial reporting agencies, as appropriate.

(5) The head of each executive agency may provide to a consumer reporting agency or commercial reporting agency information from a system of records that a person is responsible for a claim which is current, if notice required by section 552a(e)(4) of title 5 indicates that information in the system may be disclosed to a consumer reporting agency or commercial reporting agency, respectively.

(f) **(1)** The Secretary of Defense may suspend or terminate an action by the Secretary or by the Secretary of a military department under subsection (a) to collect a claim against the estate of a person who died while serving on active duty as a member of the Army, Navy, Air Force, Marine Corps, or Coast Guard during a period when the Coast Guard is operating as a service in the Navy if the Secretary determines that, under the circumstances applicable with respect to the deceased person, it is appropriate to do so.

(2) The Secretary of Homeland Security may suspend or terminate an action by the Secretary under subsection (a) to collect a claim against the estate of a person who died while serving on active duty as a member of the Coast Guard if the Secretary determines that, under the circumstances applicable with respect to the deceased person, it is appropriate to do so.

(3) The Secretary of Veterans Affairs may suspend or terminate an action by the Secretary under subsection (a) to collect a claim against the estate of a person who died while serving on active duty as a member of the Army, Navy, Air Force, Marine Corps, or Coast Guard during a period when the Coast Guard is operating as a service in the Navy if the Secretary determines that, under the circumstances applicable with respect to the deceased person, it is appropriate to do so.

(4) In this subsection, the term "active duty" has the meaning given that term in section 101 of title 10.

(g) **(1)** If a nontax debt or claim owed to the United States has been delinquent for a period of 180 days—

(A) the head of the executive, judicial, or legislative agency that administers the program that gave rise to the debt or claim shall transfer the debt or claim to the Secretary of the Treasury; and

(B) upon such transfer the Secretary of the Treasury shall take appropriate action to collect or terminate collection actions on the debt or claim.

(2) Paragraph (1) shall not apply—

(A) to any debt or claim that—

(i) is in litigation or foreclosure;

(ii) will be disposed of under an asset sales program within 1 year after becoming eligible for sale, or later than 1 year if consistent with an asset sales program and a schedule established by the agency and approved by the Director of the Office of Management and Budget;

(iii) has been referred to a private collection contractor for collection for a period of time determined by the Secretary of the Treasury;

(iv) has been referred by, or with the consent of, the Secretary of the Treasury to a debt collection center for a period of time determined by the Secretary of the Treasury; or

(v) will be collected under internal offset, if such offset is sufficient to collect the claim within 3 years after the date the debt or claim is first delinquent; and

(B) to any other specific class of debt or claim, as determined by the Secretary of the Treasury at the request of the head of an executive, judicial, or legislative agency or otherwise.

(3) For purposes of this section, the Secretary of the Treasury may designate, and withdraw such designation of debt collection centers operated by other Federal agencies. The Secretary of the Treasury shall designate such centers on the basis of their performance in collecting delinquent claims owed to the Government.

(4) At the discretion of the Secretary of the Treasury, referral of a nontax claim may be made to—

(A) any executive department or agency operating a debt collection center for servicing, collection, compromise, or suspension or termination of collection action;

(B) a private collection contractor operating under a contract for servicing or collection action; or

(C) the Department of Justice for litigation.

(5) Nontax claims referred or transferred under this section shall be serviced, collected, or compromised, or collection action thereon suspended or terminated, in accordance with otherwise applicable statutory requirements and authorities. Executive departments and agencies operating debt collection centers may enter into agreements with the Secretary of the Treasury to carry out the purposes of this subsection. The Secretary of the Treasury shall—

(A) maintain competition in carrying out this subsection;

(B) maximize collections of delinquent debts by placing delinquent debts quickly;

(C) maintain a schedule of private collection contractors and debt collection centers eligible for referral of claims; and

(D) refer delinquent debts to the person most appropriate to collect the type or amount of claim involved.

(6) Any agency operating a debt collection center to which nontax claims are referred or transferred under this subsection may charge a fee sufficient to cover the full cost of implementing this subsection. The agency transferring or referring the nontax claim shall be charged the fee, and the agency charging the fee shall collect such fee by retaining the amount of the fee from amounts collected pursuant to this subsection. Agencies may agree to pay through a different method, or to fund an activity from another account or from revenue received from the procedure described under section 3720C of this title. Amounts charged under this subsection concerning delinquent claims may be considered as costs pursuant to section 3717(e) of this title.

(7) Notwithstanding any other law concerning the depositing and collection of Federal payments, including section 3302(b) of this title, agencies collecting fees may retain the fees from amounts collected. Any fee charged pursuant to this subsection shall be deposited into an account to be determined by the executive department or agency operating the debt collection center charging the fee (in this subsection referred to in this section as the "Account"). Amounts deposited in the Account shall be available until expended to cover costs associated with the implementation and operation of Governmentwide debt collection activities. Costs properly chargeable to the Account include—

(A) the costs of computer hardware and software, word processing and telecommunications equipment, and other equipment, supplies, and furniture;

(B) personnel training and travel costs;

(C) other personnel and administrative costs;

(D) the costs of any contract for identification, billing, or collection services; and

(E) reasonable costs incurred by the Secretary of the Treasury, including services and utilities provided by the Secretary, and administration of the Account.

(8) Not later than January 1 of each year, there shall be deposited into the Treasury as miscellaneous receipts an amount equal to the amount of unobligated balances remaining in the Account at the close of business on September 30 of the preceding year, minus any part of such balance that the executive department or agency operating the debt collection center determines is necessary to cover or defray the costs under this subsection for the fiscal year in which the deposit is made.

(9) Before discharging any delinquent debt owed to any executive, judicial, or legislative agency, the head of such agency shall take all appropriate steps to collect such debt, including (as applicable)—

(A) administrative offset,

(B) tax refund offset,

(C) Federal salary offset,

(D) referral to private collection contractors,

(E) referral to agencies operating a debt collection center,

(F) reporting delinquencies to credit reporting bureaus,

(G) garnishing the wages of delinquent debtors, and

(H) litigation or foreclosure.

(10) To carry out the purposes of this subsection, the Secretary of the Treasury may prescribe such rules, regulations, and procedures as the Secretary considers necessary and transfer such funds from funds appropriated to the Department of the Treasury as may be necessary to meet existing liabilities and obligations incurred prior to the receipt of revenues that result from debt collections.

(h) **(1)** The head of an executive, judicial, or legislative agency acting under subsection (a)(1), (2), or (3) of this section to collect a claim, compromise a claim, or terminate collection action on a claim may obtain a consumer report (as that term is defined in section 603 of the Fair Credit Reporting Act (15 U.S.C. 1681a)) or comparable credit information on any person who is liable for the claim.

(2) The obtaining of a consumer report under this subsection is deemed to be a circumstance or purpose authorized or listed under section 604 of the Fair Credit Reporting Act (15 U.S.C. 1681b).

(i) **(1)** The head of an executive, judicial, or legislative agency may sell, subject to section 504(b) of the Federal Credit Reform Act of 1990 and using competitive procedures, any nontax debt owed to the United States that is delinquent for more than 90 days. Appropriate fees charged by a contractor to assist in the conduct of a sale under this subsection may be payable from the proceeds of the sale.

(2) After terminating collection action, the head of an executive, judicial, or legislative agency shall sell, using competitive procedures, any nontax debt or class of nontax debts owed to the United States, if the Secretary of the Treasury determines the sale is in the best interests of the United States.

(3) Sales of nontax debt under this subsection—

(A) shall be for—

(i) cash, or

(ii) cash and a residuary equity or profit participation, if the head of the agency reasonably determines that the proceeds will be greater than sale solely for cash,

(B) shall be without recourse, but may include the use of guarantees if otherwise authorized, and

(C) shall transfer to the purchaser all rights of the Government to demand payment of the nontax debt, other than with respect to a residuary equity or profit participation under subparagraph (A)(ii).

(4) **(A)** Within one year after the date of enactment of the Debt Collection Improvement Act of 1996, each executive agency with current and delinquent collateralized nontax debts shall report to the Congress on the valuation of its existing portfolio of loans, notes and guarantees, and other collateralized debts based on standards developed by the Director of the Office of Management and Budget, in consultation with the Secretary of the Treasury.

(B) The Director of the Office of Management and Budget shall determine what information is required to be reported to comply with subparagraph (A). At a minimum, for each financing account and for each liquidating account (as those terms are defined in sections 502(7) and 502(8), respectively, of the Federal Credit Reform Act of 1990) the following information shall be reported:

(i) The cumulative balance of current debts outstanding, the estimated net present value of such debts, the annual administrative expenses of those debts (including the portion of salaries and expenses that are directly related thereto), and the estimated net proceeds that would be received by the Government if such debts were sold.

(ii) The cumulative balance of delinquent debts, debts outstanding, the estimated net present value of such debts, the annual administrative expenses of those debts (including the portion of salaries and expenses that are directly related thereto), and the estimated net proceeds that would be received by the Government if such debts were sold.

(iii) The cumulative balance of guaranteed loans outstanding, the estimated net present value of such guarantees, the annual administrative expenses of such guarantees (including the portion of salaries and expenses that are directly related to such guaranteed loans), and the estimated net proceeds that would be received by the Government if such loan guarantees were sold.

(iv) The cumulative balance of defaulted loans that were previously guaranteed and have resulted in loans receivables, the estimated net present value of such loan assets, the annual administrative expenses of such loan assets (including the portion of salaries and expenses that are directly related to such loan assets), and the estimated net proceeds that would be received by the Government if such loan assets were sold.

(v) The marketability of all debts.

(5) This subsection is not intended to limit existing statutory authority of agencies to sell loans, debts, or other assets.

[*As amended by* Pub. L. No. 97–258, 96 Stat. 970 (1982); Pub. L. No. 97–452, 96 Stat. 2470 (1983); Pub. L. No. 98–216, 98 Stat. 4 (1984); Pub. L. No. 99–514, 100 Stat. 2095 (1986); Pub. L. No. 101–552, 104 Stat. 2746 (1990); Pub. L. No. 102–365, 106 Stat. 973 (1992); Pub. L. No. 103–272, 108 Stat. 1375 (1994); Pub. L. No. 104–106, 110 Stat. 459 (1996); Pub. L. No. 104–134, 110 Stat. 1321–359 (1996); Pub. L. No. 104–201, 110 Stat. 2635 (1996); Pub. L. No. 104–316, 110 Stat. 3834 (1996); Pub. L. No. 109–241, 120 Stat. 566 (2006); Pub. L. No. 110–389, 122 Stat. 4185 (2008)]

* * *

31 U.S.C. § 3713. Priority of government claims

(a) **(1)** A claim of the United States Government shall be paid first when—

(A) a person indebted to the Government is insolvent and—

(i) the debtor without enough property to pay all debts makes a voluntary assignment of property;

(ii) property of the debtor, if absent, is attached; or

(iii) an act of bankruptcy is committed; or

(B) the estate of a deceased debtor, in the custody of the executor or administrator, is not enough to pay all debts of the debtor.

(2) This subsection does not apply to a case under title 11.

(b) A representative of a person or an estate (except a trustee acting under title 11) paying any part of a debt of the person or estate before paying a claim of the Government is liable to the extent of the payment for unpaid claims of the Government.

[*As amended by* Pub. L. No. 97–258, 96 Stat. 970 (1982)]

* * *

31 U.S.C. § 3716. Administrative offset

(a) After trying to collect a claim from a person under section 3711(a) of this title, the head of an executive, judicial, or legislative agency may collect the claim by administrative offset. The head of the agency may collect by administrative offset only after giving the debtor—

(1) written notice of the type and amount of the claim, the intention of the head of the agency to collect the claim by administrative offset, and an explanation of the rights of the debtor under this section;

(2) an opportunity to inspect and copy the records of the agency related to the claim;

(3) an opportunity for a review within the agency of the decision of the agency related to the claim; and

(4) an opportunity to make a written agreement with the head of the agency to repay the amount of the claim.

(b) Before collecting a claim by administrative offset, the head of an executive, judicial, or legislative agency must either—

(1) adopt, without change, regulations on collecting by administrative offset promulgated by the Department of Justice, the Government Accountability Office, or the Department of the Treasury; or

(2) prescribe regulations on collecting by administrative offset consistent with the regulations referred to in paragraph (1).

(c) **(1)** **(A)** Except as otherwise provided in this subsection, a disbursing official of the Department of the Treasury, the Department of Defense, the United States Postal Service, the Department of Health and Human Services, or any other government corporation, or any disbursing official of the United States designated by the Secretary of the Treasury, shall offset at least annually the amount of a payment which a payment certifying agency has certified to the disbursing official for disbursement, by an amount equal to the amount of a claim which a creditor agency has certified to the Secretary of the Treasury pursuant to this subsection.

(B) An agency that designates disbursing officials pursuant to section 3321(c) of this title is not required to certify claims arising out of its operations to the Secretary of the Treasury before such agency's disbursing officials offset such claims.

(C) Payments certified by the Department of Education under a program administered by the Secretary of Education under title IV of the Higher Education Act of 1965 shall not be subject to administrative offset under this subsection.

(2) Neither the disbursing official nor the payment certifying agency shall be liable—

(A) for the amount of the administrative offset on the basis that the underlying obligation, represented by the payment before the administrative offset was taken, was not satisfied; or

(B) for failure to provide timely notice under paragraph (8).

(3) **(A)** **(i)** Notwithstanding any other provision of law (including sections 207 and 1631(d)(1) of the Social Security Act (42 U.S.C. 407 and 1383(d)(1)), section 413(b) of Public Law 91–173 (30 U.S.C. 923(b)), and section 14 of the Act of August 29, 1935 (45 U.S.C. 231m)), except as provided in clause (ii), all payments due to an individual under—

(I) the Social Security Act,

(II) part B of the Black Lung Benefits Act, or

(III) any law administered by the Railroad Retirement Board (other than payments that such Board determines to be tier 2 benefits),

shall be subject to offset under this section.

(ii) An amount of $9,000 which a debtor may receive under Federal benefit programs cited under clause (i) within a 12-month period shall be exempt from offset under this subsection. In applying the $9,000 exemption, the disbursing official shall—

(I) reduce the $9,000 exemption amount for the 12-month period by the amount of all Federal benefit payments made during such 12-month period which are not subject to offset under this subsection; and

(II) apply a prorated amount of the exemption to each periodic benefit payment to be made to the debtor during the applicable 12-month period.

For purposes of the preceding sentence, the amount of a periodic benefit payment shall be the amount after any reduction or deduction required under the laws authorizing the program under which such payment is authorized to be made (including any reduction or deduction to recover any overpayment under such program).

(B) The Secretary of the Treasury shall exempt from administrative offset under this subsection payments under means-tested programs when requested by the head of the respective agency. The Secretary may exempt other payments from administrative offset under this subsection upon the written request of the head of a payment certifying agency. A written request for exemption of other payments must provide justification for the exemption under standards prescribed by the Secretary. Such standards shall give due consideration to whether administrative offset would tend to interfere substantially with or defeat the purposes of the payment certifying agency's program. The Secretary shall report to the Congress annually on exemptions granted under this section.

(C) The provisions of sections 205(b)(1), 809(a)(1), and 1631(c)(1) of the Social Security Act shall not apply to any administrative offset executed pursuant to this section against benefits authorized by title II, VIII, or title XVI of the Social Security Act, respectively.

(D) This section shall apply to payments made after the date which is 90 days after the enactment of this subparagraph (or such earlier date as designated by the Secretary of Health and Human Services) with respect to claims or debts, and to amounts payable, under title XVIII of the Social Security Act.

(4) The Secretary of the Treasury may charge a fee sufficient to cover the full cost of implementing this subsection. The fee may be collected either by the retention of a portion of amounts collected pursuant to this subsection, or by billing the agency referring or transferring a claim for those amounts. Fees charged to the agencies shall be based on actual administrative offsets completed. Amounts received by the United States as fees under this subsection shall be deposited into the account of the Department of the Treasury under section 3711(g)(7) of this title, and shall be collected and accounted for in accordance with the provisions of that section.

(5) The Secretary of the Treasury in consultation with the Commissioner of Social Security and the Director of the Office of Management and Budget, may prescribe such rules, regulations, and procedures as the Secretary of the Treasury considers necessary to carry out this subsection. The Secretary shall consult with the heads of affected agencies in the development of such rules, regulations, and procedures.

(6) Any Federal agency that is owed by a person a past due, legally enforceable nontax debt that is over 180 days delinquent, including nontax debt administered by a third party acting as an agent for the Federal Government, shall notify the Secretary of the Treasury of all such nontax debts for purposes of administrative offset under this subsection.

(7) **(A)** The disbursing official conducting an administrative offset with respect to a payment to a payee shall notify the payee in writing of—

(i) the occurrence of the administrative offset to satisfy a past due legally enforceable debt, including a description of the type and amount of the payment otherwise payable to the payee against which the offset was executed;

(ii) the identity of the creditor agency requesting the offset; and

(iii) a contact point within the creditor agency that will handle concerns regarding the offset.

(B) If the payment to be offset is a periodic benefit payment, the disbursing official shall take reasonable steps, as determined by the Secretary of the Treasury, to provide the notice to the payee not later than the date on which the payee is otherwise scheduled to receive the payment, or as soon as practical thereafter, but no later than the date of the administrative offset. Notwithstanding the preceding sentence, the failure of the debtor to receive such notice shall not impair the legality of such administrative offset.

(8) A levy pursuant to the Internal Revenue Code of 1986 shall take precedence over requests for administrative offset pursuant to other laws.

(d) Nothing in this section is intended to prohibit the use of any other administrative offset authority existing under statute or common law.

(e) **(1)** Notwithstanding any other provision of law, regulation, or administrative limitation, no limitation on the period within which an offset may be initiated or taken pursuant to this section shall be effective.

(2) This section does not apply when a statute explicitly prohibits using administrative offset or setoff to collect the claim or type of claim involved.

(f) The Secretary may waive the requirements of sections 552a(o) and (p) of title 5 for administrative offset or claims collection upon written certification by the head of a State or an executive, judicial, or legislative agency seeking to collect the claim that the requirements of subsection (a) of this section have been met.

(g) The Data Integrity Board of the Department of the Treasury established under 552a(u) of title 5 shall review and include in reports under paragraph (3)(D) of that section a description of any matching activities conducted under this section. If the Secretary has granted a waiver under subsection (f) of this section, no other Data Integrity Board is required to take any action under section 552a(u) of title 5.

(h) **(1)** The Secretary may, in the discretion of the Secretary, apply subsection (a) with respect to any past-due, legally-enforceable debt owed to a State if—

(A) the appropriate State disbursing official requests that an offset be performed; and

(B) a reciprocal agreement with the State is in effect which contains, at a minimum—

(i) requirements substantially equivalent to subsection (b) of this section; and

(ii) any other requirements which the Secretary considers appropriate to facilitate the offset and prevent duplicative efforts.

(2) This subsection does not apply to—

(A) the collection of a debt or claim on which the administrative costs associated with the collection of the debt or claim exceed the amount of the debt or claim;

(B) any collection of any other type, class, or amount of claim, as the Secretary considers necessary to protect the interest of the United States; or

(C) the disbursement of any class or type of payment exempted by the Secretary of the Treasury at the request of a Federal agency.

(3) In applying this section with respect to any debt owed to a State, subsection (c)(3)(A) shall not apply.

[*As added by* Pub. L. No. 97–452, 96 Stat. 2471 (1983), *and amended by* Pub. L. No. 104–134, 110 Stat. 1321–359 (1996); Pub. L. No. 106–169, 113 Stat. 1856 (1999); Pub. L. No. 108–271, 118 Stat. 814 (2004); Pub. L. No. 110–234, 122 Stat. 1482 (2008); Pub. L. No. 110–246, 122 Stat. 2244 (2008); Pub. L. No. 110–275, 122 Stat. 2590 (2008)]

31 U.S.C. § 3717. Interest and penalty on claims

(a) **(1)** The head of an executive, judicial, or legislative agency shall charge a minimum annual rate of interest on an outstanding debt on a United States Government claim owed by a person that is equal to the average investment rate for the Treasury tax and loan accounts for the 12-month period ending on September 30 of each year, rounded to the nearest whole percentage point. The Secretary of the Treasury shall publish the rate before November 1 of that year. The rate is effective on the first day of the next calendar quarter.

(2) The Secretary may change the rate of interest for a calendar quarter if the average investment rate for the 12-month period ending at the close of the prior calendar quarter, rounded to the nearest whole percentage point, is more or less than the existing published rate by 2 percentage points.

(b) Interest under subsection (a) of this section accrues from the date—

(1) on which notice is mailed after October 25, 1982, if notice was first mailed before October 25, 1982; or

(2) notice of the amount due is first mailed to the debtor at the most current address of the debtor available to the head of the executive or legislative agency, if notice is first mailed after October 24, 1982.

(c) The rate of interest charged under subsection (a) of this section—

(1) is the rate in effect on the date from which interest begins to accrue under subsection (b) of this section; and

(2) remains fixed at that rate for the duration of the indebtedness.

(d) Interest under subsection (a) of this section may not be charged if the amount due on the claim is paid within 30 days after the date from which interest accrues under subsection (b) of this section. The head of an executive, judicial, or legislative agency may extend the 30-day period.

(e) The head of an executive, judicial, or legislative agency shall assess on a claim owed by a person—

(1) a charge to cover the cost of processing and handling a delinquent claim; and

(2) a penalty charge of not more than 6 percent a year for failure to pay a part of a debt more than 90 days past due.

(f) Interest under subsection (a) of this section does not accrue on a charge assessed under subsection (e) of this section.

(g) This section does not apply—

(1) if a statute, regulation required by statute, loan agreement, or contract prohibits charging interest or assessing charges or explicitly fixes the interest or charges; and

(2) to a claim under a contract executed before October 25, 1982, that is in effect on October 25, 1982.

(h) In conformity with standards prescribed jointly by the Attorney General, the Secretary of the Treasury, and the Comptroller General, the head of an executive, judicial, or legislative agency may prescribe regulations identifying circumstances appropriate to waiving collection of interest and charges under subsections (a) and (e) of this section. A waiver under the regulations is deemed to be compliance with this section.

(i) **(1)** The head of an executive, judicial, or legislative agency may increase an administrative claim by the cost of living adjustment in lieu of charging interest and penalties under this section. Adjustments under this subsection will be computed annually.

(2) For the purpose of this subsection—

(A) the term "cost of living adjustment" means the percentage by which the Consumer Price Index for the month of June of the calendar year preceding the adjustment exceeds the Consumer Price Index for the month of June of the calendar year in which the claim was determined or last adjusted; and

(B) the term "administrative claim" includes all debt that is not based on an extension of Government credit through direct loans, loan guarantees, or insurance, including fines, penalties, and overpayments.

[*As added by* Pub. L. No. 97–452, 96 Stat. 2472 (1983), *and amended by* Pub. L. No. 104–134, 110 Stat. 1321–359 (1996)]

31 U.S.C. § 3718. Contracts for collection services

(a) Under conditions the head of an executive, judicial, or legislative agency considers appropriate, the head of the agency may enter into a contract with a person for collection service to recover indebtedness owed, or to locate or recover assets of, the United States Government. The head of an agency may not enter into a contract under the preceding sentence to locate or recover assets of the United States held by a State government or financial institution unless that agency has established procedures approved by the Secretary of the Treasury to identify and recover such assets. The contract shall provide that—

(1) the head of the agency retains the authority to resolve a dispute, compromise a claim, end collection action, and refer a matter to the Attorney General to bring a civil action; and

(2) the person is subject to—

(A) section 552a of title 5, to the extent provided in section 552a(m); and

(B) laws and regulations of the United States Government and State governments related to debt collection practices.

(b) (1) (A) The Attorney General may make contracts retaining private counsel to furnish legal services, including representation in negotiation, compromise, settlement, and litigation, in the case of any claim of indebtedness owed the United States. Each such contract shall include such terms and conditions as the Attorney General considers necessary and appropriate, including a provision specifying the amount of the fee to be paid to the private counsel under such contract or the method for calculating that fee. The amount of the fee payable for legal services furnished under any such contract may not exceed the fee that counsel engaged in the private practice of law in the area or areas where the legal services are furnished typically charge clients for furnishing legal services in the collection of claims of indebtedness, as determined by the Attorney General, considering the amount, age, and nature of the indebtedness and whether the debtor is an individual or a business entity. Nothing in this subparagraph shall relieve the Attorney General of the competition requirements set forth in division C (except sections 3302, 3501(b), 3509, 3906, 4710, and 4711) of subtitle I of title 41.

(B) The Attorney General shall use his best efforts to enter into contracts under this paragraph with law firms owned and controlled by socially and economically disadvantaged individuals and law firms that are qualified HUBZone small business concerns (as defined in section 3(p) of the Small Business Act), so as to enable each agency to comply with paragraph (3).

(2) The head of an executive, judicial, or legislative agency may, subject to the approval of the Attorney General, refer to a private counsel retained under paragraph (1) of this subsection claims of indebtedness owed the United States arising out of activities of that agency.

(3) Each agency shall use its best efforts to assure that not less than 10 percent of the amounts of all claims referred to private counsel by that agency under paragraph (2) are referred to law firms owned and controlled by socially and economically disadvantaged individuals and law firms that are qualified HUBZone small business concerns. For purposes of this paragraph—

(A) the term "law firm owned and controlled by socially and economically disadvantaged individuals" means a law firm that meets the requirements set forth in clauses (i) and (ii) of section 8(d)(3)(C) of the Small Business Act (15 U.S.C. 637(d)(3)(C)(i) and (ii)) and regulations issued under those clauses;

(B) "socially and economically disadvantaged individuals" shall be presumed to include these groups and individuals described in the last paragraph of section 8(d)(3)(C) of the Small Business Act; and

(C) the term "qualified HUBZone small business concern" has the meaning given that term in section 3(p) of the Small Business Act.

(4) Notwithstanding sections 516, 518(b), 519, and 547(2) of title 28, a private counsel retained under paragraph (1) of this subsection may represent the United States in litigation in connection with legal services furnished pursuant to the contract entered into with that counsel under paragraph (1) of this subsection.

(5) A contract made with a private counsel under paragraph (1) of this subsection shall include—

(A) a provision permitting the Attorney General to terminate either the contract or the private counsel's representation of the United States in particular cases if the Attorney General finds that such action is for the convenience of the Government;

(B) a provision stating that the head of the executive or legislative agency which refers a claim under the contract retains the authority to resolve a dispute regarding the claim, to compromise the claim, or to terminate a collection action on the claim; and

(C) a provision requiring the private counsel to transmit monthly to the Attorney General and the head of the executive or legislative agency referring a claim under the contract a report on the services relating to the claim rendered under the contract during the month and the progress made during the month in collecting the claim under the contract.

(6) Notwithstanding the fourth sentence of section 803(6) of the Fair Debt Collection Practices Act (15 U.S.C. 1692a(6)), a private counsel performing legal services pursuant to a contract made under paragraph (1) of this subsection shall be considered to be a debt collector for the purposes of such Act.

(7) Any counterclaim filed in any action to recover indebtedness owed the United States which is brought on behalf of the United States by private counsel retained under this subsection may not be asserted unless the counterclaim is served directly on the Attorney General or the United States Attorney for the judicial district in which, or embracing the place in which, the action is brought. Such service shall be made in accordance with the rules of procedure of the court in which the action is brought.

(c) The Attorney General shall transmit to the Congress an annual report on the activities of the Department of Justice to recover indebtedness owed the United States which was referred to the Department of Justice for collection. Each such report shall include a list, by agency, of—

(1) the total number and amounts of claims which were referred for legal services to the Department of Justice and to private counsel under subsection (b) during the 1-year period covered by the report;

(2) the total number and amount of those claims referred for legal services to the Department of Justice which were collected or were not collected or otherwise resolved during the 1-year period covered by the report; and

(3) the total number and amount of those claims referred for legal services to private counsel under subsection (b)—

(A) which were collected or were not collected or otherwise resolved during the 1-year period covered by the report;

(B) which were not collected or otherwise resolved under a contract terminated by the Attorney General during the 1-year period covered by the report; and

(C) on which the Attorney General terminated the private counsel's representation during the 1-year period covered by the report without terminating the contract with the private counsel under which the claims were referred.

(d) Notwithstanding section 3302(b) of this title, a contract under subsection (a) or (b) of this section may provide that a fee a person charges to recover indebtedness owed, or to locate or recover assets of, the United States Government is payable from the amount recovered.

(e) A contract under subsection (a) or (b) of this section is effective only to the extent and in the amount provided in an appropriation law. This limitation does not apply in the case of a contract that authorizes a person to collect a fee as provided in subsection (d) of this section.

(f) This section does not apply to the collection of debts under the Internal Revenue Code of 1986 (26 U.S.C. 1 *et seq.*).

(g) In order to assist Congress in determining whether use of private counsel is a cost-effective method of collecting Government debts, the Attorney General shall, following consultation with the Government Accountability Office, maintain and make available to the Inspector General of the Department of Justice, statistical data relating to the comparative costs of debt collection by participating United States Attorneys' Offices and by private counsel.

[*As added by* Pub. L. No. 97–452, 96 Stat. 2472 (9183), *and amended by* Pub. L. No. 98–167, 97 Stat. 1104 (1983); Pub. L. No. 99–514, 100 Stat. 2095 (1986); Pub. L. No. 99–578, 100 Stat. 3305 (1986); Pub. L. No. 102–589, 106 Stat. 5135 (1992); Pub. L. No. 103–272, 108 Stat. 1362 (1994); Pub. L. No. 104–134, 110 Stat. 1321–359 (1996); Pub. L. No. 105–135, 111 Stat. 2633 (1997); Pub. L. No. 108–271, 118 Stat. 814 (2004); Pub. L. No. 111–350; 124 Stat. 3849 (2011)]

31 U.S.C. § 3719. Reports on debt collection activities

(a) In consultation with the Comptroller General of the United States, the Secretary of the Treasury shall prescribe regulations requiring the head of each agency with outstanding nontax claims to prepare and submit to the Secretary at least once each year a report summarizing the status of loans and accounts receivable that are managed by the head of the agency. The report shall contain—

(1) information on—

(A) the total amount of loans and accounts receivable owed the agency and when amounts owed the agency are due to be repaid;

(B) the total amount of receivables and number of claims at least 30 days past due;

(C) the total amount written off as actually uncollectible and the total amount allowed for uncollectible loans and accounts receivable;

(D) the rate of interest charged for overdue debts and the amount of interest charged and collected on debts;

(E) the total number of claims and the total amount collected; and

(F) the number and total amount of claims referred to the Attorney General for settlement and the number and total amount of claims the Attorney General settles;

(2) the information described in clause (1) of this subsection for each program or activity the head of the agency carries out; and

(3) other information the Secretary considers necessary to decide whether the head of the agency is acting aggressively to collect the claims of the agency.

(b) The Secretary shall analyze the reports submitted under subsection (a) of this section and shall report annually to Congress on the management of debt collection activities by the head of each agency, including the information provided the Secretary under subsection (a).

[*As added by* Pub. L. No. 97–452, 96 Stat. 2472 (9183), *and amended by* Pub. L. No. 104–134, 110 Stat. 1321–380 (1996)]

31 U.S.C. § 3720. Collection of payments

(a) Each head of an executive agency (other than an agency subject to section 9 of the Act of May 18, 1933 (48 Stat. 63, chapter 32; 16 U.S.C. 831h)) shall, under such regulations as the Secretary of the Treasury shall prescribe, provide for the timely deposit of money by officials and agents of such agency in accordance with section 3302, and for the collection and timely deposit of sums owed to such agency by the use of such procedures as withdrawals and deposits by electronic transfer of funds, automatic withdrawals from accounts at financial institutions, and a system under which financial institutions receive and deposit, on behalf of the executive agency, payments transmitted to post office lockboxes. The Secretary is authorized to collect from any agency not complying with the requirements imposed pursuant to the preceding sentence a charge in an amount the Secretary determines to be the cost to the general fund caused by such noncompliance.

(b) The head of an executive agency shall pay to the Secretary of the Treasury charges imposed pursuant to subsection (a). Payments shall be made out of amounts appropriated or otherwise made available to carry out the program to which the collections relate. The amounts of the charges paid under this subsection shall be deposited in the Cash Management Improvements Fund established by subsection (c).

(c) There is established in the Treasury of the United States a revolving fund to be known as the "Cash Management Improvements Fund". Sums in the fund shall be available without fiscal year limitation for the payment of expenses incurred in developing the methods of collection and deposit described in subsection (a) of this section and the expenses incurred in carrying out collections and deposits using such methods, including the costs of personal services and the costs of the lease or purchase of equipment and operating facilities.

[*As added by* Pub. L. No. 98–369, 98 Stat. 1152 (1984)]

31 U.S.C. § 3720A. Reduction of tax refund by amount of debt

(a) Any Federal agency that is owed by a person a past-due, legally enforceable debt (including debt administered by a third party acting as an agent for the Federal Government) shall, and any agency subject to section 9 of the Act of May 18, 1933 (16 U.S.C. 831h), owed such a debt may, in accordance with regulations issued pursuant to subsections (b) and (d), notify the Secretary of the Treasury at least once each year of the amount of such debt.

(b) No Federal agency may take action pursuant to subsection (a) with respect to any debt until such agency—

(1) notifies the person incurring such debt that such agency proposes to take action pursuant to such paragraph with respect to such debt;

(2) gives such person at least 60 days to present evidence that all or part of such debt is not past-due or not legally enforceable;

(3) considers any evidence presented by such person and determines that an amount of such debt is past due and legally enforceable;

(4) satisfies such other conditions as the Secretary may prescribe to ensure that the determination made under paragraph (3) with respect to such debt is valid and that the agency has made reasonable efforts (determined on a government-wide basis) to obtain payment of such debt; and

(5) certifies that reasonable efforts have been made by the agency (pursuant to regulations) to obtain payment of such debt.

(c) Upon receiving notice from any Federal agency that a named person owes to such agency a past-due legally enforceable debt, the Secretary of the Treasury shall determine whether any amounts, as refunds of Federal taxes paid, are payable to such person. If the Secretary of the Treasury finds that any such amount is payable, he shall reduce such refunds by an amount equal to the amount of such debt, pay the amount of such reduction to such agency, and notify such agency of the individual's home address.

(d) The Secretary of the Treasury shall issue regulations prescribing the time or times at which agencies must submit notices of past-due legally enforceable debts, the manner in which such notices must be submitted, and the necessary information that must be contained in or accompany the notices. The regulations shall specify the minimum amount of debt to which the reduction procedure established by subsection (c) may be applied and the fee that an agency must pay to reimburse the Secretary of the Treasury for the full cost of applying such procedure. Any fee paid to the Secretary pursuant to the preceding sentence may be used to reimburse appropriations which bore all or part of the cost of applying such procedure.

(e) Any Federal agency receiving notice from the Secretary of the Treasury that an erroneous payment has been made to such agency under subsection (c) shall pay promptly to the Secretary, in accordance with such regulations as the Secretary may prescribe, an amount equal to the amount of such erroneous payment (without regard to whether any other amounts payable to such agency under such subsection have been paid to such agency).

(f) **(1)** Subsection (a) shall apply with respect to an OASDI overpayment made to any individual only if such individual is not currently entitled to monthly insurance benefits under title II of the Social Security Act.

(2) **(A)** The requirements of subsection (b) shall not be treated as met in the case of the recovery of an OASDI overpayment from any individual under this section unless the notification under subsection (b)(1) describes the conditions under which the Commissioner of Social Security is required to waive recovery of an overpayment, as provided under section 204(b) of the Social Security Act.

(B) In any case in which an individual files for a waiver under section 204(b) of the Social Security Act within the 60-day period referred to in subsection (b)(2), the Commissioner of Social Security shall not certify to the Secretary of the Treasury that the debt is valid under subsection (b)(4) before rendering a decision on the waiver request under such section 204(b). In lieu of payment, pursuant to subsection (c), to the Commissioner of Social Security of the amount of any reduction under this subsection based on an OASDI overpayment, the Secretary of the Treasury shall deposit such amount in the Federal Old-Age and Survivors Insurance Trust Fund or the Federal Disability Insurance Trust Fund, whichever is certified to the Secretary of the Treasury as appropriate by the Commissioner of Social Security.

(g) In the case of refunds of business associations, this section shall apply only to refunds payable on or after January 1, 1995. In the case of refunds of individuals who owe debts to Federal agencies that have not participated in the Federal tax refund offset program prior to the date of enactment of this subsection, this section shall apply only to refunds payable on or after January 1, 1994.

(h)(1)[1] The disbursing official of the Department of the Treasury—

(1) shall notify a taxpayer in writing of—

(A) the occurrence of an offset to satisfy a past-due legally enforceable nontax debt;

(B) the identity of the creditor agency requesting the offset; and

(C) a contact point within the creditor agency that will handle concerns regarding the offset;

(2) shall notify the Internal Revenue Service on a weekly basis of—

(A) the occurrence of an offset to satisfy a past-due legally enforceable non-tax debt;

(B) the amount of such offset; and

(C) any other information required by regulations; and

(3) shall match payment records with requests for offset by using a name control, taxpayer identifying number (as that term is used in section 6109 of the Internal Revenue Code of 1986), and any other necessary identifiers.

(h)(2)[2] The term "disbursing official" of the Department of the Treasury means the Secretary or his designee.

(i) An agency subject to section 9 of the Act of May 18, 1933 (16 U.S.C. 831h), may implement this section at its discretion.

[*As added by* Pub. L. No. 98–369, 98 Stat. 1153 (1984), *and amended by* Pub. L. No. 101–508, 104 Stat. 1388–287 (1990); Pub. L. No. 102–589, 106 Stat. 5133 (1992); Pub. L. No. 103–296, 108 Stat. 1488 (1994); Pub. L. No. 104–134, 110 Stat. 1321–375 (1996)]

31 U.S.C. § 3720B. Barring delinquent Federal debtors from obtaining Federal loans or loan insurance guarantees

(a) Unless this subsection is waived by the head of a Federal agency, a person may not obtain any Federal financial assistance in the form of a loan (other than a disaster loan or a marketing assistance loan or loan deficiency payment under subtitle C of the Agricultural Market Transition Act (7 U.S.C. 7231 *et seq.*)) or loan insurance or guarantee administered by the agency if the person has an outstanding debt (other than a debt under the Internal Revenue Code of 1986) with any Federal agency which is in a delinquent status, as determined under standards prescribed by the Secretary of the Treasury. Such a person may obtain additional loans or loan guarantees only after such delinquency is resolved in accordance with those standards. The Secretary of the Treasury may exempt, at the request of an agency, any class of claims.

(b) The head of a Federal agency may delegate the waiver authority under subsection (a) to the Chief Financial Officer of the agency. The waiver authority may be redelegated only to the Deputy Chief Financial Officer of the agency.

[*As added by* Pub. L. No. 104–134, 110 Stat. 1321–365 (1996), *and amended by* Pub. L. No. 106–387, 114 Stat. 1549 (2000)]

* * *

31 U.S.C. § 3720D. Garnishment

(a) Notwithstanding any provision of State law, the head of an executive, judicial, or legislative agency that administers a program that gives rise to a delinquent nontax debt owed to the United States by an individual may in accordance with this section garnish the disposable pay of the individual to collect the amount owed, if the individual is not currently making required repayment in accordance with any agreement between the agency head and the individual.

(b) In carrying out any garnishment of disposable pay of an individual under subsection (a), the head of an executive, judicial, or legislative agency shall comply with the following requirements:

(1) The amount deducted under this section for any pay period may not exceed 15 percent of disposable pay, except that a greater percentage may be deducted with the written consent of the individual.

(2) The individual shall be provided written notice, sent by mail to the individual's last known address, a minimum of 30 days prior to the initiation of proceedings, from the head of the executive, judicial, or legislative agency, informing the individual of—

(A) the nature and amount of the debt to be collected;

(B) the intention of the agency to initiate proceedings to collect the debt through deductions from pay; and

(C) an explanation of the rights of the individual under this section.

(3) The individual shall be provided an opportunity to inspect and copy records relating to the debt.

1. So in original

2. So in original

(4) The individual shall be provided an opportunity to enter into a written agreement with the executive, judicial, or legislative agency, under terms agreeable to the head of the agency, to establish a schedule for repayment of the debt.

(5) The individual shall be provided an opportunity for a hearing in accordance with subsection (c) on the determination of the head of the executive, judicial, or legislative agency concerning—

(A) the existence or the amount of the debt, and

(B) in the case of an individual whose repayment schedule is established other than by a written agreement pursuant to paragraph (4), the terms of the repayment schedule.

(6) If the individual has been reemployed within 12 months after having been involuntarily separated from employment, no amount may be deducted from the disposable pay of the individual until the individual has been reemployed continuously for at least 12 months.

(c) **(1)** A hearing under subsection (b)(5) shall be provided prior to issuance of a garnishment order if the individual, on or before the 15th day following the mailing of the notice described in subsection (b)(2), and in accordance with such procedures as the head of the executive, judicial, or legislative agency may prescribe, files a petition requesting such a hearing.

(2) If the individual does not file a petition requesting a hearing prior to such date, the head of the agency shall provide the individual a hearing under subsection (a)(5) upon request, but such hearing need not be provided prior to issuance of a garnishment order.

(3) The hearing official shall issue a final decision at the earliest practicable date, but not later than 60 days after the filing of the petition requesting the hearing.

(d) The notice to the employer of the withholding order shall contain only such information as may be necessary for the employer to comply with the withholding order.

(e) **(1)** An employer may not discharge from employment, refuse to employ, or take disciplinary action against an individual subject to wage withholding in accordance with this section by reason of the fact that the individual's wages have been subject to garnishment under this section, and such individual may sue in a State or Federal court of competent jurisdiction any employer who takes such action.

(2) The court shall award attorneys' fees to a prevailing employee and, in its discretion, may order reinstatement of the individual, award punitive damages and back pay to the employee, or order such other remedy as may be reasonably necessary.

(f) **(1)** The employer of an individual—

(A) shall pay to the head of an executive, judicial, or legislative agency as directed in a withholding order issued in an action under this section with respect to the individual, and

(B) shall be liable for any amount that the employer fails to withhold from wages due an employee following receipt by such employer of notice of the withholding order, plus attorneys' fees, costs, and, in the court's discretion, punitive damages.

(2) **(A)** The head of an executive, judicial, or legislative agency may sue an employer in a State or Federal court of competent jurisdiction to recover amounts for which the employer is liable under paragraph (1)(B).

(B) A suit under this paragraph may not be filed before the termination of the collection action, unless earlier filing is necessary to avoid expiration of any applicable statute of limitations period.

(3) Notwithstanding paragraphs (1) and (2), an employer shall not be required to vary its normal pay and disbursement cycles in order to comply with this subsection.

(g) For the purpose of this section, the term "disposable pay" means that part of the compensation of any individual from an employer remaining after the deduction of any amounts required by any other law to be withheld.

(h) The Secretary of the Treasury shall issue regulations to implement this section.

[*As added by* Pub. L. No. 104–134, 110 Stat. 1321–369 (1996)]

31 U.S.C. § 3720E. Dissemination of information regarding identity of delinquent debtors

(a) The head of any agency may, with the review of the Secretary of the Treasury, for the purpose of collecting any delinquent nontax debt owed by any person, publish or otherwise publicly disseminate information regarding the identity of the person and the existence of the nontax debt.

(b) **(1)** The Secretary of the Treasury, in consultation with the Director of the Office of Management and Budget and the heads of other appropriate Federal agencies, shall issue regulations establishing procedures and requirements the Secretary considers appropriate to carry out this section.

(2) Regulations under this subsection shall include—

(A) standards for disseminating information that maximize collections of delinquent nontax debts, by directing actions under this section toward delinquent debtors that have assets or income sufficient to pay their delinquent nontax debt;

(B) procedures and requirements that prevent dissemination of information under this section regarding persons who have not had an opportunity to verify, contest, and compromise their nontax debt in accordance with this subchapter; and

(C) procedures to ensure that persons are not incorrectly identified pursuant to this section.

[*As added by* Pub. L. No. 104–134, 110 Stat. 1321–372 (1996)]

* * *

B.2 Federal Employee Salary Offset Statute—5 U.S.C. § 5514

Title 5—Government Organization and Employees

Part III—Employees

Subpart D—Pay and Allowances

Chapter 55—Pay Administration

Subchapter II—Withholding Pay

* * *

5 U.S.C. § 5514. Installment deduction for indebtedness to the United States

(a) **(1)** When the head of an agency or his designee determines that an employee, member of the Armed Forces or Reserve of the Armed Forces, is indebted to the United States for debts to which the United States is entitled to be repaid at the time of the determination by the head of an agency or his designee, or is notified of such a debt by the head of another agency or his designee the amount of indebtedness may be collected in monthly installments, or at officially established pay intervals, by deduction from the current pay account of the individual. The deductions may be made from basic pay, special pay, incentive pay, retired pay, retainer pay, or, in the case of an individual not entitled to basic pay, other authorized pay. The amount deducted for any period may not exceed 15 percent of disposable pay, except that a greater percentage may be deducted upon the written consent of the individual involved. If the individual retires or resigns, or if his employment or period of active duty otherwise ends, before collection of the amount of the indebtedness is completed, deduction shall be made from subsequent payments of any nature due the individual from the agency concerned. All Federal agencies to which debts are owed and which have outstanding delinquent debts shall participate in a computer match at least annually of their delinquent debt records with records of Federal employees to identify those employees who are delinquent in repayment of those debts. The preceding sentence shall not apply to any debt under the Internal Revenue Code of 1986. Matched Federal employee records shall include, but shall not be limited to, records of active Civil Service employees government-wide, military active duty personnel, military reservists, United States Postal Service employees, employees of other government corporations, and seasonal and temporary employees. The Secretary of the Treasury shall establish and maintain an interagency consortium to implement centralized salary offset computer matching, and promulgate regulations for this program. Agencies that perform centralized salary offset computer matching services under this subsection are authorized to charge a fee sufficient to cover the full cost for such services.

(2) Except as provided in paragraph (3) of this subsection, prior to initiating any proceedings under paragraph (1) of this subsection to collect any indebtedness of an individual, the head of the agency holding the debt or his designee, shall provide the individual with—

(A) a minimum of thirty days written notice, informing such individual of the nature and amount of the indebtedness determined by such agency to be due, the intention of the agency to initiate proceedings to collect the debt through deductions from pay, and an explanation of the rights of the individual under this subsection;

(B) an opportunity to inspect and copy Government records relating to the debt;

(C) an opportunity to enter into a written agreement with the agency, under terms agreeable to the head of the agency or his designee, to establish a schedule for the repayment of the debt; and

(D) an opportunity for a hearing on the determination of the agency concerning the existence or the amount of the debt, and in the case of an individual whose repayment schedule is established other than by a written agreement pursuant to subparagraph (C), concerning the terms of the repayment schedule.

A hearing, described in subparagraph (D), shall be provided if the individual, on or before the fifteenth day following receipt of the notice described in subparagraph (A), and in accordance with such procedures as the head of the agency may prescribe, files a petition requesting such a hearing. The timely filing of a petition for hearing shall stay the commencement of collection proceedings. A hearing under subparagraph (D) may not be conducted by an individual under the supervision or control of the head of the agency, except that nothing in this sentence shall be construed to prohibit the appointment of an administrative law judge. The hearing official shall issue a final decision at the earliest practicable date, but not later than sixty days after the filing of the petition requesting the hearing.

(3) Paragraph (2) shall not apply to routine intra-agency adjustments of pay that are attributable to clerical or administrative errors or delays in processing pay documents that have occurred within the four pay periods preceding the adjustment and to any adjustment that amounts to $50 or less, if at the time of such adjustment, or as soon thereafter as practical, the individual is provided written notice of the nature and the amount of the adjustment and a point of contact for contesting such adjustment.

(4) The collection of any amount under this section shall be in accordance with the standards promulgated pursuant to sections 3711 and 3716–3718 of title 31 or in accordance with any other statutory authority for the collection of claims of the United States or any agency thereof.

(5) For purposes of this subsection—

(A) "disposable pay" means that part of pay of any individual remaining after the deduction from those earnings of any amounts required by law to be withheld; and

(B) "agency" includes executive departments and agencies, the United States Postal Service, the Postal Regulatory Commission, any nonappropriated fund instrumentality described in section 2105(c) of this title, the United States Senate, the United States House of Representatives, and any court, court administrative office, or instrumentality in the judicial or legislative branches of the Government, and government corporations.

(b) **(1)** The head of each agency shall prescribe regulations, subject to the approval of the President, to carry out this section and section 3530(d) of title 31. Regulations prescribed by the Secretaries of the military departments shall be uniform for the military services insofar as practicable.

(2) For purposes of section 7117(a) of this title, no regulation prescribed to carry out subsection (a)(2) of this section shall be considered to be a Government-wide rule or regulation.

(c) Subsection (a) of this section does not modify existing statutes which provide for forfeiture of pay or allowances. This section and section 3530(d) of title 31 do not repeal, modify, or amend section 4837(d) or 9837(d) of title 10 or section 1007(b), (c) of title 37.

(d) A levy pursuant to the Internal Revenue Code of 1986 shall take precedence over other deductions under this section.

(e) An employee of a nonappropriated fund instrumentality described in section 2105(c) of this title is deemed an employee covered by this section.

[*As enacted by* Pub. L. No. 89–554, 80 Stat. 477 (1966), *and amended by* Pub. L. No. 96–54, 93 Stat. 381 (1979); Pub. L. No. 97–258, 96 Stat. 1063 (1982); Pub. L. No. 97–365, 96 Stat. 1751 (1982); Pub. L. No. 97–452, 96 Stat. 2478 (1983); Pub. L. No. 98–216, 98 Stat. 6 (1984); Pub. L. No. 104–134, 110 Stat. 1321–363 (1996); Pub. L. No. 109–435, 120 Stat. 3241 (2006); Pub. L. No. 110–181, 122 Stat. 162 (2008)]

* * *

B.3 Selected Provisions of Federal Debt Collection Procedures Act

Title 28. Judiciary and Judicial Procedure

Part VI. Particular Proceedings

Chapter 176. Federal Debt Collection Procedure

Subchapter A. Definitions and General Provisions

28 U.S.C.

§ 3001. Applicability of chapter
§ 3002. Definitions
§ 3004. Service of process; enforcement; notice
§ 3010. Co-owned property

* * *

Subchapter C. Postjudgment Remedies

28 U.S.C. § 3001. Applicability of chapter

(a) In general.—Except as provided in subsection (b), the chapter provides the exclusive civil procedures for the United States—

(1) to recover a judgment on a debt; or

(2) to obtain, before judgment on a claim for a debt, a remedy in connection with such claim.

(b) Limitation.—To the extent that another Federal law specifies procedures for recovering on a claim or a judgment for a debt arising under such law, those procedures shall apply to such claim or judgment to the extent those procedures are inconsistent with this chapter.

(c) Amounts owing other than debts.—This chapter shall not apply with respect to an amount owing that is not a debt or to a claim for an amount owing that is not a debt.

[*Added by* Pub. L. No. 101–647, tit. XXXVI, § 3611, 104 Stat. 4933 (Nov. 29, 1990)]

28 U.S.C. § 3002. Definitions

As used in this chapter:

(1) "Counsel for the United States" means—

(A) a United States attorney, an assistant United States attorney designated to act on behalf of the United States attorney, or an attorney with the United States Department of Justice or with a Federal agency who has litigation authority; and

(B) any private attorney authorized by contract made in accordance with section 3718 of title 31 to conduct litigation for collection of debts on behalf of the United States.

(2) "Court" means any court created by the Congress of the United States, excluding the United States Tax Court.

(3) "Debt" means—

(A) an amount that is owing to the United States on account of a direct loan, or loan insured or guaranteed, by the United States; or

(B) an amount that is owing to the United States on account of a fee, duty, lease, rent, service, sale of real or personal property, overpayment, fine, assessment, penalty, restitution, damages, interest, tax, bail bond forfeiture, reimbursement, recovery of a cost incurred by the United States, or other source of indebtedness to the United States, but that is not owing under the terms of a contract originally entered into by only persons other than the United States;

and includes any amount owing to the United States for the benefit of an Indian tribe or individual Indian, but excludes any amount to which the United States is entitled under section 3011(a).

(4) "Debtor" means a person who is liable for a debt or against whom there is a claim for a debt.

(5) "Disposable earnings" means that part of earnings remaining after all deductions required by law have been withheld.

(6) "Earnings" means compensation paid or payable for personal services, whether denominated as wages, salary, commission, bonus, or otherwise, and includes periodic payments pursuant to a pension or retirement program.

(7) "Garnishee" means a person (other than the debtor) who has, or is reasonably thought to have, possession, custody, or control of any property in which the debtor has a substantial nonexempt interest, including any obligation due the debtor or to become due the debtor, and against whom a garnishment under section 3104 or 3205 is issued by a court.

(8) "Judgment" means a judgment, order, or decree entered in favor of the United States in a court and arising from a civil or criminal proceeding regarding a debt.

(9) "Nonexempt disposable earnings" means 25 percent of disposable earnings, subject to section 303 of the Consumer Credit Protection Act.

(10) "Person" includes a natural person (including an individual Indian), a corporation, a partnership, an unincorporated association, a trust, or an estate, or any other public or private entity, including a State or local government or an Indian tribe.

(11) "Prejudgment remedy" means the remedy of attachment, receivership, garnishment, or sequestration authorized by this chapter to be granted before judgment on the merits of a claim for a debt.

(12) "Property" includes any present or future interest, whether legal or equitable, in real, personal (including choses in action), or mixed property, tangible or intangible, vested or contingent, wherever located and however held (including community property and property held in trust (including spendthrift and pension trusts)), but excludes—

(A) property held in trust by the United States for the benefit of an Indian tribe or individual Indian; and

(B) Indian lands subject to restrictions against alienation imposed by the United States.

(13) "Security agreement" means an agreement that creates or provides for a lien.

(14) "State" means any of the several States, the District of Columbia, the Commonwealth of Puerto Rico, the Commonwealth of the Northern Marianas, or any territory or possession of the United States.

(15) "United States" means—

(A) a Federal corporation;

(B) an agency, department, commission, board, or other entity of the United States; or

(C) an instrumentality of the United States.

(16) "United States marshal" means a United States marshal, a deputy marshal, or an official of the United States Marshals Service designated under section 564.

[*Added by* Pub. L. No. 101–647, tit. XXXVI, § 3611, 104 Stat. 4933 (Nov. 29, 1990)]

* * *

28 U.S.C. § 3004. Service of process; enforcement; notice

(a) Manner of service.—A complaint, notice, writ, or other process required to be served in an action or proceeding under this chapter shall be served in accordance with the Federal Rules of Civil Procedure unless otherwise provided in this chapter.

(b) Nationwide enforcement.—

(1) Except as provided in paragraph (2)—

(A) any writ, order, judgment, or other process, including a summons and complaint, filed under this chapter may be served in any State; and

(B) such writ, order, or judgment may be enforced by the court issuing the writ, order, or process, regardless of where the person is served with the writ, order, or process.

(2) If the debtor so requests, within 20 days after receiving the notice described in section 3101(d) or 3202(b), the action or proceeding in which the writ, order, or judgment was issued shall be transferred to the district court for the district in which the debtor resides.

(c) Notice and other process.—At such time as counsel for the United States considers appropriate, but not later than the time a prejudgment or postjudgment remedy is put into effect under this chapter, counsel for the United States shall exercise reasonable diligence to serve on the debtor and any person who the United States believes, after exercising due diligence, has possession, custody, or control of the property, a copy of the application for such remedy, the order granting such remedy, and the notice required by section 3101(d) or 3202(b).

[*Added by* Pub. L. No. 101–647, tit. XXXVI, § 3611, 104 Stat. 4936 (Nov. 29, 1990)]

* * *

28 U.S.C. § 3010. Co-owned property

(a) Limitation.—The remedies available to the United States under this chapter may be enforced against property which is co-owned by a debtor and any other person only to the extent allowed by the law of the State where the property is located. This section shall not be construed to limit any right or interest of a debtor or co-owner in a retirement system for Federal military or civilian personnel established by the United States or any agency thereof or in a qualified retirement arrangement.

(b) Definitions.—For purposes of subsection (a)—

(1) the term "retirement system for Federal military or civilian personnel" means a pension or annuity system for Federal military or civilian personnel of more than one agency, or for some or all of such personnel of a single agency, established by statute or by regulation pursuant to statutory authority; and

(2) the term "qualified retirement arrangement" means a plan qualified under section 401(a), 403(a), or 409 of the Internal Revenue Code of 1986 or a plan that is subject to the requirements of section 205 of the Employee Retirement Income Security Act of 1974.

[*Added by* Pub. L. No. 101–647, tit. XXXVI, § 3611, 104 Stat. 4937 (Nov. 29, 1990)]

* * *

28 U.S.C. § 3013. Modification or protective order; supervision of enforcement

The court may at any time on its own initiative or the motion of any interested person, and after such notice as it may require, make an order denying, limiting, conditioning, regulating, extending, or modifying the use of any enforcement procedure under this chapter.

[*Added by* Pub. L. No. 101–647, tit. XXXVI, § 3611, 104 Stat. 4938 (Nov. 29, 1990)]

28 U.S.C. § 3014. Exempt property

(a) Election to exempt property.—An individual debtor may, in an action or proceeding under this chapter, elect to exempt property listed in either paragraph (1) or, in the alternative, paragraph (2). If such action or proceeding is against debtors who are husband and wife, one debtor may not elect to exempt property listed in paragraph (1) and the other debtor elect to exempt property listed in paragraph (2). If the debtors cannot agree on the alternative to be elected, they shall be deemed to elect paragraph (1). Such property is either—

(1) property that is specified in section 522(d) of title 11, as amended from time to time; or

(2) **(A)** any property that is exempt under Federal law, other than paragraph (1), or State or local law that is applicable on the date of the filing of the application for a remedy under this chapter at the place in which the debtor's domicile has been located for the 180 days immediately preceding the date of the filing of such application, or for a longer portion of such 180-day period than in any other place; and

(B) any interest in property in which the debtor had, immediately before the filing of such application, an interest as a tenant by the entirety or joint tenant, or an interest in a community estate, to the extent that such interest is exempt from process under applicable nonbankruptcy law.

(b) Effect on assertion and manner of determination.—

(1) Statement.—A court may order the debtor to file a statement with regard to any claimed exemption. A copy of such statement shall be served on counsel for the United States. Such statement shall be under oath and shall describe each item of property for which exemption is claimed, the value and the basis for such valuation, and the nature of the debtor's ownership interest.

(2) Hearing.—The United States or the debtor, by application to the court in which an action or proceeding under this chapter is pending, may request a hearing on the applicability of any exemption claimed by the debtor. The court shall determine the extent (if any) to which the exemption applies. Unless it is reasonably evident that the exemption applies, the debtor shall bear the burden of persuasion.

(3) Stay of disposition.—Assertion of an exemption shall prevent the United States from selling or otherwise disposing of the property for which such exemption is claimed until the court determines whether the debtor has a substantial nonexempt interest in such property. The United States may not take possession of, dispose of, sell, or otherwise interfere with the debtor's normal use and enjoyment of an interest in property the United States knows or has reason to know is exempt.

(c) Debtors in joint cases.—Subject to the limitation in subsection (a), this section shall apply separately with respect to each debtor in a joint case.

[*Added by* Pub. L. No. 101–647, tit. XXXVI, § 3611, 104 Stat. 4938 (Nov. 29, 1990)]

28 U.S.C. § 3015. Discovery as to debtor's financial condition

(a) In general.—Except as provided in subsection (b), in an action or proceeding under subchapter B or C, the United States may have discovery regarding the financial condition of the debtor in the manner in which discovery is authorized by the Federal Rules of Civil Procedure in an action on a claim for a debt.

(b) Limitation.—Subsection (a) shall not apply with respect to an action or proceeding under subchapter B unless there is a reasonable likelihood that the debt involved exceeds $50,000.

[*Added by* Pub. L. No. 101–647, tit. XXXVI, § 3611, 104 Stat. 4939 (Nov. 29, 1990)]

* * *

Subchapter C. Postjudgment Remedies

28 U.S.C. § 3201. Judgment liens

(a) Creation.—A judgment in a civil action shall create a lien on all real property of a judgment debtor on filing a certified copy of the abstract of the judgment in the manner in which a notice of tax lien would be filed under paragraphs (1) and (2) of section 6323(f) of the Internal Revenue Code of 1986. A lien created under this paragraph is for the amount necessary to satisfy the judgment, including costs and interest.

(b) Priority of lien.—A lien created under subsection (a) shall have priority over any other lien or encumbrance which is perfected later in time.

(c) Duration of lien; renewal.—

(1) Except as provided in paragraph (2), a lien created under subsection (a) is effective, unless satisfied, for a period of 20 years.

(2) Such lien may be renewed for one additional period of 20 years upon filing a notice of renewal in the same manner as the judgment is filed and shall relate back to the date the judgment is filed if—

(A) the notice of renewal is filed before the expiration of the 20-year period to prevent the expiration of the lien; and

(B) the court approves the renewal of such lien under this paragraph.

(d) Release of judgment lien.—A judgment lien shall be released on the filing of a satisfaction of judgment or release of lien in the same manner as the judgment is filed to obtain the lien.

(e) Effect of lien on eligibility for Federal grants, loans or programs.—A debtor who has a judgment lien against the debtor's property for a debt to the United States shall not be eligible to receive any grant or loan which is made, insured, guaranteed, or financed directly or indirectly by the United States or to receive funds directly from the Federal Government in any program, except funds to which the debtor is entitled as beneficiary, until the judgment is paid in full or otherwise satisfied. The agency of the United States that is responsible for such grants and loans may promulgate regulations to allow for waiver of this restriction on eligibility for such grants, loans, and funds.

(f) Sale of property subject to judgment lien.—

(1) On proper application to a court, the court may order the United States to sell, in accordance with sections 2001 and 2002, any real property subject to a judgment lien in effect under this section.

(2) This subsection shall not preclude the United States from using an execution sale pursuant to section 3203(g) to sell real property subject to a judgment lien.

[*Added by* Pub. L. No. 101–647, tit. XXXVI, § 3611, 104 Stat. 4948 (Nov. 29, 1990)]

28 U.S.C. § 3202. Enforcement of judgments

(a) Enforcement remedies.—A judgment may be enforced by any of the remedies set forth in this subchapter. A court may issue other writs pursuant to section 1651 of title 28, United States Code, as necessary to support such remedies, subject to rule 81(b) of the Federal Rules of Civil Procedure.

(b) Notice.—On the commencement by the United States of an action or proceeding under this subchapter to obtain a remedy, the counsel for the United States shall prepare, and clerk of the court shall issue, a notice in substantially the following form:

"NOTICE

"You are hereby notified that this [property] is being taken by the United States Government, which has a court judgment in [case docket number and jurisdiction of court] of $[amount] for [reason of debt].

"In addition, you are hereby notified that there are exemptions under the law which may protect some of this property from being taken by the United States Government if [name of judgment debtor] can show that the exemptions apply. Below is a summary of the major exemptions which apply in most situations in the State of [State where property is located]:

"[A statement summarizing in plain and understandable English the election available with respect to such State under section 3014 and the types of property that may be exempted under each of the alternatives specified in paragraphs (1) and (2) of section 3014(a) and a statement that different property may be so exempted with respect to the State in which the debtor resides.]

"If you are [name of judgment debtor], you have a right to ask the court to return your property to you if you think the property the Government is taking qualifies under one of the above exemptions [For a default judgment:] or if you think you do not owe the money to the United States Government that it says you do.

"If you want a hearing, you must notify the court within 20 days after you receive this notice. You must make your request in writing, and either mail it or deliver it in person to the clerk of the court at [address]. If you wish, you may use this notice to request the hearing by checking the box below and mailing this notice to the court clerk. You must also send a copy of your request to the Government at [address], so the Government will know you want a hearing. The hearing will take place within 5 days after the clerk receives your request, if you ask for it to take place that quickly, or as soon after that as possible.

"At the hearing you may explain to the judge why you believe the property the Government has taken is exempt [For a default judgment:] or why you think you do not owe the money to the Government. [For a writ of execution:] If you do not request a hearing within 20 days of receiving this notice, your [property] may be sold at public auction and the payment used toward the money you owe the Government.

"If you think you live outside the Federal judicial district in which the court is located, you may request, not later than 20 days after yourl receive this notice, that this proceeding to take your property be transferred by the court to the Federal judicial district in which you reside. You must make your request in writing, and either mail it or deliver it in person to the clerk of the court at [address]. You must also send a copy of your request to the Government at [address], so the Government will know you want the proceeding to be transferred.

"Be sure to keep a copy of this notice for your own records. If you have any questions about your rights or about this procedure, you should contact a lawyer, an office of public legal assistance, or the clerk of the court. The clerk is not permitted to give legal advice, but can refer you to other sources of information."

(c) Service.—A copy of the notice and a copy of the application for granting a remedy under this subchapter shall be served by counsel for the United States on the judgment debtor against whom such remedy is sought and on each person whom the United States, after diligent inquiry, has reasonable cause to believe has an interest in property to which the remedy is directed.

(d) Hearing.—By requesting, within 20 days after receiving the notice described in section 3202(b), the court to hold a hearing, the judgment debtor may move to quash the order granting such remedy. The court that issued such order shall hold a hearing on such motion as soon as practicable, or, if so requested by the judgment debtor, within 5 days after receiving the request or as soon thereafter as possible. The issues at such hearing shall be limited—

(1) to the probable validity of any claim of exemption by the judgment debtor;

(2) to compliance with any statutory requirement for the issuance of the postjudgment remedy granted; and

(3) if the judgment is by default and only to the extent that the Constitution or another law of the United States provides a right to a hearing on the issue, to—

(A) the probable validity of the claim for the debt which is merged in the judgment; and

(B) the existence of good cause for setting aside such judgment.

This subparagraph shall not be construed to afford the judgment debtor the right to more than one such hearing except to the extent that the Constitution or another law of the United States provides a right to more than one such hearing.

(e) Sale of property.—The property of a judgment debtor which is subject to sale to satisfy the judgment may be sold by judicial sale, pursuant to sections 2001, 2002, and 2004 or by execution sale pursuant to section 3203(g). If a hearing is requested pursuant to subsection (d), property with respect to which the request relates shall not be sold before such hearing.

[*Added by* Pub. L. No. 101–647, tit. XXXVI, § 3611, 104 Stat. 4949 (Nov. 29, 1990)]

28 U.S.C. § 3203. Execution

(a) Property subject to execution.—All property in which the judgment debtor has a substantial nonexempt interest shall be subject to levy pursuant to a writ of execution. The debtor's earnings shall not be subject to execution while in the possession, custody, or control of the debtor's employer. Co-owned property shall be subject to execution to the extent such property is subject to execution under the law of the State in which it is located.

(b) Creation of execution lien.—A lien shall be created in favor of the United States on all property levied on under a writ of execution and shall date from the time of the levy. Such lien shall have priority over all subsequent liens and shall be for the aggregate amount of the judgment, costs, and interest. The execution lien on any real property as to which the United States has a judgment lien shall relate back to the judgment lien date.

(c) Writ of execution.—

(1) Issuance.—On written application of counsel for the United States, the court may issue a writ of execution. Multiple writs may issue simultaneously, and successive writs may issue before the return date of a writ previously issued.

(2) Form of writ.—

(A) General contents.—A writ of execution shall specify the date that the judgment is entered, the court in which it is entered, the amount of the judgment if for money, the amount of the costs, the amount of interest due, the sum due as of the date the writ is issued, the rate of postjudgment interest, the name of the judgment debtor, and the judgment debtor's last known address.

(B) Additional contents.—

(i) Except as provided in clauses (ii) and (iii), the writ shall direct the United States marshal to satisfy the judgment by levying on and selling property in which the judgment debtor has a substantial nonexempt interest, but not to exceed property reasonably equivalent in value to the aggregate amount of the judgment, costs, and interest.

(ii) A writ of execution issued on a judgment for the delivery to the United States of the possession of personal property, or for the delivery of the possession of real property, shall particularly describe the property, and shall require the marshal to deliver the possession of the property to the United States.

(iii) A writ of execution on a judgment for the recovery of personal property or its value shall direct the marshal, in case a delivery of the specific property cannot be had, to levy and collect such value out of any property in which the judgment debtor has a substantial nonexempt interest.

(d) Levy of execution.—

(1) In general.—Levy on property pursuant to a writ of execution issued under this section shall be made in the same manner as levy on property is made pursuant to a writ of attachment issued under section 3102(d).

(2) Death of judgment debtor.—The death of the judgment debtor after a writ of execution is issued stays the execution proceedings, but any lien acquired by levy of the writ shall be recognized and enforced by the court for the district in which the estate of the deceased is located. The execution lien may be enforced—

(A) against the executor, administrator, or personal representative of the estate of the deceased; or

(B) if there be none, against the deceased's property coming to the heirs or devisees or at their option against cash in their possession, but only to the extent of the value of the property coming to them.

(3) Records of United States marshal.—

(A) A United States marshal receiving a writ of execution shall endorse thereon the exact hour and date of receipt.

(B) The United States marshal shall make a written record of every levy, specify the property on which levy is made, the date on which levy is made, and the marshal's costs, expenses, and fees.

(C) The United States marshal shall make a written return to the court on each writ of execution stating concisely what is done pursuant to the writ and shall deliver a copy to counsel for the United States who requests the writ. The writ shall be returned not more than—

(i) 90 days after the date of issuance if levy is not made; or

(ii) 10 days after the date of sale of property on which levy is made.

(e) Appointment of receiver.—Pending the levy of execution, the court may appoint a receiver to manage property described in such writ if there is a substantial danger that the property will be removed from the jurisdiction of the court, lost, materially injured or damaged, or mismanaged.

(f) Replevy; redemption.—

(1) Before execution sale.—

(A) Before execution sale, the United States marshal may return property1 to the judgment debtor any personal property taken in execution, on—

(i) satisfaction of the judgment, interest, and costs, and any costs incurred in connection with scheduling the sale; or

(ii) receipt from the judgment debtor of a bond—

(I) payable to the United States, with 2 or more good and sufficient sureties to be approved by the marshal, conditioned on the delivery of the property to the marshal at the time and place named in the bond to be sold under subsection (g); or

(II) for the payment to the marshal of a fair value thereof which shall be stated in the bond.

(B) A judgment debtor who sells or disposes of property replevied under subparagraph (A) shall pay the United States marshal the stipulated value of such property.

(C) If the judgment debtor fails to deliver such property to the United States marshal pursuant to the terms of the delivery described in subparagraph (A)(ii)(I) and fails to pay the United States marshal the stipulated value of such property, the United States marshal shall endorse the bond "forfeited" and return it to the court from which the writ of execution issued. If the judgment is not fully satisfied, the court shall issue a writ of execution against the judgment debtor and the sureties on the bond for the amount due, not exceeding the stipulated value of the property, on which execution no delivery bond shall be taken, which instruction shall be endorsed on the writ.

(2) After execution sale.—The judgment debtor shall not be entitled to redeem the property after the execution sale.

(g) Execution sale.—

(1) General procedures.—An execution sale under this section shall be conducted in a commercially reasonable manner—

(A) Sale of real property.—

(i) In general.—

(I) Except as provided in clause (ii), real property, or any interest therein, shall be sold, after the expiration of the 90-day period beginning on the date of levy under subsection (d), for cash at public auction at the courthouse of the county, parish, or city in which the greater part of the property is located or on the premises or some parcel thereof.

(II) The court may order the sale of any real property after the expiration of the 30-day period beginning on the date of levy under subsection (d) if the court determines that such property is likely to perish, waste, be destroyed, or otherwise substantially depreciate in value during the 90-day period beginning on the date of levy.

(III) The time and place of sale of real property, or any interest therein, under execution shall be advertised by the United States marshal, by publication of notice, once a week for at least 3 weeks prior to the sale, in at least one newspaper of general circulation in the county or parish where the property is located. The first publication shall appear not less than 25 days preceding the day of sale. The notice shall contain a statement of the authority by which the sale is to be made, the time of levy, the time and place of sale, and a brief description of the property to be sold, sufficient to identify the property (such as a street address for urban property and the survey identification and location for rural property), but it shall not be necessary for the notice to contain field notes. Such property shall be open for inspection and appraisal, subject to the judgment debtor's reasonable objections, for a reasonable period before the day of sale.

(IV) The United States marshal shall serve written notice of public sale by personal delivery, or certified or registered mail, to each person whom the marshal has reasonable cause to believe, after a title search is conducted by the United States, has an interest in property under execution, including lienholders, co-owners, and tenants, at least 25 days before the day of sale, to the last known address of each such person.

(ii) Sale of city lots.—If the real property consists of several lots, tracts, or parcels in a city or town, each lot, tract, or parcel shall be offered for sale separately, unless not susceptible to separate sale because of the character of improvements.

(iii) Sale of rural property.—If the real property is not located in a city or town, the judgment debtor may—

(I) divide the property into lots of not less than 50 acres or in such greater or lesser amounts as ordered by the court;

(II) furnish a survey of such prepared by a registered surveyor; and

(III) designate the order in which those lots shall be sold. When a sufficient number of lots are sold to satisfy the amount of the execution and costs of sale, the marshal shall stop the sale.

(B) Sale of personal property.—

(i) Personal property levied on shall be offered for sale on the premises where it is located at the time of levy, at the courthouse of the county, parish or city wherein it is located, or at another location if ordered by the court. Personal property susceptible of being exhibited shall not be sold unless it is present and subject to the view of those attending the sale unless—

(I) the property consists of shares of stock in corporations;

(II) by reason of the nature of the property, it is impractical to exhibit it; or

(III) the debtor's interest in the property does not include the right to the exclusive possession.

(ii) **(I)** Except as provided in subclause (II), personal property, or any interest therein, shall be sold after the expiration of the 30-day period beginning on the date of levy under subsection (d).

(II) The court may order the sale of any personal property before the expiration of such 30-day period if the court determines that such property is likely to perish, waste, be destroyed, or otherwise substantially depreciate in value during such 30-day period.

(iii) Notice of the time and place of the sale of personal property shall be given by the United States marshal by posting notice thereof for not less than 10 days successively immediately before the day of sale at the courthouse of any county, parish, or city, and at the place where the sale is to be made.

(iv) The United States marshal shall serve written notice of public sale by personal delivery, or registered or certified mail at their last known addresses, on the judgment debtor and other persons who the marshal has reasonable cause to believe, after diligent inquiry, have a substantial interest in the property.

(2) Postponement of sale.—The United States marshal may postpone an execution sale from time to time by continuing the required posting or publication of notice until the date to which the sale is postponed, and appending, at the foot of each such notice of a current copy of the following:

"The above sale is postponed until the ______________ day of ________________, 19______, at ______ o'clock _______.M., ________________, United States Marshal for the District of ________________, by ________________, Deputy, dated ________________."

(3) Sale procedures.—

(A) Bidding requirements.—A bidder at an execution sale of property, may be required by the United States marshal to make a cash deposit of as much as 20 percent of the sale price proposed before the bid is accepted.

(B) Resale of property.—If the terms of the sale are not complied with by the successful bidder, the United States marshal shall proceed to sell the property again on the same day if there is sufficient time. If there is insufficient time, the marshal shall schedule and notice a subsequent sale of the property as provided in paragraphs (1) and (2).

(4) Rights and liabilities of purchasers.—

(A) Transfer of title after sale.—

(i) If property is sold under this subsection and the successful bidder complies with the terms of the sale, the United States marshal shall execute and deliver all documents necessary to transfer to the successful bidder, without warranty, all the rights, titles, interests, and claims of the judgment debtor in the property.

(ii) If the successful bidder dies before execution and delivery of the documents needed to transfer ownership, the United States marshal shall execute and deliver them to the successful bidder's estate. Such delivery to the estate shall have the same effect as if accomplished during the lifetime of the purchaser.

(B) Purchaser considered innocent purchaser without notice.—The purchaser of property sold under execution shall be deemed to be an innocent purchaser without notice if the purchaser would have been considered an innocent purchaser without notice had the sale been made voluntarily and in person by the judgment debtor.

(C) Liability of successful bidder who fails to comply.—A successful bidder at an execution sale who fails to comply with the terms of the sale shall forfeit to the United States the cash deposit or, at the election of the United States, shall be liable to the United States, on a subsequent sale of the property, for all net losses incurred by the United States as a result of such failure.

(h) Disposition of proceeds; further levy.—

(1) Distribution of sale proceeds.—

(A) The United States marshal shall first deliver to the judgment debtor such amounts to which the judgment debtor is entitled from the sale of partially exempt property.

(B) The United States marshal shall next deduct from the proceeds of an execution sale of property an amount equal to the reasonable expenses incurred in making the levy of execution and in keeping and maintaining the property.

(C) Except as provided in subparagraph (D), the United States marshal shall deliver the balance of the proceeds to the counsel for the United States as soon as practicable.

(D) If more proceeds are received from the execution sale than is necessary to satisfy the executions held by the United States marshal, the marshal shall pay the surplus to the judgment debtor.

(2) Further levy if execution not satisfied.—If the proceeds of the execution sale of the property levied on are insufficient to satisfy the execution, the United States marshal shall proceed on the same writ of execution to levy other property of the judgment debtor.

[*Added by* Pub. L. No. 101–647, tit. XXXVI, § 3611, 104 Stat. 4950 (Nov. 29, 1990)]

28 U.S.C. § 3204. Installment payment order

(a) Authority to issue order.—Subject to subsection (c), if it is shown that the judgment debtor—

(1) is receiving or will receive substantial nonexempt disposable earnings from self employment that are not subject to garnishment; or

(2) is diverting or concealing substantial earnings from any source, or property received in lieu of earnings;

then upon motion of the United States and notice to the judgment debtor, the court may, if appropriate, order that the judgment debtor make specified installment payments to the United States. Notice of the motion shall be served on the judgment debtor in the same manner as a summons or by registered or certified mail, return receipt requested. In fixing the amount of the payments, the court shall take into consideration after a hearing, the income, resources, and reasonable requirements of the judgment debtor and the judgment debtor's dependents, any other payments to be made in satisfaction of judgments against the judgment debtor, and the amount due on the judgment in favor of the United States.

(b) Modification of order.—On motion of the United States or the judgment debtor, and upon a showing that the judgment debtor's financial circumstances have changed or that assets not previously disclosed by the judgment debtor have been discovered, the court may modify the amount of payments, alter their frequency, or require full payment.

(c) Limitation.—

(1) An order may not be issued under subsection (a), and if so issued shall have no force or effect, against a judgment debtor with respect to whom there is in effect a writ of garnishment of earnings issued under this chapter and based on the same debt.

(2) An order may not be issued under subsection (a) with respect to any earnings of the debtor except nonexempt disposable earnings.

[*Added by* Pub. L. No. 101–647, tit. XXXVI, § 3611, 104 Stat. 4955 (Nov. 29, 1990)]

28 U.S.C. § 3205. Garnishment

(a) In general.—A court may issue a writ of garnishment against property (including nonexempt disposable earnings) in which the debtor has a substantial nonexempt interest and which is in the possession, custody, or control of a person other than the debtor, in order to satisfy the judgment against the debtor. Co-owned property shall be subject to garnishment to the same extent as co-owned property is subject to garnishment under the law of the State in which such property is located. A court may issue simultaneous separate writs of garnishment to several garnishees. A writ of garnishment issued under this subsection shall be continuing and shall terminate only as provided in subsection (c)(10).

(b) Writ.—

(1) General requirements.—The United States shall include in its application for a writ of garnishment—

(A) the judgment debtor's name, social security number (if known), and last known address;

(B) the nature and amount of the debt owed and the facts that not less than 30 days has elapsed since demand on the debtor for payment of the debt was made and the judgment debtor has not paid the amount due; and

(C) that the garnishee is believed to have possession of property (including nonexempt disposable earnings) in which the debtor has a substantial nonexempt interest.

(2) Proper garnishee for particular property.—

(A) If the property consists of a right to or share in the stock of an association or corporation, or interests or profits therein, for which a certificate of stock or other negotiable instrument is not outstanding, the corporation, or the president or treasurer of the association shall be the garnishee.

(B) If the property consists of an interest in a partnership interest, any partner other than the debtor shall be the garnishee on behalf of the partnership.

(C) If the property or a debt is evidenced by a negotiable instrument for the payment of money, a negotiable document of title or a certificate of stock of an association or corporation, the instrument, document, or certificate shall be treated as property capable of delivery and the person holding it shall be the garnishee, except that—

(i) subject to clause (ii), in the case of a security which is transferable in the manner set forth in State law, the entity that carries on its books an account in the name of the debtor in which is reflected such security shall be the garnishee; and

(ii) notwithstanding clause (i), the pledgee shall be the garnishee if such security is pledged.

(c) Procedures applicable to writ.—

(1) Court determination.—If the court determines that the requirements of this section are satisfied, the court shall issue an appropriate writ of garnishment.

(2) Form of writ.—The writ shall state—

(A) The nature and amount of the debt, and any cost and interest owed with respect to the debt.

(B) The name and address of the garnishee.

(C) The name and address of counsel for the United States.

(D) The last known address of the judgment debtor.

(E) That the garnishee shall answer the writ within 10 days of service of the writ.

(F) That the garnishee shall withhold and retain any property in which the debtor has a substantial nonexempt interest and for which the garnishee is or may become indebted to the judgment debtor pending further order of the court.

(3) Service of writ.—The United States shall serve the garnishee and the judgment debtor with a copy of the writ of garnishment and shall certify to the court that this service was made. The writ shall be accompanied by—

(A) an instruction explaining the requirement that the garnishee submit a written answer to the writ; and

(B) instructions to the judgment debtor for objecting to the answer of the garnishee and for obtaining a hearing on the objections.

(4) Answer of the garnishee.—In its written answer to the writ of garnishment, the garnishee shall state under oath—

(A) whether the garnishee has custody, control or possession of such property;

(B) a description of such property and the value of such interest;

(C) a description of any previous garnishments to which such property is subject and the extent to which any remaining property is not exempt; and

(D) the amount of the debt the garnishee anticipates owing to the judgment debtor in the future and whether the period for payment will be weekly or another specified period.

The garnishee shall file the original answer with the court issuing the writ and serve a copy on the debtor and counsel for the United States.

(5) Objections to answer.—Within 20 days after receipt of the answer, the judgment debtor or the United States may file a written objection to the answer and request a hearing. The party objecting shall state the grounds for the objection and bear the burden of proving such grounds. A copy of the objection and request for a hearing shall be served on the garnishee and all other parties. The court shall hold a hearing within 10 days after the date the request is received by the court, or as soon thereafter as is practicable, and give notice of the hearing date to all the parties.

(6) Garnishee's failure to answer or pay.—If a garnishee fails to answer the writ of garnishment or to withhold property in accordance with the writ, the United States may petition the court for an order requiring the garnishee to appear before the court to answer the writ and to so withhold property before the appearance date. If the garnishee fails to appear, or appears and fails to show good cause why the garnishee failed to comply with the writ, the court shall enter judgment against the garnishee for the value of the judgment debtor's nonexempt interest in such property (including nonexempt disposable earnings). The court may award a reasonable attorney's fee to the United States and against the garnishee if the writ is not answered within the time specified therein and a petition requiring the garnishee to appear is filed as provided in this section.

(7) Disposition order.—After the garnishee files an answer and if no hearing is requested within the required time period, the court shall promptly enter an order directing the garnishee as to the disposition of the judgment debtor's nonexempt interest in such property. If a hearing is timely requested, the order shall be entered within 5 days after the hearing, or as soon thereafter as is practicable.

(8) Priorities.—Judicial orders and garnishments for the support of a person shall have priority over a writ of garnishment issued under this section. As to any other writ of garnishment or levy, a garnishment issued under this section shall have priority over writs which are issued later in time.

(9) Accounting.—

(A) While a writ of garnishment is in effect under this section, the United States shall give an annual accounting on the garnishment to the judgment debtor and the garnishee.

(B) Within 10 days after the garnishment terminates, the United States shall give a cumulative written accounting to the judgment debtor and garnishee of all property it receives under a writ of garnishment. Within 10 days after such accounting is received, the judgment debtor or garnishee may file a written objection to the accounting and a request for hearing. The party objecting shall state grounds for the objection. The court shall hold a hearing on the objection within 10 days after the court receives the request for a hearing, or as soon thereafter as is practicable.

(10) Termination of garnishment.—A garnishment under this chapter is terminated only by—

(A) a court order quashing the writ of garnishment;

(B) exhaustion of property in the possesion,1 custody, or control of the garnishee in which the debtor has a substantial nonexempt interest (including nonexempt disposable earnings), unless the garnishee reinstates or reemploys the judgment debtor within 90 days after the judgment debtor's dismissal or resignation; or

(C) satisfaction of the debt with respect to which the writ is issued.

[*Added by* Pub. L. No. 101–647, tit. XXXVI, § 3611, 104 Stat. 4956 (Nov. 29, 1990)]

* * *

Appendix C Federal Wage Garnishment Statute and Regulations

C.1 Federal Statutory Restrictions on Garnishment

15 U.S.C. §§ 1671–1677

[*As enacted by* Pub. L. No. 90–321, 82 Stat. 163 (1968), unless otherwise noted]

TITLE 15—COMMERCE AND TRADE

Chapter 41—Consumer Credit Protection

15 U.S.C.

Subchapter II—Restrictions on Garnishment

Title 15—Commerce and Trade

* * *

Chapter 41—Consumer Credit Protection

* * *

Subchapter II—Restrictions on Garnishment

15 U.S.C. § 1671. Congressional findings and declaration of purpose

(a) Disadvantages of garnishment

The Congress finds:

(1) The unrestricted garnishment of compensation due for personal services encourages the making of predatory extensions of credit. Such extensions of credit divert money into excessive credit payments and thereby hinder the production and flow of goods in interstate commerce.

(2) The application of garnishment as a creditors' remedy frequently results in loss of employment by the debtor, and the resulting disruption of employment, production, and consumption constitutes a substantial burden on interstate commerce.

(3) The great disparities among the laws of the several States relating to garnishment have, in effect, destroyed the uniformity of the bankruptcy laws and frustrated the purposes thereof in many areas of the country.

(b) Necessity for regulation

On the basis of the findings stated in subsection (a) of this section, the Congress determines that the provisions of this subchapter are necessary and proper for the purpose of carrying into execution the powers of the Congress to regulate commerce and to establish uniform bankruptcy laws.

15 U.S.C. § 1672. Definitions

For the purposes of this subchapter:

(a) The term "earnings" means compensation paid or payable for personal services, whether denominated as wages, salary, commission, bonus, or otherwise, and includes periodic payments pursuant to a pension or retirement program.

(b) The term "disposable earnings" means that part of the earnings of any individual remaining after the deduction from those earnings of any amounts required by law to be withheld.

(c) The term "garnishment" means any legal or equitable procedure through which the earnings of any individual are required to be withheld for payment of any debt.

15 U.S.C. § 1673. Restriction on garnishment

(a) Maximum allowable garnishment

Except as provided in subsection (b) of this section and in section 1675 of this title, the maximum part of the aggregate disposable earnings of an individual for any workweek which is subjected to garnishment may not exceed

(1) 25 per centum of his disposable earnings for that week, or

(2) the amount by which his disposable earnings for that week exceed thirty times the Federal minimum hourly wage prescribed by section 206(a)(1) of Title 29 in effect at the time the earnings are payable, whichever is less. In the case of earnings for any pay period other than a week, the Secretary of Labor shall by regulation prescribe a multiple of the Federal minimum hourly wage equivalent in effect to that set forth in paragraph (2).

(b) Exceptions

(1) The restrictions of subsection (a) of this section do not apply in the case of

(A) any order for the support of any person issued by a court of competent jurisdiction or in accordance with an administrative procedure, which is established by State law, which affords substantial due process, and which is subject to judicial review.

(B) any order of any court of the United States having jurisdiction over cases under chapter 13 of Title 11.

(C) any debt due for any State or Federal tax.

(2) The maximum part of the aggregate disposable earnings of an individual for any workweek which is subject to garnishment to enforce any order for the support of any person shall not exceed—

(A) where such individual is supporting his spouse or dependent child (other than a spouse or child with respect to whose support such order is used), 50 per centum of such individual's disposable earnings for that week; and

(B) where such individual is not supporting such a spouse or dependent child described in clause (A), 60 per centum of such individual's disposable earnings for that week;

except that, with respect to the disposable earnings of any individual for any workweek, the 50 per centum specified in clause (A) shall be deemed to be 55 per centum and the 60 per centum specified in clause (B) shall be deemed to be 65 per centum, if and to the extent that such earnings are subject to garnishment to enforce a support order with respect to a period which is prior to the twelve-week period which ends with the beginning of such workweek.

(c) Execution or enforcement of garnishment order or process prohibited
No court of the United States or any State, and no State (or officer or agency thereof), may make, execute, or enforce any order or process in violation of this section.

[*As amended by* Pub. L. No. 95–30, 91 Stat. 161 (1977); Pub. L. No. 95–598, 92 Stat. 2676 (1978)]

15 U.S.C. § 1674. Restriction on discharge from employment by reason of garnishment

(a) Termination of employment
No employer may discharge any employee by reason of the fact that his earnings have been subjected to garnishment for any one indebtedness.

(b) Penalties
Whoever willfully violates subsection (a) of this section shall be fined not more than $1,000, or imprisoned not more than one year, or both.

15 U.S.C. § 1675. Exemption for state-regulated garnishments

The Secretary of Labor may by regulation exempt from the provisions of section 1673(a) and (b)(2) of this title garnishments issued under the laws of any State if he determines that the laws of that State provide restrictions on garnishment which are substantially similar to those provided in section 1673(a) and (b)(2) of this title.

[*As amended by* Pub. L. No. 95–30, 91 Stat. 161 (1977)]

15 U.S.C. § 1676. Enforcement by Secretary of Labor

The Secretary of Labor, acting through the Wage and Hour Division of the Department of Labor, shall enforce the provisions of this subchapter.

15 U.S.C. § 1677. Effect on state laws

This subchapter does not annul, alter, or affect, or exempt any person from complying with, the laws of any State

(1) prohibiting garnishments or providing for more limited garnishment than are allowed under this subchapter, or

(2) prohibiting the discharge of any employee by reason of the fact that his earnings have been subjected to garnishment for more than one indebtedness.

C.2 Department of Labor Wage Garnishment Regulations, 29 C.F.R. Part 870

The Department of Labor's wage garnishment regulations, 29 C.F.R. Part 870, reprinted below, have *not* been amended to reflect Public Law Number 110–28, 121 Stat. 188 (2007), which amended the Fair Labor Standards Act of 1938, 29 U.S.C. § 206(a)(1). The amendment increased the minimum wage to $5.85 an hour (effective July 24, 2007), to $6.55 an hour (effective July 24, 2008), and to $7.25 an hour on July 24, 2009. These changes increase the amount of wages protected from wage garnishment so that, as of July 24, 2009, $217.50 of weekly disposable earnings (thirty times the minimum wage) is protected.

The tables in the wage garnishment regulations have not been revised to reflect these changes. However, the Department of Labor does publish a fact sheet which updates the numbers. It may be found at www.dol.gov/whd/regs/compliance/whdfs30.htm.

The first table in the regulations, found at 29 C.F.R. § 870.10(c)(3), specifies the maximum amount of disposable earnings fully exempt under federal law. To reflect the current minimum wage as of July 24, 2009, it should be revised to read as follows:

Date	*Minimum amount*	*Weekly amount*	*Biweekly amount*	*Semi-monthly amount*	*Monthly rate*
July 24, 2009	$7.25	$217.50	$435.00	$471.25	$942.50

If a consumer's disposable earnings are below the levels established in a second table, found at 29 C.F.R. § 870.10(c)(4), but above the levels specified in the first table, then the consumer's disposable earnings are partially exempt. In that case less than twenty-five percent of the earnings may be garnished. To reflect the current minimum wage as of July 24, 2009, the second table should be revised to read as follows:

Date	*Minimum amount*	*Weekly amount*	*Biweekly amount*	*Semi-monthly amount*	*Monthly rate*
July 24, 2009	$7.25	$290.00	$580.00	$628.33	$1256.67

For higher wages than specified in the second table, the maximum amount to be garnished is twenty-five percent of the consumer's disposable income.

PART 870—RESTRICTION ON GARNISHMENT

Subpart A—General

29 C.F.R.

Subpart B—Determinations and Interpretations

Subpart C—Exemption for State-Regulated Garnishments

AUTHORITY: 15 U.S.C. §§ 1673, 1675, 1676, unless otherwise noted.

SOURCE: 35 Fed. Reg. 8226 (May 26, 1970), unless otherwise noted.

Subpart A—General

29 C.F.R. § 870.1 Purpose and scope

(a) This part sets forth the procedures and any policies, determinations, and interpretations of general application whereby the Secretary of Labor carries out his duties under section 303 of the CCPA dealing with restrictions on garnishment of earnings, and section 305 permitting exemptions for State-regulated garnishments in certain situations. While the Secretary's duties under section 303 include insuring that certain amounts of earnings are protected, such duties do not include establishing priorities among multiple garnishments, as such priorities are determined by other Federal statutes or by State law.

(b) Functions of the Secretary under the CCPA to be performed as provided in this part are assigned to the Administrator of the Wage and Hour Division (hereinafter referred to as the Administrator), who, under the general direction and control of the Assistant Secretary, Wage and Labor Standards Administration, shall be empowered to take final and binding actions in administering the provisions of this part. The Administrator is empowered to subdelegate any of his duties under this part. Any legal advice and assistance required for administration of this part shall be provided by the Solicitor of Labor.

[*As amended by* 44 Fed. Reg. 30,684 (May 29, 1979)]

29 C.F.R. § 870.2 Amendments to this part

The Administrator may, at any time upon his own motion or upon written request of any interested person setting forth reasonable grounds therefor, amend any rules in this part.

Subpart B—Determinations and Interpretations

29 C.F.R. § 870.10 Maximum part of aggregate disposable earnings subject to garnishment under section 303(a)

(a) Statutory provision. Section 303 (a) of the CCPA provides that, with some exceptions, the maximum part of the aggregate disposable earnings of an individual for any workweek which is subjected to garnishment may not exceed

(1) 25 per centum of his disposable earnings for that week, or

(2) the amount by which his disposable earnings for that week exceed thirty times the Federal minimum hourly wage prescribed by section 6(a)(1) of the Fair Labor Standards Act of 1938, in effect at the time the earnings are payable, whichever is less. In the case of earnings for any pay period other than a week, the Secretary of Labor shall by regulation prescribe a multiple of the Federal minimum hourly wage equivalent in effect to that set forth in paragraph (2).

(b) Weekly pay period. The statutory exemption formula applies directly to the aggregate disposable earnings paid or payable for a pay period of 1 workweek, or a lesser period. Its intent is to protect from garnishment and save to an individual earner the specified amount of compensation for his personal services rendered in the workweek, or a lesser period. Thus:

(1) The amount of an individual's disposable earnings for a workweek or lesser period which may not be garnished is 30 times the Fair Labor Standards Act minimum wage. If an individual's disposable earnings for such a period are equal to or less than 30 times the minimum wage, the individual's earnings may not be garnished in any amount. (When the minimum wage increases, the proportionate amount of earnings which may not be garnished also increases.) On April 1, 1991, the minimum wage increased to $4.25. Accordingly, the amount of disposable weekly earnings which may not be garnished is $127.50 effective April 1, 1991. (For the period April 1, 1990 through March 31, 1991, the amount that may not be garnished is $114 (30 x $3.80).)

(2) For earnings payable on or after April 1, 1991, if an individual's disposable earnings for a workweek or lesser period are more than $127.50, but less than $170.00, only the amount above $127.50 is subject to garnishment. (For earnings payable during the period April 1, 1990, through March 31, 1991, when the Fair Labor Standards Act minimum wage was $3.80, this range computes to more than $114.00, but less than $152.00.)

(3) For earnings payable on or after April 1, 1991, if an individual's disposable earnings for a workweek or lesser period are $170.00 or more, 25 percent of his/her disposable earnings is subject to garnishment. (The weekly figure was $152.00 (40 x $3.80) for the period April 1, 1990 through March 31, 1991.)

(c) Pay for a period longer than 1 week. In the case of disposable earnings which compensate for personal services rendered in a pay period longer than 1 workweek, the weekly statutory exemption formula must be transformed to a formula applicable to such earnings providing equivalent restrictions on wage garnishment.

(1) The 25 percent part of the formula would apply to the aggregate disposable earnings for all the workweeks or fractions thereof compensated by the pay for such pay period.

(2) The following formula should be used to calculate the dollar amount of disposable earnings which would not be subject to garnishment: The number of workweeks, or fractions thereof, should be multiplied times the applicable Federal minimum wage and that amount should be multiplied by 30. For example, for the period April 1, 1990 through March 31, 1991 when the Federal minimum wage was $3.80 per hour, the formula should be calculated based on a minimum wage of $3.80 ($3.80 multiplied by 30 equals $114; $114 multiplied by the number of workweeks (or fractions thereof) equals the amount that cannot be garnished). As of April 1, 1991, the $4.25 Federal minimum wage replaces $3.80 in the formula (and the amount which cannot be garnished would then be $127.50 multiplied by the number of workweeks (or fractions thereof)). For purposes of this formula, a calendar month is considered to consist of 4 workweeks. Thus, during the period April 1, 1990 through March 31, 1991 when the Federal minimum hourly wage was $3.80 an hour, the amount of disposable earnings for a 2-week period is $228.00 (2 x 30 x $3.80); for a monthly period, $494.00 (4 x 30 x $3.80). Effective April 1, 1991, such amounts increased as follows: for a two-week period, $255.00 (2 x 30 x $4.25); for a monthly period, $552.50 (4 x 30 x $4.25). The amount of disposable earnings for any other pay period longer than 1 week shall be computed in a manner consistent with section 303(a) of the act and with this paragraph.

(3) Absent any changes to the rate set forth in section 6(a)(1) of the Fair Labor Standards Act, disposable earnings for individuals paid weekly, biweekly, semimonthly, and monthly may not be garnished unless they are in excess of the following amounts:

[*table omitted*][1]

(4) Absent any changes to the rate set forth in section 6(a)(1) of the Fair Labor Standards Act, if the disposable earnings are less than the following figures, only the difference between the appropriate figures set forth in paragraph (c)(3) of this section and the individual's disposable earnings may be garnished.

[*table omitted*][2]

1. This table has not been updated to reflect Public Law No. 110–28, 121 Stat. 188 (2007), which amended the Fair Labor Standards Act of 1938, 29 U.S.C. § 206(a)(1). Please see the introduction to this subsection for updated calculations taking the current minimum wage into account.
2. This table has not been updated to reflect Public Law No. 110–28, 121 Stat. 188 (2007), which amended the Fair Labor Standards Act of 1938, 29 U.S.C. § 206(a)(1). Please see the introduction to this subsection for updated calculations taking the current minimum wage into account.

For example, in April of 1990, if an individual's disposable earnings for a biweekly pay period are $274.00, the difference between $228.00 and $274.00 (i.e., $46.00) may be garnished.

(5) If disposable earnings are in excess of the figures stated in paragraph (c)(4) of this section, 25% of the disposable earnings may be garnished.

(d) Date wages paid or payable controlling. The date that disposable earnings are paid or payable, and not the date the Court issues the garnishment order, is controlling in determining the amount of disposable earnings that may be garnished. Thus, a garnishment order in November 1990, providing for withholding from wages over a period of time, based on exemptions computed at the $3.80 per hour minimum wage then in effect, would be modified by operation of the change in the law so that wages paid after April 1, 1991, are subject to garnishment to the extent described in paragraphs (b) and (c) of this section on the basis of a minimum rate of $4.25 per hour. This principle is applicable at the time of the enactment of any further increase in the minimum wage.

AUTHORITY: Pub. L. 93–259, 88 Stat. 55 (1974).

[*As amended by* 40 Fed. Reg. 52,610 (Nov. 11, 1975); 43 Fed. Reg. 28,471 (June 30, 1978); 43 Fed. Reg. 30,276 (July 14, 1978); 44 Fed. Reg. 30,685 (May 29, 1979); 56 Fed. Reg. 32,254 (July 15, 1991); 56 Fed. Reg. 40,660 (Aug. 15, 1991)]

29 C.F.R. § 870.11 Exceptions to the restrictions provided by section 303(a) of the CCPA and priorities among garnishments

(a) **(1)** Section 303(b) of the Consumer Credit Protection Act provides that the restrictions in section 303(a) do not apply to:

(i) Any debt due for any State or Federal tax, or

(ii) Any order of any court of bankruptcy under Chapter XIII of the Bankruptcy Act.

(2) Accordingly the Consumer Credit Protection Act does not restrict in any way the amount which may be withheld for State or Federal taxes or in Chapter XIII Bankruptcy Act proceedings.

(b) **(1)** Section 303(b) provides the following restrictions on the amount that may be withheld for the support of any person (e.g. alimony or child support):

(A) Where such individual is supporting his spouse or dependent child (other than a spouse or child with respect to whose support such order is issued), 50 per centum of such individual's disposable earnings for that week; and

(B) Where such individual is not supporting such a spouse or dependent child described in clause (A), 60 per centum of such individual's disposable earnings for that week; except that, with respect to the disposable earnings of any individual for any workweek, the 50 per centum specified in clause (A) shall be deemed to be 55 per centum and the 60 per centum specified in clause (B) shall be deemed to be 65 per centum, if and to the extent that such earnings are subject to garnishment to enforce a support order with respect to a period which is prior to the twelve week period which ends with the beginning of such workweek.

(2) Compliance with the provisions of section 303(a) and (b) may offer problems when there is more than one garnishment. In that event the priority is determined by State law or other Federal laws as the CCPA contains no provisions controlling the priorities of garnishments. However, in no event may the amount of any individual's disposable earnings which may be garnished exceed the percentages specified in section 303. To illustrate:

(i) If 45% of an individual's disposable earnings were garnished for taxes, and this garnishment has priority, the Consumer Credit Protection Act permits garnishment for the support of any person of only the difference between 45% and the applicable percentage (50 to 65%) in the above quoted section 303(b).

(ii) If 70% of an individual's disposable earnings were garnished for taxes and/or a Title XIII Bankruptcy debt, and these garnishments have priority, the Consumer Credit Protection Act does not permit garnishment either for the support of any person or for other debts.

(iii) If 25% of an individual's disposable earnings were withheld pursuant to an ordinary garnishment which is subject to the restrictions of section 303(a), and the garnishment has priority in accordance with State law, the Consumer Credit Protection Act permits the additional garnishment for the support of any person of only the difference between 25% and the applicable percentage (50–65%) in the above quoted section 303(b).

(iv) If 25% or more of an individual's disposable earnings were withheld pursuant to a garnishment for support, and the support garnishment has priority in accordance with State law, the Consumer Credit Protection Act does not permit the withholding of any additional amounts pursuant to an ordinary garnishment which is subject to the restrictions of section 303(a).

[*As amended by* 44 Fed. Reg. 30,685 (May 29, 1979)]

Subpart C—Exemption for State-Regulated Garnishments

29 C.F.R. § 870.50 General provision

Section 305 of the CCPA authorizes that Secretary to "exempt from the provisions of section 303(a) garnishments issued under the laws of any State if he determines that the laws of that State provide restrictions on garnishment which are substantially similar to those provided in section 303(a)."

29 C.F.R. § 870.51 Exemption policy

(a) It is the policy of the Secretary of Labor to permit exemption from section 303(a) of the CCPA garnishments issued under the laws of a State if those laws considered together cover every case of garnishment covered by the Act, and if those laws provide the same or greater protection to individuals. Differences in text between the restrictions of State laws and those in section 303(a) of the Act are not material so long as the State laws provide the same or greater restrictions on the garnishment of individuals' earnings.

(b) In determining whether State-regulated garnishments should be exempted from section 303(a) of the CCPA, or whether such an exemption should be terminated, the laws of the State shall be examined with particular regard to the classes of persons and of transactions to which they may apply; the formulas provided for determining the maximum part of an individual's earnings which may be subject to garnishment; restrictions on the application of the formulas; and with regard to procedural burdens placed on the individual whose earnings are subject to garnishment.

(c) Particular attention is directed to the fact that subsection (a) of section 303, when considered with subsection (c) of that section, is read as not requiring the raising of the subsection (a) restrictions as affirmative defenses in garnishment proceedings.

29 C.F.R. § 870.52 Application for exemption of State-regulated garnishments

(a) An application for the exemption of garnishments issued under the laws of a State may be made in duplicate by a duly authorized representative of the State. The application shall be filed with the Administrator of the Wage and Hour Division, Department of Labor, Washington, DC 20210.

(b) Any application for exemption must be accompanied by two copies of all the provisions of the State laws relating to the garnishment of earnings, certified to be true and complete copies by the Attorney General of the State. In addition, the application must be accompanied by a statement, in duplicate, signed by the Attorney General of the State, showing how the laws of the State satisfy the policy expressed in § 870.51(a) and setting forth any other matters which the Attorney General may wish to state concerning the application.

(c) Notice of the filing of an application for exemption shall be published in the *Federal Register*. Copies of the application shall be available for public inspection and copying during business hours at the national office of the Wage and Hour Division and in the regional office of the Wage and Hour Division in which the particular State is located. Interested persons shall be afforded an opportunity to submit written comments concerning the application of the State within a period of time to be specified in the notice.

[*As amended by* 35 Fed. Reg. 14,315 (Sept. 11, 1970)]

29 C.F.R. § 870.53 Action upon an application for exemption

(a) The Administrator shall grant or deny within a reasonable time any application for the exemption of State-regulated garnishments. The State representative shall be notified in writing of the decision. In the event of denial, a statement of the grounds for the denial shall be made. To the extent feasible and appropriate, the Administrator may afford to the State representative and to any other interested persons an opportunity to submit orally or in writing data, views, and arguments on the issue of whether or not an exemption should be granted and on any subsidiary issues.

(b) If an application is denied, the State representative shall have an opportunity to request reconsideration by the Administrator. The request shall be made in writing. The Administrator shall permit argument whenever the opportunity to do so has not been afforded under paragraph (a) of this section, and may permit argument in any other case.

(c) General notice of every exemption of State-regulated garnishments and of its terms and conditions shall be given by publication in the *Federal Register*.

29 C.F.R. § 870.54 Standards governing the granting of an application for exemption

The Administrator may grant any application for the exemption of State-regulated garnishments whenever he finds that the laws of the State satisfy the policy expressed in § 870.51(a).

29 C.F.R. § 870.55 Terms and conditions of every exemption

(a) It shall be a condition of every exemption of State-regulated garnishments that the State representative have the powers and duties

> **(1)** To represent, and act on behalf of, the State in relation to the Administrator and his representatives, with regard to any matter relating to, or arising out of, the application, interpretation, and enforcement of State laws regulating garnishment of earnings;
> **(2)** To submit to the Administrator in duplicate and on a current basis, a certified copy of every enactment by the State legislature affecting any of those laws, and a certified copy of any decision in any case involving any of those laws, made by the highest court of the State which has jurisdiction to decide or review cases of its kind, if properly presented to the court; and
> **(3)** To submit to the Administrator any information relating to the enforcement of those laws, which the Administrator may request.

(b) The Administrator may make any exemption subject to additional terms and conditions which he may find appropriate to carry out the purposes of section 303(a) of the Act.

29 C.F.R. § 870.56 Termination of exemption

(a) After notice and opportunity to be heard, the Administrator shall terminate any exemption of State-regulated garnishments when he finds that the laws of the State no longer satisfy the purpose of section 303(a) of the Act or the policy expressed in § 870.51(a). Also, after notice and opportunity to be heard, the Administrator may terminate any exemption if he finds that any of its terms or conditions have been violated.

(b) General notice of the termination of every exemption of State-regulated garnishments shall be given by publication in the Federal Register.

29 C.F.R. § 870.57 Exemptions

Pursuant to section 305 of the CCPA (82 Stat. 164) and in accordance with the provisions of this part, it has been determined that the laws of the following States provide restrictions on garnishment which are substantially similar to those provided in section 303(a) of the CCPA (82 Stat. 163); and that, therefore, garnishments issued under those laws should be, and they hereby are, exempted from the provisions of section 303(a) subject to the terms and conditions of §§ 870.55(a) and 870.56:

(a) State of Virginia. Effective June 30, 1978, garnishments issued under the laws of the State of Virginia are exempt from the provisions of sections 303(a) and 303(b) of the CCPA under the following additional conditions: (1) Whenever garnishments are ordered in the State of Virginia which are not deemed to be governed by section 34–29 of the Code of Virginia, as amended, and the laws of another State are applied, sections 303(a) and 303(b) of the CCPA shall apply to such garnishments according to the provisions thereof; and (2) whenever the earnings of any individual subject to garnishment are withheld and a suspending or supersedeas bond is undertaken in the course of an appeal from a lower court decision, sections 303(a) and 303(b) of the CCPA shall apply to the withholding of such earnings under this procedure according to the provisions thereof.

[*As added by* 35 Fed. Reg. 18,527 (Dec. 5, 1970), *and amended by* 43 Fed. Reg. 28,472 (June 30, 1978)]

Appendix D Treasury Rule Protecting Electronically-Deposited Exempt Federal Benefits

This appendix reprints 31 C.F.R. §§ 212.1 through 212.12 and apps. A, B, and C (effective May 1, 2011) as promulgated by 76 Fed. Reg. 9939 (Feb. 23, 2011) and as amended by 78 Fed. Reg. 32,099 (May 29, 2013).

PART 212—GARNISHMENT OF ACCOUNTS CONTAINING FEDERAL BENEFIT PAYMENTS

31 C.F.R.

AUTHORITY: 5 U.S.C. §§ 1103, 8346, 8470; 31 U.S.C. §§ 321, 3321, 3332; 38 U.S.C. §§ 501(a), 5301(a); 42 U.S.C. §§ 405(a), 407, 659, 1383(d)(1); 45 U.S.C. §§ 231f(b), 231m, 352(e), 362(1).

SOURCE: 76 Fed. Reg. 9939 (Feb. 23, 2011); 78 Fed. Reg. 32,099 (May 29, 2013); 78 Fed. Reg. 60,695 (Oct. 2, 2013).

31 C.F.R. § 212.1 Purpose

The purpose of this part is to implement statutory provisions that protect Federal benefits from garnishment by establishing procedures that a financial institution must follow when served a garnishment order against an account holder into whose account a Federal benefit payment has been directly deposited.

31 C.F.R. § 212.2 Scope

This part applies to:

(a) *Entities*. All financial institutions, as defined in § 212.3.

(b) *Funds*. Federal benefit payments protected from garnishment pursuant to the following authorities:

(1) SSA benefit payments protected under 42 U.S.C. 407 and 42 U.S.C. 1383(d)(1);

(2) VA benefit payments protected under 38 U.S.C. 5301(a);

(3) RRB benefit payments protected under 45 U.S.C. 231m(a) and 45 U.S.C. 352(e); and

(4) OPM benefit payments protected under 5 U.S.C. 8346 and 5 U.S.C. 8470.

31 C.F.R. § 212.3 Definitions

For the purposes of this part, the following definitions apply.

Account means an account, including a master account or sub account, at a financial institution and to which an electronic payment may be directly routed.

Account holder means a natural person against whom a garnishment order is issued and whose name appears in a financial institution's records as the direct or beneficial owner of an account.

Account review means the process of examining deposits in an account to determine if a benefit agency has deposited a benefit payment into the account during the lookback period.

Benefit agency means the Social Security Administration (SSA), the Department of Veterans Affairs (VA), the Office of Personnel Management (OPM), or the Railroad Retirement Board (RRB).

Benefit payment means a Federal benefit payment referred to in § 212.2(b) paid by direct deposit to an account with the character "XX" encoded in positions 54 and 55 of the Company Entry Description field and the number "2" encoded in the Originator Status Code field of the Batch Header Record of the direct deposit entry.

Federal banking agency means the Federal Deposit Insurance Corporation, the Board of Governors of the Federal Reserve System, the Office of the Comptroller of the Currency, the Office of Thrift Supervision, or the National Credit Union Administration.

Financial institution means a bank, savings association, credit union, or other entity chartered under Federal or State law to engage in the business of banking.

Freeze or *account freeze* means an action by a financial institution to seize, withhold, or preserve funds, or to otherwise prevent an account holder from drawing on or transacting against funds in an account, in response to a garnishment order.

Garnish or *garnishment* means execution, levy, attachment, garnishment, or other legal process.

Garnishment fee means any service or legal processing fee, charged by a financial institution to an account holder, for processing a garnishment order or any associated withholding or release of funds.

Garnishment order or *order* means a writ, order, notice, summons, judgment, levy or similar written instruction issued by a court, a State or State agency, a municipality or municipal corporation, or a State child support enforcement agency, including a lien arising by operation of law for overdue child support or an order to freeze the assets in an account, to effect a garnishment against a debtor.

Lookback period means the two month period that begins on the date preceding the date of account review and ends on the corresponding date of the month two months earlier, or on the last date of the month two months earlier if the corresponding date does not exist. Examples illustrating the application of this definition are included in Appendix C to this part.

Protected amount means the lesser of the sum of all benefit payments posted to an account between the close of business on the beginning date of the lookback period and the open of business on the ending date of the lookback period, or the balance in an account when the account review is performed. Examples illustrating the application of this definition are included in Appendix C to this part.

State means a State of the United States, the District of Columbia, the Commonwealth of Puerto Rico, the Commonwealth of the Northern Mariana Islands, American Samoa, Guam, or the United States Virgin Islands.

State child support enforcement agency means the single and separate organizational unit in a State that has the responsibility for administering or supervising the State's plan for child and spousal support pursuant to Title IV, Part D, of the Social Security Act, 42 U.S.C. 654.

United States means:

(1) A Federal corporation,

(2) An agency, department, commission, board, or other entity of the United States, or

(3) An instrumentality of the United States, as set forth in 28 U.S.C. 3002(15).

31 C.F.R. § 212.4 Initial action upon receipt of a garnishment order

(a) *Examination of order for Notice of Right to Garnish Federal Benefits.* Prior to taking any other action related to a garnishment order issued against a debtor, and no later than two business days following receipt of the order, a financial institution shall examine the order to determine if the United States or a State child support enforcement agency has attached or included a Notice of Right to Garnish Federal Benefits, as set forth in Appendix B to this part.

(b) *Notice of Right to Garnish Federal Benefits is attached to or included with the order.* If a Notice of Right to Garnish Federal Benefits is attached to or included with the garnishment order, then the financial institution shall follow its otherwise customary procedures for handling the order and shall not follow the procedures in § 212.5 and § 212.6.

(c) *No Notice of Right to Garnish Federal Benefits.* If a Notice of Right to Garnish Federal Benefits is not attached to or included with the garnishment order, then the financial institution shall follow the procedures in § 212.5 and § 212.6.

31 C.F.R. § 212.5 Account review

(a) *Timing of account review.* When served a garnishment order issued against a debtor, a financial institution shall perform an account review:

(1) No later than two business days following receipt of (A) the order, and (B) sufficient information from the creditor that initiated the order to determine whether the debtor is an account holder, if such information is not already included in the order; or

(2) In cases where the financial institution is served a batch of a large number of orders, by a later date that may be permitted by the creditor that initiated the orders, consistent with the terms of the orders. The financial institution shall maintain records on such batches and creditor permissions, consistent with § 212.11(b),

(b) *No benefit payment deposited during lookback period.* If the account review shows that a benefit agency did not deposit a benefit payment into the account during the lookback period, then the financial institution shall follow its otherwise customary procedures for handling the garnishment order and shall not follow the procedures in § 212.6.

(c) *Benefit payment deposited during lookback period.* If the account review shows that a benefit agency deposited a benefit payment into the account during the lookback period, then the financial institution shall follow the procedures in § 212.6.

(d) *Uniform application of account review.* The financial institution shall perform an account review without consideration for any other attributes of the account or the garnishment order, including but not limited to:

(1) The presence of other funds, from whatever source, that may be commingled in the account with funds from a benefit payment;

(2) The existence of a co-owner on the account;

(3) The existence of benefit payments to multiple beneficiaries, and/or under multiple programs, deposited in the account;

(4) The balance in the account, provided the balance is above zero dollars on the date of account review;

(5) Instructions to the contrary in the order; or

(6) The nature of the debt or obligation underlying the order.

(e) *Priority of account review.* The financial institution shall perform the account review prior to taking any other actions related to the garnishment order that may affect funds in the account.

(f) *Separate account reviews.* The financial institution shall perform the account review separately for each account in the name of an account holder against whom a garnishment order has been issued. In performing account reviews for multiple accounts in the name of one account holder, a financial institution shall not trace the movement of funds between accounts by attempting to associate funds from a benefit payment deposited into one account with amounts subsequently transferred to another account.

31 C.F.R. § 212.6 Rules and procedures to protect benefits

The following provisions apply if an account review shows that a benefit agency deposited a benefit payment into an account during the lookback period.

(a) *Protected amount.* The financial institution shall immediately calculate and establish the protected amount for an account. The financial institution shall ensure that the account holder has full and customary access to the protected amount, which the financial institution shall not freeze in response to the garnishment order. An account holder shall have no requirement to assert any right of garnishment exemption prior to accessing the protected amount in the account.

(b) *Separate protected amounts.* The financial institution shall calculate and establish the protected amount separately for each account in the name of an account holder, consistent with the requirements in § 212.5(f) to conduct distinct account reviews.

(c) *No challenge of protection.* A protected amount calculated and established by a financial institution pursuant to this section shall be conclusively considered to be exempt from garnishment under law.

(d) *Funds in excess of the protected amount.* For any funds in an account in excess of the protected amount, the financial institution shall follow its otherwise customary procedures for handling garnishment orders, including the freezing of funds, but consistent with paragraphs (f) and (g) of this section.

(e) *Notice.* The financial institution shall issue a notice to the account holder named in the garnishment order, in accordance with § 212.7.

(f) *One-time account review process.* The financial institution shall perform the account review only one time upon the first service of a given garnishment order. The financial institution shall not repeat the account review or take any other action related to the order if the same order is subsequently served again upon the financial institution. If the financial institution is subsequently served a new or different garnishment order against the same account holder, the financial institution shall perform a separate and new account review.

(g) *No continuing or periodic garnishment responsibilities.* The financial institution shall not continually garnish amounts deposited or credited to the account following the date of account review, and shall take no action to freeze any funds subsequently deposited or credited, unless the institution is served with a new or different garnishment order, consistent with the requirements of this part.

(h) *Impermissible garnishment fee.* The financial institution may not charge or collect a garnishment fee against a protected amount. The financial institution may charge or collect a garnishment fee up to five business days after the account review if funds other than a benefit payment are deposited to the account within this period, provided that the fee may not exceed the amount of the non-benefit deposited funds.

31 C.F.R. § 212.7 Notice to the account holder

A financial institution shall issue the notice required by § 212.6(e) in accordance with the following provisions.

(a) *Notice requirement.* The financial institution shall send the notice in cases where:

(1) A benefit agency deposited a benefit payment into an account during the lookback period;

(2) The balance in the account on the date of account review was above zero dollars and the financial institution established a protected amount; and

(3) There are funds in the account in excess of the protected amount.

(b) *Notice content.* The financial institution shall notify the account holder named in the garnishment order of the following facts and events in readily understandable language.

(1) The financial institution's receipt of an order against the account holder.

(2) The date on which the order was served.

(3) A succinct explanation of garnishment.

(4) The financial institution's requirement under Federal regulation to ensure that account balances up to the protected amount specified in § 212.3 are protected and made available to the account holder if a benefit agency deposited a benefit payment into the account in the last two months.

(5) The account subject to the order and the protected amount established by the financial institution.

(6) The financial institution's requirement pursuant to State law to freeze other funds in the account to satisfy the order and the amount frozen, if applicable.

(7) The amount of any garnishment fee charged to the account, consistent with § 212.6.

(8) A list of the Federal benefit payments subject to this part, as identified in § 212.2(b).

(9) The account holder's right to assert against the creditor that initiated the order a further garnishment exemption for amounts above the protected amount, by completing exemption claim forms, contacting the court of jurisdiction, or contacting the creditor, as customarily applicable for a given jurisdiction.

(10) The account holder's right to consult an attorney or legal aid service in asserting against the creditor that initiated the order a further garnishment exemption for amounts above the protected amount.

(11) The name of the creditor, and, if contact information is included in the order, means of contacting the creditor.

(c) *Optional notice content.* The financial institution may notify the account holder named in the garnishment order of the following facts and events in readily understandable language.

(1) Means of contacting a local free attorney or legal aid service.

(2) Means of contacting the financial institution,

(3) By issuing the notice required by this part, the financial institution is not providing legal advice.

(d) *Amending notice content.* The financial institution may amend the content of the notice to integrate information about a State's garnishment rules and protections, for the purposes of avoiding potential confusion or harmonizing the notice with State requirements, or providing more complete information about an account.

(e) *Notice delivery.* The financial institution shall issue the notice directly to the account holder, or to a fiduciary who administers the account and receives communications on behalf of the account holder, and only information and documents pertaining to the garnishment order, including other notices or forms that may be required under State or local government law, may be included in the communication.

(f) *Notice timing.* The financial institution shall send the notice to the account holder within 3 business days from the date of account review.

(g) *One notice for multiple accounts.* The financial institution may issue one notice with information related to multiple accounts of an account holder.

(h) *Not legal advice.* By issuing a notice required by this part, a financial institution creates no obligation to provide, and shall not be deemed to be offering, legal advice.

31 C.F.R. § 212.8 Other rights and authorities

(a) *Exempt status.* Nothing in this part shall be construed to limit an individual's right under Federal law to assert against a creditor a further exemption from garnishment for funds in excess of the protected amount, or to alter the exempt status of funds that may be protected from garnishment under Federal law.

(b) *Account agreements.* Nothing in this part shall be construed to invalidate any term or condition of an account agreement between a financial institution and an account holder that is not inconsistent with this part.

31 C.F.R. § 212.9 Preemption of State law

(a) *Inconsistent law preempted.* Any State or local government law or regulation that is inconsistent with a provision of this part is preempted to the extent of the inconsistency. A State law or regulation is inconsistent with this part if it requires a financial institution to take actions or make disclosures that contradict or conflict with the requirements of this part or if a financial institution cannot comply with the State law or regulation without violating this part.

(b) *Consistent law not preempted.* This regulation does not annul, alter, affect, or exempt any financial institution from complying with the laws of any State with respect to garnishment practices, except to the extent of an inconsistency. A requirement under State law to protect benefit payments in an account from freezing or garnishment at a higher protected amount than is required under this part is not inconsistent with this part if the financial institution can comply with both this part and the State law requirement.

31 C.F.R. § 212.10 Safe harbor

(a) *Protection during examination and pending review.* A financial institution that complies in good faith with this part shall not be liable to a creditor that initiates a garnishment order, or for any penalties under State law, contempt of court, civil procedure, or other law for failing to honor a garnishment order, for account activity during:

(1) The two business days following the financial institution's receipt of a garnishment order during which the financial institution must determine if the United States or a State child support enforcement agency has attached or included a Notice of Right to Garnish Federal Benefits, as set forth in § 212.4; or

(2) The time between the financial institution's receipt of the garnishment order and the date by which the financial institution must perform the account review, as set forth in § 212.5.

(b) *Protection when protecting or freezing funds.* A financial institution that complies in good faith with this part shall not be liable to a creditor that initiates a garnishment order for any protected amounts, to an account holder for any frozen amounts, or for any penalties under State law, contempt of court, civil procedure, or other law for failing to honor a garnishment order in cases where:

(1) A benefit agency has deposited a benefit payment into an account during the lookback period, or

(2) The financial institution has determined that the order was obtained by the United States or issued by a State child support enforcement agency by following the procedures in § 212.4.

(c) *Protection for providing additional information to account holder.* A financial institution shall not be liable for providing in good faith any optional information in the notice to the account holder, as set forth in § 212.7(c) and (d).

(d) *Protection for financial institutions from other potential liabilities.* A financial institution that complies in good faith with this part shall not be liable for:

(1) Bona fide errors that occur despite reasonable procedures maintained by the financial institution to prevent such errors in complying with the provisions of this part;

(2) Customary clearing and settlement adjustments that affect the balance in an account, including a protected amount, such as deposit reversals caused by the return of unpaid items, or debit card transactions settled for amounts higher than the amounts originally authorized; or

(3) Honoring an account holder's express written instruction, that is both dated and provided by the account holder to the financial institution following the date on which it has been served a particular garnishment order, to use an otherwise protected amount to satisfy the order.

31 C.F.R. § 212.11 Compliance and record retention

(a) *Enforcement.* Federal banking agencies will enforce compliance with this part.

(b) *Record retention.* A financial institution shall maintain records of account activity and actions taken in response to a garnishment order, sufficient to demonstrate compliance with this part, for a period of not less than two years from the date on which the financial institution receives the garnishment order.

31 C.F.R. § 212.12 Amendment of this part

This part may be amended only by a rulemaking issued jointly by Treasury and all of the benefit agencies as defined in § 212.3.

Appendix A to Part 212—Model Notice to Account Holder

A financial institution may use the following model notice to meet the requirements of § 212.7. Although use of the model notice is not required, a financial institution using it properly is deemed to be in compliance with § 212.7.

Information in brackets should be completed by the financial institution. Where the bracketed information indicates a choice of words, as indicated by a slash, the financial institution should either select the appropriate words or provide substitute words suitable to the garnishment process in a given jurisdiction.

Parenthetical wording in italics represents instructions to the financial institution and should not be printed with the notice. In most cases, this wording indicates that the model language either is optional for the financial institution, or should only be included if some condition is met.

MODEL NOTICE:

[Financial institution name, city, and State, shown as letterhead or otherwise printed at the beginning of the notice]

IMPORTANT INFORMATION ABOUT YOUR ACCOUNT

Date:

Notice to:

Account Number:

Why am I receiving this notice?

On [date on which garnishment order was served], [Name of financial institution] received a garnishment order from a court to [freeze/remove] funds in your account. The amount of the garnishment order was for $[amount of garnishment order]. We are sending you this notice to let you know what we have done in response to the garnishment order.

What is garnishment?

Garnishment is a legal process that allows a creditor to remove funds from your [bank]/[credit union] account to satisfy a debt that you have not paid. In other words, if you owe money to a person or company, they can obtain a court order directing your [bank]/[credit union] to take money out of your account to pay off your debt. If this happens, you cannot use that money in your account.

What has happened to my account?

On [date of account review], we researched your account and identified one or more Federal benefit payments deposited in the last 2 months. In most cases, Federal benefit payments are protected from garnishment. As required by Federal regulations, therefore, we have established a "protected amount" of funds that will remain available to you and that will not be [frozen/removed] from your account in response to the garnishment order.

(Conditional paragraph if funds have been frozen) Your account contained additional money that may not be protected from garnishment. As required by law, we have [placed a hold on/removed] these funds in the amount of $[amount frozen] and may have to turn these funds over to your creditor as directed by the garnishment order.

The chart below summarizes this information about your account(s):

Account Summary as of [date of account review]

Account number	Amount in account	Amount protected	Amount subject to garnishment (now [frozen/removed])	Garnishment fee charged

(If the account holder has multiple accounts, add a row for each account.)

Please note that these amount(s) may be affected by deposits or withdrawals after the protected amount was calculated on [date of account review].

Do I need to do anything to access my protected funds?

You may use the "protected amount" of money in your account as you normally would. There is nothing else that you need to do to make sure that the "protected amount" is safe.

Who garnished my account?

The creditor who obtained a garnishment order against you is [name of creditor].

What types of Federal benefit payments are protected from garnishment?

In most cases, you have protections from garnishment if the funds in your account include one or more of the following Federal benefit payments:

- Social Security benefits
- Supplemental Security Income benefits
- Veterans benefits
- Railroad retirement benefits
- Railroad Unemployment Insurance benefits
- Civil Service Retirement System benefits
- Federal Employees Retirement System benefits

(Conditional section if funds have been frozen) What should I do if I think that additional funds in my account are from Federal benefit payments?

If you believe that additional funds in your account(s) are from Federal benefit payments and should not have been [frozen/removed], there are several things you can do.

(Conditional sentence if applicable for the jurisdiction) You can fill out a garnishment exemption form and submit it to the court.

You may contact the creditor that garnished your account and explain that additional funds are from Federal benefit payments and should be released back to you.

(Conditional sentence if contact information is in the garnishment order) The creditor may be contacted at [contact information included in the garnishment order].

You may also consult an attorney (lawyer) to help you prove to the creditor who garnished your account that additional funds are from Federal benefit payments and cannot be taken. If you cannot afford an attorney, you can seek assistance from a free attorney or a legal aid society. *(Optional sentences)* [Name of State, local, or independent legal aid service] is an organization that provides free legal aid and can be reached at [contact information]. You can find information about other free legal aid programs at [insert "http://www.lawhelp.org" or other legal aid programs website].

(Optional section) How to contact [name of financial institution].

This notice contains all the information that we have about the garnishment order. However, if you have a question about your account, you may contact us at [contact number].

Appendix B to Part 212—Form of Notice of Right to Garnish Federal Benefits

The United States, or a State child support enforcement agency, certifying its right to garnish Federal benefits shall attach or include with a garnishment order the following Notice, on official organizational letterhead.

Information in brackets should be completed by the United States or a State child support enforcement agency, as applicable. Where the bracketed information indicates a choice of words, as indicated by a slash, the appropriate words should be selected from the options.

Notice of Right to Garnish Federal Benefits

Date:

[Garnishment Order Number]/[State Case ID]:

The attached garnishment order was [obtained by the United States, pursuant to the Federal Debt Collection Procedures Act, 28 U.S.C. § 3205, or the Mandatory Victims Restitution Act, 18 U.S.C. § 3613, or other Federal statute]/[issued by (name of the State child support enforcement agency), pursuant to authority to attach or seize assets of noncustodial parents in financial institutions in the State of (name of State), 42 U.S.C. § 666].

Accordingly, the garnishee is hereby notified that the procedures established under 31 C.F.R. Part 212 for identifying and protecting Federal benefits deposited to accounts at financial institutions do not apply to this garnishment order.

The garnishee should comply with the terms of this order, including instructions for withholding and retaining any funds deposited to any account(s) covered by this order, pending further order of [name of the court]/[the name of the State child support enforcement agency].

Appendix C to Part 212—Examples of the Lookback Period and Protected Amount

The following examples illustrate this definition of *lookback period*.

Example 1: Account review performed same day garnishment order is served.

A financial institution receives garnishment order on Wednesday, March 17. The financial institution performs account review the same day on Wednesday, March 17. The lookback period begins on Tuesday, March 16, the date preceding the date of account review. The lookback period ends on Saturday, January 16, the corresponding date two months earlier.

Example 2: Account review performed the day after garnishment order is served.

A financial institution receives garnishment order on Wednesday, November 17. The financial institution performs account review next business day on Thursday, November 18. The lookback period begins on Wednesday, November 17, the date preceding the date of account review. The lookback period ends on Friday, September 17, the corresponding date two months earlier.

Example 3: No corresponding date two months earlier.

A financial institution receives garnishment order on Tuesday, August 30. The financial institution performs the account review two business days later on Thursday, September 1. The lookback period begins on Wednesday, August 31, the date preceding the date of account review. The lookback period ends on Wednesday, June 30, the last date of the month two months earlier, since June 31 does not exist to correspond with August 31.

Example 4: Weekend between receipt of garnishment order and account review.

A financial institution receives garnishment order on Friday, December 10. The financial institution performs the account review two business days later on Tuesday, December 14. The lookback period begins on Monday, December 13, the date preceding the date of account review. The lookback period ends on Wednesday, October 13, the corresponding date two months earlier.

The following examples illustrate the definition of *protected amount.*

Example 1: Account balance less than sum of benefit payments.

A financial institution receives a garnishment order against an account holder for $2,000 on May 20. The date of account review is the same day, May 20, and the balance in the account when the review is performed is $1,000. The lookback period begins on May 19, the date preceding the date of account review, and ends on March 19, the corresponding date two months earlier. The account review shows that two Federal benefit payments were deposited to the account during the lookback period totaling $2,500, one for $1,250 on Friday, April 30 and one for $1,250 on Tuesday, April 1. Since the $1,000 balance in the account when the account review is performed is less than the $2,500 sum of benefit payments posted to the account during the lookback period, the financial institution establishes the protected amount at $1,000. The financial institution is not required to send a notice to the account holder.

Example 2: Three benefit payments during lookback period.

A financial institution receives a garnishment order against an account holder for $8,000 on December 2. The date of account review is the same day, December 2, and the balance in the account when the account review is performed is $5,000. The lookback period begins on December 1, the date preceding the date of account review, and ends on October 1, the corresponding date two months earlier. The account review shows that three Federal benefit payments were deposited to the account during the lookback period totaling $4,500, one for $1,500 on December 1, another for $1,500 on November 1, and a third for $1,500 on October 1. Since the $4,500 sum of the three benefit payments posted to the account during the lookback period is less than the $5,000 balance in the account when the account review is performed, the financial institution establishes the protected amount at $4,500 and seizes the remaining $500 in the account consistent with State law. The financial institution is required to send a notice to the account holder.

Example 3: Intraday transactions.

A financial institution receives a garnishment order against an account holder for $4,000 on Friday, September 10. The date of account review is Monday, September 13, when the opening balance in the account is $6,000. A cash withdrawal for $1,000 is processed after the open of business on September 13, but before the financial institution has performed the account review, so that the balance in the account is $5,000 when the financial institution initiates an automated program to conduct the account review. The lookback period begins on Sunday, September 12, the date preceding the date of account review, and ends on Monday, July 12, the corresponding date two months earlier. The account review shows that two Federal benefit payments were deposited to the account during the lookback period totaling $3,000, one for $1,500 on Wednesday, July 21, and the other for $1,500 on Wednesday, August 18. Since the $3,000 sum of the two benefit payments posted to the account during the lookback period is less than the $5,000 balance in the account when the account review is performed, the financial institution establishes the protected amount at $3,000 and, consistent with State law, freezes the $2,000 remaining in the account after the cash withdrawal. The financial institution is required to send a notice to the account holder.

Example 4: Benefit payment on date of account review.

A financial institution receives a garnishment order against an account holder for $5,000 on Thursday, July 1. The date of account review is the same day, July 1, when the opening balance in the account is $3,000, and reflects a Federal benefit payment of $1,000 posted that day. The lookback period begins on Wednesday, June 30, the date preceding the date of account review, and ends on Friday, April 30, the corresponding date two months earlier. The account review shows that two Federal benefit payments were deposited to the account during the lookback period totaling $2,000, one for $1,000 on Friday, April 30 and one for $1,000 on Tuesday, June 1. Since the $2,000 sum of the two benefit payments posted to the account during the lookback period is less than the $3,000 balance in the account when the account review is performed, the financial institution establishes the protected amount at $2,000 and places a hold on the remaining $1,000 in the account in accordance with State law. The financial institution is required to send a notice to the account holder.

Example 5: Account co-owners with benefit payments.

A financial institution receives a garnishment order against an account holder for $3,800 on March 22. The date of account review is the same day, March 22, and the balance in the account is $7,000. The lookback period begins on March 21, the date preceding the date of account review, and ends on January 21, the corresponding date two months earlier. The account review shows that four Federal benefit payments were deposited to the account during the lookback period totaling $7,000. Two of these benefit payments, totaling $3,000, were made to the account holder against whom the garnishment order was issued. The other two payments, totaling $4,000, were made to a co-owner of the account. Since the financial institution must perform the account review based only on the presence of benefit payments, without regard to the existence of co-owners on the account or payments to multiple beneficiaries or under multiple programs, the financial institution establishes the protected amount at $7,000, equal to the sum of the four benefit payments posted to the account during the lookback period. Since $7,000 is also the balance in the account at the time of the account review, there are no additional funds in the account which can be frozen. The financial institution is not required to send a notice to the account holder.

Appendix E Selected Federal Exemption Provisions

E.1 Social Security and SSI Benefits—42 U.S.C. §§ 407, 1383

Chapter 7—Social Security

Subchapter II—Federal Old-Age, Survivors, and Disability Insurance Benefits

42 U.S.C. § 407. Assignment of benefits

(a) In general

The right of any person to any future payment under this subchapter shall not be transferable or assignable, at law or in equity, and none of the moneys paid or payable or rights existing under this subchapter shall be subject to execution, levy, attachment, garnishment, or other legal process, or to the operation of any bankruptcy or insolvency law.

(b) Amendment of section

No other provision of law, enacted before, on, or after April 20, 1983, may be construed to limit, supersede, or otherwise modify the provisions of this section except to the extent that it does so by express reference to this section.

(c) Withholding of taxes

Nothing in this section shall be construed to prohibit withholding taxes from any benefit under this subchapter, if such withholding is done pursuant to a request made in accordance with section 3402(p)(1) of the Internal Revenue Code of 1986 [26 U.S.C.A. § 3402] by the person entitled to such benefit or such person's representative payee.

* * *

[49 Stat. 624 (1935); 53 Stat. 1372 (1939); Pub. L. No. 98–21, 97 Stat. 130 (1983); Pub. L. No. 105–277, 112 Stat. 2681–911 (1998)]

Subchapter XVI—Supplemental Security Income for Aged, Blind, and Disabled

Part B—Procedural and General Provisions

42 U.S.C. § 1383. Procedure for payment of benefits

* * *

(d) Procedures applicable; prohibition on assignment of payments; representation of claimants; maximum fees; penalties for violations

(1) The provisions of section 407 of this title and subsections (a), (d), and (e) of section 405 of this title shall apply with respect to this part to the same extent as they apply in the case of subchapter II of this chapter.

* * *

[Pub. L. No. 92–603, 86 Stat. 1475 (1972); Pub. L. No. 93–233, 87 Stat. 969 (1973); Pub. L. No. 93–368, 88 Stat. 420 (1974); Pub. L. No. 94–202, 89 Stat. 1135 (1976); Pub. L. No. 94–365, 90 Stat. 990 (1976); Pub. L. No. 94–569, 90 Stat. 2700 (1976); Pub. L. No. 96–222, 94 Stat. 195 (1980); Pub. L. No. 96–265, 94 Stat. 450, 457, 459, 470 (1980); Pub. L. No. 96–473, 94 Stat. 2266 (1980); Pub. L. No. 97–35, 95 Stat. 866 (1981); Pub. L. No. 97–248, 96 Stat. 407 (1982); Pub. L. No. 98–369, 98 Stat. 1131, 1150, 1169 (1984); Pub. L. No. 98–460, 98 Stat. 1803, 1809 (1984); Pub. L. No. 99–272, 100 Stat. 288 (1986); Pub. L. No. 99–514, 100 Stat. 2918 (1986); Pub. L. No. 99–570, 100 Stat. 3207 (1986); Pub. L. No. 99–643, 100 Stat. 3576–3579 (1986); Pub. L. No. 100–203, 101 Stat. 1330 (1987); Pub. L. No. 100–647, 102 Stat. 3779 (1988); Pub. L. No. 101–239, 103 Stat. 2482, 2483, 2485 (1989); Pub. L. No. 101–508, 104 Stat. 1388 (1990); Pub. L. No. 103–296, 108 Stat. 1478, 1499, 1500, 1501, 1509, 1514, 1515, 1541, 1544 (1994); Pub. L. No. 103–387, 108 Stat. 4077 (1994); Pub. L. No. 103–432, 108 Stat. 4468–4470 (1994); Pub. L. No. 104–121, 110 Stat. 853 (1996); Pub. L. No. 104–193, 110 Stat. 2188, 2194, 2196, 2197, 2267 (1996); Pub. L. No. 105–33, 111 Stat. 622, 639 (1997); Pub. L. No. 105–306, 112 Stat. 2929 (1998); Pub. L. No. 106–169, 113 Stat. 1831, 1832, 1843, 1856 (1999); Pub. L. No. 106–170, 113 Stat. 1874, 1884 (1999); Pub. L. No. 108–203, 118 Stat. 496, 497, 500, 502, 503, 505, 506, 517, 519, 521 (2004); Pub. L. No. 109–163, 119 Stat. 3337 (2006); Pub. L. No. 109–171, 120 Stat. 154 (2006); Pub. L. No. 110–234, 122 Stat. 1095, 1097 (2008); Pub. L. No. 110–246, 122 Stat. 1664, 1857, 1858 (2008); Pub. L. No. 111–115, 123 Stat. 3029 (2009); Pub. L. No. 111–142, 124 Stat. 39 (2010)]

* * *

E.2 Veterans' Benefits—38 U.S.C. § 5301

Part IV. General Administrative Provisions

Chapter 53. Special Provisions Relating to Benefits

38 U.S.C. § 5301. Nonassignability and exempt status of benefits

(a) **(1)** Payments of benefits due or to become due under any law administered by the Secretary shall not be assignable except to the extent specifically authorized by law, and such payments made to, or on account of, a beneficiary shall be exempt from taxation, shall be exempt from the claim of creditors, and shall not be liable to attachment, levy, or seizure by or under any legal or equitable process whatever, either before or after receipt by the beneficiary. The preceding sentence shall not apply to claims of the United States arising under such laws nor shall the exemption therein contained as to taxation extend to any property purchased in part or wholly out of such payments. The provisions of this section shall not be construed to prohibit the assignment of insurance otherwise authorized under chapter 19 of this title, or of servicemen's indemnity.

(2) For the purposes of this subsection, in any case where a payee of an educational assistance allowance has designated the address of an attorney-in-fact as the payee's address for the purpose of receiving a benefit check and has also executed a power of attorney giving the attorney-in-fact authority to negotiate such benefit check, such action shall be deemed to be an assignment and is prohibited.

(3) **(A)** This paragraph is intended to clarify that, in any case where a beneficiary entitled to compensation, pension, or dependency and indemnity compensation enters into an agreement with another person under which agreement such other person acquires for consideration the right to receive such benefit by payment of such compensation, pension, or dependency and indemnity compensation, as the case may be, except as provided in subparagraph (B), and including deposit into a joint account from which such other person may make withdrawals, or otherwise, such agreement shall be deemed to be an assignment and is prohibited.

(B) Notwithstanding subparagraph (A), nothing in this paragraph is intended to prohibit a loan involving a beneficiary under the terms of which the beneficiary may use the benefit to repay such other person as long as each of the periodic payments made to repay such other person is separately and voluntarily executed by the beneficiary or is made by preauthorized electronic funds transfer pursuant to the Electronic Funds Transfers Act (15 U.S.C. 1693 *et seq.*).

(C) Any agreement or arrangement for collateral for security for an agreement that is prohibited under subparagraph (A) is also prohibited and is void from its inception.

(b) This section shall prohibit the collection by setoff or otherwise out of any benefits payable pursuant to any law administered by the Secretary and relating to veterans, their estates, or their dependents, of any claim of the United States or any agency thereof against (1) any person other than the indebted beneficiary or the beneficiary's estate; or (2) any beneficiary or the beneficiary's estate except amounts due the United States by such beneficiary or the beneficiary's estate by reason of overpayments or illegal payments made under such laws to such beneficiary or the beneficiary's estate or to the beneficiary's dependents as such. If the benefits referred to in the preceding sentence are insurance payable by reason of yearly renewable term insurance, United States Government life insurance, or National Service Life Insurance issued by the United States, the exemption provided in this section shall not apply to indebtedness existing against the particular insurance contract upon the maturity of which the claim is based, whether such indebtedness is in the form of liens to secure unpaid premiums or loans, or interest on such premiums or loans, or indebtedness arising from overpayments of dividends, refunds, loans, or other insurance benefits.

(c) **(1)** Notwithstanding any other provision of this section, the Secretary may, after receiving a request under paragraph (2) of this subsection relating to a veteran, collect by offset of any compensation or pension payable to the veteran under laws administered by the Secretary the uncollected portion of the amount of any indebtedness associated with the veteran's participation in a plan prescribed in chapter 73 of title 10.

(2) If the Secretary concerned (as defined in section 101(5) of title 37) has tried under section 3711(a) of title 31 to collect an amount described in paragraph (1) of this subsection in the case of any veteran, has been unable to collect such amount, and has determined that the uncollected portion of such amount is not collectible from amounts payable by that Secretary to the veteran or that the veteran is not receiving any payment from that Secretary, that Secretary may request the Secretary to make collections in the case of such veteran as authorized in paragraph (1) of this subsection.

(3) **(A)** A collection authorized by paragraph (1) of this subsection shall be conducted in accordance with the procedures prescribed in section 3716 of title 31 for administrative offset collections made after attempts to collect claims under section 3711(a) of such title.

(B) For the purposes of subparagraph (A) of this paragraph, as used in the second sentence of section 3716(a) of title 31—

(i) the term "records of the agency" shall be considered to refer to the records of the department of the Secretary concerned; and

(ii) the term "agency" in clauses (3) and (4) shall be considered to refer to such department.

(4) Funds collected under this subsection shall be credited to the Department of Defense Military Retirement Fund under chapter 74 of title 10 or to the Retired Pay Account of the Coast Guard, as appropriate.

(d) Notwithstanding subsection (a) of this section, payments of benefits under laws administered by the Secretary shall not be exempt from levy under subchapter D of chapter 64 of the Internal Revenue Code of 1986 (26 U.S.C. 6331 *et seq.*).

(e) In the case of a person who—

(1) has been determined to be eligible to receive pension or compensation under laws administered by the Secretary but for the receipt by such person of pay pursuant to any provision of law providing retired or retirement pay to members or former members of the Armed Forces or commissioned officers of the National Oceanic and Atmospheric Administration or of the Public Health Service; and

(2) files a waiver of such pay in accordance with section 5305 of this title in the amount of such pension or compensation before the end of the one-year period beginning on the date such person is notified by the Secretary of such person's eligibility for such pension or compensation,

the retired or retirement pay of such person shall be exempt from taxation, as provided in subsection (a) of this section, in an amount equal to the amount of pension or compensation which would have been paid to such person but for the receipt by such person of such pay.

[Pub. L. No. 85–857, 72 Stat. 1229 (1958); Pub. L. No. 94–502, 90 Stat. 2405 (1976); Pub. L. No. 95–479, 92 Stat. 1564 (1978); Pub. L. No. 97–295, 96 Stat. 1310 (1982); Pub. L. No. 99–576, 100 Stat. 3286, 3296 (1986); Pub. L. No. 101–189, 103 Stat. 1586 (1989); Pub. L. No. 102–25, 105 Stat. 120 (1991); Pub. L. No. 102–40, 105 Stat. 238, 239 (1991); Pub. L. No. 102–54, 105 Stat. 285 (1991); Pub. L. No. 102–83, 105 Stat. 403 (1991); Pub. L. No. 102–86, 102 Stat. 426 (1991); Pub. L. No. 108–183, 117 Stat. 2671 (2003)]

* * *

E.3 Exception Allowing Enforcement of Child Support Claims Against Social Security and Veterans' Benefits—42 U.S.C. § 659

Chapter 7—Social Security

Subchapter IV—Grants to States for Aid and Services to Needy Families with Children and for Child-Welfare Services

Part D—Child Support and Establishment of Paternity

* * *

42 U.S.C. § 659. Consent by the United States to income withholding, garnishment, and similar proceedings for enforcement of child support and alimony obligations

(a) Consent to support enforcement

Notwithstanding any other provision of law (including section 407 of this title and section 5301 of Title 38), effective January 1, 1975, moneys (the entitlement to which is based upon remuneration for employment) due from, or payable by, the United States or the District of Columbia (including any agency, subdivision, or instrumentality thereof) to any individual, including members of the Armed Forces of the United States, shall be subject, in like manner and to the same extent as if the United States or the District of Columbia were a private person, to withholding in accordance with State law enacted pursuant to subsections (a)(1) and (b) of section 666 of this title[1] and regulations of the Secretary under such subsections, and to any other legal process brought, by a State agency administering a program under a State plan approved under this part or by an individual obligee, to enforce the legal obligation of the individual to provide child support or alimony.

* * *

[Pub. L. No. 93–647, 88 Stat. 2357 (1975); Pub. L. No. 95–30, 91 Stat. 157 (1977); Pub. L. No. 98–21, 97 Stat. 130 (1983); Pub. L. No. 104–193, 110 Stat. 2242 (1996); Pub. L. No. 105–33, 111 Stat. 631 (1997); Pub. L. No. 106–169, 113 Stat. 1855 (1999); Pub. L. No. 109–435, 120 Stat. 3242 (2006)]

* * *

E.4 Civil Service and Federal Retirement and Disability Benefits—5 U.S.C. §§ 8130, 8346, 8470

Title 5—Government Organization and Employees

Part III—Employees

Subpart G—Insurance and Annuities

Chapter 81—Compensation for Work Injuries

Subchapter I—Generally

5 U.S.C. § 8130. Assignment of claim

An assignment of a claim for compensation under this subchapter is void. Compensation and claims for compensation are exempt from claims of creditors.
[Pub. L. No. 89–554, 80 Stat. 546 (1966)]

* * *

Chapter 83—Retirement

Subchapter III—Civil Service Retirement

5 U.S.C. § 8346. Exemption from legal process; recovery of payments

(a) The money mentioned by this subchapter is not assignable, either in law or equity, except under the provisions of subsections (h) and (j) of section 8345 of this title, or subject to execution, levy, attachment, garnishment, or other legal process, except as otherwise may be provided by Federal laws.

* * *

[Pub. L. No. 89–554, 80 Stat. 583 (1966); Pub. L. No. 94–166, 89 Stat. 1002 (1975); Pub. L. No. 95–366, 92 Stat. 600 (1978); Pub. L. No. 95–454, 92 Stat. 1224 (1978)]

* * *

1. [*Editor's Note:* 42 U.S.C. § 666 deals with procedures to improve the effectiveness of child support enforcement, including the withholding of payments.]

Chapter 84—Federal Employees' Retirement System

Subchapter VI—General and Administrative Provisions

5 U.S.C. § 8470. Exemption from legal process; recovery of payments

(a) An amount payable under subchapter II, IV, or V of this chapter is not assignable, either in law or equity, except under the provisions of section 8465 or 8467, or subject to execution, levy, attachment, garnishment or other legal process, except as otherwise may be provided by Federal laws.

* * *

[Pub. L. No. 99–335, 100 Stat. 577 (1986)]

* * *

E.5 Servicemembers' Pay—37 U.S.C. § 701

Chapter 13—Allotments and Assignments of Pay

37 U.S.C. § 701. Members of the Army, Navy, Air Force, and Marine Corps; contract surgeons

(a) Under regulations prescribed by the Secretary of the military department concerned,[2] a commissioned officer of the Army, Navy, Air Force, or Marine Corps may transfer or assign his pay account, when due and payable.

(b) A contract surgeon, or contract dental surgeon, of the Army, Navy, or Air Force, on duty in Alaska, Hawaii, the Philippine Islands, or Puerto Rico, may transfer or assign his pay account, when due and payable, under the regulations prescribed under subsection (a).

(c) An enlisted member of the Army, Navy, Air Force, or Marine Corps may not assign his pay, and if he does so, the assignment is void.

* * *

[Pub. L. No. 87–649, 76 Stat. 484 (1962); Pub. L. No. 89–718, 80 Stat. 1123 (1966); Pub. L. No. 99–145, 99 Stat. 665 (1985); Pub. L. No. 102–25, 105 Stat. 117 (1991); Pub. L. No. 104–201, 110 Stat. 2582 (1996)]

* * *

E.6 Military Annuities and Survivors' Benefits—10 U.S.C. §§ 1440, 1450

Chapter 73—Annuities Based on Retired or Retainer Pay

Subchapter I—Retired Serviceman's Family Protection Plan

* * *

10 U.S.C. § 1440. Annuities not subject to legal process

Except as provided in section 1437(c)(3)(B) of this title, no annuity payable under this subchapter is assignable or subject to execution, levy, attachment, garnishment, or other legal process.
[70A Stat. 111 (1956); Pub. L. No. 92–425, 86 Stat. 706 (1972); Pub. L. No. 98–525, 98 Stat. 2546 (1984); Pub. L. No. 99–145, 99 Stat. 739 (1985)]

2. [*Editor's Note:* No such regulations have been enacted.]

* * *

Subchapter II—Survivor Benefit Plan

10 U.S.C. § 1450. Payment of annuity: beneficiaries

* * *

(i) Annuities exempt from certain legal process

Except as provided in subsection (*l*)(3)(B), an annuity under this section is not assignable or subject to execution, levy, attachment, garnishment, or other legal process.

* * *

[Pub. L. No. 92–425, 86 Stat. 708 (1972); Pub. L. No. 94–496, 90 Stat. 2375 (1976); Pub. L. No. 95–397, 92 Stat. 845, 848 (1978); Pub. L. No. 97–22, 95 Stat. 137 (1981); Pub. L. No. 97–252, 96 Stat. 736 (1982); Pub. L. No. 98–94, 97 Stat. 653 (1983); Pub. L. No. 98–525, 98 Stat. 2546, 2548 (1984); Pub. L. No. 99–145, 99 Stat. 672, 674–677, 739 (1985); Pub. L. No. 99–661, 100 Stat. 3885, 3886, 3992 (1986); Pub. L. No. 100–26, 101 Stat. 273 (1987); Pub. L. No. 100–180, 101 Stat. 1106 (1987); Pub. L. No. 100–224, 101 Stat. 1538 (1987); Pub. L. No. 101–189, 103 Stat. 1588, 1602 (1989); Pub. L. No. 103–337, 108 Stat. 2859 (1994); Pub. L. No. 104–201, 110 Stat. 2561 (1996); Pub. L. No. 105–85, 111 Stat. 1799 (1997); Pub. L. No. 105–261, 112 Stat. 2048 (1998); Pub. L. No. 106–398,114 Stat. 1654, 1654A (2000); Pub. L. No. 110–181, 122 Stat. 157, 158 (2008); Pub. L. No. 110–417, 122 Stat. 4492 (2008); Pub. L. No. 111–31, 123 Stat. 1857 (2009); Pub. L. No. 112–239, 126 Stat. 1632 (2013)]

* * *

E.7 Student Assistance—20 U.S.C. § 1095a

Chapter 28—Higher Education Resources and Student Assistance

Subchapter IV—Student Assistance

Part F—General Provisions Relating to Student Assistance Programs

* * *

20 U.S.C. § 1095a. Wage garnishment requirement

* * *

(d) No attachment of student assistance

Except as authorized in this section, notwithstanding any other provision of Federal or State law, no grant, loan, or work assistance awarded under this subchapter and part C of subchapter I of chapter 34 of Title 42, or property traceable to such assistance, shall be subject to garnishment or attachment in order to satisfy any debt owed by the student awarded such assistance, other than a debt owed to the Secretary and arising under this subchapter and part C of subchapter I of chapter 34 of Title 42.

* * *

[Pub. L. No. 89–329, 79 Stat. 1219 (1965); Pub. L. No. 102–164, 105 Stat. 1066 (1991); Pub. L. No. 105–244, 112 Stat. 1753 (1998); Pub. L. No. 109–171, 120 Stat. 180 (2006)]

* * *

E.8 Railroad Retirement Benefits—45 U.S.C. § 231m

Chapter 9—Retirement of Railroad Employees

Subchapter IV—Railroad Retirement Act of 1974

* * *

45 U.S.C. § 231m Assignability; exemption from levy

(a) Except as provided in subsection (b) of this section and the Internal Revenue Code of 1986 [26 U.S.C.A. § 1 *et seq.*], notwithstanding any other law of the United States, or of any State, territory, or the District of Columbia, no annuity or supplemental annuity shall be assignable or be subject to any tax or to garnishment, attachment, or other legal process under any circumstances whatsoever, nor shall the payment thereof be anticipated.

(b) **(1)** This section shall not operate to exclude the amount of any supplemental annuity paid to an individual under section 231a(b) of this title from income taxable pursuant to the Federal income tax provisions of the Internal Revenue Code of 1986 [26 U.S.C.A. § 1 *et seq.*].

(2) This section shall not operate to prohibit the characterization or treatment of that portion of an annuity under this subchapter which is not computed under section 231b(a), 231c(a), or 231c(f) of this title, or any portion of a supplemental annuity under this subchapter, as community property for the purposes of, or property subject to, distribution in accordance with a court decree of divorce, annulment, or legal separation or the terms of any court-approved property settlement incident to any such court decree. The Board shall make payments of such portions in accordance with any such characterization or treatment or any such decree or settlement.

(3) **(A)** Payments made pursuant to paragraph (2) of this subsection shall not require that the employee be entitled to an annuity under section 231a(a)(1) of this title: Provided, however, That where an employee is not entitled to such an annuity, payments made pursuant to paragraph (2) may not begin before the month in which the following three conditions are satisfied:

(i) The employee has completed ten years of service in the railroad industry or, five years of service all of which accrues after December 31, 1995.

(ii) The spouse or former spouse attains age 62.

(iii) The employee attains age 62 (or if deceased, would have attained age 62).

(B) Payments made pursuant to paragraph (2) of this subsection shall terminate upon the death of the spouse or former spouse, unless the court document provides for termination at an earlier date. Notwithstanding the language in a court order, that portion of payments made pursuant to paragraph (2) which represents payments computed pursuant to section 231b(f)(2) of this title shall not be paid after the death of the employee.

(C) If the employee is not entitled to an annuity under section 231a(a)(1) of this title, payments made pursuant to paragraph (2) of this subsection shall be computed as though the employee were entitled to an annuity.

[Pub. L. No. 93–445, 88 Stat. 1345 (1974); Pub. L. No. 98–76, 97 Stat. 438 (1983); Pub. L. No. 99–514, 100 Stat. 2095 (1986); Pub. L. No. 110–458, 122 Stat. 5112 (2008)]

E.9 Merchant Seamen Wages—46 U.S.C. § 11109

Part G—Merchant Seamen Protection and Relief

Chapter 111—Protection and Relief

46 U.S.C. § 11109. Attachment of wages

(a) Wages due or accruing to a master or seaman are not subject to attachment or arrestment from any court, except for an order of a court about the payment by a master or seaman of any part of the master's or seaman's wages for the support and maintenance of the spouse or minor children of the master or seaman, or both. A payment of wages to a master or seaman is valid, notwithstanding any prior sale or assignment of wages or any attachment, encumbrance, or arrestment of the wages.

(b) An assignment or sale of wages or salvage made before the payment of wages does not bind the party making it, except allotments authorized by section 10315 of this title.

(c) This section applies to an individual employed on a fishing vessel or any fish processing vessel.

[Pub. L. No. 98–89, 97 Stat. 580 (1983); Pub. L. 98–364, 98 Stat. 450 (1984)]

* * *

E.10 Longshoremen's and Harbor Workers' Death and Disability Benefits—33 U.S.C. § 916

Chapter 18—Longshore and Harbor Workers' Compensation

* * *

33 U.S.C. § 916. Assignment and exemption from claims of creditors

No assignment, release, or commutation of compensation or benefits due or payable under this chapter, except as provided by this chapter, shall be valid, and such compensation and benefits shall be exempt from all claims of creditors and from levy, execution, and attachment or other remedy for recovery or collection of a debt, which exemption may not be waived.

[44 Stat. 1434 (1927)]

* * *

E.11 Foreign Service Retirement and Disability Benefits—22 U.S.C. § 4060

Chapter 52—Foreign Service

Subchapter VIII—Foreign Service Retirement and Disability

Part I—Foreign Service Retirement and Disability System

22 U.S.C. § 4060. Assignment and attachment of moneys

* * *

(c) Applicability of other provisions of law or remedies
None of the moneys mentioned in this part shall be assignable either in law or equity, except under subsection (a) or (b) of this section, or subject to execution, levy, attachment, garnishment, or other legal process, except as otherwise may be provided by Federal law.

[Pub. L. No. 96–465, 94 Stat. 2120 (1980); Pub. L. No. 99–335, 100 Stat. 609 (1986)]

* * *

E.12 Compensation for Injury, Death, or Detention of Employees of U.S. Contractors Outside the U.S.—42 U.S.C. § 1717

Chapter 12—Compensation for Injury, Death, or Detention of Employees of Contractors with United States Outside United States

Subchapter II—Miscellaneous Provisions

* * *

42 U.S.C. § 1717. Assignment of benefits; execution, levy, etc., against benefits

The right of any person to any benefit under subchapter I of this chapter shall not be transferable or assignable at law or in equity except to the United States, and none of the moneys paid or payable (except money paid hereunder as reimbursement for funeral expenses or as reimbursement with respect to payments of workmen's compensation or in the nature of workmen's compensation benefits), or rights existing under said subchapter, shall be subject to execution, levy, attachment, garnishment, or other legal process or to the operation of any bankruptcy or insolvency law.

[56 Stat. 1035 (1942)]

E.13 Federal Emergency Management Agency Federal Disaster Assistance—44 C.F.R. § 206.110

PART 206—FEDERAL DISASTER ASSISTANCE

* * *

44 C.F.R. § 206.110 Federal assistance to individuals and households

(a) Purpose. This section implements the policy and procedures set forth in section 408 of the Robert T. Stafford Disaster Relief and Emergency Assistance Act, 42 U.S.C. 5174, as amended by the Disaster Mitigation Act of 2000. This program provides financial assistance and, if necessary, direct assistance to eligible individuals and households who, as a direct result of a major disaster or emergency, have uninsured or under-insured, necessary expenses and serious needs and are unable to meet such expenses or needs through other means.

* * *

(g) Exemption from garnishment. All assistance provided under this subpart is exempt from garnishment, seizure, encumbrance, levy, execution, pledge, attachment, release or waiver. Recipients of rights under this provision may not reassign or transfer the rights. These exemptions do not apply to FEMA recovering assistance fraudulently obtained or misapplied.

* * *

[67 Fed. Reg. 61,452 (Sept. 30, 2002); 67 Fed. Reg. 62,896 (Oct. 9, 2002); 74 Fed. Reg. 15,348 (April 3, 2009)]

* * *

Appendix F Federal Trade Commission Credit Practices Rule

16 C.F.R. Part 444

PART 444—CREDIT PRACTICES

AUTHORITY: 15 U.S.C. § 57a; 5 U.S.C. § 552, unless otherwise noted.

SOURCE: 49 Fed. Reg. 7789 (Mar. 1, 1984), unless otherwise noted.

16 C.F.R. § 444.1 Definitions

(a) *Lender.* A person who engages in the business of lending money to consumers within the jurisdiction of the Federal Trade Commission.

(b) *Retail installment seller.* A person who sells goods or services to consumers on a deferred payment basis or pursuant to a lease-purchase arrangement within the jurisdiction of the Federal Trade Commission.

(c) *Person.* An individual corporation, or other business organization.

(d) *Consumer.* A natural person who seeks or acquires goods, services, or money for personal, family, or household use.

(e) *Obligation.* An agreement between a consumer and a lender or retail installment seller.

(f) *Creditor.* A lender or a retail installment seller.

(g) *Debt.* Money that is due or alleged to be due from one to another.

(h) *Earnings.* Compensation paid or payable to an individual or for his or her account for personal services rendered or to be rendered by him or her, whether denominated as wages, salary, commission, bonus, or otherwise, including periodic payments pursuant to a pension, retirement, or disability program.

(i) *Household goods.* Clothing, furniture, appliances, one radio and one television, linens, china, crockery, kitchenware, and personal effects (including wedding rings) of the consumer and his or her dependents, provided that the following are not included within the scope of the term "household goods":

- **(1)** Works of art;
- **(2)** Electronic entertainment equipment (except one television and one radio);
- **(3)** Items acquired as antiques; and
- **(4)** Jewelry (except wedding rings).

(j) *Antique.* Any item over one hundred years of age, including such items that have been repaired or renovated without changing their original form or character.

(k) *Cosigner.* A natural person who renders himself or herself liable for the obligation of another person without compensation. The term shall include any person whose signature is requested as a condition to granting credit to another person, or as a condition for forbearance on collection of another person's obligation that is in default. The term shall not include a spouse whose signature is required on a credit obligation to perfect a security interest pursuant to state law. A person who does not receive goods, services, or money in return for a credit obligation does not receive compensation within the meaning of this definition. A person is a cosigner within the meaning of this definition whether or not he or she is designated as such on a credit obligation.

16 C.F.R. § 444.2 Unfair credit practices

(a) In connection with the extension of credit to consumers in or affecting commerce, as commerce is defined in the Federal Trade Commission Act, it is an unfair act or practice within the meaning of Section 5 of that Act for a lender or retail installment seller directly or indirectly to take or receive from a consumer an obligation that:

- **(1)** Constitutes or contains a cognovit or confession of judgment (for purposes other than executory process in the State of Louisiana), warrant of attorney, or other waiver of the right to notice and the opportunity to be heard in the event of suit or process thereon.
- **(2)** Constitutes or contains an executory waiver or a limitation of exemption from attachment, execution, or other process on real or personal property held, owned by, or due to the consumer, unless the waiver applies solely to property subject to a security interest executed in connection with the obligation.
- **(3)** Constitutes or contains an assignment of wages or other earnings unless:
  - **(i)** The assignment by its terms is revocable at the will of the debtor, or
  - **(ii)** The assignment is a payroll deduction plan or preauthorized payment plan, commencing at the time of the transaction, in which the consumer authorizes a series of wage deductions as a method of making each payment, or
  - **(iii)** The assignment applies only to wages or other earnings already earned at the time of the assignment.
- **(4)** Constitutes or contains a nonpossessory security interest in household goods other than a purchase money security interest.

16 C.F.R. § 444.3 Unfair or deceptive cosigner practices

(a) In connection with the extension of credit to consumers in or affecting commerce, as commerce is defined in the Federal Trade Commission Act, it is:

- **(1)** A deceptive act or practice within the meaning of section 5 of that Act for a lender or retail installment seller, directly or indirectly, to misrepresent the nature or extent of cosigner liability to any person.
- **(2)** An unfair act or practice within the meaning of section 5 of that Act for a lender or retail installment seller, directly or indirectly, to obligate a cosigner unless the cosigner is informed prior to becoming obligated, which in the case of open end credit shall mean prior to the time that the agreement creating the cosigner's liability for future charges is executed, of the nature of his or her liability as cosigner.

(b) Any lender or retail installment seller who complies with the preventive requirements in paragraph (c) of this section does not violate paragraph (a) of this section.

(c) To prevent these unfair or deceptive acts or practices, a disclosure, consisting of a separate document that shall contain the following statement and no other, shall be given to the cosigner prior to becoming obligated, which in the case of open end credit shall mean prior to the time that the agreement creating the cosigner's liability for future charges is executed:

NOTICE TO COSIGNER

You are being asked to guarantee this debt. Think carefully before you do. If the borrower doesn't pay the debt, you will have to. Be sure you can afford to pay if you have to, and that you want to accept this responsibility.

You may have to pay up to the full amount of the debt if the borrower does not pay. You may also have to pay late fees or collection costs, which increase this amount.

The creditor can collect this debt from you without first trying to collect from the borrower. The creditor can use the same collection methods against you that can be used against the borrower, such as suing you, garnishing your wages, etc. If this debt is ever in default, that fact may become a part of *your* credit record.

This notice is not the contract that makes you liable for the debt.

16 C.F.R. § 444.4 Late charges

(a) In connection with collecting a debt arising out of an extension of credit to a consumer in or affecting commerce, as commerce is defined in the Federal Trade Commission Act, it is an unfair act or practice within the meaning of section 5 of that Act for a creditor, directly or indirectly, to levy or collect any delinquency charge on a payment, which payment is otherwise a full payment for the applicable period and is paid on its due date or within an applicable grace period, when the only delinquency is attributable to late fee(s) or delinquency charge(s) assessed on earlier installment(s).

(b) For purposes of this section, "collecting a debt" means any activity other than the use of judicial process that is intended to bring about or does bring about repayment of all or part of a consumer debt.

16 C.F.R. § 444.5 State exemptions

(a) If, upon application to the Federal Trade Commission by an appropriate State agency, the Federal Trade Commission determines that:

(1) There is a State requirement or prohibition in effect that applies to any transaction to which a provision of this rule applies; and

(2) The State requirement or prohibition affords a level of protection to consumers that is substantially equivalent to, or greater than, the protection afforded by this rule;

Then that provision of the rule will not be in effect in that State to the extent specified by the Federal Trade Commission in its determination, for as long as the State administers and enforces the State requirement or prohibition effectively.

(b) [*Reserved.*]

Appendix G Summaries of State Exemption Laws

What Is Included

This appendix summarizes state exemption statutes. It focuses on statutes that exempt property of consumer debtors from collection by creditors. Statutes that provide special exemption rules for child support or other family support collections, or for other special types of debts, such as reimbursements to the state, are not summarized here.

This appendix also does not summarize exemption provisions found in laws other than the state's general exemption laws. For example, statutes that create or regulate specific assets, such as public or private pensions, workers' compensation, educational savings accounts, insurance, or crime victims' compensation, often contain their own exemption language.

Whenever an asset is not listed as exempt in the state's exemption statute, the statutes that create or regulate that type of asset should also be checked. In addition, this appendix only summarizes prohibitions against waiver of exemptions that are found in the state's exemption statutes, not those in the Federal Trade Commission's Credit Practices Rule or state consumer protection laws.

In addition to exemption statutes, many states protect certain assets by common law doctrines such as ownership by the entireties.

Collier on Bankruptcy, volume 14, is a valuable reference on state exemption law. It reprints the full text of state exemption statutes, including most of those summarized here.

Exemptions in Bankruptcy Proceedings

This appendix includes a series of questions and answers for each state designed to help determine the applicable exemption law for purposes of 11 U.S.C. § 522(b)(3)(A) in a debtor's bankruptcy proceeding. Which state's exemption law applies is determined by the debtor's domicile. According to the Bankruptcy Code, the debtor's domicile for exemption purposes is the state in which the debtor's domicile has been located for the 730 days immediately preceding the petition filing date or, if the debtor's domicile has not been located in a single state for the 730-day period, the state in which the debtor was domiciled for the longer portion of the 180 days immediately preceding the 730-day period.[1]

If the domiciliary state, as determined by section 522(b)(3)(A), has not opted out of the federal exemption scheme, or if the statutory opt-out applies only to residents or domiciliaries of that state, the debtor may claim the federal bankruptcy exemptions found in section 522(d). The first question for each state therefore asks whether the state has opted out of the federal bankruptcy exemption scheme. The next question asks whether the state's opt-out is limited to residents or domiciliaries of that state.

If the effect of section 522(b)(3)(A) is to render the debtor ineligible for any exemption, the debtor may use the federal bankruptcy exemptions found in section 522(d). Such a situation could arise if the exemption law of the debtor's domicile requires the debtor to reside within the state in order to claim an exemption or if the law does not permit an exemption to be taken on property located outside the state. Thus the next question addresses whether the state exemption provisions covering homesteads and personal property may be given extraterritorial effect, thereby permitting an exemption to be used on property not located within the state.

If the language of the state exemption statute indicates that it applies only to property located in that state, or to a debtor domiciled in that state, the response is listed as "no." If the language of the state exemption statute indicates that it applies only to a resident of that state, the response is listed as "probably not," recognizing the possibility that a debtor may maintain a residence in the state even though the bankruptcy case has been filed in the state of the debtor's domicile for venue purposes. If the state exemption statute indicates that it applies to property located outside the state, or if the statute is silent but case law has construed the statute as having extraterritorial effect, the response is listed as "yes." If the statute does not clearly specify its extraterritorial effect and the issue has not been resolved by case law, the response is listed as "uncertain." In some cases, in which the statutory language or case law is inconclusive but suggests a leaning in one direction, the response is listed as "possibly yes," "possibly not," "probably yes," or "probably not."

ALABAMA

Has state opted out of federal bankruptcy exemptions? Yes. Ala. Code § 6-10-11.

Is opt out limited to residents or domiciliaries of the state? Not specified, but probably yes. Ala. Code § 6-10-11: "In cases instituted under [Title 11] there shall be exempt . . . only that property . . . exempt under the laws of Alabama and under [federal laws other than § 522(d)]." *See In re* Walley, 9 B.R. 55 (Bankr. S.D. Ala. 1981) (opt-out statute applies only to Alabama residents).

Do state's exemptions have extraterritorial application?

Homestead: No. *See In re* Carter, 213 B.R. 26 (Bankr. N.D. Ala. 1997); Sims v. Cox, 611 So. 2d 339 (Ala. 1992). *See also* Ala. Code § 6-10-2 (limited to "the homestead of every resident of this state").

Personal property: Probably not. Ala. Code § 6-10-6 limited to "the personal property of such resident."

***Wages:* Ala. Code §§ 5-19-15, 6-10-7, 6-10-120.**

Scope: Wages, salaries, or other compensation of laborers or employees, residents of Alabama, for personal services.

Amount: For consumer loans, consumer credit sales, and consumer leases, similar to federal exemptions (Ala. Code § 5-19-15); for all other debts, 75% of weekly disposable income is exempt. Ala. Code § 6-10-7. For consumer loans, disposable earnings are those left after legally required deductions. Disposable earnings do not include voluntary "periodic payments pursuant to a pension, retirement or disability program." Ala. Code § 5-19-15.

Survival after payment/deposit: Not specified in exemption statute.

Waiver: Permitted. Waiver must be in writing. Ala. Code § 6-10-120.

***Homestead:* Ala. Const. art. X, §§ 205, 206; Ala. Code §§ 6-10-2 through 6-10-4, 6-10-20, 6-10-41, 6-10-120, 6-10-122.**

Amount: $5000 per individual not exceeding 160 acres is exempt, subject to certain liens. Manufactured home explicitly included. If husband and wife own homestead jointly, each may claim the exemption separately "to the same extent and value as an unmarried individual." Exemption

1. 11 U.S.C. § 522(b)(3)(A).
For a discussion of the domiciliary requirements, see Ch. 10, *supra*.

available whether debtor owns a fee or less estate, whether in common or in severalty. Ala. Code §§ 6–10–2, 6–10–4.

Procedural requirements: Any resident may file sworn declaration with office of probate judge in county where property located. Ala. Code § 6–10–20. (This is not essential to claim of exemption; other procedure exists to claim exemptions after levy. Ala. Code § 6–10–26.)

Special provisions: If home owner dies, homestead exemption survives during the lifetime of the surviving spouse and the minority of any children. Ala. Code § 6–10–2. Married person's mortgage, deed, or other conveyance of homestead requires signature of spouse, made before an officer authorized to take acknowledgment of deeds. Ala. Code § 6–10–3. Once a homestead declaration is filed, temporary absence or leasing of homestead will not eliminate the exemption. Ala. Code § 6–10–41.

Waiver: Yes, by separate instrument in writing. Signature of spouse, if any, required, and must be made before officer authorized to take acknowledgment of deeds. Ala. Code §§ 6–10–120, 6–10–122.

***Tangible personal property:* Ala. Const. art. X, § 204; Ala. Code §§ 6–10–5, 6–10–6, 6–10–120, 6–10–121, and 6–10–126.**

Household goods: $3000. All personal property, except for wages. Ala. Code § 6–10–6.

Motor vehicles: See above.

Tools of trade: See above.

Clothing and jewelry: All necessary and proper wearing apparel of debtor and family; not covered by $3000 cap. Ala. Code § 6–10–6.

Miscellaneous and wildcard: Burial place and church pew (Ala. Code § 6–2–5), family portraits and books; not covered by $3000 cap. Ala. Code § 6–10–6.

Waiver: May be waived, in writing, either by separate instrument, or included in note or contract, *except* as to specified essential household goods, tools of trade, vehicle essential to debtor's business, wearing apparel and library. Ala. Code §§ 6–10–120, 6–10–121, 6–10–126.

***Benefits, retirement plans, insurance, judgments, and other intangibles:* Ala. Code § 6–10–8.**

Public benefits: Not specified in exemption statute.

Pensions, retirement plans, and annuities: Not specified in exemption statute.

Insurance, judgments, or other compensation for injury: Insurance policies, if spouse or children are beneficiaries. Proceeds of insurance in beneficiaries' hands are exempt as to debts of the insured. Ala. Code § 6–10–8.

Bank accounts: Not specified in exemption statute.

Alimony, child support: Not specified in exemption statute.

Tax refunds:

Survival after payment or deposit: Not specified in exemption statute.

ALASKA

Has state opted out of federal bankruptcy exemptions? No. *See In re* Tinkess, 459 B.R. 76 (Bankr. D. Alaska 2008) (finding that Alaska Stat. § 09.38.055 lacks sufficient specificity to operate as an opt-out statute).

Is opt out limited to residents or domiciliaries of the state? Not applicable.

Do state's exemptions have extraterritorial application?

Homestead: No. Alaska Stat. § 09.38.010 limited to "property in this state."

Personal property: Uncertain. Alaska Stat. § 09.38.120 provides that residents of Alaska are entitled to the exemptions provided under this chapter, and non-residents are entitled to the exemptions provided by the law of the jurisdiction of their residence. Residents are defined as persons physically present in the state who intend to maintain a permanent home there.

***Wages:* Alaska Stat. §§ 09.38.030, 09.38.050, 09.38.065, 09.38.105, 09.38.115, 09.38.500; Alaska Admin. Code tit. 8, § 95.030.**

Scope: Money received by an individual for personal services, whether denominated wages, salary, commission, or otherwise. Alaska Stat. § 98.38.500. For debtor who does not receive income weekly, semi-monthly, or monthly, cash and liquid assets up to $1890 per month; increases to $2970 per month if debtor is sole supporter of household. Alaska Admin. Code tit. 8, § 95.030.

Amount: $473 of weekly net earnings is exempt, increases to $743 if individual's wages are sole support of household. Alaska Stat. §§ 09.38.030, 09.38.050; Alaska Admin. Code tit. 8, § 95.030. Net earnings are gross earnings less sums required by law or court order to be withheld. Alaska Stat. § 09.38.030. Dollar amounts under this chapter are adjusted on October 1 of even-numbered years, in accordance with the Consumer Price Index; new amounts reported in Alaska Administrative Code. Alaska Stat. § 09.38.115. For debtor who does not receive income weekly, semi-monthly, or monthly, cash and liquid assets up to $2970 per month. Alaska Stat. § 09.38.030; Alaska Admin. Code tit. 8, § 95.030.

Survival after payment/deposit: Not specified in exemption statute.

Waiver: Waiver of exemptions given to unsecured creditor before levy is unenforceable. Alaska Stat. § 09.38.105.

***Homestead:* Alaska Stat. §§ 09.38.010, 09.38.060, 09.38.065, 09.38.105, 09.38.115; Alaska Admin. Code tit. 8, § 95.030.**

Amount: $72,900 in a principal residence; multiple owners of single homestead may claim only their *pro rata* share of this amount (that is, only one exemption per homestead); homestead is subject to certain liens. Alaska Stat. § 09.38.010. Amount adjusted for Consumer Price Index; new amounts take effect on October 30 of even-numbered years, and must be announced by the preceding June 30 at Alaska Admin. Code tit. 8, § 95.030. Alaska Stat. § 09.38.115.

Procedural requirements: Not specified.

Special provisions: Proceeds of a voluntary sale of a homestead are exempt for six months after receipt, if traceable. Alaska Stat. § 09.38.060. Proceeds of a sale or taking by eminent domain, or of compensation for damaged or destroyed property, are exempt for twelve months, if traceable. Alaska Stat. § 09.38.060.

Waiver: Waiver of exemptions given to unsecured creditor before levy is unenforceable. Alaska Stat. § 09.38.105.

***Tangible personal property:* Alaska Stat. §§ 09.38.015, 09.38.020, 09.38.025, 09.38.060, 09.38.105, 09.38.115; Alaska Admin. Code tit. 8, § 95.030 (reports new amounts adjusted for CPI).**

Household goods: $4050, including household goods, clothing, and family pictures and heirlooms. Alaska Stat. § 09.38.020; Alaska Admin. Code tit. 8, § 95.030.

Motor vehicles: $4050 in car worth not more than $27,000. Alaska Stat. § 09.38.020; Alaska Admin. Code tit. 8, § 95.030.

Tools of Trade: $3780. Alaska Stat. § 09.38.020; Alaska Admin. Code tit. 8, § 95.030.

Clothing and jewelry: Clothing included in household goods, above. Jewelry: $1350. Alaska Stat. § 09.38.020; Alaska Admin. Code tit. 8, § 95.030.

Miscellaneous and wildcard: Pets: $1350. Alaska Stat. § 09.38.020; Alaska Admin. Code tit. 8, § 95.030. Health aids, burial plot, no cap. Alaska Stat. § 09.38.015.

Waiver: Wavier of exemptions given to unsecured creditor before levy is unenforceable. Alaska Stat. § 09.38.105.

Special provisions: Dollar amounts under this chapter are adjusted on October 1 of even-numbered years, in accordance with the Consumer Price Index; new amounts reported in Alaska Administrative Code. Alaska Stat. § 09.38.115. Compensation for the loss or destruction of exempt property is exempt for twelve months, if traceable. Alaska Stat. § 09.38.060.

***Benefits, retirement plans, insurance, judgments, and other intangibles:* Alaska Stat. §§ 09.38.015, 09.38.017, 09.38.025, 09.38.030; Alaska Admin. Code tit. 8, § 95.030 (reports new amounts adjusted for CPI).**

Public benefits: Any benefits paid or payable and exempt under federal law. Alaska Stat. § 09.38.015. Benefits that are not totally exempt (including unemployment, and certain disability benefits) are treated like cash or liquid assets (see above, under Wages). Alaska Stat. § 09.38.030. Senior Care Benefits, pursuant to Alaska Stat. §§ 47.45.300 through 47.45.309 (cash and prescription drug assistance), are fully exempt. Note that the exemption for Senior Care Benefits will sunset on June 30, 2011. The act providing for sunset was repealed effective June 31, 2011, leaving the status of this provision in doubt.

Pensions, retirement plans, and annuities: Various public employees' retirement plans. Contributions to tax-qualified retirement plan or benefits paid from plan (except for contributions made within 120 days before filing bankruptcy). This section does not prevent payments from plan to alternate payee under qualified domestic relations order. Beneficiaries other than the retiree, including those who inherit IRAs, explicitly protected. Certain annuity contracts. Alaska Stat. § 09.38. 017. Certain other plans are treated like cash or liquid assets (see above, under Wages). Alaska Stat. § 09.38.030.

Insurance, judgments, or other compensation for injury: Benefits paid or payable for medical or surgical care, to the extent they are or will be used for such care. Alaska Stat. § 09.38.015. Award from violent crime victims board (or crime victims act of another jurisdiction). Alaska Stat. § 09.38.015. Certain unmatured life insurance and annuity contracts (but if accrued dividends and loan values exceed $500,000, debtor may be required to obtain payment of the lesser of the amount of the creditors claim or the amount by which these values exceed $500,000). Alaska Stat. § 09.38.025. Personal injury judgments, family support, and various insurance proceeds are treated like cash or liquid assets (see above under Wages). Alaska Stat. § 09.38.030.

Bank accounts: College tuition savings plan pursuant to Alaska Stat. §§ 14.40.802 or 14.40.809(a). Alaska Stat. § 09.38.015. Effective July 1, 2008, funds held in an escrow account for real estate taxes and insurance, pursuant to the Mortgage Lending Regulation Act, Alaska Stat. § 6.60.360, are exempt. Alaska Stat. § 09.38.015. Individual who does not receive earnings weekly, semi-monthly, or monthly may exempt $1400 ($2200 if sole support of household) in cash and other liquid assets, including bank accounts, available in any month. Alaska Stat. § 09.38.030.

Alimony, child support: Child support collections made by child support enforcement agency.

Tax refunds:

Survival after payment or deposit: Not specified in exemption statute.

ARIZONA

Has state opted out of federal bankruptcy exemptions? Yes. Ariz. Rev. Stat. Ann. § 33–1133.

Is opt out limited to residents or domiciliaries of the state? Yes. Ariz. Rev. Stat. Ann. § 33–1133: "Residents of this state are not entitled to the Federal exemptions provided in 11 U.S.C. § 522(d)." *See In re* Rody, 468 B.R. 384 (Bankr. D. Ariz. 2012) (Arizona opt-out applicable only to Arizona residents).

Do state's exemptions have extraterritorial application?

Homestead: Uncertain. Compare Ariz. Rev. Stat. Ann. § 33–1101, which limits its application to "any person . . . who resides within the state," with Ariz. Rev. Stat. Ann. § 33–1102(A), which provides procedure for debtor having more than one residence to select property as exempt. *See In re* Jarski, 301 B.R. 342 (Bankr. D. Ariz. 2003).

Personal property: Uncertain. *See In re* Rody, 468 B.R. 384 (Bankr. D. Ariz. 2012) (even if personal property exemptions have extraterritorial effect, they are limited to Arizona residents).

***Wages:* Ariz. Rev. Stat. Ann. §§ 33–1131, 33–1132, 12–1598.10(B)(5) and (F).**

Scope: Wages, salary, or compensation for personal services, including bonuses and commissions or otherwise, including payments pursuant to a pension or retirement program or a deferred compensation plan. Ariz. Rev. Stat. Ann. § 33–1131.

Amount: Similar to federal. Ariz. Rev. Stat. Ann. § 33–1131. May be reduced to 15% in case of "extreme economic hardship" to debtor or family. Ariz. Rev. Stat. Ann. § 1598.10(F). Disposable income is calculated by subtracting those amounts required by law to be withheld. Ariz. Rev. Stat. Ann. § 33–1131. Garnishment forbidden if the debt was, at the time of service of the writ, subject to an effective agreement for debt scheduling between the judgment debtor and a qualified debt counseling organization. Ariz. Rev. Stat. Ann. § 1598.10(B)(5).

Survival after payment/deposit: Not specified in exemption statute.

Waiver: Void and unenforceable. Ariz. Rev. Stat. Ann. § 33–1132.

***Homestead:* Ariz. Rev. Stat. Ann. §§ 33–1101 through 33–1104, 33–1126.**

Amount: $150,000; condominiums, co-ops, and manufactured homes (with or without land) explicitly included. Ariz. Rev. Stat. Ann. § 33–1101. Married couple may claim only one exemption. Homestead is subject to certain liens. Ariz. Rev. Stat. Ann. § 33–1101. Debtor who does not claim homestead may exempt prepaid rent or security deposit up to $2000. Ariz. Rev. Stat. Ann. § 33–1126.

Procedural requirements: No written claim or recording required. (But if debtor owns multiple properties, creditor may require debtor to designate one as homestead.) Ariz. Rev. Stat. Ann. § 33–1102.

Special provisions: Proceeds from sale of homestead are exempt for 18 months. Ariz. Rev. Stat. Ann. § 33–1101.

Waiver: By mortgage or consensual lien, or by declaration of abandonment or waiver, recorded in county where homestead located. Ariz. Rev. Stat. Ann. § 33–1104.

***Tangible personal property:* Ariz. Rev. Stat. Ann. §§ 33–1121.01, 33–1123 through 33–1125, 33–1127 through 33–1130, 33–1132.**

Household goods: $6000 furniture and appliances; consumer electronic devices explicitly included. Ariz. Rev. Stat. Ann. § 33–1123.

Motor vehicles: $6000 in one vehicle (up to $12,000 if debtor is physically disabled). Ariz. Rev. Stat. Ann. § 33–1125.

Tools of trade: $5000 (does not cover motor vehicle used only for commuting); explicitly includes telephone numbers, client contact information, marketing tools such as web sites and domain names or other intangibles or work product. $2500 farm equipment. Ariz. Rev. Stat. Ann. § 33–1130.

Clothing and jewelry: $500 clothing. Ariz. Rev. Stat. Ann. § 33–1125. $2000 wedding and engagement rings. Ariz. Rev. Stat. Ann. § 33–1125.

Miscellaneous and wildcard: $400 musical instruments; $800 animals; $250 books; a burial plot; miscellaneous items, explicitly including computers, worth $1000; materials used for instruction of youth; health aids. Ariz. Rev. Stat. Ann. § 33–1125. Food, fuel, and provisions for six months. Ariz. Rev. Stat. Ann. § 33–1124. Husband or wife may each claim personal property exemption, which may be stacked. Ariz. Rev. Stat. Ann. § 33–1121.01.

Waiver: Void and unenforceable (except for security interests, or recovery of leased property). Ariz. Rev. Stat. Ann. §§ 33–1122, 33–1131.

***Benefits, retirement plans, insurance, judgments, and other intangibles:* Ariz. Rev. Stat. Ann. § 33–1126.**

Public benefits: Not specified in exemption statute. *See* Ariz. Rev. Stat. Ann. § 46–208.

Pensions, retirement plans, and annuities: Certain public and private pensions and tax-qualified retirement plans. A 2011 amendment provides that beneficiaries of certain tax-qualified plans are protected whether their interest arises from "inheritance, designation, appointment or otherwise."

Insurance, judgments, or other compensation for injury: $20,000 life insurance proceeds in hands of surviving spouse or child. Cash surrender value of certain insurance policies, if beneficiary is debtor's spouse, child, parent or sibling. Also exempt if beneficiary is other family member who is dependent. Proceeds of fire or other insurance, or any claim for damage to or destruction of, exempt property. Proceeds of health, accident, or disability insurance, or similar program of benefits in use by any employer (certain exceptions, but no cap).

Bank accounts: $300 in one bank account. Ariz. Rev. Stat. Ann. § 33–1126. Tax-qualified college savings plan is exempt as to debts of both owner and beneficiary, *except* for funds contributed within two years before debtor files bankruptcy. Ariz. Rev. Stat. § 33–1126(10).

Alimony, child support: Court-ordered child support or spousal maintenance (no cap).

Tax refunds:

Survival after payment or deposit: Not specified in exemption statute.

ARKANSAS

Has state opted out of federal bankruptcy exemptions? No. Ark. Code Ann. § 16–66–217.

Is opt out limited to residents or domiciliaries of the state? Not applicable.

Do state's exemptions have extraterritorial application?

Homestead: Probably not. Ark. Code Ann. § 16–66–210 limited to homestead "of any resident of this state." *See* Cherokee Constr. Co. v. Harris, 122 S.W. 485 (Ark. 1909).

Personal property: Uncertain.

***Wages:* Ark. Code Ann. § 16–66–208.**

Scope: Wages of all laborers and mechanics.

Amount: $25 per week is absolutely exempt; sixty days wages are exempt if debtor's property plus the wages do not exceed the amount exempt under the state constitution (see summary of Article 9 of the state constitution under tangible personal property, *infra*).

Survival after payment/deposit: Not specified in exemption statute.

Waiver: Not specified in exemption statute.

***Homestead:* Ark. Const. art. 9, §§ 3, 4, 5; Ark. Code Ann. §§ 16–66–210, 16–66–212, 16–66–218.**

Amount: Bankruptcy only: $800 for unmarried debtor, $1250 for married. Ark. Code Ann. § 16–66–218. Non-bankruptcy (married or head of household only): 80 acres rural or one quarter acre urban, or, if this land is not worth $2500, then up to 160 acres rural or one acre urban, up to a value of $2500. Ark. Const. art. 9, §§ 3, 4, 5; Ark. Code Ann. § 16–66–210.

Procedural requirements: None stated. Right not lost by failure to schedule. Non-debtor spouse may claim if debtor fails to do so. Ark. Code Ann. § 16–66–212.

Special provisions: Continues to protect minor children after death of debtor. Ark. Code Ann. § 16–66–210.

Waiver: Not specified in exemption law.

***Tangible personal property:* Ark. Const. art. 9, §§ 1, 2; Ark. Code Ann. §§ 16–66–218, 16–66–219, 16–66–220.**

Household goods: Bankruptcy only: Personal property used as residence or burial plot, if real property not claimed, $800 unmarried or $1250 married. Ark. Code Ann. § 16–66–218. A federal court has held the personal property, motor vehicle, and tools of the trade exemptions to be contrary to, and therefore limited by, the lower ceilings in the Arkansas Constitution ($500 and apparel if married or head of household, otherwise $200 and apparel).[2]

Motor vehicles: Bankruptcy only: $1200. Ark. Code Ann. § 16–66–218.

Tools of trade: Bankruptcy only: $750. Ark. Code Ann. § 16–66–218.

Clothing and jewelry: Wedding bands, (Ark. Code Ann. §§ 16–66–218, 66–219) necessary wearing apparel.

Miscellaneous and wildcard: Any personal property: $500 married; $200 unmarried. Ark. Const. art. 9, §§ 1, 2; Ark. Code Ann. § 16–66–218.

Waiver: Not specified in exemption statute.

***Benefits, retirement plans, insurance, judgments, and other intangibles:* Ark. Code Ann. §§ 16–66–209, 16–66–218, 16–66–220.**

Public benefits: Not specified in exemption statute. But note that benefits are exempted under various other statutes (cross-referenced in Ark. Code Ann. § 16–66–218).

Pensions, retirement plans, and annuities: Certain public and private pensions and retirement plans, including IRAs and SEPs. Debtor who chooses state bankruptcy exemptions is limited to $20,000 per debtor or married couple. Ark. Code Ann. § 16–66–220.

Insurance, judgments, or other compensation for injury: Moneys paid or payable from life, health and disability insurance including a payment to the owner, insured, or beneficiary for the cash surrender value of the policy. Ark. Code Ann. § 16–66–209.

Bank accounts: Not specified in exemption statute.

Alimony, child support: Not specified in exemption statute.

Tax refunds:

Survival after payment or deposit: Not specified in exemption statute.

2. *In re* Holt, 894 F.2d 1005 (8th Cir. 1990).

CALIFORNIA

Has state opted out of federal bankruptcy exemptions? Yes. Cal. Civ. Proc. Code § 703.130 (West).

Is opt out limited to residents or domiciliaries of the state? Not specified. Cal. Civ. Proc. Code § 703.130 (West): "[T]he exemptions set forth in [§ 522(d)] . . . are not authorized in this state."

Do state's exemptions have extraterritorial application?

Homestead: Yes. *See In re* Urban, 375 B.R. 882 (B.A.P. 9th Cir. 2007) (rejecting constitutional challenge to extraterritorial application of California's exemption law to debtor's chapter 13 case filed in Montana); *In re* Arrol, 207 B.R. 662 (Bankr. N.D. Cal. 1997).

Personal property: Yes. *See In re* Urban, 375 B.R. 882 (B.A.P. 9th Cir. 2007).

***Wages:* Cal. Civ. Proc. Code §§ 703.070, 704.070, 706.011, 706.050, 706.051, 706.052 (West).**

Scope: Compensation payable by an employer to an employee for personal services whether denominated as wages, salary, commission, bonus, or otherwise. Employee is defined as a public officer or any individual who performs services subject to the right of the employer to control both what shall be done and how it shall be done. Cal. Civ. Proc. Code § 706.011 (West).

Amount: Garnishment is limited to the lesser of 25% of disposable earnings or the amount by which disposable earnings exceed 40 times the state minimum hourly wage. Cal. Civ. Proc. Code § 706.050 (West). Larger exemption if debtor can prove need: "the portion of the judgment debtor's earnings which the judgment debtor proves is necessary for the support of the judgment debtor or the judgment debtor's family supported in whole or in part by the judgment debtor is exempt from levy under this chapter." Cal. Civ. Proc. Code § 706.051 (West).

Survival after payment/deposit: Yes. Paid earnings in bank account 75% exempt (100% if already subjected to withholding order or wage assignment). Cal. Civ. Proc. Code §704.070 (West).

Waiver: Not specified in exemption statute.

***Homestead:* Cal. Civ. Proc. Code §§ 487.025, 703.110, 703.040, 704.030, 704.710 through 704.730 (West).**

Amount: $75,000. Increases to $100,000 if debtor is family member and if at least one other family member owns no interest in homestead or only a community property interest. $175,000 for debtors over age 55 if income is under $25,000 (without joint income) or $35,000 (married debtors, joint income) and if sale is involuntary. $175,000 if over age 65 or disabled; may include house, manufactured home, boat, or condominium. Cal. Civ. Proc. Code §§ 704.710, 704.730 (West). In bankruptcy, the debtor has the option of selecting the $24,060 exemption set forth at Cal. Civ. Proc. Code § 703.140 (West).

Procedural requirements: Yes. See Cal. Civ. Proc. Code §§ 704.910 through 704.995 (West), for declaration of homestead procedure.

Special provisions: Proceeds exempt for six months. Declared homestead continues to protect property after death of owner, if occupied by surviving spouse or specified family member. $3050 exemption for materials purchased in good faith for repair or improvement of homestead. Cal. Civ. Proc. Code § 704.030 (West). A 2007 amendment allows a debtor not residing in the homestead to claim homestead if a spouse or former spouse resides there, up to the time a court order divides the community property (but note that debtor may still have only one homestead). Cal. Civ. Proc. Code § 704.720 (West).

Waiver: Prior waivers void (but note that homestead declaration does not limit the right to convey or encumber the property). Cal. Civ. Proc. Code § 703.040 (West).

***Tangible personal property:* Cal. Civ. Proc. Code §§ 703.040, 703.110, 703.150, 704.010 through 704.070 (West).**

Household goods: Ordinary and necessary household furnishings, appliances, wearing apparel, and other personal effects. Cal. Civ. Proc. Code § 704.020 (West). Proceeds from execution sale of items of extraordinary value are exempt in the amount determined by the court to be sufficient to purchase ordinary and necessary replacement. Cal. Civ. Proc. Code § 704.020 (West). No doubling of exemptions. Cal. Civ. Proc. Code § 703.110 (West).

Motor vehicles: $2900 aggregate equity in motor vehicle(s); insurance or other compensation for loss or destruction of vehicle exempt for ninety days after receipt. Cal. Civ. Proc. Code § 704.010 (West).

Tools of trade: Single: $7625 (not more than $4850 commercial motor vehicle). Spouses: $15,250 (not more than $9700 commercial motor vehicle). Cal. Civ. Proc. Code § 704.060 (West).

Clothing and jewelry: Ordinary and necessary wearing apparel (Cal. Civ. Proc. Code § 704.020 (West)); $7625 jewelry, heirlooms, and works of art. Cal. Civ. Proc. Code § 704.040 (West).

Miscellaneous and wildcard: Health aids. Cal. Civ. Proc. Code § 704.050 (West). Family or cemetery plots. Cal. Civ. Proc. Code § 704.200 (West).

Waiver: Prior waivers void. Cal. Civ. Proc. Code § 703.040 (West).

Special provisions: In bankruptcy, the debtor has the option of selecting the exemptions set forth at Cal. Civ. Proc. Code § 703.140 (West), which are similar but not identical to the federal exemptions. Some personal property exemptions are adjusted every three years for the cost of living. New amounts are reported in the California Judicial Forms pamphlet, electronically published in the references and annotations to the exemptions chapter. Cal. Civ. Proc. Code § 703.150 (West).

***Benefits, retirement plans, insurance, judgments, and other intangibles:* Cal. Civ. Proc. Code §§ 703.080, 704.070 through 704.190 (West).**

Public benefits: Automatic exemption for first $1525 ($2275 for two or more depositors) of directly deposited public benefit funds, or first $3050 ($4575 for two or more depositors) of directly deposited Social Security funds. The rest of the account is exempt insofar as it consists of exempt benefits; the statute provides for notice to the depositor and a procedure for determining the amount of exempt funds. Cal. Civ. Proc. Code § 704.080 (West). Unemployment benefits (including certain payments from employer, union, or fraternal organization). Welfare benefits (see Cal. Welf. & Inst. Code §§ 10000 through 18996 (West)) or similar aid provided by charitable organization or fraternal benefit society. Cal. Civ. Proc. Code § 704.170 (West). Relocation benefits for persons displaced by certain eminent domain takings. Cal. Civ. Proc. Code § 704.180 (West). Financial aid at an institution of higher education. Cal. Civ. Proc. Code § 704.190 (West).

Pensions, retirement plans, and annuities: Public retirement benefits (except as to family support judgment) (Cal. Civ. Proc. Code § 704.110 (West)); certain private retirement plans, including but not limited to SEPs, IRAs, profit sharing plans used for retirement (except as to family support judgments). Cal. Civ. Proc. Code § 704.115 (West).

Insurance, judgments, or other compensation for injury: $11,475 unmatured life insurance policies: separate exemption for each spouse; may be stacked. Cal. Civ. Proc. Code § 704.100 (West). Health or disability insurance benefits (except as to claim of the health care creditor whose bill was the basis for the claim, or certain family support claims). Cal. Civ. Proc.

Code § 704.130 (West). Personal injury judgment or settlement, so far as needed for support (same exceptions). Cal. Civ. Proc. Code § 704.150 (West). Wrongful death judgment or settlement if debtor or spouse was dependent on victim, so far as needed for support. Cal. Civ. Proc. Code § 704.160 (West). Workers' compensation (except for family support).

Bank accounts: For a deposit account with direct benefits: Public benefits, one payee: $1575. Social Security, one payee: $3050. Public benefits, two payees: $2275. Social Security, two payees: $4575. For an inmate trust account: $1525 ($300 for restitution fine or order). Cal. Civ. Proc. Code § 704.090 (West).

Alimony, child support: Not specified in exemption statute.

Tax refunds:

Survival after payment or deposit: Yes. Cal. Civ. Proc. Code § 703.080 (West). See sections covering specific types of benefits.

Special provisions: In bankruptcy, the debtor has the option of selecting the exemptions set forth at Cal. Civ. Proc. Code § 703.140 (West), which are similar to the federal exemptions.

COLORADO

Has state opted out of federal bankruptcy exemptions? Yes. Colo. Rev. Stat. § 13–54–107.

Is opt out limited to residents or domiciliaries of the state? Yes. Colo. Rev. Stat. § 13–54–107: "[T]he exemptions in [§ 522(d)] are denied to residents of this state. Exemptions authorized to be claimed by residents of this state shall be limited to those exemptions expressly provided by the statutes of this state."

Do state's exemptions have extraterritorial application?

Homestead: No. Colo. Rev. Stat. §§ 38–41–201, 38–41–203 limited to "every homestead in the state of Colorado occupied as a home by the owner." *See In re* Kelsey, 477 B.R. 870 (Bankr. M.D. Fla. 2012); *In re* Underwood, 342 B.R. 358 (Bankr. N.D. Fla. 2006).

Personal property: Uncertain. *Compare In re* Underwood, 342 B.R. 358 (Bankr. N.D. Fla. 2006), *with In re* Kelsey, 477 B.R. 870 (Bankr. M.D. Fla. 2012).

***Wages:* Colo. Rev. Stat. § 13–54–104.**

Scope: Compensation for personal services; payments to independent contractors are protected. Also includes various insurance, disability, and other benefits.

Amount: Similar to federal, except that thirty times minimum wage refers to *state* minimum wage. Disposable earnings are defined as those left after certain voluntary health insurance deductions, as well as legally required taxes, and so forth. A higher percentage of earnings may be garnished to recover overpayments of certain state benefits.

Survival after payment/deposit: Not specified in exemption statute.

Waiver: Not specified in exemption statute.

***Homestead:* Colo. Rev. Stat. §§ 38–41–201, 38–41–201.6 through 38–41–209.**

Amount: $60,000 in a residence, or $90,000 if owner, spouse, or dependent is elderly (defined as age 60 or older) or disabled. Colo. Rev. Stat. § 38–41–201. Manufactured homes explicitly included. Colo. Rev. Stat. §§ 38–41–201.5, 38–41–201.6.

Procedural requirements: Filing of homestead declaration permitted but not required. If filed, spouse's signature will be required for sale or encumbrance of property. Colo. Rev. Stat. § 38–41–202.

Special provisions: Sale or insurance proceeds are exempt for two years if kept separate and apart from other moneys. Colo. Rev. Stat. §§ 38–41–207, 38–41–209. If the proceeds are used to purchase a new homestead, the exemption carries over to the new homestead. Colo. Rev. Stat. § 38–41–207. After death of owner, homestead exemption continues to protect surviving spouse and minor children. Colo. Rev. Stat. §§ 38–41–204, 38–41–208.

Waiver: Permitted.

***Tangible personal property:* Colo. Rev. Stat. §§ 13–54–101 through 13–54–103.**

Household goods: $3000 in household goods; $600 in food and fuel. Nonexclusive list of household goods includes computers, sound systems, cameras, bicycles, fax machines, and toys, as well as the usual furniture, dishes, and so forth. Colo. Rev. Stat. § 13–54–102.

Motor vehicles: $5000 in vehicles or bicycles ($10,000 if elderly or disabled). Colo. Rev. Stat. § 13–54–102.

Tools of trade: $20,000 in tools of trade. May not be stacked with motor vehicle exemption. $50,000 in farm tools, equipment, and animals; married couple engaged in farming may claim only one farm equipment exemption. May not be stacked with tools of trade exemption. Colo. Rev. Stat. § 13–54–102.

Clothing and jewelry: $1500 in clothing; $2000 in jewelry. Colo. Rev. Stat. § 13–54–102.

Miscellaneous and wildcard: $1500 in books and family pictures; one burial site for debtor and each dependent; health aids. $3000 for library of professional person (specifically including clergy). Colo. Rev. Stat. § 13–54–102.

Waiver: Waived by failure to timely claim.

***Benefits, retirement plans, insurance, judgments, and other intangibles:* Colo. Rev. Stat. §§ 13–54–102 through 13–54–103, 13–64–210.**

Public benefits: Tax refund attributable to earned income credit or child tax credit. *See also* Colo. Rev. Stat. § 26–2–131 (public assistance is exempt).

Pensions, retirement plans, and annuities: Military pensions. Various private retirement plans, including ERISA plans and IRAs. Public or private disability benefits due or any proceeds thereof, not otherwise provided for under law, up to $3000 per month. Claims or proceeds in excess of this amount are treated like wages. For certain types of debts (child support debt or arrearages; restitution for theft, embezzlement, or misappropriation of certain public funds; and certain willful violations of fiduciary duty to a public pension fund), public and private pensions are treated as earnings for calculating garnishment limits. Colo. Rev. Stat. § 13–54–102, 13–54–104.

Insurance, judgments, or other compensation for injury: $100,000 in cash surrender value of certain insurance; proceeds of certain life insurance. Insurance proceeds for loss of or damage to exempt property. Crime victim reparation. Periodic payments to compensate for the loss of future earnings are exempt to the same extent as wages. Colo. Rev. Stat. § 13–54–102, 13–54–104. Personal injury damages (except as to obligations incurred for such injuries or the collection of such damages). Colo. Rev. Stat. § 13–64–210.

Bank accounts: Not specified in exemption statute.

Alimony, child support: Child support payments (but exemption lost if commingled with other funds; if deposited in bank must be in special purpose account). Colo. Rev. Stat. § 13–54–102.5.

Tax refunds:

Survival after payment or deposit: Not specified (except for child support provisions described above).

CONNECTICUT

Has state opted out of federal bankruptcy exemptions? No.

Is opt out limited to residents or domiciliaries of the state? Not applicable.

Do state's exemptions have extraterritorial application?

Homestead: Uncertain.

Personal property: Uncertain.

***Wages:* Conn. Gen. Stat. §§ 52–352b(d), 52–361a.**

Scope: Earnings by reason of personal services, including any compensation payable by an employer to an employee, whether called wages, salary, commission, bonus, or otherwise.

Amount: Garnishment is limited to lesser of 25% of debtor's weekly disposable income or amount by which weekly disposable income exceeds forty times the federal or state minimum wage. Conn. Gen. Stat. § 52–361a(f). Disposable income is that left after deductions of taxes, normal retirement contributions, union dues and fees, and health or group life insurance premiums. All wages earned by a public assistance recipient under an incentive earnings program are exempt. Conn. Gen. Stat. § 52–352(d). No garnishment unless judgment debtor has failed to comply with an installment payment order. Conn. Gen. Stat. § 52–361a(a). Garnishment will be for the statutory maximum, unless the court provides otherwise pursuant to motion for modification. Conn. Gen. Stat. § 52–361a(f). No more than one garnishment at a time. Conn. Gen. Stat. § 52–361a(f). Employer may not discharge or discipline employee for garnishment unless there are more than seven wage executions in one calendar year. Conn. Gen. Stat. § 52–361a(j).

Survival after payment/deposit: Not specified in exemption statute.

Waiver: Not specified in exemption statute.

***Homestead:* Conn. Gen. Stat. §§ 53–352b(l), 52–352a, 52–352b(t).**

Amount: $75,000 excluding consensual or statutory liens; $125,000 for money judgment arising out of services provided at a hospital. Conn. Gen. Stat. § 52–352b(t). One residential security deposit, and utility deposits for one residence. Conn. Gen. Stat. § 52–352b(l). Co-ops and mobile manufactured homes explicitly included. Conn. Gen. Stat. § 52–352a.

Procedural requirements: Not specified in exemption statute.

Special provisions: Not specified in exemption statute.

Waiver: Not specified in exemption statute.

***Tangible personal property:* Conn. Gen. Stat. §§ 52–352a, 52–352b.**

Household goods: Necessary food, furniture, bedding, and appliances. Conn. Gen. Stat. §§ 52–352a, 52–352b(a).

Motor vehicles: $3500 (fair market value, less any liens and encumbrances). Conn. Gen. Stat. § 52–352b(j).

Tools of trade: Tools, books, instruments, livestock, and feed, necessary for debtor's occupation, profession, or farming. Conn. Gen. Stat. § 52–352b(b).

Clothing and jewelry: Necessary clothing. Conn. Gen. Stat. §§ 52–352a, 52–352b(a). Wedding and engagement rings. Conn. Gen. Stat. § 52–352b(k).

Miscellaneous and wildcard: Wildcard $1000 in any property. Conn. Gen. Stat. § 52–352b(r). Health aids (Conn. Gen. Stat. § 52–352b(f)), burial plot (Conn. Gen. Stat. § 52–352b(c)), certain military items, residential security deposit, and utility security deposits. Irrevocable transfers of money to an account being held by a licensed debt adjuster for the benefit of creditors.

Waiver: Not specified in exemption statute.

***Benefits, retirement plans, insurance, judgments, and other intangibles:* Conn. Gen. Stat. § 52–352b. *See* §§ 5–171, 52–321a.**

Public benefits: Public assistance payments, wages of public assistance recipient under incentive program (Conn. Gen. Stat. § 52–352b(d)), workers' compensation, Social Security, veterans' and unemployment benefits. Conn. Gen. Stat. § 52–352b(g). *See also* Conn. Gen. Stat. § 17B-86 (various types of state-administered aid exempt).

Pensions, retirement plans, and annuities: Certain public and private pensions and retirement plans. Conn. Gen. Stat. § 52–352b(m).

Insurance, judgments, or other compensation for injury: Health and disability insurance payments (Conn. Gen. Stat. § 52–352b(e)), crime victim reparations (Conn. Gen. Stat. § 52–352b(o)), benefits from certain fraternal associations (Conn. Gen. Stat. § 52–352b(p)), up to $4000 in accrued dividends or loan value of certain insurance policies (Conn. Gen. Stat. § 52–352b(s)). Insurance proceeds on exempt property exempt to same extent as the property. Conn. Gen. Stat. § 52–352b(q).

Bank accounts: Irrevocable transfers of money to an account held by a licensed debt adjuster for the benefit of creditors of the exemptioner. Conn. Gen. Stat. § 52–352b(u).

Alimony, child support: Court-approved payments for child support (Conn. Gen. Stat. § 52–352b(h)); alimony or other support treated as wages. Conn. Gen. Stat. § 52–352b(h).

Tax refunds:

Survival after payment or deposit: Not specified in exemption statute.

DELAWARE

Has state opted out of federal bankruptcy exemptions? Yes. Del. Code Ann. tit. 10, § 4914.

Is opt out limited to residents or domiciliaries of the state? Yes. Del. Code Ann. tit. 10, § 4914: "[A]n individual debtor domiciled in Delaware is not authorized or entitled to elect the Federal exemptions . . . [in § 522(d)] and may exempt only that property from the estate as set forth is subsection (b) of this section."

Do state's exemptions have extraterritorial application?

Homestead: Probably not. Del. Code Ann. tit. 10, § 4914 applies to "an individual debtor domiciled in Delaware."

Personal property: Probably not. Del. Code Ann. tit. 10, § 4902 limited to "every person residing in this state."

***Wages:* Del. Code Ann. tit. 6, § 4345; Del. Code Ann. tit. 10, § 4913.**

Scope: Salaries, commissions, and every other form of remuneration paid to an employee for labor or services; does not include payment made for services rendered by self-employed person. Del. Code Ann. tit. 10, § 4913.

Amount: 85% exempt. Del. Code Ann. tit. 10, § 4913. For debts arising from retail installment sale, totally exempt for sixty days after default on the contract or installment account. Del. Code Ann. tit. 6, § 4345. Only one garnishment at a time. Del. Code Ann. tit. 10, § 4913.

Survival after payment/deposit: Not specified in exemption statute.

Waiver: Not specified in exemption statute.

***Homestead:* Del. Code Ann. tit. 10, § 4914.**

Amount: In bankruptcy only: $75,000 in 2010; $100,000 in 2011; $125,000 in 2012. For disabled person, or a married couple of which at least one spouse is age 65 or over: $125,000 immediately.

Procedural requirements: None specified.

Special provisions: Homestead exemption not available for debts resulting from certain securities offenses or any crime, tort, or willful or reckless misconduct that caused serious physical injury or death to another individual in the preceding five years.

Waiver: None specified.

***Tangible personal property:* Del. Code Ann. tit. 10, §§ 4902, 4903, 4912, 4914, 7323.**

Household goods: Bedding. Del. Code Ann. tit. 10, § 7323.

Motor vehicles: In bankruptcy only: tools of trade and/or motor vehicle necessary to employment, $15,000. Joint debtors may stack. Del. Code Ann. tit. 10, § 4914.

Tools of trade: $50 or $75, depending on location. Del. Code Ann. tit. 10, §§ 4902, 7323. In bankruptcy only: tools of trade and/or motor vehicle necessary to employment, $15,000. Joint debtors may stack. Del. Code Ann. tit. 10, § 4914.

Clothing and jewelry: Necessary wearing apparel, no cap. Del. Code Ann. tit. 10, § 4902.

Miscellaneous and wildcard: Family bible, books and pictures, church pew, burial place, no cap. Del. Code Ann. tit. 10, § 4902. $500 wildcard for head of family. Del. Code Ann. tit. 10, § 4903. In bankruptcy only: $25,000 in personal property and/or equity in real property, other than the debtor's principal residence. Del. Code Ann. tit. 10, § 4914.

Waiver: Allowed; both spouses' signatures required. Del. Code Ann. tit. 10, § 4912.

***Benefits, retirement plans, insurance, judgments, and other intangibles:* Del. Code Ann. tit. 10, §§ 4915, 4916.**

Public benefits: Not specified in exemption statute. *See* Del. Code Ann. tit. 31, § 513 (assistance provided under state public assistance code exempt).

Pensions, retirement plans, and annuities: Certain tax-qualified retirement plans, including rollovers. Not exempt from claims of alternate payee under qualified domestic relations order. Del. Code Ann. tit. 10, § 4915.

Insurance, judgments, or other compensation for injury: Assets held or amounts payable under life insurance and annuity contracts, as defined in § 1035(b) of the Internal Revenue Code. Del. Code Ann. tit. 10, § 4915. *See also* Del. Code Ann. tit. 18, §§ 2725 through 2728 (insurance and annuities).

Bank accounts: Funds held in, or proceeds payable from, Delaware College Investment Plan Account (except when contributions in most recent year exceed $5000 or the average contribution in the two preceding years). Del. Code Ann. tit. 10, § 4916.

Alimony, child support: Payments received by alternate payee of retirement plan, pursuant to qualified domestic relations order are exempt. Del. Code Ann. tit. 10, § 4915.

Tax refunds:

Survival after payment or deposit: Not specified in exemption statute.

DISTRICT OF COLUMBIA

Has state opted out of federal bankruptcy exemptions? No.

Is opt out limited to residents or domiciliaries of the state? Not applicable.

Do state's exemptions have extraterritorial application?

Homestead: Yes (with limitations). D.C. Code § 15–501(a) provides that specified property of a head of family or householder, who resides in the District of Columbia or who earns the major portion of his livelihood there, is exempt "regardless of his place of residence."

Personal property: Yes (with limitations as noted above).

***Wages:* D.C. Code §§ 16–571 through 16–572; 16–584.**

Scope: Compensation paid or payable for personal services, whether called wages, salary, commission, bonus, or otherwise; includes periodic payments pursuant to a pension or retirement program. D.C. Code § 16–571.

Amount: Similar to federal. Only one garnishment at a time. D.C. Code § 16–572. Discharge for garnishment forbidden. D.C. Code § 16–584.

Survival after payment/deposit: Not specified in exemption statute.

Waiver: Not specified in exemption statute.

***Homestead:* D.C. Code §§ 15–501(a)(14), 15–502(a).**

Amount: Head of family or householder only: Debtor's aggregate interest in real property used as the residence of the debtor or property of the debtor or debtor's dependent in a cooperative that owns property that debtor or dependent uses as a residence. D.C. Code § 15–501(a)(14).

Procedural requirements: Not specified in exemption statute.

Special provisions: Not specified in exemption statute.

Waiver: Mortgage, deed of trust, or sale not valid unless signed by spouse or domestic partner of debtor, if debtor is living with spouse or domestic partner. D.C. Code § 15–502.

***Tangible personal property:* D.C. Code § 15–501 through 15–503.**

Household goods: $8625 aggregate, single item $425. Household goods, furnishings, wearing apparel, books, animals, crops, musical instruments. D.C. Code § 15–501(a)(2).

Motor vehicles: $2575 in one vehicle. D.C. Code § 15–501(a)(1).

Tools of trade: $1625 (D.C. Code § 15–501(a)(4)); library and office furniture of professional person, $300. D.C. Code § 15–501(a)(13).

Clothing and jewelry: Included in household goods exemption.

Miscellaneous and wildcard: $850 any property; unused homestead exemption up to $8075 (D.C. Code § 15–501(a)(3)); health aids (D.C. Code § 15–501(a)(6)); family pictures and library, $400. D.C. Code § 15–501(a)(8).

Waiver: Any sale or encumbrance of exempt property requires signature of spouse or domestic partner, if debtor is living with spouse or domestic partner.

Special provisions: All tangible and intangible personal property exemptions are for householder or head of family only.

***Benefits, retirement plans, insurance, judgments, and other intangibles:* D.C. Code §§ 15–501 through 15–503.**

Public benefits: The right to receive Social Security; veterans' benefits; disability, illness, or unemployment benefit. D.C. Code § 15–501(a)(7).

Pensions, retirement plans, and annuities: Certain retirement plans. D.C. Code §§ 15–501(a)(7), 15–501(a)(9).

Insurance, judgments, or other compensation for injury: Unmatured life insurance contract (D.C. Code § 15–501(a)(5)); life insurance payments to the extent needed for support; compensation for pain and suffering, actual pecuniary loss, or loss of future earnings; crime victim reparations; certain wrongful death judgments, to the extent needed for support. D.C. Code § 15–501(a)(11).

Bank accounts: Not specified in exemption statute.

Alimony, child support: Alimony, support, or separate maintenance to the extent needed for support. D.C. Code § 15–501(a)(7). Interest in retirement plan awarded to alternate payee under qualified domestic relations order. D.C. Code § 15–501(a)(10).

Tax refunds:

Survival after payment or deposit: Not specified in statute.

Special provisions: All tangible and intangible personal property exemptions are for householder or head of family only.

FLORIDA

Has state opted out of federal bankruptcy exemptions? Yes, except as to exemptions provided by 11 U.S.C. § 522(d)(10). Fla. Stat. §§ 222.20, 222.201.

Is opt out limited to residents or domiciliaries of the state? Yes. Fla. Stat. §§ 222.20, 222.201: "esidents of this state shall not be entitled to the Federal exemptions provided in § 522(d) [except the exemptions in § 522(d)(10)]." *See In re* Camp, 631 F.3d 757 (5th Cir. 2011) (Florida opt-out statute applicable only to residents of Florida); *In re* Battle, 366 B.R. 635 (Bankr. W.D. Tex. 2006).

Do state's exemptions have extraterritorial application?

Homestead: No. *See In re* Adams, 375 B.R. 532 (Bankr. W.D. Mo. 2007) (because Florida law was construed to provide exemptions only to residents, debtor could claim federal exemptions); *In re* Schulz, 101 B.R. 301 (Bankr. N.D. Fla. 1989). Procedure for recording a homestead declaration is available only to "any natural person residing in this state." Fla. Stat. § 222.01. *But see In re* Camp, 396 B.R. 194 (Bankr. W.D. Tex. 2008) (federal bankruptcy law requires that Florida exemptions apply to Texas property as if it were in Florida, when debtors moved from Florida to Texas).

Personal property: No. *See In re* Adams, 375 B.R. 532 (Bankr. W.D. Mo. 2007); *In re* Schulz, 101 B.R. 301 (Bankr. N.D. Fla. 1989). *But see In re* Camp, 396 B.R. 194 (Bankr. W.D. Tex. 2008) (federal bankruptcy law requires that Florida exemptions apply to Texas property as if it were in Florida, when debtors moved from Florida to Texas).

***Wages:* Fla. Stat. § 222.11.**

Scope: Earnings, defined as compensation paid or payable in money of sum certain for personal services or labor whether called wages, salary, commission, or bonus, of a head of family, defined as one who provides more than 50% of the support of a child or dependent.

Amount: Head of Family: $750 per week of disposable earnings is exempt, and amounts over $750 can be garnished only if debtor has agreed in writing. Disposable earnings are those left over after all deductions required by law. Others: same as federal.

Survival after payment/deposit: Earnings remain exempt for six months in a bank account, even if commingled with other funds, so long as earnings can be traced and properly identified.

Waiver: Wages of head of household in excess of $750 may be garnished with debtor's written permission. The consent must be in a separate document, attached to the contract to which it relates, and in the same language as that contract. The form of the waiver is prescribed by statute.

***Homestead:* Fla. Const. art. X, § 4(a)(1); Fla. Stat. §§ 222.01 through 222.03, 222.05.**

Amount: Up to one half acre inside a municipality or 160 acres outside a municipality is exempt under the Florida Constitution regardless of value, with exceptions for four types of debts (taxes, purchase money debts, services, or labor for home repair or improvement, and other labor performed on real property). By statute, a manufactured home may be a homestead, whether or not the home owner owns the land. Fla. Stat. § 222.05. In addition, if the homestead is outside a municipality and includes less than 160 acres, the debtor may exempt non-homestead land to bring the total up to 160 acres.

Procedural requirements: Permitted but not required to file declaration of homestead, may do so after levy. Fla. Stat. §§ 222.01, 222.02.

Special provisions: None specified in exemption statute.

Waiver: Not specified in exemption statute.

***Tangible personal property:* Fla. Const. art. X, § 4; Fla. Stat. §§ 222.061, 222.07, 222.25.**

Household goods: $1000 wildcard in any personal property.

Motor vehicles: Up to $1000 in any one motor vehicle. Fla. Stat. § 222.25.

Tools of trade: See above.

Clothing and jewelry: See above.

Miscellaneous and wildcard: $1000 wildcard noted above. Professionally prescribed health aids. Fla. Stat. § 222.25. For a debtor who does not claim or receive the benefits of a homestead exemption, $4000 in any personal property (this exemption does not apply to a debt for child or spousal support). Fla. Stat. § 222.25.

Waiver: Not specified in exemption statute.

***Benefits, retirement plans, insurance, judgments, and other intangibles:* Fla. Stat. §§ 222.13, 222.14, 222.18, 222.21, 222.22, 222.25. *See* Fla. Stat. § 121.131.**

Public benefits: Earned income tax credit, pursuant to the Internal Revenue Code, or a deposit in a financial institution traceable to an earned income tax credit. Fla. Stat. § 222.25. Wages, re-employment assistance, or unemployment benefits owing to a deceased employee, paid to spouse or certain other family members exempt as to debts of the deceased. Fla. Stat. §§ 222.15, 222.16.

Pensions, retirement plans, and annuities: Public pension money received within three months before the attachment; certain tax-qualified retirement plan (except as to claims of alternate payee under qualified domestic relations order). A 2011 amendment makes clear that the exemption for tax-qualified retirement accounts applies to inherited accounts. This amendment applies retroactively. Fla. Stat. § 222.21.

Insurance, judgments, or other compensation for injury: Life insurance proceeds exempt as to creditors of the insured. Fla. Stat. § 222.13. Cash surrender values of insurance policies or annuities. Fla. Stat. § 222.14. Disability income benefits under any policy of life, health, accident, or other insurance. Fla. Stat. § 222.18.

Bank accounts: Money paid into or out of a medical savings account or hurricane savings account. Monies paid into or out of prepaid postsecondary education expense trust fund are not subject to attachment, garnishment, or legal process by creditors of either purchaser or beneficiary of contract. Fla. Stat. § 222.22.

Alimony, child support: Pension funds received by alternate payee under qualified domestic relations order.

Tax refunds:

Survival after payment or deposit: Not specified in exemption statute, except as to tax refunds attributable to earned income tax credit, public pension money received within three months, or payments into or out of medical savings or prepaid college trust fund accounts.

GEORGIA

Has state opted out of federal bankruptcy exemptions? Yes. Ga. Code Ann. § 44–13–100(b).

Is opt out limited to residents or domiciliaries of the state? Yes, with limitation as to prepetition period debtor domiciled in Georgia. Ga. Code Ann. § 44–13–100(b): "an individual debtor whose domicile is in Georgia is prohibited from applying or utilizing [§ 522(d)]"; an " 'individual debtor whose domicile is in Georgia' means an individual whose domicile has been located in Georgia for the 180 days immediately preceding the date of the filing of the bankruptcy petition or for a longer portion of such 180 day period than in any other place." *See In re* Chandler, 362 B.R. 723 (Bankr. N.D. W. Va. 2007).

Do state's exemptions have extraterritorial application?

Homestead: Uncertain. Ga. Code Ann. § 44–13–100 applies to "any debtor who is a natural person."

Personal property: Not specified in exemption statute, but possibly yes. *See In re* Stockburger, 106 F.3d 402, 1997 WL 41202 (6th Cir. Jan. 31, 1997) (unpublished) (Georgia exemption applies to personal property located in Tennessee because it is the law of the debtor's domicile that controls under § 522(b), not the location of the property).

***Wages:* Ga. Code Ann. §§ 18–4–20(d) through 18–4–20(f).**

Scope: Compensation paid or payable for personal services, whether called wages, salary, commission, bonus, or otherwise, including periodic payments pursuant to a pension or retirement program. Ga. Code Ann. § 18–4–20(a)(2).

Amount: Similar to federal. Ga. Code Ann. § 18–4–20(d).

Survival after payment/deposit: Not specified in exemption statute.

Waiver: Not specified in exemption statute.

***Homestead:* Ga. Code Ann. §§ 44–13–1, 44–13–40, 44–13–100(a)(1).**

Amount: $21,500 for any property used as residence or burial plot. Ga. Code Ann. §§ 44–13–1, 44—13–100. Bankruptcy only: $43,000 if title to property is in one of two spouses who is a debtor. Ga. Code Ann. § 44–13–100(a)(1). May be waived except as to certain essential personal property. Ga. Code Ann. § 44–13–40.

Procedural requirements: None stated. Exemptions may be claimed after judgment.

Special provisions: If debtor fails to claim exemption, spouse or anyone acting on behalf of minor children or dependents may do so.

Waiver: May be waived except as to certain essential personal property.

***Tangible personal property:* Ga. Code Ann. §§ 44–13–1, 44–13–40, 44–13–100.**

Household goods: Any real or personal property in the amount of $5000. Ga. Code Ann. § 44–13–1. Bankruptcy only: up to $300 per item, $5000 total in household goods, clothing, appliances, animals, books, crops, or musical instruments. Ga. Code Ann. § 44–13–100(4).

Motor vehicles: Bankruptcy only: $5000. Ga. Code Ann. § 44–13–100(3).

Tools of trade: Bankruptcy only: $1500. Ga. Code Ann. § 44–13–100(7).

Clothing and jewelry: Bankruptcy only: $500 jewelry. Ga. Code Ann. § 44–13–100(5).

Miscellaneous and wildcard: Bankruptcy only: $600 plus unused amount of $5000 exemption (Ga. Code Ann. § 44–13–100(6)); health aids. Ga. Code Ann. § 44–13–100(10).

Waiver: Permitted, except as to wearing apparel and $300 worth of household and kitchen furniture and provisions. Waiver may be included in note or contract evidencing indebtedness. Ga. Code Ann. § 44–13–40.

***Benefits, retirement plans, insurance, judgments, and other intangibles:* Ga. Code Ann. §§ 18–4–22, 44–13–100.**

Public benefits: Bankruptcy only: Social Security; veterans' benefits; unemployment, illness, or disability benefits; local public assistance. Ga. Code Ann. § 44–13–100(2).

Pensions, retirement plans, and annuities: Certain tax-qualified retirement plans until paid to beneficiary; after payment they are treated like wages. Ga. Code Ann. § 18–4–22. Bankruptcy only: Payments from IRAs, pensions, annuities, or similar plans, as needed for support. Ga. Code Ann. § 44–12–100(2).

Insurance, judgments, or other compensation for injury: Bankruptcy only: unmatured life insurance contracts, up to $2000 in accrued dividends or cash or loan value of life insurance (Ga. Code Ann. § 44–13–100(8)); right to receive or property traceable to crime victim reparations, wrongful death award to extent needed for support, personal injury judgment up to $10,000 (not including pain and suffering or actual pecuniary loss), compensation for loss of future earnings of debtor or one on whom debtor is dependent. Ga. Code Ann. § 44–13–100(11).

Bank accounts: Not specified in exemption statute.

Alimony, child support: Bankruptcy only: alimony, support, or separate maintenance to the extent needed for support. Ga. Code Ann. § 44–13–100(2).

Tax refunds:

Survival after payment or deposit: Not specified in exemption statute.

HAWAII

Has state opted out of federal bankruptcy exemptions? No.

Is opt out limited to residents or domiciliaries of the state? Not applicable.

Do state's exemptions have extraterritorial application?

Homestead: No. Haw. Rev. Stat. § 651–92(a)(1) applies to one parcel of real property "in the state of Hawaii."

Personal property: Uncertain.

***Wages:* Haw. Rev. Stat. §§ 652–1(a), (b), 651–121, 653–3.**

Scope: Wages, salary, stipend, commissions, annuity, or net income under a trust. Haw. Rev. Stat. § 652(1)(a)(4).

Amount: 95% of first $100 earned per month, 90% of the next $100, and 80% of all sums in excess of $200 per month. Haw. Rev. Stat. § 652(1)(a)(4).

Survival after payment/deposit: Wages for thirty days prior to attachment proceedings are exempt. Haw. Rev. Stat. § 651–121(6).

Waiver: Not specified in exemption statute.

***Homestead:* Haw. Rev. Stat. §§ 651–91 through 651–93, 651–96.**

Amount: $30,000 for married person, head of family, or person over 65, and $20,000 for all others. Haw. Rev. Stat. § 651–92(a). Explicitly includes long-term leases, condos, co-ops, and any real property interest that vests immediate right of possession (Haw. Rev. Stat. § 651–92), subject to certain liens. Haw. Rev. Stat. § 651–92. Married couple may claim only one homestead; after decree of separate maintenance or interlocutory decree of divorce, each may claim individual exemption. Haw Rev. Stat. § 651–93.

Procedural requirements: None stated. May be claimed at time of levy.

Special provisions: Proceeds exempt for six months. Haw. Rev. Stat. § 651–96.

Waiver: Not specified in exemption statute.

***Tangible personal property:* Haw. Rev. Stat. §§ 651–121, 651–122.**

Household goods: Necessary furniture, appliances, and books. Haw. Rev. Stat. § 651–121(1).

Motor vehicles: $2575 (fair market value less liens and encumbrances). Haw. Rev. Stat. § 651–121(2).

Tools of trade: Tools, implements, one commercial fishing boat, motor vehicle reasonably necessary to, and used by the debtor in his or her trade, business, or profession. Haw. Rev. Stat. § 651–121(3).

Clothing and jewelry: Necessary clothing; $1000 jewelry and watches. Haw. Rev. Stat. § 651–121(1).

Miscellaneous and wildcard: Burial place. Haw. Rev. Stat. § 651–121(4). Sales and insurance proceeds of exempt property exempt for six months after receipt. Haw. Rev. Stat. § 651–121(5).

Waiver: Not specified in exemption statute.

***Benefits, retirement plans, insurance, judgments, and other intangibles:* Haw. Rev. Stat. §§ 651–124, 653–3.**

Public benefits: Not specified in exemption statute.

Pensions, retirement plans, and annuities: Pensions, annuities, retirement, disability, death benefits, or certain public employees' pension plans pursuant to certain tax-qualified plans. (Except as to claims of alternate payee under qualified domestic relations order or contributions made to a plan within three years before bankruptcy, voluntary or involuntary, or before the date a civil action is initiated against the debtor.) Haw. Rev. Stat. §§ 651–124, 653–3.

Insurance, judgments, or other compensation for injury: Not specified in exemption statute. *See* Haw. Rev. Stat. § 431:10–232, 431:10–233.

Bank accounts: Not specified in exemption statute.

Alimony, child support: Not specified in exemption statute.

Tax refunds:

Survival after payment or deposit: Not specified in exemption statute.

IDAHO

Has state opted out of federal bankruptcy exemptions? Yes. Idaho Code Ann. § 11–609.

Is opt out limited to residents or domiciliaries of the state? Not specified. Idaho Code Ann. § 11–609: "In any federal bankruptcy proceeding, an individual debtor may exempt from property of the estate only such property as is specified under the laws of this state."

Do state's exemptions have extraterritorial application?

Homestead: Not specified in exemption statute, but probably not. *See In re* Stephens, 2012 WL 3205362 (B.A.P. 9th Cir. Aug 02, 2012) (predicting that Idaho Supreme Court would limit applicability of Idaho's homestead exemption to real property located within Idaho); *In re* Capps, 438 B.R. 668 (Bankr. D. Idaho 2010) (real property located in Colorado not exempt under Idaho homestead exemption); *In re* Halpin, 1994 WL 594199 (Bankr. D. Idaho Nov. 1, 1994) (relying upon secondary authority, finds that Idaho homestead may not be used outside state).

Personal property: Probably not. Idaho Code Ann. § 11–602(1) provides that: "esidents of this state are entitled to the exemptions provided by this act. Nonresidents are entitled to the exemptions provided by the law of the jurisdiction of their residence." Idaho Code Ann. § 11–602(2) provides that the term " 'resident' means an individual who intends to maintain his home in this state." *See also In re* Footen, 2012 WL 669849 (Bankr. D. Or. Feb. 29, 2012); *In re* Almgren, 384 B.R. 12 (Bankr. D. Idaho 2007) (Idaho exemption for worker's compensation benefits did not apply to benefits payable under Tennessee's statutes).

***Wages:* Idaho Code Ann. §§ 11–206, 11–207.**

Scope: Compensation paid or payable for personal services, whether called wages, salary, commission, bonus, or otherwise, including periodic payments from pension or retirement program. Idaho Code Ann. § 11–206.

Amount: Similar to federal. Idaho Code Ann. § 11–207. Idaho law also provides that an individual is entitled to an exemption for disposable earnings, earned but not yet paid, up to $1500. This exemption shall not affect the application or operation of the garnishment restrictions in § 11–207.

Survival after payment/deposit: Not specified in exemption statute.

Waiver: Not specified in exemption statute.

***Homestead:* Idaho Code Ann. §§ 55–1001 through 55–1008.**

Amount: Lesser of $100,000 or net value of debtor's residence (includes manufactured home or unimproved lands on which a residence will be built). Idaho Code Ann. §§ 11–1001, 11–1002.

Procedural requirements: If land occupied as residence, homestead exemption is automatic; if owner wishes to claim homestead in land not yet so occupied, must record a declaration of homestead (as well as a declaration of abandonment of any previous homestead). Idaho Code Ann. § 55–1004. Owner who plans to be away from homestead for more than six months must record declaration of homestead. Idaho Code Ann. § 55–1006.

Special provisions: Sales or insurance proceeds are exempt for one year from the date of the sale or receipt; must show intent to establish new homestead. Idaho Code Ann. § 55–1008. Married couple may not stack homestead exemptions. Idaho Code Ann. § 55–1002. Exemption does not protect against judgments obtained before homestead was established. Idaho Code Ann. § 55–1005.

Waiver: Conveyance or encumbrance of homestead requires signature of both spouses. Idaho Code Ann. § 55–1007.

***Tangible personal property:* Idaho Code Ann. §§ 11–603 through 11–607.**

Household goods: $750 single item, $7500 aggregate. Furniture and appliances reasonably necessary for one household including one firearm, clothing, animals, books, and musical instruments. Idaho Code Ann. § 11–605(1).

Motor vehicles: $7000 in one vehicle. Idaho Code Ann. § 11–605(3).

Tools of trade: $2500 (Idaho Code Ann. § 11–605(3)); a 160-inch water right for irrigation of lands the debtor cultivates. Idaho Code Ann. § 11–605(7).

Clothing and jewelry: Clothing included in $7500 exemption above; $1000 jewelry. Idaho Code Ann. § 11–605(2).

Miscellaneous and wildcard: $800 wildcard for tangible personal property (Idaho Code Ann. § 11–605(11)); health aids (Idaho Code Ann. § 11–603(2)); $1000 in crops from 50 acres of land that the debtor cultivates; up to $500 per item portraits and heirlooms; military items (Idaho Code Ann. § 11–605(6)); burial plot (Idaho Code Ann. § 11–603(1)); one firearm up to $750 (Idaho Code Ann. § 11–605)(8)); provisions of food and water with storage containers and shelving, sufficient for 12 months for debtor and dependents. Idaho Code Ann. § 11–605(4). Compensation for lost, damaged, or destroyed exempt property exempt to the same extent as the property, for three months. Idaho Code Ann. § 11–606.

Waiver: Not specified in exemption statute.

***Benefits, retirement plans, insurance, judgments, and other intangibles:* Idaho Code Ann. §§ 11–603 through 11–607, 55–1011.**

Public benefits: Social Security or veterans' benefits; state, local, or federal public assistance; state unemployment (to extent provided for in Idaho Code Ann. § 72–1375). Idaho Code Ann. §§ 11–603(3), 11–603(6) *See also* Idaho Code Ann. § 56–223 (public assistance exempt).

Pensions, retirement plans, and annuities: Certain pensions and tax-qualified retirement plans, except as to claims of alternate payee under qualified domestic relations order. Idaho Code Ann. § 11–605.

Insurance, judgments, or other compensation for injury: Up to $5000 in any accrued dividend or interest under, or loan value of, an unmatured life insurance contract owned by debtor in which the insured is the debtor or a person on whom the debtor is dependent. Insurance proceeds of exempt property exempt to same extent as the property, for three months after receipt. Idaho Code Ann. §§ 11–605(8), 11–605(9). Benefits payable for medical, surgical, or hospital care. Idaho Code Ann. § 11–603(5). Exempt so far as needed for support: benefits payable by reason of disability or illness, personal injury compensation (for injury to self or one on whom dependent), wrongful death compensation (if debtor dependent on victim), life insurance proceeds (if debtor was spouse or dependent of insured). Idaho Code Ann. § 11–604.

Bank accounts: Medical savings accounts, as defined by Idaho Code Ann. § 63–3022K.

Alimony, child support: Certain retirement benefits received by alternate payee pursuant to qualified domestic relations order. Alimony, support, or separate maintenance, so far as needed for support. Idaho Code Ann. § 11–604A.

Tax refunds:

Survival after payment or deposit: Limited. Exemptions for insurance, personal injury compensation, alimony, support, separate maintenance, illness or disability benefits lost if commingled with other funds. Idaho Code Ann. § 11–604(3).

ILLINOIS

Has state opted out of federal bankruptcy exemptions? Yes. 735 Ill. Comp. Stat. § 5/12–1201.

Is opt out limited to residents or domiciliaries of the state? Yes. 735 Ill. Comp. Stat. § 5/12–1201: "esidents of this state shall be prohibited from using . . . [§ 522(d)] except as may be otherwise permitted under the laws of Illinois." *See In re* George, 440 B.R. 164 (Bankr. E.D. Wis. 2010) (finding that Illinois exemption law has an implied residency requirement). *But see In re* Shell, 478 B.R. 889 (Bankr. N.D. Ind. 2012) (question of whether Illinois opt-out statute is applicable only to residents is irrelevant when considering application of § 522(b)(3)(A)).

Do state's exemptions have extraterritorial application?

Homestead: Uncertain. *See In re* George, 440 B.R. 164 (Bankr. E.D. Wis. 2010) (Illinois exemptions are available only to current Illinois residents).

Personal property: Uncertain. *See In re* George, 440 B.R. 164 (Bankr. E.D. Wis. 2010) (Illinois exemptions are available only to current Illinois residents).

***Wages:* 735 Ill. Comp. Stat. §§ 5/12–801, 5/12–803, 5/12–813, 5/12–817, 5/12–818; 740 Ill. Comp. Stat. § 170/4.**

Scope: Wages, salary, commission, or bonus. 735 Ill. Comp. Stat. § 5/12–801.

Amount: The greater of 85% of disposable income, or 45 times the greater of the federal minimum wage, or, for wage summonses served after January 1, 2006, the wage prescribed by section 4 of the minimum wage law, is exempt. Disposable earnings are those left after all legally required withholding. 735 Ill. Comp. Stat. § 5/12–803, 740 Ill. Comp. Stat. § 170/4. One who wrongfully causes wage garnishment summons to issue is liable to the employer and the employee for damages, including reasonable attorney fees. 735 Ill. Comp. Stat. § 5/12–817. Discharge for garnishment forbidden. 735 Ill. Comp. Stat. § 5/12–818.

Survival after payment/deposit: Not specified in exemption statute.

Waiver: Wage garnishment order may not be issued on confession of judgment. 735 Ill. Comp. Stat. § 5/12–813.

***Homestead:* 735 Ill. Comp. Stat. §§ 5/12–901 through 5/12–907.**

Amount: $15,000; if property is owned by two or more persons, each may exempt proportionate share of $30,000. 735 Ill. Comp. Stat. § 5/12–901.

Procedural requirements: Not specified in exemption statute.

Special provisions: Sales proceeds are exempt for one year from the date of the sale. 735 Ill. Comp. Stat. § 5/12–906. If home owner dies, exemption survives so long as surviving spouse or minor children occupy the homestead. If spouse deserts family, exemption protects spouse who still resides in homestead. 735 Ill. Comp. Stat. § 5/12–902. Homestead exemption will not protect against drug forfeiture. 735 Ill. Comp. Stat. § 5/12–903.5. Insurance proceeds for loss or destruction of homestead, if insured in favor of a person who may claim exemption, are exempt to the extent the building would have been. 735 Ill. Comp. Stat. § 5/12–907.

Waiver: Must be in writing, and signed by spouse, if any. 735 Ill. Comp. Stat. § 5/12–904.

***Tangible personal property:* 625 Ill. Comp. Stat. § 45/3A-7; 735 Ill. Comp. Stat. § 5/12–1001.**

Household goods: Included in $4000 wildcard. 735 Ill. Comp. Stat. § 5/12–1001(b). Proceeds of sale of exempt property remain exempt to same extent as property is exempt.

Motor vehicles: $2400 in one motor vehicle. 735 Ill. Comp. Stat. § 5/12–1001(c).

Tools of trade: $1500. 735 Ill. Comp. Stat. § 5/12–1001(d).

Clothing and jewelry: Necessary clothing. 735 Ill. Comp. Stat. § 5/12–1001(a).

Miscellaneous and wildcard: $4000 in any property. 735 Ill. Comp. Stat. § 5/12–1001(b). Bible, school books, family pictures (735 Ill. Comp. Stat. § 5/12–1001(a)); health aids (735 Ill. Comp. Stat. § 5/12–1001(e)); certificate of title to watercraft over twelve feet in length is exempt, although the watercraft itself is not exempt. 625 Ill. Comp. Stat. § 45/3A-7. Personal property exemption does not apply if exempt property purchased with intent to convert non-exempt to exempt property, or in fraud of creditors. Property acquired within six months before filing bankruptcy is presumed to have been acquired in anticipation of bankruptcy. 735 Ill. Comp. Stat. § 5/12–1001.

Waiver: Not specified in exemption statute.

***Benefits, retirement plans, insurance, judgments, and other intangibles:* 735 Ill. Comp. Stat. §§ 5/12–1001, 5/12–1006. *See* 820 Ill. Comp. Stat. § 405/1300.**

Public benefits: Social Security, veterans' benefits, unemployment, public assistance. 735 Ill. Comp. Stat. §§ 5/12–1001(g), 5/12–1001(h). Waivers of exemption void as to unemployment benefits. *See also* 305 Ill. Comp. Stat. § 5/11–3 (financial aid exempt).

Pensions, retirement plans, and annuities: Certain public and private pension and retirement plans, including IRAs and SEPs. 735 Ill. Comp. Stat. § 5/12–1006.

Insurance, judgments, or other compensation for injury: Proceeds and cash values of insurance policies or annuities payable to spouse, or child, parent, or other dependent of insured, or to a revocable or irrevocable trust, the primary beneficiary of which is a spouse, child, parent, or other dependent of the insured; disability, illness, or unemployment benefit. 735 Ill. Comp. Stat. § 5/12–1001(f). Right to receive or property traceable to crime victim reparations, wrongful death (of person on whom debtor was dependent, to extent needed for support), up to $15,000 personal injury. 735 Ill. Comp. Stat. § 5/12–1001(h).

Bank accounts: Funds in accounts invested in the Illinois College Savings Pool. 735 Ill. Comp. Stat. § 5/12–1001(j).

Alimony, child support: Alimony, support, or separate maintenance, to the extent needed for support. 735 Ill. Comp. Stat. § 5/12–1001(g).

Tax refunds:

Survival after payment or deposit: Sale proceeds of exempt property exempt to same extent as property. Right to receive certain compensation (insurance, crime victim reparations, personal injury, or wrongful death) remains exempt for two years after right accrues, property traceable to certain compensation remains exempt for five years if traceable.

INDIANA

Has state opted out of federal bankruptcy exemptions? Yes. Ind. Code § 34–55–10–1.

Is opt out limited to residents or domiciliaries of the state? Yes. Ind. Code § 34–55–10–1: "an individual debtor domiciled in Indiana is not entitled to use . . . [§ 522(d) exemptions]."

Do state's exemptions have extraterritorial application?

Homestead: No. *See* Ind. Code § 34–55–10–2 (applies to the property of a "debtor domiciled in Indiana"); *In re* West, 352 B.R. 905 (Bankr. M.D. Fla. 2006).

Personal property: No. *See* Ind. Code § 34–55–10–2 (applies to the property of a "debtor domiciled in Indiana"); *In re* West, 352 B.R. 905 (Bankr. M.D. Fla. 2006).

***Wages:* Ind. Code § 24–4.5–5–105.**

Scope: Earnings of an individual, including wages, commissions, income, rents, or profits.

Amount: Similar to federal.

Survival after payment/deposit: Not specified in exemption statute.

Waiver: Not specified in exemption statute.

***Homestead:* Ind. Code §§ 34–55–10–2(c)(1), (2), and (5); §§ 34–55–10–2.5, 34–55–10–14; 750 Ind. Admin. Code § 1–1–1 (adjusted exemption amounts).**

Amount: $17,600 subject to certain liens. Ind. Code §§ 34–55–10–2(c)(1), 34–55–10–14. The exemption is individually available to joint judgment debtors if property held by them as tenants by entireties. Ind. Code § 34–55–10–2(c)(1). Additional exemption for "real estate or tangible personal property" of $9350. Ind. Code § 34–55–10–2(c)(2). As of 2010, and every six years thereafter, the Department of Financial Institutions must establish new exemption amounts, based on changes in the Consumer Price Index. Ind. Code § 34–55–10–2.5.

Procedural requirements: None stated. May claim after judgment.

Special provisions: Not specified in exemption statute.

Waiver: Not specified in exemption statute.

***Tangible personal property:* Ind. Code §§ 34–55–10–2, 34–55–10–2.5; 750 Ind. Admin. Code § 1–1–1 (adjusted exemption amounts).**

Household goods: $9350 in any tangible personal property or nonresidential real property (Ind. Code § 34–55–10–2(c)(2)) and $350 of intangible personal property, including bank accounts and cash (Ind. Code § 34–55–10–2(c)(3)); exemptions are subject to certain liens.

Motor vehicles: See above.

Tools of trade: See above.

Clothing and jewelry: See above.

Miscellaneous and wildcard: Health aids (no cap). Ind. Code § 34–55–10–2(c)(4).

Waiver: Not specified in exemption statute.

***Benefits, retirement plans, insurance, judgments, and other intangibles:* Ind. Code § 34–55–10–2.**

Public benefits: Veterans' disability benefits for service-connected disability (Ind. Code § 34–55–10–2(c)(12)); tax refund attributable to state or federal earned income credit. Ind. Code § 34–55–10–2(c)(11).

Pensions, retirement plans, and annuities: Certain retirement plans, including rollovers. Ind. Code § 34–55–10–2(c)(6).

Insurance, judgments, or other compensation for injury: Not specified in exemption statute.

Bank accounts: Medical savings accounts and certain prepaid tuition and educational savings accounts. Ind. Code §§ 34–55–10–2(c)(7) through 34–55–10–2(c)(10). Choses in action, deposit accounts, and cash up to $350. Ind. Code § 34–55–10–2.

Alimony, child support: Not specified in exemption statute.

Tax refunds:

Survival after payment or deposit: Not specified in exemption statute.

IOWA

Has state opted out of federal bankruptcy exemptions? Yes. Iowa Code § 627.10.

Is opt out limited to residents or domiciliaries of the state? Not specified, but probably not. Iowa Code § 627.10: "A debtor to whom the law of this state applies on the date of filing of a petition in bankruptcy is not entitled to elect . . . [§ 522(d) exemptions]." *See In re* Williams, 369 B.R. 470 (Bankr. W.D. Ark. 2007) (debtors residing in Arkansas are subject to Iowa opt-out statute).

Do state's exemptions have extraterritorial application?

Homestead: Not specified in exemption statute, but probably yes. *Compare In re* Stephens, 402 B.R. 1 (B.A.P. 10th Cir. 2009) (Oklahoma resident could claim Iowa homestead exemption in proceeds of former Iowa home), *and In re* Williams, 369 B.R. 470 (Bankr. W.D. Ark. 2007) (debtor could use Iowa homestead exemption for Arkansas property), *with In re* Stone, 329 B.R. 860 (Bankr. N.D. Iowa 2005) (relying on Rogers v. Raisor, 14 N.W. 317 (Iowa 1882); proceeds of an Iowa homestead reinvested in a new homestead in another state not exempt under Iowa law).

Personal property: Probably not. Iowa Code § 627.6 applies to property of a "debtor who is a resident of this state."

***Wages:* Iowa Code §§ 627.6, 642.21, 537.5105, 537.5201.**

Scope: Compensation paid or payable for personal services, whether called wages, salary, commission, bonus, or otherwise, including periodic payments from pension or retirement program. Iowa Code § 642.21(3).

Amount: Maximum garnishment ranges from $250 a year when expected earnings do not exceed $12,000 to 10% of annual earnings when such earnings exceed $50,000. Iowa Code §§ 537.5105, 642/21(1). Tax refunds and accrued wages are exempt in bankruptcy only, up to $1000 aggregate. Iowa Code § 627.6(10). In addition, if the debt arises from a consumer credit contract, greater of 75% or 40 times the minimum wage is exempt. Iowa Code § 537.5105. The Iowa Consumer Code also provides a procedure for a consumer to seek a reduction in the garnishment amount, if the funds are needed for support of the consumer or the consumer's household. Iowa Code § 537.5105. Discharge for garnishment forbidden; discharged employee has private right of action for reinstatement and up to six weeks lost wages. Iowa Code §§ 537.5201(5), 642.21(2)(c).

Survival after payment/deposit: Not specified in exemption statute.

Waiver: Not specified in exemption statute.

***Homestead:* Iowa Code §§ 561.1 through 561.3, 561.20 through 561.22, 627.6(15), 627.9.**

Amount: Up to one half acre in city or town, otherwise 40 acres; also acreage up to $500 in value (Iowa Code § 561.2); building on the property used for business purposes is exempt up to $300. Iowa Code § 561.3. Only one homestead per household unit (defined as persons who reside together, whether or not related). Homestead purchased with pension money is fully exempt. Iowa Code § 627.9. Up to $500 in the aggregate in: any residential rental deposit, held by landlord as a security deposit; pre-paid rent under an unexpired residential lease; utility security deposits; interest paid on security deposits required by law to be placed in interest-bearing account is also exempt. Iowa Code § 627.6(15).

Procedural requirements: May select homestead and cause it to be platted, but failure to do so will not destroy exemption.

Special provisions: "Owner" includes a person, or the person's surviving spouse, who occupies the homestead as a beneficiary of a trust that includes the property in the trust estate. Iowa Code § 561.1. Homestead liable for debts which predate the acquisition of the homestead (Iowa Code § 627.21), but exemption passes uninterrupted from old homestead to new, if new homestead acquired with proceeds of old. Iowa Code § 561.20. Homestead purchased with pension money is exempt even as to claims for preexisting debts. Iowa Code § 627.9. If land is annexed to a city or town, rural homestead will continue as before until the land is sold.

Waiver: Waiver of homestead of agricultural land containing forty acres or more, contained in a contract, must include prescribed language in ten-point boldface type stating that debtor knows of and voluntarily waives homestead rights. Iowa Code § 561.22.

***Tangible personal property:* Iowa Code §§ 627.6, 627.6A, 627.7.**

Household goods: $7000. Explicitly includes computers, cameras, and a wide range of electronic entertainment equipment (record, tape, CD and DVD players, satellite dishes, cable equipment, and so forth). Iowa Code § 627.6(5).

Motor vehicles: $7000 in the aggregate of one motor vehicle. Motor vehicle not exempt as to claim for damages resulting from use of the vehicle. Iowa Code §§ 627.6(9), 627.7.

Tools of trade: $10,000. Farming implements and livestock included, but may not be exempted for deficiency judgment upon foreclosure on agricultural land if debtor exercises the delay of enforcement provisions of Iowa Code § 654.6. Iowa Code §§ 627.6(11) through 627.6(13).

Clothing and jewelry: Clothing and trunks included in household goods exemption. Jewelry: $2000 (Iowa Code § 627.6(1)(b)), plus engagement or wedding rings, but if ring acquired by debtor or dependent after the date of marriage and within two years before execution issued or exemption claimed, then limit of $7000 minus any amount claimed under the jewelry exemption. Iowa Code § 627.6(1)(a)

Miscellaneous and wildcard: One shotgun and either a rifle or a musket (Iowa Code § 627.6(2)); $1000 in books and paintings (Iowa Code § 627.6(3)); professionally prescribed health aids (Iowa Code § 627.6(7)); burial space. Iowa Code § 627.6(4). Up to $500 aggregate in prepaid rent or security deposits, or utility security deposits. $1000 cash, bank accounts, or any other personal property, whether otherwise exempt or not. Iowa Code § 627.614.

Waiver: Not specified in exemption statute.

***Benefits, retirement plans, insurance, judgments, and other intangibles:* Iowa Code §§ 627.6, 627.6A, 627.8, 627.9, 627.13, 627.19. *See* Iowa Code § 96.15.**

Public benefits: Social Security, veterans' benefits, unemployment, or any public assistance benefit. Iowa Code § 627.6(8). (Waivers of exemption void as to unemployment benefits.) Iowa Code § 96.15. Financial assistance provided under Iowa Code §§ 600.17 to 600.22 (adopted child assistance). Iowa Code § 627.19. *See also* Iowa Code § 239B.6 (family assistance exempt).

Pensions, retirement plans, and annuities: Certain pension and retirement plans, including IRAs, SEPs, and Roth IRAs; rollovers explicitly included, but above-normal contributions made within one year of bankruptcy excluded. Pensions and retirement plans not exempt if claim is for family support. Iowa Code §§ 627.6(8), 627.6A, 627.8.

Insurance, judgments, or other compensation for injury: Workers' Compensation (not exempt as to family support debts). Iowa Code § 627.13. Disability or illness benefits. Iowa Code § 627.6(8). Accrued dividends, loan or cash surrender value of life insurance policy if spouse, child or dependent is beneficiary; capped at aggregate $10,000 for policies acquired or certain additions to existing policy within two years before execution is issued or exemption claimed. If insured dies, all avails of insurance policies (including life, health, accident or disability) exempt in beneficiaries' hands up to $15,000, as to debts contracted before death of insured. Iowa Code § 627.6(6). Payments, including a structured settlement, resulting from the wrongful death of a person upon whom debtor or debtor's dependents were dependent, or personal injury to debtor or dependent, so far as needed for support. Iowa Code § 627.6(16).

Bank accounts: $1000 wildcard can be applied to bank account.

Alimony, child support: Alimony, support, or separate maintenance, so far as needed for support.

Tax refunds: Bankruptcy only: accrued wages and state and federal tax refunds, up to $1000 aggregate. Iowa Code § 627.6(10).

Survival after payment or deposit: Not specified in exemption statute.

KANSAS

Has state opted out of federal bankruptcy exemptions? Yes, except as to 11 U.S.C. § 522(d)(10) (benefits, alimony, support, maintenance, certain pensions and similar payments). Kan. Stat. Ann. § 60–2312.

Is opt out limited to residents or domiciliaries of the state? Not specified. Kan. Stat. Ann. § 60–2312: "[N]o person, as an individual debtor under the [Bankruptcy Code], may elect exemptions pursuant to [§ 522(d)]."

Do state's exemptions have extraterritorial application?

Homestead: No. *See In re* Spika, 149 B.R. 181 (D. Kan. 1992); *In re* Ginther, 282 B.R. 16 (Bankr. D. Kan. 2002).

Personal property: Probably not. Kan. Stat. Ann. § 60–2304 applies to property of "every person residing in this state."

***Wages:* Kan. Stat. Ann. §§ § 60–2309 through 60–2311.**

Scope: Compensation paid or payable for personal services, whether called wages, salary, commission, bonus, or otherwise. Kan. Stat. Ann. § 60–2310(a).

Amount: Similar to federal. Kan. Stat. Ann. § 60–2310(b). If a debtor is prevented from working at his or her usual employment for two weeks because of illness of the debtor or a family member, garnishment is forbidden until the expiration of two months after recovery from the illness. Kan. Stat. Ann. § 60–2310(c). No employee may be discharged or disciplined because of wage garnishment. Kan. Stat. Ann. § 60–2311. If a debt is assigned to a person or collection agency, the assignee may not use wage garnishment (except for certain child support, tax or court restitution collections). Kan. Stat. Ann. § 60–2310(d).

Survival after payment/deposit: Not specified in exemption statute.

Waiver: Not specified in exemption statute.

***Homestead:* Kan. Stat. Ann. §§ 60–2301 through 60–2303.**

Amount: 160 acres of farm land or one acre in a town or city, subject to certain liens. Manufactured home explicitly included. Kan. Stat. Ann. § 60–2301. If land is annexed to a city or town, homestead rights shall continue as before the annexation, until the property is sold.

Procedural requirements: None stated. May be claimed at time of levy. Kan. Stat. Ann. § 60–2302.

Special provisions: Not specified.

Waiver: Sale or encumbrance requires signature of spouse, if any. Kan. Stat. Ann. §§ 60–2301, 60–2303.

***Tangible personal property:* Kan. Stat. Ann. § 60–2304.**

Household goods: Household goods, fuel, food, and clothing reasonably necessary at principal residence for one year. Kan. Stat. Ann. § 60–2304(a).

Motor vehicles: $20,000, if used regularly to commute to work; disabled (definition at Kan. Stat. Ann. § 8–1124) no limitations. Kan. Stat. Ann. § 60–2304(c).

Tools of trade: $7500. Kan. Stat. Ann. § 60–2304(e).

Clothing and jewelry: Clothing, see above; $1000 in jewelry. Kan. Stat. Ann. § 60–2304(b).

Miscellaneous and wildcard: Burial space (Kan. Stat. Ann. § 60–2304(d)); National Guard uniforms and equipment.

Waiver: Not specified in exemption statute.

***Benefits, retirement plans, insurance, judgments, and other intangibles:* Kan. Stat. Ann. §§ 60–2304, 60–2308, 60–2313, 60–2315.**

Public benefits: Public assistance, unemployment, workers' compensation. Kan. Stat. Ann. § 60–2313. *See also* Kan. Stat. Ann. § 39–717(c) (assistance under Social Welfare Act is exempt).

Pensions, retirement plans, and annuities: Certain pensions and retirement accounts, including tax-qualified IRAs. Kan. Stat. Ann. §§ 60–2308, 60–2313.

Insurance, judgments, or other compensation for injury: Life insurance; crime victim compensation; benefits from fraternal organization; certain annuities and death or disability benefits. Kan. Stat. Ann. § 60–2313.

Bank accounts: Prepaid college tuition accounts, if the beneficiary is a lineal descendant of the debtor, certain recent contributions excluded; prepaid funeral. Kan. Stat. Ann. § 60–2313.

Alimony, child support: Alimony, so far as reasonably necessary to debtor's support.

Tax refunds: Bankruptcy only: Tax refund attributable to state or Federal earned income credit.

Survival after payment or deposit: Not specified in exemption statute.

KENTUCKY

Has state opted out of federal bankruptcy exemptions? No. Ky. Rev. Stat. Ann. § 427.170 (West).

Is opt out limited to residents or domiciliaries of the state? Not applicable.

Do state's exemptions have extraterritorial application?

Homestead: No. Ky. Rev. Stat. Ann. § 427.060 (West) applies to "real or personal property . . . that such debtor or . . . dependent . . . uses as a permanent residence in this state."

Personal property: Probably not. Ky. Rev. Stat. Ann. § 427.010 (West) applies to "personal property of an individual debtor resident in this state."

***Wages:* Ky. Rev. Stat. Ann. §§ 427.005, 427.010(2), 427.140 (West).**

Scope: Compensation paid or payable for personal services, whether called wages, salary, commission, bonus, or otherwise, including periodic payments pursuant to pension or retirement program. Ky. Rev. Stat. Ann. § 427.005 (West).

Amount: Similar to federal exemptions. Ky. Rev. Stat. Ann. § 427.010(2) (West). Employee may not be discharged for garnishment. Ky. Rev. Stat. Ann. § 427.140 (West).

Survival after payment/deposit: Not specified in exemption statute.

Waiver: Not specified in exemption statute.

***Homestead:* Ky. Rev. Stat. Ann. §§ 427.060, 427.070, 427.100, 427.160 (West).**

Amount: $5000 in real or personal property used as a residence. Ky. Rev. Stat. Ann. § 427.060 (West). In bankruptcy, an additional $1000 in real property may be exempted if this sum is not applied to exempt personal property. Ky. Rev. Stat. Ann. § 427.160 (West).

Procedural requirements: None stated. May be claimed after judgment.

Special provisions: Does not apply to debts existing at time homestead established. Ky. Rev. Stat. Ann. § 427.060 (West). At debtor's death exemption preserved in hands of surviving spouse and minor children. Ky. Rev. Stat. Ann. § 427.070 (West).

Waiver: Permitted. Must be in writing, signed by spouse (if any), and recorded like a conveyance of real estate. Ky. Rev. Stat. Ann. § 427.100 (West).

***Tangible personal property:* Ky. Rev. Stat. Ann. §§ 427.005, 427.010(1), 427.030, 427.040, 427.150, 427.160 (West).**

Household goods: $3000 in household goods, clothing, and jewelry. Ky. Rev. Stat. Ann. § 427.010(1) (West). Explicitly excludes antiques, works of art, jewelry other than wedding rings, and electronic equipment except for one TV and one radio. Ky. Rev. Stat. Ann. § 427.005 (West).

Motor vehicles: $2500. Ky. Rev. Stat. Ann. § 427.010(1) (West).

Tools of trade: $300 tools of trade. $3000 farm implements and livestock. Ky. Rev. Stat. Ann. § 427.010(1) (West). $1000 office, library, and instruments and $2500 motor vehicle used by professional (for example, clergy, doctor, dentist, attorney, chiropractor, veterinarian) (Ky. Rev. Stat. Ann. § 427.040 (West)); $2500 motor vehicle if used by person who services essential mechanical, electrical, or other equipment in general use. Ky. Rev. Stat. Ann. § 427.030 (West).

Clothing and jewelry: See above.

Miscellaneous and wildcard: Health aids. Ky. Rev. Stat. Ann. § 427.010(1) (West). Bankruptcy only: $1000 in any real or personal property. Ky. Rev. Stat. Ann. § 427.160 (West).

Waiver: Not specified in exemption statute.

***Benefits, retirement plans, insurance, judgments, and other intangibles:* Ky. Rev. Stat. Ann. §§ 427.010(1), 427.110 through 427.125, 427.150, 427.160 (West).**

Public benefits: Not specified in exemption statute. *See* Ky. Rev. Stat. Ann. § 205.220 (West) (public assistance exempt).

Pensions, retirement plans, and annuities: Assets of and benefits under profit sharing, annuity, or similar plans based on debtor's age, illness, disability, or length of service; certain tax-qualified retirement plans (Ky. Rev. Stat. Ann. § 427.010(1) (West)); certain public pensions. Ky. Rev. Stat. Ann. §§ 427.020 through 427.130 (West).

Insurance, judgments, or other compensation for injury: Life insurance proceeds; benefits from fraternal organization (Ky. Rev. Stat. Ann. § 427.110 (West)); crime victim reparations; $7500 personal injury judgments. Compensation for wrongful death or loss of future earnings is exempt to the extent necessary for support of debtor or dependent. Ky. Rev. Stat. Ann. § 427.150 (West).

Bank accounts: Not specified.

Alimony, child support: Alimony, support, or separate maintenance, to the extent needed for support.

Tax refunds:

Survival after payment or deposit: Not specified in exemption statute (except that police or firefighter pension is exempt "before or after its order for distribution").

LOUISIANA

Has state opted out of federal bankruptcy exemptions? Yes. La. Rev. Stat. Ann. § 13:3881(B)(1).

Is opt out limited to residents or domiciliaries of the state? Not specified. La. Rev. Stat. Ann. § 13:3881(B)(1): "In cases instituted under [Title 11], there shall be exempt . . . only that property and income which is exempt under the laws of the state of Louisiana and under federal laws other than [§ 522(d)]."

Do state's exemptions have extraterritorial application?

Homestead: Uncertain.

Personal property: Uncertain.

***Wages:* La. Rev. Stat. Ann. § 13:3881.**

Scope: Earnings of any individual. Disposable earnings are those left after legally required deductions and deductions in usual course of business for retirement, health insurance, and life insurance. La. Rev. Stat. Ann. § 13:3881(A)(1)(b).

Amount: Similar to federal exemptions. La. Rev. Stat. Ann. § 13:3881(A)(1)(a).

Survival after payment/deposit: Not specified in exemption statute.

Waiver: Not specified in exemption statute.

***Homestead:* La. Rev. Stat. Ann. § 20:1, § 13.3851.1. *See* La. Const. art. 12, § 9.**

Amount: Residence and land, building and appurtenances on contiguous tracts of up to five acres if within a municipality, two hundred acres if not. Up to $35,000 (La. Rev. Stat. Ann. § 20:1(A)(1)), except that for expenses resulting from catastrophic or terminal illness or injury, homestead is exempt up to full value. La. Rev. Stat. Ann. §§ 20:1(A)(2), 20:1(A)(3). Some exceptions, including taxes, mortgage, certain criminal restitution. La. Rev. Stat. Ann. §20.1(C). A homestead may not be seized for consumer credit card charges, but the creditor may file a lien, so as to establish its priority in the proceeds, if the homestead is subsequently sold. The provisions of this section may be waived by a waiver "in authentic form." The homeowner may sue within one year to annul a sheriff's sale, if property is purchased by the judgment creditor and is still in the creditor's hands. Violation of this section may not, however, be asserted against a third party purchaser. La. Rev. Stat. Ann. § 13:3851.1.

Procedural requirements: Not specified.

Special provisions: Homestead exemption protects surviving spouse and minor children who continue to occupy homestead. La. Rev. Stat. Ann. § 20:1(B).

Waiver: Permitted, but requires signature of spouse, if any, recorded in mortgage records. If, however, homestead is separate property of one spouse, that spouse may waive homestead in a mortgage, without the signature of non-owner spouse. Not permitted for rendering of medical treatment, medical services, or hospitalization. La. Rev. Stat. Ann. § 20:1(D).

***Tangible personal property:* La. Rev. Stat. Ann. § 13:3881.**

Household goods: Clothing, household goods, non-sterling silverware (La. Rev. Stat. Ann. § 13:3881(A)(4)), certain retirement plans; poultry, fowl, and one cow for family use; a right of personal servitude of habitation and the usufruct under Article 223 of the Civil Code. La. Rev. Stat. Ann. § 13:3881(A)(3).

Motor vehicles: $7500 in one vehicle, used by debtor and family for any purpose. Only one motor vehicle per household. $7500 in any vehicle substantially modified, equipped or fitted for adapting its use to physical disability of debtor or family, and used for transporting such disabled person. La. Rev. Stat. Ann. §§ 13:3881(A)(7), 13:3881(A)(8).

Tools of trade: Tools, instruments, books, and one utility trailer used for trade, calling, or profession by which debtor earns living. La. Rev. Stat. Ann. § 13:3881(A)(2). Certain livestock.

Clothing and jewelry: Clothing; $5000 wedding and engagement rings. La. Rev. Stat. Ann. § 13:3881(A)(5).

Miscellaneous and wildcard: Household pets, family portraits, arms and military accoutrements, musical instruments (La. Rev. Stat. Ann. § 13:3881(A)(4)), one firearm valued up to $500. La. Rev. Stat. Ann. § 13:3881(A)(2).

Waiver: Not specified in exemption statute.

***Benefits, retirement plans, insurance, judgments, and other intangibles:* La. Rev. Stat. Ann. § 13:3881.**

Public benefits: Not specified in exemption statute. *See* La. Rev. Stat. Ann. § 46:111 (public assistance exempt). Earned income tax refund. La. Rev. Stat. Ann. § 13:3881(A)(6).

Pensions, retirement plans, and annuities: Pensions, tax-deferred arrangements (defined; includes IRAs, Roth IRA's specifically included, and SEPs), and annuities, except as to criminal fines, restitution, or incarceration expenses. La. Rev. Stat. Ann. § 13:3881(D).

Insurance, judgments, or other compensation for injury: Proceeds of any property insurance settlement received as a result of damage caused by a gubernatorially declared disaster to an asset exempt under this section, or held in an escrow account and identified as the proceeds of an exempt asset, is exempt to the same extent as the destroyed or damaged asset. La. Rev. Stat. Ann. § 13:3881(A)(9).

Bank accounts: Not specified in exemption statute.

Alimony, child support: Not specified in exemption statute.

Tax refunds:

Survival after payment or deposit: "Proceeds" of exempt pensions, tax-deferred arrangements, and annuities are exempt.

MAINE

Has state opted out of federal bankruptcy exemptions? Yes. Me. Rev. Stat. Ann. tit. 14, § 4426.

Is opt out limited to residents or domiciliaries of the state? Not specified. Me. Rev. Stat. Ann. tit. 14, § 4426: "[A] debtor may exempt from property of the debtor's estate under [Title 11], only that property exempt under [11 U.S.C. § 522(b)(2)(A) and (B)]."

Do state's exemptions have extraterritorial application?

Homestead: Uncertain.

Personal property: Uncertain.

Wages: **Me. Rev. Stat. Ann. tit. 9-A, §§ 5–105, 5–106; Me. Rev. Stat. Ann. tit. 19A, § 2356.**

Scope: Earnings of an individual. Me. Rev. Stat. Ann. tit. 9-A, § 5–105(1).

Amount: For consumer credit transaction, maximum garnishment is lesser of 25% of weekly wages or the amount by which wages exceed 40 times the state or federal minimum hourly wage, whichever is higher. Me. Rev. Stat. Ann. tit. 9-A, § 5–105(2). Disposable earnings are those left after legally required deductions. Me. Rev. Stat. Ann. tit. 9-A, § 5–105(1). Discharge for garnishment forbidden. Me. Rev. Stat. Ann. tit. 9-A, § 5–106.

Survival after payment/deposit: Not specified in garnishment statute.

Waiver: Not specified in garnishment statute.

Homestead: **Me. Rev. Stat. Ann. tit. 14, § 4422(1).**

Amount: $47,500 in real or personal property used as residence or burial plot, subject to certain exceptions; $95,000 if debtor over 60 or has mental or physical disability that prevents him or her from working and lasts at least twelve months or results in death; $95,000 if minor dependent(s) of debtor have a principal place of residence with debtor. If debtor's interest in the property is held jointly with other person or persons, then the lesser of $47,500 or the debtor's fractional share of $95,000, or, if debtor is over 60 or disabled, debtor's fractional share of $190,000. Increased exemptions for elderly or disabled do not apply to liens obtained prior to that provision's effective date, nor to tort judgments involving "other than ordinary negligence on the part of the debtor." Exemption does not protect property that has been fraudulently conveyed.

Procedural requirements: Not specified in exemption statute.

Special provisions: Proceeds from sale of exempt property remain exempt for six months from date of receipt.

Waiver: Not specified in exemption statute.

Tangible personal property: **Me. Rev. Stat. Ann. tit. 14, §§ 4422(2)–(9), (11), (15), (16).**

Household goods: Household goods, not more than $200 per item (Me. Rev. Stat. Ann. tit. 14, § 4422(3)); a cook stove, all heating equipment, and various fuels (Me. Rev. Stat. Ann. tit. 14, § 4422(6)); food and provisions for six months, all equipment necessary for harvesting food and material necessary to raise food for one growing season. Me. Rev. Stat. Ann. tit. 14, §§ 4422(7), 4422(8).

Motor vehicles: $5000. Me. Rev. Stat. Ann. tit. 14, § 4422(2).

Tools of trade: $5000 (Me. Rev. Stat. Ann. tit. 14, § 4422(5)); one fishing boat, not more than 46 feet in length. Me. Rev. Stat. Ann. tit. 14, § 4422(9). Farm equipment. Me. Rev. Stat. Ann. tit. 14, § 4422(8). Logging implements. Me. Rev. Stat. Ann. tit. 14, § 4422(9-A).

Clothing and jewelry: Clothing, not more than $200 per item (Me. Rev. Stat. Ann. tit. 14, § 4422(3)); $750 in jewelry and a wedding and engagement ring. Me. Rev. Stat. Ann. tit. 14, § 4422(4).

Miscellaneous and wildcard: Books, animals, crops, and musical instruments held for personal use but no more than $200 per individual item (Me. Rev. Stat. Ann. tit. 14, § 4422(3)); health aids. Me. Rev. Stat. Ann. tit. 14, § 4422(12); tools of trade (Me. Rev. Stat. Ann. tit. 14, §§ 4422(5)); legal awards and life insurance benefits. Me. Rev. Stat. Ann. tit. 14, §§ 4422(14). $400 in any property (Me. Rev. Stat. Ann. tit. 14, § 4422(152)); in addition, the unused residence exemption, up to $6000, may be applied to exempt household goods, clothing, furniture, tools of the trade, and awards for bodily injury (Me. Rev. Stat. Ann. tit. 14, § 4422(16).

Waiver: Not specified in exemption statute.

Special provisions: Note that Maine's Domestic Relations Code, Me. Rev. Stat. Ann. tit. 19-A, § 2203, which allows seizure and sale of property for family support debts, has its own list of exemptions. It was originally scheduled to sunset on October 1, 1998, but the sunset provision was repealed in 1997 by 1997 Me. Laws ch. 669, § 4.

Benefits, retirement plans, insurance, judgments, and other intangibles: **Me. Rev. Stat. Ann. tit. 14, §§ 4422(10), (11), (13), (14); Me. Rev. Stat. Ann. tit. 3, § 703.**

Public benefits: Social Security, veterans' benefits, unemployment, local public assistance, earned income tax credit, or additional child credit. Me. Rev. Stat. Ann. tit. 14, §§ 4422(13)(A) through 4422(13)(C). *See also* Me. Rev. Stat. Ann. tit. 22, §§ 3180 (aid to needy persons), 3766 (TANF).

Pensions, retirement plans, and annuities: Certain pensions, retirement accounts, and annuities, to the extent necessary for support. Me. Rev. Stat. Ann. tit. 14, § 4422(13)(E).

Insurance, judgments, or other compensation for injury: Property traceable to crime victim reparation, wrongful death judgment, personal injury judgment (up to $12,500), compensation for loss of future earnings. Me. Rev. Stat. Ann. tit. 14, § 4422(14). Unmatured life insurance contract; up to $4000 in accrued interest or loan value of life insurance (Me. Rev. Stat. Ann. tit. 14, §§ 4422(10), 4422(11)); disability, illness, or unemployment benefit. Me. Rev. Stat. Ann. tit. 14, § 4422(13)(C).

Bank accounts: Not specified in exemptions statute.

Alimony, child support: Alimony, support, or separate maintenance, to extent needed for support. Me. Rev. Stat. Ann. tit. 14, § 4422(13)(D).

Tax refunds:

Survival after payment or deposit: Not specified in exemption statute, but note that some exemptions refer to the "right to receive" and others to the "right to receive or property traceable to" various benefits.

MARYLAND

Has state opted out of federal bankruptcy exemptions? Yes. Md. Code Ann., Cts. & Jud. Proc. § 11–504 (West).

Is opt out limited to residents or domiciliaries of the state? Not specified, but probably not. Md. Code Ann., Cts. & Jud. Proc. § 11–504 (West): "In any bankruptcy proceeding, a debtor is not entitled to the federal exemptions provided by § 522(d) of the federal Bankruptcy Code." *See In re* Brooks, 393 B.R. 80 (Bankr. M.D. Pa. 2008) (Maryland opt-out statute is not limited to domiciliaries).

Do state's exemptions have extraterritorial application?

Homestead: Yes. *See In re* Grimes, 18 B.R. 132 (Bankr. D. Md. 1982).

Personal property: Yes, except exemption under Md. Code Ann., Cts. & Jud. Proc. § 11–504(f) (West). *See In re* Grimes, 18 B.R. 132 (Bankr. D. Md. 1982). *See also In re* Brooks, 393 B.R. 80 (Bankr. M.D. Pa. 2008) ($6000 wildcard exemption in money or property of any kind under § 11–504(b)(5) may be used by debtor in Pennsylvania case but not additional $5000 bankruptcy only wildcard exemption in real or personal property under § 11–504(f)).

***Wages:* Md. Code Ann., Com. Law §§ 15–601, 15–601.1 (West).**

Scope: All monetary remuneration paid to any employee for his or her employment. Md. Code Ann., Com. Law § 15–601 (West).

Amount: Caroline, Kent, Queen Anne's, and Worcester counties follow the federal scheme; in all other counties, the greater of $145 times the number of weeks in which wages earned or 75% of disposable wages is exempt; any medical insurance payment deducted from wages is exempt. Md. Code Ann., Com. Law § 15–601.1 (West). Note that the provisions for $145/week in certain counties have been held to be pre-empted, to the extent that they would allow garnishment greater than that permitted by the CCPA, *Marshall v. Safeway, Inc.*, 2014 WL 1227629 (Md. Mar. 26, 2014.)

Survival after payment/deposit: Not specified in exemption statute.

Waiver: Not specified in exemption statute.

***Homestead:* Md. Code Ann., Cts. & Jud. Proc. §§ 11–504, 11–507 (West).**

Amount: No explicit homestead exemption. $6000 wildcard exemption, which may be applied to any type of property. Md. Code Ann., Cts. & Jud. Proc. § 11–504(b)(5) (West). In bankruptcy, additional $5000 in owner-occupied real property (condo or co-op explicitly included) or personal property, or a manufactured home that has been converted to real property pursuant to Real Property § 8B-201. The manufactured home exemption is prospective only, and applies only to cases filed on or after October 1, 2014. These exemptions are subject to certain liens. Md. Code Ann., Cts. & Jud. Proc. § 11–507 (West). In bankruptcy only, the amount of the federal homestead exemption (11 U.S.C. § 522(d)(1), adjusted in accordance with 11 U.S.C. § 104), with certain restrictions. Md. Code Ann., Cts. & Jud. Proc. §§ 11–504(f), 11–504(g) (West).

Procedural requirements: None stated.

Special provisions: None stated.

Waiver: Not specified in exemption statute.

***Tangible personal property:* Md. Code Ann., Cts. & Jud. Proc. § 11–504 (West).**

Household goods: $1000 in goods held for family or household use. Md. Code Ann., Cts. & Jud. Proc. § 11–504(b)(4) (West). Additional $5000 in bankruptcy.

Motor vehicles: As miscellaneous and wildcard exemptions.

Tools of trade: $5000. Md. Code Ann., Cts. & Jud. Proc. § 11–504(b)(1) (West).

Clothing and jewelry: As household goods or miscellaneous and wildcard exemptions.

Miscellaneous and wildcard: $6000 in money or property of any kind; health aids. Bankruptcy only: additional $5000 in real or personal property.

Waiver: Certain provisions (including the tangible property and compensation for injury exemptions) may not be waived "by cognovit note or otherwise."

***Benefits, retirement plans, insurance, judgments, and other intangibles:* Md. Code Ann., Cts. & Jud. Proc. § 11–504 (West).**

Public benefits: Not specified in exemption statute. *See* Md. Code Ann., Hum. Serv. § 5–407. (assistance provided under state public assistance program is exempt).

Pensions, retirement plans, and annuities: Certain tax qualified retirement plans, except as to claims of alternate payee under qualified domestic relations order. Exemption for retirement plans does not apply to claims by the Dept. of Health and Mental Hygiene.

Insurance, judgments, or other compensation for injury: Money payable in the event of injury, sickness, or death, or for loss of future earnings, including insurance, judgments, arbitration awards, compensation, and relief. Md. Code Ann., Cts. & Jud. Proc. § 11–504(b)(2) (West). Twenty-five percent of the net recovery on a personal injury claim (defined as the amount left after attorney fees, medical bills, expenses, liens, and subrogation) may be reached for child support arrearages. Md. Code Ann., Cts. & Jud. Proc. § 11–504(i) (West).

Bank accounts: See Md. Code Ann., Cts. & Jud. Proc. § 11–603(1) (West) (forbidding garnishment of married couple's account for debt of one spouse, if account was held jointly on date of judgment).

Alimony, child support: Child support paid or payable in accordance with agreement or court order; spousal support exempt to same extent as wages. Md. Code Ann., Cts. & Jud. Proc. §§ 11–504(b)(6), 11–504(b)(7) (West). Payments from retirement plan to alternate payee under qualified domestic relations order.

Tax refunds:

Survival after payment or deposit: Not specified in exemption statute.

MASSACHUSETTS

Has state opted out of federal bankruptcy exemptions? No.

Is opt out limited to residents or domiciliaries of the state? Not applicable.

Do state's exemptions have extraterritorial application?

Homestead: Uncertain. Note, however, that Mass. Gen. Laws ch. 188, §§ 3 and 5, require that a declaration of homestead must be recorded in the registry of deeds for the county or district in which the property is situated or, if a manufactured home, in the city or town clerk's office in the city or town in which the manufactured home is located.

Personal property: Uncertain.

***Wages:* Mass. Gen. Laws ch. 246, § 28 and 28A; Mass. Gen. Laws ch. 235, § 34.**

Scope: Wages for personal labor or personal services. Mass. Gen. Laws ch. 246, § 28.

Amount: The greater of 85% of gross wages or 50 times state or federal minimum wage. Mass. Gen. Laws ch. 246, § 28. The full amount owing or paid to a person on public assistance is exempt. Mass. Gen. Laws ch. 235, § 15.

Survival after payment/deposit: Not specified in exemption statute.

Waiver: Not specified in exemption statute.

***Homestead:* Mass. Gen. Laws ch. 188, §§ 1 through 14; Mass. Gen. Laws ch. 235, § 34(14).**

Amount: Automatic homestead, $125,000. Recorded homestead, declaration protects equity of up to $500,000 in principal family residence. Mass. Gen. Laws ch. 188, § 1. Only owner-occupied residence can be homesteaded, and a person can have only one homestead at a time. The exemption is not effective against debts for taxes, mortgages, liens recorded prior to recordation of the homestead, declarations, orders for support of a spouse or minor children, and liens arising from a judgment based on fraud, mistake, duress, undue influence, or lack of capacity. Mass. Gen. Laws ch. 188, §§ 3, 8. A person claiming a homestead may voluntarily subordinate up to $20,000 of his or her homestead for a new line of credit under certain conditions. Mass. Gen. Laws ch. 188, § 4. Each debtor who is 62 or older, or disabled, may exempt $500,000 per individual, whether property is owned individually or jointly. Mass. Gen. Laws ch. 188, § 2. Homestead explicitly includes a single-family home, a 2–4 unit multiple dwelling, a condo or co-op unit, or a mobile or manufactured home. Owner specifically includes a life tenant or holder of beneficial interest in a trust. Mass. Gen. Laws ch. 188, § 1. Proceeds of sale and proceeds of insurance covering loss are protected for certain periods. Mass. Gen. Laws ch. 188, § 11. For debtor without homestead, the amount needed to pay rent on the dwelling unit occupied by debtor and family, not to exceed $2500/month. Mass. Gen. Laws ch. 235, § 34(14).

Procedural requirements: Yes. Homesteads recorded prior to Mar. 16, 2011 remain valid. For declared homestead, by statute after Mar. 16, 2011, homeowner must file declaration of homestead. Mass. Gen. Laws ch. 188, § 5. Disabled debtor must file copy of SSI award letter, or physician's certificate stating that debtor meets SSI eligibility requirements, at time of filing homestead declaration. The homestead declaration should state whether the owner or a family member is a servicemember protected by the SCRA, but failure to include this will not affect the validity or enforceability of the declaration. Mass. Gen. Laws ch. 188, § 5.

Special provisions: The homestead estate survives the death of the declarant, for the benefit of a surviving spouse or minor children residing in the homestead. Other protections are provided for divorced and separated spouses and other family members. Mass. Gen. Laws ch. 188, §§ 6, 7.

Waiver: Sale of homestead property or release of homestead requires the signature of the owner and spouse, if any. Mass. Gen. Laws ch. 188, § 10. Waiver up to $20,000 of homestead for certain loans.

***Tangible personal property:* Mass. Gen. Laws ch. 235, § 34; Mass. Gen. Laws ch. 246, § 28.**

Household goods: One television, computer, heating unit, stove, refrigerator, freezer, and hot water heater (unlimited value); beds; up to $500 per month for utilities; $15,000 in additional necessary household furniture (Mass. Gen. Laws ch. 235, §§ 34(1), 34(2), 34(12)); books up to $5000; $600 in provisions. Mass. Gen. Laws ch. 235, § 34(3).

Motor vehicles: One motor vehicle, worth up to $7500. For people who are disabled or over 60, motor vehicle worth up to $15,000. Mass. Gen. Laws ch. 235, § 34(16).

Tools of trade: $5000; materials and stock in trade $5000 (Mass. Gen. Laws ch. 235, §§ 34(5), 34(6)); boats and tackle of a fisher, $1500. Mass. Gen. Laws ch. 235, § 34(9).

Clothing and jewelry: Necessary wearing apparel; jewelry, $1225. Mass. Gen. Laws ch. 235, § 34(18).

Miscellaneous and wildcard: Various specified livestock and hay. Mass. Gen. Laws ch. 235, § 34(4). Wildcard of $1000 plus up to $5000 of certain unused exemptions. Mass. Gen. Laws ch. 235, § 34(17).

Waiver: Not specified in personal property exemption statute.

***Benefits, retirement plans, insurance, judgments, and other intangibles:* Mass. Gen. Laws ch. 246, §§ 28, 28A; Mass. Gen. Laws ch. 32, § 19; Mass. Gen. Laws ch. 235, §§ 34(15), 34A.**

Public benefits: All income from Massachusetts public assistance, workers compensation, unemployment benefits, and payments to families with dependent children is exempt. Any sum of money which was received by or is owing to debtor as public assistance. Mass. Gen. Laws ch. 235, § 15. *See also* Mass. Gen. Laws ch. 118, § 10.

Pensions, retirement plans, and annuities: Certain pensions and retirement plans, including IRAs; rollovers explicitly covered. Note that sums in excess of 7% of owner's income, deposited within five years before bankruptcy filing or judgment, are not exempt. This exception does not apply to rollovers or transfers. Mass. Gen. Laws ch. 235, § 34A; Mass. Gen. Laws ch. 246, § 28.

Insurance, judgments, or other compensation for injury: Not specified in exemption statute.

Bank accounts: $2500 in cash or savings or other deposit in bank account as of the date of the trustee process summons. Mass. Gen. Laws ch. 235, § 34(15); Mass. Gen. Laws ch. 246, § 28A.

Alimony, child support: Not specified in exemption statute.

Tax refunds:

Survival after payment or deposit: Not specified in exemption statute.

MICHIGAN

Has state opted out of federal bankruptcy exemptions? No.

Is opt out limited to residents or domiciliaries of the state? Not applicable.

Do state's exemptions have extraterritorial application?

Homestead: Uncertain.

Personal property: Uncertain.

***Wages:* Mich. Comp. Laws § 600.5311.**

Scope: Wages.

Amount: Householders may exempt 60% of weekly wages, but not less than $15 per week, and an extra $2 per week per dependent other than a spouse. Other debtors may exempt 40% of weekly wages, but not less than $10 per week.

Survival after payment/deposit: Not specified in exemption statute.

Waiver: Not specified in exemption statute.

***Homestead:* Mich. Const. art. X, § 3; Mich. Comp. Laws §§ 559.214, 600.6022 through 600.6024, 600.6027.**

Amount: $3500 not exceeding 40 acres rural or one lot inside city, town, or village, subject to certain liens; an equity of redemption as described in Mich. Comp. Laws § 600.6060. Mich. Comp. Laws §§ 600.6023(1)(g), 600.6023(1)(h), 600.6024. Condominiums occupied as residence explicitly included. Mich. Comp. Laws § 559.214. For state prisoners' reimbursement, $50,000 (Mich. Comp. Laws § 600.6022(4)); homestead is exempt from county prisoners' reimbursement. Mich. Comp. Laws § 600.6022(3).

Procedural requirements: If homestead has not been platted and set apart, debtor may designate at time of levy. Mich. Comp. Laws § 600.027.

Special provisions: After owner's death, exemption protects surviving spouse and minor children. Mich. Comp. Laws §§ 600.6023(1)(i), 600.6023(3).

Waiver: Not specified in exemption statute. Signature of spouse, if any, required for any mortgage except purchase money; claim for invalidity resulting from lack of signature must be filed within 25 years after recording. Mich. Comp. Laws § 600.6023(1)(g)).

***Tangible personal property:* Mich. Const. art. X, § 3; Mich. Comp. Laws § 600.6023.**

Household goods: $1000 household furniture, utensils, books, and appliances (Mich. Comp. Laws § 600.6023(1)(b)); six months of provisions and fuel (Mich. Comp. Laws § 600.6023(1)(a)); certain farm animals; six months' supply of feed; tools of trade; certain disability benefits and retirement accounts.

Motor vehicles: Not specified unless it is a tool of the debtor's trade.

Tools of trade: $1000 tools, materials, stock, vehicle for principal business or profession (Mich. Comp. Laws § 600.6023(1)(e)); for householder, certain livestock and feed. Mich. Comp. Laws § 600.6023(1)(d).

Clothing and jewelry: All clothing. Mich. Comp. Laws § 600.6023(1)(a).

Miscellaneous and wildcard: All family pictures; all arms required by law to be kept (Mich. Comp. Laws § 600.6023(1)(a)); burial place; a pew. Mich. Comp. Laws § 600.6023(1)(c).

Waiver: Not specified in exemption statute.

***Benefits, retirement plans, insurance, judgments, and other intangibles:* Mich. Comp. Laws § 600.6023.**

Public benefits: Not specified in exemption statute. *See* Mich. Comp. Laws § 400.63 (assistance provided under Social Welfare Act is exempt).

Pensions, retirement plans, and annuities: Certain pensions and tax qualified plans, including rollovers (except as to contributions made on eve of bankruptcy or claims for family support). Mich. Comp. Laws §§ 600.6023(1)(j), 600.6023(1)(k).

Insurance, judgments, or other compensation for injury: Insurance benefits paid or payable for illness or disability. Mich. Comp. Laws § 600.6023(1)(f).

Bank accounts: Certain educational savings accounts. Mich. Comp. Laws § 600.6023(1)(l).

Alimony, child support: Not specified in exemption statute.

Tax refunds:

Survival after payment or deposit: Not specified in exemption statute.

MINNESOTA

Has state opted out of federal bankruptcy exemptions? No.

Is opt out limited to residents or domiciliaries of the state? Not applicable.

Do state's exemptions have extraterritorial application?

Homestead: Yes. *See In re* Drenttel, 403 F.3d 611 (8th Cir. 2005).

Personal property: Not specified in exemption statute, but probably yes based on *In re* Drenttel, 403 F.3d 611 (8th Cir. 2005).

***Wages:* Minn. Stat. §§ 550.37(13), 550.37(14), 550.37(25), 550.136, 571.922.**

Scope: Compensation paid to an employee, who performs personal services for employer who may control both what is done and how it is done, whether called wages, salary, commission, bonus, or otherwise, including periodic payments pursuant to pension or retirement plan; compensation for the sale of certain agricultural products from family farm; maintenance as defined in the domestic relations statutes. Minn. Stat. § 550.136.

Amount: Garnishment limited to lesser of 25% of disposable earnings or amount by which disposable earnings exceed 40 times federal minimum wage. Minn. Stat. §§ 550.37(13), 571.922. Disposable earnings are those left after all deductions required by law. If the debtor has been a recipient of needs-based assistance or an inmate of a correctional institution, no garnishment is permitted for six months after return to employment and termination of all public assistance. Minn. Stat. § 550.37(14). A separate provision completely exempts proceeds of payments received by a person for labor, skill, material, or machinery contributing to an improvement in real estate. Minn. Stat. § 550.37(25). Private right of action for employee terminated because of wage garnishment.

Survival after payment/deposit: Exempt wages remain exempt for 20 days following deposit in financial institution. Statute explicitly protects against banker's right of setoff and provides for first-in first-out tracing of exempt funds. Minn. Stat. § 550.37(13).

Waiver: Not permitted.

***Homestead:* Minn. Stat. §§ 510.01, 510.02, 510.06, 510.07, 550.37(12).**

Amount: $975,000 for a farm, otherwise $390,000; home or house owned and occupied by debtor and land on which such house is situated but only a total of 160 acres. Minn. Stat. §§ 510.01, 510.02. Manufactured homes specifically included. Minn. Stat. § 550.37(12).

Procedural requirements: None stated. If homestead has not been set apart, it may be claimed at time of levy.

Special provisions: Proceeds exempt for one year. Minn. Stat. § 510.07. If home owner dies or deserts family, exemption continues to protect spouse and minor children. Minn. Stat. § 510.06.

Waiver: Not specified in exemption statute.

***Tangible personal property:* Minn. Stat. § 550.37.**

Household goods: $10,350. Household furniture and appliances, including sound systems, radios, and televisions. Minn. Stat. § 550.37(4).

Motor vehicles: $4600. If modified for disability, at a cost of no less than $4350: $46,000. Minn. Stat. § 550.37(12a).

Tools of trade: Farm implements: $13,000. Tools of trade: $11,500. Aggregate of these two exemptions may not exceed $13,000. Minn. Stat. §§ 550.37(5) through 550.37(7).

Clothing and jewelry: All clothing and one watch. $2817.50 in aggregate interest in wedding rings or other religious or culturally recognized symbols of marriage exchanged by debtor and spouse at time of marriage, and in the debtor's possession. Minn. Stat. § 550.37(4).

Miscellaneous and wildcard: Books and musical instrument; pew and burial place. Minn. Stat. § 550.37(2).

Waiver: Household goods exemption may not be waived, except for purchase money security interest or pawnbroker's possessory interest. Minn. Stat. § 550.37(4). Other exemptions may be waived by written waiver in prescribed form. Minn. Stat. § 550.37(19).

Special provisions: Note that all dollar amounts, except for farm implements and combined farm implements plus tools of trade, are indexed and therefore fluctuate periodically; amounts are adjusted on July 1 of even numbered years. Minn. Stat. § 550.37(4a).

***Benefits, retirement plans, insurance, judgments, and other intangibles:* Minn. Stat. § 550.37.**

Public benefits: All government assistance based on need and the earnings of any recipient, or anyone who has been a benefit recipient, or an inmate of a correctional institution within the past six months. Minn. Stat. § 550.37(14).

Pensions, retirement plans, and annuities: Certain pensions and retirement plans. Employee benefits, present value $69,000. Minn. Stat. § 550.37(24).

Insurance, judgments, or other compensation for injury: All money arising from any claim for damage to or destruction of exempt property (Minn. Stat. § 550.37(9)); life insurance proceeds from death of spouse or parent, up to $46,000 with additional $11,500 for each of survivor's dependents; $9200 in accrued interest or loan values of certain life insurance (Minn. Stat. §§ 550.37(10), 550.37(23)); certain benefits from fraternal associations (Minn. Stat. § 550.37(11)); rights of action for personal injuries. Minn. Stat. § 550.37(22).

Bank accounts: Not specified (but note provisions exempting traceable exempt funds).

Alimony, child support: Not specified in exemption statute.

Tax refunds:

Survival after payment or deposit: Exemptions for public benefits or the earnings of recipients continue for 60 days after deposit in financial institution. First-in, first-out tracing. Minn. Stat. § 550.37(14). Other funds (for example, insurance, compensation for damage, and so forth) remain exempt so long as traceable by first-in, first-out method. Burden on debtor to show exempt source. Minn. Stat. § 550.37(20).

MISSISSIPPI

Has state opted out of federal bankruptcy exemptions? Yes. Miss. Code Ann. § 85-3-2.

Is opt out limited to residents or domiciliaries of the state? Yes. Miss. Code Ann. § 85-3-2: "esidents of the State of Mississippi shall not be entitled to the federal exemptions . . . [in § 522(d)]."

Do state's exemptions have extraterritorial application?

Homestead: Uncertain.

Personal property: Uncertain.

***Wages:* Miss. Code Ann. §§ 85-3-1(j), 85-3-1(k), 85-3-4.**

Scope: Wages, salaries or other compensation of laborers or employees. Miss. Code Ann. § 85-3-4.

Amount: Exempt for thirty days after date of service of writ of attachment, execution, or garnishment; thereafter similar to federal (Miss. Code Ann. § 85-3-4); $5000 federal tax refund; $5000 state tax refund. Miss. Code Ann. §§ 85-3-1(i) through 85-3-1(k).

Survival after payment/deposit: Not specified in exemption statute.

Waiver: Not specified in exemption statute.

***Homestead:* Miss. Code Ann. §§ 85-3-21 through 85-3-27, 85-3-1(d).**

Amount: Householder may claim $75,000 of 160 acres owned and occupied as a residence, subject to liens. Miss. Code Ann. §§ 85-3-21, 85-3-23. $30,000 for manufactured home used as debtor's residence; debtor who has claimed a homestead exemption pursuant to Miss. Code Ann. § 85-3-21 may not claim this personal property exemption for mobile home. Miss. Code Ann. § 85-3-1(d).

Procedural requirements: Permitted but not required to record declaration of homestead. If this is not done, statute prescribes a formula for determining what land is homestead. Miss. Code Ann. §§ 85-3-25, 85-3-27.

Special provisions: Proceeds of sale or insurance are exempt. Miss. Code Ann. § 85-3-1(b), 85-3-23. Spouses, widows, or widowers over 60 may claim exemption on former residence even if they no longer reside there. Miss. Code Ann. § 85-3-21.

Waiver: Not specified in exemption statute.

***Tangible personal property:* Miss. Code Ann. § 85-3-1.**

Household goods: Tangible personal property of the following kinds to a total value of $10,000: household goods (definition similar to that of FTC rule restricting non-possessory security interests), wearing apparel, books, animals or crops, motor vehicles, implements, professional books or tools of a trade, cash on hand, professionally prescribed health aids, and any item of personal property worth less than $200. Miss. Code Ann. § 85-3-1(a).

Motor vehicles: Included in $10,000 exemption above.

Tools of trade: Included in $10,000 exemption above.

Clothing and jewelry: Included in $10,000 exemption above.

Miscellaneous and wildcard: Included in $10,000 exemption above. Additional $50,000 wildcard exemption for debtors age 70 or older. Miss. Code Ann. § 85-3-1(h).

Waiver: Not specified in exemption statute.

***Benefits, retirement plans, insurance, judgments, and other intangibles:* Miss. Code Ann. §§ 85-3-1, 85-3-11 through 85-3-19.**

Public benefits: $5000 in earned income tax credit proceeds. Miss. Code Ann. § 85-3-1(i).

Pensions, retirement plans, and annuities: Certain pensions and tax-qualified retirement plans. Miss. Code Ann. § 85-3-1(e).

Insurance, judgments, or other compensation for injury: Sale or insurance proceeds of exempt property; income from disability insurance (Miss. Code Ann. § 85-3-1(b)); certain life insurance proceeds (but not cash surrender or loan value of more than $50,000 resulting from payments or deposits within one year before writ issues) (Miss. Code Ann. § 85-3-11); $10,000 personal injury judgments. Miss. Code Ann. § 85-3-17.

Bank accounts: Assets of health savings account; moneys paid into certain educational savings accounts, or paid out from the account, for use as tuition. Miss. Code Ann. §§ 85-3-1(f), 85-3-1(g). The $10,000 wildcard for tangible personal property can be applied to cash on hand. Miss. Code Ann. § 85-3-1(a)(iv).

Alimony, child support: Not specified in exemption statute.

Tax refunds: $5000 Federal tax refund; $5000 state tax refund; $5000 earned income credit. Miss. Code Ann. §§ 85-3-1(i) through 85-3-1(k).

Survival after payment or deposit: Not specified in exemption statute.

MISSOURI

Has state opted out of federal bankruptcy exemptions? Yes. Mo. Rev. Stat. § 513.427.

Is opt out limited to residents or domiciliaries of the state? Not specified. Mo. Rev. Stat. § 513.427: "Every person [seeking] relief under Title 11 . . . , shall be permitted to exempt from property of the estate any property that is exempt from attachment and execution under the law of the state of Missouri or under federal law, other than [§ 522(d)], and no such person is authorized to claim as exempt the property that is specified under [§ 522(d)]."

Do state's exemptions have extraterritorial application?

Homestead: Yes. *In re* Woodruff, 2005 WL 1139891 (Bankr. W.D. Mo. Apr. 28, 2005) (because Missouri exemption law is silent concerning extraterritorial application, and because Missouri's exemptions must be construed liberally, Missouri homestead could be claimed for Mississippi home).

Personal property: Not specified in exemption statute, but probably yes, based on *In re* Woodruff, 2005 WL 1139891 (Bankr. W.D. Mo. Apr. 28, 2005).

***Wages:* Mo. Rev. Stat. § 525.030.**

Scope: Aggregate earnings of an individual. Mo. Rev. Stat. § 525.030(2).

Amount: Garnishment limited to 10% for head of family; otherwise similar to federal. Mo. Rev. Stat. § 525.030(2). Discharge of employee for garnishment is forbidden; violation of this provision is a misdemeanor. Mo. Rev. Stat. §§ 525.030(5), 525.030(6).

Survival after payment/deposit: Not specified in exemption statute.

Waiver: Not specified in exemption statute.

***Homestead:* Mo. Rev. Stat. §§ 513.430(6), 513.475, 513.510.**

Amount: $15,000 in residence and land used in connection with it; exemption for multiple owners may not exceed, in aggregate, $15,000. Mo. Rev. Stat. § 513.475. Manufactured home not on or attached to land in which debtor has a fee interest, used as residence and not exceeding $5000 in value is exempt. Mo. Rev. Stat. § 513.430(1)(6).

Procedural requirements: None stated. Homestead is acquired when deed recorded (or in case of inheritance, when new owner acquires title). Mo. Rev. Stat. § 513.510.

Special provisions: Does not protect against debts that pre-date acquisition of homestead. Mo. Rev. Stat. § 513.510.

Waiver: Spouse must join in any sale or encumbrance. Mo. Rev. Stat. § 513.475.

***Tangible personal property:* Mo. Rev. Stat. §§ 513.430, 513.440.**

Household goods: $3000 in household goods and furnishings, wearing apparel, appliances, books, animals, crops, or musical instruments. Mo. Rev. Stat. § 513.430(1)(1).

Motor vehicles: $3000. Mo. Rev. Stat. § 513.430(1)(5).

Tools of trade: $3000. Mo. Rev. Stat. § 513.430(1)(4).

Clothing and jewelry: Clothing included in $1000 household goods exemption. Wedding ring: $1500; other jewelry: $500. Mo. Rev. Stat. § 513.430(1)(2).

Miscellaneous and wildcard: $600 any property. Mo. Rev. Stat. § 513.430(1)(3). Additional $1250 wildcard for head of family, plus $350 for each unmarried, dependent, minor child; may not be used to exempt the non-exempt 10% of wages. Mo. Rev. Stat. §513.440. Professionally prescribed health aids. Mo. Rev. Stat. § 513.430(1)(9).

Waiver: Not specified in exemption statute.

***Benefits, retirement plans, insurance, judgments, and other intangibles:* Mo. Rev. Stat. §§ 513.430, 513.440.**

Public benefits: Right to receive Social Security, veterans' benefits, unemployment, local public assistance. Mo. Rev. Stat. § 513.430(1)(10).

Pensions, retirement plans, and annuities: Any payment under certain public and private employee benefit plans; money payable to a participant in certain retirement plans, except as to the claims of an alternate payee under a qualified domestic relations order. Inherited plans explicitly included. Mo. Rev. Stat. §§ 513.430(1)(e), 513.430(1)(f).

Insurance, judgments, or other compensation for injury: Unmatured life insurance contracts; accrued dividends and loan values of certain life insurance (in bankruptcy, $150,000 limit) (Mo. Rev. Stat. §§ 513.430(1)(7), 513.430(1)(8)); right to receive disability, illness, or unemployment benefit. Mo. Rev. Stat. § 513.430(1)(10). Right to receive, or property traceable to, wrongful death judgment for person on whom debtor was dependent, so far as needed for support. Mo. Rev. Stat. § 513.430(1)(11).

Bank accounts: Health Savings plans. Mo. Rev. Stat. § 513.430(f).

Alimony, child support: Right to receive alimony, support, or separate maintenance, up to $750 per month. Mo. Rev. Stat. § 513.430(1)(10). Payments from pension plan to alternative payee under qualified domestic relations order are exempt. Mo. Rev. Stat. §§ 513.430(1)(10)(e), 513.430(1)(10)(f).

Tax refunds:

Survival after payment or deposit: Not specified in exemption statute, but note that some exemptions refer to "right to receive" and others to "payments under" or "traceable to."

MONTANA

Has state opted out of federal bankruptcy exemptions? Yes. Mont. Code Ann. § 31–2–106.

Is opt out limited to residents or domiciliaries of the state? Not specified. Mont. Code Ann. § 31–2–106: "An individual may not exempt from the property of the estate in any bankruptcy proceeding the property specified in [§ 522(d)]."

Do state's exemptions have extraterritorial application?

Homestead: Uncertain.

Personal property: Uncertain.

***Wages:* Mont. Code Ann. §§ 25–13–601, 25–13–610, 25–13–614.**

Scope: Same as federal. Mont. Code Ann. § 25–13–614.

Amount: Similar to federal. Mont. Code Ann. § 25–13–614.

Survival after payment/deposit: Yes. Exempt for 45 days after receipt, if traceable by first-in, first-out or "any other reasonable basis for tracing." Mont. Code Ann. §§ 25–13–610(2), 25–13–610(3).

Waiver: Waiver of exemptions in unsecured promissory note is unenforceable. Mont. Code Ann. § 25–13–601.

***Homestead:* Mont. Code Ann. §§ 70–32–101 through 70–32–107, 70–32–202, 70–32–216, 70–32–301.**

Amount: $250,000 in dwelling house or manufactured home and land thereunder. Mont. Code Ann. §§ 70–32–101, 70–32–104. Claimant who owns undivided interest in property is limited to an exemption proportional to claimant's interest. Mont. Code Ann. § 70–32–104.

Procedural requirements: Declaration of homestead must be recorded. Mont. Code Ann. §§ 70–32–105 through 70–32–107. But it appears that homestead is protected against debts that precede recording, except mortgages and certain other liens. Mont. Code Ann. § 70–32–202. The main effect of recording a homestead declaration appears to be to require a spouse's signature on any sale or encumbrance thereafter.

Special provisions: Proceeds are exempt for eighteen months following sale, condemnation, or destruction of the property. Mont. Code Ann. § 70–32–216.

Waiver: If homestead declaration has been recorded, spouse must join in any sale or encumbrance. Mont. Code Ann. § 70–32–301.

***Tangible personal property:* Mont. Code Ann. §§ 25–13–601, 25–13–608, 25–13–609, 25–13–613.**

Household goods: $600 per item, or $4500 in the aggregate in furniture, appliances, jewelry, wearing apparel, books, firearms and other sporting goods, animals, feed, crops, and musical instruments. Mont. Code Ann. § 25–13–609(1).

Motor vehicles: $2500. Mont. Code Ann. § 25–13–609(2).

Tools of trade: $3000. Mont. Code Ann. § 25–13–609(3).

Clothing and jewelry: Included in $4500 household goods exemption.

Miscellaneous and wildcard: Health aids (Mont. Code Ann. § 25–13–608(1)(a)); burial place (Mont. Code Ann. § 25–13–608(1)(h)); property used to carry out government functions. Compensation for lost, damaged, or destroyed exempt property remains exempt for six months, if proceeds are traceable, for example in a bank account. Mont. Code Ann. § 25–13–613.

Waiver: Waiver of exemptions in unsecured promissory note is unenforceable. Mont. Code Ann. § 25–13–601.

***Benefits, retirement plans, insurance, judgments, and other intangibles:* Mont. Code Ann. §§ 25–13–608 through 25–13–610, 25–13–613, 31–2–106.**

Public benefits: Social Security, veterans', or local public assistance benefits that debtor has received or is entitled to receive (Mont. Code Ann. §§ 25–13–608(1)(b), 25–13–608(1)(c)); right to receive unemployment benefits.

Pensions, retirement plans, and annuities: Certain public or private pensions or tax-qualified IRAs. Mont. Code Ann. §§ 25–13–608(1)(e), 25–13–608(1)(i), 25–13–608(1)(j).

Insurance, judgments, or other compensation for injury: Disability or illness benefits (Mont. Code Ann. § 25–13–608(1)(d)); benefits paid for medical, surgical, or hospital care (Mont. Code Ann. § 25–13–608(1)(f)), to the extent they are used or will be used to pay for the care; unmatured life insurance policies. Mont. Code Ann. § 25–13–608(1)(k). Compensation for lost, damaged, or destroyed exempt property remains exempt for six months, if proceeds are traceable, for example in a bank account. Mont. Code Ann. § 25–13–610(1).

Bank accounts: Shares in certain cooperative associations having up to $500 par value. Mont. Code Ann. § 35–15–404. Sales proceeds of exempt property, or compensation for lost, damaged, or destroyed exempt property remains exempt for six months, if proceeds are traceable, for example in a bank account. Mont. Code Ann. §§ 25–13–610(1), 25–13–610(3).

Alimony, child support: Maintenance and child support. Mont. Code Ann. § 25–13–608(1)(g).

Tax refunds:

Survival after payment or deposit: Proceeds of sale or indemnification for loss of exempt property remain exempt for six months if traceable (that is, first in, first out from bank account). Note that the exemption for certain benefits refers to payments debtor has received or is entitled to receive.

NEBRASKA

Has state opted out of federal bankruptcy exemptions? Yes. Neb. Rev. Stat. § 25–15,105.

Is opt out limited to residents or domiciliaries of the state? Not specified, but may be limited to cases filed in Nebraska. Neb. Rev. Stat. § 25–15,105: "The federal exemptions provided in [§ 522(d)], are hereby rejected by . . . Nebraska. [The Nebraska personal exemptions] apply to any bankruptcy petition filed in Nebraska after April 17, 1980." *In re* Alcorn, 2013 WL 3353837 (Bankr. D.S.D. Jul 03, 2013) (opt-out limited to Nebraska residents); *In re* Long, 470 B.R. 186 (Bankr. D. Kan. 2012) (same).

Do state's exemptions have extraterritorial application?

Homestead: No. *In re* Long, 470 B.R. 186 (Bankr. D. Kan. 2012).

Personal property: No. *In re* Alcorn, 2013 WL 3353837 (Bankr. D.S.D. Jul 03, 2013).

***Wages:* Neb. Rev. Stat. § 25–1558, 25–1560 through 25–1563.**

Scope: Earnings paid or payable by an employer to an employee for personal services, whether called wages, salary, commission, bonus, or otherwise, including periodic payments from pension or retirement program. Neb. Rev. Stat. § 25–1558(4).

Amount: Head of family, 85% of disposable earnings exempt except for support obligations. Head of family is defined as anyone who actually supports and maintains one or more individuals related to him or her by blood, marriage, adoption, or guardianship and whose right to exercise family control and provide for the dependent(s) is based on some moral or legal obligation. All others, similar to federal. Neb. Rev. Stat. § 25–1558(1). Discharge of employee for garnishment forbidden. Neb. Rev. Stat. § 25–1558(6).

Survival after payment/deposit: Wages appear to be exempt for 60 days under Neb. Rev. Stat. § 25–1560.

Waiver: Assignment, transfer, mortgage, or pledge of exempt wages or salary is void and unenforceable. Neb. Rev. Stat. § 25–1558(5).

***Homestead:* Neb. Rev. Stat. §§ 40–101 through 40–103, 40–111 through 40–113, 40–115, 40–116.**

Amount: $60,000 in a dwelling located on up to 160 acres if not in city or village or two contiguous lots if in city or village (Neb. Rev. Stat. § 40–101); available only to persons age 65 or older or to heads of households, defined as married persons, surviving spouses, or anyone with a dependent residing with him or her. Neb. Rev. Stat. §§ 40–102, 40–115.

Procedural requirements: None stated. May be claimed after judgment, any time before confirmation of sale.

Special provisions: Proceeds of involuntary sale of homestead are exempt for six months to the same extent as the homestead. Neb. Rev. Stat. §§ 40–111 through 40–113.

Waiver: Spouse must join in any conveyance or encumbrance.

***Tangible personal property:* Neb. Rev. Stat. §§ 25–1552, 25–1556.**

Household goods: Immediate personal possessions of debtor and family (Neb. Rev. Stat. § 25–1556(1)); $1500 household goods, appliances, computers, books, and musical instruments. Neb. Rev. Stat. § 25–1556(3).

Motor vehicles: Tools of trade exemption applies to motor vehicle used for work or for commuting. Neb. Rev. Stat. § 25–1556(4).

Tools of trade: $2400. Neb. Rev. Stat. § 25–1556(4).

Clothing and jewelry: All necessary clothing. Neb. Rev. Stat. § 25–1556(2).

Miscellaneous and wildcard: $2500 any personal property except wages. Neb. Rev. Stat. § 25–1552. Professionally prescribed health aids. Neb. Rev. Stat. § 25–1556(5).

Waiver: Not specified in exemption statute.

***Benefits, retirement plans, insurance, judgments, and other intangibles:* Neb. Rev. Stat. §§ 25–1552, 25–1553, 25–1556, 25–1559, 25–1563.01, 25–1563.02.**

Public benefits: Not specified in exemption statute. *See* Neb. Rev. Stat. §§ 68–148 (general assistance), 68–1013 (aid to aged, blind, disabled, dependent children, medical assistance). Full amount of any federal or state earned income credit tax refund. Neb. Rev. Stat. § 25–1553.

Pensions, retirement plans, and annuities: Military disability pensions, and $2000 in property purchased or improved with funds therefrom (Neb. Rev. Stat. § 25–1559); certain employee benefits and individual retirement plans, so far as needed for support. Neb. Rev. Stat. § 25–1563.01.

Insurance, judgments, or other compensation for injury: Compensation for personal injury or death, whether lump sum or structured settlement, including interest. Neb. Rev. Stat. § 25–1563.02.

Bank accounts: Not specified in exemption statute.

Alimony, child support: Not specified in exemption statute.

Tax refunds:

Survival after payment or deposit: Note exemption for property traceable to military disability pension.

NEVADA

Has state opted out of federal bankruptcy exemptions? Yes. Nev. Rev. Stat. § 21.090(3).

Is opt out limited to residents or domiciliaries of the state? Yes. Nev. Rev. Stat. § 21.090: "Any exemptions specified in [§ 522(d)], do not apply to property owned by a resident of this State . . . ."

Do state's exemptions have extraterritorial application?

Homestead: Yes. *In re* Fernandez, 2011 WL 3423373 (W.D. Tex. Aug. 5, 2011) (permitting use of Nevada homestead exemption on property located in Texas, despite Nevada exemption law requirement that homestead be recorded in county where property located).

Personal property: Uncertain.

***Wages:* Nev. Rev. Stat. §§ 21.090, 31.295 through 31.298.**

Scope: Earnings. Nev. Rev. Stat. §§ 21.090(1)(g), 31.295(1).

Amount: Garnishment may not exceed the lesser of 25% of disposable earnings for the workweek or the amount by which disposable earnings that week exceed 50 times the federal minimum wage. Nev. Rev. Stat. §§ 21.090(1)(g), 31.295(2).

Survival after payment/deposit: Yes. Earnings are defined to include compensation received by the judgment debtor, in the possession of the judgment debtor, held in accounts in a bank or any other financial institution, or, in the case of a receivable, compensation that is due the judgment debtor. Nev. Rev. Stat. §§ 21.090(1)(g)(2), 31.295(2).

Waiver: Not specified in garnishment statute.

***Homestead:* Nev. Rev. Stat. §§ 21.090, 21.095, 115.005, 115.010, 115.040.**

Amount: $550,000 in either land and a dwelling or a manufactured home, subject to certain liens (Nev. Rev. Stat. §§ 115.005, 115.010); land held in spendthrift trust for debtor is exempt. Unlimited exemption if "allodial title" has been established. Nev. Rev. Stat. § 115.010. (Nevada residents can acquire "allodial title" to their land by buying out the property tax right from the government. Then the landowner does not have to pay property tax on the land.) Nev. Rev. Stat. §§ 21.090(1)(l), 21.090(1)(m). The primary dwelling, including a manufactured home, and land may not be executed upon for a medical bill during the lifetime of the debtor, debtor's spouse, a joint tenant who was a joint tenant at the time judgment was entered, or debtor's disabled dependent adult child, or during the minority of any child of debtor. Nev. Rev. Stat. § 21.095. A 2007 amendment added an exemption for sums reasonably deposited with a landlord, to secure the rental or lease of debtor's primary residence (except not exempt as to landlord's claims for rent). Nev. Rev. Stat. § 21.090(1)(n).

Procedural requirements: Procedure available for filing declaration of homestead. Exemption available even without declaration. Once declaration is filed, spouse must join in any encumbrance or sale.

Special provisions: None specified.

Waiver: Spouse must join in conveyance or encumbrance of declared homestead. Nev. Rev. Stat. §§ 115.010(3), 115.040.

***Tangible personal property:* Nev. Rev. Stat. §§ 21.080, 21.090, 21.100.**

Household goods: $12,000 necessary household goods, furnishings, electronics, wearing apparel, other personal effects, and yard equipment. Nev. Rev. Stat. § 21.090(1)(b).

Motor vehicles: $15,000 (Nev. Rev. Stat. § 21.090(1)(f)); no limit if specially equipped for disabled debtor or dependent. Nev. Rev. Stat. § 21.090(1)(p).

Tools of trade: $10,000 tools of trade; $4500 mining equipment; $4500 farm equipment. Nev. Rev. Stat. §§ 21.090(1)(c) through 21.090(1)(e).

Clothing and jewelry: Jewelry is included in the $5000 wildcard exemption. Nev. Rev. Stat. § 21.090(1)(a).

Miscellaneous and wildcard: $5000 in private library, works of art, musical instruments, jewelry, all family pictures, and keepsakes (Nev. Rev. Stat. § 21.090(1)(a)); health aids (Nev. Rev. Stat. § 21.090(1)(q)); property held in a spendthrift trust or a discretionary or support trust governed by chapter 163 of the Nev. Rev. Stat.; uniforms debtor is legally required to keep (Nev. Rev. Stat. § 21.090(1)(i)); one gun; a collection of metal bearing ores, geological specimens, art curiosities, or paleontological remains if the debtor catalogues them and the catalogue is kept near the collection for the free inspection of all visitors. Coin collections are not exempt. Nev. Rev. Stat. § 295.100. $1000 in any property, including accounts in a financial institution. Nev. Rev. Stat. § 21.090(1)(z).

Waiver: Not specified in exemption statute.

***Benefits, retirement plans, insurance, judgments, and other intangibles:* Nev. Rev. Stat. §§ 21.080, 21.090, 21.100, 21.105.**

Public benefits: Social Security benefits, including without limitation, retirement, survivors, SSI, and disability. Nev. Rev. Stat. § 21.090(1)(y). *See* Nev. Rev. Stat. § 422.291 (assistance awarded pursuant to public welfare administration laws is exempt). Earned income credit or any similar credit pursuant to state law. Nev. Rev. Stat. § 21.090(1)(aa). Unemployment compensation (Nev. Rev. Stat. § 21.090(1)(a)(hh)); workers' compensation (Nev. Rev. Stat. § 21.090(1)(gg)); money paid or rights existing for vocational rehabilitation pursuant to Nev. Rev. Stat. § 615.270 (Nev. Rev. Stat. § 21.090(1)(jj)); public assistance provided by the Department of Health and Human Services pursuant to Nev. Rev. Stat. §§ 422.291 and 442A.325 (Nev. Rev. Stat. § 21.090(1)(kk)); child welfare assistance pursuant to Nev. Rev. Stat. § 432.036(ll).

Pensions, retirement plans, and annuities: Up to $500,000 (present value) in tax-qualified retirement plan. Nev. Rev. Stat. § 21.090(1)(r). Benefits or refunds paid or payable from the Public Employees' Retirement System. Nev. Rev. Stat. § 21.090(1)(ii).

Insurance, judgments, or other compensation for injury: Money or benefits in any manner growing out of life insurance. Nev. Rev. Stat. § 21.090(1)(k). Proceeds from a private disability insurance plan (Nev. Rev. Stat. § 21.090(1)(ee)); money in a trust fund for funeral or burial services. Nev. Rev. Stat. § 21.090(1)(ff). Payments, up to $16,500, for personal injury to debtor or person on whom debtor is dependent (Nev. Rev. Stat. § 21.090(1)(u)); as needed for support, payments for wrongful death of person on whom debtor is dependent (Nev. Rev. Stat. § 21.090(1)(v)); so far as necessary for support, payments for loss of future earnings (Nev. Rev. Stat. § 21.090(1)(w)); restitution for criminal act. Nev. Rev. Stat. § 21.090(1)(x).

Bank accounts: If exempt funds have been electronically direct-deposited in a personal bank account within 45 days before date of service of garnishment, then the lesser of $2000 or the entire account balance is not subject to execution and must remain accessible to the judgment debtor. If exempt benefits have not been direct-deposited, then the lesser of $400 or the entire account balance is not subject to execution and must remain accessible to the judgment debtor. A judgment debtor must make a claim of exemption to exempt any larger amount of exempt funds in the account. Nev. Rev. Stat. § 21.105. Pre-paid funeral. Nev. Rev. Stat. § 21.090(1)(ff).

Tax refunds:

Alimony, child support: Court-ordered family support. Nev. Rev. Stat. §§ 21.090(1)(s), 21.090(1)(t).

Survival after payment or deposit: Not specified in exemption statute.

NEW HAMPSHIRE

Has state opted out of federal bankruptcy exemptions? No.

Is opt out limited to residents or domiciliaries of the state? Not applicable.

Do state's exemptions have extraterritorial application?

Homestead: Yes. *See In re* Varanasi, 394 B.R. 430 (Bankr. S.D. Ohio 2008) (applying New Hampshire's homestead exemption to Ohio residence; no unconstitutional taking, impairment of contract or denial of equal protection, even though New Hampshire's homestead amount was ten times Ohio's); *In re* Weza, 248 B.R. 470 (Bankr. D.N.H. 2000) (New Hampshire homestead may be claimed for property outside state because homestead statute does not limit exemption to property located in New Hampshire; homestead denied, however, because debtor did not currently reside on property).

Personal property: Not specified in exemption statute, but probably yes. *See In re* Weza, 248 B.R. 470 (Bankr. D.N.H. 2000).

***Wages:* N.H. Rev. Stat. Ann. §§ 161-C:11, 512:21.**

Scope: Wages. N.H. Rev. Stat. Ann. §§ 512.21(I), 512.21(II).

Amount: Fifty times federal minimum wage is exempt. N.H. Rev. Stat. Ann. § 512.21(II).

Survival after payment/deposit: Not specified in exemption statute.

Waiver: Not specified in exemption statute.

***Homestead:* N.H. Rev. Stat. Ann. §§ 480:1, 480:3-a, 480:4, 480:5-a, 480:9.**

Amount: $100,000. Manufactured housing explicitly included (but not the underlying land, if owned by another). N.H. Rev. Stat. Ann. § 480:1.

Procedural requirements: Procedure available for establishing homestead, but apparently not prerequisite to existence of exemption.

Special provisions: Exemption not lost by conveyance to revocable trust. N.H. Rev. Stat. Ann. § 480:9. Homestead right protects surviving spouse. N.H. Rev. Stat. Ann. § 480:3-a.

Waiver: Spouse must join in conveyance or encumbrance, with formalities used for conveyance of land. N.H. Rev. Stat. Ann. § 480:5-a.

***Tangible personal property:* N.H. Rev. Stat. Ann. § 511:2.**

Household goods: $3500 household furniture; beds and bedding; stove, utensils, refrigerator, heating unit; sewing machine; $400 provisions and fuel. N.H. Rev. Stat. Ann. §§ 511.2(II) through 511.2(VI).

Motor vehicles: $4000. N.H. Rev. Stat. Ann. § 511.2(XVI).

Tools of trade: $5000. N.H. Rev. Stat. Ann. § 511.2(IX).

Clothing and jewelry: Necessary clothing (N.H. Rev. Stat. Ann. § 511.2(I)); $500 jewelry. N.H. Rev. Stat. Ann. § 511.2(XVII).

Miscellaneous and wildcard: Wildcard exemption of $1000 plus up to $7000 from unused exemptions for furniture, provisions and fuel, library, tools of trade, motor vehicle, and jewelry. N.H. Rev. Stat. Ann. § 511.2(VIII). Burial place (N.H. Rev. Stat. Ann. § 511.2(XV)); militia uniforms and arms; $800 in books (N.H. Rev. Stat. Ann. § 511.2(VII)); various livestock (N.H. Rev. Stat. Ann. §§ 511.2(X) through 511.2(XIII)); a meeting-house pew. N.H. Rev. Stat. Ann. § 511.2(XIV).

Waiver: Not specified in exemption statute.

***Benefits, retirement plans, insurance, judgments, and other intangibles:* N.H. Rev. Stat. Ann. §§ 511:2, 512:21. *See* N.H. Rev. Stat. Ann. §§ 100-A:26, 102:23.**

Public benefits: Not specified in exemption statute. *See* N.H. Rev. Stat. Ann. § 167:25 (public assistance to blind, aged, disabled persons, or dependent children is exempt).

Pensions, retirement plans, and annuities: Federal pension or bounty funds before payment to debtor (N.H. Rev. Stat. Ann. § 512.21(IV)); certain tax-qualified retirement plans. N.H. Rev. Stat. Ann. § 511.2(XIX).

Insurance, judgments, or other compensation for injury: Damages for the conversion of exempt property (N.H. Rev. Stat. Ann. § 512.21(VII)); certain insurance proceeds while in the hands of insurance company. N.H. Rev. Stat. Ann. § 512.21(VIII).

Bank accounts: Not specified in exemption statute.

Alimony, child support: Not specified in exemption statute.

Tax refunds:

Survival after payment or deposit: Not specified in exemption statute, but note restrictive language in insurance and military pensions exemptions.

NEW JERSEY

Has state opted out of federal bankruptcy exemptions? No.

Is opt out limited to residents or domiciliaries of the state? Not applicable.

Do state's exemptions have extraterritorial application?

Homestead: No exemption.

Personal property: Uncertain.

***Wages:* N.J. Stat. Ann. §§ 2A:17–50, 2A:17–56, 2A:17–56.9, 2A:17–56.12 (West).**

Scope: Wages, debts, salary, income from trust funds, or profits, due and owing or to become due and owing. N.J. Stat. Ann. § 2A:17–50 (West).

Amount: $48/week is exempt. N.J. Stat. Ann. § 2A:17–50 (West). 90% exempt if debtor's income does not exceed 250% of the poverty level. N.J. Stat. Ann. § 2A:17–56 (West). Employer who discharges employee because of family support garnishment commits disorderly person offense and employee has private right of action for wrongful discharge. N.J. Stat. Ann. § 2A:17–56.12 (West). For a debt owing to the state, 25% of gross earnings may be garnished, if, after the execution, debtor's income will not be less than 250% of poverty level. N.J. Stat. Ann. § 2A:17–56 (West).

Survival after payment/deposit: Not specified, but note "due and owing" language.

Waiver: Not specified in exemption statute.

Homestead: None.

Amount: Not applicable.

Procedural requirements: Not applicable.

Special provisions: Not applicable.

Waiver: Not applicable.

***Tangible personal property:* N.J. Stat. Ann. §§ 2A:17–19, 2A:26–4, 38A:4–8 (West).**

Household goods: $1000 household goods and furniture. N.J. Stat. Ann. §§ 2A:17–19, 2A:26–4 (West).

Motor vehicles: Not specified.

Tools of trade: Not specified.

Clothing and jewelry: All necessary clothing. N.J. Stat. Ann. § 2A:17–19 (West).

Miscellaneous and wildcard: $1000 all personal property except clothing. N.J. Stat. Ann. § 2A:17–19 (West). Pay and other benefits due as a result of participation in the state militia. N.J. Stat. Ann. § 38A:4–8 (West).

Waiver: Not specified in exemption statute.

Benefits, retirement plans, insurance, judgments, and other intangibles:

Public benefits: Not specified in exemption statute.

Pensions, retirement plans, and annuities: Not specified in exemption statute.

Insurance, judgments, or other compensation for injury: Not specified in exemption statute.

Bank accounts: Not specified in exemption statute.

Alimony, child support: Not specified in exemption statute.

Tax refunds:

Survival after payment or deposit: Not specified in exemption statute.

NEW MEXICO

Has state opted out of federal bankruptcy exemptions? No.

Is opt out limited to residents or domiciliaries of the state? Not applicable.

Do state's exemptions have extraterritorial application?

Homestead: Uncertain.

Personal property: Uncertain.

***Wages:* N.M. Stat. Ann. § 35–12–7.**

Scope: Disposable earnings.

Amount: Greater of 75% of disposable earnings or 40 times minimum wage is exempt. Disposable earnings are those left after legally required deductions.

Survival after payment/deposit: Not specified in garnishment statute.

Waiver: Not specified in garnishment statute.

***Homestead:* N.M. Stat. Ann. §§ 42–10–9, 42–10–11.**

Amount: $60,000 in land or a dwelling if debtor owns, leases, or purchases the dwelling. N.M. Stat. Ann. § 42–10–9. Subject to certain liens. N.M. Stat. Ann. § 42–10–11. If property is jointly owned by two persons, each is entitled to a $60,000 exemption. N.M. Stat. Ann. § 42–10–9.

Procedural requirements: None specified.

Special provisions: None specified.

Waiver: Not specified in exemption statute.

***Tangible personal property:* N.M. Stat. Ann. §§ 42–10–1, 42–10–2, 42–10–10, 53–4–28, 53–10–2.**

Household goods: Furniture and books. N.M. Stat. Ann. §§ 42–10–1, 42–10–2.

Motor vehicles: $4000. N.M. Stat. Ann. §§ 42–10–1, 42–10–2.

Tools of trade: $1500. N.M. Stat. Ann. §§ 42–10–1, 42–10–2.

Clothing and jewelry: Clothing; $2500 jewelry. N.M. Stat. Ann. §§ 42–10–1, 42–10–2.

Miscellaneous and wildcard: $500 in personal property other than money; married debtors or heads of households may take $500 any personal property (N.M. Stat. Ann. §§ 42–10–1, 42–10–2). A resident without a homestead may exempt $5000 in real or personal property (N.M. Stat. Ann. § 42–10–10); health aids (N.M. Stat. Ann. §§ 42–10–1, 42–10–2); the minimum amount of shares necessary for membership in certain cooperative associations (N.M. Stat. Ann. § 42–10–10); debtor's interest in the property of an unincorporated association (N.M. Stat. Ann. § 53–10–2).

Waiver: Not specified in exemption statute.

***Benefits, retirement plans, insurance, judgments, and other intangibles:* N.M. Stat. Ann. §§ 42–10–1 through 42–10–5.**

Public benefits: Not specified in exemption statute. *See* N.M. Stat. Ann. § 27–2–21 (assistance granted under Public Assistance Act is exempt).

Pensions, retirement plans, and annuities: Interests in or proceeds from pension or retirement fund. N.M. Stat. Ann. §§ 42–10–1, 42–10–2.

Insurance, judgments, or other compensation for injury: Cash surrender value of, and payments from accident, health, and life insurance and certain annuities, exempt as to debts of both insured and beneficiary; life insurance proceeds exempt as to debts of deceased. N.M. Stat. Ann. §§ 42–10–3, 42–10–5. Up to $5000 in benefits from benevolent association, as to debts of association member but not recipient. N.M. Stat. Ann. § 42–10–4.

Bank accounts: Not specified in exemption statute.

Alimony, child support: Not specified in exemption statute.

Tax refunds:

Survival after payment or deposit: Not specified in exemption statute, but note language regarding retirement plans and insurance.

NEW YORK

Has state opted out of federal bankruptcy exemptions? Yes. N.Y. Debt. & Cred. Law §§ 282, 284 (McKinney). However, an individual debtor in a bankruptcy case may opt to use the exemptions provided under section 522(d) of the Bankruptcy Code in lieu of New York exemptions. N.Y. Debt. & Cred. Law § 285 (McKinney).

Is opt out limited to residents or domiciliaries of the state? Yes. N.Y. Debt. & Cred. Law § 282 (McKinney): "[A]n individual debtor domiciled in this state may exempt only [property specified in this statute]."

Do state's exemptions have extraterritorial application?

Homestead: No. *See In re* Crandall, 346 B.R. 220 (Bankr. M.D. Fla. 2006).

Personal property: No. *See In re* Crandall, 346 B.R. 220 (Bankr. M.D. Fla. 2006).

***Wages:* N.Y. C.P.L.R. 5205(d), 5205(e), 5231, 5252, 5241 (McKinney); N.Y. Soc. Serv. Law § 137-a (McKinney).**

Scope: Earnings for personal services.

Amount: Thirty times the federal or state minimum wage, whichever is larger, is exempt. N.Y. C.P.L.R. § 5231 (McKinney). 90% of earnings rendered 60 days before or any time after delivery of execution to the sheriff or a motion to apply the debtor's earnings to a judgment is exempt (N.Y. C.P.L.R. § 5205(d)(2) (McKinney)); wages received in addition to public assistance are exempt. Garnishment forbidden if debtor is receiving public assistance or would qualify for public assistance if the amount of the garnishment were subtracted from his or her wages. N.Y. Soc. Serv. Law § 137-a (McKinney). The pay of enlisted personnel and non-commissioned officers in the military is completely exempt, except for family support debts. N.Y. C.P.L.R. § 5205(e) (McKinney). Employer may not discipline or refuse to hire employee because of wage execution. Private right of action for six weeks lost wages, civil penalty of $500 ($1000 for repeat offense), court may order reinstatement or hiring. N.Y. C.P.L.R. § 5252 (McKinney). Private right of action if employer withholds income after being formally notified by social services official that worker is receiving or eligible for aid. N.Y. Soc. Serv. Law § 137-a (McKinney).

Survival after payment/deposit: Not specified in exemption statute.

Waiver: Not specified in exemption statute.

***Homestead:* N.Y. C.P.L.R. 5206, 5253 (McKinney).**

Amount: Beginning in 2012, amounts will be adjusted at three-year intervals for changes in the consumer price index. § 5253. Amount varies by county. $150,000 in Kings, Queens, New York, Bronx, Richmond, Nassau, Suffolk, Rockland, Westchester, and Putnam. $125,000 in Dutchess, Albany, Columbia, Orange, Saratoga, and Ulster. $75,000 in all other counties. Applies to the following types of property owned as a principal residence: a lot with a dwelling, a cooperative apartment, a condominium, or a manufactured home, unless the judgment was recovered wholly for the purchase price. N.Y. C.P.L.R. § 5206(a) (McKinney). Security deposit for rental of residence and utility deposits for residence are also exempt.

Procedural requirements: None specified in exemption statute.

Special provisions: Proceeds from a judgment sale are exempt for one year. Protection continues after owner's death, to protect surviving spouse or minor children. N.Y. C.P.L.R. § 5206(b) (McKinney). Exemption lost if premises not used as residence, except for up to one year absence if homestead is damaged or destroyed. N.Y. C.P.L.R. § 5206(c) (McKinney).

Waiver: Not specified in exemption statute.

***Tangible personal property:* N.Y. C.P.L.R. 5205, 5253 (McKinney); N.Y. Debt. & Cred. Law §§ 282, 283(1) (McKinney).**

Household goods: All stoves, home heating equipment, and fuel for 120 days (N.Y. C.P.L.R. § 5205(a)(1) (McKinney)); one sewing machine; religious texts, family pictures, school books, other books up to $500 (N.Y. C.P.L.R. § 5205(a)(2) (McKinney)); family pew (N.Y. C.P.L.R. § 5205(a)(3) (McKinney)); domestic animals and feed for 120 days to a value of $1000; a 120-day supply of food for the debtor and family (N.Y. C.P.L.R. § 5205(a)(4) (McKinney)); all wearing apparel, household furniture, one refrigerator; one radio; one television; one computer and associated equipment; one cell phone, necessary crockery, tableware, and cooking utensils. N.Y. C.P.L.R. § 5205(a)(5) (McKinney). Exemption amounts will be adjusted for inflation at three-year intervals, for changes in consumer price index. 5253. Exemption for these and other tangible personal property items is capped at $10,000 in the aggregate in bankruptcy. N.Y. Debt. & Cred. Law § 283 (McKinney).

Motor vehicles: $4000; if equipped for use by disabled debtor, $10,000. Not applicable to debts for family support. N.Y. Debt. & Cred. Law § 282(1) (McKinney); N.Y. C.P.L.R. § 5205(a)(8) (McKinney).

Tools of trade: $3000. N.Y. C.P.L.R. § 5205(a)(7) (McKinney).

Clothing and jewelry: All wearing apparel (N.Y. C.P.L.R. § 5205(a)(5) (McKinney); a wedding ring; watch, jewelry, and art up to $1000. N.Y. C.P.L.R. § 5205(a)(6) (McKinney).

Miscellaneous and wildcard: 90% of any unpaid proceeds from the sale of milk if the debtor is a farmer (N.Y. C.P.L.R. § 5205(f) (McKinney)); security deposits (N.Y. C.P.L.R. § 5205(g) (McKinney)); health aids and guide dogs (N.Y. C.P.L.R. §§ 5205(a)(5), 5205(h)(1) (McKinney)); residential rental or utility security deposits. Non-bankruptcy, in lieu of homestead, $1000 in personal property, cash, or bank account. N.Y. C.P.L.R. § 5205(a)(9) (McKinney). Beginning in 2012, amounts will be adjusted at three-year intervals for changes in the consumer price index. Bankruptcy only: Wildcard of the lesser of $5000 or the amount of certain unused exemptions, for cash, defined to include bank accounts and tax refunds). N.Y. Debt. & Cred. Law § 283 (McKinney).

Waiver: Not specified in exemption statute.

***Benefits, retirement plans, insurance, judgments, and other intangibles:* N.Y. C.P.L.R. 5205, 5222 (McKinney); N.Y. Debt. & Cred. Law §§ 282, 283(1) (McKinney).**

Public benefits: Non-bankruptcy: Note provisions above, forbidding garnishment. Bankruptcy: Right to receive Social Security, unemployment, veterans' benefits, local public assistance. N.Y. Debt. & Cred. Law § 282(2) (McKinney).

Pensions, retirement plans, and annuities: Any property held in trust for debtor and 90% of income from such trusts—this includes certain retirement plans. Note that there are separate provisions for retirement accounts in bankruptcy exemptions. N.Y. Debt. & Cred. Law § 282(2) (McKinney).

Insurance, judgments, or other compensation for injury: Judgment for loss or destruction of exempt property remains exempt for one year after judgment is satisfied (N.Y. C.P.L.R. § 5205(b) (McKinney)); certain life insurance, including right to accelerate payment or enter into viatical settlement as provided for in insurance law. N.Y. C.P.L.R. § 5205(i) (McKinney). In bankruptcy, may also exempt right to receive disability, illness, or unemployment benefits; crime victim reparations; wrongful death to extent necessary for support; $7500 personal injury (not including pain and suffering or actual pecuniary loss); loss of future earnings to extent needed for support. N.Y. Debt. & Cred. Law § 282(3) (McKinney).

Bank accounts: A bank account deposit up to 240 times the state or federal minimum hourly wage, whichever is higher, is exempt except such part as a court determines to be unnecessary for the reasonable requirements of the judgment debtor and his or her dependents. If bank account contains reasonably identifiable statutorily exempt funds that have been electronically or direct deposited within 45 days preceding the service of a restraining order, $2500 (adjusted every three years for inflation, beginning in 2012) in the debtor's account is exempt. N.Y. C.P.L.R. § 5205(l) (McKinney). Funds in a college choice tuition savings program trust fund are fully exempt as to the designated beneficiary, if a minor, and $10,000 is exempt as to the account owner. N.Y. C.P.L.R. §§ 5205(j), 5222 (McKinney). Additional exemption in bankruptcy for the lesser of $5000 or the amount of certain unused exemptions.

Alimony, child support: Court-ordered family support, to the extent needed for support (this determination to be made by court that made support order). N.Y. C.P.L.R. § 5205(d)(3) (McKinney).

Tax refunds:

Survival after payment or deposit: If reasonably identifiable statutorily exempt funds have been electronically or direct deposited within 45 days preceding the service of a restraining notice, $2500 in the debtor's account is exempt. This section does not alter the status of exempt funds, or the debtor's right to claim them exempt. The amount of this exemption is adjusted for inflation every three years, starting in 2012.

NORTH CAROLINA

Has state opted out of federal bankruptcy exemptions? Yes. N.C. Gen. Stat. § 1C-1601(f).

Is opt out limited to residents or domiciliaries of the state? Yes. N.C. Gen. Stat. § 1C-1601(f): "The exemptions provided in [§ 522(d)], are not applicable to residents of this State. The exemptions provided by this Article and by other statutory or common law of this State shall apply for purposes of [§ 522(b)]."

Do state's exemptions have extraterritorial application?

Homestead: No. *See In re* Owings, 140 F. 739 (E.D.N.C. 1905).

Personal property: Uncertain.

***Wages:* N.C. Gen. Stat. § 1–362.**

Scope: Earnings for personal services within 60 days before date of court order.

Amount: Exempt to the extent needed for family support.

Survival after payment/deposit: Not specified in exemption statute.

Waiver: Not specified in exemption statute.

***Homestead:* N.C. Const. art. X, § 2; N.C. Gen. Stat §§ 1C-1601(a)(1), 1601(e).**

Amount: $35,000 (for unmarried debtor over age 65, who formerly owned the property in tenancy by entireties or joint tenancy with person now deceased, $60,000) in residence consisting of real or personal property, including a cooperative, subject to certain liens and support claims. N.C. Gen. Stat. §§ 1C-1601(a)(1), 1C-1601(e).

Procedural requirements: None specified in exemption statute.

Special provisions: Exemption survives for the benefit of minor children and unremarried spouse. N.C. Const. art. X, §§ 2(2), 2(3). Sale or encumbrance of homestead requires signatures of both spouses. N.C. Const. art. X, § 2(4).

Waiver: Exemptions may not be waived before judgment, except by transfer of the property concerned. Waiver after judgment must be in writing and approved by court clerk or judge. May also be waived by failure to claim, after being notified to do so.[3] N.C. Gen. Stat. § 1C-1601(c).

***Tangible personal property:* N.C. Gen. Stat. § 1C-1601.**

Household goods: $5000 for debtor plus $1000 per dependent up to an additional $4000. Includes furniture, books, musical instruments, clothing, animals, crops. N.C. Gen. Stat. § 1C-1601(a)(4).

Motor vehicles: $3500. N.C. Gen. Stat. § 1C-1601(a)(3).

Tools of trade: $2000. N.C. Gen. Stat. § 1C-1601(a)(5).

Clothing and jewelry: Clothing included in household goods exemption.

Miscellaneous and wildcard: Unused homestead exemption, up to $5000. N.C. Gen. Stat. § 1C-1601(a)(2). Professionally prescribed health aids. N.C. Gen. Stat. § 1C-1601(a)(7).

Waiver: Exemptions may not be waived before judgment, except by transfer of the property concerned. Waiver after judgment must be in writing and approved by court clerk or judge. May also be waived by failure to claim, after being notified to do so. Exemptions will apply to household goods, notwithstanding any non-purchase money security interest. No exemption for tangible property purchased within 90 days before initiation of collection proceedings or filing of bankruptcy, unless the property was purchased solely with the proceeds of exempt property. N.C. Gen. Stat. §§ 1C-1601(c), 1C-1601(d).

***Benefits, retirement plans, insurance, judgments, and other intangibles:* N.C. Const. art. X, § 5; N.C. Gen. Stat. § 1C-1601.**

Public benefits: Not specified in exemption statute.

Pensions, retirement plans, and annuities: Certain tax-qualified retirement plans, including inherited plans. N.C. Gen. Stat. §§ 1C-1601(a)(9), 1C-1601(a)(11).

Insurance, judgments, or other compensation for injury: Life insurance for the benefit of spouse or children is exempt as to debts of the insured. N.C. Gen. Stat. § 1C-1601(a)(6); N.C. Const. art. X, § 5. Compensation for personal injury of debtor or person on whom debtor dependent, or wrongful death of person on whom debtor dependent (except as to claims for medical, legal, funeral, or other services arising from the accident that gave rise to the claim). N.C. Gen. Stat. § 1C-1601(a)(8).

Bank accounts: Tax-qualified college savings account, cumulative limit of $25,000. Does not apply to payments within preceding 12 months, unless these were consistent with past pattern of contributions. N.C. Gen. Stat. § 1C-1601(a)(10).

Alimony, child support: Alimony and separate maintenance to the extent needed for support of debtor and dependents. N.C. Gen. Stat. § 1C-1601(a)(12).

Tax refunds:

Survival after payment or deposit: Not specified in exemption statute.

NORTH DAKOTA

Has state opted out of federal bankruptcy exemptions? Yes. N.D. Cent. Code § 28–22–17.

Is opt out limited to residents or domiciliaries of the state? Yes. N.D. Cent. Code § 28–22–17: "esidents of this state are not entitled to the federal exemptions provided in [§ 522(d)]. The residents of this state are limited to claiming those exemptions allowable by North Dakota law."

Do state's exemptions have extraterritorial application?

Homestead: Uncertain.

Personal property: Uncertain. Note, however, that certain additional exemptions provided pursuant to N.D. Cent. Code § 28–22–03.1, including motor vehicle and wildcard ("in lieu of homestead") are available only to "resident[s] of this state."

***Wages:* N.D. Cent. Code §§ 28–22–18, 28–25–11, 32–09.1–01, 32–09.1–03.**

Scope: Compensation paid or payable for personal services, whether called wages, salary, commission, bonus, or otherwise, including military retirement pay or periodic payments pursuant to a pension or retirement program. Does not include Social Security benefits or veterans' disability (except for child support garnishment). N.D. Cent. Code § 32–09.1–01.

3. *But see* Household Fin. Corp. v. Ellis, 107 N.C. App. 262, 419 S.E.2d 592 (1992) (section is unconstitutional if it attempts to limit the claiming of constitutional exemptions to twenty days, after notice to designate is served), *aff'd*, 333 N.C. 786 (1993) (per curiam).

Amount: Greater of 75% of disposable earnings or forty times federal minimum wage is exempt, with an additional $20 for each dependent living with debtor (N.D. Cent. Code § 32–09.1–03); earnings for personal services received within sixty days preceding order are totally exempt if debtor can show earnings are necessary for use of a family supported in whole or in part by debtor. N.D. Cent. Code § 28–25–11. Disposable earnings are those left after legally required deductions. Wages are exempt only to the extent provided for in § 32–09.1–03. N.D. Cent. Code § 28–22–18.

Survival after payment/deposit: Not specified in garnishment statute.

Waiver: Not specified in garnishment statute.

***Homestead:* N.D. Cent. Code §§ 28–22–02, 28–22–03.1(1), 47–18–01, 47–18–04, 47–18–14, 47–18–16.**

Amount: $100,000 in land and dwelling but lots must be contiguous (N.D. Cent. Code § 47–18–01); or a manufactured home occupied as a residence (N.D. Cent. Code § 28–22–02(10)); exemption subject to certain liens. N.D. Cent. Code § 47–18–04.

Procedural requirements: Procedure available for filing declaration of homestead, but homestead right not impaired by failure to do so.

Special provisions: Sales or insurance proceeds are exempt for one year. N.D. Cent. Code §§ 47–18–14, 47–18–16.

Waiver: Spouse must join in any conveyance or encumbrance.

***Tangible personal property:* N.D. Cent. Code §§ 28–22–01 through 28–22–05.**

Household goods: Fuel and provisions for one year. N.D. Cent. Code § 28–22–02(6).

Motor vehicles: $2950 equity in one vehicle, or $32,000 if modified at cost of not less than $1500 to accommodate owner with permanent disability. N.D. Cent. Code § 28–22–03.1(2).

Tools of trade: Head of family may exempt $1500 tools of trade. N.D. Cent. Code § 28–22–03.1(3). All crops and grain on up to 160 acres of land occupied by debtor, either as tenant or owner, but subject to seed, thresher, and landlord's liens. N.D. Cent. Code § 28–22–02(8).

Clothing and jewelry: All wearing apparel not exceeding $5000 in value and all clothing of the debtor and the debtor's family. N.D. Cent. Code § 28–22–02(5).

Miscellaneous and wildcard: $7500 in lieu of homestead. N.D. Cent. Code § 28–22–03.1(1). This wildcard may not be claimed if the debtor, debtor's spouse, or other head of debtor's family has claimed the homestead exemption. Wildcard of $3750 for single person (N.D. Cent. Code § 28–22–05), $7500 for head of family, that is, married person or one who resides with certain dependents. N.D. Cent. Code § 28–22–03. (May not be used to exempt a real estate interest of any kind.) Head of family may choose either the wildcard, or the listed head of family exemptions above, and $1500 in books and musical instruments. Also exempted: all family pictures, a pew, family library, family bible or other family primary religious text, professionally prescribed health aids. N.D. Cent. Code §§ 28–22–02(1) through 28–22–02(04), 28–22–03.1(6).

Waiver: Not specified in exemption statute.

***Benefits, retirement plans, insurance, judgments, and other intangibles:* N.D. Cent. Code §§ 28–22–03.1, 28–22–19.**

Public benefits: Social Security, veterans' disability, aid to dependent children, crime victims' compensation, disability, illness, or unemployment benefit. N.D. Cent. Code §§ 28–22–03.1(8), 28–22–03.1(9), 28–22–19(2), 28–22–19(3).

Pensions, retirement plans, and annuities: Tax-qualified retirement funds that have been effect for at least one year, up to $100,000 in one fund and $200,000 aggregate. Dollar limit does not apply if funds are reasonably necessary for support. N.D. Cent. Code § 28–22–03.1(7). Public employees' pensions. N.D. Cent. Code § 28–22–19(1). Other pensions, annuities, etc. on account of age, illness, death, disability, or length of service, so far as reasonably necessary for support. N.D. Cent. Code § 28–22–03.1(8)(e).

Insurance, judgments, or other compensation for injury: Proceeds of insurance covering property that is protected by an absolute exemption, if the insurance benefits are in cash or have been invested in other property capable of exemption under this chapter. N.D. Cent. Code § 28–22–02(9). Any unmatured life insurance contract owned by the debtor. Up to $8000, less any amount of property transferred as specified in 11 U.S.C. 542(d), in any accrued dividend or interest under, or loan value of, any unmatured life insurance contract owned by the debtor of which the insured is the debtor or an individual on whom the debtor is dependent. N.D. Cent. Code §§ 28–22–03.1(4), 28–22–03.1(5). Right to receive compensation for wrongful death of person on whom debtor dependent, as needed for support; payment up to $18,450 for personal injury to debtor or one on whom debtor dependent (excluding pain and suffering and actual pecuniary loss); up to $18,450 as compensation for loss of future earnings, as needed for support; award under crime victim's reparation law. N.D. Cent. Code § 28–22–03.1(9).

Bank accounts: Not specified in exemption statute.

Alimony, child support: alimony, support, or separate maintenance, but not a property settlement, to the extent needed for support. N.D. Cent. Code § 28–22–03.1(8)(d).

Tax refunds:

Survival after payment or deposit: Apparently yes. Statute lists benefits "paid or payable" or "amounts received from" or "funds traceable to" various benefits.

OHIO

Has state opted out of federal bankruptcy exemptions? Yes. Ohio Rev. Code Ann. § 2329.662 (West).

Is opt out limited to residents or domiciliaries of the state? Yes. Ohio Rev. Code Ann. § 2329.662 (West): "[T]his state specifically does not authorize debtors who are domiciled in this state to exempt the property specified in [§ 522(d)]."

Do state's exemptions have extraterritorial application?

Homestead: No. Ohio Rev. Code Ann. § 2329.66 (West) applies to "every person who is domiciled in this state."

Personal property: No. Ohio Rev. Code Ann. § 2329.66 (West) applies to "every person who is domiciled in this state." *See also* Pallante v. Int'l Venture Investments, Ltd., 622 F. Supp. 667 (N.D. Ohio 1985) (domiciliary of Louisiana may not exempt wages under Ohio exemption statute).

***Wages:* Ohio Rev. Code Ann. §§ 2329.66(A)(13), 2329.661 (West).**

Scope: Personal earnings.

Amount: Similar to federal exemptions. Disposable earnings are those left after legally required deductions. Ohio Rev. Code Ann. § 2329.66(A)(13) (West).

Survival after payment/deposit: Not specified in exemption statute.

Waiver: Forbidden. Ohio Rev. Code Ann. § 2329.661(B) (West).

***Homestead:* Ohio Rev. Code Ann. §§ 2329.66(A)(1)(b), 2329.661 (West).**

Amount: $132,900 in one parcel of real or personal property used by debtor or dependent as residence, subject to certain liens. Ohio Rev. Code Ann. § 2329.66(A)(1)(b) (West). For debts for health care services or supplies, the exemption has no dollar limit; this does not preclude the creation of a lien, which may be enforced only when property is sold or otherwise transferred to someone other than a surviving spouse or surviving minor child of debtor. Ohio Rev. Code Ann. § 2329.66(A)(1)(a) (West). Starting on April 1, 2010, and at three-year intervals thereafter, dollar amounts will be adjusted for changes in the Consumer Price Index. Ohio Rev. Code Ann. § 2329.66(B) (West).

Procedural requirements: Not specified in exemption statute.

Special provisions: Not specified in exemption statute.

Waiver: Forbidden. Any promise, agreement, or contract that waives the exemption laws of the state is void insofar as it seeks to waive the exemptions. Ohio Rev. Code Ann. § 2329.661(B) (West).

***Tangible personal property:* Ohio Rev. Code Ann. § 2329.66, 2329.661 (West).**

Household goods: $575 per item, or $12,250 in the aggregate, in household furnishings, household goods, wearing apparel, appliances, books, animals, crops, musical instruments, and hunting and fishing equipment, held primarily for personal, family or household use. Ohio Rev. Code Ann. § 2329.66(A)(4)(a) (West).

Motor vehicles: $3675. Ohio Rev. Code Ann. § 2329.66(A)(2) (West).

Tools of trade: $2325. Ohio Rev. Code Ann. § 2329.66(A)(5) (West).

Clothing and jewelry: Clothing included in household goods exemption. Jewelry: $1550. Ohio Rev. Code Ann. § 2329.66(A)(4)(b) (West).

Miscellaneous and wildcard: In bankruptcy only, a wildcard exemption of $1225 (Ohio Rev. Code Ann. § 2329.66(A)(18) (West)); burial plot; health aids (Ohio Rev. Code Ann. §§ 2329.66(A)(7) (West), 2329.66(A)(8)); notary's seal and official register. Ohio Rev. Code Ann. § 2329.66(A)(15) (West).

Waiver: Forbidden. Ohio Rev. Code Ann. § 2329.661(B) (West).

Special provisions: On April 1, 2010, and on April 1 in every third calendar year thereafter, amounts are to be adjusted to reflect changes in Consumer Price Index. Ohio Rev. Code Ann. § 2329.661(B) (West).

***Benefits, retirement plans, insurance, judgments, and other intangibles:* Ohio Rev. Code Ann. §§ 2329.66, 2329.661, 3334.09, 3334.15 (West).**

Public benefits: Unemployment, workers' compensation, Work First, disability assistance, certain other public benefits. Payments under sections 24 or 32 of the Internal Revenue Code. Ohio Rev. Code Ann. § 2329.66(A)(9) (West).

Pensions, retirement plans, and annuities: Certain public and private pensions and retirement plans. Ohio Rev. Code Ann. §§ 2329.66(A)(6), 2329.66(A)(10) (West).

Insurance, judgments, or other compensation for injury: Certain life insurance, annuities, and group insurance; certain benefits from fraternal organizations; payments from health and disability insurance (Ohio Rev. Code Ann. § 2329.66(A)(6) (West)); wrongful death compensation, for person on whom debtor was dependent so far as needed for support; $23,000 personal injury compensation; compensation for loss of future earnings. Ohio Rev. Code Ann. § 2329.66(A)(12) (West). Starting on April 1, 2010, and at three-year intervals thereafter, dollar amounts will be adjusted for changes in the Consumer Price Index.

Bank accounts: An interest in a tuition credit or a payment subject to a tuition credit contract. Ohio Rev. Code Ann. §§ 2329.66(A)(16), 3334.09, 3334.15 (West). $425 in cash, money due or to become due within 90 days, tax refunds, or bank deposits. Ohio Rev. Code Ann. § 2329.66(A)(3) (West). Starting on April 1, 2010, and at three-year intervals thereafter, dollar amounts will be adjusted for changes in the Consumer Price Index. Ohio Rev. Code Ann. § 2329.66(B) (West).

Alimony, child support: Child or spousal support or maintenance, as needed for support. Payments pursuant to a qualified domestic relations order. Ohio Rev. Code Ann. §§ 2329.66(A)(10)(f), 2329.66(A)(11) (West).

Tax refunds: Included in wildcard for cash, bank accounts, etc., Ohio Rev. Code Ann. § 2329.66(A)(3)

Survival after payment or deposit: Not specified in exemption statute.

OKLAHOMA

Has state opted out of federal bankruptcy exemptions? Yes. Okla. Stat. tit. 31, § 1(B).

Is opt out limited to residents or domiciliaries of the state? Yes. Okla. Stat. tit. 31, § 1(B): "No natural person residing in this state may exempt from the property of the estate in any bankruptcy proceeding the property specified in [§ 522)d)] . . . ."

Do state's exemptions have extraterritorial application?

Homestead: Probably not. Okla. Stat. tit. 31, § 1 applies to "every person residing in the state."

Personal property: Probably not. Okla. Stat. tit. 31, § 1 applies to "every person residing in the state."

***Wages:* Okla. Stat. tit. 12, §§ 1171.1, 1171.2; Okla. Stat. tit. 31, §§ 1(18), 1.1.**

Scope: Money earned by a natural person as wages, salary, bonus, or commission for personal services.

Amount: Follows federal scheme except debtor who is supporting dependent(s) may exempt a larger percentage on a showing of hardship. Okla. Stat. tit. 12, § 1171.1; Okla. Stat. tit. 31, §§ 1(18), 1.1.

Survival after payment/deposit: Protections apply to earnings within previous 90 days. Okla. Stat. tit. 31, § 1(18).

Waiver: Not specified in garnishment statute.

***Homestead:* Okla. Const. art. XII, § 1; Okla. Stat. tit. 31, §§ 1, 2, 5.**

Amount: 160 acres not within any city or town, or annexed by a city or town after November 1, 1997, and owned, occupied, and used for both residential and commercial agricultural purposes; urban homestead exemption shall not exceed $5000 if more than 25% of the square foot area of the improvements on the land is used for business purposes or if less than 75% of square foot area of the improvements on the land is used as principal residence. Okla. Const. art. XII, § 1; Okla. Stat. tit. 31, §§ 1, 2. Subject to certain liens. Okla. Stat. tit. 31, § 5.

Procedural requirements: None specified in exemption statute.

Special provisions: Temporary rental of the homestead, without acquiring a new homestead, will not eliminate exemption.

Waiver: Not specified in exemption statute. Okla. Stat. tit. 31, § 2.

***Tangible personal property:* Okla. Stat. tit. 31, § 1.**

Household goods: All household furniture, including a personal computer and related equipment, books, portraits, and pictures. Okla. Stat. tit. 31, §§ 1(3), 1(6).

Motor vehicles: $7500 in one vehicle.

Tools of trade: $10,000 aggregate in tools of trade and farming implements. Okla. Stat. tit. 31, § 1(5).

Clothing and jewelry: $4000 clothing, $3000 in wedding and anniversary rings. Okla. Stat. tit. 31, §§ 1(7), 1(8)

Miscellaneous and wildcard: Health aids (Okla. Stat. tit. 31, § 1(9)), a limited number of poultry and livestock (Okla. Stat. tit. 31, §§ 1(10) through 1(13), 1(15), 1(16)), $2000 in guns (Okla. Stat. tit. 31, § 1(14)), and a year's supply of provisions (Okla. Stat. tit. 31, § 1(17)); burial place. Okla. Stat. tit. 31, § 1(4).

Waiver: Not specified in exemption statute.

***Benefits, retirement plans, insurance, judgments, and other intangibles:* Okla. Stat. tit. 31, §§ 1, 7.**

Public benefits: Amount received as earned income tax credit. Okla. Stat. tit. 31, § 1(23). *See also* Okla. Stat. tit. 56, § 173 (assistance received under certain statutes is exempt).

Pensions, retirement plans, and annuities: Military pensions (Okla. Stat. tit. 31, § 7); certain tax-qualified retirement plans. Okla. Stat. tit. 31, § 1(20).

Insurance, judgments, or other compensation for injury: Up to $50,000 personal injury, wrongful death, or workers' compensation (no punitive damages). Okla. Stat. tit. 31, § 1(21).

Bank accounts: Any interest in Oklahoma college tuition savings plan, created pursuant to Okla. Stat. tit. 70, §§ 3970.1 to 3970.12. Okla. Stat. tit. 31, § 1(24). Funds in a personal development account, pursuant to Title 56, §§ 251 *et seq.* Okla. Stat. tit. 31, § 1(22).

Alimony, child support: Right to receive alimony, separate support, or child support, so far as needed for support. Okla. Stat. tit. 31, § 1(19).

Tax refunds:

Survival after payment or deposit: Not specified in exemption statute.

OREGON

Has state opted out of federal bankruptcy exemptions? No. Or. Rev. Stat. § 18.300.

Is opt out limited to residents or domiciliaries of the state? Not applicable.

Do state's exemptions have extraterritorial application?

Homestead: Yes. *See In re* Stratton, 269 B.R. 716 (Bankr. D. Or. 2001) (Oregon homestead exemption applied to property in California).

Personal property: Probably yes, based on *In re* Stratton, 269 B.R. 716 (Bankr. D. Or. 2001).

***Wages:* Or. Rev. Stat. §§ 18.348, 18.375, 18.385.**

Scope: Compensation paid or payable for personal services, whether called wages, salary, commission, bonus, or otherwise, including periodic payments pursuant to pension or retirement plan. Some independent contractors are covered. Or. Rev. Stat. § 18.375.

Amount: Greater of 75% of disposable earnings or $218/week is exempt. Disposable earnings are those left over after legally required deductions. Discharge for garnishment forbidden. Or. Rev. Stat. § 18.385.

Survival after payment/deposit: Yes, if funds are traceable and not more than $7500 accumulated. Or. Rev. Stat. § 18.348.

Waiver: Waivers are void. Or. Rev. Stat. § 18.385(8).

***Homestead:* Or. Rev. Stat. §§ 18.395, 18.398, 18.402.**

Amount: $40,000 in a residence (explicitly covers purchaser's interest in a land sale contract), manufactured or floating home explicitly included (Or. Rev. Stat. §§ 18.395 (1), 18.395(9), 18–395(10)); if two members of household are debtors whose interests in homestead are subject to execution, may not exceed $50,000 (Or. Rev. Stat. § 18.395 (1)); may not exceed 160 acres if outside town or city; may not exceed one block if within town or city (Or. Rev. Stat. § 18.402); homestead exemption subject to certain liens.

Procedural requirements: None specified in exemption statute.

Special provisions: Proceeds exempt for one year if debtor intends to use them to purchase another homestead. Or. Rev. Stat. §§ 18.395 (2), 18.395(3). No homestead may be sold for a debt of $3000 or less, except for two or more judgments for the same judgment creditor that total $3000 or more. Or. Rev. Stat. §§ 18.395 (5) through 18.395(7).

Waiver: Not specified in exemption statute.

***Tangible personal property:* Or. Rev. Stat. §§ 18.345, 18.362.**

Household goods: $3000 in household goods, a 60-day supply of fuel and provisions. Or. Rev. Stat. § 18.345(1)(f).

Motor vehicles: $3000 (joint debtors may stack). Or. Rev. Stat. §§ 18.345(1)(d), 18.345(3).

Tools of trade: $5000 (joint debtors may stack). Or. Rev. Stat. §§ 18.345(1)(c), 18.345(3).

Clothing and jewelry: $1800 in wearing apparel, jewelry, and other personal items (joint debtors may stack). Or. Rev. Stat. §§ 18.345(1)(b), 18.345(3).

Miscellaneous and wildcard: $400 which can be stacked by joint debtors and applied toward any personal property, but which cannot be used to increase another exemption (Or. Rev. Stat. § 18.345(1)(p)); $600 in books, pictures, and musical instruments (joint debtors may stack) (Or. Rev. Stat. §§ 18.345(1)(a), 18.345(3)); all health aids; $1000 in animals, poultry and 60-day supply of feed (Or. Rev. Stat. § 18.345(1)(e)); and a rifle or shotgun and one pistol, the combined value of which may not exceed $1000. Or. Rev. Stat. § 18.362.

Waiver: Not specified in exemption statute.

***Benefits, retirement plans, insurance, judgments, and other intangibles:* Or. Rev. Stat. §§ 18.345, 18.348, 18.352, 18.358.**

Public benefits: The right to receive an earned income tax credit under federal law, and all moneys traceable to a payment of an earned income tax credit. Or. Rev. Stat. § 18.345(1)(n). Veterans' benefits and loans. Or. Rev. Stat. § 18.345(1)(m). Numerous other public benefits are exempted by the statutes establishing the benefit programs. *See, e.g.*, Or. Rev. Stat. § 411.760. Unemployment, workers' compensation, and most other state or Federal benefits may be reached for family support.

Pensions, retirement plans, and annuities: Certain pensions and private retirement plans and annuities, including rollovers from employee pensions to individual accounts. Or. Rev. Stat. § 18.358.

Insurance, judgments, or other compensation for injury: Right to receive, or property traceable to, award under crime victim reparation law (Or. Rev. Stat. § 18.345(1)(j)); right to receive, or property traceable to, personal injury compensation up to $10,000 (Or. Rev. Stat. § 18.345(1)(k)); right to receive, or property traceable to, compensation for loss of future earnings, to extent needed for support.

Bank accounts: Not specified in exemption statute (except as to survival of exemption in certain exempt funds). Or. Rev. Stat. § 18.348. Medical or health savings account. Or. Rev. Stat. § 18.345(1)(o).

Alimony, child support: Spousal support, child support, or separate maintenance, to the extent needed for support. Or. Rev. Stat. § 18.345(1)(i).

Tax refunds:

Survival after payment or deposit: Funds exempt under other specified statutes (including retirement plans, wages, public employees' pensions, vocational rehabilitation, college tuition savings, veterans' loans, public assistance, aid to blind or disabled, old age assistance, Medicaid, benefits for injured inmates, workers' compensation, unemployment, benefits from fraternal organizations, Social Security, and veterans' benefits) remain exempt if deposited in bank account, so long as traceable, but exemption lost if more than $7500 accumulated. The limit on accumulation does not apply to funds exempted by 42 U.S.C. § 407 (the anti-alienation provision of the Social Security law). Or. Rev. Stat. § 18.348.

PENNSYLVANIA

Has state opted out of federal bankruptcy exemptions? No.

Is opt out limited to residents or domiciliaries of the state? Not applicable.

Do state's exemptions have extraterritorial application?

Homestead: No exemption.

Personal property: Uncertain.

***Wages:* 23 Pa. Cons. Stat. § 3703; 42 Pa. Cons. Stat. § 8127.**

Scope: Wages, salaries and commissions of individuals. 42 Pa. Cons. Stat. § 8127.

Amount: Completely exempt in hands of employer, *except* for certain residential rent or damages, board for four weeks or less, family support, student loan, or criminal fine, restitution, costs. (Support 50%; landlord-tenant 10% or a sum not to place debtor's income below federal poverty guidelines, whichever is less; not specified for other exceptions.) Net wages are those left after legally required deductions, health insurance, and union dues. Garnishment for rent or damages not permitted if lessee is victim of domestic abuse. The Rules of Civil Procedure, Rules 3301 through 3304 and 3312 require notice to debtors of the exemption for income below the poverty guidelines, the guideline amount, and the procedure for preventing garnishment of exempt wages. 42 Pa. Cons. Stat. § 8127.

Survival after payment/deposit: Exempt "in the hands of the employer."

Waiver: Not specified in garnishment statute.

Homestead: No statutory homestead exemption, but common-law doctrine of tenancy by the entireties protects property owned by husband and wife from debts owed just by one spouse. *See* Sterrett v. Sterrett, 166 A.2d (Pa. 1960).

Amount: Not applicable.

Procedural requirements: Not applicable.

Special provisions: Not applicable.

Waiver: Not applicable.

***Tangible personal property:* 42 Pa. Cons. Stat. §§ 8122, 8123, 8124, 8125, 8127.**

Household goods: See miscellaneous and wildcard exemptions.

Motor vehicles: See miscellaneous and wildcard exemptions.

Tools of trade: See miscellaneous and wildcard exemptions.

Clothing and jewelry: All clothing. 42 Pa. Cons. Stat. § 8124(a).

Miscellaneous and wildcard: $300 in property including bank notes, money, securities, real property, or money due the debtor; the exemption is inapplicable to claims for support, or for board for four weeks or less, or to foreclosure judgments or certain wage claims. 42 Pa. Cons. Stat. § 8123. Bibles and schoolbooks, sewing machines if not kept for sale or hire, and certain uniforms (42 Pa. Cons. Stat. § 8124(a)); tangible personal property on exhibition at any international exhibition held under the auspices of the federal government is exempt in the hands of the authorities of such exhibition or otherwise. 42 Pa. Cons. Stat. § 8125.

Waiver: Forbidden. 42 Pa. Cons. Stat. § 8122.

***Benefits, retirement plans, insurance, judgments, and other intangibles:* 42 Pa. Cons. Stat. §§ 8123, 8124, 8125, 8127.**

Public benefits: Unemployment compensation.

Pensions, retirement plans, and annuities: Certain public or private pensions and individual retirement plans or annuities, including rollovers. (Except for rollovers, contributions in excess of $15,000 per year not exempt.) 42 Pa. Cons. Stat. § 8124(b).

Insurance, judgments, or other compensation for injury: Workers' compensation; certain life, health, and accident insurance; benefits from fraternal organizations; no-fault auto insurance recoveries. 42 Pa. Cons. Stat. § 8124(c).

Bank accounts: $300 wildcard described above may be applied to money. Note also the protection for electronically-deposited exempt funds described.

Alimony, child support: Not specified in exemption statute.

Tax refunds:

Survival after payment or deposit: Yes, at least as to exempt funds electronically direct deposited on a recurring basis and identified as exempt. Pennsylvania Rules of Civil Procedure Rule 3111.1 provides that service of a writ does not attach such funds. Rules 3252 and 3253 prescribe language for writs of execution and interrogatories to the garnishee that clearly informs creditors and garnishees that such funds should not be attached.

PUERTO RICO

Has state opted out of federal bankruptcy exemptions? No.

Is opt out limited to residents or domiciliaries of the state? Not applicable.

Do state's exemptions have extraterritorial application?

Homestead: Uncertain.

Personal property: Uncertain.

***Wages:* P.R. Laws Ann. tit. 32, § 1130.**

Scope: Earnings for personal services within 30 days before levy of execution. P.R. Laws Ann. tit. 32, § 1130(7).

Amount: 75% exempt if debtor can show earnings are necessary for use of family supported wholly or in part by debtor's labor. P.R. Laws Ann. tit. 32, § 1130(7).

Survival after payment/deposit: Not specified in exemption statute.

Waiver: Not specified in exemption statute.

***Homestead:* P.R. Laws Ann. tit. 31, §§ 1858 through 1858k.**

Amount: A parcel and the structure thereon, or a condo, which debtor lawfully owns, and is occupied by debtor or debtor's family exclusively as a principal residence. Subject to certain mortgages and debts. P.R. Laws Ann. tit. 31, §§ 1858.

Procedural requirements: Individual who acquires homestead should set forth this fact in the deed, or individual who already owns land may file homestead. Failure to do so does not destroy exemption, provided exemption is timely claimed after notice of foreclosure or attachment. P.R. Laws Ann. tit. 31, § 1858f through 1958i.

Special provisions: If home owner dies or deserts family, exemption continues to protect spouse, minor children, and certain other dependents. Leasing of the home during temporary absence resulting from work, study, military service, or illness of debtor or certain family members does not eliminate the exemption unless beneficiary obtains another principal residence. § 1858d. Sales proceeds protected for nine months, if invested in another Puerto Rico homestead. § 1858e. P.R. Laws Ann. tit. 31, §§ 1858c and 1958e.

Waiver: Forbidden (except in mortgages and certain sharecropping contracts). P.R. Laws Ann. tit. 31, § 1851.

***Tangible personal property:* P.R. Laws Ann. tit. 32, § 1130.**

Household goods: $100 in chairs, tables, desks, and books (P.R. Laws Ann. tit. 32, § 1130.1); necessary household furniture including one sewing machine; $200 in a stove, furniture, beds, bedding; provisions sufficient for one month (P.R. Laws Ann. tit. 32, § 1130(2)); iceboxes; $200 in a washing machine, $100 in a radio, $250 in a television and an electric iron. P.R. Laws Ann. tit. 32, § 1130(14).

Motor vehicles: One motor vehicle used in debtor's occupation (except for purchase money and repair debts for the vehicle). Exemption is capped at $6000 for liability for injury to third person by the motor vehicle. P.R. Laws Ann. tit. 32, § 1130(4)(a).

Tools of trade: $300 tools of trade. Various farm animals and their equipment and feed for one month; a water right not to exceed the amount used for land the debtor actually cultivates; $200 in seeds to be planted or sowed within six months; certain mining equipment, aggregate $500. P.R. Laws Ann. tit. 32, §§ 1130(3) through 1130(6).

Clothing and jewelry: All clothing. P.R. Laws Ann. tit. 32, § 1130(2).

Miscellaneous and wildcard: Artwork done by the debtor, family portraits, and their necessary frames (P.R. Laws Ann. tit. 32, § 1130(2)); $500 in shares of a homestead association if the debtor has no homestead (P.R. Laws Ann. tit. 32, § 1130(8)); uniforms the debtor is required to keep and one gun. P.R. Laws Ann. tit. 32, § 1130(10).

Waiver: Not specified in exemption statute.

***Benefits, retirement plans, insurance, judgments, and other intangibles:* P.R. Laws Ann. tit. 32, § 1130.**

Public benefits: Not specified in exemption statute.

Pensions, retirement plans, and annuities: Not specified in exemption statute.

Insurance, judgments, or other compensation for injury: Certain life insurance. P.R. Laws Ann. tit. 32, § 1130(9).

Bank accounts: Not specified in exemption statute.

Alimony, child support: Not specified in exemption statute.

Tax refunds:

Survival after payment or deposit: Not specified in exemption statute.

RHODE ISLAND

Has state opted out of federal bankruptcy exemptions? No.

Is opt out limited to residents or domiciliaries of the state? Not applicable.

Do state's exemptions have extraterritorial application?

Homestead: Probably yes. *See In re* Jevne, 387 B.R. 301 (Bankr. S.D. Fla. 2008) (Rhode Island law is silent on extraterritoriality of homestead exemption, so under principle of liberal interpretation it applies to Florida property); *In re* Franklino, 329 B.R. 363 (Bankr. D.R.I. 2005) (court accepted without discussion parties stipulation that debtor may claim Rhode Island homestead in property located in Connecticut).

Personal property: Uncertain.

***Wages:* R.I. Gen. Laws §§ 9-26-4(6), (8) and (9).**

Scope: Wages or salary.

Amount: $50 per week is exempt. R.I. Gen. Laws § 9-26-4(8). All wages are exempt if debtor is, or within one year was, "an object of relief from any state, federal, or municipal corporation or agency." R.I. Gen. Laws § 9-26-4(8). Wages due a sailor are completely exempt. R.I. Gen. Laws § 9-26-4(6).

Survival after payment/deposit: Not specified in exemption statute.

Waiver: Not specified in exemption statute.

***Homestead:* R.I. Gen. Laws § 9-26-4.1.**

Amount: $500,000 in land or buildings which debtor has a right to possess by lease or otherwise and occupies or intends to occupy as a principal residence. Life tenants and trust beneficiaries explicitly included. Lessee covered if he or she was owner of the home before its transfer to lessor. Significant exceptions: certain liens, debts owed to a federally insured depository institution or a person regulated under title 19 (financial institutions), debt contracted prior to the purchase of the residence. Only one exemption per residence (whether single or multiple owners) and only one principal residence per family.

Procedural requirements: None. "Automatic by operation of law."

Special provisions: None specified.

Waiver: Not specified in exemption statute.

***Tangible personal property:* R.I. Gen. Laws § 9-26-4.**

Household goods: Furnishings and family stores of a housekeeper, up to $9600. R.I. Gen. Laws § 9-26-4(3).

Motor vehicles: Motor vehicles with aggregate value up to $12,000. R.I. Gen. Laws § 9-26-4(13).

Tools of trade: Professional's library; tools of trade up to $2000. R.I. Gen. Laws § 9-26-4(2).

Clothing and jewelry: Necessary clothing of debtor and family (R.I. Gen. Laws § 9-26-4(1)); $2000 jewelry. R.I. Gen. laws § 9-26-4(14).

Miscellaneous and wildcard: Books up to $300; one cemetery plot (R.I. Gen. Laws §§ 9-26-4(4), 9-26-4(5)); debts secured by bills of exchange or promissory notes; $50 in holdings in consumer cooperative association. Bankruptcy-only wildcard exemption: $6500. R.I. Gen. Laws § 9-26-4(16).

Waiver: Not specified in exemption statute.

***Benefits, retirement plans, insurance, judgments, and other intangibles:* R.I. Gen. Laws §§ 9-26-4, 9-26-5.**

Public benefits: Not specified in exemption statute. (But note exemption for "other property . . . exempted . . . by general or special acts . . . or by the policy of the law.") R.I. Gen. Laws § 9-26-4(10). *See* R.I. Gen. Laws § 40-6-14 (assistance provided under Public Assistance Act is exempt); § 40-5.2-17 (assistance provided under the Rhode Island Works program is exempt).

Pensions, retirement plans, and annuities: Tax-qualified IRAs, pensions, and retirement annuities, except for certain domestic relations orders (R.I. Gen. Laws § 9-26-4(11)); police or firefighters' pensions. R.I. Gen. Laws §§ 9-26-4(12), 9-26-5.

Insurance, judgments, or other compensation for injury: Not specified in exemption statute.

Bank accounts: Account balance in prepaid tuition or tuition savings plan (as defined in R.I. Gen. Laws § 16–7–3). R.I. Gen. Laws § 9–26–4(15).

Alimony, child support: Not specified in exemption statute.

Tax refunds:

Survival after payment or deposit: Not specified in exemption statute.

SOUTH CAROLINA

Has state opted out of federal bankruptcy exemptions? Yes. S.C. Code Ann. § 15–41–35.

Is opt out limited to residents or domiciliaries of the state? Not specified. S.C. Code Ann. § 15–41–35: "No individual may exempt from the property of the estate in any bankruptcy proceeding the property specified in [§ 522(d)] except as may be expressly permitted by this chapter or by other provisions of law of this State."

Do state's exemptions have extraterritorial application?

Homestead: No. S.C. Code Ann. § 15–41–30 applies to the "real and personal property of a debtor domiciled in this state."

Personal property: No. S.C. Code Ann. § 15–41–30 applies to the "real and personal property of a debtor domiciled in this state."

***Wages:* S.C. Code Ann. §§ 15–39–410, 15–39–420.**

Scope: Personal service earnings are exempt.

Amount: Fully exempt.

Survival after payment/deposit: Not specified in exemption statute.

Waiver: Not specified in exemption statute.

***Homestead:* S.C. Code Ann. § 15–41–30(A)(1). *See* S.C. Const. art. III, § 28.**

Amount: $56,150 in real property or personal property used as residence or in cooperative used as residence or in burial plot. Multiple owners may exempt up to $112,275. Starting July 1, 2008, homestead exemption amounts are adjusted annually, according to the Consumer Price Index. New amounts are published each March 1. S.C. Code Ann. § 15–41–30(B).

Procedural requirements: Not specified in exemption statute.

Special provisions: Not specified in exemption statute.

Waiver: Not specified in exemption statute.

***Tangible personal property:* S.C. Code Ann. § 15–41–30. *See* S.C. Const. art. III, § 28.**

Household goods: $4500 in household furnishings and goods, clothing, appliances, books, animals, crops, musical instruments. S.C. Code Ann. § 15–41–30(A)(3).

Motor vehicles: $5625 in one motor vehicle. S.C. Code Ann. § 15–41–30(A)(2).

Tools of trade: $1675. S.C. Code Ann. § 15–41–30(A)(6).

Clothing and jewelry: $1125 in jewelry (S.C. Code Ann. § 15–41–30(A)(4)); clothing included in household goods exemption.

Miscellaneous and wildcard: $5625 in cash and liquid assets (including bank deposits) for those debtors without a homestead (S.C. Code Ann. § 15–41–30(A)(5)); up to $5000 in unused personal property exemptions (S.C. Code Ann. § 15–41–30(A)(7)); health aids. S.C. Code Ann. § 15–41–30(A)(10).

Waiver: Not specified in exemption statute.

Special provisions: Dollar amounts are to be adjusted on July 1st each year, to account for changes in the Consumer Price Index. S.C. Code Ann. § 15–41–30(B).

***Benefits, retirement plans, insurance, judgments, and other intangibles:* S.C. Code Ann. § 15–41–30.**

Public benefits: Right to receive or property traceable to Social Security, unemployment, local public assistance, veterans' benefits. S.C. Code Ann. § 15–41–30(A)(11).

Pensions, retirement plans, and annuities: ERISA pensions; right to receive payment under certain tax-qualified retirement plans. Retirement accounts exempt to the same extent permitted by § 522(d) of the bankruptcy law. This exemption protects persons with "an interest" in retirement plan as "participant, beneficiary, contingent annuitant, alternate payee or otherwise." S.C. Code Ann. §§ 15–41–30(A)(13), 15–41–30(A)(14).

Insurance, judgments, or other compensation for injury: Certain life insurance (S.C. Code Ann. §§ 15–41–30(A)(8), 15–41–30(A)(9)); right to receive disability, illness, or unemployment benefit; right to receive, or property traceable to, award under crime victim reparation law, payment for bodily injury to debtor or bodily injury or wrongful death of one on whom debtor is dependent (S.C. Code Ann. § 15–41–30(A)(12)), or life insurance proceeds of one on whom debtor was dependent (so far as needed for support). S.C. Code Ann. § 15–41–30(A)(2). Accrued dividend or interest, or loan value of certain insurance: $4500.

Bank accounts: Not specified in exemption statute (but note in lieu of homestead exemption).

Alimony, child support: Right to receive alimony, support, or separate maintenance. S.C. Code Ann. § 15–41–30(A)(11)(d).

Tax refunds:

Survival after payment or deposit: Note that some exemptions specify "right to receive" or "right to receive and property traceable to."

SOUTH DAKOTA

Has state opted out of federal bankruptcy exemptions? Yes. S.D. Codified Laws §§ 43–31–30, 43–45–13.

Is opt out limited to residents or domiciliaries of the state? Yes. S.D. Codified Laws §§ 43–31–30, 43–45–13: "esidents of this state are not entitled to [§ 522(d) exemptions], exemptions which this state specifically does not authorize." *See In re* Volk, 26 B.R. 457 (Bankr. D.S.D. 1983).

Do state's exemptions have extraterritorial application?

Homestead: Uncertain. Compare S.D. Codified Laws § 43–31–1, which applies to the "homestead of every family, resident in this state," with S.D. Codified Laws § 43–31–2, which defines a homestead as including "two or more houses or mobile homes thus used at different times and places."

Personal property: Uncertain.

***Wages:* S.D. Codified Laws §§ 21–18–2.1, 21–18–51 through 21–18–53.**

Scope: Compensation paid or payable for personal services whether called wages, salary, commission, bonus, or otherwise; includes periodic payments from pension or retirement plan. S.D. Codified Laws § 28–18–2.1.

Amount: Greater of 80% of disposable income or forty times minimum wage is exempt. Additional exemption of $25/week for each dependent residing with debtor. S.D. Codified Laws § 21–18–51.

Survival after payment/deposit: Not specified in garnishment statute.

Waiver: Not specified in garnishment statute.

Homestead: **S.D. Codified Laws §§ 43-31-1 through 43-31-6, 43-31-11, 43-31-13, 43-45-3.**

Amount: Dwelling exempt, subject to certain exceptions; manufactured home must be larger than 240 square feet at its base and registered in South Dakota at least six months before the claim of exemption (S.D. Codified Laws § 43-31-2); $60,000 in sale proceeds are exempt for one year after receipt but exemption is $170,000 if debtor is 70 or older or the unremarried spouse of such a person (S.D. Codified Laws § 43-31-1); limit of one acre within a town plat and 160 acres outside a town plat; if outside a town plat and acquired under U.S. laws relating to mineral lands, limit is 40 acres; if acquired as a "lode mining claim," limit is five acres. S.D. Codified Laws § 43-31-4.

Procedural requirements: Home owner may have homestead platted, but failure to do so does not destroy exemption. S.D. Codified Laws § 43-31-6.

Special provisions: Upon death of home owner, exemption continues to protect surviving spouse and minor children. S.D. Codified Laws § 43-31-15. New homestead will be exempt to the same extent and in the same manner as the old. S.D. Codified Laws § 43-31-13. Proceeds of sale of homestead exempt for one year. S.D. Codified Laws § 43-45-3.

Waiver: Both spouses must join in conveyance or encumbrance.

Tangible personal property: **S.D. Codified Laws §§ 43-45-2, 43-45-4.**

Household goods: See miscellaneous and wildcard exemptions; provisions and fuel for one year absolutely exempt. S.D. Codified Laws § 43-45-2(7).

Motor vehicles: See miscellaneous and wildcard exemptions.

Tools of trade: See miscellaneous and wildcard exemptions.

Clothing and jewelry: All clothing. S.D. Codified Laws § 43-45-2(5).

Miscellaneous and wildcard: Personal property head of family $7000, others $5000 (S.D. Codified Laws § 43-45-4); burial plot; all family pictures; a pew; health aids (S.D. Codified Laws §§ 43-45-2(1) through 43-45-2(4), 43-45-2(8)); $200 in a family library.

Waiver: Not specified in exemption statute.

Benefits, retirement plans, insurance, judgments, and other intangibles: **S.D. Codified Laws §§ 43-45-6, 43-45-15 through 43-45-18.**

Public benefits: Not specified in exemption statute. *See* S.D. Codified Laws § 28-7A-18 (TANF is exempt).

Pensions, retirement plans, and annuities: Up to $1 million and the income and distributions therefrom in employee benefit plan. Employee benefit plan is defined as certain tax-qualified plans. In the event that any court of South Dakota finds the exemption excessive, the court is directed to determine what amount is permissible under the state constitution. S.D. Codified Laws §§ 43-45-16 through 43-45-18.

Insurance, judgments, or other compensation for injury: Life insurance payments to spouse or minor children, exempt from debts of insured and beneficiaries up to $10,000. S.D. Codified Laws § 43-45-6.

Bank accounts: Not specified in exemption statute.

Alimony, child support: Not specified in exemption statute.

Tax refunds:

Survival after payment or deposit: Not specified in exemption statute.

TENNESSEE

Has state opted out of federal bankruptcy exemptions? Yes. Tenn. Code Ann. § 26-2-112.

Is opt out limited to residents or domiciliaries of the state? Yes (as to "citizens"). Tenn. Code Ann. § 26-2-112: "[C]itizens of Tennessee, . . . are not authorized to claim as exempt the property described in [§ 522(d)]."

Do state's exemptions have extraterritorial application?

Homestead: Uncertain.

Personal property: Uncertain.

Wages: **Tenn. Code Ann. §§ 26-2-102, 26-2-106 through 26-2-108.**

Scope: Compensation paid or payable for personal services, whether called wages, salary, commission, or otherwise, including periodic payments pursuant to pension or retirement program. Tenn. Code Ann. § 26-2-102.

Amount: Similar to federal, with additional $2.50 per week exemption for each dependent child under age 16. Tenn. Code Ann. §§ 26-2-106, 26-2-107. Disposable earnings are those left after legally required deductions. Tenn. Code Ann. § 26-2-102.

Survival after payment/deposit: Not specified in exemption statute.

Waiver: May be waived by written contract for "a debt secured by the homestead" (§ 26-2-302(c)) but may not be waived in a note, other instrument evidencing debt, or any other instrument not conveying property in which a homestead may be claimed (§ 26-2-301(d)).

Homestead: **Tenn. Const. art. 11, § 11; Tenn. Code Ann. §§ 26-2-301 through 26-2-306, 26-2-311.**

Amount: $5000 in real property used as principal place of residence; joint debtors may only exempt $7500 in shared home. For an unmarried individual age 62 or older, the amount is $12,500. For a couple, when one party is age 62 or over, the amount is $20,000. For a couple, when both parties are 62 or older, the amount is $25,000. For an individual who has one or more minor children in such individual's custody, the amount is $25,000. Tenn. Code Ann. § 26-2-301. Life estates and equitable estates covered, if owned by the individual and used as a residence by individual, or spouse or dependent. Tenn. Code Ann. § 26-2-302. Leased property covered if leased for not less than two or more than fifteen years. Tenn. Code Ann. § 26-2-303. Exemption protects against some criminal law seizures but not against subject to sale for payment of public taxes or satisfaction of debt for improvements. Tenn. Code Ann. § 26-2-306.

Procedural requirements: None stated. Homestead may be set apart at time of levy.

Special provisions: Insurance proceeds also exempt up to $5000. Tenn. Code Ann. § 26-2-304. After owner's death, or if owner deserts family, exemption continues to protect spouse and minor children. Tenn. Code Ann. § 26-2-311.

Waiver: Not specified in exemption statute.

Tangible personal property: **Tenn. Code Ann. §§ 8-36-111, 26-2-102 through 26-2-104, 26-2-111, 49-5-909.**

Household goods: See miscellaneous and wildcard exemptions.

Motor vehicles: See miscellaneous and wildcard exemptions.

Tools of trade: $1900. Tenn. Code Ann. § 26-2-111(4).

Clothing and jewelry: Necessary and proper clothing. Tenn. Code Ann. § 26-2-104.

Miscellaneous and wildcard: Personal property to the aggregate value of $10,000 (includes cash or bank accounts) (Tenn. Code Ann. § 26-2-103); health aids (Tenn. Code Ann. § 26-2-111(5)); family portraits and pictures; Bible and school books. Tenn. Code Ann. § 26-2-104. Burial space. Tenn. Code Ann. § 26-2-305.

Waiver: Not specified in exemption statute.

***Benefits, retirement plans, insurance, judgments, and other intangibles:* Tenn. Code Ann. §§ 8–36–111, 26–2–105, 26–2–110, 26–2–111, 49–5–909.**

Public benefits: Right to receive Social Security, unemployment, veterans' benefits. Tenn. Code Ann. § 26–2–111(1). *See also* Tenn. Code Ann. §§ 71–2–216, 71–3–121, 71–4–117, 71–4–1112 (exempting benefits under various state public assistance statutes).

Pensions, retirement plans, and annuities: Public employees' retirement benefits (Tenn. Code Ann. §§ 8–36–111, 26–2–105, 49–5–909); certain tax-qualified private retirement benefits (private retirement payments treated like wages). Tenn. Code Ann. §§ 26–2–105, 26–2–111(1).

Insurance, judgments, or other compensation for injury: Accident, health, or disability insurance benefits (Tenn. Code Ann. §§ 26–2–110, 26–2–111); certain life insurance; up to $15,000 aggregate in right to receive or property traceable to an award up to $5000 under crime victim reparations law, compensation up to $7500 for personal bodily injury, or up to $10,000 for wrongful death of person on whom debtor was dependent (Tenn. Code Ann. § 26–2–111(2)); compensation for loss of future earnings so far as necessary for the support of debtor or dependents. Tenn. Code Ann. § 26–2–111(3).

Bank accounts: Archer Medical Savings Account, or tax-qualified health savings account. See also Tangible Personal Property, above.

Alimony, child support: Right to receive certain alimony and child support. Tenn. Code Ann. §§ 26–2–111(1)(E), 26–2–111(1)(F). Funds or liquid assets owed for court-ordered child support; exempt only if immediately paid into court or attached on behalf of the obligee. Tenn. Code Ann. § 26–2–111(6).

Tax refunds:

Survival after payment or deposit: Not specified but note language in certain benefit exemptions regarding "right to receive" or "right to receive and property traceable to." State pensions remain exempt in bank account.

TEXAS

Has state opted out of federal bankruptcy exemptions? No.

Is opt out limited to residents or domiciliaries of the state? Not applicable.

Do state's exemptions have extraterritorial application?

Homestead: No. *See In re* Bingham, 2008 WL 186277 (Bankr. D. Kan. Jan. 18, 2008) (Texas homestead not available for property located in Kansas); *In re* Tate, 2007 WL 81835 (Bankr. D. Or. Jan. 8, 2007); *In re* Peters, 91 B.R. 401 (Bankr. W.D. Tex. 1988). *See also* Tex. Prop. Code Ann. § 41.002 (West) (which provides a definition of homestead that applies to "all homesteads in this state whenever created").

Personal property: Probably not. *See In re* Peters, 91 B.R. 401 (Bankr. W.D. Tex. 1988).

***Wages:* Tex. Const. art. 16, § 28; Tex. Prop. Code Ann. § 42.001 (West).**

Scope: Wages or commissions for personal services. Tex. Prop. Code Ann. §§ 42.001(b)(1), 42.001(d) (West).

Amount: Current wages for personal service are exempt from garnishment. Commissions for personal services also protected, up to 25% of aggregate limitations ($60,000 for a family, $30,000 for an individual). Tex. Prop. Code Ann. § 42.001(d) (West).

Survival after payment/deposit: Not specified in exemption statute.

Waiver: Not specified in exemption statute.

***Homestead:* Tex. Const. art. 16, §§ 50, 51; Tex. Prop. Code Ann. §§ 41.001, 41.002, 41.004, 41.005, 41.0021 (West).**

Amount: Rural homestead consists of not more than 200 acres for a family or 100 acres for an individual; an urban homestead consists of not more than ten acres (for property sold before January 1, 2000, the prior one-acre exemption applies); includes improvements; must be claimant's home which may include place of business (Tex. Const. art. 16, § 50; Tex. Prop. Code Ann. § 41.002 (West)); homestead is subject to certain liens. Tex. Const. art. 16, § 50; Tex. Prop. Code Ann. § 41.001(b) (West). Urban is defined as within municipal limits and receiving certain municipal services. Tex. Prop. Code Ann. § 41.002 (West). A homestead exemption is available for residences owned by certain kinds of trust. Tex. Prop. Code Ann. § 42.0021 (West).

Procedural requirements: Procedure available for designation of homestead, but may be done at time of levy. Tex. Prop. Code Ann. § 41.005 (West).

Special provisions: Proceeds from sale exempt for six months. Tex. Prop. Code Ann. § 41.001(c) (West).

Waiver: The Texas Constitution includes detailed restrictions and procedural requirements for loans secured by the homestead. Tex. Const. art. 16, § 50. Homestead may not be abandoned without consent of spouse. Tex. Prop. Code Ann. § 41.004 (West).

***Tangible personal property:* Tex. Prop. Code Ann. §§ 42.001 through 42.005 (West).**

Household goods: Up to $60,000 for a family, $30,000 for a single adult, of the following: household furnishings, provisions, trade implements, clothing, two firearms, sporting equipment, certain animals, certain vehicles, and pets; exemptions not applicable to a child support lien under Family Code. Tex. Prop. Code Ann. § 42.001(a) (West).

Motor vehicles: See description of wildcard under household goods, *supra*.

Tools of trade: See description of wildcard under household goods, *supra*.

Clothing and jewelry: See description of wildcard under household goods, *supra*. (Jewelry limited to 25% of aggregate amount.)

Miscellaneous and wildcard: See description of wildcard under household goods, *supra*. Health aids exempt and not included in cap. Tex. Prop. Code Ann. § 42.001(b)(2) (West). Bible, or other book of sacred writings. Tex. Prop. Code Ann. § 42.001(b)(4) (West).

Waiver: Not specified in exemption statute.

***Benefits, retirement plans, insurance, judgments, and other intangibles:* Tex. Prop. Code Ann. §§ 42.001, 42.0021, 42.0022 (West).**

Public benefits: Not specified in exemption statute. *See* Tex. Hum. Res. Code Ann. § 31.040 (West) (assistance granted under financial assistance laws is exempt).

Pensions, retirement plans, and annuities: Rights to assets held in, or to receive payments from, certain pensions, annuities, or tax-qualified retirement plans. Non-taxable rollovers and inherited accounts explicitly included. Tex. Prop. Code Ann. § 42.0021 (West).

Insurance, judgments, or other compensation for injury: Certain life insurance.

Bank accounts: Funds held in, or right to receive payments from, certain college tuition savings plans established pursuant to the Education Code; health savings accounts, as defined in Internal Revenue code. Tex. Prop. Code Ann. § 420.022 (West).

Alimony, child support: Alimony, support, or separate maintenance, received or to be received. Tex. Prop. Code Ann. § 42.001(b)(3) (West).

Tax refunds:

Survival after payment or deposit: Not specified in exemption statute.

UTAH

Has state opted out of federal bankruptcy exemptions? Yes. Utah Code Ann. § 78B-5–513.

Is opt out limited to residents or domiciliaries of the state? Yes. Utah Code Ann. § 78B-5–513: "An individual may not exempt from the property of the estate in any bankruptcy proceeding property specified in [§ 522(d) *unless the individual is a non-resident of this state and has been for the 180 days preceding the bankruptcy*."

Do state's exemptions have extraterritorial application?

Homestead: No. The exemption provided in Utah Code Ann. § 78B-5–503 applies to a homestead "consisting of property in this state." *See In re* Katseanes, 2007 WL 2962637 (Bankr. D. Idaho Oct. 9, 2007).

Personal property: Uncertain.

***Wages:* Utah Code Ann. §§ 70C-7–103, 70C-7–104, 78B-5–505(1)(b) (West).**

Scope: Compensation for personal services, whether called wages, salary, commission, bonus, or otherwise, including periodic payments pursuant to pension, disability, or retirement plan. Utah Code Ann. § 70C-7–103(1) (West).

Amount: Similar to federal. Utah Code Ann. § 70C-7–103(2) (West). Disposable earnings are those left after legally required deductions. Utah Code Ann. § 70C-7–103(1) (West). Unpaid earnings, as of the date of filing of a bankruptcy petition, are exempt up to 1/12 or 1/24 (depending on whether debtor is paid more often than once a month) of the state median income for debtor's family size. Utah Code Ann. § 78B-5–505(1)(b) (West).

Survival after payment/deposit: Not specified in exemption statute.

Waiver: Not specified in exemption statute.

***Homestead:* Utah Const. art. XXII, § 1; Utah Code Ann. §§ 78B-5–503, 78B-5–504, 78B-5–507 (West).**

Amount: Up to $30,000 for an individual or $60,000 for joint owners in the "primary personal residence" defined as a dwelling or manufactured home (whether or not debtor owns the land on which manufactured home is located) and up to one acre of land "as reasonably necessary to make use of the dwelling or mobile home." Property is defined to include an equitable interest in real property awarded by a court in divorce proceedings. If property is not the primary personal residence, exemption is limited to $5000 ($10,000 for joint owners). Utah Code Ann. § 78B-5–503 (West).

Procedural requirements: Procedure available for filing declaration of homestead; may be filed up to time stated in notice of execution. Utah Code Ann. § 78B-5–504 (West).

Special provisions: Proceeds remain exempt for one year. Utah Code Ann. § 78B-5–503(5)(b) (West). A person may not claim a homestead in property acquired as a result of criminal activity. Utah Code Ann. § 78B-5–503(2)(d) (West).

Waiver: Spouse must join in conveyance or encumbrance. Utah Code Ann. § 78B-5–503(4) (West). Waiver of exemptions in favor of unsecured creditor is unenforceable. Utah Code Ann. § 78B-5–509 (West).

***Tangible personal property:* Utah Code Ann. §§ 39–1–47, 78B-5–505 through 78B-5–511 (West).**

Household goods: Washer, dryer, refrigerator, stove, microwave, sewing machine, carpets, 12 months of provisions, beds and bedding. Utah Code Ann. § 78B-5–505(1) (West). In addition, $1000 exemptions for goods chosen from each of four categories: (1) sofas, chairs, and so forth, (2) kitchen and dining tables and chairs, (3) animals, books, and musical instruments, and (4) heirlooms or other items of sentimental value. Utah Code Ann. § 78B-5–506(1) (West).

Motor vehicles: $3000; specifically excludes recreational or off-road vehicles, except for a motorcycle or van used for daily transportation. Utah Code Ann. § 78B-5–505(3) (West).

Tools of trade: $5000, including motor vehicle to which other exemptions have not been applied, actually used in the individual's principal trade or business. Utah Code Ann. § 78B-5–505(2) (West).

Clothing and jewelry: All clothing, excluding furs and jewelry. Utah Code Ann. § 78B-5–505(1) (West).

Miscellaneous and wildcard: Health aids; burial plot (Utah Code Ann. § 78B-5–505(1) (West)); military property (Utah Code Ann. § 39–1–47 (West)); family pictures; works of art by debtor. Utah Code Ann. § 78B-5–505(1) (West). Firearms and ammunition, $250 per individual, $500 per household. Utah Code Ann. § 78B-5–505(1)(e) (West). Traceable proceeds of property sold, taken by condemnation, lost, damaged or destroyed remain exempt for one year. Utah Code Ann. § 75B-5–507 (West).

Waiver: Waiver of exemptions in favor of unsecured creditor is unenforceable. Utah Code Ann. § 78B-5–509 (West).

***Benefits, retirement plans, insurance, judgments, and other intangibles:* Utah Code Ann. §§ 78B-5–505 through 78B-5–511.**

Public benefits: Veterans' benefits; benefits received or to be received from any source on account of disability, illness, or unemployment. Utah Code Ann. § 78B-5–505(1) (West).

Pensions, retirement plans, and annuities: Certain tax-qualified retirement plans. Rollovers explicitly included; other contributions within one year of bankruptcy not exempt. Payments from plans for illness or disability fully exempt; others exempt to extent needed for support. Proceeds or benefits of certain trusts of which debtor or dependents are beneficiary. Utah Code Ann. § 78B-5–505(1) (West).

Insurance, judgments, or other compensation for injury: Benefits received or to be received from any source on account of disability, illness, or unemployment (Utah Code Ann. § 78B-5–505(1) (West)); proceeds of insurance, judgment or settlement for personal injury or wrongful death; benefits paid or payable for medical, surgical, or hospital care, so far as used to pay for that care. Proceeds or benefits of any life insurance paid or payable to debtor upon the death of debtor's spouse or children, provided that policy had been owned by debtor for a continuous unexpired period of one year; proceeds or benefits of any contracts paid or payable to spouse or children upon the death of the debtor, provided that policy has been in existence for continuous unexpired period of one year; proceeds or avails of any unmatured life insurance contracts owned by debtor, excluding any payments made during year before levy or execution. (These sections do not apply to any life insurance pledged as collateral for a loan or other legal obligation.) Utah Code Ann. § 78B-5–505(1) (West).

Bank accounts: Not specified in exemption statute.

Alimony, child support: Child support (Utah Code Ann. § 78B-5–505(1) (West)); payments from retirement plan to alternate payee under qualified domestic relations order. Alimony and separate maintenance exempt to extent needed for support. Utah Code Ann. § 78B-5–505(1) (West).

Tax refunds:

Survival after payment or deposit: Benefits remain exempt after receipt by and in possession of individual, and in any other form in which it is traceable.

VERMONT

Has state opted out of federal bankruptcy exemptions? No.

Is opt out limited to residents or domiciliaries of the state? Not applicable.

Do state's exemptions have extraterritorial application?

Homestead: Yes. *See In re* Oliver, 182 B.R. 699 (Bankr. D. Vt. 1995) (debtor may use Vermont homestead to exempt proceeds of sale of property in another state).

Personal property: Uncertain.

***Wages:* Vt. Stat. Ann. tit. 12, §§ 3170, 3172.**

Scope: Earnings.

Amount: Follows the federal scheme except for consumer credit claims when the greater of 85% of weekly disposable earnings or 40 times federal minimum wage is exempt. Vt. Stat. Ann. tit. 12, § 3170(b). No garnishment if debtor was, within two months of the garnishment hearing, a welfare recipient. Vt. Stat. Ann. tit. 12, § 3170(a). Court may reduce garnishment amount if debtor shows that weekly expenditures "reasonably incurred" for maintenance of self or dependents exceed the statutorily exempt amount. Garnishment orders may be modified from time to time. Vt. Stat. Ann. tit. 12, §§ 3170(b), 3170(c). Discharge of employee because of garnishment forbidden; discharge within 60 days after garnishment rebuttably presumed to be violation; employee has private right of action for reinstatement, back wages, damages, costs, and reasonable attorney fees. Vt. Stat. Ann. tit. 12, § 3172.

Survival after payment/deposit: Not specified in garnishment statute.

Waiver: Forbidden. Vt. Stat. Ann. tit. 12, § 3170(d).

***Homestead:* Vt. Stat. Ann. tit. 27, §§ 101, 105, 107, 109, 141.**

Amount: $125,000 in land and a dwelling, which may be a permanently sited manufactured home, including the rents, issues, and profits. Vt. Stat. Ann. tit. 27, § 101.

Procedural requirements: Deed or homestead must be recorded; exemption does not protect against debts which precede this declaration, except that new homestead acquired with proceeds of sale of former homestead is exempt as to any debts as to which former homestead was exempt. Vt. Stat. Ann. tit. 27, §§ 107, 109.

Special provisions: Homestead protects surviving spouse. Vt. Stat. Ann. tit. 27, § 105.

Waiver: Spouse must join in conveyance or encumbrance. Note, however, that one spouse or civil union partner may lose homestead right by conveyance of property to other spouse or partner. Vt. Stat. Ann. tit. 27, § 141.

***Tangible personal property:* Vt. Stat. Ann. tit. 12, §§ 2740, 3023.**

Household goods: $2500 in aggregate value in household furnishings, goods, or appliances; books; wearing apparel; animals; crop; musical instruments; one cooking stove; heating appliances; one refrigerator; one freezer; one water heater; sewing machines; various amounts of specified fuel; specified livestock and accessories (Vt. Stat. Ann. tit. 12, §§ 2740(8) through 2740(14)); health aids; proceeds of exempt property.

Motor vehicles: $2500. Vt. Stat. Ann. tit. 12, § 2740(1).

Tools of trade: $5000 tools of trade (Vt. Stat. Ann. tit. 12, § 2740(2)); $5000 in aggregate value in growing crops. Vt. Stat. Ann. tit. 12, § 2740(6).

Clothing and jewelry: Clothing included in household goods exemption, above. A wedding ring; $500 in aggregate value in other jewelry. Vt. Stat. Ann. tit. 12, §§ 2740(3), 2740(4).

Miscellaneous and wildcard: Proceeds of exempt property (Vt. Stat. Ann. tit. 12, § 3023); $400 aggregate interest in any property plus up to $7000 of unused exemptions for motor vehicles, tools of trade, jewelry, household goods, and crops (Vt. Stat. Ann. tit. 12, § 2740(7)); health aids. Vt. Stat. Ann. tit. 12, § 2740(17).

Waiver: Not specified in exemption statute.

***Benefits, retirement plans, insurance, judgments, and other intangibles:* Vt. Stat. Ann. tit. 12, § 2740. *See* Vt. Stat. Ann. tit. 3, § 476.**

Public benefits: Any property traceable to the debtor's right to receive Social Security or veterans' benefits, to the extent reasonably needed for support of debtor or dependents. *See also* Vt. Stat. Ann. tit. 33, § 124 (all moneys granted to persons as assistance are exempt).

Pensions, retirement plans, and annuities: State employees' pensions; property traceable to a pension, annuity, profit sharing, stock bonus or similar plan on account of death, disability, illness, or retirement from or termination of employment, so far as necessary for support of debtor or dependents. Vt. Stat. Ann. tit. 12, § 2740(19). Tax-qualified individual retirement plans, if contributions limited to tax-qualified amounts; contributions to a self-directed plan within one year before bankruptcy are non-exempt. Exemption for IRAs limited to $5000 for child support debts. Vt. Stat. Ann. tit. 12, § 2740(16).

Insurance, judgments, or other compensation for injury: Unmatured life insurance contract. Vt. Stat. Ann. tit. 12, § 2740(18). Any property traceable to the debtor's right to receive the following, to the extent reasonably needed for the support of debtor and dependents: disability or illness benefits, crime victim's compensation, certain insurance benefits, personal injury (including pain and suffering and actual pecuniary loss) and wrongful death recoveries, compensation for loss of future earnings. Vt. Stat. Ann. tit. 12, § 2740(19).

Bank accounts: $700. Vt. Stat. Ann. tit. 12, § 2740(15).

Alimony, child support: Any property traceable to debtor's right to receive alimony, support, or separate maintenance, to the extent needed for support. Vt. Stat. Ann. tit. 12, § 2740(19).

Tax refunds:

Survival after payment or deposit: Yes. Note "property traceable to" language in various benefits exemptions.

VIRGIN ISLANDS

Has state opted out of federal bankruptcy exemptions? No.

Is opt out limited to residents or domiciliaries of the state? Not applicable.

Do state's exemptions have extraterritorial application?

Homestead: Uncertain.

Personal property: Uncertain.

***Wages:* V.I. Code Ann. tit. 5, §§ 521, 522.**

Scope: Wages, salary, commissions, or other remuneration for services performed by an employee for his employer, including any remuneration measured partly or wholly by percentages or share of profits, or by other sums based upon work done or results produced, and any drawing account made available to an employee by his employer. V.I. Code Ann. tit. 5, § 521.

Amount: 90% of gross wages in excess of $30 per week is exempt. V.I. Code Ann. tit. 5, § 522(a).

Survival after payment/deposit: Not specified in exemption statute.

Waiver: Not specified in exemption statute.

Homestead: **V.I. Code Ann. tit. 5, § 478.**

Amount: $30,000; rural homestead may not exceed five acres and urban homestead may not exceed one quarter of an acre. V.I. Code Ann. tit. 5, § 478(a).

Procedural requirements: None stated. Homestead may be claimed at time of levy. V.I. Code Ann. tit. 5, § 478(b).

Special provisions: None specified.

Waiver: Spouse must join in encumbrance.

Tangible personal property: **V.I. Code Ann. tit. 5, § 479.**

Household goods: $3000. Head of household only. V.I. Code Ann. tit. 5, § 479(3).

Motor vehicles: None.

Tools of trade: Exempt so far as necessary to carry on trade, occupation, or profession by which debtor habitually earns a living. V.I. Code Ann. tit. 5, § 479(2).

Clothing and jewelry: Clothing. (Watches and jewelry not exempt.) V.I. Code Ann. tit. 5, § 479(1).

Miscellaneous and wildcard: None

Waiver: Not specified in exemption statute.

Benefits, retirement plans, insurance, judgments, and other intangibles:

Public benefits: Not specified in exemption statute. *See* V.I. Code Ann. tit. 34, § 13 (public assistance granted under social welfare laws is exempt).

Pensions, retirement plans, and annuities: Not specified in exemption statute.

Insurance, judgments, or other compensation for injury: Not specified in exemption statute.

Bank accounts: Not specified in exemption statute.

Alimony, child support: Not specified in exemption statute.

Tax refunds:

Survival after payment or deposit: Not specified in exemption statute.

VIRGINIA

Has state opted out of federal bankruptcy exemptions? Yes. Va. Code Ann. § 34–3.1.

Is opt out limited to residents or domiciliaries of the state? Not specified. Va. Code Ann. § 34–3.1: "No individual may exempt from the property of the estate in any bankruptcy proceeding the property specified in [§ 522(d)], except as may otherwise be expressly permitted under this title."

Do state's exemptions have extraterritorial application?

Homestead: Yes. Va. Code Ann. § 34–6 sets out the procedure for declaring a homestead for real estate located outside the state. *See also In re* McWilliams, 296 B.R. 424 (Bankr. E.D. Va. 2002) (debtor's claim of Virginia homestead exemption in North Carolina property denied because debtor failed to file homestead deed in both county in which he resided and county in which property was located as required by Virginia law).

Personal property: Uncertain.

Wages: **Va. Code Ann. §§ 34–4.2, 34–17(B), 34–29, 34–32, 34–33.**

Scope: Earnings of an individual. Va. Code Ann. § 34–29(d).

Amount: Greater of 75% or 40 times federal minimum wage is exempt. Va. Code Ann. § 34–29(a). Wages of minor fully exempt as to debts of parents. Va. Code Ann. § 34–33. Debtors with a gross household income [defined] of $1750/month or less, who support dependent children, may exempt an additional $34/week for one child, $52/week for two, or $66/week for three or more children. Va. Code Ann. § 34–4.2. "Homestead exemption," which covers real and personal property, may be used to recover garnished wages. Declaration should be filed after garnishment summons served on employer and before return date of summons. Va. Code Ann. § 34–17(B).

Survival after payment/deposit: Not specified in exemption statute.

Waiver: Void and unenforceable. Va. Code Ann. § 34–29(e).

Homestead: **Va. Code Ann. §§ 34–4, 34–4.1, 34–6, 34–14, 34–18, 34–22.**

Amount: $5000 in any property plus $500 for each dependent; $10,000 if debtor is age 65 or over (Va. Code Ann. § 34–4), profits derived from homestead property are exempt (Va. Code Ann. § 34–18); exemption subject to certain liens. Additional $10,000 in real or personal property for certain disabled veterans. Va. Code Ann. § 34–4.1.

Procedural requirements: Homestead declaration must be recorded. Va. Code Ann. §§ 34–6, 34–14.

Special provisions: None specified.

Waiver: Permitted. Va. Code Ann. § 34–22.

Tangible personal property: **Va. Code Ann. §§ 34–4, 34–4.1, 34–6, 34–14, 34–18, 34–22, 34–26 through 34–28.**

Household goods: $5000. Va. Code Ann. § 34–26(4a).

Motor vehicles: $6000. Va. Code Ann. § 34–26(8).

Tools of trade: $10,000. Does not cover motor vehicle used only for commuting. "Occupation" includes enrollment in school or college. Va. Code Ann. § 34–26(7). For debtor engaged in farming, certain livestock and farming implements. Va. Code Ann. § 34–27.

Clothing and jewelry: $1000 clothing; wedding and engagement rings. Va. Code Ann. §§ 34–26(1a), 34–26(4).

Miscellaneous and wildcard: See homestead exemption above (any real or personal property) (Va. Code Ann. §§ 34–4, 34–4.1); family bible; $5000 family portraits and heirlooms; burial place; pets; $3000 one firearm; health aids. Va. Code Ann. § 34–26.

Waiver: Permitted as to property exempted under general ("any real or personal property") homestead exemption, but note that non-possessory security interests are forbidden in certain essential property exempted by Va. Code Ann. §§ 34–26, 34–27, and 34–29. Va. Code Ann. §§ 34–22, 34–28.

Benefits, retirement plans, insurance, judgments, and other intangibles: **Va. Code Ann. §§ 34–26, 34–28.1, 34–34.**

Public benefits: Not specified in exemption statute. *See* Va. Code Ann. § 63.2–506 (public assistance exempt).

Pensions, retirement plans, and annuities: Retirement plans exempt to the same extent permitted under federal bankruptcy law. Va. Code Ann. § 34–34.

Insurance, judgments, or other compensation for injury: Personal injury or wrongful death causes of action or proceeds of judgment or settlement, except as to certain liens. Va. Code Ann. § 34–28.1.

Bank accounts: Pre-need funeral contract, up to $5000. Va. Code Ann. § 34–26(3).

Alimony, child support: Not specified in exemption statute.

Tax refunds:

Survival after payment or deposit: Not specified in exemption statute.

WASHINGTON

Has state opted out of federal bankruptcy exemptions? No.

Is opt out limited to residents or domiciliaries of the state? Not applicable.

Do state's exemptions have extraterritorial application?

Homestead: Uncertain.

Personal property: Uncertain.

***Wages:* Wash. Rev. Code §§ 6.27.010, 6.27.150, 6.27.170.**

Scope: Compensation paid or payable for personal services, whether called wages, salary, commission, bonus, or otherwise, including periodic payments pursuant to a pension or retirement program. Wash. Rev. Code § 6.27.010.

Amount: The greater of 75%, or 35 times the federal minimum wage is exempt. Wash. Rev. Code § 6.27.150.

Survival after payment/deposit: Not specified in garnishment statute.

Waiver: Not specified in garnishment statute.

***Homestead:* Wash. Rev. Code §§ 6.13.010 through 6.13.080.**

Amount: $125,000 for dwelling house or manufactured home (whether or not permanently affixed) and land, or unimproved land on which debtor intends to place dwelling house or manufactured home. Wash. Rev. Code §§ 6–13–010, 6–13–030. If debtor is married or in a state-registered domestic partnership, may consist of community property or separate property of either spouse or domestic partner, provided that the same premises cannot be claimed separately by the spouses or domestic partners with the effect of increasing the exemption in excess of the amount specified by law (Wash. Rev. Code § 6–13–020); homestead exemption subject to certain liens. Wash. Rev. Code § 6–13–080.

Procedural requirements: Homestead is automatic in land occupied as residence; declaration of homestead required to exempt unimproved land on which owner intends to build residence. Wash. Rev. Code § 6–13–040. Declaration of non-abandonment must be recorded if owner who wishes to retain homestead will be absent for more than six months. Wash. Rev. Code § 6–13–050.

Special provisions: Proceeds or insurance remain exempt for one year. Wash. Rev. Code § 6–13–070.

Waiver: Spouse or domestic partner must join in conveyance or encumbrance. Wash. Rev. Code § 6–13–060.

***Tangible personal property:* Wash. Rev. Code §§ 6.15.010 through 6.15.040 and 6.15.900.**

Household goods: $6500 ($13,000 for marital community), not more than $750 per item, household goods, appliances, and furniture. Wash. Rev. Code § 6–15–010(c)(i).

Motor vehicles: $3250 motor vehicle used for personal transportation (two vehicles, aggregate $6500, for community). Wash. Rev. Code § 6–15–010(d).

Tools of trade: $10,000. Wash. Rev. Code § 6–15–010(c)(ii).

Clothing and jewelry: All clothing (but $3500 per individual limit for furs, jewelry, or ornaments). Wash. Rev. Code § 6–15–010(a).

Miscellaneous and wildcard: $3500 for private libraries, including various kinds of electronic media; all family pictures and keepsakes (Wash. Rev. Code § 6–15–010(b)); health aids. Wash. Rev. Code § 6–15–010(c)(v). $3000 wildcard: may not be used for earnings, not more than $1500 for cash, not more than $500 ($200 for certain debts owed to state agencies) for bank accounts, stocks, or the like. Wash. Rev. Code § 6–15–010(c)(ii).

Waiver: Not specified in exemption statute.

Special provisions: Note that references to "marital community," community, spouse, etc. apply to state registered domestic partnerships.

***Benefits, retirement plans, insurance, judgments, and other intangibles:* Wash. Rev. Code §§ 6.15.010 through 6.15.040, 48.18.400 through 48.18.430.**

Public benefits: Not specified in exemption statute. *See* Wash. Rev. Code §§ 74.04.280, 74.08.210 (public assistance exempt).

Pensions, retirement plans, and annuities: Certain pensions, annuities, employee benefit plans, or tax-qualified individual retirement accounts. Wash. Rev. Code § 6–15–020.

Insurance, judgments, or other compensation for injury: $20,000 personal injury judgments; compensation for loss of future earnings, so far as needed for support. Wash. Rev. Code § 6–15–010(c)(vi). Proceeds and avails of life insurance and certain disability insurance fully exempt, as to debts of the insured, or debts of beneficiary existing at time proceeds made available. Wash. Rev. Code §§ 48.18.400 through 48.18.430. Insurance proceeds for loss or destruction of exempt property are exempt. Wash. Rev. Code § 6–15–030.

Bank accounts: $200. Prepaid college tuition units (pursuant to Wash. Rev. Code § 28B.95) purchased more than two years prior to the date of a bankruptcy filing or court judgment. Wash. Rev. Code § 6–15–010(e). Health savings account.

Alimony, child support: Child support, so long as traceable. Wash. Rev. Code § 6–15–010(c)(iv).

Tax refunds:

Survival after payment or deposit: Yes, as to certain pension and retirement benefits.

WEST VIRGINIA

Has state opted out of federal bankruptcy exemptions? Yes. W. Va. Code § 38–10–4.

Is opt out limited to residents or domiciliaries of the state? Yes. W. Va. Code § 38–10–4: "[T]his state specifically does not authorize persons who are domiciled in this state to exempt the property specified in [§ 522(d)]."

Do state's exemptions have extraterritorial application?

Homestead: Uncertain.

Personal property: Uncertain.

***Wages:* W. Va. Code §§ 38–5A-1, 38–5A-3, 38–5A-9, 38–5B-12.**

Scope: Salary and wages are given their ordinary meaning, but include compensation measured partly or wholly by commissions, percentages or share of profits, or by other sums based upon work done or results produced, whether or not debtor is given a drawing account. W. Va. Code § 38–5A-1.

Amount: Greater of 80% of wages or 30 times federal minimum hourly wage per week is exempt. W. Va. Code §§ 38–5A-3, 38–5A-9, 38–5B-12.

Survival after payment/deposit: Not specified in exemption statute, but note that it covers money "due and owing" or "to become due and owing." W. Va. Code § 38–5A-3.

Waiver: Not specified in exemption statute.

***Homestead:* W. Va. Const. art. 6, § 48; W. Va. Code §§ 38–9–1 through 38–9–6, 38–10–4.**

Amount: Bankruptcy only: $25,000 in real or personal property or a cooperative that debtor or dependent uses as a residence, or in a burial plot of debtor or dependent; $250,000 for physician's bankruptcy arising from certain medical malpractice judgments. W. Va. Code § 38–10–4(a). Non-bankruptcy: $5000, which may be claimed by a "husband, wife, parent or other head of household." W. Va. Code §§ 38–9–1, 38–9–2. For all debts and liabilities for hospital or medical expenses incurred for a catastrophic illness or injury as defined, the exemption is $7500. (Enhanced exemption does not apply to debts incurred before July 1, 1996.) W. Va. Code § 38–9–3(b).

Procedural requirements: None stated. Homestead available "by operation of law." W. Va. Code § 38–9–1.

Special provisions: After debtor's death, exemption continues to protect minor children. W. Va. Code § 38–9–5.

Waiver: Void and unenforceable except as to certain consensual security interests. W. Va. Code § 38–9–6.

***Tangible personal property:* W. Va. Code §§ 38–8–1, 38–8–3, 38–8–10, 38–8–15, 38–10–4, 46A-2-136; W. Va. Const. art. 6, § 48.**

Household goods: Bankruptcy: household goods and furnishings, clothing, books, animals, musical instruments, up to $400 in any item to an aggregate of $8000. W. Va. Code § 38–10–4(c). Non-bankruptcy: $8000. W. Va. Code § 38–8–1(a)(2). For consumer credit transactions and consumer leases, all the property listed in W. Va. Code § 38–8–1, plus all children's books, pictures, toys, and other such personal property of children, and all "medical health equipment used for health purposes" by consumer, spouse, or dependent. W. Va. Code § 46A-2–136.

Motor vehicles: Bankruptcy: $2400. W. Va. Code § 38–10–4(b). Non-bankruptcy: $5000. W. Va. Code § 38–8–1(a)(1).

Tools of trade: Bankruptcy: $1500. W. Va. Code § 38–10–4(f). Non-bankruptcy: $3000. W. Va. Code § 38–8–1(a)(3).

Clothing and jewelry: Bankruptcy: $1000 in jewelry. W. Va. Code § 38–10–4(d). (Clothing included in household goods exemption).

Miscellaneous and wildcard: Bankruptcy: $800 plus any unused household goods exemption (W. Va. Code § 38–10–4(e)); health aids. W. Va. Code § 38–10–4(i). Non-bankruptcy, head of household: $1000 any personal property. $15,000 cap on non-bankruptcy personal property exemptions including certain bank accounts. W. Va. Code § 38–8–1(b).

***Benefits, retirement plans, insurance, judgments, and other intangibles:* W. Va. Code §§ 38–8–1, 38–10–4.**

Public benefits: Bankruptcy: Right to receive Social Security, unemployment, veterans' benefits, local public assistance. W. Va. Code § 38–10–4(j). *See also* W. Va. Code § 9–5–1 (welfare assistance exempt).

Pensions, retirement plans, and annuities: Bankruptcy: Certain pensions and retirement plans; any unmeasured life insurance, and up to $8000 in accrued dividends or loan value (W. Va. Code §§ 38–10–4(g), 38–10–4(h)); right to receive any disability, illness, or unemployment benefit (W. Va. Code § 38–10–4(j)); right to receive or property traceable to crime victim reparations (W. Va. Code § 38–10–4(k)), wrongful death of person on whom debtor was dependent (W. Va. Code § 38–10–4(k)), life insurance proceeds as needed for support, up to $15,000 personal injury compensation (not including pain and suffering or actual pecuniary loss), loss of future earnings. W. Va. Code § 38–10–4(k). Non-bankruptcy: Certain IRA and Simplified Employee Pension funds are exempt. W. Va. Code § 38–8–1(a)(5).

Insurance, judgments, or other compensation for injury: Bankruptcy only: $8000 in loan value or accrued dividends of certain life insurance; $15,000 personal injury; wrongful death payment as needed for support; certain life insurance, as needed for support, compensation for loss of future earnings, as needed for support. W. Va. Code § 38–10–4(k).

Bank accounts: Bankruptcy: Payments to prepaid college tuition fund. W. Va. Code § 38–10–4(k)(6). Non-bankruptcy: "[F]unds on deposit in a federally insured financial institution, wages or salary, not to exceed" the greater of $1000 or a figure based on 125% of poverty level. W. Va. Code § 38–8–1(a)(4).

Alimony, child support: Bankruptcy: Right to receive alimony, support or separate maintenance, to the extent needed for support. W. Va. Code § 38–10–4(j).

Tax refunds:

Survival after payment or deposit: Note "property traceable to" language in certain bankruptcy exemptions.

WISCONSIN

Has state opted out of federal bankruptcy exemptions? No.

Is opt out limited to residents or domiciliaries of the state? Not applicable.

Do state's exemptions have extraterritorial application?

Homestead: Uncertain.

Personal property: Probably not. Wis. Stat. § 815.18(5) provides: "A resident is entitled to the exemptions provided by this section. A non-resident is entitled to the exemptions provided by the law of the jurisdiction of his or her residence."

***Wages:* Wis. Stat. §§ 812.30, 812.34, 812.38, 815.18(3)(h).**

Scope: Compensation paid or payable for personal services whether called wages, salary, commission, bonus, or otherwise, including periodic payments under a pension or retirement program. Wis. Stat. §§ 812.30(6), 812.30(7).

Amount: Greater of 80% of disposable earnings or the amount of the federal poverty line adjusted for family size is exempt. Wis. Stat. § 812.34(2). Disposable earnings are those left after legally required deductions. Wis. Stat. § 812.30(6). Garnishment is forbidden if debtor is eligible to receive need-based public assistance or has received it within six months or if the debtor's household income is below the poverty line. If a 20% garnishment would result in household income below the poverty line, garnishment limited to the amount by which household income exceeds the poverty line. Wis. Stat. § 812.34(2). Debtor may petition for relief, if the exemption is "insufficient to acquire the necessities of life for the debtor and his or her dependents." Wis. Stat. § 812.38. *See also* Wis. Stat. § 815.18(3)(h) (exempting 75% of wages or 30 times minimum wage from execution).

Survival after payment/deposit: Not specified in exemption statute.

Waiver: Not specified in exemption statute.

***Homestead:* Wis. Stat. §§ 815.20, 990.01(13), 990.01(14).**

Amount: $75,000 except for mortgages, taxes, and certain mechanics liens. Spouses may stack exemptions. Wis. Stat. § 815.20. This increased amount applies only to executions issued on or after December 16, 2009. Otherwise the prior limits of $40,000, which may not be stacked, will apply. Not less than one quarter acre, nor more than 40 acres, so far as reasonably necessary to use the dwelling as a home, subject to the value limitation. Wis. Stat. §§ 990.01(13), 990.01(14).

Procedural requirements: None stated. Homestead may be set apart at time of levy.

Special provisions: Sale proceeds exempt for two years, if held with intention to purchase another homestead.

Waiver: Not specified in exemption statute.

***Tangible personal property:* Wis. Stat. §§ 425.106, 815.18.**

Household goods: $12,000. For executions issued before December 16, 2009, the former limit of $5000 remains in effect. Household goods, wearing apparel, firearms, Bible, library, pew. Wis. Stat. § 815.18(3)(d). For debts that arise from a consumer credit transaction, certain specified household goods are exempt.

Motor vehicles: $4000, plus any unused household goods exemption. Wis. Stat. § 815.18(3)(g). For executions issued before December 16, 2009, the former limit of $1200 remains in effect.

Tools of trade: $15,000. A debtor who does not claim this exemption may exempt up to $15,000 in an interest in a closely held business [defined] that employs debtor, or in whose business debtor is actively involved. Wis. Stat. § 815.18(3)(b). For executions issued before December 16, 2009, the former limit of $7500 remains in effect.

Clothing and jewelry: Clothing and jewelry are included in household goods exemption.

Miscellaneous and wildcard: Provisions for burial. Wis. Stat. § 815.18(3)(a).

Waiver: Contractual waiver is void.

***Benefits, retirement plans, insurance, judgments, and other intangibles:* Wis. Stat. § 815.18. *See also* Wis. Stat. §§ 45.03(8)(b), 49.96, 108.13, 614.96.**

Public benefits: Social Security, certain other public assistance, unemployment, veterans' benefits. Wis. Stat. § 815.18(3)(ds).

Pensions, retirement plans, and annuities: Certain public and private pensions and retirement plans. Wis. Stat. §§ 815.18(3)(ef), 815.18(3)(j), 815.18(3)(n).

Insurance, judgments, or other compensation for injury: Insurance proceeds for damage to or destruction of exempt property payable to or received by debtor, for two years after date of receipt (Wis. Stat. § 815.18(3)(e)); unmatured life insurance and up to $150,000 in accrued dividends or loan value, lesser amounts if contract issued or funded within twenty-four months before the earlier of the date the exemption was claimed or the date the action was filed that gave rise to the judgment (Wis. Stat. § 815.18(3)(f)), life insurance proceeds or wrongful death judgment for person on whom debtor was dependent, to extent needed for support; up to $50,000 personal injury, including pain and suffering and actual pecuniary loss (Wis. Stat. § 815.18(3)(i)) (for executions issued before December 16, 2009, the former limit of $25,000 remains in effect); compensation for loss of future earnings; crime victim reparations; certain fraternal benefits; certain annuities.

Bank accounts: $5000 in bank account, but only to extent account is for personal rather than business use. Wis. Stat. § 815.18(3)(k). Tuition units purchased under Wis. Stat. § 14:63 or § 14:64. Wis. Stat. §§ 815.18(3)(o), 815.18(3)(p).

Alimony, child support: Child support, family support, or maintenance to extent needed for support. Wis. Stat. § 815.18(3)(c).

Tax refunds:

Survival after payment or deposit: Yes, as to property traceable to life insurance proceeds, wrongful death, personal injury, loss of future earnings, or certain retirement plans and military pensions. Property traceable to exempt property is exempt only if so specified in this section. Wis. Stat. § 815.18(4).

WYOMING

Has state opted out of federal bankruptcy exemptions? Yes. Wyo. Stat. Ann. § 1–20–109.

Is opt out limited to residents or domiciliaries of the state? Yes, to the extent that debtor is domiciled in Wyoming for specified period. Wyo. Stat. Ann. § 1–20–109: "[T]he [§ 522(d) exemptions] are not authorized in cases when Wyoming law is applicable on the date of the filing of the petition and the debtor's domicile has been located in Wyoming for the one hundred eighty (180) days immediately preceding the date of the filing of the petition or for a longer portion of the one hundred eighty (180) day period than in any other place."

Do state's exemptions have extraterritorial application?

Homestead: Uncertain.

Personal property: Uncertain.

***Wages:* Wyo. Stat. Ann. §§ 1–15–408(b), 1–15–511.**

Scope: Accrued and unpaid earnings for personal services. Wyo. Stat. Ann. § 1–15–408(a).

Amount: Similar to federal. Wyo. Stat. Ann. §§ 1–15–408(b), 1–15–511(a).

Survival after payment/deposit: No. Note "accrued and unpaid" language.

Waiver: Not specified in garnishment statute.

***Homestead:* Wyo. Const. art. 19, § 9; Wyo. Stat. Ann. §§ 1–20–101 through 1–20–104.**

Amount: $20,000, each occupant entitled to separate exemption (Wyo. Stat. Ann. §§ 1–20–101, 1–20–102); mobile home or house trailer explicitly included, whether or not wheels are removed or home is resting on immoveable support. Wyo. Stat. Ann. § 1–20–104.

Procedural requirements: Not specified in exemption statute.

Special provisions: After owner's death, exemption continues to protect surviving spouse and minor children. Wyo. Stat. Ann. § 1–20–103.

Waiver: Not specified in exemption statute.

***Tangible personal property:* Wyo. Stat. Ann. §§ 1–20–105, 1–20–106.**

Household goods: $4000. May be stacked if two or more persons in residence. Wyo. Stat. Ann. § 1–20–106(a)(iii).

Motor vehicles: $5000 in one vehicle. Wyo. Stat. Ann. § 1–20–106(a)(iv).

Tools of trade: $4000. Wyo. Stat. Ann. § 1–20–106(b).

Clothing and jewelry: $2000 in necessary clothing; no jewelry except wedding rings. Wyo. Stat. Ann. § 1–20–105.

Miscellaneous and wildcard: Family library and pictures; cemetery lot. Wyo. Stat. Ann. §§ 1–20–106(a)(i), 1–20–106(a)(ii).

Waiver: Not specified in exemption statute.

***Benefits, retirement plans, insurance, judgments, and other intangibles:* Wyo. Stat. Ann. §§ 1–20–110, 1–20–111.**

Public benefits: Not specified in exemptions statute. *See* Wyo. Stat. Ann. § 42–2–113 (public assistance exempt).

Pensions, retirement plans, and annuities: Certain public or private pensions, or retirement plans and annuities, "paid or payable." IRAs, Roth IRAs and SEP IRAs explicitly included. Wyo. Stat. Ann. § 1–20–110.

Insurance, judgments, or other compensation for injury: Not specified in exemptions statute.

Bank accounts: Contributions to a qualified medical savings account (except for debts for medical expenses), to the extent that contributions are allowable under the Internal Revenue Code. Wyo. Stat. Ann. § 1–20–111.

Alimony, child support: Not specified in exemptions statute.

Tax refunds:

Survival after payment or deposit: Note "paid or payable" language in exemption for retirement accounts.

Appendix H Online Companion Material for This Treatise

H.1 Introduction

A large number of online pleadings, primary source documents, and practice tools accompany NCLC's treatises. **In 2015, we will launch the NCLC Digital Library, an all-new website offering full digital versions of the full text of all of our consumer law treatises.** The online companion material discussed in this appendix will then be more fully integrated with the digital book content. Purchasers and subscribers to this title will be provided additional information on accessing and using the new website prior to launch. Throughout the transition, visit www.nclc.org/library to access all online material for this title.

H.2 About the Online Companion Material

Highlights of the online companion material to *Collection Actions* are more than 50 pleadings relating to consumer defenses to collection actions or consumer claims against collectors for litigation misconduct.

H.3 Locating Documents

Documents associated with this treatise can be found by three methods.

1. Search. The website offers full-text search of the online material. Enter your search term(s) in the Search box and you will be provided a list of the documents matching your search.

2. Contents. Online companion material is also listed in a hierarchical table of contents. Click an entry to expand a contents branch and browse documents.

3. Pleadings search. This flexible search option allows pleadings to be located using one or more categories: pleading type (general, class action, or bankruptcy), subject, and legal claim. For many users, this method will be the preferred way to find a pleading. For example, make one selection from "Type of Pleading—General," one from "Subject," and three from "Legal Claim" to locate all pleadings of that type and subject that contain one or more of the three legal claims selected. If this search produces insufficient results, deselect "Subject" or "Legal Claim" to find pleadings of that type in any subject area or based upon any legal claim.

H.4 Downloading and Using Documents

Click a document title in your search results or in the table of contents to download the full document. Practice aids and primary source materials are offered in PDF format and can be viewed, printed, or copy-pasted, while most pleadings can be downloaded in Microsoft Word format to easily adapt and use in a case.

H.5 Finding Additional Pleadings

Over 2000 pleadings are available in NCLC's *Consumer Law Pleadings* and can be located on the Consumer Law Pleadings website using the same finding techniques discussed above. Purchase of *Consumer Law Pleadings* includes a printed index guide.

Index

Throughout index, references are to sections